The Great Psyche Discography

Reviews for

Martin C. Strong's

The Great Rock Discography

"Illustrated with some humour and considerable expertise by Harry Horse, it's a killer tome well worth the money that Canongate are asking … as far as discographical books are concerned, this one can safely be filed under 'unbelievable' " **– Fred Dellar, N.M.E.**

"Exhaustive and refreshingly opinionated" **– The Guardian**

"Strong is rock's Leslie Halliwell" **– Scotland on Sunday**

"The book, which took ten years to compile, is a worthy rival to the Music Master catalogue" **– The Times**

"A labour of love which has produced a monumental chronicle of rock music … mighty" **– The Herald**

"Far more accurate and comprehensive than many other similar books" **– Time Out**

"Extremely well-presented and more readable than a reference book has any right to be" **– Mojo**

"If you really want to know EVERYTHING, you need *The Great Rock Discography*" **– The Sun**

"This is THE rock reference bible" **– What's On**

"A Herculean labour of love … Strong should provide hours of useful diversions for record collectors" **– Q**

"The last word in rock 'n' roll trainspotting" **– The Guardian**

"An essential tome for music obsessives" **– The Face**

The Great Psychedelic Discography

Martin C. Strong

Illustrations by Harry Horse

CANONGATE

This book is dedicated to . . .
my mother JEAN FOTHERINGHAM
(born: 6th of January, 1929,
died: 31st of August 1985)

Still missing you
and thanks for still
guiding me through all
the hard times.

* * *

First published in 1997 in Great Britain
by Canongate Books Ltd, 14 High St, Edinburgh EH1 1TE

ISBN 0 86241 726 0

British Library Cataloguing in Publication Data
A catalogue record for this book is available on request from the British Library

Typeset by TexturAL, Edinburgh

Printed and bound in Finland by WSOY

Acknowledgements

I'd like to thank the following people who have encouraged me during the last year or so. They are:- my daughters SHIRLEY and SUZANNE, my dad GERRY 'Geoff' STRONG, my granny MACKAY (who turned 90 this year), BRENDON GRIFFIN, VIC ZDZIEBLO, FORREST DUNCAN, ALAN LAWSON, DOUGIE NIVEN, MIKEY KINNAIRD, EILEEN SCOTT-MONCRIEFF (thanks for the memories), SANDY and CAROLINE McCRAE, MICHAEL FLETCHER, TED MOCHAR, DAVIE SEATH, ALAN and ELAINE BREWSTER, The McELROYS – PAUL, STEPHEN, BRIAN, MAUREEN and KEVIN, IRENE WHYTE, DEREK IRVINE, HAMISH McLEOD-PRENTICE, HUNTER WATT, IAIN JENKINS, RUSSELL MAYES, LINDA TONER, BILL FISHER, JOHN McARDLE, ANDREW RISK, KEVIN 'HAGGIS' MacKENZIE, IAN ROBERTSON, STUART ROBERTSON, BRIAN HAY, DAVIE WALKER, BOB GREENAWAY, DAVIE McPHEAT, COLIN TAYLOR, LES O'CONNOR (deceased), PETER WAUGH, TAM MORRISON, BRIAN and MARGARET HUNTER, SHUG MACKIE, PETER McGUCKIN, CHRIS HILL and LEE TAYLOR (from The N.S.A.), GARETH SHANNON (from The Society Of Authors), DREW (Europa Records, 34 The Arcade, Stirling), PAUL KLEMM, IAIN SUTHERLAND, MALCOLM STEWART (Jimpress, Hendrix fanzine), PAUL HUGHES, ALLAN MANN, and all the regulars at SMITH'S LOUNGE in Falkirk (they know who they are), DAVIE and MALKY, plus everyone from The HEBRIDES bar in Edinburgh, all at CANONGATE BOOKS, FALKIRK indie band ARAB STRAP (for just being great and sorry I couldn't quite fit you into this book).

Thanks to everyone who wrote to me over the last year:- MARTIN NISBET, BOB PARR, RICHARD-MICHAEL KUJAS, ALEXANDER KAROTSCH, NICK MORONEY, RICHARD HENNESSEY, GRAEME LARMOUR, TERRY POULTON, JOEL A. STEIN, TONY McGROGAN, JOHN SIEWERT, RICHARD JONES, GUILLAUME BARREAU-DECHERF, MICHAEL YEATES, BERTHOLD NUCHTER, DOUGLAS A. BROWN, C. BLAIR, STEWART WILLIAMSON, MARK CHAMBERLIN, DAVID CLOUTER, ANDREAS DUDA, STUART MAZDON, SAM VANDIVER, STEVE ALLEN, WOLFGANG NUCHTER, ALEXEI ROUDITCHEV, LARRY E. LARSON, STEFAN WEBER, STUART CAMERON, CHRIS CLARK, WIM VAN DER MARK, MARK O SULLIVAN, BERNARD PIERRE (Ambassador of Belgium in Prague), JOHN MACKIE, NIGEL COUZINS, TONY FARNBOROUGH, CHRIS OWEN, JOHN STEEL, GEOFF WHITE, JONATHAN and PAUL COOK, HORST LUEDTKE, FRANZ ZEIDLER, OLIVER SEIDL, AL HOLLYWOOD, ULI SCHMIDT, JOHN GREAVES, J. BENNINK, ANDREAS SCHOLLIG, SCOTT MURPHY (The Filth And The Fury fanzine), ALAN SPICER, PETER J. SMITH, AIDAN P. DOWNEY, JORG FOTH, SILVIO HELLEMANN, AXEL DREYER, ALAN OFFICER and NICK WALL.

I'd also like to give a special mention to BRENDON, who contributed his spare time collaborating with me on certain areas of the book. He'd like to thank all those, past and present, who have given him inspiration and/or support:- his family (mum ANN, brother ROBERT and dad NICKY, also GEORGE INNES, MOIRA, SUSAN, LINDA + ELIZABETH SMITH, ADELE, PAUL AND JACQUELINE) and friends, in no particular order:- PAUL AITKEN aka THE BLACK GOAT, KEITH 'CAPTAIN VAGUE' MUNRO, SUSAN 'POSH SPICE' GRANT, JIM PINKHAM, CLAIRE 'SPEECHY' BALFOUR, DARREN 'RED HAND MAN' McKENNA, ANDY 'THE GHAND MAN' GRIFFIN, DARREN ARNOLD, WILLIE PEAT (R.I.P.), JANE 'SPACE CADET' ABERCROMBY, JANE + MAL, SEAN 'I'M ALL FOR ALCOHOL' McDONALD (and accompanying Nairn characters i.e. CARBO, MARTIN, KAREN, etc.), ALIXE 'TOP MODEL BIRD' BOARDMAN, SUSAN ANDERSON, LOUISE HINTON, NADIA OUSALLAM, NICK DEWAR, NIKKY SPROTT, PHILIP HAWKES, CAROLINE PRESTON, AVRIL GRIEG, ROY DUNSIRE, GUIN WILLIAMS, DYLAN MITCHELL, CHRIS 'THE RIDDLER' BIRREL, LESLEY WOODALL, PAM RIBBECK, STEVEN AITKEN, CATH 'SEA OF KNOBCHEESE' SMITH, NEIL SMITH, SEAN McKENNA, all the Londoners – MATT, GARY, HOWARD, SIMON, BISH, BECCA, RUTH, COLEY, DELI, JODY, KATIE (BMG SPECIAL PROJECTS), ROBBO, JOE, SOPHIE, GLENN, CHRIS, SASS 'SUPERBABE' LAMPARD, and all the DCR class of '94/95 unlucky enough to be living down there. Last but definitely not least, the Europeans: SUZANNE RUFFERT, ELSBETH FRICKE, MONICA CAMPAGNOLI, MARIA MARCOS, SAMIRA EL BOUHAIRI, MARTIN + DETLEFFE, ANNE + STEPHANIE (Edinburgh), PIERRE LANGIN.

* * *

Preface

Well, here it is, "The GREAT PSYCHEDELIC DISCOGRAPHY". Yes, I know, what an original title. Must have taken weeks to come up with that one, I hear you all sarcastically ask? The honest answer is, I did put in a lot of hours on the title, mostly before I went to sleep at night (or whenever), and when I 'sort of' woke up in the morning. A couple of titles (among many) my publishers rejected were:- "COSMIC DAZE: A TRIP THROUGH THE ROCK DISCOGRAPHY" and "KALEIDOSCOPIC VISIONS", (yes both a bit pompous). The publishers let me have four words to play around with. These were:- PSYCHEDELIC, DISCOGRAPHY, GREAT and er... THE. Not surprisingly, I eventually came up with the title.

This is the 5th book/tome I have had published (alright you might say, they've all been updates!). When THE GREAT ROCK DISCOGRAPHY came out November '94, containing 1000 bands/artists, it was to say the least, a bit primitive (but it was my baby!). The 2nd EDITION (September '95) was a better affair and started to sell abroad. Last year (September '96), The 3rd EDITION sold over 25,000 copies worldwide (i.e. USA, Germany, Australia, etc.). Around thc same time, THE WEE ROCK DISCOGRAPHY (a concise version of the 3rd, with many new artists and an update) also sold well. Starting this book around September/October 1996, I came up with the idea that people (and those who wrote to me) were after more than my estimation on who are the best 1000 artists/groups of all time. Instead of writing a 4th edition for 1997 release, I decided to write three: THE GREAT PSYCHEDELIC DISCOGRAPHY (the book which you are holding right now), THE GREAT HARD & HEAVY ROCK DISCOGRAPHY and THE GREAT ALTERNATIVE & INDIE ROCK DISCOGRAPHY. I'm still working on the latter two, which should be in the shops between Spring & Summer next year (God/Canongate willing). While working on this PSYCHEDELIC project, I came across a great deal of difficulties, mostly due to me trying to perfect and select the artists I would include. It's not a 3rd EDITION out-takes book, although of course it does take artists from that, updating & correcting their work, while supplying grammatically superior and expanded biographies. The big difference you will find in this book is the inclusion of *catalogue numbers* (not just British!). This will help you order a recording, while also letting you know if you have the possibly pricey original in your collection. I've also split the book into two sections, the first contains everything psychedelic going back to The BEATLES and The ROLLING STONES, moving on to more experimental and progressive sounds to ambient music before the arrival of British punk (1976). The second and smaller part looks at groups/artists that progressed psychedelic or experimental music a step or two further (i.e. JULIAN COPE, WIRE, XTC, MY BLOODY VALENTINE), a sort of extra reward for the more contemporary fan of psychedelia. I was only allowed 390 working pages in this book, an estimation I originally went way over. Heartbroken, I painstakingly cut out lots of beat groups, R&B/blues artists and anything that was not suited (as I said it was not going to be an out-takes book). This PSYCHEDELIC book could be a little misleading as it contains a LOT more than what it suggests (i.e. GARAGE, PROGRESSIVE, EXPERIMENTAL, AMBIENT, NEW-AGE and RETRO-PSYCH). It takes an A–Z easy-going look at any group or artist who had even the slightest leanings in the world of psychedelic music (yes music, not anyone who smoked a joint and warbled out some trippy lyrics). A few more points I'd like to mention before I sign off:–

1. When is *Record Collector* going to review one of my books?
2. When am I going to meet a Rock Star? I mentioned this in my last book!
3. Is there anybody out there willing to put a bit of financial muscle into setting the book up on the internet? (no timewasters please).
4. £14.99, the history of psychedelic rock for around the same price as the new VERVE album (in Virgin that is). Can't be bad, eh!
5. Joking aside, if you see any mistakes in the book, trivial or glaring, don't be afraid to write to me (c/o CANONGATE).

P.S.- To the kind person who took £5,000 from my hard-earned royalties, I hope you're spending it wisely (as VERA LYNN used to sing...).

* * *

How To Read The Book

If you're struggling in any way how to comprehend some of the more complex parts of each discography, here are some examples to make it easier. Read below for around 10 minutes, taking a step at a time. The final lines/examples you see will give you a good guide before you proceed with the actual chronological discographies. However, I think that once you've read your own favourites you'll have a good idea. There have been no complaints so far, although this book might have a few queries regarding the introduction of catalogue numbers.

GROUP / ARTIST

Formed/Born: Where/When ... biography including style/analysis, song-writers, cover versions, trivia, etc.

Recommended: i.e. selective rating between 1 and 10 – an amalgamation of music press reviews, your letters and my own personal opinion.

SINGER (born; b. day/month/year, town/city, country) – vocals, whatever (ex-GROUP; if any) / **MUSICIAN** (b. BIRTH NAME, 8 Sep'60, Musselburgh, Scotland) – instruments / **OTHER MUSICIANS** – other instruments, vocals, etc.

UK Label US Label

date. (single, ep or album) *(UK cat.no.)* <*US cat.no.*> **THE TITLE** [ ] [ ] US date

note:- UK label – there might be a foreign label if not released in UK.
also:- Labels are only mentioned when the group signs a new contract.

note:- date is UK date – there might also be a foreign release, even an American one, if not issued in Britain.

note:- (UK catalogue number; in curved brackets) <US cat.no.; in pointed brackets>

note:- chart positions UK + US are in the boxes under the labels.

also:- the boxes in the above example have been left blank, thus it did not hit either UK or US charts.

note:- US date after the boxes indicates a variation from its UK counterpart.

also:- Any other info after the boxes (e.g. German) indicates it was not issued in the US.

date. (7") *(UK cat.no.)* **A-SIDE. / B-SIDE** [ ] [-]
US date. (7") <*US cat.no.*> **A-SIDE. / DIFFERENT B-SIDE** [-] [ ]

note:- The two examples above show that the UK + US release did not have an identical A-side & B-side, thus the chart boxes are marked with a – to indicate it was not released in either the UK or the US.

date. (7"/c-s) *(CATNO 1/+C)* **A-SIDE. / B-SIDE** [ ] [-]

note:- above had two formats with the same tracks (i.e. 7"/c-s). However, catalogue numbers will always vary among different formats – often only slightly (e.g. CATNO 1/+C). Each cat.no. would read thus:- (7")=*(CATNO 1)* and (c-s)=*(CATNO 1C)*. To save space the (/) slash comes into effect. The (/) means "or" and in this case it is prefixed with a + sign for the equivalent cassette (c-s).

date. (7"/c-s) *(example same as above)* **SEE ABOVE** [ ] [-]
(12"+=/cd-s+=) *(CATNO 1-12/1-CD)* – Extra tracks.

note:- If there are more formats with extra or different tracks, a new line would be used. Obviously there would also be alternative catalogue numbers utilising the "(/)" as before. Extra tracks would therefore mean the addition of the sign "(+=)" to each format.

date. (lp/c/cd) *(CATNO 200/+MC/CD)* <*US catno 4509*> **ALBUM TITLE** [ ] [ ]
– Track listing / Track 2 / And so on. *(re-iss. = re-issued)*

notes:- A later date, and other 'Label' are mentioned, if different from original; *new cat.no.)* (could be re-iss. many times and if "(+=)" sign occurs there will be extra tracks from the original). <could also apply to the US release if in pointed brackets>

note:- Album above released in 3 formats, thus 3 catalogue numbers are neccessary. The "long-player" lp *(CATNO 200)* is obvious. The "cassette" c = +MC *(CATNO 200MC)* or "compact disc" cd *(CATNO 200CD)*. The US <*cat.no.*> will normally be just one set of numbers (or see further below for other details).

date. (cd/c/lp) *(CD/TC+/CATNO 200)* <*UScatno 4509*> **ALBUM TITLE** [ ] [ ] US date

note:- This time a prefix is used instead of a suffix, thus the differentials appear before the standard lp catalogue number. For instance, the cd would read as *(CDCATNO 200)*.

Jun 97. (cd/c/lp) <*(5557 49860-2/-4/-1)*> **ALBUM TITLE** [1] [1] May97

note:- Some catalogue numbers don't include any letters, but instead consist of a number sequence followed by one digit which universally corresponds with the format
(i.e. 2 = cd / 4 = c / 1 = lp).

also:- If the US numbers are identical, there would be no need to list them separately, i.e. <*(the numbers)*>

note:- I've also marked down an actual date of release and its variant in the US (you'll find this fictitious album also hit No.1 in both charts "and ah've no even heard it yet, man!")

—— **NEW MUSICIAN/SINGER** (b.whenever, etc.) – instruments (ex-GROUP(s) replaced = repl. DEPARTING MUSICIAN/SINGER, who joined whatever

note:- Above denotes a line-up change.

associated GROUP/ARTIST with major name-change

note:- This would always be in grey.

UK Label US Label

Jun 97. (cd/c/lp; GROUP or ARTIST with minor change of name)
<*(5557 49860)*> **ALBUM TITLE** [1] [1] May97

– compilations, etc. –

date. (cd) *compilation Label only; (cat.no.)* **ALBUM TITLE** [100] [-]
– Track listing would be selective, only included if the release was deemed essential.

RECORD-LABEL ABBREVIATIONS

ABC Paramount – ABC Para
Alternative Tentacles. – Alt.Tent.
Amphetamine Reptile – A. Reptile
Beachheads in Space – Beachheads
Beat Goes On – B.G.O.
Beggar's Banquet – Beggar's B.
Blanco y Negro – Blanco Y N.
Castle Communications – Castle
Coast to Coast – CoastCoast
Cooking Vinyl – Cooking V.
Def American – Def Amer.
Emergency Broadcast – Emergency
Factory Benelux – Factory Ben.
Food For Thought – Food for Tht.
Hypertension – Hypertens
Les Disques Du Crepescule – Crepescule
Les Tempes Modern – Les Temps
Magnum Force – Magnum F.
Marble Arch – Marble A.
Music for Midgets – M. F. Midgets
Music for Nations – M. F. N.
Music Of Life – M.O.L.
One Little Indian – O L Indian
Pacific Jazz – Pacific J.
Paisley Park – Paisley P.
Pye International – Pye Inter
Red Rhino Europe – R.R.E.
Regal Starline – Regal Star
Regal Zonophone – Regal Zono.
Return to Sender – R. T. S.
Road Goes on Forever – Road Goes
Sacred Heart – Sacred H.
Seminal Tway – Seminal Tw
Special Delivery – Special D.
Sympathy for the Record Industry – Sympathy F.
Thunderbolt – Thunderb.
Transatlantic – Transatla.
United Artists – U.A.
Vinyl Japan – Vinyl Jap
Vinyl Solution – Vinyl Sol.
Warner Brothers – Warners
Worker's Playtime – Worker's P.
World Pacific – World Pac.
4th & Broadway – 4th & Broad.
20th Century – 20th Cent
92 Happy Customers – 92 Happy C.

Formats & Abbreviations

VINYL (black coloured unless stated)

(lp) = The (LONG PLAYER) record . . . circular 12" plays at 33⅓ r.p.m., and has photo or artwork sleeve. Approximate playing time . . . 30–50 minutes with average 10 tracks. Introduced in the mid-50's on mono until stereo took over in the mid-60's. Quadrophonic had a spell in the 70's, but only on mainly best selling lp's, that had been previously released. Because of higher costs to the manufacturer and buyer, the quad sunk around 1978. Also note that around the mid-50's, some albums were released on 10 inch.
Note:- Average cost to the customer as of July 1997 = £8.50 (new). Budget re-issues are around £5 or under. Collectors can pay anything from £1 to £500, depending on the quality of the recording. Very scratched records can be worthless, but unplayed mint deletions are worth a small fortune to the right person. Auctions and record fairs can be the place to find that long lost recording that's eluded you. This applies to all other vinyl below.

(d-lp) = The (DOUBLE–LONG PLAYER) record . . . as before. Playing time 50–90 minutes on 4 sides, with average 17 tracks. Introduced to rock/pop world in the late 60's, to complement compilations, concept & concert (aka live) albums.[1]
Compilations:- are a selection of greatest hits or rare tracks, demos, etc.
Concepts:- are near uninterrupted pieces of music, based around a theme.
Note that normal lp's could also be compilations, live or concept. Some record companies through the wishes of their artists, released double lp's at the price of one lp. If not, price new would be around £15.

(t-lp) = The (TRIPLE–LONG PLAYER) record . . . as before. Playing time over 100 minutes with normally over 20 tracks. Because of the cost to the consumer, most artists steered clear of this format. Depending on the artwork on the sleeve, these cost over £17.50. (See its replacement, the CD.)

(4-lp-box) = The (BOXED–LONG PLAYER) record (could be between 4 and 10 in each boxed-set). As the triple album would deal with live, concept or compilation side, the boxed-set would be mostly re-issues of all the artist's album material, with probably a bonus lp thrown in, to make it collectable. Could be very pricey, due to lavish outlay in packaging. They cost over £25 new.

(m-lp) = The (MINI–LONG PLAYER) record . . . playing time between 20–30 minutes and containing on average 7 tracks. Introduced for early 80's independent market, and cost around £4.
Note:- This could be confused at times with the extended-play 12" single.

(pic-lp) = The (PICTURE DISC–LONG PLAYER) record . . . as before but with album artwork/ design on the vinyl grooves. Mainly for the collector because of the slightly inferior sound quality. If unplayed, these can fetch between £10 and £250.

(coloured lp) = The (COLOURED–LONG PLAYER) record; can be in a variety of colours including . . . white/ blue/ red/ clear/ purple/ green/ pink/ gold/ silver.

(red-lp) = The (RED VINYL–LONG PLAYER) record would be an example of this.

(7") = The (7 INCH SINGLE). Arrived in the late 50's, and plays at 45 r.p.m. Before this its equivalent was the 10" on 78 r.p.m. Playing time now averages 4 minutes per side, but during the late 50's up to mid-60's, each side averaged 2½ minutes. Punk rock/new wave in 1977/78, resurrected this idea. In the 80's, some disco releases increased playing time. Another idea that was resurrected in 1977 was the picture sleeve. This had been introduced in the 60's, but mostly only in the States.
Note:- Cost in mid-97 was just under £2. Second-hand rarities can cost between 25p to £200, depending again on its condition. These also might contain limited freebies/gifts (i.e. posters, patches, stickers, badges, etc.). Due to the confusion this would cause, I have omitted this information, and kept to the vinyl aspect in this book. Another omission has been DJ promos, demos, acetates, magazine freebies, various artists' compilations, etc. Only official shop releases get a mention.

(7" m) = The (7 INCH MAXI-SINGLE). Named so because of the extra track, mostly on the B-side. Introduced widely during the early 70's; one being ROCKET MAN by ELTON JOHN.

(7" ep) = The (7 INCH EXTENDED PLAY SINGLE). Plays mostly at 33⅓ r.p.m., with average playing time 10–15 minutes and 4 tracks. Introduced in the late 50's as compilations for people to sample their albums. These had a *title* and were also re-introduced in 1977 onwards, but this time for punk groups' new songs.

(d7") = The (DOUBLE 7 INCH SINGLE). Basically just two singles combined . . . 4 tracks. Introduced in the late 70's for the "new wave/romantics", and would cost slightly more than normal equivalent.

(7" pic-d) = The (7 INCH PICTURE-DISC SINGLE). This was vinyl that had a picture on the grooves, which could be viewed through a see-through plastic cover.

(7" sha-pic-d) = The (7 INCH SHAPED-PICTURE-DISC SINGLE). Vinyl as above but with shape (i.e. gun, mask, group) around the edge of the groove. Awkward because it would not fit into the collector's singles box. Initially limited, and this can still be obtained at record fairs for over £3. Note:- However, in the book the type of shape has not been mentioned, due to the lack of space.

(7" coloured) = The (7 INCH COLOURED SINGLE). Vinyl that is not black (i.e. any other colour; red, yellow, etc.). Note:- (7" multi) would be a combination of two or more colours (i.e. pink/purple).

1: **Note: –** Interview long players mainly released on 'Babatak' label, have not been included due to the fact this book only gives artists' music discography.

(7" flexi) = The (7 INCH FLEXIBLE SINGLE). One-sided freebies, mostly given away by magazines, at concerts or as mentioned here; free with single or lp. Worth keeping in mint condition and well protected.

(12") = The (12 INCH SINGLE). Plays at 45 r.p.m., and can have extended or extra tracks to its 7" counterpart (+=) or (++=). B-side's playing speed could be at 33 r.p.m. Playing time could be between 8 and 15 minutes. Introduced in 1977 with the advent of new wave and punk. They were again a must for collectors, for the new wave of British heavy metal scene.

(12" ep) = The (12 INCH EXTENDED PLAY SINGLE). Virtually same as above but *titled* like the 7" ep. Playing time over 12 minutes, and could have between 3 and 5 tracks.

(d12") = The (DOUBLE 12 INCH SINGLE). See double 7". Can become very collectable and would cost new as normal 12", £3.50.

(12" pic-d) = The (12 INCH PICTURE-DISC SINGLE). As with 7" equivalent . . . see above.

(12" sha-pic-d) = The (12 INCH SHAPED-PICTURE-DISC SINGLE). See above 7" equivalent.

(12" colrd) = The (12 INCH COLOURED SINGLE). Not black vinyl . . . see above 7" equivalent.

(10") = The (10 INCH SINGLE). Plays at 45 r.p.m., and like the 12" can have extra tracks (+=). Very collectable, it surfaced in its newer form around the early 80's, and can be obtained in shops at £4. Note:- also (10" ep)/ (d10")/ (10" coloured)/ (10" pic-d)/ (10" sha-pic-d).

CASSETTES

(c) = The (CASSETTE) album . . . size in case 4½ inches high. Playing-time same as lp album, although after the mid-80's cd revolution, some were released with extra tracks. Introduced in the late 60's, to compete with the much bulkier lp. Until the 80's, most cassettes were lacking in group info, lyric sheets, and freebies. Note:- Cost to the consumer as of July 1997 = £9 new. But for a few exceptions, most do not increase in price, and can be bought second-hand or budget-priced for around £6.

(d-c) = The (DOUBLE-CASSETTE) album . . . as above, and would hold same tracks as d-lp or even t-lp. Price between £15 and £20.

(c-s) = The (CASSETTE-SINGLE). Now released mostly with same two tracks as 7" equivalent. The other side played the same 2 or 3 tracks. Introduced unsuccessfully in the US around the late 60's. Re-introduced there and in Britain in the mid-80's. In the States, it and its cd counterpart have replaced the charting 7" single for the 90's. Cost new is around £1–£2.50, and might well become quite collectable.

(c-ep) = The (CASSETTE-EXTENDED PLAY SINGLE). Same as above but *titled* as 12".

COMPACT DISCS

(cd) = The (COMPACT DISC) album. All 5" circular and mostly silver on its groove side. Perspex casing also includes lyrics & info, etc. Introduced late in 1982, and widely the following year (even earlier for classical music). Initially for top recording artists, but now in 1997 nearly every release is in cd format. Playing time normally over 50 minutes and containing extra tracks or mixes. Possible playing time is just under 80 minutes. Marketed as unscratchable, although if they go uncleaned, they will stick just as vinyl. Average price (mid-97) is £15, and will become collectable, possibly early in the next century if, like most predictions, they do not deteriorate with time.

(d-cd) = The (DOUBLE-COMPACT DISC) album . . . same as above although very pricey, between £16 and £25.

(cd-s) = The (COMPACT DISC-SINGLE). Mainly all 5" (but some 3" cd-s could only be played with a compatible gadget inside the normal cd player). Playing time over 15 minutes to average 25 minutes, containing 4 or 5 tracks. Introduced in 1986 to compete with the 12" ep or cassette. 99% contained extra tracks to normal formats. Cost new around over £5.00, which soon rose to over double that, after a couple years of release.

(pic-cd-s) = The (PICTURE-COMPACT DISC-SINGLE). Has picture on disc, which gives it its collectability. Also on (pic-cd-ep).

(vid-pic-s) = The (VIDEO-COMPACT DISC-SINGLE). A video cd, which can be played through stereo onto normal compatible TV screen. Very costly procedure, but still might be the format of the future. Promo videos can be seen on pub juke-boxes, which has made redundant the returning Wurlitzer style.

DIGITAL AUDIO TAPE

(dat) = The (DIGITAL AUDIO TAPE) album. Introduced in the mid-80's, and except for Japan and the rich yuppie, are not widely issued. It is a smaller version of the cassette, with the quality of the cd.

Another format (which I have not included) is the CARTRIDGE, which was available at the same time as the cassette. When the cassette finally won the battle in the early 80's, the cartridge became redundant. All car-owners of the world were happy when thieves made them replace the stolen cartridge player with the resurrected cassette. You can still buy these second-hand, but remember you'll have to obtain a second-hand 20-year-old player, with parts possibly not available.

Other abbreviations: repl. = replaced / comp. = compilation / re-iss. = re-issued / re-dist. = re-distributed

A Very Brief History of Psychedelia

Chambers 20th Century Dictionary definition of the word:–

PSYCHEDELIC: a state of relaxation and pleasure, with heightened perception and increased mental powers generally.

PSYCHEDELIC: visual effects and/or sound effects whose action on the mind is a little like that of psychedelic drugs.

PSYCHEDELIC: dazzling in pattern.

PSYCHEDELIC: drugs which cause, or are believed to cause, the taker to enter such a state.

The last of these has been dismissed from the way I came to select the artists in this book. While the choice to use drugs remains with the individual, I in no way condone the use of psychedelics which, if used the wrong way, can have extremely serious consequences.

The term 'psychedelic' means different things to different people. Whatever definition you favour, there's no shying away from the fact that the term is inextricably linked with drugs (or LSD, to be more specific), as is the music. You could argue that psychedelic music has existed for thousands of years in the form of ethnic religious music, whether it be the tribal chanting of the Native American Indians or the drone of the sitar. In the same way, psychedelic drugs are nothing new either; mushrooms, peyote etc. have probably been around as long as man himself, it's just that, until recently (well, earlier this century), there was no neatly encompassing term to file them under. That honour fell to one HUMPHRY OSMOND, a British psychiatrist who did some fine work in the field of LSD research, experimenting with the drug as a possible cure for alcoholism (there's hope for you yet, Martin). This man came up with the following little ditty to describe the ups and downs of the everyday, household trip, inventing the term 'psychedelic' in the process: 'To fathom hell or soar angelic, just take a pinch of psychedelic'. Profound sentiments indeed, but it's unlikely that OSMOND could've foreseen just how many people would take him at his word. Arguably, there could've been no psychedelic revolution without LSD and that's where ALBERT HOFFMANN comes in. Probably the only boffin ever celebrated in song, his infamous bike ride was documented by such unboffin-type bands as The BEACH BOYS ('I JUST WASN'T MADE FOR THESE TIMES') and TOMORROW ('MY WHITE BICYCLE'). Basically, the man had synthesized a unique hallucinogenic from lysergic acid, LSD-25, duly casting himself in the role of guinea pig. On the 19th of April 1963, after dissolving the drug in a glass of water, he saddled up for a rather unadvised bike ride home and...well, you can imagine the rest. The drug soon proliferated among the therapeutic/scientific community, eventually finding its way into the hands of the bohemian set. Among the warriors of the LSD vanguard were AL HUBBARD and MICHAEL HOLLINGSHEAD although it was TIMOTHY LEARY who probably did more than anyone to spread the gospel. After his pioneering research project at Harvard was eventually shut down, LEARY made it his mission to convert America, coining the tired phrase, 'Turn on, tune in, drop out'. And that was exactly what a generation of young people did, including those who were musically inclined. As the dope-smoking, jazz-loving, folk-protesting 'Beatniks' of the 50's were exposed to the delights/torture of LSD, an embryonic 'hippy' scene began to form, the name a derogatory term derived from the Beat slang, 'hip'. The hippies themselves preferred the term 'Head' or 'Freak', 'scenes' springing up all over America, the largest (and most famous) being in San Francisco. As bands who had previously been playing blues, folk, jug-band music, R&B etc., began to experiment with the drug, they sought to replicate the LSD experience with their music; psychedelic rock was born. In 1965, writer KEN KESEY (who had earlier taken part in LEARY's drug trials at Harvard) and his self-proclaimed bunch of merry pranksters dreamed up a novel way of transforming upstanding American citizens into inner-space cadets: the 'Acid Test'. Often held at KESEY's ranch, these multimedia events sought to bombard the participant with as much sensory overload as they could muster, including taped messages, strobes and a proto-psychedelic band called The Warlocks. Soon changing their name to The GRATEFUL DEAD, they were one of the most readily identifiable and enduring bands to come out of the Bay Area scene, their live shows and massive cult following becoming a phenomenon. Over in L.A., the BYRDS had already hit No.1 in the summer of '65 with a reworking of BOB DYLAN's 'MR. TAMBOURINE MAN', the dreamy, chiming guitars adding a psychedelic edge to DYLAN's already ambiguous lyrics, and while the band insisted that 'EIGHT MILES HIGH' wasn't a drug song, it's soaring harmonies and crashing guitar came close to reproducing the psychic rollercoaster ride of an LSD trip. Another hotbed of psychedelic activity was Austin, Texas, where bands like 13TH FLOOR

ELEVATORS and RED CRAYOLA were developing a much darker take on the genre, The ELEVATORS' ROKY ERICKSON later joining the alternative rock'n'roll hall of fame alongside SYD BARRETT, PETER GREEN, BRIAN WILSON etc. The latter was profoundly affected by the drug, and while it undoubtedly contributed to his deteriorating mental condition, it also inspired him to create The BEACH BOYS' masterpiece, 'PET SOUNDS'. Across the Atlantic, meanwhile, The BEATLES came up with their trippy meisterwork, 'REVOLVER'. Ironically, just as the effect of LSD on rock was bearing its most creative fruit, the drug was made illegal in America on October 7th, 1966. However, rather than stifling the burgeoning psychedelic scene, it seemed that more bands than ever were taking a trip into the unknown. While the States produced such diverse psychedelic innovators as The VELVET UNDERGROUND, The DOORS, LOVE, JEFFERSON AIRPLANE and Blighty-bound JIMI HENDRIX, Britain's dayglo ambassadors of the new counter-culture were PINK FLOYD. Fronted by the aforementioned SYD BARRETT, the band unleashed two tripped out classic 45's in 'ARNOLD LAYNE' and 'SEE EMILY PLAY', which preceded their kaleidoscopic debut album, 'THE PIPER AT THE GATES OF DAWN'. 1967, the year of flower-power and the fabled summer of love, was when all things psychedelic came to a head. By this point, the phenomenon had taken over the pop mainstream, The MONKEES, The MAMAS & THE PAPAS, SCOTT McKENZIE, The LEMON PIPERS and The LOVIN' SPOONFUL all having top hits on both sides of the Atlantic. At its height, The BEATLES released their crowning glory of the whole era with 'SGT. PEPPER'. Even rivals The STONES got in on the psychedelic act with 'THEIR SATANIC MAJESTIES REQUEST' later that year. Perhaps the most interesting British example of psychedelic experimentation came with the wigged-out folk of The INCREDIBLE STRING BAND (yes, psychedelia even reached the frozen north, i.e. Scotland). However, their appeal didn't stretch to the pop charts, where The KINKS, The WHO, The SMALL FACES, The ANIMALS and The YARDBIRDS had progressed from their R&B roots into psychedelic rock/pop. Back in the USA, artists such as FRANK ZAPPA and CAPTAIN BEEFHEART used the psychedelic scene as a vehicle for their warped avant-garde outings. 1968 saw rock getting heavier, STEPPENWOLF and IRON BUTTERFLY churning out riff-laden monsters, although their psychedelic influences were still glaringly obvious nonetheless. Soul music was also getting heavier, The CHAMBERS BROTHERS, The TEMPTATIONS and SLY & THE FAMILY STONE taking their cue from HENDRIX and cooking up a hard-hitting psychedelic stew which addressed issues of race and inequality. GEORGE CLINTON later took this equation to its ultimate funky conclusion with FUNKADELIC, PARLIAMENT, etc. In Britain, there emerged another interesting by-product in the shape of progressive rock, which mixed psychedelia with harder-edged, mellotron-laden experimentation. Following SYD BARRETT's untimely departure, PINK FLOYD evolved into the movement's flagbearer. Other outfits that were (sometimes unfairly) labelled under the prog-rock banner were YES, KING CRIMSON and EMERSON, LAKE & PALMER (GENESIS were to emerge a little later). And thus the 70's took shape, the star-spangled optimism of the 60's being replaced by bloated, over-indulgent decadence. By this time, LSD had fallen out of favour with the rock elite, although the echoes of the previous decade were still apparent in much of the musical output of the day. Progressive/Experimental rock took a particularly firm foothold in Europe, especially Germany where groups like TANGERINE DREAM, CAN and KRAFTWERK were pioneering electronic rock music. Back in the UK, glam-rock was dominating the charts, ROXY MUSIC uniquely managing to combine effortless pop hooks and bolder experimentation (on their first two albums at least). One of the band's prime movers, BRIAN ENO, soon ventured into more oblique ambient territory after a couple of more accessible solo outings. ENO was the catalyst in BOWIE's 1977 attempts to move into more leftfield experimentation, 'LOW' and 'HEROES' providing a laid-back alternative to the breakneck onslaught of punk. This musical phenomenon arose as a direct result of the overbearing pompousness of mid 70's rock, psychedelic experimentation going into enforced hibernation while punk/new wave ruled the airwaves. (See SECTION II for post-punk psychedelic activities.)

* * *

AFFINITY

Formed: England . . . late 60's by LINDA HOYLE and lads below. Signed to progressive label 'Vertigo' in 1970, but their jazz-fusion album, did little but become a collectors item later in life. LINDA HOYLE went solo but with a more introspective jazz feel. Her 1971 album 'PIECES OF ME' has also become a rare piece and can fetch over £100. • **Songwriters:** Group except; ELI'S COMING (Janis Ian) / ALL ALONG THE WATCHTOWER (Bob Dylan). HOYLE covered LONELY WOMAN (Laura Nyro) / BACKLASH BLUES (Nina Simone).

Recommended: AFFINITY (*6)

LINDA HOYLE – vocals / **LYNTON NAIFF** – organ / **MIKE JOPP** – guitar / **MO FOSTER** – bass / **GRANT SERPELL** – drums

Vertigo — not issued

Jun 70. (7") *(6059 007)* **I WONDER IF I CARE AS MUCH. / THREE SISTERS** [ ] [-]

Jun 70. (lp) *(6360 004)* **AFFINITY** [ ] [-]
– I am and so are you / Night flight / I wonder if I care as much / Mr. Joy / Three sisters / Coconut Grove / All along the watchtower. *(cd-iss.1994 on 'Repertoire'+=; REP 4349)*– Eli's coming / United states of mind.

1970. (7") *(6059 018)* **ELI'S COMING. / UNITED STATES OF MIND** [ ] [-]

—— Disbanded soon after above. SERPELL joined SAILOR and NAIFF gigged with TOE FAT and KILLING FLOOR.

– compilations, etc. –

Apr 97. (cd) *Music & Arts; (CD 940)* **THIS IS OUR LUNCH** [ ] [-]

LINDA HOYLE

—— went solo, w/ **JOHN MARSHALL** – drums + **KARL JENKINS** – piano, oboe + **CHRIS SPEDDING** – guitar + **JEFF CLYNE** – bass (all of NUCLEUS) / **COLIN PURBROOK** – piano

Vertigo — not issued

Dec 71. (lp) *(6360 060)* **PIECES OF ME** [ ] [-]
– Backlash blues / Paper tulips / Black crow / For my darling / Pieces of me / Lonely women / Hymn to Valerie Solanas / The ballad of Marty Mole / Journey's end / Morning for one / Barrelhouse music.

—— She later moved to Canada, and married PETE KING.

AGITATION FREE

Formed: Berlin, Germany . . .1967 from the ashes of two German beat groups. Tutored by avant-garde composer THOMAS KESSLER, a final line-up was formed in 1971 and the group undertook a Middle Eastern tour financed by the 'Goethe Institute'. The debut album, 'MALESCH' (1972), was heavily influenced by their trip, containing recordings of native musicians they'd played with on the tour. Combining eastern inflections, electronic experimentation and hypnotic hammond organ, the album was a progressive classic. '2ND' (1973) was just as accomplished if a little more subtle and atmospheric. After more personnel upheaval, the band split in 1974. A posthumous album was released a couple of years later entitled 'LAST'.

Recommended: MALESCH (*9) / 2ND (*7) / LAST (*7)

LUTZ ULBRICH – guitar, zither, organ / **MICHAEL GUNTHER** – bass / **JORG SCHWENKE** – guitar; repl. AX GENRICH, who joined GURU GURU / **BURGHARD RAUSCH** – drums; repl. GERD KLEMKE, who had repl. CHRISTOPH FRANKE, who joined TANGERINE DREAM / **MICHAEL HONIG** – keyboards; repl. LUTZ KRAMER / guests **ULI POPP** – bongos / **PETER-MICHAEL HAMEL** – hammond organ

Vertigo — not issued

1972. (lp) *(6360 607)* **MALESCH** [-] [-] German
– You play for us today / Sahara city / Ala Tul / Pulse / Khan El Khalili / Malesch / Ruckssturz. *(cd-iss.1990's on 'Spalax';)*

—— **STEFAN DIEZ** – drums; repl. SCHWENKE who quit due to drug problem

—— added, but only until the recording of 2nd; **DIETMAR BURMEISTER** – drums (yes another) (ex-ASH RA TEMPEL)

Nov 73. (lp) *(6360 615)* **2ND** [-] [-] German
– First communication / Dialogue and random / Laila (part 1 & 2) / In the silence of the morning sunrise / A quiet walk: Listening – Two – Not of the same king / Haunted island. *(cd-iss.1990's on 'Spalax';)*

—— **GUSTAV LUTJENS** – guitar, repl. DIEZ who became jazz guitarist

—— LUTJENS was soon repl. by the returning **JORG SCHWENKE** – guitar

—— disbanded late 1974, although one more recording surfaced below

Barclay — not issued

1976. (lp) *(80612)* **LAST** [-] [-] France
– / Looping IV. *(cd-iss.1990's on 'Spalax';)*

—— ULBRICH joined ASH RA TEMPEL in 1975. HONIG joined TANGERINE DREAM, KLAUS SCHULZE (a colloboration) before he went solo in 1978 'DEPARTURE FROM THE NORTHERN WASTELANDS' for 'Warners' *K 56464)*. Nine/Ten years later, he released follow-up 'XCEPT ONE' for 'Cinema'; *(7469191)*, then film soundtrack 'THE BLOB' on cd. RAUSCH became a professional DJ, also writing pop songs. In 1997, he and MANUEL GOTTSCH had 'EARLY WATER' released by 'Spalax'; *14536)*

– compilations, etc. –

1995. (cd) *Musique Intemporelle;* **FRAGMENTS** (unreleased) [-] [-] German

Jan AKKERMAN (see under ⇒ FOCUS)

Daevid ALLEN (see under ⇒ GONG)

ALQUIN

Formed: Netherlands . . .early 70's by FERNINAND BAKKER, DICK FRANSSEN, JOB TARENSKEEN, and others below, who signed to 'Polydor'. A group of diverse progressive rock & jazz leanings. Their debut saw them sound like FOCUS, KING CRIMSON, YES, BEATLES, etc. A more self-inspired follow-up in 1973, was laid aside, when releasing the funkier 'NOBODY CAN WAIT FOREVER'. Roger Bain produced their 1974 lp, which was also released in the States. BAKKER's off-shoot band The METEORS, were not the same as UK punkabilly group of the same name.

Recommended: MARKS (*5) / THE MOUNTAIN QUEEN (*5)

FERDINAND BAKKER – guitar, keyboards, vocals / **DICK FRANSSEN** – keyboards / **RONALD OTTENHOFF** – horns / **HEIN MARS** – bass / **PAUL WESTRATE** – drums / **JOB TARENSKEEN** – percussion, saxes

Polydor — R.C.A.

1972. (lp) *(2480 152)* **MARKS** [ ] [-]
– Oriental journey / The least you could do is send me some flowers / Soft Royce / Mr.Barnum Jr.'s magnificent & fabulous city (live) / I wish I could / You always can change / Marc's occasional showers / Catherine's wig.

1973. (lp) *(2480 179)* **THE MOUNTAIN QUEEN** [ ] [-]
– The dance / Soft-eyed woman / Convicts of the air / Mountain queen / Mr. Barnum Jr's magnificent and fabulous city / Don and Dewey.

—— added **MICHAEL VAN DIJK** – vocals (ex-EKSEPTION)

1974. (lp) *(2480 262)* *<APLI 1061>* **NOBODY CAN WAIT FOREVER** [ ] [ ] 1975
– New Guinea sunrise: Sunrise – Wake me up / Mr. Widow / Stranger: stranger – You might as well fall / Darling superstar / Farewell, Miss Barcelona / Wheel-chair groupie / Revolution's eye: Revolution's theme – Nobody can wait forever.

1975. (7") *<10414>* **MR. WIDOW. / STRANGER** [-] [ ]

—— now a 5-piece, when WESTRATE + MARS departed.

1975. (lp) *(2646 101)* **CRASH** [ ] [-]

1976. (lp) *(2925 045)* **BEST KEPT SECRET** [ ] [-]

—— added **JAN VISSER** – bass

1976. (lp) *(2441 067)* **ON TOUR (live)** [ ] [-]
– New Guinea sunrise: Sunrise – Wake me up / L.A. / Rendezvous / The dance / Amy / I wish I could / Wheel-chair groupie.

—— Disbanded after release of above. BAKKER and TARENSKEEN formed The METEORS who signed to 'EMI', releasing three albums, the first of which was 'TEENAGE HEART' (1979).

AMBOY DUKES (see under ⇒ NUGENT, Ted)

AMERICAN BLUES

Formed: Dallas, Texas, USA . . . 1967 as The WARLOCKS by DUSTY HILL, ROCKY HILL and FRANK BEARD. The latter had met the brothers after they had watched him drumming for The CELLAR DWELLERS at Pat Kirkwood's local Fort Worth Cellar nightclub. They had cut one Merseybeat-type 45 in 1967, 'BAD DAY' / 'CALL' for the independent 'Steffek' label <1921>. The WARLOCKS were a weird outfit, who were known to take lots of speed and dye their hair blue. They released 3 very limited-edition 45's, before they appropriately renamed themselves AMERICAN BLUES. An album of part psychedelia, part heavy blues was soon gathering attention, leading to a deal with 'Uni' and a second, more blues orientated album. In 1970, DUSTY and FRANK found BILLY GIBBONS, forming the megabucks band ZZ TOP.

Recommended: AMERICAN BLUES IS HERE (*6) / DO THEIR THING (*5)

DUSTY HILL – vocals, bass / **ROCKY HILL** – guitar / **FRANK BEARD** – drums (ex-CELLAR DWELLERS)

not issued Paradise

1968. (7"; as WARLOCKS) <1017> **IF YOU REALLY WANT ME TO STAY. / GOOD TIME TRIPPIN'** -

1968. (7"; as WARLOCKS) <1021> **SPLASH DAY. / LIFE'S A MYSTERY** -

not issued Ara

1968. (7"; as WARLOCKS) <1915> **ANOTHER YEAR. / POOR KID** -

— added **DOUG DAVIS** – guitar, keyboards

not issued Karma

1968. (lp) <1001> **AMERICAN BLUES IS HERE** -
– If I were a carpenter / All I saw was you / She'll be mine / Fugue for Lady Cheriff / It's gone / Keep my heart in a rage / Mercury blues / Melted like snow / Mellow.

1969. (7") <101> **IF I WERE A CARPENTER. / ALL I SAW WAS YOU** -

— now without DAVIS

not issued Uni

1969. (lp) <73004> **AMERICAN BLUES DO THEIR THING** -
– You were so close to me / Wonder man / Just plain Jane / Shady / Captain Fire / Chocolate ego / Nightmare of a wise man / Dreams / Softly to the sun. *(UK-iss.Jul87 on 'See For Miles'; SEE 99)*

— of course it's well documented that DUSTY and FRANK teamed up with BILLY GIBBONS to form ZZ TOP

AMON DUUL

Formed: Essen, Germany . . .1967 as a communal outfit, which split two ways the following year, after appearing at Song Days Festival in Essen alongside FRANK ZAPPA's MOTHERS OF INVENTION and The FUGS. While some members formed the more musical AMON DUUL II, releasing material outside Germany, AMON DUUL concentrated solely on their homeland. The prime movers behind this loosely based outfit were RAINER BAUER and ULLRICH LEOPOLD, who provided much of the material for their tentative debut 'PSYCHEDELIC UNDERGROUND' (1969). Politically-driven acid-rock, both repetitive & percussive with lengthy unproduced jams, the band's style had much in common with US outfit RED CRAYOLA. While AMON DUUL II gained a cult following, spreading to Britain in the early 70's, this lot were happy to remain relatively obscure and anonymous. After a disappointing second set, 'COLLAPSING', they returned with the more folky flavoured 'PARADIESWARTS DUUL' in 1971. This was effectively the band's swan song, after which some members moved onto AMON DUUL II.

Recommended: PSYCHEDELIC UNDERGROUND (*5) / PARADIESWARTS DUUL (*6)

RAINER BAUER – vocals, guitar / **ULRICH LEOPOLD** – bass / **WOLFGANG KRISCHKE** – percussion, piano / **ELLA BAUER (ELEONORA ROMANA)** – percussion, vocals / **HELGA FILANDA** – percussion, vocals / **ANGELICA FILANDA** – percussion, vocals / **USCHI OBERMAIER** – maracas / **PETER LEOPOLD** – drums

Metrognome not issued

1969. (lp) *(MLP 15332)* **PSYCHEDELIC UNDERGROUND** - - German
– Ein wunderhuebsches maedchen traeumt von Sandosa / Kaskados minnelied / Mama Duul und ihre sauerkrautband spielt auf / Im garten Sandosa / Der garten Sandosa im Morgentau / Bitterlings verwandlung. *(re-iss.1970's as 'THIS IS AMON DUUL'; 200146) (UK-iss.Jul80 as 'MINNELIED' on 'Brain'; 0040 149) <US-iss.1974 on 'Prophecy'> (cd-iss.Nov95 on 'Captain Trip'; CTCD 021) (cd-iss.Apr97 on 'Spalax'; 14947) (UK cd-iss.Jun97 on 'Repertoire'; REP 4616WY)*

— now w/ out PETER who joined AMON DUUL II

1969. (lp) *(SMLP 012)* **COLLAPSING** - - German
– Booster / Bass gestrichen / Tusch ff / Singvogel ruckwarts / Lua-lua-he / Shattering and fading / Nachrichten aus Cambistan / Big sound / Krawall / Blech und aufbau / Natur.

— **KLAUS ESSER** – guitar repl. WOLFGANG, ANGELIKA + USCHI

Ohr not issued

1970. (7") *(OS 57.000)* **ETERNAL FLOW. / PARAMECHANICAL WORLD** - - German

1971. (lp) *(56.008)* **PARADIESWARTS DUUL** - - German
– Love is peace / Show your thirst and Sun your open mouth / Paramechanische welt. *(cd-iss.Oct95 on 'Captain Trip'; CTCD 017)*

— originals re-formed

BASF not issued

1973. (d-lp) *(29 29079-8)* **DISASTER – LUUD NOMA** (out-takes) - - German
– Drum things / Asynchron / Yea yea yea / Broken / Somnium / Frequency / Autognomes / Chaoticolour / Expressiondiom / Attitude / Impropulsion. *(re-iss.1985 as 'EXPERIMENTE' on 'Timewind' Germany; DB 50142)*

— disbanded soon after above

– compilations, etc –

Aug 87. (lp/cd) *Thunderbolt; (THBL/CDTB 043)* **AIRS ON A SHOESTRING** -
– Hymn for the hardcore / Pioneer / One moments anger is two pints of blood / Marcus Leid / Olaf. *(cd re-iss.Apr97 on 'Spalax'; 14515)*

AMON DUUL II

Formed: Munich, Germany ... Autumn 1968 from the original AMON DUUL commune. While the aforesaid outfit remained as a separate musical entity, CHRIS KARRER set-up AMON DUUL II with JOHANNES WEINZIERL, FALK-ULRICH ROGNER, RENATE KNAUP, CHRISTIAN 'SHRAT' THIERFELD an DIETER SERFAS. Securing a deal with 'Liberty', they released their first album in 1969, 'PHALLUS DEI' (God's Penis), which introduced a further two members, PETER LEOPOLD (from AMON DUUL I) and Englishman DAVE ANDERSON. Avant-garde space-rock in the mould of PINK FLOYD and GRATEFUL DEAD, the album brought home-produced, psychedelic improvisation to the German market. 'YETI', the follow-up in 1970, was a much more structured double-set featuring some excellent acid-rock numbers including the weird but wonderful single 'ARCHANGEL'S THUNDERBIRD'. Their next effort, 'DANCE OF THE LEMMINGS' (1971), concentrated more on lengthy, segued collages, including the outrageously brilliant, 'SYNTELMAN'S MARCH OF THE ROARING SEVENTIES'. With members coming and going at their leisure, it was difficult for the band to maintain any degree of consistancy and records like 'CARNIVAL IN BABYLON' (1972), 'WOLF CITY' (1972), etc, sounded uninspired in comparison to their earlier work. Even a deal with 'Atlantic' in 1974, failed to result in a return to form. The band still exist today, WEINZEIRL having brought back past members KARRER, ROGNER, RENATE, LEOPOLD and MEID for Christmas concerts in 1992. • **Trivia:** AMON DUUL II members guested on releases by POPOL VUH and EMBRYO.

Recommended: PHALLUS DEI (*6) / YETI (*8) / DANCE OF THE LEMMINGS (*6) / WOLF CITY (*6) / ANTHOLOGY (*7)

JOHN WEINZIERL – lead guitar, vocals / **RENATE KNAUP-KROTENSCHWANZ** – vocals / **CHRIS KARRER** – violin, guitar, vocals, sax / **FALK-U ROGNER** – keyboards, synthesizers / **DAVE ANDERSON** – bass / **SCHRAT** (b. CHRISTIAN THIELE) – bongos, vocals / **PETER LEOPOLD** – drums / **DIETER SERFAS** – drums and guests / **HOLGER TRULZSCH** – percussion / **CHRISTIAN BUCHARD** – vibes

Liberty Liberty

1969. (lp) *(LSB 83279)* **PHALLUS DEI** -
– Kanaan / Dem guten' Schonen, wahren / Luzifers ghilom / Henriette Kroten schwantz / Phallus dei. *(re-iss.Feb72 on 'Sunset'; SLS 50257) (cd-iss.Nov92 on 'Repertoire' Germany; REP 4274-WY) (cd re-iss.Apr97 on 'Mantra'; MANTRA 012)*

— now without SERFAS, but with new guests **ULRICH LEOPOLD** – bass / **RAINER BAUER** – guitar, vocals (both of other AMON DUUL)

1970. (7") *(15355)* **SOAP SHOP ROCK. / ARCHANGEL'S THUNDERBIRD** - - German

1970. (7") *(15417)* **RATTLESNAKE PLUMCAKE. / BETWEEN THE EYES** - - German

1971. (7") *(15468)* **LIGHT. / LEMMINGMANIA** - - German

Sep 70. (7") *(LBF 15355)* **ARCANGEL'S THUNDERBIRD. / BURNING SISTER** -

Nov 70. (d-lp) *(LSP 101)* **YETI** -
– Soda shop rock; (a) Burning sister / (b) Halluzination guillotine / (c) Gulp a sonata / (d) Flesh-coloured anti-aircraft alarm / She came through the chimney / Archangel's thunderbird / Cerberus / The return of Ruebezahl / Eye-shaking king / Pale gallery / Yeti (improvisation) / Yeti talks to Yogi (improvisation) / Sandoz in the rain (improvisation). *(cd-iss.Nov92 on 'Repertoire' Germany; REP 4275)*

— **LOTHAR MEID** – bass, vocals repl. ANDERSON who joined HAWKWIND

— **KARL-HEINZ HAUSMANN** – keyboards repl. SCHRAT who formed SAMETI / added guests / **JIMMY JACKSON** – mellotron / **AL GROMER** – sitar / **HENRIETTE KROTENSCHWANZ** – vocals / **ROLF ZACHER** – vocals

U.A. U.A.

Jun 71. (d-lp) *(UAD 60003-4)* **DANCE OF THE LEMMINGS**
– Syntelman's march of the roaring seventies: (a) In the glass garden – (b) Pull down your mask – (c) Prayer to the silence – (d) Telephonecomplex / (a) Restless skylight – transistor child – Landing in a ditch – (b) Dehypnotized toothpaste – (c) A short stop to the Transylvanian brain surgery / Race from here to your ears: (a) Little tornados – (b) Overheated tiara – (c) The flyweighted five – (d) Riding on a cloud – (e) Paralized Paradise – (f) H.G. Well's take off / Chamsin soundtrack; The Marilyn Monroe memorial church / Chewing gum telegram / Stumbling over melted moonlight / Toxicological whispering. *(cd-iss.Nov92 on 'Repertoire' Germany; REP 4276-WY)*

— added **D. SECUNDUS FICHELSCHER** – drums, congas

Apr 72. (lp) *(UAG 29327)* **CARNIVAL IN BABYLON**
– C.I.D. in Urik / All the years round / Shimmering sands / Kronwinkl 12 / Tables are turned / Hawknose harlequin.

1972. (7") *(UA 35338)* **ALL THE YEARS ROUND. / TABLES ARE TURNED** - - German

— now w/ out HAUSMANN

Nov 72. (lp) *(UAG 29406)* **WOLF CITY**
– Surrounded by the stars / Jail-house frog / Green-bubble-raincoated man / Wolf city / Wie der wind am ende einer strasse / Deutsch Nepal / Sleepwalker's timeless bridge. *(cd-iss.Apr97 on 'Mantra'; MANTRA 013)*

1973. (lp) *(USP 102)* **LIVE IN LONDON (live)**
– Archangels thunderbird / Eye shaking king / Soap shop rock / Improvisation / Syntelman's march of the roaring seventies: (a) Pull down your mask – (b) Prayer to the silence – (c) Telephonecomplex) / (a) Restless skylight – Transistor child – Landing in a ditch – (b) Dehypnotized toothpaste – (c) A short stop at the Transylvanian brain surgery / Race from here to your ears: (a) Little tornadoes – (b) Riding on a cloud (c) Paralized paradise.

— **ROBBY HEIBL** – bass repl. MEID (although he later returned)

1974. (lp) *(UAS 29504)* **VIVE LA TRANCE**
– A morning excuse / Fly united / Jalousie / Im krater bluhn weider die baume / Mozambique (dedicated to Monika Ertt) / Apocalyptic bore / Dr. Trap / Pigman / Manana / Ladies mimikry.

1974. (7") *(UA 35466)* <419> **PIGMAN. / MOZAMBIQUE** - German

— **ROBBY HEIBL** returned to replace MEID, KRAMPER and SECUNDUS

— (signed to 'Nova' in Germany)

Atlantic Atco

1975. (lp) *(K 50136)* **HIJACK** -
– I can't wait (parts 1 & 2) / Mirror / Traveller / You're not alone / Explode like a star / Da Guadeloop / Lonely woman / Liquid whisper / Archy the robot.

1975. (7") *(6.11579)* **MIRROR. / LIQUID WHISPER** - - German

1975. (d-lp) *(K 50182)* **MADE IN GERMANY** - -

– Dreams / Ludwig / The king's chocolate waltz / Blue grotto / 5.5.55 / Emigrant song / La krautoma / Metropolis / Loosey girls / Gala gnome / Top of the mud / Mr.Kraut's jinx.

— **KARRER, WEINZIERL** and **LEOPOLD** were joined by **KLAUS EBART** – bass who repl. ROGNER and **STEFAN ZAUNER** – keyboards repl. KNAUP and BALDERSON

1976. (lp) *(622 890)* **PYRAGONY X** - - German
– Flower of the Orient / Merlin / Crystal hexagram / Lost in space / Sally the seducer / Telly vision / The only thing / Capuccino.

1977. (lp) *(623 305)* **ALMOST ALIVE** - - German
– One blue morning / Goodbye my love / Ain't today tomorrow's yesterday / Hallelujah / Feeling uneasy / Live in Jericho.

— now w/out WEINZIERL

— (signed to 'Strand' in Germany)

Vinyl — not issued

Jan 79. (lp) *(LV 1004)* **ONLY HUMAN** -
– Another morning / Don't turn to stone / Kirk Morgan / Spaniards & spacemen / Kismet / Pharaoh / Ruby lane.

1979. (7") *(6.12459)* **DON'T TURN TO STONE. / SPANIARDS & SPACEMEN** - - German

— line-up **CHRIS KARRER / RENATE ASCHAUER KNAUP / JOERG EVERS** – bass, guitar, synthesizers / **DANIEL FICHELSCHER** – drums, percussion / **FALK ROGNER** – synth / plus **JOHN WEINZIERI** – guitar / **LOTHAR MEID** – bass / **STEFAN ZAUNER** – piano, synth

Telefunken — not issued

1981. (lp) *(624 852)* **VORTEX** - - German
– Vortex / Holy west / Die 7 fetten Jahr / Wings of the wind / Mona / We are machines / Das gestern ist das heute von Morgen / Vibes in the air.

— Broke-up but reformed in the 80's with line-up below **JOHN WEINZIERL, DAVE ANDERSON, JULIE WAREING** – vocals / **ROBERT CALVERT** – vocals / **GUY EVANS** – drums (ex-VAN DER GRAAF GENERATOR)

Illuminated — not issued

Jan 83. (lp) *(JAMS 024)* **HAWK MEETS PENGUIN** -
– One moment of anger is two pints of blood / Meditative music from the third o before the producers pt.1 & 2. *(re-iss.as 'HAWK MEETS PENGUIN VOL.1' Dec85 on 'Demi-Monde'; DM 04) (cd-iss.1992 on 'Thunderbolt'; CDTB 102) (cd re-iss.Apr97 on 'Spalax'; 14848)*

Jan 85. (lp) *(JAMS 27)* **MEETING WITH MEN MACHINES** -
– Pioneer / Old one / Marcus lied / Song / Things aren't always what they seem / Burundi drummer's nightmare. *(re-iss.1985 on 'Demi-Monde'; DM 006) (cd-iss.Mar93 on 'Thunderbolt'; CDTB 107) (cd re-iss.Jun97 on 'Spalax'; 14820)*

Demi-Monde — not issued

Jan 89. (lp) *(DMLP 1013)* **FOOL MOON** -
– Fool moon / Tribe / Tik tok song / Haupmotor / Hymn for the hardcore. *(cd-iss.Nov89 on 'The CD Label'; CDTL 011) (cd re-iss.Jun97 on 'Spalax'; 14516)*

May 89. (lp; AMON DUUL & BOB CALVERT) *(DMLP 1015)* **DIE LOSUNG** -
– Big wheel / Urban Indian / Adrenalin rush / Visions of fire / Drawn to the flame / They call it home / Die losung / Drawn to the flame (part 2). *(cd-iss.Jun89 on 'The CD Label'; CDTL 009)*

— disbanded again, but re-formed for gigs late 1992 with **KARRER, WEINZIERL, ROGNER, RENATE, LEOPOLD & MEID**

Mantra — not issued

Jun 93. (cd) **SURROUNDED BY THE STARS / BARS** -
-

Mystic — not issued

Aug 96. (cd) *(MYS 106CD)* **NADA MOONSHINE** -

– compilations, others –

May 75. (lp) *United Artists; (UAS 29723)* **LEMMINGMANIA** -

Mar 87. (d-lp) *Raw Power; (RAWLP 032)* **ANTHOLOGY** -
– Soup shock rock / Burning sister / Halluzination guillotine / Gulp a sonata / Flesh-coloured anti-aircraft alarm / Kanaan / Trap / Phallus dei / Yet (improvisation) / Wolf city / C.I.D. in Uruk / Morning excuse / Apocalyptic bone / Jailhouse frog.

Nov 92. (cd) *Windsong; (WINCD 026)* **LIVE IN CONCERT (live BBC '73)** -

UTOPIA

WEINZIERI, MEID, KROTEN SCHWANTZ, FICHELSCHER, OLAF KUSLER (producer) / **ROGNER, KARRER**

U.A. — U.A.

1973. (lp) *(UAG 29438)* **UTOPIA** -
– What you gonna do / The Wolf-man Jack show / Alice / Las Vegas / Deutsch Nepal / Utopiat No. 1 / Nasi Goreng / Jazz kiste.

ANCIENT GREASE (see under ⇒ EYES OF BLUE)

Ian ANDERSON (see under ⇒ JETHRO TULL)

Jon ANDERSON (see under ⇒ YES)

ANDERSON BRUFORD WAKEMAN HOWE (see under ⇒ YES)

ANDROMEDA

Formed: London, England . . . 1966 as an R&B acid-rock act fronted by JOHN CANN, they released a self-titled album in 1969 for 'R.C.A.'. However, CANN took off for ATOMIC ROOSTER and later formed HARD STUFF. This trio were around for two albums between 1972 and 1973, before CANN returned to ATOMIC ROOSTER. Under the pseudonym of JOHN DU CANN, he later had a one-off Top 40 pop hit with 'DON'T BE A DUMMY' (1979).

Recommended: ANDROMEDA (*7)

JOHN CANN – guitar, vocals (ex-ATTACK) / **MICK HAWKSWORTH** – bass, vocals / **IAN McSHANE** – drums

R.C.A. — not issued

Jul 69. (7") *(RCA 1854)* **GO YOUR WAY. / KEEP OUT 'COS I'M DYING** -

1969. (lp) *(SF 8031)* **ANDROMEDA** -
– Too old / Day of the change / And now the Sun shines / Gold and silver turns to dust: 1. Discovery, 2. Sanctuary, 3. Determination / Return to sanity: 1. Breakdown, 2. Hope, 3. Conclusion / Reason / I can stop the Sun / When to stop: 1. Traveller, 2. Turning point, 3. Journey's end. *(cd-iss.Jun97 on 'Second Battle'; SB 042)*

— Disbanded at the end of 60's. HAWKSWORTH formed FUZZY DUCK, before he joined TEN YEARS AFTER. CANN joined ATOMIC ROOSTER, before forming HARD STUFF.

– compilations, etc. –

1990. (lp) *Music Mixture; (MM 026)* **7 LONELY STREET** -

Nov 94. (cd) *Kissing Spell; (KSCD 9592)* **ANTHOLOGY 1966-1969** -
(re-iss.Jun97; same)

Nov 95. (cd) *Kissing Spell; (KSCD 9594)* **ANDROMEDA** (sessions, demos from 67-68) -

1995. (lp) *Kissing Spell; (KSLP 9597)* **LIVE 1967** -

HARD STUFF

JOHN CANN – guitar, vocals, cello / **JOHN GUSTAFSON** – bass, piano, vocals (ex-BIG THREE, ex-MERSEYBEATS, ex-QUARTERMASS) / **PAUL HAMMOND** – drums (ex-ATOMIC ROOSTER)

Purple — Mercury

Jan 72. (lp) *(TPSA 7505)* <663> **BULLET PROOF**
– Jay time / Sinister minister / No witch at all / Taken alive / Time gambler (Rodney) / Millionaire / Monster in Paradise / Hobo / Mr. Longevity / R.I.P. / The provider (part 1).

Apr 72. (7") *(PUR 103)* **THE ORCHESTRATOR. / JAY TIME** -

Nov 73. (lp) *(TPSA 7507)* **BOLEX DEMENTIA** -
– Roll a rocket / Libel / Ragman / Spiders web / Get lost / Sick'n'tired / Mermany / Jumpin' thumpin' (ain't that somethin') / Dazzle dizzy / Bolex dementia.

Nov 73. (7") *(PUR 116)* **INSIDE YOUR LIFE. / HOW DO YOU DO IT** -

— After their split, CANN helped re-form ATOMIC ROOSTER.

ANDWELLA'S DREAM

Formed: Northern Ireland . . . 1968 as The METHOD by songwriter DAVE LEWIS, NIGEL SMITH and GORDON BARTON. They subsequently moved to London and changed their name to ANDWELLA'S DREAM, having signed to 'C.B.S.'. The debut album, 'LOVE AND POETRY', was fuelled by HENDRIX-inspired psychedelic rock and although well-received, the record was a commercial failure (incidentally, it's now a very rare collector's piece worth over £200). They then steered themselves towards the progressive rock market of the early 70's, slightly adjusting the group name, changing labels, but ultimately having no luck with two TRAFFIC-ish, R&B jazz albums 'WORLD'S END' & 'PEOPLE'S PEOPLE'.

Recommended: LOVE AND POETRY (*8) / WORLD'S END (*5) / PEOPLE'S PEOPLE (*5)

DAVE LEWIS – vocals, guitar, keyboards / **NIGEL SMITH** – bass, vocals / **GORDON BARTON** – drums

C.B.S. — not issued

Jun 69. (7") *(4301)* **SUNDAY. / MIDDAY SUN** -

Jul 69. (lp) *(63673)* **LOVE AND POETRY** -
– Days grew longer for love / Sunday / Lost a number found a king / Man without a name / Clockwork man / Cocaine / Shades of grey / High on a mountain / Andwella / Midday sun / Take my road / Felix / Goodbye. *(cd-iss.Jun97 on 'Fingerprint'; SPACD 1961)*

Aug 69. (7") *(4469)* **MRS. MAN. / FELIX** -

Nov 69. (7") *(4634)* **MR. SUNSHINE. / SHADES OF GREY** -

— as DAVID LEWIS, he made very rare 1970 lp 'SONGS OF DAVID LEWIS' *(AX 1)* now worth over £300. He's also connected with the DAVE BAXTER album 'GOODBYE DAVE' issued on 'Reflection' *(REFL 9)*

ANDWELLA

— added **DAVE McDOUGALL** – keyboards + **JACK McCULLOCH** – drums (ex-ONE IN A MILLION, ex-THUNDERCLAP NEWMAN)

Reflection — Dunhill

Aug 70. (lp) *(REF 1010)* <50095> **WORLD'S END**
– Hold on to your mind / Lady love / Michael Fitzhenry / I'm just happy to see you get her / Just how long / World's end / Back on the road / I got a woman / Reason for living / Shadow of the night.

Sep 70. (7") *(RS 1)* **EVERY LITTLE MINUTE. / MICHAEL FITZHENRY** -

Oct 70. (7") *(RS 3)* **HOLD ON TO YOUR MIND. / SHADOW OF THE NIGHT** -

1970. (7") <4275> **I GOT A WOMAN. / WORLD'S END** -

— **DAVE STRUTHERS** – bass, vocals, repl. McCULLOCH

Jan 71. (7") *(RS 6)* **ARE YOU READY. / PEOPLE'S PEOPLE** -
(re-iss.Jul71; HRS 6)

Aug 71. (lp) *(REFL 10)* <50105> **PEOPLE'S PEOPLE**
– She taught me to love / Saint Bartholomew / The world of Angelique / Mississippi water / I've got my own / Are you ready / Four days in September / Lazy days /

People's people / Behind the painted screen / All for you.

Sep 71. (7") *<4291>* **MISSISSIPPI WATER. / ALL FOR YOU** [-] [ ]

— split after above

ANIMALS

Formed: Newcastle, England ... 1960, as The ALAN PRICE COMBO. BURDON's arrival in 1962 led to tension in the ranks, no doubt a major contributing factor to the band's increasingly manic stage show. After supporting the likes of legendary bluesmen SONNY BOY WILLIAMSON and JOHN LEE HOOKER, they moved to London early in '64 and were promptly signed to EMI's 'Columbia' label by then virtually unknown producer MICKIE MOST. Re-christened The ANIMALS by the fans, the band adopted the name with glee and hit paydirt in summer '64 with the blues standard, 'HOUSE OF THE RISING SUN'. A massive hit on both sides of the Atlantic, with BURDON's ominous vocal phrasing and PRICE's wailing organ, the record remains the band's defining moment. Rarely, if ever, has the United Kingdom produced a white guy who could sing the blues like ERIC BURDON. The whisky-soaked menace of his voice sounded at times like Old Nick incarnate and was a key component in The ANIMALS feisty challenge to The ROLLING STONES' throne at the height of the 60's R&B Boom. Much like The BYRDS, The ANIMALS had an uncanny knack of covering material which, on paper, seemed less than obvious, but worked a treat on vinyl. 'DON'T LET ME BE MISUNDERSTOOD' and 'WE GOTTA GET OUT OF THIS PLACE' both went Top 5 in the UK, ensuring respectable sales of their debut album, 'ANIMAL TRACKS'. PRICE left in 1965, beginning a dispute (incredibly still ongoing after more than 30 years) with BURDON over the publishing rights to 'HOUSE OF THE RISING SUN'. With DAVE ROWBERRY as PRICE's replacement, the band cut a few more albums including the semi-classic 'ANIMALIZATION', which contained such powerful tracks as 'INSIDE – LOOKING OUT' and 'GIN HOUSE BLUES'. The original ANIMALS fell apart towards the end of '66, CHAS CHANDLER going on to manage JIMI HENDRIX. BURDON moved to San Francisco, where he immersed himself in the nascent psychedelic scene, consuming liberal quantities of LSD. Under the new and improved moniker ERIC BURDON & THE ANIMALS, he released in 1967, his paeon to the emerging hippy culture, 'WINDS OF CHANGE'. Other highlights of this period include BURDON's tribute to the narcotic delights of the Swiss pharmaceutical industry, 'A GIRL NAMED SANDOZ' and 'MONTEREY', his reverential recollection of the legendary pop festival. BURDON kept his third eye in check enough to release a handful of introspective albums before this particular version of The ANIMALS split at the end of '68. He tasted major success for the last time with soul/funk band WAR, their debut single 'SPILL THE WINE', climbing into the Top 3 in the States mid 1970. The collaboration was short-lived, however, and BURDON went solo with weak support from the public. The original ANIMALS line-up (minus PRICE, of course) re-formed in 1977 and again in '83, although the new material was met with a lukewarm response in the UK. CHAS CHANDLER, who also went onto work with SLADE and others, died of a heart attack on the 17th July '96. • **Songwriters:** BURDON lyrics / PRICE arrangements songs, with covers BOOM BOOM + DIMPLES + I'M MAD AGAIN (John Lee Hooker) / I'M IN LOVE AGAIN (Fats Domino) / TALKIN' ABOUT YOU (Ray Charles) / GONNA SEND YOU BACK TO GEORGIA (Timmy Shaw) / DON'T LET ME BE MISUNDERSTOOD (Nina Simone) / PRETTY THING (Bo Diddley) / BABY LET ME TAKE YOU HOME (Russell-Farrell) / BRING IT ON HOME TO ME (Sam Cooke) / WE'VE GOTTA GET OUT OF THIS PLACE (Mann-Weil) / DON'T BRING ME DOWN (Goffin-King) / RIVER DEEP MOUNTAIN HIGH (Phil Spector) / PAINT IT BLACK (Rolling Stones) / etc.

Recommended: SINGLES PLUS (*8)

ERIC BURDON (b.11 May'41, Walker, nr.Newcastle, England) – vocals / **ALAN PRICE** (b.19 Apr'41, Fairfield, Durham, England) – keyboards, vocals / **HILTON VALENTINE** (b.21 May'43, North Shields, England) – guitar / **CHAS CHANDLER** (b.18 Dec'38, Heaton, nr.Newcastle, England) – bass / **JOHN STEEL** (b. 4 Feb'41, Gateshead, England) – drums

Columbia M.G.M.

Apr 64. (7") *(DB 7247) <K 13242>* **BABY LET ME TAKE YOU HOME. / GONNA SEND YOU BACK TO WALKER** (US 'A'side) [21] [57] Sep64

Jun 64. (7") *(DB 7301) <K 13264>* **THE HOUSE OF THE RISING SUN. / TALKIN' 'BOUT YOU** [1] [1] Jul64

Sep 64. (7") *(DB 7354) <K 13274>* **I'M CRYING. / TAKE IT EASY** [8] [19] Oct64

Oct 64. (lp; mono/stereo) *(33SX 1669) <E/SE 4264>* **THE ANIMALS** [6] [7] Sep64
– Story of Bo Diddley / Bury my body / Dimples / I've been around / I'm in love again / The girl can't help it / I'm mad again / She said yeah / The right time / Memphis / Boom boom / Around and around. *(US diff. tracks +=>–* The house Of The Rising Sun. *(re-iss.Oct69 on 'Regal Starline'; SRS 5006)*

Nov 64. (7") *<K 13298>* **BOOM BOOM. / BLUE FEELING** [-] [43]

Jan 65. (7") *(DB 7445) <K 13311>* **DON'T LET ME BE MISUNDERSTOOD. / CLUB A-GO-GO** [3] [15] Feb65

Mar 65. (lp; mono/stereo) *<E/SE 4281>* **THE ANIMALS ON TOUR (live)** [-] [99]
– Boom boom / How you've changed / I believe to my soul / Mess around bright lights / Big city / Worried life blues / Let the good times roll / Crying dimples / She said yeah.

Apr 65. (7") *(DB 7539) <K 13339>* **BRING IT ON HOME TO ME. / FOR MISS CAULKER** [7] [32] May 65

May 65. (lp; mono/stereo) *(33SX 1708) <E/SE 4305>* **ANIMAL TRACKS** [6] [57] Sep65
– Mess around / How you've changed / Hallelujah, I love her so / I believe to my soul / Worried life blues / Roberta / I ain't got you / Bright lights, big city / Let the good times roll / For Miss Caulker / Roadrunner. *(re-iss.Sep84 on 'Fame' lp/c; FA/TCFA 413110)*

Jul 65. (7") *(DB 7639) <K 13382>* **WE'VE GOTTA GET OUT OF THIS PLACE. / I CAN'T BELIEVE IT** [2] [13] Aug65

Oct 65. (7") *(DB 7741) <K 13414>* **IT'S MY LIFE. / I'M GONNA CHANGE THE WORLD** [7] [23] Nov65

— **DAVE ROWBERRY** (b.27 Dec'43, Newcastle, England) – keyboards (ex-MIKE COTTON SOUND) repl. PRICE who went solo

Decca M.G.M.

Feb 66. (7") *(F 2332)* **INSIDE – LOOKING OUT. / OUTCAST** [12] [-]

Mar 66. (7") *<K 13468>* **INSIDE – LOOKING OUT. / YOU'RE ON MY MIND** [-] [34]

— **BARRY JENKINS** (b.22 Dec'44, Leicester, England) – drums (ex-NASHVILLE TEENS) repl. STEEL

May 66. (7") *(F 12407) <K 13514>* **DON'T BRING ME DOWN. / CHEATING** [6] [12]

May 66. (lp) *(LK 4797)* **ANIMALISMS** [4] [-]
– One monkey don't stop no show / Maudie / Outcast / Sweet little sixteen / You're on my mind / Clapping / Gin house blues / Squeeze her – Tease her / What am I living for / I put a spell on you / That's all I am to you / She'll return it.

Aug 66. (lp; mono/stereo) *<E/SE 4384>* **ANIMALIZATION** [-] [20]
– Don't bring me down / One monkey don't stop no show / You're on my mind / She'll return it / Cheating / Inside – looking out / See see rider / Gin house blues / Maudie / What am I living for / Sweet little sixteen / I put a spell on you.

Sep 66. (7") *<K 13582>* **SEE SEE RIDER. / SHE'LL RETURN IT** [-] [10]

Nov 66. (lp; mono/stereo) *<E/SE 4414>* **ANIMALISM** [-] [33]
– All night long / Shake / Other side of this life / Rock me baby / ucille / Smokestack lightning / Hey Gyp / Hit the road Jack / Outcast / Louisiana blues / That's all I am to you / Going down slow.

ERIC BURDON & THE ANIMALS

— ERIC with session musicians incl. BENNY GOULSON

Oct 66. (7") *(F 12502)* **HELP ME GIRL. / SEE SEE RIDER** [14] [-]

Dec 66. (7") *<K 13636>* **HELP ME GIRL. / THAT AIN'T WHERE IT'S AT** [-] [29]

Mar 67. (lp; mono/stereo) *<E/SE 4433>* **ERIC IS HERE** [-] [ ]
– Help me girl / In the night / Mama told me not to come / I think it's gonna rain today / This side of goodbye / That ain't where it's at / Wait till next year / Losin' control / It's not easy / Biggest bundle of them all / It's been a long time coming / True love.

— ERIC who had earlier moved to California brought back **BARRY JENKINS** in Jan '67

— recruited **VIC BRIGGS** (b.14 Feb'45, London) – guitar (ex-STEAMPACKET) to finally repl ROWBERRY / **JOHN WIEDER** (b.21 Apr'47, London) – guitar, violin repl. VALENTINE who went solo / **DANNY McCULLOCH** (b.18 Jul'45, London) – bass repl. CHANDLER who became producer

M.G.M. M.G.M.

May 67. (7") *(MGM 1340) <K 13721>* **WHEN I WAS YOUNG. / A GIRL NAMED SANDOZ** [45] [15] Apr67

Aug 67. (7") *(MGM 1344)* **GOOD TIMES. / AIN'T THAT SO** [20] [-]

Aug 67. (7") *<K 13769>* **SAN FRANCISCAN NIGHTS. / GOOD TIMES** [-] [9]

Oct 67. (lp; mono/stereo) *(C/CS 8052) <E/SE 4454>* **WINDS OF CHANGE** [ ] [42] Sep67
– San Franciscan nights / Good times / Winds of change / Poem by the sea / Paint it black / Black plague / Yes I am experienced / Man-woman / Hotel hell / Anything / It's all meat. *(re-iss.Apr71; 2354 001) (cd-iss.Oct85 on 'Polydor'; 825 717-2)*

Oct 67. (7") *(MGM 1359)* **SAN FRANCISCAN NIGHTS. / GRATEFULLY DEAD** [7] [-]

Nov 67. (7") *<K 13868>* **MONTEREY. / AIN'T IT SO** [-] [15]

Feb 68. (7") *(MGM 1373) <K 13939>* **SKY PILOT (pt.1). / SKY PILOT (pt.2)** [40] [14] Jun68

Mar 68. (7") *<K 13917>* **ANYTHING. / IT'S ALL MEAT** [-] [80]

May 68. (7") *(MGM 1412)* **MONTEREY. / ANYTHING** [ ] [-]

May 68. (lp; mono/stereo) *(C/CS 8075) <E/SE 4537>* **THE TWAIN SHALL MEET** [ ] [79] Mar68
– Just the thought / Closer to the truth / No self pity / Orange and red beans / Sky pilot / We love you Lil / All is one.

— **ZOOT MONEY** – keyboards (ex-BIG ROLL BAND, ex-DANTALIAN'S CHARIOT) / **ANDY SOMERS** (aka SUMMERS) – guitar, bass (ex-BIG ROLL BAND, ex-DANTALIAN'S CHARIOT) repl. BRIGGS and McCULLOCH

Aug 68. (lp; mono/stereo) *<E/SE 4553>* **EVERY ONE OF US** [-] [ ]
– Uppers and downers / Serenade to a sweet lady / The immigrant lad / Year of the guru / St.James infirmary / New York 1963 – America 1968 / White houses.

Nov 68. (7") *<K 14013>* **WHITE HOUSES. / RIVER DEEP MOUNTAIN HIGH** [-] [67]

Jan 69. (7") *(MGM 1461)* **RING OF FIRE. / I'M AN ANIMAL** [25] [-]

Dec 68. (lp; mono/stereo) <d-lp> *(C/CS 8105) <SE 4591-2>* **LOVE IS** [-] [ ]
– River deep, mountain high / I'm the animal / I'm dying, or am I / Gemini / The madman / Ring of fire / Coloured rain / To love somebody / As tears go passing by. *(UK re-iss.Apr71; 2354 006-007) (re-iss.1973; 2619 002)*

May 69. (7") *(MGM 1481)* **RIVER DEEP, MOUNTAIN HIGH. / HELP ME GIRL** [ ] [-]

— Split Feb69. WIEDER joined FAMILY, ZOOT went solo, JENKINS joined HEAVY JELLY, SOMERS became SUMMERS and joined KEVIN AYERS then KEVIN COYNE. He later helped form The POLICE

ERIC BURDON & WAR

ERIC BURDON – vocals, and WAR: – **LONNIE (LEROY) JORDAN** – keyboards, vocals / **HOWARD SCOTT** – guitar, vocals / **CHARLES MILLER** – saxophone, clarinet / **HAROLD BROWN** – drums, percussion / **B.B. DICKERSON** – bass / **THOMAS 'PAPA DEE' ALLEN** – keyboards / **LEE OSKAR** – harmonica

Polydor M.G.M.

Sep 70. (lp) *(2310 041) <SE 4663>* **ERIC BURDON DECLARES WAR** [50] [18] May70
– Dedication / Roll on Kirk / Tobacco road / I have a dream / Spill the wine / Blues for Memphis Slim / Birth / Mother Earth / Mr.Charlie / Danish pastry / You're no

stranger. *(re-iss.Oct79 on 'MCA'; MCF 3026) <cd-iss.Oct95 on 'Avenue'; 74321 30526-2)*

Jul 70. (7") *(2001 072) <K 14118>* **SPILL THE WINE. / MAGIC MOUNTAIN** [ ] [3]

Liberty M.G.M.

Dec 70. (7") *(LBF 15434) <K 14196>* **THEY CAN'T TAKE AWAY OUR MUSIC. / HOME COOKIN'** [ ] [50]

Feb 71. (d-lp) *(LDS 84003-4) <SE 4710-2>* **BLACK MAN'S BURDON** [ ] [82] Dec70
– Black on black in black / Paint it black / Laurel and Hardy / P.C. 3 / Black bird / Paint it black / Spirit / Beautiful new born child / Nights in white satin / Bird and the squirrel / Nuts seed and life / Out of nowhere / Sun – Moon / Pretty colours / Gun / Jimbo / Bare back ride / Home cookin' / They can't take away our music. *(re-iss.Oct79 on 'MCA'; MCSP 306) <US-cd 1993 on 'Avenue'; R2 71193>*

U.A. M.G.M.

Jun 71. (7") *(UP 35217)* **PAINT IT BLACK. / SPIRIT** [ ] [-]

ERIC BURDON & JIMMY WITHERSPOON

JIMMY WITHERSPOON – blues guitarist + WAR backing.

U.A. M.G.M.

Aug 71. (7") *(UP 35287) <K 14296>* **SOLEDAD. / HEADIN' FOR HOME** [ ] [ ]

Dec 71. (lp) *(UAG 29251) <SE 4791>* **GUILTY!** [ ] [ ]
– I've been drinking / Once upon a time / Steam roller / The laws must change / Have mercy judge / Goin' down slow / Soledad / Home dream / Wicked wicked man / Headin' for home / The time has come. *<US re-iss.1976 as 'BLACK AND WHITE BLUES' on 'LA'; GG 58001> (re-iss.Oct79 as 'BLACK AND WHITE BLUES' on 'M.C.A.'; MCF 3024)*

ERIC BURDON BAND

performed at Reading festival (Aug73), backed by **AARON BUTLER** – guitar / **RANDY RICE** – bass / **ALVIN TAYLOR** – drums. This line-up also featured on his next long awaited album

Capitol Capitol

Dec 74. (7") *<3997>* **THE REAL ME. / LETTER FROM THE COUNTRY FARM** [-] [ ]

Feb 75. (lp) *(<E-ST 11359>)* **SUN SECRETS** [ ] [51] Dec74
– It's my life / Ring of fire / Medley: When I was young – Warchild – The real me / Don't let me be misunderstood – Nina's school / Letter from the County farm / Sun secrets.

Feb 75. (7") *<4007>* **RING OF FIRE. / THE REAL ME** [-] [ ]

— added **JOHN STERLING** – guitar / **TERRY RYAN** – keyboards / **MOSES WHEELOCK** – percussion / **GEORGE SURANOVICH** – drums / and **KIM KESTERSON** – bass (repl. AARON BUTLER)

Aug 75. (lp/<lp>) *(E-ST/<SMAS 11426>)* **STOP** [ ] [ ]
– City boy / Gotta get it on / The man / I'm lookin' up / Rainbow / All I do / Funky fever / By mine / The way it should be / Stop.

ORIGINAL ANIMALS

reformed to record below **BURDON, PRICE, VALENTINE, CHANDLER + STEEL**

Barn U.A.

Aug 77. (7") *(2014 109)* **PLEASE SEND ME SOMEONE TO LOVE. / RIVERSIDE COUNTY** [ ] [-]

Aug 77. (lp/c) *(2314 104) <790>* **BEFORE WE WERE SO RUDELY INTERRUPTED** [ ] [70]
– Brother Bill (the last clean shirt) / Many rivers to cross / Lonely avenue / Please send me someone to love / Riverside county / It's all over now, baby blue / Fire on the sun / As the crow flies / Just a little bit / The fool.

Oct 77. (7") *(2014 115)* **MANY RIVERS TO CROSS. / BROTHER BILL (THE LAST CLEAN SHIRT)** [ ] [-]

Nov 77. (7") *<1070>* **FIRE ON THE SUN. / RIVERSIDE COUNTY** [-] [ ]

— PRICE returned to solo work.

ERIC BURDON

— solo with many session people.

Polydor not issued

Mar 78. (lp) *(2302 078)* **SURVIVOR** [ ] [-]
– Rocky / Woman of the rings / The kid / Tomb of the unknown singer / Famous flames / Hollywood woman / Hook of Holland / I was born to live the blues / Highway dealer / P.O. box 500.

1980. (lp) *(2344 147)* **DARKNESS – DARKNESS** [ ] [-]
– Darkness darkness / On the horizon / Rat race / Gospel singer / Ride on / Baby what's wrong / Cry to me / So much love / Ecstasy / Too late.

Ariola not issued

1981. (lp; as ERIC BURDON'S FIRE DEPT.) *(S 202 800-320)* **THE LAST DRIVE** [-] [-] German
– The last drive / Power company / Bird on the beach / The rubbing out of long hair / Atom-most-fear / Dry / Female terrorist / The last poet.

ANIMALS

reformed again in 1983.

I.R.S. I.R.S.

Sep 83. (7") *(PFP 1019) <9920>* **THE NIGHT. / NO JOHN NO** [ ] [48]
(12"+=) *(PFXS 1019)* – Melt down.

Sep 83. (lp) *(<SP 70037>)* **ARK** [ ] [66]
– Loose change / Love is for all time / My favourite enemy / Prisoner of the light / Being there / Hard times / The night / Trying to get to you / Just can't get enough / Melt down / Gotta get back to you / Crystal nights.

Nov 83. (7"/12") *(PFP/+X 1030) <9923>* **LOVE IS FOR ALL TIME. / JUST CAN'T GET ENOUGH** [ ] [ ]

Sep 84. (lp) *(<IRSA 70043>)* **RIP IT TO SHREDS – THE GREATEST HITS LIVE (live 1983)** [ ] [ ]
– It's too late / House of the rising Sun / It's my life / Don't bring me down / Don't let me be misunderstood / I'm cryin' / Bring it on home to me / O lucky man / Boom boom / We've gotta get out of this place.

— (split though they did reunion gigs)

ERIC BURDON BAND

with **JOHN STERLING + SNUFFY WALDEN** – guitar / **STEVE GOLDSTEIN + LUIS CABAZA + RONNIE BARRON** – keyboards / **BILL McCUBBIN + TERRY WILSON** – bass / **TONY BRUANAGLE** – drums

Blackline not issued

1983. (lp) *(BL 712)* **COMEBACK** [ ] [-]
– No more Elmore / The road / Crawling King Snake / Take it easy / Dey won't / Wall of silence / Streetwalker / It hurts me too / Lights out / Bird on the beach. *(UK-iss.Jun84 as 'THE ROAD' on 'Thunderbolt'; THBL 1017) (cd-iss.Sep94 on 'Line'; LICD 900058)*

Bullfrog Carrere

Mar 84. (lp) *(BDL 4006) <267.003>* **POWER COMPANY** [ ] [ ] Dec83
– Power company / Devil's daughter / You can't kill my spirit / Do you feel it (today) / Wicked man / Heart attack / Who gives a f*** / Sweet blood call / House of the rising Sun / Comeback. *<US-iss.1988 as 'WICKED MAN on 'GNP Crescendo' lp/c/cd; GNP S/C/D 2194)*

Striped Horse not issued

Aug 88. (12") *(SH12 615)* **RUN FOR YOUR LIFE (extended). / RUN FOR YOUR LIFE / RUN FOR YOUR LIFE (instrumental)** [ ] [-]
(cd-s+=) *(SHCD 615)* – Run for your life (Animal remix).

Aug 88. (cd) *<SHD 5006>* **I USED TO BE AN ANIMAL** [-] [ ]
(UK-iss.Jul94 on 'Success' cd/c;)

Rhino Rhino

1990. (c-s) *(4JM 74425)* **SIXTEEN TONS / ('A'instrumental)** [-] [ ]

– compilations, etc. –

on 'Columbia' UK / 'MGM' US, unless stated otherwise

Nov 64. (7"ep) *(SEG 8374)* **THE ANIMALS IS HERE** [ ] [-]
– The house of the rising sun / I'm crying / Gonna send you back to Walker / Baby let me take you down.

Mar 65. (7"ep) *(SEG 8400)* **THE ANIMALS** [ ] [-]
– Boom boom / Around and around / Dimples / I've been around.

Jul 65. (7"ep) *(SEG 8439)* **THE ANIMALS NO.2** [ ] [-]
– I'm in love again / Bury my body / I'm mad again / She said yeah.

Oct 65. (7"ep) *(SEG 8452)* **THE ANIMALS ARE BACK** [ ] [-]
–

Jan 66. (7"ep) Decca; *(DFE 8643)* **IN THE BEGINNING THERE WAS EARLY ANIMALS** [ ] [-]
– Boom boom / Pretty thing / I just wanna make love to you.

Feb 66. (lp; mono/stereo) *<E/SE 4324>* **THE BEST OF THE ANIMALS** [-] [6]
– It's my life / Gonna send you back to Walker / Bring it on home to me / I'm mad again / The house of the rising sun / We've gotta get out of this place / Boom boom / I'm in love again / I'm crying / Don't let me be misunderstood. *(UK iss.Mar89 on 'Crusader')*

Apr 66. (lp) *(SX 6035)* **MOST OF THE ANIMALS** [4] [-]
– The house of the rising sun / We've gotta get out of this place / Roadrunner / Let the good times roll / Hallelujah I love her so / It's going to change the world / Bring it on home to me / Worried life blues / Baby let me take you home / For Miss Caulker / I believe to my soul / How you've changed. *(re-iss.Sep71 on 'Music For Pleasure'; MFP 5218,* hit no.18) *(cd-iss.Feb92; CDMFP 5218)*

Sep 66. (7"ep) *(SEG 8499)* **ANIMAL TRACKS** [ ] [-]
–

Jun 67. (lp; mono/stereo) *<E/SE 4454>* **THE BEST OF ERIC BURDON & THE ANIMALS VOL.2** [-] [71]

Mar 69. (lp) *<SE 4602>* **THE GREATEST HITS OF ERIC BURDON & THE ANIMALS** [-] [ ]

1971. (d-lp) *M.G.M.;* **POP HISTORY** [-] [ ]

1971. (d-lp) *M.G.M.;* **STAR PORTRAIT** [-] [ ]
– Good times / Sky pilot / We love you Lil / Hey Gyp, dig the slowness / San Franciscan nights / Paint it black / When I was young / See see rider / Ring of fire / River deep, mountain high / True love (comes only once in a lifetime) / Inside – looking out / I'm an animal / Monterey / To love somebody / Anything / I'm dying, or am I?. *(cd-iss. Jul 88)*

Mar 71. (7") *(2006 028)* **GOOD TIMES. / SAN FRANCISCAN NIGHTS** [ ] [-]
(re-iss.Nov82 flipped over on 'Polydor'; POSP 534)

Sep 72. (7"m) *R.A.K.; (RR 1)* **THE HOUSE OF THE RISING SUN. / DON'T LET ME BE MISUNDERSTOOD / I'M CRYING** [25] [-]
(re-iss.Sep82 7",7"pic-d; RR/+P 1, hit UK No.11)

Oct 75. (lp) *Polydor; (2356 142)* **ERIC BURDON & THE ANIMALS** [ ] [-]

Apr 76. (lp) *Polydor; (2368 106)* **ERIC BURDON AND THE ANIMALS** [ ] [-]

Apr 76. (lp) *D.J.M.; (DJSL 069)* **IN CONCERT FROM NEWCASTLE (live '63)** [ ] [-]
(re-iss.Dec 76 as 'LIVE IN NEWCASTLE'; DJB 26069) (re-iss.Jan 77 as 'NEWCASTLE '63 on 'Charly'; CR 30016) (re-iss.Feb81; CR 30197) (re-iss.Nov88 as 'LIVE AT THE CLUB A GO GO, NEWCASTLE' on 'Decal'; LIK 88) (cd-iss.Feb93 on 'Charly'; CDCD 1037) (cd re-iss.Jun97 on 'Spalax'; 14550)

Nov 76. (lp; by ERIC BURDON & WAR) *A.B.C.; (ABCL 5207) <ABCD 988>* **LOVE IS ALL AROUND** (out-takes) [ ] [ ]
<US-cd-iss 1993 on 'Avenue'; R2 71218>

Jan 77. (7"; by ERIC BURDON & WAR) *A.B.C.; <(12244)>* **MAGIC MOUNTAIN / HOME DREAM** [ ] [ ]

Jan 77. (lp) *Charly; (CR 30018)* **SONNY BOY WILLIAMSON AND THE ANIMALS (live '63)** [ ] [-]
(re-iss.Dec81 as 'THE ANIMALS WITH SONNY BOY WILLIAMSON'; CR 30199) (re-iss.Nov88 on 'Decal'; LIK 45) (cd-iss.Jul90; CDCHARLY 215)

Sep 83. (lp) *Polydor; (SPELP 40)* **ERIC BURDON AND THE ANIMALS** [ ] [-]
(cd-iss.Nov90; 847 046-2)

Oct 87. (lp/c) *E.M.I.; (746605-1/-4)* **THE SINGLES** [ ] [-]
(first 10 singles 'A' & 'B') *(cd-iss.Aug88; CZ 10)*

Apr 88. (lp/c) *Platinum; (PLAT/PLAC 006)* **GREATEST HITS : ERIC BURDON – THE ANIMALS** [ ] [-]

Dec 85. (cd) *In-Akustik; (INAK 854CD)* **THAT'S LIVE (live by "ERIC BURDON & BAND")** [ ] [-]

1988. (cd) *Pair; <PCD 2-4791>* **ERIC BURDON SINGS THE ANIMALS' GREATEST** [-] [ ]
<re-iss.Oct95 on 'Avenue'; R2 71708>

Dec 88. (lp/c/cd) *See For Miles; (SEE/+K/CD 244)* **THE EP COLLECTION** [ ] [-]
Jun 90. (cd) *Nightriding; (KNCD 10013)* **GOLDEN DECADE** [ ] [-]
Jul 90. (d-cd/d-c/d-lp) *E.M.I.; (CD/TC+/EM 1367)* **THE COMPLETE ANIMALS** [ ] [-]
Oct 90. (7"/c-s) *E.M.I.; (EM/TCEM 154)* **WE'VE GOTTA GET OUT OF THIS PLACE. / THE HOUSE OF THE RISING SUN** [ ] [-]
(12"+=) *(12EM 154)* – Baby let me follow you down.
(cd-s++=) *(CDEM 154)* – Blue feeling.
Dec 90. (cd/c/lp) *Decal; (CD/C+/LIK 72)* **TRACKIN' THE HITS** [ ] [-]
Mar 91. (cd/d-lp) *Sequel; (NEXCD/NEDLP 153)* **INSIDE LOOKING OUT (THE 1965-1966 SESSIONS)**(cd+= extra tracks) [ ] [-]
1992. (cd) *Blue Wax; <117>* **THE UNRELEASED** [ ] [-]
1992. (7") *Old Gold; (OG 8000)* **HOUSE OF THE RISING SUN. / WE'VE GOTTA GET OUT OF THIS PLACE** [ ] [-]
Oct 92. (cd; ERIC BURDON) *Thunderbolt; (CDTB 017)* **CRAWLING KING SNAKE** [ ] [-]
Sep 92. (cd/c) *Prestige; (PRC DSP/ASSP 500)* **RARITIES** [ ] [-]
Sep 93. (cd/c) *Spectrum; (550119-2/-4)* **INSIDE OUT** [ ] [-]
1993. (cd; ERIC BURDON) *Avenue; <R2 71219>* **SUN SECRETS / STOP** [-] [ ]
Jul 93. (cd; ERIC BURDON) *Polydor; (511778-2)* **GOOD TIMES** [ ] [ ]
May 94. (cd; ANIMALS AND SONNY BOY WILLIAMSON) *Sixteen; (CD 9011)* **16 GREAT HITS** [ ] [-]
Apr 95. (cd; ERIC BURDON) *Jet; (JETCD 1011)* **LOST WITHIN THE HALLS OF TIME** [ ] [-]
Oct 95. (cd; ERIC BURDON) *Aim; (AIM 1054)* **MISUNDERSTOOD** [ ] [-]
Aug 96. (cd; ERIC BURDON) *S.P.V.; (SPV 0858999-2)* **RARE MASTERS VOL.1** [ ] [-]
Aug 96. (cd; ERIC BURDON) *S.P.V.; (SPV 0854423-2)* **RARE MASTERS VOL.2** [ ] [-]
Jul 96. (cd; ERIC BURDON) *Receiver; (RRCD 220)* **ERIC BURDON LIVE (live)** [ ] [-]
Feb 97. (cd; ERIC BURDON) *Thunderbolt; (CDTB 180)* **SOLDIER OF FORTUNE** [ ] [-]
Apr 97. (cd; ERIC BURDON) *B.R.Music; (RM 1542)* **GREATEST HITS** [ ] [-]

AORTA

Formed: Chicago, Illinois, USA . . . 1968 by former ROTARY CONNECTION members JIM NYEHOLT and JIM DONLINGER. Their first album was well-received, featuring some excellent tight organ/guitar interplay on some of the more acid/psychedelic tinged numbers; 'CATALYPTIC', 'WHAT'S IN MY MIND'S EYE' & 'SLEEP TIGHT'. Unfortunately however, their second release introduced DONLINGER's brother TOM, although it was a big let down leading to the group folding.

Recommended: AORTA (*7)

JIM DONLINGER – vocals, guitar (ex-ROTARY CONNECTION) / **BOBBY JONES** – bass / **JIM NYEHOLT** – keyboards (ex-ROTARY CONNECTION) / **BILLY HERMAN** – drums, vocals

not issued / Atlantic

1968. (7") *<2545>* **SHAPE OF THINGS TO COME. / STRANGE** [-] [ ]

not issued / Columbia

1969. (7") *<44870>* **STRANGE. / ODE TO MISSY MTFZSPKIK** [-] [ ]
1969. (lp) *<CS 9785>* **AORTA** [-] [ ]
– Main vein 1 / Heart attack / What's in my mind's eye / Magic bed / Main vein 2 / Sleep tight / Catalyptic / Main vein 3 / Sprinkle Road to Cork Street / Ode to Missy Mtfzospkik / Strange / A thousand thoughts / Thoughts and feelings / Main vein 4.

— **MIKE BEEN** – bass, guitar, vocals; repl. JONES

— **TOM DONLINGER** – drums, percussion (ex-ROTARY CONNECTION) repl. HERMAN

not issued / Happy Tiger

1970. (7") *<567>* **SAND CASTLES. / WILLIE JEAN** [-] [ ]
1970. (lp) *<1010>* **AORTA 2** [-] [ ]

— when they split, MIKE BEEN and JIM DONLINGER joined (H.P.) LOVECRAFT

APHRODITE'S CHILD (see under ⇒ VANGELIS)

APPLE

Formed: London, England . . . 1968 by DENIS REGAN, ROB INGRAM, JEFFREY HARROD and DAVID BRASSINGTON. Signed to 'Page One' in 1968, they released two heavy, R&B-tinged psychedelic 45's. They have since become very collectable, as has their first and only album 'AN APPLE A DAY', which is worth over £500. The record featured two YARDBIRDS covers, 'PSYCHO DAISIES' & 'ROCK ME BABY', along with a re-working of The LOVIN' SPOONFUL's 'SPORTING LIFE'. They also released a US-only cover of SCAFFOLD's big UK hit 'THANK YOU VERY MUCH'.

Recommended: AN APPLE AN DAY (*8)

DENIS REGAN – vocals / **ROB INGRAM** – guitar / **JEFFREY HARROD** – bass / **DAVID BRASSINGTON** – drums

Page One / Page One

Oct 68. (7") *(POF 101) <21012>* **LET'S TAKE A TRIP DOWN THE RHINE. / BUFFALO BILLYCAN** [ ] [ ]
Dec 68. (7") *(POF 110)* **DOCTOR ROCK. / THE OTHERSIDE** [ ] [-]

Page One / Smash

Jan 69. (7") *<S-2143>* **THAN YOU VERY MUCH. / YOUR HEART IS FREE JUST LIKE THE WIND** [-] [ ]
Feb 69. (lp) *(POLS 016)* **AN APPLE A DAY . . .** [ ] [-]
– Let's take a trip down the Rhine / Doctor Rock / The otherside / Mr. Jones / The Mayville line / Queen of hearts blues / Rock me baby / Buffalo Billycan / Photograph / Psycho daisies / Sporting life / Pretty girl love you. *(cd-iss.1994 on 'Repertoire'+= single mixes; RR 4366-WP)*– Let's take a trip down the Rhine / Buffalo Billycan / Doctor Rock / The otherside.

— split after above

ARC (see under ⇒ SKIP BIFFERTY)

ARGENT

Formed: London, England . . . 1969 by ROD, who introduced BALLARD, HENRIT and cousin RODFORD. The eponymous debut album, released in 1970, sounded like a heavier version of ROD's old band The ZOMBIES. The hypnotic keyboard sound was still in evidence, although guitarist RUSS BALLARD's rifferama added weight to the proceedings. While the album was a commercial failure, it did provide a U.S. hit ('LIAR') for THREE DOG NIGHT. A couple of years later they scored their own hit with the classic 70's rock of 'HOLD YOUR HEAD UP'. Their sound became increasingly heavy and self-indulgent on later albums and the overblown pomp of 'GOD GAVE ROCK 'N' ROLL TO YOU' (1973) was their last single to hit the charts. (The song was later given a hilarious reworking by KISS). Although the subsequent 'IN DEEP' (1973) album was a relative success, chart action eluded them for the remainder of their career. After a final flop album for 'R.C.A.', the band split, ROD going off to a more mainstream solo career. • **Songwriters:** BALLARD or ARGENT / WHITE. • **Trivia:** BALLARD went on to produce LEO SAYER and ROGER DALTREY, and write for many others.

Recommended: THE BEST OF ARGENT – AN ANTHOLOGY (*7)

ROD ARGENT (b.14 Jun'45, St.Albans, England) – keyboards, vocals (ex-ZOMBIES) / **RUSS BALLARD** (b.31 Oct'47, Waltham Cross, England) – vocals, guitar (ex-ROULETTES) / **JIM RODFORD** (b. 7 Jul'45, St.Albans) – bass (ex-ZOMBIES) / **BOB HENRIT** (b. 2 May'45, Broxbourne, England) – drums (ex-ROULETTES)

Epic / Date

Jan 70. (lp) *(EPC 63781) <26525>* **ARGENT** [ ] [ ]
– Like honey / Liar / Be free / Schoolgirl / Dance in the smoke / Lonely hard road / The feeling's inside / Freefall / Stepping stone / Bring you joy. *(re-iss.Sep91 on 'Beat Goes On'; BGOCD 110)*
1970. (7") *<1659>* **LIAR. / SCHOOLGIRL** [-] [ ]

Epic / Epic

Nov 70. (7") *<10718>* **REJOICE. / SWEET MARY** [-] [ ]
Jan 71. (7") *(EPC 5423) <10746>* **CELEBRATION. / KINGDOM** [ ] [ ]
Feb 71. (lp) *(EPC 64190) <30128>* **RING OF HANDS** [ ] [ ]
– Celebration / Sweet Mary / Cast your spell Uranus / Lothlorien / Chained / Rejoice / Pleasure / Sleep won't help me / Where are we going wrong.
Nov 71. (7") *(EPC 9135) <10852>* **HOLD YOUR HEAD UP. / CLOSER TO HEAVEN** [ ] [5] May72
Feb 72. (7") *(EPC 7786)* **HOLD YOUR HEAD UP. / KEEP ON ROLLIN'** [5] [-]
Apr 72. (lp) *(EPC 64962) <31556>* **ALL TOGETHER NOW** [13] [23]
– Hold your head up / Keep on rollin' / Tragedy / I am the dance of ages / Be my lover, be my friend / He's a dynamo / Pure love: a) Fantasia, (b) Prelude, (c) Pure love, (d) Finale. *(cd-iss.Aug94; 477377-2) (cd re-iss.Jun97 on 'Koch Int.'; 37941-2)*
Jun 72. (7") *(EPC 8115)* **TRAGEDY. / REJOICE** [34] [-]
Aug 72. (7") *<10919>* **TRAGEDY. / HE'S A DYNAMO** [-] [ ]
Mar 73. (7") *(EPC 1243) <10972>* **GOD GAVE ROCK AND ROLL TO YOU. / CHRISTMAS FOR THE FREE** [18] [ ]
Mar 73. (lp) *(EPC 65475) <32195>* **IN DEEP** [49] [90]
– God gave rock and roll to you / It's only money (part 1 & 2) / Losing hold / Be glad / Christmas for the free / Candles on the river / Rosie. *(cd-iss.Jun95; 480529-2)*
Jul 73. (7") *(EPC 1628)* **IT'S ONLY MONEY (part 2). / CANDLE ON THE RIVER** [ ] [-]
Aug 73. (7") *<11019>* **IT'S ONLY MONEY (part 2). / LOSING HOLD** [-] [ ]
Feb 74. (7") *(EPC 2147)* **THUNDER AND LIGHTNING. / KEEPER OF THE FLAME** [ ] [-]
Feb 74. (lp) *(EPC 65924) <32573>* **NEXUS** [ ] [ ]
– The comming of Kohoutek / Once around the Sun / Infinite wanderer / Love / Music from the spheres / Thunder and lightning / Keeper of the flame / Man for all reasons / Gonna meet my maker.
May 74. (7") *(EPC 2448) <11137>* **MAN FOR ALL REASONS. / MUSIC FROM THE SPHERES** [ ] [ ]
Jul 74. (7") *<50025>* **THUNDER AND LIGHTNING. / COMING OF KOHOUTEK** [-] [ ]
Nov 74. (d-lp) *(EPC 88063) <33079>* **ENCORE (live)** [ ] [ ]
– The coming of Kohoutec / It's only money (parts 1 & 2) / God gave rock and roll to you / Thunder and lightning / Music from the spheres / I don't believe in miracles / I am the dance of ages / Keep on rollin' / Hold your head up / Time of the season. *(cd-iss.Nov93 on 'Beat Goes On';)*
Nov 74. (7") *(EPC 2849)* **KEEP ON ROLLIN' (live). / I AM THE DANCE OF AGES (live)** [ ] [ ]

— (May74) **JOHN GRIMALDI** (b.25 May'55, St.Albans) – lead guitar, mandolin, violin, cello and **JOHN VERITY** (b. 3 Jul'49, Bradford, England) – guitar, bass, vocals (ex-Solo) repl. BALLARD who went solo, + composer

Apr 75. (lp) *(EPC 80691) <33422>* **CIRCUS** [ ] [ ]
– Circus / Highwire / Clown / Trapeze / Shine on sunshine / The ring / The jester.
Jun 75. (7") *(EPC 3407)* **HIGHWIRE. / CIRCUS** [ ] [ ]

Good Earth / U.A.

Oct 75. (lp) *(RS 1020) <LA 560G>* **COUNTERPOINT** [ ] [ ]
– On my feet again / I can't remember / But yes / Time / Waiting for the yellow one / It's off / Be strong / Rock & roll show / Butterfly / Road back home.
Oct 75. (7") *(RCA 2624)* **ROCK'N'ROLL SHOW. / IT'S FALLEN OFF** [ ] [ ]

— Disbanded Jun76, when GRIMALDI quit. The rest formed PHOENIX apart from

ROD ARGENT who went solo, etc.

- compilations, others, etc. -

on 'Epic' unless mentioned otherwise

Feb 76. (7") *(152332)* **HOLD YOUR HEAD UP. / GOD GAVE ROCK AND ROLL TO YOU** ☐ ☐
(re-iss.Jul84 on 'C.B.S.'; A 4580)

Apr 76. (lp/c) *(EPC/40 81321)* <33955> **AN ANTHOLOGY - THE BEST OF ARGENT** ☐ ☐
– School girl / It's only money / Pleasure / Hold your head up / Thunder and lightning / Liar / God gave rock'n'roll to you / Keep on rollin'. *(re-iss.Sep84 lp/c; EPC/40 32517) (cd-iss.Apr90 on 'CBS Collectors'; 902293-2)*

Jun 76. (7") *(EPC 4321)* **HOLD YOUR HEAD UP. / IT'S ONLY MONEY** ☐ ☐

Apr 78. (lp) *Embassy; (CBS 31640)* **HOLD YOUR HEAD UP** ☐ -

Feb 79. (7") *(EPC 7062)* **HOLD YOUR HEAD UP. / TRAGEDY** ☐ ☐

Jul 82. (7") *Old Gold; (OG 9187)* **HOLD YOUR HEAD UP. / DANCE IN THE SMOKE** ☐ -

Nov 88. (7") *Old Gold;* **GOD GAVE ROCK AND ROLL TO YOU. / TRAGEDY** ☐ -

May 91. (cd)(c) *Elite;* **MUSIC FROM THE SPHERES** ☐ -
(re-iss.Sep93; same)

Mar 95. (cd) *Windsong; (WINCD 067)* **BBC RADIO 1 LIVE IN CONCERT (live)** ☐ -

ROD ARGENT

M.C.A. M.C.A.

May 77. (7") *(MCA 294)* **GYMNOPEDIES No.1. / LIGHT FANTASTIC** ☐ -

May 78. (7"; as SAN JOSE featuring RODRIGUEZ ARGENTINA) *(MCA 369)* **ARGENTINE MELODY (CANCION DE ARGENTINA). / ('A'version)** 14 -

—— ROD composed this theme tune to for the soccer World Cup.

Sep 78. (7") *(MCA 393)* **HOME. / No.1** ☐ -

Oct 78. (lp/c) *(MCF/+C 2854)* **MOVING HOME** ☐ -
– Home / Silence / I'm in the mood / Summer / No.1 / Tenderness / Well, well, well / Pastorius mentioned / Smiling / Recollection. *(re-iss.Jul82; MCL 1695)*

Jan 79. (7") *(MCA 403)* **SILENCE. / RECOLLECTION** ☐ -

Jan 82. (7")(12"; by ROD ARGENT & BARBARA THOMPSON) *()* **WITH YOU. / GHOSTS** ☐ -

Feb 82. (lp; by ROD ARGENT & BARBARA THOMPSON) *(MCF 3125)* **GHOSTS** ☐ -
– Poltergeist / With you / Secret soul / All alone / Ghosts / Little girl / Falling stars / Moving on / Sweet spirit.

M.M.C. not issued

Nov 83. (lp/c; by ROD ARGENT & BARBARA THOMPSON) *(TM/ZCTM 3)* **SHADOWSHOW** ☐ -
– Secure in you / Down on your luck / Sleepwalker / Siren / Manhattan midnite / It's over / Echoes / Moving in the morning sun / Doing what must be done / Midday riser / Times past.

Jun 88. (lp/c/cd) *(LP/TC/CD MMC 1012)* **RED HOUSE** ☐ -
– Teenage years / Salvation song / A 4th gymnopedie / Helpless / Sweet Russian / In memory / Baby don't you cry no more / First touch / Suite T / Spirits.

Sep 88. *(7") (MMCS 1)* **BABY DON'T YOU CRY NO MORE. / TEENAGE YEARS** ☐ -

Weekend not issued

Mar 90. (7"; by ROD ARGENT & PETER VAN HOOKE featuring CLEM CLEMPSON) *(WEEK 100)* **NOT WITH A BANG. / THE PIGLET FILES** ☐ -

ART (see under ⇒ SPOOKY TOOTH)

ART & LANGUAGE (see under ⇒ RED CRAYOLA)

ART BEARS (see under ⇒ HENRY COW)

ARTWOODS

Formed: Ealing, London, England . . .1964 by ART WOOD, older brother of guitarist RONNIE WOOD (now of The ROLLING STONES). Since the late 50's, ART had been playing professionally in a 9-piece swing / big band outfit ART WOOD COMBO. In 1962, he joined ALEXIS KORNER's BLUES INCORPORATED alongside stars-to-be CYRIL DAVIES, LONG JOHN BALDRY, GINGER BAKER plus future members of The ROLLING STONES; JAGGER, RICHARDS, WYMAN and WATTS. He then formed The NEW ART WOOD COMBO, who comprised; DON WILSON – bass, vocals / DEREK GRIFFITHS – guitar / JON LORD – piano / REG DUNNAGE – drums. Tragically, while on tour their van crashed and DON suffered two broken legs, thus ending his musical career. MALCOLM POOL was recruited just in time to play a residency in the now famous 100 Club. On the strength of this gig they were signed by 'Decca', although DUNNAGE was unwilling to commit himself full-time and left soon after. His replacement was temporarily filled by MITCH MITCHELL (future JIMI HENDRIX EXPERIENCE), although after a few gigs he was ousted in favour of KEEF HARTLEY (fresh from a stint with RORY STORM & THE HURRICANES, filling in for RINGO STARR). MIKE VERNON, producer for Decca, soon suggested the name The ARTWOODS after taking the idea from The MANFREDS (aka MANFRED MANN). Their debut release, 'SWEET MARY', was critically well-received, although it was the first of several commercial flops, despite an appearance on the first edition of cult TV pop show 'Ready, Steady, Go!'. In 1965, they backed American blues singer MAE MERCER on tours alongside BO DIDDLEY, HOWLIN' WOLF and LITTLE WALTER. After being introduced to the new Hammond organ in 1966, LORD's keyboard work became more polished, although their first and only album 'ART GALLERY', was given the thumbs down by critics and public alike due to a lack of original material. After one more 45 for 'Decca', they signed for 'Parlophone' but were dropped in early '67. Around the same time, HARTLEY was sacked prior to a tour of Denmark and COLIN MARTIN was called in. A change of group name (see below) didn't change their fortunes and they quickly disintegrated. • **Style:** White blues/ mod outfit. • **Songwriters:** LORD wrote most, except SWEET MARY (Leadbelly) / IF I EVER GET MY HANDS ON YOU (Carter-Lewis) / OH MY LOVE (Fox-Smith) / HOOCHIE COOCHIE MAN (Muddy Waters) / WHAT SHALL I DO (Marvin Jenkins) / I TAKE WHAT I WANT (Sam & Dave) / THESE BOOTS ARE MADE FOR WALKING (hit; Nancy Sinatra) / A TASTE OF HONEY (Bobby Scott) / OUR MAN FLINT (?) / etc.

Recommended: 100 OXFORD STREET (*6)

ART WOOD – vocals, harmonica / **JON LORD** – keyboards / **DEREK GRIFFITHS** – guitar / **MALCOLM POOL** – bass (ex-ROADRUNNERS) / **KEEF HARTLEY** – drums (ex-RORY STORM & THE HURRICANES)

Decca not issued

Oct 64. (7") *(F 12015)* **SWEET MARY. / IF I EVER GET MY HANDS ON YOU** ☐ -

Feb 65. (7") *(F 12091)* **OH MY LOVE. / BIG CITY** ☐ -

Aug 65. (7") *(F 12206)* **GOODBYE SISTERS. / SHE KNOWS WHAT TO DO** ☐ -

Apr 66. (7") *(F 12384)* **I TAKE WHAT I WANT. / I'M LOOKING FOR A SAXOPHONIST DOUBLING FRENCH HORN WEARING SIZE 37 BOOTS** ☐ -

Jun 66. (lp) *(LK 4830)* **ART GALLERY** ☐ -
– Can you hear me / Down in the valley / Things get better / Walk on the wild side / I keep forgettin' / Keep lookin' / One more heartache / Work, work, work / Be my lady / If you gotta make a fool of somebody / Stop and think it over / Don't cry no more. *(re-iss.Apr70 on 'Decca Eclipse'; ECS 2025)*

Aug 66. (7") *(F 12465)* **I FEEL GOOD. / MOLLY ANDERSON'S COOKERY BOOK** ☐ -

Parlophone not issued

Jan 67. (7") *(R 5590)* **WHAT SHALL I DO. / IN THE DEEP END** ☐ -

—— **COLIN MARTIN** – drums repl. HARTLEY who joined JOHN MAYALL and later went solo

Fontana not issued

Nov 67. (7"; as ST. VALENTINE'S DAY MASSACRE) *(TF 883)* **BROTHER CAN YOU SPARE A DIME./ AL'S PARTY** ☐ -

—— Disbanded not long after the disaster of above. ART WOOD inherited from the break-up of The SMALL FACES and formed QUIET MELON. This highly hyped supergroup also consisted of RON WOOD, KENNY JONES, IAN McLAGAN plus ROD STEWART and KIM GARDNER (ex-CREATION). Although they played several gigs in late 1969, four tracks they recorded never made the shops. Of course all but ART and KIM went onto become The FACES. Meanwhile, LORD found deserved success with bubblegum hitmakers The FLOWERPOT MEN ('Let's Go To San Francisco') before co-forming heavy rock giants DEEP PURPLE. GRIFFITHS joined LUCAS then The MIKE COTTON SOUND, before re-joining KEEF HARTLEY in DOG SOLDIER. MALCOLM POOL joined COLOSSEUM then the DON PARTRIDGE BAND.

- compilations, etc. -

Apr 66. (7"ep) *Decca; (DFE 8654)* **JAZZ IN JEANS** ☐ -
– These boots are made for walkin' / A taste of honey / Our man Flint / Routine.

1973. (lp) *Spark; (SRLM 2006)* **THE ARTWOODS** ☐ -
– Don't cry no more / Our man Flint / I take what I want / Work, work, work / Be my lady / One more heartache / Can you hear me / Walk on the wild side / Things get better / I keep forgettin' / A taste of honey / Routine.

Mar 83. (lp) *Edsel; (ED 107)* **100 OXFORD STREET** ☐ -
– Sweet Mary / If I ever get my hands on you / Goodbye sisters / Oh my love / I take what I want / Big city / She knows what to do / I'm looking for a saxophonist doubling / Keep lookin' / I keep forgettin' / I feel good / One more heartache / Down in the valley / Be my lady / Stop and think it over / Don't cry no more. *(cd-iss.Mar91; EDCD 107)*

ARZACHEL (see under ⇒ EGG)

ASH RA TEMPEL

Formed: Berlin, Germany . . .early 70's by MANUEL GOTTSCHING and HARTMUT ENKE. Having been influenced by the blues and classical music from an early age, GOTTSCHING subsequently became inspired by PINK FLOYD's psychedelic experimentation. They were joined by others, including KLAUS SCHULZE, who had just quit TANGERINE DREAM. Their debut self-titled album, released in March '71, borrowed heavily from the trippy ambience of both these bands. In September that year, SCHULZE left to pursue a solo career, while the remainder completed a follow-up, 'SCHWINGUNGEN'. By the time of its release in the summer of '72, they had met 60's acid-guru/preacher TIMOTHY LEARY in Switzerland. The resulting acid-fried, collaborative album, 'SEVEN UP', was named after the fizzy drink which they lovingly spiked with LSD before each show.
Following this, they met up with another "underground" philosopher; the painter/artist WALTER WEGMULLER, who collaborated on their next project 'JOIN INN'. In 1976, they signed to Richard Branson's 'Virgin', where they made three albums under the new ASHRA tag. They were now more keyboard-orientated, breaking free from their exotic Eastern-styled psychedelia of old.

On subsequent releases, GOTTSCHING further diversified into new-age ambience.

Recommended: ASH RA TEMPEL (*6) / SCHWINGUNGEN (*6) / SEVEN UP (*7) / SUN RAIN (*7 compilation)

MANUEL GOTTSCHING – guitar, vocals, electronics / **HARTMUT ENKE** – bass / **KLAUS SCHULZE** – drums, percussion, electronics (ex-TANGERINE DREAM)

Ohr / not issued

1971. (lp) *(OMM 556013)* **ASH RA TEMPEL** [-] [-] German
– Amboss / Traummaschine.

— **WOLFGANG MUELLER** – drums, vibes, repl. SCHULZE who went solo

1972. (lp) *(OMM 556020)* **SCHWINGUNGEN** [-] [-] German
– Light and darkness: Light – Look at your sun – Darkness – Flowers must die – Schwingungen: Suche – Liebe.

— **ROSIE MUELLER** – vocals, harp, repl. WOLFGANG

— KLAUS SCHULZE also returned for below album

1972. (lp) *(OMM 556032)* **JOIN INN** [-] [-] German
– Freak'n'roll / Jenseits.

— added **DIETER DIERKS** – bass, percussion + numerous

Kosmischen Kuriere / not issued

1973. (lp; ASH RA TEMPEL & TIMOTHY LEARY) *(KM 58001)* **SEVEN UP (live)** [-] [-] German
– Space / Time. *(UK cd-iss.Oct96 on 'Spalax'; 14249)*

— **HARALD GROSSKOPF** – drums, repl. ENKE

1973. (lp) *(KM 58007)* **STARRING ROSIE** [-] [-] German
– Laughter loving / Day-dream / Schizo / Cosmic tango / Interplay of forces / The fairy dance / Bring me up. *(UK cd-iss.Feb97 on 'Spalax'; 14247)*

— were just basically **GOTTSCHING** – guitars, electronics

1974. (lp) *(KM 58015)* **INVENTIONS FOR ELECTRIC GUITAR** [-] [-] German
– Echo waves / Quasarsphere / Pluralis.

ASHRA

Virgin / not issued

Feb 77. (lp) *(V 2080)* **NEW AGE OF EARTH** [ ] [-]
– Sunrain / Ocean of tenderness / Deep distance / Nightdust. *(re-iss.1984; OVED 45) (cd-iss.Jun90; CDV 2080) (cd re-iss.Apr97 on 'Spalax'; 14505)*

— added guest UDI ARNDT – guitar

Nov 77. (lp) *(V 2091)* **BLACKOUTS** [ ] [-]
– 77 slightly delayed / Midnight on Mars / Don't trust the kids / Blackouts / Shuttle cock / Lotus (parts 1-4). *(re-iss.Aug88; OVED 193)*

— added guest LUTZ ULBRICH – guitar

Mar 79. (lp) *(V 2117)* **CORRELATIONS** [ ] [-]
– Ice train / Club Cannibal / Oasis / Bamboo sands / Morgana da capo / Pas de trois / Phantasus.

1980. (lp) *(202 284)* **BELLE ALLIANCE** [-] [-] German

Thunderbolt / not issued

Apr 90. (cd/lp) *(CDTB/THBL 086)* **WALKIN' THE DESERT** [ ] [-]
– First movement / Second movement / Third movement / Fourth movement.

1992. (cd) *(CDTB 138)* **TROPICAL HEAT** [ ] [-]
– Mosquito dance / Tropical heat / Pretty papaya / Nights in sweat / Don't stop the fan / Monsoon.

– compilations, etc –

Nov 90. (3xcd-box) *Virgin; (TPAK 12)* **COLLECTOR'S EDITION** [ ] [-]
– (BLACKOUTS / + Edgar Froese – Aqua / Klaus Schulze – Timewind)

Jan 96. Virgin; (cd) *(CDOVD 463)* **SUNRAIN** [ ] [-]

ASYLUM CHOIR

Formed: Los Angeles, California, USA . . . by duo of LEON RUSSELL and MARC BENNO. They took a hugely unsuccessful psychedelic trip on their debut album, 'LOOK INSIDE THE ASYLUM CHOIR'. A second album was knocked back by Mercury subsidiary 'Smash' and of course, both went on to solo careers. While BENNO carved out a small niche, LEON became a top songwriter and session man, later forming his own label 'Shelter'.

Recommended: LOOK INSIDE THE ASYLUM CHOIR (*4) / THE ASYLUM CHOIR II (*5)

LEON RUSSELL – vocals, guitar, keyboards / **MARC BENNO** – vocals, drums

Mercury / Smash

1968. (7") *<2188>* **SOUL FOOD. / WELCOME TO HOLLYWOOD** [-] [ ]

1969. (7") *<2204>* **INDIAN STYLE. / ICICLE STAR TREE** [-] [ ]

1969. (lp) *(SMCL 20141) <67107>* **LOOK INSIDE THE ASYLUM CHOIR** [ ] [ ] 1968
– Welcome to Hollywood / Soul food / Icicle star tree / Death of the flowers / Indian style / Episode containing three songs: N.Y. op – Land of dog / Mr. Henri the clown / Thieves in the choir / Black sheep boogaloo. *(re-iss.Jun71; 6338 049)*

— split and both went solo after recording below album

A&M / Shelter

1971. (7") *<7313>* **STRAIGHT BROTHER. / TRYIN' TO STAY ALIVE** [-] [ ]

1972. (lp) *(AMLS 68089) <SW 8910>* **THE ASYLUM CHOIR II** [ ] [ ] 1971
– Sweet home Chicago / Down on the base / Hello, little friend / Salty candy / Tryin' to stay 'live / . . .Intro to Rita . . . / Straight brother / Learn how to boogie / Ballad for a soldier / When you wish upon a fag / Lady in waiting.

– compilations, etc. –

Apr 91. (cd) *Sequel; (NEXCD 152)* **ASYLUM CHOIR** [ ] [-]
– (mostly all material)

ATLANTIS (see under ⇒ FRUMPY)

ATOMIC ROOSTER

Formed: London, England . . . mid-'69 by VINCENT CRANE, CARL PALMER and NICK GRAHAM. The former two had enjoyed No.1 success with ARTHUR BROWN ('Fire') and signed to 'B&C' label for early 1970 eponymous debut. This breached the Top 50, but CRANE was left on his own, when PALMER co-founded EMERSON, LAKE & PALMER, while GRAHAN joined SKIN ALLEY. Their replacements JOHN CANN and PAUL HAMMOND, helped create a new heavy/progressive sound, which led to two massive hits; 'TOMORROW NIGHT' & 'DEVIL'S ANSWER'. This period also produced two Top 20 albums 'DEATH WALKS BEHIND YOU' & 'IN HEARING OF'; the latter adding PETE FRENCH (from LEAF HOUND & CACTUS). Went through yet another split soon after, although CRANE found new but experienced voxman CHRIS FARLOWE (had 1996 hit with 'OUT OF TIME'). Also in this 1972 line-up was RICK PARNELL (son of orchestra leader JACK PARNELL), but fans "flocked-off" to heavier pastures. The albums 'MADE IN ENGLAND' & 'NICE 'N' GREASY' plummetted badly, CRANE going off to work with ARTHUR BROWN again. He did resurrect the band a few times later in '79 and 1983, but this was put aside when he was invited to boost KEVIN ROWLAND & DEXYS on 1985's 'Don't Stand Me Down'. Suffering from a long depression, CRANE took his own life in 1989.

Recommended: IN SATAN'S NAME – THE DEFINITIVE COLLECTION (*7)

VINCENT CRANE (b. VINCENT CHEESMAN, 1945) – keyboards, vocals, bass-pedal / **CARL PALMER** (b. 20 Mar'51, Birmingham, England) – drums, percussion (both ex-CRAZY WORLD OF ARTHUR BROWN) / **NICK GRAHAM** – bass, guitar, flute, vocals

B&C / Elektra

Feb 70. (lp) *(CAS 1010)* **ATOMIC ROOSTER** [49] [-]
– Friday the 13th / And so to bed / Broken wings / Before tomorrow / Banstead / S.L.Y. / Winter / Decline and fall. *(re-iss.Oct86 on 'Charisma'; CHC 58) (cd-iss.Aug91 & Jul93 on 'Repertoire' lp/c/cd; REP 4135WZ)*

Mar 70. (7") *(CB 121)* **FRIDAY THE 13th. / BANSTEAD** [ ] [-]

— **JOHN CANN** – vocals, guitar (ex-ANDROMEDA) repl. NICK joined SKIN ALLEY **PAUL HAMMOND** – drums, percussion repl. CARL who joined EMERSON, LAKE & PALMER

Dec 70. (7") *(CB 131) <45727>* **TOMORROW NIGHT. / PLAY THE GAME** [11] [ ]

Jan 71. (lp) *(CAS 1026) <EKS 74094>* **DEATH WALKS BEHIND YOU** [12] [90]
– Death walks behind you / Vug / Tomorrow night / Seven streets / Sleeping for years / I can't take no more / Nobody else / Gershatzer. *(cd-iss.Aug91 & Jul93 on 'Repertoire'; REP 4069WZ)*

— added **PETE FRENCH** – vocals (ex-LEAF HOUND, CACTUS)

Jul 71. (7") *(CB 157) <45745>* **DEVIL'S ANSWER. / THE ROCK** [4] [ ]
(re-iss.Jun76)

Pegasus / Elektra

Aug 71. (lp) *(PEG 1) <EKS 74109>* **IN HEARING OF ATOMIC ROOSTER** [18] [ ]
– Breakthrough / Break the ice / Decision – indecision / A spoonful of bromide helps the pulse rate go down / Black snake / Head in the sky / The rock / The price. *(cd-iss.Aug91 & Jul93 & Jul95 on 'Repertoire'; REP 4068WZ)*

— **CRANE** now with newcomers **CHRIS FARLOWE** (b.1940) – vocals (ex-COLOSSEUM, ex-Solo, etc.) replaced FRENCH who joined LEAFHOUND / **STEVE BOLTON** – guitar repl. CANN (to HARD STUFF) as JOHN DU CANN had 1979 hit / **RICK PARNELL** – drums repl. HAMMOND (to HARD STUFF) added / **BILL SMITH** – bass / **LIZA STRIKE** and **DORIS TROY** – backing vocals

Dawn / Elektra

Sep 72. (7") *(DNS 1027) <45800>* **STAND BY ME. / NEVER TO LOSE** [ ] [ ] 1973

Oct 72. (lp) *(DNLS 3038) <EKS 75039>* **MADE IN ENGLAND** [ ] [ ]
– Time take my life / Stand by me / Little bit of inner air / Don't know what went wrong / Never to lose / Introduction / Breathless / Space cowboy / People you can't trust / All in Satan's name / Close your eyes. *(cd-iss.May91 on 'Sequel'; NENCD 610)*

Nov 72. (7") *(DNS 1029) <45766>* **SAVE ME. / CLOSE YOUR EYES** [ ] [ ]

Jan 73. (7"; VINCENT CRANE & CHRIS FARLOWE) *(DNS 1034)* **CAN'T FIND A REASON. / MOODS** [ ] [-]

— **JOHNNY MANDELA** – guitar repl. STEVE, BILL, LIZA and DORIS

1973. (lp) *(DNLS 3049) <EKS 75074>* **NICE'N'GREASY** <US-title 'ATOMIC ROOSTER IV'> [ ] [ ]
– All across the country / Save me / Voodoo in you / Goodbye planet Earth / Take one take / Can't find a reason / Ear in the snow / What you gonna do. *(cd-iss.Jul91 on 'Sequel'; NEMCD 611)*

— now without FARLOWE who returned to a solo career.

Decca / not issued

Mar 74. (7"; as VINCENT CRANE'S ATOMIC ROOSTER) *(FR 13503)* **TELL YOUR STORY (SING YOUR SONG). / O.D.** [ ] [-]

— CRANE teamed up with ARTHUR BROWN and split band.

— re-formed 1980, with **JOHN DU CANN** – guitar / **PRESTON HEYMAN** – drums

E.M.I. / not issued

Jun 80. (7"/ext.12") *(EMI/12EMI 5084)* **DO YOU KNOW WHO'S LOOKING FOR YOU? / THROW YOUR LIFE AWAY** [ ] [-]

Sep 80. (lp) *(EMC 3341)* **ATOMIC ROOSTER** [ ] [-]
– They took control of you / She's my woman / He did it again / Where's the show? / In the shadows / Do you know who's looking for you? / Don't lose your mind / Watch out / I can't stand it / Lost in space. *(re-iss.Oct86 on 'Charisma')*

— **PAUL HAMMOND** – drums repl. PRESTON

Polydor / not issued

Sep 81. (7") *(POSP 334)* **PLAY IT AGAIN. / START TO LIVE** [ ] [-]
(12"+=) *(POSPX 334)* – Devil's answer (live).

Feb 82. (7") *(POSP 408)* **END OF THE DAY. / LIVING UNDERGROUND** [ ] [-]

(12"+=) *(POSPX 408)* – Tomorrow night (live).

— guests **BERNIE TORME and DAVID GILMOUR** repl. HAMMOND and CANN

Towerbell / not issued

Jun 83. (lp/c) *(TOWLP/ZCTOW 004)* **HEADLINE NEWS**
– Hold your fire / Headline news / Taking a chance / Metal minds / Land of freedom / Machine / Dance of death / Carnival / Time. *(cd-iss.Nov94 on 'Voiceprint'; VP 171CD) (cd re-iss.Jun97 on 'Blueprint'; BP 171CD)*

— Finally split 1983. VINCENT CRANE joined/guested for DEXY'S MIDNIGHT RUNNERS in 1985. He committed suicide 20 Feb'89, after suffering recurring depression. In his latter days, he had also written for pop star KIM WILDE.

– compilations, others, etc. –

1974. (lp) *B&C; (CS 9)* **ASSORTMENT**
1977. (d-lp) *Mooncrest; (CDR 2)* **HOME TO ROOST**
– Death walks behind you / Vug / Seven sheets / Sleeping for years / Can't take no more / Nobody else / Friday the 13th / And so to bed / Broken wings / Before tomorrow / Banstead / Winter / Breakthrough / Decision – Indecision / Devil's answer / Black snae / Head in the sky / A spoonful of bromide helps the pulse go down / Tomorrow night / Break the ice. *(re-iss.1983; same) (re-iss.Dec86 on 'Raw Power' d-lp/d-c/cd; RAW LP/TC/CD 027)*
Aug 80. (7"m) *B&C; (BCS 21)* **DEVIL'S ANSWER. / TOMORROW NIGHT / CAN'T TAKE NO MORE**
Jun 84. (7") *Old Gold; (OG 9391)* **DEVIL'S ANSWER. / TOMORROW NIGHT**
Apr 89. (cd-ep) *Old Gold; (OG 6136)* **DEVIL'S ANSWER / TOMORROW NIGH / ('Natural Born Boogie' by Humble Pie)**
Jun 89. (lp/cd) *Demi-Monde; (DM LP/CD 1020)* **THE BEST OF ATOMIC ROOSTER**
Sep 89. (lp/cd) *Receiver; (RR LD/DCD 003)* **DEVIL'S ANSWER**
Dec 89. (cd/c) *Action Replay; (CDAR/ARLC 100)* **THE BEST AND THE REST OF . . .**
Feb 90. (cd/lp) *Demi-Monde; (DM CD/LP 1023)* **THE DEVIL HITS BACK**
Feb 93. (cd) *Sahara; (SARCD 001-2)* **THE BEST OF VOLS 1 & 2**
Oct 93. (cd) *Windsong; (WINCD 042)* **BBC LIVE IN CONCERT**
Jul 94. (cd/c) *Success;* **THE BEST OF ATOMIC ROOSTER**
Apr 96. (cd) *Laserlight; (12666)* **THE BEST OF ATOMIC ROOSTER**
Jun 97. (d-cd) *Snapper; (SMDCD 128)* **IN SATAN'S NAME – THE DEFINITIVE COLLECTION**
– Banstead / An so to bed / Friday 13th / Broken wings / Tomorrow night / Play the game / Vug / Sleeping for years / Death walks behind you / Devil's answer / Rock / Breakthrough / Break the ice / Spoonful of bromide / Stand by me / Never to lose / Don't know what went wrong / Space cowboy / People you can't trust / All in Satan's name / Close your eyes / Save me / Can't find a reason / All across the country / Voodoo in you / Goodbye Planet Earth / Satan's wheel/

ATTACK

Formed: London, England . . . 1966 initially as The SOUL SYSTEM by RICHARD SHERMAN and GERRY ANDERSON. The first single in early '67, 'TRY IT', was a reworking of The STANDELLS garage track 'TRY IT'. Their follow-up, 'HI HO SILVER LINING' was deprived of a chart position by JEFF BECK's hit version. They then released 'CREATED BY CLIVE' which had a rival version cut by The SYN, although this time both versions failed to chart. A final 45 flopped, forcing them to abandon the proposed album, 'ROMAN GODS OF WAR', in March '68.

Recommended: MAGIC IN THE AIR (*6)

RICHARD SHERMAN – vocals / **JOHN CANN** – guitar, vocals / **DAVID O'LIST** – lead guitar / **GERRY HENDERSON** – bass / **ALAN WHITEHEAD** – drums

Decca / London

Jan 67. (7") *(F 12550)* **TRY IT. / WE DON'T KNOW**
Mar 67. (7") *(F 12578) <1013>* **HI HO SILVER LINING. / ANYMORE THAN I DO**

— DAVEY O'LIST joined The NICE, while WHITEHEAD went to MARMALADE. They were replaced by **BRIAN DAVIDSON + KEVIN FLANAGAN**

Jun 67. (7") *(F 12631)* **CREATED BY CLIVE. / COLOUR OF MY MIND**
Jan 68. (7") *(F 12725)* **NEVILLE THUMBCATCH. / LADY ORANGE PEEL**

— CANN formed FIVE DAY WEEK STRAW PEOPLE, who made an eponymous album, before he joined ANDROMEDA, while DAVIDSON was another to join The NICE

– compilations, others, etc. –

Oct 72. (7") *Decca; (F 13353)* **HI HO SILVER LINING. / ANYMORE THAN I DO**
1990. (lp) *Reflection; (MM 08)* **MAGIC IN THE AIR**
(cd-iss.Apr94 on 'Aftermath'; AFT 1001)

AUDIENCE

Formed: London, England . . .1968 by HOWARD WERTH. After their debut eponymous album for 'Polydor' and a support slot on LED ZEPPELIN's tour, they signed to Tony Stratton-Smith's emerging 'Charisma' label. In 1970, they contributed to the film soundtrack 'Bronco Bullfrog' and released their follow-up, 'FRIEND'S FRIEND'S FRIEND', another progressive jazz-rock hybrid that drew from VAN DER GRAAF and ZEPPELIN. After SHEL TALMY (famous for his WHO productions) had dropped out at the last minute, tunesmith WERTH employed the services of GUS DUDGEON to produce their 1971 effort 'THE HOUSE ON THE HILL'. The record featured two cover versions, the better of the two being 'I PUT A SPELL ON YOU', made famous in the 50's by SCREAMIN' JAY HAWKINS. A final album, 'LUNCH', was served up in 1972, after a reasonably successful tour supporting The FACES.

Recommended: AUDIENCE UNCHAINED (*6)

HOWARD WERTH – vocals, guitar / **TREVOR WILLIAMS** – bass, vocals / **TONY CONNOR** – drums, percussion, piano / **KEITH GEMMELL** – saxophone

Polydor / not issued

1970. (lp) *(583 065)* **AUDIENCE**
– Banquet / Poet / Waverley stage coach / River boat queen / Harlequin / Heaven was an island / Too late I'm gone / Maidens cry / Pleasant convalescence / Leave it unsaid / Man on the box / House on the hill. *(cd-iss.Dec95 on 'RPM'; RPM 148)*

Charisma / Elektra

Jun 70. (7") *(CB 126)* **BELLADONNA MOONSHINE. / THE BIG SPELL**
Aug 70. (lp) *(CAS 1012)* **FRIEND'S FRIEND'S FRIEND**
– Nothing you do / Belladonna moonshine / It brings a tear / Raid / Right on their side / Ebony variations / Priestess / Friend's friend's friend. *(re-iss.Aug76; same) (cd-iss.Jun92; CASCD 1012)*
Feb 71. (7"m) *(CB 141)* **INDIAN SUMMER. / IT BRINGS A TEAR / PRIESTESS**
May 71. (7") *(CB 156)* **YOU'RE NOT SMILING. / EYE TO EYE**
May 71. (lp) *(CAS 1032) <EKS 74100>* **THE HOUSE ON THE HILL**
– Jackdaw / You're not smiling / I had a dream / Raviole / Nancy / Eye to eye / I put a spell on you / The house on the hill. *(re-iss.Aug76; same) (re-iss.Aug82 lp/c; CHC/+MC 4) (cd-iss.Oct90; CASCD 1032)*
1971. (7") *<45756>* **NANCY. / I PUT A SPELL ON YOU**
Apr 72. (lp) *(CAS 1054) <EKS 75026>* **LUNCH**
– Stand by the door / Seven more bruises / Hula girl / Ain't the man you need / In accord / Barracuda Dan / Hunder and lightnin' / Party games / Trombone gulch / Buy me an island. *(re-iss.Aug76; same) (re-iss.Aug88 lp/c; CHC/+MC 36) (cd-iss.Dec90 & Mar94; CASCD 1054)*
1972. (7") *(CB 185)* **STAND BY THE DOOR. / THUNDER AND LIGHTNIN'**
1972. (7") *<45788>* **STAND BY THE DOOR. / SEVEN MORE BRUISES**

— **PATRICK NEUBERGH** – saxophone + **NICK JUDD** – keyboards, repl. GEMMELL who joined STACKRIDGE. Disbanded when CONNOR joined HOT CHOCOLATE and WILLIAMS to JONATHAN KELLY.

– compilations, etc. –

1973. (lp) *Charisma; (CS 7)* **YOU CAN'T BEAT THEM**
– Trombone gulch / Thunder and lightnin' / Raviole / Elixir of youth / I had a dream / You're not smiling / Ain't the man you need / It brings a tear / Indian summer / Jackdaw / Nancy.
1973. (7") *Charisma; (CB 204)* **YOU'RE NOT SMILING. /**
Dec 92. (cd) *Virgin; (CDVM 9007)* **AUDIENCE UNCHAINED**

HOWARD WERTH & THE MOONBEAMS

— with **MIKE MORAN** – keyboards / **FRED GANDY** – bass / **ROGER POPE** – drums / **BOB WESTON** – slide guitar / + session

Charisma / Rocket

Feb 74. (7") *(CB 225)* **LUCINDA. / JOHAN**
Jun 75. (7") *(CB 256)* **COCKTAIL SHAKE. / SAMMY LEE LANE**
Oct 75. (lp) *(CAS 1104)* **KING BRILLIANT**
– Cocktail shake / Got to unwind / The embezzler / A human note / Ugly water / Midnight flyer / Fading star / dear John / Roulette / The Aleph. *(cd-iss.Dec92; CASCD 1104)*
Nov 75. (7") *(CB 269)* **DEAR JOHN. / ROULETTE**
Apr 76. (7") *<40555>* **DEAR JOHN. / MIDNIGHT FLYER**

HOWARD WERTH

Metabop / not issued

1983. (7") *(WERTH 1)* **4D MAN. / WHAT'S HOPPIN'**

Demon / not issued

Jan 84. (lp) *(SIXOF 1)* **SIX OF ONE AND HALF A DOZEN OF THE OTHER**
– Hovering / 4D man / Individual / Meek power / Astro logic / What's hoppin'? / Respectable / I keep forgettin' / Little bitty pretty one / Dancing little thing / Smokestack lightning / One more heartache / Show me. *(cd-iss.Jul92 on 'Mau Mau'; MAUCD 620)*

— Retired from music business.

Brian AUGER

Born: 18 Jul'39, Bihar, India / raised . . . London, England, where he gained an early schooling on the piano. In 1964, with jazz and R&B much in vogue, he formed a short-lived outfit called The TRINITY, with JOHN McLAUGHLIN, RICK LAIRD and PHIL KINNORA. The former two musicians later formed The MAHAVISHNU ORCHESTRA, AUGER enlisting new musicians and singers to complete his loosely assembled STEAMPACKET. These vocalists included legendary and semi-legendary future stars, ROD STEWART, LONG JOHN BALDRY and JULIE DRISCOLL. They released one single for 'Columbia', before AUGER teamed up with JULIE DRISCOLL to form a re-vamped TRINITY. Together they plucked DYLAN's obscure 'THIS WHEEL'S ON FIRE', from the (as yet) unreleased "Basement Tapes". Marking a significant departure from AUGER's familiar R&B sound, the track was a one-off trip into psychedelic territory and the UK Top 5 in 1968. Their next effort failed to emulate the success of its predecessor and following

DRISCOLL's departure, AUGER's personal/personnel problems resulted in The TRINITY's eventual break-up. In the early 70's, he returned with a new act, the jazz-orientated OBLIVION EXPRESS. They were basically targetted at the US market, where they enjoyed healthy sales for the albums, 'CLOSER TO IT!' (1973) and 'STRAIGHT AHEAD' (1974). By this time, AUGER had relocated to San Francisco, where he continued to work until the next decade.

Recommended: AUGERNIZATION – THE BEST OF BRIAN AUGER (*5)

BRIAN AUGER TRINITY

BRIAN AUGER – organ / **RICK BROWN** or **ROGER SUTTON** – bass / **MICKY WALLER** or **CLEM CATTINI** – drums / **VIC BRIGGS** – guitar

Columbia not issued?

Jun 65. (7") *(DB 7590)* **FOOL KILLER. / LET'S DO IT TONIGHT** [ ] [-]
Oct 65. (7") *(DB 7715)* **'65 GREEN ONIONS. / KIKO** [ ] [-]
Mar 67. (7"; solo) *(DB 8163)* **TIGER. / OH BABY, WON'T YOU COME BACK HOME TO CROYDON, WHERE EVERYBODY BEEDLE'S AND BO'S** [ ] [-]

— with **JULIE DRISCOLL** – vocals / **DAVE AMBROSE** (b.11 Aug'46) – bass / **CLIVE THACKER** (b.13 Feb'40, Enfield, England) – drums / **GARY BOYLE** (b. Bihar, India) – guitar

Marmalade Atco

Oct 67. (7"; as BRIAN AUGER & TRINITY) *(598 003)* **RED BEANS AND RICE. / (part 2)** [ ] [-]

JULIE DRISCOLL, BRIAN AUGER & TRINITY

Apr 68. (7") *(598 006) <6593>* **THIS WHEEL'S ON FIRE. / A KIND OF LOVE-IN** [5] [ ]
May 68. (lp) *(607 002) <33256>* **OPEN** [12] [ ]
– In and out / Isola Natale / Black cat / Lament for Miss Baker / Goodbye jungle telegraph / Tramp / Why (am I treated so bad) / Kind of love in / Break it up / Season of the witch.
Jul 68. (7") *<6611>* **IN AND OUT. / BLACK CAT** [-] [ ]

— added a brass section + a string trio.

Sep 68. (7") *(598 011)* **ROAD TO CAIRO. / SHADES OF YOU** [ ] [ ]

BRIAN AUGER TRINITY

1969. (7") *<6656>* **A DAY IN THE LIFE. / BUMPIN' ON SUNSET** [ ] [-]
Apr 69. (lp) *(607 003) <33273>* **DEFINITELY WHAT!** [ ] [ ]
– A day in the life / George Bruno money / Far horizon / John Brown's body / Red beans and rice / Bumpin' on sunset / If you live / Definitely what. *(cd-iss.Sep94 on 'One Way'; OW 30012)*
May 69. (7") *(598 015)* **WHAT YOU GONNA DO? / BUMPIN' ON SUNSET** [ ] [ ]

JULIE DRISCOLL with THE BRIAN AUGER TRINITY

Jul 69. (d-lp) *(608 005-6) <2701>* **STREET NOISE** [ ] [ ]
– Tropic of capricorn / Czechoslovakia / Medley / Take me to the water / I'm going back home / A word about colour / Light my fire / Indian rope Man / When I was a young girl / Flesh failures (Let the sunshine in) / Ellis Island / In search of the sun / Finally you found out / Looking in the eye of the world / Vauxhall to Lambeth Bridge / All blues / I've got life / Save the country. *(also released in 2 parts Jan70; 608 014/015)*
1969. (7") *(598 018)* **TAKE ME TO THE WATER. / INDIAN ROPE MAN** [ ] [ ]
1969. (7") **THE FLESH FAILURES (LET THE SUNSHINE IN). / SAVE THE COUNTRY** [-] [ ]

— added **BOYLE + SUTTON / + BARRY REEVES + COLIN ALLEN** – drums

R.C.A. R.C.A.

Oct 70. (7") *<0381>* **LISTEN HERE. / I WANNA TAKE YOU HIGHER** [-] [100]
1970. (7") *(RCA 1947)* **I WANT TO TAKE YOU HIGHER. / JUST ME JUST YOU** [ ] [ ]
Jul 70. (lp) *(SF 8101) <4372>* **BEFOUR** [ ] [-]
– I wanna take you higher / Pavane / No time to live / Maiden voyage / Listen here / Just you and me. *(cd-iss.Sep95 on 'One Way';)*

BRIAN AUGER TRINITY with OBLIVION EXPRESS

with **ROBBIE McINTOSH** – drums / **BARRY DEAN** – guitar, bass / **JIM MULLEN** – guitar

Jun 71. (lp) *(SF 8101) <4462>* **OBLIVION EXPRESS** [ ] [ ]
– Dragon song / Total eclipse / The light on the road / The sword / Oblivion express.

BRIAN AUGER'S OBLIVION EXPRESS

Polydor R.C.A.

Aug 71. (7") *(2058 133)* **MARIE'S WEDDING. / TOMORROW CITY** [ ] [-]
Aug 71. (7") *<0579>* **MARIE'S WEDDING. / TROUBLE** [-] [ ]
Oct 71. (lp) *(2383 062) <4540>* **A BETTER LAND** [ ] [ ]
– Dawn of another day / Marie's wedding / Trouble / Women of the seasons / Fill your head with laughter / On thinking it over / Tomorrow city / All the time there is / A better land.

— added **ALEX LIGERTWOOD** – vocals

May 72. (lp) *(2383 104) <4703>* **SECOND WIND** [ ] [ ]
– Truth / Don't look away / Somebody help us / Freedom jazz dance / Just you, just me / Second wind. *(cd-iss.Nov95 on 'One Way';)*
May 72. (7") *<0735>* **SECOND WIND. / FREEDOM JAZZ DANCE** [-] [ ]

— **JACK MILLS** – guitar repl. MULLEN / **LENNOX LAINGTON** – bass repl. LIGERTWOOD

— **GODFREY McLEAN** – drums repl. ROBBIE who joined AVERAGE WHITE BAND

C.B.S. R.C.A.

Jun 73. (7") *<0085>* **HAPPINESS IS JUST AROUND THE BEND. / INNER CITY BLUES** [-] [ ]
Jul 73. (lp) *(CBS 65625) <0140>* **CLOSER TO IT!** [ ] [64]
– Whenever you're ready / Happiness is just around the bend / Light on the path / Compared to what / Inner city blues / Voices of other times.
Aug 73. (7") *(CBS 1444)* **INNER CITY BLUES. / LIGHT ON THE PATH** [ ] [-]

— **STEVE FERRONE** – drums (of AVERAGE WHITE BAND) repl. McLEAN

Apr 74. (7") *(CBS 2309)* **STRAIGHT AHEAD. / CHANGE** [ ] [-]
Apr 74. (7") *<0282>* **STRAIGHT AHEAD. / BEGINNING AGAIN** [-] [ ]
May 74. (lp) *(CBS 80058) <0454>* **STRAIGHT AHEAD** [ ] [45] Apr74
– Beginning again / Bumpin' on sunset / Straight ahead / You'll stay in my heart.

— **LIGERTWOOD** returned to repl. LAINGTON

Dec 74. (lp) *<0645>* **LIVE OBLIVION VOL.1 (live)** [-] [51]
– Beginning again / Don't look away / Bumpin' on sunset / Truth // Freedom jazz dance / Happiness is just around the bend / Maiden voyage / Second wind / Whenever you're ready / Inner city blues / Straight ahead / Compared to what.
Oct 75. (7") *<10534>* **BRAIN DAMAGE. / FOOLISH GIRL** [-] [ ]
Oct 75. (lp) *<1210>* **REINFORCEMENTS** [-] [ ]
– Thoughts from afar / Something out of nothing / Plum / Foolish girl / Brain damage / Big yin / Future pilot.
Mar 76. (d-lp) *<1230>* **LIVE OBLIVION VOL.2 (live)** [-] [ ]
– Freedom jazz dance / Happiness is just around the bend / Maiden voyage / Second wind / Whenever you're ready / Inner city blues / Straight ahead / Compared to what.

BRIAN AUGER

with **LIGERTWOOD, MILLS, LAINGTON** plus **CLIVE CHAMAN** – bass / **LENNY WHITE** – drums

Warners Warners

Feb 77. (lp) *(K 56326) <BS 2981>* **HAPPINESS HEARTACHES** [ ] [ ]
– Back street bible class / Spice island / Gimme a funky break / Never gonna come down / Happiness heartaches / Got to be born again / Paging Mr. McCoy.

— next with (aka DRISCOLL, who had married KEITH TIPPETTS). **DAVID McDANIELS** – bass / **DAVE CRIGGER** – drums / **GEORGE DOERING** – guitar

Apr 78. (lp; by BRIAN AUGER & JULIE TIPPETTS) *(K 56458) <BSK 3153>* **ENCORE (live)** [ ] [ ]
– Spirit / Don't let me be misunderstood / Git up / Freedom highway / Future pilot / Rope ladder to the Moon / No time to live / Nothing will be as it was / Lock all the gates.

not issued Headfirst

1981. (lp) *<9702>* **SEARCH PARTY** [-] [ ]
– Planet Earth calling / Red alert / Sea of tranquility / Voyager 3 / I'm gone / Golden gate.

— Retired until he recorded solo album in Italy 1984.

Polydor Blue Flame

Jul 85. (lp) *(823 753-1/-4)* **HERE AND NOW** [-] [ ] France
– Night train to nowhere / They say nothing lasts forever / Searching for your love / Heart of the hunter / The hurricane / Call me / Happiness is just around the bend / Downtown hookup.

– compilations, others, etc. –

on 'Polydor' unless mentioned otherwise

Aug 68. (lp; shared with JULIE DRISCOLL) *Music For Pleasure; (MFP 1265)* **JOOLS / BRIAN** [ ] [-]
1970. (lp) *(2334 004)* **BEST OF BRIAN AUGER TRINITY** [ ] [ ]
Jun 71. (7"; BRIAN AUGER & JULIE DRISCOLL) *(2058 119)* **THIS WHEEL'S ON FIRE. / ROAD TO CAIRO** [ ] [-]
1972. (lp) *(26680)* **POP HISTORY** [ ] [-]
Mar 73. (lp) *Flashback Series; (2384 062)* **JULIE DRISCOLL, BRIAN AUGER TRINITY** [ ] [-]
Jan 77. (lp; BRIAN AUGER & JULIE DRISCOLL) *Charly; (CR 30019)* **LONDON 64-67** [ ] [-]
Jan 77. (lp; STEAMPACKET) *Charly;* **FIRST OF THE SUPERGROUPS; EARLY DAYS** [ ] [-]
Apr 77. (lp) *R.C.A.; <2249>* **THE BEST OF BRIAN AUGER** [-] [ ]
1978. (d-lp) *(2625 008)* **STAR PORTRAIT** [ ] [-]
Nov 80. (d-lp) **GREATEST HITS** [ ] [ ]
Jul 84. (7") *Old Gold; (OG 9427)* **THIS WHEEL'S ON FIRE. / (b-side by "Crazy World Of Arthur Brown")** [ ] [-]
Apr 89. (lp/c; by JULIE DRISCOLL / BRIAN AUGER) *Decal; (LIK/TCLIK 51)* **THE ROAD TO VAUXHALL 1967-69** [ ] [-]
Jul 95. (cd/d-lp) *Tongue & Groove; (TNG CD/LP 008)* **AUGERNIZATION – THE BEST OF BRIAN AUGER** [ ] [-]

Kevin AYERS

Born: 16 Aug'45, Herne Bay, Kent, England; raised in Malaysia. Left school and moved to Canterbury, where he and ROBERT WYATT helped form SOFT MACHINE in 1966. Burned out after a gruelling American tour supporting JIMI HENDRIX, the singer/songwriter decamped in 1968 to Ibiza to write material for the fledgling 'Harvest' label, the fruits of his labour being the following years' 'JOY OF A TOY' (title taken from an ORNETTE COLEMAN track). The album's idiosyncratic flair was indicative of the direction AYERS would take in his later work and contained some of his most enduring songs. In 1970, he hooked up with a young MIKE OLDFIELD to form KEVIN AYERS AND THE WHOLE WIDE WORLD. The unit, including saxophonist LOL COXHILL and keyboardist DAVID BEDFORD, released the experimental classic 'SHOOTING FOR THE MOON', setting the standard for the emergent progressive rock of the 70's. Critics complained that his monotone vox lay too close to SYD BARRETT, NICK DRAKE or even NICO, although he did manage to retain a distinctive character on such songs as 'CLARENCE IN WONDERLAND' and 'COLORES PARA DOLORES'. While 'WHATEVERSHEBRINGSWESING' (1972) and 'BANANAMOUR' (1973) contained moments of inspired exprimentation, AYERS began to move towards more straightforward writing. He appeared on the 'Island' live recording 'JUNE 1, 1974' alongside JOHN CALE, ENO and NICO, but he increasingly shied away from from publicity. The quality of his recorded output became inconsistent and directionless throughout the rest of the 70's and 80's, although he retained a diehard cult following. On the 1976 album 'YES WE HAVE NO MANANAS', he unwisely chose to record an appalling version of 'FALLING IN LOVE AGAIN' (made famous in the 30's by MARLENE DIETRICH). • **Trivia:** In 1987, he contributed vocals to a MIKE OLDFIELD song, 'FLYING START', from the album 'ISLANDS'. AYERS had also largely contributed to an album (LINGUISTIC LEPROSY) in 1974 by friend and Deia neighbour LADY JUNE.

Recommended: BANANA PRODUCTIONS – BEST OF . . . (*8)

KEVIN AYERS – vocals, guitar (ex-SOFT MACHINE, ex-WILDE FLOWERS) / with **DAVID BEDFORD** – keyboards / **MIKE RATLEDGE** – keys / **HUGH HOPPER** – bass / **ROB TAIT** and **ROBERT WYATT** – drums / etc.

Harvest **not issued**

Nov 69. (lp) *(SHVL 763)* **JOY OF A TOY** [ ] [-]
– Joy of a toy . . . / Town feeling / Clarietta rag / Girl on a swing / Song for insane times / Stop this train again doing it / Eleanor's cake which ate her / Lady Rachel / Oleh olah bandu bandong / All this crazy gift of time. *(re-iss.Jun89 on 'Beat Goes On' lp/cd; BGO LP/CD 78)*

Feb 70. (7") *(HAR 5011)* **SINGING A SONG IN THE MORNING. / ELEANOR'S CAKE WHICH ATE HER** [ ] [-]

— After being augmented on last single by CARAVAN members, he formed backing group The WHOLE WIDE WORLD, which included **DAVID BEDFORD** – keyboards / **MIKE OLDFIELD** – bass / **LOL COXHILL** – saxophone / **MICK FINCHER** – drums

Oct 70. (lp; as KEVIN AYERS & THE WHOLE WORLD) *(SHSP 4005)* **SHOOTING AT THE MOON** [ ] [-]
– May I / Rheinhardt and Geraldine / Colores para Dolores / Lunatics lament / Pisser dans un violin / The oyster and the flying fish / Underwater / Clarence in wonderland / Red, green and you, blue / Shooting at the Moon. *(re-iss.Jun89 on 'Beat Goes On' lp/cd; BGO LP/CD 13)*

Oct 70. (7") *(HAR 5027)* **BUTTERFLY DANCE. / PUIS-JE?** [ ] [-]

Aug 71. (7") *(HAR 5042)* **STRANGER IN BLUE SUEDE SHOES. / STARS** [ ] [-]

— The WHOLE WIDE WORLD were augmented by GONG members **DIDIER MALHERBE** – sax / **STEVE HILLAGE** – guitar / also session drummers **WYATT, DUFORT & TONY CARR**

Jan 72. (lp) *(SHVL 800)* **WHATEVERSHEBRINGSWESING** [ ] [-]
– There is loving – Among us – There is loving / Margaret / Oh my / Song from the bottom of a well / Whatevershebringswesing / Stranger in blue suede shoes / Champagne cowboy blues / Lullaby. *(re-iss.Jun89 on 'Beat Goes On' lp/cd; BGO LP/CD 11)*

— **ARCHIE LEGGAT** – bass (ex-WONDERWHEEL) repl. OLDFIELD who went solo / **EDDIE SPARROW** – drums / etc.

Nov 72. (7") *(HAR 5064)* **OH! WOT A DREAM. / CONNIE ON A RUBBER BAND** [ ] [-]

Harvest **Sire**

Apr 73. (7") *(HAR 5071)* **CARIBBEAN MOON. / TAKE ME TO TAHITI** [ ] [ ]
(re-iss.Jul75; HAR 5100) (re-iss.May76; HAR 5109)

May 73. (lp) *(SHVL 807)* <SAS 7406> **BANANAMOUR** [ ] [ ]
– Don't let it get you down / Shouting in a bucket-blues / When your parents go to sleep / Interview / International anthem / Decadence / Oh! wot a dream / Hymn / Beware of the dog. *<US-iss.+=)–* CARIBBEAN MOON (lp). *(re-iss.May86 on 'E.M.I.'; EMS 1124) (cd-iss.Oct92 on 'Beat Goes On'; BGOCD 142)*

— His touring '747' band incl. **HENRY CRALLAN** – keyboards / **FREDDIE SMITH** – drums / **CAL BATCHELOR** – guitar. In the studio he now used many session people.

Island **not issued**

Apr 74. (7") *(WIP 6194)* **THE UP SONG. / EVERYBODY'S SOMETIMES AND SOME PEOPLE'S ALL THE TIME BLUES** [ ] [-]

May 74. (lp) *(ILPS 9263)* **THE CONFESSIONS OF DR.DREAM AND OTHER STORIES** [ ] [-]
– Day by day / See you later / Didn't feel lonely till I thought of you / Everybody's sometimes and some people's all the time blues / It begins with a blessing, but it ends with a curse / Once I awsheared / Ball bearing blues / The confessions of Dr.Dream (a) Irreversible neural damage, (b) Invitation, (c) The one chance dance, (d) Doctor Dream theme, (e) Two into 4 goes. *(re-iss.Nov90 on 'Beat Goes On' cd/lp; BGO CD/LP 86)*

Jul 74. (7") *(WIP 6201)* **AFTER THE SHOW. / THANK YOU VERY MUCH** [ ] [-]

— He was credited alongside ENO, NICO and JOHN CALE on 'Island' Various Artists album 'JUNE 1st, 1974'; *ILPS 9291*, released that month. *(cd-iss.Feb90; IMCD 92)*

— He formed backing group, which included **ZOOT MONEY** – keyboards / **RICK WILLS** – bass / **TONY NEWMAN** – drums / **OLLIE HALSALL** – guitar

Mar 75. (lp) *(ILPS 9322)* **SWEET DECEIVER** [ ] [-]
– Observations / Guru banana / City waltz / Toujours la voyage / Sweet deceiver / Diminished but not finished / Circular lather / Once upon an ocean / Farewell again / Another dawn. *(cd-iss.Oct92 on 'Beat Goes On'; BGOCD 98)*

Feb 76. (7") *(WIP 6271)* **FALLING IN LOVE AGAIN. / EVERYONE KNOWS THE SONG** [ ] [-]

— Retained ZOOT, calling in **ANDY SOMERS** – guitar / **CHARLIE McCRACKEN** – bass / **ROB TOWNSEND** – drums

Harvest **A.B.C.**

Feb 76. (7") *(HAR 5107)* **STRANGER IN BLUE SUEDE SHOES. / FAKE MEXICAN TOURIST BLUES** [ ] [-]

Jun 76. (lp) *(SHSP 4057)* **YES WE HAVE NO MANANAS** [ ] [ ]
– Star / Mr.Cool / The owl / Love's gonna turn you 'round / Falling in love again (ich bin von kopf bis fuss duf liebe eingesteldt) / Help me / Ballad of Mr. Snake / Everyone knows the song / Yes I do / Blue. *(cd-iss.Apr93 on 'Beat Goes On'; BGOCD 143)*

1976. (7") <12303> **MR. COOL. /** [-] [ ]

Apr 77. (7") *(HAR 5124)* **STAR. / THE OWL** [ ] [-]

— **BILL LIVESY** – keyboards repl. ZOOT, etc.

Apr 78. (lp/c) *(SHSP/TC-SHSP 4085)* **RAINBOW TAKEAWAY** [ ] [-]
– Blaming it all on love / Ballad of a salesman who sold himself / A view from a mountain / Rainbow takeaway / Waltz for you / Beware of the dog 2 / Strange song / Goodnight goodnight / Hat song. *(cd-iss.May93 on 'Beat Goes On';)*

Feb 80. (lp/c) *(SHSP/TC-SHSP 4106)* **THAT'S WHAT YOU GET, BABE** [ ] [-]
– That's what you get, babe / Where do I go from here / You never outrun your heart / Given and taken / Idiots / Super salesman / Money, money, money / Miss Hanagal / I'm so tired / Where do the stars end. *(cd-iss.Jun93 on 'Beat Goes On'; BGOCD 190)*

Feb 80. (7") *(HAR 5198)* **MONEY, MONEY, MONEY. / STRANGER IN BLUE SUEDE SHOES** [ ] [-]

— Retired to Majorca in Spain. Still retained **FOLLIE** + employed new Spanish musicians.

not issued **Columbia**

1982. (7") *(MO 2113)* **ANIMALS. / DON'T FALL IN LOVE WITH ME** [-] [-] Spain

Charly **not issued**

Jun 83. (lp) *(CR 30224)* **DIAMOND JACK AND THE QUEEN OF PAIN** [ ] [-]
– Madame Butterfly / Lay lady lay / Who's still crazy / You keep me hangin' on / You are a big girl / Steppin' out / My speeding heart / Howling man / Give a little bit / Champagne and valium.

Jul 83. (7") *(CYZ 7107)* **MY SPEEDING HEART. / CHAMPAGNE AND VALIUM** [ ] [-]

Blau **not issued**

1984. (lp) *(A-014)* **DEIA VU** [-] [-] Spain

Illuminated **not issued**

May 86. (7"promo) *(LEV 71)* **STEPPING OUT. / ONLY HEAVEN KNOWS** [-] [-]

Jun 86. (lp) *(AMA 25)* **AS CLOSE AS YOU THINK** [ ] [-]
– Heaven only knows / Wish I could fall / etc.

Virgin **not issued**

Feb 88. (lp/c/cd) *(V/TCV/CDV 2510)* **FALLING UP** [ ] [-]
– Saturday night (in Deya) / Flying start / The best we have / Another rolling stone / Do you believe? / That's what we did / Night fighters / Am I really Marcel?.

Permanent **not issued**

Feb 92. (cd/c/lp) *(PERM CD/MC/LP 5)* **STILL LIFE WITH GUITAR** [ ] [-]

– compilations, others, etc. –

on 'Harvest' unless mentioned otherwise

Jun 75. (d-lp) *(SHDW 407)* **JOY OF A TOY / SHOOTING AT THE MOON** [ ] [-]

Feb 76. (lp) *(SHSM 2005)* **ODD DITTIES** [ ] [-]

Jul 83. (lp) *(SHSM 2005)* **THE KEVIN AYERS COLLECTION** [ ] [-]
(re-iss.Jun86; same) (re-iss.Jul90 & Jun97 lp/cd; same/SEECD 117)

Jun 89. (d-lp/c)(cd) *(EM/TC-EM 2032)(CZ 176)* **BANANA PRODUCTIONS – THE BEST OF KEVIN AYERS** [ ] [-]
– Butterfly dance / Girl on a swing / Soon soon soon / Sweet deceiver / Caribbean moon / Decadence *[not on cd]* / Irreversible neural damage / Gemini child / The lady Rachel / Toujours le voyage *[not on cd]* / Stranger in blue suede shoes / There is loving – Among us – There is loving / The Clarietta rag / Reinhardt & Geraldine – Colores para Dolores / Stars / Don't let it get you down / Hat song / Singing a song in the morning / Ballad of a salesman who sold himself / Clarence in Wonderland / Diminished but not finished / Blue *[not on cd]* / Song from the bottom of a well.

Jul 92. (cd) *Windsong; (WINCD 018)* **THE BBC RADIO LIVE IN CONCERT (live)** [ ] [-]

Oct 92. (cd) *Connoisseur; (CSAPCD 110)* **DOCUMENT SERIES PRESENTS (CLASSIC ALBUM & SINGLE TRACKS 1969-1980)** [ ] [-]

BABE RUTH

Formed: Hatfield, Hertfordshire, England . . . 1971 as SHACKLOCK by namesake ALAN SHACKLOCK, who soon found singer JENNY HAAN. She was raised in the States as a teenager, which probably inspired them to take the new name BABE RUTH (after the legendary baseball player). They were basically a hard-driving progressive-rock act, front-girl HAAN taking most of the plaudits. The debut album, 'FIRST BASE', didn't even hit that mark in the UK, but went gold in Canada, paving the way for a minor success in the States with their third album. However, by 1975, they had lost the two core members SHACKLOCK and HAAN, replacing them with BERNIE MARSDEN and ELLIE HOPE.

Recommended: THE BEST OF BABE RUTH (*6)

JANITA 'JENNY' HAAN (b.Edgeware, England) – vocals / **ALAN SHACKLOCK** – guitar, vocals, organ, percussion / **DAVE HEWITT** – bass / **JEFF ALLEN** – drums / **DAVE PUNSHON** – piano

Decca / not issued

Sep 71. (7") *(F 13234)* **RUPERT'S MAGIC FEATHER. / FLOOD** [ ] [-]

— **DICK POWELL** – drums repl. JEFF ALLEN

Harvest / Harvest

Nov 72. (7") *(HAR 5061)* <3553> **WELLS FARGO. / THEME FROM 'A FEW DOLLARS MORE'** [ ] [ ]

Nov 72. (lp) *(SHSP 4022)* <11151> **FIRST BASE** [ ] [ ]
– Wells Fargo / The runaways / King Kong / Black dog / The mexican / Joker.

Apr 73. (7") *(HAR 5072)* **AIN'T THAT LIVIN'. / WE ARE HOLDING ON** [ ] [-]

— **ED SPEVOCK** – drums (ex-PETE BROWN'S PIBLOKTO) repl. POWELL + PUNSHON

Mar 74. (lp) *(SHVL 812)* <1275> **AMAR CABALERO** [ ] [ ]
– Lady / Broken cloud / Gimme some leg / Baby pride / Cool jerk / We are holding on / Doctor ove / Amar Cabalero: El Cabalero de la reina Isabella – Hombre de la guitarra – El testament de Amelia.

May 74. (7") *(HAR 5082)* **IF HEAVEN'S ON BEAUTY'S SIDE. / DOCTOR LOVE** [ ] [-]

— added **STEVE GURL** – keyboards (ex-WILD TURKEY)

Oct 74. (7") *(HAR 5087)* **WELLS FARGO. / THE MEXICAN** [ ] [-]

Jan 75. (7") *(HAR 5090)* **PRIVATE NUMBER. / SOMEBODY'S NOBODY** [ ] [ ]

Feb 75. (lp) *(SHSP 4039)* <11367> **BABE RUTH** [ ] [75]
– Dancer / Somebody's nobody / Theme from 'A Few Dollars More' / We people darker than blue / Jack O'Lantern / Private number / Turquoise / Sad but rich / The duchess of Orleans.

Oct 75. (7"m) *(SPSR 377)* **THE DUCHESS OF ORLEANS. / THE JACK O'LANTERN / TURQUOISE** [ ] [-]

— **BERNIE MARSDEN** – guitar (ex-WILD TURKEY) repl. SHACKLOCK

Capitol / Capitol

Nov 75. (lp) <*(EST 11451)*> **STEALIN' HOME** [ ] [ ]
– It'll happen in time / Winner takes all / Fascination / Two thousand sunsets / Elusive / Can you feel it / Say no more / Caught at the plate / Tomorrow.

Apr 76. (7") *(CL 15689)* <4219> **ELUSIVE. / SAY NO MORE** [ ] [ ]

— **SPEVOCK, MARSDEN + GURL** recruited **ELLIE HOPE** – vocals + **RAY KNOTT** – bass to repl. HAAN + HEWITT who formed JENNY HAAN'S LION. She went solo in 1979.

Apr 76. (lp) *(EST 23739)* <EST 11515> **KID'S STUFF** [ ] [ ]
– Oh, dear what a shame / Welcome to the show / Since you went away / Standing in the rain / Sweet, sweet surrender / Oh, doctor / Nickelodeon / Keep your distance / Living a lie.

— **ALLAN ROSS + SID TWINEHAM** – guitar repl.MARSDEN who joined PAICE, ASHTON & LORD. He later formed ALASKA and others, and joined WHITESNAKE. BABE RUTH disbanded in 1977, and some moved on to disco outfit LIQUID GOLD.

– compilations, etc. –

Oct 77. (lp) *Harvest; (SHSM 2019)* **THE BEST OF BABE RUTH** [ ] [ ]
– Wells Fargo / Ain't that livin' / Theme from 'A Few Dollars More' / Private number / Joker / Dancer / The Duchess of Orleans / Black dog / If Heaven's on beauty's side / Lady / Jack O'Lantern. *(re-iss.Aug86 on 'Revolver' lp/c; WKFM LP/MC 81)*

BALLOON FARM

Formed: based – New York, USA . . . 1967 by former Floridians (see below). Their excellent garage/psych debut 45, 'A QUESTION OF TEMPERATURE' (produced by HUGO & LUIGI) soon rose up the US charts, finally hitting the Top 40 in the Spring of '68. It was characterised by fuzzy punk guitar work that didn't quite gel on their follow-up 'FARMER BROWN'.

Recommended: the debut single

D. HENNY / J. SAKS / M. APPEL / E. SCHINUG

London / Laurie

Mar 68. (7") *(HLP 10185)* <3405> **A QUESTION OF TEMPERATURE. / HURTIN' FOR YOUR LOVE** [ ] [37] Feb68

Jun 68. (7") <3445> **FARMER BROWN. / HURRY UP SUNDOWN** [-] [ ]

— some of the members evolved into the more subdued outfit HUCK FINN

Peter BANKS (see under ⇒ FLASH)

Tony BANKS (see under ⇒ GENESIS)

BARCLAY JAMES HARVEST

Formed: Oldham, Lancashire, England . . . Autumn 1966 by art school students JOHN LEES and STUART WOLSTENHOLME. After their initial 45 on 'Parlophone', EMI subsequently found a new home for them on their aptly named 'Harvest' label. In 1970, their eponymous debut album was recorded with a full orchestra conducted by ROBERT GODFREY, their typically prog-rock sound proving a hit with the student fraternity. However their heavy use of mellotron proved none too popular with the critics of the day, who at times lambasted them for their neo-classical pretentions. In fact they were unfairly described by the music press as "the poor man's MOODY BLUES". Their 1971 follow-up 'ONCE AGAIN', featured what was to become their finest song, 'MOCKINGBIRD', a combination of both tender harmonies and quality instrumentation. They carried on in the same vein with two other albums 'BJH AND OTHER SHORT STORIES' & 'BABY JAMES HARVEST', leading to a contract with 'Polydor' in 1974. Finally gaining wide-scale recognition upon the releases of their 4th album 'EVERYONE IS EVERYBODY ELSE', it remains a mystery to most why it didn't chart. By this stage their live appeal was such that 'Polydor' subsequently released a double live set, a piece of work that encompassed everything they'd been working towards during their career. Although Britain and the States had somehow ignored them, they won many converts in Europe, especially Germany, who were always interested in anything prog-rock or symphonic. With the onset of the "new wave" explosion, they were forced into the margins, although they retained a loyal family of fans.
• **Trivia:** A CONCERT FOR THE PEOPLE was recorded near the Berlin Wall and was transmitted live on German TV and radio.

Recommended: THE COMPACT BARCLAY JAMES HARVEST (*8) / BARCLAY JAMES HARVEST LIVE (*8) / ONCE AGAIN (*7) / EVERYONE IS EVERYBODY ELSE (*8)

STUART 'WOOLY' WOLSTENHOLME (b.15 Apr'47) – keyboards, vocals / **JOHN LEES** (b.13 Jan'48) – guitar, vocals, wind / **LES HOLROYD** (b.12 Mar'48, Bolton, England) – bass, vocals / **MELVIN PRITCHARD** (b.20 Jan'48) – drums

Parlophone / Sire

Apr 68. (7") *(R 5693)* <4105> **EARLY MORNING. / MR. SUNSHINE** [ ] [ ]

Harvest / Sire

Jun 69. (7") *(HAR 5003)* <4112> **BROTHER THRUSH. / POOR WAGES** [ ] [ ]

Jun 70. (lp) *(SHVL 770)* <SES 97026> **BARCLAY JAMES HARVEST** [ ] [ ]
– Taking some time on / Mother dear / The sun will never shine / When the world was waken / Good love child / The iron maiden / Dark now my sky.

Aug 70. (7") *(HAR 5025)* **TAKING SOME TIME ON. / THE IRON MAIDEN** [ ] [-]

Feb 71. (lp) *(SHVL 788)* <4904> **ONCE AGAIN** [ ] [ ]
– She said / Happy old world / Song for dying / Galadriel / Mockingbird / Vanessa Simmons / Ball and chain / Lady loves. *(quad-lp Jul73; Q4SHVL 788) (re-iss.Jul83 on 'Fame' lp/c; FA/TCFA 3073)*

Feb 71. (7") *(HAR 5034)* **MOCKINGBIRD. / VANESSA SIMMONS** [ ] [-]

Nov 71. (lp) *(SHVL 794)* <5904> **BJH AND OTHER SHORT STORIES** [ ] [ ]
– Ow / Harry's song / Ursula / Little lapwing / Song with no meaning / Blue John's blues / The poet / After the day.

Apr 72. (7") *(HAR 5051)* **I'M OVER YOU. / CHILD OF MAN** [ ] [-]

Sep 72. (7"; as BOMBADIL) *(HAR 5056)* **BREATHLESS. / WHEN THE CITY SLEEPS** [ ] [-]
(re-iss.Mar75; HAR 5095)

Harvest / Harvest

Oct 72. (7") *(HAR 5058)* <3501> **THANK YOU. / MEDICINE MAN** [ ] [ ]

Oct 72. (lp) *(SHSP 4023)* <11145> **BABY JAMES HARVEST** [ ] [ ] Feb73
– Crazy (over you) / Delph town morn / Summer soldier / Thank you / One hundred thousand smiles out / Moonwater. *(re-iss.May85 on 'E.M.I.' lp/c; ATAK/TC-ATAK 8) (re-iss.Mar87 on 'Fame' lp/c; FA/TC-FA 3172)*

May 73. (7") *(HAR 5060)* **ROCK AND ROLL WOMAN. / THE JOKER** [ ] [ ]

Polydor / Capitol

May 74. (7") *(2058 474)* **POOR BOY BLUES. / CRAZY CITY** [ ] [-]

Jun 74. (lp)(c) *(2383 286)(3170 186)* <PD 6508> **EVERYONE IS EVERYBODY ELSE** [ ] [ ]

– Child of the universe / Negative Earth / Paper wings / The great 1974 mining disaster / Crazy city / See me see you / Poor boy blues / Mill boys / For no one. *(re-iss.Aug83 lp/c; SPE LP/MC 11) (cd-iss.Nov87 & Feb92; 833 448-2)*

Jul 74. (7") *<15104>* **CHILD OF THE UNIVERSE. / CRAZY CITY** [-] [ ]

Nov 74. (d-lp) *(2683 052)* **BARCLAY JAMES HARVEST – LIVE (live)** [40] [-]
– Summer soldier / Medicine man / Crazy city / After the day / The great 1974 mining disaster / Galadriel / Negative Earth / She said / Paper wings / For no one / Mockingbird. *(cd-iss.Jul91 on 'Connoisseur; VSOPCD 164)*

Oct 75. (lp) *(2383 361) <6617>* **TIME HONOURED GHOSTS** [32] [ ]
– In my life / Sweet Jesus / Titles / Jonathan / Beyond the grave / Song for you / Hymn for the children / Moon girl / One night. *(re-iss.Aug83 lp/c; SPE LP/MC 12) (cd-iss.Apr87 & Feb92; 831 543-2)*

Nov 75. (7") *(2058 660) <15118>* **TITLES. / SONG FOR YOU** [ ] [ ]

Polydor M.C.A.

Oct 76. (lp) *(2442 144) <2234>* **OCTOBERON** [19] [ ]
– Polk street rag / Suicide? / May day / Ra / Believe in me / The world goes on / Rock'n'roll star. *(re-iss.Aug83 lp/c; SPE LP/MC 13) (cd-iss.Jun84 & Feb92; 821 930-2)*

Nov 76. (7") *<40690>* **POLK STREET RAG. / ROCK'N'ROLL STAR** [-] [ ]

Mar 77. (7"ep) *(2229 198)* **LIVE EP (live)** [49] [-]
– Rock'n'roll star / Medicine man (part 1 & 2).

Jul 77. (7") *(2058 904) <40795>* **HYMN. / OUR KID'S KID** [ ] [ ]

Sep 77. (lp)(c) *(2442 148)(3170 460) <2302>* **GONE TO EARTH** [30] [ ]
– Hymn / Love is like a violin / Friend of mine / Poor man's Moody Blues / Hard hearted woman / Sea of tranquility / Spirit on the water / Leper's song / Taking me higher. *(cd-iss.Mar83; 800 092-2)*

Mar 78. (7") *(2059 002)* **FRIEND OF MINE. / SUICIDE** [ ] [ ]

Apr 78. (d-lp/d-c) *(PODV/+C 2001)* **LIVE TAPES (live)** [ ] [-]
– Child of the universe / Rock'n'roll star / Poor man's Moody Blues / Mockingbird / Hard hearted woman / One night / Take me higher / Suicide? / Crazy city / Jonathan / For no one / Polk street rag / Hymn. *(d-cd.iss.Feb85; 821 523-2)*

Polydor Polydor

Sep 78. (lp/c) *(POLD/+C 5006) <6173>* **XII** [31] [ ]
– Fantasy: Loving is easy / Berlin / Classics: A tale of two sixties / Turning in circles / Fact: The closed shop / In search of England / Sip of wine / Harbour / Science fiction: Nova Lepidoptera / Giving it up / Fiction: The streets of San Francisco. *(cd-iss.Jan85; 821 941-2)*

Nov 78. (7",7"blue) *(POSP 012)* **LOVING IS EASY. / POLK STREET RAG** [ ] [-]

Jan 79. (7") **LOVING IS EASY. / TURNING IN CIRCLES** [-] [ ]

—— Trimmed to a trio plus session men when WOLSTENHOLME went solo / **KEVIN McALEA** – keyboards (ex-BEES MAKE HONEY, ex-KATE BUSH)

Nov 79. (lp/c) *(POLD/+C 5029) <6267>* **EYES OF THE UNIVERSE** [ ] [ ]
– Love on the line / Alright get down boogie (Mu ala rusic) / The song they love to sing / Skin flicks / Sperratus / Capricorn / Play to the world. *(cd-iss.Jun84; 821 591-2)*

Dec 79. (7") *(POSP 97)* **LOVE ON THE LINE. / ALRIGHT GET DOWN BOOGIE (MU ALA RUSIC)** [63] [ ]

Feb 80. (7") *(POSP 140)* **CAPRICORN. / BERLIN** [ ] [ ]

Nov 80. (7") *(POSP 195)* **LIFE IS FOR LIVING. / SHADES OF B. HILL** [61] [ ]

May 81. (lp/c) *(POLD/+C 5040)* **TURN OF THE TIDE** [55] [-]
– Waiting on the borderline / How do you feel now / Back to the wall / Highway for fools / Echoes and shadows / Death of the city / I'm like a train / Doctor doctor / Life is for living / In memory of the martyrs. *(cd-iss.Mar83 & Feb92; 800 013-2)*

Jun 82. (lp/c) *(POLD/+C 5052)* **A CONCERT FOR THE PEOPLE (BERLIN)** [15] [-]
– Berlin / Loving is easy / Mockingbird / Sip of wine / Nova Lepidoptera / In memory of the martyrs / Life is for living / Child of the universe / Hymn. *(cd-iss.Mar83 & Feb92; 800 026-2)*

May 83. (lp/c)(cd) *(POLH/+C 3)(811 638-2)* **RING OF CHANGES** [36] [-]
– Fifties child / Looking from the outside / Teenage heart / High wire / Midnight drug / Waiting for the right time / Just a day away / Paradiso dos cavalos / Ring of changes. *(cd-iss.Feb92 cd/c; 811 638-2/-4)*

May 83. (7") *(POSP 585)* **JUST A DAY AWAY. / ROCK'N'ROLL LADY (live)** [68] [ ]
(7"sha-pic-d) *(POPPX 585)* – ('A'side) / Looking from the outside.

Oct 83. (7") *(POSP 640)* **WAITING FOR THE RIGHT TIME. / BLOW ME DOWN** [ ] [ ]
(12"+=) *(POSPX 640)* – ('A'extended).

Mar 84. (7"/7"sha-pic-d) *(POSP/+P 674)* **VICTIMS OF CIRCUMSTANCE. / ('A'instrumental)** [ ] [ ]
(ext.12"+=) *(POSPX 674)* – Love on the line (live).

Apr 84. (lp/c)(cd) *(POLD/+C 5135)(817 950-2)* **VICTIMS OF CIRCUMSTANCE** [33] [-]
– Sideshow / Hold on / Rebel woman / Say you'll stay / For your love / Victim of circumstance / Inside my nightmare / Watching you / I've got a feeling.

Sep 84. (7") *(POSP 705)* **I'VE GOT A FEELING. / REBEL WOMAN** [ ] [ ]

Nov 86. (7") *(POSP 834)* **HE SAID LOVE. / ON THE WINGS OF LOVE** [ ] [ ]
(12"+=) *(POSPX 834)* – Hymn (live).

Feb 87. (lp/c)(cd) *(POLD/+C 5209)(831 483-2)* **FACE TO FACE** [65] [ ]
– Prisoner of your love / He said love / Alone in the night / Turn the key / Guitar blues / African / Following me / All my life / Panic / Kiev. *(cd+=)*– On the wings of love.

Apr 88. (lp/c)(cd) *(POLD/+C 5219)(835 590-2)* **GLASNOST (live)** [ ] [ ]
– Berlin / Alone in the night / Hold on / African / On the wings of love / Poor man's Moody Blues / Love on the line / Medicine man / Kiev / Hymn / Turn the key / He said love.

Feb 90. (7"; as BJH) *(PO 67)* **CHEAP THE BULLET. / BERLIN** [ ] [ ]
(12"+=) *(PZ 67)* – Shadows on the sky.
(cd-s+=) *(PZCD 67)* – Alone in the night / Hold on.

Mar 90. (cd/c/lp; as BJH) *(841 751-2/-4/-1)* **WELCOME TO THE SHOW** [ ] [ ]
– The life you lead / Lady Macbeth / Cheap the bullet / Welcome to the show / John Lennon's guitar / African nights / Psychedelic child / Where do we go / If love is king / Halfway to freedom.

May 92. (7")(c-s) **STAND UP. / LIFE IS FOR LIVING** [ ] [-]
(cd-s+=) – John Lennon's guitar / Play to the world.
(cd-s+=) – Alone in the night / Poor man's Moody Blues.

Jun 93. (cd/c) *(519 303-2/-4)* **CAUGHT IN THE LIGHT** [ ] [ ]
– Who do we think we are? / Knoydart / Copii Romania / Back to Earth / Cold war / Forever yesterday / The great unknown / Spud-u-like / Silver wings / Once more / A matter of time / Ballad of Denshaw Mill.

—— look to have disbanded after above.

– compilations, etc. –

on 'Harvest' unless otherwise mentioned

Sep 72. (lp) *EMI Starline; (SRS 5126)* **EARLY MORNING ONWARDS** [ ] [-]
– Early morning / Poor wages / Brother Thrush / Mr. Sunshine / Taking some time on / Mother dear / Mockingbird / Song with no meaning / I'm over you / Child of man / After the day.

Mar 75. (7") *(HAR 5094)* **MOCKINGBIRD. / GALADRIEL** [ ] [ ]

Jan 77. (lp) *(SHSM 2013)* **THE BEST OF BARCLAY JAMES HARVEST** [ ] [-]
(re-iss.Aug86 on 'E.M.I.' lp/c; ATAK/TC-ATAK 95)

Sep 79. (lp) *(SHSM 2023)* **THE BEST OF BARCLAY JAMES HARVEST VOL.2** [ ] [-]

Feb 81. (lp) *(SHSM 2033)* **THE BEST OF BARCLAY JAMES HARVEST VOL.3** [ ] [-]

Nov 85. (cd) *Polydor; (825 895-2)* **THE COMPACT STORY OF BARCLAY JAMES HARVEST** [ ] [ ]

Oct 87. (cd) *E.M.I.; (CDP 746 709-2)* **ANOTHER ARABLE PARABLE** [ ] [-]

Dec 90. (cd/c) *Connoisseur; (VSOP CD/MC 140)* **ALONE WE FLY** [ ] [-]
– Crazy city / For no one / Mockingbird / Hymn / Our kid's kid / Berlin / Loving is easy / Love on the line / Rock'n'roll lady / Shades of B Hill / Fifties child / Waiting for the right time / Blow me down / Sideshow / He said love / Guitar blues.

Mar 91. (d-cd/d-c/d-lp) *Harvest; (CD/TC+/EN 5014)* **THE HARVEST YEARS** [ ] [-]

Jun 92. (cd) *Polydor; (513 587-2)* **THE BEST OF BARCLAY JAMES HARVEST** [ ] [-]

Dec 92. (cd) *Beat Goes On; (BGOCD 152)* **BARCLAY JAMES HARVEST / ONCE AGAIN** [ ] [-]
(re-iss.Oct95 on 'One Way';)

Dec 92. (cd) *Beat Goes On; (BGOCD 160)* **BJH & OTHER SHORT STORIES / BABY JAMES HARVEST** [ ] [-]
(re-iss.Oct95 on 'One Way';)

May 93. (cd/c) *Spectrum; (550029-2/-4)* **SORCERERS & KEEPERS** [ ] [-]

Feb 96. (4xcd-box) *EMI-Barclay; (CDBARCLAY 1)* **FOUR ORIGINALS** [ ] [-]
– (first 4 albums)

Aug 96. (cd) *Connoisseur; VSOPCD 228)* **ENDLESS DREAM** [ ] [-]

Mar 97. (cd) *Disky; (DC 86721-2)* **MOCKINGBIRD** [ ] [-]

JOHN LEES

Polydor not issued

Sep 74. (7") *(2058 513)* **BEST OF MY LOVE. / YOU CAN'T GET IT** [ ] [-]

—— The next 2 releases were recorded in '73

Harvest Capitol

Jul 77. (lp) *(SHSM 2018)* **A MAJOR FANCY** [ ] [ ]
– Untitled No.1 – Heritage / Untitled No.2 / Untitled No.3 / Child of the universe / Kes (a major fancy) / Long ships / Sweet faced Jane / Witburg night.

Jul 77. (7") *(HAR 5132)* **CHILD OF THE UNIVERSE. / KES (A MAJOR FANCY)** [ ] [-]

Syd BARRETT

Born: ROGER KEITH BARRETT, 6 Jan'46, Cambridge, England. Earned the nickname SID (which he later changed to SYD), after regulars at the local Riverside Jazz Club found out his surname and christened him after an old drummer from the area, SID BARRET. SYD was talented enough to secure a place at the prestigious Camberwell Art School in 1963 and once in London, he teamed up with his old friend ROGER WATERS, who had asked him to join his band The SCREAMING ABDABS. At SYD's suggestion, the band renamed themselves PINK FLOYD after two Georgia bluesmen featured on an old record he owned. Turned onto LSD by a friend, he became fascinated by the mysteries of the Universe, even carrying around a Times Astronomical Atlas. This obsession would later inspire such FLOYD classics as 'ASTRONOMY DOMINE' and 'INTERSTELLAR OVERDRIVE'. The latter's main riff was famously derived from a chord pattern SYD worked out after hearing manager PETER JENNER attempting to hum LOVE's version of BURT BACHARACH's 'My Little Red Book'. The 1967 album 'THE PIPER AT THE GATES OF DAWN' on which these two tracks appeared, made the group and especially BARRETT, major league pop stars. This was something that did SYD's increasingly erratic mental health no good whatsoever. By the time of the album's release, he had moved into the infamous Cromwell Road flat in London, living on a daily diet of hallucinogenics and was beginning to develop a piercing stare, which would scare even the most hardened person in his company. At EMI's request, BARRETT recorded two further tracks, 'SCREAM THY LAST SCREAM' and 'VEGETABLE MAN', which were unsurprisingly rejected, EMI staff producer NORMAN SMITH dubbing them "lunatic ravings". His penultimate offering for FLOYD, 'APPLES AND ORANGES', flopped, and SYD's mental condition deteriorated further. After missing some shows and performances, WATERS eventually made it clear he was surplus to requirement. His last effort with PINK FLOYD, 'JUGBAND BLUES', appeared after his departure, on the second FLOYD album 'A SAUCERFUL OF SECRETS' (mid-68). It was his last poignant statement for FLOYD, a self-diagnosis of his encroaching schizophrenia. EMI (actually 'Harvest') still had enough confidence in SYD to offer him a solo deal, as he set about recording his debut, 'THE MADCAP LAUGHS'. Released early in 1970 after a laborious year in the studio, it featured drummer NICK MASON and other FLOYD-ians, thus its brief entry into the UK Top 40. Despite SYD being high on the tranquiliser Mandrax, the album had its moments, with the likes of 'OCTOPUS', 'DARK GLOBE', 'TERRAPIN', 'NO GOOD TRYIN' and 'LONG GONE', making up for the other lost-in-the-ether tracks. The hastily recorded 'BARRETT', released later the same year, used a band featuring DAVE GILMOUR (the friend who replaced him in PINK FLOYD), RICK

WRIGHT and JERRY SHIRLEY, giving him some cohesion, and although it was more assured in depth, it lacked the fragility of its predecessor. The album was poorly received and SYD retreated to the cellar of his mother's home in Cambridge. He resurfaced in 1972 as part of the doomed STARS project (with TWINK & JACK MONK), before finally giving up music altogether. He never fully recovered from his debilitating mental illness and tragically, at the time of writing, he's become almost blind due to diabetes related problems. Whether the drugs actually caused his decline or merely assisted it is something that will no doubt continue to be debated long into the future, although you can be sure SYD won't care to listen. A flawed genius whose legend and influence grows stronger with each passing year, SYD BARRETT was the whimsical child-like star, burning brightly in a kaleidoscope of technicolour sound, before dropping out into a haze of drug-induced psychosis. He has since been tributed and stylised by many, including TELEVISION PERSONALITIES, ROBYN HITCHCOCK and The LEGENDARY PINK DOTS. • **Trivia:** PINK FLOYD paid homage to SYD on their album SHINE ON YOU CRAZY DIAMOND track from album 'WISH YOU WERE HERE'. SYD attended these sessions but didn't contribute.

Recommended: THE MADCAP LAUGHS (*8) / BARRETT (*6) / OPEL (*6)

SYD BARRETT – vocals, guitar; augmented by **DAVID GILMOUR + ROGER WATERS** with **MIKE RATLEDGE** – keyboards / **HUGH HOPPER** – bass / **ROBERT WYATT** – drums (all of SOFT MACHINE) plus **JOHN 'WILLIE' WATSON + JERRY SHIRLEY** – rhythm (latter of HUMBLE PIE)

Harvest Harvest

Oct 69. (7") *(HAR 5009)* **OCTOPUS. / GOLDEN HAIR** [ ] [ ]

Jan 70. (lp) *(SHVL 765) <SABB 11314>* **THE MADCAP LAUGHS** [40] [ ]
– Terrapin / No good trying / Love you / No man's land / Dark globe / Here I go / Octopus / Golden Hair / Long gone / She took a long cold look / Feel / If it's in you / Late night. *(cd-iss.Oct87; CDP 746 607-2) (re-iss.cd Jun94; CDGO 2053) (re-iss.Feb97 on 'E.M.I.'; LPCENT 1)*

— SYD retained GILMOUR, SHIRLEY + WILSON adding **RICK WRIGHT** – keyboards (of PINK FLOYD) and guest on one **VIC SAYWELL** – tuba

Nov 70. (lp) *(SHSP 4007)* **BARRETT** [ ] [-]
– Baby lemonade / Love song / Dominoes / It is obvious / Rats / Maisie / Gigolo aunt / Waving my arms in the air / Wined and dined / Wolfpack / Effervescing elephant / I never lied to you. *(cd-iss.May87; CDP 746 606-2) (re-iss.cd Jun94; CDGO 2054)*

— His solo career ended and he formed short-lived STARS early in '72, with **TWINK** – drums (ex-PINK FAIRIES) + **JACK MONK** – bass (they made no recordings)

— In 1982, he was living with his mother having hung up guitar.

– compilations, others, etc. –

Sep 74. (d-lp) *Harvest; (SHDW 404)* **SYD BARRETT** [ ] [-]
– (THE MADCAP LAUGHS & BARRETT).

Jan 88. (12"ep) *Strange Fruit; (SFPS/+CD 043)* **THE PEEL SESSIONS (24.2.70)** [ ] [-]
– Terrapin / Gigolo aunt / Baby lemonade / Two of a kind / Effervescing elephant. *(cd re-iss.Sep95; same)*

Oct 88. (cd)(c/lp) *Harvest; (CDP 791 206-2)(TC+/SHSP 4126)* **OPEL** (recorded 68-70) [ ] [ ]
– Opel / Clowns and daggers (Octopus) / Rats / Golden hair (vocal) / Dollyrocker / Word song / Wined and dined / Swan Lee (Silas Lang) / Birdie hop / Let's split / Lanky (part 1) / Wouldn't you miss me / Golden hair (instrumental). *(re-iss.cd Jun94; CDGO 2055)*

Apr 93. (3xcd-box) *E.M.I.; (SYDBOX 1)* **CRAZY DIAMOND – THE COMPLETE SYD BARRETT** [ ] [ ]
– (all 3 albums above)

Apr 94. (cd) *Cleopatra; (CLEO 5771-2)* **OCTOPUS** [ ] [-]

Peter BAUMANN

Born: 1953, Berlin, Germany. After leaving The ANTS, he joined TANGERINE DREAM in 1971, although after several successful albums, he decided to go solo. Visiting America in 1976, he conducted a series of laser shows and recorded his first album 'ROMANCE 76', a collection of atmospheric, synthesized music. After the follow-up two years later, BAUMANN built a studio in Berlin where he produced some up and coming European acts. Relocating to Manhattan, New York at the turn of the decade, he built a custom made studio in his East Side apartment, subsequently recruiting Brooklyn vocalist ELI HOLLAND, to augment him on his 1984 project, BAUMANN. • **Trivia:** His 3rd album was produced by ROBERT PALMER.

Recommended: PHASE BY PHASE (*6)

PETER BAUMANN – keyboards, synthesizers (ex-TANGERINE DREAM)

Virgin Virgin

Feb 77. (lp) *(V 2069)* **ROMANCE '76** [ ] [ ]
– Bicentennial present / Romance / Phase by phase / Meadow of infinity (part 1) / The glass bridge / Meadow of infinity (part 2). *(re-iss.1988 lp/c; OVED/+C 197)*

— In 1978 (Nov), he recorded and released lp 'BAUMANN/ KOEK', with said German instrumentalist on the 'Jaguar' label.

— added **WOLFGANG THIERFELDT** – drums / **B. JOBSKI** – horns / **W. ROPER** – recorder

1979. (lp) *(V 2124)* **TRANS-HARMONIC NIGHTS** [ ] [ ]
– This day / White beach and black beach / Chasing the dream / Biking up the Strand / Phase day / Meridian moorland / The third site / Dance at dawn. *(re-iss.1988 lp/c; OVED/+C 198) (cd-iss.Oct90; CDV 2124)*

— now w/ **RITCHIE FLIEGLER + JOHN TROPEA** – guitar / **CARSTEN BOHN + MIKE DAWE** – drums / **LINDSAY KAY BRYNAN** – vocals

Virgin Portrait

Sep 81. (lp) *(V 2214)* **REPEAT REPEAT** [ ] [ ]
– Repeat repeat / Home sweet home / Decca dance / Real times / M.A.N. series two / Daytime logic / Brain damage / Kinky Dinky / What is your use? / Playland pleasure. *(re-iss.1988 lp/c OVED/+C 199)*

Sep 81. (7") *(VS 446)* **REPEAT REPEAT. / HOME SWEET HOME** [ ] [ ]

— w/ **FLIEGLER / BRUCE BRODY** – synth / **ELI HOLLAND** – vocals / **RICH TEETER** – drums

Arista Arista

Jan 84. (7"; as BAUMANN) *(ARIST 556)* **STRANGERS IN THE NIGHT. / WELCOME** [ ] [-]
(12"+=) *(ARIST12 556)* – Strangers in the night (part 2).

Feb 84. (lp; as BAUMANN) *(205970)* **STRANGERS IN THE NIGHT** [ ] [ ]
– Strangers in the night / Metro man / King of the jungle / Be mine / Time machine / Taxi / Cash / Glass house / Ground zero / Welcome.

– compilation –

Jan 96. (cd) *Virgin; (CDOVD 464)* **PHASE BY PHASE** [ ] [-]

B.B. BLUNDER (see under ⇒ BLOSSOM TOES)

BEACH BOYS

Formed: Hawthorne, Los Angeles, California, USA . . . 1961 by WILSON brothers BRIAN, DENNIS and CARL, who were soon joined by their cousin MIKE LOVE and neighbour AL JARDINE. They went through a series of cringe-inducing names before being individually christened The BEACH BOYS by a local DIY studio, who had released their first single 'SURFIN' on their small 'Candix' label. As sales of the record mushroomed, the band decided to keep the name. MURRAY WILSON, the brothers' tyrannical father, seized the opportunity to become their manager, producer and song publisher; not exactly a healthy combination and one which the band would come to regret when financial troubles dogged them throughout the next decade and beyond. For the moment however, on the surface at least, everything was hunky dory, the band riding the commercial crest of their surfing wave as they signed to 'Capitol' in 1962 and became the very essence the sun-tanned, Californian dream. The hits came thick and fast with the prodigiously talented BRIAN writing most of the material. Songs like 'SURFIN SAFARI' and 'SURFIN U.S.A.' were effervescent feelgood anthems, their jaw dropping vocal harmonies framing images of surf, sea and beautiful girls. Early glimpses of BRIAN's penchant for introspection are evident on tracks like the poignant 'IN MY ROOM', co-written with GARY USHER, the first of many songwriters BRIAN would collaborate with during the course of his career. The execrable sentiments of songs like 'BE TRUE TO YOUR SCHOOL', were a result of a period of collaboration with lyricist ROGER CHRISTIAN, although this partnership also created livlier gems like 'LITTLE DEUCE COUPE' and 'I GET AROUND'. The latter song was probably the highlight of 'ALL SUMMER LONG', the 1964 album which saw the band make the leap from being primarily a singles act to creating consistent long players. By Christmas of that year, however, the strain of their horrendous recording/touring treadmill was too much for BRIAN and he suffered a series of nervous breakdowns. Producing and arranging 6 albums in just over 2 years as well as writing over 60 songs in the same period would've been too much for the hardiest of souls, let alone the painfully shy and sensitive BRIAN. This episode signalled the end of BRIAN's live commitment to the band, allowing him to concentrate solely on composing and recording. 'BEACH BOYS – TODAY' and 'SUMMER DAYS (AND SUMMER NIGHTS)' represented a career high with breathtaking material highlighting BRIAN's preoccupation with achieving the perfect sound. He had become obsessed with outdoing The BEATLES who he saw as a threat, a paranoia that grew stronger after his first forays into the world of LSD. He first took the drug in the summer of '65 and it changed his aproach to music, to his whole life in fact, with BRIAN later stating that his mind was opened and it scared the shit out of him. BRIAN then enlisted the unlikely help of erstwhile ad sloganeer TONY ASHER to express the lyrical mood of these new pieces, and the result was 'PET SOUNDS'. Released in May '66, it still holds the coveted "best album of all-time" position among many critics, with fragile highlights being 'GOD ONLY KNOWS', 'WOULDN'T IT BE NICE' and 'CAROLINE NO', which perfectly evoked BRIAN's turbulent emotional state. Reportedly devastated at the album's lack of success in his home country (yes, it did hit Top 10) and feeling outdone by The BEATLES' 'Revolver' and DYLAN's 'Blonde On Blonde', he upped his drug use and vowed to go one better, dreaming of the ultimate studio masterpiece. Initially pencilled in for inclusion on 'PET SOUNDS' in its earliest incarnation, 'GOOD VIBRATIONS' was released in October that year and soon became their biggest ever selling single. With its pioneering use of the theramin and complex vocal arrangements, its success vindicated BRIAN's vision of grand sonic tapestrys over the formulaic pop that other members (most notably MIKE LOVE and his father) wanted to churn out. Around this time, BRIAN began working on his masterpiece (with self-styled L.A. boho scenester/songwriter VAN DYKE PARKS), which had a working title of 'DUMB ANGEL', later changing to 'SMILE'. The sessions that resulted are the stuff of legend, with BRIAN's mental condition deteriorating rapidly under the weight of his own expectation. Among BRIAN's more whimsical foibles were having a box filled with sand so he could play piano barefoot "like on the beach, man" (Surf's Up, indeed). More worrying was the pathological superstition which saw him attempt to destroy tapes of the abandoned 'SMILE' album, although these did surface later on albums 'SMILEY SMILE', 'HEROES AND VILLAINS' and 'SURF'S UP'. From this point on, BRIAN retreated even further from the world at large and spent much of the following decade in bed. A string of average, occasionally good albums followed with DENNIS emerging as a fairly talented songwriter. Recorded after the band's acrimonious split with 'Capitol', 1971's 'SURF'S UP' was the highlight of this period with its 'SMILE'-era title track and spirited contributions from other band members. DENNIS WILSON's association with the infamous CHARLES MANSON, albeit before he went on his killing spree in 1969, probably brought more attention than any music the band released at this time. With the exception of one outstanding BRIAN-penned song 'SAIL ON SAILOR' from the disappointing 'HOLLAND' set, much of the 70's material was creatively bland to say the least. On the 4th June 1973, their father died and eventually MIKE LOVE's brothers STAN and STEVE were removed from management after STEVE was found guilty of embezzling around $1 million. 1977's 'BEACH BOYS LOVE YOU' album saw BRIAN return to take the reins again for the first time in 10 years, and included some fine material. From here on in, The BEACH BOYS became nothing more than a nostalgic novelty act, living on past glories while producing stagnant albums for the over 40's. On the 28th December '83, tragedy struck when DENNIS drowned during a diving trip in Marina Del Ray. The band struggled on minus BRIAN who'd been sacked a year earlier. The band scored a surprise US No.1 hit in 1988 with the soppy 'KOKOMO', which was co-written with former MAMAS & THE PAPAS singer JOHN PHILLIPS. Meanwhile, BRIAN released a competent, not to mention long-awaited solo album under the guidance of his controversial therapist EUGENE LANDY. He even recorded a second album, which was strangely turned down by his new label 'Sire', despite garnering rave reviews from critics who'd heard the pre-release tapes. 1995 saw the release of BRIAN's 'I JUST WASN'T MADE FOR THESE TIMES', an album project combining re-working of older and rare material. A year later The BEACH BOYS scraped the barrel of banality when they did a nauseating run through of their 60's hit 'FUN, FUN, FUN' with STATUS QUO. This was surely the end of the sandy road for the once inspirational outfit. • **Covered:** THE TIMES THEY ARE A-CHANGIN' (Bob Dylan) / PAPA OOM MOW MOW (Rivingtons) / I CAN HEAR MUSIC (Ronettes) / BARBARA ANN (Regents) / LOUIE LOUIE (Kingsmen) / WHY DO FOOLS FALL IN LOVE? (Frankie Lymon & the Teenagers) / MONSTER MASH (Bobby Pickett) / JOHNNY B. GOODE (Chuck Berry) / DO YOU WANNA DANCE (Bobby Freeman) / YOU'VE GOT TO HIDE YOUR LOVE AWAY + I SHOULD HAVE KNOWN BETTER (Beatles) / ALLEY OOP (Hollywood Argyles) / BLUEBIRDS OVER THE MOUNTAIN (Ersel Hickey) / THEN I KISSED HER (Crystals) / COME GO WITH ME (Del-Vikings) / CALIFORNIA DREAMIN' (Mamas & The Papas) / THE WANDERER (Dion) / ROCK AND ROLL MUSIC (Chuck Berry) / BLUEBERRY HILL (Fats Domino) / MONA (Bo Diddley) / PEGGY SUE (Buddy Holly) / THE AIR THAT I BREATHE (Hollies) / HOT FUN IN THE SUMMERTIME (Sly & The Family Stone) / WALKING IN THE SAND (Shangri-la's) / UNDER THE BOARDWALK (Drifters) / etc.

Recommended: THE VERY BEST OF THE BEACH BOYS (*8) / PET SOUNDS (*10) / THE BEACH BOYS – TODAY (*6) / SURF'S UP (*6) / SMILEY SMILE (*6)

BRIAN WILSON (b.20 Jun'42, Inglewood, California) – vocals, percussion / **CARL WILSON** (b.21 Dec'46) – guitar, vocals / **DENNIS WILSON** (b. 4 Dec'44) – vocals, drums / **MIKE LOVE** (b.15 Mar'44, Baldwin Hills, California) – vocals / **AL JARDINE** (b. 3 Sep'42, Lima, Ohio) – vocals, guitar

not issued Candix

Dec 61. (7") *<301>* **SURFIN'. / LUAU** – □
Feb 62. (7") *<331>* **SURFIN'. / LUAU** – 75

—— **DAVID MARKS** – vocals repl. JARDINE who became a dentist

Capitol Capitol

Aug 62. (7") *(CL 15273) <4777>* **SURFIN' SAFARI. / 409** □ 14 / 76
Nov 62. (lp) *<T 1808>* **SURFIN' SAFARI** – 32
– Surfin' safari / County fair / Ten little indians / Chug-a-lug / Little girl (you're my Miss America) / 409 / Surfin' * / Heads you win – tails I lose / Summertime blues / Cuckoo clock * / Moon dawg / The shift. *(UK-iss.Apr63; SY 4572) (re-iss.Jun81 on 'Greenlight'; GO 2014)*– omitted *
Jan 63. (7") *(CL 15285) <4880>* **TEN LITTLE INDIANS. / COUNTY FAIR** □ 49 Nov62
(re-iss.Jun79; CL 16041)
Mar 63. (7") *(CL 15305) <4932>* **SURFIN' U.S.A.. / SHUT DOWN** 34 3 / 23
(re-iss.Jun79; CL 16042)
Apr 63. (lp; stereo/mono) *<S+/T 1890>* **SURFIN' U.S.A.** – 2
– Surfin' U.S.A. / Farmer's daughter / Misirlou / Stoked / Lonely sea / Shut down / Noble surfer / Honky tonk / Lana / Surf jam / Let's go trippin' / Finders keepers. *(UK-iss.Aug65; same); hit No.17)*

—— **AL JARDINE** – vocals returned to repl. MARKS

Jul 63. (7") *<5009>* **SURFER GIRL. / LITTLE DEUCE COUPE** – 7 / 15
Sep 63. (lp; stereo/mono) *<S+/T 1981>* **SURFER GIRL** – 7
– Surfer girl / Catch a wave / Surfer Moon / South bay surfer / Rocking surfer / Little deuce Coupe / In my room / Hawaii / Surfer's rule / Our car club / Your summer dream / Boogie woogie. *(UK-iss.Mar67; same); hit No.13) (re-iss.Aug86 lp/c; EMS/TC-EMS 1175)*
Oct 63. (lp; stereo/mono) *<(S+/T 1998)>* **LITTLE DEUCE COUPE** □ 4
– Little deuce Coupe / Ballad of ole' Betsy / Be true to your school / Car crazy cutie * / Cherry, cherry Coupe / 409 / Shut down / Spirit of America / Our car club * / No-go showboat / A young man is gone / Custom machine. *(re-iss.Jun81 on 'Greenlight'; GO 2025)*– omitted * *(re-iss.Aug86 lp/c; EMS/TC-EMS 1174)*
Nov 63. (7") *<5069>* **BE TRUE TO YOUR SCHOOL. / IN MY ROOM** – 6 / 23
Dec 63. (7") *<5096>* **LITTLE SAINT NICK. / THE LORD'S PRAYER** – □
Jan 64. (7"; as SURVIVORS) *<5102>* **PAMELA JEAN. / AFTER THE GAME** – □
Mar 64. (7") *(CL 15339) <5118>* **FUN, FUN, FUN. / WHY DO FOOLS FALL IN LOVE** □ 5 Feb64
(re-iss.Jun79; CL 16043)
Jul 64. (lp; stereo/mono) *<(S+/T 2027)>* **SHUT DOWN, VOLUME 2** □ 13 Apr64
– Fun, fun, fun / Don't worry baby / In the parkin' lot / "Cassius" Love vs "Sonny" Wilson / The warmth of the sun / This car of mine / Why do fools fall in love / Pom-pom play girl / Keep an eye on summer / Shut down (pt.II) / Louie louie / Denny's drum. *(re-iss.May89 on 'C5'; C5-535)*

—— Note:- 'SHUT DOWN' was a various artists surf US-lp issued Jul63 reaching No.7. It contained two BEACH BOYS tracks; 409 / Shut down.

Jun 64. (7") *(CL 15350) <5174>* **I GET AROUND. / DON'T WORRY BABY** 7 1 May64
(re-iss.Jun79; CL 16044)
Jul 64. (lp; stereo/mono) *<S+/T 2110>* **ALL SUMMER LONG** – 4
– I get around / All summer long / Hushabye / Little Honda / We'll run away / Carl's big chance / Wendy / Do you remember? / Girls on the beach / Drive-in / Our favourite recording session / Don't back down. *(UK-iss.Jun65; same) (re-iss.Jul73 on 'Music For Pleasure'; MfP 50065) (re-iss.Aug86 lp/c; EMS/TC-EMS 1176)*
Oct 64. (7") *(CL 15361) <5245>* **WHEN I GROW UP (TO BE A MAN). / SHE KNOWS ME TOO WELL** 27 9 Aug64
(re-iss.Jun79; CL 16045)
Oct 64. (7"ep) *<R-5267>* **LITTLE HONDA / DON'T BACK DOWN. / WENDY / HUSHABYE** – 65 / 44
Dec 64. (7") *<5312>* **THE MAN WITH ALL THE TOYS. / BLUE CHRISTMAS** – □
Jan 65. (7") *(CL 15370) <5306>* **DANCE, DANCE, DANCE. / THE WARMTH OF THE SUN** 24 8 Oct64
(re-iss.Jun79; CL 16046)
Feb 65. (lp; stereo/mono) *<(S+/T 2198)>* **BEACH BOYS CONCERT (live)** □ 1 Nov64
– Fun, fun, fun / The little old lady from Pasadena / Little deuce Coupe / Long tail Texan / In my room / Monster mash / Let's go trippin' / Papa-oom-mow-mow / The wanderer / Hawaii / Graduation day / I get around / Johnny B. Goode. *(re-iss.Jun81 on 'Greenlight' lp/c; GO/TCGO 2005)*

—— **GLEN CAMPBELL** – vocals (on tour) repl. BRIAN who suffered breakdown. However BRIAN did stay as writer/producer (6th member)

Feb 65. (7") *<5372>* **DO YOU WANNA DANCE?. / PLEASE LET ME WONDER** – 12 / 52
Mar 65. (7") *(CL 15384)* **ALL SUMMER LONG. / DO YOU WANNA DANCE?** □ –
(re-iss.Jun79; CL 16047)
Mar 65. (lp; stereo/mono) *<(S+/T 2269)>* **THE BEACH BOYS TODAY!** – 4
– Do you wanna dance? / Good to my baby / Don't hurt my little sister / When I grow up (to be a man) / Help me, Rhonda / Dance, dance, dance / Please let me wonder / I'm so young / Kiss me baby / She knows me too well / In the back of my mind / She knew me too well. *(UK-iss.Apr66; same); hit No.6) (re-iss.Jan72 as 'DO YOU WANNA DANCE' on 'Music For Pleasure'; MFP 5235)*

—— **BRUCE JOHNSTON** – vocals (ex-his combo) repl. GLEN CAMPBELL who went solo

May 65. (7") *(CL 15392) <5395>* **HELP ME, RHONDA. / KISS ME BABY** 27 1 Apr65
(re-iss.Jun79; CL 16048)
Jul 65. (lp; stereo/mono) *<(S+/T 2354)>* **SUMMER DAYS (AND SUMMER NIGHTS!!)** – 2
– The girl from New York City / Amusements parks U.S.A. / Then I kissed her / Salt Lake City / Girl don't tell me / Help me Rhonda / Let him run wild / You're so good to me / Summer means new love / I'm bugged at my ol' man / And your dream comes true. *(UK-iss.Jul66; same); hit No.4) (re-iss.Jun78; CAPS 1023) (re-iss.Aug86 lp/c; EMS/TC-EMS 1178)*
Aug 65 (7") *(CL 15409) <5464>* **CALIFORNIA GIRLS. / LET HIM RUN WILD** 26 3 Jul65
(re-iss.Jun79; CL 16049)
Dec 65. (7") *(CL 15425) <5540>* **THE LITTLE GIRL I ONCE KNEW. / THERE'S NO OTHER (LIKE MY BABY)** □ 20 Nov65
(re-iss.Jun79; CL 16050)
Feb 66. (7") *(CL 15432) <5561>* **BARBARA ANN. / GIRL DON'T TELL ME** 3 2 Dec65
(re-iss.Jun79; CL 16051)
Feb 66. (lp; stereo/mono) *<(S+/T 2398)>* **BEACH BOYS' PARTY!** 3 6 Nov65
– Hully gully / I should have known better / Tell me why / Papa-oom- mow-mow / Mountain of love / You've got to hide your love away / Devoted to you / Alley oop / There's no other (like my baby) / I get around – Little deuce Coupe / The times they are a-changin' / Barbara Ann. *(re-iss.Aug86 lp/c; EMS/TC-EMS 1177)*
Apr 66. (7"; by BRIAN WILSON *(CL 15438) <5610>* **CAROLINE, NO. / SUMMER MEANS NEW LOVE** □ 32 Mar66
Apr 66. (7") *(CL 15441) <5602>* **SLOOP JOHN B. / YOU'RE SO GOOD TO ME** 2 3 Mar66
(re-iss.Jun79; CL 16052)
May 66. (lp; stereo/mono) *<(S+/T 2458)>* **PET SOUNDS** 2 10
– Wouldn't it be nice / You still believe in me / That's not me / Don't talk (put your head on my shoulder) / I'm waiting for the day / Let's go away for awhile / Sloop John B. / God only knows / I know there's no answer / Here today / I just wasn't made for these times / Pet sounds / Caroline, no. *(re-iss.Jun81 on 'Greenlight'; GO 2002) (re-iss.May82 on 'Fame'; FA 3018) (re-iss.Aug86 lp/c; EMS/TC-EMS 1179) <(cd-iss.Jun90; 7-48421)>*– Hang on to your ego / Trombone Dixie. *(re-iss.Nov93 on 'Fame' cd/c; CD/TC FA 3298)*
Jul 66. (7") *(CL 15459) <5706>* **GOD ONLY KNOWS. / WOULDN'T IT BE NICE** 2 39 / 8
(re-iss.Jun79; CL 16053)
Oct 66. (7") *<5676>* **GOOD VIBRATIONS. / LET'S GO AWAY FOR AWHILE** – 1
Oct 66. (7") *(CL 15475)* **GOOD VIBRATIONS. / WENDY** 1 –
(re-iss.Jun79; CL 16054)
Apr 67. (7") *(CL 15502)* **THEN I KISSED HER. / MOUNTAIN OF LOVE** 4 –
(re-iss.Jun79; CL 16055)

Capitol Brother

Aug 67. (7") *(CL 15510) <1001>* **HEROES AND VILLAINS. / YOU'RE WELCOME** 8 12 Jul67

(re-iss.Jun79; CL 16056)

Sep 67. (7"; BRIAN WILSON & MIKE LOVE) *(CL 15513) <1002>* **GETTIN' HUNGRY. / DEVOTED TO YOU** [ ] [ ]

Nov 67. (lp; stereo/mono) *<(S+/T 9001)>* **SMILEY SMILE** [9] [41] Sep67
– Heroes and villains / Vegetables / Fall breaks and back to winter / She's goin' bald / Little pad / Good vibrations / With me tonight / Wind chimes / Gettin' hungry / Wonderful / Whistle in.

Capitol Capitol

Nov 67. (7") *(CL 15521) <2028>* **WILD HONEY. / WIND CHIMES** [29] [31]
(re-iss.Jun79; CL 16057)

Dec 67. (7") *<2068>* **DARLIN'. / HERE TODAY** [-] [19]

Jan 68. (7") *(CL 15527)* **DARLIN'. / COUNTRY AIR** [11] [-]
(re-iss.Jun79; CL 16058)

Mar 68. (lp; stereo/mono) *<(S+/T 2859)>* **WILD HONEY** [7] [24] Dec67
– Wild honey / Aren't you glad / I was made to love her / Country air / A thing or two / Darlin' / I'd love just once to see you / Here comes the night / Let the wind blow / How she boogalooed it / Mama says.

May 68. (7") *(CL 15545) <2160>* **FRIENDS. / LITTLE BIRD** [25] [47]
(re-iss.Jun79; CL 16059)

Jul 68. (7") *(CL 15554) <2239>* **DO IT AGAIN. / WAKE THE WORLD** [1] [20]
(re-iss.Jun79; CL 16060)

Sep 68. (lp; stereo/mono) *<(S+/T 2895)>* **FRIENDS** [13] [ ] Jun68
– Meant for you / Friends / Wake the world / Be here in the mornin' / When a man needs a woman / Passing by / Anna Lee, the healer / Little bird / Be still / Busy doing nothin' / Diamond head / Transcendental meditation.

Dec 68. (7") *(CL 15572) <2360>* **BLUEBIRDS OVER THE MOUNTAIN. / NEVER LEARN NOT TO LOVE** [33] [61]
(re-iss.Jun79; CL 16061)

Feb 69. (7") *(CL 15584) <2432>* **I CAN HEAR MUSIC. / ALL I WANT TO DO** [10] [24]
(re-iss.Jun79; CL 16062)

Feb 69. (lp) *<(EST 133)>* **20/20** [3] [68]
– Do it again / I can hear music / Bluebirds over the mountain / Be with me / All I want to do / The nearest faraway place / Cottonfields / I went to sleep / Time to get alone / Never learn not to love / Our prayer / Cabinessence.

Jun 69. (7") *(CL 15598) <2530>* **BREAK AWAY. / CELEBRATE THE NEWS** [6] [63]
(re-iss.Jun79; CL 16063)

Stateside Reprise

Feb 70. (7") *<0894>* **ADD SOME MUSIC TO YOUR DAY. / SUSIE CINCINATTI** [-] [64]

Sep 70. (7") *<0929>* **SLIP ON THROUGH. / THIS WHOLE WORLD** [-] [ ]

Nov 70. (7") *(SS 2181) <0957>* **TEARS IN THE MORNING. / IT'S ABOUT ME** [ ] [ ]

Nov 70. (lp) *(SSL 8251) <6382>* **SUNFLOWER** [29] [ ] Sep70
– Slip on through / This whole world / Add some music to your day / Got to know the woman / Deirdre / It's about time / Tears in the morning / All I wanna do / Forever / Our sweet love / At my window / Cool, cool water. *(re-iss.Nov80 on 'Caribou'; 31773>–* Cottonfields. *(re-iss.Jul91 on 'Epic' cd/c; 467836-2/-4)*

Dec 70. (7"; by DENNIS WILSON & RUMBO) *(SS 2184)* **SOUND OF FREE. / LADY** [ ] [-]

Feb 71. (7") *<0998>* **COOL, COOL WATER. / FOREVER** [-] [ ]

Jun 71. (7") *(SS 2190) <1015>* **LONG PROMISED ROAD. / DEIRDRE** [ ] [ ]

Oct 71. (7") *<1047>* **LONG PROMISED ROAD. / TILL I DIE** [-] [89]

Nov 71. (7") *(SS 2194)* **DON'T GO NEAR THE WATER. / STUDENT DEMONSTRATION TIME** [ ] [ ]

Nov 71. (lp) *(SSL 10313) <6453>* **SURF'S UP** [15] [29] Aug71
– Don't go near the water / Long promised road / Take a load off your feet / Disney girls (1957) / Student demonstration time / Feel flows / Lookin' at tomorrow / A day in the life of a tree / 'Til I die / Surf's up. *<re-iss.Nov80 on 'Caribou'; 31774> (re-iss.Jul91 on 'Epic' cd/c; 467835-2/-4)*

Nov 71. (7") *<1058>* **SURF'S UP. / DON'T GO NEAR THE WATER** [-] [ ]

— **BLONDIE CHAPLIN** – guitar repl. JOHNSTON who later went solo
added **RICKY FATAAR** – drums (DENNIS now just vocals)

Reprise Reprise

May 72. (7") *(K 14173) <1091>* **YOU NEED A MESS OF HELP TO STAND ALONE. / CUDDLE UP** [ ] [ ]

Jun 72. (d-lp) *(K 44184) <2083>* **CARL AND THE PASSIONS – SO TOUGH** [25] [50] May72
– You need a mess of help to stand alone / Here she comes / He come down / Marcella / Hold on dear brother / Make it good / All this is that / Cuddle up. *(w/ 'PET SOUNDS') (re-iss.Jul91 on 'Epic' cd/c; 468349-2/-4)*

Aug 72. (7") *<1101>* **MARCELLA. / HOLD ON DEAR BROTHER** [-] [ ]

Jan 73. (lp) *(K 54008) <2118>* **HOLLAND** [20] [36]
– Sail on sailor / Steamboat / California saga (on my way to sunny Californ-i-a (medley):- Big surf – Beaks of eagles – California / The trader / Leaving this town / Only with you / Funky pretty. *(7"ep free-w/a) <2118>* **MOUNT VERNON AND FAIRWAY (A FAIRY TALE)** – Better get back in bed / Magic transistor radio / Mount Vernon and Fairway / I'm the pied piper / Radio King Dom. *(re-iss.Jul91 on 'Epic' cd/c; 467837-2/-4)*

Feb 73. (7") *<1138>* **SAIL ON SAILOR. / ONLY WITH YOU** [-] [79]

Feb 73. (7") *(K 14232)* **CALIFORNIA SAGA: CALIFORNIA. / SAIL ON SAILOR** [37] [-]

May 73. (7") *<1156>* **CALIFORNIA SAGA (ON MY WAY TO SUNNY CALIFORN-I-A). / FUNKY PRETTY** [-] [84]

Nov 73. (d-lp) *(K 84001) <6484>* **THE BEACH BOYS IN CONCERT (live)** [ ] [25]
– Sail on sailor / Sloop John B. / The trader / You still believe me / California girls / Darlin' / Marcella / Caroline, no / Leaving this town / Heroes and villains / We got love / Don't worry baby / Surfin' U.S.A. / Good vibrations / Fun, fun, fun / Funky pretty / Let the wind blow / Help me Rhonda / Surfer girl / Wouldn't it be nice. *(re-iss.Jun91 on 'Epic' cd/c; 468345-2/-4)*

Jul 74. (7") *<1310>* **I CAN HEAR MUSIC (live). / LET THE WIND BLOW (live)** [-] [ ]

Aug 74. (7"ep) *(K 14346)* **CALIFORNIA SAGA: CALIFORNIA / SAIL ON SAILOR. / MARCELLA / I'M THE PIED PIPER** [ ] [-]

— **JAMES GUERICO** – bass (on tour) repl. BLONDIE and RICKY / **DENNIS** returned to his drums

Jun 75. (7") *(K 14394) <1325>* **SAIL ON SAILOR. / ONLY WITH YOU** [ ] [49]

Dec 75. (7"w-drawn) *(K 14411) <1321>* **CHILD OF WINTER. / SUSIE CINCINNATI** [-] [ ] Dec74

— **BRIAN** returned to live work

— After this point, The BEACH BOYS abandoned even the slightest attempts to push their own musical boundaries, Instead relying upon tired retreads of their earlier sound. For details of their recordings from 1976 onwards, seek out The GREAT ROCK DISCOGRAPHY.

– compilations, exploitations, etc. –

on 'Capitol' unless stated otherwise

1963. (7"ep) *(EAP 1-20540)* **SURFIN' U.S.A.** [ ] [-]

1964. (7"ep) *(EAP 1-20603)* **FUN, FUN, FUN** [ ] [-]

1964. (7"ep) *(EAP 5267)* **FOUR BY THE BEACH BOYS** [ ] [-]

1964. (7"ep) *(EAP 4-2198)* **BEACH BOYS CONCERT** [ ] [-]

1964. (7"ep) *(EAP 1-20781)* **THE BEACH BOYS HITS** [ ] [-]

Nov 64. (lp; stereo/mono) *(S+/T 2164)* **BEACH BOYS CHRISTMAS ALBUM** [ ] [ ]
(re-iss.Oct94 on 'Music For Pleasure' cd/c; CD/TC MFP 6150)

Oct 66. (lp; stereo/mono) *(S+/T 20856) <2545>* **THE BEST OF THE BEACH BOYS** [2] [8]

1967. (7"ep) *(EAP 6-2458)* **GOD ONLY KNOWS** [ ] [-]

Oct 67. (lp; stereo/mono) *(S+/T 20956) <2706>* **THE BEST OF THE BEACH BOYS VOL.2** [3] [50] Aug67

Nov 68. (lp; stereo/mono) *(S+/T 21142) <2905>* **THE BEST OF THE BEACH BOYS VOL.3** [3] [ ] Sep68

Aug 69. (d-lp) *<253>* **CLOSE UP** [-] [ ]
– (SURFIN' U.S.A. / ALL SUMMER LONG)

Mar 70. (lp) *Regal Starline; (SRS 5014)* **BUG-IN** [ ] [-]

May 70. (7") *(CL 15640) <2765>* **COTTONFIELDS. / THE NEAREST FARAWAY PLACE** [5] [ ]

Sep 70. (lp) *(T 21628)* **GREATEST HITS** [5] [-]

Jul 71. (lp) *Regal Starline; (SRS 5074)* **THE BEACH BOYS** [ ] [-]

Aug 72. (7"m) *(CMS 1)* **WOULDN'T IT BE NICE. / FUN FUN FUN / CALIFORNIA GIRLS** [ ] [-]

Aug 72. (lp) *(ST 21715) <11584>* **LIVE IN LONDON (live 1969)** [ ] [75] Dec76
(re-iss.Sep77 on 'Music For Pleasure'; 50345)

Nov 72. (7"m) *(CMS 2)* **BARBARA ANN. / DANCE DANCE DANCE / YOU'RE SO GOOD TO ME** [ ] [-]

Nov 73. (7") *(CL 15772)* **LITTLE SAINT NICK. / THE LORD'S PRAYER** [ ] [-]

May 74. (7") *(CL 15781)* **ALL SUMMER LONG. / SURFIN' SAFARI** [ ] [-]

Jul 74. (d-lp) *<2166>* **WILD HONEY / 20-20** [-] [50]

Aug 74. (7") *<3924>* **SURFIN' U.S.A. / THE WARMTH OF THE SUN** [-] [36]

Nov 74. (d-lp) *<(EA-ST 11307)>* **ENDLESS SUMMER** [ ] [1] Jul74
(re-iss.Sep81 on 'Music For Pleasure'; MfP 50528) (cd-iss.Feb87 on 'E.M.I.'; CDP 746 467-2)

Oct 74. (d-lp) *<2167>* **FRIENDS / SMILEY SMILE** [-] [ ]

Apr 75. (d-lp) *(VMP 1007) <SVBB 11384>* **SPIRIT OF AMERICA** [ ] [8]
(cd-iss.Jun87; CDP7 746 618-2)

May 75. (d-lp) *(ESTSP 14)* **WILD HONEY / FRIENDS** [ ] [-]

Jun 75. (7") *(CL 15822)* **BREAK AWAY. / CELEBRATE THE NEWS** [ ] [-]

Oct 75. (lp) *Music For Pleasure; (MFP 50234) / Brother; <2223>* **GOOD VIBRATIONS – THE BEST OF BEACH BOYS** [ ] [25] Jul75

Jun 76. (7") *(CL 15875)* **GOOD VIBRATIONS. / WOULDN'T IT BE NICE** [18] [-]

Jul 76. (lp/c) *E.M.I.; (EMTV/TC-EMTV 1)* **20 GOLDEN GREATS** [1] [ ]
(cd-iss.Nov87; CDEMTV 1) (re-iss.1979 blue-lp; same) (re-iss.cd+c Sep94)

Dec 76. (lp) *(EST 24009)* **STACK O' TRACKS** [ ] [ ]

Nov 77. (7") *(CL 15954)* **LITTLE SAINT NICK. / SANTA CLAUSE IS COMING TO TOWN / ('A'instrumental)** [ ] [-]

May 78. (7") *(CL 15969)* **LITTLE DEUCE COUPE. / (B-side by SUNRAYS and SUPERSTOCKS)** [ ] [-]

Jun 78. (7") *(CL 15991)* **CALIFORNIA GIRLS. / YOU'RE SO GOOD TO ME / DO IT AGAIN** [ ] [-]

Jun 79. (26x7"box) *(BBP 26)* **SINGLES COLLECTION** [ ] [ ]
(7"free-w/a) – (as "The SURVIVORS" – Pamela Jean / After the game.

Jun 80. (7"m) *(CL 16148)* **GOD ONLY KNOWS. / GIRLS ON THE BEACH / IN MY ROOM** [ ] [-]

Jun 80. (lp/c) *(CAPS/TC-CAPS 1037)* **GIRLS ON THE BEACH** [ ] [ ]

Dec 80. (7"m) *Creole; (CR 214)* **SURFIN' SAFARI. / SURFIN' / SURFER GIRL** [ ] [-]

Jan 81. (7xlp-box) *World Records; (WRC SM 651-657)* **THE CAPITOL YEARS** [ ] [-]

Jan 81. (7xlp-box) *WRC; (SM 651/657)* **THE CAPITOL YEARS** [ ] [-]

Aug 81. (7") *(CL 213) <5030>* **BEACH BOYS MEDLEY. / GOD ONLY KNOWS** [47] [12]

Jun 82. (lp) *<12220>* **SUNSHINE DREAM** [-] [ ]

Jul 83. (d-lp) *(BBTV 1867193)* **THE VERY BEST OF THE BEACH BOYS** [1] [ ]
– Surfin' safari / Surfin' U.S.A. / Shut down / Little deuce Coupe / In my room / Fun, fun, fun / I get around / Don't worry baby / When I grow up (to be a man) / Wendy / Little Honda / Dance dance dance / All summer long / Do you wanna dance / Help me Rhonda / California girls / Little girl I once knew / Barbara Ann / You're so good to me / Then I kissed her / Sloop John B. / God only knows / Wouldn't it be nice / Here today / Good vibrations / Heroes and villains / Wild honey / Darlin' / Country air / Here comes the night / Friends / Do it again / Bluebirds over the mountain / I can hear music / Break away / Cottonfields.

1983. (d-c) *Cambra; (CRT 009)* **BEACH BOYS** [ ] [-]

Oct 83. (lp/c) *(EST/TC-EST 7122931)* **THE BEACH BOYS' RARITIES** [ ] [-]
(re-iss.1985 lp/c; ATAK/TC-ATAK 6)

Mar 84. (7") *EMI Gold; (G45 10)* **BARBARA ANN. / GOD ONLY KNOWS** [ ] [-]

Oct 84. (c) *Audio Fidelity; (ZCGAS 720)* **BEACH BOYS** [ ] [-]

Nov 84. (lp/c) *Topline; (TOP/KTOP 109)* **SURFER GIRL** (different) [ ] [-]

Dec 84. (d-lp/d-c) *C.B.S.; (22178) / Caribou; <37445>* **TEN YEARS OF HARMONY (1970-1980)** [ ] [ ] Dec81

Aug 86. (cd/c/d-lp) *(CD/TC+/EN 5005) <12396>* **MADE IN THE U.S.A.** [ ] [96] Jul86

Oct 86. (lp) *Meteor; (MTM 022)* **WIPE OUT** [ ] [-]

Oct 86. (lp/c) *Music For Pleasure; (MFP/TC-MFP 5763)* **DO IT AGAIN** [ ] [-]

Jul 87. (cd; with JAN & DEAN) *Bescol; (CD 34)* **15 GREATEST HITS** [ ] [-]

Nov 87. (cd; with JAN & DEAN) *Timeless Treasures; (MC 1635)* **16 ORIGINAL HITS** [ ] [-]

May 88. (cd-s) *Rhino; (R 373001)* **LIL' BIT OF GOLD: THE BEACH BOYS** [ ] [ ]
– California girls / Help me Rhonda / Wouldn't it be nice / Good vibrations.

Jun 90. (7") *(CL 579)* **WOULDN'T IT BE NICE. / I GET AROUND** [58] [ ]
(12"+=/cd-s+=) *(12/CD CL 579)* – Medley of hits.

Jun 90. (cd)(c/d-lp) *(CDP7 94620-2)(TC+/EMTVD 51)* **SUMMER DREAMS** [2] [-]

Jun 90. (cd) *(CDP7 93691-2)* **SURFIN' SAFARI / SURFIN' U.S.A.** [ ] [ ]
(contains extra tracks) (c-iss.Jul91; C 493691)

Jun 90. (cd) *(CDP7 93692-2)* **SURFER GIRL / SHUT DOWN, VOLUME 2** [ ] [ ]
(contains extra tracks) (c-iss.Jul91; C 493692)

Jul 90. (cd) *(CDP7 93693-2)* **LITTLE DEUCE COUPE / ALL SUMMER LONG** [ ] [ ]
(contains extra tracks) (c-iss.Aug91; C 493693)

Aug 90. (cd) *(CDP7 93694-2)* **TODAY / SUMMER DAYS (AND SUMMER NIGHTS!!)** [ ] [ ]
(contains extra tracks) (c-iss.Aug91; C 493694)

Aug 90. (cd) *(CDP7 93695-2)* **BEACH BOYS' CONCERT / LIVE IN LONDON** [ ] [ ]
(contains extra tracks) (c-iss.Aug91; C 493695)

Aug 90. (cd) *(CDP7 93696-2)* **WILD HONEY / SMILEY SMILE** [ ] [ ]
(contains extra tracks) (c-iss.Aug91; C 493696)

Aug 90. (cd) *(CDP7 93697-2)* **FRIENDS / 20-20** [ ] [ ]
(contains extra tracks) (c-iss.Aug91; C 493697)

Aug 90. (cd) *(CDP7 93698-2)* **BEACH BOYS' PARTY / STACK O-TRACKS** [ ] [ ]
(contains extra tracks) (c-iss.Aug91; C 493698)

Jun 91. (7"/c-s) *E.M.I.; (EM/+C 1)* **DO IT AGAIN. / GOOD VIBRATIONS** [61] [ ]
(cd-s+=) *(EMCT 1)* – Wouldn't it be nice.

Jun 93. (cd/c) *Fame; (CD/TC FA 3294)* **CRUISIN'** [ ] [ ]

Jul 93. (5xcd-box) *(CDS 789936-2)* **GOOD VIBRATIONS – 30 YEARS OF THE BEACH BOYS** [ ] [ ]

Jul 94. (cd/c; with JAN & DEAN) *Success;* **BEACH PARTY** [ ] [-]

Feb 95. (cd) *B.A.M.;* **PEARLS OF THE PAST** [ ] [-]

Jun 95. (d-cd/d-c) *E.M.I.; (CD/TC ESTVD 3)* **THE BEST OF THE BEACH BOYS** [26] [ ]

Mar 97. (cd) *Disky; (DC 878682)* **ALL SUMMER LONG** (diff.) [-] [ ]

Mar 97. (3xcd-box) *(CDOMB 018)* **TODAY / SUMMER DAYS AND SUMMER NIGHTS / SMILEY SMILE** [ ] [-]

BRIAN WILSON

Sire Sire

May 87. (7") *<28350>* **LET'S GO TO HEAVEN IN MY CAR. / TOO MUCH SUGAR** [-] [ ]

Jul 88. (lp/c)(cd) *(WX 157/+C)(925669-2) <25669>* **BRIAN WILSON** [ ] [54]
– Love and mercy / Walkin' the line / Melt away / Baby let your hair grow long / Little children / One of the boys / There's so many / Night time / Let it shine / Rio Grande / Meet me in my dreams tonight. *(re-iss.cd Dec95; 7599 25669-2)*

Aug 88. (7") *(W 7814) <27814>* **LOVE AND MERCY. / HE COULDN'T GET HIS POOR OLD BODY TO MOVE** [ ] [ ]
(12"+=/3"cd-s+=) *(W 7814 T/CD)* – One for the boys.

Nov 88. (7") *(W 7787)* **NIGHT TIME. / ONE FOR THE BOYS** [ ] [-]
(12"+=/3"cd-s+=) *(W 7787 T/CD)* – Being with the one you love.

Feb 89. (7") *<27694>* **MELT AWAY. / BEING WITH THE ONE YOU LOVE** [-] [ ]

— with musicians **JIM KELTNER** – drums / **JAMES HUTCHINSON** – bass / **BENMONT TENCH** – keyboards / **MARK GOLDENBERG + WADDY WACHTEL** – guitar / **DAVID McMURRAY** – sax, flute

M.C.A. M.C.A.

Sep 95. (cd) *(MCD 11270)* **I JUST WASN'T MADE FOR THOSE TIMES** [59] [ ]
– Meant for you / This whole world / Caroline, no / Let the wind blow / Love and mercy / Do it again / The warmth of the sun / Wonderful / Still I dream of it / Melt away / 'Til I die.

WEA WEA

Nov 95. (cd/c; BRIAN WILSON & VAN DYKE PARKS) *(9362 45427-2/-4)* **ORANGE CRATE ART** [ ] [ ]

— For MIKE LOVE, DENNIS WILSON and CARL WILSON solo releases, see The GREAT ROCK DISCOGRAPHY

BEACON STREET UNION

Formed: Boston, Massachusetts, USA . . .1967 by PAUL TARTACHNY, JOHN LINCOLN WRIGHT, WAYNE ULAKY, RICHARD WEISBERG and ROBERT RHODES. They were part of the "Bosstown Sound", which grew up in their hometown, a fusion of acid-blues and psychedelia. In 1968, their debut album 'THE EYES OF . . .' came to be regarded as a mini-masterpiece, selling well enough to reach the US Top 75. The second album 'THE CLOWN DIED IN MARVIN GARDENS' (released the same year) contained their version of CARL PERKINS' 'BLUE SUEDE SHOES', plus a 16-minute re-working of BIG JOE WILLIAMS' 'BABY PLEASE DON'T GO'. When they split the following year, three of their members formed the short-lived EAGLE.

Recommended: THE EYES OF THE BEACON STREET UNION (*7) / THE CLOWN DIED IN MARVIN GARDENS (*7)

JOHN LINCOLN WRIGHT – vocals / **PAUL TARTACHNY** – guitar, vocals / **WAYNE ULAKY** – bass, vocals / **ROBERT RHODES** – keyboards, brass / **RICHARD WEISBERG** – drums

M.G.M. M.G.M.

Feb 68. (lp) *(CS 8069) <SE 4517>* **THE EYES OF THE BEACON STREET UNION** [ ] [75]
– Recitation / My love is / Beautiful Delilah / Sportin' life / Four hundred and five / Mystic mourning / Sadie said no / Speed kills / Blue avenue / South End incident (speed kills) / Green destroys the gold / The prophet.

May 68. (7") *(MGM 1416) <13935>* **BLUE SUEDE SHOES. / FOUR HUNDRED AND FIVE** [ ] [ ]

Sep 68. (lp) *<SE 4568>* **THE CLOWN DIED IN MARVIN GARDENS** [-] [ ]
– The clown died in Marvin Gardens / The clown's overture / Angus of Aberdeen / Blue suede shoes / Not very August afternoon / Now I taste the tears / King of the jungle / May I light your cigarette / Baby please don't go.

Sep 68. (7") *<14012>* **MAY I LIGHT YOUR CIGARETTE? / MAYOLA** [-] [ ]

— soon evolved into below outfit

EAGLE

WRIGHT, RHODES + ULAKY recruited **J. JAMES** – guitar, vocals

Pye Inter.. Janus

1970. (lp) *(NSPL 28138) <JLS 3011>* **COME UNDER NANCY'S TENT** [ ] [ ]
–

Sep 70. (7") *(7N 25530) <113>* **KICKIN' IT BACK TO YOU. / COME IN, IT'S ALL FOR FREE** [-] [ ] May70

Oct 70. (7") *<135>* **BROWN HAIR. / WORKING MAN** [-] [ ]

— disappeared from the scene

BEATLES

Formed: Liverpool, England . . . by JOHN LENNON and PAUL McCARTNEY as schoolboy band The QUARRYMEN in 1957. GEORGE HARRISON joined up the following year, although they split late '59. They reformed in the Spring of 1960 as The SILVER BEATLES, adding PETE BEST and STU SUTCLIFFE. Dropping the SILVER part of their name, they employed manager Alan Williams, who secured them local gigs. Later that year, they toured Hamburg, West Germany, although they had to return when HARRISON was deported for being under eighteen. On the 21st of March '61, they debuted at Liverpool's 'Cavern Club', preceding another 3-month stint in Hamburg. While there, they recorded for 'Polydor' records, backing cabaret-type pop singer TONY SHERIDAN. (These recordings were later released, when the band were at the peak of their popularity). Around mid-'61, STU stayed in Hamburg to get married and study art. There, he was to tragically die of a brain haemorrhage on the 10th April of 1962. With PAUL now on bass and BRIAN EPSTEIN as their new manager, they laid down a demo for 'Decca', which was subsequently disregarded by DICK ROWE. Instead he signed BRIAN POOLE & THE TREMELOES (!), although he soon found consolation when he contracted rivals-to-be The ROLLING STONES. Summer '62 brought sunshine when George Martin introduced them to EMI's 'Parlophone' label. During rehearsals BEST was fired and replaced by the more experienced drummer RINGO STARR. By the end of 1962 their debut single 'LOVE ME DO' was in the UK Top 20. The follow-up 'PLEASE PLEASE ME' (1963) reached No.2 and The BEATLES had arrived, their breezy, fresh-faced pop striking a chord in a music scene that was crying out for a band with the effortless charisma of the cheeky Scousers. More, their mop-toppped, sharp-suited image (courtesy of BRIAN EPSTEIN) remains one of the most enduring impressions in the history of pop culture. And thus did that dog-eared cliche of a phenomenon, 'BEATLEMANIA' tighten its grip as the band toured above ROY ORBISON later that year to unprecedented scenes of teenage delirium. They also found time to knock out a debut album, 'PLEASE PLEASE ME' (1963), produced by their mentor George Martin and featuring a heady cocktail of live wig-outs ('I SAW HER STANDING THERE', 'TWIST AND SHOUT'etc.) and LENNON/McCARTNEY originals. This precocious songwriting partnership was entering its golden period as the band notched up an incredible string of No.1 singles in quick succession, 'FROM ME TO YOU' (1963), 'SHE LOVES YOU' (1963), 'I WANT TO HOLD YOUR HAND' (1963) and 'CAN'T BUY ME LOVE' (1964). The BEATLES finished 1963 in fine style; a No.1 follow-up album, 'WITH THE BEATLES', the biggest selling single in British history, 'SHE LOVES YOU' and a performance before the Queen Mother at the Royal Command Variety Performance. With British domination well under way, the band flew to America in February 1964, droves of hysterical fans greeting them upon their landing at New York's Kennedy Airport. They made a legendary appearance on the 'Ed Sullivan Show' and by April The BEATLES held the top five positions in the American Billboard singles charts (i.e. No.1:- CAN'T BUY ME LOVE, 2:- TWIST AND SHOUT, 3:- SHE LOVES YOU, 4:- I WANT TO HOLD YOUR HAND, 5:- PLEASE PLEASE ME). Flying high, that summer saw the release of The BEATLES' first movie and accompanying soundtrack, 'A HARD DAY'S NIGHT'. The band proved themselves as compelling on screen as on stage, and the film's revolutionary shooting technique created the blueprint for decades of rockumentaries to come. The same year also saw the release of the band's third album, 'BEATLES FOR SALE', a record which included some of the last genuine LENNON/McCARTNEY collaborations. Each were developing their own particular style and although all their songs continued to be credited as joint efforts, by the following year the pair seldom wrote together. 'HELP' (1965), a filmic follow-up to 'A HARD DAY'S NIGHT', featured some of LENNON and McCARTNEY's most focused songwriting to date (notably the title track and 'YESTERDAY') and was filmed at various locations around the globe. The BEATLES performed before a record number of fans at New York's Shea Stadium in August, the same month as 'HELP' was opened in the U.S. By this point The BEATLES were undoubtedly the biggest pop/rock band in the world, unique in their abilty to produce music that seemingly crossed all

boundaries of age, race, class and gender. Even so, it was a shock to the rock world when the Queen announced in the summer of '65 that the band were each to receive an M.B.E.. It was almost unthinkable that bad boy rivals The ROLLING STONES would be given such a (dubious) honour, and while the two bands were poles apart musically, LSD and the burgeoning psychedelic culture brought them together briefly. 'RUBBER SOUL' (1965), written and recorded in just over a month, was the sound of The BEATLES in flux, shedding their clean cut image and interpreting the influence of BOB DYLAN's pioneering folk-rock experiments. Despite the transformation taking place, the sound was more fluid and assured, the songwriting more mature. LENNON's 'IN MY LIFE' was beautifully bittersweet while McCARTNEY almost equalled 'YESTERDAY' with 'MICHELLE' and the lilting 'NORWEGIAN WOOD' saw HARRISON's first forays into sitar work. The album was sandwiched between pioneering double A-sided singles 'DAY TRIPPER' / 'WE CAN WORK IT OUT' (1965) and 'PAPERBACK WRITER' / 'RAIN' (1966). 'RAIN' was the first overtly psychedelic BEATLES record, innovative in its use of rhythm and featuring an undulating LENNON vocal (a style much mimicked by many of todays crop of young bands). Its potential was fully realised on 'REVOLVER' (1966), oft cited as The BEATLES' pinnacle achievement and as one of the best albums ever made. McCARTNEY excelled himself with the string-cloaked melancholy of 'ELEANOR RIGBY', while HARRISON's biting 'TAXMAN' kicked off the album in strident style. But it was the psychedelic numbers which made most impact. 'SHE SAID SHE SAID' was a swirling piece of trip-pop, while 'TOMMORROW NEVER KNOWS' remains one of the most bizarre and enigmatic songs in The BEATLES' canon. With a working title of 'THE VOID', the song was based on one of LENNON's first profound acid trips and was partly inspired by the ancient religious text beloved of hippies at the time, 'The Tibetan Book Of The Dead'. With a hypnotic drum sound that many have since tried and failed to recreate, backwards guitar that sounded like a flock of screeching pterodactyls and LENNON's mantra-like vocals, the record set a precedent in psychedelic rock. At this stage The BEATLES were already preoccupied with the possibilities of the recording studio and significantly, the band played their last gig in San Francisco's Candlestick Park the same month 'REVOLVER' was released. Ensconced in Abbey Road Studios, the band came up with the double A-side, 'PENNY LANE' / 'STRAWBERRY FIELDS FOREVER'. Released in February '67, the single's effects-laden innovation was a taster for The BEATLES' much heralded psychedelic concept album 'SGT. PEPPER'S LONELY HEARTS CLUB BAND'. Its release coinciding perfectly with the fabled 1967 'Summer Of Love', the record was a landmark in new studio technique. Utilising the (then) pioneering four-track recording process, the band painstakingly pieced together ornate pieces of sonic intricacy that set new standards. It contained many classics such as 'LUCY IN THE SKY WITH DIAMONDS' (wrongly thought by many to be about L.S.D.), 'SHE'S LEAVING HOME' and the never-ending 'A DAY IN THE LIFE', complete with prolonged intentionally stuck-in-the-groove outro. Fans and critics alike made it "their greatest album of all time", although many others thought it too overblown as well as overproduced. A month later, the anthemic 'ALL YOU NEED IS LOVE' gave them another No.1, helped no doubt by its simultaneous worldwide TV broadcast. The death of BRIAN EPSTEIN cast a shadow over the celebrations but the band moved on, filming/recording 'MAGICAL MYTERY TOUR' (1967). A trippy film and soundtrack inspired by KEN KESEY and his bunch of technicolour minstrels, it contained the infamous LENNON-penned surrealism of 'I AM THE WALRUS'. Screened on British TV on Boxing Day 1967, the film was almost universally panned. Unbowed, The BEATLES decamped to India for spiritual retreat with the Maharishi Mahesh Yogi, during which time they accumulated much of the material that would form the 'WHITE ALBUM'. Upon their return to English shores, they set about forming the 'Apple Corporation', which would handle all the business dealings of the band as well as functioning as a label for The BEATLES and likeminded talent. The first release was 'HEY JUDE' / 'REVOLUTION' (1968), the former a rousing torch song, the latter a stinging attack by LENNON on would-be radicals. Eventually released in November '68, 'THE BEATLES (White Album)' was a sprawling double set recorded in an environment of tension and breakdown of inter-band communications. Yet it contained some of The BEATLES finest songs, 'HARRISON's solemn 'WHILE MY GUITAR GENTLY WEEPS', LENNON's gorgeous 'DEAR PRUDENCE' and 'JULIA', a moving tribute to his mother. The album also included the cryptic genius of LENNON's 'HAPPINESS IS A WARM GUN' while 'REVOLUTION No.9' was The BEATLES at their most defiantly experimental. Nevertheless, the recording had strained relationships within the band to breaking point and the subsequent back to basics sessions in 1969 (eventually emerging as the 'LET IT BE' album) broke down in disarray. Incredibly, the band got it together one last time for 'ABBEY ROAD' (1969), a breathtaking sweep through the diverse styles of each of the songwriters. GEORGE HARRISON contributed two of his best tracks, 'SOMETHING' and the pastoral beauty of 'HERE COMES THE SUN'. McCARTNEY penned most of the medley which formed a sizeable chunk of the album and which included one of his most heartbreakingly lovely songs, 'GOLDEN SLUMBERS'. 'LET IT BE', eventually released in 1970 was hardly a fitting epitaph for The BEATLES, PHIL SPECTOR's production coming in for some flak. It did, however, contain such definitive BEATLES moments as the deeply reflective title track, the sleepy 'ACROSS THE UNIVERSE' and the beguiling 'THE LONG AND WINDING ROAD'. The BEATLES had officially split a couple of months before the album's release in April 1970, estranged amid personal rows and more serious business disagreements. LENNON, McCARTNEY and HARRISON all went on to resepectable solo careers, although none of the subsequent recordings had quite the same impact as The BEATLES' material. The band remain one of the greatest cultural icons of the 20th Century with a back catalogue that even OASIS will never be able to match. • **Covered:** TWIST AND SHOUT (Isley Brothers) / A TASTE OF HONEY (Bobby Scott) / THERE'S A PLACE / MONEY (Barrett Strong) / ROLL OVER BEETHOVEN + ROCK AND ROLL MUSIC (Chuck Berry) / YOU REALLY GOT A HOLD OF ME (Miracles) / PLEASE MR. POSTMAN (Marvelettes) / KANSAS CITY (Wilbert Harrison) / WORDS OF LOVE (Diamonds) / CHAINS (Cookies) / BABY IT'S YOU (Shirelles) / etc. • **Trivia:** They form own label 'Apple' in 1968. Release own records and sign others including BADFINGER, MARY HOPKINS, JAMES TAYLOR, etc.

Recommended: SGT. PEPPER'S LONELY HEARTS CLUB BAND (*10) / REVOLVER (*9) / THE BEATLES 'White Album' (*10) / THE BEATLES 1967-70 (*10) / THE BEATLES 1962-66 (*10) / LIVE AT THE BBC (*8) / RUBBER SOUL (*9) / PLEASE PLEASE ME (*6) / WITH THE BEATLES (*7) / A HARD DAY'S NIGHT (*7) / BEATLES FOR SALE (*6) / HELP (*6) / ABBEY ROAD (*9) / LET IT BE (*7)

JOHN LENNON (b. JOHN WINSTON LENNON, 9 Oct'40) – vocals, rhythm guitar / **PAUL McCARTNEY** (b. JAMES PAUL McCARTNEY, 18 Jun'42) – vocals, guitar / **GEORGE HARRISON** (b.25 Feb'43) – vocals, lead guitar/ **STU SUTCLIFFE** (b. STUART, 23 Jun'40, Edinburgh, Scotland) – bass/ **PETE BEST** (b.1941) – drums

		Polydor	Decca	
Jan 62.	(7"; as TONY SHERIDAN & THE BEATLES) *(NH 66-833) <31382>* **MY BONNIE. / THE SAINTS**			Apr62

(re-iss.May63 hit UK No.48; same) (re-iss.Feb64; same) <US re-iss.Jan64 on 'M.G.M.'; K 13213>; hit No. 26) (above A-side was released Aug61 in Germany as TONY SHERIDAN & The BEAT BROTHERS)

— Were a quartet at the time, STU stayed in Germany, died 10 Apr'62 of brain haemorrhage. McCARTNEY now on bass and vocals.

— (Aug62) **RINGO STARR** (b.RICHARD STARKEY, 7 Jul'40) – drums (ex-RORY STORM & THE HURRICANES)repl. BEST

		Parlophone	not issued
Oct 62.	(7") *(R 4949)* **LOVE ME DO. / P.S. I LOVE YOU**	17	-

(re-iss.Feb63; same) *<US-iss.Apr64 on 'Tollie'; 9008>*; hit Nos. 1+10> *<US re-iss.Aug64 on 'Oldies'; 45 OL 151> <US re-iss.Oct65 on 'Capitol Starline'; 6062> (re-iss.Oct82; same); hit No.4) (re-iss.cd-s.1989) (re-iss.Oct92; same); hit No.53)*

Parlophone Vee Jay

Jan 63. (7") *(R 4983) <VJ 498>* **PLEASE PLEASE ME. / ASK ME WHY** [2] [ ]
(re-iss.Feb63; same) (re-iss.Jan83; same); hit 29) (re-iss.cd-s.1989)

Mar 63. (lp; mono)(lp; stereo) *(PMC 1202)(PCS 3042)* **PLEASE PLEASE ME** [1] [-]
– I saw her standing there / Misery / Anna (go to him) / Chains / Boys / Ask me why / Please please me / Love me do / P.S. I love you / Baby, it's you / Do you want to know a secret / A taste of honey / There's a place / Twist and shout. *(c-iss.1970's) (cd-iss.Feb87; CDP 746435-2); hit 32) (re-iss.Nov88 lp/c; PMC/TC-PMC 1202)*

Apr 63. (7") *(R 5015) <VJ 522>* **FROM ME TO YOU. / THANK YOU GIRL** [1] [ ]
(re-iss.Apr83; same); hit No.40) (re-iss.cd-s.1989)

Jul 63. (lp) *<1062>* **INTRODUCING . . . THE BEATLES** [-] [2] Feb64
– (tracks nearly same as UK debut)

Aug 63. (7") *(R 5055) <Swan; S-4152>* **SHE LOVES YOU. / I'LL GET YOU** [1] [1] Sep63
(re-iss.Aug83; same); hit No.45) (re-iss.cd-s.1989)

Nov 63. (lp; mono)(lp; stereo) *(PMC 1206)(PCS 3042)* **WITH THE BEATLES** [1] [-]
– It won't be long / All I've got to do / All my loving / Don't bother me / Little child / Till there was you / Please Mr.Postman / Roll over Beethoven / Hold me tight / You really got a hold of me / I wanna be your man / Don't bother me / Little child / Roll over Beethoven / Devil in her heart / Not a second time / Money. *(c-iss.1970's) (cd-iss.Feb87; CDP 746436-2); hit No.40) (re-iss.Nov88 lp/c; PMC/TC-PMC 1206)*

Nov 63. (7") *(R 5084)* **I WANT TO HOLD YOUR HAND. / THIS BOY** [1] [-]
(re-iss.Nov83; same); hit No.62) (re-iss.cd-s.1989)

Jan 64. (7") *<VJ 581>* **PLEASE PLEASE ME. / FROM ME TO YOU** [-] [3]
<US re-iss.Aug64 on 'Oldies'; 45 OL 150> <US re-iss.Oct65 on 'Capitol Starline'; 6063>

Parlophone Capitol

Jan 64. (7") *<5112>* **I WANT TO HOLD YOUR HAND. / I SAW HER STANDING THERE** [-] [1] [14]

Jan 64. (lp) *<2047>* **MEET THE BEATLES!** [-] [1]
– I want to hold your hand / I saw her standing there / This boy / It won't be long / All I've got to do / All my loving / Don't bother me / Little child / Till there was you / Hold me tight / I wanna be your man / Not a second time.

Mar 64. (7") *(R 5114) <5150>* **CAN'T BUY ME LOVE. / YOU CAN'T DO THAT** [1] [1]
(re-iss.Mar84; same); hit No.53) (re-iss.cd-s.1989)

Apr 64. (lp) *<2080>* **THE BEATLES' SECOND ALBUM** [-] [1]
– Roll over Beethoven / Thank you girl / You really got a hold on me / Devil in her heart / Money / You can't do that / Long tall Sally / I call your name / Please Mr. Postman / I'll get you / She loves you.

Jul 64. (7") *(R 5160)* **A HARD DAY'S NIGHT. / THINGS WE SAID TODAY** [1] [-]
(re-iss.Jul84; same); hit No.52) (re-iss.cd-s.1989)

Jul 64. (7") *<5222>* **A HARD DAY'S NIGHT. / I SHOULD HAVE KNOWN BETTER** [-] [1] [53]

Jul 64. (lp; mono)(lp; stereo) *(PMC 1230)(PCS 3058) <6366>* **A HARD DAY'S NIGHT (Soundtrack)** [1] [1]
– A hard day's night / I should have known better / If I fell / I'm happy just to dance with you / And I love her / Tell me why / Can't buy me love / Anytime at all / I'll cry instead / Things we said today / When I get home / You can't do that / I'll be back. *(re-iss.Jan71; same); hit 39) (cd-iss.Feb87; CDP 746437-2); hit No.30) (re-iss.Nov88 lp/c; PMC/TC-PMC 1230)*

Aug 64. (7") *<5234>* **I'LL CRY INSTEAD. / I'M HAPPY JUST TO DANCE WITH YOU** [-] [25] [95]

Aug 64. (7") *<5235>* **AND I LOVE HER. / IF I FELL** [-] [12] [53]

Sep 64. (7") *<5255>* **MATCHBOX. / SLOW DOWN** [-] [17] [25]

Nov 64. (7") *(R 5200) <5327>* **I FEEL FINE. / SHE'S A WOMAN** [1] [1] [4]
(re-iss.Nov84; same) ; hit No.65) (re-iss.cd-s.1989)

Dec 64. (lp; mono)(lp; stereo) *(PMC 1240)(PCS 3062)* **BEATLES FOR SALE** [1] [-]
– No reply / I'm a loser / Baby's in black / Rock and roll music / I'll follow the sun / Mr. Moonlight / Kansas City / Eight days a week / Words of love / Honey don't / Every little thing / I don't want to spoil the party / What you're doing / Everybody's trying to be my baby. *(c-iss.1970's) (cd-iss.Feb87; CDP 746438-2); hit No.45) (re-iss.Nov88 lp/c; PMC/TC-PMC 1240)*

Jan 65. (lp) *<2228>* **BEATLES '65** [-] [1]
– (track listing near as above)

Feb 65. (7") *(5371>* **EIGHT DAYS A WEEK. / I DON'T WANT TO SPOIL THE PARTY** [-] [1] [39]

Apr 65. (7") *(R 5265) <5407>* **TICKET TO RIDE. / YES IT IS** [1] [1]
(re-iss.Apr85; same); hit No.70) (re-iss.cd-s.1989)

Jul 65. (lp) *<2358>* **BEATLES VI** [-] [1]
– Kansas City / Eight days a week / You like me too much / Bad boy / I don't want to spoil the party / Words of love / What you're doing / Yes it is / Dizzy Miss Lizzy / Tell me what you see / Every little thing.

Jul 65. (7") *(R 5305) <5476>* **HELP!. / I'M DOWN** [1] [1]
(re-iss.Apr76; same); hit No.37) *(re-iss.Jul85; same) (re-iss.cd-s.1989)*

Jul 65. (lp; mono)(lp; stereo) *(PMC 1255)(PCS PCS 3071) <2386>* **HELP! (Soundtrack)** [1] [1] Aug65
– Help! / The night before / You've got to hide your love away / I need you / Another girl / You're gonna lose that girl / Ticket to ride / Act naturally / It's only love / You like me too much / Tell me what you see / I've just seen a face / Yesterday / Dizzy Miss Lizzy. *(re-iss.Jul71 lp/c; same); hit No.33) (cd-iss.Apr87; CDP 746439-2); hit No.61) (re-iss.Nov88 lp/c; PMC/TC-PMC 1255)*

Sep 65. (7") *<5498>* **YESTERDAY. / ACT NATURALLY** [-] [1]

Dec 65. (7") *(R 5389) <5555>* **DAY TRIPPER. / WE CAN WORK IT OUT** [1] [5] [1]
(re-iss.Dec85; same) (re-iss.cd-s.1989)

Dec 65. (lp; mono)(lp; stereo) *(PMC 1267)(PCS 3075) <2442>* **RUBBER SOUL** [1] [1]
– Drive my car / Norwegian wood (this bird has flown) / You won't see me / Nowhere man / Think for yourself / The word / Michelle / What goes on? / Girl / I'm looking through you / In my life / Wait / If I needed someone / Run for your life. *(c-iss.1970's) (cd-iss.Apr87; CDP 746440-2); hit UK No.60) (re-iss.Nov88 lp/c; PMC/TC-PMC 1267)*

Feb 66. (7") *<5587>* **NOWHERE MAN. / WHAT GOES ON** [-] [3] [81]

Jun 66. (7") *(R 5452) <5651>* **PAPERBACK WRITER. / RAIN** [1] [1] [23]
(re-iss.Mar76; same); hit No.23) (re-iss.Jun86; same) (re-iss.cd-s.1989)

Aug 66. (7") *(R 5493) <5715>* **YELLOW SUBMARINE. / ELEANOR RIGBY** [1] [2] [11]
(re-iss.Aug86; same); hit No.63) (re-iss.cd-s.1989)

Aug 66. (lp; mono/stereo) *(PMC/PCS 7009) <2576>* **REVOLVER** [1] [1]
– Taxman / I love you to / I want to tell you / Eleanor Rigby / Here, there and everywhere / Good day sunshine / For no one / Got to get you into my life / I'm only sleeping / She said she said / And your bird can sing / Doctor Robert / Tomorrow never knows / Yellow submarine. *(c-iss.1970's) (cd-iss.Apr87; CDP 746441-2); hit UK No.55) (re-iss.Nov88 lp/c; PMC/TC-PMC 7009)*

Feb 67. (7") *(R 5570) <5810>* **PENNY LANE. / STRAWBERRY FIELDS FOREVER** [2] [1] [8]
(re-iss.Mar76; same); hit No.32) (re-iss.Feb87; same); hit No.65) (re-iss.cd-s.1989)

Jun 67. (lp; mono/stereo) *(PMC/PCS 7027) <2653>* **SGT. PEPPER'S LONELY HEARTS CLUB BAND** [1] [1]
– Sgt.Pepper's lonely hearts club band / With a little help from my friends / Lucy in the sky with diamonds / Getting better / Fixing a hole / She's leaving home / Being for the benefit of Mr.Kite / Within you without you / When I'm sixty-four / Lovely Rita / Good morning, good morning / Sgt. Pepper's lonely hearts club band (reprise) / A day in the life. *(c-iss.1970's) (cd-iss.Jun87; CDP 746442-2); hit UK No.3) (re-iss.Nov88 lp/c; PMC/TC-PMC 7027) (re-iss.Jun92; same); hit UK No.6)*

Jul 67. (7") *(R 5620) <5964>* **ALL YOU NEED IS LOVE. / BABY YOU'RE A RICH MAN** [1] [1] [34]
(re-iss.Jul87; same); hit No.47) (re-iss.cd-s.1989)

Nov 67. (7") *(R 5655) <2056>* **HELLO GOODBYE. / I AM THE WALRUS** [1] [1] [56]
(re-iss.Nov87; same); hit No.63) (re-iss.cd-s.1989)

Dec 67. (d7"ep; stereo/mono) *(S+/MMT 1)* **MAGICAL MYSTERY TOUR** [2] [-]
– Magical mystery tour / Your mother should know / Flying / Fool on the hill / Blue Jay way / I am the walrus.

Dec 67. (lp) *(imported) <2835>* **MAGICAL MYSTERY TOUR (Soundtrack)** [31] [1]
– (above UK-ep, plus 1967 singles) *(UK-iss.Oct76, cd-iss.Sep87; CDP 748 062-2); hit UK 52)*

Mar 68. (7") *(R 5675) <2138>* **LADY MADONNA. / THE INNER LIGHT** [1] [4] [96]
(re-iss.Mar88; same); hit No.67) (re-iss.cd-s.1989)

Apple Apple

Aug 68. (7") *(R 5722) <2276>* **HEY JUDE. / REVOLUTION** [1] [1] [12]
(re-iss.Mar76; same); hit No.12) (re-iss.Aug88; same); hit No.52) (re-iss.cd-s.1989)

Nov 68. (d-lp; mono/stereo) *(PMC/PCS 7067-8) <101>* **THE BEATLES (White Album)** [1] [1]
– Back in the U.S.S.R / Dear Prudence / Glass onion / Ob-la-di-ob-la-da / Wild honey pie / The continuing story of Bungalow Bill / While my guitar gently weeps / Happiness is a warm gun / Martha my dear / I'm so tired / Blackbird / Piggies / Rocky raccoon / Don't pass me by / Why don't we do it in the road / I will / Julia / Birthday / Yer blues / Mother nature's son / Everybody's got something to hide except me and my monkey / Sexy Sadie / Helter skelter / Long long long / Revolution 1 / Honey pie / Savoy truffle / Cry baby cry / Revolution 9 / Good night. *(re-iss.Sep78 white-lp; same) (cd-iss.Aug87; CDP CDS 746443-2); hit UK No.18) (re-iss.Nov88 lp/c;)*

Jan 69. (lp; mono/stereo) *(PMC/PCS 7070) <153>* **YELLOW SUBMARINE (Soundtrack)** [4] [2]
– Yellow submarine / Only a northern song / All together now / Hey bulldog / It's all too much / All you need is love / Pepperland / Sea of time / Sea of holes / Sea of monsters / March of the Meanies / Pepperland laid waste / Yellow submarine in Pepperland. (with GEORGE MARTIN ORCHESTRA) *(re-iss.Aug87; CDP 746445-2); hit UK 60) (re-iss.Nov88 lp/c; PCS/TC-PCS 7070)*

Apr 69. (7"; by BEATLES with BILLY PRESTON) *(R 5777) <2490>* **GET BACK. / DON'T LET ME DOWN** [1] [1] [35]
(re-iss.Mar76; same); hit No.28) (re-iss.Apr89; same); hit 74) (re-iss.cd-s.1989)

May 69. (7") *(R 5786) <2531>* **THE BALLAD OF JOHN AND YOKO. / OLD BROWN SHOE** [1] [8]
(UK re-iss.May89) (re-iss.cd-s.1989)

Sep 69. (lp/c) *(PCS/TC-PCS 7088) <383>* **ABBEY ROAD** [1] [1]
– Come together / Maxwell's silver hammer / Something / Oh darling / Octopus's garden / I want you (she's so heavy) / Here comes the sun / Because / You never gave me your money / Sun king / Mean Mr.Mustard / Polythene Pam / She came in through the bathroom window / Golden slumbers / Carry that weight / The end / Her majesty. *(UK re-iss.Oct87; CDP 746 446-2); hit No.30) (re-iss.Nov88 lp/c; PCS/TC-PCS 7088)*

Oct 69. (7") *(R 5814) <2654>* **SOMETHING. / COME TOGETHER** [4] [3] [1]
(UK re-iss.Oct89) (re-iss.cd-s.1989)

Mar 70. (7") *(R 5833) <2764>* **LET IT BE. / YOU KNOW MY NAME (LOOK UP MY NUMBER)** [2] [1]
(UK re-iss.Mar90) (re-iss.cd-s.1989)

May 70. (lp/c) *(PCS/TC-PCS 7096) <34001>* **LET IT BE** [1] [1]
– Two of us / Dig a pony / Across the universe / I me mine / Dig it / Let it be / Maggie Mae / I've got a feeling / One after 909 / The long and winding road / For you blue / Get back. *(cd-iss.Oct87; CDP 746 447-2); hit No.50) (re-iss.Nov88 lp/c;*

PCS/TC-PCS 7096)

May 70. (7") *<2832>* **THE LONG AND WINDING ROAD. / FOR YOU BLUE** [-] [1]

— Officially disbanded April 1970. All 4 had released, or were due to release, own albums. See **Paul McCARTNEY ⇒ , John LENNON ⇒ , George HARRISON ⇒ , Ringo STARR ⇒ .**

– compilations, others, etc. –

on 'Parlophone' UK / 'Capitol' US unless otherwise mentioned

Jul 63. (7"ep) *(GEP 8880)* **TWIST AND SHOUT** [2] [-]
– Twist and shout / A taste of honey / Do you want to know a secret / There's a place.

Sep 63. (7"ep) *(GEP 8882)* **THE BEATLES HITS** [14] [-]
– From me to you / Thank you girl / Please please me / Love me do.

Nov 63. (7"ep) *(GEP 8883)* **THE BEATLES (No.1)** [19] [-]
– I saw her standing there / Misery / Chains / Anna (go to him).

Jan 64. (7"; by TONY SHERIDAN & THE BEATLES) *Polydor; (NH 52-906)* **SWEET GEORGIA BROWN. / NOBODY'S CHILD** [ ] [-]

Feb 64. (7"ep) *(GEP GEP 8891)* **ALL MY LOVING** [12] [-]
– All my loving / Ask me why / Money / P.S. I love you.

Mar 64. (7"; by TONY SHERIDAN & THE BEATLES) *M.G.M.; <K 13227>* **WHY. / CRY FOR A SHADOW** [-] [88]

Mar 64. (7") *Tollie; <9001>* **TWIST AND SHOUT. / THERE'S A PLACE** [-] [2]

Apr 64. (7") *Vee Jay; <VJ 587>* **DO YOU WANT TO KNOW A SECRET. / THANK YOU GIRL** [-] [74] [2]

May 64. (7") *Swan; <S-4182>* **SIE LIEBT DICH. / I'LL GET YOU** [-] [35] [97]

May 64. (7"; by TONY SHERIDAN & THE BEATLES) *Polydor; (NH 52-317)* **AIN'T SHE SWEET. / IF YOU LOVE ME BABY** [29] [-]

Jun 64. (lp; by TONY SHERIDAN & THE BEATLES) *Polydor Special; (236 201)* **THE BEATLES' FIRST** [ ] [-]
(re-iss.Jun71 as THE EARLY YEARS on 'Contour') (re-iss. as 'THE FIRST ALBUM' cd+c May93 on 'Spectrum', credited to TONY SHERIDAN & THE BEATLES)

Jun 64. (7"; by TONY SHERIDAN & THE BEATLES) *Atco; <6302>* **SWEET GEORGIA BROWN. / TAKE OUT SOME INSURANCE ON ME BABY** [-] [ ]

Jun 64. (7"ep) *(GEP 8913)* **LONG TALL SALLY** [14] [-]
– Long tall Sally / I call your name / Slow down / Matchbox.

Jun 64. (7"ep) *<EAP 2121>* **FOUR BY THE BEATLES** [-] [92]
– All my loving / This boy / Roll over Beethoven / Please Mr.Postman.

Jul 64. (7"; by TONY SHERIDAN & THE BEATLES) *Atco; <6308>* **AIN'T SHE SWEET. / NOBODY'S CHILD** [-] [19]

Aug 64. (lp) *<2108>* **SOMETHING NEW** [-] [2]

Aug 64. (7") *Oldies; <45 OL 149>* **DO YOU WANT TO KNOW A SECRET. / THANK YOU GIRL** [-] [ ]
<US re-iss.Oct65 on 'Capitol Starline'; 6064>

Aug 64. (7") *Oldies; <45 OL 152>* **TWIST AND SHOUT. / THERE'S A PLACE** [-] [ ]
<US re-iss.Oct65 on 'Capitol Starline'; 6061>

Nov 64. (7"ep) *(GEP 8920)* **EXTRACTS FROM THE FILM 'A HARD DAY'S NIGHT'** [34] [-]
– I should have known better / If I fell / Tell me why / And I love her.

Dec 64. (7"ep) *(GEP 8924)* **EXTRACTS FROM THE ALBUM 'A HARD DAY'S NIGHT' 2** [ ] [-]
– Anytime at all / I'll cry instead / Things we said today / When I get home.

Dec 64. (lp) *<2222>* **THE BEATLES' STORY (narrative)** [-] [7]

Feb 65. (7"ep) *<R 5365>* **4-BY THE BEATLES** [-] [ ]
– Honey don't / I'm a loser / Mr.Moonlight / Everybody's trying to be my baby.

Apr 65. (7"ep) *(GEP 8931)* **BEATLES FOR SALE** [ ] [-]
– No reply / I'm a loser / Rock and roll music / Eight days a week.

Jun 65. (7"ep) *(GEP 8938)* **BEATLES FOR SALE (NO.2)** [ ] [-]
– I'll follow the sun / Baby's in black / Words of love / I don't want to spoil the party.

Oct 65. (7") *Capitol Starline; <6065>* **ROLL OVER BEETHOVEN. / MISERY** [-] [ ]

Oct 65. (7") *Capitol Starline; <6066>* **BOYS. / KANSAS CITY** [-] [ ]

Dec 65. (7"ep) *(GEP 8946)* **THE BEATLES' MILLION SELLERS** [ ] [-]
– She loves you / Can't buy me love / I feel fine / I want to hold your hand.

Mar 66. (7"ep) *(GEP 8948)* **YESTERDAY** [ ] [-]
– Yesterday / Act naturally / You like me too much / It's only love.

Jul 66. (lp) *(2553>* **YESTERDAY . . . AND TODAY** [-] [1]

Jul 66. (7"ep) *(GEP 8952)* **NOWHERE MAN** [ ] [-]
– Nowhere man / Drive my car / Michelle / You won't see me.

Dec 66. (lp) *(PMC/PCS 7016)* **A COLLECTION OF BEATLES OLDIES** [7] [-]
– She loves you / From me to you / We can work it out / Help! / Michelle / Yesterday / I feel fine / Yellow submarine / Can't buy me love / Bad boy / Day tripper / A hard day's night / Ticket to ride / Paperback writer / Eleanor Rigby / I want to hold your hand. *(re-iss.Oct83 on 'Fame' lp/c; FA/TC-FA 3081)*

Mar 70. (lp) *Apple; <385>* **HEY JUDE** [-] [2]
(UK-iss.May79 on 'Parlophone' lp/c; PCS/TC-PCS 7184)

Apr 73. (d-lp/d-c) *Apple; (PCSP/TC2-PCSP 717) <3403>* **THE BEATLES 1962-1966** [3] [3]
– Love me do / Please please me / She loves you / From me to you / She loves you / I want to hold your hand / All my loving / Can't buy me love / A hard day's night / And I love her / Eight days a week / I feel fine / Ticket to ride / Yesterday / Help! / You've got to hide your love away / We can work it out / Day tripper / Drive my car / Norwegian wood (this bird has flown) / Nowhere man / Michelle / In my life / Girl / Paperback writer / Eleanor Rigby / Yellow submarine. *(re-iss.Sep78 & Feb94 red-lp) (d-cd-iss.Jul91;) (re-iss.d-cd Sep93 on 'Apple-Parlophone', hit UK No.3)*

Apr 73. (d-lp/d-c) *Apple; (PCSP/TC2-PCSP 718) <3404>* **THE BEATLES 1967-1970** [2] [1]
– Strawberry fields forever / Penny lane / Sgt. Pepper's lonely hearts club band / With a little help from my friends / Lucy in the sky with diamonds / A day in the life / All you need is love / I am the Walrus / Hello, goodbye / The fool on the hill / Magical mystery tour / Lady Madonna / Hey Jude / Revolution / Back in the U.S.S.R / While my guitar gently weeps / Ob-la-di, ob-la-da / Get back / Don't let me down / The ballad of John and Yoko / Old brown shoe / Here comes the sun / Come together / Something / Octopus's Garden / Let it be / Across the universe / The long and winding road. *(re-iss.Sep78 & Feb94 blue-lp) (d-cd-iss.Jul91;) (re-iss.d-cd Sep93 on 'Apple-Parlophone', hit UK No.4)*

Mar 76. (7") *(R 6013)* **YESTERDAY. / I SHOULD HAVE KNOWN BETTER** [8] [-]

Jun 76. (lp/c) *(PCSP/TC-PCSP 719) <11537>* **ROCK'N'ROLL MUSIC** [11] [2]
(re-iss.Nov80 as . . . VOL.1 / . . . VOL.2 both on 'MfP')

Jun 76. (7") *<4274>* **GOT TO GET YOU INTO MY LIFE. / HELTER SKELTER** [-] [7]

Jul 76. (7") *(R 6016)* **BACK IN THE U.S.S.R. / TWIST AND SHOUT** [19] [-]

Aug 76. (d-lp) *Polydor; (2683 068)* **THE BEATLES TAPES (interviews)** [45] [-]

Nov 76. (7") *<4347>* **OB-LA-DI, OB-LA-DA. / JULIA** [-] [49]

Apr 77. (d-lp/d-c) */ Lingasong; <7001>* **LIVE AT THE STAR CLUB, HAMBURG, GERMANY 1962** [ ] [ ]

May 77. (lp/c) *(EMTV/TC-EMTV 4) <11638>* **THE BEATLES AT THE HOLLYWOOD BOWL (live)** [1] [2]
(UK re-iss.Sep84 on 'MfP')

Dec 77. (d-lp/d-c) *(PCSP/TC-PCSP 721) <11711>* **LOVE SONGS** [7] [24]

Sep 78. (7") *(R 6022) <4612>* **SGT. PEPPER'S LONELY HEARTS CLUB BAND – WITH A LITTLE HELP FROM MY FRIENDS. / A DAY IN THE LIFE** [63] [71]

Nov 78. (14xlp-box) **THE BEATLES COLLECTION** [ ] [ ]
– (all original albums boxed)

Oct 79. (lp/c) *(PCM/TC-PCM 1001) <12060>* **RARITIES** [71] [21] Apr80

Nov 80. (lp/c) *(PCS/TC-PCS 7214)* **BEATLES BALLADS** [17] [ ]

Dec 81. (14x7"ep's) **THE BEATLES EP COLLECTION** [ ] [ ]
– (all ep's above plus new SHE'S A WOMAN)
– She's a woman / Baby you're a rich man / This boy / The inner light.

Apr 82. (lp/c) *() <12199>* **REEL MUSIC** [ ] [19]

May 82. (7") *(R 6055) <5107>* **BEATLES MOVIE MEDLEY. / I'M HAPPY JUST TO DANCE WITH YOU** [10] [12] Mar82
– ('A'medley); Magical Mystery Tour – All You Need Is Love – You've Got To Hide Your Love Away – I Should Have Known Better – A Hard Day's Night – Ticket To Ride – Get Back.

Oct 82. (d-lp/d-c) *(PCTC/TC-PCTC 260) <12245>* **20 GREATEST HITS** [10] [50]

Feb 88. E.M.I./ US= Capitol; (d-lp)(c)(cd) **PAST MASTERS VOL.1** [49] [ ]

Feb 88. E.M.I./ US= Capitol; (d-lp)(c)(cd) **PAST MASTERS VOL.2** [46] [ ]

Oct 88. (box-lp)(box-c)(box-cd) **THE ULTIMATE BOX SET** [ ] [ ]

Aug 91. E.M.I.; (c-s x all) **THE SINGLES** [ ] [-]
– (all 7"singles boxed)

Jun 92. (cd-ep x14-box) **COMPACT DISC EP'S** [ ] [-]

Jul 81. (lp) *Phoenix; (PHX 1004)* **EARLY MUSIC VOL.1** [ ] [-]

Jul 81. (lp) *Phoenix; (PHX 1005)* **EARLY MUSIC VOL.2** [ ] [-]

Feb 82. (lp) *Phoenix; (PHX 1011)* **RARE BEATLES** [ ] [-]

Aug 81. (d-lp)(c) *Audio Fidelity;* **HISTORIC BEATLES** [ ] [-]

Sep 82. (lp/c) *Audio Fidelity;(AFELP/ZCALP 1047)* **THE COMPLETE SILVER BEATLES** [ ] [-]

Jul 82. (10"lp) *Charly; (CFM 701)* **THE SAVAGE YOUNG BEATLES** [ ] [-]
(re-iss.as THE BEATLES FEATURING TONY SHERIDAN, HAMBURG on 'Topline, cd-iss.Feb93 on 'Charly')

Sep 83. (lp) *Audio Fidelity;* **COMETS** [ ] [-]

Nov 83. (lp) *Berkeley;* **AUDITION TAPES** [ ] [-]

Dec 83. Breakaway; (lp) **HAMBURG TAPES VOL.1** [ ] [-]

Dec 83. Breakaway; (lp) **HAMBURG TAPES VOL.2** [ ] [-]

Dec 83. Breakaway; (lp) **HAMBURG TAPES VOL.3** [ ] [-]

Apr 86. (lp/c) *Showcase; (SHLP/SHTC 130)* **LIVE BEATLES VOL.1 (live)** [ ] [-]

Apr 86. (lp/c) *Showcase; (SHLP/SHTC 131)* **LIVE BEATLES VOL.2 (live)** [ ] [-]

Oct 87. (lp/c)(cd) *Topline; (TOP/KTOP 181)(TOPCD 523)* **THE DECCA SESSIONS (1/1/62)** [ ] [-]

Jun 92. (cd/c) *Columbia; (468950-2/-4)* **ROCKIN' AT THE STAR-CLUB (live)** [ ] [ ]

Dec 94. (d-cd/d-c/d-lp) *Apple; (CD/TC+/PCSP 726)* **LIVE AT THE BBC (live)** [1] [3]
– Beatle greetings / From us to you / Riding on a bus / I got a woman / Too much monkey business / Keep your hands off my baby / I'll be on my way / Young blood / A shot of rhythm and blues / Sure to fall (in love with you) / Some other guy / Thank you girl / Sha la la la la! / Baby it's you / That's all right (mama) / Carol / Soldier of love / A little rhyme / Clarabella / I'm gonna sit right down and cry (over you) / Crying, waiting, hoping / Dear Wack! / You really got a hold on me / To know her is to love her / A taste of honey / Long tall Sally / I saw her standing there / The honeymoon song / Johnny B Goode / Memphis, Tennessee / Lucille / Can't buy me love / From Fluff to you / Till there was you // Crinsk Dee night / A hard day's night / Have a banana! / I wanna be your man / Just a rumour / Roll over Beethoven / All my loving / Things we said today / She's a woman / Sweet little sixteen / 1882! / Lonesome tears in my eyes / Nothin' shakin' / The hippy hippy shake / Glad all over / I just don't understand / So how come (no one loves me) / I feel fine / I'm a loser / Everybody's trying to be my baby / Rock and roll music / Ticket to ride / Dizzy Miss Lizzy / Medley: Kansas City – Hey! hey! hey! hey! / Set fire to that lot! / Matchbox / I forgot to remember to forget / Love these Goon shows! / I got to find my baby / Ooh! my soul / Ooh! my arms / Don't ever change / Slow down / Honey don't / Love me do.

Mar 95. (c-s/7") *Apple; (TC+/R 6406)* **BABY IT'S YOU / I'LL FOLLOW THE SUN** [7] [67]
(cd-s+=) *(CDR 6406)* – Devil in her heart / Boys.

Nov 95. (d-cd/d-c/t-lp) *Apple; (CD/TC+/PCSP 727)* **ANTHOLOGY 1** [2] [1]
– Free as a bird / Speech (by JOHN LENNON) / That'll be the day / In spite of all the danger / Sometimes I'd borrow (speech by PAUL McCARTNEY) / Hallelujah I love her so / You'll be mine / Cayenne / First of all (speech by PAUL) / My Bonnie (w/ TONY SHERIDAN) / Ain't she sweet / Cry for a shadow / Brian was a beautiful guy (speech by JOHN) / Secured them an audition (speech by BRIAN EPSTEIN) / Searchin' / Three cool cats / The Sheik of Araby / Like dreamers do / Hello little girl / Well, the recording test (speech by BRIAN) / Besame mucho / Love me do / How do you do it? / Please please me / One after 909 (sequence) / One after 909 (complete) / Lend me your comb / I'll get you / We were performers (speech by JOHN) / I saw her standing there / From me to you / Money (that's what I want) / You really got a hold on me / Roll over Beethoven / She loves you / Till there was you (music man) / Twist and shout / This boy / I want to hold your hand / Boys, what I was thinking (speech by The BEATLES and MORECAMBE & WISE) / Moonlightbay (w/ MORECAMBE & WISE) / Can't buy me love / All my loving / You can't do that / And I love her / A hard day's night / I wanna be your man / Long tall Sally / Boys / Shout / I'll be back (take 2) / I'll be back (take 3) / You know what to do /

No reply (demo) / Mr.Moonlight / Leave my kitten alone / No reply / Eight days a week (sequence) / Eight days a week (complete) / Kansas City – hey, hey, hey.

— (below single was recently re-recorded from JOHN LENNON's 1977 cut)

Dec 95. (c-s/7") *Apple; (TC+/R 6422)* **FREE AS A BIRD. / CHRISTMAS TIME (IS HERE AGAIN)** [2] [6]
(cd-s+=) *(CDR 6422)* – I saw her standing there (take 9) / This boy (take 13).

Mar 96. (c-s/7") *Apple; (TC+/R 6425)* **REAL LOVE / BABY'S IN BLACK** [4] [11]
(cd-s+=) *(CDR 6425)* – Yellow submarine / Here, there and everywhere.

Mar 96. (d-cd/d-c/t-lp) *(CD/TC+/PCSP 728)* **ANTHOLOGY 2** (compilation) [1] [2]

Oct 96. (d-cd/d-c/t-lp) *(CD/TC+/PCSP 729)* **ANTHOLOGY 3** [4] [1]

Feb 97. (7"red/cd-s; BEATLES featuring TONY SHERIDAN) *Presstige 2; (GECK 06/+CD)* **CRY FOR A SHADOW. / LET'S DANCE** [ ] [-]

Feb 97. (7"blue/cd-s; BEATLES featuring TONY SHERIDAN) *Presstige 2; (GECK 07/+CD)* **IF YOU LOVE ME BABY. / WHAT'D I SAY** [ ] [-]

Feb 97. (7"green/cd-s; BEATLES featuring TONY SHERIDAN) *Presstige 2; (GECK 08/+CD)* **SWEET GEORGIA BROWN. / RUBY RUBY** [ ] [-]

Feb 97. (7"yellow/cd-s; BEATLES featuring TONY SHERIDAN) *Presstige 2; (GECK 09/+CD)* **YA YA. / WHY** [ ] [-]

Apr 97. (cd/c) *Presstige 2; (SYB 1 CD/MC)* **CRY FOR A SHADOW – THE SAVAGE YOUNG BEATLES** [ ] [-]

May 97. (d-cd) *Metro; (OTR 1100026)* **THE LOST FAB FOUR TAPES** [ ] [-]

BEAU BRUMMELS

Formed: Bay Area, San Francisco, USA . . . mid'64 by SAL VALENTINO, RON ELLIOTT, RON MEAGHER and JOHN PETERSEN. After attracting a cult local following, they gained a brief member DECLAN MULLIGAN, prior to signing for Tom Donahue and Bob Mitchell's 'Autumn' label. With help from producer SLY STONE, they had a hit with 'LAUGH LAUGH', a flawless piece of Merseybeat-styled pop, highlighting VALENTINO's crystal clear vocals. After their hits dried up, they evolved into a more manufactured folk-pop outfit that briefly deviated into psychedelia with the enchanting 'MAGIC HOLLOW' from the 1967 set 'TRIANGLE'. Following MEAGHER's departure, the duo of ELLIOTT and VALENTINO cut a country album, 'BRADLEY'S BARN', before splitting. They reformed in 1974, although the resulting eponymous album was an abysmal set of watered down country-pop. • **Songwriters:** Group compositions, except MR. TAMBOURINE MAN + ONE TOO MANY MORNINGS (Bob Dylan) / YOU'VE GOT TO HIDE YOUR LOVE AWAY + YESTERDAY (Beatles) / LOUIE LOUIE (Kingsmen) / HOMEWARD BOUND (Simon & Garfunkel) / THESE BOOTS ARE MADE FOR WALKING (Nancy Sinatra) / PLAY WITH FIRE (Rolling Stones) / MONDAY, MONDAY (Mamas & The Papas) / HANG ON SLOOPY (McCoys) / MRS.BROWN YOU'VE A LOVELY DAUGHTER (Herman's Hermits) / WOMAN (Peter & Gordon) / etc. • **Trivia:** ELLIOTT later sessioned for RANDY NEWMAN, EVERLY BROTHERS, etc.

Recommended: AUTUMN IN SAN FRANCISCO (*7)

RON ELLIOTT (b.21 Oct'43, Healdsberg, Calif.) – vocals, guitar / **SAL VALENTINO** (b.SAL SPAMPINATO, 8 Sep'42) – vocals / **RON MEAGHER** (b. 2 Oct'41, Oakland, Calif.) – guitar then bass / **JOHN PETERSEN** (b. 8 Jan'42, Rudyard, Mich.) – drums / **DECLAN MULLIGAN** (b.County Tipperary, Ireland) – bass (left before first)

Pye Int. / Autumn

Feb 65. (7") *(7N 25293)* <8> **LAUGH, LAUGH. / STILL IN LOVE WITH YOU BABY** [ ] [15] Dec64

May 65. (7") *(7N 25306)* <10> **JUST A LITTLE. / THEY'LL MAKE YOU CRY** [ ] [9] Mar65

Jun 65. (lp) *(NPL 28062)* <SLP 103> **INTRODUCING THE BEAU BRUMMELS** [ ] [24] May65
– Laugh, laugh / Still in love with you baby / Just a little / Just wait and see / Oh lonesome me / Ain't that loving you baby / Stick like glue / They'll make you cry / That's if you want me to / I want more loving / I would be happy / Not too long ago. *<cd-iss.Mar95 on 'Sundazed'; SC 6039>*

Sep 65. (7") *(7N 25318)* <16> **YOU TELL ME WHY. / I WANT YOU** [ ] [38] Jun65

Nov 65. (7") *(7N 25333)* <20> **DON'T TALK TO STRANGERS. / IN GOOD TIME** [ ] [52] Sep65

Jan 66. (7") *(7N 25342)* <24> **GOOD TIME MUSIC. / SAD LITTLE GIRL** [ ] [97] Nov65

Jan 66. (lp) <SLP 104> **VOLUME 2** [-] [ ]
– You tell me why / I want you / Doesn't matter / That's alright / Sometime at night / Can it be / Sad little girl / Woman / Don't talk to strangers / I've never known / When it comes to your love / In good time. *<cd-iss.Mar95 on 'Sundazed'; SC 6040>*

not issued / Warners

May 66. (7") <5813> **ONE TOO MANY MORNINGS. / SHE REIGNS** [-] [95]

Jul 66. (lp) <WS 1644> **BEAU BRUMMELS '66** [-] [ ]
– You've got to hide your love away / Mr. Tambourine man / Louie Louie / Homeward bound / These boots are made for walking / Yesterday / Bang bang / Hang on Sloopy / Play with fire / Woman / Mrs.Brown you've got a lovely daughter / Monday, Monday. *(UK cd-iss.Mar96 on 'WEA'; 7599 26885-2)*

Sep 66. (7") <5848> **FINE WITH ME. / HERE WE ARE AGAIN** [-] [ ]

— **ELLIOTT, VALENTINO + MEAGHER** were now joined by session man **VAN DYKE PARKS** – keyboards. PETERSON later joined HARPERS BIZARRE.

Oct 67. (lp) <WS 1692> **TRIANGLE** [-] [ ]
– Are you happy? / Only dreaming now / Painter of women / Keeper of time / It won't get better / Nine pound hammer / Magic hollow / All I've seen her / Triangle / Wolf of velvet fortune / Old Kentucky home. *(UK cd-iss.Mar96 on 'WEA'; 7599 26886-2)*

1967. (7") <7014> **DON'T MAKE PROMISES. / TWO DAYS 'TIL TOMORROW** [-] [ ]

1967. (7") <7079> **MAGIC HOLLOW. / LOWER LEVEL** [-] [ ]

1968. (7") <7204> **ARE YOU HAPPY. / LIFT ME** [-] [ ]

— now duo (**ELLIOTT + VALENTINO**) + sessioners **KENNY BUTTREY** – drums / **JERRY REED** – guitar / **DAVID BRIGGS** – keyboards / **NORMAN PUTTNAM** – bass

1968. (lp) <WS 1760> **BRADLEY'S BARN** [-] [ ]
– Turn around / An added attraction / Deep water / Long walking down to misery / Little bird / Cherokee girl / I'm a sleeper / The loneliest man in town / Love can fall a long way down / Jessica / Bless you California. *(UK-iss.Apr85 on 'Edsel'; ED 151) (cd-iss.Mar96 on 'WEA'; 7599 26887-2)*

1968. (7") <7218> **I'M A SLEEPER. / LONG WALKING DOWN TO MISERY** [-] [ ]

1968. (7") <7260> **CHEROKEE GIRL. / DEEP WATER** [-] [ ]

— Disbanded Dec'68

RON ELLIOTT

not issued / Warners

1970. (lp) <WS 1833> **THE CANDLESTICKMAKER** [-] [ ]
– Molly in the middle / Lazy day / All time green / To the city, to the sea / Deep river runs blue / The candlestickmaker suite: Dark into down – Questions.

— He later joined PAN who released self-named album in 1973 on 'Columbia'.

— SAL VALENTINO formed STONEGROUND in 1971. They released 3 albums on 'Warners'.

BEAU BRUMMELS

original 1965 line-up and **DAN LEVITT** – guitar

not issued / Warners

Apr 75. (lp) <WS 2842> **THE BEAU BRUMMELS** [-] [ ]
– First in line / Goldrush / Today by day / Tennessee walker / Gate of hearts / Wolf / Down to the bottom / You tell me why / Singing cowboy / The lonely side.

May 75. (7") <8119> **DOWN TO THE BOTTOM. / YOU TELL ME WHY** [-] [ ]

— Disbanded again mid'75.

– compilations, others, etc. –

1967. (lp) *Vault;* <LPS 114> **THE BEST OF THE BEAU BRUMMELS** [-] [ ]

1968. (lp) *Vault;* <LPS 121> **VOL.44** [-] [ ]

1975. (lp) *J.A.S.; (JAS 5000)* **THE ORIGINAL HITS OF . . . 1964** [-] [ ]

1981. (lp) *Rhino;* <101> **THE BEST OF THE BEAU BRUMMELS 1964-68** [-] [ ]

Jul 85. (lp) *Edsel; (ED 141)* **AUTUMN IN SAN FRANCISCO** [ ] [-]
– Laugh, laugh / Just a little / You tell me why / Don't talk to strangers / In good time / Sad little girl / Still in love with you baby / Stick like glue / That's if you want me to / Can it be / When it comes to your love / Gentle wanderin' ways / I grow old / Lonely man / She sends me. *(cd-iss.Jul90; EDCD 141)*

Feb 94. (cd) *Big Beat; (CDWIKD 127)* **AUTUMN OF THEIR YEARS** [ ] [-]

Jun 97. (cd) *Spotlight; (HADCD 213)* **60's GEMS** [ ] [-]

BEAVER & KRAUSE

Formed: San Francisco, California, USA . . . late 60's, by PAUL BEAVER, who had played in several jazz outfits, while BERNARD KRAUSE was a member of the more folk-orientated WEAVERS. They met at 'Elektra' records, where KRAUSE worked as a staff producer. They premiered with the low-key 'RAGNAROCK' late in '68, and its pioneering electronic explorations/soundscapes led to film work, notably 'Rosemary's Baby', 'Catch 22' & 'Performance'. They also sessioned for The BEATLES, SIMON & GARFUNKEL, The ROLLING STONES, NEIL YOUNG and BEACH BOYS. By this time (1970), a new album 'IN A WILD SANCTUARY', surfaced for the 'Warner Brothers' label. It gained wide appraisal from many in the business, but a live gem 'GANDHARVA' (A Celestial Music) superseded this the following year. Their third outing for the label, 'ALL GOOD MEN', saw them fall from grace. However, it was all over anyway when PAUL BEAVER died of a heart attack on the 16th of January '75.

Recommended: RAGNAROCK – ELECTRONIC FUNK (*6) / IN A WILD SANCTUARY (*7) / GANDHARVA (*8)

PAUL BEAVER (b. 1925) – electronics, Moog synthesizers, organ / **BERNARD KRAUSE** (b. Detroit, Michigan) – electronics, Moog

not issued / Limelight

1968. (lp) <86069> **RAGNAROCK – ELECTRONIC FUNK** [-] [ ]
– Peace three / Signal generators / Control generators / Frequency modulation / Amplitude modulation / Ring modulation / Filtering / Tape delay / Peace three. *(UK-iss.1975 as 'THE NONESUCH GUIDE TO ELECTRONIC MUSIC' on 'Nonesuch'; HC 73018)*

— added **DAVE GRUISIN** – keyboards / **HOWARD ROBERTS** – guitar / **MILT HOLLAND** – percussion / **BUD SHANK** – flute

Warners / Warners

1970. (lp) <WS 1850> **IN A WILD SANCTUARY** [-] [ ]
– Another part of time / And there was morning / Spaced / So long as the waters flow / Aurora hominis / Salute to the vanishing bald eagle / People's park / Walking green algae blues / Sanctuary.

1970. (7") <7414> **PEOPLE'S PARK. / SALUTE TO THE VANISHING BALD EAGLE** [-] [ ]

— below with many incl. **MIKE BLOOMFIELD + RONNIE MONTROSE** – guitar / **GERRY MULLIGAN** – saxophone

1971. (7") <7485> **WALKIN' BY THE RIVER. / SAGA OF THE BLUE BEAVER** [-] [ ]

Jan 72. (lp) *(K 46130)* <WS 1909> **GANDHARVA (live)** [ ] [ ]
– Soft-white / Saga of the blue beaver / Nine moons in Alaska / Walkin' / Walkin' by the river / Gandharva / By your grace / Good places / Short film for David /

Bright shadows. *(cd-iss.1990's on 'WEA'; 9362 45472-2)*

1972. (7") *<7642>* **A REAL SLOW DRAG. / BLUEBIRD CANYON STOMP**

1972. (lp) *(K 46184) <BS 2624>* **ALL GOOD MEN**
– A real slow drag / Legend days are over / Loves of Col. Evol / Sweet William / Bluebird canyon stomp / Looking back now / Prelude / Child of the morning sun / Between the sun and the rain / All good men / Waltz me around again Willie – Real slow drag.

— split after above and both went into session work. PAUL BEAVER completed a solo album 'PERCHANCE TO DREAM' early '75, just prior to his death.

BE-BOP DELUXE (see under ⇒ NELSON, Bill)

David BEDFORD

Born: c.1950, London, England. He studied at The Royal Academy Of Music before becoming a member of KEVIN AYERS & THE WHOLE WORLD from the late 60's to August '71. He then teamed up with LOL COXHILL to make a one-off 45 for 'Polydor', 'PRETTY LITTLE GIRL'; (2001 253). There was also a COXHILL-BEDFORD b-side, 'MOOD', on the flip of WILL DANDY & THE DANDYLETTES' 'Dandelion' 45; (2058 214). This was released at the same time as his solo debut. For the next few years, he worked with his friend MIKE OLDFIELD on the milestone 'TUBULAR BELLS' album. Simultaneously he completed his first solo effort, 'NURSES SONG WITH ELEPHANTS', issued early '72 on John Peel & Clive Selwood's 'Dandelion' label. BEDFORD moved to 'Virgin' in 1974 for the release of follow-up 'STAR'S END', structurally owing much to the aforementioned TUBULAR BELLS. Prior to his next theme/project, 'THE RIME OF THE ANCIENT MARINER', BEDFORD, OLDFIELD and The ROYAL PHILHARMONIC ORCHESTRA, hit the UK Top 20 with 'THE ORCHESTRAL TUBULAR BELLS'. Over the course of the next few years, 'Virgin' issued a further couple of albums in the same vein, 'THE ODYSSEY' (1976) and 'INSTRUCTIONS FOR ANGELS' (1977). BEDFORD kept a lower profile in the 80's, although the 1985 concept album, 'RIGEL 9', was a beautiful sci-fi musical, which should have furnished DAVID with his first success (maybe one day they might adapt into a TV play or even a film). • **Style:** Classical multi-instrumentalist composer taking themes from; COLERIDGE's poem 'RIME OF THE ANCIENT MARINER' which included TIELMAN SUSATO's 16th Century classical 'La Mourisque' and a sea shanty 'The Rio Grande'. 1976's 'THE ODYSSEY' was inspired from HOMER's work/ 'INSTRUCTIONS FOR ANGELS' from a poem by KENNETH PATCHEN. • **Trivia:** Worked on/arranged albums by ROY HARPER, EDGAR BROUGHTON BAND, etc.

Recommended: NURSES SONG WITH ELEPHANTS (*5) / STAR'S END (*6) / THE RIME OF THE ANCIENT MARINER (*6) / THE ODYSSEY (*5) / INSTRUCTIONS FOR ANGELS (*5) / STAR CLUSTERS (*5) / RIGEL 9 (*7)

DAVID BEDFORD – piano, organ, percussion, violin, flute, etc. with **MIKE OLDFIELD** – bass / **KEVIN AYERS** – vox / + The SEBASTIAN BELL ENSEMBLE / OMEGA PLAYERS & The PIPE TWIRLERS

Dandelion not issued

Mar 72. (lp) *(2310 165)* **NURSES SONG WITH ELEPHANTS**
– It's easier than it looks / Nurses song with elephants / Some bright stars for Queen's College / Sad and lonely faces. *(cd-iss.Sep96 on 'Blueprint'; BP 116CD)*

— next performed by The ROYAL PHILHARMONIC ORCHESTRA conducted by VERNON HANDLEY / + **MIKE OLDFIELD** – guitar, bass, co-producer / **CHRIS CUTLER** – percussion

Virgin Virgin

Nov 74. (lp) *(V 2020)* **STAR'S END**
– Side One / Side Two. *(cd-iss.Jun97; CDV 2020)*

— Jan'85, credited on MIKE OLDFIELD's 'THE ORCHESTRAL TUBULAR BELLS'.

— w/ **MIKE OLDFIELD** – guitar / actor **ROBERT POWELL** – narrator / **DIANA COULSON + LUCY BLACKBURN** – vocals plus classes 2 & 3 from Queen's College London.

Sep 75. (lp) *(V 2038)* **THE RIME OF THE ANCIENT MARINER**
– The rime of the ancient mariner / The Rio Grande. *(re-iss.Aug88; OVED 152) (cd-iss.Apr94; CDOVD 443)*

— w/ Queen's College Choir; on 'The Sirens'; **VICKY COOPER, SOPHIE DICKSON, MEGAN POWELL, JUDY PLANT, DAISY GOODWIN, SERENA MACREADY-SELLERS + MIA DICKSON / MIKE OLDFIELD + ANDY SUMMERS** – guitar / **ANNE MURRAY + ROSALIND KANDLER** – recorder / **LAYNE HOLSTEAD** – oboe / **NICOLETTE ALVEY** – synthesizers, wine glasses + **ELLY LEMOS**

Sep 76. (lp) *(V 2070)* **THE ODYSSEY**
– (i) Penelope's shroud / King Aeolus / (ii) Penelope's shroud / The Phaeacian Games / (iii) Penelope's shroud / The sirens / Scylla and Charybdis / (iv) Penelope's shroud / Circe's island / Penelope's shroud completed / The battle in the hall. *(re-iss.1988; OVED 153) (cd-iss.Apr94; CDOVD 444)*

— now w/ **MIKE OLDFIELD** – guitar / **MIKE RATLEDGE** – synths / LEICESTERSHIRE SCHOOLS SYMPHONY ORCHESTRA / **JEFF BRYANT, MICK BAINES, ROBIN DAVIS** – french horns / **JIM DOUGLAS** – oboe / **SOPHIE DICKSON, DIANA COULSON** – vocals / **JENNIFER ANGEL, JULIA FOGUEL, CELIA HUTCHISON, MARY ROSE LILLINGTON + FIONA LOFTS** – flutes

Nov 77. (lp) *(V 2090)* **INSTRUCTIONS FOR ANGELS**
– Theme / Variation 1 & 2: "Wanderers of the pale wood. Parts 1 & 2 / Variation 3: 'The dazzling burden" / Variation 4: "Be music, night" / Variation 5: "First came the lion-rider" / Variation 6: "Instructions for angels" / Finale: "The valley-sleeper, the children, the snakes and the giant". *(cd-iss.Jun97; CDV 2090)*

— **BEDFORD** – keyboards with **MIKE RATLEDGE** – keyboards / **MIKE OLDFIELD** – producer

1983. (lp) *(206 344)* **STAR CLUSTERS, NEBULAE & PLACES IN DEVON / THE SONG OF THE WHITE HORSE**
– (as titled above)

— with **URSULA LE GUIN** – lyrics / **ADRIAN LEVENE, BILL BENHAM + BELINDA BUNT** – violin / **DANIEL WOODGATE** – drums (of MADNESS) / **MARK BEDFORD** – bass (of MADNESS) / **CLEM CLEMPSON** – guitar / **PETE KING** – sax / **ENN REITEL** – plays "Anders" & "Lee" / **GERARD KENNY** – vocals "Anders" / **SARAH DUTHIE "The Red One" / LORIN STEWART "Kapper" / STRAWBERRY SWITCHBLADE – funeral leaders / The BARNET SCHOOLS CHOIR + THE COUNTY OF AVON SCHOOLS SYMPHONIC WINDBAND**

Charisma not issued

Jun 85. (lp/c; by DAVID BEDFORD / URSULA LE GUIN) *(RIGEL/CRIGEL 9)* **RIGEL 9**
– OVERTURE: SCENE 1 (a) The forest, (b) Anders and The Red One, (c) Anders' capture / SCENE 2 (a) The city, (b) Anders and The Red One / SCENE 3 (a) Kapper and Lee in the forest, (b) The death of The Orange One, (c) The funeral procession / SCENE 4 (a) Anders alone in the city, (b) The ritual song, (c) Anders' flight through the forest, (d) At the ship: Countdown – Lift off, (e) Finale. *(re-iss.Jun88 lp/c; CHC/+MC 77) (cd-iss.Jun97; CDOVD 484)*

BEEFEATERS (See under ⇒ BYRDS)

BEGGARS OPERA

Formed: Glasgow, Scotland . . .late 60's originally as The SYSTEM. In 1970, they had a hit in Europe with 'SARABANDE'. At the same time, the debut album, 'ACT ONE', took centre stage for the spiralling progressive label 'Vertigo'. A few more albums pandering to YES & ELP-style indulgence failed to make the grade, while their pomp prog-rock covers of 'MacARTHUR PARK' and 'CLASSICAL GAS', couldn't match their predecessors RICHARD HARRIS / JIM WEBB and MASON WILLIAMS respectively. • **Songwriters:** Group or SCOTT / ERSKINE. ERSKINE's role was taken over by GARDINER, with PARK and GRIFFITHS also contributing.

Recommended: ACT ONE (*6) / WATERS OF CHANGE (*5) / PATHFINDER (*5)

MARTIN GRIFFITHS – vocals / **RICKY GARDINER** – guitar, vocals / **ALAN PARK** – organ / **MARSHALL ERSKINE** – bass, flute / **RAYMOND WILSON** – drums / (also co-writer VIRGINIA SCOTT)

Vertigo Vertigo

Jan 71. (7") *(6059 026)* **SARABANDE. / THINK**

Jan 71. (lp) *(6360 018) <5080>* **ACT ONE**
– Poet and peasant / Passacaglia / Memory / Raymond's road / Light cavalry.

— added **GORDON SELLER** – bass, guitar, vocals / **VIRGINIA SCOTT** – keyboards, vocals

Nov 71. (lp) *(6360 054)* **WATERS OF CHANGE**
– Time machine / Lament / I've no idea / Nimbus / Festival / Silver peacock / Impromptu / The fox. *(cd-iss.Apr95 on 'Repertoire'; IMS 7029)*

— now w/out ERSKINE + SCOTT (although latter still co-writer on some)

1972. (7") *(6059 060)* **HOBO. / PATHFINDER**

Aug 72. (lp) *(6360 073)* **PATHFINDER**
– Hobo / MacArthur Park / The witch / Pathfinder / From shark to haggis / Stretcher / Madame Doubtfire. *(cd-iss.1989 on 'Line'; LICD 9.00728 0) (cd re-iss.Apr95 on 'Repertoire'; IMS 7028)*

— **LINNIE PETERSON** – vocals (ex-WRITING ON THE WALL) + **COLIN FAIRLEY** – drums, percussion, vocals repl.GRIFFITHS

Sep 73. (7") *(6059 088)* **TWO TIMING WOMAN. / LADY OF HELL FIRE**

1973. (lp) *(6360 090)* **GET YOUR DOG OFF ME!**
– Get your dog off me! / Freestyle ladies / Open letter / Morning day / Requiem / Classical gas / Sweet blossom woman / Turn your money green / La-di-da / Working man.

Jul 74. (7") *(6059 105)* **CLASSICAL GAS. / SWEET BLOSSOM WOMAN**

— **RICKY GARDINER** brought back wife-to-be **VIRGINIA (SCOTT). PARK became CLIFF RICHARD's musical director.**

Jupiter not issued

1974. (lp) *(88907)* **SAGITTARY** German
– Sagittary / Something to lose / World crisis blues / Smiling in a summer dress / Freedom song / I'm the music man / Just twenty one / Jack the ripper / Love of my own / Simplicity.

— **PETE SCOTT** – vocals + **CLEM CATTINI** – drums repl. FAIRLEY

1975. (lp) *(27702)* **BEGGARS CAN'T BE CHOOSERS** German
– I'm a roadie / Beggars can't be choosers / Hungry man / You're not welcome / Young blood man / Union card / We must love / Keep climbing / Bar room pearl / Death.

— split when RICKY joined DAVID BOWIE on tour. Re-formed for below.

Vertigo not issued

1979. (lp) *(6350 060)* **LIFELINE** German
– Lifeline / I gave you love / You never believe I'm human / Showman in a showman / Yes I need someone / Lost in space / Now you're gone / Bad dreams / Four moons.

— Folded for the last time.

BELL & ARC (see under ⇒ SKIP BIFFERTY)

BETWEEN

Formed: based Germany . . . 1970 as BETWEEN THE CHAIRS by PETER-MICHAEL HAMEL. Shortening their name to BETWEEN, this cosmopolitan band cut their debut album, 'EINSTEIG' in 1971. The record reflected the differing musical backgrounds of the various BETWEEN members but wasn't entirely successful at creating an effective hybrid. After some line-up alterations, 'Vertigo' released 'AND THE WATERS OPENED' in 1973, an all acoustic affair which more fully realised founder HAMMEL's vision of creating something musically unique. 'DHARANA' (1974) was a symphonic piece of improvisation while 1978's 'CONTEMPLATION' was more similar in style to the debut. The band finally split after the 'SILENCE BEYOND TIME' album in 1980.

Recommended: EINSTIG (*6) / AND THE WATERS OPENED (*7)

PETER-MICHAEL HAMEL – piano, organ / **ULRICH STRANZ** – viola / **ROBERT ELISCU** (b. USA) – oboe, flute / **COTCH BLACK** (b. USA) – tabla, percussion / **ROBERTO DETREE** (b. Argentina) – guitar, bass / **JAMES GALWAY** (b. Eire) – flute

Wergo / not issued

Oct 71. (lp) *(WER SM 1001)* **EINSTIEG** [-] [-] German
– Katakomben / Two trees / Volkstanz / Primary – Stage / Flight of ideas / Triumphzug Kaiser Maximillian / Barcelona rain / Memories / Space ship / Try Bach.

— **FABIAN ARKUS** – synthesizer; repl. STRANZ who went classical

— **DURU OMSON** – flute, percussion, vocals; repl. GALWAY who became a classical flautist and had many UK hit albums and a one-hit-wonder; a version of JOHN DENVER's 'ANNIE'S SONG', which made No.3.

— while BETWEEN convalesced, HAMEL issued his first solo album (see below) and guested for AGITATION FREE, while ELISCU guested on the first of several POPOL VUH albums

Vertigo / not issued

1973. (lp) *(6360 612)* **AND THE WATERS OPENED** [-] [-] German
– And the waters opened / Uroboros / Syn devotion / Happy stage / Samum.

— **CHARLES CAMPBELL** – congas; repl. OMSON + ARKUS

1974. (lp) *(6360 619)* **DHARANA** [-] [-] German
– Joy . . . sadness . . . joy / Om namo Buddhaya / Sunset / Listen to the light / Dharana. *(re-iss.May78 on 'Wergo'; WER SM 1011)*

— now without BLACK, who was repl. by guests; actor **GERD WESTPHAL HESEE** – poems / **AL GROMER** – sitar (ex-POPOL VUH, ex-AMON DUUL II) / **TOM VAN DER GELD** – vibraphone / **GARY TODD + JERZY ZIEMBROWSKI** – bass / **HOLGER BRANDT** – drums / **PETER MULLER** – sarangi / **BOBBY JONES** – saxes / **FRANZ LEHRNDORFER** – organ

Electrola / not issued

1975. (lp) *(062-29546)* **HESSE BETWEEN MUSIC** [-] [-] German
– Om namo Buddhaya / Whistlin' / From Tom's diary / Glueck / Chinesische legende / Suicide / When you're smiling / Zarathustra / Variationen uber "Eisenach" / Leb wohl, Frau Welt / Govinda / Lachen, lachen, lachen. *(re-iss.May78 on 'Wergo'; WER SM 1015)*

— **HAMEL, ELISCU, DETREE, VAN DER GELD, MULLER + TODD** added **JEFFREY BIDDEAU** – congas / **ILONA PEDERSON** – English-horn / **SANKHA KUMAR CHATTERJEE** – tabla

Wergo / not issued

May 78. (lp) *(WER SM 1012)* **CONTEMPLATION** [-] [-] German
– Contemplation / Watch the trees / Circle / Ivory and steel / Orphikon / State of sound.

— **ROGER JANNOTA** – wind; repl. PEDERSON

— **CHARLIE CAMPBELL** – congas; repl. VAN DER GELD

1980. (lp) *(WER SM 1023)* **SILENCE BEYOND TIME** (German 'STILLE UBER DIE ZEIT') [-] [-] German
– Brain wave / Two alone by the waterphone / Back to the roots / Das molekuel / Silence beyond time / Peaceful piece / Movens / Last flight.

— HAMEL continued with his solo outings

PETER-MICHAEL HAMEL

-vocals, piano, organ

Vertigo / not issued

1972. (d-lp) *(6641 055)* **HAMEL** [-] [-] German
– Storm over Asia and calm * / Bolivia (part 1 & 2) / Fire of holy eyes * / Song of the dolphins * / Sinking sangsara / Aura * / Gomorrhaga / Cathedral on "C". *(iss.1981 as lp 'AURA' * tracks on 'Wergo'; WER SM 1009)*

1973. (lp) *(6360 613)* **VOICE OF SILENCE** [-] [-] German
– Pantra tantra / The voice of silence.

Harmonia Mundi / not issued

1975. (d-lp) *(2922 292)* **BUDDHIST MEDITATION** [-] [-] German

— added **ULRICH KRAUS** – synth, producer / **ANATOL KRAUS** – electronics

Wergo / not issued

1977. (lp) *(WER SM 1013)* **NADA** [-] [-] German
– Nada / Silence / Slow motion / Beyond the wall of sleep.

— now without ANATOL

Kuckuck / not issued

1980. (lp) *(046)* **COLOURS OF TIME** [-] [-] German
– Colours of time (part 1) / Colours of time (part 2).

1981. (lp) *(048)* **BARDO** [-] [-] German
– Dorian Dervishes / Bardo.

1983. (d-lp) *(063-064)* **TRANSITION** [-] [-] German
– Transition / Mandala / Let it play / Transpersonal / Apotheosis.

1985. (lp) *(885295)* **ORGANUM** [-] [-] German
– Organum (pt.1) / Organum (pt.2) / Organum (pt.3) / Organum (pt.4).

1987. (d-lp) *(078)* **LET IT PLAY** (compilation 1979-1983) [-] [-] German

BIG BOY PETE (see under ⇒ MILLER)

BIG BROTHER & THE HOLDING CO.

Formed: San Francisco, California, USA . . .late '65 by SAM ANDREW, PETER ALBIN, DAVE ESKERSON and CHUCK JONES. Shortly after, the latter two were replaced by JAMES GURLEY and DAVID GETZ respectively. Through promoter CHET HELMS, they enlisted Texan JANIS JOPLIN, who had just turned down an opportunity to join The 13th FLOOR EVEVATORS. Signing to 'Mainstream' records in 1967, they turned in an excellent Monterey festival performance, just prior to releasing their eponymous debut album. However, their blistering set caught the attention of 'Columbia', who subsequently released 'CHEAP THRILLS' album, which hit No.1 in the States for 7 weeks in the fall of '68. This roughshod and at times ramshackle affair, nevertheless captured the tremendous vocal talent of JOPLIN on soul-wrenching numbers such as 'PIECE OF MY HEART' (a Top 20 hit) and 'BALL AND CHAIN' (blues rock for acid heads). Her star rating outstriped her backing band at a rate of knots, and it was inevitable that she would take off for a solo career (see own entry). This all but killed any further success for BIG BROTHER, although they continued, releasing two further lacklustre albums in the early 70's. In 1987 however, GETZ, ANDREW, GURLEY and ALBIN recruited new singer MICHELLE BASTIAN for a series of low-key gigs. • **Style:** Powerful bluesy rock, that gave light to tremendous vocal talent of JANIS JOPLIN. In the 70's, they mellowed with her absence. • **Note:** Nothing whatsoever to do with 80's outfit BIG BROTHER, who released 12" 'Adventures In Success'.

Recommended: BIG BROTHER AND THE HOLDING CO. (*5) / CHEAP THRILLS (*7)

SAM ANDREW (b.18 Dec'41, Taft, California) – guitar, vocals / **PETE ALBIN** (b. 6 Jun'44) – bass, vocals / **JAMES GURLEY** (b.22 Dec'39, Detroit, Mich.) – guitar repl. DAVE ESKERSON (left Nov65) / **DAVID GETZ** (b.24 Jan'40, Brooklyn, N.Y.) – drums repl. CHUCK JONES (left Feb66) also on occasion / **ED BOGAS** – violin (left before Summer'66, to NEW RIDERS OF THE PURPLE SAGE)

— (Jun66) added **JANIS JOPLIN** (b.19 Jan'43, Port Arthur, Texas) – vocals

Fontana / Mainstream

Jul 67. (7") <657> **BLIND MAN. / ALL IS LONELINESS** [-] [ ]

Sep 67. (7") <662> **DOWN ON ME. / CALL ON ME** [-] [ ]
<hit US No.43 in Aug'68> (UK-iss.Sep68 on 'London'; HLT 10226)

Nov 67. (lp; stereo/mono) *(S+/TL 5457)* *<6099>* **BIG BROTHER & THE HOLDING COMPANY** [ ] [60] Aug67
– Bye bye baby / Easy rider / Intruder / Light is faster than sound / Call on me / Women is losers / Blind man / Down on me / Caterpillar / All is loneliness. *(re-iss.1969 on 'London' mono/stereo; HA-T/SH-T 8377) <US re-iss.May71 on 'Columbia'; 30631>*– Coo Coo / The last mile. *(cd-iss.Apr93 as 'FIRST ALBUM' on 'Sony Europe';)*

Nov 67. (7") <666> **BYE BYE BABY. / INTRUDER** [-] [ ]

Dec 67. (7") *(TF 881)* **BYE BYE BABY. / ALL IS LONELINESS** [ ] [-]

Feb 68. (7") <675> **WOMEN IS LOSERS. / LIGHT IS FASTER THAN SOUND** [-] [ ]

C.B.S. / Columbia

Aug 68. (7") *(CBS 3683)* <44626> **PIECE OF MY HEART. / TURTLE BLUES** [ ] [12]

Sep 68. (lp) *(CBS 63392)* <PC 9700> **CHEAP THRILLS** [ ] [1] Aug68
– Combination of the two / I need a man to love / Summertime / Piece of my heart / Turtle blues / O sweet Mary / Ball and chain. *<US re-iss.Mar81; > (cd-iss.Jan91 & Jun92 on 'Columbia'; CD 32004)*

— Folded late 1968. JANIS JOPLIN went solo, taking SAM ANDREW. In Aug69 GETZ and ALBIN re-formed BIG BROTHER & THE HOLDING COMPANY with **NICK GRAVENITES** – vocals / **MIKE PRENDERGAST** – guitar / **TED ASHBURTON** – piano

— soon split again, GETZ was also in NU BUGALOO EXPRESS.

— **GETZ, GURLEY, ALBIN, SAM ANDREW + NICK GRAVENITES** – vocals re-grouped **BIG BROTHER & THE HOLDING COMPANY** with **KATHI McDONALD** – vocals / **MIKE FINNEGAN** – keyboards / **DAVID SCHALLOCK** – guitar (both ex-NU BUGALOO EXPRESS)

Jan 71. (lp) *(CBS 64118)* <PC 30222> **BE A BROTHER** [ ] [ ] Nov70
– Keep on / Joseph's coat / Home on the strange / Someday / Heartache people / Sunshine baby / Mr. Natural / Funkie Jim / I'll change your flat tire Merle / Be a brother.

Jan 71. (7") <45284> **KEEP ON. / HOME ON THE STRANGE** [-] [ ]

Aug 71. (lp) <KC 30738> **HOW HARD IT IS** [-] [ ]
– How hard it is / You've been talkin' 'bout me, baby / House on fire / Black widow spider / Last band on side one / Nu Boogaloo jam / Maui / Shine on / Buried alive in the blues / Promise her anything but give her Arpeggio.

Sep 71. (7") <45502> **NU BOOGALOO JAM. / BLACK WIDOW SPIDER** [-] [ ]

— Split Feb'72. ALBIN rejoined COUNTRY JOE (McDONALD) & THE FISH. He and GETZ were part of them in 1969. FINNEGAN played live with STEPHEN STILLS etc. GRAVENITES tried to revitalise ELECTRIC FLAG.

– compilations, etc. –

Nov 68. (7") *Mainstream;* <678> **COO COO. / THE LAST MILE** [-] [84]

Jan 84. (lp) *Edsel; (ED 135)* **CHEAPER THRILLS** (live 26th July '66) [ ] [-]
(cd-iss.Sep90; EDCD 135)

Apr 86. (lp) *Edsel; (ED 170)* **JOSEPH'S COAT** (best of 71's two albums) [ ] [-]

BIG STAR (see under ⇒ BOX TOPS)

BIG SLEEP (see under ⇒ EYES OF BLUE)

BIRDS

Formed: West Drayton, Middlesex, England . . . 1964 as The THUNDERBIRDS by quintet below. The band included future stars RONNIE WOOD (Faces & Stones) and KIM GARDNER (Creation). They caused a minor stir, when, for a publicity stunt, they served an injunction on US future stars The BYRDS on their use of the name. Their second 45, the mod-ish/R&B-style 'LEAVIN' HERE', broke into the UK Top 50, although they soon faded from 3 minute fame. • **Songwriters:** GARDNER – WOOD. • **Trivia:** They featured in the film 'The Deadly Bees' (1967). Their singles are worth over 50 quid, the most pricy being 200 for the one-off BIRD'S BIRDS art-pop attempt.

Recommended: THESE BIRDS ARE DANGEROUS (*5)

ALI McKENZIE – vocals / **RONNIE WOOD** – guitar, vocals / **TONY MUNROE** – guitar, vocals / **KIM GARDNER** – bass, vocals / **PETE McDANIELS** – drums

Decca / not issued

Oct 64. (7") *(F 12031)* **YOU'RE ON MY MIND. / YOU DON'T LOVE ME (YOU DON'T CARE)** [ ] [–]
Apr 65. (7") *(F 12140)* **LEAVING HERE. / NEXT IN LINE** [45] [ ]
Oct 65. (7") *(F 12257)* **NO GOOD WITHOUT YOU. / HOW CAN IT BE** [ ] [ ]

Reaction / not issued

Sep 66. (7"; as BIRD'S BIRDS) *(591 005)* **SAY THOSE MAGIC WORDS. / DADDY DADDY** [ ] [–]

— Disbanded late '66 when GARDNER had already took off to join CREATION. He later became part of ASHTON, GARDNER & DYKE. RONNIE WOOD joined JEFF BECK before also later joining CREATION (mid'68). As said above, he became more famous in The FACES and mid-70's ROLLING STONES.

- compilations, etc. -

1979. (7") *Decca; (FR 13864)* **LEAVING HERE. /** [ ] [–]
1985. (m-lp) *Edsel; (NEST 901)* **THESE BIRDS ARE DANGEROUS** [ ] [–]
– (first 3 singles)

BLACK CAT BONES (see under ⇒ LEAFHOUND)

Peter BLEGVAD (see under ⇒ SLAPP HAPPY)

BLIND FAITH

Formed: London, England . . . May '69 . . . as supergroup of musicians ERIC CLAPTON, GINGER BAKER, STEVE WINWOOD and RIC GRECH. They introduced their accomplished style of roots blues at the BRIAN JONES memorial concert in Hyde Park, supporting The ROLLING STONES. Their first and only album recorded virtually live in the studio, was a massive seller on both sides of the Atlantic and included some stellar moments ('CAN'T FIND MY WAY HOME', 'PRESENCE OF THE LORD'). They subsequently undertook a promotional tour of the States that Autumn, although to the disappointment of many fans, the project was abruptly aborted. • **Songwriters:** CLAPTON and WINWOOD, with cover WELL ALL RIGHT (Buddy Holly). • **Trivia:** GINGER BAKER's 11 year-old daughter was controversially used posing topless on UK album sleeve. This was soon banned in the States.

Recommended: BLIND FAITH (*7)

STEVE WINWOOD (b.12 May'48, Birmingham, England) – vocals, keyboards (ex-TRAFFIC, ex-SPENCER DAVIS GROUP) / **ERIC CLAPTON** (b.30 Mar'45, Ripley, England) – guitar, vocals (ex-CREAM, ex-JOHN MAYALL . . . , ex-YARDBIRDS, etc) / **RIC GRECH** (b. 1 Nov'46, Bordeaux, France) – bass (ex-FAMILY) / **GINGER BAKER** (b.19 Aug'39, Lewisham, England) – drums (ex-CREAM, ex-GRAHAM BOND ORGANISATION, ex-BLUES INC.)

Polydor / R.S.O.

Aug 69. (lp) *(583-059) <304>* **BLIND FAITH** [1] [1] Jul69
– Had to cry today / Can't find my way home / Well all right / Presence of the Lord / Sea of joy / Do what you like. *<US re-iss.Feb77 on 'R.S.O.'; 3016> (re-iss.Nov77 on 'R.S.O.'; 2394 142) (re-iss.Aug83 on 'R.S.O.'; SPELP 14) (cd-iss.Apr86+=; 825 094-2) (cd re-iss.Sep95)*– Exchange and mart / Spending all my days.

— Disbanded later 1969. GINGER BAKER formed AIRFORCE with STEVE WINWOOD. The latter returned to TRAFFIC before carving out a solo career. RIC GRECH went solo. As did ERIC CLAPTON who also formed DEREK & THE DOMINOES in 1970.

- compilations, others, etc. -

Obviously none were released but some BLIND FAITH tracks did surface on ERIC CLAPTON compilations CROSSROADS and THE HISTORY OF ERIC CLAPTON (see ⇒)

BLODWYN PIG

Formed: Luton, England . . . late 1968, by MICK ABRAHAMS, veteran of The HUSTLERS, SCREAMING LORD SUTCH, NEIL CHRISTIAN'S CRUSADERS and JETHRO TULL. He played bass for the latter on one album, 'TIME WAS', before quickly deciding where his roots lay. Having re-signed for the 'Island' label (home of JETHRO TULL), BLODWYN PIG had two surprise entries into the Top 10 album listings. 'AHEAD RINGS OUT' (1969) and 'GETTING TO THIS' (1970) consisted largely of progressive roots blues, with touches of jazz experimentation, not too dissimilar to JETHRO TULL or even ROY HARPER. They disbanded when ABRAHAMS formed his own solo outfit, although he did re-form the group briefly in the mid-70's and then again in the 90's. An album in 1993, 'LIES', was simply a retread of past glories, although it did produce a version of DR. JOHN & DOC POMUS' 'THE VICTIM'. • **Trivia:** Albums now worth in excess of £30 each.

Recommended: AHEAD RINGS OUT (*7) / GETTING TO THIS (*6)

MICK ABRAHAMS (b. 7 Apr'43) – vocals, guitar (ex-JETHRO TULL, ex-McGREGOR'S ENGINE) / **JACK LANCASTER** – saxophone / **ANDY PYLE** – bass (ex-McGREGOR'S ENGINE) / **RON BERG** – drums

Island / A&M

May 69. (7") *(WIP 6059)* **DEAR JILL. / SWEET CAROLINE** [ ] [–]
Aug 69. (lp) *(ILPS 9101) <AM 4210>* **AHEAD RINGS OUT** [9] [ ]
– It's only love / Dear Jill / Walk on the water / The modern alchemist / See my way / Summer day / The change song / Backwash / Ain't ya coming home babe? *(re-iss.Mar89 on 'Beat Goes On' lp/cd; BGO LP/CD 54) (cd re-iss.Oct94; same)*
Sep 69. (7") *(WIP 6069)* **SUMMER DAY. / WALK ON THE WATER** [ ] [–]
Oct 69. (7") *<1158>* **DEAR JILL. / SUMMER DAY** [–] [ ]

Chrysalis / A&M

Jan 70. (7") *(WIP 6078)* **SAME OLD STORY. / SLOW DOWN** [ ] [–]
Apr 70. (lp) *(ILPS 9122) <AM 4243>* **GETTING TO THIS** [8] [96] Jun70
– Drive me / Variations on Nainos / Meanie Morney / Long bomb blues / The squirreling must go on / San Francisco sketches:- (a) Beach scape, (b) Fisherman's wharf, (c) Telegraph hill, (d) Close the door I'm falling out of the room / Worry / Toys / Send your son to die. *(re-iss.Oct90 on 'Beat Goes On' lp/cd; BGO LP/CD 81) (cd re-iss.Oct94; same)*

— (Sep70) **PETE BANKS** – guitar, vocals (ex-YES) repl. ABRAHAMS who went solo. Released two 'Chrysalis' lp's in 1971 and 1972 respectively; '(A MUSICAL EVENING WITH) THE MICK ABRAHAMS BAND' *(CHR 9147)* & 'AT LAST' *CHR 1005)* (now both respectively on cd Sep92 & Sep91) on 'Beat Goes On'; *BGOCD 95)* & 'Edsel'; *EDCD 335).* In 1974 he released another 'HAVE FUN LEARNING THE GUITAR WITH MICK ABRAHAMS' on 'SRT'; *(73313).* In the 90's, he was back with 'ALL SAID AND DONE' for 'Elite' cd; *(007CD).*

— Meanwhile the remaining members changed group name to **LANCASTER'S BOMBER** (Dec70) **LARRY WALLIS** – guitar, vocals repl. BANKS who formed FLASH

— Disbanded again WALLIS joined UFO. ANDY PYLE joined SAVOY BROWN and then JUICY LUCY where he was reunited with RON BERG. They both rejoined SAVOY BROWN.

— Early 1974 to mid '74, BLODWYN PIG reunited (LANCASTER, PYLE and ABRAHAMS) plus CLIVE BUNKER – drums (ex-JETHRO TULL). PYLE joined CHICKEN SHACK. They re-formed in Apr'89, with ABRAHAMS once again at the helm.

— Re-formed by **ABRAHAMS / MIKE SUMMERLAND** – bass (ex-GEORGIE FAME) / **GRAHAM WALKER** – drums (ex-GARY MOORE) / **DAVE LENNOX** – keyboards

A New Day / Viceroy

Jun 94. (cd) *(AND CD3)* **LIES** [ ] [ ]
– Lies / Tonight is gone / Recession blues / Latin girl / Gnatz / Funny money / Witness / Aby's lean / The victim (born in the country) / Won't let you down / Dead man's hill / Maggie Rose.

Indigo / not issued

1995. (cd) *(IGOCD 2011)* **ALL TORE DOWN – LIVE (live)** [ ] [–]

A New Day / not issued

Mar 97. (cd; as MICK ABRAHAMS & BLODWYN PIG) *(ANDCD 10)* **PIG IN THE MIDDLE** [ ] [–]

- compilations, etc. -

Apr 97. (cd) *Indigo; (IGOXCD 507)* **THE MODERN ALCHEMIST** [ ] [–]

BLONDE ON BLONDE

Formed: London, England . . . 1968 by RALPH DENYER, LES HICKS, RICHARD HOPKINS and GARETH JOHNSON. They signed to 'Pye' that year and played their blend of underground psychedelia at The Isle Of Wight festival in 1969. Many fans who attended that day witnessed what was possibly the birth of progressive rock, although some described them simply as another MOODY BLUES. The album 'CONTRASTS', containing a cover of BEATLES' 'ELEANOR RIGBY', was a little too commercial for some tastes, although it has become quite collectable. They moved to 'Ember' records in the early 70's, but two more albums did nothing to shift people's opinions. • **Note:** Two other outfits of the same name came forth in the latter half of the 70's.

Recommended: CONTRASTS (*6)

RALPH DENYER – vocals, guitar / **GARETH JOHNSON** – guitar, sitar / **RICHARD HOPKINS** – bass, keyboards / **LES HICKS** – percussion, drums

Pye / Janus

Nov 68. (7") *(7N 17637)* **ALL DAY ALL NIGHT. / COUNTRY LIFE** [ ] [–]
(re-iss.Dec69; same)
1969. (lp) *(NSPL 18288) <JLS 3003>* **CONTRASTS** [ ] [ ]
– Ride with Captain Max / Spinning wheel / No sleep blues / Goodbye / I need my friend / Mother Earth / Eleanor Rigby / Conversationally making the grade / Regency / Island on an island / Don't be too long / Jeanette Isabella. *(cd-iss.Aug94 on 'See For Miles'+=; SEECD 406)*– All day all night / Country life.

— **DAVE THOMAS** – vocals, harmonica, bass, guitar, repl. DENYER

— **RICHARD JOHN** – bass, repl. HOPKINS

Ember / not issued

Apr 70. (7") *(EMB 279)* **CASTLES IN THE SKY. / CIRCLES** [ ] [–]
May 70. (lp) *(NR 5049)* **REBIRTH** [ ] [–]
– Castles in the sky / Broken hours / Hearts without a home / Time is passing / Circles / November / Colour question / You'll never know me – reprise.

— **GRAHAM DAVIS** – vocals, banjo, guitar, bass + **KIP** – mellotron, repl. RICHARD JOHN

1971. (lp) *(NR 5058)* **REFLECTIONS ON A LIFE** [ ] [-]
– Gene machine / I don't care / Love song / Bar room blues / Sad song for an easy lady / Ain't it sad too / Bargain / Rut / Happy families / No.2 psychological decontamination unit / Chorale (forever).

1972. (7") *(EMB 316)* **SAD SONG FOR AN EASY LADY. / HAPPY FAMILIES** [ ] [-]

— all went back into the wilderness after above

BLOSSOM TOES

Formed: London, England . . . as The INGOES 1967 by BRIAN GODDING, JIM CREGAN, BRIAN BELSHAW and KEVIN WESTLAKE. Their quirky English-pop was sought out by GIORGIO GOMELSKY, who had founded his new label 'Marmalade'. Coming on like a fusion of The BEATLES with The MOVE, they were launched with the album 'WE ARE EVER SO CLEAN', which surely should have fared better in the commercial stakes. The experimental pop of the single, 'WHAT ON EARTH', was "one-that-got-away" in 1968. A year later, they treaded heavier ground with the much lawded 'PEACE LOVIN' MAN', which was taken from the 'IF ONLY FOR A MOMENT' set. CREGAN then formed a new heavy group STUD, and the rest took on the task of becoming B.B. BLUNDER (one of the silliest names in pop/rock), not surprisingly a failure. • **Covered:** I'LL BE YOUR BABY TONIGHT (Bob Dylan).

Recommended: THE COMPLETE (*7) / B.B. Blunder:- WORKER'S PLAYTIME (*6)

BRIAN GODDING – vocals, guitar, keyboards / **JIM CREGAN** – guitar, vocals / **BRIAN BELSHAW** – bass, vocals / **KEVIN WESTLAKE** – drums

Marmalade / not issued

Oct 67. (7") *(598 002)* **WHAT ON EARTH. / MRS. MURPHY'S BUDGERIGAR** [ ] [-]

Nov 67. (lp) *(607/8 001)* **WE ARE EVER SO CLEAN** [ ] [-]
– Look at me, I'm you / I'll be late for tea / The remarkable saga of the frozen dog / Telegram Tuesday / Love is / What's it for / People of the royal parks / What on Earth / Mrs. Murphy's budgerigar / I will bring you this and that / Mister watchmaker / When the alarm clock rings / The intrepid balloonist's handbook 1 / You / Track for speedy freaks.

— **POLI PALMER** (r.n. JOHN) – drums, repl. WESTLAKE who with GARY FARR released a 45 'EVERYDAY' / 'GREEN' for 'Marmalade'; *598 007)*

Mar 68. (7") *(598 009)* **I'LL BE YOUR BABY TONIGHT. / LOVE IS** [ ] [-]

Oct 68. (7") *(598 012)* **POST CARD. / EVERYONE'S LEAVING ME NOW** [ ] [-]

— **BARRY REEVES** – drums, percussion, repl. PALMER (later to FAMILY)

Apr 69. (7") *(598 014)* **PEACE LOVIN' MAN. / UP ABOVE MY HOBBY HORSE'S HEAD** [ ] [-]

Aug 69. (lp) *(608 010)* **IF ONLY FOR A MOMENT** [ ] [ ]
– Peace lovin' man / Kiss of confusion / Listen to the silence / Love bomb / Billy Boo the gunman / Indian summer / Just above my hobby horse's head / Wait a minute.

Oct 69. (7") *(598 022)* **NEW DAY. / LOVE BOMB** [ ] [-]

— Broke up early 1970. CREGAN formed STUD and later joined COCKNEY REBEL and ROD STEWART's band.

B.B. BLUNDER

GODDING, BELSHAW rejoined **WESTLAKE** with **BRIAN AUGER, JULIE DRISCOLL, MICK TAYLOR** + guests **MARK CHARIG, NICK EVANS, CHRIS KIMSEY, BARRY JENKINS** + **GRAHAM SMITH**

U.A. / U.A.

Apr 71. (7") *(UP 35203)* **STICKY LIVING. / ROCKY YAGBAG** [ ] [-]

Jun 71. (lp) *(UAG 20156)* **WORKERS' PLAYTIME** [ ] [ ]
– Sticky living / You're so young / Lost horizons / Research / Rocky yagbag / Seed / Put your money where your mouth is / Rise / Moondance / New day. *(re-iss.Feb89 by BLOSSOM TOES II; as 'NEW DAY' on 'Decal' lp/c; LIKD/TCLIKD 48)*

— were also credited on REG KING (ex-ACTION) single 'LITTLE BOY' issued on 'United Artists' *(UP 35204)*

— split after above.

– compilations, etc. –

Oct 88. (d-lp/c) *Decal; (LIKD/TCLIKD 43)* **THE COMPLETE BLOSSOM TOES** [ ] [-]

BLUE CHEER

Formed: San Francisco, California . . .early 1967 originally as a 6-piece, The SAN FRANCISCO BLUES BAND. They trimmed down to a trio (DICKIE PETERSON, LEIGH STEPHENS and PAUL WHALEY) soon after witnessing The JIMI HENDRIX EXPERIENCE at the Monterey Pop Festival, signing to 'Philips' that year and later moving to Boston. In 1968, they had a resounding US Top 20 smash with a souped-up version of EDDIE COCHRAN's 'SUMMERTIME BLUES'. Although its parent lp nearly made Top 10, they failed to consolidate their success with further releases. However, they did claim to be the loudest band in the world and their CREAM similarities gained them a cult Hell's Angels following. In fact, they were actually managed by a fully paid-up member of the gang and were part of the late 60's drug scene, having taken their name from a particular mindbending brand of LSD. They reformed in the late 80's, although this failed to win them any new converts, most heavy-metal kids opting for their higher octane descendents (i.e. METALLICA, SLAYER, ANTHRAX, etc.) • **Songwriters:** PETERSON and group, except other covers, PARCHMENT FARM (Mose Allison) / (I CAN'T GET NO) SATISFACTION (Rolling Stones) / THE HUNTER (Booker T. & The MG's).

Recommended: THE BEST OF BLUE CHEER (*7)

DICKIE PETERSON (b.1948, Grand Forks, N.Dakota) – vocals, bass (ex-GROUP 'B')/ **LEIGH STEPHENS** – guitar, vocals/ **PAUL WHALEY** – drums (ex-OXFORD CIRCLE)

Philips / Philips

Mar 68. (7") *(BF 1646) <40516>* **SUMMERTIME BLUES. / OUT OF FOCUS** [ ] [14] Jan68

Jul 68. (lp; stereo/mono) *(S+/BL 7839) <600/200 264>* **VINCEBUS ERUPTUM** [ ] [11] Mar 68
– Summertime blues / Rock me baby / Doctor please / Out of focus / Parchment farm / Second time around. *(German cd-iss.Aug92 on 'Line'; LMCD 9.51075 Z) (cd-iss.Nov94 on 'Repertoire';)*

Jul 68. (7") *(BF 1684) <40541>* **JUST A LITTLE BIT. / GYPSY BALL** [ ] [92] Jun68

— added on some **RALPH BURNS KELLOGG** – keyboards

Oct 68. (7") *(BF 1711) <40561>* **FEATHERS FROM YOUR TREE. / SUN CYCLE** [ ] [ ]

Oct 68. (lp) *(SBL 7860) <600 278>* **OUTSIDEINSIDE** [ ] [90] Sep68
– Feathers from your tree / Sun cycle / Just a little bit / Gypsy ball / Come and get it / (I can't get no) Satisfaction / The hunter / Magnolia caboose babyfinger / Babylon. *(German cd-iss.Aug92 on 'Line'; LMCD 9.51076 Z) (cd-iss.Nov94 on 'Repertoire';)*

— **RANDY HOLDEN** – guitar (ex-OTHER HALF, ex-SONS OF ADAM) repl. LEIGH due to his deafness. He went solo before joining SILVER METRE and then PILOT (U.S.). Solo single; 1969 'RED WEATHER / SAKI ZWADOO' *Philips <40628>* / albums; 1969 'RED WEATHER' *Philips (SBL 7897) <PHS-600 294>* / Sep71 'LEIGH STEPHENS & A CAST OF THOUSANDS' *Charisma <CAS 1040>*

May 69. (7") *<40602>* **WHEN IT ALL GETS OLD. / WEST COAST CHILD OF SUNSHINE** [-] [ ]

Jul 69. (lp) *(SBL 7896) <600 305>* **NEW! IMPROVED! BLUE CHEER** [ ] [84] Apr 69
– When it all gets old / West Coast child of sunshine / I want my baby back / Aces'n eights / As long as I live / It takes a lot of love, it takes a train to cry / Peace of mind / Fruit & icebergs / Honey butter love. *(cd-iss.Nov94 on 'Repertoire' +=; IMS-7025)–* All night long / Fortunes.

— **NORMAN MAYELL** (b.1942, Chicago, Illinois) – drums repl. WHALEY

— **GARY YODER** – guitar, vocals (ex-OXFORD CIRCLE) repl. HOLDEN

Nov 69. (7") *<40651>* **ALL NIGHT LONG. / FORTUNES** [-] [ ]

Feb 70. (lp) *(6336 001) <600 333>* **BLUE CHEER** [ ] [ ]
– Fool / You're gonna need someone / Hello L.A., bye bye, Birmingham / Saturday freedom / Ain't that the way (love's supposed to be) / Rock and roll queens / Better when we try / Natural man / Lovin' you's easy / The same old story. *(German cd-iss.Aug92 on 'Line'; LMCD 9.51078 Z)*

Feb 70. (7") *<40664>* **HELLO, L.A., BYE BYE, BIRMINGHAM. / NATURAL MEN** [-] [ ]

Jun 70. (7") *<40682>* **FOOL. / AIN'T THAT THE WAY (LOVE'S SUPPOSED TO BE)** [-] [ ]

— **BRUCE STEPHENS** (b.1946) – guitar + **RALPH** repl.YODER

Nov 70. (lp) *(6336 004) <600 347>* **B.C. £5 THE ORIGINAL HUMAN BEINGS** [ ] [ ]
– Good times are hard to find / Love of a woman / Make me laugh / Pilot / Babaji (twilight raga) / Preacher / Black Sun / Tears by my bed / Man on the run / Sandwich / Rest at ease. *(German cd-iss.Aug92 on 'Line'; LMCD 9.51079 Z)*

Apr 71. (7") *(6051 010) <40691>* **PILOT. / BABAJI (TWILIGHT RAGA)** [ ] [ ] Oct70

Nov 71. (lp) *<600 350>* **OH! PLEASANT HOPE** [-] [ ]
– Highway man / Believer / Money troubles / Traveling man / Oh! pleasant hope / I'm the light / Ecological blues / Lester the arrester / Heart full of soul. *(German cd-iss.Aug92 on 'Line'; LMCD 9.51080 Z)*

— Disbanded 1971, but briefly did reunions 1975 & 1979. In 1984 they returned to studio. (WHALEY and PETERSON, + TONY RAINIER – guitar)

not issued / Megaforce

1985. (lp) *<MRI 1069>* **THE BEAST IS BACK** [-] [ ]
– Nightmares / Summertime blues / Ride with me / Girl next door / Babylon / Heart of the city / Out of focus / Parchment farm.

— Toured again in the late 80's/early 90's.

— now **PETERSON** plus **ANDREW DUCK McDONALD** – guitar / **DAVID SALCE** – drums

Thunderbolt / not issued

Sep 90. (cd/lp) *(CDTB/THBL 091)* **BLITZKREIG OVER NUREMBERG (live)** [ ] [-]
– Babylon – Girl next door / Ride with me / Just a little bit / Summertime blues / Out of focus / Doctor please / The hunter / Red house.

Nibelung / not issued

Nov 90. (lp) *(23010-413)* **HIGHLIGHTS AND LOWLIVES** [-] [-] Germ'y
– (new recordings of old material?) *(cd-iss.1991 on 'Thunderbolt'; CDTB 125)*

1991. (cd) **DINING WITH SHARKS** [-] [-] Germ'y

– compilations, others, etc. –

Oct 82. (lp/c) *Philips;* **THE BEST OF BLUE CHEER** [-] [-] Europe

1986. (lp) *Rhino; <RNLP 70130>* **LOUDER THAN GOD: THE BEST OF BLUE CHEER** [-] [ ]

BLUES MAGOOS

Formed: The Bronx, New York, USA . . .mid-60's originally gigging as BLOOS MAGOOS around Greenwich Village, they were soon opening for HERMAN'S HERMITS and The WHO. They subsequently inked a deal with 'Mercury', after a one-off 45 for 'Verve Folkways'; 'SO I'M WRONG AND YOU ARE RIGHT'. Their quasi-psychedelic leanings were more apparent in their sound than their image, although later in their stage act they dazzled their audience with neon-tinted suits that lit up under the spotlight. Late in 1966, the group started to climb the charts with a brilliant 3rd single, '(WE AIN'T GOT) NOTHING YET'. Its parent album, 'PSYCHEDELIC LOLLIPOP', also sold well, having included a version of J.D. LOUDERMILK's 'TOBACCO ROAD' (their previous 45). The BLUES MAGOOS struggled to make another major impact in the charts, although their second album, 'ELECTRIC COMIC BOOK', was a garage/psych nugget. The record was characterised by some fine guitar work, notably on 'PIPE DREAM' (a minor hit), 'JUST A CHER O'BOWLIES' and a cover of (VAN MORRISON's) 'GLORIA'. Three more albums succeeded this, although none were of great interest to the public or the music press, especially after poor versions of 'I CAN HEAR THE GRASS GROW' (Move), 'HEARTBREAK HOTEL' (Elvis) and a dismal festive JINGLE BELLS effort. • **Trivia:** BALANCE's BOB KULICK was brother of BRUCE from KISS.

Recommended: PSYCHEDELIC LOLLIPOP (*6) / ELECTRIC COMIC BOOK (*8)

RALPH SCALA (b.12 Dec'47) – vocals, organ / **EMIL THIELHELM** (b.16 Jun'49; aka PEPPY CASTRO) – vocals, rhythm guitar / **MIKE ESPOSITO** – lead guitar / **RON GILBERT** (b.25 Apr'46) – bass, vocals / **GEOFF DAKING** (b. 8 Dec'47, Delaware) – drums

not issued — Verve Folkways

Jun 66. (7") *(5006)* **SO I'M WRONG AND YOU ARE RIGHT. / PEOPLE HAD NO FACES** [-] [ ]
<re-iss.1967; same>

Mercury — Mercury

Sep 66. (7") *<72590>* **TOBACCO ROAD. / SOME TIMES I THINK ABOUT YOU** [-] [ ]

Nov 66. (7") *(MF 954) <72622>* **(WE AIN'T GOT) NOTHIN' YET. / GOTTA GET AWAY** [ ] [5]

Fontana — Mercury

Dec 66. (lp; stereo/mono) *(S+/TL 5402) <61096>* **PSYCHEDELIC LOLLIPOP** (UK-title 'BLUES MAGOOS') [ ] [21] Nov66
– (We ain't got) Nothin' yet / Love seems doomed / Tobacco Road / Queen of my nights / I'll go crazy / Gotta get away / Something I think about / One by one / Worried life blues / She's coming home. *(cd-iss.1994 on 'Repertoire'; REP 4194)*

Mar 67. (7") *<72660>* **THERE'S A CHANCE WE CAN MAKE IT. / PIPE DREAM** [-] [81] [60]

Apr 67. (lp) *<61104>* **ELECTRIC COMIC BOOK** [-] [74]
– Pipe dream / There's a chance we can make it / Life is just a Cher O'Bowles / Gloria / Intermission / Albert Common is dead / Baby, I want you / Summer is the man / Let's get together / Take my love / Rush hour / That's all folks.

Jun 67. (7") *<72692>* **ONE BY ONE. / DANTE'S INFERNO** [-] [71]

Jul 67. (7") *(TF 848)* **ONE BY ONE. / LOVE SEEMS DOOMED** [ ] [-]

Sep 67. (7") *<72707>* **I WANNA BE THERE. / SUMMER IS THE MAN** [-] [ ]

Nov 67. (7") *<72729>* **LIFE IS JUST CHER O'BOWLIES. / THERE SHE GOES** [-] [ ]

Dec 67. (7") *<72762>* **JINGLE BELLS. / SANTA CLAUS IS COMING TO TOWN** [-] [ ]

Jan 68. (lp) *<SR 61167>* **BASIC BLUES MAGOOS** [-] [ ]
– Sybil Green (of the inbetween) / I can hear the grass grow / All the better to see you with / Yellow rose / I wanna be there / I can move a mountain / President's council on psychedelic fitness / Scarecrow's love affair / There she goes / Accidental meditation / You're getting old / Sublimal sonic laxitive / Chicken wire lad.

Feb 68. (7") *<72838>* **I CAN HEAR THE GRASS GROW. / YELLOW ROSE** [-] [ ]

— **THEILHELM** recruited entire new band **ERIC KAZ** – keyboards, vocals, harmonica (ex-BEARS) / **JOHN LIELLO** – vibes, percussion / **ROGER EATON** – bass, vocals / **HERB LOVELL** – drums / **RICHIE DICKON** – percussion / **DEAN EVANSON** – flute / **SOTO** – sax / **TITO** – congas

ABC-Probe — A.B.C.

1969. (7") *<11226>* **HEARTBREAK HOTEL. / I CAN FEEL IT (FEELIN' TIME)** [-] [ ]

1969. (lp) *<ABCS 697>* **NEVER GOING BACK TO GEORGIA** [-] [ ]
– Heartbreak Hotel / Heartattack / The hunter / I can feel it / Gettin' of / Never going back to Georgia / Broke down piece of man / Nobody knows you when you're down and out.

1969. (7") *<11250>* **NEVER GOIN' BACK TO GEORGIA. / FEELIN' TIME (I CAN FEEL IT)** [-] [ ]

— **JIM PAYNE** – drums / **COOKER LOPRESTI** – bass / **PEE WEE ELLIS + DADDY YA YA** – percussion repl. LOVELL, EATON, EVANSON, SOTO + TITO

1970. (7") *<11283>* **GULF COAST BOUND. / SEA BREEZE EXPRESS** [-] [ ]

Mar 71. (lp) *(SPB 1024) <ABCS 710>* **GULF COAST BOUND** [ ] [ ]
– Gulf Coast bound / Slow down sundown / Can't get enough of you / Magoo's blues / Tonight / The sky's about to cry / Sea breeze express / Never goin' back to Georgia.

Apr 71. (7") *(PRO 522)* **CAN'T GET ENOUGH OF YOU. / SEA BREEZE EXPRESS** [ ] [-]

— When they split, KAZ went solo & into sessions. He later joined AMERICAN FLYER, alongside CRAIG FULLER. THIELHELM formed the more pop orientated BARNABY BYE with the ALESSI brothers.

Marc BOLAN

Born: MARC FELD, 30 Sep'47, London, England. He began his performing career under the improbable moniker of TOBY TYLER, before ditching it and signing to 'Decca'. After 3 flop singles, he enjoyed a brief stint with JOHN'S CHILDREN ('Desdemona') before teaming up in 1968 with bongo player STEVE PEREGRINE TOOK to form TYRANNOSAURUS REX. Far from the hoary, chest-beating proto-metal that name might imply, the band's sound was a folky melange of acoustic guitar, manic bongos and pop melodies. Unfortunately the band were victims of their era and prone to lyrical flights of fancy that often broke down into hippy cliche, just check out the title of their debut mid-68 album 'MY PEOPLE WERE FAIR AND HAD SKY IN THEIR HAIR . . . BUT NOW THEY'RE CONTENT TO WEAR STARS IN THEIR BROWS'. A bit of a hippy himself at the time, Radio One DJ JOHN PEEL championed their first single 'DEBORAH', as well as material from their next 3 albums. They became a big draw on the underground circuit, helping the albums gain minor placings in the UK charts. MARC's ex-model features and effeminate charisma did no harm in making him an object of hippy chick lust, and it was about time the band had a sexier name to match. Just before the group became T.REX, TOOK was replaced by MICKEY FINN, as they gradually adopted an all-electric sound. The spanking new single 'RIDE A WHITE SWAN', nearly nailed the No.1 spot in October 1970 and made BOLAN a fully fledged pop idol. A jaunty little number with a stabbing guitar-line, it heralded the band's strident new sound, although it retained the quasi-mystical lyrical schtick. STEVE CURRY and BILL LEGEND were drafted in and the band notched up 8 consecutive Top 3 hits, including 4 UK chart-toppers. The celebratory 'HOT LOVE' and the timeless 'GET IT ON' both hit the top spot as did the 'ELECTRIC WARRIOR' album, displaying a welcome move to raunchier (but often equally silly) lyrics. BOLAN then set up his own label through EMI after 'JEEPSTER' was re-issued without his consent. He almost single handedly invented the "glam-rock" phenomenon, achieving the rare feat of being a rock idol and pop star at the same time. 'TELEGRAM SAM', 'METAL GURU' and the evergreen'20th CENTURY BOY' are still guarenteed to get you dusting down your 6" platforms a quarter of a century on. After the single 'THE GROOVER' was released in 1973 and after splitting with his wife JUNE CHILD, BOLAN brought in his new girlfriend GLORIA JONES to record 'TRUCK ON (TYKE)'. This was the first single by T.REX not to make the Top 10. His creativity was ebbing and he moved to America to record some lacklustre formulaic material in a variety of styles. Like early fan JOHN PEEL, BOLAN embraced the subsequent punk takeover and had a new deal with 'R.C.A.' before he met his untimely end on 16th September 1977. In yet another bizarre rock'n'roll death, his girlfriend crashed their car into a tree near Barnes Common, which soon became a shrine. Since his death, obsessive fans and curious observers alike have lapped up a stream of documentaries, greatest hits packages, tributes and re-issues (mostly on fan club label 'Marc On Wax'), which show no sign of abating. • **Covers:** SUMMERTIME BLUES (Eddie Cochran) / DO YOU WANNA DANCE (Bobby Freeman) / DOCK OF THE BAY (Otis Redding) / TO KNOW HIM IS TO LOVE HIM (Teddy Bears) / RIP IT UP (Little Richard) / ENDLESS SLEEP (Joey Reynolds) / A TEENAGER IN LOVE (Dion).

Recommended: THE ULTIMATE COLLECTION (*9) / MY PEOPLE WERE FAIR . . . (*6) / PROPHETS, SEERS . . . (*6) / UNICORN (*7) / A BEARD OF STARS (*6).

Marc BOLAN

— solo, using session men

Decca — not issued

Nov 65. (7") *(F 12288)* **THE WIZARD. / BEYOND THE RISING SUN** [ ] [-]

Jun 66. (7") *(F 12413)* **THE THIRD DEGREE. / SAN FRANCISCO POET** [ ] [-]

Parlophone — not issued

Dec 66. (7") *(R 5539)* **HIPPY GUMBO. / MISFIT** [ ] [-]

— BOLAN then joined JOHN'S CHILDREN before forming own band

TYRANNOSAURUS REX

MARC – vocals, guitars / **STEVE PEREGRINE TOOK** (b.28 Jul'49, London) – bongos, vocals

Regal Zonophone — A&M

Apr 68. (7") *(RZ 3008)* **DEBORA. / CHILD STAR** [34] [ ]

Jun 68. (lp; stereo/mono) *(S+/LRZ 1003)* **MY PEOPLE WERE FAIR AND HAD SKY IN THEIR HAIR . . . BUT NOW THEY'RE CONTENT TO WEAR STARS ON THEIR BROWS** [15] [ ]
– Red hot mama / Scenesof / Child star / Strange orchestras / Chateau in Virginia Waters / Dwarfish trumpet blues / Mustang Ford / Afghan woman / Knight / Graceful fat shake / Weilder of words / Frowning Atahuallpa. *(re-iss.May85 on 'Sierra' lp/c; FEDB/CFEDB 5013)*

Regal Zonophone — Blue Thumb

Aug 68. (7") *(RZ 3011)* **ONE INCH ROCK. / SALAMANDA PALAGANDA** [28] [ ]

Oct 68. (lp; stereo/mono) *(S+/LRZ 1005)* **PROPHETS, SEERS AND SAGES, THE ANGELS OF THE AGES** [ ] [ ]
– Deboraarobed / Stacey grove / Wind quartets / Conesuala / Trelawny lawn / Aznagell the mage / The friends / Salamanda Palaganda / Our wonderful brownskin man / Oh Harley (the Saltimbanques) / Eastern spell / The travelling tragition / Juniper suction / Scenes of dynasty. *(re-iss.May85 on 'Sierra' lp/c; FEDB/CFEDB 5022) (cd-iss.Oct94 on 'Disky'; CUCD 10)*

Jan 69. (7") *(RZ 3016)* **PEWTER SUITOR. / WARLORD OF THE ROYAL CROCODILES** [ ] [ ]

May 69. (lp; stereo/mono) *(S+/LRZ 1007)* **UNICORN** [12] [ ]
– Chariots of silk / 'Pon a hill / The seal of seasons / The throat of winter / Cat black (the wizard's hat) / Stones of Avalon / She was born to be my unicorn / Like a white star, tangled and far, Tulip that's what you are / Warlord of the royal crocodiles / Evenings of Damask / The sea beasts / Iscariot / Nijinsky hind / The pilgrim's tale / The misty coast of Albany / Romany soup. *(re-iss.May85 on 'Sierra' lp/c; FEDB/CFEDB 5024) (cd-iss.Oct94 on 'Disky'; CUCD 11)*

Jul 69. (7") *(RZ 3022)* **KING OF THE RUMBLING SPIRES. / DO YOU REMEMBER?** [44] [ ]

— **MICKEY FINN** (b. 3 Jan'47) – bongos, vocals repl. TOOK who joined PINK

with
my Les paul
I Know I'm SMALL
But I enjoy
living anyway
Harry Horse

FAIRIES (He died Nov80)

Jan 70. (7") *(RZ 3025)* **BY THE LIGHT OF THE MAGICAL MOON. / FIND A LITTLE WOOD** [ ] [ ]

Mar 70. (lp) *(SLRZ 1013)* **A BEARD OF STARS** [21] [ ]
– Prelude / A day laye / The woodland bop / First heart mighty dawn dart / Pavillions of sun / Organ blues / By the light of the magical Moon / Wind cheetah / A beard of stars / Great horse / Dragon's ear / Lofty skies / Dove / Elemental child. *<US-import had free 7"; BLUE THING> (re-iss.May85 on 'Sierra' lp/c; FEDB/CFEDB 5035)*

T.REX

Fly BlueThumb

Oct 70. (7"m) *(BUG 1) <121>* **RIDE A WHITE SWAN. / IS IT LOVE / SUMMERTIME BLUES** [2] [76] Jan71

— added **STEVE CURRY** (b.21 May'47, Grimsby, England) – bass / **BILL LEGEND** (b. 8 May'44, Essex, England) – drums

Fly Reprise

Dec 70. (lp/c) *(HIFLY/ZCFLY 2) <6440>* **T.REX** [13] [ ] Apr71
– The children of Rarn / Jewel / The visit / Childe / The time of love is now / Diamond meadows / Root of star / Beltane walk / Is it love / One ich rock / Summer deep / Seagull woman / Sun eye / The wizard / The children of Rarn (reprise). *(re-iss.Mar78 + Oct81; same) (re-iss.May85 on 'Sierra' lp/c; FEDB/CFEDB 5010) (cd-iss.May92 on 'Castle';)*

Feb 71. (7"m) *(BUG 6)* **HOT LOVE. / WOODLAND ROCK / KING OF THE MOUNTAIN COMETH** [1] [-]

Apr 71. (7"m) *<1006>* **HOT LOVE. / ONE INCH ROCK / SEAGULL WOMAN** [-] [72]

Jul 71. (7"m) *(BUG 10)* **GET IT ON (BANG A GONG). / THERE WAS A TIME / RAW RAMP** [1] [-]

Sep 71. (lp/c) *(HIFLY/ZCFLY 6) <6466>* **ELECTRIC WARRIOR** [1] [32] Oct71
– Mambo sun / Cosmic dancer / Jeepster / Monolith / Lean woman blues / Get it on (bang a gong) / Planet queen / Girl / The motivator / Life's a gas / Rip off. *(re-iss.Mar78 + Oct81; same) (cd-iss.May87 on 'Sierra; CDTR 2) (re-iss.Apr90 on 'Castle' c/cd+=; CLA MC/CD 180)*– Hot love / Deborah.

Nov 71. (7") *(BUG 16)* **JEEPSTER. / LIFE'S A GAS** [2] [-]

Nov 71. (7") *<1056>* **JEEPSTER. / RIP OFF** [-] [-]

Dec 71. (7") *<1032>* **BANG A GONG (GET IT ON). /** [-] [10]

E.M.I. Reprise

Jan 72. (7"m) *(T REX 1) <1078>* **TELEGRAM SAM. / CADILLAC / BABY STRANGE** [1] [67] Apr72
(re-iss.Mar82; same); hit No.69)

May 72. (lp/c) *(HIFLY/ZCFLY 8)* **BOLAN BOOGIE** (compilation) [1] [ ]
– Get it on (bang a gong) / The king of the mountain cometh / She was born to be my unicorn / Dove / Woodland bop / Ride a white swan / Raw ramp / Jeepster / First heart mighty dawn dart / By the light of the magical Moon / Summertime blues / Hot love. *(re-iss.Mar78 & Oct81; same) (re-iss.Apr89 on 'Castle' lp/c/cd; CLA LP/MC/CD 145)*

May 72. (7"m) *(MARC 1) <1095>* **METAL GURU. / LADY / THUNDERWING** [1] [ ]

Jul 72. (lp/c) *(BLN/ 5001) <2095>* **THE SLIDER** [4] [17] Aug72
– Metal guru / Mystic lady / Rock on / The slider / Baby boomerang / Spaceball ricochet / Buick MacKane / Telegram Sam / Rabbit fighter / Baby strange / Ballrooms of Mars / Chariot choogle / Main man. *(re-iss.Nov89 on 'Marc On Wax' lp/c/cd; MARC L/K/D 503) (cd re-iss.Jul94 on 'Edsel'; EDCD 390)*

Jul 72. (7") *<1122>* **THE SLIDER. / ROCK ON** [-] [ ]

Sep 72. (7"m) *(MARC 2)* **CHILDREN OF THE REVOLUTION. / JITTERBUG LOVE / SUNKEN RAGS** [2] [ ]

Dec 72. (7") *(MARC 3)* **SOLID GOLD EASY ACTION. / BORN TO BOOGIE** [2] [ ]

Mar 73. (7") *(MARC 4)* **20th CENTURY BOY. / FREE ANGEL** [3] [ ]

Mar 73. (lp/c) *(BLN/ 5002) <2132>* **TANX** [4] [ ]
– Tenement lady / Rapids / Mister mister / Broken hearted blues / Shock rock / Country honey / Electric Slim and the factory man / Mad Donna / Born to boogie / Life is strange / The street and the babe shadow / Highway knees / Left hand Luke and the beggar boys. *(re-iss.Oct87 on 'Marc On Wax' lp/pic-lp/c/cd; RAP/+D/C/CD 504) (re-iss.Nov89 lp/c/cd; MARC L/K/D 504) (cd re-iss.Jul94 on 'Edsel'; EDCD 391)*

Jun 73. (7") *(MARC 5)* **THE GROOVER. / MIDNIGHT** [4] [-]

Jun 73. (7") **THE GROOVER. / BORN TO BOOGIE** [-] [ ]

— added **JACK GREEN** – guitar (plus 3 female backing singers incl. **GLORIA JONES**)

Nov 73. (7") *(MARC 6)* **TRUCK ON (TYKE). / SITTING HERE** [12] [-]

— (T.REX = FINN, CURRIE, GREEN, JONES – keyboards, vocals) / **DAVY LUTTON** – drums (ex-HEAVY JELLY), repl. LEGEND (2 more female singers)

Feb 74. (7"; as MARC BOLAN & T.REX) *(MARC 7)* **TEENAGE DREAM. / SATISFACTION PONY** [13] [ ]

Mar 74. (lp/c; as MARC BOLAN & T.REX) *(BNLA 7751)* **ZINC ALLOY AND THE EASY RIDERS OF TOMORROW** [12] [ ]
– Venus loon / Sound pit / Explosive mouth / Galaxy / Orange / Nameless wildness / Teenage dream / Liquid gang / Carsmile Smith & the old one / You've got to jive to stay alive – Spanish midnight / Interstellar soul / Painless persuasion and the meathawk / Immaculate / The avengers (superbad) / The leopards (featuring Gardinia and The Mighty Slug). *(re-iss.Oct87 on 'Marc On Wax' lp/pic-lp/c/cd; RAP/+D/C/CD 505) (re-iss.Nov89 lp/c/cd; MARC L/K/D 505) (cd re-iss.Jul94 on 'Edsel'; EDCD 392)*

Jul 74. (7") *(MARC 8)* **LIGHT OF LOVE. / EXPLOSIVE MOUTH** [22] [-]

— added **DINO DINES** – keyboards

Nov 74. (7") *(MARC 9)* **ZIP GUN BOOGIE. / SPACE BOSS** [41] [-]

Feb 75. (lp/c) *(BNLA/ 7752)* **BOLAN'S ZIP GUN** [ ] [ ]
– Light of love / Solid baby / Precious star / Zip gun boogie / Token of my love / Think zine / 'Till dawn / Girl in the thunderbolt suit / I really love you baby / Golden belt. *(re-iss.Jul87 on 'Marc On Wax' lp/pic-lp/c/cd; RAP/+D/C/CD 506) (re-iss.Nov89 lp/c/cd; MARC L/K/D 506) (cd re-iss.Jul94 on 'Edsel'; EDCD 393)*

— members FINN and GREEN departed. The latter to PRETTY THINGS. Now 5-piece comprising **BOLAN, JONES, CURRIE, LUTTON + DINES**

Jul 75. (7") *(MARC 10)* **NEW YORK CITY. / CHROME SITAR** [15] [-]

— next with **BILLY PRESTON** – keyboards

Oct 75. (7"m; as T.REX DISCO PARTY) *(MARC 11)* **DREAMY LADY. / DO YOU WANNA DANCE / DOCK OF THE BAY** [30] [-]

Feb 76. (lp/c) *(BLNA/ 5004)* **FUTURISTIC DRAGON** [50] [ ]
– Futuristic dragon / Jupiter lion / All alone / Chrome sitar / New York City / My little baby / Calling all destroyers / Theme for a dragon / Sensation boulevard / Ride my wheels / Dreamy lady / Dawn storm / Casual agent. *(re-iss.Oct87 on 'Marc On Wax' lp/pic-lp/c/cd; RAP/+D/C/CD 507) (re-iss.Nov89 lp/c/cd; MARC L/K/D 507) (cd re-iss.Jul94 on 'Edsel'; EDCD 394)*

Feb 76. (7") *(MARC 13)* **LONDON BOYS. / SOLID BABY** [40] [-]

Jun 76. (7") *(MARC 14)* **I LOVE TO BOOGIE. / BABY BOOMERANG** [13] [-]

Sep 76. (7") *(MARC 15)* **LASER LOVE. / LIFE'S AN ELEVATOR** [41] [-]

Jan 77. (7"; by MARC BOLAN & GLORIA JONES) *(EMI 2572)* **TO KNOW HIM IS TO LOVE HIM. / CITY PORT** [ ] [-]

— now comprised BOLAN and DINES who brought in **MILLER ANDERSON** – guitar (ex-SAVOY BROWN) repl. GLORIA JONES who went solo / **HERBIE FLOWERS** – bass repl. CURRIE who went into sessions **TONY BRENNAN** – drums repl. LUTTON who joined WRECKLESS ERIC

Mar 77. (7") *(MARC 16)* **THE SOUL OF MY SUIT. / ALL ALONE** [42] [-]

Mar 77. (lp/c) *(BLNA 5005)* **DANDY IN THE UNDERWORLD** [26] [ ]
– Dandy in the underworld / Crimson moon / Universe / I'm a fool for you / I love to boogie / Visions of Domino / Jason B. Sad / Groove a little / Hang-ups / The soul of my suit / Pain and love / Teen riot structure. *(re-iss.Oct87 on 'Marc On Wax'; lp/pic-lp/c/cd; RAP/+D/C/CD 508) (re-iss.Nov89 lp/c/cd; MARC L/K/D 508) (cd re-iss.Jul94 on 'Edsel'; EDCD 395)*

May 77. (7") *(MARC 17)* **DANDY IN THE UNDERWORLD. / GROOVE A LITTLE** [ ] [-]

Aug 77. (7") *(MARC 18)* **CELEBRATE SUMMER. / RIDE MY WHEELS** [ ] [-]

— On 16th Sep'77 MARC BOLAN died when his car driven by GLORIA hit a tree. ANDERSON joined SOUTHSIDE JOHNNY and FLOWERS formed SKY.

Apr 78. (7") *(MARC 19)* **CRIMSON MOON. / JASON B. SAD** [ ] [-]

– compilations, others, etc. –

On 'Fly' UK / 'Reprise' US unless mentioned otherwise.

Aug 71. (lp/c) *(TON/CTON 2)* **THE BEST OF T.REX** [21] [ ]

Mar 72. (d-lp/d-c) *(TOOFA/ZCTOF 3-4) / A&M; <3514>* **PROPHETS, SEERS AND SAGES, THE ANGELS OF THE AGES / MY PEOPLE WERE FAIR . . .** <US-title 'TYRANNOSAURUS REX – A BEGINNING'> [1] [ ]
(re-iss.Oct81; same)

Mar 72. (7"ep) *Magni Fly; (ECHO 102)* **DEBORA / ONE INCH ROCK. / WOODLAND BOP / SEAL OF SEASONS** [7] [ ]

1973. (7") *<1150>* **BANG A GONG. / TELEGRAM SAM** [-] [ ]

1973. (7") *<1151>* **METAL GURU. / JEEPSTER** [-] [ ]

1973. (7") **HOT LOVE. / RIP OFF** [-] [ ]

Oct 72. (lp/c) *Music For Pleasure;* **RIDE A WHITE SWAN** [ ] [-]

Dec 72. (d-lp/d-c) *Cube; (TOOFA/ZCTOF 9-10)* **A BEARD OF STARS / UNICORN** [44] [ ]
(re-iss.Mar78 + Oct81; same) (re-iss.Sep88 on 'That's Original' d-lp/c/cd;) (re-iss.cd Oct94 on 'Disky';)

Sep 73. (7"; as BIG CARROT) *E.M.I.; (EMI 2047)* **BLACKJACK. / SQUINT EYE MANGLE** [ ] [-]

Nov 73. (lp/c) *E.M.I.; (BLN/ 5003)* **GREAT HITS** [32] [ ]

Jun 74. (lp; by MARC BOLAN) *Track; (2410 201)* **THE BEGINNING OF DOVES** [ ] [-]
(re-iss.Aug89 on 'Media Motion' lp/c/cd; MEDIA/+C/CD 2) (cd-iss.Oct91 on 'Receiver';)

Jun 74. (7"m; by MARC BOLAN) *Track; (2094 013)* **JASPER C. DEBUSSY. / HIPPY GUMBO / THE PERFUMED GARDEN OF GULLIVER SMITH** [ ] [-]

Nov 74. (lp) *Sounds Superb; (90059)* **GET IT ON** [ ] [-]
(re-iss.Jun86 on 'Fame'; FA/TC-FA 3154)

Apr 76. (7") *Cube; (BUG 66)* **HOT LOVE. / GET IT ON** [ ] [-]

Sep 77. (7"ep) *Cube; (ANT 1)* **BOLAN'S BEST PLUS ONE** [ ] [-]
– Ride a white swan / Motivator / Jeepster / Demon queen.

Mar 78. (7"m) *Cube; (ANT 2)* **HOT LOVE. / RAW RAMP / LEAN WOMAN BLUES** [ ] [-]

Apr 78. (d-lp) *Cube; (HIFLD 1)* **MARC, THE WORDS AND MUSIC OF MARC BOLAN** [ ] [-]
(with free interview disc; BINT 1)

Apr 78. (d-lp) *Pickwick; (PDA 044)* **THE T.REX COLLECTION / GREATEST HITS** [ ] [-]
(d-c-iss.Feb80; PDC 044)

Jun 78. (lp/c) *Hallmark; (SHM/+C 953)* **GREATEST HITS VOL.1** [ ] [-]
(re-iss.Jan87 as 'THE VERY BEST OF VOLUME 1' lp/c; SMH/HSC 3204)

Jun 79. (lp/c) *E.M.I.; (NUT 5)* **SOLID GOLD T.REX** [51] [ ]
(re-iss.May82 on 'Fame' lp/c; FA/TC-FA 3005)

Jul 79. (12"ep) *Cube; (ANTS 001)* **LIFE'S A GAS / FIND A LITTLE WOOD. / ONCE UPON THE SEAS OF ABYSSINIA / BLESSED WILD APPLE GIRL** [ ] [-]
(re-iss.Jul82 on 'Rarn'; MBFS RAP 1)

Sep 80. (lp/c) *E.M.I.; (NUT/TC-NUT 28)* **THE UNOBTAINABLE T.REX** [ ] [-]

Mar 81. (12"pic-ep/12"clear-ep) *Rarn; (MBFS 001 C/P)* **THE RETURN OF THE ELECTRIC WARRIOR** [50] [-]
– Sing me a song / Endless sleep (extended) / The lilac hand of Menthol Dan. *(re-iss.7"pic-d.Jul82;)*

Aug 81. (pic-lp; 2 diff) *Marc; (ABOLAN 1P)* **T.REX IN CONCERT (live)** [35] [-]

Sep 81. (7"/7"pic-d; by MARC BOLAN) *Cherry Red; (CHERRY/+P 29)* **YOU SCARE ME TO DEATH. / THE PERFUMED GARDEN OF GULLIVER SMITH** [51] [-]

Oct 81. (pic-lp/lp; by MARC BOLAN) *Cherry Red; (P+/ERED 20)* **YOU SCARE ME TO DEATH** [88] [-]
(re-iss.Nov94 on 'Emporio' cd/c; EMPR CD/MC 545)

Oct 81. (7"; by MARC BOLAN) *Cherry Red; (CHERRY 32)* **CAT BLACK. / JASPER C. DEBUSSY** [ ] [-]

Nov 81. (d-lp/c) *Countdown; (PLAT/ZCPLAT 1002)* **THE PLATINUM COLLECTION OF T.REX** [ ] [-]

Jan 82. (lp/pic-lp; as MARC BOLAN & T.REX) *Cube; (ICS/+X 1004)* **ACROSS THE AIRWAVES** [ ] [-]

Jan 82. (7"blue) *Marc; (SBOLAN 13)* **MELLOW LOVE. / FOXY BOX / LUNACY'S BACK** [ ] [-]
(12"+=) *(SBOLAN 13)* – Rock me.

May 82. (7"m; by MARC BOLAN) *Cherry Red; (CHERRY 39)* **THE WIZARD. / BEYOND THE RISING SUN / RINGS OF FORTUNE** ☐ -
Jun 82. (10"ep) *Marc On Wax; (ABOLAN 2)* **CHILDREN OF RARN SUITE** ☐ -
(free one-side 7"w-above)– MISTER MOTION
Jul 82. (12"blue) *Rarn; (MBFS RAP 2)* **DEEP SUMMER. / OH BABY / ONE INCH ROCK** ☐ -
Jul 82. (7") *Old Gold; (OG 9230)* **GET IT ON. / JEEPSTER** ☐ -
Jul 82. (7"ep) *E.M.I.; (MARC 20)* **CHILDREN OF THE REVOLUTION / I LOVE TO BOOGIE. / LONDON BOYS / SOLID GOLD EASY ACTION** ☐ -
Aug 82. (7") *Dakota; (BAK 3)* **HOT LOVE. / JEEPSTER** ☐ -
Aug 82. (7") *Dakota; (BAK 4)* **GET IT ON. / DEBORA** ☐ -
Aug 82. (7") *Dakota; (BAK 5)* **RIDE A WHITE SWAN. / ONE INCH ROCK** ☐ -
Aug 82. (7") *Old Gold; (OG 9229)* **HOT LOVE. / RIDE A WHITE SWAN** ☐ -
Aug 82. (7") *Old Gold; (OG 9230)* **GET IT ON. / JEEPSTER** ☐ -
Aug 82. (7") *Old Gold; (OG 9234)* **DEBORA. / ONE INCH ROCK** ☐ -
Sep 82. (7"ep) *E.M.I.; (MARC 22)* **TRUCK ON (TYKE) / ZIP GUN BOOGIE. / TEENAGE DREAM / LIGHT OF LOVE** ☐ -
Sep 82. (7"ep) *E.M.I.; (MARC 23)* **TELEGRAM SAM / THE SOUL OF MY SUIT. / METAL GURU / LASER LOVE** ☐ -
Oct 82. (lp/c) *Countdown; (COUNT/ZCCNT 11)* **T.REX** ☐ -
Dec 82. (7"ep) *Marc; (SBOLAN 1)* **CHRISTMAS BOP. / SHY BOY / RIDE A WHITE SWAN** ☐ -
(12"ep+=/12"pic-d-ep+=) *(SBOLAN 12/+EP)* – King of the rumbling spires / Savage Beethoven.
Jun 83. (7"pic-d) *Marc; (SBOLAN 14PD)* **THINK ZINC. / MAGICAL MOON / TILL DAWN** ☐ -
(12") – ('A'side) / Rip it up / A teenager in love.
Aug 83. (7") *Cube; (BUG 90)* **JEEPSTER. / GET IT ON** ☐ -
Sep 83. (lp/c; by MARC BOLAN) *Marc On Wax; (MARC L/K 501)* **DANCE IN THE MIDNIGHT** 83 -
(re-iss.Apr85; same)
Apr 84. (d-lp/d-c; by MARC BOLAN) *Cambra; (CR/+T 115)* **BEYOND THE RISING SUN** ☐ -
Jun 84. (7"promo' by MARC BOLAN) *Cube; (BUG 99)* **SAILOR OF THE HIGHWAY. / DO YOU REMEMBER** ☐ -
(12"+=) **RARE MAGIC EP** (HBUG 99) – Demon queen / Pewtor suitor / The wizard.
Aug 84. (red-lp/c) *Marc On Wax; (MARC L/K 500)* **BILLY SUPER DUPER** ☐ -
(re-iss.Apr85 lp/c; same)
Aug 84. (lp) *Marc On Wax; (ABOLAN 5)* **T.REXTASY** ☐ -
(free 12"w-above) *(ABOLAN 5F)* JAM (live). / ELEMENTAL CHILD (live)
Nov 84. (lp/c) *Sierra; (FEDD/CFEDD 1000)* **OFF THE RECORD WITH T.REX** ☐ -
Jan 85. (7") *Old Gold; (OG 9505)* **METAL GURU. / CHILDREN OF THE REVOLUTION** ☐ -
Jan 85. (7") *Old Gold; (OG 9506)* **TELEGRAM SAM. / I LOVE TO BOOGIE** ☐ -
Jan 85. (7") *Old Gold; (OG 9507)* **SOLID GOLD EASY ACTION. / THE GROOVER** ☐ -
Mar 85. (d-lp/d-c) *Cambra; (CR/+T 5161)* **THE MAIN MAN** ☐ -
(7"pic-d. w/above) – TEENAGE DREAM. / SOLID GOLD SEGUE
Apr 85. (d-lp/d-c; as MARC BOLAN & T.REX) *K-Tel; (NE/CE 1297)* **THE BEST OF THE 20th CENTURY BOY** 5 -
(cd-iss.Oct87; NCD 3325)
May 85. (12"ep) *Sierra; (FED 12)* **GET IT ON / THERE WAS A TIME. / RAW RAMP / ELECTRIC BOOGIE** ☐ -
May 85. (7"ep) *Marc On Wax; (TANX 1)* **MEGAREX 1 (medley). / CHARIOT CHOOGLE / LIFE'S AN ELEVATOR** 72 -
(12"+=) *(12TANX 1)* – Solid baby.
May 85. (7"pic-ep) *Marc On Wax; (PTANX 1)* **MEGAREX 2 (medley). / TAME MY TIGER / CHROME SITAR / SOLID BABY**
(MEGAREX 3: was a 12"sha-pic-ep; STANX 1)
Jul 85. (7"m) *Marc On Wax; (TANX 2)* **SUNKEN RAGS. / JITTERBUG LOVE / DOWN HOME LADY** ☐ -
(12"+=) *(12TANX 2)* – Funky London / Childhood.
Jul 85. (lp/c; as MARC BOLAN & T.REX) *Dojo; (DOJO LP/TC 12)* **A CROWN OF JEWELS** ☐ -
Nov 85. (lp/c/cd) *Marc On Wax; (MARC L/K/D 509)* **TILL DAWN** ☐ -
(cd-iss.Oct91 on 'Castle'; CLACD 247)
Jun 86. (12"ep) *Archive 4; (TOF 102)* **CLASSIC CUTS** ☐ -
– Jeepster / Ride a white swan / Get it on / Hot love.
Feb 87. (7") *Marc On Wax;* **CHILDREN OF THE REVOLUTION (remix). / THE SLIDER (remix) / TEAR FOR THE HIGH STAR** (by 'Dave Ashby') ☐ -
(12"+=) – Free angel (TV remix).
Mar 87. (d-lp/d-c/d-cd) *Marc On Wax; (MARC L/K/CD 510)* **THE SINGLES COLLECTION** ☐ -
May 87. (7"; as MARC BOLAN & T.REX) *Marc On Wax; (MARC 10)* **GET IT ON. / JEEPSTER** 54 -
(12"+=/c-s+=/cd-s+=) *(MARC B/C/CD 10)* – Cadillac.
May 87. (cd; as T.REX & MARC BOLAN) *Sierra; (CDTR 1)* **GREATEST HITS** ☐ -
Aug 87. (12"ep) *Strange Fruit; (SFPS 031)* **THE PEEL SESSIONS** (27.10.70) ☐ -
– Jewel / Ride a white swan / Elemental child / Sun eye. *(cd-ep-iss.Dec94; SFPSCD 031)*
1987. (lp/c/cd; as MARC BOLAN & T.REX) *Connoisseur; (VSOP LP/MC/CD 100)* **STAND BY ME** ☐ -
Sep 87. (7"m; as MARC BOLAN & T.REX) *Marc On Wax; (MARC 11)* **I LOVE TO BOOGIE. / RIDE A WHITE SWAN / HOT LOVE** ☐ -
(12"+=/cd-s+=) *(12MARC/MARCD 11)* – Hot George.
Oct 87. (lp/c; as MARC BOLAN & T.REX) *Hallmark; (SHM/HSC 3217)* **TEENAGE DREAM** ☐ -
(cd-iss.Oct87 on 'Pickwick'; PWK 040)
Jan 88. (3"cd-ep) *Special Edition; (CD3-13)* **HOT LOVE / GET IT ON / TELEGRAM SAM / METAL GURU** ☐ -
1988. (lp) *Fun; (FUN 9029)* **18 GREATEST HITS** ☐ -
Jul 88. (lp/c/cd) *Knight; (KN LP/MC/CD 10003)* **NIGHTRIDING** ☐ -
Mar 89. (cd-s) *Old Gold; (OG 6130)* **TELEGRAM SAM / METAL GURU / CHILDREN OF THE REVOLUTION** ☐ -
May 89. (cd-s) *Old Gold; (OG 6134)* **SOLID GOLD EASY ACTION / 20th CENTURY BOY / THE GROOVER** ☐ -
Aug 89. (lp/c/cd) *Marc On Wax; (MARC L/K/D 513)* **THE MARC SHOWS** (Granada TV shows) ☐ -
1990. (4xlp-box) *Rhino;* **WHERE THERE'S CHAMPAGNE** - ☐
Apr 91. S.P.S.; (lp)(cd) **RARITIES VOLUME ONE** ☐ -
Jun 91. (cd/c) *Music Club; (MC CD/TC 030)* **THE VERY BEST OF MARC BOLAN & T.REX** ☐ -
(gold-cd-iss.Mar96; MCCDSE 030)
Aug 91. (7"/c-s; as MARC BOLAN & T.REX) *Marc On Wax; (MARC/+ 501)* **20th CENTURY BOY. / MIDNIGHT / THE GROOVER** 13 -
(12"+=)(cd-s+=) – Telegram Sam.
Sep 91. (cd/c/lp; MARC BOLAN & T.REX) *Telstar; (TCD// 2539)* **THE ULTIMATE COLLECTION** 4 -
– 20th century boy / Metal guru / I love to boogie / Deborah / New York City / Telegram Sam / Hot love / Dreamy lady / One inch rock / The soul of my suit / London boys / Ride a white swan / Get it on / Light of love / Children of the revolution / Jeepster / Laser love / Zip gun boogie / The groover / King of the rumbling spires / Plateau skull / Truck on (Tyke) / Solid gold easy action / Teenage dream. *(cd has 4 extra above)*
Oct 91. Marc On Wax; (7"/c-s; as MARC BOLAN & T.REX) **METAL GURU. / THUNDERWIND / BOLAN'S ZIP GUN** ☐ -
(12"+=/cd-s+=) – Solid baby (remix).
Nov 91. (cd; by MARC BOLAN) *Cherry Red; (CBRED 70)* **LOVE AND DEATH** ☐ -
Nov 91. (7") *Marc On Wax;* **SLEEPY MAURICE. / (1968 interview)** ☐ -
Dec 91. (cd/c/d-lp) *Marc On Wax; (MARC CD/MC/LP 514)* **BORN TO BOOGIE (live & poetry)** ☐ -
Dec 91. (cd) *Dojo;* **THE EARLY YEARS** ☐ -
(re-iss.+lp+c)
Dec 91. (3xcd-box; as MARC BOLAN & T.REX) *Essential; (ESBCD 965)* **ANTHOLOGY** ☐ -
– (THE EARLY YEARS / THE SINGLES A'S & B'S / GLAM ROCK TO FAST PUNK 1972-1977)
Feb 92. (cd) *Castle; (CLABX 909)* **3 ORIGINALS** ☐ -
– (T.REX / BOLAN BOOGIE / ELECTRIC WARRIOR)
Jun 92. (cd/c) *Action Replay; (CDAR/ARLC 1031)* **THE BEST OF THE REST OF MARC BOLAN** ☐ -
Apr 93. (cd; TYRANNOSAURUS REX) *Windsong; (WINCD 032)* **BBC RADIO 1 LIVE IN CONCERT (live)** ☐ -
Apr 93. (cd-ep) *Deram;* **THE WIZARD / BEYOND THE RISIN' SUN / THE THIRD DEGREE / SAN FRANCISCO POET** ☐ -
Jun 93. (cd) *Deram;* **THE WIZARD** ☐ -
Jun 93. (cd-ep) *Zinc Alloy;* **BLOWIN' IN THE WIND / THE ROAD I'M ON (GLORIA) / BLOWIN' IN THE WIND (session version)** ☐ -
Sep 93. (cd) *Sequel; (NEXCD 250)* **THE DEFINITIVE TYRANNOSAURUS REX** ☐ -
Nov 93. (cd) *Soundwind; (ACD 105106)* **16 GREATEST HITS** ☐ -
Apr 94. (cd) *Remember;* **20th CENTURY BOY** ☐ -
Oct 94. (cd) *Edsel; (EDCD 401)* **GREAT HITS (1972-1977: THE A SIDES)** ☐ -
Oct 94. (cd) *Edsel; (EDCD 402)* **GREAT HITS (1972-1977: THE B SIDES)** ☐ -
Oct 94. (cd) *Edsel; (EDCD 403)* **RABBIT FIGHTER (THE ALTERNATIVE SLIDER)** ☐ -
Oct 94. (cd) *Edsel; (EDCD 404)* **MESSING WITH THE MYSTIC** ☐ -
May 95. (cd) *Edsel; (EDCD 410)* **LEFT HAND LUKE (THE ALTERNATIVE TANX)** ☐ -
May 95. (cd) *Edsel; (EDCD 413)* **LIGHT OF LOVE** ☐ -
Jun 95. (cd; MARC BOLAN & T.REX) *Edsel; (EDCD 411)* **UNCHAINED: VOLUME 1 (UNRELEASED RECORDINGS 1972)** ☐ -
Jun 95. (cd; MARC BOLAN & T.REX) *Edsel; (EDCD 412)* **UNCHAINED: VOLUME 2 (UNRELEASED RECORDINGS 1972)** ☐ -
Aug 95. (cd-s) *Old Gold;* **TELEGRAM SAM / 20th CENTURY BOY** ☐ -
Sep 95. (cd/c; as MARC BOLAN & T.REX) *Polygram TV; (525 961-2/-4)* **THE ESSENTIAL COLLECTION** 24 -
Sep 95. (cd/c) *Emporio; (EMPR CD/MC 589)* **PREHISTORIC** ☐ -
Oct 95. (cd; MARC BOLAN & T.REX) *Edsel;* **UNCHAINED: VOLUME 3 (UNRELEASED RECORDINGS 1973 PART 1)** ☐ -
Oct 95. (cd; MARC BOLAN & T.REX) *Edsel;* **UNCHAINED: VOLUME 4 (UNRELEASED RECORDINGS 1973 PART 2)** ☐ -
Oct 95. (cd; as MARC BOLAN & T.REX) *Edsel; (EDCD 440)* **CHANGE (THE ALTERNATIVE ZINC ALLOY)** ☐ -
Jun 96. (cd) *Edsel; (EDCD 443)* **PRECIOUS STAR (THE ALTERNATIVE BOLAN'S ZIP GUN)** ☐ -
Jun 96. (cd; MARC BOLAN & T.REX) *Edsel; (EDCD 444)* **UNCHAINED: VOLUME 5 (UNRELEASED RECORDINGS 1974)** ☐ -
Jun 96. (cd; MARC BOLAN & T.REX) *Edsel; (EDCD 445)* **UNCHAINED: VOLUME 6 (UNRELEASED RECORDINGS 1975)** ☐ -
Jun 96. (cd) *Band Of Joy; (BOJCD 016)* **LIVE AT THE BBC** ☐ -
Sep 96. (cd/c) *Telstar; (TCD/STAC 2858)* **ACOUSTIC WARRIOR** ☐ -
Jan 97. (cd; as MARC BOLAN & T.REX) *Burning Airlines; (PILOT 4)* **ELECTRIC WARRIOR SESSIONS** ☐ -
(lp-iss.Mar97 on 'Get Back'; GET 502)
May 97. (cd-s) *BMG; (MASSCD 1000)* **GET IT ON** ☐ -
May 97. (cd/c) *BMG; (MASQ CD/MC 1010)* **GET IT ON** ☐ -

Jun 97. (cd) *Edsel; (EDCD 522)* **DAZZLING RAIMENT (THE ALTERNATIVE FUTURISTIC DRAGON)** [ ] [-]
Jun 97. (cd) *Edsel; (EDCD 524)* **UNCHAINED: UNRELEASED RECORDINGS VOL.7** [ ] [-]
Jun 97. (d-cd) *Edsel; (EDCD 530)* **LIVE** [ ] [-]

BONZO DOG BAND

Formed: London, England ... 1965 by art students RODNEY SLATER and ROGER 'RUSKIN' SPEAR, who soon enlisted fellow eccentrics VIV STANSHALL, NEIL INNES and 'LEGS' LARRY SMITH. Their flexible line-up also numbered VERNON DUDLEY BOHAY-NOWELL, SAM SPOONS and BOB KERR. They took elements of The NEW VAUDEVILLE BAND and The TEMPERANCE SEVEN to a more modern conclusion, much in evidence on two early 'Parlophone' 45's in 1966. A year later, they released their debut album, 'GORILLA', on 'Liberty' and performed on The BEATLES' film 'MAGICAL MYSTERY TOUR'. The album skillfully parodied 20's Englishness on comic tracks like 'JOLLITY FARM', 'THE INTRO AND THE OUTRO' and 'DEATH CAB FOR CUTIE', STANSHALL and INNES being the main protagonists behind the surreal humour. Early in 1968 they secured a weekly slot on the satirical London Weekend TV show, 'Do Not Adjust Your Set'. By the end of the year, they were at No.5 with the surprise novelty hit, 'I'M THE URBAN SPACEMAN', which was produced by PAUL McCARTNEY under the pseudonym of APOLLO C. VERMOUTH. They released a further clutch of albums over the course of the next few years, some incorporating a more rock-based format, more convincingly executed by US counterparts, The MOTHERS OF INVENTION. After their final split in 1972, INNES and STANSHALL went onto greater things. INNES wrote for his GRIMMS project with a plethora of artists such as The SCAFFOLD. After a TV comedy, 'RUTLAND WEEKEND TELEVISION' (1976), with ERIC IDLE (of MONTY PYTHON), he later worked on children's television such as The Raggy Dolls. Meanwhile, STANSHALL released his first solo album, 'MEN OPENING UMBRELLAS AHEAD' (1974), and set to task on his finest hour, 'SIR HENRY AT RAWLINSON END' (1978), an excellent production of comic genius that was played to death each night on the John Peel show before being made into a film. Sadly, VIVIAN STANSHALL died in a fire at his home on the 3rd of March 1995. Two days later early member VERNON also died. • **Covered:** ALLEY OOP (Hollywood Argyles) / Monster Mash (Bobby Pickett) / etc. STANSHALL solo:- SUSPICION (Elvis Presley) / YOUNG ONES (Cliff Richard).

Recommended: THE BEAST OF THE BONZO DOG BAND (*6) / Vivian Stanshall: SIR HENRY AT RAWLINSON'S END (*9)

BONZO DOG DOO-DAH BAND

VIVIAN STANSHALL (b.21 Mar'43, Shillingford, England) – vocals, trumpet / **NEIL INNES** (b. 9 Dec'44, Essex, England) – piano, vocals, guitar / **'LEGS' LARRY SMITH** (b.18 Jan'44, Oxford, England) – drums / **RODNEY SLATER** (b. 8 Nov'44, Lincolnshire, England) – horns / **ROGER RUSKIN SPEAR** (b.29 Jun'43, London) – tenor sax, kazoo, objects / **VERNON DUDLEY BOHAY-NOWELL** (b.29 Jul'32, Plymouth, England) – bass, banjo, guitar / **SAM SPOONS** (b. MARTIN STAFFORD ASH, 8 Feb'42, Bridgewater, England) – percussion

Stateside not issued

Apr 66. (7") *(R 5430)* **MY BROTHER MAKES THE NOISES FOR THE TALKIES. / I'M GONNA BRING A WATERMELON TO MY GAL TONIGHT** [ ] [-]
Sep 66. (7") *(R 5499)* **ALLEY OOP. / BUTTON UP YOUR OVERCOAT** [ ] [-]

Liberty Imperial

Oct 67. (lp; mono/stereo) *(LBL/LBS 83056) <12370>* **GORILLA** [ ] [ ]
– Cool Britannia / Equestrian statue / Jollity farm / I left my heart in San Francisco / Look out, there's a monster coming / Jazz, delicious hot, disgusting cold / Death cab for Cutie / Narcissus / The intro and the outro / Mickey's son and daughter / Big shot / Music for head ballet / Piggy bank love / I'm bored / The sound of music. *(re-iss.Nov70 on 'Sunset'; SLS 50160) (re-iss.Aug80; LBR 1019) (cd-iss.Jul95 on 'Beat Goes On';)*
Nov 67. (7") *(LBF 15040)* **EQUESTRIAN STATUE. / THE INTRO AND THE OUTRO** [ ] [ ]

— **DENNIS COWAN** (b. 6 May'47, London) – bass repl. BOHAY-NOWELL. Also SPOONS departed. For a short while BOB KERR "the nearly unknown" played sax.

Oct 68. (7") *(LBF 15144) <66345>* **I'M THE URBAN SPACEMAN. / THE CANYONS OF YOUR MIND** [5] [ ]
<US re-iss.1972 on 'United Artists'; 50809>

BONZO DOG BAND

Nov 68. (lp; mono/stereo) *(LBL/LBS 83158E)* **THE DOUGHNUT IN GRANNY'S GREENHOUSE** [40] [ ]
– We are normal / Postcard / Beautiful Zelda / Can blue men sing the whites / Hello Mabel / Kama Sutra / Humanoid boogie / The trouser press / My pink half of the drainpipe / Rockaliser baby / Rhinocratic oaths / Eleven mustachioed daughters. *(re-iss.Mar71 on 'Sunset'; SLS 50210) (re-iss.Mar87 on 'Edsel'; XED 209)*
Jul 69. (7") *(LBF 15201) <66373>* **MR. APOLLO. / READY MADES** [ ] [ ]
Aug 69. (lp) *(LBS 83257) <12445>* **TADPOLES** [36] [ ]
– Hunting tigers out in 'Indiah' / Shirt / Tubas in the moonlight / Dr. Jazz / Monster mash / I'm the urban spaceman / Ali Baba's camel / Laughing blues / By a waterfall / Mr. Apollo / Canyons of your mind. *(re-iss.Sep73 as 'URBAN SPACEMAN' on 'Sunset'; SLS 50350) (re-iss.May86 on 'Edsel'; ED 186)*
Nov 69. (7") *(LBF 15273)* **I WANT TO BE WITH YOU. / WE WERE WRONG** [ ] [-]
Nov 69. (lp) *(LBS 83290) <12457>* **KEYNSHAM** [ ] [ ]
– You done my brain in / Keynsham / Quiet talks and summer walks / Tent / We were wrong / Joke shop man / The bride stripped bare by "The Bachelors" / Look at me, I'm wonderful / What do you do? / Mr. Slater's parrot / Sport (the odd boy) / I want to be with you / Noises for the leg / "Busted". *(re-iss.Nov75 on 'Sunset'; SLS 50375) (re-iss.Dec80; LBR 1041) (re-iss.Sep87 on 'Edsel'; XED 235)*
Feb 70. (7") *(LBF 15314)* **YOU DONE MY BRAIN IN. / MR. SLATER'S PARROT** [ ] [-]

— Split early 1970 with each member doing own disastrous projects. **STANSHALL, INNES, SMITH, RUSKIN-SPEAR and COWAN** re-formed late '71. Also using session people **HUGHIE FLINT** – drums / **BUBS WHITE** – guitar / **ANDY ROBERTS** – guitar / **DAVE RICHARDS** – bass / **DICK PARRY** – woodwind

U.A. U.A.

Mar 72. (lp) *(UAS 29288)* **LET'S MAKE UP AND BE FRIENDLY** [ ] [-]
– The strain / Turkeys / King of scurf / Waiting for the wardrobe / Straight from my heart / Rusty / Rawlinson End / Don't get me wrong / Fresh wound / Slush / Bad blood. *(re-iss.May78 on 'Sunset'; SLS 50418) (re-iss.Apr87 on 'Awareness' lp/c; AWL/AWT 1004)*
May 72. (7") *<50943>* **SLUSH. /** [-] [ ]

— NEIL INNES joined GRIMMS before going solo. He then augmented the MONTY PYTHON team (part-time) before actually appearing in their films. He also created the Beatles spoof The RUTLES. He went on to host an under-5 children's TV show. LARRY SMITH went on tour with ELTON JOHN and ERIC CLAPTON. RUSKIN-SPEAR formed his KINETIC WARDROBE. SLATER became a government officer. STANSHALL narrating on MIKE OLDFIELD's "Tubular Bells" album, while also going solo. In 1978, he released the side-splitting 'SIR HENRY AT RAWLINSON END'.

– compilations, others, etc. –

on 'United Artists' unless mentioned otherwise

Aug 70. (lp) *Liberty; (LBS 83332) <5517>* **THE BEAST OF THE BONZOS** [ ] [ ]
Oct 73. (7") *(UP 35602)* **THE INTRO AND THE OUTRO. / HELLO MABEL** [ ] [-]
(re-iss.1975; UP 36002)
Mar 74. (7") *(UP 35662)* **MR. SLATER'S PARROT. / NOISES FOR THE LEG** [ ] [-]
Apr 74. (d-lp) *(UAD 60071-2) <LA 321>* **THE HISTORY OF THE BONZOS** [42] [ ]
May 78. (7"m) *(UP 36397)* **I'M THE URBAN SPACEMAN. / THE INTRO AND THE OUTRO / STRAIN** [ ] [ ]
Jul 84. (7") *EMI Golden 45's; (G 4533)* **I'M THE URBAN SPACEMAN. / THE INTRO AND THE OUTRO** [ ] [-]
Oct 84. (lp/c) *M.F.P.; (MFP/TCMFP 5680)* **THE VERY BEST OF THE BONZO DOG DOO-DAH BAND** [ ] [-]
Jul 88. (12"ep) *Strange Fruit; (SFPS 051)* **THE PEEL SESSIONS (29.7.69)** [ ] [-]
– We're going to bring it on home / Sofa Head / Tent / Monster mash.
Apr 90. (cd)(c/lp) *E.M.I.; (CDP 792675-2)(TC+/EMS 1335)* **THE BEASTIALITY OF THE BONZOS** [ ] [-]
– The intro and the outro / Canyons of your mind / Trouser press / Postcard / Mickey's son and daughter / Sport (the odd boy) / Tent / I'm the urban spaceman / Mr. Apollo / Shirt / Bad blood / Ready mades / Rhinocratic oaths / Can blue men sing the whites / Mr.Slater's parrot / The strain / We are normal / My pink half of the drainpipe / Jazz, delicious hot, disgusting cold / Big shot / Jollity farm / Humanoid boogie.
Jul 91. (cd) *Rhino;* **THE BEST OF THE BONZOS** [ ] [ ]
Apr 92. (cd-ep) *China; (WOKCD 2021)* **NO MATTER WHO YOU VOTE FOR, THE GOVERNMENT ALWAYS GETS IN / URBAN SPACEMAN / THE INTRO / Neil Innes: THEM** [ ] [-]
Jul 92. (cd) *E.M.I.; (CDP 799596-2)* **THE INTRO** [ ] [-]
Jul 92. (cd) *E.M.I.; (CDP 799597-2)* **THE OUTRO** [ ] [-]
(cd re-iss.Mar97 on 'Music For Pleasure'; CDMFP 6311)
Jul 92. (cd) *E.M.I.; (CDP 799598-2)* **DOG-ENDS** [ ] [-]
Aug 92. (3xcd-box) *E.M.I.; (CDDOG 1)* **CORNOLOGY** [ ] [-]
– (THE INTRO / THE OUTRO / DOG-ENDS)
Jun 95. (cd) *Strange Fruit; (SFRCD 134)* **UNPEELED** [ ] [-]
Feb 96. (4xcd-box) *E.M.I.; (CDBONZO 1)* **FOUR BONZO ORIGINALS** [ ] [-]

David BOWIE

Born: DAVID ROBERT JONES, 8 Jan'47, Brixton, London. In 1964 he formed The KING BEES with schoolmate GEORGE UNDERWOOD but after one single they split when BOWIE joined The MANNISH BOYS. They also lasted half a year, DAVID going solo with backing from The LOWER THIRD. In early 1966, he became DAVID BOWIE and signed to 'Pye' although commercial success continued to elude him. After three years of trying, he finally charted with 'SPACE ODDITY', a classic that introduced his "MAJOR TOM" character. That year (1969) his father died, but he was compensated by the introduction to ANGIE, his future wife. Although he was regarded as one of the top newcomers to the rock/pop scene, it took him until 1972 to finally establish himself as *the* rock star. He formed his now famous backing band, The SPIDERS, and announced his bisexuality to the music press. The single, 'STARMAN', and parent album, 'ZIGGY STARDUST' (an archetype alter-ego), were to hit the UK top 10. By this stage he'd come a long way from being a 60's ANTHONY NEWLEY copyist, innovating a risque, glam rock style and pioneering the 'feathercut', make-up for men and stage-mime (the latter being learnt from LINDSEY KEMP). Signed to R.C.A., the company duly re-issued his past three albums which all broke into the U.K. charts and 'ALADDIN SANE' (1973) was the first of his many No.1 albums. 'DIAMOND DOGS' (1974) represented the finale of his futuristic concept work and bore the hit single, 'REBEL, REBEL', while the follow-up concert album, 'DAVID LIVE' (1974), documented the mammoth tour that followed. With 'YOUNG AMERI-

CANS' in 1975, his music took a dramatic and not entirely well-recieved turn towards Philadelphia soul/disco. Nevertheless, the album hit No.2 in the UK and a collaborative single with JOHN LENNON, 'FAME', gave him a US No.1. BOWIE then made yet another about face; dallying briefly with themes of fascism and dictatorship, he recorded the stark 'STATION TO STATION' (1976) album, before relocating to Berlin with BRIAN ENO and continuing his move towards experimental/avant-garde rock. The resulting albums, 'LOW' and 'HEROES', both released in 1977, were fairly successful in the UK despite containing some of BOWIE's most uncommercial work to date. After a final album with ENO, BOWIE returned to more conventional rock, gaining another No.1 hit with his resurrection of Major Tom on 'ASHES TO ASHES' (1980). After a two and a half year hiatus, he returned with the NILE RODGERS-produced 'LET'S DANCE' album. A typically polished, 80's-sounding record, it featured the single 'CHINA GIRL', complete with controversial video (in 1977, BOWIE had originally collaborated on the track with IGGY POP for the wild man's 'The Idiot' album). The rest of BOWIE's 80's output was hardly essential and at the turn of the decade he set up the embaressing TIN MACHINE project, a misguided attempt at a return to spontaneous rock'n'roll. Ignoring the critical barbs, he carried on with this set up until 1991 but couldn't sunstantiate any major hits. The release of 'OUTSIDE' (1995), (a collaboration with his old mucker ENO) saw BOWIE back in critical favour, while more recently 'EART HL ING' (1997) was an admirable attempt to incorporate cutting edge dance styles into his music, collaborating with drum 'n' bass don A GUY CALLED GERALD. • **Songwriters:** He wrote all his own material even managing some for others (e.g. ALL THE YOUNG DUDES for (Mott The Hoople) / OH YOU PRETTY THINGS (Peter Noone) / THE MAN WHO SOLD THE WORLD / (Lulu) / PINK ROSE (Adrian Belew) / etc. He produced 'RCA' acts LOU REED (Transformer) / MICK RONSON (Slaughter on Tenth Avenue) / etc. BOWIE's cover album PIN-UPS featured SORROW (Merseys) / ROSALYN (Pretty Things) / HERE COMES THE NIGHT (Them) / SHAPES OF THINGS (Yardbirds) / FRIDAY ON MY MIND (Easybeats) / ANYWAY ANYHOW ANYWHERE + I CAN'T EXPLAIN (Who) / SEE EMILY PLAY (Pink Floyd) / WHERE HAVE ALL THE GOOD TIMES GONE (Kinks) / DON'T BRING ME DOWN + I WISH YOU WOULD (Pretty Things) / EVERYTHING'S ALRIGHT (Mojos) /. Other covers:- LET'S SPEND THE NIGHT TOGETHER (Rolling Stones) / KNOCK ON WOOD (Eddie Floyd) / ALABAMA SONG (Brecht-Weill) / DANCING IN THE STREET (Martha & The Vandellas). I FEEL FREE (Cream) / NITE FLIGHT (Scott Walker) / I KNOW IT'S GONNA HAPPEN SOMEDAY (Morrissey) / DON'T LET ME DOWN & DOWN (Tacha-Valmont) / THE SEEKER (Who). – TIN MACHINE :- He co-wrote with GABRELS except MAGGIE'S FARM (Bob Dylan) / WORKING CLASS HERO (John Lennon, who also co-wrote FAME for BOWIE in 1975) / IF THERE IS SOMETHING (Roxy Music). • **Trivia:** BOWIE'S acting career started in 1976 with the film 'THE MAN WHO FELL TO EARTH' and 'JUST A GIGOLO' (1978). After starring in stage production of ELEPHANT MAN in 1980, he returned to films THE HUNGER (1982) / MERRY XMAS MR. LAWRENCE (1983) / LABYRINTH (1986) / ABSOLUTE BEGINNERS (1986) / THE LAST TEMPTATION OF CHRIST (1989). In 1985, he was one of the major stars of LIVE AID concert, and co-sang on 'DANCIN' IN THE STREET' with MICK JAGGER.

Recommended: CHANGESONEBOWIE (*10) / ZIGGY STARDUST (*10) / ALADDIN SANE (*9) / THE MAN WHO SOLD THE WORLD (*9) / LOW (*10) / HUNKY DORY (*8) / HEROES (*9) / SPACE ODDITY (*6) / STATION TO STATION (*8) / SCARY MONSTERS (*7) / DIAMOND DOGS (*6) / PIN-UPS (*5) / YOUNG AMERICANS (*5) / LODGER (*4) / LET'S DANCE (*6) / TIN MACHINE (*4) / BLACK TIE, WHITE NOISE (*5) / OUTSIDE (*6) / EART HL ING (*6)

DAVID BOWIE – vocals, acoustic guitar

Vocalion / not issued

Jun 64. (7"; as DAVIE JONES with The KING BEES) *(Pop V 9221)* **LIZA JANE. / LOUIE LOUIE GO HOME** [ ] [-]
(re-iss.Sep78 on 'Decca'; F 13807)

Parlophone / not issued

Mar 65. (7"; as The MANNISH BOYS) *(R 5250)* **I PITY THE FOOL. / TAKE MY TIP** [ ] [-]

Aug 65. (7"; as DAVY JONES) *(R 5315)* **YOU'VE GOT A HABIT OF LEAVING. / BABY LOVES THAT WAY** [ ] [-]

Pye / Warners

Jan 66. (7"; as DAVID BOWIE with The LOWER THIRD) *(7N 17020) <5814>* **CAN'T HELP THINKING ABOUT ME. / AND I SAID TO MYSELF** [ ] [ ]

Apr 66. (7") *(7N 17079)* **DO ANYTHING YOU SAY. / GOOD MORNING GIRL** [ ] [-]

Aug 66. (7") *(7N 17157)* **I DIG EVERYTHING. / I'M NOT LOSING SLEEP** [ ] [-]

Deram / Deram

Dec 66. (7") *(DM 107)* **RUBBER BAND. / THE LONDON BOYS** [ ] [-]

Feb 67. (7") *<85009>* **RUBBER BAND. / THERE IS A HAPY LAND** [-] [ ]

Apr 67. (7") *(DM 123)* **THE LAUGHING GNOME. / THE GOSPEL ACCORDING TO TONY DAY** [ ] [-]
(re-iss.Sep73; same); hit UK No.6 (re-iss.Jun82)

Jun 67. (lp; mono/stereo) *(DML/SML 1007)* **DAVID BOWIE** [ ] [-]
– Uncle Arthur / Sell me a coat / Rubber band / Love you till Tuesday There is a happy land / We are hungry men / When I live my dream / Little bombadier / Silly boy blue / Come and buy me toys / Join the gang / She's got medals / Maids of Bond Street / Please Mr. Gravedigger. *(re-iss.Nov69 on 'Philips'; SBL 7912) (re-iss.Aug84 lp/c; DOA 1) (cd-iss.Oct88; 800 087-2)*

Jul 67. (7") *(DM 135) <85016>* **LOVE YOU TILL TUESDAY. / DID YOU EVER HAVE A DREAM** [ ] [ ]

—— (Jul68-Feb69) **BOWIE** formed FEATHERS with girlfriend **HERMOINE FARTHINGALE + JOHN HUTCHINSON** – bass. BOWIE went solo, recording solo album with session players **RICK WAKEMAN** – keyboards

Philips / Mercury

Jul 69. (7") *(BF 1801) <72949>* **SPACE ODDITY. / THE WILD EYED BOY FROM FREECLOUD** [5] [ ]

Nov 69. (lp) *(SBL 7912)* **DAVID BOWIE – MAN OF WORDS MAN OF MUSIC** [ ] [-]
– Space oddity / Unwashed and somewhat slightly dazed / Letter to Hermione / Cygnet committee / Janine / An occasional dream / The wild eyed boy from Freecloud / God knows I'm good / Memory of a free festival. *(re-iss.Nov72 as 'SPACE ODDITY' on 'RCA' lp/c; LSP/PK 4813) (hit No.17 UK + No.16 US; <ST 61246>) (re-iss.Oct84 on 'RCA' lp/c/cd; PL/PK/PD 84813) (re-iss.Apr90 on 'EMI' cd/c/lp; CD/TC+/EMC 3571) (+=)–* Conversation piece / Don't sit down. *(hit UK No.64)*

—— **BOWIE** formed backing band **HYPE** with **TONY VISCONTI** – bass / **MICK RONSON** – guitar / **JOHN CAMBRIDGE** – drums

Mercury / Mercury

Mar 70. (7") *(MF 1135)* **THE PRETTIEST STAR. / CONVERSATION PIECE** [ ] [-]

—— **MICK 'Woody' WOODMANSEY** – drums repl. CAMBRIDGE

Jun 70. (7") *(6052 026) <73075>* **MEMORY OF A FREE FESTIVAL (part 1). / (part 2)** [ ] [ ]

Jan 71. (7") *(6052 049)* **HOLY HOLY. / BLACK COUNTRY ROCK** [ ] [-]

Apr 71. (lp) *(6338 041) <61325>* **THE MAN WHO SOLD THE WORLD** [ ] [ ]
– The width of a circle / All the madmen / Black country rock / After all / Running gun blues / Saviour machine / She took me cold / The man who sold the world / The supermen. *(re-iss.Nov72 on 'RCA' lp/c; LSP/PK 4816) (hit No.26 UK) (re-iss.Apr83 on 'RCA' lp/c; INTS/INTK 5237) (hit UK 64) (re-iss.Oct84 on 'RCA Int.' lp/c/cd; NL/NK/PD 84654) (re-iss.Apr90 on 'EMI' cd/c/lp; CD/TC+/EMC 3573) (+=)–* Lightning frightening / Moonage daydream / Holy holy / Hang on to yourself. *(hit UK No.66)*

Jun 71. (7") *<73175>* **ALL THE MADMEN. /** [-] [ ]

—— Became **SPIDERS FROM MARS (BOWIE, RONSON, WOODMANSEY), TREVOR BOULDER** – bass repl. VISCONTI

R.C.A. / R.C.A.

Dec 71. (lp/c) *(SF/PK 8244) <AFL-1 4623>* **HUNKY DORY** [ ] [93]
– Changes / Oh! you pretty things / Eight line poem / Life on Mars? / Kooks / Quicksand / Fill your heart – Andy Warhol / Song for Bob Dylan / Queen bitch / The Bewlay Brothers. *(re-dist.Sep72 reached No.3 UK) (re-iss.Jan81 lp/c; INTS/INTK 5064) (hit No.32 UK) (pic-lp Apr84; BOPIC 2) (re-iss.Oct84 on 'RCA Int.' lp/c/cd; NL/NK/PD 83844) (re-iss.Apr90 on 'EMI' cd/c/lp; CD/TC+/EMC 3572) (+=)–* Bombers / The supermen (alt.) / Quicksand (demo) / The Bewlay Brothers (alt.). *(hit UK No.39)*

Jan 72. (7") *(RCA 2160) <74-0605>* **CHANGES. / ANDY WARHOL** [ ] [66] Apr72
(re-iss.Dec74; same); reached No.41 UK

Apr 72. (7") *(RCA 2199) <74-0719>* **STARMAN. / SUFFRAGETTE CITY** [10] [65] Jun72

Jun 72. (lp/c) *(SF/PK 8267) <AFL-1 4702>* **THE RISE AND FALL OF ZIGGY STARDUST AND THE SPIDERS FROM MARS** [5] [75]
– Five years / Soul love / Moonage daydream / Starman / It ain't easy / Lady Stardust / Star / Hang on to yourself / Ziggy Stardust / Suffragette city / Rock'n'roll suicide. *(re-iss.Jan81 lp/c; INTS/INTK 5063) (hit No.33 UK) (pic-lp Apr84; BOPIC 3) (re-iss.Oct84 on 'RCA Int.' lp/c/cd; NL/NK/PD 83843) (re-iss.Apr90 on 'EMI' cd+=/c+=/lp; CD/TC+/EMC 3577) <re-iss.Jun90 on 'Rykodisc'+=; 10134>; hit No.93.* – John, I'm only dancing (demo) / Velvet goldmine / Sweet head / Ziggy Stardust (demo) / Lady Stardust (demo). *(hit UK No.25) (re-iss.Feb97 on 'E.M.I.'; LPCENT 4)*

Sep 72. (7") *(RCA 2263)* **JOHN, I'M ONLY DANCING. / HANG ON TO YOURSELF** [12] [-]

Nov 72. (7") *(RCA 2302)* **THE JEAN GENIE. / ZIGGY STARDUST** [2] [-]

Nov 72. (7") *<74-0838>* **THE JEAN GENIE. / HANG ON TO YOURSELF** [-] [71]

Jan 73. (7") *<74-0876>* **SPACE ODDITY. / THE MAN WHO SOLD THE WORLD** [-] [15]

Apr 73. (7") *(RCA 2352)* **DRIVE-IN-SATURDAY. / ROUND AND ROUND** [3] [-]

—— with guests **MIKE GARSON** – piano / **KEN FORDHAM** and **BUX** – saxophone, flute

Apr 73. (lp/c) *(RS/PK 1001) <AFL-1 4852>* **ALADDIN SANE** [1] [17] May73
– Watch that man / Aladdin Sane (1913-1938-197?) / Drive-in Saturday / Panic in Detroit / Cracked actor / Time / The prettiest star / Let's spend the night together / The Jean genie / Lady grinning soul. *(re-iss.Feb81 on 'RCA Int.' lp/c; INTS/INTK 5067) (hit No.49 UK Feb82) (re-iss.Mar84 on 'RCA Int.' lp/c; NL/NK 83890) (pic-lp Apr84; BOPIC 1) (cd-iss.Jun85; PD 83890) (re-iss.Jul90 on 'EMI' cd/c/lp; CD/TC+/EMC 3579)(+=)–* (other rare tracks). *(hit UK No.43)*

Jun 73. (7") *<APBO 0001>* **TIME. / THE PRETTIEST STAR** [-] [ ]

Jun 73. (7") *(RCA 2316)* **LIFE ON MARS. / THE MAN WHO SOLD THE WORLD** [3] [-]

Aug 73. (7") *<APBO 0028>* **LET'S SPEND THE NIGHT TOGETHER. / LADY GRINNING SOUL** [-] [ ]

—— **AYNSLEY DUNBAR** – drums repl. WOODY

Oct 73. (7") *(RCA 2424) <APBO 0160>* **SORROW. / AMSTERDAM** [3] [ ] Nov73

Oct 73. (lp/c) *(RS/PK 1003) <AFL-1 0291>* **PIN-UPS** [1] [23]
– Rosalyn / Here comes the night / I wish you would / See Emily play / Everything's alright / I can't explain / Friday on my mind / Sorow / Don't bring me down / Shapes of things / Anyway anyhow anywhere / Where have all the good times gone!. *(re-iss.Sep81 lp/c; RCA LP/K 3004) (re-iss.Apr83 on 'RCA Int.' lp/c; INTS/INTK 5236) (hit UK 57) (pic-lp Apr84; BOPIC 4) (re-iss.Jul90 on 'EMI' cd/c/lp; CD/TC+/EMC 3580) (hit No.52)*

—— **DUNBAR** and **TONY NEWMAN** – drums / **HERBIE FLOWERS** – bass / **MIKE GARSON** – keyboards

Feb 74. (7") *(LPBO 5009)* **REBEL REBEL. / QUEEN BITCH** [5] [-]

Apr 74. (7") *(LPBO 5021)* **ROCK'N'ROLL SUICIDE. / QUICKSAND** [22] [-]

May 74. (7") *<APBO 0287>* **REBEL REBEL. / LADY GRINNING SOUL** [-] [64]

May 74. (lp/c; as BOWIE) *(<APL/APK 1-0576>)* **DIAMOND DOGS** [1] [ ]
– Future legend / Diamond dogs / Sweet thing / Candidate / Sweet thing (reprise) / Rebel rebel / Rock'n'roll with me / We are the dead / 1984 / Big brother (including 'Chant of the ever circling skeletal family'). *(re-iss.Feb81 on 'RCA Int.' lp/c; INTS/INTK 5068) (hit UK 60 in May83) (re-iss.Mar84 on 'RCA Int.' lp/c/cd; NL/NK/PD 83889) (pic-lp Apr84; BOPIC 5) (re-iss.Jun90 on 'E.M.I.' cd/c/lp;*

CD/TC+/EMC 3584) (+=)– Dodo / Candidate. *(hit UK No.67)*

Jun 74. (7") *(<APBO 0293>)* **DIAMOND DOGS. / HOLY HOLY** [21] [ ]

— added **EARL SLICK** – guitar / **DAVID SANBORN** – saxophone

Sep 74. (7") *(RCA 2466)* **KNOCK ON WOOD (live). / PANIC IN DETROIT (live)** [10] [-]

Oct 74. (7") *<10026>* **1984 (live). / QUEEN BITCH** [-] [ ]

Nov 74. (d-lp/c) *(<APL/APK 2-0771>)* **DAVID LIVE (live at the Tower theatre Philadelphia '74)** [2] [8]
– 1984 / Rebel rebel / Moonage daydream / Sweet thing / Changes / Suffragette city / Aladdin Sane (1913-1938-197?) / All the young dudes / Cracked actor / Rock'n'roll with me / Watch that man / Knock on wood / Diamond dogs/ Big brother / The width of a circle / The Jean genie / Rock'n'roll suicide. *(re-iss.May84 lp/c; PL/PK 80771) (re-iss.Jun90 on 'EMI' cd/c/d-lp+=; CD/TC+/DBLD 1)*– (band intro) / Here today, gone tomorrow / Time. *(re-iss.d-cd Jun95 on 'EMI'; same)*

Dec 74. (7") *<10105>* **ROCK'N'ROLL WITH ME (live). / PANIC IN DETROIT (live)** [-] [ ]

— **ANDY NEWMARK** – drums / **WILLIE WEEKS** – bass / **CARLOS ALOMAR** – guitar / **EARL SLICK** – guitar / guests **LUTHER VANDROSS + JOHN LENNON** – backing vocals

Feb 75. (7") *(RCA 2523)* **YOUNG AMERICANS. / SUFFRAGETTE CITY** [18] [-]

Mar 75. (7") *<10152>* **YOUNG AMERICANS. / KNOCK ON WOOD (live)** [-] [28]

Mar 75. (lp/c) *(APL/APK 1-1006) <0998>* **YOUNG AMERICANS** [2] [9]
– Young Americans / Win / Fascination / Right / Somebody up there like me / Across the universe / Can you hear me / Fame. *(re-iss.Sep81 lp/c; RCA LP/K 3009) (re-iss.Oct84 lp/c/cd; PL/PK/PD 80998) (re-iss.Apr91 on 'E.M.I.' cd+=/c+=/lp; CD/TC+/EMD 1021)*– Who can I be now? / John, I'm only dancing (again) (1975) / It's gonna be me. *(hit UK No.54)*

Jul 75. (7") *(RCA 2579) <10320>* **FAME. / RIGHT** [17] [1] Jun75

Sep 75. (7"m) *(RCA 2593)* **SPACE ODDITY. / CHANGES / VELVET GOLDMINE** [1] [-]

— retained **SLICK + ALOMAR**

— **GEORGE MURRAY** – bass + **DENNIS DAVIS** – drums repl. WEEKS + NEWMARK

Nov 75. (7") *(RCA 2640) <10441>* **GOLDEN YEARS. / CAN YOU HEAR ME** [8] [10]

Jan 76. (lp/c) *(<APL/APK 1-1327>)* **STATION TO STATION** [5] [3]
– Station to station / Golden years / Word on a wing / TVC 15 / Stay / Wild is the wind. *(re-iss.Sep81 lp/c; RCA LP/K 3013) (re-iss.Oct84 lp/c/cd; PL/PK/PD 81327) (re-iss.Apr91 on 'E.M.I.' cd/c/lp; CD/TC+/EMD 1020) (+=)*– Word on the wing (live) / Stay (live). *(hit UK No.57)*

May 76. (7") *(RCA 2682) <10664>* **TVC 15. / WE ARE THE DEAD** [33] [64]

Jun 76. (lp/c) *(RS/PK 1055) <1732>* **CHANGESONEBOWIE** (compilation) [2] [10]
– Space oddity / John, I'm only dancing / Changes / Ziggy Stardust / Suffragette city / The Jean genie / Diamond dogs / Rebel rebel / Young Americans / Fame / Golden years. *(re-iss.May84 lp/c/cd; PL/PK/PD 81732)*

Jul 76. (7") *(RCA 2726)* **SUFFRAGETTE CITY. / STAY** [ ] [-]

Aug 76. (7") *<10736>* **STAY. / WORD ON A WING** [-] [ ]

— now collaborated with **BRIAN ENO** – synthesizers

— **RICKY GARDINER** – guitar repl. SLICK

Jan 77. (lp/c) *(PL/PK 12030) <2030>* **LOW** [2] [11]
– Speed of life / Breaking glass / What in the world / Sound and vision / Always crashing in the same car / Be my wife / A new career in a new town / Warszawa / Art decade / Weeping wall / Subterraneans. *(re-iss.Dec80 on 'RCA Int.' lp/c; INTS/INTK 5065) ;hit UK 85 in Jun83) (re-iss.Mar84 on 'RCA Int.' lp/c/cd; NL/NK/PD 83856) (re-iss.Aug91 on 'E.M.I.' cd/c/lp; CD/TC+/EMD 1027) (+=)*– (bonus tracks). *(hit UK No.64)*

Feb 77. (7") *(PB 0905) <10905>* **SOUND AND VISION. / A NEW CAREER IN A NEW TOWN** [3] [69]

Jun 77. (7") *(PB 1017) <11017>* **BE MY WIFE. / SPEED OF LIFE** [ ] [ ]

— next guest **ROBERT FRIPP** – guitar who repl. RICKY GARDINER.

Oct 77. (7") *(PB 1121) <11121>* **HEROES. / V2-SCHNEIDER** [24] [ ]

Oct 77. (lp/c) *(PL/PK 12522) <2522>* **"HEROES"** [3] [35]
– Beauty and the beast / Joe the lion / Heroes / Sons of the silent age / Blackout / V-2 Schneider / Sense of doubt / Moss garden / Neukoln / Black out / The secret life of Arabia. *(re-iss.Dec80 lp/c; INTS/INTK 5066) (hit UK 75 in Jun83) (re-iss.Nov84 lp/c/cd; NL/NK/PD 83857) (re-iss.Apr91 on 'E.M.I.' cd/c/lp; CD/TC+/EMD 1025) (+=)*– Joe the Lion (1991 remix) / Abolumajor.

Jan 78. (7") *(PB 1190) <11190>* **THE BEAUTY AND THE BEAST. / SENSE OF DOUBT** [39] [ ]

— added **ADRIAN BELEW** – guitar / **SIMON HOUSE** – violin (ex-HIGH TIDE, ex-HAWKWIND) / **SEAN MAYES** – piano

Sep 78. (d-lp,yellow-d-lp/d-c) *(PL/PK 02913) <2913>* **STAGE (live)** [5] [44]
– Hang on to yourself / Ziggy Stardust / Five years / Soul love / Star / Station to station / Fame / TVC 15 / Warszawa / Speed of life / Art decade / Sense of doubt / Breaking glass / Heroes / What in the world / Blackout / Beauty and the beast. *(re-iss.Jul84 d-lp/cd; PL/PD 89002) (re-iss.Feb92 on 'EMI' d-cd/c; CD/TC EMD 1030)*– (bonus tracks).

Oct 78. (7"ep) *(BOW 1)* **BREAKING GLASS (live). / ZIGGY STARDUST (live) / ART DECADE (live)** [54] [-]

Apr 79. (7") *(BOW 2) <11585>* **BOYS KEEP SWINGING. / FANTASTIC VOYAGE** [7] [ ]

May 79. (lp/c) *(BOW LP/K 1) <3254>* **LODGER** [4] [20]
– Fantastic voyage / African night flight / Move on / Yassassin / Red sails / D.J. / Look back in anger / Boys keep swinging / Repetition / Red money. *(re-iss.May82 on 'RCA Int.' lp/c; INTS/INTK 5212) (re-iss.Mar84 on 'RCA Int.' lp/c/cd; NL/NK/PD 84234) (re-iss.Aug91 on 'E.M.I.' cd/c/lp; CD/TC+/EMD 1026)*– (2 tracks).

Jul 79. (7",7"green) *(BOW 3)* **D.J. / REPETITION** [29] [-]

Aug 79. (7") *<11661>* **D.J. / FANTASTIC VOYAGE** [-] [ ]

Oct 79. (7") *<11724>* **LOOK BACK IN ANGER. / REPITITION** [-] [ ]

Dec 79. (7"/ext.12") *(BOW 4/12-4)* **JOHN, I'M ONLY DANCING (AGAIN) (1975). / JOHN, I'M ONLY DANCING (1972)** [12] [-]

Jan 80. (7") *<11887>* **JOHN, I'M ONLY DANCING (1972). / JOE THE LION** [-] [ ]

Feb 80. (7") *(BOW 5)* **ALABAMA SONG. / SPACE ODDITY** [23] [ ]

— guest **ROBERT FRIPP** – guitar repl. BRIAN ENO

Aug 80. (7") *(BOW 6)* **ASHES TO ASHES. / MOVE ON** [1] [-]

Sep 80. (7") *<12078>* **ASHES TO ASHES. / IT'S NO GAME** [-] [ ]

Sep 80. (lp/c) *(BOW LP/K 2) <3647>* **SCARY MONSTERS** [1] [12]
– It's no game (No.1) / Up the hill backwards / Scary monsters (and super creeps) / Ashes to ashes / Fashion / Teenage wildlife / Scream like a baby / Kingdom come / Because you're young / It's no game (No.2). *(re-iss.Oct84 lp/c/cd; PL/PK/PD 83647) (re-iss.Jun92 on 'EMI' cd/c; CD/TC EMD 1029) (+=)*– Space oddity / Panic in Detroit / Crystal Japan / Alabama song.

Oct 80. (7"/12") *(BOW/+T 7) <12134>* **FASHION. / SCREAM LIKE A BABY** [5] [70]

Jan 81. (7"/c-s) *(BOW/+C 8)* **SCARY MONSTERS (AND SUPER CREEPS). / BECAUSE YOU'RE YOUNG** [20] [-]

Mar 81. (7"/c-s) *(BOW/+C 9)* **UP THE HILL BACKWARDS. / CRYSTAL JAPAN** [32] [-]

— (next single "UNDER PRESSURE" was a No.1 collaboration w/ "QUEEN")

Nov 81. (7"/12") *(BOW/+T 10)* **WILD IS THE WIND. / GOLDEN YEARS** [24] [-]

Nov 81. (lp/c) *(BOW LP/K 3) <4202>* **CHANGESTWOBOWIE** (compilation) [24] [68]
– Aladdin Sane / Oh you pretty things / Starman / 1984 / Ashes to ashes / Sound and vision / Fashion / Wild is the wind / John, I'm only dancing (again) (1975) / D.J. *(re-iss.May84 lp/c/cd; PL/PK/PD 84202)*

Feb 82. (7"ep) *(BOW 11)* **BAAL'S HYMN** [29] [-]
– Baal's hymn / Remembering Marie / Ballad of the adventurers / The drowned girl / The dirty song.

Apr 82. (7"/ext.12") *(MCA/+T 770) <52024>* **CAT PEOPLE (PUTTING OUT FIRE). / PAUL'S THEME (by GIORGIO MORODER)** [26] [67]

— (above single taken from the feature film of the same name on 'MCA-UK' / 'Backstreet' US)

Nov 82. (7"/12"; by DAVID BOWIE & BING CROSBY) *(BOW/+T 12) <13400>* **PEACE ON EARTH – LITTLE DRUMMER BOY. / FANTASTIC VOYAGE** [3] [ ]

— now with **NILE RODGERS + STEVIE RAY VAUGHAN** – guitar / **BERNARD EDWARDS + CARMINE ROJAS** – bass / **OMAR HAKIM + TONY THOMPSON** – drums / **SAMMY FIGUEROA** – percussion

EMI America / EMI America

Mar 83. (7"/12"/c-s) *(EA/12EA/45-TCEA 152) <8158>* **LET'S DANCE. / CAT PEOPLE (PUTTING OUT FIRE)** [1] [1]

Apr 83. (lp/pic-lp/c) *(AML/AMLP/TCAML 3029) <17093>* **LET'S DANCE** [1] [4]
– Modern love / China girl / Let's dance / China girl / Without you / Ricochet / Criminal world / Cat people (putting out fire) / Shake it. *(cd-iss.Jan84; CDP 7460022) (re-iss.cd Nov95 on 'Virgin American'; CDVUS 96)*

Jun 83. (7"/7"pic-d/12") *(EA/EAP/12EA 157) <8165>* **CHINA GIRL. / SHAKE IT** [2] [10]

Sep 83. (7"/12") *(EA/12EA 158) <8177>* **MODERN LOVE. / MODERN LOVE (live)** [2] [14]

Feb 84. (7") *<8190>* **WITHOUT YOU. / CRIMINAL WORLD** [-] [73]

— retained **HAKIM, ROJAS, FIGUEROA** / brought back **ALOMAR** and recruited **DEREK BRAMBLE** – bass, snyths, etc.

Sep 84. (7"/12") *(EA/12EA 181) <8231>* **BLUE JEAN. / DANCING WITH THE BIG BOYS** [6] [8]

Sep 84. (lp/c)(cd) *(DB/TCDB 1)(CDP 746047-2) <17138>* **TONIGHT** [1] [11]
– Loving the alien / Don't look down / God only knows / Tonight / Neighbourhood threat / Blue Jean / Tumble and twirl / I keep forgetting / Dancing with the big boys. *(re-iss.cd Nov95 on 'Virgin American'; CDVUS 97)*

Nov 84. (7") *(EA 187) <8246>* **TONIGHT. / TUMBLE AND TWIRL** [53] [53]
(12") *(12EA 187)* – ('A'vocal dance mix) / ('B'extended dance mix) / ('A'dub mix).

— (next single, from the film "Falcon And The Snowman")

Jan 85. (7"/12"; by DAVID BOWIE with The PAT METHENY GROUP) *(EA 190) <8251>* **THIS IS NOT AMERICA. / ('A'instrumental by The PAT METHENY GROUP)** [14] [32]

May 85. (7"/7"pic-d) *(EA/+P 195) <8271>* **LOVING THE ALIEN. / DON'T LOOK DOWN** [19] [ ]
(ext.12"+=/ext.12"sha-pic-d+=) *(12EA/+P 195)* – ('A'extended dub mix).

Sep 85. (7"; by DAVID BOWIE & MICK JAGGER) *(EA 204) <8288>* **DANCING IN THE STREET (Clearmountain mix). / ('A'instrumental)** [1] [7]
(12") *(12EA 204)* – ('A'-Steve Thompson mix) / ('A'dub version) / ('A'edit).

— (below single from 'Virgin' records film & album of the same name, cont. 3 BOWIE tracks, album reached No.19 UK)

Mar 86. (7"/7"sha-pic-d)(ext.12") *(VS/+S 838)(VS 838-12) <8308>* **ABSOLUTE BEGINNERS. / ('A'dub version)** [2] [53]
(re-iss.3"cd-s Nov88; CDT 20)

— (below single from the feature film "Labyrinth" which cont. 5 BOWIE tracks, album reached No.38 UK)

— now with **ALOMAR, ROJAS + ERDAL KIZILCAY** – keyboards / **PHILIPPE SAISSE** – keyboards, etc. / **PETER FRAMPTON** – guitar

Jun 86. (7"/7"sha-pic-d) *(EA/+P 216) <8323>* **UNDERGROUND. / ('A'instrumental)** [21] [ ]
(ext.dance-12"+=) *(VS 906-12)* – ('A'dub).

— (the next, was from animated film of the same name on 'Virgin')

Nov 86. (7"/7"sha-pic-d) *(VS/+S 906)* **WHEN THE WIND BLOWS. / ('A'instrumental)** [44] [-]
(12"+=) *(VS 906-12)* – ('A'dub).

Mar 87. (7"/7"red) *(EA/+X 230) <8380>* **DAY-IN DAY-OUT. / JULIE** [17] [21]
(ext.dance-12"+=/remix-12"+=)(ext.dance c-s+=) *(12EA/+X 230)(TCEA 230)* – ('A'extended dub).

Apr 87. (lp/c/cd) *(AMLS/TCAMLS/CDAMLS 3117) <17267>* **NEVER LET ME DOWN** [6] [34]
– Day-in day-out / Time will crawl / Beat of your drum / Never let me down / Zeroes / Glass spider / Shining star (makin' my love) / New York's in love / '87 and cry / Bang bang / Too dizzy. *(cd+=)*– Time will crawl (extended dance) / Never let me down (version) / Day-in day-out (Groucho mix).*(re-iss.cd Nov95 on 'Virgin American'; CDVUS 98)*

Jun 87. (7"/7"w-poster) *(EA/+P 237) <43020>* **TIME WILL CRAWL. / GIRLS** [33] [ ]

(12") *(12EA 237)* – ('A'extended dance mix) / ('A'version) / ('B'extended).
(12") *(12EAX 237)* – ('A'dance crew mix) / ('A'dub) / ('B'-Japanese version).
Aug 87. (7"/7"pic-d) *(EA/+P 239) <43031>* **NEVER LET ME DOWN. / '87 AND CRY** [34] [27]
(c-s+=) *(TCEA 239)* – Time will crawl (extended dance mix) / Day-in day-out (Groucho mix).
(ext.dance-12"+=) *(12EA 239)* – ('A'dub) / ('A'acappella).

TIN MACHINE

was the name of **BOWIE's** next project/band. **DAVID BOWIE** – vocals, saxophone / **REEVES GABRELS** – lead guitar / **TONY SALES** – bass / **HUNT SALES** – drums (both ex-IGGY POP, ex-TODD RUNDGREN RUNT)plus p/t member **KEVIN ARMSTRONG** – guitar

Manhattan Manhattan

May 89. (cd/c/lp) *(CD/MC+/MTLS 1044) <91990>* **TIN MACHINE** [3] [28]
– Heaven's in here / Tin machine / Prisoner of love / Crack city / I can't read / Under the god / Amazing / Working class hero / Bus stop / Pretty thing / Video crimes / Run * / Sacrifice yourself * / Baby can dance. *(cd+= *) (re-iss.cd Nov95 on 'Virgin American'; CDVUS 99)*
Jun 89. (7"/c-s) *(MT/TCMT 68)* **UNDER THE GOD. / SACRIFICE YOURSELF** [51] [ ]
(10"+=/12"+=/cd-s+=) *(10/12/CD MT 68)* – (the interview).
Aug 89. (7"/7"s/7"sha-pic-d/c-s) *(MT/MTG/MTPD/TCMT 73)* **TIN MACHINE. / MAGGIE'S FARM (live)** [48] [ ]
(12"+=) *(12MT 73)* – I can't read (live).
(cd-s++=) *(CDMT 73)* – Bus stop (live country version).
Oct 89. (7"/7"s/7"sha-pic-d/c-s) *(MT/MTS/MTPD/TCMT 76)* **PRISONER OF LOVE. / BABY CAN DANCE (live)** [ ] [ ]
(12"+=) *(12MT 76)* – Crack city (live).
(cd-s++=) *(CDMT 76)* – ('A'version).

London Victory

Aug 91. (7"/12") *(LON/+X 305)* **YOU BELONG IN ROCK'N'ROLL. / AMLAPURA** [33] [ ]
(pic-cd+=) *(LONCD 305)* – Stateside / Hammerhead.
Sep 91. (cd/c/lp) *(828 272-2/-4/-1) <511216>* **TIN MACHINE II** [23] [ ]
– Baby universal / One shot / You belong in rock'n'roll / If there is something / Amlapura / Betty wrong / You can't talk / Stateside / Shopping for girls / Big hurt / I'm sorry / Goodbye Mr. Ed / Hammerhead.
Oct 91. (7"/c-s) *(LON/+CS 310)* **BABY UNIVERSAL. / YOU BELONG IN ROCK'N'ROLL** [48] [ ]
(12") *(LONT 310)* – ('A'side) / A big hurt (live) / ('A'live).
(cd-s) *(LONCD 310)* – ('A'side) / Stateside (live) / If there is something (live) / Heaven's in here (live).

— In Feb'92, BOWIE's song 'SOUND AND VISION (remix)' was re-done with himself and 808 STATE on label 'Tommy Boy'.

Jul 92. (cd/c/lp) *(828 328-2/-4/-1)* **TIN MACHINE LIVE – OY VEY, BABY (live)** [ ] [ ]
– If there is something / Amazing / I can't read / Stateside / Under the god / Goodbye Mr. Ed / Heaven's in here / You belong in rock'n'roll.

DAVID BOWIE

(solo again) and starred in the film 'THE LINGUINI INCIDENT'.

Warners Warners

Aug 92. (7"/c-s) *(W 0127/+C)* **REAL COOL WORLD. / ('A'instrumental)** [53] [ ]
(12") *(W 0127T)* – ('A'club) / ('A'dub thing 1 & 2) / ('A'dub overture).
(cd-s+=) *(W 0127CD)* – (2 more 'A'mixes).

— with **NILE RODGERS** – guitar, co-producer / **DAVE RICHARDS + RICHARD HILTON + PHILIPPE SAISSE + RICHARD TEE** – keyboards / **BARRY CAMPBELL + JOHN REGAN** – bass / **PUGI BELL + STERLING CAMPBELL** – drums / **GERADO VELEZ** – percussion. Plus guests **MICK RONSON** – guitar / **LESTER BOWIE** – trumpet / **REEVES GABRELS** – guitar / **MIKE GARSON** – piano / **AL B.SURE!** – vocals / **WILD T.SPRINGER** – guitar

Savage-BMG Savage-BMG

Mar 93. (c-s) *(74321 139424)* **JUMP THEY SAY. / PALLAS ATHENA (Don't Stop Praying Mix)** [9] [ ]
(cd-s+=) *(74321 139422)* – ('A'-Hard Hands mix) / ('A'-JAE-E remix).
(cd-s) *(74321 139432)* – ('A'-Brothers In Rhythm mix) / ('A'-Brothers In Rhythm instrumental) / ('A'-Leftfield vocal) / ('A'ext).
(12") *(74321 139424-1)* – ('A'-Hard Hands mix) / ('A'version) / ('A'-Leftfield vocal) / ('A'-dub oddity mix).
Apr 93. (cd/c/lp) *(<74321 13697-2/-4/-1>)* **BLACK TIE WHITE NOISE** [1] [39]
– The wedding / You've been around / I feel free / Black tie white noise / Jump they say / Nite flight / Pallas Athena / Miracle tonight / Don't let me down & down / Looking for Lester / I know it's gonna happen someday / The wedding song / Jump they say (alternate mix) / Lucy can't dance.
Jun 93. (7"/c-s) *(74321 14868-7/-4)* **BLACK TIE WHITE NOISE. / YOU'VE BEEN AROUND (Jack Dangers remix)** [36] [ ]
(cd-s+=) *(74321 14868-2)* – ('A'extended remix) / ('A'-Urban).
(12") *(74321 14868-1)* – ('A'extended) / ('A'trance mix) / ('A'version) / ('A'club mix with AL B.SURE!) / ('A'extended urban mix).
Oct 93. (7"/c-s) *(74321 16226-7/-4)* **MIRACLE TONIGHT. / LOOKING FOR LESTER** [40] [ ]
(cd-s+=) *(74321 16226-2)* – ('A'-Philly mix) / ('A'-Masereti mix).
(12") *(74321 16226-1)* – ('A'-Blunted mix) / ('A'-Make believe mix) / ('A'-Philly mix) / ('A'dance dub).
Nov 93. (7"/c-s) *(74321 17705-7/-4)* **BUDDHA OF SUBURBIA. / DEAD AGAINST IT** [35] [ ]
(cd-s+=) *(74321 17705-2)* – South horizon / ('A'-Lenny Kravitz rock mix).
Nov 93. (cd/c) *(74321 17004-2/-4)* **BUDDHA OF SUBURBIA (TV soundtrack)** [ ] [-]
– Buddah of suburbia / Sex and the church / South horizon / The mysteries / Bleed like a craze, dad / Strangers when we meet / Read against it / Untitled No.1 / Ian Fish / UK heir / Buddah of suburbia (featuring LENNY KRAVITZ).

— now with **ENO** – synthesizers, co-writer (on most) / **REEVES GABRELS / ERDAL KIZILCAY / MIKE GARSON / STERLING CAMPBELL / CARLOS ALOMAR / JOEY BARON / YOSSI FINE**

R.C.A. Arista

Sep 95. (c-s/cd-s) *(74321 30703-4/-2)* **THE HEARTS FILTHY LESSON / I AM WITH NAME** [35] [92]
(cd-s+=) *(74321 30703-2)* – ('A'-Bowie mix) / ('A'-Trent Reznor alt.remix) / ('A'-Tony Maserati remix).
(12"pic-d) *(74321 30703-1)* – (5-'A'mixes; Bowie / alt. / Rubber / Simple text / Filthy).
Sep 95. (cd/c/d-lp) *(<74321 30702-2/-4/-1>)* **OUTSIDE** [8] [21]
– THE NATHAN ADLER DIARIES: A Hyper Cycle:- Leon takes us outside / Outside / The hearts filthy lesson / A small plot of land / segue – Baby Grace (a horrid cassette) / Hallo spaceboy / The motel / I have not been to Oxford Town / No control / segue – Algeria touchshriek / The voyeur of utter destruction (as beauty) / segue – Ramona A. Stone – I am with name / Wishful beginnings / We prick you / segue – Nathan Adler / Strangers when we meet.
Nov 95. (7"/c-s) *(74321 32940-7/-4)* **STRANGERS WHEN WE MEET. / THE MAN WHO SOLD THE WORLD (live)** [39] [ ]
(cd-s+=) *(74321 32940-2)* – ('A'side again) / Get real.
(12") *(74321 32940-1)* – ('A'side) / The seeker / Hang ten high.
Feb 96. (7"pink/c-s) *(74321 35384-7/-4)* **HALLO SPACEBOY. / THE HEARTS FILTHY LESSON** [12] [ ]
(cd-s+=) *(74321 35384/-2)* – Moonage daydream (live) / Under pressure (live).

— below a collaboration with A GUY CALLED GERALD. His main band:- REEVES GABRELS, MIKE GARSON + ZACHARY ALFORD + GAIL ANN DORSEY – vocals

Nov 96. (12"/cd-s) *(74321 39741-1/-2)* **TELLING LIES /** [ ] [ ]
Jan 97. (12"/cd-s) *(74321 45207-1/-2)* **LITTLE WONDER. / ('A'mix) / TELLING LIES** [14] [ ]
(cd-s) *(74321 45208-2)* – ('A'mixes) / Jump they say.
Feb 97. (cd/c) *(<74321 44944-2/-4>)* **EART HL ING** [6] [39]
– Little wonder / Looking for satellites / Battle for Britain (the letter) / Seven years in Tibet / Dead man walking / Telling lies / Last thing you should do / I'm afraid of Americans / Law (earthlings on fire).
Apr 97. (12"/cd-s) *(74321 47584-1/-2)* **DEAD MAN WALKING. / TELLING LIES** [32] [ ]
(cd-s) *(74321 47585-2)* – ('A'mixes) / I'm deranged / Heart's filthy lesson.

– compilations, etc. –

Note; All below on 'RCA' unless otherwise mentioned

Mar 70. (lp; mono/stereo)(c) *Decca; (PA/SPA 58)(KCSP 58)* **THE WORLD OF DAVID BOWIE** [ ] [-]
(re-iss.Feb73)
Oct 72. (7"ep) *Pye; (7N 8002)* **DO ANYTHING YOU SAY / CAN'T HELP THINKING ABOUT ME. / I DIG EVERYTHING / I'M NOT LOSING SLEEP** [ ] [-]
May 75. (d-lp) *Decca; (DPA 3017-8) / London; <628-9>* **IMAGES 66-67** [ ] [ ]
May 75. (7") *Decca; (F 13579)* **THE LONDON BOYS. / LOVE YOU TILL TUESDAY** [ ] [-]
Mar 79. (7"ep) *E.M.I.; (EMI 2925)* **I PITY THE FOOL / TAKE MY TIP. / YOU'VE GOT A HABIT OF LEAVING / BABY LOVES THAT WAY** [ ] [-]
(re-iss.Nov82 on 'Charly'; CYM 1)
Dec 80. (lp/c) *K-Tel; (NE/+C 1111)* **THE BEST OF DAVID BOWIE** [3] [-]
Apr 81. (lp/c) *Decca; (TAB/KTAB 17)* **ANOTHER FACE** [ ] [-]
Apr 81. (lp) *(BL 43606)* **CHRISTIANE F. – WIR KINDER VOM BAHNHOF ZOO (soundtrack)** [-] [-] Europe
Jun 81. (10"m-lp/c) *P.R.T.; (DOW/ZCDOW 1)* **DON'T BE FOOLED BY THE NAME** [ ] [-]
Dec 82. (10x7"pic-d-singles) *(BOW 100)* **FASHIONS** [ ] [-]
– SPACE ODDITY / LIFE ON MARS / THE JEAN GENIE / REBEL REBEL / SOUND & VISION / DRIVE-IN SATURDAY / SORROW / GOLDEN YEARS / BOYS KEEP SWINGING / ASHES TO ASHES
Jan 83. (lp/c) *(PL/PK 45406)* **RARE** [34] [-]
Aug 83. (lp/c) *(BOW LP/K 004) <4792>* **GOLDEN YEARS (live recent)** [33] [99]
Aug 83. (lp) *Decca Rock Echoes; (TAB 71)* **A SECOND FACE** [ ] [-]
Oct 83. (d-lp/d-c) *(PL/PK 84862) <4862>* **ZIGGY STARDUST – THE MOTION PICTURE (live '73 film)** [17] [89]
(cd-iss.Sep92 on 'EMI'; CDP 780411-2)
Oct 83. (7") *(RCA 372) <13660>* **WHITE LIGHT WHITE HEAT (live). / CRACKED ACTOR (live)** [46] [ ]
Jan 84. (7") *<13769>* **1984. / TVC 15** [-] [ ]
Apr 84. (lp/c/cd) *(PL/PK/PD 84919) <4919>* **FAME AND FASHION (ALL TIME GREATEST HITS)** [40] [ ]
May 84. (lp/c) *Deram; (BOWIE/BOWMC 1)* **LOVE YOU TILL TUESDAY (soundtrack)** [53] [-]
May 85. (12"ep; by ARNOLD CORNS & THE SPIDERS FROM MARS) *Krazy Kat; (PAST 2)* **HANG ON TO YOURSELF. / LOOKING FOR A FRIEND / MAN IN THE MIDDLE** [ ] [-]
Nov 85. (d-lp/c) *Castle; (CCS LP/MC 118)* **THE COLLECTION** [ ] [-]
(cd-iss.Aug92; CCSCD 118)
Apr 86. (lp/c) *Showcase; (SHLP/SHTC 137)* **RARE TRACKS** [ ] [-]
Aug 86. (12"ep) *Archive 4; (TOF 105)* **ARCHIVE 4** [ ] [-]
– London boys / Love you till Tuesday / Laughing gnome / Maid of Bond Street.
Oct 87. (m-lp/c/cd) *P.R.T.; (PYL/PYM/PYC 6001)* **1966: DAVID BOWIE** [ ] [-]
(pic-m-lp Jun88; PYX 6001) (re-iss.Dec89 on 'Castle' lp/c/cd; CLA LP/MC/CD 154)
Jan 89. (cd) *Deram; (820 570-2)* **CHAMELEON** [ ] [-]
Sep 89. Rykodisc; <0120> **SOUND + VISION** [-] [97]
Mar 90. (c-s/7") *EMI-USA; (TC+/FAME 90)* **FAME 90 (Gass mix). / ('A'-Queen Latifah's version)** [28] [ ]
(cd-s+=) *(CDFAME 90)* – ('A'house mix) / ('A'hip hop mix).
(12") *(12FAME 90)* – ('A'side) / ('A'house) / ('A'hip hop).
(7"pic-d) *(FAMEPD 90)* – ('A'side) / ('A'-bonus beats mix).
Apr 90. (cd/c/d-lp) *E.M.I.; (CD/TC+/DBTV 1) / Rykodisc; <20171>* **CHANGESBOWIE** [1] [39]
– Space oddity / John, I'm only dancing / Changes / Ziggy stardust / Suffragette city / The Jean genie / Diamond dogs / Rebel rebel / Young Americans / Fame ('90 remix) / Golden years / Heroes / Ashes to ashes / Fashion / Let's dance / China girl / Modern love / Blue Jean.
Apr 91. (cd/c) *Rino;* **EARLY ON (1964-66)** [-] [ ]
May 93. (cd/c) *Spectrum; (550021-2/-4)* **THE GOSPEL ACCORDING TO DAVID BOWIE** [ ] [-]

Nov 93. (d-cd/d-c/t-lp) *E.M.I.; (7243 828099-2/-4/-1)* **THE SINGLES COLLECTION** [9] [ ]
(re-iss.Nov95 d-cd/d-c/t-lp; CD/TC+/EM 1512)
May 94. (cd/c/d-lp) *Trident; (GY/+MC/LP 002)* **SANTA MONICA '72 (live)** [74] [-]
Jul 95. (cd) *Trident; (GY 014)* **RARESTONEBOWIE** [ ] [-]
Mar 96. (cd/c) *Spectrum; (551706-2/-4)* **LONDON BOY** [ ] [-]
Jun 97. (d-cd) *O.T.R.; (OTR 1100048)* **EARTH CALLING ZIGGY** [ ] [-]

BOXER (see under ⇒ PATTO)

BOX OF FROGS (see under ⇒ YARDBIRDS)

BOX TOPS

Formed: Memphis, Tennessee, USA ... 1967 originally as RONNIE & THE DeVILLES. They signed to 'Bell' label offshoot 'Mala', and with the legendary DANN PENN producing, the band soon topped the US chart with their debut 45, 'THE LETTER', which subsequently became a well covered standard for many artists. Throughout the 60's, they had a large number of hits, with CHILTON virtually taking over the reins just prior to their 1969 demise. CHILTON headed back to Memphis, where he hooked up with his old schoolfriend CHRIS BELL to form the hugely influential but desperately unlucky BIG STAR. The first two albums sounded like a rougher take on the pop sensibilities of The BEATLES and The BEACH BOYS, with the 1972 debut 'NO.1 RECORD', especially, having great commercial potential. Guitarist BELL acted as a foil for CHILTON's inspired outpourings and the album contained such acoustic gems as 'BALLAD OF EL GOODOO'. Despite garnering rave reviews, the album failed to sell, due almost wholly to the distribution problems of their label 'Ardent' (a 'Stax' offshoot). BELL left at the end of '72, after a fallout with CHILTON over live work, the upshot being that BIG STAR became CHILTON's "power-pop" baby. Generally thought to be his artistic peak, 1973's 'RADIO CITY' had a gloriously raw spontaneity, with 'SEPTEMBER GURLS' proving the pained highlight. Distribution problems continued to dog Ardent and as the record stiffed, BIG STAR gradually broke-up. Although released under the BIG STAR moniker, 'BIG STAR's THE THIRD ALBUM', later re-released as 'SISTER LOVERS', was more or less the work of CHILTON. A difficult album, although none the less rewarding, it showcased a vulnerable man exorcising his demons in haunting and deeply introspective songs. CHRIS BELL's similarly downbeat 'I AM THE COSMOS', was recorded around the time of his death in a car accident in 1978, and was posthumously released by 'Rykodisc' in the early 90's. In 1979, CHILTON re-surfaced after a quiet period in New York, where his makeshift band toured with the likes of TELEVISION and The CRAMPS, whom he went on to produce. That same year saw him record the folk-punk 'BANGKOK' single and 'FLIES ON SHERBET', a cult classic which featured a hotch-potch of inspired covers and CHILTON originals. In the 80's, he worked with TAV FALCO under the name The PANTHER BURNS before releasing a solo album 'HIGH PRIEST' in 1987, a fairly enjoyable romp through a patchwork of ragged styles. The praise lavished upon BIG STAR by the likes of PRIMAL SCREAM and TEENAGE FANCLUB, brought about a renaissance of sorts, and CHILTON re-formed the band in 1993. He also released a further solo album in 1995, 'A MAN CALLED DESTRUCTION'.

Recommended: THE BEST OF THE BOX TOPS (*5) / DOCUMENT (*5 ALEX CHILTON) / RECORD RADIO CITY (*7; Big Star) / SISTER LOVERS (*8; Big Star) / I AM THE COSMOS (*8; Chris Bell)

ALEX CHILTON (b.28 Dec'50) – vocals, guitar / **JOHN EVANS** – organ / **GARY TALLEY** (b.17 Aug'47) – guitar / **BILL CUNNINGHAM** (b.23 Jan'50) – bass, piano / **DANNY SMYTHE** – drums

Stateside Mala-Bell

Sep 67. (7") *(SS 2044)* <565> **THE LETTER. / HAPPY TIMES** [5] [1] Jul67
Nov 67. (7") *(SS 2070)* <580> **NEON RAINBOW. / SHE KNOWS HOW** [ ] [24]
Jan 68. (lp; stereo/mono) *(S+/SL 10218)* <6011> **THE LETTER – NEON RAINBOW** [ ] [87] Nov67
– The letter / She knows how / Trains & boats & planes / Break my mind / A whiter shade of pale / Everything I am / Neon rainbow / People make the world / I'm your puppet / Happy times / Gonna find somebody / I pray for rain.

Bell Mala

Mar 68. (7") *(BLL 1001)* <593> **CRY LIKE A BABY. / THE DOOR YOU CLOSED ON ME** [15] [2]
Apr 68. (lp; mono/stereo) *(M/S BLL 105)* <6017> **CRY LIKE A BABY** [ ] [59]
– Cry like a baby / Deep in Kentucky / I'm the one for you / Weeping Analeah / Every time / Fields of clover / Trouble with Sam / Lost / Good morning dear / 727 / You keep me hanging on / The door you closed to me.
May 68. (7") *(BLL 1017)* <12005> **CHOO CHOO TRAIN. / FIELDS OF CLOVER** [ ] [26]

— **RICK ALLEN** (b.28 Jan'46, Little Rock, Arkansas) – organ, drums repl. EVANS **TOM BOGGS** (b.16 Jul'47, Wynn, Arkansas) – drums repl. SMYTHE (both return to college)

Sep 68. (7") *(BLL 1035)* <12017> **I MET HER IN CHURCH. / PEOPLE GONNA TALK** [ ] [37]
Oct 68. (lp; mono/stereo) *(M/S BLL 108)* <6023> **NON-STOP** [ ] [ ]
– Choo choo train / I'm movin' on / Sandman / She shot a hole in my soul / People gonna talk / I met her in church / Rock me baby / Rollin' in my sleep / I can dig it / Yesterday / Where's my mind / If I had let you in.
Dec 68. (lp) <6025> **SUPER HITS** (compilation) [-] [45]
– The letter / Trains & boats & planes / Break my mind / A whiter shade of pale / She sot a hole in my soul / Neon rainbow / Cry like a baby / I'm your puppet / I met her in church / You keep me hanging on / Choo choo train. *(UK-iss.1970 mono/stereo; M/S BLL 129)*
Jan 69. (7") *(BLL 1045)* <12035> **SWEET CREAM LADIES, FORWARD MARCH. / SANDMAN** [ ] [28] Dec68
Mar 69. (7") *(BLL 1063)* <12038> **I SHALL BE RELEASED. / I MUST BE THE DEVIL** [ ] [67]

— **JERRY RILEY** – guitar repl. TALLEY

Jul 69. (7") *(BLL 1068)* <12040> **SOUL DEEP. / HAPPY SONG** [22] [18]
Oct 69. (7") *(BLL 1084)* <12042> **TURN ON A DREAM. / TOGETHER** [ ] [58]
Oct 69. (lp) *(SBLL 120)* <6032> **DIMENSIONS** [ ] [77] Sep69
– Soul deep / I shall be released / Midnight angel / Together / I'll hold out my hand / I must be the Devil / Sweet cream ladies, forward march / The happy song / Ain't no way / Rock me baby.
Jul 70. (7") *(BLL 1097)* <865> **YOU KEEP TIGHTENING UP ON ME. / COME ON HONEY** [ ] [92] Mar70

— CHILTON (now the only original member), ALLEN, BOGGS and RILEY brought in **SWAIN SCHAEFER** – piano / **HAROLD CLOUD** – bass (both) repl. CUNNINGHAM

Sep 71. (lp) *(BELLS 149)* **BOX TOPS** [ ] [-]
– The letter / Cry like a baby / Soul deep / I'm movin' on / Lost / A whiter shade of pale / Together / The happy song / Fields of clover / Weeping Analeah / I'll hold out my hand / I pray for rain.

– UK compilations etc. –

Jan 73. (7") *London; (HLU 10402)* **SUGAR CREEK WOMAN. / IT'S ALL OVER** [ ] [-]
Jun 74. (lp) *Sound Superb; (SPR 90051)* **THE BEST OF THE BOX TOPS** [ ] [-]
May 78. (7") *Stiff; (BUY 28)* **CRY LIKE A BABY. / THE LETTER** [ ] [-]
Mar 82. (7") *J.B.; (JB 04)* **THE LETTER. / CRY LIKE A BABY** [ ] [-]
Jul 82. (7") *Old Gold; (OG 9116)* **THE LETTER. / CRY LIKE A BABY** [ ] [-]
Aug 82. (7"m) *Creole; (CR 178)* **THE LETTER. / (2 tracks by other artists)** [ ] [-]
Aug 82. (7"m) *Creole; (CR 179)* **CRY LIKE A BABY. / (2 tracks by other artists)** [ ] [-]
1988. (cd) *Warner Super Savers; (WSP 27611)* **THE ULTIMATE BOX TOPS** [ ] [-]
Nov 88. (lp) *Decal; (LIK 41)* **THE BEST OF THE BOX TOPS featuring ALEX CHILTON** [ ] [-]
– The letter / Neon rainbow / I pray for rain / The door you closed to me / Cry like a baby / Deep in Kentucky / Fields of clover / You keep me hangin' on / Choo choo train / I can dig it / Yesterday where's my mind / Soul deep / I shall be released / Together / I must be the Devil / Sweet cream ladies, forward march / Happy song.
Jun 89. Arista; (cd-ep) *(162071)* **THE LETTER / HAPPY TIMES / CRY LIKE A BABY / THE DOOR YOU CLOSED ON ME** [ ] [-]

BIG STAR

were formed in 1971 by singer/ songwriter/ guitarist **CHRIS BELL** (b.12 Jan'51, Memphis) plus **ALEX CHILTON / ANDY HUMMEL** (b.26 Jan'51) – bass / **JODY STEPHENS** (b. 4 Oct'52) – drums

not issued Ardent

Apr 72. (lp) <*ADS 1501*> **#1 RECORD** [-] [ ]
– Feel / The ballad of El Goodo / In the street / Don't lie to me / Thirteen / The India song / When my baby's beside me / My life is right / Give me another chance / Try again / Watch the sunrise / St 100-6. *(re-iss.Nov86 & Jan90 on 'Big Beat' lp/c; WIK/+C 53)*
Apr 72. (7") <2902> **IN THE STREET. / WHEN MY BABY'S BESIDE ME** [-] [ ]
Jul 72. (7") <2904> **DON'T LIE TO ME. / WATCH THE SUNRISE** [-] [ ]

— now trio when BELL left to go solo, He's killed in car crash 27th Dec'78.

Feb 74. (lp) <*ADS 2803*> **RADIO CITY** [-] [ ]
– O, my soul / Life is white / Way out west / What's going on / You got what you deserve / Mod Lang / Back of a car / Daisy glaze / She's a mover / September gurls / Morpha too – I'm in love with a girl. *(re-iss.Nov86 & Mar95 on 'Big Beat' lp/c; WIK/+C 54)*
Feb 74. (7") <2909> **O, MY SOUL. / MORPHATOO – I'M IN LOVE WITH A GIRL** [-] [ ]
May 74. (7") <2912> **SEPTEMBER GIRLS. / MOD LANG** [-] [ ]
(UK-iss.Sep78 on 'Stax'; *STAX 504)*
1974. (7"; as BOX TOPS) <0199> **WILLOBEE AND DALE. / I'M GONNA BE ALRIGHT** [-] [ ]

— ALEX CHILTON now sole BIG STAR with session people, incl. STEPHENS + STEVE CROPPER. In 1975, after recording below album, they disbanded. It was finally released.

Aura P.V.C.

Jul 78. (lp) *(AUL 703)* <7903> **BIG STAR'S THE THIRD ALBUM** [ ] [ ]
– Stroke it Noel / For you / Kizza me / You can't have me / Nightime / Blue moon / Take care / Jesus Christ / Femme fatale / O Dana / Big black car / Holocaust / Kangaroo / Thank you friends. *(re-iss.1987 on 'Dojo' lp/cd; DOJO LP/CD 55) <US re-iss.Nov87 lp/c/cd; PVC/+C/CD 8917> (UK cd-iss.Mar92 & Apr97 on 'Rykodisc'; RCD 10220) (cd re-iss.Oct94 on 'Line'; LICD 900492)*
Jul 78. (7") *(AUS 103)* **KIZZA ME. / DREAM LOVER** [ ] [-]
Dec 78. (7") *(AUS 107)* **JESUS CHRIST. / BIG BLACK CAR** [ ] [-]

– (BIG STAR) compilations etc. –

Jul 78. (d-lp) *Stax; (SXSP 302)* **£1 RECORD / RADIO CITY** [ ] [ ]
(cd-iss.Jun87 & Jan90 on 'Big Beat'; CDWIK 910)– (omits; In the street / St 100-6.
1988. (lp) *Line; (LILP 400509)* **BIG STAR'S BIGGEST** [-] [-] German
– The ballad of El Goodo / In the street / Don't lie to me / When my baby's beside me / Try again / Watch the sunrise / Life is white / What's goin' ahn / Back of a car / She's a mover / Way out west / September gurls / Jesus Christ / O'Dana / Holocaust / Kangaroo / Big black car / Thank you friends. *(UK cd-iss.Oct94; LICD 900509)*
Mar 92. Rykodisc; (cd) *(RCD 10221)* **LIVE** [ ] [-]
(re-iss.Apr97; same)

ALEX CHILTON

went solo in 1977, with **RICHARD ROSEBROUGH** – drums / etc.

not issued / Ork

1977. (lp) <81978> **ONE DAY IN NEW YORK**
1977. (12"ep) **SINGER NOT THE SONG**

Aura / Peabody

Feb 80. (lp) *(AUL 710)* **LIKE FLIES ON SHERBET**
– Boogie shoes / My rival / Hey! little child / Hook or crook / I've had it / Rock hard / Girl after girl / Waltz across Texas / Alligator man / Like flies on sherbet. *(cd-iss.Sep92 on 'Great Expectations'+=;)*– No more the Moon shines on Lorena. *(cd re-iss.Oct94 on 'Line'; LICD 900486) (cd re-iss.Jan96 on 'Cooking Vinyl'; COOKCD 095)*

Jun 80. (7") *(AUS 117)* **HEY! LITTLE CHILD. / NO MORE THE MOON SHINES ON LORENA**

— with **KNOX** – guitar / **MATTHEW SELIGMAN** – bass + **MORRIS WINDSOR** – drums

Line / not issued

1981. Line; (lp) <OLLP 5081> **BACH'S BOTTOM** (rec.1975) German
– Take me home / Make me like it / Everytime I close my eyes / All of the time / Oh baby I'm free / I'm so tired (parts 1 & 2) / Free again / Jesus Christ / The singer not the song / Summertime blues / Take me home again. *(cd-iss.Nov87; LICD 900091) (cd re-iss.Mar97 on 'Razor & Tie'; RE 2010)*

Jan 83. (lp) *(OLLP 5264)* **LIVE IN LONDON (live)**
– Bangkok / Tramp / In the street / Hey little child / Nightime / Rock hard / Alligator man / The letter / Train kept a rollin' / Kanga roo / My rival / Stranded on a dateless night / September gurls / No more the Moon shines on Lorena. *(cd-iss.May93 on 'Rev-Ola'; CREV 015CD)*

New Rose / Big Time

Jul 85. (lp) *(ROSE 68)* **FEUDALIST TARTS** France
(cd-iss.1986 as 'STUFF'; ROSE 68CD)– (with 10 extra tracks).

May 86. (7") *(NEW 068)* **NO SEX. / UNDERCRASS** France
(12"+=) *(NEW12 068)* – Wild kingdom.
(d7"+=) *(NEW 69)* – September gurls / I'm gonna make you mine (live Paris'85).

Nov 87. (7") *(NEW 96)* **MAKE A LITTLE MOVE. / LONELY WEEKENDS** France

Nov 87. (lp/c/cd) *(ROSE 130/+C/CD)* **HIGH PRIEST** France
– Take it off / Let me get close to you / Dalai Lama * / Volare / Thing for you / Forbidden love / Make a little love / Trouble don't last / Don't be a drag / Nobody's fool / Come by here / Raunchy / Junkyard * / Lonely weekends / Margie * / Rubber room *. *(cd+= *)*

Feb 88. (d7"-ltd) *(NEW 102)* **DALAI LAMA. / MARGIE / / JUNKYARD. / RUBBER ROOM** France

Jan 90. (m-lp/cd) *(ROSE 194/+CD)* **BLACKLIST** France
– Little GTO / Guantanamerika / Jailbait / Baby baby baby / Nice and easy does it / I will turn your money green.

(above cont.some covers). In 1992 CHILTON resurrected BIG STAR (see below).

New Rose / Ardent

Feb 94. (cd) **CLICHES**

Ruf

Jun 95. (cd) *(RRCD 90131-2)* **A MAN CALLED DESTRUCTION**

Shoeshine / not issued

Oct 96. (7") *(SHOE 005)* **MARGIE. /**

– (ALEX CHILTON) compilations etc. –

Sep 85. (lp/cd) *Aura;* **DOCUMENT**
– Kizza me / Downs / Holocaust / Big black car / Kangaroo / Dream lover / My rival / Hey little child / Hook or crook / Like flies on sherbet / Bangkok / September gurls / In the street.

Mar 86. (d-lp) *Fan Club; (FC 015)* **LOST DECADE (1969-77)** France
May 91. (cd) *Rhino;* **19 YEARS (1969-87)**
Feb 92. New Rose; (cd) **ALEX CHILTON**
Mar 96. (cd) *Rev-ola; (CREV 044CD)* **1970**
Mar 97. (cd) *Razor & Tie; (RE 2032)* **FEUDALISTIC TARTS / NO SEX**
Mar 97. (cd) *Razor & Tie; (RE 2033)* **HIGH PRIEST / BLACKLIST**
May 97. (d-cd) *Arcade; (302108-2)* **TOP 30**

BIG STAR

re-formation with **CHILTON / JONATHAN BAUER** – guitar, vocals / **KEN STRINGFELLOW** – guitar, bass

Zoo / Zoo

Sep 93. (cd/c) **LIVE AT MISSOURI UNIVERSITY (4.25.93) (live)**
– In the street / Don't lie to me / When my baby's beside me / I am the cosmos / The ballad of El Goodo / Back of a car / Way out west / Daisy glaze / Baby strange / For you / Fool / September gurls / Thank you friends / Slut / Jeepster.

— CHILTON teamed up with VEGA (from SUICIDE) and BEN VAUGHN on album 'CUBIST BLUES' for 'Last Call'; (7422466)

BRAINBOX (see under ⇒ FOCUS)

BRINSLEY SCHWARZ

Formed: Turnbridge Wells, England . . . 1965 as the beat/psychedelic combo KIPPINGTON LODGE by SCHWARZ and NICK LOWE. After 5 flop singles between '67 & '69 (the first 'SHY BOY', should have been a hit), they renamed themselves in Autumn '69. They came under the wing of DAVID ROBINSON, former tour manager for JIMI HENDRIX, who now headed the Famepushers Agency. On 3rd April '70, he chartered a plane to fly 150 music journalists to New York to see them support VAN MORRISON at East Fillmore. This proved to be a six-figure sum disaster, due to an admittedly dodgy performance. Predictably, the press ignored their debut album for 'United Artists' and not surprisingly it bombed. Unbowed, they went off to take stock and write new material, resurfacing late in the year with follow-up 'DESPITE IT ALL'. The preceding single 'COUNTRY GIRL' was reminiscent of 'SWEETHEART OF THE RODEO'-era BYRDS and was as fine an example of country-rock as anything coming out of America at the time. Pioneers of the genre in the UK, the band went on to experiment with many other areas of American roots music, evidenced on their 1972 album, 'NERVOUS ON THE ROAD'. Their interest in the "down home" sound had deepened upon seeing American bar band EGGS OVER EASY playing at the Tally Ho club in London. The venue had become a focus for the burgeoning "pub rock" scene of which The BRINSLEY'S would soon be such an integral part, along with acts such as BEES MAKE HONEY and DUCKS DELUXE. As well as digging the band's R&B boogie, BRINSLEY SCHWARZ were heavily influenced by EGGS OVER EASY's freewheeling attitude which didn't give a fig for the banks of Marshall stacks and sprawling concept albums which were de rigeur in the early 70's. The same back to basics spirit that inspired the BRINSLEY's to scale down the length of their songs and cut their hair, laid the foundations for the punk explosion later in the decade as well as breaking such important figures as ELVIS COSTELLO and JOE STRUMMER (101'ERS). For the moment though, the band had found a comfortable niche and the track 'HAPPY WHAT WE'RE DOING', from the 'NERVOUS ON THE ROAD' set seemed to confirm this. Another two excellent albums followed, showcasing LOWE's comprehensive songwriting talent on such classic tracks as '(WHAT'S SO FUNNY 'BOUT) PEACE, LOVE AND UNDERSTANDING'. Ironically, no commercial breakthrough came and the band split amicably in 1975, with NICK LOWE going on to a successful solo career, while BRINSLEY and keyboard player BOB ANDREWS helped to form The RUMOUR (GRAHAM PARKER's backing band). • **Covered:** (The Beatles') I SHOULD HAVE KNOWN BETTER. / TELL ME WHY as 'The LIMELIGHT' in '75. • **Trivia:** In 1974, they were featured as The ELECTRICIANS (with DAVE EDMUNDS; their sometimes producer) in the film 'Stardust'.

Recommended: SURRENDER TO THE RHYTHM (THE BEST OF . . .) (*7)

KIPPINGTON LODGE

BRINSLEY SCHWARZ – guitar, sax / **NICK LOWE** (b.25 Mar'49, Woodbridge, England) – vocals, bass / **BARRY LANDERMAN** – organ / **PETE WHALE** – drums

Parlophone / Capitol

Oct 67. (7") *(R 5645)* **SHY BOY. / LADY ON A BICYCLE**
Mar 68. (7") *(R 5677)* <2236> **RUMOURS. / AND SHE CRIED**
(above 4 tracks re-iss.Nov78.7"ep on 'EMI')

— **BOB ANDREWS** (b.20 Jun'49) – organ, vox repl. BARRY to VANITY FARE

Aug 68. (7") *(R 5717)* **TELL ME A STORY. / UNDERSTAND A WOMAN**
Dec 68. (7") *(R 5750)* **TOMORROW TODAY. / TURN OUT THE LIGHT**
May 69. (7") *(R 5776)* **IN MY LIFE. / I CAN SEE HER FACE**

BRINSLEY SCHWARZ

(BRINSLEY, NICK and BOB) recruited **BILLY RANKIN** – drums to repl. PETE

U.A. / Capitol

Apr 70. (lp) *(UAS 29111)* <SWBC 11869> **BRINSLEY SCHWARZ**
– Hymn to me / Shining brightly / Rock & roll women / Lady constant / What do you suggest / Mayfly / Ballad of a has-been beauty queen. *(cd-iss.Feb94 on 'Repertoire'; REP 4421WY)*

May 70. (7") *(UP 35118)* **SHINING BRIGHTLY. / WHAT DO YOU SUGGEST**
Jun 70. (7") <3004> **HYMN TO ME. / ROCK & ROLL WOMAN**

Liberty / not issued

Nov 70. (7") *(LBY 15419)* **COUNTRY GIRL. / FUNK ANGEL**
(re-iss.1972 on 'United Artists'; UP 35312)

Dec 70. (lp) *(LBG 83427)* **DESPITE IT ALL**
– Country girl / The slow one / Funk angel / Piece of home / Love song / Starship / Ebury down / Old Jarrow.

— added **IAN GOMM** (b.17 Mar'47) – guitar, vocals

U.A. / U.A.

Oct 71. (lp) *(UAS 29217)* <5566> **SILVER PISTOL**
– Dry land / Merry go round / One more day / Nightingale / Silver pistol / The last time I was fooled / Unknown number / Range war / Egypt / Niki Hoeke speedway / Ju ju man / Rockin' chair. *(re-iss.Apr86 on 'Edsel'; ED 190) (cd-iss.Sep90; EDCD 190)*

Jan 72. (7") <50915> **SILVER PISTOL. / NIGHTINGALE**

— Contributed 5 tracks to 'GREASY TRUCKERS' live lp, Apr72.

Sep 72. (lp) *(UAS 29374)* <5647> **NERVOUS ON THE ROAD**
– It's been so long / Happy doing what we're doing / Surrender to the rhythm / Don't lose your grip on love / Nervous on the road (but can't stay at home) / Feel a little funky / I like it like that / Brand new you, brand new me / Home in my hand / Why, why, why, why, why. *(re-iss.Dec80 on 'Liberty'; LBR 1040) (cd-iss.Oct95 on 'Beat Goes On'; BGOCD 289)*

Oct 72. (7") <50976> **NERVOUS ON THE ROAD. / HARRY DOING WHAT WE'RE DOING**
May 73. (7"; as The HITTERS) *(UP 35530)* **THE HYPOCRITE. / THE VERSION**
Aug 73. (7") *(UP 35588)* **SPEEDO. / I WORRY**
Oct 73. (lp) *(UAS 29489)* **PLEASE DON'T EVER CHANGE**
– Hooked on love / Why do we hurt the one we love? / I worry ('bout you baby) / Don't ever change / Home in my hand / Play that fast thing (one more time) / I won't make it without you / Down in Mexico / Speedo / Hypocrite (the version). *(re-iss.Jan88 on 'Edsel'; ED 237) (cd-iss.Sep90; EDCD 237)*

Mar 74. (7") *(UP 35642)* **I'VE CRIED MY LAST TEAR. / (IT'S GONNA BE A) BRINGDOWN**
May 74. (7") *(UP 35700)* **(WHAT'S SO FUNNY 'BOUT) PEACE, LOVE AND UNDERSTANDING. / EVER SINCE YOU'RE GONE**
Jul 74. (lp) *(UAS 29641)* **THE NEW FAVOURITES OF BRINSLEY SCHWARZ**

– Peace, love and understanding / Ever since you're gone / Ugly things / I got the real thing / Look what's in your eye tonight / Now's the time / Small town, big city / Trying to live my life without you / I like you I don't love you / Down in the dive. *(re-iss.Aug80 on 'Liberty'; LBR 1033)*

Jan 75. (7") *(UP 35768)* **I LIKE YOU, I DON'T LOVE YOU. / EVERYBODY** [ ] [-]
Jan 75. (7"; as LIMELIGHT) *(UP 35779)* **I SHOULD HAVE KNOWN BETTER. / TELL ME WHY** [ ] [-]
Mar 75. (7") *(UP 35812)* **THERE'S A CLOUD IN MY HEART. / I GOT THE REAL THING** [ ] [-]

— Disbanded Mar75. SCHWARZ and RANKIN joined DUCKS DELUXE, The former later joining with ANDREWS in GRAHAM PARKER & THE RUMOUR. IAN GOMM later went solo, as did NICK LOWE.

– compilations, others, etc. –

on 'United Artists' unless mentioned otherwise

Mar 74. (lp) *(USP 101)* **ORIGINAL GOLDEN GREATS** [ ] [-]
Jun 76. (7"m) *(UP 36409)* **COUNTRY GIRL. / HOOKED ON LOVE / SURRENDER TO THE RHYTHM** [ ] [-]
Jul 78. (lp) *(UAK 30177)* **FIFTEEN THOUGHTS OF BRINSLEY SCHWARZ** [ ] [-]
Sep 78. (7") *(UP 36466)* **PEACE, LOVE AND UNDERSTANDING. / I'VE CRIED MY LAST TEAR** [ ] [-]
1978. (7"ep; by KIPPINGTON LODGE) *E.M.I.; (NUT 2894)* **KIPPINGTON LODGE** [ ] [-]
May 88. (lp/c)(cd on 'Charly') *Decal; (LIK/TCLIK 22)(CDCHARLY 22)* **IT'S ALL OVER NOW** [ ] [-]
Jul 91. (cd/c/lp) *E.M.I.; (CD/TC+/EMS 1407)* **SURRENDER TO THE RHYTHM (THE BEST OF BRINSLEY SCHWARZ)** [ ] [-]
– Country girl / Surrender to the rhythm / Ugly things / Happy what we're doing / The look what's in your eyes / Last time I was fooled / Silver pistol / Nightingale / Hypocrite / Trying to live my life without you / I like it like that / Nervous on the road / Down in Mexico / I worry ('bout you baby) / Play that fast thing (one more time) / Don't lose your grip on love / Ju Ju man / Down in the dive / Home in my hand.
Jul 94. (cd) *Beat Goes On; (BGOCD 239)* **BRINSLEY SCHWARZ / DESPITE IT ALL** [ ] [-]
Dec 95. (cd) *Beat Goes On; (BGOCD 289)* **NERVOUS ON THE ROAD / THE NEW FAVOURITES OF . . .** [ ] [-]

Dave BROCK (see under ⇒ HAWKWIND)

Edgar BROUGHTON BAND

Formed: Warwick, England . . . 1968 by EDGAR and his brother STEVE. They moved to London in 1970, having already signed to 'Harvest'. After the 1969 album, 'WASA WASA', chart success ensued with the anthemic 'OUT DEMONS OUT' (a FUGS cover). The band's HAWKWIND-style hippie-metal was perfectly suited to the burgeoning free festival circuit, although this didn't always translate well to vinyl. Nevertheless, they still managed two Top 30 albums and a popular minor hit, 'APACHE DROPOUT', which fused the famous SHADOWS hit with a more obscure CAPTAIN BEEFHEART number. The remainder of the 70's was largely taken up by managerial and record company disagreements, although some patchy albums did surface. • **Trivia:** STEVE BROUGHTON drummed on MIKE OLDFIELD's 'Tubular Bells'.

Recommended: AS WAS – THE BEST OF THE EDGAR BROUGHTON BAND (*6)

EDGAR BROUGHTON (b. ROBERT EDGAR BROUGHTON, 24 Oct'47) – vocals, guitar / **STEVE BROUGHTON** (b.20 May'50) – drums / **ARTHUR GRANT** (b.14 May'50) – bass, vocals / **VICTOR UNITT** (b. 5 Jul'46) – guitar

Harvest | not issued

Jun 69. (7") *(HAR 5001)* **EVIL. / DEATH OF AN ELECTRIC CITIZEN** [ ] [-]
Jul 69. (lp) *(SHVL 757)* **WASA WASA** [ ] [-]
– Death of an electric citizen / American boy soldier / Why can't somebody love me / Neptune / Evil / Crying / Love in the rain / Dawn crept away. *(cd-iss.Mar92 on 'Beat Goes On'; BGOCD 129)*

— Became a trio early in 1970 when VICTOR joined The PRETTY THINGS

Mar 70. (7") *(HAR 5015)* **OUT DEMONS OUT. / MOMMA'S REWARD** [39] [-]
May 70. (7") *(HAR 5021)* **UP YOURS!. / OFFICER DAN** [ ] [-]
Jun 70. (lp) *(SHVL 772)* **SING BROTHER SING** [18] [-]
– There's no vibrations but wait / The moth; (a) The moth, (b) People, (c) Peter / Momma's reward (keep them freaks a-rollin') / Refugee / Officer Dan / Old Gopher / Aphrodite / Granma / The psychopath; (a) The psychopath, (b) Is for butterflies / It's falling away. *(re-iss.Jan89 on 'Beat Goes On'; BGOLP 7) (cd-iss.May92; BGOCD 7)*

— **VICTOR UNITT** – guitar, vocals returned.

Nov 70. (7") *(HAR 5032)* **APACHE DROPOUT. / FREEDOM** [33] [-]
May 71. (lp) *(SHVL 791)* **THE EDGAR BROUGHTON BAND** [28] [-]
– Evening over rooftops / The birth / Piece of my own / Poppy / Don't even know which day it is / House of turnabout / Madhatter / Getting hard / What is a woman for / Thinking of you / For Dr.Spock (parts 1 & 2). *(cd-iss.Mar94 on 'Repertoire';)*
Jun 71. (7") *(HAR 5040)* **HOTEL ROOM. / CALL ME A LIAR** [ ] [-]
Mar 72. (7") *(HAR 5049)* **GONE BLUE / SOMEONE. / MR. CROSBY** [ ] [-]
Jul 72. (lp) *(SHTC 252)* **IN SIDE OUT** [ ] [-]
– Get out of bed / There's nobody there / Side by side / Sister Angela / I got mad / They took it away / Homes fit for heroes / Gone blue / Chilly morning momma / The rake / Totin' this guitar / Double agent / It's not you / Rock and roll. *(re-iss.Sep89 on 'Beat Goes On';) (cd-iss.Apr94 on 'Repertoire';)*
May 73. (lp) *(SHVL 810)* **OORA** [ ] [-]
– Hurricane man – Rock'n'roller / Roccococooler / Eviction / Oh you crazy noy! / Things on my mind / Exhibits from a new museum – Green lights / Face from a window – Pretty – Hijack boogie – Slow down / Capers. *(cd-iss.Sep91 on 'Beat Goes On'; BGOCD 114)*

— **JOHN THOMAS** – guitar repl. UNITT

NEMS | not issued

May 76. (lp) *(NEL 6006)* **BANDAGES** [ ] [-]
– Get arise / Speak down the wires / John Wayne / The whale / Germany / Love gang / One to seven / Lady life / Signal injector / Fruehling flowers / I want to lie. *(cd-iss.May92 on 'Castle'; CLACD 261)*

— added **TERRY COTTAM** – guitar, vocals

— Disbanded Nov'76, after recording below album

B.B. | not issued

1979. (lp) *(201009)* **LIVE HITS HARDER (live)** [-] [-] China
– There's nobody there / Love in the rain / One to seven / Hotel room / Evening over rooftops / Freedom / Poppy / Signal injector / Smokestack. *(UK-iss.Dec95 on 'C.T.E.' cd/c; 08/00 84948906)*

The BROUGHTONS

were formed by **EDGAR & STEVE** plus **ARTHUR GRANT** – bass / **RICHARD DeBASTION** – keyboards / **TOM NORDEN** – guitar / **PETE TOLSEN** – guitar

Infinity | not issued

Oct 79. (lp) *(INS 3027)* **PARLEZ-VOUS ENGLISH?** [ ] [-]
– Little one / Waiting for you / Drivin' to nowhere / Meglamaster / Didecoi / April in England / Revelations one / Anthem / Down in the jungle / Ventasong / Young boys / All I want to be.
Oct 79. (7") *(INT 597)* **LITTLE ONE. / DOWN IN THE JUNGLE** [ ] [-]

Harvest | not issued

Jan 80. (7") *(HAR 5199)* **ALL I WANT TO BE. / MEGLAMASTER** [ ] [-]

— The BROUGHTONS were once again a trio, plus **NORDEN + DENNIS HAINES** – keyboards

Sheet | not issued

Mar 82. (7") *(BULL 2)* **GOODBYE ANCIENT HOMELAND. / DO YOU WANNA BE IMMORTAL / LAST ELECTIONEER** [ ] [-]
Jun 82. (lp) *(SHEET 2)* **SUPERCHIP** [ ] [-]
– Metal Sunday / Superchip / Who only fade away / Curtain / Outrageous bahaviour / Not so funny farm / Night hogs / Pratfall / OD 476600/1162/11180 / Do you wanna be immortal / Subway information / The last electioneer / Goodbye ancient homeland / Innocent bystanders. *(cd-iss.1996 on 'See For Miles'+=; SEECD 464)*– The virus.

— EDGAR became a youth worker, until Spring '89 when he re-formed band with **STEVE** – drums / **ARTHUR GRANT** – guitar / **ANDREW BRISTOW** – bass

– compilations, others, etc. –

on 'Harvest' unless mentioned otherwise

Apr 75. (lp) *(SHSM 2001)* **A BUNCH OF 45's** [ ] [ ]
Apr 86. (lp/c) *E.M.I.; (EMS/TCEMS 1122)* **OUT DEMONS OUT – THE BEST OF THE EDGAR BROUGHTON BAND** [ ] [-]
Sep 88. (cd) *E.M.I.; (CDP 790963-2)* **AS WAS – THE BEST OF EDGAR BROUGHTON BAND** [ ] [-]
– Out demons out / Love in the rain / Green lights / Sister Angela / I got mad / Hotel room / Thinking of you / For Dr.Spock (part 2) / American boy soldier / Call me a liar / Roccocoooler / Evening over rooftops / Momma's reward (keep them freaks a rollin') / Refugee / Evil / House of turnabout / Up yours / Apache drop out / Homes fit for heroes / Things on my mind.
Nov 92. (cd) *Connoisseur; (CSAPCD 109)* **DOCUMENT SERIES PRESENTS . . . CLASSIC ALBUM & SINGLE TRACKS 1969-1973** [ ] [-]
May 93. (cd) *Beat Goes On; (BGOCD 179)* **EDGAR BROUGHTON BAND / IN SIDE OUT** [ ] [-]

Arthur BROWN

Born: ARTHUR WILTON, 24 Jun'44, Whitby, Yorkshire, England. In 1965, ARTHUR made his debut recording with The DIAMONDS, on a free Reading University flexi-disc; 'YOU DON'T KNOW'. Two years later, he formed The CRAZY WORLD OF ARTHUR BROWN together with VINCENT CRANE and DRACHEN THEAKER. After gigs at the pivotal UFO Club in London, they signed to 'Track' records. Their 2nd outing for the label, the CRANE-composed 'FIRE', set the charts alight, hitting No.1 on the 14th of August 1968. The single's success was largely down to a Top Of The Pops appearance in which ARTHUR took shock-rock to bizarre new heights, his helmeted head theatrically ablaze as the stunned audience stood with jaws agape in bewilderment. The record also hit the US Top 3, the disappointing parent album (which included a cover of SCREAMIN' JAY HAWKINS' 'I PUT A SPELL ON YOU') cited as the reason BROWN became a one-hit-wonder. In the early 70's BROWN incorporated the use of a drum machine (said to be first ever rock group to use one), as his KINGDOM COME tried in vain to recreate earlier glories. In 1974, he returned with a solo album, 'DANCE', which featured a fair version of The ANIMALS' 'WE GOTTA GET OUT OF THIS PLACE'. Twenty years on, BROWN was stll touting his madcap act around the country, releasing a live cd, 'ORDER FROM CHAOS' (1994).

Recommended: THE CRAZY WORLD OF ARTHUR BROWN (*5)

The CRAZY WORLD OF ARTHUR BROWN

ARTHUR BROWN – vocals with **VINCENT CRANE** – keyboards / **DRACHEN THEAKER** – drums (JON HISEMAN – on below 'A' side)

Track | Atlantic

Sep 67. (7") *(604008)* **DEVIL'S GRIP. / GIVE HIM A FLOWER** [ ] [ ]

— added **SEAN NICHOLAS** (aka NICK GREENWOOD) – bass (on tour)

Jun 68. (7") *(604022)* <2556> **FIRE. / REST CURE** [1] [2] Sep68
(re-iss.Nov74; 2094 017) (re-iss.Jul84 on 'Old Gold'; OG 9427)

— (below used session drummers AYNSLEY DUNBAR, JOHN MARSHALL or

PAUL JONES)

Jun 68. (lp) *(612005)* *<8198>* **THE CRAZY WORLD OF ARTHUR BROWN** [2] [7] Sep68
– Prelude – nightmare / Fanfare – fire poem / Fire / Come and buy / Time / I put a spell on you / Spontaneous / Apple creation / Rest cure / I've got money / Child of my kingdom. *(re-iss.Nov70 as 'BACKTRACK'; 2407 012) (cd-iss.Feb91 on 'Polydor'; 833736-2)*

— **JEFF CUTLER** – drums repl. THEAKER / **DICK HENNINGHAM** – organ repl. CRANE

— (Jul68) **BROWN and GREENWOOD** recruited **CARL PALMER** – drums repl. CUTLER

PETE SOLLEY – keyboards repl. HENNINGHAM

— (Oct68) **VINCENT CRANE** – organ returned to repl. SOLLEY

Nov 68. (7") *(604026)* **NIGHTMARE. / WHAT'S HAPPENING** [ ] [ ]

— **JOHN MARSHALL** – drums repl. PALMER who formed ATOMIC ROOSTER: **McCULLOCH** – keyboards repl. CRANE who formed ATOMIC ROOSTER / **DENNIS TAYLOR** – bass repl. GREENWOOD / **ARTHUR BROWN** went solo for a while with GEORGE KHAN, BUTCH POTTER and JOHN MITCHELL in session. Recorded as "The PUDDLETOWN EXPRESS" and "RUSTIC HINGE" (see further on)

KINGDOM COME

ARTHUR BROWN – vocals / **ANDY DALBY** – guitar / **MICHAEL HARRIS** – keyboards / **PHIL SHUTT** – bass / **MARTIN STEER** – drums

Polydor Polydor

Sep 71. (7") *(2001 234)* **GENERAL MESSENGER. / I D SIDE TO BE B-SIDE THE C-SIDE** [ ] [ ]

Oct 71. (lp) *(2310 130)* **GALACTIC ZOO DOSSIER** [ ] [-]
– General messenger / Space plucks / Galactic zoo / Metal monster / Simple man / Night of the pigs / Sunrise / Trouble / Brains / Creep / Creation / Gypsy escape / No time. *(cd-iss.Apr93 on 'Voiceprint'+=; VP 135CD)*

Oct 72. (lp) *(2310 178)* **ARTHUR BROWN'S KINGDOM COME** [ ] [ ]
– The teacher / A scientific experiment (featuring Lower colonic irrigation) / The whirlpool / The hymn / Water / City melody / Traffic light song / Love is (the spirit that will never die). *(cd-iss.Apr93 on 'Voiceprint'; VP 136CD)*

— **VICTOR PERAINO** – keyboards, synthesizer repl. HARRIS / **TONY UTER** – percussion repl. STEER

Polydor Passport

Jan 73. (7") *(2001 416)* **SPIRIT OF JOY. / COME ALIVE** [ ] [ ]

Apr 73. (lp) *(2310 254)* *<98003>* **JOURNEY** [ ] [ ]
– Time captives / Triangles / Gypsy / Superficial roadblocks; (a) Lost time, (b) Superficial roadblocks, (c) Corpora supercelestia / Conception / Spirit of joy / Come alive. *(cd-iss.Apr93 on 'Voiceprint'; VP 137CD) (cd re-iss.Mar97 on 'Blueprint'; BP 137CD)*

ARTHUR BROWN

— solo with loads of session people, incl. ANDY DALBY

Gull Gull

Sep 74. (7") *(GULS 4)* **GYPSIES. / DANCE** [ ] [-]

Sep 74. (lp) *(GULP 1008)* *<6-405>* **DANCE** [ ] [ ]
– We gotta get out of this place / Helen with the sun / Take a chance / Crazy / Hearts and minds / Dance / Out of time / Quietly with tact / Soul garden / The Lord will find a way / Is there nothing beyond God. *(cd-iss.Sep92 on 'Line'; LICD 900002)*

May 75. (7") *(GULS 13)* **WE GOTTA GET OUT OF THIS PLACE. / HERE I AM** [ ] [ ]

— **VINCENT CRANE** rejoined

Feb 78. (lp) *(GULP 1023)* **CHISOLM IN MY BOSOM** [ ] [-]
– Need to know / Monkey walk / I put a spell on you / She's on my mind / Let a little sunshine (into your life) / The lord is my saviour / Chisholm in my bosom. *(cd-iss.Sep92 on 'Line'; 900344)*

— teamed up with KLAUS SCHULTZ on some recordings

WEA not issued

1980. (lp; by ARTHUR BROWN & VINCENT CRANE) *(58088)* **FASTER THAN THE SPEED OF LIGHT** [-] [-] Dutch
– Storm clouds / Nothing we can do / No / Bright gateway / Timeship / Come and join the fun / Stormwind / Storm / This is it / Tightrope / Balance / Faster than the speed of light.

— now living in Austin, Texas + with band **SCOTT MORGAN** – synth / **STERLING SMITH** – mellotron / **D.ALDRIDGE** – percussion

Remote not issued

1982. (lp) *(REM 101)* **REQUIEM** [ ] [-]
– Requiem / Mechanical masseur / Busha busha / 2024 / Chant-shades / Animal people / Spirits / Gabriel. *(cd-iss.Feb93 on 'Voiceprint'; VP 125CD)*

Voiceprint not issued

Feb 93. (cd) *(VPCD 124CD)* **SPEAK NO TECH** [ ] [-]
– King of England / Conversations / Strange romance / Not fade away / Morning was cold / Speak no tech / Names are names / Love lady / Big guns don't lie / Take a picture / You don't know / Old friend my colleage / Lost my soul in London / Joined forever / Mandala / Desert floor.

Mar 94. (cd) *(VP 144CD)* **ORDER FROM CHAOS – LIVE 1993 (live)** [ ] [-]
– When you open the door (part 1 & 2) / King of England / Juices of love / Nightmare / Fire poem / Fire / Come and buy / Pick it up / Mandela / Time captains / I put a spell on you. *(re-iss.Sep96 on 'Blueprint'; BP 144CD)*

– compilations etc. –

Sep 77. (d-lp; as ARTHUR BROWN'S KINGDOM COME) *Gull; (GUD 2003-4)* **THE LOST EARS** [ ] [-]

May 88. (lp) *Reckless; (RECK 2)* **STRANGELANDS** [ ] [-]
(cd-iss.1989 +=; CDRECK 2)– RUSTIC HINGE

Jul 88. (lp) *Reckless; (RECK 3)* **RUSTIC HINGE** [ ] [-]

Sep 95. (cd) *See For Miles; (SEECD 431)* **CHISHOLM IN MY BOSOM / DANCE** [ ] [-]

Jun 97. (cd; KINGDOM COME) *Blueprint; (BP 163CD)* **JAM** [ ] [-]

Michael BROWN (see under ⇒ LEFT BANKE)

BUBBLE PUPPY

Formed: San Antonio, Texas, USA . . . 1967 out of bands WILLOWDALE HANDCAR and The NEW SEEDS. ROD PRINCE, ROY COX, DAVID FORE and TODD POTTER chose the name BUBBLE PUPPY from the Aldous Huxley book 'Brave New World', having taken yet another acid trip. They signed to 'International Artists' (home of 13th FLOOR ELEVATORS, GOLDEN DAWN and LOST & FOUND), moving to Houston in 1968 to record debut album 'A GATHERING OF PROMISES'. To promote it, they issued their first 45 'HOT SMOKE & SASSAFRAS', which surprised many by hitting the US Top 20 early in '69. It was basically a hard-rock effort embelished with vocal harmonies and a hint of psychedelia, which remained astonishingly unissued in Britain. The album sold well enough to reach the Top 200, but further 45's disappointed new converts. During a tour supporting STEPPENWOLF, NICK ST. NICHOLAS persuaded them to move to California, where they changed their name to DEMIAN. An album surfaced with some re-worked versions of their oldies, but nothing came out of it.

Recommended: A GATHERING OF PROMISES (*6)

ROD PRINCE – vocals, guitar / **TODD POTTER** – guitar / **ROY COX** – bass / **DAVID FORE** – drums

not issued Inter. Artists

Jan 69. (7") *<128>* **HOT SMOKE & SASSAFRAS. / LONELY** [-] [14]

Apr 69. (7") *<133>* **BEGINNING. / IF I HAD A REASON** [-] [ ]

May 69. (7") *<IA-LP 10>* **A GATHERING OF PROMISES** [-] [ ]
– Hot smoke & sassafras / Todd's tune / I've got to reach you / Lonely / Gathering of promises / Hurry sundown / Elizabeth / It's safe to say / Road to St. Stephens / Beginning. *(re-iss.Mar88 on 'Decal'; LIK 33) (cd-iss.Jun94 on 'Eva'; 642038)*

Jul 69. (7") *<136>* **DAYS OF OUR TIME. / THINKIN' ABOUT THINKIN'** [-] [ ]

Oct 69. (7") *<138>* **WHAT DO YOU SEE. / WHEN I WAS KING** [-] [ ]

— they changed their name to DEMIAN and released an eponymous album in 1971 for 'ABC'; <718>.

– compilations, etc. –

Aug87. (lp) *One Big Guitar; (OBGLP 9004)* **WHEELS GO ROUND** [ ] [-]

Tim BUCKLEY

Born: 14 Feb'47, Washington DC, USA. Signed to 'Elektra' in 1966 by FRANK ZAPPA manager HERB COHEN, who'd discovered him playing folk clubs around L.A. He recorded an eponymous debut with ZAPPA's musicians backing him up, before moving to New York where he was influenced by Greenwich Village troubadour FRED NEIL (whose 'DOLPHINS', he would later cover on 1973 album 'SEFRONIA'). 1967's 'GOODBYE AND HELLO', wore its influences on its sleeve but won critical plaudits for its cascading vocal versatility and meandering grace. Released a couple of years later, 'HAPPY / SAD's introspective intimations abandoned conventional song structures for abstract folk-jazz workouts. Desite their more experimental nature, the songs retained a tangible warmth of feeling, especially the lovely 'BUZZIN' FLY'. A frenetic period of creativity followed in 1970, with BUCKLEY releasing three albums in the space of a year. 'BLUE AFTERNOON' carried on in much the same vein while he took a further sidestep into improvisation with 'LORCA', culminating in the uncompromising 'STARSAILOR'. In true BUCKLEY fashion, he veered wildly into new territory with the sexually explicit 1972 album 'GREETINGS FROM L.A.', which exhibited an interest in black music. The doomed singer recorded two final rather patchy and self-indulgent albums before he died of an accidental drug overdose on 29th June '75. His poetic awareness and uncompromising efforts to push musical boundaries, had taken him down a solitary path that bypassed commercial success and eventually led to disillusionment and death, although he left behind a musical legacy of shimmering beauty. In 1990, 'DREAM LETTER', an album of live material from 1968, was unearthed to critical acclaim and along with various other re-issues, has only served to feed the myth of one of rock's greatest enigmas. • **Covered:** SALLY GO ROUND THE ROSES (Jaynettes). • **Trivia:** His songs were later recorded by (This Mortal Coil) – SONG TO THE SIREN / (Blood, Sweat & Tears) – MORNING GLORY, etc. • **Legacy:** In 1994, his son JEFF BUCKLEY signed to 'Big Cat' and also appeared at Reading Festival in that August. A debut EP release 'LIVE AT SIN-E' was issued prior to debut 'Columbia' album 'GRACE' which cracked UK Top 50. However, just like his father before him, he was to meet an untimely death, tragically drowning in early 1997. (his own bio/discography is being prepared as this goes to press)

Recommended: BEST OF TIM BUCKLEY (1983 US-import lp; *8) / HAPPY SAD (*8) / GREETINGS FROM L.A. (*7) / DREAM LETTER (*7)

TIM BUCKLEY – vocals, guitar with **LEE UNDERWOOD** – guitar, keyboards / **BILLY MUNDI** – drums / **JIM FIELDER** – bass / **VAN DYKE PARKS** – piano / **JACK NITZSCHE** – string arrangements

Elektra Elektra

Nov 66. (7") *<45606>* **GRIEF IN MY SOUL. / WINGS** [-] [ ]

Dec 66. (lp; mono/stereo) *(EKL/EKS 4004)* *<74004>* **TIM BUCKLEY** [ ] [ ] Oct66
– I can't see you / Wings / Song of the magician / Strange street affair under blue /

Valentine melody / Aren't you the girl / Song slowly sung / It happens every time / Song for Jainie / Grief in my soul / She is / Understand your man. *<re-iss.Jul71 & Mar75; same)*

Jan 67. (7") *(EKSN 45008) <45612>* **AREN'T YOU THE GIRL. / STRANGE STREET AFFAIR UNDER BLUE**

— BUCKLEY retained only UNDERWOOD, recruiting **CARTER C. COLLINS** – congas

Aug 67. (7") *<45618>* **LADY GIVE ME YOUR HEART. / ONCE UPON A TIME**

Oct 67. (7") *<45623>* **MORNING GLORY. / ONCE I WAS** -

Nov 67. (7") *(EKSN 45018)* **MORNING GLORY. / KNIGHT-ERRANT** -

Dec 67. (lp; mono/stereo) *(EKL/EKS 318) <7318>* **GOODBYE AND HELLO** Oct67

– No man can find the war / Carnival song / Pleasant street / Hallucinations / I never asked to be your mountain / Once I was / Phantasmagoria in two / Knight-Errant / Goodbye and hello / Morning glory. *(re-iss.Jul71; K 42070) (re-iss.Mar93 & Sep95 on 'Warners' cd/c; 7559 60896-2/-4)*

Jan 68. (7") *(EKSN 45023)* **ONCE I WAS. / PHANTASMAGORIA IN TWO** -

Mar 68. (7") *(EKSN 45031)* **WINGS. / I CAN'T SEE YOU**

— added **JOHN MILLER** – acoustic & electric bass / **DAVID FREEDMAN** – vibes, percussion

Oct 68. (7") *(EKSN 45041)* **PLEASANT STREET. / CARNIVAL SONG**

Jul 69. (lp) *<(EKS 74045)>* **HAPPY - SAD** 81

– Strange feeling / Buzzin' fly / Love from room 109 at the Islander (on Pacific Coast Highway) / Dream letter / Gypsy woman / Sing a song for you. *(re-iss.Jul71; K 42072) (cd-iss.Feb93; 7559 74045-2)*

— added **JIMMY MADISON** – drums

Straight Straight

Feb 70. (7") *(S 4799)* **HAPPY TIME. / SO LONELY**

Feb 70. (lp) *<(STS 1060)>* **BLUE AFTERNOON**

– Happy time / Chase the blues away / I must have been blind / The river / So lonely / Cafe / Blue melody / Train. *<US re-iss.Jul71 on 'Warners'; WS 1842>*

— BUCKLEY retained only UNDERWOOD and COLLINS, recruiting **JOHN BLAKIN** – bass

Elektra Elektra

Oct 70. (lp) *(2410 005) <EKS 74074>* **LORCA**

– Lorca / Anonymous proposition / I had a talk with a woman / Driftin' / Nobody walkin'. *<US re-iss.Jul71; K 42053> (re-iss.Mar75; same)*

— BUCKLEY retained only UNDERWOOD and BALKIN, recruiting co-write **LARRY BECKETT / MAURI BAKET** – timpani / **BUZZ GARDNER and BUNK GARDNER on wind and horns**

Straight Straight

Jan 71. (lp) *<(STS 1064)>* **STARSAILOR**

– Come here woman / I woke up / Monterey / Moulin Rouge / Song to the siren / Jungle fire / Starsailor / The healing festival / Down by the borderline. *<US re-iss.Jul71 on 'Warners'; WS 1881>*

— from now on BUCKLEY used loads of session people plus past friends.

Warners Warners

Oct 72. (7") *<7623>* **MOVE WITH ME. / NIGHTHAWKIN'** -

Oct 72. (lp) *(K 46176) <BS 2631>* **GREETINGS FROM L.A.**

– Move with me / Get on top / Sweet surrender / Nighthawkin' / Devil eyes / Hong Kong bar / Make it right. *<cd-iss.Jul89 on 'Disc Int.'; EN 73506> (cd-iss.Feb96; 7599 27261-2)*

Discreet-Warners Discreet-Warners

May 74. (lp) *(K 49201) <MS 2157>* **SEFRONIA**

– Dolphins / Honeyman / Because of you / Peanut man / Martha / Quicksand / I know I'd recognise your face / Stone in love / Sefronia – After Asklepiades, after Kafka / Sefronia – The King's chain / Sally go 'round the roses. *(re-iss.Oct89 on 'Edsel' lp/cd; ED/+CD 277) (cd re-iss.Feb97 on 'Manifesto'; PT 340701)*

May 74. (7") *<1187>* **STONE IN LOVE. / QUICKSAND** -

Jul 74. (7") *<1189>* **HONEYMAN. / DOLPHINS** -

Nov 74. (lp) *(K 59204) <DS 2201>* **LOOK AT THE FOOL**

– Look at the fool / Bring it on up / Helpless / Freeway blues / Tijuana moon / Ain't it peculiar / Who could deny you? / Mexicali voodoo / Down in the street / Wanda Lu. *(re-iss.Oct89 on 'Edsel' lp/cd; ED/+CD 294) (cd re-iss.Feb97 on 'Manifesto'; PT 340702)*

Nov 74. (7") *<1311>* **WANDA LU. / WHO COULD DENY YOU** -

— TIM died 29 Jun'75 (see biog.)

– compilations, etc. –

Sep 76. (7") *Elektra; (K 12223)* **MORNING GLORY. / ONCE I WAS**

Jun 90. (d-lp/d-cd) *Demon; (DFIEND/+CD 200)* **DREAM LETTER – LIVE IN LONDON 1968 (live)** -

(cd re-iss.Feb97 on 'Manifesto'; PT 340703)

Aug 91. (12"ep/cd-ep) *Strange Fruit;* **THE PEEL SESSIONS** -

– Morning glory / Coming home to you / Sing a song for you / Hallucinations / Troubadour / Once I was.

Mar 94. (cd) *Demon; (EDCD 400)* **LIVE AT TROUBADOUR 1969 (live)** -

(re-iss.May97 on 'Manifesto'; PT 340705)

Aug 94. (cd) *Band Of Joy; (BOJCD 009)* **MORNING GLORY** -

Sep 95. (cd) *Edsel; (EDCD 450)* **HONEYMAN** (live 27th Nov'73) -

BUFFALO SPRINGFIELD

Formed: Los Angeles, California, USA . . . March '66. In a well-documented incident, STEPHEN STILLS and guitarist RICHIE FUREY were caught in a traffic jam on Sunset Strip, when by pure chance, STILLS recognised the driver of a black hearse, NEIL YOUNG. Along with bass player and fellow Canadian BRUCE PALMER, YOUNG had travelled down to Hollywood to try his luck in the fabled City of Angels. This fated get-together also led to another member being recruited, drummer DEWEY MARTIN. STILLS and YOUNG clashed right from the off, but it was essentially this tension that fuelled the band's creative spark in a JAGGERS/RICHARDS kind of fashion. Taking their name from a type of steamroller, and with the help of the SONNY & CHER management team of CHARLIE GREENE and BRIAN STONE, the band were signed to Atlantic offshoot 'Atco' in a matter of months. With the combined talent of STILLS and YOUNG's soaring harmonies and driving rhythm, the band often came on like a country-fied BEATLES, although their albums are notable for their striking stylistic diversity. The ambitiously eccentric, YOUNG-penned debut single, 'NOWADAYS CLANCY CAN'T EVEN SING', did nothing, while 'BURNED', the 2-minute pop thrill of a follow-up, fared equally badly. But then STILLS struck gold with the famous protest anthem 'FOR WHAT IT'S WORTH', released in the same month as the band's fine eponymous debut album. The song concerned itself with the previous summer's riots whereby a coterie of businessmen had threatened Sunset Strip's nightlife by proposing the building of a business district. Of course the students were none too happy, especially when 300 protesters were arrested. The song was duly adopted by rebels everywhere as a general mascot for fighting the good fight, and its vaguely psychedelic, menacing tone perfectly evoked the feelings of persecution felt by the emerging flower children. Throughout 1967, the band was rocked by internal squabbling with various members coming and going. An album, 'STAMPEDE', was recorded but never quite completed. It later surfaced as a bootleg and one track from it, 'DOWN TO THE WIRE', featuring an impassioned YOUNG vocal, was included on his, 'DECADE' (1976) compilation. YOUNG also missed the bands slot at the Monterey Pop Festival, DAVID CROSBY taking his place. Despite all this, the band completed a follow-up, 'BUFFALO SPRINGFIELD AGAIN', which was issued in late '67. Opinions on the album are mixed with some critics deeming it a classic of its time, others criticising its watered down production. The best moments are YOUNG's JACK NITZSCHE-arranged numbers, 'BROKEN ARROW' and 'EXPECTING TO FLY', the latter possessed a haunting, lysergic quality. STILL's compositions, 'BLUEBIRD' and 'ROCK AND ROLL WOMAN', lack the sophistication of YOUNG's surreal epics but are enjoyable none the less. The tension between YOUNG and STILLS eventually finished the band (DAVID CROSBY once commenting that they used their guitars as weapons, on stage and off!) with a final album, 'LAST TIME AROUND', released after the split. YOUNG contributed the fragile 'I AM A CHILD' and one other song before leaving the band early on during the sessions. YOUNG went on to an erratic, often mercurial career, while STILLS went off to help form CROSBY, STILLS and NASH (re-united with YOUNG in 1970). FURAY meanwhile, went off to join country rockers POCO. Along with The BYRDS and LOVE, BUFFALO SPRINGFIELD were one of the most influential, if somewhat short-lived bands to come out of L.A.

Recommended: BUFFALO SPRINGFIELD (*7) / BUFFALO SPRINGFIELD AGAIN (*8) / LAST TIME AROUND (*6) / THE BEST OF . . . RETROSPECTIVE (*8)

STEPHEN STILLS (b. 3 Jan'45, Dallas, Texas) – lead guitar, vocals / **NEIL YOUNG** (b.12 Nov'45, Toronto, Canada) – lead guitar, vocals / **RICHIE FURAY** (b. 9 May'44, Dayton, Ohio) – vocals, guitar / **BRUCE PALMER** (b. 1944, Liverpool, Canada) – bass repl. KEN KOBLUN / **DEWEY MARTIN** (b.30 Sep'42, Chesterfield, Canada) – drums (ex-DILLARDS)

Atlantic Atco

Oct 66. (7") *<6428>* **NOWADAYS CLANCY CAN'T EVEN SING. / GO AND SAY GOODBYE** -

Dec 66. (7"w-drawn) *<6452>* **BURNED. / EVERYBODY'S WRONG** -

Jan 67. (lp; stereo/mono) *(588/587 070) <SD+/33-200>* **BUFFALO SPRINGFIELD** Dec66

– Don't scold me (*) / Go and say goodbye / Sit down I think I love you / Nowadays Clancy can't even sing / Everybody's wrong / Hot dusty roads / Flying on the ground / Burned / Do I have to come right out and say it? / Leave / Pay the price / Out of my mind. *<re-iss.Feb67 stereo/mono; SD+/33-200-A>* – For what it's worth (repl.track (*); hit US No.80> *(re-iss.1971; K 30028) (cd-iss.Feb93; 7567 90389-2)*

Jan 67. (7") *(584 077) <6459>* **FOR WHAT IT'S WORTH. / DO I HAVE TO COME RIGHT OUT AND SAY IT?** 7

— on stage **KEN KOBLUN** and **JIM FIELDER**, latter of The MOTHERS, repl. PALMER, although PALMER did return occasionally. / **DOUG HASTINGS** – guitar repl. YOUNG (also DAVID CROSBY guested at Monteray)

— **BOB WEST** – bass & CHARLIE CHIN – banjo deputise for above reshuffles

Jul 67. (7") *<6499>* **BLUEBIRD. / MR. SOUL** - 58

— **STILLS, FURAY, MARTIN** and the returning **YOUNG** recruit **JIM MESSINA** (b. 5 Dec'47, Maywood, Calif.) – bass repl. FIELDER who joined BLOOD SWEAT & TEARS

Oct 67. (7") *(584 145) <6519>* **ROCK'N'ROLL WOMAN. / A CHILD'S CLAIM TO FAME** 44 Sep67

Jan 68. (lp; stereo/mono) *(588/587 091) <SD+/33-226>* **BUFFALO SPRINGFIELD AGAIN** 44 Nov67

– Mr. Soul / A child's claim to fame / Everydays / Expecting to fly / Bluebird / Hung upside down / Sad memory / Good time boy / Rock'n'roll woman / Broken arrow. *(re-iss.1971; K 40014) (cd-iss.Jul88; 790-391-2)*

Feb 68. (7") *(584 165) <6545>* **EXPECTING TO FLY. / EVERYDAYS** 98 Jan68

Jun 68. (7") *(584 189) <6572>* **UNO MUNDO. / MERRY-GO-ROUND**

Aug 68. (7") *<6602>* **KIND WOMAN. / SPECIAL CARE** -

— with original line-up they recorded another album, but they had split by May'68. MESSINA who had always been their sound recordist posthumously assembled line-up

Oct 68. (7") *<6615>* **ON THE WAY HOME. / FOUR DAYS GONE** - 82

Dec 68. (lp) *(228 024) <SD33-256>* **LAST TIME AROUND** 42 Aug68

– On the way home / It's so hard to wait / Pretty girl why / Four days gone / Carefree country day / Special care / The hour of not quite rain / Questions / I am a child / Merry-go-round / Uno mundo / Kind woman. *(re-iss.1971; K 40077) (cd-iss.Mar94 on 'Atco'; 7567 90393-2)*

— After their split, NEIL YOUNG went solo and joined STEPHEN STILLS in

CROSBY, STILLS NASH & YOUNG. FURAY formed POCO adding later MESSINA. DEWEY MARTIN tried in vain to use BUFFALO SPRINGFIELD name.

- compilations, etc. -

on 'Atlantic' UK / 'Atco' US; unless otherwise mentioned

Mar 69. (lp) *(228 012) <SD33-283>* **RETROSPECTIVE - THE BEST OF BUFFALO SPRINGFIELD** [ ] [42] Feb69
– For what it's worth / Mr. Soul / Sit down I think I love you / Kind woman / Bluebird / On the way home / Nowadays Clancy can't even sing / Broken arrow / Rock'n'roll woman / I am a child / Go and say goodbye / Expecting to fly. *(re-iss.1971; K 40071) (cd-iss.Jul88; 790 417-2)*

Oct 69. (7") *Atco; (226 006)* **PRETTY GIRL WHY / QUESTIONS** [ ] [-]

Oct 70. (lp) *(K 2462 012)* **EXPECTING TO FLY** [ ] [-]

Oct 72. (7"ep) *(K 10237)* **BLUEBIRD / MR. SOUL. / ROCK'N'ROLL WOMAN / EXPECTING TO FLY** [ ] [-]

Dec 73. (d-lp) *(K 70001) <SD2 806>* **BUFFALO SPRINGFIELD** [ ] [-]

— some BUFFALO SPRINGFIELD live tracks appeared on NEIL YOUNG's compilation lp 'JOURNEY THROUGH THE PAST', and two on his 'DECADE' triple in '77.

BULLDOG BREED

Formed: England . . . early '69 out of The FLIES. They released three singles between 1966 and '68, the first being a version of the BOYCE/HART number made famous by The MONKEES; 'I'M NOT YOUR STEPPING STONE'. BULLDOG BREED (with KEITH CROSS & BERNARD JINKS) signed to the fashionable 'Deram' label in 1969, but only managed to squeeze out one single, 'PORTCULLIS GATE'. Moving to the more obscure 'Nova' subsidiary, they released an album of progressive PINK FLOYD-ish psychedelia. CROSS and JINKS then teamed up with ex-FLIES drummer PETER DUNTON to form T.2. They were likened to CREAM due to their powerhouse trio approach, although they were a lot more progressive, especially on the 20-minute track 'MORNING' (from their only album, 'IT'LL ALL WORK OUT IN BOOMLAND'). Made a successful appearance at the Isle Of Wight Festival before disbanding. They re-formed and recorded another shelved lp later in the 70's. • **Trivia:** The FLIES singles are worth over £50 as is the T.2. album, while BULLDOG BREED releases fetch just under that price.

Recommended: MADE IN ENGLAND (*5) / T.2.:- IT'LL ALL WORK OUT IN BOOMLAND (*7)

FLIES

PETER DUNTON – drums, vocals / (+ others)

Decca | not issued

1966. (7") *(F 12533)* **I'M NOT YOUR STEPPING STONE. / TALK TO ME** [ ] [-]

1966. (7") *(F 12594)* **HOUSE OF LOVE. / IT HAD TO BE YOU** [ ] [-]

R.C.A. | not issued

Oct 68. (7") *(RCA 1757)* **THE MAGIC TRAIN. / GENTLY AS YOU FEEL** [ ] [-]

— **PETER DUNTON soon joined GUN, then T.2. (see further below)**

BULLDOG BREED

KEITH CROSS – vocals, keyboards, guitar / **BERNARD JINKS** – bass, vocals / **LOUIS FARRELL** – drums

Deram | not issued

Sep 69. (7") *(DM 270)* **PORTCULLIS GATE. / HALO IN MY HAIR** [ ] [-]

Deram Nova | not issued

Jan 70. (lp; stereo/mono) *(S+/DN 5)* **MADE IN ENGLAND** [ ] [-]
– Paper man / Sheba's broomstick ride / I flew / Eileen's haberdashery store / Folder men / Dougal / When the sun stands still / Reborn / Friday hill / Silver / You / Top o the pops cock / Revenge – Austin Osmanspare. *(cd-iss.Jun97 on 'World Wide Records'; WWR-CD 0052)*

T.2.

CROSS + JINKS / + PETER DUNTON

Decca | not issued

Aug 70. (lp) *(SKL 5050)* **IT'LL ALL WORK OUT IN BOOMLAND** [ ] [-]
– In circles / J.L.T. / No more white horses / Morning. *(cd-iss.1992 on 'World Wide Records'+=; WWR-CD 0032)–*

— the shelved album 'SECOND BITE' was issued 1992; *WWR-CD 0033)*

CROSS & ROSS

KEITH CROSS + PETER ROSS – guitar, vocals / with on session CHRIS STEWART, NICK LOWE, TONY CARR + JIMMY HASTINGS

Decca | London

Sep 71. (7") *(F 13224) <20069>* **CAN YOU BELIEVE IT? / BLIND WILLIE JOHNSON** [ ] [ ]

May 72. (7") *(F 13316) <20073>* **PEACE IN THE END. / PROPHETS GUILDERS** [ ] [ ]

Aug 72. (7") *(SKL 5129)* **BORED CIVILIANS** [ ] [-]
– Last ocean rider / Bored civilians / Peace in the end / Story to a friend / Loving you takes so long / Pastels / Dead salute / Boo Radley / Fly home.

— both virtually disappeared from view.

Eric BURDON (see under ⇒ ANIMALS)

BYRDS

Formed: Los Angeles, California, USA . . . 1964 as The JETSET by JIM McGUINN, GENE CLARK and DAVID CROSBY. All three had come from folky backgrounds, McGUINN having toured with The CHAD MITCHELL TRIO as a teenager and CLARK already having proved an accomplished songwriter with The NEW CHRISTY MINSTRELS. CROSBY, meanwhile was an ambitious singer/songwriter who'd performed with LES BAXTER'S BALLADEERS. The JETSET recorded a one-off flop single for 'Elektra', 'PLEASE LET ME LOVE YOU', under the pseudonym of The BEEF-EATERS. Later the same year, they recruited expert bluegrass player CHRIS HILLMAN, previously of The HILLMEN, who'd incorporated his instrumental dexterity on the mandolin into his bass playing. Drummer MICHAEL CLARKE, with his chiselled, BRIAN JONES-esque looks, completed the line-up, initially playing on cardboard boxes when the band were too hard-up to afford a real drum-kit! Profoundly influenced by The BEATLES, they soon changed their name to The BYRDS (the mis-spelling a tribute to their heroes), and set about realising their vision of marrying the fab four's electric energy to the folk music which was their stock in trade. With the help of long-time manager JIM DICKSON and the unlikely recommendation of MILES DAVIS, the band signed to 'Columbia'. At the insistence of DICKSON and producer TERRY MELCHER, the reluctant BYRDS eventually agreed to re-work their earlier demo of 'MR. TAMBOURINE MAN' (this and other demos later surfaced on 'PREFLYTE'). It was a canny decision which did nothing less than change the course of pop/rock history. The resulting song's unforgettable euphoric rush charged DYLAN's lyrics with a youthful romanticism, encapsulating in 3 minutes, what it was to be young and have the world at your feet. It soon hit No.1 on both sides of the Atlantic and it still sounds as fresh today as it did then, a timeless slice of hypnotic, bittersweet pop with McGUINN's delivery forging an affecting DYLAN / LENNON hybrid. Much has since been made of the fact that only one BYRD, McGUINN, actually played on the record, with MELCHER hiring session musicians like LEON RUSSELL, LARRY KNECHTAL and HAL BLAINE. However, any doubts about The BYRDS ability as a band were dispelled with the self-titled debut album, a folk-rock classic. It was a case of more of the same really, with the band turning in a dazzling string of DYLAN covers, making the songs distinctly their own. 'CHIMES OF FREEDOM' was a ringing, hippy call to arms, fuelled by a starry-eyed optimism and they even managed to transform the Welsh mining disaster ballad 'BELLS OF RHYMNEY', into an effervescent swirl. GENE CLARK was the band's chief songwriter at this stage, contributing the classic BEATLES-esque originals 'FEEL A WHOLE LOT BETTER', 'I KNEW I'D WANT YOU' and 'HERE WITHOUT YOU'. In the summer of '65, they played a residency at Ciro's nightclub on Sunset Strip, often cited as the origin of the L.A. hippy movement (described by The L.A. Times as being frequented by people who looked like they'd been dragged from Sherwood Forest!). They were back at No.1 by the end of 1965, when they managed to transform PETE SEEGER's Book Of Ecclestiastes-adaptation 'TURN! TURN! TURN!' into a classic pop record, a miracle of biblical proportions. Very early the next year, the second album boasted two more DYLAN covers, an uninspiring update of 'THE TIMES THEY ARE A-CHANGIN' and 'LAY DOWN YOUR WEARY TUNE', apparently the song that finally persuaded DYLAN that The BYRDS were doing something above and beyond mere imitation. McGUINN contributed two songs, one of which was his tribute to the assassinated JOHN F. KENNEDY, 'HE WAS A FRIEND OF MINE', while CLARK offered three originals, including the classic 'SET YOU FREE THIS TIME'. Recorded the previous January, 'EIGHT MILES HIGH' pioneered psychedelic rock, predating the efforts of The BEATLES, The BEACH BOYS and the San Franciscan bands. The JOHN COLTRANE-inspired track was promptly vetoed by radio stations on its spring '66 release, amid allegations that the song was an explicit account of an LSD trip. After the completion of the third album 'FIFTH DIMENSION', CLARK departed, citing his paranoia-fuelled fear of flying and CROSBY's digs regarding his tambourine playing. The new album heralded a move away from sparkling pop to a more complex, ambitious and intelligent sound. Influenced heavily by Indian sitar player RAVI SHANKAR, and modal jazz, the record didn't fulfill the promise of the preceding single but still contained some memorable moments. McGUINN's 'MR SPACEMAN' hinted at the country sound the band would later embrace. Just prior to releasing the fourth album, 'YOUNGER THAN YESTERDAY', the band issued 'SO YOU WANT TO BE A ROCK'N'ROLL STAR', a sarcastic reaction to manufactured bands by a group that had fallen out of favour with the Hollywood set. The album was an assorted bag of styles, with HILLMAN emerging as a talented songwriter on the likes of 'TIME BETWEEN' and 'THOUGHTS AND WORDS', while CROSBY had his finest moment with the haunting 'EVERYBODY'S BEEN BURNED'. Despite the melange of styles, the album predated 'SGT PEPPER', once again proving that The BYRDS were ahead of their time. By the time of 'THE NOTORIOUS BYRD BROTHERS' in 1968, CROSBY's dictational manner had led to his ejection from the band, along with MICHAEL CLARKE. A contender for the The BYRDS best album, the record was again stylistically diverse but included possibly the band's finest moment in the GOFFIN/KING number, 'GOIN' BACK' (later a hit for DUSTY SPRINGFIELD). It's wistful musings on the passage from childhood to maturity were set against a backdrop of heavenly harmonies and celestial pedal steel while 'WASN'T BORN TO FOLLOW' (another GERRY GOFFIN-CAROLE KING cover), was a triumphant clarion call of phased, psychedelic country. With the addition of GRAM PARSONS and HILLMAN's cousin KEVIN KELLEY, the band steered radically away from the studio-enhanced sound of 'NOTORIOUS', straight into the heart of country, once again staying one step ahead of their peers and foreshadowing the country-rock boom of the early 70's. 'SWEETHEART OF THE RODEO', with its purist sound, confounded the hippies and despite playing a show at the Grand Ole Opry, and even, God forbid, cutting their hair! for the occasion, the country crowd remained suspicious of their druggy image, thereby ensuring little commercial success. Released in '68, PARSONS was the driving force behind the album, contributing beautiful songs like 'HICKORY WIND' and 'ONE HUNDRED YEARS FROM NOW', which sat majestically alongside covers of LOUVIN BROTHERS and DYLAN material. The gypsy-like PARSONS soon left, taking HILLMAN with him to form The FLYING BURRITO BROTHERS. McGUINN (who'd now changed his name to ROGER, following his immersion in the Indonesian religion, Subud) recruited country guitar maestro CLARENCE WHITE along with a cast of other musicians. The albums that followed were inconsistent, although they contained a few BYRDS classics and highlighted WHITE's virtuoso guitar playing. 'DR BYRDS & MR HYDE', featured the ironic stab at the country establishment, 'DRUG STORE TRUCK DRIVING MAN', while 'THE BALLAD OF EASY RIDER's gentle meandering title track was a minor classic. The half live/half studio set, 'UNTITLED', from 1970, included an impassioned performance from WHITE on 'LOVER ON THE BAYOU' and a lovely version of LOWELL GEORGE's 'TRUCK STOP GIRL'. Probably the strongest set of the latter day BYRDS, it also included the single 'CHESTNUT MARE', and the evocative McGUINN and JACQUES LEVY song 'ALL THE THINGS'. Much of McGUINN's songs during this period came from the abandoned 'Gene Tryp' project which he had begun with New York psychologist LEVY to chart the history of American music. The last few albums weren't quite as ambitious in their scope, but 'BYRDMANIAX' and 'FARTHER ALONG' were enjoyable despite having the weight of such an illustrious career on their shoulders. McGUINN did the right thing and called it a day at last in mid-72, later joining up with the original BYRDS for an uninspired album a year later. Two of the BYRDS most talented members died in separate incidents in the early 70's, CLARENCE WHITE killed by a drunken driver, GRAM PARSONS from a heroin overdose. CROSBY survived a descent into free-base cocaine addiction and a liver transplant to record songs in Nashville with McGUINN and HILLMAN in 1990. A proposed tour never happened but the tracks are included on the wonderful 'Columbia' boxed set released the same year. More recently, McGUINN was sighted running through some old numbers on 'Later With Jools (Holland)' in true troubadour style. An endless list of artists and bands (TOM PETTY, R.E.M., LONG RYDERS, SMITHS, PRIMAL SCREAM, RIDE, etc), have kept alive the spirit of The BYRDS in their own particular style, while the band's own recordings remain timeless treasures.

Recommended: MR. TAMBOURINE MAN (*8) / TURN! TURN! TURN! (*8) / FIFTH DIMENSION (*6) / YOUNGER THAN YESTERDAY (*7) / THE BYRDS' GREATEST HITS (*10) / NOTORIOUS BYRD BROTHERS (*9) / SWEETHEART OF THE RODEO (*8) / GREATEST HITS VOL.2 (*8) / UNTITLED (*7)

GENE CLARK (b.HAROLD EUGENE CLARK, 17 Nov'41, Tipton, Missouri, USA) – vocals, tambourine / **JIM McGUINN** (b.JAMES JOSEPH McGUINN, 13 Jul'42, Chicago, Illinois, USA) – guitar, vocals / **DAVID CROSBY** (b.DAVID VAN CORTLAND, 14 Aug'41, L.A.) – guitar, vocals

Pye Inter. Elektra

Nov 64. (7"; as BEEFEATERS) *(7N 25277)* *<45013>* **PLEASE LET ME LOVE YOU. / DON'T BE LONG** [ ] [ ] Sep64

— added **CHRIS HILLMAN** (b. 4 Dec'42, L.A.) – bass, vocals (ex-HILLMEN) / **MICHAEL CLARKE** (b. 3 Jun'43, New York City) – drums

C.B.S. Columbia

Jun 65. (7") *(201765)* *<43271>* **MR. TAMBOURINE MAN. / I KNEW I'D WANT TO** [1] [1] May65

Aug 65. (7") *(201796)* *<43332>* **ALL I REALLY WANT TO DO. / I'LL FEEL A WHOLE LOT BETTER** [4] [40] Jul65

Aug 65. (lp; stereo/mono) *(S+/BPG 62571)* *<9172>* **MR. TAMBOURINE MAN** [7] [6] Jun65
– Mr. Tambourine man / I'll feel a whole lot better / Spanish Harlem incident / You won't have to cry / Here without you / The bells of Rhymney / All I really want to do / I knew I'd want you / It's no use / Don't doubt yourself, babe / Chimes of freedom / We'll meet again. *(re-iss.Jul77; CBS/40 31503)*

Oct 65. (7") *(202008)* *<43424>* **TURN! TURN! TURN!. / SHE DON'T CARE ABOUT TIME** [26] [1]

Feb 66. (7") *(202037)* *<43501>* **SET YOU FREE THIS TIME. / IT WON'T BE WRONG** [ ] [79] [63]

Mar 66. (lp; stereo/mono) *(S+/SPG 62652)* *<9254>* **TURN! TURN! TURN!** [11] [17] Dec65
– Turn! Turn! Turn! / It won't be wrong / Set you free this time / Lay down your weary tune / He was a friend of mine / The world turns all around her / Satisfied mind / If you're gone / The times they are a-changin' / Wait and see / Oh! Susannah. *(re-iss.Jul77; CBS/40 31526)*

— trimmed to a quartet when GENE CLARK went solo

Apr 66. (7") *(202067)* *<43578>* **EIGHT MILES HIGH. / WHY?** [24] [14]

Jul 66. (7") *(202259)* *<43702>* **5D (FIFTH DIMENSION). / CAPTAIN SOUL** [ ] [44]

Sep 66. (lp; stereo/mono) *(S+/BPG 62783)* *<9349>* **FIFTH DIMENSION** [27] [24] Aug66
– 5D (Fifth Dimension) / Wild mountain thyme / Mr. Spaceman / I see you / What's happening?!?! / I come and stand at every door / Eight miles high / Hey Joe / John Riley / Captain Soul / 2-4-2 Foxtrot (the Lear jet song). *(re-iss.Jul83 lp/c; CBS/40 32284) (cd-iss.May96 on 'Sony'; 483707-2)*

Oct 66. (7") *(202295)* *<43766>* **MR. SPACEMAN. / WHAT'S HAPPENING?!?!** [ ] [36] Sep66

Feb 67. (7") *(202559)* *<43987>* **SO YOU WANT TO BE A ROCK'N'ROLL STAR. / EVERYBODY'S BEEN BURNED** [ ] [29] Jan67

Apr 67. (lp; stereo/mono) *(S+/BPG 62988)* *<9442>* **YOUNGER THAN YESTERDAY** [37] [24] Mar67
– So you want to be a rock'n'roll star / Have you seen her face / C.T.A. – 102 / Renaissance fair / Time between / Everybody's been burned / Thoughts and words / Mind gardens / My back pages / The girl with no name / Why. *(re-iss.Mar87 on 'Edsel' cd/c/lp; CD/C+/ED 227) (re-iss.Oct94 & May96 on 'Columbia' cd/c; 483708-2)*

May 67. (7") *(2648)* *<44054>* **MY BACK PAGES. / RENAISSANCE MAN** [ ] [30] Mar67

Jun 67. (7") *<44157>* **HAVE YOU SEEN HER FACE. / DON'T MAKE WAVES** [-] [74]

Sep 67. (7") *<44230>* **LADY FRIEND. / OLD JOHN ROBERTSON** [-] [82]

Sep 67. (7") *(2924)* **LADY FRIEND. / DON'T MAKE WAVES** [ ] [-]

Oct 67. (lp; stereo/mono) *(S+/BPG 63107)* *<9516>* **THE BYRDS' GREATEST HITS** (compilation) [ ] [6] Aug67
– Mr. Tambourine man / I'll feel a whole lot better / Bells of rhymney / Turn! turn! turn! / All I really want to do / Chimes of freedom / Eight miles high / Mr.Spaceman / 5D (Fifth Dimension) / So you want to be a rock'n'roll star / My back pages. *(re-iss.Jan84; CBS/40 32068) (cd-iss.Jun89; CD 32068) (REMASTERED cd.Feb91; 467843-2) (cd re-iss.May96 on 'Sony'; 483705-2)*

— **GENE CLARK** – guitar, vocals returned to repl. DAVID who formed CROSBY, STILLS and NASH (JIM also changed name to ROGER McGUINN)

Dec 67. (7") *(3093)* *<44362>* **GOIN' BACK. / CHANGE IS NOW** [ ] [89] Nov67
(re-iss.Jun77; 5300)
Now a trio of **McGUINN, HILLMAN and CLARKE** (GENE continued solo career)

Apr 68. (lp; stereo/mono) *(S+/BPG 63169)* *<9575>* **THE NOTORIOUS BYRD BROTHERS** [12] [47] Jan68
– Artificial energy / Goin' back / Natural harmony / Draft morning / Wasn't born to follow / Get to you / Change is now / Old John Robertson / Tribal gathering / Dolphin's smile / Space odyssey. *(re-iss.Aug88 on 'Edsel' cd/lp; CD+/ED 262) (cd re-iss.Mar97 on 'Columbia'; 486751-2)*

— **KEVIN KELLEY** (b.1945, California) – drums (ex-RISING SONS) repl. MICHAEL who joined DILLARD & CLARK. Also added **GRAM PARSONS** (b.INGRAM CECIL CONNOR III, 5 Nov'46, Winterhaven, Florida) – guitar, vocals, keyboards (ex-INTERNATIONAL SUBMARINE BAND) / guests on album – **SNEAKY PETE** – pedal steel guitar / **DOUG DILLARD** – banjo

May 68. (7") *(3411)* *<44499>* **YOU AIN'T GOING NOWHERE. / ARTIFICIAL ENERGY** [45] [74]

Sep 68. (lp) *(63353)* *<9670>* **SWEETHEART OF THE RODEO** [ ] [77] Aug68
– You ain't going nowhere / I am a pilgrim / The Christian life / You're still on my mind / Pretty Boy Floyd / You don't miss your water / Hickory wind / One hundred years from now / Blue Canadian Rockies / Life in prison / Nothing was delivered. *(re-iss.Jun87 on 'Edsel' cd/lp; CD+/ED 234) (cd re-iss.Mar97 on 'Columbia'; 486752-2)*

Oct 68. (7") *(3752)* *<44643>* **PRETTY BOY FLOYD. / I AM A PILGRIM** [ ] [ ]

— **CARLOS BERNAL** – guitar played on US tour replacing GRAM who joined FLYING BURRITO BROTHERS alongside HILLMAN and SNEAKY PETE. Soon McGUINN recruited entirely new members **CLARENCE WHITE** (b. 6 Jun'44, Lewiston, Maine, USA) – guitar, vocals (ex-NASHVILLE WEST) repl. BERNAL / **GENE PARSONS** (b. 9 Apr'44) – drums, vocals (ex-NASHVILLE WEST) repl. KELLEY / **JOHN YORK** – bass, vocals repl. HILLMAN

Mar 69. (7") *(4055)* *<44746>* **BAD NIGHT AT THE WHISKEY. / DRUG STORE TRUCK DRIVIN' MAN** [ ] [ ]

Apr 69. (lp) *(63545)* *<9755>* **DR. BYRDS AND MR.HYDE** [15] [ ] Mar69
– This wheel's on fire / Old blue / Your gentle way of loving me / Child of the universe / Nashville West / Drug store truck drivin' man / King Apathy III / Candy / Bad night at the Whiskey / My back pages – B.J.blues – Baby what you want me to do. *(cd-iss.Aug91 on 'Beat Goes On'; BGOCD 107) (cd re-iss.Mar97 on 'Columbia'; 486753-2)*

Jun 69. (7") *(4284)* *<44868>* **LAY LADY LAY. / OLD BLUE** [ ] [ ]

Sep 69. (7") *(4572)* **WASN'T BORN TO FOLLOW. / CHILD OF THE UNIVERSE** [ ] [-]

Oct 69. (7") *<44990>* **THE BALLAD OF EASY RIDER. / WASN'T BORN TO FOLLOW** [-] [5]

Jan 70. (lp) *(63795)* *<9942>* **THE BALLAD OF EASY RIDER** [41] [36] Dec69
– The ballad of Easy Rider / Fido / Oil in my lamp / Tulsa County / Jack Tarr the sailor / Jesus is just alright / It's all over now, baby blue / There must be someone / Gunga Din / Deportee (plane wreck at Los Gatos) / Armstrong, Aldrin and Collins. *(cd-iss.Mar97 on 'Columbia'; 486751-2)*

Feb 70. (7") *(4753)* *<45071>* **JESUS IS JUST ALRIGHT. / IT'S ALL OVER NOW, BABY BLUE** [ ] [97]

— **SKIP BATTIN** (b. 2 Feb'34, Gallipolis, Ohio) – bass, repl. YORK

Nov 70. (d-lp) *(66253)* *<30127>* **UNTITLED (1/2 live)** [11] [40] Oct70
– Lover of the bayou / Positively 4th Street / Nashville West / So you want to be a rock'n'roll star / Mr.Tambourine man / Mr.Spaceman / Eight miles high / Chestnut mare / Truck stop girl / All the things / Yesterday's train / Hungry planet / Just a season / Take a whiff (on me) / You all look alike / Well come back home.

Dec 70. (7") *(5322)* *<45259>* **CHESTNUT MARE. / JUST A SEASON** [19] [ ]

May 71. (7") *(7253)* **I TRUST (EVERYTHING'S GONNA WORK OUT FINE). / THIS IS MY DESTINY** [ ] [-]

Aug 71. (lp) *(64389)* *<30640>* **BIRDMANIAX** [ ] [46] Jul71
– Glory, glory / Pale blue / I trust / Tunnel of love / Citizen Kane / I wanna grow up to be a politician / Absolute happiness / Green apple quick step / My destiny / Kathleen's song / Jamaica say you will. *(cd-iss.Sep90 on 'Line'; CLCD 900930)*

Oct 71. (7") *(7501)* *<45440>* **GLORY, GLORY. / CITIZEN KANE** [ ] [ ]

Oct 71. (lp) *(64650)* *<31795>* **THE BYRDS' GREATEST HITS VOLUME 2** (compilation) <US title 'THE BEST OF THE BYRDS (GREATEST HITS, VOLUME II'> [ ] [ ] Dec72
– The ballad of Easy rider / Jesus is just alright / Chestnut mare / You ain't goin' nowhere / I am a pilgrim / Goin' back / I trust / Lay lady lay / Wasn't born to follow / The times they are a-changin' / Drug store truck drivin' man / Get to you.

Jan 72. (lp) *(64676)* *<31050>* **FARTHER ALONG** [ ] [ ] Dec71
– Tiffany queen / Get down your line / B.B. class road / Bugler / America's great national pastime / Antique Sandy / Precious Kate / So fine / Lazy waters / Bristol

steam convention blues / Farther along.
Jan 72. (7") *(7712) <45514>* **AMERICA'S GREAT NATIONAL PASTIME. / FARTHER ALONG**

— They split mid '72, SKIP joined NEW RIDERS OF THE PURPLE SAGE. CLARENCE WHITE was killed in a road accident 14 Jul'73. / **JOHN GUERRIN** – drums (session men) took over briefly when reforming

— **McGUINN** then re-formed the original **"BYRDS"** Himself, **CROSBY, CLARK, HILLMAN + CLARKE**

Asylum Asylum

Apr 73. (lp) *(SYLA 8754) <5058>* **THE BYRDS** 31 20 Mar73
– Full circle / Sweet Mary / Changing heart / For free / Born to rock'n'roll / Things will be better / Cowgirl in the sand / Long live the King / Borrowing time / Laughing / (See the sky) about to rain. *(cd-iss.Feb93 on 'Warners; 7559 60955-2)*
May 73. (7") *(AYM 516)* **THINGS WILL BE BETTER. / FOR FREE** -
Jun 73. (7") *(AYM 517) <11016>* **FULL CIRCLE. / LONG LIVE THE KING** Apr73
Jul 73. (7") *<11019>* **COWGIRL IN THE SAND. / LONG LIVE THE KING** -

— McGUINN, HILLMAN and CLARK all went solo, later teaming up together on album. CROSBY re-formed CROSBY, STILL and NASH. Sadly, MICHAEL CLARKE was to die of liver failure 19th December '93. For all their solo work; see The GREAT ROCK DISCOGRAPHY

– (BYRDS) compilations, etc. –

On 'CBS' / 'Columbia' unless mentioned otherwise.
Feb 66. (7"ep) *(EP 6069)* **THE TIMES ARE A-CHANGING** 15 -
Oct 66. (7"ep) *(EP 6077)* **EIGHT MILES HIGH** 18 -
Aug 69. (lp) *Together; <ST-T 1001>* **PREFLYTE (demo recordings of '64)** -
<re-iss.1973 on 'Columbia'; C 32183> (UK-iss.Sep73 on 'Bumble'; GEXP 8001)
Dec 69. (lp) *Together; <ST-T 1019>* **EARLY L.A.** -
May 73. (d-lp) *(68242)* **THE HISTORY OF THE BYRDS** 47 -
– Mr. Tambourine man / Turn! turn! turn! / She don't care about time / Wild mountain thyme / Eight miles high / Mr.Spaceman / 5D (Fifth Dimension) / So you want to be a rock'n'roll star / Time between / My back pages / Lady friend / Goin' back / Old John Robertson / Wasn't born to follow / You ain't goin' nowhere / Hickory wind / Nashville West / Drug store truck drivin' man / Gunga Din / Jesus is just alright / The ballad of Easy Rider / Chestnut mare / Yesterday's train / Just a season / Citizen Kane / Jamaica say you will / Tiffany queen / America's great national pastime. *(re-iss.Sep87 d-lp/c; 460115-1/-4)*
Jul 73. (7") *(8210)* **MR. TAMBOURINE MAN. / TURN! TURN! TURN!** -
(re-iss.Feb78; 5951)
Aug 75. (7") *Asylum; (AYM 545)* **FULL CIRCLE. / THINGS WILL BE BETTER**
Feb 76. (7") *(3952)* **CHESTNUT MARE. / ALL I REALLY WANT TO DO**
Jul 76. (7") *(4411)* **TURN! TURN! TURN!. / YOU AIN'T GOIN' NOWHERE**
Jul 76. (d-lp) *(22040)* **SWEETHEART OF THE RODEO / THE NOTORIOUS BYRD BROTHERS**
Feb 80. (lp/c) *(CBS/40 31795)* **THE BYRDS PLAY DYLAN**
(cd-iss.Apr94 & Feb96 on 'Sony'; 476757-2)
Aug 80. (lp/c) *(CBS/40 31851)* **THE ORIGINAL SINGLES 1965-1967**
(re-iss.Nov81 lp/c; CBS/40 32069)
Feb 82. (lp/c) *(CBS/40 32103)* **THE ORIGINAL SINGLES 1967-1969**
Jul 82. (7") *Old Gold; (OG 9182)* **CHESTNUT MARE. / WASN'T BORN TO FOLLOW** -
Sep 83. (7"ep/c-ep) *Scoop 33; (7SR/7SC 5016)* **6-TRACK HITS**
– Lay lady lay / Turn! turn! turn! / Goin' nowhere / So you want to be a rock'n'roll star / Chestnut mare / All I really want to do.
Jul 84. (7") *Epic; (EPCA 4575)* **MR. TAMBOURINE MAN. / WASN'T BORN TO FOLLOW**
Sep 86. (d-lp/c) *Castle; (CCS LP/MC 151)* **THE BYRDS COLLECTION** -
(cd-iss.1988; CCSCD 151)– (omits some tracks).
Jan 88. (7") *Old Gold; (OG 9747)* **MR. TAMBOURINE MAN. / TURN! TURN! TURN!** -
May 88. (lp) *Murray Hill; <MH 70318>* **NEVER BEFORE** -
<cd-iss.Aug89; D 22808>
1988. (lp/cd) *Rhino; <R1/R2 70244>* **IN THE BEGINNING** -
1989. (3"cd-ep) **MR. TAMBOURINE MAN / TURN! TURN! TURN!. / ALL I REALLY WANT TO DO / LAY LADY LAY**
Nov 90. (4xcd-box) *Columbia; (467611-2) <46773>* **THE ULTIMATE BYRDS**
– (above included 4 new songs)
1990. (7"ep) *Columbia;* **FOUR DIMENSIONS**
– Eight miles high / Mr.Tambourine man / Turn! turn! turn! (to everything there is a season) / I feel a whole lot better
Feb 91. (cd/c) *Raven; (RV CD/CA 10)* **FULL FLYTE 1965-1970** -
Jul 91. (3xcd-box) *Columbia; (468338-2)* **MR. TAMBOURINE MAN / TURN! TURN! TURN! / YOUNGER THAN YESTERDAY** -
Mar 93. (cd/c) *Columbia; (471665-2/-4)* **20 ESSENTIAL TRACKS**
Oct 94. (cd) *Columbia;* **THE BEST**
Oct 94. (cd-ep) *Columbia;* **TURN! TURN! TURN!. / (other artists)**
Jun 97. (d-cd) *Columbia; (487995-2)* **THE VERY BEST OF THE BYRDS** -
(above from the soundtrack of Oscar winning film 'Forrest Gump')

— For ROGER McGUINN and other solo releases; see GREAT ROCK DISCOGRAPHY

BYSTANDERS (see under ⇒ MAN)

CACTUS (see under ⇒ VANILLA FUDGE)

John CALE

Born: 9 Mar'42, Cwmamman, Garnant, Wales. He studied classical piano and later viola at London's Guildhall School Of Music. As an 8 year old schoolboy prodigy, he'd already composed music for the BBC. In 1963, he moved to New York on a scholarship, and under JOHN CAGE and LaMONTE YOUNG's tuition, he experimented with avant-garde music. In 1965, he met LOU REED, and formed the legendary VELVET UNDERGROUND, CALE's wailing viola and white noise experimentation meshing with REED's pop sensibilties and dark lyrics to create their distinctive sound. After being fired by the band in 1968, he went solo, releasing a couple of albums for 'Columbia'. His debut in 1970 'VINTAGE VIOLENCE', saw him exhibiting a more traditional side to his enigmatic persona, with gentle folky songs. A collaboration entitled 'CHURCH OF ANTHRAX', with minimalist composer TERRY RILEY, followed in 1971. CALE continued the trend towards his roots with 'ACADEMY OF PERIL', before returning once more to the songwriter format of his first album. With LITTLE FEAT members LOWELL GEORGE and RICHIE HAYWARD among his backing band, he cut the classic 'PARIS 1919', which infused his melancholic songwriting with a disturbing unease. This was the template for much of CALE's 70's output with 1974's 'FEAR' also introducing a more aggressive element. 'HELEN OF TROY' (1975), featured a version of 'HEARTBREAK HOTEL' guarenteed to send a shiver up anyone's spine, although the album was generally disappointing overall. In 1976, he cemented his reputation by producing the legendary PATTI SMITH album, 'HORSES', having previously worked on the classic blast of primal noise that was THE STOOGES first album. His career went into a bit of a slump in the latter half of the 70's, and after an infamous incident in which he allegedly beheaded a chicken onstage (!), he had a brief dalliance with the New York punk scene. He regained his footing with 1982's 'MUSIC FOR A NEW SOCIETY', an intelligent, minimalistic affair. The mid-80's saw him sign to British label 'Beggars Banquet', and release the more mainstream 'ARTIFICIAL INTELLIGENCE'. 'WORDS FOR THE DYING', released in 1989, was a return to the classical field which included a collaboration with BRIAN ENO. They also teamed up on the sparse 'WRONG WAY UP' from 1990. 'SONGS FOR DRELLA' (a tribute to mentor ANDY WARHOL), saw CALE hook up once more with his old sparring partner LOU REED, together producing an album that outshone CALE's more recent solo outings. He and REED re-united with the others in VELVET UNDERGROUND for live work which resulted in the comeback album 'LIVE MCMXCIII'. A year later, another collaboration, this time with BOB NEUWIRTH, was largly ignored by the public. Throughout his career, he also sessioned for others, including ENO, and produced MODERN LOVERS (JONATHAN RICHMAN), SQUEEZE, etc. • **Style:** Described initially as 'Baroque'n'roll', he drifted back into avant-garde. As an 'Island' artist, he shifted into more accessible rock forms, becoming one of the genre's most gifted and influential artists. His vocal monotone drew comparisons with stablemate like NICK DRAKE or even KEVIN AYERS.

Recommended: GUTS (*6) / PARIS 1919 (*8) / SLOW DAZZLE (*7)

JOHN CALE – vocals, viola, keyboards, bass, guitar with session people

C.B.S. / Columbia

Nov 70. (7") *<45154>* **FAIRWEATHER FRIEND. / CLEO**

Dec 70. (lp) *(64256) <CS 1037>* **VINTAGE VIOLENCE**
– Hello there / Gideon's bible / Adelaide / Big white cloud / Cleo / Please / Charlemange / Bring it on up / Amsterdam / Ghost story / Fairweather friend. *(re-iss.May87 on 'Edsel' lp/cd; ED/+CD 230) (cd-iss.Sep94 on 'Columbia'; 477356-2)*

Jan 71. (7") *<45266>* **GIDEON'S BIBLE. / BIG WHITE CLOUD**

Apr 71. (lp; JOHN CALE & TERRY RILEY) *(64259) <CS 30131>* **CHURCH OF ANTHRAX**
– Church of anthrax / The hall of mirrors in the palace at Versailles / The soul of Patrick Lee / Ides of March / The protege. *(cd-iss.Oct93 on 'Sony Europe';) (cd re-iss.Mar96 on 'Columbia'; 476640-2)*

Reprise / Reprise

Apr 72. (lp) *(K 44212) <MS 2079>* **ACADEMY IN PERIL**
– The philosopher / Brahms / Legs Larry at Television Centre / Academy in peril / Intro: days of steam / 3 orchestral pieces: (a) Faust, (b) The balance, (c) Capt. Morgan's lament / King Harry / John Milton. *(re-iss.Apr86 on 'Edsel'; XED 182) (cd-iss.Apr89; EDCD 182) (cd-iss.Oct93 on 'Warners'; 7599 26930-2)*

May 72. (7") *<1108>* **DAYS OF STEAM. / LEGS LARRY AT TELEVISION CENTER**

Mar 73. (lp) *(K 44239) <MS 2131>* **PARIS 1919**
– Child's Christmas in Wales / Hanky panky nohow / The endless plain of fortune / Andalucia / Macbeth / Paris 1919 / Graham Greene / Half past France / Antartica starts here. *(cd-iss.Oct93 on 'Warners'; 7599 25926-2)*

— Around this time he contributed to album 'JUNE 1st, 1974' on 'Island' with others ENO, NICO, KEVIN AYERS. *(ILPS 9291)*

— now with **ENO** – synth / **PHIL MANZANERA** – guitar / **ARCHIE LEGGAT** – bass / **FRED SMITH** – drums guest on below 'A'side **JUDY NYLON** – vocals

Island / A&M

Jul 74. (7") *(WIP 6202)* **THE MAN WHO COULDN'T AFFORD TO ORGY. / SYLVIA SAID**

Sep 74. (lp) *(ILPS 9301)* **FEAR**
– Fear is a man's best friend / Buffalo ballet / Barracuda / Emily / Ship of fools / Gun / The man who couldn't afford to orgy / You know more than I know / Momamma scuba. *(re-iss.Aug91 cd)(c; IMCD 140)(ICM 9301)*

— with **CHRIS SPEDDING + PHIL MANZANERA** – guitar / **PAT DONALDSON** – bass / **TIMI DONALD + GERRY CONWAY** – drums / **ENO** – synthesizer / **CHRIS THOMAS** – violin, electric piano

Apr 75. (lp) *(ILPS 9317)* **SLOW DAZZLE**
– Mr. Wilson / Taking it all away / Dirty ass rock'n'roll / Darling I need you / Rollaroll / Heartbreak hotel / Ski patrol / I'm not the loving kind / Guts / The jeweller. *(cd-iss.Jun88; CID 9317) (re-iss.cd Aug94; IMCD 202)*

— **PHIL COLLINS** – drums repl. CONWAY, MANZANERA + THOMAS.

Nov 75. (lp) *(ILPS 9350)* **HELEN OF TROY**
– My Maria / Helen of Troy / China sea / Engine / Save us / Cable Hogue / I keep a close watch / Pablo Picasso / Leaving it up to you * / Baby what you want me to do? / Sudden death. *(some copies repl.* by)*– Coral Moon'. *(cd-iss.Apr94; IMCD 177)*

Feb 77. (lp) *(ILPS 9459)* **GUTS** (compilation)
– Guts / Mary Lou / Helen of Troy / Pablo Picasso / Leaving it up to you / Fear is a man's best friend / Gun / Dirty ass rock 'n' roll / Heartbreak hotel. *(cd-iss.Aug94; IMCD 203)*

— with **RITCHIE FLIEGLER** – lead guitar / **BRUCE BRODY** – mogg synthesizer / **JIMMY BAIN** – bass / **KEVIN CURRIE** – drums

Illegal / not issued

Sep 77. (7"ep) *(ILL 003)* **ANIMAL JUSTICE**
– Chicken shit / Memphis / Hedda Gabbler.

— with **MARK AARON** – guitar / **JOE BIDWELL** – keyboards / **GEORGE SCOTT** – bass / **DOUG BROWN** – drums / **DEERFRANCE** – vocals

not issued / Spy

Dec 79. (lp) *<SP 004>* **SABOTAGE (live)**
– Mercenaries (ready for war) / Baby you know / Evidence / Dr.Mudd / Walkin' the dog / Captain Hook / Only time will tell / Sabotage / Chorale.

not issued / I.R.S.

1980. (7") *<9008>* **MERCENARIES (READY FOR WAR). / ROSEGARDEN FUNERAL OF SORES**

— with **STURGIS NIKIDES** – guitar, vocals / **JIM GOODWIN** – keyboards, synth. / **PETER MUNY** – bass / **ROBERT MEDECI** – drums

A&M / A&M

Mar 81. (lp) *(AMLH 64849)* **HONI SOIT**
– Dead or alive / Strange times in Casablanca / Fighter pilot / Wilson Joliet / Streets of Laredo / Honi soit (la premiere Lecon de Francaise) / Riverbank / Russian roulette / Magic & lies. *(cd-iss.Jul94; CDMID 1936)*

Apr 81. (7") *(AMS 8130)* **DEAD OR ALIVE. / HONI SOIT**

— now w/ **ALAN LANIER** – keyboards / **D. J. YOUNG** – guitar / **DAVID LICHTENSTEIN** – drums / **JOHN WONDERLING / MIKE McCLINTOCK / ROBERT ELK**

Ze-Island / Ze

Aug 82. (lp/c) *(ILPS/ICT 7019)* **MUSIC FOR A NEW SOCIETY**
– Taking your life in your hands / Thoughtless kind / Sanities / If you were still around / Close watch / Mama's song / Broken bird / Chinese envoy / Changes made / Damn life / Rise, Sam and Rimsky Korsakov. *(cd-iss.Mar94 on 'Yellow Moon'; YMCD 003)*

Apr 83. (7") *(IS 113)* **I KEEP A CLOSE WATCH. / CLOSE WATCH (instrumental)**

— **ANDY HEERMANS** – bass, vocals repl. LANIER

Jun 83. (lp/c) *(ILPS/ICT 7024)* **CARIBBEAN SUNSET**
– Hungry for love / Experiment number 1 / Model Beirut recital / Caribbean sunset / Praetorian underground / Magazines / Where there's a will / The hunt / Villa Albani.

Aug 84. (7") *(IS 197)* **OOH LA LA. / MAGAZINES**

Sep 84. (lp/c) *(ILPS/ICT 7026)* **JOHN CALE COMES ALIVE (live)**
– Ooh la la / Evidence / Dead or alive / Chinese envoy / Leaving it up to you / Dr. Mudd / Waiting for the man / Heartbreak hotel / Fear / Never give up on you.

— with **DAVID YOUNG** – guitar / **JAMES YOUNG** – keyboards / **GRAHAM DOWDALL** – percussion

Beggars Banquet / Warners

Jul 85. (7"/12") *(BEG 145/+T)* **DYING ON THE VINE. / EVERYTIME THE DOGS BARK**

Nov 85. (lp/c) *(BEG A/C 68)* **ARTIFICIAL INTELLIGENCE**
– Everytime the dogs bark / Dying on the vine / The sleeper / Vigilante lover / Chinese takeaway (Hong Kong 1997) (medley) / Song of the valley / Fade away tomorrow / Black rose / Satellite walk. *(re-iss.Jan89 on 'Lowdown-Beggars Banquet' lp/c; BBL/+C 68) (cd-iss.Mar96; BBL 68CD)*

Nov 85. (12"m) *(BEG 153T)* **SATELLITE WALK. / DYING ON THE VINE / CRASH COURSE IN HARMONICS**

— now w/ **BRIAN ENO** – synthesizers, keyboards / **NEIL CATCHPOLE** – viola, violin / choir

Land / Warners

Oct 89. (lp/c/cd) *(LAND/+C/CD 009)* **WORDS FOR THE DYING**
– The Falkland suite:- Introduction-There was a saviour – Interlude I / On a wedding anniversary – Interlude II – Lie still, sleep becalmed – Do not go gentle into that

good night / Songs without words 1 & 2 / The soul of Carmen Miranda. *(re-iss.cd Oct95 on 'All Saints'; ASCD 009)*

— Apr'90, CALE & Lou REED⇒, collaborated on Andy Warhol tribute album SONGS FOR DRELLA. On 'Warners' records lp/c//cd*WX 345/+C //7599 26140-2*. It was CALE's first excursion into the Top 30.

— Oct'90, he teamed up with ENO (see –), on album 'WRONG WAY UP' on 'Land' and a single 'ONE WORD'.

Delabel / not issued

Nov 91. (cd) **PARIS S'EVEILLE, SUIVI D'AUTRES COMPOSITIONS** [-] [-] France
– Paris S'eveille, suivi d'autres / Sanctus (four etudes for electronic orchestra) / Animals at night / The cowboy laughs at round-up / Primary motive 1) Factory speech, 2) Strategy session, 3) Closing titles / Antartica starts here / Booker T. (by VELVET UNDERGROUND) *(UK-iss.Mar93 on 'Crepuscule';) (re-iss.Nov95 on 'Yellow Moon'; YMCD 007)*

Crepuscule / not issued

Nov 93. (cd) *(TWI 9542) <<bfiMDNMflLA NAISSANCE DE L'AMOUR* [ ] [-]
– La naissance de l'amour / If you love me no more / And if I love you still / Judith / Converging themes / Opposites attract / I will do it, I will keep it / Keep it to yourself / Walk towards the sea / Unquiet heart / Waking up to love / Mysterious relief / Never been so hapy / Beyond expectations / Conversations in the garden / La naissance de l'amour II / Secret dialogue / Roma / On the dark side / La naissance de l'amour III / Eye to eye / Maria's car crash and hotel rooms / La naissance de l'amour IV.

M.C.A. / M.C.A.

May 94. (cd; JOHN CALE / BOB NEUWIRTH) **LAST DAY ON EARTH (Soundtrack)** [ ] [ ]
– Overture- a) A tourist, b) A contract, c) A prisoner / Cafe Shabu / Pastoral angst / Who's in charge? / Short of time / Angel of death / Paradise Nevada / Old China / Ocean life / Instrumental / Modern world / Streets come alive / Secrets / Maps of the world / Broken hearts / The high and the mighty road.

Hannibal / not issued

Sep 96. (cd) *(HNCD 1395)* **WALKING ON LOCUSTS** [ ] [-]
– Dancing undercover / Set me free / So what / Crazy Egypt / So much for love / Tell me why / Indistinct notion of cool / Secret corrida / Circus / Gatorville and points east / Some friends / Entre nous.

Jun 97. (cd) *(HNCD 1407)* **EAT / KISS – MUSIC FOR THE FILMS OF ANDY WARHOL** [ ] [-]
– KISS:- Infinite guitar, quartet / Frozen warning, Jimmy, metal-violin solo – Daid Tiye (backing vocal) / B.J., quartet, Moe / Violin solo – Todd, Tiye, quartet / Harpsichord, infinite guitar / Quartet, Moe – Harpsichord, Tiye – percussion / Quartet, cello solo – Dawn, harpsichord / B.J., quartet, electric piano / B.J., quartet, electric piano / Quartet solo / Solo Tiye, strings // EAT:- B.J., 12-string guitar intro – David / Reading from 'Melanethon' (Swedenborg) / Todd solo, 12-string, Moe / Piano, B.J.

– compilations, etc. –

Jul 91. (c) *Danceteria; (DANCD 113)* **EVEN COWBOYS GET THE BLUES (live 1978-79 at CBGB's)** [ ] [ ]
(cd-iss.Jun97; same)

Oct 92. (cd) *Hannibal; (HNCD 1372)* **FRAGMENTS OF A RAINY SEASON (live)** [ ] [-]

Oct 92. (cd) *Traditional Line; (TL 001326)* **BROKEN HEARTS LIVE 1984-1992 (live)** [ ] [-]

Nov 93. (cd) *Crepuscule;* **23 SOLO PIECES FOR LA NAISSANCE DE L'AMOUR** [ ] [-]
(re-iss.Nov95 on 'Yellow Moon'; YMCD 007)

1994. (d-cd) *Rhino;* **SEDUCING DOWN THE DOOR: A JOHN CALE COLLECTION** [-] [ ]

Sep 96. (d-cd) *Island; (524235-2)* **THE ISLAND YEARS ANTHOLOGY** [ ] [-]

Randy CALIFORNIA (see under ⇒ SPIRIT)

Robert CALVERT (see under ⇒ HAWKWIND)

CAMEL

Formed: London, England . . . 1972 by R&B veteran PETE BARDENS, plus ex-backing band of PHILIP GOODHAND-TAIT; DOUG FERGUSON, ANDY WARD and ANDY LATIMER. Their first recording, 'GOD OF LIGHT REVISITED – PARTS ONE, TWO, THREE', featured on 1 side of a various double album, 'Greasy Truckers – Live At Dingwalls'. The following year, they issued their eponymous debut on 'M.C.A.', before moving to 'Deram' for the follow-up, 'MIRAGE' (1974). CAMEL really came into their own with their conceptual interpretation of Paul Gallico's 'THE SNOW GOOSE'. A Top 30 breakthrough, it was dominated by excellent instrumental pieces which perfectly translated Gallico's children story into a prog-rock framework. However, Gallico served a writ against the group for copyright infringement. Unbowed, CAMEL came up with yet another successful album, 'MOONMADNESS', this time utilising vocals which took them a stage further in their musical development. Another Top 20 album followed in 1977, 'RAIN DANCES', a softer, more conventional affair, as was the 1978 studio follow-up, 'BREATHLESS'. Although they retained a loyal fan-base within the college fraternity, the onset of more hip sounds (i.e. punk & new wave) effectively swept them under the carpet. They disbanded in '84, but re-formed seven years later. Their comeback album, 'DUST AND DREAMS' (1992), was inspired by John Steinbeck's book ,'The Grapes Of Wrath'.

Recommended: THE SNOW GOOSE (*8) / MOONMADNESS (*6) / RAIN DANCES (*6) / THE COLLECTION (*7)

PETER BARDENS – keyboards, vocals (ex-THEM, ex-solo, ex-SHOTGUN EXPRESS) / **ANDY LATIMER** – vocals, guitar / **DOUG FERGUSON** – bass / **ANDY WARD** – drums, percussion

M.C.A. / not issued

Nov 72. (7") *(MU 1177)* **NEVER LET GO. / CURIOSITY** [ ] [-]

Dec 73. (lp) *(MUPS 477)* **CAMEL** [ ] [-]
– Slow yourself down / Mystic queen / Six ate / Separation / Never let go / Curiosity / Arubaluba. *(re-iss.1974; MCF 2065) (re-iss.Aug81 lp/c; MCL/+C 1601) (re-iss.Nov82 on 'Fame' lp/c; FA/TCFA 3054) (cd-iss.Jul93 on 'Camel Prod.'; CP 002CD)*

Deram / Janus

1974. (lp) *(SML 1107) <7009>* **MIRAGE** [ ] [ ]
– Freefall / Supertwister / Nimrodel: – The procession – The white rider / Earthrise / Lady fantasy: – Encounter – Smiles for you – Lady fantasy. *(cd-iss.Jun89; 820 613-2)*

Decca / Janus

May 75. (lp/c) *(SKLR/KSKC 5207) <7016>* **THE SNOW GOOSE** [22] [ ]
– The great marsh – Rhayader – Rhayader goes to town – Sanctuary – Fritha – The snow goose – Friendship – Migration – Rhayader alone / Flight of the snow goose – Preparation – Dunkirk – Epitaph – Fritha alone – La princesse Perdue – The great marsh. *(re-iss.Nov76; same) (cd-iss.Jul88; 800 080-2)*

May 75. (7") *(FR 13581)* **FLIGHT OF THE SNOW GOOSE. / RHAYADER** [ ] [-]

Sep 75. (7") *(FR 13603)* **THE SNOW GOOSE. / FREEFALL** [ ] [-]

Apr 76. (lp/c) *(TXSR/KTXCR 115) <7024>* **MOONMADNESS** [15] [ ]
– Aristillus / Song within a song / Chord change / Spirit of the water / Another night / Air born / Lunar sea. *(cd-iss.1983 & Jul89; 810 879-2)*

Jun 76. (7") *(FR 13656) <262>* **ANOTHER NIGHT. / LUNAR SEA** [ ] [ ]

— **RICHARD SINCLAIR** – bass (ex-CARAVAN) repl. FERGUSON

Sep 77. (lp/c) *(TXSR/KTXCR 124) <7035>* **RAIN DANCES** [20] [ ]
– First light / Metrognome / Tell me / Highways of the sun / Unevensong / One of these days I'll get an early night / Elke / Skylines / Rain dances. *(cd-iss.Dec91 on 'London'+=; 820 725-2)*– Highways of the sun (single edit).

Sep 77. (7") *(FR 13729)* **HIGHWAYS OF THE SUN. / TELL ME** [ ] [-]

— added **MEL COLLINS** – saxophone (ex-KING CRIMSON etc.) **/ DAVE SINCLAIR** – keyboards (ex-CARAVAN etc.)

Apr 78. (d-lp/d-c) *(DBCR/KBC 7-8)* **A LIVE RECORD (live)** [ ] [-]
– Never let go / Song within a song / Lunar sea / Skylines / Lady fantasy: Encounter – Smiles for you – Lady fantasy / The great marsh – Rhayader – Rhayader goes to town – Sanctuary – Fritha – The snow goose – Friendship – Migration – Rhayader alone / Flight of the snow goose: – Preparation – Dunkirk – Epitaph – Fritha alone – La princesse Perdue – The great marsh / Ligging at Louis'.*(re-iss.Jul93 cd/c;)*

Decca / Arista

Sep 78. (lp/c) *(TXSR/KTXSR 132) <4206>* **BREATHLESS** [26] [ ]
– Breathless / Echoes / Wing and a prayer / Down on the farm / Starlight ride / Summer lightning / You make me smile / The sleeper / Rainbow's end. *(re-iss.Aug92 on 'Deram' cd/c; 820 726-2/-4)*

— **COLIN BASS** – bass, vocals repl. RICHARD who later rejoined CARAVAN / **KIT WATKINS** – keyboards, flute repl. PETER who went solo then LATIMER, WARD

Sep 79. (lp/c) *(TXSR/KTXSR 137) <4254>* **I CAN SEE YOUR HOUSE FROM HERE** [45] [ ]
– Wait / Your love is no stronger than mine / Eye of the storm / Who are we / Survival / Hymn to her / Neon magic / Remote romance. *(cd-iss.Jan89 & Oct93 on 'London'; 820 614-2)*

Oct 79. (7") *(FR 13871)* **YOUR LOVE IS NO STRONGER THAN MINE. / NEON MAGIC** [ ] [-]

Feb 80. (7") *(FR 13879)* **REMOTE ROMANCE. / RAINBOW'S END / TELL ME** [ ] [-]

— **DUNCAN MACKAY** – keyboards (ex-COCKNEY REBEL) repl. KIT

Jan 81. (lp/c) *(SKL/KSKC 5323)* **NUDE** [36] [-]
– City life / Nude / Drafted / Docks / Beached / Landscapes / Changing places / Pomp and circumstance / Please come home / Reflections / Captures / The homecoming / Lies / The last farewell / The birthday cake / Nude's return. *(cd-iss.1987; 810 880-2)*

— **JAN SCHELHAAS** – keyboards (ex-CARAVAN) repl. MACKAY who joined BUDGIE

Decca / Passport

May 82. (lp/c) *(SKL/KSKC 5328) <PB 6013>* **THE SINGLE FACTOR** [57] [ ]
– No easy answer / You are the one / Heroes / Selva / Manic / Lullaby / Sasquatch / Camelogue / Today's goodbye / A heart's desire / End piece. *(cd-iss.1983 & May94; 800 081-2)*

— **PAUL BURGESS** – drums, percussion repl. WARD (who joined MARILLION)

Mar 84. (lp/c)(cd) *(SKL/KSKC 5334)(820 020-2)* **STATIONARY TRAVELLER** [57] [-]
– Pressure points / Refugee / Copos / Cloak and dagger man / Stationary traveller / West Berlin / Fingertips / Missing / Afterwords / Long goodbyes. *(cd re-iss.Jul89; same)*

Mar 84. (7"/12") *(CAMEL/CAMEX 1)* **CLOAK AND DAGGER MAN. / PRESSURE POINTS** [ ] [-]

— **LATIMER, BASS + BURGESS** with returning guests **MEL COLLINS & PETER BARDENS** brought in **TOM SCHERPENZEEL** – keyboards / **RICHIE CLOSE** – keyboards + **CHRIS RAINBOW** – vocals, keyboards

Nov 84. (lp/c)(cd) *(SKL/KSKC 5338)(823 812-2)* **PRESSURE POINTS – CAMEL LIVE** (live 11th May'84) [ ] [-]
– West Berlin / Pressure points / Drafted / Captured / Lies / Rhayader goes to town / Sasquatch / Fingertips / Rhayader / Wait. *(cd re-iss.1987 on 'London'; 820 166-2)*

— CAMEL disbanded in '84, but re-formed again in 1991.

Camel / not issued

Sep 92. (cd/c) *(CP 001 CD/C)* **DUST AND DREAMS** [ ] [-]
– Dust bowl / Go west / Dusted out / Mother road / Needles / Rose of Sharon / End of the line / Storm clouds / Cotton camp / Broken ranks / Sheet rain / Whispers / Little rivers and little Rose / Hopeless anger / Whispers in the rain. *(cd re-iss.Jul93; same)*

Nov 93. (d-cd) *(CP 004CD)* **NEVER LET GO (live '92)** [ ] [-]

Jan 96. (cd) *(CP 006CD)* **HARBOUR OF TEARS** [ ] [-]

– compilations etc. –

Sep 81. (lp/c) *Decca; (SKL/KSKC 5325)* **CHAMELEON** [ ] [-]

Nov 85. (d-lp/c/cd) *Castle; (CCS LP/MC/CD 116)* **THE COLLECTION** [ ] [-]
– Aristilus / Freefall / Supertwister / Spirit of the water / Lunar sea / The white rider / Earthrise / Song within a song / Rhayader – Rhayader goes to town – Migration – Rhayader alone – La princesse Perdue – The great marsh / Drafted / Captured / Sasquatch / Rain dances / Highways of the sun / First light.

May 91. (cd/c) *Elite;* **LANDSCAPE** ☐ -
Jul 93. (cd) *Camel Prod.; (CP 003CD)* **CAMEL ON THE ROAD 1972 (live)** ☐ -
Nov 94. (cd) *Deram; (844 340-2)* **ECHOES** ☐ -
Jan 95. (cd) *Camel Prod.; (CP 005CD)* **CAMEL ON THE ROAD 1982 (live)** ☐ -
Mar 97. (cd) *Camel Prod.; (CP 007CD)* **CAMEL ON THE ROAD 1981 (live)** ☐ -
— In Jul 94, PETE BARDENS released cd 'BIG SKY' for 'H.T.D.'.

Jimmy CAMPBELL (see under ⇒ 23rd TURNOFF)

Patrick CAMPBELL-LYONS (see under ⇒ NIRVANA (Ire-UK)

CAN

Formed: Cologne, Germany ... 1968 initially as INNER SPACE by HOLGER CZUKAY and IRMIN SCHMIDT. MICHAEL KAROLI and JAKI LEIBEZEIT were soon recruited along with DAVID JOHNSON and black American vocalist MALCOLM MOONEY. Later that year, JOHNSON bailed out prior to their debut album, 'MONSTER MOVIE' (1970). Having studied under KARL-HEINZ STOCKHAUSEN, CZUKAY and SCHMIDT (who were also influenced by JOHN CAGE, TERRY RILEY and The VELVET UNDERGROUND) pioneered their own take on avant-garde minimalism, creating a hypnotic, free-form sound, relentless in its intensity. The album included a 20-minute piece, 'YOU DOO RIGHT', extracted from a marathon improv-session and highlighting the very real dementia of MOONEY's ravings. He suffered a nervous breakdown soon after and was subsequently replaced by the Japanese 'vocalist' DAMO SUZUKI prior to recording 'SOUNDTRACKS'. More improvised beauty was evidenced on their next set, the German Top 40 classic, 'TAGO MAGO' (1971), a sprawling double-set that featured two of their more hypnotic tracks, 'HALLELUWAH' and 'MUSHROOM'. On their next two releases, 'EGE BAMYASI' and 'FUTURE DAYS', CAN explored even more ritualistic textures alongside SUZUKI's partly-spoken tri-lingual ramblings. SUZUKI subsequently returned to Japan to become a Jehovah's Witness, after a final gig at the 1973 Edinburgh Festival. Vocal duties were now shared by KAROLI and SCHMIDT on the more percussive 'SOON OVER BABALUMA' album (1974). They signed to Richard Branson's innovative 'Virgin' label the following year, 'LANDED' being a prime example of British-influenced avant-garde rock. In 1976, they surprised many by having a Top 30 hit, 'I WANT MORE', penned by PINK FLOYD's DAVID GILMOUR. With the addition of ROSKO GEE and sessionman REEBOP KWAKU BAAH, they moved in a more African/reggae influenced direction; CZUKAY having already withdrawn from most of the proceedings. Their final efforts were of little significance, the 1979 album interesting only for its re-hash of Offenbach's 'CAN-CAN', which had previously been released as a single. KAROLI, SCHMIDT and CZUKAY all continued in the 80's as solo artists, the latter teaming up once again with LEIBEZEIT (and JAH WOBBLE) on the 1982 album 'FULL CIRCLE'. The original line-up reformed in 1986 for an album, 'RITE TIME', but the record lacked the inspiration and originality that characterised CAN's earlier work. The band remain highly regarded, cited as a major influence by artists as diverse as CARL CRAIG and PRIMAL SCREAM. Even The FALL payed homage to them by crediting a song as 'I AM DAMO SUZUKI'.

Recommended: CANNIBALISM (*8) / TAGO MAGO (*9) / EGE BAMYASI (*7) / FUTURE DAYS (*7) / SOON OVER BABALUMA (*6)

IRMIN SCHMIDT (b.29 May'37, Berlin, Germany) – keyboards / **HOLGER CZUKAY** (b.24 Mar'38, Danzig, Germany) – bass, electronics / **DAVID JOHNSON** – flute / **MICHAEL KAROLI** (b.29 Apr'48, Straubing, Germany) – guitar, violin / **JAKI LEIBEZEIT** (b.26 May'38, nr.Dresden, Germany) – drums / **MALCOLM MOONEY** – vocals

Music Factory | not issued

Nov 68. (7"; by IRMIN SCHMIDT) **KAMA SUTRA. /** - - German
— Now a quintet when JOHNSON departed (below issued Germany Aug'69)

U.A. | U.A.

May 70. (lp) *(UAS 29094)* **MONSTER MOVIE** ☐ -
– Father cannot yell / Mary, Mary so contrary / You doo right / Outside my door. *(cd-iss.Jun89 on 'Spoon-Mute'; SPOONCD 004)*
— **KENJI 'DAMO' SUZUKI** (b.16 Jan'50, Japan) – vocals repl.MOONEY who suffered a nervous breakdown
Sep 70. Liberty; (7") **SOUL DESERT. / SHE BRINGS THE RAIN** - - German
Sep 71. (lp) *(UAS 29283)* **SOUNDTRACKS** ☐ -
– Deadlock / Tango whiskeyman / Don't turn the light off / Leave me alone / Soul desert / Mother sky / She brings the rain. *(cd-iss.Jun89 on 'Spoon-Mute'; SPOONCD 005)*
1971. (7") **TURTLES HAVE SHORT LEGS. / HALLELUWAH (edit)** - - German
1971. (7") **SPOON. / SHIKAKO MARU TEN** - - German
Feb 72. (d-lp) *(UAD 60009-10)* **TAGO MAGO** ☐ -
– Paperhouse / Mushroom / Oh yeah / Halleluwah / Aumgn / Peking O / Bring me coffee or tea. *(cd-iss.Jul89 on 'Spoon-Mute'; SPOONCD 006-007)*
Nov 72. (lp) *(UAS 29414) <063>* **EGE BAMYASI** ☐ ☐
– Pinch / Sing swan song / One more night / Vitamin C / Soup / I'm so green / Spoon. *(cd-iss.Jun89 on 'Spoon-Mute'; SPOONCD 008)*
Feb 73. (7") *(UP 35506)* **SPOON. / I'M SO GREEN** ☐ -
Jun 73. (lp) *(UAS 29505) <213>* **FUTURE DAYS** ☐ ☐
– Future days / Spray / Moonshake / Bel Air. *(cd-iss.Jun89 on 'Spoon-Mute'; SPOONCD 009)*
Oct 73. (7") *(UP 35596) <446>* **MOONSHAKE. / FUTURE DAYS (edit)** ☐ ☐
— trimmed to a quartet when DAMO SUZUKI left to become a Jehovah's Witness. Now **SCHMIDT / KAROLI** (shared vocals) **CZUKAY + LIEBEZEIT**
Nov 74. (lp) *(UAG 29673) <343>* **SOON OVER BABALUMA** ☐ ☐
– Dizzy dizzy / Come sta, la luna / Splash / Chain reaction / Quantum physics. *(cd-iss.Jun89 on 'Spoon-Mute'; SPOONCD 010)*
Dec 74. (7") *(UP 35749)* **DIZZY DIZZY. / SPLASH** ☐ -

Virgin | Polydor

Sep 75. (lp) *(V 2041)* **LANDED** ☐ ☐
– Full moon on the highway / Half past one / Hunters and collectors / Vernal equinox / Red hot Indians / Unfinished. *(cd-iss.Jun87; CDV 2041) (re-iss.Aug88; OVED 194)*
— approx Mar76, tried two vocalists one a Malayan, the other **MICHAEL COUSINS** (English). added **DAVID GILMOUR** – guest/composer (3) b.vocals of PINK FLOYD
Jul 76. (7") *(VS 153)* **I WANT MORE. / ... AND MORE** 26 ☐
Oct 76. (lp) *(V 2071)* **FLOW MOTION** ☐ ☐
– I want more / Cascade waltz / Laugh till you cry ... live till you die / ...And more / Babylonian pearl / Smoke (E.F.S. No.59) / Flow motion. *(cd-iss.Jun87; CDV 2071) (re-iss.Aug88; OVED 88)*
Nov 76. (7") *(VS 166)* **SILENT NIGHT. / CASCADE WALTZ** ☐ -
— added **ROSKO GEE** – bass + **REEBOP KWAKU BAAH** (b. Konongo, Ghana) – percussion (both ex-TRAFFIC) (HOLGER now synths., samplers)
Mar 77. (lp) *(V 2079)* **SAW DELIGHT** ☐ ☐
– Don't say no / Sunshine day and night / Call me / Animal waves / Fly by night. *(cd-iss.Jun87; CDV 2079) (re-iss.Aug88; OVED 195)*
Apr 77. (7") *(VS 172)* **DON'T SAY NO. / RETURN** ☐ -
— HOLGER went on a few holidays (& solo). The rest of the band below (**SCHMIDT, KAROLI, LIEBEZEIT, BAAH & GEE**) recorded album.

Lightning | Peters Int.

Jun 78. (7") *(LIG 545)* **CAN-CAN. / CAN BE** ☐ -
Jul 78. (lp) *(LIP 4) <9024>* **OUT OF REACH** ☐ ☐
– Serpentine / Pauper's daughter and I / November / Seven days awake / Give me no roses / Like Inobe God / One more day. *(re-iss.Jun86 on 'Thunderbolt'; THBL 025) (cd-iss.Nov88; CDTB 025)*

Laser | not issued

Jul 79. (lp) *(LASL 2)* **CAN** ☐ -
– All gates open / Safe / Sunday jam / Sodom / Aspectacle / E.F.S. No.99: "can can" / Ping pong / Can be. *(re-iss.Feb85 as 'INNER SPACE' on 'Thunderbolt'; THBL 020) (cd-iss.Jun87; THBL 020)*
— had already split late '78. JAKI formed PHANTOM BAND and collaborated with HOLGER. IRMIN went solo and formed BRUNO SPOERRI. MICHAEL in '84 went solo. All their releases were mainly German only. **CAN** reformed 1969 line-up 20 years on.

Mercury | not issued

Oct 89. (lp/c/cd) *(838 883-1/-4/-2)* **RITE TIME** ☐ -
– On the beautiful side of a romance / The without law man / Below this level (patient's song) / Movin' right along / Like a new world / Hoolah hoolah / Give the drummer some / In the distance lies the future. *(cd-iss.Oct94 on 'Spoon-Mute'; SPOONCD 029)*

White Label | not issued

Sep 90. (cd)(c)(lp) **FISHERMAN'S FRIEND REMIXES** ☐ -

– compilations, others, etc. –

on 'United Artists' unless otherwise mentioned
Aug 74. (lp) *(USP 103)* **LIMITED EDITION** ☐ -
May 76. (d-lp) *Caroline; (CAD 3001)* **UNLIMITED EDITION** ☐ -
Nov 76. (lp) *Sunset; (SLS 50400)* **OPENER** (71-74 material) ☐ -
Oct 78. (d-lp) *(UDM 105-6)* **CANNIBALISM** ☐ -
May 81. (7") *Virgin; (VS 422) / Polydor;* **I WANT MORE. / ... AND MORE** ☐ ☐
(12"+=) *(VS 422-12)* – Silent night.
1981. (lp) *(SPOON 012)* **DELAY 1968** - - German
– Butterfly / Pnoom / 19th century man / Thief / Man named Joe / Uphill / Little star of Bethlehem. *(cd-iss.Jun89 on 'Spoon-Mute'; SPOONCD 012)*
Oct 81. (lp) *Virgin; (OVED 3)* **INCANDESCENCE** ☐ -
1982. (c) *Pure Freude; (PF 23)* **ONLYOU** - - German
Mar 83. (12"ep) *Cherry Red; (12CHERRY 57)* **MOONSHAKE. / TURTLES HAVE SHORT LEGS / ONE MORE NIGHT** ☐ -
Jan 85. (c) *Tago Mago; (TM 4755)* **PREHISTORIC FUTURE** - - France
Jun 91. (cd) *Spoon-Mute; (SPOONCD 23-24)* **UNLIMITED EDITION** (new collection) ☐ -
Nov 92. (cd) *Spoon-Mute; (SPOONCD 021)* **CANNIBALISM II** ☐ -
– Uphill / Pnoom / Connection / Mother Upduff / Little star / T.V. spot / Doko E. / Turtles have short legs / Shikaku maru ten / Gomorrha / Blue bag / Red hot Indians / Half past one / Flow motion / Smoke / I want more . . .and more / Laugh till you cry / Aspectacle animal waves / Sunshine day and night / E.F.S. No.7 / Melting away.
Oct 94. (cd) *Spoon-Mute; (SPOONCD 3031)* **ANTHOLOGY** ☐ -
Feb 95. (cd) *Spoon-Mute; (SPOONCD 022)* **CANNIBALISM III** ☐ -
– (solo work 1979-1991 from CZUKAY, SCHMIDT, LIEBEZEIT & KAROLI)
Oct 95. (cd) *Strange Fruit; (SFRCD 135)* **LIVE AT THE BBC (Peel sessions)** ☐ -
May 97. (t-lp/d-cd) *Grey Area; (SPOON/+CD 39-40)* **SACRILEGE** ☐ -

HOLGER CZUKAY

Music Factory | not issued

1968. (lp; by HOLGER CZUKAY with ROLF DAMMERS) *(SRS 002)* **CANAXIS 5** - - German
– Boat woman song / Canaxis. *(re-iss.1981 on 'Spoon'; SPOON 015) (cd-iss.Feb95 on 'Spoon-Mute'; SPOONCD 015)*
— CZUKAY with other CAN members augenting

E.M.I. | not issued

Nov 79. (7") *(EMI 5005)* **COOL IN THE POOL. / OH LORD GIVE US MORE MONEY** ☐ -

(re-iss.Jul83; same)

Jan 80. (lp) *(EMC 3319)* **MOVIES** [ ] [-]
– Cool in the pool / Oh Lord give us some money / Persian love / Hollywood symphony.

—— 1980, CZUKAY released 12"ep 'LES VAMPYRETTES' in Germany with CONRAD PLANK & AXEL GROS on 'Electrola'; *(F 667.226)*

—— mid'81, CZUKAY teamed up with JAH WOBBLE and JAKI LIEBEZEIT to releases 12"ep 'HOW MUCH ARE THEY?' for 'Island'; *(12WIP 6701)*

—— most of the tracks appeared on below 'Virgin' German album.

Feb 82. (lp/c) *(EMC/TC-EMC 3394)* **ON THE WAY TO THE PEAK OF NORMAL** [ ] [-]
– Ode to perfume / On the way to the peak of normal / Witches multiplication table / Two bass shuffle / Hiss'n'listen.

Mar 82. (7") *(EMI 5280)* **ODE TO PERFUME. / PERSIAN LOVE** [ ] [-]

Virgin not issued

1982. (lp; by HOLGER CZUKAY, JAH WOBBLE & JAKI LIEBEZEIT) *(205 866-320)* **FULL CIRCLE** [-] [-] German
– How much are they? / Where's the money? / Full circle R.P.S. (No.7) / Mystery R.P.S. (No.8) / Trench warfare / Twilight world. *(cd-iss.May92 on 'Virgin'; CDOVD 437)*

—— In Oct'83, he teamed up with JAH WOBBLE (again) & The EDGE (U2), to release mini-album 'SNAKE CHARMER' for 'Island'; *(IMA 1)*

May 84. (lp/c) *(V/TCV 2307)* **DER OSTEN IST ROT** [ ] [-]
– The photo song / Bankel rap '82 / Michy / Rhonrad / Collage / Esperanto socialiste / Der osten ist rot / Das massenmedium / Schaue vertrauensvoll in die zukunft / Traum mal wieder. *(re-iss.Apr86 lp/c; OVED/+C 161)*

May 84. (7") *(VS 671)* **THE PHOTO SONG. / DAS MASSENMEDIUM** [ ] [-]
(12"+=) *(VS 671-12)* – Biomutanten.

Jan 87. (lp/c) *(V/TCV 2408)* **ROME REMAINS ROME** [ ] [-]
– Hey ba ba re bob / Blessed Easter / Sudentenland / Hit hit flop flop / Perfect world / Music in the air. *(cd-iss.Jan88+=; CDV 2408)*– DER OSTEN IST ROT (lp)

—— (Mar'88) collaborated next with DAVID SYLVIAN on album 'PLIGHT AND PREMONITION' for 'Venture' cd/c/lp; *(CD/TC+/VE 11)*

—— next with **SHELDON ANCEL** – vocals / **M.KAROLI** – guitar / **J.LIEBEZEIT** – drums

Jan 91. (cd/c/lp) **RADIO WAVE SURFER** [ ] [-]
– Rhine water / It ain't no crime / I get weird dreams / Saturday night movie / Dr.Oblivion / We can fight all night / Get it sweet / Ride a radio wave / Atmosphere tuning / Voice of Bulgaria / Late night radio / Through the freezing snow / Encore.

Mute not issued

May 93. (cd) *(CDSTUMM 125)* **MOVING PICTURES** [ ] [-]
– Longing for daydreams / All night long / Radio in an hourglass / Dark moon / Floatspace / Rhythms of a secret life.

JAKI LEIBEZEIT

PHANTOM BAND

with others **DOMINIK VON SENGER** – guitar / **HELMUT ZERLETT** – keyboards / **OLEK GELBA** – percussion / **ROSKO GEE** – bass, vocals

Sky not issued

1980. (lp) *(048)* **PHANTOM BAND** [-] [-] German
– You inspired me / I'm the one / For M. / Phantom drums / Absolutely straight / Rolling / Without desire / No more fooling / Pulsar / Latest news. *(UK cd-iss.Feb95 on 'Spoon-Mute'; SPOONCD 017)*

—— **SHELDON ANCEL** – vocals repl. GEE

1981. (lp) *(065)* **FREEDOM OF SPEECH** [-] [-] German
– Freedom of speech / E.F.1 / Brain police / No question / Relax / Gravity / Trapped again.

—— In 1981 he and CZUKAY teamed up with PHEW on lp 'PHEW'

—— now without OLEK

Spoon not issued

1983. (lp) *(SPOON 017)* **NOWHERE** [-] [-] German
– Loading zone / Planned obsolescene / Mind probe / Morning alarm / Weird love / Neon man / Positive day / Nervous breakdown / The party / George the space monster / This is the rule / Cricket talk / Nowhere. *(cd-iss.Feb95; SPOONCD 17)*

IRMIN SCHMIDT

Spoon not issued

1980. (lp) *(SPOON 003)* **FILM MUSIK** [-] [-] German

1981. (lp; with BRUNO SPOERRI) *(SPOON 011)* **TOY PLANET** [-] [-] German
– The seven game / Toy Planet / Two dolphins go dancing / Yom tov / Spring lite rite / Rapido de noir / When the workers came to life. *(UK-iss.Apr90 on 'Venture' cd/c/lp; CD/TC+/VE 48)*

1982. (lp) *(SPOON 013)* **FILM MUSIK VOL.2** [-] [-] German

—— In 1983 he issued other German album 'ROTE ERDE' on 'Teldec'.

Jun 84. (d-lp) *(SPOON 018-019)* **FILM MUSIK VOLS. 3 & 4** [-] [-] German

W.E.A. not issued

1987. (lp/cd) *(242010-1/-2)* **MUSIC AT DUSK** [-] [-] German
– Cliff into silence / Love / Roll on, Euphrates / The great escape / Villa wunderbar / The child in history / Alcohol. *(UK cd-iss.Nov92 on 'Fine Line-Mute'; IRMIN 1CD)*

Virgin not issued

1990. (cd) *(209919)* **FILM MUSIK VOL.5** [-] [-] German

Mute not issued

Nov 92. (cd) *(IRMIN 2CD)* **IMPOSSIBLE HOLIDAYS** [ ] [-]
– Dreamtime / Le weekend / Surprise / Shudder of love / Lullaby big / Time the dreamkiller / German ghast drift.

Spoon not issued

Oct 94. (cd) *(SPOONCD 3233)* **ANTHOLOGY / SOUNDTRACK** [ ] [-]

MICHAEL KAROLI & POLLY ESTES

—— with **POLLY ESTES** – vocals / **KAI ALTHOFF** – percussion

Spoon not issued

1984. (lp) *(SPOON 016)* **DELUGE** [-] [-] German
– One thing (or the other) / Fear of losing control / Home truths / Sentimental / The lake / Deluge (the river). *(UK cd-iss.Mar95 on 'Spoon'; SPOONCD 016)*

—— In 1984, DAMO SUZUKI's featured on 'IN THE NIGHT' album by band DUNKELZIFFER. It was released inbetween 2 other German albums 'COLOURS AND SOUL' and 'SONGS FOR EVERYONE', which I'm not sure if he appeared on.

CAPTAIN BEEFHEART AND HIS MAGIC BAND

Formed: Los Angeles, California, USA . . . 1964 by DON VAN VLIET, a child-prodigy sculptor who, between the ages of five and thirteen, had his clay animals featured on a weekly TV show hosted by Portuguese sculptor Augustino Rodriguez. An opportunity to develop his art skills were halted when his parents declined a scholarship on his behalf to study art in Europe, preferring instead to move to Lancaster in the Mojave desert. Here he met FRANK ZAPPA at the local high school, setting up a few local bands while ZAPPA started to write a script for a B-movie 'CAPTAIN BEEFHEART MEETS THE GRUNT PEOPLE'. When FRANK went to Los Angeles to form The MOTHERS OF INVENTION, he adopted the name CAPTAIN BEEFHEART and set about recruiting The MAGIC BAND. They signed to 'A&M' in 1964, releasing their version of BO DIDDLEY's 'DIDDY WAH DIDDY', which sold enough copies to encourage the label to buy studio time for an album. When completed, president Jerry Moss rejected the tapes, citing it too strange and anti-commercial. Undaunted, VAN VLIET and a new set of musicians, including RY COODER, re-recorded most of these masters, the album 'SAFE AS MILK' finally surfacing in 1967 on the 'Buddah' label. This was a masterpiece of its time, full of BEEFHEART on a HOWLIN' WOLF-style trip; the great tracks being 'ELECTRICITY', 'ABBA ZABA', 'AUTUMN CHILD' & 'ZIG ZAG WANDERER'. However, RY COODER departed for more safer pastures when VAN VLIET/BEEFHEART left the stage halfway through their set at the 1967 Monterey Pop Festival, leaving the band to play to a bewildered but carefree hippy audience. BEEFHEART often showed signs of outlandish behaviour which split the band up as much as his personality. Late in 1968, they recorded another album, 'MIRROR MAN', although this was shelved until his popularity had grown in the early 70's. However, one album did appear that year, 'STRICTLY PERSONAL', which BEEFHEART slammed for its radical remix by producer BOB KRASNOW. This riled him so much that he signed a new contract with old friend ZAPPA who gave him complete artistic control on his new 'Straight' label. Having wrote about 30 songs in a day, BEEFHEART took his new bunch of weirdo musicians (ANTENNAE JIMMY SEMENS, DRUMBO, ART TRIPP III, ZOOT HORN ROLLO and THE MASCARA SNAKE) to rehearse in a house which was close-by an old friend JIMMY CARL BLACK (drummer for ZAPPA). They stayed there for a full eight months, only one of them at a time venturing out if the band was in need of food & drink, etc. This was VAN VLIET's tyrannical way of keeping the band tight, so as to establish virtuoso musicianship while he got on with the weird vocals. The resulting album (a double!) 'TROUT MASK REPLICA' was handed to ZAPPA, much to his surprise, after four and a half hours in the studio. When released at the turn of the decade, it was initially given the thumbs down by many critics and fans. Those hardy enough to give it a few tolerant spins, however, were convinced of its genius. The record surprisingly nearly made the UK Top 20, having been played to death on John Peel's radio one night-time show. Its virtual insanity was literally not of this world, utilising the complex structures of jazz legend ORNETTE COLEMAN; the best tracks to break through – to the sane among us, were 'THE BLIMP', 'PENA', 'DALI'S CAR', 'ELLA GURU' & 'OLD FART AT PLAY'. It has since become regarded as a classic, although it should never be played to someone not of your generation. He returned a thank-you to ZAPPA, when he sang a track, 'WILLIE THE WIMP', on his 'Hot Rats' album, although their friendship was fraying with every meeting, two egos too big for one room. In 1970, he settled down to a more conventional avant-garde Delta-blues album 'LICK MY DECALS OFF, BABY' (compared that is, to their last). It was another excellent set; combing through the depths of his unearthly roots to find tracks such as 'DOCTOR DARK', 'I LOVE YOU, YOU BIG DUMMY' and the title track. 1972 saw another great album 'THE SPOTLIGHT KID', featuring the delights of 'CLICK CLACK', 'I'M GONNA BOOGLARIZE YOU BABY' & 'WHEN IT GROWS IT STACKS'. Their next, 'CLEAR SPOT' covered new territory on softer tracks like 'TOO MUCH TIME' & 'MY HEAD IS ONLY A HOUSE UNLESS IT RAINS', tempting the MAGIC BAND to bail out and form their own outfit, MALLARD. The album did, however, include another powerful BEEFHEART special in the shape of 'BIG EYED BEANS FROM VENUS'. In 1974, with a new line-up, he signed to UK's 'Virgin' label but his work at this point, especially on the albums 'UNCONDITIONALLY GUARENTEED' & 'BLUEJEANS AND MOONBEAMS', was poor. He tried to escape yet another restrictive deal; it was said he would sign anything, and teamed up with his old pal FRANK ZAPPA and The MOTHERS. Their collaboration, 'BONGO FURY', set the ball rolling for a litigation battle between him and Virgin' UK, resulting in another deal!, this time with 'Warner Brothers' for the 1978 album 'SHINY BEAST (BAT CHAIN PULLER)', a marked return to form on some tracks. Virgin won the rights to this album, which gained a UK release in early 1980. Two other records surfaced in the next two years; 'DOC AT RADAR STATION' and the considerably better 'ICE CREAM FOR CROW', the latter

Icecream for CROW

containing the excellent title track, his final epitaph. He retired from the music business and set up home with his wife JAN at a trailer park in the Mojave desert. Still an avid sculptor and painter, with the help of fan Julian Schnabel, he began exhibiting his primitive canvases which made him more money than his records ever did. In the mid-80's, a host of young British indie acts including STUMP, McKENZIES, The SHRUBS, etc, took on the mantle of the BEEFHEART sound. Always asked if he would return, BEEFHEART has repeatedly refused to get back on the bandwagon (having fallen into ill-health, both physically and mentally, a return to the recording studio is unlikely to say the least). A remarkable figure of his time, DON VAN VLIET examplified the glory of not worrying about the exploitation of the music industry, only happy with his own, and of course the MAGIC BAND's work. Let's just hope he's around for several more years to enjoy whatever he creates. • **Trivia:** He also covered JACK NITZCHE's 'HARD WORKIN' MAN' on the 1978 film 'Blue Collar', which starred Harvey Keitel.

Recommended: SAFE AS MILK (*9) / TROUT MASK REPLICA (*10 or *2; depending on your taste) / MIRROR MAN (*7) / LICK MY DECALS OFF, BABY (*8) / THE SPOTLIGHT KID (*8) / CLEAR SPOT (*7) / SHINY BEAST (BAT CHAIN PULLER (*6) / DOC AT RADAR STATION (*5) / ICE CREAM FOR CROW (*6)

CAPTAIN BEEFHEART (b. DON VAN VLIET, 15 Jan'41, Glendale, California) – vocals, harmonica, occasional guitar, wind instruments / **ALEX ST. CLAIRE** – guitar / **DOUG MOON** – guitar / **JERRY HANDLEY** – bass / **PAUL BLAKELY** – drums

A&M A&M

1966. (7") *<794>* **DIDDY WAH DIDDY. / WHO DO YOU THINK YOU'RE FOOLING** -

1966. (7") *<818>* **MOONCHILD. / FRYING PAN** -

1968. (7") *(AMS 726)* **MOONCHILD. / WHO DO YOU THINK YOU'RE FOOLING** -

— **The CAPTAIN** recruited an entire new band . . . **RY COODER** – slide guitar repl. MOON + ST.CLAIRE (they later joined DENNY KING) / **HERB BERMANN** – bass, co-composer repl. HANDLEY / **JOHN FRENCH** (DRUMBO) – drums repl. BLAKELY

Pye Int. Kama Sutra

Jan 68. (7") *(7N 25443)* **YELLOW BRICK ROAD. / ABBA ZABA**

Feb 68. (lp) *(NPL 28110) <BDS 5001>* **SAFE AS MILK** 1967
– Sure 'nuff 'n yes I do / Zig zag wanderer / Call on me / Dropout boogie / I'm glad / Electricity / Yellow brick road / Abba zaba / Plastic factory / Where there's woman / Plastic factory / Grown so ugly / Autumn child. *(re-iss.1968 on 'Marble Arch' 2 tracks less; MAL 1117) (re-iss.1970 on 'Buddah' stereo; 623 171) (re-iss.Jan82 on 'P.R.T.'; NCP 1004) (re-iss.Jul85 on 'Buddah' lp/c; 252260-1/-4) (cd-iss.May91 on 'Castle'; CLACD 234)*

— **JEFF COTTON** (ANTENNAE JIMMY SEMENS) **-guitar** repl. COODER who went solo

not issued Buddah

1968. (lp) *<BDS 5077>* **MIRROR MAN** (rec.1965) -
– Tarot plane / Kandy korn / 25th century Quaker / Mirror man. *(UK-iss.May71 on 'Buddah'; 2365 002); reached No.49) (re-iss.May82 on 'P.R.T.'; NCP 1006) (re-iss.Apr86 on 'Edsel'; ED 184) (cd-iss.May91 on 'Castle'; CLACD 235)*

Liberty BlueThumb

Dec 68. (lp; mono/stereo) *(LBL/LBS 83172) <BTS 1>* **STRICTLY PERSONAL**
– Ah feel like acid / Safe as milk / Trust us / Son of Mirror Man – Mere man / On tomorrow / Beatles bones 'n' smokin' stones / Gimme that harp boy / Kandy korn. *(re-iss.Nov79 lp/c; LBR/TCR 1006) (cd-iss.Aug94 on 'E.M.I.'; CZ 529)*

— **The CAPTAIN** retained **DRUMBO** and **ANTANNAE** plus new members **ZOOT HORN ROLLO** (b.BILL HARKLEROAD) – brass, narrator, guitar, flute / **ROCKETTE NORTON** (b.MARK BOSTON) – bass, narrator repl. HERB / **THE MASCARA SNAKE** (b.VICTOR HAYDEN) – clarinet / guest **DOUG MOON** returned

Straight Straight

Nov 69. (d-lp) *(STS 1053) <RS 2027>* **TROUT MASK REPLICA** 21
– Frownland / The dust blows forward 'n dust blows back / Dachau blues / Ella guru / Hair pie: bake 1 / Moonlight on Vermont / Hair pie: bake 2 / Pena / Well / When big Joan sets up / Fallin' ditch / Sugar 'n spikes / Ant man bee / Pachuco cadaver / Bills corpse / Sweet sweet bulbs / Neon meate dream of an octafish / China pig / My human gets me blues / Dali's car / Orange claw hammer / Wild life / She's too much for my mirror / Hobo chang ba / The blimp (mousetrap replica) / Steal softly thru snow / Old fart at play / Veteran's day poppy. *(re-iss.May75 on 'Reprise'; K 64026) (re-iss.cd Sep94 on 'WEA'; K 927 196-2)*

— **ED MARIMBA** (ART TRIPP) – marimba (ex-MOTHERS OF INVENTION) repl. THE MASCARA SNAKE

Jan 71. (lp) *(STS 1063) <RS 6240>* **LICK MY DECALS OFF, BABY** 20
– Lick my decals off, baby / Doctor Dark / I love you, you big dummy / Peon / Bellerin' plain / Woe-is-uh-me-bop / Japan in a dishpan / I wanna find a woman that'll hold my big toe till I have a go / Petrified forest / One rose that I mean / The Buggy boogie woogie / The Smithsonian Institute blues (or the big dig) / Space-age couple / The clouds are full of wine (not whiskey or rye) / Flash Gordon's ape. *(re-iss.Jul73 on 'Reprise')*

— **THE WINGED EEL FINGERLING** (r.n. ELLIOT INGBER) – guitar, etc. (ex-MOTHERS etc.) repl. SEMENS who had already formed MU

Reprise Reprise

Jan 72. (7") *<1068>* **CLICK CLACK. / I'M GONNA BOOGLARIZE YOU BABY** -

Feb 72. (lp; by CAPTAIN BEEFHEART) *(K 44162) <RS 2050>* **THE SPOTLIGHT KID** 44
– I'm gonna booglarize you baby / White jam / Blabber 'n smoke / When it blows its stacks / Alice in Blunderland / The spotlight kid / Click clack / Grow fins / There ain't no Santa Claus on the evenin' stage / Glider.

— **ROY 'OREJON' ESTRADA** – bass (ex-LITTLE FEAT, ex-MOTHERS OF INVENTION) repl. INGBER. ROCKETTE moved to guitar, and augmented by backing vocals The **BLACKBERRIES / RUSS TITELMAN** – guitar (guested, as he did on "Safe as Milk")

Nov 72. (lp) *(K 54007) <MS 2115>* **CLEAR SPOT**
– Low yo yo stuff / Nowadays a woman's gotta hit a man / Too much time / Circumstances / My head is my only a house unless it rains / Sun zoom sparks / Clear spot / Crazy little thing / Long neck bottles / Her eyes are a blue million miles / Big eyed beans from Venus / Golden birdies.

Mar 73. (7") *(K 14233) <1133>* **TOO MUCH TIME. / MY HEAD IS MY ONLY HOUSE UNLESS IT RAINS**

— **ALEX ST.CLAIRE** – guitar returned to repl. ROY. Added **MARK MERCELLO** – keyboards

Virgin Mercury

Apr 74. (lp) *(V 2015) <SRMI 709>* **UNCONDITIONALLY GUARENTEED**
– Upon the my-oh-my / Sugar bowl / New electric ride / Magic be / Happy love song / Full Moon, hot Sun / I got love on my mind / This is the day / Lazy music / Peaches. *(re-iss.Aug82 + Aug85 on 'Fame' lp/c; FA/TCFA 3034) (re-iss.Aug88; OVED 66) (cd-iss.Jun88; CDV 2015)*

Apr 74. (7") *(VS 110)* **UPON THE MY-OH-MY. / MAGIC BE** -

Apr 74. (7") *<73494>* **UPON THE MY-OH-MY. / I GOT LOVE ON MY MIND** -

— **ELLIOT INGBER** – guitar returned to repl. ST.CLAIRE plus session men **MARK GIBBONS, MICHAEL SMOTHERMAN, JIMMY CARAVAN** – all keyboards repl. MARCELLO.

— **DEAN SMITH** – guitar / **BOB WEST** – bass / **GENE PELLO** – drums / **TV GRIMES** – percussion

Nov 74. (lp) *(V 2123)* **BLUEJEANS AND MOONBEAMS**
– Party of special things do / Same old blues / Observatory crest / Pompadour swamp / Captain's holiday / Rock'n'roll's evil doll / Further than we've gone / Twist ah luck / Bluejeans and moonbeams. *(re-iss.Mar84; OVED 19) (cd-iss.Jun88; CDV 2023)*

— Late '75 **BEEFHEART** collaborated with **FRANK ZAPPA** on **"BONGO FURY"** album. This was a near live album with 2 studio tracks.

— His new touring band featured past members **ELLIOT, INGBER** and **JOHN FRENCH** plus **DENNY WHALLEY** – slide guitar / **BRUCE FOWLER** – trombone (both on bongos)

— His '76 band were **DRUMBO, WHALLEY, JEFF MORRIS TEPPER** – guitar, and **JOHN THOMAS** – piano. They recorded first sessions for the next album

— **ERIC DREW FELDMAN** – keyboards, bass repl. THOMAS / **ROBERT WILLIAMS** – drums repl. DRUMBO / **RICHARD REDISS** – slide guitar repl. WHALLEY / **ART TRIPP** – marimba returned from MALLARD. **BRUCE FOWLER** also returned.

Virgin Warners

Feb 80. (lp) *(V 2149) <BSK 3256>* **BAT CHAIN PULLER** (US-title 'SHINY BEAST') 1978
– The floppy boot stomp / Tropical hot dog night / Ice rose / Harry Irene / You know you're a man / Bat chain puller / When I see mommy I feel like a mummy / Owed t'Alex / Candle mambo / Love lies / Suction prints / Apes-ma. *(re-iss.Aug88; OVED 67) (cd-iss.Jun87; CDV 2149)*

— **GARY LUCAS** – guitar repl. REDISS

Virgin Virgin

Aug 80. (lp) *(V 2172)* **DOC AT RADAR STATION**
– Hot head / Ashtray heart / A carrot is as close as a rabbit gets to a diamond / Run paint run run / Sue Egypt / Brickbats / Dirty blue Gene / Best batch yet / Telephone / Flavour bud living / Sheriff of Hong Kong / Making love to a vampire with a monkey on my knee. *(re-iss.Aug88; OVED 68) (cd-iss.Jun88; CDV 2172)*

— The CAPTAIN brought in **HATSIZE SNYDER, CLIFF MARTINEZ, WILLIAMS, LAMBOURNE FOWLER and DRUMBO**

Aug 82. (12") *(VS 534-12) <03190>* **LIGHT REFLECTED OFF THE OCEANS OF THE MOON. / ICE CREAM FOR CROW**

Virgin Epic

Sep 82. (lp) *(V 2237)* **ICE CREAM FOR CROW** 90
– Ice cream for crow / The host, the ghost, the most holy-o / Semi-multi-(coloured) caucasian / Hey Garland, I dig your tweed coat / Evening bell / Cardboard cut-out sundown / The past is sure tense / Ink mathematics / The witch doctor life / "81" poop hatch / The thousand and tenth day of the human totem pole / Skeleton makes good. *(re-iss.Aug88; OVED 121) (cd-iss.Apr88; CDV 2237)*

— He retired from music business to concentrate on painting/sculpting in his recently bought Mojave desert home.

– compilations etc. –

Jul 70. (lp) *Buddah; (2349 002)* **DROPOUT BOOGIE** -
(a re-iss. of "SAFE AS MILK" 2 tracks less)

1975. (lp) *WRMB;* **WHAT'S ALL THIS BOOGA-BOOGA MUSIC (live)** -

Aug 76. (d-lp) *Reprise; (K 84006)* **TWO ORIGINALS OF . . .**
– LICK MY DECALS OFF, BABY / THE SPOTLIGHT KID.

Nov 77. (d-lp/d-c) *Pye; (FILD/ZCFILD 008)* **THE CAPTAIN BEEFHEART FILE** (first 2-lp's)

1978. (d-lp) *Impossible;* **EASY TEETH** - -

Jan 78. (7") *Buddah; (BDS 466)* **SURE 'NUFF 'N' YES I DO. / ELECTRICITY** -

May 78. (7") *M.C.A.; (MCA 366)* **HARD WORKIN' MAN (by Jack Nitzsche featuring Captain Beefheart). / Coke Machine (by Jack Nitzche)** -

— Above also features RY COODER – on guitar

1978. (7"pic-ep) *Virgin; (SIXPACK 1)* **SIX-PACK / SIX TRACK** -
– Sugar bowl / Same old blues / Upon the My-Oh-My / Magic be / Rock'n'roll's evil doll / New electric ride.

Jul 83. (10"lp/c) *P.R.T.; (DOW/ZCDOW 15)* **MUSIC IN SEA MINOR** -

Jul 84. (lp/pic-lp) *Design; (PIL/+P 4)* **TOP SECRET** -

Oct 84. (m-lp) *A&M; (AMY 226)* **THE LEGENDARY SESSIONS** -
– Diddy wah diddy / Who do you think you're folling / Moonchild / Frying pan / Here I am, I always am. *(re-iss.Oct86 on 'Edsel'; BLIMP 902) (cd-iss.Mar92; BLIMPCD 902)*

Jun 88. (d-lp)(c)(d-cd) *That's Original; (TFO LP/MC/CD 11)* **SAFE AS MILK / MIRROR MAN** -
(re-iss.d-cd.May91 on 'Castle')

Feb 91. (d-cd) *Reprise; (7599 26249-2)* **THE SPOTLIGHT KID / CLEAR SPOT** -

Jul 91. (cd) *The Collection; (ORO 146)* **ZIG ZAG WANDERER** -

Jun 92. (cd) *Sequel; (NEXCD 215)* **I MAY BE HUNGRY BUT I SURE AIN'T WEIRD - THE ALTERNATIVE CAPTAIN BEEFHEART** [ ] [-]
Jun 93. (cd) *Virgin; (CDVM 9028)* **A CARROT IS AS CLOSE AS A RABBIT GETS TO A DIAMOND** [ ] [-]
Nov 93. (cd) *Movieplay Gold; (MPG 74025)* **LONDON 1974 (live)** [ ] [-]

CARAVAN

Formed: Canterbury, England . . .1967. Stalwarts of that well-documented scene, PYE HASTINGS, RICHARD COUGHLAN and cousins DAVE and RICHARD SINCLAIR soon evolved into CARAVAN. They had all stemmed from The WILDE FLOWERS, a pioneering band that'd seen SOFT MACHINE luminaries ROBERT WYATT, KEVIN AYERS and HUGH HOPPER pass through its ranks. As SOFT MACHINE developed its distinctive psychedelic jazz-rock, CARAVAN's eponymous debut album, released in 1968 on 'Verve', highlighted the band's wistful melody and extended workouts that scuplted moods rather than songs. They signed to 'Decca', releasing 'IF I COULD DO IT ALL OVER AGAIN, I'D DO IT ALL OVER YOU' in 1970. The albums unfortunate title belied a quality set of melancholy prog-rock that extended the ideas of their debut. 1971 saw the band release 'IN THE LAND OF THE GREY AND PINK', probably their best effort, once again featuring the Hammond organ that was CARAVAN's trademark. A series of line-up changes began with DAVE SINCLAIR leaving for ROBERT WYATT'S MATCHING MOLE, the band relacing him with STEVE MILLER (alas, not he of 'The Joker' fame) for the 'WATERLOO LILY' album. MILLER's stay was brief, as he and RICHARD SINCLAIR took off to form HATFIELD & THE NORTH. By the next album, 1973's 'FOR GIRLS WHO GROW PLUMP IN THE NIGHT', they recruited new line-up (see below) plus the returning DAVE SINCLAIR. The original sleeve artwork was knocked back by the record company for its depiction of a pregnant naked woman. The record was released amid an extended period of live work, the group recording an album on tour with the New Symphonia. The even more unfortunately titled 'CUNNING STUNTS' album displayed a distinct lack of any material even remotely stunning, the band becoming a bit bogged-down in the prog-rock quagmire. However it did breach the UK Top 50 in 1975, setting the scene for another unworthy follow-up, 'BLIND DOG AT ST. DUNSTANS'. The onset of Punk obviously did nothing for their cause, although PYE bravely struggled on with a series of half-baked albums, struggled in vain to capture the mellow CARAVAN vibe of old. The four originals reconvened for 1982's 'BACK TO FRONT' and then signed off until the early 90's when neo-psychedelic crusty bands like OZRIC TENTACLES, wearing their influences proudly, led to a bit of a CARAVAN renaissance. Various members under various monikers recorded 'CARAVAN OF DREAMS' (1992) and 'THE BATTLE OF HASTINGS' (1995). • **Songwriters:** All group compositions.

Recommended: CANTERBURY TALES – THE BEST OF CARAVAN (*8) / IN THE LAND OF THE GREY AND PINK (*6).

RICHARD SINCLAIR – vocals, bass (ex-WILDE FLOWERS) / **PYE HASTINGS** – guitar, vocals (ex-WILDE FLOWERS) / **RICHARD COUGHLAN** – drums, precussion (ex-WILDE FLOWERS) / **DAVE SINCLAIR** – keyboard, vocals with guests **JIMMY HASTINGS** – flute, arrangements / **BRIAN HOPPER** – horns

Verve / Verve Folk

Oct 68. (lp; stereo/mono) *(S+/VLP 6011)* **CARAVAN** [ ] [-]
– A place of my own / Ride / Policeman / Love song with flute / Cecil runs / Magic man / Granma's lawn / Where but for Caravan would I be. *(re-iss.Jun72 on 'M.G.M.'; 2353 058) (re-iss.1979 on 'Polydor'; 2353 058) (cd-iss.Sep96 on 'H.T.D.'; HTDCD 65)*
Jan 69. (7") *(VS 1518) <5102>* **A PLACE OF MY OWN. / RIDE** [ ] [ ]

Decca / London

Sep 70. (7") *(F 13063)* **IF I COULD DO IT ALL OVER AGAIN, I'D DO IT ALL OVER YOU. / HELLO HELLO** [ ] [-]
Oct 70. (lp) *(SKL 5052) <PS 582>* **IF I COULD DO IT ALL OVER AGAIN, I'D DO IT ALL OVER YOU** [ ] [ ]
– If I could do it all over again, I'd do it all over you / And I wish I were stoned / Don't worry / As I feel I die / With an ear to the ground I can make it: Martinian – Only Cox – Reprise / Hello, hello / Asforteri / Can't be long now – Francoise – For Richard – Warlock / Limits. *(cd-iss.Jan89 on 'London'; 820 521-2) (re-iss.c Jul93; 820 521-4) (re-iss.Apr96 on 'H.T.D.' cd/c; HTD CD/MC 57) (cd re-rec.Apr97+=; HTDCD 57L)*
Feb 71. (7") *(F 23125) <20065>* **LOVE TO LOVE YOU (AND TONIGHT PIGS WILL FLY). / GOLF GIRL** [ ] [ ]

— with guests **JIMMY HASTINGS** – wind / **DAVID GRINSTEAD** – percussion

Deram / London

May 71. (lp) *(SDL-R 1) <PS 593>* **IN THE LAND OF GREY AND PINK** [ ] [ ]
– Golf girl / Winter wine / Love to love you (and tonight pigs will fly) / In the land of grey and pink / Nine feet underground: Nigel blows a tune – Love's a friend – Make it 76 – Dance of the seven paper hankies – Hold grandad by the nose – Honest I do – Disassociation – 100% proof. *(cd-iss.Apr89; 820 520-2) (re-iss.c Jul93; 820 520-4)*

— **STEVE MILLER** – keyboards (ex-DYBLE, COXHILL & THE MILLER BROTHERS') repl. DAVE who joined ROBERT WYATT'S MATCHING MOLE / with guests **JIMMY HASTINGS, LOL COXHILL** – saxophone / **MIKE COTTON** – trumpet / **PHIL MILLER** – guitar

Apr 72. (lp) *(SDL 8) <PS 615>* **WATERLOO LILY** [ ] [ ]
– Waterloo Lily / Nothing at all – It's coming soon / Songs and signs / Aristocracy / The love in your eye / To catch me a brother / Subsultus – Debouchement – Tilbury kecks / The world is yours. *(cd-iss.Jul90; 820 919-2) (re-iss.c Jul93; 820 919-4)*

— **DEREK AUSTIN** – keyboards repl. STEVE MILLER who formed DELIVERY / **STUART EVANS** – bass repl. RICHARD SINCLAIR who joined HATFIELD & THE NORTH added **PETER GEOFFREY RICHARDSON** – electric viola to founders **HASTINGS & COUGHLAN. DAVE HASTINGS** returned to repl. AUSTIN / **JOHN G. PERRY** – bass, vocals (ex-SPREADEAGLE) repl. EVANS

Oct 73. (lp) *(SDL 12) <PS 627>* **FOR GIRLS WHO GROW PLUMP IN THE NIGHT** [ ] [ ]
– Memory Lain, Hugh / Headloss / Hoedown / Surprise, surprise / E'Thlu Thlu / The dog, the dog, he's at it again / Be all right / Chance of a lifetime / L'auberge du sanglier / A hunting we shall go / Pengola / Backwards / A hunting we shall go (reprise). *(cd-iss.Aug91; 820 971-2) (re-iss.c Jul93; 820 971-4)*
Nov 73. (7") *<20080>* **HEADLOSS. /** [ ] [-]

— **MARTYN FORD** – conducted orchestra, SIMON JEFFES – arrangements

Apr 74. (lp) *(SKLR 1110) <PS 650>* **CARAVAN AND THE NEW SYMPHONIA (LIVE AT DRURY LANE) (live)** [ ] [ ]
– (introduction) / Mirror of the day / The love in your eye / Virgin on the ridiculous / For Richard. *(re-iss.Jun92 cd/c; 844 125-2/-4)*

— **MIKE WEDGWOOD** – bass (ex-CURVED AIR) repl. PERRY (to QUANTUM JUMP)

Decca / B.T.M.

Aug 75. (lp) *(SKLR 5210) <BTM 5000>* **CUNNING STUNTS** [50] [ ]
– The show of your lives / Stuck in a hole / Lover / No back stage pass / Welcome the day / The Dabsong conshirtoe:- The mad Dabsong – Ben Karratt rides again – Pro's and con's / Wraiks and ladders – Sneakin' out the bare square – All sorts of unmentionable things / The fear and loathing in Tollington Park rag. *(cd-iss.Dec88 on 'Beat Goes On';) (re-iss.Apr93 on 'Deram' cd/c; 844 126-2/-4) (cd re-iss.Sep94 on 'Repertoire';) (cd re-iss.Jan96 on 'H.T.D.'; HTDCD 52)*
Sep 75. (7") *(FR 13599)* **STUCK IN A HOLE. / LOVER** [ ] [ ]

— **JAN SCHELHAAS** – keyboards (ex-GARY MOORE) repl. DAVE SINCLAIR

B.T.M. / Arista

Apr 76. (lp) *(BTM 1007) <4088>* **BLIND DOG AT ST. DUNSTANS** [53] [ ]
– Here I am / Chiefs and Indians / A very smelly, grubby little oik / Bobbing wide / Come on back / A very smelly, grubby little oik (reprise) / Jack and Jill / CAn you hear me / All the way (with John Wayne's single-handed liberation of Paris). *(cd-iss.Sep94 on 'Repertoire';) (cd re-iss.May96 on 'H.T.D.'; HTDCD 60)*
Jul 76. (7") *(SBT 104)* **ALL THE WAY (WITH JOHN WAYNE'S SINGLE-HANDED LIBERATION OF PARIS). / CHIEFS AND INDIANS** [ ] [ ]

— **DEK MESSECAR** – bass (ex-DARRYL WAY'S WOLF) repl. WEDGEWOOD who went solo (above now alongside **HASTINGS, COUGHLAN, RICHARDSON** and **SCHELHAAS**)

Arista / Arista

May 77. (7") *(ARIST 110)* **BETTER BY FAR. / SILVER STRINGS** [ ] [ ]
Aug 77. (lp/c) *(SPARTY/TCARTY 1008) <AB 4134>* **BETTER BY FAR** [ ] [ ]
– Feelin' alright / Behind you / Better by far / Silver strings / The last unicorn / Give me more / Man in the car / Let it shine / Nightmare.

— **DAVE SINCLAIR** – keyboards returned from CAMEL (tour) to repl. DEK. Now a quartet when JAN joined CAMEL in '79

Kingdom / not issued

Oct 80. (7") *(KV 8009)* **HEARTBREAKER. / IT'S NEVER TOO LATE** [ ] [-]
Oct 80. (lp/c) *(KVL/+X 9003)* **THE ALBUM** [ ] [-]
– Heartbreaker / Corner of my eye / Watcha gonna tell me / Piano player / Make yourself at home / Golden mile / Bright shiny day / Piano player / Clera blue sky / Keepin' up de fences. *(re-iss.1983 lp/c; KVL/CKVL 9003) (cd-iss.Aug92; CDKVL 9003)*
Mar 81. (7") *(KV 8014)* **KEEPIN' UP DE FENCES. / GOLDEN MILE** [ ] [-]

— **RICHARD SINCLAIR** – vocals, bass returned from CAMEL, joined all founders, repl. RICHARDSON who went into sessions etc.

also added **MEL COLLINS** – saxophone (ex-KING CRIMSON, etc., etc.,)

Jun 82. (lp) *(KVS 5011)* **BACK TO FRONT** [ ] [-]
– Back to Herne Bay front / Betcha wanna take it all / Hold on hold on / A.A. man / Videos of Hollywood / Sally don't change it / All aboard / Taken my breath away / Proper job / Back to front. *(cd-iss.Aug92; CDKVS 5011)*

— Disbanded but reformed in 1990. In 1992, they became . . .

RICHARD SINCLAIR'S CARAVAN OF DREAMS

with also **DAVE SINCLAIR + JIMMY HASTINGS** / plus **ANDY WARD** (ex-CAMEL)

H.T.D. / not issued

Jul 92. (cd/c) *(HTD CD/MC 7)* **CARAVAN OF DREAMS** [ ] [-]
– Going for a song / Cruising / Only the brave / Plan it Earth / Heather / Keep.
Jan 94. (d-cd) *(HTDCD 17)* **AN EVENING OF MAGIC (live)** [ ] [-]
– In the land of grey and pink / Only the brave – Plan it Earth / Share it / Videos / Heather / Going for a song / O Caroline / Nine feet underground / Felafel shuffle / Keep on caring / Cruising / Emily / Halfway between Heaven and Earth – It didn't matter anyway / Golf girl.

RICHARD SINCLAIR

R.S.S. / not issued

Jul 94. (cd) *(RSSCD 001)* **R.S.V.P.** [ ] [-]

- compilations etc. -

Nov 76. (d-lp) *Decca; (DKLR 81-82)* **CANTERBURY TALES** [ ] [-]
– If I could do it all over again I'd do it all over you / Aristocracy / Can't be long now – Francoise – For Richard – Warlock / Nine feet underground: Nigel blows a tune – Love's a friend – Make it 76 – Dance of the seven paper hankies – Hold grandad by the nose – Honest I do – Disassociation – 100 proof / Golf girl / Hoedown / The love in your eye / Subsultus – Debouchement – Tilbury kecks / Memory Laine, Hugh / Headloss / Virgin on the ridiculous / The dog, the dog, he's at it again.
1978. (lp) *London; <50011>* **THE BEST OF CARAVAN** [-] [ ]
(UK-iss.Sep87 on 'C5' lp/c; C5/+K 505) (cd-iss.1990 & Apr93; C5CD 505X)
Jul 81. (lp) *Rock Roots; (TAB 23)* **THE SHOW OF OUR LIVES** [ ] [-]
Sep 84. (lp) *Kingdom; (KVC 6003)* **THE CANTERBURY COLLECTION** ('80-'82 material) [ ] [-]
(cd-iss.Jan87; CDKVL 9028)
Apr 85. (lp) *See For Miles; (SEE 46)* **AND I WISH I WERE STONED, DON'T WORRY** [ ] [-]
May 91. (cd/c) *Elite; (ELITE 002 PCD/PMC)* **SONGS AND SIGNS** [ ] [-]

(originally only available in 1979 on German 'Decca'; 623668)
Aug 91. (cd/c) Elite; (ELITE 017 CDP/MCP) **WITH AN EAR TO THE GROUND**
Oct 91. (cd) Windsong; (WINCD 003) **IN CONCERT (live)** -
Mar 93. (cd) Code 90; (NINETY 2) **LIVE 1990 (live)** -
Apr 94. (cd) H.T.D.; (HTDCD 18) **COOL WATER** -
– Cool water / Just the way you are / Tuesday is rock and roll nite / The crack of the willow / Ansaphone / Cold fright / Side by side / You woke me up in one of those / To the land of my fathers / Poor Molly / Send reinforcements.
Nov 94. (cd) Deram; (515 524-2) **ANTHOLOGY** -
Oct 95. (cd/lp) H.T.D.; (HTD CD/LP 41) **BATTLE OF HASTINGS** -
Apr 96. (cd/c) H.T.D.; (HTD CD/MC 57) **ALL OVER YOU** -

Walter CARLOS

Born: 1939, Pawtucket, Rhode Island, USA. He worked for several years as a pharmacist while writing TV jingles, until being introduced to the MOOG synthesizer by it's creator Dr. ROBERT A.MOOG. With the guidance of another friend, musicologist BENJAMIN FOLKMAN, he released a remarkable tribute to J.S. BACH; 'SWITCHED-ON BACH' (1968). Early the next year, it made the US Top 10, staying in the Top 100 for over a year and earning 3 Grammy Awards for 'Best Classical Album', 'Best Performance By An Instrumental Soloist' and 'Best Engineering Recording'. His subsequent attempts to re-create this work failed to convince the buying public and purists alike, although critically (especially retrospectively), he/she has received worldwide acclaim for keeping the MOOG alive. In 1992 after around 20 years known as WENDY, he finally became a fully-fledged woman so-to-speak, when his much publicised sex-change operation! went ahead. To mark the occasion, he re-recorded his debut and re-released it as 'SWITCHED-ON BACH II' by of course, WENDY CARLOS.

Recommended: SWITCHED ON BACH (*5)

WALTER CARLOS – Moog synthesizer

C.B.S. / Columbia

Nov 68. (lp) (63501) <MS-7194> **SWITCHED-ON BACH** 10
– Bach: Sinfonia to Cantata No.29 / Air on a G string / Two-part invention in F major / Two-part invention in B flat major / Two-part invention in D minor / Jesu, Joy of man's desiring / Prelude and fugue No.7 in E flat major / Prelude and fugue No.2 in C minor / Chorale prelude "Wachet Auf" / Brandenburg concerto No.3 in G minor.
Dec 69. (7") (CBS 4296) <45033> **BRANDENBURG CONCERTO No.3 IN G MAJOR. / SCARLATTI: SINFONIA TO CANTATA No.29**
Dec 69. (lp) (CBS 63656) <MS-7286> **THE WELL-TEMPERED SYNTHESIZER**
– Scarlatti: Sonata in G major, L. 209 – Sonata in D major, L. 164 / Handel: Water music – Bouree _ Air – Allegro de Cisco / Scarlatti: Sonata in E major, L.430 – Sonata in D major, L. 465 / Bach: Brandenburg concerto No.4 in G major, BWV 1049 / Monteverdi: Domine ad Adjuvandum.
Mar 72. (7") (K 16145) <7547> **MARCH FROM 'A CLOCKWORK ORANGE'. / (part 2)**
— above from 'Warners' UK film 'A CLOCKWORK ORANGE'; WB 56127)
Jul 72. (lp) (CBS 65048) <31480> **WALTER CARLOS' CLOCKWORK ORANGE**
– Timesteps / Title music march from 'A Clockwork Orange' / Rossini: La gazza landra (the thieving magpie), abridged / Theme from 'A Clockwork Orange' / Beethoven: Ninth Symphony – second movement (Scherzo) / Rossini: William Tell overture, abridged / Country lane.
Jul 72. (d-lp) (CBS 67267) <31234> **SONIC SEASONINGS**
– Spring / Summer / Fall / Winter. (with RACHEL ELLKIND – vocals)
1972. (7") <45741> **ELEANOR RIGBY. / WHAT'S NEW PUSSYCAT** -
Mar 74. (lp/c) (CBS/40 63501) <KM-32659> **SWITCHED-ON BACH II**
– Selections from Suite No.2 in B minor BWV 1067: Badinerie – Minuet – Bouree – Two part invention in A minor, BWV. 784 / Two part invention in A major, BWV. 783 / Sheep may safely graze – From Cantana No.208, BWV. 208 / Suite from Anna Magdalena's notebook: Musette in D major, ANH. 216 / Minuet in G major, ANH. 114 / Bist du bei mir, MWV. 508 / Marche in D major, ANH. 122 / Brandenburg Concerto No.5 in D major, BWV. 1050: Allegro – Affet tuoso – Allegro. (cd-iss.1992;)
Sep 75. (7") (3590) **WHAT'S NEW PUSSYCAT?. / DANCE OF THE REED PIPES**
Jan 77. (lp/c) (CBS/40 73163) <M-32088> **BY REQUEST**
– Three dances from "The Nutcracker Suite": Russian dance – Dance of the Sugar-plum fairy – Dance of the reed pipes / Dialogues for piano and two loudspeakers / Episodes for piano and electronic sound / Brandenburg Concerto No.2 in F major (first movement) / Pomp and circumstance march, OP. 39, No.1 (excerpt) / What's new pussycat? / Eleanor Rigby / Little fugue in G minor / Geodesic dance / Minuet / Wedding march (based on the bridal chorus from "Lohengrin") / Pompous circumstances (with apologies to Sir Edward Elgar, Bart).
1977. (lp) (CBS 73395) **BRANDENBURG CONZERTOS 3-5**
– Konzert Nr.3 in G major: Andante – Adagio – Allegro / Konzert Nr.4 in G major: Allegro – Andante – Presto – Konzert Nr.5 in D major: Allegro – Affet tuoso – Allegro.
— Officially became WENDY CARLOS (see above). In 1980, he contributed 2 tracks 'Main Title' & 'Rocky Mountains' to the film soundtrack of 'THE SHINING' (starring Jack Nicholson) for 'Warners'; (K 56827) <23449>
1981. (lp) <HM-45950> **SWITCHED-ON BRANDENBURGS, VOL.1** -
— In Nov82, another film 'TRON' featured his music, 'CBS'; (70223) <SM-37782>
1984. (lp) <M-39340> **DIGITAL MOONSCAPES** -

not issued / Audion

Nov 86. (lp/c/cd) <SYN/+C/CD 200> **BEAUTY IN THE BEAST** -

– compilations, etc –

Aug 83. (lp) C.B.S.; (CBS 74110) **THE BEST OF CARLOS**
– Theme from 'A Clockwork Orange' / What's new pussycat? / Eleanor Rigby / La gazza ladra / WAter music / Jesu, joy of man's desiring / Air on a G string / Brandenburg No.3.

Ian CARR (see under ⇒ NUCLEUS)

CASTAWAYS

Formed: Richfield, Minnesota, USA . . . 1962 (to play at a fraternity party) by DENNY CRASWELL, DICK ROBY and ROY HENSLEY. The line-up was completed by JIM DONNA and BOB FOLSCHOW, the former providing the domineering "garage" organ for their debut smash hit, 'LIAR, LIAR' in 1965. However, this was their only chart triumph, further attempts on the local label 'Soma', (no connection to Glasgow's top dance label!) sinking without trace. No album was ever released, and when CRASWELL joined CROW in 1969, the band were left to play sporadic gigs, soldiering on with this occasional live work well into the 80's. Their profile was boosted when their one hit wonder, 'LIAR, LIAR', made the soundtrack of 'Good Morning Victnam'.

Recommended: first 45

ROY HENSLEY – guitar / **DENNY CRASWELL** – drums / **DICK ROBY** – bass / **JIM DONNA** – keyboards / **BOB FOLSCHOW** – guitar

London / Soma

Nov 65. (7") (HL 10003) <1433> **LIAR, LIAR. / SAM** 12 Jul65
1966. (7") <1442> **GOODBYE BABE. / A MAN'S GOTTA BE A MAN** -
1966. (7") <1461> **GIRL IN LOVE. / SHOULD HAPPEN TO ME** -

– compilations, others –

1960's. (7") Soma; <1469> **LIAR, LIAR. / Trashmen: Surfin' Bird** -
— now a quartet when CRASWELL left to join CROW

CATAPILLA

Formed: England . . .early 70's by (see below).This short-lived jazz rock aggregation peddled progressive fare with a distinctly sinister resonance and while the songs were often typically drawn out affairs, they avoided the worst pitfalls of instrumental indulgence. While the self-titled debut (1971) was largely vocal-led, the follow-up, 'CHANGES' (1972) was more instrumental, the music losing none of its unsettling intensity. This was the band's final recording, after which they retired from the music scene. Apart from CALVERT that is, who now owns 'CATAPILLA' records in DEVON. • **Trivia:** CALVERT was not the same as HAWKWIND's lyricist. ANNA is the sister of JO MEEK (Julian's Treatment).

Recommended: CATAPILLA (*6) / CHANGES (*5)

ANNA MEEK – vocals / **ROBERT CALVERT** – saxophone / **GRAHAM WILSON** – guitar / **THIERRY REINHARDT** – wind / **DAVE TAYLOR** – bass / **MALCOLM FRITH** – drums / **HUGH EAGLESTONE** – sax

Vertigo / Vertigo

Jul 71. (lp) (6360 029) <1006> **CATAPILLA**
– Naked death / Tumble weed / Promises / Embryonic fusion.
— **MEEK, CALVERT + WILSON** plus **RALPH ROLINSON** – keyboards / **CARL WASSARD** – bass / **BRIAN HANSON** – drums
Aug 72. (lp) (6360 074) **CHANGES** -
– Reflection / Charing Cross / Thank Christ for George / It could only happen to me.
— All retired from music, bar CALVERT who now owns 'Catapilla' records of Devon.

CHAMBERS BROTHERS

Formed: Lee County, Mississippi, USA . . . 1959 by brothers LESTER, WILLIE, JOE and GEORGE. In 1961, they relocated to Los Angeles, touring as a black gospel/folk outfit, although they increasingly incorporated R&B into their sound. After cutting a version of CURTIS MAYFIELD's 'PEOPLE GET READY', they were picked up by 'Vault' records. They were now augmented by drummer BRIAN KEENAN and began to fashion their pioneering blend of psychedelic soul. In 1966, they moved up a step to 'Columbia' records, where they flopped with four 45's. The first of these, 'TIME HAS COME TODAY', was given another lease of life in the summer of '68 when it bubbled under the US Top 10, having been embraced by the hippie fraternity. They followed this with another hit, 'I CAN'T TURN YOU LOOSE', and two widely accepted albums. They moved with the times in the early 70's, when funk was at its loose-limbed height, although this didn't bear any commercial fruit. • **Songwriters:** The brothers, except SHOUT (Isley Brothers) / I CAN'T TURN YOU LOOSE (Otis Redding) / + loads, etc. • **Trivia:** LESTER had learned harmonica from the legendary SONNY TERRY.

Recommended: THE TIME HAS COME (*6)

LESTER CHAMBERS (b.13 Apr'40) – vocals, harmonica / **WILLIE CHAMBERS** (b. 2 Mar'38) – guitar, vocals / **JOE CHAMBERS** (b.22 Aug'52) – guitar, vocals / **GEORGE CHAMBERS** (b.26 Sep'31) – bass, vocals

Vocalion Vault

1966. (lp) *(SAVL 8058)* <9003> **PEOPLE GET READY** [ ] [ ] 1965
– Yes, yes, yes / Tore up over you / Reconsider baby / You've got me running / People get ready / Money / You can run / Hooka tooka / Call me / Summertime / Your old lady / It's all over now.

Mar 66. (7") *(V 9267)* **LOVE ME LIKE THE RAIN. / PRETTY GIRLS EVERYWHERE** [ ] [ ]

Jul 66. (7") *(V 9276)* **CALL ME. / SEVENTEEN** [ ] [ ]

— added **BRIAN KEENAN** (b.28 Jan'44) – drums (ex-MANFRED MANN)

1966. (lp) <115> **THE CHAMBERS BROTHERS – NOW (live)** [ ] [ ]
– Introduction to / High heel sneakers / Baby, please don't go / What'd I say / Long tall Sally / Bony Moronie / It's groovin' time / You don't have to go / C.C. rider / So fine.

C.B.S. Columbia

1966. (7") <43816> **TIME HAS COME TODAY. / DINAH** [-] [ ]

1967. (7") *(202 565)* <43957> **ALL STRUNG OUT OVER YOU. / FALLING IN LOVE** [ ] [ ]

1967. (7") <44080> **PLEASE DON'T LEAVE ME. / I CAN'T STAND IT** [-] [ ]

Direction Columbia

Jan 68. (7") *(3215)* <44296> **UPTOWN. / LOVE ME LIKE THE RAIN** [ ] [ ]

Aug 68. (7") *(3671)* <44414> **THE TIME HAS COME TODAY. / PEOPLE GET READY** [ ] [11]
(re-iss.Sep68; 3760)

Nov 68. (lp) *(63407)* <9522> **THE TIME HAS COME** [ ] [4] Jan68
– All strung out over you / People get ready / I can't stand it / Romeo and Juliet / In the midnight hour / So tired / Uptown / Please don't leave me / What the world needs now is love / Time has come today.

Nov 68. (7") *(3865)* <44679> **I CAN'T TURN YOU LOOSE. / DO YOUR THING** [ ] [37]

Nov 68. (lp) *(63451)* <9671> **A NEW TIME – A NEW DAY** [ ] [16]
– I can't turn you loose / Guess who / Do your thing / Where have all the flowers gone / Love is all I have / You got the power . . . to turn me on / I wish it would rain / Rock me mama / No, no, no, don't say goodbye / Satisfy you / A new time – a new day.

May 69. (7") *(4098)* <44779> **ARE YOU READY? / YOU GOT THE POWER TO TURN ME ON** [ ] [ ]

Jun 69. (7") *(4318)* **PEOPLE GET READY. / NO, NO, NO, DON'T SAY GOODBYE** [ ] [-]

Aug 69. (7") *(4367)* <44890> **WAKE UP. / EVERYBODY NEEDS SOMEONE** [ ] [92] Jun69

— (above from the film 'The April Fools')

— The rest of their releases were more soul or gospel orientated

– compilations, others, etc. –

1968. (lp) *Liberty; (LBS 83272) / Vault; <120>* **SHOUT** [ ] [ ]

1968. (7") *Vault;* **GIRLS WE LOVE YOU. / JUST A CLOSER WALK WITH THEE** [-] [ ]

Dec 68. (7") *Vault; <945>* **SHOUT (part 1). / (part 2)** [-] [83]

1969. (7") *Vault;* **HOUSE OF THE RISING SUN. / BLUES GET OFF MY SHOULDER** [-] [ ]

1970. (lp) *Liberty; (LBS 83296) / Vault; <128>* **FEELIN' THE BLUES** [-] [ ]

Nov 70. (d-lp) *Vault; <135>* **GREATEST HITS** [-] [ ]

Nov 71. (lp) *C.B.S.; (64598) <30871>* **THE CHAMBERS BROTHERS' GREATEST HITS** [ ] [ ]
– Funky / In the midnight hour / Time has come today / I can't turn you loose / People get ready / Let's do it / All strung out / Are you ready / Love, peace and happiness.

1975. (7") *C.B.S.; (13-33136)* **TIME HAS COME TODAY. / I CAN'T TURN YOU LOOSE** [ ] [-]

CHARLATANS

Formed: Haight-Ashbury, San Francisco, California, USA . . . 1964 by former draftsman GEORGE HUNTER, MIKE WILHELM and RICHARD OLSEN. They were soon aided by MICHAEL FERGUSON and SAM LINDE, the latter deposed by DAN HICKS. The band fashioned a distinctive image, dressing up in turn-of-the-century costumes, either Western or Victorian. This helped them gain a residency in the summer of '65 at the Red Dog Saloon, a bar in Virginia City, Nevada. For this, FERGUSON designed the billboard (first ever psychedelic rock poster!), which led to them sharing future bills with GRATEFUL DEAD (i.e. WARLOCKS) and JEFFERSON AIRPLANE. They played a variety of styles, including jug-band, folk & blues, but they returned to 'Frisco having had their demos for the 'Autumn' label rejected. 'M.G.M.' offered them a deal, subsequently handing them over to 'Kama Sutra' in 1966. They shelved an album's worth of material and released a single, 'THE SHADOW KNOWS', without their permission, before the band decided to bail out. The next few years saw FERGUSON, then HICKS (who had become their guitarist) and finally HUNTER, take off, disgruntled at the band's lacklustre efforts, while WILHELM and OLSEN persevered with new recruits. This led to the release of an eponymous album in 1969, which, if issued a few years previously, might have made an impact, at least in the States. All originals became quite creative in the 70's, WILHELM fronting LOOSE GRAVEL and later joining The FLAMIN' GROOVIES, OLSEN becoming a producer at Pacific High Studios. HUNTER was the sleeve artist on the 1969 albums by IT'S A BEAUTIFUL DAY, QUICKSILVER MESSENGER SERVICE and CANNED HEAT.

Recommended: THE CHARLATANS (*6)

GEORGE HUNTER – vocals, autoharp, tambourine / **MIKE WILHELM** – guitar, vocals / **RICHARD OLSEN** – bass, clarinet, vocals / **MICHAEL FERGUSON** – piano / **DAN HICKS** (b. 9 Dec'41, Little Rock, Arkansas) – drums, repl. SAM LINDE

not issued Kama Sutra

1966. (7") <230> **THE SHADOW KNOWS. /** [-] [ ]

— **WILHELM + OLSEN** introduced **TERRY WILSON** – drums, who repl. HICKS (he formed own DAN HICKS & HIS RED HOT LICKS)

— DARREL DeVORE – piano, repl. PATRICK GOGERTY, who had repl. FERGUSON (he joined Red Dog Saloon barmaid LYNNE HUGHES, in the band TONGUE & GROOVE). HUNTER also departed in 1968 (see above)

Philips Philips

1969. (lp) *(SBL 7903)* <600 309> **THE CHARLATANS** [ ] [ ]
– High coin / Easy when I'm dead / Ain't got the time / Folsom prison blues / The blues ain't nothin' / Time to get straight / When I go sailin' by / Doubtful waltz / Wabash cannonball / Alabama bound / When the movies are over.

— split just after the release of above. MIKE WILHELM released an eponymous album for the 'ZigZag' magazine in 1976. He also fronted LOOSE GRAVEL and joined The FLAMIN' GROOVIES.

– compilations, etc. –

1982. (m-lp) *Line; (LMS 3025)* **THE AUTUMN DEMOS** [-] [-] German
– Baby won't you tell me / The blues ain't nothing / Number one / Jack of diamonds.

1980's. (lp) *Eva; (12017)* **ALABAMA BOUND** [-] [-] France
– Alabama bound / Codeine / I saw her / Devil / Long come a viper / By hook or by crook / Baby won't you tell me / Side track / The shadow knows / 32-20 / I saw her (instrumental) / Codeine blues / Alabama bound (live).

Jun 94. (cd) *Eva; (842020)* **CHARLATANS / ALABAMA BOUND** [ ] [-]

Aug 96. (cd) *Big Beat; (CDWIKD 138)* **THE AMAZING CHARLATANS** [ ] [-]

CHICAGO LINE (see under ⇒ PATTO, Mike)

Alex CHILTON (see under ⇒ BOX TOPS)

CHOCOLATE WATCH BAND

Formed: San Jose, California, USA . . .1964 by NED TORNEY, MARK LOOMIS, JO KEMLING, TOM ANTONE and GARY ANDRIJASEVICH. By the following year, only LOOMIS and ANDRIJASEVICH remained, the rest going off to form The OTHER SIDE. CWB mark II was completed by DAVE AGULIAR, DAVE 'SEAN' TOLBY and BILL FLORES, who were soon under the wing of manager ED COBB (former boss of STANDELLS). He insisted on studio session men and a substitute vocalist DON BENNETT, who played on most of the master recordings between '66 and '68, much to the anguish of the band. After a clutch of psychedelic garage albums, the band split although their cult appeal has grown stronger with each passing decade.

Recommended: 44 (*6)

DAVE AGUILAR – vocals; repl. JO KEMLING / **SEAN TOLBY** – guitar (ex-OTHER SIDE); repl. NED TORNEY / **MARK LOOMIS** – guitar, vocals / **BILL FLORES** – bass; repl. TOM ANTONE / **GARY ANDRIJASEVICH** – drums

not issued Uptown

1966. (7") <740> **SWEET YOUNG THING. / BABY BLUE** [-] [ ]

1966. (7"; as The HOGS) <HBR 511> **BLUE THEME. / LOOSE LIP SYNC SHIP** [-] [ ]
<above released on the 'HBR' label>

1966. (7") <749> **MISTY LANE. / SHE WEAVES A TENDER TRAP** [-] [ ]

not issued Tower

1967. (7") <373> **ARE YOU GONNA BE THERE (AT THE LOVE-IN). / NO WAY OUT** [-] [ ]

1967. (lp) <ST 5096> **NO WAY OUT** [-] [ ]
– Let's talk about girls / In the midnight hour / Come on / Dark side of the mushroom / Hot dusty road / Are you gona be there (at the love-in) / Gone and passes by / No way out / Expo 2000 / Gossamer wings. *(cd-iss.Jun93 on 'Big Beat' . . .PLUS +=; CDWIKD 118)*– Sweet young thing / Baby blue / Misty lane / She weaves a tender trap / Milk cow blues / Don't let the Sun catch you crying / Since you broke my heart / Misty lane (remix).

1968. (lp) <ST 5106> **THE INNER MYSTIQUE** [-] [ ]
– Voyage of the Trieste / In the past / The inner mystique / I'm not like everybody else / Medication / Let's go, let's go, let's go / Baby blue / I ain't no miracle worker. *(cd see compilations)*

— **DANNY PHAY** – guitar (ex-OTHER SIDE) repl. AGULIAR

1969. (lp) <ST 5153> **ONE STEP BEYOND** [-] [ ]
– Uncle Moris / How ya been / Devil's motorcycle / I don't need no doctor / Flowers / Fireface / And she's lonely. *(cd see compilations)*

— **PHIL STOMA** – lead guitar; repl. LOOMIS

— split and little was heard of them since

– compilations, etc. –

1983. (lp) *Eva; (12030)* **LET'S TALK ABOUT GIRLS** [-] [-] France

1983. (lp) *Eva; (12048)* **ARE YOU GONNA BE THERE** [-] [-] France

1983. (lp) *Rhino; <RNLP 108>* **THE BEST OF CHOCOLATE WATCH BAND** [-] [ ]
– Let's talk about girls / Sweet young thing / No way out / Baby blue / Expo 2000 / In the past / I'm not like everybody else / Are you gonna be there (at the love-in) / Don't need your lovin' / Misty lane / She weaves a tender trap / Sitting there standing / Milkcow blues / I ain't no miracle worker. *<US re-iss.Jun88; same>*

Oct 84. (lp) *Big Beat; (WIKA 25)* **44** [ ] [-]
– Don't need your lovin' / No way out / Baby blue / I'm not like everybody else / Misty lane / Loose lip sync ship / Are you gonna be there (at the love-in) / Gone and passes by / Sitting there standing / She weaves a tender trap / Sweet young thing / I ain't no miracle worker / Blues theme. *(cd-iss.May90; CDWIK 25)*

Apr 93. (cd) *Big Beat; (CDWIKD 111)* **THE INNER MYSTIQUE / ONE STEP BEYOND** [ ] [-]

CHOCOLATE WATCH BAND

Formed: London, England . . . early 1967 by duo GARY OSBORNE and JACK OLIVER. They subsequently signed to 'Decca', releasing the catchy pop tune, 'THE SOUND OF THE SUMMER'. Like its psychedelic follow-up, 'REQUIEM', the single failed to break through and the band faded into obscurity.

Recommended: 2nd 45, both are worth over £20.

JACK OLIVER – vocals, guitar / **GARY OSBORNE** – vocals, guitar

Decca not issued

Aug 67. (7") *(F 12649)* **THE SOUND OF THE SUMMER. / THE ONLY ONE IN SIGHT** -

Dec 67. (7") *(F 12704)* **REQUIEM. / WHAT'S IT TO YOU** -

— unheard of again from 1968

CHOSEN FEW (see under ⇒ SKIP BIFFERTY)

CLARK – HUTCHINSON

Formed: London, England ... 1969 by ANDY CLARK and MICK HUTCHISON. Having bailed out of The SAM GOPAL DREAM in 1967 with bassist PETE SEARS, they formed their own outfit VAMP, releasing a couple of 45's for 'Atlantic'. In 1969, a German-only album, 'BLUES', was released although the official CLARK-HUTCHINSON debut, 'A = MH2', came out in 1970. This was an instrumental slice of progressive-rock with Eastern overtones and delightful guitar work, clocking in at just over 50 minutes. A few more albums materialized during the early 70's but they never sold in any substantial ammount. CLARK subsequently took off with new bassman STEPHEN AMAZING to form UPP. The group issued a few progressive funk albums in the mid 70's, the first featuring producer and guitarist JEFF BECK and interestingly described as EMERSON, LAKE & PALMER backing ISAAC HAYES.

Recommended: A = MH2 (*6) / RETRIBUTION (*6) / GESTALT (*5)

VAMP

ANDY CLARK – organ / **MICK HUTCHINSON** – lead guitar / **PETE SEARS** – bass / **VIV PRINCE** – drums (ex-PRETTY THINGS, ex-BUNCH OF FIVES)

Atlantic not issued

Sep 68. (7") *(584 213)* **FLOATIN'. / THINKIN' TOO MUCH** -

1969. (7"w-drawn) *(584 263)* **GREEN PEA. / WAKE UP AND TELL ME** - -

CLARK-HUTCHINSON

ANDY CLARK – keyboards, bass drum, bagpipes, saxophones, flute, guitar / **MICK HUTCHINSON** – guitar, bass, percussion, flute / plus **WALT MONAHAN** – bass / **FRANCO** – drums

Little Wing not issued

1968. (lp) *(LW 2042)* **BLUES** - - German

Decca Nova Sire

Jan 70. (lp; stereo/mono) *(S+/DN-R2) <97021>* **A = MH2**
– Improvisation on a modal scale / Acapulco gold / Impromtu in "E" monir / Textures in 3'4 / Improvisation on an Indian scale.

— added **DEL COVERLEY** – drums, percussion / **STEPHEN AMAZING** – bass

Deram Deram

Nov 70. (lp) *SML 1076) <18055>* **RETRIBUTION**
– Free to be stoned / After hours / In best suit / Death the lover.

— now without STEPHEN

May 71. (lp) *(SML 1090)* **GESTALT** -
– Man's best friend / Love is the light / The light burns on / Come up here / Disorientated (part one) / A boat in the mist / Orientated / First reminder / Mix elixir / Poison / Disorientated (part two).

— both went into sessions, CLARK being the more prolific

UPP

ANDY CLARK – keyboards, vocals / **STEPHEN AMAZING** – bass / **JIM COPLEY** – drums (ex-SPREADEAGLE) / + guest **JEFF BECK** – guitar (solo artist)

Epic Epic

1975. (lp) *(EPC 80625) <33439>* **UPP**
– Bad stuff / Friendly street / It's a mystery / Get down in the dirt / Give it to you / Jeff's one / Count to ten.

— **DAVID BUNCE** – guitar repl. BECK

Apr 76. (7") *(EPC 4204)* **DANCE YOUR TROUBLES AWAY. / I DON'T WANT NOTHING (TO CHANGE)**

1976. (lp) *(EPC 81322)* **THIS WAY UPP**
– Never turn my back on you / Groovin' mood / Say goodbye / Dance your troubles away / I don't want nothing (to change) / There's still hope / Nitto / Get to the bottom.

Acrobat not issued

Nov 79. (7") *(BAT 14)* **NERVOUS. / THURSDAY** -

— CLARK back into sessions while COPLEY later turned up as session man for TEARS FOR FEARS and GO WEST

CLEAR BLUE SKY

Formed: England . . .1970 as a youthful trio (see below). Spotted at a youth club gig by NIRVANA's PATRICK CAMPBELL-LYONS, he insisted they should record for 'Vertigo'. 1970 saw the release of their excellent eponymous album, a hard hitting set of progressive power-rock which was unfairly ignored. They carried on touring for a few more years, going into the studio to record another (as yet unreleased) album before splitting. • **Style:** Youthful trio of heavy progressive power-rock. • **Songwriters:** Group. • **Trivia:** Expect to pay over 60 quid for an original mint copy of the debut.

Recommended: CLEAR BLUE SKY (*8)

JOHN SIMMS – guitar / **MARK SHEATHER** – bass / **KEN WHITE** – drums

Vertigo not issued

Jan 71. (lp) *(6360 013)* **CLEAR BLUE SKY** -
– Journey to the inside of the Sun: Sweat leaf – The rocket ride – I'm comin' home / You mystify / Tool of my trade / My heaven / Birdcatcher. *(cd-iss.1995 on 'Repertoire'; REP 4110)*

— split soon after above

George CLINTON

Born:22 Jul'40, Kannapolis, North Carolina, USA. Raised in Newark, New Jersey, CLINTON's love of doo-wop inspired him to form The PARLIAMENTS. They released a couple of singles in 1955, before moving to Detroit and recording for 'Gordy (Tamla Motown)' in 1962. The band made little progress, although GEORGE wrote songs for Motown artists such as The JACKSON 5 and DIANA ROSS. In 1965, unsuccessful in their attempts to land a deal, they issued a one-off 45, 'THAT WAS MY GIRL', for 'Golden World'. In 1967, he created the earliest incarnations of his future psychedelic image and added new musicians such as EDDIE HAZEL and BERNIE WORRELL. Signing to 'Revilot' in the States, they then hit Top 20 with single '(I WANNA) TESTIFY'. After a series of flops, he was stopped temporarily by Motown writers HOLLAND-DOZIER-HOLLAND from using PARLIAMENT'S name. Meanwhile, CLINTON was being heavily influenced by The MC5, JIMI HENDRIX, SLY & THE FAMILY STONE, the primal throb of The STOOGES and radical politics, not to mention a hefty dose of LSD. By the late 60's, his group had evolved into FUNKADELIC and signed to 'Westbound'. The eponymous debut album of 1970 set the scene with its marriage of skintight rhythm, slow burning vocals and searing psychedelic guitar freakouts. Meanwhile, CLINTON had been given back the rights to The PARLIAMENTS moniker, changing it simply to PARLIAMENT, and signing to 'Invictus'. More or less the same line-up that'd recorded 'FUNKADELIC', worked on 'OSMIUM', PARLIAMENT's 1971 debut. While this album was more in keeping with the free range psychedelia of FUNKADELIC, PARLIAMENT became a vehicle for the more groove-orientated instalments in the P-FUNK saga. The 'PARLIAFUNKADELICAMENT THANG' effect was akin to a mind-bending 60's trip put through the blender of 70's excess with a soundtrack that combined soul, blues, gospel, psychedelic rock, sex and politics to create P-FUNK. Over the coming years the collective would grow into a large musical corporation which featured over 35 members, releasing such classic albums as FUNKADELIC's 'MAGGOT BRAIN' (1971) and 'COSMIC SLOP' (1973), while PARLIAMENT's first two dancefloor friendly albums, 'UP FOR THE DOWN STROKE' (1974) and 'CHOCOLATE CITY' (1975), set the scene for the landmark 'MOTHERSHIP CONNECTION', an interstellar concept piece from the inner galaxy of CLINTON's fevered mind. His re-definition of the black man's past and sci-fi vision of the future was underpinned by the precocious instrumental precision of former JB's trio BOOTSY COLLINS, BERNIE WORRELL and FRED WESLEY. CLINTON furthered his conceptual reach with 1977's 'FUNKENTELECHY VS THE PLACEBO SYNDROME', in which he presented his ideas of the Man keeping the kids oppressed through material dependency. In the meantime, FUNKADELIC had signed to 'Warners' and 1978's anthemic celebration of P-Funk, 'ONE NATION UNDER A GROOVE,' saw them reach a commercial and artistic peak, having already hit the US Top 30 two years previously with 'TEAR THE ROOF OFF THE SUCKER'. By the turn of the decade, there were so many side projects taking up the creative energy of the P-FUNK posse (BOOTSY'S RUBBER BAND, PARLET, HORNY HORNS, etc), that both PARLIAMENT and FUNKADELIC fizzled out, the latter releasing the last decent effort in 1981's 'ELECTRIC SPANKING OF WAR BABIES'. CLINTON went on to a solo career, offering the excellent 'COMPUTER GAMES' album and accompanying canine madness of the 'ATOMIC DOG' single. In the 90's, the ageing, dayglo warrior guested on records by PRIMAL SCREAM and ICE CUBE, as well as playing to sold out shows worldwide with The P-FUNK ALLSTARS. CLINTON's unswerving belief in the power of the funk to set people free (in every sense) lends his music a delirious, hedonistic quality, which, together with his synthesis of disparate musical styles and technology, is an ever present influence on a diverse range of artists, not leaset the P-FUNK sampling hip-hop community. • **Songwriters:** He covered SUNSHINE OF YOUR LOVE (Cream). • **Trivia:** In 1985, he collaborated with THOMAS DOLBY on 'DOLBY'S CUBE' single 'May The Cube Be With You'. Note: – An entirely different George Clinton surprised us with 'ABC' release 'Please Don't Run From Me'.

Recommended: PARLIAMENT LIVE – P FUNK EARTH TOUR (*7) /

FUNKADELIC (*7) / ELECTRIC SPANKING OF WAR BABIES (*7) / COSMIC SLOP (*7) / CHOCOLATE CITY (*8) / MAGGOT BRAIN (*7)

— For The PARLIAMENTS' releases between 1959-1969, see GREAT ROCK DISCOGRAPHY.

FUNKADELIC

— **CLINTON + RAYMOND DAVIS** – vocals / **CLARENCE 'Fuzzy' HASKINS** – vocals / **EDDIE HAZEL** – lead guitar / **TAWL ROSS** – rhythm guitar / **TKI FULTON** – drums / **MICKEY ATKINS** – some organ

BERNIE WORRELL – keyboards repl. ATKINS

Pye Int. Westbound

1969. (7") *<148>* **MUSIC FOR MY MOTHER. / ('A'instrumental)** [-] [ ]

Sep 69. (7") *<150>* **I'LL BET YOU. / QUALIFY AND SATISFY** [-] [63]

Apr 70. (7") *(7N 25519) <158>* **I GOT A THING, YOU GOT A THING, EVERYBODY'S GOT A THING. / FISH, CHIPS & SWEAT** [ ] [80] Feb70

Sep 70. (lp) *(NSPL 28137) <2000>* **FUNKADELIC** [ ] [ ] Mar70
– Mommy, what's a Funkadelic? / I'll bet you / Music for my mother / I got a thing, you got a thing, everybody's got a thing / Good old music / Quality and satisfaction / What is soul?. *(re-iss.Aug89 on 'Westbound' lp/c/cd; SEW/SEWC/CDSEW 010)*

Dec 70. (7") *<167>* **I WANNA KNOW IF IT'S GOOD TO YOU. / ('A'instrumental)** [-] [81]

1971. (lp) *(NSPL 28137) <2001>* **FREE YOUR MIND . . . AND YOUR ASS WILL FOLLOW** [ ] [92] Oct70
– Free your mind and your ass will follow / Friday night, August 14th / Funky dollar bill / I wanna know if it's good to you / Some more / Eulogy and light. *(re-iss.Feb90 on 'Westbound' lp/c/cd; SEW/SEWC/CDSEW 012)*

Apr 71. (7") *(7N 25548) <175>* **YOU & YOUR FOLKS, ME & MINE. / FUNKY DOLLAR BILL** [ ] [91] Feb71

PARLIAMENT

(i.e. **CLINTON & FUNKADELIC** musicians) + **R.DAVIS / G.THOMAS / F.HASKINS / C.SIMON**

Invictus Invictus

Dec 70. (7") *<9077>* **I CALL MY BABY PUSSYCAT. / LITTLE OLE COUNTRY BOY** [-] [ ]
(UK-iss.Dec84 on 'H.D.H.'; HDH 457)

Feb 71. (7") *<9091>* **RED HOT MAMA. / LITTLE OLE COUNTRY BOY** [-] [ ]

Jul 71. (lp) *(SVT 1004) <7302>* **OSMIUM** [ ] [ ] Dec70
– The breakdown / Call my baby Pussycat / Little ole country boy / Moonshine Heather / Oh Lord – why Lord – prayer / Red hot mama / My automobile / Nothing before me but thang / Funky woman / Come on in out of the rain / The silent boatman. *(re-iss.Feb90 as 'RHENIUM' on 'H.D.H.' cd/c/lp; HDH CD/MC/LP 008)–* (extra tracks) *(cd-iss.Jul93;)*

Jul 71. (7") *(INV 513)* **LIVIN' THE LIFE. / THE SILENT BOATMAN** [ ] [-]

Jul 71. (7") *<9095>* **THE BREAKDOWN. / LITTLE OLE COUNTRY BOY** [-] [ ]

Sep 71. (7") *<9123>* **COME IN OUT OF THE RAIN. / LITTLE OLE COUNTRY BOY** [ ] [ ]

FUNKADELIC

Now without NELSON + ROSS. Replaced by **GARY SHIDER** – guitar

Westbound Westbound

Sep 71. (7") *<185>* **CAN YOU GET TO THAT. / BACK IN OUR MINDS** [-] [93]

Sep 71. (lp) *(6310 200) <2007>* **MAGGOT BRAIN** [ ] [ ] Aug71
– Maggot brain / Can you get to that / Hit it and quit it / You and your folks, me and mine / Super stupid / Back in our minds / Wars of armageddon. *(re-iss.Aug89 lp/c/cd; SEW/SEWC/CDSEW 002)*

— added **WILLIAM BOOTSY COLLINS** – bass / **CATFISH COLLINS** – guitar / **FRANKIE 'Kash' WADDY** – drums (all of The J.B.'s, ex-JAMES BROWN)

Jul 72. (d-lp) *<2020>* **AMERICA EATS IT'S YOUNG** [-] [ ]
– You hit the nail on the head / If you don't like the effects / Don't produce the cause / Everybody is going to make it this time / A joyful process / We hurt too / Loose booty / Philmore / I call my baby Pussycat / America eats its young / Biological speculation / That was my girl / Balance / Miss Lucifer's love / Wake up. *(UK cd-iss.Jul90 cd/c/lp; CDSEWD/SEWC2/SEW2 029)*

1972. (7") *<197>* **I MISS MY BABY. / BABY I OWE YOU SOMETHING GOOD** [-] [ ]

1972. (7") *<198>* **HIT AND QUIT IT. / A WHOLE LOT OF BS** [-] [ ]

1973. (7") *<205>* **LOOSE BOOTY. / A JOYFUL PROCESS** [-] [ ]

Jul 73. (lp) *<2022>* **COSMIC SLOP** [-] [ ]
– Happy dug out / You can't miss what you can't measure / March to the witches castle / Let's make it last / Cosmic slop / No compute (alias spit don't make no babies) / Broken heart / Trash a go-go / Can't stand the strain. *(UK-iss.Feb91 cd/c/lp; CDSEW/SEWC/SEWA 035)*

1973. (7") *<218>* **COSMIC SLOP. / YOU DON'T LIKE THE EFFECTS, DON'T PRODUCE THE CAUSE** [-] [ ]

— added **FRED WESLEY & MACEO PARKER** – horns (both of J.B.'s)

Nov 74. (lp) *<1001>* **STANDING ON THE VERGE OF GETTING IT ON** [-] [ ] Sep74
– Red hot mama / Alice in my fantasies / I'll stay / Sexy ways / Standing on the verge of getting it on / Jimmy's got a little bit of bitch in him / Good thoughts, bad thoughts. *(re-iss.Aug91 cd/c/lp; CDSEW/SEWC/SEWA 040)*

Nov 74. (7") *<224>* **(STANDING) ON THE VERGE OF GETTING IT ON. / JIMMY'S GOT A LITTLE BIT OF BITCH IN HIM** [-] [ ]

1975. (7") *<5000>* **RED HOT MAMA. / VITAL JUICES** [-] [ ]

1975. (lp) *<1004>* **FUNKADELIC'S GREATEST HITS** (compilation) [-] [ ] Jul74

20th Cent Westbound

Jun 75. (lp) *(215)* **LET'S TAKE IT TO THE STAGE** [-] [ ]
– Good to your earhole / Better by the pound / Be my beach / No head no backstage pass / Let's take it to the stage / Get off your ass and jam / Baby I owe you something good / Stuffs & things / The song is familiar / Atmosphere. *(UK re-iss.Mar92 cd/c/lp; CDSEW/SEWC/SEWA 044)*

Oct 75. (7") *<5014>* **BETTER BY THE POUND. / STUFFS AND THINGS** [-] [99]

Jan 76. (7") *<5026>* **LET'S TAKE IT TO THE STAGE. / BIOLOGICAL SPECULATION** [-] [ ]

— **MIKE HAMPTON** – guitar repl. EDDIE HAZEL who went solo

1976. (lp) *<227>* **TALES OF KIDD FUNKADELIC** [-] [ ]
– Butt to butt resuscitation / Let's take it to the people / Undisco kid / Take your dead ass home / I'm never gonna tell it / Takes of Kidd Funkadelic / How do yeaw view you. *(UK re-iss.Mar93 cd/lp; CDSEW/SEWA 054)*

1976. (7") *<5029>* **UNDISCO KIDD. / HOW DO YEAW VIEW YOU** [-] [ ]

— After one more compilation 'THE BEST OF FUNKADELIC EARLY YEARS, VOL.1' in 1977, COLLINS continued with BOOTSY'S RUBBER BAND. Also leaving were HASKINS, SIMON and DAVIS who were to form own FUNKADELIC in the early 80's. They and 'Lax' label issued album CONNECTIONS AND DISCONNECTIONS (without CLINTON).

— Meanwhile in the mid-70's,

PARLIAMENT

(**CLINTON, etc.**) were signed to . . .

Casablanca Casablanca

Dec 74. (7") *<0003>* **THE GOOSE (pt.1). / (pt.2)** [-] [ ]

Dec 74. (lp) *(CAL 2011) <7002>* **UP FOR THE DOWN STROKE** [ ] [ ] Aug74
– Up for the down stroke / Testify / The goose / I can move you (if you let me) / I just got back / All your goodies are gone / Whatever makes baby feel good / Presence of a brain. *(re-iss.May77 & Nov78; same)*

Feb 75. (7") *(CBX 505) <0013>* **UP FOR THE DOWN STROKE. / PRESENCE OF A BRAIN** [ ] [63] Aug74

Feb 75. (7") *<811>* **TESTIFY. / I CAN MOVE YOU (IF YOU LET ME)** [-] [ ]

May 75. (7") *<831>* **CHOCOLATE CITY. / ('A'long version)** [-] [94]

Jun 75. (lp) *(CAL 2012) <7014>* **CHOCOLATE CITY** [ ] [91] Apr75
– Chocolate city / Ride on / Together / Side effects / What comes funky / Let me be / If it don't fit (don't force it) / Misjudged you / Big footin'. *(re-iss.May77; same)*

Nov 75. (7") *<843>* **RIDE ON. / BIG FOOTIN'** [-] [ ]

Jun 76. (7") *<852>* **P. FUNK (WANTS TO GET FUNKED UP). / NIGHT OF THE THUMPASORUS PEOPLES** [-] [ ]

Jun 76. (lp) *(CAL 2013) <7022>* **MOTHERSHIP CONNECTION** [ ] [13] Feb76
– P. Funk (wants to get funked up) / Mothership connection (star child) / Unfunky UFO / Supergroovalisticprosifunkstication (the thumps bump) / Handcuffs / Tear the roof off the sucker (give up the funk) / Night of the thumpasorus people. *(re-iss.May77; same) (re-iss.Aug87; 824 502-1/-4)*

Jun 76. (7") *(CBX 518) <856>* **TEAR THE ROOF OFF THE SUCKER (GIVE UP THE FUNK). / P. FUNK (WANTS TO GET FUNKED UP)** [ ] [15] May76

1976. (7") *<864>* **STAR CHILD. / SUPERGROOVALISTICPROSIFUNKSTACATION (THE THUMPS BUMB)** [-] [ ]

Oct 76. (7",12") *<871>* **DO THAT STUFF. / HANDCUFFS** [-] [ ]

May 77. (lp) *(CAL 2001) <7034>* **THE CLONES OF DR. FUNKENSTEIN** [ ] [20] Oct76
– Prelude / Gamin' on ya / Dr. Funkenstein / Children of productions / Gettin' to know you / Do that stuff / Everything is on the one / I've been watching you (move your sexy body) / Funkin' for fun. *(re-iss.Feb91 cd/c/lp; 842620-2)*

Jan 77. (7") *<875>* **DR. FUNKENSTEIN. / CHILDREN OF PRODUCTION** [-] [ ]

May 77. (7"m) *(CAN 103)* **TEAR THE ROOF OFF THE SUCKER (GIVE UP THE FUNK). / DR. FUNKENSTEIN / P. FUNK (WANTS TO GET FUNKED UP)** [ ] [-]

Jun 77. (d-lp) *(CALD 5002) <7053>* **PARLIAMENT LIVE – P.FUNK EARTH TOUR (live)** [ ] [29] May77
– P. Funk (wants to get funked up) / Dr. Funkenstein's supergroovalisticprosifunkstication / Medley: (a) Let's take it to the stage, (b) Take your dead ass home, (c) Say som'n nasty / Do that stuff / The landing (of the holy mothership) / The undisco Kidd (the girl is bad) / Children of production / Mothership connection (star child) / Swing down, sweet chariot / This is the way we funk with you (featuring Mike Hampton; lead snare) / Dr. Funkenstein / Gamin' on you / Tear the roof off the sucker medley:- (a) Give up the funk (tear the roof off the sucker) (b) Get off your ass and jam / Night of the thumpasorus people / Fantasy is reality.

1977. (7") *<892>* **FANTASY IS REALITY. / THE LANDING (OF THE HOLY MOTHERSHIP)** [-] [ ]

Dec 77. (lp) *(CALN 2021) <7084>* **FUNKENTELECHY VS. THE PLACEBO SYNDROME** [ ] [13]
– Bop gun (endangered species) / Sir Nose D'voidoffunk / Pay attention B-3M / Wizard of finance / Funkentelechy / Placebo syndrome / Flash light.

Jan 78. (7") *(CAN 115) <900>* **BOP GUN (ENDANGERED SPECIES). / I'VE BEEN WATCHING YOU (MOVE YOUR SEXY BODY)** [ ] [ ] Nov77
(12"+=) *(CANL 115)* – Do that stuff. *<US-12" has 2 'A'mixes>*

Apr 78. (7") *(CAN 123) <909>* **FLASH LIGHT. / SWING LOW, SWEET CHARIOT (live)** [ ] [16] Feb78
(US-12") *<same>* – (2 'A'mixes).

1978. (7") *<921>* **FUNKENTELECHY (part 1). / (part 2)** [-] [ ]

— Early '78, other PARLIAMENT / FUNKADELIC off-shoots "PARLET" (vocalists MALLIA FRANKLIN, JEANETTE WASHINGTON and SHIRLEY HAYDEN) released album 'THE PLEASURE PRINCIPLE'. Another album 'INVASIONS OF THE BODY SNATCHERS' was further issued Jul 79. "The BRIDES OF FUNKENSTEIN" (vocalists LYNN MABRY and DAWN SILVA) released album 'FUNK OR WALK' on 'Atlantic' late 1978.

FUNKADELIC

meanwhile had reappeared signing to . . .

Warners Warners

1977. (7") *<8309>* **COMIN' ROUND THE MOUNTAIN. / IF YOU GOT FUNK, YOU GOT STYLE** [-] [ ]

Feb 78. (lp) *(K 56299) <2973>* **HARDCORE JOLLIES** [ ] [96] Nov77
– Osmosis phase one / Comin' round the mountain / Smokey / If you got funk, you got style / Hardcore jollies / Terribitus phase two / Sould mate / Cosmic slop / You scared the lovin' outta me / Adolescent funk. *(re-iss.Jul93 on 'Charly' cd/lp; CDGR/LPGR 101)*

Feb 78. (7") *<8367>* **SMOKEY. / SOUL MATE** [-] [ ]

— add **JEROME BRAILEY** – drums (who had joined PARLIAMENT mid '76) / **WALTER 'JUNIE' MORRISON** – keyboards (ex-OHIO PLAYERS)

Nov 78. (7"/12") *(K 17246/+T)* <8618> **ONE NATION UNDER A GROOVE (part 1). / (part 2)** 9 28 Oct78

Dec 78. (lp) *(K 56539)* <3209> **ONE NATION UNDER A GROOVE** 56 16 Sep78
– One nation under a groove / Groovallegience / Who says a funk band can't play rock / Promentalashitbackwashipsychosisenema squad / Into you / Cholly (funk getting ready to roll) / Lunchmeat and phobia / P.E.squad / Doodoo chasers / Maggot brain. *(re-iss.Jul93 on 'Charly' cd/lp; CDGR/LPGR 100)*

Apr 79. (7") *(K 17321)* <8735> **CHOLLY (FUNK GETTING READY TO ROLL). / INTO YOU**
(US-12") <same> – (2-'A'mixes).

— drummer BRAILEY left to form own group MUTINY.

Oct 79. (lp) *(K 56712)* <3371> **UNCLE JAM WANTS YOU** 18
– Freak of the week / (Not just) Knee deep / Uncle Jam / Field manoeuvres / Cholly wants to go to California / Foot soldiers. *(re-iss.Jun93 on 'Charly' cd/lp; CDGR/LPGR 103)*

Jan 80. (7") *(K 17494)* <49040> **(NOT JUST) KNEE DEEP. / (part 2)** 77 Oct79

1980. (7") <49117> **UNCLE JAM. / (part 2)** -

Aug 81. (7"/12") *(K 17786/+T)* <49667> **THE ELECTRIC SPANKING OF WAR BABIES. / THE ELECTRIC SPANKING (instrumental)**

Apr 81. (lp) *(K 56874)* <3482> **THE ELECTRIC SPANKING OF WAR BABIES**
– The electric spanking of war babies / Electrocuties / Funk gets stronger / Brettino's bounce / She loves you / Shockwaves / Oh, I / Laka-prick. *(re-iss.Jun93 on 'Charly' cd/lp; CDGR/LPGR 102)*

1981. (7") <49807> **SHOCKWAVES. / BRETTINO'S BOUNCE** -

— (above featured CLINTON's long-time friend SLY STONE)

— The FUNKADELIC project had now been abandoned, due to splinter band.

PARLIAMENT

were still around simultaneously with FUNKADELIC and continued throughout the 80's.

Casablanca Casablanca

Dec 78. (7") *(CAN 136)* <950> **AQUA BOOGIE (A PSYCHOALPHADISCOBETABIOQUADOLOOP). / (YOU'RE A FISH AND I'M A) WATER SIGN** 89

Dec 78. (lp/pic-lp) *(CAL N/H 2043)* <7125> **MOTOR-BOOTY AFFAIR** 23
– Mr. Wiggles / Rumpopsteelskin / (You're a fish and I'm a) Water sign / Aqua boogie (a psychoalphadiscobetabioquadoloop) / One of those funky things / Liquid sunshine / Motor-booty affair / Deep. *(re-iss.Feb91 cd/c/lp; 842621-2)*

1979. (7") <976> **RUMPOFSTEELSKIN. / LIQUID SUNSHINE** -

Jul 79. (7"/12") *(CAN/+L 154)* **DEEP. / FLASH LIGHT** -

Dec 79. (lp) <(NBLP 7195)> **GLORYHALLASTOOPID – OR PIN THE TALE ON THE FUNKY** - 44
– Party people / Big bang theory / Freeze (sizzaleenmean) / Colour me funky / Theme from the black hole / May we bang you / Gloryhallastoopid (or pin the tale on the funky).

Jan 80. (12") *(CANL 188)* **THEME FROM THE BLACK HOLE. / THE BIG BANG THEORY** -

Apr 80. (7") <(NR 2222)> **PARTY PEOPLE. / PARTY PEOPLE (reprise)** Dec79
(12") – ('A'side) / Tear the roof off the sucker (give up the funk) / Flash light.

1980. (7") <2235> **THEME FROM THE BLACK HOLE. / (YOU'RE A FISH AND I'M A) WATER SIGN** -

Apr 81. (7"/12") *(CAN/+L 223)* <2250> **AGONY OF DE FEET. / THE FREEZE (SIZZALEENMEAN)**

Apr 81. (lp) <(NBLP 7249)> **TROMBIPULATION** 61 Jan81
– Trombipulation / crush it / Long way round / Agony of de feet / Now doo review / Let's play house / Body language / Peck-a-groove. *(cd-iss.Feb91; 842623-2)*

— PARLIAMENT were also defunkt, leaving behind a few exploitation releases

1981. (12") <NBD 20235> **CRUSH IT. / BODY LANGUAGE** -

GEORGE CLINTON

(solo) with numerous session people and **BOOTSY COLLINS / FRED WESLEY**

— another GEORGE CLINTON issued 1979 single 'Please Don't Run From Me'

Capitol Capitol

Nov 82. (lp/c) <(EST/TCEST 12246)> **COMPUTER GAMES** 40
– Get dressed / Man's best friend / Loopzilla / Pot sharing tots / Computer games / Atomic dog / Free alterations / One fun at a time. *(re-iss.May95 on 'MCI' cd/c; MUS CD/MC 511) (cd-iss.Apr97 on 'E.M.I.'; REPLAYCD 45)*

Nov 82. (7") *(CL 271)* <5160> **LOOPZILLA. / POT SHARING TOTS** 57
(12"+=) *(12CL 271)* – ('A'-broadcast version).
(US-12") <8538> – (2-'A'versions).

Feb 83. (7")(12") *(CL 280)* <5201><8556> **ATOMIC DOG. / MAN'S BEST FRIEND**
(12"+=) *(12CL 280)* <8544> – ('A'instrumental).

1983. (7") <5222> **GET DRESSED. / FREE ALTERATIONS** -

Dec 83. (7"/12") *(CL 319)* <5296><8572> **NUBIAN NUT. / FREE ALTERATIONS**
(12") <9039> – (2-'A'versions).

Jan 84. (lp/c) <(EST/TCEST 12308)> **YOU SHOULDN'T NUF BIT FISH** Dec83
– Nubian nut / Quickie / Last dance / Silly millameter / Stingy / You shouldn't – Nuf bit fish. *(cd-iss.Sep91 on 'E.M.I.'; CZ 469)*

1984. (7")(12") <5324><8580> **QUICKIE. / LAST DANCE** -

1984. (7")(ext-12") <5332><9065> **LAST DANCE. / LAST DANCE (version)** -

Jul 85. (7") *(CL 365)* <5473> **DOUBLE OH-OH. / BANGLADESH**
(12") <8642> – (2-'A'versions).

Sep 85. (lp/c) *(CLINT/TC-CLINT 1)* <12417> **SOME OF MY BEST JOKES ARE FRIENDS** Aug85
– Some of my best jokes are friends / Double oh-oh / Bulletproof / Pleasures of exhaustion (do it till I drop) / Bodyguard / Bangladesh / Thrashin' / Some of my best jokes are friends – reprise.

Dec 85. (7")(12") <5504><8653> **BULLETPROOF. / SILLY MILLAMETER** -

Apr 86. (7") *(CL 402)* **DO FRIES GO WITH THAT SHAKE. / PLEASURES OF EXHAUSTION (DO IT TILL I DROP)** 57
(UK-12"+=) *(12CL 402)* – Scratch medley.
(US-12") <15219> – (2-'A'versions).

— Did he release IRON EAGLE (Soundtrack) album around this time?

May 86. (7") <5602> **HEY GOOD LOOKIN'. / ('A'mix)** -
(12"+=) <15263> – ('A'extended).

May 86. (lp) <12481> **R&B SKELETONS (IN THE CLOSET)** -
– Hey good looking / Do fries go with that shake / Mix master suite – Startin' from scratch – Counter irritant – Nothing left to burn – Electric Pygmies – Intense – Cool Joe – R&B Skeleton (in the closet). *(UK cd-iss.Sep91 on 'E.M.I.'; CZ 470)*

1986. (7") <5642> **R&B SKELETONS IN THE CLOSET. / NUBIAN NUT** -

1987. (lp) <12534> **THE BEST OF GEORGE CLINTON & THE MOTHERSHIP CONNECTION LIVE FROM HOUSTON (live)** -
– Atomic dog / R&B skeletons (in the closet) / Quickie / Do fries go with that shake / Hey good lookin' / Double oh-oh / Nubian nut / Last dance.

Paisley P. Paisley P.

Jul 89. (7"/12") *(W 7557/+T)* <27557> **WHY SHOULD I DOG U OUT (part 1). / (part 2)**

Aug 89. (lp/c/cd) *(K 925994-1/-4/-2)* <25994> **THE CINDERELLA THEORY**
– Airbound / Tweakin' / The Cinderella theory / Why should I dog you out? / Serious slammin' / There I go again / (She's got it) Goin' on / The banana boat song / French kiss / Rita bewitched / Kredit-Kard / Airbound (reprise).

1989. (7") <22190> **TWEAKIN'. / FRENCH KISS** -
(12") <21337> – ('A'side) / Hysterical / ('A'remix).

Oct 93. (cd/c) *(7599 25518-2/-4)* **HEY MAN, SMELL MY FINGER**
– Martial law / Paint the White House black / Way up / Dis beat disrupts / Get satisfied / Hollywood / Rhythm and rhyme / The big pump / If true love / High in my hello / Maximumisness / Kickback / The flag was still there / Martial law (hey man . . . smell my finger) (single version). *(re-iss.Mar95 on 'New Power Generation' cd/c; NPG 6053-2/-4)*

— CLINTON guested for PRIMAL SCREAM on their early 1994 album 'GIVE OUT BUT DON'T GIVE UP'. To start the second half of '94, he featured on ICE CUBE single 'BOP GUN (ONE NATION) ', a re-indition of his old FUNKADELIC number.

Essential Rykodisc

Feb 95. (cd) *(ESSCD 280)* **FIFTH OF FUNK**
– Flatman and Robin / Count Funkula (I didn't know that funk was loaded) / Thumparella (Oh Kay) / Eyes of a dreamer / I found you / Ice melting in your heart / Clone ranger / Who do you love / Up up up and away / Can't get over losing you / Rat kissed the cat / Too tight for light / Every little bit hurts. *(re-iss.Apr97; ESMCD 490)*

P-FUNK ALL STARS

— another CLINTON aggregation

not issued Hump

1982. (7") <1> **HYDRAULIC PUMP. / (part 2)** -

1982. (7") <3> **ONE OF THOSE SUMMERS. / IT'S TOO FUNKY IN HERE** -

not issued CBS

1983. (7") <04032> **GENERATOR POP. / (part 2)** -

not issued Uncle Jam

1983. (lp) <39168> **URBAN DANCEFLOOR GUERRILLAS** -

Westbound Westbound

Oct 90. (d-cd/d-c/d-lp) *(CDSEW2/SEWC2/SEW2 031)* **P-FUNK ALL STARS LIVE (live at The Beverly Theater 1983)**

Jun 95. (cd/lp) *(CD+/SEWD 097)* **HYDRAULIC FUNK** (early material) -
– Pump up and down / Pumpin' it up / Copy cat / Throw your hand up in the air / Generator pop / Acupuncture / One of those summers / Catch a keeper / Pumpin' you is so easy / Generator pop (mix).

PARLIAMENT, FUNKADELIC & THE P-FUNK ALL STARS

Hot Hands Hot Hands

Apr 95. (12"/cd-s) *(12/CD HOTH 1)* **FOLLOW THE LEADER. / ('A'-D&S radio mix) / ('A'-Kool az phuk mix)**

May 95. (cd/c) *(HOTH CD/CD/MC/LP 1)* **DOPE DOGS**
–

GEORGE CLINTON & THE P-FUNK ALLSTARS

MJJ-Epic MJJ-Epic

May 96. (c-s) *(663321-4)* **IF ANYBODY'S GONNA GET FUNKED UP /**
(12"/cd-s) *(663321-6/-2)* –

Jun 96. (cd/c/lp) *(483833-2/-4/-1)* **T.A.P.O.A.F.O.M.**
– If anybody gets funked up (it's gonna be you) / Summer swim / Funky kind (gonna knock it down) / Mathematics / Hard as steel / New spaceship / Underground angel / Let's get funky / Flatman and Bobbin / Sloppy seconds / Rock the party / Get your funk on / T.A.P.O.A.F.O.M. (fly away).

— also P-FUNK singles on UK 'Frontline' in 1995; 'P-FUNK ERA' & 'RETURN OF THE GANGSTA'

– (GEORGE CLINTON compilations) –

Aug 92. (cd/c/lp; Various) *Esential; (ESS CD/MC/LP 185)* **GEORGE CLINTON FAMILY SERIES – VOL.1** -
(cd re-iss.Jul96; ESMCD 383)

Jan 93. (cd/c/lp; Various) *Esential; (ESS CD/MC/LP 189)* **GEORGE CLINTON FAMILY SERIES – VOL.2** -
(cd re-iss.Jul96; ESMCD 384)

Feb 93. (cd/lp) *Music Of Life; (MOL CD/LP 026)* **SAMPLE SOME OF DISC, SAMPLE SOME OF DAT** -
(re-iss.Nov94 cd/lp; MOL CD/LP 36)

Jun 93. (cd/c/lp; Various) *Esential; (ESS CD/MC/LP 190)* **GEORGE CLINTON FAMILY SERIES PART 3 – P IS THE FUNK** -
(cd re-iss.Jul96; ESMCD 385)

Sep 93. (cd/c/lp; Various) *Esential; (ESS CD/MC/LP 198)* **GEORGE CLINTON FAMILY SERIES – VOL.4** -

Oct 93. (cd/lp) *Music For Life; (MOL CD/LP 33)* **SAMPLE SOME OF DISC, SAMPLE SOME OF DAT, VOL.II** [ ] [-]
Mar 97. (d-lp/cd) *EMI Premier; (PRMD/+CD 20)* **THE GREATEST FUNKIN' HITS** [ ] [-]

- (PARLIAMENT) compilations -

Sep 86. (lp/c) *Club; (JAB B/C 18)* **UNCUT FUNK – THE BOMB (THE BEST OF PARLIAMENT)** [ ] [-]
May 93. (d-cd) *Mercury; (514417-2)* **TEAR THE ROOF OFF: 1974-80** [ ] [ ]
(re-iss.Sep95; same)
Oct 94. (cd; PARLIAMENTS) *Goldmine; (GSCD 052)* **I WANNA TESTIFY** [ ] [ ]
Sep 95. (cd) *Mercury; (526995-2)* **GIVE UP THE FUNK** [ ] [-]
Jun 97. (cd) *Deepbeats; (DEEPMO 23)* **PARLIAMENT – THE EARLY YEARS** [ ] [-]

- (FUNKADELIC) compilations, etc -

1989. (12") *M.C.A.; <23953>* **BY THE WAY OF THE DRUM. / ('A'edit) / ('A'instrumental)** [-] [ ]
Aug 90. (4xpic-cd-box) *Westbound; (WBOXPD 1)* **FUNKADELIC PICTURE DISC BOX SET** [ ] [-]
Oct 92. (d-cd/d-c/d-lp) *Westbound; (CDSEW/SEWC/SEW 2055)* **MUSIC FOR YOUR MOTHER (the singles)** [ ] [ ]
Mar 94. (4xpic-cd-box) *Westbound; (WBOXPD 5)* **PICTURE DISC BOXED SET VOLUME 2** [ ] [ ]
– (COSMIC SLOP / TALES OF KIDD FUNKADELIC / LET'S TAKE IT TO THE STAGE / STANDING ON THE VERGE OF GETTING IT ON)
Mar 94. (cd/lp) *Charly; (CDGR/LPGR 104)* **THE BEST OF FUNKADELIC 1976-1981** [ ] [-]
Nov 94. (cd) *Charly; (CPCD 8064)* **HARDCORE FUNK JAM** [ ] [-]
Oct 94. (4xcd-box) *Sequal; (NEFCD 273)* **PARLIAMENT / FUNKADELIC LIVE (live)** [ ] [-]
Apr 96. (c-s/12"/cd-s) *Charly; (MC/12/CD NATION 1)* **ONE NATION UNDER A GROOVE** [ ] [-]
Apr 96. (cd) *Westbound; (CDSEWD 108)* **FUNKADELIC LIVE (live Rochester 1971)** [ ] [ ]
May 97. (cd/c) *Southbound; (CD+/SEWD 115)* **FINEST** [ ] [ ]

CLOUDS

Formed: Edinburgh, Scotland . . . 1968 by IAN ELLIS, HARRY HUGHES and BILLY RITCHIE. They had previously cut their teeth in R&B combo The PREMIERS, before forming underground act 1-2-3. They signed to 'Island' with the help of impresario TERRY ELLIS, who brought in orchestra arranger DAVID PALMER (his past credits included JETHRO TULL). Their debut 45, 'MAKE NO BONES ABOUT IT', duly arrived in March '69, with their debut album following five months later. The aptly named 'SCRAPBOOK' was a directionless collection of ambitious, lyrically dour, group-penned songs, redeemed to a certain extent by sporadic bursts of humour. The title track was released as a second single although it was a further two years before they released the follow-up album, 'WATERCOLOUR DAYS'. The record attempted to blend together pop and progressive rock, again failing to strike a chord with the majority of the buying public. They played their final gig in October '71, with only IAN and HARRY re-showing on unheard demos of BOWIE's 'Hunky Dory'.
Recommended: SCRAPBOOK (*5) / WATERCOLOUR DAYS (*4)

BILLY RITCHIE – keyboards, vocals, guitar / **IAN ELLIS** – guitar, vocals, bass / **HARRY HUGHES** – drums

Island | Deram

Mar 69. (7") *(WIP 6055)* **MAKE NO BONES ABOUT IT. / HERITAGE** [ ] [-]
Aug 69. (lp) *(ILPS 9100) <DES 18044>* **SCRAPBOOK** <US title 'UP ABOVE OUR HEADS'> [ ] [ ]
– Introduction – Scrapbook / The carpenter / The colours have run / I'll go girl / Grandad / Ladies and gentlemen / Humdrum / Union Jack / Old man / Waiter, there's something in my soup / Scrapbook.
Sep 69. (7") *(WIP 6067)* **SCRAPBOOK. / THE CARPENTER** [ ] [-]
1971. (lp) *(ILPS 9151)* **WATERCOLOUR DAYS** [ ] [ ]
– Watercolour days / Cold sweat / Lighthouse / Long time / Mind of a child / I know better than you / Leavin' / Get off my farm / I am the melody.
—— split later in 1971, RITCHIE and group becoming anonymous again

- compilations, etc. -

Jul 96. Beat Goes On; (cd) *(BGOCD 317)* **SCRAPBOOK / WATERCOLOUR DAYS** [ ] [-]

CLUSTER

Formed: East Berlin, Germany . . . 1969 as KLUSTER by HANS-JOACHIM ROEDELIUS, DIETER MOEBIUS and CONRAD SCHNITZLER. After two neo-psychedelic albums they altered their name slightly to CLUSTER in the early 70's, releasing a further couple of lush, quirky electronic gems, 'CLUSTER' & 'CLUSTER II'. In 1974, before their third album 'ZUCKERZEIT', they teamed up with MICHAEL ROTHER (of NEU!) to complete a clutch of albums under the HARMONIA moniker. This trio were more versatile, utilising electronic percussion, pianos and other pieces of synths on 2 mid-70's albums, 'HARMONIA' & 'DE LUXE'. In 1976, ROEDELIUS and MOEBIUS re-formed CLUSTER as a duo and made a triumphant return with 'SOWIESOSO'. By the late 70's, they were collaborating with long-time ambient exponent BRIAN ENO on the albums 'CLUSTER AND ENO' and 'AFTER THE HEAT'. The following decade, ROEDELIUS and MOEBIUS worked on their own solo albums, as well as working on further material with ENO. Around the same time, ROEDELIUS moved to Blumau in Austria where he revived the Cluster moniker (slightly!), after MOEBIUS guested on 'APROPOS CLUSTER' (1990). This highly rated outfit remain one of Germany's more interesting electronic pioneers, especially beloved of Kraut-rock afficiondo JULIAN COPE.

Recommended: KLUSTER: KLOPFZEICHEN (*6) / KLUSTER ZWEI: OSTEREI (*6) / CLUSTER (*7) / CLUSTER 2 (*6) / HARMONIA (*5) / DE LUXE: HARMONIA (*6) / ZUCKERZEIT (*7)

KLUSTER

KONRAD SCHNITZLER (PLANK) (ex-TANGERINE DREAM), **HANS-JOACHIM ROEDELIUS, DIETER MOEBIUS** – instruments / **CHRISTA RUNGE** – vocals

Schwann | not issued

Feb 70. (lp) *(AMS 511)* **KLOPFZEICHEN** [-] [-] German
Nov 70. (lp) *(AMS 512)* **KLUSTER ZWEI: OSTEREI** [-] [-] German

CLUSTER

MOEBIUS (b. 16 Jan'44) – organ, guitar, electronics / **ROEDELIUS** (b.24 Oct'34) – organ, cello, electronics / **CONRAD PLANK** – electronics

Philips | not issued

Sep 71. (lp) *(6305 074)* **CLUSTER** [-] [-] German
– 15:43 / 7:42 / 21:32. *(UK cd-iss.Feb97 on 'Soul Static Sound; SOUL 17)*
—— now all on synthesizers

Brain | not issued

Apr 72. (lp) *(1006)* **CLUSTER 2** [-] [-] German
– Plas / Im suden / Fuer die katz / Live in der fabrik / Georgel / Nabitte. *(UK-iss.1979 on 'Logo'; 0001 006) (cd-iss.Oct96 on 'Spalax'; 14864)*
—— **MICHAEL ROTHER** – guitar (of NEU!), repl. PLANK who went into production
1974. (lp) *(1065)* **ZUCKERZEIT** [-] [-] German
– Hollywood / Caramel / Rote kiki / Rosa / Caramba / Fotschi tong / James / Marzipan / Rotor / Heisse lippen. *(re-iss.1980; 0040.116) (UK cd-iss.Oct96 on 'Spalax'; 14865)*

HARMONIA

MOEBIUS, ROEDELIUS + ROTHER
1974. (lp) *(1044)* **MUSIK VON HARMONIA** [-] [-] German
– Watussi / Sehr komisch / Sonnenschein / Dino / Ohrwurm / Ahoi / Veterano / Hausmusik. *(re-iss.1980 as 'DINO'; 0040 123)*
1975. (lp) *(1073)* **HARMONIA DELUXE** [-] [-] German
– De luxe / Walky-talky / Monster / Notre Dame / Gollum / Kekse.

CLUSTER

—— now duo of **MOEBIUS + ROEDELIUS**

Sky | not issued

1976. (lp) *(005)* **SOWIESOSO** [-] [-] German
– Sowiesoso / Halwa / Dem wanderer / Umleitung / Zum wohl / Es war einmal / In Ewigkeit. *(cd-iss.Oct 93 ; SKYCD 3005)*
—— added **BRIAN ENO** – synthesizers (solo artist) / **HOLGER CZUKAY** – bass (of CAN)
May 78. (lp) *(010)* **CLUSTER AND ENO** [ ] [-]
– Ho renomo / Schoene haende / Steinsame / Wehrmut / Mit Siamaen / Selange / Die bunge / One / Fuer Louise. *(cd-iss.Oct93; SKY3 010)*
Sep 78. (lp; CLUSTER & FARNBAUER) *(015)* **LIVE IN VIENNA (live)** [-] [-] German
Mar 79. (lp; as ENO, MOEBIUS & ROEDELIUS) *(021)* **AFTER THE HEAT** [-] [-] German
– Oil / Foreign affairs / Luftschloss / The shade / Old land / Base & apex / Light arms / Broken head / The belldog / Tzima N'arki. *(cd-iss.Oct93; SKY3 021)*
—— duo once again
Dec 79. (lp) *(027)* **GROSSES WASSER** [-] [-] German
– Avanti / Prothese / Isodea / Breitengrad 20 / Manchmal / Grosses wasser.
1981. (lp) *(063)* **CURIOSUM** [-] [-] German
– Oh Odessa / Proantipro / Seltsame gegend / Hello melange / Tristan in der bar / Charlic / Ufer.
Sep 84. (lp) *(SKY 093)* **STIMMUNGEN** [-] [-] German
—— Disgrouped and both carried on solo work

MOEBIUS

—— with **HOLGER CZUKAY** – keyboards, synths, etc
1980. (lp; MOBIUS & PLANK) *(039)* **RASTAKRAUT PASTA** [-] [-] German
– New / Rastakraut pasta / Feedback 66 / Missi Cacadou / Two oldtimers / Solar plexus / Landebahn.
1981. (lp; on 'Sesam') *(1005)* **PART OF ART** [-] [-] German
1981. (lp; MOBIUS & PLANK) *(067)* **MATERIAL** [-] [-] German
– Conditionierer / Infiltration / Toll kuehn / Osmo fantor / Nordoestliches gefuehl.
1982. (lp) *(071)* **STRANGE MUSIC** [-] [-] German
– Subito / White house / Fortschritt / Clarks shiraz / Yingyang / 883 / Glucose.
1983. (lp) *(083)* **TONSPUREN** [-] [-] German
– Contramio / Hasenheide / Rattenwiesel / Transport / Etwas / Nervoes / B 36 / Furbo / Sinister / Immerhin.
Mar 84. (lp; MOEBIUS, PLANK & NEUMEIER) *(SKY 085)* **ZERO SET** [ ] [-]
– Speed display / Load / Pitch control / All repro / Recall / Search zero. *(cd-iss.1990's; SKYCD3 085)*

Apr 84. (lp; ENO, MOEBIUS, ROEDELIUS, PLANK) *(SKY 090)* **BEGEGNUNGEN** [ ] [-]
– Johanneslust / Two oldtimers / The belldog / Nervoes / Pitch control / Dem wanderer / Schoene haende. *(cd-iss.Oct93; SKY3 090)*
1984. (lp; MOBIUS & BEERBOHM) *(091)* **DOUBLE CUT** [-] [-] German
1985. (lp; ENO, MOEBIUS, ROEDELIUS, PLANK) *(SKY 095)* **BEGEGNUNGEN II** (compilation) [ ] [-]
– Conditionierer / Speed display / Mr. Livingstone I suppose / Broken head / Langer atem / Hasenheide / Es war einmal / Fur Louise. *(cd-iss.Oct93; SKY3 095)*
Jan 86. (lp; CLUSTER & ENO) *(SKY 105)* **OLD LAND** [ ] [-]
Aug 86. (lp) *(SKY 109)* **BLUE MOON** [ ] [-]
X / not issued
1985. (lp) *(624 560)* **MIRROR OF INFINITY** [-] [-] German
Rocke / not issued
Oct 93. (cd/c) *(ROC CD/MC 001)* **AUGUST** [ ] [ ]

ROEDELIUS

— with **MOEBIUS, PLANK / + JOSO CHRISTO** – guitar, bass

Sky / not issued
1978. (lp) *(SKY 014)* **DURCH DIE WUSTE** [-] [-] German
– Am rockzipfel / Durch die wuste / Johanneslust / Glaubersalz / Mr. Livingstone I suppose / Regenmacher.
1979. (lp; on 'Egg') *(90291)* **JARDIN AU FOU** [-] [-] French

— now completely solo.

1979. (lp) *(028)* **SELBSTPORTRAIT** (rec.1973-77) [-] [-] German
– In liebe dein / Girlande / Inselmoos / Fabelwein / Prinzregent / Kamee / Herold / Halmharfe / Arcona / Staunen im Fjord / Minne.
1980. (lp) *(040)* **SELBSTPORTRAIT II** (rec.1973-79) [-] [-] German
– Signal / Gewiss / Aufbruch / Schoenheitsfecken / Alle jahre wieder / Uebern fluss / Tee fuer die geisha / Kichererbsen / Grundlsee / Regenwurm / Thronfolge / Signal.
1980. (lp) *(044)* **SELBSTPORTRAIT III – REISE DURCH ARCADIEN** [-] [-] German
– Sonntags / Geburtstag / Fieber / Hochzeit / Geradewohl / Erinnerung / Zuversicht / Stimmung.
1981. (lp) *(058)* **LUSTWANDEL** [-] [-] German
– Lustwandel / Legende / Ansinnen / Betrachtung / Draussen vorbei / Harlekin / Von ferne her / Vom fliegen / Willkommen / Pirouette / Dein antlitz / Langer atem / Die andere blume. *(cd-iss.1993; SKYCD 3058)*
1981. (lp) *(064)* **WENN DER SUDWIND WEHT** [-] [-] German
– Wenn der sudwind weht / Veilchenwurzein / Mein Freund Farouk / Mutee / Freudentanz / Goldregen / Auf leisen sohlen / Saumpfad / Sonnengeflecht / Felix Austria. *(cd-iss.1990's; SKYCD 3064)*
1982. (lp) *(072)* **OFFENDE TUREN** [-] [-] German
– Abenteurliche begegnung / Besucher im traum / Mit offenem visier / Von osten her / Der sieger / Auf der hoehe / Allemande / Spiegelung / Husche / Stufe um stufe / Zeremoniell / Wende.
1982. (lp) *(078)* **FLIEG VOGEL, FLIEGE** [-] [-] German
– Uber Berg und Tai / Klares wasser / Baer im honig / Flieg vogel, fliege / Kleines glueck / Lange weile / Oh, du gruene Neune / Meilenstein / Salzpfaumen / Auf auf und davon / Wanderung.

— added **ERIC SPITZER-MARLYN** – guitar, bass, vocals / **ALEXANDER CZJZEK** – sax

Schaliter / not issued
1983. (lp) *(204686)* **WASSER IM WIND** [-] [-] German
– Der ruf aus der ferne / Am stadtrand / Zwei sind eins / Auf des tigers spur / Immergruen / Wasser im wind / Kundmachung / Heilsamer Brunnen / Fenster im schnee.
E.G. / not issued
1984. (lp) *(EGED 34)* **GESCHENK DES AUGENBLICKS** [ ] [-]
– Geschenk des augenblicks (Gift of the moment) / Adieu quichotte / Troubadour / Kleine blume irgendwo (Little flower somewhere) / Ohn unterlass (Continuously) / Gefundene zeit (Time regained) / Sehnsucht ich will dich lassen (To be free and yearning) / Das sanfte (Mellowness) / Tag fur tag (Day by day) / Zu fussen der berge am ufer des sees / Wurzein des glucks (Roots of joy). *(re-iss.Jan87; same) (cd-iss.Jun97; CDOVD 483)*
Cicada / not issued
1986. (lp) *(004)* **WIE DAS WISPERN DES WINDES** [-] [-] Dutch
Polydor / not issued
1987. (lp/cd) *(831627-1/-2)* **WEITES LAND** [-] [-] German
– Einklang / Sonniger Morgen / Beruhung / Ballade / Weibt du noch / Nahe / Weites land / Hoffnung.

— still with **CZJZEK**

Venture / not issued
Jul 87. (cd/c/lp) *(CD/TC+/VE 4)* **MOMENTI FELICI** [ ] [-]
– Im Fruhtau / Leicht zu fuss / Anima mundi / Uber den wolken / Anfgewacht / Capriccio / Guten morgen / Am weiher / Pas de deux.
Jul 89. (cd/c/lp) *(CD/TC+/VE 42)* **BASTIONEN DER LIEBE (FORTRESS OF LOVE)** [ ] [-]
– Happy birthday / Im revier des tigers / Five stations / Harmonia / Ciao Maurice / An einer quelle / Lokomotion / Smile / Life is a treasure od . . . / Allegra / Feu doux / Ordre du coeur.

– compilations, etc. –

Sep 84. (lp) *Sky; (SKY 094)* **AUF LEISEN SOHLEN** [ ] [-]

CLUSTER

— were a duo once more

Clear Spot / not issued
1993. (cd) **APROPOS CLUSTER** [ ] [-]
Dec 96. (cd) *(105865)* **ONE HOUR** [ ] [-]
Cleopatra / not issued
Mar 97. (d-cd) *(CLP 9933)* **FIRST ENCOUNTER TOUR (live)** [ ] [-]
May 97. Marginal Talent; (cd) *(MT 365)* **ERUPTION** [ ] [-]

COLOSSEUM

Formed: London, England ... Sep'68 by JON HISEMAN, DICK-HECKSTALL-SMITH, DAVE GREENSLADE, JIM ROCHE and TONY REEVES (most stemming from JOHN MAYALL and GRAHAM BOND). Early the following year (after ROCHE was releaced by JAMES LITHERLAND), they scored a Top 20 album with 'THOSE WHO ARE ABOUT TO DIE SALUTE YOU', its avant-garde hybrid of progressive jazz and rock a revelation to those outwith the psychedelic sphere. They then shifted to the more credible 'Vertigo' label (like 'Fontana', also part of the Phonogram group), where they recorded their second Top 20 album, 'VALENTYNE SUITE'. LITHERLAND was then replaced by DAVE CLEMPSON, REEVES later superseded by MARK CLARKE. Seasoned R&B singer CHRIS FARLOWE was also invited to join for their third set, 'DAUGHTER OF TIME', which eschewed their complex jazz in favour of a more rock-based approach. Nevertheless, the album sold quite well, as did their final live set in 1971. HISEMAN and CLARKE created TEMPEST, although the former returned in 1976 with COLOSSEUM II, which featured GARY MOORE on guitar. Three albums in a heavier vein surfaced between 1976 and 1977. HISEMAN continued to work as a session man in the 80's, re-forming COLOSSEUM for a series of concerts in 1994. • **Songwriters:** Each contributed music with HISEMAN lyrics. Initial lyrics were by poet PETE BROWN, who also went solo. They covered WALKING IN THE PARK (Graham Bond). TEMPEST covered PAPERBACK WRITER (Beatles). • **Trivia:** In 1969, COLOSSEUM appeared in the rock film 'Supersession'.

Recommended: EPITAPH (*6)

JON HISEMAN (b.21 Jun'44, Blackheath, London) – drums (ex-GRAHAM BOND, ex-JOHN MAYALL) / **DAVE GREENSLADE** – keyboards (ex-CHRIS FARLOWE's THUNDERBIRDS) / **TONY REEVES** – bass (ex-JOHN MAYALL'S BLUESBREAKERS) / **DICK HECKSTALL-SMITH** (b.26 Sep'34, Ludlow, England) – sax (ex-GRAHAM BOND, ex-JOHN MAYALL) / **JAMES LITHERLAND** – guitar, vocals repl. JIM ROCHE

Fontana / Dunhill
Mar 69. (lp) *(STL 5510)* **THOSE WHO ARE ABOUT TO DIE SALUTE YOU** [15] [-]
– Walking in the park / Plenty hard luck / Mandarin / Debut / Beware the Ides of March / The road she walked before / Backwater blues / Those who are about to die.
May 69. (7") *(TF 1029)* **WALKING IN THE PARK. / THOSE WHO ARE ABOUT TO DIE** [ ] [-]
Vertigo / Dunhill
Nov 69. (lp) *(VO 1)* **VALENTYNE SUITE** [15] [-]
– The kettle / Elegy / Butty's blues / The machine demands a sacrifice / The Valentyne suite: a) January's search, b) February's Valentyne, c) The grass is always greener. *(re-iss.Oct77 on 'Bronze')*
Nov 69. (7") **THE KETTLE. / PLENTY HARD LUCK** [-] [ ]
Jan 70. (lp) **THE GRASS IS GREENER** [-] [ ]
– Jumping off the sun / Lost Angeles / Elegy / Butty's blues / Rope ladder to the Moon / Bolero / The machine demands a sacrifice / The grass is greener.

— **DAVE CLEMPSON** (b. 5 Sep'49) (had played on US version of 2nd lp) – guitar, vocals (ex-BAKERLOO) repl. LITHERLAND who joined MOGUL THRASH. In 1970, DICK + GEN were credited on lp 'THINGS WE LIKE' with JACK BRUCE + JOHN McLAUGHLIN.

— (Sep70) **MARK CLARKE** – bass, vocals repl. REEVES (later to GREENSLADE) / added **CHRIS FARLOWE** (b.JOHN DEIGHTON) – vocals (ex-Solo artist)

Nov 70. (lp) *(6360 017)* **DAUGHTER OF TIME** [23] [ ]
– Three score and ten, amen / Time lament / Take me back to Doomsday / The daughter of time / Theme for an imaginary western / Bring out your dead / Downhill and the shadows / The time machine. *(re-iss.Jul94 on 'Success' cd/c;)*
Bronze / Warners
Jun 71. (d-lp) *(ICD 1)* **COLOSSEUM LIVE (live)** [17] [ ]
– Rope ladder to the Moon / Walking in the park / Skellington / Tanglewood 63 / Encore / Stormy Monday blues / Lost Angeles. *(re-iss.Oct77; BRSP 2) (re-iss.Mar87 on 'Castle'; CLALP 122) (cd-iss.Jun92 on 'Sequel'; NEXCD 201)*
Nov 71. (lp) *(ILPS 9173)* **THE COLLECTOR'S COLOSSEUM** (compilation) [ ] [-]
– Jumping off the Sun / Those about to die / I can't live without you / Beware the Ides Of March / Walking in the park / Bolero / Rope ladder to the Moon / The grass is greener. *(re-iss.Oct77; BRON 173)*

— split Oct'71. DAVE formed GREENSLADE. CLEMPSON joined HUMBLE PIE and FARLOWE joined ATOMIC ROOSTER. CLARKE joined URIAH HEEP until mid-72.

TEMPEST

— were formed by **HISEMAN & CLARKE** plus **PAUL WILLIAMS** – vocals (ex-JUICY LUCY, ex-ZOOT MONEY, ex-JOHN MAYALL) / **ALLAN HOLDSWORTH** – guitar

Bronze / not issued
Jan 73. (lp) *(ILPS 9220)* **JON HISEMAN'S TEMPEST** [ ] [-]
– Gorgon / Foyers of fun / Dark house / Brothers / Up and on / Grey and black / Strange her / Upon tomorrow.

— **OLLIE HALSALL** – guitar repl. WILLIAMS (HOLDSWORTH joined SOFT MACHINE)

Mar 74. (lp) *(ILPS 9267)* **LIVING IN FEAR** [ ] [-]
– Funeral empire / Paperback writer / Stargazer / Dance to my tune / Living in fear / Yeah, yeah, yeah / Waiting for a miracle / Turn around. *(both above on cd Feb91 on 'Sequel';)*

COLOSSEUM II

— was formed by **HISEMAN** in May75. **MIKE STARR** – vocals / **DON AIREY** –

keyboards / **NEIL MURRAY** – bass / **GARY MOORE** – guitar, vocals (ex-THIN LIZZY, ex-SKID ROW)

Bronze Warners

Apr 76. (lp) *(ILPS 9356)* **STRANGE NEW FLESH** -
– Dark side of the moog / Down to you / Gemini and Leo / Secret places / On second thoughts / Winds. *(re-iss.Apr86 on 'Castle' lp/cd; CLA LP/CD 104)*

— with MOORE now on some lead vocals, **NEIL MOLE** – bass repl. STARR who joined LUCIFER'S FRIEND. Also NEIL MURRAY left (later to WHITESNAKE)

M.C.A. M.C.A.

Jan 77. (lp) *(MCF 8200)* **ELECTRIC SAVAGE**
– Am I / Intergallactic strut / Put it this way / All skin and bone / Rivers / The scorch / Lament / Desperado. *(re-iss.Jul82; MCL 1696)*

Aug 77. (7") *(MCA 311)* **LAMENT. / THE SCORCH** -

Oct 77. (lp) *(MCF 8217)* **WARDANCE**
– War dance / Put it that way / Major key / Castles / Fighting talk / Quaser / Inquisition / Star maidens / Mysteriouso / Last exit. *(re-iss.Aug81; MCL 1603)*

— **KEITH AIREY** – guitar repl. GARY MOORE who joined THIN LIZZY. But they soon split late 1978. DON AIREY joined RAINBOW. HISEMAN joined his wife BARBARA THOMPSON in the band PARAPHERNALIA.

JON HISEMAN

Kuckluck not issued

1981. (lp) **NIGHT IN THE SUN** - - German
– Tropeiro / The hearts of carnival / Sun roof / A night in the sun / Eunice / Makenna Beach / Walking on air.

Temple not issued

Sep 86. (lp/cd) *(TM 08/+2)* **ABOUT TIME TOO!** -
– Solo Berlin: Ganz schon heiss, man / Solo Hanover: Ganz schon heiss, man

COLOSSEUM

— **FARLOWE / HECKSTALL-SMITH + CLARKE** re-formed in 1994

Intuition not issued

May 95. (cd) **THE REUNION CONCERTS 1994 (live)** -
– January's search – February's valentyne – The grass is always greener (the valentyne suite) / Those about to die we salute you / Elegy / Theme for an imaginary western / The machine demands another sacrifice / Solo Colonia / Lost Angeles / Stormy Monday blues.

– other compilations, etc. –

Apr 86. (lp/c/cd) *Raw Power; (RAW LP/MC/CD 014)* **EPITAPH** -
– Walking in the park / Bring out your dead / Those about to die / Beware the ides of March / Daughter of time / Valentyne suite.

Jun 90. (cd) *Knight; (KNCD 10016)* **THE GOLDEN DECADE OF COLOSSEUM** -

Jan 91. (cd) *Sequel; (NEXCD 161)* **THOSE WHO ARE ABOUT TO DIE SALUTE YOU / VALENTYNE SUITE** -

May 91. (cd/d-lp) *Castle; (CCS CD/LP 287)* **THE COLOSSEUM COLLECTION** -

May 95. (cd) *Spectrum;* **THE IDES OF MARCH** -

COSMIC EYE

Formed: London, England . . . 1971 as an ensemble of cosmopolitan musicians. Together, they created what was probably one of the first "new-age" records in the concept album, 'DREAM SEQUENCE'. It consisted of just one track split over two sides and was too ambitious for many with its freeform collision of ethnic and bebop jazz. Despite this, the record remains a much sought after piece of work, fetching around £100.

Recommended: DREAM SEQUENCE (*5)

AMANCIO D'SILVA – guitar / **VIRAM JASANI** – sitar / **JOHN MAYER** – violin / **RAY SWINFIELD + DEREK GROSSMAN + C. TAYLOR** – flutes / **ALAN BRANSCOMBE** – sax / **TONI CAMPO** – bass / **KESH SATI** – tabla / **D. WRIGHT** – drums

Regal Zonophone not issued

1972. (lp) *(SLRZ 1030)* **DREAM SEQUENCE** -
– Dream sequence.

COUNT FIVE

Formed: San Jose, California, USA . . .1965 by (see below). After signing to L.A. label 'Double Shot', they released their debut single 'PSYCHOTIC REACTION', a garage-psych classic which hit the US Top 5 in late 1966. Borrowing heavily from The YARDBIRDS, the track later gained cult status after being featured on LENNY KAYE's seminal 1972 garage-punk compilation, 'NUGGETS'. After a disappointing debut album and a string of flop singles, the group disbanded in 1968. Apparently, they were reputed to have given up $1,000,000 worth of bookings so they could return to school (truly psychotic!). • **Songwriters:** Group. • **Trivia:** In the early 80's, The CRAMPS revived 'PSYCHOTIC REACTION'.

Recommended: PSYCHOTIC REACTION (*7)

KEN ELLNER (b.1948, Brooklyn, N.Y.) – vocals, harmonica / **SEAN BYRNE** (b.1947, Dublin, Ireland) – guitar, vocals / **JOHN 'Mouse' MICHALSKI** (b.1949, Cleveland, Ohio) – lead guitar / **ROY CHANEY** (b.1948, Indianapolis, Indiana) – bass / **CRAIG 'Butch' ATKINSON** (b.1947, Springfield, Missouri, USA) – drums

Pye Inter. Double Shot

Oct 66. (7") *(7N 25393)* *<104>* **PSYCHOTIC REACTION. / THEY'RE GONNA GET YOU** 5 Sep66

Nov 66. (lp) *<DSM 1001>* **PSYCHOTIC REACTION** -
– Double-decker bus / Pretty big mouth / The world / My generation / She's fine / Psychotic reaction / Peace of mind / They're gonna get you / The morning after / Can't get your lovin' / Out in the street. *(cd-iss.May92 on 'Repertoire';)*

Jan 67. (7") *<106>* **PEACE OF MIND. / THE MORNING AFTER** -

Mar 67. (7") *<110>* **YOU MUST BELIEVE ME. / TEENY BOPPER, TEENY BOPPER** -

May 67. (7") *<115>* **MERRY-GO-ROUND. / CONTRAST** -

Jan 68. (7") *<125>* **DECLARATION OF INDEPENDENCE. / RELEATION IN SLOW MOTION** -

Jun 68. (7") *<141>* **MAILMAN. / PRETTY BIG MOUTH** -

— Disbanded in 1968. BYRNE returned to Ireland and joined PUBLIC FOOT THE ROMAN for one album in 1973. Five years later his group LEGOVER issued album 'WAIT TILL NIGHTIME'.

compilations, others

Oct 87. (lp) *Edsel; (ED 225)* **PSYCHOTIC REACTION** -
– PSYCHOTIC REACTION lp tracks + / You must believe me / Teeny bopper, teeny bopper / Merry-go-round / Contrast / Revelation in slow motion / Declaration of independence. *(cd-iss.Mar91; ED 225CD)*

COUNTRY JOE AND THE FISH (see under ⇒ McDONALD, Country Joe)

(see under ⇒ McDONALD, Country Joe)

Kevin COYNE

Born: 21 Jan'44, Derby, England. At 19, after attending a local art college, he worked as a social therapist at a mental hospital in Preston. COYNE moved to London in 1968, where he was initially employed as a social worker in Camden, while moonlighting on vocal duties for local act SIREN. Signing to John Peel's 'Dandelion' label, they released two competent albums between 1969 and 1971, the eponymous debut containing some fine numbers including, 'GET RIGHT CHURCH', 'AND I WONDER' and 'ASYLUM'. In 1972, COYNE left his job and the band to go solo full-time, releasing 'CASE HISTORY' the same year. A more acoustic set, his throaty, mannered vocal chords (described as a cross between ROGER CHAPMAN or JOE COCKER) went hand-in-hand with the records heavy subject material (i.e. 'UGGY'S SONG', 'EVIL ISLAND' & 'MAD BOY'). In 1973, he was ppicked up by Richard Branson's new 'Virgin' label, where he released the seminal critically-acclaimed double-set 'MARJORY RAZORBLADE', a disturbing double-set drawing on his past experiences dealing with mental patients. His subsequent work for 'Virgin' continued to make no concessions to commerciality and a final outing, 'SANITY STOMP' (1980), was backed by punk/dub outfit, The RUTS. Throughout the 80's and beyond, he released several albums, some only finding favour in Germany where he has resided for several years. • **Songwriters:** COYNE wrote all, except some with CLAGUE. In 1980, he wrote with PAUL WICKENS. Covered KNOCKIN' ON HEAVEN'S DOOR (Bob Dylan) / OL' MAN RIVER (Paul Robeson) / ONE FINE DAY (Chiffons).

Recommended: THE DANDELION YEARS (*8) / MARJORY RAZORBLADE (*8) / IN LIVING BLACK AND WHITE (*7) / SIGN OF THE TIMES (*7)

SIREN

KEVIN COYNE – vocals, guitar / **DAVID CLAGUE** – bass, guitar, producer / **NICK CUDWORTH** – guitar, piano / **JOHN CHICHESTER** – lead guitar / **TAT MEAGER** – drums / with guests **COLIN WOOD** – keyboards, flute / **DAVID GIBBONS / ALISTAIR CAMPBELL**

Dandelion Elektra

1969. (7"; as CLAGUE with KEVIN COYNE) *(S 4493)* **BOTTLE UP AND GO. / MANDY LEE** -

1969. (lp) *(63755)* **SIREN**
– Ze-ze-ze-ze / Get right church / Rock me baby / Wake up my children / Wasting my time / Sixteen women / First time I saw your face / Gardener man / And I wonder / The war is over / Asylum / Bertha Lee / I wonder where.

Sep 69. (7"; as COYNE-CLAGUE) *(S 4494)* **THE STRIDE. / I WONDER WHERE** -

1970. (7") *<45714>* **ZE-ZE-ZE-ZE. / AND I WONDER** -

— **MICK GRATTON** – guitar, repl. CHICHESTER.

Jan 71. (lp) *(DAN 8001)* **STRANGE LOCOMOTION** -
– Relaxing with Bonnie Lou / Some dark day / Hot potato / Soon / Gigolo / I'm all aching / Strange locomotion / Shake my hand / Lonesome ride / Fetch me my woman / Fat moaning Minnie / Squeeze me.

May 71. (7") *(DAN 7002)* **STRANGE LOCOMOTION. / I'M ALL ACHING** -

KEVIN COYNE

solo, retaining **CLAGUE,** (+ with session people)

1972. (lp) *(2310 228)* **CASE HISTORY** -
– God bless the bride / White horse / Uggy's song / Need somebody / Evil Island home / Araby / Mad boy / My message to the people / Sand all yellow. *(cd-iss.Sep94 on 'See For Miles'; SEECD 410)*

Polydor not issued

1972. (7") *(2001 357)* **CHEAT ME. / FLOWERING CHERRY** -

Virgin Virgin

1973. (d-lp) <lp> *(VD 2501)* **MARJORY RAZORBLADE**
– Marjory Razorblade / Marlene / Talking to no one / Eastbourne ladies / Old soldiers / I want my crown / Nasty, lonesome valley / House on the hill / Cheat me / Jackie and Edna / Everybody says / Mummy / Heaven in my view / Karate king / Dog Latin / This is Spain / Chairman's ball / Good boy / Chicken wing. *(cd-iss.Oct90+=; CDVM 2501)*– Lovesick fool / Sea of love.

Aug 73. (7") *(VS 102)* **MARLENE. / EVERYBODY SAYS**
Nov 73. (7") *(VS 104)* **LOVESICK FOOL. / SEA OF LOVE**
1974. (lp) *(V 2012)* **BLAME IT ON THE NIGHT**
– River of sin / Sign of the times / I believe in love / Don't delude me / Wanting you is not easy / Take a train / Blame it on the night / Poor swine / Light up you little light / Choose / Witch / Right on her side. *(cd-iss.Apr91;)*
1974. (7") *(VS 107)* **I BELIEVE IN LOVE. / QUEENIE QUEENIE CAROLINE**

— His band were **GORDON SMITH** – slide guitar / **ANDY SUMMERS** – guitar / **TIM PENN** – keyboards / **PETER WOOLF** – drums / **ARCHIE LEGGAT** – bass

Apr 75. (lp) *(V 2033)* **MATCHING HEAD AND FEET**
– Saviour / Lucy / Lonely lover / Sunday morning sunrise / Rock'n'roll hymn / Mrs. Hooley go home / It's not me / Turpentine / Tulip / One fine day. *(cd-iss.Jun91; CDV 2033)*
Apr 75. (7") *(VS 119)* **ROCK'N'ROLL HYMN. / IT'S NOT ME**

— **STEVE THOMPSON** – bass repl. LEGGAT who went solo. **ZOOT MONEY** – keyboards, vocals (ex-ERIC BURDON) repl. PENN and SMITH

Nov 75. (7") *(VS 126)* **LORNA. / SHANGRI-LA**
Feb 76. (7") *(VS 136)* **DON'T MAKE WAVES. / MONA WHERE'S MY TROUSERS**
Feb 76. (lp) *(V 2047)* **HEARTBURN**
– Strange locomotion / Don't make waves / Happy band / I love my mother / Shangri-la / America / Big white bird / Games games games / My mother's eyes / Daddy. *(cd-iss.Apr91;)*
May 76. (7") *(VS 148)* **WALK ON BY. / SHANGRI-LA**

— ZOOT & ANDY joined KEVIN AYERS. The latter formed The POLICE.

Oct 76. (7") *(VS 160)* **FEVER. / DADDY**
Jan 77. (d-lp) *(VD 2505)* **IN LIVING BLACK AND WHITE (live)**
– Case history No.2 / Fat girl / Talking to no-one / My mother's eyes / Ol' man river / Eastbourne ladies / Sunday morning sunrise / One fine day / Marjory Razorblade / Coconut Island / Turpentine / House on the hill / Knockin' on Heaven's door / Saviour / Mummy / Big white bird / America. *(cd-iss.Feb91; CDVM 2505)*
Apr 77. (7") *(VS 175)* **MARLENE. / ENGLAND IS DYING**
Jan 78. (7") *(VS 203)* **AMSTERDAM. / I REALLY LOVE YOU**
Feb 78. (lp) *(V 2095)* **DYNAMITE DAZE**
– Dynamite daze / Brothers of mine / Lunatic / Are we dreaming / (Take me back to) Dear old Blighty / I really live round here (fake friends) / I am / Amsterdam / I only want to see you smile / Juliet and Mark / Woman, woman, woman / Cry / Dance of the bourgeoisie. *(cd-iss.Jun91 & Mar94; CDV 2096)*
1978. (lp) *(V 2110)* **MILLIONAIRES AND TEDDYBEARS**
– People / Having a party / I'll go too / I'm just a man / Pretty park / Let me be with you / Marigold / Don't blame Mandy / Little Miss Portobello / Wendy's dream / The world is full of fools. *(cd-iss.Apr91;)*
Mar 79. (7") *(VS 255)* **I'LL GO TOO. / HAVING A PARTY**
Aug 79. (lp; KEVIN COYNE & DAGMAR KRAUSE) *(V 2128)* **BABBLE**
– Are you deceiving me? / Come down here / Dead, dying, gone / Stand up / Lonely man / I really love you / Sun shines down on me / I confess / Sweetheart / Shaking hands with the Sun / My mind's joined forces / It's my mind / Love together / Happy homes / It really doesn't matter / We know who we are. *(cd-iss.Mar91;)*
Feb 80. (lp) *(V 2151)* **BURSTING BUBBLES**
– The only one / Children's crusade / No melody / Learn to swim – learn to drown / Mad boy No.2 / Dark dance hall / Don't know what to do / A little piece of Heaven / Day to day / Golden days / The old fashioned love song. *(cd-iss.Mar91;)*

— next release had backing by punk group The **RUTS.**

1980. (d-lp) *(V 3504)* **SANITY STOMP**
– Fat man / The monkey man / How strange / When (see you again) / Taking on the world / No romance / Too dark (one for the hero) / Admit you're wrong / Formula eyes / New motorway / A lovin' hand / Fear of breathing / In silence / Take on the Bowers / Wonderful wilderness / My wife says / The world speaks / You can't kill us. *(cd-iss.Apr91+=;)*– Somewhere in my mind.

— with **BRIAN GODDING** – guitar / **STEVE BULL** – synthesizers / **STEVE LAMB** – bass / **DAVE SHEEN** – drums, vocals

Cherry Red — not issued

Oct 81. (lp) *(RED 23)* **POINTING THE FINGER**
– There she goes / As I recall / Children of the deaf / One little moment / Let love reside / Sleeping – Waking / Pointing the finger / You can't do that / Song of the womb / Old lady.

— **PETER KIRTLEY** – guitar + **JIM WOODLAND** – vocals repl.GODDING / LAMB + SHEEN although the latter 2 returned in 1983

1982. (lp) *(BRED 30)* **POLITICZ**
– Your holiness / Liberation / Fun flesh / Flashing back / Tell the truth / Banzai / Poisoning you / Magnolia street / I've got the photographs.
Nov 82. (7") *(CHERRY 49)* **SO STRANGE. / FATHER DEAR FATHER**

Rough Trade — not issued

Feb 84. (lp) *(RTD 22)* **LEGLESS IN MANILA**
– Big money man / Gina's song / Money machine / Raindrop on the river / Nigel in Napoli / Zoo wars / Black clouds / Legless in Manila / Don't raise an argument / Cycling. *(cd-iss.Nov94 on 'Golden Hind')*

— **PETER KIRTLEY** – guitar, returned to repl. HOPE-EVANS

On — not issued

1985. (lp) *(12-1250)* **ROUGH – LIVE (live)** — German
– The house on the hill / Singing the blues / Gina's song / Lucille / Pretty park / Dark dance hall / A loving hand / The monkey man / The old fashioned love song / I wander (poem).

— with **HANS PUKKE** – guitar / **ROBERT STEINHART** – bass / **FALK STEFFEN** – drums

Line — not issued

1987. (lp/cd; as KEVIN COYNE BAND) *(LILP/842 438)* **STUMBLING ON TO PARADISE** — German
– I'm still here / Pack of lies / How is your luck / Sunshine home / Tear me up / No revolution / Victoria smiles / Charming / Winter into summer / Love for five minutes / Back home boogie. *(re-iss.cd Nov 94 on 'Golden Hind')*

Ind.M.S. — not issued

1989. (lp/cd; by KEVIN COYNE & THE PARADISE BAND) *(/57218023)* **EVERYBODY'S NAKED** — German
– The millionaires song / I couldn't love you / Not the way / We don't talk too much / Here comes the morning / City crazy / Take me back in your arms / Last time blues / The slave / Old hippie / Radio / Everybody's naked. *(re-iss.cd Dec 94 on 'Zabo')*

Golden Hind — not issued

Jun 94. (cd) **TOUGH AND SWEET**
– Little Miss Dynamite / Precious love / Burning head II / Really in love / Pony tail song / Elvis is dead / Totally naked II / Walls have ears / Baby blue / Talking money / Slow burner / All the loving / No lullabies / It's amazing II / Tell me Tony / Now's the time / Getting old / Some day / Love and money / Let's get romantic / Creeper.
Nov 94. (cd) **WILD TIGER LOVE**
– The bungalow / Sensual / Cafe crazy / Looking in your eyes / Open up the gates / Go Sally go / American girls / Fish brain / Fooled again / Don't you look (that way) / Raindrops on the window / Passion's pleasure.
Dec 94. (cd) **ROMANCE – ROMANCE**
– Ready for love / Happy, happy / Chances / It's all over / The 17th floor / Theresa / No kindness, no pity / The Heaven song / Lovers and friends / Wild eyes / Best friend / Impossible child / Neighbourhood girl.

Blueprint — not issued

Oct 95. (cd) *(CD 388701724-2)* **THE ADVENTURES OF CRAZY FRANK**

– compilations, others, etc. –

1978. (lp) *Virgin; (V 2527)* **BEAUTIFUL EXTREMES**
– Something gone wrong / Looking for the river / Roses in your room / Face in the mirror / All the battered babies / Right in hand / Love in your heart / Hello friends, hello everyone / Mona, where's my trousers / So strange / Rainbow curve / Fool fool fool. *(re-iss.Feb83 on 'Cherry Red'; MRED 43)*
Feb 82. (3xlp-box) *Butt; (BUTBOX 1)* **THE DANDELION YEARS**
– (SIREN / STRANGE LOCOMOTION / CASE HISTORY lp's)
Feb 91. (d-cd) *Virgin;* **MARJORY RAZORBLADE / MILLIONAIRE AND TEDDY BEARS**
Mar 91. (cd/lp) *Strange Fruit; (SFR CD/LP 112)* **THE PEEL SESSIONS (73-79)**
– Marlene / Cheat me / By up me duck / The miner's song / Evil island home / Araby / Dance of the bourgenoise / Do not shout at me father / Need somebody / Poor swine / Rivers of blood / Lunatic / I only want to see you smile / That's rock'n'roll / A leopard never changes its spots / I couldn't love you.
Mar 94. (cd) *Virgin; (CDVM 9029)* **SIGN OF THE TIMES**
– Marjory razorblade / Marlene / Eastbourne ladies / House on the hill / Dog Latin / Good boy / Karateking / Fat girl / Saviour / Brothers of mine / Dynamite daze / Having a party / I'm just a man / The only one / Children's crusade / Mona, where's my trousers / Sign of the times / Witch / Blame it on the night.
Aug 94. (cd) *Mau Mau; (MAUCD 640)* **POINTING THE FINGER / POLITCZ**
Oct 94. (cd; by SIREN) *Voiceprint; (DJC 001)* **RABBITS**
Dec 94. (cd; by SIREN) *See For Miles;* **STRANGE LOCOMOTION / SIREN**
Mar 95. (cd) *Golden Hind* **ELVIRA: SONGS FROM THE ARCHIVES 1979-83**
Sep 95. (cd; SIREN & KEVIN COYNE) *Blueprint; (DJC 002CD)* **LET'S DO IT**

CRAZY WORLD OF ARTHUR BROWN

(see under ⇒ BROWN, Arthur)

CREAM

Formed: London, England . . . mid '66 as earliest ever supergroup by ERIC CLAPTON, GINGER BAKER and JACK BRUCE, who'd all cut their their teeth with top-flight R&B outfits earlier in the decade. This fine pedigree led to Robert Stigwood signing them to his newly-founded 'Reaction' label, after their lauded debut at The National Jazz & Blues Festival in Windsor on the 3rd of July '66. Their initial 45, 'WRAPPING PAPER', gave them the first of many Top 40 hits, a number that didn't inspire much critical praise. To end the year, they issued a debut album, 'FRESH CREAM', lifting from it, the breezy psychedelic single, 'I FEEL FREE', a number which united BRUCE and poet/lyricist PETE BROWN in a new songwriting partnership. It also gave CREAM their biggest hit to date, reaching No.11 in the UK. Alongside original material, the album featured updated blues standards, 'SPOONFUL' (Willie Dixon), 'ROLLIN' & TUMBLIN' (Muddy Waters) and 'I'M SO GLAD' (Skip James). Over the course of the next six months, they became increasingly influenced by the pioneering psychedelic blues of JIMI HENDRIX. This was much in evidence on the next 45, 'STRANGE BREW', a slow-burning piece of sinister psych-blues. One of the highlights of their second album, 'DISRAELI GEARS', this record also featured such enduring CREAM classics as, 'SUNSHINE OF YOUR LOVE' (a US-only Top 5 hit), 'TALES OF BRAVE ULYSSES' & 'WORLD OF PAIN'. In fact every track was fantastic and the album remains an essential purchase for any self-respecting record collector. Their 3rd set, 'WHEELS OF FIRE', recorded in San Francisco and New York, consisted of two records, one studio – one live. The former featured an omninous cover of BOOKER T's 'BORN UNDER A BAD SIGN', while the live disc included a definitive re-working of ROBERT JOHNSON's 'CROSSROADS'. However, the album (which was soon split into two single lp's) failed to garner the same critical praise as its predecessor, pandering too heavily to commerciality. They played their farewell tour in November '68, culminating in a legendary sell-out show on the 26th at The Royal Albert Hall. They were already in the US Top 10 with the GEORGE HARRISON and CLAPTON-penned 'WHITE ROOM', the song later becoming a fitting epitaph after it was given a UK release early '69. All went on to high profile solo careers, the most obvious being ERIC 'God' CLAPTON.

Recommended: DISRAELI GEARS (*8) / STRANGE BREW – THE VERY BEST

OF CREAM (*9) / WHEELS OF FIRE (*7) / (also CREAM tracks on CLAPTON comps.)

ERIC CLAPTON (b.ERIC PATRICK CLAPP, 30 May'45, Ripley, Surrey, England) – guitar, vocals (ex-YARDBIRDS, ex-JOHN MAYALL'S BLUESBREAKERS) / **JACK BRUCE** (b.JOHN BRUCE, 14 May'43, Glasgow, Scotland) – vocals, bass (ex-GRAHAM BOND, ex-JOHN MAYALL'S BLUESBREAKERS, ex-MANFRED MANN) / **GINGER BAKER** (b.PETER BAKER, 19 Aug'39, Lewisham, London, England) – drums (ex-GRAHAM BOND ORGANISATION, ex-ALEXIS KORNER'S BLUES INCORPORATED)

Reaction | Atco

Oct 66. (7") *(591 007)* **WRAPPING PAPER. / CAT'S SQUIRREL** 34 | -

Dec 66. (lp; mono/stereo) *(593/594 001)* <33206> **FRESH CREAM** 6 | 39
– N.S.U. / Sleepy time time / Dreaming / Sweet wine / Spoonful / Cat's squirrel / Four until late / Rollin' and tumblin' / I'm so glad / Toad. *(re-iss.Feb69; stereo); reached No.7 UK. (re-iss Oct70 as 'FULL CREAM'; 2447 010) (re-iss.Mar75 as 'CREAM' on 'Polydor'+=; 2384 067); 2 tracks) (cd-iss.Jan84+=; 827 576-2)–* Wrapping paper / The coffee song.

Dec 66. (7") *(591 011)* <6462> **I FEEL FREE. / N.S.U.** 11 |

Jun 67. (7") *(591 015)* <6488> **STRANGE BREW. / TALES OF BRAVE ULYSSES** 17 |

Nov 67. (7") <6522> **SPOONFUL. / (part 2)** - |

Nov 67. (lp; mono/stereo) *(593/594 003)* <33232> **DISRAELI GEARS** 5 | 4
– Strange brew / Sunshine of your love / World of pain / Dance the night away / Blue condition / Tales of brave Ulysses / S.W.L.A.B.R. / We're going wrong / Outside woman blues / Take it back / Mother's lament. *<US re-iss.Feb77 on 'R.S.O.'; 3010> (re-iss.Nov77 on 'R.S.O.'; 239 412-2) (cd-iss.Jan84 on 'Track'; 823 636-2)*

Polydor | Atco

Jan 68. (7") <6544> **SUNSHINE OF YOUR LOVE. / S.W.L.A.B.R.** - | 5
(UK-iss.Sep68; 56286); hit No.25)

May 68. (7") *(56258)* <6575> **ANYONE FOR TENNIS. / PRESSED RAT AND WARTHOG** 40 | 64

— **FELIX PAPPALARDI** – producer, instruments guested as 4th p/t member

Aug 68. (d-lp; mono/stereo) *(582/583 031-2)* <2-700> **WHEELS OF FIRE** 3 | 1 Jul68
(re-iss.1972; 2612 001) <US re-iss.Feb77 on 'R.S.O.'; 3802> (re-iss.Jan84 on 'R.S.O.'; 3216 036) (cd-iss.Jan84; 8254 142) (cd re-iss.Feb89; 827 658-2)

Aug 68. (lp; mono/stereo) *(582/583 033)* **WHEELS OF FIRE – IN THE STUDIO** 7 | - •
– White room / Sitting on top of the world / Passing the time / As you said / Pressed rat and warthog / Politician / Those were the days / Born under a bad sign / Deserted cities of the heart. *(re-iss.Nov77 on 'R.S.O.'; 2394 136)*

Aug 68. (lp; mono/stereo) *(582/583 040)* **WHEELS OF FIRE – LIVE AT THE FILLMORE (live)** | -
– Crossroads / Spoonful / Traintime / Toad. *(re-iss.Nov77 on 'R.S.O.'; 2394 137)*

Jan 69. (7") *(65300)* <6617> **WHITE ROOM. / THOSE WERE THE DAYS** 28 | 6 Sep68

— They split around mid-'68. The rest of their releases were posthumous and CLAPTON went solo after forming BLIND FAITH with BAKER. He also went solo. JACK BRUCE went solo, etc.

– compilations, others, etc. –

either 'Polydor' in UK and 'Atco' in the US.

Jan 69. (7") <6646> **CROSSROADS. / PASSING THE TIME** - | 28

Mar 69. (lp) *(583 053)* <7001> **GOODBYE** 1 | 2
– I'm so glad (live) / Politician (live) / Sitting on top of the world (live) / Badge / Doing that scrapyard thing / What a bringdown. *(re-iss.Nov77 & Aug84 on 'R.S.O.'; 2394 178) (cd-iss.Jan84.+=; 823 660-2)–* Anyone for tennis.

Apr 69. (7") *(56315)* <6668> **BADGE. / WHAT A BRINGDOWN** 18 | 60 Mar69
(re-iss.Oct72; 2058 285)

Nov 69. (lp) *(583 060)* <291> **BEST OF CREAM** 6 | 3 Jul69
(re-iss.Nov77 on 'R.S.O.'; 3216 031) (re-iss.Apr86 on 'Arcade'; ADAH 429)

Jun 70. (lp) *(2383 016)* <33-328> **LIVE CREAM (live)** 4 | 15 Apr70
– N.S.U. / Sleepy time time / Lawdy mama / Sweet wine / Rollin' and tumblin'. *(re-iss.Nov77 & Mar85 on 'R.S.O.' lp/c; SPE LP/MC 93) (cd-iss.May88; 827 577-2)*

Jul 70. (7") **LAWDY MAMA (live). / SWEET WINE (live)** - |

Jul 71. (7") **I FEEL FREE. / WRAPPING PAPER** |
(re-iss.Jul84 on 'Old Gold'; OG 9423)

Jun 72. (lp) *(2383 119)* <7005> **LIVE CREAM VOL.2** 15 | 27 Mar72
– Deserted cities of the heart / White room / Politician / Tales of brave Ulysses / Sunshine of your love. *(re-iss.Nov77 on 'R.S.O.';) (cd-iss.May88; 823 661-2)*

Apr 73. (d-lp) *(2659 022)* <3502> **HEAVY CREAM** | Oct72

Oct 80. (6xlp-box) *(2658 142)* **CREAM BOX SET** |

Oct 83. (lp)(c) *(2479 212)(3215 038)* **THE STORY OF CREAM VOL.1** |

Oct 83. (lp)(c) *(2479 213)(3215 039)* **THE STORY OF CREAM VOL.2** | -

Apr 78. (lp)(c) *R.S.O.; (3228 005)* **CREAM VOLUME TWO** |

Feb 83. (lp/c) *R.S.O.; (RSD/TRSD 5021)* **STRANGE BREW – THE VERY BEST OF CREAM** |
– Badge / Sunshine of your love / Crossroads / White room / Born under a bad sign / Swlabr / Strange brew / Anyone for tennis / I feel free / Tales of brave Ulysses / Politician / Spoonful. *(cd-iss.Nov87 on 'Polydor';)*

Aug 82. (7") *R.S.O.; (RSO 91)* **BADGE. / TALES OF BRAVE ULYSSES** |
(12"+=) *(RSOX 91)* – White room.

Jul 86. (7") *(POSP 812)* **I FEEL FREE. / BADGE** |

Jul 84. (7") *Old Gold; (OG 9425)* **WHITE ROOM. / BADGE** | -

Jul 84. (7") *Old Gold; (OG 9426)* **SUNSHINE OF YOUR LOVE. / ANYONE FOR TENNIS** | -

Feb 89. (cd) *Koine; (K 880803)* **LIVE 1968 (live)** | -

Dec 91. (cd; w/booklet) *U.F.O.;* **IN GEAR** | -

Nov 92. (cd) *I.T.M.; (ITM 960002)* **THE ALTERNATIVE ALBUM** | -
(re-iss.Jan97 on 'Masterplan'; MP 42009)

Dec 92. (cd/c) *Pickwick; (PWK S/MC 4127P)* **DESERTED CITIES: THE CREAM COLLECTION** | -

Feb 95. (cd/c) *(523 752-2/-4)* **THE VERY BEST OF CREAM** |

CREATION

Formed: Middlesex, England . . . 1961 as 5-piece! MARK FOUR by KENNY PICKETT, JACK JONES and EDDIE PHILLIPS. Under the guidance of manager ROBERT STIGWOOD they released a couple of flop singles for 'Mercury'. Following a further two stiffs for 'Decca' and 'Fontana' respectively, they changed their line-up in mid-66 and became The CREATION. They also employed new manager TONY STRATTON-SMITH who found American producer SHEL TALMY and a new label, 'Planet'. Things started looking up when the group unleashed 2 superb 45's in 1966, 'MAKING TIME' and 'PAINTER MAN', both hitting the UK Top 50 (aided by alleged chart hyping from TONY). The former marked their finest moment, a blistering combination of searing R&B and psychedelia while the latter hit No.1 in Germany. When they moved to 'Polydor' in 1967, however, they ran out of steam and split the year after. Unfortunately their only lp release had been in Germany, where they had found some degree of success. • **Trivia:** PHILLIPS was the first person to play guitar with a violin bow, a feat later achieved by JIMMY PAGE of LED ZEPPELIN. • **Songwriters:** PICKETT or PHILLIPS plus covers:- ROCK AROUND THE CLOCK (Bill Haley) / TRY IT BABY (Marvin Gaye) / LIKE A ROLLING STONE (Bob Dylan) / BONY MORONIE (Larry Williams) / HEY JOE (hit; Jimi Hendrix). • **Trivia:** In 1970, PICKETT co-wrote UK No.1 hit 'Grandad' for CLIVE DUNN (Dad's Army) with HERBIE FLOWERS. PICKETT was later to write 'TEACHER TEACHER' for DAVE EDMUNDS, before he co-wrote some more songs with BILLY BREMNER. **Legacy:** PAINTER MAN was a 1979 UK Top 10 hit for BONEY M, while much later The GODFATHERS (in 1990) and RIDE (in 1994) covered HOW DOES IT FEEL TO FEEL. Many have been inspired by them including TELEVISION PERSONALITIES / TIMES / BIFF BANG POW and the label 'Creation'.

Recommended: HOW DOES IT FEEL TO FEEL (*8) / THE CREATION (*7)

MARK FOUR

KENNY PICKETT (b. 3 Sep'47, Ware, England) – vocals / **EDDIE PHILLIPS** (b.EDWIN, 15 Aug'45, Leytonstone, England) – lead guitar / **MICK THOMPSON** – rhythm guitar / **JOHN DALTON** – bass / **JACK JONES** (b. 8 Nov'44, Northampton, England) – drums

Mercury | not issued

May 64. (7") *(MF 815)* **ROCK AROUND THE CLOCK. / SLOW DOWN** | -

Aug 64. (7") *(MF 825)* **TRY IT BABY. / CRAZY COUNTRY HOP** | -

Decca | not issued

Aug 65. (7") *(F 12204)* **HURT ME IF YOU WILL. / I'M LEAVING** | -

Fontana | not issued

Feb 66. (7") *(TF 664)* **WORK ALL DAY (SLEEP ALL NIGHT). / GOING DOWN FAST** | -

— Split after final gig on 6th June 1966. DALTON joined The KINKS.

CREATION

BOB GARNER – bass (ex-TONY SHERIDAN BAND) repl. THOMPSON

Planet | Planet

Jun 66. (7") *(<PLF 116>)* **MAKING TIME. / TRY AND STOP ME** 49 |

Oct 66. (7") *(<PLF 119>)* **PAINTER MAN. / BIFF BANG POW** 36 |

KIM GARDNER – bass (ex-BIRDS) repl. GARNER

Polydor | Decca

Jun 67. (7") *(56177)* **IF I STAY TOO LONG. / NIGHTMARES** |

Oct 67. (7") *(56207)* **LIFE IS JUST BEGINNING. / THROUGH MY EYES** | -

Nov 67. (7") <32227> **HOW DOES IT FEEL TO FEEL. / LIFE IS JUST BEGINNING** - |

Jan 68. (7") *(56230)* **HOW DOES IT FEEL TO FEEL. / TOM TOM** | -

RON WOOD – guitar (ex-BIRDS) repl. DIGGER who had briefly repl. PICKETT. **PICKETT** returned to repl. PHILLIPS + GARDNER

May 68. (7") *(56246)* **MIDWAY DOWN. / THE GIRLS ARE NAKED** | -

— Disbanded soon after above. PICKETT continued to write for SHEL TALMY and he also became road manager for LED ZEPPELIN in America. RON WOOD joined The FACES and later became a member of The ROLLING STONES. GARDNER co-formed ASHTON, GARDNER & DYKE who had a 1970 Top 3 hit with 'RESURRECTION SHUFFLE'. He later formed BADGER. JACK JONES drifted into cabaret session work.

— CREATION re-formed in the mid-80's with **PHILLIPS, PICKETT, NOBBY DALTON** – bass (ex-KINKS) + **MICK AVORY** – drums (ex-KINKS).

Jet | not issued

Apr 87. (7") *(JET 7-047)* **A SPIRIT CALLED LOVE. / MAKING TIME** | -
(12"+=) *(JET 12-047)* – Mumbo jumbo.

— **PHILLIPS**, etc, without PICKETT formed pub band CUCKOOS NEST. In 1994, The CREATION re-formed with **PICKETT, JONES + PHILLIPS.**

Creation | Rykodisc

Jul 94. (7") *(CRE 200)* **CREATION. / SHOCK HORROR** | -
(cd-s+=) *(CRECD 200)* – Power surge.

Mar 96. (cd/lp) *()* **THE CREATION** |

— On the 10th Jan'97, KENNY PICKETT died of a heart attack in his home.

– compilations, etc. –

Sep 73. (lp) *Charisma; (CS 8)* **CREATION '66-67** | -

Oct 73. (7") *Charisma; (CB 213)* **MAKING TIME. / PAINTER MAN** | -
(re-iss.Nov77 on 'Raw'; RAW 4)

Sep 82. (lp) *Edsel; (ED 106)* **HOW DOES IT FEEL TO FEEL** | -
– How does it feel to feel / Life is just beginning / Through my eyes / Ostrich man / I am the walker / Tom Tom / The girls are naked / Painter man / Try and stop me / Biff bang pow / Making time / Cool jerk / For all that I am / Nightmares / Midway

down / Can I join your band?. *(cd-iss.Aug90; EDCD 106)*– Uncle Bert / Like a rolling stone / If I stay too long / Hey Joe.

1983. (lp) *Eva; (12005)* **THE MARK FOUR / THE CREATION** *(cd-iss.1992; EVA B16)*

May 84. (7") *Edsel; (E 5006)* **MAKING TIME. / UNCLE BERT**

1985. (7"ep; by MARK FOUR) *Bam Caruso; (OPRA 037)* **LIVE AT THE BEAT SCENE CLUB**
– Hurt me if you will / Got my mojo working / That's how strong my love is.

Apr 93. (m-lp) *Edsel; (NESTCD 904)* **PAINTER MAN**

Oct 93. (cd/lp) *Cohesion; (COCRD/COCRL 1)* **LAY THE GHOST (live)**

CRESSIDA

Formed: London, England . . .late 60's by ANGUS CULLEN, IAN CLARKE, PETER JENNINGS, KEVIN McCARTHY and JOHN HEYWORTH. They were a mysterious outfit who were critically well received, and although their two 'Vertigo' albums sold poorly, they've since become highly sought after collector's items. From the melancholic eponymous debut (featuring excellent track 'SPRING'), to their more elaborately arranged follow-up 'ASYLUM' (in 1971), they provided inspiration for the progressive mellotron-wielding faction of the rock world. Similar in style to BARCLAY JAMES HARVEST, KING CRIMSON or CARAVAN, they had the potential to break through to a wider audience.

Recommended: CRESSIDA (*8) / ASYLUM (*7)

ANGUS CULLEN – vocals, guitar / **JOHN HEYWORTH** – guitar / **PETER JENNINGS** – keyboards, harps / **KEVIN McCARTHY** – bass / **IAN CLARKE** – drums, percussion

Vertigo not issued

Feb 70. (lp) *(VO 7)* **CRESSIDA**
– To play your little game / Winter is coming again / Time for bed / Cressida / Home and where I long to be / Depression / One of a group / Lights in my mind / The only earthman in town / Spring '69 / Down down / Tomorrow is a whole new day. *(cd-iss.1994 on 'Repertoire'; REP 4299)*

— **JOHN CULLEY** – guitar + **HAROLD McNAIR** – flute, repl. HEYWORTH

Mar 71. (lp) *(6360 025)* **ASYLUM**
– Asylum / Munich / Goodbye Post Office Tower goodbye / Survivor / Reprieved / Lisa / Summer weekend of a lifetime / Let them come when they will. *(cd-iss.1994 on 'Repertoire'; REP 4105)*

— split 1972. CULLEY later joined BLACK WIDOW, while CLARKE joined URIAH HEEP.

CROCHETED DOUGHNUT RING

Formed: London, England ... 1960 as The WHIRLWINDS by RON GENT, PETE GOSLING, BERT PULHAM, DAVE OSBOURNE and DAVE SKATES. They subsequently opted for a new moniker in 1962; The FORCE FIVE, playing cover versions at local gigs until they signed to 'United Artists' a few years later. They debuted with the 45, 'DON'T MAKE MY BABY BLUE', then followed it with another catchy freakbeat song 'YEAH, I'M WAITING', aired on TV's 'Ready Steady Go' in 1965. Three more singles turned up during the next year, none of which made any chart progress. With new singer RICK MILLS, they soon evolved into the West Coast and SMALL FACES influenced CROCHETED DOUGHNUT RING, signing to 'Polydor' in 1967 for their debut, 'TWO LITTLE LADIES'. Later in the year, they moved to the more psychedelic-biased label 'Deram', and hit the shops with 'HAVANA ANNA'. While the single flopped in the UK, it was a surprise Top 3 hit in Japan. They were unable to undertake a promotional tour due to financial problems and things went from bad to worse. A classically-inspired follow-up 'MAXINE'S PARLOUR', remains their finest hour and the band split later that year as Pulham went off to join GULLIVER'S PEOPLE.

Recommended: no albums as yet but should have a combined effort later in the 90's.

FORCE FIVE

RON GENT – vocals / **PETE GOSLING** – guitar / **BERT PULHAM** – lead guitar / **DAVE OSBOURNE** – bass / **DAVE SKATES** – drums

U.A. Ascot

Apr 64. (7") *(UP 1051)* **DON'T MAKE MY BABY BLUE. / SHAKING POSTMAN**

May 65. (7") *(UP 1089)* **YEAH, I'M WAITING. / I DON'T WANT TO SEE YOU AGAIN**

Aug 65. (7") *(UP 1102)* **BABY DON'T CARE. / COME DOWN TO EARTH**

Dec 65. (7") *(UP 1118)* <2206> **I WANT YOU BABE. / GEE TOO TIGER** 1966

1966. (7") *(UP 1141)* **DON'T KNOW WHICH WAY TO TURN. / BABY LET YOUR HAIR DOWN**

CROCHETED DOUGHNUT RING

— **RICK MILLS** – vocals (ex-FINGERS, ex-solo artist) repl. GENT

— **GEORGE BIRD** – bass, repl. OSBOURNE

Polydor not issued

Oct 67. (7"m) *(56204)* **TWO LITTLE LADIES. / AZEILA AND RHODODENDREN / NICE**

Deram not issued

Dec 67. (7") *(DM 169)* **HAVANA ANNA. / HAPPY CASTLE**

Mar 68. (7") *(DM 180)* **MAXINE'S PARLOUR. / GET OUT YOUR ROCK AND ROLL SHOES**

Nov 68. (7"; as DOUGHNUT RING) *(DM 215)* **DANCE AROUND JULIE. / THE BANDIT**

— folded when PULHAM joined GULLIVER'S PEOPLE. DAVE SKATES died sometime in the 70's or 80's, while BIRD is a driving instructor.

CROSBY, STILLS, NASH (& YOUNG)

Formed: Los Angeles, California, USA ... Summer 1968 as a superband trio (DAVID) CROSBY, (STEPHEN) STILLS and (GRAHAM) NASH. Their eponymous first offering was released in Summer '69 and soon broke into the US Top 10. Featuring the distinctive songwriting talent of each member respectively on 'GUINNEVERE', 'SUITE: JUDY BLUE EYES' and 'MARRAKESH EXPRESS', the album introduced the close harmonising that would come to characterise the band. Later that year the trio recruited NEIL YOUNG (ex-BUFFALO SPRINGFIELD) who'd played an electric set on their mid-'69 gigs and who'd already embarked on his successful solo career. The newly augmented line-up played Woodstock as well as supporting The ROLLING STONES at their ill-fated Altamont concert which, ironically, saw the dreams of the Woodstock generation shatter. Nevertheless the band were adopted as hippy flagbearers and after lifting the coveted 'Best Newcomers' award at The Grammys, they released their magnum opus, 'DEJA VU' (1970). With YOUNG contributing the achingly gorgeous 'HELPLESS' and the sublime 'COUNTRY GIRL' suite, his intensity, both vocal and instrumental was a towering influence although STILLS offered a powerful cover of JONI MITCHELL's 'WOODSTOCK'. NASH's 'TEACH YOUR CHILDREN' and 'OUR HOUSE' were slighter in comparison but rounded out the record perfectly. Blighted by ego problems with drug habits to match, the band split the same month as YOUNG's ominous 'OHIO' single was released, an inpired protest against the killing of four students by the National Guard during an anti-war demo at Kent State University. The patchy, posthumous live album 'FOUR-WAY STREET' (1971) was hardly a fitting epitaph although predictably it sold in bucketloads. While YOUNG continued with his mercurial solo career, STILLS released a follow-up to his well-recieved debut solo album and later recorded with the country-inflected MANASSAS. CROSBY and NASH, meanwhile, worked as a duo, releasing their eponymous debut in 1972. Minus STILLS and YOUNG, the record was pleasant if hardly essential, lacking the tension that had made CSN&Y so compelling. The inevitable reunion took place in 1974 and the biggest personality clash in rock toured the world to ecstatic audiences although the band couldn't keep it together long enough to record anything concrete in the studio (the fact that YOUNG travelled in his own tourbus didn't bode too well). STILLS and YOUNG recorded the 'LONG MAY YOU RUN' album in 1976 which boasted the wistful charm of the title track and the exquisite 'FONTAINEBLEU' but was otherwise fairly lacklustre. The following year CROSBY, STILLS and NASH reformed and recorded the million selling 'CSN', again another inoffensive collection which lacked the focus YOUNG had brought to the group in the past. Indeed, while CSN were touring their particular brand of polite folk-Pop, YOUNG was interpreting punk with his 'LIVE RUST' and 'RUST NEVER SLEEPS' albums, outstripping CSN creatively and commercially. 'DAYLIGHT AGAIN' (1982) spawned the American singles 'WASTED ON THE WAY' and 'SOUTHERN CROSS' while the band split later the same year as CROSBY was sentenced to five years for drugs and firearms offences. In the event, he was allowed to attend a rehabilitation program as an alternative which he later reneged on and did actually serve some time during the mid-'80's. Out on bail, he appeared live with STILLS, NASH and YOUNG at Live Aid and the quartet made a long-awaited second album in 1988, 'AMERICAN DREAM'. Although it eclipsed most of the YOUNG-less CSN material, it was hardly the masterpiece people had waited almost two decades for. The standout track was CROSBY's 'COMPASS', a song borne of his drug-induced hardships. NEIL YOUNG subsequently refused to tour the record and that, more or less, was that. CSN continued unbowed, even after CROSBY underwent a liver transplant following the release of the 'AFTER THE STORM' (1994) album. With YOUNG now almost in the 30th year of a solo career which shows no sign of letting up (even if his recent output has been under par), it doesn't appear likely that he'll make another record with his old sparring partners though given his infamous contrariness, anything is possible! • **Songwriters:** All 4 took a hand individually and later together in all songs. Also covered; WOODSTOCK (Joni Mitchell) / DEAR MR.FANTASY (Traffic) / and a few more. • **Miscellaneous:** CROSBY's late 60's drug problem was to rear its ugly head again in 1982, when he was arrested twice for possessing cocaine and a gun. The following year, he was convicted and sentenced to 5 years, but after an appeal was sent to a drug rehabilitation center to recover. In Mar'85, he reneged on agreement and was sent to jail. He was released a couple of years later and soon married long-time girlfriend Jan Dance. Early in 1989, he was back again with a solo album 'OH YES WE CAN', which followed a re-union CROSBY, STILLS, NASH & YOUNG comeback album 'AMERICAN DREAM'.

Recommended: DEJA VU (*8) / THE BEST OF CROSBY & STILLS, (*5) / STILL STILLS – THE BEST OF STEPHEN STILLS (*6) / (best solo:-) GRAHAM NASH – SONGS FOR BEGINNERS (*7)

For NEIL YOUNG, albums and reviews, see own discography ⇒.

CROSBY, STILLS & NASH

DAVID CROSBY (b. DAVID VAN CORTLAND, 14 Aug'41, Los Angeles, Calif.) – vocals, guitar (ex-BYRDS) / **STEPHEN STILLS** (b. 3 Jan'45, Dallas, Texas)– vocals, guitar, bass, keyboards (ex-BUFFALO SPRINGFIELD) / **GRAHAM NASH** (b. 2 Feb'42, Blackpool, England)– vocals, guitar (ex-HOLLIES)
with **DALLAS TAYLOR** – drums

Atlantic Atlantic

Jun 69. (lp) *(588 189)* <8229> **CROSBY, STILLS & NASH** [25] [6]
– Suite: Judy blue eyes / Marrakesh express / Guinnevere / You don't have to cry / Pre-road downs / Wooden ships / Lady of the island / Helplessly hoping / Long time gone / 49 bye-byes. *(re-iss.1972; K 40033) (cd-iss.Jul87; K2 40033)*

Jul 69. (7") *(584 283)* <2652> **MARRAKESH EXPRESS. / HELPLESSLY HOPING** [17] [28]

Oct 69. (7") *(584 304)* <2676> **SUITE: JUDY BLUE EYES. / LONG TIME GONE** [ ] [21] Sep69

CROSBY, STILLS, NASH & YOUNG

— added **NEIL YOUNG** (b.12 Nov'45, Toronto, Canada) – guitar, vocals (ex-BUFFALO SPRINGFIELD) also **GREG REEVES** – bass

Mar 70. (lp) *(2401 001)* <7200> **DEJA VU** [5] [1]
– Carry on / Teach your children / Almost cut my hair / Helpless / Woodstock / Deja vu / Our house / 4 + 20 / Country girl: Whiskey boot hill – Down, down, down – Country girl / Everybody I love you. *(re-iss.1972 lp/c; K/K4 50001) (cd-iss.May87; K2 50001)*

Apr 70. (7") *(2091 002)* **TEACH YOUR CHILDREN. / COUNTRY GIRL** [ ] [-]

May 70. (7") *(2091 010)* <2723> **WOODSTOCK. / HELPLESS** [ ] [11] Mar70

May 70. (7") <2735> **TEACH YOUR CHILDREN. / CARRY ON** [-] [16]

Aug 70. (7") *(2091 023)* <2740> **OHIO. / FIND THE COST OF FREEDOM** [ ] [14] Jun70

Nov 70. (7") *(2091 039)* <2760> **OUR HOUSE. / DEJA VU** [ ] [30] Sep70

— (May'70) **CALVIN 'FUZZY' SAMUELS** – bass repl. REEVES **JOHN BARBATA** – drums (ex-TURTLES) repl. TAYLOR

— (Aug'70) split before release of posthumous album below with last line-up

Apr 71. (d-lp) *(2657 007)* <2-902> **FOUR-WAY STREET (live)** [5] [1]
– On the way home / Teach your children / Triad / The Lee shore / Chicago / Right between the eyes / Cowgirl in the sand / Don't let it bring you down / 49 bye-byes / Love the one you're with / Pre-road downs / Long time gone / Southern man / Ohio / Carry on / Find the cost of freedom. *(re-iss.1972 lp/c; K/K4 60003) (cd-iss.Jul87; K2 60003) (d-cd re-iss.Aug92)*

— Their solo recordings, excluding NEIL YOUNG's, are below

STEPHEN STILLS

— - vocals, guitar with **STEPHEN FROMHOLTZ** – guitar / **PAUL HARRIS** – keyboards / **DALLAS TAYLOR** – drums / **CALVIN SAMUELS** – bass / **plus Memphis Horns**

Atlantic Atlantic

Nov 70. (lp) *(2401 004)* <7202> **STEPHEN STILLS** [30] [3]
– Love the one you're with / Do for the others / Church (part of someone) / Old times, good times / Go back home / Sit yourself down / To a flame / Black queen / Cheroke / We are not helpless. *(cd-iss.Oct95; 7567 82809-2)*

Dec 70. (7") *(2091 046)* <2778> **LOVE THE ONE YOU'RE WITH. / TO A FLAME** [37] [14]

May 71. (7") *(2091 069)* <2790> **SIT YOURSELF DOWN. / WE ARE NOT HELPLESS** [ ] [37] Mar71

Jul 71. (lp) *(2401 013)* <7206> **STEPHEN STILLS II** [22] [8]
– Change partners / Nothin' to do but today / Fishes and scorpions / Sugar babe / Know you got to run / Open secret / Relaxing town / Singin' call / Ecology song / Word game / Marianne / Bluebird revisited. *(re-iss.1978;)*

Jul 71. (7") *(2091 117)* <2806> **CHANGE PARTNERS. / RELAXING TOWN** [ ] [43] Jun71

Sep 71. (7") *(2091 141)* <2820> **MARIANNE. / NOTHIN' TO DO BUT TODAY** [ ] [42] Aug71

STEPHEN STILLS & MANASSAS

STILLS retained **SAMUELS, HARRIS** and **TAYLOR,** brought in **CHRIS HILLMAN** – guitar, vocals / **AL PERKINS** – steel guitar, guitar / **JOE LALA** – percussion / **KENNY PASSARELLI** – bass (ex-JOE WALSH) repl. SAMUELS

Atlantic Atlantic

May 72. (d-lp/c) *(K/K4 60021)* <2-903> **MANASSAS** [30] [4] Apr72
– Fallen eagle / Jesus gave love away for free / Colorado / So begins the task / Hide to the deep / Don't look at my shadow / It doesn't matter / Johnny's garden / Bound to fall / How far / Move around / The love gangster / Song of love / Rock'n'roll crazies – Cuban bluegrass / Jet set (sigh) / Anyway / Both of us (bound to lose) / What to do / Right now / The treasure (take one) / Blues man. *(cd-iss.Feb93 & Oct95; 7567 82808-2)*

May 72. (7") <2876> **IT DOESN'T MATTER. / ROCK'N'ROLL CRAZIES – CUBAN BLUEGRASS** [-] [61]

Aug 72. (7") *(K 10147)* **IT DOESN'T MATTER. / FALLEN ANGEL** [ ] [-]

Nov 72. (7") <2888> **ROCK'N'ROLL CRAZIES. / COLORADO** [-] [92]

May 73. (lp/c) *(K/K4 40440)* <7250> **DOWN THE ROAD** [33] [26]
– Isn't it about time / Lies / Pensamiento / So many times / Business on the street / Do you remember the Americans / Down the road / City junkies / Guaguanco de Vero / Rollin' my stone. *(cd-iss.Nov93; 7567 81424-2)*

May 73. (7") *(K 10306)* <2959> **ISN'T IT ABOUT TIME. / SO MANY TIMES** [ ] [56] Apr73

Jul 73. (7") *(K 10340)* <2917> **GUAGUANCO DE VERO. / DOWN THE ROAD** [ ] [ ] Feb73

— (Sep73) **HARRIS, PERKINS and HILLMAN joined SOUTHERN HILLMAN FURAY BAND. STEPHEN STILLS** formed his own band, retaining **PASSARELLI** and **LALA** plus **DONNIE DACUS** – guitar / **JERRY AIELLO** – keyboards / **HUSS KUNKEL** – drums

CROSBY, STILLS NASH & YOUNG

— (May'74) re-formed, mainly for concerts. Augmented by **TIM DRUMMOND** – bass / **RUSS KUNKEL** – drums / **JOE LALA** – percussion

STEPHEN STILLS

— went solo again (Feb75) with new band **LALA, DACUS, AIELLO** plus **GEORGE PERRY** – bass / **RONNIE ZIEGLER** – drums

C.B.S. Columbia

Jun 75. (lp/c) *(69146)* <33575> **STILLS** [31] [19]
– Turn back the pages / My favorite changes / My angel / In the way / Love story / To mama Christopher and the old man / First things first / New mama / As I come of age / Shuffle just as bad / Cold cold world / Myth of Sisyphus.

Jul 75. (7") *(3497)* <10179> **TURN BACK THE PAGES. / SHUFFLE JUST AS BAD** [ ] [84]

— added **RICK ROBERTS** – guitar, vocals (of FIREFALL)

Apr 76. (7") <10369> **BUYIN' TIME. / SOLDIER** [-] [ ]

May 76. (lp/c) *(81330)* <34148> **ILLEGAL STILLS** [54] [30]
– Buyin' time / Midnight in Paris / Different tongues / Closer to you / Soldier / The loner / Stateline blues / No me nieges / Ring of love / Circlin'.

Jul 76. (7") *(4416)* **THE LONER. / STATELINE BLUES** [ ] [-]

STILLS-YOUNG BAND

STEPHEN STILLS – vocals, guitar / **NEIL YOUNG** – vocals, guitar with **AIELLO, PERRY, VITALE + LALA**

Reprise Reprise

Sep 76. (7") *(K 14446)* <1365> **LONG MAY YOU RUN. / 12:8 BLUES** [ ] [ ]

Oct 76. (lp/c) *(K/K4 54081)* <2253> **LONG MAY YOU RUN** [12] [26]
– Long may you run / Make love to you / Midnight on the bay / Black coral / Ocean girl / Let it shine / 12/8 blues (all the same) / Fontainebleau / Guardian angel. *(cd-iss.Jul93; K2 54081)*

Dec 76. (7") <1370> **MIDNIGHT ON THE BAY. / BLACK CORAL** [-] [ ]

— CROSBY, STILLS & NASH re-formed in '77 (see further on for more solo STILLS)

DAVID CROSBY

with loads of session people, too numerous to mention.

Atlantic Atlantic

Feb 71. (lp) *(2401 005)* <SD 7203> **IF I COULD ONLY REMEMBER MY NAME** [12] [12]
– Music is love / Cowboy movie / Tamalpais High (at about 3) / Laughing / What are their names / Traction in the rain / Song with no name (tree with no leaves) / Orleans / I'd swear there was somebody here. *(re-iss.1972 lp/c; K/K4 40320) (cd-iss.Nov93; 56781415-2)*

Apr 71. (7") <2792> **MUSIC IS LOVE. / LAUGHING** [-] [95]

Jul 71. (7") <2809> **ORLEANS. / TRACTION IN THE RAIN** [-] [ ]

GRAHAM NASH & DAVID CROSBY

duo (DAVID & GRAHAM with more sessioners and left over GRATEFUL DEAD members which were included on DAVID's debut solo album.

May 72. (lp/c) *(K/K4 50011)* <7220> **GRAHAM NASH & DAVID CROSBY** [13] [4] Apr72
– Southbound train / Whole cloth / Black notes / Strangers room / Where will I be / Page 43 / Frozen smiles / Games / Girl to be on my mind / The wall song / Immigration man.

May 72. (7") <2873> **IMMIGRATION MAN. / WHOLE CLOTH** [-] [36]

Jul 72. (7") **SOUTHBOUND TRAIN. / WHOLE CLOTH** [ ] [-]

Jul 72. (7") <2892> **SOUTHBOUND TRAIN. / THE WALL SONG** [-] [99]

— after CROSBY, STILLS, NASH & YOUNG reunion May74-Feb75

— resurrected partnership, with steady band members **CRAIG DOERGE** – keyboards / **LEE SKLAR + TIM DRUMMOND** – bass / **DANNY KOOTCH & RUSS KUNKEL** – drums / **DAVID LINDLEY** – guitar, violin.

Polydor A.B.C.

Jan 76. (lp) *(2310 428)* <902> **WIND ON THE WATER** [ ] [6] Oct75
– Carry me / Mama lion / Bittersweet / Take the money and run / Naked in the rain / Love work out / Low down payment / Cowboy of dreams / Homeward through the haze / Fieldworker / To the last whale. *(cd-iss.Nov91 on 'Thunderbolt'; CDTB 128) (cd re-iss.Mar97 on 'Nectar'; NTMCD 550)*

Nov 75. (7") <12140> **CARRY ME. / MAMA LION** [ ] [52]

Mar 76. (7") <12165> **TAKE THE MONEY AND RUN. / BITTERSWEET** [-] [ ]

May 76. (7") <12185> **LOVE WORK OUT. / BITTERSWEET** [-] [ ]

Jul 76. (lp) *(2319 468)* <956> **WHISTLING DOWN THE WIRE** [ ] [26]
– Spotlight / Broken bird / Time after time / Dancer / Mutiny / J.B.'s blues / Marguerita / Taken at all / Foolish man / Out of the darkness.

Aug 76. (7") **OUT OF THE DARKNESS. / LOVE WORK OUT** [ ] [-]

Aug 76. (7") <12199> **OUT OF THE DARKNESS. / BROKEN BIRD** [-] [89]

Oct 76. (7") <12217> **SPOTLIGHT. / FOOLISH MAN** [-] [ ]

— CROSBY STILLS & NASH re-formed '77 (see further on)

GRAHAM NASH

solo using C,S & N past members plus GRATEFUL DEAD main men

Atlantic Atlantic

Jun 71. (lp) *(2401 011)* <SD 7204> **SONGS FOR BEGINNERS** [13] [15]
– Military madness / Better days / Wounded bird / I used to be a king / Be yourself / Simple man / Man in the mirror / There's only one / Sleep song / Chicago / We can change the world. *(cd-iss.Feb93; 7567 81416-2)*

Jun 71. (7") *(2091 096)* <2804> **CHICAGO. / SIMPLE MAN** [ ] [35] May71

Aug 71. (7") <2827> **MILITARY MADNESS. / SLEEP SONG** [-] [73]

Sep 71. (7") *(2091 135)* **MILITARY MADNESS. / I USED TO BE A KING** [ ] [-]

Nov 71. (7") *<2840>* **I USED TO BE A KING. / WOUNDED BIRD** [-] [ ]
Nov 73. (7") *<2990>* **PRISON SONG. / HEY YOU (LOOKING AT HTE MOON)** [-] [ ]
Mar 74. (lp/c) *(K/K4 50025) <SD 7288>* **WILD TALES** [ ] [34] Dec73
– Wild tales / Hey you (looking at the Moon) / Prison song / You'll never be the same / And so it goes / Oh! Camil (the winter soldier) / I miss you / On the line / Another sleep song.
Mar 74. (7") *(K 10425)* **ON THE LINE. / I MISS YOU** [ ] [-]
Aug 74. (7") *(K 10470)* **GRAVE CONCERN. / ANOTHER SLEEP SONG** [ ] [-]
— GRAHAM rejoined below and had more solo releases later.

CROSBY, STILLS & NASH

reformed in '77, with various session men.

Atlantic Atlantic
Jun 77. (lp/c) *(K 50369) <19104>* **CSN** [23] [2]
– Shadow captain / See the changes / Carried away / Fair game / Anything at all / Cathedral / Dark star / Just a song before I go / Cold rain / In my dreams / I give you give blind.
Jun 77. (7") *(K 10947) <3401>* **JUST A SONG BEFORE I GO. / DARK STAR** [ ] [7] May77
Oct 77. (7") *(K 11024) <3432>* **FAIR GAME. / ANYTHING AT ALL** [ ] [43] Sep77
Dec 77. (7") *<3453>* **CARRIED AWAY. / I GIVE YOU GIVE BLIND** [-] [ ]

STEPHEN STILLS

more solo releses with session people & his tour band **DALLAS TAYLOR** – drums / **GEORGE PERRY** – bass / **MIKE FINNEGAN** – keyboards / **JERRY TOLMAN & BONNIE BRAMLETT** – b.vocals

C.B.S. Columbia
Sep 78. (7") *(6662) <10804>* **CAN'T GET NO BOOTY. / LOWDOWN** [ ] [ ]
Oct 78. (lp) *(82859) <35380>* **THOROUGHFARE GAP** [ ] [83]
– You can't dance alone / Thoroughfare gap / We will go / Beaucoup yumbo / What's the game / Midnight rider / Woman Lleva / Lowdown / Not fade away / Can't get no booty.
Nov 78. (7") *<10872>* **THOROUGHFARE GAP. / LOWDOWN** [-] [ ]

GRAHAM NASH

solo, with usual and past session people + CROSBY, STILLS & YOUNG

Capitol Capitol
Jan 80. (7") *<4812>* **IN THE 80'S. / T.V. GUIDE** [-] [ ]
Mar 80. (7") *<4849>* **OUT ON THE ISLAND. / HELICOPTER SONG** [-] [ ]
Mar 80. (lp) *(12014)* **EARTH & SKY** [-] [ ]
– Earth & sky / Love has come / Out on the island / Skychild / Helicopter song / Barrel of pain / T.V. guide / It's alright / Magical child / In the 80's.
May 80. (7") *<4879>* **EARTH & SKY. / MAGICAL CHILD** [-] [ ]

CROSBY, STILLS & NASH

re-formed mid '82, with session men

Atlantic Atlantic
Jul 82. (lp/c) *(K/K4 50896) <19360>* **DAYLIGHT AGAIN** [ ] [8]
– Turn your back on love / Wasted on the way / Southern cross / Into the darkness / Delta / Since I met you / Too much love to hide / Song for Susan / You are alive / Might as well have a good time / Daylight again. *(cd-iss.Oct94; 7567 82672-2)*
Nov 82. (7") *(K 11747) <4058>* **WASTED ON THE WAY. / DELTA** [ ] [9] Jul82
Nov 82. (7") *(K 11749) <89969>* **SOUTHERN CROSS. / INTO THE DARKNESS** [ ] [18] Sep82
Jan 83. (7") *<89888>* **TOO MUCH LOVE TO HIDE. / SONG FOR SUSAN** [-] [69]
Jun 83. (lp) *(78-0075-1) <80075>* **ALLIES (live)** [ ] [43]
– War games / Raise a voice / Turn your back on love / Barrel of pain / Shadow captain / Dark star / Blackbird / He played real good for free / Wasted on my way / For what it's worth. *(cd-iss.1984; 780 075-2)*
Jul 83. (7") *(A 9818) <89812>* **WAR GAMES (live). / SHADOW CAPTAIN (live)** [ ] [45] Jun83
(12") *(A 9818T)* – ('A'side) / Dark Star (live) / Keep your . . .
Sep 83. (7") *<89775>* **RAISE A VOICE (live). / FOR WHAT IT'S WORTH (live)** [-] [ ]
— split Aug'82, when CROSBY was sentenced to 5 years for drugs. He got leniency, when he agreed to rehabilitate himself in a drug hospital Dec'84.

STEPHEN STILLS

solo again (2nd single featured WALTER FINNEGAN)

W.E.A. Atlantic
Aug 84. (7") *<89633>* **STRANGER. / NO HIDING PLACE** [-] [61]
Sep 84. (lp/c) *(780 177-1) <80177>* **RIGHT BY YOU** [ ] [75] Aug84
– 50/50 / Stranger / Flaming heart / Love again / No problem / Can't let go / Grey to green / Only love can break your heart / No hiding place / Right by you. *(cd-iss.Nov93; 7567 80177-2)*
Oct 84. (7") *<89611>* **CAN'T LET GO. / GREY TO GREEN** [-] [67]
— (above as STEPHEN STILLS featuring MICHAEL FINNIGAN)
Dec 84. (7") *<89597>* **ONLY LOVE CAN BREAK YOUR HEART. / LOVE AGAIN** [-] [ ]

not issued Goldhill
1990. (cd) **STILLS ALONE** [-] [ ]
– Isn't it so / Everybody's talkin' / Just isn't like you / In my life / Ballad of Hollis Brown / Singin call / The right girl / Blind fiddler medley / Amazonia / Treetop flyer.

GRAHAM NASH

solo, he had rejoined The HOLLIES between Sep81-Apr83.

Atlantic Atlantic
Apr 86. (7") *(A 9434) <89434>* **INNOCENT EYES. / I GOT A ROCK** [ ] [84]
Apr 86. (lp/c) *(781-633-1/-4) <81633>* **INNOCENT EYES** [ ] [ ]
– See you in Prague / Keep away from me / Innocent eyes / Chippin' away / Over the wall / Don't listen to the rumours / Sad eyes / Newday / Glass and steel / I got a rock.
Jul 86. (7") *<89396>* **SAD EYES. / NEWDAY** [-] [ ]
Oct 86. (7") *<89373>* **CHIPPIN' AWAY. / NEWDAY** [-] [ ]

CROSBY, STILLS, NASH & YOUNG

re-formed yet again

Atlantic Atlantic
Nov 88. (7") *<88966>* **GOT IT MADE. / THIS OLD HOUSE** [-] [69]
Nov 88. (lp/c)(cd) *(WX 233/+C)(781 886-2) <81888>* **AMERICAN DREAM** [ ] [16]
– American dream / Got it made / Name of love / Don't say goodbye / This old house / Nighttime for the generals / Shadowland / Drivin' thunder / Clear blue skies / That girl / Compass / Soldiers of peace / Feel your love / Night song.
Jan 89. (7") *(A 9003) <88966>* **AMERICAN DREAM. / COMPASS** [55] [ ]
(12"+=) *(A 9003T)* – Soldiers of peace.
(12"g-f++=) *(A 9003TX)* – Ohio.

DAVID CROSBY

solo again

A&M A&M
Feb 89. (lp/c/cd) *<(AMA/AMC/CDA 5232)>* **OH YES I CAN** [ ] [ ]
– Drive my car / Melody / Monkey and the underdog / In the wide ruin / Tracks in the dust / Drop down mama / Lady of the harbour / Distances / Flying man / Oh yes I can / My country 'tis of thee.
Feb 89. (7") *(AM 500)* **DRIVE MY CAR. / TRACKS IN THE DUST** [ ] [ ]
(12"+=) *(AMY 500)* – Flying men.
Apr 89. (7"/12") *(AM/+Y 502)* **LADY OF THE HARBOR. / DROP DOWN MAMA** [ ] [ ]
— with band **LELAND SKLAR** – bass / **RUSSELL KUNKEL + JEFF PORCARO** – drums / **CRAIG DOERGE** – keyboards / **ANDY FAIRWEATHER-LOWE** – guitar / **DEAN PARKS** – guitar, flute / **BERNIE LEADON** – acoustic guitar / **C.J. VANSTON** – keyboards / with many guests **JACKSON BROWNE + DON WAS** plus outside writers + on session **PHIL COLLINS, JONI MITCHELL, MARC COHN, JIMMY WEBB, PAUL BRADY, STEPHEN BISHOP, JOHN HIATT, BONNIE HAYES + NOEL BRAZIL.**

Atlantic Atlantic
May 93. (7"/c-s; by DAVID CROSBY featuring PHIL COLLINS) *<87360>* **HERO. / COVERAGE** [ ] [44]
(cd-s+=) – Fare thee well.
Jun 93. (cd/c) *(7567 82484-2/-4)* **THOUSAND ROADS** [ ] [ ]
– Hero / Too young to die / Old soldier / Through your hands / Yvette in English / Thousand roads / Columbus / Helpless heart / Coverage / Natalie.
Mar 95. (cd/c) *(7567 82620-2/-4)* **IT'S ALL COMING BACK TO ME NOW (live '93)** [ ] [ ]
– In my dreams / Rusty and blue / Hero / Till it shines on you / 1000 roads / Cowboy movie / Almosy cut my hair / Deja vu / Long time gone / Wooden ships.

CROSBY, STILLS & NASH

with **JOE VITALE** – drums, organ, synth bass / **LELAND SKLAR** – bass / **CRAIG DOERGE** – keyboards / **MIKE LANDAU** – guitar / **MIKE FISHER** – percussion.

East West Atlantic
Jun 90. (cd/c/lp) *(7567 82101-2/-4/-1) <82107>* **LIVE IT UP** [ ] [57]
– Live it up / If anybody had a heart / Tomboy / Haven't we lost enough / Yours and mine / (Got to keep) Open / Straight line / House of broken dreams / Arrows / After the dolphin.
Jul 90. (7") *<87909>* **LIVE IT UP. / CHUCK'S LAMENT** [-] [ ]
Aug 94. (cd/c) *(7567 82654-2/-4)* **AFTER THE STORM** [ ] [98]
– Only waiting for you / Find a dream / Camera / Unequal love / Till it shines / It won't go away / These empty days / In my life / Street to lean on / Bad boyz / After the storm / Panama.

– their compilations etc. –

on 'Atlantic' unless mentioned otherwise
Aug 74. (lp/c) *(K/K4 50023) <18100>* **SO FAR – THE BEST OF . . .** [25] [1]
– Woodstock / Marrakesh express / You don't have to cry / Teach your children / Love the one you're with / Almost cut my hair / Wooden ships / Dark star / Helpless / Chicago – We can change the world / Cathedral / 4 + 20 / Our house / Change partners / Just a song before I go / Ohio / Wasted on the way / Southern cross / Suite: Judy blue eyes / Carry on – Questions / Horses through a rainstorm / Johnny's garden / Guinnevere / Helplessly hoping / The Lee Shore / Taken it all / Shadow captain / As I come of age / Drive my car / Dear Mr. Fantasy / In my dreams / Yours and mine / Haven't we lost enough? / After the dolphin / Find the cost of freedom. *(cd-iss.Jan87; K2 50023) (cd re-iss.Oct94; 7567 82648-2)*
Oct 75. (d-lp) *(K 60063)* **TWO ORIGINALS OF STEPHEN STILLS (1st 2 lp's)** [ ] [-]
Dec 75. (lp) *(K 50214) <18156>* **STEPHEN STILLS – LIVE (live)** [ ] [ ]
Jan 77. (lp) *(K 50327) <18201>* **STEPHEN STILLS – THE BEST OF STEPHEN STILLS** [ ] [ ]
– Love the one you're with / It doesn't matter / We are not helpless / Marianne / Bound to fall / Isn't it about time / Change partners / Go back home / Johnny's garden / Rock and roll crazies – Cuban bluegrass / Sit yourself down.
Nov 77. (lp; CROSBY & NASH) *Polydor; (2310 565) / A.B.C.; <1042>* **LIVE (live)** [ ] [52]
Jan 79. (lp; CROSBY & NASH) *Polydor; (2310 626) / A.B.C.; <1102>* **THE BEST OF CROSBY & NASH** [ ] [ ] Oct78
(re-iss.Nov80)
Nov 80. (lp/c) *Atlantic; (K/K4 50766) <16026>* **REPLAY** [ ] [ ] Sep80
– Carry on / Marrakesh express / Just a song before I go / First things first / Shadow captain / To the last whale / Love the one you're with / Pre-road downs / Change partners / I give you give blind / Cathedral. *(cd-iss.Oct94; 7567 82648-2)*
Dec 91. (d-cd/d-c) *(7567 80487-2/-4)* **CARRY ON** [ ] [ ]
Dec 91. (4xcd-box/4xc-box) *East West; (7567 82319-2/-4)* **THE BEST OF CROSBY, STILLS & NASH** [ ] [-]
Feb 92. (7"/c-s) *East West;* **OUR HOUSE. / MARRAKESH EXPRESS** [ ] [ ]

(12"+=/cd-s+=) – Carry on / Dear Mr. Fantasy (STEPHEN STILLS / GRAHAM NASH).

— (above A-side was re-actified on a famous building society TV ad).

CROSS & ROSS (see under ⇒ BULLDOG BREED)

CUPID'S INSPIRATION

Formed: Stamford, Lincolnshire, England . . . 1967 initially as The ENDS by TERRY RICE-MILTON, WYNDHAM GEORGE, LAUGHTON JAMES and ROGER GRAY. They picked an old LITTLE ANTHONY & THE IMPERIALS song, 'YESTERDAY HAS GONE', for their debut, the single going top 5 in mid-'68. By this point they had added GARFIELD TONKIN, who played on their Top 40 follow-up 'MY WORLD'. Unable to repeat their earlier success, a newfound progressive sound helped make their decline even speedier. RICE-MILTON attempted a solo career, reviving a CILLA BLACK cover (!), and even new bassman GORDON HASKELL left to do his own thing.

Recommended: YESTERDAY HAS GONE (*5)

T. (TERRY) RICE-MILTON (b. 5 Jun'46) – vocals / **WYNDHAM GEORGE** (b.20 Feb'47) – guitar / **LAUGHTON JAMES** (b.21 Dec'46) – bass / **ROGER GRAY** (b.29 Apr'49) – drums

Nems

Jun 68. (7") *(56 3500)* **YESTERDAY HAS GONE. / DREAM** [4] [ ]

— added **GARFIELD TONKIN** (b.28 Sep'46) – piano

Sep 68. (7") *(56 3702)* **MY WORLD. / EVERYTHING IS MEANT TO BE** [33] [ ]

1969. (lp; CUPID'S INSPIRATION featuring T. RICE-MILTON) *(6-63553)* **YESTERDAY HAS GONE** [ ] [-]

— **BERNARD LEE** – guitar, repl. GEORGE

— **GORDON HASKELL** – bass (ex-FLEUR DE LYS), repl. JAMES + TONKIN

Bell / not issued

1969. (7") *(BLL 1069)* **THE SAD THING. / LOOK AT ME** [ ] [-]

— now without HASKELL, who quickly went solo, later joining KING CRIMSON

C.B.S. / not issued

Jan 70. (7") *(4722)* **WITHOUT YOUR LOVE. / DIFFERENT GUY** [ ] [-]

Mar 70. (7") *(4994)* **ARE YOU GROWING TIRED OF MY LOVE. / SUNSHINE** [ ] [-]

— split after above, when RICE-MILTON took to the cabaret circuit.

– compilations, others, etc –

Apr 74. (7") *D.J.M.; (DJS 10300)* **YESTERDAY HAS GONE. / MY WORLD** [ ] [-]

Apr 87. (7") *N.B.; (NB 51)* **YESTERDAY HAS GONE. / MY WORLD** [ ] [-]

May 87. (7") *M.B.S.; (MBS 001)* **YESTERDAY HAS GONE. / MY WORLD** [ ] [-]

CURVED AIR

Formed: London, England . . . early 1970 by Royal College of Music violinist DARRYL WAY and FRANCIS MONKMAN (ex-SISYPHUS). When asked to perform the musical 'Who The Murderer Was', the band found ex-British 'Hair' musical singer SONJA KRISTINA (who had also recently spent time playing solo folk festivals). She had also released a single in 1968 'LET THE SUNSHINE IN' / 'FRANK MILLS' for 'Polydor'; (56299). They took the name CURVED AIR from a Terry Riley album, and after another tour signed to 'Warners'. In late 1970, they issued their debut album, 'AIR CONDITIONING' (the first rock group on picture disc), which crashed into the Top 10 due to this marketing ploy. The record was an ambitious effort, the track 'VIVALIDI' based on the composer's "Four Seasons" masterpiece. Their 1971 US tour was quickly followed by their first UK single success, 'BACK STREET LUV'. Although the sultry SONJA was the main focal point, their sound was of the quasi-classical variety, DARRYL WAY's perspex electric violin something of a unique novelty. Their third album, 'PHANTASMAGORIA', was their last to break the Top 20, the substition of 17 year-old EDDIE JOBSON for solo bound DARRYL WAY taking them into more eclectic synth territory. DARRYL returned in 1974 for a live set, while STEWART COPELAND joined on drums a year later. He was to marry SONJA the same year, although the group had now become a stale parody of its former self.

Recommended: THE BEST OF CURVED AIR (*6)

SONJA KRISTINA (b.14 Apr'49, Brentwood, Essex, England) – vocals / **DARRYL WAY** (b.17 Dec'48, Taunton, Somerset, England) – violin, vocals / **FRANCIS MONKMAN** (b. 9 Jun'49, Hampstead, London, England) – keyboards (ex-SISYPHUS) / **ROBERT MARTIN** – bass / **FLORIAN PILKINTON-MIKSA** (b. 3 Jun'50, Roehampton, London) – drums (both ex-SISYPHUS)

Warners / Warners

Nov 70. (pic-lp)(lp) (WSX 3012)(K 56004) <3012><1903> **AIR CONDITIONING** [8] [ ]
– It happened today / Stretch / Screw / Blind man / Vivaldi / Hide and seek / Propositions / Rob one / Situations / Vivaldi (with cannons). *(cd-iss.Jun94 on 'Line'; LECD 9010230) (cd re-iss.Apr96; 7599 26433-2)*

Jan 71. (7"m) *(WB 8023)* **IT HAPPENED TODAY. / VIVALDI / WHAT HAPPENS WHEN YOU BLOW YOURSELF UP?** [ ] [ ]

— **IAN EYRE** – bass repl. ROBERT

Jul 71. (7") *(WB 8029)* **BACK STREET LUV. / EVERDANCE** [4] [ ]
(re-iss.1974; K 16092)

Sep 71. (lp) *(K 46092) <1951>* **SECOND ALBUM** [11] [ ]
– Young mother / Back street luv / Jumbo / You know / Puppets / Everdance / Bright summer's day '68 / Piece of mind. *(cd-iss.Apr96; 7599 26434-2)*

— **MIKE WEDGWOOD** (b.19 May'56, Derby, England) – bass repl. IAN

Mar 72. (7") *(K 16164)* **SARAH'S CONCERN. / PHANTASMAGORIA** [ ] [ ]

Apr 72. (lp) *(K 46158) <2628>* **PHANTASMAGORIA** [20] [ ]
– Marie Antoinette / Melinda (more or less) / Not quite the same / Cheetah / Ultra-Vivaldi / Phantasmagoria / Whose shoulder are you looking over anyway / Over and above / One a ghost, always a ghost.

— **SONJA & MIKE** brought in new members **EDDIE JOBSON** (b.28 Apr'55, Billingham, England) – violin, synthesizers repl. DARRYL who formed his WOLF
KIRBY GREGORY – guitar repl. FRANCIS who went into sessions
JIM RUSSELL – drums repl. FLORIAN who joined KIKI DEE

Apr 73. (lp) *(K 46224)* **AIR CUT** [ ] [-]
– The purple speed queen / Elfin boy / Metamorphosis / World / Armin / U.H.F. / Two-three-two / Easy.

— Split mid-'73. Re-formed Autumn '74. SONJA the sole survivor recruited past members **DARRYL WAY** – violin returned to repl. JOBSON who joined ROXY MUSIC in '73. **FRANCIS MONKMAN** – keyboards repl. GREGORY / **FLORIAN PILKINTON-MISK** – drums repl. RUSSELL and **PHIL KOHN** – bass repl. WEDGWOOD who joined CARAVAN.

Deram / not issued

Feb 75. (lp) *(SML 1119)* **CURVED AIR LIVE (live)** [ ] [-]
– It happened today / Marie Antoinette / Back street luv / Propositions / Young mother / Vivaldi / Everdance. *(cd-iss.Jan95 on 'Repertoire'; REP 4514-WY) (cd re-iss.Nov95 on 'H.T.D.'; HTDCD 49)*

Mar 75. (7") *(DM 426)* **BACK STREET LUV (live). / IT HAPPENED TODAY (live)** [ ] [-]

— **MICK JAQUES** – guitar repl. FRANCIS MONKMAN who joined 801, then SKY **STEWART COPELAND** (b.16 Jul'52) – drums repl. FLORIAN. **JOHN PERRY** – bass (ex-CARAVAN) repl. PHIL / also guest **PETE WOODS** – keyboards

B.T.M. / not issued

Sep 75. (lp) *(BTM 1005)* **MIDNIGHT WIRE** [ ] [-]
– Woman on a one night stand / Day breaks my heart / The fool / Pipe of dreams / Orange Street blues / Dance of love / Midnight wire. *(cd-iss.Jan95 on 'Repertoire'; REP 4499-WY) (cd re-iss.Nov95 on 'H.T.D.'; HTDCD 50)*

— **TONY REEVES** – bass (ex-GREENSLADE) repl. PERRY who joined QUANTUM JUMP (above now with **SONJA, DARRYL, STEWART + MICK**)

Jun 76. (lp) *(BTM 1008)* **AIRBORNE** [ ] [-]
– Desiree / Kids to blame / Broken lady / Juno / Touch of tequila / Moonshine / Heaven (never seemed so far away) / Hot and bothered / Dazed. *(cd-iss.Sep94 on 'Repertoire';)*

Aug 76. (7") *(SBT 103)* **DESIREE. / KIDS TO BLAME** [ ] [-]

Oct 76. (7") *(SBT 106)* **BABY PLEASE DON'T GO. / BROKEN LADY** [ ] [-]

— **ALEX RICHMAN** – keyboards (ex-BUTTS BAND) repl. DARRYL WAY who went solo They split early '77. STEWART COPELAND formed The POLICE, TONY REEVES re-formed GREENSLADE, SONJA KRISTINA went solo forming group ESCAPE. In the 80's she toured Scotland with heavy band TUNIS who were based in High Wycombe.

SONJA KRISTINA

(solo with said band?) and featuring DARRYL WAY, etc, etc.

Chopper / not issued

Apr 80. (7") *(CHOP 101)* **ST. TROPEZ. / MR. SKIN** [ ] [-]

Aug 80. (lp) *(CHOPE 5)* **SONJA KRISTINA** [ ] [-]
– Street run / Man the colour / Colder than a rose in the snow / Breaking out in smiles / Mr. Skin / Roller coaster / Full time woman / The comforter / St. Tropez / Fade away.

— In '84 **SONJA** and **DARRYL** re-formed

CURVED AIR

Pearl Key / not issued

Jul 84. (7") *(PK 07350)* **RENEGADE. / WE'RE ONLY HUMAN** [ ] [-]

— They again re-formed for some gigs in 1988 & Summer 1990.

Essential / not issued

Aug 90. (cd/c/lp) *(ESS CD/MC/LP)* **LOVECHILD** [ ] [-]
– Exsultate jubilate / Lovechild / Seasons / The flasher / Joan / The dancer / The widow / Paris by night. *(cd re-iss.May94 on 'Castle'; CLACD 342)*

— split soon after above

– compilations, etc. –

1974. (7"ep) *Warners; (K 16412)* **BACK STREET LUV / IT HAPPENED TODAY. / MARIE ANTOINETTE / ULTRA VIVALDI** [ ] [-]

Apr 76. (lp) *Warners; (K 36015)* **THE BEST OF CURVED AIR** [ ] [-]
– It happened today / Vivaldi / You know / Back street luv / Melinda (more or less) / Cheetah / Metamorphosis / The purple speed queen.

Oct 81. (7") *Decca; (F 13911)* **BACK STREET LUV. / IT HAPPENED TODAY** [ ] [-]

Dec 95. (cd) *Band Of Joy; (BOJCD 014)* **BBC SESSIONS (live)** [ ] [-]

SONJA KRISTINA

Fruithouse / not issued

May 91. (cd/c/lp; as SONJA KRISTINA with TY-LOR & FRIENDS) *(FH CD/MC/LP 1)* **SONGS FROM THE ACID FOLK** [ ] [-]

H.T.D. / not issued

Apr 95. (cd) *(HTDCD 34)* **HARMONICS OF LOVE** [ ] [-]

Holger CZUKAY (see under ⇒ CAN)

DANTALIAN'S CHARIOT

Formed: London, England . . . 1967, after ZOOT MONEY had split his BIG ROLL BAND. They gigged frequently at London's 'Middle Earth' club, the line-up including ANDY SUMMERS, PAT DONALDSON and COLIN ALLEN. Their one and only 45, 'THE MADMAN RUNNING THROUGH THE FIELDS' (penned by MONEY & SUMMERS), was a definitive piece of British psychedelia, now highly collectable and fetching up to £60. The record was given a new lease of life when ERIC BURDON borrowed it for his 'Love Is' album, ZOOT and ANDY having joined the new ANIMALS. The flip side was a TONY COTTON and RAY SMITH ballad, its style not in keeping with their positively cosmic stage show (they used to dress in white robes). They recorded enough material for an album, later shelved when ZOOT returned to solo work (his discography due for inclusion in a forthcoming edition of The GREAT ROCK DISCOGRAPHY). The other members also went on to greater things, SUMMERS becoming famous for his part in The POLICE.

Recommended: the single

ZOOT MONEY (b. GEORGE BRUNO MONEY, 17 Jul'42, Bournemouth, England) – vocals, keyboards (ex-BIG ROLL BAND) / **ANDY SUMMERS** – guitar / **PAT DONALDSON** – bass / **COLIN ALLEN** – drums

Columbia / not issued

Aug 67. (7") *(DB 8260)* **THE MADMAN RUNNING THROUGH THE FIELDS. / THE SUN CAME BURSTING THROUGH MY CLOUD** [ ] [-]

— when they split, MONEY continued solo. ANDY SUMMERS joined KEVIN COYNE and later The POLICE. ALLEN joined JOHN MAYALL and STONE THE CROWS.

- compilations, etc. -

Mar 97. Tenth Planet; (cd) *(TP 015)* **CHARIOT RISING** [ ] [-]
(re-iss.Mar97 on 'Wooden Hill'; WHCD 005)

DARK

Formed: Northampton, England . . . 1968 by singer/guitarist STEVE GILES, although it was a further three years before he found stable members; bassman COLIN BUSH and drummer CARL, who was soon replaced by CLIVE THORNYCROFT. They were initially a covers band on the local gig circuit, although they premiered their own songs while supporting STATUS QUO. Becoming involved with music entrepeneur ALAN BOWLEY, they recorded their first acetate 'R.C.8' / 'IN THE SKY' in the spring of 1970. The following year, they replaced BUSH with RON JOHNSON and second guitarist MARTIN WEAVER, the team that subsequently cut and released the legendary rare/very limited album, 'DARK ROUND THE EDGES' (now worth over a staggering 1,000 quid). They had the opportunity of signing for 'Island' in 1972, deciding to reject the offer for personal reasons. GILES and JOHNSON were joined by R.STRYJECK, a single in 1974, 'WATCH OUT FOR THE NIGHT' / 'ALL THE LOVING I NEED' was shelved. • **Style:** Pioneers of atmospheric gothic progressive rock. • **Songwriters:** GILES, some with others. • **Trivia:** MARTIN's first band WICKED LADY have also attracted some interest in the 90's, with a cd release of their 'THE AXEMAN COMETH' for the 'Kissing Spell' label in '93.

Recommended: DARK ROUND THE EDGES (*?; have you heard it?)

STEVE GILES – vocals, guitar / **MARTIN WEAVER** – guitar (ex-WICKED LADY) / **RON JOHNSON** – bass / **CLIVE THORNYCROFT** – drums

S.I.S. / not issued

1972. (lp) *(0102)* **DARK ROUND THE EDGES** [ ] [-]
– *(re-iss.1990 on 'Swank') (cd-iss.Nov92 & Jun97 on 'Kissing Spell'; KSCD 9204)*– In the sky / Watch out for the night / All the loving I need.

— disbanded in 1974 after WEAVER and THORNYCROFT departed.

Dave DAVIES (see under ⇒ KINKS)

Sandy DAVIS (see under ⇒ GRACIOUS)

Spencer DAVIS GROUP

Formed: Birmingham, England . . . August 1963, DAVIS meeting PETER YORK and the WINWOOD brothers STEVE and MUFF at a local jazz club. It was soon apparent that the veterans (in the early 20's), were being overshadowed by the precocious 15-year old multi-talented STEVE. After a year on the circuit, they signed to 'Fontana' records with the aid of 'Island' owner CHRIS BLACKWELL, who had recommended the act. Their early 45's failed to distinguish them from the R&B pack (having only achieved minor placings) and it was only with the release of JACKIE EDWARDS' 'KEEP ON RUNNING' that the band exploded onto the scene. It topped the chart for one week in January 1966, a year that also saw the rejuvenation of 'THE FIRST LP' (which hit Top 10), a follow-up 45, 'SOMEBODY HELP ME' (another No.1) and STEVE's first self-penned hit, 'WHEN I COME HOME'. A prolific period for the band, they ended the year on a high, having scored with another Top 10 album and their third slice of genius, 'GIMME SOME LOVIN' (denied pole position by The Four Tops' 'Reach Out I'll Be There'). Still only 17, STEVE's 'Motown'-influenced vocal talent increasingly began to outlive the basic R&B backing the rest of the band were providing. Breaking away from the group, he took a more psychedelic approach with his new outfit, TRAFFIC. SPENCER DAVIS soldiered on with a new line-up, but it was clear the spark had been extinguished and the hits soon dried up. • **Other covers:** DIMPLES (John Lee Hooker) / EVERY LITTLE BIT HURTS (Brenda Holloway) / etc. • **Trivia:** Late in 1967, they made a small cameo appearance in the film 'HERE WE GO ROUND THE MULBURRY BUSH'.

Recommended: THE BEST OF THE SPENCER DAVIS GROUP (*7)

SPENCER DAVIS (b.17 Jul'42, Swansea, Wales) – guitar, vocals, harmonica (ex-SAINTS) / **STEVE WINWOOD** (b.12 May'48, Birmingham) – vocals, keyboards, guitar / **MUFF WINWOOD** (b.MERVYN, 14 Jun'43) – bass, vocals / **PETER YORK** (b.15 Aug'42, Middlesborough, England) – drums

Fontana / Fontana

Aug 64. (7") *(TF 471)* **DIMPLES. / SITTIN' AND THINKIN'** [ ] [-]
Oct 64. (7") *(TF 499)* <1960> **I CAN'T STAND IT. / MIDNIGHT TRAIN** [47] [ ] Mar65
Jan 65. (7") *(TF 530)* **EVERY LITTLE BIT HURTS. / IT HURTS ME SO** [41] [-]
May 65. (7") *(TF 571)* **STRONG LOVE. / THIS HAMMER** [44] [-]
Jul 65. (lp) *(TL 5242)* **THEIR FIRST LP** (hit-Jan66) [6] [-]
– My babe / Dimples / Searchin' / Every little bit hurts / I'm blue (gong gong song) / Sittin' and thinkin' / I can't stand it / Here right now / Jump back / It's gonna work out fine / Midnight train / It hurts me so. *(re-iss.1968 as 'EVERY LITTLE BIT HURTS' on 'Wing'; WL 1165)*

Fontana / Atco

Nov 65. (7") *(TF 632)* <6400> **KEEP ON RUNNING. / HIGH TIME BABY** [1] [76]
Jan 66. (lp) *(TL 5295)* **THE SECOND ALBUM** [2] [-]
– Look away / Keep on running / This hammer / Georgia on my mind / Please do something / Let me down easy / Strong love / I washed my hands in muddy water / Since I met you baby / You must believe me / Hey darling / Watch your step.
Mar 66. (7") *(TF 679)* <6416> **SOMEBODY HELP ME. / STEVIE'S BLUES** [1] [ ]
Aug 66. (7") *(TF 739)* **WHEN I COME HOME. / TRAMPOLINE** [12] [-]
Sep 66. (lp) *(TL 5359)* **AUTUMN '66** [4] [-]
– Together till the end of time / Take this hurt off me / Nobody knows you when you're down and out / Midnight special / When a man loves a woman / When I come home / Mean woman blues / Dust my blues / On the green light / Neighbour, neighbour / High time baby / Somebody help me.

Fontana / U.A.

Oct 66. (7") *(TF 762)* <50108> **GIMME SOME LOVING. / BLUES IN F** [2] [7] Jan67
(above 'A'side was different remix in the States)
Jan 67. (7") *(TF 785)* <50144> **I'M A MAN. / CAN'T GET ENOUGH OF IT** [9] [10] Mar67
Mar 67. (lp; mono/stereo) <UAL3/UAS6 578> **GIMME SOME LOVIN'** [-] [54]
– Keep on running / When a man loves a woman / Take this hurt off me / Georgia on my mind / You must believe me / Here right now / When I get home / I'm a man. *(UK-iss 1988 on 'Capitol';)*
Jun 67. (7") <50162> **SOMEBODY HELP ME. / ON THE GREEN LIGHT** [-] [47]

— **EDDIE HARDIN** (b.EDWARD HARDING, 19 Feb'49) – organ, vocals replaced STEVE who joined TRAFFIC and later BLIND FAITH then solo. / **PHIL SAWYER** (b.8 Mar'47) – lead guitar replaced MUFF who became A&R man, / also **CHARLIE McCRACKEN** – bass (guest)

Jul 67. (lp; mono/stereo) <UAL3/UAS6 589> **I'M A MAN** [-] [83]
– Dimples / Every little bit hurts / Stevie's blues / On the green light / Searchin' / Midnight train / My babe / Georgia on my mind / I can't get enough of it / I'm a man / I can't stand it / Look away.
Jul 67. (7") *(TF 854)* <50202> **TIME SELLER. / DON'T WANT YOU NO MORE** [30] [100]

U.A. / U.A.

Dec 67. (7") *(UP 1203)* **MR. SECOND CLASS. / SANITY INSPECTOR** [35] [-]
Dec 67. (7") <50286> **AFTER TEA. / LOOKING BACK** [-] [ ]
Mar 68. (7") *(UP 2213)* **AFTER TEA. / MOONSHINE** [ ] [-]
Apr 68. (lp; stereo/mono) *(S+/ULP 1192)* **WITH THEIR NEW FACE ON** [ ] [-]
– With his new face on / Mr. Second class / Alec in transitland / Sanity inspector / Feel your way / Morning sun / Moonshine / Don't want you no more / Time seller / Stop me, I'm fallin'.

— (Nov68) **DEE MURRAY** – bass / **NIGEL OLSSON** – drums repl. HARDIN & YORK who formed self named duo.

1969. (lp) <UAS 6691> **HEAVIES**
– Please do something / Waltz for lum umba / I'm blue (gong gong song) / Hey darling / Mean woman blues / Watch your step / Drown in my own tears / Together til' the end of time / Take this hurt off me / Back into my life again.

— (signed to 'CBS/Columbia' and copies of album 'LETTERS FROM EDITH' surfaced; US title 'FUNKY')

— Split mid '69. MURRAY and OLSSON joined ELTON JOHN's Band.

1971. (lp; by SPENCER DAVIS & PETER JAMESON) *(UAS 29177)* **IT'S BEEN SO LONG**
– It's been so long / Crystal river / One hundred years ago / Balkan blues / Brother can you make up your mind / Mountain lick / Jav's tune / King of her / It's too late now.

1972. (lp; by SPENCER DAVIS) *(UAS 29361)* **MOUSETRAP**
– Rainy season / Listen to the rhythm / What can I be / Tried / Easy rider / Tumbledown tenement row / Sunday walk in the rain / I washed my hands in muddy water / Sailor's lament / Hollywood Joe / In the hills of Tennessee / Ella speed.

1972. (7"; by SPENCER DAVIS) <50922> **LISTEN TO THE RHYTHM. / SUNDAY WALK IN THE RAIN**

1972. (7"; by SPENCER DAVIS) <50993> **RAINY SEASON. / TUMBLE-DOWN TENEMENT ROW**

— now group re-united w / **HARDIN, YORK, FENWICK + CHARLIE McCRACKEN** – bass

Vertigo Vertigo

Mar 73. (7") *(6059 076)* **CATCH YOU ON THE REBOB. / THE EDGE**

May 73. (lp) *(6360 088)* **GLUGGO**
– Catch you on the Moon / Don't it let it bring you down / Alone / Today Gluggo, tomorrow the world / Feeling rude / Legal eagle shuffle / Trouble in mind / Mr.Operator / Tumbledown tenement row.

May 73. (7") <110> **DON'T LET IT BRING YOU DOWN. / TODAY GLUGGO, TOMORROW THE WORLD**

Jun 73. (7") *(6059 082)* **MR. OPERATOR. / TOUCHING CLOTH**

Oct 73. (7") *(6059 087)* <112> **LIVIN' IN A BACK STREET. / SURE NEED A HELPING HAND**

Jun 74. (lp) *(6360 105)* **LIVIN' IN A BACK STREET**
– Living in a backstreet / One night / Hanging around / No reason / Fasted thing / On four wheels / Backstreet boys / Another day / Sure need a helping hand / We can give it a try / Let's have a party.

— SPENCER retired from solo work until 1983.

Allegience not issued

Apr 84. (lp/c) *(ALE/+C 5603)* **CROSSFIRE**
– Blood runs hot / Don't want you no more / Love is on a roll / Crossfire / Private number / Just a gigolo / Careless love / A pretty girl is like a melody / When the day is done / Hush-a-bye. *(cd-iss.Dec92 as 'NOW' on 'Kenwest'; SPCD 352)*

May 84. (7"; by SPENCER DAVIS & DUSTY SPRINGFIELD) *(ALES 3)* **PRIVATE NUMBER. / DON'T WANT YOU NO MORE**

— SPENCER became an executive at Island records in the mid 70's. In mid-80's, **SPENCER DAVIS BAND** reformed with others **DON KIRKPATRICK, EDDIE TREE** – guitars / **RICK SERATTE** – keys / **CHARLIE HARRISON** – bass / **BRYAN HITT** – drums (ex-WANG CHUNG)

In Akustik not issued

1988. (cd) *(INAK 8410)* **LIVE TOGETHER**
(above recorded 1984) (re-iss.Mar95; same)

1988. (cd) *(INAK 8590)* **24 HOURS – LIVE IN GERMANY**
(above recorded 1985) (re-iss.Mar95; same)

– compilations, others, etc. –

1965. (7"ep) *Fontana; (TE 17444)* **SHE PUT THE HURT ON ME**
– She put the hurt on me / I'm getting better / I'll drown in my own tears / Goodbye Stevie.

Aug 65. (7"ep) *Fontana; (TE 17450)* **EVERY LITTLE BIT HURTS**
– Every little bit hurts / It hurts me so / I can't stand it / Midnight train.

Jun 66. (7"ep) *Fontana; (TE 17463)* **SITTIN' AND THINKIN'**
– Sittin' and thinkin' / Jump back / Dimples / Searching.

Mar 68. (lp; mono/stereo) *Island; (ILP/+S 9070)* **THE BEST OF THE SPENCER DAVIS GROUP FEATURING STEVIE WINWOOD**
(re-iss.Oct86; same) (cd-iss.May88; CID 9070) (re-iss.cd Mar93; IMCD 151)

Mar 68. (lp) *United Artists;* <UAS 6641> **SPENCER DAVIS' GREATEST HITS**

1969. (c-ep) *Philips; (MCF 5003)* **THE HITS OF THE SPENCER DAVIS GROUP**

Aug 76. (7") *Island; (WIP 6318)* **GIMME SOME LOVING. / GIMME SOME LOVING '76**

May 78. (7"ep) *Island; (IEP 10)* **THE SPENCER DAVIS GROUP**
– Keep on running / Somebody help me / Every little bit hurts / I'm a man.

1985. (cd) *E.M.I.; (CDP 746 598-2)* **THE BEST OF THE SPENCER DAVIS GROUP**

1986. (lp) *Rhino;* <RNLP 70172> **GOLDEN ARCHIVE SERIES**

Dec 88. (c) *Capitol; (4XLL 9055)* **GIMME SOME LOVIN'**

Mar 91. (cd) *O.N.N. Range; (ONNCD 82)* **SPENCER DAVIS**

May 91. (7") *Island; (IS 487)* **KEEP ON RUNNING. / HIGH TIME BABY**
(12"+=/cd-s+=) *(12IS/CID 487)* – Somebody help me / This hammer.

Aug 92. (cd) *Success; (22511CD)* **KEEP ON RUNNING**

May 93. (cd/c) *Royal Collection; (RC 82149)* **KEEP ON RUNNING**

Aug 93. (cd) *Pilz; (448215-2)* **I'M A MAN**

Feb 94. (cd) *Javelin; (HADCD 123)* **SPOTLIGHT ON SPENCER DAVIS**

Mar 94. (cd-ep) *Pilz; (447523-2)* **I'M A MAN**
– Keep on running / Somebody help me / I'm a man / Gimme some loving / Crossfire.

Apr 94. (cd) *Music De-Luxe; (MSCD 4)* **KEEP ON KEEPING ON**

Jun 94. (cd) *R.P.M.; (RPMCD 127)* **TAKING OUT TIME 1967-69**

Oct 94. (cd) *Charly; (CDCD 1193)* **KEEP ON RUNNING**

Jun 95. (cd) *R.P.M.; (RPMCD 150)* **CATCH YOU ON THE REBOP – LIVE IN EUROPE 1973**

Mar 96. (d-cd) *Island Chronicles; (CRNCD 5)* **EIGHT GIGS A WEEK – THE STEVE WINWOOD YEARS**

Jun 97. (cd/c) *Hallmark; (30431-2/-4)* **GIMME SOME LOVIN'**

— (also look out for STEVE WINWOOD compilations 'KEEP ON RUNNING' & 'THE FINER THINGS', which have a batch of SDG hits.

Pete DELLO (see under ⇒ HONEYBUS)

DETROIT (see under ⇒ RYDER, Mitch)

DEVIANTS (see under ⇒ PINK FAIRIES)

DIGA RHYTHM BAND (see under ⇒ GRATEFUL DEAD)

DOG THAT BIT PEOPLE (see under ⇒ LOCOMOTIVE)

DON AND THE GOODTIMES (see under ⇒ TOUCH)

DONOVAN

Born: DONOVAN PHILIP LEITCH, 10 May'46, Maryhill, Glasgow, Scotland. At the age of 10, his family moved to Hatfield, England. In 1964, while playing small gigs in Southend, he was spotted by Geoff Stephens and Peter Eden, who became his managers. Later that year, after performing on the 'Ready Steady Go!' pop show over three consecutive weeks, the denim-clad beatnik signed to 'Pye'. His debut single, 'CATCH THE WIND' (issued the same time as DYLAN's 'The Times They Are A-Changin'), saw him break into the Top 5, later reaching Top 30 in America where he was enjoying the fruits of a burgeoning career. His follow-up, 'COLOURS', also made the Top 5 in the summer of '65, as did the debut album, 'WHAT'S BIN DID AND WHAT'S BIN HID'. Later in the year, the 'UNIVERSAL SOLDIER' EP saw DONOVAN begin to develop his uncompromising anti-war stance, a theme which he touched on with his second album, 'FAIRYTALE'. Initially heralded as Britain's answer to BOB DYLAN, he began to build on his folk/pop roots, progressing into flower-power with 'SUNSHINE SUPERMAN' in 1966. The album of the same name (issued only in the States) saw DONOVAN hit a creative high point and included the much revered, 'SEASON OF THE WITCH'. At the beginning of '67, the single 'MELLOW YELLOW' was riding high in the American hit parade, and 'EPISTLE TO DIPPY' soon followed suit. In the meantime, 'MELLOW YELLOW', was given a belated UK release (making Top 10), while its similarly titled parent album (again only issued in the US), hit No.14. 'SUNSHINE SUPERMAN', a UK compilation lp of both aforementioned albums, made the Top 30 in the middle of '67. His label, 'Pye', followed the same marketing strategy with his next UK album, the double 'A GIFT FROM A FLOWER TO A GARDEN', which was in actual fact, two US-only lp's in one. During this highly prolific period, which saw him inspired by the transcendental meditation of guru Maharishi Mahesh Yogi, he released two sublime pieces of acid-pop in 'THERE IS A MOUNTAIN' and 'JENNIFER JUNIPER'. The momentum continued with, 'HURDY GURDY MAN', another classic sojourn into psychedelia which hit Top 5 on both sides of the Atlantic. In 1969, he collaborated with The JEFF BECK GROUP on 'GOO GOO BARABAJAGAL', although this was his final 45 to make a major chart appearance. An album, 'OPEN ROAD' (1970), named after his new band, surprised many by cracking the US & UK charts. In 1971, he recorded a double album of children's songs 'H.M.S. DONOVAN', which led to a critical backlash from the music press. After a 3-year exile in Ireland for tax reasons, he set up home in California with his wife Linda Lawrence and daughters Astrella and Oriole. He has fathered two other children with his new American wife, Enid; DONOVAN LEITCH JNR. (star of the film 'Gas, Food, Lodging') and IONE SKYE, the latter said to be none too bothered about her famous father. DONOVAN enjoyed something of a renaissance in the early 90's when HAPPY MONDAYS' mainman SHAUN RYDER (now of BLACK GRAPE) sang his praises, leading to a comeback album, 'DONOVAN RISING'. He is still going strong today, releasing a well-received album, 'SUTRAS', for the RCA affiliated 'American' label in 1996. • **Songwriters:** Self-penned except, UNIVERSAL SOLDIER (Buffy Sainte-Marie) / LONDON TOWN (Tim Hardin) / REMEMBER THE ALAMO (Jane Bowes) / CAR CAR (Woody Guthrie) / GOLDWATCH BLUES (Mick Softley) / DONNA DONNA (Kevess-Secunda-Secanta-Schwartz-Zeitlin) / OH DEED I DO+ DO YOU HEAR ME NOW (Bert Jansch) / CIRCUS OF SOUR (Paul Bernath) / LITTLE TIN SOLDIER (Shawn Phillips / LORD OF THE DANCE (Sydney Carter) / ROCK'N'ROLL WITH ME (David Bowie-Warren Peace) / MY SONG IS TRUE (Darell Adams) / NO MAN'S LAND (Eric Bogle) / WIND IN THE WILLOWS (Eddie Hardin) / NEWEST BATH GUIDE + MOIRA McCAVENDISH (John Betjeman) / THE SENSITIVE KIND (J. J. Cale) / traditional:- KEEP ON TRUCKIN' + YOU'RE GONNA NEED SOMEBODY + CANDY MAN + THE STAR + COULTER'S CANDY + HENRY MARTIN + THE HEIGHTS OF ALMA + YOUNG BUT GROWING + STEALIN'. He also put music to words/poetry by; William Shakespeare (UNDER THE GREENWOOD TREE) / Gypsy Dave (A SUNNY DAY) / Lewis Carroll (WALRUS AND THE CARPENTER + JABBERWOCKY) / Thora Stowell (THE SELLER OF STARS + THE LITTLE WHITE ROAD) / Fifida Wolfe (LOST TIME) / Lucy Diamond (THE ROAD) / Agnes Herbertson (THINGS TO WEAR) / Edward Lear (THE OWL AND THE PUSSYCAT) / Eugene Field (WYNKEN, BLYNKEN AND NOD) / W. B. Yeats (THE SONG OF WANDERING AENGUS) / Natalie Joan (A FUNNY MAN) / Thomas Hood

(QUEEN MAB) / Astella Leitch (MEE MEE I LOVE YOU) / Warwick Embury (ONE NIGHT IN TIME) / Note; HURLEY GURLEY MAN originally had a verse by GEORGE HARRISON but this was not recorded and he only added this for live appearences. • **Trivia:** Sang co-lead on title track from ALICE COOPER's 1973 lp 'Billion Dollar Babies'.

Recommended: SUNSHINE SUPERMAN (US version; *7) / A GIFT FROM A FLOWER TO A GARDEN (*7) / GREATEST HITS AND MORE (*8)

DONOVAN – vocals, acoustic guitar, harmonica with **BRIAN LOCKING** – bass / **SKIP ALLEN** – drums / **GYPSY DAVE** (b. DAVID MILLS) – kazoo, etc.

Pye Hickory

Mar 65. (7") *(7N 15801) <1309>* **CATCH THE WIND. / WHY DO YOU TREAT ME LIKE YOU DO** [4] [23] Apr65
May 65. (7") *(7N 15866) <1324>* **COLOURS. / TO SING FOR YOU** [4] [61] Jun65
May 65. (lp) *(NPL 18117) <123>* **WHAT'S BIN DID AND WHAT'S BIN HID** <US title 'CATCH THE WIND'> [3] [30]
– Josie / Catch the wind / Remember the Alamo / Cuttin' out / Car car * (riding in my car) / Keep on truckin' / Goldwatch blues / To sing for you / You're gonna need somebody on your bond / Tangerine puppet / Donna Donna * / Ramblin' boy *(re-iss.Jul68 on 'Marble Arch';)* – (omitted *)
Sep 65. (7") *<1338>* **UNIVERSAL SOLDIER. / DO YOU HEAR ME** [-] [53]
Sep 65. (7"ep) *(NEP 24219)* **THE UNIVERSAL SOLDIER EP** [13] [-]
– Universal soldier / The ballad of a crystal man / Do you hear me now* / The war drags on.
Oct 65. (lp) *(NPL 18128)* **FAIRYTALE** [20] [85] Dec 65
– Colours * / To try for the sun / Sunny Goodge street / Oh deed I do / Circus of sour / The summer day reflection song / Candy man / Jersey Thursday / Belated forgiveness plea / Ballad of a crystal man / Little tin soldier * / Ballad of Geraldine. *(re-iss.Mar69 on 'Marble Arch';)*– (omitted *). *(re-iss.Feb91 on 'Castle' cd/c; CLA CD/MC 226)*
Nov 65. (7") *(7N 15984)* **TURQUOISE. / HEY GYP (DIG THE SLOWNESS)** [30] [-]
Nov 65. (7") *<1375>* **YOU'RE GONNA NEED SOMEBODY ON YOUR BOND. / THE LITTLE TIN SOLDIER** [-] [ ]
Jan 66. (7") *<1402>* **TO TRY FOR THE SUN. / TURQUOISE** [-] [ ]
Feb 66. (7") *(7N 17067)* **JOSIE. / LITTLE TIN SOLDIER** [ ] [-]
Apr 66. (7") *(7N 17088)* **REMEMBER THE ALAMO. / THE BALLAD OF A CRYSTAL MAN** [ ] [-]

— **DONOVAN** plus **JOHN CAMERON** – piano, harpsicord / **HAROLD McNAIR** – flute

Pye Epic

Jul 66. (7") *(7N 17241) <10045>* **SUNSHINE SUPERMAN. / THE TRIP** [2] [1] Jun66
Sep 66. (lp; mono><stereo) *<LN 24217><BN 26217>* **SUNSHINE SUPERMAN** [-] [11]
– Sunshine Superman / Legend of a girl child Linda / The observation / Guinevere / Celeste / Writer in the Sun / Season of the witch / Hampstead incident / Sand and foam / Young girl blues / Three kingfishers / Bert's blues. *(UK-iss.Feb91 on 'Beat Goes On' cd/c; BGO CD/MC 68) (cd re-iss.Oct96 on 'EMI Gold'; CDGOLD 1066)*
Nov 66. (7") *<10098>* **MELLOW YELLOW. / SUNNY SOUTH KENSINGTON** [-] [2]
Jan 67. (7") *<10127>* **EPISTLE TO DIPPY. / PREACHIN' LOVE** [-] [19]
Feb 67. (7") *(7N 17267)* **MELLOW YELLOW. / PREACHIN' LOVE** [8] [-]
Feb 67. (lp; mono><stereo) *<LN 24239><BN 26239>* **MELLOW YELLOW** [-] [14]
– Mellow yellow / Writer in the Sun / Sand and foam / The observation / Bleak city woman / House of Jansch / Young girl blues / Museum / Hampstead incident / Sunny South Kensington. *(cd-iss.Oct93 on 'Sony Europe';)*
Jun 67. (lp) *(NPL 18181)* **SUNSHINE SUPERMAN** [25] [-]
– (compilation of last 2 US albums)
Oct 67. (7") *(7N 17403) <10212>* **THERE IS A MOUNTAIN. / SAND AND FOAM** [8] [11] Sep67

— **DONOVAN** retained **HAROLD** and in came **TONY CARR** – percussion / **CANDY JOHN CARR** – bongos **CLIFF BARTON** – bass / **KEITH WEBB** – drums / **MIKE O'NEIL** – keyboards / **MIKE CARR** – vibraphone / **ERIC LEESE** – electric guitar

Dec 67. (7") *<10253>* **WEAR YOUR LOVE LIKE HEAVEN. / OH GOSH** [-] [23]
Dec 67. (lp; mono><stereo) *<LN 24349><BN 26349>* **WEAR YOUR LOVE LIKE HEAVEN** [-] [60]
– Wear your love like Heaven / Mad John's escape / Skip-a-long Sam / Sun / There was a time / Oh gosh / Little boy in corduroy / Under the greenwood tree / The land of doesn't have to be / Someone's singing / Song of the naturalist's wife / The enchanted gypsy.

— **KEN BALDOCK** – bass repl. BARTON, LEESE, WEBB, O'NEIL + MIKE CARR

Dec 67. (lp; mono><stereo) *<LN 24350><BN 26350>* **FOR LITTLE ONES** [-] [ ]
– Voyage into the golden screen / Isle of Islay / The mandolin man and his secret / Lay of the last tinker / The tinker and the crab / Widow with shawl (a portrait) / The lullaby of spring / The magpie / Starfish-on-the-toast / Epistle to Derroll.
Feb 68. (7") *(7N 17457) <10300>* **JENNIFER JUNIPER. / POOR COW** [5] [26]
Apr 68. (d-lp-box; mono/stereo) *(NPL/NSPL 20000) <L2N6/B2N 171>* **A GIFT FROM A FLOWER TO A GARDEN** [13] [19]
– (contains 2 US Dec67 albums boxed) *(cd-iss.Jul93 & Jun97 on 'Beat Goes On'; BGOCD 194)*
May 68. (7") *(7N 17537) <10345>* **HURDY GURDY MAN. / TEEN ANGEL** [4] [5]
Sep 68. (lp; mono/stereo) *(NPL/NSPL 18237) <BN 26420>* **DONOVAN IN CONCERT (live)** [ ] [18] Jul68
– Isle of Islay / Young girl blues / There is a mountain / Poor cow / Celeste / The fat angel / Guinevere / Widow with shawl (a portrait) / Preachin' love / The lullaby of Spring / Writer in the Sun / Rules and regulations / Pebble and the man / Mellow yellow. *(re-iss.May91 & Apr97 on 'Beat Goes On' cd/c/lp; BGO CD/MC/LP 90) (cd-iss.Nov94 on 'Start';) (re-iss.cd Jan96 on 'Happy Price'; HP 93432)*
Oct 68. (7") *<10393>* **LALENA. / AYE, MY LOVE** [-] [33]
Oct 68. (lp) *<BN 26420>* **HURDY GURDY MAN** [-] [20]
– Jennifer Juniper / Hurdy gurdy man / Hi, it's been a long time / Peregrine / The entertaining of a shy girl / Tangier / As I recall it / Get thy bearings / West Indian lady / Teas / The river song / The Sun is a very magic fellow / A sunny day.
Nov 68. (7") *(7N 17660)* **ATLANTIS. / I LOVE MY SHIRT** [23] [-]
Feb 69. (7") *<10434>* **ATLANTIS. / TO SUSAN ON THE WEST COAST WAITING** [-] [7] [35]
Mar 69. (lp) *(NPL/NSPL 18283) <BXN 26439>* **DONOVAN'S GREATEST HITS** (compilation) [ ] [4]
– Epistle to Dippy / Sunshine Superman / There is a mountain / Jennifer Juniper / Wear your love like Heaven / Season of the witch / Mellow yellow / Colours / Hurdy gurdy man / Catch the wind / Lalena. *<re-iss.1972; PE 26439> <re-iss.1973; BN 26836> (re-iss.Sep79 on 'CBS-Embassy' lp/c; CBS/40 31759) (cd-iss.Aug90 on 'Epic';)*
Jun 69. (7"; DONOVAN with The JEFF BECK GROUP) *(7N 17778)* **GOO GOO BARABAJAGAL (LOVE IS HOT). / BED WITH ME** [12] [-]
Sep 69. (7"; DONOVAN with The JEFF BECK GROUP) *<10510>* **GOO GOO BARABAJAGAL (LOVE IS HOT). / TRUDI** [-] [36]
Sep 69. (lp; DONOVAN with The JEFF BECK GROUP) *<BN 26481>* **BARABAJAGAL** [-] [ ]
– Barabajagal / Superlungs my supergirl / I love my shirt / The love song / To Susan on the West Coast waiting / Atlantis / Trudi / Pamela Jo / Happiness runs. *(cd-iss.Oct93 on 'Sony Europe';)*

— with **JOHN CARR** – drums, vocals / **MIKE THOMPSON** – bass, vocals / **MIKE O'NEILL** – piano

Dawn Epic

Sep 70. (lp) *(DNLS 3009) <30125>* **OPEN ROAD** [30] [16] Jul70
– Changes / Song for John / Curry land / Joe Bean's theme / People used to / Celtic rock / Riki tiki tavi / Clara clairvoyant / Roots of oak / Season of farewell / Poke at the Pope / New Year's resovolution.
Sep 70. (7"; DONOVAN with OPEN ROAD) *(DNS 1006) <10649>* **RIKI TIKI TAVI. / ROOTS OF OAK** [ ] [55]

— (DANNY – double bass)

Dec 70. (7"; DONOVAN with DANNY THOMPSON) *(DNA 1007)* **CELIA OF THE SEALS. / MR.WIND** [ ] [-]
Feb 71. (7") *(10694>* **CELIA OF THE SEAS. / THE SONG OF THE WANDERING AENGUS** [-] [84]
Jul 71. (d-lp) *(DNLD 4001)* **H.M.S. DONOVAN** [ ] [-]
– The walrus and the carpenter / Jabberwocky / The seller of the stars / Lost time / The little white road / The star / Coulter's candy / The road / Things to wear / The owl and the pussycat / Homesickness / Fishes in love / Mr.Wind / Wynken, Bylnken and Nod / Celia of the seas / The pee song / The voyage to the Moon / The unicorn / Lord of dance / Little Ben / Can ye dance / In an old fashioned picture book / The song of the wandering Aengus / A funny man / Lord of the reedy river / Henry Martin / Queen Mab / La moor.

— with guests **CHRIS SPEDDING** – guitar / **JOHN 'RABBIT' BUNDRICK** – keyboards / **JIM HORN** – bass / **COZY POWELL** – drums

Epic Epic

Mar 73. (lp) *(SEPC 65450) <32156>* **COSMIC WHEELS** [15] [25]
– Cosmic wheels / Earth sign man / Sleep / Maria Magenta / Wild witch lady / Sleep / The music makers / The intergallactic laxative / I like you / Only the blues / Appearances. *(cd-iss.Sep94 on 'Epic-Rewind'; 477378-2)*
Apr 73. (7") *(EPC 1471) <10983>* **I LIKE YOU. / EARTH SIGN MAN** [ ] [66]
Jun 73. (7") *(EPC 1644) <11023>* **MARIA MAGENTA. / THE INTERGALLACTIC LAXATIVE** [ ] [ ]

— now with **STEVE MARRIOT, PETER FRAMPTON** and **NICKY HOPKINS**

Nov 73. (7") *(EPC 1960)* **SAILING HOMEWARD. / LAZY DAZE** [ ] [-]
Dec 73. (lp) *(SEPC 69050) <32800>* **ESSENCE TO ESSENCE** [ ] [-]
– Operating manual for spaceship Earth / Lazy daze / Life goes on / There is an ocean / Dignity of man / Yellow star / Divine daze of deathless delight / Boy for every girl / Saint Valentine's angel / Life is a merry-go-round / Sailing homeward.
Jan 74. (7") *<11108>* **SAILING HOMEWARD. / YELLOW STAR** [-] [ ]

— Mainly used session musicians from now on.

Sep 74. (7") *(EPC 2661) <50016>* **ROCK'N'ROLL WITH ME. / THE DIVINE DAZE OF DEATHLESS DELIGHT** [ ] [ ] Nov74
Nov 74. (lp) *(SEPC 69104) <33245>* **7-TEASE** [ ] [ ]
– Rock and roll souljer / Your broken heart / Salvation stomp / The ordinary family / Ride-a-mile / Sadness / Moon rok / Love of my life / The voice of protest / How silly / The great song of the sky / The quest.
Jan 75. (7") *<50077>* **ROCK AND ROLL SOULJER. / HOW SILLY** [-] [ ]
Feb 75. (7") *(EPC 3037)* **ROCK AND ROLL SOULJER. / LOVE OF MY LIFE** [ ] [-]
Jun 76. (lp) *(SEPC 86011) <33945>* **SLOW DOWN WORLD** [ ] [ ]
– Dark-eyed blue jean angel / Cryin' shame / The mountain / Children of the world / My love is true (love song) / A well known has-been / Black widow / Slow down world / Liberation rag.
Jun 76. (7") *<50237>* **A WELL-KNOWN HAS-BEEN. / DARK EYED BLUE JEAN ANGEL** [-] [ ]

Rak Arista

Aug 77. (7") *<0280>* **DARE TO BE DIFFERENT. / THE INTERNATIONAL MAN** [-] [ ]
Oct 77. (lp) *(SRAK 528)* **DONOVAN** [ ] [-]
– Brave new world / Local boy chops wood / Kalifornia kids / International man / Lady of the stars / Dare to be different / Mijah's dance / The light / Astral angel.
Nov 77. (7") *(RAK 265)* **THE LIGHT. / THE INTERNATIONAL MAN** [ ] [-]
Feb 78. (7") *(RAK 269)* **DARE TO BE DIFFERENT. / SING MY SONG** [ ] [-]

— (note:- on above US singles [Jan 73, Jan 75, Jun 76, Aug 77] the 'B' side was mono version on 'A').

Luggage-R.C.A. Allegiance

Aug 80. (lp) *(PL 28429)* **NEUTRONICA** [ ] [-]
– Shipwreck / Only to be expected / Comin' to you / No hunger / Neutron / Mee Mee I love you / The heights of Alma / No man's land / We are one / Madrigalinda / Harmony.

— with **DANNY THOMPSON** – double bass / **JOHN STEPHENS** – drums / **TONY ROBERTS** – multi-wind instruments / and his 9 year-old daughter **ASTELLA** – dual vocals

Oct 81. (lp) *(PL 28472)* **LOVE IS ONLY FEELING** [ ] [-]
– Lady of the flowers / Lover o lover / The actor / Half Moon bay / The hills of Tuscany / Lay down Lassie / She / Johnny Tuff / Love is only feeling / Marjorie

Margerine.

Oct 81. (7") *(7-LUG 03)* **LAY DOWN LASSIE. / LOVE IS ONLY FEELING**

Jan 84. (lp) *(PL 70060) <72857>* **LADY OF THE STARS**
– Lady of the stars / I love you baby / Seasons of the witch / Bye bye girl / Every reason / Boy for every girl / Local boy chops wood / Sunshine superman / Til I see you again / Living for the lovelight.

After nearly 7 years in the wilderness, he returned on new label

Permanent Permanent

Nov 90. (cd/c/lp) *(PERM CD/MC/LP 2)* **DONOVAN RISING**
– Jennifer Juniper / Catch the wind / The hurdy gurdy man / Sunshine superman / Sadness / Universal soldier / Cosmic wheels / Atlantis / Wear your love like heaven / Colours / To Susan on the west coast waiting / Young girl blues / Young but growing / Stealing / Sailing homeward / Love will find a way / Lalena.

— He had also credited on The SINGING CORNER's (Nov90) single version of his JENNIFER JUNIPER.

Silhouette not issued

Apr 92. (cd-ep) *(MDCDKR 3)* **NEW BATH GUIDE / MOIRA McCAVENDISH / BROTHER SUN, SISTER MOON**

American-RCA American

Oct 96. (cd) *(74321 39743-2)* **SUTRAS**
– Please don't bend / Give it all up / Sleep / Everlasting sea / High your love / The clear-browed one / The way / Deep peace / Nirvana / Eldorado / Be mine / Lady of the lamp / The evernow / Universe am I.

– compilations, others, etc. –

on 'Pye' UK / 'Hickory' (70's 'Epic') US unless otherwise mentioned

Dec 65. (7"ep) *(NEP 24229)* **COLOURS**
– Catch the wind / Why do you treat me like you do / Colours / To sing for you.

Mar 66. (7"ep) *(NEP 24239)* **DONOVAN VOL.1**
– Sunny Goodge Street / Oh deed I do / Jersey Thursday / Hey Gyp (dig the slowness).

Jul 66. (7") *<1417>* **HEY GYP (DIG THE SLOWNESS). / THE WAR DRAGS ON**

Oct 66. (7") *<1470>* **SUNNY GOODGE STREET. / SUMMER DAY REFLECTION SONG**

Sep 66. (lp) *<135>* **THE REAL DONOVAN** 96

Jan 67. (7") *<193>* **CATCH THE WIND. / UNIVERSAL SOLDIER**

Oct 67. (lp) *Marble Arch; (MAL 718)* **UNIVERSAL SOLDIER** 5
(re-iss.Feb83 on 'Spot'; SPR/SPC 8514)

Feb 68. (7"ep) *(NEP 24287)* **CATCH THE WIND**
– Catch the wind / Remember the Alamo / Josie / Rambling Rose.

Apr 68. (lp) *<143>* **LIKE IT IS, WAS AND EVERMORE SHALL BE**

1968. (7") *<1492>* **DO YOU HEAR ME NOW. / WHY DO YOU TREAT ME LIKE YOU DO**

Aug 68. (7"ep) *(NEP 24299)* **HURDY GURDY DONOVAN**
– Jennifer juniper / Hurdy gurdy man / Mellow yellow / There is a mountain. *(re-iss.Nov71; PMM 104)*

Jun 69. (lp) *United Artists; (UAS 29044)* **IF IT'S TUESDAY IT MUST BE BELGUIM (Soundtrack)**

Nov 69. (lp) *<149>* **THE BEST OF DONOVAN**

1970. (lp) *Marble Arch; (MAL 1168)* **THE WORLD OF DONOVAN**

Oct 70. (7") *Janus; <A-501>* **COLORS. / JOSIE**

Oct 70. (7") *Janus; <A-502>* **CATCH THE WIND. / WHY DO YOU TREAT ME LIKE YOU DO**

Oct 70. (7") *Janus; <A-503>* **CANDY MAN. / HEY GYP (DIG THE SLOWNESS)**

Nov 70. (d-lp) *Janus; <3022>* **DONOVAN P.LEITCH** (early work)

1971. (lp) *Golden Hour; (GH 506)* **THE GOLDEN HOUR OF DONOVAN**

1971. (lp) *Hallmark; (HMA 200)* **CATCH THE WIND**
(re-iss.Apr86 on 'Showcase' lp/c; SH LP/TC 133)

1972. (lp) *Hallmark; (HMA 241)* **COLOURS**
(re-iss.Oct87 on 'P.R.T.' lp/c/cd; PYL/PYM/PYC 7004)

1972. (7") *Memory Lane; <15-2251>* **SUNSHINE SUPERMAN. / MELLOW YELLOW**

1972. (7") *Memory Lane; <15-2280>* **JENNIFER JUNIPER. / HURDY GURDY MAN**

1973. (4xlp-set) *(11PP 102)* **FOUR SHADES OF DONOVAN / OPEN ROAD / DONOVAN'S GREATEST HITS/ / H.M.S. DONOVAN**

Nov 77. (d-lp/c) *(FILD/ZCFLD 004)* **THE DONOVAN FILE**

Jul 78. (7") **COLOURS. / UNIVERSAL SOLDIER**

Jul 80. (7"ep) *Flashback; (FBEP 107)* **EP**
– Catch the wind / Turquoise / Colours / Universal soldier.

Oct 81. (lp/c) *P.R.T.; (SPOT/ZCSPT 1017)* **SPOTLIGHT ON DONOVAN**

Jul 82. (7") *Old Gold; (OG 9134)* **CATCH THE WIND. / COLOURS**

Jul 83. (10"lp/c) *P.R.T.; (DOW/ZCDOW 13)* **MINSTREL BOY**

Feb 85. (7") *EMI Gold; (G 4545)* **MELLOW YELLOW. / SUNSHINE SUPERMAN**

Aug 89. (7") *E.M.I.; (EM 98)* **SUNSHINE SUPERMAN. / JENNIFER JUNIPER**
(ext.12"+=) *(12EM 98)* – Wear your love like Heaven.
(cd-s++=) *(CDEM 98)* – Mellow yellow.

Sep 89. (cd)(c/lp) *E.M.I.; (CZ 193)(TC+/EMS 1333)* **GREATEST HITS AND MORE**
– Sunshine Superman / Wear your love like Heaven / Jennifer Juniper / Barabajagal (love is hot) / Hurdy gurdy man / Epistle to Dippy / To Susan on the West Coast waiting / Catch the wind / Mellow yellow / There is a mountain / Happiness runs / Season of the witch / Superlungs – My Supergirl / Lalena / Atlantis. *(cd+=)*– Preachin' love / Poor cow / Teen angel / Aye my love.

1990. Marble Arch; (cd) **JOSIE**
(re-iss.Jul94 on 'Success')

Oct 90. (lp/c/cd) *See For Miles; (SEE/+K/CD 300)* **THE EP COLLECTION**

Dec 90. (cd/c) *Castle; (CCS CD/MC 276)* **THE COLLECTION**

Feb 91. (d-cd/d-c/d-lp) *E.M.I.; (CD/TC+/EM 1385)* **THE TRIP** (1964-1968 material)

Mar 91. (7") *Gulf Peace Team; (GPT 1)* **UNIVERSAL SOLDIER. / CATCH THE WIND**
(12"+=) *(GPT 001T)* – I'll try for the sun.

Jun 91. (cd)(c) *Mammoth; (MMCD 5717)(MMMC 4717)* **THE HITS**

Jul 91. (cd) *The Collection; (ORO 155)* **TILL I SEE YOU AGAIN**
(re-iss.Jul94 on 'Success')

Mar 93. (cd) *Dojo-Castle; (EARLD 13)* **THE EARLY YEARS**

Sep 93. (cd) *Remember; (RMB 7/4 5059)*

Dec 93. (cd) *Disky; (GOLD 206)* **GOLD: GREATEST HITS**

May 94. (cd) *Music DeLuxe; (MDCD 6)* **COLOURS**

Oct 94. (cd) *Charly; (CDCD 1206)* **SUNSHINE SUPERMAN**

Nov 94. (4xcd-box) *E.M.I.; (DONOVAN 1)* **ORIGINALS**

Jan 95. (cd/c) *Spectrum; (550 721-2/-4)* **UNIVERSAL SOLDIER**

Dec 95. Javelin; (cd) **SUNSHINE SUPERMAN**

Aug 96. (cd/c) *Hallmark; (30501-2/-4)* **SUNSHINE TROUBADOR**

Nov 96. (cd) *Experience; (EXP 013)* **DONOVAN**

Apr 97. (cd) *Artful; (ARTFULCD 5)* **THE VERY BEST OF**

May 97. (cd) *C.M.C.; (100082)* **SUNSHINE SUPERMAN**

DOORS

Formed: Los Angeles, California, USA . . . July 1965 by RAY MANZAREK and JIM MORRISON. In 1966, after some personnel changes, they soon settled with JOHN DENSMORE and ROBBY KRIEGER and became The DOORS. They were released from a 'Columbia' recording contract, when ARTHUR LEE (of LOVE), recommended them to his 'Elektra' label boss Jac Holzman. Early in 1967, their eponymous debut album was issued, which soon climbed to US No.2 after an edited version of 'LIGHT MY FIRE' hit No.1 in July '67. The single and album showcased MORRISON's overtly sexual vocal theatrics against a backdrop of organ-dominated, avant-garde blues. The classic debut also contained two cover versions (see below), the lucid psychedelia of 'THE CRYSTAL SHIP', plus the extremely disturbing 11-minute epic, 'THE END' (which was later used on the soundtrack for the 1979 Francis Ford Coppola film, 'Apocalypse Now'). While other bands of the era were into peace and love, The DOORS found their salvation in a much darker vision, again in evidence on the follow-up (also in '67), 'STRANGE DAYS'. This was another classic, tracks like, 'LOVE ME TWO TIMES', 'YOU'RE LOST LITTLE GIRL' and 'PEOPLE ARE STRANGE' further enhancing the band's powerful mystique. As MORRISON's drink and drugs antics became increasingly problematic, he was arrested many times (on stage and off), mostly for lewd simulation of sexual acts and indecent exposure. Nevertheless, in the late summer of '68, they found themselves at the top of the US charts again with the 45, 'HELLO I LOVE YOU' and the album, 'WAITING FOR THE SUN'. A disappointing 4th album, 'THE SOFT PARADE' (1969), did, however, contain a classic US Top 3 hit, 'TOUCH ME'. More controversy was generated, when, in November '69, MORRISON was accused of interfering with an airline stewardess while a flight was in progress. He was later acquitted, but the following year, was given eights months hard labour after being found guilty of indecent exposure and profanity. He was freed on appeal and began work on 1970's, 'MORRISON HOTEL / HARD ROCK CAFE', a return to rawer, more basic rock'n'roll. After the recording of 'L.A. WOMAN', he relocated to Paris in the Spring of '71 with his girlfriend Pamela, amid rumours of an imminent split from the group. The aforementioned album was delivered in June, a masterpiece that carried on the re-evaluation of their blues roots. His over-indulgence in drugs and booze, had given his vocal chords a deeper resonance, showcased on such classics as, 'RIDERS ON THE STORM' (a Top 30 hit), 'LOVE HER MADLY', the JOHN LEE HOOKER cover 'CRAWLING KING SNAKE' and the freewheeling title track. Ironically, just as the band seemed to have found their feet again, JIM MORRISON was found dead in his bathtub on the 3rd of July 1971. Speculation was rife at the time, but it later became apparent he had died from a drugs/drink induced heart attack. He was also buried in Paris, his grave becoming a shrine to all but his parents, who disowned him in 1967. The others continued as a trio for the next two years, but sadly the public refused to acknowledge them as the real DOORS. The "god-like" cult of MORRISON has mushroomed to incredible proportions in the years following his death, rumours continuing, Elvis-like, to circulate that he is still alive. There have been many imitators over the last quarter of a century, although none have matched his/their dark majesty. • **Songwriters:** MORRISON – words/poetry (under the influence of explorative narcotics), Group/MANZAREK compositions. Covered; ALABAMA SONG (Brecht-Weill) / BACK DOOR MAN (Howlin' Wolf) / WHO DO YOU LOVE (Bo Diddley) / LITTLE RED ROOSTER (Willie Dixon) / BEEN DOWN SO LONG (J.B. Lenoir). • **Trivia:** In 1968, they featured on a UK TV documentary 'The Doors Are Open', which was later issued on video. In 1991, Oliver Stone released a feature film 'THE DOORS', with Val Kilmer playing the role of MORRISON.

Recommended: THE DOORS (*9) / STRANGE DAYS (*8) / WAITING FOR THE SUN (*6) / THE SOFT PARADE (*5) / MORRISON HOTEL (*8) / ABSOLUTELY LIVE (*6) / L.A. WOMAN (*9) / WEIRD SCENES INSIDE THE GOLDMINE (*8) / BEST OF THE DOORS (*8)

JIM MORRISON (b. 8 Dec'43, Melbourne, Florida) – vocals / **RAY MANZAREK** (b.12 Feb'35, Chicago, Illinois) – keyboards, bass pedal / **ROBBY KRIEGER** (b. 8 Jan'46) – guitar / **JOHN DENSMORE** (b. 1 Dec'45) – drums / also guest **DOUG LUBAHN** – bass (of CLEAR LIGHT)

Elektra Elektra

Feb 67. (7") *(EKSN 45009) <45611>* **BREAK ON THROUGH (TO THE OTHER SIDE). / END OF THE NIGHT** Jan67

Mar 67. (lp; mono/stereo) *<(EKL/EKS 74007)>* **THE DOORS** 1 Mar 67

Lizard King

– Break on through (to the other side) / Soul kitchen / The crystal ship / Twentieth century fox / Alabama song (whiskey song) / Light my fire / Back door man / I looked at you / End of the night / Take it as it comes / The end. *(re-iss.Nov71 lp/c; K/K4 42012) (cd-iss.Jan84; K2 42012) (re-iss.cd Feb89; 974007-2) (re-hit UK No.43 in Apr91)*

Apr 67. (7") *(EKSN 45012)* **ALABAMA SONG (WHISKEY BAR). / TAKE IT AS IT COMES** [ ] [-]

Jul 67. (7") *(EKSN 45014) <45615>* **LIGHT MY FIRE (edit). / THE CRYSTAL SHIP** [49] [1] Jun67
(re-iss.Jul71; same)

Sep 67. (7") *(EKSN 45017) <45621>* **PEOPLE ARE STRANGE. / UNHAPPY GIRL** [ ] [12]

Dec 67. (lp; mono/stereo) *<(EKL/EKS 74014)>* **STRANGE DAYS** [ ] [3] Nov67
– Strange days / You're lost little girl / Love me two times / Unhappy girl / Horse latitudes / Moonlight drive / People are strange / My eyes have seen you / I can't see your face in my mind / When the music's over. *(re-iss.Nov71 lp/c; K/K4 42016) (cd-iss.Jan86; K2 42016) (cd re-iss.Feb89; 974014-2)*

Dec 67. (7") *(EKSN 45022) <45624>* **LOVE ME TWO TIMES. / MOONLIGHT DRIVE** [ ] [25]

Apr 68. (7") *(EKSN 45030) <45628>* **THE UNKNOWN SOLDIER. / WE COULD BE SO GOOD TOGETHER** [ ] [39] Mar68
(re-iss.Jun71; K 12004)

Aug 68. (7") *(EKSN 45037) <45635>* **HELLO, I LOVE YOU. / LOVE STREET** [15] [1] Jul68

— **LEROY VINEGAR** – acoustic bass repl. LABAHN

Sep 68. (lp; mono/stereo) *<(EKL/EKS 74024)>* **WAITING FOR THE SUN** [16] [1] Aug68
– Hello I love you / Love street / Not to touch the Earth / Summer's almost gone / Wintertime love / The unknown soldier / Spanish caravan / My wild love / We could be so good together / Yes, the river flows / Five to one. *(re-iss.Nov71 lp/c; K/K4 42041) (cd-iss.Jan86; K2 42041) (cd re-iss.Feb89; 974024-2)*

Dec 68. (7") *(EKSN 45050) <45646>* **TOUCH ME. / WILD CHILD** [ ] [3]

May 69. (7") *(EKSN 45059) <45656>* **WISHFUL SINFUL. / WHO SCARED YOU** [ ] [44] Mar69

Aug 69. (7") *(EKSN 45065) <45663>* **TELL ALL THE PEOPLE. / EASY RIDE** [ ] [57] Jun69

Sep 69. (lp) *<(EKS 75005)>* **THE SOFT PARADE** [ ] [6] Aug69
– Tell all the people / Touch me / Shaman's blues / Do it / Easy ride / Wild child / Runnin' blue / Wishful sinful / The soft parade. *(re-iss.Nov71 lp/c; K/K4 42079) (cd-iss.Feb89; 975005-2)*

Sep 69. (7") *<45675>* **RUNNIN' BLUE. / DO IT** [-] [64]

— guest **LONNIE MACK** – bass repl. LUBAHN

Apr 70. (7") *<45685>* **YOU MAKE ME REAL. / ROADHOUSE BLUES** [-] [50]

Apr 70. (7") *(2101 004)* **YOU MAKE ME REAL. / THE SPY** [ ] [-]

Apr 70. (lp) *<(EKS 75007)>* **MORRISON HOTEL / HARD ROCK CAFE** [12] [4] Mar70
– Land ho! / The spy / Queen of the highway / Indian summer / Maggie McGill / Roadhouse blues / Waiting for the sun / You make me real / Peace frog / Blue Sunday / Ship of fools. *(re-iss.Nov71 lp/c; K/K4 42080) (cd-iss.Apr86; K2 42080) (re-iss.cd.Feb89; 975007-2)*

Jul 70. (7") *(2101 008)* **ROADHOUSE BLUES. / BLUE SUNDAY** [ ] [-]

Sep 70. (d-lp) *(2665 002) <9002>* **ABSOLUTELY LIVE (live)** [69] [8] Aug70
– Who do you love medley: Alabama song – Back door man – Love hides – Five to one / Build me a woman / When the music's over / Close to you / Universal mind / Break on through (to the other side) / The celebration of the lizard / Soul kitchen. *(re-iss.Nov71 d-lp; K 62005) (d-cd-iss.Mar87 w-drawn; 2665 002)*

Oct 70. (7") *<45708>* **UNIVERSAL MIND. / THE ICEWAGON FLEW** [-] [ ]

Mar 71. (lp/c) *(K/K4 42062) <74079>* **13** (compilation) [ ] [25] Dec70
– Light my fire / People are strange / Back door man / Moonlight drive / The crystal ship / Roadhouse blues / Touch me / Love me two times / You're lost little girl / Hello, I love you / Land ho / Wild child / The unknown soldier.

— guest **JERRY SCHEFF** – bass repl. MACK

May 71. (7") *<(EK 45726)>* **LOVE HER MADLY. / (YOU NEED MEAT) DON'T GO NO FURTHER** [ ] [11] Apr71

Jun 71. (lp/c) *(K/K4 42090) <75011>* **L.A. WOMAN** [26] [9] May71
– The changeling / Love her madly / Been down so long / Cars hiss by my window / L.A. woman / L'America / Hyacinth house / Crawling King Snake / The wasp (Texas radio and the big beat) / Riders on the storm. *(cd-iss.1984; K2 42090) (cd re-iss.Feb89 & Apr91; 975011-2)*

Jul 71. (7") *(K 12021) <45738>* **RIDERS ON THE STORM (edit). / THE CHANGELING** [22] [14]

— **RAY** – vocals, ROBBIE and JOHN carried on when JIM MORRISON died 3rd Jul'71 of a mysterious heart attack. The trio continued (MANZAREK now on vox). Used guest session bassmen **WILLIE RUFF, WOLFGANG MERTZ** and **JACK CONRAD**

Nov 71. (7") *(K 12036) <45757>* **TIGHTROPE RIDE. / VARIETY IS THE SPICE OF LIFE** [ ] [71]

Dec 71. (lp/c) *(K/K4 42104) <75017>* **OTHER VOICES** [ ] [31] Nov71
– In the eye of the sun / Variety is the spice of life / Ships w.sails / Tightrope ride / Down on the farm / I'm horny, I'm stoned / Wandering musician / Hang on to your life

May 72. (7") *(K 12048) <45768>* **SHIP W. SAILS. / IN THE EYE OF THE SUN** [ ] [ ]

— bass sessions **J. CONRAD, CHARLES LARKEY, LEE SKLAR and CHRIS ETHRIDGE.**

Aug 72. (7") *(K 12059) <45793>* **GET UP AND DANCE. / TREETRUNK** [ ] [ ]

Aug 72. (lp/c) *(K/K4 42116) <75038>* **FULL CIRCLE** [ ] [68]
– Get up and dance / Four billion souls / Verdilac / Hardwood floor / Good rockin' / The mosquito / The piano bird / It slipped my mind / The Peking king and the New York queen.

Sep 72. (7") *<45807>* **THE MOSQUITO. / IT SLIPPED MY MIND** [-] [85]

Dec 72. (7"w-drawn) **THE PIANO BIRD. / GOOD ROCKIN'** [-] [-]

— They finally split 1973. MANZAREK went solo and KRIEGER & DENSMORE formed The BUTTS BAND. With JESS RODEN as lead singer / **PHILIP CHEN** – bass / **ROY DAVIS** – keyboards, they made 2 albums for ~'Blue Thumb' records; 'THE BUTTS BAND' (1974) / 'HEAR AND NOW' (1975).

– compilations, etc. –

Note; All on 'Elektra' until mentioned otherwise

Mar 72. (d-lp/d-c) *(K/K4 62009) <6001>* **WEIRD SCENES INSIDE THE GOLD MINE** [50] [55] Feb72
– Break on through (to the other side) / Strange days / Shaman's blues / Love street / Peace frog / Blue Sunday / The wasp (Texas radio and the big beat) / End of the night / Love her madly / Ship of fools / The spy / The end / Take it as it comes / Running blue / L.A. woman / Five to one / Who scared you? / Don't go no further / Riders on the storm / Maggie McGill / Horse latitudes / When the music's over.

Sep 74. (lp/c) *(K/K4 42143) <5035>* **THE BEST OF THE DOORS** [ ] [ ]

Feb 76. (7") *(K 12203)* **RIDERS ON THE STORM. / L.A. WOMAN** [33] [-]

Sep 76. (7") *(K 12227)* **LIGHT MY FIRE. / THE UNKNOWN SOLDIER** [ ] [-]

Sep 76. (7") *(K 12228)* **LOVE HER MADLY. / TOUCH ME** [ ] [-]

Nov 78. (lp/c; by JIM MORRISON) *(K/K4 52111) <502>* **AN AMERICAN PRAYER** (poetry recorded 8 Nov'70 with some DOORS tapes) [ ] [54]
– Awake / Ghost song / Dawn's highway / Newborn awakening / To come of age / Black polished chrome / Latino chrome / Angels and sailors / Stoned immaculate / The poet's dreams / The movie / Curses invocations / World on fire / American night / Roadhouse blues / Lament / The hitchhiker / An American prayer. *(re-iss.May95 cd/c/lp;)*

Jan 79. (7") *(K 12215)* **LOVE ME TWO TIMES. / HELLO I LOVE YOU** [ ] [-]
(w/ free 7"+=) *(SAM 94)* – GHOST SONG. / ROADHOUSE BLUES

Jan 79. (7") **ROADHOUSE BLUES. / AN AMERICAN PRAYER** [-] [ ]

Jan 80. (7")<12"> *(K 12400) <ELK 22032>* **THE END. / (b-side 'Delta' not by The DOORS)** [ ] [-]

Oct 80. (lp/c) *(K/K4 52254) <515>* **GREATEST HITS** [ ] [17]
– Hello, I love you / Light my fire / People are strange / Love me two times / Riders on the storm / Break on through / Roadhouse blues / Touch me / L.A. woman / Love her madly / The ghost song / The end. *(cd-iss.Oct95 cd/c; 7559 61860-2/-4)*

Oct 80. (7") **PEOPLE ARE STRANGE. / NOT TO TOUCH THE EARTH** [-] [ ]

Oct 82. (d-c) *(K4 62034)* **MORRISON HOTEL / L.A. WOMAN** [ ] [-]

Oct 83. (7") *<60269>* **GLORIA (live). / MOONLIGHT DRIVE (live)** [-] [71]

Oct 83. (12") *(E 9774T)* **GLORIA (live). / LOVE ME TWO TIMES (live)** [ ] [-]

Oct 83. (lp/c) *(960269-1/-4) <60269>* **ALIVE SHE CRIED (live)** [36] [23]
– Gloria / Light my fire / You make me real / The wasp (Texas radio and the big beat) / Love me two times / Little red rooster / Moonlight drive. *(cd-iss.Jul84; 960269-2)*

Aug 84. (d-c) *(K4 62040)* **THE SOFT PARADE / AN AMERICAN PRAYER** [ ] [ ]

Jun 85. (lp/c) *(EKT 9/+C) <60417>* **CLASSICS** [ ] [ ]

Sep 85. (7") *Old Gold; (OG 9520)* **RIDERS ON THE STORM. / LIGHT MY FIRE** [ ] [-]

Nov 85. (d-lp/c/cd) *(EKT 21/+C/CD) <60345>* **BEST OF THE DOORS** [ ] [ ]
– Break on through (to the other side) / Light my fire / The crystal ship / People are strange / Strange days / Love me two times / Five to one / Waiting for the Sun / Spanish caravan / When the music's over / Hello, I love you / Roadhouse blues / L.A. woman / Riders on the storm / Touch me / Love her madly / The unknown soldier / The end. (cd+=) – Alabama song (whiskey bar). *(re-iss.Apr91 hit UK No.17 & US No.32)*

Jun 87. (m-lp/c)(cd) *(EKT 40/+C)(960741-2) <60741>* **LIVE AT THE HOLLYWOOD BOWL (live)** [ ] [ ]
– Wake up / Light my fire / The unknown soldier / A little game / The hill dwellers / Spanish caravan.

Mar 91. (lp/c)(cd) *(EKT 85/+C)(961047) <61047>* **THE DOORS: A FILM BY OLIVER STONE - MUSIC FROM THE ORIGINAL SOUNDTRACK** [11] [8]

Apr 91. (7") *(EKR 121)* **BREAK ON THROUGH. / LOVE STREET** [64] [ ]
(12"+=/cd-s+=) *(EKR 125 TW/CD)* – Hello I love you / Touch me.

May 91. (7") *(EKR 125)* **LIGHT MY FIRE. / PEOPLE ARE STRANGE** [7] [ ]
(ext; 12"+=/cd-s+=) *(EKR 125 TW/CD)* – Soul kitchen.

May 91. (t-lp/d-c)(d-cd) *(EKT 88/+C)(7559 61082) <61082>* **THE DOORS: IN CONCERT (live)** [24] [50]

Jul 91. (7") *(EKR 131)* **RIDERS ON THE STORM. / LOVE ME TWO TIMES (live)** [68] [ ]
(12"+=/cd-s+=) *(EKR 131 TW/CD)* – Roadhouse blues (live).

Jun 95. (c-s; by JIM MORRISON & THE DOORS) *(EKR 205C)* **THE GHOST SONG. / (interview)** [ ] [ ]
(cd-s+=) *(EKR 205CD)* – Love me two times (live) / Roadhouse blues (live).

Bob DOWNES

Born: London, England. A virtuoso flautist, his first record 'ELECTRIC CITY' was released by progressive label 'Vertigo' in 1970. It was a pleasurable listen, shifting between progressive rock and avant-garde jazz. His next work, 'DEEP DOWN HEAVY' (also in 1970), turned up on the cheapo 'Music For Pleasure' label, surprisingly well-received in view of its combined music and poetry (the latter being provided by ROBERT COCKBURN). The track 'POPLAR CHEAM' was a nifty example, with references to more than forty London underground stations in its verse. DOWNES recorded another album, 'OPEN MUSIC' (worth now over £75), before he set up his own 'Ophenian' label. He also went on to compose for the ballet 'Rambert', later moving to the continent at the end of the 80's.

Recommended: ELECTRIC CITY (*6) / DEEP DOWN HEAVY (*6) / BOB DOWNES' OPEN MUSIC (*6)

BOB DOWNES – vocals, flute, saxophones / with a plethora of musicians on first including NUCLEUS the band

Vertigo — not issued

Mar 70. (lp) *(6360 005)* **ELECTRIC CITY** [ ] [-]
– No time like the present / Keep off the grass / Don't let tomorrow get you down / Dawn until dawn / Go find time / Walking on / Crush hour / West 2 / In your eyes / Piccadilly circles / Gonna take a journey. *(cd-iss.1994 on 'Repertoire'; REP 4451-WP)*

Sep 70. (7") *(6059 011)* **NO TIME LIKE THE PRESENT. / KEEP OFF THE GRASS**

— on next now with poet **ROBERT COCKBURN** – poetry

Music For Pleasure / not issued

Oct 70. (lp) *(MFP 1412)* **DEEP DOWN HEAVY**

Philips / not issued

Feb 71. (lp) *<SBL 7922>* **BOB DOWNES' OPEN MUSIC**
– Dream journey / Birth of a forest / Integration / Contact / Ghosts in space / Desert haze / Electric city.

Ophenian / not issued

Jan 74. (lp) *(BDOM 001)* **DIVERSIONS**
Nov 74. (lp) *(BDOM 002)* **EPISODES AT 4 A.M.**
Oct 75. (lp) *(BDOM 003)* **HELLS ANGELS**

— as said, worked with the ballet 'Rambert'.

DOWNLINERS SECT

Formed: Twickenham, London, England ... 1963 initially as The DOWNLINERS by DON CRAINE, who met various musicians from R&B clubs around London, gaining a residency at the Studio 51 club. They recorded a rare and now very collectable EP 'A NITE AT GT. NEWPORT STREET'm which captured their raw R&B sound. Signed to 'Columbia' soon after, and debuted with a brazen version of JIMMY REED's 'BABY WHAT'S WRONG'. Their follow-up 'LITTLE EGYPT' (from The COASTERS) was another to flop, although it hit No.1 in Sweden! CRAINE's everpresent deer-stalker hat, was a turn-off for the younger UK audiences on a diet of beat, mod & R&B. So too was their 'COUNTRY SECT' album of 1965, confusing most in its diverse experimental country and folk overtones. Members also came and went very quickly, leaving CRAINE to abandon Britain for Sweden in 1968, where he recorded jukebox 45's 'SPIDER', 'LORD OF THE RING' & EP 'WHITE CATERPILLAR'. In 1976, CRAINE and mainstay KEITH GRANT re-formed the band and on the crest of a pub-rock/punk 1976/77, they had an indie hit on 'Raw' records; 'SHOWBIZ'. CRAINE was still going strong in the early 90's, with The BRITISH INVASION ALL-STARS after nearly 30 years in the business. • **Songwriters:** CRAINE except other covers GREEN ONIONS (Booker T & The MG's) / TOO MUCH MONKEY BUSINESS (Chuck Berry) / COPS AND ROBBERS (Bo Diddley) / DON'T LIE TO ME (Fats Domino) / MAY THE BIRD OF PARADISE FLY UP YOUR NOSE (Jimmy Dickens) / LITTLE EGYPT (Coasters) / WHY DON'T YOU LOVE ME (Lou Reed-John Cale) / etc.

Recommended: THE DEFINITIVE DOWNLINERS SECT – SINGLES A's & B's (*6)

DON CRAINE – vocals, rhythm guitar / **TERRY GIBSON** – lead guitar / **KEITH GRANT** – vocals, bass / **JOHNNY SUTTON** – drums

Contrast Sound / not issued

Jan 64. (7"ep) *(RBCSP 001)* **NITE IN GT. NEWPORT STREET**

— added **RAY STONE** – harmonica

Columbia / Smash

Jun 64. (7") *(DB 7300)* **BABY WHAT'S WRONG. / BE A SECT MANIAC**
Sep 64. (7") *(DB 7347) <1954>* **LITTLE EGYPT. / SECT APPEAL**
(re-iss.Dec76 on 'Charly'; CYS 1020)
Nov 64. (7") *(DB 7415)* **FIND OUT WHAT'S HAPPENING. / INSECTICIDE**
Dec 64. (lp) *(33SX 1658)* **THE SECT**
– Hurt by love / One ugly child / Lonely and blue / Our little rendezvous / Guitar boogie / Too much monkey business / Sect appeal / Baby what's on your mind / Cops and robbers / Easy rider / Bloodhound / Bright lights / I wanna put a tiger in your tank / Be a sect maniac. *(re-iss.Apr77 on 'Charly'; CR 30122)*
Mar 65. (7") *(DB 7509)* **WRECK OF THE OLD '97. / LEADER OF THE SECT**
Jun 65. (7") *(DB 7597)* **I GOT MINE. / WAITING IN HEAVEN SOMEWHERE**
Jul 65. (lp) *(33SX 1745)* **THE COUNTRY SECT**
– If I could just go back / Rocks in my bed / Ballad of the hounds / Little play soldiers / Hard travellin' / Wait for the light to shine / I got mine / Waiting in Heaven / Above and beyond / Bad storm coming / Midnight special / Wolverton mountain. *(re-iss.Nov77 on 'Charly'; CR 30137)*
Jul 65. (7"ep) *(SEG 8438)* **THE SECT SING SICK SONGS**
– I want my baby back / Leader of the sect / Midnight hour / Now she's dead.
Oct 65. (7") *(DB 7712)* **BAD STORM COMING. / LONELY AND BLUE**
Jan 66. (7") *(DB 7817)* **ALL NIGHT WORKER. / HE WAS A SQUARE**

— without STONE

Apr 66. (lp) *(SCX 6028)* **THE ROCK SECT'S IN**
– Hang on Sloopy / Fortune teller / Hey hey hey hey / Everything I've got to give / Outside / I'm hooked on you / Comin' home baby / Why don't you smile now / Don't lie to me / May the bird of Paradise fly up your nose / He was a square / I'm looking for a woman / The rock sect's in again / Brand new Cadillac. *(re-iss.Jul78 on 'Charly'; CR 30140)*
Jun 66. (7") *(DB 7939)* **GLENDORA. / I'LL FIND OUT**

— now a duo of **CRAINE + GRANT**

Sep 66. (7") *(DB 8008)* **THE COST OF LIVING. / EVERYTHING I'VE GOT TO GIVE**

— **BOB TAYLOR** – lead guitar + **KEVIN FLANAGAN** – drums + **BARRY COOPER** – keyboards repl. GIBSON + SUTTON + brief member MATTHEW FISHER who joined PROCOL HARUM

Pye / not issued

Feb 67. (7"; DON CRAINE'S NEW DOWNLINERS SECT) *(7N 17261)* **I CAN'T GET AWAY FROM YOU. / ROSES**

— Disbanded in 1968. CRAINE formed duo FINNEGAN'S WAKE and later LOOSE END. Re-formed DOWNLINERS SECT in 1976.

— **CRAINE, GRANT, GIBSON / PAUL TILLER** – mouth harp, vocals / **PAUL HOLM** – drums

Raw / not issued

Nov 77. (7") *(RAW 10)* **SHOWBIZ. / KILLING ME**

Sky / not issued

Feb 80. (lp) *(SKY 301)* **SHOWBIZ** – German
– Showbiz / Let's ride / Break up / Frustration / Out of school / Playing my guitar / Richmond rhythm & blues / Looser ends / Wild time / Red hot mama / Blue coupe de ville / Mismanagement.

— Re-formed again in the mid 80's.

not issued / Inner Mystique

1985. (7") *<IM 5082>* **COLOR CODED RED. / YOU AIN'T DOING ME RIGHT**

— In 1990, CRAINE backed THEE HEADCOATS on EP 'THEE HEADCOATS SECT' on 'Hangman'; *(LYNCH 1EP)*. CRAINE + GRANT featured for BRITISH INVASION ALL-STARS on 1991 cd/c 'REGRESSION'; on 'Promised Land'; *(82152)*. In 1991 on same label 'UNITED' cd; *(246890)*.

— **CRAINE + GRANT** with **DEL DWYER** – guitar / **ALAN BROOKES** – drums

Promised Land / not issued

Sep 91. (cd/c) **SAVAGE RETURN**
– Bad girls looking for fun / Piccadilly run / Ain't I got you / Hard case / Midnight call / Pan American boogie / Eel Pie memories / Down the road apiece / Talkin' 'bout you / Studio 51 / Bad penny / Who do you love / Cadillac / Bye bye Johnny / Some say they do / Before you accuse me. *(re-iss.May94 on 'Kingdom'; CDKVL 9033)*

Carveyliner / not issued

Dec 91. (video-s) **BAD GIRLS. / MIDNIGHT CALL**

Hangman / not issued

1992. (lp) *(HANG 42UP)* **THE BIRTH OF SUAVE**
(cd-iss.Sep94; HOG 002)

– compilations, others

Sep 79. (7") *Lava; (LC 5649)* **CADILLAC. / ROLL OVER BEETHOVEN** – German
1983. (lp) *Line; (OLLP 5183AS)* **BE A SECT MANIAC**
May 87. (lp) *Decal; (LIK 10)* **CROSS SECTION**
(re-iss.Jan91 as 'LIVE' on 'Beat City'; BC 86003)
Apr 94. (cd) *See For Miles; (SEECD 398)* **THE DEFINITIVE DOWNLINERS SECT – SINGLES A'S & B'S**
(re-iss.May97; same)

Nick DRAKE

Born: 19 Jun'48, Burma. He moved to Britain in the mid 50's, first to Tamworth-in-Ardon then Stratford. Already a budding singer-songwriter by the time he reached Cambridge University, he was discovered playing a gig by ASHLEY HUTCHINGS of Fairport Convention, who, in turn, introduced him to Witchseason Productions head JOE BOYD. Bowled over by his talent, BOYD helped him sign to 'Island', who released debut album 'FIVE LEAVES LEFT' in '69. The album highlighted his precocious talent and painful sensitivity, the music possessing a remarkable maturity not in keeping with DRAKE's young years. The melancholic resonance of DRAKE's voice and his crystalline guitar playing were complimented by delicate string arrangements, the effect one of understated intensity. After moving to London, DRAKE recorded the classic 'BRYTER LAYTER' in 1970 with BOYD again producing a cast of musicians that included RICHARD THOMPSON and JOHN CALE. The album boasted a jazzier flavour which saw DRAKE in a slightly more positive frame of mind. Ironically, like its predecessor, the album failed to sell in any great quantity. Due to his crippling shyness, DRAKE found live work too difficult, passing up the opportunity to promote his music. He fell into a deep depression, no doubt frustrated at his lack of success and inability to do something about it. After a spell in Europe he returned to record his tortured masterpiece, 'PINK MOON'. Recorded in just two nights, its spare, haunting songs were cloaked in regret and dissillusionment. The bleak tone only let up occasionally as DRAKE attemted to exorcise his demons over a skeletal acoustic backing. Once again, the album was a commercial failure and DRAKE's mood blackened further, although he did begin work on a new album in 1973. He spent time in France with singer/friend FRANCOISE HARDY and his bouts of depression diminished when he decided to live there permanently. However, this didn't last long and he sadly overdosed on anti-depressants on 25th November 1974, a tragic end to a troubled but brilliant career. A questionable coroner's verdict was "Death By Suicide". The subsequent interest in DRAKE's work led to various compilations being released, including the excellent 'FRUIT TREE' boxed set. His music entrances more listeners with each passing year, a belated recognition that recently saw him grace the cover of 'Mojo' magazine. • **Trivia:** His sister Gabrielle was a semi-successful TV actress in the 70's/80's 'Crossroads' soap.

Recommended: FIVE LEAVES LEFT (*8) / BRYTER LAYTER (*9) / FIVE LEAVES LEFT (*8) / PINK MOON (*8)

NICK DRAKE – vocals, guitar, piano with **RICHARD THOMPSON** – guitar / **DANNY THOMPSON** – double bass / **PAUL HARRIS** – keyboards / **CLAIRE LOWTHER** and **ROCKY DZIDZORNU**, plus 15-piece orchestra.

Island / Antilles

Sep 69. (lp) *(ILPS 9105) <AN 7010>* **FIVE LEAVES LEFT**
– Time has told me / River man / Three hours / Day is done / Way to blue / Cello song / The thoughts of Mary Jane / Man in a shed / Fruit tree / Saturday sun. *(cd-*

iss.Feb87; CID 9195) (re-iss.cd May89; IMCD 8)

— retained **RICHARD** bringing in other (FAIRPORT CONVENTION members: **DAVE PEGG** – drums / **DAVE MATTACKS** – bass. Also sessioned **PAUL HARRIS, RAY WARLEIGH, CHRIS McGREGOR.**

Nov 70. (lp) *(ILPS 9134) <7028>* **BRYTER LAYTER** ☐ ☐
– Introduction / Hazey Jane II / At the chime of a city clock / One of these things first / Hazey Jane I / Bryter layter / Fly / Poor boy / Northern sky / Sunday. *(cd-iss.May87; CID 9134) (re-iss.cd Oct89; IMCD 71)*

— **NICK DRAKE** – vocals, guitar (totally solo)

Feb 72. (lp) *(ILPS 9184)* **PINK MOON** ☐ -
– Pink moon / Place to be / Road / Which will / Horn / Things behind the sun / Know / Parasite / Ride / Harvest breed / From the morning / Voice from the mountain / Rider on the wheel / Black eyed dog / Hanging on a star. *(cd-iss.Apr90; IMCD 94)*

— He had put down some tracks for new album, when on 25th Nov'74, he overdosed on medication/drugs.

– compilations, others, etc. –

1972. (lp) *Island; <9307>* **NICK DRAKE** (69-70 material) - ☐
Apr 79. (3xlp-box) *Island; (NDSP 100)* **FRUIT TREE – THE COMPLETE RECORDED WORKS** ☐ -
– (contains all 3 albums)
May 85. (lp/c) *Island; (ILPS 9826)* **HEAVEN IN A WILD FLOWER** ☐ ☐
(cd-iss.Apr90; IMCD 91)
Aug 86. (4xlp-box) *Hannibal / Rykodisc; (HNBX 5302)* **FRUIT TREE** ☐ ☐
– (all 3 lp's, plus 1987 album) *(4xcd-box-iss.Dec91; HNCD 5402)(+=)*– TIME OF NO REPLY / Fruit tree / Fly / Man in a shed / Thoughts of Mary Jane.
Mar 87. (lp/cd) *Hannibal / Rykodisc; (HN BL/CD 1318)* **TIME OF NO REPLY** ☐ ☐
Jun 94. (cd)(c/lp) *Island; (IMCD 196)(ICM/ILPM 2082)* **WAY TO BLUE – AN INTRODUCTION TO NICK DRAKE** ☐ ☐

DREAM POLICE

Formed: Glasgow, Scotland . . . 1969 by DAVE BATCHELOR, TED McKENNA, ONNIE McINTYRE and HAMISH STUART. They were recommended to 'Decca' by JUNIOR CAMPBELL (ex-MARMALADE), their debut in 1970, 'I'LL BE HOME', a mixture of orchestrated post quasi-psychedelia. The flip-side, 'LIVING IS EASY', in contrast, had more of a progressive feel. It sold poorly, as did their follow-up, 'OUR SONG'. For their third that year, 'I'VE GOT NO CHOICE', they chose to follow a more country-rock direction, a decision which split the band in two (see below).

Recommended: no albums, but first 45 worth searching out

DAVE BATCHELOR – vocals / **TED McKENNA** – keyboards / **ONNIE McINTYRE** – guitar, vocals / **HAMISH STUART** – guitar, vocals

Decca / Parrot
Mar 70. (7") *(F 12998) <3024>* **I'LL BE HOME. / LIVING IS EASY** ☐ ☐
Sep 70. (7") *(F 13079)* **OUR SONG. / MUCH TOO MUCH** ☐ -
Nov 70. (7") *(F 13105)* **I'VE GOT NO CHOICE. / WHAT'S THE CURE FOR HAPPINESS** ☐ -

— turned in their badges, when BATCHELOR and McKENNA joined TEAR GAS. They were soon to join The SENSATIONAL ALEX HARVEY BAND, BATCHELOR only as producer. They were replaced by JOE BREEN and MATT IRVING, who were later involved in session work, BREEN solo and IRVING for PAUL YOUNG. McINTYRE and STUART formed The AVERAGE WHITE BAND, the latter moving onto PAUL McCARTNEY in the 80's.

DR. STRANGELY STRANGE

Formed: Ireland . . .1969 by trio of TIM GOULDING, TIM BOOTH and TIM PAWLE. Signed to the progressive 'Island' label, they introduced themselves with the JOE BOYD-produced album, 'KIP OF THE SERENES'. Its individually composed songs drew comparisons to The INCREDIBLE STRING BAND, and showed an eerie beauty, encapsulated on the psychedelic track, 'STRANGELY STRANGE BUT ODDLY NORMAL' (also included on the label's compilation, 'Nice Enough To Eat'). In 1970, a second album, 'HEAVY PETTING', appeared. Released on 'Vertigo', it featured a very young GARY MOORE on guitar and rock drumming by DAVE MATTACKS. Folk man ANDY IRVINE (from SWEENEY'S MEN) also played mandolin on what was described as a more confident set.

Recommended: KIP OF THE SERENES (*6)

IVAN PAWLE – vocals, bass, fiddle, percussion / **TIM GOULDING** – vocals, keyboards, harmonica, recorder, violin / **TIM BOOTH** – vocals, guitar, mandolin, percussion / augmented on all by **LINUS** – percussion, vocals / **JAY MYRDAL** – glockenspiel

Island / not issued
Aug 69. (lp) *(ILPS 9106)* **KIP OF THE SERENES** ☐ -
– Strangely strange but oddly normal / Dr. Dim & Dr. Strange / Roy Rogers / Dark-haired lady / On the west cork hack / A tale of two orphanages / Strings in the earth and air / Ship of fools / Frosty mornings / Donnybrook Fair.

— added guests **GARY MOORE** – guitar / **DAVE MATTACKS** – drums, percussion / **BRENDAN SHIELS** – bass / **ANDY IRVINE** – mandolin / **HEATHER WOODS** – vocals / etc.

Vertigo / not issued
Oct 70. (lp) *(6360 009)* **HEAVY PETTING** ☐ -
– Ballad of the wasps / Summer breeze / Kilmanoyadd stomp / I will lift up my eyes / Sign of the mind / Gave my love an apple / Jove was at home / When Adam delved / Ashling / Mary Malone of Moscow / Friends. *(re-iss.1986 on 'Frizzbee' Dutch; 5) (cd-iss.Nov92 on 'Repertoire'; REP 4273)*

— the trio were to be guests on MIKE HERON's 'Smiling Men' album, while previous to this IVAN featured on INCREDIBLE STRING BAND's 'Changing Horses'.

DRUID

Formed: England . . .. 1974 by DANE, ANDREW McCRORIE-SHAND, NEIL BREWER and CEDRIC SHARPLEY. An unusual bunch, they delivered progressive pop in a recycled style that was more YES than even YES themselves. Their mainly group-penned compositions found their way onto their debut 'TOWARD THE SUN' album in 1975. However, it was lambasted for its unfashionable self-indulgence. The follow-up was frankly forgettable and thankfully, the band returned to their day jobs.

Recommended: TOWARD THE SUN (*5)

DANE – guitar, vocals / **ANDREW McCRORIE-SHAND** – keyboards / **NEIL BREWER** – bass / **CEDRIC SHARPLEY** – drums, percussion

E.M.I. / not issued
1975. (lp) *(EMC 3081)* **TOWARD THE SUN** ☐ -
– Voices / Remembering / Theme / Toward the sun / Red carpet for an Autumn / Dawn of evening / Shangri-la.
1976. (lp) *(EMC 3128)* **FLUID** ☐ -
– Razor truth / Painters clouds / FM 145 / Nothing but morning / Crusade / Barnaby / Kestrel / Left to find / The fisherman's friend.

— disbanded after above.

DR. Z

Formed: North Wales, UK . . .1970 by professor KEITH KEYES. Under the moniker of DR.Z, he issued a very rare 45, 'LADY LADYBIRD'. Never having performed live, he and his cohorts finally released their debut album in 1971 for 'Vertigo'. It was recorded under the guidance of producer PATRICK CAMPBELL-LYONS (NIRVANA), to whom KEYES had initially sent a demo tape. The record's failure to sell more than 100 copies led it to becoming a much sought after collector's item, now worth nearly £200.

Recommended: 3 PARTS TO MY SOUL (*6)

KEITH KEYES – vocals, keyboards, harps

Fontana / not issued
Jul 70. (7") *(6007 023)* **LADY LADYBIRD. / PEOPLE IN THE STREET** ☐ -

— added guests **ROB WATSON** – bass / **BOB WATKINS** – drums, percussion

Vertigo / not issued
Nov 71. (lp) *(6360 048)* **3 PARTS TO MY SOUL – SPIRITUS MANES ET UMBRA** ☐ -
– Evil woman's manly child / Spiritus / Manes et umbra / Summer for the roses / Burn in anger / Too well satisfied / In a token of despair.

— KEYES faded without trace.

Bob DYLAN

Born: ROBERT ALLAN ZIMMERMAN, 24 May'41, Duluth, Minnesota, USA. In 1960 he left his local university, changing his name to BOB DYLAN. He also began a trek to New York where he played his first gig supporting JOHN LEE HOOKER on 11 April '61 at Gerde's Folk City. Soon after, he enjoyed harmonica session work for folk songstress Caroline Hester. Her employers 'Columbia' records, through John Hammond Snr., signed him in October '61. His eponymous debut album in 1962 gained sparse attention, although his live work created critical appraisal. In 1963 he unleashed 'THE FREEWHEELIN' BOB DYLAN', and after PETER, PAUL & MARY lifted a million seller from it, 'BLOWIN' IN THE WIND', the record gained enough respect to give him a US Top 30 album. The record also saw a pronounced development in DYLAN's songwriting dexterity on tracks like the cutting 'MASTERS OF WAR'. While his untrained, nasal vocals could be something of an acquired taste, they communicated the lyrics in a way that lent them greater depth and resonance. But DYLAN really hit his stride with 'THE TIMES THEY ARE A-CHANGIN' the following year, an album that represented his most pointed protest writing. On subsequent albums, DYLAN shied away from direct missives like 'WITH GOD ON OUR SIDE' and 'ONLY A PAWN IN THEIR GAME'. 'ANOTHER SIDE OF BOB DYLAN' (1964) was contrastingly personal in tone, 'I DON'T BELIEVE IN YOU' and 'IT AIN'T ME BABE' venting DYLAN's spleen on matters of the heart rather than the soapbox. The lyrics also began to assume an air of enigmatic suggestiveness, 'MY BACK PAGES' and 'CHIMES OF FREEDOM' boasting striking, lucid imagery which The BYRDS would later complement with their incandescent, chiming guitars and ringing harmonies. Influenced by the British R&B boom (especially The BEATLES), DYLAN stunned folk purists with the half electric/half acoustic 'BRINGING IT ALL BACK HOME' (1965). The newly plugged in DYLAN was a revelation and with the likes of the stream-of-consciousness 'SUBTERRANEAN HOMESICK BLUES', the album influenced in turn the bands DYLAN had taken his cue from. The acoustic tracks on the second side such as 'MR. TAMBOURINE MAN' and 'IT'S ALL OVER NOW BABY BLUE' rank among DYLAN's finest, the former giving The BYRDS their breakthrough hit. While the folk faithful dissed DYLAN at that summer's Newport Festival, he wowed the rock world with the masterful 'LIKE A ROLLING STONE' single and followed it up with the seminal 'HIGHWAY 61 REVISITED' (1965). A free flowing hybrid of blues, folk and R&B that used such esteemed musicians as AL KOOPER and PAUL BUTTERFIELD, rock music had never been graced with such complex, expansive lyrics. Backed by members of The HAWKS (who'd supported DYLAN on his recent tour and later become The BAND) and a posse of crack Nashville sessioneers, DYLAN recorded another rock milestone with 'BLONDE ON BLONDE' (1966). 'VISIONS OF JOHANNA' was DYLAN at his most lysergic, casting surreal lyrical spells with hypnotic ease. After a motorcycle accident that summer he sustained severe neck injuries and went in to semi-retirement, looking after his family and holing up in Woodstock with The BAND. These sessions eventually saw the light of day in 1975 as 'THE BASEMENT TAPES', a classic double album of experimental roots rock. Upon his return to the music scene, DYLAN's vocals were slightly altered and his music had taken a distinct turn towards country-rock on 'JOHN WESLEY HARDING' (1968). The following year's 'NASHVILLE SKYLINE' was stone country, even featuring a bittersweet duet with JOHNNY CASH. After a lean spell, DYLAN returned with two harder-edged rock classics, 'BLOOD ON THE TRACKS' (1975) and 'DESIRE' (1975), providing him with a much needed boost in credibility both with the critics and the buying public. From 1979 on through the 80's his work mellowed into more spiritual themes as a result of his new found Christianity. Only the DANIEL LANOIS produced 'OH MERCY' (1989) came close to capturing the magic of old, the outtakes/rarities compilations 'BIOGRAPH' (1985) and 'THE BOOTLEG SERIES' (1991) of more interest to DYLAN fans than much of his new material. • **Songwriters:** 99% DYLAN compositions except; HOUSE OF THE RISING SUN + IN MY TIME OF DYIN' (trad.) / TAKE A MESSAGE TO MARY (Everly Brothers) / THE BOXER (Simon & Garfunkel) / EARLY MORNIN' RAIN (Gordon Lightfoot) / A FOOL SUCH AS I + CAN'T HELP FALLING IN LOVE (hits; Elvis Presley) / BIG YELLOW TAXI (Joni Mitchell) / MR.BOJANGLES (Jerry Jeff Walker) / LET'S STICK TOGETHER (Wilbert Harrison) / SPANISH IS THE LOVING TONGUE + SHENANDOAH (trad.) / ANGELS FLYING TOO CLOSE TO THE GROUND (Willie Nelson) / etc. **Writing credits/hits:** BLOWIN' IN THE WIND + DON'T THINK TWICE, IT'S ALRIGHT (Peter, Paul & Mary; 1963) / ALL I REALLY WANT TO DO (Cher; 1965) / IT AIN'T ME BABE (Turtles; 1965) / MR. TAMBOURINE MAN + ALL I REALLY WANT TO DO + MY BACK PAGES (Byrds; 1965-1967) / IT'S ALL OVER NOW, BABY BLUE + FAREWELL ANGELINA (Joan Baez; 1965) / IF YOU GOTTA GO, GO NOW + JUST LIKE A WOMAN + MIGHTY QUINN (Manfred Mann; 1965/66/68) / TOO MUCH OF NOTHING (Peter, Paul & Mary; 1967) / THIS WHEEL'S ON FIRE (Julie Driscoll, Brian Auger & The Trinity; 1968) / ALL ALONG THE WATCHTOWER (Jimi Hendrix; 1968) / IF NOT FOR YOU (Olivia Newton-John; 1971) / A HARD RAIN'S A-GONNA FALL (Bryan Ferry; 1973) / KNOCKIN' ON HEAVEN'S DOOR (Eric Clapton; 1975 / Guns n' Roses; 1992) / I'LL BE YOUR BABY TONIGHT (UB40 & Robert Palmer; 1990) / & some minor hits. **Filmography:** DON'T LOOK BACK (1965 documentary) / EAT THE DOCUMENTARY (1971 docu-film) / PAT GARRETT & BILLY THE KID (1973) / RENALDO AND CLARA (1978) / HEARTS OF FIRE (1987). • **Trivia:** On the 22 Nov'65, BOB married Sara Lowndes, but she divorced him in 1977. (Band members in discography are selective)

Recommended: BOB DYLAN (*7) / THE FREEWHEELIN' BOB DYLAN (*9) / THE TIMES THEY ARE A-CHANGIN' (*7) / ANOTHER SIDE OF BOB DYLAN (*8) / BRINGING IT ALL BACK HOME (*9) / HIGHWAY 61 REVISITED (*10) / BLONDE ON BLONDE (*10) / GREATEST HITS (*10) / JOHN WESLEY HARDING (*6) / NASHVILLE SKYLINE (*6) / SELF PORTRAIT (*4) / NEW MORNING (*4) / MORE GREATEST HITS (*7) / PAT GARRETT AND BILLY THE KID (*5) / PLANET WAVES (*6) / BEFORE THE FLOOD (*7) / BLOOD ON THE TRACKS (*10) / DESIRE (*10) / THE BASEMENT TAPES (*9) / HARD RAIN (*6) / SLOW TRAIN COMING (*5) / STREET LEGAL onwards (see future edition of GREAT ROCK DISCOGRAPHY)

BOB DYLAN – vocals, guitar, harmonica

C.B.S. Columbia

Mar 62. (7") *<42656>* **MIXED UP CONFUSION. / CORRINA CORRINA** [-] [ ]

Jun 62. (lp; stereo/mono) *(S+/BPG 62022) <8579>* **BOB DYLAN** [ ] [ ] Mar62
– She's no good / Talkin' New York / In my time of dyin' / Man of constant sorrow / Fixin' to die blues / Pretty Peggy-o / Highway 51 blues / Gospel plow / Baby, let me follow you down / House of the risin' sun / Freight train blues / Song to Woody / See that grave is kept clean. *(re-dist.May65, hit No.13) (re-iss.Mar81 lp/c; CBS/40 32001) (cd-iss.Nov89; CD 32001)*

—— added musicians **HOWARD COLLINS** – guitar / **GEORGE BARNES** – bass / **HERB LOVELL** – drums / **LEONARD GASKIN** – bass / etc.

Nov 63. (lp; stereo/mono) *(S+/BPG 62193) <8786>* **THE FREEWHEELIN' BOB DYLAN** [16] [22] May63
– Blowin' in the wind / Girl from the North Country / Masters of war / Down the highway / Bob Dylan's blues / A hard rains a-gonna fall / Don't think twice, it's all right / Bob Dylan's dream / Oxford Town / / Talking World War III blues / Corrina, Corrina / Honey, just allow me one more chance / I shall be free. *(re-dist.Apr65, hit No.1) (re-iss.Mar81 lp/c; CBS/40 62193) (cd-iss.Nov89; 32390)*

Jan 64. (7") *<42856>* **BLOWIN' IN THE WIND. / DON'T THINK TWICE IT'S ALRIGHT** [-] [ ]

Jun 64. (lp; stereo/mono) *(S+/BPG 62251) <8905>* **THE TIMES THEY ARE A-CHANGIN'** [20] [20] Mar64
– The times they are a-changin' / Ballad of Hollis Brown / With God on our side / One too many mornings / North country blues / Only a pawn in their game / Boots of Spanish leather / When the ship comes in / The lonesome death of Hattie Carroll / Restless farewell. *(re-dist.Apr65, hit No.4) (re-iss.Mar81 lp/c; CBS/40 32021) (cd-iss.Nov89; CD 32021)*

Nov 64. (lp; stereo/mono) *(S+/BPG 62429) <8993>* **ANOTHER SIDE OF BOB DYLAN** [8] [43] Sep64
– All I really want to do / Black crow blues / Spanish Harlem incident / Chimes of freedom / I shall be free No.10 / To Ramona / Motorpsycho nitemare / I don't believe you / Ballad in plain D / It ain't me babe. *(re-iss.Mar81 lp/c; CBS/40 32034) (cd-iss.Nov89; CD 32034)*

Mar 65. (7") *(201751)* **THE TIMES THEY ARE A-CHANGIN'. / HONEY, JUST ALLOW ME ONE MORE CHANCE** [9] [-]
(re-iss.May82; 1751)

—— with **BOBBY GREGG** – drums / **JOHN SEBASTIAN** – bass / **BRUCE LANGHORNE** – guitar

Apr 65. (7") *(201753) <43242>* **SUBTERRANEAN HOMESICK BLUES. / SHE BELONGS TO ME** [9] [39] Mar65

May 65. (lp; stereo/mono) *(S+/BPG 62515) <9128>* **BRINGING IT ALL BACK HOME** [1] [6] Apr65
– Subterranean homesick blues / She belongs to me / Maggie's farm / Love minus zero – No limit / Outlaw blues / On the road again / Bob Dylan's 115th dream / Mr. Tambourine man / Gates of Eden / It's alright, ma (I'm only bleeding) / It's all over now, baby blue. *(re-iss.Jul83 lp/c; CBS/40 32344) (cd-iss.Jul87; CD 62515) (cd re-iss.Jul89 as 'SUBTERRANEAN HOMESICK BLUES'; CD 32344)*

Jun 65. (7") *(201781)* **MAGGIE'S FARM. / ON THE ROAD AGAIN** [22] [-]

—— now with **AL KOOPER** – organ / **PAUL BUTTERFIELD** – guitar / **PAUL GRIFFIN** – keyboards / **CHARLIE McCOY** – guitar / **RUSS SAVAKUS** – bass

Aug 65. (7") *(201811) <43346>* **LIKE A ROLLING STONE. / GATES OF EDEN** [4] [2] Jul65
(re-iss.May82; 1811)

Sep 65. (lp; stereo/mono) *(S+/BPG 62572) <9189>* **HIGHWAY 61 REVISITED** [4] [3]
– Like a rolling stone / Tombstone blues / It takes a lot to laugh, it takes a train to cry / From a Buick 6 / Ballad of a thin man / Queen Jane approximately / Highway 61 revisited / Just like Tom Thumb's blues / Desolation row. *(re-iss.Dec85 lp/c; CBS/40 62572) (cd-iss.Nov89; CD 62572)*

Oct 65. (7") *(201824) <43389>* **POSITIVELY 4th STREET. / FROM A BUICK 6** [8] [7] Sep65

Jan 66. (7") *(201900) <43477>* **CAN YOU PLEASE CRAWL OUT YOUR WINDOW? / HIGHWAY 61 REVISITED** [17] [58] Dec65

Apr 66. (7") *(202053) <43541>* **ONE OF US MUST KNOW (SOONER OR LATER). / QUEEN JANE APPROXIMATELY** [33] [ ] Feb66

—— Now augmented by members of The **BAND:- ROBBIE ROBERTSON** – guitar / **RICHARD MANUEL** – keyboards / **LEVON HELM** – drums / **RICK DANKO** – bass / **GARTH HUDSON** – keyboards plus also **KENNY BUTTREY** – drums

May 66. (7") *(202307) <43592>* **RAINY DAY WOMEN NOS.12 & 35. / PLEDGING MY TIME** [7] [2] Apr66

Jul 66. (7") *(202258) <43683>* **I WANT YOU. / JUST LIKE TOM THUMB'S BLUES (live)** [16] [20] Jun66

Aug 66. (d-lp; stereo/mono) *(S+/66012) <841>* **BLONDE ON BLONDE** [3] [9] Jul66
– Rainy day women Nos.12 & 35 / Pledging my love / Visions of Johanna / One of us must know (sooner or later) / Most likely you go your way (and I'll go mine) / Temporary like Achilles / Absolutely sweet Marie / 4th time around / Obviously 5 believers / I want you / Stuck inside of Mobile with the Memphis blues again / Leopard-skin pill-box hat / Just like a woman / Sad eyed lady of the lowlands. *(re-iss.May82 d-lp/d-c; CBS/40 22130) (d-cd-iss.Jul87; CD 66012) (d-cd re-iss.Jun89; CD 22130) (d-cd re-iss.Feb95; CK 64411)*

Sep 66. (7") *<43792>* **JUST LIKE A WOMAN. / OBVIOUSLY 5 BELIEVERS** [-] [33]

Jan 67. (lp; stereo/mono) *(S+/BPG 62847) <9463>* **BOB DYLAN'S GREATEST HITS** (compilation) <US diff.tracks> [6] [10] Apr67
– Blowin' in the wind / It ain't me babe / The times they are a-changin' / Mr. Tambourine man / She belongs to me / It's all over now, baby blue / Subterranean homesick blues / One of us must know (sooner or later) / Like a rolling stone / Just like a woman / Rainy day women Nos. 12 & 35. *(re-iss.Mar88; 460907) (cd-iss.Nov89; 450882-2) (re-iss.Feb91 & Apr97 on 'Columbia'; 460907-2) (re-iss.cd Oct94 as 'BEST OF . . .';)*

May 67. (7") *(202700) <44069>* **LEOPARD-SKIN PILL-BOX HAT. / MOST LIKELY YOU GO YOUR WAY (AND I'LL GO MINE)** [ ] [81]

—— now with **BUTTREY, McCOY** and **PETE DRAKE** – sitar, guitar

Feb 68. (lp; stereo/mono) *(S+/BPG 63252) <9604>* **JOHN WESLEY HARDING** [1] [2] Jan68
– John Wesley Harding / As I went out one morning / I dreamed I saw St. Augustine / All along the watchtower / The ballad of Frankie Lee and Judas Priest / Drifter's escape / Dear landlord / I am a lonesome hobo / I pity the poor immigrant / The wicked messenger / Down along the cove / I'll be your baby tonight. *(re-iss.Nov89 lp/c/cd; 463359-1/-4/-2)*

—— next featured **CHARLIE DANIELS** – bass, guitar / **etc.**

May 69. (7") *(4219) <44826>* **I THREW IT ALL AWAY. / DRIFTER'S ESCAPE** [30] [85]

May 69. (lp) *(63601) <9825>* **NASHVILLE SKYLINE** [1] [3] Apr69
– Girl from the North country (with JOHNNY CASH) / Nashville skyline rag / To be alone with you / I threw it all away / Pegy Day / Lady lady lay / One more night / Tell me that it isn't true / Country pie / Tonight I'll be staying here with you. *(re-iss.May87 lp/c; CBS/40 32675) (cd-iss.Jan86; CD 63601)*

Sep 69. (7") *(4434) <44926>* **LAY LADY LAY. / PEGGY DAY** [5] [7] Jul69

Dec 69. (7") *(4611) <45004>* **TONIGHT I'LL BE STAYING HERE WITH YOU. / COUNTRY PIE** [ ] [50] Oct69

Jul 70. (d-lp) *(66250) <30050>* **SELF PORTRAIT** [1] [4] Jun70
– All the tired horses / Alberta £1 / I forgot more than you'll ever know / Days of 49 / Early mornin' rain / In search of little Sadie / Let it be me / Little Sadie / Woogie boogie / Belle isle / Living the blues / Like a rolling stone (version) / Copper kettle (the pale moonlight) / Gotta travel on / Blue Moon / The boxer / The mighty Quinn (Quinn, the eskimo) / Take me as I am / Take a message to Mary / It hurts me too / Minstrel boy / She belongs to me / Wigwam / Alberta £2. *(re-iss.Sep87 d-lp/c; 460112-1/-4) (re-iss.Feb91 on 'Columbia' cd/c; 460112-2/-4)*

Jul 70. (7") *(5122) <45199>* **WIGWAM. / COPPER KETTLE (THE PALE MOONLIGHT)** [ ] [41]

Nov 70. (lp) *(69001) <30290>* **NEW MORNING** [1] [7]
– If not for you / Day of the locusts / Time passes slowly / Went to see the gypsy / Winterlude / If dogs ran free / New morning / Sign on the window / One more weekend / The man in me / Three angels / Father of the night. *(re-iss.Sep83 lp/c;*

Ain't it just like the night to play tricks when you're
trying to be so quiet - Lights flicker from the opposite loft
Just Louise and her lover so entwined - and these visions
of Johanna they conquer my mind But she just makes it
all so concise and clear - that Johanna's not here - THE
GHOST OF ELECTRICITY HOWLS IN THE BONES OF HER FACE
Little Boy lost he takes himself so seriously - he brags of
his misery he likes to live dangerously He's sure got a lot
of gall - to be so useless and all INSIDE THE MUSEUMS
INFINITY GOES UP ON TRIAL - VOICES ECHO THIS IS WHAT
SALVATION MUST BE LIKE AFTER A WHILE - BUT MONA LISA
MUST HAVE HAD THE HIGHWAY BLUES - YOU CAN TELL BY THE WAY
SHE SMILES - See the primitive wallflower freeze and the
jelly faced women all sneeze and the one with the moustache
say jeez I can't find my knees. Oh jewels and binoculars hang
from the head of the mule - But THESE VISIONS OF JOHANNA
they make it all seem so cruel - The peddler now speaks
to the Countess who's pretending to care for him - SAYING -
NAME ME SOMEONE WHO'S NOT A PARASITE AND I'LL GO OUT AND
SAY A PRAYER FOR HIM - BUT LIKE LOUISE ALWAYS SAYS YOU
CAN'T LOOK AT MUCH CAN YA MAN AS SHE HERSELF PREPARE FOR HIM - AND
MADONNA SHE STILL HAS NOT SHOWED WE SEE THIS EMPTY CAGE
NOW CORRODE - WHERE HER CAPE ON THE STAGE ONCE IT FLOWED -
THE FIDDLER HE NOW STEPS TO THE ROAD - HE WRITES EVERYTHING'S
BEEN RETURNED THAT WAS OWED ON THE BACK OF THE FISH TRUCK THAT LOADS WHILE
MY CONSCIENCE EXPLODES - HARMONICAS PLAY THE
SKELETON KEYS IN THE RAIN - AND THESE VISIONS OF JOHANNA
ARE ALL THAT REMAIN

CBS/40 32267) (re-iss.Feb91 & Feb94 on 'Columbia' cd/c; CD 32267)

Mar 71. (7") *(7092)* **IF NOT FOR YOU. / NEW MORNING** [ ] [-]

Jun 71. (7") *(7329)* <45409> **WATCHING THE RIVER FLOW. / SPANISH IS THE LOVING TONGUE** [24] [41]

Dec 71. (7") *(7688)* <45516> **GEORGE JACKSON (acoustic). / GEORGE JACKSON (big band version)** [ ] [33] Nov71

Dec 71. (d-lp/c) *(CBS/40 67239)* <31120> **MORE BOB DYLAN GREATEST HITS** <US-title 'BOB DYLAN'S GREATEST HITS, VOL.II'> (compilation) [12] [14]
– Watching the river flow / Don't think twice, it's alright / Lay lady lay / Stuck inside Mobile with the Memphis blues again / I'll be your baby tonight / All I really want to do / My back pages / Maggie's farm / Tonight I'll be staying here with you / Positively 4th Street / All along the watchtower / The mighty Quinn (Quinn, the eskimo) / Just like Tom Thumb's blues / A hard rain's a-gonna fall / If not for you / New morning / Tomorrow is a long time / When I paint my masterpiece / I shall be released / You ain't goin' nowhere / Down in the flood. *(cd-iss.Oct87; CD 67239) (cd re-iss.Aug92 on 'Columbia'; 467851-2) (re-iss.Mar93 on 'Columbia' cd/c; 471243-2/-4)*

Sep 73. (lp/c) *(CBS/40 69042)* <32460> **PAT GARRETT AND BILLY THE KID (Soundtrack)** [29] [16] Jul73
– Mmain title theme / Cantina theme (working for the law) / Billy 1 / Bunkhouse theme / River theme / Turkey chase / Knockin' on Heaven's door / Final theme / Billy 4 / Billy 7. *(re-iss.Mar82 lp/c; CBS/40 32098) (re-iss.Feb91 on 'Columbia' cd/c;)*

Sep 73. (7") *(1762)* <45913> **KNOCKIN' ON HEAVEN'S DOOR. / TURKEY CHASE** [14] [12] Aug73

Dec 73. (lp/c) *(CBS/40 69049)* <32747> **DYLAN** (rec.1970) [ ] [17]
– Lily of the west / Can't help falling in love / Sarah Jane / The ballad of Ira Hayes / Mr. Bojangles / Mary Ann / Big yellow taxi / A fool such as I / Spanish is the loving tongue. *(re-iss.Mar83) (cd+c-iss.Feb91 on 'Columbia')*

Jan 74. (7") *(2006)* <45982> **A FOOL SUCH AS I. / LILY OF THE WEST** [ ] [55] Dec73

Island **Asylum**

Feb 74. (lp/c) *(ILPS/ICT 9261)* <1003> **PLANET WAVES** [7] [1]
– On a night like this / Going going gone / Tough mama / Hazel / Something there is about you / Forever young / Dirge / You angel you / Never say goodbye / Wedding song. *(re-iss.Sep82 lp/c; CBS/40 32154) (cd-iss.Nov89 on 'C.B.S.'; CD 21154)*

Feb 74. (7") <11033> **ON A NIGHT LIKE THIS. / YOU ANGEL YOU** [-] [44]

Feb 74. (7") *(WIP 6168)* **ON A NIGHT LIKE THIS. / FOREVER YOUNG** [ ] [-]

Apr 74. (7") **SOMETHING THERE IS ABOUT YOU. / GOING GOING GONE** [-] [ ]

Asylum **Asylum**

Jul 74. (d-lp/d-c; as BOB DYLAN & THE BAND) *(IBD 1)* <201> **BEFORE THE FLOOD** (tracks by The BAND) [8] [3]
– Most likely you go your way (and I'll go mine) / Lay lady lay / Rainy day women Nos.12 & 35 / Knockin' on Heaven's door / It ain't me babe / The ballad of a thin man / Up on Cripple Creek * / I shall be released / Endless highway * / The night they drove old Dixie down * / Stage fright * / Don't think twice, it's all right / Just like a woman / It's alright ma (I'm only bleeding) / The shape I'm in * / When you awake * / The weight * / All along the watchtower / Highway 61 revisited / Like a rolling stone / Blowin' in the wind. *(re-iss.Sep82 on 'C.B.S.' d-lp/d-c; CBS/40 22137) (cd-iss.Jul87 + Nov89 + Jun96; CD 22137)*

— The BAND had been his backing group from the mid '60's.

Aug 74. (7") <11043> **MOST LIKELY YOU GO YOUR WAY (AND I'LL GO MINE) (live). / STAGE FRIGHT (The BAND live)** [-] [66]

Nov 74. (7") **ALL ALONG THE WATCHTOWER (live). / IT AIN'T ME BABE (live)** [-] [ ]

C.B.S. **Columbia**

Feb 75. (lp/c) *(CBS/40 69097)* <32235> **BLOOD ON THE TRACKS** [4] [1]
– Tangled up in blue / Simple twist of fate / You're a big girl now / Idiot wind / You're gonna make me lonesome when you go / Meet me in the morning / Lily, Rosemary and the Jack of Hearts / If you see her, say hello / Shelter from the storm / Buckets of rain. *((cd-iss.Dec85; CD 69097) (re-iss.Sep93 on 'Columbia' cd/c; 467842-2/-4)*

Mar 75. (7") *(3160)* <10106> **TANGLED UP IN BLUE. / IF YOU SEE HER, SAY HELLO** [ ] [31]

Jul 75. (d-lp/c) *(CBS/40 88147)* <33682> **THE BASEMENT TAPES** (rec.1967) [8] [7]
– Odds and ends / Orange juice blues (blues for breakfast) / Million dollar bash / Yazoo street scandal / Goin' to Acapulco / Katie's been gone / Lo and behold / Bessie Smith / Clothes line saga / Apple suckling tree / Please Mrs. Henry / Tears of rage / Too much of nothing / Yea! heavy and a bottle of wine / Ain't no more Cane / Crash on the levee (down in the flood) / Ruben Remus / Tiny Montgomery / You ain't goin' nowhere / Don't ya tell Henry / Nothing was delivered / Open the doors, Homer / Long distance operator. *(cd-iss.Nov89; 466137-2)*

Oct 75. (7") *(3665)* **MILLION DOLLAR BASH. / TEARS OF RAGE** [ ] [ ]

— next featured **EMMYLOU HARRIS** – vocals / **SCARLET RIVIERA** – violin / **RONNE BLAKELY** – vocals / **HOWIE WYTHE** – drums / **ROB STONER** – bass / **STEVEN SOLES** – guitar

Jan 76. (7") *(3879)* <10245> **HURRICANE (part 1). / HURRICANE (full version)** [43] [33] Nov75

Jan 76. (lp/c) *(CBS/40 86003)* <33893> **DESIRE** [3] [1]
– Hurricane / Isis / Mozambique / One more cup of coffee / Oh, sister / Joey / Romance in Durango / Black diamond bay / Sara. *(re-iss.Apr85 lp/c; CBS/40 32570) (cd-iss.Jul87; 86003) (cd re-iss.Jun89; CD 32470)*

Apr 76. (7") *(4113)* <10298> **MOZAMBIQUE. / OH, SISTER** [ ] [54] Mar76

— His HARD RAIN tour added **MICK RONSON** – guitar / **DAVID MANSFIELD** – keyboards

Sep 76. (lp/c) *(CBS/40 86016)* <34349> **HARD RAIN (live)** [3] [17]
– Maggie's farm / One too many mornings / Stuck inside of Mobile with the Memphis blues again / Lay lady lay / Shelter from the storm / You're a big girl now / I threw it all away / Idiot wind. *(re-iss.Apr83 lp/c; CBS/40 32308) (cd-iss.Nov89; CD 32308)*

Feb 77. (7") *(4859)* <10454> **RITA MAY. / STUCK INSIDE OF MOBILE WITH THE MEMPHIS BLUES AGAIN (live)** [ ] [ ]

— Admittedly, BOB DYLAN's later work could in no way be considered as pioneering as his past recordings. However, it would be a shame to leave out the rest of the great man's releases due to his towering influence on rock music in general.

May 78. (7"/12") *(7/12 6499)* <10805> **BABY STOP CRYING. / NEW PONY** [13] [ ]

Jun 78. (lp/c) *(CBS/40 86067)* <35453> **STREET-LEGAL** [2] [11]
– Changing of the guards / New pony / No time to think / Baby stop crying / Is your love in vain / Senor (tales of Yankee power) / True love tends to forget / We better talk this over / Where are you tonight (journey through dark heat). *(cd-iss.Mar86; CD 86087) (re-iss.May95 cd/c; 403289)*

Oct 78. (7"/12") *(7/12 6718)* **IS YOUR LOVE IN VAIN. / WE BETTER TALK THIS OVER** [56] [-]

Dec 78. (7") *(6935)* <10851> **CHANGING OF THE GUARDS. / SENOR (TALES OF YANKEE POWER)** [ ] [ ]

1978. (7"ep) **4 SONGS FROM "RENALDO AND CLARA"** [-] [ ]
– People get ready / Never let me go / Isis / It ain't me babe.

May 79. (d-lp/d-c) *(CBS/40 96004)* <36067> **BOB DYLAN AT BUDOKAN (live)** [4] [13]
– Mr. Tambourine man / Shelter from the storm / Love minus zero – No limit / Ballad of a thin man / Don't think twice, it's all right / Maggie's farm / One more cup of coffee / Like a rolling stone / I shall be released / Oh sister / Is your love in vain? / Going going gone / Blowin' in the wind / Just like a woman / Simple twist of fate / All along the watchtower / I want you / All I really want to do / Knockin' on Heaven's door / It's alright ma (I'm only bleeding) / Forever young / The times they are a-changin'. *(cd-iss.Jul87; CD 96004)*

Jun 79. (7"m) *(7473)* **FOREVER YOUNG (live). / ALL ALONG THE WATCHTOWER (live) / I WANT YOU (live)** [ ] [-]

Aug 79. (7") *(7828)* **PRECIOUS ANGEL. / TROUBLE IN MIND** [ ] [-]

Sep 79. (lp/c) *(CBS/40 86095)* <36120> **SLOW TRAIN COMING** [2] [3]
– Gotta serve somebody / Precious angel / I believe in you / Slow train / Gonna change my way of thinking / Do right to me baby (do unto others) / When you gonna wake up / Man gave names to all the animals / When he returns. *(re-iss.Nov85 lp/c; CBS/40 32524) (cd-iss.Mar86; CD 86095) (cd re-iss.Apr89; CD 32524)*

Sep 79. (7") <11072> **GOTTA SERVE SOMEBODY. / TROUBLE IN MIND** [-] [24]

Oct 79. (7") *(7970)* **MAN GAVE NAMES TO ALL THE ANIMALS. / WHEN HE RETURNS** [ ] [-]

Jan 80. (7") <11168> **MAN GAVE NAMES TO THE ANIMALS. / WHEN YOU GONNA WAKE UP** [-] [ ]

Jan 80. (7") *(8134)* **GOTTA SERVE SOMEBODY. / GONNA CHANGE MY WAY OF THINKING** [ ] [-]

Mar 80. (7") <11235> **SLOW TRAIN. / DO RIGHT TO ME BABY (DO UNTO OTHERS)** [-] [ ]

May 80. (7") <11318> **SOLID ROCK. / COVENANT WOMAN** [-] [ ]

Jun 80. (lp/c) *(CBS/40 83113)* <36553> **SAVED** [3] [24]
– A satisfied mind / Saved / Covenant woman / What can I do for you? / Solid rock / Pressing on / In the garden / Saving Grace / Are you ready. *(reiss.Sep86 lp/c; CBS/40 32742) (re-iss.Feb91 & Mar93 on 'Columbia' cd/c; 403274-2/-4)*

Jun 80. (7") *(8743)* <11370> **SAVED. / ARE YOU READY** [ ] [ ]

Jun 81. (7") <02510> **HEART OF MINE. / THE GROOM'S STILL WAITING AT THE ALTAR** [-] [ ]

Jul 81. (7") *(A 1406)* **HEART OF MINE. / LET IT BE ME** [ ] [-]

Aug 81. (lp/c) *(CBS/40 85178)* <37496> **SHOT OF LOVE** [6] [33]
– Shot of love / Heart of mine / Property of Jesus / Lenny Bruce / Watered down love / Dead man, dead man / In the summertime / Trouble / Every grain of sand. *(re-iss.Feb91 on 'Columbia' cd+=/c+=; 467839-2/-4)*– The groom's still waiting at the altar. *(re-iss.cd Jun94 on 'Sony Europe'; 983338-2)*

Sep 81. (7") *(A 1460)* **LENNY BRUCE. / DEAD MAN, DEAD MAN** [ ] [-]

Oct 83. (7") *(A 3916)* **UNION SUNDOWN. / I AND I** [ ] [ ]

Nov 83. (lp/c) *(CBS/40 25539)* <38819> **INFIDELS** [9] [20]
– Jokerman / Sweetheart like you / Neighbourhood bully / License to kill / Man of peace / Union sundown / I and I / Don't fall apart on me tonight. *(cd-iss.Jul87; Cd 25539) (re-iss.Dec89 lp/c/cd; 460727-1/-4/-2)*

Dec 83. (7") <04301> **SWEETHEART LIKE YOU. / UNION SUNDOWN** [-] [55]

May 84. (7") <04425> **JOKERMAN. / ISIS** [-] [ ]

Jun 84. (7") *(A 4055)* **JOKERMAN. / LICENSE TO KILL** [ ] [-]

Dec 84. (lp/c/cd) *(CBS/40/CD 26334)* <39944> **REAL LIVE (live)** [54] [ ]
– Highway 61 revisited / Maggie's farm / I and I / License to kill / It ain't me babe / Tangled up in blue / Masters of war / Ballad of a thin man / Girl from the North country / Tombstone blues. *(re-iss.Feb91 on 'Columbia' cd/c; 467841-2/-4)*

Jan 85. (7"/7"g-f) *(A/GA 5020)* **HIGHWAY 61 REVISITED (live). / IT AIN'T ME BABE (live)** [ ] [ ]

Jun 85. (7") *(A 6303)* <04933> **TIGHT CONNECTION TO MY HEART. / WE'D BETTER TALK THIS OVER** [ ] [ ]

Jun 85. (lp/c/cd) *(CBS/40/CD 86313)* <40110> **EMPIRE BURLESQUE** [11] [33]
– Tight connection to my heart (has anybody seen my love) / Seeing the real you at last / I'll remember you / Clean cut kid / Never gonna be the same again / Trust yourself / Emotionally yours / When the night comes falling from the sky / Something's burning, baby / Dark eyes. *(re-iss.cd.1988; Cd 86313) (re-iss.Feb91 on 'Columbia' cd/c; 467840-2/-4)*

Aug 85. (7"/ext.12") *(A/TA 6469)* **WHEN THE NIGHT COMES FALLING FROM THE SKY. / DARK EYES** [ ] [-]

— In Apr'86, he was credited next on the TOM PETTY ⇒ single 'BAND OF THE HAND'.

Oct 85. (7") <05697> **WHEN THE NIGHT COMES FALLING FROM THE SKY. / EMOTIONALLY YOURS** [-] [ ]

Jul 86. (lp/c/cd) *(CBS/40/CD 86326)* <40439> **KNOCKED OUT LOADED** [35] [53]
– You wanna ramble / They killed him / Driftin' too far from shore / Precious memories / Maybe someday / Brownsville girl / Got my mind made up / Under your spell. *(re-iss.Feb91 & Mar93 on 'Columbia' cd/c; 467040-2/-4)*

Oct 86. (7") *(651148-7)* **THE USUAL. / GOT MY MIND MADE UP** [ ] [ ]
(12"+=) *(651148-6)* – Precious memories / Driftin' too far from shore.

Jun 88. (lp/c/cd) *(460267-1/-4/-2)* <40957> **DOWN IN THE GROOVE** [32] [61]
– Let's stick together / When did you leave Heaven? / Sally Sue Brown / Death is not the end / Had a dream about you, baby / Ugliest girl in the world / Silvio / Ninety miles an hour (down a dead end street) / Shenandoah / Rank strangers to me.

Jul 88. (7") **SILVIO. / DRIFTIN' TOO FAR FROM SHORE** [-] [ ]

Jul 88. (7") *(651406-7)* **SILVIO. / WHEN DID YOU LEAVE HEAVEN?** [ ] [-]
(12"+=) *(651406-6)* – Driftin' too far from shore.

— Later in '88 & onwards, he was also part of supergroup TRAVELING WILBURYS

Feb 89. (lp/c/cd; BOB DYLAN & GRATEFUL DEAD) *(463381/-1/-4/-2) <45056>* **DYLAN & THE DEAD (live July'87)** [38] [37]
– Slow train / I want you / Gotta serve somebody / Queen Jane approximately / Joey / All along the watchtower / Knockin' on Heaven's door. *(re-iss.May94 on 'Columbia' cd/c; 463381-2/-4)*

Oct 89. (lp/c/cd) *(465800-1/-4/-2) <45281>* **OH MERCY** [6] [30]
– Political world / Where teardrops fall / Everything is broken / Ring them bells / Man in the long black coat / Most of the time / What good am I? / Disease of conceit / What was it you wanted / Shooting star.

Oct 89. (7") **EVERYTHING IS BROKEN. / DEAD MAN, DEAD MAN** [-] [ ]

Oct 89. (7") *(655358-7)* **EVERYTHING IS BROKEN. / DEATH IS NOT THE END** [ ] [-]
(12"/12"w-print) *(655358-6/-8)* – ('A'side) / Dead man, dead man / I want you (live).
(cd-s) *(655358-2)* – ('A'side) / Where the teardrops fall / Dead man, dead man (live) / Ugliest girl in the world (live).

Feb 90. (7") *(655643-7)* **POLITICAL WORLD. / RING THEM BELLS** [ ] [ ]
(12"+=/cd-s+=) *(655643-6/-2)* – Silvio / All along the watchtower (live).
(cd-s) *(655643-5)* – ('A'side) / Caribbean wind / You're a big girl now / It's all over now, baby blue.

Sep 90. (cd/c/lp) *(467188-2/-4/-1) <46794>* **UNDER THE RED SKY** [13] [38]
– Wiggle wiggle / Under the red sky / Unbelievable / Born in time / TV talkin' time / 10,000 men / 2x2 / God knows / Handy Dandy / Cat's in the well.

Sep 90. (7") *(656304-7)* **UNBELIEVABLE. / 10,000 MEN** [ ] [ ]
(cd-s+=) *(656304-2)* – In the summertime / Jokerman.

Feb 91. (7"/c-s) *(656707-7/-4)* **SERIES OF DREAMS. / SEVEN CURSES** [ ] [ ]
(cd-s+=) *(656707-5)* – Tangled up in blue / Like a rolling stone.

— totally solo DYLAN

Columbia Columbia

Nov 92. (cd/c/lp) *(472710-2/-4/-1) <53200>* **GOOD AS I BEEN TO YOU** [18] [51]
– Frankie & Albert / Jim Jones / Blackjack Davey / Canadee-i-o / Sittin' on top of the world / Little Maggie / Hard times / Step it up and go / Tomorrow night / Arthur McBride / You're gonna quit me / Diamond Joe / Froggie went a courtin'.

— In Aug93, a host of artists released a live tribute d-cd,d-c 'ANNIVERSARY CONCERT', which hit US No.30. Below all traditional tunes.

Nov 93. (cd/c) *(474857-2/-4)* **WORLD GONE WRONG** [35] [70]
– World gone wrong / Ragged and dirty / Love Henry / Blood in my eyes / Delia / Broke down engine / Two soldiers / Stack A Lee / Jack A Roe / Love pilgrim.

— with **TONY GARNIER** – bass / **JOHN JACKSON** – guitar / **BUCKY BAXTER** – pedal steel, dobro / **WINSTON WATSON** – drums / **BRENDAN O'BRIEN** – hammond organ

Apr 95. (cd/c/lp) *(478374-2/-4/-1)* **MTV UNPLUGGED** [10] [23]
– Tombstone blues / Shooting star / All along the watchtower / The times they are a-changin' / John Brown / Desolation row / Rainy day women £ 12 & 35 / Love minus zero – No limit / Dignity / Knockin' on Heaven's door / Like a rolling stone / With God on our side.

May 95. (c-s) *(662076-4)* **DIGNITY / JOHN BROWN** [33] [ ]
(cd-s+=) *(662076-5)* – It ain't me babe (live).
(cd-s) *(662076-2)* – ('A'side) / A hard rain's a-gonna fall.

— To end '96, 'KNOCKIN' ON HEAVEN'S DOOR' hit UK No.1 for DUNBLANE; Scottish musicians and children of the town where psycho Thomas Hamilton murdered 16 children and a teacher earlier in the year. This added another verse, highlighting the need to outlaw guns in Britain.

– compilations, others, etc. –

on 'CBS / Columbia' unless otherwise mentioned

Nov 65. (7"ep) *(EP 6051)* **DYLAN** [ ] [-]

Apr 66. (7"ep) *(EP 6070)* **ONE TOO MANY MORNINGS** [ ] [-]
– One too many mornings / Spanish Harlem incident / Oxford town / She belongs to me.

Jun 66. (7"ep) *(EP)* **DON'T THINK TWICE IT'S ALRIGHT** [ ] [-]
– Don't think twice it's alright / Blowin' in the wind / Corrina, Corrina / When the ship comes.

Oct 66. (7"ep) *(EP 6078)* **MR. TAMBOURINE MAN** [ ] [-]
– Mr. Tambourine man / Subterranean homesick blues / It's all over now, baby blue.

Mar 73. (7") *(1158)* **JUST LIKE A WOMAN. / I WANT YOU** [ ] [-]

Feb 76. (7") *(3945)* **LAY LADY LAY. / I THREW IT ALL AWAY** [ ] [-]

Oct 83. (lp/c) *Go International; (GLP/GMC 1)* **HISTORICAL ARCHIVES VOL.1** [ ] [-]

Oct 83. (lp/c) *Go Internationals; (GLP/GMC 2)* **HISTORICAL ARCHIVES VOL.2** [ ] [-]

Nov 85. (5xlp-box/3xc-box/3xcd-box) *(CBS/40/CD 66509) <38830>* **BIOGRAPH** [ ] [33]

— (above contains 16 unreleased tracks)

Sep 87. (cd) *Compact Collection; (76025)* **THE GASLIGHT TAPES** [ ] [-]

1988. (lp) *Joker; (SM 4123)* **THE BEST OF BOB DYLAN** [ ] [-]

May 88. (lp/c) *Big Time; (22/21 15531)* **DON'T THINK TWICE, IT'S ALRIGHT** [ ] [-]

May 88. (lp/c) *Big Time; (22/21 15551)* **BLOWIN' IN THE WIND** [ ] [-]

1988. (d-c) *(CDBD 241)* **DESIRE / BLOOD ON THE TRACKS** [ ] [-]

Apr 91. (3xcd/3xc/6xlp) *(468086-2/-4/-1) <47382>* **THE BOOTLEG SERIES VOLUMES 1-3 (RARE & UNRELEASED) 1961-1991** [32] [49]

Aug 92. (d-cd) *(466831-2)* **HIGHWAY 61 REVISITED / JOHN WESLEY HARDING** [ ] [-]

Oct 93. (3xcd-box) *(471621-2)* **BLONDE ON BLONDE / JOHN WESLEY HARDING / SELF PORTRAIT** [ ] [-]

Nov 94. (cd/c/d-lp) *Columbia; (477805-2/-4/-1)* **GREATEST HITS VOLUME III** [ ] [ ]
– Tangled up in blue / Changing the guards / The groom's still waiting at the altar / Hurricane / Forever young / Jokerman / Dignity / Silvio / Ring them bells / Gotta serve somebody / Series of dream / Brownsville girl / Under the red sky / Knockin' on Heaven's door.

Jun 97. (d-cd/d-c) *Sony; (SONYTV 28 CD/MC)* **THE BEST OF BOB DYLAN** [8] [ ]
– Blowin' in the wind / The times they are a-changin' / Don't think twice, it's alright / Mr. Tambourine man / Like a rolling stone / Just like a woman / All along the watchtower / Lay lady lay / If not for you / Knockin' on Heaven's door / Forever young / Tangled up in blue / Shelter from the storm / I shall be released / Oh sister / Gotta serve somebody / Jokerman / Everything is broken.

DZYAN

Formed: Germany ... early 1972 by JOCHEN LENSCHNER, DIETER KRAMER, GERD EHRMANN, REINHARD KARWATKY and LUDWIG BRAUM. They quickly recorded their self-titled debut and inspired by prog-rock in the shape of KING CRIMSON and other British bands of their ilk, the album featured the excellent 'KABISRAIN' track. On their next two releases, they explored a more jazz/ethnic direction, much in the same vein as AGITATION FREE and BETWEEN.

Recommended: DZYAN (*5) / TIME MACHINE (*6) / ELECTRIC SILENCE (*5)

JOCHEN LENSCHNER – vocals / **REINHARD KARWATKY** – bass / **GERD EHRMANN** – sax / **LUDWIG BRAUM** – drums, percussion / **HARRY KRAMER** – guitar

Aronda not issued

Apr 72. (lp) *(AS 10006)* **DZYAN** [-] [-] German
– Emptiness / The bud awakes / The wisdom / Fohat's work / Hymn / Dragonsong / Things we're looking for / Back to earth.

— LOTHAR SCHARF played live gigs, before he left for VIRGO

— sole survivor **KARWATKY** recruited **EDDY MARRON** – guitar, saz, vocals / **PETER GIGER** – drums, percussion

Bacillus not issued

Nov 73. (lp) *(BLPS 19161)* **TIME MACHINE** [-] [-] German
– Kabisrain / Magika / Light shining out of darkness / Time machine. *(cd-iss.1994)*

Dec 74. (lp) *(BLPS 19202)* **ELECTRIC SILENCE** [-] [-] German
– Back to where we come from / A day in my life / The road not taken / Khali / For earthly thinking / Electric silence. *(cd-iss.1994)*

— split late '74 when KARWATKY departed. GIGER and MARRON recruited GUNTER LENZ recorded one album in 1976 'GIGER, LENZ & MARRON' for 'Nagara'; *(MIX 1011-N)* PETER GIGER had already released a solo album 'FAMILY OF PERCUSSION' *(MIX 1010-N)* Others:- 1978 'WHERE THE HAMMER HANGS' *(MIX 1015-N)* & 1982 'FOR DRUMMERS ONLY' *(MIX 1022-N)*. MARRON solo in 1978 'POR MARCO' *(MIX 1017)*

EAGLE (see under ⇒ BEACON STREET UNION)

EARTH & FIRE

Formed: Netherlands . . .early 70's by KOERTS brothers. A progressive rock outfit, changing to a more pop-orientated sound after their brilliant eponymous debut. Ex-GOLDEN EARRING drummer JAAP EGGERMONT took over production until 1977, but it was clear they were going nowhere. • **Trivia:** Their debut featuring a sleeve by artist ROGER DEAN, is worth over £150 mint.

Recommended: EARTH AND FIRE (*7)

JERNEY KAAGMAN – vocals / **CHRIS KOERTS** – guitar, vocals / **GERARD KOERTS** – keyboards, flute, vocals / **HANS ZIECH** – bass / **TON VAN DER KLEIJ** – drums, percussion

Polydor not issued

Mar 70. (7") *(56790)* **SEASONS. / PARADISE** -

Nephentha Redbullet

Jun 71. (7") *(6129 001)* **INVITATION. / WILD AND EXCITING** -

Jun 71. (lp) *(6437 004) <3000>* **EARTH AND FIRE**
– Wild and exciting / Twlight dreamer / Ruby is the one / You know the way / Vivid shady Ian / 21st century show / Seasons / Love quiver / What's your name.

Polydor Polydor

1972. (lp) *(2925 003)* **SONG OF THE MARCHING CHILDREN** -
– Carnaval of the animals / Ebbtide / Storm and thunder / Song of the marching children: a) Theme of the marching children, b) Opening of the seal, c) Childhood, d) Affliction, e) Damnation, f) Purification, g) The march.

1973. (lp) *(2925 013)* **ATLANTIS / MAYBE TOMORROW MAYBE TONIGHT** -
– Atlantis: Prelude – Prologue (don't know) / Rise and fall (under a cloudy sky) – Theme of Atlantis – The threat (suddenly) – Destructions (rumbling from inside the Earth) – Epilogue (don't know) / Maybe tomorrow maybe tonight / Interlude / Fanfare / Theme from Atlantis / Please close the door / Prelude.

1973. (7") *<15073>* **ATLANTIS. / MAYBE TOMORROW MAYBE TONIGHT** -

— **THEO HURTS** – bass, guitar, repl. ZIECH

Jul 74. (7") *(2121 235)* **LOVE OF LIFE. / TUFTY THE CAT** -

1975. (lp) *(2925 033)* **TO THE WORLD A FUTURE** -
– To the world a future / How time flies / The last seagull / Only time will tell / Voice from yonder / Love of life / Circus.

1976. (lp) *(2925 044)* **THE STORY OF EARTH AND FIRE** (compilation) -

1977. (lp) *(2925 065)* **GATE TO INFINITY** -
– Recognition / A princess in Egypt / The joyous untruth / Infinity / A lifetime before / 78th Avenue / Smile / Green Park station / Dizzy raptures / Driftin'.

— **BERT RUITER** – bass / **AL TAMBOER** – drums, repl. HURTS + KLEIJ

Aug 80. (7") *(POSP 156)* **WEEKEND. / ANSWER ME** -

Vertigo not issued

1980. (lp) *(6360 642)* **REALITY FILLS FANTASY** - - Dutch
– People come people go: Movement 13 / Fire of love / Weekend / Can't live without it anymore / Where were you / Season of the falling leaves / Answer me / Reprise.

— **RONNIE MEYJES** – guitar, repl. CHRIS

1981. (lp) *(6399 271)* **ANDROMEDA GIRL** - - Dutch
– Dream / Singer in the rain / Andromeda girl / What more could you desire / Tell me why / Love is an ocean / You / From shore to shore / Just one chance.

Polydor not issued

1982. (lp) *(810079-1)* **IN A STATE OF FLUX** - - Dutch
– Twenty-four hours / Jack is back / The two of us / Wish you were here / Strange town / Love is to give away / I don't know why / Hide away / In a state of flux / Dona nobis pacem.

— split after above

– compilations, others, etc. –

1979. (lp) *Polydor; (2499 109)* **ROCK SENSATION** -
– Maybe tomorrow maybe tonight / Theme from Atlantis / From the end till the beginning / Carnaval of the animals / Song of the marching children: Theme of the marching children – Opening of the seal – Childhood – Affliction – Damnation – Purification – The march.

May 83. (lp/c) *Polydor; (8105 101/104)* **EARTH AND FIRE** -
– Memories / Seasons / Ruby is the one / Wild and exciting / Invitation / Storm and thunder / Maybe tomorrow, maybe tonight / Love of life / Only time will tell / Thanks for the love / What difference does it make / 78th Avenue / Smile / Green park station.

1988. (cd) *Star; (CD 840252)* **THE VERY BEST OF . . .** - - Dutch
– Weekend / Ruby is the one / Maybe tomorrow maybe tonight / Memories / Storm and thunder / Wild and exciting / Love of life / Seasons / Fire of love / Thanks for the love / Invitation / Only time will tell / What difference does it make / 78th Avenue / Weekend (remix '88).

EARTH OPERA

Formed: Boston, Massachusetts, USA . . .1967 by PETER ROWAN and DAVID GRISMAN, both veterans of various bluegrass outfits. They only released a couple of electric folk albums, tinted with a little psychedelia, before they went their separate ways. GRISMAN subsequently played on GRATEFUL DEAD's legendary 'American Beauty' album, while PETER formed The ROWAN BROTHERS. • **Trivia:** JOHN CALE guested on their 2nd PETER K. SIEGEL produced lp.

Recommended: EARTH OPERA (*5) / THE GREAT AMERICAN EAGLE TRAGEDY (*5)

PETER ROWAN – vocals, guitar, saxophone / **DAVID GRISMAN** – mandocello, mandolin, saxophone, vocals / **JOHN NAGY** – bass, cello / **BILL STEVENSON** – keyboards, vibes / **PAUL DILLON** – drums, percussion, guitar, vocals

Elektra Elektra

Sep 68. (7") *(EKSN 45035)* **CLOSE YOUR EYES AND SHUT THE DOOR. / DREAMLESS** -

Sep 68. (lp) *<(EKS 74016)>* **EARTH OPERA**
– The Red Sox are winning / As it is before / Dreamless / To care at all / Home of the brave / The child bride / Close your eyes and shut the door / Time and again / When you were full of wonder / Death by fire.

— now without STEVENSON

Feb 69. (7") *(EKSN 45049) <45636>* **THE AMERICAN EAGLE TRAGEDY. / WHEN YOU WERE FULL OF WONDER**

1969. (lp) *<(EKS 74038)>* **THE GREAT AMERICAN EAGLE TRAGEDY**
– Home to you / Mad Lydia's waltz / Alfie Finney / Sanctuary from the law / All winter long / The American eagle tragedy / Roast beef love / It's love.

May 69. (7") *(EKSN 45061) <45650>* **HOME TO YOU. / ALFIE FINNEY** 97 Apr69

— When they split ROWAN joined SEATRAIN for 2 albums ('SEATRAIN' and 'MARBLEHEAD MESSENGER'), before joining The ROWAN BROTHERS.

EAST OF EDEN

Formed: Brighton, England . . .1967 by GEOFF NICHOLSON, DAVE ARBUS, RON CAINES, RON CAINES and DAVE DUFORT. They debuted with the 'KING OF SIAM' single in 1968 for 'Atlantic', although their progressive leanings became more apparent on the 'Deram' single, 'NORTHERN HEMISPHERE'. This track was lifted from their early '69 album, 'MERCATOR PROJECTED'. In 1970, with their hard progressive rock sound embellished by ARBUS's wild violin playing, they hit the Top 30 with the album, 'SNAFU'. It was followed by an instrumental track not included on the album, 'JIG-A-JIG', which made the Top 10. However, this was effectively a novelty hit, and the band's growing audience could no longer take them seriously. They became more countrified by 1971, obviously influenced by AREA CODE 615 and other American outfits of that ilk. Yhey soon moved to the 'Harvest' stable', becoming a little more successful in Germany, where they were still releasing albums in the late 70's.

Recommended: SNAFU (*6)

GEOFF NICHOLSON – guitar, vocals / **DAVE ARBUS** – violin, flute, sax, bagpipes / **RON CAINES** – saxophones, organ, vocals / **STEVE YORK** – bass, harmonica, piano / **DAVE DUFONT** – drums, percussion

Atlantic not issued

Jul 68. (7") *(584 198)* **KING OF SIAM. / BALLAD OF HARVEY KAYE** -

Deram Deram

Feb 69. (lp) *(DML/SML 1038) <18023>* **MERCATOR PROJECTED**
– Northern hemisphere / Isadora / Waterways / Centaur woman / Bathers / Communion / Moth / In the stable of the Sphinx.

Mar 69. (7") *(DM 242) <85042>* **NORTHERN HEMISPHERE. / COMMUNION**

— **ANDY SNEDDON** – bass, repl. YORK who joined MANFRED MANN CHAPTER III

— **GEOFF BRITTON** – drums, percussion, repl. DUFONT who joined KEVIN AYERS

Feb 70. (lp) *(SML 1050) <18043>* **SNAFU** 29
– Have to whack it up / Leaping beauties for Rudy / Marcus Junior / Xhorkham / Ramadhan / In the snow for a blue / Boehm constrictor / Better git in your soul / Uno transito ciapori / Gum Arabic / Confucius / Nymphenburger / Habibi baby / Beast of Sweden / Traditional.

Apr 70. (7") *(DM 297) <85075>* **JIG-A-JIG. / MARCUS JUNIOR** 7

Dec 70. (7"ep) *(DM 338)* **RAMADHAN / IN THE SNOW FOR A BLOW. / BETTER GIT IT IN YOUR SOUL / HAVE TO WHACK IT UP A BIT** -

— **JEFF ALLEN** – drums, repl. BRITTON who later joined ROUGH DIAMOND

Harvest Harvest

Jul 71. (lp) *(SHVL 792) <806>* **EAST OF EDEN**
– Wonderful feeling / Goodbye / Drazy Daisy / Here comes the day / Take what you need / No time / To Mrs V.

— **GARTH WATT-ROY** – guitar, vocals / **MARTIN FISHER** – bass / **JIM ROCHE** – guitar / **DAVE WELLER** – saxophone, repl. NICHOLSON, SNEDDON + CAINES

Nov 71. (lp) *(SHVL 796)* **NEW LEAF** -
– Bradshaw the bison hunter / Ain't gonna do no harm / Get happy / Don't be afraid /

Man said / Song for no one / Nothin' to do / Road song / Home blues.

Sep 72. (7") *(HAR 5055)* **BOOGIE WOOGIE FLU. / LAST DANCE OF THE CLOWN** -

U.A. not issued

Jun 73. (7") *(UP 35567)* **SIN CITY GIRLS. / ALL OUR YESTERDAYS** -

— Disbanded but re-formed for releases in Germany.

— **JOE O'DONNELL** – violin (ex-MUSHROOM), repl. ROCHE who joined MAJOR SURGERY

Harvest not issued

1975. (lp) *(062-97101)* **ANOTHER EDEN** - - German
– Mandarin's daughter / Hey Zimmerman / Kensington cowboy / Catalina troubadour / What's happening / Summer days / Hey baby / Fancy Nancy.

— now w/ out any originals **LES DAVIDSON** – guitar / **PETER FILLEUL** – keyboards / **DAVID JACKS** – bass / **DAVE WELLER** – sax, repl. WATT-ROY, ARBUS, O'DONNELL + FISHER. ARBUS was to join ROGER DALTREY's band, and become a teacher.

Dec 76. (lp) *(062-98065)* **HERE WE GO AGAIN** - - German
– Like a plate / All is said and done / Fallin' down / Talkin' on the telephone / Merci merci / Here we go again / Spain / Heaven knows / You can find the star / Let's find some time.

— **DYL KATZ** – bass + **IAN LYNN** – keyboards, vibes, vocals, repl. FILLEUL

E.M.I. not issued

Jan 78. (lp) *(064-61810)* **IT'S THE CLIMATE** - - German
– Rock'n'roll king / It's the climate / This time / Walnut / Sensible shoes / If you go / Patterns / Down and out / You.

Nov 78. (lp) *(064-62639)* **SILVER PARK** - - German
– Low moan / What fun / Calypso / Silver park / Strawberry pie / Burnin' / Look what you've done / Rock reggae / Bad weather / Road work.

— Disbanded for the final time.

– compilations, others

Jun 71. (lp) *Decca; (SPA 157)* **WORLD OF EAST OF EDEN** -
1975. (d-lp) *Deram; (SDM 3013 1/2)* **SNAFU / MERCATOR PROJECTED** - -
1976. (d-lp) *Nova; (628367)* **THINGS** - - German

EASYBEATS

Formed: Sydney, Australia ... 1963 by 3 ex-UK compatriots STEVIE WRIGHT, GEORGE YOUNG and GORDON FLEET, plus Dutch immigrants HARRY VANDA and DICK DIAMONDE, who had all met in a migrant youth hostel. They took the group name from a Brian Matthews radio show, and were soon signed by Ted Albert of 'Parlophone' Australia. Their second 45, 'SHE'S SO FINE', hit No.1 down under, followed by a string of Australian chartbusters. In mid-66, they signed a worldwide deal with 'United Artists', soon hitting Top 20 on both sides of the Atlantic with 'FRIDAY ON MY MIND'. They found it hard to emulate this classic pop song, and by the late 60's they had parted company. GEOGE and HARRY formed PAINTBOX in 1970, before they finally appeared as hitmakers again with FLASH & THE PAN. • **Style:** Ranged from being easy-listening pop to dippy psychedelic pop. • **Songwriters:** WRIGHT-YOUNG or VANDA-YOUNG, except HIT THE ROAD JACK (Ray Charles) / CAN'T TAKE MY EYES OFF YOU (Frankie Valli; hit) / etc. • **Trivia:** After moving back to Australia, GEORGE YOUNG produced JOHN PAUL YOUNG, who had UK + US Top 10 hit with 'Love Is In The Air'. GEORGE had previously galvanised two of his other brothers ANGUS and MALCOLM, to form their own heavy-metal outfit, AC/DC.

Recommended: THE COLLECTION (*5)

(LITTLE) STEVIE WRIGHT (b.20 Dec'48, Leeds, England) – vocals / **HARRY VANDA** (b. HARRY VANDENBERG, 22 Mar'47, The Hague, Netherlands) – guitar (ex-STARFIGHTERS) / **GEORGE YOUNG** (b. 6 Nov'47, Glasgow, Scotland) – guitar / **DICK DIAMONDE** (b.28 Dec'47, Hilversum, Netherlands) – bass / **GORDON 'SNOWY' FLEET** (b.16 Aug'45, Liverpool, England) – drums (ex-MOJOS)

Parlophone Ascot

Mar 65. (7") *(8146)* **FOR MY WOMAN. / SAY THAT YOU'RE MINE** - - Aust.
May 65. (7") *(8157)* **SHE'S SO FINE. / THE OLD OAK TREE** - - Aust.
Jun 65. (lp) *(PMEO 9484)* **EASY** - - Aust.
– It's so easy / I'm a madman / I wonder / She said alright / I'm gonna tell everybody / Hey girl / She's so fine / You got it off me / Cry, cry, cry / A letter / Easy beat / You'll come back again / Girl on my mind / Ya can't do that.

Jul 65. (7") *(8168)* **WEDDING RING. / ME OR YOU** - - Aust.
Sep 65. (7") *(8171)* **EASY AS CAN BE. / SAD & LONELY & BLUE** - - Aust.
Jan 66. (7") *(8186) <2214>* **WOMEN (MAKE YOU FEEL ALRIGHT). / IN MY BOOK** - Aust.
Jan 66. (lp) *(PMCO 7530)* **IT'S 2 EASY** - - Aust.
– Let me be / You are the light / Women (make you feel alright) / Come and see her / I'll find somebody to take your place / Someway, somewhere / Easy as can be / I can see / Sad and lonely blue eyes / Somethin' wrong / In my book / What about our love / Then I'll tell you goodbye / Wedding ring. *cd-iss.Mar93 on 'Repertoire')*

Jun 66. (lp) *(PMCO 7537)* **VOLUME 3** - - Aust.
– Sorry / Funny feeling / Say you want me / You said that / Goin' out of my mind / Not in love with you / Promised things / The last day of Mary / Today / My my my / Dance of the lovers / What do you want babe / Can you leave her?. *(cd-iss.Mar93 on 'Repertoire')*

Aug 66. (7") *(8224)* **SORRY. / FUNNY FEELING** - - Aust.

— Group had earlier moved to London, England. Still signed to 'Parlophone' Australia.

U.A. U.A.

Jun 66. (7") *(UP 1144)* **COME AND SEE HER. / WOMEN (MAKE YOU FEEL ALRIGHT)** -
Oct 66. (7") *(UP 1157) <50106>* **FRIDAY ON MY MIND. / MADE MY BED, GONNA LIE ON IT** 6 16 Mar67
Mar 67. (7") *(UP 1175)* **WHO'LL BE THE ONE?. / SATURDAY NIGHT** -

— (In Australia, above 'B'side was DO YOU HAVE A SOUL)

Apr 67. (lp) *(ULP 1167) <UAS 3588>* **GOOD FRIDAY** (US-title 'FRIDAY ON MY MIND')
– Saturday night / Happy is the man / Do you have a soul / River deep mountain high / Hound dog * / Pretty girl / Friday on my mind / Who'll be the one / Made my bed gonna lie in it / Remember Sam. *<US 'Women' repl. *> <US version re-iss.Nov85 on 'Fan Club'> (re-cd-iss.Feb92 on 'Repertoire' US title; REP 4162WZ)*

— (Mar67) **FREDDIE SMITH** – drums repl. FLEET who returned to Australia. Later **TONY CAHILL** repl. SMITH more permanently after recording of below lp.

Jun 67. (7") *(UP 1183) <50187>* **HEAVEN AND HELL. / PRETTY GIRL**
Nov 67. (7") *<50206>* **FALLING OFF THE EDGE OF THE WORLD. / REMEMBER SAM** -
Jan 68. (7") *(UP 1201)* **MUSIC GOES ROUND MY HEAD. / COME IN YOU'LL GET PNEUMONIA** -
Mar 68. (7") *(UP 2205)* **HELLO, HOW ARE YOU? / FALLING OFF THE EDGE OF THE WORLD** 20 -
Mar 68. (7") *<50289>* **HELLO, HOW ARE YOU? / COME IN YOU'LL GET PNEUMONIA** -
May 68. (lp) *(ULP 1193) <UAS 6667>* **VIGIL** <Us title 'FALLING OFF THE EDGE OF THE WORLD'>
– Good times / What in the world / Falling off the edge of the world / Music goes round my head / Can't take my eyes off you / Sha la la / Come on in you'll get pneumonia / See saw / Land of make believe / Fancy seeing you here / Hello how are you / Hit the road Jack / We all live happily together / I can't stand it. *(cd-iss.Feb92 on 'Repertoire')*

Jun 68. (7") *(UP 2219)* **THE LAND OF MAKE BELIEVE. / WE ALL LIVE HAPPILY TOGETHER** -
Sep 68. (7") *(UP 2243) <50488>* **GOOD TIMES. / LAY ME DOWN AND DIE**

— (Australian 'B'side 'THE LAND OF MAKE BELIEVEi)

Dec 68. (7") *(8571)* **LAY ME DOWN AND DIE. / SEE LINE WOMAN** - - Aust.

Polydor Rare Earth

Oct 69. (7") *(56335) <5009>* **ST. LOUIS. / CAN'T FIND LOVE** 100
Nov 69. (lp) *(2482 010)* **FRIENDS** -
– St. Louis / Who are my friends / Watching the world go by / Can't find love / Holding on / I love Marie / Rock and roll boogie / Tell your mother / Train song / What becomes of you my love / Woman you're on my mind. *(cd-iss.Nov92 on 'Repertoire')*

Jan 70. (7"; by HARRY VANDA) *(56357)* **I LOVE MARIE. / GONNA MAKE IT** -
Apr 70. (7") *(2001 028)* **FRIENDS. / ROCK'N'ROLL BOOGIE** -

— Disbanded early 1970. CAHILL joined PYTHON LEE JACKSON then RAY CHARLES.

– compilations, others, etc. –

on 'Parlophone' Australia unless mentioned otherwise

1965. (7"ep) *(GEPO 70024)* **SHE'S SO FINE** - - Aust.
1965. (7"ep) *(GEPO 70028)* **EASY AS CAN BE** - - Aust.
1965. (7"ep) *(GEPO 70032)* **EASY FEVER** - - Aust.
1966. (7"ep) *(GEPO 70041)* **FRIDAY ON MY MIND** - - Aust.
1966. (lp) *(PMEO 9958)* **THE BEST OF THE EASYBEATS, PLUS PRETTY GIRL** - - Aust.
1967. (7"ep) *(GEPO 70046)* **HEAVEN AND HELL** - - Aust.
1967. (7"ep) *(GEPO 70048)* **EASY FEVER VOLUME 2** - - Aust.
1970. (7") *(8892)* **PECULIAR HOLE IN THE SKY. / H.P. MAN** - - Aust.
1970s. (7"ep) *Raven; (RV 01)* **MEAN OLD LOVIN'** - - Aust.
1970s. (7"ep) *Raven; (RV 08)* **SON OF EASY FEVER** - - Aust.
1978. (lp) *Albert; (APLP 026)* **THE SHAME JUST DRAINED** - - Aust.
(cd-iss.Mar93 on 'Repertoire')
1980. (d-lp) *Albert; (APLP 046)* **ABSOLUTE ANTHOLOGY** - - Aust.
1985. (7") *New Rose; (EASY 1)* **FRIDAY ON MY MIND. / HELLO, HOW ARE YOU** -
Jan 87. (lp) *Fan Club; (FC 019)* **EASY AS CAN BE – THE BEST OF THE EASYBEATS VOLUME 2** - -
Jan 86. (lp) *Rhino; (RNLP 124)* **THE BEST OF THE EASYBEATS** - -
(cd-iss.May95 on 'Repertoire'; RNCD 124)
Feb 85. (7") *EMI Gold; (G45 37)* **FRIDAY ON MY MIND. / HELLO, HOW ARE YOU** -
(re-iss.Jun88 on 'Old Gold'; OG 9548)
(above 'A'side also on flip of ZOMBIES 45)
Dec 89. (cd) *Impact; <9.00823>* **THE COLLECTION** -
Jan 95. (cd) *BR Music; (BRCD 118)* **VERY BEST OF THE EASYBEATS** -
Oct 95. (cd) *Raven; (RVCD 40)* **LIVE – STUDIO AND STAGE** -

PAINTBOX

— were formed by **GEORGE + HARRY**

Youngblood not issued

1970. (7") *(YB 1013)* **GET READY FOR LOVE. / CAN I GET TO KNOW YOU** -
(re-iss.Oct71; YB 1029)

— became TRAMP then WHATWHAT.

HAFFY'S WHISKY SOUR

Deram not issued

Nov 71. (7") *(DM 345)* **SHOT IN THE HEAD. / BYE BYE BLUEBIRD** -

— Yet again they change name to

MARCUS HOOK ROLL BAND

after brief spell as GRAPEFRUIT with GEORGE ALEXANDER.

Regal Zonophone Capitol

Aug 72. (7") *(RZ 3061)* **NATURAL MAN. / BOOGALOOING IS FOR WRONG**

Mar 73. (7") *(RZ 3072)* **LOUISIANA LADY. / HOOCHIE COOCHIE HAR KAU** [ ] [ ]

Apr 73. (lp) *<11991>* **FEATURING VANDA & YOUNG** [-] [ ]
– Can't stand the heat / Goodbye Jane / Quick reaction / Silver shoes / Watch her do it now / People and the power / Red revolution / Shot in the head / Ape man / Louisiana lady.

E.M.I. | not issued

Mar 74. (7") *(EMI 2119)* **CAN'T STAND THE HEAT. / MOONSHINE BLUES** [ ] [-]

— VANDA and YOUNG returned to Australia, where YOUNG also became producer for little brothers band AC/DC. He also sessioned for them in 1974. They formed pop outfit FLASH & THE PAN in 1979.

EGG

Formed: London, England ... 1968 out of URIEL by CLIVE BROOKS, DAVE STEWART and MONT CAMPBELL, an outfit that also included STEVE HILLAGE. A year later, they became ARZACHEL although their only release was an eponymous album which has since become a collector's item (now worth over £200). The record was a spaced-out, psychedelic affair full of weird sound effects, very reminiscent of PINK FLOYD. When HILLAGE took off for other pursuits (i.e. KHAN, GONG, solo), the trio re-formed as EGG. For the next three and a half years, they honed their esoteric jazz music over a couple of albums. After a period with HILLAGE in KHAN, both returned for a third and final outing, 'THE CIVIL SURFACE' (1974). DAVE STEWART was later famous for his partnership with singer BARBARA GASKIN on the No.1 single, 'IT'S MY PARTY'.

Recommended: ARZACHEL (*7) / EGG (*6) / THE POLITE FORCE (*6) / THE CIVIL SURFACE (*7)

ARZACHEL

HUGO MARTIN MONTGOMERY-CAMPBELL – bass, vocals, keyboards / **DAVE STEWART** – piano, organ / **STEVE HILLAGE** – guitar / **CLIVE BROOKS** – drums

Evolution | Roulette

1969. (lp) *(Z 1003) <42036>* **ARZACHEL** [ ] [ ]
– Garden of earthly delights / Azathoth / Queen St. gang / Leg / Clean innocent fun / Metempsychosis. *(cd-iss.Aug94 on 'Drop Out'; DOCD 1983)*

— HILLAGE joined GONG before after a stint with KHAN. He later went solo and in the 90's formed SYSTEM 7.

EGG

HUGO / DAVE / CLIVE

Deram | Deram

Aug 69. (7") *(DM 269)* **SEVEN IS A JOLLY GOOD TIME. / YOU ARE ALL PRINCESS** [ ] [-]

1970. (lp) *(Nova SDN 14) <18039>* **EGG** [ ] [ ]
– Bulb / While growing my hair / I will be absorbed / Fugue in D-minor / They laughed when I sat down at the piano / the song of McGillicudie the pusillanimous (or don't worry James, your socks are hanging in the coal cellar with Thomas) / Boilk / Symphony No.2: Movement 1 – Movement 2 – Blane – Movement 4. *(re-iss.Oct88 as 'SEVEN IS A JOLLY GOOD TIME' on 'See For Miles' lp/cd+=; SEE 47/220C)–* Seven is a jolly good time / You are all princess.

Jan 71. (lp) *(SML 1074)* **THE POLITE FORCE** [ ] [-]
– A visit to Newport hospital / Contra song / Boilk (incl. Bach: Durch Adams fall ist ganz verderbt) / Long piece No.3 (part 1-4).

— STEWART joined KHAN with HILLAGE.

Caroline | not issued

1974. (lp) *(C 1510)* **THE CIVIL SURFACE** [ ] [-]
– Germ patrol / Wind quartet 1 / Enneagram / Prelude / Wing at the ground loosely now / Nearch / Wind quartet 2. *(cd-iss.Oct90 on 'Charisma'; CACD 1510)*

— Split 1974. CLIVE BROOKS joined The GROUNDHOGS. DAVE STEWART had already formed HATFIELD + THE NORTH and NATIONAL HEALTH.

– compilations, etc. –

1992. (cd) *Deram; (844 168-2)* **EGG FEATURING DAVE STEWART** [ ] [-]

EIRE APPARENT

Formed: Ireland ... 1967 by ERNIE GRAHAM, DAVY LUTTON, HENRY MCULLOCH and CHRIS STEWART (MICK COX and then PETER TOLSON also contributed guitar). After securing the services of top manager CHAS CHANDLER, they supported JIMI HENDRIX on his Stateside tour, the great man going on to produce their psychedelic-tinged debut album in '69. Previously they had surfaced with a one-off 'Track' single, 'FOLLOW ME'. After its relative failure, all became more visible after joining higher profile bands (see below).

Recommended: SUN RISE (*6)

ERNIE GRAHAM – vocals / **HENRY McCULLOCH** – guitar / **CHRIS STEWART** – bass / **DAVY LUTTON** – drums

Track | not issued

Jan 68. (7") *(604 019)* **FOLLOW ME. / HERE I GO AGAIN** [ ] [-]

Buddah | Buddah

Mar 69. (7") *(201 039)* **ROCK'N'ROLL BAND. / YES I NEED SOMEONE** [ ] [-]
(re-iss.Mar72; 2011 117)

Apr 69. (lp) *(203 021) <BDS 5031>* **SUN RISE** [ ] [ ]
– Yes I need someone / Got to get away / The clown / Mr. Guy Fawkes / Someone is sure to (want you) / Rock'n'roll band / Morning glory / Magic carpet / Captive in the sun / Let me stay / 1026. *(cd-iss.Feb92 on 'Sequel'; NEXCD 199)*

1969. (7") *<67>* **LET ME STAY. / YES I NEED SOMEONE** [-] [ ]

— Disbanded after above. ERNIE joined CLANCY then HELP YOURSELF, while McCULLOCH went off to The GREASE BAND and then PAUL McCARTNEY & WINGS. STEWART later joined SPOOKY TOOTH and LUTTON went to ELLIS.

ELECTRIC PRUNES

Formed: Seattle, Washington, USA ... 1965 by JIM LOWE, KEN WILLIAMS, WEASEL SPANGOLA, MARK TULIN and PRESTON RITTER. That year they also moved to Los Angeles where they signed to 'Reprise' records. After an initial flop, they soon broke into the charts late 1966 with bad trip anthem, 'I HAD TOO MUCH TO DREAM LAST NIGHT'. Overnight this classic piece of deranged garage-psych won them a cult following among the emerging underground scene. Another Annette Tucker & Nancie Mantz written song, 'GET ME TO THE WORLD ON TIME', also charted on both sides of the Atlantic in Spring 1967. When their albums failed to bear any commercial fruit, their most recent member, DAVID AXELROD, took over. With no original members left, the new look ELECTRIC PRUNES found it difficult to gel. Their 1968 album, 'MASS IN F MINOR', was a complete disaster, abandoning their garage roots in favour of a dubious concept rock opera based on a Latin Gregorian chant. 'RELEASE OF AN OATH' was similarly overblown while their swansong, 'JUST GOOD OLD ROCK'N'ROLL' was an embarassing piece of tired good-time rock. • **Songwriters:** LOWE-TULIN, except as mentioned and AXELROD in '68.

Recommended: LONG DAY'S FLIGHT (*6).

JIM LOWE (b. San Luis Obispo, California) – vocals / **KEN WILLIAMS** (b. Long Beach, California) – lead guitar / **WEASEL SPANGOLA** (b. Cleveland, Ohio) – rhythm guitar / **MARK TULIN** (b. Philadelphia, Pennsylvania) – bass / **PRESTON RITTER** (b. Stockton, California) – drums

Reprise | Reprise

May 66. (7") *<0473>* **AIN'T IT HARD. / LITTLE OLIVE** [-] [ ]

Nov 66. (7") *(RS 20532) <0532>* **I HAD TOO MUCH TO DREAM (LAST NIGHT). / LUVIN'** [49] [11]
(re-iss.Mar79 UK on 'Radar'; ADA 16)

Apr 67. (7") *(RS 205 64) <0564>* **GET ME TO THE WORLD ON TIME. / ARE YOU LOVIN' ME MORE (BUT ENJOYING IT LESS)** [42] [27] Mar67

Apr 67. (lp; mono/stereo) *<(RLP/RSLP 6248)>* **ELECTRIC PRUNES** [ ] [ ]
– I had too much to dream last night / Bangles / Onie / Are you lovin' me more / Train for tomorrow / Sold to the highest bidder / Get me to the world on time / About a quarter to nine / The king is in the counting house / Luvin' / Try me on for size / The Toonerville trolley.

— **QUINT** – drums repl. RITTER

May 67. (7") *<0594>* **DR. DOGOOD. / HIDEAWAY** [-] [ ]

Jul 67. (7") *(RS 20607) <0607>* **THE GREAT BANANA HOAX. / WIND-UP TOYS** [ ] [ ]

Aug 67. (lp) *<RS 6262>* **UNDERGROUND** [-] [ ]
– The great banana hoax / Children of rain / Wind-up toys / Antique doll / It's not fair / I happen to love you / Dr. Dogood / I / Hideaway / Big city / Capt. Glory / A long day's flight.

Dec 67. (7") *(RS 23212)* **A LONG DAY'S FLIGHT. / THE KING IN HIS COUNTING HOUSE** [ ] [-]

1968. (7") *(RS 20652) <0652>* **EVERYBODY KNOWS YOU'RE NOT IN LOVE. / YOU NEVER HAD IT BETTER** [ ] [ ]

— added **DAVID AXELROD** – conductor / **RON MORGAN** – guitar repl. SPANGOLA / **BRETT WADE** (b. Vancouver, Canada) – bass, vocals, flute repl. MARK TULIN + **RICHARD WHETSTONE** (b. Hutchinson, Kansas) – drums (on session until '69) repl. QUINT

— **MARK KINCAID** (b. Topeka, Kansas) – vocals, guitar repl. JIM LOWE / also **JOHN HERREN** (b. Elk City, Oklahoma) – keyboards repl. WILLIAMS (above 2 amalgamating with **MORGAN, WADE** and **WHETSTONE)** There were now no original members left, even AXELROD went solo

Mar 68. (lp; mono/stereo) *<(RLP/RSLP 6275)>* **MASS IN F MINOR** [ ] [ ] Jan68
– Kyrie Eleison / Gloria / Credo / Sanctus / Benedictus / Agnus Dei.

Nov 68. (lp) *<(RSLP 6316)>* **RELEASE OF AN OATH** [ ] [ ]
– Kol Nidre / Holy are you / General confession / Individual confessional / Our father, our king / Adoration / Closing hymn.

— now without HERREN

Jun 69. (7") *<0756>* **HEY MR. PRESIDENT. / FLOWING SMOOTHLY** [-] [ ]

Jun 69. (lp) *<RS 6342>* **JUST GOOD OLD ROCK'N'ROLL** [-] [ ]
– Tracks / 14 year old funk / Sell / Sing to me / Silver passion mine / Love grows / So many people to tell / Finders keepers, losers weepers / Giant sunhouse / Violent rose / Thorjan.

– compilations etc. –

1968. (7") *Reprise; <0704>* **I HAD TOO MUCH TO DREAM LAST NIGHT. / GET ME TO THE WORLD ON TIME** [-] [ ]

1973. (7") *Elektra; (K 12102)* **I HAD TOO MUCH TO DREAM (LAST NIGHT). / ('Lies' by The Knickerbockers)** [ ] [-]

May 86. (lp/c) *Edsel; (ED/CED 179)* **LONG DAY'S FLIGHT** (66-67) [ ] [-]
– Ain't it hard / Little Olive / I had too much to dream (last night) / Luvin' / Get me to the world on time / Are you lovin' me more (but enjoying it less) / Bangles / Train for tomorrow / Sold to the highest bidder / Try me on for size / Doctor Do-good / Hideaway / The great banana hoax / Children of rain / Antique doll / I happen to love you / A long day's flight / You never had it better. *(cd-iss.Apr89; EDCD 179)*

May 97. (cd) *Heartbeat; (CDHB 67)* **STOCKHOLM 1967** [ ] [-]

ELIAS HULK

Formed: London, England ... 1969 PETER THORPE, GRANVILLE FRAZER, NEIL TATUM, JAMES HAINES and BERNARD JAMES. They released only one bluesy hard-rock album, 'UNCHAINED', which also dabbled with progressive rock. It sold extremely poorly, thus its now collectable value (nearly £200). Nothing has been heard of them since.

Recommended: UNCHAINED (*4)

PETER THORPE – vocals / **GRANVILLE FRAZER** – guitar / **NEIL TATUM** – guitar / **JAMES HAINES** – bass / **BERNARD JAMES** – drums

Youngblood / not issued

1970. (lp) *(SSYB 8)* **UNCHAINED** [ ] [-]
– Anthology of dreams / Nightmare / Been around too long / Yesterday's trip / We can fly / Free / Delhi blues / Ain't got you. *(re-iss.Jan90 on 'See For Miles' lp/cd; SEE/+CD 286)*

— as said split after above

Cass ELLIOT (see under ⇒ MAMAS & THE PAPAS)

ELOY

Formed: Hanover, Germany ... early '69 by FRANK BORNEMANN, who took the name from the futuristic race in HG Wells' 'The Time Machine'. BORNEMANN and the rest (ERICH SCHRIEVER, MANFRED WIECZORKE, WOLFGANG STOCKER and HELMUTH DRAHT) won a talent contest, resulting in a record deal with 'Philips'. Their eponymous debut in 1971 (written mostly by SCHRIEVER and WIECZORKE), was basically bloated, over-weight progressive rock and its relative failure led to BORNEMANN taking over control. They returned in 1973 on 'Harvest' records with a markedly improved second set, 'INSIDE', which contained the spaced-out 17-minute 'LAND OF NO BODY'. Their next, 'FLOATING' (1974) was a lot heavier than its predecessor, leading to a tour of the States. In 1975, BORNEMANN again changed direction, this time to a full-blown HG Wells-type concept piece, 'POWER AND THE PASSION', but it was lambasted for being over-produced and self-indulgent. ELOY continued in this vein for the next few albums until 1979's 'SILENT CRIES AND MIGHTY ECHOES' took on a more mid-70's PINK FLOYD or HAWKWIND approach. The sci-fi biased 80's albums were outdated slices of symphonic rock, although synthesizers were always present. They were finally rewarded with a UK contract in 1982 for the release of the album, 'PLANETS'. Another change of direction, this time to an even heavier progressive sound, won them a new audience, although this didn't improve their critical standing. • **Trivia:** All their 70's German lp's were issued on cd by 'Harvest' in the 90's.

Recommended: INSIDE (*7) / METROMANIA (*6) / PLANETS (*6) / CHRONICLES VOL.1 (*6) / CHRONICLES VOL.2 (*6)

FRANK BORNEMANN – lead guitar, vocals, percussion / **MANFRED WIECZORKE** – keyboards, vocals / **E. SCHRIEVER** – / **H. DRAHT** –

Philips / not issued

1971. (lp) *(6305 089)* **ELOY** [-] [-] German
– Today / Something yellow / Eloy / Song of a paranoid soldier / Voice of revolution / Isle of Sun / Dillus roady.

— **WOLFGANG STOECKER** – bass / **FRITZ RANDOW** – drums, percussion, flute, guitar, repl. SCHRIEVER + DRAHT

Electrola / Janus

1973. (lp) *(IC 062-29479)* <3062> **INSIDE** [-] [ ] German
– Land of nobody / Inside / Future city / Up and down.

— **LUITJEN JANSSEN** – bass repl. STOECKER

1974. (lp) *(IC 062-29521)* <7018> **FLOATING** [-] [ ] German
– Floating / The light from deep darkness / Castle in the air / Plastic girl / Madhouse.

— added **DETLEV SCHWAAR** – guitar

1975. (lp) *(IC 062-29602)* **POWER AND THE PASSION** [-] [-] German
– Introduction / Journey into / Lover over six centuries / Mutiny / Imprisonment / Daylight / Thoughts of home / The zany magician / Back into the present / Notre Dame.

— **BORNEMANN** with complete new line-up **DETLEV SCHMIDTCHEN** – keyboards, guitar / **KLAUS-PETER MATZIOL** – bass, vocals / **JUERGEN ROSENTHAL** – drums, percussion

1976. (lp) *(IC 062-31787)* **DAWN** [-] [-] German
– Awakening / Between the times: Memory – Flash – Appearance of the voice – Return to the voice / The Sun-song / The dance in doubt and fear / Lost (introduction) / Lost (the decision) / The midnight fight / The victory of mental force / Gliding into light and knowledge / Le reveil du soleil / The dawn.

1977. (lp) *(IC 064-32596)* **OCEAN** [-] [-] German
– Poseidon's creation / Incarnation of Logos / Decay of Logos / Atlantis agony at June 5th, 8498, 13 p.m. Gregorian Earthtime.

1978. (lp) *(IC 064-45269)* **SILENT CRIES AND MIGHTY ECHOES** [-] [-] German
– Astral entrance / Master of sensation / The apocapyse: Silent cries divide the nights – The vision – Burning – Force majeure / Pilot to Paradise / De labore solis / Mighty echoes.

1979. (d-lp) *(IC 164-32934/5)* **LIVE (live)** [-] [-] German
– Poseidon's creation / Incarnation of Logos / The Sun-song / The dance in doubt and fear / Mutiny / Gliding into light and knowledge / Inside / Atlantis agony at June 5th, 8498, 13 p.m., Gregorian Earthtime.

— **FRANK + KLAUS-PETER** added **HANNES ARKONA** – guitar / **HANNES FOLBERTH** – keyboards / **JIM McGILLIVRAY** – drums, percussion

1980. (lp) *(IC 064-45936)* **COLOURS** [-] [-] German
– Horizons / Illuminations / Giant / Impressions / Child migration / Galery / Silhouette / Sunset.

Heavy Metal / not issued

Jul 82. (lp/pic-lp/c) *(HMI LP/PD/MC 1) (IC 064-46483)* **PLANETS** [ ] [-]
– On the verge of darkening lights / Point of no return / Mysterious monolith / Queen of the night / At the gates of dawn / Sphinx / Carried by cosmic winds.

— **FRITZ RANDOW** – drums, percussion, returned to repl. McGILLIVRAY

Jan 83. (clear-lp/c) *(HMI LP/MC 3) (IC 064-46548)* **TIME TO TURN** [ ] [-]
– Through a somber galaxy / Behind the walls of imagination / Magic mirrors / Time to turn / End of an odyssey / The flash / Say, is it really true.

Apr 83. (lp/pic-lp/c) *(HMI LP/PD/MC 12) (IC 064-46714)* **PERFORMANCE** [ ] [-]
– In disguise / Shadow and light / Mirador / Surrender / Heartbeat / Fools / A broken frame.

Nov 83. (7"/7"pic-d) *(HM INT/PD 1)* **FOOLS. / HEARTBEAT** [ ] [-]

— (In 1984, they moved to 'E.M.I.' label in Germany only)

Sep 84. (lp/pic-lp/c/cd) *(HMI LP/PD/MC/XD 21) (792502-1)* **METROMANIA** [ ] [-]
– Escape to the heights / Follow the light / All life is one / Nightriders / Seeds of creation / Metromania / The stranger.

— **BORNEMANN** added **MICHAEL GERLACH** – keyboards, synthesizers + sessioners

— (Moved to 'S.P.V.' label in Germany only)

FM Revolver / not issued

Aug 89. (lp/pic-lp/c/cd) *(REV LP/PD/MC/XD 120)* **RA** [ ] [-]
– Voyager of the future race / Sensations / Dreams / Invasion of a megaforce / Rainbow / Hero. *(cd re-iss.Jan95 & Jan97 on 'SPV'; SPV 085-48022)*

S.P.V. / not issued

Dec 94. (cd) *(SPV 084-48202)* **THE TIDE RETURNS FOREVER** [ ] [-]
(re-iss.Jan97; same)

Jan 95. (cd) *(SPV 085-48082)* **DESTINATION** [ ] [-]
(re-iss.Jan97; same)

compilations, etc

Jul 94. (cd) *S.P.V.; (SPV084-48182)* **CHRONICLES VOL.1** [ ] [-]
Jul 94. (cd) *S.P.V.; (SPV084-48192)* **CHRONICLES VOL.2** [ ] [-]

EMBRYO

Formed: Munich, Germany ... 1969 by CHRISTIAN BURCHARD and EDGAR HOFMANN, who had both previously been in jazz outfit The CONTEMPORARY TRIO. In 1967, the two discovered free jazz, playing alongside CHRIS KARRER, PETER LEOPOLD, JIMMY JACKSON and DIETER SERFAS, who all went on to form AMON DUUL II. BURCHARD featured as a guest on their 1969 debut album, 'PHALLUS DEI', while he and HOFMANN were both members of The MAL WALDRON QUARTET (an American who had worked with jazz giants JOHN COLTRANE and BILLIE HOLIDAY). LOTHAR MEID soon joined and EMBRYO was born. Other early members came and went, until LOTHAR also departed, having been replaced by RALPH FISCHER and JOHN KELLY. This line-up completed the memorable 'OPAL' debut, a mixture of everything under the sun; jazz, psychedelia, rock, blues, soul, etc. It took continental music to a new depth, even coming with a free balloon as a gimmick. However, the record was the last to feature the great guitar work of JOHN KELLY, highlighted on one of the tracks, 'YOU DON'T KNOW WHAT'S HAPPENING'. BURCHARD and HOFMANN continued to work with many musicians over the next two decades; one of them, the 19 year-old ROMAN BUNKA, played on their classic follow-up, the ethnically fused 'EMBRYO'S RACHE'. The record was also graced with some splendid electric violin work from HOFMANN. BUNKA was to come and go over the next three albums, and didn't feature on the semi-classic 1972 release, 'FATHER, SON & HOLY GHOST'. Just prior to this, two albums, 'STEIG AUS' and 'ROCKSESSION', were to have been released by 'United Artists', although the label wanted a more conventional approach to their material. In the event, the albums subsequently surfaced the following year on the 'Brain' label. These were the last great pieces of EMBRYO for some time, featuring a re-working of the WALDRON 18-minute composition 'CALL', although they still failed to gain a British release (like everything they did!, & why?!). In 1974, BURCHARD & EMBRYO returned with 'WE KEEP ON', which, with its long studio jam sessions (provided by American jazzman CHARLIE MARIANO), didn't live up to their previous work. With MARIANO's involvement, the album found some recognition in the States where it had finally been released. EMBRYO subsequently became funkier, taking a lighter jazz-rock direction, forced on them by their label 'BASF'. This resulted in them forming their own 'April' label in 1975 alongside SPARIFANKAL, TON STEIN SCHERBEN and CHECKPOINT CHARLIE. A female vocalist, MARIA ARCHER, featured on their next two albums, the second of which was a disappointing live effort recorded in Austria. They exchanged a number of musicians and singers with the group MISSUS BEASTLEY, one of them being MARIA. In 1976, they set off for India, where BUNKA laid down most of the material for the 1977 album, 'APO CALYPSO'. This proceeds from this album financed another long journey (with family and friends) to Pakistan and Afghanistan. They came back with over 40 hours of tapings, resulting in the late 1979 release of 'EMBRYO'S REISE', a fantastic return of progressive ethnic rock. It featured the acid-speedster, 'ES IST, WIE'S IST', plus 'LOST SCOOTERS'. In the 80's, they completed more albums for 'Schneeball' & the Italian 'Materiali Sonori', although none of these could match anything from the last decade. They subsequently toured Third World countries, recruiting some fine African musicians. Upon their return, this new found ethnic sound introduced them to a more jazz-rock orientated audience.

Recommended: OPAL (*7) / EMBRYO'S RACHE (*8) / FATHER, SON & HOLY GHOST (*7) / STEIG AUS (*7) / ROCKSESSION (*7) / WE KEEP ON (*6) / EMBRYO'S REISE (*8)

CHRISTIAN BURCHARD – drums, vibraphone, keyboards / **EDGAR HOFMANN** – saxophone, violin, flute / **RALPH FISCHER** – bass, keyboards, vocals + **JOHN KELLY** – guitar; repl. LOTHAR MEID who joined DOLDINGER'S MOTHERHOOD and later AMON DUUL II (other early members before recording; JIMI JACKSON – keyboards / WOLFGANG PAAP – drums, percussion / DIETER SERFAS – drums, percussion / INGO SCHMIDT – sax) (guests on below album; **BETTSY ALLEH** – vocals / **ROBERTO DETREE** – motocello / **HOLGER TRULTZCH** – bongos (the latter two later joined BETWEEN and POPOL VUH respectively)

Ohr / not issued

1970. (lp) *(OMM 56.003)* **OPAL** [-] [-] German
– Opal / You don't know what's happening / Revolution / Glockenspiel / Got no name / Call / End of soul / People from Outer Space. *(re-iss.Nov88 on Italian 'Materiali Sonori' lp/cd; MASO 33046/+CD)*

— **HANSI FISCHER** – flute, vocals (ex-XHOL) repl. KELLY

— **ROMAN BUNKA** – bass; repl. RALPH

— guests; **HERMANN BREUERS** – keyboards / **FRANZ BONTGEN** – vocals / **JIMI JACKSON** – organ, mellotron (joined for 'STEIG AUS' & 'ROCKSESSION' albums)

U.A. / not issued

1971. (lp) *(UAS 29239)* **EMBRYO'S RACHE** [-] [-] German
– Tausendfuessler / Time:- 1. I can't wait – 2. Eva's wolke / Revenge / Espangna si, Franco no / Sittin' at the moon / Verwandlung.

— **DAVE KING** – bass, vocals, flute; repl. JORG EVERS (appeared on 'STEIG AUS' & 'ROCKSESSION' albums) and repl. ROMAN

— **SIEGFRIED SCHWAB** – guitar; repl. MAL WALDRON – piano (appeared on 'STEIG AUS' & 'ROCKSESSION' albums) and repl. HANSI

1972. (lp) *(UAS 29344)* **FATHER, SON AND HOLY GHOST** [-] [-] German
– The special trip / Nightmares / King Insano / Free / The sun song / Marimbaroos / Forgotten sea.

Brain / not issued

1973. (lp) *(1023)* **STEIG AUS** [-] [-] German
– Radio Marrakesh / Orient-express / Dreaming girls / Call: part 1; Organ walk – Marimba villagecall – part 2; Embryo. *(re-iss.1978; 40.121)*

Dec 73. (lp) *(1036)* **ROCKSESSION** [-] [-] German
– A place to go / Entrances / Warm canto / Dirge. *(UK-iss.1979 on 'Logo'; 0201.109)*

— **BURCHARD** assembled new line-up:- **ROMAN BUNKA** – saz (Turkish stringed instrument! (re-joined) / **DIETER MIEKAUTSCH** – keyboards (of MISSUS BEASTLEY, ex-MISSING LINK) / American **CHARLIE MARIANO** – saxophones, flute

BASF / BASF

1974. (lp) *(<20.21865-1>)* **WE KEEP ON** [-] [ ]
– No place to go / Flute and saz / Ehna, Ehna, Abu Lele / Hackbrett dance / Abdul Malek / Don't come tomorrow.

— **UWE MULLRICH** – bass (ex-LOKOMOTIVE KREUZBERG) repl. MIEKAUTSCH who joined MISSUS BEASTLEY. (**HOFMANN** guest on following albums)

Jan 75. (lp) *(<17.22385-3>)* **SURFIN'** [-] [ ]
– You can turn me on / Music of today / Secret / Surfin' / New ridin' / In my lunamatic / Dance of some broken glasses / Side track.

— added **DIETER MIEKAUTSCH** – keyboards (returned) / **MARIA ARCHER** – vocals

April / not issued

1976. (lp) *(00005)* **BAD HEADS AND BAD CATS** [-] [-] German
– Layed back / Nina Kupenda / Bad heads / Road song / After the rain / Klondykenetti / Tag X. *(re-iss.1979; same)*

1976. (lp) *(0003)* **LIVE (live)** [-] [-] German
– Bamboo railway / You can turn me on / Tiflis / Road song / After the rain / Bambule / No more love / Sho do Ima / The orange man. *(re-iss.1979; same)*

— **MICHAEL WEHMEYER** – keyboards; repl. ARCHER who joined MISSUS BEASTLEY / **BUTZE FISCHER** – drums, percussion (ex-MISSUS BEASTLEY) repl. MIEKAUSTCH (album guests; TRILOK GURTU – sitar + SHOBA GURTU – vox)

1977. (lp) *(0010)* **APO CALYPSO** [-] [-] German
– Break into pieces / Endless feeling / Together / Knast-funk / Amnesty total / Getalongwithasong. *(re-iss.1979; same)*

— line-up now; **BURCHARD, WEHMEYER, BUNKA, MULLRICH, HOFMANN / + REMI DREXLER** – guitar (ex-OUT OF FOCUS) / **FRIEDMANN JOSCH** – flutes, sax (ex-MISSUS BEASTLEY)

Schneeball / not issued

Nov 79. (d-lp) *(0020)* **EMBRYO'S REISE** [-] [-] German
– Strasse nach asien / Paki funk / Lost scooters / Anar, anar / Es ist, wie's ist / Kurdistan / Far East / Chan Delawar Khan / Farid / Cello, cello / Rog de quadamuna achna / Hymalaya radio / Maharaj / Lassie, lassie. *(cd-iss.May97; 30202)*

— added guests **CHARLIE MARIANO** – saxes / + KARNATAKA COLLEGE OF PERCUSSION

Oct 80. (lp) *(0023)* **LIFE! (live)** [-] [-] German

Nov 80. (lp) *(ASS 5)* **ANTHOLOGY 1970-1979** (unreleased tracks) [-] [-] German

— WEHMEYER, JOSCH + MULLRICH left to form DISSIDENTEN. They were repl. by **GERALD LUCIANO** – bass (ex-KATHARGO, ex-GURU GURU) / the returning **ROMAN BUNKA** (ex-MISSUS BEASTLEY, & solo) – guitar / **FREDDY SETZ** – drums (ex-AERA) / **JAY ZIER** – guitar (repl. DREXLER) / guests:- WERNER ALDINGER – bassoon / ULLI BASSENGE – vocals / ROLF SILVESTER / CHRIS KARRER – guitar, etc.

Dec 82. (d-lp) *(0028)* **LA BLAMA SPAROZZI** [-] [-] German
– Abart / Report / Xingu / La blama sparozzi / Jay / Computer killer / Cimbalero / Zapata pasteta / Kehlig sehlig / Duo / Mundbogen 9 / El Moro / Fun bahia / Auf gottes auge wachst kein gras / Evas zimmer / Nigeria Karnataka / Pia Pia / Wasserrader / Egypt Straat / Grace.

— now without SETZ + ZIER (**WEHMEYER** returned)

1984. (lp) *(33026)* **ZACK GLUCK** [-] [-] Italy
– Che Mangerai domani, vipera / Dage django / Zack gluck / Hoer, spiel, vergiss / Electraunico / Montespertoli / Che mangerai domani, vipera (part 2) / U-bahn / Ali Baba.

— (above album released on 'Materiali Sonori')

— now quartet of **BURCHARD, HOFMANN, LUCIANO** + new member **JULIUS GOLOMBECK** – guitar / plus a host of African percussionists

1985. (lp) *(1043)* **EMBRYO & YORUBA DUN DUN ORCHESTRA** [-] [-] German
– Welt-ab-originale aye-aye / Bata solo / Mix 3 / Just landed / Dun-dun solo / Dschamilija / Dun-dun solo / A-ara-eche-kalo.

— **BURCHARD, BUNKA, HOFMANN, WEHMEYER / + DIETER SERFAS** – drums / **LOKKO RICHTER** – bass (ex-MISSUS BEASTLEY, ex-AERA) / plus the African musicians again

Mar 87. (lp) *(33036)* **AFRICA** [-] [-] Italy
– Djangedi / Sango / Mao in Afrique (parts 1 & 2) / Konga / Yulius's song / Dun dun mix / Bush / Wole Alade / Lagune musik crossriver xylophone.

— (above album on 'Materiali Sonori')

— below was a 20th anniversary celebration with **BURCHARD** + a host of present & past members

Jan 89. (lp) *(1045)* **TURN PEACE** [-] [-] German

— above was their final release

– compilations, etc. –

Dec 74. (lp) *Brain; (200 152)* **THIS IS EMBRYO** [-] [-] German

Jan 76. (d-lp) *United Artists; (UAS 29774)* **CLASSIC GERMAN ROCK SCENE** (2nd & 3rd albums) [-] [-] German

EMERSON, LAKE & PALMER

Formed: London, England . . . mid-1970 by KEITH EMERSON, GREG LAKE and CARL PALMER, who had all cut their teeth in late 60's acts/combos (see below). After an aborted collaboration with HENDRIX (just prior to his death) and an appearance at the Isle Of Wight festival on the 29th August '70, they signed to 'Island'. Later in the year, they unleashed their eponymous debut, which immediately established the band as one of the leading purveyors of 70's prog-rock. In fact, they focused more on the classical side of things, proving that rock could be adapted for more high-brow tastes (EMERSON had previously explored this field while with The NICE). Next-up was 'TARKUS' (1971), a misguided concept piece which was based around a battle between a Manticore (a mythical beast) and a mechanicanized armadillo (!). Riding on the coat-tails of their debut success, it nevertheless reached No.1 (Top 10 in the States). Their third album was a live adaptation of Mussorgsky's 'PICTURES AT AN EXHIBITION', a fine effort which was let down by the closing track, a pointless cover of B.BUMBLE & THE STINGERS' early 60's hit 'NUTROCKER'. In 1972, they fulfilled their early potential with 'TRILOGY', an album that also made the Top 3, showcasing their most accomplished work to date on tracks such as 'THE ENDLESS ENIGMA', 'LIVING SIN' and 'ABADDON'S BOLERO'. The following year, ELP created the label 'Manticore', its first release being the 'BRAIN SALAD SURGERY' album which consolidated their position as one of the 70's leading bands, at least in commercial terms. Once again, former part-time KING CRIMSON member PETE SINFIELD was drafted in to collaborate on the lyrics. Tracks like the romantic 'STILL . . . YOU TURN ME ON' and the grandiose epic, 'KARN EVIL 9' were skillfully placed side by side with an arresting re-working of the hymn 'JERUSALEM'. While the band took a 2-year hiatus, they released a stop-gap triple live set entitled, 'WELCOME BACK MY FRIENDS' that was a little too overblown, pricey and pretentious for many. In 1975, the fans cringed when a solo GREG LAKE returned with the festive 'I BELIEVE IN FATHER CHRISTMAS' which hit No.2. The multi-talented keyboard maestro, KEITH EMERSON, also had a solo outing, a surprisingly basic rock'n'roll cover of Meade Lux Lewis' 'HONKY TONK TRAIN BLUES'. In 1977, ELP eventually returned with the double album, 'WORKS 1', a patchy affair which nevertheless spawned an inspired cover of Aaron Copeland's 'FANFARE FOR THE COMMON MAN'. In its edited form, the track gave the band a near No.1 in the UK. This however, was to be their last work of any relevance. All went solo in the 80's, and when PALMER formed PM, ELP conviently found a replacement (P) in the guise of Cozy POWELL. This set-up was short-lived although the original EMERSON, LAKE & PALMER re-formed once more in 1991. They were found floundering on past glories with the mediocre 'BLACK MOON' album the following year. • **Trivia:** 'Manticore', the label they formed in 1973, also signed PETE SINFIELD, P.F.M. and LITTLE RICHARD!

Recommended: EMERSON, LAKE & PALMER (*6) / PICTURES AT AN EXHIBITION (*6) / TRILOGY (*8) / BRAIN SALAD SURGERY (*8)

KEITH EMERSON (b. 2 Nov'44. Todmorden, England) – keyboards (ex-NICE, ex-GARY FARR & THE T-BONES / **GREG LAKE** (b.10 Nov'48, Bournemouth, England) – vocals, guitar, bass (ex-KING CRIMSON) / **CARL PALMER** (b.20 Mar'47, Birmingham, England) – drums, percussion (ex-ATOMIC ROOSTER, ex-CRAZY WORLD OF ARTHUR BROWN)

Island / Cotillion

Nov 70. (lp/c) *(ILPS/ILPC 9132)* **EMERSON, LAKE & PALMER** [4] [18]
– The barbarian / Take a pebble / Knife edge / The three fates:- Clotho – Lachesis – Acropus / Tank / Lucky man. *(re-iss.Dec73 on 'Manticore' lp/c; K/K4 43503) (cd-iss.1988 on 'WEA') (re-iss.cd Dec93 on 'Victory')*

Mar 71. (7") *<44106>* **LUCKY MAN. / KNIFE EDGE** [-] [48]
<US re-iss.Jan73 on 'Atlantic'; 13153> hit No.51>

Jun 71. (lp/c) *(ILPS/ILPC 9155)* **TARKUS** [1] [9]
– Tarkus:- Eruption – Stones of years – Iconoclast – The mass – Manticore – Battlefield – Aquatarkus – (conclusion) / Jeremy Bender / Bitches crystal / The

only way / Infinite space / A time and a place / Are you ready Eddy?. *(re-iss.Dec73 on 'Manticore' lp/c; K/K4 43504) (cd-iss.Sep89 on 'WEA') (re-iss.cd Dec93 on 'Victory')*

Sep 71. (7") *<44131>* **STONES OF YEARS. / A TIME AND A PLACE** [-] [ ]

Nov 71. (lp/c) *(HELP/HELC 1)* **PICTURES AT AN EXHIBITION** [3] [10]
– Promenade: The gnome – Promenade – The sage – The old castle – Blues variation – Promenade / The hut of Baba Yaga – The curse of Baba Yaga – The hut of Baba Yaga – The great gates of Kiev – Nutrocker. *(re-iss.Dec73 on 'Manticore' lp/c; K/K4 33501) (cd-iss.1988 on 'Cotillion' & Sep89 on 'WEA') (re-iss. Dec93 on 'Victory')*

Mar 72. (7") *<44151>* **NUTROCKER. / THE GREAT GATES OF KIEV** [-] [70]

Jul 72. (lp/c) *(ILPS/ILPC 9186)* **TRILOGY** [2] [5]
– The endless enigma (part 1) – Fugue – The endless enigma (part 2) / From the beginning / The sheriff / Hoedown / Trilogy / Living sin / Abaddon's bolero. *(re-iss.Dec73 on 'Manticore' lp/c; K/K4 43505) (cd-iss.Jun89 on 'Atlantic') (re-iss.cd Dec93 on 'Victory')*

Aug 72. (7") *<44158>* **FROM THE BEGINNING. / LIVING SIN** [-] [39]

Manticore Manticore

Dec 73. (lp/c) *(K/K4 53501)* **BRAIN SALAD SURGERY** [2] [11]
– Jerusalem / Toccata / Still . . .you turn me on / Benny the bouncer / Karn evil 9. 1st impression – part 1 & 2 – 2nd impression – 3rd impression. *(cd-iss.Jun89 on 'WEA') (re-iss.cd Dec93 on 'Victory')*

Dec 73. (7") *(K 13503)* **JERUSALEM. / WHEN THE APPLE BLOSSOM BLOOMS IN THE WINDMILLS OF YOUR MIND, I'LL BE YOUR VALENTINE** [ ] [-]

Dec 73. (7") *<2003>* **BRAIN SALAD SURGERY. / STILL YOU TURN ME ON** [-] [ ]

Aug 74. (t-lp/d-c) *(K/K4 63500)* **WELCOME BACK MY FRIENDS, TO THE SHOW THAT NEVER ENDS – LADIES AND GENTLEMEN . . . EMERSON, LAKE & PALMER (live)** [5] [4]
– Hoedown / Jerusalem / Toccata / Tarkus:- Eruption – Stones of years – Iconoclaust – The mass – Manticore – Battlefield – Epitaph – Aquatarkus – (conclusion) / Take a pebble – Piano improvisations – Take a pebble (conclusion) / Jeremy Bender / The sheriff / Karn evil 9. 1st impression – 2nd impression – 3rd impression. *(re-iss.cd Dec93 on 'Victory')*

Nov 75. (7"; by GREG LAKE) *(K 13511) <3305>* **I BELIEVE IN FATHER CHRISTMAS. / HUMBUG** [2] [ ]
(re-iss.Nov82 hit 72, & Dec83 hit 65) (re-iss.Nov92 on 'Atlantic'; A 7393)

Apr 76. (7"; by KEITH EMERSON) *(K 13513)* **HONKY TONK TRAIN BLUES. / BARREL HOUSE SHAKE DOWN** [21] [-]

Atlantic Atlantic

Mar 77. (d-lp/d-c) *(K/K4 80009)* **WORKS 1** [9] [12]
– Piano concerto No.1 – 1st movement: Allegro giojoso / 2nd movement: Andante molto cantabile / 3rd movement: Toccata con fuoco / Lend your love to me tonight / C'est la vie / Hallowed by thy name / Nobody loves you like I do / Closer to believing / The enemy God dances with the black spirits / L.A. nights / New Orleans / Bach: Two part invention in D minor / Food for your soul / Tank / Fanfare for the common man / Pirates. *(cd-iss.Jun89) (re-iss.d-cd Dec93 on 'Victory')*

Jun 77. (7"/12") *(K 10946/+T) <3398>* **FANFARE FOR THE COMMON MAN (edit). / BRAIN SALAD SURGERY** [2] [ ]

Aug 77. (7"; A-side by GREG LAKE) *(K 10990) <3405>* **C'EST LA VIE. / JEREMY BENDER** [ ] [ ]

Nov 77. (lp/c) *(K/K4 50422)* **WORKS 2** (compilation of rare and demo work) [20] [37]
– Tiger in a spotlight / When the apple blossoms bloom in the windmills of your mind, I'll be your valentine / Bullfrog / Brain salad surgery / Barrel house shake down / Watching over you / So far to fall / Maple leaf rag / I believe in Father Christmas / Close but not touching / Honky tonk train blues / Show me the way to go home. *(cd-iss.Jun89) (re-iss.cd Dec93 on 'Victory')*

Jan 78. (7"; A-side by GREG LAKE) **WATCHING OVER YOU. / HALLOWED BE THY NAME** [ ] [ ]

Nov 78. (lp/c) *(K/K4 50552)* **LOVE BEACH** [48] [55]
– All I want is you / Love beach / Taste of my love / The gambler / For you / Canario / Memoirs of an officer and a gentleman – Prologue – The education of a gentleman / Love at first sight / Letters from the front / Honourable company. *(cd-iss.Jun89) (re-iss.cd Dec93 on 'Victory')*

Nov 78. (7") *(K 11225)* **ALL I WANT IS YOU. / TIGER IN A SPOTLIGHT** [ ] [ ]

— (disbanded Dec78)

Oct 79. (lp/c) *(K/K4 50652)* **EMERSON, LAKE & PALMER IN CONCERT (live 1978)** [ ] [73]
– (introductory fanfare) / Peter Gunn / Tiger in a spotlight / C'est la vie / The enemy god dances with the black spirits / Knife edge / Piano concerto No.1 / Pictures at an exhibition.

Dec 79. (7") *(K 11416)* **PETER GUNN (live). / KNIFE EDGE (live)** [ ] [ ]

KEITH EMERSON

Atlantic Atlantic

Sep 80. (7") *(K 11612)* **TAXI RIDE (ROME). / MATER TENEBRARUM** [ ] [ ]

Atlantic Cinevox

Dec 80. (lp) *(K 50753)* **INFERNO (Soundtrack)** [ ] [ ]
– Inferno / Rose's descent into a cellar / The taxi ride / The library / Sarah in the library vaults / Bookbinder's delight / Rose leaves the apartment / Rose gets it / Elisa's story / A cat attic attack / Kazanian's tarantella / Mark's discovery / Matter tenebarum / Inferno (finals) / Ices, cigarettes, etc. *(re-iss.Mar90 on 'Cinevox'; CIA 5022)*

— added **NEIL SYMONETTE** – drums / **TRISTAN FRY** – percussion / **GREG BOWEN** – trumpet / **JEROME RICHARDSON** – sax / **PAULETTE McWILLIAMS** – vocals

M.C.A. Backstreet

Apr 81. (7") *(MCA 697)* **I'M A MAN. / NIGHTHAWKS MAIN TITLE THEME** [ ] [ ]

Apr 81. (lp) *(MCF 3107)* **NIGHTHAWKS (Soundtrack)** [ ] [ ]
– Nighthawks – main title theme / Mean stalkin' / The bust / Nighthawking / The chase / I'm a man / The chopper / tramway / I'm comin' in / Face to face / The flight of the hawk. *(re-iss.Jan89; MCA 1521)*

Red Bus not issued

Dec 83. (7") *(RBUS 85)* **UP THE ELEPHANT AND ROUND THE CASTLE. / ('A'instrumental)** [ ] [-]

— (above featured comedian JIM DAVIDSON)

Chord not issued

Apr 85. (lp) *(ESP 1)* **THE BEST OF KEITH EMERSON** (compilation) [ ] [-]

Apr 85. (lp/cd) *(CHORD/+CD 001)* **BEST REVENGE (Soundtrack with JOHN COLEMAN)** [ ] [-]
– Dream runner / The runner / Wha 'dya mean / Straight between the eyes / Orchestral suite to "Best Revenge" / Playing for keeps (main title theme). *(re-iss.Nov86)*

— **MOTT** – guitar / **DICK MORRISSEY + ANDREW BRENNAN + PETE KING** – saxophone

Apr 85. (lp/cd) *(CHORD/+CD 002)* **HONKY** [ ] [-]
– Hello sailor / Bach before the mast / Salt cay / Green ice / Intro-juicing / Big horn breakdown / Yancey special / Rum-a-thing / Jesus loves me. *(re-iss.May86)*

Apr 85. (lp) *(CHORD 003)* **HARMAGEDON / CHINA FREE FALL (Soundtracks; b-side by DEREK AUSTIN)** [ ] [-]
– Theme from Floi / Joe and Micheko / Children of the light / Funny's skate state / Zamedy stomp / Challenge of the psonic fighters. *(re-iss.Feb87)*

— Some with **DOREEN CHANTER** – vocals / **MIKE SEBBAGE** – vocals / **TOM NICOL + DEREK WILSON** – drums / **MICHAEL SHEPPARD** – bass, guitar, co-producer

May 86. (lp/cd) *(CHORD/+CD 004)* **MURDEROCK (soundtrack)** [ ] [-]
– Murderock / Tonight is your night / Streets to blame / Not so innocent / Prelude to Candice / Don't go in the shower / Coffee time / Candice / New York dash / Tonight is not your night / The spill one.

— next with The National Philharmonic Orchestra, plus **BRAD DELP, LEVON HELM.**

Dec 86. (cd) *(CDCOLL 1)* **THE EMERSON COLLECTION** (compilation) [ ] [-]

Priority not issued

Nov 88. (lp/c/cd) *(KEITH LP/MC/CD 1)* **EMERSON – THE CHRISTMAS ALBUM** [ ] [-]
(cd-iss.Jun93 & Dec95 on 'Amp';)

Emerson not issued

Dec 88. (7") *(KEITH 1)* **WE THREE KINGS OF ORIENT ARE. / CAPTAIN STARSHIP HOPKINS** [ ] [-]

Amp not issued

Apr 95. (cd) *(AMPCD 026)* **CHANGING STATES** [ ] [-]

Dec 95. (cd-s) **TROIKA (THE CHRISTMAS SINGLE). /** [ ] [-]

GREG LAKE BAND

GREG LAKE – vocals, guitar, bass with **TOMMY EYRE** – keyboards / **GARY MOORE** – guitar (ex-solo artist ex-THIN LIZZY ex-COLOSSEUM) / **TRISTRAM MARGETTS** – bass / **TED McKENNA** – drums (ex-SENSATIONAL ALEX HARVEY BAND)

Chrysalis Chrysalis

Sep 81. (7") *(CHS 2553)* **LOVE YOU TOO MUCH. / SOMEONE** [ ] [ ]

Oct 81. (lp/c) *(CHR/ZCHR 1357)* **GREG LAKE** [62] [62]
– Nuclear attack / Love you too much / It hurts / One before you go / Loving goodbye / Retribution drive / Black and blue / Let me love you once / The lies / For those who dare.

Dec 81. (7") **LET ME LOVE YOU ONCE. /** [-] [48]

Feb 82. (7") *(CHS 2567)* **IT HURTS. / RETRIBUTION DRIVE** [ ] [ ]

Jul 83. (lp/c) *(CHR/ZCHR 1392)* **MANOEUVRES** [ ] [ ]
– Manoeuvres / Too young to love / Paralysed / A woman like you / I don't want to lose your love tonight / It's you, you've got to believe / Famous last words / Slave to love / Haunted / I don't know why I still love you.

— LAKE joined ASIA with PALMER

PM

CARL PALMER with **TODD COCHRAN** – keyboards / **BARRY FINNERTY** – guitar, vocals / **JOHN NITZINGER** – guitar, vocals / **ERIK SCOTT** – bass, vocals

Ariola Ariola

May 80. (lp/c) *(ARL/ZCARL 5048)* **1 PM** [ ] [ ]
– Dynamite / You've got me rockin' / Green velvet splendour / Dreamers / Go on carry on / D'ya go all the way / Go for it / Madeleine / You're too much / Children of the air age.

Apr 80. (7") *(ARO 217)* **YOU GOT ME ROCKIN'. / GO FOR IT** [ ] [ ]

Jul 80. (7") *(ARO 234)* **DYNAMITE. / D'YA GO ALL THE WAY** [ ] [ ]

— (Jan81) PALMER joined ASIA.

EMERSON, LAKE & POWELL

are the new set up **COZY POWELL** (b.29 Dec'47, Cirencester, England) – drums, (ex-solo artist, ex-RAINBOW, etc.)

Polydor Polydor

Jul 86. (lp/c)(cd) *(POLD/+C 5191)(829 297-2)* **EMERSON, LAKE & POWELL** [35] [23] Jun 86
– Mars, the bringer of war / The score / Learning to fly / Touch and go / Miracle / Love blind / Step aside / Lay down your guns.

Jul 86. (7") *(POSP 804)* **TOUCH AND GO. / LEARNING TO FLY** [ ] [60] Jun 86
(12"+=) *(POSPX 804)* – The locomotion.

Sep 86. (7") **LAY DOWN YOUR GUNS. / ?** [-] [ ]

— (1987 originals reformed but disbanded Oct87)

3

was the unit formed by **EMERSON, PALMER** and American **ROBERT BERRY** – vocals (ex-HUSH)

Geffen Geffen

Feb 88. (lp/c/cd) *(924 181-1/-4/-2)* **TO THE POWER OF THREE** [ ] [ ]
– Talkin' about / Lover to lover / Chains / Desde la vida / Eight miles high / Runaway / You do or you don't / On my way home.

Feb 88. (7") **TALKIN' ABOUT. / LA VISTA** [-] [ ]

EMERSON, LAKE & PALMER

re-formed 1992.

Victory-London Victory-..

Apr 92. (cd/c/lp) *(828 318-2/-4/-2)* **BLACK MOON** [ ] [78]

– Black Moon / Paper blood / Affairs of the heart / Romeo and Juliet / Farewell to arms / Changing states / Burning bridges / Close to home / Better days / Footprints in the snow. *(cd re-iss.Apr97 on 'Essential'; ESMCD 506)*

London London

May 92. (7") *(LON 320)* **BLACK HOLE. / MILES IZ DEAD**
(12"+=/cd-s+=) *(LON X/CD 320)* – A blade of grass.

Nov 92. (7"/c-s) *(LON/+C 327)* **AFFAIRS OF THE HEART. / BETTER DAYS**
(cd-s+=) *(LONCD 327)* – A blade of grass / Black moon.
(cd-s) *(LOCDP 327)* – ('A'side) / Black moon (radio) / Fanfare for the common man / Jerusalem.

Feb 93. (cd/c) *(828 933-2/-4)* **LIVE AT THE ROYAL ALBERT HALL (live)**
– 1st impression part 2 / Tarkus: Eruption – Stones of years – Iconoclast / Knife edge / Paper blood / Romeo & Juliet / Creole dance / Still . . . you turn me on / Lucky man / Black moon / The pirates / Finale / Fanfare for the common man / America / Blue rondo A la Turk. *(cd re-iss.Apr97 on 'Essential'; ESMCD 504)*

Nov 93. (4xcd-box) *(828 459-2)* **RETURN OF THE MANTICORE** (old & new material)

Dec 93. (cd) *(828 477-2)* **WORKS LIVE (live)**

Sep 94. (cd/c) *(828 554-2/-4)* **IN THE HOT SEAT**
– Hand of truth / Daddy / One by one / Heart on ice / Thin line / Man in the long black coat / Change / Give me a reason to stay / Gone too soon / Street war. *(cd+=)*– Pictures at an exhibition: a) Promenade – b) The gnome – c) Promenade – d) The sage – e) The hut of Baba Yaga – f) The great gates of Kiev.

- compilations, others, etc. -

Nov 80. (lp/c) *Atlantic; (K/K4 50757)* **THE BEST OF EMERSON, LAKE & PALMER**
– Hoedown / Lucky man / Karn evil 9 / Trilogy / Fanfare for the common man / Still . . .you turn me on / Tiger in a spotlight / Jerusalem / Peter Gunn. *(cd-iss.1983; K2 50757)*

Jul 92. (cd/c/lp) *Atlantic;* **THE ATLANTIC YEARS**

Apr 97. (d-cd; GREG LAKE) *Essential; (ESDCD 522)* **FROM THE BEGINNING: THE GREG LAKE RETROSPECTIVE** -

EMTIDI

Formed: Germany . . . 1970 by MAIK HIRSCHFELDT and Canadian DOLLY HOLMES. Their eponymous debut album was issued a very limited edition for the 'Thorofon' label, although this was basically an acoustic folk set. In 1972, after working with DIETER DIERKS in his studio, they returned with the remarkable acid-folk set, 'SAAT'. Its many highlights included 'WALKIN' IN THE PARK' and the title track. They fused STEELEYE SPAN and The FAIRPORTS with ASH RA TEMPEL or even KLAUS SCHULZE. Sadly this was their final release.

Recommended: EMTIDI (*5) / SAAT (*9)

DOLLY HOLMES – vocals, guitar, bouzouki / **MAIK HIRSCHFELDT** – guitar, flute, vocals

Thorofon not issued

1971. (lp) *(7626374)* **EMTIDI** - - German
– Lookin' for people / Shadow on your face / Long long journey / No turn back / Space age / Let the joint go 'round / Yvonne's dream / Birds on a graveyard / Flute piece.

— DOLLY now vocals, keyboards + MAIK now multi + synths / added guests **DIETER DIERKS** – percussion, bass, mellotron

Pilz not issued

1972. (lp) *(20 29077-8)* **SAAT** - - German
– Walkin' in the park / Traume / Touch the sun / Long time rain / Saat / Die reise. *(cd-iss.1988 on 'Galaxis'; CD 9019)*

— split after above

END

Formed: Surrey, England . . . late '64 by COLIN GIFFIN and DAVE BROWN, who were originally called The INNOCENTS. They had previously had one skirmish with the UK Top 30 in 1961, guesting on BOBBY ANGELO & THE TUXEDOS' single, 'BABY SITTIN'. By 1965, the line-up was completed by NICKY GRAHAM, JOHN HORTON and ex-TUXEDOS drummer ROGER GROOM. Signing to 'Philips', they debuted with the GLYN JOHNS-produced beat 45, 'I CAN'T GET ANY JOY'. Early in 1967, without a contract in Britain, they had two big hits in Spain; 'YOU BETTER BELIEVE IT, BABY' and 'WHY'. They returned to England late in '67, soon unleashing a new psychedelic-styled 45, 'SHADES OF ORANGE'. This hit the attention of Rolling Stone BILL WYMAN, who wanted to produce their debut album, 'INTROSPECTION'. Unfortunately, his other commitments delayed its release, which was also hindered by their split. They found a new vocalist TIM HENDERSON, becoming the more creatively fruitful TUCKY BUZZARD. By 1973, they were re-united with WYMAN on their final fling, 'BUZZARD', released on the (Deep) 'Purple' label. • **Songwriters:** BROWN – GIFFIN, except YOU BETTER BELIEVE IT, BABY (Joe Tex) / PLEASE DO SOMETHING (Don Covay) / etc.

Recommended: INTROSPECTION (*6)

COLIN GIFFIN – vocals, guitar / **DAVE BROWN** – vocals, bass / **JOHN HORTON** – sax / **NICK GRAHAM** – keyboards, vocals / **ROGER GROOM** – drums

Philips Philips

Oct 65. (7") *(BF 1444)* <40323> **I CAN'T GET ANY JOY. / HEY LITTLE GIRL**

— **HUGH ATTWOOLL** – drums, repl. GROOM who joined NASHVILLE TEENS

— **GORDIE SMITH** – sax, repl. HORTON

Sonoplay not issued

Jan 67. (7") *(SN 20.002)* **YOU BETTER BELIEVE IT, BABY. / PLEASE DO SOMETHING** - - Spain

Mar 67. (7") *(SN 20.014)* **WHY. / YO-YO** - - Spain

Sep 67. (7") *(SN 20.0??)* **MORNING DEW. / NEW ORLEANS** - - Spain

Jan 68. (7") *(SN 20.054)* **LOVING, SACRED LOVING. / WE'VE GOT IT MADE** - - Spain

Decca London

Mar 68. (7") *(F 22750)* <1016> **SHADES OF ORANGE. / LOVING, SACRED LOVING** May68

— **TERRY TAYLOR** – guitar (ex-MODE), repl. SMITH

Dec 69. (lp; stereo/mono) *(S+/LK-R 5015)* <PS 560> **INTROSPECTION**
– Dreamworld / Under the rainbow / Shades of orange / Bromley Common / Cardboard watch / Introspection (part 1) / What does it feel like / Linen draper / Don't take me / Loving, sacred loving / She said yeah / Jacob's bladder / Introspection (part 2).

— had already split. GIFFIN released one-off single 'CHANGES IN OUR TIME' / 'WHEN I WAS SO YOUNG' for 'CBS' *(CBS 4030)*

- compilation -

Nov 96. (cd) *Tenth Planet; (TP 025)* **IN THE BEGINNING . . . THE END** -

TUCKY BUZZARD

TIM HENDERSON – vocals (ex-MODE) / **TERRY TAYLOR** – guitar / **NICK GRAHAM** – keyboards / **DAVE BROWN** – bass / **PAUL FRANCIS** – drums

Capitol Capitol

1969. (lp) <E-ST 787> **WARM SLASH** -
– Time will be your doctor / Stainless steel lady / Sally shotgun / Gu gu gu / My friend / Pisces apple lady / She's meat / Ace the face / Whiskey eyes / Rolling cloud.

Jun 71. (7") *(CL 15687)* **SHE'S A STRIKER. / HEARTBREAKER**

Jul 71. (lp) <(E-ST 864)> **COMING ON AGAIN**
– Mistreating woman / She's a striker / Fill you in / Need your love / Which way, when for why / Burnin' / Sky balloon / Ain't too soon.

— **RON TAYLOR** – guitar, repl. NICK

— **CHRIS JOHNSON** – drums, percussion, repl. PAUL

Purple Passport

Mar 73. (7") *(PUR 113)* **GOLD MEDALLIONS. / FAST BLUESY WOMAN**

Mar 73. (7") *(TPSA 7510)* <97001> **ALRIGHT ON THE NIGHT**
– Can't live without it / ast bluesy woman / Gold medallions / All I want is your love / Rainbow rider / "Rudi" movie star / Pictures / Last war.

— **PHIL TALBOT** – guitar, repl. RON

Nov 73. (lp) *(TPSA 7512)* <98001> **BUZZARD**
– Who do you love / Run in the mornin' / Hanging on in there (waiting for you to come) / Superboy rock'n'roller / Bo-bo's Hampton / Wine & wimmin' / Superfine lady / Near to me / Shy boy.

— split 1974.

Aug 77. (7") *(PUR 134)* **GOLD MEDALLIONS. / SUPERBOY ROCK'N'ROLLER** -

ENID

Formed: Finchden Manor, England . . .1974 by ROBERT JOHN GODFREY, FRANCIS LICKERISH and STEPHEN STEWART. In the late 60's, after leaving The Royal Academy Of Music, GODFREY became the orchestral musical director for BARCLAY JAMES HARVEST. In 1973, he released a solo album, 'THE FALL OF HYPERION', for 'Charisma', before adopting the group name, The ENID, a school in-joke. After a number of successful live shows, their debut, 'IN THE REGION OF THE SUMMER STARS' surfaced in '76. Similar to STEVE HACKETT's solo work at the time, this was a powerful concept piece, full of melancholy romantic breaks on tracks, 'THE FOOL . . . THE FALLING TOWER', 'THE DEVIL' and 'THE LOVERS'. The record earned them a break for 'Pye' records, the label itself going broke in 1980. This resulted in a few fallow years during which some of the members could be found backing KIM WILDE to earn a crust. 1983 saw the art-rockers make a comeback of sorts with a self-financed album, 'SOMETHING WICKED THIS WAY COMES'. The band reached a creative peak in 1986 when they showcased their 'SALOME' album in the form of a ballet at London's Hammersmith Odeon. In 1990, GODFREY re-surfaced as writer/manager for a fledgling band, COME SEPTEMBER.

Recommended: IN THE REGION OF THE SUMMER STARS (*7)

ROBERT JOHN GODFREY – keyboards / **FRANCIS LICKERISH** – guitar / **STEPHEN STEWART** – guitar, percussion (ex-PAVANQ; w/ TOM ROBINSON) / **GLENN TOLLETT** – bass, keyboards, tuba / **ROBBIE DOBSON** – drums

Buk Buk

Feb 76. (lp) *(BULP 2014)* <52001> **IN THE REGION OF THE SUMMER STARS** 1977
– The fool . . .the falling tower / Death, the reaper / The lovers / The Devil / The Sun / The last judgement / In the region of the summer stars. *(re-iss.Jul77 on 'EMI International'; INS 3005) (re-iss.Nov84 on 'EMI International'; 2603 231) (re-iss.Jun84 on 'Enid'; ENID 7) (cd-iss.1988; ENIDCD 7) (cd re-iss.May94 on 'Mandella'; MNTLCD 7)*

May 76. (7") *(BUK 3002)* **THE LOVERS. / IN THE REGION OF THE SUMMER STARS** -

— **CHARLIE ELSTON** – keyboards / **TERRY PACK** – bass + **DAVID STOREY** – drums, percussion, repl. TOLLETT, DOBSON + last lp guest trumpeter DAVE HANCOCK

EMI International EMI Inter..

May 77. (7") *(INT 534)* **JUBILEE. / OMEGA** -

Sep 77. (7") *(INT 540)* **GOLDEN EARRINGS. / OMEGA**
Nov 77. (lp/c) *(INS/TC-INS 3012)* **AERIE FAERIE NONSENSE**
– Prelude / Mayday Galliard / Ondine / Childe Roland / Fand: 1st movement – 2nd movement. *(re-iss.Nov84 on 'EMI International'; 2603 241) (re-iss.Jun84 on 'Enid'; ENID 6) (cd-iss.1988; ENIDCD 6) (cd re-iss.May94 on 'Mandella'; MNTLCD 6)*

—— **WILLIAM GILMOUR** – keyboards, repl. ELSTON

Pye / not issued

Feb 79. (lp) *(NSPH 18593)* **TOUCH ME**
– Charades: Humouresque – Cortege – Elegy (Touch Me) – Gallavant / Albion fair (pts.1 & 2). *(re-is.Feb84 on 'Enid'; ENID 5) (cd-iss.Feb90; ENIDCD 5) (cd re-iss.May94 on 'Mandella'; MNTLCD 5)*

—— **MARTIN RUSSELL** – keyboards, bass + **ROBBIE DOBSON** – drums (latter returned) to repl. PACK + STOREY

Aug 79. (7"colrd) *(7P 106)* **DAMBUSTERS MARCH – LAND OF HOPE AND GLORY. / THE SKYEBOAT SONG**
Oct 79. (lp) *(NH 116)(ZCNH 116)* **SIX PIECES**
– Sanctus / Once she was / Ring master / Punch and Judy man / Hall of mirrors / Dreamer. *(re-iss.Apr84 on 'Enid'; ENID 4) (cd-iss.Feb90; ENIDCD 4) (cd re-iss.May94 on 'Mandella'; MNTLCD 4)*
Jun 80. (7") *(7P 187)* **THE FOOL. / TITO**
Oct 80. (d-lp) *(18619)* **RHAPSODY IN ROCK** (w/ orchestra)
– God save the Queen / Dies Irae / Song of Fand / Punch and Judy man / Humouresque / Cortege / Wild thing / Sanctus / Hall of mirors / Dreamer.

E.M.I. / not issued

1980. (7") *(EMI 5109)* **GOLDEN EARRINGS. / 665 – THE GREAT BEAN**

—— Trimmed to duo of **GODFREY + STEWART** after they were off the road between 1981-82.

Bronze / not issued

Jul 81. (7") *(BRO 127)* **WHEN YOU WISH UPON A STAR. / JESSICA**
Nov 81. (7") *(BRO 134)* **HEIGH HO. / TWINKLE TWINKLE LITTLE STAR**

R.A.K. / not issued

Aug 82. (7") *(RAK 349)* **AND THEN THERE WERE NONE. / LETTER FROM AMERICA**
(re-iss.12" Oct84 on 'EMI'+=; EMI 5505)– Raindown.

Enid / not issued

Feb 83. (lp) *(ENID 3)* **SOMETHING WICKED THIS WAY COMES**
– Raindown / Jessica / And then there were none / Evensong / White star / Song for Europe / Something wicked this way comes / Letter from America / The Sun / Judgement / The dreamer. *(cd-iss.Jan87; ENIDCD 3) (cd re-iss.May94 on 'Mandella'; MNTLCD 1)*
Jan 84. (lp/c; mail order) *(ENID 1/+C)* **LIVE AT HAMMERSMITH VOL.1 (live 1979)**
– God save the Queen / The last judgement / In the region of the summer stars / Fand.
Jan 84. (lp/c; mail order) *(ENID 2/+C)* **LIVE AT HAMMERSMITH VOL.II (live 1979)**
(cd-iss.May94 on 'Mandella'; MNTLCD 10)
– Mayday Galliard / Humouresque / Cortege / Albion fair / Encore.
Oct 84. (d-lp) *(ENID 8)* **THE SPELL**
– Winter / Spring / Summer / Autumn / Elephants never die / The sentimental side of Mrs.James / For the family and friends of Mark / The song of Fand. *(cd-iss.Feb90; ENIDCD 8) (re-iss.May94 on 'Mandella'; MNTLCD 8)*
Apr 85. (lp) *(ENID 9)* **FAND SYMPHONIC TONE POEM**
– Fand (the music & words).
Mar 86. (lp) *(ENID 10)* **SALOME**
– O Salome / Sheets of blue / The change / The Jack / Flames of power. *(re-iss.cd May94 on 'Mandella'; MNTLCD 9)*

Dojo / not issued

Aug 86. (d-lp) *(DOJOLP 24)* **LOVERS AND FOOLS** (compilation)
– Hall of mirrors / Sheets of blue / The lovers / Evensong / Bright star / The flame of power / The fool . . .the falling tower / Something wicked this way comes / Summer / The flood / In the region of the summer stars / Fantasy on Scarborough fair.

Sedition / not issued

Sep 86. (7"/12") *(EDIT/+L 3314)* **ITCHYCOO PARK. / SHEETS OF BLUE**

Enid / not issued

1988. (cd) *(ENID 11)* **THE SEED AND THE SOWER**
– Children crossing / Bar of shadow / La rage / Longhome / Earth born. *(re-iss.May94 on 'Mandella'; MNTLCD 2)*
Feb 90. (cd) *(ENIDCD 12)* **FINAL NOISE**
– Childe Roland / Hall of mirrors / Song for Europe / Something wicked this way comes / Sheets of blue / Chaeldean crossing / La rage / Earthborn / Jerusalem.
1990. (7"/12") *(ENID 7/6 999)* **SALOME. / SALOMEE**

Mandella / not issued

Nov 94. (cd) *(MNTLCD 11)* **TRIPPING THE LIGHT FANTASTIC**
Oct 95. (cd) *(MNTLCD 12)* **SUNDIALER**
Aug 96. (d-cd) *(MNTLCD 13)* **ANARCHY ON 45**

Also issued a number of fan club/ bootlegs & associated releases released on 'The Stand' unless mentioned otherwise

1984. (lp) *(STAND 1)* **THE STAND 1984**
1985. (lp) *(STAND 2)* **THE STAND 1985**
1986. (lp; GLEN BAKER) *(STAND 3)* **BRIEF ENCOUNTER**
1986. (lp) *(LE 1)* **LIVERPOOL**
1987. (c) *(HAM 1)* **AT HAMMERSMITH 17th OCTOBER 1986 (live)**
1988. (c) *(HAM 2)* **AT HAMMERSMITH 30th October 1987 (live)**
1988. (lp/c; GODFREY & STEWART) *(HEART LP/C)* **JOINED BY THE HEART**
1988. (c; WILLIAM ARKLE, aka R.J. GODFREY) *(WAM 1)* **THE MUSIC OF WILLIAM ARKLE**
1989. Nuage; (c; ROBERT JOHN GODFREY) *(MM 1)* **REVERBERATIONS**
1989. Nuage; (c) *(MM 2)* **INNER PIECES**
1989. Nuage; (c) *(MM 3)* **INNER VISIONS**
Mar 95. Newt; (lp) *(AHOE 1)* **AN ALTERNATIVE HISTORY VOL.1**
Mar 95. Newt; (cd) *(AHOE 2)* **AN ALTERNATIVE HISTORY VOL.2**
Mar 95. Newt; (cd) *(AHOE 3)* **AN ALTERNATIVE HISTORY VOL.3**

ROBERT JOHN GODFREY

Charisma / not issued

1974. (lp) *(CAS 1084)* **FALL OF HYPERION**
– Raven / Mountains / Water song / End of side one / Isault / Daemon of the world – Arrival of the Phoenix – Across the abyss – Daemon – Wanderer – IHS – Tuba mirum.

Brian ENO

Born: BRIAN PETER GEORGE ST.JOHN LE BAPTISTE DE LA SALLE ENO, 15 May'48, Suffolk, England. After leaving art school, where he fronted heavy group MAXWELL DEMON, he joined ROXY MUSIC in 1971. Contributing greatly to their image and sound on the albums, 'ROXY MUSIC' & 'FOR YOUR PLEASURE', he left due to a dispute over their increasingly pop-rock orientated direction. His first post-ROXY venture was '(NO PUSSYFOOTING)' in 1973 with ROBERT FRIPP (of KING CRIMSON). This was nothing more than extreme experimentation of synth-electronics and treated guitar. However, it did provide art lovers with a photo-shot of ENO & FRIPP in a multi-mirrored room. His first solo work in early 1974, 'HERE COME THE WARM JETS', disappointed the critics, who gave it the thumbs down, bar one gem, 'BABY'S ON FIRE'. He released two more greatly improved efforts for 'Island' before he formed his own label in 1975, appropriately titled 'Obscure'. Preceding this, in a fit of depression, he joined The WINKIES for a short tour during Feb-Mar'74, but departed after being diagnosed with a collapsed lung. He recovered to find himself on an 'Island records' concert bill on '1st JUNE, 1974', alongside stablemates KEVIN AYERS, NICO and JOHN CALE. The following year, he was hit by a car, which caused slight but not lasting brain damage. 1975's 'ANOTHER GREEN WORLD' represented the fruition of ENO's aural experimentation, sculpting instrumental, insidiously melodic soundscapes while the title track was subsequently used as the theme tune for the BBC TV arts series, 'Arena'. 'BEFORE AND AFTER SCIENCE' (1977) was an equally brilliant, if colder sounding, tapestry of sonic delights. Around this time, ENO began working with DAVID BOWIE on a trilogy of lp's that included 'LOW' (1977) and 'HEROES' (1977), while the following year he hooked up with TALKING HEADS, producing three of their albums during the period 1978-'80. He also collaborated with DAVID BYRNE on the ethnic-flavoured 'MY LIFE IN THE BUSH OF GHOSTS' (1981). With 'AMBIENT 1: MUSIC FOR AIRPORTS' (1978), ENO created an innovative classic while 'APOLLO: ATMOSPHERS AND SOUNDTRACKS' (1983) was a beguiling fusion of country and ambient, the gorgeous 'DEEP BLUE DAY' belatedly cropping up on the 'TRAINSPOTTING' (1996) soundtrack. After initially collaborating with Canadian producer/engineer DANIEL LANOIS for production duties on such early 80's projects as 'THE PEARL' (a HAROLD BUDD/ENO album), the two worked wonders on U2's seminal 'UNFORGETTABLE FIRE' (1984). ENO clocked up further U2 production credits on 'THE JOSHUA TREE' (1987) and 'ACHTUNG BABY' (1991), scooping a joint Grammy (with LANOIS) in 1992 for the latter. The same year saw the release of a long awaited ENO solo album, 'NERVE NET', which took its cue from the burgeoning ambient techno scene. Throughout the 90's, this electronic auteur has continued to work on a dizzying array of music and other multi media projects, even publishing a volume of diaries in 1996, 'A YEAR WITH SWOLLEN APPENDICES'. The balding genius once described himself as a non-musician who just turned dials and swiches. Maybe, but he happens to turn the right dials and switches, and this technically brilliant ambient experimentalist's obscure new musak is possibly a direct link to what listeners will appreciate in the 21st century. • **Songwriters:** All composed by ENO. • **Trivia:** His 1977 song 'KING'S LEAD HAT' was in fact an anagram of TALKING HEADS. ENO has also done session and production work for JOHN CALE (1974-75), ROBERT WYATT (1975), ROBERT CALVERT (1975), DAVID BOWIE (1977) / DEVO (1978) / TALKING HEADS (1978-80) / U2 (1985-91 with Daniel Lanois) / etc.

Recommended: DESERT ISLAND SELECTION (*7) / HERE COME THE WARM JETS (*7) / ANOTHER GREEN WORLD (*9) / TAKING TIGER MOUNTAIN BY STRATEGY (*7) / NERVE NET (*6) / MY LIFE IN THE BUSH OF GHOSTS (*8) with DAVID BYRNE / APOLLO (*8) / WRONG WAY UP (*7) with JOHN CALE.

FRIPP & ENO

ROBERT FRIPP – guitar of KING CRIMSON / **BRIAN ENO** – synthesizers, instruments

Island-Help / Antilles

Nov 73. (lp) *(HELP 16) <7007>* **(NO PUSSYFOOTING)**
– The heavenly music corporation / Swastika girls. *(re-iss.Oct77 on 'Polydor'; 2343 095) (re-iss.Jan87 on 'E.G.' lp/cd; EGED/EEGCD 2)*

ENO

now solo with guest session people, including ROXY MUSIC musicians and ROBERT FRIPP, CHRIS SPEDDING, PAUL RUDOLPH and others.

Island / Island

Jan 74. (lp/c) *(ILPS/ICT <9268>)* **HERE COME THE WARM JETS** [26]
– Needles in the camel's eye / The paw paw Negro blowtorch / Baby's on fire / Cindy tells me / Driving me backwards / On some faraway beach / Black rank / Dead finks don't talk / Some of them are old / Here come the warm jets. *(re-iss.Mar77 on 'Polydor'; 2302 063) (re-iss.Jan87 on 'E.G.' lp/c/cd; EG LP/MC/CD 11) (cd re-iss.Mar91; same)*
Mar 74. (7") *(WIP 6178)* **SEVEN DEADLY FINNS. / LATER ON**

—— guests incl. PORTSMOUTH SINFONIA ORCHESTRA, PHIL COLLINS –

drums / etc.

Nov 74. (lp/c) *(ILPS/ICT <9309>)* **TAKING TIGER MOUNTAIN (BY STRATEGY)**
– Burning airlines give you so much more / Back in Judy's jungle / The fat lady of Limbourg / Mother whale eyeless / The great pretender / Third uncle / Put a straw under baby / The truth wheel / China my China / Taking tiger mountain. *(re-iss.Mar77 on 'Polydor'; 2302 068) (re-iss.Jan87 on 'E.G.' lp/c/cd; EG LP/MC/CD 17) (cd re-iss.Mar91; same)*

Aug 75. (7") *(WIP 6233) <036>* **THE LION SLEEPS TONIGHT (WIMOWEH). / I'LL COME RUNNING**

— now with **FRIPP** (3) / **COLLINS** (3) / **JOHN CALE** – viola (2) / **PAUL RUDOPLH** (3) / **PERCY JONES** – bass (3) / **ROD MELVIN** – piano (3) / **BRIAN TURRINGTON** – bass, piano (1)

Sep 75. (lp/c) *(ILPS/ICT <9351>)* **ANOTHER GREEN WORLD**
– Sky saw / Over Fire Island / St. Elmo's fire / In dark trees / The big ship / I'll come running / Another green world / Sombre reptiles / Little fishes / Golden hours / Becalmed / Zawinul – Lava / Everything merges with the night. *(re-iss.Mar77 on 'Polydor'; 2302 069) (re-iss.Jan87 & Mar91 on 'E.G.' lp/c/cd; EG LP/MC/CD 21)*

Obscure Antilles

Nov 75. (lp) *(OBS 3) <7030>* **DISCREET MUSIC**
– Discreet music 1 & 2 / Three Variations on canon in D major; a) Fullness of wind – b) French catalogues – c) Brutal ardour. *(re-iss.Jan87 on 'EG-Editions' lp/c/cd; EGED/EGEDC/EEGCD 23)*

FRIPP & ENO

collaborate again.

Help-Island Antilles

Dec 75. (lp) *(HELP 22) <7018>* **EVENING STAR**
– Wind on water / Evening star / Evensong / Wind on wind / An index of metals. *(re-iss.Oct77 on 'Polydor'; 2343 094) (re-iss.Jan87 on 'E.G.' lp/cd;* EGED/EEGCD 3)

— For the next couple of years he worked with 801 (PHIL MANZANERA's band). He also produced his own 'Obscure' label, discovering people including PENGUIN CAFE ORCHESTRA, MICHAEL NYMAN, MAX EASTLEY & DAVID TOOP, HAROLD BUDD plus JAN STEELE / JOHN CAGE. More commercially he also played on and produced 1977 albums by DAVID BOWIE, TALKING HEADS, ULTRAVOX.

BRIAN ENO

Polydor Island

Dec 77. (lp) *(2302 071) <9478>* **BEFORE AND AFTER SCIENCE**
– No one receiving / Backwater / Kurt's rejoiner / Energy fools the magician / King's lead hat / Here he comes / Julie with . . . / By this river / Through hollow lands / Spider and I. *(re-iss.Jan87 on 'E.G.' lp/c/cd; EG LP/MC/CD 32) (cd re-iss.Mar91; same)*

Jan 78. (7") *(2001 762)* **KING'S LEAD HAT. / R.A.F. (by "ENO & SNATCH")**

Polydor E.G.

Sep 78. (lp) *(2310 623) <EGS 105>* **MUSIC FOR FILMS** 55
– M386 / Aragon / From the same hill / Inland sea / Two rapid formations / Slow water / Sparrowfall 1 / Sparrowfall 2 / Sparrowfall 3 / Quartz / Events in dense fog / There is nobody / A measured room / Patrolling wire borders / Task force / Alternative 3 / Strange light / Final sunset. *(privately pressed 1976 on 'EG'; EGM 1) (re-iss.Jan87 on 'E.G.' lp/c/cd; EGED/EGEDC/EEGCD 5)*

Ambient P.V.C.

Mar 79. (lp/c) *(AMB/+C 001) <7908>* **AMBIENT 1: MUSIC FOR AIRPORTS**
– 1'1 / 2'1 / 1'2 / 2'2. *(re-iss.Jan87 on 'E.G.' lp/c/cd; EGED/EGEDC/EEGCD 17)*

— Early in '79, ENO and MOEBIUS & ROEDILIUS (from CLUSTER) released album 'AFTER THE HEAT' *(Sky 021)*

— Late in 1979, ENO collaborated with trumpeter JON HASSELL on album 'FOURTH WORLD VOL.1: POSSIBLE MUSICS' on 'E.G.'; *EGED 007)*

— next with **HAROLD BUDD** – piano

E.G.-Ambient E.G.

Apr 80. (lp; ENO & BUDD) *(EGAMB 002) <EGS 107>* **AMBIENT 2: THE PLATEAUX OF MIRRORS**
– First light / Steal away / The plateau of mirror / Above Chiangmai / An arc of doves / Not yet remembered / The chill air / Among fields of crystal / Wind in lonely fences / Failing light. *(re-iss.Jan87 on 'EG')*

— next with DAVID BYRNE, vocalist and instrumentalist w/ TALKING HEADS

E.G. Sire

Feb 81. (lp/c; BRIAN ENO & DAVID BYRNE) *(EG LP/MC 48) <6093>* **MY LIFE IN THE BUSH OF GHOSTS** 29 44
– America is waiting / Mea culpa / Regiment / Help me somebody / The Jezebel spirit / Qu'ran / Moonlight in glory / The carrier / A secret life / Come with us / Mountain of needles. *(re-iss.Jan87 on 'E.G.' lp/c/cd; EG LP/MC/CD 48)*

May 81. (7"; BRIAN ENO & DAVID BYRNE) *(EGO 1)* **THE JEZEBEL SPIRIT. / REGIMENT**
(12"+=) *(EGOX 1)* – Very very hungry (Qu'ran).

Mar 82. (lp/c) *('EG-Editions'; EGED/+C 20)* **AMBIENT (4): ON LAND** 93 -
– Lizard point / The lost day / Tal coat / Shadow / Lantern marsh / Unfamiliar wind / A clearing / Dunwich Beach, Autumn 1960. *(cd-iss.Jan87 on 'E.G.'; EEGCD 20)*

Jul 83. (lp; BRIAN ENO with DANIEL LANOIS & ROGER ENO) *(EGLP 53)* **APOLLO: ATMOSPHERES & SOUNDTRACKS** -
– Under stars / The secret place / Matta / Signals / An ending (ascent) / Under stars II / Drift / Silver morning / Deep blue day / Weightless / Always returning / Stars. *(re-iss.Jan87 & Mar91 on 'E.G.' lp/c/cd; EG LP/MC/CD 53)*

EG-Editions not issued

Aug 84. (lp; HAROLD BUDD & BRIAN ENO with DANIEL LANOIS) *(EGED 37)* **THE PEARL** -
– Late October / A stream with bright fish / The silver ball / Against the sky / Lost in the humming air / Dark-eyed sister / Their memories / The pearl / Foreshadowed / An echo of night / Still return. *(re-iss.Jan87 on 'E.G.' lp/c/cd; EG LP/MC/CD 37)*

— In 1984, he released 2 albums 'BEGEGNUNGEN I & II' with MOEBIUS, ROEDILUS & PLANK.

Aug 85. (lp/c; MICHAEL BROOK with BRIAN ENO & DANIEL LANOIS) *('EG-Editions'; EGED/+C 41)* **HYBRID** -
– Hybrid / Distant village / Mimosa / Pond life / Ocean motion / Midday / Earth floor / Vacant. *(re-iss.Nov86 on 'E.G.' lp/c/cd; EG LP/MC/CD 41)*

Aug 85. (lp; ROGER ENO with BRIAN ENO) *('EG-Editions'; EGED 42)* **VOICES** -
– A place in the wilderness / The day after / At the water's edge / Grey promenade / A paler sky / Through the blue / Evening tango / Recalling winter / Voices / The old dance / Reflections on I.K.B. *(re-iss.Jan87 on 'E.G.' lp/c/cd; EG LP/MC/CD 42)*

Jan 87. (lp/cd) *(EG LP/CD 64)* **THURSDAY AFTERNOON** -
– Thursday afternoon. *(1 track only) (re-iss.cd Mar91; same)*

ENO / CALE

— (collaboration **JOHN CALE** – vocals, multi-)with **ROBERT AHWAI** – rhythm guitar / **DARYL JOHNSON** – bass / **NEIL CATCHPOLE** – violin / **RONALD JONES** – drums, tabla / **DAVE YOUNG** – guitars, bass

Land Opal-Warner

Oct 90. (lp/c/cd) *(AS/+C/CD 12)* **WRONG WAY UP**
– Lay my love / One word / In the backroom / Empty frame / Cordoba / Spinning away / Footsteps / Been there done that / Crime in the desert / The river. *(re-iss.Jul92; same)*

Nov 90. (12"ep/cd-ep) **ONE WORLD. / GRANDFATHER'S HOUSE / PALAQUIN** -

BRIAN ENO

Opal-WEA Opal-Warner

Jul 92. (7") **FRACTIAL ZOOM. / ('A'-Moby mix)**
(12"+=) – (4 mixes).
(cd-s++=) – (another mix) / The roil, the choke.

Sep 92. (cd/c) *(9362 45033-2/-4)* **NERVE NET** 70
– Fractial zoom / Wire shock / What actually happened? / Pierre in mist / My squelchy life / Decentre / Juju space jazz / The roil, the choke / Ali click / Distributing being / Web.

Oct 92. (7") **ALI CLICK (Beirut mix). / ('A'-Rural mix)**
(12"+=) – ('A'-Markus Draws + Grid mixes).
(cd-s) – ('A'side) / ('A'-Markus Draws + Grid mixes) / ('A'-trance long darkly mad mix) / ('A'-trance instrumental).

Nov 92. (cd/c) *(9362 45010-2/-4)* **THE SHUTOV ASSEMBLY**
– Triennale / Alhondiga / Markgraph / Lanzarote / Francisco / Riverside / Innocenti / Stedelijk / Ikebukero / Cavallino.

— (above music inspired by Moscow painter Sergei Shutov)

— Around the same time as above, he lectured at Sadler's Wells, and is the brunt of NME jokes as Professor Eno.

All Saints Gyroscope

Jun 93. (cd) *(ASCD 015)* **:NEROLI:**
– :Neroli:.

— Above long piece of music, was used in hospitals for childbirth!

— Sep 94; he was credited on JAMES' ltd.album 'WAH WAH'.

Oct 95. (lp/c/cd; BRIAN ENO & JAH WOBBLE) *(AS/+C/CD 023)* **SPINNER** 71
– Where we lived / Like organza / Steam / Garden recalled / Marine radio / Unusual balance / Space diary 1 / Spinner / Transmitter and trumpet / Left where it fell.

Jun 97. (cd) *(ASCD 032)* **THE DROP**
– Slip dip / But if / Belgium drop / Cornered / Black drop / Out-out / Swanky / Coasters / Blissed / M.C. Organ / Boomcubist / Hazard / Rayonism / Dutch blur / Back clack / Dear world / Iced world.

– his compilations, others, etc. –

on 'E.G.' unless mentioned otherwise

Apr 82. (d-c; FRIPP & ENO) *(EGDC 2)* **NO PUSSYFOOTIN' / EVENING STAR** -

Nov 83. (10xlp-box) *(EGBS 002)* **WORKING BACKWARDS 1983-1973** -
– (first 9 lp's, plus MUSIC FOR FILMS VOL.2 / + RARITIES m-lp:- Seven deadly finns / The lion sleeps tonight / Strong flashes of light / More volts / Mist rhythm)

Mar 86. (lp/c) *(EG LP/MC 65)* **MORE BLANK THAN FRANK** -
(cd-iss.Jun87 & Mar91; EGCD 65)

Jan 87. (cd) *(EGCD 65)* **DESERT ISLAND SELECTION** -
– Here he comes / Everything merges with the night / I'll come running (edit) / On some faraway beach (edit) / Spirits drifting / Back in Judy's jungle / St. Elmo's fire / No one receiving / Julie with . . . / Taking tiger mountain (edit) / 1'1.

Jan 87. (lp/c) *EG-Editions; (EGED/+C 35)* **MUSIC FOR FILMS 2** -
– The dove / Roman twilight / Matta / Dawn, marshland / Climate study / The secret place / An ending (ascent) / Always returning 1 / Signals / Under stars / Drift / Study / Approaching Taidu / Always returning 2.

Mar 89. (cd-s) *(CDT 41)* **ANOTHER GREEN WORLD / DOVER BEACH / DEEP BLUE DAY / 2'1** -

Dec 89. (3xc-box)(3xcd-box) *(EG BM/BC 7)* **ISLAND VARIOUS ARTISTS** -
– (ANOTHER GREEN WORLD / BEFORE AND AFTER SCIENCE / APOLLO)

Nov 93. (3xcd-box) *Virgin; (ENOBX 1)* **BRIAN ENO** (collaborations) -

Nov 93. (3xcd-box) *Virgin; (ENOBX 2)* **BRIAN ENO 2** (collaborations) -

Feb 94. (cd/c) *Venture; (CD/TC VE 920)* **THE ESSENTIAL FRIPP AND ENO** -

Oct 94. (3xcd-box) *Virgin; (TPAK 36)* **THE COMPACT COLLECTION** -

— ENO contributed 2 tracks on live lp 'JUNE 1st, 1974' with KEVIN AYERS, NICO and JOHN CALE. He also with brother ROGER and DANIEL LANOIS provided one track to DUNE film (1984). For albums by CLUSTER & ENO; see CLUSTER.

EPIDAURUS

Formed: Germany . . . 1976 as a studio outfit. This obscure band recorded only one album, the seminal 'EARTHLY PARADISE' (1977). Featuring hypnotic displays of instrumental dexterity (moog, clarinet, mellotron etc.), the album became an instant classic among afficiondos and fans can only wonder at what 'EPIDAURUS' might've produced had they been more prolific. As it stands, their debut has since become something of a cult item and is highly sought after by collectors.

Recommended: EARTHLY PARADISE (*8)

CHRISTIANE WARD – vocals / **GUNTHER HENNE** – organ, mellotron, moog, clavinet, piano / **GERD LINKE** – organ, mellotron, moog, clavinet, piano / **HEINZ KUNERT** – bass / **MANFRED STRUCK + VOLKER OEHMIG** – drums, percussion

Gema / not issued

1977. (lp) *(PL 1004)* **EARTLY PARADISE** [-] [-] German
– Actions and reactions / Silas Marner / Wings of the dove / Andas / Mitternachstraum.

— never returned to the studio

EPISODE SIX

Formed: Harrow, England . . . 1965 by sister and brother SHEILA and GRAHAM CARTER-DIMMOCK plus vocalist ANDY ROSS (all ex-LIGHTNINGS), who recruited (ex-MADISONS); HARVEY SHIELDS, TONY LANDER and in 1964; ROGER GLOVER. In April '65, ROSS quit and was replaced by IAN GILLAN. Soon they were snapped up by 'Pye', who brought out The BEATLES-influenced debut, 'PUT YOURSELF IN MY PLACE', in early '66. However several 45's later (notably the psychedelic 'I CAN SEE THROUGH YOU'), the band split, GILLAN and GLOVER of course going on to greater and heavier things; DEEP PURPLE. • **Songwriters:** GLOVER wrote most except some by GRAHAM or HARVEY. Covered; PUT YOURSELF IN MY PLACE (Elgins) / I HEAR TRUMPETS BLOW (Tokens) / HERE, THERE AND EVERYWHERE (Beatles) / I WILL BREAK YOUR HEART (Charles Aznavour) / BABY BABY BABY (Cliff Bennett & The Rebel Rousers) / MORNING DEW (Tim Rose) / etc.

Recommended: PUT YOURSELF IN MY PLACE (*6)

IAN GILLAN – vocals / **SHEILA CARTER-DIMMOCK** – organ, vocals / **GRAHAM CARTER-DIMMOCK** – rhythm guitar, vocals / **TONY LANDER** – lead guitar / **ROGER GLOVER** – bass / **HARVEY SHIELDS** – drums

Pye / not issued

Jan 66. (7") *(7N 17018)* **PUT YOURSELF IN MY PLACE. / THAT'S ALL I WANT** [ ] [-]
Apr 66. (7") *(7N 17110)* **I HEAR TRUMPETS BLOW. / TRUE LOVE IS FUNNY THAT WAY** [ ] [-]
Aug 66. (7") *(7N 17147)* **HERE, THERE AND EVERYWHERE. / MIGHTY MORRIS TEN** [ ] [-]
Nov 66. (7"; SHEILA CARTER & EPISODE SIX) *(7N 17194)* **I WILL WARM YOUR HEART. / INCENSE** [ ] [-]
Feb 67. (7") *(7N 17244)* **LOVE, HATE, REVENGE. / BABY BABY BABY** [ ] [-]
Jun 67. (7") *(7N 17330)* **MORNING DEW. / SUNSHINE GIRL** [ ] [-]
Sep 67. (7"; as NEO MAYO) *(7N 17371)* **I WON'T HURT YOU. / U.F.O.** [ ] [-]

— above was actually a solo single by GRAHAM under above pseudonym.

— **JOHN KERRISON** – drums, repl.

Oct 67. (7") *(7N 17376)* **I CAN SEE THROUGH YOU. / WHEN I FALL IN LOVE** [ ] [ ]

M.G.M. / M.G.M.

May 68. (7"; as EPISODE) *(1409)* **LITTLE ONE. / WIDE SMILES** [ ] [ ]

— **MICK UNDERWOOD** – drums (ex-HERD), repl. KERRISON

Chapter One / Chapter One

Oct 68. (7") *(CH 103)* <2902> **LUCKY SUNDAY. / MR. UNIVERSE** [ ] [ ]
Jan 69. (7") *(CH 104)* **MOZART VERSUS THE REST. / JAK D'OR** [ ] [-]

— Finally finished their last chapter in June '69. They did however leave behind another track 'GENTLEMEN OF THE PARK' used on the film 'Les Bicyclettes De Belsize'. Only available Mar69 on 'Polydor' shared soundtrack 'MUSIC FROM TWISTED NERVE & LES BICYCLETTES DE BELSIZE'; *(583 728)*. GILLAN and GLOVER joined heavy heroes DEEP PURPLE, while UNDERWOOD joined QUATERMASS. SHEILA and GRAHAM worked in Beirut, before returning to England.

compilations, others

Sep 87. (lp/cd) *P.R.T.; (PYL/PYC 6026)* **PUT YOURSELF IN MY PLACE** [ ] [-]
– (all the singles 1966-1967 except GRAHAM's solo)
Jul 91. (cd) *Sequel; (NEXCD 156)* **THE ROOTS OF DEEP PURPLE: THE COMPLETE EPISODE SIX (THE COMPLETE PYE SESSIONS)** [ ] [-]

EPITAPH

Formed: Dortmund, Germany . . . 1969 by CLIFF JACKSON. Comprising an Anglo-Germanic blend of musicians, and drawing on early 70's English heavy rock, the band's self-titled debut was released in 1971 on Polydor. Both this album and 1972's 'STOP, LOOK AND LISTEN' were heavily progressive in style while 'OUTSIDE THE LAW' (1974) saw the band adopting a more basic heavy rock sound. Signed to American label 'Billingsgate', the band were primed to break into the lucrative U.S. market when disaster struck and the company went bankrupt. This effectively finished off the band although CLIFF JACKSON recruited a new cast of musicians, finally emerging with the 'RETURN TO REALITY' album in 1979 after inking a deal with 'Brain' records. Neither this album nor any subsequent efforts matched the quality of the band's earlier output and even a reformation of the original EPITAPH line-up in the early 80's failed to repeat past glories.

Recommended: EPITAPH (*6) / STOP, LOOK AND LISTEN (*7)

CLIFF JACKSON (b. England) – vocals, guitar / **BERND KOLBE** – bass, vocals / **KLAUS WALZ** – guitar, vocals / **JIM McGILLIVRAY** – drums

Polydor / not issued

1971. (lp) *(2371 225)* **EPITAPH** [-] [-] German
1972. (7") **LONDON GIRL. /** [-] [-] German
1972. (7") **I'M TRYING. / CHANGING WORLD** [-] [-] German
1972. (lp) *(2371 274)* **STOP, LOOK AND LISTEN** [-] [-] German
– Crossroads / Nightingale / Uptight / Fly / Stop, look and listen.

Zebra-Polydor / not issued

Jan 73. (7") *(2047 003)* **AUTUMN '71. / ARE YOU READY** [-] [-] German
Apr 73. (7") *(2047 005)* **WE LOVE YOU ALICE. / PARADISE FOR SALE** [-] [-] German

— **ACHIM WIELERT** – drums, percussion; repl. McGILLIVRAY

Membran / Billingsgate

1974. (lp) *(22-131-1)* <BG 1009> **OUTSIDE THE LAW** [-] [ ]
– Reflexion / Woman / Big city / In your eyes / Outside the law / Tequila shuffle / Fresh air. *(re-iss.1979 on 'Babylon'; 80.001)*

— **NORBERT LEHMANN** – drums (ex-KARTHAGO) repl. ACHIM

— split **JACKSON** but re-formed new line-up in 1977; **HEINZ GLASS** – guitar / **MICHAEL KARCH** – keyboards / **HARVEY JANSSEN** – bass / **FRITZ RANDOW** – drums

Brain / not issued

1979. (lp) *(60.185)* **RETURN TO REALITY** [-] [-] German
– Set your spirit free / Strangers / We can get together / Summer sky / On the road / Return to reality / Spread your wings.

— KARSCH departed during recording of below

1980. (lp) *(60.274)* **SEE YOU IN ALASKA** [-] [-] German
– Do you believe in love / Hold on / Bad feeling / Fantasy / See you in Alaska / When I lose your love / Keep on moving / Tonight / Telephone line.
1981. (lp) *(60.385)* **LIVE (live)** [-] [-] German
– Still alive / Hard life / Kamikaze / Tequila Fritz / Goin' to Chicago / Die high / On the road / What about me / Do you feel right.

— **JACKSON** re-united original members; *KLAUS WALZ* – guitar, vocals / **BERNIE KOLBE** – bass, vocals / **NORBERT LEHMANN** – drums, vocals

Rockport / not issued

1982. (lp) *(RO 14)* **DANGER MAN** [-] [-] German
– Long live the children / Heartless / High wire / Snake charmer / Small town girl / Ain't no liar / Let me know / The daughter.

— split after aboves attempt

– compilations, etc. –

1979. (d-lp) *Babylon; (80.002)* **HANDICAP** [-] [-] German

EPSILON

Formed: Germany. The band were considerably influenced by English psychedelic, art-rock and progressive bands, their 1971 self-titled debut notable for ORTEL's distinctive organ playing. By the release of 1972's 'MOVE ON', the band had adopted a looser, suppler sound that shied away from the symphonic strainings of the debut. The new sound complimented ORTEL's soul based vocal and the album marked the creative highpoint of EPSILON's career. Ironically, ORTEL and ERTL had already left the band by this point and a slightly modified EPSILON cut the average 'OFF' album for 'Philips' in 1974. With success continuing to elude them, the band recorded another couple of flop singles for 'Ariola' in 1975 before splitting, WINZOWSKI forming the MICHAEL WYNN band and later recruiting DAANSEN.

Recommended: EPSILON (*5) / MOVE ON (*7)

WALTER ORTEL – organ, piano, vocals / **MICHAEL WINZKOWSKI** – guitar, vocals / **MICHAEL ERTL** – bass / **HAERTMUT PFANNMULLER** – drums, percussion

Bacillus / not issued

Apr 71. (lp) *(6494 001)* **EPSILON** [-] [-] German
– Two-2-II / 2-Four-4 / Every day's pain / Before / Between midnight / Paint it black . . . or white / Hurry up. *(re-iss.1972 on 'Bellaphon'; BLPS 19070) (re-iss.1977; BAC 2002) (re-iss.1982; 260-09-017) (cd-iss.1990's)*

— with guests **CURT CRESS** – drums, percussion (ex-ORANGE PEEL) / **CHRISTIAN FELKE** – flute (ex-NOSFERATU) / **RAINER MARZ** – guitar, vocals (ex-JERONIMO) / **PETE BENDER** – backing vocals

Bellaphon / not issued

Feb 72. (lp) *(BLPS 19078)* **MOVE ON** [-] [-] German
– Walkin' on my way / She belongs to me / Feelings / What about a future / Move on / Reichelsheim / Hear me crying / Waiting / Don't know why. *(re-iss.1977 on 'Bacillus'; BAC 2004) (re-iss.1982 on 'Bacillus'; 260-09-012) (cd-iss.1990's)*

— **HEINRICH MOHN** – bass (ex-ORANGE PEEL) repl. ERTL

— **JOHAN DAANSEN** – guitar, keyboards, vocals; repl. ORTEL

— added for live shows **PETER KOCH** – percussion (ex-JERONIMO)

Philips / not issued

1974. (lp) *(6305 216)* **OFF** [-] [-] German
– I've been moving / A new day / On the ode to John / Behind the border / Logo motive / Let's sit down / Open your eyes / Sadness / I know now.

— released two singles for 'Ariola' in 1975. WINZOWSKI became MICHAEL WYNN and formed his own band with DAANSEN

Roky ERICKSON
(see under ⇒ 13th FLOOR ELEVATORS)

EULENSPYGEL

Formed: Germany ... 1970 as The ROYAL SERVANTS by DETLEF NOTTRODT and MATTHIAS MAIER. Changing their name to EULENSPYGEL, the band released the album '2' in 1971, a more progressive offering than 'WE', blending a diverse array of musical styles with the vocals sung this time around in the band's native German. The album caused controversy with its eminently distasteful cover shot of a slowly sizzling chick, later withdrawn after a barrage of complaints. Unbowed, the band returned with the 'AUSSCHUSS' album in 1972. Similarly progressive in content, the record was the last offering from the group until 1979 when NOTTRODT re-emerged with a different line-up on the self-titled 'EULENSPYGEL'. The band recorded a final album in 1983 before fading into obscurity.

Recommended: 2 (*8)

DETLEV 'KEUCHER' NOTTRODT – vocals, guitars / **MATTHIAS 'JAMES' THUROW** – guitars, violin / **MANFRED MAIER** – vocals / **RONALD LIBAL** – bass / **REINHARD** – organ / **GUNTER KLINGER** – drums, percussion

Elite Special — not issued

1970. (lp; ROYAL SERVANTS) *(PLPS 30130)* **WE** [-] [-] German

— **NOTTRODT, THUROW, LIBAL + KLINGER** recruited **MULO MAULBETSCH** – vocals, harmonica / **KARLHEINZ GROSSHANS** – organ, vocals / **CORNELIUS HAUPTMANN** – flute

Spiegelei — not issued

Sep 71. (lp) *(28760-7U)* **2** [-] [-] German
– Till / Son my / Konsumgewasche / Staub auf deinem haar / Die wunde bleibt / Das lied vom ende: Erstans – Alt – Jung sein – Hastig und kaputt – Das ende vom lied.

— now without CORNELIUS

Jul 72. (lp) *(28780-5U)* **AUSSCHUSS** [-] [-] German
– Abfall / Menschenmacher / Teufelskreis / Herzliches beileid / Der fremde / Untertanenfabrik. *(re-iss.1972 with new non-offensive cover; 28770-6U)*

— **NOTTRODT** re-surfaced with new line-up; **GUNTER MAREK** – guitar / **PETER WEBER** – bass / **PETER GARATTONI** – drums, percussion

Bellaphon — not issued

1979. (lp) *(BBS 2584)* **EULENSPYGEL** [-] [-] German
– Boogie / Spaziergang / Mir reicht's / Liebeslied / Maedchen / Till Eulenspygel / Mein freund Hans / Kinderlied / Begegnung / Ich flipp' aus.

Neue Welt — not issued

1983. (lp) *(NW 9009)* **LAUT UND DEUTLICH** [-] [-] German
– Gib mir deine liebe / No future generation / Mei neuer job / Elvira / Heut wird's passieren / Eiszeit / Dompteur / / Jetzt han i's g'schafft / Dr. Fool / Du bist soo wunderschon.

— disappeared once again

EXPLORERS
(see under ⇒ ROXY MUSIC)

EYES

Formed: Ealing, West London, England ...1962/3 as The RENEGADES. They changed their name to GERRY HART & THE HARTBEATS before becoming The EYES late in '64, a blinding R&B act who played garage sounding covers. Signing to 'Mercury', the band releaed a string of well-received 45's, the flipside of the second, 'MY DEGENERATION', being written as an answer to The WHO's 'My Generation'. A further two singles surfaced in 1966, a version of The EVERLY BROTHERS' 'MAN WITH MONEY' and yet another cover, The BEATLES' 'GOOD DAY SUNSHINE'. They soon lost sight of their creative muse, although they did reform as The PUPILS to record a ROLLING STONES tribute album. • **Songwriters:** NOLDER except aforementioned and SHAKIN' ALL OVER (Johnny Kidd & The Pirates).

Recommended: SCENE BUT NOT HEARD (*6)

TERRY NOLDER – vocals / **CHRIS LOVEGROVE** – guitars / **PHIL HEATLEY** – guitars / **BARRY ALLCHIN** – bass / **BRIAN CORCORAN** – drums, repl. KEN GIRVAN

Mercury

Nov 65. (7") *(MF 881)* **WHEN THE NIGHT FALLS. / I'M ROWED OUT** [ ] [-]
Jan 66. (7") *(MF 897)* **THE IMMEDIATE PLEASURE. / MY DEGENERATION** [ ] [-]
1966. (7"ep) *(10035 MCE)* **THE ARRIVAL OF THE EYES** [ ] [-]
– (first 2 singles; 4 tracks)
May 66. (7") *(MF 910)* **MAN WITH MONEY. / YOU'RE TOO MUCH** [ ] [-]
Aug 66. (7") *(MF 934)* **GOOD DAY SUNSHINE. / PLEASE DON'T CRY** [ ] [-]

PUPILS

(same line-up)

Wing — not issued

Dec 66. (lp) *(WL 1150)* **A TRIBUTE TO THE ROLLING STONES** [ ] [-]
– I wanna be your man / Not fade away / If you need me / 19th nervous breakdown / As tears go by / (I can't get no) Satisfaction / Route 66 / The last time / Play with fire / Get off of my cloud / Little red rooster / It's all over now. *(re-iss.1969 on 'Fontana'; SFL 13087)*

— **STEVE VALENTINE** – guitar, repl. HEATLEY

— Split 2 months later in 1967. NOLDER joined ANDROMEDA before The ENTIRE SIOUX NATION in 1969.

– compilations, others

Jun 84. (m-lp) *Bam Caruso; (KIRI 028)* **BLINK** [ ] [-]
– (all the 45's from mid-60's + PUPILS)
Feb 87. (m-lp) *Bam Caruso; (MARI 038)* **SCENE BUT NOT HEARD** (demos) [ ] [-]
– When the night falls (take 1) / I'm rowed out / The immediate pleasure / Radio London jingle / Shakin' all over / When the night fals (take 2).

EYES OF BLUE

Formed: Swansea, Wales ...1966 by GARY PICKFORD-HOPKINS, RITCHIE FRANCIS, PHIL RYAN, TAFF WILLIAMS and WYNDHAM REESE. Their first 45, 'UP AND DOWN', came from the newly run stable of 'Deram', and was penned by the same songwriting team that gave us LOS BRAVOS' 'Black Is Black'. However, follow-up hits were not forthcoming and a few more light pop psychedelic excursions did nothing. Two albums appeared for 'Mercury' in 1969, although they didn't exactly set the progressive-rock fraternity alight. All of the group went on to better Welsh rock outfits; ANCIENT GREASE and BIG SLEEP, while most became involved with MAN.

Recommended: THE CROSSROADS OF TIME (*5) / IN FIELDS OF ARDATH (*5) / Ancient Grease:- WOMEN AND CHILDREN FIRST (*6) / Big Sleep:- BLUEBELL WOOD (*5)

GARY PICKFORD-HOPKINS – vocals / **RICK (RITCHIE) FRANCIS** – guitar / **PHIL RYAN** – keyboards / **RAY 'Taff' WILLIAMS** – bass / **WYNDHAM REESE** – drums

Deram — Deram

Nov 66. (7") *(DM 106) <85001>* **UP AND DOWN. / HEART TROUBLE** [ ] [ ]
Feb 67. (7") *(DM 114) <85003>* **SUPERMARKET FULL OF CANS. / DON'T ASK ME TO MEND YOUR BROKEN HEART** [ ] [-]

— **RAY BENNETT** – bass, repl. WILLIAMS who joined BYSTANDERS (MAN)

— **JOHN WEATHERS** – drums, repl. REES

Mercury — Mercury

Aug 68. (7") *(MF 1049)* **LARGO. / YESTERDAY** [ ] [-]
Feb 69. (lp) *(SMCL 20134)* **THE CROSSROADS OF TIME** [ ] [ ]
– Crossroads of time / Never care / I'll be your friend / 7 and 7 is / Prodigal son / Largo / Love is the law / Yesterday / I wonder why / World of emotion / Inspiration of a new day.
1969. (lp) *(SMCL 20164)* **IN FIELDS OF ARDATH** [ ] [ ]
– Merry go round / The light we see / Souvenirs (tribute to Django) / Ardath / Spanish blues / Door (the child that is born on the sabbath day) / Little bird / After the war / Extra hour / Chances / Apache '69.
1969. (7") *<72911>* **APACHE '69. / Q III** [-] [ ]

— When BENNETT + FRANCIS departed, they became ...

ANCIENT GREASE

PICKFORD-HOPKINS, RYAN + WEATHERS recruited **MICHAEL 'WILL' YOUATT** – bass

Mercury — not issued

May 71. (lp) *(6338 033)* **WOMAN AND CHILDREN FIRST** [ ] [-]
– Freedom train / Don't want / Odd song / Eagle song / Where the snow lies forever / Mother grease the cat / Time to die / Prelude to a blind man / Mystic mountain / Woman and children first.

BIG SLEEP

— were virtually original EYES OF BLUE line-up ...

PICKFORD-HOPKINS – vocals, guitar / **RYAN** – keyboards / **WEATHERS** – drums / **WILLIAMS** – now guitar / **FRANCIS** – now bass, piano, vocals

Pegasus — not issued

Aug 71. (lp) *(PEG 4)* **BLUEBELL WOOD** [ ] [-]
– Death of a hope / Odd song / Free life / Aunty James / Saint and sceptic / Bluebell Wood / Watching love grow / When the Sun was out.

— Split in 1971, WEATHERS joined GENTLE GIANT, then MAN, alongside RYAN. PICKFORD-HOPKINS sessioned for DEKE LEONARD (MAN), then ANDY FAIRWEATHER-LOW. In 1983, he released solo single 'WHY?' for 'Spartan' records.

RITCHIE FRANCIS

Pegasus — not issued

Mar 72. (lp) *(PEG 11)* **SONGBIRD** [ ] [-]

FACTORY (see under ⇒ FRATERNITY OF MAN

FACTORY

Formed: Surrey, England ... 1968 initially as The SOUVENIR BADGE FACTORY by JACK BRAND, BILL MacLEOD and IAN OATES. After they shortened their name, the fresh, young school leavers were sought out by sound engineer turned producer, BRIAN CARROLL, who worked on their debut, 'PATH THROUGH A FOREST'. It was a fantastic slice of psychedelia, a hybrid of CREAM and PINK FLOYD, backed on the flip by a cover of PAUL REVERE & THE RAIDERS' 'GONE'. It has since become a very rare collector's item worth over £100, as was the long-awaited follow-up 'TRY A LITTLE SUNSHINE'. This was written by a friend of CARROLL's, JOHN PANTRY, who was the main man behind PETER & THE WOLVES (ex-NORMAN CONQUEST). It's very brief drug connotations led to the BBC and other stations knocking it back from their "safe" airwaves, causing their backers CARROLL and DAMON LYON-SHAW to find alternative protegies in FIVE DAY RAIN. On a much sought-after compilation album released in 1995, they covered MR LACEY (Fairport Convention) and SECOND GENERATION WOMAN (Family).

Recommended: PATH THROUGH THE FOREST (*8)

JACK BRAND – vocals, bass / **IAN OATES** – lead guitar / **BILL MacLEOD** – drums

M.G.M. | not issued

Oct 68. (7") *(MGM 1444)* **PATH THROUGH THE FOREST. / GONE** [ ] [-]

C.B.S. | not issued

Oct 69. (7") *(CBS 4540)* **TRY A LITTLE SUNSHINE. / RED CHALK HILL** [ ] [-]

—— split when their producers found somebody else to work with.

– compilations, etc.

1995. (cd) *Bri-Tone; (BFT 101)* **PATH THROUGH THE FOREST** [ ] [-]
– Path through the forest / Gone / Try a little sunshine / Red chalk hill / Mr. Lacey / Second generation woman. *(lp-iss.Aug96 on 'Heads Together'+=;)–* (extra track).

FAIRFIELD PARLOUR (see under ⇒ KALEIDOSCOPE (UK)

FAMILY

Formed: Leicester, England ... 1967 by CHARLIE WHITNEY, ROGER CHAPMAN, JIM KING and RIC GRECH. They had stemmed from The FARINAS, a band who existed for 5 years and who issued one single in 1964 for 'Fontana'; YOU'D BETTER STOP / I LIKE IT LIKE THAT. After moving to London, the band made their debut at The Royal Albert Hall in July '67 supporting TIM HARDIN. Signing to 'Reprise' in 1968, following a one-off 7" for 'Liberty', FAMILY's DAVE MASON & JIMMY MILLER produced the debut album, 'MUSIC FROM A DOLL'S HOUSE', which made the UK Top 40. CHAPMAN's unmistakable, frog-in throat vocal style, complimented by WHITNEY's distinctive guitar and GRECH's violin, created an enduring classic and soon marked the band out as cult favourites. The follow-up, 'ENTERTAINMENT', included 'WEAVER'S ANSWER', a song which went on to become a staple of the band's infamous live show. Soon after the album's release, GRECH departed for BLIND FAITH, being replaced by JOHN WEIDER. The band also recruited POLI PALMER on keyboards in place of saxophonist KING before releasing two Top 10 albums within a year, 'A SONG FOR ME' & 'ANYWAY'. Unusually for a prog-rock outfit, FAMILY were no strangers to hit singles, the classic 'IN MY OWN TIME' (from 'ANYWAY') reaching No.4, following on from the memorable successes 'NO MULES FOOL' and 'STRANGE BAND'. During the next three years the band went through yet more personnel shifts, perhaps accounting for the inconsistency of their last two albums. While 'FEARLESS' was quite impressive, 'BANDSTAND' was patchy, although it did spawn one of their last hits, 'BURLESQUE'. FAMILY then moved to the 'Raft' label where they recorded their final, slightly disappointing effort, 'IT'S ONLY A MOVIE', in 1973. The album was a complete flop and the band broke up, CHAPMAN and WHITNEY going on to form the more basic STREETWALKERS. CHAPMAN has released numerous solo albums, beginning with 'CHAPPO' in '79.

Recommended: THE BEST OF FAMILY (*9) / MUSIC IN A DOLL'S HOUSE (*7) / ENTERTAINMENT (*6) / A SONG FOR ME (*6) / FEARLESS (*6) / BANDSTAND (*5) / THE BEST OF STREETWALKERS (*5)

ROGER CHAPMAN (b. 8 Apr'44) – vocals / **CHARLIE WHITNEY** (b. 4 Jun'44) – guitar, vocals / **JIM KING** (b.1945) – saxophone, flute / **RICK GRECH** (b. 1 Nov'46, Bordeaux, France) – bass / **HARRY OVENALL** – drums

Liberty | not issued

Sep 67. (7") *(LBF 15031)* **SCENE THRU THE EYE OF A LENS. / GYPSY WOMAN** [ ] [-]

—— **ROB TOWNSEND** (b. 7 Jul'47) – drums repl. HARRY

Reprise | Reprise

Jun 68. (7") *(RS 23270)* **ME AND MY FRIEND. / HEY MR. POLICEMAN** [ ] [ ]

Jul 68. (7") *<0786>* **OLD SONGS NEW SONGS. / HEY MR. POLICEMAN** [-] [ ]

Jul 68. (lp; mono/stereo) *(<RLP/RSLP 6312>)* **MUSIC IN A DOLL'S HOUSE** [35] [ ]
– The chase / Mellowing grey / Never like this / Me and my friend / Variation on a theme of Hey Mr. Policeman / Winter / Old songs new songs / Variation on a theme of the breeze / Hey Mr. Policeman / See through windows / Variation on a theme of me and my friend / Peace of mind / Voyage / The breeze / 3 x time. *(re-iss.Sep87 on 'See For Miles' lp/c/cd; SEE/+K/CD 100)*

Nov 68. (7") *(RS 23315) <0809>* **SECOND GENERATION WOMAN. / HOME TOWN** [ ] [ ]

Mar 69. (lp; mono/stereo) *(<RLP/RSLP 6340>)* **FAMILY ENTERTAINMENT** [6] [ ]
– The weaver's answer / Observations from a hill / Hung up down / Summer '67 / How-hi-the-li / Second generation woman / From past archives / Dim / Processions / Face in the crowd / Emotions. *(re-iss.Sep87 on 'See For Miles' lp/c/cd; SEE/+K/CD 200)*

—— **JOHN WEIDER** (b.21 Apr'47) – bass, violin (ex-ERIC BURDON & ANIMALS) repl. GRECH who joined BLIND FAITH

Oct 69. (7") *(RS 27001) <0881>* **NO MULE'S FOOL. / GOOD FRIEND OF MINE** [29] [ ]

—— **POLI PALMER** (b. JOHN, 25 May'43) – keyboards, vibes (ex-ECLECTION) repl. KING who joined RING OF TRUTH

Jan 70. (lp) *(RSLP 9001) <6384>* **A SONG FOR ME** [4] [ ]
– Drowned in wine / Some poor soul / Love is a sleeper / Stop for the traffic (through the heart of me) / Wheels / Song for sinking lovers / Hey let it rock / The cat and the rat / 93's ok J. / A song for me. *(re-iss.Nov88 on 'See For Miles' lp/cd; SEE/+CD 240) (cd re-iss.Nov93 on 'Castle'; CLACD 376)*

Apr 70. (7") *(RS 27005)* **TODAY. / SONG FOR SINKING LOVERS** [ ] [ ]

Aug 70. (7"m) *(RS 27009)* **STRANGE BAND. / THE WEAVER'S ANSWER / HUNG UP DOWN** [11] [ ]

Reprise | U.A.

Nov 70. (lp) *(RSX 9005) <5527>* **ANYWAY ...** (half live) [7] [ ]
– Good news bad news / Holding the compass / Strange band / Willow tree / Part of the load / Anyway / Normans / Lives and Ladies. *(re-iss.Nov88 on 'See For Miles' lp/cd; SEE/+CD 245) (re-iss.cd May94 on 'Castle'; CLACD 375)*

Mar 71. (lp) *(RMP 9007) <6413>* **OLD SONGS NEW SONGS** (compilation remixed) [ ] [ ]
– Hung up down / Today / Observations from a hill / Good friend of mine / Drowned in wine / Peace of mind / Home town / The cat and the rat / No mule's fool / See through windows / The weaver's answer. *(cd-iss.Mar92 on 'See For Miles'; SEECD 334)*

Jun 71. (7") *(K 14090) <50832>* **IN MY OWN TIME. / SEASONS** [4] [ ]

—— **JOHN WETTON** (b.12 Jul'49, Derby, England) – bass, vocals (ex-MOGUL THRASH) repl. WEIDER who joined STUD

Oct 71. (lp) *(K 54003) <5562>* **FEARLESS** [14] [ ]
– Between blue and me / Sat'd'y barfly / Larf and sing / Spanish tide / Save some for thee / Take your partners / Children / Crinkly grin / Blind / Burning bridges. *(re-iss.cd May94 on 'Castle';)*

Nov 71. (7") *<50882>* **BETWEEN BLUE AND ME. / LARF & SING** [-] [ ]

Sep 72. (7") *(K 14196) <50951>* **BURLESQUE. / THE ROCKIN' R'S** [13] [ ]

Sep 72. (lp) *(K 54006) <5644>* **BANDSTAND** [15] [ ]
– Burlesque / Bolero babe / Coronation / Dark eyes / Broken nose / My friend the sun / Glove / Ready to go / Top of the hill. *(re-iss.Nov88 on 'See For Miles' lp/cd; SEE/+CD 241) (cd re-iss.Mar94 on 'Castle'; CLACD 322)*

Jan 73. (7") *(K 14218) <171>* **MY FRIEND THE SUN. / GLOVE** [ ] [ ]

—— CHAPMAN, WHITNEY and TOWNSEND were joined by **JIM CREGAN** – bass, guitar (ex-STUD) repl. WETTON who joined KING CRIMSON / **TONY ASHTON** (b. 1 Mar'46, Blackburn, England) – keyboards (ex-ASHTON, GARDNER and DYKE) repl. PALMER

Raft | U.A.

Apr 73. (7") *(RA 18501)* **BOOM BANG. / STOP THIS CAR** [ ] [ ]

Sep 73. (7") *(RA 18503)* **SWEET DESIREE. / DRINK TO YOU** [ ] [ ]

Sep 73. (lp) *(RA 58501) <UALA 181>* **IT'S ONLY A MOVIE** [30] [ ]
– It's only a movie / Leroy / Buffet tea for two / Boom bang / Boots 'n' roots / Banger / Sweet Desiree / Suspicion / Check out.

Oct 73. (7") *<416>* **IT'S ONLY A MOVIE. / SUSPICION** [-] [ ]

—— They split late '73 with TOWNSEND joining MEDICINE HEAD and CREGAN went to COCKNEY REBEL, ASHTON went into production. ROGER and CHARLIE formed CHAPMAN / WHITNEY STREETWALKERS, who released a number of albums before ROGER went solo in 1979 (see GREAT ROCK DISCOGRAPHY)

– compilations, others, etc. –

on 'Reprise' UK, or 'United Artists' in the States

Sep 74. (lp) *Reprise; (K 54023)* **THE BEST OF FAMILY** [ ] [-]
– Burlesque / My friend the Sun / The chase / Old songs, new songs / Part of the load / In my own time / It's only a movie / Sweet desiree / Sat'd'y barfly / Children / No mule's fool / The weaver's answer. *(re-iss.Nov91 on 'See For Miles' lp/cd+=;) (cd re-iss.Jul94 on 'Line'; CRCD 901238)*
Nov 74. (7") *(K 14378)* **MY FRIEND THE SUN. / BURLESQUE** [ ] [-]
May 78. (7"ep) *(K 14487)* **BURLESQUE. / IN MY OWN TIME / THE WEAVER'S ANSWER** [ ] [-]
Oct 81. (lp) *Rebecca; (BEC 777)* **RISE ... VERY BEST OF FAMILY** [ ] [-]
Jan 82. (7") *Rebecca; (BECS 77)* **BURLESQUE. / MY FRIEND THE SUN** [ ] [-]
Nov 88. (12"ep/cd-ep) *Strange Fruit; (SFPS/+CD 061)* **THE PEEL SESSIONS** (8.5.73) [ ] [-]
Aug 89. (d-lp/d-c/d-cd) *That's Original; (TFO LP/MC/CD 22)* **IT'S ONLY A MOVIE / FEARLESS** [ ] [-]
Oct 91. (cd) *Windsong; (WINCD 001)* **BBC RADIO 1 LIVE IN CONCERT** [ ] [-]
Nov 92. (cd) *Castle; (CCSCD 354)* **THE COLLECTION – THE SINGLES A's & B's** [ ] [-]
Mar 93. (cd/c) *Castl; (CCS CD/MC 374)* **THE BEST OF FAMILY** [ ] [-]
Mar 93. (cd) *Dutch East India; (DEI 8333-2)* **THE PEEL SESSIONS** [ ] [-]

Merrell FANKHAUSER (see under ⇒ MU)

FANTASY

Formed: Gravesend, England ...1970 as CHAPEL FARM, by DAVE METCALFE, PAUL LAWRENCE, DAVE READ, BRIAN CHATHAM (drums) and BOB VANN (guitar). Not long after their formation, tragedy struck when VANN died after falling off a cliff during his 18th birthday celebrations at Cliftonville Hotel. When CHATHAM left the band a year later, he was replaced by PETE JAMES and JON WEBSTER. After a few gigs as FIREQUEEN supporting the likes of PINK FAIRIES and EDGAR BROUGHTON BAND, they became FANTASY, the name suggested by their label, 'Polydor'. The debut single, 'POLITELY INSANE', flopped although it was quickly followed by the excellent 'PAINT A PICTURE' album (which has become rare enough to fetch over £250 mint). The record was comprised of progressive rock in the mould of CARAVAN or GENESIS, fusing together keyboard-orientated PROCOL HARUM-style rock and neo-gothic, mystical influences. In 1974, they returned to the studio with producer PETER SAMES and cut a second lp, 'BEYOND THE BEYOND'. However, this was shelved when METCALFE quit and the band folded. • **Songwriters:** METCALFE and group.

Recommended: PAINT A PICTURE (*7)

PAUL LAWRENCE – vocals, guitar / **DAVE METCALFE** – keyboards, vocals / **PETE JAMES** – guitar, vocals / **DAVE READ** – bass, vocals / **JON WEBSTER** – drums, vocals

Polydor | not issued

Oct 73. (7") *(2058 405)* **POLITELY INSANE. / I WAS ONCE AWARE** [ ] [-]
Nov 73. (lp) *(2383 246)* **PAINT A PICTURE** [ ] [-]
– Paint a picture / Circus / The award / Politely insane / Widow / Icy river / Thank Christ / Young man's fortune / Gnome song / Silent mime. *(re-iss.1990 by 'Second Battle' Germany; 843 263-1) (Japanese cd-iss.1991 on 'Polydor'; KK ERC-29229)*

— Disbanded in Autumn 1974.

– others, etc. –

Feb 92. (cd) *Audio Archives; (AACD 001)* **BEYOND THE BEYOND** [ ] [-]

FAPARDOKLY (see under ⇒ MU)

Don FARDON (see under ⇒ SORROWS)

Mick FARREN (see under ⇒ PINK FAIRIES)

FAT MATTRESS

Formed: London, England . . .early 1969 by NOEL REDDING, formerly of the great JIMI HENDRIX EXPERIENCE. He brought together some semi-established session men (NEIL LANDON, JIM LEVERTON and ERIC DILLON) and released two bluesy psychedelic albums for 'Polydor' at the turn of the decade. CHRIS WOOD of TRAFFIC played flute on the eponymous debut, an album that also featured their finest track, 'MR. MOONSHINE'.

Recommended: FAT MATTRESS (*6) / FAT MATTRESS II (*5)

NOEL REDDING – guitar, vocals / **NEIL LANDON** – vocals (ex-FLOWERPOT MEN) / **JIM LEVERTON** – brass, harps, organ, vocals / **ERIC DILLON** – drums, percussion

Polydor | Atco

Sep 69. (7") *(BM 56352)* **NATURALLY. / IREDESCENT BUTTERFLY** [ ] [ ]
Sep 69. (lp) *(583 056) <33309>* **FAT MATTRESS** [ ] [ ]
– All night drinker / I don't mind / Bright new way / Petrol pump assistant / Mr. Moonshine / Magic forest / Walking through a garden / Everything's blue / She came in the morning / How can I live. *(re-iss.Dec69; same) (cd-iss.Jun92 on 'Sequel'+=; NEXCD 196)*– Little girl in white / Margerita / Which way to go / Future days / Cold wall of stone.
Nov 69. (7") *(BM 56367)* **MAGIC LANTERNS. / BRIGHT NEW WAY** [ ] [ ]

— added **STEVE HAMMOND** – guitar / **MICK WEAVER** – organ (ex-AMEN CORNER), repl. REDDING who went to the States to form ROAD

Sep 70. (7") *(2058 053)* **HIGHWAY. / BLACK SHEEP OF THE FAMILY** [ ] [ ]
Oct 70. (lp) *(2383 025) <33347>* **FAT MATTRESS II** [ ] [ ]
– The storm / Anyway you want / Leafy lane / Naturally / Roamin' / Happy my love / Childhood dream / She / Highway / At the ball / People. *(cd-iss.Jul92 on 'Sequel'+=; NEXCD 197)*– Hall of kings / Long red / Words / The river.

— Disbanded. LEVERTON joined JUICY LUCY, and later became a member of SAVOY BROWN.

FAUST

Formed: Hamburg, Germany . . . 1970 by producer UWE NETTELBECK, who was given money to assemble a collective of musicians in his Wumme studios. These numbered RUDOLF SOSNA, HANS JOACHIM IRMLER, JEAN HERVE PERON, GUNTHER WUSTHOFF and ARNULF MEIFERT; the latter being replaced by RICHARD DIERMAYER in 1971. Following in the footsteps of CAN, TANGERINE DREAM and AMON DUUL II, they became an integral part of the burgeoning underground "krautrock" scene. Early recordings for 'Polydor', although strikingly innovative, failed to gain any widespread commercial appeal outside Germany. However, 'THE FAUST TAPES' (a 'Virgin' sampler of unreleased tunes) introduced them to the UK and sold a respectable quantity due to its 49p price-tag. This unfortunately disqualified it from chart returns. Inspired by a myriad of influences that took in everything from KARL-HEINZ STOCKHAUSEN to The BEATLES to The MOTHERS OF INVENTION, they left conventional song structures at the starting gate. Instead they opted for a continuous collage of musical set pieces which nevertheless had the potential to be great 3-minute songs. Alternately delighting and disgusting audiences, they were prone to playing pinball machines and weilding pneumatic drills on stage. They toured this bizarre spectacle around Europe after Richard Branson's 'Virgin' issued 'FAUST IV' while in 1974, they recorded an album with American minimalist TONI CONRAD (he had earlier been in The DREAM SYNDICATE; part of JOHN CALE's pre-VELVET days). Eventually FAUST faded away into obscurity but were recalled for a one-off gig at London's Marquee on the 25th of October '92. Their comeback album, 'RETURN OF A LEGEND', was issued in June '97 and they were lined up for another rare live appearance at the Edinburgh Festival. • **Trivia:** UWE also produced for SLAPP HAPPY. Were and still are one of JULIAN COPE's (ex-TEARDROP EXPLODES) fave bands.

Recommended: SO FAR (*8) / THE FAUST TAPES (*5 at the time / *8 now!)

RUDOLF SOSNA – guitar / **HANS JOACHIM IRMLER** – guitar / **WERNER DIERMAIER** – drums; repl. ARNULF MEIFERT / **JEAN HERVE PERON** – bass / **GUNTHER WUSTHOFF** – saxophone

Polydor | not issued

Jul 72. (lp) *(2310 142)* **FAUST** [ ] [-]
– Why don't you eat carrots / Meadow meal / Miss Fortune. *(re-iss.Oct79 as 'FAUST ONE' on 'Recommended'; RRA 1)*

— MEIFERT departed around same time, but still contributed later

1972. (lp) *(2310 196)* **FAUST SO FAR** [ ] [-]
– It's a rainy day, sunshine girl / On the way to Abamae / No harm / So far / Mamie is blue / I've got my car and my T.V. / Picnic on a frozen river / Me back space . . . / . . . In the spirit. *(re-iss.Oct79 on 'Recommended'; R.R.TWO)*
1972. (7") *(2001 299)* **SO FAR** [ ] [-]

Caroline | not issued

1972. (lp; by TONI CONRAD & FAUST) *(C 1501)* **OUTSIDE DREAM SYNDICATE** [ ] [-]
(cd-iss.Feb94 on 'Lithium')

— added **PETER BLEGVAD** – guitar, clarinet, vocals

Virgin | not issued

1973. (lp) *(V 2004)* **FAUST IV** [ ] [-]
– Krautrock / The sad skinhead / Jennifer / Just a second / Picnic on a picnic river / Deuxieme tableux / Giggy smile / Laeuft . . . heisst dass es laeuft oder es kommt bald . . . laeuft / It's a bit of a pain. *(cd-iss.Oct92; CDV 2004)*
1973. (lp) *(VC 501)* **THE FAUST TAPES** (rec.1971-73) [ ] [-]
– (no song titles) *(re-iss.1980 on 'Recommended'; RRA 6) (cd-iss.Apr91 as 'THE LAST LP' + Feb94 + Jun 96 on 'Recommended'; RERF 2CD)*

— Disbanded in 1973. PETER BLEGVAD went solo. However, they did re-form for London Marquee gig on 25 Oct'92.

Recommended | not issued

Jun 97. (cd) *(RER 25)* **RETURN OF A LEGEND** [ ] [-]

– compilations, etc –

on 'Recommended' unless mentioned otherwise

Mar 80. (7"ep) *(RRI 15)* **EXTRACTS FROM FAUST PARTY 3** [ ] [-]
1980. (lp) *(RR 5)* **CASABLANCA MOON** [ ] [-]
Nov 92. (cd) *(RERF 1CD)* **THE FAUST TAPES (71 MINUTES OF FAUST)** [ ] [-]
(re-iss.Feb94 + Jun96; same)
Jan 97. (cd) *(RERF 3CD)* **YOU KNOW FAUST** [ ] [-]

FEVER TREE

Formed: Houston, Texas . . . early '67 out of the group BOSTWICK VINE, by DENNIS KELLER, ROB LANDES, E.E. WOLFE, MICHAEL KNUST and JOHN TUTTLE. Signing to Chicago's 'Mainstream' records, they released two flop 45's before moving to the 'Uni' label. A transitional period, they progressed from garage-psyche to more conventional psychedelic rock, underpinned by symphonic strains. Their 1968 eponymous album, was soon followed by a minor US hit, 'SAN FRANCISCO GIRLS (RETURN OF THE NATIVE)' (like much of their material, it was penned by co-producers SCOTT and VIVIAN HOLTZMAN), which gained airplay on John Peel's 'Top Gear' radio show. The album, which was introduced by a piece from classical composer BACH, also included a few covers, notably a segued version of The BEATLES' 'DAY TRIPPER' & 'WE CAN WORK IT OUT', a worthy effort. The second album, 'ANOTHER TIME, ANOTHER PLACE', opened with a near IRON BUTTERFLY-type re-working of 'MAN WHO PAINTS THE PICTURES', showing a murkier, heavier side of the band. However, the album was blighted by a poor choice of cover versions (i.e. PEGGY LEE's 'FEVER'). The third album, 'CREATION', contained another new version of an old song, 'IMITATION SITUATION'. The album was a creative disaster, although it did feature a guest appearance by BILLY GIBBONS (of MOVING SIDEWALKS; later ZZ TOP). In the early 70's, they moved to the California coast and signed to 'Ampex' for a last dismal effort, 'FOR SALE'. Yes, they had indeed sold out, the album reviving early 'Mainstream' singles, 'HEY MISTER' & 'GIRL OH GIRL'. In the 70's, MICHAEL KNUST resurrected a new FEVER TREE, although this was short-lived. • **Songwriters:** KNUST or LANDES and the HOLTZMANS, except NOWADAYS CLANCY CAN'T EVEN SING (Buffalo Springfield) / NINETY-NINE AND ONE HALF (Wilson Pickett – Steve Cropper) / GRAND CANDY YOUNG SWEET (. . . Davis) / PEACE OF MIND (Woods) / I PUT A SPELL ON YOU (Screaming Jay Hawkins) / HEY JOE (hit; Jimi Hendrix) / SHE COMES IN COLORS (Love).

Recommended: FEVER TREE (*9) / ANOTHER TIME ANOTHER PLACE (*7)

DENNIS KELLER – vocals / **MICHAEL KNUST** – lead guitar / **ROB LANDES** – keyboards, flute, multi / **E.E. WOLFE III** – bass / **JOHN TUTTLE** – drums, percussion

not issued | Main-stream

1967. (7") *<661>* **HEY MISTER. / I CAN BEAT YOUR DRUM** [-] [ ]
1967. (7") *<665>* **GIRL OH GIRL (DON'T PUSH ME). / STEVE LENORE** [-] [ ]

M.C.A. | Uni

Aug 68. (lp) *(UNLS 102) <73024>* **FEVER TREE** [ ] [ ] May68
– Imitation situation I (Toccata and Fugue) / Where do you go? / San Francisco girls (return of the native) / Ninety-nine and one half / Man who paints the pictures / Filigree & shadow / The sun also rises / Day tripper – We can work it out / Nowadays Clancy can't even sing / Unlock my door / Come with me (rainsong). *(re-iss.Jun86 as 'SAN FRANCISCO GIRLS' on 'See For Miles'+=; SEE 71)*– Man who paints the pictures – part II / Peace of mind / Death is the dancer.
Oct 68. (7") *(MU 1043) <55060>* **SAN FRANCISCO GIRLS (RETURN OF THE NATIVE). / COME WITH ME** [ ] [91] May68
Dec 68. (lp) *(MUPS 374) <73040>* **ANOTHER TIME, ANOTHER PLACE** [ ] [83]
– Man who paints the pictures – part II / What time did you say it is in Salt Lake City? / Don't come crying to me girl / Fever / Grand candy young sweet / Jokes are for sad people / I've never seen evergreen / Peace of mind / Death is the dancer.
Feb 70. (lp) *<73067>* **CREATION** [-] [97]
– Woman, woman (woman) / Love makes the sunrise / Catcher in the rye / Wild woman ways / Fever blue / Run past my window / Imitation situation II / Time is now / The God game.

— **GRANT JOHNSON** – keyboards + **KEVIN KELLEY** – drums, repl. on some LANDES + TUTTE

not issued | Ampex

1970. (7") *<11013>* **SHE COMES IN COLORS. / YOU'RE NOT THE SAME BABY** [-] [ ]
1970. (lp) *<A-10113>* **FOR SALE** [-] [ ]
– I put a spell on you / You're not the same baby / She comes in colors / Hey mister / Come on in / Girl don't push me / Hey Joe, where you gonna go.
1970. (7") *<11028>* **I PUT A SPELL ON YOU. / HEY JOE, WHERE YOU GONNA GO** [-] [ ]

— Disbanded in 1970, although MICHAEL re-formed for another outing. His new band comprised; **KENNETH BLANCHETT, PAT BRENNAN + ROBBIE PARRISH**

not issued | Buttermilk

1970's. (7"ep) **FEVER TREE RETURN** [-] [ ]
– Mama hang around / Nowadays Clancy can't even song / +2

– compilations, etc –

1985. (lp) *M.C.A.;* **THE BEST OF FEVER TREE** [-] [ ]
Mar 93. (cd) *See For Miles; (SEECD 364)* **FEVER TREE / ANOTHER TIME ANOTHER PLACE** [ ] [-]
(re-iss.Jun97; same)

John FIDDLER (see under ⇒ MEDICINE HEAD)

FIRE

Formed: Hounslow, Middlesex, England . . . 1966 by DAVID LAMBERT, DICK DUFALL and BOB VOICE. Their first single, 'FATHER'S NAME IS DAD', released in 1968, was an excellent psychedelic pop tune showing prodigious promise. The follow-up, 'ROUND THE GUM TREE', was a slight disappointment, although its predecessor has since become very pricey at around £100. In 1969, they started recording their album, 'THE MAGIC SHOEMAKER', which, when unleashed the following year, impressed the few hundred who bothered to buy it. Its LAMBERT-narrated concept material, based on a fairytale about a group of children on a coach journey, had fine moments, including 'CHILDREN OF IMAGINATION' and the psyche/R&B coloured 'I CAN SEE THE SKY'. However, after its release, LAMBERT, DUFALL and VOICE were poached by worthier bands.

Recommended: THE MAGIC SHOEMAKER (*7)

DAVID LAMBERT – vocals, guitar, keyboards / **DICK DUFALL** – bass, vocals / **BOB VOICE** – drums, vocals

Decca | not issued

Mar 68. (7") *(F 12753)* **FATHER'S NAME IS DAD. / TREACLE TOFFEE WORLD** [ ] [-]
Nov 68. (7") *(F 12856)* **ROUND THE GUM TREE. / TOOTHIE RUTHIE** [ ] [-]

Pye | not issued

1970. (lp) *(NSPL 18343)* **THE MAGIC SHOEMAKER** [ ] [-]
– Children of imagination / Tell you a story / Magic shoes / Reason for everything / Only a dream / Flies like a bird / Like to halp you if I can / I can see the sky / Shoemaker / Happy man I am / Children of imagination. *(re-iss.May90 on 'See For Miles' lp/cd; SEE/+CD 294)*

— LAMBERT joined The STRAWBS and recorded an unreleased solo lp 'FRAMED' in 1979. VOICE and DUFALL joined PAUL BRETT'S SAGE.

FIVE AMERICANS

Formed: Dallas, Texas, USA . . . mid-60's by Oklahoma-raised MICHAEL RABON, JOHN DURRILL, JIMMY WRIGHT and two others. In 1965, they released three singles for the local 'Abnak' label, one of which, 'I SEE THE LIGHT', was picked up by 'H.B.R.'. The song became a Top 30 hit early the next year. 'EVOL – NOT LOVE' was another to crack the charts, although 'Abnak' were to take control again in 1967. They subsequently amassed another three DALE HAWKINS-produced Top 40 hits, beginning with the near-million seller, 'WESTERN UNION'. They had previously cut two albums, followed-up by another two hard-edged psyche pop efforts. These were unmitigated flops in the late 60's, something they never quite recovered from. • **Covered:** TWIST AND SHOUT (Isley Brothers) / GIMME SOME LOVIN' (Spencer Davis Group) / I PUT A SPELL ON YOU (Screaming Jay Hawkins) / WHAT'D I SAY (Ray Charles) / etc.

Recommended: I SEE THE LIGHT (*6)

MICHAEL RABON – vocals / **JOHN DURRILL** – keyboards / **JIMMY WRIGHT** – / 2 others

not issued | Abnak

1965. (7") *<109>* **I SEE THE LIGHT. / THE OUTCASTS** [-] [ ]
1965. (7") *<114>* **SYMPATHY./ REALITY** [-] [ ]
1965. (7") *<116>* **IF I COULD. / NOW THAT IT'S OVER** [-] [ ]

Pye Int . . . | H.B.R.

Feb 66. (7") *(7N 25354) <HBR 454>* **I SEE THE LIGHT. / THE OUTCASTS** [ ] [26] Dec65
Apr 66. (lp) *<HBR 9503>* **I SEE THE LIGHT** [-] [ ]
– I see the light / Losing game / Goodbye / I know they lie / Twist and shout / She's-a-my-own / The train / It's a crying shame / I'm so glad / Don't blame me / The outcasts / What'd I say. *(UK cd-iss.Apr94 on 'Sundazed'+=; CDSC 6018)*– The train / Good times.
Jun 66. (7") *(7N 25373) <HBR 468>* **EVOL – NOT LOVE. / DON'T BLAME ME** [ ] [52] Apr66

Stateside | Abnak

Apr 67. (7") *(SS 2012) <118>* **WESTERN UNION. / NOW THAT IT'S OVER** [ ] [5] Feb67
May 67. (7") *(SS 2036) <120>* **SOUND OF LOVE. / SYMPATHY** [ ] [36]
Jun 67. (lp) *<2067>* **WESTERN UNION** [-] [ ]
– Western union / Big cities / If I could / Now that it's over / Reality / Sound of love / Sympathy / Husbands and wives / I put a spell on you / Gimme some lovin' / See-saw man / Tell Ann I love her.
Aug 67. (7") *<123>* **ZIP CODE. / SWEET BIRD OF YOUTH** [-] [36]
Nov 67. (7") *<125>* **STOP LIGHT. / TELL ANN I LOVE HER** [-] [ ]
Feb 68. (7") *(SS 2097) <126>* **7.30 GUIDED TOUR. / SEE-SAW MAN** [ ] [96] Jan68
Feb 68. (lp) *<2069>* **PROGRESSIONS** [-] [ ]
1968. (7") *<128>* **NO COMMUNICATION. / THE RAINMAKER** [-] [ ]
1968. (7") *<131>* **LOVIN' IS LOVIN'. / CON MAN** [-] [ ]
1968. (7") *<132>* **GENERATION GAP. / THE SOURCE** [-] [ ]
1969. (lp) *<2071>* **NOW & THEN** [-] [ ]
1969. (7") *<134>* **VIRGINIA GIRL. / CALL ON ME** [-] [ ]
1969. (7") *<137>* **IGNERT WOMAN. / SCROOGE** [-] [ ]
1969. (7"; as MICHAEL RABON & THE FIVE AMERICANS) *<139>* **I SEE THE LIGHT '69. / RED CAPE** [-] [ ]
1970. (7") *<142>* **SHE'S TOO GOOD TO ME. / MOLLY BACK** [-] [ ]

— split and RABON formed GLADSTONE. DURRILL later wrote hit music for CHER, notably 'Dark Lady'. WRIGHT married stable mate ROBIN from outfits JON & ROBIN and The IN-CROWD.

FLAMIN' GROOVIES

Formed: Bay Area, San Francisco, California, USA . . . 1965 originally as The CHOSEN FEW and then The LOST AND FOUND, by CYRIL JORDAN, ROY LONEY, GEORGE ALEXANDER and TIM LYNCH. In 1967, they issued a self-financed debut lp, the 10" 'SNEAKERS', which resulted in a deal with 'Epic'. After one poorly promoted lp, 'SUPERSNAZZ', they left to join the roster of the 'Kama Sutra' label, aided by producer Richard Robinson in 1970. There, they issued two well-received albums, 'FLAMINGO' and 'TEENAGE HEAD', before again moving stables to 'United Artists' in '72. Ctitically acclaimed, the albums highlighted The 'GROOVIES' characteristic high-energy rock'n'roll, updating 50's material into 60's-style garage punk. The following years resulted in many personnel changes, and after touring Europe in 1976, they finally released the DAVE EDMUNDS-produced 'Sire' comeback, 'SHAKE SOME ACTION' (he had previously worked on their 1972 album, 'SLOW DEATH'). Although the band were associated with the embryonic new wave/punk movement, the album's power-pop harmonies found little credibility with this scene. The band released a further two albums in the same vein before splitting then re-forming for the live comeback lp, 'ONE NIGHT STAND' (1987). • **Songwriters:** JORDAN-LONEY, until the latter's departure in '71. Recorded many covers including; SOMETHIN' ELSE (Eddie Cochran) / PISTOL PACKIN' MAMA (Gene Vincent) / SHAKIN' ALL OVER (Johnny Kidd) / THAT'LL BE THE DAY (Buddy Holly) / KEEP A KNOCKIN' (Little Richard) / MOVE IT (Cliff Richard) / FEEL A WHOLE LOT BETTER (Byrds) / PAINT IT BLACK + JUMPIN' JACK FLASH + 19th NERVOUS BREAKDOWN (Rolling Stones) / MARRIED WOMAN (Frankie Lee Sims) / TEENAGE CONFIDENTIAL (Jerry Lee Lewis) / WEREWOLVES OF LONDON (Warren Zevon) / ABSOLUTELY SWEET MARIE (Bob Dylan) / TALLAHASSEE LASSIE (Freddy Cannon) / KICKS (Mann-Weill) / CALL ME LIGHTNING (Who) / MONEY (Barrett Strong) / PLEASE PLEASE ME + MISERY + THERE'S A PLACE (Beatles) / etc. • **Trivia:** Long-time fan GREG SHAW, issued 1975 single 'YOU TORE ME DOWN', for his own 'Bomp' magazine label.

Recommended: GROOVIES GREATEST GROOVES (*6)

ROB LONEY (b.13 Apr'46) – vocals / **CYRIL JORDAN** (b. 1948) – lead guitar / **TIM LYNCH** (b.18 Jul'46) – rhythm guitar / **GEORGE ALEXANDER** (b.18 May'46, San Mateo, Calif.) – bass / **DANNY MIHM** – drums (ex-WHISTLING SHRIMP) repl. RON GRECO

not issued Snazz

1967. (10"m-lp) *<2371>* **SNEAKERS**
– The slide / I'm drowning / Babes in the sky / Love time / My yada / Golden clouds / Prelude in A flat to afternoon of a plad. *<US re-iss.1975 on 'Skydog'; FGG 803>*

not issued Epic

1968. (7") *<10501>* **ROCKIN' PNEUMONIA AND THE BOOGIE WOOGIE FLU. / THE FIRST ONE'S FREE**
1968. (7") *<10564>* **SOMETHIN' ELSE. / LAURIE DID IT**
1970. (lp) *<26487>* **SUPERSNAZZ**
– Love have mercy / The girl can't help it / Laurie did it / Apart from that / Rockin' pneumonia and the boogie woogie flu / The first one's free / Pagan Rachel / a) Somethin' else, b) Pistol packin' mama / Brushfire / Bam balam / Around the corner. *(UK-rel.Feb86 on 'Edsel'; ED 173) (cd-iss.Aug93 on 'Columbia'; 467073-2)*

Kama Sutra Kama Sutra

1971. (lp) *<KSBS 2021>* **FLAMINGO**
– Roadhouse / Headin' for the Texas border / Gonna rock tonite / Comin' after you / Sweet roll me on down / Keep a knockin' / Second cousin / Childhood's end / Jailbait. *(UK cd-iss.Jan90 on 'Big Beat'+=; CDWIK 925)*– Walkin' the dog / Somethin' else / My girl Josephine / Louie Louie / Rockin' pneumonia and the boogie woogie flu / Going out theme (version 2).
1971. (d-lp) *<KSBS 2031>* **TEENAGE HEAD**
– Teenage head / Whiskey women / Yesterday's numbers 32:20 / High flyin' baby / City lights / Have you seen my baby / Evil-hearted Ada / Doctor Boogie / Rumble / Shakin' all over / That'll be the day / Round and round / Going out theme. *('FLAMINGO' + 'TEENAGE HEAD' iss.UK as 'FLAMIN' GROOVIES' on 'Kama Sutra' d-lp; 2683 003) (UK re-iss.1989 on 'Dojo' lp/cd; DOJO LP/CD 58) (cd re-iss.Jan90 on 'Big Beat'; CDWIK 926)*

Aug 71. (7") *(2013 031)* **TEENAGE HEAD. / EVIL-HEARTED ADA**
Mar 72. (7"ep) *(2013 042)* **GONNA ROCK TONITE / KEEP A-KNOCKIN'. / (3 others by 'Sha Na Na')**

— **CHRIS WILSON** (b.10 Sep'52, Waltham, Massachusetts, USA) – vocals (ex-LOOSE GRAVEL) repl. LONEY / **JAMES FARRELL** – guitar (ex-LOOSE GRAVEL) repl. LYNCH who formed HOT KNIVES. — changed to The DOGS for a short while, before returning to same

U.A. U.A.

Jun 72. (7") *(UP 35392)* **SLOW DEATH. / TALAHASSIE LASSIE**
Jun 72. (lp) **SLOW DEATH**
– Sweet little rock'n'roller / Doctor Boogie / Walking the dog / Roadhouse / Teenage head / Slow death / Shakin' all over / Louie Louie / Have you seen my baby / Can't explain.
Jan 73. (7") *(UP 35464)* **MARRIED WOMAN. / GET A SHOT OF RHYTHM & BLUES**

— **JORDAN, WILSON, FARRELL and ALEXANDER** recruited new member **DAVID WRIGHT** – drums repl. TERRY RAE who had repl. MIHM (to HOT KNIVES)

Skydog not issued

1974. (7") *()* **JUMPIN' JACK FLASH. / BLUES FROM PHILLYS** France
(re-iss.'77 on 12";)
1974. (7"ep) *<>* **GREASE** France
– Let me rock / Dog meat / Sweet little rock'n'roller.

Philips not issued

1975. (7") *()* **LET THE BOY ROCK'N'ROLL. / YES IT'S TRUE** France

not issued Bomp

1975. (7") *<101>* **YOU TORE ME DOWN. / HIM OR ME**

Sire Sire

Jun 76. (lp) *(9103 251)* **SHAKE SOME ACTION**
– Shake some action / Sometimes / Yes it's true / St. Louis blues / You tore me down / Please please girl / Let the boy rock'n'roll / Don't you lie to me / She said yeah / I'll cry alone / Misery / I saw her / Teenage confidential / I can't hide. *(re-iss.Sep78; SRK 6021) (cd-iss.Sep93 on 'Aim'; AIMCD 1017)*
Jul 76. (7"m) *(6198 086)* **DON'T YOU LIE TO ME. / SHE SAID YEAH / SHAKE SOME ACTION**
Nov 76. (7") *(6078 602)* **SHAKE SOME ACTION. / TEENAGE CONFIDENTIAL**
Nov 76. (7") *<731>* **TEENAGE CONFIDENTIAL. / I CAN'T HIDE**

— **MIKE WILHELM** – guitar repl. FARRELL who joined PHANTOM MOVERS

Apr 78. (lp) *(9103 333)* **THE FLAMIN' GROOVIES NOW!**
– Feel a whole lot better / Bewteen the lines / Ups and downs / There's a place / Take me back / Reminiscing / Good laugh man / Yeah my baby / House of blue lights / All I wanted / Blue turns to grey / When I heard your name / Move it / Don't put me on. *(re-iss.Sep78; SRK 7059)*
Apr 78. (7"m,12"m) *(6078 619)* **FEEL A WHOLE LOT BETTER. / PAINT IT BLACK / SHAKE SOME ACTION**
Aug 78. (7") *(SIR 4002)* **MOVE IT. / WHEN I HEARD YOUR NAME**
Jun 79. (lp) *(SRK 6067)* **JUMPING IN THE NIGHT**
– Please please girl / Next one crying / Down down down / Tell me again / Absolutely sweet Marie / (You're my) Wonderful one / Jumpin' in the night / 19th nervous breakdown / Boys / 5D / First plane home / Lady friend / In the U.S.A. *<US-different tracks>*
1979. (7"m) *(SIR 4018)* **ABSOLUTELY SWEET MARIE. / WEREWOLVES OF LONDON / NEXT ONE CRYING**

— **DANNY MIHM** – drums (ex-PHANTOM MOVERS) re-repl. WRIGHT before split CHRIS WILSON joined BARRACUDAS in '82, **CYRIL JORDAN** re-formed **FLAMIN' GROOVIES** in 1986

— **JACK JOHNSON** – guitar + **PAUL ZAHL** – drums repl.WILSON, WRIGHT + WILHELM

A.B.C. not issued

Jul 87. (7") *(ABCS 015)* **SHAKE SOME ACTION (live). / ?**
Jul 87. (lp) *(ABCLP 10)* **ONE NIGHT STAND (live)**
– Kicks / Bittersweet / I can't hide / Money / Call me Lightning / Shake some action / Slow death / Teenage head / Slow down / Tallahassee lassie. *(cd-iss.Apr89; ABCD 10) (re-iss.Sep93 on 'Aim' cd/c; AIM CD/C 1008)*

– compilations etc. –

Jun 76. (7") *Kama Sutra; (KSS 707)* **TEENAGE HEAD. / HEADIN' FOR TEXAS BORDER**
Nov 76. (7"ep) *United Artists; (REM 406)* **SLOW DEATH EP**
– Slow death / Talahassie lassie / Married woman / Get a shot of rhythm & blues.
May 84. (lp) *Skydog; (SK 12226)* **SUPERGREASE** France
1980's. (7") *Skydog;* **I CAN'T EXPLAIN. / LITTLE QUEENIE** France
Nov 84. (lp) *Eva; (12044)* **'68 (live)** France
Nov 84. (lp) *Eva; (12045)* **'70 (live)** France
Jul 85. (lp/c) *Buddah; (252262-1/-4)* **STILL SHAKIN'**
May 86. (lp/c) *Edsel; (ED/CED 183)* **ROADHOUSE**
– (compilation of 'FLAMINGO' + 'TEENAGE HEAD').
Aug 88. (lp) *Voxx; (200009)* **BUCKET OF BRAINS**
(UK cd-iss.Apr95 on 'E.M.I.'; CZ 542)
Aug 89. (lp/c/cd) *Sire; (K 925948-1/-4/-2)* **GROOVIES GREATEST GROOVES**
– Shake some action / Teenage head / Slow death / Tallahassie lassie / Yeah my baby / Yes it's true / First plane home / In the U.S.A. / Between the lines / Don't you lie to me / Down down down / I'll cry alone / You tore me down / Please please girl / Yes I am / Teenage confidential / I can't hide / Absolutely sweet Marie / Don't put me on / I saw her / All I wanted / Jumpin' in the night / There's a place / River deep, mountain high. *(cd re-iss.Jan96 on 'Warners'; 7599 25948-2)*
Nov 89. (lp) *Aim; (COLLECT 2)* **ROCKFIELD SESSIONS**
Apr 93. (cd/lp) *Marilyn;* **RARE DEMOS & LIVE RECORDINGS**
Sep 93. (cd/c) *Ain; (AIM CD/C 1030)* **STEP UP**
Oct 93. (cd) *Aim; (COLLECT 1-2)* **SNEAKERS / ROCKFIELD SESSIONS**
Nov 93. (cd) *Mystery;* **ROCKIN' AT THE ROUNDHOUSE – LIVE IN LONDON 1976/78 (live)**
May 94. (cd) *Eva; (842070)* **LIVE 68/70 (live)**
Nov 94. Bomp; (10"lp) **EP**
Apr 95. (cd) *Aim; (AIM 1051CD)* **LIVE AT THE FESTIVAL OF THE SUN BARCELONA (live)**
Apr 97. (cd) *Aim; (AIM 2001CD)* **OLDIES BUT GOLDIES: BEST OF**

ROY LONEY

solo with all original FLAMIN' GROOVIES

not issued Solid Smoke

1978. (7"ep) **ARTISTIC AS HELL**

— **ROY** formed **PHANTOM MOVERS** with **DANNY, MIHM** and **JAMES FARRELL + LARRY LEA** – guitar, vocals / **MAURICE TANI** – bass / **NICK BUCK** – keyboards.

Sep 79. (lp) *<SS 9001>* **OUT AFTER DARK**
– Born to be your fool / Used hoodoo / Phantom mover / Neat petite / Return to sender / People people / Rockin' in the graveyard / I love it / Scum city / Trophy / She run away / San Francisco girls.
1980. (m-lp) *<SS 9002>* **PHANTOM TRACKS**
– Emmy Emmy / Down the road apiece / Act of love / You ain't gettin' out / Hundred miles an hour / I must behave / Don't believe those lies / Poor tuxedo.

— **JOHN KALDOR** – guitar / **JOHNNY SURRELL** – drums repl. FERRELL + MIHM

1981. (lp) *<SS 9003>* **CONTENTS UNDER PRESSURE**
– Sorry / We're all heroes / Dead ringer / Different kind / Swinging single / Too funky to live / She's no lady / Heart full of soul / Cinema girls / Last time I'll cry / Intrigue indeed / Contents under pressure.

Rockhouse Solid Smoke

Nov 82. (lp) *(LPL 8203) <SS 9006>* **ROCK & ROLL DANCE PARTY**
– Ain't got a thing / My baby comes to me / Gonna rock tonite / Magdalena / Slip, slide and stomp / Doctor Boogie / Panic to a manic degree / Oh pretty woman / Double dare / Lovin' machine / Lana Lee / Don't start cryin' now / Goodnight Alcatraz.
Apr 83. (7"m) *(SP 8211)* **LANA LEE. / MAGDALENA / GOODNIGHT**

Lolita not issued

Jun 84. (lp) *(LOLITA 5017)* **FAST AND LOOSE**
Jun 84. (lp) *(LOLITA 5018)* **ROY LONEY LIVE (live)**

Aim not issued

Sep 93. (cd) *(AIMCD 1025)* **SCIENTIFIC BOMBS AWAY**
– Chicken run around / Bip bop boom / Run your shoes / Deviled eyes / Nervous Slim / Boy, man! / Bad news travels fast / Your best friend's number / Here comes Curly / Cry like the wind / Nobody / Feel so fine.

– his compilations, etc

Sep 93. (cd/c) *Marilyn;* **ACTION SHORTS**

FLAMING YOUTH

Formed: London, England ... 1969 by GORDON SMITH, BRIAN CHATTON, RONNIE CARYL and PHIL COLLINS (yes! that one). Under the wing of songwriters KEN HOWARD and ALAN BLAKLEY (famous for pop groups The HERD and DAVE DEE, DOZY, BEAKY, MICK & TICH), they arranged their enterprisingly packaged concept album, 'ARK 2'. However, the group fell apart after the flop of their third 45, 'FROM NOW ON', when their talented young drummer successfully auditioned for GENESIS.

Recommended: ARK 2 (*6)

GORDON SMITH – guitar, bass, vocals / **BRIAN CHATTON** – keyboards, vocals / **RONNIE CARYL** – bass, guitar, vocals / **PHIL COLLINS** – drums, percussion, vocals

Fontana not issued

Oct 69. (lp) *(STL 5533)* **ARK 2** [ ] [-]
– Guide me Orion / Earthglow / Weightlessness / Mars / Jupiter / Saturn / Uranus / The magician / Neptune / The mystic / From now on / Changes / In the light of love / Space child / Pulsar.

Oct 69. (7") *(TF 1057)* **GUIDE ME ORION. / FROM NOW ON (IMMORTAL INVISIBLE)** [ ] [-]

Jun 70. (7") *(6001 002)* **EVERY MAN, WOMAN AND CHILD. / DRIFTING** [ ] [-]

Dec 70. (7") *(6001 003)* **FROM NOW ON. / SPACE CHILD** [ ] [-]

— Disbanded when PHIL COLLINS joined GENESIS. CHATTON joined JACKSON HEIGHTS for their second album '5TH AVENUE BUS' in 1972.

FLASH

Formed: London, England . . .1972 by guitarist PETER BANKS, veteran of BLODWYN PIG, YES and the latter's acid-embryo, The SYN. He also featured on a NEAT CHANGE b-side, 'I LIED TO AUNTIE MAY', in 1968 for 'Decca'. In 1972, on a staple diet of fast and furious progressive rock (not unlike YES), FLASH were surprise hitmakers in the US with their debut 45, 'SMALL BEGINNINGS'. They subsequently supported ALICE COOPER on his successful 1972 world tour, while their eponymous album was riding high in the US Top 50. However, this was their last entry into charts, as their next album, 'FLASH IN THE CAN', suggested. BANKS completed a solo album before he faded into obscurity for nigh on two decades. In 1993, having nearly re-joined YES for one of their re-union tours, he completed the instrumental album, 'INSTINCT'. • **Songwriters:** BANKS-CARTER or BENNETT. 2nd/3rd album – BENNETT, CARTER or BANKS-BENNETT.

Recommended: FLASH (*7) / IN THE CAN (*6) / OUT OF OUR HANDS (*5)

COLIN CARTER – vocals / **PETER BANKS** – guitars, synthesiser, vocals (ex-BLODWYN PIG, ex-YES, ex-MABLE GREER'S TOYSHOP, ex-SYN) / **RAY BENNETT** – bass, vocals, rhythm guitar / **MIKE HOUGH** – drums, percussion / **TONY KAYE** – organ, piano synthesizers (ex-YES)

Sovereign Capitol

Feb 72. (lp) *(SVNA 7251) <11040>* **FLASH** [ ] [33] May72
– Small beginnings / Morning haze / Children of the universe / Dreams of Heaven / The time it takes. *(cd-iss.Sep94 on 'One Way'; OWS 2117796)*

Mar 72. (7") *(SOV 105) <3345>* **SMALL BEGINNINGS. / MORNING HAZE** [ ] [29] Jun72

Jun 72. (7") *<3496>* **CHILDREN OF THE UNIVERSE. / LIFETIME** [-] [ ]

— Reduced to a quartet, when KAYE formed BADGER

Nov 72. (lp) *(SVNA 7255) <11115>* **FLASH IN THE CAN** [ ] [ ]
– Lifetime / Monday morning eyes / Black and white / Stop that banging / There no more. *(cd-iss.Sep94 on 'One Way'; OWS 2156841)*

Jan 73. (7") *(SOV 116)* **WATCH YOUR STEP. / LIFETIME** [ ] [ ]

Oct 73. (lp) *(SVNA 7260) <11218>* **OUT OF OUR HANDS** [ ] [ ] Aug73
– Open sky / None the wiser (King) / Farewell number one (Pawn) / Man of honour (Knight) / Dead ahead (Queen) / The bishop / Psychosync (Escape) – (Farewell number two) – (Conclusion) / Manhattan morning (Christmas '72) / Shadows (It's you). *(cd-iss.Sep94 on 'One Way'; OWS 2117414)*

— Split early in 1974, after BANKS had went solo.

PETER BANKS

with **STEVE HACKETT + JAN AKKERMAN** – guitar / **RAY BENNETT + JOHN WETTON** – bass / **MIKE HOUGH + PHIL COLLINS** – drums

Sovereign Sovereign

Sep 73. (lp) *(SVNA 7256) <SMAS 11217>* **TWO SIDES OF PETER BANKS** [ ] [ ]
– Vision of the King / The white horse: (a) On the hill, (b) Lord of the dragon / Knights: (a) The falcon, (b) The bear / Battles / Knights – reprise / Last eclipse / Beyond the loneliest sea / Stop that / Get out of my fridge. *(cd-iss.Sep94 on 'One Way'; OWS 2118009)*

— He then formed own group EMPIRE, who recorded 3 unreleased lp's, before he moved to L.A. in 1976. Returned to the fold in the 90's.

— **PETER BANKS** – guitars, synthesizers / with co-writers & players **GERALD GOFF + BILL FORTH**

H.T.D. not issued

Feb 93. (cd) *(HTDCD 11)* **INSTINCT** (instrumental) [ ] [-]
– No place home / All points south / Fogbound / Sticky wicket / Shortcomings / Code blue / Angels / Anima Mundi / Swamp report / Instinctive behavour / Dominating factor / Never the same.

Blueprint not issued

Jun 97. (cd) *(BP 235CD)* **LIVE** [ ] [-]
– Small beginnings / Room with a view / Children of the universe / Dreams of Heaven / Dead again / Psycho synch.

FLEETWOOD MAC

Formed: London, England . . . July 1967, by MICK FLEETWOOD, PETER GREEN and BOB BRUNNING. They quickly inducted JEREMY SPENCER and made live debut at prestidgeous Windsor Jazz & Blues Festival on 12 Aug'67. They replaced BRUNNING with another ex-BLUESBREAKERS member JOHN McVIE, and signed to 'Blue Horizon'. Billed at first as PETER GREEN'S FLEETWOOD MAC, they flopped late '67 with first 45 'I BELIEVE MY TIME AIN'T LONG'. Around the same time, they became in-house band for blues artists like OTIS SPANN and DUSTER BENNETT. Early in '68, their debut lp 'PETER GREEN'S FLEETWOOD MAC', hit the Top 5, and was soon pursued by Top 40 singles 'BLACK MAGIC WOMAN' & 'NEED YOUR LOVE SO BAD'. Their 2nd lp 'MR. WONDERFUL', also cracked the UK Top 10, and was followed by million-selling UK No.1 instrumental 'ALBATROSS'. Out of contract, they signed one-off deal with 'Immediate', who issued another Top 3 gem 'MAN OF THE WORLD' early '69. In the Autumn, yet another classic 'OH WELL' (in 2 parts), hit No.2 for new label 'Reprise', and at the same time lp 'THEN PLAY ON' made UK Top 10. On Apr'70, GREEN departed group, due to increasing state of mental health. He left behind another haunting Top 10 single 'THE GREEN MANALISHI', which showed his deep lyrical attitude at the time. Without him, the group failed to emulate earlier success, and had rough period until the mid-70's. Newcomers LINDSEY BUCKINGHAM and STEVIE NICKS, came into the fold alongside CHRISTINE McVIE (member and wife of JOHN McVIE since Aug'70) and MICK FLEETWOOD. Early in 1976 now residents of California, USA, they had 3 US Top 20 hits, and a self-titled album, that eventually rose to the top that year. Their much anticipated 1977 follow-up 'RUMOURS' surpassed its predecessor, topping both US & UK charts, before going on to sell over 15 million copies. Although the McVIE's separation quickly followed, the break-up of BUCKINGHAM and NICKS sealed the band's fate. The group, however, continued to be massive attraction for the rest of the 70's & 80's. All had own solo sideline, with the beautiful STEVIE being the most prolific in the 80's until her departure. • **Style:** Pioneers of the white blues boom of the late 60's, they progressed into sophisticated husband-wife AOR team, ready-made for FM radio. • **Songwriters:** GREEN compositions, except early covers; NEED YOUR LOVE SO BAD (Little Willie John) / NO PLACE TO GO (Howlin' Wolf) / DUST MY BROOM (Robert Johnson) / etc. • **Trivia:** Late 1973, their manager Clifford Davis, put together a bogus FLEETWOOD MAC, which resulted in a legal court battle, in which they won. The bogus group became STRETCH, and had a late '75 UK Top 20 hit with 'Why Did You Do It'.

Recommended: GREATEST HITS (*9; 1971 version) / not counting RUMOURS for this book, and of course their other later GREATEST HITS

JEREMY SPENCER (b. 4 Jul'48, Hartlepool, England) – guitar, vocals / **PETER GREEN** (b. PETER GREENBAUM, 29 Oct'49) – guitar, vocals (ex-JOHN MAYALL'S BLUESBREAKERS, ex-SHOTGUN EXPRESS) / **MICK FLEETWOOD** (b.24 Jun'42, Redruth, England) – drums (ex-JOHN MAYALL'S BLUESBREAKERS) / **JOHN McVIE** (b.26 Nov'45) – bass (ex-JOHN MAYALL'S BLUESBREAKERS) repl. BOB BRUNNING who formed SUNFLOWER BLUES BAND after recording B-side)

Blue Horizon Epic

Nov 67. (7"; as PETER GREEN'S FLEETWOOD MAC) *(57-3051)* **I BELIEVE MY TIME AIN'T LONG. / RAMBLING PONY** [ ] [-]
(re-iss.1969 on 'C.B.S.'; 3051)

Feb 68. (lp; stereo/mono) *(S+/7-63200) <26402>* **PETER GREEN'S FLEETWOOD MAC** <US-title 'FLEETWOOD MAC'> [4] [ ] Aug68
– My heart beat like a hammer / Merry go round / Long grey mare / Shake your moneymaker / Looking for somebody / No place to go / My baby's good to me / I love another woman / Cold black night / The world keep on turning / Got to move. *(re-iss.Oct73 on 'CBS-Embasssy'; EMB 31036) (re-iss.Jul77 on 'CBS' lp/c; CBS/40 31494) (cd-iss.Aug94 as 'FLEETWOOD MAC' on 'Columbia Rewind'; 477 358-2)*

Mar 68. (7") *(57-3138)* **BLACK MAGIC WOMAN. / THE SUN IS SHINING** [37] [-]

Apr 68. (7") *<10351>* **BLACK MAGIC WOMAN. / LONG GREY MARE** [-] [ ]

Jul 68. (7") *(57-3139) <10386>* **NEED YOUR LOVE SO BAD. / STOP MESSIN' ROUND** [31] [ ]

Aug 68. (lp) *(7-63025)* **MR. WONDERFUL** [10] [-]
– Stop messin' round / Coming home / Rollin' man / Dust my broom / Love that burns / Doctor Brown / Need your love tonight / If you be my baby / Evenin' boogie / Lazy poker blues / I've lost my baby / Trying so hard to forget. *(re-iss.Nov89 on 'Essential' lp/c/cd; ESS LP/MC/CD 010) (re-iss.cd on 'Castle'; CCSCD 368)*

— added **DANNY KIRWAN** (b.13 Mar'50) – guitar, vocals (ex-BOILERHOUSE)

Nov 68. (7") *(57-3145) <10436>* **ALBATROSS. / JIGSAW PUZZLE BLUES** [1] [ ]
(re-iss.Nov71 on 'C.B.S.'; CBS 3145)

Feb 69. (lp) *<BN 26446>* **ENGLISH ROSE** [-] [ ]
– Stop messin' round / Jigsaw puzzle blues / Doctor Brown / Something inside of me / Evenin' boogie / Love that burns / Black magic woman / I've lost my baby / One sunny day / Without you / Coming home / Albatross.

Immediate not issued

Apr 69. (7"; b-side by EARL VINCE & THE VALIENTS) *(IM 080)* **MAN OF THE WORLD. / SOMEBODY'S GONNA GET THEIR HEAD KICKED IN TONIGHT** [2] [-]
(re-iss.Feb83; same)

Reprise Reprise

Sep 69. (7") *<0860>* **RATTLESNAKE SHAKE. / COMING YOUR WAY** [-] [ ]

Sep 69. (7") *(RS 27000) <0883>* **OH WELL (Pt.1). / OH WELL (Pt.2)** [2] [55] Jan70

— (note that SPENCER, for some reason did not play on the below album)

Sep 69. (lp) *(RSLP 9000) <6368>* **THEN PLAY ON** [6] [ ]
– Coming your way / Closing my eyes / Showbiz blues / Underway / Oh well / Although the sun is shining / Rattlesnake shake / Searching for Madge / Fighting for Madge / Closing my eyes / When you say / One sunny day / Although the sun is shining / Like crying / Before the beginning. *(re-iss.Jul71 lp/c; K/K4 44103) ;re-iss.Apr77) (cd-iss.Jun88 with extra tracks; 927 448-2)*

May 70. (7") *(RS 27007) <0925>* **THE GREEN MANALISHI (WITH THE TWO-PRONG CROWN). / WORLD IN HARMONY** [10] [ ]

— Now a quartet of **FLEETWOOD, McVIE, SPENCER and KIRWAN** when GREEN went solo

Sep 70. (lp) *(RSLP 9004)* *<6408>* **KILN HOUSE** [39] [69]
– This is the rock / Station man / Blood on the floor / Hi ho silver / Jewel eyed Judy / Buddy's song / Earl Grey / One together / Tell me all the things you do / Mission bell. *(re-iss.Jul71 lp/c; K/K4 54001) (cd-iss.Feb93 on 'Warners'; 7599 27453-2)*

Jan 71. (7") *<0984>* **JEWEL EYED JUDY. / STATION MAN** [-] [ ]

— added **CHRISTINE** (PERFECT) **McVIE** (b.12 Jul'43, Birmingham, England) – keyboards, vocals (ex-CHICKEN SHACK) (she had already guested on 'MR. WONDERFUL' album)

Mar 71. (7") *(RS 27010)* **DRAGONFLY. / PURPLE DANCER** [ ] [-]

— **BOB WELCH** (b.31 Jul'46, Los Angeles, Calif.) – guitar, vocals (ex-HEAD WEST) repl. SPENCER who formed CHILDREN OF GOD

Sep 71. (lp/c) *(K/K4 44153)* *<6465>* **FUTURE GAMES** [ ] [91]
– Women of 1000 years / Morning rain / What a shame / Future games / Sands of time / Sometimes / Lay it all down / Show me a smile. *(re-iss.Apr77; same) (cd-iss.Feb93 on 'Warners'; 7599 27458-2)*

Sep 71. (7") *<1057>* **SANDS OF TIME. / LAY IT ALL DOWN** [-] [ ]

Apr 72. (lp/c) *(K/K4 44181)* *<2080>* **BARE TREES** [ ] [70]
– Child of mine / The ghost / Homeward bound / Sunny side of Heaven / Bare trees / Sentimental lady / Danny's chant / Spare me a little of your love / Dust / Thoughts on a grey day. *(re-iss.Apr77; same) (cd-iss.Feb93 on 'Warners'; 7599 27240-2)*

Aug 72. (7") *<1093>* **SENTIMENTAL LADY. / SUNNY SIDE OF HEAVEN** [-] [ ]

Aug 72. (7") *(K 14194)* **SPARE ME A LITTLE OF YOUR LOVE. / SUNNY SIDE OF HEAVEN** [ ] [-]

— **DAVE WALKER** – vocals (ex-SAVOY BROWN) repl. KIRWAN who went solo / added **BOB WESTON** – guitar, vocals (ex-LONG JOHN BALDRY) (above two now with FLEETWOOD, J. McVIE, C. McVIE and WELCH)

May 73. (7") *<1157>* **REMEMBER ME. / DISSATISFIED** [-] [ ]

May 73. (lp/c) *(K/K4 44235)* *<2138>* **PENGUIN** [ ] [49] Apr73
– Remember me / Bright fire / Dissatisfied / (I'm a) Road runner / The derelict / Revelation / Did you ever love me / Night watch / Caught in the rain. *(re-iss.Apr77; same) (cd-iss.Feb93 on 'Warners'; 7599 26178-2)*

Jun 73. (7") *<1172>* **DID YOU EVER LOVE ME. / REVELATION** [-] [ ]

Jun 73. (7") *(K 14280)* **DID YOU EVER LOVE ME. / THE DERELICT** [ ] [-]

— Reverted to a quintet when WALKER departed forming HUNGRY FIGHTER

Jan 74. (lp/c) *(K/K4 44248)* *<2158>* **MYSTERY TO ME** [ ] [67] Nov73
– Emerald eyes / Believe me / Just crazy love / Hypnotized / Forever / Keep on going / The city / Miles away / Somebody / The way I feel / Good things come to those who wait / Why / For your love. *(re-iss.Apr77; same) (cd-iss.Feb93 on 'Warners'; 7599 25982-2)*

Mar 74. (7") *(K 14315)* *<1188>* **FOR YOUR LOVE. / HYPNOTIZED** [ ] [ ]

— Trimmed to quartet when WESTON also left

Sep 74. (lp/c) *(K/K4 54026)* *<2196>* **HEROES ARE HARD TO FIND** [ ] [34]
– Heroes are hard to find / Coming home / Angel / The Bermuda Triangle / Come a little bit closer / She's changing me / Bad loser / Silver heels / Prove your love / Born enchanter / Safe harbour. *(cd-iss.Feb93 on 'Warners'; 7599 27216-2)*

Feb 75. (7") *(K 14388)* *<1317>* **HEROES ARE HARD TO FIND. / BORN ENCHANTER** [ ] [ ]

— **LINDSEY BUCKINGHAM** (b. 3 Oct'47. Palo Alto, Calif.) – guitar, vocals (as below; ex-BUCKINGHAM-NICKS) repl. WELCH / added **STEVIE NICKS** (b. STEPHANIE NICKS, 26 May'48, Phoenix, Arizona) – vocals

Aug 75. (lp,white-lp/c) *(K/K4 54043)* *<2225>* **FLEETWOOD MAC** [ ] [1]
– Monday morning / Warm ways / Blue letter / Rhiannon / Over my head / Crystal / Say you love me / Landslide / World turning / Sugar daddy / I'm so afraid. *(Nov76 hit UK No.23) (cd-iss.1983; 2281-2) (cd-iss.Dec85 on 'Warners'; K2 54043) (re-iss.Feb93 cd/c/lp; 7599 27241-2/-4/-1)*

Oct 75. (7") *(K 14403)* **WARM WAYS. / BLUE LETTER** [ ] [-]

Feb 76. (7") *(K 14413)* *<1339>* **OVER MY HEAD. / I'M SO AFRAID** [ ] [20] Nov75

Apr 76. (7") *(K 14430)* *<1345>* **RHIANNON. / SUGAR DADDY** [ ] [11] Feb76
(re-iss.Feb78 reached UK-No.46)

Sep 76. (7") *(K 14447)* *<1356>* **SAY YOU LOVE ME. / MONDAY MORNING** [40] [11] Jun76

Warners Warners

Jan 77. (7") *(K 16872)* *<8304>* **GO YOUR OWN WAY. / SILVER SPRINGS** [38] [10]

Feb 77. (lp,white-lp/c) *(K/K4 56344)* *<3010>* **RUMOURS** [1] [1]
– Second hand news / Dreams / Never going back again / Don't stop / Go your own way / Songbird / The chain / You make loving fun / I don't want to know / Oh daddy / Gold dust woman. *(cd-iss.Dec83; K2 56344) (re-iss.Jun88 lp/c; K/K4 56344) (re-iss.Feb93 cd/c/lp; 7599 27313-2/-4/-1)*

Apr 77. (7") *(K 16930)* *<8413>* **DON'T STOP. / GOLD DUST WOMAN** [32] [3] Jul77

Jun 77. (7") *(K 16969)* *<8371>* **DREAMS. / SONGBIRD** [24] [1] Apr77

Sep 77. (7") *(K 17013)* **YOU MAKE LOVING FUN. / NEVER GOING BACK AGAIN** [45] [-]

Oct 77. (7") *<8483>* **YOU MAKE LOVING FUN. / GOLD DUST WOMAN** [-] [9]

Sep 79. (7") *(K 17468)* *<49077>* **TUSK. / NEVER MAKE ME CRY** [6] [8]

Oct 79. (d-lp/c) *(K/K4 66088)* *<3350>* **TUSK** [1] [4]
– Over & over / The ledge / Think about me / Save me a place / Sara / What makes you think you're the one / That's all for everyone / Not that funny / Sisters of the Moon / Angel / That's enough for me / Brown eyes / Never make me cry / I know I'm not wrong / Honey hi / Beautiful child / Walk a thin line / Tusk / Never forget. *(cd-iss.Mar87; K2 66088) (re-iss.Feb93 cd/c/d-lp; 7599 27395-2/-4/-1)*

Dec 79. (7") *(K 17533)* *<49150>* **SARA. / THAT'S ENOUGH FOR ME** [37] [7]

Feb 80. (7") *(K 17577)* **NOT THAT FUNNY. / SAVE ME A PLACE** [ ] [-]

Mar 80. (7") *<49196>* **THINK ABOUT ME. / SAVE ME A PLACE** [-] [20]

Mar 80. (7") *(K 17614)* **THINK ABOUT ME. / HONEY HI** [ ] [-]

Jun 80. (7") *<49500>* **SISTERS OF THE MOON. / WALK A THIN LINE** [-] [86]

Nov 80. (d-lp/c) *(K/K4 66097)* *<3500>* **FLEETWOOD MAC LIVE (live)** [31] [14]
– Monday morning / Say you love me / Dreams / Oh well / Over & over / Sara / Not that funny / Never going back again / Landslide / Fireflies / Over my head / Rhiannon / Don't let me down again / One more night / Go your own way / Don't stop / I'm so afraid / The farmer's daughter.

Jan 81. (7") *<49660>* **FIREFLIES. / OVER MY HEAD** [-] [60]

Feb 81. (7") *(K 17746)* **THE FARMER'S DAUGHTER (live). / DREAMS (live)** [ ] [-]

Mar 81. (7") *<49700>* **THE FARMER'S DAUGHTER (live). / MONDAY MORNING (live)** [-] [ ]

Jul 82. (7") *(K 17965)* *<29966>* **HOLD ME. / EYES OF THE WORLD** [ ] [4] Jun82

Jul 82. (lp/c) *(K/K4 56952)* *<23607>* **MIRAGE** [5] [1]
– Love in store / Can't go back / That's alright / Book of love / Gypsy / Only over you / Empire state / Straight back / Hold me / Oh Diane / Eyes of the world / Wish you were here. *(cd-iss.Dec83; K2 56952) (re-iss.Feb93 cd/c/lp; 7599 23607-2/-4/-1)*

Sep 82. (7") *(K 17997)* *<29918>* **GYPSY. / COOL WATER** [46] [12] Aug82

Nov 82. (7") *<29848>* **LOVE IN STORE. / CAN'T GO BACK** [-] [22]

Dec 82. (7"/7"pic-d) *(FLEET 1/+P)* **OH DIANE. / ONLY OVER YOU** [9] [-]
(12"+=) *(FLEET 1T)* – The chain.

Feb 83. (7") *<29698>* **OH DIANE. / THAT'S ALRIGHT** [-] [ ]

Apr 83. (7") *(W 9848)* **CAN'T GO BACK. / THAT'S ALRIGHT** [ ] [-]
(12") *(W 9848T)* – ('A'side) / Rhiannon / Tusk / Over and over.

Mar 87. (7"/ext.12"/ext.12"pic-d) *(W 8398/+T/TP)* *<28398>* **BIG LOVE. / YOU AND I, PART 1** [9] [5]
(d7"+=) *(W 8398F)* – The chain / Go your own way.

Apr 87. (lp/c)(cd) *(WX 65/+C)(925 471-2)* *<25471>* **TANGO IN THE NIGHT** [1] [7]
– Big love / Seven wonders / Everywhere / Caroline / Tango in the night / Mystified / Little lies / Family man / Welcome to the room . . . Sara / Isn't it midnight / When I see you again / You and I, part II.

Jun 87. (7") *(W 8317)* *<28317>* **SEVEN WONDERS. / BOOK OF MIRACLES (instrumental)** [56] [19]
(ext-remix.12"+=/ext-remix.12"pic-d+=) *(W 8317T/+P)* – ('A'dub).

Aug 87. (7") *(W 8291)* *<28291>* **LITTLE LIES. / RICKY** [5] [4]
(ext.c-s+=/ext.12"+=/ext.12"pic-d+=) *(W 8291/+C/T/TP)* – ('A'dub).

Nov 87. (7") *(W 8114)* *<28114>* **FAMILY MAN. / DOWN ENDLESS STREET** [54] [90] Mar88
(7"box/12") *(W 8114 B/T)* – ('A'extended vocal remix) / Family party bonus beats / You and I, part II.

Feb 88. (7") *(W 8143)* *<28143>* **EVERYWHERE. / WHEN I SEE YOU AGAIN** [4] [14] Nov 87
(12"+=) *(W 8143T)* – ('A'extended) / ('A'dub version).
(3"cd-s+=) *(W 8143CD)* – Rhiannon / Say you love me.

Jun 88. (7") *(W 7860)* **ISN'T IT MIDNIGHT. / MYSTIFIED** [60] [-]
(12"+=/3"cd-s+=) *(W 7860 T/CD)* – Say you love me / Gypsy.

Nov 88. (7") *(W 7644)* *<27644>* **AS LONG AS YOU FOLLOW. / OH WELL (live)** [66] [43]
(12"+=/3"cd-s+=) *(W 7644 T/CD)* – Gold dust woman.

Nov 88. (lp/c)(cd) *(WX 221/+C)(925 838-2)* *<25801>* **FLEETWOOD MAC'S GREATEST HITS** (compilation) [3] [14]
– As long as you follow / No questions asked / Rhiannon / Don't stop / Go your own way / Hold me / Everywhere / Gypsy / Say you love me / Dreams / Little lies / Sara / Tusk. *(c+=/cd+=)*– Oh Diane / Big love / You making loving fun / Seven wonders.

Feb 89. (7") *(W 7528)* **HOLD ME. / NO QUESTIONS ASKED** [ ] [-]
(12"+=/3"cd-s+=) *(W 7528 T/CD)* – I loved another woman (live).

— (Jul88) When BUCKINGHAM departed, he was repl. by **RICK VITO** (b.13 Oct'49, Darby, Pennsylvania) – guitar / **BILLY BURNETT** (b. 8 May'53, Memphis, Tenn.) – guitar (ex-MICK FLEETWOOD'S ZOO)

Apr 90. (7"/c-s) *(W 9866/+C)* *<19866>* **SAVE ME. / I LOVED ANOTHER WOMAN (live)** [53] [33]
(12"+=/cd-s+=/s-cd-s+=) *(W 9866 T/CD/CDX)* – Everywhere (live).

Apr 90. (cd/cd-box w-pic-d)(lp/c) *(7599 26111/26206-2)(WX 335/+C)* *<26111-2/-4>* **BEHIND THE MASK** [1] [18]
– Skies the limit / In the back of my mind / Do you know / Save me / Affairs of the heart / When the Sun goes down / Behind the mask / Stand on the rock / Hard feelings / Freedom / When it comes to love / The second time. *(re-iss.cd Feb95)*

Aug 90. (7"/c-s) *(W 9739/+C)* **IN THE BACK OF MY MIND. / LIZARD PEOPLE** [58] [-]
(12"/cd-s) *(W 9739 T/CD)* – ('A'side) / Little lies (live) / The chain (live).
(s-cd-s+=) *(W 9739CDX)* – Lizard people.

Nov 90. (7"/c-s) *(W 9740/+C)* **SKIES THE LIMIT. / LIZARD PEOPLE** [ ] [-]
(12"/cd-s) *(W 9740 T/CD)* – ('A'side) / Little lies (live) / The chain (live).

Feb 91. (7") **SKIES THE LIMIT. / THE SECOND TIME** [-] [ ]

— (late 1990) STEVIE NICKS left to go solo, and CHRISTINE departed due to MICK's new book allegations.

Jan 93. (7"/c-s) *(W 0145/+C)* **LOVE SHINES. / THE CHAIN (alt.mix)** [ ] [ ]
(cd-s+=) *(W 0145CD)* – The chain (Not That Funny live version) / Isn't it midnight (alt.version).

— **MICK FLEETWOOD, JOHN McVIE, CHRISTINE McVIE** (departed in '94, but on below) + **BILLY BURNETTE** added **DAVE MASON** (b.10 May'46, Worcester, England) – vocals, guitars (ex-TRAFFIC, ex-solo artist)/ **BEKKA BRAMLETT** (b.19 Apr'68, Westwood, Calif.) – vocals (daughter of DELANEY & BONNIE)

Oct 95. (cd/c) *(<9362 45920-2/-4>)* **TIME** [47] [ ]
– Talkin' to my heart / Hollywood (some other kind of town) / Blow by blow / Winds of change / I do / Nothing without you / Dreamin' the dream / Sooner or later / I wonder why / Nights in Estoril / I got it in for you / All over again / These strange times.

– (with PETER GREEN) compilations, others, etc. –

Note all 'Blue Horizon' releases were on 'Epic' US.

Jul 69. (7") *Blue Horizon; (57-3157)* **NEED YOUR LOVE SO BAD. / NO PLACE TO GO** [32] [-]

Aug 69. (lp) *Blue Horizon; (7-63215)* **PIOUS BIRD OF GOOD OMEN** [18] [-]
– Need your love so bad / Coming home / Rambling pony / The big boat / I believe my time ain't long / The sun is shining / Albatross / Black magic woman / Just the blues / Jigsaw puzzle blues / Looking for somebody / Stop messin' around. *(re-iss.Jun81 on 'C.B.S.'; CBS 32050) (cd-iss.Jun95 on 'Columbia-Rewind'; 480 524-2)*

Note all CBS releases were on 'Epic' US.

May 71. (lp) *C.B.S.; (63875)* **THE ORIGINAL FLEETWOOD MAC BEFORE THE SPLIT** [ ] [ ]
(re-iss.+c/cd.Jun90 on 'Castle')

Jun 71. (d-lp) *Blue Horizon; <3801>* **FLEETWOOD MAC IN CHICAGO** [-] [ ]
<US-iss.Nov75 on 'Sire'; SASH 37152> <re-iss.1977; 2XS 6009>

Oct 71. (d-lp) *Epic; <KE 30632>* **BLACK MAGIC WOMAN** [-] [ ]
– (US lp's; 'FLEETWOOD MAC' (1968) & 'ENGLISH ROSE')

Nov 71. (lp/c) *C.B.S.; (CBS/40 69011)* **GREATEST HITS** [36] [ ]
– The green Manalishi (with the two-pronged crown) / Oh well (part 1 & 2) / Shake your moneymaker / Need your love so bad / Rattlesnake shake / Dragonfly / Black magic woman / Albatross / Man of the world / Stop messin' around / Love that burns. *(re-iss.Feb88 lp/c; CBS 460 704-1/4) (cd-iss.Apr89; 460 704-2) (re-iss.cd Dec94 on 'Columbia-Rewind'; 477 512-2)*

May 72. (7") *Reprise; (K 14174)* **THE GREEN MANALISHI (WITH THE TWO-PRONG CROWN). / OH WELL (Pt.1)** [ ] [ ]
(re-iss.Mar73 & Nov76; same)

May 73. (7") *C.B.S.; (CBS 8306)* **ALBATROSS. / NEED YOUR LOVE SO BAD** [2] [ ]
(re-iss.Feb78; CBS 5957) (re-iss.Nov90 on 'Old Gold'; OG 9955)

Aug 73. (7") *C.B.S.; (CBS 1722)* **BLACK MAGIC WOMAN. / STOP MESSIN' ROUND** [ ] [ ]

Jun 75. (d-lp) *C.B.S.; (CBS 22025)* **THE ORIGINAL FLEETWOOD MAC / ENGLISH ROSE** [ ] [ ]
(re-iss.Jun76; 81308-9) (re-iss.Jun90 on 'Essential' cd/c/lp; ESS CD/MC/LP 026) (re-iss.cd May94 on 'Castle'; CLACD 344)

Oct 75. (7"; b-side by DANNY KIRWAN) *D.J.M.; (DJS 10620)* **MAN OF THE WORLD. / SECOND CHAPTER** [ ] [-]
(re-iss.Feb76 & Jun78 on 'Epic'; EPC 6466)

Mar 77. (d-lp/c) *C.B.S. / Sire; (CBS/40 88227) <3706>* **VINTAGE YEARS** [ ] [ ]
(re-iss.May82 as 'THE VINTAGE YEARS: HISTORY OF FLEETWOOD MAC'; CBS 22122)

Aug 77. (lp) *Embassy; (EMB 31569)* **ALBATROSS** (1 side by 'CHRISTINE PERFECT') [ ] [-]
(cd-iss.Feb91 on 'Columbia'; CD 31569)

Sep 78. (lp/c) *C.B.S.; (CBS/40 83110)* **MAN OF THE WORLD** [ ] [-]
Feb 80. (lp) *C.B.S.; (CBS 31798)* **BLACK MAGIC WOMAN** [ ] [-]
Aug 83. (c) *C.B.S.; (40-22163)* **FLEETWOOD MAC / THE PIOUS BIRD OF GOOD OMEN** [ ] [-]
Jul 84. (7") *C.B.S.; (A 4578)* **ALBATROSS. / MAN OF THE WORLD** [ ] [-]
Jan 85. (lp) *Shanghai; (HAI 107)* **LIVE IN BOSTON (live)** [ ] [-]
(re-iss.May88 on 'Line'; IMLP 400129) (cd-iss.Oct85 on 'Shanghai'; HAI 400) (cd-iss.Oct89 on 'Castle')

Aug 85. (d-lp/c) *Shanghai; (HAI/HAC 300)* **CERULEAN (LIVE IN BOSTON Part II)** [ ] [-]
Sep 85. (7") *Old Gold; (OG 9529)* **MAN OF THE WORLD. / ('Natural Born boogie' by Humble Pie)** [ ] [-]
Oct 85. (lp) *Platinum; (24076)* **RATTLESNAKE SHAKE** [ ] [-]
Oct 85. (lp) *Platinum;(24077)* **MADISON BLUES** [ ] [-]
Dec 85. (lp) *Platinum; (24082)* **OH WELL** [ ] [-]
Apr 86. (lp) *Commander; (LP 39006)* **RATTLESNAKE SHAKE LIVE** [ ] [-]
Apr 86. (lp) *Commander; (LP 39007)* **OH WELL LIVE** [ ] [-]
Apr 86. (lp) *Commander; (LP 39008)* **GREEN MANALISHI LIVE** [ ] [-]
Nov 86. (cd) *Commander; (CD 99011)* **FLEETWOOD MAC LIVE (live 1968)** [ ] [-]
(re-iss.May88; same) (re-iss.May94//Nov94 on 'Arc'; MEC 949020//MO 3016) (re-iss.Aug95 on 'Abracadabra'; AB 3017)

Nov 86. (lp/c/cd) *Thunderbolt; (THBL/THBC/CDTB 1.038)* **LONDON LIVE '68 (live)** [ ] [-]
Jul 87. (d-lp/c/cd) *Castle; (CCS LP/MC/CD 157)* **THE COLLECTION** [ ] [-]
(re-iss.cd Jan94)

Sep 87. (lp) *Commander; (224 821-7)* **GREATEST HITS LIVE** [ ] [-]
(re-iss.Dec89 lp/c/cd; 264 821-7/-4/-2) (re-iss.cd Apr93 on 'Zillion'; 261 0992)

1988. (lp) *Varrick; <VR 020>* **JUMPING AT SHADOWS** [-] [ ]
– (same as above)

Feb 89. (7") *C.B.S.; (654 613-7)* **ALBATROSS. / MAN OF THE WORLD** [ ] [-]
(12"+=/cd-s+=) *(654 613-6/-2)* – Black magic woman / Love that burns.

Apr 89. (lp/c/cd) *Castle; (CCS LP/MC/CD 216)* **THE BLUES COLLECTION** [ ] [-]
1989. (3"cd-ep) *C.B.S.; (655 171-3)* **ALBATROSS / BLACK MAGIC WOMAN / NEED YOUR LOVE SO BAD / I'D RATHER GO BLIND** [ ] [-]
Oct 89. (lp/c/cd) *Castle; (CLA LP/MC/CD 152)* **BOSTON LIVE** [ ] [-]
Nov 89. (lp/c/cd) *Mainline; (264 824-1/-4/-2)* **OH WELL** [ ] [-]
Nov 89. (lp/c) *Hallmark; (SHM/HSC 3268)* **LOOKING BACK ON FLEETWOOD MAC** [ ] [-]
(cd-iss.May90 on 'Pickwick'; PWKS 533)

Jul 90. (cd) *Marble Ach; (CMACD 125)* **FLEETWOOD MAC LIVE (live)** [ ] [-]
Feb 91. (3xcd/5xlp) *Essential; (ESB CD/LP 138)* **THE BLUES YEARS** [ ] [-]
Jun 91. (cd/c) *Elite; (ELITE 008 MC/CD)* **LIKE IT THIS WAY** [ ] [-]
(re-iss.Sep93; same)

Mar 92. (cd/lp; as PETER GREEN'S FLEETWOOD MAC) *Reciever; (RR CD/LP 157)* **LIVE AT THE MARQUEE (live)** [ ] [-]
(re-iss.cd Jun92 on 'Sunflower'; SF-CD 104)

Sep 92. (cd; as PETER GREEN'S FLEETWOOD MAC) *Dojo Early Years; (EARLD 5)* **THE EARLY YEARS** [ ] [-]
Feb 93. (cd) *Castle; (SSLCD 207)* **LIVE** [ ] [-]
Jun 93. (cd) *Point; (261 0202)* **21 GREATEST HITS LIVE** [ ] [-]
Mar 94. (cd) *Castle; (MACCD 187)* **MADISON BLUES LIVE** [ ] [-]
May 94. (cd) *Castle; (MATCD 266)* **THE BLUES YEARS** [ ] [-]
Jul 94. (cd/c) *Success;* **LIVE (live)** [ ] [-]
Jun 95. (cd) *Renaissance; (551 776-2)* **FLEETWOOD MAC** [ ] [-]
Sep 95. (d-cd/d-c; as PETER GREEN'S FLEETWOOD MAC) *Fleetwood; (EDF CD/MC 297)* **LIVE AT THE BBC** [48] [-]

– (without GREEN) compilations, others, etc

1978. (lp/c) *Repise; (K/K4 44138)* **THE BEST OF FLEETWOOD MAC** [ ] [-]
Oct 82. (c) *Warners; (K4 66103)* **RUMOURS / FLEETWOOD MAC** [ ] [ ]
Nov 92. (4xcd/4xc) *Warners; (9362 45129-2/-4)* **25 YEARS – THE CHAIN** [ ] [ ]
Feb 93. (d-cd) *Warners; (9362 45188-2)* **25 YEARS – SELECTIONS FROM THE CHAIN** [ ] [-]

— for more mainstream solo work, see GREAT/WEE ROCK DISCOGRAPHY

FLEUR-DE-LYS

Formed: Southampton, England . . . Autumn '64 as LES FLEUR DE LYS by ALEX CHAMBERLAIN, GARY CHURCHILL, FRANK SMITH and KEITH GUSTER. The latter retained the group name, after their debut single, 'MOONDREAMS' (a BUDDY HOLLY cover) was recorded with a very young JIMMY PAGE. GUSTER recruited new members GORDON HASKELL, PHIL SAWYER and PETE SEARS to record their gutsy psychedelic version of PETE TOWNSHEND's 'CIRCLES'. In 1966, they signed to 'Polydor', adding former child actor CHRIS ANDREWS for the single, 'MUD IN YOUR EYE'. This also included some fine fret-work from new guitarist BRYN HAWORTH. A year later, they split once again when their producer/manager FRANK FENTER invited them to back SHARON TANDY in the studio and for live work. His own project, RUPERT'S PEOPLE, needed writers and musicians, leading to ANDREWS joining up. In 1968, they started to work on an album, while the HASKELL-written 45, 'GONG WITH A LUMINOUS NOSE', was another flop. The album remained unreleased, although they did augment singer JOHN BROMLEY on his 'SING' album. They lost yet another member, this time HASKELL, to the more productive KING CRIMSON, and it was clear the band were getting nowhere. Their last effort, 'YOU'RE JUST A LIAR', was very American in sound, possibly due to their label 'Atlantic'. The company also released their penultimate heavily Stax-influenced single, 'STOP CROSSING THE BRIDGE'.

Recommended: REFLECTIONS (*7)

FRANK SMITH – vocals, guitar / **ALEX CHAMBERLAIN** – organ / **GARY CHURCHILL** – bass / **KEITH GUSTER** – drums

Immediate / not issued

Nov 65. (7"; as LES FLEUR DE LYS) *(IM 20)* **MOONDREAMS. / WAIT FOR ME** [ ] [-]

— **GORDON HASKELL** – bass repl. CHURCHILL

— **PHIL SAWYER** – guitar repl. SMITH

— **PETE SEARS** – keyboards repl. CHAMBERLAIN

Apr 66. (7") *(IM 32)* **CIRCLES. / SO COME ON** [ ] [-]

— added **CHRIS ANDREWS** – vocals

— **BRYN HAWORTH** – guitar repl. SAWYER + SEARS (latter to SAM GOPAL)

Polydor / not issued

Nov 66. (7") *(56124)* **MUD IN YOUR EYE. / I'VE BEEN TRYING** [ ] [-]

— CHRIS ANDREWS left to concentrate on own project RUPERT'S PEOPLE. Others became backing band for South African singer SHARON TANDY on her single 'Hold On'. HAWORTH took over vocal duties.

Sep 67. (7") *(56200)* **I CAN SEE A LIGHT. / PRODIGAL SON** [ ] [-]
Sep 67. (7"; as SHYSTER) *(56202)* **TICK TOCK. / THAT'S A HOE DOWN** [ ] [-]
May 68. (7") *(56251)* **GONG WITH THE LUMINOUS NOSE. / HAMMER HEAD** [ ] [-]

— backed WILLIAM E. KIMBER on his WAYGOOD ELLIS single 'I Like What I'm Trying To Do'.

— **GUSTER + HAWORTH** recruited new members **TONY HEAD** – vocals / **TAGO BYERS** – bass, to repl. HASKELL who joined KING CRIMSON

Atlantic / not issued

Jan 68. (7"; as CHOCOLATE FROG) *(584 027)* **BUTCHERS AND BAKERS. / I FORGIVE YOU** [ ] [-]
Jun 68. (7") *(584 193)* **STOP CROSSING THE BRIDGE. / BRICK BY BRICK (STONE BY STONE)** [ ] [-]
Feb 69. (7") *(584 243)* **YOU'RE JUST A LIAR. / ONE CITY GIRL** [ ] [-]

— added **GRAHAM MAITLAND** – guitar (ex-SCOTS OF ST. JAMES), although the band were to split soon after. MAITLAND later joined FIVE DAY RAIN, while HAWORTH took off to the West Coast and went solo

– compilations, etc. –

May 97. (cd) *Blueprint; (BP 256CD)* **REFLECTIONS** [ ] [-]
– Circles / Mud in your eye / Gong with the luminous nose / Sugar love / Hold on / Prodigal son / One city girl / Daughter of the sun / Tick tock / I can see the light / Liar / I forgive you / So come on / Hammerhead / Stop crossing the bridge / I like what I'm trying to do / Hold on / Butchers and bakers / Wait for me / Reflections of Charlie Brown / Brick by brick / I've ben trying / Moondreams / So many things.

FLIES (see under ⇒ BULLDOG BREED)

FLO & EDDIE (see under ⇒ TURTLES)

FLOH DE COLOGNE

Formed: Cologne, Germany . . . 1966. Originally a loose troupe of performance artists, this politically minded band's first foray into the murky waters of the music business was on 1968's 'VIETNAM'. After signing to 'Ohr' records, the band cut the seminal 'FLIESSBANDBABYS BEATSHOW' (1970), a uniquely German send up of rock music with its tongue planted firmly in cheek. 1971's 'PROFITGEIER' carried on in much the same fashion, pushing their serious political message through a satirical, cabaret style concept. After a live album, 1973's 'LUCKY STREIK', the band recorded the mock rock symphony of 'GEIER SYMPHONIE' (1973). 'MUMIEN' (1974) was a heavily politicised concept album relating to events in South America while 'TILT' (1975) focused on events closer to their German home. By this point, the music had ceased to match the lyrical dexterity and when WOLLSCHON left after 'TILT', the band lost the main drive behind their sharply observed lyrics. They struggled on for another four albums before finally splitting in the early 80's.

Recommended: VIETNAM (*6) / FLIESSBANDBABYS BEATSHOW (*8) / PROFITGEIER (*8) / LUCKY STREIK (*6) / GEIER SYMPHONIE (*7)

GERD WOLLSCHON – lyrics, organ / **BRITTA BALTRUSCHAT** – voice / **HANS-JORG FRANK** – drums, organ / **MARKUS SCHMIDT** – bass, guitar / with **DIETER SUVERKRUP** – guitar, vocals (solo artist)

Plane not issued

1968. (lp; FLOH DE COLOGNE & DIETER SUVERKRUP) *(S 33101)* **VIETNAM** [-] [-] German
– Fuehrung / Ansprache / Zuerst kommen / Tango / Western – ballade / Kinderlied: 1. McNamara 62 – 2. Partisanenbekampfung – 3. Interview / Hexenverbrennung / Vater unser / Technisches / Zitat / Viet-test / Fuehrung / Wirtschaftsbericht / Kapitalismus (tiel 1) / Jack Miller / Kapitalismus (tiel 2).

— collaborator DIETER was repl. by **DIETER KLEMM** – drums, bass

— **DICK STADTLER** – guitar; repl. BRITTA

Ohr not issued

Jul 70. (lp) *(OMM 56.000)* **FLIESSBANDBABYS BEATSHOW** [-] [-] German
– Fliessbandbaby / Fliessbandbaby manchmal traume' ich / Komm mit mir ins wegschmeisswunderland / Sei ruhig, fliessbandbaby / Ford Capri / He Johnny / Arbeit macht frei / Wenn springer mal ruelpst / Armer junger Krupp / Die oberen 10,000 / Fliessbandbaby / Wir sind wieder wer / Maedchen mach die beine breit / Fliessbandbaby, du sitzt im gefaengnis.

1971. (lp) *(OMM 56.010)* **PROFITGEIER** [-] [-] German
– He, halo stift / Die einen kommen erster klasse zur welt / Wir stehen am rande / Bekenntnis der unpolitischen vaeter / Auf dem arbeitsmarkt / Der kapitalismus stinkt / Wir brauchen keine millionaere / Die luft gehoert denen, die sie atmen / Profitgeier / Wir werden immer mehr.

— added **THEO KOENIG** – wind, vocals

1973. (d-lp) *(OMM 2/56 029-030)* **LUCKY STREIK (live)** [-] [-] German
– Countdown / Schoen ist der jugendtraum / Sozialpartner-blues / Streikposten / Kalte wut / Wenn ich einmal reich bin / Streikposten / Gonzales / Karl liest ein flugblatt / Die wirtschaft ist jetzt in gefahr / Der imker / Streikposten / Deine freheit / Vergleiche / Der loewenthaler / Was ein kommunist trinken darf / Streikposten / Wenn es brennt / Streikposten / Luege zum abschied / Freie marktwirtschaft / Wenn dich jemand fragt / Fuer die zukunft sehen wir rot / Unternehmerraetsel / Saurier / Aktionseinheit / Wir sind millionenmal so stark.

1973. (lp) *(OMM 556 033)* **GEIER SYMPHONIE** [-] [-] German
– La grande tristesse (requiem) / Danse macabre (Totentanz) / Serenade des vautours (Leichenschmaus).

—' **VRIDOLIN ENXING** – keyboards, guitar, bass; repl. SCHMIDT

Plane not issued

1974. (lp) *(S 99201)* **MUMIEN** [-] [-] German
– Widmung / Marsch der mumien I / Und die reichen / Marsch der mumien II / Pp etc. / Oktober '73 / Fruehling in Chile / Zeugen / Du siehst das leid / Freiheitskaempfer / Salvador allende / Gegen den hunger / Marsch der mumien III / Des volkes fesseln.

1975. (lp) *(S 99202)* **TILT** [-] [-] German
– Tilt / Und trittst du in das leben raus / In dem arbeitsamt / Graefin Thyssen, Onkel Herbert und etwas zum abwischen / Kohlrock / Hey Johnny / Bravo schicksalsstory / Es steht ein haus in Schwaebisch hall / Verfassungs-honky-tonky / Nachruf auf Karl / Zug der zeit.

— now without WOLLSCHON

1977. (lp) *(K 20905)* **ROTKAPCHEN** [-] [-] German

1978. (lp) *(S 90239)* **PRIMA FREHEIT** [-] [-] German
– Ich kenne ein land / Ich steh' so rum / Ballade vom studenten aus den kleinen verhaeltnissen / Zwischenspiel / Eddie, der baer / Was ist fortschritt / Prima freheit.

1980. (lp) *(S 88230)* **(LIEDER AUS DER) ROCKOPER KOSLOWSKI** [-] [-] German
– Ein polnischer knecht / Familiengschichten / Paradiesvogel / Und weil er jung und kraeftig war / Dreck unterm nagel / Die prinessin auf der nadel / Schlackenfahrer – Schorsch / Koslowsky / schlaegt zu / P.S.

— now without THEO KLEMM

1983. (lp) *(S 88319)* **FAATERLAND** [-] [-] German
– Nicht so eng sehn / Kopf an die wand / Die drei / Erkennst du dich nicht / Die erste million / Faaterland / Stalingrader appell / Der anti-ami / Der Amerikanische freund / Dann ist es erreicht / Ballade von samstag auf sonntag / Es gab eine zeit.

— split after a farewell tour with former collaborator DIETER SUVERKRUP

FOCUS

Formed: Amsterdam, Netherlands ... late 1969 by THIJS VAN LEER, HANS CLEUVER and MARTIN DRESDEN, who became backing band for the Dutch version of the musical 'HAIR'. In 1970, they enlisted virtuso guitarist JAN AKKERMAN, who had previously departed from BRAINBOX. Signing to the 'Bovema' label in Holland, their first lp, 'IN AND OUT OF FOCUS', hit the shelves. Following the European success of the 'HOUSE OF THE KING' track, 'Blue Horizon' picked it up for release in the UK and it subsequently provided the theme tune for many a British TV documentary. Their 2nd album, 'MOVING WAVES', was a more progressively innovative set, containing the extended version of 'HOCUS POCUS', furnishing them with a surprise UK Top 20 hit for new label 'Polydor'. It was described by some as a novelty single due to LEER's strangulated yodel intermittently punctuating AKKERMAN's blistering guitar-work. Fairly unrepresentative of the FOCUS sound, the majority of the band's material was characterised by more pronounced neo-classical and jazz-rock leanings. They consolidated this early chart success with 'SYLVIA', a less frantic, more melodic piece, which fared even better than its predecessor. The single was gleaned from the 1972 double-set, 'FOCUS 3', another album which surprised many by also hitting the charts Stateside. However, after a stop-gap live album recorded at The Rainbow, the band disappointed critics and fans alike with the more conventional 'HAMBURGER CONCERTO' in 1974. From then on the band chose jazz-fusion as their raison d'etre, leading to a sharp commercial decline and inevitable split. AKKERMAN and VAN LEER had already moonlighted with solo outings, going full-time after FOCUS's demise. • **Songwriters:** AKKERMAN & VAN LEER, except TOMMY (Tom Barlage). • **Trivia:** On Apr'90, FOCUS of late'72 re-formed for Dutch TV special.

Recommended: MOVING WAVES (*7) / FOCUS III (*6)

BRAINBOX

JAN AKKERMAN – guitar, organ / **KAZIMIRZ LUX** – vocals, percussion / **ANDRE REYNEN** – bass / **PIERRE VAN DER LINDEN** – drums

Parlophone Elektra

Jun 69. (7") *(R 5775)* <45673> **WOMAN'S GONE. / DOWN MAN** [ ] [ ]

Parlophone Capitol

1969. (lp) *(PCS 7094)* <ST 596> **BRAINBOX** [ ] [ ] 1970
– Dark rose / Reason to believe / Baby, what you want me to do / Scarborough Fair / Summertime / Sinner's prayer / Sea of delight. *(cd-iss.Jun97 by BRAINBOX & JAN AKKERMAN on 'Oseudonym'; CDP 1033DD)*

May 70. (7") *(R 5842)* **TO YOU. / SO HELPLESS** [ ] [-]

FOCUS

THIJS VAN LEER (b.31 Mar'48) – organ, flute, some vocals / **JAN AKKERMAN** (b.24 Dec'46) – lead guitar, lute (ex-HUNTERS) / **MARTIN DRESDEN** – guitar / **HANS CLEUVER** – drums

Polydor Sire

Jan 71. (lp) *(2344 003)* <97027> **IN AND OUT OF FOCUS** [ ] [ ]
– Focus (instrumental) / Why dream / Happy nightmare (mescaline) / Anonymous / Black beauty / Sugar Island / House of the king / Focus (vocal). *<US re-iss.Jun73; 7404> (re-iss.Dec73; same as above)*

Jan 71. (7") *(2001 134)* **HOUSE OF THE KING. / BLACK BEAUTY** [ ] [ ]

— **PIERRE VAN DER LINDEN** (b.19 Feb'46) – drums (ex-BRAINBOX, ex-HUNTERS) repl. CLEUVER / **CYRIL HAVERMANS** – bass, vocals repl. DRESDEN

Blue Horizon Sire

Oct 71. (lp) *(2931 002)* <7401> **MOVING WAVES** [ ] [ ]
– Hocus pocus / Le clochard ("bread") / Janus / Moving waves / Focus II / Eruption: Orpheus – Pupilla – Tommy – Pupilla – Answer – The bridge – Euridice – Dayglow – Endless road – Answer – Orfeus – Euridice. *(re-dist.Nov72 by 'Polydor' lp/c; same); hit No.2) <US re-dist.Nov72; same>*

Oct 71. (7") *(2094 006)* **HOCUS POCUS. / JANIS** [ ] [-]

Jan 72. (7") *(2094 008)* **TOMMY. / FOCUS II** [ ] [-]

Polydor Sire

Oct 72. (7") *(2001 211)* **HOCUS POCUS. / JANIS** [20] [ ]

— **BERT RUITER** (b.26 Nov'46) – bass, vocals repl. CYRIL who went solo

Nov 72. (d-lp/c) *(2659/ 016)* <3901> **FOCUS III** [6] [35] Mar73
– Round goes the gossip / Love remembered / Sylvia / Carnival fugue / Focus III / Answers? questions! questions? answers! / Anonymous II (part 1) / Elspeth of Nottingham / House of the king.

Dec 72. (7") *(2001 422)* **SYLVIA. / HOUSE OF THE KING** [4] [-]

Feb 73. (7") <704> **HOCUS POCUS (pt.1). / HOCUS POCUS (pt.2)** [-] [9]

Jul 73. (7") <708> **SYLVIA. / LOVE REMEMBERED** [-] [89]

Oct 73. (lp/c) *(2443/ 118)* <7408> **FOCUS AT THE RAINBOW (live)** [23] [ ]
– Focus III / Answers? questions! questions? answers! / Focus II / Eruption: Orfeus – Answer – Pupilla – Tommy – Pupilla / Hocus pocus / Sylvia / Hocus pocus (reprise). *(cd-iss.Apr97 on 'E.M.I.'; REPLAYCD 40)*

— (Oct73) **COLIN ALLEN** – drums (ex-STONE THE CROWS, ex-JOHN MAYALL) repl. LINDEN (He later briefly returned)

Polydor Atco

Apr 74. (7") *(2058 466)* **HAREM SCAREM. / EARLY BIRTH** [ ] [ ]

May 74. (lp/c) *(2442/ 124)* <36-100> **HAMBURGER CONCERTO** [20] [66]
– Delitiae musicae / Harem scarem / La cathedrale de Strasbourg / Birth / Hamburger concerto:- Starter – Rare – Medium I – Medium II – Well done – One for the road.

Jul 75. (lp) *(2384 070)* **FOCUS** (compilation) [23] [-]

— (mid'75) **DAVID KEMPER** (b.USA) – drums repl. ALLEN

Oct 75. (lp/c) *(2302/ 036)* <36-117> **MOTHER FOCUS** [ ] [ ]
– Mother Focus / I need a bathroom / Bennie Helder / Soft vanilla / Hard vanilla / Tropic bird / Focus IV – Someone's crying . . .what! / All together . . .oh that! / No hang ups / My sweetheart / Father Bach. *(cd-iss.Apr97 on 'E.M.I.'; REPLAYCD 41)*

Mar 76. (7") *(2001 640)* **HOUSE OF THE KING. / O AVENDROOD** [ ] [-]

— (Mar76) **PHILIP CATHERINE** (b.27 Oct'42, London) – guitar (ex-JEAN LUC PONTY, ex-JOHN McLAUGHLIN) repl. JAN AKKERMAN who went solo / **STEVE SMITH** – drums (ex-JEAN LUC PONTY) repl. VAN DER LINDEN / added **EEF ALBERS** – guitar

Harvest Sire

Sep 77. (lp) *(SHSP 4068)* <7531> **SHIP OF MEMORIES** (rare 1973) [ ] [ ]
– P's march / Can't believe my eyes / Focus V / Out of Vesuvius / Glider / Red sky at night / Spoke the Lord Creator / Crackers / Ship of memories.

Jan 78. (lp) *(SHSP 11721)* **FOCUS CON PROBY** [ ] [-]
– Wingless / Orion / Night flight / Eddy / Sneezing bull / Brother / Tokyo Rose / Maximum / How long.

— They split around the same time but managed to leave a collaboration with 60's pop star **P.J.PROBY** above

— **RICHARD JAMES** – drums repl. SMITH who joined JOURNEY. THIJS VAN LEER continued his solo career, further below.

— **AKKERMAN + VAN LEER** re-formed for Dutch gigs and album (with **TATO GOMEZ + RUUS JACOBS** – bass / **ED STARING** – synthesizers / **SERGIO CASTILLO** – drums / **USTAD ZAMIR AHMED KHAN** – tabla

Vertigo not issued

Aug 85. (lp/cd) *(824 524-1/-2)* **FOCUS** [ ] [-]
– Russian roulette / King Kong / Le tango / Indian summer / Beethoven's revenge / Ole Judy / Who's calling.

— In April 1990, the 1972/73 line-up were back again

- compilations, others, etc. -

Feb 75. (lp) *Sire; <7505>* **DUTCH MASTERS – A SELECTION OF THEIR FINEST RECORDINGS 1969-1973**
Sep 84. (lp/c) *Fame; (FA 41 3112-1/-4)* **GREATEST HITS OF FOCUS**
– Focus / Moving waves / Focus II / Tommy / Hocus pocus / House of the king / Sylvia / Janis.
Feb 85. (7") *Golden 45's; (G 4539)* **SYLVIA. / HOCUS POCUS**
Apr 87. (7") *Old Gold; (OG 9696)* **SYLVIA. / HOCUS POCUS**
May 94. (cd) *E.M.I.;* **HOCUS POCUS – THE BEST OF FOCUS**

THIJS VAN LEER

C.B.S. Columbia

Nov 72. (lp) *(CBS 64589) <32346>* **INTROSPECTION**
– Pavane / Rondo / Agnus dei / Focus 1 / Erbarme dich / Focus 2 / Introspection.

— next arranged by **ROGER VAN OTTERLOO** / voice by **LETTY DE JONG**

Dec 75. (lp) *(CBS 65915)* **INTROSPECTION 2**
– Goyeseas No.IV / Rondo II / Introduction / Siciliano / Focus III / Larghetto & Allegro / Introspection II / Sheep may safely graze / Mild wild Rose / Bist du bei hair / Carmes elysium.
Dec 75. (7") *(CBS 1024)* **RONDO. / SICILIANO**

— In Apr76, he issued 'O MY LOVER' lp on 'Philips'; *6303 143)*

Dec 76. (lp) *(CBS 69239)* **MUSICA PER LA NOTTE DI NATALE**
– O Jesulein suess / Coventry carol / Hark, the herald angels sing / Es ist ein Ros' entsprungen / Mafia die zoude naaar Bethlehem gaan / Vom Himmel hoch, da komm ich her / Er is een Kindeke Geboren Op Aard / Away in a manger / Ich steh' an deiner Krippe hier / Hoe leit dit kindeke / God rest ye merry gentleman.
Nov 77. (7") *(CBS 5804)* **PAVANE. / COVERNTY CAROL**
Feb 79. (lp) *(CBS 86034)* **INTROSPECTION 3**
– Reigen se liger / Rondeau / Adagio / Elazotta / Brother / Siciliano / Rondo III / He shall feed his flock / Focus V.
Aug 79. (lp) *(CBS 86059)* **NICE TO HAVE MET YOU**
– My sweetheart / Nice to have met you (concrete) / Pastorale / Bahama mama / Hocus pocus / Tonight beneath the sky / Rosebud / Super frishell.
Oct 79. (7") *(CBS 6446)* **BAHAMA MAMA. /**

PEDAL POINT

— were formed by **THIJS VAN LEER / TATO GOMEZ** – vocals, bass, percussion / **PAUL SHICIHARA** – guitar / **MARIO AREANDONAG** – drums, percussion, vocals.

C.B.S. Euro / not issued

1981. (lp) *(CBS 88531)* **DONA NOBIS PACEM**
– Kyrie, kyrie Eleison 1 – Christe Eleison – Kyrie Eleison 2 / Credo: introduction Credo 1 & 2 – Et in umum – Et incarnatus est – Crucifixus / Credo (continued): Et resuurexit – Et resurrexit 2 – Et in spiritum sanctum: Sanctus – Osanna / Agnus dei / Pater noster.

VAN LEER BAND

— Co-produced by PHIL WARD-LARGE, who now works for BBC on Johnnie Walker show.

Ariola / not issued

1987. (lp) *(688465)* **I HATE MYSELF**

JAN AKKERMAN

— In 1972 'E.M.I.' re-iss.1969 Dutch lp, 'TALENT FOR SALE'; *Imperial 5C048 51105)* as 'GUITAR FOR SALE'; *EMI 048 51105.*

Harvest / Sire

Apr 73. (7") *(HAR 8069)* **BLUE BOY. / MINSTREL-FARMERS DANCE**
May 73. (lp) *(SHSP 4026) <7407>* **PROFILE** Sep73
– Fresh air / Must be my land / Wrestling to get out / Back again / The fight / Fresh air – blue notes for listening / Water and skies are telling me / Happy Gabriel / Andante sostenute / Maybe just a dream / Elude / Kemps jig / Blue boy / Minstrel-farmers dance / Stick.

Atlantic / Atco

Jan 74. (lp) *(K 40522) <7032>* **TABERNAKEL**
– Brittania / Coranto for Mrs. Muircroft / The Earl of Derby / Hid galliard / House of the king / A galliard / A pavan / Javeh / A fantasy / Lammy / I am asleep, half asleep / Awak – she is Lammy / We are / The last will and testament / Amen.
Jan 74. (7") *(K 10427)* **HOUSE OF THE KING. / JAVEH**
Feb 77. (lp; by JAN AKKERMAN with KAZ LUX) *(K 50320)* **ELI**
– Eli / Guardian angel / Tranquilizer / Can't fake a good time / There he still goes / Striadberg / Wings of strings / Naked actress / Fairytale.
Feb 78. (7") *(K 11014)* **CRACKERS. / WINGS OF STRINGS**
Feb 78. (lp) *(K 50420) <19159>* **JAN AKKERMAN**
– Crackers / Angel watch / Pavane / Street walker / Skydancer / Floatin' / Gate to Europe.
May 78. (7") *(K 11131)* **CRACKERS. / ANGELS WATCH**
Aug 78. (lp) *(CBS 81843)* **ARUNJUEZ**
– Adagio from 'Concerto de Aranjuez' / Nightwings / Madinha / Espandeta / Pavane pour une infante defunte / Love remembered / The seed of God / Bachranas Brasileiras No.5.

— (above with CLAUS OGERMAN on arrangements of orchestra) (on 'CBS')

Mar 79. (lp) *(K 50660)* **LIVE (live)**
– Transitory / Skydancer / Pavane / Crackers / Tommy / Azimuth.
1979. Bovena Negrum; (lp) **A PHENOMENON** (compilation) Dutch
Dec 79. (lp) *(K 50664)* **3**
– Stingray / Wait and see / She's so divine / Funk me / This is the one / Night prayer / Time out of mind.
Jan 80. (7") *(K 11374)* **SHE'S SO DEVINE. / SKYDANCER**

Polydor / not issued

1981. (lp; by JAN AKKERMAN & KAZ LUX) *(2417 141)* **TRANSPARENTAL** German
– Inspiration / Apocalypso / Concentrate don't hesitate / Transparental / I don't make it much longer / Marsha / You're not the type / The party is over.

C.N.R. / not issued

1981. (lp) *(60480)* **OIL IN THE FAMILY** German
– Oil in the family / Formula none / Discoasis / No doubt about it / Family – reprise / Blue in the shadow.

W.E.A. / not issued

1982. (lp) *(58441)* **PLEASURE POINT** German
– Valdez / Heavy pleasure / Cool in the shadow / Visions of blue / C.S. / Bird island. *(UK-iss.Jul87 on 'Decal' lp/c; LIK/TCLIK 13) (cd-iss.Jul87 on 'Charly'; CDCHARLY 90) (re-iss.cd Nov91;)*

Polydor / not issued

1982. (lp) *(2374210)* **IT COULD HAPPEN TO YOU** German
– Old tennis shoe / Come closer / Funkology: (a) Baby start (b) One way (c) Free / It could happen to you. *(UK-iss.Dec85 on 'Charly'; CR 30246)*

Metrognome / not issued

1983. (lp) *(815715-1)* **CAN'T STAND NOISE** German
– Pietons / Everything must change / Back to the factory / Journey (a real elegant gipsy) / Heavy treasure / Just because / Who knows. *(UK-iss.May86 on 'Charly'; CR 30250) (last 2 albums on cd Jun86 as 'THE COMPLETE GUITARIST'; CDCHARLY 17) (cd re-iss.1992)*

C.B.S. / not issued

1984. (lp) *(CBS 26094)* **FROM THE BASEMENT** German
– Headbanger / All along the watchtower / Dark rose / Wallenberg / From the basement / P.C.B. chicken / Status quo.

Sound Products / not issued

1987. (cd) *(JACD 7)* **HEARTWARE**
– My pleasure / Just because, so / Lost & found / Heartware / Winter born / Lyric / Lonely street of dreams / Firenze.

Inak / not issued

1988. (cd; by JAN AKKERMAN & JOACHIM KUEHN) *(INAK 868CD)* **LIVE! (live)**
– (part 1 in Kiel / part 2 in Stutgart).

FORCEFIELD

AKKERMAN with **RAY FENWICK & COZY POWELL / + MO FOSTER** – bass / **PETE PRESENT** – vocals

— Covered TIRED OF WAITING . . . (Kinks) + many others.

President / not issued

Feb 87. (7"/ext.12") *(PT 551/12-551)* **SMOKE ON THE WATER. / SHINE IT ON ME**
Sep 87. (lp/cd) *(PTLS/PCOM 1088)* **FORCEFIELD**
–
Aug 88. (7") *(PT 578)* **HEARTACHE. / I LOSE AGAIN (instrumental)**
Aug 88. (lp/cd) *(PTLS/PCOM 1095)* **FORCEFIELD II: THE TALISMAN**
– The talisman / Year of the dragon / Tired of waiting for you / Heartache / Good is good / Carrie / Without your love / I lose again / The mercenary. *(cd+=)–* Black night / Strange kind of woman / I lose again (instrumental).
Sep 89. (lp/cd) *(PTLS/PCOM 1100)* **FORCEFIELD III: TO OZ AND BACK**
– Hit and run / Always / Stay away / Desire / Tokyo / Who'll be next in line / Wings on my feet / Fire power / hold on / Rendezvous.
Nov 90. (cd/lp) *(PCOM/PTLS 1110)* **FORCEFIELD IV: LET THE WILD RUN FREE**
–
Nov 90. (cd) *(PCOM 1122)* **INSTRUMENTALS** (compilation)

JAN AKKERMAN

I.R.S. / E.M.I.

Jun 90. (lp/c/cd) *(EIRSA/+MC/CD 1026)* **THE NOISE OF ART**
– Trojan horse / You can't keep a bad man up / Bonnaville / Shame on you / Prelude: friends always / Prima Donna / Having fun / Akkerman's sombrero / My pleasure / Quiet storm.

Inak / Inak

Dec 94. (cd) **PUCCINI'S CAFE**

FORCEFIELD II (see under ⇒ FOCUS)

FORCE FIVE (see under ⇒ CROCHETED DOUGHNUT RING)

The FOX

Formed: based London, England . . . 1970 by musicians below. They had a tuneful style as simple as NIRVANA (UK), or even US band AORTA. In fact, their only album, 'FOR FOX SAKE' (subtle as a sledgehammer!), was even released there. It was a much sought-after piece of post-psychedelia, featuring an epic finale in 'MADAME MAGICAL'. • **Trivia:** Not to be confused with a number of other groups of the same name.

Recommended: FOR FOX SAKE (*6)

STEVE BRAYNE – guitar / **WINSTON WEATHERALL** – guitar, sitar / **ALEX LANE** – keyboards / **DAVE WINDROSS** – bass, piano / **TIM REEVES** – drums

Fontana / Panda

Jun 70. (7") *(6007 016)* **SECOND HAND LOVE. / BUTTERFLY**
1970. (lp) *(6309 007) <CR 1336>* **FOR FOX SAKE**
– Secondhand love / Lovely day / As she walks away / Glad I could / Butterfly / Look in the sky / Good time music / Mr. Blank / Man in a fast car / Birthday card / Madame magical. *(cd-iss.May97 on 'Flash'; FLASH 34)*

— split not long after above

Ritchie FRANCIS (see under ⇒ EYES OF BLUE)

FRANZ K.

Formed: Germany . . . late 1969 by MICK HANNES and brothers PETER and STEFAN JOSEFUS. Taking their name from the famous Czech writer, the band's debut two track album, 'SENSEMANN' (1972) was as dark, dense and edgy as the paranoid prose of their namesake; proto-space rock with a typically German political edge. By the following year, however, the band had straightened out somewhat and on 1973's 'ROCK IN DEUTSCH', both the music and lyrics were less explicit. This shift in style was even more pronounced on 1977's 'WIR HABEN BOCK AUF ROCK', wherein the band were churning out rock by numbers. They continued in this vein throughout the 80's, the last album to date, 'ZIEH DEINE SCHWARZEN SCHUHE AN' being released in 1989.

Recommended: SENSEMANN (*6)

PETER JOSEFUS – vocals, bass / **MICK HANNES** – guitar / **STEFAN JOSEFUS** – drums

Philips / not issued

1972. (lp) *(6305 127)* **SENSEMANN** [-] [-] German
– Das goldene Reich / Sensemann.

Zebra / not issued

1973. (lp) *(2949 014)* **ROCK IN DEUTSCH** [-] [-] German
– Scheiss und marschier / Cabora bassa / Peterlied / Raeder / Big boss / Mackie messer / Rita B.

Aladin / not issued

1977. (lp) *(ALA 056-32663)* **WIR HABEN BOCK AUF ROCK** [-] [-] German
– Wir haben bock auf rock / Bye bye Johnny / Eh, mann / Der Koenig / Tiger / Halt mich fest / Condor.

1978. (lp) *(ALA 056-45078)* **GEHT ZUM TEUFEL** [-] [-] German
– Geh zum teufel / Samstang um halb vier / Rock lady / Rock in Schessel / Blues / Denn sie war / Fernsehstar.

1979. (lp) *(ALA 84356)* **GEWALT IST SCHNITT** [-] [-] German
– Immer wieder und wieder / Vergiss es / Mann kann nicht alles haben / Gewalt ist schitt / Renn, bruder Renn / Seht ihr den clown / Clownerie / Der trinker.

1980. (lp) *(ALA 84654)* **TROTZDEM HART** [-] [-] German
– Der erste krach in deinem leben / Er ist ein held / Ap inne disco / Marmor, Stein und eisen bricht / Lang lebe rockmusik / Der rebell / Engel in jeans.

1981. (lp) *(ALA 85377)* **WILDER TANZ** [-] [-] German
– Randale / Peter Gunn / Wilder tanz / Dies ist auch mein land / Rockband.

C.B.S. / not issued

1982. (lp) *(25196)* **LIVE BOCK AUF ROCK (live)** [-] [-] German
– Tiger / Vergiss es / Der erste krach in deinem leben / Renn, bruder Renn / Rock in Scheessel / Wir haben bock auf rock / Bye bye Johnny.

1983. (lp) *(25357)* **SCHOENE AUSSICHTEN** [-] [-] German
– Heilsarmee / Keine knete / Lieb mich jetze / Cha cha cha / Es ist vorbei / Arbeit muss her / Es ist schon hart / er politiker / Nur rock.

Steps / not issued

1985. (lp) *(720 001)* **EWIG UND DREI TAGE** [-] [-] German
– Vulkan unterm eis / Dr. Basic / Der diplomat / Zieh deine schwarzen Schuhe an / Die 7. dimension / Walkman / Deutschland, Deutschland / Ewig und drei tage / Schwarzfahrn / Tempo 2000.

E.M.I. / not issued

1986. (lp) *(1C066-156907-1)* **LANG LEBE ROCK MUSIK** [-] [-] German
– Tiger / Lang lebe rock musik / Zieh deine schwarzen schuhe an / Geh zum teufel / Arbeit muss her / Wir haben bock auf rock / Der erste krach in deinem leben / Rock in scheessel / Bye, bye Johnny.

Musicraft / not issued

1989. (lp) *(57210103)* **ZIEH DEINE SCHWARZEN SCHUHE AN** [-] [-] German
– Zieh deine schwarzen schuhe an / Heute nicht / Wasser in der wuste / Purer wahnsinn / Vulkan unterm els / Ewig und drei tae / Extra-mischung / Dr. Basic / Rebellen der liebe / Die 7. dimension.

— nothing was heard of them in the 90's

FRATERNITY OF MAN

Formed: California, USA . . .1968 by LAWRENCE WAGNER, ELLIOTT INGBER, MARTIN KIBBEE and RICHIE HAYWARD (the latter had featured in US group The FACTORY alongside LOWELL GEORGE; an embryonic LITTLE FEAT). That year, their eponymous debut did little to penetrate the American market, although one of its fun-country tracks, 'DON'T BOGART ME', was used to better effect on the soundtrack of the cult 1969 film 'Easy Rider' (people know the song as 'Don't Bogart That Joint'). A second album appeared in '69, and included most future members of LITTLE FEAT (see below). • **Style:** Comic acid-country outfit, with tinges of avant-garde folk! • **Songwriters:** Group except a cover of FRANK ZAPPA's 'OH NO'.

Recommended: FRATERNITY OF MAN (*6) / GET IT ON! (*5)

FACTORY

LOWELL GEORGE – lead guitar / **WARREN KLEIN** – guitar / **MARTIN KIBBEY** – bass / **DALLAS TAYLOR** – drums

not issued / Uni

1967. (7") *<55005>* **WHEN I WAS AN APPLE. / SMILE LET YOUR LIFE BEGIN** [-] [ ]

— **RITCHIE HAYWARD** – drums; repl. TAYLOR, who joined CLEAR LIGHT

1967. (7"; with EMIL RICHARDS) *<55027>* **NO PLACE I'D RATHER BE. /** [-] [ ]

FRATERNITY OF MAN

— formed by **KLEIN, KIBBEY + TAYLOR**

LARRY WAGNER – vocals, guitar; repl. LOWELL GEORGE who joined The MOTHERS OF INVENTION and later formed LITTLE FEAT

— added **ELLIOT INGBER** – guitar (ex-MOTHERS OF INVENTION)

not issued / A.B.C.

1968. (lp) *<ABCS 647>* **FRATERNITY OF MAN** [-] [ ]
– Candy striped lion's tail / Bikini baby / In the morning / Last call for alcohol / Wispy Paisley skies / Field day / Plastic rat / Stop me, citate me / Oh no / I don't believe it / Blue guitar / Don't bogart me / Just doin' our job. *(UK cd-iss.Oct95 on 'Edsel'; EDCD 437)*

1968. (7") *<11106>* **DON'T BOGART ME. / WISPY PAISLEY SKIES** [-] [ ]
(UK-iss.Mar70 on 'Stateside'; SS 2166)

— on next they were joined by **LOWELL GEORGE + BILL PAYNE**

not issued / Dot

1969. (lp) *<25955>* **GET IT ON!** [-] [ ]
– Boo man / Don't start me talkin' / Pool of tears / The throbber / Cat's squirrel / Too high to eat / Forget her / Coco lollipop / rick bag / Mellow token. *(UK cd-iss.Oct95 on 'Edsel'; EDCD 438)*

— Split in 1969, when INGBER (as WINGED EEL FINGERLING) joined CAPTAIN BEEFHEART. RICHIE, LOWELL and PAYNE formed LITTLE FEAT.

FREEDOM

Formed: London, England . . . late '67 by sacked PROCOL HARUM members RAY ROYER and BOBBY HARRISON. Following an out-of-court settlement with their previous band, they were commissioned by the Italian film director, Dino de Laurentiis, to write a score for his movie, 'Nerosubianco'. Although the project was shelved due to lack of finances, it later surfaced in Italy circa mid-'69. A few singles and a German-only album came out around the same time, most of which are now highly sought-after by collectors. After their UK debut lp in 1971, they signed for progressive label, 'Vertigo', where they made two rare albums. These were more progressive in nature, moving away from the heavy blues of their earlier work. • **Songwriters:** HARRISON and ROYER, until latters departure in 1970. • **Trivia:** Their last album is worth over £75.

Recommended: THROUGH THE YEARS (*5) / FREEDOM IS MORE THAN A WORD (*5)

BOBBY HARRISON – vocals, drums (ex-PROCOL HARUM) / **RAY ROYER** – guitar (ex-PROCOL HARUM) / **MIKE LEASE** – keyboards / **STEVE SHIRLEY** – bass, vocals

Mercury / not issued

Jun 68. (7") *(MF 1033)* **WHERE WILL YOU BE TONIGHT. / TRYING TO GET A GLIMPSE OF YOU** [ ] [-]

Plexium / not issued

Jan 69. (7") *(PXM 3)* **ESCAPE WHILE YOU CAN. / KANDY KAY** [ ] [-]

Atlantic / not issued

1969. (lp) *(ATL 08028)* **NEROSUBIANCO (soundtrack)** [-] [-] Italy
(UK-iss.'Nerosubianco' Apr95 on 'Tenth Planet'; TP 011)

— **PETER DENNIS** – vocals, bass, keyboards, repl. STEVE

— **ROGER SAUNDERS** – vocals, guitar, keyboards, repl. MIKE + RAY

Metrognome / not issued

Jul 69. (lp) *(MLP 15371)* **AT LAST** [-] [-] German

— added 4th member **STEVE JOLLY** – guitar

Probe / A.B.C.

Oct 70. (7") *(PRO 504)* **FRUSTRATED WOMAN. / MAN MADE LAWS** [ ] [-]

Nov 70. (lp) *(SBPA 6252)* **FREEDOM** [ ] [-]
– Nobody / In search of something / Dusty track / Man made laws / Ain't no chance to score / Pretty woman / Freedom / Frustrated woman.

Vertigo / Cotillion

Sep 71. (lp) *(6360 050)* *<SD 9048>* **THROUGH THE YEARS** [ ] [ ]
– Freestone / Through the years / Get yourself together / London City / Thanks / Toe grabber. *(cd-iss.1991 on 'Repertoire'; REP 4226)*

Sep 71. (7") *(6059 051)* **THANKS. / MISS LITTLE LOUISE** [ ] [-]

— **MATT MONOGHAN** – bass, repl. DENNIS

Jul 72. (lp) *(6360 072)* **IS MORE THAN A WORD** [ ] [-]
– Together / Miss little Louise / Sweaty feet / Brainbox jam / Direction / Going down / Dream / Ladybird.

— MONOGHAN joined MICK ABRAHAMS BAND. BOBBY HARRISON joined SNAFU after solo outing.

Peter FRENCH (see under ⇒ LEAFHOUND)

FRIJID PINK

Formed: Detroit, Michigan, USA . . .early 1967 by school mates KELLY GREEN, GARY RAY THOMPSON, RICH STEVENS, LARRY ZELANKA (keyboards) and TOM HARRIS (bass). The latter two were replaced a year later by THOMAS BEAUDRY. In 1969, they signed to 'Parrot', where their hard-rocking, tripped-out re-working of 'HOUSE OF THE RISING SUN' hit the US Top 10. After it became a massive success in Britain & Germany, their career took a sharp decline, only the singles, 'SING A SONG OF FREEDOM' and ELVIS's 'HEARTBREAK HOTEL' making any chart impact. In 1972, producers VINNY TESTA + CLYDE STEVENS brought in new musicians to add to RICH STEVENS.

Recommended: FRIJID PINK (*7)

KELLY GREEN – vocals / **GARY RAY THOMPSON** – guitar / **THOMAS BEAUDRY** – bass / **RICH STEVENS** – drums

Deram Parrot

Aug 69. (7") <334> **TELL ME WHY. / CRYING SHAME** [-] [ ]

Dec 69. (7") <340> **GOD GAVE ME YOU. / DRIVIN' BLUES** [-] [ ]

Feb 70. (7") *(DM 288)* <341> **HOUSE OF THE RISING SUN. / DRIVIN' BLUES** [4] [7]

Mar 70. (lp) *(1062)* <71033> **FRIJID PINK** [ ] [11] Jan70
– God gave me you / Crying shame / I'm on my way / Drivin' blues / Tell me why / End of the line / House of the rising sun / I want to be your lover / Boozin' blues. *(cd-iss.1990's on 'Repertoire'+=;)*– Heartbreak hotel / Music for the people.

Jul 70. (7") *(DM 309)* <349> **SING A SONG OF FREEDOM. / END OF THE LINE** [ ] [55]

Nov 70. (lp) *(1077)* <71041> **DEFROSTED** [ ] [ ] Oct70
– Black lace / Sing a song for freedom / I'll never be lonely / Bye bye blues / Pain in my heart / Sloony / I'm movin' / I haven't got the time.

Dec 70. (7") *(DM 321)* <352> **HEARTBREAK HOTEL. / BYE BYE BLUES** [ ] [72]

Apr 71. (7") *(DM 332)* <355> **MUSIC FOR THE PEOPLE. / SLOONY** [ ] [ ]

Jun 71. (7") *(DM 336)* <358> **WE'RE GONNA BE THERE (WHEN JOHNNY COMES MARCHING HOME). / SHORTY KLINE** [ ] [ ]

Dec 71. (7") *(DM 347)* <360> **LOST SON. / I LOVE HER** [ ] [ ]

— **STEVENS** was virtually left to recruit members; **JON WEARING** – vocals / **LARRY ZELANKA** – piano, organ / **CRAIG WEBB** – guitar / **TOM HARRIS** – bass

not issued Lion

Nov 72. (7") <115> **EARTH OMEN. / LAZY DAY** [-] [ ]

Jan 73. (lp) <1004> **EARTH OMEN** [-] [ ]
– Miss Evil / Sailor / Earth omen / Lazy day / Train woman / Eternal dream / New horizon / Rainbow rider / Mr. Blood. *(cd-iss.Jan95 on 'Repertoire'+=; REP 4456-WY)*– (2 tracks).

1972. (7") <136> **GO NOW. / LAZY DAY** [-] [ ]

1974. (7") <158> **SHADY LADY. / BIG BETTY** [-] [ ]

not issued Fantasy

1975. (lp) <9464> **ALL PINK INSIDE** [-] [ ]

— Split around the mid-70's.

– others, etc. –

Sep 85. (7") *Old Gold; (OG 9533)* **HOUSE OF THE RISING SUN. / (other artist)** [ ] [-]

Robert FRIPP (see under ⇒ KING CRIMSON)

Fred FRITH (see under ⇒ HENRY COW)

Edgar FROESE (see uner ⇒ TANGERINE DREAM)

FRUMPY

Formed: Germany ...1969 by CARSTEN BOHN together with JEAN-JAQUES KRAVETZ, KARL-HEINZ SCHOTT and INGA RUMPF. They had all been members of The CITY PREACHERS, who numbered DAGMAR KRAUSE among their ranks (later of SLAPP HAPPY). Their debut album, 'ALL WILL BE CHANGED' (1970), was an early prog-rock gem, dominated by organ solos and accomplished rhythmic flurries. The follow-up, 'FRUMPY 2' was more guitar orientated with a marked symphonic feel, much in evidence on the final track 'DUTY'. The quality of the instrumental breaks and songwriting marked it out as a career peak while 'BY THE WAY' (1972) was more pedestrian in comparison. The band split later that summer, although 'Philips' released a double live album the following year. SCHOTT, KRAVETZ and RUMPF formed ATLANTIS in 1972, releasing a series of more commercial albums throughout the 70's. BAUMANN went solo until a FRUMPY reformation in 1990.

Recommended: ALL WILL BE CHANGED (*7) / FRUMPY 2 (*8) / BY THE WAY (*6)

FRUMPY

CARSTEN BOHN – drums, percussion / **JEAN-JAQUES KRAVETZ** – organ / **KARL-HEINZ SCHOTT** – bass / **INGA RUMPF** – vocals

Philips not issued

1970. (lp) <6305 067> **ALL WILL BE CHANGED** [-] [-] German
– Life without pain / Rosalie (part 1) / Otium / Rosalie (part II) / Indian rope man / Morning / Floating (part 1) / Baroque / Floating (part II). *(cd-iss.1991 on 'Repertoire'+=; RR 4146WZ)*– (2 extra).

1971. (7") <15034> **LIFE WITHOUT PAIN. / MORNING** [-] [ ]

— added **RAINER BAUMANN** – guitar

1971. (lp) *(6305 098)* **FRUMPY 2** [-] [-] German
– Good winds / How the gypsy was born / Take care of illusion / Duty. *(cd-iss.1993 on 'Repertoire'; REP 4339WP)*

— KRAVETZ left for a solo album in 1972, but returned after **ERWIN KANIA** had repl. him on half of below album

Vertigo not issued

1972. (lp) *(6360 604)* **BY THE WAY** [-] [-] German
– Goin' to the country / By the way / Singing songs / I'm afraid, big moon / Release / Keep on going.

Philips not issued

1973. (d-lp) *(662302-2)* **LIVE (live)** [-] [-] German
– Keep on going / Singing songs / Blackwater blues / Duty / Release / Take care of illusion / To my mother.

ATLANTIS

— were already formed by **INGA RUMPF, JEAN-JACQUES + KARL-HEINZ** plus **FRANK DIETZ** – guitar / **CURT CRESS** – drums / **JACKIE DIETZ** – vocals / **REEBOP KWAKU BAAH** – percussion / **JEAN ROUSSEL** – keyboards

Vertigo Vertigo

1973. (lp)(c) *(6360 609)(7142 002)* *<VEL 1016>* **ATLANTIS** [ ] [-]
– Get up / Big brother / Rock & roll preacher / Maybe it's useless / Let's get on the road again / Living at the end of time / Words of love.

— **RAINER SCHNELLE** – keyboards / **RINGO FUNK** – drums / **GASPAR LAWAL** – percussion; repl. FRANK, JACKIE, REEBOP + CURT

1974. (lp) *(6360 614)* **IT'S GETTING BETTER** [ ] [-]
– It's getting better / Drifting winds / Days of giving / Changed it all / Fighter of truth / Woman's truth / A simple song.

— **ALEX CONTI** – guitar, vocals + **ADRIAN ASKEW** – keyboards; repl. SCHNELLE, KRAVETZ, ROUSSEL + LAWAL

Vertigo Venus

1974. (lp) *(6360 621)* *<1009>* **OOH BABY** [ ] [ ]
– Brother / Son of a bitch's son / Waiting and longing / Mr. Bigshot / The way I choose / Ooh baby / Smiling people / New York City / Godfather / Leave it to the Devil.

1974. (d-lp) *(6623 900)* *<1010>* **ATLANTIS LIVE (live)** [ ] [ ]
– Friends / Ooh baby / Somewhere / It's getting better / Waiting and longing / Brother / Rock & roll preacher / New York City / Mr. Bigshot / Mainline Florida / Godfather / Going to the country / Rock me baby / Leave it to the Devil.

1974. (7") *<15016>* **OOH BABY. / MAINLINE FLORIDA** [-] [ ]

— **RAINER MARZ + FRANK DIETZ** – guitars, repl. CONTI + ASKEW

1975. (lp) *(6360 630)* *<1011>* **GET ON BOARD** [-] [ ]
– Get on board / Change my mind / The man / Let me stay for a while / Keep the music / Going on / Chartbuster / The captain and the ship / If I couldn't sing / Tried to climb a mountain.

— with members from 1975-78

1978. (lp) *(F 1002)* **TOP OF THE BILL** [-] [-] German
– He's got a gun in his hand / Hot rocks / Out of tune / Don't out the lady down / Northern bounty / Haven't you heard / Just blues.

— disbanded in 1978. CARSTEN his BANDSTAND, while BAUMAN formed his own band.

FRUMPY

re-formed original line-up

Mercury not issued

1990. (cd) *<842517-2>* **FRUMPY NOW** [-] [-]
– What is it / When I fall in love / Good good feeling / We can sing a song / One world / Come on / Pirate style / Come together / Now and forever / All we need is music / Living in a madhouse / Love train / Now the gypsy is born.

– compilations, etc. –

1975. (lp) *Fontana; (6434 163)* **ATTENTION** [-] [-] German

1976. (lp) *Fontana; (6434 301)* **IN AND OUT OF STUDIOS** [-] [-] German

1976. (lp) *Fontana; (6434 304)* **ATTENTION! FRUMPY 2** [-] [-] German

1982. (lp) *Vertigo; (6449 103)* **MOTIVE** [-] [-] German

FRUUPP

Formed: Belfast, N.Ireland ... 1972 by VINCENT McCUSKER, along with PETER FARRELLY, STEPHEN HOUSTON and MARTIN FOYE. They signed to the UK label, 'Dawn' (home of MUNGO JERRY), issuing progressive pomp-rock debut, 'FUTURE LEGENDS', after which they relocated to London in 1973. Overweight jazzy-rock solos drew comparisons with GENESIS or YES, although the follow-up, 'SEVEN SECRETS', was more classically-tinged. Their fourth and final effort, 'MODERN MASQUERADES' was produced by saxophonist IAN McDONALD, who also contributed two tracks. • **Songwriters:** Group or McCUSKER or HOUSTON.

Recommended: FUTURE LEGENDS (*7) / SEVEN SECRETS (*6) / PRINCE OF HEAVEN'S EYES (*6) / MODERN MASQUERADES (*7)

PETER FARRELLY – vocals, bass, guitar / **STEPHEN HOUSTON** – keyboards, oboe, vocals / **VINCENT McCUSKER** – guitar, vocals / **MARTIN FOYE** – drums, percussion

Dawn not issued

1973. (lp) *(DNLS 3053)* **FUTURE LEGENDS** [ ] [-]
– Future legends / Decision / As day breaks with dawn / Graveyard epistle / Lord of the incubus / Olde tyme future / Song for a thought / Future legends.

1974. (lp) *(DNLS 3058)* **SEVEN SECRETS** [ ] [-]
– Faced with Skekinah / Wise as wisdom / White eyes / Garden lady / Three spires / Elizabeth.

1974. (lp) *(DNLH 2)* **THE PRINCE OF HEAVEN'S EYES** [ ] [-]
– It's all up now / Prince of Heaven / Jaunting car / Annie Austere / Knowing you / Crystal brook / Seaward sunset / The perfect wish.

Oct 74. (7") *(DNS 1087)* **PRINCE OF HEAVEN. / JAUNTING CAR** [ ] [-]

— **JOHN MASON** – keyboards, vibes, vocals; repl. HOUSTON (guest on next album **IAN McDONALD** – sax

1975. (lp) *(DNLS 3070)* **MODERN MASQUERADES** [ ] [-]
– Misty morning way / Masquerading with dawn / Gormenghast / Mystery night / Why / Janet planet / Sheba's song.

— Split in 1976.

– compilations, etc. –

Mar 92. (cd) *Sequel; (NEXCD 203)* **SONGS FOR A THOUGHT** [ ] [-]
– Future legends – intro / It's all up now / Garden lady / Three spires / Wise as

wisdom / Prince of darkness / Graveyard epistle / Janet planet / Prince of Heaven / White eyes / On a clear day / Decision / Lord of the incubus / The seventh secret.

Aug 96. (cd) *C5; (C5HCD 645)* **FUTURE LEGENDS / SEVEN SECRETS** [ ] [-]

Aug 96. (cd) *C5; (C5HCD 646)* **THE PRINCE OF HEAVEN'S EYES / MODERN MASQUERADES** [ ] [-]

(above 2 cd's omitted 1 track each)

FUGS

Formed: Greenwich Village, New York, USA . . . 1964 by poets/satirists ED SANDERS, KEN WEAVER and TULI KUPFERBERG. Beginning life at the local McDougall Theatre, they built up a reputation for translating WILLIAM BLAKE works into outrageously crude pieces of avant-garde rock. In 1965, they signed to jazz label, 'E.S.P.', unleashing the "first album". It contained the political satire of 'KILL FOR PEACE', the drug orientated 'NEW AMPHETAMINE SHRIEK' and the sex-angled 'COCA COLA DOUCHE'. Not surprisingly, they were shunned by "respectable" American citizens, although they mellowed somewhat with their next lp, 'FUGS'. Their underground brand of performance rock could be described as satirist LENNY BRUCE being backed by The VELVET UNDERGROUND. After a few more offensive productions, they signed to 'Reprise' in 1967, and might have scored a hit 45 with 'OUT DEMONS OUT'. It remained unreleased, only surfacing later as a hit 45 for The EDGAR BROUGHTON BAND. Orginally part of the beatnik scene they later embraced hippy ideals, galvanising new pacifist anti-war activity around New York. They returned in the 80's for some low-key live outings and a couple of albums, none of which possessed the intensity of old. • **Songwriters:** SANDERS or KUPFERBERG words and FUGS music.

Recommended: VIRGIN FUGS (*6)

ED SANDERS (b.Kansas City, Missouri) – vocals, guitar / **TULI KUPFERBERG** – vocals, percussion / **KEN WEAVER** (b. Galveston, Texas) – drums, vocals / **PETER STAMPFEL** – guitar, banjo, vocals / **STEVE WEBER** – guitar (both ex-HOLY MODAL ROUNDERS) / **VINNY LEARY** – guitar, bass / **JOHN ANDERSON** – bass / **PETE KEARNEY** – guitar

not issued | Broadside

Jan 66. (lp) *<1018>* **FIRST ALBUM** [-] [ ]
– Slum Goddess / Ah, sunflower weary of time / Supergirl / Swineburne stomp / I couldn't get high / How sweet I roamed from field to field / Seize the day / My baby done left me / Boobs a lot / Nothing. *(UK-iss.1969 on 'Fontana' stereo/mono; S+/TL 5513) (cd-iss.Jun93 on 'Big Beat'+=; CDWIKD 119)– (lp re-iss.Jun97; same)*

not issued | E.S.P.

— WEBER left to re-join The HOLY MODAL ROUNDERS with STAMPFEL, and was repl. by **LEE CRABTREE** – piano + **PETE KEARNEY** – guitar (ANDERSON also missing)

Dec 66. (7") *<4507>* **FRENZY. / I WANT TO KNOW** [-] [ ]

Jan 67. (lp) *<1028>* **THE FUGS** (alias 'THE FUGS SECOND ALBUM') [-] [95]
– Frenzy / I want to know / Skin flowers / Group grope / Coming down / Dirty old man / I kill for peace / Morning, morning / Doin' all right / Virgin forest. *(UK-iss.1969 as 'FUGS II' on 'Fontana' stereo/mono; S+/TL 5524) (cd-iss.Sep93 on 'Ace';)*

Jun 67. (lp) *<1038>* **VIRGIN FUGS** [-] [ ]
– We're the fugs / New amphetamine shriek / Saran wrap / The ten commandments / Hallucination horrors / I command the house of the Devil / C.I.A. man / Coco Cola douche / My bed is getting crowded / Coca rocka / I saw the best of my generation rot. *(UK-iss.1969 on 'Fontana' stereo/mono; S+/TL 5501) (UK cd-iss.Jun97; same)*

— **SANDERS, KUPFERBERG & WEAVER** recruit new members **CHARLIE LARKEY** – drums / **KEN PINE** – guitar, vocals / **DANNY KORTCHMAR** – guitar

Transatlantic | Reprise

Jan 68. (lp) *(TRA 180) <RS 6280>* **TENDERNESS JUNCTION** [ ] [ ]
– Turn on, tune in, drop out / Knock knock / The garden is open / Wet dream / Hare Krishna / Exorcising the Devil spirits from the Pentagon / War song / Dover beach / Fingers of the Sun / Aphrodite mass: Litany of the street grope genuflection at the temple . . . – Petals in the sea – Sappho's hymn to Aphrodite – Homage to throb thrills. *(re-iss.Jan89 on 'Edsel'; ED 298)*

— added **BOB MASON** – 2nd drummer

Sep 68. (lp) *(TRA 181) <RS 6305>* **IT CRAWLED INTO MY HAND, HONEST** [ ] [ ]
– Crystal liason / Ramases II is dead, my love / Burial waltz / Wide wide river / Life is strange / Johnny Pissoff meets the red angel – Marijuana – Leprechaun – When the mode of the music changes – Whimpers from the jello – Divine toe (part 1) – We're both dead now, Alice – Life is funny – Grope need (part 1) – Tuli, visited by the ghost of Plotinus / More grope need (Grope need part 2) – Robinson Crusoe – Claude Pelieu and J.J.Lebel discuss the early Verlaine bread crust fragments – The national Haiku contest – The divine toe (part 2) – Irene.

Sep 68. (7") *(BIG 115)* **CRYSTAL LIASON. / WHEN THE MODE OF THE MUSIC CHANGES** [ ] [-]

— **DAN HAMBURG** – guitar repl. DANNY

Reprise | Reprise

Nov 69. (lp) *(<RSLP 6359>)* **THE BELLE OF AVENUE A** [ ] [ ]
– Bum's song / Dust devil / Chicago / Four minutes to twelve / Mr.Mack / The belle of Avenue A / Queen of the Nile / Flower children / Yodeling yippie / Children of the dream.

— **CARL LYNCH** – guitar repl. DAN added **HOWARD JOHNSON** – tuba / **JULIUS WATKINS** – horns / **RICHARD TEE** – organ

1970. (lp) *<RS 6396>* **GOLDEN FILTH ALIVE AT HTE FILLMORE EAST (live '68)** [-] [ ]
– Slum goddess / CCD / How sweet I roamed / I couldn't get high / Saran wrap / I want to know / Homemade / Nothing / Supergirl. *(re-iss.Feb87 on 'Edsel'; ED 217)*

— disbanded early 1970. LARKEY later married and played bass for CAROLE KING. In 1984, **SANDERS + KUPFERBERG** re-formed the **FUGS** w/ **STEVE TAYLOR** – vocals, guitar / **COBY BATY** – vocals, drums, percussion / **VINNIE LEARY** – guitar / **MARK KRAMER** – bass, keyboards (SHOCKABILLY)

New Rose | S.P.V.

Apr 85. (lp) *(ROSE 56)* **REFUSE TO BE BURNT-OUT (live in the 80's)** [ ] [-]
– The five feet / If you were to be President / Nova slum goddess / Nicaragua / Fingers of the sun / Wide wide river / How sweet I roamed / Refuse to be burnt-out / Country punk / C.I.A. man / Ban the bomb / Keeping the issues alive. *(cd-iss.Mar95 on 'Big Beat';)*

— Now without **KRAMER** who joined BUTTHOLE SURFERS then BONGWATER.

Mar 86. (lp/cd) *(ROSE 79/+CD)* **NO MORE SLAVERY** [ ] [-]

— **SANDERS, KUPFERBERG, TAYLOR, BATY,** plus **SCOTT PETITO** – bass, guitar, synth / **MARILYN GRISPELL** – piano, synth / **LARRY BRODY + ANNE JACOBSON + LESLIE RITTER** – vocals

Jun 87. (d-lp/cd) *(ROSE 115/+CD)* **STAR PEACE (A MUSICAL DRAMA IN 3 ACTS)** [ ] [-]
– Act 1, Scene 1: Mr. President, this is the greatest hour – Dazzle the sky – The wagon trains – This evil empire – Go for it – La traison des journalists – the prayer / Hymn to America / Act 1, Scene 2: Rose petals veiled in smoke – the President's in my pocket / Act 1, Scene 3: Technology is going to act us free – There's a dim bulb burning – The pax coel: America / Slapping leather in strange, strange skies – The great spasm – the battle in the sky – I see Lois / Act 2, Scene 1: Da Vinci once thought of a secret weapon – A nuke free world – I believe in destiny / Act 2, Scene 2: The threat, the threat – How much do you really know about those whom you hate – the metastasis – The peer jeer – He was such a scientist / Act 2, Scene 3: Protest and survive – World wide green – Till the wormwood fell from the sky no more / Act 3, Scene 1: The rapture song – The sharing mind – Talking in nuke tongue – The list from Plymouth rock / Act 3, Scene 3: Liberty not war – The secret agenda / Act 3, Scene 3: She must die – The terrible things / Act 3, Scene 4: A death in the mountains – Oh the pain – Do not mourn for me.

– compilations, others, etc. –

Jun 75. (lp) *E.S.P.; <2018>* **FUGS 4, ROUNDERS SCORE** (out-takes some with HOLY MODAL ROUNDERS) [-] [ ]

Jun 94. (cd) *Ace;* **LIVE FROM THE 60's (live)** [ ] [-]

Oct 95. (cd) *Big Beat;* **THE REAL WOODSTOCK FESTIVAL (live)** [ ] [-]

(above originally released in Sweden 1993)

TULI KUPFERBERG

not issued | E.S.P.

1967. (lp,gold-lp) *<1035>* **NO DEPOSIT, NO RETURN** [-] [ ]
– Pubol / Social studies / The hidden dissuaders lifetime guarentee / The art science / Want ads 1 / Rangoon / Rambler purina lanoflo / The hyperemiator / The sap glove / The bunny mother / Auto-da-fe / Fields matrimonial service / Want ads 2 / Howard Johnsons army / No deposit, no return.

Shimmy Disc | Shimmy Disc

1989. (lp/cd) *<SHIMMY 020/+CD>* **TULI AND FRIENDS** [-] [ ]
(cd+=)– (bonus tracks).

— In the 80's KUPFERBERG became director of the 'Revolting Theater' New York, after earlier surviving a jump off of Brooklyn Bridge.

ED SANDERS

not issued | Reprise

1971. (lp) *<RS 6374>* **SANDERS' TRUCK STOP** [-] [ ]
– Jimmy Joe / The hippybilly boy / The maple court tragedy / Heartbreak crash pad / Banshee / The plaster song / The illiad / Breadtray mountain / The A.B.M. machine / They're cuttin' my coffin at the sawmill / Homesick blues / Pindar's revenge.

1972. (lp) *<RS 2105>* **BEER CANS ON THE MOON** [-] [ ]

— ED SANDERS retired from music scene, but became underground writer, also managing to write a best-seller (The Family) about the Charles Manson case.

FUNKADELIC (see under ⇒ CLINTON, George)

FURS & FROHLING (see under ⇒ SCHICKE, FURS & FROHLING)

FUZZY DUCK

Formed: London, England . . . 1970 by MICK HAWKSWORTH and ROY SHARLAND. They released only one very limited heavy/progressive rock album in 1971, splitting soon after. Two singles also surfaced for 'M.A.M.' (the home of GILBERT O'SULLIVAN), although they failed to break through commercially.

Recommended: FUZZY DUCK (*6)

MICK HAWKSWORTH – bass (ex-ANDROMEDA, ex-FIVE DAY WEEK STRAW PEOPLE) / **ROY SHARLAND** – organ (ex-SPICE; aka URIAH HEEP, ex-ARTHUR BROWN) / **GARTH WATT-ROY** – vocals, guitar / **PAUL FRANCIS** – drums

M.A.M. | not issued

Aug 71. (7") *(MAM 37)* **DOUBLE TIME WOMAN. / JUST LOOK AROUND YOU** [ ] [-]

Sep 71. (lp) *(MAM-AS 1005)* **FUZZY DUCK** [ ] [-]
– Time will be your doctor / Mrs. Prout / Just look around you / Afternoon out / More than I am / Country boy / In our time / A word from Big D. *(re-iss.1990 on 'Reflection'; MM 05)(w/ free 7"+=)*– DOUBLE TIME WOMAN. / ONE MORE HOUR *(re-iss.1993 on 'Aftermath'; AFT 1003) (cd-iss.1993 on 'Repertoire'+=; REP 4352-WP)*– Double time woman / Big brass band / One more hour / No name face.

Nov 71. (7") *(MAM 51)* **BIG BRASS BAND. / ONE MORE HOUR** [ ] [-]

— When they folded late 1971, GARTH returned to The GREATEST SHOW ON EARTH

Peter GABRIEL

Born: 13 May'50, Cobham, Surrey, England. After 8 years as leader of GENESIS, he left in May'75 to pursue a solo career, releasing the first of his four self-titled studio albums in 1977. Produced by BOB EZRIN (more often found working with heavy-rock acts), the album's overwrought feel found GABRIEL struggling for a musical identity despite including such enduring songs as the classic 'SOLISBURY HILL', a Top 20 hit single, and its creepy flipside, 'MORIBUND THE BURGERMEISTER'. 1978's follow-up boasted ROBERT FRIPP at the production helm, and a somewhat pared-down sound, GABRIEL illustrating his admiration for the punk ethos on 'D.I.Y.' and rocking out on the raging 'ON THE AIR'. His third, in 1980, moved towards a radically different style of songwriting, based around rhythm rather than chord sequences. With the use of a pioneering sampler, the Fairlight CMI, GABRIEL was able to construct tracks around the rhythm, adding instrumentation to enhance the sound. With STEVE LILLYWHITE producing and a cast of collaborators including FRIPP, KATE BUSH and PHIL COLLINS, he created a compelling set of minimalistic songs, the hypnotic anti-war single 'GAMES WITHOUT FRONTIERS', taking GABRIEL into the Top 5. The album also included his inspired tribute to murdered black South African activist (STEVE) 'BIKO'. This introduced GABRIEL's growing interest in world music, an area he would explore further on his fourth album (released in the States as 'SECURITY'). Incorporating ethnic sounds and rhythms into his distictive songwriting technique, GABRIEL discovered a new found artistic freedom, creating one of his most accomplished and inventive albums in the process. Highlights included the single, 'SHOCK THE MONKEY', the African tribal drumming of 'RHYTHM OF THE HEAT', and the exotic 'THE FAMILY AND THE FISHING NET'. His increasing immersion in all things ethnic saw him become involved with the newly conceived WOMAD festival in 1982, highlighting music from the furthest flung corners of the globe. After a shaky start, the festival has now become an annual event with an affiliated world music label, 'Real World'. The 80's also saw GABRIEL record two soundtrack albums, Alan Parker's 'BIRDY' (1985) and Martin Scorsese's 'THE LAST TEMPTATION OF CHRIST' (1989). The former was made-up largely of revamped tracks from his earlier work, the original songs transformed into atmospheric mood pieces to impressive effect, while the latter was an eerily affecting collage of folksy, world music stylings. Sandwiched between these two, was the album which finally marked his arrival as a major league rock star. 'SO', released in 1986, saw GABRIEL incorporating his ethnic experimentation into the pop format with remarkable dexterity. The track, 'SLEDGEHAMMER', with its polished funk and famous, award winning video, shot into the upper regions of the charts, propelling the album to No.1 in the UK (No.2 in America). The record was a free ranging world trip, showcasing strong melodies ('DON'T GIVE UP' with KATE BUSH) against exotic backdrops, the culmination of his work to date. The long awaited "proper" follow-up, 'US' was eventually released in 1992, just held off the top spot on both sides of the Atlantic. The album was a markedly more downbeat, introspective affair, the single 'DIGGING IN THE DIRT', highlighting GABRIEL's return to more personal songwriting. It was also inspired by his mid-80's divorce from childhood sweetheart JILL MOORE and the split with his girlfriend, actress ROSANNA ARQUETTE. GABRIEL continues to devote much of his time to the 'Real World' label, although he did find some time for a tour and a live album, 'SECRET WORLD' in 1994. • **Covered;** STRAWBERRY FIELDS FOREVER (Beatles) / SUZANNE (Leonard Cohen). • **Trivia:** In 1982, he co-wrote & produced 'Animals Have More Fun' for JIMMY PURSEY (ex-SHAM 69). He has also guested for ROBBIE ROBERTSON (his 1987 album) & JONI MITCHELL (her 1991 album).

Recommended: SHAKIN' THE TREE: SIXTEEN GOLDEN GREATS (*9).

PETER GABRIEL – vocals, keyboards (ex-GENESIS, ex-GARDEN WALL) with **TONY LEVIN** – bass / **STEVE HUNTER** – guitar / **LARRY FAST** – keyboards / **JIMMY MAELEN** – percussion / **ALAN SCHWARTZBERG** – drums / **ROBERT FRIPP** – guitar

Charisma | Atco

Feb 77. (lp/c) *(CDS/+MC 4006) <36-147>* **PETER GABRIEL** [7] [38]
– Moribund the burgermeister / Solisbury Hill / Modern love / Excuse me / Humdrum / Slowburn / Waiting for the big one / Down the Dolce Vita / Here comes the flood. *(cd-iss.May83; CDSCD 4006) (re-iss.Aug88 lp/c; CHC/+MC 38) (cd re-iss.May87; PGCD 1)*

Mar 77. (7") *(CB 301) <7079>* **SOLISBURY HILL. / MORIBUND THE BURGERMEISTER** [13] [68]

Jun 77. (7") *(CB 302)* **MODERN LOVE. / SLOWBURN** [ ] [ ]

— now with **FRIPP,** plus **JERRY MAROTTA** – drums / **ROY BITTAN** – piano / **SID McGINNIS** – guitar / **BAYETE** – keyboards

May 78. (7") *(CB 311)* **D.I.Y. / PERSPECTIVE** [ ] [-]
(12"w-drawn) *(CB 319)* – ('A'remix) / Mother of violence / Teddy bear.

Charisma | Atlantic

Jun 78. (lp/c) *(CAS/+MC 4013) <19181>* **PETER GABRIEL** [10] [45]
– On the air / D.I.Y. / Mother of violence / A wonderful day in a one-way world / White shadow / Indigo / Animal magic / Exposure / Flotsam and jetsam / Perspective / Home sweet home. *(re-iss.Mar84 lp/c; CHC/+MC 24) (cd-iss.May87; PGCD 2)*

Jun 78. (7") **D.I.Y. / MOTHER OF VIOLENCE** [-] [ ]

Charisma | Mercury

Feb 80. (7"m) *(CB 354)* **GAMES WITHOUT FRONTIERS. / THE START / I DON'T REMEMBER** [4] [-]

May 80. (7") *(CB 360)* **NO SELF CONTROL. / LEAD A NORMAL LIFE** [33] [-]

Jul 80. (7") *<76086>* **GAMES WITHOUT FRONTIERS. / LEAD A NORMAL LIFE** [-] [48]

Sep 80. (7") *<76086>* **I DON'T REMEMBER. /** [-] [ ]

— now with **FRIPP, LEVIN + MAROTTA** plus guests **PHIL COLLINS** – drums / **KATE BUSH + PAUL WELLER** – vocals

May 80. (lp/c) *(CAS/+Mc 4019) <3848>* **PETER GABRIEL** [1] [22]
– Intruder / No self control / Start / I don't remember / Family snapshot / And through the wire / Not one of us / Lead a normal life / Biko. *(re-iss.Sep83 lp/c; CDS/+MC 4019) (cd-iss.May87; PGCD 3)*

Aug 80. (7"/12") *(CB 370/+12)* **BIKO. / SHOSHOLOZA / JETZT KOMMT DIE FLUT** [38] [ ]

— guests on next incl. **DAVID LORD** – synthesizers, co-producer / **JOHN ELLIS** – guitar / + some of last line-up

Charisma | Geffen

Sep 82. (lp/c) *(PG/+MC 4) <2011>* **PETER GABRIEL** <US-title 'SECURITY'> [6] [28]
– The rhythm of the heat / San Jacinto / I have the touch / The family and the fishing net / Shock the monkey / Lay your hands on me / Wallflower / Kiss of life. *(re-iss.Sep83 lp/c; same) (cd-iss.1986; PGCD 4)*

Sep 82. (7"/7"pic-d/12") *(SHOCK 1/+22/12) <29883>* **SHOCK THE MONKEY. / SOFT DOG (instrumental)** [58] [29]
(7"/12") *(SHOCK 1/350)* – ('A'side) / ('B'-instrumental).

Dec 82. (7") *(CB 405)* **I HAVE THE TOUCH. / ACROSS THE RIVER** [ ] [-]

Jun 83. (d-lp/c) *(PGD L/MC 1) <4012>* **PETER GABRIEL PLAYS LIVE (live)** [8] [44]
– The rhythm of the heat / I have the touch / Not one of us / Family snapshot / D.I.Y. / The family and the fishing net / Intruder / I go swimming / San Jacinto / Solisbury Hill / No self control / I don't remember / Shock the monkey / Humdrum / On the air / Biko. *(cd-iss.Jun85; PGDLD 1) (cd re-iss.1988; CDPGD 100)*– (omits 4 tracks).

Jun 83. (7") *(GAB 1)* **I DON'T REMEMBER (live). / SOLISBURY HILL (live)** [62] [-]
(12"+=) *(GAB 12)* – Kiss of life (live).
(free-12"w- 12") *(GAB 122)* – GAMES WITHOUT FRONTIERS (live). / SCHNAPPSCHUSS (EIN FAMILIENFOTO)

Virgin | Geffen

Nov 83. (7") *<29542>* **SOLISBURY HILL (live). / I GO SWIMMING (live)** [-] [84]

May 84. (7") *(VS 689)* **WALK THROUGH THE FIRE. / THE RACE (by Larry Carlton)** [69] [ ]
(12"+=) *(VS 689-12)* – I have the touch (remix).

Mar 85. (lp/c/cd) *(CAS/+MC/CD 1167) <24070>* **BIRDY – MUSIC FROM THE FILM (soundtrack)** [51] [ ]
– At night / Floating dogs / Quiet and alone / Close up / Slow water / Dressing the wound / Birdy's flight / Slow marimbas / The heat / Sketchpad with trumpet and voice / Under lock and key / Powerhouse at the foot of the mountain. *(re-iss.Apr90 on 'Virgin' lp/c; OVED/+C 283)*

— with **MAROTTA, LEVIN** plus **DANIEL LANOIS** – guitar, co-producer / **MANU KATCHE** – percussion / **YOUSSOU N'DOUR + KATE BUSH** – guest vocals / **STEWART COPELAND** – drums /**etc.**

Apr 86. (7") *(PGS 1)* **SLEDGEHAMMER. / JOHN HAS A HEADACHE** [4] [-]
(12"+=) *(PGS 112)* – Don't break this rhythm / ('A'dance mix).
('A'dance-12"+=) *(PGS 113)* – Biko (extended) / I have the touch ('85 remix).

May 86. (7") *<28718>* **SLEDGEHAMMER. / DON'T BREAK THIS RHYTHM** [-] [1]

May 86. (lp/c/cd) *(PG/+MC/CD 5) <24088>* **SO** [1] [2]
– Red rain / Sledgehammer / Don't give up / That voice again / In your eyes / Mercy street / Big time / We do what we're told. *(pic-cd.Dec88+=; PGCDP 5)* – This is the picture (excellent birds). *(re-iss.Feb97 on 'E.M.I.'; LPCENT 16)*

Sep 86. (7") *<28622>* **IN YOUR EYES. / ('A'-Special mix)** [-] [26]
<US re-iss.May89 on 'W.T.G.'; WTG 68936>; reached 41>

Oct 86. (7"; PETER GABRIEL & KATE BUSH) *(PGS/+P 2)* **DON'T GIVE UP. / IN YOUR EYES (special mix)** [9] [-]
(12"+=) *(PGS 2-12)* – This is the picture (excellent birds).

Jan 87. (7") *<28503>* **BIG TIME. / WE DO WHAT WE'RE TOLD** [-] [8]

Mar 87. (7") *(PGS 3)* **BIG TIME. / CURTAINS** [13] [-]
(12"+=) *(PGS 312)* – ('A'extended).
('A'ext-c-s) *(PGT 312)* – Across the river / No self control (live). *(re-iss.3"cd-s.1989; GAIL 312)*

Mar 87. (7"; PETER GABRIEL & KATE BUSH) *<28463>* **DON'T GIVE UP / CURTAINS** [-] [72]

Jun 87. (7") *(PGS 4)* **RED RAIN. / GA GA (I GO SWIMMING(** [46] [ ]
(12"+=/c-s+=) *(PGS/+C 412)* – Walk through the fire.

Jan 88. (7"/c-s) *(PGS/+C 6)* **BIKO (live). / NO MORE APARTEID** [49] [-]
(12"+=/cd-s+=) *(PGS/CDPGS 6-12)* – I have the touch ('85 remix).

— In May 89, PETER ws credited with YOUSSOU N'DOUR on minor hit single

'SHAKIN THE TREE' *(VS/+T/CD 1167)*

Real World | Geffen

Jun 89. (d-lp/c/cd) *(RW LP/MC/CD 1) <24206>* **PASSION (Soundtrack film 'The Last Temptation Of Christ')** [29] [60]
– The feeling begins / Gethsemane / Of these, hope / Lazarus raised / Of these, hope – reprise / In doubt / A different drum / Zaar / Troubled / Open* / Before night falls / With this love / Sandstorm / Stigmata** / Passion / With this love – choir / Wall of breath / The promise of shadows / Disturbed / It is accomplished / Bread and wine. *(*= with SHANKAR) (**= with MAHMOUD TABRIZI ZADEH)*

Sep 92. (7")(c-s) *(PGS/+C 7) <19136>* **DIGGING IN THE DIRT. / QUIET STEAM** [24] [52]
(cd-s+=) *(PGSDG 7)* – ('A'instrumental).
(cd-s++=) *(PGSCD 7)* – Bashi-bazouk.

Oct 92. (lp/c/cd) *(PG/+MC/CD 7) <24473>* **US** [2] [2]
– Come talk to me / Love to be loved / Blood of Eden / Steam / Digging in the dirt / Fourteen black paintings / Kiss that frog / Secret world.

Jan 93. (7"/c-s) *(PGS/+C 8) <19145>* **STEAM. / ('A'-Carter ... mix)** [10] [32] Nov92
(cd-s) *(PGSDG 8 / PGSDX 8)* – ('A' mix) / Games without frontiers (mix) / (2 'A' extended + dub mix or Games (other mix)

Mar 93. (7"/c-s) *(PGS/+C 9)* **BLOOD OF EDEN. / MERCY STREET** [43] [ ]
(cd-s+=) *(PGSDG 9)* – ('A'-special mix)
(cd-s+=) *(PGCDX 9)* – Sledgehammer.

Sep 93. (7"/c-s) *(PGS/+C 10)* **KISS THAT FROG. / ('A'- mindblender mix)** [46] [ ]
(cd-s+=) *(PGSDG 10)* – Digging in the dirt.
(cd-s+=) *(PGSDX 10)* – Across the river / Shaking the tree (Bottrill remix).

— Below single, another from 'Philadelphia' film on 'Epic' records.

Jun 94. (7"/c-s) *(660480-7/-4)* **LOVE TOWN. / LOVE TO BE LOVED** [49] [ ]
(cd-s+=) *(660480-2)* – Different drum.

— live with **TONY LEVIN** – bass, vocals / **DAVID RHODES** – guitar, vocals / **MANU KATCHE** – drums / **PAULA COLE** – vocals / **JEAN CLAUDE NAIMRO** – keyboards, vocals / **RAVI SHANKAR** – violin, vocals / **LEVON MINASSIAN** – doudouk

Aug 94. (c-s) *(PGSC 11)* **SECRET WORLD (live). / COME TALK TO ME** [39] [ ]
(cd-ep) *(PGSCD 11)* – ('A'live) / Red rain (live) / San Jacinto (live) / Mercy Street (live).

Sep 94. (d-cd/d-c) *(PG DCD/MC 8)* **SECRET WORLD LIVE (live)** [10] [23]
– Come talk to me / Steam / Across the river / Slow marimbas / Shaking the tree / Red rain / Blood of Eden / Kiss that frog / Washing of the water / Solisbury Hill / Digging in the dirt / Sledgehammer / Secret world / Don't give up / In your eyes.

– compilations, etc. –

on 'Virgin' UK / 'Geffen' US, unless mentioned otherwise

Jan 83. (7") *Old Gold; (OG 9265)* **SOLISBURY HILL. / GAMES WITHOUT FRONTIERS** [ ] [-]

Mar 83. (d-c) *Charisma; (CASMC 102)* **PETER GABRIEL 1 / PETER GABRIEL 2** [ ] [-]

1988. (3"cd-ep) *(CDT 33)* **SOLISBURY HILL / MORIBUND THE BURGERMEISTER / SOLISBURY HILL (live)** [ ] [-]
(re-iss.Apr90; VVCS 8)

Jun 88. (cd) *XCDSD 4018)* **PETER GABRIEL 3 (German version)** [ ] [-]

Oct 90. (3xcd-box) *(TPAK 9)* **PETER GABRIEL 1 / 2 / 3** [ ] [ ]

Nov 90. (lp/c/cd) *(PGTV/+C/D 6) <24326>* **SHAKING THE TREE – SIXTEEN GOLDEN GREATS** [11] [48]
– Solisbury Hill / I don't remember / Sledgehammer / Family snapshot / Mercy Street / Shaking the tree / Don't give up / Here comes the flood / Games without frontiers / Shock the monkey / Big time / Biko. *(cd+=/c+=)*– San Juanito / Red rain / I have the touch / Zaar.

Dec 90. (7"/c-s) *(VS/+C 1322)* **SOLISBURY HILL. / SHAKING THE TREE** (w/ YOUSSOU N'DOUR) [57] [-]
(12"+=/cd-s+=) *(VS T/CD 1322)* – Games without frontiers.

GALLIARD

Formed: London, England ... 1969 as a 6-piece including singer GEOFF BROWN. They released a couple of albums, more jazzy than progressive, although their second, 'NEW DAWN', (with HARRY BECKETT in tow), became a collector's item, now worth over £70.

Recommended: STRANGE PLEASURE (*5) / NEW DAWN (*5)

GEOFF BROWN – vocals, guitar, keyboards / **RICHARD PANNELL** – guitar, sitar, vocals / **DAVE CASWELL** – woodwind, vocals / **JOHN SMITH** – woodwind / **ANDY ABBOTT** – bass, accordion, vocals / **LES PODRAZA** – drums, percussion, vocals

Deram Nova | not issued

Feb 70. (lp) *(SDN 4)* **STRANGE PLEASURE** [ ] [-]
– Modern day fairy tale / Pastorale / I wrapped her in ribbons / Children of the sun / Got to make it / Frog Galliard / Blood / Hear the colours / I wanna be back home.

— JOHN SMITH was repl. by **HAROLD BECKETT** – woodwind / **LYLE JENKINS** – saxophones / **JOHN HUGHES** – trombone / **TONY ROBERTS** – woodwind / **JOHN MORTON** – piano / **DAVE GRAY** – alto sax

Deram | not issued

Jul 70. (7") *(DM 306)* **I WRAPPED HER IN RIBBONS. / HERMIT AND THE KNIGHT** [ ] [-]

Dec 70. (lp) *(SML 1075)* **NEW DAWN** [ ] [-]
– New dawn breaking / Ask for nothing / Winter – Spring – Summer / Open up your mind / And smile again / Something's going on / Premonition / In your minds eye.

— split after above , HAROLD BECKETT went solo

GANDALF

Formed: based- New York, USA ... 1968 by main writer PETE SANDO. Their one and only album in 1969 was given a low-key release but should have been given more of a push, the record since becoming a "lost" classic. From its gem of an opening track, 'GOLDEN EARRINGS' (also a rare 45; and actually a 1948 hit for BING CROSBY!) to the more sedate finale 'I WATCH THE MOON', it oozed pop sensibility with psychedelic and progressive leanings. Produced by KOPPELMAN and RUBIN (who had worked with THE SOPWITH CAMEL and LOVIN' SPOONFUL), it featured spacey laid back versions of TIM HARDIN's 'HANG ON TO A DREAM' and HARRY BELAFONTE's 'SCARLET RIBBONS'.

Recommended: GANDALF (*8)

PETE SANDO – vocals, guitars / **FRANK HUBACH** – keyboards / **BOB MULLER** – bass / **DAVID BAUER** – drums

not issued | Capitol

1969. (7") *<P-2400>* **GOLDEN EARRINGS. / NEVER TOO FAR** [-] [ ]

1969. (lp) *<ST 121>* **GANDALF** [-] [ ]
– Golden earrings / Hang on to a dream / Never too far / Scarlet ribbons / You upset the grace of living / Can you travel alone / Nature boy / Tiffany rings / Me about you / I watch the moon. *(UK cd-iss.Jul91 & Jun 97 on 'See For Miles'; SEECD 326)*

— went to ground after above

— not sure of another GANDALF who released in Jul'95 a cd 'COLOURS OF THE EARTH' *(SKV 080CD)*

GANDALF THE GREY

Formed: New York, USA . . . 1972 as a studio project by . . . well, er . . . I just don't know. A bit mysterious this one, although it deserves a mention for its post-psychedelic guitar work fused with progressive folk-rock on his/their only album 'THE GREY WIZARD I AM'. It gained a UK release in 1986 and is very rare, best tracks being the title track and 'FROM THE GREY HAVENS'. The UK version could also get very pricey; it's worth about £25 at the moment, while the US original is still rocketing.

Recommended: THE GREY WIZARD I AM (*6)

GANDALF THE GREY – guitar, vocals, etc

not issued | Grey Wizard

1972. (lp) *<S-7>* **THE GREY WIZARD I AM** [-] [ ]
– The grey wizard I am / My elven home / From the grey havens / Here on 8th Street / Go and see / The Christmas song / Old town church / The home coming / I don't know why the people / Mr. Joe's / Sunshine down the line. *(UK-iss.1986 on 'Heyoka'; HEY 207)*

Elmer GANTRY'S VELVET OPERA (see under ⇒ VELVET OPERA)

Jerry GARCIA (see under ⇒ GRATEFUL DEAD)

Ron GEESIN

Born: 1943, Ayrshire, Scotland. In 1961, he joined the Crawley-based jazz combo, The ORIGINAL DOWNTOWN SYNCOPATORS, who issued a few EP's as well as a very limited 10" album. In 1965, he recorded a solo EP, before he started to write music for documentaries and TV commercials. Living in Notting Hill, London, he built up recording equipment for his next outing; the 1967 album 'A RAISE OF EYEBROWS'. The album highlighted GEESIN's eclectically experimental avant-garde jazz. In 1969, he toured alongside folkies ROY HARPER and RALPH McTELL, while he worked on his next project, 'THE BODY'. This was a collaboration with ROGER WATERS (of PINK FLOYD), who had previously invited RON to augment and co-write on PINK FLOYD's 'ATOM HEART MOTHER' album. In 1971/72, he sessioned and produced albums for BRIDGET ST. JOHN and ARMORY KANE respectively, 'Songs For The Gentle Man' and 'Just To Be There'. In 1973, he set up his own-named label, for which he issued three albums in the mid-70's. At the same time, he issued some library-only albums, although he was to drop out of the music scene in the late 70's and 80's. In 1990, after working on various BBC TV and radio productions, he surfaced once again with the cd-album, 'FUNNY FROWN'. • **Trivia:** In 1969, he appeared on lp 'JOHN PEEL PRESENTS TOP GEAR' with track 'Agitation In Anticipation Of Offspring, Parts W, X & Y'.

Recommended: A RAISE OF EYEBROWS (*6) / AS HE STANDS (*5)

ORIGINAL DOWNTOWN SYNCOPATORS

RON GEESIN – piano / + ?

V.J.M. | not issued

1962. (7"ep) *(VEP 14)* **ORIGINAL DOWNTOWN SYNCOPATORS** [ ] [-]
– Sensation rag / Skeleton jangle / Mojo stomp / Indiana.

John R.T. Davis | not issued

1963. (10"lp) *(DAVLP 301-2)* **THE ORIGINAL DOWNTOWN SYNCOPATORS** [ ] [-]

Columbia | not issued

1964. (7"ep) *(SEG 8293)* **IT'S JASS** [ ] [-]

RON GEESIN

-vocals, keyboards, synthesizers, etc

		no label	not issued
1965.	(ltd-7"ep) *(RRG 319-320)* **RON GEESIN**		-

		Transatlantic	not issued
Jun 67.	(lp; stereo/mono) *(S+/TRA 161)* **A RAISE OF EYEBROWS**		-

– A raise of eyebrows / Freedom for four voices and me / Psychedelia / Positives / It's all very new, you know / A female / Certainly random / The eye that nearly saw / Two fifteen string guitars for nice people / From an electric train / A world of too much sound / Another female / We're all going to Liverpool / Ha! ha! but reasonable. *(check)*

— In 1970, he worked with PINK FLOYD on their album 'ATOM HEART MOTHER'. The groups' main man returned the favour on below.

		Harvest	Harvest
Dec 70.	(lp; by RON GEESIN & ROGER WATERS) *(SHSP 4008)* *<SW 751>* **MUSIC FROM THE BODY (soundtrack)**		

– Our song / Sea shell and stone / Red staff writhe / Gentle breeze blew through life / Lick your partners / Bridge passage for three plastic teeth / Cain of life / Womb bit / Embryo thought / March past of the embryos / More than seven dwarfs in Penis land / Dance of the red corpuscles / Body transport / Breathe old folks ascension / Bedtime – Dream – Clime / Piddle in perspex / Embryonic womb talk / Mrs. Throat goes walking / Sea shell and soft stone / Give birth to a smile. *(cd-iss.1989 on 'E.M.I.'; CDP7 92548-2) (cd re-iss.Feb96; CZ 178)*

		Ron Geesin	not issued
May 73.	(lp) *(RON 28)* **AS HE STANDS**		-

– Roll 'em, bowl 'em-in three movements / Duet for two and a street market / On-through-out-up / Waiting for life / The middle of whose night? / Wrap a keyboard round a plant / Twist and knit for two guitars / Up above my heart / A cymbal and much electronics / To Roger Waters wherever you are / Mr. Pugeot's trot / Upon compositions / Concrete line up / Rise up Sebastian! / Looming view / Can't you stop that thing. *(check)*

1975.	(lp) *(RON 31)* **PATRUNS**		-

– B-wink / Octave creep / Double octave ripple / A, D & G black major throb / White note of calm / Dripped chromatic essence / Smoke hips (the time dance) / Grand E minor opening / E minor paint splash slap lash / E minor, lie down still / Pastrun spread / Platform twitch / Romanian rag tome shut / Chromatic trashers / Grand B major ending wink.

1977.	(lp) *(RON 323)* **RIGHT THROUGH**		-

		Headscope	not issued
1991.	(cd) *(HEDCD 001)* **FUNNY FROWN**		-
1993.	(cd) *(HEDCD 002)* **BLUEFUSE**		-

– compilations, etc

on 'K.P.M.' unless mentioned otherwise

1972.	(ltd-lp) *(KPM 1102)* **ELECTROSOUND**	-	- Library
1975.	(ltd-lp) *(KPM 1154)* **ELECTROSOUND VOL.2**	-	- Library
1977.	(ltd-lp) *(KPM 1201)* **ATMOSPHERES**	-	- Library
1988.	(ltd-cd) *Themes Int.; (TIM 11CD)* **MAGNIFICENT MACHINES**	-	- Library
Mar 94.	(cd) *Cherry Red; (CDBRED 110)* **HYSTERY – THE RON GEESIN STORY**		-

– Ron's adress / Parallel bar / Throat sweat / Mental passage / Whistling heart / Go! / Foretease / Twisted pair / Big imp / Morecambe Bay / Sit down, mamma / T'mith / Throb thencewards thrill / Smoked hips (the time dance) / Frenzy / Animal autos / Where daffodils do thrive / Upon composition / Can't you stop that thing / Vocal chords / Syncopot / Song of the wire / Affections for string quartet / With a smile up his nose, they entered / Three vignettes / Certainly random / A raise of eyebrows / No.8 Scalpel incision foxtrot.

Sep 95.	See For Miles; (cd) *(SEECD 433)* **A RAISE OF EYEBROWS / AS HE STANDS**		-

GENESIS

Formed: Godalming, Surrey, England . . . early 1967 by Charterhouse public school boys PETER GABRIEL and TONY BANKS (both ex-The GARDEN WALL). They teamed up with former members of The ANON; MICHAEL RUTHERFORD, ANTHONY PHILLIPS and CHRIS STEWART. Still at school, they signed to 'Decca', having sent demos to solo artist and producer JONATHAN KING. Their first 2 singles flopped, as did their 1969 MOODY BLUES-styled album, 'FROM GENESIS TO REVELATION', which only sold around 500 copies. Early in 1970, they were seen live by TONY STRATTON-SMITH, who became their manager after signing them to his 'Charisma' label. Their second album, 'TRESPASS', failed to break through, although it contained the live favourite and edited 45, 'THE KNIFE'. After its release, they found new members PHIL COLLINS and STEVE HACKETT, who replaced recent additions JOHN MAYHEW and ANTHONY PHILLIPS. Late in '71, they issued their set, 'NURSERY CRYME', which featured another two gems, 'THE MUSICAL BOX' and 'THE RETURN OF THE GIANT HOGWEED'. By this point the band transformed into one of the leading purveyors of progressive rock, bizarre extrovert GABRIEL proving a compelling, theatrical focus for the critically-lauded group. It was also the brief debut on lead vox for COLLINS, who sang on the track, 'FOR ABSENT FRIENDS'. A year later, with many gigs behind them, they had their first taste of chart success when 'FOXTROT' hit the UK Top 20. This contained the excellent concept piece, 'SUPPER'S READY', which lasted all of 23 minutes. In 1973, a live album of their best work so far, hit the Top 10, as did their studio follow-up, 'SELLING ENGLAND BY THE POUND'. This boasted another epic track, 'THE BATTLE OF EPPING FOREST', plus another COLLINS lead vocal in 'MORE FOOL ME'. Lifted from it, was a near Top 20 single, 'I KNOW WHAT I LIKE (IN YOUR WARDROBE)'. Late in 1974, they again made Top 10, with the concept double album, 'THE LAMB LIES DOWN ON BROADWAY', which was their first US Top 50 placing, the band performing the album in its entirety as part of a worldwide live show. Shortly after a last concert in May '75, GABRIEL left for a solo career, COLLINS taking over the vocal duties. Surprisingly, this did not harm the commercial appeal of the group when they returned in 1976 with the Top 3 album, 'A TRICK OF THE TAIL'. His drum-stool was filled for live gigs by the seasoned BILL BRUFORD, then CHESTER THOMPSON, who appeared on the 1977 live double album, 'SECONDS OUT'. This was also the last album to feature STEVE HACKETT, who also left for a lucrative solo career. In 1978, their next album, appropriately titled ' . . . AND THEN THERE WERE THREE' (COLLINS, BANKS & RUTHERFORD), hit No.3 and also climbed into the US Top 20. The 80's were even more fruitful for the band, as they hit the top spot in the UK with each successive album, also amassing a number of hit singles over the same period. During this era, PHIL COLLINS (who had moonlighted in his own BRAND X) scored a number of easier-listening hit singles and albums. Although they remain one of the stadium rock circuit's largest grossing bands, the band have lost all trace of their pioneering 70's sound. With PHIL COLLINS now out of the picture, BANKS and RUTHERFORD took on the relatively younger Scotsman, RAY WILSON, who had previously fronted chart-toppers, STILTSKIN. TONY BANKS also released some solo work, as did MIKE RUTHERFORD, who made coffee-table pop/rock with his outfit, MIKE + THE MECHANICS.
• **Songwriters:** GABRIEL lyrics and group compositions. From 1978, the trio collaborated on all work.

Recommended: NURSERY CRYME (*8) / TRESPASS (*6) / FOXTROT (*9) / GENESIS LIVE (*7) / SELLING ENGLAND BY THE POUND (*8) / THE LAMB LIES DOWN ON BROADWAY (*8) / A TRICK OF THE TAIL (*7) / WIND & WUTHERING (*6) / . . . AND THEN THERE WERE THREE (*6) / DUKE (*6) / ABACAB (*5) / GENESIS (*5) / INVISIBLE TOUCH (*5)

PETER GABRIEL (b.13 May'50, London, England) – vocals / **TONY BANKS** (b.27 Mar'51, East Heathly, Sussex, England) – keyboards, vocals / **ANTHONY PHILLIPS** (b.Dec'51, Putney, England) – guitar, vocals / **MICHAEL RUTHERFORD** (b. 2 Oct'50, Guildford, Surrey, England) – bass, guitar / **CHRIS STEWART** – drums

		Decca	Parrot
Feb 68.	(7") *(F 12735)* *<3018>* **THE SILENT SUN. / THAT'S ME**		
May 68.	(7") *(F 12775)* **A WINTER'S TALE. / ONE-EYED HOUND**		-

— **JOHN SILVER** – drums repl. CHRIS

Mar 69.	(lp; mono/stereo) *(LK/SKL 4990)* **FROM GENESIS TO REVELATION**		

– Where the sour turns to sweet / In the beginning / Fireside song / The serpent / Am I very wrong? / In the wilderness / The conqueror / In hiding / One day / Window / In limbo / The silent sun / A place to call my own. *(re-iss.1974 as 'IN THE BEGINNING'; same) (re-iss.Oct93 on 'Music Club' cd/c;)*

Jun 69.	(7") *(F 12949)* **WHERE THE SOUR TURNS TO SWEET. / IN HIDING**		-

— (Jul69) **JOHN MAYHEW** – drums repl. JOHN SILVER

		Charisma	Impulse
Oct 70.	(7"w-drawn) *(GS 1)* **LOOKING FOR SOMEONE. / VISIONS OF ANGELS**	-	-
Oct 70.	(lp) *(CAS 1020)* *<9295>* **TRESPASS**		

– Looking for someone / White mountain / Visions of angels / Stagnation / Dusk / The knife. *<US re-iss.1974 on 'ABC'; 816> (re-iss.Mar83; CHC/+MC 12)(hit 98; Apr84) (cd-iss.Jun88; CASCD 1020) (cd re-iss.Aug94; CASCDX 1020)*

Jun 71.	(7") *(CB 152)* **THE KNIFE (part 1). / THE KNIFE (part 2)**		-

— (Dec70) **GABRIEL, BANKS + RUTHERFORD** recruited new members **PHIL COLLINS** (b.31 Jan'51, Chiswick, London, England) – drums, vocals (ex-FLAMING YOUTH) repl. MAYHEW / **STEVE HACKETT** (b.12 Feb'50, London) – guitar (ex-QUIET WORLD) repl. ANTHONY PHILLIPS who went solo

		Charisma	Charisma
Nov 71.	(lp)(c) *(<CAS 1052>)(7208 552)* **NURSERY CRYME**		

– The musical box / For absent friends / The fountain of Salmacis / Seven stones / Harold the barrel / Harlequin / The return of the giant hogweed. *(hit UK No.39 May74) (re-iss.Feb84 lp/c; CHC/+MC 22); hit 68) (cd-iss.Sep85; CASCD 1052) (cd re-iss.Aug94; CASCDX 1052)*

May 72.	(7") *(CB 181)* **HAPPY THE MAN. / SEVEN STONES**		
Oct 72.	(lp)(c) *(<CAS 1058>)(7208 553)* **FOXTROT**	12	

– Get 'em out by Friday / Time-table / Watcher of the skies / Can-utility and the coastliners / Horizon / Supper's ready; (i) Lover's leap, (ii) The guaranteed eternal sanctuary man, (iii) Ikhaton and Itsacon and their band of merry men, (iv) How dare I be so beautiful, (v) Willow farm, (vi) Apocalypse in 9/8 co-starring the delicious talents of Gabble Ratchet, (vii) As sure as eggs is eggs (aching men's feets). *(re-iss.Sep83 lp/c; CHC/+MC 38) (cd-iss.Jul86; CASCD 1058) (cd re-iss.Aug94; CASCDX 1058)*

Feb 73.	(7") *<103>* **WATCHER OF THE SKIES. / WILLOW FARM**	-	
Jul 73.	(lp)(c) *(CLASS 1)(7299 288)* *<1066>* **GENESIS LIVE (live)**	9	May74

– Watcher of the skies / Get 'em out by Friday / The return of the giant hogweed / The musical box / The knife. *(re-iss.Feb86 lp/c; CHC/+MC 23) (cd-iss.Jul87; CLACD 1) (cd re-iss.Aug94; CLACDX 1)*

Oct 73.	(lp)(c) *(CAS 1074)(7208 554)* *<6060>* **SELLING ENGLAND BY THE POUND**	3	70

– Dancing in the moonlight knight / I know what I like (in your wardrobe) / Firth of fifth / More fool me / The battle of Epping Forest / After the ordeal / The cinema show / Aisle of plenty. *(re-iss.Oct86 lp/c; CHC/+MC 46) (cd-iss.Feb86; CASCD 1074) (cd re-iss.Aug94; CLACDX 1074) (re-iss.Feb97 on 'E.M.I.'; LPCENT 17)*

Mar 74.	(7") *(CB 224)* *<26002>* **I KNOW WHAT I LIKE (IN YOUR WARDROBE). / TWILIGHT ALEHOUSE**	21	

		Charisma	Atco
Nov 74.	(d-lp)(d-c) *(CGS 101)(7599 121)* *<401>* **THE LAMB LIES DOWN ON BROADWAY**	10	41

– The lamb lies down on Broadway / Fly on a windshield / Broadway melody of 1974 / Cuckoo cocoon / In the cage / The grand parade of lifeless packaging / Back in N.Y.C. / Hairless heart / Counting out time / Carpet crawlers / The chamber of 32 doors / / Lilywhite Lilith / The waiting room / Anyway / Here comes the supernatural anaesthetist / The lamia / Silent sorrow in empty boats / The colony of Slippermen (The arrival – A visit to the doktor – Raven) / Ravine / The light dies down on Broadway / Riding the scree / it. *(re-iss.Sep83 d-lp/c; CGS/+MC 101) (d-cd-iss.Feb86; CGSCD 1) (cd re-iss.Aug94; CGSCDX 1)*

Nov 74.	(7") *(CB 238)* **COUNTING OUT TIME. / RIDING THE SCREE**		-
Dec 74.	(7") *<7013>* **COUNTING OUT TIME. / THE LAMB LIES DOWN ON BROADWAY**	-	

Apr 75. (7") *(CB 251)* **CARPET CRAWLERS. / THE WAITING ROOM (evil jam) (live)** [ ] [-]

—— Now just a quartet when PETER GABRIEL left to go solo.

Feb 76. (lp)(c) *(CDS 4001) <129>* **A TRICK OF THE TAIL** [3] [31]
– Dance on a volcano / Entangled / Squonk / Mad mad Moon / Robbery, assault and battery / Ripples / A trick of the tail / Los endos. *(re-iss.Sep83 lp/c; CDS/+MC 4001) (cd-iss.Apr86; CDSCD 4001) (re-iss.Apr90 on 'Virgin' lp/c; OVED/+C 306) (cd re-iss.Oct94; CDSCDX 4001)*

Mar 76. (7") *(CB 277)* **A TRICK OF THE TAIL. / RIPPLES** [ ] [-]
Mar 76. (7") *<7050>* **RIPPLES. / ENTANGLED** [-] [ ]
Jan 77. (lp)(c) *(CDS 4005)(7208 611) <144>* **WIND AND WUTHERING** [7] [26]
– Eleventh Earl of Mar / One for the vine / Your own special way / Wot gorilla? / All in a mouse's night / Blood on the rooftops / Unquiet slumbers for the sleepers . . .In that quiet Earth / Afterglow. *(re-iss.Sep83 lp/c; CDS/+MC 4005) (cd-iss.Apr86; CDSCD 4005) (re-iss.Apr90 on 'Virgin' lp/c; OVED/+C 332) (cd re-iss.Oct94; CDSCDX 4005)*

Feb 77. (7") *(CB 300)* **YOUR OWN SPECIAL WAY. / IT'S YOURSELF** [43] [-]
Feb 77. (7") *<7076>* **YOUR OWN SPECIAL WAY. / . . .IN THAT QUIET EARTH** [-] [62]
May 77. (7"ep) *(GEN 001)* **SPOT THE PIGEON** [14] [-]
– Match of the day / Inside and out / Pigeons. *(cd-ep-iss.1988 on 'Virgin'; CDT 40)*

—— added **BILL BRUFORD** – drums (ex-YES, ex-KING CRIMSON) **CHESTER THOMPSON** – drums (ex-FRANK ZAPPA) they were both used on live album below, with CHESTER augmenting on tours.

Oct 77. (d-lp)(d-c) *(GE 2001)(7649 067) <9002>* **SECONDS OUT (live)** [4] [47]
– Sqounk / Carpet crawlers / Robbery, assault and battery / Afterglow / Firth of fifth / I know what I like (in your wardrobe) / The lamb lies down on Broadway / The musical box / Supper's ready / The cinema show / Dance on a volcano / Los endos. *(re-iss.Sep83 d-lp/d-c; GE/+MC 2001) (d-cd-iss.Nov85; GECD 2001) (d-cd re-iss.Oct94; GECDX 2001)*

—— (Jun77) Now a trio of **COLLINS, BANKS & RUTHERFORD** when STEVE HACKETT continued solo career.

Charisma Atlantic

Mar 78. (7") *(CB 309)* **FOLLOW YOU FOLLOW ME. / BALLAD OF BIG** [7] [-]
Mar 78. (7") *<3474>* **FOLLOW YOU FOLLOW ME. / INSIDE AND OUT** [-] [23]
Apr 78. (lp)(c) *(CDS 4010)(7208 619) <19173>* **. . .AND THEN THERE WERE THREE** [3] [14]
– Down and out / Undertow / Ballad of big / Snowbound / Burning rope / Deep in the motherlode / Many too many / Scene from a night's dream / Say it's alright Joe / The lady lies / Follow you follow me. *(re-iss.Sep83 lp/c; CDS/+MC 4010) (cd-iss.May83; 800 059-2) (re-iss.Aug91 on 'Virgin' lp/c; OVED/+C 368) (cd re-iss.Oct94; CDSCDX 4010)*

Jun 78. (7") *(CB 315)* **MANY TOO MANY. / THE DAY THE LIGHT WENT OUT IN VANCOUVER** [43] [-]
Jul 78. (7") *<3511>* **SCENE FROM A NIGHT'S DREAM. / DEEP IN THE MOTHERLODE** [-] [ ]
Mar 80. (7") *(CB 356)* **TURN IT ON AGAIN. / BEHIND THE LINES (part 2)** [8] [-]
Mar 80. (lp/c) *(CBR/+C 101) <16014>* **DUKE** [1] [11]
– Behind the lines / Duchess / Guide vocal / Man of our time / Misunderstanding / Heathaze / Turn it on again / Alone tonight / Cul-de-sac / Please don't ask / Duke's end / Duke's travels. *(re-iss.Sep83 lp/c; CBR/+C 101) (cd-iss.Apr85; CBRCD 101) (re-iss.Mar91 on 'Virgin' lp/c; OVED/+C 345) (cd re-iss.Oct94; CBRCDX 101)*

May 80. (7") *(CB 363)* **DUCHESS. / OPEN DOOR** [46] [-]
May 80. (7") *<3662>* **MISUNDERSTANDING. / BEHIND THE LINES** [-] [14]
Sep 80. (7") *(CB 369)* **MISUNDERSTANDING. / EVIDENCE OF AUTUMN** [42] [-]
Sep 80. (7") *<3751>* **TURN IT ON AGAIN. / EVIDENCE OF AUTUMN** [-] [58]
Aug 81. (7") *(CB 388)* **ABACAB. / ANOTHER RECORD** [9] [-]
Sep 81. (lp/c) *(CBR/+C 102) <19313>* **ABACAB** [1] [7]
– Abacab / No reply at all / Me and Sarah Jane / Kep it dark / Dodo / Lurker / Who dunnit? / Man on the corner / Like it or not / Another record. *(cd-iss.May83; 800 044-2) (re-iss.Mar91 on 'Virgin' lp/c; OVED/+C 344) (cd re-iss.Oct94; CBRCDX 102)*

Oct 81. (7") *(CB 391)* **KEEP IT DARK. / NAMINANU** [33] [-]
(12"+=) *(CB 391-12)* – Abacab (long version).
Oct 81. (7") *<3858>* **NO REPLY AT ALL. / HEAVEN LOVE MY LIFE** [-] [29]
Jan 82. (7") *<3891>* **ABACAB. / WHO DUNNIT?** [-] [26]
Feb 82. (7") *(CB 393) <4025>* **MAN IN THE CORNER. / SUBMARINE** [41] [40] Mar82
May 82. (7") *<4053>* **PAPERLATE. / YOU MIGHT RECALL** [-] [32]
May 82. (7"ep) *(GEN 1)* **3 X 3 E.P.** [10] [-]
– Paperlate / You might recall / Me and Virgil.
Jun 82. (d-lp/d-c) *(GE/+MC 2002) <2000>* **THREE SIDES LIVE (live except ***)** [2] [10]
– Turn it on again / Dodo / Abacab / Behind the lines / Duchess / Me and Sarah Jane / Follow you follow me / Misunderstanding / In the cage / Afterglow / One for the vine * / Fountain of Salmacis * / Watcher of the skies * / It * / Paperlate *** / You might recall *** / Me and Virgil *** / Evidence of Autumn *** / Open door *** / You might recall II ***. *(cd-iss.Apr85; GECD 2002) <US-cd.repl.* w/ The cinema show + The colony of Slippermen> (re-iss.Apr92 d-lp/c; DOVD/+C 2) (cd re-iss.Oct94; GECDX 2002)*

Virgin Atco

Aug 83. (7"/ext.12") *(MAMA 1/+12) <89770>* **MAMA. / IT'S GONNA GET BETTER** [4] [73]
(cd-ep.iss.Jun88; CDT 5)
Oct 83. (lp/c/cd) *(GEN LP/MC/CD 1) <80116>* **GENESIS** [1] [9]
– Mama / That's all / Home by the sea / Second home by the sea / Illegal alien / Taking it all too hard / Just a job to do / Silver rainbow / It's gonna get better. *(re-iss.Jul87; same)*

Nov 83. (7") *(TATA 1)* **THAT'S ALL. / TAKING IT ALL TOO HARD** [16] [-]
(12"+=) *(TATAY 1)* – Firth of fifth (live).
Nov 83. (7") *<89724>* **THAT'S ALL. / SECOND HOME BY THE SEA** [-] [6]
Feb 84. (7"/7"sha-pic-d) *(AL/+S 1) <89698>* **ILLEGAL ALIEN. / TURN IT ON AGAIN (live)** [46] [44]
(12"+=) *(AL 1-12)* – ('A'extended).

Jun 84. (7") *<89656>* **TAKING IT ALL TOO HARD. / SILVER RAINBOW** [-] [50]
May 86. (7",7"clear) *(GENS 1)* **INVISIBLE TOUCH. / THE LAST DOMINO** [15] [1]
(12"+=) *(GENS 1-12)* – ('A'extended).
Jun 86. (lp/c/cd) *(GEN LP/MC/CD 2) <81641>* **INVISIBLE TOUCH** [1] [3]
– Invisible touch / Tonight, tonight, tonight / Land of confusion / In too deep / Anything she does / Domino:- In the glow of the night – The last domino / Throwing it all away / The Brazilian. *(pic-cd.Dec88; GENCDP 2)*

Aug 86. (7"/12") *(GENS 2/+12)* **IN TOO DEEP. / DO THE NEUROTIC** [19] [-]
Aug 86. (7") *<89372>* **THROWING IT ALL AWAY. / DO THE NEUROTIC** [-] [4]
Nov 86. (7") *(GENS 3) <89336>* **LAND OF CONFUSION. / FEEDING THE FIRE** [14] [4] Oct86
(12"+=) *(GENS 3-12)* – Dance the neurotic.
(cd-s++=) *(SNEG 3-12)* – ('A'extended).
Mar 87. (7"/12") *(GENS 4/+12)* **TONIGHT, TONIGHT, TONIGHT. / IN THE GLOW OF THE NIGHT** [18] [3] Feb87
(12"+=/cd-s+=) *(GENS/DRAW 4-12)* – Paperlate / ('A'ext.remix).
(cd-s+=) *(CDEP 1)* – Invisible touch (extended) / ('A'-John Potoker remix).
Apr 87. (7") *<89316>* **IN TOO DEEP. / I'D RATHER BE WITH YOU** [-] [3]
Jun 87. (7") *(GENS 5)* **THROWING IT ALL AWAY. / I'D RATHER BE WITH YOU** [22] [-]
(12"+=/c-s+=) *(GENS/+C 5-12)* – Invisible touch (live).
Oct 91. (7"/c-s) *(GENS/+C 6) <87571>* **NO SON OF MINE. / LIVING FOREVER** [6] [13]
(12"+=/cd-s+=) *(GENS/GENCD 6)* – Invisible touch (live).
Nov 91. (cd/c/d-lp) *(GEN CD/MC/LP 3) <82344>* **WE CAN'T DANCE** [1] [4]
– No son of mine / Jesus he knows me / Driving the last spike / I can't dance / Never a time / Dreaming while you sleep / Tell me why / Living forever / Hold on my heart / Way of the world / Since I lost you / Fading lights.

Jan 92. (7"/c-s) *(GENS/+C 7) <87532>* **I CAN'T DANCE. / ON THE SHORELINE** [7] [7]
(cd-s+=) *(GENDG 7)* – In too deep (live) / That's all (live).
(cd-s+=) *(GENDX 7)* – ('A'-sex mix).
Apr 92. (7"/c-s) *(GENS/+C 8) <87481>* **HOLD ON MY HEART. / WAY OF THE WORLD** [16] [12]
(cd-s+=) *(GENDG 8)* – Your own special way (live).
(cd-s+=) *(GENDX 8)* – Home by the sea.
Jul 92. (7"/c-s) *(GENS/+C 9) <87454>* **JESUS HE KNOWS ME. / HEARTS OF FIRE** [20] [23]
(cd-s+=) *(GENDG 9)* – I can't dance (mix).
(cd-s+=) *(GENDX 9)* – Land of confusion (rehearsal version).
Nov 92. (cd/c/d-lp) *(GEN CD/MC/LP 4) <82452>* **THE WAY WE WALK VOLUME 1: THE SHORTS (live)** [3] [35]
– Land of confusion / No son of mine / Jesus he knows me / Throwing it all away / I can't dance / Mama / Hold on my heart / That's all / In too deep / Tonight, tonight, tonight / Invisible touch.

Nov 92. (7"/c-s) *(GENS/+C 10)* **INVISIBLE TOUCH (live). / ABACAB (live)** [7] [-]
(cd-s+=) *(GENDG 10)* – The Brazilian.
Nov 92. (c-s/cd-s) *<87411>* **NEVER A TIME. / ?** [-] [21]
Jan 93. (cd/c/lp) *(GEN CD/MC/LP 5)* **LIVE / THE WAY WE WALK VOLUME 2: THE LONGS (live)** [1] [ ]
– Old medley: Dance on a volcano – Lamb lies down on Broadway – The musical box – Firth of fifth – I know what I like . . . / Driving the fast spike / Domino: part I – In the glow of the night, part II – The last domino / Home by the sea – Second home by the sea / Drum duet.

Feb 93. (7"/c-s) *(GENS/+C 11)* **TELL ME WHY. / DREAMING WHILE YOU SLEEP** [40] [ ]
(cd-s+=) *(GENDG 11)* – Tonight, tonight, tonight.

– compilations etc. –

on 'Charisma' unless mentioned otherwise

May 74. (d-lp-box) *(CGS 102)* **GENESIS COLLECTION VOLUME ONE** [ ] [-]
– (TRESPASS / NURSERY CRYME)
May 74. (d-lp-box) *(CGS 103)* **GENESIS COLLECTION VOLUME TWO** [ ] [-]
– (FOXTROT / SELLING ENGLAND BY THE POUND)
May 76. (lp/c) *Decca; (ROOTS/KRTC 1)* **ROCK ROOTS: GENESIS** [ ] [-]
– (debut lp + early 45's)
Mar 83. (d-c) *(CASMC 112)* **FOXTROT / SELLING ENGLAND BY THE POUND** [ ] [-]
Apr 86. (lp/pic-lp) *Metal Masters; (MACHM/+P 4)* **WHEN THE SOUR TURNS TO SWEET** [ ] [-]
(cd-iss.Oct87; MACD 4) (re-iss.Jul91;)
Mar 87. (cd) *London; (820496-2)* **AND THE WORLD WAS** (early) [ ] [-]
Jun 88. (7") *Old Gold; (OG 9263)* **I KNOW WHAT I LIKE (IN YOUR WARDROBE). / COUNTING OUT TIME** [ ] [-]
Jun 88. (7") *Old Gold; (OG 9264)* **FOLLOW YOU FOLLOW ME. / A TRICK OF THE TAIL** [ ] [-]
Nov 90. Virgin; (pic-cd-box) *(TPAK 1)* **GENESIS CD COLLECTORS EDITION** [ ] [ ]
– (TRESPASS / NURSERY CRYME / FOXTROT)

—— PHIL COLLINS solo pop material (see book GREAT ROCK DISCOGRAPHY)

TONY BANKS

Charisma Charisma

Oct 79. (7") *(CB 344)* **FOR A WHILE. / FROM THE UNDERTOW** [ ] [-]
Oct 79. (lp/c) *(CAS/+MC 1148) <2207>* **A CURIOUS FEELING** [21] [ ]
– From the undertow / Lucky me / The lie / After the lie / A curious feeling / Forever morning / You / Somebody else's dream / The waters of Lethe / For a while / In the dark. *(re-iss.Oct86 lp/c; CHC/+MC 42) (cd-iss.1988; CASCD 1148)*

Jul 80. (7") *(CB 365)* **A CURIOUS FEELING. / FOR A WHILE** [ ] [-]
Apr 83. (7"/12") *(BANKS 1/+12)* **THIS IS LOVE. / CHARM** [ ] [-]
May 83. (7") *(A 9825)* **THE WICKED LADY. / (part 2)** [ ] [-]

—— (above from the film soundtrack 'THE WICKED LADY; on 'WEA')

Jun 83. (lp/c) *(TB/+MC 1)* **THE FUGITIVE** [50] [ ]

– This is love / Man of spells / And the wheels keep turning / Say you'll never leave me / Thirty three's / By you / At the edge of night / Charm / Moving under. *(re-iss.Oct86 lp/c; CHC/+MC 43) (cd-iss.1988; TBCD 1)*

Aug 83. (7") *(BANKS 2)* **AND THE WHEELS KEEP TURNING. / MAN OF SPELLS** [ ] [-]
(12"+=) *(BANKS 2/+12)* – Sometime never.

— (below with JIM DIAMOND and TOYAH on vocals)

Sep 85. (7"ep) *(CBEP 415)* **TONY BANKS** [ ] [-]
– Red wing (instrumental) / You call this victory / Line of symmetry.

Oct 86. (7"; by FISH & TONY BANKS) *(CB 426)* **SHORT CUT TO NOWHERE. / SMILIN JACK CASEY** [ ] [-]
(12"+=) *(CB 426-12)* – K.2.

Jul 87. (cd) *(CASCD 1173)* **SOUNDTRACKS** ('Quicksilver' // 'Lorca And The Outlaws') [ ] [ ]
– Short cut to nowhere / Smilin' Jack Casey / Quicksilver suite: Rebirth – Gypsy – Final chase // You call this victory / Lion of symmetry / Redwing suite: Redwing – Lorca – Kid and Detective Droid – Lift off – Death of Abby. *(re-iss.Nov89 lp/c; CHC/+MC 82)*

BANKSTATEMENT

TONY BANKS with friends, etc.

Virgin / Atlantic

Jul 89. (7") *(VS 1200)* **THROWBACK. / THURSDAY THE 12th** [ ] [-]
(12"+=/cd-s+=) *(VS T/CD 1200)* – This is love.

Aug 89. (lp/c/cd) *(V/TCV/CDV 2600)* **BANKSTATEMENT** [ ] [ ]
– Throwback / I'll be waiting / Queen of darkness / That night / Raincloud / he border / Big man / A house needs a roof / The more I hide it. *(cd+=)*– Diamonds aren't so bad / Thursday the 12th.

Oct 89. (7") *(VS 1208)* **I'LL BE WAITING. / DIAMONDS AREN'T SO BAD** [ ] [-]
(12"+=/cd-s+=) *(VS T/CD 1208)* – And the wheels keep turning.

TONY BANKS

solo, with guest vocals **ANDY TAYLOR, FISH, JAYNEY KLIMEK**

May 91. (7"/c-s) **I WANNA CHANGE THE SCORE. / HERO FOR AN HOUR** [ ] [-]
(12"+=) – Big man (BANKSTATEMENT).
(cd-s++=) – The waters of Lethe.

Jun 91. (cd/c/lp) *(CD/TC+/V 2658)* **STILL** [ ] [ ]
– Red day on blue street / Angel face / The gift / Still it takes me by surprise / Hero for an hour / I wanna change the score / Water out of wine / Another murder of a day / Back to back / The final curtain.

MIKE RUTHERFORD

Charisma / Passport

Jan 80. (7") *(CB 353)* **WORKING IN LINE. / COMPRESSION** [ ] [-]

Feb 80. (lp) *(CAS 1149)* <9843> **SMALLCREEP'S DAY** [13] [ ]
– Smallcreep's day: Between the tick and the tock – Working in line – After hours – Cats and rats in the neighbourhood – Smallcreep alone – Out into the daylight – At the end of the day / Moonshine / Time and time again / Romani / Every road / Overnight job. *(re-iss.Oct86 lp/c; CHC/+MC 53) (cd-iss.Jun89; CASCD 1149)*

Mar 80. (7") **WORKING IN LINE. / MOONSHINE** [-] [ ]

Jul 80. (7") *(CB 364)* **TIME AND TIME AGAIN. / AT THE END OF THE DAY** [ ] [-]

W.E.A. / Atlantic

Aug 82. (7") *(K 79331)* <89976> **HALFWAY THERE. / A DAY TO REMEMBER** [ ] [ ] Nov82

Aug 82. (7") <89981> **A DAY TO REMEMBER. / MAXINE** [-] [ ]

Sep 82. (lp/c) *(K/K4 99249)* <80015> **ACTING VERY STRANGE** [23] [ ]
– Acting very strange / A day to remember / Maxine / Halfway there / Who's fooling who / Couldn't get arrested / I don't wanna know / Hideaway.

Oct 82. (7"/12") *(RUTH 1/+T)* **ACTING VERY STRANGE. / COULDN'T GET ARRESTED** [ ] [-]

Jan 83. (7") *(U 9967)* **HIDEAWAY. / CALYPSO** [ ] [-]

— MIKE then formed the pop outfit MIKE + THE MECHANICS (see book GREAT ROCK DISCOGRAPHY)

GENTLE GIANT

Formed: Portsmouth, England ... 1966 as SIMON DUPREE & THE BIG SOUND, by SHULMAN brothers DEREK, RAY and PHIL. Early in '67, they had a UK Top 50 hit with 'I SEE THE LIGHT'. By the end of the year, 'KITES', gave them a Top 10 smash, although they soon opted out of the psychedelic pop market in favour of the burgeoning prog-rock scene. Late in 1969, the three brothers, with three new recruits (KERRY MINEAR, GARY GREEN and MARTIN SMITH), re-launched themselves as the more experimental GENTLE GIANT. A year later, they appeared on the pivotal 'Vertigo' label, their eponymous debut album regaining support from stalwart Radio One DJ, ALAN 'Fluff' FREEMAN. Their fourth album, 'OCTOPUS' (1972), although not a major success in Britain, it hit the Top 200 in North America. They might have built upon this Stateside interest, but for Columbia's decision not to release their next project, 'IN A GLASS HOUSE'. However, in 1974, they finally cracked the Top 100 with their much-improved, 'THE POWER AND GLORY'. Signing a new deal in Britain with 'Chrysalis' records, their seventh album, 'FREE HAND', again only found a paying audience across the water. However, it did contain more impressive vocal gymnastics, much in evidence on the opening two tracks, 'JUST THE SAME' and 'ON REFLECTION'. The band was subsequently crushed under the jack-booted heels of punk rock, although they did soldier on under 1980. DEREK moved to New York, becoming an A&R executive and going on to sign hard-rock acts, CINDERELLA and KINGDOM COME. • **Songwriters:** MINNEAR and the SHULMANS collaborated on most recordings. SIMON DUPREE covered; DAY TIME, NIGHT TIME (Mike Hugg of Manfred Mann). • **Trivia:** MINNEAR had graduated from the Royal Academy Of Music in the late 60's.

Recommended: GIANT STEPS ...THE FIRST FIVE YEARS (*6) / FREE HAND (*6)

SIMON DUPREE & THE BIG SOUND

DEREK SHULMAN (b. 2 Feb'47, Glasgow, Scotland) – vocals / **RAY SCHULMAN** (b. 8 Dec'49, Portsmouth, England) – lead guitar / **PHIL SCHULMAN** (b.27 Aug'37, Glasgow) – saxophone, trumpet / **ERIC HINE** – keyboards / **PETE O'FLAHERTY** – bass / **TONY RANSLEY** – drums

Parlophone / Tower

Dec 66. (7") *(R 5542)* **I SEE THE LIGHT. / IT IS FINISHED** [45] [-]

Feb 67. (7") *(R 5574)* <347> **RESERVATIONS. / YOU NEED A MAN** [ ] [ ]

May 67. (7") *(R 5594)* <427> **DAY TIME, NIGHT TIME. / I'VE SEEN IT ALL BEFORE** [ ] [ ]

Aug 67. (lp; mono/stereo) *(PCM/PCS 7029)* <T 5097> **WITHOUT RESERVATIONS** [39] [ ]
– Medley: Sixty minutes of your love – A lot of love / Love / Get off my Bach / There's a little playhouse / Day time, night time / I see the light / What is soul / Teacher, teacher / Amen / Who cares / Reservations. *(re-dist.1969; same)*

Oct 67. (7") *(R 5646)* **KITES. / LIKE THE SUN LIKE THE FIRE** [9] [ ]

Mar 68. (7") *(R 5670)* **FOR WHOM THE BELL TOLLS. / SLEEP** [43] [ ]

May 68. (7") *(R 5697)* **PART OF MY PAST. / THIS STORY NEVER ENDS** [ ] [ ]

Sep 68. (7") *(R 5727)* **THINKING ABOUT MY LIFE. / VELVET AND LACE** [ ] [ ]

Nov 68. (7"; as The MOLES) *(R 5743)* **WE ARE THE MOLES (part 2) / (part 2)** [ ] [-]

Feb 69. (7") *(R 5757)* **BROKEN HEARTED PIRATES. / SHE GAVE ME THE SUN** [ ] [-]

— **GERRY KENWORTHY** – keyboards repl. HINE

Nov 69. (7") *(R 5816)* **THE EAGLE FLIES TONIGHT. / GIVE IT ALL BACK** [ ] [-]

— Split late '69. The SHULMAN's formed GENTLE GIANT while the others left the business.

– compilations etc. –

Nov 78. (7"ep) *E.M.I.; (EMI 2893)* **SIMON DUPREE & THE BIG SOUND** [ ] [-]
– Kites / For whom the bells toll / Reservations / I see the light.

Mar 82. (lp/c) *See For Miles; (CM/+K 109)* **AMEN** [ ] [-]
– Kites / Like the sun like the fire / Sleep / For whom the bells toll / Broken hearted pirates / 60 Minutes of your love / A lot of love / Love / Get off my Bach / There's a little picture playhouse / Day time, night time / I see the light / What is soul / Amen / Who cares / She gave me the sun / Thinking about my life / It is finished / I've seen it all before / You need a man / Reservations. *(re-iss.Dec86 as 'KITES'; same) (cd-iss.May93 & May97 as 'KITES' on 'See For Miles'; SEECD 368)*

Mar 87. (7") *Old Gold; (OG 9655)* **KITES. / (b-side by other artist)** [ ] [-]

GENTLE GIANT

DEREK SHULMAN – vocals, bass, saxophone / **RAY SHULMAN** – guitar, bass, violin, keyboards, drums / **PHIL SHULMAN** – saxophone, trumpet / **KERRY MINNEAR** (b.2 Apr'48, Salisbury, England) – keyboards, vocals (ex-RUST) / **GARY GREEN** (b.20 Nov'50, Stroud Green, England) – guitar, vocals / **MARTIN SMITH** – drums (ex-MOJOS)

Vertigo / Vertigo

Nov 70. (lp) *(6360 020)* **GENTLE GIANT** [ ] [-]
– Giant / Funny ways / Alucard / Isn't it quiet and cold / Nothing at all / Why not? / The Queen. *(cd-iss.Aug89 on 'Line'; LICD 900722) (cd re-iss.Nov94 on 'Repertoire';) (cd re-iss.Feb97 on 'Mercury'; 842624-2)*

Aug 71. (lp) *(6360 041)* <1005> **ACQUIRING THE TASTE** [ ] [ ]
– Pantagruel's nativity / Edge of twilight / The house, the street, the room / Acquiring the taste / Wreck / The Moon is down / Black cat / Plain truth. *(cd-iss.Oct89 on 'Line'; LICD 900726) (cd re-iss.Aug90; 842917-2) (cd re-iss.Feb97 on 'Mercury'; 842917-2)*

— **MALCOLM MORTIMER** – drums repl. MARTIN

Vertigo / Columbia

Jul 72. (lp) *(6360 070)* <31649> **THREE FRIENDS** [ ] [ ]
– (prologue) / Schooldays / Working all day / Peel the paint / Mister Class and quality? / Three friends. *(cd-iss.Oct89 on 'Line'; LICD 900730)*

— **JOHN WEATHERS** (b.Wales) – drums (ex-GRAHAM BOND, ex-EYES OF BLUE, ex-ANCIENT GREASE, ex-PETE BROWN, etc.) repl. MALCOLM

Dec 72. (lp) *(6360 080)* <32022> **OCTOPUS** [ ] [ ]
– The advent of Panurge / Raconteur troubadour / A cry for everyone / Knots / The boys in the band / Dog's life / Knots / Think of me with kindness / River. *(cd-iss.Oct89 on 'Line'; LICD 900736) (cd re-iss.Nov94 on 'Repertoire';) (cd re-iss.Feb97 on 'Mercury'; 842694-2)*

— now quintet of **DEREK, RAY, KERRY, GARY + JOHN** when PHIL left.

W.W.A. / Capitol

Dec 73. (lp) *(WWA 002)* **IN A GLASS HOUSE** [ ] [-]
– The runaway / An inmate's lullaby / Way of life / A reunion / Experience / In a glass house / Index. *(cd-iss.Dec92 on 'Road Goes On Forever'; RGFCD 1001) (cd re-iss.Jul94 on 'Terrapin Truckin'; TRUCKCD 1)*

Jan 74. (7") *(WWP 1001)* **IN A GLASS HOUSE. / AN INMATE'S LULLABY** [ ] [-]

Oct 74. (lp) *(WWA 010)* <11337> **THE POWER AND THE GLORY** [ ] [78]
– Proclamation / So sincere / Aspirations / Playing the game / Cogs in cogs / No god's a man / The face / Valedictory. *(cd-iss.Dec92 on 'Road Goes On Forever'; RGFCD 1002)*

Nov 74. (7") *(WWS 017)* **THE POWER AND THE GLORY. / PLAYING THE GAME** [ ] [-]

Chrysalis Capitol

Aug 75. (lp/c) *(CHR/ZCHR 1093) <11428>* **FREE HAND** 48
– Just the same / On reflection / Free hand / Time to kill / His last voyage / Talybont / Mobile. *(cd-iss.Aug93 on 'Road Goes On Forever'; RGFCD 1004) (cd-iss.Jul94 on 'Terrapin Truckin'; TRUCKCD 4)*

Apr 76. (lp/c) *(CHR/ZCHR 1115) <11532>* **INTERVIEW**
– Interview / Give it back / Design / Another show / Empty city / Timing / I lost my head. *(cd-iss.Mar93 on 'Road Goes On Forever'; RGFCD 1005) (cd-iss.Jul94 on 'Terrapin Truckin'; TRUCKCD 5) (cd re-iss.Oct95 on 'One Way';)*

Jan 77. (d-lp/d-c) *(CTY/ZCTY 1133) <11592>* **PLAYING THE FOOL – LIVE (live)** 89
– Just the same / Proclamation / On reflection / Excerpts from Octopus (Boys in the band, etc) / Funny ways / In a glass house / So sincere / Free hand / Sweet Georgia Brown (breakdown in Brussels) / Peel the paint / I lost my head. *(re-iss.May89 on 'Essential' d-lp/cd; ESS LP/CD 006) (cd re-iss.Dec94 on 'Terrapin Truckin'; TRUCKCD 9)*

Aug 77. (lp/c) *(CHR/ZCHR 1152) <11696>* **THE MISSING PIECE** 81
– Two weeks in Spain / I'm turning around / Betcha thought we couldn't do it / Who do you think you are? / Mountain time / As old as you're young / Memories of old days / Winning / For nobody. *(cd re-iss.Aug93 on 'Road Goes On Forever'; RGFCD 1006) (cd-iss.Jul94 on 'Terrapin Truckin'; TRUCKCD 6)*

Aug 77. (7") *(CHS 2160)* **I'M TURNING AROUND. / JUST THE SAME (live)** -

Sep 77. (7") *<4484>* **I'M TURNING AROUND. / COGS IN COGS** -

Oct 77. (7") *(CHS 2181)* **TWO WEEKS IN SPAIN. / FREE HAND** -

Sep 78. (7") *(CHS 2245)* **THANK YOU. / SPOOKY BOOGIE** -

Sep 78. (lp/c) *(CHR/ZCHR 1186) <11813>* **GIANT FOR A DAY**
– Word from the wise / Thank you / Giant for a day / Spooky boogie / Take me / Little brown bag / Friends / No stranger / It's only goodbye / Rock climber. *(cd-iss.Aug93 on 'Road Goes On Forever'; RGFCD 7) (cd-iss.Jul94 on 'Terrapin Truckin'; TRUCKCD 7)*

Jan 79. (7") *(CHS 2270)* **WORD FROM THE WISE. / NO STRANGER** -

Jan 79. (7") *<4652>* **WORD FROM THE WISE. / SPOOKY BOOGIE** -

Chrysalis Columbia

Aug 80. (lp/c) *(CHR/ZCHR 1285)* **CIVILIAN**
– Convenience / All through the night / Shadows on the street / Number one / Underground / I'm a camera / Inside out / It's not imagination. *(cd-iss.Jul94 on 'Terrapin Truckin'; TRUCKCD 8)*

— Split 1980. RAY SHULMAN went into production. WEATHERS joined MAN.

– compilations, others, etc. –

on 'Vertigo' unless otherwise mentioned

Nov 75. (d-lp) *(6641 334)* **GIANT STEPS . . . (THE FIRST FIVE YEARS) 1970-75** -
– Giant / Alucard / Nothing at all / Plain truth / Prologue / A cry for everyone / Why not / Peel the paint / Mister Class and quality? / River / The face / The runaway / Power and the glory / Playing the game / In a glass house.

Oct 77. (d-lp) *(6641 629)* **PRETENTIOUS (FOR THE SAKE OF IT)** -

Aug 81. (lp/c) *(6381/7215 045)* **GREATEST HITS** - - Dutch

Apr 94. (cd) *Terrapin Truckin'; (TRUCKCD 1010)* **THE LAST TIME (LIVE 1980)** -

Dec 94. (cd) *Windsong; (WINCD 066)* **IN CONCERT (live)** -

Jul 96. (cd) *Strange Fruit; (BOJCD 018)* **LIVE IN CONCERT (live)** -

Sep 96. (cd) *Red Steel; (RMCCD 0205)* **LAST STEPS (live 1980)** - -

GHOST

Formed: Birmingham, England . . ..1969 by former MASTER SINGERS and OPPOSITE LOOK member SHIRLEY KENT. In 1966, she and the singers released an EP, 'THE MASTER SINGERS AND SHIRLEY KENT FOR CHAREC 67' (Keele University 103). It included two of her songs; 'ONE DAY OLD' & 'BACK'. In 1969, they released their debut 45, 'WHEN YOU'RE DEAD', clearly influenced by the US West Coast sound. The following year's similarly titled album (now worth over £100) was more a fusion of psychedelic-tinted blues and folk, KENT drawing comparisons to SANDY DENNY. After one more single, however, the band split, KENT later returning in 1975 with a new folk outfit, VIRGINIA TREE.

Recommended: WHEN YOU'RE DEAD – ONE SECOND (*6)

SHIRLEY KENT – vocals, acoustic guitar / **PAUL EASTMONT** – vocals, guitar (ex-VELVETT FOGG) / **TERRY GUY** – keyboards / **DANIEL MacGUIRE** – bass / **CHARLIE GRIMA** – drums

Gemini not issued

Dec 69. (7") *(GMS 007)* **WHEN YOU'RE DEAD. / INDIAN MAID** -

Jan 70. (lp) *(GME 1004)* **WHEN YOU'RE DEAD – ONE SECOND** -
– Too late to cry / Hearts and flowers / Time is my enemy / For one second / In Heaven / When you're dead / etc. *(re-iss.May87 on 'Bam Caruso'; KIRI 077)*

Aug 70. (7") *(GMS 014)* **I'VE GOT TO GET TO KNOW YOU. / FOR ONE SECOND** -

— SHIRLEY vacated to re-join The OPPOSITE LOOK and they evolved into RESURRECTION then below reformation . . .

VIRGINIA TREE

(aka **SHIRLEY KENT, PAUL EASTMONT, TERRY GUY** + 3)

Minstrel not issued

1975. (lp-ltd.) *(0001)* **FRESH OUT** -
– I'm glad there is you / Let us go dancing / Hiding there / Harlequin and Columbine / Make believe girl / In my garden. *(re-iss.1989 by SHIRLEY KENT as 'FOREVER A WILLOW' on 'Magic Spell'+=; 0001)–* A dedication to Bertram George Tipping / My dad / In my garden (orchestral).

— SHIRLEY gave up this project in 1977 and went into production work.

SHIRLEY KENT

Tadpole not issued

1980. (7") *(TAD 001)* **MY DAD. / MARIANNE** -

GILA

Formed: Stuttgart, Germany . . . 1969 by CONNY VEIT, FRITZ SCHEILING, WALTER WIEDERKEHR and DANIEL ALLUNO. They recorded their eponymous debut at DIETER DIERK's studio in 1971. A remarkable concept piece hovering between PINK FLOYD-like psychedelia, space-rock and continental progressive-rock, it showed off VEIT's climactic and cosmic guitar playing. However, they split soon after, VEIT taking off for rivals POPOL VUH. Ensuring his heartfelt desire to still play live, VEIT borrowed some of the PV musicians, who, along with vocalist SABINE MERBECH, recorded a second GILA album, 'BURY MY HEART AT WOUNDED KNEE', a concept based on the book of the same name, which detailed the systematic genocide of the native Americans. It was another meisterwork, disgarding at times the electricity of the last album for a more sullen acoustic-folk style, highlighted on the opening tracks, 'THIS MORNING' and 'IN A SACRED MANNER'. These were pieces of lush, dream-like beauty, the album climaxing with a percussion-pounding, final track, 'THE BUFFALO ARE COMING'. Sadly, no other GILA recordings were ever made.

Recommended: GILA (*9) / BURY MY HEART AT WOUNDED KNEE (*8)

CONNY VEIT – guitar, vocals, tabla / **FRITZ SCHEILING** – keyboards / **WALTER WIEDERKEHR** – bass / **DANIEL ALLUNO** – drums, bongos, tabla

BASF not issued

Aug 71. (lp) *(20.21110-9)* **GILA** - - German
– Aggression / Kommunkation / Kollaps / Kontakt / Kollektivitaet / Individualitaet. *(cd-iss.1990's on 'Second Battle';)*

— split until **VEIT** re-formed new line-up; **FLORIAN FRICKE** – mellotron, grand piano (of POPOL VUH, ex-TANGERINE DREAM) / **DANIEL SECUNDUS FICHELSCHER** – drums, percussion, bass (of POPOL VUH, ex-AMON DUUL II) / **SABINE MERBACH** – vocals

Warners not issued

1973. (lp) *(K 46234)* **BURY MY HEART AT WOUNDED KNEE** - - German
– This morning / In a sacred manner / Sundance chant / Young coyote / Black kettle's battle / Little smoke / The buffalo are coming. *(re-iss.1982; same)*

— finally came apart, when VEIT briefly joined GURU GURU

GILES, GILES & FRIPP (see under ⇒ KING CRIMSON)

Philip GLASS

Born: 31 Jan'37, Baltimore, Maryland, USA. He studied violin from the age of six before taking up the flute, graduating to Julliard in '58. Subsequently winning many awards including the coveted BMI prize, he went on to meet Indian sitar luminary, RAVI SHANKAR, who hired him to notate Eastern music. In 1968, GLASS formed a septet/ensemble and began to create his own characteristic style of classical minimalism, which encompassed both Eastern and Western influences. Founding his own 'Chatham' label in '71, he started to release his work on vinyl. He continued in much the same fashion, eventually forming the 'Tomato' label in '78. As Through the turn of the decade and beyond, GLASS adopted an increasingly "new age"-style sound, being commissioned by Francis Ford Coppola to score the soundtrack for his 1983 docu-film, 'KOYAANISQATSI'. Hitting the classical chart with 'EINSTEIN ON THE BEACH', he subsequently ventured into the rock world on his 1986 album, 'SONGS FROM LIQUID DAYS'. It featured such high profile rock and pop artists such as DAVID BYRNE, LAURIE ANDERSON, SUZANNE VEGA and PAUL SIMON, who each contributed set pieces of prose. A lifelong BOWIE fan (in particular his 1977 work), he later re-worked 'LOW' (1993) and 'HEROES' (1997) in his own inimitable orchestral style.

Recommended: MUSIC IN TWELVE PARTS (*5) / LOW (*6)

PHILIP GLASS – organ, with **JON GIBSON + RICHARD LANDRY** – flute, soprano sax / **RICHARD PECK** – saxophones / **MICHAEL RIESMAN + JOAN LA BARBARA** – organs

Chatham Square Chatham Square

1971. (d-lp) *(LP 1001/2)* **MUSIC FOR CHANGING PARTS**

1972. (lp) *(LP 1003)* **MUSIC IN FIFTHS / MUSIC IN A SIMILAR MOTION**

Folkways Folkways

1974. (lp) *(FTS 33902)* **TWO PAGES**

Cardine not issued

1976. (lp; by The PHILIP GLASS ENSEMBLE) *(LA 2010)* **MUSIC IN TWELVE PARTS – PARTS 1 & 2** -
– Side 1 / Side 2. *(re-iss.Oct86 on 'Charisma' lp/c/cd; CA/TCA/CACD 2010) (re-iss.Jan89 on 'Venture' lp-box/c-box/cd-box; VEBX/TCCBX/CDVBX 32) (cd-box re-iss.Oct96 on 'Nonesuch'; 7559 79324-2)*

Shandar Shandar

Mar 78. (lp) *(SHAN 83515)* **SOLO MUSIC**

— **PAUL ZUKOFSKY** – violin, repl. JOAN

C.B.S. Tomato

1979. (q-lp) *<TOM 4-2901>* **EINSTEIN ON THE BEACH**
– Knee play 1; Act 1, Scene 1:- Train / Act 1, Scene 2:- Trial / Knee play 2; Act 2, Scene 1:- Dance 1 / Act 2, Scene 2:- Night train / Knee play 3; Act 3, Scene 1:- Trial-Prison / Act 3, Scene 2:- Dance 2 / Knee play 4; Act 4, Scene 1:- Building train / Act

4, Scene 2:- Bed / Act 4, Scene 3:- Spaceship / Knee play 5.

— **SHARON MOE + LARRY WECHSLER** – French horns + **JACK KRIPL** – flute, saxes, clarinet, repl. LANDRY + ZUKOFSKY

Epic Columbia

Apr 82. (lp/c) *(CBS/40 73640) <37265>* **GLASSWORKS** □ □
– Opening / Floe / Islands / Rubric / Facades / Closing. *(cd-iss.May85; MK 73640)*

Jun 82. (7") *<02734>* **FACADES. / RUBRIC** - □

— In 1983, he was credited on RAY MANZAREK (ex-DOORS) album 'CARMINA BURANA'.

Jun 83. (lp/c) *(CBS/40 25480)* **THE PHOTOGRAPHER** □ □
– A gentleman's honor (vocal) / Act II / A gentleman's honor (instrumental) / Act III. *(cd-iss.Feb86 on 'CBS'; MK 37849)*

Jun 83. (7") *(EPCA 3481)* **A GENTLEMAN'S HONOUR. / FACADES** □ □

Island Antilles

Jul 83. (lp/c) *(ISTA/ICT 4) <AN/+CD 8707>* **KOYAANISQATSI** □ □
– Opening / Vessel / Cloud / Pruitt egoe 5.15 / Closing. *(cd-iss.Sep86; CID 120) (cd re-iss.Apr90 on 'Antilles'; IMCD 98)*

— retained **MICHAEL RIESMAN** – conductor, producer

— added **KURT MUNKACSI** – producer

Nonesuch-Elektra Nonesuch-Elektra

Dec 85. (lp/c)(cd) *(EKT 23/+C)(<979 113-2>)* **MISHIMA (Soundtrack)** □ □
– Mishima – Opening / November 25: Morning / 1934: Grandmother & Kimitake / Temple of the pavillion (like some enormous music) / Osamu's theme: Kyoko's house / 1937: Saint Sebastian / Kyoko's house (stage blood is not enough) / November 25: Ichigaya / 1957: Award montage / Runaway horses (poetry written with a splash of blood) / 1962: Body building / November 25: The last day / F-104: Epilogue from Sun and steel / Mishima – closing.

C.B.S. Portrait

May 86. (7"/12") *(A/TA 7166)* **FREEZING. / LIGHTNING** □ □

— above with LINDA RONSTADT on vocals

Jun 86. (lp/c/cd) *(FM/FMT/MK <39564>)* **SONGS FROM LIQUID DAYS** □ 91
– Changing opinion / Lightning / Freezing / Liquid days (part 1) / Open the kingdom (liquid days, part 2) / Forgetting.

May 87. (lp/c/cd) *(FM/FMT/MK <39539>)* **DANCE PIECES** (recorded 1979-84) □ □
– In the upper room / Dance I / Dance II / Dance V / Dance VII / Dance IX / Glasspieces: Glasspiece £1 / Glasspiece £2 / Glasspiece £3.

1987. (d-cd) *(MK <39672>)* **SATYAGRAHA** □ □
– Satyagraha: Act 1 – Tolstoy: Scene 1/2/3 – Act II – Tagore: Scene 1/2/3 – Act III – King: Part 1/2/3.

1987. (lp) *<(42457)>* **AKHNATEN** □ □
– Hymn to the sun / Akhnaten & Nefertiti / Window of appearances / Epilogue.

1988. (cd) *<M2K 44765>* **DANCE NOS.1-5** - □

Virgin Virgin

Oct 86. (lp/c) *(OVED/+C 151)* **NORTH STAR** □ -
– Etoile Polaire (North star) / Victor's lament / River run / Mon pere, mon pere / Are years what? (for Marianne Moore) / Lady day / Ange des orages / Ave / Ikook / Montage. *(cd-iss.May88; CDV 2085)*

Nonesuch Nonesuch

Aug 88. (lp/c/cd) *<K 979 192-1/-4/-1>* **POWAQQATSI** □ □

Apr 89. (lp/c/cd) *(K 979 209-1/-4/-2)* **THE THIN BLUE LINE (Soundtrack)** □ □
– Opening credits / Interrogation (part 1) / Turko (part 1) / Vidor / Adam's story / Defense atorney's / The judge / The trial (part 2) / The mystery eyewitness (part 2) / The thin blue line / Defense attorney's (part 2 / Harris' crimes (part 2) / Hell on Earth / The confession / Prologue / Interrogation (part 2) / Turko (part) / Harris' story / Comets and Vegas / Harris' crimes (part 2) / The trial (part 1) / The mystery eyewitness (part 2) / The electric chair / Harris' testimony / The mystery eyewitness (part 5) / Harris' childhood / End credits.

Venture

Feb 89. (cd/c/lp) *(CD/TC+/VE 39)* **1000 AIRPLANES ON THE ROOF** □ □
– 1000 airplanes on the roof / City walk / Girlfriend / My building disappeared / Screens of memory / What time is grey / Labyrinth / Return to the hive / Three truths / The encounter / Grey cloud over New York / Where have you been as the doctor / A normal man running.

C.B.S. Columbia

1989. (cd) *<45576>* **SOLO PIANO** - □
– Metamorphosis one – five / Mad rush / Wichita sultra vortex.

1989. (cd) *<45570>* **SONGS FROM THE TRILOGY** - □
– Protest / Evening song / Hymn to the Sun / Trial – Prison / Akhnaten & Nefertiti / Kuru field of justice / Knee 1 / Tolstoy farm / Window of appearances / Bed / Epilogue / Knee 5.

Private Private

Sep 90. (cd/c; RAVI SHANKAR & PHILIP GLASS) *(260/410 947)* **PASSAGES** □ □
– Offering / Channels and winds / Meetings along the edge /Sadhanipa / Ragas in minor scale / Prashanti.

Point-Philips

Mar 93. (cd/c/lp) *(438150-2/-4/-1)* **LOW** □ □
–

— next with ATLANTA SYMPHONY ORCHESTRA & CHORUS – ROBERT SHAW

Sony Classical Sony Classical

1993. (cd) **ITAIPU / THE CANYON** □ □
– Itaipu:- (I) Mato grosso, (II) The lake, (III) The dam, (IV) To the sea / The canyon.

Nonesuch Nonesuch

Oct 93. (cd) *(7559 79329-2)* **ANIMA MUNDI** (soundtrack) □ □

Point Point

Feb 97. (cd/c) *(454388-2/-4)* **HEROES SYMPHONY (THE MUSIC OF BOWIE AND ENO)** □ □

– compilations, etc. –

Apr 97. (3xcd-box) *Sony; (SM3K 62960)* **GLASSMASTERS** □ □
– Window of appearances III / The dam / Vow / Open the kingdom / Attack and fall / Confrontation and rescue / Funeral of Amenhotep III / Floe / Dance No.5 / Spaceship / Photographer (act III) / Building-train / Knee play 3 / Facades / Akhnanten act III.4 epilogue / Freezing / Akhnanten's hymn to the Aten / Satyagaha act.III 3 evening song / Knee play 5 / Mad rush.

GLOBAL VILLAGE TRUCKING CO.

Formed: London, England . . . 1972 by communal hippies, JON OWEN, JAMES LASCELLES, JOHN McKENZIE, MIKE MEDORA and SIMON STEWART. They gained a brief bit of fame after sharing the 'Greasy Truckers – Live At Dingwalls' double-lp with HENRY COW, GONG and CAMEL. The tracks on one side were; 'LOOK INTO ME', 'EARL STONHAM (THE GUNSLINGER)', 'YOU'RE A FLOOZY MADAME KARMA (BUT I LOVE YOUR LOWDOWN WAYS)' & 'EVERYBODY NEEDS A GOOD FRIEND'. More effective on the fesitval circuit, they only managed to cobble together one workman-like album in 1976.

Recommended: GLOBAL VILLAGE TRUCKING CO. (*5)

JON OWEN – vocals, guitar / **MICHAEL MEDORA** – guitar, harmonica / **JOHN McKENZIE** – bass, vocals / **JAMES LASCELLES** – keyboards, vocals / **SIMON STEWART** – drums / plus guests **PETE KIRTLEY** – guitar, vocals / **JIM CUOMO** – saxophone / **CAROMAY DIXON + MONICA GARRELTS** – backing vox

Caroline not issued

1976. (lp) *(C 1516)* **GLOBAL VILLAGE TRUCKING CO.** □ -
– On the judgement day / Lasga's farm / Love your neighbour / Short change / Tall story / Smiling revolution / Love will find a way / If you don't mind (me saying) / The inevitable fate of Ms. Danya Sox / Watch out there's a mind about.

— Returned to more successful live festival work for the next few years.

Robert John GODFREY (see under ⇒ ENID)

GODS

Formed: Hatfield, England . . .1965 by MICK TAYLOR, KEN HENSLEY and brothers JOHN and BRIAN GLASCOCK. They took the names of THOR, HERMES, OLYMPUS and MARS on their much delayed debut, 'COME ON DOWN TO MY BOAT BABY' in 1967 (now rare and worth over £50 mint). When it flopped, TAYLOR joined his hero JOHN MAYALL in the BLUESBREAKERS, before joining The ROLLING STONES in the Spring of '69. The GODS were re-incarnated by KEN HENSLEY in the Autumn of '67 and were rewarded, after many college gigs, with a new contract for 'Columbia'. However, bass player PAUL NEWTON formed SPICE (later URIAH HEEP) and was deposed by GREG LAKE, although he also left to join KING CRIMSON and later EMERSON, LAKE & PALMER. 1968 saw The GODS first album in the shops, appropriately titled 'GENESIS' (now worth £100). Flop singles were superseded by their second experimental album, 'TO SAMUEL A SON' (worth over £75). By the time of its release, HENSLEY had joined The CLIFF BENNETT BAND, which evolved into TOE FAT (featuring virtually all The GODS). HENSLEY was soon drafted into URIAH HEEP in early 1970. • **Songwriters:** Group.

Recommended: GENESIS (*6) / TO SAMUEL A SON (*6)

MICK TAYLOR – guitar / **KEN HENSLEY** – keyboards, vocals / **JOHN GLASCOCK** – bass, vocals / **BRIAN GLASCOCK** – drums

Polydor not issued

Jun 67. (7") *(BM 56168)* **COME ON DOWN TO MY BOAT BABY. / GARAGE MAN** □ -

— **KEN HENSLEY / + LEE KERSLAKE** – drums / **JOE KNAS** – guitar, vocals / + **JOHN GLASCOCK** – bass, vocals, returned to repl. GREG LAKE who had repl. PAUL NEWTON

Columbia

Oct 68. (7") *(DB 8486)* **BABY'S RICH. / SOMEWHERE IN THE STREET** □ -

Oct 68. (lp) *(SCX 6286)* **GENESIS** □ -
– Toward the skies / Candles getting shorter / You're my life / Looking glass / Misleading colours / Radio show / Plastic horizon / Farthing man / I never knew / Time and eternity. *(cd-iss.1990's on 'Repertoire'; REP 4418)*– Baby's rich / Somewhere in the streets / Hey! bulldog / Real love guarenteed.

Feb 69. (7") *(DB 8544)* **HEY! BULLDOG. / REAL LOVE GUARENTEED** □ -

May 69. (7") *(DB 8572)* **LONG TIME, SAD TIME, BAD TIME. / MARIA** □ -

Feb 70. (lp) *(SCX 6372)* **TO SAMUEL A SON** □ -
– To Samuel a son / Eight o'clock in the morning / He's growing / Sticking wings on flies / Lady lady / Penny dear / Long time, sad time, bad time / Five to three / Autumn / Yes I cry / Groozy / Momma I need / Candlelight / Lovely Anita.

— Had already disbanded some time in 1969 (see above biog. details)

compilations, etc

Nov 76. Harvest; (lp) *(SHSM 2011)* **THE GODS: FEATURING KEN HENSLEY** □ -

GODZ

Formed: New York, USA . . . mid 60's by JAY DILLON, LARRY KESSLER, JIM McCARTHY and PAUL THORNTON. Drawing comparisons to labelmates The FUGS, they released a clutch of avant-garde albums which combined elements of anarchic psychedelia and acid-folk. Their penultimate set, 'THE THIRD TESTAMENT', finally won them a small cult following, the best track being, 'NEET STREET'. • **Trivia:** Not to be confused with US outfit of the late 70's.

Recommended: GODZ II (*5) / THE THIRD TESTAMENT (*6)

JAY DILLON – vocals, keyboards / **JIM McCARTHY** – guitar, vocals / **LARRY KESSLER** – bass, violin / **PAUL THORNTON** – drums, percussion

Fontana E.S.P.

1966. (lp) *(STL 5500)* <*1037*> **CONTACT HIGH WITH THE GODZ**
– Turn on / White cat heat / Na na naa / Eleven / 1+1=? / Lay in the Sun / Squeek / Godz / May you never be alone.

1967. (lp) *(STL 5512)* <*1047*> **GODZ II**
– Radar eyes / Riffin' / Where / New song / Squeek / Soon the Moon / Crusade / You won't see me / Travelin' salesman / Permanent green light.

— now without DILLON

1968. (lp) <*1077*> **THE THIRD TESTAMENT** -
– Ruby red / Eeh ooh / Down by the river / First multitude / ABC / Walking guitar blues / Neet street / Womban / Kim / Like a sparrow / Quack.

1969. (lp) <*2017*> **GODZHUNHEIT** -

— Disbanded after above which included many session people.

GOLDEN DAWN

Formed: Austin, Texas, USA . . . 1967 by GEORGE KINNEY, a former school mate of ROKY ERICKSON (of 13th FLOOR ELEVATORS), who he also played together with, in his first band, The FUGITIVES. Taking the name from Aleister Crowley's book 'The Sect Of The Golden Dawn', KINNEY teamed up together with members of local band CHELSEA, signing for 'International Artists' (also home of RED CRAYOLA, 13th FLOOR ELEVATORS and LOST & FOUND). An album, 'POWER PLANT', surfaced in 1967, although it failed miserably due to poor promotion. It was, however, a fine piece of work, featuring heavy duty lyrics and some great acid-psych instrumentation. Sadly, it was their only vinyl outing, KINNEY going on to publish ROKY's book, 'Openers', while ROKY languished in Rusk State hospital. In 1978, with new wave/avant-garde at the forefront in the UK, GOLDEN DAWN played an 'International Artists' reunion gig at London's Hope & Anchor alongside their old labelmates (see above). An EP combining a track from each group (they contributed 'STARVATION') was given away free at the door by 'Radarscope' (RAD 88).

Recommended: POWER PLANT (*7)

GEORGE KINNEY – vocals / **JIMMY BIRD** – guitar / **TOM RAMSEY** – guitar / **BILL HALLMAN** – bass / **BOBBY RECTOR** – drums

not issued Int.Artists

1967. (lp) <*IALP-4*> **POWER PLANT** -
– Evolution / This way please / Starvation / I'll be around / Seeing is believing / My time / A nice surprise / Every day / Tell me why / Reaching out to you. *(UK-iss.Mar88 on 'Decal'; LIK 24) (cd-iss.May94 on 'Eva'; 824969)*

— disbanded after KINNEY fell out with label and moved to California

GONG

Formed: Paris, France . . . c.1970 by Australian DAEVID ALLEN, who had been part of the embryonic Canterbury beatnik scene in England since the mid-60's. Previous to this, he had hung-out with the likes of WILLIAM BURROUGHS and ALLEN GINSBERG at the famous Beat Hotel in Paris, cultivating his bohemian leanings and free-form poetry skills. He hitched back to England and soon met a young ROBERT WYATT while lodging at his parent's house. Through WYATT, he was introduced to MIKE RATLEDGE and HUGH HOPPER, with whom he subsequently formed the jazz-influenced WILDE FLOWERS. A prototype SOFT MACHINE, they also numbered another youngster; KEVIN AYERS. ALLEN remained for a one-off 45, 'Love Makes Sweet Music', in 1967, while he was subsequently refused re-entry into Britain after a gig in St. Tropez. This effectively ended his tenure with the group, providing the impetus to set up his own commune of hippies who later evolved into GONG. A flexible outfit at this stage, they provided the backing for two albums, 'MAGICK BROTHER, MYSTIC SISTER' & 'BANANA MOON', the latter being credited to ALLEN. Theirs was an enchanting blend of whimsical, unconventional psychedelia that combined spaced-out rock and weird experimentation. 1971 produced the excellent 'CAMEMBERT ELECTRIQUE', which crystalised their innovative sound, the album finally being issued in the UK when Richard Branson's newly formed 'Virgin' label virtually gave it away for 49p. Titles like 'SQUEEZING SPONGES OVER POLICEMEN'S HEADS', 'WET CHEESE DELIRIUM' and the not-so ridiculously named 'TRIED SO HARD', were perfect examples of GONG's acid-fried humour. They had been part of the Glastonbury scene following a slot at the 1971 festival, although ALLEN broke up the band soon after. A year later, they reformed with a slightly altered line-up; GILLI SMYTH, DIDIER MALHERBE, LAURIE ALLEN, CHRISTIAN TRITSCH and FRANCIS MOZE, along with new space-cadets STEVE HILLAGE and TIM BLAKE. Now on 'Virgin', the band began work on a trilogy of albums entitled 'RADIO GNOME INVISIBLE', beginning with 'THE FLYING TEAPOT'. The second and third of these; 'ANGEL'S EGG' and 'YOU', came out the following year, ALLEN later decamping to Majorca. With their leading light gone, the band went through a dizzying series of personnel changes; HILLAGE went solo, while MOERLEN left a couple of times before he finally took control of the reins in 1976. This resulted in the creatively poor NICK MASON-produced set, 'SHAMAL'. Another, 'GAZEUSE!', was just as bad, the group taking some time to recover from the stagnant jazz-rock they peddled during the MOERLEN period. Meanwhile, ALLEN was carving out his own solo career; the punk-rock number, 'OPIUM FOR THE PEOPLE', in 1978 introducing a harder edge, while PLANET GONG and MOTHER GONG (GILLI's outfit) was as zany as anything the original GONG had ever produced. By the late 80's, GONG (and occasionally GONG MAISON) was again under the control of ALLEN, who had (predictably!) set up home in Glastonbury.

Recommended: CAMEMBERT ELECTRIQUE (*8) / THE FLYING TEAPOT (*7) / ANGEL'S EGG (*6) / YOU (*6) / THE BEST OF GONG (*8) / LIVE FLOATING ANARCHY (*7)

DAEVID ALLEN (b.Australia) – guitar, vocals (ex-SOFT MACHINE) / **GILLI SMYTH** (b.France) – whispered vocals / **DIDIER MALHERBE** – sax, flute / **RACHID HOUARI** – drums, tabla / **DIETER GEWISSLER** – contrabass / **CARL FREEMAN** – contrabass / **BARE PHILLIPS** – contrabass / **BURTON GREEN** – piano, piano harp / **TASMIN SMYTH** (Gilli's daughter) – vocals

Byg Actuel not issued

Feb 70. (lp) *(5-529 029)* **MAGICK BROTHER, MYSTIC SISTER** - - France
– Mystick sister, Magick brother / Glad to say to say / Rational anthem / Chainstore chant – Pretty Miss Titty / Fable of a Fredfish – Hope you feel o.k.? / Ego / Gong song / Princess dreaming / 5 & 20 schoolgirls / Cos you got green hair. *(UK-iss.Nov77 on 'Charly'; CRL 5052) (cd-iss.Nov86 on 'Decal'; CDLIK 31)*

1970. (7") *(129021)* **EST-CE-QUE JE SUIS. / HIP HIPNOTIZE YOU** - - France

— now with Englishmen **PIP PYLE, CHRISTIAN TRITSCH + ROBERT WYATT**

1971. (lp; by DAEVID ALLEN) *(45 529 345)* **BANANA MOON** - - France
– Time of our life / Memories / All I want is out of here / Fred the fish / White rock blues and cabin code / Stoned innocent / Frankenstein, and his adventures in the land of Flip / I am a bowl. *(UK-iss.Jul75 on 'Caroline'; C 1512) (re-iss.May79 on 'Charly'; CR 30165) (cd-iss.May90 on 'Decal'; CDLIK 63)*

— **CHRISTIAN TRITSCH** – bass / **GERRY FIELDS** – violin / **DANIEL LALOU** – multi horns, percussion repl. **FREEMAN, GREEN, PHILLIPS** and **T. SMYTH**

1971. (lp) *(45 529 533)* **CAMEMBERT ELECTRIQUE** - - France
– Radio gnome / You can't kill me / I've bin stone before / Mister long shanks: O mother – I am your fantasy / Dynamite: I am your animal / Wet cheese delirium / Squeezing sponges over policemen's heads / Fohat digs holes in space / Tried so hard / Tropical fish: Selene / Gnome the second. *(UK-iss.Jun74 on 'Caroline'; VC 502) (re-iss.1982 on 'Charly'; CRM 2003) (cd-iss.Mar86 on 'Decal'; CDLIK 11) (re-iss.cd 1988 on 'Caroline'; C 1520) (re-iss.cd Mar90 on 'Decal'; CDLIK 64) (cd-iss.Nov94 on 'Gas'; AGASCD 001) (re-iss.Sep95 on 'Spalax';)*

Jan 71. (lp; Philips UK) *(6332 033)* **CONTINENTAL CIRCUS (Soundtrack)** -
– Blues for Findlay / Continental circus world / What do you want / Blues for Findlay (instrumental). *(cd-iss.May96 on 'Mantra'; 642089)*

— **LAURIE ALLEN** (b.England) – drums repl. PYLE who joined HATFIELD + THE NORTH / added **FRANCIS MOZE** – bass (ex-MAGMA)

— Disbanded early '72 after Glastonbury Fayre, but re-formed by end of year. Added **STEVE HILLAGE** (b. 2 Aug'51, England) – guitar (ex-KEVIN AYERS, ex-KHAN, ex-URIEL) / **TIM BLAKE** (b.England) – synthesizers

Virgin Virgin

May 73. (lp) *(V 2002)* **FLYING TEAPOT (RADIO GNOME INVISIBLE PART 1)** -
– Radio gnome invisible / Flying teapot / The pot head pixies / The octave doctors and the crystal machine / Zero to hero and the witch's spell / Witch's song / I am your pussy. *(re-iss.Jan82 on 'Charly'; CR 30202) (re-iss.Mar84; OVED 14) (cd-iss.May91 on 'Decal'; CDLIK 67) (re-iss.cd Sep95 on 'Spalax';)*

— Although DAEVID and GILLI moved to Majorca, Spain, they returned mid 1973. / **PIERRE MOERLEN** (b.Colmar, France) – drums repl. LAURIE / **MIKE HOWLETT** (b.Fiji) – bass, vocals repl. MOZE

Dec 73. (lp) *(V 2007)* **ANGEL'S EGG (RADIO GNOME INVISIBLE PART 2)** -
– Other side of the sky / Sold to the highest Buddha / Castles in the clouds / Prostitute poem / Givin' my luv to you / Selene / Flute salad / Oily way / Outer temple – Inner temple / Percolations / Love is how you make it / I never glid before / Eat the phone book code. *(re-iss.Aug82 on 'Charly'; CR 30219) (re-iss.Mar84; OVED 15) (cd-iss.1989; CDV 2007) (re-iss.cd Apr91 on 'Decal'+=; CDLIK 75)*– Ooby-Stooby doomsday or The D-Day DJs got the DDT blues.

— **MIQUETTE GIRAUDY** – keyboards repl. GILLI

Oct 74. (lp) *(V 2019)* **YOU**
– Thoughts for nought / A.P.H.P.'s advice / Magick mother invocation / Master builder / A sprinkling of clouds / Perfect mystery / The isle of everywhere / You never blow your trip forever. *(re-iss.Aug82 on 'Charly'; CR 30220) (re-iss.Mar84; OVED 16) (cd-iss.1989; CDV 2019) (re-iss.cd Aug91 on 'Decal'; CDLIK 76)*

— Virtually break-up, when DAEVID and GILLI move to Spain again. In May'76, DAEVID continued solo career and re-formed GONG in the late 80's. Meanwhile back in 1975, after he recorded solo FISH RISING album, STEVE HILLAGE also became solo artist using most of GONG!.

GONG

re-formed with only one original **DIDIER MALHERBE.** He recruited **JORGE PINCHEVSKY** – violin / **MIQUETTE GIRAUDY** – keyboards / **MIKE HOWLETT** – drums / **MIREILLE BAUER** – percussion, xylophone, etc. / **PATRICE LEMOINE** – keyboards

— (HOWLETT went on to become producer of A FLOCK OF SEAGULLS, etc)

Feb 76. (lp) *(V 2046)* **SHAMAL**
– Wingful of eyes / Chandra / Bambooji / Cat in Clark's shoes / Mandrake / Shamal. *(re-iss.Mar84; OVED 17) (cd-iss.1989; CDV 2046)*

— **PIERRE MOERLEN** returned to repl. BRIAN DAVISON (ex-REFUGEE) who had toured with them in 1976 after BILL BRUFORD left to join GENESIS, ZAPPA, etc. / **ALLAN HOLDSWORTH** – guitar (ex-SOFT MACHINE, etc) / **FRANCIS MOZE**

– bass returned / **BENOIT MOERLEN** – keyboards / **MINO CINELOU** – percussion / **DIDIER & MIREILLE** also

Feb 77. (lp) *(V 2074)* **GAZEUSE!** (US title 'EXPRESSO')
– Expresso / Night illusion / Percolations part 1 & 2 / Shadows of Mireille. *(re-iss.Mar84; OVED 18) (cd-iss.Jun90; CDV 2074)*

— Disbanded again Spring 1977 (aargghh!!!). Left behind retrospective below (all line-ups).

Aug 77. (d-lp) *(VGD 3501)* **LIVE! ETC. (live)** -
– You can't kill me / Zero the hero and the witches spell / Flying teapot / Dynamite: I am your animal / 6/8 (coit) / Est ce que je suis / Ooby Scooby doomsday or the D-day DJ's got the DDT blues / Radio gnome invisible / Oily way / Outer temple – Inner temple / Where have all the flowers gone / Isle of everywhere / Get it inner / Master builder / Flying teapot. *(cd-iss.Jun90; CDVM 3501)*

— **PIERRE MOERLEN** retained group name with **HOLDSWORTH, BENOIT MOERLEN, BAUER** (on next lp only), plus **DARYL WAY** – violin (ex-CURVED AIR) / **HANNY ROWE** – bass / **FRANCOISE CHAUSSE** – percussion / **BON LOZANGA** – percussion

Feb 78. (lp) *(V 2099)* **EXPRESSO II** -
– Heavy tune / Golden dilemma / Sleepy / Soli / Burning / Three blind mice. *(re-iss.1986; OVED 65) (cd-iss.Jun90; CDV 2099)*

PIERRE MOERLEN'S GONG

Arista Arista

Feb 79. (lp) *(SPART 1080)* **DOWNWIND**
– Aeroplane / Crooscurrents / Downwind / Jin go la ba / What you know / Emotions / Xtasea. *(re-iss.Jul91 on 'Great Expectations' cd/lp; PIP CD/LP 025)*

Oct 79. (lp) *(SPART 1105)* **TIME IS THE KEY**
– And na greine / Earthrise / Supermarket / Faerie steps / An American in England / The organ grinder / Sugar street / The bender / Arabesque intro / Esnuria two / Time is the key. *(re-iss.Nov90 on 'Great Expectations' cd/lp; PIP CD/LP 018)*

Jul 80. (lp) *(SPART 1130)* **PIERRE MOERLEN'S GONG LIVE (live)** -
– Downwind / Mandrake / Golden dilemma / Soli / Drum solo / Esnurio / Crosscurrents. *(re-iss.Nov90 on 'Great Expectations' cd/lp; PIP CD/LP 019)*

— (featured **MIKE OLDFIELD** – guitar)

— **BRIAN HOLLOWAY** – guitar repl. HOLDSWORTH (to various groups)

1981. (lp) *(202955)* **LEAVE IT OPEN** - - Dutch
– Leave it open / How much better it has become / I woke up this morning felt like playing the guitar / It's about time / Stok stok stok sto-gak / Adrien.

Eulenspiegel not issued

1986. (lp/c/cd) *(EU LP/MC/CD 1053)* **BREAKTHROUGH** - - Dutch
– Breakthrough / Spaceship disco / Rock in seven / Six 8 / Poitou / Children's dreams / Portrait / The road out / Romantic punk / Far east.

Line not issued

1988. (lp) *(LIDLP 5.0003)* **SECOND WIND** -
– Second wind / Time and space / Say no more / Deep end / Crystal funk / Exotic / Beton / Alan Key / Crash and co. *(cd-iss.Nov92 on 'Line'+=; LICD 900698)*– Crash and co. (# 2 & 3).

– compilations, others –

Jan 87. (cd) *Virgin; (COMCD 1)* **A WINGFUL OF EYES** -
(re-iss.Jan96; CDOVD 462)

Apr 89. (lp) *Demi-Monde; (DMLP 018)* **THE MYSTERY AND THE HISTORY OF THE PLANET GONG** (rarities 1971-72) -
(cd-iss.1989 & 1993 on 'Thunderbolt'; CDTL 010 & CDTB 116) (cd-iss.Jun97 on 'Spalax'; 14518)

Nov 95. (cd) *Nectar; (NTMCD 517)* **THE BEST OF GONG** -

Dec 95. (3xcd-box) *Spalax;* **THE RADIO GNOME TRILOGY** -

Dec 95. (cd) *Strange Fruit; (SFRCD 137)* **PRE MODERNIST WIRELESS ON RADIO** -

May 96. (cd) *Mantra; (890025)* **LIVE AU BATACLAN 1973 (live)** -

May 96. (cd) *Mantra; (890042)* **LIVE AT SHEFFIELD 1974 (live)** -

Jun 96. (cd; as GONG MAISON) *Gas; (AGASCD 004)* **GLASTONBURY 1989 (live)** -

Jun 96. (cd) *Summit; (SUMCD 4117)* **THE VERY BEST OF GONG** -

DAEVID ALLEN

DAEVID + PEPSI MILAN – guitar, mandolin / **ANA CAMPS** – vocals / **TONI PASCUAL** – synths, keyboards / **TONI ARES** – bass / **TONI FREE FERNANDEZ** – guitar / with GONG guests; **MIKE HOWLETT** – bass / **PIERRE MOERLEN** – percussion

Virgin not issued

May 76. (lp; by DAEVID ALLEN & EUTERPE) *(V 2054)* **GOOD MORNING!** -
– Children of the new world / Good morning! / Spirit / Song of satisfaction / Have you seen my friend / French garden / Wise man in your heart / She doesn't she. *(cd-iss.Jun90; CDV 2054) (+=)*– Euterpe gratitude piece.

DAEVID + PEPSI + JUAN BIBLIONI – guitar / **SAM GOPAL** – percussion, synthesizers / **VICTOR PERAINO** – synth, keyboards / **MARIANNE OBERASCHER** – harp

Affinity not issued

Nov 77. (lp) *(AFF 3)* **NOW IS THE HAPPIEST TIME OF YOUR LIFE** -
– Flamenco zero / Why do we treat ourselves like we do / Tally & Orlando / Meet the cockpit pixie / See you on the moontower / Poet for sale / Crocodile nonsense poem / Only make love if you want to / I am / Deya goddess. *(cd-iss.Nov90 on 'Decal'; CDLIK 69) (re-iss.cd Dec95 on 'Spalax'; 542825)*

PLANET GONG

DAEVID ALLEN + HERE AND NOW (London musicians); **GILLIE SMYTH** – vocals / **PROF. S.SHARPSTRINGS** – guitar, vocals / **KEITH MISSILE** – bass / **KIF KIF LE BATTEUR** – drums / **GAVIN DA BLITZ** – synthesizers / **SUZA DA BLOOZ + ANNI WOMBAT** – vocals

Feb 78. (7") *(AF 5101)* **OPIUM FOR THE PEOPLE. / POET FOR SALE** -

Charly not issued

Apr 78. (10") *(CYX 202)* **OPIUM FOR THE PEOPLE. / STONED INNOCENT FRANKENSTEIN** -

Apr 78. (lp) *(CRM 2000)* **LIVE FLOATING ANARCHY 77 (live)** -
– Psychological overture / Floating anarchy / Stoned innocent Frankenstein / New age transformation / Try no more sages / Opium for the people / Allez Ali Baba blacksheep have you any bullshit – Mama mya mantram. *(cd-iss.Oct90 on 'Decal'; CDLIK 68) (re-iss.cd Dec95 on 'Spalax';)*

— with **PEPSI + CHRIS CUTLER** – percussion / **GEORGE BISHOP** – sax, clarinet / **ANGEL ADUANO** – banjo / **BRIAN DAMAGE** – drums / **RONALD WALTHERN** – pipes

May 79. (lp; by DAEVID ALLEN) *(CRL 5015)* **N'EXISTE PAS!** -
– Professor Sharpstrings says / The freedom of the city in a suitable box / The say the say / Something tells me / H's a fine air for fliss / But it's really not real / Because barroom philoshers / 333 / No other than the mother is my song / Theme from hashish to ashes / The turkeybirds breakfast / Rajneesh with thanks / No God will not go on or the wrong way to be right / O man you.

NEW YORK GONG

DAEVID ALLEN + MATERIAL; BILL LASWELL – bass / **MICHAEL BEINHORN** – synthesizers / **DON DAVIS** – alto sax / **FRED MAHER** – drums / **CLIFF CULTRERI** – guitar / + **BILL BACON** – drums / **MARK KRAMER** – organ / **GARY WINDO** – tenor sax

Jan 80. (7") *(CY 51056)* **MUCH TOO OLD. / I AM A FREUD** -

Apr 80. (lp) *(CRL 5021)* **ABOUT TIME** -
– Preface / Much too old / Black September / Materialism / Strong woman / I am a freud / O my photograph / Jungle windo(w) / Hours gone. *(cd-iss.Dec90 on 'Decal'; CDLIK 73)*

1980. (10"ep) *(CYX 203)* **JUNGLE WINDO(W). / MUCH TOO OLD / MATERIALISM** -

DAEVID ALLEN

HARRY WILLIAMSON – bass, sax (repl.DAVIS, WINDO + KRAMER)

1981. (lp) *(CR 30218)* **DIVIDED ALIEN PLAYBAX '80** -
– When / Well / Bell / Boon / Dab / Gray / Rude / Disguise / Pearls / Bodygas / Froghello / Fastfather / Smile. *(cd-iss.Dec95 on 'Spalax'; 14837)*

May 83. (12"ep) *(CY 2101)* **ALIEN IN NEW YORK** -
– Bananareggae / Are you ready / Oo lala / Side windo.

— with **MARK KRAMER** – piano / **ELIZABETH MIDDLETON** – piano, vocals / **W.S. BURROUGHS**

Shanghai not issued

Nov 82. (m-lp) *(HAI 201)* **THE DEATH OF ROCK AND OTHER ENTRANCES** -
– Death of rock / Poet for sale / Tally's birthday song / You never existed at all / Afraid. *(cd-iss.Jan93 on 'Voiceprint'+=; VP 114CD) (cd re-iss.Aug96 on 'Blueprint'; BP 114CD)*

— He returned to Australia and teamed up with DAVID TOLLEY

Aug 86. (m-lp; as The EX) *(HAI 202)* **DON'T STOP** -
– Do / Eat / Work / Dinosaur / What they say.

Invisible not issued

1987. (7"; as INVISIBLE OPERA COMPANY OF TIBET) *(INV 001)* **TRIAL BY HEADLINE. / TRIAL BY HEADLINE** - - Aust.

Demi Monde not issued

Oct 89. (lp/cd) *(DM LP/CD 1019; one-side by MOTHER GONG)* **THE OWL AND THE TREE** -
– The owly song / I am my own lover / I am a tree / Lament for the future of the forest / Hands / Unseen alley / La dee Madri.

GONG

DAEVID + GRAHAM CLARKE – violin / **DIDIER MALHERBE / KEITH MISSILE** – bass

Dec 89. (cd/lp; as GONG MAISON) *(DM CD/LP 1022)* **GONG MAISON** -
– Flying teacup / 1989 / Titti-caca / Tatlas Logorythique / Negotiate / We circle around. *(cd+=)*– (1 track).

— In 1991, their touring line-up of GONG MAISON was **DAEVID ALLEN, DIDIER MALHERBE, GRAHAM CLARKE** – violin / **SHYAMAL MAITRA + KEITH MISSILE**

Celluloid not issued

Oct 92. (cd) *(66914-2)* **SHAPESHIFTER** - - France
– Flying teacup / 1989 / Titti-caca / Tatlas Logorythique / Negotiate / We circle around. *(re-iss.Jan97 on 'Viceroy'; VIC 80392)*

Code 90 not issued

Mar 93. (cd) *(NINETY 2)* **LIVE ON TV 1990 (live)** -
– Planetary introduction / You can't kill me / I've bin stoned before – Long Shanks – Omotha / Radio gnome invisible / Pot-head pixies / Voix lactee / Outer vision / Inner vision / Gorbachev cocktail – I am your animal / Flying teacup / I am you.

Sep 95. (d-cd) *(VPGAS 101CD)* **25th BIRTHDAY PARTY – OCTOBER 8-9, 1994, THE FORUM (live)** -
– Thom intro / Floating into a birthday gig / You can't kill me / adio gnome 25 / I am your pussy / ot head pixies / Never glid before / Eat that phonebook / Gnomic address / Flute salad / Oily way. *(re-iss.Mar97; same)*

Sep 95. (m-cd; as GONG GLOBAL FAMILY) *(VPGASCD 102)* **HOW TO NUKE THE EIFFEL TOWER** -
– Away away (South Pacific version) / Away away (twelve selves version) / Nuclear megawaste / Chernobyl rain.

Mar 97. Gas; (cd) *(AGASCD 001)* **CAMEMBERT ELECTRIQUE (Not What You Think . . . Unreleased studio tracks)** -

May 97. Sound & Media; (cd) *(SUMCD 4117)* **THE VERY BEST OF GONG** -

Daevid ALLEN

Demi Monde not issued

Feb 90. (cd/lp) *(DM CD/LP 1025)* **AUSTRALIA AQUARIA / SHE** -
– Gaia / Peaceful warrior / Australia aquaria / She / Isis is calling / Slave queen / Voice of Om / Voice of Om dub. *(re-iss.cd Feb91 as 'THE AUSTRALIAN YEARS' on 'Voiceprint'+=; VP 101)*– Don't stop.

Amp not issued

1990. (cd; by DAEVID ALLEN, HARRY WILLIAMSON & GILLI SMYTH) *(CD 011)* **STROKING THE TAIL OF THE BIRD** -

– (part 1) / (part 2).

Voiceprint | not issued

Feb 91. (cd) *(VPCD 102)* **THE SEVEN DRONES** [ ] [-]
– C drone (muladhara) / D drone (swadhishthana) / E drone (manipura) / F drone (anahata) / G drone (visuddha) / A drone (njna) / B drone (sahaiara) / Hello me.

1991. (cd; as INVISIBLE OPERA COMPANY OF TIBET) *(VP 106CD)* **JEWEL IN THE LOTUS** [ ] [-]
(re-iss.Apr96 on 'Gas'; AGASCD 006)

— Next with; **GRAHAM CLARK + MARK ROBSON**

1992. (cd; by DAEVID ALLEN & THE MAGICK BROTHERS) *(VP 107CD)* **LIVE AT THE WITCHWOOD 1991 (live)** [ ] [-]
– Wise man in your heart / etc.

Shimmy Disc | Shimmy Disc

Nov 92. (lp/cd; by DAEVID ALLEN & KRAMER) *(SHIMMY 060/+CD)* **WHO'S AFRAID** [ ] [ ]

— (above was augmented by label boss & BONGWATER man MARK KRAMER)

Voiceprint | not issued

Nov 93. (cd) *(VP 111CD)* **TWELVE SELVES** [ ] [-]
– Introdrone / Mystico fanatico / Away away away / Colage – Bellyphone of telephone / She – Isis is calling / Colage patafisico – Divided alien manifesto / I love sex but / Wargasm / Children of the new world / O Wichito / Sexual blueprint / Gaia / My heart's song.

Mar 97. (cd; as INVISIBLE OPERA COMPANY OF TIBET) *(VP 147CD)* **GLISSANDO SPIRIT** [ ] [-]
– Landing / Uluwatu / Electric bird / Baliman energy / Cosmic dancer / Inner voice / High mountains dance / Dreaming / Moon in the sky / Mirage / Distant shore / Stars can frighten you / 7 keys / Wizard's garden / Eastside.

– his compilations, etc

Feb 94. (m-cd) *Voiceprint; (VPR 012CD)* **VOICEPRINT RADIO SESSION** [ ] [-]

Mar 94. (cd; DAEVID ALLEN TRIO) *Voiceprint; (VP 122CD)* **LIVE 1963 (live)** [ ] [-]

Mar 95. (cd) *Legend; (KZLM 1505-1)* **BANANA MOON GONG** (late 60's material) [ ] [-]

May 96. (cd) *Gas; (AGASCD 007)* **DREAMING A DREAM** [ ] [-]

MOTHER GONG

with DAEVID ALLEN – producer, guitar, vocals / **DIDIER MALHERBE** – sax, flute / **PIP PYLE** – drums / **PEPSI MILAN** – guitar / **VERA BLUM** – violin / **TONY PASCUAL** – keyboards / etc

Charly | not issued

Jun 78. (lp; by GILLI SMYTH) *(CRL 5007)* **MOTHER** [ ] [-]
– I am a fool / Back to the womb / Mother / Shakti Yoni / Next time ragtime / Time of the goddess / Taliesin / Keep the children free / Prostitute poem (street version) / O.k. man / This is your world.

— **GILLI + HARRY WILLIAMSON** – guitar (+ others)

Nov 79. (lp) *(CRL 5018)* **FAIRY TALES** [ ] [-]
– Wassilissa: Three riders / The Baba Yaga's collage / The forbidden room / Time machine / Flying / Wassilissa returns home / Through the machine again / The Baba Yaga / The three tongues: The shoemaker's son / Land of dogs / The frog / An Irish inn in Rome / The arena / Turtles / Birds / The feast / The Pied Piper: Hamelin / Rats amok / An angry crowd / Rat-rock / A thousand guilders / Children / Magic land.

— settled line-up; **GILLI, HARRY, DIDIER / + GUY EVANS** – drums (ex-VAN DER GRAAF) / **DAYNE CRANENBURG** – bass / **YAN EMERIC** – slide guitar / **HUGH HOPPER** – bass

Butt | not issued

Jan 81. (lp) *(BUTT 003)* **ROBOT WOMAN** [ ] [-]
– Disco at the end of the world / Womans place / Robot woman / Machine song / The sea / Listen . . . / Searching the airwaves / Billi Bunker's blues / Military procession / Customs man / Red alert / Stars / Australia.

— **DAVE SAWYER** – percussion (repl.EMERIC + HOPPER)

Shanghai | not issued

Sep 84. (lp) *(HAI 100)* **ROBOT WOMAN II** [ ] [-]
– Suggestive station / This train / I wanna be with you / The moving walkway / The upwardly mobile song / Tigers or elephants / Mirror / You can touch the sky / 1999 / Crazy town / Angry song / Looking for / Leotards.

Dec 86. (lp) *(HAI 109)* **ROBOT WOMAN III** [ ] [-]
– It's you and me baby / Faces of woman / Desire / War / Children's song / Lady's song / Woman of streams / I'm sorry / Men cry / Solutions / Magenta part one.

— **GILLI + HARRY / + ROBERT CALVERT** – sax (ex-CATAPILLA)

Mothermusic | not issued

1992. (cd) *(MM 101CD)* **LIVE 1991** [-] [-] Aust.

Voiceprint | not issued

May 93. (cd) *(VP 134CD)* **SHE MADE THE WORLD – MAGENTA** [ ] [-]
– Magenta / Water / She made the world / Weather / Malicious sausage / Sea horse / Spirit calling / Tattered jacket / Warm / When the show is over / I am a witch / Spirit of the bush / Blessed be.

Jun 93. (cd; by GILLI SMYTH) *(VP 139CD)* **EVERY WITCHES WAY** [ ] [-]
– Simple / Bold and brazen / Show is over / We who were raging / Beltaine / Four horsemen / Medicine woman / Animal / Magic / Llammas / I am witch / Lady Wise / Simples.

Demi Monde | not issued

Feb 94. (cd) *(DMCD 1026)* **WILD CHILD** [ ] [-]

Voiceprint | not issued

Sep 94. (cd) *(VP 176CD)* **EYE** [ ] [-]
– Fanfare / She's the mother of / Sunday / Beds / Time is a hurrying dog / Ancient / Zen / Quantum / Spirit canoe / What if we were gods and godesses / Auction / Little boy / Magic stories / Excuses / Sax canoe / Fairy laughter / Virtual relity.

– her compilations, etc. –

Oct 94. Voiceprint; (cd) *(VP 007CD)* **THE VOICEPRINT RADIO SESSIONS** [ ] [-]

— In France, DIDIER MALHERBE issued 1979 lp 'BLOOM' (Sonopresse) and 1980 single 'DANSEKORLA. / BONG' (Sonopresse). In 1987 'Cryonic' of France released 'FATON BLOOM'. In 1990 'Mantra' issued 'FETISH'. Sep92; 'Tangram' issued 'ZEFF'.

GOOD RATS

Formed: Long Island, New York, USA . . . 1964 by college students PEPPI and MICKEY MARCHELLO. A debut album finally appeared in 1968, blending an amalgam of rock'n'roll and progressive rock. This failed to create any stir, and they went underground for nigh on five years. They returned in 1973/4 with an extended line-up (see below), recording the 'Warner Brothers' album, 'TASTY'. Dropped by the label, they formed their own 'Ratcity', for which they subsequently released the album, 'RATCITY IN BLUE'. With FLO & EDDIE (MARK VOLMAN & HOWARD KAYLAN) at the helm (also providing some of the higher-range vocals), their fourth album, 'FROM RATS TO RICHES', was picked up by UK label, 'Radar' for release in 1978. Despite featuring guests MANFRED MANN, MEL COLLINS and LARRY FAST, the 'BIRTH COMES TO US ALL' album was a commercial disaster, two more dismal outings leaving the band with no choice but to drop out of the music scene.

Recommended: THE GOOD RATS (*6) / FROM RATS TO RICHES (*6)

PEPPI MARCHELLO – vocals, mouth-harp / **MICKEY MARCELLO** – guitar, vocals

London | Kapp

Dec 68. (lp) <KS 3580> **THE GOOD RATS** [-] [ ]
– We are the Good Rats / Joey Ferrari / For the sake of anyone / Anybody got the time / My back is achin' (and my mind is no better) / The hobo / If you stay by me / Gotta get back / The truth is gone / Family portrait.

Jan 69. (7") *(HLR 10237)* <946> **THE HOBO. / TRUTH IS GONE** [ ] [ ]

— added **JOHN 'THE CAT' GATTO** – guitar, keyboards / **LENNY KOTKE** – bass / **JOE FRANCO** – drums

not issued | Warners

1974. (lp) <2813> **TASTY** [-] [ ]
– Back to my music / Injun Joe / Tasty / Papa poppa / Klask-ka-bob / Fireball express / Fred upstairs & Ginger snappers / Joo boys / Phil Fleish / Songwriter. *<re-iss.1978 on 'Ratcity'; RCR 8002>*

Philips | Ratcity

1976. (lp) *(6310 625)* <RCR 8004> **RATCITY IN BLUE** [ ] [ ]
– Does it make you feel good / Boardwalk slasher / Ratcity in blue / Almost anything goes / The room / Mean mother / Writing the pages / Reason to kill / Advertisement in the voice / Yellow flower / Tough guys / Hour glass.

Radar | Passport

Dec 77. (7") <7912> **JUST FOUND A LADY. / COO COO COO BLUES** [-] [ ]

Feb 78. (lp) *(RAD 5)* <PB 9825> **FROM RATS TO RICHES** [ ] [ ] 1977
– Taking it to Detroit / Just found me a lady / Mr. Mechanic / Dear sir / Let me / Victory in space / Coo coo coo blues / Don't hate the ones who bring you rock & roll / Could be tonight / Local zero.

May 78. (7") *(ADA 9)* **MR. MECHANIC. / VICTORY IN SPACE** [ ] [-]

1978. (lp) <PB 9830> **BIRTH COMES TO US ALL** [-] [ ]
– You're still doing it / City liners / Cherry river / Ordinary man / Man or a fish / School days / Juvenile song / Gino / Bed and a bottle / Birth comes to us all.

not issued | Arista

1980. (lp) <SP 20> **RATS THE WAY YOU LIKE IT – LIVE AT LAST (live)** [-] [ ]
– Taking it to Detroit / Does it make you feel good / Tasty / Ratcity in blue / Beat up rambler / Fireball express / Coo coo coo blues / Dear sir / Reason to kill / Local zero.

— **BRUCE KULICK** – guitar + **SCHULYLER DEALE** – bass; repl. GATTO

Logo | Ratcity

1981. (lp) *(1027)* <RCR 8003> **GREAT AMERICAN MUSIC** [ ] [ ]
– New York survivor / Julie / Hollywood ending / Great American music halls / Yes or no / Ice cold / On my way to school / Oh so good / Rock & roll point of view.

— split after above

Sam GOPAL

Born: India. He formed The SAM GOPAL DREAM in 1967, an imaginative underground outfit numbering ANDY CLARK, MICK HUTCHINSON and PETE SEARS. They played the famous UFO club in London, before having a demo featured on John Peel's 'Perfumed Garden' pirate radio show. This short-lived outfit failed to release any product and were subsequently joined by VIV PRINCE for a farewell gig at the Middle Earth club, the others forming VAMP for a one-off 45. Later, CLARK and HUTCHINSON started their own duo, while SEARS went off to the West Coast, joining US bands STONEGROUND, COPPERHEAD and finally JEFFERSON STARSHIP. GOPAL formed another Eastern-orientated band, which included LEMMY (later of HAWKWIND and MOTORHEAD). They released a TREVOR WATTS-produced album in 1969, 'ESCALATOR', which contained a version of DONOVAN's 'SEASON OF THE WITCH' alongside classic cuts 'COLD EMBRACE', 'THE DARK LORD' and LEMMY's psychedelic title track.

Recommended: ESCALATOR (*7)

SAM GOPAL – tabla, percussion / **IAN 'LEMMY' WILLIS** – vocals, guitars / **ROGER D'ELIA** – guitars / **PHIL DUKE** – bass

Stable | not issued

Jan 69. (lp) *(SLE 8001)* **ESCALATOR** [ ] [-]
– Cold embrace / The dark lord / The sky is burning / You're alone now / Grass / It's only love / Escalator / Angry faces / Midsummer nights dream / Season of the witch / Yesterlove.

1969. (7"ep; sampler) *(SLE 8001)* **ESCALATOR / COLD EMBRACE. / SKY IS BURNING / ANGRY FACES** [-] [-]

1969. (7") *(STA 5602)* **HORSE. / BACK DOOR MAN**

— split after above. LEMMY joined HAWKWIND and later formed MOTORHEAD. SAM GOPAL later turned up for DAEVID ALLEN (GONG).

GRACIOUS

Formed: Esher, Surrey, England . . . 1966 as SATAN'S DISCIPLES by school friends ALAN COWDEROY and PAUL 'Sandy' DAVIS. They were soon joined by MARTIN KITCAT, MARK LAIRD and ROBERT LIPSON. Bass player LAIRD left, and was replaced by road manager TIM WHEATLEY. With the help of manager DAVID BOOTH, they found a new name, GRACIOUS!. They recruited a temporary 6th member, KEITH IRELAND, to sing harmony on a German tour. Songwriters DAVIS and KITCAT scored an ambitious conceptual "suite" about the seasons of the year, duly sending the demo to Norrie Paramour (producer to CLIFF RICHARD & THE SHADOWS). In 1969, with Mellotron in tow, they played a double bill alongside KING CRIMSON, which led to a private cinema rendition of the piece in front of Mr. Paramour. Although it wasn't his "cup of tea", TIM RICE (yes that one!) agreed to work on their debut 'Polydor' single, 'BEAUTIFUL'. This also led to PAUL DAVIS sessioning on RICE's 'Jesus Christ Superstar', and the group signing for progressive label 'Vertigo' in 1970. An slightly self-indulgent album (known as the exclamation mark, and now worth over £50 due to the label's famous hypnotic swirl on the vinyl's centre), was released that summer, although it sold poorly. A follow-up was scheduled by the label in 1971, but its delay and lack of money, led to them disbanding. 'THIS IS . . . GRACIOUS!!' did surface, however, as a budget release on the 'Philips' label the following year.

Recommended: GRACIOUS! (*6) / THIS IS . . . GRACIOUS!! (*6)

PAUL DAVIS – vocals, 12-string guitar, timpani / **MARTIN KITCAT** – Mellotron, pianos, vocals / **ALAN COWDEROY** – guitar, vocals / **TIM WHEATLEY** – bass / **ROBERT LIPSON** – drums

Polydor / not issued

Jun 69. (7") *(BM 56333)* **BEAUTIFUL. / WHAT A LOVELY RAIN**

Vertigo / Capitol

Aug 70. (7") *(6059 009)* **ONCE ON A WINDY DAY. / FUGUE IN D MINOR**

Aug 70. (lp) *(6360 002) <602>* **GRACIOUS!**
– Introduction / Heaven / Hell / Fugue in 'd' minor / The dream. *(cd-iss.1990's on 'Repertoire'; REP 4060)*

Philips / not issued

May 72. (lp) *(6382 004)* **THIS IS . . . GRACIOUS!!**
– Supernova: (a) Arrival of the traveller, (b) Blood red sun, (c) Say goodbye to love, (d) Prepare to meet thy maker / C.B.S. / What's come to be / Blue skies and alibis / Hold me down.

— Had already split prior to above album. WHEATLEY later joined TAGGETT, who made one eponymous lp in 1974 for 'E.M.I.', before he became involved with running 'Vertigo' for three years. COWDEROY later got a job for 'Stiff' records in 1976/77, before landing an executive job for 'A&M'. He now co-manages DEL AMITRI. KITCAT also worked in the business, before settling in America and selling his much-prized Mellotron. PAUL DAVIS went solo, but due to another artist of the same name he opted for his nickname.

– compilations, etc –

Mar 95. (d-cd) *Beat Goes On; (BGOCD 256)* **GRACIOUS! / THIS IS . . . GRACIOUS!!**

SANDY DAVIS

with **COWDEROY / MARTIN BRILEY** – guitar / **ANDREW BRYCE JACKMAN** – keyboards / **PETER SKELLERN** – piano

E.M.I. / not issued

Nov 73. (7") *(EMI 2097)* **MY FAVOURITE LADY. / SNUGGLE UP**
Mar 74. (7") *(EMI 2130)* **I GOT FRIENDS. / LAST OF MY GOODBYES**
Apr 74. (lp) *(EMC 3029)* **INSIDE EVERY FAT MAN**
– Inside every fat man / I got friends / Rocker box man / Show a little love / Snuggle up / Up high / Really move it / Sunny day / My favourite lady / Last of my goodbyes / Lend me a fiver / He gives us all his love.
Jul 74. (7") *(EMI 2181)* **INSIDE EVERY FAT MAN. / SHARE A LITTLE LOVE**

— with **GORDON HUNTER** – guitar / **DELISLE HARPER** – bass / **ROY DAVIES** – keyboards / **CHRIS MERCER** – saxophone / **STEVE FERRONE** – drums / plus AVERAGE WHITE BAND on harmony

Feb 75. (7") *(EMI 2261)* **ONLY LOVE CAN LAST FOREVER. / EUGENE BABY**
Mar 75. (lp) *(EMC 3070)* **BACK ON MY FEET AGAIN**
– Back on my feet again / Baby I do / Wild woman / Who knows / Step in the right direction / Sweet little rock'n'roller / Only love can last forever / You and I / He's just a heartbreaker.

GRANNY'S INTENTIONS

Formed: London, England . . . 1967 by JOHNNY DUNCAN, JOHNNY HOCKEDY, JOHN RYAN, PETE CUMMINGS and PAT NASH. They released four progressive, blues-based 45's for 'Deram', before finally getting around to an album, 'HONEST INJUN', in 1970. A very youthful GARY MOORE guested on the album, before being asked to join up full-time.

Recommended: HONEST INJUN (*4)

JOHNNY DUNCAN – vocals / **JOHNNY HOCKEDY** – guitar, mandolin / **JOHN RYAN** – keyboards / **PETE CUMMINGS** – bass, flute / **PAT NASH** – drums

Deram / Deram

Nov 67. (7") *(DM 158)* **THE STORY OF DAVID. / SANDY'S ON THE PHONE AGAIN**
Apr 68. (7") *(DM 184)* **JULIE DON'T LOVE ME ANYMORE. / ONE TIME LOVERS**
Oct 68. (7") *(DM 214) <85037>* **NEVER AN EASY THING. / HILDA THE BILDA**

— **GARY MOORE** – guitar repl. HOCKEDY

Apr 70. (7") *(DM 293)* **TAKE ME BACK. / MAYBE**
1970. (lp) *(SML 1060)* **HONEST INJUN**

— split in 1970. GARY MOORE joined SKID ROW before going solo.

GRATEFUL DEAD

Formed: San Francisco, California, USA . . . 1965 by JERRY GARCIA, who had spent 9 months of 1959 in the army before finding ROBERT HUNTER, lyricist extrordinaire, and forming folk outfit The THUNDER MOUNTAIN TUB THUMPERS. Along the way, this loose collective of musicians included soon-to-be GRATEFUL DEAD members BOB WEIR and RON McKERNAN (aka PIGPEN), JERRY going on to make demos in 1963 as duo JERRY & SARAH GARCIA. It wasn't until 1965 that the earliest incarnation of The GRATEFUL DEAD, The WARLOCKS, set out on their "golden road to unlimited gigging", when they took centre stage as house band for KEN KESEY's (author of 'One Flew Over The Cuckoo's Nest') legendary acid tests. Created by KESEY and his band of merry pranksters, the main objective of these psychedelic shindigs was to bombard the tripping hordes with as much sensory overload as posible; flashing lights, pre-recorded chants, hidden speakers hissing subversive messages and of course, the ear splitting racket of The WARLOCKS. With crowd and band liberally dosed with LSD courtesy of acidmeister AUGUSTUS STANLEY III, the events were clearly a formative part of their career. By this time, the band had gone electric, inspired by the raucous rock'n'roll of The BEATLES, bolstering the sound with drummer BILL KREUTZMANN and bassist PHIL LESH. Changing their name to the equally hoary sounding GRATEFUL DEAD (picked at random from a dictionary), the band toured California alongside JEFFERSON AIRPLANE. In 1966, they issued a one-off 45, 'DON'T EASE ME IN' for 'Fantasy' off-shoot label 'Scorpio', which led to 'Warners' signing them up in 1967. Recorded in three amphetamine-fuelled days, 'THE GRATEFUL DEAD' was released to the expectant hippy faithful in December of the same year, an admirable but untimately doomed attempt to recreated their fabled live sound in the studio. After an impromptu guest spot at one of their early shows, drummer MICKEY HART augmented the band's rhythm section, creating a more subtly complex rather than powerful sound. The group also recruited keyboardist TOM CONSTANTEN, whose avant-garde influences included JOHN CAGE and STOCKHAUSEN. Adding to the DEAD's psychedelic stew, these two further inspired the band's live improviation, partly captured on 'ANTHEM OF THE SUN' in 1968. An ambitious collage of live and studio pieces, the album was another flawed attempt to seize the essence of the elusive beast that was the band's live show. It did however, contain bizarrely experimental sections with wonderful cod-hippy titles like, 'CRYPTICAL ENVELOPMENT' and 'THE FASTER WE GO, THE ROUNDER WE GET', these worth the admission price alone. The experimentation continued with 'AOXOMOXOA' in 1969, GARCIA's old mate ROBERT HUNTER marking his first collaboration with the band and helping to contain the explorations inside defined song structures. Highlights included 'MOUNTAINS OF THE MOON', with its celestial harpsicord and 'ST STEPHEN', a song that would go on to become a staple of the band's live set. With the release of 'LIVE DEAD' in 1970, The GRATEFUL DEAD finally did itself justice on vinyl, silencing the critics of their previous output who couldn't understand why the band were held in such high esteem by their fiercely loyal San Franciscan fanbase. On the track 'DARK STAR', the band crystallised their free-flowing improvisation in breathtaking style, while the celebratory 'TURN ON YOUR LOVE LIGHT', was also a standard of the band's now legendary live shows. Attracting multitudes of tye-dyed freaks, affectionately nicknamed "Deadheads", the band's gigs became communal gatherings, where both the crowd and band could lose themselves in the spaced-out jams which would often stretch songs over an hour or more. Forget 15 minutes of fame (as ANDY WARHOL once gave us all), the DEAD needed 15 minutes just for the intro! Ironically the band's next two studio albums marked a radical new direction with pared-down sets of harmony laden country-folk. With CONSTANTEN out of the picture by early 1970 and mounting debts, the group went for a simpler sound, clearly influenced by CROSBY, STILLS and NASH and GARCIA's part-time dabblings with The NEW RIDERS OF THE PURPLE SAGE. 'WORKINGMAN'S DEAD' was symptomatic of the times as bands began to move away from the psychedelic claustrophobia of the late 60's (note 'NEW SPEEDWAY BOOGIE' about the end of the hippy dream; the Altamont Festival which a ROLLING STONES fan was killed by a drug-crazed Hell's Angel). 'AMERICAN BEAUTY' carried on where the previous album left off, 'SUGAR MAGNOLIA' and 'RIPPLE' being the highlights of this highly regarded piece of roots rock. By 1971, HART had departed and the band were reduced to five core members. Two live albums followed, the double 'GRATEFUL DEAD' and 'EUROPE 72', the latter stretching to three slabs of vinyl. 1972 also saw the release of WEIR's solo album, 'ACE', actually a GRATEFUL DEAD album in all but name. It

DARK STAR
JERRY GARCIA

included the glorious tongue-in-cheek romp, 'MEXICALI BLUES' and also saw WEIR begin writing with JOHN PERRY BARLOW, a partnership that would see HUNTER's input diminish over the following years. Years of alcohol abuse led to PIGPEN dying on 8th May '73 and he was replaced by KEITH GODCHAUX, who had toured with them the previous year. His wife DONNA also joined, taking up vocal duties. Around this time the band set up their own label, imaginatively titled 'Grateful Dead Records', releasing 'WAKE OF THE FLOOD' in July '73. The album was their most successful to date, containing the melancholy 'STELA BLUE', although ironically, profits were lost to bootleggers. 'BLUES FOR ALLAH', from 1975, signalled a jazzier, fuller sound, though by this juncture the band were in financial deep water and signed with 'United Artists'. The source of much of their money problems was a concert movie which ate up most of their resources. 'STEAL YOUR FACE' was next in line and was intended for the movie, although it remained in the can due to the album's relative critical failure. Signing to 'Arista' and drafting in KEITH OLSEN on production duties they released 'TERRAPIN STATION' in 1977, an album which showcased a lusher, fuller sound. For '78's 'SHAKEDOWN STREET', the band collaborated with LOWELL GEORGE, and what could have been an interesting pairing, came out sounding limp and uninspiring; a pale reflection of what the DEAD were capable of. Despite the inconsistent quality of their studio work, the DEAD were always a safe live bet and they played the gig to surely top all gigs with their series of dates at the Pyramids in Egypt. Still carrying a hippy torch (even through the punk days), they filled large venues wherever they played and became a multi-million dollar industry in their own right. However, as they concentrated on live work, their studio outings suffered, their 1980 album 'GO TO HEAVEN' being particularly disappointing athough it spawned their first success in the US singles chart with 'ALABAMA GETAWAY'. Another two live sets followed in 1981, 'DEAD SET' and 'RECKONING'. The latter was an acoustic album featuring classics like 'RIPPLE' and 'CASSIDY'. Soon after their release, GARCIA became a full blown heroin addict, narrowly escaping death when he fell into a diabetic coma in in 1986. Once he rehabilitated, the DEAD came back to life with 'IN THE DARK', a spirited set that reached the Top 10 in the US chart, even resulting in top selling 45, 'TOUCH OF GREY'. Their tribute to growing old with pride, it was a first when the band agreed to make a video for MTV. The awful 'DYLAN & THE DEAD' (yes with Mr. Zimmerman) was muted and dull, as was the studio 1989 offering, 'BUILT TO LAST'. Tragedy hit the band yet again, when keyboardist BRENT MYDLAND (who himself had replaced KEITH GODCHAUX in '79) was killed by a hard drugs cocktail. BRUCE HORNSBY (yes that solo geezer) was drafted in temorarily for touring commitments, while VINCE WELNICK joined full-time. The band released yet another live album the same year, the hardly dangerous 'WITHOUT A NET' and also started issuing the DICK'S PICKS series of archive recordings from great days of yore. On 9th August, 1995, the ailing JERRY GARCIA died of heart failure in a rehab unit after his arteries clogged up. It seemed inevitable that the long strange trip of The GRATEFUL DEAD had come to an end, GARCIA's guiding light relocating to find his "Dark Star" once again. The DEAD left behind a rich musical legacy, including numerous solo outings and off-shoot projects, but will always be remembered, by the 'Deadheads' at least, for their transcendental live performances. • **Songwriters:** Most by HUNTER-GARCIA or WEIR, LESH and some by others, including JOHN BARLOW. Covered; GOOD MORNING LITTLE SCHOOLGIRL (Don & Bob) / NEW MINGLEWOOD BLUES + SAMSON AND DELILAH (trad.) / JOHNNY B. GOODE (Chuck Berry) / NOT FADE AWAY (Buddy Holly) / ME AND BOBBY McGEE (Kris Kristofferson) / BIG BOSS MAN (Bo Diddley) / DANCING IN THE STREET (hit; Martha & The Vandellas) / STAGGER LEE (Lloyd Price) / LITTLE RED ROOSTER (Willie Dixon) / DEAR MR. FANTASY (Traffic) / WALKIN' BLUES (Robert Johnson) / NEXT TIME YOU SEE ME (Junior Parker) / etc. GARCIA covered; IT TAKES A LOT TO LAUGH + POSITIVELY 4TH STREET + KNOCKIN' ON HEAVEN'S DOOR (Bob Dylan) / LET'S SPEND THE NIGHT TOGETHER + WILD HORSES (Rolling Stones) / HE AIN'T GIVE YOU NONE (Van Morrison) / THAT'S ALL RIGHT MAMA (Arthur Crudup) / MY FUNNY VALENTINE / WHEN THE HUNTER GETS CAPTURED BY THE GAME (Smokey Robinson) / LET IT ROCK (Chuck Berry) / RUSSIAN LULLABY (Irving Berlin) / MIDNIGHT TOWN (Kahn-Hunter) / I SAW HER STANDING THERE (Beatles) / etc. • **Trivia:** An edited 'DARK STAR', was used as theme in the US 70's series of 'Twilight Zone'.

Recommended: THE GRATEFUL DEAD (*6) / ANTHEM OF THE SUN (*8) / AOXOMOXOA (*6) / LIVE/DEAD (*7) / WORKINGMAN'S DEAD (*8) / AMERICAN BEAUTY (*10) / WHAT A LONG STRANGE TRIP IT'S BEEN (*8) / GRATEFUL DEAD (*6) / EUROPE '72 (*6) / TERRAPIN STATION (*6)

JERRY GARCIA (b. JEROME JOHN GARCIA, 1 Aug'42) – vocals, lead guitar / **BOB WEIR** (b. ROBERT HALL, 6 Oct'47) – rhythm guitar / **RON 'PIGPEN' McKERNAN** (b. 8 Sep'45, San Bruno, Calif.) – keyboards, vocals, mouth harp / **PHIL LESH** (b. PHILIP CHAPMAN, 15 Mar'40, Berkeley, Calif.) – bass / **BILL KREUTZMANN** (b. 7 Apr'46, Palo Alto, Calif.) – drums (DAN MORGAN left before recording)

not issued / Scorpio

Jun 66. (7") <003-201> **DON'T EASE ME IN. / STEALIN'** [-] [ ]

Warners / Warners

Feb 67. (7") <7016> **THE GOLDEN ROAD (TO UNLIMITED DEVOTION). / CREAM PUFF WAR** [-] [ ]

Dec 67. (lp; mono/stereo) *(<W/+S 1689>)* **THE GRATEFUL DEAD** [ ] [73] Feb67
– The golden road (to unlimited devotion) / Cold rain and snow / Good morning little schoolgirl / Beat it on down / Sitting on top of the world / Cream puff war / Morning dew / New, new Minglewood blues / Viola Lee blues. *(re-iss.Mar87 on 'Edsel'; ED 221) <US cd-iss.1987; 2-1689> (cd-iss.Jul88 on 'Atlantic'; K 259302) (cd-iss.Feb93 & Oct95)*

— added **TOM CONSTANTEN** – keyboards / **MICKEY HART** (b.1950, Long Island, N.Y.) – percussion and returning lyricist **ROBERT HUNTER**

Oct 68. (7") *(WB <7186>)* **BORN CROSS-EYED. / DARK STAR** [ ] [ ]

Nov 68. (lp) *(<WS 1749>)* **ANTHEM OF THE SUN** [ ] [87] Aug 68
– That's it for other one:- Cryptical envelopment – Quadlibet for tender feet – The faster we go, the rounder we get – We leave the castle / New potato caboose / Born cross-eyed / Alligator / Caution (do not stop on the tracks). *(re-iss.Jul71; K 46021) <US cd-iss.1987; 2-1749> (re-iss.Jul88 on 'WEA' lp/cd; K2 4602-1/2) (re-iss.cd 1992; 7599 27173-2)*

Oct 69. (lp) *(<WS 1790>)* **AOXOMOXOA** [ ] [73] Jun 69
– St. Stephen / Dupree's diamond blues / Rosemary / Doin' the rag / Mountains of the Moon / China cat sunflower / What's become of the baby / Cosmic Charlie. *(re-iss.Jul71; K 46027) ;re-iss.Jan77) <US cd-iss.1987; 2-1790> (re-iss.Jun89 on 'WEA' c/cd; K4 46027/ K927 128-2)*

Oct 69. (7") <7324> **DUPREE'S DIAMOND BLUES. / COSMIC CHARLIE** [-] [ ]

Feb 70. (d-lp) <2(WS 1830)> **LIVE/DEAD (live in the studio)** [ ] [64] Dec 69
– Dark star / Death don't have no mercy / Feedback / And we bid you goodnight / St. Stephen / The eleven / Turn on your love light. *(re-iss.Jul71; K 66002) <US cd-iss.1987; 2-1830> (cd-iss.Jun89 on 'WEA'; K927 181-2)*

— **DAVID NELSON** – acoustic guitar repl. CONSTANTEN / added guest **JOHN DAWSON** – guitar, vocals (on some)

— above pairing also formed off-shoot band The NEW RIDERS OF THE PURPLE SAGE, who initially toured as support to DEAD, with GARCIA in their ranks.

Sep 70. (lp) *(<WS 1869>)* **WORKINGMAN'S DEAD** [ ] [27] Jun 70
– Uncle John's band / High time / Dire wolf / New speedway boogie / Cumberland blues / Black Peter / Easy wind / Casey Jones. *(re-iss.Jul71; K 46049) <US cd-iss.1987; 2-1889> (re-iss.1988 lp/c) (cd-iss.Jun89 on 'WEA'; K2 46049)*

Aug 70. (7") *(WB <7410>)* **UNCLE JOHN'S BAND. / NEW SPEEDWAY BOOGIE** [ ] [69]

— added guest **DAVID TORBERT** – bass (1)

Dec 70. (lp) *(<WS 1893>)* **AMERICAN BEAUTY** [ ] [30]
– Box of rain / Friend of the Devil / Sugar magnolia / Operator / Candyman / Ripple / Brokedown palace / Till the morning comes / Attics of my life / Truckin. *(re-iss.Jul71; K 46074) ;re-iss.Jan77) <US cd-iss.1987; 2-1893> (re-iss.Jun89 on 'WEA' c/cd; K2/K4 46074)*

Jan 71. (7") <7464> **TRUCKIN. / RIPPLE** [-] [64]

— Now **GARCIA, WEIR, LESH, KREUTZMANN** and **'PIGPEN'** with new members **MERL SAUNDERS** – keyboards (repl. PIGPEN for a while when he was ill) all guests had departed, incl. HART and NELSON.

Oct 71. (d-lp) *(K 66009)* <2WS 1935> **GRATEFUL DEAD** (SKULL & ROSES) (live) [ ] [25]
– Bertha / Mama tried / Big railroad blues / Playing in the band / The other one / Me & my uncle / Big boss man / Me & Bobby McGhee / Johnny B. Goode / Wharf rat / Not fade away / Goin' down road feeling bad. *<US cd-iss.1987; 2-1935> (cd-iss.1988; 927 192-2) (re-iss.cd 1992; 7599 27192-2)*

Jan 72. (7") **JOHNNY B. GOODE. / SO FINE (by 'Elvin Bishop')** [-] [ ]

— added on tour **KEITH GODCHAUX** (b.14 Jul'48) – keyboards (ex-DAVE MASON band) and **DONNA GODCHAUX** (b.22 Aug'47) – vocals (They both repl. SAUNDERS)

Dec 72. (t-lp) *(K 66019)* <3WS 2668> **EUROPE '72 (live)** [ ] [24] Nov 72
– Cumberland blues / He's gone / One more Saturday night / Jack Straw / You win again / China cat sunflower / I know you rider / Brown-eyed woman / Hurts me too / Ramble on Rose / Sugar magnolia / Mr. Charlie / Tennessee Jed / Truckin' / (epilog) / (prelude) / (Walk me out in the) Morning dew. *(cd-iss.Oct95;)*

Dec 72. (7") <7667> **SUGAR MAGNOLIA (live). / MR. CHARLIE (live)** [-] [91]

— Now just basic 4 of **GARCIA, WEIR, LESH, KREUTZMANN** and both **GODCHAUX'S.** ('PIGPEN' sadly died 8 May'73 after a long and threatening bout of illness) note that ROBERT HUNTER was still writing their lyrics, next 2 albums also included ten or more session people.

Warners / Grateful Dead

Jul 73. (lp/c) *(K/K4 49301)* <GD 01> **WAKE OF THE FLOOD** [ ] [18] Oct 73
– Mississippi half-step uptown toodeloo / Let me sing your blues away / Row Jimmy / Stella blue / Here comes sunshine / Eyes of the world / Weather Report suite (part 1; Prelude – part 2; Let it grow). *(re-iss.Jan76 on 'United Artists'; UAS 29903) (<re-iss.Apr89 on 'Grateful Dead' lp/c/cd; GDV/GDTCGDCD 4002>) (pic-cd Feb90; GDPD 4002)*

Nov 73. (7") *(K 19301)* <01> **LET ME SING YOUR BLUES AWAY. / HERE COMES SUNSHINE** [ ] [ ]

Jan 74. (7") <02> **EYES OF THE WORLD. / WEATHER REPORT SUITE (part 1; PRELUDE)** [-] [ ]

Jul 74. (lp/c) *(K/K4 59302)* <GD 102> **FROM THE MARS HOTEL** [47] [16]
– Scarlet begonias / Ship of fools / Pride of Cucamonga / Loose Lucy / U.S. blues / Unbroken chain / China doll / Money money. *(re-iss.Jan76 on 'United Artists'; UAS 29904) <US cd-iss.Dec85 on 'Mobile Fidelity'; MFCD 830> (re-iss.Mar89 on 'Grateful Dead' lp/c/cd; GDV/GDTCGDCD 4007) (pic-cd Feb90; GDPD 4007)*

Aug 74. (7") *(UP 36030)* <03> **U.S. BLUES. / LOOSE LUCY** [ ] [ ]

— added the returning **MICKEY HART** – percussion

U.A. / Grateful Dead

Oct 75. (lp) *(UAS 29895)* <LA 494> **BLUES FOR ALLAH** [45] [12] Sep 75
– Help on the way / Slipknot / Franklin's tower / King Solomon's marbles / Stronger than dirt or milkin' the turkey / The music never stopped / Crazy fingers / Sage & spirit / Blues for Allah / Sand castles & glass camels / Unusual occurances in the desert. *(<re-iss.Mar89 on 'Grateful Dead' lp/c/cd; GDV/GDTCGDCD 4001>) (pic-cd Feb90; GDPD 4001)*

Oct 75. (7") <718> **THE MUSIC NEVER STOPPED. / HELP IS ON THE WAY** [-] [81]

Jun 76. (d-lp) *(UAD 60131-2)* <LA 620> **STEAL YOUR FACE (live)** [42] [56]
– The promised land / Cold rain and snow / Around and around / Stella blue / Mississippi half-step uptown toodeloo / Ship of fools / Beat it down the line / Big river / Black-throated wind / U.S. blues / El Paso / Sugaree / It must have been the roses / Casey Jones. *(re-iss.Mar89 on 'Grateful Dead' lp/c/cd; GDV2/GDTCGDCD2 4006) (pic-cd Feb90; GDPD2 4006)*

1976. (7") <762> **FRANKLIN'S TOWER. / HELP IS ON THE WAY** [-] [ ]

Arista Arista

Aug 77. (lp/c) *(SPART/TC-ARTY 1016)* <*AL 7001*> **TERRAPIN STATION** 28
– Estimated prophet / Samson and Delilah / Passenger / Dancing in the street / Sunrise / Terrapin station. *(re-iss.1983; SPARTY 1016) (re-iss.Jan87 lp/c; 201/401 190)* <*US cd-iss.1986; ARCD 8065*> *(cd-iss.Nov90; 260175)*

Oct 77. (12")<7"> *(DEAD 1)* <*0276*> **DANCING IN THE STREETS. / TERRAPIN STATION**

Feb 78. (7") <*0291*> **PASSENGER. / TERRAPIN STATION** -

Dec 78. (lp/c) *(ARTY/TC-ART 159)* <*AB 4198*> **SHAKEDOWN STREET** 41
– Good lovin' / France / Shakedown street / Serangetti / Fire on the mountain / I need a miracle / From the heart of me / Stagger Lee / New, new Minglewood blues / If I had the world to give. <*US cd-iss.1986; ARCD 4198*> *(cd-iss.Jun91; 251 133)*

Dec 78. (7") *(ARIST 236)* <*0383*> **GOOD LOVIN'. / STAGGER LEE**

Mar 79. (7") <*0410*> **SHAKEDOWN STREET. / FRANCE** -

— **BRENT MYDLAND** (b.1953, Munich, Germany) – keyboards repl. both GODCHAUX'S (KEITH was killed in car crash 23 Jul'80)

May 80. (lp/c) *(SPART/TCART 1115)* <*AL 9508*> **GO TO HEAVEN** 23
– Far from home / Althea / Feel like a stranger / Alabama getaway / Don't ease me in / Easy to love you / Lost sailor / Saint of circumstance. <*US cd-iss.1986; ARCD 9508*>

Jun 80. (7") <*0519*> **ALABAMA GETAWAY. / FAR FROM ME** - 68

Jan 81. (7") <*0546*> **DON'T EASE ME IN. / FAR FROM ME** -

Apr 81. (d-lp) *(DARTY 9)* <*A2L 8604*> **RECKONING (live)** (all line-ups) 43
– Dire wolf / The race is on / Oh babe it ain't no lie / It must have been the roses / Dark hollow / China doll / Been all around the world / Monkey and the engineer / Jack-a-roe / Deep Elam blues / Cassidy / To lay me down / Rosalie McFall / On the road again / Bird song / Ripple.

1981. (7") <*116*> **ALABAMA GETAWAY. / SHAKEDOWN STREET** -

Sep 81. (d-lp) *(DARTY 11)* <*A2L 8606*> **DEAD SET (live)** 29
– Samson and Delilah / Friend of the Devil / New, new Minglewood blues / Deal / Candyman / Little red rooster / Loser / Passenger / Feel like a stranger / Franklin's tower / Fire on the mountain / Rhythm devils / Greatest story ever told / Brokedown palace. <*US cd-iss.1986; ARCD 8112*>

Sep 87. (7"/12") <cd-s/7",7"grey> *(RIS/+T 35)* <*ASCD+/9606*> **TOUCH OF GREY. / MY BROTHER ESAU** 9 Jul 87

Oct 87. (lp/c/cd) *(208/408/258 564)* <*AL/AC/ARCD 8452*> **IN THE DARK** 57 6 Jul 87
– Touch of grey / Hell in a bucket / When push comes to shove / West L.A. fadeaway / Tons of steel / Throwing stones / Black muddy river. *(re-iss.Nov90 cd/lp; 261/211 145)*

Nov 87. (cd-s/7") <*ASCD+/9643*> **THROWING STONES. / WHEN PUSH COMES TO SHOVE** -

— Late '87, they recorded live album 'DYLAN AND THE DEAD' with BOB DYLAN, which was released early 1989, and hit US No.37.

Nov 89. (lp/c/cd) *(210/410/260 326)* <*AL/AC/ARCD 875*> **BUILT TO LAST** 27
– Foolish heart / Just a little light / Built to last / Blow away / Standing on the Moon / Victim or the crime / We can run / Picasso moon / I will take you home.

Nov 89. (cd-s/7") <*ASCD+/9899*> **FOOLISH HEART. / WE CAN RUN** -

Oct 90. (d-cd/t-lp) *(303/353 935)* <*ACD2 8634*> **WITHOUT A NET (live)** 43
– Feel like a stranger / Mississippi half-step uptown toodeloo / Walkin' blues / Althea / Cassidy / Let it grow / China cat sunflower – I know you rider / Looks like rain / Eyes of the world / Victim or the crime / Help on the way – Slipknot! – Franklin's tower / Bird song / One more Saturday night / Dear Mr. Fantasy.

— BRETT MYDLAND died 26 Jul'90 of a drug overdose. Replaced by **VINCE WELNICK** (b.22 Feb'52, Phoenix, Arizona) – keyboards (ex-TUBES, ex-TODD RUNDGREN)

– compilations etc. –

on 'Grateful Dead' records unless mentioned otherwise

Apr 72. (lp) *Polydor; (2310 171) / Sunflower;* <*SNF 5004*> **HISTORIC DEAD** (rare '66) Jun71

Apr 72. (lp) *Polydor; (2310 172) / Sunflower;* <*SUN 5001*> **VINTAGE DEAD (live '66)** Oct70

1972. (lp) *Pride;* <*PRD 0016*> **THE HISTORY OF GRATEFUL DEAD** -

Sep 73. (lp) *Warners; (K 46246)* <*BS 2721*> **HISTORY OF THE DEAD – BEAR'S CHOICE (live rarities)** 60 Jul73
<*US cd-iss.1988; 2721-2*>

Mar 74. (lp) *Warners; (K 56024)* <*BS 2674*> **SKELETONS FROM THE CLOSET** 75
(re-iss.Oct86 on 'Thunderbolt' lp/c/cd; THBL/THBCCDTB 018) <*US cd-iss.1988; 2764-2*>

Apr 74. (7") *Warners;* <*WB 21988*> **SUGAR MAGNOLIA. / MR. CHARLIE** -

— All below on 'Grateful Dead' US records, unless otherwise mentioned.

Feb 77. (d-lp) *United Artists; (UDM 103-4)* **WAKE OF THE FLOOD / FROM MARS HOTEL**

Feb 78. (d-lp) *Warners; (K 66073)* **WHAT A LONG STRANGE TRIP IT'S BEEN: THE BEST OF GRATEFUL DEAD** Nov 77
– New, new Minglewood blues / Cosmic Charlie / Truckin' / Black Peter / Born cross-eyed / Ripple / Doin' that rag / Dark star / High time / New speedway boogie / St. Stephen / Jack Straw / Me & my uncle / Tennessee Jed / Cumberland blues / Playing in the band / Brown-eyed woman / Ramble on Rose. <*US cd-iss.1989; 3091-2*>

1987. (6xcd-box) *Arista;* <*ACD6 8530*> **DEAD ZONE: THE GRATEFUL DEAD CD COLLECTION 1977-1987** -
– (Arista albums from 77-87)

1987. (cd) *Pair;* <*ARP2 1053*> **FOR THE FAITHFUL** -

Jun 91. (d-cd/d-c/t-lp) *(GDCD2/GDTC2/GDV2 4015)* **ONE FROM THE VAULT** (live 13 Aug'75, Great American Music Hall, San Francisco) May91
– (introduction) / Help on the way / Franklin's tower / Music never stopped / It must have been the roses / Eyes of the world – drums / King Solomon's marbles / Around and around / Sugaree / Big river / Crazy fingers – drums / The other one / Sage and spirit / Goin' down the road feeling bad / U.S. blues / Blues for Allah.

Jan 92. (cd) *(GDCD 4016)* **INFRARED ROSES (live)**
– Crowd sculpture / Parallelogram / Little Nemo in Lightland / Riverside rhapsody / Post-modern highrise table top stomp / Infrared roses / Silver apples of the Moon / Speaking in swords / Magnesium night light / Sparrow hawk row / River of nine sorrows / Apollo at the Ritz.

Aug 92. (d-cd/d-lp) *(GDCD2/GDV2 4018)* **TWO FROM THE VAULT** (live 23/24 Aug'68, Shrine Auditorium, L.A.) May92
– Good morning little schoolgirl / Dark star / St. Stephen / The eleven / Death don't have no mercy / The other one / New potato caboose / Turn on your lovelight / Morning dew.

Dec 93. (d-cd) *(GDCD 4019)* **DICK'S PICK VOL.ONE: TAMPA, FLORIDA 12/19/73 (live)**
– Here comes sunshine / Big river / Mississippi half-step uptown toodeloo / Weather report suite (Prelude – part 1, Let it grow – part 2) / Big railroad blues / Playing in the band / He's gone / Truckin' / Nobody's fault but mine / Jam / The other one / Jam / Stella blue / Around and around.

Jan 94. (cd/c) *Dare International; (DIL CD/C 1001)* **RISEN FROM THE VAULTS**

Jun 95. (cd) *(GDCD 4020)* **DICK'S PICKS VOL.TWO: COLUMBUS, OHIO 10/3/71 (live)**
– Dark star / Jam / Sugar magnolia / St. Stephen / Not fade away / Going down the road feeling bad / Not fade away.

Oct 95. (d-cd/d-c) *(GD CD/MC 24021)* **HUNDRED YEAR HALL** (live 26th April 1972, Jahrhundert Halle, Frankfurt) 26
– Bertha / Me & my uncle / The next time you see me / China cat sunflower / I know you rider / Jack Straw / Big railroad blues / Playing in the band / Turn on your love light / Going down the road feeling bad / One more Saturday night / Truckin' / Cryptical envelopment / Comes a time / Sugar magnolia.

Oct 96. (d-cd/d-c) *Arista;* <*(07822 18934-2/-4)*> **THE ARISTA YEARS 1977-95** 95

Jan 97. (3xcd-box) <*(GDCD 34024)*> **DOZIN' AT THE KNICK** 74 Nov96

Jan 97. (3xcd-box) <*(GDCD 34026)*> **DICK'S PICKS VOL.6**

Apr 97. (3xcd-box) <*(GDCD3 4027)*> **DICK'S PICKS VOL.7 (Alexandra Palace 9-11 Sep'74)**

May 97. (cd) *Metro; (OTR 1100024)* **NIGHT OF THE GRATEFUL DEAD** -

Jun 97. (d-cd) <*(GDCD2 4052)*> **FALLOUT FROM THE PHIL ZONE** 83

Jun 97. (cd) *Swell Artifact; (SA 1969)* **GRAYFOLDED**

Jun 97. (cd; MICKEY & THE HEARTBEATS) *Anthology; (ANT 2912)* **HARTBITS VOL.2**

JERRY GARCIA

solo used session men from the DEAD plus others

C.B.S. Douglas

Jul 71. (lp; by HOWARD WALES & JERRY GARCIA) *(69013)* <*KZ 30859*> **HOOTEROLL?**
– South side strut / A trip to what next / Up from the desert / DC-502 / One a.m. approach / Uncle Martin's / Da bird song. *(cd-iss.Oct87 & Jul92 on 'Rykodisc';* <*RCD 10052*>*)* <*US cd+=*> – Morning in Marin / Evening in Marin.

Jan 72. (7"; by HOWARD WALES & JERRY GARCIA) <*7-6501*> **SOUTH SIDE STRUT. / UNCLE MARTIN'S** -

Warners Warners

Jan 72. (lp) *(K 46139)* <*BS 2582*> **GARCIA** (aka 'The Wheel') 35
– Deal / Bird song / Sugaree / Loser / Late for supper / Spiderdawg / Eep hour / To lay me down / An odd little place / The wheel. *(<re-iss.Feb89 as 'THE WHEEL' on 'Grateful Dead' lp/c/cd; GDV/GDTC/<GDCD 4003>)*

1973. (7") <*7551*> **THE WHEEL. / DEAL** -

1973. (7") <*7569*> **SUGAREE. / EEP HOUR** -

not issued Fantasy

Dec 73. (d-lp) <*F 79002*> **LIVE AT THE KEYSTONE (live with MERLE SAUNDERS)** -
– Let's spend the night together / It takes a lot to laugh, it takes a train to cry / The harder they come / That's all right mama / He ain't give you none / Positively 4th street / My funny valentine / etc.

Round Round

Jun 74. (lp) *(RX 59301)* <*RX 102*> **GARCIA** (aka 'Compliments Of Garcia') 49
– Let it rock / When the hunter gets captured by the game / That's what love will make us do / Russian lullabye / Turn on the bright lights / He ain't give you none / What goes around / Let's spend the night together / Mississippi moon / Midnight town. *(<re-iss.Apr89 as 'COMPLIMENTS OF GARCIA' on 'Grateful Dead' lp/c/cd; GDV/GDC/<GDCD 4011>)*

Jul 74. (7") <*4504*> **LET IT ROCK. / MIDNIGHT TOWN** -

— **GARCIA, DAVID GRISMAN, PETER ROWAN, JOHN KAHN, VASSAR CLEMENTS**

Mar 75. (lp; by OLD & IN THE WAY) <*RX 103*> **OLD AND IN THE WAY** -
– Pig in a pen / Midnight moonlight / Old and in the way / Knockin' on your door / The hobo song / Panama red / Wild horses / Kissimmee kid / White dove / Land of the Navajo. *(UK-iss.Feb85 on 'Sugarhill' lp/cd; SH/+CD 3746)* <*US cd-iss.1987 on 'Rykodisc'; RCD 1009*> *(re-iss.cd 1990 on 'Grateful Dead'; GDCD 4014)*

U.A. Round

Feb 76. (lp) *(UAG 29921)* <*RX 107*> **REFLECTIONS** 42
– Might as well / Mission in the rain / They love each other / I'll take a melody / It must have been the roses / Tore up over you / Catfish John / Comes a time. *(re-iss.Feb89 on 'Grateful Dead' lp/cd; GDV/GDTC/GDCD 4008)*

Arista Arista

Apr 78. (lp; by JERRY GARCIA BAND) *(SPART 1053)* <*AB 4160*> **CATS UNDER THE STARS**
– Rubin and Cherise / Love in the afternoon / Palm Sunday / Cats under the stars / Rhapsody in red / Rain / Down home / Gomorrah. <*US cd-iss.1988; ARCD 8535*>

Nov 82. (lp) *(1204973)* <*AL 9603*> **RUN FOR THE ROSES**
– Run for the roses / I saw her standing there / Without love / Midnight getaway / Leave the little girl alone / Valerie / Knockin' on Heaven's door. <*US cd-iss.1986; ARCD 8557*>

not issued Fantasy

1988. (lp) <*MPF 4533*> **KEYSTONE ENCORES VOLUME 1** -

1988. (cd) <*FCD 7701-2*> **LIVE AT KEYSTONE VOLUME 1** -

1988. (lp) <*MPF 4534*> **KEYSTONE ENCORES VOLUME 2** -

1988. (cd) <*FCD 7702-2*> **LIVE AT KEYSTONE VOLUME 2** -

1988. (cd) <*FCD 7703-2*> **KEYSTONE ENCORES** (compilation of above) -

— (above credited with MERLE SAUNDERS; lp/cd's with diff.titles)

Grateful Dead / Grateful Dead

Mar 89. (lp/c/cd; as JERRY GARCIA ACOUSTIC BAND) *(GDV/GDC/GDCD 4005)* **ALMOST ACOUSTIC**
– Swing low, sweet chariot / Deep Elam blues / Blue yodel £9 (standing on the corner) / Spike driver blues / I've been all around this world / I'm here to get my baby out of jail / I'm troubled / Oh, the wind and the rain / The girl at the Crossroads bar / Oh babe it ain't no lie / Casey Jones / Diamond Joe / Gone home / Ripple.

— with **JOHN KAHN** – bass / **DAVID KEMPER** – drums / **MARVIN SEALS** – keyboards / and backing vocalists **JACKIE LA BRANCH** and **GLORIA JONES**

Arista / Arista

Sep 91. (d-cd) *(354284)* <*18690-2*> **JERRY GARCIA BAND (live)** 97
– The way you do the things you do / Waiting for a miracle / Simple twist of fate / Get out of my life / My sister and brothers / I shall be released / Dear Prudence / Deal / Stop that train / Senor (tales of Yankee power) / Evangeline / The night they drove old Dixie down / Don't let go / That lucky old Sun / Tangled up in blue.

not issued / Acoustic Disc

1993. (cd; by DAVID GRISMAN / JERRY GARCIA) <*ACD-9*> **NOT FOR KIDS ONLY** -

Apr 97. (cd; JERRY GARCIA & DAVID GRISMAN) <*(ACD-21)*> **SHADY GROVE**

Grateful Dead / Grateful Dead

May 97. (cd; JERRY GARCIA BAND) *(GDCD 4051)* **HOW SWEET IT IS** 81 Apr97

BOB WEIR

solo, with DEAD session men

Warners / Warners

Mar 72. (7") <*7611*> **ONE MORE SATURDAY NIGHT. / CASSIDY** -

Apr 72. (7"; by GRATEFUL DEAD with BOBBY ACE) *(WB 7611)* **ONE MORE SATURDAY NIGHT. / BERTHA** -

Aug 72. (lp) *(K 46165)* <*BS 2627*> **ACE** May72
– The greatest story ever told / Black-throated wind / Walk in the sunshine / Playing in the band / Looks like rain / Mexicali blues / One more Saturday night / Cassidy. *(<re-iss.Apr89 on 'Grateful Dead' lp/c/cd; GDV/GDTC/<GDCD 4004>)*

KINGFISH

with **BOB WEIR** and **DAVE TORBERT** plus DEAD and other sessioners

U.A. / Round

Apr 76. (lp) *(UAG 29922)* <*RX 108*> **KINGFISH** 50 Mar 76
– Lazy lightnin' / Supplication / Wild northland / Asia minor / Home to Dixie / Jump for joy / Goodbye yer honor / Big iron / This time / Hypnotize / Bye and bye. *(re-iss.Nov89 on 'Grateful Dead' lp/cd; GDV/GDCD 4012)*

May 76. (7") <*794*> **HYPNOTIZE. / SUPPLICATION** -

U.A. / Jet

Jun 77. (lp) *(UAG 30080)* <*LA 732-G*> **LIVE'N'KICKIN'** May 77
– Goodbye yer honor / Juke / Mule skinner blues / I hear you knockin' / Hypnotize / Jump for joy / Overnight bag / Jump back / Shake and fingerpop / Action and around. *(re-iss.Feb79 on 'Jet')*

— (BOB appears rarely on above)

Nov 77. (7"m) *(<UP 36314>)* **GOODBYE YER HONOR. / JUMP FOR JOY / I HEAR YOU KNOCKIN'**

— BOB left KINGFISH before they released another album 'TRIDENT' in '78 on 'Jet' US.

compilation

1985. (lp) *Relix;* <*RRLP 2005*> **KINGFISH** -
(UK cd-iss.May93; CCRCD 108)

BOB WEIR

continued solo career as well as returning to the DEAD

Arista / Arista

Mar 78. (7") <*AS 0315*> **BOMBS AWAY. / EASY TO SLIP** - 70

Apr 78. (lp) *(SPART 1044)* <*AB 4155*> **HEAVEN HELP THE FOOL** 69 Jan 78
– Easy to slip / I'll be doggone / Wrong way / Heaven help the fool / Shade of grey / This time forever / Salt Lake City / Bombs away.

Jun 78. (7") <*AS 0336*> **I'LL BE DOGGONE. / SHADE OF GREY** -

BOBBY & THE MIDNITES

BOB WEIR – vocals, guitar / **BILLY COBHAM** – drums, vocals / **BOBBY COCHRAN** – guitar / **ALPHONSO JOHNSON** – bass / **BRENT MYLAND** – keyboards / **MATTHEW KELLY** – harmonica

Nov 81. (lp) <*AL 9568*> **BOBBY AND THE MIDNITES** -
– Book of rules / Me without you / Josephine / Fly away / Carry me / Festival. *(UK cd-iss.1986; ARCD 8558)*

Nov 81. (7") <*TOO MANY LOSERS. / HAZE* -

— **DAVE GARLAND** – keyboards, synths + **KENNY GRADNEY** – bass, vocals repl. JOHNSON, MYLAND + JOHNSON

C.B.S. / Columbia

Dec 84. (lp) *(26046)* <*BFC 39276*> **WHERE THE BEAT MEETS THE STREET**
– (I want to live in) America / Where the beat meets the street / She's gonna win your heart / Ain't that peculiar / Lifeguard / Rock in the 80's / Lifeline / Falling / Thunder and lightning / Gloria Monday.

SEASTONES

PHIL LESH with **NED LAGIN**, plus DEAD session men and others

not issued / Round

Oct 75. (lp) <*RX 106*> **SEASTONES** -

(UK cd-iss.1991 extended on 'Rykodisc'; RCD 40193)

MICKEY HART

Warners / Warners

Oct 72. (lp) *(K 46182)* <*BS 2635*> **ROLLING THUNDER**
– Rolling thunder – Shoestone invocation / The main ten (playing in the band) / Fletcher Carnaby / The chase (progress) / Blind John / Young man / Deep wide and frequent / Pump song / Granma's cookies / Hangin' on. *<re-iss.1986 on 'Relix' some colrd vinyl; RRLP 2026> (cd-iss.Mar89 on 'Grateful Dead'; GDCD 4009)*

Dec 72. (7") <*7644*> **BLIND JOHN. / THE PUMP SONG** -

not issued / Celestial.

1983. (lp) <*003*> **YAMANTAKA** -
– Yamantaka (parts 1-7) / The revolving mask of Yamantaka.

— (above with NANCY HENNINGS & HENRY WOLFF) (below with FLORA PURIM & AIRTO MOREIRA)

not issued / Reference

1983. (lp) <*12*> **DAFOS** -
– Dry sands of the desert / Ice of the north / Reunion (1, 2, 3) / Saudacao popular / Psychopomp / Subterranean caves of Kronos / The gates of Dafos / Passage. *(UK cd-iss.Nov91 on 'Rykodisc'; RCD 10108) (re-iss.Nov94)*

Rykodisc / not issued

Mar 91. (cd) *(RCD 005)* **AT THE EDGE** -
– Four for Garcia / Sky water / Slow sailing / Lonesome hero / Fast sailing / Cougar run / Eliminators / Brainstorm / Pigs in space. *(re-iss.cd Jul91 & Mar97; RCD 10124)*

Nov 91. (cd; by MICKEY & TARO HART) *(RCD 20112)* **MUSIC TO BE BORN BY** -
– Music to be born by.

Nov 94. (cd) *(RCD 10206)* **PLANET DRUM** -

DIGA RHYTHM BAND

MICKEY HART – drums, plus 10 percussionists

U.A. / U.A.

1976. (7") <*843*> **HAPPINESS IS DRUMMING. / RAZOOLI** -

U.A. / Round

Mar 76. (lp) *(UAG 29975)* <*RX 110*> **DIGA**
– Razooli / Happiness is drumming / Tal Mala / Sweet sixteen / Magnificent sevens. *(cd-iss.Oct90 on 'Rykodisc'; RCD 10101)*

RHYTHM DEVILS

with HART, LESH and KREUTZMANN plus more percussionists

not issued / Passport

1980. (lp) <*PB 9844*> **RHYTHM DEVILS PLAY RIVER MUSIC: APOCALYPSE NOW SESSIONS** -
– Compound / Trenches / Street gang / The beast / Steps / Tar / Lance / Cave / Napalm for breakfast / Hell's bells. *(re-iss.Mar89 on 'Rykodisc' lp/c;)*

ROBERT HUNTER

solo with numerous session people incl. GRATEFUL DEAD folk

not issued / Round

Jun 74. (lp) <*RX 101*> **TALES OF THE GREAT RUM RUNNERS** -
– Lady simplicity / That train / Dry dusty road / I heard you singing / Rum runners / Children's lament / Maybe she's a bluebird / Boys in the barroom / It must have been the roses / Arizona lightning / Standing at your door / Mad / Keys to the rain. *(UK-iss.May89 on 'Grateful Dead' lp/cd; GDV/GDCD 4013)*

Jul 74. (7") <*RX 4505*> **RUM RUNNERS. / IT MUST HAVE BEEN THE ROSES** -

Mar 75. (lp) <*RX 105*> **TIGER ROSE** -
– Tiger rose / One thing to try / Rose of Sharon / Wild Bill / Dance a hole / Cruel white water / Over the hills / Last flash of rock'n'roll / Yellow Moon / Ariel. *(re-iss.& remixed May89 on 'Grateful Dead' lp/cd; GDV/GDCD 4010)*

Dark Star / Relix

Apr 81. (lp) *(DSLP 8001)* <*RRLP 2001*> **JACK O'ROSES**
– Box of rain / Book of Daniel / Friend of the Devil / etc.

1982. (lp,pic-lp) <*RRLP 2002*> **PROMONTORY RIDER: A RETROSPECTIVE COLLECTION** (74-75 rare material) -
(UK cd-iss.Jun93 on 'Relix'; CCRCD 110)

1984. (d-lp) <*RRLP 2003*> **AMAGAMALIN ST.** -
– Roseanne / Amagamalin Street / Gypsy parlor ight / Rambling ghost / Ithaca / Don't be deceived / Taking Maggie home / Out of the city / Better bad luck / Streetwise / Where did you go / 13 roses. *(UK cd-iss.Jun93 on 'Relix'; CCRCD 101)*

Feb 85. (lp) <*RRLP 2006*> **LIVE '85 (live)** -

Dec 85. (lp) <*RRLP 2009*> **THE FLIGHT OF MARIE HELENA** -

Relix / Relix

1986. (7") <*RR45 1*> **AIM AT THE HEART. / WHO, BABY, WHO?** -

Mar 89. (lp) <*(RRLP 2019)*> **ROCK COLUMBIA** Aug86
– Eva / End of the road / I never see you / Aim at the heart / Kick it on down / What'll you raise? / Who, baby, who? / Rock Columbia. *(cd-iss.Jun93; CCRCD 102)*

Mar 89. (lp) <*(RRLP 2029)*> **LIBERTY** Mar88
– Liberty / Cry down the years / Bone alley / Black shamrock / The song goes on / Do deny / Worried song / Come and get it / When a man loves a woman.

Rykodisc / Rykodisc

Sep 91. (cd) <*(RCD 10214)*> **A BOX OF RAIN (live)**
(re-iss.Mar94)

Dec 93. (cd) <*(RCD 20265)*> **SENTINEL**

KEITH & DONNA

with GARCIA plus more sessioners

not issued / Round

1975. (lp) <*RX 104*> **KEITH AND DONNA GODCHAUX** -
– River deep, mountain high / Sweet baby / Woman make you / When you start to move / Showboat / My love for you / Farewell Jack / Who was John / Every song I sing.

— They later formed The HEART OF GOLD BAND with MICKEY HART

— also 'SAMPLER FOR DEAD HEADS' m-lp's featuring various solo material.

GRAVY TRAIN

Formed: Lancashire, England . . .1970 by NORMAN BARRATT (who had replaced JIMMY PAGE; future LED ZEPPELIN, in the band of LORD SUTCH and HEAVY FRIENDS). Similar to the early folk/blues sound of JETHRO TULL, they released for 'Vertigo', the hard rocking self-titled debut. Their second for the company, 'BALLAD OF A PEACEFUL MAN' (complete with spiral label & gatefold sleeve now worth over £150 mint) was a more accomplished set featuring the charming, 'HOME AGAIN'. Their third and fourth albums, in 1973 and '74 respectively, took a downward course, leading to their demise. However, the swansong boasted some fine artwork from ROGER DEAN (more famous for his YES sleeves).

Recommended: GRAVY TRAIN (*5) / BALLAD OF A PEACEFUL MAN (*7)

NORMAN BARRATT – vocals, guitar / **LES WILLIAMS** – bass, vocals / **J.D. HUGHES** – flute, keyboards, vocals / **BARRY DAVONPORT** – drums

Vertigo / not issued

Jan 71. (lp) *(6360 023)* **GRAVY TRAIN** [ ] [-]
– The new one / Dedication to Syd / Coast road / Enterprise / Think of life / Earl of Pocket Nook. *(cd-iss.1990's on 'Repertoire'; REP 4063)*

Oct 71. (7") *(6059 049)* **ALONE IN GEORGIA. / CAN ANYBODY HEAR ME** [ ] [-]

Dec 71. (lp) *(6360 051)* **BALLAD OF A PEACEFUL MAN** [ ] [-]
– Alone in Georgia / (A ballad of) A peaceful man / Jule's delight / Messenger / Can anybody hear me / Old tin box / Won't talk about it / Home again. *(cd-iss.1990's on 'Repertoire'; REP 4122)*

Dawn / not issued

1973. (lp) *(DNLS 3046)* **SECOND BIRTH** [ ] [-]
– Morning coming / Peter / September morning news / Motorway / Fields and factories / Strength of a dream / Tolpuddle episode / Second birth. *(cd-iss.1990's on 'Nemesis'+=; NEM 612)–* Good time thing.

1973. (7") *(DNS 1036)* **STRENGTH OF A DREAM. / TOLPUDDLE EPISODE** [ ] [-]

— **JIM FRANK** – drums, percussion / **PETE SOLLEY + MARY ZINOVIEFF** – synthesizers / **LES WILLIAMS** – bass / **RUSSELL CORDWELL** – drums / **P.P. ARNOLD + BOBBY HARRISON** – vocals, repl. DAVONPORT

Feb 74. (7") *(DNS 1058)* **STARBRIGHT STARLIGHT. / GOOD TIME THING** [ ] [-]

1974. (lp) *(DNLH 1)* **STAIRCASE TO THE DAY** [ ] [-]
– Starbright starlight / Bring my life on back to me / Never wanted you / Staircase to the day / Going for a quick one / The last day / Evening of my life / Busted in Schenectady. *(cd-iss.1990's on 'Nemesis'+=; NEM 613)–* Climb aboard the gravy train / Sanctuary.

Jul 75. (7") *(DNS 1115)* **MY WHOLE WORLD ENDED. / BABY DON'T KNOCK** [ ] [-]

— Disbanded in 1975 and BARRATT guested for The MANDALA BAND and numerous Christian rock acts.

GREATEST SHOW ON EARTH

Formed: London, England . . . 1968 as soul outfit The LIVING DAYLIGHTS, by brothers NORMAN and GARTH WATT-ROY, along with New Orleans-born OZZIE LANE and others (see below). However, when LANE returned to America, they found new British-born vocalist COLIN HORTON-JENNINGS and signed to progressive label, 'Harvest'. Early in 1970, their bluesy debut album, 'HORIZONS', surfaced, and a single from it, 'REAL COOL WORLD', became popular in Europe. Later that year, they squeezed out another album, but it was clear their success was going to lie elsewhere. NORMAN found fame (after GLENCOE) with IAN DURY's band The BLOCKHEADS. • **Songwriters:** WATT-ROY – WATT-ROY.

Recommended: HORIZONS (*5)

COLIN HORTON-JENNINGS – vocals, guitar, flute; who repl. LANE / **GARTH WATT-ROY** – guitar, vocals / **NORMAN WATT-ROY** – bass, vocals / **MIKE DEACON** – keyboards, vocals / **RON PRUDENCE** – drums, percussion / DICK HANSON + TEX PHILPOTTS + IAN AITCHISON – brass, percussion

Harvest / not issued

Feb 70. (7") *(HAR 5012)* **REAL COOL WORLD. / AGAIN AND AGAIN** [ ] [-]

Mar 70. (lp) *(SHVL 769)* **HORIZONS** [ ] [-]
– Sunflower morning / Angelina / Skylight man / Day of the lady / Real cool world / I fought for love / Horizons / Again and again. *(cd-iss.Nov94 on 'Repertoire'; REP 4484)*

Sep 70. (7") *(HAR 5026)* **TELL THE STORY. / MOUNTAIN SONG** [ ] [-]

Nov 70. (lp) *(SHVL 783)* **THE GOING'S EASY** [ ] [-]
– Borderline / Magic woman touch / Story times and nursery rhymes / The leader / Love magnet / Tell the story. *(cd-iss.Nov94 on 'Repertoire'+=; REP 4483)–* Mountain song.

— When they finished the show DEACON joined VINEGAR JOE then DARTS and SUZI QUATRO. JENNINGS formed TAGGETT with ex-GRACIOUS and DADDY LONGLEGS members. GARTH joined FUZZY DUCK and later EAST OF EDEN / MARMALADE / BONNIE TYLER / PAUL YOUNG. NORMAN formed GLENCOE, which became LOVING AWARENESS before evolving into IAN DURY's BLOCKHEADS.

– compilations, others –

1975. (lp) *Harvest; (SHSM 2004)* **GREATEST SHOW ON EARTH** [ ] [-]

Jul 77. (7") *Harvest; (HAR 5129)* **MAGIC WOMAN TOUCH. / AGAIN AND AGAIN** [ ] [-]

GREAT SOCIETY

Formed: San Francisco, California, USA . . .1965 by man and wife JERRY and GRACE SLICK. Together with his brother DARBY plus PETER VANDERGELDER and DAVID MINOR, they debuted on the 22nd September '65 at The Coffee Gallery. Around six weeks later TOM DONAHUE released their one and only 45, 'SOMEBODY TO LOVE' (possibly the first ever psychedelic recording), for Autumn subsidiary, 'North Beach'. The single surfaced once more, along with another of their songs, 'WHITE RABBIT', for GRACE's next outfit, the pivotal JEFFERSON AIRPLANE. • **Songwriters:** Band members except; FREE ADVICE (John Phillips / Michelle Gilliam) / OUTLAW BLUES (Bob Dylan) / SALLY GO ROUND THE ROSES (Jaynettes). • **Trivia:** Also appear on Various Artists collections; 'SAN FRANCISCO ROOTS' (US Vault) & 'THE AUTUMN STORY' (Edsel).

GRACE SLICK (b.GRACE WING, 30 Oct'39, Chicago) – vocals / **DARBY SLICK** – lead guitar / **DAVID MINOR** – rhythm guitar / **PETER VANDERGELDER** – bass, sax / **JERRY SLICK** – drums

not issued / North Beach

Nov 65. (7") *<NB 1001>* **SOMEONE TO LOVE. / FREE ADVICE** [-] [ ]

— Disbanded in Sep66 after recording 2 albums worth with GRACE before she joined JEFFERSON AIRPLANE. All but JERRY (who joined The FINAL SOLUTION) journeyed to Calcutta studying under Ali Akbar Khan.

– others, etc. –

on 'C.B.S.' / 'Columbia' unless mentioned otherwise

Mar 68. (lp; as GRACE SLICK & THE GREAT SOCIETY) *(CBS 63476) <CS 9624>* **CONSPICUOUS ONLY IN IT'S ABSENCE** [ ] [ ]
– Sally go 'round the roses / Didn't think so / Grimly forming / Somebody to love / Father Bruce / Outlaw blues / Often as I may / Arbitration / White rabbit. *<re-iss.1970 on 'Harmony'; 30391> (UK re-iss.1981 on 'CBS-Embassy'; 31800)*

1968. (7") *<44583>* **SALLY GO ROUND THE ROSES. / DIDN'T THINK SO** [-] [ ]

Sep 68. (lp) *<CS 9702>* **HOW IT WAS** [-] [ ]
– That's how it is / Darkly smiling / Nature boy / You can't try / Daydream nightmare / Everybody knows / Born to be burned / Father. *<re-iss.as 'THE GREAT SOCIETY' on 'Harmony'; 30459>*

1988. (d-lp) *Edsel; (DED 280)* **LIVE AT THE MATRIX (live)** [ ] [-]
(cd-iss.Mar91; EDCD 280)

Norman GREENBAUM

Born: 20 Nov'42, Malden, Massachusetts, USA. In the mid-60's, he formed West Coast psychedelic outfit DR. WEST'S MEDICINE SHOW & JUNK BAND and had a near US Top 50 novelty hit with 'THE EGGPLANT THAT ATE CHICAGO' in late 1966. After time spent running a dairy farm, he surfaced again in 1970 with the No.1 smash 'SPIRIT IN THE SKY'. This piece of psychedelic pop/rock introduced fuzz guitar and handclapping over GREENBAUM's cosmic vocals. • **Songwriters:** Self-penned with a few covers thrown in. • **Trivia:** DOCTOR AND THE MEDICS returned 'SPIRIT IN THE SKY' to UK No.1.

Recommended: SPIRIT IN THE SKY (*5)

DR. WEST'S MEDICINE SHOW & JUNK BAND

NORMAN GREENBAUM – vocals / **BONNIE WALLACH** – guitar, vocals / **JACK CARRINGTON** – guitar, percussion, vocals / **EVAN ENGBER** – drums

C.B.S. / Go Go

1967. (7") *(202492) <100>* **THE EGGPLANT THAT ATE CHICAGO. / YOU CAN'T FIGHT CITY HALL BLUES** [ ] [52] Nov66

1967. (7") *(202658)* **GONOLIERS, SHAKESPEARS, OVERSEERS. / DADDY I KNOW** [ ] [ ]
(re-iss.Jul70 on 'Page One'; POF 176)

Page One / Gregor

Apr 68. (7") *(POF 23061)* **BULLETS LA VERNE. / JIGSAW** [ ] [ ]

Feb 69. (lp) *<001>* **THE EGG PLANT THAT ATE CHICAGO** [-] [ ]
– Patent medicine / Summer love song / How Lew sin ate / Dominating baby / Look at her now / The eggplant that ate Chicago / Modern day fish / Nora / Old fruit peddler / Weird. *(UK-iss.Jul70 as 'WITH DR.WEST'S MEDICINE SHOW AND JUNK BAND' on 'Page One'; POLS 017)*

NORMAN GREENBAUM

— with **RUSSELL DASHIEL** – guitar / **NORMAN MAYELL** – drums / **DOUG KILMER** – bass / **WILLIAM TRUCKAWAY** – synthesizers

Reprise / Reprise

1969. (7") *<0739>* **SPIRIT IN THE SKY. / CANNED HAM** [-] [ ]

1969. (7") *<0752>* **SCHOOL FOR SWEET TALK. / CHILDREN OF PARADISE** [-] [ ]

1969. (7") *<0818>* **MARCY. / CHILDREN OF PARADISE** [-] [ ]

Oct 69. (7") *(RS 20846) <0846>* **JUBILEE. / SKYLINE** [-] [ ]

Feb 70. (7") *(RS 20885) <0885>* **SPIRIT IN THE SKY. / MILK COW** [1] [3]
(re-iss.Nov73; K 14025) (re-iss.May86 on 'Old Gold'; OG 9550)

May 70. (lp) *(RSLP 6365) <6365>* **SPIRIT IN THE SKY** [ ] [23] Feb70
– Junior Cadillac / Spirit in the sky / Skyline / Jubilee / Alice Bodine / Tars of India / The power / Good lookin' woman / Milk cow / Marcy.

Jul 70. (7") *(RS 20919) <0919>* **CANNED HAM. / JUNIOR CADILLAC** [ ] [46] Jun70

Jan 71. (7") *<0956>* **RHODE IALND RED. / I.J. FOXX** [-] [ ]

May 71. (7") *(RS 21000) <1008>* **CALIFORNIA EARTHQUAKE. / RHODE ISLAND RED** [ ] [93]

1971. (lp) <6422> **BACK HOME AGAIN**
– Back home again / Rhode Island red / Canned ham / Titfield thunder / Miss Fancy / Lucille got stealed / Circulate / Hook and ladder / Damper / I.J. Foxx.
1973. (7") <1134> **PETULAMA. / DALRY QUEEN**
1973. (lp) <2084> **PETULAMA**

Surrey

Jun 74. (7") *(SIT 5010)* **NANCY WHISKEY. / TWENTIETH CENTURY FOX**

— Retired from music business in 1974.

– compilations, etc. –

Feb 96. (cd) *Edsel; (EDCD 470)* **SPIRIT IN THE SKY / BACK HOME AGAIN**

GREENSLADE

Formed: London, England . . . late '72 by former COLOSSEUM members DAVE GREENSLADE and TONY REEVES. After two moderately-received, keyboard-orientated albums in 1973, they made the UK Top 40 lists with their third set, 'SPYGLASS GUEST'. Its progressive leanings drew comparisons with CAMEL and CARAVAN, the record also featuring the ornate artwork of Roger Dean (famous for his YES covers). In 1975, they released what was to many fans, their best effort in 'TIME & TIDE'. They disbanded with the advent of punk rock, DAVE continuing to score TV themes (including the 'Gangsters' drama).

Recommended: SPYGLASS GUEST (*6) / TIME AND TIDE (*6)

DAVE GREENSLADE – keyboards, vibes (ex-COLOSSEUM, ex-CHRIS FARLOWE, etc) / **DAVE LAWSON** – vocals, keyboards, clarinet, flute (ex-ALAN BOWN, ex-EPISODE SIX) / **TONY REEVES** – bass (ex-COLOSSEUM) / **ANDREW McCULLOCH** – drums (ex-KING CRIMSON, ex-CRAZY WORLD OF ARTHUR BROWN)

Warners Mercury

Mar 73. (lp) *(K 46207)* **GREENSLADE**
– Feathered friends / An English western / Drowning man / Temple song / Melange / What are you doin' to me / Sun dance.
Jun 73. (7") *(K 16264)* **TEMPLE SONG. / AN ENGLISH WESTERN**
Nov 73. (lp) *(K 46259)* **BEDSIDE MANNERS ARE EXTRA**
– Bedside manners are extra / Pilgrim's progress / Time to dream / Drum folk / Sunkissed you're not / Chalkhill.

— added **DAVE CLEMPSON** – guitar (ex-HUMBLE PIE, ex-COLOSSEUM) / **GRAHAM SMITH** – violin (ex-STRING DRIVEN THING, etc.)

Jul 74. (lp/c) *(K/K4 56055)* **SPYGLASS GUEST** 34
– Spirit of the dance / Little red fry-up / Rainbow / Siam see saw / Joie de vivre / Red light / Melancholy race / Theme for an imaginary western.

— **MARTIN BRILEY** – bass repl. REEVES who joined CURVED AIR

Jul 75. (lp/c) *(K/K4 56126)* **TIME AND TIDE**
– Animal farm / Newsworth / Time / Tide / Catalan / The flattery stakes / Waltz for a fallen idol / The ass's ears / Doldrums / Gangsters.
Jul 75. (7") *(K 16584)* **CATALAN. / ANIMAL FARM**

— Disbanded early 1976.

DAVE GREENSLADE

Warners Warners

Sep 76. (7") *(K 16828)* **GANGSTERS. / RUBBER FACE, LONELY EYES**
Nov 76. (lp/c) *(K/K4 56306)* **CACTUS CHOIR**
– Pedro's party / Gettysburg / Swings and roundabouts / Time takes my time / Cactus choir / Forever and ever / Country dance – finale.

— DAVE re-formed GREENSLADE early '77 with **TONY REEVES** – bass / **MICK RODGERS** – vocals, guitar / **JON HISEMAN** – drums (ex-COLOSSEUM) before DAVE went solo again.

E.M.I. not issued

Dec 79. (d-lp) *(EMSP 332)* **THE PENTATEUCH OF THE COSMOGONY**
– Introit / Moondance / Bel tempest / Glass / Three brides / Birds bats and dragonflies / Nursery hymn / The minstrel / Fresco – Kahrinn / Bascarole / Dryland / Forest kingdom / Vivat Regina / Scream but not heard / Mischief – War / Lament for the sea / Miasma generator / Exile / Jubilate / The tiger and the dove. *(re-iss.1994;)*
Jan 80. (7") *(EMI 5034)* **THE PENTATEUCH OVERTURE. / MISCHIEF – WAR**

— DAVE did sparse recordings, and went into further TV work).

Virgin not issued

Apr 94. (cd/c) **FROM THE DISCWORLD**
– A-Tuin the turtle / Octane the colour of magic / The luggage / The shades of Ankhmorpork / Wyrd sisters / The unseen university – The librarian / Death / A wizard's staff has a knob on the end / Dryads / Pyramids / Smell gods / Stick and bucket dance / The one horseman and three pedestrians of the apocalypse / Hollywood dreams.

GROBSCHNITT

Formed: Germany . . . early 1970 out of The CREW, by EROC, WILDSCHWEIN and LUPO. Released on the up and coming 'Brain' label, their debut album was a competent prog-rock affair, with distinctive symphonic leanings and complex electronic effects. By the release of 'BALLERMAN', a couple of years later, HARLOS and QUETTING had jumped ship and keyboardist VOLKER 'MIST' KAHRS was recruited to flesh out the sound. The double album documented their characteristically German take on rock theatre and made for fascinating listening if you avoided the worst excesses of teutonic 'humour'. UHLERMANN left soon after and was replaced by WOLFGANG 'PEPE' JAEGAR for 1975's 'JUMBO'. But GROBSCHNITT's finest hour is generally regarded as coming with 1977's 'ROCKPOMMEL'S LAND', a prog-rock concept classic which centred on the fantasy dreamworld of a bored kid. After a live album, 'SOLAR MUSIC' (1978), the band began to lose their focus and the 80's saw them struggling to keep abreast of current musical trends. EROC's albums, until his split in 1982, included GROB members.

Recommended: GROBSCHNITT (*8) / BALLERMANN (*7) / JUMBO (*7) / ROCKPOMMEL'S LAND (*9) / SOLAR MUSIC – LIVE (*6) / MERRY-GO-ROUND (*5) / ILLEGAL (*6)

STEFAN 'WILDSCHWEIN' DANELIAK – vocals, guitar / **JOACHIM 'EROC' EHRIG** – drums, percussion / **GERD OTTO 'LUPO' KUHN** – guitars, vocals / **AXEL 'FELIX' HARLOS** – drums / **BERNHARD 'BAR' UHLEMANN** – bass, flute, percussion / **HERMANN 'QUICKSILVER' QUETTING** – keyboards

Brain not issued

Aug 72. (lp) *(1008)* **GROBSCHNITT** German
– Symphony: Introduction – Modulation – Variation – Finale / Travelling / Wonderful music / Sun trip: Am Oelberg – On the way – Battlefield – New era.

— **VOLKER 'MIST' KAHRS** – keyboards; repl. HARLOS + QUETTING

Feb 74. (d-lp) *(2-1050)* **BALLERMANN** German
– Sahara / Nickel-Odeon / Drummer's dream / Morning song / Magic train / Solar music (part 1 & 2).

— **WOLFGANG 'PEPE' JAEGAR** – bass; repl. UHLEMANN

1975. (lp) *(1076)* **JUMBO** German
– Jupp / The excursion of Father Smith / The clown / Dream and reality / Sunny Sunday's sunset / Auf wiedersehen.
1976. (lp) *(1081)* **JUMBO (Deutsch version)** German
1977. (lp) *(60.041)* **ROCKPOMMEL'S LAND** German
– Ernie's reise / Severity town / Anywhere / Rockpommel's land.
1978. (lp) *(60.139)* **SOLAR MUSIC – LIVE (live)** German
– Solar music 1 / Food sicore / Solar music 2 / Muhlheim special / Otto pank rock / Golden mist / Solar music 3.

— added **TONI MOGG MOLLO** – vocals

1979. (lp) *(60.224)* **MERRY-GO-ROUND** German
– Come on people / Merry-go-round / A.C.Y.M. / Du schaffst das nicht / Coketrain / May day.
1980. (lp) *(60.291)* **VOLLE MOLLE (live)** German
– Snowflakes / A.C.Y.M. / Wuppertal punk / Beifall / Waldeslied / Coketrain show / Rockpommel's land.

— **MILLA KAPOLKE** – bass, guitar, vocals; repl. JAEGAR

1981. (lp) *(60.365)* **ILLEGAL** German
– The sniffer / Space-rider / Mary Green / Silent movie / Joker / Illegal / Simple dimple / Raintime.

— now without KAHRS

1982. (lp) *(60.510)* **RAZZIA** German
– Wir wollen sterben / Der alte freund / Razzia / Remscheid / Schweine im weltall / Poona-express / Wir wollen leben.

— **JURGEN CRAMER** – keyboards + **PETER JURIET** – drums, percussion; repl. EROC who went solo

1984. (lp) *(817 836)* **KINDER UND NARREN** German
– Paradox / Orakel / Geradeaus / Keine angst / Ich liebe dich / Augenstern / Wie der wind / Die kinder ziehn zum strand / Koenige der welt.

— **TARZAN WASSKONIG** – keyboards; repl. CRAMER

1985. (lp) *(827 734)* **SNONNENTANZ – LIVE (live)** German
– Explosionen / Polar traum / Sonnentanz / Neonherz / Wir sind die sonne / Uhrkampf / Solar energie.
1987. (lp) *(826 439)* **FANTASTEN** German
– Auf dem seil / Fantasten / Unser Himmel / Hallo mama / Sous le tapis / Mein leben / Mauerblumen / Komm' und tanz' / Film im kopf / Der weh nach haus.

— (above released on 'Teldec')

— **LUPO, WILDSCHWEIN + MOLLO** recruited new members (some prior to below?); **SUGAR ZUCKERMANN** – keyboards / **HARRY STULLE PORTIER** – bass / **ADMIRAL TOP SAHNE** – drums

1990. (cd/lp) *(843 106-2/-1)* **LAST PART – LIVE (live)** German
– Keine angst / Space rider / Razzia – Illegal / Silent movie / Raintime / Lupo's marchenstunde / Wie der wind / Mary Green / Anywhere / Simple dimple / Unglaublich / Silent movie (part 2).

— nothing heard of them in the 80's.

GROUNDHOGS

Formed: New Cross, London, England . . . 1963 by TONY McPHEE, who named them after a JOHN LEE HOOKER track. In 1964, they signed with Mickie Most's Anglo-American agency, soon having their debut 45, 'SHAKE IT', issued on 'Interphon'. Around the same time, they recorded an lp, 'LIVE AT THE AU-GO CLUB, NEW YORK', with their hero HOOKER. They returned to England in 1965 and subsequently went through a series of false starts before finally stablising their line-up in 1968. Just prior to this, McPHEE had teamed up with JOHN DUMMER BLUES BAND, who released two singles for 'Mercury'. However, with advice from Andrew Lauder of 'United Artists', the new GROUNDHOGS took-off with (their) debut, 'SCRATCHING THE SURFACE'. In 1969, the single 'BDD' (Blind Deaf Dumb) flopped in the UK, although it bizarrely hit the top spot in Lebanon! In the early 70's, they scored with two UK Top 10 lp's, 'THANK CHRIST FOR THE BOMB' (which caused controversy with its sarcastic praise of the nuclear deterrent) and 'SPLIT' (which they always seemed to do, from then on). One of the tracks from the latter, 'CHERRY RED', featured on Top Of The Pops (22nd of April '71). Although they had lost none of their white-boy Chicago blues elements, the aforementioned couple of albums moved towards a more mellotron-based prog-rock sound. Two albums in 1972, 'WHO WILL SAVE THE WORLD?' and 'HOGWASH', revisited their blues roots. 1974's 'SOLID' album, meanwhile, saw a return to the charts, a feat TONY McPHEE & his GROUNDHOGS couldn't emulate with further releases. They are still going strong well into the 90's, releasing albums for the diserning blues connoisseur. • **Songwriters:** McPHEE penned except; EARLY IN THE MORNING (Sonny Boy Williamson) / STILL A FOOL (Muddy Waters) / MISTREATED (Tommy Johnson) / etc. • **Trivia:** TONY McPHEE appeared on JOHN DUMMER BAND releases between 1968-69. Around the same time he guested on BIG JOE WILLIAMS recordings.

Recommended: DOCUMENT SERIES PRESENTS . . . THE GROUNDHOGS (*8) / THANK CHRIST FOR THE BOMB (*8) / SPLIT (*7).

TONY McPHEE (b.22 Mar'44, Lincolnshire, England) – guitar, vocals, keyboards / **JOHN CRUIKSHANK** – vocals, mouth harp / **PETE CRUIKSHANK** (b. 2 Jul'45) – bass / **DAVID BOORMAN** – drums / on session **TOM PARKER** – piano repl. BOB HALL

not issued | Interphon

Jan 65. (7") <7715> **SHAKE IT. / ROCK ME** | - |

JOHN LEE'S GROUNDHOGS

HOOKER – solo blues guitarist **TERRY SLADE** – drums repl. BOORMAN + added 3-piece brass section

Planet | Planet

Jan 66. (7") (<PLF 104>) **I'LL NEVER FALL IN LOVE AGAIN. / OVER YOU BABY**

— TONY McPHEE joined The TRUTH for a short stint before sessioning for CHAMPION JACK DUPREE on his '66 single 'Get Your Head Happy'

T.S. McPHEE

– solo with **PETE CRUICKSHANK / BOB HALL /** and **VAUGHN REES** – drums / **NEIL SLAVEN** – guitar

Purdah | not issued

Aug 66. (7") (45-3501) **SOMEONE TO LOVE ME. / AIN'T GONNA CRY NO MO'** | | -

— This band also backed JO-ANN KELLY. In summer McPHEE formed HERBAL MIXTURE around the same time he joined JOHN DUMMER BLUES BAND on two 1966 singles.

GROUNDHOGS

re-formed (**TONY McPHEE** and **PETE CRUICKSHANK**) recruited **STEVE RYE** – vocals, mouth harp / **KEN PUSTELNIK** – drums

Liberty | World Pacific

Nov 68. (lp; mono/stereo) *(LBL/LBS 83199E) <21892>* **SCRATCHING THE SURFACE (live)**
– Man trouble / Married men / Early in the morning / Come back baby / You don't love me / Rocking chair / Walkin' blues / No more daggin' / Still a fool. *(re-iss.Sep88 & Apr97 on 'Beat Goes On' lp/cd+=; BGO LP/CD 15)*– Oh death / Gasoline / Rock me / Don't pass the hat around.

Dec 68. (7") *(LBF 15174)* **YOU DON'T LOVE ME. / STILL A FOOL**

— trimmed to a trio when RYE left due to illness

Liberty | Imperial

Jul 69. (lp) *(LBS 83253) <12452>* **BLUES OBITUARY**
– BDD / Daze of the weak / Times / Mistreated / Expressman / Natchez burning / Light was the day. *(re-iss.Jan89 on 'Beat Goes On' lp/cd; BGO LP/CD 6)*

Aug 69. (7") *(LBF 15263)* **BDD. / Tony McPhee: GASOLINE**

Liberty | Liberty

May 70. (lp) *(LBS 83295) <7644>* **THANK CHRIST FOR THE BOMB** | 9 |
– Strange town / Darkness is no friend / Soldier / Thank Christ for the bomb / Ship on the ocean / Garden / Status people / Rich man, poor man / Eccentric man. *(re-iss.1975 on 'Sunset'; 50376) (re-iss.May86 on 'Fame' lp/c; FA41/TCFA 3152) (re-iss.Dec89 on 'Beat Goes On' lp/cd; BGO LP/CD 67)*

1970. (7") *(LBF 15346)* **ECCENTRIC MAN. / STATUS PEOPLE** | | -

1970. (7") **SHIP ON THE OCEAN. / SOLDIER** | - |

Liberty | U.A.

Mar 71. (lp) *(LBS 83401) <UA 5513>* **SPLIT** | 5 |
– Split (parts 1-4) / Cherry red / A year in the life / Junkman / Groundhog. *(re-iss.Aug80; LBR 1017) (re-iss.Mar86 on 'E.M.I.' lp/c; ATAK/TC-ATAK 73) (re-iss.Dec89 on 'Beat Goes On'; BGO LP/CD 76)*

U.A. | U.A.

Mar 72. (lp) *(UAG 29347) <UA 5570>* **WHO WILL SAVE THE WORLD? THE MIGHTY GROUNDHOGS**
– Earth is not room enough / Wages of peace / Body in mind / Music is the food of thought / Bog roll blues / Death of the sun / Amazing Grace / The grey maze. *(re-iss.Dec89 & Apr91 on 'Beat Goes On' lp/cd; BGO LP/CD 77)*

— **CLIVE BROOKS** – drums (ex-EGG) repl. PUSTELNIK

Oct 72. (lp) *(UAG 29419) <UA 008>* **HOGWASH**
– I love Miss Ogyny / You had a lesson / The ringmaster / 3744 James Road / Sad is the hunter / S'one song / Earth shanty / Mr. Hooker, Sir John. *(re-iss.Apr89 on 'Beat Goes On' lp/cd; BGO LP/CD 44) (cd re-iss.May91;)*

W.W.A. | W.W.A.

Oct 73. (lp; T.S. McPHEE; solo) *(WWA 1)* **THE TWO SIDES OF TONY (T.S.) McPHEE** | | -
– Three times seven / All my money, alimoney / Morning's eyes / Dog me, bitch / Take it out / The hurt. *(cd-iss.Dec92 on 'Castle';)*

Nov 73. (7") *(WWS 006)* **SAD GO ROUND. / OVER BLUE**

Jun 74. (lp) *(WWA 004)* **SOLID** | 31 |
– Light my light / Free from all alarm / Sins of the father / Sad go round / Corn cob / Plea sing – plea song / Snow storm / Joker's grave. *(cd-iss.Oct91 on 'Castle'; CLACD 266)*

Aug 74. (7") *(WWS 012)* **PLEA SING – PLEA SONG. / Tony McPhee: DOG ME BITCH**

— **McPHEE** brought back **PETE CRUIKSHANK** – rhythm guitar, / plus new members **DAVE WELLBELOVE** – guitar / **MARTIN KENT** – bass / **MICK COOK** – drums

U.A. | U.A.

Feb 76. (lp) *(UAG 29917) <LA 603>* **CROSSCUT SAW**
– Crosscut saw / Promiscuity / Boogie with us / Fulfilment / Live a little lady / Three way split / Mean mistreater / Eleventh hour.

Mar 76. (7") *(UP 36095)* **LIVE A LITTLE LADY. / BOOGIE WITHUS**

— **RICK ADAMS** – rhythm guitar repl. PETE

Oct 76. (lp) *(UAG 29994) <LA 680>* **BLACK DIAMOND**
– Body talk / Fantasy partner / Live right / Country blues / Your love keeps me alive / Friendzy / Pastoral future / Black diamond.

Oct 76. (7"; as TONY McPHEE & GROUNDHOGS) *(UP 36177)* **PASTORAL FUTURE. / LIVE RIGHT**

— split '77. **McPHEE** formed **TERRAPLANE,** with **ALAN FISH** – bass / **WILGUR CAMPBELL** – drums. They appeared on album CHECKIN' IT OUT by 'BILLY BOY ARNOLD'. (1979 split) **TONY** formed TURBO ('79-'83) with **CLIVE BROOKS** – drums / **PAUL RAVEN**

TONY McPHEE BAND

with **MICK MIRTON** – drums / **STEVE TOWNER** – bass

T.S. | not issued

May 83. (7"; sold at gigs) *(TS 001)* **TIME OF ACTION. / BORN TO BE WITH YOU** | | -

GROUNDHOGS

McPHEE with **ALAN FISH** – bass / **MICK MIRTON** – drums

Conquest | not issued

May 85. (lp) *(QUEST 1)* **RAZOR'S EDGE** | | -
– Razor's edge / I confess / Born to be with you / One more chance / The protector / Superseded / Moving fast, standing still / I want you to love me. *(re-iss.Nov89 on 'Landslide';)*

— (Early'86) **DAVE THOMPSON** – bass repl. FISH who joined DUMPY'S RUSTY NUTS / **KEN PUSTELNIK** – drums returned to repl. MIRTON who joined DUMPY'S RUSTY NUTS. They gigged several times and appeared on Radio 2's 'Rhythm and Blues'.

— **DAVE ANDERSON** – bass (ex-AMON DUUL II, ex-HAWKWIND) repl. THOMPSON / **MIKE JONES** – drums repl. PUSTELNIK

Demi-Monde | not issued

May 87. (lp) *(DMLP 1014)* **BACK AGAINST THE WALL** | | -
– Back against the wall / Not to submission / Blue boar blues / Waiting in shadows / Ain't no slaver / Stick to your guns / In the meantime / 54156. *(cd-iss.Jul87 on 'The CD Label'; CDTL 005)*

— ANDERSON re-formed AMON DUUL II, taking with him McPHEE as guest

TONY McPHEE and the GROUNDHOGS

recorded album below

Apr 88. (d-lp) *(DMLP 1016)* **HOGS ON THE ROAD (live)** | | -
– Express man / Strange town / Eccentric man / 3744 James Road / I want you to love me / Split (part IV) / Soldier / Back against the wall / Garden / Split / Waiting in shadows / Light my light / Me and the Devil / Mistreated / Groundhogs blues / Cherry red. *(cd-iss.Aug88 on 'The CD Label'; CDTL 008) (cd re-iss.Mar94 on 'Thunderbolt'; CDTB 114)*

H.T.D. | not issued

Aug 89. (lp/cd) *(HTD LP/CD 2)* **NO SURRENDER** | | -
– Razor's edge / 3744 James Road / Superseeded / Light my light / One more chance / Garden. *(cd+=)*– Split (pt.2) / Eccentric man / Strange town / Cherry red. *(re-iss.Dec90 cd/lp; same)*

Feb 93. (cd; TONY McPHEE) *(HTDCD 10)* **FOOLISH PRIDE** | | -
– Foolish pride / Every minute / Devil you know / Masqueradin' / Time after time / On the run / Took me by surprise / Whatever it takes / Been there done that / I'm gonna win.

Dec 94. (cd; as TONY (T.S.) McPHEE) *(HTDCD 26)* **SLIDE T.S. SLIDE** | | -

– compilations etc. –

Sep 74. (d-lp) *United Artists; (UDF 31) <60063-4>* **GROUNDHOGS' BEST 1969-1972**
– Groundhog / Strange town / Bog roll blues / You had a lesson / Eccentric man / Earth is not room enough / BDD / Split part 1 / Cherry red / Mistreated / 3744 James Road / Soldier / ad is the hunter / Garden / Split part 4. *(re-iss.Mar88 on 'Beat Goes On' d-lp/cd; BGO DLP/MC 1) (cd-iss.Mar90 on 'E.M.I.'; CDP 7-90434-2)*

Apr 84. (d-lp) *Psycho; (PSYCHO 24)* **HOGGIN' THE STAGE** | | -
(with free 7") (cd-iss.Nov95 on 'Receiver'; RRCD 207)

May 86. (d-lp/c) *Raw Power; (RAW LP/TC 021)* **MOVING FAST, STANDING STILL** | | -
– RAZOR'S EDGE' & 'THE TWO SIDES OF T.S. McPHEE', incl. 4 extra 'Immediate' 45's)

Jun 92. (cd) *Beat Goes On; (BGOCD 131)* **CROSSCUT SAW / BLACK DIAMOND** | | -

Dec 92. (cd/c) *Connoisseur; (CSAP CD/MC 112)* **DOCUMENT SERIES PRESENTS (CLASSIC ALBUM CUTS 1968-1976)** | | -
– Still a fool / Walking blues / Mistreated / Express man / Eccentric man / Status people / Cherry red / Split (part IV) / Wages of peace / Amazing Grace / Love you Miss Ogyny / Earth shanty / Live a little lady / Boogie with us / Pastoral future / Live right.

Jul 93. (d-cd) *H.T.D.; (HTDCD 12)* **GROUNDHOG NIGHT – GROUNDHOGS LIVE (live)** | | -

Sep 94. (cd) *Windsong; (WINCD 064)* **BBC RADIO 1 LIVE IN CONCERT** | | -

Feb 96. (4xcd-box) *E.M.I.; (CDHOGS 1)* **FOUR GROUNDHOGS ORIGINALS** | | -
– (SCRATCHING THE SURFACE / BLUES OBITUARY / THANK CHRIST FOR THE BOMB / SPLIT)

Feb 97. (cd) *EMI Gold; (CDGOLD 1074)* **THE BEST OF** | | -

Jun 97. (cd; with HERBAL MIXTURE) *Distortions; (D 1012)* **PLEASE LEAVE MY MIND** | | -

TONY McPHEE

also released other solo work.

1968. (lp) *Liberty; (LBS 83190)* **ME AND THE DEVIL**
(contributed some tracks to below compilation)

1969. (lp) *Liberty; (LBS 83252)* **I ASKED FOR WATER, SHE GAVE ME GASOLINE**

— Next credited with **JO-ANN KELLY**

1971. (lp) *Sunset; (SLS 50209)* **SAME THING ON THEIR MINDS**

GRYPHON

Formed: London, England ... 1971 out of SPELLTHORN by BRIAN GULLAND and RICHARD HARVEY, who had been students at The Royal College Of Music. Initially a baroque folk outfit similar to STEELEYE SPAN or FAIRPORT CONVENTION, they released their eponymous debut in 1973. With lengthier compositions (e.g. the 19-minute title trac), they moved further into the rock field on 'MIDNIGHT MUSHRUMPS', another album highlighting their minstrel-like virtuosity. By their third album, 'RED QUEEN TO GRYPHON THREE', they had now developed a wholly instrumental style, influenced by the burgeoning progressive scene (YES – RICK WAKEMAN, CAMEL or GREENSLADE). With the advent of punk in '76/'77, GRYPHON's olde England folk/prog hybrid seemed glaringly out of time. After a further GRYPHON album, 'TREASON', HARVEY took off for the world of commercial jingles and TV soundtracks, notably 'G.B.H.', which he co-wrote with ELVIS COSTELLO. • **Songwriters:** Traditional olde England anonymous tunes arranged by TAYLOR or GULLAND, until they or HARVEY or group took over in 1974. 'PASTIME WITH GOOD COMPANY' was written by HENRY VIII. • **Trivia:** GRAEME TAYLOR, MALCOLM BENNETT and DAVID OBERLE appeared on STEVE HOWE's 'Beginnings' album.

Recommended: THE COLLECTION (*7)

RICHARD HARVEY (b.25 Sep'53, Enfield, Middlesex, England) – recorder, krumhorn, keyboards, guitar, mandolin / **BRIAN GULLAND** (b. 30 Apr'51, Maidstone, Kent, England) – bassoon, krumhorn, recorder, keyboards, vocals / **GRAEME TAYLOR** (b. 2 Feb'54, Stockwell, London) – guitars, keyboards, vocals, recorder / **DAVID OBERLE** (b. 9 Jan'53, Farnborough, Kent) – drums, percussion, vocals, tympani

Transatlantic Arista

1973. (lp) *(TRA 262)* **GRYPHON**
– Kemp's jig / Sir Gavin Grimbold / Touch and go / Three jolly butchers / Pastime with good company / The Linquiet grave / Estambie / Crossing the stiles / The astrologer / Tea wrecks / Juniper suite / The Devil and the farmer's wife. *(cd-iss.May95 on 'Curio'; ITEMCD 4)*

— added **PHILIP NESTOR** – bass

May 74. (lp) *(TRA 282)* **MIDNIGHT MUSHRUMPS**
– Midnight mushrumps / The ploughboy's dream / The last flash of Gaberdine tailor / Gulland rock / Dubbel Dutch / Ethelion. *(re-iss.Aug86 on 'Conifer';) (cd-iss.May95 on 'Curio'; ITEMCD 5)*

— + guests on next **PETE REDDING** – acoustic bass / **ERNEST HART** – organ

Nov 74. (lp) *(TRA 287) <4018>* **RED QUEEN TO GRYPHON THREE** 1975
– Opening move / Second spasm / Lament / Checkmate. *(cd-iss.May95 on 'Curio'; ITEMCD 6)*

— **MALCOLM BENNETT** – bass repl. NESTOR

Sep 75. (lp) *(TRA 302)* **RAINDANCE**
– Down the dog – Raindance / Mother Nature's son / Le cambrioleur est dans le mouchoir / Ormolu / Continental version / Wallbanger / Don't say go / (Ein klein) Helden Leben. *(cd-iss.May95 on 'Curio'; ITEMCD 7)*

— **HARVEY, B.GULLAND + OBERLE** recruited **JONATHAN DAVIE** – bass, repl. BENNETT

— **BOB FOSTER** – guitar, repl. TAYLOR who joined ASHLEY HUTCHINGS + ALBION BAND

— added **ALEX BAIRD** – drums (ex-CONTRABAND)

Harvest not issued

Apr 77. (lp) *(SHSP 4063)* **TREASON**
– Spring song / Round and round / Flash in the pantry / Falero lady / Snakes and ladders / The fall of the leaf / Major disaster. *(cd-iss.Jun93 & Apr97 on 'C5'; C5CD 602)*

Jul 77. (7") *(HAR 5125)* **SPRING SONG. / THE FALL OF THE LEAF**

— Disbanded and HARVEY joined GORDON GILTRAP, MIKE HERON on session. After several solo releases, he later (Jul91) re-appeared with ELVIS COSTELLO on soundtrack to TV serial 'G.B.H.'. ALEX BAIRD joined The JAGS, who had a minor hit 'BACK OF MY HAND' in 1978. BRIAN GULLAND joined French band MALICORNE.

– compilations, etc. –

Oct 91. (cd/c) *Curio; (ITEM 1 CD/MC)* **THE COLLECTION**
– Kemp's jig / Pastime with good company / Touch and go / The astrologer / Estampie / Unquiet grave / Juniper suite / Midnight mushrumps (excerpt) / Ploughboy's dream / Ethelion / Lament (excerpt) / Raindance / Don't say go / Ormolu / Ein klien heldenieben (excerpt).

May 95. (cd) *Curio; (ITEMCD 3)* **THE COLLECTION II**

Jan 96. (cd) *Essential; (ESMCD 356)* **GRYPHON / MIDNIGHT MUSHRUMPS**

Feb 97. (cd) *Essential; (ESMCD 460)* **RED QUEEN TO GRYPHON THREE / RAINDANCE**

GTO's

Formed: Los Angeles, California, USA ...mid-1967 by PAMELA MILLER, who was introduced to DON VLIET (CAPTAIN BEEFHEART) through school-friend VICTOR HAYDON (later THE MASCARA SNAKE in BEEFHEART's MAGIC BAND). Around 1967, she became groupie/friend of more famous stars including CHRIS HILLMAN (Byrds) and JIM MORRISON (Doors). She soon met other music lovers; a Puerto Rican from New York, LUCY, plus SPARKY, SANDRA and CHRISTINE FRKA. All were re-christened (with MISS before their name) by weirdo singer TINY TIM, subsequently meeting FRANK ZAPPA in Spring '68. He invited them to back-up his MOTHERS on tour as dancers. SANDRA and LUCY were also deposed by MISS MERCY and MISS CYNDERELLA as thet took the name GTO's (GIRLS TOGETHER OUTRAGEOUSLY). The fun-loving girls recorded their one and only lp, 'PERMANENT DAMAGE', for ZAPPA's 'Straight' records. It almost never saw the light of day, as they were busted for drug use. During 1969, each quit, starting with LUCY, when the anti-drug ZAPPA finally issued their album later that year. PAMELA and MERCY went into session work, singing 'Hippie Boy' for The FLYING BURRITO BROTHERS on their lp, 'The Gilded Palace Of Sin'. CHRISTINE surfaced the following year on ZAPPA's 'Hot Rats' album, before she died in 1972 from an overdose of prescription drugs (used to kill the pain from her crooked back). MISS CYDERELLA soon became Mrs. JOHN CALE (ex-VELVET UNDERGROUND), while PAMELA provided vocals on The PINK FAIRIES tour in October 1970 as well as ZAPPA's'200 Motels' before meeting MICHAEL DES BARRES, later marrying him. She wrote a book, 'I'M WITH THE BAND', detailing her "Confessions Of A Groupie". • **Songwriters:** Individually. • **Trivia:** NICKY HOPKINS and JEFF BECK played on their album.

Recommended: PERMANENT DAMAGE (*6)

MISS PAMELA DES BARRES (b.PAMELA MILLER) – vocals / **MISS SPARKY** (b. LINDA SUE PARKER) – vocals / **MISS MERCY FONTENTOT** – vocals, repl. MISS SANDRA LEANOR / **MISS CYDERELLA** – vocals, repl. MISS LUCY / **MISS CHRISTINE FRKA** – vocals

Straight Straight

Nov 69. (7") *<STS 104>* **CIRCULAR CIRCULATION. / MERCY'S TUNE**

Apr 70. (lp) *(STS 1059) <RS 6390>* **PERMANENT DAMAGE** Nov69
– The Eureka Springs garbage lady / The captain's fat Theresa shoes / I'm in love with the ooo-ooo man / Circular circulation / Shock treatment / etc. *<US cd-iss.1990 on 'Enigma'; >*

— Disbanded sometime in 1969.

G.T.R. (see under ⇒ HACKETT, Steve)

GURU GURU

Formed: Munich, Germany . . . 1968 as GURU GURU GROOVE by MANI NEUMAIER and ULI TREPTE. Both had been members of the freeform jazz outfit, The IRENE SCHWEITZER TRIO, before recruiting vocalist HANS SACHS to play at the 'Holy Hill Festival' in Heidelberg. When SACHS departed the following Spring, they shortened the name and recruited a series of guitarists, ending up with AX GENRICH in April 1970 (who replaced JIM KENNEDY). Later in the year, they unleashed their "spaced-out" debut, 'UFO', a brilliant heavy psychedelic rock album, the colourful MANI taking PINK FLOYD or ASH RA TEMPEL as his inspirational source. The next year, they came up with another great piece, 'HINTEN', full of HENDRIX and CREAM-like guitar passages and featuring MANI's excellent percussion work. Their third album, 'KAN GURU', was their finest achievement, highlighting a long undisciplined jam, 'OXYMORON'. They lost the place a bit when TREPTE left, evidence on the patchy eponymous album in '73. MANI and a series of backing musicians, singers, etc, signed to the British branch of 'Atlantic', their work evolving into more accessible jazz-rock. They split in July '74, MANI spending time in the studio, during the next 12 months, with various musicians from CLUSTER / HARMONIUM, KATHARGO, KRAAN. Several albums resulted from these sessions, 'MANI UND SEINE FREUNDE' being released under the GURU GURU moniker. The colourful MANI again assembled a new bunch of musicians, releasing two albums incorprating various styles and their characteristic German sense of humour. These were, 'TANGO FANGO' (1976) & 'GLOBETROTTER' (1977). They returned in fine style with the 1979-recorded 'HEY DU!', sporting a slight change of name; GURU GURU SUNBAND. The 80's were largely disappointing to even the most ardent of fans, 1983's reggae/new wave/jazzy effort 'NEUE STREICHE' a particular low-point. Little or nothing has been heard of MANI NEUMAIER during the 90's.

Recommended: UFO (*8) / HINTEN (*7) / KAN GURU (*8) / GURU GURU (*5) / TANGO FANGO (*6) / GLOBETROTTER (*6) / HEY DU! (*6) / MANI IN GERMANI (*5)

MANI NEUMEIER (b.31 Dec'40, Munich) – drums, percussion, vocals / **AX GENRICH** – guitar, vocals (ex-AGITATION FREE) / **ULI TREPTE** – bass, vocals

Ohr not issued

Aug 70. (lp) *(556 005)* **UFO** German
– Stone in / Girl call / Next time see you at the Dalai Lahma / UFO / Der LSD marsch. *(cd-iss.1990's)*

Sep 71. (lp) *(556 017)* **HINTEN** German
– Electric junk / The meaning of meaning / Bo Diddley / Space ship.

Brain not issued

1972. (lp) *(1007)* **KANGURU** German
– Oxymoron / Immer lustig / Baby cake walk / Ooga booga.

— **BRUNO SCHAAB** – bass, vocals (ex-NIGHT SUN) repl. TREPTE who went into solo sessions (see below), TOMORROW'S GIFT, FAUST, KICKBIT

INFORMATION and settling with own group SPACEBOX

1973. (lp) *(50022)* **GURU GURU** [-] [-] German
– Samantha's rabbit / Medley: Rocken mit Eduard – Something else – Weekend – Twenty flight rock / Woman drum / Der elektrolurch / The story of life.

— **HANS HARTMANN** – bass, piano repl. BRUNO

Atlantic not issued

Nov 73. (lp) *(K 50022)* **DON'T CALL US, WE'LL CALL YOU** [ ] [-]
– Africa steels / The show round dance / 200 cliches / Das zwickmaschinchen / Guru Guru Ltd.

— **HOUSCHANG NEJADEPOUR** – guitar (ex-EILIFF) repl. AX

Jun 74. (lp) *(K 50044)* **DANCE OF THE FLAMES** [ ] [-]
– Dagobert Duck's 100th birthday / The girl from Hirschorn / The day of timestop / Dance of the flames / Samba das Rosa S / Rallulli / At the juncture of light and dark / God's endless love for men.

— **MANI** brought in **AX GENRICH** – guitar / **HELMUT HATTLER** – bass (of KRAAN) / **JAN FRIDE** – percussion (of KRAAN) / **DIETER MOEBIUS** – synthesizer (of CLUSTER) / **HANS-JOACHIM ROEDELIUS** – organ (of CLUSTER) / **INGO BISCHOF** – keyboards (of KARTHAGO) / **SEPP JANDRISITS** – guitar / **TOMMY GOLDSCHMITT** – percussion (of KARTHAGO) / **JURGEN 'JOGI' KARPENKIEL** – bass (ex-KOLLEKTIV) / **GERD DUDECK** – sax, flute / **PETER WOLBRANDT** – guitar

1975. (lp) *(K 50157)* **MANI UND SEINE FREUNDE** [ ] [-]
– Sunrise is everywhere / Chicken rock / It's your turn / Walking / Eating my hot dog / Fly easy / From another world Woodpecker's dream / 1,2,3,4 marsch'n'rock / Drink wine.

— **MANI, SEPP, JOGI, (part-time INGO + TOMMY)** recruited **ROLAND SCHAEFFER** – saxophones, guitar, vocals (ex-BRAINSTORM)

Brain not issued

1976. (lp) *(1089)* **TANGO FANGO** [-] [-] German
– Tomorrow / Tango fango / Soba soave bossanova / Un, deux, trois / Nightbear / Banana flip / L. Torro / Salto Mortadella / Das lebendige / Radio: O Uhr 69 / Wir machen musik – Der Kaiser Jodler / Schnaderhopferl bye bye Johnny.

— **PETER KUHNSTEDT** – bass repl. KARPENKIEL (still featured on below)

1977. (lp) *(60.039)* **GLOBETROTTER** (live/studio) [-] [-] German
– Rolling through the city / I am really into rock'n'roll, man / Moroso / When the lights go out / Da wee / May dream / Simba ka limba / Globetrotter.

— **DIETER BORNSCHLEGAL** – guitar, percussion (ex-ATLANTIS) repl. SEPP

1978. (d-lp) *(80.018)* **LIVE (live)** [-] [-] German
– Transylvania express / As long the music's flowing / Formentera / Conga jam / What's the matter with the kids / Herzflimmern / Ooga booga special: Ooga booga kick – It's a kind of . . . – Yahumba drum – Hunky punky / Der elektrolurch / Moroso / Medicin man's overdose: Cohelo suave – Dance for Mescalito.

— **NEUMEIER, SCHAEFFER, BISCHOF** brought in **WOLFGANG 'BUTZE' FISCHER** – drums (ex-SPARIFANKAL, ex-MISSUS BEASTLEY, ex-EMBRYO) / **GERALD LUCIANO HARTWIG** – bass (ex-KARTHAGO)

Jan 80. (lp; as GURU GURU SUNBAND) *(60.187)* **HEY DU!** [-] [-] German
– Starway / Does war I / Was fuer'ne welt / Girl fushi / Hey du! / Taoma / Atommolch.

— added **HEINZ GEMBUS** – bass

GeeBeeDee not issued

1981. (lp) *(8)* **MANI IN GERMANI** [-] [-] German
– Andrea / Stamp out reality / Jupiter god / Komm lutsch mal / Heitgen lind'schtod / Der zweifache weg / Fuer biene maya / Blue huhn / Lurchis abenteuer.

— **NEUMEIER** recruited **WOLBRANDT / PHILIP MEIER** – bass / **TOMMY BALUFF** – keyboards

Bieber not issued

1983. (lp) *(BI 6190)* **NEUE STREICHE** [-] [-] German

— NEUMEIER AND FRIENDS (with KONRAD PLANK + DIETER MOEBIUS) released two albums 'ZERO SET' (1983) & 'L.S. BEARFORCE' (1984). The latter introduced **EDMUND HEIMANN** – guitar / **LOTUS SCHMIDT** – drums / **EDGAR HOFMANN** – flute

Casino not issued

1987. (lp) *(87302)* **JUNGEL** [-] [-] German

1988. (lp) *(300 009)* **LIVE '88 (live)** [-] [-] German

— MANI retired GURU GURU

– compilations, etc. –

1974. (d-lp) *Brain; (002-1057)* **DER ELEKTROLURCH** [-] [-] German
– (virtually 'KANGURU' & 'GURU GURU')

1974. (lp) *2001; (200.145)* **THIS IS GURU GURU** [-] [-] German

1980. (lp) *Brain; (40.115)* **THE STORY OF LIFE** [-] [-] German

Jun 87. (lp; GURU GURU / ULI TREPTE) *United Dairies; (UD 024)* **HOT ON SPOT / INBETWEEN**(live 1972 / solo July '74) [ ] [-]
– United dish / Sitting in the sun / White line fever / Earmike song. *(cd-iss.1988 on 'TTE'; 002)*

Dec 95. (cd) *Think Progressive; (EFA 035002)* **WAH WAH** [ ] [-]

Jan 96. (cd) *Think Progressive; (EFA 035012)* **LIVE** [ ] [-]

GYPSY

Formed: Leicester, England . . .1969 out of the group LAGAY, by former school friends ROBIN PIZER, MOTH SMITH, ROD READ, JOHN KNAPP and DAVID McCARTHY. They signed to 'United Artists' in 1970 and surfaced with the conventional hippy-rock of their eponymous debut album the following year. After another West-Coast influenced effort in 1972, they hit the road again when sales virtually dried up. • **Songwriters:** PIZER.

Recommended: GYPSY (*6)

ROBIN PIZER – vocals, guitar / **ROD READ** – vocals, guitar / **DAVID McCARTHY** – vocals, guitar / **MOTH SMITH** – drums, percussion / **JOHN KNAPP** – vocals, 12-string guitar, keyboards

United Artists United Artists

Apr 71. (7") *(UP 35202)* **WHAT MAKES A MAN A MAN. / I WANT TO BE BESIDE YOU** [ ] [-]

Jun 71. (lp) *(UAS 29155)* **GYPSY** [ ] [ ]
– What makes a man a man / Keep on trying / I don't care, do you mind / Turning wheel / Feel about the country fine / Standing alone / Feel so bad / I want to be beside you / Please don't stay / Let me take you home / Pony ride.

Aug 71. (7") *(UP 35272)* **CHANGES COMING. / DON'T CRY ON ME** [ ] [-]

— **RAY MARTINEZ** – guitar, vocals, repl. ROD

Nov 72. (7") *(UP 35462)* **BRAND NEW CAR. / YOU KNOW BETTER THAN ME** [ ] [-]

1972. (lp) *(UAS 29420)* **BRENDA AND THE RATTLESNAKE** [ ] [-]
– You know better than me / Brand new car / Shame shame / Who's cheating / Without you / Universe / Comes a time / Let's roll / Midnight fighter / Change your mind.

May 73. (7") *(UP 35546)* **LET'S ROLL. / WITHOUT YOU** [ ] [-]

— Gave up the long road to success after above.

Steve HACKETT

Born: 12 Feb'50, London, England. In the late 60's, after periods with CANTERBURY GLASS and SARABANDE, he formed QUIET WORLD, making one album in 1970, 'THE ROAD'. By the end of the year, he had taken up guitar duties for GENESIS, playing on a string of albums from 'NURSERY CRYME' (1971) to 'SECONDS OUT' (1977). While still part of GENESIS in 1975, he released the first in a long series of solo albums, 'VOYAGE OF THE ACOLYTE', which reached the UK Top 30. By the time of his follow-up, 'PLEASE DON'T TOUCH', HACKETT had left GENESIS to concentrate wholly on his solo career. The album broke away from its predecessors neo-classical conceptualism, opting for a more accomplished rock set. He continued to score with successive albums until he signed a deal with 'Lambourghini' in '83. The resulting album, 'BAY OF KINGS', was a more acoustic based affair, going down none too well with a large section of his fanbase. In 1986, he once again saw some chart action with the pomp-rock supergroup, GTR, which also numbered STEVE HOWE of YES. In 1988, HACKETT was back on the solo trail with another classical guitar set, 'MOMENTUM'. In the 90's, he combined some of these styles, even incorporating a blues element on the 1994 album, 'BLUES WITH A FEELING'. • **Covered;** BORN IN CHICAGO (Nick Gravenites) / THE STUMBLE (King-Thompson) / BLUES WITH A FEELING (. . .Jacobs).

Recommended: VOYAGE OF THE ACOLYTE (*8) / DEFECTOR (*7) / SPECTRAL MORNINGS (*6) / CURED (*6).

STEVE HACKETT – guitar, vocals, keyboards (ex-GENESIS, ex-QUIET WORLD) with **JOHN HACKETT** – flute, keyboards / **JOHN ACOCK** – keyboards / **SALLY OLDFIELD** – vocals / **NIGEL WARREN GREEN** – cello / **ROBIN MILLER** – wind / guests **MICHAEL RUTHERFORD, JOHN GUSTAFSON + PERCY JONES** – all bass / **PHIL COLLINS** – drums, vocals

Charisma Chrysalis

Oct 75. (lp)(c) *(CAS 1111)(7208 555) <1112>* **VOYAGE OF THE ACOLYTE** [26] [ ]
– Ace of wands / Hands of the priestess (part I) / A tower struck down / Hands of the priestess (part II) / The hermit / Star of Sirius / The lovers / Shadow of the Hierophant. *(re-iss.Oct86; CHC 47) (cd-iss.May88; CASCD 1111)*

— STEVE left GENESIS (deciding on full-time career). Retained only his brother JOHN and friend JOHN ACOCK. Guest vocalists were **RICHIE HAVENS, RANDY CRAWFORD** and **STEVE WALSH,** also **CHESTER THOMPSON** – drums, percussion / **JAMES BRADLEY** – percussion / **PHIL EHART** – percussion / **TOM FOWLER** – bass / **DAVE LEBOLT** – keyboards / **GRAHAM SMITH** – violin.

Apr 78. (lp)(c) *(CDS 4012)(7208 620) <1176>* **PLEASE DON'T TOUCH** [38] [ ]
– Narnia / Carry on up the vicarage / Racing in A / Kim / How can I? / Hoping love will last / Land of a thousand autumns / Please don't touch / The voice of Necam / Icarus ascending. *(cd-iss.May88; CDSCD 4012)*

May 78. (7") *(CB 312)* **HOW CAN I?. / KIM** [ ] [-]

Oct 78. (7") *(CB 318)* **NARNIA. / PLEASE DON'T TOUCH** [ ] [ ]

— Steve and brother with **PETER HICKS** – vocals / **DICK CADBURY** – bass / **NICK MAGNUS** – keyboards / **JOHN SHEARER** – drums

May 79. (lp) *(CDS 4017) <1223>* **SPECTRAL MORNINGS** [22] [ ]
– Every day / The virgin and the gypsy / The red flower of Tachai blooms everywhere / Clocks – the angel of Mons / The ballad of the decomposing man / Lost time in Cordoba / Tigermoth / Spectral mornings. *(re-iss.Sep83; same) (re-iss.Aug88 lp/c; CHC/+MC 67) (cd-iss.1987; CDSCD 4017)*

Jun 79. (7") *(CB 334)* **EVERY DAY. / LOST TIME IN CORDOBA** [ ] [ ]

Sep 79. (7") *(CB 341)* **CLOCKS – THE ANGELS OF MONS. / ACOUSTIC SET** [ ] [ ]
(12"+=) *(CB 341-12)* – Tigermoth.

Charisma Charisma

Mar 80. (7") *(CB 357)* **THE SHOW. / HERCULES UNCHAINED** [ ] [ ]

Jun 80. (lp/c) *(CDS/+MC 4018) <3103>* **DEFECTOR** [9] [ ]
– The Steppes / Time to get out / Slogans / Leaving / Two vamps as guests / Jacuzzi / Hammer in the sand / The toast / The show / Sentimental institution. *(re-iss.Mar83 lp/c; CHC/+MC 15) (cd-iss.Apr89 on 'Virgin'; CDSCD 4018)*

Aug 80. (7") *(CB 368)* **SENTIMENTAL INSTITUTION. / THE TOAST** [ ] [ ]

— added **KIM POOR** – vocals / **BIMBO ACOCK** – sax

Charisma Epic

Aug 81. (7") *(CB 385)* **HOPE I DON'T WAKE. / TALES OF THE RIVERBANK** [ ] [-]

Aug 81. (lp)(c) *(CDS 4021)(7144 153) <37632>* **CURED** [15] [ ]
– Hope I don't wake / Picture postcard / Can't let go / The air-conditioned nightmare / Funny feeling / A cradle of swans / Overnight sleeper / Turn back time. *(re-iss.Mar84 lp/c; CHC/+MC 21) (cd-iss.Apr89 on 'Virgin'; CDSCD 4021)*

Oct 81. (7") *(CB 390)* **PICTURE POSTCARD. / THEME FROM "SECOND CHANCE"** [ ] [ ]

Nov 81. (7") *<02609>* **HOPE I DON'T WAKE. / A CRADLE OF SWANS** [-] [ ]

— **CHRIS LAWRENCE** – bass / **NIGEL WARREN GREEN** – cello / **IAN MOSLEY** – drums (returned)

Apr 83. (7") *(CELL 1)* **CELL 151. / TIME LAPSE AT MILTON KEYNES** [66] [ ]
(12"+=) *(CELL 12)* – Air conditioned nightmare.
(free ltd-12" w/a *(CELL 13)* **CLOCKS – THE ANGEL OF MONS. / ACOUSTIC SET / TIGERMOTH**

Apr 83. (lp/c) *(HACK/HAKC 1) <38515>* **HIGHLY STRUNG** [16] [ ]
– Camino royale / Cell 151 / Always somewhere else / Walking through walls / Give it away / Weightless / India rubber man / Hackett to pieces. *(re-iss.Aug88 lp/c; CHC/+MC 40) (cd-iss.Apr89 on 'Virgin'; HAKCD 1) (cd-iss.Mar94 on 'Virgin')*

— **STEVE HACKETT** now totally solo on guitars

Lambourghini not issued

Nov 83. (lp/c) *(LMGLP/ZCLGP 3000)* **BAY OF KINGS** [70] [-]
– Bay of kings / The journey / Kim / Marigold / St.Elmo's fire / Petropolis / Second chance / Cast adrift / Horizons / Black light / The barren land / Calamaria. *(re-iss.Jun89 on 'Start' lp/c/cd; STL/STC/SCD 10) (re-iss.cd Jun94 on 'Permanent'; PERMCDL 20)*

— now with **NICK MAGNUS + FERNAND MOURA** – keyboards / **IAN MOSLEY** – drums / **KIM POOR** – vocals / **RONALDO DIAMANTE** – bass / etc

Aug 84. (7") *(LMG 16)* **A DOLL THAT'S MADE IN JAPAN. / A DOLL THAT'S MADE IN JAPAN (instrumental)** [ ] [-]
(12") *(12LMG 16)* – ('A'side) / Just the bones.

Sep 84. (lp/c/cd) *(LMGLP/ZCLMG/CDLMG 4000)* **TILL WE HAVE FACES** [54] [-]
– Duel / Matilda Smith-Williams' home for the aged / Let me count the ways / A doll that's made in Japan / Myopia / What's my name / The Rio connection / Taking the easy way out / When you wish upon a star. *(re-iss.Oct89 on 'Start' lp/c/cd; STL/STC/SCD 11) (cd re-iss.Jun94 on 'Permanent'; PERMCDL 19)*

G.T.R.

formed by **STEVE HACKETT** – guitar / **STEVE HOWE** – guitar (YES) / **MAX BACON** – vocals (ex-NIGHTWING, ex-BRONZ) / **PHIL SPALDING** – bass / **JONATHAN MOVER** – drums (ex-MARILLION, ex-S.O.S.)

Arista Arista

May 86. (7"/7"pic-d) *(GTR/+SD 1) <9470>* **WHEN THE HEART RULES THE MIND. / REACH OUT (NEVER SAY NO)** [ ] [14]
(12"+=) *(GTR12 1)* – Sketches in the sun / Hackett to bits.

Jul 86. (lp/c/cd) *(207/407/257 716) <8400>* **G.T.R.** [41] [11]
– When the heart rules the mind / The hunter / Here I wait / Sketches in the sun / Jeckyl and Hyde / You can still get through / Reach out (never say no) / Toe the line / Hackett to bits / Imagining. *(re-iss.Apr88 lp/c/cd; 208/408/258 980)*

Aug 86. (7") *<9512>* **THE HUNTER. / SKETCHES IN THE SUN** [-] [85]
(12") – ('A'side) / Hackett to bits.

STEVE HACKETT

returned to solo work, retained **JOHN HACKETT** – flute, + brought in **FUDGE SMITH** – drums / **JULIAN COLBECK** – keyboards, bass

Start not issued

Apr 88. (lp/c/cd) *(STL/STC/SCD 15)* **MOMENTUM** [ ] [-]
– Cavalcanti / The sleeping sea / Portrait of a Brazilian lady / When the bells break / A bed, a chair & a guitar / Concert for Munich / Last rites of innocence / Troubled spirit / Variations on theme by Chopin / Pierrot / Momentum. *(cd re-iss.Jun94 on 'Permanent'; PERMCDL 21)*

Permanent not issued

May 93. (cd/c) *(PERM CD/MC 13)* **GUITAR NOIR** [ ] [-]
– Take these pearls / Dark as the grave / Paint your picture / There are many sides to the night / Like an arrow / Walking away from rainbows / Sierra quemada / Lost in your eyes / Little America / In the heart of the city / Vampyre with a healthy appetite / Tristesse.

Jun 94. (cd) *(PERMCDL 22)* **TIME LAPSES** [ ] [-]

— now w / **SINCLAIR / DEGENHARDT / COLBECK**(co-writer some)

Virgin Virgin

Oct 94. (cd/c) *(PERM CD/MC 27)* **BLUES WITH A FEELING** [ ] [ ]
– Born in Chicago / The stumble / Love of another kind / Way down south / A blue part of town / Footloose / Tombstone roller / Blues with a feeling / Big Dallas sky / The 13th floor / So many roads / Solid ground.

EMI Classics not issued

Apr 97. (cd; STEVE HACKETT & THE ROYAL PHILHARMONIC ORCHESTRA) *(CDC 556348-2)* **A MIDSUMMER NIGHT'S DREAM** [ ] [-]

– compilations, etc. –

Mar 83. (d-c) *Charisma; (CASMC 105)* **VOYAGE OF THE ACOLYTE / PLEASE DON'T TOUCH** [ ] [-]

Oct 92. (cd) *Virgin; (CDVM 9014)* **THE UNAUTHORISED BIOGRAPHY** [ ] [ ]
– Narnia / Hackett to pieces / Don't fall away from me / Spectral mornings / The steppes / The virgin and the gypsy / The air-conditioned nightmare / Cell 151 / Slogans / Icarus ascending / Prayers and dreams / Star of Sirius / Hammer in the sand / Ace of wands / Hoping love will last. *(with 2 new songs)*;– Players and dreams / Don't fall away from me)

Norman HAINES BAND (see under ⇒ LOCOMOTIVE)

Peter-Michael HAMEL (see under ⇒ BETWEEN)

Claire HAMILL

Born: JOSEPHINE CLARE HAMILL, 4 Aug'54, Port Clarence, Middlesborough, England – eldest of seven children. She started to write her own material from an early age, later winning a talent contest, which gained her a record deal with 'Island'. Initially a folk singer, she released her debut album, 'ONE HOUSE LEFT STANDING' in 1971, featuring JOHN MARTYN on guitar. After her follow-up a couple of years later, 'OCTOBER', she ventured into the rock circuit, supporting the likes of JETHRO TULL and PROCOL HARUM. Around the same time in '74, after working on the West Coast, she signed with RAY DAVIES' (Kinks) newly-formed 'Konk' records. He produced her third set, 'STAGE DOOR JOHNNIES', which featured her re-working of MICHAEL MURPHY's 'GERONIMO'S CADILLAC'. On her next album, 'ABRACADABRA', she covered DAVIES' 'CELLULOID HEROES', although again the critics showed little interest. In 1976, she had a brief stint as the vocalist with RICK GRECH's S.D.M. (Square Dance Machine), but this proved to be unfruitful and she retired for a while. HAMILL subsequently started writing for a few groups, even joining WISHBONE ASH for one 1982 album, 'Two Barrels Burning'. She returned in her own right in 1984, with the multi-layered, 'TOUCHPAPER'. This was followed by her first real venture into "new age" music, 'VOICES' (1986). Another of that ilk surfaced in '88, 'LOVE IN THE AFTERNOON'.

Recommended: ONE HOUSE LEFT STANDING (*5) / OCTOBER (*5) / VOICES (*6)

CLAIRE HAMILL – vocals, guitar, piano, with many session people

Island / Island

Feb 72. (7") *(WIP 6122)* **WHEN I WAS A CHILD. / ALICE IN THE STREETS OF DARLINGTON** [ ] [-]

Feb 72. (lp) *(ILPS 9182)* **ONE HOUSE LEFT STANDING** [ ] [-]
– When I was a child / The man who cannot see tomorrow's sunshine / Consummation / The river / Where are your smiles at / Baseball blues / Urge for going / Flowers for grandma / The phoenix / Smile your blues away. *(re-iss.Mar83 on 'Beggars Banquet' lp/c; BOP A/C 4) (cd-iss.Jun97 on 'Blueprint'; BP 239CD)*

1972. (7") *(WIP 6133)* **BASEBALL BLUES. / SMILE YOUR BLUES AWAY** [ ] [-]

1972. (7") *<1202>* **BASEBALL BLUES. / FLOWERS FOR GRANDMA** [-] [ ]

1973. (lp) *(ILPS 9225)* **OCTOBER** [ ] [-]
– Island / To the stars / Please stay tonight / Wall to wall carpeting / Speedbreaker / I don't get any older / Warrior of the water / The artist / Baby what's wrong (with you) / Sidney Gorgeous / Crying under the bed clothes / Peaceful. *(re-iss.Mar83 on 'Beggars Banquet' lp/c; BOP A/C 5) (cd-iss.Apr97 on 'Blueprint'; BP 238CD)*

1973. (7") *(WIP 6154)* **SPEEDBREAKER. / THE ARTIST** [ ] [-]

Konk / not issued

Jan 75. (lp) *(KONK 101)* **STAGE DOOR JOHNNIES** [ ] [-]
– We gotta get out of this place / Oh daddy / All the cakes she baked him / Trying to work it all out / Geronimo's Cadillac / Something to believe in / You know how ladies are / You take my breath away / Go now / Luck of the draw / Stage door Johnnies.

Jan 75. (7") *(KOS 1)* **GERONIMO'S CADILLAC. / LUCK OF THE DRAW** [ ] [-]

— now with members of CAFE SOCIETY (incl. TOM ROBINSON)

Sep 75. (7") *(KOS 3)* **RORY. / ONE SUNDAY MORNING** [ ] [-]

Nov 75. (lp) *(KONK 104)* **ABRACADABRA** [ ] [-]
– Rory / Forbidden fruit / One Sunday morning / I love you so / For sailors / Jamaica / Under a piece of glass / You dear / Maybe it is / In so deep / Celluloid heroes.

— She retired for a while.

W.E.A. / not issued

Feb 81. (7") *(K 18440)* **FIRST NIGHT IN NEW YORK. / ULTRAVIOLET LIGHT** [ ] [-]

— In the early 80's, she surprisingly joined WISHBONE ASH.

Beggars Banquet / not issued

Apr 83. (7") *(BEG 90)* **24 HOURS FROM TULSA. / WHEN I WAS A CHILD** [ ] [-]
(12"+=) *(BEG 90T)* – Speedbreaker.

Coda / not issued

Nov 83. (7") *(CODS 2)* **IN THE PALM OF MY HAND. / JUMP** [ ] [-]
(12"+=) *(CODST 2)* – Jump (club mix).

May 84. (7"/12") *(CODS/+T 5)* **THE MOON IS A POWERFUL LOVER. / ONCE IS NOT ENOUGH** [ ] [-]

Jul 84. (7"/12") *(CODS/+T 8)* **DENMARK. / TWO FOOLS IN A STORM** [ ] [-]

Sep 84. (lp/cd)(c) *(CODA 8/+CD)(COCA 8)* **TOUCHPAPER** [ ] [-]
– The moon is a powerful lover / Denmark / Two fools in a storm / First night in New York / Come along brave lads / Jump / In the palm of my hand / Gonna be the one / Ultraviolet light / Once is not enough.

May 85. (7"/12") *(CODS/+T 14) BIF YOU'D ONLY TALK TO ME. / DON'T PROLONG THE AGONY* [ ] [-]

Mar 86. (7") *(CODS 18)* **SPRING . . . AWAKEN, LARKRISE. / SPRING . . . MOSS** [ ] [-]

Apr 86. (lp/c)(cd) *(NAGE/+C 8)(NAGE 8CD)* **VOICES** [ ] [-]
– Spring . . . awaken, larkrise / Tides / Spring . . . moss / Summer afternoon in a wheatfield / Stars / Autumn / Leaf fall / Mist on the ridge / Harvest winter / Icicle rain / Sleep. *(re-iss.Jan93 cd)(c; NAGE 103CD)(NAGEC 103)*

Nov 86. (7") *(CODS 21)* **THE DOOMSDAY. / SPRING . . . MOSS** [ ] [-]
(7"ep+=) *(CODEP 21)* – Glastonbury (Jerusalem) / Tides / Spring . . . awaken, larkrise / Stars.

Apr 88. (7") *(CODS 24)* **GLASTONBURY. / THE CROSSING** [ ] [-]

May 88. (lp/c)(cd) *(NAGE/+C 18)(NAGE 18CD)* **LOVE IN THE AFTERNOON** [ ] [-]
– Glastonbury / Japanese lullaby / The crossing / Calling to you / Horses / Trees / Liverpool theme / Love in the afternoon / The beauty of England.

Landscape / not issued

1989. (7")(7") *(PENGUINS 1)(PENGUIN BW1)* **SOMEDAY WE WILL BE TOGETHER. / ('A'instrumental)** [ ] [-]
(cd-s/cd-s) *(PENGUIN CD 1/2)* –

— retired from the music scene after above's failure

Peter HAMMILL (see under ⇒ VAN DER GRAAF GENERATOR)

Bo HANSSON

Born: Sweden. Something of a multi-instrumentalist, his first recordings were in the late 60's with drummer RUNE KARLSSON. The second of these, 'MAN IN THE MOON' (1969) was obviously about the recent Moon landing and similar cosmic themes. In 1972, his first solo outing, 'LORD OF THE RINGS' (based on J.R.R. Tolkien's classic book) caused a minor stir in the progressive rock world, hitting the Top 40 and also making the US Top 200 lists!. However, a move into more jazz-orientated material on his next work, 'THE MAGICIAN'S HAT', was ill advised. After another effort in the same vein, 'ATTIC THOUGHTS' (1975), he adapted Richard Adams' 'WATERSHIP DOWN', which was given the thumbs down by the critics. He retired from the UK music scene, having never surpassed his musical rival, MIKE OLDFIELD.

Recommended: LORD OF THE RINGS (*6)

BO HANSSON – organ, guitar, moog synthesizer, bass / **RUNE KARLSSON** – drums, congas

Polydor / not issued

1967. (lp; by HANSSON & KARLSSON) *(184 196)* **SWEDISH UNDERGROUND** [-] [-] Sweden

1969. (lp; by HANSSON & KARLSSON) *(583 564)* **MAN AT THE MOON** [ ] [-]
– Pick-up / Space / Time / Brain / Discovering / In the beginning God / Peace on Earth / Cosmos / Space within / Life / Cordially yours.

— added **GUNNAR BERGSTEN** – saxophone / **STEN BERGMAN** – flute

Charisma / P.V.C.

Sep 72. (lp) *(CAS 1059) <7907>* **LORD OF THE RINGS** [34] [ ]
– Leaving shire / The old forest / Tom Bombadil / Fog on the Barrow- Downs / The black riders / Flight to the Ford / At the house of Elrond / The Ring goes south / A journey in the dark / Lothlorien / Shadowfax / The horns of Rohan / The battle of the Pelennor Fields / Dreams in the house of healing / Homeward bound / The scouring of the shire / The grey havens. *(re-iss.Aug82, re-dist.Sep83; same) (re-iss.Mar90 on 'M.N.W.P.' lp/c/cd; SR/+S/CD 4600) (cd-iss.Nov93 on 'Resource'; RES 508CD)*– (11 extra tracks from next 2 albums). *(cd re-iss.Jun96 on 'Edsel'; EDCD 493)*

— added **KENNY HAKANSSON** – guitar

Charisma / Charisma

Apr 74. (lp) *(CAS 1073) <6062>* **THE MAGICIAN'S HAT** [ ] [ ]
– The city / Divided reality / Elidor / Before the rain / Fylke / Playing downhill into the downs / Findhorn's song / Awakening / Wandering song / The Sun / Excursion with complications. *(re-iss.Aug82 lp/c; CHC/+MC 8) (re-dist.Sep83; same) (cd-iss.Nov93 on 'Resource'; RES 509CD)*

May 74. (7") *(CB 230)* **WANDERING SONG. / THE BLACK RIDERS – FLIGHT TO THE FORD** [ ] [-]

— Later in 1974, he appeared as Othello in the musical 'CATCH MY SOUL', in which he also sang six songs.

— **GORAN LAGERBERG** – bass, acoustic guitar / **THOMAS NETZLER** – bass / **MATS GLENNGARD** – violin / **ROLF SCHERRER** – acoustic guitar / **FINN SJOBERG** – guitar, repl. BERGMAN

Charisma / Sire

Dec 75. (lp) *(CAS 1113) <7525>* **ATTIC THOUGHTS** [ ] [ ]
– Attic thoughts; Repose – Wandering / Time and space / Waiting / Waltz for Interbeings / Time for great achievements / The Hybills / Rabbit music; Intro – Fiver / Day and night / A happy prank. *(cd-iss.Jul95 on 'Resource'; SRS 3625CD)*

— **FREDRIK NOREN + BO SKOGLUND** – drums, repl. KARLSSON

— **STEN BERGMAN + TORBJORN EKLUND** – flute / **PONTUS OLSSON** – piano, repl. BERGSTEN, GLENNGARD + SCHERER

Sep 77. (lp) *(CAS 1132) <6044>* **MUSIC INSPIRED BY WATERSHIP DOWN** [ ] [-]
– Migration / Master Rabbit / Fiver / Hazel / General Blackworth / Silflay / Migration continued / Patrol / The forest / The escape / Watership Down. *(re-iss.1989; CHC 49)*

1978. (lp) **EL-AHRAIHAH** [-] [ ]
– Born of the gentle south / Allegro for Arescue / Legend and light / Trialand adversity / The twice victory / The kingdom brightly smiles.

— Retired or just disappeared from music business.

– compilations, etc. –

Apr 83. (lp) *Charisma; (9290 425)* **THE BEST OF BO HANSSON** [ ] [-]

HAPSHASH & THE COLOURED COAT

Formed: England . . .1967 by MICHAEL ENGLISH and NIGEL WEYMOUTH together with manager GUY STEVENS. The debut album was an acid-fried frenzy of psychedelic experimentation featuring the likes of 'A MIND BLOWN IS A MIND SHOWN' (quite!). Following its release, ENGLISH and WEYMOUTH returned to their day jobs and a modified line-up recorded the more conventional 'WESTERN FLYER' (1969), before the band split later the same year.

Recommended: HAPSHASH & THE COLOURED COAT FEATURING . . . (*5)

MICHAEL ENGLISH – vocals, percussion / **NIGEL WAYMOUTH** – vocals, percussion / **GUY STEVENS** – vocals, percussion, plus **EDDIE TRIPP** – bass / **TONY McPHEE** – guitar, vocals (of GROUNDHOGS) / **MICHAEL MAYHEW** – guitar / **MIKE BATT** – piano, producer / **FREDDIE BALLERINI** – violin

Minit Minit

Nov 67. (lp) *(MLS <40001E)>* **HAPSHASH & THE COLOURED COAT FEATURING THE HUMAN HOST AND THE HEAVY METAL KIDS**
– H-O-P-P-Why? / A mind blown is a mind shown / The new Messiah coming 1985 / Aoum / Empires of the sun. *(cd-iss.1990's on 'Repertoire'; REP 4404WY)*

— **ANDY RENTON** – drums + **MICHAEL RAMSDEN** – vocals + **MICKEY FINN** – guitar, repl. GUY STEVENS + McPHEE + WAYMOUTH + ENGLISH

Liberty Imperial

Feb 69. (7") *(LBF 15188)* **COLINDA. / THE WALL**

Mar 69. (lp) *(LBL/LBS 83212R) <LP 12430>* **WESTERN FLYER**
– Telephone budreaux / Colinda / Chicken run / Big Bo Peep / Blue Narcissus / Car car / Milk shake knock / The wall / You for Ophelia / Fare you well. *(cd-iss.Mar94 on 'Repertoire'; REP 4415WY)*

— Split in 1969.

HARDIN & YORK

Formed: Birmingham, England . . . 1969 by breakaway ex-SPENCER DAVIS GROUP musicians EDDIE HARDIN and PETE YORK. Their first effort together, 'TOMORROW TODAY', was a mixed bag of R&B pop which made little impact commercially. A year later, they released their second album, 'THE WORLD'S SMALLEST BIG BAND', which highlighted the more encouraging 8-minute epic, 'THE PIKE', alongside a selection of similarly organ-dominated, progressive rock/pop. However, a quality performance at The Marquee in June '71 (with RAY FENWICK in tow) couldn't prevent their imminent split. They left behind a third poorly-rated album, 'FOR THE WORLD'. EDDIE took off for a solo career, although HARDIN & YORK did re-surface together in 1974 for an album featuring CHARLY McCRACKEN. • **Songwriters:** Duo except; JAILHOUSE ROCK (hit; Elvis Presley) / MEAN WOMAN BLUES (?) / RIP IT UP (Little Richard) / LADY MADONNA + NORWEGIAN WOOD (Beatles) / LIKE A ROLLING STONE (Bob Dylan).

Recommended: TOMORROW TODAY (*5) / THE WORLD'S SMALLEST BIG BAND (*6) / FOR THE WORLD (*4) / LIVE AT THE MARQUEE (*7)

EDDIE HARDIN – vocals, keyboards / **PETE YORK** – drums, percussion, with session men on debut; **MIKE HURST + VIC FLICK** – guitar / **HERBIE FLOWERS** – bass / **MEL THORPE** – horns / **REX MORRISSEY** – sax / **RON HILL** – cornet

Bell Bell

May 69. (7") *(BLL 1064) <799>* **TOMORROW TODAY. / CANDLELIGHT**

May 69. (lp) *(SBLL 125) <6043>* **TOMORROW TODAY**
– Tomorrow today / 100 years from now / I'm lost / Drinking my wine / Candlelight / Beautiful day / Mountains of sand / Can't keep a good man down / Listen everyone. *(cd-iss.Jun94 on 'R.P.M.'+=; RPMCD 128)*– All I see is you / Mulberry place / Sunday morning / Rock and roll music / Can't find my way home / Just a case of time. *(cd re-iss.Nov94 on 'Repertoire'+=; REP 4481)*– Parking meters / Tomorrow today (live) / The pike (live).

Jul 70. (lp) *(SBLL 136)* **THE WORLD'S SMALLEST BIG BAND** [ ] [-]
– Just a case of time / Can't find my way home / Love, a song for you / Rock'n'roll medley; Jailhouse rock – Mean woman blues – Rip it up / The pike / Northern melody; Lady Madonna – Norwegian wood. *(cd-iss.Jun94 on 'R.P.M.'+=; RPMCD 129)*– The pike / If I could just make it to Heaven / David difficult / Tomorrow today / Candlelight / Little Miss Blue / Can't keep a good man down. *(cd re-iss.Nov94 on 'Repertoire'+=; REP 4482)*– Cowboy / Everyone I know.

Mar 71. (lp) *(SBLL 141)* **FOR THE WORLD**
– Deep in my despair / Have mercy woman / For the world / Some places are better to be / Extension 345 / Cowboy / I'll be back again / Feeling – Seeing – Hearing / Natural gas / Take away today. *(re-iss.Jul71 on 'Decca'; SKL 5095) <US-iss.1971 on 'London'; 602> (re-iss.Jan85 on 'See For Miles'; SEE 41)*

EDDIE HARDIN

Decca not issued

Nov 71. (7") *(F 13252)* **DRIVING. / WHERE I'M GOING TO SLEEP TONIGHT** [ ] [-]

Apr 72. (lp) *(TXS 106)* **HOME IS WHERE YOU FIND IT** [ ] [-]
– Driving / Strange people / Gone is the sunshine / Home is where you find it / Let me comfort you / Sunshine / Brother we can surely work it out / We can give it a try / Soul's awoken / When there's not you / I don't like it / California Sun / Spend your money honey.

Apr 72. (7") *(F 13307)* **SPEND YOUR MONEY HONEY. / WHY DOES EVERYBODY PUT ME DOWN** [ ] [-]

— with drummer **IAN PAICE** (DEEP PURPLE) / **DEE MURRAY** – bass

Decca not issued

1973. (lp; as PETE YORK PERCUSSION BAND) *(TXS 109)* **PERCUSSION BAND** [ ] [-]
– Keep on running / Nothing yet / Cold night in the city / Sombrero Sam / Mel's blues / Moles hawk / Stroke / Arrival of the Queen of Shiva / Points / It's over.

HARDIN & YORK

— next with **CHARLY McCRACKEN** – bass

Vertigo not issued

1974. (lp) *(6360 622)* **HARDIN & YORK WITH CHARLY McCRACKEN** [ ] [ ]
– Ain't no breeze / Back row movie star / Freedom / Wish I'd never joined a band / Clubtrop / Some sweet dream / Loving you's so easy. *(cd-iss.Apr94 on 'Repertoire'; REP 4452WY)*

— above was 'heir last effort as a duo (or even a trio!)

EDDIE HARDIN

— with session people.

Mercury not issued

Aug 74. (7") *(6008 008)* **S'EASY. / STRANGE TIMES** [ ] [-]

G.T.O. not issued

Jun 75. (7") *(GT 24)* **SUMMER DAYS. / SEEMS I'M ALWAYS GOING TO LOVE YOU** [ ] [-]

Attic not issued

1977. (lp) *(LAT 1023)* **YOU CAN'T TEACH AN OLD DOG NEW TRICKS** [ ] [-]
– Oh what a day it's been / Strange times / Drinking / Glad to be home / Moving / S'easy / Give me freedom / Think I'll wait another day / Settling down / Here there and everywhere. *(cd-iss.Nov94 on 'Repertoire'+=; REP 4464)*– Bet you all wish it was Sunday / Credit card city / Still a few pages left.

R.C.A. not issued

1982. (lp) *(PL 30101)* **CIRCUMSTANTIAL EVIDENCE** [-] [-] German
– Little teaser / Mine tonight / Maybe I'm amazed / That's what the lady said / Long tall Sally / California / It won't be long / Universal dream / Maybe baby / Mess of blues.

Coda not issued

Apr 86. (lp/c)(cd) *(NAGE/+C 9)(NAGE 9CD)* **DAWN TILL DUSK** [ ] [-]
– Awakening / Morning sky / Realisation / Looking outward / Another day / Image of tomorrow / Endless dream / Lightning scheme / Dreaming / Conclusion.

Sep 88. (lp/c)(cd) *(NAGE/+C 19)(NAGE 19CD)* **SURVIVAL** [ ] [-]
– Innocent victims / Lost childhood / Seeds of suspicion / Schools of thought / Perfect survivor / Lessons to learn / Where do we go from here / A slice of Paradise / Never again / Rules we can't ignore.

President not issued

Jun 85. (lp; EDDIE HARDIN & ZAK STARKEY) *(PTLS 1078)* **WIND IN THE WILLOWS** [ ] [-]
– Wind in the willows / Good morning to you / I'd forgotten how to smile / The wildwood / The badger / I'm looking forward to tomorrow / Mr.Toad / Piper at the gates of dawn / Wayfarers all.

Sep 85. (7") *(PT 538)* **GOOD MORNING TO YOU. / WAYFARERS ALL** [ ] [-]

Jul 87. (7") *(PT 561)* **RED NOSE CITY. / CARIBBEAN NIGHTS** [ ] [-]

Feb 88. (lp) *(PTLS 1089)* **SITUATIONS** [ ] [-]
– Red nose city / Don't thank the bank / When the going gets tough / Caribbean nights / Till summer / Friends / Situations / Just another song / Sometime never / Every night / The morning after.

C.S.A. not issued

Dec 89. (lp/c/cd) *(BIRTH LP/MC/CD 4)* **MUSIC OF THE STARS – AQUARIUS** [ ] [-]

Sep 95. (cd) *(CSA 106)* **STILL A FEW PAGES LEFT** [ ] [-]

In-Akustik not issued

May 97. (cd) *(INAK 11005)* **WHEN WE WERE YOUNG** [ ] [-]

Angel Air not issued

Jun 97. (cd) *(SJPCD 009)* **WIZARD'S CONVENTION** [ ] [-]
– Hot head of steam / Sernatitus blues / Happening all the time / Here I go again / Someone sings / Talking ain't cheap / Try a little tenderness / Sultana / Brickmaker blues / Can't let you go / I think it's going to rain today / As long as I still have you / Before we say goodbye / Lucille / What a way to spend a day.

— Meanwhile, in 1980, PETE YORK formed his NEW YORK band and released German-only lp's; 1980 'INTO THE FURNACE' *(Teldec 624463)* / 1981 'WHAT'S THE RACKET' *(Teldec 624504)* + 1981 with 'HARDIN & NEW YORK' *(Teldec 624595)* + solo 1982 'OPEN ROAD' *(Teldec 624910)*. He went solo in 1984 'LIVE TOGETHER' *(In-Akustik CD 8410)* / 1985 'STEAMING' *(In-Akustik CDINAK 855)*. From 1987, he made a series of five or more 'SUPER DRUMMING' cd volumes for 'Global Satellite'.

– their compilations, etc

Oct 94. (cd) *R.P.M.; (RPM 135)* **LIVE AT THE MARQUEE** [ ] [-]

HARD STUFF (see under ⇒ ANDROMEDA)

Colin HARE (see under ⇒ HONEYBUS)

HARMONIA (see under ⇒ CLUSTER)

Roy HARPER

Born: 12 Jun'41, Manchester, England. He was raised by his father, following his mother's death during childbirth. His step-mother was a Jehovah's Witness, leading to him becoming anti-religious. As a young teenager, he played in a skiffle group with his brother DAVID, but at 15, after leaving school, he joined the R.A.F. Not finding it to his liking, he feigned madness to escape further service. Roy then underwent ECT treatment at a mental hospital, later being institutionalised in Lancaster Moor. He then spent a year in jail at Walton Prison, Liverpool. In 1964, after busking around Europe, he moved to London and gained a solo residency at LES COUSINS' folk club in Soho. In 1966, he was signed to Peter Richards's 'Strike' records, who issued his debut lp, 'THE SOPHISTICATED BEGGAR'. The record encompassed his best pieces of poetry, only using a simple revox machine as backing. The following year, he signed to 'C.B.S.', issuing a second flop 45, which preceded the album, 'COME OUT FIGHTING, GENGHIS SMITH'. This featured an 11-minute track, 'CIRCLE' another of his highly personal folk/blues confessionals. In the summer of '68, he played free concerts at London's Hyde Park, which brought him a new underground audience. In 1969, he released the album, 'FOLKJOKEOPUS', which also featured a similarily lengthy track, the 15-minute 'McGOOGHAN'S BLUES'. Signing to 'Harvest' early in 1970, he released his fourth album in as many years, 'FLAT, BAROQUE AND BESERK' (it featured an uncredited guest spot from The NICE on the track, 'HELL'S ANGEL'). ROY then embarked on a US tour, but after arriving there drunk and jet-lagged he was arrested for abusive behavior. He slept on West Coast beaches, while playing many gigs. In 1971, he released the highly regarded 'STORMCOCK' set, which hosted DAVID BEDFORD on orchestration and friend JIMMY PAGE (of LED ZEPPELIN) on the first of many guitar sessions for him. PAGE had already written an ode, 'Hats Off To Harper' for their LED ZEPPELIN III album. In 1972, he made his acting debut in the low-budget British film, 'Made', alongside Carol White. Most of the music from the film appeared in his next project, 'LIFEMASK', which was written as his last will and testament, following a near fatal, recurring blood disorder. On the 14th of February '74, he released the appropriately titled, 'VALENTINE', which gave him his first entry into the UK album chart. It was premiered at a concert on Valentine's Day at London's Rainbow theatre, with backing from PAGE, BEDFORD, KEITH MOON and JOHN BONHAM. Later in 1974, he formed the band TRIGGER (with BILL BRUFORD – drums / CHRIS SPEDDING – guitar & DAVE COCHRAN – bass), and supported PINK FLOYD at Knebworth. In 1975, he sang lead vox on PINK FLOYD's 'Have A Cigar', featured on the album, 'Wish You Were Here'. FLOYD had already guested on his next album, 'HQ', which, like its 1977 follow-up, 'BULLINAMINGVASE', hit the UK Top 40. In between the aforementioned projects, he had briefly resided in the States. In 1982 with MARK THOMPSON, he set up his own 'Public' records, who issued ROY's return to form with the 'WORK OF HEART' album. Early in 1985, he scored his last UK Top 50 album, the JIMMY PAGE collaboration, 'WHATEVER HAPPENED TO JUGULA'. He continued to take an active part in the music scene, the album, 'DEATH OR GLORY' being his last effort in 1992. • **Trivia:** PAUL and LINDA McCARTNEY guested on his 'ONE OF THOSE DAYS IN ENGLAND' album. Meanwhile, KATE BUSH guested on ROY's 'THE UNKNOWN SOLDIER' album, returning the compliment by appearing on her hit 45, 'Breathing'.

Recommended: THE SOPHISTICATED BEGGAR (*8) / STORMCOCK (*8) / HQ (*7) / BULLINAMINGVASE (*7) / WORK OF HEART (*6) / ROY HARPER 1970-75 (*6)

ROY HARPER – vocals, guitar (see above for famous session people)

Strike / not issued

Mar 66. (7") *(JH 304)* **TAKE ME IN YOUR EYES. / PRETTY BABY** [ ] [-]

Dec 66. (lp) *(JHL 105)* **THE SOPHISTICATED BEGGAR** [ ] [-]
– China girl / Goldfish / Sophisticated beggar / My friend / Big fat silver aeroplane / Blackpool / Legend / Girlie / October the twelfth / Black clouds / Mr. Station master / Forever / Committed. *(re-iss.Aug70 & 1972 as 'RETURN OF THE SOPHISTICATED BEGGAR' on 'Youngblood' and 'Birth' respectively; SSYB 7 & RAB 3) (re-iss.1977 on 'Big Ben'; BBX 502) (re-iss.Jan89 on 'Sundown' lp/cd; SDLP/CDSM 051) (cd re-iss.Oct94 on 'J.H.D.'; JHDCD 064) (cd re-iss.Oct96 on 'Science Friction'; HUCD 007)*

C.B.S. / not issued

Oct 67. (7") *(CBS 203001)* **MIDSPRING DITHERING. / ZENGEM** [ ] [-]

Jan 68. (lp) *(CBS 63184)* **COME OUT FIGHTING GHENGIS SMITH** [ ] [-]
– Freak street / You don't need money / Ageing raver / In a beautiful rambling mess / All you need is / What you have / Circle / Highgate Cemetary / Come out fighting Ghengis Smith / Zaney Janey / Ballad of songwriter / Midspring dithering / Zenjem / It's tomorrow and today is yesterday / Francesca / She's the one / Nobody's got any money in the summer. *(re-iss.Jun77 as 'THE EARLY YEARS' on 'CBS-Embassy'; EMB 31544) (re-iss.Sep91 on 'Awareness' lp/cd;) (cd re-iss.Nov94 & Oct96 on 'Science Friction'; HUCD 006)*

Apr 68. (7") *(CBS 3371)* **LIFE GOES BY. / NOBODY'S GOT ANY MONEY IN THE SUMMER** [ ] [-]

Liberty / World Pacific

Apr 69. (lp; mono/stereo) *(LBL/LBS 83231) <21888>* **FOLKJOKEOPUS** [ ] [ ]
– Sergeant Sunshine / She's the one / In the time of water / Composer of life / One for all / Exercising some control / McGoohan's blues / Manana. *(re-iss.Sep77 on 'Sunset'; SLS 50373) <US re-iss.1978 on 'Chrysalis'; 1160> (re-iss.Aug86 & Nov88 on 'Awareness' lp/c; AWL/AWT 1003) (cd-iss.Oct89; AWCD 1003) (cd re-iss.Oct94 & Oct96 on 'Science Friction'; HUCD 009)*

Harvest / Harvest

Jun 70. (lp) *(SHVL 766) <418>* **FLAT, BAROQUE AND BERSERK** [ ] [ ]
– Don't you grieve / I hate the white man / Feelin' all the Saturday / How does it feel / Goodbye / Another day / Davey / East of the sun / Tom Tiddler's ground / Francesca / Song of the ages / Hell's angels. *(re-iss.Jul85 lp/c; 260585-1/-4) (cd-iss.1992 & Jun94 on 'Hard Up' respectively; HUCD 003 & HUP 3LTDCD)*

May 71. (lp) *(SHVL 789)* **STORMCOCK** [ ] [-]
– Hors d'oeuvres / The same old rock / One man rock and roll band / Me and my woman. *<US-iss.1978 on 'Chrysalis'; 1161> (re-iss.Apr87 on 'Awareness' lp/c; AWL/AWT 2001) (cd re-iss.Oct94 & Oct96 on 'Science Friction'; HUCD 004)*

Oct 72. (7") *(HAR 5059)* **BANK OF THE DEAD (VALERIE'S SONG). / LITTLE LADY** [ ] [-]

Feb 73. (lp) *(SHVL 808)* **LIFEMASK** (music from film soundtrack 'MADE') [ ] [-]
– Highway blues / All Ireland / Little lady / Bank of the dead (Valerie's song) / South Africa / The Lord's prayer: Poem – Modal song (part 1-4) – Front song – Middle song – End song – Front song (reprise). *<US-iss.1978 on 'Chrysalis'; 1162> (re-iss.Apr87 on 'Awareness' lp/c; AWL/AWT 1007)*– (4 tracks). *(cd-iss.Sep94 & Oct96 on 'Science Friction'; HUCD 005)*

Feb 74. (7") *(HAR 5080)* **(DON'T YOU THINK WE'RE) FOREVER. / MALE CHAUVINIST PIG BLUES** [ ] [-]

Feb 74. (lp) *(SHSP 4027)* **VALENTINE** [27] [-]
– Forbidden fruit / Male chauvinist pig blues / I'll see you again / Twelve hours of sunset / Acapulco gold / Commune / Magic woman / Che / North country / (Don't you think we're) Forever. *<US-iss.1978 on 'Chrysalis'; 1163> (re-iss.Apr89 on 'Awareness' lp/c/cd; AWL/AWT/AWCD 1015)*– Home (studio) / Too many movies / Home (live). *(cd re-iss.Nov94 & Oct96 on 'Science Friction'; HUCD 015)*

Oct 74. (7") *(HAR 5089)* **HOME (live). / HOME (studio)** [ ] [-]

Nov 74. (d-lp) *(SHDW 405)* **FLASHES FROM THE ARCHIVES OF OBLIVION (live)** [ ] [-]
– Home / Commune / Don't you grieve / Twelve hours of sunset / Kangaroo blues / All Ireland / Me and my woman / South Africa / Interference / Highway blues / One man rock and roll band / Another day / M.C.P. blues / Too many movies / Home (studio version) *<US-iss.1978 on 'Chrysalis'; 1164> (re-iss.Apr89 on 'Awareness' d-lp/c/cd; AW CD/TD/LD 1012) (cd re-iss.Sep94 & Oct96 on 'Science Friction'; HUCD 010)*

Harvest / Chrysalis

May 75. (lp) *(SHSP 4046) <1105>* **HQ** <US-title 'WHEN AN OLD CRICKETER LEAVES THE CREASE'> [31] [ ] Feb 76
– The game (part I-V) / The spirit lives / Grown-ups are just silly children / Referendum / Forget-me-not / Hallucinating light / When an old cricketer leaves the crease / Referendum. *(re-iss.Mar86 on 'E.M.I.' lp/c; ATAK/TCATAK 68) (cd-iss.Aug95 & Oct96 on 'Science Friction'; HUCD 019)*

May 75. (7") *(HAR 5096)* **WHEN AN OLD CRICKETER LEAVES THE CREASE. / HALLUCINATING LIGHT (acoustic)** [ ] [ ]

Oct 75. (7") *(HAR 5102)* **GROWN-UPS ARE JUST SILLY CHILDREN. / REFERENDUM (LEGEND)** [ ] [-]

Feb 77. (lp) *(SHSP 4060)* **BULLINAMINGVASE** [25] [ ]
– One of those days in England / These last days / Cherishing the lonesome / Naked flame / Watford Gap * / One of those days in England (parts 2-10). *(free 7"w/a) (PSR 407)* REFERENDUM / ANOTHER DAY (live). / TOM TIDDLER'S GROUND (live) *(lp re-iss.Mar77, track * repl. by;* – Breakfast in bed. *(re-iss.Apr87 on 'E.M.I.' lp/c; EMS/TCEMS 1259)*

Mar 77. (7") *(HAR 5120)* **ONE OF THOSE DAYS IN ENGLAND. / WATFORD GAP** [ ] [-]

Nov 77. (7"; as ROY HARPER'S BLACK SHEEP) *(HAR 5140)* **SAIL AWAY. / CHERISHING THE LONESOME** [ ] [-]

Mar 80. (7") *(HAR 5203)* **PLAYING GAMES. / FIRST THING IN THE MORNING** [ ] [-]

Jun 80. (lp) *(SHVL 820)* **THE UNKNOWN SOLDIER** [ ] [-]
– Playing games / I'm in love with you / The flycatcher / You / Old faces / Short and sweet / First thing in the morning / The unknown soldier / Ten years ago / True story.

Jun 80. (7"m) *(HAR 5207)* **SHORT AND SWEET. / WATER SPORTS (live) / UNKNOWN SOLDIER (live)** [ ] [-]

Public / not issued

Oct 82. (7") *(PUBS 1001)* **NO ONE EVER GETS OUT ALIVE. / CASUALITY (live)** [ ] [-]

Nov 82. (lp/c) *(PUBLP/TCPUBLP 5001)* **WORK OF HEART** [ ] [-]
– Drawn to the flames / Jack of hearts / I am a child / Woman / I still care / Work of heart; (i) No one ever gets out alive – (ii) Two lovers in the Moon – (iii) We are the people – (iv) All us children (so sadly far apart) – (v) We are the people (reprise) – (vi) No one ever gets out alive (finale). *(re-iss.Nov86 on 'Awareness' lp,c; AWL 1002) (lp w/ free 7"x2; PUBS 1001/1002; 2nd very ltd) (cd-iss.Oct89; AWCD 1002)*

Mar 83. (7") *(PUBS 1002)* **I STILL CARE. / GOODBYE LADYBIRD** [ ] [-]

Hardup / not issued

1984. (lp; ltd) *(PUB 5002)* **BORN IN CAPTIVITY** (demos) [ ] [-]
– Stan / Drawn to the flames / Come to bed eyes / No woman is safe / I am a child / Elizabeth / Work of heart; (i) No one ever gets out alive – (ii) Two lovers on the Moon – (iii) We are the people – (iv) All us children (so sadly far apart) – (v) We are the people (reprise) – (vi) No one ever gets out alive (finale). *(re-iss.Jul85 & Nov88 on 'Awareness' lp/c; AWL/AWT 1001) (cd-iss.Apr89; AWCD 1001) (cd re-iss.Oct96 on 'Blueprint'; HUCD 008)*

ROY HARPER and JIMMY PAGE

with **JIMMY PAGE** – guitar (ex-LED ZEPPELIN)

Beggars Banquet / P.V.C.

Feb 85. (lp/c) *(BEGA/BEGC 60)* **WHATEVER HAPPENED TO JUGULA** [44] [ ]
– Nineteen forty-eightish / Hangman / Elizabeth / Advertisement / Bad speech / Hope / Twentieth century man. *(re-iss.Aug88 & Jul91 on 'Lowdown – Beggars Banquet' lp/c/cd; BBL/+C 60/+CD)*

Mar 85. (7") *(BEG 131)* **ELIZABETH. / ADVERTISEMENT** [ ] [ ]
(12"+=) *(BEG 131T)* – (I hate the) White man (live).

ROY HARPER

E.M.I. / not issued

Jun 86. (d-lp/c) *(EM/TCEM 5004)* **IN BETWEEN EVERY LINE (live)** [ ] [-]
– One of those days in England / Short and sweet / True story / Referendum / Highway blues / One man rock and roll band / The game / Hangman. *(cd-iss.Nov94 & Oct96 on 'Science Friction'; HUCD 018)*

Mar 88. (7") *(EM 46)* **LAUGHING INSIDE. / LAUGHING INSIDE (acoustic)** [ ] [-]

—— (above single was also released as 3 promos in the disguise of palindromes; RORY PHARE / HARRY ROPE / PER YARROH; *(Regal Zonophone; RP 1 / HP 1 / PY 1)*

Mar 88. (cd/c/lp) *(CD/TC+/EMC 3524)* **DESCENDANTS OF SMITH** [ ] [-]
– Laughing inside / Garden of uranium / Still life / Pinches of salt / Desert island / Government surplus / Surplus liquorice / Liquorice alltime / Maile lei / Same shoes / Descendants of Smith. *(cd+=)*– Laughing inside (rough and ready version). *(cd-iss.Sep94 & Oct96 as 'GARDEN OF URANIUM' on 'Science Friction' respectively; HUCD 014)*

—— below featured DAVE GILMOUR, KATE BUSH & STEVE BROUGHTON

Awareness / I.R.S.

May 90. (cd/c/lp) *(AW CD/T/L 1018)* **ONCE** [ ] [ ] 1991
– Once / Once in the middle of nowhere / Nowhere to run to / Black cloud of Islam / If / Winds of change / Berliners / Sleeping at the wheel / For longer than it takes / Ghost dance. *(cd re-iss.Oct94 on 'Line'; LICD 900892) (cd re-iss.Oct96 on 'Science Friction'; HUCD 011)*

Nov 90. (cd/c/lp) **BURN THE WORLD** [ ] [-]
– Burn the world (studio) / Burn the world (live). *(cd re-iss.Oct94 & Oct96 on 'Science Friction'; HUCD 013)*

Nov 92. (cd/c/lp) **DEATH OR GLORY** [ ] [-]
– Death or glory / War came home / Tonight duty / Waiting for Godot / Part zed next

to me / Man kind / Tallest tree / Miles remains / Fourth world / Why / Cardboard city / One more tomorrow / Plough / On summer day / If I can. *(cd re-iss.Dec94 & Oct 96 on 'Science Friction'; HUCD 012)*

– compilations etc. –

May 78. (7") *Harvest; (HAR 5160)* **WHEN AN OLD CRICKETER LEAVES THE CREASE. / HOME (studio)**

May 78. (lp) *Harvest; (SHSM 2025)* **ROY HARPER 1970-75** [ ] [-]
– Don't you grieve / (I hate the) White man / Tom Tiddler's ground / Me and my woman / Little lady / South Africa / Forbidden fruit / I'll see you again / Commune / Another day / When an old cricketer leaves the crease / Home.

Dec 88. (lp/c/cd) *Awareness; (AWL/AWT/AWCD 1011)* **LOONY ON THE BUS** (rare) [ ] [-]
– No change (ten years ago) / Sail away / / Playing prison / I wanna be part of the news / Burn the world / Casuality / Cora / Loony on the bus / Come up and see me / The flycatcher / Square boxes.

1992. (c) *Hard Up; (HU 2)* **BORN IN CAPTIVITY II (live)** [ ] [-]

Nov 94. (cd) *Awareness; (cd)* **BORN IN CAPTIVITY / WORK OF HEART** [ ] [-]
(re-iss.cd Nov94 on 'Science Friction';)

Dec 94. (cd) *Awareness;* **COMMERCIAL BREAKS** (unreleased from 1977 on 'Harvest'; *SHSP 4077)* [ ] [-]
– My little girl / I'm in love with you / Ten years ago / Sail away / I wanna be part of the news / Cora / Come up and see me / The flycatcher / Too many movies / Square boxes / Burn the world (part 1) / Playing prisons. *(re-iss.Feb95 & Oct96 on 'Science Friction'; HUCD 016)*

Dec 94. (cd) *Awareness;* **AN INTRODUCTION TO ROY HARPER** [ ] [-]
– Legend / She's the one / Tom Tiddler's ground / Highway blues / Che / Hallucinating light / One of those days in England / You / Nineteen forty-eightish / Pinches of salt / Ghost dance / The tallest tree / Miles remains. *(re-iss.Feb95 & Oct96 on 'Science Friction'; HUCD 017)*

Aug 95. (cd) *Griffin;* **UNHINGED** [ ] [-]
– Descendants of Smith / Legend / North country / When an old cricketer leaves the crease / Three hundred words / Hope / Naked flame / Commune / South Africa / Back to the stones / Frozen moment / Highway blues / The same old rock. *(re-iss.Oct96 on 'Blueprint'; HUCD 020)*

May 96. (cd) *Blueprint; (BP 220CD)* **LIVE AT LES COUSINS (live)** [ ] [-]
Apr 97. (cd) *Science Friction; (HUCD 022)* **LIVE AT THE BBC VOL.1** [ ] [-]
Apr 97. (cd) *Science Friction; (HUCD 023)* **LIVE AT THE BBC VOL.2** [ ] [-]
Jun 97. (cd) *Science Friction; (HUCD 024)* **LIVE AT THE BBC VOL.3** [ ] [-]
Jun 97. (cd) *Science Friction; (HUCD 025)* **LIVE AT THE BBC VOL.4** [ ] [-]
Jun 97. (cd) *Science Friction; (HUCD 026)* **LIVE AT THE BBC VOL.5** [ ] [-]
Jun 97. (cd) *Science Friction; (HUCD 027)* **LIVE AT THE BBC VOL.6** [ ] [-]

George HARRISON

Born: 25 Feb'43, Wavertree, Liverpool, England. Released in late 1968, HARRISON's 'WONDERWALL' was the first solo release by a BEATLE, although it flopped in the UK. He followed it up with a classic piece of late 60's self-indulgence, the awful 'ELECTRONIC SOUNDS' (released on his own 'Zapple' label). While HARRISON's pioneering sitar work was praiseworthy, the same experimental spirit applied to a Moog synthesizer, (strung out over a whole album), was downright dull. Despite being overshadowed by the writing partnership of LENNON and McCARTNEY, HARRISON's songs rank among the BEATLES' best, not least 'SOMETHING' and 'HERE COMES THE SUN'. When the BEATLES officially split in 1969, it was perhaps an opportunity for GEORGE to really go for it and prove his writing skills over a whole album. Not content with two sides of vinyl, he went for six, releasing the triple-set 'ALL THINGS MUST PASS' in 1970. The Herculean task of keeping a consistently high standard over three albums was beyond even the mercurial talent of HARRISON, although the peaks definitely outweigh the troughs. PHIL SPECTOR's legendary production skills enhance the gorgeous melodies of 'MY SWEET LORD' and DYLAN's 'IF NOT FOR YOU', while HARRISON's well-documented spirituality is given a voice in the title track and 'THE ART OF DYING'. The aforementioned 'MY SWEET LORD' was released as a single in early '71 topping the charts on both sides of the Atlantic. Success was bittersweet though, as BRIGHT TUNES (owners of songwriter RONNIE MACK's estate) claimed the song plagiarised their CHIFFONS song, 'HE'S SO FINE'. Five years later, the court gave 6-figure royalties to the plaintiff. HARRISON helped to organise a huge famine relief benefit gig in New York, playing alongside a cast of musicians that included his old mucker RINGO STARR as well as BOB DYLAN. The gig was released on another triple-set in 1972 as 'CONCERT FOR BANGLADESH'. May '73 saw yet another No.1 US single, 'GIVE ME LOVE (GIVE ME PEACE ON EARTH)' taken from the similarly successful album, 'LIVING IN THE MATERIAL WORLD'. If HARRISON was riding the crest of a wave, then he was soon to be dallying listlessly in a stagnant creative pond. In 1974, he set up his own 'Dark Horse' label, releasing the clueless album of the same name as well as signing up artists like RAVI SHANKAR and SPLINTER. He and his wife PATTI were divorced in June '77, after her much publicised affair with ERIC CLAPTON. In 1979, he founded his own 'Homemade' film productions, which released the 80's movies: 'Life Of Brian', 'The Long Good Friday', 'Time Bandits', 'The Missionary', 'Mona Lisa', 'A Private Function', 'Water', and 'Shanghai Surprise'. Mediocre albums were his forte at the turn of the decade, and even the tribute to LENNON, 'ALL THOSE YEARS AGO', (from 1981's 'SOMEWHERE IN ENGLAND'), seemed uninspired. HARRISON teamed up with ELO's JEFF LYNNE for 1987's 'CLOUD NINE'; his production, along with the hit, 'GOT MY MIND SET ON YOU', helping to make the record HARRISON's most successful of the 80's (and 90's for that matter). In the decade since, HARRISON has been involved in the relatively brief TRAVELING WILBURYS project (with LYNNE, DYLAN, PETTY & ROY ORBISON under various brotherly guises) as well as releasing 'LIVE IN JAPAN' in 1992, culled from a series of Japanese concerts with CLAPTON. In the mid-90's, he was involved in the archive project which saw the release of a BEATLES documentary, rarities/outtakes albums and even a "new" single, 'FREE AS A BIRD'. As ever though, the man remains an enigma, the quintessential rock star hermit content to do his own thing with a minimum of fuss. • **Covered:** I'D HAVE YOU ANYTIME + I DON'T WANT TO DO IT (Bob Dylan) / BYE BYE LOVE (Everly Brothers) / GOT MY MIND SET ON YOU (James Ray) / ROLL OVER BEETHOVEN (Chuck Berry).

Recommended: ALL THINGS MUST PASS (*8) / THE BEST OF GEORGE HARRISON (*7) / THE BEST OF DARK HORSE 1976-89 (*6)

GEORGE HARRISON – instruments (no vocals) (of-BEATLES)

Apple Apple

Nov 68. (lp; stereo/mono) *(S+/APCOR 1) <3350>* **WONDERWALL MUSIC (Soundtrack)** [ ] [49] Jan69
– Microbes / Red lady too / Tabla and Pavajak / In the park / Drilling a hole / Guru Vandana / Greasy legs / Ski-ing / Gat Kirwani / Dream scene / Party Seacombe / Love scene / Crying / Cowboy music / Fantasy sequins / On the bed / Glass box / Wonderwall to be here / Singing om. *(cd-iss.Jun92; CDSAPCOR 1)*

—— **GEORGE** – moog synthesizer (no vocals)

Zapple Zapple

May 69. (lp) *(02) <3358>* **ELECTRONIC SOUND** [ ] [ ]
– Under the Mersey wall / No time or space.

—— He became in-house 'Apple' producer, before gigging with DELANEY & BONNIE late 1969. The BEATLES break-up, and he went solo again with vocals, etc, with **DEREK & THE DOMINOES** (Eric Clapton and his band) / **BADFINGER / BILLY PRESTON** – keyboards / **RINGO STARR, GINGER BAKER** – drums / etc.

Apple Apple

Nov 70. (t-box-lp) *(<STCH 639>)* **ALL THINGS MUST PASS** [4] [1]
– I'd have you anytime / My sweet Lord / Wah-wah / Isn't it a pity / What is life / If not for you / Behind that locked door / Let it down / Run of the mill / Beware of darkness / Apple scruffs / Ballad of Frankie Crisp (let it roll) / Awaiting on you all / All things must pass / I dig love / Art of dying / Isn't it a pity / Hear me Lord / Out of the blue / It's Johnny's birthday / Plug me in / I remember Jeep / Thanks for the pepperoni. *(d-cd.iss.May87 on 'E.M.I.'; CDS 746688-2)*

Nov 70. (7") *<2995>* **MY SWEET LORD. / ISN'T IT A PITY** [-] [1]
Jan 71. (7") *(R 5884)* **MY SWEET LORD. / WHAT IS LIFE** [1] [-]
(re-iss.Nov76; same)
Feb 71. (7") *<1828>* **WHAT IS LIFE. / APPLE SCRUFFS** [-] [10]
Jul 71. (7") *(R 5912) <1836>* **BANGLA-DESH. / DEEP BLUE** [10] [23]

—— In Jan72, he with other artists released live triple album 'CONCERT FOR BANGLADESH'; *(<STCX 3385>)*. It hit UK No.1 & US No.2. *(re-iss.Aug91 d-cd/d-c; 468835-2/-4)*

—— **GEORGE** now with various session people

May 73. (7") *(R 5988) <1862>* **GIVE ME LOVE (GIVE ME PEACE ON EARTH). / MISS O'DELL** [8] [1]

Jun 73. (lp/c) *(PAS 10006) <3410>* **LIVING IN THE MATERIAL WORLD** [2] [1]
– Give me love (give me peace on earth) / Sue me, sue you blues / The light that has lighted the world / Don't let me wait too long / Who can see it / Living in the material world / The Lord loves the one (that loves the Lord) / Be here now / Try some buy some / The day the world gets 'round / That is all. *(cd-iss.Jan92 on 'E.M.I.'; CDPAS 10006)*

Dec 74. (7") *(R 6002) <1879>* **DING DONG; DING DONG. / I DON'T CARE ANYMORE** [38] [36] Jan75

Dec 74. (lp/c) *(PAS 10008) <3418>* **DARK HORSE** [ ] [4]
– Hari's on tour (express) / Simply shady / So sad / Bye bye love / Maya love / Ding dong; ding dong / Dark horse / Far East man / Is it he (Jai Sri Krishna). *(re-iss.Dec80 on 'Music For Pleasure'; MFP 50510) (cd-iss.Jan92 on 'E.M.I.'; CDPAS 10008)*

Feb 75. (7") *(R 6001) <1877>* **DARK HORSE. / HARI'S ON TOUR (EXPRESS)** [ ] [15] Nov74
Sep 75. (7") *(R 6007) <1884>* **YOU. / WORLD OF STONE** [38] [20]

Oct 75. (lp/c) *(PAS 10009) <3420>* **EXTRA TEXTURE (READ ALL ABOUT IT)** [16] [8]
– The answer's at the end / This guitar (can't keep from crying) / You / Ooh baby (you know that I love you) / World of stone / A bit more of you / Can't stop thinking about you / Tired of midnight blue / Grey cloudy lies / His name is legs (ladies & gentlemen). *(cd-iss.Jan92 on 'E.M.I.'; CDPAS 10009)*

Feb 76. (7") *(R 6012) <1885>* **THIS GUITAR (CAN'T KEEP FROM CRYING). / MAYA LOVE** [ ] [ ]

Apple Capitol

Oct 76. (lp/c) *(PAS 10011) <11578>* **THE BEST OF GEORGE HARRISON** (compilation) [ ] [31]
– Something (BEATLES) / If I needed someone (BEATLES) / Here comes the sun (BEATLES) / Taxman (BEATLES) / Think for yourself (BEATLES) / While my guitar gently weeps (BEATLES) / For you blue (BEATLES) / My sweet Lord / Give me love (give me peace on Earth) / You / Bangla-Desh / Dark horse / What is life. *(re-iss.Oct81 on 'Music For Pleasure' lp/c; MFP 50523) (cd-iss.May87 on 'Parlophone'; CDP 746682-2)*

Dark Horse Dark Horse

Nov 76. (7") *(K 16856) <8294>* **THIS SONG. / LEARNING HOW TO LOVE YOU** [ ] [25]

Nov 76. (lp/c) *(K/K4 56319) <3005>* **THIRTY-THREE AND A THIRD** [35] [11]
– Woman don't you cry for me / Dear one / Beautiful girl / This song / See yourself / It's what you value / True love / Pure Smokey / Crackerbox palace / Learning how to love you.

Jan 77. (7") *<8313>* **CRACKERBOX PALACE. / LEARNING HOW TO LOVE YOU** [-] [19]
Feb 77. (7") *(K 16896)* **TRUE LOVE. / PURE SMOKEY** [ ] [-]
Jun 77. (7") *(K 16967)* **IT'S WHAT YOU VALUE. / WOMAN DON'T YOU CRY FOR ME** [ ] [-]
Feb 79. (7") *<8763>* **BLOW AWAY. / SOFT-HEARTED HANA** [-] [16]
Feb 79. (7") *(K 17327)* **BLOW AWAY. / SOFT TOUCH** [51] [-]
Feb 79. (lp/c) *(K/K4 56562) <3255>* **GEORGE HARRISON** [39] [14]
– Love comes to everyone / Not guilty / Here comes the moon / Soft- hearted Hana /

Blow away / Faster / Your love is forever / Dark sweet lady / Soft touch / If you believe.

Apr 79. (7") *(K 17284)* **LOVE COMES TO EVERYONE. / SOFT-HEARTED HANA** [ ] [-]

Apr 79. (7") *<8844>* **LOVE COMES TO EVERYONE. / SOFT TOUCH** [-] [ ]

Jul 79. (7"/7"pic-d) *(K 17423/+P)* **FASTER. / YOUR LOVE IS FOREVER** [ ] [-]

May 81. (7") *(K 17807) <49725>* **ALL THOSE YEARS AGO. / WRITING'S ON THE WALL** [13] [2]

Jun 81. (lp/c) *(K/K4 56870) <3492>* **SOMEWHERE IN ENGLAND** [13] [11]
– Blood from a clone / Unconsciousness rules / Life itself / All those years ago / Baltimore oriole / Teardrops / That which I have lost / Writing's on the wall / Hong Kong blues / Save the world.

Jul 81. (7") *(K 17837) <49785>* **TEARDROPS. / SAVE THE WORLD** [ ] [ ]

Oct 82. (7") *(929864-2) <29864>* **WAKE UP MY LOVE. / GREECE** [ ] [53]

Nov 82. (lp/c) *(K 923734-1/-4) <23734>* **GONE TROPPO** [ ] [ ]
– Wake up my love / That's the way it goes / I really love you / Greece / Gone troppo / Mystical one / Unknown delight / Baby don't run away / Dream away / Circles.

Jan 83. (7") *<29744>* **I REALLY LOVE YOU. / CIRCLES** [-] [ ]

— Took long time off from solo career to establish his film production work. Returned after nearly five years with new session people.

Sep 87. (lp/c)(cd) *(WX 123/+C)(925643-2) <25643>* **CLOUD NINE** [10] [8] Nov87
– Cloud 9 / That's what it takes / Fish on the sand / Just for today / This is love / When we was fab / Devil's radio / Someplace else / Wreck of the Hesperus / Breath away from Heaven / Got my mind set on you.

Oct 87. (7") *(W 8178) <28178>* **GOT MY MIND SET ON YOU. / LAY HIS HEAD** [2] [1]
(12"+=/12"pic-d+=) *(W 8178T/+P)* – ('A'extended).

Feb 88. (7") *(W 8131) <28131>* **WHEN WE WAS FAB. / ZIGZAG** [25] [23]
(12"+=/12"pic-d+=/3"cd-s+=) *(W 8131 T/TX/CD)* – That's the way it goes (remix) / ('A'mix).

Jun 88. (7") *(W 7913) <27913>* **THIS IS LOVE. / BREATH AWAY FROM HEAVEN** [55] [ ]
(12"+=) *(W 7913T)* – All those wasted years ago.
(3"cd-s++=) *(W 7913CD)* – Hong Kong blues.

— Later in 1988, HARRISON teamed up with BOB DYLAN, ROY ORBISON, JEFF LYNNE and TOM PETTY in The TRAVELLING WILBURYS. He also continued solo work below.

Oct 89. (lp/c)(cd) *(WX 312/+C)(K 925643-2) <25726>* **THE BEST OF DARK HORSE (1976-1989)** (compilation) [ ] [ ]
– Poor little girl / Blow away / That's the way it goes / Cockamamie business / Wake up my love / Life itself / Got my mind set on you / Here comes the Moon / Gone troppo / When we was fab / Love comes to everyone / All those years ago / Cheer down. *(c+=/cd+=)*– Crackerbox Palace.

Nov 89. (7") *(W 2696)* **CHEER DOWN. / POOR LITTLE GIRL** [ ] [-]
(12"+=/cd-s+=) *(W 2696 T/CD)* – Crackerbox palace.

Jul 92. (cd/c) *(7599 26964-2/-4) <26964>* **LIVE IN JAPAN (with ERIC CLAPTON AND BAND)** [ ] [ ]
– I want to tell you / Old brown shoe / Taxman / Give me love (give me peace on Earth) / If I needed someone / Something / What is life / Dark horse / Piggies / Got my mind set on you / Cloud nine / Here comes the Sun / My sweet Lord / All those years ago / Cheer down / Devil's radio / Isn't it a pity / While my guitar gently weeps / Roll over Beethoven.

– compilations etc. –

Oct 82. (d-cd) *Dark Horse; (K 466101)* **THIRTY-THREE AND A THIRD / GEORGE HARRISON** [ ] [-]

Mickey HART (see under ⇒ GRATEFUL DEAD)

Annie HASLAM (see under ⇒ RENAISSANCE)

HATFIELD AND THE NORTH

Formed: Canterbury, England . . .early '72 by ex-CARAVAN members RICHARD and DAVE SINCLAIR, plus former DELIVERY musicians PHIL MILLER and PIP PYLE. DAVE soon returned to CARAVAN early 1973 and was replaced by DAVE STEWART, before they recorded an eponymous album for 'Virgin'. Their quirky sound was inspired by the avant-garde jazz-rock of SOFT MACHINE, a direction they developed further on their more melodic second set, 'THE ROTTERS CLUB' (1975). They split soon after, however, STEWART and MILLER forming NATIONAL HEALTH. RICHARD returned to CARAVAN, later joining CAMEL. He later turned up in the early 90's with his new project, RICHARD SINCLAIR'S CARAVAN OF DREAMS.

Recommended: HATFIELD AND THE NORTH (*5) / THE ROTTER'S CLUB (*5)

RICHARD SINCLAIR (b. 6 Jun'48, Canterbury, Kent) – vocals, bass (exCARAVAN) / **PHIL MILLER** (b.22 Jan'49, Barnet, Hertfordshire) – guitar (ex-DELIVERY) / **DAVE STEWART** (b.30 Dec'50, Waterloo, London) – keyboards (ex-EGG, ex-KHAN) / **PIP PYLE** (b. 4 Apr'50, Sawbridgeworth, Hertfordshire) – drums (ex-DELIVERY), with guest vocalists **BARBARA GASKIN, AMANDA PARSONS, ANN ROSENTHAL + ROBERT WYATT** plus **GEOFF LEIGH** – sax, flute / **JEREMY BAINES** – pixiephone

Virgin — not issued

Mar 74. (lp) *(V 2008)* **HATFIELD AND THE NORTH** [ ] [-]
– The Stubbs effect / Big jobs / Going up to the people and tinkling / Calyx / Son of 'There's no place like Homerton' / Aigrette / Rifferama / Fol de Rol / Shaving is boring / Licks for the ladies / Bossa nochance / Big jobs No.2 / Lobster in cleavage probe / Gigantic land-crabs in Earth takeover bid / The other Stubbs effect. *(re-iss.Aug88; OVED 131) (cd-iss.Jul87 +=; CDV 2008)*– Let's eat (real soon) / Fitter stoke has a bath.

Nov 74. (7") *(VS 116)* **LET'S EAT (REAL SOON). / FITTER STOKE HAS A BATH** [ ] [-]

— now with same 3 guest female vocalists plus **JIMMY HASTINGS** – flute, saxes / **LINDSAY COOPER** – bassoon, oboe / **TIM HODGKINSON** – clarinet / **HUGH MONTGOMERY CAMPBELL** – French horn

Mar 75. (lp) *(V 2030)* **THE ROTTER'S CLUB** [43] [-]
– Share it / Lounging there trying / (Big) John Wayne socks psychology on the jaw / Chaos at the greasy spoon / The yes 'no interlude / Fitter Stoke has a bath / Didn't matter anyway / Underdub / Mumps / Your majesty is like a cream donut / Lumps / Prenut. *(re-iss.Aug88; OVED 132) (cd-iss.Jun88 +=; CDV 2030)*– Halfway between Heaven and Earth / Oh, Len's nature / Lything and gracing.

— Disbanded mid 1975 and RICHARD SINCLAIR retired until re-forming a near CARAVAN in his CARAVAN OF DREAMS of the early 90's.

– compilations, others –

Mar 80. (lp) *Virgin; (VR 5)* **AFTERS** (rec.1973-1975) [ ] [-]
– Let's eat (real soon) / Fitter Stoke has a bath / Mumps / Share it / Lounging there trying / The Stubbs effect / Big jobs (poo poo extract) / Going up to the people and tinkling / Calyx / (Big) John Wayne socks psychology on the jaw / Chaos at the greasy spoon / Halfway between Heaven and Earth / Oh, Len's nature / Lything and gracing / Prenut / Your majesty is like a cream donut (loud). *(re-iss.1988; OVED 196)*

May 93. (cd) *Code 90; (NINETY 6)* **LIVE 1990** [ ] [-]

NATIONAL HEALTH

DAVE STEWART – keyboards / **PHIL MILLER** – guitar / **PIP PYLE** – drums, percussion / **JIMMY HASTINGS** – wind / **NEIL MURRAY** – bass, repl. MONT CAMPBELL / **AMANDA PARSONS** – vocals / **ALAN GOWEN** – synthesizers / **JOHN MITCHELL** – percussion / **BILL BRUFORD** – drums

Affinity — Visa

Feb 78. (lp) *(AFF 6) <IMP 7002>* **NATIONAL HEALTH** [ ] [ ]
– Tenemos roads / Brujo / Borogoves / Elephants. *(cd-iss.Jun90 on 'Decal'; CDLIK 66) (cd re-iss.Jun97 on 'Spalax'; 14827)*

— **JOHN GREAVES** – bass, piano (ex-COLOSSEUM II), repl. NEIL MURRAY, PARSONS, MITCHELL, GOWEN + guest BRUFORD

Charly — not issued

1978. (lp) *(CRL 5010)* **OF QUEUES AND CURES** [ ] [-]
– The Bryden 2-step (for amphibeans) (part 1) / The collapso / Squarer for Maud / Dreams wide awake / Binoculars / Phlakatoen / The Bryden 2-step (part 2). *(cdiss.Oct90 on 'Decal'; CDLIK 70)*

— now with guests **RICHARD SINCLAIR, ANNIE WHITEHEAD, ELTON DEAN, TED EMMETT, JIMMY HASTINGS, AMANDA PARSONS + BARBARA GASKIN**

Lounging — Europa

Mar 83. (lp) *(LA 02) <JP 2008>* **D.S. AL CODA** [ ] [ ]
– Portrait of a shrinking man / Tntfx / Black hat / I feel a night coming on / Arriving twice / Shining water / Tales of a damson knight / Flanagan's people / Toad of Toad Hall. *(cd-iss.Sep96 on 'Blueprint'; BP 129CD)*

– compilations, etc. –

Nov 96. (cd) *Voiceprint; (VP 113CD)* **MISSING PIECES** [ ] [-]

HATFIELD AND THE NORTH

re-formed for one-off gig.

May 93. Code 90; (cd) *(NINETY 6)* **LIVE 1990 (live)** [ ] [-]
– Share it / Shipwrecked / Underdub / Blott / Going for a song / Cauliflower ears / Halfway between Heaven & Earth / 5-4 intro / It didn't matter anyway.

Helmut HATTLER (see under ⇒ KRAAN)

HAWKWIND

Formed: London, England . . . mid-69 as GROUP X, by ex-FAMOUS CURE members DAVE BROCK and MICK SLATTER who were joined by NIK TURNER, TERRY OLLIS, DIK MIK and JOHN HARRISON. They soon became HAWKWIND ZOO but SLATTERY opted out for a gypsy lifestyle in Ireland after they signed to 'United Artists'in late '69. Now as HAWKWIND and after many free concerts (mostly at open-air festivals) they released their eponymous debut in late summer 1970. While this album was a melange of bluesy, heavy psychedelic rock, the band added more personnel for the follow-up, 'IN SEARCH OF SPACE' (1971), including synth player DEL DETTMAR and vocalist/poet ROBERT CALVERT. His sci-fi musings featured heavily on the album, while the scattered electronic stabs and saxaphone honking merged with the driving rhythm section to create their own tripped out take on space rock. The record saw HAWKWIND break into the album chart top 20 while the following summer they smashed into the top 3 with the classic 'SILVER MACHINE' (1972) single, LEMMY KILMISTER's pile driving bass fuelling the beast with a turbo-charged power. It had previously featured on the live various artists 'GREASY TRUCKERS' PARTY' album, as well as appearing on the similar 'GLASTONBURY FAYRE' compilation. The success of the single secured the band top 20 placings on all four of their future albums for 'United Artists' although come 1975, after the classic 'WARRIOR ON THE EDGE OF TIME' album, LEMMY had departed to form MOTORHEAD and CALVERT had been replaced by sci-fi writer MICHAEL MOORCOCK. The band signed to 'Charisma' and despite continuing moderate success, were dogged by legal battles over the HAWKWIND name towards the end of the decade. With a substantially altered line-up, HAWKWIND continued to release albums on their own 'Flicknife' label throughout the 80's. Tragedy struck when CALVERT died from a heart attack in 1988 although yet another line-up saw HAWKWIND into the 90's with the 'SPACE BANDITS' (1990) album. The band continue to attract a loyal following of die-hard hippies

and the emergence of the psychedelic/crusty techno scene has done them no harm, many young stoners citing HAWKWIND as a prominent influence.
• **Songwriters:** Mostly by BROCK or CALVERT until the latter's departure, ALAN DAVEY eventually replacing him. Other various personnel over the years also took part in writing.

Recommended: IN SEARCH OF SPACE (*8) / SPACE RITUAL (*8) / WARRIOR ON THE EDGE OF TIME (*6) / STASIS – THE U.A. YEARS 1971-1975 (*7)

DAVE BROCK (b. Islesworth, England) – vocals, guitar / **NIK TURNER** (b. Oxford, England) – vocals, saxophone / **HUW-LLOYD LANGTON** – guitar repl. MICK SLATTERY (Oct69, when as HAWKWIND ZOO) **JOHN HARRISON** – bass / **TERRY OLLIS** – drums / **DIK MIK** (b. S. McMANUS, Richmond, England) – electronics engineer, synthesizers

Liberty U.A.

Jul 70. (7") *(LBF 15382)* **HURRY ON SUNDOWN. / MIRROR OF ILLUSION**

Aug 70. (lp) *(LBS 83348)* **HAWKWIND**
– Hurry on sundown / The reason is / Be yourself / Paranoia (part 1 & 2) / Seeing it as you really are / Mirror of illusion. *(re-iss.Sep75 on 'Sunset'; SLS 50374) (re-iss.Feb80 as 'ROCKFILE' on 'United Artists'; LBR 1012) (re-iss.Feb84 on 'E.M.I.' lp/pic-lp; SLS/+P 1972921) (hit UK 75) (cd-iss.Feb94 on 'Repertoire';)*

— (Sep70) **THOMAS CRIMBLE** – bass repl. JOHN HARRISON / **DEL DETTMAR** – synthesizer repl. LANGTON (partway through next album)

— (May71) **DAVE ANDERSON** – bass (ex-AMON DUUL II) repl. CRIMBLE On stage they also added on vocals **ROBERT CALVERT** (b. Pretoria, South Africa) – poet, vocals, **MICHAEL MOORCOCK** – sci-fi writer and **STACIA** – exotic dancer

U.A. U.A.

Oct 71. (lp) *(UAG 29202)* **IN SEARCH OF SPACE** [18]
– You shouldn't do that / You know you're only dreaming / Master of the universe / We took the wrong step years ago / Adjust me / Children of the sun. *(re-iss.Jan81 on 'Liberty'; LBG 29202) (re-iss.Jun85 on 'Liberty-EMI' lp/c; ATAK/TCATAK 9) (re-iss.Oct87 on 'Fame' lp/c; FA/TCFA 3192) (cd-iss.May89 & Dec95 on 'Fame'; CDFA 3192)*

— (Sep71) **LEMMY** (b. IAN KILMISTER, 24 Dec'45, Stoke-On-Trent, England) – bass, vocals repl. ANDERSON

— (Jan72) **SIMON KING** – drums (ex-OPAL BUTTERFLY) repl. OLLIS (group now **KING, LEMMY, BROCK, TURNER, DIK MIK, DETTMAR, CALVERT, STACIA** and p/t **MOORCOCK**)

Jun 72. (7") *(UP 35381)* <50949> **SILVER MACHINE. / SEVEN BY SEVEN** [3]
(re-iss.'76) (re-iss.Oct78, hit UK 34) (re-hit 67 when re-iss.Dec82 7"/7"pic-d/12"; UP/UPP/12UP 35381)

Nov 72. (lp) *(UAG 29364)* **DOREMI FASOL LATIDO** [14]
– Brainstorm / Space is deep / Down through the night / One change / Lord of light / Time we left this world today / The watcher. *(re-iss.1979) (re-iss.Jun85 on 'Liberty-EMI') (US cd-iss.Jul91 on 'One Way')*

May 73. (d-lp) *(UAD 60037-8)* **SPACE RITUAL – RECORDED LIVE IN LIVERPOOL AND LONDON (live)** [9]
– Earth calling / Born to go / Down through the night / The awakening / Lord of light / The black corridor / Space is deep / Electronic No.1 / Orgone accumulator / Upside down / 10 seconds of forever / Brainstorm / 7 by 7 / Sonic attack / Time we left this world today / Master of the universe / Welcome to the future. *(re-iss.1979)*

Aug 73. (7") *(UP 25566)* <314> **URBAN GUERILLA. / BRAINBOX POLLUTION** [39]

— Now a trim sex/septet when DIK MIK and CALVERT departed. The latter going solo. (Apr74) **SIMON HOUSE** – keyboards, synthesizers, violin (ex-THIRD EAR BAND, ex-HIGH TIDE) repl. DETTMAR who emigrated to Canada

Aug 74. (7") *(UP 35715)* **PSYCHEDELIC WARLORDS (DISAPPEAR IN SMOKE). / IT'S SO EASY**

Sep 74. (lp/c) *(UAG/UAC 29672)* **HALL OF THE MOUNTAIN GRILL** [16]
– Psychedelic warlords (disappear in smoke) / Wind of change / D-rider / Web weaver / You'd better believe it / Hall of the mountain grill / Lost Johnnie / Wind of change / Goat willow / Paradox. *(re-iss.Jan81 on 'Liberty'; LBG 29672) (re-iss.Jun85 on 'Liberty-EMI';) (re-iss.Sep85 on 'Fame'; FA41 3133-1) (cd-iss.May89 & Dec95; CD-FA 3133)*

— added **ALAN POWELL** – 2nd drums (ex-STACKRIDGE, ex-CHICKEN SHACK, etc)

Charisma Atco

Mar 75. (7") *(UP 35808)* **KINGS OF SPEED. / MOTORHEAD**

May 75. (lp/c) *(UAG/UAC 29766)* **WARRIOR ON THE EDGE OF TIME** [13]
– Assault and battery – part one / The golden void – part two / The wizard blew his horn / Opa-Loka / The demented man / Magnu / Standing at the edge / Spiral galaxy 28948 / Warriors / Dying seas / Kings of speed. *(re-iss.1979)(re-iss.Jan81 + Jun85 on 'Liberty-EMI')*

— **PAUL RUDOLPH** – bass (ex-PINK FAIRIES) repl. LEMMY who formed MOTORHEAD **BOB CALVERT** – vocals returned, STACIA the dancer left to get married. **CALVERT** and **RUDOLPH** now with **BROCK, TURNER, KING, HOUSE** and **POWELL**. note also that MOORCOCK left to form his DEEP FIX

Charisma Charisma

Jul 76. (7") *(CB 289)* **KERB CRAWLER. / HONKY DORKY** [-]

Aug 76. (lp/c) *(CDS 4004)* **ASTOUNDING SOUNDS AND AMAZING MUSIC** [33] [-]
– Reefer madness / Steppenwolf / City of lagoons / The aubergine that ate Rangoon / Kerb crawler / Kadu flyer / Chronoglide skyway. *(re-iss.Mar83; CHC 14) (cd-iss.Apr89 on 'Virgin'; CDSCD 4004)*

Jan 77. (7") *(CB 299)* **BACK ON THE STREETS. / THE DREAM OF ISIS**

— **ADRIAN SHAW** – bass TURNER who formed SPHINX then INNER CITY BLUES

Jun 77. (lp/c) *(CDS/CDC 4008)* **QUARK, STRANGENESS AND CHARM** [30] [-]
– Spirit of the age / Damnation alley / Fable of a failed race / Quark, strangeness and charm / Hassan I Sah Ba / The forge of Vulcan / Days of the underground / Iron dream. *(re-iss.Oct86 lp/c; CHC/MC 50) (cd-iss.Apr89 on 'Virgin'; CDSCD 4008)*

Jul 77. (7") *(CB 305)* **QUARK, STRANGENESS AND CHARM. / THE FORGE OF VULCAN** [-]

— **PAUL HAYLES** – keyboards repl. HOUSE who joined DAVID BOWIE on tour

HAWKLORDS

BROCK and **CALVERT** recruiting new members **STEVE SWINDELLS** – keyboards (ex-STRING DRIVEN THING, ex-PILOT) / **HARVEY BAINBRIDGE** – bass / **MARTIN GRIFFIN** – drums

Oct 78. (lp/c) *(CDS/CDC 4014)* **25 YEARS ON** [48] [-]
– Psi-power / Free fall / Automotion / 25 years / Flying doctor / The only ones / The dead dreams of the cold war kid / The age of the micro man. *(re-iss.Aug82; CHC 10) (cd-iss.Apr89 on 'Virgin'; CDS4014)*

Oct 78. (7") *(CB 323)* **PSI-POWER. / DEATH TRAP** [-]

Dec 78. (7") <*CAS 701*> **PSI-POWER. / ('A'extended)** [-]

Mar 79. (7") *(CB 332)* **25 YEARS. / (ONLY) THE DEAD DREAMS OF A COLD KID**
(12"grey+=) *(CB 332-12)* – PXR 5.

HAWKWIND

recorded '78 by **BROCK, TURNER, SHAW, KING / + HAYLES**

May 79. (lp/c) *(CDS 4016)* **PXR 5** [59]
– Death trap / Jack of shadows / Uncle Sam's on Mars / Infinity / Life form / Robot / High rise / PXR 5. *(re-iss.Mar84; CHC 25) (cd-iss.Apr89 on 'Virgin'; CDSCD 4016)*

— **HAWKWIND** in 1979 were **SIMON KING** – drums returned from QUASAR, to repl. GRIFFITHS in Dec78 (CALVERT left to go solo). **TIM BLAKE** – keyboards (ex-GONG)repl. SWINDELLS who went solo, added **HUW-LLOYD LANGTON** – guitar who returned from QUASAR, band now – **BROCK, LANGTON, BAINBRIDGE, KING** and **BLAKE**

Bronze not issued

Jul 80. (lp/c) *(BRON/TCBRON 527)* **LIVE 1979 (live)** [15]
– Shot down in the night / Motorway city / Spirit of the age / Brainstorm / Lighthouse / Master of the universe / Silver machine. *(cd-iss.Feb92 on 'Castle'; CLACD 243)*

Jul 80. (7") *(BRO 98)* **SHOT DOWN IN THE NIGHT (live). / URBAN GUERILLA (live)** [59] [-]

— **GINGER BAKER** – drums (ex-CREAM, ex-BLIND FAITH, ex-AIRFORCE etc) repl. KING who teamed up with SWINDELLS

Nov 80. (7") *(BRO 109)* **WHO'S GONNA WIN THE WAR. / NUCLEAR TOYS**

Nov 80. (blue-lp/c) *(BRON/TCBRON 530)* **LEVITATION** [21]
– Levitation / Motorway city / Psychosis / World of tiers / Prelude / Who's gonna win the war / Space chase / The 5th second forever / Dust of time. *(re-iss.Jul87 on 'Castle' lp/cd; CLA/+CD 129)*

— **MARTIN GRIFFIN** – drums returned to repl. BAKER / **KEITH HALE** – keyboards repl. BLAKE

RCA Active not issued

Oct 81. (7") *(RCA 137)* **ANGELS OF DEATH. / TRANS-DIMENSIONAL** [-]

Oct 81. (lp/c) *(RCA LP/K 6004)* **SONIC ATTACK** [19] [-]
– Sonic attack / Rocky paths / Psychosonia / Virgin of the world / Angels of death / Living on the edge / Coded language / Disintigration / Streets of fear / Lost chances.

May 82. (lp/c) *(RCA LP/K 9004)* **CHURCH OF HAWKWIND** [26] [-]
– Angel voices / Nuclear drive / Star cannibal / The phenomena of luminosity / Fall of Earth city / The church / The joker at the gate / Some people never die / Light specific data / Experiment with destiny / The last Messiah / Looking in the future. *(cd-iss.Jun94 on 'Dojo')*

— **NIK TURNER** – vocals, saxophone returned to repl. HALE

Aug 82. (7"/7"pic-d) *(RCA/+P 267)* **SILVER MACHINE (remix). / PSYCHEDELIC WARLORDS (remix)** [-]

Oct 82. (lp/c) *(RCA LP/K 6055)* **CHOOSE YOUR MASQUES** [29] [-]
– Choose your masques / Dream worker / Arrival in Utopia / Silver machine / Void city / Solitary mind games / Fahrenheit 451 / The scan / Waiting for tomorrow.

Flicknife not issued

Oct 83. (lp) *(SHARP 014)* **ZONES** (live, with other 80's line-ups) [57] [-]
– Zones / Dangerous vision / Running through the back brain / The island / Motorway city / Utopia 84 / Society alliance / Sonic attack / Dream worker / Brainstorm. *(re-iss.Mar84 on pic-lp; PSHARP 014)*

Oct 83. (7") *(FLS 025)* **MOTORWAY CITY (live). / MASTER OF THE UNIVERSE (live)** [-]

Jan 84. (7") *(7FLEP 104)* **NIGHT OF THE HAWKS. / GREEN FINNED DEMON** [-]
(12"ep+=) *(FLEP 104)* **-THE EARTH RITUAL PREVIEW** – Dream dancers / Dragons + fables.

Nov 84. (lp) *(SHARP 022)* **STONEHENGE: THIS IS HAWKWIND, DO NOT PANIC** [-]
– Psi power / Levitation / Circles / Space chase / Death trap / Angels of death / Shot down in the night / Stonehenge decoded / Watching the grass grow. *(cd-iss.May92 on 'Anagram'; CDM GRAM 54)*

— **ALAN DAVEY** – bass, vocals repl. BAINBRIDGE and TURNER / **CLIVE DEAMER** – drums repl. GRIFFIN

Nov 85. (lp/c/cd) *(SHARP 033/+C/CD)* **CHRONICLE OF THE BLACK SWORD** [65] [-]
– Song of the swords / Shade gate / Sea king / Pulsing cavern / Elric the enchanter / Needle gun / Zarozinia / Demise / Sleep of a thousand tears / Chaos army / Horn of destiny. *(cd-iss.w / 3 extra tracks) (re-iss.cd Aug92 on 'Dojo'; DPJPCD 72)*

Nov 85. (7") *(FLS 032)* **NEEDLE GUN. / ARIOCH** [-]
(12"+=) *(FLST 032)* – Song of the swords.

Mar 86. (7") *(FLS 033)* **ZAROZINIA. / ASSAULT AND BATTERY** [-]
(12"+=) *(FLST 033)* – Sleep of a 1000 tears.

— **HAWKWIND** are now **BROCK**, as DR. HASBEEN – vocals, guitar, keyboards, synthesizers, **LANGTON, DAVEY, BAINBRIDGE** now vocals, keyboards, synthesizer and **DANNY THOMPSON** – drums, percussion, vocals

G.W.R. Roadrunner

May 88. (lp/c/cd) *(GW/+C/CD 26)* **THE XENON CODEX** [79] 1989
– The war I survived / Wastelands of sleep / Neon skyline / Lost chronicles / Tides / Heads / Heads / Mutation zone / E.M.C. / Sword of the east / Good evening. *(US-iss. on pic-d)*

— **BROCK, BAINBRIDGE, DAVEY** plus **SIMON HOUSE, RICHARD CHADWICK &**

BRIDGETT WISHART

Oct 90. (lp/c/cd) *(GW/+C/CD 103)* **SPACE BANDITS** [70] [-]
– Images / Black elk speaks / Wings / Out of the shadows / Realms / Ship of dreams / TV suicide. *(re-iss.cd Feb92 on 'Castle'; CLACD 282)*

Essential not issued

May 92. (cd/c/d-lp) *(ESSCD/ESSMC/ESSD 181)* **ELECTRIC TEEPEE** [53] [-]
– L.S.D. / Blue shift / Death of war / The secret agent / Garden pests / Space dust / Snake dance / Mask of the morning / Rites of Netherworld / Don't understand / Sadness runs deep / Right to decide / Going to Hawaii / Electric teepee. *(re-iss.Jul95 on 'Dojo')*

Oct 93. (cd/c/lp) *(ESS CD/MC/LP 196)* **IT'S THE BUSINESS OF THE FUTURE TO BE DANGEROUS** [75] [ ]
– It's the business of the future to be dangerous / Space is their (Palestine) / Tibet is not China (pt.1 & 2) / Let barking dogs lie / Wave upon wave / Letting in the past / The camera that could lie / 3 or 4 erections during the course of the night / Technotropic zone exists / Give me shelter / Avante.

Emergency not issued

Sep 94. (12"ep/cd-ep) *(EBS T/D)* **QUARK, STRANGENESS & CHARM / UNCLE SAM'S ON MARS / BLACK SUN** [ ] [-]

Sep 94. (cd/c/d-lp) *(EBS CD/MC/LP 111)* **THE BUSINESS TRIP** [ ] [-]
– Altair / Quark strangeness and charm / LSD / The camera that would lie / Green finned demon / Do that / The day a wall came down / Berlin axis / Void of golden light / Right stuff / Wastelands / The dream goes on / Right to decide / The dream has ended / The future / Terra mystica.

Sep 95. (12"ep/cd-ep) *(EB T/CD 107)* **AREA S.4.** [ ] [-]
– Alien / Sputnik Stan / Medley: Death trap – Wastelands of sleep – Dream has . . . .

Oct 95. (cd/lp) *(EB SCD/LP 118)* **ALIEN 4** [ ] [-]
– Abducted / Alien (I am) / Reject your human touch / Blue skin / Beam me up / Vega / Xenonorph / Journey / Sputnik Stan / Kapal / Festivals / Deah trap / Wastelands / Are you losing your mind.

May 96. (cd)(lp) *()* **LOVE IN SPACE (live October 1995)** [ ] [-]

– compilations, etc. –

1973. (d7") *United Artists;* **HURRY ON SUNDOWN. / MASTER OF THE UNIVERSE/ / SILVER MACHINE. / ORGONE ACCUMULATOR** [-] [ ]

Apr 76. (lp) *United Artists; (UAK 29919)* **ROADHAWKS (live in the 70's)** [34] [ ]
– Hurry on sundown / Paranoia / You shouldn't do that / Silver machine / Urban guerilla / Space is deep / Wind of change / The golden void. *(re-iss.Apr84 on 'Fame' lp/c; FA 413096-1/-4)*

Feb 77. (lp) *United Artists; (UAG 30025)* **MASTERS OF THE UNIVERSE** [ ] [-]
– Master of the universe / Brainstorm / Sonic attack / Orgone accumulator / It's so easy / Lost Johnnie. *(re-iss.May82 on 'Fame' lp/c; FA/C 3008) (re-iss.Jun87 & Dec95 on 'Liberty' lp/c; EMS/TCEMS 1258) (re-iss.May89 on 'Fame' lp/c/cd; FA/TCFA/CDFA 3220) (re-iss.Jul90 on 'Marble Arch' c/cd; CMA/+CD 129) (re-iss.Jul94 on 'Success' cd/c;) (cd-iss.Apr97 on 'Spalax'; 14972)*

Sep 80. (lp/c) *Charisma; (BG/+C 2)* **REPEAT PERFORMANCE** [ ] [-]
– Kerb crawler / Back on the streets / Quark strangeness and charm / Spirit of the age / Steppenwolf / 25 years / PSI power / The only ones / High rise / Uncle Sam's on Mars.

May 81. (12"ep; as HAWKWIND ZOO) *Flicknife; (FLEP 100)* **HURRY ON SUNDOWN. / KINGS OF SPEED / SWEET MISTRESS OF PAIN** [ ] [-]
(re-iss.Dec83)

Jul 81. (7"/12") *Flicknife; (FLS/+EP 205)* **MOTORHEAD. / VALIUM TEN** [ ] [-]
(re-iss.12" Oct82)

Nov 81. (12"ep; as SONIC ASSASSINS) *Flicknife; (FLEP 101)* **OVER THE TOP. / FREEFALL / DEATH TRAP** [ ] [-]

Mar 82. (lp) *Flicknife; (SHARP 001)* **FRIENDS & RELATIONS** (1/2 live '77-78, 1/2 studio '82) [ ] [-]
(re-iss.Nov83) (re-iss.Nov94 on 'Emporio' cd/c)

Jun 82. (7"; as HAWKLORDS) *Flicknife; (FLS 209)* **WHO'S GONNA WIN THE WAR. / TIME OFF** [ ] [-]

Feb 83. (7") *Flicknife; (FLS 14)* **HURRY ON SUNDOWN. / LORD OF THE HORNETS / DODGEM DUKE** [ ] [-]

Mar 83. (d-c) *Charisma; (CASMC 110)* **QUARK, STRANGENESS & CHARM / PXR 5** [ ] [-]
(re-iss.'88)

1983. (lp) *Flicknife; (SHARP 107)* **TWICE UPON A TIME: HAWKWIND FRIENDS AND RELATIONS VOL.2** [ ] [-]

Jul 83. (d-lp) *Illuminated; (JAMS 29)* **TEXT OF FESTIVAL (live '70-72)** [ ] [-]
(1-lp re-iss.Jul85 as 'IN THE BEGINNING' on 'Demi Monde'; DM 005) (re-iss.cd Mar94 on 'Charly') (re-iss.Dec88 on 'Thunderbolt'; THBL 2.068) (cd-iss.first 3 sides) (cd re-iss.Mar97; CDTB 068)

Jun 84. (10"m-lp) *Flicknife; (SHARP 109)* **INDEPENDENTS DAY** [ ] [-]

Nov 84. (d-lp/d-c) *A.P.K.; (APK/+C 8)* **SPACE RITUAL 2 (live)** [ ] [-]
(cd-iss.1987 on 'The CD Label'; CDTL 003)

Feb 85. (lp) *Demi-Monde; (DM 002)* **BRING ME THE HEAD OF YURI GAGARIN** (live '73 Empire Pool) [ ] [-]
(cd-iss.Nov86 on 'Charly'; CDCHARLY 40) (cd-iss.Nov92 on 'Thunderbolt'; CDTB 101) (cd re-iss.Apr97 on 'Spalax'; 14846)

Feb 85. (lp) *Flicknife; (SHARP 024)* **HAWKWIND, FRIENDS AND RELATIONS VOL.3** [ ] [-]
(c-iss.Apr84 with VOL.1 on reverse; *SHARP C1024) (other c-iss.Apr84 with VOL.2 on reverse; SHARP C2024)*

Jul 85. (lp) *Dojo; (DOJOLP 11)* **LIVE 70-73 (live)** [ ] [-]

May 85. (lp) *Mausoleum; (SKULL 8333369)* **UTOPIA 84** [ ] [-]

Nov 85. (lp) *Mausoleum; (SKULL 83103)* **WELCOME TO THE FUTURE** [ ] [-]

Nov 85. (lp) *Obsession; (OBLP 1)* **RIDICULE** [ ] [-]
(re-iss.of disc 2 of 'SPACE RITUAL') (re-iss.1990 cd/lp; OBSESS CD/LP 1)

Nov 85. (lp/pic-lp)(cd) *Samurai; (SAMR 038/+PD)(SAMRCD 038)* **ANTHOLOGY - HAWKWIND VOL.1** [ ] [-]
(cd+=)– Silver machine. (re-iss.pic-lp.Nov86 as 'APPROVED HISTORY OF HAWKWIND'; SAMR 046) (re-iss.Apr90 as 'ACID DAZE 1' on 'Receiver'; RR 125)

Mar 86. (lp/cd)(c) *Samurai; (SAMR/+CD 039)(TCSAMR 039)* **ANTHOLOGY - HAWKWIND VOL. 2** [ ] [-]
(cd-iss.1986 extra 4 tracks) (re-iss.Apr90 as 'ACID DAZE 2' on 'Receiver'; RR 126)

May 86. (7"/7"sha-pic-d) *Samurai; (HW 7001/001)* **SILVER MACHINE. / MAGNU** [ ] [-]
(12"+=) *(HW12-001)* – Angels of death.

Jul 86. (7") *Flicknife; (FLS 034-A)* **MOTORHEAD. / HURRY ON SUNDOWN** [ ] [-]

Jul 86. (lp/c) *Samurai; (SAMR 040/+TC)* **ANTHOLOGY - HAWKWIND VOL.3** [ ] [-]
(re-iss.Apr90 as 'ACID DAZE 3' on 'Receiver'; RR 127)

Jul 86. (lp) *Hawkfan; (HWFB 2)* **HAWKFAN 12** [ ] [-]

Sep 86. (d-lp/d-c/cd) *Castle; (CCS LP/MC/CD 148)* **THE HAWKWIND COLLECTION (Pts. 1 & 2)** [ ] [-]
(cd-iss.Dec86 omits some tracks)

Nov 86. (lp/c) *Flicknife; (SHARP 036/+C)* **INDEPENDENTS DAY VOL.2** [ ] [-]

Jan 87. (lp/c) *R.C.A.; (NL/NK 71150)* **ANGELS OF DEATH** [ ] [-]

Apr 87. (lp/c/cd) *Flicknife; (SHARP 040/+C/CD)* **OUT AND INTAKE** [ ] [-]
(cd+=) – (2 extra tracks).

Sep 87. (lp/c/cd) *Start; (STF L/C/CD 2)* **BRITISH TRIBAL MUSIC** [ ] [-]

Oct 87. (3xbox-pic-lp) *Flicknife; (HWBOX 1)* **OFFICIAL PICTURE LOGBOOK** [ ] [-]
– ('STONEHENGE' / 'BLACK SWORD' / 'OUT & INTAKE' / '(interview)' lp *(cd-iss.Nov94 on 'Dojo';)*

Dec 87. (lp/c) *Thunderbolt; (THBL/THBC 044)* **EARLY DAZE (THE BEST OF HAWKWIND)** [ ] [-]
(cd-iss.Jun88; CDTB CDTB 044)

Sep 88. (cd) *Virgin; (COMCD 8)* **SPIRIT OF THE AGE** [ ] [-]
(re-iss.Oct91 on 'Elite'; ELITE 021CD) (re-iss.Sep 93)

Nov 88. (cd) *Flicknife; (SHARP 1422CD)* **ZONES / STONEHENGE** [ ] [-]

Nov 88. (cd) *Flicknife; (SHARP 1724CD)* **BEST OF HAWKWIND, FRIENDS & RELATIONS** [ ] [-]

Dec 88. (d-lp/cd) *Flicknife; (SHARP 2045/+CD)* **THE TRAVELLERS AID TRUST** [ ] [-]

Dec 88. (d-lp/d-cd) *That's Original; (TFO 17/+CD)* **LEVITATION / HAWKWIND LIVE** [ ] [-]

Mar 89. (cd) *Avanti; (ISTCD 004)* **IRONSTRIKE** [ ] [-]

May 89. (lp) *Legacy; (GWSP 1)* **LIVE CHRONICLES** [ ] [-]
(re-iss.Feb92 cd/c on 'Castle'; CCS CD/MC 123)

May 89. (lp/c/cd) *Powerhouse; (POW/+C/CD 5502)* **NIGHT OF THE HAWKS** [ ] [-]
(cd-iss. has 3 extra tracks)

1990. (cd/c) *Action Replay; (ARLC/CDAR 1018)* **BEST AND THE REST OF HAWKWIND** [ ] [-]

Mar 90. (2xcd-box)(3xlp-box) *Receiver; (RRDCD 1X)(RRBX 1)* **ACID DAZE (re-issue)** [ ] [-]
(3 VOLUMES re-iss.cd Jul93)

May 90. (cd)(c/lp) *E.M.I.; (CDP 746694-2)(TC+/NTS 300)* **STASIS, THE U.A. YEARS 1971-1975** [ ] [-]
– Urban guerilla / Psychedelic warlords (disappear in smoke) / Brainbox pollution / 7 by 7 / Paradox / Silver machine / You'd better believe it / Lord of light / The black corridor (live) / Space is deep (live) / You shouldn't do that (live). *(re-iss.cd Dec95 on 'Fame')*

Dec 90. (12"blue-ep) *Receiver; (REPLAY 3014)* **THE EARLY YEARS LIVE** [ ] [-]
– Silver machine / Spirit of the age / Urban guerilla / Born to go.

1990. (c) *Capitol; <4XLL 57286>* **METAL CLASSICS 2: BEST OF HAWKWIND** [-] [ ]

1990. (cd/c) *Knight; (KN CD/MC 10017)* **NIGHT RIDING** [ ] [-]

Jun 91. (lp/c/cd) *G.W.R.; (GW/+MC/CD 104)* **PALACE SPRINGS** [ ] [-]
– (remixed tracks from 'WARRIORS . . . ' & 'XENON . . .) *(re-iss.cd Jul92 on 'Castle'; CLACD 303)*

Oct 91. (cd/c) *Windsong; (WIN CD/MC 007)* **BBC RADIO 1 LIVE IN CONCERT (live)** [ ] [-]

Feb 92. (3xcd-box) *Castle; (CLABX 911)* **3 ORIGINALS** [ ] [-]

Feb 92. (cd) *Raw Fruit; (FRSCD 005)* **THE FRIDAY ROCK SHOW SESSIONS (live '86)** [ ] [-]

Jun 92. (cd) *Anagram; (GRAM 53)* **MIGHTY HAWKWIND CLASSICS 1980-1985** [ ] [-]

Aug 92. (cd) *Dojo; (DOJOCD 71)* **HAWKLORDS LIVE** [ ] [-]

Jun 93. (12"ep/c-ep/cd-ep) *4 Real; (4R 1 T/CS/D)* **SPIRIT OF THE AGE (The Solstice remixes)** [ ] [-]

Nov 93. (12"ep/cd-ep) *4 Real; (4R 2 T/D)* **DECIDE YOUR FUTURE. / ?** [ ] [-]

Mar 94. (lp) *Emergency Broadcast;* **UNDISCLOSED FILES** [ ] [-]

Apr 94. (cd) *Cleopatra; (CLEO 57732)* **LORD OF LIGHT** [ ] [-]

Apr 94. (cd) *Cleopatra; (CLEO 57412)* **PSYCHEDELIC WARLORDS** [ ] [-]

Dec 94. (cd) *Cyclops; (CYCL 021)* **CALIFORNIA BRAINSTORM** [ ] [-]

Feb 95. (cd) *Emergency Broadcast; (EBSCD 114)* **UNDISCLOSED FILES - ADDENDUM** [ ] [-]

Mar 95. (cd) *Anagram; (CDMGRAM 91)* **THE RARITIES . . .** [ ] [-]

May 95. (cd) *Spectrum; (550764-2)* **SILVER MACHINE** [ ] [-]

Oct 95. (cd) *Anagram; (CDGRAM 94)* **INDEPENDENTS DAY VOLUMES 1 & 2** [ ] [-]

Mar 97. (cd) *Emporio; (EMPRCD 710)* **ONWARD FLIES THE BIRD - LIVE AND RARE** [ ] [-]

DAVE BROCK

Hawkfan not issued

Jun 83. (7"; as DR. TECHNICAL & THE MACHINES) *(HWFB 1)* **ZONES. / PROCESSED** [ ] [-]

Flicknife not issued

Sep 83. (7",7"pic-d) *(FLS 024)* **SOCIAL ALLIANCE. / RAPING ROBOTS IN THE STREET** [ ] [-]

Apr 86. (lp) *(SHARP 018)* **EARTHED TO THE GROUND** [ ] [-]
– Earth to the ground / Assassination / Green finned demon / Spirits / Sweet obsession / Oscillations / Machine dreams / Now is the winter of our discontent / On the case.

Apr 88. (lp) *(SHARP 042)* **AGENT OF CHAOS** [ ] [-]
– High tech cities / A day in the office / Hades deep / Words of a song / Heads / Nocturn / Wastelands of sleep / Empty dreams / Into the realms / Mountain in the sky.

May 89. (cd) *(SHARP 1842CD)* **DAVE BROCK & THE AGENTS OF CHAOS**
– (2 albums above minus a few tracks)

Emergency not issued

Jul 95. (cd) **STRANGE TRIPS AND PIPE DREAMS**
– Hearing aid test / White zone / UFO line / Space / Pipe dream / Self / Something's going on / Bosnia / Parasites are here on Earth / Gateway / It's never too late / La forge / Encounters.

HUW LLOYD-LANGTON GROUP

with **KENNY WILSON** – bass / **JON CLARK** – drums, percussion

Flicknife not issued

Jul 83. (7") *(FLS 021)* **WIND OF CHANGE. / OUTSIDE THE LAW**
Dec 83. (lp) *(SHARP 015)* **OUTSIDE THE LAW**
– Outside the law / Five to four / Talk to you / Rocky paths / Space chase / Waiting for tomorrow / Mark of gain / Psychedelic warlords. (incl. 2 'Hawkwind' tracks). *(free 7" w/a) (FREE 001)*– WORKING TIME. / I SEE YOU

Ultra Noise not issued

Jul 84. (12") *(12HUW 1)* **DREAMS THAT FADE AWAY. / OUTSIDE THE LAW**
Mar 85. (lp) *(SHARP 026)* **NIGHT AIR**

Gas not issued

Apr 86. (lp) *(GAS 4014)* **LIKE AN ARROW . . . (THROUGH THE HEART)**
– Strange times / I could cry / Like an arrow / So long waiting / On the move / No man's land / Voices that fade / Wars are the hobby there / Take a back step / In their eyes / Can you feel.

G W.R. not issued

Aug 88. (lp) *(GW 27)* **TIME SPACE AND LLG**

He released other album in 1991 'ELEGY', after departure from HAWKWIND. In 1994 he issued 'RIVER RUN' for 'Allegro' records.

ROBERT CALVERT

U.A. U.A.

May 74. (lp) *(UAG 29507)* **CAPTAIN LOCKHEED AND THE STARFIGHTERS**
– Franz Joseph Strauss / The aerospace inferno / Aircraft salesman / The widow maker / Test pilots / The right stuff / Board meeting / The song of the gremlin / Ground crew / Hero with a wing / Ground control to pilot / Ejection / Interview / I resign / The song of the gremlin (part 2) / Bier garten / Catch a falling starfighter (the gremlin). *(re-iss.Jan87 on 'Beat Goes On' lp/cd; BGO/+CD 5)*
Jun 74. (7"; as CAPTAIN LOCKHEED AND THE STARFIGHTERS) *(UP 35543)* *<297>* **CATCH A FALLING STARFIGHTER (THE GREMLIN). / EJECTION**
Sep 75. (lp) *(UAG 29852)* **LUCKY LIEF AND THE LONGSHIPS**
– Ship of fools / The lay of the surfers / Brave new world / Voyaging to inland / The making of Midgare / Moonshine in the mountains / Magical potion / Stormchant of the Skraelings / Volstead o vodeo do / Phase locked lopp / Ragna rock. *(re-iss.Mar87 on 'Beat Goes On'; BGO 2) (cd-iss.Jan89; BGOCD 2)*

Wake Up not issued

Jul 79. (7"green-flexi; as ROBERT CALVERT and the 1st X1) *(WUR 5)* **CRICKET STAR**

Flicknife not issued

1981. (7") *(FLS 204)* **LORD OF THE HORNETS. / THE GREENFLY & THE ROSE**

A-side not issued

Sep 81. (m-lp) *(IF 0311)* **HYPE (THE SONGS OF TOM MAHLER)**
– Over my head / Ambitious / It's the same / Hanging out on the seafront / Sensitive / Evil rock / We like to be frightened / Teen ballad of Deano / Flight 105 / The luminous green glow of the dials of the dashboard (at night) / The greenfly & the rose / Lord of the hornets. *(re-iss.Dec89 on 'See For Miles' lp/cd; SEE/+CD 278)*

Flicknife not issued

Sep 84. (m-lp) *(SHGARP 021)* **FREQ**
– Ned Ludd / Acid rain / All the machines are quiet / Picket line / The cool courage of the bomb squad / Work song. *(cd-iss.Jun92 as 'FREQ REVISITED' on 'Anagram' +=; CDMGRAM 55)* – Lord of the hornets / The greenfly & the rose.

Demi-Monde not issued

Apr 86. (lp) *(DM 1010)* **TEST-TUBE CONCEIVED**
– Telekinesis / I hear voices / Fanfare for the perfect race / On line / Save them from the scientists / Fly on the wall / Thanks to the scientists / ? / In vitro / Breed / The rah rah band. *(cd-iss.Aug87 on 'The CD Label'; CDTL 007)*

— On 14 Aug'88, ROBERT CALVERT died of a heart attack.

– (CALVERT) posthumous, etc. –

Aug 89. (lp; mail-order) *Clear; (BLACK 1)* **ROBERT CALVERT AT THE QUEEN ELIZABETH HALL (live)**
(cd-iss.May93 on 'Beat Goes On';)
Oct 92. (cd) *Beat Goes On; (BGOCD 135)* **BLUEPRINTS FROM THE CELLAR**

MICHAEL MOORCOCK & DEEP FIX

(whilst a member of HAWKWIND)

U.A. U.A.

May 75. (lp) *(UAG 29732)* **THE NEW WORLDS FAIR**
–
(cd-iss.Jun95 on 'Dojo';)

Flicknife not issued

Dec 80. (7") *(FLS 200)* **DODGEM DUDE. / STARCRUISHER**
1982. (7"ltd; solo) *(none)* **THE BROTHEL OF ROSENSTRASSE. / TIME CENTRE**

— He and label 'Cyborg' released in May92 a cassette 'BROTHEL IN ROSENSTRASSE'.

NIK TURNER

("SPHYNX")with **TIM BLAKE & MIQUETTE GIRAUDY** – synthesizers / **MORRIS PERT & ALAN POWELL** – percussion / **MIKE HOWLETT** – bass / **STEVE HILLAGE** – guitar

Charisma not issued

Jun 78. (lp) *(CDS 4011)* **XITINTODAY**
– The awakening / Pyramid spell / Tha hall of double truth / Anabus Thoth / Horos, Isis & Nepthys.

— ("INNER CITY UNIT") with **MICK STUPP** – drums / **BAZ MAGENTO** – bass / **DEAD FRED** – keyboards, vocals **TREN THOMAS** – guitar, vocals

Riddle not issued

Oct 79. (7") *(RID 001)* **SOLITARY ASHTRAY. / SO TRY AS ID**
1980. (lp) *(RID 002)* **PASS OUT (THE 360<< >> PSYCHO DELERIA SOUND)**
(cd-iss.Feb90 on 'Oldhitz', w/2 extra; OLD 001)
Jul 80. (7") *(RID 003)* **PARADISE BEACH. / AMYL NITRATE**

— **DON FERARI** – drums repl. STUPP / **RAY BURNS** (CAPTAIN SENSIBLE) – guitar repl. BAZ added **BILL BOSTON** – horns / **MAX WALL** – vocals

Avatar not issued

May 81. (lp) *(AALP 5004)* **THE MAXIMUM EFFECT**
Sep 81. (7"red) *(AAA 113)* **BEER, BACCY, BINGO, BENIDORM. / IN THE MOOD (NUDE)**
Feb 82. (7") *(AAA 119)* **BONES OF ELVIS. / SID'S SONG**

Flicknife not issued

Jul 82. (lp)(c) *(SHARP 103)* **PUNKADELIC**
– Watching the grass grow / Space invaders / God disco / Disco tango / Polythene / Cars eat with autoface / Gas money / Blue mine haggard robot / Alright on the flight / Bildeborg.

— with other line-up

Demi Monde not issued

Dec 84. (lp) *(DM 001)* **NEW ANATOMY**
– Young girls / Convoy / Beyond the stars / Help shark / Hectic electric / Birdland / Lonesome train / Forbidden planet / Stop the city / Doctor Strange / Wild hunt. *(cd-iss.Mar93 on 'Thunderb.')*

Flicknife not issued

Sep 85. (lp) *(SHARP 031)* **THE PRESIDENT'S TAPES**

Jettisound not issued

Oct 85. (12"ep) *(JZ 5)* **BLOOD AND BONES**
– Blood and bones / Little black egg / Paint your windows white / Help sharks.

— TURNER later issued 'PROPHETS OF TIME' in 1994 for 'Cleopatra'. Two others in May'97 'PAST OR FUTURE'; Cleopatra (CLP 96852) 'SPHYNX' compilation; Cleopatra (CLEO 21352).

NIK TURNER / ROBERT CALVERT

Pompadour not issued

1982. (lp) *(POMP 001)* **ERSATZ**

STEVE SWINDELLS

(80's with SIMON KING, HUW-LLOYD LANGTON, and NIC POTTER

R.C.A. not issued

1974. (lp) *(LPL1 5057)* **MESSAGES**
– Miles away again / Energy crisis / The Earl's Court case / Living in sin / I don't like eating meat / Shake up your soul / Surrender / I can't see where the light switch is / Messages from Heaven.

Atco not issued

Oct 80. (7") *(K 11532)* **SHOT DOWN IN THE NIGHT. / IT'S ONLY ONE NIGHT IN YOUR LIFE**
Oct 80. (lp) *(K 50738)* **FRESH BLOOD**
– Turn it on, turn it off / Fresh blood / I feel alive / Is it over now / Low life Joe / Bitter and twisted / I don't wait on the stairs / Down on Love street / Figures of authority / Shot down in the night.
Dec 80. (7") *(K 11605)* **TURN IT ON, TURN IT OFF. / LOW LIFE JOE**

TIM BLAKE

— also had solo releases, mainly in France 1977 + 1978. CRYSTAL MACHINE lp + BLAKE'S NEW JERUSALEM lp on 'Egg' records. The later was issued UK Nov78 on 'Barclay Towers'. The cds were given light there in 1992 on 'Mantra' label. He issued 'MAGICK' cd in US 1991 on 'Voiceprint'.

ALAN DAVEY

Hawkfan not issued

Oct 87. (d7") *(HWFB 3-4)* **THE ELF EP**
– Solar jug / Cosmic dawn / Chinese whispers / Ode to a brass assassin / The switch (don't touch).

HELP YOURSELF

Formed: Wales . . .1969 by MALCOLM MORLEY (ex-SHADES OF MORLEY BROWN; who issued one 1968 single 'SILLY GIRL'./ 'PRETTY BLUE BIRD' for 'Mercury'; (MF 1054). He and co-founder DAVE CHARLES had emerged from the ashes of SAM APPLE PIE and were soon joined by KEN WHALEY and RICHARD TREECE. Signed to 'Liberty', their eponymous debut in '71 was a patchy affair, a collection of bland mainstream progressive rock. A second, more West Coast-influenced set, 'STRANGE AFFAIR' was a lot better, the track, 'AMERICAN WOMAN' being the highlight (newcomers ERNIE GRAHAM, PAUL BURTON and JO JO GLEMSER making the difference). They released their second album of the year, 'BEWARE OF THE SHADOW', before KEN WHALEY returned on the

1973 effort, appropriately titled, 'THE RETURN OF KEN WHALEY'. They split soon after, all except MORLEY joining DEKE LEONARD's ICEBERG, although he did join DEKE's great band MAN (as did WHALEY). • **Covers:** JOHNNY B. GOODE (Chuck Berry).

Recommended: STRANGE AFFAIR (*7) / BEWARE OF THE SHADOW (*6)

MALCOLM MORLEY – guitar, vocals / **RICHARD TREECE** – guitar, vocals / **KEN WHALEY** – bass / **DAVE CHARLES** – drums, vocals

Liberty Liberty

Apr 71. (7") *(LBF 15459)* **RUNNING DOWN DEEP. / PAPER LEAVES** ☐ ☐

May 71. (lp) *(LBS 83484) <5583>* **HELP YOURSELF** ☐ ☐
– I must see Jesus for myself / To Katherine they fell / Your eyes are looking down / Old man / Look at the view / Paper leaves / Running down deep / Deborah / Street songs. *(re-iss.Oct89 on 'Beat Goes On'; BGOLP 52)*

— **PAUL BURTON** – bass, guitar, vocals / **ERNIE GRAHAM** – vocals, guitar / **JO JO GLEMSER** – guitar, repl. WHALEY who joined inception of DUCKS DELUXE

U.A. U.A.

Mar 72. (7") *(UP 35355)* **HEAVEN ROW. / BROWN LADY** ☐ ☐

Mar 72. (lp) *(UAS 29287) <5591>* **STRANGE AFFAIR** ☐ ☐
– Strange affair / Brown lady / Movie star / Deanna Call and Scotty / Heaven row / Excerpts from 'The All For For Electric Trapper' / Many ways of meeting.

May 72. (7") *<50973>* **MOVIE STAR. / STRANGE AFFAIR** [-] ☐

— now without GRAHAM and GLEMSER

1972. (lp) *(UAS 29413) <079>* **BEWARE OF THE SHADOW** ☐ ☐
– Alabama lady / Reaffirmation / Colapso / She's my girl / Molly bake bean / American mother / Passing through.

Dec 72. (7") *(UP 35466)* **MOMMY WON'T BE HOME FOR CHRISTMAS./ JOHNNY B. GOODE** ☐ [-]

— **KEN WHALEY** – bass, returned to repl. BURTON

1973. (lp) *(UAS 29487)* **THE RETURN OF KEN WHALEY** ☐ [-]
– Who killed Paradise / Amy / Man we're glad we know you / Pioneers of the west in the head / Candy Kane / Blown away / The golden handshake / It has to be. *(free lp in box with above) (UDG 4001)* **HAPPY DAYS** – Jesus what are little kids for / Virginia / Waiting at the station / Seashell / I've got beautiful you / My friend / Elephants by my side.

— free lp augmented by **PAUL BURTON / MARTIN ACE** – bass, vocals (ex-MAN) / **GEORGINA ACE** – guitar, vocals / **VIVIAN MORRIS** – guitar, vocals

— Unfortunately this was their last new recording. All main members except MORLEY joined DEKE LEONARD's ICEBERG in 1973, with WHALEY and MORLEY soon joined the re-formed MAN. Guest MARTIN ACE also returned to aforementioned bands.

Jimi HENDRIX

Born: JOHNNY ALLEN HENDRIX, 27 Nov'42, Seattle, Washington, USA. He was raised by a part Cherokee Indian mother and black father, who, at age 3, changed his forenames to JAMES MARSHALL and bought him his first guitar. Being left-handed, he turned it upside down and reversed the strings, teaching himself by listening to blues and rock'n'roll artists such as ROBERT JOHNSON, MUDDY WATERS, B.B. KING and CHUCK BERRY. In the early 60's, he enlisted in the paratroopers, thus avoiding the draft into the US army. He was subsequently discharged for medical reasons in 1962, after injuring himself during a jump. Two years later, he moved to New York and backed acts LITTLE RICHARD, The ISLEY BROTHERS, IKE & TINA TURNER. He soon struck up a partnership with soul singer CURTIS KNIGHT, also obtaining a contract with Ed Chalpin. He is said to have written 'The Ballad Of Jimi' in 1965, after JIMI told him he would die in 1970! Early in 1966, JIMMY JAMES & THE BLUE FLAMES were born. With JIMI's reputation now spreading, he was seen by ex-ANIMALS bassman CHAS CHANDLER, who invited him to London. After auditions, they found a rhythm section of NOEL REDDING and MITCH MITCHELL, smashing their way into the UK Top 10 in early '67 with the 'Polydor' one-off 45, 'HEY JOE'. Chandler then set up a deal with Kit Lambert's new 'Track' label, and The JIMI HENDRIX EXPERIENCE exploded onto the scene. Their first Hendrix-penned 45, the thundering acid-fever of 'PURPLE HAZE', made the UK Top 3, as did the scintillating debut album 'ARE YOU EXPERIENCED?'. This was released hot on the heels of their 3rd Top 10 single, 'THE WIND CRIES MARY'. Hendrix was a revelation, a black super-freak whose mastery of the guitar was above and beyond anything previously heard. In fact, he virtually re-invented the instrument, duly illustrating various methods of on-stage abuse (biting it i.e. playing it with his teeth, shagging it and even setting fire to it!). He was duly booked on the Monterey International Pop Festival bill, where he played an orgasmic version of 'WILD THING'. The following month saw a wholly inappropriate US support tour with The MONKEES, leaving both him and teenybop audiences baffled, but no doubt entertained, for 7 nights. After another classic UK hit, 'THE BURNING OF THE MIDNIGHT LAMP', he released his 2nd lp, 'AXIS: BOLD AS LOVE', which made the Top 5 early in '68, and was the first to chart and hit the Top 3 in his native U.S.A. In the Autumn of '68, he revived and transformed BOB DYLAN's 'ALL ALONG THE WATCHTOWER', which broke into the US Top 20 and UK 5. It was trailed by a superb UK Top 10 double-lp, 'ELECTRIC LADYLAND', which went No.1 in US, and featured the now famous controversial naked women sleeve, which some shops sold in a brown cover!. In 1969, he was busted for drugs, leading to the split of his band. They played together for the last time on 29 June at the Denver Pop Festival. REDDING had already formed FAT MATTRESS, but MITCHELL returned with other musicians BILLY COX and LARRY LEE. They played the Woodstock Festival 17-18 August '69, performing an excellent version of 'STAR SPANGLED BANNER' that went down in the folklore of rock music. To end the year, he was found not guilty of an earlier charge of heroin and marijuana possession and at the same time, he formed all-black outfit BAND OF GYPSYS, with COX and drummer BUDDY MILES. They released the live album, 'BAND OF GYPSYS' in May'70 (recorded at FILLMORE EAST, New Year's Eve/Day 1969/70). This hit Top 5 in the States, and, following a court order, he paid ex-manager Ed Chalpin $1m in compensation and percentage of royalties. Tragically, after a few more open-air festival concerts and some bad drugs trips, he died in London on 18th Sep'70. He was said to have left a phoned message to Chandler saying "I need help bad, man". The official cause of death was an inhalation of vomit, due to barbiturate intoxication, leading to a coroner's decision of an open verdict. To many rock music buffs, he remains the greatest axegrinder of all-time and who knows what he might have become had he survived the heady sixties. • **Songwriters:** HENDRIX except other covers; HEY JOE (William Roberts) / JOHNNY B.GOODE (Chuck Berry) / GLORIA (Them) / SGT. PEPPER (Beatles) / HANG ON SLOOPY (McCoys) / TUTTI FRUTTI + LUCILLE (LIttle Richard) / BO DIDDLEY (Bo Diddley) / PETER GUNN (Henry Mancini) / HOOCHIE COOCHIE MAN (Muddy Waters) / BLUE SUEDE SHOES (Carl Perkins) / etc. • **Trivia:** In Jan'69, he and band play live tribute of CREAM's 'Sunshine Of Your Love' on The LULU Show, much to annoyance of TV controllers.

Recommended: ARE YOU EXPERIENCED? (*10) / AXIS: AS BOLD AS LOVE (*9) / ELECTRIC LADYLAND (*10) / BAND OF GYPSYS (*8) / THE CRY OF LOVE (*7) / THE ULTIMATE EXPERIENCE (compilation *10)

JIMI HENDRIX – vocals, lead guitar (ex-CURTIS KNIGHT) with **NOEL REDDING** (b.DAVID REDDING, 25 Dec'45, Folkstone, Kent, England) – bass / **MITCH MITCHELL** (b.JOHN MITCHELL, 9 Jun'47, Ealing, London, England) – drums

Polydor Reprise

Dec 66. (7"; as JIMI HENDRIX) *(56139)* **HEY JOE. / STONE FREE** [6] [-]
(re-iss.Jul84 on 'Old Gold')

Track Reprise

Mar 67. (7") *(604 001)* **PURPLE HAZE. / 51ST ANNIVERSARY** [3] [-]

Mar 67. (7") *<0572>* **HEY JOE. / 51st ANNIVERSARY** [-] ☐

May 67. (7") *(604 004)* **THE WIND CRIES MARY. / HIGHWAY CHILE** [6] [-]

May 67. (lp; mono/stereo) *(612/613 001) <6261>* **ARE YOU EXPERIENCED** [2] [5] Aug67
– Foxy lady / Manic depression / Red house / Can you see me / Love or confusion / I don't live today / May this be love / Fire / Third stone from the sun / Remember / Are you experienced. *(re-iss.Nov70;) (re-iss.Nov81; 612 001) (re-iss.Sep85 on 'Polydor' lp/c; SPE LP/MC 97) (cd-iss.Jun91 & Oct93 cd/c; 521036-2/-4) (re-iss.Apr97 on 'MCA' cd/c; MCD/MCC 11608)*

Aug 67. (7") *<0597>* **PURPLE HAZE. / THE WIND CRIES MARY** [-] [65]

Aug 67. (7") *(604 007)* **THE BURNING OF THE MIDNIGHT LAMP. / THE STARS THAT PLAY WITH LAUGHING SAM'S DICE** [18] [-]

Dec 67. (7"; by JIMI HENDRIX) *<0641>* **FOXY LADY. / HEY JOE** [-] [67]

Dec 67. (lp; mono/stereo) *(612/613 003) <6281>* **AXIS: BOLD AS LOVE** [5] [3] Feb68
– Experience / Up from the skies / Spanish castle magic / Wait until tomorrow / Ain't no telling / Little wing / If six was nine / You've got me floating / Castles made of sand / She's so fine / One rainy wish / Little Miss Lover / Bold as love. *(re-iss.Nov70;) (re-iss.Aug83 on 'Polydor' lp/c; (SPE LP/MC 71) (cd-iss.1987 on 'Polydor'; 813 572-2) (re-iss.Jul91 & Oct93 on 'Polydor' lp/c/cd; 847243-1/-4/-2) (re-iss.Apr97 on 'MCA' cd/c; MCD/MCC 11601)*

Feb 68. (7") *<0665>* **UP FROM THE SKIES. / ONE RAINY WISH** [-] [82]

Apr 68. (lp; mono/stereo) *(612/613 004) <2025>* **SMASH HITS** (compilation) [4] [6] Jul69
– Purple haze / Fire / The wind cries Mary / Can you see me / 51st anniversary / Hey Joe / Stone free / The stars that play with laughing Sam's dice / Manic depression / Highway chile / The burning of the midnight lamp / Foxy lady. *(re-iss.Jun73 on 'Polydor';) (re-iss.Aug83 on 'Polydor' lp/c; SPE LP/MC 3) (cd-iss.Feb85; 813 572-2)*

May 68. (7") *<0728>* **FOXY LADY. / PURPLE HAZE** [-] ☐

Jul 68. (7") *<0742>* **ALL ALONG THE WATCHTOWER. / CROSSTOWN TRAFFIC** [-] ☐

— JIMI now brought in old session campaigners **AL KOOPER** and **STEVE WINWOOD** – keyboards plus **JACK CASADY** – bass / **BUDDY MILES** – drums / (to repl. MITCHELL and REDDING)

Sep 68. (7") *<0767>* **ALL ALONG THE WATCHTOWER. / BURNING OF THE MIDNIGHT LAMP** [-] [20]

Oct 68. (7") *(604 025)* **ALL ALONG THE WATCHTOWER. / LONG HOT SUMMER NIGHT** [5] [-]

Nov 68. (d-lp) *(613 008-9) <6307>* **ELECTRIC LADYLAND** [6] [1] Oct68
– And the gods made love / (Have you ever been to) Electric Ladyland / Crosstown traffic / Voodoo chile / Rainy day, dream away / 1983 (a merman I should turn to be) / Moon, turn the tide . . . gently gently away / Little Miss Strange / Long hot summer night / Come on / Gypsy eyes / The burning of the midnight lamp / Still raining still dreaming / House burning down / All along the watchtower / Voodoo chile (slight return). *(also iss.lp/lp; 613 010/017) (re-iss.Jun73 on 'Polydor';) (re-iss.Jan84 on 'Polydor'; 350011-2) (re-iss.Jul91 & Oct93 on 'Polydor' lp/c/cd; 847233-1/-4/-2) (re-iss.Apr97 on 'MCA' cd/c; MCD/MCC 11600)*

Apr 69. (7") *(604 029) <0798>* **CROSSTOWN TRAFFIC. / GYPSY EYES** [37] [52] Nov68

Oct 69. (7") *(604 033)* **(LET ME LIGHT YOUR) FIRE. / THE BURNING OF THE MIDNIGHT LAMP** [-] ☐

Feb 70. (7") *<0853>* **STONE FREE. / IF 6 WAS 9** [-] ☐

Apr 70. (7") *<0905>* **STEPPING STONE. / IZABELLA** [-] ☐

JIMI HENDRIX

retained **BUDDY MILES** + recruited **BILLY COX** – bass

Track Capitol

Jun 70. (lp) *(2406 002) <472>* **BAND OF GYPSYS (live)** [6] [5] Apr70
– Who knows / Machine gun / Changes / Power of soul / Message to love / We gotta live together. *(re-iss.Aug83 on 'Polydor'; SPELP 16) (cd-iss.May88; 821 933-2) (re-iss.Dec89 & Jul91 on 'Polydor' lp/c/cd; 847 237-1/-4/-2) (re-iss.Apr97 on 'MCA'*

cd/c; MCD/MCC 11607)

— On 18th Sep'70 HENDRIX died of a drug overdose (see above)

- compilations etc. -

on 'Polydor' unless mentioned otherwise / 'Reprise' US

Feb 68. (lp; with CURTIS KNIGHT) *London; (HA 8349) / Capitol; <2856>* **GET THAT FEELING (live 1964)** | 39 | 75

Nov 68. (lp) *London; / Capitol;* **STRANGE THINGS**
(re-iss.Apr86 on 'Showcase' lp/c; SHLP/SHTC 101)

Note; All below 'Track' releases were issued on 'Reprise' US.

Sep 67. (7") *Track; (604 009)* **HOW WOULD YOU FEEL. / YOU DON'T WANT ME** | | -

May 70. (lp) *Track;* **BACKTRACK:4 (shared with The WHO)**

May 70. (lp) *Track;* **BACKTRACK:8 (shared with The WHO**

- posthumous albums / singles (some exploitation) -

Oct 70. (7"; JIMI HENDRIX with CURTIS KNIGHT) *London; (HLZ 10321)* **BALLAD OF JIMI. / GLOOMY MONDAY**

Sep 70. (lp) *Reprise; <2029>* **MONTEREY INTERNATIONAL POP FESTIVAL (live soundtrack)** | - | 16

Oct 70. (7"m) *Track; (2095 001)* **VOODOO CHILE (SLIGHT RETURN). / HEY JOE / ALL ALONG THE WATCHTOWER** | 1 | -

Mar 71. (lp) *Track; (2408 101) <2034>* **THE CRY OF LOVE** | 2 | 3
– Freedom / Drifting / Ezy rider / Night bird flying / My friend / Straight ahead / Astro man / Angel / In from the storm / Belly button window. *(re-iss.Jun73 on 'Polydor' lp)(c; 2302 023)(3194 025) (re-iss.Sep85 on 'Polydor' lp/c; SPE LP/MC 98) (cd-iss.Mar89; 829 926-2) (re-iss.Jul91 & Mar93 on 'Polydor' cd/c/lp; 847242-2/-4/-1)*

Apr 71. (7") *Track; (2094 007)* **NIGHT BIRD FLYING. / FREEDOM** | | -

Mar 71. (7") *Reprise; <1000>* **FREEDOM. / ANGEL** | - | 59

Oct 71. (7") *Reprise; <1044>* **DOLLY DAGGER. / STAR SPANGLED BANNER** | - | 74

Oct 71. (7"ep) *Track; (2094 010)* **GYPSY EYES. / REMEMBER / PURPLE HAZE / STONE FREE** | 35 |

Nov 71. (lp) *(2302 016)* **JIMI HENDRIX AT THE ISLE OF WIGHT (live)** | 17 | -
– Midnight lightning / Foxy lady / Lover man / Freedom / All along the watchtower / In from the storm. *(re-iss.Apr84 lp/c; SPE LP/MC 71) (cd-iss.Mar89; 831 813-2) (re-iss.Jul91 & Mar93 cd/c/lp; 847 236-2/-4/-1)*

Jan 72. (lp) *(2302 018) <2049>* **HENDRIX IN THE WEST (live)** | 7 | 12
– Johnny B. Goode / Lover man / Blue suede shoes / Voodoo chile (slight return) / The queen / Sergeant Pepper's lonely hearts club band / Little wing / Red house.

Jan 72. (7") *Reprise; <1082>* **JOHNNY B. GOODE. / LOVERMAN** | - |

Feb 72. (7") *(2001 277)* **JOHNNY B. GOODE. / LITTLE WING** | 35 | -

May 72. (7") *Reprise;* **LITTLE WING. / THE WIND CRIES MARY** | - |

Nov 72. (lp) *(2302 020) <2103>* **WAR HEROES** | 23 | 48
– Bleeding heart / Highway chile / Tax free / Peter Gunn / Catastrophe / Stepping stone / Midnight / 3 little bears / Beginning / Izabella. *(re-iss.Aug83 on 'Polydor' lp/c; SPE LP/MC 4) (cd-iss.Mar89; 813 573-2) (re-iss.Jul91 cd/c/lp;) (re-iss.cd+c Mar93)*

Oct 73. (d-lp) **ARE YOU EXPERIENCED / AXIS: BOLD AS LOVE** | | -

Feb 74. (lp) *(2310 301)* **LOOSE ENDS** | | -
– Come down hard on me / Blue suede shoes / Jam 292 / The stars that play with laughing Sam's dice / Drifter's escape / Hoochie koochie man / (Have you ever been to) Electric Ladyland. *(cd-iss.Mar89; 837 574-2)*

Mar 75. (lp) *(2343 080)* **JIMI HENDRIX** | 35 | -

Sep 75. (lp) *(2310 398) <2204>* **CRASH LANDING** | 35 | 5 Mar75
– Message to love / Somewhere over the rainbow / Crash landing / Coming down hard on me / Peace in Mississippi / With the power / Stone free again / Captain Coconut. *(re-iss.Mar83 lp/c; SPE LP/MC 94) (cd-iss.Mar89;) (cd-iss.Jun91 & Mar93 cd/c/lp; 847263-2/-4/-1)*

Nov 75. (lp) *(2310 415) <2229>* **MIDNIGHT LIGHTNING** | 46 | 43
– Trashman / Midnight lightning / Hear my train a-coming / Gypsy boy / Blue suede shoes / Machine gun / Once I had a woman / Beginnings. *(re-iss.Mar89 lp/c/cd; 825 166-1/-4/-2)*

Oct 76. (lp) **JIMI HENDRIX VOL.2** | | -

Jul 78. (d-lp)(d-c) *(261 2034)(350 0122) <2245>* **THE ESSENTIAL JIMI HENDRIX**
(with free one-sided 33rpm 7" **GLORIA**

Jun 80. (lp) *<2299>* **NINE TO THE UNIVERSE** | - |

Jun 80. (lp) *(2343 114)* **STONE FREE**
(re-iss.Nov83 lp/c; SPE LP/MC 51)

Sep 80. (7") **VOODOO CHILE. / GLORIA**

Sep 80. (6x7"-box) **6 SINGLES BOXED** (1st 6)

Sep 80. (12xlp-box) *(2625 038)* **10th ANNIVERSARY BOXED SET**

Jan 81. (lp) *(2311 014) <2293>* **THE ESSENTIAL JIMI HENDRIX VOLUME 2** | | Aug79

Nov 81. (12"ep) *(POSPX 401)* **ALL ALONG THE WATCHTOWER. / FOXY LADY / PURPLE HAZE / MANIC DEPRESSION**

Jun 82. (lp) *(234 3115)* **VOODOO CHILE**
(re-iss.Nov83 lp/c; SPE LP/MC 52)

Sep 82. (12"ep) *(POSPX 608)* **VOODOO CHILE. / GIPSY EYES / HEY JOE / 3RD STONE FROM THE SUN**

Feb 83. (lp/c) *(PODV/+C 6)* **SINGLES ALBUM** | 77 | -

Jun 83. (d-c) *(TWOMC 3)* **CRASH LANDING / MIDNIGHT LIGHTNING**

Nov 84. (lp/c/cd) *(823 704-1/-4/-2)* **KISS THE SKY**
(re-iss.Jun91 cd/c/lp;) (re-iss.Mar93 cd/c)

Feb 86. (lp/c/cd) *(827 990-1/-4/-2)* **JIMI PLAYS MONTEREY (live)**
(re-iss.Jun91 & Mar93 cd/c/lp; 847 244-2/-4/-1)

1986. Capitol; (lp,cd) *<SJ 12416>* **BAND OF GYPSYS 2** | - |

Jul 87. (lp/c/cd) *(833 004-1/-4/-2) / Rykodisc; <RCD 20038>* **LIVE AT WINTERLAND (live)**
(re-iss.Jun91 & Mar93 cd/c/lp; 847 238-2/-4/-1)

Jan 89. (7") *(PO 33)* **PURPLE HAZE. / 51ST ANNIVERSARY**
(12"+=) *(PZ 33)* – All along the watchtower.

(cd-s+=) *(PZCD 33)* – Hey Joe.

1989. (4xcd-box) **BOXED SET**
– ARE YOU EXPERIENCED? / WAR HEROES / IN THE WEST / BAND OF GYPSIES

Nov 89. (cd) *Hal Leonard; <HL 00660036>* **FUZZ, FEEDBACK & WAH-WAH (live)** -

Nov 89. (cd) *Hal Leonard; <HL 00660038>* **WHAMMY BAR & FINGER GREASE (live)** -

Nov 89. (cd) *Hal Leonard; <HL 00660040>* **RED HOUSE: VARIATIONS ON A THEME (live)** -

Nov 89. (cd) *Hal Leonard; <HL 00660041>* **OCTAVIA & UNIVIBE (live)** -

Mar 90. (7"/c-s) *(PO/+CS 71)* **CROSSTOWN TRAFFIC. / PURPLE HAZE** 61
(12"+=) *(PZ 71)* – All along the watchtower.
(cd-s++=) *(PZCD 71)* – Have you ever been (to Electric Ladyland).

1990. (cd) **THE JIMI HENDRIX EXPERIENCE**

Oct 90. (cd/c/lp) *(847 231-2/-4/-1)* **CORNERSTONES (1967-1970, FOUR YEARS THAT CHANGED THE MUSIC) (live)** 5
– Hey Joe / Foxy lady / Purple haze / The wind cries Mary / Have you ever been to (Electric Ladyland) / Crosstown traffic / All along the watchtower / Voodoo chile (slight return) / Star spangled banner / Stepping stone / Room full of mirrors / Ezy rider / Freedom / Drifting / In from the storm / Angel. *(cd+=/c+=)*– Fire (live) / Stone free (live).

Oct 90. (7"ep) *(PO 100)* **ALL ALONG THE WATCHTOWER. / VOODOO CHILE / HEY JOE** 52
(12"+=/c-s+=) *(POCS/PZCD 100)* – Crosstown traffic.

Nov 90. (4xcd-box) *<9-26435-2>* **LIFELINES: THE JIMI HENDRIX STORY (live)** -

Feb 91. (4xcd-box) **SESSIONS BOX – ARE YOU EXPERIENCED? / AXIS: BOLD AS LOVE / ELECTRIC LADYLAND / CRY OF LOVE**

Mar 91. (4xcd-box) *(847 235-2)* **FOOTLIGHTS (live)**
– JIMI PLAYS MONTEREY / ISLE OF WIGHT / BAND OF GYPSIES / LIVE AT WINTERLAND

Feb 92. (4xcd-box) *(511 763-2)* **STAGES (live)**
– (Stockholm 5 Sep'67 / Paris 29 Jan'68 / San Diego 24 May'69 / Atlanta 4 Jul'70)

Nov 92. (cd/c) *Polygram TV; (517235-2/-4)* **THE ULTIMATE EXPERIENCE** 25 72 Jul93
– All along the watchtower / Purple haze / Hey Joe / The wind cries Mary / Angel / Voodoo chile (slight return) / Foxy lady / Burning of the midnight lamp / Highway chile / Crosstown traffic / Castles made of sand / Long hot summer night / Red house / Manic depression / Gypsy eyes / Little wing / Fire / Wait until tomorrow / Star spangled banner (live) / Wild thing (live). *(re-iss.Sep95; same)*

Feb 94. (cd) *I.T.M.; (ITM 960004)* **PURPLE HAZE IN WOODSTOCK (live)**

Apr 94. (3xcd-box) *Pulsar; (PULSE 301)* **GREATEST HITS** -

'Polydor' (the ones not mentioned), were issued on 'M.C.A.' in US.

Apr 94. (cd/c) *(521037-2/-4)* **BLUES** 10 45

Aug 94. (cd/c) **WOODSTOCK (live)** 32 37

May 94. (cd) *Ramble Tamble;* **LIVE AT THE 'SCENE' CLUB N.Y., N.Y. (live)** -

Aug 94. (cd) *Charly;* **BEFORE THE EXPERIENCE** -

Oct 94. (cd) *Charly; (CDCD 1189)* **THE EARLY YEARS** -

Oct 70. (7"; with CURTIS KNIGHT) *R.C.A.;* **NO SUCH ANIMAL (part 1). / (part 2)**

Apr 71. (lp) *Saga; (6307)* **JIMI HENDRIX**

1972. (lp) *Saga; (6313)* **JIMI HENDRIX AT HIS BEST VOL.1**

1972. (lp) *Saga; (6314)* **JIMI HENDRIX AT HIS BEST VOL.2**

1972. (lp) *Saga; (6315)* **JIMI HENDRIX AT HIS BEST VOL.3**

Apr 71. (lp; with CURTIS KNIGHT) *Hallmark;* **THE ETERNAL FIRE OF JIMI HENDRIX** -

1973. (lp; with CURTIS KNIGHT) *Hallmark; (SHM 791)* **THE WILD ONE** -

Aug 71. (lp) *Ember; (NE 5057)* **EXPERIENCE (live)** 9 -
– (opening jam) / Room full of mirrors / C-blues / Smashing of amps. *(re-iss.Sep79 on 'Bulldog'; BDL 4002) (cd-iss.Jan87 & Nov91; BDCD 40023) (cd-iss.Mar95 on 'Nectar';)*

Mar 72. (lp) *Ember; (NR 5061)* **MORE EXPERIENCE (live)** -
(re-iss.Sep79 & Jul82 on 'Bulldog')

Feb 75. (lp) *Ember; (EMB 3428)* **LOOKING BACK WITH JIMI HENDRIX (live)** -

Oct 73. (lp) *Ember; (NR 5068)* **IN THE BEGINNING (live)** -
(re-iss.1984 on 'Everest'; CBR 1031)

1974. (lp) *Ember;* **FRIENDS FROM THE BEGINNING (with 'LITTLE RICHARD')** -
(re-iss.Jan77)

Nov 71. (lp) *Reprise; (K 44159) <2040>* **RAINBOW BRIDGE (live soundtrack)** 16 15 Oct71
– Dolly dagger / Earth blues / Pali gap / Room full of mirrors / Star spangled banner / Look over yonder / Hear my train a-comin' / Hey baby. *(cd-iss.Mar87; K2 44159) (cd re-iss.Apr89; 831 312-2)*

Jun 73. (7") *Reprise;* **HEAR MY TRAIN A-COMIN'. / ROCK ME BABY**

Jul 73. (d-lp) *Reprise; (K 64017)* **SOUNDTRACK RECORDINGS FROM THE FILM 'JIMI HENDRIX'** 37

Jun 82. (7") *Reprise;* **FIRE. / LITTLE WING** -

Jul 72. (lp) *Music For Pleasure; (MFP 5278)* **WHAT'D I SAY (live)** -

Sep 84. (lp) *Music For Pleasure; (MFP 50053)* **THE BIRTH OF SUCCESS (live)** -

Nov 72. (lp) *Enterprise; (ENTF 3000)* **RARE HENDRIX** -

Dec 72. (lp) *Enterprise;* **JIMI HENDRIX IN SESSION** -

1973. (lp) *Enterprise; (ENTF 1030)* **HENDRIX '66** -

1973. (lp) *Boulevard; (41060)* **JIMI HENDRIX 1964** -

Nov 75. (lp) *D.J.M.; (DJLMD 8011)* **FOR REAL** -

(re-iss.Feb82 on 'Audio Fidelity';)
Aug 79. (lp) *Bulldog; (BDL 2010) / Douglas;* **20 GOLDEN PIECES OF JIMI HENDRIX (live)** ☐ -
Sep 79. (lp) *Bulldog; (BDL 4003)* **MORE ESSENTIAL** ☐ -
Oct 80. (lp) *Red Lightnin'; (RL 0015)* **WOKE UP THIS MORNING AND FOUND MYSELF DEAD (live)** ☐ -
(cd-iss.Nov86; RLCD 0068) (pic-lp.Oct88; RLP 0048) (cd-iss.1992 on 'Point'; 262033-2)
Jun 81. (lp) *Audio Fidelity; (1002)* **COSMIC TURNAROUND** ☐ -
Oct 81. (4xlp-box) *Audio Fidelity;* **THE GENIUS OF HENDRIX** ☐ -
Mar 82. (lp) *Audio Fidelity;* **HIGH, LIVE AND DIRTY** ☐ -
Dec 82. (cd) *Bulldog; (BDL 2027)* **20 GOLDEN PIECES OF JIMI HENDRIX VOL.2 (live)** ☐ -
Oct 84. (c) *Audio Fidelity; (ZCGAS 703)* **JIMI HENDRIX VOL.1** ☐ -
Oct 84. (c) *Audio Fidelity; (ZCGAS 704)* **JIMI HENDRIX VOL.2** ☐ -
Oct 84. (c) *Audio Fidelity; (ZCGAS 732)* **JIMI HENDRIX VOL.3** ☐ -
Nov 81. (lp) *Phoenix; (PHX 1012)* **FREE SPIRIT** ☐ -
(re-iss.Jun87 on 'Thunderbolt'; THBM 006)
Sep 82. (lp) *Phoenix; (PHX 1020)* **MOODS** ☐ -
Sep 82. (lp) *Phoenix; (PHX 1026)* **ROOTS OF HENDRIX** ☐ -
Aug 82. (d-lp) *C.B.S.; (88592) / Reprise; <22306>* **THE JIMI HENDRIX CONCERTS (live)** 16 79
– Fire / I don't live today / Red house / Stone free / Are you experienced? / Little wing / Voodoo chile (slight return) / Bleeding heart / Hey Joe / Wild thing / Hear my train a-comin'. *(re-iss.Aug89 on 'Media Motion' lp/c/cd; MEDIA/+C/CD 1) (re-iss.Feb90 on 'Castle' lp+=/c+=/cd+=; CCS LP/MC/CD 235)–* Foxy lady.
Aug 82. (7"/12") *C.B.S.; (A/+13 2749)* **FIRE (live). / ARE YOU EXPERIENCED (live)** ☐ -
Oct 82. (lp) *Dakota;* **THE BEST OF JIMI HENDRIX** ☐ -
Nov 83. (lp/c) *Contour; (CN/+4 2067)* **THE JIMI HENDRIX ALBUM** ☐ -
Jul 84. (7") *Old Gold; (OG 9430)* **PURPLE HAZE. / THE WIND CRIES MARY** ☐ -
Jul 84. (7") *Old Gold; (OG 9431)* **VOODOO CHILE (SLIGHT RETURN). / BURNING OF THE MIDNIGHT LAMP** ☐ -
Jul 84. (7") *Old Gold; (OG 9432)* **ALL ALONG THE WATCHTOWER. / FOXY LADY** ☐ -
Jul 85. (lp/c) *Topline; (TOP/KTOP 124)* **GANGSTER OF LOVE** ☐ -
Apr 86. (lp/c) *Arcade; (ADAH/+C 430)* **THE LEGEND** ☐ -
May 86. (lp/c) *Sierra; (FEDB/CFEDB 5032)* **REPLAY OF JIMI HENDRIX** ☐ -
Aug 86. (lp/c) *Fame; (FA/TC-FA 3160)* **JOHNNY B. GOODE (live)** ☐ -
May 87. (cd) *E.M.I.; (CDP 746 485-2)* **THE BEST OF JIMI HENDRIX** ☐ -
May 88. (lp/c/cd) *Big Time; (261 525-1/-4/-2)* **16 GREAT CLASSICS** ☐ -
Jun 88. (cd; shared with TINA TURNER) *Thunderbolt; (CDTBD 001)* **VOICES IN THE WIND** ☐ -
Nov 88. (12"ep/cd-ep) *Strange Fruit; (SFPS/+CD 065)* **THE PEEL SESSIONS** ☐ -
– Radio One theme / Day tripper / Wait until tomorrow / Hear my train a'comin' / Spanish castle magic. *(cd re-iss.Apr96; same)*
Feb 89. (d-lp/c/cd) *Castle; (CCS LP/MC/CD 212) / Rykodisc; <RALP 00782>* **THE RADIO ONE SESSIONS** 30 ☐
– Stone free / Radio one theme / Day tripper / Killing floor / Love or confusion / Catfish blues / Drivin' south / Wait until tomorrow / Hear my train a-comin' / Hound dog / Fire / Hoochie coochie man / Purple haze / Spanish castle magic / Hey Joe / Foxy lady / The burning of the midnight lamp.
Nov 89. (5xlp/3xc/3xcd-box) *Castle; (HB LP/MC/CD 100)* **LIVE AND UNRELEASED – THE RADIO SHOWS (live)** ☐ -
Feb 89. (cd) *Koine; (K 880 802)* **JAM SESSIONS** ☐ -
Jan 90. (cd) *Zeta; (ZET 517)* **THE LAST EXPERIENCE CONCERT (live)** ☐ -
Apr 90. (cd/lp) *Thunderbolt; (CDTB/THBL 075)* **NIGHT LIFE** ☐ -
Dec 90. (pic-lp) *Discussion; (IFSIXWAS 9)* **WELL I STAND NEXT TO A MOUNTAIN** ☐ -
Feb 91. (cd/c) *Action Replay; (CDAR/ARLC 1022)* **THE BEST & THE REST OF JIMI HENDRIX** ☐ -
Dec 91. (cd/lp) *U.F.O.;* **IN 1967 (free w/booklet)** ☐ -
Nov 92. (7"/c-s) *East West;* **THE WIND CRIES MARY. / FIRE** ☐ -
(12"+=/cd-s+=) – Foxy lady / May this be love.
Dec 92. (cd) *Univibes;* **CALLING LONG DISTANCE** ☐ -
Apr 93. (d-cd/d-c) *Deja Vu; (R2CD 4003)* **THE GOLD COLLECTION** ☐ -
(re-iss.Jun95; same)
Apr 93. (cd) *Pulsar;* **HIS FINAL LIVE PERFORMANCE (live)** ☐ -
Sep 93. (cd) *I.T.M.; (ITM 960008)* **JIMI HENDRIX AT THE MONTEREY POP FESTIVAL, 1967 (live)** ☐ -
Dec 93. (cd) *Entertainers;* **FIRE** ☐ -
Jan 95. (cd) *Collection; (COL 017)* **THE COLLECTION** ☐ -
Mar 95. (cd) *Top Masters; (3179)* **THE EARLY JIMI HENDRIX** ☐ -
Apr 95. (cd/c) *Muskateer; (MU 5/4 018)* **LIVE IN NEW YORK** ☐ -
Apr 95. (cd/c) *(527 520-2/-4)* **VOODOO SOUP** ☐ 66
– The new rising sun / Belly button window / Stepping stone / Freedom / Angel / Room full of mirrors / Midnight / Night bird flying / Drifting / Ezy rider / Pali gap / Message to love / Peace in Mississippi / In from the storm.
May 95. (cd) *Thunderbolt; (CDTB 075)* **NIGHT LIFE** ☐ -
Jun 95. (cd) *Receiver; (RRCD 200)* **SUNSHINE OF YOUR LOVE** ☐ -
Aug 95. (cd) *Voiceprint; (844200-2)* **SUPERSESSION** ☐ -
Sep 95. (cd) *Strawberry; (SRCD 115)* **THE LAST EXPERIENCE** ☐ -
Nov 95. (cd) *The Collection;* **GREATEST HITS** ☐ -
— On April 5th 1996, JIMI's girlfriend at the time of his death; MONIKA DANNEMAN, committed suicide (carbon monoxide poisoning). In her book 'The Inner Life Of Jimi Hendrix', she had recently broke an injunction, involving a libellous statement made to JIMI's other one-time girlfriend KATHY ETCHINGHAM.
Apr 96. (cd/c) *Hallmark; (30418-2/-4)* **EARLY DAZE** ☐ -
Aug 96. (d-cd) *Natural Collection; (TNC 96205)* **REAL ROCK STANDARDS** ☐ -
Feb 97. (cd) *S.P.V.; (SPV 0854468-2)* **BALLAD OF JIMI: THE AUTHENTIC PPX RECORDINGS VOLUME 3** ☐ -
Feb 97. (cd) *S.P.V.; (SPV 0854469-2)* **LIVE AT GEORGE'S CLUB: THE AUTHENTIC PPX RECORDINGS VOLUME 4** ☐ -
Apr 97. (cd) *Arcade; (300455-2)* **THE DIAMOND COLLECTION** ☐ -
Apr 97. (cd/c) *M.C.A.; (MCD/MCC 11599)* **RAYS OF THE RISING SUN** ☐ 49
May 97. (d-cd) *Metro; (OTR 1100030)* **IN WORDS AND MUSIC** ☐ -
Jun 97. (cd) *BR Music; (RM 1536)* **PSYCHO** ☐ -

HENRY COW

Formed: based Cambridge University, England . . .1968 by FRED FRITH and TIM HODGKINSON. They played The Edinburgh Fesival in Sep'72 using the name CABARET VOLTAIRE (later used by the infamous Sheffield outfit). Running the Explorer's Club alongside DEREK BAILEY, LOL COXHILL, etc., they soon issued their avant-garde debut album, 'LEGend', before augmenting MIKE OLDFIELD's live version of 'TUBULAR BELLS'. The band had already featured on the 'GREASY TRUCKERS – LIVE AT DINGWALLS' double album with tracks 'OFF THE MAP', 'CAFE ROYAL', KEEPING WARM IN THE WINTER' & 'SWEET HEART OF MINE', subsequently touring Europe with similarly unconventional acts CAPTAIN BEEFHEART and FAUST before their dual lp with SLAPP HAPPY; 'DESPERATE STRAIGHTS'. HENRY COW then collaborated with The ART BEARS, FRITH also releasing many solo albums over the following two decades. • **Songwriters:** Group compositions. • **Trivia:** Took their name from early 20th century composer HENRY COWELL.

Recommended: LEGend (*6) / UNREST (*6) / IN PRAISE OF LEARNING (*5)

FRED FRITH (b.17 Feb'49, Heathfield, England) – guitar, violin, piano, vox / **CHRIS CUTLER** (b. 4 Jan'47, Washington DC, USA) – drums, piano, percussion / **TIM HODGKINSON** (b. 1 May'49, Salisbury, England) – organ, alto sax, clarinet / **JOHN GREAVES** (b.23 Feb'50, Prestatyn, Clwyd, Wales) – bass, piano, vocals / **GEOFF LEIGH** – saxophone, flute, recorder, vocals

Virgin Virgin
May 73. (lp) *(V 2005) <13107>* **LEGend** ☐ ☐
– Nirvana for mice / Amygdala / Teenbeat introduction / Teenbeat / Extract from 'With The Yellow Half Moon and blue star / Teenbeat reprise / The tenth Chaffinch / Nine funerals of the citizen king. *(cd-iss.Nov93 on 'R.E.R.'; ESD 80502)*
— **LINDSAY COOPER** (b. 3 Mar'51, Hornsey, London, England) – bassoon, oboe, recorder, vocals (ex-COMUS) repl. LEIGH
May 74. (lp) *(V 2011)* **UNREST** ☐ -
– Bitter storm over Ulm / Half asleep – Half awake / Ruins / Solemn music Lingvaphonie / Upon entering the Hotel Adlon / Arcades / Deluge. *(re-iss.Jun88 on 'Broadcast'; BC 4)*
— Early in 1975, they teamed up with SLAPP HAPPY (aka DAGMAR KRAUSE, PETER BLEGVAD and ANTHONY MOORE) to make a 'Virgin' album; 'DESPERATE STRAIGHTS' *(V 2024)*. They stayed to augment and co-produce on next HENRY COW album below.
May 75. (lp) *(V 2027)* **IN PRAISE OF LEARNING** ☐ -
– War / Living in the heart of the beast / Beginning / The long march / Beautiful as the Moon / Terrible as an army with banners / Morning star. *(re-iss.Mar86 on 'Broadcast'; BC 3) (cd-iss.Sep93 on 'R.E.R.'; ESD 80502)*
— added **DAGMAR KRAUSE** – vocals, piano / + guest **ROBERT WYATT** – drums

Caroline not issued
Jun 76. (d-lp) *(CAD 3002)* **CONCERTS (live)** ☐ -
– Beautiful as the Moon / Bad alchemy / Nirvana for mice / Little red riding hood hits the road / Ottowa song / Ruins / Groningen / Udine / Gloria Gloom / Groningen again / Oslo / Terrible as an army with banners.
— **GEORGIE BORN** – bass, cello / **ANNE-MARIE ROELOFS** – trombone, violin / **IRENE SCHWEIZER** – piano, repl. GREAVES and KRAUSE who both went solo

Broadcast not issued
Oct 78. (lp) *(BC 1)* **WESTERN CULTURE** ☐ -
– History & prospects: In dusty – The decay of cities – On the raft – Day by day: Falling away – Gretel's tale – Look back – 1'2 the sky. *(cd-iss.Jan93 on 'R.E.R.'; BCD 1)*

– compilations, etc. –

Jan 93. (cd) *R.E.R.; (CSB 1)* **THE VIRGIN YEARS** ☐ -
Sep 93. (cd/c) *R.E.R.; (ESD 80492/80502)* **UNREST / IN PRAISE OF LEARNING** ☐ -

ART BEARS & HENRY COW

FRITH / CUTLER / KRAUSE + guests **COOPER, HODGKINSON + BORN**

Recommended not issued
1978. (lp) *(RE 2188)* **HOPES AND FEARS** ☐ -
– Aha: Palace courtyard; a) On suicide, b) The dividing line, c) Joan, d) Maze, e) In two minds / Mer: Irrigated land; a) Terrain, b) The tube, c) The dance, d) Pirate song, e) Labyrinth, f) Riddle, g) Moeris, dancing, h) Piers.
— LINDSAY COOPER was to join DAVID THOMAS & THE PEDESTRIANS (1982-85)

ART BEARS

Recommended Ralph
Oct 79. (lp) *(RE 0618) <RR 7905>* **WINTER SONGS** ☐ ☐
– The bath of stars / First things first / Gold / The summer wheel / The slave / The hermit / Rats and monkeys / The skeleton / The winter wheel / Man and boy / Winter and war / Force / 3 figures / 3 wheels. *(cd-iss.Jun93 on 'R.E.R.'; ABCD 1)*
1981. (lp) *(RE 6622)* **THE WORLD AS IT IS TODAY** ☐ -
– The song of investment capital overseas / Truth / Freedom / (Atmed) Peace / Civilization / Democracy / The song of the martyrs / Law / The song of the monopolists / The song of the dignity of labour under capital / Albion awake. *(w/ free live 1-sided clear-7"ep)* **CODA TO 'MAN AND BOY'**

R.E.R. not issued
Apr 93. (cd) *(ABCD 2)* **HOPES & FEARS** ☐ -

NEWS FROM BABEL

KRAUSE, CUTLER, COOPER, BORN / + ZEENA PARKINS – harp / **PHIL MINTON** – trumpet

Recommended not issued

1984. (lp) *(RE 6116)* **WORK RESUMED ON THE TOWER**
– Sirens & silences: Odysseus – Auschwitz Babel – Klein's bottle black gold – Devils – Dry leaf / Work resumed on the tower: Arcades (of glass) – Victory – Anno mirabilis (in the year of miracles). *(cd-iss.Apr97 +=; RERNFBCD)*– LETTER HOME

FRED FRITH

Caroline not issued

Oct 74. (lp) *(C 1508)* **GUITAR SOLOS**
– Hello music / Glass – Steel ghosts / Out of their heads (on locoweed) / Not forgotten / Hollow music / Heat – Moment / No birds. *(cdiss.May93 on 'R.E.R.'; DBC 904)*

— added other guitarists **DEREK BAILEY, HANS REICHEL + G.F. FITZGERALD**

Jan 76. (lp) *(C 1518)* **GUITAR SOLOS II**
– Water / Struggle / The north / Only reflect / Brixton winter / 1976 / Avantelove / Vain yookts / Donner kuhle / Virglane / Praxis / The lost chord.

— now with other guitarists **HENRY KAISER, EUGENE CHADBOURNE, DAVEY WILLIAMS, CHIP HANDY, PETER CUSACK, AKIRA JIJIMA + KEITH ROWE**

Red Rift

1979. (lp) *(008) <RIFT 1>* **GUITAR SOLOS III**
– Robert Louis Stevenson / Dien da / For Eign music / Little missy / Total babes / Whistling with guitar accompaniment / For 'A' / Alienated industrial seagulls etc. / Song of river nights / Should old Arthur / Memories of Hanover Lodge / Memories of Wildey Road / Ezekiel / Coming No.4.

— he now used many session people

not issued Ralph

1980. (lp) *<8057>* **GRAVITY**
– The Boys beats the Rams / Spring any day now / Don't cry for me / The hands of the juggler / Norrgarden nyvla / Year of the monkey / What a dilemma / Crack in the concrete / Come across / Dancing in the street / My enemy is a bad man / Slap dance / A career in real estate / Dancing in Rockville Maryland. *(cd-iss.May93 on 'R.E.R.'; DBC 901)*

1981. (lp) *<8106>* **SPEECHLESS**
– Kick the can (part 1) / Carnival on Wall St. / Ahead in the sand / Laughing matter / Esperanza / Women speak to men, men speak to women / A spit in the ocean / Navajo / Balance / Saving grace / Speechless / Conversations with white care / Domaine de Planousset / Kick the can (part II).

— now with **PHIL MINTON** – vocals / **BOB OSTERTAG** – synthesizers, tapes, radio

not issued Rift

1982. (lp) *<RIFT 4>* **VOICE OF AMERICA (live)**
– Que hacen los extranos / Sandinista dialogue / Song: Revolution / Chronology of the chilean coup / Let's make a deal / T.V. coverage of the return of the Teheran hostages / The Super Bowl / Savadoran national guard chanting slogans while training / Chaquito, a small boy, speaking at his father's funeral on the Chinchontepec volcano / Small girl singing at a ceremony to mark the end of the literacy campaign in Esteli / Song: Mourn not the dead.

— multi FRED with **BILL LASWELL + TINA CURRAN** – bass / **PAUL SEARS + FRED MAHER + FRANK WUYTS + HANS BRUNIUSSON** – drums

Recommended Ralph

1983. (lp) *<FF 8356>* **CHEAP AT HALF THE PRICE**
– Some clouds don't / Cap the knife / Evolution / Too much, too little / The welcome / Same old me / Some clouds do / Instant party / Walking song / Flying in the face of facts / Heart bares / Absent friends / The great healer.

Jun 87. (lp; by FRED FRITH & RENE LUISER) *(VICT 01)* **NOUS AUTRE**

Recommended S.S.T.

Dec 87. (lp/cd; FRITH & KAISER) *<(SST 147/+CD)>* **WITH ENEMIES LIKE THESE, WHO NEEDS FRIENDS** (rec.1979-83, originally issued on 'Metrolanguage' *ML 107)*
– The trace / Three languages / Love in Hell / Twisted memories . . . / One of nature's mistakes / Roy Rogers / It sings / Drowsy Maggie / The Kirghiz light / The golden eighties / Objects everyday / The changing of names / It moves / One-eyed theater / Dog puppet born out of a sock / Hard time killin' floor blues.

— In Nov87 and 1990, he was credited on FRENCH FRITH KAISER THOMPSON albums on 'Demon'; 'LIVE, LOVE, LARF & LOAF' lp/cd *(F102)* & 'INVISIBLE MEANS' cd/lp *(F199)*.

Mar 88. (d-lp/cd) *(REC REC/DEC 20) <SST 172/+CD>* **THE TECHNOLOGY OF TEARS**

— with **ANNE BOURNE** – cello, accordion / **JANE SIBERRY** – vocals, acoustic guitar / **KEN MYHR** – slide guitar / **CHRISTIE MacFADYEN** – vocals / **JEAN DEROME** – saxes

Made To Measure

1989. (cd) *(MTM 21) <7570>* **THE TOP OF HIS HEAD**
– Title theme / Driving to the train / Wheels within / Hold on hold / Lucy leaves a note / Gus escapes / Gravity's a rule / Channel change / Orbit / Fall to call / Underwater dream / This old Earth / Donuts / The long drive / Lucy / The premonition / Questions and answers / The performance.

I.T.M. not issued

Oct 90. (cd; by FRED FRITH, ZEENA PERKINS & ELLIOTT SHARP) *(ITM 1454)* **NAD**

R.E.R. not issued

Apr 93. (cd) *(DEC 40)* **HELTER SKELTER**

May 93. (cd) *(DBC 30)* **STEP ACROSS THE BORDER**

Tzadik not issued

Feb 97. (cd) *(TZA 7503)* **EYE TO EAR**

HERD

Formed: London, England ... early 1965 by pop entrepreneurs KEN HOWARD and ALAN BLAIKLEY. They had already provided songwriting services for 60's beat groups The HONEYCOMBS and DAVE DEE, MICKY, BEAKY, MICK & TICH. The pair then brought in 5 local musicians although the newly formed unit didn't achieve anything until the arrival of a young PETER FRAMPTON. He gave the band their image, as well as furnishing them with two 1967 UK Top 20 hits, 'FROM THE UNDERWORLD' & 'PARADISE LOST'. The singles showcased HERD's orchestrated psychedelic pop, and were included on the 1968 debut album. After a further Top 5 smash, 'I DON'T WANT OUR LOVIN' TO DIE', they fell out of favour, although band members went on to greater things, especially PETER FRAMPTON.

Recommended: PARADISE AND UNDERWORLD (*5)

TERRY CLARK – vocals / **GARY TAYLOR** – guitar / **ANDY BOWN** – bass / **LEWIS RICH** – organ / **MICK UNDERWOOD** – drums repl.TONY CHAPMAN.

Parlophone not issued

May 65. (7") *(R R 5284)* **GOODBYE BABY, GOODBYE. / HERE COMES THE FOOL**

Oct 65. (7") *(R 5353)* **SHE WAS REALLY SAYING SOMETHING. / IT'S BEEN A LONG TIME BABY**

Feb 66. (7") *(R 5413)* **SO MUCH IN LOVE. / THIS BOY'S ALWAYS BEEN TRUE**

— **BOWN** (now keyboards) + **TAYLOR** (now bass) recruited in Autumn '66 / **PETER FRAMPTON** – vocals, guitar who repl. TERRY CLARK and LEWIS RICH / **ANDREW STEELE** – drums repl. UNDERWOOD who joined EPISODE SIX, etc. etc.

Fontana Fontana

Apr 67. (7") *(TF 819)* **I CAN FLY. / DIARY OF A NARCISSIST**

Jun 67. (7") *<1588>* **I CAN FLY. / UNDERSTAND ME**

Aug 67. (7") *(TF 856) <1602>* **FROM THE UNDERWORLD. / SWEET WILLIAM** 6

Dec 67. (7") *(TF 887) <1610>* **PARADISE LOST. / COME ON – BELIEVE ME** 15

Mar 68. (lp; stereo/mono) *(S+/TL 5458)* **PARADISE LOST** 38
– From the underworld / On my way home / I can fly / Goodbye groovy / Mixed up minds / Impressions of Oliver / Paradise lost / Sad / Something strange / On your own / She loves me, She loves me not / Fare thee well / Sweet William / Come on believe me / I don't want our loving to die / Our fairy tale *(re-iss.1989;)*

May 68. (7") *(TF 925) <1618>* **I DON'T WANT OUR LOVING TO DIE. / OUR FAIRY TALE** 5

Sep 68. (7") *(TF 975)* **SUNSHINE COTTAGE. / MISS JONES**

1968. (lp) *<67579>* **LOOKING THRU YOU (compilation)**
– I don't want our loving to die / Come on – believe me / Our fairy tale / On my way home / Goodbye / Groovy / From the underworld / Paradise lost / Sweet William / I can fly / Understand me.

May 69. (7") *(TF 1011) <1646>* **THE GAME. / BEAUTY QUEEN**

— **HENRY SPINETTI** – drums repl. STEELE (also FRAMPTON left in Mar'69 to join HUMBLE PIE before going solo)

— Now a trio **BOWN, TAYLOR and SPINETTI**

B&C not issued

Jun 71. (7") *(CB 154)* **YOU'VE GOT ME HANGIN' FROM YOUR LOVIN' TREE. / I DON'T WANNA GO TO SLEEP AGAIN**

— Caved in finally after BOWN formed JUDAS JUMP with SPINETTI. He later went solo, making around 4 albums. TAYLOR was soon to re-appear with pop band FOX.

- compilations, etc - -

Aug 72. Bumble; (7"m) *(GEX 1)* **FROM THE UNDERWORLD. / PARADISE LOST / ON MY WAY HOME**

Jan 73. Bumble; (lp) *(GEMP 5001)* **NOSTALGIA**

1973. Bumble; (7") *(GE 120)* **I DON'T WANT OUR LOVIN' TO DIE. / THE GAME**

Jul 82. Old Gold; (7") *(OG 9236)* **FROM THE UNDERWORLD. / PARADISE LOST**

Jul 82. Old Gold; (7") *(OG 9245)* **I DON'T WANT OUR LOVIN' TO DIE. /**

Aug 92. Repertoire; (cd) *(REP)* **PARADISE AND UNDERWORLD** *(was German release in 1969 on 'Hansa')*

Oct 95. BR Music; (cd) *(BX 4512)* **FROM THE UNDERWORLD (THE SINGLES AND MORE)**

HIGH TIDE

Formed: London, England ...1969 by TONY HILL (ex-MISUNDERSTOOD, SIMON HOUSE, PETER PAVLI and ROGER HADDEN. They signed to 'Liberty' although their subsequent attempts to break into the progressive rock market didn't bear fruit. Their two albums, 'SEA SHANTIES' (1969) and 'HIGH TIDE' (1970), showcased a studied conceptual fusion of JIM MORRISON-like vocals, intricate, heavy guitar and violin, more palatable to continental audiences (Both albums are now worth over $35 mint). SIMON HOUSE was later to find a wee bit fame with HAWKWIND, then DAVID BOWIE. • **Songwriters:** Group. • **Trivia:** Before HILL joined The MISUNDERSTOOD, his group, The ANSWERS, released two 1966 'Columbia' 45's, 'IT'S JUST A FEAR'./ 'YOU'VE GOTTA BELIEVE ME' and 'THAT'S WHAT YOU'RE DOING TO ME'./ 'GOT A LETTER FROM MY BABY'.

Recommended: SEA SHANTIES (*6) / HIGH TIDE (*5)

TONY HILL – vocals, guitar (ex-ANSWERS, ex-MISUNDERSTOOD) / **PETER PAVLY** – bass / **SIMON HOUSE** – violin / **ROGER HADDEN** – drums

Liberty Liberty

1969. (lp) *(LBS 83264) <7638>* **SEA SHANTIES**
– Futilist's lament / Death warmed up / Pushed, but not forgotten / Walking down their outlook / Missing out / Nowhere. *(re-iss.May84 on 'Psycho'; PSYCHO 26)*

1970. (lp) *(LBS 83294)* **HIGH TIDE** [ ] [-]
– Blankman cries again / The joke / saneonymous. *(re-iss.May84 on 'Psycho'; PSYCHO 27)*

—— Folded in 1970 and all augmented DENNY GERRARD on his only lp 'SINISTER MORNING' for 'Deram Nova' *(SDN 10)*. HOUSE eventually joined HAWKWIND before moving to DAVID BOWIE band in 1978.

—— They re-formed in the 80's and recorded some more mail-order lp's including 'INTERESTING TIMES' (1986) / 'THE FLOOD' / 'ANCIENT GATES' / 'A FIERCE NATIVE'. TONY HILL completed a solo cd in 1991 'PLAYING FOR TIME'.

- compilations, etc. -

Aug 94. (cd) *E.M.I.; (CZ 530)* **SEA SHANTIES / HIGH TIDE** [ ] [-]

Steve HILLAGE

Born: 2 Aug'51, London, England. While at school he joined the short-lived URIEL for six months in early 1968. They became EGG after his departure to university, and made two albums in the early 70's, one of which, 'ARACHEZ' (issued on 'Evoluton'), is now worth over £200. After returning to London in the Spring of '71, HILLAGE formed the equally short-lived KHAN with ex-URIEL member DAVE STEWART (who was also leading the aforementioned EGG at the same time). KHAN released one album, 1972's 'SPACE SHANTY', before HILLAGE joined KEVIN AYERS' touring band, playing alongside French-based uber-hippies GONG. 1973 saw him hooking up with the communal space cadets, helping to focus their freaky meanderings over the course of three albums. When GONG splintered in 1975, HILLAGE went solo with his girlfriend MIQUETTE GIRAUDY; enlisting assorted GONG members for his debut, 'FISH RISING'. The TODD RUNDGREN-produced follow-up, 'L', was a consumate development of his quasi-psychedelic guitar ambience and "New Age" musings while 1977's 'MOTIVATION RADIO' was produced by synthesizer innovator MALCOLM CECIL (ex-TONTO'S EXPANDING HEAD BAND). While "Punk" was telling the kids there was no future, or at least a rather unpleasant one, HILLAGE was bravely pushing on with the hippy tenets of love, peace and spirituality. He released a clutch of trippy ambient rock albums in the late 70's, as well as having a hand in the 1979 revival of The Glastonbury Fayre, now just plain old Glastonbury. The highlight of his recorded output during this period was 1979's 'RAINBOW DOME MUSICK', a dreamy slice of instrumental ambience. Throughout the 80's, HILLAGE was an in-house producer for 'Virgin', working with the likes of SIMPLE MINDS and ROBYN HITCHCOCK, having previously worked with The SKIDS and others. He then teamed up with ALEX PATERSON of The ORB when the dance scene was in its optimistic infancy back in 1989. This meeting led to the formation of SYSTEM 7, a laid back collective with HILLAGE and GIRAUDY as its prime movers, enlisting the aid of respected players like the aforementioned PATERSON and PAUL OAKENFOLD along the way. SYSTEM 7's self-titled debut was a tentative step towards their new ambient-techno sound, more fully realised on the relatively successful '777' in 1993. The act were perfect for the neo-psychedelic clubs which were emerging, becoming a live favourite at Club Dog and Whirly-Gig events. Like JAM & SPOON'S 'Tripomatic Fairytales', SYSTEM 7's next album, 'POINT 3', was released in two halves, 'THE FIRE ALBUM', which was a rhythmic trance opus and 'THE WATER ALBUM', an ambient version of the same tracks. Things had come full circle, HILLAGE was back in his element producing soundtracks for people to lose themselves to, chemically or otherwise, a new generation of pseudo-hippies. 1996's 'POWER OF SEVEN' saw SYSTEM 7 work with DERRICK MAY on a harder set of Detroit-influenced techno. • **Covered:** NOT FADE AWAY (Buddy Holly) / HURDY GURDY MAN (Donovan) / IT'S ALL TOO MUCH + GETTING BETTER (Beatles).

Recommended: FISH RISING (*6) / LIVE HERALD (*7) / SYSTEM 7 (*6) / RAINBOW DOME MUSICK (*7) / POINT 3 (*7) / POWER OF SEVEN (*6)

KHAN

STEVE HILLAGE – guitar, vocals (ex-GONG, ex-URIEL, ex-KHAN) / **DICK HENNINGHAM** – organ (ex-ARTHUR BROWN) / **NICK GREENWODD** – bass (ex-ARTHUR BROWN) / **ERIC PEACHEY** – drums

Deram P.V.C.

May 72. (lp) *(DSL 11)* **SPACE SHANTY** [ ] [-] 1978
– Space shanty / Stranded effervescent psychonovelty No.5 / Mixed up man of the mountains / Driving to Amsterdam / Stargazers / Hollow stone escape of the space pirates. *(re-iss.Feb77; same) (cd-iss 1991 on 'Mantra' France)*

—— **DAVE STEWART** – organ (ex-EGG, ex-URIEL) repl. HENNINGHAM / **NIGEL SMITH** – bass repl. GREENWOOD. (DAVE moved to HATFIELD + THE NORTH) Late 1972, HILLAGE joined KEVIN AYERS Band on tour. In 1973, he joined GONG making 3 lp's **FLYING TEAPOT** (1973), **ANGEL'S EYES** (1973), **YOU** (1974). He guested for EGG on their Nov74 album 'THE CIVIL SURFACE'.

STEVE HILLAGE

went solo with some GONG members.

Virgin Atlantic

Apr 75. (lp/c) *(V/TCV 2031)* **FISH RISING** [33] [ ]
– Solar musick suite:- (i) Sun song – (ii) Canterbury sunrise – (iii) Hiram afterglid meets the Dervish – (iv) Sun song (reprise) / Fish / Meditation of the snake / The salmon song:- (i) Salmon pool – (ii) Solomon's Atlantis – (iii) Swimming with the salmon – (iv) King of the fishes / Afterglid:- (i) Sun moon surfing – (ii) Great wave and the boat of Hermes – (iii) The silver ladder – (iv) Astral meadows – (v) The Lafta yoga song – (vi) Gliding – (vii) Golden vibe – the outglid. *(re-iss.Mar84; OVED 28) (cd-iss.Jun87; CDV 2031)*

—— Next used TODD RUNDGREN'S UTOPIA as backing alongside others.

Sep 76. (lp/c) *(V/TCV 2066)* **'L'** [10] [ ]
– Hurdy gurdy man / Hurdy gurdy glissando / Electrick gypsies / Om nama Shivaya / Luna musick suite / It's all too much. *(re-iss.Mar84; OVED 29) (cd-iss.Jun87; CDV 2066) (cd re-iss.Apr97 on 'Virgin-VIP'; CDVIP 184)*

Oct 76. (7") *(VS 161)* **IT'S ALL TOO MUCH. / SHIMMER** [ ] [-]

Feb 77. (7") *(VS 171)* <3384> **HURDY GURDY MAN. / OM NAMA SHIVAYA** [ ] [ ]

Sep 77. (lp/c) *(V/TCV 2777)* **MOTIVATION RADIO** [28] [ ]
– Mellow dawn / Motivation / Light in the sky / Radio / Wait one moment / Saucer surfing / Searching for the spark / Ovtave doctors / Not fade away (glide forever). *(re-iss.Mar84; OVED 32) (cd-iss.Jun88; CDV 2777)*

Dec 77. (7") *(VS 197)* **NOT FADE AWAY (GLIDE FOREVER). / SAUCER SURFING** [ ] [ ]

Apr 78. (lp,green-lp/c) *(T/TCV 2098)* **GREEN** [30] [-]
– Sea nature / Ether ships / Musick of the trees / Palm trees (love guitar) / Unidentified (flying being) / U.F.O. over Paris / Leyliness to Glassdom / Crystal city / Activation meditation / The glorious om riff. *(re-iss.Mar84; OVED 30) (cd-iss.Jun90; CDV 2098)*

May 78. (7") *(VS 212)* **GETTING BETTER. / PALM TREES (LOVE GUITAR)** [ ] [ ]

Feb 79. (d-lp/c) *(V/TCV 3502)* **LIVE HERALD (live)** [54] [-]
– The salmon song / The Dervish riff / Castle in the clouds / Hurdy gurdy man / Light in the sky / Searching for the spark / Electrick gypsies / Radiom / Lunar musick suite / Meditation of the dragon / It's all too much / The golden vibe / Talking to the sun / 1988 aktivator / New age synthesis (unzipping the zype) / Healing feeling. *(cd-iss.Jun90, omits side 4; CDVM 3502)*

Apr 79. (lp,clear-lp) *(VR 1)* **RAINBOW DOME MUSICK** [52] [-]
– Garden of Paradise / Four ever rainbow. *(re-iss.1984; same) (cd-iss.Jun88; CDVR 1)*

Sep 79. (lp/c) *(V/TCV 2135)* **OPEN** [71] [-]
– Day after day / Getting in tune / Open / Definite activity / Don't dither, do it / The fire inside / Earthrise. *(re-iss.Mar84; OVED 31) (cd-iss.Jun90 as 'OPEN FEATURING STUDIO HERALD'; CDV 2135)*

Nov 79. (7") *(VS 313)* **DON'T DITHER, DO IT. / GETTING IN TUNE** [ ] [ ]

—— Took time off for sessions, etc., until his return in 1982

Jan 83. (7"/12") *(VS 574/+12)* **KAMIKAZE EYES. / BEFORE THE WORLD WAS MADE** [ ] [ ]

Feb 83. (lp/c) *(V/TCV 2244)* **FOR TO NEXT** [48] [-]
– These uncharted lands / Kamikaze eyes / Alone / Anthems for the blind / Bright future / Frame by frame / Waiting / Glory. *(free instrumental-lp w/a 'AND NOT OR')* – Before the storm / Red Admiral / Serotonin / And not or / Knights templar / Still golden. *(re-iss.Dec83; OVED 13) (re-iss.Aug88; OVED 123) (cd-iss.Jul90 with free album; CDV 2244) (re-iss.cd Mar94;)*

Apr 83. (7") *(VS 551)* **ALONE. / FRAME BY FRAME** [ ] [-]
(12"+=) *(VS 551-12)* – Timelines.

—— HILLAGE went more into production for SIMPLE MINDS, ROBYN HITCHCOCK, etc. In the 90's, he guested with ALEX PATERSON in The ORB and founded his own ambient group SYSTEM 7.

- compilations, others, etc. -

1979. (12"pic-ep) *Virgin; (SIXPACK 2)* **SIX PACK** [ ] [-]
– The salmon song / It's all too much / The golden vibe / Not fade away / Elektric gypsies / Radio.

1983. (lp) *Aura; <AURA 1>* **AURA** [-] [ ]

Aug 92. (cd) *Windsong; (WINCD 014)* **BBC RADIO 1 LIVE IN CONCERT (live)** [ ] [-]

SYSTEM 7

STEVE HILLAGE – guitar / **with ALEX PATERSON** (Orb) / **YOUTH** / **DERRICK MAY** / **STEVE WADDINGTON** (Beloved) / **PAUL OAKENFIELD** / **MICK McNEIL** (ex-Simple Minds) / **MIQUETTE GIRAUDY** (ex-Gong) / **OLU ROWE** – vocals / **ZOE THRASH** (Orb) / **ANDY FALCONER** (engineer)

Ten-Virgin Virgin

Nov 90. (12") *(TENX 335)* **SUNBURST (Flutter mix). / SUNBURST (Paradise mix)** [ ] [-]

—— now w/ **ANIFF COUSINS** (Chapter and the Verse) / + **MONDAY MICHIRU** – vocals

Sep 91. (cd/c/d-lp) *(DIXCD/CDIX/DIX 102)* **SYSTEM 7** [ ] [ ]
– Sunburst / Freedom fighters / Habibi / Altitude / Bon humeur / Fractal liaison / Dog / Thunderdog / Listen / Strange quotations / Miracle / Over and out.

Oct 91. (12"/cd-s) *(TEN X/CD 385)* **HABIBI (Another World mix). / MIRACLE / HABIBI (edit)** [ ] [ ]
(12"clear) *(TENY 385)* – ('A'-Tex mix) / ('A'-Legian Beach mix) / Mia (Ultraworld Colony mix).

Feb 92. (7") *(TEN 394)* **FREEDOM FIGHTERS (new style). / DEPTH DISCO** [ ] [ ]
(12"clear+=/cd-s+=) *(TEN X/CD 394)* – ('A'-Praying by the sea mix) / ('A'-Freedom void mix).
(pic-cd-s+=) *(TENCX 394)* – ('A'-Praying by the sea mix) / Mia (the fisherman mix).

Jun 92. (d12"ep) *(TENG 403)* **ALTITUDES** (8 mixes) [ ] [ ]

Big Life Big Life

Feb 93. (12"ep/cd-ep) *(BFL T/X 2)* **7:7 EXPANSION (mixes)** [39] [ ]

Feb 93. (cd/c) *(BFL CD/MC 1)* **777** [30] [ ]
– 7:7 expansion / A cool dry place / Desire (ghost mix) / On the seventh night / Sinbad / Ship of the desert / Fay deau deau.

Jul 93. (12"ep/cd-ep) *(BFL T/D 8)* **SINBAD. / QUEST** [ ] [ ]

Oct 94. (12"ep/cd-ep) *(BFL T/D 20)* **SIRENES. / ('A'-Marshall Jefferson mix) / ('A'-Laurent Garnier mix) / Coltrane (water mix)** [ ] [ ]
(cd-ep+=) – Alpha wave / Gliding in two-tone curves (water edit).

Oct 94. (cd/c/d-lp) *(BFL CA/MA/LA 11)* **POINT 3: THE FIRE ALBUM** [ ] [ ]
– Sirenes / Alpha wave (water edit) / Mysterious traveler / Coltrane (remix) / Radiate / Overview / Gliding on duo-tone curves / Jupiter! / Dr. Livingstone I pressume / Batukau.

Oct 94. (cd/c) *(BFL CD/MD 11)* **POINT 3: THE WATER ALBUM** [ ] [ ]

Apr 95. (12"ep/cd-ep) *(BKL T/D 25)* **ALPHA WAVE (Plastikman acid house mix). / ('A'-Alpha mix) / ('A'-That sound mix)** [ ] [ ]

Jan 96. (12"ep/cd-ep) *(BFL T/D 30)* **INTERSTATE / ('A'-David Holmes mix) / ('A'-Doc Scott mix)** [ ] [ ]

Feb 96. (cd/c/lp) *(BFL CD/MC/LP 16)* **POWER OF 7** [ ] [ ]

Jul 96. (12"ep/cd-ep) *(BFL T/D 38)* **HANGAR 84 /** [ ] [ ]

Oct 96. (cd/t-lp) *(BFL CD/LP 21)* **SYSTEM EXPRESS** [ ] [ ]

Jun 97. (12"/cd-s) *(BFL T/D 42)* **RITE OF SPRING. /** [ ] [-]

Jon HISEMAN (see under ⇒ COLOSSEUM)

H.M.S. BOUNTY (see under ⇒ MU)

HOELDERLIN

Formed: Germany ... late 1970 as HOLDERLIN by brothers CHRISTIAN and JOCHEN GRUMBKOW together with NANNY DE RUIG. They were soon joined by CHRISTOPH NOPPENEY, PETER KASEBERG and MICHAEL BRUCHMANN. Signing to the 'Pilz' label, then run by ROLF-ULRICH KAISER, he provided them with recording time at DIETER DIERK's studio early in '72. From these sessions came their progressive-folk debut album, 'HOLDERLIN'S TRAUM'. Full of expert, complex instrumentation and British folk roots (i.e. INCREDIBLE STRING BAND, PENTANGLE & FAIRPORT CONVENTION), it was, and still is, regarded as a classic of its time. However a follow-up was delayed due to the demise of their label and also 'Ohr', who they were to record for. They found a home at 'Spiegelei' in '75, and under the direction of KONRAD PLANK, (now without NANNY who was replaced with PETER's brother JOACHIM) recorded the eponymous 'HOELDERLIN'. This attempted to break away from folk to a more progressive-rock stance, influenced no doubt by the British success of GENESIS. If one track stood out more than any other, it was the 17-minute 'DEATHWATCHBEETLE', a concept suite of pristine quality. They were back in the studio within a year, recording the weird concept, 'CLOWNS AND CLOUDS', the best tracks being 'STREAMING' and 'PHASING' from the "Clouds" side. The KASEBERG's subsequently left and were soon replaced by HANS BAAR, who played on their European tour. This turned out to be a gruelling affair that led to CHRISTIAN retiring from live and studio work, concentrating solely on the lyrics and their management. Spaniard PABLO WEEBER was duly drafted in to complete their 4th album, 'RARE BIRDS', which further fuelled the GENESIS comparisons. After a live double album recorded in the autumn of '77, the GRUMBKOW's and HANS BAAR brought in a fresh line-up which completed the appropriately titled, but disappointing, 'NEW FACES' in 1979. Their final effort, 'FATA MORGANA', was even worse and they decided to split after an up and down 10 years in the business.

Recommended: HOLDERLIN'S TRAUM (*9) / HOELDERLIN (*8) / CLOWNS AND CLOUDS (*7) / RARE BIRDS (*6) /

NANNY DE RUIG – vocals / **CHRISTIAN GRUMBKOW** – guitar / **JOCHEN GRUMBKOW** – keyboards, cello, flute, mellotron, clavinet / **CHRISTOPH NOPPENEY** – violin, viola, flute / **PETER KASEBERG** – bass, guitar / **MICHAEL BRUCHMANN** – drums, percussion / guests on the album; **PETER BURSCH** – sitar (of BROSELMASCHINE) / **MIKE HELLBACH** – tabla (of BROSELMASCHINE) / **WALTER WESTRUPP** – recorder

Pilz | not issued

Apr 72. (lp; as HOLDERLIN) *(20 21314-5)* **HOLDERLIN'S TRAUM** [-] [-] German
– Waren wir / Peter / Strohhalm / Requiem fur einen wicht / Erwachen / Wetterbericht / Traum. *(re-iss.1981; same) (cd-iss.1990's;)*

— **JOACHIM KASEBERG** – guitar repl. NANNY

Spiegelei | not issued

May 75. (lp) *(26511-6U)* **HOELDERLIN** [-] [-] German
– Schwebebahn / I love my dog / Honeypot / Nuernberg / Deathwatchbeetle. *(re-iss.1981; INT 160.601)*

— **HANS BAAR** – bass, vocals, guitar repl. PETER + JOACHIM KASEBERG

Apr 76. (lp) *(26605-6U)* **CLOWNS AND CLOUDS** [-] [-] German
– Mad house / Your eyes / Circus / Tango Mili / Marching / Sensations / Streaming / Phasing. *(re-iss.1981; INT 160.607)*

— **PABLO WEEBER** – guitar repl. CHRISTIAN who stayed on as lyricist and part-manager

Oct 77. (lp) *(INT 160.608)* **RARE BIRDS** [-] [-] German
– Haektik intergalaktik / Sky-lift / Before you lay down rough and thorny / Rare bird / Necronomicon / Sun rays.

Feb 78. (d-lp) *(INT 180.602)* **LIVE TRAUMSTADT (live)** [-] [-] German
– Intro / Schwebebahn / Haektik intergalaktik / Circus / Phasing / Streaming / Die stadt / Mad house / Sun rays / Soft landing.

— **JOACHIM + HANS (+ CHRISTIAN** lyrics) recruited **TOMMY L'OHR** – synthesizer, vocals, guitars / **RUDIGER ELZE** – guitars / **EDUARD SCHICKE** – drums, percussion

Aug 79. (lp) *(INT 145.605)* **NEW FACES** [-] [-] German
– Somebody's callin' / I want you / Cold winds / Gentle push / High in Shanghai / The shouter / Footsteps / Weekend.

— guest on last album; **BERND KOENIG** – keyboards, vocals; repl. ELZE

1981. (lp) *(INT 145.626)* **FATA MORGANA** [-] [-] German
– Fata Morgana / Lena / Hallo / Manchmal / Supermarket / Laerm / Kamikaze / Das alte lied.

— split after above

HOLLIES

Formed: Manchester, England . . . 1961 by ALLAN CLARKE and GRAHAM NASH, who quickly found DON RATHBONE and ERIC HAYCOCK. In 1963, they signed to EMI's 'Parlophone' label, adding a 5th member, TONY HICKS. Their debut 45, '(AIN'T THAT) JUST LIKE ME', made the UK Top 30, being followed by 'SEARCHIN'', their first of 21 consecutive Top 20 hits until 1971's 'LITTLE WILLY' failed to register. During the early part of their career, The HOLLIES were basically a pop industry beat group, jumping on the psychedelic bandwagon in 1968 with the mythical pretentiousness of 'KING MIDAS IN REVERSE'. However, following the departure of NASH, they increasingly moved into the cabaret scene. They regained a bit of credibility in late 1969, however, with the much-loved ballad, 'HE AIN'T HEAVY'. In August '71, CLARKE left for the first time, returning in mid-73 after his Swedish replacement MICHAEL RICKFORS failed to impress the buying public. They immediately reinstated themselves when a Top 30 hit, was followed by near No.1 smash, 'THE AIR THAT I BREATHE'. Although future hits were few and far between, they plugged on throughout the 70's & 80's. • **Songwriters:** CLARKE-HICKS-NASH, until latter's departure to CROSBY, STILLS & NASH. HOLLIES covered; (AIN'T THAT) JUST LIKE ME + SEARCHIN' (Coasters) / STAY (Maurice Williams & The Zodiacs) / JUST ONE LOOK (Doris Troy) / YES I WILL (Goffin-Titelman) / I'M ALIVE (Clint Ballard Jr.) / LOOK THROUGH ANY WINDOW + BUS STOP (Graham Gouldman) / IF I NEEDED SOMEONE (George Harrison; Beatles) / I CAN'T LET GO + THE BABY (Chip Taylor) / SORRY SUZANNE (T.MacAuley & G.Stephens) / GASOLINE ALLEY BRED (T.MacAuley-R.Cook-R.Greenaway) / WHEN THE SHIP COMES IN (Bob Dylan) / JESUS WAS A CROSSMAKER (Judee Sill) / SANDY (Bruce Springsteen) / STOP IN THE NAME OF LOVE (Supremes) / SOLDIER'S SONG (Mike Batt) / CARRIE (John Miles) / STAND BY ME (Ben E.King) / SHINE SILENTLY (Nils Lofgren) / etc. Also cover albums 'HOLLIES SING (Bob) DYLAN' and 'BUDDY HOLLY'. KENNY LYNCH collaborated on several with HICKS on 1971's 'DISTANT LIGHT'. • **Trivia:** In 1988 after exposure on Miller lite UK TV ad, the 1969 hit 'HE AIN'T HEAVY, HE'S MY BROTHER' re-charted, hitting No.1.

Recommended: THE AIR THAT I BREATHE (THE BEST OF THE HOLLIES) (*6)

ALLAN CLARKE (b. 5 Apr'42, Salford, Manchester, England) – vocals / **TONY HICKS** (b.16 Dec'43, Nelson, Lancashire, England) – lead guitar / **GRAHAM NASH** (b. 2 Feb'42, Blackpool, England) – guitar / **ERIC HAYDOCK** (b. 3 Feb'43) – bass / **DON RATHBONE** – drums

Parlophone | Liberty

May 63. (7") *(R 5030)* **(AIN'T THAT) JUST LIKE ME. / HEY WHAT'S WRONG WITH ME** [25] [-]

Aug 63. (7") *(R 5052)* **SEARCHIN'. / WHOLE WORLD OVER** [12] [-]

— **BOBBY ELLIOTT** (b. 8 Dec'42, Burnley, England) – drums (ex-SHANE FENTON & THE FENTONES) repl. RATHBONE (still on next single b-side and album track – *)

Nov 63. (7") *(R 5077)* <55674> **STAY. / NOW'S THE TIME** [8] [ ] Mar64

Jan 64. (lp) *(PMC 1220)* **STAY WITH THE HOLLIES** [2] [-]
– Little lover / Memphis / Talkin' 'bout you / It's only make believe / Rockin' Robin / Mr. Moonlight / You better move on / Watcha gonna do 'bout it / What king of girl are you / Candy man / What kind of boy. *(re-iss.Oct87 on 'Beat Goes On'; BGOLP 4) (cd-iss.Oct88; BGOCD 4)*

Parlophone | Imperial

Feb 64. (7") *(R 5104)* <66026> **JUST ONE LOOK. / KEEP OFF THAT FRIEND OF MINE** [2] [98] Apr64

May 64. (7") *(R 5137)* **HERE I GO AGAIN. / BABY THAT'S ALL** [4] [-]

Jul 64. (7") <66044> **HERE I GO AGAIN. / LUCILLE** [-] [ ]

Sep 64. (7") *(R 5178)* <66070> **WE'RE THROUGH. / COME ON BACK** [7] [ ] Oct64

Nov 64. (lp) *(PMC 1235)* **IN THE HOLLIES STYLE** [ ] [-]
– The time for love / Don't you know / You'll be mine / It's in her kiss / Come on home / Set me free / Too much monkey business / I thought of you last night / Nitty gritty; something's got a hold of me. *(re-iss.Mar88 & Apr97 on 'Beat Goes On' lp/cd; BGO LP/CD 8)*

Jan 65. (7") *(R 5232)* **YES I WILL. / NOBODY** [9] [-]

May 65. (7") *(R 5287)* **I'M ALIVE. / YOU KNOW HE DID** [1] [-]

Aug 65. (7") *(R 5322)* <66134> **LOOK THROUGH ANY WINDOW. / SO LONELY** [4] [32] Nov65

Sep 65. (lp) *(PMC 1261)* <12312> **THE HOLLIES** [8] [ ] Jun66
– Put yourself in my place / When I come home to you / That's my desire / Mickey's monkey / Very last day / Down the line / Lawdy Miss Clawdy / You must believe me / Too many people / Fortune teller / I've been wrong. *(re-iss.Nov69 as 'REFLECTION' on 'Regal Starline'; SRS 5008) (re-iss.Jul88 on 'Beat Goes On'; BGOLP 25) (cd-iss.Apr91; BGOCD 25)*

Dec 65. (7") *(R 5392)* **IF I NEEDED SOMEONE. / I'VE GOT A WAY OF MY OWN** [20] [-]

Jan 66. (lp) <12299> **HEAR! HERE!** [-] [ ]
– I'm alive / Very last day / You must believe me / Put yourself in my place / Down the line / That's my desire / Look through any window / Lawdy Miss Clawdy / When I come home to you / Lonely / I've been wrong / Too many people.

Feb 66. (7") *(R 5409)* <66158> **I CAN'T LET GO. / I'VE GOT A WAY OF MY OWN** [2] [42] Mar66

Jun 66. (lp; mono/stereo) *(PMC/PCS 7008)* <12330> **WOULD YOU BELIEVE?** <US-title 'BUS STOP'> [16] [75] Oct66
– Stewball / Take your time / Don't you even care / Oriental sadness / I take what I want / Hard hard year / Fifi the flea / That's how strong my love is / I am a rock / Sweet little sixteen. *(re-iss.Oct88 on 'Beat Goes On'; BGOLP 24) (cd-iss.Apr91; BGOCD 24)*

— **BERNIE CALVERT** (b.16 Sep'43, Burnley) – bass repl. HAYDOCK who formed HAYDOCK'S ROADHOUSE **JOHN PAUL JONES** – bass sessioned on the next b-side. (Later to LED ZEPPELIN)

Jun 66. (7") *(R 5469)* <66186> **BUS STOP. / DON'T RUN AND HIDE** [5] [5] Jul66

— in Aug'66, they teamed up with actor/comedian PETER SELLERS on single 'AFTER THE FOX', from the film on 'United Artists'

Oct 66. (7") *(R 5508)* <66214> **STOP! STOP! STOP!. / IT'S YOU** [2] [7]

Oct 66. (lp; mono/stereo) *(PMC/PCS 7011)* <12339> **FOR CERTAIN BECAUSE** <US-title 'STOP! STOP! STOP!'> [23] [91] Feb67

– Don't even think about changing / Peculiar situation / Tell me to my face / Suspicious look in your eyes / Pay you back with interest / Clown / It's you / Crusader / What's wrong with the way I live / What went wrong / High classed. *(re-iss.Dec71 as 'STOP! STOP! STOP!' on 'Regal Starline'; SRS 5088) (re-iss.Apr88 on 'Beat Goes On' lp/c; BGO MC/CD 9) (cd-iss.Dec89; BGOCD 9)*

Feb 67. (7") *(R 5562)* <66231> **ON A CAROUSEL. / ALL THE WORLD IS LOVE** [4] [11] Mar67

May 67. (7") <66240> **PAY YOU BACK WITH INTEREST. / WHAT'CHA GONNA DO ABOUT IT** [-] [28]

— Between 22nd Feb'67 and 16th Jan'68 used session drummer **DOUGIE WRIGHT** to repl. ELLIOT who had taken ill, also **CLEM CATTINI** guested

Parlophone Epic

May 67. (7") *(R 5602)* <10180> **CARRIE-ANNE. / SIGNS THAT WILL NEVER CHANGE** [3] [9] Jun67

Jun 67. (lp; mono/stereo) *(PMC/PCS 7022)* <26315> **EVOLUTION** [13] [43] Jul67

– When your light's turned on / Have you ever loved somebody / Lullaby to Tim / The games we play / Leave me / Rain on the window / Then the heartaches begin / Ye olde coffee shoppe / You need love / Stop right there / Water on the brain / Heading for a fall. *(re-iss.Feb72 as 'HOLLIES' on 'Music For Pleasure'; MFP 5252) (re-iss.1989 on 'Beat Goes On'; BGOLP 80) (cd-iss.Jun93; BGOCD 80)*

Sep 67. (7") *(R 5637)* **KING MIDAS IN REVERSE. / EVERYTHING IS SUNSHINE** [18] [-]

Sep 67. (7") <10234> **KING MIDAS IN REVERSE. / WATER ON THE BRAIN** [-] [51]

Oct 67. (lp; mono/stereo) *(PMC/PCS 7039)* **BUTTERFLY** [ ] [-]

– Try it / Wish you a wish / Step inside / Pegasus the flying horse / Dear Eloise / Away away away / Elevated observations / Would you believe / Butterfly / Maker / Charlie and Fred. *(re-iss.1989 on 'Beat Goes On' lp/cd; BGO LP/CD 79)*

Nov 67. (7") <10251> **DEAR ELOISE. / WHEN YOUR LIGHTS TURNED ON** [-] [50]

Mar 68. (7") *(R 5680)* **JENNIFER ECCLES. / OPEN UP YOUR EYES** [11] [-]

Mar 68. (7") <10298> **JENNIFER ECCLES. / TRY IT** [-] [40]

Jun 68. (7") <10361> **DO THE BEST YOU CAN. / ELEVATED OBSERVATIONS** [-] [93]

Sep 68. (7") *(R 5733)* **LISTEN TO ME. / DO THE BEST YOU CAN** [11] [-]

Sep 68. (7") <10400> **LISTEN TO ME. / EVERYTHING IS SUNSHINE** [-] [ ]

— **TERRY SYLVESTER** (b. 8 Jan'45, Liverpool, England) – vocals, guitar (ex-SWINGING BLUE JEANS) repl. NASH who joined CROSBY, STILLS & NASH. (**ELLIOT** also returned)

— without NASH, the band seemed to lose the slight quasi-psychedelic sparkle they had achieved in the recent recordings. See GREAT ROCK DISCOGRAPHY for further details of the 70's, 80's & compilations.

HOLY MODAL ROUNDERS

Formed: Greenwich Village, New York, USA . . .1963 by STAMPFEL and WEBER who, after a few lp's for 'Prestige', joined The FUGS. In 1967, they resumed their partnership for the album, 'INDIAN WAR WHOOP', an avant-garde hybrid of country blues and folk music. The record featured playwright/actor and drummer SAM SHEPARD, who subsequently played with his duo, The MORAY EELS, on the collaborative project, 'THE MORAY EELS EAT THE HOLY MODAL ROUNDERS'. It contained the unique 'BIRD SONG', later featured on the 1970 soundtrack from cult biker film, 'EASY RIDER'.

Recommended: HOLY MODAL ROUNDERS (*6) / HOLY MODAL ROUNDERS 2 (*5)

PETER STAMPFEL (b.29 Oct'38, Wauwautosa, Wisconsin, USA) – vocals, banjo, violin / **STEVE WEBER** (b.22 Jun'44, Philadelphia, USA) – guitar, vocals

not issued Prestige

1964. (lp) <PRST 7720> **HOLY MODAL ROUNDERS** [-] [ ]

– Blues in the bottle / Give the fiddler a drum / The cuckoo / Euphoria / Long John / Hesitation blues / Hey hey baby / Reuben's train / Mister Spaceman / Moving day / Better things for you / Same old man / Hop high ladies / Bound to lose. *(UK-iss.1970 on 'Transatlantic'; TRA 7451) (UK re-iss.May88 on 'Big Beat'; WIK 75)*

1965. (lp) <PRST 7410> **HOLY MODAL ROUNDERS 2** [-] [ ]

– Flop eared mole / Black eyed Susie / Sail away ladies / Clinch mountain backstep / Fishing blues / Statesboro blues / Junko partner / Mole in the ground / Hot corn cold corn / Down the Old Plank Road / Chevrolet 6 / Crowley waltz / Bully of the town. *(UK-iss.1970 on 'Transatlantic'; TRA) (UK re-iss.Oct88 on 'Big Beat'; WIK 79)*

— added **SAM SHEPARD** – drums / + **LEE CRABTREE** – keyboards

Fontana E.S.P.

1967. (lp) *(STL 5517)* <ESPS 1068> **INDIAN WAR WHOOP** [ ] [ ]

– Indian war whoop / Sweet apple cider soldier's boy / Cocaine blues / Sky divers / Radar blues / The J.W.W. song / Football blues / Bay rum blues / Morning glory. *(re-iss.Apr97 on 'Get Back'; GET 1009)*

— **RICHARD TYLER** – piano / **JOHN WESLEY ANNIS** – bass, repl. CRABTREE

Elektra Elektra

1968. (lp) *(EKL 4026)* <EKS 74026> **MORAY EELS EAT THE HOLY MODAL ROUNDERS** [ ] [ ]

– Birdsong / One will do for now / Take-off artist song / Werewolf / Interlude / Dame Fortune / Mobile line / Duji song / My mind capsized / S.T.P. song / Interlude 2 / Half a mind / Pledge.

— **MICHAEL McCARTY** – drums / **ROBIN REMAILLY** – guitar, mandolin, fiddle, vocals, repl. SHEPARD (who became successful actor and writer) + TYLER

not issued Metromedia

1971. (lp) <740> **GOOD TASTE IS TIMELESS** [-] [ ]

1971. (7") <223> **BOOBS A LOT. / LOVE IS THE CLOSEST THING** [-] [ ]

1974. (7") <0201> **BOOBS A LT. / BLACK BOTTOM** [-] [ ]

not issued Fantasy

1972. (d-lp) <24711> **STAMPFEL & WEBER** (compilation) [-] [ ]

— Re-formed in mid'70's. **LUKE FAUST** repl. McCARTY + ANNIS

not issued Rounder

1975. (lp) <ROUNDER 3004> **ALLEGED IN THEIR OWN TIME** [-] [ ]

– Low down dog / Don't seem right / New Reuben's train / Voodoo Queen Marie / Chittlin' cookin' time in Cheatham County / Nova / Sally in the alley / She's more to be pitied / Rocky road / Across the alley from the Alamo / Synergy / Red rocking chair / Random canyon / Monday morning / Shoot that turkey buzzard. <re-iss.1988>

not issued Adelphi

1978. (lp) <AD 1030> **LAST ROUND** [-] [ ]

(imp.into UK May81)

STAMPFEL & WEBER

not issued Rounder

1982. (lp) <3051> **GOIN' NOWHERE FAST** [-] [ ]

(imp.into UK Aug88)

PETER STAMPFEL AND THE BOTTLECAPS

Rounder Rounder

May 87. (lp/c) *(REU 1016)* <ROUNDER 9003/+C> **PETER STAMPFEL & THE BOTTLECAPS** [ ] [ ] 1988

– Drink American / Surfer angel / Random violence / Lonely junkie / Screaming industrial breakdown / Everything must go / Oh what a night for love / Impossible groove / Funny the first time / Trials, troubles, tribulations / Paraphernalia / Press on.

HOME

Formed: Britain . . .early 70's by MICK COOK, LAURIE WISEFIELD, MICK STUBBS, CLIFF WILLIAMS, WILL WEIDER and CLIVE JOHN. After signing to 'C.B.S.', they released 'PAUSE FOR A HOARSE HORSE' in 1971, a set that made little impact although it posessed a charming, melodic West Coast sound. Their eponymous second set (which hit UK Top 50), showed a little more variation, LAURIE WISEFIELD's fluent guitar style giving the album more of a bite. Their third album, the concept, 'THE ALCHEMIST', was a completely different affair, progressive rock with emotive lyrics. However, this was their final outing, WISEFIELD going on to WISHBONE ASH.

Recommended: PAUSE FOR A HOARSE HORSE (*5) / HOME (*6) / THE ALCHEMIST (*7)

MICK STUBBS – vocals, guitar, keyboards / **LAURIE WISEFIELD** – guitar, vocals, steel guitar / **CLIFF WILLIAMS** – bass, vocals / **MICK COOK** – drums, percussion / **CLIVE JOHN** – keyboards / **WILL WEIDER** – violin

C.B.S. Epic

Dec 71. (lp) *(CBS 64356)* <31146> **PAUSE FOR A HOARSE HORSE** [ ] [ ]

– Tramp / Family /Pause for a hoarse horse / Red E. Lewis and the red caps / In my time / How would it feel / Bad days / Mother / Moses / Welwyn Garden City blues / You're no good.

— now without CLIVE and WILL

Feb 72. (7") *(CBS 7809)* **FANCY LADY, HOLLYWOOD CHILD. / SHADY LADY** [ ] [ ]

Nov 72. (lp) *(CBS 64752)* **HOME** [41] [ ]

– Dreamer / Knave / Fancy lady, Hollywood child / Rise up / Dear Lord / Baby friend of mine / Western front / Lady of the birds. *(cd-iss.Jul96 on 'Columbia'; 484440-2)*

1973. (lp) *(CBS 65550)* **THE ALCHEMIST** [ ] [ ]

– School days / The old man dying / Time passes by / The old man calling (save the people) / The disaster / The sun's revenge / A secret to keep / The brass band played / Rejoicing / The disaster returns (devastation) / The death of the alchemist. *(cd-iss.Aug95 on 'Columbia'; 480971-2)*

— Split soon after recording shelved lp (untitled; test pressings worth over £150 mint). WISEFIELD joined WISHBONE ASH, while COOK joined The GROUNDHOGS. WILLIAMS joined BANDIT in 1977 alongside Scotsman JIM DIAMOND. However after an eponymous album for 'Arista', he quit and joined AC/DC.

HONEYBUS

Formed: London, England . . .Spring 1967 by PETE DELLO and manager TERRY NOON. Previously, they had played together in The YUM YUM BAND and had also backed singer STEVE DARBYSHIRE. DELLO recruited writing partner RAY CANE, who had previously penned for The APPLEJACKS ('Boom Boom Boom Boom – Everybody Fall Down' & 'Baby Jane'). They were quickly snapped up by Decca subsidiary, 'Deram', who issued their debut 45, 'DELIGHTED TO SEE YOU'. This was a directionless piece of pop/rock, which, like the bulk of their output, touched on R&B, psychedelia, folk and even tempered jazz. After another flop, they scored in 1968 with a Top 10 UK hit, 'I CAN'T LET MAGGIE GO'. Unfortunately, in the summer of that year, the band lost their main contributor and producer, DELLO, subsequently floundering without him. • **Songwriters:** DELLO (until his departure after hit) or CANE. The group wrote more together as the 60's faded. • **Trivia:** Their only hit was used for a famous 'Nimble' bread TV advert.

Recommended: AT THEIR BEST (*5)

PETE DELLO (b. PETER BLUMSON) – vocals, guitar, keyboards / **RAY CANE** (b.RAYMOND BYART) – guitar, bass, keyboards / **COLIN HARE** – vocals, guitar, bass / **PETER KIRCHER** – drums (ex-LOVING KIND with Noel Redding)

Deram Deram

Jun 67. (7") *(DM 131)* **DELIGHTED TO SEE YOU. / THE BREAKING UP SCENE** [ ] [-]

Oct 67. (7") *(DM 152)* **DO I FIGURE IN YOUR LIFE. / THROW MY LOVE AWAY** [ ] [-]

Mar 68. (7") *(DM 182)* **I CAN'T LET MAGGIE GO. / TENDER ARE THE ASHES** [8] [-]
(re-iss.Mar82 on 'Decca'; F 13915)

Apr 68. (7") <7520> **I CAN'T LET MAGGIE GO. / (DO I FIGURE) IN YOUR LIFE** [-] [ ]

— now without DELLO who later went solo. He was replaced by **JIM KELLY** – guitar

Sep 68. (7") *(DM 207)* <7522> **GIRL OF INDEPENDENT MEANS. / HOW LONG** [ ] [ ]

May 69. (7") *(DM 254)* **SHE SOLD BLACKPOOL ROCK. / WOULD YOU BELIEVE** [ ] [-]

— Group had already split in the Summer of '69, but had recorded below.

Mar 70. (lp) *(SML 1056)* **STORY** [ ] [ ]
– Story / Black mourning band / Scarlet lady / Fresher than the sweetness in water / He was Colombus / Ceilings Nos.1 / Under the silent tree / She's out there / She said yes / I remember Caroline / How long / Ceilings Nos.2.

Mar 70. (7") *(DM 289)* **STORY. / THE NIGHT TO CHOOSE** [ ] [-]

COLIN HARE

Penny Farthing not issued

Oct 71. (lp) *(PELS 516)* **MARCH HARE** [ ] [-]
– Get up the road / Bloodshot eyes / For where have you been / Find me / Underground girl / To my maker / Alice / Nothing to write home about / New day / Cowboy Joe (saga) / Just like me / Charlie Brown's time. *(re-iss.Sep89 on 'See For Miles'+=; SEE/+CD 261)*– Grannie, grannie / Fighting for peace.

PETE DELLO

Page One not issued

Feb 69. (7") *(POF 135)* **I'M A GAMBLER. / GO AWAY** [ ] [-]

— (above was credited to LACE, while below was to MAGIC VALLEY)

Penny Farthing not issued

Aug 69. (7") *(PEN 701)* **TAKING THE HEART OUT OF LOVE. / UPTIGHT BASIL** [ ] [-]

— For same label 'Penny Farthing', DELLO augmented JOHN KILLIGREW on 1971 self-titled lp *(PELS 513)*.

— Next with all of HONEYBUS

Nepthena not issued

Aug 71. (lp; by PETER DELLO & FRIENDS) *(6437 001)* **INTO YOUR EARS** [ ] [-]
– It's what you've got / There's nothing that I can do for you / I'm a gambler / Harry the earwig / Do I still figure in your life / Uptight Basil / Hear me only / Taking the heart out of love / On a time said Sylvie / A good song / It's the way / Arise Sir Henry / Madame chairman of the committee. *(re-iss.Dec89 on 'See For Miles' lp/cd; SEE/+CD 257)*– I'm a gambler (LACE) / Go away (LACE) / Taking the heart out of love (MAGIC VALLEY) / Uptight Basil (MAGIC VALLEY).

HONEYBUS

— re-formed late 1971 with originals **DELLO, CANE, HARE + KIRCHER**

Bell not issued

Jan 72. (7") *(BLL 1205)* **SHE IS THE FEMALE TO MY SOUL. / FOR WHERE HAVE YOU BEEN** [ ] [-]

Warners not issued

Mar 73. (7") *(K 16250)* **FOR YOU BABY. / LITTLE LOVELY ONE** [ ] [-]

Apr 73. (lp; w/drawn) *(K 46248)* **RECITAL** [-] [-]
– Be thou my side / Julie in my heart / Big ship / Cross-channel ferry / Lady's not for burning / She's a lady / Little lovely one / Lute girl / Writing's on the wall / Baroque'n'roll / Lovely Vanessa / I can't say it but I can sing it.

— When they split again, KIRCHER became a member of SHANGHAI, before moving to The ORIGINAL MIRRORS in 1976 (a support band for STATUS QUO, whom he joined in 1983 but left 3 years later)

— **DELLO** re-united group in 1976 for re-recording & new song

Decca not issued

Apr 76. (7") *(F 13631)* **I CAN'T LET MAGGIE GO. / JULIE IN MY HEART** [ ] [-]

– compilations, etc. –

Oct 83. (7") *Old Gold; (OG 9347)* **I CAN'T LET MAGGIE GO. / Jesamine (by the Casuals)** [ ] [-]

Aug 89. (lp/cd) *See For Miles; (SEE/+CD 264)* **AT THEIR BEST** [ ] [-]
– Story / Fresher than the sweetness in water / Ceilings Nos.1 / She said yes / I can't let Maggie go / The right to choose / Delighted to see you / Tender are the ashes / She sold Blackpool rock (French version) / Black mourning band / He was Columbus / Under the silent tree / I remember Caroline / Julie in my heart / Do I figure in your life? / Would you believe? / How long? *(cd re-iss.Jun97; same)*

Oct 93. (cd) *Disky; (PACD 7014)* **OLD MASTERS, HIDDEN TREASURES** [ ] [-]

HOOK (see under ⇒ LEAVES)

HOT TUNA

Formed: San Francisco, California, USA . . . 1969 by JORMA KAUKONEN and JACK CASADY as an off-shoot to their JEFFERSON AIRPLANE. They originally called themselves HOT SHIT (in reference to dope, rather than excrement), but thought better when record company 'RCA' decided to issue an eponymous album in 1970. By this time, they had added mouth-harpist WILL SCARLET, drummer JOEY COVINGTON and guitarist PAUL ZIEGLER. The album subsequently scraped into the US Top 30, a pared-down set of acoustic country-folk. It marked a complete departure from the elaborate psychedelia of JEFFERSON AIRPLANE, although the band were augmented by many other JEFFERSON renegades throughout an eight year campaign. On subsequent releases HOT TUNA turned up their amps, although they were constantly dogged by critiscism of KAUKONEN's laissez faire attitude. Though hardly groundbreaking, the bulk of the band's output consisted of listenable roots rock. • **Songwriters:** KAUKONEN and CASADY except a few covers. • **Trivia:** CASADY produced KAUKONEN's first solo outing in 1974 'QUAH'.

Recommended: TRIMMED AND BURNING (*6)

JORMA KAUKONEN (b.23 Dec'40, Washington, D.C.) – vocals, lead guitar / **JACK CASADY** (b.13 Apr'44, Washington) – bass (both of JEFFERSON AIRPLANE) / **WILL SCARLETT** – mouth harp with **JOEY COVINGTON** – drums (new of JEFFERSON AIRPLANE) / **PAUL ZIEGLER** – guitar

R.C.A. R.C.A.

Aug 70. (lp) *(SF 8125)* <LSP 4353> **HOT TUNA** [ ] [30] Jul70
– Hesitation blues / How long blues / Uncle Sam blues / Don't you leave me here / Death don't have no mercy / Know you rider / Search my heart / Winin' boy blues / New song (for the morning) / Mann's fate. *(cd-iss.Jul91 on 'Edsel'; EDCD 331)*

— **PAPA JOHN CREACH** (b.28 May 1917, Beaver Falls, Pennsylvania) – violin (new of JEFFERSON AIRPLANE) repl. ZIEGLER / **SAMMY PIAZZA** – drums repl. COVINGTON who also left JEFFERSON AIRPLANE (Apr72) and joined BLACK KANGAROO and later his own FAT FANDANGO.

SEp 71. (7") <0528> **CANDY MAN. / BEEN SO LONG** [-] [ ]

Oct 71. (lp) <(LSP 4550)> **FIRST PULL UP, THEN PULL DOWN (live)** [-] [ ] Jun71
– John's other / Candy man / Been so long / Want you to know / Keep your lamps trimmed and burning / Never happen no more / Come back baby.

— **RICHARD TALBOTT** – guitar, vocals repl. WILL

Grunt Grunt

Apr 72. (lp) *(FTR 1004)* <0921> **BURGERS** [ ] [68] Mar72
– True religion / Highway song / 99 blues / Sea child / Keep on truckin' / Water song / Ode for Billy Dean / Let us get together right down here / Sunny day strut. *(re-iss.Jul84 on 'R.C.A.'; NL 37729)*

Apr 72. (7") *(65-0502)* **KEEP ON TRUCKIN'. / WATER SONG** [ ] [ ]

— **KAUKONEN** and **CASADY** had now (Aug72) departed from JEFFERSON AIRPLANE. The HOT TUNA trio was completed by **SAMMY PIAZZA** – drums. (PAPA went solo)

Feb 74. (lp) <(BFL 1-0348)> **THE PHOSPHORESCENT RAT** [ ] [ ]
– I see the light / Letter to the North Star / Easy now / Corners without exits / Day to day out the window blues / In the kingdom / Living just for you / Seaweed strut / Solilquy for 2 / Sally, where'd you get your liquor from.

— **BOB STEELER** – drums repl. SAMMY

Jul 75. (lp) *(FTR 2003)* <BFL 1-0348> **AMERICA'S CHOICE** [ ] [75] May75
– Sleep song / Funky £7 / Invitation / Walkin' blues / Hit single £1 / Serpent of dreams / I don't wanna go / Great divide: revisited.

— added **JOHN SHERMAN** – guitar / also **NICK BUCK** – keyboards, synths

Aug 75. (7") <10443> **HOT JELLYROLL BLUES. / SURPHASE TEN SION** [-] [ ]

Oct 75. (lp) <BFL 1-1238> **YELLOW FEVER** [-] [97]
– Baby what you want me to do / Hot jelly roll blues / Free rein / Sunrise dance with the Devil / Song for the fire maiden / Bar room crystal ball / Half-time saturation / Surphase tension.

Sep 76. (7") *(RCG 1002)* <10776> **IT'S SO EASY. / I CAN'T BE SATISFIED** [ ] [ ]

Nov 76. (lp) *(FTR 2006)* <BFL 1-1920> **HOPPKORV** [ ] [ ]
– Santa Claus retreat / Watch the north wind rise / It's so easy / Bowlegged woman, knock kneed man / Drivin' around / I wish you would / I can't be satisfied / Talking 'bout you / Extrication love song / Song from the stainless cymbal.

Mar 78. (d-lp) *(FLO 2545)* <CYL 2-2545> **DOUBLE DOSE (live)** [ ] [92]
– Winin' boy blues / Keep your lamps trimmed and burning / Embryonic journey / Killing time in the crystal city / I wish you would / Genesis / Extracation love song / Talking 'bout you / Funky £7 / Serpent of dreams / Bowlegged woman, knock kneed man / I see the light / Watch the north wind rise / Sunrise dance with the Devil / I can't be satisfied. *(cd-iss.Dec94 on 'Edsel'; EDCD 397)*

— Broke-up early 1978. CASADY and BUCK formed S.V.T. in 1980 (NO REGRETS lp)

– compilations, etc. –

Feb 80. (lp) *Grunt; (FLI 3357)* <3357> **FINAL VINYL** [ ] [ ]
– Hesitation blues / Candy man / Ja da / Water song / Day to day out the window blues / Easy now / Funky No.7 / Hot jelly roll blues / Song from the stainless cymbal / I wish you would.

Jul 87. (lp) *Relix;* <RRCD 2011> **HISTORIC (live electric)** [-] [ ]
(cd-iss.Jun93;)

Oct 84. <US-pic-lp> *Relix;* **SPLASHDOWN (live acoustic '75)** [-] [ ]

Aug 94. (cd) *Edsel; (EDCD 396)* **TRIMMED AND BURNING** [ ] [-]
– Keep your lamps trimmed and burning / Ben so long / Sunny day strut / Water song / Soliloquy for 2 / Corners without exits / In the kingdom / Hit single 1 / Sleep song / Serpent of dreams / Bar rom crystal bal / I can't be satisfied / Watch the north wind rise / Song from the stainless cymbal / Embryonic journey / Killing time in the crystal city.

Dec 94. (cd) *Relix;* <RBRS 0006> **RELIX BAY ROCK SHOP 6: HOT TUNA SPECIAL No.1** [-] [ ]

Dec 94. (cd) *Relix;* <RBRS 0007) **RELIX BAY ROCK SHOP 7: HOT TUNA SPECIAL No.2** [-] [ ]

JORMA KAUKONEN

with sessioners

R.C.A. / Grunt

Feb 75. (lp) <BFL 1-0209> **QUAH** [-] [ ]
– Genesis / I'll be all right / Song for the North star / I'll let you know before I leave / Flying clouds / Another man done gone / I am the light of this world / Police dog blues / Blue prelude / Sweet Hawaiian sunshine / Hamar promenade.

Jan 80. (lp) *(PL 13446)* *<1-3446>* **JORMA** [ ] [ ] Oct79
– Straight ahead / Roads and roads / Valley of tears / Song for the high mountain / Wolves and lambs / Too long out, too long in / Requiem for an angel / Vampire woman / Da-ga-da-ga.

— (next with backing group VITAL PARTS)

1980. (lp) *<1-3727>* **BARBEQUE KING** [-] [ ]
– Runnin' with fast crowd / Man for all seasons / Starting over again / Milkcow blues boogie / Roads and roads / Love is strange / To hate is to stay young / Rockabilly shuffle / Snout psalm / Barbeque king.

not issued / Relix

Apr 85. (lp) **MAGIC** [-] [ ]
– Walkin' blues / Winnin' boy blues / I'll be alright some day / Embryonic journey / Candyman / Roads and roads / Good shepherd / Man's fate.

Jul 87. (lp) *<RRCD 2012>* **TOO HOT TO HANDLE** [-] [ ]
– Broken highway / Too many years / Radical sleep / Killing time in the crystal city / Ice age / Waking blues / Death don't have no mercy / Too hot to handle.

KBC BAND

(aka **JORMA KAUKONEN, MARTY BALIN, JACK CASADY**)

Arista / Arista

Feb 87. (lp/c/cd) *(208/408/258 021)* *<8440>* **KBC BAND** [ ] [75] Nov86
– Mariel / It's not you, it's not me / Hold me / America / No more heartaches / Wrecking crew / When love comes / Dream motorcycle / Sayonara.

I.R.S. / Arista

Feb 87. (7"/12") *(IRS/+T 4)* **IT'S NOT YOU, IT'S NOT ME. / DREAM MOTORCYCLE** [ ] [-]
Feb 87. (7") **WRECKING CREW. / AMERICA** [-] [ ]
Apr 87. (7") **MARIEL. / HOLD ME** [-] [ ]

— (in 1994, KAUKONEN & TOM CONSTANTEN released 'EMBRYONIC JOURNEY' for 'Relix'; *RRCD 2067)*

HOT TUNA

re-formed **KAUKONEN + CASADY** plus **MICHAEL FALZARANO** – guitar, mandolin, vocals, harmonica

not issued / Relix

1990. (cd) **AIR A DICE FOUND** [-] [ ]
1992. (cd) **LIVE AT SWEETWATER (live)** [-] [ ]
1993. (cd) **LIVE AT SWEETWATER TWO (live)** [-] [ ]

Steve HOWE (see under ⇒ YES)

Linda HOYLE (see under ⇒ AFFINITY)

H.P. LOVECRAFT

Formed: Chicago, Illinois, USA . . .1967 (named after the famous horror writer), by GEORGE EDWARDS and DAVID MICHAELS. They had just left an outfit, The ROVIN' KIND, who had covered 'ANYWAY THAT YOU WANT ME'. The song subsequently became H.P. LOVECRAFT's first single and by this point, three other musicians had been added together with a 9-piece orchestra. It failed to register a chart placing, as did their follow-up, debut album, 'SAILING ON THE WHITE SHIP'. Nevertheless, the band became regulars at Fillmore West and Winterland concerts alongside The GRATEFUL DEAD and JEFFERSON AIRPLANE. In 1968, before their 2nd set, they recruited JEFF BOYAN (from BLACKSTONES) to boost their live performances. They split in '69, however, only EDWARDS and TEGZA resurrecting the name LOVECRAFT, on a 1971 album, 'VALLEY OF THE MOON'. • **Style:** Atmospheric acid-folk-rock outfit with two contrasting songwriters / vocalists; EDWARDS – the folk troubadour / MICHAELS – classically trained with 4-octave range. • **Songwriters:** Covered; ANYWAY THAT YOU WANT ME (Chip Taylor; hit- Troggs) / LET'S GET TOGETHER (Dino Valentine) / I'VE BEEN WRONG BEFORE (Randy Newman) / etc.

Recommended: AT THE MOUNTAINS OF MADNESS (*8)

GEORGE EDWARDS – vocals, guitar / **DAVID MICHAELS** – vocals, keyboards, woodwind / **TONY CAVALLARI** – lead guitar, vocals / **JERRY McGEORGE** – bass, vocals (ex-SHADOWS OF KNIGHT) / **MICHAEL TEGZA** – drums, percussion, vocals

Philips / Philips

Feb 67. (7") *<40464>* **ANYWAY THAT YOU WANT ME. / IT'S ALL OVER FOR YOU** [-] [ ]
Nov 67. (7") *(BF 1620)* *<40491>* **WAYFARING STRANGER. / THE TIME MACHINE** [ ] [ ]
Jan 68. (7") *<40506>* **THE WHITE SHIP. / (part 2)** [-] [ ]
Feb 68. (lp) *(SBL 7830)* *<PHS 600-252>* **SAILING ON THE WHITE SHIP** (UK-title 'H.P. LOVECRAFT') [ ] [ ]
– Wayfaring stranger / Let's get together / I've been wrong before / The drifter / That's the bag I'm in / The white ship / Country boy and Bleaker Street / The time machine / That's how much I love you, baby (more or less) / Gloria Patria. *(re-iss.1972 as 'THIS IS H.P. LOVECRAFT'; 6336 210)*

Feb 68. (7") *(BF 1639)* **THE WHITE SHIP. / I'VE BEEN WRONG BEFORE** [ ] [-]

— **JEFFREY BOYLAN** – bass; repl. McGEORGE

1968. (7") *<40578>* **KEEPER OF THE KEYS. / BLUE JACK OF DIAMONDS** [-] [ ]
1968. (lp) *(SBL 7872)* *<PHS 600-279>* **H.P. LOVECRAFT 2** [ ] [ ]
– Spin spin spin / It's about time / Blue Jack of Diamonds / Electralentando / At the mountains of madness / Mobius trip / High flying bird / Nothing's boy / Keeper of the keys. *(re-iss.Jul72 as 'THIS IS H.P. LOVECRAFT VOL.2'; 6336 213) (cd-iss.Jun97 on 'Britonic'; 10)*

— Folded later in 1968.

LOVECRAFT

GEORGE EDWARDS + MICHAEL TEGZA + JIM DONLINGER – guitar, vocals / **MICHAEL BEEN** – bass, keyboards, vocals / **MARTY GREBB** – guitar, bass, vocals

Reprise / Reprise

Jan 71. (lp) *(K 44117)* *<RS 6419>* **VALLEY OF THE MOON** [ ] [ ]
– We can have it altogether / Brother I wonder / Love has come to me / Will I know when my time comes / Two step tussle / Take me by the hand / Lady come softly / The dawn / Never gonna go back / Dear / Hopefully we'll all remain together.

Feb 71. (7") *<0996>* **WE CAN HAVE IT ALTOGETHER. / WIIL I KNOW WHEN MY TIMES COMES?** [-] [ ]

— **TEGZA** + new recruits **LALOMIE WASHBURN** – vocals, percussion / **FRANK CAPEK + JORGE RODRIGUEZ** – guitar / **MARK JUSTIN** – keyboards, synthesizers / **CRAIG GIGSTAD** – bass / **GEORGE AGOSTO** – percussion

not issued / Mercury

1975. (7") *<73698>* **I FEEL BETTER. / FLIGHT** [-] [ ]
1975. (lp) *<SRMI 1031>* **WE LOVE YOU WHOEVER YOU ARE** [-] [ ]
1975. (7") *<73707>* **AIN'T GETTIN' NONE. / WE LOVE YOU (WHOEVER YOU ARE)** [-] [ ]

— Finally folded after above.

– compilations, others, etc

Oct 88. (d-lp) *Edsel; (DED 256)* **AT THE MOUNTAINS OF MADNESS** [ ] [-]
– (contains debut US single and first 2 lp tracks)

Jan 92. (cd) *Edsel; (EDCD 345)* **LIVE – MAY 11, 1968 (live)** [ ] [-]
– Wayfaring stranger / The drifter / It's about time / The white ship / At the mountains of madness / The bag I'm in / I've never been wrong before / Country boy & Bleeker Street.

HUMAN BEINZ

Formed: Youngstown, Cleveland, Ohio, USA ... 1966 as The HUMAN BEINGZ, by JOHN RICHARD BELLEY, JOE MARKULIN, JOHN PACHUTA and MIKE TATMAN. They were initially a British-invasion influenced cover versions outfit, before signing to the 'Capitol' label. 'NOBODY BUT ME' became a massive hit in early 1968, the song's bar-room, psychedelic pop taking the band into the US top 10. This was also the name of their second album, which breached the lower reaches of the American album charts later the same year. • **Songwriters:** Group except; MY GENERATION (Who) / EVIL HEARTED YOU (Yardbirds) / HEY JOE (trad.) / THE TIMES THEY ARE A-CHANGIN' (Bob Dylan) / GLORIA (Them) / NOBODY BUT ME (Isley Brothers).

Recommended: NOBODY BUT ME (*6)

JOHN RICHARD BELLEY – vocals, lead guitar / **JOE 'TING' MARKULIN** – rhythm guitar / **MEL PACHUTA** – bass / **MIKE TATMAN** – drums

not issued / Elysian

1966. (7"; as HUMAN BEINGZ) *<820F 8687>* **MY GENERATION. / EVIL HEARTED YOU** [-] [ ]
1967. (7"; as HUMAN BEINGZ) *<3376>* **HEY JOE. / SPIDER MAN** [-] [ ]

not issued / Gateway

1967. (7") *<828>* **THE TIMES THEY ARE A-CHANGIN'. / GLORIA** [-] [ ]
1967. (lp) *<GLP 3012>* **HUMAN BEINZ / MAMMALS** [-] [ ]
1967. (7") *<838>* **PIED PIPER. / MY GENERATION** [-] [ ]

Capitol / Capitol

Jan 68. (7") *(CL 15529)* *<5990>* **NOBODY BUT ME. / SUENO** [ ] [8] Nov67
Mar 68. (lp) *<2906)* **NOBODY BUT ME** [-] [65]
– Nobody but me / Black is the color of my true love's hair / Flower grave / Sueno / Turn on your lovelight / Serenade to Sarah / The Shaman / Dance on through / Foxy lady / It's fun to be clean / This lonely town. *(UK cd-iss.Sep91 on 'See For Miles'; SEECD 327)*

Apr 68. (7") *(CL 15542)* *<2119>* **TURN ON YOUR LOVELIGHT. / IT'S FUN TO BE CLEAN** [ ] [80] Mar68
Jun 68. (7") *<2198>* **EVERY TIME WOMAN. / THE FACE** [-] [ ]
Oct 68. (lp) *<ST 2926>* **EVOLUTION** [-] [ ]
– The face / My animal / Every time woman / Close your eyes / If you don't mind Mrs. Applebee / Cement / Two of a kind / April 15th. *(UK-iss.Oct86 on 'Decal'; LIK 5)*

Nov 68. (7") *<2431>* **I'VE GOT TO KEEP ON PUSHING. / THIS LITTLE GIRL OF MINE** [-] [ ]

— Disbanded after above.

HUMAN INSTINCT

Formed: New Zealand . . .mid 60's originally as The FOUR FOURS, by DAVE HARTSTONE, FRANK HAYES, BILL WARD and MAURICE GREER. They left for England in the Autumn of '66, securing a deal with 'Mercury'. The label issued their debut single, 'CAN'T STOP AROUND', later the same year. The single failed to make the charts as did two further releases that year. Their fourth 45, 'A DAY IN MY MIND'S MIND', was an intense piece of psychedelia, while their last single, 'RENAISSANCE FAIR', was a re-working of The BYRDS classic. The group duly returned to their homeland, where they recorded a number of albums. • **Trivia:** All their singles are now worth over £25.

Recommended: the two 'Deram' singles.

DAVE HARTSTONE – / **FRANK HAYES** – / **BILL WARD** – / **MAURICE GREER** – drums

		Mercury	Mercury
Dec 66.	(7") *(MF 951)* **CAN'T STOP AROUND. / I WANT TO BE LOVED BY YOU**	☐	☐
Mar 67.	(7") *(MF 972)* **RICH MAN. / ILLUSIONS**	☐	☐
Jun 67.	(7") *(MF 990)* **GO-GO. / I CAN'T LIVE WITHOUT YOU**	☐	☐
		Deram	Time
Dec 67.	(7") *(DM 167)* **A DAY IN MY MIND'S MIND. / DEATH OF THE SEASIDE**	☐	-
Feb 68.	(7") *(DM 177)* <503> **RENAISSANCE FAIR. / PINK DAWN**	☐	☐

— returned to New Zealand after above. They made three albums there which were compiled below

– compilations, etc. –

1988.	(t-lp) *Little Wing; (LW 4002-3-4)* **1969-1971**	-	- New Z.

- compilations, etc. -

1973. (lp) *Sunset; (SLS 50354)* **ON WITH THE SHOW**
– Skeleton and the roundabout / Going home / Reminds me of you / Imposters of life's magazine / I like my toys / Hurry up John / Come with me / Knocking nails into my house / On with the show / (Don't put your boys in the army) Mrs. Ward / Please no more sad songs / Follow me, follow / Sitting in my tree / Birthday / Days of the broken arrows / End of the road.

Jan 76. (7") *United Artists; (UP 36060)* **THE SKELETON AND THE ROUNDABOUT. / THE MORNING SUNSHINE**

Dec 85. (lp) *See For Miles; (SEE 60)* **LIGHT AT THE END OF THE ROAD**
– End of the road / The morning sunshine / The lady who said she could fly / Happy birthday – The birthday / Girl at the window / Big chief Wooly Bosher / Here we round the lemon tree / My father's son / The skeleton and the roundabout / Come with me / Going home / Mr. Crow and Sir Norman / Please no more sad songs / Follow me, follow / On with the show / Lucky man / Imposters of life's magazine / Days of the broken arrows. *(cd-iss.1990 as 'THE BEST OF THE IDLE RACE FEATURING JEFF LYNNE'; SEECD 60)*

May 96. (d-cd) *Premier; (PRDCD 2)* **BACK TO THE STORY**

— Also in 1993 'Harvest' cd 'THE JEFF LYNNE YEARS 1968/73: MESSAGE FROM THE COUNTRY' was issued & contained seven IDLE RACE tracks; *CDP 92585-2)*

IDLE RACE

Formed: Birmingham, England . . .Spring '66, evolving from MIKE SHERIDAN & The NIGHTRIDERS (who included ROY WOOD). After splitting with the aforementioned outfit, GREG MASTERS, DAVE PRITCHARD, ROGER SPENCER and (the ex-VIKINGS') guitarist JOHNNY MANN formed The NIGHTRIDERS. The latter departed after a few months and was replaced by JEFF LYNNE (yes that one!). After one 45 for 'Polydor', they became The IDLE RACE having signed to 'Liberty' in 1967. Unfortunately several singles later, they had still not breached the charts, resulting in JEFF looking for success elsewhere, first with The MOVE, then E.L.O. Having progressed from quasi-psychedelia to prog-rock, the IDLE RACE version of MUNGO JERRY's 'IN THE SUMMERTIME' subsequently hit No.1 in Argentina! Their follow-up was also a cover; HOTLEGS' 'NEANDERTHAL MAN'. • **Songwriters:** LYNNE wrote bulk of material by 1967 and even produced their eponymous second lp. ROY WOOD wrote 'HERE WE GO ROUND THE LEMON TREE'.

Recommended: THE BEST OF THE IDLE RACE FEATURING JEFF LYNNE (*7)

JEFF LYNNE – vocals, guitar / **DAVE PRITCHARD** – rhythm guitar, vocals / **GREG MASTERS** – bass, vocals / **ROGER SPENCER** – drums, vocals

Polydor — not issued

Nov 66. (7"; by NIGHTRIDERS) *(56116)* **IT'S ONLY THE DOG. / YOUR FRIEND** — -

Liberty — Liberty

Sep 67. (7") <55997> **HERE WE GO ROUND THE LEMON TREE. / MY FATHER'S SON** — -

Oct 67. (7") *(LBF 15026)* **IMPOSTERS OF LIFE'S MAGAZINE. / SITTING IN MY TREE**

Mar 68. (7") *(LBF 15054)* **SKELETON AND THE ROUNDABOUT. / KNOCKING NAILS INTO MY HOUSE**

Jun 68. (7") *(LBF 15101)* **END OF THE ROAD. / THE MORNING SUNSHINE**

Sep 68. (7"w-drawn) *(LBF 15129)* **I LIKE MY TOYS. / THE BIRTHDAY** — - — -

Oct 68. (lp; stereo/mono) *(LBS/LBL 83132)* <LST 7603> **THE BIRTHDAY PARTY**
– Skeleton and the roundabout / Happy birthday – The birthday / I like my toys / Morning sunshine / Follow me, follow / Sitting in my tree / On with the show / Lucky man / (Don't put your boys in the army) Mrs.Ward / Pie in the sky / Lady who said she could fly / End of the road. *(re-iss.1976 on 'Sunset'; SLS 50381) (re-iss.May89 on 'C5'; C5-536)*

May 69. (7") *(LBF 15218)* **DAYS OF BROKEN ARROWS. / WARM RED CARPET**

Jul 69. (7") *(LBF 15242)* **COME WITH ME. / REMINDS ME OF YOU**

Nov 69. (lp) *(LBS 83221)* **IDLE RACE** — -
– Come with me / Days of broken arrows / Worn red carpet / Mr. Crow and Sir Norman / Reminds me of you / Big chief Wooly Bosher / Going home / Please no more sad songs / Hurry up John.

— (Jan70) **DAVE WALKER** – vocals repl. ROY CULLOM who had repl. for 2 months JEFF (who finally joined The MOVE, before forming The ELECTRIC LIGHT ORCHESTRA)

— added **MIKE HOPKINS** – lead guitar (ex-DIPLOMATS)

Jun 70. (7") *(1273)* **IN THE SUMMERTIME. / TOLD YOU TWICE** — - — - Europe

Nov 70. (7") *(1295)* **NEANDERTHAL MAN. / VICTIM OF CIRCUMSTANCE** — - — - Europe

Regal Zonophone — not issued

May 71. (7") *(RZ 3036)* **DANCING FLOWER./ BITTER GREEN** — -

May 71. (lp) *(SLRZ 1017)* **TIME IS** — -
– Dancing flower / Sad o'sad / Clock / I will see you / By the Sun / Alcatraz / And the rain / She sang hymns out of tune / Bitter green / We want it all.

— When they split early '72, mostly all joined the teething STEVE GIBBONS BAND, having earlier backed KING BISCUIT BOY. WALKER joined SAVOY BROWN then CHICKEN SHACK, before being given a free transfer to FLEETWOOD MAC. ROGER became OLLIE SPENCER and worked as a comedian. PRITCHARD went onto WILLY & THE POOR BOYS, and much later HOPKINS joined QUARTZ.

IHRE KINDER

Formed: Nuremberg, Germany . . . mid-60's as JONAH & THE WHALES by drummer JONAS PORST. After a one-off single for the 'VOGUE' label, HENNIG, PORST and MEYER formed IHRE KINDER, recruiting MUCK GROH, KARL MACK and PETER SCHMIDT. The new band eventually secured a deal with 'Philiips' who released their self-titled debut in 1969. A folky, politically aware collection, it pioneered German language rock. 'LEERE HANDE' (1970) was musically more accomplished, the newly recruited ERNST SCHULTZ embellishing the folk based sound with flute and guitar. The progressive influences evident on the album were consolidated on '2375 008' (1970) and this is generally regarded as their creative peak. HENNIG left soon after for a solo career although he guested on 1971's 'WERDOHL'. The group spintered after SCHULTZ pursued a solo career although HENNIG subsequently reformed the group for the lacklustre 'ANFANG OHNE ENDE' (1972). The band finally split in 1973 although various members continued to release albums under differing musical guises.

Recommended: LEERE HANDE (*7) / 2375 004 (*8)

SONNY HENNIG – vocals / **ERNST SCHULTZ** – guitar / **GEORGIE MEYER** – violin / **THOMMY RODER** – bass / **JONAS PORST** – drums

Vogue — not issued

1966. (7"; as JONAH & THE WHALES) *(DVS 14511)* **IT AIN'T ME BABE. /** — - — - German

— **PORST** – producer, manager / **SONNY HENNIG** – vocals, keyboards / **GEORGIE MEYER** – flute, vocals / **now recruited new name & line-up; MUCK GROH** – guitar / **OLDERS FRENZEL** – drums; repl. PETER SCHMIDT / **WALTI SCHNEIDER** – bass, vocals; repl. KARL MACK / added **JUDITH BRIGGER** – vocals

Philips — not issued

Oct 69. (lp) *(844 393)* **IHRE KINDER** — - — - German
– Maedchen / Kinderspiel / Madame / Der clown / Vergissmeinnicht / Schwarzer engel / Was kann ich denn dafaur / Der kleine Koenig / Schwarzer Peter / Wenn liebe das ist / Plastiki und Plastika.

— now without JUDITH + PORST (just manager)

Kuckuck — not issued

Apr 70. (lp) *(2375 001)* **LEERE HANDE** — - — - German
– Hilf mir / Es wird ein Tag Sein / Nimm deine Liese / Pedro der Pfau / Nie vergess ich wie es war / Wuerfelspiel / Ich kann dir nichts geben / Suedafrika apartheit express / Strasse ohne Ziel / Das Paradies muss auf Erden sein / Leere Haende. *(UK-iss.Jan71 as 'EMPTY HANDS' on 'Polydor' + English; 2371 165)*

— **TOMMI ROEDER** – bass, saxophone, vocals; repl. SCHNEIDER

— added **ERNST SCHULTZ** – guitar, flute, vocals

Nov 70. (lp) *(2375 004)* **2375 004** — - — - German
– Komm zu mir / Hexenhammer / Mutter bekommt ein kind / Leben sie wohl / Weisser Schnee, schwarze nacht / Menschen wie sand am meer / Mantel im wind / Strassenkind.

Aug 71. (lp; by SONNY HENNIG) *(2375 008)* **TRANENGAS** — - — - German
– 1000 tips zum uberleben / Schwarze nacht nr.2 / Kranke / Toten um Gottes Willem / Kopfgeldjaeger / Pik as / Wermuthliebe / Mensch, wo bist du geblieben / Tranengas.

— above album with SCHNEIDER, STORCH, FRANK DIEZ, SCHULTZ, ROEDER + ECKHARDT RAHN

Nov 71. (lp) *(2375 013)* **WERDOHL** — - — - German
– Babylon / Rosa rot / Unterwegs – 8 vor 2 / Worte / Komm wir fahr'n aufs land / Werdohl / Die graue Stadt / Kennst du den Mann / Schlaflied.

— **HENNIG, ROEDER** + the returning **SCHNEIDER** brought in new members; **WOLF STUMM** – guitar / **GUNTER STORCH** – drums (MUCK GROH formed AERA in 1972 and completed a solo album 'MUCKEFUCK' in 1979 for 'Erlkonig' *(INT 148.412)* Meanwhile, SCHULTZ released his solo effort 'PARANOIA PICKNICK' early 1972 *(2375 014). It included many members of IHRE KINDER, although they were missing on his 1977 and 1981 folk efforts 'IRGENDSO EIN LIED' (Erlkonig; ERL 2009)* & 'GLUCKLICHE VERLIERER' *(Hor Zu; 203 755)*

1972. (lp) *(2375 0016)* **ANFANG OHNE ENDE** — - — - German
– Fliessbandlied / Ein lied fur Ddich / Fur dich und mich / Auf dem Schachbrett / Albtraum / In Ewigkeit amen / Unny Wersal und seine band / Wer hat angst vorm schwarzen mann / Anfang ohne ende.

— split in 1973, although they did concerts the following year **HENNIG, SCHULTZ, FRENZEL + ULLI GRUN** – guitar / **HEINZ HOFF** – drums. HENNIG + GRUN formed The POWERFUL TRAMPS before they re-formed as MEISTERSINGER & IHRE

KINDER with **ULI GRUEN** – vocals, synthesizer, guitar / **ALFRED SCHMUCKER** – bass, vocals / **AXEL GOLSER** – drums / **ERDMUTHE SINGER** – flute / **RALF ROSCHER + UWE KORN** – vocals / **FRITZ SCHMIDT** – effects

Meistersinger | not issued

1979. (lp; as MEISTERSINGER & IHRE KINDER) *(01004)* **DIE FAHRT ZUM MOND** [-] [-] German
– Die Mondkalb – Affaere / Die fahrt zum mond / Summsemann / Das vollmondgesicht / Mondschein – Symphonie / Mondfrau.

— **HENNIG, SCHULTZ, GROH, ROEDER, SCHNEIDER + FRENZEL**

Ohr Today | not issued

1982. (lp) *(OMM 560001)* **LIVE '82 (live)** [-] [-] German
– Leere haende / Wuerfelsiel / Strasse ohne ziel / Komm zu dir / Hexenhammer / Weiser Schnee, Schwarze nacht / Toter soldat / Schwarzer Peter / Nie vergass ich wie es war.

— **HENNIG + SCHULTZ** employed new members **ALF SCHMUCKER** – bass, vocals / **HELMUT KOERBER** – bass / **AXEL GOLSER** – drums / **HANS GRASSER + KELLI KEILHOFER + HANS PUKKE** – guitars / + others

Virgin | not issued

1984. (lp) *(206 678)* **HEUTE** [-] [-] German
– Kalanderblatt / Die letzte oper / Jetanzt / Meister der angst / Beklava / Tief unter der erde / Beim zahnarzt / Aussteiger – blues / Ganz bestimmt.

— split after above

ILLUSION

Formed: USA ...1968 by Italian-Americans JOHN VINCI, CHUCK ADLER, RICHIE CERNIGLIA, MIKE MANISCALCO and MICHAEL RICCIARDELLA. 'DID YOU SEE HER EYES?' (their debut 45), was re-issued in 1969, hitting the US Top 40. It was a mountainous piece of psychedelia, a hybrid of the heavy sounds around at that time. However, this success was never surpassed, the group only managing to scrape into the US Hot 100 with two more 45's, 'TOGETHER' and 'LET'S MAKE EACH OTHER HAPPY'. • **Note:** Not to be confused with ILLUSION of 1977/78 featuring ex-YARDBIRDS members. An eponymous ILLUSION album + 'OUT OF THE MIST' were issued by this group.

Recommended: ILLUSION (*5)

JOHN VINCI – vocals / **MIKE MANISCALCO** – guitar, keyboards / **RICHIE CERNIGLIA** – guitars / **CHUCK ADLER** – bass / **MIKE RICCIARDELLA** – drums

Dot | Steed

Mar 69. (7") *(DOT 122)* <712> **DID YOU SEE HER EYES? / FALLING IN LOVE** [ ] [ ] Jan69
May 69. (7") <717> **I LOVE YOU, YES I DO. / RUN RUN RUN** [-] [ ]
Jun 69. (7") <718> **DID YOU SEE HER EYES? / FALLING IN LOVE** [-] [32]
Oct 69. (lp) *(S)LPD 531)* <ST 37003> **ILLUSION** [ ] [69] May69
– Did you see her eyes? / Takin' sweet talkin' soul / Just imagine / Medley:- Run run run – Willy Gee (Miss Holy Lady) / I love you, yes I do / Alone / Charlena / Medley:- Why, tell me why – Real thing / You made me what I am.
Nov 69. (7") <721> **HOW DOES IT FEEL? / ONCE IN A LIFETIME** [-] [ ]
Jan 70. (7") *(DOT 133)* <722> **TOGETHER. / DON'T PUSH IT** [ ] [80] Dec69
Apr 70. (lp) *(SLPD 537)* <ST 37005> **TOGETHER (AS A WAY OF LIFE)** [ ] [ ]
– How does it feel / Happy days / Bright eyes / Don't push it / Once in a lifetime / Love me girl / Lila / Angel / Peace pipe / Naked blues / Little boy / Together.

Paramount | Steed

Jul 70. (7") *(PARA 3007)* <726> **LET'S MAKE EACH OTHER HAPPY. / BESIDE YOU** [ ] [98] Jun70
Jan 71. (lp) *(SPFL 264)* <ST 37006> **IF IT'S SO** [ ] [ ]
– Man / Let's make each other happy / When I metch baby / Collection / If it's so / Life cycle theme / Dr. Stone / Excerpt from Recuverdas de Alhambra.
Jan 71. (7") <732> **COLLECTION. / WAIT A MINUTE** [-] [ ]

— disappeared in 1971.

INCREDIBLE STRING BAND

Formed: Glasgow, Scotland ... early 1966 by ROBIN WILLIAMSON, CLIVE PALMER and MIKE HERON. From the early 60's, WILLIAMSON had played London gigs alongside BERT JANSCH (future PENTANGLE), before he returned to Glasgow. In April 1961, he formed a duo with Englishman PALMER, although they found it difficult to establish themselves, that is, until 1965 when PALMER set up the 'Incredible' folk club in Sauchiehall Street. That same year, the pair performed at the Edinburgh Folk Festival, catching the eye of Nathan Joseph of 'Transatlantic' records who recorded them for the concert's Various Artists compilation. After their folk club was shut down by the police, they became a trio, adding MIKE HERON to become The INCREDIBLE STRING BAND. After months tracking them down, American producer JOE BOYD finally found them and duly signed them to 'Elektra'. He subsequently took them to London, where they recorded their eponymous debut album (summer '66). With this well-received record under their belt, PALMER departed for Afghanistan. When he returned he declined to re-join the act, who were now broke but under the management of BOYD. Upon ROBIN's return from Morocco, the duo (augmented by some friends), played an 'Elektra' records package alongside TOM PAXTON and JUDY COLLINS, at The Royal Albert Hall. It helped promote their second album, '5,000 SPIRITS OR THE LAYERS OF THE ONION', which made the UK Top 30 in 1967. Their underground blend of psychedelic folk was crystallised on such charming tracks as, 'CHINESE WHITE', 'FIRST GIRL I LOVED' and 'PAINTING BOX'. In Spring '68, they surprisingly crashed into the UK Top 5 with their third set, 'THE HANGMAN'S BEAUTIFUL DAUGHTER'. The album's witty lyrics (alternately penned by HERON or WILLIAMSON) and ethnic multi-instrumentation was embellished with the vocals of the duo's girlfriends, LICORICE and ROSE. The highlights of this album, arguably the group's finest hour, were 'A VERY CELLULAR SONG', 'THE MINOTAUR'S SONG' and 'KOEEOADDI THERE'. Late that year, they issued 2 single lp's as a double-set, 'WEE TAM' & 'THE BIG HUGE'. However, this brilliant but confused package failed to sell. Over the next two years, they released three UK Top 40 albums ('I LOOKED UP', a collection of baroque eclecticism – 'U' verging on pantomine), but after a move to 'Island' in 1971, they soon faded from the commercial limelight. Nevertheless, the second 'Island' album, 'LIQUID ACROBAT AS REGARDS THE AIR', hit the Top 50, boasting the spine-tingling melancholy of the 11-minute 'DARLING BELLE'. HERON and WILLIAMSON went their separate ways in the mid-70's, the former writing 'DON'T KILL IT CAROL' (later a hit for MANFRED MANN'S EARTH BAND), the latter becoming something of a self-styled cosmic folk story-teller (complete with harp).

Recommended: 5,000 SPIRITS (*7) / THE HANGMAN'S BEAUTIFUL DAUGHTER (*7) / WEE TAM & THE BIG HUGE (*8) / SEASONS THEY CHANGE – THE BEST OF THE INCREDIBLE STRING BAND (*8).

ROBIN WILLIAMSON (b.24 Nov'43, Edinburgh, Scotland) – vocals, guitars, etc. / **CLIVE PALMER** (b. England) – guitar, banjo, vocals / **MIKE HERON** (b.12 Dec'42) – vocals, rhythm guitar, sitar, etc.

Elektra | Elektra

Jun 66. (lp) *(EUK 254)* *<EKS 7322>* **THE INCREDIBLE STRING BAND** [ ] [ ]
– Maybe someday / October song / When the music starts to play / Schaeffer's jig / Womankind / The tree / Whistle tune / Dandelion blues / How happy am I / Empty pocket blues / Smoke shovelling song / Can't keep me here / Good as gone / Footsteps of the heron / Niggertown / Everything's fine right now. *(re-iss.Jul68; EKL 254); hit No.34) (cd-iss.Jul93; 7559 61547-2) (cd re-iss.Jun94 on 'Hannibal'; HNCD 4437)*

— Now a duo when PALMER went to Afghanistan. He later formed FAMOUS JUG BAND added **CHRISTINA 'LICORICE' McKENNA** – some vocals, organ (a guest on below) plus guests **DANNY THOMPSON** – double bass (of PENTANGLE) / **JOHN HOPKINS** – piano

Jul 67. (lp; mono/stereo) *(EUK/+S7 257)* *<EKS 74010>* **THE 5,000 SPIRITS OR THE LAYERS OF THE ONION** [26] [ ]
– Chinese white / No sleep blues / Painting box / The Mad Hatter's song / Little cloud / The eyes of fate / Blues for the muse / The hedgehog's song / First girl I loved / You know that you could be / My name is death / Gently tender / Way back in the 1960's. *(re-iss.1968; EKS 7257) (re-iss.Jan73 + 1976; K 42001) (cd-iss.Mar92; 7559 60913-2) (cd re-iss.Jun94 on 'Hannibal'; HNCD 4438)*
Mar 68. (7") *(EKSN 45028)* **PAINTING BOX. / NO SLEEP BLUES** [ ] [ ]
Mar 68. (lp; mono/stereo) *(EUK/+S7 258)* *<EKS 74021>* **THE HANGMAN'S BEAUTIFUL DAUGHTER** [5] [ ] Jun68
– Koeeoaddi there / The minotaur's song / Witches hat / A very cellular song / Mercy I cry city / Waltz of the new Moon / The water song / Three is a green crown / Swift as the wind / Nightfall. *(re-iss.Jan73 + 1976; K 42002) (cd-iss.Mar92; 7559 60835-2) (cd re-iss.Jun94 on 'Hannibal'; HNCD 4437)*

— **MIKE, ROBIN** and his girlfriend **LICORICE** introduced MIKE'S girlfriend **ROSE SIMPSON** – some vocals, bass, percussion, violin

Oct 68. (d-lp; mono/stereo) *(EKL/EKS7 4036-7)* **WEE TAM / THE BIG HUGE** [ ] [-]
(d-cd-iss.Nov94 on 'Hannibal'; HNCD 4802)
Oct 68. (lp; mono/stereo) *(EKL/<EKS7 4036>)* **WEE TAM** [ ] [ ] Mar69
– Job's tears / Puppies / Beyond the see / The yellow snake / Log cabin home in the sky / You get brighter / The half-remarkable question / Air / Ducks on a pond. *(re-iss.Jan73 + 1976; K 42021) (cd-iss.Feb92; 7559 60914-2)*
Oct 68. (lp; mono/stereo) *(EKL/<EKS7 4037>)* **THE BIG HUGE** [ ] [ ] Mar69
– Maya / Greatest friend / The son of Noah's brother / Lordly nightshade / The mountain of God / Cousin caterpillar / The iron stone / Douglas Traherne Harding / The circle is unbroken. *(re-iss.Jan73 + 1976; K 42022) (cd-iss.Jul93; 7559 61548-2)*

— LICORICE was now a full-time member

Oct 69. (7") *(EKSN 45074)* **BIG TED. / ALL WRIT DOWN** [ ] [-]
Nov 69. (lp) *(<EKS 74057>)* **CHANGING HORSES** [30] [ ]
– Big Ted / White bird / Dust be diamonds / Sleepers, awake! / Mr. & Mrs. / Creation. *(cd-iss.Jul93; 7559 61549-2) (cd-iss.Dec94 on 'Hannibal'; HNCD 4439)*

— added guest **DAVE MATTACKS** – drums of FAIRPORT CONVENTION

Apr 70. (lp) *(<EKS 7401>)* **I LOOKED UP** [30] [ ] Jul70
– Black Jack Davy / The letter / Pictures in a mirror / This moment / When you find out who you are / Fair as you. *(re-prom.1970; 2469 002) (cd-iss.Dec94 on 'Hannibal'; HNCD 4440)*
Apr 70. (7") *(2101 003)* **THIS MOMENT. / BLACK JACK DAVY** [ ] [-]
May 70. (7") *<45696>* **THIS MOMENT. / BIG TED** [-] [ ]

— augmented by **JANET SHANKMAN** – b.vocals (ROBIN married her Dec70) **PETE GRANT** – banjo / **GREG HART** – sitar (of STONE MONKEY) plus guest **MALCOLM LE MAISTRE** – keyboards, bass (of EXPLODING GALAXY)

Oct 70. (d-lp) *(2665 001)* *<7E 2002>* **"U"** [34] [ ] Jan71
– El wool suite / The juggler's song / Time / Bad Sadie Lee / Queen of love / Partial belated overture / Light in the time of darkness – Glad to see you / Walking along with you / Hirem pawn Itof – Fairies' hornpipe / Bridge theme / Bridge song / Astral plane theme / Invocation / Robot blues / Puppet song / Cutting the strings / I know you / Rainbow. *(re-iss.Jan73; K 62002)*

— Back to basic duo of **ROBIN + MIKE** plus **LICORICE + ROSE**

Island | Elektra

Apr 71. (lp) *(ILPS 9140)* **BE GLAD FOR THE SONG HAS NO ENDING** [ ] [-]
– Come with me / All writ down / Vishangro / See all the people / Waiting for you / (Be glad for) The song has no ending.

— **MALCOLM LE MAISTRE** – keyboards, bass, vocals returned to repl. ROSE

Oct 71. (lp) *(ILPS 9172)* *<74112>* **LIQUID ACROBAT AS REGARDS THE AIR** [46] [ ] Feb72
– Talking of the end / Dear old battlefield / Cosmic boy / Worlds they rise and fall / Evloution rag / Painted chariot / Adam and Eve / Red hair / Here till here is there / Tree / Jigs: Eyes like leaves – Sunday is my wedding day – Drops of whiskey – Grumbling old men / Darling Belle. *(re-iss.Aug91 cd)(c; IMCD 130)(ICM 9172)*

— added **GERARD DOTT** – clarinet, saxophone (he played on HERON's 1972 solo album) and guest on one **STUART GORDON** – viola

Oct 72. (lp) *(ILPS 9211)* **EARTH SPAN** [ ] [-]
– My father was a lighthouse keeper / Antoine / Restless night / Sunday song / Black Jack David / Banks of sweet Italy / The actor / Moon hang low / The sailor and the dancer / Seagull. *(cd-iss.Dec92 on 'Edsel'; EDCD 360)*

Nov 72. (7") *(WIP 6145)* **BLACK JACK DAVID. / MOON HANG LOW** [ ] [-]

— **STAN LEE** – bass repl. LICORICE who joined WOODY WOODMANSEY Band **JACK INGRAM** – drums (added to ROBIN, MIKE, MALCOLM, GERARD and STAN)

Island Reprise

Feb 73. (7") *(WIP 6158)* **AT THE LIGHTHOUSE DANCE. / JIGS** [ ] [-]
Feb 73. (lp) *(ILPS 9229) <2139>* **NO RUINOUS FEUD** [ ] [ ]
– Explorer / Down before Cathy / Saturday maybe / Jigs / Old Bouccaneer / At the lighthouse dance / Second fiddle / Circus girl / Turquoise blue / My blue tears / Weather the storm / Little girl. *(cd-iss.Nov92 on 'Edsel'; EDCD 367)*

— **GRAHAM FORBES** – electric guitar (ex-POWERHOUSE) repl. GERARD / **JOHN GILSTON** – drums repl. INGRAM

Mar 74. (lp) *(ILPS 9270) <2198>* **HARD ROPE & SILKEN TWINE** [ ] [ ]
– Maker of islands / Cold February / Glancing love / Dreams of no return / Dumb Kate / Ithkos. *(cd-iss.Feb93 on 'Edsel'; EDCD 368)*

— WILLIAMSON + HERON went onto solo careers

– compilations etc. –

Mar 71. (lp) *Elektra; (EKS 74065) / Reprise; <7E 2004>* **RELICS OF THE INCREDIBLE STRING BAND** [ ] [ ]
Nov 76. (d-lp) *Island; (ISLD 9)* **SEASONS THEY CHANGE – BEST OF THE INCREDIBLE STRING BAND** [ ] [-]
– Black Jack David / Blues for the muse / Nightfall / Puppies / Cold days of February / Worlds they rise and fall / Chinese white / Empty pocket blues / When the music starts to play / Saturday maybe / Red hair / The circle is unbroken / First girl I loved / Cosmic boy / Darling Belle / My father was a lighthouse keeper / Queen Juanita and her fisherman lover.
Oct 91. (cd/lp) *Band Of Joy; (BOJ CD/LP 004)* **ON AIR (live)** [ ] [-]
Nov 92. (cd) *Windsong; (WINCD 029)* **BBC RADIO 1 LIVE IN CONCERT** [ ] [-]
Jun 97. (cd) *Blueprint; (PWMD 5003)* **CHELSEA SESSIONS 1967** [ ] [-]

— HERON and WILLIAMSON also released solo albums before their split. HERON = 'SMILING MEN WITH BAD REPUTATIONS' and WILLIAMSON = 'MYRRH'. Plus they went onto solo careers in 1975. (see GREAT ROCK DISCOGRAPHY)

IRON BUTTERFLY

Formed: San Diego, California, USA ... 1966 by DOUG INGLE, RON BUSHY, DANNY WEIS, JERRY PENROD and DARRYL DeLOACH. They soon moved to Los Angeles and after being spotted at the Whiskey A-Go-Go, they signed to Atlantic subsidiary label 'Atco'. Early 1968, they issued the 'HEAVY' album, which bulldozed its way into the lower regions of the US Top 100. In the summer of '68, WEIS and PENROD departed, superseded by LEE DORMAN and ERIK BRAUN. This line-up subsequently recorded the organ-driven, progressive proto-metal of 'IN-A-GADDA-DA-VIDA' (aka 'The Garden of Life'), a classic album which hit the US Top 5, going on to sell over 3 million copies. The edited title track (trimmed from 17-minute lp version) gave them additional success in the singles chart. With the aforementioned album still riding high in the charts, their 1969 'BALL' album bounced into the Top 3. In 1970, they introduced the twin-guitar assault of MIKE PIERA and LARRY REINHARDT, who featured on their Top 20 set, 'METAMORPHOSIS'. They split soon after, only to surface again in 1975 with two poor efforts, 'SCORCHING BEAUTY' and 'SUN AND STEEL'. • **Songwriters:** INGLE and BUSHY were main contributors, until addition then departure of BRAUN and DORMAN. • **Trivia:** In 1968, 2 tracks 'OSSESSION' & 'UNCONSCIOUS POWER' were used on the film soundtrack of 'The Savage Seven'.

Recommended: IN-A-GADDA-DA-VIDA (*8) / LIGHT AND HEAVY – THE BEST OF . . . (*7)

DOUG INGLE (b. 9 Sep'46, Omaha, Nebraska) – keyboards, vocals /**JERRY PENROD** – guitar / **DANNY WEIS** – guitar (both ex-DAVID ACKLES band) / **RON BUSHY** (b.23 Sep'45, Washington, D.C.) – drums, vocals / **DARRYL DeLOACH** – bass, vocals

Atco Atco

Feb 68. (lp) *(2465 015) <33227>* **HEAVY** [ ] [78]
– Possession / Unconscious power / Get out of my life, woman / Gentle as it may seem / You can't win / So-lo / Look for the sun / Fields of sun / Stamped ideas / Iron butterfly theme. *(cd-iss.1992 on 'Repertoire'+=;)*– I can't help but deceive you little girl / To be alone.

Atlantic Atco

Jun 68. (7") *(584 188) <6573>* **POSSESSION. / UNCONSCIOUS POWER** [ ] [ ] May68

— **ERIK BRAUN** (b.11 Aug'50, Boston, Mass.) – lead guitar, vocals repl. WEIS and PENROD who formed RHINOCEROS / **LEE DORMAN** (b.19 Sep'45, St.Louis, Missouri) – bass, multi repl. DeLOACH

Jul 68. (lp; mono/stereo) *(587/588 116) <33250>* **IN-A-GADDA-DA-VIDA** [ ] [4]
– Most anything you want / Flowers and beads / My mirage / Termination / Are you happy / In-a-gadda-da-vida. *(re-iss.Jan73; K 40022) (cd-iss.Jul87 & Jun93; K2 40022) (re-iss.cd deluxe version Nov95 on 'Rhino'; 8122 72196-2)*
Aug 68. (7") *<6606>* **IN-A-GADDA-DA-VIDA (edit). / IRON BUTTERFLY THEME** [-] [30]
Feb 69. (lp) *(228 011) <33280>* **BALL** [ ] [3]
– In the time of our lives / Soul experience / Lonely boy / Real fright / In the crowds / It must be love / Her favourite style / Filled with fear / Belda-beast.
Mar 69. (7") *(584 254) <6647>* **SOUL EXPERIENCE. / IN THE CROWDS** [ ] [75] Feb69
Jul 69. (7") *<6676>* **IN THE TIME OF OUR LIVES. / IT MUST BE LOVE** [-] [96]
Nov 69. (7") *<6712>* **I CAN'T HELP BUT DECEIVE YOU LITTLE GIRL. / TO BE ALONE** [-] [ ]
Apr 70. (lp) *(2400 014) <33318>* **IRON BUTTERFLY LIVE (live)** [ ] [20]
– In the time of our lives / Filled with fear / Soul experience / You can't win / Are you happy / In-a-gadda-da-vida. *(re-iss.1972; K 40086)*
Jul 70. (7") *(2091 024)* **IN-A-GADDA-DA-VIDA (edit). / TERMINATION** [ ] [-]

— **INGLE, BUSHY and DORMAN** recruited new members **MIKE PINERA** (b.29 Sep'48, Tampa, Florida) – guitar, vocals (ex-BLUES IMAGE) repl. BRAUN who later formed FLINTWHISTLE / added **LARRY REINHARDT** (b. 7 Jul'48, Florida) – guitar

Oct 70. (7") *<6782>* **EASY RIDER (LET THE WIND PAY THE WAY). / SOLDIER IN OUR TOWN** [-] [66]
Feb 71. (7") *<6818>* **SILLY SALLY. / STONE BELIEVER** [-] [ ]
Apr 71. (lp) *(2401 003) <33339>* **METAMORPHOSIS** [ ] [16] Aug70
– Free flight / New day / Shady lady / Best years of our lives / Slower than guns / Stone believer / Soldier in our town / Easy rider (let the wind pay the way) / Butterfly bleu. *(cd-iss.Jun92 on 'Repertoire';)*

— Disbanded Spring '71, with DORMAN and REINHARDT forming CAPTAIN BEYOND. PINERA formed RAMATAM before later joining ALICE COOPER (1981-82). Re-formed 1974, as 4-piece with **BUSHY, BRAUN** and newcomers **HOWARD REITZES** (b.22 Mar'51, Southgate, Calif.) – keyboards, vocals / **PHIL KRAMER** (b.12 Jul'52, Youngstown, Ohio) – bass, vocals

M.C.A. M.C.A.

Feb 75. (lp) *(MCF 2694) <465>* **SCORCHING BEAUTY** [ ] [ ]
– 1975 overture / Hard miseree / High on a mountain top / Am I down / People of the world / Searchin' circles / Pearly Gates / Lonely hearts / Before you go. *(cd-iss.Jun95 on 'Repertoire';)*
Feb 75. (7") *<40379>* **SEARCHIN' CIRCLES. / PEARLY GATES** [-] [ ]

— **BILL DeMARTINES** – keyboards repl. REITZES

Dec 75. (lp) *(MCF 2738) <2164>* **SUN AND STEEL** [ ] [ ]
– Sun and steel / Lightnin' / Beyond the Milky Way / Free / Scion / Get it out / I'm right, I'm wrong / Watch the world goin' by / Scorching beauty. *(cd-iss.Mar95 on 'Edsel'; EDCD 408)*
Jan 76. (7") *(MCA 221) <40494>* **BEYOND THE MILKY WAY. / GET IT OUT** [ ] [ ]

— Broke up again in 1976, BUSHY formed JUICY GROOVE.

— In May'89, IRON BUTTERFLY reformed w/**DORMAN, BRAUN, REINHARDT** and new men **STEVE FELDMANN** – vocals / **DEREK HILLARD** – keyboards / **KENNY SUAREZ** – drums

– compilations, others, etc. –

on 'Atlantic' UK & 'Atco' US unless mentioned otherwise

Jan 72. (lp) *(K 40298) <33369>* **EVOLUTION – THE BEST OF IRON BUTTERFLY** [ ] [ ] Dec71
– Iron Butterfly theme / Possession / Unconscious power / Flowers and beads / Termination / In-a-gadda-da-vida / Soul experience / Stone believer / Belda-beast / Easy rider (let the wind pay the way) / Slower than guns.
1973. (lp) *(30038)* **STAR COLLECTION** [ ] [-]
Oct 75. (d-lp) *(K 80003)* **TWO ORIGINALS OF . . .** [ ] [-]
– (BALL / METAMORPHISIS)
Feb 93. (cd) *Rhino; (8122 71166-2)* **LIGHT AND HEAVY: THE BEST OF IRON BUTTERFLY** [ ] [ ]

ISOTOPE

Formed: London, England ... 1973 by veteran 60's session man GARY BOYLE (credits included MILLIE and DUSTY SPRINGFIELD). In 1974, after enlisting JEFF CLYNE, BRIAN MILLER and NIGEL MORRIS, their eponymous debut was released by 'Gull', a laboured progressive jazz-rock effort. Their POLI PALMER (Family)-produced follow-up, 'ILLUSION', introduced new members, notably former SOFT MACHINE bassman HUGH HOPPER. A third and final set, 'DEEP END', was another mixture of MAHAVISHNU (John McLaughlin)-type avant-jazz.

Recommended: THE BEST OF ISOTOPE (*5)

GARY BOYLE (b.24 Nov'41, Patna, India) – guitar (ex-BRIAN AUGER, ex-ECLECTION) / **BRIAN MILLER** (b.28 Apr'47, St.Neots, Huntingdonshire, England) – keyboards / **JEFF CLYNE** (b.29 Jan'47, London) – bass / **NIGEL NORRIS** (b.20 Jun'48, Dalston, London) – drums

Gull not issued

1974. (lp/c) *(GULP/ZCGUL 1002)* **ISOTOPE** [ ] [-]
– Then there were four / Do the business / Oh little fat man / Sunshine park / Bite on this / Upward curve / Retrasing my steps / Windmills and waterfalls / Honkey donkey. *(re-iss.Sep77; same)*

— **HUGH HOPPER** – bass (ex-SOFT MACHINE, ex-Solo artist), repl. CLYNE / **LAURENCE SCOTT** – keyboards, repl. MILLER

Jan 75. (lp/c) *(GULP/ZCGUL 1006)* **ILLUSION** [ ] [-]
– Illusion / Rangoon creeper / Spanish sun / Edorian / Frog / Sliding dogs / Lion sandwich / Golden section / Marin country girl / Lily Kong / Temper tantrum. *(re-iss.Sep77;)*

— added **ZOE KRONBERGER** – vocals, + guests **MORRIS PERT** – percussion / **NEVILLE WHITEHEAD + DAN K. BROWN** – bass / **FRANK ROBERTS** – keyboards

Jun 76. (lp/c) *(GULP/ZCGUL 1017)* **DEEP END** [ ] [-]
– Attila / Deep end / Mr.M's picture / Crunch cake / Fonebone / Black sand / Another side / Pipe dream. *(re-iss.Sep77; same)*

— Folded and HOPPER went solo as did BOYLE

– compilations, etc. –

Jan 78. (lp/c) *Gull; (GULP/ZCGUL 1024)* **THE BEST OF ISOTOPE** [ ] [-]
Sep 95. (cd) *See For Miles; (SEECD 432)* **ISOTOPE / ILLUSION** [ ] [-]

GARY BOYLE

with various session people

Gull | not issued

Jul 77. (lp) *(GULP 1020)* **THE DANCER** [ ] [-]
– Cowshed shuffle / The dancer / Now that we're alone / Lullabye for a sleepy dormouse / Almond burfi / Pendle mist / Apple crumble / Maiden voyage.

Aug 78. (lp) *(GULP 1028)* **ELECTRIC GLIDE** [ ] [-]
– Snap crackle / Electric glide / Gaz / Hayabusa / Grumble / Morning father joys / Brat No.2 / It's almost light again. *(cd-iss.Apr97 on 'Naim Audio'; NAIMCD 002)*

— now with **PAUL BIRCHELL** – keyboards / **GARY CULSHAW** – bass / **GRAHAM DEAN** – drums

Pickup | not issued

1980. (lp) *(80305)* **STEP OUT** [ ] [-]
– Jeanies dance / Numb thumb / Step out / Periscope / Fuchie ce pesta / Thinking of you / Gitte / So many times before.

— GARY went into session work.

IT'S A BEAUTIFUL DAY

Formed: San Francisco, California, USA . . .mid '67, by classically trained violinist DAVID LA FLAMME. They released their eponymous debut on the local 'Sound' label in 1968, before signing to 'Columbia'. The focus of the band was undoubtably songwriter LA FLAMME's custom-built five-string electric violin, which gave the group a highly individual style. When 'Columbia' re-released the album in May '69, it breached both the UK and US charts, the classic single, 'WHITE BIRD', becoming a regular fixture on FM radio. Drawing comparisons with early JEFFERSON AIRPLANE, the band nevertheless posessed a bewitching, atmospheric appeal which ran through tracks like 'BOMBAY CALLING' and 'TIME IS'. The follow-up, 'MARRYING MAIDEN', was almost as good as its predecessor, an eclectic collection of quasi-psychedelic stylings which once again nudged into both Top 50's. This was the beginning of the end though, as subsequent offerings like 'CHOICE QUALITY STUFF' and 'TODAY' paled into insignificance. The band finally split in 1974, as a result of a drawn out managerial dispute.

Recommended: IT'S A BEAUTIFUL DAY (*8)/ MARRYING MAIDEN (*7)

DAVID LA FLAMME (b. 5 Apr'41, Salt Lake City, Utah) – electric violin / **PATTIE SANTOS** (b.16 Nov'49) – vocals / **BILL GREGORY** – guitar / **MITCHELL HOLMAN** (b. Denver, Colorado) – bass / **VAL FUENTES** (b.25 Nov'47, Chicago, Illinois) – drums / plus guest (wife) **LINDA LA FLAMME** – keyboards, co-composer

not issued | San Franciscan Sound

1968. (7") <7> **BULGARIA. / AQUARIAN DREAM** [-] [ ]

C.B.S. | Columbia

May 69. (lp) *(CBS 63722)* <9768> **IT'S A BEAUTIFUL DAY** [58] [47]
– White bird / Hot summer day / Wasted union blues / Girl with no eyes / Bombay calling / Bulgaria / Time is. *(hit UK chart May70) (re-iss.Sep79; CBS 83787)*

Aug 69. (7") *(CBS 4457)* <44928> **WHITE BIRD. / WASTED UNION BLUES** [ ] [ ]

Feb 70. (7") <45152> **SOAPSTONE MOUNTAIN. / GOOD LOVIN'** [-] [ ]

Apr 70. (7") *(CBS 4933)* **SOAPSTONE MOUNTAIN. / DO YOU REMEMBER THE SUN** [ ] [-]

Jul 70. (lp) *(CBS 64065)* <1058> **MARRYING MAIDEN** [45] [28]
– Don and Dewey / The dolphins / Essence of now / Hoedown / Soapstone mountain / Waiting for the song / Let a woman flow / It comes right down to you / Good lovin' / Galileo / Do you remember the sun. *(re-iss.Apr82 lp/c; CBS/40 32132)*

Aug 70. (7") <45309> **THE DOLPHINS. / DO YOU REMEMBER THE SUN** [-] [ ]

— **HAL WAGENET** (b. Willits, Calif.) – guitar repl. GREGORY / **TOM FOWLER** – bass repl. JOHN NICHOLAS who had repl. HOLMAN / added **FRED WEBB** (b. Santa Rosa, Calif.) – keyboards

Jan 72. (7") <45536> **ANYTIME. / APPLE AND ORANGES** [-] [ ]

Feb 72. (lp) *(CBS 64314)* <30734> **CHOICE QUALITY STUFF / ANYTIME** [ ] [ ] Dec71
– Creed of love / Bye bye baby / The Grand Camel Suite / No word for glad / Lady love / Words / Place of dreams / Oranges & apples / Anytime / Bitter wine / Misery love / Company.

Dec 72. (lp) *(CBS 64929)* <31338> **AT CARNEGIE HALL (live)** [ ] [ ]
– Give your woman what she wants / A hot summer day / Angels and animals / Bombay calling / Going to another party / Good lovin' / The Grand Camel suite / White bird. *(cd-iss.Aug95 on 'Columbia'; 480970-2)*

Feb 73. (7") <45788> **WHITE BIRD (live). / WASTED UNION BLUES (live)** [-] [ ]

— **BUD COCKRELL – bass** repl. FOWLER who later joined FRANK ZAPPA

Apr 73. (lp) *(CBS 65483)* <32181> **. . .TODAY** [ ] [ ]
– Ain't that lovin' you baby / Child / Down on the bayou / Watching you watching me / Mississippi Delta / Ridin' thumb / Time / Lie to me / Burning low / Creator.

Apr 73. (7") *(CBS 1625)* <45853> **AIN'T THAT LOVIN' YOU BABY. / TIME** [ ] [ ]

Feb 74. (lp) *(CBS 658 12)* <32660> **1,001 NIGHTS (live)** [ ] [ ]
– White bird / Ain't that lovin' you baby / Ridin' thumb / Bombay calling / A hot summer day / Soapstone mountain / The dolphins / Don and Dewey / Bye bye baby / Hoedown. *(re-iss.Mar82 lp/c; CBS/40 32133)*

— Broke-up 1974. BUD joined PABLO CRUISE around mid'73.

DAVID LA FLAMME

eventually went solo + **MITCHELL FROOM** – keyboards, producer / **JAMES RALSTON** – guitar / **DOUG KILMER** – bass / **PETER MILO** – drums / **DOMINIQUE DELACROIX** – vocals

not issued | Amherst

Nov 76. (lp) <AMH 1007> **WHITE BIRD** [-] [ ]
– White bird / Hot summer day / Swept away / Easy woman / This man / Baby be wise / Spirit of America.

Nov 76. (7") <717> **WHITE BIRD. / SPIRIT OF AMERICA** [-] [89]

Feb 77. (7") <721> **EASY WOMAN. / BABY BE WISE** [-] [ ]

1978. (lp) <AMH 1012> **INSIDE OUT** [-] [ ]
– Who's gonna love me? / My life / Nightsong / Forever and a day / Somewhere down the road / Where flamingos fly / Need somebody / The day you went away / Can't wait until tomorrow. *(cd-iss.Sep95 with 'WHITE BIRD' Sep95 on 'Edsel'; EDCD 419)*

— DAVID retired from music scene the same year. PATTIE SANTOS with BUD COCKRELL issued lp 'NEW BEGINNINGS' in 1978 on 'A&M'. She died in a car crash on 14 Dec'89.

JACKSON HEIGHTS

Formed: London, England ...1969 by namesake LEE JACKSON, former vocalist/bassist with symphonic prog rockers The NICE. The debut album, 'KINGS PROGRESS' (1970), showcased a more mainstream sound than The NICE while further albums, '5TH AVENUE BUS' (1972), 'RAGAMUFFIN'S FOOL' (1973) and 'BUMP AND GRIND' (1973), struck a balance between art-rock pretension and consumer friendly pop.

Recommended: KINGS PROGRESS (*6) / THE FIFTH AVENUE BUS (*6)

LEE JACKSON (b. 8 Jan'43, Newcastle-Upon-Tyne, England) – vocals, bass, guitar, harmonica (ex-NICE) / **CHARLIE HARCOURT** – guitar, keyboards, vocals / **COVARRUBIAS TAPIA** – guitar, vocals / **MARIO ENRIQUE** – bass / **TOMMY SLONE** – drums, percussion

Charisma Mercury

1970. (7") *(JH 1)* **DOUBTING THOMAS. / INSOMNIA**

Sep 70. (lp) *(CAS 1018)* *<SR 61331>* **KINGS PROGRESS**
– Mr. Screw / Since I last saw you / Sunshine freak / Kings progress / Doubting Thomas / Insomnia / Cry of Euegene.

— JACKSON sacked everyone and recruited **JOHN McBURNIE** – guitar / **BRIAN CHATTON** – keyboards / **MIKE GILES** – drums

Vertigo Vertigo

Apr 72. (lp) *(6360 067)* **THE FIFTH AVENUE BUS**
– Tramp / Dog got bitten / Autumn brigade / Long time dying / Sweet hill tunnel / Laughing gear / House in the country / Rent a friend / Luxford / Pastor Roger. *(cd-iss.1990's on 'Repertoire'; REP 4365)*

— session people repl. pianists LAWRIE WRIGHT + DAVE WATTS.

1973. (lp) *(6360 077)* **RAGAMUFFIN'S FOOL**
– Maureen / Oh you beauty / As she starts / Beebop catch a thief / Ragamuffin's fool choral / Chips and chicken / Poor Peter / Fool of water.

1973. (7") *<108>* **A WINTER'S TALE. / THE DEMON TRUCKER**

1973. (lp) *<V6 5089>* **JACKSON HEIGHTS** (cont. comp of above 2)

1973. (lp) *(6360 092)* **BUMP AND GRIND**
– I could be your orchestra / Spaghetti sunshine / Long naked lady / Public romance / Bump and grind / Cumberland country / It's a shame / Lady's in the chorus / Whatever happened to the conversations.

— Soon disbanded, when JACKSON formed ...

REFUGEE

LEE JACKSON – vocals, bass / **PATRICK MORAZ** (b.24 Jun'48, Morges, Switzerland) – keyboards / **BRIAN DAVISON** – drums

Charisma Charisma

1974. (lp) *(CAS 1087)* **REFUGEE**
– Papillion / Someday / Grand Canyon / Ritt Mickley / Credo.

— When they split JACKSON returned to being a painter and decorator. MORAZ went solo and joined YES.

JADE WARRIOR

Formed: 1968 as JULY by TONY DUHIG, TOM NEWMAN and JON FIELD. They released one 'Sgt.Pepper'-type eponymous album, before their untimely demise. NEWMAN subsequently became a producer for Richard Branson's 'Virgin' label in 1971, working on MIKE OLDFIELD's classic debut, 'Tubular Bells'. Meanwhile, DUHIG and FIELD formed JADE WARRIOR, supplying listeners with three albums of pioneering "new age" ambient-rock. The third of these, the meditative 'LAST AUTUMN'S DREAM', spawned their only single, 'THE DEMON TRUCKER'. A fourth set, 'ECLIPSE', was withdrawn by their label, 'Vertigo' and remains unreleased. They then shifted to the more sympathetic 'Island' records in 1973, issuing a further clutch of uncommercial albums. They re-emerged periodically throughout the 80's, although DUHIG was to die of heart failure on the 11th of November 1990, aged 49.

• **Trivia:** Their JULY lp, is now worth in excess of £250 mint.

Recommended: JULY (*7) / JADE WARRIOR (*5) / LAST AUTUMN'S DREAM (*7)

JULY

TOM DUHIG – guitar / **JON FIELD** – percussion, flute / **TOM NEWMAN** – vocals, guitar, organ, mandolin, bass, tabla

Major Minor not issued

Jun 68. (7") *(MM 568)* **MY CLOWN. / DANDELION SEEDS**

Jul 68. (lp; mono/stereo) *(MM/SM LP 29)* **JULY**
– My clown / Dandelion seeds / Jolly Mary / Hello to me / You missed it all / Way / To be free / Move on sweet flower / Crying is for writers / I see / Friendly man / Bird lived.

Oct 68. (7") *(MM 580)* **HELLO, WHO'S THERE? / THE WAY**

— Split when TOM NEWMAN went solo, then into production and sessions for MIKE OLDFIELD. He went solo for 'Virgin' in 1975; 'FINE OLD TOM' + unreleased 1976 'LIVE AT THE ARGONAUT'. Other albums; 'FAERIE SYMPHONY' (1977 'Decca') / 'BAYOU MOON' (1985 'Coda') / 'ASPECTS' (1985 'Coda'). Some of these featured JON FIELD.

JADE WARRIOR

TONY DUHIG – guitar / **JON FIELD** – percussion, flute / **GLYN HAVARD** – vocals, bass

Vertigo Vertigo

Jun 71. (lp) *(6360 033)* *<1007>* **JADE WARRIOR**
– The traveller / A prenormal day at Brighton / Masai morning: Casting the bones / The hunt – A ritual of kings / Windweaver / Dragonfly day: Metamorphosis – Dance of the sun spirit / Death / Petunia / Telephone girl / Psychiatric sergeant / Slow ride / Sundial song. *(cd-iss.Sep94 on 'Line'; LICD 900548)*

— added guests **DAVE CONNORS** – saxes, flute / **ALLAN PRICE** – drums

Jan 72. (lp) *(6360 062)* *<1009>* **RELEASED**
– Three-horned dragon king / Eyes on you / Bride of summer / Water curtain love / Minna Moto's dream / We have reason to believe / Barazinbar / Yellow eyes.

Mar 72. (7") *<106>* **WE HAVE REASON TO BELIEVE. / BARAZINBAR**

— **DAVID DUHIG** – guitar, repl. CONNORS

Nov 72. (7") *(6059 069)* **THE DEMON TRUCKER. / SNAKE**

Nov 72. (lp) *(6360 079)* *<1012>* **LAST AUTUMN'S DREAM**
– A winter's tale / Snake / Dark river / Joanne / Obedience / Morning hymn / May queen / The demon trucker / Lady of the lake / Borne on the solar wind. *(cd-iss.Jul94 on 'Line'; LICD 900563)*

Jan 73. (7") *<108>* **THE DEMON TRUCKER. / A WINTER'S TALE**

— In 1973, Vertigo opted not to release 'ECLIPSE'. HAVARD departed to later join YACHTS, then JANE AIRE & THE BELVEDERES.

— **FIELD + DUHIG** brought in session people **DAVID DUHIG** – guitar / **COLDRIDGE GOOD** – bass / **SKAILA KANGA** – harp / **GRAHAM DEACON + CHRIS KARAN** – drums

Island Antilles

1974. (lp) *(ILPS 9290)* **FLOATING WORLD**
– Clouds / Mountain of fruit and flowers / Red lotus / Clouds / Rain flower / Easty / Monkey chant / Memories of a distant sea / Quba. *(cd-iss.Apr90; IMCD 99)*

— now w/ guests **STEVE WINWOOD** – keyboards / **MAGGIE THOMAS** – recorder / **GRAHAM MORGAN** – drums

1975. (lp) *(ILPS 9318)* **WAVES**
– Waves (part 1) / Waves (part 2).

— duo now w/ guests **GOODE + MORGAN** plus **FRED FRITH** – viola / **JOE O'DONNELL + DEBBIE HALL** – violin / **ROGER BRYSON + JEFF WESTLEY** – piano / **PETE GIBSON** – brass

1976. (lp) *(ILPS 9393)* **KITES**
– Songs of the forest / Wind song / The emperor's kite / Wind borne / Kite song / Land of the warrior / Quietly by the riverbank / Arrival of the emporer: What does the venerable sir do / Teh ch'eng: Do understand this / Arrival of Chia Shan: Discourse and liberation / Towards the mountains / The last question.

— now w/ guests **KANGA + MORGAN** plus **JOHN DENITH + GODFREY McLEAN** – drums / **DICK CUTHELL** – horn, flute / **BILL SMITH** – bass / **GOWAN TURNBULL** – sax / **KUMA HARADA** – bass

1978. (lp) *(ILPS 9552)* *<7068>* **WAY OF THE SUN**
– Sun Ra / Sun child / Moontears / Heaven stone / Way of the Sun / River song / Carnival / Dance of the Sun / Death of Ra. *(cd-iss.Apr90; IMCD 100)*

1978. (7") *(JAD 1)* **WAY OF THE SUN. / SUN RA**

— Split 1979.

Butt not issued

Mar 82. (lp) *(BUTT 001)* **REFLECTIONS** (compilation 1971-73)
– English morning / Lady of the lake / Borne on the solar wind / Morning hymn / Bride of summer / Soldiers song / A winter's tale / Yellow eyes / Dark river / House of dreams.

— duo re-formed in 1984 w/ guests **DAVID DUHIG** – guitar / **GOWAN TURNBULL** – sax, flute / **BRAD LANG** – bass / **JEFF BARAK** – drums / **ANISSE HADEED** – various percussion

Pulse not issued

1984. (lp) *(005)* **HORIZEN**
– Images of Dune: Prescient dawn / Endless desert ... endless lives ... the maker: The freeman / People of the sand ... spice ritual ... sietch tabre: Journey on a dream / Giant beneath the sand ... the prophet ... riding the maker / Caribbean wave / Horizon / East wind / Grey lake, red mountain / Long wait at Mount Li.

— Went separate ways again after above, and sadly DUHIG was to die late in 1990.

(JULY) compilation, etc.

1987. (lp) *Bam Caruso; (KIRI 097)* **DANDELION SEEDS**

Tommy JAMES & THE SHONDELLS

Formed: Niles, Michigan, USA ... 1960 by TOMMY JAMES, initially as

TOMMY & THE TORNADOES. His/their first single, 'LONG PONY TALE', was recorded when he was only 13, having learned the guitar four years earlier. He then formed The SHONDELLS, who were concocted to fulfil after-school gigs. They then signed with the local 'Snap' label in 1962 and after a flop debut, they recorded a JEFF BARRY-ELLIE GREENWICH number, 'HANKY PANKY'. It was a regional hit in 1963 and upon its re-issue two years later, it was caned by Pittsburg DJ BOB MACK. By the summer of '66, it had climbed to the top of charts, soon selling over a million copies for their new label, 'Roulette'. A new SHONDELLS were put together by TOMMY JAMES; EDDIE GRAY, RONNIE ROSSMAN, MIKE VALE and PETE LUCIA (mainstays over the next 5 years). He also employed the songwriting talents of producers RITCHIE CORDELL and BO GENTRY, which resulted in a string of neo-bubblegum Top 50 hits. One of them, 'MONY MONY', in 1968, was even a massive No.1 garage-style giant in the UK, leading to TOMMY taking full control of the writing, producing and arranging of all their work. Now psychedelic rather than bubblegum, they took the US charts by storm again early in 1969. 'CRIMSON AND CLOVER' became another No.1 (selling over 5 million copies) and two successive singles, 'SWEET CHERRY WINE' & 'CRYSTAL BLUE PERSUASION' also made the Top 10. Over the next year, they enjoyed more Top 50 US hits, but, exhausted, the drug-taking JAMES retreated to a farm in New York to contemplate a solo career. After producing ALIVE AND KICKING's version of his 'TIGHTER, TIGHTER', he made his pop comeback. In the 70's, he had a number of hit US singles, many minor, although the biggest by a long shot was the Top 5, 'DRAGGIN' THE LINE', in the summer of '71. Early in 1980, he returned to the Top 20 with an AOR million-seller, 'THREE TIMES IN LOVE'. He virtually retired a year later, although his work has since been covered (i.e. 'CRIMSON AND CLOVER' by JOAN JETT – 'MONY MONY' by BILLY IDOL and 'I THINK WE'RE ALONE NOW' by pop starlet TIFFANY).

Recommended: ANTHOLOGY (*6)
Although he/they were only briefly associated with psychedelia, a full discography is listed due to their ommision from editions 1-3.

TOMMY JAMES (b. THOMAS GREGORY JACKSON, 29 Apr'47, Dayton, Ohio) – vocals / **LARRY COVERDALE** – guitar / **CRAIG VILLENEUVE** – keyboards / **LARRY WRIGHT** – bass / **JIM PAYNE** – drums

not issued | Selsom

1960. (7"; as TOMMY & THE TORNADOES) <101> **LONG PONY TALE** [-] [ ]
1962. (7"; as The SHONDELLS) <102> **WHY DO FOOLS FALL IN LOVE. / UPSETTER OF HER HEART** [-] [ ]

not issued | Snap

Feb 63. (7"; as The SHONDELLS) <102> **HANKY PANKY. / THUNDERBOLT** [-] [ ]
<re-iss.Dec 65 on 'Red Fox'; 110>

— **TOMMY** with new line-up; **RONALD ROSSMAN** (b.28 Feb'45) – keyboards / **MICHAEL VALE** (b.17 Jul'47) – bass / **GEORGE MAGURA** – saxophone, organ, bass / **VINCENT PIETROPAOLI** – drums

Roulette | Roulette

Jun 66. (7") *(RK 7000)* <4686> **HANKY PANKY. / THUNDERBOLT** [38] [1] May66
Jun 66. (lp) <25336> **HANKY PANKY** [-] [46]
– Hanky panky / I'll go crazy / I'm so proud / The lover / Love makes the world go 'round / Good lovin' / Say I am (what I am) / Cleo's mood / Don't throw our love away / Shake a tail feather / Soul searchin' baby / Lots of pretty girls.
Jul 66. (7") <4695> **SAY I AM (WHAT I AM). / LOTS OF PRETTY GIRLS** [-] [21]

— **EDDIE GRAY** (b.27 Feb'48) – guitar, repl. MAGURA

— **PETE LUCIA** (b. 2 Feb'47) – drums, repl. PIETROPAOLI

Pye Inter.. | Roulette

Nov 66. (7") *(7N 25398)* <4710> **IT'S ONLY LOVE. / YA! YA!** [ ] [31] Oct66
Nov 66. (lp) <25344> **IT'S ONLY LOVE** [-] [ ]
– It's only love / Hold on a little bit longer / I'm so lonesome I could cry / It's alright / Juanita / Ya! ya! / We'll have a world / Don't let my love pass you by / Fanny Mae / Some.

Major Minor | Roulette

Apr 67. (7") *(MM 511)* <4720> **I THINK WE'RE ALONE NOW. / GONE GONE GONE** [ ] [4] Feb67
Apr 67. (lp) <25353> **I THINK WE'RE ALONE NOW** [-] [74]
– I like the way / (Baby, baby) I can't take it no more / I think we're alone now / California sun / Baby let me down / Gone, gone, gone / Mirage / Shout / Trust each other in love / Run, run, baby, run / Let's be lovers / What I'd give to see your face again.
Apr 67. (7") <4736> **MIRAGE. / RUN, RUN, BABY, RUN** [-] [10]
Jun 67. (7") <4756> **I LIKE THE WAY. / (BABY, BABY) I CAN'T TAKE IT NO MORE** [-] [25]
Aug 67. (7") <4762> **GETTIN' TOGETHER. / REAL GIRL** [-] [18]
Sep 67. (lp) <25357> **GETTIN' TOGETHER** [-] [ ]
Jan 68. (7") *(MM 548)* <4775> **OUT OF THE BLUE. / LOVE'S CLOSING IN ON ME** [ ] [43] Oct67
Mar 68. (7") *(MM 558)* <7000> **GET OUT NOW. / WISH IT WERE YOU** [ ] [48] Jan68
May 68. (lp; mono/stereo) *(MM/SM LP 27)* <25355> **SOMETHING SPECIAL! (THE BEST OF TOMMY JAMES & THE SHONDELLS)** (compilation) [ ] [ ] Feb68
– Out of the blue / Say I am / Gettin' together / Run, run, baby, run / I like the way / Love's closin' in on me / I think we're alone now / Real girl / Mirage / Don't let my love pass you by / It's only love / Hanky panky.
May 68. (7") *(MM 567)* <7008> **MONY MONY. / ONE TWO THREE AND I FELL** [1] [3] Mar68

Roulette | Roulette

Jul 68. (7") <7016> **SOMEBODY CARES. / DO UNTO ME** [-] [53]
Sep 68. (lp; mono/stereo) *(RR/SR LP 1)* <RS 42012> **MONY MONY** [ ] [ ] Jul68
– Mony Mony / Do unto me / (I'm) Taken / Nightime (I'm a lover) / Run away from me / Somebody cares / Get out now / I can't go back to Denver / Some kind of love / Gingerbread man / One two three and I fell.
Sep 68. (7") <7024> **DO SOMETHING TO ME. / GINGERBREAD MAN** [-] [38]
Sep 68. (7") *(RO 500)* **DO SOMETHING TO ME. / SOMEBODY CARES** [ ] [-]
Jan 69. (7") *(RO 502)* <7028> **CRIMSON AND CLOVER. / SOME KIND OF LOVE** [ ] [1] Dec68
Feb 69. (lp; mono/stereo) *(RS/SR LP 2)* <RS 42023> **CRIMSON AND CLOVER** [ ] [8] Jan69
– Crimson and clover / Kathleen McArthur / I am a tangerine / Do something to me / Crystal blue persuasion / Sugar on Sunday / Breakaway / Smokey roads / I'm alive.
Apr 69. (7") *(RO 506)* <7039> **SWEET CHERRY WINE. / BREAKAWAY** [ ] [7]
Jun 69. (7") *(RO 507)* <7050> **CRYSTAL BLUE PERSUASION. / I'M ALIVE** [ ] [2] May69
Oct 69. (7") *(RO 511)* <7060> **BALL OF FIRE. / MAKIN' GOOD TIME** [ ] [19] Sep69
Dec 69. (lp; mono/stereo) *(RR/SR LP 3)* <RS 42030> **CELLOPHANE SYMPHONY** [ ] [ ] Oct69
– Cellophane symphony / Makin' good time / Evergreen / Sweet cherry wine / Papa rolled his own / Changes / Loved one / I know who I am / The love of a woman / On behalf of the entire staff & management.
Dec 69. (lp) <42040> **THE BEST OF TOMMY JAMES & THE SHONDELLS** (compilation) [-] [21]
Feb 70. (7") *(RO 513)* <7066> **SHE. / LOVED ONE** [ ] [23] Dec69
Feb 70. (7") <7071> **GOTTA GET BACK TO YOU. / RED ROVER** [-] [45]
Apr 70. (lp) <SR 42044> **TRAVELIN'** [-] [91]
– Bloody water / Red rover / Candy makers / She / Talkin' and signifyin' / Travelin' / Gotta get back to you / Early in the mornin' / Moses & me / Kelly told Anne.
Jun 70. (7") *(RO 516)* <7076> **COME TO ME. / TALKIN' AND SIGNIFYIN'** [ ] [47] May70

— split when TOMMY JAMES was now solo. The other 4 became HOG HEAVEN and released an eponymous US album in 1971 on 'Roulette'; *<42057>*

TOMMY JAMES

— with a plethera of session people

Sep 70. (7") *(RO 518)* <7084> **BALL AND CHAIN. / CANDY MAKERS** [ ] [57] Jul70
Dec 70. (7") <7093> **CHURCH STREET SOUL REVIVAL. / DRAGGIN' THE LINE** [-] [62]
Jan 71. (lp) <42051> **TOMMY JAMES** [-] [ ]
– Mony Mony / Ball of fire / Nightime (I'm a lover) / I can't go back to Denver / Gingerbread man / Crimson and clover / Hanky panky / Mirage / Crystal blue persuasion / Sugar on Sunday / I think we're alone now / Makin' good time.
Mar 71. (7") <7100> **ADRIENNE. / LIGHT OF DAY** [-] [93]
May 71. (7") *(2097 001)* **ADRIENNE. / CHURCH STREET SOUL REVIVAL** [ ] [-]
Aug 71. (7") *(2097 003)* <7103> **DRAGGIN' THE LINE. / BITS & PIECES** [ ] [4] Jun71
Sep 71. (lp) <3001> **CHRISTIAN OF THE WORLD** [-] [ ]
– Christian of the world / Rings and things / I'm coming home / Sing, sing, sing / Draggin' the line / Sail a happy ship / Light of day / Bits and pieces / I believe in love / Church Street soul revival / Another hill to climb / Adrienne / Silk, satin, carriage waiting.
Nov 71. (7") <7114> **NOTHING TO HIDE. / WALK A COUNTRY MILE** [-] [41]
Jan 72. (7") *(2097 005)* <7110> **I'M COMING HOME. / SING, SING, SING** [ ] [40] Sep71
Feb 72. (7") <7119> **TELL 'EM WILLIE BOY'S A'COMIN'. / FORTY DAYS AND FORTY NIGHTS** [-] [89]
Jun 72. (7") <7126> **CAT'S EYE IN THE WINDOW. / DARK IS THE NIGHT** [-] [90]
Aug 72. (7") <7130> **LOVE SONG. / KINGSTON HIGHWAY** [-] [67]
Aug 72. (lp) *(2432005)* <3007> **MY HEAD, MY BED & MY RED GUITAR** [ ] [ ]
– Walk a country mile / Who's gonna cry / Forty days and forty nights / Kingston highway / I live to love a woman / Fortunata / Dark is the night / Nothin' to hide / Tell 'em Willie Boy's a'comin' / White horses / The last one to know / Rosalee / Paper flowers.
Oct 72. (7") <7135> **CELEBRATION. / THE LAST ONE TO KNOW** [-] [95]
Feb 73. (7") <7140> **BOO, BOO, DON'T CHA BE BLUE. / RINGS AND THINGS** [-] [70]
May 73. (7") <7147> **CALICO. / HEY, MY LADY** [-] [ ]

M.C.A. | M.C.A.

Sep 74. (7") *(MCA 158)* <40289> **GLORY GLORY. / COMIN' DOWN** [ ] [ ]

not issued | Fantasy

1976. (7") <761> **I LOVE YOU LOVE ME LOVE. / DEVIL GATE DRIVE** [-] [ ]
1976. (7") <776> **TIGHTER, TIGHTER. / COMIN' DOWN** [-] [ ]
1976. (lp) <9509> **IN TOUCH** [-] [ ]
– Tighter, tighter / Devil gate drive / Touch me / Don't want to fall away from you / Treat me nice / One track mind / Calico / The magician / I love you love me love / Comin' down.
1978. (7") <811> **LOVE IS GONNA FIND A WAY. / I DON'T LOVE YOU ANYMORE** [-] [ ]
1978. (lp) <9532> **MIDNIGHT RIDER** [-] [ ]
– Love is gonna find a way / I don't love you anymore / Bobby don't leave me alone / Midnight rider / Double or nothin' / Still got a thing for you / What happened to the girl / Keep it in the groove.
1979. (7") <886> **TIGHTER, TIGHTER. / COMIN' DOWN** [-] [ ]

R.C.A. | Millenium

Mar 80. (7") *(FB 1785)* <11785> **THREE TIMES IN LOVE. / I JUST WANNA PLAY THE MUSIC** [ ] [19] Jan80
Mar 80. (lp) <7748> **THREE TIMES IN LOVE** [-] [ ]
– You got me / Long way down / Three times in love / Lady in white / Everything I am / It's magic / I just wanna lay the music / Let it slide / It's all right (for now).
Apr 80. (7") <11787> **NO HAY DOS SIN TRES (THREE TIMES IN LOVE). / I JUST WANNA PLAY THE MUSIC** [-] [ ]
Jun 80. (7") <11788> **IT'S ALL RIGHT (FOR NOW). / YOU GOT ME** [-] [ ]

May 81. (7") *<11802>* **YOU'RE SO EASY TO LOVE. / HALFWAY TO HEAVEN** [-] [58]
1981. (lp) *<7758>* **EASY TO LOVE** [-] [ ]
1981. (7") *<11814>* **LADY IN WHITE. / PAYIN' FOR MY LOVER'S MISTAKE** [-] [ ]

Polydor 21 Records

Mar 83. (7") *(POSP 564) <105>* **SAY PLEASE. / TWO TIME LOVER** [ ] [ ]

– compilations, etc. –

Sep 73. (7") *Concord; (CON 30)* **MONY MONY. / DRAGGIN' THE LINE / CRYSTAL BLUE PERSUASION** [ ] [-]
Sep 75. (7") *Pye International; (7N 25694)* **MONY MONY. / BABY BABY I CAN'T TAKE NO MORE** [ ] [-]
Jan 76. (7") *Contempo; (CS 9038)* **I THINK WE'RE ALONE NOW. / MIRAGE** [ ] [-]
1977. (7"ep) *Buddah; (BD 117)* **MONY MONY / CRYSTAL BLUE PERSUASION. / HANKY PANKY / CRIMSON AND CLOVER** [ ] [-]
1978. (lp/c) *Pye International; (NSPL/ZCP 28260)* **20 GENUINE U.S. CHARTBUSTERS** [ ] [-]
Jul 80. (7") *Flashback; (FBEP 101)* **MONY MONY / CRIMSON AND CLOVER. /** [ ] [-]
Apr 83. (10"lp/c) *P.R.T.; (DOW/ZCDOW 6)* **SHORT SHARP SHOTS** [ ] [-]
Apr 84. (7") Old Gold; (OG 9410) **MONY MONY. / CRIMSON AND CLOVER** [ ] [-]
Jul 88. (lp/c) *Exel; (XEL LP/MC 113)* **I THINK WE'RE ALONE NOW** [ ] [-]
Jan 90. (cd/c/lp) *Roulette; (CD/TC+/ROU 5004)* **ANTHOLOGY** [ ] [-]
– Hanky panky / Say I am (what I am) / It's only love / I think we're alone now / Baby baby I can't take it no more / Mirage / I like the way / Run, run, baby, run * / Gettin' together / Real girl * / Love's closin' in on me * / Out of the blue / Get out now / I'm taken * / One two three and I fell / Mony Mony / Somebody cares / Do something to me / Crimson and clover / Sugar on Sunday / Crystal blue persuasion / Sweet cherry wine / Loved one * / Ball of fire / She / Gotta get back to you * / draggin' the line. *(cd+= *)*
1991. (cd) *Rhino;* **TOMMY JAMES: THE SOLO YEARS 1970-1981** [-] [ ]
Nov 93. (cd) *Sequel; (NEMCD 646)* **HANKY PANKY / MONY MONY** [ ] [-]
Nov 93. (cd) *Sequel; (NEMCD 647)* **CRIMSON & CLOVER / CELLOPHANE** [ ] [-]

JANE

Formed: Germany ... 1970. The band signed with the 'Brain' label in 1971, releasing their debut, 'TOGETHER', the following year. Despite the monotonous vocals of BERND PULST, the album was a commercially orientated collection of dramatic, keyboard dominated heavy rock. With PULST ousted and MAUCHER ill, the band enlisted WOLFGANG KRANTZ for the 1973 album, 'HERE WE ARE', a similarly commercial slice of progressive space rock. By the release of 'JANE III' (1974), NADOLNY had quit and the band's characteristic organ sound was replaced by a more guitar-led heavy rock approach. Later that summer, MARTIN HESSE and GOTTFRIED JANKO replaced the departed MAUCHER and KRANTZ. JANKO led the band in a poppier direction for 1975's 'LADY', although with NADOLNY back in the fold for 'FIRE, WATER, EARTH AND AIR' (1976), the band employed synthesizer for the first time, resulting in a sweeping, orchestral feel. After NADDNY quit shortly after the album's release, MANFRED WIECZORKE was recruited, his distinctive keyboard style forming the basis of 1978's 'AGE OF MADNESS'. He departed the following year, however, and although the band struggled on through the 80's amid continually fluctuating personnel, it was clear JANE were well past their sell by date.

Recommended: TOGETHER (*7) / HERE WE ARE (*8)

BERND PULST – vocals / **KLAUS HESS** – guitar, vocals, bass, keyboards / **WERNER NADOLNY** – keyboards, flute / **CHARLY MAUCHER** – bass, vocals / **PETER PANKA** – drums, percussion

Brain Capitol

Feb 72. (lp) *(1002)* **TOGETHER** [-] [-] German
– Daytime / Wind / Try to find / Spain / Together / Hangman.

—— now without PULST

—— **WOLFGANG KRANTZ** – bass, guitar, vocals; repl. MAUCHER who fell ill

Mar 73. (lp) *(1032)* **HERE WE ARE** [-] [-] German
– Redskin / Out in the rain / Dandelion / Moving / Waterfall / Like a queen / Here we are.

—— **CHARLY MAUCHER** – guitar, keyboards; repl. NADOLNY

May 74. (lp) *(1048) <11425>* **JANE III** [-] [ ]
– Comin' again / Mother, you don't know / I need you / Way to Paradise / Early in the morning / Jane – session / Rock'n'roll star / King of Thule / Baby, what you're doin'.

—— MAUCHER + KRANTZ left to form HARLIS and were repl. by **GOTTFRIED JANKO** – keyboards, vocals / **MARTIN HESSE** – bass (both ex-DULL KNIFE)

Mar 75. (lp) *(1066)* **LADY** [-] [-] German
– Waiting for the sunshine / Scratches on your back / Music machine / Make me feel better / Lady / Lord love / Midnight mover / Silver knickers / So, so long.

—— **WERNER NADOLNY** – organ, piano, synthesizer (returned) repl. JANKO

Jan 76. (lp) *(1084)* **FIRE, WATER, EARTH & AIR** [-] [-] German
– Fire, water, earth & air / Air & the end. *(cd-iss.1989; 831748-2)*

—— **PANKA + HESS** recruited **MANFRED WIECZORKE** – keyboards, vocals (ex-ELOY) + **MARTIN HESS** – bass, vocals

Oct 76. (d-lp) *(80.001)* **JANE LIVE (live)** [-] [-] German
– All my friends / Lady / Rest of my life / Expectation / River / Out in the rain / Hangman / Fire, water, earth & air / Another way / Daytime / Hightime for crusader / Windows.

1977. (lp) *(60.055)* **BETWEEN HEAVEN AND HELL** [-] [-] German
– Between Heaven and Hell / Twilight / Voice in the wind / Your circle.

1978. (lp) *(60.124)* **AGE OF MADNESS** [-] [-] German
– Age of madness / Memory / Symphonie / Auroville / Lovesong / Bad game / Get this power / With her smile / Meadow / Age of madness (part 2). *(UK cd-iss.Jun97 on 'epertoire'; RR 7047)*

—— now without MANFRED

Feb 80. (lp) *(60.218)* **SIGN NO.9** [ ] [-]
– No. 9 / That's the way / Love can't wait / Henry goes married / Say hello / Moonstone / Love on earth / Letter to Mariann / I know one day. *(UK-iss.on 'Logo'; 0060.218)*

—— added **PEDJA** – vocals, strings

Mar 81. (lp) *(60.354)* **JANE** [ ] [-]
– On my way / New man in town / Stay with me / Stop the clock / Rockin' around / Intro – Easy going / Love your life / Dynamite / Cadillac rider / Out on the street.

—— **CHARLY MAUCHER** – bass, vocals returned to repl. MARTIN + PEDJA

Jul 83. (lp) *(60.519)* **GERMANIA** [-] [-] German
– Germania / Rock and roll revolution / Got no shadows / Cool and collected / Get back to you / No future / I'm so down / Driving me crazy / When I went to the scene / Southern line.

—— KLAUS HESS disbanded group at the end of '82, while PANKA and MAUCHER became part of the 'Warlock' rock opera, which included past member NADOLNY. They also toured as LADY JANE, while KLAUS released solo album in 1983 'STERNENTANZ'. JANE re-formed in 1987.

Sky not issued

1987. (lp) *(111)* **BEAUTIFUL LADY** [-] [-] German
1988. (lp) *(130)* **LIVE '88 (live)** [-] [-] German

Brain not issued

1990. (cd) *(843071-2)* **JANE LIVE '89 (live)** [-] [-] German
– All my friends / Lady / Medley 1 / Energy (drum solo) / I need you / Way to Paradise / Beautiful lady / Out in the rain / Daytime / Hangman / Medley 2 / Rest of my life / So, so long.

—— nothing heard from them since

JASON CREST

Formed: Tonbridge, Kent, England ... 1967 by TERRY CLARKE, and TERRY DOBSON, initially as The SPURLYWEEVES, then The GOOD THING BRIGADE, the latter getting to the demo stage. They were found by former FOUR PENNIES bassist turned 'Philips' A&R man, FRITZ FRYER, who secured them a deal on the strength of their self-penned number, 'THE COLLECTED WORKS OF JUSTIN CREST'. With a slight adjustment, they took the name for the group, debuting with 'TURQUOISE TANDEM CYCLE' in 1968. The slow PROCOL HARUM-type ballad was full of neo-classical overtones, although it wasn't a hit. Another flop resulted in the record company employing the services of The MOVE's ROY WOOD to produce their third 45, a version of his song, 'THE LEMON TREE'. FRYER's composition, 'WATERLOO ROAD', was yet another disaster, causing him to quit in 1969 after the release of the heavy/pop psychedelic fifth single, 'BLACK MASS'. The band then evolved into early 70's progressive acts; HIGH BROOM and HOLY MACKEREL, the latter finally releasing a slightly countrified album!
• **Covered:** YOU REALLY GOT A HOLD ON ME (Smokey Robinson).
• **Trivia:** The first and fifth 45's are worth over £50.

Recommended: THE BLACK MASS (*6)

TERRY CLARKE – vocals / **TERRY DOBSON** – guitar / **DEREK SMALLCOMBE** – guitar / **RON FOWLER** – bass / **ROGERY SIGGERY** – drums

Philips not issued

Jan 68. (7") *(BF 1633)* **TURQUOISE TANDEM CYCLE. / GOOD LIFE** [ ] [-]
Apr 68. (7") *(BF 1650)* **JULIANO THE BULL. / TWO BY THE SEA** [ ] [-]
Aug 68. (7") *(BF 1687)* **THE LEMON TREE. / PATRICIA'S DREAM** [ ] [-]
Feb 69. (7") *(BF 1752)* **WATERLOO ROAD. / EDUCATION** [ ] [-]

—— **JOHN SELLEY** – bass (or before), repl. FOWLER

Jul 69. (7") *(BF 1809)* **BLACK MASS. / PLACE IN THE SUN** [ ] [-]

—— split when DOBSON quit the music biz.

—— **BRIAN BENNETT** – guitar (ex-MIKE STUART SPAN), repl. DOBSON

Aug 70. (7"; as HIGH BROOM) *(WI 6088)* **DANCING IN THE MOONLIGHT. / PERCY'S ON THE RUN** [ ] [-]
(re-iss.1973 on 'Columbia'; DB 8969)

—— SMALLCOMBE spent 1971 with band SAMUEL PROBY, who released one eponymous album, before he returned to the fold

—— **CHRIS WARE** – guitar repl. BENNETT

—— **TONY WOOD** – bass repl. SELLEY

C.B.S. not issued

1972. (lp; as HOLY MACKEREL) *(65297)* **HOLY MACKEREL** [ ] [-]

—— split after above, CLARKE re-surfacing a decade later in VENDETTA

– compilations, etc. –

1993. Scanner Dots; (lp; ltd) *<unknown>* **THE BLACK MASS** [-] [ ]

JEFFERSON AIRPLANE

Formed: San Francisco, California, USA ... early 1965 by MARTY BALIN and PAUL KANTNER. They recruited others and signed to 'RCA' in late '65, releasing a flop debut single, 'IT'S NO SECRET'. In September '66, their first album, ' . . . TAKES OFF', was finally issued, a competent hybrid of folk-rock and blues notable for the powerful singing of second vocalist SIGNE

ANDERSON. By the time of the album's release, however, ANDERSON had left to have a baby and was replaced by GRACE SLICK (formerly of The GREAT SOCIETY). SKIP SPENCE also left and the drum stool was filled by SPENCER DRYDEN. The potential of this all-playing, all-writing group was fulfilled on the follow-up lp, 'SURREALISTIC PILLOW' (1967). A psychedelic classic, the record spawned two top 10 singles in the U.S., 'SOMEBODY TO LOVE' (1967) and 'WHITE RABBIT' (967), SLICK having brought both songs with her from her previous band. Her vocal's were even stronger than ANDERSON's and her commanding clarity stamped itself indelibly on every song, particularly 'WHITE RABBIT', a neo classical, lysergic nursery rhyme (inspired by the Lewis Carroll book 'Alice In Wonderland') that managed to sound at once sinister and insidiously catchy. Even KAUKONEN's blistering guitar work and CASSADY's relentlessly inventive bass playing sounded more assured, the album going on to sell half a million copies. The band then took psychedelic experimentation ever further with 'AFTER BATHING AT BAXTER'S' (1968). Comprising a number of free-form song 'suites', the album was hard going; the melodies were still in there, they were just harder to find among the wilful weirdness and extended instrumental jams. 'R.C.A.' must have breathed a sigh of relief when the band came up with the relatively more accessible 'CROWN OF CREATION' (1968). A more conventional set of songs, it featured the scary 'THE HOUSE AT POONEIL CORNERS', SLICK's haunting 'LATHER' and a cover of DAVID CROSBY's menage-a-trois elegy, 'TRIAD'. After a thundering live set, 'BLESS ITS POINTED LITTLE HEAD' (1969), the band recorded the last album to feature the classic JEFFERSON line-up, 'VOLUNTEERS' (1970). It featured the unflinching politicism of 'WE CAN BE TOGETHER' and though the title track was used in the 'Woodstock' movie, the band's own performance wasn't filmed. Soon after the album's release, DRYDEN left to join The NEW RIDERS OF THE PURPLE SAGE and was replaced by JOEY COVINGTON. BALIN also departed around this time after a prolonged period of tension with SLICK, violinist PAPA JOHN CREACH (was this the man behind MADONNA's 'Papa Don't Preach' we ask ourselves?) taking up the slack. The subsequent 'BARK' (1971) and 'LONG JOHN SILVER' (1972) albums (released on the band's newly formed 'Grunt' label) bore none of the intensity of The 'AIRPLANE's earlier work and the band's final effort, the live 'THIRTY SECONDS OVER WINTERLAND' (1973) was similarly underwhelming. By this point, JOHN BARBATA had replaced sticksman COVINGTON while DAVID FRIEBERG (ex-QUICKSILVER MESSENGER SERVICE) had been recruited on vocals. While CASSADY and KAUKONEN went full-time with their side project, HOT TUNA, SLICK and KANTNER formed JEFFERSON STARSHIP with the remaining 'AIRPLANE members. The name was taken from an earlier, KANTNER sci-fi inspired project that released one album, 1971's '(IT'S A FRESH WIND THAT) BLOWS AGAINST THE NORTH'. The debut JEFFERSON STARSHIP album, 'DRAGONFLY' (1974), was well written and skillfully executed but it was clear the band were headed towards the mainstream and with 'RED OCTOPUS' (1975), the band's sleek sound was crystallised, the album shifting a cool four million copies. MARTY BALIN was also back in the fold by this point and his song, 'MIRACLES', went Top 3 later the same year. Disillusioned with the new direction, SLICK soon left for a low key solo career while JEFFERSON STARSHIP continued to notch up hit albums. She later rejoined, although by 1984 even KANTNER had become tired of the group's commercial sound, leaving and taking the JEFFERSON part of the name with him. As STARSHIP, the SLICK fronted band went on to even bigger success, reeling off hits like 'WE BUILT THIS CITY ON ROCK 'N' ROLL' (1985) and the nauseous pop slush of 'NOTHING'S GONNA STOP US NOW' (1987). Incredibly/inevitably there was a full reunion of the classic JEFFERSON AIRPLANE line-up in 1989 which produced an eponymous album. A pointless exercise in crusty nostalgia, it was almost as dull as the dishwater STARSHIP were peddling. • **Songwriters:** KANTNER or BALIN, plus SLICK.

Recommended: SURREALISTIC PILLOW (*8) / AFTER BATHING AT BAXTER'S (*7) / CROWN OF CREATION (*7) / VOLUNTEERS (*6) / GREATEST HITS (TEN YEARS AND CHANGE 1979-1991) (STARSHIP *5)

MARTY BALIN (b. MARTYN JEREL BUCHWALD, 30 Jan'43, Cincinnati, Ohio, USA) – vocals, guitar (ex-solo) / **PAUL KANTNER** (b.12 Mar'42, San Francisco) – guitar, vocals / **JORMA KAUKONEN** (b.23 Dec'40, Washington, D.C.) – lead guitar / **SIGNE TOLY ANDERSON** (b.15 Sep'41, Seattle, Wash.) – vocals / **JACK CASADY** (b.13 Apr'44, Washington, D.C.) – bass repl. BOB HARVEY / **SKIP SPENCE** (b.18 Apr'46, Ontario, Canada) – drums (ex-QUICKSILVER MESSENGER SERVICE) repl. JERRY PELOQUIN

R.C.A. R.C.A.

Feb 66. (7") *<8679>* **IT'S NO SECRET. / RUNNIN' ROUND THIS TABLE** [-] [ ]

May 66. (7") *<8848>* **COME UP THE YEARS. / BLUES FROM AN AEROPLANE** [-] [ ]

Sep 66. (lp) *<LSP 3584>* **JEFFERSON AIRPLANE TAKES OFF** [-] [ ]
– Blues from an airplane / Let me in / It's no secret / Bringing me down / Tobacco road / Coming up the years / Run around / Let's get together / Don't slip away / Chauffeur blues / And I like it. *(UK-iss.Oct71; SF 8195) (re-iss.Jun74;)*

Sep 66. (7") *<8967>* **BRINGING ME DOWN. / LET ME IN** [-] [ ]

— **GRACE SLICK** (b. GRACE BARNETT WING, 30 Oct'39, Chicago, Illinois) – vocals (ex-GREAT SOCIETY) repl. SIGNE who left to look after her baby / **SPENCER DRYDEN** (b. 7 Apr'38, New York City) – drums (ex-PEANUT BUTTER CONSPIRACY, ex-ASHES) repl. SKIP who formed MOBY GRAPE

Dec 66. (7") *<9063>* **MY BEST FRIEND. / HOW DO YOU FEEL** [-] [ ]

Sep 67. (lp; mono/stereo) *(RD/SF 7889) <LSP 3766>* **SURREALISTIC PILLOW** [ ] [3] Feb67
– She has funny cars / Somebody to love / My best friend / Today / Comin' back to me / How do you feel / 3/5 mile in 10 seconds / D.C.B.A. – 25 / Embryonic journey / White rabbit / Plastic fantastic lover. *(UK-rel.had different tracks) (cd-iss.Sep84; PD 83766) (cd re-iss.Oct87; ND 83738)*

May 67. (7") *(RCA 1594) <9140>* **SOMEBODY TO LOVE. / SHE HAS FUNNY CARS** [ ] [5] Feb67

Sep 67. (7") *(RCA 1631) <9248>* **WHITE RABBIT. / PLASTIC FANTASTIC LOVER** [ ] [8] Jun67

Nov 67. (7") *(RCA 1647) <9297>* **BALLAD OF YOU AND ME AND POONEIL. / TWO HEADS** [ ] [42] Sep67

Jun 68. (lp; mono/stereo) *(RD/SF 7926) <LSP 1511>* **AFTER BATHING AT BAXTERS** [ ] [17] Dec67
– (Streetmasse): / Ballad of you and me and Pooneil – A small package of value will come to you, shortly – Young girl Sunday blues / (The war is over): / Martha – Wild thyme / (Hymn to an older generation): / The last wall of the castle – Rejoyce / How sweet it is:- Watch her ride – Spare chaynge / Shizoforest love suite: Two heads – Won't you try – Saturday afternoon. *(re-iss.Dec88 lp/c; NL/NK 84718)*

Jan 68. (7") *<9389>* **WATCH HER RIDE. / MARTHA** [-] [61] Dec67

Jun 68. (7") *(RCA 1711) <9496>* **GREASY HEART. / SHARE A LITTLE JOKE** [ ] [98] Mar68

Sep 68. (7") *(RCA 1736)* **IF YOU FEEL LIKE CHINA BREAKING. TRIAD** [ ] [-]

Oct 68. (7") *<9644>* **CROWN OF CREATION. / TRIAD** [-] [64]

Dec 68. (lp; mono/stereo) *(RD/SF 7976) <LSP 4058>* **CROWN OF CREATION** [ ] [6] Sep68
– Lather / In time / Triad / Star track / Share a little joke / Chushingura / If you feel / Crown of creation / Ice cream Phoenix / Greasy heart / The house at Pooh Corner. *(re-iss.Oct85 lp/c; NL/NK 83797) (cd-iss.Jun88; ND 83660)*

Jun 69. (lp; mono/stereo) *(RD/SF 8019) <LSP 4133>* **BLESS ITS POINTED LITTLE HEAD (live)** [38] [17] Feb69
– Clergy / 3/5 of a mile in 10 seconds / Somebody to love / Fat angel / Rock me baby / The other side of this life / It's no secret / Plastic fantastic lover / Turn out the lights / Bear melt.

Jul 69. (7") *<0150>* **PLASTIC FANTASTIC LOVER (live). / THE OTHER SIDE OF THIS LIFE (live)** [-] [ ]

Feb 70. (lp) *(SF 8164) <LSP 4238>* **VOLUNTEERS** [34] [13] Nov69
– We can be together / Good shepherd / The farm / Hey Frederick / Turn my life down / Wooden ships / Eskimo blue day / A song for all seasons / Meadowlands / Volunteers. *(re-iss.Oct85)*

Mar 70. (7") *(RCA 1933) <0245>* **VOLUNTEERS. / WE CAN BE TOGETHER** [ ] [65] Nov69

— **JOEY COVINGTON** – drums repl. DRYDEN who joined NEW RIDERS OF THE PURPLE SAGE (above new with **SLICK, CASADY, BALIN** and **KAUKONEN**) (note also DRYDEN played on below 'A' side)

Aug 70. (7") *(RCA 1989) <0343>* **MEXICO. / HAVE YOU SEEN THE SAUCERS?** [ ] [ ]

— At this time various members, mainly KAUKONEN and CASADY side lined HOT TUNA. PAUL KANTNER then recorded album with what was then p/t JEFFERSON STARSHIP (see further below and his late '71 co-credit with GRACE SLICK

— **PAPA JOHN CREACH** (b.28 May 1917, Beaver Falls, Pennsylvania) – violin (of HOT TUNA) finally repl. BALIN who left earlier.

Grunt Grunt

Oct 71. (lp) *<(FTR 1001)>* **BARK** [42] [11] Sep71
– When the Earth moves again / Feel so good / Crazy Miranda / Pretty as you feel / Wild turkey / Law man / Rock and roll island / Third week in Chelsea / Never argue with a German if you're tired or European song / Thunk / War movie. *(re-iss.Jul84; NL 84386)*

Oct 71. (7") *<(65-0500)>* **PRETTY AS YOU FEEL. / WILD TURKEY** [ ] [60]

— **JOHN BARBATA** – drums (ex-CROSBY & NASH, ex-TURTLES) repl. JOEY

Jun 72. (lp) *<(FTR 1007)>* **LONG JOHN SILVER** [30] [20]
– Long John Silver / Aerie (gang of eagles) / Twilight double leader / Milk train / Son of Jesus / Easter? / Trial by fire / Alexander the medium / Eat starch mom.

Sep 72. (7") *<(65-0506)>* **LONG JOHN SILVER. / MILK TRAIN** [ ] [ ]

1972. (7") *<(65-0511)>* **TWILIGHT DOUBLE DEALER. / TRIAL BY FIRE** [ ] [ ]

— **DAVID FREIBERG** (b.24 Aug'38, Boston, Mass.) – vocals (ex-QUICKSILVER MESSENGER SERVICE) (They made last album recorded between 71-72)

Apr 73. (lp) *<(FTR 0147)>* **30 SECONDS OVER WINTERLAND (live)** [ ] [52]
– Have you seen the saucers / Feel so good / Crown of creation / When the Earth moves again / Milk train / Trial by fire / Twilight double leader. *(re-iss.Oct85 lp/c; NL/NK 83867)*

— Now non-recording quintet of SLICK, KANTNER, FREIBERG, BARBATA and CREACH. CASADY and KAUKONEN made HOT TUNA their full-time band.

PAUL KANTNER & JEFFERSON STARSHIP

with JERRY GARCIA, DAVID CROSBY, GRAHAM NASH, MICKEY HART

R.C.A. R.C.A.

Jan 71. (7") *<0426>* **A CHILD IS COMING. / LET'S GO TOGETHER** [-] [ ]

Apr 71. (lp) *(SF 8163) <LSP 4448>* **(IT'S A FRESH WIND THAT) BLOWS AGAINST THE NORTH** [ ] [20] Nov70
– Mau mau (Amerikon) / The baby tree / Let's go together / A child is coming / Sunrise / Hijack / Home / Have you seen the stars tonite / X-M / Starship.

PAUL KANTNER & GRACE SLICK

Grunt Grunt

Dec 71. (lp) *<(FTR 1002)>* **SUNFIGHTER** [ ] [89]
– Silver spoon / Diana (part 1) / Sunfighter / Titanic / Look at the wood / When I was a boy I watched the wolves / Million / China / Earth mother / Diana (part 2) / Universal Copernican mumbles / Holding together. *(re-iss.Apr89 on 'Essential' lp/cd; ESS LP/CD 001)*

Jan 72. (7") *<0503>* **SUNFIGHTER. / CHINA** [-] [ ]

— KANTNER later released a US only album 'THE PLANET EARTH ROCK AND ROLL ORCHESTRA iss.Aug83. After leaving JEFFERSON STARSHIP he formed KBC with BALIN and CASADY (ex-AIRPLANE members). They released a single and album early '83.

PAUL KANTNER, GRACE SLICK, DAVID FREIBERG

with guests **JORMA KAUKONEN** – guitar / **JACK CASADY** – bass / **CHAQUICO** – guitar / **JERRY GARCIA** ('Grateful Dead') / **DAVID CROSBY** ('Crosby, Stills & Nash')

Grunt Grunt

Jun 73. (lp) *<(BFL 1-0148)>* **BARON VON TOLBOOTH & THE CHROME NUN** □ □
– Ballad of the chrome nun / Fat / Flowers of the night / Walkin' / Your mind has left your body / Across the board / Harp tree lament / White boy (transcaucasian airmachine blues) / Fishman / Sketches of China.

Jun 73. (7") *<0094>* **BALLAD OF THE CHROME NUN. / SKETCHES OF CHINA** [-] □

— For JEFFERSON STARSHIP + STARSHIP recordings (which had nothing whatsoever to do with psychedelia) see The GREAT ROCK DISCOGRAPHY.

JEFFERSON AIRPLANE

were reformed with **SLICK, KANTNER, KAUKONEN, CASADY and BALIN.** Augmented by **KENNY ARONOFF** – drums / **PETER KAUKONEN and RANDY JACKSON** – guitar (ex-ZEBRA)

Epic Epic

Oct 89. (lp/c/cd) *(465 659-1/-4/-2) <45271>* **JEFFERSON AIRPLANE** □ [85]
– Planes / Solidarity / Summer of love / The wheel / True love / Now is the time / Panda / Freedom / Ice age / Madeleine Street / Common market madrigal / Upfront blues / Too many years.

Oct 89. (7") *<73044>* **SUMMER OF LOVE. / PANDA** [-] □

Jan 90. (c-s) *<73080>* **TRUE LOVE /** [-] □

— JEFFERSON STARSHIP ("the next generation") were formed after above.

– (AIRPLANE) compilations, etc. –

on 'R.C.A.' unless mentioned otherwise

Jun 70. (7") *(RCA 1964)* **WHITE RABBIT. / SOMEBODY TO LOVE** □ □

Nov 70. (lp) *(SF 8164) <4459>* **THE WORST OF JEFFERSON AIRPLANE** □ [12]
(re-iss.Sep86 on 'Fame' lp/c; FA/TC-FA 3167)

Apr 74. (lp) *Grunt; <(APL 1-0437)>* **EARLY FLIGHT** □ □

Apr 76. (7"m) *(RCA 2676)* **WHITE RABBIT. / SOMEBODY TO LOVE / CROWN OF CREATION** □ □

Dec 76. (d-lp) *(SF 7889) <1255>* **FLIGHT LOG** (1966-76 work) □ [37]

Apr 79. (12") *RCA Gold; (GOLD 4)* **WHITE RABBIT. / SOMEBODY TO LOVE** □ [-]

Jul 80. (lp/c) *(INT S/K 5030) <42727>* **THE BEST OF JEFFERSON AIRPLANE** □ □
(re-iss.1984 lp/c; NL/NK 89186)

Nov 86. (7") *Old Gold; (OG 9631)* **WHITE RABBIT. / SOMEBODY TO LOVE** □ [-]

1987. (7") *<5156>* **WHITE RABBIT. / PLASTIC FANTASTIC LOVER** □ [-]

May 87. (7") *Ariola; (JEFF 1)* **WHITE RABBIT. / SOMEBODY TO LOVE** □ □
(12"+=) *(JEFFT 1)* – She has funny cars / Third week in Chelsea.

Jul 87 (d-lp/c/d-cd) *(NL/NK/ND 90036) <5724>* **2400 FULTON STREET – AN ANTHOLOGY** □ □
– It's no secret / Come up the years / My best friend / Somebody to love / Comin' back to me / Embryonic journey / She has funny cars / Plastic fantastic lover / Wild tyme / The ballad of you & me & Pooneil – A small package of value will come to you, shortly / White rabbit / Won't you try Saturday afternoon / Lather / We can be together / Crown of creation / Mexico / Wooden ships / Rejoyce / Volunteers / Pretty as you feel / Martha / Today / Third week in Chelsea. *(d-cd+=)*– Let's get together / Blues from an airplane / J.P.P. McStep B. Blues / Fat angel / Greasy heart / We can be together / Have you seen the saucers / Eat starch mom / Good shepherd / Eskimo blue day / The Levi commercials. *(re-iss.d-cd.1992;)*

Oct 88. (d-lp/c/cd) *Castle; (CCS LP/MC/CD 200)* **THE COLLECTION** □ [-]
<US cd-iss.Oct92; >

1989. (3"cd-ep) *(PD 49463)* **WHITE RABBIT / PLASTIC FANTASTIC LOVER / SOMEBODY TO LOVE / SHE HAS FUNNY CARS** □ [-]

May 90. (cd/lp) *Thunderbolt; (CDTB/THBL 074)* **LIVE AT THE MONTEREY FESTIVAL (live)** □ [-]

Nov 92. (3xcd-box) **JEFFERSON AIRPLANE LOVES YOU** □ [-]

Apr 93. (cd) *Pulsar;* **WOODSTOCK REVIVAL** □ [-]

Sep 93. (cd/c) *Remember; (RMB 7/4 5065)* **WHITE RABBIT (featuring GRACE SLICK)** □ [-]

Aug 96. (cd) *B.M.G. Special; <74321 40057-2>* **JOURNEY (THE BEST OF JEFFERSON AIRPLANE)** □ [-]

Sep 96. (cd; w-free pic-cd) *Experience; (EXP 021)* **JEFFERSON AIRPLANE LIVE** □ [-]

Jan 97. (cd) *Stampa Alternativa; (SB 03)* **WE ARE ALL ONE** □ □

— for GRACE SLICK solo releases, see GREAT ROCK DISCOGRAPHY

JETHRO TULL

Formed: London, England . . . late 1967 by Scots-born IAN ANDERSON and GLENN CORNICK, who had both been in Blackpool band, JOHN EVANS' SMASH for four years alongside school friends EVANS and JEFFREY HAMMOND-HAMMOND. IAN and GLENN brought in former McGREGORY'S ENGINE members MICK ABRAHAMS plus CLIVE BUNKER, adopting the 18th Century name of an English agriculturist/inventor, JETHRO TULL. It was often mistaken by the uninitiated, as the name of the lead singer, IAN ANDERSON. Early in 1968, through agents Terry Ellis & Chris Wright, 'M.G.M.' issued their debut single, 'SUNSHINE DAY', mistakenly credited as JETHRO TOE at the pressing plant (it has since changed hands for over £100 at record fairs). On the 29th of June '68, after a residency at the Marquee Club, they supported PINK FLOYD at a free rock concert in Hyde Park, London. Following another enthusiastically received concert at Sunbury's Jazz & Blues Festival in August, they signed to 'Island'. By the end of the year, their debut album, 'THIS WAS', had cracked the UK Top 10, even managing to break into the American Top 75. Early in '69, they hired TONY IOMMI (future BLACK SABBATH) and DAVID O'LIST (of The NICE), for a few gigs following the departure of ABRAHAMS. In May '69, with the addition of MARTIN BARRE, they secured a UK Top 3 placing with the classic 'LIVING IN THE PAST' single. This was quickly followed by the UK No.1 album, 'STAND UP', which also made the Top 20 in the States. They then signed to associate label, 'Chrysalis', scoring two more UK Top 10 singles in 'SWEET DREAM' and 'THE WITCHES PROMISE'. By this juncture, the band were moving away from their early blues-orientated sound into the murky waters of progressive rock, ANDERSON's songwriting voice becoming more vocal with each successive release. With his fevered, one- legged flute playing and laughably outlandish vagrant garb, ANDERSON gave the group its visual trademark, for many people he was *JETHRO TULL*. After a series of line-up changes and continued success in America, the band released 'AQUALUNG' (1971), a million selling concept album through which ANDERSON expressed his contempt for organised religion. This was nothing, however, compared to the contempt which ANDERSON himself would be subject to from a volatile music press whose patience was wearing thin. If the ambitious 'THICK AS A BRICK' (1972) received a less than enthusiastic response from the press, then 'PASSION PLAY's whimsical self-indulgence was met with a critical mauling. As is often the case, the public ignored the reviews and queued up in droves for a copy, especially in America. 'WAR CHILD' and 'MINSTREL IN THE GALLERY' heralded a return to more traditional song structures but by this time, the critics had it in for the band. 'TULL did little to improve the situation by releasing the execrable 'TOO OLD TO ROCK'N'ROLL, TOO YOUNG TO DIE' (1976). Cast into the ghetto of eternal unhipness with the onslaught of punk, JETHRO TULL carried on unhindered, their live shows attracting hordes of die-hard fans. While their recorded output took on a more folky bent with 'SONGS FROM THE WOOD' and 'HEAVY HORSES', the beast that was the 'TULL live phenomenon was beamed around the world by satellite from a show at New York's Madison Square Garden in 1978. ANDERSON began working on a solo album in 1980 with ex-members of ROXY MUSIC and FAIRPORT CONVENTION, the finished article, "A", eventually being released as an official JETHRO TULL album. While the record was greeted with enthusiasm from fans, the follow-up ANDERSON solo lp, 'WALK INTO THE LIGHT' (1983) and subsequent group project 'UNDER WRAPS' (1984) tested even the most ardent 'TULL devotees with their cod-electronica. After a few years break, the band released 'CREST OF A KNAVE' (1987), a harder rocking affair and a return to form of sorts. 'ROCK ISLAND' (1989) and 'CATFISH RISING' (1991) were disappointing in comparison while the live 1992 album, 'A LITTLE LIGHT MUSIC', saw the band in refreshing semi-acoustic mode. 1995 marked a fair solo effort by ANDERSON and a well received 'TULL album, 'ROOTS TO BRANCHES'. While the band's studio output continues to be inconsistent at best, the prospect of a JETHRO TULL live show still has old prog die-hards parting with their hard-earned cash. • **Songwriters:** ANDERSON lyrics / group compositions, except BOUREE (J.S.Bach) / JOHN BARLEYCORN (trad.) / CAT'S SQUIRREL (Cream). • **Trivia:** ANDERSON still controls his trout-farming business in Northern Scotland. In 1974, he produced STEELEYE SPAN's 'Now We Are Six' album.

Recommended: AQUALUNG (*8) / A PASSION PLAY (*7) / LIVING IN THE PAST (*7) / THE VERY BEST OF JETHRO TULL (*8)

IAN ANDERSON (b.10 Aug'47, Edinburgh, Scotland) – vocals, flute / **GLENN CORNICK** (b.24 Apr'47, Barrow-in-Furness, England) – bass / **MICK ABRAHAMS** (b. 7 Apr'43, Luton, England) – guitar, vocals (ex-McGREGORY'S ENGINE) / **CLIVE BUNKER** (b.12 Dec'46) – drums (ex-McGREGORY'S ENGINE)

M.G.M. not issued

Mar 68. (7"; as JETHRO TOE) *(MGM 1384)* **SUNSHINE DAY. / AEROPLANE** □ [-]

Island Reprise

Aug 68. (7") *(WIP 6043)* **A SONG FOR JEFFREY. / ONE FOR JOHN GEE** □ [-]

Oct 68. (lp; mono/stereo) *(ILP/+S 985) <6336>* **THIS WAS** [10] [62] Feb69
– My Sunday feeling / Some day the sun won't shine for you / Beggar's farm / Move on alone / Serenade to a cuckoo / Dharma for one / It's breaking me up / Cat's squirrel / A song for Jeffrey / Round. *(re-iss.Jan74 lp/c; CHR/ZCHR 1041) (cd-iss.1986; CCD 1041)*

Dec 68. (7") *(WIP 6048)* **LOVE STORY. / A CHRISTMAS SONG** [29] [-]

Mar 69. (7") *<0815>* **LOVE STORY. / A SONG FOR JEFFREY** [-] □

— **MARTIN BARRIE** (b.17 Nov'46) – guitar repl. MICK ABRAHAMS who formed BLODWYN PIG

May 69. (7") *(WIP 6056)* **LIVING IN THE PAST. / DRIVING SONG** [3] [-]

Jul 69. (lp) *(ILPS 9103) <6360>* **STAND UP** [1] [20] Oct69
– A new day yesterday / Jeffrey goes to Leicester Square / Bouree / Back to the family / Look into the sun / Nothing is easy / Fat man / We used to know / Reasons for waiting / For a thousand mothers. *(re-iss.Nov83 on 'Fame' lp/c; FA/TCFA 413086-1/-4) (cd-iss.Jan89; CCD 1042) (re-iss.Feb97 on 'E.M.I.'; LPCENT 8)*

Chrysalis Reprise

Oct 69. (7") *(WIP 6070)* **SWEET DREAM. / 17** [9] [-]

Oct 69. (7") *<0886>* **SWEET DREAM. / REASONS FOR WAITING** [-] □

Jan 70. (7") *(WIP 6077) <0899>* **THE WITCH'S PROMISE. / TEACHER** [4] □

— augmented by **JOHN EVAN** (b.28 Mar'48) – keyboards (he later joined full-time)

Apr 70. (lp) *(ILPS 9123) <6400>* **BENEFIT** [3] [11]
– With you there to help me / Nothing to say / Alive and well and living in / Son / For Michael Collins, Jeffrey and me / To cry you a song / A time for everything /

Inside / Play in time / Sossity; you're a woman. *(re-iss.Jan74 lp/c; CHR/ZCHR 1043) (cd-iss.Jun87; CPCD 1043)*

May 70. (7") *(WIP 6081)* **INSIDE. / ALIVE AND WELL AND LIVING IN** [ ] [-]

Jul 70. (7") *<0927>* **INSIDE. / A TIME FOR EVERYTHING** [-] [ ]

— **JEFFREY HAMMOND-HAMMOND** (b.30 Jul'46) – bass repl. CORNICK who formed WILD TURKEY

Mar 71. (lp) *(ILPS 9145) <2035>* **AQUALUNG** [4] [7] Apr 71
– Aqualung / Cross-eyed mary / Cheap day return / Mother goose / Wond'ring aloud / Up to me / My God / Hymn £43 / Slipstream / Locomotive breath / Wind-up. *(re-iss.Jan74 lp/c; CHR/ZCHR 1044) (cd-iss.1988; CCD 933-2) (re-iss.cd Mar94;)*

Jul 71. (7") *<1024>* **HYMN #43. / MOTHER GOOSE** [-] [91]

— **ANDERSON, BARRE, HAMMOND-HAMMOND** and **EVAN** were joined by **BARRIEMORE BARLOW** (b.10 Sep'49) – drums (ex-JOHN EVAN'S SMASH) who repl. BUNKER who joined BLODWYN PIG

Sep 71. (7"ep) *(WIP 6106)* **LIFE IS A LONG SONG / UP THE POOL. / DR. BOGENBROOM / FOR LATER / NURSIE** [11] [-]

Oct 71. (7") *<1054>* **LOCOMOTIVE BREATH. / WIND** [-] [ ]

Chrysalis Reprise

Mar 72. (lp) *(CHR 1003) <2071>* **THICK AS A BRICK** [5] [1] May72
– Thick as a brick (side 1) / Thick as a brick (side 2). *(re-iss.Jan74 lp/c; CHR/ZCHR 1003) (cd-iss.1986; ACCD 1003) (cd-re-iss.Apr89 on 'Mobile Fidelity'; UDCD 510) (cd re-iss.as part of 25th Anniversary on 'E.M.I.'+=; CDCNTAV 5)*– Thick as a brick (live at Madison Square Gardens 1978) / (interview).

Apr 72. (7") *<1153>* **THICK AS A BRICK (edit £1). / HYMN £43** [-] [ ]

Chrysalis Chrysalis

Jul 72. (d-lp) *(CJT 1) <2106>* **LIVING IN THE PAST** (live / studio compilation) [8] [3] Nov72
– By kind permission of / Dharma for one / Wond'ring again / Locomotive breath / Life is a long song / Up the pool / Dr.Bogenbroom / For later / Nursie / A song for Jeffrey / Love story / Christmas song / Teacher / Living in the past / Driving song / Bouree / Sweet dream / Singing all day / Teacher / The witches promise / Inside / Just trying to be. *(cd-iss.Oct87; CCD 1035) (re-iss.Mar94 cd/c;)*

Oct 72. (7") *<2006>* **LIVING IN THE PAST. / CHRISTMAS SONG** [-] [11]

May 73. (7") *<2012>* **A PASSION PLAY (edit £8). / A PASSION PLAY (edit £9)** [-] [80]

Jul 73. (lp) *(<CHR/ZCHR 1040>)* **A PASSION PLAY** [13] [1]
– A passion play (part 1; including 'The story of the hare who lost his spectacles' part 1)- /- (part 2) / A passion play (part 2). *(cd-iss.Jan89; CCD 1040)*

Aug 73. (7") *<2017>* **A PASSION PLAY (edit £6). / A PASSION PLAY (edit £10)** [-] [ ]

Oct 74. (7") *(CHS 2054) <2101>* **BUNGLE IN THE JUNGLE. / BACK-DOOR ANGELS** [ ] [12]

Oct 74. (lp/c) *(<CHR/ZCHR 1067>)* **WAR CHILD** [14] [2]
– War child / Queen and country / Ladies / Back-door angels / Sea lion / Skating away on the thin ice of a new day / Bungle in the jungle / Only solitaire / The third hooray / Two fingers.

Jan 74. (7") *<2103>* **SKATING AWAY ON THE THIN ICE OF A NEW DAY. / SEA LION** [-] [ ]

Sep 75. (lp/c) *(<CHR/ZCHR 1082>)* **MINSTREL IN THE GALLERY** [20] [7]
– Minstrel in the gallery / Cold wind to Valhalla / Black satin dancer / Requiem / One white duck / 0x10 = Nothing at all – Baker St. Muse (including Pig-me and the whore – Nice little tune – Crash barrier waltzer – Mother England reverie) / Grace. *(cd-iss.1986; CCD 1082)*

Oct 75. (7") *(CHS 2075) <2106>* **MINSTREL IN THE GALLERY. / SUMMER DAY SANDS** [ ] [79]

— **JOHN GLASCOCK** (b.1953) – bass (ex-CHICKEN SHACK, ex-TOE FAT) repl. HAMMOND-HAMMOND

Mar 76. (7") *(CHS 2086)* **TOO OLD TO ROCK'N'ROLL, TOO YOUNG TO DIE. / RAINBOW BLUES** [ ] [-]

Mar 76. (lp/c) *(<CHR/ZCHR 1111>)* **TOO OLD TO ROCK'N'ROLL, TOO YOUNG TO DIE** [25] [14] May76
– Quizz kid / Crazed institution / Salamander / Taxi grab / From a dead beat to an old greaser / Bad-eyed and loveless / Big dipper / Too old to rock'n'roll, too young to die / Pied piper / The chequered flag (dead or alive). *(cd-iss.1986; CCD 1111)*

Apr 76. (7") *<2114>* **TOO OLD TO ROCK'N'ROLL, TOO YOUNG TO DIE. / BAD- EYED AND LOVELESS** [-] [ ]

— added **DAVID PALMER** – keyboards (He had been their past orchestrator)

Nov 76. (7"ep) *(CXP 2)* **RING OUT, SOLSTICE BELLS / MARCH THE MAD SCIENTIST. / A CHRISTMAS SONG / PAN DANCE** [28] [-]

Jan 77. (7") *(CHS <2135>)* **THE WHISTLER. / STRIP CARTOON** [ ] [59] Apr 77

Feb 77. (lp/c) *(<CHR/ZCHR 1132>)* **SONGS FROM THE WOOD** [13] [8]
– Songs from the wood / Jack-in-the-green / Cup of wonder / Hunting girl / Ring out, solstice bells / Velvet green / The whistler / Pibroch (cap in hand) / Fire at midnight. *(cd-iss.1986; ACCD 1132)*

Apr 78. (7") *(CHS 2214)* **MOTHS. / LIFE IS A LONG SONG** [ ] [-]

Apr 78. (lp/c) *(<CHR/ZCHR 1175>)* **HEAVY HORSES** [20] [19]
– . . .And the mouse police never sleeps / Acres wild / No lullaby / Moths / Journeyman / Rover / One brown mouse / Heavy horses / Weathercock. *(cd-iss.1986; CCD 1175)*

Nov 78. (7",7"white) *(CHS 2260)* **A STITCH IN TIME. / SWEET DREAM (live)** [ ] [-]

Nov 78. (d-lp/c) *(CJT/ZCJT 4) <1201>* **LIVE-BURSTING OUT** [17] [21] Oct78
– No lullaby / Sweet dream / Skating away on the thin ice of a new day / Jack-in-the-green / One brown mouse / A new day yesterday / Flute solo improvisation – God rest ye merry gentlemen / Bouree / Songs from the wood / Thick as a brick / Hunting girl / Too old to rock'n'roll, too young to die / Conundrum / Cross-eyed Mary / Quatrain / Aqualung / Locomotive breath / The dambuster's march – medley. *(cd-iss.1990)*

Sep 79. (7") *(CHS 2378)* **NORTH SEA OIL. / ELEGY** [ ] [ ]

Sep 79. (lp/c) *(<CDL/ZCDL 1238>)* **STORMWATCH** [27] [22]
– North Sea oil / Orion / Home / Dark ages / Warm sporran / Something's on the move / Old ghosts / Dun Ringill / Flying Dutchman / Elegy. *(cd-iss.Jan89; CCD 1238)*

Nov 79. (7") *<2387>* **HOME. / WARM SPORRAN** [-] [ ]

Nov 79. (7"ep) *(CHS 2394)* **HOME / KING HENRY'S MADRIGAL (THEME FROM MAINSTREAM). / WARM SPORRAN / RING OUT SOLSTICE BELLS** [ ] [-]

— ANDERSON for what was supposed to be a solo album retained **BARRE** / plus new **DAVE PEGG** (b. 2 Nov'47, Birmingham, England) – bass (ex-FAIRPORT CONVENTION) repl. GLASCOCK who died. / **EDDIE JOBSON** (b.28 Apr'55, England) – keyboards (ex-ROXY MUSIC, ex-CURVED AIR, etc) repl. EVANS and PALMER who took up session work / **MARK CRANEY** (b. Los Angeles, Calif.) – drums repl. BARLOW who went solo.

Aug 80. (lp/c) *(<CDL/CDC 1301>)* **"A"** [25] [30] Sep 80
– Crossfire / Fylingdale flyer / Working John, working Joe / Black Sunday / Protect and survive / Batteries not included / 4.W.D. (low ratio) / The Pine Marten's jig / And further on.

Oct 80. (7") *(CHS 2468)* **WORKING JOHN, WORKING JOE. / FYLINGDALE FLYER** [ ] [-]

— **PETER JOHN VITESSE** – keyboards repl. JOBSON who went solo / **GERRY CONWAY** – drums (ex-STEELEYE SPAN) repl. CRANEY

Apr 82. (lp/c) *(<CDL/CDC 1380>)* **BROADSWORD AND THE BEAST** [27] [19] May82
– Beastie / Clasp / Fallen on hard times / Flying colours / Slow marching band / Broadsword / Pussy willow / Watching me watching you / Seal driver / Cheerio. *(cd-iss.Apr83; CCD 1380)*

May 82. (7") *<2613>* **PUSSY WILLOW. / FALLEN ON HARD TIMES** [-] [ ]

May 82. (7"/7"pic-d) *(CHS/+P 2616)* **BROADSWORD. / FALLEN ON HARD TIMES** [ ] [-]

— **DOANNE PERRY** – drums repl. CONWAY

Sep 84. (lp/pic-lp/c/cd) *(CDL/CDLP/ZCDL/CCD 1461) <1-/0-/4-/2-1461>* **UNDER WRAPS** [18] [76]
– Lap of luxury / Under wraps I / European legacy / Later that same evening / Saboteur / Radio free Moscow / Nobody's car / Heat / Under wraps II / Paperazzi / Apogee. *(c+=/cd+=)*– Automatic engineering / Astronomy / Tundra / General crossing.

Sep 84. (7") *(TULL 1)* **LAP OF LUXURY. / ASTRONOMY** [70] [ ]
(d7"+=/12"+=) *(TULL D/X 1)* – Tundra / Automatic engineering.

Jun 86. (7") *(TULL 2)* **CORONIACH. / JACK FROST AND THE HOODED CROW** [ ] [ ]
(12"+=) *(TULLX 2)* – Living in the past / Elegy.

— **ANDERSON, BARRE, PEGG** and **PERRY** recruited new member **MARTIN ALLCOCK** – keyboards (ex-FAIRPORT CONVENTION) repl. VITESSE

Sep 87. (lp/c/cd) *(CDL/ZCDL/CCD 1590) <1-/4-/2-1590>* **CREST OF A KNAVE** [19] [32]
– Steel monkey / Farm on the freeway / Jump start / Said she was a dancer / Dogs in midwinter * / Budapest / Mountain men / The waking edge * / Raising steam. *(cd+= *)*

Oct 87. (7"/7"pic-d) *(TULL/+P 3)* **STEEL MONKEY. / DOWN AT THE END OF YOUR ROAD** [ ] [ ]
(12"+=)(c-s+=) *(TULLX/ZTULL 3)* – Too many too / I'm your gun.

Dec 87. (7"/7"pic-d) *(TULL/+P 4)* **SAID SHE WAS A DANCER. / DOGS IN MIDWINTER** [55] [ ]
(12"+=) *(TULLX 4)* – The waking edge.
(cd-s+=) *(TULLCD 4)* – Down at the end of your road / Too many too.

Aug 89. (lp/pic-lp/c/cd) *(CHR/CHRP/ZCHR/CCD 1708) <1-/0-/4-/2-21708>* **ROCK ISLAND** [18] [56]
– Kissing Willie / The rattlesnake trail / Ears of tin / Undressed to kill / Rock Island / Heavy water / Another Christmas song / The whalers dues / Big Riff and Mando / Strange avenues.

Aug 89. (c-s) **KISSING WILLIE. / EARS OF TIN** [-] [ ]

Nov 89. (7") *(TULL 5)* **ANOTHER CHRISTMAS SONG. / SOLSTICE BELLS** [ ] [ ]
(12"+=) *(TULLX 5)* – Jack Frost.
(cd-s) *(TULLCD 5)* – ('A'side) / Intro – A Christmas song – Cheap day return – Mother goose – Outro – Locomotive breath (live).

— **ANDY GIDLINGS** – keyboards (3) / **MATT PEGG** – bass (3) / etc. repl. ALLCOCK

Aug 91. (7"/c-s) *(TULL/+XMC 6)* **THIS IS NOT LOVE. / NIGHT IN THE WILDERNESS** [ ] [ ]
(12"+=/cd-s+=) *(TULL X/CD 6)* – Jump start (live).

Sep 91. (cd/c/lp) *(CCD/ZCHR/DCHR 1886) <2-/4-/1-1863>* **CATFISH RISING** [27] [88]
– This is not love / Occasional demons / Rocks on the road / Thinking round corners / Still loving you tonight / Doctor to my disease / Like a tall thin gin / Sparrow on the schoolyard wall / Roll yer own / Goldtipped boots, black jacket and tie. *(free 12"ep)*– WHEN JESUS CAME TO PLAY. / SLEEPING WITH THE DOG / WHITE INNOCENCE

— **DAVID MATTACKS** – drums, percussion, keyboards repl. PERRY and guests

Mar 92. (12"pic-d) *(TULLX 7)* **ROCKS ON THE ROAD. / JACK-A-LYNN (demo) / AQUALUNG – LOCOMOTIVE BREATH (live)** [47] [ ]
(c-s) *(TULLMC 7)* – ('A'side) / Bouree (live) / Mother goose – Jack-a-Lyn (live).
(2xbox-cd-s++=) *(TULLCD 7)* – Tall thin god (live) / Fat man (live).

Sep 92. (cd/c/d-lp) *(CCD/ZCHR/CHR 1954) <2-/4/-1-1954>* **A LITTLE LIGHT MUSIC (live in Europe '92)** [34] [ ]
– Someday the sun won't shine for you / Living in the past / Life is a long song / Under wraps / Rocks on the road / Nursie / Too old to rock and roll, too young to die / One white duck / A new day yesterday / John Barleycorn / Look into the sun / A Christmas song / From a dead beat to an old greaser / This is not love / Bouree / Pussy willow / Locomotive breath.

— **PERRY** returned to repl.MATTACKS. Bass playing was provided by **DAVE PEGG / STEVE BAILEY**

Sep 95. (cd/c/d-lp) *(CCD/ZCHR/CHR 6109) <2-/4-/1-6109>* **ROOTS TO BRANCHES** [20] [ ]
– Roots to branches / Rare and precious chain / Out of the noise / This free will / Wounded, old and reacherous / Dangerous veils / Beside myself / Valley / At last, forever / Stuck in the August rain / Another Harry's bar.

– compilations, others, etc. –

on 'Chrysalis' unless mentioned otherwise

Jan 76. (7") *(CHS 2081)* **LIVING IN THE PAST. / REQUIEM** [ ] [ ]

Jan 76. (lp/c) *(<CHR/ZCHR 1078>)* **M.U. – THE BEST OF JETHRO TULL** [44] [13]
– Teacher / Aqualung / Thick as a brick (edit £1) / Bungle in the jungle / Locomotive breath / Fat man / Living in the past / A passion play (£8) / Skating away on the thin ice of a new day / Rainbow blues / Nothing is easy. *(cd-iss.Dec85; ACCD 1078)*

Feb 76. (7") *<2110>* **LOCOMOTIVE BREATH. / FAT MAN** [-] [62]
Nov 77. (lp/c) *(<CHR/ZCHR 1135>)* **REPEAT – THE BEST OF JETHRO TULL VOL.2** [ ] [94]
– Minstrel in the gallery / Cross-eyed Mary / A new day yesterday / Bouree / Thick as a brick (edit £1) / War child / A passion play (edit £9) / To cry you a song / Too old to rock'n'roll, too young to die / Glory row. *(cd-iss.Apr86;)*
Dec 82. (d-c) *(ZCDP 105)* **M.U. / REPEAT** [ ] [-]
Oct 85. (lp/c/cd) *(JTTV/ZJTTV/CCD 1515)* **ORIGINAL MASTERS** [63] [ ]
Aug 87. (7") *Old Gold; (OG 9637)* **LIVING IN THE PAST. / THE WITCHES' PROMISE** [ ] [-]
Jun 88. (5xlp-box/3xc-box/3xcd-box) *(T/MC/CD BOX 1) <41653>* **20 YEARS OF JETHRO TULL** [78] [97]
– THE RADIO ARCHIVES:- A song for Jeffrey / Love story * / Fat man / Bouree / Stormy Monday blues * / A new day yesterday * / Cold wind to Valhalla / Minstrel in the gallery / Velvet green / Grace * / The clasp / / Pibroch (pee-break) – Black satin dancer (instrumental) * / Fallen on hard times // THE RARE TRACKS:- Jack Frost and the hooded crow / I'm your gun / Down at the end of your road / Coronach * / Summerday sands * / Too many too / March the mad scientist * / Pan dance / Strip cartoon / King Henry's madrigal / A stitch in time / 17 / One for John Gee / Aeroplane / Sunshine day // FLAWED GEMS:- Lick your fingers clean * / The Chateau Disaster Tapes: Scenario – Audition – No reheasal / Beltane / Crossword * / Saturation * / Jack-A-Lynn * / Motoreyes * / Blues instrumental (untitled) / Rhythm in gold // THE OTHER SIDES OF TULL:- Part of the machine * / Mayhem, maybe * / Overhang * / Kelpie * / Living in these hard times / Under wraps II * / Only solitaire / Cheap day return / Wond'ring aloud * / Dun Ringill * / Salamander / Moths / Nursie * / Life is a long song * / One white duck – 0x10 = Nothing at all // THE ESSENTIAL TULL:- Songs from the wood / Living in the past * / Teacher * / Aqualung * / Locomotive breath * / The witches promise * / Bungle in the jungle / Farm on the freeway / Thick as a brick / Sweet dream. *(re-iss.Aug88 as d-lp/d-c/d-cd; tracks *; CHR/ZCHR/CCD 1655)*
Jun 88. (pic-cd) *(TULLPCD 1)* **PART OF THE MACHINE / STORMY MONDAY BLUES (live) / LICK YOUR FINGERS CLEAN (live) / MINSTREL IN THE GALLERY (live) / FARM ON THE FREEWAY (live)** [ ] [-]
Jan 91. (cd/c/lp) *Raw Fruit; (FRS CD/MC/LP 004)* **LIVE AT HAMMERSMITH 1984 (live)** [ ] [-]
Apr 93. (4xcd-box) *(CDCHR 60044)* **25th ANNIVERSARY BOXED SET** [ ] [ ]
– REMIXED (CLASSIC SONGS) / CARNEGIE HALL N.Y. (RECORDED LIVE NEW YORK CITY 1970) / THE BEACON'S BOTTOM (TAPES) / POT POURRI (LIVE ACROSS THE WORLD AND THROUGH THE YEARS)
May 93. (7") *(CHS 3970)* **LIVING IN THE PAST. / HARD LINER** [32] [ ]
(12") *(12CHS 3970)* – ('A'side) / ('A'club)/ ('A'dub ravey master) / ('A'dub N.Y. mix).
(d-cd-s) *(23970-1)* – Living in the (slightly more recent) past / Silver river turning / Rosa on the factory floor / I don't want to be me / ('A'side) / Truck stop runner / Piece of cake / Man of principle.
May 93. (d-cd/d-c) *(CDCHR/ZCHR 6001)* **THE VERY BEST OF JETHRO TULL – THE ANNIVERSARY COLLECTION** [ ] [ ]
– A song for Jeffrey / Beggar's farm / A Christmas song / A new day yesterday / Bouree / Nothing is easy / Living in the past / To cry you a song / Teacher / Sweet dream / Cross-eyed Mary / Mother goose / Aqualung / Locomotive breath / Life is a long song / Thick as a brick (extract) / Skating away on the thin ice of a new day / Bungle in the jungle/ / Minstrel in the gallery / Too old to rock'n'roll / Songs from the wood / Jack in the green / The whistler / Heavy horses / Dun Ringill / Fylingdale flyer / Jack-a-Lynn / Pussy willow / Broadsword / Under wraps II / Steel monkey / Farm on the freeway / Jump start / Kissing Willie / This is not love.
Nov 93. (d-cd) *(CDCHR 6057)* **NIGHTCAP – THE UNRELEASED MASTERS 1973-1991** [ ] [ ]
– CHATEAU D'ISASTER – First post / Animelee / Tiger Moon / Look at the animals / Law of the bungle part II / Left right / Solitaire / Critique oblique / Post last / Scenario / Audition / No rehearsal/ / UNRELEASED & RARE TRACKS – Paradise steakhouse / Sealion II / Piece of cake / Quartet / Silver river turning / Crew nights / The curse / Rosa on the factory floor / A small cigar / Man of principle / Commons brawl / No step / Drive on the young side of life / I don't want to be me / Broadford bazaar / Lights out / Truck stop runner / Hard liner.
Apr 95. (cd) *Windsong; (WINCD 070)* **IN CONCERT (live)** [ ] [-]
Feb 97. (cd) *EMI Gold; (CDGOLD 1079)* **THROUGH THE YEARS** [ ] [-]
Mar 97. (cd) *Disky; (DC 87861-2)* **THE JETHRO TULL COLLECTION** [ ] [-]
Apr 97. (3xcd-box) *(CDOMB 021)* **THE ORIGINALS** [ ] [-]
– (THIS WAS / STAND UP / BENEFIT)

IAN ANDERSON

solo album augmented by **PETER JOHN VITESSE** – synth, keyboards

Chrysalis Chrysalis

Nov 83. (7") *(CHS 2746)* **FLY BY NIGHT. / END GAME** [ ] [ ]
Nov 83. (lp/c) *(CDL/ZCDL 1443)* **WALK INTO LIGHT** [78] [ ]
– Fly by night / Made in England / Walk into light / Trains / End game / Black and white television / Toad in the hole / Looking for Eden / User-friendly / Different Germany. *(cd-iss.Jun97 on 'Beat Goes On'; BGOCD 350)*

JOHN'S CHILDREN

Formed: Leatherhead, Surrey, England . . . May '66 as SILENCE, by ANDY ELLISON, GEOFF McCLELLAND, JOHN HEWLETT and CHRIS TOWNSON. In September '66, they became JOHN'S CHILDREN, signing a record deal with 'Columbia' through manager Simon Napier-Bell. They issued two R&B/YARDBIRDS-type singles at the turn of '66, nearly coming to prominence in March '67 when MARC BOLAN arrived for four months (as a replacement for McCLELLAND). Their third 45, 'DESDEMONA' (on the 'Track' label), became a psychedelic underground classic, although it was laughably banned from daytime radio play, due to the lyrics, "lift up your skirt and fly". When BOLAN left to form the legendary TYRANNOSAURUS REX (T.REX), however, the band lost momentum. They had previously recorded an album, 'ORGASM', early in '67, which although withdrawn in the UK, was released in the States for the 'White Whale' label (September 1970). ELLISON subsequently went solo, later returning in '74 with JET. By 1977, he/they had evolved into pop/punk The RADIO STARS, scoring a UK Top 40 hit with 'NERVOUS WRECK'. **Songwriters:** ELLISON wrote most. The RADIO STARS covered DEAR PRUDENCE + NORWEGIAN WOOD (Beatles).

Recommended: THE LEGENDARY ORGASM ALBUM (1982 lost 'ORGASM' lp)

ANDY ELLSION – vocals / **GEOFF McLELLAND** – guitar, vocals / **JOHN HEWLETT** – bass / **CHRIS TOWNSON** – drums

Columbia not issued

Oct 66. (7") *(DB 8030)* **THE LOVE I THOUGHT I'D FOUND. / STRANGE AFFAIR** [ ] [-]
Feb 67. (7") *(DB 8124)* **JUST WHAT YOU WANT – JUST WHAT YOU'LL GET. / BUT SHE'S MINE** [ ] [-]

— **MARC BOLAN** – guitar, vocals (ex-solo) repl. McLELLAND

Track not issued

May 67. (7") *(604 003)* **DESDEMONA. / REMEMBER THOMAS A'BECKETT** [ ] [-]

— **CHRIS COLVILLE** – drums repl. BOLAN who formed TYRANNOSAURUS REX **TOWNSON** switched to guitar (ELLISON and HEWLETT still remained)

Aug 67. (7") *(604 005)* **COME AND PLAY WITH ME IN THE GARDEN. / SARA CRAZY CHILD** [ ] [-]
Oct 67. (7") *(604 010)* **GO GO GIRL. / JAGGED TIME LAPSE** [ ] [-]
Jan 68. (7"; as ANDY ELLISON on A-side) *(604 018)* **IT'S BEEN A LONG TIME. / ARTHUR GREEN** [ ] [-]

— They split Autumn '67. The original line-up did record an album '67 but due to its title 'ORGASM' it was not released for over 15 years.

– compilations, etc. –

May 82. (lp) *Cherry Red; (BRED 31)* **THE LEGENDARY ORGASM ALBUM** [ ] [-]
– Smashed blocked (live & studio) / Just what you want, just what you'll get (live & studio) / Killer Ben / Jagged time lapse / Not the sort of girl / You're a nothing / Cold on me / Leave me alone / Let me know / Why do you lie / Strange affair / But she's mine. *(cd-iss.Jun88; CDMRED 31)*
Nov 87. (lp/cd) *Bam Caruso; (KIRI 095/+CD) MIDSUMMER NIGHT'S SCENE* [ ] [-]
Dec 90. (m-lp) *Zinc Alloy;* **PLAYING WITH THEMSELVES** [ ] [-]
May 91. (m-lp) *Zinc Alloy;* **PLAYING WITH THEMSELVES VOL.2** [ ] [-]
Jun 97. (cd) *Burning Airlines; (PILOT 012)* **SMASHED BLOCKED** [ ] [-]

— JOHN'S CHILDREN tracks appeared on BOLAN's 'BEGINNING OF DOVES' album. After split drummer TOWNSON later joined The JOOK in '71, he later joined JET with ANDY. They later evolved into The RADIO STARS (see GREAT ROCK DISCOGRAPHY)

ANDY ELLISON

had went straight into solo career in '67.

S.N.B. not issued

Feb 68. (7") *(55-3308)* **YOU CAN'T DO THAT. / CASBAH (or) CORNFLAKE ZOO** [ ] [-]

C.B.S. not issued

Apr 68. (7") *(CBS 3357)* **FOOL FROM UPPER EDEN. / ANOTHER LUCKY LIE** [ ] [-]

JON & VANGELIS (see under ⇒ VANGELIS)

Janis JOPLIN

Born: 19 Jan'43, Port Arthur, Texas, USA. In the early 60's, she hitched to California and San Francisco, where she sang in The WALLER CREEK BOYS trio alongside future 13th FLOOR ELEVATORS member R.POWELL ST.JOHN. In 1963, she subsequently appeared opposite JORMA KAUKONEN (later JEFFERSON AIRPLANE) at local night spots. In 1966, after nearly giving up singing and her hippy drug-taking ways for a life of domesticity, she returned to Texas where she briefly rehearsed with The 13th FLOOR ELEVATORS. That same year, she again ventured to San Francisco, this time joining BIG BROTHER & THE HOLDING COMPANY. They released two albums, the second of which, 'CHEAP THRILLS', stayed at the top of the US charts for 8 weeks. When they temporary folded late in '68, she went solo, although her alcohol and drug abuse was becoming increasingly pronounced. After three major concerts; London's Royal Albert Hall, Newport Festival and New Orleans Pop Festival, she unleashed her 1969 solo debut, 'I GOT DEM OL' KOSMIC BLUES AGAIN', which made the US Top 5. In May '70, she formed her new backing group, The FULL-TILT BOOGIE BAND, beginning work on an album in the Autumn of 1970. Before it was completed, however, on the 4th of October 1970, JANIS was found dead in her Hollywood hotel room. The coroner's verdict reported that her death was due to an accidental drug overdose. Early in 1971, her last recording, 'PEARL' was issued, topping the US charts for 9 weeks, also giving her a first taste of UK chart action. She again hit pole position in the States with a great version of KRIS KRISTOFFERSON's 'ME AND BOBBY McGEE'. But for her death, she would probably have become the greatest female singer of all-time, her powerful 3-octave vocals having the capacity to transform the most run-of-the-mill tune into a tour de force. • **Songwriters:** She used many outside writers, including JERRY RAGAVOY, and covered; PIECE OF MY HEART (hit; Erma Franklin) / MAYBE (Chantells) / TO LOVE SOMEBODY (Bee Gees) / etc. • **Trivia:** In 1979, a film, 'The Rose', was released based on her life, featuring BETTE MIDLER in her role.

Recommended: JANIS JOPLIN'S GREATEST HITS (*8)

JANIS JOPLIN – vocals (ex-BIG BROTHER & THE HOLDING COMPANY) / **SAM ANDREW** – guitar (ex-BIG BROTHER & THE HOLDING COMPANY) / others in her KOZMIC BLUES BAND were **BRAD CAMPBELL** (aka KEITH CHERRY) – bass / **TERRY CLEMENTS** – saxophone / **RICHARD KERMODE** – organ repl. BILL KING (Feb69) / **LONNIE CASTILLE** – drums repl. ROY MARKOWITZ (Apr69) / **TERRY HENSLEY** – trumpet repl. MARCUS DOUBLEDAY (Apr69) / added **SNOOKY FLOWERS** – saxophone (Feb69)

—— (Jul69) **JOHN TILL** – guitar, vocals repl. SAM ANDREW / **MAURY BAKER** – drums repl. CASTILLE / **DAVE WOODWARD** – trumpet repl. GASCA who repl. HENSLEY

		C.B.S.	Columbia
Oct 69.	(lp) *(CBS 63546) <9913>* **I GOT DEM OL' KOZMIC BLUES AGAIN MAMA!** – Try (just a little bit harder) / Maybe / One good man / As good as you've been to this world / To love somebody / Kozmic blues / Little girl blue / Work me, Lord. *(re-iss.1983 lp/c; CBS/40 32063) (cd-iss.1988; CD 63546) (cd re-iss.Jan91;)*		5
Nov 69.	(7") *<45023>* **KOZMIC BLUES. / LITTLE GIRL BLUE**	-	41
Dec 69.	(7"w-drawn) *(CBS 3683)* **TURTLE BLUES. / PIECE OF MY HEART**	-	-
Jan 70.	(7") *<45080>* **TRY (JUST A LITTLE BIT HARDER). / ONE GOOD MAN**	-	
Apr 70.	(7") *<45128>* **MAYBE. / WORK ME, LORD**	-	

—— JANIS JOPLIN & THE FULL TILT BOOGIE BAND

retained **CAMPBELL** and **TILL** / added **RICHARD BELL** – piano / **KEN PEARSON** – organ / **CLARK PIERSON** – drums/ On the 4th Oct70, JANIS died of a drug overdose. She had just recorded below album

		C.B.S.	Columbia
Jan 71.	(lp) *(CBS 64188) <30322>* **PEARL** – Move over / Cry baby / A woman left lonely / Half Moon / Buried alive in the blues / My baby / Me and Bobby McGee / Mercedes Benz / Trust me / Get it while you can. *(re-iss.Jan84 lp/c; CBS/40 32064) (cd-iss.1988; CD 64188) (cd re-iss.Jan91 & Jul95 on 'Columbia'; 480415-2)*	50	1
Jan 71.	(7") *(CBS 7019) <45314>* **ME AND BOBBY McGEE. / HALF MOON**		1
May 71.	(7") *(CBS 7217) <45379>* **CRY BABY. / MERCEDES BENZ**		42
Sep 71.	(7") *<45433>* **GET IT WHILE YOU CAN. / MOVE OVER**	-	78

– other posthumous JANIS JOPLIN releases –

on 'CBS' UK / 'Columbia' US unless mentioned otherwise

Oct 71.	(7"ep) *(CBS 9136)* **MOVE OVER / CRY BABY. / TRY (JUST A LITTLE BIT HARDER) / PIECE OF MY HEART**		
Jul 72.	(d-lp) *(CBS 67241) <31160>* **JANIS JOPLIN IN CONCERT (live half with BIG BROTHER & THE HOLDING COMPANY / half with FULL TILT BOOGIE BAND)** – Down on me / Bye, bye baby / All is loneliness / Piece of my heart / Road block / Flower in the sun / Summertime / Ego rock / Half moon / Kozmic blues / Move over / Try (just a little bit harder) / Get it while you can / Ball and chain. *(re-iss.Sep87; 460128-1/4) (cd-iss.Aug93; 466838-2)*	30	4 May72
Jul 72.	(7") *(CBS 8241) <45630>* **DOWN ON ME (live). / BYE, BYE BABY (live)**		91
Jul 73.	(lp) *(CBS 65470) <32168>* **JANIS JOPLIN'S GREATEST HITS** – Piece of my heart / Summertime / Try (just a little bit harder) / Cry baby / Me and Bobby McGee / Down on me / Get it while you can / Bye, bye baby / Move over / Ball and chain. *(re-iss.Sep82 & May90 lp/c; CBS/40 32190) (cd-iss.1988; 831 726-2) (cd re-iss.Oct94 on 'Sony'; 476555-2)*		37
May 75.	(d-lp) *(CBS 88115) <33345>* **JANIS (soundtrack)** (includes rare 1963-65 material)		54
1975.	(7") *(13-33205)* **ME AND BOBBY McGHEE. / GET IT WHILE YOU CAN**		-
Mar 76.	(7") *(CBS 3960)* **PIECE OF MY HEART. / KOZMIC BLUES**		-
Jul 80.	(d-lp) *<(CBS 88492)>* **ANTHOLOGY** *(d-cd-iss.Jun97 on 'Columbia'; 467 405-2)*		
Feb 82.	(lp) *(CBS 85354)* **FAREWELL SONG**		
Nov 84.	(d-c) **PEARL / CHEAP THRILLS**		

Jun 86. (lp/c) *(CBS/40 54731)* **GOLDEN HIGHLIGHTS OF JANIS JOPLIN** ☐ -
Dec 90. (3xcd-box) *(467387-2)* **CHEAP THRILLS / PEARL / I GOT DEM OL' KOZMIC BLUES AGAIN** ☐ -
Sep 92. (d-cd) *Sony; (4610202)* **PEARL / I GOT DEM OL' KOZMIC BLUES AGAIN!** ☐ ☐
Nov 92. (cd) *I.T.M.; (ITM 960001)* **MAGIC OF LOVE** ☐ -
Sep 93. (cd) *I.T.M.; (ITM 960007)* **LIVE AT WOODSTOCK, 1969 (live)** ☐ ☐
Jan 94. (3xcd-box) *Legacy; (CD 48845-2)* **JANIS** ☐ ☐
Dec 94. (cd) *Columbia;* **THE BEST** ☐ ☐
Apr 95. (cd) *Legacy; (478515-2)* **18 ESSENTIAL SONGS** ☐ -

JUICY LUCY (see under ⇒ MISUNDERSTOOD)

JULIAN'S TREATMENT

Formed: London, England . . . 1969 by poet/writer JULIAN JAY SAVARIN, who was augmented by singer/narrator CATHY PRUDEN on the 1970 concept double album, 'A TIME BEFORE THIS'. It was a keyboard-laden progressive rock affair, characterised by touches of cosmic jazz intertwined with softly spoken melodramas. The record was dominated by the excellent tracks, 'COMING OF THE MULE' and 'PHANTOM CITY'. SAVARIN subsequently returned with a solo album, 'WAITERS ON THE DANCE' (1971), a prosaic piece of work based on the book, 'Lemmus, A Time Trilogy – Waiters On The Dance'. It was a further 15 years before his comeback, although the single, 'SUMMER LOVE', was hardly worth the wait. Both albums are now worth £75 & £175 respectively.

Recommended: A TIME BEFORE THIS (*7)

JULIAN JAY SAVARIN – keyboards, vocals / **CATHY PRUDEN** – vocals / etc.

Youngblood Decca

Mar 70. (7") *(YB 1009)* **PHANTOM CITY. / ALDA, DARK LADY OF THE OUTER WORLDS** ☐ -
Jul 70. (d-lp) *(SYB 2) <DL 75224>* **A TIME BEFORE THIS** ☐ ☐
– First oracle / The coming of the mule / Phantom city / The black tower / Alda, dark lady of the outer worlds / Altarra, princess of the blue women / Second oracle / Twins of the Centauri – Alkon, planet of Centauri / The Terran / Fourth from the sun / Strange things / A time before this. *(re-iss.Mar90 on 'See For Miles' lp/cd+=; SEE/+CD 288)*– Child of the night / Stranger / The death of Alda / Cycles / Soldiers of time.

JULIAN JAY SAVARIN

Birth not issued

1971. (lp) *(RAB 2)* **WAITERS ON THE DANCE** ☐ -
(re-iss.1987 on '5 Hours Back'; TOCK 002)

— in the 70's he made a 'Lyntone' comic books sampler 45 'I AM YOU'. / 'KIZEESH' *(LYN 3426)*

Square Biz not issued

Aug 86. (12"; as JULIAN JAY) *(12SUJ 110)* **SUMMER LOVE. / I DON'T THINK SHE'S IN LOVE ANYMORE** ☐ -
Apr 89. (12"/7"; as JULIAN JAY) *(12+/SUJ 116)* **WAS IT WORTH IT. /** ☐ -

— went back for treatment (so to speak!)

JULY (see under ⇒ JADE WARRIOR)

JUST FOUR MEN (see under ⇒ WIMPLE WINCH)

KAK (see under ⇒ OXFORD CIRCLE)

KALEIDOSCOPE

Formed: California, USA ... 1963 by ex-RODENTS player DAVID LINDLEY. The RODENTS released one US 'Pequod' 45, 'AND YOUR BIRD CAN SING'. / 'COME AND LIVE ME', before breaking up in early '66. LINDLEY soon found others; SOLOMON FELDHOUSE, CHRIS DARROW, CHARLES CHESTER CRILL, FENRUS EPP and JOHN VIDICAN, forming The BAGHDAD BLUES BAND, who quickly became KALEIDOSCOPE. With the help of producer Barry Freidman (alias Frazier Mohawk), they signed to 'Epic', subsequently failing commercially with everything but their minor 1969 album, 'INCREDIBLE KALEIDOSCOPE'. By this time, they had relocated to New York, playing the 1969 Newport Folk Festival. • **Style:** Ecletic R&B outfit, with Eastern influences blending together acid-rock, cajun and new heavy blues for the disappointing 'BERNICE' set. • **Songwriters:** LINDLEY and group, except MINNIE THE MOOCHER (Cab Calloway). • **Trivia:** Group backed LEONARD COHEN on his 1968 debut lp. In 1969 the group recorded two tracks, 'Brother Mary' & 'Mickey's Tune', for the Various Artists film soundtrack 'Zabriskie Point'.

Recommended: BACON FROM MARS (*7) / A BEACON FROM MARS (*6) / SIDE TRIPS (*6)

DAVID LINDLEY (b.1944, San Marino, Calif.) – banjo, fiddle, guitar (ex-RODENTS, ex-MAD RAMBLERS) / **SOLOMON FELDTHOUSE** (b. Turkey) – vocals, guitar types, kazoo repl. JOHN WELSH – guitar / **CHRIS DARROW** – mandolin, bass (ex-DRY CITY PLAYERS) repl. RICK O'NEILL – bass / **CHARLES CHESTER CRILL** – harmonica, keyboards, fiddle repl. BRIAN MONSOUR (CRILL's aliases were CONNIE / **FENRUS EPP / MAX**(WELL) **BUDA / TEMPLETON PARCELY) / JOHN VIDICAN** – drums

not issued / Epic

Dec 66. (7") *<10117>* **PLEASE. / ELEVATOR MAN**

Jun 67. (7") *<10219>* **WHY TRY. / LITTLE ORPHAN ANNIE**

Jun 67. (lp) *<26304>* **SIDE TRIPS**
– Egyptian gardens / If the night / Hesitation blues / Please / Keep your mind open / Pulsating dreams / Oh death / Come on in / Why try / Minnie the moocher. *(UK-rel.Jul88 on 'Edsel'; ED 284) (cd-iss.Feb91; EDCD 284) (cd re-iss.Mar94 on 'Line'; LCCD 9009250)*

Sep 67. (7") *<10239>* **I FOUND OUT. / RAMPE RAMPE**

Jan 68. (lp) *<26333>* **A BEACON FROM MARS**
– I found out / Greenwood sidee / Life will pass you by / Taxim / Baldheaded end of a broom / Louisiana man / You don't love me / Beacon from Mars. *(UK-iss.Oct88 on 'Edsel'; ED 288) (cd-iss.Feb91; EDCD 288)*

— **STUART BROTMAN** – bass repl. DARROW who joined NITTY GRITTY DIRT BAND **PAUL LAGOS** – drums repl. JOHN VIDICAN

May 68. (7") *<10332>* **HELLO TROUBLE. / JUST A TASTE**

Jun 69. (7") *<10481>* **KILLING FLOOR** (alt. title TEMPE ARIZONA). / LIE TO ME

Jun 69. (lp) *<26467>* **INCREDIBLE KALEIDOSCOPE**
– Lie to me / Let the good love flow / Tempe Arizona (or) Killing floor / Petite fleure / Banjo / Cuckoo / Seven-ate sweet. *(UK-iss.Oct88 on 'Edsel'; ED 292) (cd-iss.Feb91; EDCD 292)*

— **ROB JOHNSON** – bass repl. BROTMAN

— added **JEFF KAPLAN** – guitar, vocals (died of drug o.d. late '70)

C.B.S. / Columbia

Mar 70. (lp; in UK as AMERICAN KALEIDOSCOPE) *(CBS 64005)* *<26508>* **BERNICE**
– Chocolate whale / Another lover / Sneakin' thru the ghetto / To know is not to be / Lulu Arfin nanny / Lie & hide / Ballad of Tommy Udo / Bernice / Soft ann easy / New blue ooze.

— **RICHARD APLAN** – fiddle repl. FELDTHOUSE and CRILL before they split late '70. DAVID LINDLEY worked with TERRY REID then sessions with WARREN ZEVON, MARIA MULDAUR, AMERICA, LINDA RONSTADT, RY COODER, etc. Below was a reunion album which featured DARROW, FELDTHOUSE, BROTMAN, CRILL as 'PARCELY + BUDA' and the heavily disguised DAVID LINDLEY as 'DePARIS LETANTE'

Island / Pacific Arts

Jan 77. (lp) *(ILPS 9462)* *<102>* **WHEN SCOPES COLLIDE** Sep76
– Ghost riders in the sky / Canun tune / Younever Cantell / Little Egypt / My love comes softly / Your love / Black and tan fantasy / Hard on the trail / Stu's balkan blues / Man of constant sorrow / It's long you're after / So long.

— DARROW and PARCEL (CRILL) teamed up forming The RANK STRANGERS, they released one eponymous US album in '77 on 'Pacific Arts'. In 1988, KALEIDOSCOPE re-formed to release album 'GREETINGS FROM KARTOONISTA ... WE AIN'T DEAD YET' for 'Gifthorse-Curb'. LINDLEY went solo (see GREAT ROCK DISCOGRAPHY)

– compilations, etc. –

Oct 67. (7") *Okeh; <7300>* **NOBODY. / (Find Yourself Someone To Love by 'Larry Williams & Johnny 'Guitar' Watson')**

Aug 83. (lp) *Edsel; (XED 115)* **BACON FROM MARS** (1967-69)
– Egyptian gardens / If the night / Please / Keep your mind open / Pulsating dream / Oh death / Why try / I found out / Life will pass you by / Lie to me / Petite fleure / Banjo / Cuckoo / Nobody / Elevator man / Hello trouble.

Jun 84. (lp) *Edsel; (ED 138)* **RAMPE RAMPE** (rarities)

Nov 90. (cd) *Demon; (FIENDCD 188)* **GREETINGS FROM KARTOONISTAN**

Aug 93. (cd) *Edsel; (EDCD 375)* **BLUES FROM BAGDHAD – THE VERY BEST OF KALEIDOSCOPE**
– BACON FROM MARS tracks + / Rampe rampe / Greenwood sidee / Beacon from Mars / Seven-ate sweet.

KALEIDOSCOPE

Formed: West London, England ... 1964 initially as The SIDE KICKS by EDDIE PUMER, DAN BRIDGEMAN, PETER DALTREY and STEVE CLARK. They moved from being an R&B influenced covers group, subsequently becoming The KEY. Early in 1967, with help of music publisher Dick Leahy (who became their producer), they signed to 'Fontana'. Their first DALTREY and PUMER-penned single, 'FLIGHT FROM ASHIYA' (complete with rare pic-sleeve) flopped, although it was soon followed by the cult late 1967 album, 'TANGERINE DREAM'. This was comprised of dreamy collages of PINK FLOYD-ish material, as was their 1969 follow-up, 'FAINTLY BLOWING'. In 1970, after they became FAIRFIELD PARLOUR, they shifted to a more progressive-rock style, much in evidence on the only album, 'FROM HOME TO HOME'. They also worked on the film soundtrack of 'Eye Witness', which starred Mark Lester. Radio One DJ and future TV comedy celebrity, KENNY EVERETT was a noted fan of the band. 'TANGERINE DREAM', has been known to change hands for over £100. In fact anything from the quartet is known to be worth lots of dosh.

Recommended: DIVE INTO YESTERDAY (*8) / FROM HOME TO HOME (*6; FAIRFIELD PARLOUR)

EDDIE PUMER – guitar / **PETE DALTREY** – vocals, keyboards / **DAN BRIDGEMAN** – drums, percussion / **STEVE CLARKE** – bass, flute

Fontana / not issued

Sep 67. (7") *(TF 863)* **FLIGHT FROM ASHIYA. / HOLIDAYMAKER**

Nov 67. (lp; stereo/mono) *(S+/TL 5448)* **TANGERINE DREAM**
– Kaleidoscope / Please excuse my face / Drive into yesterday / Mr. Small, the watch repairer man / Flight from Ashiya / The murder of Lewis Tollani / (Further reflections) In the room of percussion / Dear Nellie Goodrich / Holidaymaker / A lesson, perhaps / The sky children. *(re-iss.Mar87 on '5 Hours Back'; TOCK 005)*

Jan 68. (7") *(TF 895)* **A DREAM FOR JULIE. / PLEASE EXCUSE MY FACE**

Sep 68. (7") *(TF 964)* **JENNY ARTICHOKE. / JUST HOW MUCH YOU ARE**

Mar 69. (7") *(TF 1002)* **DO IT AGAIN FOR JEFFREY. / POEM**

Apr 69. (lp) *(STL 5491)* **FAINTLY BLOWING**
– Faintly blowing / Poem / Snapdragon / A story from Tom Bitz / (Love song) For Annie / If you so wish / Opinion / Bless the executioner / Black fjord / The feathered tiger / I'll kiss you once / Music. *(re-iss.Mar87 on '5 Hours Back'; TOCK 006)*

Jul 69. (7") *(TF 1048)* **BALLOON. / IF YOU SO WISH**

— recorded "lost" album below in 1970.

– compilations, others, etc. –

Jul 91. (cd) *Blast From The Past; (BFTP 001CD)* **WHITE-FACED LADY**
– Overture / Broken mirrors / Dear Elvis Presley ... (angel's song) / Nursey, nursey / Small song – Heaven in the back row / Burning bright / The matchseller / The coronation of the fledgling / All hail to the hero / White faced lady / Freefall / Standing / The Indian head (diary song) / Song from Jon / Long way down / The locket / Picture with conversation / Angel (epitaph).

Sep 96. (cd) *Fontana; (534003-2)* **DIVE INTO YESTERDAY**
– Dive into yesterday / Mr. Small, the watch repairer man / Flight from Ashiya / Murder of Lewsis Tollani / (Further reflections) In the room of percussion / Dear Nellie Goodrich / The sky children / Dream for Julie / Faintly blowing / Poem / Snapdragon / A story from Tom Bitz / (Love song) For Annie / If you so wish / Opinion / Jenny Artichoke / Just how much you are / Bless the executioner / Black fjord / Feathered tiger / I'll kiss you once / Do it again for Jeffrey / Music.

FAIRFIELD PARLOUR

(same line-up)

Vertigo / R.C.A.

Apr 70. (7") *(6059 003)* *<0482>* **BORDEAUX ROSE. / CHALK ON THE WALL**

Aug 70. (lp) *(6360 001)* **FROM HOME TO HOME**
– Aries / In my box / By your bedside / Soldier of the flesh / I will always feel the same / Free / Emily / Chalk on the wall / Glorious house of Arthur / Monkey / Sunny side circus / Drummer boy of Shiloh. *(re-iss.Jul91 on 'Blast From The Past' lp/cd+=; BFTP 003 LP/CD)*– Just another day / Caraminda / I am all the animals / Songs for you.

Jul 70. (7"m) *(6059 008)* **JUST ANOTHER DAY / CARAMINDA. / I AM ALL THE ANIMALS / SONGS FOR YOU**

Philips / not issued

Aug 70. (7"; as I LUV WIGHT) *(6006 043)* **LET THE WORLD WASH IN. / MEDIAEVAL MASQUERADE** [ ] [-]

Prism / not issued

Apr 76. (7") *(PRI 1)* **BORDEAUX ROSE. / BABY STAY FOR TONIGHT** [ ] [-]

— When they split late '70, only DAN cropped up as FREEN BEANS to make one-off single 'BLISTER BOOGIE'.

Paul KANTER & Grace SLICK (see under ⇒ JEFFERSON AIRPLANE)

KARTHAGO

Formed: Berlin, Germany . . . 1970 by JOEY ALBRECHT and GERALD LUCIANO HARTWIG, who toured as a duo under the moniker of BLUES MACHINE. Recruiting percussionist THOMAS GOLDSHMITT, they assumed the name KARTHAGO and inked a deal with 'BASF'. INGO BISCHOFF and WOLFGANG BROCK completed the line-up and the band recorded their self-titled debut in late 1971, a lavishly packaged collection of heavy, funk-inflected rock that drew comparisons with SANTANA. These influences were more pronounced on the follow-up, 'SECOND STEP' (1973), which emphasized the inherent instrumental synergy the group possessed. A succession of personnel changes saw KONNI BOMMARIUS and GLEN CORNICK join for 1975's 'ROCK'N'ROLL TESTAMENT'. Recorded in England and produced by 'Bacillus' head Peter Hawke, the album introduced a more polished prog-rock sound. Although the set was well-received, the band split after a 1976 live album. ALBRECHT briefly reformed the band for the lightweight 1978 album, 'LOVE IS CAKE' (yeah, right!).

Recommended: KARTHAGO (*7) / SECOND STEP (*7)

JOEY ALBRECHT – vocals, guitar / **GERALD LUCIANO HARTWIG** – bass, vocals / **THOMAS GOLDSCHMITT** – hand percussion / **INGO BISCHOF** – keyboards, vocals / **WOLFGANG BROCK** – drums

BASF / not issued

Dec 71. (lp) *(20.21185-1)* **KARTHAGO** [-] [-] German
– String rambler / I don't live tomorrow / But I know / Morning surprise / I give you everything you want / I know what you can do my babe / Why don't you stop buggin' me / Black fire / Nos vamos. *(re-iss.1979 on 'Brain'; 40.087)*

— **NORBERT LEHMANN** – drums; repl. BROCK who joined The RATTLES

May 73. (lp) *(20.21780-9)* **SECOND STEP** [-] [-] German
– Pacemaker / I don't care / Crosswords and intermissions / Don't send me your money, send me your heart / Wild river / Lamento juvenil / California gigging / Oberbaum bridge.

— **KONNI BOMMARIUS** – drums (ex-2066 & THEN, ex-ABACUS) repl. LEHMANN who joined EPITAPH

— **GLENN CORNICK** – bass (ex-JETHRO TULL, ex-WILD TURKEY) repl. HARTWIG

Bacillus / not issued

Feb 75. (lp) *(BLPS 19201)* **ROCK'N'ROLL TESTAMENT** [-] [-] German
– Hard-loving woman / We gonna keep it together / Now the irony keeps me company / Rock'n'roll testament / The creeper / Back again / Sound in the air / Highway five / For Kathy / See you tomorrow in the sky.

— **GERALD HARTWIG** (returned) to repl. CORNICK

— **RINGO FUNK** – drums (ex-ATLANTIS, ex-JERONIMO) + **REINHARD BOPP** – guitar, vocals (ex-HARDCAKE SPECIAL) repl. BOMMARIUS

Apr 76. (d-lp) *(BDA 7506)* **LIVE AT THE ROXY (live)** [-] [-] German
– The world is like a burning fire / Sound in the air / Rock'n'roll testament / We gonna keep it together / Thema in "C" / The second string rambler / Wild river / Highway seeker / We give you everything you need / Going down / See you tomorrow in the sky.

— split until **ALBRECHT** re-formed with **RINGO / + CHICO DE LOS REYES** – piano, vocals / **JOCHEN ROTH** – guitar / **ERNST KEINZ** – bass

Crystal / not issued

Feb 78. (lp) *(064CRY 32769)* **LOVE IS A CAKE** [-] [-] German
– Rock'n'roll man / The friend / Rosie / Remember / I will love / Love is a cake / Woman / Dreams of love / Doing the best I can / Crazy woman / Ira Lee.

— split after disaster above

– compilations, etc. –

1977. (lp) *Bacillus; (BAC 2042)* **LIVE (live)** [-] [-] German
1978. (d-lp) *Bacillus; (BAC 2055)* **BEST OF KARTHAGO** [-] [-] German

Jorma KAUKONEN (see under ⇒ HOT TUNA)

John KAY (see under ⇒ STEPPENWOLF)

KAYAK

Formed: Netherlands . . .1973 by MAX WERNER, TON SCHERPENZEEL, JOHAN SLAGER, CEES VAN LEEUWEN and PIM KOOPMAN. After a spell with the UK label, 'Harvest' (between 73-75), this English-language avant-garde outfit released two albums, 'SEE SEE THE SUN' and 'KAYAK'. They subsequently enjoyed some mild success in the States, their best seller being the 1978 album, 'STARLIGHT DANCER', which contained the hit single ,' I WANT YOU TO BE MINE'.

Recommended: SEE SEE THE SUN (*6) / KAYAK (*5) / ROYAL RED BOUNCER (*6)

MAX WERNER (b. WERLEROFZOIETS) – vocals, mellotron, percussion / **TON SCHERPENZEEL** – keyboards, synthesizers, percussion, accordion, harps, vocals / **JOHAN SLAGER** – guitar / **CEES VAN LEEUWEN** – bass, percussion / **PIM KOOPMAN** – drums, percussion

Harvest / Harvest

Apr 74. (lp) *(SHSP 4033)* <11305> **SEE SEE THE SUN** [ ] [ ]
– Reason for it all / Lyrics / Mouldy wood / Lovely Luna / Hope for alive / Ballet of the cripple / Forever is a lonely thought / Mammoth / See see the sun. *(cd-iss.Jun97 on 'Pseudonym'; CDP 1024DD)*

Aug 74. (7") *(HAR 5084)* **WINTERTIME. / SERENADE** [ ] [-]

Oct 74. (lp) *(SHSP 4036)* **KAYAK** [ ] [-]
– Alibi / Wintertime / Mountain too rough / They get to know me / Serenade / Woe and alas / Mireille / Trust in the machine / His master's noise.

Jul 75. (7") *(HAR 5099)* **WE ARE NOT AMUSED. / GIVE IT A NAME** [ ] [-]

— **BERT VELDKAMP** – bass, vocals, repl. LEEUWEN

Vertigo / Janus

Jan 76. (lp) *(6360 530)* <7023> **ROYAL RED BOUNCER** [ ] [ ]
– Royal red bouncer / Life of gold / (You're so) Bizarre / Bury the world / Chance for a lifetime / If this is your welcome / Moments of joy / Patricia Anglaia / Said no word / My heart never changed. *(cd-iss.Jun97 on 'Pseudonym'; CDP 1012DD)*

1976. (lp) *(6360 854)* **THE LAST ENCORE** [ ] [-]
– Back to the Front / Nothingless / Love of a victim / Land on the water / The last encore / Do you care / Still my heart cries for you / Relics from a distant age / Love me tonight / Get on board / Evocation / Raid your own house / Well done.

— **THEO DE JONG** – bass + **CHARLES LOUIS SCHOUTEN** – drums, repl. VELDKAMP + KOOPMAN

Feb 78. (lp) *(6360 856)* <7034> **STARLIGHT DANCER** [ ] [ ]
– I want you to be mine / Ballad for a lost friend / Turn the tide / Nothingless / Still my heart cries for you / Starlight dancer / Love of a victim / Land on the water / Do you care / Back to the Front / Irene.

Apr 78. (7") <274> **I WANT YOU TO BE MINE. / IRENE** [-] [55]

— **MAX** now drums alongside **TON + JOHAN** + incoming **PETER SCHERPENZEEL** – bass / **EDWARD REEKERS** – vocals / **IRENE LINDERS** – vocals / **KATHERINE LAPTHORN** – vocals

Feb 79. (7") <278> **KEEP THE CHANGE. / IVORY DANCE** [-] [ ]

Feb 79. (lp) *(6413 507)* <7039> **PHANTOM OF THE NIGHT** [-] [ ] German
– Winning ways / Keep the change / Ruthless queen / Crime of passion / First signs of Spring / Daphine (Laurel tree) / The poet and the one man band / No man's land / Journey through time / Phantom of the night.

Vertigo / Mercury

1980. (lp) *(6413 960)* <SRMI 3824> **PERISCOPE LIFE** [-] [ ] German
– Atral aliens / What's in a name / Stop that song / If you really need me now / Periscope life / Beggar's can't be choosers / The sight / Lost blue of Chartres / Anne / One way or another / Sad to say farewell.

1981. (lp) *(6399 115)* **MERLIN** [-] [-] Euro
– Merlin / Tintagel / The sword in the stone / The king's enchanter / Niniane (lady of the lake) / Seagull / Boogie heart / Now that we've come this far / Can't afford to lose / Love's a glow.

— now without IRENE + KATHERINE

Bellaphon / not issued

1982. (lp) *(26007053)* **EYEWITNESS (live)** [-] [-] German
– Eyewitness / Periscope life / Ruthless queen / Want you to be mine / Lyrics / Chance for a lifetime / Who's fooling who / Irene / Only you and I know / Winning ways / Starlight dancer / No man's land.

– compilations, imports. –

1978. (lp) *E.M.I.; (25828)* **THE BEST OF KAYAK** [-] [-] Dutch

KBC BAND (see under ⇒ HOT TUNA)

KENNY AND THE KASUALS

Formed: Dallas, Texas, USA . . . 1965 as The KEN DANIEL COMBO. When MARK LEE discovered them playing at the La Fontaine Club in Dallas, he decided he wanted to become their manager, renaming them KENNEY AND THE KASUALS. They recorded their debut, 'NOTHIN' BETTER TO DO', on his small independent label, 'Mark', although this single and the subsequent two 45's gained scant recognition. In 1966, LEE secured them gigs at The Studio Club in Dallas and a limited-edition, purportedly live, album was released during this period. In fact, the record was recorded virtually live one afternoon in a local studio, having fooled many in the process. It contained many fine cover versions of standards such as 'MONEY', 'GLORIA' and 'BABY PLEASE DON'T GO', soon becoming a rare collector's piece. They then moved on from their garage sound to more acid-psych, much in evidence on their local hit 45, 'JOURNEY TO THYME', which gained wider distribution from 'United Artists'. After another fine single, 'SEE SAW RIDE', they relocated to New York. Constant rows between KENNY and other members, led to their demise in the Autumn of '67, more or less sealed when KENNY was drafted. Without him, they became The TRUTH, failing with their only single, 'CHIMES ON 42nd STREET', in 1968. In 1978, KENNY AND THE KASUALS were back in the recording studio to lay down some tracks for an EP and a long-awaited second album, 'GARAGE KINGS'.

Recommended: TEEN DREAMS (*6)

KENNY DANIEL – vocals / **PAUL ROACH** – keyboards / **TOMMY NICHOLS** – lead guitar / **LEE LIGHTFOOT** – bass / **DAVID BLACKLEY** – drums

not issued / Mark

1965. (7") <911> **NOTHIN' BETTER TO DO. / FLOATIN'** [-] [ ]
1965. (7") <1002> **DON'T LET YOUR BABY GO. / THE BEST THING AROUND** [-] [ ]

1965. (lp) *<5000>* **IMPACT** -
– Chicago 60616 / Money / All the day and all the night / You make me feel so good / I'm not talking / Empty heart / It's all right / Gloria / You better move on / Baby, please don't go / Got a good thing going / Farmer John. *(UK cd-iss.May97 on 'Flash'; FLASH 26)*

1966. (7") *<1003>* **IT'S ALL RIGHT. / YOU MAKE ME FEEL SO GOOD** -

1966. (lp; as KENNEY AND THE KASUALS) *<5000>* **LIVE AT THE STUDIO CLUB (live)** -
<re-iss.1977; same>

— **JERRY SMITH** – lead guitar; repl. NICHOLS

1966. (7") *<1004>* **RAINDROP TO TEARDROPS. / STRINGS OF TIME** -

1967. (7") *<1006>* **JOURNEY TO THYME. / I'M GONNA MAKE IT** -
<above was also issued nationwide by 'United Artists'; 50085>

1967. (7") *<1008>* **SEE SAW RIDE. / AS I KNEW** -

— **RICHARD BORGENS** – lead guitar (ex-BRIKS) repl. ROACH

— when KENNY got drafted, they renamed themselves below . . .

1968. (7"; as TRUTH) *<1009>* **CHIMES ON 42nd STREET. / WHEN WAS THEN** -

— split after KENNY returned for a farewell gig April 1968. In 1978, **KENNY + JERRY** re-formed with new members **DAN GREEN** – guitar / **GREG DANIELS** – bass / **RON MASON** – drums / + augmented by **KARL TOMORROW** – keyboards

Line | Mark

1978. (7"ep) *<400>* **THE KASUALS ARE BACK** -

1979. (lp) *(LLP 5020) <700>* **GARAGE KINGS (live in the studio)** - German
– (C'mon) Shake it / Out of control / Makes no difference / Everybody's making it / Disco goer / Candy, little girl / I love to go flying / Why did we ever call it love / Lost woman (live) / (Jesus) Arms of love / Live at Casa Chaos:- Rock'n'roll medley.

— above was brief reformation

- compilations, etc. -

1978. (lp) *Mark; <6000>* **TEEN DREAMS** -
1982. (lp) *Eva; (12011)* **NOTHING BETTER TO DO** - - French
1983. (lp) *Eva; (12031)* **THINGS GET BETTER** -

Shirley KENT (see under ⇒ GHOST)

KHAN (see under ⇒ HILLAGE, Steve)

KING CRIMSON

Formed: Bournemouth, England . . . summer 1967 by ROBERT FRIPP, plus brothers MIKE and PETE GILES, who formed the soft-rock trio BRAIN, then GILES, GILES & FRIPP. After signing to 'Deram' early in '68, and adding couple IAN McDONALD and JUDY DYBLE, they issued flop album, 'THE CHEERFUL INSANITY OF . . . ' in September of that year. With IAN now replacing PETE, the trio soon became KING CRIMSON, adding new vocalist GREG LAKE, who debuted at The Speakeasy on 9th of April '69. Three months later, they supported The ROLLING STONES at Hyde Park's free concert, which attracted the attention of the 'Island' label. In October '69, they unleashed 'IN THE COURT OF THE CRIMSON KING', a masterful debut album which made UK Top 5 and US Top 30. During the early 70's, however, they were in turmoil once more when a couple of group members departed, leaving FRIPP and lyricist/road manager, PETE SINFIELD, to work things out. Eventually, with augmentation from session men and ex-members, they recorded the 1970 follow-up album, 'IN THE WAKE OF POSEIDON'. An aggregation of KING CRIMSON members had earlier performed the weird, 'CAT FOOD' single on 'Top Of The Pops'. FRIPP and group went through even more upheavals, although they still scored with astounding album successes until they split for the first time late in '74. FRIPP had already been a prolific session man for the likes of VAN DER GRAAF GENERATOR and (BRIAN) ENO. With the latter, he was co-credited on two experimental budget lp's, 'NO PUSSYFOOTIN' (1973) and 'EVENING STAR' (1975). He then moved to New York and worked with PETER GABRIEL on his first three albums, at the same time working with BOWIE on 'Heroes'. In 1979, FRIPP released his debut solo album, 'EXPOSURE', which featured many of his close friends handling vocals (see below). The following year, his instrumental set, 'GOD SAVE THE QUEEN / UNDER HEAVY MANNERS', was followed by a short-lived project/band, The LEAGUE OF GENTLEMEN. In 1981, he re-formed KING CRIMSON with BILL BRUFORD, ADRIAN BELEW and TONY LEVIN. They made three more fruitful albums, before FRIPP was again left contemplating a revived solo career. During the period, 1982-84, FRIPP collaborated on two albums, 'I ADVANCE MASKED' and 'BEWITCHED', with ANDY SUMMERS (ex-POLICE). Like many of their contemporaries, KING CRIMSON re-formed in 1994, issuing a series of studio and live albums. • **Style:** Progressive neo-classical rock outfit, whose initial MOODY BLUES' mellotron-sound was swapped for the distinctive self-indulgent guitar-mastery of FRIPP. In the early 70's, KING CRIMSON advanced with a jazz-rock tinted fusion, while in the 80's they took a more modern, solid and basic approach. Solo, FRIPP, often experimented with electronics, which were dubbed "Frippertronics" in the early 80's. • **Songwriters:** FRIPP music, lyrics SINFIELD (until departure). Newcomer ADRIAN BELEW collaborated with FRIPP in the 80's. • **Trivia:** In the mid-80's, FRIPP married singer/actress TOYAH WILLCOX, even collaborating on an album, 'THE LADY OR THE TIGER', in 1987.

Recommended: IN THE COURT OF THE CRIMSON KING (*9) / IN THE WAKE OF POSEIDON (*6) / LIZARD (*6) / ISLANDS (*7) / LARK'S TONGUE'S IN ASPIC (*8) / RED (*8) / STARLESS & BIBLE BLACK (*8) / FRAME BY FRAME – THE CONCISE . . . (*9) / NETWORK (*7)

GILES, GILES & FRIPP

PETE GILES – bass / **MICHAEL GILES** (b.1942)– drums / **ROBERT FRIPP** (b.16 May'46, Wimbourne, Dorset, England)– guitar, mellotron

C.B.S. | not issued

May 67. (7"; as BRAIN) *(R 5595)* **NIGHTMARES IN RED. / KICK THE DONKEY** -

Deram | not issued

Jun 68. (7") *(DM 188)* **ONE IN A MILLION. / NEWLY-WEDS** -

— added **IAN McDONALD** (b.25 Jun'46, London) – keyboards / and guest **JUDY DYBLE** – vocals (ex-FAIRPORT CONVENTION) also featured as did KING CRIMSON lyricist **PETE SINFIELD**

Sep 68. (lp; mono/stereo) *(DML/SML 1022)* **THE CHEERFUL INSANITY OF GILES, GILES & FRIPP** -
– The Saga of Rodney Toady / One in a million / Just George / Thursday morning / North meadow / Call tomorrow / Newly-weds / Digging my lawn / Suite No.1 / Little children / The crukster / How do you know / The sun is shining / Brudite eyes / Elephant song. *(re-iss.1970; SPA 423) (re-iss.Apr82 on 'Editions-EG'; EGED 16) (re-iss.Aug93 cd/c+=; 820 965-2/-4)*– (extra versions).

— IAN now on vocals (JUDY left to join TRADER HORNE)

Sep 68. (7") *(DM 210)* **THURSDAY MORNING. / ELEPHANT SONG** -

KING CRIMSON

ROBERT, IAN + MIKE recruited **GREG LAKE** (b.10 Nov'48) – vocals, bass (ex-GODS)

Island | Atlantic

Oct 69. (7") *(WIP 6071) <2703>* **THE COURT OF THE CRIMSON KING (part 1). / (part 2)** 80 Dec69

Oct 69. (lp) *(ILPS 9111) <8245>* **IN THE COURT OF THE CRIMSON KING** 5 28 Dec69
– 21st century schizoid man (including; Mirrors) / I talk to the wind / Epitaph (including; March for no reason – Tomorrow and tomorrow) / Moonchild (including; The dream – The illusion) / The court of the Crimson King (including; The return of the fire witch – The dance of the puppets). *<US re-iss.1970; SD 19155> (re-iss.Mar77 on 'Polydor' lp)(c; 2302 057)(3100 357) (cd-iss.May83 on 'Polydor'; 800 030-2) (re-iss.Jan87 & Nov91 on 'E.G.' lp/c/cd; EG LP/MC/CD 1)*

— **PETE GILES** – bass (ex-GILES, GILES & FRIPP) repl. IAN who with MIKE had formed McDONALD & GILES. IAN later formed FOREIGNER. MIKE appeared below. Added **KEITH TIPPET** – piano (other two were FRIPP & LAKE)

Mar 70. (7") *(WIP 6080)* **CAT FOOD. / GROON** -

— added **MEL COLLINS** – saxophone (ex-CIRCUS) / plus guest on 1 track **GORDON HASKELL** – vocals

May 70. (lp) *(ILPS 9127) <8266>* **IN THE WAKE OF POSEIDON** 4 31 Sep70
– Peace – a beginning / Pictures of a city (including; 42nd at Treadmill) / Cadence and cascade / In the wake of Poseidon (including; Libra's theme) / Peace – a theme / Cat food / The Devil's triangle: Merday morn – Hand of Sceiron – Garden of worm / Peace – an end. *(re-iss.Mar77 on 'Polydor' lp)(c; (2302 058)(3100 358) (re-iss.Jan87 & Nov91 on 'E.G.' lp/c/cd; EG LP/MC/CD 2)*

— **GORDON HASKELL** (now full-time) repl. GREG who formed EMERSON, LAKE & PALMER (earlier). FRIPP had also retained **MEL COLLINS / ANDY McCULLOCH** – drums repl. MIKE

Dec 70. (lp) *(ILPS 9141) <8278>* **LIZARD** 30
– Cirkus (including; Entry of the chameleons) / Indoor games / Happy family / Lady of the dancing water / Lizard suite: Prince Rupert awakes – Bolero-The peacock's tale – The battle of glass tears; (a) Dawn song – (b) Last skirmish – (c) Prince Rupert's lament / Big top. *(re-iss.Apr77 on 'Polydor' lp)(c; 2302 059)(3100 359) (re-iss.Jan87 & Nov91 on 'E.G.' lp/c/cd; EG LP/MC/CD 4)*

— **BOZ BURRELL** (b. RAYMOND, 1946, Lincoln, England) – vocals, bass repl. HASKELL who went solo / **IAN WALLACE** (b.29 Sep'46, Bury, England) – drums repl. McCULLOCH who joined GREENSLADE

Dec 71. (lp) *(ILPS 9175) <7212>* **ISLANDS** 30 76
– Formentera lady / The sailor's tale / Letters / (prelude) / Song of the gulls – Islands / Ladies of the road. *(re-iss.Apr77 on 'Polydor' lp)(c; 2302 060)(3100 360) (re-iss.Jan87 on 'E.G.' lp/c/cd; EG LP/MC/CD 5)*

— FRIPP was sole survivor (lyricist PETE SINFIELD left early '72, to go into production for ROXY MUSIC's debut and be lyricist for Italians P.F.M.) / **JOHN WETTON** (b.12 Jul'49, Derby, England) – vocals, bass (ex-FAMILY) repl. BOZ who formed BAD COMPANY / **BILL BRUFORD** (b.17 May'48, London, England) – drums (ex-YES) repl. WALLACE who joined STREETWALKERS / **DAVID CROSS** (b.1948, Plymouth, England) – violin, flute repl. COLLINS who later joined CAMEL + sessions / added **JAMIE MUIR** – percussion and new lyricist **RICHARD PALMER-JAMES**

Mar 73. (lp) *(ILPS 9230) <7263>* **LARKS' TONGUES IN ASPIC** 20 61
– Larks' tongues in aspic (part one) / Book of Saturday / Exiles / Easy money / The talking drum / Larks' tongues in aspic (part two). *(re-iss.Apr77 on 'Polydor' lp)(c; 2302 061)(3100 361) (re-iss.Jan87 & Nov91 on 'E.G.' lp/c/cd; EG LP/MC/CD 7)*

— Reverted to a quartet when JAMIE became a Tibetan monk

Feb 74. (7") *(WIP 6189) <3016>* **THE NIGHT WATCH. / THE GREAT DECEIVER**

Feb 74. (lp) *(ILPS 9275) <7298>* **STARLESS AND BIBLE BLACK** 28 64
– The great deceiver / Lament / We'll let you know / The night watch / Trio / The mincer / Starless and bible black / Trio / Fracture. *(re-iss.Apr77 on 'Polydor' lp)(c; 2302 065)(3100 365) (re-iss.Jan87 & Nov91 on 'E.G.' lp/c/cd; EG LP/MC/CD 12)*

— now just basically a trio of FRIPP, WETTON and BRUFORD with old guests **MEL COLLINS, IAN McDONALD** and the departing **CROSS** augmenting on a track

Oct 74. (lp) *(ILPS 9308) <18110>* **RED** 45 66
– Red / Fallen angel / One more red nightmare / Providence / Starless. *(re-iss.Apr77 on 'Polydor' lp/c; 2302 066)(3100 366) (re-iss.Jan87 & Nov91 on 'E.G.' lp/c/cd; EG LP/MC/CD 15)*

— Split just before last album. Next live album was recorded with DAVID CROSS

Apr 75. (lp) *(ILPS 9316) <18136>* **U.S.A. (live)**
– Larks' tongues in aspic (part II) / Lament / Exiles / Asbury park / Easy money / 21st century schizoid man. *(re-iss.Dec79 on 'Polydor'; 2302 067) (re-iss.Jan87 on 'E.G.' lp/c/cd; EG LP/MC/CD 18)*

— JOHN WETTON joined BRIAN FERRY, then URIAH HEEP and later ASIA etc. As above BILL BRUFORD went solo and formed UK, after GONG stints.

ROBERT FRIPP

solo adding keyboards and a number of friends **PETER GABRIEL, PETER HAMILL & DARYL HALL** on vox, plus **PHIL COLLINS, BARRY ANDREWS, TONY LEVIN & MICHAEL NARADA WALDEN** – other instruments

E.G. | E.G.-Polydor

Apr 79. (lp/c) *(EG LP/MC 101) <6201>* **EXPOSURE** [71] [79]
– (prelude) / You burn me up I'm a cigarette / Breathless / Disengage / North star / Chicago / NY3 / Mary / Exposure / Haaaden two / Urban landscape / I may not have had enough of me but I've had enough of you / (first inaugural address to the J.A.C.E. Sherborne House) / Water music I / Here comes the flood / Water music II / Postscript. *(cd-iss.Jan87 & Apr89; EGCD 41)*

Mar 80. (lp/c) *(EG LP 105) <PL 6266>* **GOD SAVE THE QUEEN / UNDER HEAVY MANNERS (instrumental)**
– Under heavy manners / The zero of the signified / Red two scorer / God save the Queen / 1983. *(re-iss.Jan87 lp/c/cd; EG LP/MC/CD 45)*

E.G.-Editions | not issued

Apr 81. (lp/c) *(EGED/+C 10)* **LET THE POWER FALL (FRIPPERTRONICS)** [-]
– 1984 / 1985 / 1986 / 1987 / 1988 / 1989. *(cd-iss.Jan87; EEGCD 10)*

LEAGUE OF GENTLEMEN

FRIPP retained **BARRY ANDREWS** adding **SARA LEE** – bass (ex-JANE AIRE) / **JOHNNY TOOBAD** – drums

E.G.-Editions | Polydor

Dec 80. (7") *(EGEND 1)* **HEPTAPARAPARSHINOKH. / MARRIAGEMUZIC** [-]

Mar 81. (lp) *(EGED 9) <16317>* **LEAGUE OF GENTLEMEN (instrumental)**
– Indiscreet / Inductive recurrance / Minor man / Heptaparaparshinokh / Dislocated / Pareto optimum 1 / Eye needles / Indiscreet II / Pareto optimum 2 / Cognitive dissonance / H.G. Wells / Trap / Ochre / Indiscreet III.

Mar 81. (7") *(EGEND 2)* **DISLOCATED. / 1984** [-]

KING CRIMSON

FRIPP along with past member BRUFORD recruits newcomers **ADRIAN BELEW** (b. ROBERT STEVEN BELEW, 23 Dec'49, Covington, Kentucky) – guitar, vocals (ex-TOM TOM CLUB) / **TONY LEVIN** (b. 6 Jun'46, Boston, Mass.) – bass (ex-session man including PETER GABRIEL)

E.G. | Warners

Sep 81. (lp/c) *(EG LP/MC 49) <BSK 3629>* **DISCIPLINE** [41] [45]
– Elephant talk / Frame by frame / Matte Kudasai / Indiscipline / Thelahun ginjeet / The sheltering sky / Discipline. *(re-iss.Jan87 & Nov91 lp/c/cd; EG LP/MC/CD 49)*

Nov 81. (7") *(EGO 2)* **MATTE KUDASAI. / ELEPHANT TALK** [-]

Jun 82. (lp/c) *(EG LP/MC 51) <23692-1>* **BEAT** [39] [52]
– Neal and Jack and me / Heartbeat / Sartori in Tangier / Waiting man / Neurotica / Two hands / The howler / Requiem. *(cd-iss.Apr84 on 'Polydor'; 821 194-2) (re-iss.Jan87 & Nov91 lp/c/cd; EG LP/MC/CD 51)*

Jun 82. (7") *(EGO 6) <29964>* **HEARTBEAT. / REQUIEM (excerpt)**

Feb 84. (7") *(EGO 15) <29309>* **SLEEPLESS. / NUAGES**
(12") *(EGOX 15)* – ('A'side) / ('A'instrumental & dance mixes).

Mar 84. (lp/c/cd) *(EG LP/MC/CD 55) <25071>* **THREE OF A PERFECT PAIR** [30] [58]
– Three of a perfect pair / Model man / Sleepless / Man with an open heart / Nuages (that which passes, passes like clouds) / Industry / Dig me / No warning / Lark's tongues in aspic (part three). *(re-iss.Jan87 & Nov91; same)*

— FRIPP disbanded KING CRIMSON project for a decade.

– compilations, others, etc. –

Jun 72. (lp) *Help-Island; (HELP 6)* **EARTHBOUND (live)** [-]
– 21st century schizoid man / Peoria / The sailor's tale / Earthbound / Groon. *(re-iss.Oct77 on 'Polydor' lp)(c; 2343 092)(3192 385) (re-iss.Apr82 on 'EG')*

Feb 76. (d-lp) *Island; (ISLP 7)* **A YOUNG PERSON'S GUIDE TO KING CRIMSON** [-]
– Epitaph (including; (a) March for no reason – (b) Tomorrow and tomorrow / Cadence and cascade / Ladies of the road / I talk to the wind / Red / Starless / The night watch / Book of Saturday / Peace – a beginning / Cat food / Coda from Larks' tongues in aspic part 2 / Moonchild; (a) Mirrors – (b) The illusion / Trio / The court of the crimson king (including; (a) The return of the fire witch – (b) Dance of the puppets / 21st century schizoid man. *(re-iss.Mar77 on 'Polydor' d-lp/c; 2612 035)(3500 123) (cd-iss.1986 on 'E.G.'; EGCD 22)*

Feb 76. (7") *Island; (WIP 6274)* **21st CENTURY SCHIZOID MAN. / EPITAPH** [-]

Dec 80. (d-lp) *Polydor;* **IN THE COURT OF THE CRIMSON KING / LARKS' TONGUES IN ASPIC** [-]

Dec 86. (cd/d-lp/d-c) *E.G.; (EG CD/MC/LP 68)* **THE COMPACT KING CRIMSON**

Apr 87. (7"; by BRAIN) *Bam Caruso; (OPRA 63)* **NIGHTMARES IN RED. / (other artist)** [-]

Dec 89. (3xcd-box/3xc-box/3xlp-box) *E.G.; (EGBC/EGBM/EGBL 6)* **KING CRIMSON BOXED SET** [-]
– (IN THE COURT OF THE CRIMSON KING / LARKS' TONGUES IN ASPIC / DISCIPLINE)
(above 3 albums were packaged with other 'Island' artists)

1991. (cd-ep) *Virgin;* **THE ABBREVIATED KING CRIMSON – HEARTBEAT (medley)** [-]
– The King Crimson barber shop – 21st century schizoid man (abbreviated) – In the court of the crimson king (abbreviated) – Elephant talk (edit) – Matte Kudesai – Heartbeat (edit).

Dec 91. (4xcd-box) *Virgin; (KCBOX 1)* **FRAME BY FRAME: THE ESSENTIAL KING CRIMSON** [-]

Nov 92. (4xcd-box) *Virgin; (KCDIS 1)* **THE GREAT DECEIVER** [-]

Sep 93. (cd/c) *Virgin; (CDV/TCV 2721)* **SLEEPLESS: THE CONCISE KING CRIMSON**
– 21st century schizoid man / Epitaph / In the court of the crimson king / Cat food / Ladies of the road / Starless (abridged) / Red / Fallen angel / Elephant talk / Frame by frame / Matte Kudasai / Heartbeat / Three of a perfect pair / Sleepless.

Dec 93. (3xcd-box) *Virgin;* **IN THE COURT OF THE CRIMSON KING / IN THE WAKE OF POSEIDON / LIZARD** [-]

Apr 97. (d-cd) *Discipline; (DGM 9607)* **EPITAPH (live in 1969)** [-]

ROBERT FRIPP / LEAGUE OF GENTLEMEN

EG-Editions | E.G.

Jun 85. (lp/c) *(EGED/+C 9)* **GOD SAVE THE KING**
– God save the King / Under heavy manners / Heptaparparshinokh / Inductive resonance / Cognitive dissonance / Dislocated / HG Wells / Eye needles / Trap. *(cd-iss.Jan87; EEGCD 9)*

Nov 86. (lp/c/cd) *(EGED/+C 43)* **ROBERT FRIPP AND THE LEAGUE OF CRAFTY GUITARISTS: LIVE! (live)**
– Guitar craft theme 1: Invocation / Tight muscle party at Love Beach / The chords that bind / Guitar craft theme 3: Eye of the needle / All or nothing II / Guitar craft theme 2: Aspiration / All or nothing I / Circulation / A fearful symmetry / The new world / Crafty march. *(cd-iss.Jan87; EEGCD 43)*

— Late 1988, FRIPP / FRIPP (TOYAH) toured augmented by **TREY GUNN** – stick bass / **PAUL BEAVIS** – percussion, drums

— In mid'93, ROBERT FRIPP collaborated with ex-JAPAN singer DAVID SYLVIAN on near UK Top 20 album 'THE FIRST DAY'.

— In Aug'94, FRIPP was part of FFWD alongside THOMAS FEHLYN, KRIS WESTON + Dr.ALEX PATTERSON of The ORB. In Sep'94, FRIPP again teamed up with DAVID SYLVIAN on album 'DAMAGE'.

KING CRIMSON

FRIPP / BRUFORD / BELEW / LEVIN / GUNN / MASTELOTTO

Discipline | Virgin

Dec 94. (cd) *(DGM 0004)* **VROOOM**
– Vrooom / Sex, sleep, eat, drink, dream / Cage / Thrak / When I say stop, continue / One time.

Apr 95. (cd/cd/c) *(KC CDX/CDY/MC 1)* **THRAK** [58] [83]
– Vrooom / Coda: Marine 475 / Dinosaur / Walking on air / B'boom / Thrak / Inner garden I / People / Radio I / One time / Radio II / Inner garden II / Sex, sleep, eat, drink, dream / Vrooom vrooom / Vrooom vrooom coda.

Aug 95. (d-cd) *(DGM 9503)* **B'BOOM: OFFICIAL SOUNDTRACK – LIVE IN ARGENTINA (live** [-]
– Vrooom / Frame by frame / Sex, sleep, eat, drink, dream / Red / One time / B'boom / Thrak / Improv – Two sticks / Elephant talk / Indiscipline // Vrooom vrooom / Matte Kudesai / The talking drum / Lark's tongues in aspic (part 2) / Heartbeat / Sleepless / People / B'boom / Thrak.

May 96. (cd) *(DGM 9604)* **THRAKATTAK** [-]

Sep 96. (cd) *(DGMVC 1)* **LIVE IN JAPAN 1995 (live)** [-]
– Frame by frame / Dinosaur / One time / Red / B'room / Thrak / Matte kudasai / Three of a perfect pair / Vroom vroom / Sex, sleep, eat, drink, dream / Elephant talk / Indiscipline / Talking drum / Larks' tongues in aspic part II / People / Walking on air.

ROBERT FRIPP

Discipline | Virgin

Nov 94. (cd; ROBERT FRIPP STRING QUARTET) *(DGM 9303)* **THE BRIDGE BETWEEN**

Feb 95. (cd) *(DGM 9402-2)* **1999 SOUNDSCAPES – LIVE IN ARGENTINA (live)** [-]
– 1999 (part one) / 2000 / 2001 / Interlude / 2002.

Aug 95. (cd) *(DGM 9506)* **A BLESSING OF TEARS** [-]

Sep 95. (cd) **1995 SOUNDSCAPES – VOLUME TWO – LIVE IN CALIFORNIA (live)** [-]
– The cathedral of tears / First light / Midnight blue / Reflection 1 / Second light / A blessing of tears / Returning I / Returning II.

Oct 95. (cd) *(DGM 9502)* **INTERGALACTIC BOOGIE EXPRESS – LIVE IN EUROPE 1991** (live with The LEAGUE OF CRAFTY GUITARISTS) [-]
– A Connecticut Yankee in the court of King Arthur / Rhythm of the universe / Lark's hrak / Circulation 1 / Intergalactic boogie express / G force / Eye of the needle / Corrente / Driving force / Groove penetration / Flying home / Circulation II / Fireplace / Fragments of skylab / Asturias / Prelude circulation / Cheeseballs / Prelude in c minor / Wabash cannonball / Fractual Jazn / Ashesis. *(re-iss.Mar97; same)*

Mar 96. (cd) *(DGM 9505)* **1995 SOUNDSCAPES VOL.1 (LIVE IN ARGENTINA)** [-]

May 96. (cd; LEAGUE OF GENTLEMEN) *(DGM 9602)* **THRANG THRANG GOZINBULX**

Sep 96. (cd) *(DGM 9507)* **THAT WHICH PASSES**
– On acceptance / On the approach of doubt / Worm in Paradise / New worlds / On triumph / On awe / This too shall pass / Fear of light / Time to die.

Jun 97. (cd-ep) *(DGM 9704)* **PIE JESU /** [-]

– FRIPP compilations, etc. –

Jan 87. (10"m-lp/c) *E.G.; (EGM LP/MC 4)* **NETWORK**
– North star / (i) Water music 1 – (ii) Here comes the flood / God save the king / Under heavy manners.

May 91. (cd; ROBERT FRIPP & LEAGUE OF CRAFTY GUITARISTS) *E.G.; (EEG 21022)* **SHOW OF HANDS**

KINGDOM COME (see under ⇒ BROWN, Arthur)

KINGFISH (see under ⇒ GRATEFUL DEAD)

KINGSMEN

Formed: Portland, Oregon, USDA . . . 1958 by schoolboys LYNN EASTON and JACK ELY, who soon enlisted MIKE MITCHELL, BOB NORDBY and DON GALLUCCI. In May '63, after tours supporting PAUL REVERE & THE RAIDERS, they gained studio time, recording the classic garage cover of RICHARD BERRY's 'LOUIE LOUIE'. This was soon given a release on 'Jerden', becoming a hit in Boston before it was re-issued on 'Wand'. Although banned in certain states, it soared to No.2 in the American charts, becoming a standard for many future rock/pop groups. At the time of its success, the group went through turmoil when EASTON took over both the leadership and vocals of the group (this led to his friend ELY departing). On American TV, EASTON was seen miming to ELY's raunchy vocals. They continued in the same vein covering many standards in their inimitable garage-punk style. See ⇒ • **Covers:** LOUIE LOUIE (Richard Berry) / MONEY (Barrett Strong) / LITTLE LATIN LUPE LU (Righteous Brothers) / KILLER JOE (Rocky Fellers) / etc.

Recommended: LOUIE LOUIE – GREATEST HITS (*5)

LYNN EASTON – saxophone, vocals / **JACK ELY** – vocals, guitar / **MIKE MITCHELL** – lead guitar / **BOB NORDBY** – bass / **DON GALLUCCI** – organ

		not issued	Jalynne	
1962.	(7") <108> **DIG THIS. / LADY'S CHOICE**	-		
		not issued	Jerden	
Jun 63.	(7") <712> **LOUIE LOUIE. / HAUNTED CASTLE**	-		
		Pye Int.	Wand	
Jan 64.	(7") *(7N 25231)* <143> **LOUIE LOUIE. / HAUNTED CASTLE** *<US re-iss.May66; same>; hit No.97>*	26	2	Sep63

— (Aug63) **EASTON** took over vox from **ELY** who moved to drums! just before he departed / **GARY ABBOTT** – drums repl. ELY. **NORM SUNDHOLM** – bass repl. NORDBY

Jan 64.	(lp) *(NPL 28050)* <657> **LOUIE LOUIE: THE KINGSMEN IN PERSON (live Portland)** – Louie Louie / The waiting / Mojo workout / Fever / Money / Bent scepter / Long tall Texan / You can't sit down / Twist & shout / J.A.J. / Night train / Mashed potatoes.		20	
Mar 64.	(7") <150> **MONEY. / BENT SCEPTER**	-	16	

— **BARRY CURTIS** – organ repl. **DON DICK PETERSON** – drums repl. GARY

Jul 64.	(7") *(7N 25262)* <157> **LITTLE LATIN LUPE LU. / DAVID'S MOOD**		46	
Sep 64.	(7") *(7N 25273)* <164> **DEATH OF AN ANGEL. / SEARCHING FOR LOVE**		42	
Feb 65.	(7") *(7N 25292)* <172> **THE JOLLY GREEN GIANT. / LONG GREEN**		4	Jan65
Feb 65.	(lp) *(NPL 28054)* <659> **THE KINGSMEN, VOLUME II (live)** – Kingsmen introduction / Little Latin Lupe Lu / Long green / Do you love me / New Orleans / Walking the dog / David's mood / Something's got a hold on me / Come on baby, let the good times roll / Ooh poo pah doo / Great balls of fire / Linda Lou / Earth of an angel.		15	Sep64
Feb 65.	(lp) <662> **THE KINGSMEN, VOLUME 3 (live)** – The jolly green giant / Over you / That's cool, that's trash / Don't you just know it / I go crazy / La-do-dada / Long green / Mother-in-law / Shout / Searching for love / Tall cool one / Comin' home baby.	-	22	
Jun 65.	(7") *(NPL 25311)* <183> **THE CLIMB. / WAITING**		65	May65
Jul 65.	(7") <189> **ANNIE FANNY. / GIVE HER LOVIN'**	-	47	
Aug 65.	(7") *(NPL 25322)* **ANNIE FANNY. / SOMETHING'S GOT A HOLD ON ME**		-	
Feb 66.	(7") <1107> **(YOU GOT) THE GAMMA GOOCHE. / IT'S ONLY THE DOG**	-		
Mar 66.	(lp) *(NPL 28068)* <670> **THE KINGSMEN ON CAMPUS (live)** – Annie Fanny / Rosalie / A hard day's night / I like it like that / Stand by me / Little green thing / The climb / Sticks and stones / Peter Gunn / Some times / Shotgun / Genevieve.		68	Oct65
Jun 66.	(7") *(7N 25370)* <1115> **KILLER JOE. / LITTLE GREEN THING**		77	Mar66
Jun 66.	(7") **THE KRUNCH. / THE CLIMB**	-		
Sep 66.	(lp) *(NPL 28085)* <674> **THE KINGSMEN'S GREATEST HITS** <US-title '15 GREAT HITS'> (compilation & new) – Killer Joe / Good lovin' / Jenny take a ride / Ooh poo pah doo / Fever / Quarter to three / Poison Ivy / Satisfaction / Twist and shout / Money / Searchin' / Hang on Sloopy / Do you love me / Shout / New Orleans.		87	Aug66
Sep 66.	(7") <1127> **LITTLE SALLY TEASE. / MY WIFE CAN'T COOK**	-		
Nov 66.	(7") <1137> **IF I NEEDED SOMEONE. / THE GRASS IS GREEN**	-		
Jan 67.	(7") *(7N 25406)* <1147> **DAYTIME SHADOWS. / TROUBLE**			
		Wand	Wand	
Jan 67.	(lp) <(WNS 6)> **UP AND AWAY** – Trouble / If I needed someone / Grass is green / Tosin' and turnin' / Under my thumb / Wild thing / (I have found) Another girl / Daytime shadows / Shake a tailfeather / Children's caretaker / Land of a thousand dances / Mustang Sally / Little Sally tease / Hushabye.			
Mar 67.	(7") <1154> **THE WOLF OF MANHATTAN. / CHILDREN'S CARETAKER**	-		
Jul 67.	(7") <1157> **DON'T SAY NO. / ANOTHER GIRL (I HAVE FOUND)**	-		

— In Jul'67, EASTON left group as they soon dissolved.

1968.	(7") <1164> **BO DIDDLEY BACH. / JUST BEFORE THE BREAK OF DAY**	-		
1968.	(7") <1174> **GET OUT OF MY LIFE WOMAN. / SINCE YOU'VE BEEN GONE**	-		
1968.	(7") **I GUESS I WAS DREAMIN'. / ON LOVE**	-		

— split in Sep'68. Re-formed in 1972 with **FREDDIE DENNIS** – bass / **STEVE FRIEDSON** – keyboards (added to MIKE MITCHELL, DICK PETERSON + BARRY CURTIS)

– compilations, etc. –

on 'Pye International'; unless mentioned otherwise

1964.	(7"ep) *(NEP 44023)* **THE KINGSMEN**		
1965.	(7"ep) *(NEP 44040)* **MOJO WORKOUT**		
1966.	(7"ep) *(NEP 44063)* **FEVER**		
Apr 66.	(7") *(7N 25366)* **LITTLE LATIN LUPE LU. / LOUIE LOUIE**		-
1969.	Marble Arch; (lp) *(MAL 829)* **THE KINGSMEN'S GREATEST HITS**		-
1971.	Wand; (7") *(WN 14)* **LOUIE LOUIE. / IF I NEEDED SOMEONE**		-
1972.	Scepter; (lp) <18002> **THE BEST OF THE KINGSMEN** *(re-iss.Jan86 on 'Rhino'; RNLP 126) (cd-iss.Sep91)*	-	
1980.	Piccadilly; (lp) <3329> **A QUARTER TO THREE**	-	
1980.	Piccadilly; (lp) <3330> **YA YA**	-	
1980.	Piccadilly; (lp) <3346> **HOUSE PARTY**	-	
1980.	Piccadilly; (lp) <3348> **GREAT HITS**	-	
Jul 81.	Old Gold; (7") *(OG 9054)* **LOUIE LOUIE. / THE JOLLY GREEN GIANT**		-
Jan 87.	Decal; (lp) *(LIK 6)* **LOUIE LOUIE – GREATEST HITS** – Louie Louie / Money (that's what I want) / The jolly green giant / Death of an angel / The climb / Get out of my life woman / Little Latin lupe lu / Killer Joe / Annie Fanny / Long green / Little Sally tease / Trouble / If I needed someone.		-
Jan 96.	Instant; (cd) *(CPCD 8160)* **LOUIE LOUIE**		-

KINKS

Formed: Muswell Hill, London, England . . . 1963 by brothers RAY and DAVE DAVIES, who recruited PETER QUAIFE from The RAVENS. With help from managers Robert Wace and Grenville Collins, they met Larry Page who gave them the name KINKS late '63. He also arranged demos, which were soon heard by American SHEL TALMY, securing them a deal with 'Pye' early '64. Two singles flopped, but the third, 'YOU REALLY GOT ME', stormed the top spot in the UK, soon breaking into US Top 10. With its scuzzy, propulsive guitar riff, the song is oft cited as one of the first real "heavy rock" records, although it's debatable whether RAY DAVIES would admit to inspiring a multitude of poodle maned Van Halen soundalikes. A top selling eponymous lp followed, as did a series of Top 10 sixties singles, including two more UK No.1's, 'TIRED OF WAITING FOR YOU' and 'SUNNY AFTERNOON'. As RAY's songwriting developed, the band moved to a quieter, more reflective sound, his camp, semi-detached vocals complementing the wry observations and quintessential Englishness of the lyrical themes. Come 1967, when every band worth their weight in spiked sugarcubes were looking towards the 'East', Davies looked no further than his proverbial back garden. 'SOMETHING ELSE', with its heartfelt eulogies to a mythical England past, still stands as the Kinks' greatest moment, the aching melancholy of 'WATERLOO SUNSET' its crowning glory. Davies' nostalgic bent continued on 1968's 'THE KINKS ARE THE VILLAGE GREEN PRESERVATION SOCIETY', an enchanting concept album that reached ever further into a faded history of rural simplicity. It also included the KINKS' sole dalliance with psychedelia, 'WICKED ANNABELLA', a Brothers Grimm-like fairytale come nightmare fantasy. DAVIES' lyrical obsessions were given centre stage once more on 'ARTHUR (OR THE DECLINE OF THE ROMAN EMPIRE)' (1969) wherein the rosy hue of the past was contrasted with the grey decline of modern day Britain. The mood lightened somewhat with 1970's surprise No.2 hit single, 'LOLA', a tongue in cheek tribute to a male cross-dresser and the standout track from the subsequent album, 'LOLA VERSUS POWERMAN AND THE MONEYGOROUND PART 1'. 1971's 'MUSWELL HILLBILLIES' echoed ~'VILLAGE GREEN's collection of storybook vignettes although the band were beginning to lose their focus and the hits were about to dry up. 'SUPERSONIC ROCKETSHIP' went top 20 in 1972 but the follow-up, 'CELLULOID HEROES', failed to chart. Both songs were taken from the album, 'EVERYBODY'S IN SHOWBIZ', and were high points in an otherwise unremarkable affair. The remainder of the 70's saw the KINKS become bogged down in ill-advised concept albums and self-parody although while the band were virtually ignored in the UK, they still had a sizeable following in America, hitting the US Top 30 with the patchy 'SLEEPWALKER' album in 1977. With the release of the harder rocking 'LOW BUDGET' a couple of years later, the band were embraced fully by the US rock fraternity and hitched a lucrative ride on the stadium rock circuit as well as gaining a sizeable piece of chart action. While the early 80's albums, 'GIVE THE PEOPLE WHAT THEY WANT' and 'STATE OF CONFUSION' were competent albeit largely uninspired, the Americans lapped them up and the band even found themselves back in the UK Top 20 with the classic 'COME DANCING' single. Throughout the 80's the band once again descended into inconsistency and commercial wilderness, their live shows being the sole factor in keeping the KINKS' spirit intact. Fast forward to 1995 and BLUR were riding high on the 'Britpop' wave with their heavily KINKS-influenced 'Parklife' album. Overrated and trailing in the KINKS shadows, the album's success nevertheless gave Blur mainman DAMON ALBORN the opportunity to express his admiration for his hero RAY DAVIES and perform a poignant TV duet with the great man on 'WATERLOO SUNSET'. The renewed interest also resulted in a TV documentary on the KINKS and a solo tour by Ray, not to mention autobiographies by both RAY and DAVE. • **Songwriters:** RAY DAVIES wrote all of work, except covers; LONG TALL SALLY (Ernie Johnson) / TOO MUCH MONKEY

BUSINESS (Chuck Berry) / GOT LOVE IF YOU WANT IT (Slim Harpo) / MILK COW BLUES (Elvis Presley) / etc. • **Trivia:** RAY produced 1969 lp 'Turtle Soup' for The TURTLES. He was married on the 12th December '64 to Rasa Dicpetri, but later divorced her (see KINKS biography by Johnny Rogan). In 1981, he divorced his second wife Yvonne. (RAY had a relationship with CHRISSIE HYNDE of The PRETENDERS for three years). She gave him a daughter, Natalie, in February '83, although they separated when she started dating JIM KERR (of SIMPLE MINDS). In 1986, RAY appeared in the film musical, 'Absolute Beginners'.

Recommended: FACE TO FACE (*8) / SOMETHING ELSE (*7) / VILLAGE GREEN PRESERVATION SOCIETY (*8) / ARTHUR (*8) / THE ULTIMATE COLLECTION (*9) / COME DANCING WITH THE KINKS – THE BEST OF . . . 1977-1986 (*7).

RAY DAVIES (b.21 Jun'44) – vocals, guitar / **DAVE DAVIES** (b. 3 Feb'47) – guitar, vocals / **PETER QUAIFE** (b.31 Dec'43, Tavistock, Devon) – bass with session drummers

Pye / Cameo

Mar 64. (7") *(7N 15611)* <308> **LONG TALL SALLY. / I TOOK MY BABY HOME** [ ] [ ] Apr64
<US re-iss.Nov64; 345>

May 64. (7") *(7N 15636)* **YOU STILL WANT ME. / YOU DO SOMETHING TO ME** [ ] [-]

Pye / Reprise

Aug 64. (7") *(7N 15673)* <0306> **YOU REALLY GOT ME. / IT'S ALRIGHT** [1] [7] Sep64

—— **MICK AVORY** (b.15 Feb'44) – drums was now used although he joined 9 months previously

Oct 64. (lp) *(NPL 18096)* <6143> **THE KINKS** <US-title 'YOU REALLY GOT ME'> [3] [29] Dec64
– Beautiful Delilah / So mystifying / Just can't go to sleep / Long tall Shorty / You really got me / Cadillac / Bald headed woman / Revenge / Too much monkey business / Revenge / I've been driving on Bald mountain / Stop your sobbing / Got love if you want it. *(re iss.Jan67 on 'Golden Guinea'; GGL 0357) (re-iss.May80 as 'YOU REALLY GOT ME'; NSPL 18615) (re-iss.Oct87 on 'P.R.T.' lp/c/cd; PYL/PYM/PYC 6002) (cd re-iss.Dec89 on 'Castle'; CLACD 155)*

Oct 64. (7") *(7N 15714)* <0334> **ALL DAY AND ALL OF THE NIGHT. / I GOTTA MOVE** [2] [7] Dec64
(re-iss.Oct84 on 'P.R.T.'; KIS 003) (re-iss.Jan88 on 'P.R.T.'; PYS 4)

Jan 65. (7") *(7N 15759)* <0347> **TIRED OF WAITING FOR YOU. / COME ON NOW** [1] [6] Mar65

Mar 65. (lp) <6158> **KINKS-SIZE** [-] [13]
– Tired of waiting for you / Louie Louie / I've got that feeling / Revenge / I gotta move / Things are getting better / I gotta go now / I'm a lover not a fighter / Come on now / All day and all of the night.

Mar 65. (lp) *(NPL 18112)* <6173> **KINDA KINKS** [3] [60] Aug65
– Look for me baby / Got my feet on the ground / Nothin' in the world can stop me worryin' 'bout that girl / Naggin' woman / Wonder where my baby is tonight / Tired of waiting for you / Dancing in the street / Don't ever change / Come on now / So long / You shouldn't be sad / Something better beginning. *(re-iss.Oct87 on 'P.R.T.' lp/c/cd; PYL/PYM/PYC 6003) (cd re-iss.Dec89 on 'Castle'; CLACD 156)*

Mar 65. (7") *(7N 15813)* <0366> **EVERYBODY'S GONNA BE HAPPY. / WHO'LL BE THE NEXT IN LINE** [11] [ ] Apr65
<above 45 flipped over in the States with B-side hitting No.34>

May 65. (7") *(7N 15854)* <0379> **SET ME FREE. / I NEED YOU** [9] [23] Jun65

Jul 65. (7") *(7N 15919)* <0409> **SEE MY FRIEND. / NEVER MET A GIRL LIKE YOU BEFORE** [10] [ ]

Nov 65. (7") <0420> **A WELL RESPECTED MAN. / MILK COW BLUES** [-] [13]

Nov 65. (7") *(7N 15981)* <0454> **TILL THE END OF THE DAY. / WHERE HAVE ALL THE GOOD TIMES GONE** [6] [50] Mar66

Nov 65. (lp) *(NPL 18131)* <6197> **THE KINK KONTROVERSY** [9] [95] Apr66
– Milk cow blues / Ring the bells / Gotta get the first plane home / When I see that girl of mine / Till the end of the day / The world keeps going round / I'm on the island / Where have all the good times gone / It's too late / What's in store for me / You can't win. *(re-iss.Oct87 on 'P.R.T.' lp/c/cd; PYL/PYM/PYC 6004) (cd re-iss.Dec89 on 'Castle'; CLACD 157)*

Dec 65. (lp) <6184> **KINKS KINKDOM** [-] [47]
– Well respected man / Such a shame / Wait 'til the summer comes along / Naggin' woman / Who'll be the next in line / Don't you fret / I need you / It's all right / Louie Louie.

Feb 66. (7") *(7N 17064)* <0471> **DEDICATED FOLLOWER OF FASHION. / SITTING ON MY SOFA** [4] [36] May66

—— **JOHN DALTON** – bass deputised on tour for QUAIFE while injured

Jun 66. (7") *(7N 17125)* <0497> **SUNNY AFTERNOON. / I'M NOT LIKE EVERYBODY ELSE** [1] [14] Aug66

Aug 66. (lp) <6217> **THE KINKS GREATEST HITS** (compilation) [-] [9]
– Dedicated follower of fashion / Tired of waiting for you / All day and all of the night / You really got me / Well respected man / Who'll be the next in line / Everybody's gonna be happy / Till the end of the day / Set me free / Something better beginning.

—— **JOHN DALTON** sessioned between 66-69, QUAIFE's photo on covers

Oct 66. (lp; mono/stereo) *(NPL/NSPL 18145)* <6228> **FACE TO FACE** [12] [ ] Feb67
– Party line / Rosy won't you please come home / Dandy / Too much on my mind / Session man / Rainy day in June / House in the country / Sunny afternoon / Holiday in Waikiki / Most exclusive residence for sale / Fancy / Little Miss Queen of Darkness / You're looking fine / I'll remember. *(re-iss.Oct87 on 'P.R.T.' lp/c/cd; PYL/PYM/PYC 6005) (cd re-iss.Dec89 on 'Castle'; CLACD 158)*

Nov 66. (7") *(7N 17125)* <0540> **DEAD END STREET. / BIG BLACK SMOKE** [5] [73] Jan67

May 67. (7") *(7N 17321)* **WATERLOO SUNSET. / ACT NICE AND GENTLE** [2] [-]

May 67. (lp; mono/stereo) *(NPL/NSPL 18191)* <6260> **LIVE AT KELVIN HALL (live in Glasgow)** <US-title 'THE LIVE KINKS'> [ ] [ ] Sep67
– Till the end of the day / I'm on an island / You really got me / All day and all of the night / A well respected man / You're looking fine / Sunny afternoon / Dandy / Come on now / Milk cow blues – Batman theme – Tired of waiting for you. *(re-iss.Oct87 on 'P.R.T.' lp/c/cd; PYL/PYM/PYC 6007) (cd re-iss.Dec89 on 'Castle'; CLACD 160)*

Jun 67. (7") <0587> **MR. PLEASANT. / HARRY RAG** [-] [80]

Sep 67. (7") <0612> **WATERLOO SUNSET. / TWO SISTERS** [-] [ ]

Oct 67. (lp; mono/stereo) *(NPL/NSPL 18193)* <6279> **SOMETHING ELSE BY THE KINKS** [35] [ ] Feb68
– David Watts / Death of a clown / Two sisters / No return / Harry Rag / Tin soldier man / Situation vacant / Love me till the sun shines / Lazy old sun / Afternoon tea / Funny face / End of the season / Waterloo sunset. *(re-iss.Oct87 on 'P.R.T.' lp/c/cd; PYL/PYM/PYC 6006) (cd re-iss.Dec89 on 'Castle'; CLACD 159)*

Oct 67. (7") *(7N 17400)* <0647> **AUTUMN ALMANAC. / MR. PLEASANT** [3] [ ]

Apr 68. (7") *(7N 17468)* <0691> **WONDERBOY. / POLLY** [37] [ ]

Jul 68. (7") *(7N 17573)* <0762> **DAYS. / SHE'S GOT EVERYTHING** [12] [ ]

Jul 68. (lp; mono/stereo) *(NPL/NSPL 18233)* <6327> **THE KINKS ARE THE VILLAGE GREEN PRESERVATION SOCIETY** [ ] [ ]
– Village green preservation society / Do you remember Walter / Picture book / Johnny Thunder / The last of the steam powered trains / Big sky / Sitting by the riverside / Animal farm / Village green / Starstruck / Phenomenal cat / All my friends were there / Wicked Annabella / Monica / People take pictures of each other. *(re-iss.Nov85 on 'Flashback-PRT'; FBLP 8091) (re-iss.Oct87 on 'P.R.T.' lp/c/cd; PYL/PYM/PYC 6008) (cd re-iss.Oct89 on 'Castle'; CLACD 161) (cd re-iss.Feb97 on 'Original Recordings'; ORRLP 005)*

Apr 69. (7") *(7N 17724)* <0743> **PLASTIC MAN. / KING KONG** [31] [ ]

Apr 69. (7") <0806> **STARSTRUCK. / PICTURE BOOK** [-] [ ]

—— **JOHN DALTON** (b.21 May'43) – bass officially repl. QUAIFE

Jun 69. (7") <0847> **WALTER. / VILLAGE GREEN PRESERVATION SOCIETY** [-] [ ]

Jun 69. (7"; b-side by KINKS featuring DAVE DAVIES) <7N 17776> **DRIVIN'. / MINDLESS CHILD OF MOTHERHOOD** [ ] [-]

Sep 69. (7") *(7N 17812)* **SHANGRI-LA. / THIS MAN HE WEEPS TONIGHT** [ ] [-]
(above initially had 'LAST OF THE STEAM-POWERED TRAINS' on B-side)

Oct 69. (lp) *(NSPL 18317)* <6366> **ARTHUR (OR THE DECLINE AND FALL OF THE BRITISH EMPIRE** [ ] [ ]
– Victoria / Yes sir, no sir / Some mother's son / Brainwashed / Australia / Shangri-la / Mr. Churchill says / She bought a hat like Princess Marina / Young and innocent days / Nothing to say / Arthur. *(re-iss.Oct87 on 'P.R.T.' lp/c/cd; PYL/PYM/PYC 6009) (cd re-iss.Oct89 on 'Castle'; CLACD 162)*

Dec 69. (7") *(7N 17865)* **VICTORIA. / MR. CHURCHILL SAYS** [33] [-]

Jan 70. (7") <0863> **VICTORIA. / BRAINWASHED** [-] [62]

Jun 70. (7") *(7N 17961)* **LOLA. / BERKELEY MEWS** [2] [-]

Aug 70. (7") <0930> **LOLA. / MINDLESS CHILD OF MOTHERHOOD** [-] [9]

Nov 70. (lp) *(NSPL 18359)* <6423> **LOLA VERSUS POWERMAN & THE MONEYGOROUND, PART ONE** [ ] [35]
– The contenders / Strangers / Denmark Street / Get back in line / Lola / Top of the pops / The moneygoround / This time tomorrow / A long way from home / Rats / Apeman / Powerman / Got to be free. *(re-iss.Oct87 on 'P.R.T.' lp/c/cd; PYL/PYM/PYC 6010) (cd re-iss.Oct89 on 'Castle'; CLACD 163)*

Nov 70. (7") *(7N 45016)* <0979> **APEMAN. / RATS** [5] [45] Jan71

Mar 71. (lp) *(NSPL 18365)* **(SOUNDTRACK FROM THE FILM) "PERCY"** [ ] [-]
– God's children / Lola / The way love used to be / Completely / Running round town / Moments / Animals in the zoo / Just friends / Helga / Willesden Green / God's children – end. *(re-iss.Oct87 on 'P.R.T.' lp/c/cd; PYL/PYM/PYC 6011) (cd re-iss.Oct89 on 'Castle'; CLACD 164)*

Apr 71. (7") *(7N 8001)* **GOD'S CHILDREN. / MOMENTS** [ ] [-]
(7"m+=) *(7NX 8001)* – The way love used to be / Dreams.

Apr 71. (7") <1017> **GOD'S CHILDREN. / THE WAY LOVE USED TO BE** [-] [ ]

—— added **JOHN GOSLING** – keyboards (he guested on 'LOLA' album), plus **LAURIE BROWN** – trumpet / **JOHN BEECHAM** – trombone / **ALAN HOLMES** – saxophone recruited from The MIKE COTTON SOUND. The three became full-time members '73, adding to **R. DAVIES, D. DAVIES, AVORY and DALTON**

R.C.A. / R.C.A.

Nov 71. (lp) *(SF 8243)* <LSP 4644> **MUSWELL HILLBILLIES** [ ] [100]
– 20th century man / Acute schizophrenia paranoia blues / Holiday / Skin and bone / Alcohol / Complicated life / Here come the people in the grey / Have a cuppa tea / Holloway jail / Oklahoma U.S.A. / Uncle son / Muswell hillbilly.

Feb 72. (7") <74-0620> **20th CENTURY MAN. / SKIN AND BONE** [-] [ ]

May 72. (7") *(RCA 2211)* <74-0807> **SUPERSONIC ROCKET SHIP. / YOU DON'T KNOW MY NAME** [16] [ ]

Aug 72. (d-lp) *(DPS 2035)* <6065> **EVERYBODY'S IN SHOWBIZ** [ ] [70]
– Here comes yet another day / Maximum consumption / Unreal reality / Hot potatoes / Sitting in my hotel / You don't know my name / Supersonic rocket ship / Look a little on the sunny side / Celluloid heroes / Motorway. / **EVERYBODY'S A STAR (live)** – Top of the pops / Brainwashed / Mr. Wonderful / Acute schizophrenia paranoia blues / Holiday / Muswell Hillbilly / Alcohol / Banana boat song / Skin and bone / Baby face / Lola.

Nov 72. (7") *(RCA 2299)* <74-0852> **CELLULOID HEROES. / HOT POTATOES** [ ] [ ]

Jun 73. (7") <74-0940> **ONE OF THE SURVIVORS. / SCRAPHEAP CITY** [-] [ ]

Jun 73. (7") *(RCA 2387)* **SITTING IN THE MIDDAY SUN. / ONE OF THE SURVIVORS** [ ] [-]

Sep 73. (7") *(RCA 2418)* **SWEET LADY GENEVIEVE. / SITTING IN MY HOTEL** [ ] [-]

Sep 73. (7") <5001> **SWEET LADY GENEVIEVE. / SITTING IN THE MIDDAY SUN** [-] [ ]

Dec 73. (d-lp) *(SF 8392)* <LPL 5002> **PRESERVATION ACT I** [ ] [ ]
– Morning song / Daylight / Sweet Lady Genevieve / There's a change in the weather / Where are they now / One of the survivors / Cricket / I am your man / Here comes Flash / Sitting in the midday Sun / Demolution.

—— next 45 only contained **RAY & DAVE DAVIES**, before full 5 + 3 again

Apr 74. (7") *(RCA 5015)* **MIRROR OF LOVE. / CRICKET** [ ] [-]

Jun 74. (7") <0275> **MONEY TALKS. / HERE COMES FLASH** [-] [ ]

Jun 74. (d-lp) <(LPL2 5040)> **PRESERVATION ACT II**
– (announcement) / Introduction to solution / When a solution comes / Money talks / (announcement) / Shepherds of the nation / Scum of the Earth / Secondhand car spiv / He's evil / Mirror of love / (announcement) / Nobody gives / Oh where oh where is love? / Flash's dream / Flash's confession / Nothing lasts forever / (announcement) /

Artificial man / Scrapheap city / (announcement) / Salvation Road.

Jul 74. (7") *(RCA 5042) <APBO 10019>* **MIRROR OF LOVE. / HE'S EVIL** [ ] [ ]

Oct 74. (7") *(RCA 2478)* **HOLIDAY ROMANCE. / SHEPHERDS OF THE NATION** [ ] [-]

Oct 74. (7") *<APBO 10121>* **PRESERVATION. / SALVATION** [-] [ ]

Apr 75. (7") *<APBO 10251>* **ORDINARY PEOPLE. / STAR MAKER** [-] [ ]

Apr 75. (7") *(RCA 2546)* **DUCKS ON THE WALL. / RUSH HOUR BLUES** [ ] [-]

May 75. (lp) *(SF 8411) <LPI 5081>* **SOAP OPERA** [ ] [51]
– Everybody's a star (starmaker) / Ordinary people / Rush hour blues / Nine to five / When work is over / Have another drink / Underneath the neon sign / Holiday romance / You make it all worth while / Ducks on the wall / Face in the crowd / You can't stop the music. *(re-iss.Jul84)*

May 75. (7") *(RCA 2567)* **YOU CAN'T STOP THE MUSIC. / HAVE ANOTHER DRINK** [ ] [-]

Nov 75. (lp) *(RS 1028) <FLI 5102>* **SCHOOLBOYS IN DISGRACE** [ ] [45]
– Schooldays / Jack the idiot dunce / Education / The first time we fall in love / I'm in disgrace / Headmaster / The hard way / The last assembly / No more looking back / (finale).

Nov 75. (7") *<10551>* **THE HARD WAY. / I'M IN DISGRACE** [-] [ ]

Jan 76. (7"m) *(RCM 1)* **NO MORE LOOKING BACK. / JACK THE IDIOT DUNCE / THE HARD WAY** [ ] [-]

— Now down to basic 5-piece after the 3 brass section members departed

Arista Arista

Feb 77. (lp/c) *(SP/TC ARTY 1002) <AL 4106>* **SLEEPWALKER** [ ] [21]
– Life on the road / Mr. Big man / Sleepwalker / Brother / Juke box music / Sleepless night / Stormy sky / Full moon / Life goes on.

Mar 77. (7") *(ARIST 97) <0240>* **SLEEPWALKER. / FULL MOON** [ ] [48]

Jun 77. (7") *(ARIST 114)* **JUKE BOX MUSIC. / SLEEPLESS NIGHT** [ ] [-]

Jun 77. (7") *<0247>* **JUKE BOX MUSIC. / LIFE GOES ON** [-] [ ]

— **ANDY PYLE** – bass (ex-BLODWYN PIG, ex-SAVOY BROWN, etc) repl. DALTON

Dec 77. (7") *(ARIST 153) <0296>* **FATHER CHRISTMAS. / PRINCE OF THE PUNKS** [ ] [ ]

May 78. (lp/c) *(SP/TC ART 1055) <AL 4167>* **MISFITS** [ ] [40]
– Misfits / Hay fever / Live life / Rock'n'roll fantasy / In a foreign land / Permanent waves / Black Messiah / Out of the wardrobe / Trust your heart / Get up.

May 78. (7") *(ARIST 189) <0342>* **ROCK'N'ROLL FANTASY. / ARTIFICIAL LIGHT** [ ] [30] Jul78

Jul 78. (7") *(ARIST 199)* **LIVE LIFE. / IN A FOREIGN LAND** [ ] [-]

Jul 78. (7") *<0372>* **LIVE LIFE. / BLACK MESSIAH** [-] [ ]

Sep 78. (7") *(ARIST 210)* **BLACK MESSIAH. / MISFITS** [ ] [-]

— RAY DAVIES, DAVE DAVIES and MICK AVORY recruited new members **GORDON EDWARDS** – keyboards (ex-PRETTY THINGS) repl. GOSLING (to NETWORK) / **JIM RODFORD** (b. 7 Jul'45, St. Albans, England) – bass (ex-ARGENT, ex-PHOENIX) repl. PYLE (to NETWORK)

Jan 79. (7"/12") *(ARIST/+12 240)* **(WISH I COULD FLY LIKE) SUPERMAN. / LOW BUDGET** [ ] [-]

— **IAN GIBBON** – keyboards repl. EDWARDS

Apr 79. (7") *<0409>* **(WISH I COULD FLY LIKE) SUPERMAN. / PARTY LINE** [-] [41]

Sep 79. (7") *(ARIST 300)* **MOVING PICTURES. / IN A SPACE** [ ] [-]

Sep 79. (lp/c) *(SP/TC ART 1099) <AB 4240>* **LOW BUDGET** [ ] [11] Jul79
– Attitude / Catch me now I'm falling / Pressure / National health / (I wish I could fly like) Superman / Low budget / In a space / Little bit of emotion / Gallon of gas / Misery / Moving pictures. *(cd-iss.Apr88; 251 146)*

Sep 79. (7") *<0448>* **GALLON OF GAS. / LOW BUDGET** [-] [ ]

Nov 79. (7") *<0458>* **CATCH ME NOW I'M FALLING. / LOW BUDGET** [-] [ ]

Nov 79. (7") *(ARIST 321)* **PRESSURE. / NATIONAL HEALTH** [ ] [-]

Jul 80. (d-lp) *(DARTY 6) <8401>* **ONE FOR THE ROAD (live)** [ ] [14] Jun80
– The hard way / Catch me now I'm falling / Where have all the good times gone / Lola / Pressure / All day and all of the night / 20th century man / Misfits / Prince of the punks / Stop your sobbing / Low budget / Attitude / (Wish I could fly like) Superman / National health / Till the end of the day / Celluloid heroes / You really got me / Victoria / David Watts.

Jul 80. (7"ep) *(ARIST 360)* **WHERE HAVE ALL THE GOOD TIMES GONE (live)** [ ] [-]
– Where have all the good times gone / Victoria / Attitude / David Watts.

Aug 80. (7") *<0541>* **LOLA (live). / CELLULOID HEROES (live)** [-] [81]

Oct 80. (7") *<0577>* **YOU REALLY GOT ME (live). / ATTITUDE (live)** [-] [ ]

Jun 81. (lp/c) *(SP/TC ART 1171) <9567>* **GIVE THE PEOPLE WHAT THEY WANT** [ ] [15]
– Around the dial / Give the people what they want / Killer's eyes / Predictable / Add it up / Destroyer / Yo-yo / Back to front / Art lover / A little bit of abuse / Better things.

Jun 81. (7") *(ARIST 415)* **BETTER THINGS. / MASSIVE REDUCTIONS** [46] [-]
(d7"+=) *(KINKS 1)* – Lola / David Watts.

Oct 81. (7",7"pic-d) *(ARIST 426)* **PREDICTABLE. / BACK TO FRONT** [ ] [ ]

Oct 81. (7") *<0619>* **DESTROYER. / BACK TO FRONT** [-] [85]

Nov 81. (7") *<0649>* **BETTER THINGS. / YO-YO** [-] [92]

Jun 83. (lp/c) *(205/405 275) <8018>* **STATE OF CONFUSION** [ ] [12]
– State of confusion / Definite maybe / Labour of love / Come dancing / Property / Don't forget to dance / Young Conservatives / Heart of gold / Cliches of the world (B movie) / Bernadette. *(cd-iss.1988 on 'Ariola')*

Jul 83. (7"/12") *(ARIST/+12 502) <1054/9016>* **COME DANCING. / NOISE** [12] [6] May83

Aug 83. (7") *<9075>* **DON'T FORGET TO DANCE. / YOUNG CONSERVATIVES** [-] [29]

Sep 83. (7",12") *(ARIST 524)* **DON'T FORGET TO DANCE. / BERNADETTE** [58] [-]

Mar 84. (7") *(ARIST 560)* **STATE OF CONFUSION. / HEART OF GOLD** [ ] [-]
(12"+=) *(ARIST12 560)* – 20th century man (live) / Lola (live).

Jul 84. (7") *(ARIST 577)* **GOOD DAY. / TOO HOT** [ ] [ ]
(ext.12"+=) *(ARIST12 577)* – Don't forget to dance.

Nov 84. (lp/c) *(206/406 685) <8264>* **WORD OF MOUTH** [ ] [57]
– Do it again / Word of mouth / Good day / Living on a thin line / Sold me out / Massive reductions / Guilty / Too hot / Missing persons / Summer's gone / Going solo. *(cd-iss.Jun88; 259 047)*

Apr 85. (7") *(ARIST 617) <9309>* **DO IT AGAIN. / GUILTY** [ ] [41] Dec84
(12"+=) *(ARIST12 617)* – Summer's gone.

Apr 85. (7") *<9334>* **SUMMER'S GONE. / GOING SOLO** [-] [ ]

Oct 86. (d-lp/c) *(302/502 778) <8428>* **COME DANCING WITH THE KINKS – THE BEST OF THE KINKS 1977-1986** (compilation) [ ] [ ] Jul86

— Returned to original line-up of **RAY, DAVE + MICK,** plus sessioners. (RODFORD and GIBBONS departed).

London M.C.A.

Nov 86. (7") *<52960>* **ROCK'N'ROLL CITIES. / WELCOME TO SLEAZY TOWN** [-] [ ]

Nov 86. (lp/c)(cd) *(LON LP/C 27)(828 030-2) <5822>* **THINK VISUAL** [ ] [81]
– Working at the factory / Lost and found / Repetition / Welcome to Sleazy Town / The video shop / Rock'n'roll cities / How are you / Think visual / Natural gift / Killing time / When you were a child.

Dec 86. (7") *(LON 119)* **HOW ARE YOU. / KILLING TIME** [ ] [-]
(12"+=) *(LONX 119)* – Welcome to Sleazy town.

Mar 87. (7") *(LON 132) <53015>* **LOST AND FOUND. / KILLING TIME** [ ] [ ]
(12"+=) *(LONX 132)* – (Ray Davies interview).

May 87. (7") *<53093>* **HOW ARE YOU. / WORKING AT THE FACTORY** [-] [ ]

Feb 88. (7") *(LON 165)* **THE ROAD. / ART LOVER** [ ] [ ]
(ext.12"+=) *(LONX 165)* – Come dancing.

May 88. (lp/c)(cd) *(LON LP/C 49)(828 078-2) <42107>* **THE ROAD (live / studio *)** [ ] [ ] Feb88
– The road * / Destroyer / Apeman / Come dancing / Art lover / Cliches of the world (B-movie) / Living on a thin line / Lost and found / It * / Around the dial / Give the people what they want.

— **BOB HENRIT** (b. 2 May'45)- drums repl. AVORY / added **MARK HALEY** – keyboards, vocals

Sep 89. (7") *(LON 239)* **DOWN ALL THE DAYS (TILL 1992). / YOU REALLY GOT ME (live)** [ ] [-]
(12"+=/cd-s+=) *(LON X/CD 239)* – Entertainment.

Oct 89. (lp/c/cd) *(828 165-1/-4/-2) <6337>* **UK JIVE** [ ] [ ]
– Aggravation / How do I get close / UK jive / Now and then / What are we doing / Entertainment / War is over / Down all the days (till 1992) / Loony balloon / Dear Margaret. *(c+=/cd+=)*– Bright lights / Perfect strangers. *(re-iss.Apr91;)*

Feb 90. (7") *(LON 250)* **HOW DO I GET CLOSE. / DOWN ALL THE DAYS (TILL 1992)** [ ] [-]
(12"+=/cd-s+=) *(LON X/CD 250)* – War is over.

Mar 90. 7") *<53699>* **HOW DO I GET CLOSE. / WAR IS OVER** [-] [ ]

Columbia Columbia

Mar 93. (cd/c) *(472489-2/-4)* **PHOBIA** [ ] [ ]
– Opening / Wall of fire / Drift away / Still searching / Phobia / Only a dream / Don't / Babies / Over the edge / Surviving / It's alright (don't think about it) / The informer / Hatred (a duet) / Somebody stole my car / Close to the wire / Scattered. *(cd+=)*– Did ya.

Jul 93. (cd-s) **SCATTERED. / HATRED (A DUET) / DAYS** [ ] [ ]

Nov 93. (7") *(659922-7)* **ONLY A DREAM (Radio Version) / SOMEBODY STOLE MY CAR** [ ] [ ]
(cd-s+=) *(659922-2)* – Babies.

Konk not issued

Oct 94. (cd/c/lp) *(KNK CD/MC/LP 1)* **TO THE BONE (live)** [ ] [-]
– All day and all of the nigt / Apeman / Tired of waiting for you / See my friend / Death of a clown / Waterloo sunset / Muswell hillbillies / Better things / Don't forget to dance / Autumn almanac / Sunny afternoon / Dedicated follower of fashion / You really got me.

Oct 94. (cd-ep) *(KNKD 2)* **WATERLOO SUNSET E.P. (live)** [ ] [-]
– Waterloo sunset / You really got me / Elevator man / On the outside.

When! not issued

Jan 97. (c-ep/cd-ep) *(WEN M/X 1016)* **DAYS EP** [35] [-]
– Days / You really got me / Dead end street / Lola.

– compilations etc. –

on 'Pye' UK / 'Reprise' US, unless mentioned otherwise

Nov 64. (7"ep) *(NEP 24200)* **KINKSIZE SESSION** [ ] [-]
– I've gotta go now / I've got that feeling / Things are getting better / Louie Louie.

Jan 65. (7"ep) *(NEP 24203)* **KINKSIZE HITS** [ ] [-]
– You really got me / It's alright / All day and all of the night / I gotta move.

Sep 65. (7"ep) *(NEP 24221)* **KWYET KINKS** [ ] [-]
– Wait till the summer / Such a shame / A well respected man / Don't you fret.

Jun 66. (lp) *Marble Arch; (MAL 612)* **WELL RESPECTED KINKS** [5] [-]

Jul 66. (7"ep) *(NEP 24258)* **DEDICATED KINKS** [ ] [-]
– Dedicated follower of fashion / Till the end of the day / See my friend / Set me free.

Sep 67. (lp) *Marble Arch; (MAL 716)* **SUNNY AFTERNOON** [9] [-]

Apr 68. (7"ep) *(NEP 24296)* **SOMETHING ELSE** [ ] [-]
– David Watts / Two sisters / Lazy old sun / Situation.

Feb 69. (lp) *Marble Arch; (MAL 1100)* **KINDA KINKS** [ ] [-]

Feb 70. (d-lp) *(NPL 18326)* **THE KINKS** [ ] [-]

Aug 71. (7"ep) *(PMM 100)* **YOU REALLY GOT ME. / WONDERBOY / SET ME FREE / LONG TALL SALLY** [ ] [-]

Oct 71. (lp) *Golden Hour; (GH 501)* **THE GOLDEN HOUR OF THE KINKS** [21] [-]
(cd-iss.Apr89 on 'Castle'; GHCD 1)

Oct 71. (lp) *Hallmark; (HMA 201)* **LOLA** [ ] [-]

Apr 72. (lp) *<6454>* **THE KINK KRONICLES** [-] [94]

Feb 73. (lp) **THE GREAT LOST KINKS ALBUM** [-] [ ]

Jun 73. (lp) *(GH 558)* **THE GOLDEN HOUR OF THE KINKS VOL.2** [ ] [-]
(cd-iss.Apr91 on 'Knight'; KGHCD 148)

1973. (lp) *Hallmark; (HMA 244)* **THE KINKS** [ ] [-]

Nov 73. (4xlp-box) **ALL THE GOOD TIMES** [ ] [-]
– (THE KINKS double / ARTHUR / THE KINKS PART 1).

Dec 73. (7") *(7N 45313)* **WHERE HAVE ALL THE GOOD TIMES GONE. / LOLA** [ ] [-]

Oct 74. (d-lp) *Golden Hour; (GHD 50)* **LOLA, PERCY AND THE POWERMAN COME FACE TO FACE WITH THE VILLAGE GREEN PRESERVATION SOCIETY – SOMETHING ELSE!** [ ] [-]

May 75. (7") *(7N 45482)* **SUNNY AFTERNOON./. SITTING ON MY SOFA** [ ] [-]
Jun 76. (lp/c) *R.C.A.; (RS/+C 1059) <1743>* **CELLULOID HEROES – THE KINKS GREATEST** [ ] [ ]
May 77. (12"ep) *Big Deal; (BD 105)* **LOLA / SUNNY AFTERNOON. / WATERLOO SUNSET / DEDICATED FOLLOWER OF FASHION** [ ] [-]
Nov 77. (d-lp) *(FILD 001)* **THE KINKS FILE** [ ] [-]
Jul 78. (7") *(7N 46102)* **DEDICATED FOLLOWER OF FASHION. / WATERLOO SUNSET** [ ] [-]
(re-iss.Mar82 on 'Old Gold'; OG 9140)
Oct 78. (d-lp) *Ronco-Pye; (RPL 2031)* **THE KINKS 20 GOLDEN GREATS** [19] [-]
Nov 78. (7"ep) **EP** [ ] [-]
– Long tall Sally / I took my baby home / You still want me / You do something to me.
Apr 79. (7") *Flashback; (FBS 1)* **YOU REALLY GOT ME. / ALL DAY AND ALL OF THE NIGHT** [ ] [-]
(re-iss.Feb80 on 'Pye'; RK 1027) (re-iss.Jun84 on 'Old Gold'; OG 9408)
Jun 80. (7"ep) *Flashback; (FBEP 104)* **WATERLOO SUNSET / DAVID WATTS. / A WELL RESPECTED MAN / STOP YOUR SOBBIN'** [ ] [-]
Jul 80. (lp) *Pickwick; (PDA 072)* **THE KINKS COLLECTION** [ ] [-]
Oct 80. (d-lp) *P.R.T.; (SPOT 1009)* **SPOTLIGHT ON THE KINKS** [ ] [-]
Jun 82. (c) *P.R.T.; (ZCTON 102)* **100 MINUTES OF . . .** [ ] [-]
Oct 82. (d-lp) *P.R.T.; (SPOT 1029)* **SPOTLIGHT ON THE KINKS VOL.2** [ ] [-]
Feb 83. (7") *Flashback; (FBS 15)* **SUNNY AFTERNOON. / TIRED OF WAITING FOR YOU** [ ] [-]
Apr 83. (lp) *P.R.T.; (DOW 4)* **SHAPE OF THINGS TO COME** [ ] [-]
Jul 83. (lp) *P.R.T.; (DOW 12)* **CANDY FROM MR. DANDY** [ ] [-]
Oct 83. (d-lp) *P.R.T.; (KINK 1)* **KINKS' GREATEST HITS – DEAD END STREET** [96] [-]
Oct 83. (7"/7"pic-d) *P.R.T.; (KD/KPD 1)* **YOU REALLY GOT ME. / MISTY WATER** [47] [-]
(12"pic-d+=) *(DKL 1)* – All day and all of the night.
Oct 84. (cd/c/lp) *P.R.T.; (CD/TC+/KINK 7251)* **THE KINKS GREATEST HITS** [ ] [-]
Nov 84. (lp) *P.R.T.; (KINK 7252)* **KOLLECTABLES** [ ] [-]
Nov 84. (lp) *P.R.T.; (KINK 7253)* **KOVERS** [ ] [-]
Nov 84. (3xlp-box) *P.R.T.; (KINKX 7254)* **THE KINKS BOX SET** [ ] [-]
Nov 85. (d-lp/c) *Castle; (CCS LP/MC 113)* **THE COLLECTION** [ ] [-]
(cd-iss.1988; CCS CD 113) (cd re-iss.Jul92 on 'BMG-RCA';)
Dec 85. (d-lp/c)(cd) *Starblend; (TRACK/+K 1)(CDTRACK 1)* **BACKTRACKIN' – THE DEFINITIVE COLLECTION** [ ] [-]
Mar 86. (7"pic-d) *P.R.T.; (7P 355)* **DEDICATED FOLLOWER OF FASHION. / AUTUMN ALMANAC** [ ] [-]
(re-iss.Mar88; PYS 7)
Mar 86. (7") *Old Gold; (OG 9577)* **SUNNY AFTERNOON. / TIRED OF WAITING FOR YOU** [ ] [-]
(re-iss.Jul87 on 7"pic-d 'P.R.T.'; PYS 2)
Mar 86. (7") *Old Gold; (OG 9579)* **LOLA. / APEMAN** [ ] [-]
Oct 87. (lp/c/cd) *P.R.T.; (PYL/PYM/PYC 4001)* **HIT SINGLES** [ ] [-]
Oct 87. (d-lp/d-c/d-cd) *P.R.T.; (PYL/PYM/PYC 7001)* **THE KINKS ARE WELL RESPECTED MEN** [ ] [-]
Nov 88. (cd-ep) *Old Gold; (OG 6102)* **YOU REALLY GOT ME / ALL DAY AND ALL OF THE NIGHT / TIRED OF WAITING FOR YOU** [ ] [-]
Feb 89. (cd-ep) *Old Gold; (OG 6117)* **WATERLOO SUNSET / SUNNY AFTERNOON / LOLA** [ ] [-]
Apr 89. (c) *Legacy; (C 901)* **C90 COLLECTOR** [ ] [-]
May 89. (lp/c)(cd) *Pickwick; (SHM/HSC 3265)(PWKS 527)* **THE BEST OF THE KINKS – 1964-66** [ ] [-]
Sep 89. (lp/c/cd) *Castle; (CTV LP/MC/CD 001)* **THE ULTIMATE COLLECTION** [35] [-]
– You really got me / All day and all of the night / Tired of waiting for you / Everybody's gonna be happy / Set me free / Till the end of the day / Dedicated follower of fashion / Sunny afternoon / Dead end street / Waterloo sunset / Autumn almanac / Wonder boy / Days / Plastic man / Victoria / Lola / Apeman / David Watts / Where have all the good times gone / Well respected man / I'm not like everybody else / End of the season / Death of a clown (DAVE DAVIES) / Suzannah's still alive (DAVE DAVIES).
Jun 90. (lp/c/cd) *See For Miles; (SEE/+K/CD 295)* **THE EP COLLECTION** [ ] [-]
1990. (cd) *Nightriding; (KNCD 10019)* **THE KINKS** [ ] [-]
Jan 91. (d-cd) *Decal; (CDLIK 74)* **THE SINGLES COLLECTION 1964-1970** [ ] [-]
Aug 91. (cd/c) *Pickwick; (PWK S/MC 4075)* **THE BEST OF THE KINKS 1966-67** [ ] [-]
Sep 91. (d-cd) *Rhino;* **PRESERVATION (A PLAY IN TWO ACTS)** [ ] [-]
Nov 91. (cd/c) *Castle; (CCS CD/MC 300)* **THE COMPLETE COLLECTION** [ ] [-]
Feb 92. (cd/c) *See For Miles; (SEE CD/K 329)* **THE EP COLLECTION VOL.2** [ ] [-]
Apr 93. (cd) *Arista; (74321 13687-2)* **THE BEST OF THE BALLADS** [ ] [-]
Sep 93. (cd/c) *Polygram TV; (516 465-2/-4)* **THE DEFINITIVE COLLECTION – THE KINKS' GREATEST HITS** [18] [-]
(re-iss.Mar97; same)
Dec 93. (cd) *Gold-Disky; (GOLD 205)* **GOLD: GREATEST HITS** [ ] [-]
May 94. (cd/c) *B.R.Music; (BR CD/MC 15)* **GREATEST HITS** [ ] [-]
May 94. (cd/c) *Prima; (PMM 0569-2/-4)* **DANDY** [ ] [-]
Jul 94. (cd) *Spectrum; (550 722-2)* **YOU REALLY GOT ME** [ ] [-]
Feb 95. (cd) *Essential; (ESBCD 288)* **REMASTERED** [ ] [-]
Aug 95. (cd) *Spectrum; (550 723-2)* **LOLA** [ ] [-]
Apr 97. (cd/c) *Polygram TV; (537554-2/-4)* **THE VERY BEST OF THE KINKS** [42] [-]

DAVE DAVIES

Pye / Reprise
Jul 67. (7") *(7N 17356) <0614>* **DEATH OF A CLOWN. / LOVE ME TILL THE SUN SHINES** [3] [ ] Aug67
Nov 67. (7") *(7N 17429) <0660>* **SUSANNAH'S STILL ALIVE. / FUNNY FACE** [21] [ ]
Aug 68. (7") *(7N 17514)* **LINCOLN COUNTY. / THERE IS NO LOVE WITHOUT LIFE** [ ] [ ]
Jan 69. (7") *(7N 17678)* **HOLD MY HAND. / CREEPING JEAN** [ ] [ ]
R.C.A. / R.C.A.
Sep 80. (7") *<PB 12089>* **IMAGINATION'S REAL. / WILD MAN** [-] [ ]
Sep 80. (lp/c) *(PL/PK 13603) <AFL-1-3603; the US title>* **DAVE DAVIES** [ ] [42] Jul80
– Where do you come from / Doing the best for you / Move over / Visionary dreamer / Nothin' more to lose / Imagination real / In you I believe / See the beast / Run / The world is changing hands.
Nov 80. (7") *<PB 12147>* **DOING THE BEST FOR YOU. / NOTHING MORE TO LOSE** [-] [ ]
Dec 80. (7") *(PB 9620)* **DOING THE BEST FOR YOU. / WILD MAN** [ ] [-]
Oct 81. (lp/c) *(RCA LP/K 6005) <AFL-1-4036>* **GLAMOUR** [ ] [ ] Jul81
– Is this the only way / Reveal yourself / World of our own / Two serious / Glamour / 7th channel / Body / Eastern eyes / Body.
Warners / Warners
Sep 83. (lp/c) *(92-3917-1/-4) <23917-1/-4>* **CHOSEN PEOPLE** [ ] [ ] Aug 83
– Mean disposition / Love gets you / Take one more / True story / Danger zone / Tapes / Freedom lies / Fire burning / Cold winter / Matter of decision / Is it any wonder / Charity / Chosen people.
Sep 83. (7") *<7-29509>* **LOVE GETS YOU. / ONE NIGHT WITH YOU** [-] [ ]
Nov 83. (7") *<7-29425>* **MEAN DISPOSITION. / COLD WINTER** [-] [ ]

– DAVE DAVIES compilations etc. –

Apr 68. (7"ep) *Pye; (NEP 24289)* **DAVE DAVIES HITS** [ ] [ ]
Aug 82. (7") *Old Gold; (OG 9128)* **DEATH OF A CLOWN. / SUSANNAH'S STILL ALIVE** [ ] [-]
Feb 88. (lp/c) *P.R.T.; (PYL/PYK 6012)* **DAVE DAVIES – THE ALBUM THAT NEVER WAS** [ ] [-]
– (1960's singles)
Jul 92. (cd) *Mau Mau; (MAUDCD 617)* **DAVE DAVIES / GLAMOUR** [ ] [-]

RAY DAVIES

— In 1984, the lp 'RETURN TO WATERLOO' was withdrawn.
(below from film 'Absolute Beginners')

Virgin / Virgin
May 86. (7"/12") *(VS 865/+12)* **QUIET LIFE. / VOICES IN THE DARK** [ ] [ ]

KIPPINGTON LODGE (see under ⇒ BRINSLEY SCHWARZ)

KLAATU

Formed: Canada . . .1976 by TERRY DRAPER, DEE LONG and JOHN WOLOSCHUCK. Taking their name from the alien robot in the 1951 sci-fi film, 'The Day The Earth Stood Still', the anonymity of their eponymous debut lp release led to speculation of it being the work of the re-formed BEATLES (it was also on 'Capitol' label, former home of the fab four). This led to it shifting enough copies in the States to reach the Top 40, a double A-side 'SUB-ROSA SUBWAY'./ 'CALLING OCCUPANTS' also breeching radio play. Subsequent releases during the next 3 years failed to emulate this fruitful beginning.

Recommended: KLAATU (*6)

TERRY DRAPER – vocals, bass / **DEE LONG** – guitar / **JOHN WOLOSCHUCK** – drums

not issued / Island
1976. (7") *<011>* **CALIFORNIA JAM. / DOCTOR MARVELLO** [-] [ ]
Capitol / Capitol
Jan 77. (7") *<4377>* **DOCTOR MARVELLO. / CALLING OCCUPANTS** [-] [ ]
Mar 77. (7") *<4412>* **SUB-ROSA SUBWAY. / CALLING OCCUPANTS** [-] [62]
Apr 77. (lp) *(E-ST <11542>)* **KLAATU** [ ] [32] Mar77
– Calling occupants / California jam / Anus of Uranus / Sub-rosa subway / True life hero / Doctor Marvello / Sir Bodsworth Rugglesby III / Little Neutrino. *(cd-iss.Apr97 on 'E.M.I.'; REPLAYCD 32)*
Apr 77. (7") *(CL 15918)* **SUB-ROSA SUBWAY. / ANUS OF URANUS** [ ] [-]
Oct 77. (7") *(CL 15947)* **CALLING OCCUPANTS. / LONELIEST OF CREATURES** [ ] [-]
Oct 77. (lp) *(E-ST <11633>)* **HOPE** [ ] [83]
– We're off you know / Madman / Around the universe in eighty days / Long live / Politzania / The loneliest of creatures / Prelude / So said the lighthouse keeper / Hope.
Feb 78. (7") *(CL 15966) <4516>* **AROUND THE UNIVERSE IN EIGHTY DAYS. / WE'RE OFF YOU KNOW** [ ] [ ]
Oct 78. (7") *<4627>* **DEAR CHRISTINE. / OLDER** [-] [ ]
Nov 78. (lp) *(E-ST <11836>)* **SIR ARMY SUIT** [ ] [ ]
– A routine day / Juicy Lucy / Everybody took a holiday / Older / Dear Christine / Mister Manson / Tokeymor field / Perpetual motion machine / Cherie / Silly boys.
Jul 80. (lp/c) *(EST/TC-EST <12080>)* **ENDANGERED SPECIES** [ ] [ ]
– I can't help it / Knee deep in love / Paranoia / Howl at the Moon / Set the world on fire / Hot box city / Dog star / Sell out / All good things.
Jul 80. (7") *<4866>* **KNEE DEEP IN LOVE. / DOG STAR** [-] [ ]

— Disappeared without trace once again in the early 80's.

KOLLEKTIV

Formed: Hamburg, Germany . . . 1972. This short-lived band recorded an influential one-off jazz-rock album. A self-titled set released in the summer of 1973, it featured only four tracks, the sonic explorations of the 'GAGEG' suite taking up a whole side of vinyl alone. Bassist JURGEN KARPENKIEL later joined space-jazz pioneers GURU GURU in the mid-70's.

Recommended: KOLLEKTIV (*7)

JURGEN HAVIX – guitar, zither / **KLAUS DAPPER** – flute, sax / **JURGEN 'JOGI' KARPENKIEL** – bass / **WALDEMAR KARPENKIEL** – drums

Brain / not issued

Jun 73. (lp) *(1034)* **KOLLEKTIV** [-] [-] German
– Rambo zambo / Baldrian / Forsterlied / Gageg: Andante – Allegro – Pressluft.

—— split and JOGI joined GURU GURU for three albums between 1975-77

KOOBAS

Formed: Liverpool, England ... 1962 out of The THUNDERBEATS and The MIDNIGHTERS, by KEITH ELLIS, TONY O'RILEY, ROY MORRIS and STU LEATHERWOOD. Managed by BRIAN EPSTEIN, they toured with The BEATLES and appeared in the film, 'FERRY CROSS THE MERSEY', alongside GERRY & THE PACEMAKERS. In 1965/66, they released two singles for 'Pye', the second being a KIM WESTON / Motown song, 'YOU'D BETTER MAKE UP YOUR MIND'. They shifted to 'Columbia' in the spring of '66, but never quite hit the mark, until that is, their quasi-psychedelic version of CAT STEVENS' 'THE FIRST CUT IS THE DEEPEST' in 1968.

Recommended: THE KOOBAS (*6)

STU LEATHERWOOD – guitar / **ROY MORRIS** – guitar / **KEITH ELLIS** – bass / **TONY O'RILEY** – drums

Columbia / not issued

Jan 65. (7"; KUBAS) *(DB 7451)* **I LOVE HER. / MAGIC POTION** [ ] [-]

Pye / not issued

Dec 65. (7") *(7N 17012)* **TAKE ME FOR A LITTLE WHILE. / SOMEWHERE IN THE NIGHT** [ ] [-]

Apr 66. (7") *(7N 17087)* **YOU'D BETTER MAKE UP YOUR MIND. / A PLACE I KNOW** [ ] [-]

Columbia / Capitol

Aug 66. (7") *(DB 7988)* **SWEET MUSIC. / FACE** [ ] [-]

Jan 67. (7") *(DB 8013)* **SALLY. / CHAMPAGNE AND CAVIAR** [ ] [-]

May 67. (7") *(DB 8187)* **GYPSY FRED. / CITY GIRL** [ ] [-]

May 68. (7") *(DB 8419)* *<2416>* **THE FIRST CUT IS THE DEEPEST. / WALKING OUT** [ ] [ ]

1969. (lp) *(SCX 6271)* **THE KOOBAS** [ ] [-]
– Royston Rose / Where are the friends / Constantly changing / Here's a day / Fade forever / Barricades / A little piece of my heart / Gold leaf tree / Mr. Claire / Circus. *(re-iss.Jun88 as 'BARRICADES' on 'Bam Caruso'; KIRI 047) (cd-iss.1994 on 'Essex'+=; ESSEX 10004CD)–* Sweet music / Face.

—— had already split before above. ELLIS joined VAN DER GRAAF GENERATOR.

MARCH HARE

STU LEATHERWOOD – guitar, vocals / **PETER SKELLERN** – vocals / **BARRY GUARD** – saxophone, drums

Chapter One / not issued

May 68. (7") *(CH 101)* **CRY MY HEART. / WITH MY EYES CLOSED** [ ] [-]

Deram / not issued

Jun 69. (7") *(DM 258)* **I COULD MAKE IT THERE WITH YOU. / HAVE WE GOT NEWS FOR YOU** [ ] [-]

—— LEATHERWOOD joined GARY & STU, who released an album in 1971 'HARLAN FARE' on 'Carnaby'; *6302 012).* SKELLERN became a successful easy listening solo star.

KRAAN

Formed: Ulm, Stuttgart, Germany . . . 1970. With most of the members having served their time on the free jazz scene, KRAAN's self-titled debut (1972) was a trippy, ethnic inflected take on the jazz-rock fusion that proliferated during the 70's. Focussing on inspired instrumental improvisation, the album contained some of KRAAN's best material, songs that became staples of their live set. 'WINTRUP' (1973) and 'ANDY NOGGER' (1974) followed the same blueprint but the band really came into its own in the live arena, 1975's 'LIVE' a classic document of their inspired musical anarchy. Ex-Kathargo keyboardist, INGO BISCHOFF, joined for the below par 'LET IT OUT' (1975), after which he left along with PAPPERT. BISCHOFF couldn't stay away for long and returned for 1977's 'WEIDERHOREN'. HELLMUT HATTLER released a well recieved solo album the same year, 'BASSBALL', using most of the KRAAN musicians. 'FLYDAY', realeased the following year, marked a departure from the hectic improvisation of old with a somewhat more tranquil jazz-rock ebb and flow. KRAAN continued throughout the 80's in similar fashion, HATTLER and BISCHOFF the constants in an ever changing musical cast.

Recommended: KRAAN (*7) / LIVE (*6)

PETER WOLBRANDT – guitar, vocals / **HELLMUT HATTLER** – bass / **JAN FRIEDE** – drums, congas / **JOHANNES PAPPERT** – saxophone

Spiegelei / not issued

1972. (lp) *(9U-28778)* **KRAAN** [-] [-] German
– Sarah's ritt durch den Schwarzwald / M.C. Esher / Kraan Arabia / Head / Sarah auf der gaenswies'.

1973. (lp) *(9U-28523)* **WINTRUP** [-] [-] German
– Silver wings / Mind quake / Backs / Gut und richtig / Wintrup / Jack Steam.

Gull / Passport

Jan 75. (lp) *(1009)* *<98006>* **ANDY NOGGER** [ ] [ ]
– Stars / Andy Nogger / Nam nam / Son of the sun / Holiday am Matterhorn / Home / Yellow bamboo. *(German-iss.1974; 0U-26439)*

May 75. (d-lp) *(GUD 2001-2)* **KRAAN LIVE (live)** [ ] [-]
– Jerk of life / Nam nam / Holiday am Matterhorn (incl. Gipfelsurm) / Sarah's ritt durch den Schwarzwald / Andy Nogger (Andy Nogger – Gutter king) / Hallo jaja I don't know / Lonesome liftboy / Kraan Arabia. *(German-iss.1975; 8U-26440)*

—— added **INGO BISCHOF** – keyboards (ex-KARTHAGO)

Dec 75. (lp) *(1013)* *<98015>* **LET IT OUT** [ ] [ ]
– Bandits in the woods / Luftpost / Degado / Prima Klima / Let it out / Die maschine / Heimweh nach ubersee / Pic nic international. *(German-iss.1975; 1U-26542)*

Harvest / not issued

Apr 77. (lp) *(064-32110)* **WIEDERHOREN** [-] [-] German
– Just one way / Vollgas ahoi / Silky way / Rendezvous in blue / Let's take a ride / Rund um die uhr / Yaqui yagua / Wiederhoren.

—— **UDO DAHMEN** – drums; repl. JAN + TOMMY

Feb 79. (lp) *(064-45210)* **FLYDAY** [-] [-] German
– Far west / My brother said / Ausflug / Gaya Gaya / You're right / Young kings song / Buy buy / Flyday.

1980. (lp) *(064-45931)* **TOURNEE (live)** [-] [-] German
– Borgward / Almrausch / Peterchens reise / Vollgas ahoi / Yaqui yagua / Silky way.

—— added **GERRY BROWN** – drums

GeeBeeDee / not issued

1982. (lp) *(28)* **NACHTFAHRT** [-] [-] German
– Wintruper echo / Faust 2000 / Elfenbein / Nachtfahrt / Praying for you / Viel zu heiss / Normal / Paper stars / Luna Park.

—— **HATTLER, BISCHOF + BROWN** recruited **MARK McMILLEN** – keyboards / **EFF ALBERS** – guitar

T.I.S. / not issued

1983. (lp) *(6623 241)* **X** [-] [-] German
– Nice try / No problem / (Watch that) You say / Almost close / Night has a way / You say (so I don't).

—— re-formed line-up; **HATTLER, WOLBRANDT, FREIDE / + JOO KRAUS** – keyboards, synthesizer, electric drums

Intercord / not issued

1988. (lp/cd) *(971820-1/-2)* **LIVE '88 (live)** [-] [-] German
– Rush hour / Dinner for two / Vollgas ahoi / You're right / Wintruper echo / Nam nam / Holiday am Matterhorn / Air basses / Nachtfahrt / Favourite land / Jerk of life / Kunststuck / Kraan Arabia '88.

1989. (lp/cd) *(986921-1/-2)* **DANCING IN THE SHADE** [-] [-] German
– Rockets / Good enough / Egyptian cha cha / Polarity / Dancing in the shade / Banana moon / Is this the way / Middle East beat / One day. *(cd+=)–* Kraan mooloo / Soldier drums.

—— nothing heard of them in the 90's

HELLMUT HATTLER

with all of KRAAN, plus **ROLAND SCHAEFFER** – sax (of GURU GURU) / **JOEY ALBRECHT** – guitar (ex-KARTHAGO) / **CURT CRESS** – drums

Harvest / not issued

1977. (lp) *(064-32523)* **BASSBALL** [-] [-] German
– Sunday walk / Wenn die kraaniche zieh'n / Penguins on Broadway / Bassball / How and why / My U.S. aunt / Mutabor / Toujours too sure.

KRAFTWERK

Formed: Dusseldorf, Germany ... 1969 as ORGANISATION by RALF HUTTER, FLORIAN SCHNEIDER-ESLEBEN and 3 others, BUTCH HAUF, FRED MONICKS and BASIL HAMMOND. After one Conrad Plank produced album, 'TONE FLOAT', for 'R.C.A.' in 1970, the pair broke away to form KRAFTWERK (German for POWERPLANT), with KLAUS DINGER and THOMAS HOMANN. After one album for 'Philips', RALF & FLORIAN became KRAFTWERK and released a 1973 album (titled after their Christian names) for 'Vertigo'. In 1974, they added KLAUS ROEDER & WOLFGANG FLUR, issuing their magnus-opus 'AUTOBAHN'. This UK & US Top 5 album contained a 22 minute title track, which, edited into 3 minutes, also became a hit. The next album, 'RADIO ACTIVITY' (which was also now issued on own 'Kling Klang' label in Germany), disappointed most and failed to secure a Top 50 placing. In 1978, they were back in the UK Top 10 at least, with excellent return to form, 'THE MAN MACHINE'. In the early 80's, they enjoyed another hit album, 'COMPUTER WORLD', and a run of UK hit singles, one of which, 'THE MODEL' (from 1978 lp) made the top spot. A projected album by the name of 'TECHNOPOP', was pencilled in for release in 1983 and allegedly E.M.I. were even supplied with artwork. The record never appeared, and of course, given KRAFTWERK's reclusive reticence, no explanation was offered. The same year, however, the band did release a one-off 12" single, 'TOUR DE FRANCE', no doubt inspired by HUTTER's preoccupation with cycling. It was to be another three years before the band released a full album, the disappointing 'ELECTRIC CAFE'. By this point the band were starting to tread water, an assumption that seemed to be confirmed when fans had to wait another five years for 'new' material. 'THE MIX', released in 1991, was actually an album of reworkings of old tracks, a bit of a hit and miss affair which failed to deliver any original pieces per se. Both BARTOS and FLUR had left the band before the album's release, allegedly sick of the laboriously slow and detailed recording process and the band's reclusive inertia. Despite a reputation for a disciplined working ethos, the band remain defiantly distant from the music industry. Their studio apparently possesses neither fax nor phone, they've no management and they've turned down all offers of remix work and collaborations. Whether they can remain on the cutting edge in such a vacuum remains to be seen and for the moment, their Guru-like status is based on past glories, sounds that continue to permeate almost all strands of pop culture, now more than ever. It's testament to their towering influence that despite releasing no new material for more than a decade, they recently headlined the Tribal Gathering dance festival. • **Style:** Robotic electronic rock act, with minimalist synth-tunes at times being twiddled by dummies. They were more inspirational than contemporaries TANGERINE DREAM, being a a major influence on ULTRAVOX!, GARY NUMAN, DAVID BOWIE '77, JEAN-MICHEL JARRE, SIMPLE MINDS, OMD, etc. • **Songwriters:** RALF & FLORIAN. • **Trivia:** They have been sampled by many, including AFRIKA BAMBAATAA on his single, 'Planet Rock'.

Recommended: AUTOBAHN (*7) / RADIOACTIVITY (*4) / TRANS-EUROPE EXPRESS (*8) / THE MAN MACHINE (*8) / COMPUTER WORLD (*6)

ORGANISATION

RALF HUTTER (b.1946, Krefeld, Germany) – electric organ, strings / **FLORIAN SCHNEIDER-ESLEBEN** (b.1947, Dusseldorf)– flute, echo unit, strings / **BUTCH HAUF** – bass, percussion / **FRED MONICKS** – drums / **BASIL HAMMOND** – percussion, vocals

R.C.A. | not issued

Aug 70. (lp) *(SF 8111)* **TONE FLOAT** [ ] [-]
– Tone float / Milk float / Silver forest / Rhythm salad / Noitasinagro.

KRAFTWERK

HUTTER + SCHNEIDER with **KLAUS DINGER** – guitar, keyboards / **THOMAS HOMANN** – percussion

Philips | not issued

1971. (lp) *(6305 058)* **KRAFTWERK** [-] [-] German
– Ruckzuck / Stratowargius / Megaherz / Vom Himmel hoch.

— **HUTTER + SCHNEIDER** trimmed to a duo. (DINGER and HOMANN formed NEU!)

1972. (lp) *(6305 117)* **KRAFTWERK 2** [-] [-] German
– Klingklang / Atem / Strom / Spule 4 / Wellenlange / Harmonika.

Vertigo | Vertigo

Nov 72. (d-lp) *(6641 077)* **KRAFTWERK** (2 German lp's combined) [ ] [-]
Nov 73. (lp) *(6360 616)* **RALF & FLORIAN** [ ] [-]
– Elektrisches roulette (Electric roulette) / Tongebirge (Mountain of sound) / Kristallo (Crystals) / Heimatklange (The bells of home) / Tanzmusik (Dance music) / Ananas symphonie (Pineapple symphony). *<US-iss.Sep75; 2006>*

— added **KLAUS ROEDER** – violin, guitar / **WOLFGANG FLUR** – percussion

Nov 74. (lp/c) *(6360/ 620) <2003>* **AUTOBAHN** [4] [5]
– Autobahn / Kometenmelodie 1 & 2 (Comet melody) / Mitternacht (Midnight) / Morgenspaziergang (Morning walk). *(re-iss.Mar82 on 'E.M.I.' lp/c; EMC/TC-EMC 3405); hit 61 UK) (re-iss.Jun85 on 'Parlophone' lp/c; AUTO/TCAUTO 1) (cd-iss.Jun87 & Aug95 on 'E.M.I.'; CDP 746153-2)*
Feb 75. (7") *(6147 012)* **AUTOBAHN. / KOMETENMELODIE** [11] [-]
Feb 75. (7") *<203>* **AUTOBAHN. / MORGENSPAZIERGANG** [-] [25]
Jul 75. (7") *(6147 015)* **KOMETENMELODIE 2. / KRISTALLO** [ ] [-]
Jul 75. (7") *<204>* **KOMETENMELODIE 2. / MITTERNACHT** [-] [ ]

— In Oct'75, **KARL BARTOS** – percussion repl. ROEDER

Capitol | Capitol

Nov 75. (lp/c) *(<EST/TC-EST 11457>)* **RADIO-ACTIVITY** [ ] [ ]
– Geiger counter / Radio-activity / Radioland / Airwaves / (intermission) / News / The voice of energy / Antenna / Radio stars / Uran / Transistor / Ohm sweet ohm. *(re-iss.Jun84 on 'Fame' lp/c; FA 413103-1/-4) (re-iss.1985 on 'E.M.I.' lp/c; EMS/TC-EMS 1256) (cd-iss.May87 on 'E.M.I.'; CDP 746474-2) (re-iss.Aug87 on 'E.M.I.' lp/c; ATAK/TCATAK 104) (re-iss.cd Apr94 on 'Cleopatra';) (re-iss.cd Apr95 on 'E.M.I.';)*
Feb 76. (7") *(CL 15853) <4211>* **RADIO-ACTIVITY. / ANTENNA** [ ] [ ]
Apr 77. (lp/c) *(<EST/TC-EST 11603>)* **TRANS-EUROPE EXPRESS** [ ] [ ]
– Europe endless / The hall of mirrors / Showroom dummies / Trans-Europe express / Metal on metal / Franz Schubert / Endless endless. *(in Feb82, they hit UK No.49 Feb82) (re-iss.1985 on 'E.M.I.' lp/c; ATAK/TCATAK 5) (re-iss.Jun86 on 'Fame' lp/c; FA 413151-1/-4) (cd-iss.May87 on 'E.M.I.'; CDP 746473-2) (re-iss.cd Apr94 on 'Cleopatra';)*
Apr 77. (7") *(CL 15917)* **TRANS-EUROPE EXPRESS. / EUROPE ENDLESS** [ ] [-]
Aug 77. (7") *(CLX 104)* **SHOWROOM DUMMIES. / EUROPE EXPRESS** [ ] [ ]
May 78. (7") *<4460>* **TRANS-EUROPE EXPRESS. / FRANZ SCHUBERT** [-] [67]
May 78. (lp/c) *(<EST/TC-EST 11728>)* **THE MAN MACHINE** [9] [ ]
– The robots / Spacelab / Metropolis / The model / Neon lights / The man machine. *(re-iss.Mar85 on 'Fame' lp/c; 413118-1/-4) (re-iss.Jul88 on 'Fame' cd/c/lp; CD/TC+/FA 3118) (re-iss.cd Apr94 on 'Cleopatra'; CLEO 5877CD) (re-iss.cd/c Apr95 on 'E.M.I.'; CD/TC EMS 1520) (cd re-iss.Jun97 on 'E.M.I.'; CDCNTAV 4)*
May 78. (7") *(CL 15981)* **THE ROBOTS (edit). / SPACELAB** [ ] [ ]
Jun 78. (7") *<4620>* **NEON LIGHTS. / THE ROBOTS** [-] [ ]
Sep 78. (7"/12"luminous) *(CL/12CL 15998)* **NEON LIGHTS. / TRANS-EUROPE EXPRESS / THE MODEL** [53] [ ]
Nov 78. (12"m) *(CL 16098)* **SHOWROOM DUMMIES. / EUROPE ENDLESS / SPACELAB** [ ] [-]

E.M.I. | Warners

Apr 81. (7") *(EMI 5175) <49723>* **POCKET CALCULATOR. / DENTAKU** [39] [ ]
(12"+=) *(12EMI 5175)* – Numbers.
(c-s) *(TCEMI 5175)* – ('A'extended) / ('A'side) / Numbers.
May 81. (lp/c) *(EMC/TC-EMC 3370) <3549>* **COMPUTER WORLD** [15] [72]
– Pocket calculator / Numbers / Computer-world / Computer love / Home computer / It's more fun to compute. *(re-iss.Apr95 cd/c; CD/TC EMS 1547)*
Jun 81. (7"/12") *(EMI/12EMI 5207)* **COMPUTER LOVE. / THE MODEL** [36] [-]
(Dec81; flipped over, hit UK No.1) (re-iss.May84; G45 16)
Jun 81. (7") *<49795>* **COMPUTER LOVE. / NUMBERS** [-] [ ]
Feb 82. (7") *(EMI 5272)* **SHOWROOM DUMMIES. / NUMBERS** [25] [-]
(12"+=) *(12EMI 5272)* – Pocket calculator.

— (In May'83, they had album 'TECHNO POP' cancelled)

Jul 83. (7") *(EMI 5413) <29342>* **TOUR DE FRANCE. / TOUR DE FRANCE (instrumental)** [22] [ ]
(c-s+=/12"+=) *(TC/12 EMI 5413)* – ('A'version).
Aug 84. (7") *(EMI 5413)* **TOUR DE FRANCE (remix). / TOUR DE FRANCE** [24] [-]
(12"+=) *(12EMI 5413)* – ('A'instrumental).
Oct 86. (7"/ext.12") *(EMI/12EMI 5588)* **MUSIQUE NON-STOP. / MUSIQUE NON STOP (version)** [ ] [ ]
Nov 86. (lp/c)(cd) *(EMD/TC-EMD 3370)(CDP 746416-2) <25525>* **ELECTRIC CAFE** [58] [ ]
– Boom boom tschak / Techno pop / Musique non stop / The telephone call / Sex object / Techno pop / Electric cafe. *(cd re-iss.Aug95; CDEMS 1546)*
Feb 87. (7") *(EMI 5602) <28441>* **THE TELEPHONE CALL. / DER TELEFON ANRUF** [ ] [ ]
(12"+=) *(12EMI 5602)* – House phone.

— **FRITZ HIJBERT** repl. WOLFGANG FLUR

May 91. (c-s/7") *(TC+/EM 192)* **THE ROBOTS (re-recorded). / ROBOTRONIK** [20] [ ]
(12"+=) *(12EM 192)* – ('A'album version).
(cd-s+=) *(CDEM 192)* – Robotnik.
Jun 91. (cd/c/d-lp) *(CD/TC+/EM 1408)* **THE MIX** ('91 remixes) [15] [ ]
– The robots / Computer love / Pocket calculator / Dentaku / Autobahn / Radioactivity / Trans-Europe express / Abzug / Metal on metal / Homecomputer / Musique non-stop. *(cd re-iss.Aug95; CDEM 1408)*
Oct 91. (c-s/7") *(TC+/EM 201)* **RADIOACTIVITY (Francois Kevorkian remix). / ('A'-William Orbit mix)** [43] [ ]
(12"+=/cd-s+=) *(12/CD EM 201)* – ('A'extended).

— In Jul'91, BARTOS and FLUR formed own project ELEKTRIC.

– compilations, others, etc. –

on 'Vertigo' unless mentioned otherwise

Oct 75. (lp) *(6360 629)* **EXCELLER 8** [ ] [-]
Oct 80. (7") *(CUT 108)* **AUTOBAHN. / (b-side by BEGGAR'S OPERA)** [ ] [-]
Apr 81. (lp) *(6449 066)* **ELEKTRO KINETIC** [ ] [-]
May 81. (7") *(VER 3)* **KOMETENMELODIE 2. / VON HIMMEL HOCH** [ ] [-]

— <In the US compilation lp 'THE ROBOTS' on 'Capitol'; *9445*>

Apr 94. (cd) *Cleopatra; (CLEO 6843CD)* **SHOWROOM DUMMIES** [ ] [-]
(re-iss.May97; same)
Apr 94. (cd) *Cleopatra; (CLEO 5761-2)* **THE MODEL (The Best Of Kraftwerk 1975-1978)** [ ] [-]
Mar 97. (12") *Discopromo; (D 762)* **NUMBERS** [ ] [-]
Mar 97. (12") *Discopromo; (D 801)* **TOUR DE FRANCE** [ ] [-]
May 97. (d-cd) *Cleopatra; (CLEO 9416-2)* **THE CAPITOL YEARS** [ ] [-]

Wayne KRAMER (see under ⇒ MC5)

Dagmar KRAUSE (see under ⇒ SLAPP HAPPY)

Sonja KRISTINA (see under ⇒ CURVED AIR)

Tuli KUPFERBERG (see under ⇒ FUGS)

LA DUSSELDORF

Formed: Dusseldorf, Germany . . . 1975 by KLAUS DINGER, his brother THOMAS and HANS LAMPE, all previous members of NEU!. They completed their eponymous debut in 1976, leading to a deal with WEA subsidiary, 'Radar', who finally issued it a year later. Their next electronic set, 'VIVA', in 1978, should have given them deserved exposure, but for the advent of avant-garde in British punk (i.e. WIRE, SIOUXSIE, MAGAZINE). • **Songwriters:** DINGERS + LAMPE.

Recommended: LA DUSSELDORF (*7) / VIVA (*7)

KLAUS DINGER – vocals, guitar (ex-NEU!) / **THOMAS DINGER** – percussion, vocals / **HANS LAMPE** – percussion, synthesizers, keyboards / **HARALD KONIETZO** – bass / **NIKOLAUS VAN RHEIN** – keyboards

Decca / not issued

Jan 77. (lp) *(SKLR 3252)* **LA DUSSELDORF** [ ] [-]
– Dusseldorf / La Dusseldorf / Silver cloud / Time. *(originally issued Germany on 'Nova'; 6-22550) (UK-iss.Dec77 on 'Radar'; RAD 7)*

— added **ANDREAS SCHELL** – piano

Radar / not issued

1978. (7"w-drawn) *(RAD 5)* **LA DUSSELDORF. / SILVER CLOUD** [-] [-]
Feb 79. (lp) *(RAD 10)* **VIVA** [ ] [-]
– Viva / White overalls / Rheinita / Vogel / Geld / Cha cha 2000. *(originally rel. Germany 1978 on 'Strand'; 6-23626)*

— now without HARALD + NIKOLAUS

Teldec / not issued

Jan 81. (lp) *(6-24524)* **INDIVIDUELLOS** [-] [-] German
– Menschen 1 / Individuellos / Menschen 2 / Sentimental / Lieber Honig 1981 / Dampfriemen / Tintarra Di . . . / Flashback / Das Yvonnchen.

— split after above

– compilations, others, etc. –

Jun 97. (cd) *Captain Trip; (CTCD 051)* **LA NEU DUSSELDORF** [ ] [-]

David LA FLAMME (see under ⇒ IT'S A BEAUTIFUL DAY)

LEAF HOUND

Formed: London, England . . . 1969 as BLACK CAT BONES by PETER FRENCH. He was a veteran of several pub-rock blues outfits, including BRUNNING SUNFLOWER BLUES BAND with BOB BRUNNING. They made one album, 'BULLEN ST. BLUES' with FRENCH and MICK HALLS co-writing most of the material. BLACK CAT BONES (who wanted a replacement for PAUL KOSSOFF) invited FRENCH to join them for the recording of an album, 'BARBED WIRE SANDWICH'. The outfit soon evolved into LEAF HOUND after the introduction of cousin MICK HALLS (with whom he'd been a member of mid-60's band, SWITCH). In 1971, their heavy touring schedule paid off with a deal for 'Decca', who released the album, 'GROWERS OF MUSHROOM', later that year. It failed to sell, although it was regarded by many rock critics as a classic of its genre; heavy progressive-blues in the mould of FREE or LED ZEPPELIN. LEAF HOUND subsequently went to Germany and Scandinavia to promote both the album and the single, 'DROWNED MY LIFE IN FEAR', which never gained a UK release. The album was delayed in Britain, and by the time of its unveiling, FRENCH had already joined ATOMIC ROOSTER. He featured on one album, 'IN HEARING OF', which hit the Top 20, but fed up with the lack of money, he joined Americans CACTUS (formerly VANILLA FUDGE). He then moved to the States in 1972, recording the album, 'OT 'N' SWEATY'. When they split to form BECK, BOGART & APPICE, he was left to recruit new members, although this idea was soon abandoned. Back on British soil and out of work, he answered an ad from the German band RANDY PIE, who in 1977, gave him a new lease of life. They had already released three albums, now gaining an American release with their fourth, 'FAST FORWARD'. Departing after only one album, he was subsequently offered a solo deal with the German 'Polydor' label, bringing back HALLS to augment him on the album, 'DUCKS IN FLIGHT'. He was then involved in the controversial 'DER FUHRER' rock opera, which was masterminded by German group PARZIVAL and was actually an anti-Hitler farce. In 1981, he teamed up with BIDDU, gaining his first UK hit!, 'STATUS ROCK' as The HEADBANGERS. • **Style:** Heavy progressive blues outfit similar to LED ZEPPELIN or FREE. • **Songwriters:** FRENCH + HALLS on most. • **Trivia:** The BLACK CAT BONES lp is worth £75, while 1971 lp is worth nearly 10 times that!.

Recommended: GROWERS OF MUSHROOM (*7)

BLACK CAT BONES

PETER FRENCH – vocals / **DEREK BROOKS** – guitar / **STU BROOKS** – bass / **BOB WESTON** – guitar / **ROD PRICE** – guitar, vocals / **STEVE MILLINER** + **ROBIN SYLVESTER** – piano / **PHIL LENOIR** – drums / **BRIAN SHORT** – vocals

Decca Nova / not issued

Nov 69. (lp) *(SDN 15)* **BARBED WIRE SANDWICH** [ ] [-]
– Chauffeur / Death valley blues / Feelin' good / Please tell my baby / Coming back / Save my love / Four women / Sylvester's blues / Good lookin' woman. *(cd-iss.Aug94 on 'See For Miles'; SEECD 405)*

— **MICK HALLS** – guitar (ex-SWITCH), repl. PRICE who joined FOGHAT

LEAF HOUND

FRENCH / BROOKS / BROOKS / HALLS / + KEITH YOUNG – drums

Decca / not issued

Oct 71. (lp) *(SKL-R 5094)* **GROWERS OF MUSHROOM** [ ] [-]
– Freelance fiend / Sad road to the sea / Drowned my life in fear / Work my body / Stray / With a minute to go / Growers of mushroom / Stagnant pool / Sawdust Caesar. *(cd-iss.Jul94 on 'See For Miles'+=; SEECD 403)–* It's going to get better.

— FRENCH had already left to join ATOMIC ROOSTER, but after recording one charting lp 'IN HEARING OF'. In 1972, FRENCH joined American rock band CACTUS, who contained former members of VANILLA FUDGE. They made one lp with him; 'OT 'N' SWEATY'. He returned to the UK in 1974 to do unfruitful auditions for DEEP PURPLE, MANFRED MANN'S EARTH BAND and URIAH HEEP. In 1977, he joined German outfit RANDY PIE to record on their 4th German/US lp 'FAST FORWARD'. He also featured on European double-lp 'ROCK OPERA – DER FUHRER' for 'Harvest' *(1C 188-32508/9)*. He dressed as Josef Goebbels and it also featured MARTI WEBB as Eva Braun. In 1977, he went solo and released 'DUCKS IN FLIGHT', but he made only one more appearance in novelty STATUS QUO pastische poutfit The HEADBANGERS, in which he sang like FRANCIS ROSSI.

PETER FRENCH

— with **BRIAN ROBERTSON** – guitar (of THIN LIZZY) / **DAVE MARKEE** – bass / **KENNY JONES** – drums (ex-FACES)

Polydor / not issued

1977. (7") *(2042 025)* **GIVE ME YOUR LOVE. / SAME OLD QUESTIONS** [-] [-] German
1978. (lp) *(2417 117)* **DUCKS IN FLIGHT** [-] [-] German

— FRENCH formed The HEADBANGERS in '81 and issued hit 45 'STATUS ROCK'

LEAGUE OF GENTLEMEN (see under ⇒ KING CRIMSON)

LEAVES

Formed: Los Angeles, California, USA . . . 1964, out of college based frat-band The ROCKWELLS, by JIM PONS and BILL RINEHART, who soon enlisted ROBERT LEE REINER, JIMMY KERN and singer JOHN BECK. In 1965, they were awarded a residency at a Sunset Strip club, which led to TV appearances and a contract for 'Mira'. After three flops, they finally broke into US Top 40 in mid-'66, with a fresher, folk-rock version of 'HEY JOE'. This annoyed both The BYRDS and LOVE, who thought they'd stolen the traditional song. It received a UK release (their only 45 to achieve this), but after its failure, the band carried on unsuccessfully in the States. • **Songwriters:** PONS + RINEHART penned, until latter's departure. Covered; YOU BETTER MOVE ON (Arthur Alexander) / LOVE MINUS ZERO + HE WAS A FRIEND OF MINE (Bob Dylan) / CODINE (Buffy Sainte-Marie) / TRY FOR THE SUN (Donovan) / etc. • **Trivia:** HEY JOE was later made famous by JIMI HENDRIX, who made the UK charts.

Recommended: 1966 (*7)

JOHN BECK – vocals (added to quartet 1965) / **BILL RINEHART** – lead guitar / **ROBERT LEE REINER** – guitar / **JIM PONS** – bass / **TOM RAY** – drums repl. JIMMY KERN

Fontana / Mira

Sep 65. (7") <202> **TOO MANY PEOPLE. / LOVE MINUS ZERO** [-] [ ]
Nov 65. (7") <207> **HEY JOE, WHERE YOU GONNA GO?. / BE WITH YOU** [-] [ ]
Jan 66. (7") <213> **YOU BETTER MOVE ON. / A DIFFERENT STORY** [-] [ ]

— **BOB ARLIN** – lead guitar (ex-CATALINAS) repl. RINEHART (to GENE CLARK)

Mar 66. (7"w-drawn) <220> **FUNNY LITTLE WORLD. / BE WITH YOU** [-] [ ]
Apr 66. (7") <222> **HEY JOE. / GIRL FROM THE EAST** (or) **FUNNY LITTLE WORLD** [-] [31]

Jun 66. (7") *(TF 713)* **HEY JOE. / FUNNY LITTLE WORLD** [ ] [-]
Aug 66. (lp) *<3005>* **HEY JOE** [-] [ ]
– Dr. Stone / Just a memory / Get out of my life woman / Girl from the East / He was a friend of mine / Hey Joe / Words / Back on the avenue / War of distortion / Tobacco Road / Goodbye, my lover / Too many people. *(re-iss.'67 on 'Surrey';)*
Sep 66. (7") *<227>* **TOO MANY PEOPLE. / GIRL FROM THE EAST** [-] [ ]
Nov 66. (7") *<231>* **GET OUT MY LIFE WOMAN. / GIRL FROM THE EAST** [-] [ ]

— Now quartet of **BECK** (now guitar), **ARLIN, PONS and RAY**, when REINER left

not issued | Capitol

1967. (7") *<5799>* **TWILIGHT SANCTUARY. / LEMON PRINCESS** [-] [ ]
1967. (lp) *<ST 2638>* **ALL THE GOOD THAT'S HAPPENING** [-] [ ]
– Codine / Try for the sun / etc.

— Disbanded '67. PONS had left to join The TURTLES. He was later to join FRANK ZAPPA'S MOTHERS

- compilations, etc. -

1982. (7"pic-d) *Panda;* **HEY JOE. / (group interview)** [-] [ ]
Feb 84. (lp) *Line; (LLP 5144)* **HEY JOE** [-] [-] German
May 84. (lp) *Fan Club; (FC 006)* **1966: LEAVES** [ ] [ ] 1982
(cd-iss.Apr91; FC 006CD)

— **ARLIN** and **BECK** formed **The NEW LEAVES** with **BUDDY SKLAR** – bass / **CRAIG BOYD** – drums. Soon became trio when BECK left. Changed group name to . . .

The HOOK

ARLIN, SKLAR plus **DALE LOYALE** – drums / **DENNIS PROVISOR** – keyboards

Uni | Uni

1968. (7") *<55057>* **SON OF FANTASY. / PLUG YOUR HEAD IN** [-] [ ]
1968. (7") *<55077>* **HOMES. / LOVE THEME IN E MINOR** [-] [ ]
1968. (lp) *<73023>* **THE HOOK WILL GRAB YOU** [-] [ ]
– Homes / Lookin' for you / You know I do / Turn your head / Son of fantasy / Dr.B and his friends / Plug your head in / Everything's groovy / Garbage man / Dimples.

— **CRAIG BOYD** – drums returned to repl. LOYALE and PROVISOR
1968. (7") *(UN 505) <55149>* **IN THE BEGINNING. / SHOW YOU THE WAY** [ ] [ ]
1969. (lp) *<73038>* **HOOKED** [-] [ ]

— Disbanded 1970

Arthur LEE (see under ⇒ LOVE)

John LEES (see under ⇒ BARCLAY JAMES HARVEST)

LEFT BANKE

Formed: New York City, New York, USA . . . early '66, by classically-trained MICHAEL BROWN. He had previously written for the one-off project, CHRISTOPHER & THE CHAPS, who issued a February single, 'IT'S ALRIGHT MA (I'M ONLY BLEEDING)' / 'THEY JUST DON'T CARE', for 'Philips'. He then assembled a group with STEVE MARTIN, TOM FINN, JEFF WINFIELD and GEORGE CAMERON, in his father Harry's studio. Their first 45, 'WALK AWAY RENEE', hit the US Top 5, quickly pursued by the Top 20 smash, 'PRETTY BALLERINA'. Theirs was a unique style of baroque'n'roll, the group fusing heavy orchestration and bubblegum psychedelia. The rest of the band then split from MICHAEL, who was left with the group name. BROWN and two newly recruited members, only managed to issue one 45, 'IVY IVY', before his old cohorts returned to the fold. They scraped out a further two singles, before BROWN formed his own outfit, MONTAGE. Without mainman BROWN, they failed with several subsequent releases, folding a few years later. In 1972, BROWN resurrected his career, hitting the US Top 50 with a new band, The STORIES, a rockier outfit, who nonetheless maintained a keen sense of melody. The following year, they topped the US charts with a rousing version of 'BROTHER LOUIE' (more familiar in the UK, to fans of HOT CHOCOLATE). BROWN again jumped ship, leaving the band to continue on their own, while he formed another outfit, The BECKIES. The LEFT BANKE re-grouped in 1978, releasing a one-off 45, 'QUEEN OF PARADISE'. • **Songwriters:** BROWN contributed most to early LEFT BANKE, and used some outside writers in The STORIES. • **Trivia:** The FOUR TOPS had a massive hit in 1969 with their 'WALK AWAY RENEE'.

Recommended: AND FINALLY IT'S . . . THE LEFT BANKE (*6).

MICHAEL BROWN (b. MICHAEL LOOKOFSKY, 25 Apr'49, Brooklyn, N.Y.) – keyboards / **STEVE MARTIN** – vocals / **JEFF WINFIELD** – guitar / **TOM FINN** – bass (ex-MAGIC PLANETS) / **GEORGE CAMERON** – drums

Philips | Smash

Sep 66. (7") *(BF 1517) <2041>* **WALK AWAY RENEE. / I HAVEN'T GOT THE NERVE** [ ] [5] Jul66
Jan 67. (7") *(BF 1540) <2074>* **PRETTY BALLERINA. / LAZY DAY** [ ] [15] Dec66

— **RICK BRAND** – guitar (ex-SPYDERS) repl. WINFIELD
Apr 67. (lp) *(BL 7773) <SRS 67088>* **WALK AWAY RENEE . . . PRETTY BALLERINA** [ ] [67] Mar67
– Pretty ballerina / She may call you up tonight / Barterers and their wives / I've got something on my mind / Let go of you girl / Evening gown / Walk away renee / What do you know / Shadows breaking over my head / I haven't got the nerve / Lazy day *<US re-iss.1970 on 'Mercury'; same>*

— BROWN split from rest of band, but retained name LEFT BANKE. The other 4 members disputed this and soon got radio stations to boycott following 45. Meanwhile BROWN had recruited **TOM FEHER** – vocals / **BERT SOMNER** – guitar

Jun 67. (7") *(BF 1575) <2089>* **IVY IVY. / AND SUDDENLY** [ ] [ ] Mar67

— (above was soon withdrawn, as others patch up dispute with BROWN)
Jun 67. (7") *<2097>* **SHE MAY CALL YOU UP TONIGHT. / BATTERERS AND THEIR WIVES** [-] [ ]
Oct 67. (7") *(BF 1614) <2119>* **DESIREE. / I'VE GOT SOMETHING ON MY MIND** [ ] [98]

— More confusion, upset proceedings, as BROWN (to MONTAGE) and BRAND break. This left others (**FINN, MARTIN + CAMERON**) with what they wanted; LEFT BANKE.
Jun 68. (7") *<2165>* **DARK IS THE BARK. / MY FRIEND TODAY** [-] [ ]
Nov 68. (7") *<2198>* **GOODBYE HOLLY. / SING LITTLE BIRD SING** [-] [ ]
Feb 69. (7") *<2209>* **BRYANT HOTEL. / GIVE THE MAN A HAND** [-] [ ]
Mar 69. (lp) *<SRS 67113>* **THE LEFT BANKE TOO** [-] [ ]
– Goodbye Holly / There's gonna be a storm / Sing little bird sing / Nice to see you / Give the man a hand / Bryant Hotel / Desiree / Dark is the bark / In the morning light / My friend today.
Jun 69. (7") *<2226>* **NICE TO SEE YOU. / THERE'S GONNA BE A STORM** [-] [ ]
Nov 69. (7") *<2243>* **MYRAH. / PEDESTAL** [-] [ ]

— Disbanded early 1970. STEVE MARTIN went solo recording one 45 for 'Buddah'.

— Meanwhile, **MICHAEL BROWN** had formed MONTAGE

MONTAGE

— in 1968 with **BOB STEURER** – vocals / **MIKE SMYTH** – guitar / **LANCE CORNELIUS** – bass / **VANCE CHAPMAN** – drums

not issued | Laurie

Mar 68. (7") *<3438>* **I SHALL CALL HER MARY. / AN AUDIENCE WITH MISS PRISCILLA GRAY** [-] [ ]
Jun 68. (7") *<3453>* **WAKE UP JIMMY. / TINSEL AND IVY** [-] [ ]
Jan 69. (lp) *<SLP 2049>* **MONTAGE** [-] [ ]
– She's alone / Grand pianist / Men are building sand / Desiree / The song is love / My love / I shall call her Mary / Tinsel & Ivy / An audience with Miss Priscilla Grey / Wake up Jimmy (something's happening outside). *(UK-iss.Jan87 on 'Bam Caruso'; KIRI 055)*

— Disbanded in '69

STORIES

BROWN with **IAN LLOYD** – vocals / **STEVEN LOVE** – guitar / **BRIAN MALDEN** – drums

Kama Sutra | Kama Sutra

May 72. (7") *<KAS 545>* **I'M COMING HOME. / YOU TOLD ME** [-] [42]
Jul 72. (7") *<KAS 558>* **TOP OF THE CITY. / STEP BACK** [-] [ ]
Nov 72. (lp) *(2319 017) <KSBS 2051>* **STORIES** [ ] [ ] Jun72
– Hello people / I'm coming home / Winter scenes / Step back / You told me / St.James / Kathleen / Take cover / Nice to have you here / High and low.
Dec 72. (7") *<KAS 563>* **CIRCLES. / PREMONITION** [-] [ ]
Apr 73. (7") *(2013 061) <KAS 566>* **DARLING. / TAKE COVER** [ ] [ ] Jan73
Mar 73. (7") *<KAS 574>* **LOVE'S IN MOTION. / CHANGES HAVE BEGUN** [-] [ ]
Mar 73. (lp) *<KSBS 2068>* **ABOUT US** [-] [ ]
– Brother Louie / Darling / Don't ever let me down / Love is in motion / Hey France / Please, please / Changes have begun / Circles / Believe me / Words / Top of the city / Down time blooze / What comes after. *<US re-iss.Aug73; hit No.29> (+=)*– Brother Louie.
May 73. (7") *<KAS 577>* **BROTHER LOUIE. / WHAT COMES AFTER** [-] [1]
Sep 73. (7") *(2013 073)* **BROTHER LOUIE. / DARLING** [ ] [-]

— BROWN left to be replaced by **KENNY AARONSON** – bass / **KEN BISCHEL** – keyboards
Oct 73. (7") *<KAS 584>* **MAMMY BLUE. / TRAVELLING UNDERGROUND** [-] [50]
Feb 74. (lp) *<KSBS 2078>* **TRAVELLING UNDERGROUND** [-] [ ]
– Soft rain / Hard when you're so far away / If it feels good, do it / Mamy blue / Stories untold / I can't understand it / Earthbound / Freefall / Travelling underground.
Mar 74. (7") *<KAS 588>* **CIRCLES. / IF IT FEELS GOOD (by IAN LLOYD)** [-] [ ]
Jun 74. (7") *<KAS 594>* **ANOTHER LOVE. / LOVE IS IN MOTION** [-] [ ]

— When they finally split, IAN LLOYD went solo releasing albums IAN LLOYD (1976 'Polydor') / GOOSE BUMPS (1979 'Scotti Bros') / 3 WC (1980 'Scotti Bros'). BROWN formed The BECKIES

LEFT BANKE

— re-formed in 1978, but without BROWN. Line-up was **MARTIN, FINN + CAMERON.**

not issued | Camerica

Sep 78. (7") *<CS 0005>* **QUEEN OF PARADISE. / AND ONE DAY** [-] [ ]

— Disbanded after an album was recorded but was shelved, (see further below)

- compilations, others, etc. -

1970. (7") *Smash; <1416>* **WALK AWAY RENEE. / PRETTY BALLERINA** [-] [ ]
Feb 84. (lp) *Bam Caruso; (KIRI 021)* **AND SUDDENLY IT'S . . . THE LEFT BANKE** [ ] [-]
– Walk away Renee / There's gonna be a storm / Desiree / Myrah / Shadows breaking over my head / Let go of you girl / Sing little bird sing / I haven't got the nerve / Goodbye Holly / Dark is the bark / I've got something on my mind / Pretty ballerina / In the morning light / She may call you up tonight / My friend tonight / Batterers and their wives / Pedestal / Foggy waterfall. *(re-iss.Feb88 +=; same)*– (2 extra tracks) *(cd-iss.Nov88 as 'AND FINALLY IT'S . . . THE LEFT BANKE'; KIRI 021CD)*
Feb 84. (7"ep) *Bam Caruso; (NRIC 022)* **WALK AWAY RENEE / EVENING GOWN. / BRYANT HOTEL / NICE TO SEE YOU** [ ] [-]
Mar 86. (lp) *Bam Caruso; (KIRI 045)* **VOICES CALLING** (1978 album) [ ] [-]

Mar 86. (7") *Bam Caruso; (NRIC 041)* **AND ONE DAY. / I CAN FLY** [ ] [-]
May 86. (m-lp) *Bam Caruso; (PABL 036)* **WALK AWAY RENEE** [ ] [-]
Aug 85. (lp) *Rhino; <RNLP 123>* **THE HISTORY OF THE LEFT BANKE** [-] [ ]
Aug 86. (lp) *Rhino;* **STRANGERS ON A TRAIN** [-] [ ]
Feb 89. (lp/c/cd; by The STORIES) *See For Miles; (SEE/+K/CD 238)*
WALK AWAY FROM THE LEFT BANKE [ ] [-]
(cd+=)– (4 extra tracks).

LEMON PIPERS

Formed: Oxford, Ohio, USA ... early '67 by IVAN BROWNE, BILL BARTLETT, REG NAVE, STEVE WALMSLEY and BILL ALBAUGH. They soon relocated to New York when songwriters/producers PAUL LEKA and SHELLY PINZ took them under their wing. After one flop, they scored a massive selling US No.1 hit, with their second single, 'GREEN TAMBOURINE' (early '68), a breezy piece of psychedelic bubblegum. Its infectious refrain soon spread to the UK; where it made the Top 10. Sadly, after few minor hits and two critically lambasted albums, they split from the scene early '69. It was a bitter end to what should have been a fruitful career (sorry!?).

Recommended: GREEN TAMBOURINE (*4)

IVAN BROWNE – vocals, rhythm guitar / **BILL BARTLETT** – lead guitar / **REG NAVE** (b. South Harrow, Middlesex, England) – keyboards / **STEVE WALMSLEY** – bass / **BILL ALBAUGH** – drums

Pye Int. / Buddah

Oct 67. (7") *<11>* **TURN AROUND AND TAKE A LOOK. / DANGER** [-] [ ]
Jan 68. (7") *(7N 25444) <23>* **GREEN TAMBOURINE. / NO HELP FROM ME** [7] [1] Dec67
Feb 68. (lp) *(NPL 28112) <BDS 5009>* **GREEN TAMBOURINE** [ ] [90]
– Green tambourine / Rice is nice / Turn around and take a look / Through with you / Shoeshine boy / Blueberry blue / Ask me if I care / Fifty year void / The shoemaker of Leatherwear Square / Stragglin' behind / Rainbow tree. *(re-iss.1970 on 'Buddah'; 2349 006) (cd-iss.1990's on 'Repertoire'; REP 4016)*
Apr 68. (7") *(7N 25454) <31>* **RICE IS NICE. / BLUEBERRY BLUE** [41] [46] Mar68
Jun 68. (7") *(7N 25464) <41>* **JELLY JUNGLE (OF ORANGE MARMALADE). / SHOESHINE BOY** [ ] [51] May68
Jul 68. (lp) *(NSPL 28118) <BDS 5016>* **JUNGLE MARMALADE** [ ] [ ]
– Jelly jungle (of orange marmalade) / I was not born to follow / Everything is you / Catch me falling / Hard core / Love beads and meditation / I need someone (the painter) / Mirrors / Wine and violet / Dead end street – Half light.
Aug 68. (7") *<63>* **WINE AND VIOLET. / LONELY ATMOSPHERE** [-] [ ]
Nov 68. (7") *<136>* **RAINBOW TREE. / I WAS NOT BORN TO FOLLOW** [-] [ ]

not issued / Carol

1969. (7") *<107>* **QUIET PLEASE. / MONAURAL 78** [-] [ ]

— Disbanded when above sales quickly plummeted. BARLETT later formed heavies RAM JAM and returned into the charts with classy 'BLACK BETTY'.

– compilations, etc. –

1968. (7"ep) *Pye International; (NEP 44091)* **PRESENTING ... (also 2 tracks by 1910 FRUITGUM CO.)** [ ] [-]
Feb 75. (7") *Buddah; (BDS 422)* **GREEN TAMBOURINE. / JELLY JUNGLE (OF ORANGE MARMALADE)** [ ] [-]
1977. (12"ep) *Buddah-Pye; (BD 106)* **RICE IS NICE. / (3 other artists)** [ ] [-]
Jul 80. (7"ep) *Flashback; (FBEP 102)* **GREEN TAMBOURINE / BLUEBERRY BLUE. / RICE IS NICE / JELLY JUNGLE (OF ORANGE MARMALADE)** [ ] [-]
May 84. (7") *Old Gold; (OG 9415)* **GREEN TAMBOURINE. / (b-side by Lovin' Spoonful)** [ ] [-]
1969. (lp) *Marble Arch; (MAL 1120)* **LEMON PIPERS** [ ] [-]
(cd-iss.Jul90 on Sequel'; NEXCD 131)

John LENNON

Born: JOHN WINSTON LENNON, 9 Oct'40, Liverpool, England. While still a member of The BEATLES (late 1968), he teamed up with his new girlfriend at the time, YOKO ONO, to record the controversial, 'UNFINISHED MUSIC NO.1: TWO VIRGINS'. The cover-shot displayed a full-frontal nude photo of the couple and the album was subsequently sold in brown paper wrapping to apparently save embarrassment to both the customers and the retailers! During Spring next year, its follow-up, 'UNFINISHED MUSIC NO.2: LIFE WITH THE LIONS', hit the shops and continued their anti-commercial, free-form direction, the songs mainly recorded on a small cassette player. Now divorced from his wife CYNTHIA, JOHN married YOKO on the 20th March '69, even changing by deed poll, his middle name from WINSTON to ONO. After the LENNON's completed an 8-day peace protest by publicly lying/sitting in a hotel bed, they released The PLASTIC ONO BAND's debut hippy anthem, 'GIVE PEACE A CHANCE'. This gave JOHN his first non-BEATLES hit, rising into the UK Top 3 and US Top 20. Later that year, 'COLD TURKEY' (a drug withdrawal song), also gave him a Top 30 smash on both sides of the Atlantic. Late 1969, he unveiled two albums, one, another avant-garde collaboration with YOKO, 'THE WEDDING ALBUM', and the other a more standard commercial product from The PLASTIC ONO BAND, 'LIVE IN TORONTO 1969', a record which breached the US Top 10. They also scored with another UK/US Top 5 hit, 'INSTANT KARMA', which was produced by PHIL SPECTOR early in 1970. In May that year, The BEATLES officially split prior to the release of another No.1 album, 'Let It Be'. JOHN then concentrated wholly on his solo career, returning with the album, 'JOHN LENNON: PLASTIC ONO BAND'. This was followed by another Top 20 anthem, 'POWER TO THE PEOPLE'. On the 3rd of September '71, he went to New York to live with YOKO and a month later, his classic album, 'IMAGINE', topped the charts in both the US and the UK (its US-only released title track, hitting No.3). In 1971, he failed in a bid to have a Christmas hit in the States with 'HAPPY XMAS (WAR IS OVER)', although this reached the UK Top 5 a year later. During the next three years, during which he released three albums, he fought to stay in America after being ordered by immigration authorities to leave. During this period, in which he temporarily split from YOKO, he went through drinking bouts with his buddy HARRY NILSSON, the pair recording an album, 'PUSSY CATS', together. On the 9th of October '75, YOKO gave birth to their first child, SEAN. LENNON then went into retirement to look after the boy in their Manhattan apartment, leaving behind a charting greatest hits, 'SHAVED FISH'. He was soon to receive his green card, allowing him to permanently reside in the States. However, in 1980 he returned to the studio once again, David Geffen offering to release an album on his self-titled label. In November that year, 'DOUBLE FANTASY' was released, soon topping both US and UK album charts. There was also a return to the singles chart, when the appropriately titled '(JUST LIKE) STARTING OVER' made the Top 10. Tragically on the 8th of December 1980, JOHN was shot five times by a deranged fan, Mark Chapman, outside the LENNON's apartment block. He died shortly afterwards at Roosevelt hospital. Not surprisingly, his previous 45 climbed back up the charts and peaked at No.1, with a re-issue of 'IMAGINE' following it to the top early in 1981. His killer was sent to a mental institution for the rest of his life, and we can only ponder what the 40-year-old might have achieved in the 80's & 90's had he lived. He remains a much revered genius, an artist who attempted to alienate the pop industry with non-conventional music styles. He was also a peaceful man, whose outbursts and human faults seemed to be portrayed falsely by the media, especially in his BEATLES days. His love of YOKO was undoubtably a turning point, finding both himself and the world around him a happier place to live. Although some of his songs exploded into frenetic rock anthems of anti-war and anti-government sentiments, his music, in its many facets, showed a poetic beauty and untouched romance. • **Songwriters:** LENNON, except covers album 'ROCK'N'ROLL' which contained;- BE-BOP-A-LULA (Gene Vincent) / STAND BY ME (Ben E.King) / PEGGY SUE (Buddy Holly) / AIN'T THAT A SHAME (Fats Domino) / SWEET LITTLE SIXTEEN + YOU CAN'T CATCH ME (Chuck Berry) / BONY MORONIE (Larry Williams) / BRING IT HOME TO ME + SEND ME SOME LOVIN' (Sam Cooke) / JUST BECAUSE (Lloyd Price) / YA YA (Lee Dorsey) / RIP IT UP + SLIPPIN' AND SLIDIN' + READY TEDDY (Little Richard) / DO YOU WANT TO DANCE (Bobby Freeman). • **Trivia:** In 1967, JOHN acted in the movie, 'How I Won The War', also appearing in many zany films with The BEATLES. In 1975, he co-wrote 'Fame' with DAVID BOWIE, which topped the US charts. His son from his first marriage, JULIAN, has previously enjoyed chart action, while SEAN has also been more visible, appearing at benefits, etc.

Recommended: IMAGINE (*8) / MIND GAMES (*7) / THE JOHN LENNON COLLECTION (*9)

JOHN LENNON & YOKO ONO

JOHN LENNON – vocals, guitar, etc. / **YOKO ONO** (b.18 Feb'33, Tokyo, Japan) – wind, vocals

Apple / Apple

Nov 68. (lp; stereo/mono) *(S+/APCOR 2) <5001>* **UNFINISHED MUSIC NO.1: TWO VIRGINS** [ ] [ ]
– Section 1, 2, 3, 4, 5, 6 / Side 2. *(cd-iss.Jan93 on'Rock Classics';) (cd re-iss.Jun97 on 'Rykodisc'; RCD 10411)*

Zapple / Zapple

May 69. (lp) *(ZAPPLE 01) <3357>* **UNFINISHED MUSIC NO.2: LIFE WITH THE LIONS (1/2 live)** [ ] [ ]
– Cambridge 1969 / No bed for Beatle John / Baby's heartbeat / Two minutes silence / Radio play. *(cd-iss.Jun97 on 'Rykodisc'; RCD 10412)*

The PLASTIC ONO BAND

Apple / Apple

Jul 69. (7") *(APPLE 13) <1809>* **GIVE PEACE A CHANCE. / REMEMBER LOVE** [2] [14]
(re-iss.Jan81, reached UK No.33)
Oct 69. (7") *(APPLES 1001) <1813>* **COLD TURKEY. / DON'T WORRY KYOKO (MUMMY'S ONLY LOOKING FOR A HAND IN THE SNOW)** [14] [30] Dec69
Dec 69. (lp; as JOHN ONO LENNON & YOKO ONO LENNON) *(SAPCOR 11) <3361>* **WEDDING ALBUM** [ ] [ ]
– John and Yoko / Amsterdam. *(cd-iss.Jun97 on 'Rykodisc'; RCD 10413)*

— JOHN and YOKO hired the following musicians **ERIC CLAPTON** – guitar (ex-YARDBIRDS, ex-CREAM, ex-BLUESBREAKERS) / **KLAUS VOORMAN** – bass (ex-MANFRED MANN) / **ALAN WHITE** – drums

Dec 69. (lp) *(CORE 2001) <3362>* **THE PLASTIC ONO BAND – LIVE PEACE IN TORONTO 1969 (live 13 Sep'69)** [ ] [10] Jan70
– Blue Suede shoes / Money (that's what I want) / Dizzy Miss Lizzy / Yer blues / Cold turkey / Give peace a chance / Don't worry Kyoko / John John (let's hope for peace).
Feb 70. (7"; LENNON / ONO WITH PLASTIC ONO BAND) *(APPLES 1003) <1818>* **INSTANT KARMA!. / Yoko Ono: WHO HAS SEEN THE WIND?** [5] [3]

JOHN LENNON & THE PLASTIC ONO BAND

The **LENNON's** retained only **KLAUS / RINGO STARR** – drums (ex-BEATLES) repl. WHITE who later joined YES

Dec 70. (lp) *(SAPCOR 17) <3372>* **JOHN LENNON: PLASTIC ONO BAND** [11] [6]
– Mother / Hold on / I found out / Working class hero / Isolation / Remember / Love / Well well well / Look at me / God / My mummy's dead. *(re-iss.Jul84 on 'Fame' lp/c; 41-3102-1/-4) (cd-iss.Apr88 on 'E.M.I.'; CDP 746770-2) (cd re-iss.Dec94 on 'Fame'; CDFA 3310)*

Dec 70. (7") *<1827>* **MOTHER. / WHY (Yoko Ono)** [-] [43]

— next single also credited with **YOKO ONO**

Mar 71. (7") *(R 5892)* **POWER TO THE PEOPLE. / OPEN YOUR BOX** [7] [-]

Mar 71. (7") *<1830>* **POWER TO THE PEOPLE. / Yoko Ono: TOUCH ME** [-] [11]

Oct 71. (lp) *(PAS 10004) <3379>* **IMAGINE** [1] [1] Sep71
– Imagine / Crippled inside / Jealous guy / It's so hard / I don't want to be a soldier / Give me some truth / Oh my love / How do you sleep? / How? / Oh Yoko!. *(also on quad-lp Jun72; Q4PAS 10004) (cd-iss.May87 on 'Parlophone'; CDP 746641-2)*

Oct 71. (7") *<1840>* **IMAGINE. / IT'S SO HARD** [-] [3]

May 72. (7") *<1848>* **WOMAN IS THE NIGGER OF THE WORLD. / Yoko Ono: SISTERS, OH SISTERS** [-] [57]

— with ELEPHANT'S MEMORY & FLUX / INVISIBLE STRINGS and lots of guests including **FRANK ZAPPA, ERIC CLAPTON,** etc.

Sep 72. (d-lp; JOHN & YOKO / PLASTIC ONO BAND) *(PCSP 7161) <3392>* **SOMETIME IN NEW YORK CITY (live)** [11] [48]
– Woman is the nigger of the world / Sisters o sisters / Attica state / Born in a prison / New York City / Sunday bloody Sunday / The luck of the Irish / John Sinclair / Angela / We're all water / (w/ CAST OF THOUSANDS); Cold turkey / Don't worry Kyoko / (w/ The MOTHERS); Jamrag / Scumbag / Au. *(re-iss.Feb86 on 'Parlophone'; see LIVE IN NEW YORK CITY')*

— Next single credited as **JOHN & YOKO / PLASTIC ONO BAND** with **The HARLEM COMMUNITY CHOIR**

Nov 72. (7",7"green) *(R 5970)* **HAPPY XMAS (WAR IS OVER). / LISTEN THE SNOW IS FALLING** [4] [ ] Nov71
(re-iss.Dec74; same); hit No.48) (re-iss.Dec80; same); No.2) (re-iss.Dec81; same); No.28) (re-iss.Dec82; ; hit 56)

JOHN LENNON

Nov 73. (7") *(R 5994) <1868>* **MIND GAMES. / MEAT CITY** [26] [18]

Nov 73. (lp/c; JOHN LENNON & PLASTIC U.F.ONO BAND) *(PCS/TC-PCS 7165) <3414>* **MIND GAMES** [13] [9]
– Mind games / Tight a $ / Aisumasen (I'm sorry) / One day (at a time) / Bring on the Lucie (Freeda people) / Nutopian international anthem / Intuition / Out of the blue / Only people / I know (I know) / You are here / Meat city. *(re-iss.Oct80 on 'Music For Pleasure' lp/c; MFP/TCMFP 50509) (cd-iss.Aug87 & Sep91 on 'Parlophone'; CDP 746769-2)*

Oct 74. (7"; JOHN LENNON & THE PLASTIC ONO NUCLEAR BAND featuring ELTON JOHN) *(R 5998) <1874>* **WHATEVER GETS YOU THRU' THE NIGHT. / BEEF JERKY** [36] [1] Sep74

Oct 74. (lp/c) *(PC/+TC 253) <3416>* **WALLS AND BRIDGES** [6] [1]
– Going down on love / Whatever gets you thru the night / Old dirt road / What you got / Bless you / £9 dream / Surprise surprise (sweet bird of Paradise) / Steel and glass / Beef jerky / Nobody loves you (when you're down and out) / Ya-ya / Scared. *(re-iss.Jan85 on 'Parlophone' lp/c; ATAK/TC-ATAK 43) (cd-iss.Jul87; CDP 746768-2)*

Jan 75. (7") *(R 6003) <1878>* **£9 DREAM. / WHAT YOU GOT** [23] [9]

Feb 75. (lp/c) *(PCS/TC-PCS 7169) <3419>* **ROCK'N'ROLL** [6] [6]
– Be-bop-a-lula / Stand by me / Medley: Rip it up – Ready Teddy / You can't catch me / Ain't that a shame / Do you want to dance / Sweet little sixteen / Slippin' and slidin' / Peggy Sue / Medley: Bring it on home to me – Send me some lovin' / Ya ya / Just because. *(re-iss.Nov81 on 'Music For Pleasure' lp/c; MFP/TCMFP 50522) (cd-iss.Jul87 on 'Parlophone'; CDP 746 707-2) (re-iss.Feb97 on 'E.M.I.'; LPCENT 9)*

Apr 75. (7") *(R 6005) <1881>* **STAND BY ME. / MOVE OVER MS. L** [30] [20] Mar75
(re-iss.Apr81; same)

Oct 75. (7") *(R 6009)* **IMAGINE. / WORKING CLASS HERO** [6] [-]
(re-iss.Dec80; same); hit No.1)

Nov 75. (lp/c) *(PCS 7173) <3421>* **SHAVED FISH** (compilation) [8] [12]
– Give peace a chance / Cold turkey / Instant karma / Power to the people / Mother / Woman is the nigger of the world / Imagine / Whatever gets you thru the night / Mind games / £9 dream / Happy Xmas (war is over) / Give peace a chance (reprise). *(cd-iss.May87 on 'E.M.I.'; CDP 746642-2)*

— JOHN was also credited on a few singles by ELTON JOHN – Feb75 'I Saw Her Standing There' which was also realeased Mar81 with 2 other. In Jul71 a rare single 'GOD SAVE US'/'DO THE OZ' was released by him and Plastic Ono Band backing 'BILL ELLIOT AND THE ELASTIC OZ BAND'

JOHN LENNON & YOKO ONO

returned after a long break

Geffen Geffen

Oct 80. (7") *(K 79186) <49604>* **(JUST LIKE) STARTING OVER. / KISS KISS KISS (Yoko Ono)** [1] [1]

Nov 80. (lp/c) *(K/K4 99131) <2001>* **DOUBLE FANTASY** [1] [1]
– (Just like) Starting over / Every man has a woman who loves him (YOKO ONO) / Clean up time / Give me something (YOKO ONO) / I'm losing you / I'm moving on (YOKO ONO) / Beautiful boy (darling boy) / Watching the wheels / I'm your angel (YOKO ONO) / Dear Yoko / Beautiful boys (YOKO ONO) / Kiss kiss kiss (YOKO ONO) / Woman / Hard times are over (YOKO ONO). *(re-iss.Jan89 on 'Capitol' cd)(c/lp; CDP 791 425-2)(TC+/EST 2083)*

Jan 81. (7"/c-s) *(K/MK 79195) <49644>* **WOMAN. / Yoko Ono: BEAUTIFUL BOYS** [1] [2]

Mar 81. (7"/c-s) *(K/MK 79207) <49695>* **WATCHING THE WHEELS. / Yoko Ono: YES, I'M YOUR ANGEL** [30] [10]

— His last two singles were released after his tragic murder 8th Dec'80

JOHN & YOKO

had recorded one more album prior to his death.

Polydor Polydor

Jan 84. (lp) *(<817 238-1>)* **A HEART PLAY: UNFINISHED DIALOGUE** (interview with Playboy) [ ] [ ]

Jan 84. (7") *(POSP 700) <817254>* **NOBODY TOLD ME. / O SANITY** [6] [5]

Jan 84. (lp/pic-lp/c)(cd) *(POLH/+P/C 5)(<817160-2>)* **MILK AND HONEY** [3] [11]
– I'm stepping out / Sleepless night (YOKO ONO) / I don't wanna face it / Don't be scared (YOKO ONO) / Nobody told me / O'sanity (YOKO ONO) / Borrowed time / Your hands (YOKO ONO) / (Forgive me) My little flower princess / Let me count the ways (YOKO ONO) / Grow old with me / You're the one (YOKO ONO).

Mar 84. (7") *(POSP 701)* **BORROWED TIME. / YOUR HANDS (Yoko Ono)** [32] [ ]
(12"+=) *(POSPX 701)* – Never say goodbye.

Jul 84. (7") *(POSP 702) <821107>* **I'M STEPPING OUT. / SLEEPLESS NIGHT (Yoko Ono)** [ ] [55]
(12"+=) *(POSPX 702)* – Loneliness.

Nov 84. (7") *(POSP 712)* **EVERY MAN HAS A WOMAN WHO LOVES HIM. / IT'S ALRIGHT** [ ] [ ]
(above from various compilation 'B'-side by his son SEAN ONO LENNON)

– posthumous releases, etc. –

on 'Parlophone' UK /'Capitol' US, unless mentioned otherwise

Jun 81. (8xlp-box) *Apple; (JLB 8)* **JOHN LENNON (BOXED)** [ ] [ ]
– (all lp's from LIVE PEACE – SHAVED FISH) *(4xcd-box-iss.Oct90; LENNON 1)*

Nov 82. (lp/c) *E.M.I.; (EMTV/TC-EMTV 37) / Geffen; <GHSP 2023>* **THE JOHN LENNON COLLECTION** [1] [33]
– (nearly as 'SHAVED FISH') *(re-iss.Jun85; same) (cd-iss. Oct89; CDEMTV 37)–* (2 extra tracks).

Nov 82. (7") *(R 6059)* **LOVE. / GIVE ME SOME TRUTH** [41] [ ]

Mar 84. (7") *EMI Gold; (G45 2)* **GIVE PEACE A CHANCE. / COLD TURKEY** [ ] [-]

Nov 85. (7") *(R 6117)* **JEALOUS GUY / GOING DOWN ON LOVE** [65] [ ]
(12"+=) *(12R 6117)* – Oh Yoko!

Feb 86. (lp/c)(cd) *(PCS/TC-PCS 7301)(CDP 746 196-2) <12451>* **LIVE IN NEW YORK CITY (live)** [55] [41]

Nov 86. (lp/c/cd) *(PCS/TCPCS/CDPCS 7308) <12533>* **MENLOVE AVE.** (sessions 74-75) [ ] [ ]
– Here we go again / Rock'n'roll people / Angel baby / Since my baby left me / To know her is to love her / Steel and glass / Scared / Old dirt road / Nobody loves you (when you're down and out).

May 87. (7") *Antar;* **TWO MINUTES SILENCE. / TWO MINUTES SILENCE (dub!)** [ ] [ ]

Aug 87. (cd) **LIVE JAM** (half of SOMETIME lp) [ ] [ ]

Oct 88. (cd/d-c/d-lp) *(CD/TC+/PCSP 722) <90803>* **IMAGINE: THE MOVIE** (Music from the Motion Picture; with some songs by The BEATLES) [64] [31]
– Real love / Twist and shout / Help! / In my life / Strawberry fields forever / A day in the life / Revolution / The ballad of John & Yoko / Julia / Don't let me down / Give peace a chance / How? / Imagine (rehearsal) / God / Mother / Stand by me / Jealous guy / Woman / Beautiful boy (darling boy) / (Just like) Starting over / Imagine.

Oct 88. (cd-s) *<44230>* **JEALOUS GUY** [-] [80]

Nov 88. (7"/7"pic-d) *(R/RP 6199)* **IMAGINE. / JEALOUS GUY** [45] [-]
(12"+=/12"pic-d+=) *(12R/+P 6199)* – Happy Xmas (war is over).
(cd-s+=) *(CDR 6199)* – Give peace a chance.

Deke LEONARD (see under ⇒ MAN)

Jaki LIEBEZEIT (see under ⇒ CAN)

LIGHTNING

Formed: Ann Arbor, Michigan, USA . . . 1969 as WHITE LIGHTNING by TOM CAPLAN. Their only 45 under this moniker was something of a psychedelic punk beauty, highlighting some wonderful lyrics side by side with treble/fuzz riffs. 'WILLIAM' was released three times during 1969, even failing on its last attempt on 'Atco'. After shortening to LIGHTNING, they branched out into the hard-rock field, releasing a competent eponymous album before splitting.

Recommended: LIGHTNING (*5)

TOM CAPLAN – lead guitar (ex-LITTER) / **MICK STANHOPE** – vocals / **RONNIE ROBERTS** – guitar, vocals / **WOODY WOODRICH** – bass / **BERNIE PERSHEY** – percussion

not issued Hexagon

Jan 69. (7"; as WHITE LIGHTNING) *<944>* **WILLIAM. / OF PAUPERS AND POETS** [-] [ ]
<re-iss.1969; 6801> <re-iss.1969 on 'Atco'; 6660>

not issued P.I.P.

1969. (7") *<8923>* **FREEDOM. / HIGHWAY** [-] [ ]

1969. (lp) *<6807>* **LIGHTNING** [-] [ ]

LIGHT OF DARKNESS

Formed: Scotland . . . 1970, soon based in Germany due to their German drummer MANFRED BEBERT. The band's output consisted of a sole self-titled album of raw garage rock that was notable primarily for the manic vocals of JOHN LATIMER. A cult classic, the album is highly sought after in its original form.

Recommended: LIGHT OF DARKNESS (*8)

JOHN LATIMER – vocals, piano, organ, percussion / **BYRON GRANT** – guitars, fiddle / **MIKE REOCH** – bass, flute, piano, harmonica / **MANFRED BEBERT** – drums, percussion

Philips / not issued

1971. (lp) *(6305 062)* **LIGHT OF DARKNESS** [-] [-] German
– Movin' along / Love in your heart / Ain't no place where I belong / Soul Francisco / Freedom's fight / Time / Down out. *(re-iss.1981 on 'ZYX') (re-iss.1991 on 'Second Battle'; SB 019LP) (cd-iss.Jun97; SB 019)*

— split after above

LIGHTSHINE

Formed: Emmerich, Germany . . . 1972. This oddball group recorded only one album, the obscure classic, 'FEELING' (1973). Combining flowing melodies, trippy instrumental passages and general outbreaks of inspired madness (instrumental and vocal), this record has become a cult collectors item.

Recommended: FEELING (*8)

JOE – guitar, vocals / **ULLI** – guitar, flute, vocals / **OLLI** – synthesizer / **WOLFGANG** – bass / **EGON** – drums

Trepiton / not issued

1973. (lp) *(1049)* **FEELING** [-] [-] German
– Sword in the sky / King and queen / Nightmare / Lory / Feeling. *(cd-iss.1994 on 'Pehner')*

— faded out soon after above

LIMBUS

Formed: Heidelberg / Karlsruhe, Germany . . . 1969. Under the moniker of LIMBUS 3, this band cut 'COSMIC MUSIC EXPERIENCE' in 1969, an innovative improvisation piece that utilised all manner of exotic, ethnic instrumentation. With the addition of MATTHIAS KNIEPER, the band became LIMBUS 4 and cut their final album, 'MANDALAS', the following year on the 'Ohr' label.

Recommended: COSMIC MUSIC EXPERIENCE (*6) / MANDALAS (*5)

ODYSSEUS ARTNER – multi / **BERND HENNINGER** – multi / **GERD KRAUS** – multi

C.P.M. / not issued

1969. (lp; as LIMBUS 3) *(LPS 1)* **COSMIC MUSIC EXPERIENCE** [-] [-] German
– / New-Atlantis.

— added **MATTHIAS KNIEPER** – multi

Ohr / not issued

1970. (lp; as LIMBUS 4) *(OMM 56.001)* **MANDALAS** [-] [-] German
– Dhyana / Kundalini / Heiku / Plasma.

— split and another to disappear

LINCOLN ST. EXIT (see under ⇒ XIT)

LITTER

Formed: Minneapolis, Minnesota, USA . . .1967 by DENNY WAITE, DAN RINALDI, TOM CAPLAN, JIM KANE and TOM MURRAY. They were basically a covers band, giving the psych/garage treatment to songs of UK R&B groups such as The WHO, The SPENCER DAVIS GROUP and The YARDBIRDS. Two albums ('DISTORTIONS' & '$100') were issued during the next year, full of punk energy and fuzz highlighted on the opening second album track, 'MINDBREAKER'. In 1969, they re-grouped for a third effort, 'EMERGE', although this was more of a safe, hard-rock attempt for a major label.

Recommended: DISTORTIONS (*7) / $100 (*8)

DENNY WAITE – vocals, organ / **DAN RINALDI** – guitar, vocals / **TOM CAPLAN** – guitar / **JIM KANE** – bass / **TOM MURRAY** – drums

not issued / Warick

1967. (7") <6710> **ACTION WOMAN. / A LEGAL MATTER** [-] [ ]
1967. (7") <6711> **SOMEBODY HELP ME. / I'M A MAN** [-] [ ]
1967. (lp) <671> **DISTORTIONS** [-] [ ]
– Action woman / Whatcha gonna do about it / Codine / Somebody help me / Substitute / I'm so glad / A legal matter / Rack my mind / Soul searchin' / I'm a man. *(UK cd-iss.Jan94 on 'Taxim'; TX 2003CD)*
1967. (7") <6712> **ACTION WOMAN. / WHATCHA GONNA DO** [-] [ ]

not issued / Hexagon

1968. (lp) <HX 681> **$100 FINE** [-] [ ]
– Here I go again / Morning sun / Mindbreaker / Tallyman / Eagle / Kaleidoscope / Apologies to 2069 / Blues 1 / She's not there. *(UK cd-iss.Jan94 on 'Taxim'; TX 2004CD)*

— **MARK GALLAGHER** – vocals (ex-TROYS) + **RAY MELINA** – lead guitar, vocals; repl. WAITE + CAPLAN (latter to WHITE LIGHTNING)

Probe / Probe

1969. (lp) *(SPB 1004) <CLPS 4504>* **EMERGE** [ ] [ ] Aug69
– Journeys / Feeling / Silly people / Blue ice / For what it's worth / Little red book / Breakfast at Gardenson's / Future of the past. *(re-iss.Mar88 on 'Big Beat'; WIK 68)*
1969. (7") <461> **FEELING. / SILLY PEOPLE** [-] [ ]
1969. (7") <467> **BLUE ICE. / ON OUR MINDS** [-] [ ]

— Disbanded in 1970.

– compilations, etc. –

1983. (lp) *Eva; (12013)* **RARE TRACKS** [-] [-] France
May 94. (cd) *Eva; (842077)* **DISTORTIONS / $100 FINE** [ ] [-]

LIVERPOOL SCENE

Formed: Liverpool, England . . . 1967 by poetry-reading trio of ROGER McGOUGH, ADRIAN HENRI and BRIAN PATTEN. These writers featured on TV's 'Look Of The Week', leading to a brief liaison with 'C.B.S.' on the album, 'THE INCREDIBLE NEW LIVERPOOL SCENE' (mostly without PATTEN). The record introduced guitarist ANDY ROBERTS, an album that was quite underground and unusual for the time. Radio One DJ, JOHN PEEL, soon became interested, producing their follow-up in 1968, 'THE AMAZING ADVENTURES OF . . .'. By this time, they had added a host of poets and musicians (see below), creating a rockier feel. They made a big impact on the audience of the 1969 Isle Of Wight Festival, although they still surprisingly failed to gain any commercial success with subsequent efforts.

Recommended: THE INCREDIBLE NEW LIVERPOOL SCENE (*6) / RECOLLECTIONS (*6)

ROGER McGOUGH – poems / **ADRIAN HENRI** – poems / **BRIAN PATTEN** – poems (on some; left after below to go solo; 3 albums) / **ANDY ROBERTS** – vocals, guitar (ex-CLAYTON SQUARES)

C.B.S. / not issued

1967. (lp) *(63045)* **THE INCREDIBLE NEW LIVERPOOL SCENE** [ ] [-]

— without McGOUGH who joined The SCAFFOLD. Added **MIKE HART** – vocals, guitar (ex-CLAYTON SQUARES) / **MIKE EVANS** – poetry, tenor sax / **PERCY JONES** – bass / **BRIAN DODSON** – drums

R.C.A. / R.C.A.

Nov 68. (7") *(RCA 1762)* **SON SON. / BABY** [ ] [ ]
Jan 69. (lp) *(SF 7995) <LSP 4189>* **THE AMAZING ADVENTURES OF THE LIVERPOOL SCENE** [ ] [ ]
– Tramcar to Frankenstein / The amazing adventures of Che Guevara / Gliders and parks / The amazing adventures of Che Guevara – part 2 / Universes / Batpoem / The amazing adventures of Che Guevara – part 3 / Percy Parslow's hamster farm / Happy burial blues / Palms / The amazing adventures of Che Guevara – part 4 / Love story.
Apr 69. (7") *(RCA 1816)* **THE WOO-WOO. / LOVE IS** [ ] [ ]

— HART left to go solo in 1970 for the 'Dandelion' label

Sep 69. (lp) *(SF 8057) <LSP 4287>* **BREAD ON THE NIGHT** [ ] [ ]
– The day we danced at the dole / The raven / C.B.S. blues / The entry of Christ into Liverpool / 64 / Come into the perfumed garden, Maud / See the conkering heroine comes / Winter poem / I've got those Fletwood Mac, Chicken Shack, John Mayall, can't fail blues.

— **PETE CLARKE** – drums, repl. DODSON

May 70. (lp) *(SF 8100)* **ST. ADRIAN AND CO. BROADWAY & 3RD** [ ] [-]
– Made in U.S.A. / Human tapeworm / Night song / Bomb commercials / Colours / Baby.
Dec 70. (lp) *(SF 8134)* **HEIRLOON** (live/studio out-takes) [ ] [-]
– Love is / Gunner from Dakar / The morning the sky went away / Moon king / I'm just a simple boy / The woo-woo / Mental astronaut / Tramcar to Frankenstein / The little car / The boathouse / Wildwest.

— split in 1970 when ANDY ROBERTS went solo. He also joined PLAINSONG and re-united with HENRI in the outfit GRIMMS

– compilations, etc. –

1972. (lp) *Charisma; (CS 3)* **RECOLLECTIONS** [ ] [-]
– The woo-woo / The day we danced at the dole / Bat poem / 64 / Colours / I've got these Fleetwood Mac, Chicken Shack, John Mayall, can't fail blues / Love is / The entry of Christ into Europe / Love story.

ANDY ROBERTS

— with **DAVE RICHARDS** – bass / **ROGER POWELL** – drums / + others

R.C.A. / Ampex

Jan 71. (lp) *(SF 8086) <10120>* **HOME GROWN** <US diff.tracks> [ ] [ ]
– Home grown / Just for the record / Applecross / John the revelator / Moths and lizards in Detroit / Creepy John / Gig song / Queen of the moonlight world / Lonely in the crowd / The one-armed boatman and the giant squid. *(re-iss.1971 on 'Charisma'; CAS 1034)*
1971. (7") <11040> **HOME GROWN. / KEEP MY CHILDREN WARM** [-] [ ]

— joined EVERYONE alongside DAVE RICHARDS, BOB SARGEANT, JOHN PORTER and JOHN PEARSON. ROBERTS had already made a single and eponymous album in 1970 for 'Charisma'; *CAS 1028)* <on 'Ampex' US>

Pegasus / Philips

Jan 72. (lp) *(PEG 5) <6303 039>* **NINA AND THE DREAM TREE** [ ] [ ]
– Keep my children war / I've seen the movie / 25 hours a day / Breakdown / Welcome home / Good time Charlie / Dream tree sequence.

— joined IAN MATTHEWS in the 'Elektra' outfit PLAINSONG, who released one 1972 album 'IN SEARCH OF AMELIA EARHART'.

Elektra / not issued

1973. (7") *(K 42139)* **URBAN COWBOY** [ ] [-]
– Charlie / Big city tension / New Karenski / Urban cowboy / Elaine / Home at last / All around my grandmother's floor / Richmond / Baby, baby / Poison apple lady.
Nov 73. (7") *(K 12127)* **53 MILES FROM SPANISH TOWN. / CLOWNS ON THE ROAD** [ ] [-]
1973. (lp) *(K 42151)* **ANDY ROBERTS AND THE GREAT STAMPEDE** [ ] [-]
– Speed well / Clowns of the road / Lord of the groves / Bottom of the garden / Kid jealousy / Great stampede / High time / Home in the sun / 53 miles from Spanish town.

Virgin not issued

Apr 84. (7") *(VS 663)* **LOOSE CONNECTIONS. / HARRY** -

Apr 84. (lp) *(V 2306)* **LOOSE CONNECTIONS (soundtrack)** -
– Loose connections / Ain't just stars (that fall) / I'm holding you responsible / Living apart together / Got all the woman / Harry / I like country music / High noon / Ten feet tall and bulletproof / Ballad of the teen-age queen / Songs of the stars / You win again / Night to day.

– compilations, etc. –

Mar 92. (cd/c) *Mooncrest; (CREST CD/MC 014)* **THE BEST OF ANDY ROBERTS** -

Huw LLOYD-LANGTON (see under ⇒ HAWKWIND)

LOCOMOTIVE

Formed: Birmingham, England . . .1967 by JIM SIMPSON, who hooked up with BRUMBEATS guitarist NORMAN HAINES. They lost CHRIS WOOD to TRAFFIC, HAINES then switching to lead vocals and keyboards. Their debut single, 'BROKEN HEART', was a typical R&B/soul ballad, although it was flipped over by DJ's for the Jamaican-styled, 'RUDY, A MESSAGE TO YOU'. It flopped, although it was thought that their "white-boy" ska sound showed greater promise. HAINES penned the follow-up, 'RUDY'S IN LOVE', a surprise Top 30 hit in 1968. This became something of a burden, when they tried for a change in direction. Their next 45, 'MR. ARMAGEDDON', was a doom-laden affair, the single not going down too well at the dance clubs they were booked into. An album, the more heavily progressive 'WE ARE EVERYTHING YOU SEE', appeared in the summer of '69, and although it was recorded at Abbey Road with GUS DUDGEON, it bombed. HAINES dug his heels in once more, this time with EARTH, the band later becoming BLACK SABBATH. LOCOMOTIVE released their final 45, the more commercial 'ROLL OVER MARY' in 1970. HAINES then took some "real" jobs to pay the taxman, although he was soon back again with a single and an album, the impressive 'DEN OF INIQUITY' (1971). The remaining members of the band, BOB LAMB and MICK HINCKS, released an album under the silly alias of THE DOG THAT BIT PEOPLE. In the 90's, HAINES returned to the circuit, re-recording 'BROKEN HEART'. • **Trivia:** All associated lp's are worth over £150, HAINES' over £500!.

Recommended: WE ARE EVERYTHING YOU SEE (*6)

NORMAN HAINES – vocals, keyboards / **JIM SIMPSON** – trumpet / **MICK HINCKS** – bass / **BOB LAMB** – drums, repl. JIMMY SKIDMORE who had repl. CHRIS WOOD (to TRAFFIC)

Direction not issued

Dec 67. (7") *(58-3114)* **BROKEN HEART. / RUDY A MESSAGE TO YOU** -

Parlophone Bell

Aug 68. (7") *(R 5718)* *<754>* **RUDY'S IN LOVE. / NEVER SET ME FREE** 25
(re-iss.Jan80 on 'E.M.I.'; EMI 5033)

Jan 69. (7") *(R 5758)* *<778>* **MR. ARMAGEDDON. / THERE'S GOT TO BE A WAY**

Aug 69. (lp) *(PCS 7093)* **WE ARE EVERYTHING YOU SEE** -
– Overture / Mr. Armageddon / Now is the end – The end is when / Lay me down gently / Nobody asked you to come / You must be joking / Day in shining armour / Loves of Augustine Abbey (parts 1-3) / Rain / Coming down / Love song for the dead Che / Times of light and darkness. *(cd-iss.Mar95 on 'Shoestring'+=; BL 004)–* (extra single tracks etc)

Sep 69. (7") *(R 5801)* **I'M NEVER GONNA LET YOU GO. / YOU MUST BE JOKING** -

— now without HAINES who went solo. Formed SACRIFICE, who evolved into NORMAN HAINES BAND.

Mar 70. (7") *(R 5835)* **ROLL OVER MARY. / MOVIN' DOWN THE LINE** -

– compilations, etc. –

Aug 71. (7") *Parlophone; (R 5915)* **RUDI'S IN LOVE. / YOU MUST BE JOKING** -

May 79. (7"ep) *E.M.I.; (EMI 2960)* **RUDI'S IN LOVE / MR. ARMAGEDDON. / THERE'S GOT TO BE A WAY / NEVER SET ME FREE** -

THE DOG THAT BIT PEOPLE

LAMB + **HINCKS** + ?

Parlophone not issued

Jan 71. (7") *(R 5880)* **LOVELY LADY. / MERRY-GO-ROUND** -

Mar 71. (lp) *(PCS 7125)* **THE DOG THAT BIT PEOPLE** -
– Goodbye country / The monkey and the sailor / Lovely lady / Sound of thunder / Cover me in roses / Someone, somewhere / Snapshot of Rex / Red queen's dance / Mr. Sunshine / Tin soldier / Reptile man. *(cd-iss.Mar95 on 'Shoestring'; BL 003)*

THE NORMAN HAINES BAND

— with **NEIL CLARKE** – guitar / **ANDY HUGHES** – bass / **JIMMY SKIDMORE** – drums / – sax

Parlophone not issued

Jan 71. (7"; as NORMAN HAYNES BAND) *(R 5871)* **DAFFODIL. / AUTUMN MOBILE** -

Sep 71. (lp) *(PCS 7130)* **DEN OF INIQUITY** -
– Life is so unkind / Rabbits / Mr. Armageddon / etc. *(cd-iss.1993 on 'Shoestring'+=;)–* Daffodil / Autumn mobile / Give it to the girl / Elaine / I really need a friend.

Jul 72. (7"; as NORMAN HAINES) *(R 5960)* **GIVE IT TO YOU GIRL. / ELAINE** -

LOKOMOTIVE KREUZBERG

Formed: Berlin, Germany . . .1972 by a group of left-leaning activists as a vehicle for their political satire. Much like FLOH DE COLOGNE, the band were big on cabaret style performance and albums such as 'JAMES BLOND' (1973) were mock concept affairs that parodied a gamut of rock stylings. 'FETTE JAHRE' (1975) is generally considered to be their best effort and the band subsequently quit after 1977's 'MOUNTAIN TOWN'.

Recommended: FETTE JAHRE (*6)

ANDREAS BAUER – vocals, keyboards, electric violin, synthesizer / **VOLKER HIEMANN** – vocals, guitar / **UWE HOLZ** – vocals, drums, harmonica / **FRANZ POWALLA** – vocals, bass / **KALLE SCHERFLING** – vocals

Plane not issued

1972. (lp) *(S 99101)* **KOLLEGE KLATT** - - German
– Abfahrt / Ein mann geht die strasse lang – 1 / Was glaubst du was du bist / Wenn ick nach de arbeit / Ich konnt / Ein kommunist wohl sein / Ein mann geht die strasse lang – 2 / Lohnpredigt / Geldsack / Solidaritaetslied.

— *MANFRED PRAEKER* – vocals, bass, guitar; repl. POWALLA

1973. (lp) *(S 99103)* **JAMES BLOND** - - German
– Criminalis / J.B. sjuperman / Guten morgen, herr Blond / Arbeitsunfall / Streiklied / Wohlfundierte Thesen / Burdas ball / Speed, king & co.

— **UWE MULLRICH** – guitar; repl. HIEMANN

1974. (7") **CHILE '73. / HEY MR. AMERIKA** - - German

— **BERNHARD POTSCHKA** – guitar; repl. UWE MULLRICH to EMBRYO

1975. (lp) *(S 99104)* **FETTE JAHRE** - - German
– Rondo / Comeback / Requiem / Fette Jahre / Nostalgie / Leise sohlen / Verfassungslied / Parlamentsmarsch.

1976. (7") **ARBEITSLOS. / TEDDY TEX** - - German

— **HERWIG MITTEREGGER** – drums, percussion; repl. SCHERFLING

1977. (lp) *(S 99105)* **MOUNTAIN TOWN** - - German
– Mountain town song / Fruhmorgens / Herr Quittegelb / Marie P. / Billie der Bulle / Tempo man.

— left the business after above

Ray LONEY (see under ⇒ FLAMIN' GROOVIES)

LOST AND FOUND

Formed: Houston, Texas, USA . . . 1965, by PETER BLACK, JIMMY FROST, JAMES HARRELL and STEVE WEBB (having changed their name from The MISFITS). They secured a 6-month residency at their local Living Eye club, soon becoming friendly with ROKY ERICKSON (13th FLOOR ELEVATORS) who set them up with 'International Artists' in 1966. The following year, their debut album, 'EVERYBODY'S HERE', surfaced unearthing some excellent fuzztones, including their re-working of The 13th FLOOR ELEVATORS' 'DON'T FALL DOWN'. However, after a second 45, 'WHERE WILL YOU COME THROUGH', which was to precede another album, they folded. A month touring with The MUSIC MACHINE was cited as the reason. Ten years later, they were back for a one-off get-together gig at London's Hope & Anchor, where punters were given a freebie EP which included their finest track, 'THERE WOULD BE NO DOUBT'.

Recommended: EVERYBODY'S HERE (*7)

PETER BLACK – vocals, bass / **JIMMY FROST** – lead guitar / **JAMES HARRELL** – bass / **STEVE WEBB** – drums

not issued Int.Artists

1967. (7") *<120>* **FOREVER LASTING PLASTIC WORDS. / EVERYBODY'S HERE** -

1967. (lp) *<IALP-3>* **EVERYBODY'S HERE** -
– Forever lasting plastic words / Everybody's here / There would be no doubt / Don't fall down / Zig zag blues / Let me be / I realize / 2 stroke blues / I'm so hip to pain / Living eye. *(UK-iss.Mar88 as 'LOST & FOUND' on 'Decal'; LIK 23) (cd-iss.Jan95 as 'FOREVER LASTING PLASTIC WORDS' on 'Eva'; 642420342)*

1968. (7") *<125>* **WHERE WILL YOU COME THROUGH. / PROFESSOR BLACK** -

— disbanded after above and BLACK soon joined ENDLE ST. CLOUD

LOTHAR & THE HAND PEOPLE

Formed: Denver, Colorado, USA . . . 1965, although the band quickly relocated to New York. Drop-out JOHN ARTHUR EMELIN was joined by TOM LYLE, RUSTY FORD, RICHARD LEWIS and WILLIAM C. WRIGHT. The latter two were ousted in favour of KIM KING and PAUL CONLY, prior to their debut single, 'L-O-V-E'. EMELIN's eerie sounding theremin (once used for films and The BEACH BOYS' 'Good Vibrations'), was a feature of their 1968 album, 'PRESENTING . . .'. Electronic psychedelic-rock combining technology with peace and love, it contained the excellent synth classic, 'MACHINES'. Characterised by robotic rhythm, it might have been an influence on the young GARY NUMAN before he formed TUBEWAY ARMY (who knows?). Produced by ROBERT MARGOULEFF (TONTO'S EXPANDING HEAD BAND), the album preceded their rush-released final recording, 'SPACE HYMNS'. • **Trivia:** 90's acid-techno pioneers, The CHEMICAL BROTHERS sampled the band on their 1997 album, 'Dig Your Own Hole'.

Recommended: THIS IS IT, MACHINES (*7)

JOHN ARTHUR EMELIN – vocals, theremin / **KIM KING** – Moog, guitar, tapes / **PAUL CONLEY** – keyboards, Moog / **RUSTY FORD** – bass / **TOM FLYE** – percussion

Capitol Capitol

1967. (7") *<5874>* **L-O-V-E. / ROSE COLORED GLASSES** [-] [ ]
1967. (7") *<5945>* **EVERY SINGLE WORD. / COMIC STRIP** [-] [ ]
1967. (7") *<2008>* **HAVE MERCY. / LET THE BOY PRETEND** [-] [ ]
Nov 68. (7") *<2376>* **MACHINES. / MILKWEED LOVE** [-] [ ]
1968. (lp) *<2997>* **PRESENTING . . . LOTHAR & THE HAND PEOPLE** [-] [ ]
– Machines / This is it / This may be goodbye / That's another story / Ha (ho) / Sex and violence / Bye bye love / You won't be lonely / It comes on anyhow. *(cd-iss.Sep94 on 'One Way'; OW 52117960)*
1969. (7") *<2556>* **MIDNIGHT RANGER. / YES, I LOVE YOU** [-] [ ]
Sep 69. (7") *(CL 15610)* **SDRAWKCAB (BACKWARDS). / TODAY IS ONLY YESTERDAY'S TOMORROW** [ ] [-]
Jan 70. (lp) *<(E-ST 247)>* **SPACE HYMN** [ ] [ ] 1969
– Yes, I love you / Today is only yesterday's tomorrow / Midnight ranger / Sister lonely / Wedding night for those who love / Heat wave / Say, I do / What grows on your head / Sdrawkcab (backwards) / Space hymn.

— another to blow the fuse before the 70's electric-age

– compilations, etc. –

Aug 86. (lp) *See For Miles; (SEE 75)* **THIS IS IT, MACHINES** [ ] [-]
– (nearly all of above). *(re-iss.Jun91 lp/cd; SEE/+CD 75)*

y as The GRASS … YAN MacLEAN. … NKA (the latter … e same … zman's … arach's … ith The … LOVE … fter, an … verthe- … the two … ss with … 67, they … ious 20- … SKIES', … E CAS- … he band … e of the … acoustic … st every … album's … to chart. … sition of … brilliant … E sacked … formed … FAYAD, … e-up cut … with two … ally LEE … he album … -created … mmercial … e-unions … e going … -formed … current … agnosed … ence for … AN until … initiate … OD and … album, … n illegal

…commended: LOVE (*6) / DA CAPO (*8) / FOREVER CHANGES ([illegible]) / COMES IN COLOURS (*8)

ARTHUR LEE (b. ARTHUR TAYLOR PORTER, 1945, Memphis, Tennessee) – vocals, guitar (ex-LAG'S, ex-AMERICAN FOUR) / **BRYAN MacLEAN** (b.1947) – guitar, vocals / **JOHN ECHOLS** (b.1945, Memphis) – lead guitar (ex-LAG'S) / **KEN FORSSI** (b.1943, Cleveland, Ohio) – bass (ex-SURFARIS) / **ALBAN 'SNOOPY' PFISTERER** (b.1947, Switzerland) – drums repl. DON CONKA

London Elektra

Mar 66. (7") *<45603>* **MY LITTLE RED BOOK. / A MESSAGE TO PRETTY** [-] [52]
Jun 66. (7") *(HLZ 10053)* **HEY JOE. / MY LITTLE RED BOOK** [ ] [-]
Sep 66. (7") *(HLZ 10073) <45605>* **7 AND 7 IS. / NO. FOURTEEN** [ ] [33] Aug66

Elektra Elektra

Sep 66. (lp; mono/stereo) *<(EKL/EKS 7-4001)>* **LOVE** [ ] [57] Jul66
– My little red book / A message to Pretty / Softly to me / Emotions / Gazing / Signed D.C. / Mushroom clouds / Can't explain / My flash on you / No matter what you do / You I'll be following / Hey Joe / Coloured bells falling / And more. *(re-iss.Jan72 lp/c; K/K4 42068) (re-iss.Feb87 on 'Edsel'; ED 218) (cd-iss.Feb93 & Dec93; 755974001-2)*

— added **MICHAEL STUART** – drums (ex-SONS OF ADAM) ('SNOOPY' now on keyboards) + **TJAY CANTRELLI** – saxophone

Dec 66. (7") *(EKSN 45010) <45608>* **SHE COMES IN COLOURS. / ORANGE SKIES** [ ] [ ]
Feb 67. (lp; mono/stereo) *<(EKL/EKS 7-4005)>* **DA CAPO** [ ] [80]
– Stephanie knows who / Orange skies / Que vida / 7 and 7 is / The castle / She comes in colors / Revelation. *(re-iss.Jan72 lp/c; K/K4 42011) (cd-iss.1989 on 'WEA'; 974005-2)*
Mar 67. (7") *<45613>* **QUE VIDA (edit). / HEY JOE** [-] [ ]
Sep 67. (7") *(EKSN 45016)* **THE CASTLE. / SOFTLY TO ME** [ ] [-]

— Reverted to a quintet when 'SNOOPY' and TJAY left. (latter to DOMINIC TROIANO)

Jan 68. (7") *<45629>* **ALONE AGAIN OR (edit). / A HOUSE IS NOT A MOTEL** [-] [ ]
Jan 68. (7") *(EKSN 45024)* **ALONE AGAIN OR. / BUMMER IN THE SUMMER** [ ] [-]
(re-iss.Oct70; 2101-019)
Feb 68. (lp; mono/stereo) *<(EKL/EKS 7-4013)>* **FOREVER CHANGES** [24] [ ] Jan68
– Alone again or / A house is not a motel / The Daily planet / Andmoreagain / Old man / The red telephone / Between Clark and Hilldale / Live and let live / Good honor man / Everything like this / Bummer in the summer / You set the scene. *(re-iss.Jan72 lp/c; K/K4 42015) (cd-iss.Jul88 on 'WEA'; 960656-2)*
Mar 68. (7") *(EKSN 45024)* **ANDMOREAGAIN. / THE DAILY PLANET** [ ] [-]
Sep 68. (7") *(EKSN 45038) <45633>* **YOUR MIND AND WE BELONG TOGETHER. / LAUGHING STOCK** [ ] [ ]

— ARTHUR LEE dismissed others and recruited new people below **JAY DONELLAN** (LEWIS) – guitar / **JIM HOBSON** – keyboards / **FRANK FAYAD** – bass / **GEORGE SURANOVICH** – drums

— augmented by **PAUL MARTIN** and **GARY ROWLES** – guitar plus **DRACKEN THEAKER** – keyboards (ex-CRAZY WORLD OF ARTHUR BROWN)

Nov 69. (lp) *<(EKS 74049)>* **FOUR SAIL** [ ] [ ] Sep69
– August / Your friend and mine – Neil's song / I'm with you / Good times / Singing cowboy / Dream / Robert Montgomery / Nothing / Talking in my sleep / Always see your face. *(re-iss.Jan72 lp/c; K/K4 42030) (re-iss.Nov87 on 'Thunderbolt'; THBL 047) (cd-iss.Jun88; CDBT 047)*
Mar 70. (7") *(EKSN 45086)* **I'M WITH YOU. / ROBERT MONTGOMERY** [ ] [-]

Harvest Blue Thumb

May 70. (d-lp) *(SHDW 3-4) <BTS 9000>* **OUT HERE** [29] [ ] Dec69
– I'll pray for you / Abalony / Signed D.C. / Listen to my song / I'm down / Stand out / Discharged / Doggone / I still wonder / Love is more than words or better late than never / Nice to be / Car lights on in the day time blues / Run to the top / Willow willow / Instra-mental / You are something / Gather round. *(re-iss.Jul88 on 'Big Beat' lp; WIKA 69) (cd-iss.Jul90; CDWIKA 69)*
May 70. (7") *<BLU-7 106>* **I'LL PRAY FOR YOU. / STAND OUT** [-] [ ]
Nov 70. (7") *(HAR 5030) <BLU-7 116>* **KEEP ON SHINING. / THE EVERLASTING FIRST** [ ] [ ]

— **GARY ROWLES** now full time , repl. JAY

Jan 71. (lp) *(SHVL 787) <BTS 8822>* **FALSE START** [ ] [ ] Dec 70
– The everlasting first / Flying / Gimi a little break / Stand out / Keep on shining / Anytime / Slick Dick / Love is coming / Feel daddy feel good / Ride that vibration. *(cd-iss.Jul92 on 'Beat Goes On'; BGOCD 127) (cd re-iss.Apr94 on 'One Way'; MCAD 22029)*
Mar 71. (7") *(HAR 5014)* **STAND OUT. / DOGGONE** [ ] [-]

ARTHUR LEE

— a solo venture with BAND AID: **FAYAD** and new men **CHARLES KARP** – guitar / **CRAIG TARWATER** – guitar / **CLARENCE McDONALD** – keyboards / **DON PONCHA** – drums / + guest **DAVID HULL** – bass

A&M A&M

Aug 72. (lp) *(AMLS 64356) <SP 4356>* **VINDICATOR** [ ] [ ]
– Sad song / You can save up to 50% / Love jumped through my window / Find somebody / He said she said / Everytime I look up / Everybody's gotta live / He knows a lot of good women / You want change for your re-run / Hamburger breath stinkfinger / Ol' morgue mouth / Busted feet. *(cd-iss.Apr97; 540697-2)*
Aug 72. (7") *<1361>* **EVERYBODY'S GOT TO LIVE. / LOVE JUMPED THROUGH MY WINDOW** [-] [ ]
Nov 72. (7") *<1381>* **SAD SONG. / YOU WANT TO CHANGE FOR YOUR RE-RUN** [-] [ ]

LOVE

— **ARTHUR LEE** recruited **MELVIN WHITTINGTON** + **JOHN STERLING** – guitar / **SHERWOOD AKUNA** + **ROBERT ROZENO** – bass / **JOE BLOCKER** – drums

R.S.O. R.S.O.

Dec 74. (7") *<SO 502>* **TIME IS LIKE A RIVER. / WITH A LITTLE ENERGY** [-] [ ]
Jan 75. (7") *(2090 151)* **TIME IS LIKE A RIVER. / YOU SAID YOU WOULD** [ ] [-]
Jan 75. (lp) *(2394 145) <SO 4804>* **REEL TO REAL** [ ] [ ]
– Time is like a river / Stop the music / Who are you? / Good old fashioned love / Which witch is which / With a little energy / Singing cowboy / Be thankful for what you got / You said you would / Busted feet / Everybody's gotta live.
Mar 75. (7") *<SO 506>* **YOU SAID YOU WOULD. / GOOD OLD FASHIONED DREAM** [-] [ ]

ARTHUR LEE

— solo again, using loads of session people

Da Capo / not issued

1977. (7"ep) *(CAP 001)* **I DO WONDER / JUST US. / DO YOU KNOW THE SECRET? / HAPPY YOU** [ ] [-]

Beggars Banquet / Rhino

Jul 81. (lp) *(BEGA 26) <RNLP 020>* **ARTHUR LEE** [ ] [ ]
– One / I do wonder / Just us / Happy you / Do you know the secret / One and one / Seven and seven is / Mr. Lee / Bend down / Stay away from evil / Many rivers to cross.

— LOVE re-formed in Autumn '91, with **ARTHUR LEE, DON CONKA, SHUGGIE OTIS** – guitar / **MELLAN WHITTINGTON** – guitar / **SHERWOOD AKUNA** – bass

New Rose / not issued

May 92. (cd/lp) *(ROSE CD/LP 288)* **ARTHUR LEE AND LOVE** [ ] [-]
(re-iss.May94; 422214)

— ARTHUR was diagnosed with Parkinson's Disease in the early 90's (see biog above)

- LOVE compilations etc. -

on 'Elektra' unless mentioned otherwise

Aug 70. (7") *<45700>* **ALONE AGAIN OR. / GOOD TIMES** [-] [99]
Dec 70. (lp) *(2469 009) <EKS 74049>* **LOVE REVISITED** [ ] [ ] Aug70
(re-iss.Jan72 lp/c; K/K4 42091)
Feb 73. (lp/c) *(K/K4 32002)* **LOVE MASTERS** [ ] [-]
– My little red book / Signed D.C. / Hey Joe / 7 and 7 is / Stephanie knows who / Orange skies / Que vida / The castle / She comes in colours / Laughing stock / Your mind / And we belong together / Old man / The Daily Planet / A house is not a motel / Andmoreagain / Alone again or.
Jul 73. (7") *(K 12113)* **ALONE AGAIN OR. / ANDMOREAGAIN** [ ] [-]
(re-iss.Apr84; E 9740)
Sep 76. (7") *(K 12231)* **ALONE AGAIN OR. / THE CASTLE** [ ] [ ]
1980. (lp) *Rhino; <RNLP 800>* **THE BEST OF LOVE** [-] [ ]
1981. (pic-lp) *Rhino; <RNDF 251>* **LOVE LIVE (live)** [-] [ ]
1982. (lp) *M.C.A.; <27025>* **STUDIO / LIVE** [-] [ ]
(UK cd-iss.Apr94 on 'One Way'; MCAD 22036)
1986. (lp) *Rhino; <RNLP 70175>* **GOLDEN ARCHIVE** [-] [ ]
Jan 93. (cd) *Raven; (RVCD 29)* **COMES IN COLOURS** [ ] [-]
– My little red book / Can't explain / Message to pretty / Softly to me / Hey Joe / Signed D.C. / And more / 7 and 7 is / No.14 / Stephanie knows who / Orange skies / Que vida / The castle / She comes in colors / Alone again or / Andmoreagain / Old man / A house is not a motel / Daily planet / Live and let live / Laughing stock / Your mind and we belong together / August / (Arthur Lee interview).

LOVECRAFT (see under ⇒ H.P. LOVECRAFT)

LOVING AWARENESS (see under ⇒ SKIP BIFFERTY)

LOVIN' SPOONFUL

Formed: Greenwich Village, New York, USA ... early '65 by JOHN SEBASTIAN and ZAL YANOVSKY. They had been part of the N.Y. folk scene during '63-'64 and had played in bands The HALIFAX THREE and The MUGWUMPS, the latter featuring DENNY DOHERTY and CASS ELLIOT (future MAMAS & THE PAPAS). Via producer ERIK JACOBSEN, they secured a deal with the 'Kama Sutra' label, issuing debut 45, 'DO YOU BELIEVE IN MAGIC', which hit the US Top 10. A string of hits followed, including a 1966 US No.1, 'SUMMER IN THE CITY'. Its jaunty momentum was preceded by the meandering 'DAYDREAM', a No.2 on both sides of the Atlantic and the perfect soundtrack for "rolling a fat one" on a lazy mid-summer's afternoon. Unfortunately for the band and especially YANOVSKY, the LOVIN' SPOONFUL had a renowned penchant for doing just that, amid other more serious narcotic dabblings. After a bust, he was allegedly sent packing by the rest of the band in 1967 for informing on his dealer. The next album, 'EVERYTHING PLAYING', lacked the effervescent sparkle of their previous material and stiffed big style. With nary a hit single in sight, the band struggled on with, ironically, YANOVSKY replacing the recently departed SEBASTIAN for a final lacklustre album. While the band's vaguely psychedelic pop was fine in 1966, by the following year's 'Summer of love' the 'SPOONFUL's happy go lucky ditties appeared a bit lukewarm in contrast to the cosmic soul searching of many other bands, especiallly their L.A. counterparts THE BYRDS and LOVE. Nevertheless, their jug-band pop/rock still has the power to put a smile on the glummest of faces and as well as the hits there were more than a few sweetly charming tracks like 'DARLIN' COMPANION' tucked away on their albums. SEBASTION was the only member to have any kind of solo success although the band regrouped fleetingly in 1980 for a guest appearance on Paul Simon's 'One Trick Pony'. • **Songwriters:** SEBASTIAN (with some traditional arrangements of 30's songs) until his departure when BUTLER was virtually going solo under LOVIN' SPOONFUL banner, although using pensmiths BONNER and GORDON. Covered; YOU BABY (Ronettes) / OTHER SIDE OF THIS LIFE (Fred Neil) / ALMOST GROWN (Chuck Berry) / SEARCHIN' (Coasters) / NEVER GOING BACK (John Stewart) / etc.

Recommended: THE COLLECTION (*7)

JOHN SEBASTIAN (b.17 Mar'44, New York City, N.Y.) – vocals, guitar, harmonica, autoharp / **ZALMAN YANOVSKY** (b.19 Dec'44, Toronto, Canada) – guitar, vocals / **STEVE BOONE** (b.23 Sep'43, Camp Lejeune, New Connecticut) – bass, vocals / **JOE BUTLER** (b.16 Sep'43, Long Island, N.Y.) – drums, vocals

Pye Int. / Kama Sutra

Oct 65. (7") *(7N 25327) <201>* **DO YOU BELIEVE IN MAGIC. / ON THE ROAD AGAIN** [ ] [9] Jul65
Jan 66. (7") *(7N 25344) <205>* **YOU DIDN'T HAVE TO BE SO NICE. / MY GAL** [ ] [10] Nov65
Mar 66. (lp; mono/stereo) *(NPL 28069) <KLP/+S 8050>* **DO YOU BELIEVE IN MAGIC** [ ] [32] Nov65
– Do you believe in magic / Blues in the bottle / Sportin' life / My gal / You baby / Fishin' blues / Did you ever have to make up your mind / Wild about my lovin' / Other side of this life / Younger girl / On the road again / Night owl blues.
Apr 66. (7") *(7N 25361) <208>* **DAYDREAM. / NIGHT OWL BLUES** [2] [2] Feb66
May 66. (lp; mono/stereo) *(NPL 28078) <KLP/+S 8051>* **DAYDREAM** [8] [10] Mar66
– Daydream / There she is / It's not time now / Warm baby / Day blues / Let the boy rock and roll / Jug band music / Didn't want to have to do it / You didn't have to be so nice / Bald headed Lena / Butchie's tune / Big noise from Speonk. *(re-iss.1990 on 'Castle' lp/cd; CLA/+CD 194)*
May 66. (7") *<209>* **DID YOU EVER HAVE TO MAKE UP YOUR MIND. / DIDN'T WANT TO HAVE TO DO IT** [-] [2]

Kama Sutra / Kama Sutra

Jul 66. (7") *<211>* **SUMMER IN THE CITY. / BUTCHIE'S TUNE** [-] [1]
Jul 66. (7") *(KAS 200)* **SUMMER IN THE CITY. / BALD HEADED LENA** [8] [-]
Sep 66. (lp; mono/stereo) *<KLP/+S 8053>* **WHAT'S UP, TIGER LILY (Soundtrack)** [-] [ ]
– (introduction to Flick) / POW / Gray prison blues / POW revisited / Unconscious minuet / Fishin' blues / Respoken / A cool million / Speakin' of spoken / Lookin' to spy / Phil's love theme / (end title).
Oct 66. (7") *<216>* **RAIN ON THE ROOF. / POW** [-] [10]
Oct 66. (7") *(KAS 201)* **RAIN ON THE ROOF. / WARM BABY** [ ] [-]
Dec 66. (lp; mono/stereo) *(KLP 401) <KLP/+S 8054>* **HUMS OF THE LOVIN' SPOONFUL** [ ] [14] Nov66
– Sittin' here lovin' you / Bes' friends / Voodoo in the basement / Darlin' companion / Henry Thomas / Full measure / Rain on the roof / Coconut grove / Nashville cats / 4 eyes / Summer in the city. *(re-iss.1990 on 'Castle' lp/cd; CLA/+CD 195)*
Dec 66. (7") *(KAS 204) <219>* **NASHVILLE CATS. / FULL MEASURE** [26] [8] [87]
Feb 67. (7") *(KAS 207) <220>* **DARLING BE HOME SOON. / DARLIN' COMPANION** [44] [15]
Apr 67. (7") *<225>* **SIX O'CLOCK. / YOU'RE A BIG BOY NOW** [-] [18]
May 67. (lp; mono/stereo) *(KLP 402) <KLP/+S 8058>* **YOU'RE A BIG BOY NOW (Soundtrack)** [ ] [ ] Apr67
– You're a big boy now / Lonely (Amy's theme) / Wash her away / Kite chase / Try and be happy / Peep show percussion / Girl, beautiful girl / Darling be home soon / Dixieland big boy / Letter to Barbara / Barbara's theme / Miss Thing's thang / March / The finale.
May 67. (lp; mono/stereo) *(KLP 403) <KLP/+S 8056>* **THE BEST OF THE LOVIN' SPOONFUL** (compilation) [ ] [3] Mar67
– Do you believe in magic / Did you ever have to make up your mind / Butchie's tune / Jug band music / Night owl blues / You didn't have to be so nice / Daydream / Blues in the bottle / Didn't want to have to do it / Wild about my lovin' / Younger girl / Summer in the city. *(re-iss.Mar69 on 'Marble Arch'; MAL 1115)*
May 67. (7") *(KAS 208)* **SIX O'CLOCK. / THE FINALE** [ ] [-]
Jul 67. (7") *<231>* **YOU'RE A BIG BOY NOW. / LONELY (AMY'S THEME)** [-] [ ]

— **JERRY YESTER** – guitar, vocals (ex-MODERN FOLK QUARTET) repl. YANOVSKY who was ostracized by rest, after reportedly being busted for drugs and incriminating others to avoid prosecution and deportation back to Canada.

Oct 67. (7") *(KAS 210) <239>* **SHE IS STILL A MYSTERY. / ONLY PRETTY, WHAT A PITY** [ ] [27]
Nov 67. (7") *(KAS 211) <241>* **MONEY. / CLOSE YOUR EYES** [ ] [48]
Mar 68. (lp) *(KLP 404) <KLPS 8061>* **EVERYTHING PLAYING** [ ] [ ] Jan68
– She is still a mystery / Priscilla millionaira / Boredom / Six o'clock / Forever / Darling be home soon / Younger generation / Money / Old folks / Only pretty, what a pity / Try a little bit / Close your eyes. *(cd-iss.Feb97 on 'Wooden Hill'; (HILLCD 11)*
May 68. (lp; mono/stereo) *(KLP/+S 405) <KLPS 8064>* **THE BEST OF THE LOVIN' SPOONFUL VOL. 2** (compilation) [ ] [ ] Mar68
– Money / She is still a mystery / Younger generation / Six o'clock / Darling be home soon / lovin' you / Boredom / Full measure / Nashville cats / Rain on the roof / Darlin' companion. *(re-iss.Mar69 on 'Marble Arch'; MAL 1116)*

— Now a trio (BUTLER now vocals) after SEBASTIAN left to go solo.

Oct 68. (7") *(KAS 213) <250>* **NEVER GOING BACK. / FOREVER** [ ] [73] Jul68
Oct 68. (7") *<251>* **(TIL I) RUN WITH YOU. / REVELATION** [-]
Jan 69. (7") *<255>* **ME ABOUT YOU. / AMAZING AIR** [-] [91]
Jun 69. (lp; by The LOVIN' SPOONFUL featuring JOE BUTLER) *(620 009) <8073>* **REVELATION: REVOLUTION '69** [ ] [ ] Mar69
– Amazing air / Never going back / The prophet / Only yesterday / War games / (Til I) Run with you / Jug of wine / Revelation: revolution '69 / Me about you / Words.

— BUTLER was virtually solo, with BONNER & GORDON the main songwriters.

— In 1969, BUTLER packed in group name. 20 years later BUTLER, BOONE, JERRY YESTER and brother JIM YESTER re-formed for US concerts.

- more compilations, etc. -

on 'Kama Sutra' unless mentioned

Jun 66. (7"ep) *(KEP 300)* **DID YOU EVER HAVE TO MAKE UP YOUR MIND** [ ] [-]
Aug 66. (7"ep) *(KEP 301)* **JUG BAND MUSIC** [ ] [-]
Oct 66. (7"ep) *(KEP 302)* **SUMMER IN THE CITY** [ ] [-]
Feb 67. (7"ep) *(KEP 303)* **DAY BLUES** [ ] [-]
Apr 67. (7"ep) *(KEP 304)* **NASHVILLE CATS** [ ] [-]
Jun 67. (7"ep) *(KEP 305)* **LOVIN' YOU** [ ] [-]
Oct 67. (7"ep) *(KEP 306)* **SOMETHING IN THE NIGHT** [ ] [-]
Dec 68. (7") *(KAS 215)* **SUMMER IN THE CITY. / DAYDREAM** [ ] [-]

(re-iss.Sep73; 2013 072) (re-iss.Jan83 on 'Flashback'; FBS 22) (re-iss.1985 on 'WEA'; U 9023) (re-iss.Oct88 on 'Old Gold'; OG 9799)

Jun 70. (7") *(2013 009)* **DARLING BE HOME SOON. / NEVER GOING BACK**

Jun 71. (7"m) *(2013 023)* **SUMMER IN THE CITY. / DAYDREAM / DO YOU BELIEVE IN MAGIC?**

Dec 71. (lp) *(2361 002)* **ONCE UPON A TIME**

Jan 72. (lp) *(2361 003)* **JOHN SEBASTIAN SONGBOOK**

Oct 73. (d-lp) *(2683 034)* **GOLDEN SPOONFUL**
(re-iss.Aug74; KSMD 9001)

Aug 74. (lp) *(2683 042)* **MORE GOLDEN SPOONFUL**
(re-iss.Aug74; KSMD 9002)

1974. (lp/c) *Golden Hour; (GH 838)* **GOLDEN HOUR OF THE LOVIN' SPOONFUL'S GREATEST HITS**
(re-iss.1990 on 'Knight' cd/c; KGH CD/MC 109)

Jul 75. (7") *(KSS 705)* **DAYDREAM. / YOU BABY**

May 76. (d-lp) *<2608>* **THE BEST OF THE LOVIN' SPOONFUL VOLS.1 & 2**

1977. (d-lp) *Pye; (FILD 009)* **THE FILE SERIES**

1977. (12"ep) *Buddah; (BD 118)* **SUMMER IN THE CITY / NASHVILLE CATS. / DAYDREAM / DO YOU BELIEVE IN MAGIC**

1978. (7") *Buddah; (BDS 474)* **SUMMER IN THE CITY. / NASHVILLE CATS**

Jun 80. (7"ep) *Pye Flashback; (FBEP 100)* **SUMMER SOUNDS**

1983. (lp) *Breakaway; (BWY 67)* **DISTANT ECHOES**

Apr 83. (10"lp/c) *P.R.T.; (DOW/ZCDOW 9)* **BEST IN THE WEST**

Apr 83. (7") *Old Gold; (OG 9291)* **DAYDREAM. / DO YOU BELIEVE IN MAGIC**

Mar 84. (7"ep/c-ep) *Scoop;* **6 TRACK HITS**

Jul 84. (7") *Old Gold; (OG 9415)* **SUMMER IN THE CITY. / (B-side by "Lemon Pipers")**

Jul 85. (lp/c) *Buddah; (252274-1/-4)* **GREATEST HITS**

1986. (lp) *Edsel; (ED 178)* **JUG BAND MUSIC**

1987. (c) *Design; (DSK 109)* **NASHVILLE CATS**

May 88. (lp/c/cd) *See For Miles; (SEE/+K/CD 229)* **THE EP COLLECTION**

1988. (d-lp/d-c/d-cd) *That's Original; (TFO LP/MC/CD 12)* **DO YOU BELIEVE IN MAGIC / EVERYTHING PLAYING**

Aug 88. (d-lp/c/cd) *Castle; (CCS LP/MC/CD 187)* **THE COLLECTION**
– Do you believe in magic / Did you ever have to make up your mind / Younger girl / Jug band music / Didn't want to have to do it / Daydream / You're a big boy now / Wash her away / Girl beautiful girl (Barbara's theme) / Bespoken / Darling be home soon / Lookin' to spy / You didn't have to be so nice / Sittin' here lovin' you / Darlin' companion / Rain on the roof / Coconut grove / Summer in the city / She is still a mystery / Boredom / Six o'clock / Younger generation / Till I run with you / Never going back.

1988. (cd-ep) *Special Edition; (CD3-11)* **THE LOVIN' SPOONFUL**

Sep 89. (lp/c/cd) *Mainline; (261530-1/-4/-2)* **20 GREATEST HITS**

1989. (lp) *Success; (2183)* **SUMMER IN THE CITY**
(cd-iss.1990 on 'Movieplay'; MP 74003) (re-iss.Apr93 on 'Pulsar';) (re-iss.cd Jan95 on 'Spectrum'; 550 736-2)

1991. (cd) *Sequel; (NEXCD 176)* **THE LOVIN' SPOONFUL GO TO THE MOVIES**

Dec 93. (cd) *Disky;* **GOLD: GREATEST HITS**

Sep 95. (cd-s) *R.C.A.;* **SUMMER IN THE CITY /**

— a various compilation WHAT'S SHAKIN' featured 4 songs was released Apr66 on 'Elektra'; *EKS 4002>) (re-iss.1988 on 'Edsel'; ED 249)*

LYRICS

Formed: Oceanside, San Diego, California . . . 1959 as a surf act by BILLY GARCIA and STEVE KHAILER. After a series of personnel changes, they settled their line-up in 1964 with BILLY enlisting brother DANNY, along with CRAIG CARLL, MICHAEL ALLEN, GARY NEVES and CHRIS GAYLORD (who had recently substituted GREG LEINHART). Their debut 45, 'SO WHAT!', was a typically earthy, garage-type song that highlighted the raw vox and harmonica of BILLY. He subsequently took off after they signed a new deal with 'Crescendo' in 1966. Three further singles appeared, although none had the appeal of their debut, most supplanting rawness for poppy harmonies.

Recommended: the debut 45

CRAIG CARLL – vocals / **CHRIS GAYLORD** – vocals, harmonica, keyboards / **STEVE KHAILER** – vocals / **BILLY GARCIA** – lead guitar / **MICHAEL ALLEN** – guitar / **DANNY GARCIA** – bass / **GARY NEVES** – drums

not issued Era

1965. (7") *<3153>* **SO WHAT! / THEY CAN'T HURT ME**

— **CLAUDE MATHIS** – drums; repl. NEVES, KHAILER (GAYLORD + ALLEN joined The MAGIC MUSHROOMS)

not issued GNP Crescendo

1966. (7") *<381>* **MY SON. / SO GLAD**

— **JACK FLANERY** – drums; repl. MATHIS

— added **DAVE COMPTON** – keyboards

1967. (7") *<393>* **MR. MAN. / WAIT**

not issued Feather

1968. (7") *<1968>* **WAKE UP TO MY VOICE. / CAN'T SEE YOU ANYMORE**

— after above they split

MAD RIVER

Formed: Antioch College, Yellow Springs, Ohio, USA . . .early '67 by LAWRENCE HAMMOND, DAVID ROBINSON, TOM MANNING and GREG DEWEY. During this time, a rare EP, 'WIND CHIMES' was recorded, the disc including an embryonic version of 'AMPHETAMINE GAZELLE'. They soon moved to Washington, before settling in San Francisco where they recorded an eponymous debut for 'Capitol'. A unique blend of acid folk and country psychedelia, it featured the warbling vocals of HAMMOND, the highlight being 'THE WAR GOES ON'. The second album, 'PARADISE BAR AND GRILL' (now without MANNING), was a more countrified affair, although it still featured acid-fried overtones.

Recommended: MAD RIVER (*7) / PARADISE BAR AND GRILL (*7)

THOMAS MANNING – vocals, guitar, bass / **LAWRENCE HAMMOND** (b. Berkeley, Calif.) – bass, mouth harp, recorder, vocals / **DAVID ROBINSON** – guitar / **GREGORY DEWEY** – drums / **RICK BOCHNER** – guitar, repl. GREG DRUIAN

not issued — Wee

1967. (7"ep) *<10021>* **MAD RIVER** [-] [ ]

Capitol — Capitol

Oct 68. (lp) *<(ST 2985)>* **MAD RIVER** [ ] [ ]
– Merciful monks / High all the time / Amphetamine gazelle / Eastern light / Wind chimes / The war goes on / Hush, Julian. *(re-iss.Mar85 on 'Edsel'; ED 140) (cd-iss.Sep90; EDCD 140)*

Oct 68. (7") *<2310>* **AMPHETAMINE GAZELLE. / HIGH ALL THE TIME** [-] [ ]

— MANNING only guested on below having departed near release date.

Jul 69. (lp) *<ST 185>* **PARADISE BAR AND GRILL** [-] [ ]
– Harfy Magnum / Paradise bar and grill / Love's not the way to treat a friend / Leave me – Stay / Copper plates / Equinox / They brought sadness / Revolution's in my pockets / Academy Cemetery / Cherokee queen. *(re-iss.May86 on 'Edsel'; ED 188) (cd-iss.Feb91; EDCD 188)*

Aug 69. (7") *<2559>* **COPPER PLATES. / HARFY MAGNUM** [-] [ ]

— Folded in Aug'69. DEWEY joined COUNTRY JOE & THE FISH. HAMMOND later formed The WHIPLASH BAND in 1976 and released 'Takoma' US lp 'COYOTE'S DREAM'.

MAGIC MIXTURE

Formed: London, England . . . 1967 by JIM THOMAS, JACK COLLINS, STAN CURTIS and MERVYN HACKER. They only managed to squeeze out one semi-psychedelic classic, 'THIS IS' (1968), which highlighted the fine, '(I'M SO) SAD'. When they split, the record went on to be quite a collector's item, while THOMAS went into session work.

Recommended: THIS IS (*7)

JOM THOMAS – vocals, guitar / **STAN CURTIS** – organ / **MERVYN HACKER** – bass / **JACK COLLINS** – drums

Saga — not issued

1968. (lp) *(FID 2125)* **THIS IS** [ ] [-]
(re-iss.1988 on 'Bat' Germany; 4215) (cd-iss.1992 on 'Merlin' Germany; MER 1)

— as said they disappeared after above

MAGMA

Formed: Paris, France . . .late 60's by CHRISTIAN VANDER – a man on an interstellar trip, vastly influenced by the legendary jazz saxophonist JOHN COLTRANE. VANDER also cited other greats such as STRAVINSKY, STOCKHAUSEN and another jazz giant, ORNETTE COLEMAN. He collected together a fine array of musicians, including KLAUS BLASQUIZ, to work on his conceptual eponymous double album in 1970. This and the follow-up piece, '1001 DEGREES CENTIGRADE', were to have been the first two parts of a nine-album magnus-opus entitled, THESUK HAMTAAHK, a project which he worked on over the next seven years. Its theme was a self-penned story based on a war/rivalry between Earth and the imaginary planet of KOBAIA, a fantasy world for which he also invented a new language. However, with a new deal for 'A&M' and personnel changes a-plenty by 1973, he cut it to a trilogy, having ended the world (so-to-speak) on the finale of a third album, 'MEKANIK DESTRUCTIV KOMANDOH'. VANDER, his wife STELLA, and his constant, KLAUS BLASQUIZ, set off on a new journey, leading to the creation of a fourth album, 'KOHNTARKOSZ'. This was an ambitious and complex work criticised for its pretentiousness by some sections of the music press, although their appeal remained strong in France; a concert (and double album) at The Taverne de L'Olympia in Paris highlighting why. CHRISTIAN continued to write more sophisticated, if not great work, throughout the latter half of the 70's and 80's. • **Trivia:** The No.1 group of former six-times world snooker champion STEVE DAVIS (mmm . . . very interesting).

Recommended: MAGMA (*8) / 1001 DEGREES CENTIGRADE (*8) / MEKANIK DESTRUCTIV KOMANDOAH (*7) / KOHNTARKKOSK (*6) / MAGMA LIVE (*7)

CHRISTIAN VANDER – drums, percussion, keyboards, vocals / **KLAUS BLASQUIZ** – vocals, percussion / **FRANCOIS CAHEN** – keyboards / **FRANCIS MOZE** – bass / **CLAUDE ENGEL** – guitar, vocals / **LOUIS SARKISSIAN** – saxophone / **STELLA VANDER** – vocals / **TEDDY LASRY** – clarinet, flute, saxophone / **RICHARD RAUX** – flute, saxophone

Philips — not issued

1970. (d-lp) *(6332 007)* **MAGMA** [-] [-] France
– Kobaia / Aina / Malaria / Sohia / Sckxyss / Aurae / Thaud Zaia / Naeu Ektila / Stoah / Muh. *(UK-iss.1974; 63595 1/2) (d-cd-iss.Mar93 on 'Seventh' France; REX 4-5)*

— **JEFF SEFFER** – sax + **LOUIS TOESCA** – trumpet, repl. RAUX, VANDER + ENGEL

1971. (lp) *(6397 031)* **1.001<< >> CENTIGRADES** [-] [-] France
– Riah Sahiltaahk / Iss lansei Doia / Ki lahl oe liahk. *(UK-iss.Mar74; 9101 286) (cd-iss.Apr93 on 'Seventh' France; REX 6)*

— **JANNIK TOP** – bass / **BENOIT WIDEMANN** + **JEAN LUC VANDERLIER** – keyboards / **CLAUDE OLMOS** – guitar / **RENE GARBES** – clarinet, vocals / + 6 female vocalists incl. the return of **STELLA VANDER** (all repl. MOZE, CAHEN, SEFFER + TOESCA)

A&M — A&M

Feb 73. (lp) *(AMLH 64397) <4397>* **MEKANIK DESTRUCTIV KOMMANDOH** [ ] [ ] Dec74
– Hortz fur dehn stekehn west / Ima su ri dondai / Kobaia is de huendin / Da zuhl wortz mekanik / Nebehr gudahtt / Mekanik kommandoh / Kreuehn kohrmahn iss de hundîn. *(re-iss.Nov76; same) (cd-iss.Apr93 on 'Seventh' France; REX 7)*

— **GERALD BIKAILO** + **MICHAEL GRAILLIER** – keyboards / **BRIAN GODDING** – guitar / **ALAIN CHARLERY** – trumpet, repl. MANDERLIER, GARBES, OLMOS, LASRY + WILDMANN

Jun 74. (lp) *(AMLH 88260) <3650>* **KOHNTARKOSZ** [ ] [ ]
– Kohntarkosz (part 1) / Ork alarm / Kohn Tarkosz (part 2) / Mekanik machine / Coltrane sundia. *(re-iss.Nov76; same) (cd-iss.Apr93 on 'Seventh' France; REX 8)*

Jul 74. (7") *(AMS 7119)* **MEKANIK MACHINE. / ('A'instrumental)** [ ] [ ]

— **GABRID FEDEROW** – guitar / **BERNARD PAGANOTTI** – bass, percussion, vocals / **DIDIER LOCKWOOD** – violin / **JEAN-POL ASSELINE** – keyboards, repl. SARKISSIAN, CHARLERY, GRAILLER, BIKAILO + GODDING

Tapioca — not issued

Jan 75. (lp) *(TP 10001)* **IHEDITS** [-] [-] France
– Sowilio – KMX – E XII – Opus 3 / KMX – B XII – Opus 7 / Om Zanka / Gamma / Terrien si je t'ai convoque / Gamma anteria. *(UK cd-iss.Jun97 on 'Seventh'; REX 19)*

— next album with all previous members.

Utopia — Utopia

Jun 75. (d-lp) *(CYL 2-1245) <TOM 2-7008>* **MAGMA LIVE (live at the Tavern de O'Olympia, Paris)** [ ] [ ] Mar79
– Kohntark (parts 1 & 2) / Kobah / Lihns / H hai / Mekanik zain. *(re-iss.Jul88 on 'Decal' lp/c; LIKD/TCLIKD 31) (cd-iss.Jul88 'Charly'; CDCHARLY 118) (re-iss.Dec88 on 'Jaro'; JARO 4122/23) (d-cd re-iss.Apr93 on 'Seventh' France; REX 10-11) (cd re-iss.Jun96 on 'Charly'; CPCD 8171)*

— **PATRICK GAUTHIER** – piano, etc / **ALAIN HATOT** – sax, flute / **PIERRE DUTOUR** – trumpet / + 4 female vocalists, repl. FEDEROW, LOCKWOOD, WIDEMANN + ASSELINE

Utopia — Tomato

1976. (lp) *(1730) <TOM 6001>* **UDU WUDU** [ ] [ ] Mar79
– Udu wudu / Weidorje / Troller tanz (Ghost dance) / Soleil d'ork (Ork'sun) / Zombies / De futura. *(re-iss.Feb88 on 'Decal' lp/c; LIK/TCLIK 18) (cd-iss.Feb88 on 'Charly'; CDCHARLY 105) (cd re-iss.Mar93 on 'Seventh' France; REX 12) (cd re-iss.Apr96 on 'Charly'; CPCD 8169)*

— **CHRISTIAN** + **KLAUS** recruited entire new band; **KAHAL NEGUMUEHRAAHT** – keyboards, synthesizers / **OURGON** + **WURD GORGO** – bass / **THAUD** + **SIHNN** – vocals

R.C.A. — Tomato

1978. (lp) *(200685) <7021>* **ATTAHK** [-] [ ] France
– The last seven minutes (1970-71, phase II) / Spiritual (Negro song) / Rind (Eastern song) / Liriik necronomicus kahnt / Maahnt / Dondai (to an eternal love) / Nono. *(re-iss.Apr88 on 'Decal' lp/c; LIK/TCLIK 26) (cd-iss.Jun88 on 'Charly'; CDCHARLY 111) (cd re-iss.Mar93 on 'Seventh' France; REX 13) (cd re-iss.Apr96 on 'Charly'; CPCD 8170)*

— **VANDER** now brought in past members + numerous others

1981. (lp) **RETROSPECTIVE VOL.1 & 2** (compilation) [-] [-] France
– Mekanik destruktiv kommandoeh / Theusz hamtaahk. *(d-cd-iss.Oct94 on 'Seventh' France; REXXV 1)*

1981. (lp) **RETROSPECTIVE VOL.3** (compilation) [-] [-] France
– Retrovision / H hai / La dawotsin. *(cd-iss.Mar93 on 'Seventh' France; REX 15)*

Jaro — not issued

1985. (lp/cd) *(JARO/+260 4120)* **MERCI** [ ] [-]
– I must return / Eliphas Levi / The night we died / Call from the dark / Do the music / Otis / Otis (ending). *(cd-iss.Apr93 on 'Seventh' France; REX 3)*

Dec 88. (d-lp) *(JARO 4129/30)* **OFFERING** [ ] [-]

A.K.T. — not issued

Nov 92. (cd) *(AKT 1)* **LES VOIX – CONCERT 1992 (live)** [ ] [-]

— must have been their final outing

- compilations, etc. -

Mar 93. (cd) *Seventh; (REX 14)* **MYTHES ET LEGENDES** (early material) [-] [-] France
Nov 94. (d-cd) *Akt IV; (HMCD 70X2)* **THEATRE DU TAUR – CONCERT 1975 – TOULOUSE (live)** [ ] [-]
Aug 95. (cd) *Akt IV; (AKT 5)* **BOBINO 1981 (live)** [ ] [-]

MALLARD

Formed: Glendale, California, USA . . .1975 by ex-CAPTAIN BEEFHEART & HIS MAGIC BAND members; BILL HARKLEROAD (aka ZOOT HORN ROLLO), MARK BOSTON (aka ROCKETTE MORTON) and ART TRIPP III (aka ED MARIMBA). They recruited an unknown frontman SAM GALPIN, who had apparently never heard of BEEFHEART (!), working in a London studio on what was to be their eponymous debut for UK label, 'Virgin'. BEEFHEART (aka Don Van Vliet) held the copyright to anything The MAGIC BAND recorded, so they came up with the name, MALLARD, HARKLEROAD having once described their sound as like the movement of a duck. A second album, 'IN A DIFFERENT CLIMATE', surfaced in 1977, and although it showed an improvement (having been recorded without the departing TRIPP), it was their last outing. • **Trivia:** JOHN 'RABBIT' BUNDRICK guested on debut, while JOHN McFEE was on 2nd.

Recommended: MALLARD (*6) / IN A DIFFERENT CLIMATE (*7)

BILL HARKLEROAD – guitar / **MARK BOSTON** – bass, vocals / **ART TRIPP III** – drums, percussion / **SAM GALPIN** – vocals, piano

Virgin Virgin

Feb 76. (lp) *(V 2045)* **MALLARD** [ ] [-]
– Back on the pavement / She's long she's lean / Road to Morroco / One day once yellow / Desperados waiting for a train / A piece of me / Reign of pain / South of the valley / Winged tuskadero / Peon.

— **GEORGE DRAGGOTA** – drums + **JOHN THOMAS** – keyboards repl. TRIPP

Jan 77. (lp) *(V 2077) <34489>* **IN A DIFFERENT CLIMATE** [ ] [ ]
– Green coyote / Your face on someone else / Harvest / Mama squeeze / Heart strings / Old Mangrey / Texas weather / Big foot.
Feb 77. (7") *(VS 168)* **HARVEST. / GREEN COYOTE** [ ] [-]
Feb 77. (7") *<9514>* **HARVEST. / MAIN SQUEEZE** [-] [ ]

— Ducked out of the limelight after above.

- compilations, etc. -

Apr 94. (cd) *Virgin; (CDDVD 442)* **MALLARD / IN A DIFFERENT CLIMATE** [ ] [-]

MAMAS AND THE PAPAS

Formed: St.Thomas, Virgin Islands, USA . . . 1964 as The NEW JOURNEYMAN by DENNY DOHERTY, and two JOURNEYMEN; JOHN PHILLIPS and MICHELLE GILLIAM. They soon brought in the larger-than-life CASS ELLIOT, relocating to California where they became The MAMAS & THE PAPAS (Mama being Hell's Angels slang for girlfriend). They were introduced to producer and owner of 'Dunhill' records Lou Adler, by 'Eve Of Destruction'-man, BARRY McGUIRE. He contracted them initially as backing singers for McGUIRE's 1965 album, 'Precious Time', which included PHILLIPS' 'CALIFORNIA DREAMIN'. The following year, this classic piece of harmony-orientated folk-pop became their debut 45, hitting the US Top 5. Their follow-up, 'MONDAY MONDAY', topped the charts (No.3 in the UK), succeeded by a string of hits, abruptly halted by the split of the group in '68. This was the result of the eventual marriage break-up of JOHN and MICHELLE, as well as drug busts and alleged record company rip-offs. All subsequently took off on solo ventures, often re-uniting for one-off concerts, etc. Tragically on the 29th of July '74, CASS ELLIOT died of a heart attack while choking on food. In 1982, the three remaining members re-grouped with a new singer, SPANKY McFARLANE (ex-SPANKY & HER GANG). MICHELLE had already began an acting career, that has since seen her in US TV dramas such as 'Knot's Landing'. • **Songwriters:** PHILLIPS penned most. Covered; DANCING IN THE STREET (Martha & The Vandellas) / DEDICATED TO THE ONE I LOVE (Shireles) / DO YOU WANNA DANCE (Bobby Freeman) / I CALL YOUR NAME (Beatles) / etc. In 1967, PHILLIPS wrote No.1 smash, 'SAN FRANCISCO', for late 80's PAPA-to-be SCOTT McKENZIE. Twenty years later, JOHN co-wrote US No.1, 'Kokomo', with The BEACH BOYS. • **Trivia:** On the 31st October 1970, MICHELLE, now divorced from JOHN, married cult actor DENNIS HOPPER (but only for a week!).

Recommended: CREEQUE ALLEY: HISTORY OF . . . (*7)

JOHN PHILLIPS (b.30 Aug'35, Parris Island, South Carolina) – vocals / **CASS ELLIOT** (b. ELLEN NAOMI COHEN, 19 Sep'41, Baltimore, Maryland) – vocals / **MICHELLE GILLIAM** (b. HOLLY MICHELLE GILLIAM, 4 Jun'45, Long Beach, Calif.) – vocals (ex-JOURNEYMEN, with PHILLIPS) (ELLIOT ex-MUGWUMPS with DOHERTY) / **DENNY DOHERTY** (b.29 Nov'41, Halifax, Nova Scotia, Canada) – vocals

R.C.A. Dunhill

Jan 66. (7") *(1503) <4020>* **CALIFORNIA DREAMIN'. / SOMEBODY GROOVY** [23] [4] Dec65
May 66. (7") *(1516) <4026>* **MONDAY MONDAY. / GOT A FEELIN'** [3] [1] Apr66
Jun 66. (lp; mono/stereo) *(RD 7803) <D/DS 50001>* **IF YOU CAN BELIEVE YOUR EYES AND EARS** [3] [1] Feb66
– Do you wanna dance / Go where you wanna go / California dreamin' / Spanish harlem / Somebody groovy / Hey girl / You baby / In crowd / Monday, Monday / Straight shooter / Got a feelin' / I call your name. *(cd-iss.1990 on 'MCA';)*
Jul 66. (7") *(1533) <4031>* **I SAW HER AGAIN. / EVEN IF I COULD** [11] [5] Jun66

— **JILL GIBSON** – vocals repl. MICHELLE for a while

Oct 66. (7") *(1551) <4050>* **LOOK THRU MY WINDOW. / ONCE THERE WAS A TIME I THOUGHT** [ ] [24]

— **MICHELLE** returned when she reconciled with husband JOHN

Jan 67. (lp; mono/stereo) *(RD/SF 7834) <D/DS 50010>* **CASS JOHN MICHELLE DENNY** [24] [4] Sep66
– No salt on her tail / Trip, stumble and fall / Dancing bear / Words of love / My heart stood still / Dancing in the steet / I saw her again / Strange young girl / I can't wait / Even if I could / That kind of girl / Once was a time I thought.
Jan 67. (7") *(1564) <4057>* **WORDS OF LOVE. / DANCING IN THE STREET** [47] [5] / [75] Nov66
Mar 67. (7") *(1576) <4077>* **DEDICATED TO THE ONE I LOVE. / FREE ADVICE** [2] [2] Feb67
Apr 67. (7") *<4083>* **CREEQUE ALLEY. / NO SALT IN HER TAIL** [-] [5]
Jun 67. (lp; mono/stereo) *(RD/SF 7880) <D/DS 50014>* **DELIVER** [4] [2] Mar67
– Dedicated to the one I love / My girl / Creeque Alley / Sing for your supper / Twist and shout / Free advice / Look through any window / Boys and girls together / String man / Frustration / Did you ever want to cry / John's music box.
Jul 67. (7") *(1613)* **CREEQUE ALLEY. / DID YOU EVER WANT TO CRY** [9] [-]
Sep 67. (7") *(1630) <4099>* **12:30 (YOUNG GIRLS ARE COMING TO THE CANYON). / STRAIGHT SHOOTER** [ ] [20] Aug67
Dec 67. (7") *(1649) <4107>* **GLAD TO BE UNHAPPY. / HEY GIRL** [ ] [26] Oct67
Dec 67. (lp; mono/stereo) *<D/DS 50025>* **FAREWELL TO THE FIRST GOLDEN ERA** (compilation) [ ] [5] Oct67
– Dedicated to the one I love / Go where you wanna go / Words of love / Look through any window / Dancing in the street / Monday Monday / Creeque Alley / Got a feelin' / 12:30 (young girls are coming to the canyon) / I call your name / I saw her again last night / California dreamin'.
Dec 67. (7") *<4113>* **DANCING BEAR. / JOHN'S MUSIC BOX** [-] [51]
Jun 68. (7") *(1710) <4125>* **SAFE IN MY GARDEN. / TOO LATE** [ ] [53] May68
Sep 68. (lp; mono/stereo) *(RD/SF 7960) <DS 50031>* **. . .PRESENTING THE PAPAS AND THE MAMAS** [ ] [15] May68
– Dream a little dream of me / Gemini child / Ivy / Mansions / Meditation mama (transcendental woman travels) / Midnight voyage / Nothing's too good for my little girl / Rooms / Safe in my garden / The right somebody to love / Too late / Twelve thirty.
Sep 68. (7") *(1744) <4150>* **FOR THE LOVE OF IVY. / STRANGE YOUNG GIRLS** [ ] [81]
Nov 68. (7") *<4171>* **DO YOU WANNA DANCE. / MY GIRL** [-] [76]

— (Jul68) Disbanded, when JOHN and MICHELLE broke up. JOHN PHILLIPS later went solo, as did DENNY and MICHELLE.

MAMA CASS

had already gone solo.

R.C.A. Dunhill

Aug 68. (7") *(1726) <4145>* **DREAM A LITTLE DREAM OF ME (live). / MIDNIGHT VOYAGE** [11] [12] Jul68
(above also credited with The MAMAS AND THE PAPAS)

Stateside Dunhill

Nov 68. (7") *(SS 8002) 4166>* **CALIFORNIA EARTHQUAKE. / TALKIN' TO YOUR TOOTHBRUSH** [ ] [67] Oct68
Dec 68. (lp; stereo/mono) *(S+/SL 5004) <DS 50040>* **DREAM A LITTLE DREAM** [ ] [87] Oct68
– Dream a little dream of me / California earthquake / The room nobody lives in / Talkin' to your toothbrush / Blues for breakfast / You know who I am / Rubber band / Long time loving you / Jane, the insane dog lady / What was I thinking of / Burn your hatred / Sweet believer.
Feb 69. (7") *<4184>* **MOVE IN A LITTLE BIT CLOSER. / ALL FOR ME** [-] [58]
Mar 69. (7") *(SS 8014)* **MOVE IN A LITTLE BIT CLOSER. / I CAN DREAM, CAN'T I** [ ] [-]
Jul 69. (7") *(SS 8021) <4195>* **IT'S GETTING BETTER. / WHO'S TO BLAME** [8] [30] May69
Nov 69. (lp; stereo/mono) *(S+/SL 5014) <DS 50055>* **BUBBLEGUM, LEMONADE AND . . . SOMETHING FOR MAMA** [ ] [91] Jun69
– Blow me a kiss / It's getting better / Easy come, easy go / I can dream, can't I / Welcome to the world / Lady Love / He's a runner / Move in a little closer, baby / When I just wear my smile / Who's to blame / Sour grapes. *<US re-iss.Nov69 as 'MAKE YOUR OWN KIND OF MUSIC'; DS 50071>*– Make your own kind of music.

MAMA CASS ELLIOT

Nov 69. (7") *(SS 8031) <4114>* **MAKE YOUR OWN KIND OF MUSIC. / LADY LOVE** [ ] [36] Oct69
Mar 70. (7") *(SS 8039) <4225>* **NEW WORLD COMING. / BLOW ME A KISS** [ ] [42] Jan70
Mar 70. (7") *<4226>* **SOMETHING TO MAKE YOU HAPPY. / NEXT TO YOU** [-] [ ]
Sep 70. (7") *(SS 8057) <4244>* **A SONG THAT NEVER COMES. / I CAN DREAM, CAN'T I?** [ ] [99] Jul70
Nov 70. (7") *(4253>* **DON'T LET THE GOOD TIMES PASS YOU BY. / A SONG THAT NEVER COMES** [-] [ ]
Mar 71. (lp) *(SPB 1020) <DS 50093>* **MAMA'S BIG ONES** (compilation) [ ] [ ]
– Dream a little dream of me / Make your own kind of music / It's getting better / Easy come, easy go / Words of love / Move in a little closer, baby / Song that never comes / One way ticket / Ain't nobody else like you / Don't let the good life pass you by / The good times are coming / New world coming. *(re-iss.Oct74 on 'A.B.C.'; ABCL 5011)*

— Late 1970-early 1971, MAMA CASS teamed up with DAVE MASON on some releases.

MAMAS AND THE PAPAS

re-united.

Probe / Dunhill

Nov 71. (lp) *(SPB 1048) <DS 50106>* **PEOPLE LIKE US** [ ] [84] Oct 71
– Dream a little dream of me / Make your own kind of music / It's getting better / Easy come, easy go / Words of love / Move in a closer, baby / Song that never comes / One way ticket / Ain't nobody else like you / Don't let the good life pass you by / The good times are coming / New world coming. *(re-iss.Oct74 on 'A.B.C.'; ABCL 5017) (re-iss.Nov76 on 'Music For Pleasure'; 50299)*

Jan 72. (7") *<4301>* **STEP OUT. / SHOOTING STAR** [-] [81]

Feb 72. (7") *(PRO 552)* **SHOOTING STAR. / NO DOUGH** [ ] [-]

— Break-up, once again for final time. All try-out solo careers.

CASS ELLIOT

went solo again.

R.C.A. / R.C.A.

1972. (7") *(2179) <74-0644>* **BABY I'M YOURS. / CHERRIES JUBILEE** [ ] [ ]

Feb 72. (lp) *<(LSP 4619)>* **CASS ELLIOT** [ ] [ ]
– Introduction – Dream a little dream of me / Extraordinary / I think a lot about you / Don't call me Mama anymore / My love / I'm coming to the best part of my life / The torchsong medley: I came here to sing a torchsong – I got a right to sing the blues – I've got it bad and that ain't good – Mean to me – Why was a born – I came here to sing a torchsong (reprise) / The night before / I like what I like / I'll be seeing you / Closing – I don't call me Mama anymore (reprise).

1972. (7") *<74-0693>* **THAT SONG. / WHEN IT DOESN'T WORK OUT** [-] [ ]

1972. (7") *<74-0764>* **DISNEY GIRLS (1957). / BREAK ANOTHER HEART** [-] [ ]

1973. (7") *<74-0830>* **DOES ANYBODY LOVE YOU. / THE ROAD IS NO PLACE FOR A LADY** [-] [ ]

1973. (lp) *(SF 8306) <LSP 4753>* **THE ROAD IS NO PLACE FOR A LADY** [ ] [ ]
–

1973. (7") *<74-0957>* **LISTEN TO THE WORLD. / I THINK A LOT ABOUT YOU** [-] [ ]

Jul 74. (7") *(LPB 07521)* **IF YOU'RE GONNA BREAK ANOTHER HEART. / DON'T CALL ME MAMA ANYMORE** [ ] [-]

Jul 74. (lp) *<(APL1-0303)>* **DON'T CALL ME MAMA ANYMORE** [ ] [ ]
– Introduction – Dream a little dream of me / Extraordinary / I think a lot about you / Don't call me Mama anymore / My love / I'm coming to the best part of my life / The torchsong medley: I came here to sing a torchsong – I got a right to sing the blues – I've got it bad and that ain't good – Mean to me – Why was a born – I came here to sing a torchsong (reprise) / The night before / I like what I like / I'll be seeing you / Closing – I don't call me Mama anymore (reprise).

— On July '74, CASS ELLIOT died of a heart attack.

– (MAMAS & PAPAS) compilations, etc. –

below on 'Stateside' UK / 'Dunhill' US unless mentioned otherwise

1966. (7"ep) *<50006>* **IF YOU CAN BELIEVE YOUR EYES AND EARS** [-] [ ]

Dec 68. (lp; stereo/mono) *(S+SL 5002) <DS 50038>* **GOLDEN ERA, VOL.2** [ ] [53] Sep68

Feb 69. (7") *(SS 8009)* **YOU BABY. / MY GIRL** [ ] [-]

Apr 69. (lp; stereo/mono) *(S+/SL 5007)* **HITS OF GOLD** [7] [-]
(re-iss.Oct74 on 'A.B.C.'; ABCL 5003) (re-iss.Aug81 on 'M.C.A.'; MCL 1614)

Sep 69. (lp) *<DS 50064>* **16 OF THEIR GREATEST HITS** [-] [61]

Sep 70. (7") *(SS 8058)* **GO WHERE YOU WANNA GO. / NO SALT ON HER TAIL** [ ] [-]

below releases on 'Probe' UK/ 'Dunhill' US unless mentioned otherwise

Oct 70. (d-lp) *(SPB 1013-4) <DS 50073>* **A GATHERING OF FLOWERS** [ ] [ ]

1971. (lp) *<DS 50100>* **MONTEREY INTERNATIONAL POP FESTIVAL (live)** [-] [ ]

Jun 72. (7") *(GFF 102)* **CALIFORNIA DREAMIN'. / DEDICATED TO THE ONE I LOVE** [ ] [-]

1972. (7"ep) *M.C.A.; <50106>* **PEOPLE LIKE US** [-] [ ]

May 73. (d-lp) *(GTSP 200) <DS 50145>* **20 GOLDEN HITS** [ ] [ ] Feb73
(re-iss.Oct74 on 'A.B.C.'; ABCL 5003) (re-iss.Oct80 on 'Music For Pleasure'; 50493) (re-iss.Mar82 on 'M.C.A.'; MCLD 613) (cd-iss.Dec92 on 'Music For Pleasure'; CDMFP 50493)

Sep 73. (7") *(GFF 124)* **MONDAY MONDAY. / CREEQUE ALLEY** [ ] [-]
(re-iss.Sep76 on 'A.B.C.'; 4131)

Jan 74. (lp) *Music For Pleasure; (SPR 90025)* **MONDAY MONDAY** [ ] [-]

Sep 74. (lp) *Music For Pleasure; (SPR 90050)* **CALIFORNIA DREAMING** [ ] [-]
(re-iss.Apr79 on 'Marks & Spencer'; MO 101225)

1976. (lp) *M.C.A.; <30005>* **THE ABC COLLECTION: GREATEST HITS** [-] [ ]

May 77. (lp) *Arcade; (ADEP 30)* **THE BEST OF THE MAMAS AND THE PAPAS** [6] [-]

Jun 80. (7"ep) *M.C.A.; (601)* **MONDAY MONDAY / CALIFORNIA DREAMIN'. / CREEQUE ALLEY / I SAW HER AGAIN** [ ] [-]

Jul 82. (7") *Old Gold; (OG 9175)* **DEDICATED TO THE ONE I LOVE. / CREEQUE ALLEY** [ ] [-]

Jul 82. (7") *Old Gold; (OG 9176)* **CALIFORNIA DREAMIN'. / MONDAY MONDAY** [ ] [-]

Jul 85. (lp) *M.C.A.; (MCM 5001)* **GOLDEN GREATS** [ ] [-]
(cd-iss.Dec88;)

Mar 88. (lp) *Platinum; (PLAT 302)* **THE VERY BEST OF THE MAMAS & THE PAPAS** [ ] [-]

Jun 88. (d-lp/c/cd) *Connoisseur; (VSOP LP/MC/CD 119)* **ELLIOT, PHILLIPS, GILLIAM, DOHERTY** [ ] [-]

Jun 88. (7"; MAMA CASS) *Old Gold; (OG 9796)* **IT'S GETTING BETTER. / DREAM A LITTLE DREAM OF ME** [ ] [-]

Sep 88. (cd) *Pickwick; (PWKS 509)* **THE VERY BEST OF MAMAS & THE PAPAS** [ ] [-]

Nov 88. (d-lp/c/cd) *Castle; (CCS LP/MC/CD 173)* **THE COLLECTION** [ ] [-]

Jul 89. (cd) *Object;* **THE MAMAS & THE PAPAS (live)** [ ] [-]

May 91. (d-cd) *M.C.A.; (MCAD2-10195)* **CREEQUE ALLEY: THE HISTORY OF THE MAMAS & PAPAS** [ ] [ ]
– Wild women / Winken', blinkin' and nod / I'll remember tonight / I don't wanna know / This precious time / (John Phillips dialogue) / California dreamin' / Go where you wanna go / Monday, Monday / You baby / Do you wanna dance / I call your name / Spanish harlem / Straight shooter / Got a feelin' / I saw her again last night / Look through my window / Words of love / Dancing in the street / (Mama Cass dialogue) / Once was a time I thought / No salt in her tail / Trip, stumble and fall / Dancing bear / Dedicated to the one I love / Creeque Alley / My girl / Twist and shout / I call your name / Twelve thirty (young girls are coming to the canyon) / Glad to be unhappy / For the love of Ivy / Safe in my garden / Midnight voyage / Dream a little dream of me / California earthquake / It's getting better / Mississippi / Watcha gonna do / (Mama Cass dialogue) / Step out / The achin' kind.

Jun 92. (cd/c) *See For Miles; (SEE CD/K 333)* **THE EP COLLECTION** [ ] [-]

Nov 93. (d-cd) *Double Platinum; (DBP 102003)* **ALL TIME GREATEST HITS** [ ] [-]

Jul 94. (cd/c) *Success;* **GREATEST HITS LIVE (live)** [ ] [-]

Dec 94. (cd/c) *Polygram TV; (523 973-2/-4)* **CALIFORNIA DREAMING – THE VERY BEST OF THE MAMAS & THE PAPAS** [14] [-]

— JOHN PHILLIPS released a solo album 'THE WOLFKING OF L.A.' in 1970.

— DENNY DOHERTY and MICHELLE PHILLIPS also released solo recordings around the mid 70's. MICHELLE appeared in the TV films 'Dillinger' & 'Valentino' 1977. Early in 1982, the remaining members plus SPANKY McFARLANE (ex-SPANKY & OUR GANG) reformed The MAMAS & THE PAPAS, but only revived 60's circuit. MICHELLE had also been replaced by MacKENZIE PHILLIPS, daughter of JOHN.

MAMMUT

Formed: Germany ... 1971 by KLAUS SCHNUR, PETER SCHNUR, RAINER HOFFMAN, THILO HERRMANN and GUNTHER SEIER. This short-lived band made one of German rock's most sought after albums, an eponymous concept affair, released in 1971. A heady combination of scathing, acid-drenched guitar, elaborate instrumental parts and sound effects, the record was underlaid by a neo classical feel. Incredibly, the album was a one-off and the band released no further material.

Recommended: MAMMUT (*9)

KLAUS SCHNUR – guitars, vocals / **PETER SCHNUR** – guitars, vocals / **RAINER HOFFMAN** – organ, piano / **THILO HERMANN** – bass, flute, vocals / **GUNTHER SEIER** – drums, percussion

Mouse Trick / not issued

1971. (lp) *(none)* **MAMMUT** [-] [-] German
– Bird Mammut / Classical Mammut / Mammut ecstasy / Footmachine Mammut / Short Mammut / Schizoid Mammut / Nagarn Mammut / Mammut opera. *(cd-iss.1992 on 'Ohrwaschl')*

— sadly their only recorded excursion.

MAN

Formed: Merthyr Tydfil, nr. Swansea, Wales . . . 1964 as The BYSTANDERS by MICKY JONES, CLIVE JOHN, RAY WILLIAMS and JEFFREY JONES. They released many 45's during a 4-year period, one of them, '98.6', hitting the Top 50 in early '67. The following year, they amalgamated with another Welsh group, The DREAM, locating singer/guitarist DEKE LEONARD. Signing to 'Pye' in 1969, MAN released their debut album, 'REVELATION', a conceptual affair which contained the European hit, 'EROTICA' (banned in the UK for its simulated orgasm sounds). Their subsequent effort, '2 OZS. OF PLASTIC WITH A HOLE IN THE MIDDLE', was another to embrace the West Coast sound of bands like QUICKSILVER MESSENGER SERVICE. Early in 1970, MARTIN ACE and TERRY WILLIAMS were drafted in to replace RAY and JEFFREY, the new line-up featuring on their eponymous third, rather self-indulgent set. Already established as a consummate live act, they released a fourth album, 'DO YOU LIKE IT HERE NOW, ARE YOU SETTLING IN?', which contained the acid-tinged classic, 'MANY ARE CALLED, BUT FEW GET UP'. The 1972 set (which didn't include the departed DEKE), 'BE GOOD TO YOURSELF AT LEAST ONCE A DAY', boasted yet another lengthy jewel, 'BANANAS'. They finally reached the Top 30 in 1973, with 'BACK TO THE FUTURE', before DEKE returned for an equally successful follow-up, 'RHINOS, WINOS AND LUNATICS'. During the first half of the 70's, MAN were continually dogged by personnel changes, the most recent member, MALCOLM MORLEY, leaving after the aforementioned album. The most astonishing of these personnel upheavals came with the addition of QUICKSILVER MESSENGER SERVICE figurehead/hero, JOHN CIPPOLINA. He stayed for only one album, the Top 30 live-set, 'MAXIMUM DARKNESS'. In 1976, they charted for the final time, with the disappointing, 'WELSH CONNECTION'. They split soon after, DEKE continuing a solo career (with MAN members) until he, MICKEY JONES, MARTIN ACE and JOHN WEATHER reformed the group in 1983. In 1995, they were still going strong, an album, 'CALL DOWN THE MOON, testament to their longevity. • **Songwriters:** Group penned from the 70's, except covers; CODINE (Buffy Sainte-Marie) / I'M GONNA LEAVE YOU (Quicksilver Messenger Service) / LET THE GOOD TIMES ROLL (Shirley & Lee) / etc. • **Trivia:** MAN also featured on the live Various Artists albums, 'GREASY TRUCKERS PARTY VOL.1' and 'CHRISTMAS AT THE PATTI', both on the 'United Artists' label (1972 + 1973).

Recommended: PERFECT TIMING (THE U.A. YEARS 1970-75) (*8) MAXIMUM DARKNESS (*7) / DO YOU LIKE IT HERE NOW, ARE YOU SETTLING IN? (*7)

THE BYSTANDERS

VIC OAKLEY – vocals / **MICKY JONES** – guitar, vocals / **CLIVE JOHN** – keyboards, vocals / **RAY 'TAFF' WILLIAMS** – bass (ex-EYES OF BLUE) / **JEFFREY JONES** – drums

Pylot — not issued

1965. (7") *(WD 501)* **THAT'S THE END. / THIS TIME** — -

Piccadilly — not issued

Jun 66. (7") *(7N 35330)* **(YOU'RE GONNA) HURT YOURSELF. / HAVE I OFFENDED THE GIRL** — -

Oct 66. (7") *(7N 35351)* **MY LOVE – COME HOME. / IF YOU WALK AWAY** — -

Dec 66. (7") *(7N 35363)* **98.6. / STUBBORN KIND OF FELLOW** 45 -

May 67. (7") *(7N 35382)* **ROYAL BLUE SUMMER SUNSHINE DAY. / MAKE UP YOUR MIND** — -

Jul 67. (7") *(7N 35399)* **PATTERN PEOPLE. / GREEN GRASS** — -

Pye — not issued

Feb 68. (7") *(7N 17476)* **WHEN JEZAMINE GOES. / CAVE OF CLEAR LIGHT** — -

Apr 68. (7") *(7N 17540)* **THIS WORLD IS MY WORLD. / PAINTING THE TIME** — -

— (disbanded 1968)

MAN

DEKE LEONARD – guitar, vocals (ex-The DREAM) / **MICKY JONES** – vocals, guitar / plus **CLIVE, RAY + JEFFREY**

Pye — Philips

Jan 69. (7") *(7N 17684)* **SUDDEN LIFE. / LOVE** — -

Jan 69. (lp) *(NSPL 18275)* **REVELATION** (US-title 'MANPOWER')
– And in the beginning . . . / Sudden life / Empty room / Puella! Puella! (woman! woman!) / Love / Erotica / Blind man / And castles rise in children's eyes / Don't just stand there (come in out of the rain) / The missing pieces / The future hides its face. *(re-iss.Oct89 on 'See For Miles' lp/cd; SEE/+CD 274) (cd re-iss.Aug91 on 'Repertoire'; REP 4024WZ)*

Dawn — Philips

Sep 69. (lp) *(DNLS 3003)* **2 OZS OF PLASTIC WITH A HOLE IN THE MIDDLE**
– (prelude) – The storm / It is as it might be / Spunk box / My name is Jesus Smith / Parchment and candles / Brother Arnold's red and white striped tent. *(re-iss.Oct89. on 'See For Miles' lp/cd; SEE/+CD 273)*

— **MARTIN ACE** – bass (ex-The DREAM) repl. RAY who joined The BIG SLEEP / **TERRY WILLIAMS** – drums (ex-The DREAM) repl. JEFFREY

Liberty — U.A.

Oct 70. (lp) *(LBG 83464) <9803>* **MAN**
– Romain / Country girl / Would the Christians wait five minutes? the lions are having a draw / Daughter of the fireplace / The alchemist. *(re-iss.Feb76 as 'MAN 1970' on 'Sunset'; SLS 50380)*

Mar 71. (7") *(LBF 15448)* **DAUGHTER OF THE FIREPLACE. / COUNTRY GIRL**

U.A. — U.A.

Nov 71. (lp) *(UAS 29236) <1032>* **DO YOU LIKE IT HERE NOW, ARE YOU SETTLING IN?**
– Angel easy / All good clean fun / We're only children / Many are called but few get up / Manillo / Love your life. *(re-iss.Aug80 on 'Liberty'; LBR 16-032)*

— now a quartet when CLIVE joined PORWITH, PRITCHARD & THE NEUTRONS

Sep 72. (lp) *(USP 100)* **LIVE AT THE PADGET ROOMS, PENARTH (live)**
– Many are called, but few get up / Daughter of the fireplace / "H" / Samuel.

— **MICKY + TERRY** + the returning **CLIVE** – guitar / recruited **PHIL RYAN** – keyboards (ex-EYES OF BLUE) repl. DEKE who went solo / **MICHAEL 'WILL' YOUATT** – bass (ex-ANCIENT GREASE) repl. MARTIN

Oct 72. (lp) *(UAG 29417) <077>* **BE GOOD TO YOURSELF AT LEAST ONCE A DAY**
– C'mon / Keep on crinting / Bananas / Life on the road. *(re-iss.May88 & Apr97 on 'Beat Goes On'; BGOLP 14) (cd-iss.Feb92; BGOCD 14)*

— **ALAN 'TWEKE' LEWIS** – keyboards (ex-WILD TURKEY) repl. RYAN (in studio)

Sep 73. (d-lp) *(UAD 60053-4) <170>* **BACK INTO THE FUTURE** (half live / half studio) 23
– A night in dad's bag / Just for you / Back into the future / Don't go away / Ain't their fight / Never say nups to Nepalese / Sospan fack (featuring The Gwalia male choir) / C'mon / Jam up jelly tight. *(cd-iss.Dec93 on 'Beat Goes On'+=; BGOCD 211)–* Oh no, not again (spunk rock '73).

Sep 73. (7") *<341>* **DON'T GO AWAY. / BACK TO THE FUTURE** -

— **MICKY & TERRY** added the returning **DEKE LEONARD** – guitar, vocals / **MALCOLM MORLEY** – keyboards (ex-HELP YOURSELF) repl. WILL (to NEUTRONS) / **KEN WHALEY** – bass (ex-HELP YOURSELF, ex-BEES MAKE HONEY) repl. CLIVE and TWEKE

May 74. (lp) *(UAG 29631) <247>* **RHINOS, WINOS AND LUNATICS** 24
– Taking the easy way out again / The thunder and lightning kid / California silks and satins / Four day Louise / Intro / Kerosene / Scotch corner / Exit. *(cd-iss.Nov93 on 'Beat Goes On'; BGOCD 208)*

Jul 74. (7") *(UP 35703) <505>* **TAKING THE EASY WAY OUT AGAIN. / CALIFORNIA SILKS AND SATINS**

— trimmed to a quartet when MALCOLM departed.

Oct 74. (7") *(UP 35739)* **DAY AND NIGHT. / HARD WAY TO LIVE (live)**

Nov 74. (lp) *(UAG 29675) <345>* **SLOW MOTION**
– Hard way to die / Grasshopper / Rock & roll you out / You don't like us / Bedtime bone / One more chance / Rainbow eyes / Day and night. *(cd-iss.Nov93 on 'Beat Goes On'; BGOCD 209)*

Nov 74. (7") *<611>* **DAY AND NIGHT. / RAINBOW EYES** -

— **MARTIN ACE** – bass returned to replace KEN who joined TYLA GANG. added American **JOHN CIPPOLINA** – guitar (ex-QUICKSILVER MESSENGER SERVICE)

Sep 75. (lp) *(UAG 29872)* **MAXIMUM DARKNESS (live)** 25 -
– Codine / 7171-551 / Babe I'm gonna leave you / Many are called, but few get up / Bananas. *(re-iss.Mar89 & Apr 97 on 'Beat Goes On'; BGOLP 43) (cd-iss.Feb92; BGOCD 43)*

— **PHIL RYAN** – keyboards returned to replace CIPPOLINA / **JOHN McKENZIE** – bass (of GLOBAL VILLAGE TRUCKING CO.) repl. MARTIN ACE who joined The MOTORS

M.C.A. — M.C.A.

Mar 76. (lp) *(MCF 2753) <2190>* **THE WELSH CONNECTION** 40
– The ride and the view / Out of your head / Love can find a way / The Welsh connection / Something is happening / Cartoon / Born with a future.

Mar 76. (7") *(MCA 236) <40539>* **OUT OF YOUR HEAD. / I'M A LOVE TAKER**

— (disbanded Spring '76)

Nov 77. (lp) *(MCF 2815)* **ALL'S WELL THAT ENDS WELL (live farewell gigs)** -
– Let the good times roll / The Welsh connection / The ride and the view / A hard way to live / Born with a future / Spunk Rock / Romain.

— TERRY WILLIAMS continued in DAVE EDMUNDS' ROCKPILE, before joining The MOTORS and later DIRE STRAITS. PHIL RYAN joined PETE BROWN Band.

DEKE LEONARD

— solo with ICEBERG at times with MAN members **MICKY JONES, MARTIN ACE, KEN WHALEY + TERRY WILLIAMS** / Others incl. **TOMMY RILEY** – drums, etc.

U.A. — U.A.

Feb 73. (7") *(UP 35494)* **DIAMOND ROAD. / CIRCLES AND SQUARES**

Jul 73. (lp) *(UAG 29464)* **ICEBERG**
– Razor blade and rattlesnake / I just can't win / Lisa / Nothing is happening / Looking for a man / A hard way to live / Broken ovation / Jesse / Ten thousand takers / The ghost of Musket flat / Jesse / Crosby (second class citizen blues) / 7171 551. *(re-iss.Dec80 on 'Liberty'; LBR 1042) (cd-iss.Nov95 on 'Beat Goes On' with next album;)*

Sep 73. (7") *(UP 35556)* **A HARD WAY TO LIVE. / THE ACHING IS SO SWEET** -

Oct 73. (7") **A HARD WAY TO LIVE. / JESSE (live)** -

Mar 74. (lp) *(UAG 29544)* **KAMIKAZE** 50
– Cool summer rain / Jayhawk special / Sharpened claws / Taking the easy way out / The black gates of death / Stacia / Broken glass and limejuice / April the third / Louisiana hoedown / In search of Sarah and twenty-six horses / The Devil's gloves.

Apr 74. (7") *(UP 35668)* **LOUISIANA HOEDOWN. / SHE'S A CAR**

Feb 79. (7") *(UP 36488)* **MAP OF INDIA. / LADY IN THE BLUE TUXEDO** -

Mar 81. (lp) *(UAG 30240)* **BEFORE YOUR VERY EYES** -
– Someone is calling / Fools like me / Marlene / Oh / When am I coming back / Get off the line / Hiding in the darkness / Big hunk of love / I feel like a pill / The world exploded in my face / What am I gonna do when the money runs out / Bad luck.

Jun 81. (7") *(BP 400)* **BIG HUNK OF LOVE. / MARLENE** -

MAN

— reformed briefly 1983. **MICKY JONES, DEKE LEONARD, MARTIN ACE** plus **JOHN WEATHERS** – drums (ex-EYES OF BLUE, ex-GENTLE GIANT)

Picasso — not issued

Dec 83. (lp/c) *(PIK/+C 001)* **FRIDAY THE 13th (live Marquee, May '83)** -
– C'mon / Talk about a morning / Kerosene / A hard way to die / Back into the future / The ride and the view / Romain. *(cd-iss.Aug93 on 'Great Expectations';)*

Omox-ROR. — not issued

1984. (7") **WHAT A NIGHT. / THE LAST BIRTHDAY PARTY** - - German

— (1987 reformed again but only to do gigs) **TERRY WILLIAMS** – drums had returned to replace WEATHERS.

Road Goes On Forever — not issued

Feb 93. (cd/c) *(RGF CD/MC 1003)* **THE TWANG DYNASTY** -
– A feather on the scales of justice / Mad on her / Jumpin' like a kangaroo / The chimes at midnight / Circumstances / The price / Women / The Chinese cut / Out of the darkness / Fast and dangerous / The wings of Mercury.

Hypertension — not issued

May 95. (cd) *(HYCD 200154)* **CALL DOWN THE MOON** -
– Call down the Moon / If I were you / Dream away / Blackout / The man with x-ray eyes / Heaven and Hell / The girl is trouble / Drivin' around / Burn my workin' clothes.

– compilations, others, etc. –

Oct 73. (lp) *Pye; (GH 569)* **GOLDEN HOUR OF MAN** -

Nov 76. (7"ep) *United Artists; (REM 408)* **BANANAS (part 1). / BANANAS (part 2)** -

Nov 86. (lp) *Latymer; (DLATE 1)* **GREEN FLY** -

Aug 90. (lp/cd; BYSTANDERS) *See For Miles; (SEE/+CD 301)* **BIRTH OF MAN** -

Feb 91. (cd) *Worldwide;* **LIVE AT THE RAINBOW 1972 (live)** -

Jun 91. (cd/c/lp) *E.M.I.; (CD/TC+/EMS 1403)* **PERFECT TIMING (THE U.A. YEARS: 1970-1975)** -
(cd+=/c+=)– (3 extra tracks).

Mar 93. (cd) *Raw Fruit; (FRSCD 010)* **LIVE AT READING '83 (live)** -

Oct 93. (cd; 1-side by DEKE LEONARD'S ICEBERG) *Windsong;* **BBC RADIO 1 LIVE IN CONCERT** (live) -

Nov 93. (cd) *Great Expectations; (PIPCD 055)* **LIVE AT THE MARQUEE (live)** -

Oct 95. (cd; DEKE LEONARD) *Beat Goes On; (BGOCD 288)* **ICEBERG / KAMIKAZE** □ -
Apr 97. (cd) *Think Progressive; (EFA 035052)* **LIVE OFFICIAL BOOTLEG (live)** □ -

Harvey MANDEL

Born: 11 Mar'45, Detroit, Michigan, USA. Blues guitarist, who spent his formative years in Chicago and the West Coast. His early sessions included work for The VENTURES, BARRY GOLDBERG and CHARLIE MUSSELWHITE. A debut album, 'CRISTO REDENTOR', in 1968, showed traces of psychedelia, highlighted in his hypnotic version of RAMSEY LEWIS's 'WADE IN THE WATER'. He then recorded a follow-up, 'RIGHTEOUS', which squeezed into the US Top 200 in May '69. Around the same period, while backstage at the Fillmore Auditorium, he was asked by CANNED HEAT to fill in for HENRY VESTINE who had just walked out. Now more blues committed, he was soon fitting in alongside BOB 'THE BEAR' HITE and AL 'BLIND OWL' WILSON at the Woodstock Festival. His most memorable playing was surely on the 1970 hit, 'LET'S WORK TOGETHER'. His third solo album, 'GAMES GUITARS PLAY', was also released around the same time, although he soon jumped ship to play for JOHN MAYALL's new US backing band. Signing to 'Janus' in '71, he returned with another instrumental, 'BABY BATTER' (initially titled, 'ELECTRONIC PROGRESS'), which found new friends in the jazz-rock field. Next up, 'THE SNAKE', was another that sold moderately, while 1973's 'SHANGRENADE', was the last for the 'Janus' label. He then formed the disappointing PURE FOOD & DRUG ACT (nice name!?), who bombed commercially with the 'CHOICE CUTS' album. He subsequently went into session work (notably for LOVE), auditioning unsuccessfully for the vacant ROLLING STONES job (left by MICK TAYLOR). He did, however, appear on a few tracks from their 1976 album, 'BLACK & BLUE'.

Recommended: CRISTO REDENTOR (*6) / RIGHTEOUS (*5)

HARVEY MANDEL – guitar; with **EDDIE HOH** – drums / and many on session

Philips Philips

1968. (lp) *(SBL 7873)* <600-281> **CRISTO REDENTOR** □ □
– Cristo redentor / Before six / The lark / Snake / Long wait / Wade in the water / Lights out / Bradley's barn / You can't tell me / Nashville 1 a.m. *<US re-dist.Sep69, after becoming CANNED HEAT member> (re-iss.Aug89 on 'Editions EG' lp/c/cd; EGED/EGEDC/EEGCD 62)*

May 69. (lp) *(SBL 7904)* <600-306> **RIGHTEOUS** □ □
– Righteous / Jive samba / Love of life / Poontang / Just a hair more / Summer sequence / Short's stuff / Boo-bee-doo / Campus blues.

— with **HOH / LARRY TAYLOR** – bass (of CANNED HEAT) / **RUSSELL DASHIEL** – guitar, keyboards

1970. (lp) *(SBL 7915)* <600-325> **GAMES GUITARS PLAY** □ □
– Leavin' trunk / Honky tonk / I don't need no doctor / Dry your eyes / Ridin' high / Capurange / Senor blues / Games people play.

— he had also left CANNED HEAT to join JOHN MAYALL

Dawn Janus

Mar 71. (lp) *(DNLS 3015)* <3017> **BABY BATTER** □ □
– Baby batter / Midnight sun / One way street / Morton groove mama / Freedom ball / El Stinger / Hank the ripper. *(cd-iss.Feb95 on 'Beat Goes On'; BGOCD 252)*

Apr 71. (7") <144> **BABY BATTER. / MIDNIGHT SUN** - □

Janus Janus

Oct 72. (7") <198> **UNO INO. / PEGASUS** - □
Nov 72. (lp) *(6310 210)* <3037> **THE SNAKE** □ □ Jul72
– The divining rod / Pegasus / Lynda Love / Peruvian flake / The snake / Uno ino / Ode to the owl / Levitation / Bite the electric eel.

1973. (lp) *(6499 831)* <3047> **SHANGRENADE** □ □
– What the funk / Fish walk / Shangrenade / Midnight Sun / Million dollar feeling / Green apple quickstep / Frenzy / Sugarloaf.

Apr 74. (7") *(6146 024)* **UNO INO. / SHANGRENADE** □ □
1974. (lp) <3067> **FEEL THE SOUND OF HARVEY MANDEL** - □
– Got to be bad / Sore throat / Just wanna be there / Candles by the bedside / Feel the sound / I got your slot / Rankachank blues / Forever and forever.

— Went back into session work and nearly joined The ROLLING STONES. e returned for a one-one during the 90's. The album was named after a rough-and-tumble bar in Chicago's West Side known as Curley's Twist City. He was joined by a plethera of musicians including vocalist **MARK SKYER**

not issued ZYX

1990's. (cd) <20332-2> **TWIST CITY** - □

– compilations, etc. –

1973. (lp) *London; (SHU 8426) / Ovation; <1415>* **GET OFF IN CHICAGO** □ □
– Check me out / Highway blues / Highest fish line / Race track daddy / Jelly roll / Local days / Sweet Lynda / I'm a lonely man / Springfield Station theme.

1975. (lp) *Janus; <7014>* **THE BEST OF HARVEY MANDEL** - □

PURE FOOD & DRUG ACT

MANDEL – guitar / **DON 'SUGARCANE' HARRIS** – violin, vocals / **RANDY RESNICK** – guitar, vocals / **COLEMAN HEAD** – guitar, vocals / **VICTOR CONTE** – bass / **PAUL LAGOS** – drums

Epic Epic

1972. (lp) *(65197)* <31401> **CHOICE CUTS** □ □
– Introduction / Jim's message / My soul's on fire / Till the day I die / Eleanor Rigby / A little soul food / Do it yourself / Where is my sunshine / What comes around goes around.

1972. (7") <10907> **ELEANOR RIGBY. / MY SOUL'S ON FIRE** - □

Manfred MANN

Formed: London, England ... late '62, initially as The MANN-HUGG BLUES BAND, subsequently naming themselves MANFRED MANN after the band's keyboard player. MANN and HUGG then recruited DAVE RICHMOND, PAUL JONES and MIKE VICKERS, playing local gigs which secured them a deal with the 'H.M.V.' label. Early in 1964, after two flop singles, they had their first chart success, hitting the Top 5 with the harmonica-fuelled R&B classic, '5-4-3-2-1'. They continued to storm the charts throughout the 60's, reaching pole position three times with 'DOO WAH DIDDY DIDDY' (1964), 'PRETTY FLAMINGO' (1966) and 'THE MIGHTY QUINN' (1968). The latter was fronted by MIKE D'ABO, who had replaced the solo bound PAUL JONES. In 1969, MANN and HUGG churned out commercial jingles for Michelen tyres and Ski yogurt before forming the heavier jazz-rock outfit, MANFRED MANN CHAPTER THREE. They delivered a couple of albums for 'Vertigo', soon reverting back to their original name in 1971. The following year, they re-emerged minus HUGG, with the more ambitious and progressive MANFRED MANN'S EARTH BAND. They struggled initially, although they created their own take on GUSTAV HOLST's "Jupiter suite" (from 'The Planets') in the form of 'JOYBRINGER' (a top 10 hit in 1973). A dry period of three years ensued, during which time they released three accessible rock albums, 'SOLAR FIRE', 'THE GOOD EARTH' and 'NIGHTINGALES AND BOMBERS'. The band saw a return to chart action with a cover of BRUCE SPRINGSTEEN's, 'BLINDED BY THE LIGHT', which also hit No.1 in America. Their albums fared a lot better from this point on, another SPRINGSTEEN re-hash, 'SPIRIT IN THE NIGHT', denting the US Top 40 in 1977. In the 80's (and 90's!), his EARTH BAND continued to tread the same ground, releasing a plethora of mediocre cover versions for the coffee-table set. One particular song, 'THE RUNNER', saw them sprinting back into the US Top 30 early in 1984. • **Songwriters:** MANN-HUGG until latter's departure in '71. Covered; DOO WAH DIDDY DIDDY (Exciters) / SHA LA LA (Shirelles) / OH NO NOT MY BABY (Goffin-King) / SMOKESTACK LIGHTNING (Howlin' Wolf) / MY LITTLE RED BOOK (Bacharach-David) / WITH GOD ON OUR SIDE + IF YOU GOTTA GO, GO NOW + JUST LIKE A WOMAN + THE MIGHTY QUINN + PLEASE, MRS.HENRY + others (Bob Dylan) / SWEET PEA (Tommy Roe) / SO LONG DAD + LIVING WITHOUT YOU (Randy Newman) / MY NAME IS JACK (John Simon) / etc. His EARTH BAND covered FATHER OF DAY, FATHER OF NIGHT + YOU, ANGEL YOU + SHELTER FROM THE STORM (Bob Dylan) / SPIRIT IN THE NIGHT + BLINDED BY THE LIGHT + FOR YOU (Bruce Springsteen) / DON'T KILL IT CAROL (Mike Heron) / REDEMPTION SONG (Bob Marley) / DO ANYTHING YOU WANNA DO (Eddie & The Hot Rods) / GOING UNDERGROUND (Jam) / BANQUET (Joni Mitchell) / PLAY WITH FIRE (Rolling Stones) / NOTHING EVER HAPPENS (Del Amitri) / PLEASURE + PAIN (Chapman-Knight) / TUMBLING BALL (M. Spiro) / THE PRICE I PAY (Robert Cray) / LOSE THE TOUCH (C. Schumann) / THE COMPLETE HISTORY OF SEXUAL JEALOUSY (Momus) / 99 LBS (D Bryant) / etc. • **Trivia:** MIKE HUGG wrote 'SHAPES OF THINGS' in 1966 for fellow R&B hitmakers, The YARDBIRDS. MANFRED played Moog synthesizer on URIAH HEEP's 1971 album, 'Look At Yourself'. The 'GLORIFIED MAGNIFIED' track was used for the theme to Radio 1's 'Sound Of The 70's'.

Recommended: AGES OF MANN (22 CLASSICS OF THE 60s) (*7) / 20 YEARS OF MANFRED MANN'S EARTH BAND (*6)

MANFRED MANN (b. MANFRED LUBOWITZ, 21 Oct'40, Johannesburg, South Africa) – keyboards / **PAUL JONES** (b.PAUL POND, 24 Feb'42, Portsmouth, England) – vocals, harmonica / **MIKE VICKERS** (b.18 Apr'41, Southampton, England) – guitar / **DAVE RICHMOND** – bass / **MIKE HUGG** (b.11 Aug'42, Andover, England) – drums

H.M.V. Prestige

Jul 63. (7") *(POP 1189)* **WHY SHOULD WE NOT. / BROTHER JACK** □ -
Oct 63. (7") *(POP 1225)* **COCK-A-HOOP. / NOW YOU'RE NEEDING ME** □ -

— **TOM McGUINESS** (b. 2 Dec'41, Wimbledon, London, England) – bass (ex-ROOSTERS) repl. RICHMOND

Jan 64. (7") *(POP 1252)* **5-4-3-2-1. / WITHOUT YOU** 5 □ Mar64

H.M.V. Ascot

Apr 64. (7") *(POP 1282)* <2151> **HUBBLE BUBBLE TOIL AND TROUBLE. / I'M YOUR KINGPIN** 11 □
Jul 64. (7") *(POP 1320)* <2157> **DOO WAH DIDDY DIDDY. / WHAT YOU GONNA DO** 1 1 Aug64
(re-iss.Oct82; PMS 1003)
Sep 64. (lp) *(CLP 1731)* **THE FIVE FACES OF MANFRED MANN** 3 -
– Smokestack lightning / Don't ask me what I say / It's gonna work out fine / Sack of wool / What you gonna do / I'm your kingpin / Hoochie coochie / Down the road apiece / I've got my mojo working / Mr. Analles / Untie me / Bring it to Jerome / Without you / You've got to take it. *(cd-iss.Jun97 on 'E.M.I.'; DORIG 121)*
Oct 64. (7") *(POP 1346)* <2165> **SHA LA LA. / JOHN HARDY** 3 12 Nov64
Nov 64. (lp) <16015> **THE MANFRED MANN ALBUM** - 35
– Do wah diddy diddy / Sack o' woe / Don't ask me what I say / What you gonna do / Got my mojo working / I'm your hoochie coochie man / Smokestack lightning / It's gonna work out fine / Down the road apiece / Untie me / Bring it to Jerome / Without you.
Jan 65. (7") *(POP 1381)* <2170> **COME TOMORROW. / WHAT DID I DO WRONG** 4 50 Feb65
Mar 65. (lp) <ALS 16018> **THE FIVE FACES OF MANFRED MANN** - □
– Sha la la / Come tomorrow / She / Can't believe it / John Hardy / Did you have to do that / Watermelon man / I'm your kingpin / Hubble bubble (toil and trouble) / You've got to take it / Dashing away with the smoothing iron / Groovin'.

Apr 65. (7") *(POP 1413)* **OH NO NOT MY BABY. / WHAT AM I DOING WRONG** [11] [-]

Apr 65. (7") *<2181>* **POISON IVY. / I CAN'T BELIEVE WHAT YOU SAY** [-] [ ]

Jun 65. (7") *<2184>* **MY LITTLE RED BOOK. / WHAT AM I DOING WRONG** [-] [ ]
<re-iss.1966; 2241>

Jul 65. (lp) *<ALS 16201>* **MY LITTLE RED BOOK OF WINNERS** [-] [ ]
– My little red book / Oh no, not my baby / What am I to do / One in the middle / You gave me somebody to love / You're for me / Poison Ivy / Without you / Brother Jack / Love like yours / I can't believe what you say / With God on your side.

Sep 65. (7") *(POP 1466)* **IF YOU GOTTA GO, GO NOW. / STAY AROUND** [2] [-]

Oct 65. (lp) *(CLP 1911) <ALS 16024>* **MANN MADE** [7] [ ]
– Since I don't have you / You're for me / Look away / L.S.D. / The abominable snowman / Watch your step / The way you do the things you do / Stormy Monday blues / Hi lili hi lo / I really do believe / Bear Hugg / You don't know me / I'll make it up to you. *(re-iss.Nov69 on 'Regal Starline'; SRS 5007)*

Oct 65. (7") *<2194>* **IF YOU GOTTA GO, GO NOW. / THE ONE IN THE MIDDLE** [-] [ ]

Jan 66. (7") *<2210>* **HI LILI, HI LO. / SHE NEEDS COMPANY** [-] [ ]

— (PETE BURFORD and DAVID HYDE deputised for VICKERS on tour until) / **JACK BRUCE** (b.14 May'43, Lanarkshire, Scotland) – bass (ex-JOHN MAYALL, ex-GRAHAM BOND) repl. VICKERS / added **LYN DOBSON** – saxophone / **HENRY LOWTHER** – trumpet (McGUINESS now guitar)

H.M.V. U.A.

Apr 66. (7") *(POP 1523) <50040>* **PRETTY FLAMINGO. / YOU'RE STANDING BY** [1] [29] Jun66

— **MANN, HUGG** and **McGUINESS** added new members **MIKE D'ABO** (b. 1 Mar'44, Bethworth, England) – vocals (ex-BAND OF ANGELS) repl. JONES who went solo, etc. / **KLAUS VOORMAN** (b.29 Apr'42, Berlin, Germany) – bass repl. JACK BRUCE who formed CREAM.

Jun 66. (7") *(POP 1541)* **YOU GAVE ME SOMEBODY TO LOVE. / POISON IVY** [36] [-]

Sep 66. <50066> **DO YOU HAVE TO DO THAT. / WHEN WILL I BE LOVED** [-] [ ]

Fontana Mercury

Jul 66. (7") *(TF 730) <72607>* **JUST LIKE A WOMAN. / I WANNA BE RIGHT** [10] [ ]

Oct 66. (7") *(TF 757) <72629>* **SEMI-DETACHED SUBURBAN MR. JAMES. / MORNING AFTER THE PARTY** [2] [ ]

Oct 66. (lp; stereo/mono) *(S+/TL 5377)* **AS IS** [22] [-]
– Trouble and tea / A now and then thing / Each other's company / Box office draw / Dealer dealer / Morning after the party / Another kind of music / As long as I have lovin' / Autumn leaves / Superstitious guy / You're my girl / Just like a woman.

Dec 66. (lp) *<6549>* **PRETTY FLAMINGO** [-] [ ]
– Pretty flamingo / Let's go get stoned / Tired of trying / Bored with living / Scared of dying / I put a spell on you / It's getting late / You're standing by / Machines / Stay around / Tennessee waltz / Drive man / Do you have to do that.

Mar 67. (7") *(TF 812) <72676>* **HA! HA! SAID THE CLOWN. / FEELING SO GOOD** [4] [ ]

May 67. (7") *(TF 828)* **SWEET PEA. / ONE WAY** [36] [-]

Sep 67. (7") *(TF 862)* **SO LONG DAD. / FUNNIEST GIG** [ ] [-]

Jan 68. (lp) *(TL 5460)* **UP THE JUNCTION (Soundtrack)** [ ] [-]
– Up the junction (vocal) / Sing songs of love / Walking around up the junction (instrumental) / Love theme (instrumental) / Up the junction (vocal & instrumental) / Just for me / Love theme (instrumental) / Sheila's dance / Belgravia / Wailing horn / I need your love / Up the junction (vocal). *(re-iss.1970; 6852 005)*

Fontana Mercury

Jan 68. (7") *(TF 897) <72770>* **MIGHTY QUINN. / BY REQUEST EDWIN GARVEY** [1] [10]
(re-iss.Jun82 on 'Old Gold'; OG 9252)

Mar 68. (lp) *(SFL 13003)* **WHAT A MANN** (compilation) [ ] [-]
– Funniest gig / Sunny / Get away / With a girl like you / Sweet pea / Wild thing / The morning after the party / Feeling so good / One way / So long dad.

Mar 68. (7") *(TF 908)* **THEME – UP THE JUNCTION. / SLEEPY HOLLOW** [ ] [ ]

May 68. (lp) *<61168>* **MIGHTY QUINN** [-] [ ]
– Mighty Quinn / Ha! ha! said the clown / Every day another hair turns grey / It's so easy falling / Big Betty / Cubist town / Country dancing / Semi-detached suburban Mr. James / The vicar's daughter / Each and every day / No better, no worse.

Jun 68. (lp; stereo/mono) *(S+/TL 5470)* **MIGHTY GARVEY!** [ ] [-]
– Happy families / No better, no worse / Each and every day / Country dancing / It's so easy falling / Happy families / Mighty Quinn / Big Betty / The vicar's daughter / Every day another hair turns grey / Cubist town / Ha! ha! said the clown / Harry the one-man band / Happy families.

Jun 68. (7") *(TF 943) <72872>* **MY NAME IS JACK. / THERE IS A MAN** [8] [ ]

Dec 68. (7") *(TF 985) <72879>* **FOX ON THE RUN. / TOO MANY PEOPLE** [5] [97]

May 69. (7") *(TF 1013) <72921>* **RAGAMUFFIN MAN. / A 'B' SIDE** [8] [ ]

— split mid 69. TOM formed McGUINESS FLINT. D'ABO went solo, and VOORMAN joined JOHN LENNON's PLASTIC ONO BAND

MANFRED MANN'S CHAPTER III

MANFRED retained **MIKE HUGG** – vocals, electric piano. — Recruited **BRIAN HUGG** – guitar / **STEVE YORK** – bass plus session singers, drummers and wind section

Vertigo Polydor

Nov 69. (lp) *(VO 3) <4013>* **MANFRED MANN CHAPTER THREE** [ ] [ ]
– Travelling lady / Snakeskin garter / Konekuf / Sometimes / Devil woman / Time / One way glass / Mister you're a better man than I / Ain't it sad / A study in inaccuracy / Where am I going. *(cd-iss.Feb94 on 'Cohesion'; MFMCD 14)*

Mar 70. (7") *<14026>* **SNAKESKIN GARTER. / SOMETIMES** [-] [ ]

— on session **CHRIS SLADE** – drums (alongside others)

Sep 70. (7") *(6059 012)* **HAPPY BEING ME. / DEVIL WOMAN** [ ] [-]

Oct 70. (lp) *(6360 012)* **MANFRED MANN CHAPTER III, VOL.2** [ ] [-]
– Lady Ace / I ain't laughing / Poor sad Sue / Jump before you think / It's good to be alive / Happy being me / Virginia. *(cd-iss.Feb94 on 'Cohesion'; MFMCD 15)*

MANFRED MANN'S EARTH BAND

— His new band now featured **CHRIS SLADE** – drums (now a full time member) / **MICK ROGERS** – vocals, guitar repl. MIKE HUGG / **COLIN PATTENDEN** – bass repl. STEVE YORK and BRIAN HUGG

Philips Polydor

Jun 71. (7"; as MANFRED MANN; w-drawn) *<14074>* **CALIFORNIA COASTLINE. / PART TIME** [-] [ ]

Jun 71. (7"; as MANFRED MANN) *(6006 122) <14113>* **LIVING WITHOUT YOU. / TRIBUTE** [ ] [69] Jan72

Sep 71. (7"; as MANFRED MANN) *(6006 251)* **MRS HENRY. / PRAYER** [ ] [ ]

Feb 72. (lp) *(6308 086) <5015>* **MANFRED MANN'S EARTH BAND** [ ] [ ]
– California coastline / Captain Bobby Stout / Sloth / Living without you / Tribute / Mrs Henry / Jump sturdy / Prayer / Part time man / I'm up and leaving. *(re-iss.Apr77 & 1981 on 'Bronze'; BRON 252) (re-iss.Jan90 on 'Castle' lp/cd; CLA LP/CD 150) (re-iss.Jan91 on 'Cohesion' lp/cd; COMME/+T/CD 6)*

Mar 72. (7") *<14130>* **PART TIME MAN. / I'M UP AND LEAVING** [-] [ ]

Sep 72. (lp) *(6308 125) <5031>* **GLORIFIED MAGNIFIED** [ ] [ ]
– Meat / Look around / One way glass / I'm gonna have you all / Down home / Our friend George / Ashes to the wind / It's all over now, baby blue / Glorified magnified. *(re-iss.Apr77 & 1981 on 'Bronze') (cd-iss.Dec93 on 'Cohesion'; MFMCD 11)*

Nov 72. (7") *(6006 251)* **MEAT. / GLORIFIED MAGNIFIED** [ ] [-]

Feb 73. (7") *<14164>* **IT'S ALL OVER NOW, BABY BLUE. / ASHES TO THE WIND** [-] [ ]

Vertigo Polydor

Apr 73. (7"; as EARTH BAND) *(6059 078)* **GET YOUR ROCKS OFF. / SADJOY** [ ] [-]

Jun 73. (lp) *(6360 087) <5050>* **MESSIN'** <US-title 'GET YOUR ROCKS OFF'> [ ] [ ]
– Buddah / Messin' / Cloudy eyes / Get your rocks off / Sadjoy / Black and blue / Mardi Gras day. *(re-iss.Apr77 & 1981 on 'Bronze'; BRON 261) (re-iss.Jan90 on 'Castle' lp/cd; CLA LP/CD 151) (re-iss.Jan91 on 'Cohesion' lp/cd; COMME/+T/CD 7)*

Jun 73. (7") *<14173>* **MARDI GRAS DAY. / SADJOY** [-] [ ]

Aug 73. (7") *<14191>* **GET YOUR ROCKS OFF. / ASHES TO THE WIND** [-] [ ]

Aug 73. (7") *(6059 083)* **JOYBRINGER. / CAN'T EAT MEAT** [9] [-]

Sep 73. (7") *<14205>* **JOYBRINGER. / CLOUDY EYES** [-] [ ]

Bronze Polydor

Nov 73. (lp) *(ILPS 9265) <6019>* **SOLAR FIRE** [ ] [96]
– Father of night, in the beginning / Pluto the dog / Solar fire / Saturn (Mercury) / Earth the circle (pts.1 & 2). *(re-iss.Apr77 & 1981; BRON 265) (re-iss.Nov87 on 'Legacy' lp/c/cd; LLP/LLK/LLCD 121) (re-iss.Jan91 on 'Cohesion' lp/c/cd; COMME/+T/CD 1)*

Mar 74. (7") **FATHER OF DAY, FATHER OF NIGHT. / SOLAR FIRE 2** [ ] [-]

Bronze Warners

Oct 74. (7") *(BRO 13)* **BE NOT TOO HARD. / EARTH HYMN (part 2a)** [ ] [-]

Oct 74. (lp/c) *(ILPS/ICT 9306) <BS 2826>* **THE GOOD EARTH** [ ] [ ]
– Give me the good earth / Launching place / I'll be gone / Earth hymn (pts.1 & 2) / Sky high / Be not too hard. *(re-iss.Apr77 + 1981; BRON 306) (cd-iss.Dec93 on 'Cohesion'; MFMCD 12)*

Jul 75. (7") *(BRO 18) <8152>* **SPIRIT IN THE NIGHT. / AS ABOVE SO BELOW (part 2)** [ ] [ ]

Aug 75. (lp/c) *(ILPS/ICT 9337) <BS 2877>* **NIGHTINGALES AND BOMBERS** [ ] [ ]
– Spirit in the night / Countdown / Time is right / Crossfade / Visionary mountains / Nightingales and bombers / Fat Nelly / As above so below. *(re-iss.Apr77 + 1981; BRON 337) (re-iss.1987 on 'Castle' lp/cd; CLA LP/CD 137) (re-iss.Jan91 on 'Cohesion' lp/c/cd; COMME/+T/CD 8)*

Feb 76. (7") *<8176>* **SPIRIT IN THE NIGHT. / AS ABOVE SO BELOW** [-] [97]

— **CHRIS THOMPSON** – vocals repl. ROGERS who later formed AVIATOR / added **DAVE FLETT** – guitar

Aug 76. (7") *(BRO 29) <8252>* **BLINDED BY THE LIGHT. / STARBIRD No.2** [6] [1]

Aug 76. (lp/c) *(ILPS/ICT 9357) <BS 3055>* **THE ROARING SILENCE** [10] [10]
– Blinded by the light / Singing the dolphin through / Waiter, there's a yawn in my ear / The road to Babylon / This side of Paradise / Starbird / Questions. *(re-iss.Apr77 + 1981; BRON 357) (re-iss.Nov87 on 'Legacy' lp/c/cd; LLP/LLK/LLCD 122) (re-iss.Jan91 on 'Cohesion' lp/c/cd; COMME/+T/CD 2)*

Nov 76. (7") *(BRO 34)* **QUESTIONS. / WAITER, THERE'S A YAWN IN MY EAR No.2** [ ] [-]

Dec 76. (7") *<8355>* **QUESTIONS. / SPIRIT IN THE NIGHT** [-] [ ]

— **PAT KING** – bass (ex-SHANGHAI, etc.) repl. PATTENDEN (to TERRA NOVA)

Jun 77. (7") *<8355>* **SPIRIT IN THE NIGHT (remix). / ROAD TO BABYLON** [-] [40]

Nov 77. (7") *(BRO 48)* **CALIFORNIA. / CHICAGO INSTITUTE** [ ] [-]

Feb 78. (lp/c) *(BRON/+C 507) <BS 3157>* **WATCH** [33] [83]
– Circles / Drowning on dry land / Fish soup / California / Chicago institute / Davy's on the road again / Martha's madman / The mighty Quinn. *(re-iss.1981; same) (re-iss.Nov87 on 'Legacy'; LLCD 123) (re-iss.Jan91 on 'Cohesion' lp/c/cd; COOME/+T/CD 3)*

Mar 78. (7") *(BRO 51)* **THE MIGHTY QUINN. / TINY** [ ] [-]

Apr 78. (7") *(BRO 52) <8620>* **DAVY'S ON THE ROAD AGAIN. / BOUILLABAISE** [6] [ ] Sep78

Jul 78. (7") *<8574>* **CALIFORNIA. / BOUILLABAISE** [-] [ ]

— After a short split, MANN reformed band retaining **THOMPSON + KING / STEVE WALLER** – guitar (ex-GONZALES) repl. FLETT / **GEOFF BRITTON** – drums (ex-EAST OF EDEN, ex-WINGS, ex-ROUGH DIAMOND, ex-CHAMPION) repl. CHRIS SLADE who joined URIAH HEEP. He later joined The FIRM (see; LED ZEPPELIN)

Feb 79. (7") *(BRO 68)* **YOU ANGEL YOU. / OUT IN THE DISTANCE** [54] [-]

Mar 79. (lp/c) *(BRON/+C 516) <3302>* **ANGEL STATION** [30] [ ]

– Don't kill it Carol / You angel you / Hollywood town / Belle of the Earth / Platform end / Angels at my gate / You are I am / Waiting for the rain / Resurrection. *(re-iss.Nov87 on 'Legacy' lp/c/cd; LLP/LLK/LLCD 124) (re-iss.Jan91 on 'Cohesion' lp/c/cd; COMME/+T/CD 4)*

May 79. (7") *<8850>* **YOU ANGEL YOU. / BELLE OF THE EARTH** [-] [58]

Jun 79. (7"/7"pic-d) *(BRO/BPO 77)* **DON'T KILL IT CAROL. / BLINDED BY THE LIGHT** [45] [ ]

— **JOHN LINGWOOD** – drums repl. BRITTON who became ill. / guests included **PETER MARSH, WILLY FINLAYSON.** (vocals – **CHRIS THOMPSON**)

Oct 80. (lp/c) *(BRON/+C 529) <BSK 3498>* **CHANCE** [ ] [87]
– Lies (through the 80's) / On the run / For you / Adolescent dream / Fritz the blank / Stranded / This is your heart / No guarentee / Heart on the street. *(re-iss.1987 on 'Castle' lp/cd; CLA LP/CD 133) (re-iss.Jan91 on 'Cohesion' lp/c/cd; COMME/+T/CD 9)*

Nov 80. (7") *(BRO 103) <49762>* **LIES (THROUGH THE 80'S). / ADOLESCENT DREAM** [ ] [ ] Jun81

Jan 81. (7") *(BRO 113) <49678>* **FOR YOU. / A FOOL I AM** [ ] [ ]

— **MATT IRVING** – bass (ex-DREAM POLICE, ex-BABYS, ex-LONGDANCER) repl. KING

Nov 81. (7") *(BRO 137)* **I (WHO HAVE NOTHING). / MAN IN JAM** [ ] [-]

Bronze Arista

Feb 82. (7") *(BRO 141)* **EYES OF NOSTRADAMUS. / HOLIDAY'S END** [ ] [-]
(12"+=) *(BROX 141)* – Man in jam.

Jun 82. (7") *(BRO 150)* **REDEMPTION SONG (NO KWAZULU). / WARDREAM** [ ] [-]

Nov 82. (7") *(BRO 157)* **TRIBAL STATISTICS. / WHERE DO THEY SEND THEM** [ ] [-]

Jan 83. (lp/c) *(BRON/C 543) <8194>* **SOMEWHERE IN AFRIKA** [87] [40] Mar84
– Tribal statistics / Eyes of Nostradamus / Third world service / Demolition man / Brothers and sisters of Azania:- (a) Afrika suite – (b) Brothers and sisters of Afrika – (c) To ban Tustan – (d) Koze Kobenini (how long must we wait?) / Lalela / Redemption song (no Kwazulu) / Somewhere in Afrika. *(re-iss.Nov87 on 'Legacy' lp/c/cd; LLP/LLK/LLCD 125) (re-iss.Jan91 on 'Cohesion' lp/c/cd; COMME/+T/CD 1)*

Jan 83. (7") *(BRO 161)* **DEMOLITION MAN. / IT'S STILL THE SAME** [ ] [-]

Feb 84. (7") *(BRO 177)* **DAVY'S ON THE ROAD AGAIN (live). / THE MIGHTY QUINN (live)** [ ] [-]
(12"+=) *(BROX 177)* – Don't kill it Carol (live).

Feb 84. (lp/c) *(BRON/+C 550)* **BUDAPEST (live)** [ ] [ ]
– Spirits in the night / Demolition man / For you / Davy's on the road again / Lies (through the 80's) / Blinded by the light / Redemption song (no Kwazulu) / The mighty Quinn. *(cd-iss.1988 on 'Ariola'; ACD 610163) (re-iss.Jan91 on 'Cohesion' lp/c/cd; COMME/+T/CD 10)*

— **MICK RODGERS** – vocals, guitar returned to repl. WALLER (MANN, THOMPSON, LINGWOOD) also still in band. (IRVING left to join LORDS OF THE NEW CHURCH. He later joined PAUL YOUNG band).

Jan 84. (7") *(BRO 180)* **(THE) RUNNER. / NO TRANSKEI** [ ] [-]
(12"+=) *(BROX 180)* – Lies (through the 80's).

Jan 84. (7") *<9143>* **(THE) RUNNER. / WHERE DO THEY SEND THEM** [-] [22]

Jun 84. (7") *<9203>* **REBEL. / FIGURES ON A PAGE** [-] [ ]

10-Virgin Virgin

Mar 86. (7"/12") *(TEN 115/+12)* **DO ANYTHING YOU WANNA DO. / CROSSFIRE** [ ] [ ]

May 86. (7"/12") *(TEN/+T 121)* **GOING UNDERGROUND. / I SHALL BE RESCUED** [ ] [ ]

Jun 86. (lp/c/cd) *(XID/CXID/DIXCD 17)* **CRIMINAL TANGO** [ ] [ ]
– Going underground / Who are the mystery kids / Banquet / Killer on the loose / Do anything you wanna do / Rescue / You got me through the heart / Hey bulldog / Crossfire.

— **MAGGIE RYDER** – vocals repl. CHRIS THOMPSON who went solo (guests incl.**FRANK MEAD** – saxophone / **DENNY NEWMAN** – bass, vocals on 1)

Oct 87. (7"/12") *(TEN/+T 196)* **GERONIMO'S CADILLAC. / TWO FRIENDS** [ ] [ ]

Nov 87. (lp/c/cd) *(DIX/CDIX/DIXCD 69)* **MASQUE** [ ] [ ]
– Joybringer (from 'Jupiter') / Billies orno bounce (including Billies bounce) / What you give is what you get (start) / Rivers run dry / Planets schmanets / Geronimo's Cadillac / Sister Billies bounce (including Sister Sadie & Billies bounce) / Telegram to Monica / A couple of mates (from 'Mars' & 'Saturn') / Neptune *Icebringer) / The hymn (from 'Jupiter') / We're going wrong.

Kaz Priority

Aug 92. (cd) *(KAZCD 902)* **PLAINS MUSIC** [ ] [ ]

— **MANFRED MANN** with **CHRIS THOMPSON + NOEL McCALLA** – vocals / **MICK ROGERS** – guitars / **STEVE KINCH** – bass / **CLIVE BUNKER + DAVID FARMER** – drums / + guests

Grapevine not issued

Jun 96. (cd/c) *(GRA CD/MC 213)* **SOFT VENGEANCE** [ ] [-]
– SOFT: Pleasure and pain / Play with fire / Nothing ever happens / Shelter from the storm / Tumbling ball / The price I pay / Lose the touch / Adults only / Wherever love drops (part one) / (interval 10 seconds) / VENGEANCE: The complete history of sexual jealousy / 99 lbs / Miss you / Nature of the beast / Wherever love drops (part two).

– compilations, others, etc. –

Jul 77. (lp) *Vertigo; (9199 107)* **MANFRED MANN'S EARTH BAND 1971-73** [ ] [-]

Oct 90. (7") *Cohesion;* **DAVY'S ON THE ROAD AGAIN. / BLINDED BY THE LIGHT** [ ] [-]

Jan 91. (cd/c/lp) *Cohesion; (BOMME 1 CD/MC/LP)* **20 YEARS OF MANFRED MANN'S EARTH BAND 1971-1991** [ ] [-]
– Blinded by the light / California / Joybringer / Tribal statistics / Somewhere in Africa / Davy's on the road again / You angel you / The runner / Questions / The mighty Quinn / Angels at the gate / For you / Demolition man.

Nov 92. (10xlp-box/10xc-box/10xcd-box) *Cohesion; (COMME/+T/CD 6)* **MANFRED MANN'S EARTH BAND** [ ] [-]
– (albums from 1972-1986) *(free-12"+=)–*

– (MANFRED MANN) compilations etc. –

on 'H.M.V.' unless otherwise mentioned

Apr 64. (7"ep) *(7EG 8848)* **MANFRED MANN'S COCK-A-HOOP WITH 5-4-3-2-1** [ ] [-]
– Cock-a-hoop / 5-4-3-2-1 / Why should we not / Without you.

Dec 64. (7"ep) *(7EG 8876)* **GROOVIN' WITH MANFRED MANN** [ ] [-]
– Do wah diddy diddy / etc.

Jul 65. (7"ep) *(7EG 8908)* **ONE IN THE MIDDLE** [6] [-]
– With God on our side / Watermelon man / What am I to do / One in the middle.

Sep 65. (7"ep) *(7EG 8922)* **NO LIVING WITHOUT YOU** [ ] [-]
– Let's go get stoned / I put a spell on you / Tired of trying / (1).

Apr 66. (7"ep) *(7EG 8942)* **MACHINES** [ ] [-]
– She needs company / Machines / Tennessee waltz / When will I be loved.

Jun 66. (7"ep) *(7EG 8949)* **INSTRUMENTAL ASYLUM** [ ] [-]

Sep 66. (lp) *(CLP 3559)* **MANN MADE HITS** [11] [-]
– Pretty flamingo / The one in the middle / Oh no not my baby / John Hardy / Spirit feel / Come tomorrow / Do wah diddy diddy / With God on our side / There's no living without your loving / Groovin' / I'm your kingpin / Sha la la / 5-4-3-2-1 / If you gotta go, go now.

Oct 66. (7"ep) *(7EG 8962)* **AS WAS** [ ] [-]

Dec 66. (7"ep) *Fontana; (TE 17483)* **INSTRUMENTAL ASSASSINATION** [ ] [-]
– Wild thing / With a girl like you / Sunny / Get away.

Jan 67. (lp; mono/stereo) *(CLP/CSD 3594)* **SOUL OF MANN** (instrumentals) [40] [-]
– The abominable snowman / I got you babe / Bare Hugg / Spirit feel / Why should we not / L.S.D. / (I can't get no) Satisfaction / God rest ye merry gentlemen / My generation / Mr. Anello / Still I'm sad / Tengo tango / Brother Jack / Sack o' woe. *(re-iss.Jul85 on 'See For Miles'; SEE 52)*

Jan 67. (7") *Ascot;* **MY LITTLE RED BOOK. / I CAN'T BELIEVE WHAT YOU SAY** [-] [ ]

1971. (lp) *Music For Pleasure; (MFP 5269)* **THE GREATEST HITS OF MANFRED MANN** [ ] [-]

Nov 71. (lp) *Philips; (6382 020)* **THIS IS . . . MANFRED MANN** [ ] [-]

Jul 76. (lp) *Sonic; (SON 016)* **MANNERISMS** [ ] [-]

Jul 77. (lp) *E.M.I.; (NUT 7)* **THE BEST OF MANFRED MANN** [ ] [-]

Jul 77. (7"ep) *Philips; (6006 575)* **HA! HA! SAID THE CLOWN / MIGHTY QUINN. / SEMI-DETACHED SUBURBAN MR. JAMES / A 'B' SIDE** [ ] [-]

Aug 77. (7"m) *E.M.I.; (EMI 2644)* **PRETTY FLAMINGO. / THE ONE IN THE MIDDLE / GOT MY MOJO WORKING** [ ] [-]

Sep 79. (d-lp/c) *E.M.I.; (EMTV/TC-EMTV 19)* **SEMI-DETACHED SUBURBAN (20 GREAT HITS OF THE SIXTIES)** [9] [-]
– Do wah diddy diddy / 5-4-3-2-1 / Sha la la / Hubble bubble, toil and trouble / Hi lili hi lo / One in the middle / Got my mojo working / With God on our side / Come tomorrow / If you gotta go, go now / Pretty flamingo / Semi-detached suburban Mr. James / There's no living without your loving / Just like a woman / Oh no not my baby / Ha ha said the clown / My name is Jack / Fox on the run / Ragamuffin man / Mighty Quinn.

May 82. (lp/c) *E.M.I.; (CM/+K 105)* **THE R&B YEARS** [ ] [-]
(re-iss.Nov86; same)

Aug 83. (d-lp) *E.M.I.; (EDP 1546363)* **THE FIVE FACES OF MANFRED MANN / MANN MADE** [ ] [-]

Oct 83. (7") *Old Gold; (OG 9376)* **PRETTY FLAMINGO. / 5-4-3-2-1** [ ] [-]

May 84. (7") *E.M.I.; (G45 15)* **5-4-3-2-1. / PRETTY FLAMINGO** [ ] [-]

Feb 86. (lp/c) *E.M.I.; (EMS/TC-EMS 1121)* **THE SINGLES ALBUM** [ ] [-]
(cd-iss.Jul87 as 'THE SINGLES ALBUM PLUS'; CDP 746603-2)

Apr 86. (lp/c) *Fontana; (PRICE/PRIMC 66)* **HIT RECORDS 1966-69** [ ] [-]

Apr 87. (7") *Old Gold; (OG 9697)* **PRETTY FLAMINGO. / COME TOMORROW** [ ] [-]

Jun 89. (lp/c/cd) *E.M.I.; (SEE/+K/CD 252)* **THE EP COLLECTION** [ ] [-]
(re-iss.cd Nov94; same)

Jul 90. (cd/c/d-lp) *Castle; (CCS CD/MC/LP 245)* **THE COLLECTION** [ ] [-]

Sep 92. (cd-ep) *Old Gold;* **PRETTY FLAMINGO / IF YOU GOTTA GO, GO NOW / COME TOMORROW** [ ] [-]

Jan 93. (cd/c/lp) *Polygram TV; (514362-2/-4/-1)* **AGES OF MANN (22 CLASSICS OF THE 60's)** [23] [-]
(re-iss.Sep95 cd/c; same)

Jun 93. (cd) *E.M.I.; (CDEMS 1500)* **THE BEST OF THE EMI YEARS 1963-1965** [ ] [-]

Dec 93. (cd/c) *Music For Pleasure; (CD/TC MFP 5994)* **THE BEST OF MANFRED MANN 1964-1966** [ ] [-]

Aug 94. (cd/c) *Arcade; (ARC 31001-62/-74)* **THE VERY BEST OF MANFRED MANN'S EARTH BAND** [69] [-]

Jun 97. Chronicles; (d-cd) *(534806-2)* **THE ASCENT OF MANN** [ ] [-]

Phil MANZANERA / 801 (see under ⇒ ROXY MUSIC)

MARCH HARE (see under ⇒ KOOBAS)

MARK FOUR (see under ⇒ CREATION)

MARSUPILAMI

Formed: London, England . . . late 60's by brothers FRED HASSON and LEARY HASSON, alongside DAVE LAVEROCK and JESSICA STANLEY CLARKE. Their eponymous debut album, showed much promise in the progressive rock scene, while a second concept set, 'ARENA' (about The Coliseum b.c.) saw them take on a more adventurous approach. PETE BARDENS (later CAMEL) produced and guested on some of the tracks. Both albums are now worth over £50.

Recommended: MARSUPILAMI (*5) / ARENA (*6)

FRED HASSON – vocals, harmonica / LEARY HASSON – keyboards / **DAVE LAVEROCK** – guitar / **JESSICA STANLEY CLARKE** – flute, vocals / **RICHARD HICKS** – bass / **MIKE FOURACRE** – drums

Transatlantic not issued

1970. (7") *(TRA 213)* **MARSUPILAMI** [ ] [-]
– Dorian deep / Born to be free / And the eagle chased the dove to its ruin / Ab inito ad finem (The opera) / Facilis descensus averni.

— added some guests (see above)

1971. (lp) *(TRA 230)* **ARENA** [ ] [-]
– Prelude to the arena (the undertones of violence in a drifting generation) / Peace of Rome (they manufactured death to keep the peace) / The arean (the fighting, the killing, the mother of fornication) / Time shadows (lay low the past, the future brings hope) / Spring.

— disappeared after above

Nick MASON (see under ⇒ PINK FLOYD)

MATCHING MOLE (see under ⇒ WYATT, Robert)

Country Joe McDONALD (& THE FISH)

Born: 1 Jan '42, Washington, D.C., USA. In the early 60's, McDONALD joined the navy, although he left after his service period was over. In 1964, he augmented fellow troubadour, BLAIR HARDIMAN, on his very rare 'GOODBYE BLUES' album, forming COUNTRY JOE & THE FISH the following year. The band cut a few EP's for the local 'Rag Baby' magazine, and, through its editor Ed Denson, they signed a recording contract with folk label, 'Vanguard'. In the summer of '67, after a much heralded Monterey Pop Festival outing, their debut album, 'ELECTRIC MUSIC FOR THE MIND AND BODY', breached the US Top 40. McDONALD was the quintessential urban folk-country star, whose satrical politico-drugs and anti-war themes induced many to identify with his anarchic outfit during the 60's. In 1968, they released a second set, 'I-FEEL-LIKE-I'M-FIXIN'-TO-DIE', which featured his ode to his ex-girlfriend, JANIS JOPLIN and the anti-nuke anthem, 'THE BOMB SONG'. The band issued a third album, 'TOGETHER', although this was their last to secure a major chart placing. Other albums followed, some solo, although in 1970, he was convicted and fined $500 for obscenity, inciting anti-social crowd behaviour after chanting 'Gimme a F.*.*.*.'. This 'Fish Cheer' had been an audience participation ritual since the mid-60's. In the 70's, he took the country element in his music to its natural conclusion, with a string of rootsy albums. • **Trivia:** In 1971, he joined actors JANE FONDA and DONALD SUTHERLAND, in a 'Free The Army' revue. In 1976, he campaigned to 'SAVE THE WHALES', even writing a single with that title.

Recommended: THE COLLECTED COUNTRY JOE & THE FISH (*7)

COUNTRY JOE & THE FISH

JOE McDONALD – vocals, guitar / **BARRY 'THE FISH' MELTON** (b.1947, Brooklyn, New York) – guitar, vocals / **CARL SHRAGER** – washboard / **BILL STEEL** – bass / **MIKE BEARDSLEE** – harp, vocals

not issued Rag Baby

Oct 65. (7"ep) *<1001>* **COUNTRY JOE & THE FISH** [-] [ ]
– I-feel-like-I'm-fixin'-to-die rag / Superbird. / PETER KRUG: Fire in the city / Johnny's gone to war.

— **McDONALD + MELTON** introduced **BRUCE BARTHOL** (b.1947, Berkeley, Calif.) – bass / **DAVID COHEN** (b.1942, Brooklyn, N.Y.) – electric guitar / **CHICKEN HIRSCH** (b.1940, Calif.) – drums / **PAUL ARMSTRONG** – harp / **JOHN FRANCIS GUNNING** – drums

Jun 66. (7"ep) *<1002>* **RAG BABY** [-] [ ]
– Bass strings / Section 43 / (Thing called) Love.

— **MARK RYAN** repl. BRUCE

Fontana Vanguard

Jul 67. (7") *<35052>* **NOT SO SWEET MARTHA LORRAINE. / THE MASKED MARAUDER** [-] [95]

Oct 67. (lp; stereo/mono) *(S+/TFL 6081) <VSD 79244>* **ELECTRIC MUSIC FOR THE MIND AND BODY** [ ] [39] Apr67
– Flying high / Not so sweet Martha Lorraine / Death sound blues / Porpoise mouth / Section 43 / Superbird / Sad and lonely times / Love / Bass strings / The masked marauder / Grace. *(re-iss.Mar69 & Feb72 on 'Vanguard'; SVRL 19026) (re-iss.Mar89 on 'Start' lp/c/cd; VM5/TC6/CD6 301) (cd re-iss.Oct95; VMD 79244)*

Nov 67. (7") *(TF 882)* **NOT SO SWEET MARTHA LORRAINE. / LOVE** [ ] [-]

Nov 67. (7") *<35059>* **JANIS. / JANIS (instrumental)** [-] [ ]

Jan 68. (7") *<35061>* **WHO AM I? / THURSDAY** [-] [ ]

Mar 68. (lp; stereo/mono) *(S+/TFL 6086) <VSD 79266>* **I-FEEL-LIKE-I'M-FIXIN'-TO-DIE** [ ] [67] Nov67
– (the fish cheer) / I-feel-like-I'm-fixin'-to-die rag / Who am I / Pat's song / Rock coast blues / Magoo / Janis / Thought dream / Thursday / Eastern jam / Colors for Susan. *(re-iss.Mar69 & Feb72 on 'Vanguard'; SVRL 19029) (re-iss.Jul89 on 'Start' lp/c/cd; VM LP5/TC6/CD7 306) (cd re-iss.Oct95; VMD 79266)*

Vanguard Vanguard

Jul 68. (7") *<35068>* **ROCK AND SOUL MUSIC. / (part 2)** [-] [ ]

Nov 68. (lp) *(SVRL 19006) <VSD 79277>* **TOGETHER** [ ] [23] Jul68
– Rock and soul music / Susan / Mojo navigator / Bright suburban Mr. & Mrs. Clean machine / Good guys – bad guys cheer / The streets of your town / The fish moan / The Harlem song / Waltzing in the moonlight / Away bounce my bubbles / Cetacean / An untitled protest. *(cd re-iss.Oct95; VMD 79277)*

— **JOE + BARRY** recruited new members **MARK KAPNER** – keyboards to replace COHEN (He joined BLUES PROJECT). **PETER ALBIN** – bass (ex-BIG BROTHER & THE HOLDING COMPANY) / **DAVID GETZ** – drums (ex-BIG BROTHER & THE HOLDING COMPANY) repl. others.

Jun 69. (7") *<35090>* **HERE I GO AGAIN. / BABY YOU'RE DRIVING ME CRAZY** [-] [ ]

Sep 69. (lp) *(STVL 19048) <VSD 79299>* **HERE WE ARE AGAIN** [ ] [ ] Jun69
– Here I go again / Donovan's reef / It's nice to have love / Baby, you're driving me crazy / Crystal blues / For no reason / I'll survive / Maria / My girl / Doctor of electricity.

Oct 69. (7") *(VA 3)* **HERE I GO AGAIN. / IT'S SO NICE TO HAVE LOVE** [ ] [-]

— **DOUG METZNER** – bass repl. ALBIN / **GREG DEWEY** – drums (ex-MAD RIVER) repl. GETZ who went solo.

Jun 70. (7") *<35112>* **I FEEL LIKE I'M FIXIN' TO DIE RAG. / JANIS** [-] [ ]

Jun 70. (7") *(6076 250)* **I FEEL LIKE I'M FIXIN' TO DIE RAG. / MARIA** [ ] [-]

Oct 70. (lp) *(6359 002) <VSD 6555>* **C.J. FISH** [ ] [ ] Apr70
– Sing sing sing / She's a bird / Mara / Hang on / The baby song / Hey Bobby / Silver and gold / Rocking 'round the world / The love machine / The return of sweet Lorraine / Hand of man. *(re-iss.Feb72; same)*

— They split Autumn 1970

COUNTRY JOE McDONALD

had solo releases between 69-71. with **HAROLD BRADLEY** – guitar, bass / **RAY EDENTON** – guitar / **GRADY MARTIN** – guitar / **NORMAN PUTMAN** – bass / **BUDDY HARMON** – drums / **HARGUS 'PIG' ROBBINS** – percussion

Vanguard Vanguard

Apr 70. (lp; stereo/mono) *(S+/VRL 19057) <VSD 6546>* **THINKING OF WOODY GUTHRIE** [ ] [ ] Dec69
– Pastures of plenty / Talkin' dust bowl / Blowing down that old dusty road / So long it's been good to know yuh / Tom Joad / The sinking of Rueben James / Roll on Columbia / Pretty Boy Floyd / When the curfew blows / This land is your land. *(re-iss.Feb72;) (re-iss.Sep89 on 'Start' cd/c; CDVMD/MCCV 6546)*

Jan 71 (lp) *(6359 004) <VSD 6557>* **TONIGHT I'M SINGING JUST FOR YOU** [ ] [ ] Mar70
– Ring of fire / Tennessee stud / Heartaches by the number / Tiger by the tail / Crazy arms / You've done me wrong / All of me belongs to you / Oklahoma hills / Tonight I'm singing just for you / Friend, lover, woman, wife / Six days on the road. *(re-iss.Feb72;)*

— solo releases now post-FISH, were augmented by some UK session men

Jan 71. (7") *<35133>* **HOLD ON IT'S COMING. / PLAYING WITH FIRE** [-] [ ]

Sep 71. (lp) *<(VSD 79314)>* **HOLD ON IT'S COMING** [ ] [ ] Apr71
– Hold on it's coming / Air Algiers / Only love is worth this pain / Playing with fire / Travelling / Joe's blues / Mr. Big pig / Balancing on the edge of time / Jamila / Hold on it's coming No.2.

Sep 71. (7") *(6076 252)* **HOLD ON IT'S COMING. / (take 2)** [ ] [-]

— with **ANNA RIZZO** – vocals / **GREG DEEY** – drums / **NACKO DEWEY** – harp / **JOHN REWIND** – guitar / **VIC SMITH** – bass

1971. (7"ep) *>1003>* **COUNTRY JOE McDONALD & GROOTNA** [-] [ ]
– Kiss my ass / Tricky Dicky / Free some day.

— (above was issued in the States on his 'Rag Baby' label.

Jan 72. (lp) *<(VSD 79315)>* **WAR WAR WAR** [ ] [ ] Aug71
– The call / Forward / Young fellow, my lad / The man from Aphabaska / The munition maker / The twins / Jean Desprez / War widow / The march of the dead.

1972. (7") *<35150>* **HANG ON. / HAND OF MAN** [-] [ ]

Jul 72. (lp) *<(VSD 79316)>* **INCREDIBLE! LIVE! COUNTRY JOE!** [ ] [ ] Feb72
– Entertainment is my business / Sweet Marie / Kiss my ass / Living in the future in a plastic dome / Walk in Santiago / Tricky Dicky / You know what I mean / Fly so high / Deep down in our hearts / Free some day / I'm on the road again.

COUNTRY JOE

formed his ALL-STAR BAND with **PETER ALBIN** – bass / **DAVID GETZ** – drums / **TUCKI BAILEY** – saxophone / **DOROTHY MOSCOWITZ** – vocals, piano (ex-UNITED STATES OF AMERICA) / **PHIL MARSH** – guitar repl. BARRY MELTON / **ANNA RIZZO** – drums repl. SALLY HENDERSON – vocals / **SEBASTIAN NICHOLSON** – congas repl. **SUSAN LYDON** – vocals

Vanguard Vanguard

Apr 73. (7") *<35161>* **FANTASY. / I SEE A ROCKET** [-] [ ]

Aug 73. (lp) *<(VSD 79328)>* **PARIS SESSIONS** [ ] [ ]
– Fantasy / Movieola / I'm so tired / Moving / I don't know why / Zombies in a house of madness / Sexist pig / Colorado Town / Coulene Anne / St. Tropez.

Oct 73. (7") *(VAN 1006)* **FANTASY. / HOLD ON IT'S COMING** [ ] [-]

— **GINNY WHITTAKER** – drums, repl. GETZ, BAILEY, MARSH + NICHOLSON

— (Feb'74) **COUNTRY JOE** toured as duo with BARRY MELTON. Still solo below.

Nov 74. (7") *<35181>* **DR. HIP. / SATISFACTORY** [-] [ ]

Apr 75. (lp) *<(VSD 79348)>* **COUNTRY JOE** [ ] [ ] Dec74
– Dr. Hip / Old Joe Corey / Making money in Chile / You messed over me / Memories / Chile / Pleasin' / Jesse James / Satisfactory / It's finally over.

Apr 75. (7") *<35184>* **JESSE JAMES. / CHILE** [-] [ ]

COUNTRY JOE McDONALD

also augmented by ENERGY CRISIS (below)**PHIL MARSH** – guitar / **BRUCE BARTHOL** – bass / **JOHN BLAKELEY** – guitar / **PETER MILIO** – drums / **TED ASHFORD** – keyboards

Fantasy Fantasy

Oct 75. (lp) *(FTA 3002) <9495>* **PARADISE WITH AN OCEAN VIEW** [ ] [ ]
– Tear down the walls / Holy roller / Lost my connection / The limit / Save the whales / Oh! Jamaica / Lonely on the road / Tricks / Breakfast for two.

Jan 76. (7") *(FTC 123) <758>* **BREAKFAST FOR TWO. / LOST MY CONNECTION** [ ] [92] Nov75

Apr 76. (7") *(FTC 130) <765>* **SAVE THE WHALES. / OH! JAMAICA** [ ] [ ]

Aug 76. (lp) *(FTA 3005) <9511>* **LOVE IS A FIRE** [ ] [ ]
– It won't burn / You're the song / In love naturally / Oh no / Baby baby / True love at last / Who's gonna fry your eggs / Colortone / I need you (this and that) /

Love is a fire.
Oct 76. (7") <780> **I NEED YOU. / LOVE IS A FIRE** -
Oct 76. (7") *(FT 135)* **IN LOVE NATURALLY. / WHO'S GONNA FRY YOUR EGGS** -
— next solo albums used BARRY MELTON and session people.
Apr 77. (lp) *(FT 529)* <9525> **GOODBYE BLUES**
– Copiapo / Thought dreams / Goodbye blues / Let's go ridin' in the car / Blood on the ice / Primitive people / TV blues / Dark clouds / Little blue whale / Wilderness trail.
Oct 77. (7") *(FT 143)* **LA DI DA. / RING OF FIRE** -
May 78. (lp) *(FT 539)* <9544> **ROCK'N'ROLL MUSIC FROM PLANET EARTH** Feb78
– Coyote / Bring back the sixties man / Sunshine through my window / Rock & roll again / Dark ship / Y.O.U. / Southern cross / Space patrol / U.F.O. / Get it together.
Mar 78. (7") *(FTC 154)* <814> **COYOTE. / SOUTHERN CROSS**
Jul 78. (7") <822> **SUNSHINE THROUGH MY WINDOW. / BRING BACK THE 60'S MAN** -
— (Sep78) **COUNTRY JOE** reformed THE FISH, with **BARRY MELTON** – guitar, vocals / **PETER ALBIN** – bass / **BOB FLURIE** – guitar / **HAROLD ACEVES** – drums
— continued solo work.
Dec 79. (lp) *(FT 565)* <9586> **LEISURE SUITE**
– Private parts / Take this time out / Doo-wop-oh / Hard work no play / La di da / Sure cure for the blues / Reaching for the stars. *(cd-iss.late'90 on 'Rag Baby'; RBCD900317)*
Dec 79. (7") **TAKE THIS TIME OUT. / PRIVATE PARTS** -

Rag Baby Rag Baby
Aug 81. (lp) *(RAG 1012)* <147 406> **ON MY OWN** (totally solo)
– Standing at the crossroads / Calamity Jane / Give some love, get some back / C-O-U-N-T-R-Y / The Halloween tree / Slide trombone blues / Your last few records just didn't make it / Power plant blues / A Vietnam veteran still alive / Yankee doodle / Darlin' Dan.
— now with ever-changing personnel.
Jun 82. (d-lp) <RAG 2001> **INTO THE FRAY (live)** -
– Kiss my ass / Quiet days in Clichy / Sexist pig / Here I go again / Breakfast for two / Love is a fire / Picks and lasers / Coyote / Hold on it's coming / Entertainment is my business / Holy roller / Not so sweet Martha Lorraine / Janis / Get it all together / A Vietnam veteran still alive / Breakfast for two / Fixin'-to-die-rag / Save the whales / Ring of fire. *(UK-iss.Feb89; same) (cd-iss.late'90; RBCD 900603)*
Oct 83. (lp) <RAG 1018> **CHILDS PLAY** -
– Not in a Chinese restaurant / Power plant blues / Picks and lasers / Ice pack / One more good year of good times / Vietnam never again / America my home / Star Yeck: Voyage of the good ship Undersize / Mi Corazon. *(UK-iss.Feb89; same)*

Line not issued
Feb 85. (lp) *(RB 9.00068)* **PEACE ON EARTH** - - German
– Live in peace / Sunshine / Let it rain / You can get it if you really want / War hero / Feeling better / The girl next door / Darlin' man (the rocket man) / Pledging my love / Garden of Eden / Space lovin' / Peace on Earth. *(cd-iss.Feb89 & Oct94 on 'Rag Baby'; RBCD 9.00068)*
1986. (d-lp) *(LI 9.00418)* **VIETNAM EXPERIENCE** - - German
– I-feel-like-I'm-fixin'-to-die rag / Foreign policy blues / Agent Orange song / The girl next door (combat nurse) / Kiss my arse / Secret agent / Vietnam veteran still alive / Vietnam never again / Mourning blues / Welcome home / Vietnam requiem – part 1:- The beginning, part 2:- The end. *(cd-iss.Jun89; LICD 9.00418)*
— Returned in 1990 to recording studio.

Rykodisc Rykodisc
Jan 91. (cd) <(RBCD 90094-2)> **SUPERSTITIOUS BLUES** -

Line Rykodisc
Jan 95. (cd) *(90130-2)* **CARRY ON**
– Picks and lasers / Lady with the lamp / Joe's blues / Hold on to each other / Stolen heart blues / Trilogy / Going home / Carry on / My last song.

– compilations, etc. (with the FISH *) –

Mar 70. (lp) *Vanguard; (SVRL 19058)* <VSD 6545> **COUNTRY JOE & THE FISH / GREATEST HITS** 74 Dec69
Nov 73. (d-lp) *Vanguard; (VSD 27-28)* **THE LIFE AND TIMES OF COUNTRY JOE AND THE FISH FROM HAIGHT – ASHBURY TO WOODSTOCK** Oct71
Jul 76. (d-lp) *Vanguard; (VSD 85-86)* **THE ESSENTIAL COUNTRY JOE McDONALD**
Mar 77. (lp/c) *Golden Hour-Pye; (GH/ZCGH 865)* **THE GOLDEN HOUR OF COUNTRY JOE McDONALD** -
Jun 76. (lp) *Fantasy;* <9530> **REUNION** (live '67-'69 line-up) -
Jun 81. (lp) *Rag Baby;* <AMR 3309> **THE EARLY YEARS** -
– (tracks as below)
Jul 81. (lp) *Rag Baby; (RAG 1000)* **COLLECTOR'S ITEMS – THE FIRST THREE EP'S**
(re-iss.Mar87 on 'New World'; NEW 87) (re-iss.Apr87 on 'Decal'; LIK 8) (cd-iss.1992 on 'Sequel';)
Aug 83. (lp) *Animus; (FEEL 1)* **ANIMAL TRACKS**
Sep 83. (7") *Animus; (TOUCH 1)* **BLOOD ON THE ICE. / (no b-side)**
— (also appeared on Various Artists compilations WOODSTOCK, QUIET DAY IN CLICHY, CELEBRATION – BIG SUE FESTIVAL (live), A TRIBUTE TO WOODY GUTHRIE, ZACHARIAH (Soundtrack).
Jun 91. (cd) *Pickwick; (VCD 111)* **COLLECTED COUNTRY JOE & THE FISH** -
– Superbird / Bass strings / Section 43 / Flying high / Not so sweet Martha Lorraine / Death sound blues / Porpoise mouth / Sad and lonely times / The fish cheer – I-feel-like-I'm-fixin'-to-die rag / Rock coast blues / Janis / Eastern jam / Good guys – bad guys cheer / Rock and roll music / An unlimited protest / Here I go again / Maria, my own / Crystal blues / Rockin' round the world.
Jul 92. (cd) *Big Beat; (CDWIK 108)* **CLASSICS** -
Aug 96. (cd) *Volt; (VCD 139)* **LIVE AT THE FILLMORE WEST 1969**

MC5

Formed: Detroit, Michigan, USA ... 1965 by TYNER, SMITH and KRAMER. After 2 limited singles releases, MC5 (MOTOR CITY FIVE) signed a contract with 'Elektra' in mid'68, helped by counter-cultural activist and DJ, John Sinclair. In addition to becoming the band's manager, he heavily influenced their political extremism and warped takes on free jazz improvisation. Reflecting the harsher geographical and economic climate of Detroit, the band espoused revolution and struggle as opposed to the love and peace ethos of the sun-kissed Californian flower children. The riotous proto-punk of their legendary, acid-fuelled live show was captured on the controversial debut, 'KICK OUT THE JAMS'. Recorded in late October '68, it eventually hit the shops in May '69 and while the original uncensored pressings contained the line 'Kick out the jams, motherfuckers!', the offending word was later supplanted with the milder 'Brothers and sisters'. Unfortunately, this wasn't enough to prevent some record stores from refusing to stock the lp and after the band explicitly aired their views on one of the aforementioned dealers in a local newspaper, they were duly given the boot by Elektra. Nevertheless, the album reached No.30 in America and although it sounds a bit dated to modern ears, it was way radical for the time, remaining an inspiration to each new generation of noiseniks. After a split with Sinclair, the band signed with Atlantic and began to move away from the overtly subversive nature of their earlier material to a more straightahead rock approach, evidenced on their Jon Landau-produced follow-up album, 'BACK IN THE U.S.A.'. Wired rock'n'roll of an impeccable degree, the record didn't fare well in the laid-back, doped-up climate of the early 70's. An ambitious third album in 1971, 'HIGH TIME', featuring horns and even Salvation Army musicians still failed to cut any commercial ice and the band split in 1972. KRAMER subsequently spent five years in jail for cocaine dealing before embarking on a low key solo career while former manager Sinclair was sentenced to ten years in the early 70's for a minor dope charge, serving only two after appeal. Tragically, ROB TYNER died from a heart attack in 1991 aged only 46. Pioneers in the true sense of the word, the MC5 together with the STOOGES were the first real punk bands, the originators who were never bettered. **Songwriters:** Group compositions, except; I CAN ONLY GIVE YOU EVERYTHING (Them) / TUTTI FRUTTI (Little Richard).

Recommended: KICK OUT THE JAMS (*9) / BACK IN THE USA (*8).

ROB TYNER (b. ROBERT DERMINER, 12 Dec'44) – vocals, harmonica / **WAYNE KRAMER** (b.30 Apr'48) – guitar, vocals, keyboards / **FRED 'SONIC' SMITH** (b. West Virginia) – guitar / **MICHAEL DAVIS** – bass / **DENNIS THOMPSON** – drums

not issued A.M.G.
1966. (7") <AMG 1001> **I CAN ONLY GIVE YOU EVERYTHING. / I JUST DON'T KNOW** -
(above credited to MOTOR CITY FIVE)

not issued A2.
Mar 68. (7") <A2 333> **LOOKING AT YOU. / BORDERLINE** -
— added 6th member **Brother J.C.CRAWFORD** – rapper / narrative

Elektra Elektra
May 69. (7") *(EKSN 45056)* <EK 45648> **KICK OUT THE JAMS. / MOTOR CITY IS BURNING** 82 Mar 69
May 69. (lp) *(mono/stereo; EKL/EKS 74042)* **KICK OUT THE JAMS** 30 Mar 69
– Ramblin' rose / Kick out the jams / Come together / Rocker reducer No.62 / Borderline / Motor city is burning / I want you right now / Starship. *(re-iss.May77.) (re-iss.+cd.Nov91) (re-iss.cd+c Mar93 on 'Pickwick') (re-iss.cd/c Sep95 on 'Warners')*
Aug 69. (7") *(EKSN 45067)* **RAMBLIN' ROSE. / BORDERLINE** -

Atlantic Atlantic
Oct 70. (7") <2678> **TONIGHT. / LOOKING AT YOU** -
Nov 70. (lp) *(2400 016)* <SD 8247> **BACK IN THE U.S.A.** Feb 70
– Tutti frutti / Tonight / Teenage list / Looking at you / Let me try / High school / Call me animal / The American ruse / Shakin' Street / The human being lawnmower / Back in the U.S.A. *(re-iss.Feb77.) (cd-iss.May93 on 'Rhino-Atlantic')*
1970. (7") <2724> **SHAKIN' STREET. / THE AMERICAN RUSE** -
Oct 71. (lp) *(2400 123)* <SD 8285> **HIGH TIME**
– Sister Anne / Baby won't ya / Miss X / Gotta keep movin' / Future – Now / Poison / Over nnd over / Skunk (sonically speaking). *(cd-iss.May93 on 'Rhino-Atlantic')*
— (split early '72 when DAVIS departed) THOMPSON, SMITH and DAVIS formed short-lived ASCENSION. FRED SMITH married PATTI SMITH and later formed SONIC'S RENDEZVOUS BAND. TYNER was credited on HOT RODS single, late'77. (see ⇒ EDDIE & THE HOT RODS).

– compilations, etc. –

1969. (7") *A.M.G.;* <AMG 1001> **I CAN ONLY GIVE YOU EVERYTHING. / ONE OF THE GUYS** -
Jul 83. (c) *R.O.I.R.;* <A 122> **BABES IN ARMS** -
(re-iss.Apr90 & Dec92 on 'Danceteria' lp/cd; DAN LP/CD 031)
May 94. (cd) *Receiver; (RRCD 185)* **BLACK TO COMM** -
Oct 94. (10"lp/cd) *Alive; (ALIVE 005/+CD)* **POWER TRIP** -
Nov 94. (cd) *Receiver; (RRCD 193)* **LOOKING AT YOU** -
Feb 95. (10"lp/cd) *Alive; (NER/+CD 2001)* **THE AMERICAN RUSE** -
Feb 95. (cd) *Skydog;* **THUNDER EXPRESS – ONE DAY IN THE STUDIO** -
Mar 95. (10"lp) *Alive; (ALIVE 008)* **ICE PICK SLIM** -
(cd-iss.Feb97; ALIVECD 8)
Sep 95. (10"ep/cd) *Alive; (ALIVE 0010/+CD)* **FRIDAY, THE 13TH** -
Mar 97. (lp) *Alive; (NER 3008)* **TEENAGE LUST** -

WAYNE KRAMER

— went solo after spending 5 years in prison for cocaine dealing.

Stiff-Chiswick not issued
Oct 77. (7") *(DEA-SUK 1)* **RAMBLIN' ROSE. / GET SOME** -

Radar not issued
Jul 79. (7") *(ADA 41)* **THE HARDER THEY COME. / EAST SIDE GIRL** -

not issued | Pure&Easy

1983. (7") *<PE 017>* **NEGATIVE GIRLS. / STREET WARFARE** [-] [ ]

— GANG WAR formed in 1980 with **JOHNNY THUNDERS** – vocals

Zodiac | not issued

1987. (7"ep; WAYNE KRAMER'S GANG WAR) *(800)* **GANG WAR (live at Max's May 1980)** [ ] [-]

May 90. (lp) *(LP 1001)* **GANG WAR** (live/studio) [ ] [-]

— WAYNE had joined the DEVIANTS in 1984 for their album HUMAN GARBAGE.

Curio | Curio

1987. (7"; as WAYNE KRAMER'S DEATH TONGUE) **SPIKE HEELS. / ?** [-] [ ]

— (WAYNE played late 80's with DAS DAMEN and G.G. ALLIN)

Nov 91. (d-cd/d-lp) *(ITEM 2 CD/LP)* **DEATH TONGUE** [ ] [ ]
– Take your clothes off / Sike heels / Spend the rent / Negative girls / Death tongue / Leather skull / The scars never show / McArthur Park / Fun in the final days / Who shot you Dutch.

— In Sep'91, ROB TYNER was found dead after suffering heart attack. He was 46.

Epitaph | Epitaph

Dec 94. (cd/c/lp) *<(E 86447-2/-4/-1)>* **THE HARD STUFF** [ ] [ ]

Feb 96. (cd/lp) *(86458-2/-1)* **DANGEROUS MADNESS** [ ] [ ]

May 97. (cd) *(6488-2)* **CITIZEN WAYNE** [ ] [ ]
– Stranger in the house / Back when dogs could talk / Revolution in apt.29 / Down on the ground / Shining Mr. Lincoln's shoes / Dope for democracy / No easy way out / You don't know my name / Count time / Snatched defeat / Doing the work / Farewell to whiskey.

— MC5 are about to reform with KRAMER, DAVIS + THOMSON

Barry McGUIRE

Born: 15 Oct'37, Oklahoma City, USA. This singer/songwriter's first break in the music business came via The NEW CHRISTY MINSTRELS, a relatively succesful 60's folk troupe who, at one point, numbered future BYRD, GENE CLARK among their ranks. (Coincidentally, the song that gave McGUIRE his fifteen minutes of fame, 'EVE OF DESTRUCTION', was turned down by The BYRDS) Signing a solo deal with 'DUNHILL' records, McGUIRE hit paydirt with the aforementioned P.F. SLOAN-penned protest smash. Earnest it may have been, but this apocalyptic folk-rock prophecy was rendered utterly compelling by McGUIRE's ferocious delivery and remains a definitive 60's anthem. The similarly titled 1965 album and its follow-up, 'THIS PRECIOUS TIME' (1966) didn't exactly capitalise on the single's success and sadly, McGUIRE fell into that much maligned of musical bargain bins, the one hit wonder. After 'BARRY McGUIRE AND THE DOCTOR' (1971), the singer converted to Christianity and thereafter worked on gospel albums. • **Songwriters:** EVE OF DESTRUCTION (P.F. Sloan / feat. Grass Roots) / CLOUDY SUMMER AFTERNOON (Bud & Travis).

Recommended: EVE OF DESTRUCTION (*5)

BARRY McGUIRE – vocals, guitar

Ember | not issued

Feb 65. (7") *(EMBS 208)* **SO LONG STAY WELL. / FAR SIDE OF THE HILL** [ ] [-]

Apr 65. (7") *(EMBS 224)* **GREENBACK DOLLAR. / ONE BY ONE** [ ] [-]

— with **P.F. SLOAN + TOMMY TEDESCO** – guitar / **LARRY KNETCHEL** – bass / **HAL BLAINE** – drums / **STEVE BARRI** – percussion

RCA Vic. | Dunhill

Aug 65. (7") *(RCA 1469)* *<4009>* **EVE OF DESTRUCTION. / WHAT EXACTLY IS THE MATTER WITH ME** [3] [1]

Oct 65. (lp) *(RD 7751)* *<DS 50003>* **EVE OF DESTRUCTION** [ ] [37] Sep65
– Eve of destruction / She belongs to me / You never had it so good / Sloop John B. / Baby blue / The sins of the family / Try to remember / Mr.Man on the street / You were on my mind / Ain't no way I'm gonna change my mind / What's exactly's the matter with me / Why not stop and dig it while you can.

Nov 65. (7") *(RCA 1493)* *<4014>* **CHILD OF OUR TIME. / UPON A PAINTED OCEAN** [ ] [72] Oct65

— **JOE OSBOURNE** – bass; repl. LARRY / The MAMAS & THE PAPAS repl. TEDESCO

Jan 66. (7") *(RCA 1497)* *<4019>* **THIS PRECIOUS TIME. / DON'T YOU WONDER WHERE IT'S AT** [ ] [ ]

Apr 66. (lp) *<DS 50005>* **THIS PRECIOUS TIME** [-] [ ]
– This precious time / California dreamin' / Let me be / Do you believe in magic / Yesterday / Hang on Sloopy / Just like Tom Thumb's blues / Upon a painted ocean / You've got to hide your love away / I'd have to be outta my mind / Child of our times / Don't you wonder where it's at.

Apr 66. (7") *(RCA 1508)* **WALKING MY CAT NAMED DOG. / I'D HAVE TO BE OUTTA MY MIND** [ ] [-]

May 66. (7") *<4028>* **CLOUDY SUMMER AFTERNOON (RAINDROPS). / I'D HAVE TO BE OUTTA MY MIND** [-] [62]

Jul 66. (7") *(RCA 1525)* **CLOUDY SUMMER AFTERNOON. / YOU'VE GOT TO HIDE YOUR LOVE AWAY (with MAMAS & THE PAPAS)** [ ] [-]

— **TEDESCO** returned to repl. OSBOURNE + BARRI

1967. (7") *<4048>* **THERE'S NOTHING ELSE ON MY MIND. / WHY NOT STOP AND DIG IT WHILE YOU CAN** [-] [ ]

1967. (7") *(RCA 1638)* *<4098>* **MASTERS OF WAR. / WHY NOT STOP AND DIG IT WHILE YOU CAN** [ ] [ ]

1968. (lp) *<DS 50033>* **THE WORLD'S LAST PRIVATE CITIZEN** [-] [ ]
– Top o' the hill / Cloudy summer afternoon / Secret saucer man / There's nothin' else on my mind / Walkin' my cat named dog / Hang on Sloopy / Masters of war / Inner manipulations / The grasshopper song / This precious time / Why not stop and dig it while you can / Eve of destruction.

1968. (7") *<4116>* **INNER MANIPULATIONS. / LOLLIPOP TRAIN** [-] [ ]

1968. (7") *<4124>* **THE GRASSHOPPER SONG. / TOP O' THE HILL** [-] [ ]

— next with **ERIC HORD** – guitar, vocals / **CHRIS HILLMAN** – bass / **MICHAEL CLARKE** – drums / **BERNIE LEADON** – guitar / **BILLY MUNDI** – drums / **SNEAKY PETE** – steel / etc

A&M | Ode

1970. (7") *<66010>* **THE OLD FARM. / SOUTH OF THE BORDER** [-] [ ]

1971. (lp; by BARRY McGUIRE & ERIC HORD *(AMLS 2008)* *<77004>* **BARRY McGUIRE AND THE DOCTOR** [ ] [ ]
– South of the border / The old farm / Too much city / Train / Electric train / Meet me at the bottom.

— McGUIRE continued with solo career, his first record 'SEEDS' was in 1974 on religious 'Myrrh' label.

Scott McKENZIE

Born: PHILIP BLONDHEIM, 1 Oct'39, Jacksonville, Florida, USA – raised in Arlington, Virginia. He was initially part of New Yorkers, The JOURNEYMEN, alongside JOHN PHILLIPS (who was soon to join The MAMAS & THE PAPAS). After cutting a few songs for 'Capitol', McKENZIE relocated to Los Angeles, keeping his association with PHILLIPS when he recorded his number, 'SAN FRANCISCO (BE SURE TO WEAR FLOWERS IN YOUR HAIR)'. With PHILLIPS also at the production helm, it became the flower-power folk anthem of summer 1967, hitting No.4 in the States and No.1 in the UK. It inspired a flux of young hippies to head for San Francisco and try out a different peace-loving culture. He scored a second hit (also with PHILLIPS) later in the year, although things dried up by 1970 due to an abysmal country-rock effort in 1970, which did, however, feature guitar work by RY COODER. He continued to work in drug education, helping people to become aware of its dangers. He later surfaced in a re-formed MAMAS & THE PAPAS and went on to co-write 'KOKOMO' for The BEACH BOYS.

Recommended: THE VOICE OF SCOTT McKENZIE (*4)

SCOTT McKENZIE – vocals (& session musicians)

not issued | Epic

1967. (7"; as SCOTT McKENZIE'S MUSICIANS) *<10124>* **NO, NO, NO, NO, NO. / I WANT TO BE ALONE** [-] [ ]

C.B.S. | Ode

Jun 67. (7") *(2816)* *<103>* **SAN FRANCISCO (BE SURE TO WEAR FLOWERS IN YOUR HAIR). / WHAT'S THE DIFFERENCE** [1] [4] May67

Oct 67. (7"; as The Voice Of SCOTT McKENZIE) *(3009)* *<105>* **LIKE AN OLD TIME MOVIE. / WHAT'S THE DIFFERENCE (CHAPTER II)** [50] [24]

Dec 67. (lp; stereo/mono) *(S+/BPG 63157)* *<44002>* **THE VOICE OF SCOTT McKENZIE** [ ] [ ] Nov67
– San Francisco (be sure to wear flowers in your hair) / Celeste / It's not time now / What's the difference (chapter II) / Reason to believe / Like an old time movie / No, no, no, no, no / Don't make promises / Twelve-thirty / Rooms / What's the difference (chapter I).

Apr 68. (7") *(3393)* *<107>* **HOLY MAN. / WHAT'S DIFFERENCE (CHAPTER III)** [ ] [ ] Mar68

1970. (7") *<66012>* **GOING HOME AGAIN. / TAKE A MOMENT** [-] [ ]

1970. (lp) *<SP 77007>* **STAINED GLASS MORNING** [-] [ ]
– Look in the mirror / Yves / Crazy man / 1969 (enemies and friends) / Dear sister / Goin' home again / Stained glass morning / Illusion / Take a moment.

— returned briefly below

Soul Stop | not issued

Mar 84. (7") *(SS 3007)* **SECRET HOME. / OPEN SECRET** [ ] [-]

– compilations, etc. –

Aug 67. (7") *Capitol; (7") (CL 15509)* *<5961>* **LOOK IN YOUR EYES? / ALL I WANT IS YOU** [ ] [ ]

Aug 74. (7") *C.B.S.; (1168)* **SAN FRANCISCO (BE SURE TO WEAR FLOWERS IN YOUR HAIR). / REASON TO BELIEVE** [ ] [-]
(re-iss.Jan78; 5964)

1975. (7") *Epic; (152312)* **SAN FRANCISCO (BE SURE TO WEAR FLOWERS IN YOUR HAIR). / JUST LIKE AN OLD TIME MOVIE** [ ] [-]
(re-iss.Apr83 on 'Old Gold'; OG 9305)

Tony McPHEE (see under ⇒ GROUNDHOGS)

David McWILLIAMS

Born: 4 Jul'45, Cregagh, Belfast, Northern Ireland. After a flop debut, 'GOD AND MY COUNTRY', for 'CBS', he signed to the 'Major Minor' label. He was the subject of a massive publicity stunt by manager PHIL SOLOMON, resulting in a succession of NME cover stories which heralded the birth of a new talent. In 1967, the heavily produced acid-folk song, 'DAYS OF PEARLY SPENCER', by rights, should have been a hit. A poignant, swirling, string accompanied masterpiece, lyrically haunting, it was a hit 25 years on, albeit for MARC ALMOND. McWILLIAMS' albums at the time did fare better, all three volumes reaching the Top 40 in the space of nine months. A follow-up single, '3 O'CLOCK FLAMINGO STREET', was just as dynamic, although he couldn't shake off the "hype" tag. His dislike of appearing on stage, also became his albatross, and it didn't help when his manager raved about him being better than VAN MORRISON (statements that would haunt McWILLIAMS over the next three decades). In 1969, he was dropped by the label, re-surfacing in the early 70's with the credible 'LORD OFFALY' album. He continued with his blend of folk-rock, although commercially, he never achieved his deserved breakthrough.

Recommended: DAVID McWILLIAMS VOL.2 (*5) / LORD OFFALY (*5) / THE BEST OF THE E.M.I. YEARS (*5)

DAVID McWILLIAMS – vocals, guitar

C.B.S. Columbia

Sep 66. (7") *(202348) <43793>* **GOD AND MY COUNTRY. / BLUE EYES**

Major Minor not issued

Jun 67. (lp) *(MMLP 2)* **SINGING SONGS BY DAVID McWILLIAMS** [38] [-]
– God and my country / Redundancy blues / Silence is shattered / Time of trouble / Hiroshima / Question of identity / Echo of my heart / Early hours of the morning / I'll be home / Leaves that fall / Twilight / Hey Sally Sally / Reaching for the sun / Sheelo gone so long / Midnight sun / Pretty bird.

Sep 67. (7") *(MM 533)* **THE DAYS OF PEARLY SPENCER. / HARLEM LADY**
(re-iss.Feb71 on 'Parlophone'; R 5886)

Oct 67. (lp) *(SMLP 10)* **DAVID McWILLIAMS VOL.2** [23] [-]
– Days of Pearly Spencer / Can I get there / For Josephine / How can I be free / Marlena / Brown-eyed gal / For a little while / Lady Helen / Time will not wait / What's the matter with me / No lock upon my door / Tomorrow's like today.

Mar 68. (lp) *(SMLP 11)* **DAVID McWILLIAMS VOL.3** [39] [-]
– 3 o'clock Flamingo Street / Harlem lady / Four seasons / Turn homeward stranger / Letter to my love / City blues / Reflections / Poverty street / And I'm free / September winds / Born to ramble / Young man's dream.

May 68. (7") *(MM 561)* **THIS SIDE OF HEAVEN. / MISTER SATISFIED**

Jan 69. (7") *(MM 592)* **THE STRANGER. / FOLLOW ME**

Jun 69. (7") *(MM 616)* **OH MAMA ARE YOU MY FRIEND? / I LOVE SUSIE IN THE SUMMER**

Regal Star. not issued

Aug 71. (lp) *(SRS 5075)* **THE DAYS OF PEARLY SPENCER** (compilation) [-]
– Days of Pearly Spencer / Can I get there by candlelight / 3 o'clock Flamingo Street / Turn homeward stranger / Poverty street / How can I be free / Reflections / Oh mama are you my friend / The stranger / I'll be home / Mr. Satisfied / Marlena / This side of Heaven / Harlem lady.

Dawn Pye

Aug 72. (lp) *(DNLS 3039) <3302>* **LORD OFFALY**
– Go on back to momma / She was a lady / I will always be your friend / Heart of the roll / I would be confessed / Spanish hope / Blind mens stepping stones / Lord Offaly / The prisoner / The gypsy.

Oct 73. (7") *(DNS 1044)* **LOVE LIKE A LADY. / DOWN BY THE DOCKYARD** [-]

1973. (lp) *(DNLS 3047)* **THE BEGGAR AND THE PRIEST** [-]
– Cross the line / Na-na / Down by the dockyard / Bells of time / Lady Margaret / Daddy lonesome / Morning that looks like rain / Pharisee / Horseman / Leave the bottles on the floor.

Apr 74. (7") *(DNS 1064)* **YOU'VE ONLY BEEN A STRANGER. / SHIPS IN THE NIGHT** [-]

1974. (lp) *(DNLS 3059)* **LIVING'S JUST A STATE OF MIND** [-]
– Singer in the band / You wear it like a crown / Twenty golden years ago / Sad dark eyes / As I used to know her / You've only been a stranger / Please come home / Sweet Lil / Living's just a state of mind / Epitaph.

E.M.I. not issued

Jul 75. (7") *(EMI 2319)* **THE DAYS OF PEARLY SPENCER. / HARLEM LADY** [-]

Feb 77. (7") *(EMI 2586)* **BY THE LIGHTS OF CYRIAN. / TOBY** [-]

May 77. (7") *(EMI 2617)* **LOVE WALKED IN. / DON'T NEED YOUR BLUES** [-]

1977. (lp) *(EMC 3169)* **DAVID McWILLIAMS** [-]
– By the lights of Cyrian / Love walked in / North side of town / Jo Anne / Lay it on the line / The key to Heaven / Don't drink the water / If you love me yesterday / Don't need your blues / The singer and the song / Toby / Money can't buy you everything.

Jul 78. (7") *(EMI 2827)* **THE DAYS OF PEARLY SPENCER. / BY THE LIGHTS OF CYRIAN** [-]

Nov 78. (7") *(EMI 2845)* **DON'T DO IT FOR LOVE. / MARKO THE MAGICIAN** [-]

Jan 79. (lp) *(EMC 3208)* **DON'T DO IT FOR LOVE** [-]
– Just like strangers / Sweet songs baby / I will rock you / Don't be afraid of the rain / Don't do it for love / Carry me home / You'll be mine tonight / Lady midnight / Farewell to Harlem / Drink talkin' / Fat man / Sweetheart of the rodeo.

Prisma not issued

1980. (lp) *(064CRY 26305)* **WHEN I WAS A DANCER** [-] [-] German
– Overture – Candlelight / Dusty bluebells / Laugh of the clown / Slip slidin' away / Alone / When I was a dancer / Circles / Are you lonely / Dream street Rose / Come on.

Carmel not issued

Jan 82. (lp) *(CAR 1001LP)* **WOUNDED** [-]

1982. (7") *(CAR 1001)* **BLACK VELVET. / EVERY TIME** [-]

—— retired from music business after above

– compilations, etc. –

Jun 92. (cd/c) *E.M.I.; (CD/TC EMS 1457)* **DAVID McWILLIAMS: BEST OF THE E.M.I. YEARS** [-]

MEDICINE HEAD

Formed: Staffordshire, England . . .late 60's by long-time friends, JOHN FIDDLER and PETER HOPE-EVANS. Playing an informal gig at a party, they were introduced to DJ, John Peel, who later aired their demo tape on his Radio One show. One of the songs, 'HIS GUIDING HAND', was issued in 1970 on Peel's 'Dandelion' label. He also co-produced their first album, 'NEW BOTTLES OLD MEDICINE', a progressive-folk effort which became a favourite with the college brigade. Ex-Yardbird, KEITH RELF, produced their next set, 'HEAVY ON THE DRUM', even joining up along with JOHN DAVIES, following HOPE-EVANS' departure. This was after a 1971 hit single, '(AND THE) PICTURES IN THE SKY', which again drew comparisons with TYRANNOSAURUS REX. HOPE-EVANS was soon back in the line-up for the TONY ASHTON-produced second hit, 'ONE AND ONE IS ONE', which made the Top 3. By '73, they become a 5-piece band, charting with another two hippie-folk 45's, 'RISING SUN' and 'SLIP AND SLIDE' over the next six months, although the latter part of the 70's were less fruitful. The 'WWA' label subsequently fell apart and Chas Chandler signed them to his 'Barn' label. FIDDLER joined The BRITISH LIONS with ex-MOTT (THE HOOPLE) stars, later joining BOX OF FROGS (ex-YARDBIRDS), before going solo.

Recommended: NEW BOTTLES OLD MEDICINE (*7) / BEST OF MEDICINE HEAD (*7)

JOHN FIDDLER – vocals, guitar, keyboards, bass drum / **PETER HOPE-EVANS** – harmonica, jew's-harp

Dandelion Warners

Nov 69. (7") *(S 4661)* **HIS GUIDING HAND. / THIS LOVE OF OLD** [-]

May 70. (lp) *(63757)* **NEW BOTTLES, OLD MEDICINE** [-]
– When night falls / Ooee baby / Next time the sun comes round / This love of old / Home's odyssey / Oh my heart to peace / Do it now / Be it as we are / Fire under mountain / Two man now / Crazy 'bout you baby / Goin' home / His guiding hand / Walkin' blues. *(cd-iss.Nov94 on 'See For Miles'+=; SEECD 411)*– Pictures in the sky / Natural sight / Just like Tom Thumbs blues (live) / Blue suede shoes (live) / To train time (live). *(cd-iss.1995 on 'Repertoire'+=; (REP 4080)*– Pictures in the sky (single version) – (reverberation version) – (home recorded demo version).

Jul 70. (7") *(S 5075)* **COAST TO COAST. / ALL FOR TOMORROW** [-]

1971. (lp) *(DAN 8005) <49005>* **HEAVY ON THE DRUM**
– There's always a light / Any day now / Medicine pony / Thou shalt not pass / Expectation blues / To train time / Call on you saviour (and sing with the drum) / Have no fear / You got me rockin' and rollin' / Once there was a day / (Sometimes) Even the Moon has no face.

Jun 71. (7") *(DAN 7003) <K 19002>* **(AND THE) PICTURES IN THE SKY. / NATURAL SIGHT** [22] Jan72

—— **KEITH RELF** – bass, producer (ex-YARDBIRDS) / **JOHN DAVIES** – drums, repl. EVANS

Polydor Polydor

Jan 72. (7") *(2001 276)* **KUM ON. / ON THE LAND** [-]

Apr 72. (7") *(2001 325)* **ONLY TO DO WHAT IS TRUE. / SITTIN' IN THE SUN** [-]

1972. (lp) *(2310 166)* **DARK SIDE OF THE MOON** [-]
– Back to the wall / In your eyes / Sittin' in the Sun / On this road / You and me / Kum on / Only to do what is true / You can make it here.

—— **EVANS** returned to repl. RELF + DAVIES. The original duo added **PAT DONALDSON** – bass / **TONY ASHTON** – keyboards, producer + **ROY DYKE** – drums (ex-ASHTON, GARDNER & DYKE) / **CLIVE THACKER** – drums / **BRIAN PARISH + MICK LIBER** – guitar

Nov 72. (7") *(2001 383)* **HOW DOES IT FEEL. / MORNING LIGHT** [-]

Dec 72. (lp) *(2310 166) <5532>* **ONE & ONE IS ONE**
– Out on the street / How does it feel / Instant karma kid / Another lay / Blue suede shoes / To train time / One & one is one / Morning light / I know why / All the fallen teenangels.

Feb 73. (7") *(2001 432) <15076>* **ONE & ONE IS ONE. / OUT ON THE STREET** [3] Apr73

—— **FIDDLER, EVANS + ASHTON** added **ROB TOWNSEND** – drums (ex-FAMILY) / **ROGER SAUNDERS** – guitar, vocals / **GEORGE FORD** – bass, vocals

Jul 73. (7") *(2058 389) <15083>* **RISING SUN. / BE MY FLYER** [11]

Jan 74. (7") *(2058 436)* **SLIP AND SLIDE. / CAJUN KICK** [22]

Feb 74. (lp) *(2383 272)* **THRU' A FIVE** [-]
– Cajun kick / Slip and slide / Take two steps / The season and the sign / Changin' man / Epitaph blues / Rising Sun / White dove / In the palm of your hand / Rain / Indian queen.

Apr 74. (7") *(6008 009)* **ALRIGHT. / PART OF THE DAY**

W.W.A. not issued

Sep 74. (7") *(WWS 15)* **MAMA COME OUT. / COME ON OVER**

—— original duo now with session men **ASHTON + SAUNDERS / CHARLIE McCRACKEN** – bass (ex-SPENCER DAVIS GROUP, ex-TASTE) / **MORGAN FISHER** – keyboards (ex-MOTT THE HOOPLE) / **B.J. COLE** – steel guitar (ex-PROCOL HARUM)

Barn-Polydor not issued

Jul 76. (7") *(2014 102)* **IT'S NATURAL. / MOON CHILD** [-]

Oct 76. (lp) *(2314 102)* **TWO MAN BAND** [-]
– It's natural / Wishin' and wishin' / Give it away / Si belle / Mother love / I'm your man / Sun's sinkin' low / Over you / River of tears / Shake me / Too much love.

Nov 76. (7") *(2014 103)* **ME AND SUZIE (HIT THE FLOOR). / MIDNIGHT** [-]

—— Disbanded. FIDDLER joined BRITISH LIONS (a splinter of MOTT THE HOOPLE) + EVANS sessioned for EDGAR BROUGHTON / ROGER CHAPMAN / PETE TOWNSHEND. They re-formed for one-off in 1980.

Harvest not issued

Jul 80. (7") *(HAR 5209)* **CAN'T GET OVER YOU. / TENDERHOOKS** [-]

– compilations, etc. –

Jul 75. (lp) *Polydor-Super; (2384 069)* **MEDICINE HEAD** [-]

Sep 81. (lp)(c) *Polydor; (2485 204)(3201 278)* **THE BEST OF MEDICINE HEAD** [-]
(re-iss.Sep90 cd/c; 843901-2/-4)

Oct 88. (7") *Old Gold; (OG 9809)* **ONE & ONE IS ONE. /** [-]

Sep 95. (cd) *Red Steel; (RMOCD 0201)* **TIMEPEACE (BOOM, HOWL AND MOAN)** [-]

Aug 96. (cd) *Red Steel; (RMCCD 0201)* **MEDICINE HEAD LIVE** [-]

JOHN FIDDLER

Harvest not issued

Jun 80. (7") *(HAR 5204)* **LOOK DON'T TOUCH. / YOU'VE GOT EVERYTHING** ☐ -

— He later (1984) joined BOX OF FROGS (a splinter of The YARDBIRDS).

Red Steel not issued

May 96. (cd) *(RMCCD 0197)* **RETURN OF THE BUFFALO** ☐ -

MELLOW CANDLE

Formed: Ireland ... 1968 as a 5-piece with young singers, CLODAGH SIMONDS and ALISON WILLIAMS at the forefront. That year, they issued a one-off single, 'FEELING HIGH', an excellent piece of psychedelic folk that was lyrically profound and musically reminiscent of early FAIRPORT CONVENTION. It was four years before they resurfaced with the album, 'SWADDLING SONGS', which again featured compelling lyrics but sold poorly (subsequently making it 'Deram's most pricey artifact, selling upwards of 400 quid).

Recommended: SWADDLING SONGS (*8)

CLODAGH SIMONS (b.1953) – vocals, keyboards / **ALISON WILLIAMS** – vocals / **DAVID WILLIAMS** – guitar, vocals / **FRANK BOYLAN** – bass / **WILLIAM MURRAY** drums

S.N.B.-CBS not issued

Aug 68. (7") *(55-3645)* **FEELING HIGH. / TEA WITH THE SUN** ☐ -

Deram not issued

Mar 72. (7") *(DM 357)* **DAN THE WING. / SILVERSONG** ☐ -

May 72. (lp) *(SDL 7)* **SWADDLING SONGS** ☐ -

– Heaven heath / Sheep season / Silversong / The poet and the witch / Messenger birds / Dan the wing / Reverend sisters / Break your token / Buy or beware / Vile excess / Lonely man / Boulders on my grave. *(cd-iss.Aug94 on 'See For Miles'; SEECD 404)*

— split after above, CLODAGH sang backing vocals on the JADE WARRIOR album, 'Kites', while both girls sang for THIN LIZZY.

– compilations, etc. –

Jun 97. (cd) *Kissing Spell; (KSCD 9520)* **VIRGIN PROPHET** ☐ -

MILLER

Born: PETE MILLER, Norwich, England. He was initially part of a backing band for US singer, MILTON, before joining PETER JAY AND THE JAYWALKERS. In 1965, he released 'THE GIRL WITH THE CASTLE' for the local 'Oak' label, the single later being picked up by 'Columbia'. The company subsequently released its B-side, 'BABY I'VE GOT NEWS FOR YOU', as the main track (thought to be the first ever psychedelic track), the single subsequently becoming a very rare collector's piece, now changing hands for £100 (both versions). He then joined The NEWS, releasing two singles, the second, 'THIS IS THE MOMENT', being produced by CHRIS ANDREWS. MILLER returned with another piece of classic psychedelia in the shape of 'COLD TURKEY', although this was under the alias BIG BOY PETE.

Recommended: their debut & final 45

MILLER – vocals

Oak not issued

1965. (7") *(RGJ 190)* **THE GIRL WITH THE CASTLE. / BABY I'VE GOT NEWS FOR YOU** ☐ -

Columbia not issued

1965. (7") *(DB 7735)* **BABY I GOT NEWS FOR YOU. / THE GIRL WITH THE CASTLE** ☐ -

NEWS

PETE MILLER – vocals, repl. ANDY FIELDS / **IVAN ZAGNI** – guitar / **HARVEY PLATT** – bass / **DENNY ROYAL** – drums

Decca not issued

Mar 66. (7") *(F 12356)* **THE ENTERTAINER. / I COUNT THE TEARS** ☐ -

Aug 66. (7") *(F 12477)* **THIS IS THE MOMENT. / YA YA DA DA** ☐ -

BIG BOY PETE

PETE MILLER under a pseudonym

Camp not issued

Feb 68. (7") *(602 005)* **COLD TURKEY. / MY LOVE IS LIKE A SPACESHIP** ☐ -

— MILLER went off to the States to retire

Steve MILLER

Born: 5 Oct'43, Milwaukee, Wisconsin, USA; raised in Dallas, Texas. After forming school band, The MARKSMAN COMBO, with BOZ SCAGGS, he later played for bluesman JIMMY REED at a 1957 gig. In the early 60's, he and SCAGGS joined The ARDELLS, who, along with BEN SIDRAN, became The FABULOUS NIGHT TRAIN. In 1964, after a brief spell in Denmark, he moved to Chicago, where he sessioned for MUDDY WATERS, HOWLIN' WOLF and PAUL BUTTERFIELD. The following year, he partnered BARRY GOLDBERG in the group, The WORLD WAR III BAND, who issued a one-off 45, 'THE MOTHER SONG' (Epic 9865) as The GOLDBERG-MILLER BAND. Late in '66, he moved to San Francisco and formed The MILLER BAND with JAMES 'Curly' COOKE, LONNIE TURNER and TIM DAVIS, later adding JIM PETERMAN, and replacing COOKE with SCAGGS. After a June appearance at The Monterey Pop Festival, they signed to 'Capitol', recording three songs for the 'Revolution' film soundtrack, which eventually hit the shops late in '69. Their debut album, 'CHILDREN OF THE FUTURE', was issued in the Spring of '68, making all of No.134 in the US charts. Its mild success, was overshadowed by the follow-up, 'SAILOR', which introduced his trademark 'GANGSTER OF LOVE' motif. The album gave them their first of many entries into US Top 30, although with each successive release, they moved further away from the neo-psychedelic experimentation which had characterised their earlier releases. In 1973, after a lean couple of years, they hit US No.1 with 'THE JOKER', a song that lyrically revived his "Gangster Of Love". Although it was regarded as a classic in the UK, it still failed to chart (that is, until 1990, when it topped the charts after being given fresh exposure on a Levi jeans TV ad). The single was the title track of the album, which became his biggest selling album to date, hitting US No.2 and staying in the chart for nine months. After a prolonged break, MILLER returned with his most accessible and commercial album to date, 1976's 'FLY LIKE AN EAGLE'. The record showcased a more straightforward approach with finely crafted songs and strong hooks, spawning a slew of hit singles that even reached the UK Top 20. Its title track was a return to the laid-back psychedelia MILLER had flirted with back in the 60's (more recently it was a hit for SEAL). The next effort, 'BOOK OF DREAMS', was almost as big; No.2 stateside and No.12 in Britain. Following another hiatus, the band released 'CIRCLE OF LOVE' (1981), a collection of radio-friendly rockers that stuck more or less to MILLER's proven formula. The title track of the band's 1982 album, 'ABRACADABRA' was a worldwide smash, its quirky jack-in-the-box feel making it a quintessential 80's record, although the album sounded somewhat laboured. After a live album and a disappointing couple of studio sets, MILLER went solo in 1988, going back to his roots on 'BORN 2 B BLUE' and releasing a further solo album in 1993, 'WIDE RIVER'. • **Songwriters:** MILLER and BEN SIDRAN compositions, except covers on 87 & 88 albums. • **Trivia:** On '69 song 'MY DARK HOUR', PAUL McCARTNEY played bass under psuedonym MARK RAMON.

Recommended: CHILDREN OF THE FUTURE (*6) / SAILOR (*7) / BRAVE NEW WORLD (*6) / YOUR SAVING GRACE (*6) / NUMBER FIVE (*6) / LIVING IN THE U.S.A. (*7) / ROCK LOVE (*5) / RECALL THE BEGINNING ... (*5) / ANTHOLOGY / THE BEST OF STEVE MILLER BAND 1968-1973 (*8) / THE JOKER (*6) / FLY LIKE AN EAGLE (*7) / BOOK OF DREAMS (*6)

The STEVE MILLER BAND

STEVE MILLER – vocals, guitar / **LONNIE TURNER** (b.24 Feb'47, Berkeley, Calif.) – bass, vocals / **BOZ SCAGGS** (b. 8 Jun'44, Ohio) – guitar / **JIM PETERMAN** – organ, vocals / **TIM DAVIS** – drums

Capitol Capitol

Apr 68. (7") *(CL 15539)* <2156> **SITTIN' IN CIRCLES. / ROLL WITH IT** ☐ ☐

Sep 68. (lp; stereo/mono) *(S+/T 2920)* <718> **CHILDREN OF THE FUTURE** ☐ ☐ Apr68

– Children of the future / Pushed me to it / You've got the power / In my first mind / The beauty of time is that it's snowing / Baby's callin' me home / Steppin' stone / Roll with it / Junior saw it happen / Fanny Mae / Key to the highway. *<re-iss.1980; SN 16262> (cd-iss.Apr97 on 'E.M.I.'; REPLAYCD 19)*

Oct 68. (7") *(CL 15564)* <2287> **LIVING IN THE U.S.A. / QUICKSILVER GIRL** ☐ 94

Jan 69. (lp; stereo/mono) *(S+/T 2984)* <719> **SAILOR** ☐ 24 Oct68

– Song for our ancestors / Dear Mary / My friend / Living in the U.S.A. / Quicksilver girls / Lucky man / Gangster of love / You're so fine / Overdrive / Dime-a-dance romance. *(re-iss.Nov83 on 'Fame' lp/c; FA41/TCFA 3085-1/-4) (re-iss.Apr91 cd/c/lp; CD/TC+/FA 3254) (cd re-iss.Apr97 on 'E.M.I.'; REPLAYCD 17)*

Jan 69. (7") <2447> **DEAR MARY. / SITTIN' IN CIRCLES** - ☐

— Trimmed to a trio of **MILLER, TURNER** and **DAVIS** with session men. (PETERMAN left just after SCAGGS who went solo) **BEN SIDRAN** – keyboards (joined briefly)

— (Mar69) **NICKY HOPKINS** – keyboards (ex-JEFF BECK GROUP) repl. SIDRAN

Sep 69. (lp) <*(E-ST 184)*> **BRAVE NEW WORLD** ☐ 22 Jun69

– Brave new world / Space cowboy / Got love 'cause you need it / It's a midnight dream / Can't you hear daddy's heartbeat / Celebration song / Seasons / Kow kow calculator / My dark hour. *(re-iss.Feb84 on 'E.M.I.'; IC 038 80117) (cd-iss.Apr97 on 'E.M.I.'; REPLAYCD 20)*

Jul 69. (7") *(CL 15604)* <2520> **MY DARK HOUR. / SONG FOR OUR ANCESTORS** ☐ ☐

Nov 69. (7") *(CL 15618)* <2638> **LITTLE GIRL. / DON'T LET NOBODY TURN YOU AROUND** ☐ ☐

Mar 70. (lp) <*(E-ST 331)*> **YOUR SAVING GRACE** ☐ 38 Nov69

– Little girl / Just a passin' fancy in a midnite dream / Don't let nobody turn you around / Baby's house / Motherless children / The last wombat in Mecca / Feel so glad / Your saving grace. *(cd-iss.May91 on 'E.M.I.'; CZ 434) (cd re-iss.Apr97 on 'E.M.I.'; REPLAYCD 21)*

— **BOBBY WINKLEMAN** – bass, vocals repl. TURNER and HOPKINS who joined QUICKSILVER MESSENGER SERVICE

Nov 70. (lp) <*(EA-ST 436)*> **NUMBER 5** ☐ 23 Jul70

– Good morning / I love you / Going to the country / Hot chili / Tokin's / Going to Mexico / Steve Miller's midnight tango / Industrial military complex hex / Jackson-Kent blues / Never kill another man. *(cd-iss.Apr97 on 'E.M.I.'; REPLAYCD 18)*

Sep 70. (7") *(CL 15665)* <2878> **GOING TO THE COUNTRY. / NEVER KILL ANOTHER MAN** ☐ 69 Aug70

Dec 70. (7") <2945> **GOING TO MEXICO. / STEVE MILLER'S MIDNIGHT TANGO** - ☐

— **STEVE MILLER** recruited entire new band **ROSS VALORY** – bass, vocals repl. WINKLEMAN / **JACK KING** – drums, vocals repl. DAVIS who went solo

Sep 71. (7") *<3228>* **ROCK LOVE. / LET ME SERVE YOU** – □

Nov 71. (lp) *<(EA-ST 748)>* **ROCK LOVE** □ □ Oct71
– The gangster is back / Blues without blame / Love shock / Let me serve you / Rock love / Harbor lights / Deliverance.

— **GERALD JOHNSON** – bass, vocals repl. VALORY who later joined JOURNEY / added **DICKY THOMPSON** – keyboards / **ROGER ALAN CLARK** – 2nd drummer

May 72. (lp) *<EST 11022>* **RECALL THE BEGINNING . . . A JOURNEY FROM EDEN** □ □ Mar72
– Welcome / Enter Maurice / High on you mama / Heal your heart / The sun is going down / Somebody somewhere help me / Love's riddle / Fandango / Nothing lasts / Journey from Eden. *(re-iss.Feb84 on 'E.M.I.'; 1C 062 81099)*

May 72. (7") *<3344>* **FANDANGO. / LOVE'S RIDDLE** – □

— (Mar72) **JOHN KING** – drums repl. JACK and ROGER / **LONNIE TURNER** – bass, vocals returned to repl. JOHNSON who joined BOZ SCAGGS

Oct 73. (7") *(CL 15765) <3732>* **THE JOKER. / SOMETHING TO BELIEVE IN** □ 1

Oct 73. (lp) *<(EST 11235)>* **THE JOKER** □ 2
– Sugar babe / Mary Lou / Loving cup / Shu ba da du ma ma / Your cash ain't nothin' but trash / The joker / Lovin' cup / Come on into my kitchen / Evil / Something to believe in. *(re-iss.Oct80; same) (re-iss.Jan83 on 'E.M.I.'; 1C 062 81514) (re-iss.Oct90 on 'Fame' cd/c/lp; CD/TC+/FA 3250)*

Feb 74. (7") *<3837>* **YOUR CASH AIN'T NOTHIN' BUT TRASH. / EVIL** – 51

— (May74) **STEVE MILLER** retired for a while, when THOMPSON and KING departed.

— (Jul75) **MILLER** retained **TURNER** and recruited for Knebworth festival **LES DUDEK** – guitar, vocals / **DOUG CLIFFORD** – drums (ex-CREEDENCE CLEARWATER REVIVAL)

— (1976) **GARY MALLABER** (b.11 Oct'46, Buffalo, N.Y.) – drums repl. CLIFFORD and DUDEK

Mercury Capitol

May 76. (7") *(6078 800) <4260>* **TAKE THE MONEY AND RUN. / SWEET MARIE** □ 11 Apr76

May 76. (lp)(c) *(9286 177)(7100 925) <11497>* **FLY LIKE AN EAGLE** 11 3
– (Space intro) / Fly like an eagle / Wild mountain honey / Serenade / Dance, dance, dance / Mercury blues / Take the money and run / Rock'n'me / You send me / Blue odyssey / Sweet Marie / The window. *(re-iss.Nov84 lp/c; PRICE/PRIMC 75) (re-iss.Jun92 on 'Arcade' cd/c; ARC 94710-2/-4)*

Aug 76. (7") *<4323>* **ROCK'N'ME. / LIVING IN THE U.S.A.** – 1

Aug 76. (7") *(6078 802)* **FLY LIKE AN EAGLE. / MERCURY BLUES** □ –

Oct 76. (7") *(6078 804)* **ROCK'N'ME. / THE WINDOW** 11 –

Dec 76. (7") *<4372>* **FLY LIKE AN EAGLE. / LOVIN' CUP** – 2

Jan 77. (7") *(6078 808)* **SERENADE. / DANCE, DANCE, DANCE** □ –

— (Oct76) added **DAVID DENNY** – guitar, vocals (ex-TERRY & THE PIRATES) / **BYRON ALLRED** – keyboards / **NORTON BUFFALO** – harmonica, vocals

Apr 77. (7") *(6078 811) <4424>* **JET AIRLINER. / BABES IN THE WOOD** □ 8

May 77. (lp)(c) *(9286 455)(7299 393) <11630>* **BOOK OF DREAMS** 12 2
– Threshold / Jet airliner / Winter time / Swingtown / True fine love / Wish upon a star / Jungle love / Electro lux imbroglio / Sacrifice / The stake / My own space / Babes in the wood. *(re-iss.Jan85 lp/c; PRICE/PRIMC 78) (re-iss.Jun92 on 'Arcade' cd/c; ARC 94730-2/-4)*

Sep 77. (7") *(6078 812) <4466>* **JUNGLE LOVE. / WISH UPON A STAR** □ 23 Jul77

Jan 78. (7") *(6078 813) <4496>* **SWINGTOWN. / WINTER TIME** □ 17 Oct77

— trimmed to a quintet of **MILLER, MALLABER, ALLRED, DOUGLAS** and **BUFFALO**

Oct 81. (lp/c) *(6302/7144 061) <ST 12121>* **CIRCLE OF LOVE** □ 26
– Heart like a wheel / Get on home / Baby wanna dance / Circle of love / Macho city. *(re-iss.Jun92 on 'Arcade' cd/c; ARC 94730-2/-4)*

Oct 81. (7") *<5068>* **HEART LIKE A WHEEL. / TRUE FINE LOVE** – 24

Nov 81. (7"m) *(STEVE 1)* **HEART LIKE A WHEEL. / JET AIRLINER / THRESHOLD** □ –

Jan 82. (7") *<5086>* **CIRCLE OF LOVE. / (part 2)** – 55

Feb 82. (7") *(STEVE 2)* **MACHO CITY. / FLY LIKE AN EAGLE** □ –

— **KENNY LEWIS** – guitar / **JOHN MASSARO** – guitar both repl. DOUGLAS

May 82. (7") *<5126>* **ABRACADABRA. / GIVE IT UP** – 1

Jun 82. (7") *(STEVE 3)* **ABRACADABRA. / NEVER SAY NO** 2 –
(re-iss.Oct84;)

Jun 82. (lp/c) *(6302/7144 204) <ST 12216>* **ABRACADABRA** 10 3
– Keeps me wondering why / Abracadabra / Something special / Give it up / Never say no / Things I told you / Young girl's heart / Cool magic / While I'm waiting. *(cd-iss.Jan83; 800090-2) (re-iss.Jun92 on 'Arcade' cd/c; ARC 94740-2/-4)*

Aug 82. (7") *(STEVE 4)* **KEEPS ME WONDERING WHY. / GET ON HOME** 52 □
(12"+=) *(STEVE 4-12)* – Abracadabra.

Oct 82. (7") *(STEVE 5)* **GIVE IT UP. / ROCK'N'ME** □ –

Oct 82. (7") *<5162>* **COOL MAGIC. / YOUNG GIRL'S HEART** – 57

Dec 82. (7") *<5194>* **GIVE IT UP. / HEART LIKE A WHEEL** – 60

Mar 83. (7") *<5223>* **LIVING IN THE U.S.A. (live). / BUFFALO SERENADE** – □

Apr 83. (lp/c)(cd) *(MERL/+C 18)(811020-2) <12263>* **THE STEVE MILLER BAND LIVE! (live)** 79 □
– Gangster of love / Rock'n'me / Living in the U.S.A. / Fly like an eagle / Jungle love / The joker / Mercury blues / Take the money and run / Abracadabra / Jet airliner. *(cd+=)*– Buffalo serenade.

Apr 83. (7") *(STEVE 6)* **TAKE THE MONEY AND RUN (live). / THE JOKER (live)** □ –
(12"+=) *(STEVE 6-12)* – Buffalo serenade (live).

— Now without MASSARO

Oct 84. (7") *(STEVE 7) <5407>* **SHANGRI-LA. / CIRCLE OF LOVE** □ 57
(12"+=) *(STEVE 7-12)* – Abracadabra.

Nov 84. (lp/c)(cd) *(MERL/+C 50)(822823-2) <12339>* **ITALIAN X-RAYS** □ □
– Radio 1 / Italian x-rays / Daybreak / Shangri-la / Who do you love / Harmony of the spheres 1 / Radio 2 / Bongo bongo / Out of the night / Golden opportunity / The Hollywood dream / One in a million / Harmony of the spheres 2. *(re-iss.Jun92 on 'Arcade' cd/c; ARC 94750-2/-4)*

Jan 85. (7") *(STEVE 8) <5442>* **BONGO BONGO. / GET ON HOME** □ 84

Mar 85. (7") *<5476>* **ITALIAN X-RAYS. / WHO DO YOU LOVE** – □

— **MILLER** with **MALLABER** and **BUFFALO** bring back **LES DUDEK** – guitar

Capitol Capitol

Jan 87. (lp/c)(cd) *(EST/TC-EST 2027)(CDP 746326-2)* **LIVING IN THE 20TH CENTURY** □ 65 Nov86
– Nobody but you baby / I want to make the world turn around / Slinky / Living in the 20th century / Maelstrom / I wanna be loved / My babe / Big boss man / Caress me baby / Ain't that lovin' you baby / Behind the barn.

Mar 87. (7"/12") *(CL/12CL 444) <5646>* **I WANT TO MAKE THE WORLD TURN AROUND. / SLINKY** □ 97 Nov86

Apr 87. (7") *<5671>* **NOBODY BUT YOU BABY. / MAELSTROM** – □

Jun 87. (7") *<5704>* **I WANNA BE LOVED. / (part 2)** – □

STEVE MILLER

solo with **BEN SIDRAN** – keyboards / **BILLY PATERSON** – bass / **GORDY KNUDTSON** – drums

Sep 88. (7") *(CL 506)* **YA YA. / FILTHY McNASTY** □ □
(12"+=) *(12CL 506)* – ('A'remix by Steve Weiss).

Sep 88. (cd/c/lp) *(CD/TC+/EST 2072) <48303>* **BORN 2B BLUE** □ □
– Zip-a-dee-doo-dah / Ya ya / God bless the child / Filthy McNasty / Born to be blue / Mary Ann / Just a little bit / When Sunny gets blue / Willow weep for me / Red top.

Polydor Sailor

Jul 93. (cd/c) *(519441-2/-4)* **WIDE RIVER** □ 85
– Wide river / Midnight train / Blue eyes / Lost in your eyes / Perfect world / Horse and rider / Circle of fire / Conversation / Cry cry cyr / Stranger blues / Walks like a lady / All your love (I miss loving).

Jul 93. (c-s/cd-s) *<85919-4/-2>* **WIDE RIVER /** – 64

Aug 93. (7"/cd-s) **WIDE RIVER. / STRANGER BLUES** □ □

– compilations, etc. –

on 'Capitol' unless mentioned otherwise

Feb 72. (7"ep) *(33RPM 7)* **MY DARK HOUR. / SONG FOR OUR ANCESTORS / THE GANGSTER IS BACK** □ –

Mar 73. (d-lp) *(ESTSP 12) <11114>* **ANTHOLOGY** □ 56 Nov72

1973. (d-lp) *(STBB 717)* **CHILDREN OF THE FUTURE / LIVING IN THE U.S.A.** □ □

Jun 74. (7") *(CL 15786) <3884>* **LIVING IN THE U.S.A. / KOW KOW CALQULATOR** □ 49 May74

Oct 75. (lp) *(VMP 1008)* **THE LEGEND** □ –

Mar 77. (lp) *(EST 24058)* **THE BEST OF THE STEVE MILLER BAND 1968-73** □ □
– Living in the U.S.A. / I love you / Don't let nobody turn you around / Seasons / Shu ba da du ma ma ma / Kow kow calculator / The joker / Going to the country / My dark hour / Your saving grace / Celebration song / Space cowboy. *(re-iss.May82 on 'Fame' lp/c; FA/TC-FA 3030) (re-iss.Aug86 on 'E.M.I.' lp/c; ATAK/TCATAK 86) (re-iss.Sep90; EST 2133) (hit UK No.34)(cd+=)*– (4 extra).

Oct 78. (7") *(6078 815)* **THE JOKER. / THE STAKE** □ □

Nov 78. (lp)(c) *(9199 916)(7299 883) <11822>* **GREATEST HITS 1974-78** □ 18
– *(cd-iss.Jan83; 800 058-2) (re-iss.Aug85 on 'Mercury' lp/c; PRICE/PRIMC 86)*

Jan 83. (7") *(CL 258)* **THE JOKER. / MY DARK HOUR. / LIVING IN THE U.S.A.** □ –

May 87. Mercury; (lp/c)(cd) *(MERH/+C 105)(830978-2)* **GREATEST HITS - A DECADE OF AMERICAN MUSIC (1976-1986)** □ □

Aug 90. (7"/c-s) *(CL/TCCL 583)* **THE JOKER. / DON'T LET NOBODY TURN YOU AROUND** 1 □
(12"+=) *(12CL 583)* – Shu ba da du ma ma ma.
(cd-s++=) *(CDCL 583)* – Living in the U.S.A.

Oct 91. Arcade; (7"/cd-s) *(AR 91621-7/-2)* **SPACE INTRO. / FLY LIKE AN EAGLE** □ –

MISUNDERSTOOD

Formed: Riverside, California, USA . . . 1965. After one US independent 45, they moved to London and signed to 'Fontana' in 1966. John Ravenscroft (aka JOHN PEEL) became their manager, the band recording a number of tracks before they were all deported back to the States. Two of these tracks were released as singles, 'I CAN TAKE YOU TO THE SUN' (1966) and 'CHILDREN OF THE SUN' (1969). The latter (released after the band had left Britain), was a psychedelic classic, skull- shakingly heavy and featuring a blistering slide guitar. Back in America, a revamped line-up recorded a couple of lighter R&B singles before evolving into the heavier JUICY LUCY. This bunch scored a 1970 UK chart hit with an astounding version of BO DIDDLEY's 'WHO DO YOU LOVE'. The psychedelic material The MISUNDERSTOOD recorded in England was given a full posthumous release on 'Cherry Red' in 1982. • **Songwriters:** Group compositions except; I'M NOT TALKING (Yardbirds) / LITTLE RED ROOSTER (Willie Dixon) / etc. JUICY LUCY covered; WHO DO YOU LOVE (Bo Diddley) / etc.

Recommended: BEFORE THE DREAM FADED (*8) / THE BEST OF JUICY LUCY (*5)

RICK BROWN – vocals / **GREG TREADWAY** – guitar / **GLENN ROSS CAMPBELL** – steel guitar / **STEVE WHITING** – bass / **RICK MOE** – drums

not issued Blues Sound

1966. (7") **YOU DON'T HAVE TO GO. /** – □

— **GUY EVANS** – drums repl. MOE **TONY HILL** – guitar (ex-ANSWER) repl.

TREADWAY

Fontana Fontana

Dec 66. (7") *(TF 777)* **I CAN TAKE YOU TO THE SUN. / WHO DO YOU LOVE** [ ] [ ]

— Disbanded when BROWN was drafted into US army. In 1969, **GLENN ROSS** reformed a new line-up (on same label), completed by **STEVE HOARD** – vocals / **NEIL HUBBARD** – guitar (ex-GRAHAM BOND ORGANISATION, ex-GREASY BAND) / **CHRIS MERCER** – saxophone, keyboards (ex-JOHN MAYALL'S BLUESBREAKERS) / **NIC POTTER** – bass / **GUY EVANS** – drums (EVANS joined VAN DER GRAAF . . .) **TONY HILL** later joined HIGH TIDE.

Feb 69. (7") *(TF 998)* **CHILDREN OF THE SUN. / I UNSEEN** [ ] [ ]

May 69. (7") *(TF 1028)* **(YOU'RE) TUFF ENOUGH. / LITTLE RED ROOSTER** [ ] [ ]

Jul 69. (7"; as MISUNDERSTOOD featuring GLENN "FERNANDO" CAMPBELL) *(TF 1041)* **NEVER HAD A GIRL (LIKE YOU BEFORE). / GOLDEN GLASS** [ ] [ ]

— Group evolved into JUICY LUCY, except POTTER who joined VAN DER GRAAF . . .

– compilations, others, etc. –

May 81. (7"m) *Cherry Red; (CHERRY 22)* **CHILDREN OF THE SUN. / WHO DO YOU LOVE / I'LL TAKE YOU TO THE SUN** [ ] [-]

Apr 82. (lp) *Cherry Red; (BRED 32)* **BEFORE THE DREAM FADED** [ ] [-]
– COLOR OF THEIR SOUND:- Children of the sun / My mind / Who do you love? / I unseen / Find a hidden door / I can take you to the sun / BLUE DAY IN RIVERSIDE:- I'm not talkin' / I need your love / You don't have to go / I cried my eyes out / Like I do. *(cd-iss.May92; CDBRED 32)*

Jun 84. (7"m/12"m) *Cherry Red; (THYME 1/+12)* **GOLDEN GLASS. / SHAKE YOUR MONEY MAKER / I'M NOT TALKING** [ ] [-]

Aug 84. (lp) *Time Stood Still; (TSSLP 1)* **GOLDEN GLASS** [ ] [-]
– Never had a girl (like you before) / Golden glass / I don't want to discuss it (you're my girl) / Little red rooster / (You're) Tuff enough / Flamingo music / Freedom / Keep on running / I'm cruisin'.

Mar 97. (cd) *Cherry Red; (CDBRED 142)* **THE LEGENDARY GOLD STAR / GOLDEN GLASS** [ ] [-]

JUICY LUCY

were formed by **RAY OWEN** – vocals / **PETE DOBSON** – drums / **NEIL HUBBARD** – guitar / **GLENN ROSS CAMPBELL** – steel guitar, mandolin / **CHRIS MERCER** – saxophone, keyboards / **KEITH ELLIS** – bass (ex-VAN DER GRAAF GENERATOR)

Vertigo Atco

Jan 70. (lp) *(VO 2) <33267>* **JUICY LUCY** [41] [ ]
– Mississippi woman / Who do you love? / She's mine / She's young / Just one time / Chicago North-Western / Train / Nadine / Are you satisfied?. *(re-iss.Dec75 on 'Bronze')*

Feb 70. (7") *(VI-6059 001)* **WHO DO YOU LOVE?. / WALKING DOWN THE HIGHWAY** [14] [ ]

— **PAUL WILLIAMS** – vocals, keyboards repl. OWEN / **ROD COOMBES** – drums repl. DOBSON / **MICK MOODY** – guitar repl. HUBBARD

Oct 70. (7") *(6059 015)* **PRETTY WOMAN. / I AM A THIEF** [44] [ ]

Nov 70. (lp) *(6360 014) <33345>* **LIE BACK AND ENJOY IT** [53] [ ]
– Thinking of my life / Built for comfort / Pretty woman / Whisky in my jar / Hello L.A. bye bye Birmingham / Changed my mind / That woman's got something / Willie the wimp / Lie back and enjoy it. (cd+=) – Walking down the highway / I'm a thief. *(cd-iss.Jan94 on 'Repertoire')*

— **JIM LEVERTON** – bass repl. ELLIS

Bronze Atco

Aug 71. (lp) *(ILPS 9157) <33367>* **GET A WHIFF A THIS** [ ] [ ]
– Mr. Skin / Midnight Sun / Midnight rider / Harvest / Mr. A. Jones / Sunday morning / Big Lil / Jessica / Future days. *(cd-iss.Jan94 on 'Repertoire')*

— JEAN ROUSSELL – keyboards (was added soon after above). The last JUICY LUCY line-up with JEAN, were **PAUL WILLIAMS, MICK MOODY,** plus newcomers **ANDY PYLE** – bass (ex-SAVOY BROWN, ex-BLODWYN PIG) who repl. JIM to HEMLOCK / **RON BERG** – drums repl. COOMBES to STEALER'S WHEEL (CAMPBELL and MERCER also left to surface later in other bands)

Polydor not issued

Mar 72. (7") *(2001 279)* **IT AIN'T EASY. / PROMISED LAND** [ ] [-]

May 72. (lp) *(2310 160)* **PIECES** [ ] [-]
– Promised land / Cuckoo / All my life / It ain't easy / Suicide pilot / Why can't it happen to me / Dead flowers in the mirror / Prospector man / How can a poor man stand these times and live.

— Broke up after CHRIS STEWART repl. PYLE who joined SAVOY BROWN with RON BERG. MICK MOODY was later to join WHITESNAKE. PAUL WILLIAMS joined TEMPEST.

– compilations, others, etc. –

1973. (lp) *Bronze; (85814)* **THE BEST OF JUICY LUCY** [ ] [-]
– Who do you love / Midnight rider / Pretty woman / That woman's got something / Jessica / Willie the wimp – Lie back and enjoy it / Changed my mind / Changed my sign / Just one time / I'm a thief / Built for comfort / Mr. Skin / Mr. A. Jones. *(re-iss.Mar90 on 'Sequel' lp/cd+=; NEX LP/CD 105)*– Future days / Chicago North Western / Hello L.A. bye bye Birmingham / Thinking of my life.

Mar 81. (7") *Bronze; (BRO 72)* **WHO DO YOU LOVE. / CHICAGO NORTH WOMAN** [ ] [-]

Jan 95. (cd) *H.T.D.; (HTDCD 28)* **HERE SHE COMES AGAIN** [ ] [-]
– Pretty woman / Try my love / Who do you love / Voodoo child / Saturday night / Up to the tracks / Talk to me / Drug squad.

May 95. (cd) *Spectrum; (550766-2)* **PRETTY WOMAN** [ ] [-]

Jun 95. (cd) *Beat Goes On; (BGOCD 279)* **JUICY LUCY / LIE BACK AND ENJOY IT** [ ] [-]

MOBY GRAPE

Formed: San Francisco, California, USA . . . September '66 by manager/self-styled scenester MATTHEW KATZ (who'd previously worked with JEFFERSON AIRPLANE) and ex-'AIRPLANE drummer turned guitarist SKIP SPENCE. Unknowns PETER LEWIS, BOB MOSELEY, JERRY MILLER and DON STEVENSON were drafted in and the fledgling GRAPES apparently took their name from a (pathetic) joke doing the rounds at the time: 'What's purple and lives at the bottom of the sea?' (who said the Americans don't have a sense of humour?!) KATZ himself wasn't exactly a laugh a minute, allegedly harassing the band into signing an outrageous contract that gave him complete control over the personnel in the band as well as the name MOBY GRAPE. After signing to Columbia, the band released their self-titled debut just as the "summer of love" was fermenting in June 1967. The album showcased the distinctive guitar triumvirate of SPENCE, LEWIS and MILLER, a sound that enhanced the fertile songwriting and close-knit harmonies. So confident were the record company in the band's profit making potential, they released five singles simultaneously. All the tracks could've been hits in their own right, but this foolhardy gesture was seen as a blatant attempt to hype the band, the result being a severe dent in their credibility and a lowly No.88 chart placing for the classic 'OMAHA'. The other four singles stiffed without trace. It didn't help matters when three of the band were caught with under-age girls on the night of the album launch. Nevertheless, the album reached the US Top 30 and the band's psychedelic mesh of country, rock, folk and blues made them favourites on the Bay Area scene. The sessions for the unfortunately titled follow-up, 'WOW', were beset with problems, not least SKIP SPENCE running amok with an axe and being carted off to hospital in a straitjacket. Unsurprisingly, the record was a patchy affair bolstered with gimmicks like the 'GRAPE JAM' disc, given away free with the album. With SPENCE out of the picture, the band released another two albums that mined a rootsier seam, 'MOBY GRAPE '69' and 'TRULY FINE CITIZEN', although the absence of SPENCE's incendiary genius was glaringly apparent. The band called it a day in 1969 only to reform in 1971, a process that'd be repeated over the following decade amid ever shifting line-ups. Due to the dodginess of their aforementioned management contract, KATZ retained the MOBY GRAPE name and set up his own version of the band in the early 70's, all very confusing, and although some decent stuff was produced, none of the various incarnations met with any commercial success. SKIP SPENCE, meanwhile, released a one-off solo album of sublime psychedelic country in 1969, 'OAR', before fading into obscurity. All in all, yet another case of what might have been, had not drugs, bad luck and even worse deals not prematurely snuffed out their talent. • **Songwriters:** Individually penned, either SPENCE, MOSLEY, MILLER & STEVENSON or LEWIS. • **Trivia:** Watch out for a track on the original 'WOW' lp, which spins at 78 rpm (impossible to play on most modern turntable).

Recommended: MOBY GRAPE (*8) / WOW (*6).

SKIP SPENCE (b. ALEXANDER, 18 Apr'46, Windsor, Ontario, Canada) – vocals, guitar (ex-JEFFERSON AIRPLANE) / **PETER LEWIS** (b.15 Jul'45, Los Angeles, Calif.) – guitar, vocals (ex-CORNELLS) / **JERRY MILLER** (b.10 Jul'43, Tacoma, Washington) – guitar, vocals (ex-FRANTICS) / **BOB MOSELEY** (b. 4 Dec'42, Paradise Valley, Calif.) – bass (ex-MISFITS) / **DON STEVENSON** (b.15 Oct'42, Seattle, Washington) – drums (ex-FRANTICS) repl. KENT DUNBAR

C.B.S. Columbia

Jun 67. (7") *<44170>* **CHANGES. / FALL ON YOU** [-] [ ]

Jun 67. (7") *<44171>* **SITTING BY THE WINDOW. / INDIFFERENCE** [-] [ ]

Jun 67. (7") *<44172>* **8:05. / MISTER BLUES** [-] [ ]

Jun 67. (7") *(CBS 2953) <44173>* **OMAHA. / HEY GRANDMA** [ ] [88]

Jun 67. (7") *<44174>* **COME IN THE MORNIG. / HEY GRANDMA** [-] [ ]
(above 5 singles released similtaneously)

Jun 67. (lp; stereo/mono) *(S+/BPG 63090) <9498/2698>* **MOBY GRAPE** [ ] [24]
– Hey grandma / Mr. Blues / Fall on you / 8:05 / Come in the morning / Omaha / Naked, if I want to / Someday / Ain't no use / Sitting by the window / Changes / Lazy me / Indifference. *(re-iss.Sep84 on 'Edsel'; ED 137) (cd-iss.Apr89; EDCD 137)*

Jul 68. (lp) *(63271) <9613>* **WOW** [ ] [20] Apr68
– The place and the time / Murder in my heart for the judge / Bitter wind / Can't be so bad / Just like Gene Autry; a foxtrot *[plays at 78 rpm]* / He / Motorcycle Irene / Three-four / Funky-tunk / Rose colored eyes / Miller's blues / Naked, if I want to. *<US +free live-lp>* **GRAPE JAM** *<CXS 3>* – Never / Boysenberry jam / Black currant jam / Marmalade / The lake.

— above featured AL KOOPER & MIKE BLOOMFIELD.

Jul 68. (7") *<44567>* **CAN'T BE SO BAD. / BITTER WIND** [-] [ ]

Jul 68. (7") *(CBS 3555)* **CAN'T BE SO BAD. / MURDER IN MY HEART FOR THE JUDGE** [ ] [-]

— SPENCE became a serious drug addict, and left, going into a mental hospital for six months. He went solo later in 1969, releasing OAR album (see further below). He is now under residential-care at his home in San Jose, California.

Feb 69. (lp) *(63430) <9696>* **MOBY GRAPE '69** [ ] [ ]
– Ooh mama ooh / Ain't that a shame / I am not willing / It's a beautiful day today / Hoochie / Trucking man / If you can't learn from my mistakes / Captain Nemo / What's to choose / Going nowhere / Seeing. *(re-iss.Aug76; same)*

Feb 69. (7") *<44789>* **TRUCKING MAN. / IF YOU CAN'T LEARN FROM MY MISTAKES** [-] [ ]

Feb 69. (7") *(CBS 3945)* **TRUCKING MAN. / OOH MAMA OOH** [ ] [-]

Jun 69. (7") **OOH MAMA OOH. / IT'S SO BEAUTIFUL TODAY** [-] [ ]

— session man **BOB MOORE** – bass repl. MOSLEY who joined the US marines. He issued a self-titled album for 'Reprise' in 1972.

Sep 69. (lp) *(63698) <9912>* **TRULY FINE CITIZEN** [ ] [ ]
– Changes, circles spinning / Looper / Truly fine citizen / Beautiful is beautiful /

Love song / Right before my eyes / Open up your heart / Now I know high / Treat me bad / Tongue-tied / Love song (part 2).

— MOBY GRAPE had already split Spring 1969. For nearly 2 years, MILLER and STEVENSON joined The RHYTHM DUKES. Original quintet re-formed with newcomer **GORDON STEVENS** – viola, mandolin

Reprise Reprise

Sep 71. (7") <1040> **GYPSY WEDDING. / APOCAYPSE** [-] [ ]
Nov 71. (7") <1055> **GOIN' DOWN TO TEXAS. / ABOUT TIME** [-] [ ]
Jan 72. (lp) *(K 44152)* <6460> **20 GRANITE CREEK** [ ] [ ] Sep71
– Gypsy wedding / I'm the kind of man that baby you can trust / About time / Goin' down to Texas / Road to the Sun / Apocalypse / Chinese song / Roadhouse blues / Ode to the man at the end of the bar / Wild oats moan / Horse out in the rain. *(re-iss.May86 on 'Edsel' lp/c; ED/CED 176)*
Jul 72. (7"; as BOB MOSLEY & MOBY GRAPE) <1096> **GONE FISHING. / GYPSY WEDDING** [-] [ ]

— In the early 70's, their manager Matthew Katz had put together a fake **MOBY GRAPE** with **FRANK RECARD** – vocals, guitar / **TOMMY SPURLOCK** – guitar / **DANNY TIMMS** – keyboards / **BOB NEWKIRK** – drums. BOB MOSLEY had gone solo Mar'72 releasing eponymous album on 'Warner Bros.'. The real MOBY GRAPE re-formed late 1973-Spring'75 with **LEWIS, MILLER, MOSLEY,** plus **JEFF BLACKBURN** – guitar + JOHN CRAVIOTTA – drums. With no new record deal, they broke again and **LEWIS, MILLER, CRAVIOTTA** and **MICHAEL BEAN** – guitar (ex-H.P. LOVECRAFT) formed **FINE WINE**. They issued one eponymous album in Germany mid'75. With NEIL YOUNG; MOSLEY, CRAVIOTTA and BLACKBURN formed the shortly defunct DUCKS (mid'77).

— **MOBY GRAPE** re-formed again, this time with **SKIP SPENCE** returning with **MILLER + LEWIS,** plus newboys **CORNELIUS BUMPUS** – keyboards / **CHRISTIAN POWELL** – bass / **JOHN OXENDINE** – drums

not issued Escape

Apr 78. (lp) <JAM 95018> **LIVE GRAPE (live)** [-] [ ]
– The last horizon / Here I sit / Honk tonk / Cuttin' in / Must be goin' now dear / Your rider / Up in the air / Set me down easy / Love you so much / You got everything I need. *(UK-iss.Jun87 on 'Line'; 400 335)*

— Finally let go around the late 70's, although some releases surfaced.

not issued San Fran Sound

1984. (lp) **MOBY GRAPE '83** [-] [ ]
1989. (lp; as MOSLEY GRAPE) **LIVE AT INDIGO RANCH (live)** [-] [ ]

— They re-formed mid 1990 as The MELVILLES, then The LEGENDARY GRAPE; released eponymous cassette in 1991 on 'Herman'. Line-up:- MILLER, LEWIS, MOSLEY, STEVENSON + DAN ABERTNATHY – guitar + KIRT TUTTLE – drums. In 1993, JERRY MILLER issued cassette 'NOW I SEE' for 'Herman'.

– compilations, others, etc. –

on 'CBS / Columbia' unless mentioned otherwise

Jun 74. (lp) *(64743)* <31098> **GREAT GRAPE** [ ] [ ]
Jun 76. (lp) *(53371)* **THE BEST OF MOBY GRAPE** [-] [-] Europe
Feb 86. (lp) *Edsel; (ED 171)* **MURDER IN MY HEART** (2nd-4th lp's) [ ] [-]
– Murder in my heart for the judge / He / Can't be so bad / Motorcycle Irene / Three-four / Rose coloured eyes / Bitter wind / I am not willing / It's a beautiful day today / If you can't learn from my mistakes / What's to choose / Seeing / Changes, circles spinning / Right before my eyes.
Nov 93. (d-cd) *Legacy; (CD 53041)* **VINTAGE: THE VERY BEST OF MOBY GRAPE** [ ] [ ]
(re-iss.Jun96 on 'Columbia; 483958-2)

ALEXANDER SKIP SPENCE

solo (all instruments)

not issued Columbia

Oct 69. (lp) <CS 9831> **OAR** [-] [ ]
– Little hands / Cripple creek / Diana / Margaret – Tiger rug / Weighted down (the prison song) / War in peace / Broken heart / All come to meet her / Book of Moses / Dixie peach promenade / Lawrence of Euphoria / Grey / Afro. *(UK-iss.Sep88 on 'Edsel'; ED 282) (cd-iss.Feb91; EDCD 282)*

Dieter MOEBIUS (see under ⇒ CLUSTER)

MOGUL THRASH

Formed: Dundee, Scotland ... Sep'69 as The DUNDEE HORNS then JAMES LITHERLAND'S BROTHERHOOD. They moved to London, found a bass player JOHN WETTON and quickly signed to 'R.C.A.', where they made one brassy single and an eponymous, progressive jazz-rock album. This was fairly popular in Europe, although only moderately successful on home shores. They subsequently broke up due to legal problems with their management, most members finding fame in other directions (see below).

Recommended: MOGUL THRASH (*5)

JOHN WETTON – vocals, bass / **JAMES LITHERLAND** – guitar / **MOLLY DUNCAN** – sax / **ROGER BALL** – sax / **MIKE ROSEN** – trumpet / **BILL HARRISON** – drums

R.C.A. not issued

Dec 70. (7") *(RCA 2030)* **SLEEPING IN THE KITCHEN. / ST. PETER** [ ] [-]
1971. (lp) *(SF 8156)* **MOGUL THRASH** [ ] [-]
– Something sad / Elegy / Dreams of glass and sand / Going north / Going west / St. Peter / What's this I hear.

— split early 1971. WETTON joined FAMILY, then a string of bands; KING CRIMSON, ROXY MUSIC, URIAH HEEP, BRYAN FERRY, U.K., ASIA, etc. Meanwhile LITHERLAND formed BANDIT, and DUNCAN and BALL joined AVERAGE WHITE BAND.

MONKEES

Formed: Los Angeles, California, USA . . . 1965, the brainchild of Hollywood TV producers, BOB RAFELSON and BERT SCHNEIDER. The pair had wanted to make a sit-com based around The BEATLES' film, 'A Hard Day's Night' and in September of that year, they ran a wanted ad for four boys aged between 17 and 21. Out of over four hundred applicants, they picked the lucky DAVY JONES, MICKEY DOLENZ, MIKE NESMITH & PETER TORK, signing them to the 'Colpix' label. All had fairly notable previous experience (see below), and were duly sent for acting/grooming lessons early in '66. Following difficulties on the songwriting front, BOB & BERT brought in pensmiths TOMMY BOYCE and BOBBY HART (on appointment from 'Screen Gems' top man, Don Kirshner), who also became the group's producers. Other writers were brought in, namely NEIL DIAMOND, GERRY GOFFIN & CAROLE KING, NEIL SEDAKA plus BARRY MANN & CYNTHIA WEIL. On the 12th of September 1966, "The MONKEES" TV show premiered on NBC, and although not an overnight success, became a teenage favourite. A month later, their debut 45, 'LAST TRAIN TO CLARKSVILLE', was released, showcasing their BEACH BOYS-style harmonies and soon climbing to US No.1. Their follow-up, 'I'M A BELIEVER' (penned by NEIL DIAMOND), also hit the top, and with their show now on BBC TV, it repeated the feat in Britain. Another DIAMOND composition, 'A LITTLE BIT ME, A LITTLE BIT YOU', made both Top 3's in March '67 (two of their albums also having amassed cross-Atlantic success). The aforementioned 45's virtually turned the group into an overnight pop phenomenon, their boyish good looks and "zany" antics endearing their bubblegum psychedelia to the nation's teenyboppers (although their music has surprisingly stood the test of time, giving them cult status). For the remainder of the 60's (with NESMITH increasingly dominating the songwriting), they carried on with further TV series' (one featuring ZAPPA, another with TIM BUCKLEY) and some major hits. Their show was axed towards the end of the decade, by which time they had gone into the movies, making the box-office disaster, 'HEAD', with writers BOB RAFELSON and JACK NICHOLSON (yes that one!). • **Covered;** DAYDREAM BELIEVER (John Sebastian) / D.W. WASHBURN (Leiber-Stoller) / etc. • **Trivia:** In 1967, their 'RANDY SCOUSE GIT' (taken from the character Alf Garnett in British sit-com 'Til Death Us Do Part') was banned by the BBC, and later given the 'ALTERNATIVE TITLE' motif.

Recommended: HEY HEY IT'S THE MONKEES – GREATEST HITS (*7)

DAVY JONES (b.30 Dec'46, Manchester, England) – vocals, rhythm guitar (ex-apprentice jockey, actor UK TV 'Coronation Street' & 'Z Cars' / solo artist) / **MICKEY DOLENZ** (b. GEORGE MICHAEL DOLENZ JR., 8 Mar'45, Tarzana, Calif.) – drums, vocals (child actor 'Circus Boy' as Corky, 'Peyton Place', etc.) / **MIKE NESMITH** (b. ROBERT MICHAEL NESMITH, 30 Dec'42, Houston, Texas) – guitar, vocals (ex-folk solo act as MICHAEL BLESSING on 'Colpix' label) / **PETER TORK** (b. PETER THORKELSON, 13 Feb'44, Washington, D.C.) – bass, vocals (ex-AU GO GO SINGERS with RICHIE FURAY / recommended by STEPHEN STILLS)
Session men on discs were; JAMES BURTON, GLEN CAMPBELL, LEON RUSSELL, HAL BLAINE + DAVID GATES.

RCA Vic. Colgems

Oct 66. (7") *(RCA 1547)* <1001> **LAST TRAIN TO CLARKSVILLE. / TAKE A GIANT STEP** [ ] [1] Sep66
(late Jan'67; – debut single hit UK No.23)
Dec 66. (7") *(RCA 1560)* <1002> **I'M A BELIEVER. / I'M NOT YOUR STEPPING STONE** [1] [1] [20]
Jan 67. (lp; mono/stereo) *(RD/SF 7844)* <101> **THE MONKEES** [1] [1] Oct66
– Theme from The Monkees / Saturday's child / I wanna be free / Tomorrow's gonna be another day / Papa Gene's blues / Take a giant step / Last train to Clarksville / This just doesn't seem to be my day / Let's dance on / I'll be true to you / Sweet young thing / Gonna buy me a dog. *<re-iss.Aug86 on 'Rhino' hit No.92; 70140> (cd-iss.Apr88 on 'Arista'; 258773) (cd-iss.Dec94 on 'Warners'; 4509 97655-2)*
Mar 67. (7") *(RCA 1580)* <1004> **A LITTLE BIT ME, A LITTLE BIT YOU. / THE GIRL I KNEW SOMEWHERE** [3] [2] [39]
Apr 67. (lp; mono/stereo) *(RD/SF 7868)* <102> **MORE OF THE MONKEES** [1] [1] Feb67
– When love comes knockin' (at your door) / She / Mary, Mary / Hold on girl / Your Auntie Grizelda / (I'm not you) Steppin' stone / Look out (here comes tomorrow) / The kind of girl I could love / The day we fell in love / Sometime in the morning / Laugh / I'm a believer. *<re-iss.Aug86 on 'Rhino' hit No.96; 70142> (cd-iss.Jun88 on 'Arista'; 259052) (cd-iss.Dec94 on 'Warners'; 4509 97658-2)*
Jun 67. (7") *(RCA 1604)* **ALTERNATIVE TITLE. / FORGET THAT GIRL** [2] [-]

— (above was to have been called 'RANDY SCOUSE GIT')

Jul 67. (lp; mono/stereo) *(RD/SF 7868)* <103> **HEADQUARTERS** [2] [1] Jun67
– You told me / I'll spend my life with you / Forget that girl / Band 6 / You just may be the one / Shades of grey / I can't get her off my mind / For Pete's sake / Mr. Webster / Sunny girlfriend / Zilch / No time / Early morning blues and greens / Randy Scouse git. *<re-iss.Aug86 on 'Rhino'; 70143> (cd-iss.Feb95 on 'Warners'; 4509 97662-2)*
Jul 67. (7") *(RCA 1620)* 1007> **PLEASANT VALLEY SUNDAY. / WORDS** [11] [3] [11]
Nov 67. (7") *(RCA 1645)* <1012> **DAYDREAM BELIEVER. / GOING DOWN** [5] [1]
Jan 68. (lp; mono/stereo) *(RD/SF 7912)* <104> **PISCES, AQUARIUS, CAPRICORN AND JONES LTD.** [5] [1] Nov67
– Salesman / She hangs out / The door into summer / Love is only sleeping / Cuddly toy / Words / Hard to believe / What am I doing hangin' round? / Peter Percival Patterson's pet pig Porky / Pleasant Valley Sunday / Daily nightly / Don't call on me / Star collector. *<re-iss.Aug86 on 'Rhino'; 70141> (cd-iss.Feb95 on 'Warners'; 4509 97663-2)*

Mar 68. (7") *(RCA 1673) <1019>* **VALLERI. / TAPIOCA TUNDRA** 12 3 / 34

May 68. (lp; mono/stereo) *(RD/SF 7948) <109>* **THE BIRDS, THE BEES & THE MONKEES** [ ] 3
– Dream world / Auntie's municipal court / We were made for each other / Tapioca tundra / Daydream believer / Writing wrongs / I'll be back on my feet / The poster / P.O. Box 9847 / Magnolia Simms / Valleri / Zor and Zam. *<re-iss.Aug86 on 'Rhino'; 70144> (cd-iss.Dec94 on 'Warners'; 4509 97665-2)*

Jun 68. (7") *(RCA 1706) <1023>* **D.W. WASHBURN. / IT'S NICE TO BE WITH YOU** 17 19 / 51

Sep 68. (7") *<1031>* **THE PORPOISE SONG. / AS WE GO ALONG** - 62

— now down to trio when TORK departed. (he still appeared on below s/track)

Mar 69. (7") *(RCA 1802) <5000>* **TEARDROP CITY. / A MAN WITHOUT A DREAM** 46 56 Feb69

May 69. (lp; mono/stereo) *(RD/SF 8016) <113>* **INSTANT REPLAY** [ ] 32 Feb69
– Through the looking glass / Don't listen to Linda / I won't be the same without her / Me without you / Just a game / Don't wait for me / You and I / While I cry / Teardrop city / The girl I left behind me / Man without a dream / Shorty Blackwell. *<re-iss.Oct86 on 'Rhino'; 70147> (cd-iss.Feb95 on 'Warners'; 4509 97661-2)*

Jun 69. (7") *(RCA 1824) <5004>* **SOMEDAY MAN. / LISTEN TO THE BAND** 47 81 / 63

Aug 69. (7") *(RCA 1862)* **DADDY'S SONG. / THE PORPOISE SONG** [ ] [ ]

Sep 69. (lp; mono/stereo) *(RD/SF 8051) <5008>* **HEAD (Soundtrack)** [ ] 45 Dec68
– Opening ceremony / The porpoise song / Ditty Diego-war chant / Circle sky / Supplicio / Can you dig it / Gravy / Superstitious / As we go along / Dandruff / Daddy's song / Poll / Long title: Do I have to do this all over again / Swami-plus strings. *<re-iss.Oct86 on 'Rhino'; 70146> (cd-iss.Dec94 on 'Warners'; 4509 97659-2)*

Sep 69. (7") *(RCA 1887) <5005>* **GOOD CLEAN FUN. / MOMMY AND DADDY** [ ] 82

Oct 69. (lp) *<117>* **THE MONKEES PRESENT . . .** - 100
– Little girl / Good clean fun / If I knew / Bye bye baby bye bye / Never tell a woman yes / Looking for the good times / Ladies Aid Society / Listen to the band / French song / Mommy and daddy / Oklahoma backroom dancer / Pillow time. *<re-iss.Nov86 on 'Rhino'; 70147> (cd-iss.Dec94 on 'Warners'; 4509 97660-2)*

— now down to **JONES + DOLENZ** duo when NESMITH left to go solo.

Jun 70. (7") *(RCA 1958) <5011>* **OH MY MY. / LOVE YOU BETTER** [ ] 98

1970. (lp) *<119>* **CHANGES** - [ ]
– Oh my my / Ticket on a ferry ride / You're so good to me / It's got to be love / Acapulco sun / 99 pounds / Tell me love / Do you feel it too / I love you better / All alone in the dark / Midnight train / I never thought it peculiar. *<re-iss.Aug86 on 'Rhino'; 70148> (cd-iss.Dec94 on 'Warners'; 4509 97657-2)*

DOLENZ AND JONES

not issued / Bell

Apr 71. (7") **DO IT IN THE NAME OF LOVE. / LADY JANE** - [ ]

— After short solo careers DOLENZ and JONES reformed . . .

DOLENZ, JONES, BOYCE & HART

— recruited new members **TOMMY BOYCE** – guitar / **BOBBY HART** – bass, (past and present co-songwriters)

not issued / Capitol

Apr 76. (lp) *<11513>* **DOLENZ, JONES, BOYCE AND HART** - [ ]

Apr 76. (7") **I REMEMBER THE FEELING. / YOU AND I** - [ ]

Jul 76. (7") **I LOVE YOU (AND I'M GLAD I SAID IT). / SAVIN' MY LOVE FOR YOU** - [ ]

MICKY DOLENZ / DAVEY JONES & London Cast

M.C.A. / M.C.A.

Jan 78. (lp/c) *(MCF/TC-MCF 2826)* **THE POINT (Soundtrack)** [ ] [ ]

1978. (7") **LIFE LINE. / IT'S A JUNGLE OUT THERE. / GOTTA GET UP** [ ] [ ]

— They finally split shortly after The Point. DOLENZ went into children's TV productions noteably writing 'Metal Mickey'. In 1983, he released solo single 'TOMORROW' / 'FAT SAM'.

MONKEES

— re-formed with **DOLENZ, JONES + TORK** and session people.

Arista / Arista

Oct 86. (7"pic-d-4/7") *(ARIST 1/2/3/4+/673) <9505>* **THAT WAS THEN, THIS IS NOW. / THEME FROM THE MONKEES** 68 20 Jul86
(12"+=) *(ARIST 12-673)* – Pleasant valley Sunday / Last train to Clarksville.

Oct 86. (lp/c/cd) *(207/407/257 874) <8432>* **THEN & NOW . . . THE BEST OF THE MONKEES** (w/ 3 new) [ ] 21 Jul86
– Then and now / Tripwire / Theme from The Monkees / Last train to Clarksville / Take a giant step / I'm a believer / I'm not your stepping stone / A little bit me, a little you / Anytime, anyplace, anywhere / That was then, this is now / The girl I knew somewhere / Pleasant valley Sunday / What am I doing hangin' 'round / Daydream believer / Valeri / Kicks.

Oct 86. (7") *<9532>* **DAYDREAM BELIEVER. / RANDY SCOUSE GIT** - 79

Rhino / Rhino

Aug 87. (7") *<74408>* **HEART AND SOUL. / M.G.B.G.T.** - 87

Aug 87. (lp/c/cd) *<(RN IN/IC/CD 70706)>* **POOL IT!** [ ] 72
– Heart and soul / (I'd go the) Whole wide world / Long way home / Secret heart / Gettin' in / (I'll) Love you forever / Every step of the way / Don't bring me down / Midnight / She's movin' in with Rico / Since you went away / Counting on you. *(cd-iss.Nov95;)*

Nov 87. (7") **EVERY STEP OF THE WAY. / I LOVE YOU FOREVER** - [ ]

— the original four re-formed in 1996

Artful / Artful

Jan 97. (cd/c) *(ARTFUL CD/MC 6)* **JUSTUS** [ ] [ ]

– compilations, etc. –

Jun 69. (lp) *Colgems; <115>* **GREATEST HITS** - 89

1971. (lp) *Colgems; <329>* **GOLDEN HITS** - [ ]

1972. (lp) *Colgems; <1001>* **BARREL FULL OF MONKEES** - [ ]

1973. (d-lp) *Laurie House; <8009>* **THE MONKEES** - [ ]

1974. (lp) *Bell; <6081>* **RE-FOCUS** - [ ]

May 74. (7") *Bell; (BLL 1354)* **MONKEES THEME. / I'M A BELIEVER** [ ] -
(re-iss.Mar90 on 'Old Gold'; OG 9123)

Sep 74. (c) *Sounds Superb; (SPR 80032)* **THE MONKEES** [ ] -

1974. (c) *Bell; (TCBEL 148)* **25 HITS** [ ] -

Aug 76. (lp) *Arista; <4089>* **THE MONKEES' GREATEST HITS** - 58

Feb 80. (7"ep) *Arista; (ARIST 326)* **THE MONKEES** 33 [ ]
– Daydream believer / Last train to Clarksville / I'm a believer / A little bit me, a little bit you.

Jun 81. (7"ep) *Arista; (ARIST 402)* **THE MONKEES VOL.2** [ ] [ ]
– I'm not your stepping stone / Pleasant valley Sunday / Alternative title (Randy Scouse git) / What am I doing.

Jun 81. (d-lp/d-c) *Arista; (DARTY/TCDAR 12)* **THE MONKEES** 99 [ ]

Jun 81. (lp/c) *Music For Pleasure; (MFP/TCMFP 50499)* **THE BEST OF THE MONKEES** [ ] -

Aug 82. (7"ep) *Arista; (ARIST 487)* **I'M A BELIEVER** [ ] [ ]
– I'm a believer / Don't listen to Linda / Last train to Clarksville / Theme from 'The Monkees'.

Jul 82. (7") *Old Gold; (OG 9117)* **DAYDREAM BELIEVER. / LAST TRAIN TO CLARKSVILLE** [ ] -

Oct 82. (lp/c) *Ronco; (RTL/4CRTL 2085)* **20 GOLDEN GREATS** [ ] -

Jun 84. (7"ep/c-ep) *Scoop; (7SR/7SC 5035)* **6 TRACK HITS** [ ] -
– I'm a believer / Valleri / Alternative title (Randy Scouse git) / Somebody man / A little bit you, a little bit me / Pleasant valley Sunday.

Jul 84. (lp) *Rhino; <RNLP 113>* **MONKEE FLIPS** - [ ]

1984. (lp/pic-lp) *Rhino;* **MONKEE BUSINESS** - [ ]

Nov 84. (lp/c) *Platinum; (PLAT/PLAC 05)* **THE MONKEES' GREATEST HITS** [ ] -
(cd-iss.1988; PLATCD 05)

Oct 87. (lp/c/cd) *Rhino; (RN LP/C/CD 70139)* **LIVE 1967 (live)** - [ ]

Oct 87. (lp/c) *Rhino; (RN LP/C 70150)* **MISSING LINKS** (rare) - [ ]

Jun 88. (7") *Old Gold; (OG 9117)* **DAYDREAM BELIEVER. / LAST TRAIN TO CLARKSVILLE** [ ] -

Mar 89. (7"ep/3"cd-ep) *Arista; (112/662 157)* **THE MONKEES** 62 [ ]
– Daydream believer / A little bit me, a little bit you / Theme from The Monkees.

Apr 89. (7"ep/3"cd-ep) *Arista; (112/662 158)* **THE MONKEES VOL.2** [ ] [ ]
– Last train to Clarksville / I'm a believer / Pleasant valley Sunday.

Apr 89. (lp/c/cd) *K-Tel; (NE1/CD2/NCD3 432)* **HEY HEY IT'S THE MONKEES – GREATEST HITS** 12 -
– Theme from The Monkees / Pleasant valley Sunday / The girl I knew somewhere / D.W. Washburn / Last train to Clarksville / A little bit me, a little bit you / teardrop city / Some day man / What am I doing hangin' 'round / Daydream believer / I'm not your stepping stone / Alternative title (randy scouse git) / Words / I'm a believer / Listen to the band / Valeri / Tapioca tundra / That was then, this is now.

Apr 94. (cd/c) *Movieplay Gold; (MPV/+4 5544)* **GREATEST HITS** [ ] -

Mar 97. Telstar; (cd/c) *(954835218-2/-4)* **HERE THEY COME: THE GREATEST HITS OF THE MONKEES** 15 -

MONKS

Formed: (based) Germany . . . mid-60's by GARY BURGER, LARRY CLARK, EDDIE SHAW and ROGER JOHNSTON, who had all originated from England. They signed to 'Polydor' records, unleashing the now forgotten, classic garage album, 'BLACK MONK TIME'. It is also possible they might have issued a German 45, 'CUCKOO' / 'I CAN'T GET OVER YOU'. • **Trivia:** In the early 90's, The FALL re-hashed 'I HATE YOU' as 'BLACK MONK THEME' on their 'Extricate' album.

Recommended: BLACK MONK TIME (*6)

GARY BURGER – guitar / **LARRY CLARK** – organ / **EDDIE SHAW** – bass / **ROGER JOHNSTON** – drums

Polydor / not issued

1966. (lp) *(2417 129)* **BLACK MONK TIME** [ ] -
– Monk time / Shut up / Boys are boys and girls are choice / Higgle-dy-piggle-dy / I hate you / Oh, how to do now / Complication / We do wie du / Drunken Maria / Love came tumblin' down / Blast off! / That's my girl. *(re-iss.Jun88 on 'Bam Caruso'; KIRI 079) (re-iss.Jun90 on 'Israphon'; ISR 003) (cd-iss.Jul91+=; ISR 003CD)*– Cuckoo / I can't get over you.

— disappeared into psychedelic oblivion

MOODY BLUES

Formed: Birmingham, England . . . May '64 by DENNY LAINE (who had just dissolved his DIPLOMATS band), MIKE PINDER, RAY THOMAS, CLINT WARWICK and GRAEME EDGE. They hooked up with manager, Tony Secunda, who subsequently secured them a deal with 'Decca' records. Their debut 45, 'LOSE YOUR MONEY', bombed, but by early '65 they were at the top spot with the BESSIE BANKS cover, 'GO NOW'. They tried desperately to emulate its success, and although they scored a few minor chart hits, they disbanded in October '66. The band quickly re-united a month later, after finding JUSTIN HAYWARD and JOHN LODGE to replace DENNY LAINE and recent member ROD CLARKE. Late in the summer of '67, they switched to the more adventurous 'Deram', immediately hitting with the concept album, 'DAYS OF FUTURE PASSED'. It broke from their mid-60's R&B/pop sound, to a more ambitious hybrid of rock and orchestral pop. A haunting piece from it, 'NIGHTS IN WHITE SATIN', became a massive seller and an all-time classic in the process. After a rare concert at London's Queen Elizabeth Hall, they issued a follow-up concept album, 'IN SEARCH OF THE LOST CHORD'. Another massive seller, it was succeeded by their first No.1 album, 'ON THE THRESHOLD OF A DREAM', in 1969. Later that year they founded their own label, 'Threshold', continuing the winning formula on a further clutch of early 70's albums, in addition to some finely crafted 45's, including 'QUESTION', 'ISN'T LIFE STRANGE' and 'I'M JUST A SINGER (IN A ROCK AND ROLL BAND)'. In the mid-70's, The MOODY BLUES was put on ice while they ventured into side projects. All had a relative degree of success, most notably the BLUE JAYS (aka HAYWARD & LODGE) who had a more mainstream sounding pop hit, 'BLUE GUITAR' (1975). With new Swiss-born keyboard wizard PATRICK MORAZ on board (fresh from a spell with YES), they released the comeback album, 'OCTAVE', in 1978, the record subsequently returning them to platinum status. Although early 80's album, 'LONG DISTANCE VOYAGER', went Top 10 on both sides of the Atlantic (No.1 in the US), creatively, the band were becoming stale. • **Songwriters:** LAINE wrote most of material, until LODGE or HAYWARD took over late '66. Also covered; I DON'T WANT TO GO ON WITHOUT YOU (Drifters) / IT AIN'T NECESSARILY SO (Gershwin) / TIME IS ON MY SIDE (Rolling Stones) / BYE BYE BIRD (Sonny Boy Williamson) / etc. • **Trivia:** 10 CC produced 1975 BLUE JAYS (HAYWARD & LODGE)'s album.

Recommended: VOICES IN THE SKY – THE BEST OF (*8)

DENNY LAINE (b. BRIAN HINES, 29 Oct'44, Jersey, England) – vocals, guitar (ex-DIPLOMATS) / **MIKE PINDER** (b.12 Dec'41) – keyboards, vocals (ex-CREWCATS) / **RAY THOMAS** (b.29 Dec'42, Stourport-on-Severn, England) – flute, vocals, harmonica / **CLINT WARWICK** (b. CLINTON ECCLES, 25 Jun'39) – bass, vocals / **GRAHAM EDGE** (b.30 Mar'42, Rochester, England) – drums (ex-GERRY LEVENE AND THE AVENGERS)

Decca London

Aug 64. (7"; as MOODYBLUES) *(F 11971)* **STEAL YOUR HEART AWAY. / LOSE YOUR MONEY (BUT DON'T LOSE YOUR MIND)** [ ] [-]

Nov 64. (7") *(F 12022)* **GO NOW! / IT'S EASY CHILD** [1] [-]

Feb 65. (7") *(F 12095)* **I DON'T WANT TO GO ON WITHOUT YOU. / TIME IS ON MY SIDE** [33] [ ]

Feb 65. (7") *<9726>* **GO NOW! / LOSE YOUR MONEY (BUT DON'T LOSE YOUR MIND)** [-] [10]

May 65. (7") *(F 12166) <9764>* **FROM THE BOTTOM OF MY HEART (I LOVE YOU). / AND MY BABY'S GONE** [22] [93]

Jul 65. (lp) *(LK 4711) <LP 428>* **THE MAGNIFICENT MOODIES** <US-title 'GO NOW! – THE MOODY BLUES'> [ ] [ ]
– I'll go crazy / Something you got / Go now! / Can't nobody love you / I don't mind / I've got a dream / Let me go / Stop! / Thank you baby / It ain't necessarily so / True story / Bye bye bird. *(cd-iss.Nov88 & Jan93 on 'Decca'; 820 758-2) (re-iss.Mar93 on 'Repertoire' +=;)–* Steal your heart away / Lose your money (but don't lose your mind) / It's easy child / I don't want to go on without you (come back) / Time is on my side / From the bottom of my heart (I love you) / And my baby's gone.

Oct 65. (7") *(F 12266)* **EVERYDAY. / YOU DON'T (ALL THE TIME)** [44] [ ]

Mar 66. (7") *<9810>* **STOP! / BYE BYE BIRD** [-] [98]

—— (Jul66) **ROD CLARKE** – bass repl. WARWICK

Oct 66. (7") *(F 12498)* **BOULEVARD DE LA MADELAINE. / THIS IS MY HOUSE (BUT NOBODY CALLS)** [ ] [ ]

—— (Nov'66) **JUSTIN HAYWARD** (b.14 Oct'46, Swindon, England) – vocals, guitar (ex-WILDE THREE, ex-solo artist) repl. DENNY who went solo (and later to WINGS) / **JOHN LODGE** (b.20 Jul'45) – bass, vocals (ex-EL RIOT & THE REBELS) repl. CLARKE

Jan 67. (7"; w-drawn after a day) *(F 12543)* **LIFE'S NOT LIFE. / HE CAN WIN** [-] [-]

May 67. (7") *(F 12607)* **FLY ME HIGH. / REALLY HAVEN'T GOT THE TIME** [ ] [ ]

Aug 67. (7") *(F 12670)* **LOVE AND BEAUTY. / LEAVE THIS MAN ALONE** [ ] [ ]

Deram Deram

Nov 67. (7") *(DM 161) <85023>* **NIGHTS IN WHITE SATIN. / CITIES** [19] [ ]
<re-iss.Jul72; same>; hit No.2> (re-iss.Nov72; same); hit No.9) (re-iss.Mar76; same) (re-iss.Oct79; same); hit No.14) (re-iss.Oct83 & Jun88 on 'Old Gold'; OG 9349)

Nov 67. (lp; mono/stereo) *(DML/SML 707) <18012>* **DAYS OF FUTURE PASSED** [27] [3] Apr68
– The day begins / Dawn:- Dawn is a feeling / The morning:- Another morning / Lunch break:- Peak hour / The afternoon:- Forever afternoon (Tuesday) / Time to get away / Evening:- The sunset / Twilight time / The night:- Nights in white satin. *<US re-iss.Sep72 hit No.3> (cd-iss.1983 on 'Threshold'; 800 082-2) (re-iss.Nov84 lp/c; DOA/KDOAC 6) (re-iss.Apr91 cd/c/lp; 820006-2/-4/-1)*

Jul 68. (7") *<85028>* **TUESDAY AFTERNOON (FOREVER AFTERNOON). / ANOTHER MORNING** [-] [24]

Jul 68. (7") *(DM 196)* **VOICES IN THE SKY. / DR. LIVINGSTONE, I PRESSUME** [23] [-]

Jul 68. (lp; mono/stereo) *(DML/SML 711) <18017>* **IN SEARCH OF THE LOST CHORD** [5] [23] Sep68
– Departure / Ride my see-saw / Dr. Livingstone, I pressume / House of four doors (part 1) / Legend of a mind / House of four doors (part 2) / Voices in the sky / The best way to travel / The actor / The word / Om. *(re-iss.Nov84 lp/c; DOA/KDOAC 7) (cd-iss.Aug86 & Apr91 on 'London'; 820 168-2)*

Oct 68. (7") *<85033>* **RIDE MY SEE-SAW. / VOICES IN THE SKY** [-] [61]

Nov 68. (7") *(DM 213)* **RIDE MY SEE-SAW. / A SIMPLE GAME** [42] [-]

Apr 69. (7") *(DM 247) <85044>* **NEVER COMES THE DAY. / SO DEEP WITHIN YOU** [ ] [91]

Apr 69. (lp; mono/stereo) *(DML/SML 1035) <18025>* **ON THE THRESHOLD OF A DREAM** [1] [20] May69
– In the beginning / Lovely to see you / Dear diary / Send me no wine / To share our love / So deep within you / Never comes the day / Lazy day / Are you sitting comfortably / The dream / Have you heard (part 1) / The voyage / Have you heard (part 2). *(cd-iss.Aug86 on 'London'; 820 170-2)*

Threshold Threshold

Oct 69. (7") *(TH 1)* **WATCHING AND WAITING. / OUT AND IN** [ ] [-]

Nov 69. (lp; mono/stereo) *(<THM/THS 1>)* **TO OUR CHILDREN'S CHILDREN'S CHILDREN** [2] [14] Jan70
– Higher and higher / Eyes of a child (part 1) / Floating / Eyes of a child (part 2) / I never thought I'd live to be a hundred / Beyond / Out and in / Gypsy / Eternity road / Candle of life / Sun is still shining / I never thought I'd live to be a million / Watching and waiting. *(cd-iss.Aug86 on 'London'; 820 364-2)*

Apr 70. (7") *(TH 4) <67004>* **QUESTION. / CANDLE OF LIFE** [2] [21]
(re-iss.Oct83 on 'Old Gold'; OG 9348)

Aug 70. (lp) *(<TH 3>)* **A QUESTION OF BALANCE** [1] [3] Sep70
– Question / How is it (we are here) / And the tide rushes in / Don't you feel small / Tortoise and the hare / It's up to you / Minstrel's song / Dawning is the day / Melancholy man / The balance. *(cd-iss.Aug86 & Jul92 on 'London'; 820 211-2)*

Jul 71. (lp) *(<TH 5>)* **EVERY GOOD BOY DESERVES FAVOUR** [1] [2] Aug71
– Procession / The story in your eyes / Our guessing game / Emily's song / After you came / Riches more than these / Nice to be here / You can never go home / My song. *(cd-iss.Aug86 & Apr91 on 'London'; 820 160-2)*

Aug 71. (7") *<67006>* **THE STORY IN YOUR EYES. / MELANCHOLY MAN** [-] [23]

Apr 72. (7") *(TH 9) <67009>* **ISN'T LIFE STRANGE. / AFTER YOU CAME** [13] [29]

Nov 72. (lp) *(<TH 7>)* **SEVENTH SOJOURN** [5] [1]
– Lost in a lost world / New horizons / For my lady / Isn't life strange / You and me / The land of make-believe / When you're a free man / I'm just a singer (in a rock'n'roll band). *(cd-iss.Sep86 on 'London'; 820 159-2)*

Jan 73. (7") *(TH 13) <67012>* **I'M JUST A SINGER (IN A ROCK'N'ROLL BAND). / FOR MY LADY** [36] [12]

—— Split early '73 but only for a 5 year trial period, releasing own solos released (2) compilations while they split

Nov 74. (d-lp) *(MB 1-2) <2-12-13>* **THIS IS THE MOODY BLUES** [14] [11]
– Question / The actor / The word / Eyes of a child / Dear diary / Legend of a mind / In the beginning / Lovely to see you / Never comes the day / Isn't life strange / The dream / Have you heard / Voyage / Ride my see-saw / Tuesday afternoon / And the tide rushes in / New horizons / Simple game / Watching and waiting / I'm just a singer (in a rock'n'roll band) / For my lady / Story in your eyes / Melancholy man / Nights in white satin. *(d-cd-iss.Aug89; 820 007-2)*

Decca London

Apr 77. (d-lp) *(MB 3-4) <690-1>* **CAUGHT LIVE + 5** (live '69 +1 studio side) [ ] [26] Jun77
– Gypsy / The sunset / Dr. Livingstone, I pressume / Never comes the day / Peak hour / Tuesday afternoon / Are you sitting comfortably / Have you heard (part 1) / The voyage / Have you heard (part 2) / Nights in white satin / Legend of a mind / Ride my see-saw / Gimme a little somethin' / Please think about it / Long summer day / King and Queen / What am I doing here.

—— re-formed mid 1978; **(HAYWARD, LODGE, EDGE, PINDER** and **THOMAS)**

Decca London

Jun 78. (lp/blue-lp/c) *(TX/+S/C 129) <PS 708>* **OCTAVE** [6] [13]
– Steppin' in a slide zone / Under moonshine / Had to fall in love / I'll be level with you / Driftwood / Top rank suite / I'm your man / Survival / One step into the light / The day we meet again. *(cd-iss.Oct86 & Jan93; 820 329-2)*

Jul 78. (7") *(F 13790) <270>* **STEPPIN' IN A SLIDE ZONE. / I'LL BE LEVEL WITH YOU** [ ] [39]

Oct 78. (7") *(F 13809) <273>* **DRIFTWOOD. / I'M YOUR MAN** [ ] [59]

—— **PATRICK MORAZ** (b.24 Jun'48, Morges, Switzerland) – keyboards (ex-YES, solo artist, ex-REFUGEE) repl. PINDER

Threshold Threshold

May 81. (lp/c) *(TXS 139) <TRL-1 2901>* **LONG DISTANCE VOYAGER** [7] [1] Jun81
– The voice / Talking out of turn / Gemini dream / In my world / 22,000 days / Nervous / Painted smile / Reflection smile / Veteran cosmic rocker. *(cd-iss.Oct86; 820 105-2)*

Jun 81. (7") *(TH 27) <601>* **GEMINI DREAM. / PAINTED SMILE** [ ] [12]

Jul 81. (7") *(TH 33) <602>* **THE VOICE. / 22,000 DAYS** [ ] [15]

Nov 81. (7"/7"pic-d) *(TH/+PD 29) <603>* **TALKING OUT OF TURN. / VETERAN COSMIC ROCKER** [ ] [65]

Aug 83. (7") *(TH 30)* **BLUE WORLD. / GOING NOWHERE** [35] [-]

Sep 83. (lp/c)(cd) *(TXS/+C 140)(810119-2) <2902>* **THE PRESENT** [15] [26]
– Blue world / Meet me halfway / Sitting at the wheel / Going nowhere / Hole in the world / Under my feet / It's cold outside of your heart / Running water / I am / Sorry. *(cd re-iss.Apr91 on 'London'; same)*

Sep 83. (7") *<604>* **SITTING AT THE WHEEL. / GOING NOWHERE** [-] [27]

Oct 83. (7") *(TH 31)* **SITTING AT THE WHEEL. / SORRY** [ ] [-]
(12"+=) *(THX 31)* – Gemini dream.

Nov 83. (7") *<605>* **BLUE WORLD. / SORRY** [-] [62]

Feb 84. (7") *<606>* **UNDER MY FEET. / RUNNING WATER** [-] [ ]

Polydor Polydor

Mar 86. (7"/12") *(POSP/+X 787) <883906>* **YOUR WILDEST DREAMS. / TALKIN' TALKIN'** [ ] [9] Apr86

May 86. (lp/c)(cd) *(POLD/+C 5190)(829179-2) <829179>* **OTHER SIDE OF LIFE** [24] [9]
– Your wildest dreams / Talkin' talkin' / Rock'n'roll over you / I just don't care / Running out of love / The other side of life / The spirit / Slings and arrows / It may be a fire. *(cd re-iss.Feb97; same)*

Aug 86. (7") *(POSP 830) <885201>* **THE OTHER SIDE OF LIFE. / NIGHTS IN WHITE SATIN (live)** [ ] [58]
(12"+=) *(POSPX 830)* – The spirit. *<US; b-side>*

May 88. (7") *(POSP 921) <887600>* **I KNOW YOU'RE OUT THERE SOMEWHERE. / MIRACLE** [52] [30]
(12"+=) *(POSPX 921)* – ('A'extended).
(cd-s+=) *(POCD 921)* – Rock'n'roll over you (live).

Jun 88. (lp/c)(cd) *(POLH/+C 43)(<835756-2>)* **SUR LA MER** [21] [38]
– I know you're out there somewhere / Want to be with you / River of endless love / No more lies / Here comes the weekend / Vintage wine / Breaking point / Miracle / Love is on the run / Deep. *(cd re-iss.Feb97; same)*

Dec 88. (7") *(PO 27)* **NO MORE LIES. / RIVERS OF ENDLESS LOVE** [ ] [ ]
(12"+=) *(PZ 27)* – The other side of life.

Jun 91. (7"/c-s) **SAY IT WITH LOVE. / LEAN ON ME (TONIGHT)** [ ] [ ]
(12"+=/cd-s+=) – Highway.

Aug 91. (cd/c/lp) *(<849433-2/-4/-1>)* **KEYS OF THE KINGDOM** [54] [94]

– Say it with love / Bless the wings (that bring you back) / Is this Heaven? / Say what you mean (pt.1 & 2) / Lean on me (tonight) / Hope and pray / Shadows on the wall / Celtic sonant / Magic / Never blame the rainbows for the rain. *(re-iss.Jan93; same)*

Mar 93. (cd/c) *(517977-2/-4)* **LIVE AT RED ROCKS (live)** [ ] [ ]
– Overture / Late lament / Tuesday afternoon (forever afternoon) / For my lady / Lean on me (tonight) / Lovely to see you / I know you're out there somewhere / The voice / Your wildest dreams / Isn't life strange / The other side of life / I'm just a singer (in a rock and roll band) / Nights in white satin / Question / Ride my see-saw. *(cd re-iss.Fen97; 517977-2)*

– compilations, etc. –

May 65. (7"ep) *Decca; (DFE 8622)* **THE MOODY BLUES** [ ] [-]
– Go now / Lose your money (but don't lose your mind) / Steal your heart away / I don't want to go on without you.

Nov 84. (7") *Threshold; (TH 33)* **THE VOICE. / GEMINI DREAM** [ ] [-]
(12"+=) *(TH/+X 33)* – Nights in white satin.

Nov 84. (lp/c)(cd) *Threshold; (SKL/KSKC 5341) <820155>* **VOICES IN THE SKY – THE BEST OF THE MOODY BLUES** [ ] [ ] Mar85
– Ride my see-saw / Talking out of turn / Driftwood / Never comes the day / I'm just a singer (in a rock and roll band) / Gemini dream / The voice / After you came / Question / Veteran cosmic rocker / Isn't life strange / Nights in white satin. *(cd re-iss.Apr91)*

Oct 79. (lp/c) *K-Tel; (NE/+C 1051)* **OUT OF THIS WORLD** [15] [-]
Sep 83. (lp/c) *A.K.A.;* **GO NOW** [ ] [-]
Sep 85. (7") *Old Gold; (OG 9509)* **GO NOW. / I DON'T WANT TO GO ON WITHOUT YOU** [ ] [-]
Sep 85. (d-lp/c) *Castle; (CCS LP/MC/CD 105)* **THE MOODY BLUES COLLECTION** [ ] [-]
Sep 87. (cd) *London; (820 517-2)* **PRELUDE** [ ] [-]
Nov 89. (lp/c/cd) *Polydor; (<840 659-1/-4/-2>)* **GREATEST HITS** [71] [ ]
(re-iss.Feb97; same)
Sep 90. (cd/c/lp) *Pickwick; (PWK S/MC/LP 4022P)* **BLUE** [ ] [-]
Sep 93. (cd/c) *Laserlight; (CD1/MC7 2209)* **GO NOW** [ ] [-]
Sep 94. (5xcd-box) *Polydor; (516436-2)* **TIME TRAVELLER** [ ] [ ]
(re-iss.Feb97; 535223-2)
Sep 96. (cd/c) *Polygram TV; (535 800-2/-4)* **THE VERY BEST OF** [13] [-]
Jun 97. (cd) *O.T.R.; (OTR 1100025)* **IN WORDS AND MUSIC** [ ] [-]

— solo work, etc. they released during 5 year trial split.

— see GREAT ROCK DISCOGRAPHY for solo material

Michael MOORCOCK (see under ⇒ HAWKWIND)

Anthony MOORE (see under ⇒ SLAPP HAPPY)

MOTHERS (OF INVENTION) (see under ⇒ ZAPPA, Frank)

MOUSE

Formed: London, England . . . 1972 by main writer RAY RUSSELL, plus AL CLARE, JEFF WATTS and AL RUSHTON. They released only one progressive rock album, 'LADY KILLER', which has since become very collectable (over £100). RAY's acid-guitar work was the main features were, 'ASHEN BESHER', 'EAST OF THE SUN' and a version of MEDICINE HEAD's 'ALL THE FALLEN TEEN-ANGELS' (a failed single in '74).

Recommended: LADY KILLER (*7)

RAY RUSSELL – vocals, guitar / **AL CLARE** – vocals, keyboards / **JEFF WATTS** – bass / **AL RUSHTON** – drums

Sovereign / not issued

1973. (7") *(SOV 122)* **WE CAN MAKE IT. / IT'S HAPPENING TO ME AND YOU** [ ] [-]
1974. (lp) *(SVNA 7262)* **LADY KILLER** [ ] [-]
– Going out tonite / You don't know / Electric lady / All the fallen teen-angels / Ashen Besher / We can make it / East of the sun / It's hapening to me and you / Sunday / Just came back.
1974. (7") *(SOV 127)* **ALL THE FALLEN TEEN-ANGELS. / JUST CAME BACK** [ ] [-]

— when they disbanded, WATTS joined STEEL MILL.

MOUSE AND THE TRAPS

Formed: Tyler, Texas, USA . . . 1965 by RONNIE 'MOUSE' WEISS, DAVE STANLEY and JERRY HOWELL, who had all escaped from JERRY VEE & THE CATALINAS. They were initially a DYLAN-sounding garage act, much in evidence on their debut single, 'A PUBLIC EXECUTION', which, for a while, bubbled under the Hot 100. They made several 45's between 1966 and 1968, but none were given much promotion by their small 'Fraternity' label. Their sound had developed from garage punk to a more psyche-acid sound, which didn't help them break through outside their local fanbase. An album was shelved prior to them signing a better deal with 'Bell', although two DALE HAWKINS-produced singles in 1969 didn't help their cause and they soon disbanded.

Recommended: THE FRATERNITY YEARS (*6)

RONNIE 'MOUSE' WEISS – vocals, guitar / **JERRY HOWELL** – keyboards / **KNOX 'BUGS' HENDERSON** – lead guitar (ex-SENSORS) / **DAVE STANLEY** – bass / **KEN 'NARDO' MURRAY** – drums

not issued / Fraternity

1966. (7"; as MOUSE) *<956>* **A PUBLIC EXECUTION. / ALL FOR YOU** [-] [ ]
1966. (7") *<966>* **MAID OF SUGAR, MAID OF SPICE. / I AM THE ONE** [-] [ ]
1966. (7"; as MOUSE) *<971>* **WOULD YOU BELIEVE? / LIKE I KNOW YOU DO** [-] [ ]
1967. (7"; as MOUSE) *<973>* **DO THE BEST YOU CAN. / PROMISES PROMISES** [-] [ ]
1967. (7"; as CHRIS ST. JOHN) *<983>* **I'VE GOT HER LOVE. / AS FAR AS THE SEA** [-] [ ]
1967. (7") *<989>* **CRYIN' INSIDE. / YA YA** [-] [ ]

— they also recorded 'PSYCHOTIC REACTION' with singer JIMMY RABBIT as POSITIVELY THIRTEENTH O'CLOCK

— (around this time) **DOUG RHONE** – lead guitar; repl. BUGS

1967. (7") *<1000>* **L.O.V.E. LOVE. / LIE, BEG, BORROW AND STEAL** [-] [ ]
1968. (7") *<1005>* **SOMETIMES YOU JUST CAN'T WIN. / CRYIN' INSIDE** [-] [ ]
1968. (7") *<1011>* **I SATISFY. / GOOD TIMES** [-] [ ]
1968. (7") *<1015>* **REQUIEM FOR SARAH** [-] [ ]

— (around this time) **BOBBY DALE** – keyboards; repl. HOWELL

not issued / Bell

1969. (7") *<850>* **WICKER VINE. / AND I BELIEVE HER** [-] [ ]
1969. (7") *<870>* **KNOCK ON MY DOOR. / WHERE'S THE LITTLE GIRL** [-] [ ]

— went back into hiding after above although in 1972, WEISS, STANLEY, MURRAY and DALE re-formed for a brief spell

– compilations, etc. –

1981. (lp) *Eva; <12001>* **PUBLIC EXECUTION** [-] [-] French
May 97. (cd) *Big Beat; (CDWIKD 171)* **THE FRATERNITY YEARS** [ ] [-]
– Public execution / Maid of sugar, maid of spice / Nobody cares / Cryin' inside / I'm a man (CHRIS ST. JOHN) / Lie, beg, borrow and steal / I've got her love (CHRIS ST. JOHN) / I am the one / Like I know you do / Sometimes you just can't win / All for you / Do the best you can / Look at the sun / You don't love me (you don't care) (CHRIS ST. JOHN) / Promises promises / I satisfy / Requiem for Sarah / L.O.V.E. love / Ya ya / Good times / Hand in hand / You are my sunshine / I wonder where the birds fly / Mohair Sam / As far as the sea (CHRIS ST. JOHN).

MOVE

Formed: Birmingham, England . . . early 1966 by ROY WOOD, CARL WAYNE, TREVOR BURTON, ACE KEFFORD and BEV BEVAN. By that summer, they had found manager Tony Secunda, who helped them sign to 'Deram'. Early the next year, their debut 45, 'NIGHT OF FEAR' (based on the 1812 Overture), had crashed into the UK Top 3. After another Top 5 hit, their third single, 'FLOWERS IN THE RAIN' (the first record to be played on the newly launched BBC Radio 1), was another to make the Top 3 in October '67 on the recently formed 'Regal Zonophone' label. Their fourth successive Top 5 hit arrived in early '68 with 'FIRE BRIGADE', quickly followed by the Top 20 self-titled album. The aforementioned singles were, for the most part, classy bubblegum psychedelia penned by the multi-talented WOOD. After a surprise flop, they scored their first No.1 early in '69 with the single, 'BLACKBERRY WAY'. They never emulated this, WOOD becoming increasingly involved with his new project, The ELECTRIC LIGHT ORCHESTRA, in 1970. He subsequently departed, JEFF LYNNE taking over the leadership, while he ended The MOVE on a high-note in mid-'72 with the Top 10 hit, 'CALIFORNIA MAN'. Remaining at 'Harvest' records, WOOD formed the 50's pastiche rock'n'roll outfit, WIZZARD (the band making their live debut at Wembley's Rock'n'roll festival in June '72). They hit the Top 10 with their first 45, 'BALL PARK INCIDENT', following it with two chart toppers, 'SEE MY BABY JIVE' and 'ANGEL FINGERS'. Around the same time (mid-'73), WOOD entered the album charts with his solo (in every sense of the word), 'BOULDERS' album. He continued to work on both projects simultaneously, scoring many Top 20 chart hits. Following his signed to the 'Jet' label in 1975, the hits (bar a few minor ones) duly dried up. • **Style:** WIZZARD were part of the glam-rock scene, Englishman ROY the group's focal point, with his tartan troosers and multi-coloured robe, topped with face-paint and a multi-coloured hair-do. • **Covered;** LOVELY RITA + POLYTHENE PAM (Beatles). • **Trivia:** ROY also produced and wrote for DARTS, etc.

Recommended: THE BEST OF THE MOVE (*6)

ROY WOOD (b. ULYSSES ADRIAN WOOD, 8 Nov'46) – guitar, vocals (ex-MIKE SHERIDAN & NIGHTRIDERS, ex-GERRY LEVENE & THE AVENGERS) / **TREVOR BURTON** (b. 9 Mar'44) – guitar, vox (ex-DANNY KING & THE MAYFAIR SET) / **CARL WAYNE** (b.18 Aug'44) – vocals (ex-CARL WAYNE & THE VIKINGS) / **CHRIS "ACE" KEFFORD** (b.10 Dec'46) – bass, vox (ex-CARL WAYNE & THE VIKINGS) / **BEV BEVAN** (b.24 Nov'44) – drums (ex-CARL WAYNE & THE VIKINGS, ex-DENNY LAINE & THE DIPLOMATS)

Deram / Deram

Dec 66. (7") *(DM 109) <7504>* **NIGHT OF FEAR. / DISTURBANCE** [2] [ ]
Apr 67. (7") *(DM 117) <7506>* **I CAN HEAR THE GRASS GROW. / WAVE THE FLAG, STOP THE TRAIN** [5] [ ]

Regal Zonophone / A&M

Sep 67. (7") *(RZ 3001)* **FLOWERS IN THE RAIN. / (HERE WE GO ROUND) THE LEMON TREE** [2] [-]
Feb 68. (7") *(RZ 3005)* **FIRE BRIGADE. / WALK UPON THE WATER** [3] [-]
Mar 68. (lp; stereo/mono) *(S+/LRZ 1002)* **THE MOVE** [15] [-]

– Yellow rainbow / Kilroy was here / (Here we go round) The lemon tree / Weekend / Walk upon the water / Flowers in the rain / Useless information / Zing went the strings of my heart / The girl outside / Fire brigade / Mist on a Monday morning / Cherry blossom clinic. *(cd-iss.Nov92 on 'Repertoire'+=;)*– (8 bonus tracks).

— quartet, (**BURTON** – bass, vocals) when KEFFORD formed ACE KEFFORD STAND

Jul 68. (7") *(RZ 3012)* **WILD TIGER WOMAN. / OMNIBUS** [ ] [-]

Sep 68. (7"ep) *(TRZ 2001)* **SOMETHING ELSE FROM THE MOVE** [ ] [-]
– Stephanie knows who / So you want to be a rock 'n' roll star / Something else / It'll be me / Sunshine help me.

Sep 68. (7") *<966>* **SOMETHING. / YELLOW RAINBOW** [-] [ ]

— added **RICHARD TANDY** – hapsicord, keyboards (of The UGLYS)

Jan 69. (7") *(RZ 3015) <1020>* **BLACKBERRY WAY. / SOMETHING** [1] [ ]

— **RICK PRICE** (b.10 Jun'44) – bass (ex-SIGHT'N'SOUND) repl. BURTON + TANDY whom became part of The UGLYS

Aug 69. (7") *(RZ 3021) <1119>* **CURLY. / THIS TIME TOMORROW** [12] [ ]

Feb 70. (lp) *(SLRZ 1012) <SP 4259>* **SHAZAM** [ ] [ ]
– Hello Susie / Beautiful daughter / Cherry blossom clinic revisited / Fields of people / Don't make my baby blue / The last thing on my mind. *(re-iss.1982 on 'Cube';) (cd-iss.Mar93 on 'Repertoire' +=;)*– Stephanie knows who / So you want to be a rock'n'roll star / Something else / It'll be me / Sunshine help me.

— now trio of **WOOD, PRICE** and **BEVAN.** (WAYNE became cabaret singer)

Mar 70. (7") *(RZ 3026) <1197>* **BRONTOSAURUS. / LIGHTNING NEVER STRIKES TWICE** [7] [ ]

— added **JEFF LYNNE** (b.30 Dec'47) – vocals, guitar, keys (ex-IDLE RACE)

Fly Capitol

Sep 70. (7") *(BUG 2)* **WHEN ALICE COMES BACK TO THE FARM. / WHAT?** [ ] [ ]

Oct 70. (lp) *(HIFLY 1) <ST 658>* **LOOKING ON** [ ] [ ]
– Looking on / Turkish tram conductor blues / What? / When Alice comes back to the farm / Open up said the world at the door / Brontosaurus / Feel too good. *(cd-iss.Mar93 on 'Repertoire'+=;)*– Blackberry way / Something / Curly / This time tomorrow / Lightning never strikes twice.

Harvest Capitol

May 71. (7"; unissued) *(HAR 5036)* **ELLA JAMES. / NO TIME** [-] [-]

Jun 71. (7") *(HAR 5038) <3126>* **TONIGHT. / DON'T MESS ME UP** [11] [ ]

Jul 71. (lp) *(SHSP 4013) <ST 811>* **MESSAGE FROM THE COUNTRY** [ ] [ ]
– Message from the country / Ella James / No time / Don't mess me up / Until your moma's gone / It wasn't my idea to dance / The minister / Ben Crawley Steel Company / The words of Aaron / My Marge. *(cd-iss.Jul94 on 'Beat Goes On'; BGOCD 238)*

Harvest U.A.

Oct 71. (7") *(HAR 5043) <50876>* **CHINATOWN. / DOWN ON THE BAY** [23] [ ]

— (Aug71) Now a trio when RICK PRICE left to go solo. The other three (WOOD, LYNNE and BEVAN) continued with The MOVE although they formed ELECTRIC LIGHT ORCHESTRA. The MOVE made one more single below before ROY WOOD also undertook solo career and formed WIZZARD.

May 72. (7"m) *(HAR 5050) <50928>* **CALIFORNIA MAN. / DO YA / ELLA JAMES** [7] [ ]

– compilations, etc. –

Mar 71. (lp) *Fly; (TON 3)* **THE BEST OF THE MOVE** [ ] [-]

Apr 72. (7"ep) *MagniFly; (ECHO 104)* **FIRE BRIGADE / I CAN HEAR THE GRASS GROW. / FLOWERS IN THE RAIN / NIGHT OF FEAR** [ ] [-]

Feb 73. (7") *United Artists; <202>* **TONIGHT. / MY MARGE** [-] [ ]

Feb 73. (lp) *United Artists; <UAS 5666>* **SPLIT ENDS** [-] [ ]

May 74. (lp) *A&M; <SP 3625>* **THE BEST OF THE MOVE** [-] [ ]

Jun 74. (7") *A&M;* **WILD TIGER WOMAN. / ZING WENT THE STRINGS OF MY HEART** [-] [ ]

Jul 74. (lp) *Music For Pleasure; (MFP 50158)* **ROY WOOD AND THE MOVE** [ ] [-]

Sep 74. (7") *Harvest; (HAR 5086) / United Artists; <50928>* **DO YA. / NO TIME** [ ] [93] Oct72

Oct 74. (lp) *Harvest; (SHSP 4035)* **CALIFORNIA MAN** [ ] [-]

Mar 78. (d-lp) *Cube; (TOOFA 5-6)* **SHAZAM / THE MOVE** [ ] [-]

May 78. (lp) *Hallmark; (SHM 952)* **THE GREATEST HITS VOL.1** [ ] [-]

Sep 79. (lp) *Harvest; (SHSM 2029)* **THE MOVE SHINES ON** [ ] [-]

Oct 81. (d-lp/d-c) *Platinum; (PLAT/+C 1001)* **THE PLATINUM COLLECTION** [ ] [-]

Jul 82. (7") *Old Gold; (OG 9227)* **NIGHT OF FEAR. / I CAN HEAR THE GRASS GROW** [ ] [-]

Aug 82. (7") *Dakota; (BAK 6)* **BLACKBERRY WAY. / I CAN HEAR THE GRASS GROW** [ ] [-]

Aug 82. (7") *Dakota; (BAK 7)* **NIGHT OF FEAR. / FIRE BRIGADE** [ ] [-]

Aug 82. (7") *Dakota; (BAK 8)* **FLOWERS IN THE RAIN. / BRONTOSAURUS** [ ] [-]

Nov 84. (d-lp/c) *Sierra; (FEDD/CFEDD 1005)* **OFF THE RECORD WITH THE MOVE** [ ] [-]

Apr 86. (d-lp/c/cd) *Castle; (CCS LP/MC/CD 135)* **THE COLLECTION** [ ] [-]

Sep 86. (12"ep) *Archive; (TOF 111)* **ARCHIVE 4** [ ] [-]
– I can hear the grass grow / Flowers in the rain / Fire brigade / Blackberry way.

Jul 88. (lp/c) *Knight; (KN LP/MC 10011)* **NIGHTRIDING** [ ] [-]

Mar 90. (7") *Old Gold; (OG 9226)* **FLOWERS IN THE RAIN. / FIRE BRIGADE** [ ] [-]

Mar 91. (cd/c) *Music Club; (MC CD/TC 009)* **THE BEST OF THE MOVE** [ ] [-]

Nov 92. (cd) *Dojo; (EARLD 7)* **THE EARLY YEARS** [ ] [-]

Oct 94. (cd) *Disky;* **THE MOVE** [ ] [-]

Mar 95. (cd) *Band Of Joy; (BOJCD 011)* **BBC SESSIONS** [ ] [-]

MU

Formed: Canoga Park, California, USA ...late 60's by MERRELL FANKHAUSER, who claimed to be the writer of The SURFARIS' 'Wipe Out' hit. He and JEFF COTTON (aka ANTENNAE JIMMY SEMENS and member of CAPTAIN BEEFHEART & HIS MAGIC BAND), formed MU after FANKHAUSER had spent the 60's in FAPARDOKLY (which later evolved into HMS BOUNTY). In 1971, they recruited three other West Coast musicians, recording at Wally Heider's DIY studio. The results, 'LEMURIAN MUSIC', surfaced three years later, after obscure/experimental music became the "in-thing", the album a quintessential underground rock classic, containing freaky guitar, dreamy clarinet and BEACH BOY-like harmonies. However, the group had by then bought a banana and papaya plantation in Maui, Hawaii, to subsidise more 'MU' recordings, these not seeing the light of day for another decade. In 1987, following a concert at Pismo Beach, FANKHAUSER suffered a heart attack, although he was soon to recover, moving into mainstream MOR. • **Songwriters:** FANKHAUSER / COTTON. • **Trivia:** Took their name MU, from the legend of the lost tribe of Lemuria. • **Tip:** Worth searching out debut (at £20-25) as it could well become pricey in future.

Recommended: THE BEST OF MU (*8)

FAPARDOKLY

MERRELL FANKHAUSER – guitar / **BILL DODD** – lead guitar / **JOHN OLIVER** – bass / **DICK LEE** – drums

not issued U.L.P.

1966. (lp) *<ULP 2250>* **FAPARDOKLY** [-] [ ]
(UK-iss.1983 on 'Psycho'; PSYCHO 5) (re-iss.1987 on '5 Hours Back'; 003)

H.M.S. BOUNTY

FANKHAUSER + DODD with **LARRY MEYERS + JACK JORDAN**

not issued Shamely

1968. (7") *<44008>* **I'M FLYING HOME. / GIRL** [-] [ ]
(UK-iss.Jun85 on 'Cherry Red'; CHERRY 88)

1968. (lp) *<SS 701>* **THINGS** [-] [ ]
– Things (goin' round in my mind) / Girl (I'm waiting for you) / What does she see in you / Lost in the city / Your painted lives / Drivin' sideways (down a one-way street) / In a minute not too soon / A visit with Ashiya / The big grey sky / Rich man's fable / Ice cube island / Madame Silky / I'm flying home. *(UK-iss.1985 on 'Time Stood Still'; TSSLP 2) (cd-iss.Jun97 on 'Sundazed'; SC 6094)*

1969. (7") *<44019>* **TAMPA RUN. / EVERYBODY'S TALKING** [-] [ ]

MU

MERRELL FANKHAUSER – vocals, guitar, bass / **JEFF COTTON** – vocals, slide guitar, bass-clarinet / **JEFF PARKER** – bass, vocals / **RANDY WIMER** – drums, vocals

not issued Mantra

1971. (7") *<101> BALLAD OF BROTHER LEW. / NOBODY WANTS TO SHINE* [-] [ ]

not issued Mu

1972. (7") *<101-2>* **ONE MORE DAY. / YOU'VE BEEN HERE BEFORE** [-] [ ]

1973. (7") *<103-4>* **TOO NAKED FOR DEMETRIUS. / ON OUR WAY TO HANA** [-] [ ]

U.A. R.T.V.

1974. (lp) *(UAG 29709) <300>* **LEMURIAN MUSIC** (rec-1971) [ ] [ ]
– Ain't no blues / Ballad of Brother Lew / Blue form / Interlude / Nobody wants to shine / Eternal thirst / Too naked for Demetrius / Numbela baye tu la / Clouds went that way.

— added **MARY LEE** – violin

Appaloosa not issued

1982. (lp) *(AP 017)* **THE LAST ALBUM** (rec.1974) [-] [-] Italy
– The land of Mu / Make a joyful noise / Haleakala / Blue Jay blue / Who will write this song / Too naked for Demetrius / One more day / On our way to Hana / You've been here before / Waiting for the Sun / In Mu / You and I / Drink from the fountain / End of an era.

— allegedly folded after they came across flying saucers and the volcano people! COTTON bought a dry cleaning business and had vowed never to play again.

– compilations, etc. –

1985. (lp) *Blue Form; <BF 1>* **CHILDREN OF THE RAINBOW** [-] [ ]

Apr 88. (lp) *Reckless; (RECK 4)* **THE BEST OF MU** [ ] [-]
(cd-iss.1990's; CDRECK 4)

Jun 88. (lp) *Reckless; (RECK 7)* **END OF AN ERA** (rare) [ ] [-]
– Land of Mu / Waiting for the sun / Haleakala / Children of the rainbow / Calling from a star / Drink from the fountain / Make a joyful noise / End of an era / Odd TV occurence / On our way to Hana / Who'll write this song / Daybreak sunshine / Blue Jay blue / The love we bare / Showering rain / You're not the only one / The awakening.

Jun 97. (cd) *Xotic Mind; (XMCD 1)* **THE BAND FROM THE LOST CONTINENT** [ ] [-]

MERRELL FANKHAUSER

with numerous session people incl. **MARY LEE + JOHN CIPOLLINA**

Full Blast not issued

1987. (lp) *(FBLP 400164)* **DOCTOR FANKHAUSER** (rec.1983) [-] [-] German
– Who can you call / Don't give up the rock / Some of them escaped it all / Buddy, Elvis and John / Maybe you can call be honey / Thought I heard a melody / That's alright mama; blues medley / Time of the day / Stone Indians pray / Cocaine and aeroplanes. *(UK cd-iss.Feb95 on 'Legend Music'; LM 9010)*

Reckless not issued

Dec 88. (lp) *(RECK 10)* **THE MAUI ALBUM** [ ] [-]
– Lovely lady / I saw your photograph / We were all free / On our way to Hanah / It's love that sings the song / In Mu / You and I / One more day / Garden in the rain / Waterfall / Lala does the boo ru / Sail it over the ocean / Love is all there is / The

source / Make a joyful noise.

		Legend Music	Legend Music
1991.	(cd) *<(LM 9002)>* **FLYING TO MACHU PICCHU**		
1994.	(cd) *<(LM 9015)>* **JUNGLE LO LO BAND**		

- others, etc. -

Feb 95.	(cd; by MERRELL AND THE EXILES) *Legend Music; (LM 9006)* **EARLY YEARS 1964-1967**		
Feb 95.	(cd) *Legend Music; (LM 9007) CALIFORNIA LIVE* (studio 1989)		

MURPHY BLEND

Formed: Berlin, Germany ... 1970 by WOLF-RODIGER UHLIG, WOLFGANG RUMLER, ANDREAS SCHOLZ and ACHIM SCHMIDT. This quartet released the sublime 'FIRST LOSS' album in 1972, a progressive rock gem which was written mainly by UHLIG. Classically trained, his symphonic organ riffs dominated the album alongside RUMLER's leaden guitar, a pioneering sound that influenced many acts throughout the 70's. The band split shortly after the album's release, ANDREAS SCHOLZ joining BLACKWATER PARK.

Recommended: FIRST LOSS (*8)

WOLF-RODIGER UHLIG – organ, cembalo, grand piano, vocals / **WOLFGANG RUMLER** – guitar, vocals / **ANDREAS SCHOLZ** – bass / **ACHIM SCHMIDT** – drums

		Kuckuck	not issued
Mar 71.	(lp) *(2375 005)* **FIRST LOSS**	-	- German

– At first / Speed is coming back / Past has gone / Praludium – Use your feet / First loss / Funny guys / Happiness. *(cd-iss.1991)*

— disbanded after above recording, SCHOLZ joined BLACKWATER PARK, while UHLIG guested on FRUMPY's 1972 album.

MUSIC MACHINE

Formed: Los Angeles, California, USA . . .mid-60's by SEAN BONNIWELL, who had sang in folk group, The WAYFARERS. He/they released their debut 45, 'TALK TALK', which hit US Top 20 late in 1966. An album soon followed, which contained a few covers, including NEIL DIAMOND's 'CHERRY CHERRY', The BEATLES' 'TAXMAN and the traditional 'HEY JOE'. However, after a minor hit, 'THE PEOPLE IN ME', their fans lost interest and it wasn't long before the singer formed his own BONNIWELL MUSIC MACHINE. In 1968/69, they released several 45's and an album, before BONNIWELL jettisoned the MUSIC MACHINE moniker.

Recommended: BEST OF (*6)

SEAN BONNIWELL – vocals, guitar (ex-WAYFARERS) / **DOUG RHODES** – organ, vocals / **MARK LANDON** – guitar / **KEITH OLSEN** – bass / **RON EDGAR** – drums (ex-GOLDBRIARS)

		Pye	Original Sound
Jan 67.	(7") *(7N 25407) <OS 61>* **TALK TALK. / COME ON IN**		15 Oct66
Jan 67.	(lp) *<OSRLPS 5015>* **(TURN ON) THE MUSIC MACHINE**	-	76

– Talk talk / See see rider / 96 tears / Hey Joe / Come on in / Cherry Cherry / Wrong / Taxman / Trouble / The people in me / Masculine intuition / Some other drum. *(UK-iss.Jul83 on 'Big Beat'; WIK 17)*

Mar 67.	(7") *(7N 25414) <OS 67>* **THE PEOPLE IN ME. / MASCULINE INTUITION**		66 Jan67
Apr 67.	(7") *<OS 71>* **DOUBLE YELLOW LINE. / ABSOLUTELY POSITIVELY**	-	

— (above single was in name only, as EDGAR, OLSEN and RHODES became MILLENIUM). BONNIWELL was now sole survivor and used MUSIC MACHINE tag.

Jul 67.	(7") *<OS 75>* **THE EAGLE NEVER HUNTS THE FLY. / I'VE LOVED YOU**	-	
Sep 67.	(7") *<OS 82>* **HEY JOE. / WRONG**	-	

(next aka SEAN w/engineer PAUL BUFF) on same label

1968.	(7"; as FRIENDLY TORPEDOS) *<OS 85>* **NOTHING'S TOO GOOD FOR MY CAR. / SO LONG AGO**	-	

— Manager BRIAN ROSS bought rights to group name. So in late summer 1967, SEAN with session men became . . .

BONNIWELL MUSIC MACHINE

with **HOLLY McKINLEY, JOE BROELY, ALAN WISDOM, FRED THOMAS + JERRY HARRIS**

		not issued	Warners
Sep 67.	(7") *<7093>* **BOTTOM OF MY SOUL. / ASTROLOGICALLY INCOMPATIBLE**	-	
Nov 67.	(lp) *<1732>* **BONNIWELL MUSIC MACHINE**	-	

– Double yellow line / The eagle never hunts the fly / Bottom of my soul / Talk me down / The day today / Me, myself and I / Soul love / etc.

Jan 68.	(7") *<7162>* **ME, MYSELF AND I. / SOUL LOVE**	-	
May 68.	(7") *<7188>* **YOU'LL LOVE ME AGAIN. / IN MY NEIGHBOURHOOD**	-	
Jul 68.	(7") *<7199>* **YOU'LL LOVE ME AGAIN. / TO THE LIGHT**	-	
Sep 68.	(7") *<7234>* **TIME OUT (FOR A DAYDREAM). / TIN CAN BEACH**	-	

		not issued	Bell
Mar 69.	(7"; as MUSIC MACHINE) *<764>* **ADVICE AND CONSENT. / MOTHER NATURE FATHER EARTH**	-	

T.S. BONNIWELL

		not issued	Capitol
Jul 69.	(7") *<2551>* **WHERE AM I TO GO? / SLEEP**	-	
Jul 69.	(lp) *<ST 277>* **CLOSE**	-	

— SEAN retired, but re-emerged in the 80's with Christian band HEAVEN SENT

- (MUSIC MACHINE) compilations, etc. -

Feb 85.	(lp) *Rhino; <RNLP 119>* **THE BEST OF THE MUSIC MACHINE**	-	

– Talk talk / The people in me / Masculine intuition / Trouble / Come on in / Advise and consent / Mother Nature – Father Earth / The eagle never hunts the fly / Double yellow line / Absolutely positively / You'll love me again / Everything is everything / Black snow / Dark white.

Jun 97.	(7"; MUSIC MACHINE & SEAN BONNIWELL) *Sundazed; (SEP 131)* **POINT OF NO RETURN. / KING MIXER**		-

MY SOLID GROUND

Formed: Germany . . . early 1971 as a one-off studio project by BERNHARD RENDEL, INGO WERNER, KARL-HEINRICH DORFER and ANDREAS WURSCHING. An album of legendary stature, their PETER HAWKE-produced, self-titled debut was released in early 1971. Drawing comparisons with the hallucinogenic space-rock of PINK FLOYD at their exploratory best, the album employed hypnotic guitar and keyboard riffs to startling effect, most notably on the opening track, 'DIRTY YELLOW MIST' and 'THE EXECUTIONER'. Incredibly, none of the band members recorded any further material of any significance.

Recommended: MY SOLID GROUND (*9)

BERNHARD RENDEL – vocals, guitar / **INGO WERNER** – piano, organ, mellotron / **KARL-HEINRICH DORFER** – bass / **ANDREAS WURSCHING** – drums

		Bacillus	not issued
Jul 71.	(lp) *(6494 008)* **MY SOLID GROUND**	-	- German

– Dirty yellow mist / Flash part IV / That's you / The executioner / Melancholie / Handful of grass / Devonshire Street W1 / "X". *(UK cd-iss.Jun97 on 'Second Battle'; SB 035)*

— all returned to wilderness

MYSTERY TREND

Formed: San Francisco, California, USA . . . 1966 by RON NAGLE, BOB CUFF, LARRY BENNETT, LARRY WEST and JOHN LUBY. They took their name, mistakenly, from a misheard line ('Mystery Tramp') in DYLAN's 'Like A Rolling Stone'. Part of the 'Frisco scene, they performed their style of flower-power folk-psych many times, but only one single surfaced for 'Verve'; 'JOHNNY WAS A GOOD BOY' in 1967. The members bailed out one by one, until only the solo bound RON NAGLE was left.

Recommended: no albums released by the band

RON NAGLE – vocals / **LARRY WEST** – lead guitar / **BOB CUFF** – guitar / **LARRY BENNETT** – bass / **JOHN LUBY** – drums

		not issued	Verve
Mar 67.	(7") *<10499>* **JOHNNY WAS A GOOD BOY. / A HOUSE ON THE HILL**	-	

— WEST, then CUFF departed, being both replaced by **JOHN GREGORY** but they split in 1968, and he went off to SEATRAIN

RON NAGLE

— with session people including **RY COODER, SAL VALENTINO + JACK NITZSCHE**

		Warners	Warners
1971.	(lp) *(46079) <WS 1902>* **BAD RICE**		

– 61 clay / Marijuana hell / Frank's store / Party in L.A. / That's what friends are for / Sister Cora / Something's gotta give now / Family style / House of Mandia.

— He went into producing and session work, notably for PAUL KANTNER (of JEFFERSON AIRPLANE) and JOHN HIATT. In 1979, he was part of The DUROCS who released one eponymous album for 'Capitol' *<11981>*

MYTHOS

Formed: Germany ... 1969 by STEPHEN KASKE, HAROLD WEISSE and THOMAS HILDEBRAND. Signing to 'Ohr' records, their eponymous debut hit the shops in January 1972. The band's progressive rock sound was characterised by KASKE's virtuoso flute playing and the album is generally regarded as something of a classic. The band split later that year although KASKE subsequently reformed MYTHOS at the end of 1973 with ROBBY LUIZAGA and HANZ-JURGEN PUTZ. This line-up recorded the trippier 'DREAMLAB' album for 'Kosmiche Musik' in 1975 although KASKE soon rejigged the line-up yet again. Focussing on more classically orientated pop rock, the albums 'STRANGE GUYS' and 'CONCRETE CITY' were released in 1977 and 1978 respectively. KASKE proceeded to disband MYTHOS once again although he kept the name for a couple of solo albums on 'Sky' records, 'QUASAR' (1981) and 'GRAND PRIX' (1982). Throughout the 80's he was gainfully employed in production work, making a comeback with a 3CD set of easy listening synth music.

Recommended: MYTHOS (*9)

STEPHAN KASKE – flute, keyboards, vocals, guitar, synthesizer / **HARALD WEISS** – bass, guitar, effects / **THOMAS HOLDEBRAND** – drums

Ohr / not issued

Jan 72. (lp) *(OMM 556.019)* **MYTHOS** [-] [-] German
– Mythoett / Oriental journey / Hero's death / Encyclopedia terrae. *(cd-iss.1990's;)*

— split late 1972, but re-formed a year later by **STEPHAN KASKE** and new members; **ROBBY LUIZAGA** – bass, acoutic guitar, mellotron / **ANS-JURGEN PUTZ** – drums, percussion

Kosmische Musik / not issued

1975. (lp) *(KM 58016)* **DREAMLAB** [-] [-] German
– Dedicated to Wernher von Braun / Message (part 1 & 2) / Expeditions / Mythalgia / Dreamlab: Echophase – Quite amazed – Going to meet my lady / Eternity. *(cd-iss.1990's;)*

— **KASKE** recruited another line-up; **SVEN DOHROW** – guitar / **EBERHARD P. SEIDLER** – bass / **RONNIE SCHREINZER** – drums

Venus / not issued

Jan 78. (lp) *(V78MY-F 1003)* **STRANGE GUYS** [-] [-] German
– Aeronaut / Strange guys / Mysterious scene / Powerslide / Terry incognita / Backstage fumble.

Jan 79. (lp) *(V78MY-B 1012)* **CONCRETE CITY** [-] [-] German
– Harry Chanceless / Concrete city / Flamenco bay / Neutron bomb / Ulysses B. Smart / Yukon.

— **KASKE** virtually solo, but aided on next by **MARKUS WORBS** – drums

Sky / not issued

Jan 81. (lp) *(046)* **QUASAR** [-] [-] German
– Quasar / Nurse robot / Flut-E-Quenzer: The knight – Duel – Lamentation conjuration – Rebirth / Flut-E-Sizer / Didn't notice, didn't mind / Nothing but your dream / Just a part / When the show's just begun.

Jan 82. (lp) *(066)* **GRAND PRIX** [-] [-] German
– Grand prix / Transamazonia / Transatlantik non-stop / Video / Jet set / Bermuda dreieck / Robot secret agents / Mayday.

— KASKE went into production, before he returned in 1990

Evil Omen / not issued

Feb 95. (cd) *(EOR 0002)* **PAIN AMPLIFIER** [ ] [-]
(above was compiled from 3xcd-box released in Germany 1990)

Ron NAGLE (see under ⇒ MYSTERY TREND)

Graham NASH (see under ⇒ CROSBY, STILLS, NASH & YOUNG)

NASHVILLE TEENS

Formed: Weybridge, Surrey, USA ... 1962 by ART SHARP, RAY PHILLIPS, MICHAEL DUNFORD, JOHN HAWKEN, PETE SHANNON and ROGER GROOM, the latter two being deposed in 1963 by JOHN ALLEN and BARRY JENKINS. A 7th member, TERRY CROW (a 3rd vocalist!), was part of the line-up that backed JERRY LEE LEWIS on his Hamburg tour (chronicled on his 'Live At The Star Club'). They were soon under the wing of former singer turned producer, MICKIE MOST, who was responsible for their classy debut Top 10 single, 'TOBACCO ROAD', in the summer of '64. Another, 'GOOGLE EYE', soon ascended to similar heights, although the single marked the end of their association with the man. Minor hits with ANDREW LOOG OLDHAM and SHEL TALMY, respectively, couldn't boost their flagging R&B sound. JENKINS departed for The ANIMALS, and a single; RANDY NEWMAN's 'THE BIGGEST NIGHT OF HER LIFE', also flopped. More cover 45's, notably DYLAN's 'ALL ALONG THE WATCH-TOWER', failed to gain any credibility, most people no doubt waiting for a "real" version by HENDRIX. PHILLIPS was soon to be the only original member left, as others bailed out to more profitable pastures. He and some made-up NASHVILLE TEENS still tread the cabaret circuit; Butlins, Pontins & Blackpool, I was told.

Recommended: BEST OF THE NASHVILLE TEENS 1964-1969 (*5)

ART SHARP (b. ARTHUR, 26 May'41) – vocals / **RAY PHILLIPS** (b. RAMON JOHN PHILLIPS, 16 Jan'44, Tiger Bay, Cardiff, Wales) / **JOHN HAWKEN** (b. 9 May'40, Bournemouth, England) – piano / **PETE SHANNON** (b. PETER SHANNON HARRIS, 23 Aug'41, Antrim, N. Ireland) – bass / **JOHN ALLEN** (b. JOHN SAMUEL ALLEN, 23 Apr'45, St. Albans, England) – guitar; repl. MICHAEL DUNFORD who later joined RENAISSANCE / **BARRY JENKINS** (b.22 Dec'44, Leicester, England) – drums; repl. ROGER GROOM

		Decca	London	
Jun 64.	(7") *(F 11930)* <9689> **TOBACCO ROAD. / I LIKE IT LIKE THAT**	6	14	Aug64
Oct 64.	(7") *(F 12000)* <9712> **GOOGLE EYE. / T.N.T.**	10		
Nov 64.	(lp) <3407> **TOBACCO ROAD**	-		
Feb 65.	(7") *(F 12089)* <9736> **FIND MY WAY BACK HOME. / DEVIL-IN-LAW**	34	98	Mar65
May 65.	(7") *(F 12143)* **THIS LITTLE BIRD. / WHATCHA GONNA DO?**	38		
Oct 65.	(7") *(F 12255)* **I KNOW HOW IT FEELS TO BE LOVED. / SOON FORGOTTEN**			
Jan 66.	(7") *(F 12316)* **THE HARD WAY. / UPSIDE DOWN**	45		

— BARRY JENKINS (to ANIMALS) was repl. by

Date	Release	Decca	London
Aug 66.	(7") *(F 12458)* **FORBIDDEN FRUIT. / REVIVED 45 TIME**		
Jan 67.	(7") *(F 12542)* **THAT'S MY WOMAN. / WORDS**		
Mar 67.	(7") *(F 12580)* **I'M COMING HOME. / SEARCHING**		
Sep 67.	(7") *(F 12657)* **THE BIGGEST NIGHT OF HER LIFE. / LAST MINUTE**		
Mar 68.	(7") *(F 12754)* **ALL ALONG THE WATCHTOWER. / SUN DOG**		

		Major Minor	not issued
1969.	(7") *(MM 599)* **THE LAMENT OF THE CHEROKEE RESERVATION INDIAN. / LOOKING FOR YOU**		-

— JOHN HAWKEN joined RENAISSANCE in 1969

		Parlophone	U.A.
Nov 71.	(7") *(R 5925)* <50880> **ELLA JAMES. / TENNESSEE WOMAN**		-
Jul 72.	(7"; w-drawn) *(R 5961)* **YOU SHOULDN'T HAVE BEEN SO NICE. / TELL THE PEOPLE**	-	-

— **PHILLIPS** was virtually left on his own with other musicians (prior/or/future)

		Enterprise	not issued
1972.	(7") *(ENT 001)* **LAWDY MISS CLAWDY. / LET IT ROCK: BREAK UP**		-

		Sky	not issued
Mar 77.	(7") *(1007)* **TOBACCO ROAD. / CHIPS AND PEAS**		-

— early 80's line-up; **RAY PHILLIPS** – vocals / **PETER AGATE** – guitar, vocals / **LEN SURTEES** – bass, vocals / **ADRIAN METCALFE** – drums, vocals

		Butt	not issued
Mar 82.	(7") *(GO 2)* **MIDNIGHT. / LIVE FOR THE SUMMER**		-
Feb 84.	(7"ep) **(FUNEP 4) TOBACCO ROAD '84. / FIND MY WAY BACK HOME / BORN TO BE WILD**		-

Date	Release	Shanghai	not issued
Nov 84.	(m-lp) *(HAI 200)* **LIVE AT THE RED HOUSE (live '82)**		-

- compilations, etc. -

Jan 65.	(7"ep) *Decca; (DFE 8600)* **THE NASHVILLE TEENS** – I need you, baby / Parchment farm / Bread and butter man / How deep is the ocean.		-
May 69.	(7") *Decca; (F 12754)* **TOBACCO ROAD. / ALL ALONG THE WATCHTOWER**		-
Dec 75.	(lp) *New World; (NW 6002)* **THE NASHVILLE TEENS**		-
Feb 85.	(7") *EMI Gold; (G45 43)* **TOBACCO ROAD. / GOOGLE EYE**		-
Apr 93.	(cd) *E.M.I.; (CDEMS 1474)* **THE BEST OF THE NASHVILLE TEENS 1964-1969** – Tobacco road / Mona (I need you baby) / T.N.T. / Parchman farm / Need you / La bamba / Bread and butter man / Google eye / Hoochie coochie man / How deep is the ocean / Find my way back home / Devil-in-law / Too much / Hurtin' inside / I like it like that / Searching / Soon forgotten / This little bird / I'm coming home / The hard way / Words / That's my woman / Lament of the Cherokee Reservation Indian / Looking for you.		-

NATIONAL HEALTH (see under ⇒ HATFIELD & THE NORTH)

NAZZ (see under ⇒ RUNDGREN, Todd)

NEKTAR

Formed: based Germany ...early 70's by English ex-patriots including frontman ROYE ALBRIGHTON. Art-rockers of a heavier persuasion than most in the genre, the band decamped to that haven of all things progressive, Germany. They cut their concept debut in 1972 for the 'Bellaphon' label, the gloriously titled 'JOURNEY TO THE CENTRE OF THE EYE'. With titles like 'DEATH OF THE MIND', 'BURN OUT MY EYES' and 'LOOK INSIDE YOURSELF, you knew these guys were partial to a few sugarcubes with their P.G. Tips. But in spite of the cliched lyrical fare, the band were surprisingly sharp instrumentally and the songs seldom deteriorated into formless noodling. The follow-up, 'A TAB IN THE OCEAN' (1972) was more of the same, while 1973's 'SOUNDS LIKE THIS' was as spontaneous and raw as you'd expect for an album that was recorded in a matter of days. Later the same year, the band broke in the U.S. top 20 with 'REMEMBER THE FUTURE' while 'DOWN TO EARTH' (1974) also breached the American chart in early '75. Later albums such as 'RECYCLED' (1976) and 'MAGIC IS A CHILD' (1977) were more studied, synth dominated affairs that lacked the spark of NEKTAR's earlier work. After a final lacklustre album, 'MAN IN THE MOON' (1980), the band split.

Recommended: JOURNEY TO THE CENTRE OF THE EYE (*6)

ROYE ALBRIGHTON – vocals, guitar / **ALLAN FREEMAN** – keyboards, vocals / **DEREK MOORE** – bass, mellotron, vocals / **RON HOWDEN** – drums, percussion

Date	Release	Bellaphon	not issued	
Mar 72.	(lp) *(BLPS 19064)* **JOURNEY TO THE CENTRE OF THE EYE** – Prelude / Astronaut's nightmare / Countenance / The nine lifeless daughters of the Sun / Warp oversight / The dream nebula (part 1 & 2) / It's all in the mind / Burn out my eyes / Void of vision / Pupil of the eye / Look inside yourself / Death of the mind.	-	-	German
Sep 72.	(lp) *(BLPS 19118)* **A TAB IN THE OCEAN** – A tab in the ocean / Desolation valley / Waves / Cryin' in the dark / King of the twilight. *(UK-iss.1974 on 'United Artists'; UAS 29499)* *<US-iss.Sep76 on 'Passport'; 98017>*	-	-	German

Date	Release	U.A.	Passport	
Apr 73.	(d-lp) *(UAD 60041-2) SOUNDS LIKE THIS* – Good days / New day dawning / What ya gonna do? / 1-2-3-4 / Do you believe in magic / Cast your fate / Day in the life of a preacher / Wings / Odyssee.		-	
Jun 73.	(7") *(NEK 1)* **WHAT YA GONNA DO? / DAY IN THE LIFE OF A PREACHER (part one)**		-	
Oct 73.	(lp) *(UAG 29545)* <98002> **REMEMBER THE FUTURE** – Remember the future parts 1 & 2 – Images of the past / Path of light / Tomorrow never comes / Confusion / Let it grow / Questions and answers / Recognition / Returning light / Wheel of time. *(correct order this lp)*		19	Jun74
1974.	(7") <7902> **REMEMBER THE FUTURE. / CONFUSION**	-		

— In 1974, German 'Bellaphon' label released live lp 'LIVE AT THE ROUNDHOUSE'; *(BLPS 19182)*. Contained tracks; Desolation valley / A day in the life of a preacher featuring the birth of Oh Willy / Oops / Mundetango / Summer breeze.

Date	Release	U.A.	Passport	
Jul 74.	(7") *(UP 35706)* **FIDGETY QUEEN. / LITTLE BOY**		-	
Oct 74.	(lp) *(UAG 29680)* <98005> **DOWN TO EARTH** – Astral man / Nelly the elephant / Early morning clown / That's life / Fidgety queen / Oh Willy / Little boy / Show me the way / (finale).		32	Jan75
Jul 75.	(7") *(UP 35853)* <7904> **ASTRAL MAN. / NELLY THE ELEPHANT**		91	Apr75

Date	Release	Decca	Passport
Mar 76.	(lp) *(SKL-R 5250)* <98011> **RECYCLED** – Recycle / Cybernetic consumption / Recycle countdown / Automaton horrorscope / Recycling / Flight to reality / Unendless imaginations / Sao Paolo sunrise / Costa Del Sol / Marvellous Moses / It's all over.		89

— In 1977, this line-up recorded a couple of live albums for German label 'Bacilus'; 'LIVE IN NEW YORK' a double (BAC 2004)/ 'MORE LIVE IN NEW YORK' *(BAC 2058)*. Just prior to the latter in 1978, the same label compiled 'THE BEST OF NEKTAR' (BAC 2056), which was issued US as 'THRU THE EARS'; *(Visa 9001)*.

— **DAVE NELSON** – guitar, vocals / **LARRY FAST** – synthesizers, repl. ROY

Bacilus / Polydor

Oct 77. (lp) *(BAC 2050) <PD 6115>* **MAGIC IS A CHILD** [-] [ ]
– Eeerie Lackawanna / Midnite lite / Love to share / Train from nowhere / Listen / On the run / Spread your wings.

— **FREEMAN** brought back former leader **ALBRIGHTON** + recruited **CARMINE ROJAS** – bass, keyboards / **DAVID PRATER** – drums, vocals

Ariola / not issued

1980. (lp) *(202215)* **MAN IN THE MOON** [-] [-] German
– Too young to die / Angel / Telephone / Far away torraine / Can't stop you now / We / You're alone / Man in the moon.

— Disbanded after above.

Bill NELSON

Born: 18 Dec'48, Wakefield, Yorkshire, England. In the late 60's, after a job as a government officer, he joined local groups, GLOBAL VILLAGE TRUCKING COMPANY and GENTLE REVOLUTION. He then released an obscure and limited solo album, 'NORTHERN DREAM', on his own label in 1971, the record soon finding its way to Radio 1 DJ, John Peel, who gave it night-time airplay. That year, NELSON formed BE-BOP DELUXE, alongside IAN PARKIN, ROBERT BRYAN, NICHOLAS CHATTERTON-DEW and RICHARD BROWN and after one single, they signed to 'Harvest'. Their first album, 'AXE VICTIM' (1974), showcased the talent of the gifted NELSON, a dextrous multi-instrumentalist and guitarist, its release swiftly followed by a tour supporting COCKNEY REBEL. In August '74, NELSON split the band up, subsequently re-forming the group with unhappy ex-REBELS. After a well-received album, 'FUTURAMA', they followed it early next year with a UK Top 30 hit single, 'SHIPS IN THE NIGHT', taken from the hit parent album, 'SUNBURST FINISH'. They enjoyed a couple of years in the big league, until NELSON decided to form another project, RED NOISE. After a promising 1979 album, 'SOUND ON SOUND', NELSON went solo, subsequently hitting the Top 10 with an adventurous, experimental double-set, 'QUIT DREAMING AND GET ON THE BEAM' (1981). Throughout the 80's and 90's, NELSON released a plethora of albums, mostly for his own obscure 'Cocteau' label. Having also worked with The SKIDS, The ASSOCIATES, YELLOW MAGIC ORCHESTRA and DAVID SYLVIAN, on collaborative efforts and production work, he subsequently released his best work for some time in 1996, 'AFTER THE SATELLITE SINGS'. • **Trivia:** His younger brother IAN (of RED NOISE), also had a minor hit with FIAT LUX.

Recommended: RAIDING THE DIVINE ARCHIVES (*8; BE BOP DELUXE) / SOUND ON SOUND (*7; RED NOISE) / QUIT DREAMING AND GET ON THE BEAM (*9) / CHIMERA (*7) / DUPLEX: THE BEST OF BILL NELSON (*7) / AFTER THE SATELLITE SINGS (*7)

BILL NELSON – vocals, lead guitar

Smile / not issued

1971 (lp) *(LAF 2182)* **NORTHERN DREAM** [ ] [-]
– Photograph (a beginning) / Everyone's hero / House of sand / End of the seasons / Rejoice / Love's a way / Northern dreamer (1957) / Bloo blooz / Sad fellings / See it through / Smiles / Chymepeace (an ending). *(re-iss.Feb81, Mar82 & Aug86 on 'Butt'; BUTT 002) (cd-iss.Mar96 on 'Blueprint'; SM 777CD)*

BE-BOP DELUXE

were formed by **BILL NELSON** plus **IAN PARKIN** – rhythm guitar / **ROBERT BRYAN** – bass / **NICHOLAS CHATTERTON-DEW** – drums / **RICHARD BROWN** – keyboards

Smile / not issued

Jan 73. (7") *(LAFS 001)* **TEENAGE ARCHANGEL. / JETS AT DAWN** [ ] [-]

— became trio, when BROWN departed.

Harvest / Harvest

May 74. (7") *(HAR 5081)* **JET SILVER (AND THE DOLLS OF VENUS). / THIRD FLOOR HEAVEN** [ ] [-]

Jun 74. (lp) *(SHVL 813) <SM 11689>* **AXE VICTIM** [ ] [ ]
– Axe victim / Love is swift arrows / Jet Silver (and the dolls of Venus) / Third floor Heaven / Night creatures / Rocket cathedrals / Adventures in a Yorkshire landscape / Jets at dawn / No trains to Heaven / Darkness (l'immoralise). *(cd-iss.Feb91; CZ 327)*– (3 extra).

— Aug74, **NELSON** recruited entire new line-up **MILTON REAME-JAMES** – keyboards (ex-COCKNEY REBEL) repl. IAN / **PAUL AVRON JEFFRYS** – bass (ex-COCKNEY REBEL) repl. ROBERT / **SIMON FOX** – drums (ex-HACKENSHACK) repl. NICHOLAS

— (late 1974) **BILL** and **SIMON** were joined by **CHARLIE TUMAHAI** (b. New Zealand) – bass who repl. MILTON & PAUL

Feb 75. (7"; w-drawn) *(HAR 5091)* **BETWEEN THE WORLDS. / LIGHTS** [-] [-]

May 75. (lp) *(SHSP 4045) <ST 11432>* **FUTURAMA** [ ] [ ]
– Stage whispers / Love with the madman / Maid in Heaven / Sister seagull / Sound track / Music in Dreamland / Jean Cocteau / Between the worlds / Swan song. *(cd-iss.Feb91; CZ 328) (cd re-iss.Apr97 on 'E.M.I.'; REPLAYCD 27)*

Jun 75. (7") *(HAR 5098)* **MAID IN HEAVEN. / LIGHTS** [ ] [-]

Jul 75. (7") *<4151>* **MAID IN HEAVEN. / SISTER SEAGULL** [-] [ ]

— added **ANDREW CLARKE** – keyboards

Jan 76. (7") *(HAR 5104) <4244>* **SHIPS IN THE NIGHT. / CRYING TO THE SKY** [23] [ ]

Jan 76. (lp/c) *(SHSP/TC-SHSP 4053) <St 11478>* **SUNBURST FINISH** [17] [96]
– Fair exchange / Heavenly homes / Ships in the night / Crying to the sky / Sleep that burns / Beauty secrets / Life in the air age / Like an old blues / Crystal gazing / Blazing apostles. *(re-iss.Mar82 on 'Fame' lp/c; FA/TC-FA 3004) (re-iss.Jun86 on 'Revolver' lp/c; REV LP/MC 71) (cd-iss.Feb91 +=; CZ 329)*– Shine / Speed of the wind / Blue as a jewel.

Aug 76. (7") *(HAR 5110)* **KISS OF THE LIGHT. / Funky Phaser Unearthly Merchandise: SHINE** [ ] [-]

Sep 76. (lp/c) *(SHSP/TC-SHSP 4058) <ST 11575>* **MODERN MUSIC** [12] [88]
– Orphans of Babylon / Twilight capers / Kiss of the light / The bird charmer's destiny / The gold at the end of my rainbow / Bring back the spark / Modern music / Dancing in the moonlight / Honeymoon on Mars / Lost in the neon world / Dance of the Uncle Sam humanoids / Modern music / Forbidden lovers / Down on Terminal street / Make the music magic. *(cd-iss.Feb91; CZ 330)*– (3 extra). *(cd re-iss.Apr97 on 'E.M.I.'; REPLAYCD 28)*

Jul 77. (white-lp) *(SHVL 816) <11666>* **LIVE IN THE AIR AGE (live)** [10] [65]
– Life in the air age / Ships in the night / Piece of mine / Fair exchange / Mill street junction / Adventures in a Yorkshire landscape / Blazing apostles. *(free-7"ep)* **SHINE. / SISTER SEAGULL / MAID IN HEAVEN** *(cd-iss.Feb91; CZ 331)*– (3 extra ep tracks).

Sep 77. (7") *(HAR 5135)* **JAPAN. / FUTURIST MANIFESTO** [ ] [-]

Feb 78. (7") *(HAR 5147) <4571>* **PANIC IN THE WORLD. / BLUE AS A JEWEL** [ ] [ ]

Feb 78. (lp/c) *(SHSP/TC-SHSP 4091) <ST 11750>* **DRASTIC PLASTIC** [22] [95]
– Electrical language / New precision / New mysteries / Surreal estate / Love in flames / Panic in the world / Dangerous stranger / Superenigmatix (lethal appliances for the home) / Islands of the dead / Visions of endless hopes / Possession / Islands of the dead. *(cd-iss.Feb91; CZ 332)*– (3 extra tracks). *(cd re-iss.Apr97 on 'E.M.I.'; REPLAYCD 29)*

May 78. (7") *(HAR 5158)* **ELECTRICAL LANGUAGE. / SURREAL ESTATE** [ ] [-]

— Disbanded Spring 1978. TUMAHAI joined The DUKES, SIMON joined JACK GREEN. CLARKE joined NICO's band.

– compilations, others, etc. –

on 'Harvest' unless mentioned otherwise

Oct 76. (7"ep) *(HAR 5117)* **HOT VALVES** [36] [ ]
– Maid in Heaven / Blazing apostles / Jet Silver and the dolls of Venus / Bring back the spark.

Nov 78. (d-lp) *(SHDW 410)* **THE BEST OF AND THE REST OF BE-BOP DELUXE** [ ] [ ]
(cd-iss.May90; 794 158-2)

May 81. (lp/c) *(SHSM/TC-SHSM 2034)* **THE SINGLES A's & B's** [ ] [-]
(cd-iss.Feb92 on 'See For Miles'; SEECD 336)

Aug 83. (7"m) *Cocteau; (COQ 7)* **PANIC IN THE WORLD. / MAID IN HEAVEN / ELECTRICAL LANGUAGE** [ ] [-]
(re-iss.Jul85 as 12"m; COQT 7)

Sep 83. (d-lp) *(EDP 154 6793)* **AXE VICTIM / FUTURAMA** [ ] [-]

May 84. (7") *EMI Gold; (G45 21)* **SHIPS IN THE NIGHT. / MAID IN HEAVEN** [ ] [-]

Aug 86. (lp) *Dojo; (DOJOLP 42)* **BOP TO THE RED NOISE** [ ] [-]

Mar 87. (lp/c) *(EMS/TC-EMS 1130)* **RAIDING THE DIVINE ARCHIVES** [ ] [-]
– Jet silver (and the dolls of Venus) / Adventures in a Yorkshire landscape / Maid in Heaven / Ships in the night / Life in the air age / Kiss of light / Sister seagull / Modern music / Japan / Panic in the world / Bring back the spark / Forbidden lovers / Electrical language. *(re-iss.Apr90 on 'E.M.I.'+=; CDP 794 158-2)*– Fair exchange / Sleep that burns / Between the worlds / Music in Dreamland.

Sep 94. (cd) *Windsong; (WINCD 065)* **RADIOLAND – BBC RADIO 1 LIVE IN CONCERT (live)** [ ] [-]

BILL NELSON'S RED NOISE

BILL NELSON with **ANDREW CLARKE** – keyboards / **RICK FORD** – drums / brother **IAN NELSON** – saxophone / **STEVE PEER** – drums

Harvest / Harvest

Feb 79. (7"red) *(HAR 5176)* **FURNITURE MUSIC. / WONDERTOYS THAT LAST FOREVER / ACQUITTED BY MIRRORS** [59] [ ]

Feb 79. (lp/c) *(SHSP/TC-SHSP 4095)* **SOUND ON SOUND** [33] [ ]
– Don't touch me, I'm electric / For young moderns / Stop – go – stop / Furniture music / Radar in my heart / Stay young / Out of touch / A better home in the phantom zone / Substitute flesh / The atom age / Art – Empire – Industry / Revolt into style. *(re-iss.Nov85 on 'Cocteau' lp/c; JC/CJC 14)*

Apr 79. (7"blue) *(HAR 5183)* **REVOLT INTO STYLE. / OUT OF TOUCH** [69] [ ]

BILL NELSON

solo, with **TOM KELLICHAN** – drums / with sessioners

Cocteau / not issued

Jun 80. (7"ep) *(COQ 1)* **DO YOU DREAM IN COLOUR?** [52] [-]
– Do you dream in colour? / Ideal homes / Instantly yours / Atom Man loves Radium Girl.

Crepescule / not issued

Mar 81. (7") **ROOMS WITH BRITTLE VIEWS. / DADA GUITARS** [-] [-] Belguim

Mercury / Mercury

Mar 81. (7") *(WILL 1)* **BANAL. / MR. MAGNETISN HIMSELF** [ ] [ ]
(12"+=) *(WILL 1-12)* – Turn to fiction.

May 81. (lp)(c) *(6359 055)(7557 010)* **QUIT DREAMIMG AND GET ON THE BEAM** [7] [ ]
– Banal / Living in my limousine / Vertical games / Disposable / False alarms / Decline and fall / Life runs out like sand / A kind of loving / Do you dream in colour? / U.H.F. / Youth of nation on fire / Quit dreaming and get on the beam. *(w/ free-lp)* **SOUNDING THE RITUAL ECHO** – Annuciation / The ritual echo / Sleep / Near east / Emak bakia / My intricate image / Endless orchids / The heat in the room / Another willingly opened window / Vanishing parades / Glass fish (for the final aquarium) / Cubical domes / Ashes of roses / The shadow garden (opium). *(iss.on own.Jun85 on 'Cocteau'; JCS 12) (cd-iss.on own.Sep89; JCCD 12) (cd-iss.Jul86 on 'Cocteau'+=; JCCD 15)*– White sound.

Jun 81. (7") *(BILL 2)* **YOUTH OF NATION ON FIRE. / BE MY DYNAMO** [73] [ ]

(d7"+=) *(WILL 22)* – Rooms with brittle views / All my wives were iron.

Sep 81. (7") *(WILL 3)* **LIVING IN MY LIMOUSINE. / BIRDS OF TIME**
(12"+=) *(WILL 3-12)* – Love in the abstract / White sound.

Apr 82. (7") *(WILL 4)* **EROS ARRIVING. / HAUNTING IN MY HEAD** -
(d7"+=) *(WILL 44)* – Flesh / He and sleep were brothers.

Jun 82. (d-lp/d-c) *(WHIRL/CURL 3)* **THE LOVE THAT WHIRLS** 28
– Empire of the senses / Hope for the heartbeat / Waiting for the voices / Private view / Eros arriving / Bride of Christ in Autumn / When your dream of perfect beauty comes true / Flaming desire / Portrait of Jan with flowers / Crystal escalator in the palace of God department store / Echo in her eyes / October man. *(re-iss.Jul86 on 'Cocteau', cd+=)* – Flesh / He and sleep were brothers.

Jul 82. (7"/12") *(WILL 5/+12)* **FLAMING DESIRE. / THE PASSION** -

May 83. (lp/c) *(MERB/+C 19)* **CHIMERA** 30
– The real adventure / Acceleration / Every day feels like another new drug / Tender is the night / Glow world / Another day, another ray of hope. *(cd-iss.Sep87 on 'Cocteau', re-iss.Apr89)*

Cocteau Portrait

Aug 83. (7"m) *(COQ 10)* **TOUCH AND GLOW. / DANCING IN THE WILD / LOVE WITHOUT FEAR**

Dec 83. (m-lp) *(JCM 3)* **SAVAGE GESTURES FOR CHARMS SAKE** -
– The man in the exine suit / Watching my dream boat go down in flames / The meat room / Another happy thought (carved forever in your cortex) / Portrait of Jan with Moon and stars. *(re-iss.Feb85)*

Aug 84. (7") *(COQ 15)* **ACCELERATION. / HARD FACTS FROM THE FICTION DEPARTMENT** -
(12"pic-d+=) *(COQT 15)* – ('A'short) / ('A'long).

Oct 84. (lp) **VISTAMIX** -
– The real adventure / Flaming desire / Acceleration / Empire of the senses / Everyday feels like another new drug / Do you dream in color? / A kind of loving / Tender is the night / Glow world / Another day, another ray of hope.

Portrait Portrait

Mar 86. (7"/12") *(A/TA 6928)* **WILDEST DREAMS. / SELF IMPERSONATION**

Apr 86. (lp/c) *(PRT/40 26602)* **GETTING THE HOLY GHOST ACROSS** 91
– Suvasini / Contemplation / Theology / Wildest dreams / Lost in your mystery / Rise like a fountain / Age of reason / Hidden flame / Because of you / Living for the spangled moment / Word for word / Illusions of you / Heart and soul / Finks and stooges of the spirit. *(cd-iss.1988 on 'C.B.S.'; CDCBS 26602)*

Cocteau Enigma

Jun 86. (lp) *(JC 7)* **CHAMBER OF DREAMS** -
– The blazing memory of innuendo / Into the luminous future / Dip in the swimming pool / Reactor / Tomorrowland (the threshold of 1947) / Listening to lizards / Endless torsion / My sublime perversion / Eros in Autumn / Sleeplessness / The latest skyline / Train of thought / Packs and fountains clouds and trees / Golden bough / Forever Orpheus / In arcadia / Sentimental / Autumn fires / Wild blue yonder. *(cd-iss.Aug89; JCCD 7)*

Oct 86. (lp/c) *(JC/TCJC 6)* **SUMMER OF GOD'S PIANO** -
– Antennae two / N.B.C.97293 / The sleep of Hollywood / The celestial bridegroom / Under the red arch / Orient pearl / Sacrament / Falling blossoms / The difficulty of being / Zanoni / The Chinese nightingale / Soon September (another enchantment) / Rural shires / Perfido incanto / The lost years / The charm of transit / Night thoughts (twilight radio) / Wysteria / Swing / Snowfall / Real of dusk / Over ocean. *(cd-iss.Aug89; JCCD 6)*

Jan 87. (lp/c/cd) *(JC/TCJC/JCCD 19)* **MAP OF DREAMS** -
– Legions of the endless night / Spinning creatures / At the gates of the singing garden / Heavenly message No.1, 2 & 3 / Fellini's picnic / Dark angel / Infernal regions / Dance of the fragrant woman / The alchemy of ecstasy / Aphrodite adorned / The wheel of fortune and the hand of fate / Forked tongues, mixed blessings / Another tricky mission for the celestial pilot / Water of life (transfiguration).

May 87. (12"; by SCALA: BILL NELSON & DARYL RUNSWICK) *(COQT 21)* **SECRET CEREMONY (theme from 'BROND'). / WIPING A TEAR FROM THE ALLSEEING EYES** -

Nov 87. (d-lp/c/cd) *(JEAN/+TC/CD 20)* **CHANCE ENCOUNTERS IN THE GARDEN OF LIGHT** -
– My dark demon / The dove consumed (the serpent slumbers) / Calling Heaven, calling Heaven overs / Path of return / Theurgia / Staircase to no place / Evocation of a radiant childhood / The kingdom of consequence / Divine raptures of a radiant childhood / Bright star (moonlight over the ocean blue) / A bird of the air shall earn the voice / Clothed in light amongst the stars / Hastening the chariot of my hearts desire / Transcendant conversation / West deep / The spirit cannot fail / Pilots of kite / Phantom gardens / The angel of hearth and home / Villefranche interior / Night tides / First memory / Azure extention / Radiant spires / Evening peal / Thremodia / Short drink for a certain fountain / Body of light / At the centre / Self-initiation / The word that became flesh / The hermetic garden / Revolving globes / The four square citadel / Orient of Memphis / Little daughters of light / Angel at the western window.

Sep 88. (lp/c/cd; as BILL NELSON ORCHESTRA ARCANA) *(JC/+TC/CD 21)* **OPTIMISM**
– Exactly the way you want it / Why be lonely / Everyday is a better day / The receiver and the fountain pen / Welcome home Mr. Kane / This is true / Greeting a new day / The breath in my father's saxophone / Our lady of apparations / The whole city between us / Deva dance / Always looking forward to tomorrow / Profiles, hearts, stars / Alchemia.

Dec 88. (7") *(COQ 22)* **LIFE IN YOUR HANDS. / DO YOU DREAM IN COLOUR** -
(12"+=/cd-s+=) *(COQ T/CD 22)* – Get out of that hole / Drean demon.

Aug 89. (lp/cd) *(JC/+CD 8)* **PAVILLIONS OF THE HEART AND SOUL** -
– Gift of the August tide / Loving tongues / Blue nude / In the realms of bells / Your nebulous smile / The glance of a glittering stranger / Another kiss for your slender neck / The warmth of women's eyes / Seduction (ritual with roses) / Dreamed entrances / Four pieces for imaginary strings:- Herself with her shadow – The exquisite corpse – Ardent hands – Her laughing torso / Migrating angels / Les amoureaux / Meshes of the afternoon / Mountains of the heart / Willow silk / Tender encounters (states of grace) / Melancholia / The eternal female.

Aug 89. (lp/cd) *(JC/+CD 9)* **CATALOGUE OF OBSESSIONS** -
– Sex party six / Tune in Tokyo / Promise of perfume / View from a balcony / Test of affection / Birds in two hemispheres / Wider windows for the walls / The boy pilots of Bangkok / Talk technique / Glass breakfast / Edge of tears / Erotikon.

Sep 90. (cd/c) *(JCCD/TCJC 24)* **CHIMES AND RINGS** -
– Lady you're a strange girl / Kiss goodbye / Call of the wild / Lost to me / Dangerous lady / Working man / Giving it all away / Ice and fire / Wonder where we go / Dreams of yesterday / Sell my soul / Back to dreams / I wait for you / Walk away from Paradise / Playing Jesus to her Judas / Something's going on / The miracle belongs to you.

Sep 90. (cd/c) *(JCCD/TCJC 25)* **NUDITY** -
– Feels like up to me / Prize of years / Still waiting / Lover boy at heart / The wonder of it all / Devil in me / A little more time / What's it all about / Thunder on the wing / Shake it up / Love to win / Running / If love were gold / I want you / Kiss it off / Angel like you / Crying all night / Only love can tell.

Sep 90. (cd/c) *(JCCD/TCJC 26)* **HEARTBREAKLAND** -
– You know how to hurt / Broken / You make me cry / Mess around / Why? / Insanity / Confused / Heartbreakland / Lucky star / Heartbreak thru' the telephone / One day at a time / Tip the wink / Shadow haunting me / Raining / Love's immortal shining angel.

Sep 90. (cd/c) *(JCCD/TCJC 27)* **DETAILS** -
– Maybe it's the future / Wondering / Wasted lives / The best of you / Stay with me / Love and a bucket full of holes / Prisoner of love / Don't wait / Man on fire / Visionary / The world to me / Strong enough / Everything permitted / Aeroplane wings / One for you / Let it all pass you by.

Imaginary not issued

Apr 91. (cd/c) **LUMINOUS** -

Venture Virgin

Aug 92. (cd/c) *(CD/TC VE 912)* **BLUE MOONS AND LAUGHING GUITARS**
– Ancient guitars / Girl from another planet / Spinnin' around / Shaker / God man slain / The dead we wake with upstairs drum / New moon rising / The glory days / Wishes / Angel in my system / Wings and everything / Boat to forever / The invisible man and the unforgettable girl / So it goes / Fires in the sky / Dream ships set sail.

All Saints not issued

Mar 95. (cd) *(ASCD 022)* **PRACTICALLY WIRED** -
– Roses and rocketships / Spinning planet / Thousand fountain island / Piano 45 / Pink buddha blues / Kid with cowboy tie / Royal ghosts / Her presence in flowers / Big noise in Twangtown / Tiny little thing / Wild blue cycle / Every moment infinite / Friends from Heaven / Eternal for Eniko.

Resurgence not issued

Feb 95. (cd) *(RES 104CD)* **CRIMSWORTH (FLOWERS STONES FOUNTAINS AND FLAMES)** -
– (part 1) / (part 2). *(re-iss.Oct96 & Apr97; same)*

Nov 95. (cd; CULTUREMIX & BILL NELSON) *(RES 113CD)* **CULTUREMIX** -
– Luna park / Radio head / Housewives on drugs / Dancematic / Four postcards home / Zebra / Exile / Tangram / Cave paintings. *(re-iss.Apr97; same)*

Oct 96. (cd) *(RES 114CD)* **AFTER THE SATELLITE SINGS** -
– Deeply dazed / Tomorrow yesterday / Flipside / Streamliner / Memory babe / Skull baby cluster / Zoom sequence / Rocket to Damascus / Beautiful nudes / Old goat / Squirm / Wow it's scootercar sexkitten / Phantom sedan / Ordinary idiots / V-ghost / Blink agog.
(re-iss.Apr97; same)

Populuxe not issued

Apr 97. (cd) *(POPU 003CD)* **ELECTRICITY MADE US ANGELS** -

Apr 97. (cd) *(POPU 004CD)* **BUDDHA HEAD** -
– My philosophy / Killing my desires / Buddha head / Way / Big river / Karma kisses / We will rise / Signs and signals / Lotus in the stream / Enlightenment / Eternally / Duality / Perfect world / Heart has its reasons / Sun will rise / Big illumination / Life as we know it.

Jun 97. (cd) *(POPU 005CD)* **DEEP DREAM DECODER** -
– Things to come / God bless me / Rise (above these things) / Snowing outside / It's all true / Head full of lights and a hat full of haloes / Girls I've loved / Amazing things / Deep dream decoder / Disolve / Year 44 (the birthday song) / Wing and a prayer / Dreamnoise and angel / Tired eyes / Golden girl / Spark.

– compilations, specials, others –

— on 'Cocteau' unless mentioned otherwise

Nov 81. (lp) *(JC 2)* **DAS KABINET (OF DR. CAGLIARI)** -
– The asylum / Waltz / The fairground / Doctor Cagliari / Cesare the somnabulist / Murder / The funeral / The somnabulist and the children / The children / Cagliari disciplines Cesare / Cagliari opens the cabinet / Jane discovers Cesare / The attempted murder of Jane / The dream dance of Jane and the somnabulist / Escape over the rooftops / The unmasking / The shot / The cabinet closes.

1982. (lp) **LA BELLE ET LA BETE (THE BEAUTY AND THE BEAST)** -
– Overture / The family / Sisters and Sedan chairs / In the forest of storms / The castle / The gates / The corridor / The great hall / Dreams (the merchant sleeps) / The rose and the beast / Magnificent (the white horse) / Beauty enters the castle / The door / The mirror / Candelabra and the gargoyles / Beauty and the beast / Transition No.1, 2 – The gift / The garden / Transitions No.3, 4 – The tragedy / Transitions No.5 – The enchanted glove / Tears as diamonds (the gift reverses) / The beast in solitude / Return of the magnificent / Transition No.6-The journey / The pavillion of Diana / Transformation No.1 & 2 / The final . . . *(above 2 albums re-iss.Jun85; JCCD 4)*

Nov 82. (5x7"box) *(JEAN 1)* **PERMANENT FLAME** -

Jan 85. (4xlp-box) *(JEAN 2)* **TRIAL BY INTAMACY** -
– (DAS KABINET / BEAUTY & THE BEAST / CHAMBER OF DREAMS / SUMMER OF GOD'S PIANO)

Feb 85. (cd) *(JCCD 10)* **THE TWO-FOLD ASPECT OF EVERYTHING** -
(d-lp-iss.Sep89; JC 10)

Nov 86. (lp/c; as ORCHESTRA ARCANA) *(JC/TCJC 18)* **ACONOGRAPHY** -

Sep 87. (d-cd) *(JCCD 17)* **CHIMERA / SAVAGE GESTURES FOR CHARMS SAKE** -

Aug 89. (lp/cd) *(JC/+CD 9)* **CATALOGUE OF OBSESSIONS** -

Sep 89. (cd/c/d-lp) *(CD/TC+/JCD 22)* **DUPLEX: THE BEST OF BILL NELSON** -
– Flaming desire / Acceleration (remix) / hope for the heartbeat (remix) / Here and now / Life in your hands / Glow world / The blazing memory of the innuendo / The angel at the western window / The man in the Rexine suit / Right then left / Half asleep in the hall of mirrors / Opening / Metaphysical jerks / Loving tongues / Radiant spires / Do you dream in clour / Living in my limousine (remix) / October man / Private view / Contemplation / Another day, another ray of hope / Another tricky mission / Portrait of Jan with flowers / Wiping a tear from the all-seeing eye / Secret ceremony (theme from 'Brond') / Broadcast news (from 'Right To Reply') / Loosening up with lady luck / The garden / Burning the groove of Satyre / Set me a seal upon thine heart.

Dec 89. (4xcd-box) *(JEANCD 89)* **DEMONSTRATIONS OF AFFECTION** -

Aug 92. (3xcd-box) *Magpie; (MAGPIE 3)* **QUIT DREAMING AND GET ON THE BEAM / CHIMERA – SAVAGE GESTURES / THE LOVE THAT WHIRLS** [] [-]
Dec 95. (4xcd-box) *Resurgence; (RES 111CD)* **BOX SET** [] [-]
(re-iss.Oct96; same)

NEU!

Formed: Dusseldorf, Germany . . .Autumn 1971 by breakaway KRAFTWERK members KLAUS DINGER and THOMAS HOMANN. The latter was soon deposed by MICHAEL ROTHER who appeared on their eponymous 1972 debut. Live gigs were augmented by EBERHARD KRAKNENN, who had also guested for KRAFTWERK. After only three acclaimed underground albums, they split in the mid-70's when ROTHER went solo. Encompassing repetitive trance-rock and avant-garde improvisation, they mined similar territory to early KRAFTWERK, AMON DUUL II or HAWKWIND (DAVE BROCK was a great fan). Along with the likes of CAN and FAUST, the band are held in high esteem by Krautrock connoisseurs. • **Songwriters:** ROTHER-DINGER. • **Trivia:** Produced by CONNY PLANK except 2nd lp.

Recommended: NEU! (*8) / NEU II (*8) / NEU '75 (*9) / BLACK FOREST GATEAU (*9)

MICHAEL ROTHER – guitar, bass, keyboards, synths, percussion / **KLAUS DINGER** – guitar, vocals, drums, keyboards (ex-KRAFTWERK)

U.A. Billingsgate

1972. (lp) *(UAS 29396) <1001>* **NEU!** [] []
– Hallo Gallo / Sonderangebot / Weissensee / Jahresuebersicht / Im glueck / Negativland / Lieber honig. *(re-iss.May80 as 'HALLO GALLO' on 'Brain' Germany; 0040 145)*
Jan 73. (7") *(UP 35485)* **SUPER. / NEUSCHNEE** [] [-]
1973. (lp) *(UAS 29500)* **NEU II** [] [-]
– Fur immer / Spitzenqualitat / Gedenkminute / Lila engel / Neuschnee / Super 16 / Neuschnee / Cassetto / Super 78 / Hallo exentrico / Super.

— ROTHER joined HARMONIA, with CLUSTER members MOEBIUS + ROEDELIUS. They made two albums 'MUSIK VON HARMONIA' *(Brain; 1044)* & 'HARMONIA DELUXE' *(Brain 1073)*, before he returned to NEU!

— added **HANS LAMPE + THOMAS DINGER** – drums (ex-KRAFTWERK)

Jun 75. (7") *(UP 35874)* **ISI. / AFTER EIGHT** [] [-]
1975. (lp) *(UAS 29782)* **NEU '75** [] [-]
– Isi / Seeland / Leb' wohl / Hero / E-Musik / After eight.

— Split after above. The DINGERS + LAMPE formed LA DUSSELDORF

– compilations, others, etc. –

Nov 82. (lp) *Cherry Red; (BRED 27)* **BLACK FOREST GATEAU** [] [-]
– Hallo Gallo / Isi / E-Musik / Negativland / Seeland / Leb' wohl / After eight.

MICHAEL ROTHER

with **JAKI LIEBEZEIT** – drums (ex-CAN) (debut was w/drawn by UK 'Radar'; *RAD 8)*

Sky not issued

1977. (lp) *(SKY 007)* **FLAMMENDE HERZEN** [-] [-] German
– Flammende herzen / Zyklodrom / Karussell / Feuerland. *(cd-iss. on 'Polydor'; 823838-2)*
1978. (lp) *(SKY 013)* **STERNTALER** [-] [-] German
– Sonnenrad / Blauer Regen / Stromlinien / Sterntaler / Fontana di luna / Orches trion.
1979. (lp) *(SKY 033)* **KATZENMUSIK** [-] [-] German
– Katzenmusik (1-12). *(cd-iss. on 'Polydor'; 825614-2)*

Polydor not issued

1982. (lp) *(2372 111)* **FERNWARME** [-] [-] German
– Silberstrei F / Elfenbein / Erikoenig / Fortuna / Klangkoerper / Hohe luft / Fernwarme.

— now without JAKI who was solo artist before slight return to CAN

1984. (lp) *(815 469-1)* **LUST** [-] [-] German
– Palmengarten / Primadonna / Dynamotron / Lust / Cascadia / Pulsar. *(cd-iss.1988; 815 469-2)*
Aug 85. (lp) *(825 619-1)* **SUSSHERZ UND TIEFENSCHARFE** [-] [-] German
– Sussherz / Tiefenscharfe / Glitzerglanz / Rapido / Daisy / Blaus licht. *(cd-iss. on 'Steamhammer-SPV'; 85-7562)*
1987. (lp/cd) *(833 685-1/-2)* **TRAUMREISEN** [-] [-] German
– Sudseewellen / Reiselust / Schwarze augen / Lucky stars / Lichtermeer / Gloria / Happy end.

— Seems to have retired from recording.

Tom NEWMAN

Born: England – half Irish. In the early 60's, he was vocalist with skiffle outfit, The PLAYBOYS, which duly evolved into R&B group, The TOMCATS. The other members were; CHRIS JACKSON (guitar), ALAN JAMES (bass) and PETE COOK (drums). They were around for a further five years, releasing four Spanish-only EP's for 'Philips' in 1966. A couple of years later, he formed the psychedelic outfit, JULY, alongside JON FIELD and TONY DUHIG. They released two singles and the now very collectable JULY album for the 'Major Minor' label; (MMLP 29). When the other band members teamed up to form JADE WARRIOR, TOM set up his own Manor Studios with young entrepreneur-to-be, RICHARD BRANSON. They worked on MIKE OLDFIELD's 'Tubular Bells', which, when finally issued, was the first release on 'Virgin'. Early in 1975, TOM's debut, 'FINE OLD TOM', also appeared on Virgin, featuring guests: OLDFIELD, FRED FRITH, CHRIS CUTLER, LOL COXHILL, HUGHIE FLINT and NEIL INNES. In 1976, he created the new Little Venice studios, issuing the album, 'FAERIE SYMPHONY', the following year. In the mid-80's, he returned with new age/ambient style albums, while still working with/producing MIKE OLDFIELD.

Recommended: FINE OLD TOM (*6)

TOM NEWMAN – vocals, guitar, organ, etc (with session people)

Virgin Antilles

Feb 75. (7") *(VS 120)* **SAD SING. / ALI'S GOT A BROKEN BONE** [] [-]
Feb 75. (lp) *(V 2022) <AN 7042>* **FINE OLD TOM** [] [-]
– Sad sing / Nursery rhyme / Song for S.P. / Superman / Alison says / Day of the Percherons / Suzie / Poor Bill / Will you be mine in the morning / Ma song / Penny's whistle boogie / She said, she said. *(cd-iss.May95 on 'Voiceprint'+=; VP 166CD) (cd re-iss.Jun97 on 'Blueprint'+=; BP 16CD)*– Ma song (demo) / Superman (demo) / Oh Susie (demo) / Poor Bill (demo) / She said she said (demo).
Nov 75. (7") *(VS 130)* **DON'T TREAT YOUR WOMAN BAD. / WHY DOES LOVE HURT SO BAD** [] [-]
Nov 75. (lp; w/drawn) *(V 2042)* **LIVE AT THE ARGONAUT** [] [-]
– Don't treat your woman bad / Kentucky / It don't come easy / Entropy / amblin' man / For the old times / Tales from Brendan's beard / Roving gambler / Draught Guinness / Paperback writer / Give a little, take a little / Aeiough. *(cd-iss.Mar95 on 'Voiceprint'; VP 168CD)*
Jan 76. (7") *(VS 133)* **SLEEP. / DARLING COREY** [] [-]
Mar 76. (7") *(VS 141)* **EBONY EYES. / DRAUGHT GUINNESS** [] [-]

Decca not issued

Oct 77. (7") *(F 13735)* **DANCE OF THE THEENA SHEE (DAOINE SIDHE). / THE UNSEELIE COURT** [] [-]
Nov 77. (lp) *(TXS 123)* **FAERIE SYMPHONY** [] [-]
– The woods / Foidin seachrain / Bean si / Little voices of the Tarans / The flutter / The Seelie court / The spell breaks / The faerie song / Dance of the Theena Shee (Daoine Sidhe) / Memories of Culchulainn / Aillen Mac Hidna / The Unseelie court / The woods of . . .

Landscape not issued

Jan 86. (lp/c)(cd) *(NAGE/+C 2)(NAGE 2CD)* **BAYOU MOON** [] [-]
– Concierto de mango in E major / Straw dogs / Gumbo fling / Fur traders descending the Misouri / Gumbo fling II / Moonrise / Voodoo de bayou / Gumbo fling III / Alligator walk / Gumbo fling IV.
Jan 86. (lp/c)(cd) *(NAGE/+C 7)(NAGE 7CD)* **ASPECTS** [] [-]
– Beach scene / The Tower of Babel / The stonemason's yard / The fighting temeraire / The Rokeby Venus / Stonehenge / The dream / Samson and Delilah.

— in 1988, recorded unissued album 'OZYMANDIAS', which was finally given light late '95 on 'Voiceprint' cd; *VP 185CD)*

Voiceprint not issued

1995. (cd) *(VP 164CD)* **HOUND OF ULSTER** [] [-]

— In Apr'95, with old buddies DAVID BEDFORD and MIKE OLDFIELD, he released cd 'VARIATIONS ON A RHYTHM OF MIKE OLDFIELD' for 'Voiceprint'; *VP 191CD)*

Mar 97. (cd) *(VP 195CD)* **BLUES AT THE HOTEL SPLENDIDE** [] []

NEWS (see under ⇒ MILLER)

NEWS FROM BABEL (see under ⇒ HENRY COW)

NICE

Formed: London, England . . . Oct'67 by ex-GARY FARR & THE T-BONES members, KEITH EMERSON and LEE JACKSON, who, along with DAVID O'LIST and BRIAN DAVIDSON, had backed-up British black soul singer, P.P.ARNOLD. Being part of Andrew Loog Oldham's 'Immediate' label, they moved in a different musical direction with their first 45, 'THOUGHTS OF EMERLIST DAVJACK'. This flopped, as did the similarly titled 1968 debut album containing their show-stopper, 'RONDO'. That summer, they surprised many when their rendition of Leonard Bernstein's 'AMERICA' (from 'West Side Story'), nearly hit the UK Top 20. It was banned in the States, however, where offence was taken to their promotional poster featuring the recently deceased Martin Luther King, Bobby and John F.Kennedy. During a subsequent performance at The Royal Albert Hall, NICE burned an American flag, riling Bernstein enough to prevent the 45 being issued in the States. Although their follow-up album, 'ARS LONGA VITA BREVIS' (1968) failed, subsequent efforts, 'THE NICE' (1969) and 'FIVE BRIDGES SUITE' (1970) both went Top 5. Pioneers of orchestral rock, NICE deconstructed classical music, arranging new interpretations around the keyboard-stabbing showman, KEITH EMERSON. This esteemed ivory-tinkler subsequently went on to even greater success with EMERSON, LAKE & PALMER. • **Songwriters:** Group compositions, using first letters of forenames (aka 'EMERLIST DAVJACK' until O'LIST left in 1968). Covered; AMERICA (Sondheim / Bernstein) / INTERMEZZO FROM KARELIA SUITE (Sibelius) / HANG ON TO A DREAM (Tim Hardin) / SHE BELONGS TO ME + MY BACK PAGES + COUNTRY PIE (Bob Dylan) / and other classical re-inditions.

Recommended: THE NICE COLLECTION (*8)

KEITH EMERSON (b. 2 Nov'44, Todmorden, England) – keyboards / **DAVID O'LIST** – guitar, vocals / **BRIAN DAVIDSON** (b.25 May'42, Leicester, England) – drums / **LEE JACKSON** (b. 8 Jan'43, Newcastle-upon-Tyne, England) – vocals, bass

Immediate Immediate

Nov 67. (7") *(IM 059)* **THE THOUGHTS OF EMERLIST DAVJACK. / AZRIAL (ANGEL OF DEATH)** [] []
Dec 67. (lp; mono/stereo) *(IMLP/IMSP 016) <52004>* **THE THOUGHTS OF EMERLIST DAVJACK** [] []

– Flower king of flies / The thoughts of Emerlist Davjack / Bonnie K. / Rondo / War and peace / Tantalising Maggie / Dawn / The cry of Eugene / Angel of death / America: 1A (adapted from 'West Side Story') – 1B second amendment / The diamond hard apples of the Moon. *(re-iss.Jul68; same) (re-iss.1978 on 'Charly'; CR 3000021) (cd-iss.1988 on 'Line'; IMCD 900228) (cd re-iss.Feb94 on 'Charly'; CDIMM 010)*

Jun 68. (7") *(IM 068)* **AMERICA (2nd Amendment). / THE DIAMOND HARD APPLES OF THE MOON** 21
(re-iss.Dec82; same)

—— now a trio, when O'LIST departed, later joining ROXY MUSIC

Dec 68. (lp) *(IMSP 020) <52020>* **ARS LONGA VITA BREVIS**
– Daddy, where did I come from? / Little Arabella / Happy Freuds / Intermezzo from Karelia / Don Edito el Gruva / Ars longa vita brevis – Prelude: 1st movement – Wakening ; 2nd movement – Realisation ; 3rd movement – Acceptance – Brandenburger ; 4th movement – Denial / Coda – Extention to the big note. *(re-iss.Dec86 on 'Castle' lp/c/cd; CLA LP/MC/CD 120)*

Dec 68. (7") *(IM 072)* **BRANDENBURGER. / HAPPY FREUDS** -
Jul 69. (7") **SHE BELONGS TO ME. / ('A'version)** -
Aug 69. (lp) *(IMSP 026) <52022>* **THE NICE** 3
– Azrael revisited / Hang on to a dream / Diary of an empty day / For example / Rondo 69 / She belongs to me. *(cd-iss.1990's on 'Repertoire';)*

Charisma Mercury

Jun 70. (lp) *(CAS 1014) <SR 61295>* **FIVE BRIDGES SUITE** 2
– The five bridges suite:- Fantasia, 1st bridge – 2nd bridge – Choral, 3rd bridge – High level fugue, 4th bridge – Finale, 5th bridge / Intermezzo Karelia suite:- Pathetique, 'Symphony No.6. 3rd movement' / Country pie – Bach: Brandenburg concerto No.6 / One of those people. *(cd-iss.Feb91; CASCD 1014)*

Jul 70. (7") *(CB 132) <73114>* **COUNTRY PIE. / ONE OF THOSE PEOPLE**

—— Disbanded mid 1970. KEITH formed EMERSON, LAKE & PALMER. LEE and BRIAN later surfaced as REFUGEE and made one eponymous album in 1974 for 'Charisma', which featured future YES man, PATRICK MORAZ.

– compilations, others, etc. –

Apr 71. (lp) *Charisma; (CAS 1030) / Mercury; <SR 61324>* **ELEGY (live)** 5
– Hang on to a dream / My back pages / 3rd movement – Pathetique / America (from 'West Side Story'). *(re-iss.Sep83 lp/c; CHC/+MC 1) (cd-iss.Feb91 & Jun93 +=; CASCD 1030)*– Diamonds blue apples of the Moon / Dawn / Tantalising Maggie / The cry of Eugene / Daddy, where did I come from? / Aziral.

Feb 72. (d-lp) *Mercury; <SRM2 6500>* **KEITH EMERSON WITH THE NICE** (4th + 5th albums) -
(cd-iss.UK 1988; 830 457-2)

Mar 72. (7"; as KEITH EMERSON & THE NICE) *Mercury; <73272>* **COUNTRY PIE – BRANDENBERG No.6. / FINALE – 5th BRIDGE** -

1972. (lp) *Charisma; (CS 1)* **AUTUMN 67 SPRING 68** -
Mar 76. (lp) *Immediate; (IML 1003)* **AMOENI REDIVI** -
Jan 78. (lp) *Immediate; (IML 2003)* **THE NICE GREATEST HITS** -
Mar 83. (d-c) *Charisma; (CASMC 163)* **FIVE BRIDGES SUITE / AUTUMN 67 AND SPRING 68** -
Nov 85. (d-lp/c/cd) *Castle; (CCS LP/MC/CD 106)* **THE NICE COLLECTION** -
– America 1A (adapted from 'West Side Story') – 1B Second amendment / Happy Freuds / The cry of Eugene / The thoughts of Emerlist Davjack / Rondo / Daddy, where did I come from? / Little Arabella / Intermezzo from Karelia / Hang on to a dream / The diamond hard apples of the Moon / Angel of death / Ars longa vita brevis – Prelude:- 1st movement – Wakening, 2nd movement – Realisation, 3rd movement – Acceptance, Brandenburger, 4th movement – Denial / Coda – Extention to the big note. *(re-iss.cd Apr94; same)*

Aug 87. (lp/c) *Seal; (SLP/SC 002)* **THE 20th ANNIVERSARY OF THE NICE** -
(re-iss.Apr88 on 'Bite Back' lp/c/cd; BTE L/C/CD 2)

Dec 93. (cd) *Immediate; (CSL 6032)* **THE BEST OF THE NICE – AMERICA** -
Mar 94. (cd) *Laserlight; (CD 12334)* **AMERICA** -
Nov 95. (3xcd-box) *Charly; (CDIMMBOX 2)* **THE IMMEDIATE YEARS** -
Jul 96. (cd) *Receiver; (RRCD 224)* **AMERICA – THE BBC SESSIONS** -

NICO

Born: CHRISTA PAFFGEN, 16 Oct'38, Cologne, Germany. Her father died in a concentration camp, and, as a girl, she travelled throughout Europe with her mother. Developing a fondness for opera, she learned to play classical piano and harmonium. In 1959, while vacationing in Italy, she was introduced by new friends to film director Federico Fellini and following a bit-part in 'La Dolce Vita', she became a top model, appearing in Vogue magazine. In the early 60's, while working in films, she became the girlfriend of French actor Alain Delon. She later give birth to his son, having already borne a daughter to actor/dancer Eric Emerson. In 1963, she fell in love with up and coming folk-star BOB DYLAN, who wrote a song for her, 'I'LL KEEP IT WITH MINE'. In 1965, at his suggestion, she moved to London and signed for Andrew Loog Oldham's new label, 'Immediate'. A single, 'I'M NOT SAYING' (written by GORDON LIGHTFOOT) was issued, although the record subsequently flopped, even after an appearance on 'Ready Steady Go'. She then moved to New York, where she met pop-artist ANDY WARHOL. He asked her to feature in an avant-garde film, 'Chelsea Girl', also asking her to join LOU REED, JOHN CALE, MO TUCKER, etc. in his managerial group, The VELVET UNDERGROUND. Together they made one glorious late 1966 album, 'THE VELVET UNDERGROUND AND NICO', NICO leaving soon after for a return to solo work. Decribed as 'The Edith Piaf of the Blank Generation', she was an avant-garde, moody songstress who was anti-pop music in every sense. After a liason with BRIAN JONES of The ROLLING STONES, she became the opposite number of teenager and new pensmith JACKSON BROWNE who wrote songs for her debut 1968 album, 'CHELSEA GIRL' (notebly 'THESE DAYS'). Regarded as an artistic triumph, she nevertheless disagreed with producer Tom Wilson's string arrangements. Subsequently moving to Los Angeles, she started writing material for her follow-up 'Elektra' album, 'THE MARBLE INDEX'. She travelled constantly between America and Europe, starring in another underground film, 'La Cicatrice Interieupe' for Philippe Garrel. In 1971, she cut the JOHN CALE-produced 'DESERTSHORE', the track 'Le Petit Chevalier' featuring her son. Fleeing New York for France after she was involved in a bottle fight with a female Black Panther member, she later appeared at The Rainbow, London on 1st of June '74 alongside JOHN CALE, ENO and KEVIN AYERS. A track, 'THE END', was recorded, and 'Island' records promptly signed her for an album of the same name, with ENO and PHIL MANZANERA at the production helm. That year, she also contributed vocals to KEVIN AYERS' album, 'Confessions Of Dr. Dream', although she subsequently retired from music to live between Berlin, Los Angeles and Spain. In 1981, she made a comeback album, appropriately titled 'DRAMA OF EXILE', but after poor audience response on a SIOUXSIE & THE BANSHEES support slot, she again went AWOL, shacking up in Manchester, England with her live-in-boyfriend / poet JOHN COOPER CLARKE. After another dismissed vinyl return in 1985, she again retired, only to re-appear at a 1987 ANDY WARHOL tribute. Tragically on 18 Jul'88, on a holiday in Ibiza with CLARKE, she fell off her bike and died of a brain haemorrhage. • **Songwriters:** As said, and other covers; THE END (Doors) / DEUTSCHLAND UBER ALLES (German national anthem) / HEROES (David Bowie) / etc. Plus there are obviously a number of VELVET UNDERGROUND re-inditions littered about. • **Trivia:** In 1974, she joined LOU REED and JOHN CALE for a French filmed VELVET UNDERGROUND reunion.

Recommended: CHELSEA GIRL (*7) / THE MARBLE INDEX (*8) / THE BLUE ANGEL (*8).

NICO – vocals (plus session people)

Immediate not issued

Aug 65. (7") *(IM 003)* **I'M NOT SAYIN'. / THE LAST MILE** -
(re-iss.May82; IMS 003)

—— (above 'B'side featured JIMMY PAGE as guitarist/writer)

—— In 1966, she teamed up with The VELVET UNDERGROUND on their eponymous lp. Breaking from them the following year, she returned to solo work, augmented by JOHN CALE + LOU REED. Her beau JACKSON BROWNE at the time also became her main songwriter.

not issued Verve

Feb 68. (lp) *<2353 025>* **CHELSEA GIRL** -
– The fairest of the seasons / These days / Little sister / Winter song / It was a pleasure then / Chelsea girls / I'll keep it with mine / Somewhere there's a father / Wrap your troubles in dreams / Eulogy to Lenny Bruce. *(UK-iss.Sep71 on 'MGM Select'; 2353 025) (re-iss.1974 on 'Polydor'; same) (cd-iss.May88 & Apr94; 835 209-2)*

—— Retained JOHN CALE as producer, etc.

Elektra Elektra

Jul 69. (lp) *<(EKL 4029)>* **THE MARBLE INDEX**
– Prelude / Lawns of dawns / No one is there / Ari's song / Facing the wind / Julius Caesar (memento Hodie) / Frozen warnings / Evening of light. *(cd-iss.Apr91 on 'WEA'+=; 7559 61096-2)*– Roses in the snow / Nibelungen.

Reprise Reprise

Jan 71. (lp) *<(RSLP 6424)>* **DESERTSHORE**
– Janitor of lunacy / Falconer / My only child / Le petit chevalier / Abschied / Afraid / Mutterlein / All that is my own. *(re-iss.1974; K 44102) (cd-iss.Apr91 on 'WEA'; 7599 25870-2)*

—— She retained **CALE** and brought in **ENO** – synthesizer / **PHIL MANZANERA** – guitar / **STERLING MORRISON** – guitar

Island not issued

Oct 74. (lp) *(ILPS 9311)* **THE END** -
– It has not taken long / Secret side / You forgot to answer / Innocent and vain / Valley of the kings / We've got the gold / The end / Das lied der Deutschen. *(cd-iss.Apr94; IMCD 174)*

—— now with **ANDY CLARKE** – keyboards / **MUHAMMED HADI** – guitar / **DAVEY PAYNE** – sax / **STEVE CORDONA** – drums / **PHILIPPE QUILICHINI** – bass

Aura not issued

Jul 81. (lp) *(AUL 715)* **DRAMA OF EXILE** -
– Genghis Khan / Purple lips / One more chance / Henry Hudson / I'm waiting for the man / Sixty forty / The sphinx / Orly flight / Heroes. *(cdiss.Mar88 on 'Line'; LILP 400106) (cd re-iss.Jul92 on 'Great Expectations'; PIPCD 037) (cd re-iss.Aug96 on 'See For Miles'; SEECD 449)*

Flicknife not issued

Sep 81. (7") *(FLS 206)* **VEGAS. / SAETA** -

Half not issued

Jul 82. (7") *(1/2 1)* **PROCESSION. / ALL TOMORROW'S PARTIES** -
(12"+=) *(1/2 1-12)* – Secret side (live) / Femme fatale (live).

Aura not issued

Jun 83. (7") *(AUS 137)* **HEROES. / ONE MORE CHANCE** -

—— with **JAMES YOUNG** – keyboards / **GRAHAM DIDS** – percussion

Beggars Banquet not issued

Jun 85. (7"/12"; as NICO & THE FACTION) **MY FUNNY VALENTINE. / MY HEART IS EMPTY** -
Jun 85. (lp/c/cd; as NICO & THE FACTION) *(BEG A/C/CD 63)* **CAMERA OBSCURA** -
– Camera obscura / Tananore / Win a few / My funny valentine / Das lied von einsamen Madchens / Fearfully in danger / My heart is empty / Into the arena / Konig. *(re-iss.Jan89 on 'Beggars Banquet-Lowdown' lp/c)(cd; BBL/+C 63)(BBL 63CD)*

—— added **ERIC RANDOM** – percussion, etc / **TOBY TOMAN** – drums

Dojo not issued

Apr 86. (d-lp/c/cd) *(DOJO LP/TC/CD 27)* **BEHIND THE IRON CURTAIN (live 1985)** -
– All saints night from a Polish motorway / One more chance / Frozen warnings /

The song of the lonely girl / Win a few / Konig / Purple lips / All tomorrow's parties / Fearfully in danger / The end / My funny valentine / 60-40 / Tananoori / Janitor of lunacy / My heart is empty / Femme fatale.

1987. (lp) *(DOJOLP 50)* **LIVE IN TOKYO, JAPAN (live)** ☐ [-]
– My heart is empty / Purple lips / Tananore / Janitor of lunacy / You forgot to answer / 60-40 / My funny valentine / Sad lied von einsannen madchens / All tomorrow's parties / Femme fatale / The end. *(cd-iss.1988 & Jun95; DOJOCD 50)*

— NICO died 18th Jul'88 (see info above).

– compilations, others, etc. –

1983. (c) *R.O.I.R.; <A 117>* **DO OR DIE** [-] ☐
(cd-iss.May93; RE 117CD)

Sep 85. (lp/c/cd) *Aura; (AU L/C/CD 731)* **THE BLUE ANGEL** (best of) ☐ ☐
– Femme fatale / All tomorrow's parties / I'll keep it with mine / Chelsea girls / Janitor of lunacy / Heroes / One more chance / Sixty forty / Waiting for the man / The end.

Oct 85. (7") *Aura; (AUS 147)* **I'M WAITING FOR THE MAN. / PURPLE LIPS (live)** ☐ [-]

Feb 87. (12"ep) *Archive 4; (TOF 110)* **LIVE (live)** ☐ [-]

Mar 87. (pic-lp) *V.U.; (NICO 1)* **LIVE IN DENMARK (live)** ☐ [-]

May 88. (c) *Half; (1/2 CASS 2)* **EN PERSONNE EN EUROPE** ☐ [-]

Nov 88. (12"ep/cd-ep) *Strange Fruit; (SFPS/+CD 064)* **THE PEEL SESSIONS** (2/2/71) ☐ [-]
– Secret side / No one is there / Janitor of lunacy / Frozen warnings.

Jun 89. (lp/cd) *Performance; (PERF 385/+CD)* **LIVE HEROES (live)** ☐ [-]

Nov 90. (cd/c/lp) *Emergo; (EM 9349-2/-4/-1)* **HANGING GARDENS** ☐ [-]

Jul 92. (cd) *Great Expectations; (PIPCD 039)* **CHELSEA GIRL LIVE (live)** ☐ [-]
(re-iss.Jun94 on 'Cleopatra'; CLEO 61062) (cd re-iss.Nov96 on 'See For Miles'; SEECD 461)

Sep 94. (cd) *Anagram; (CDMGRAM 85)* **HEROINE** ☐ [-]

Sep 96. (cd) *Cherry Red; (VICD 008)* **JANITOR OF LUNACY** ☐ [-]

Sep 96. (cd) *S.P.V.; (SPV 0849620-2)* **NICO'S LAST CONCERT (FATA MORGANA – DESERTSOUNDS IN THE PLANETARIUM) (live)** ☐ [-]

NINE DAYS' WONDER

Formed: Germany . . .1970 by WALTER SEYFFER. The band's first album was the DIETER DIRKS/PETER HAWKE-produced 'NINE DAYS' WONDER', released on 'HARVEST' in 1971. Overtly influenced by English progressive rock, it also bore the hallmark of ZAPPA/BEEFHEART style eccentricity and was heavy on squalling jazz improvisation. For 1973's follow-up, 'WE NEVER LOST CONTROL', SEYFFER recruited a completely new line-up, having disbanded the original group in 1972. The album was less manic than its predecessor although it was again produced by HAWKE. The following year, the band went through a further shift in personnel for the 'ONLY THE DANCERS' album, the most commercial NINE DAYS' WONDER release to date. Incredibly, the band went through another whole-sale shift in staff for 1976's concept album, 'SONNET TO BILLY FROST'. The group were finally disbanded when SEYFFER and UNGER formed WINTERGARDEN, releasing their self-titled debut in 1979 and 'THE LAND OF MILK AND HONEY' the following year.

Recommended: NINE DAYS' WONDER (*6)

WALTER SEYFFER – vocals, percussion, effects / **JOHN EARLE** – vocals, saxophones, guitar, flute / **ROLF HENNING** – guitar, piano / **KARL MUTSCHLECHNER** – bass / **MARTIN ROSCOE** – drums

Harvest not issued

Oct 71. (lp) *(SHSP 4014)* **NINE DAYS' WONDER** ☐ [-]
– Fermillion / Fermillion himself / Monotony / Dilemma. *(originally released in Germany on 'Bacillus'; BLPS 19073)*

— **WALTER** recruited entire new band; **FREDDIE MUENSTER** – sax, keyboards, synths / **HANS FRAUENSCHUH** – guitar / **MICHAEL BUNDT** – bass / **'Hyazintus' KARL-HEINZ WEILER** – drums (JOHN EARLE later joined GNIDROLOG, THIN LIZZY, GRAHAM PARKER, etc.)

Bacillus not issued

1973. (lp) *(BLPS 19163)* **WE NEVER LOST CONTROL** [-] [-] German
– Days in bright light / Fisherman's dream / Andromeda nomads / The great game / Angels due to arrive / We grasp the naked meat / Armaranda.

— **SEYFFER, BUNDT** + (returning) **HENNING** recruited **STEVE ROBINSON** – keyboards / **DAVID JACKSON** – saxophone, flute / **SIDHARTA GATAMA** – drums

1975. (lp) *(BLPS 19200)* **ONLY THE DANCERS** [-] [-] German
– Long distance line / Only the dancers / It's not my fault / Frustration / Hovercraft queen / Time is due / The way I'm living / Moment.

— **BERND UNGER + PETER OEHLER** – guitar, vocals, repl. HENNING, JACKSON + ROBINSON

— **RAINER SAAM** – bass, repl. BUNDT

— guests were **CHRISTIAN KOLONOVITS** – keyboards, synths / **GERD KOETHE** – wind

1976. (lp) *(BLPS 19234)* **SONNET TO BILLY FROST** [-] [-] German
– Alchemists / I need a rest / In memory of Sir Hilary / Five minute musical / Turn and go on / Sonnet to Billy Frost / Empty frame / Almost October / Jamie / You're always all alone with the things you love / I need a rest (part 2).

— Split after above. **SEYFFER + UNGER** formed . . .

WINTERGARDEN

with also **RAINER HERZOG** – keyboards, vocals / **CHRISTIAN SCHIMANSKI** – guitars, steel guitar / **CHUCK THOMAS TSCHESCHNER** – bass / **CHARLES ESPOSITO** – drums, congas / **WALTER QUINTUS** – violin, glockenspiel / **DIETER ARENDT** – drums / **IAN CUSSICK + PETER FRENCH** – vocals

Harvest not issued

1979. (lp) *(064-45265)* **WINTERGARDEN** [-] [-] German
– Judy's Blue Monday Cafe / Up and down the road / Blame it on these endless nights / The lady on the one pound note / Josephine / Khaki eyes / The way we were.

— **SEYFFER, UNGER, HERZOG + SCHIMANSKI** recruited **WOLFGANG BIERSCH** – guitar, glockenspiel / **NORBY HAAM + JOSHI DINIER** – bass / **ARMIN RUEHL + VAL HARGREAVES** – drums / **LOTHAR KRIST** – alto sax

1980. (lp) *(064-46131)* **THE LAND OF MILK & HONEY** [-] [-] German
– Anything left to share / Au pair girl / Gun that motor, boy / Swan song / The land of milk and honey / Sweet rollin' train / Face to face / And your bird can sing / The land of milk and honey (part 2).

— Disassembled after above.

NIRVANA

Formed: Based in London, England . . . 1967 by former Trinity College, Dublin student, PATRICK CAMPBELL-LYONS. After a brief spell in R&B groups, SECOND THOUGHTS (who became JULY) and HAT & TIE, he studied film-making at St. Martin's school. He founded a partnership with ALEX SPYROPOULOS and RAY SINGER (he issued 5 mid-60's solo 45's), becoming NIRVANA. They interested MUFF WINWOOD (Steve's brother), and signed to 'Island' records in '67. Two singles were issued that year, one of them, 'PENTECOST HOTEL', going to No.1 in parts of Scandanavia where they attracted a major following. Their debut album, the concept sci-fi pantomine, 'THE STORY OF SIMON SIMOPATH', was released in early '68, but did little apart from gain airplay on John Peel's~~~ Perfumed Garden radio 1 show. In April that year, they had their first and only UK Top 40 hit with the trippy, pastel-hued 'RAINBOW CHASER', although come 1969 they were dropped by their label. That year they had trimmed to a duo when RAY departed, and after their 1970 'Pye' album, 'TO MARKOS III', ALEX thought it better to exit. This left PATRICK to control activities, as his future flitted between NIRVANA and solo releases. • **Songwriters:** SPYROPOULOS & CAMPBELL-LYONS. • **Trivia:** CAMPBELL-LYONS was also a noted early 70's producer of CLEAR BLUE SKY, JADE WARRIOR and SUNBURST.

Note:- Nothing whatsoever to do with grunge-metal US stars NIRVANA, whom PATRICK thought of sueing for the rights to the group name.

Recommended: TRAVELLING ON A CLOUD (*7)

PATRICK CAMPBELL-LYONS (b. Waterford, Ireland) – vocals, keyboards, multi / **ALEX SPYROPOULOS** (b. Greece) – keyboards, choral arrangements, multi / **RAY SINGER** – guitar / with **BRIAN HENDERSON** – bass / **MICHAEL COE** – viola, French horn / **SYLVIA SCHUSTER** – cello / + on session **PETER KESTER** – drums

Island Bell

Jul 67. (7") *(WIP 6016)* **TINY GODDESS. / I BELIEVE IN MAGIC** ☐ [-]

Sep 67. (7") *(WIP 6020)* **PENTECOST HOTEL. / FEELIN' SHATTERED** ☐ [-]

Feb 68. (lp; mono/stereo) *(ILP/+S 9059)* **THE STORY OF SIMON SIMOPATH** ☐ ☐
– Wings of love / Lonely boy / We can help you / You are just the one / Satellite jockey / In the courtyard of the stars / Pentecost hotel / I never had a love like this before / Take this hand / 1999. *(cd-iss.Jan96 on 'Edsel'; EDCD 465)*

Mar 68. (7") *(WIP 6029)* **RAINBOW CHASER. / FLASHBULB** [34] ☐

May 68. (7") *<715>* **PENTECOST HOTEL. / WE CAN HELP YOU** [-] ☐

Sep 68. (lp) *(ILPS 9087)* **ALL OF US** ☐ ☐
– Rainbow chaser / Tiny goddess / All of us (the touchables) / Melanie blue / Trapeze / The show must go on / Girl in the park / Miami masquerade / Frankie the great / You can try it / Everybody loves the clown / St. John's Wood affair. *(cd-iss.Jan96 on 'Edsel'; EDCD 466)*

Sep 68. (7") *(WIP 6038)* **GIRL IN THE PARK. / C SIDE IN OCHO RIOS** ☐ [-]

Oct 68. (7") *<730>* **GIRL IN THE PARK. / YOU ARE JUST THE ONE** [-] ☐

Nov 68. (7") *(WIP 6045) <739>* **ALL OF US (THE TOUCHABLES). / TRAPEZE** ☐ ☐ Dec68

Jan 69. (7") *(WIP 6052)* **WINGS OF LOVE. / REQUIEM TO JOHN COLTRANE** ☐ [-]

— Now down to basic duo of PATRICK and ALEX. (RAY went into producing)

Mar 69. (7") *(WIP 6057)* **OH! WHAT A PERFORMANCE. / DARLING DARLENE** ☐ [-]

— added guests on 1 each; **BILLY BREMNER** – guitar / **LESLIE DUNCAN** – backing vocals

Pye Inter. Metromedia

Jan 70. (lp) *(NSPL 28132) <1018>* **TO MARKOS III** <US-title 'NIRVANA'> ☐ ☐
– The world is cold without you / Excerpt from "The Blind And The Beautiful" / I talk to my room / Christopher Lucifer / Aline Cherie / Tres tres bien / It happened two Sundays ago / Black flower / Love suite / Illinois. *(re-iss.May87 as 'BLACK FLOWER' on 'Bam Caruso'; KIRI 061) (cd-iss.Oct93 as 'BLACK FLOWER' on 'Edsel'+=; EDCD 378)*– Shine / Pentecost hotel (1993 version).

Feb 70. (7") *(7N 25525)* **THE WORLD IS COLD WITHOUT YOU. / CHRISTOPHER LUCIFER** ☐ [-]

— NIRVANA were now just PATRICK CAMPBELL-LYONS and session people, incl. JADE WARRIOR + MEL COLLINS (ALEX went on to do TV work, and produce AQUILA) He formed PICA, who released a single in Sep'70; 'TAKE THE BARRIERS DOWN'. / INSURANCE MAN' for 'Polydor'; *2058 056)*. Another was issued in Aug'71; 'RAINBOW CHASER'. / 'AD LIB' for 'Philips'; *6006 129)*

Vertigo not issued

Mar 71. (lp) *(6360 031)* **LOCAL ANAESTHETIC** ☐ [-]
– Modus operandi (method of work) / Home:- Salutation – Construction – Destruction – Re-construction – Fanfare. *(cd-iss.Aug91 & Jul93 on 'Repertoire'; REP 4109WP)*

Mar 71. (7") *(6059 035)* **THE SADDEST DAY OF MY LIFE. / (I WANNA GO) HOME** ☐ [-]

Philips not issued

Jul 71. (7") *(6006 127)* **PENTECOST HOTEL. / LAZY DAY DRIFT** ☐ [-]

Oct 71. (7") *(6006 166)* **STADIUM. / PLEASE BELIEVE ME** ☐ [-]

Feb 72. (lp) *(6308 089)* **SONGS OF LOVE AND PRAISE** ☐ -
– Rainbow chaser / Please believe me / Lord up above / She's lost it / Nova sketch / Pentecost hotel / I need your love tonight / Will there be me / Stadium. *(cd-iss.Sep95 on 'Background';)*

PATRICK CAMPBELL-LYONS

went solo with session players and a choir

Sovereign Capitol

Jan 73. (7") *(SOV 115)* **EVERYBODY SHOULD FLY A KITE. / I THINK I WANT HIM TOO** ☐ -
Feb 73. (lp) *(SVNA 7258)* **ME AND MY FRIEND** ☐ -
– Out of nowhere / Friends / Mother England / Everybody should fly a kite / Tomorrow I'll make you smile / Me and my friend / Jesus Christ Junior / I think I want him too / 1974 / Watch out Cassius Clay.
May 73. (7") *(SOV 119)* <3707> **OUT ON THE ROAD. / ME AND MY FRIEND** ☐ ☐

Decca not issued

Sep 73. (7"; as ROCK O'DOODLE) *(F 13450)* **QUEEN OF ROCK & ROLL. / WOMAN** ☐ -

Chrysalis not issued

Apr 74. (7"; as PATRICK O'MAGICK) *(CHS 2041)* **YOU'RE A WINNER. / THE PROPOSAL** ☐ -
— NIRVANA re-formed sporadically in name only by sole member PATRICK

Bradleys not issued

Feb 76. (7"; as NIRVANA) *(BRAD 7602)* **TWO OF A KIND. / BEFORE MIDNIGHT** ☐ -
— again went solo, augmented by ARTHUR BROWN + ALIKI ASHMAN.

Electric not issued

Mar 77. (7") *(WOT 12)* **THAT'S WHAT MY GURU SAID LAST NIGHT. / THE WHISTLING FIDDLER** ☐ -

U.A. not issued

Oct 78. (7"; as NIRVANA) *(UP 36461)* **LOVE IS. / PASCALE** ☐ -
Apr 79. (7"; as NIRVANA) *(UP 36538)* **RESTLESS WIND. / THANK YOU AND GOODNIGHT** ☐ -

Harvest not issued

Sep 80. (7"; as EREWHON) *(HAR 5213)* **TINY GODDESS. / THE HERO (I MIGHT HAVE BEEN)** ☐ -

Public Shanachie

1981. (lp) *(PUBL 1)* **THE ELECTRIC PLOUGH (concept)** <US-title 'THE HERO I MIGHT HAVE BEEN'> ☐ ☐
Nov 81. (7") *(PUB 006)* **NAKED ROBOTS. / WATCHING BREAKFAST TV** ☐ -

Zilch not issued

Sep 81. (7"; as NIRVANA) *(ZILCH 8)* **THE PICTURE OF DORIAN GRAY. / NO IT ISN'T** ☐ -
Feb 82. (7"; as NIRVANA) *(ZILCH 15)* **BLACK AND WHITE OR COLOUR. / TALL TREES** ☐ -
— PATRICK retired from recording, although he tried to keep NIRVANA name alive, especially after formation of the US grunge band.

– compilations, etc. –

Aug 76. (7") *Island; (WIP 6180)* **RAINBOW CHASER. / TINY GODDESS** ☐ -
Apr 87. (7") *Bam Caruso; (OPRA 45)* **BLACK FLOWER. / (WIMPLE WICH: Save My Soul)** ☐ -
Sep 92. (cd) *Island; (510974-2)* **TRAVELLING ON A CLOUD** ☐ -
Feb 95. (cd) *Edsel; (EDCD 407)* **SECRET THEATRE** ☐ -
Jun 96. (cd) *Edsel; (EDCD 485)* **ORANGE & BLUE** ☐ -

NOIR

Formed: London, England . . . early 70's by BARRY FORD, TONY COLE, GORDON HUNTE and ROY WILLIAMS. After signing to 'Dawn' records (home of MUNGO JERRY, etc), they managed only one album, 'WE HAD TO LET YOU HAVE IT', which did not have the quality to better other progressive rock acts of the time. To collector's, it is only worth £25 mint.

Recommended: WE HAD TO LET YOU HAVE IT (*5)

GORDON HUNTE – guitar, vocals / **TONY COLE** – keyboards / **ROY WILLIANS** – bass / **BARRY FORD** – drums, vocals

Dawn not issued

1971. (lp) *(DNLS 3029)* **WE HAD TO LET YOU HAVE IT** ☐ -
– Rain / Hard labour / Beggar man / In memory of Lady X / How long / System / Indian rope man / Ju ju man.
— after their split, FORD joined CLANCY, then MERGER

NORTHWIND

Formed: Glasgow, Scotland . . . early 70's by BRIAN YOUNG, HUGH BARR, TOM BRANNAN, COLIN SOMERVILLE and DAVE SCOTT (the latter had previously been The ELASTIC BAND, alongside future SWEET member ANDY SCOTT). Their one and only album, 'SISTER, BROTHER, LOVER' was a gentle piece of "progressive" acoustic rock, which now changes for over £150. The stand-out tracks were the mellow, 'HOME FOR FROZEN ROSES' and 'ACIMO AND NOIRAM'.

Recommended: SISTER, BROTHER, LOVER (*5)

BRIAN YOUNG – guitar, vocals / **HUGH BARR** – guitar / **COLIN SOMERVILLE** – keyboards / **TOM BRANNAN** – bass, vocals / **DAVE SCOTT** – drums

Regal Zonophone not issued

1971. (lp) *(SLRZ 1020)* **SISTER, BROTHER, LOVER** ☐ -
– Home for frozen roses / Acimon and Noiram / Castanettes / Guten abend / Peaceful / Many tribesmen / Quill.
— split soon after above, YOUNG initiated the Ca Va studio.

NOVALIS

Formed: Hamburg, Germany . . . 1972 by HEINO SCHUNZEL, JURGEN WENZEL, LUTZ RAHN and HARTWIG BIEREICHEL, debuting live at 'The Fabrik' in Hamburg. Their blend of symphonic rock was finally given a vinyl debut on the well-received 'BANISHING BRIDGE' in 1973. It featured the melancholic but excellent title track, which combined excerpts of bird whistles, pioneering ambience and their P.F.M.-styled "romantic rock". In 1974, WENZEL departed after some arguments, DETLEF JOB and CARLO KARGES replacing him for the eponymous follow-up in 1975. This was a markedly different affair due to German lyrics sung by HEINO. ACHIM REICHEL produced this memorable effort (and the subsequent four albums), the sound shifting between folk and classical with the latter style providing the backdrop for 'IMPRESSIONEN', a track based on BRUCKER's 5th Symphony. Their third, 'SOMMERABEND', also a beautifully lush album, was embellished with more romantic themes, culminating with the finale of a title track. Following a good live effort, 'KONZERTE', 'Brain' released their 5th album, 'BRANDUNG', featuring the side-long sequel to 'SOMMERABEND', 'SONNENWENDE'. This was their last great quality record, as 'VIELLEICHT BIST DU EIN CLOWN' let most of their fans down, incredibly outselling its predecessors. REICHEL set up a new label, 'Ahorn', which released another poor album, 'FLOSSENENGEL' in 1979. The 80's saw NOVALIS move to 'Vertigo', even finally gaining a British release for the patchy 'NEUMOND' album.

Recommended: BANISHED BRIDGE (*7) / NOVALIS (*6) / SOMMERABEND (*8) / KONZERTE (*6) / BRANDUNG (*6) / AUGENBLICKE (*6)

JURGEN WENZEL – vocals, guitar / **LUTZ RAHN** – keyboards / **HEINO SCHUNZEL** – bass / **HARTWIG BIEREICHEL** – drums (ex-GREENLIGHT)

Brain not issued

May 73. (lp) *(1029)* **BANISHED BRIDGE** - - German
– Banished bridge / High evolution / Laughing / Inside of me. *(re-iss.1981; 60.535) (UK-iss.May79 on 'Logo'; 0061 029)*
— **DETLEF JOB** – guitar + **CARLO KARGES** – guitar, keyboards (ex-TOMORROW'S GIFT) repl. WENZEL
May 75. (lp) *(1070)* **NOVALIS** - - German
– Sonnengeflecht / Wer schmetterlinge lachen hoert / Dronsz / Impressionen / Es faerbte sich die wiese gruen. *(UK-iss.Jan78; same)*
— now without KARGES, who joined new wave/pop band NENA
May 76. (lp) *(1087)* **SOMMERABEND** - - German
– Aufbruch / Wunderschaetze / Sommerabend. *(UK-iss.May79 on 'Logo'; 001 087)*
— added **FRED MUHLBOCK** – vocals, guitar, flute
Jun 77. (lp) *(60.065)* **KONZERTE (live)** - - German
– Bolero / Dronsz / Es faerbte sich die wiese gruen / Impressionen / Wer schmetterlinge lachen hoert / Wunderschaetze / Sommerabend. *(re-iss.May79 on 'Logo'; 0060 065)*
Dec 77. (lp) *(60.094)* **BRANDUNG** - - German
– Irgendwo, irgendwann / Wenn nicht mehr Zahlen und Figuren / Astralis / Sonnenwende / Brandung / Feuer bricht die zeit / Sonnenfinsternis / Daemmerung. *(UK-iss.May79 on 'Logo'; 0060.094)*
1978. (lp) *(60.164)* **VIELLEICHT BINS DU EIN CLOWN?** - - German
– Der geigenspieler / Zingaresca / Manchmal faelt der Regen eben lang / Vielleicht bin ich ein clown / City Nord / Die welt wird alt und wieder jung. *(UK-iss.Mar79 on 'Logo'; 0060 164)*

Ahorn not issued

1979. (lp) *(6.23980)* **FLOSSENENGEL** - - German
– Atlanto / Im brunnen der erde / Brennende freiheit / Im netz / Flossenengel / Walzer fuer einen verlorenen traum / Sklavenzoo / Alle wollen leben / Rueckkehr / Ob tier, ob mensch, ob baum.
1980. (lp) *(69.109)* **AUGENBLICKE** - - German
– Danmark / Ich hab noch nicht gelernt zu lieben / Cassandra / Herbstwind / Mit den zugvoegeln / Sphinx / Als kleiner junge / Magie einer nacht / Begegnungen.
— now without HEINO, replaced by **HEINZ FROHLING** – bass

Vertigo not issued

1982. (lp) *(6435 150)* **NEUMOND** ☐ -
– Anakonda / Oft sagt man mehr, wenn man schweigt / Fruehsport im sachsenwald / Du bist schoen / Kein frieden / Neumond / Nachttraum / Blauer Morgen.
1983. (lp) *(812 597)* **STERNTAUCHER** - - German
– Faehrmann / Ich will hier 'raus / Abschied / Keiner kann gewinnen / Klein wenig mehr / Sterntaucher / Grenzen / Sinus.
— **ERNST HERZNER** – vocals; repl. FROELICH
1985. (lp) *(824 645)* **NACH UNS DIE FLUT** - - German
– Die show ist aus / Im neonlicht der nacht / Drachen im wind / Nach uns die flut / Wo sind die sieger am ende der nacht / . . .Und wenn die Gitarren brennen / Hamburg (ertrinken mochte ich nicht in dir) / Heute oder nie / Gingst vorbei / 100 tage und nachte verloren in Altona / Wohn willst du gehn / Applaus applaus.

– compilations, etc. –

1980. (lp) *Brain; (40.173)* **SONNENWENDE** - - German
1980. (lp) *Brain; (60.219)* **WER SCHMETTERLINGE LACHEN HORT** (1977/78) - - German
1983. (lp) *Metrognome; (811 535)* **VISIONEN** - - German

NUCLEUS

Formed: London, England . . .1969 by self-taught trumpeter IAN CARR, a veteran of jazz outfits; NEW JAZZ ORCHESTRA, JOE HARRIOT QUARTET and DON RENDELL groups. The latter had been his partner since the mid-60's, making seven albums for 'Columbia' as The DON RENDELL & IAN CARR QUINTET; 'SHADES OF BLUE' (33SX 1733) / 'PHASE III' (S(C)X 6214) / 'LIVE' (S(C)X 6316) / 'CHANGE IS 1' (SCX 6368) / 'CHANGE IS 2' (unknown) / 'DUSK FIRE' (SX 6404) / 'GREEK VARIATIONS' (SCX 6414), with NEIL ARDLEY. All these are worth over £40 mint, the latter boasting a £65 tag. However, in 1970, CARR signed to 'Vertigo' with NUCLEUS, who also included CHRIS SPEDDING, KARL JENKINS, JOHN MARSHALL, JEFF CLYNE and BRIAN SMITH. Their debut album, 'ELASTIC ROCK' was well-received and entered the UK Top 50 for a week. They continued to surface each year, although incoming/ outgoing members seemed to be bred for another similar outfit; SOFT MACHINE. Most of their albums consisted of innovative jazz-rock, similar to COLOSSEUM and the aforementioned SOFT MACHINE, re-standardising the British contemporary musicianship of the 70's. • **Songwriters:** CARR on most. • **Trivia:** JON HISEMAN (of COLOSSEUM) produced their 1975 effort.

Recommended: ELASTIC ROCK (*6) / WE'LL TALK IT ABOUT LATER (*6)

IAN CARR (b.21 Apr'33, Dumfries, Scotland) – trumpet, flugelhorn / **CHRIS SPEDDING** – guitar (ex-PETE BROWN'S BATTERED ORNAMENTS) / **KARL JENKINS** – keyboards, wind / **JOHN MARSHALL** – drums, percussion / **JEFF CLYNE** – bass / **BRIAN SMITH** – wind

Vertigo | not issued

Jun 70. (lp) *(6360 008)* **ELASTIC ROCK** [46] [-]
– 1916 / Elastic rock / Striation / Taranaki / Twisted track / Crude blues (part 1 & 2) / 1916 (Battle of Boogaloo) / Torrid zone / Stonescape / Earth mother / Speaking for myself personally in my own opinion I think / Persephones jive.

Mar 71. (lp) *(6360 027)* **WE'LL TALK ABOUT IT LATER** [ ] [-]
– Song for the bearded lady / Sun child / Lullaby for a lonely child / We'll talk about it later / Oasis / Ballad for Joe Pimp / Easter 1916.

— below was to have been solo album, although he added to above; **RON MATHESON** – bass / **KENNY WHEELER + HAROLD BECKETT** – trumpet / **TONY ROBERTS** – wind / **CHRIS KARAN** – percussion / **KEITH WINTER** – keyboards (guest)

Jul 71. (lp; IAN CARR'S NUCLEUS) *(6360 039)* **SOLAR PLEXUS** [ ] [-]
– Clements (part 1 & 2) / Changing times / Bedrock deadlock / Spirit level / Torso / Snakeship's dream.

IAN CARR

CARR retained only **SMITH**, when SPEDDING went solo and JENKINS + MARSHALL were first to be recruited to ever-changing SOFT MACHINE

— added **ROY BABBINGTON** – bass (ex-OVARY LODGE, ex-DELIVERY / CAROL GRIMES) / **GORDON BECK + DAVE MacCRAE** – keyboards / **ALAN HOLDSWORTH** – guitar / **CLIVE THACKER** – drums / **TREVOR TOMPKINS** – percussion

1972. (lp) *(6360 076)* **BELLADONNA** [ ] [-]
– Bella Donna / Summer rain / Rema Dione / Mayday / Suspension / Hector's house.

NUCLEUS

PADDY KINGSLAND – synthesizer / **TONY LEVIN** – drums / **TONY COE** – wind / **NORMA WINSTONE** – vocals, repl. HOLDSWORTH (another to SOFT MACHINE)

1973. (lp) *(6360 091)* **LABYRINTH** [ ] [-]
– Origins / Bull-dance / Ariadne / Arena / Exultation / Naxos.

— **ROGER SUTTON** – bass, repl. BABBINGTON (to SOFT MACHINE)

— **JOCELYN PITCHEN** – guitar, repl. KINGSLAND, COE, BECK + WHEELER

— **AUREO DE SOUZA** – percussion, drums, repl. TOMPKINS + LEVIN

— **JOY YATES** – vocals, repl. WINSTONE

1973. (lp) *(6360 100)* **ROOTS** [ ] [-]
– Roots / Images / Caliban / Whapatiti / Capricorn / Odo Kamona / Southern roots and celebration.

— **BOB BERTLES** – saxophones / **KEN SHAW** – guitar / **GEOFF CASTLE** – keyboards / **BRYAN SPRING** – drums / **KIERAN WHITE** – vocals, repl. SMITH, MacCRAE, THACKER, DE SOUZA + YATES

1974. (lp) *(6360 110)* **UNDER THE SUN** [ ] [-]
– Addison trip / Feast Alfresco / In procession / New life / Pastoral graffiti / Rites of man / Sarsparilla / Taste of Sarsparilla.

— **ROGER SELLERS** – drums, percussion, repl. SPRING

Vertigo | Sire

1975. (lp) *(6360 119)* <7508> **SNAKE HIPS ETCETERA** [ ] [ ]
– Rat's bag / Alive and kicking / Rachel's tune / Snake hips etcetera / Pussyfoot / Hey day.

— added the returning **TREVOR TOMPKINS** – percussion

Nov 75. (lp) *(6360 124)* **ALLEY CAT** [ ] [-]
– Alley cat / Nosegay / Phaideaux corner / Splat / You can't be sure.

May 76. (lp; as IAN CARR, NUCLEUS) *(9286 019)* **DIRECT HITS** (compilation) [ ] [-]
– Bull-dance / Crude blues / Roots / Sarsparilla / Song for the bearded lady / Suspension / Taste of sarsparilla / Torso.

— **BRIAN SMITH** – sax / **BILL KRISTIAN** – bass, repl. BERTLES + SUTTON + SHAW

Capitol | not issued

Jul 77. (lp) *(11771)* **IN FRAGRANTI DELICTO** [ ] [-]
– Gestalt / Mysteries / Hey day / In flagranti delicto.

Feb 79. (lp; as IAN CARR NUCLEUS) *(11916)* **OUT OF THE LONG DARK** [ ] [-]
– Gone with the weed / Lady Bountiful / Solar wind / Selina / Out of the long dark / Sassy / Simply this / Black ballad / For Liam.

— **CHUCHO MERCHAN** – bass / **NIC FRANCE** – drums, repl. KRISTIAN + SELLERS

Mood | not issued

1980. (lp) *(24000)* **AWAKENING** [ ] [-]
– Awakening / Midnight oil / Mutatis mutandis / White City blues / Things past / You can't be serious – You must be joking.

— **CARR** folded band but re-formed for live outing with; **MARC WOOD** – guitar / **JOHN MARSHALL** – drums / **DIL KATZ** – bass / **PHIL TODD** – sax

1985. (lp) *(28650)* **LIVE AT THE THEATERHAUS (live)** [ ] [-]
– Dawn choruses / Bouquets pour ma belle / For miles and miles / Easy does it now / Something for Mister Jelly Roll.

IAN CARR

M.M.C. | not issued

Oct 88. (lp/c/cd) **OLD HEARTLAND** [ ] [-]
– Open country / Interiors / Disjunctive boogie / Spirit of place / Full fathom five / Old heartland / Things past.

— CARR went on to collaborate in 1990 with solo artist SIMON THOUMIRE on lp/c 'HOOTZ!' *(Black Crow; CRO 225/+MC)*. In 1994, he teamed up with KAREN TWEED on couple of albums 'TWEED & CARR' *(Tweed & Carr; TWEED 001C)*, 'SHHH!' *(Hypertension; HY 147 CD/C)*

– others, etc. –

1974. (lp; by NEIL ARDLEY with IAN CARR, STAN TRACEY & MIKE GIBBS) *Argo; (ZDA 164/5)* **WILL POWER** [ ] [-]

May 89. (d-cd) *Beat Goes On; (BGOCD 47)* **ELASTIC ROCK / WE'LL TALK ABOUT IT LATER** [ ] [-]
(re-iss.Apr94; same)

Ted NUGENT / AMBOY DUKES

Born: 13 Dec'48, Detroit, Michigan, USA. In 1966, he formed garage/psych-rock Chicago band, The AMBOY DUKES. They quickly signed to 'Mainstream' US, releasing a debut single, 'BABY PLEASE DON'T GO', in 1967. Their eponymous 1968 debut album broke into the US Top 200, and by the summer, the classic psychedelic single, 'JOURNEY TO THE CENTER OF THE MIND', was in the US Top 20. Ironically enough, NUGENT was a vehement non-drug taker, sacking anyone in the band who dabbled with them. He prefered hunting animals instead and his love of blood sports was well-publicised. Although they toured constantly in the US for the next couple of years, the band only managed minor chart placings. In 1971, they evolved into TED NUGENT & THE AMBOY DUKES, snapped up by FRANK ZAPPA's 'Discreeet' label, subsequently unleashing two albums in the mid-70's before dissolving. In 1975, NUGENT secured a solo deal with 'Epic', hitting the US Top 30 with an eponymous Tom Werman-produced debut in early '76. By this point, NUGENT had come a long way from his 60's roots, adopting a heavy metal axe-hero style. His next album in 1977, 'FREE FOR ALL' (which featured MEAT LOAF) ventured further, the first to earn him a Top 40 placing in the UK. • **Songwriters:** NUGENT penned, except BABY PLEASE DON'T GO (Big Joe Williams). • **Trivia:** In 1973, while working on a new record deal, he featured alongside other stars MIKE PINERA (Iron Butterfly), WAYNE KRAMER (MC5) and FRANK MARINO (Mahogany Rush), on the 'battle of the guitarists' stage shows. Early in 1978, he enscribed his name with a bowie knife on the arm of a fan!

• **Note:** There was another group of the same name in the UK called The AMBOY DUKES, who released several singles on 'Polydor', around the mid-60's to '68.

Recommended: JOURNEYS & MIGRATIONS (*7) / GREAT GONZOS (*6)

AMBOY DUKES

TED NUGENT – guitar, vox / plus **JOHN DRAKE** – vocals / **STEVE FARMER** – rhythm guitar / **BILL WHITE** – bass / **RICK LOBER** – keyboards / **DAVID PALMER** – drums

Fontana | Mainstream

1967. (7") <676> **BABY PLEASE DON'T GO. / PSALMS OF AFTERMATH** [-] [ ]

1967. (7") *(TF 971)* **LET'S GO GET STONED. / IT'S NOT TRUE** [ ] [-]

1968. (lp; stereo/mono) *(S+/TL 5468)* <6104> **THE AMBOY DUKES** [ ] [ ] Jan68
– Baby please don't go / I feel free / Young love / Psalms of aftermath / Colors / Let's go get stoned / Down on Philips escalator / The lovely lady / Night time / It's not true / Gimme love. *(cd-iss.Dec92 on 'Repertoire'+=;)*– J.B. special.

— **RUSTY DAY** – vocals repl. DRAKE + FARMER / **ANDY SOLOMAN** – keyboards repl. LOBER / **GREG ARAMA** – bass repl. WHITE

In the UK, they were now called The AMERICAN AMBOY DUKES

London | Mainstream

Jul 68. (7") <684> **JOURNEY TO THE CENTER OF THE MIND. / MISSISSIPPI MURDERER** [-] [16]

Oct 68. (7") <693> **SCOTTISH TEA. / YOU TALK SUNSHINE, I BREATHE FIRE** [-] [ ]

Feb 69. (lp; stereo/mono) *(SH-T/HA-T 8378)* <6112> **JOURNEY TO THE CENTER OF THE MIND** [ ] [74] Aug68
– Mississippi murderer / Surrender to your kings / Flight of the Byrd / Scottish tea / Dr. Slingshot / Journey to the center of the mind / Ivory castles / Why is a carrot more orange than an orange? / Missionary Mary / Death is life / Saint Philips friend / I'll prove I'm right / (Conclusion). *(cd-iss.Dec92 on 'Repertoire'+=; MDCD 0911)*– You talk sunshine, I breathe fire.

1969. (7") <700> **PRODIGAL MAN. / GOOD NATURED EMMA** [-] [ ]

1969. (lp; stereo/mono) *(SH-T/HA-T 8392)* <6118> **MIGRATION** [ ] [ ]
– Migration / Prodigal man / For his namesake / I'm not a juvenile delinquent / Good natured Emma / Inside the outside / Shades of green and grey / Curb your elephant / Loaded for bear. *(cd-iss.Dec92 on 'Repertoire'+=;)*– Sobbin' in my mug of bear.

1969. (7") *<704>* **FOR HIS NAMESAKE. / LOADED FOR BEAR** [-] [ ]
1969. (7") *<711>* **MIGRATION. / FLIGHT OF THE BIRDS** [-] [ ]
1969. (lp) *<6125>* **THE BEST OF THE ORIGINAL AMBOY DUKES** (compilation) [-] [ ]

Polydor Polydor

Mar 70. (lp) *<4012>* **MARRIAGE ON THE ROCKS – ROCK BOTTOM** [-] [ ]
– Marriage:- (a) Part 1 – Man / (b) Part 2 – Woman / (c) Part 3 – Music / Breast-fed 'gator (bait) / Get yer guns / Non-conformist wilderbeast man / Today's lesson / Children of the woods / Brain games of the yesteryear / The inexhaustable quest for the cosmic garbage (part 1 & 2) / (excerpt from Bartok).

— **NUGENT** brought in new members **BOB GRANGE** – bass / **KJ KNIGHT** – drums retaining also **ANDY SOLOMAN** (RUSTY DAY joined CACTUS)

TED NUGENT & THE AMBOY DUKES

Mar 71. (lp) *<4035>* **SURVIVAL OF THE FITTEST** (live) [-] [ ]
– Survival of the fittest / Rattle my snake / Mr. Jones' hanging party / Papa's will / Slidin' on / Prodigal man. *(UK-iss.1974 on 'Polydor'; 2675 141)*

— Disbanded in the early 70's, but re-formed with others **BOB GRANGE** – bass / **ANDY JEZOWSKI** – vocals / **GABRIEL MAGNO** – keyboards / **VIC MASTRIANNI** – drums

Discreet Discreet

Jun 74. (lp) *(K 59203) <2181>* **CALL OF THE WILD** [ ] [ ]
– Call of the wild / Sweet revenge / Pony express / Ain't it the truth / Renegade / Rot gut / Below the belt / Cannon balls. *(re-iss.Oct89 on 'Edsel' lp/cd; ED/+CD 278)*

Jun 74. (7") *(K 19200)* **SWEET REVENGE. / AIN'T IT THE TRUTH** [ ] [ ]

— **Rev.ATROCIOUS THEODOLIUS** – guitar, vocals repl. MAGNO

1975. (lp) *(K 59203) <2203>* **TOOTH FANG & CLAW** [ ] [ ]
– No holds barred / Sacha / The great white buffalo / Maybelline / Free flight / Hibernation / Living in the woods / Lady luck. *(re-iss.Oct89 on 'Edsel'; lp/cd; ED/+CD 295)*

— TED finally gave up AMBOY DUKES in 1975.

– compilations, etc. –

Apr 75. (d-lp) *Polydor; <2801>* **JOURNEYS & MIGRATIONS** [-] [ ]
(UK-iss.Feb83 on 'Audio Fidelity'; MRD 5008)

Jun 77. (d-lp) *Polydor; <2664 344)* **MARRIAGE ON THE ROCKS – ROCK BOTTOM / SURVIVAL OF THE FITTEST (AMBOY DUKES)** [ ] [-]

1977. (d-lp) *Warners; (K 69202)* **TWO ORIGINALS OF . . . (AMBOY DUKES)** [ ] [-]
– (CALL OF THE WILD & TOOTH, FANG & CLAW) albums

1991. (cd/c) *Thunderbolt; (CDTB/THBC 097)* **ON THE EDGE** (early AMBOY DUKES material) [ ] [-]

May 91. (cd/c) *Thunderbolt; (CDTB/THBC 120)* **OVER THE TOP** (early AMBOY DUKES material) [ ] [-]

— for TED NUGENT solo work; see GREAT ROCK DISCOGRAPHY

OBLIVION EXPRESS (see under ⇒ AUGER, Brian)

OCTOPUS

Formed: Hatfield, England . . . 1968 as The CORTINAS, by brothers PAUL and NIGEL GRIGGS. One single appeared under this moniker, until their discovery by TONY MURRAY (ex-PLASTIC PENNY / of The TROGGS), who produced the debut OCTOPUS album, 'RESTLESS NIGHT' (1969). Two previous 45's had flopped and its release wasn't exactly met with great anticipation, its bizarre artwork not doing the record any favours (it's now worth over £200!). Within its grooves, the listener was subjected to some patchy post-psychedelia and directionless progressive pop, although it did have its moments (i.e. 'COUNCIL PLANS', 'TIDE' and one of the aforementioned singles, 'THE RIVER'). A resurrected band re-surfaced for a one-off single in 1973, although this sounded dated.

Recommended: RESTLESS NIGHT (*5)

PAUL GRIGGS – vocals, guitar, piano / **NIGEL GRIGGS** – bass, guitars / + drummer

Polydor / not issued

May 68. (7"; as CORTINAS) *(56255)* **PHOEBE'S FLOWER SHOP. / TOO MUCH IN LOVE** [ ] [-]

Penny Farthing / not issued

Dec 69. (7") *(PEN 705)* **LAUGH AT THE POOR MAN. / GIRLFRIEND** [ ] [-]
May 70. (7") *(PEN 716)* **THE RIVER. / THIEF** [ ] [-]
Jun 70. (lp) *(PELS 508)* **RESTLESS NIGHT** [ ] [-]
– The river / Summer / Council plans / Restless night / Thief / Queen and the pauper / I say / John's rock / Rainchild / Tide. *(cd-iss.Sep91 on 'See For Miles'+=; SEECD 328)*– Girlfriend / Laugh at the poor man. *(re-iss.Aug96 on 'Essex'; ESSEX 1013LP)*

Mooncrest / not issued

1973. (7") *(MOON 7)* **HEY NA NA. / FUTURE FEELINGS** [ ] [-]

— went back to oblivion after above

Mike OLDFIELD

Born: 15 May'53, Reading, England. He started playing guitar at the age of seven, and by 1968, had formed SALLYANGIE with sister SALLY. They signed to folk-orientated label, 'Transatlantic', who issued the lp, 'CHILDREN OF THE SUN'. After releasing a single, 'TWO SHIPS'. / 'COLOURS OF THE WORLD', in Sep69, they split their partnership to concentrate on other projects. After a spell in the short-lived BAREFOOT, MIKE became the bassist for KEVIN AYERS' band, The WHOLE WORLD, in March 1970. He subsequently appeared on two of his albums, 'SHOOTING AT THE MOON' and 'WHATEVERSHEBRINGSWESING', between 1971 and 1972, before they dissolved. Around this time, MIKE started work on his own solo project, gaining financial support in 1972 from Richard Branson's newly formed 'Virgin' label (the same year, MIKE also contributed session work for EDGAR BROUGHTON BAND and DAVID BEDFORD). 'TUBULAR BELLS' finally saw the light of day in May '73, soon garnering critical acclaim from the music press. A near 50-minute concept piece, overdubbed many times by multi-instrumentalist, MIKE, it went into the Top 3 a year later. Aided by a surprise US Top 10 single (an album excerpt), used in the horror movie, 'The Exorcist', 'TUBULAR BELLS' repeated the feat Stateside. In September '74, his follow-up, 'HERGEST RIDGE', was completed, going straight in at No.1. Critically lambasted by some critics as "Son of Tubular Bells", it only managed to hit No.87 in America. After an orchestral Tubular Bells (conducted by DAVID BEDFORD) was panned by the rock press, although the period between 1975 and 1978 saw him branch into African and folk-type origins on the albums, 'OMMADAWN' and 'INCANTATIONS'. At the same time, he embarressed his rock following by releasing mainly festive hit 45's, although his contribution to the 70's, in both the classical and rock fields, was only matched by PINK FLOYD. The early 80's brought OLDFIELD a succession of more mainstream pop/rock albums, culminating with 1983's Top 10 'CRISES' album, which spawned his biggest ever hit single, 'MOONLIGHT SHADOW' (it featured the celestial vocal chords of MAGGIE REILLY; part of his band and new co-writing team). His next single, 'SHADOW ON THE WALL', surprisingly bombed, although it raised the profile of ex-FAMILY frontman, ROGER CHAPMAN. He continued to achieve reasonable chart success throughout the remainder of the decade, even scoring the soundtrack to the seminal Vietnam movie, 'THE KILLING FIELDS'. Although he never quite regained the ground he had broken with his debut, he nevertheless returned in 1992 with a belated "follow-up" in the form of the almost identical, but still appealling, 'TUBULAR BELLS II'. This seemed to breathe more life into OLDFIELD's flagging career, his most recent work (1996) taking on the "space-race" theme with, 'VOYAGER'. • **Covered:** SAILOR'S HORNPIPE (trad.) / IN DULCE JUBILO (R.L. Pearsall) / WILLIAM TELL OVERTURE (Korsokov) / BLUE PETER (BBC copyright) / ARRIVAL (Abba) / WONDERFUL LAND (Shadows) / ETUDE (Franscisco Tarrega). • **Trivia:** In the mid-70's, MIKE also had time to session on albums by Virgin artists; DAVID BEDFORD (Star's End) / ROBERT WYATT (Rock Bottom) / TOM NEWMAN (Fine Old Tom). MIKE's sister, SALLY, also went on to have a UK Top 20 hit with, 'MIRRORS' (late '78).

Recommended: TUBULAR BELLS (*10) / HERGEST RIDGE (*7) / OMMADAWN (*8) / INCANTATIONS (*8) / FIVE MILES OUT (*6) / CRISES (*6) / THE KILLING FIELDS (*7) / TUBULAR BELLS II (*6)

MIKE OLDFIELD – guitar, bass, everything with **TOM NEWMAN** – guitar / **JON FIELD** – flute / **STAN BROUGHTON** – drums / **LINDSAY COOPER** – wind; plus master of ceremonies, **VIVIAN STANSHALL (ex-BONZO DOG BAND)**

Virgin / Virgin

May 73. (lp/c) *(T/TCV 2001)* *<105>* **TUBULAR BELLS** [1] [3] Nov73
– Tubular bells (side 1) / Tubular bells (side 2). *(hit top Oct74) (iss.quad-lp.Jul74; QV 2001) (pic-lp Dec78; VP 2001) (cd-iss.Jun83; CDV 2001); hit UK No.28) (re-iss.Feb97 on 'E.M.I.'; LPCENT 18)*
Feb 74. (7") *<55100>* **TUBULAR BELLS (edit). / TUBULAR BELLS (excerpt)** [-] [7]
Jun 74. (7") *(VS 101)* **MIKE OLDFIELD'S SINGLE (theme from Tubular Bells). / FROGGY WENT A-COURTIN'** [31] [-]

— now with **TERRY OLDFIELD** – wind / etc.

Sep 74. (lp/c) *(V/TCV 2013)* *<109>* **HERGEST RIDGE** [1] [87]
– Hergest ridge (side 1) / Hergest ridge (side 2). *(re-iss.Apr86 lp/c; OVED/+C 163) (cd-iss.Apr86; CDV 2013)*
Jan 75. (lp/c) *(V/TCV 2026)* **THE ORCHESTRAL TUBULAR BELLS (WITH THE ROYAL PHILHARMONIC ORCHESTRA)** (live & conducted by DAVID BEDFORD with guitar by OLDFIELD) [17] [-]
– The orchestral Tubular Bells part 1 / The orchestral Tubular Bells part 2. *(cd-iss.Jul87; CDV 2026) (re-iss.Sep89 on 'VIP-Virgin' lp/c/cd; VVIP/+C/D 101)*
Feb 75. (7") *(VS 112)* **DON ALFONSO. / IN DULCE JUBILO** [ ] [-]

— back-up were **JUBULA** (African musicians) / **PIERRE MOERLEN** (of GONG) / backing vocals by sister **SALLY OLDFIELD + CLODAGH SIMMONDS**

Nov 75. (lp/c) *(V/TCV 2043)* *<33913>* **OMMADAWN** [4] [ ]
– Ommadawn (side 1) / Ommadawn (side 2). *(quad-lp Feb76; QV 2043) (cd-iss.1986; CDV 2043) (cd re-iss.Apr97 on 'Virgin-VIP'; CDVIP 185)*
Nov 75. (7") *(VS 131)* **IN DULCI JUBILO. / ON HORSEBACK** [4] [-]
Nov 75. (7") *<9508>* **OMMADAWN (excerpt). / ON HORSEBACK** [-] [ ]
Oct 76. (7") *(VS 163)* **PORTSMOUTH. / SPEAK (THO' YOU ONLY SAY FAREWELL)** [3] [-]
Nov 76. (7") *<9510>* **PORTSMOUTH. / ALGIERS** [-] [ ]
Feb 77. (7") *(VS 167)* **THE WILLIAM TELL OVERTURE. / ALGIERS** [ ] [-]
Dec 77. (7") *(VS 198)* **THE CUCKOO SONG. / PIPE TUNE** [ ] [-]

— added from last album; (see most musicians from following live album)

Nov 78. (d-lp/d-c) *(VDT/TCVDT 101)* **INCANTATIONS** [14] [ ]
– Incantations (part 1) / Incantations (part 2) / Incantations (part 3) / Incantations (part 4). *(cd-iss.Feb87; CDVD 101); omits last of 4 minutes side 3) (re-iss.Apr92 cd/c; OVED CD/C 417)*
Apr 79. (7") *(VS 245)* **GUILTY. / INCANTATIONS (excerpt)** [22] [-]
(12"blue) *(VS 245-12)* – ('A'side) / Guilty (live).

— MIKE with **PIERRE MOERLEN** – drums, percussion / **RINGO McDONOUGH** – bodhran / **MIKE FRYE, BENOIT MOERLEN, DAVID BEDFORD** (also string arrangements) / **NICO RAMSDEN** – guitar / **PHIL BEER** – guitar, vocals / **PEKKA POHJOLA** – bass / **RAY GAY, RALPH IZEN, SIMO SALMINEN, COLIN MOORE** – trumpets / **SEBASTIAN BELL, CHRIS NICHOLLS** – flutes / **PETE LEMER, TIM CROSS** – keyboards / **MADDY PRIOR** – vocals / **JONATHAN KAHAN, DICK STUDT, BEN CRUFT, JANE PRYCE, LIZ EDWARDS, NICOLA HURTON** – violins / **VANESSA PARK, DAVID BUCKNALL, JESSICA FORD, NIGEL WARREN-GREEN** – cellos / **NICK WORTERS, JOE KIRBY** – bass / **DON McVAY, PAULINE MACK, DANNY DAGGERS, MELINDA DAGGERS, LIZ BUTLER, ROSS COHEN** – vocals, plus 11 piece choir.

Aug 79. (d-lp/d-c) *(VD/TCVD 2511)* **EXPOSED (live)** [16] [-]
– Incantations (parts 1 and 2) / Incantations (parts 3 and 4) / Tubular bells (part 1) / Tubular bells (part 2) / Guilty. *(d-cd-iss.Jul86; CDVD 2511)*

— trimmed backing group down.

Nov 79. (7") *(VS 317)* **BLUE PETER. / WOODHENGE** [19] [-]
Dec 79. (lp/c) *(V/TCV 2141)* **PLATINUM** [24] [-]
– Platinum:- Airborne – Platinum – Charleston North star – Platimun finale / Woodhenge / Sally / Punkadiddle / I got rhythm. *(cd-iss.1986; CDV 2141) (re-iss.1989 lp/c; OVED/C 233)*

— next featured **PHIL COLLINS** – drums

Virgin / Epic

Sep 80. (7") *(VS 374)* **ARRIVAL. / POLKA** [ ] [-]
Oct 80. (lp/c) *(V/TCV 2181)* *<FE 37358>* **QE2** [27] [ ]
– Taurus I / Sheba / Conflict / Arrival / Wonderful land / Mirage / QE2 / Celt / Molly. *(cd-iss.1986; CDV 2181) (re-iss.1989 lp/c; OVED/+C 235)*
Nov 80. (7") *(VS 387)* **SHEBA. / WONDERFUL LAND** [ ] [-]
Dec 80. (d-lp/d-c) **AIRBORNE** [-] [ ]
– (see PLATINUM tracks, except 'Guilty' repl. – / / Tubular bells live part 1 /

Incantations (segue of 20+ mins. studio and live recordings)

— MIKE brought in **MAGGIE REILLY** – vocals (ex-CADO BELLE) / **TIM CROSS** – keyboards / **MORRIS PERT** – percussion, drums (ex-BRAND X) / **RICK FENN** – bass, guitar / **PIERRE MOERLEN** – drums, percussion returned to repl. MIKE FRYE / added **TIM RENWICK** – bass, guitar

Mar 82. (7"/7"pic-d) *(VS/+Y 464)* **FIVE MILES OUT. / LIVE PUNKADIDDLE** [43] [ ]

Mar 82. (lp/c) *(V/TCV 2222) <FE 37983>* **FIVE MILES OUT** [7] [ ]
– Taurus II / Family man / Orabidoo / Mount Teidi / Five miles out. *(cd-iss.1983; CDV 2222) (re-iss.Apr90 lp/c; OVED/+C 293) (re-iss.Oct94 on 'Virgin-VIP' cd/c;)*

Virgin Virgin

Jun 82. (7"/7"pic-d) *(VS/+Y 489) <02877>* **FAMILY MAN. / MOUNT TEIDI** [45] [ ]

Sep 82. (7"/7"pic-d) *(VS/+Y 541)* **MISTAKE. / WALDBERG (THE PEAK)** [ ] [-]

— MIKE retained REILLY + MOERLEN. New members were **SIMON PHILLIPS** – drums / **PHIL SPALDING** – bass / **GRAEME PLEETH** – keyboards / **SIMON HOUSE** – violin

May 83. (7"/7"pic-d)(12") *(VS/+Y 586)(VS 586-12)* **MOONLIGHT SHADOW. / RITE OF MAN** [4] [ ]

May 83. (cd/c/lp) *(CD/TC+/V 2262)* **CRISES** [6] [-]
– Crises / Moonlight shadow / In high places / Foreign affair / Taurus III / Shadow on the wall. *(re-iss.Mar91 cd/c; OVED CD/C 351) (re-iss.May94 on 'Virgin-VIP' cd/c; CD/TC VIP 118)*

— (below vocals by ROGER CHAPMAN, ex-FAMILY)

Sep 83. (7"/ext.12") *(VS 625/+12)* **SHADOW ON THE WALL. / TAURUS III** [ ] [ ]

Jan 84. (7"/ext.12") *(VS 648/+12)* **CRIME OF PASSION. / JUNGLE GARDENIA** [61] [ ]

— retained **REILLY, PHILLIPS + SPALDING** – adding guitar / plus **BARRY PALMER** – vocals / **MICKEY SIMMONDS** – keyboards / **HAROLD ZUSCHRADER** – synth.

Jun 84. (7") *(VS 686)* **TO FRANCE. / IN THE POOL** [48] [ ]
(ext.12"+=) *(VS 686-12)* – Bones.

Jul 84. (cd/c/lp) *(CD/TC+/V 2308)* **DISCOVERY** [15] [-]
– To France / Poison arrows / Crystal gazing / Tricks of the light / Discovery / Talk about your life / Saved by a bell / The lake. *(re-iss.Apr92 cd/c; OVED CD/C 421)*

Sep 84. (7") *(VS 707)* **TRICKS OF THE LIGHT. / APEMAN** [ ] [ ]
(12"+=) *(VS 707-12)* – ('A'instrumental).

Nov 84. (7"/ext.12") *(VS 731/+12)* **ETUDE. / EVACUATION** [ ] [ ]

Dec 84. (cd/c/lp) *(CD/TC+/V 2328)* **THE KILLING FIELDS (Soundtrack)** [97] [ ]
– Pran's theme / Requiem for a city / Evacuation / Pran's theme 2 / Capture / Execution / Bad news / Pran's departure / Worksite / The year zero / Blood sucking / The year zero 2 / Pran's escape – The killing fields / The trek / The boy's burial – Pran sees the red cross / Good news / Etude. *(re-iss.Jun88 lp/c; OVED/+C 183)*

— **ANITA HEGERLAND + ALED JONES** – vocals repl. REILLY

Nov 85. (7") *(VS 836)* **PICTURES IN THE DARK. / LEGEND** [50] [ ]
(ext.12") *(VS 836-12)* – The trap.

Apr 86. (7"/7"sha-pic-d)(ext.12") *(VS/+S 863)(VS 863-12)* **SHINE. / THE PATH** [ ] [ ]

May 87. (7") *(VS 955)* **IN HIGH PLACES. / POISON ARROWS** [ ] [-]
(12"+=) *(VS 955-12)* – Jungle Gardenia.

— vocalists – **JON ANDERSON / KEVIN AYERS / BONNIE TYLER**

Sep 87. (7") *(VS 990)* **ISLANDS. / THE WIND CHIMES (part one)** [ ] [ ]
(c-s+=/ext.12"+=)(cd-s+=) *(VS/+C 990-12)(CDEP 6)* – When the night's on fire.

Oct 87. (cd/c/lp) *(CD/TC+/V 2466) <90645>* **ISLANDS** [29] [ ]
– The wind chimes (parts 1 & 2) / Islands / Flying start / North point / Magic touch / The time has come. *(cd+=)–* When the night's on fire. *(re-iss.Apr92 cd/c; OVED CD/C 418)*

Nov 87. (7") *(VS 1013)* **THE TIME HAS COME. / (final extract from) THE WIND CHIMES** [ ] [-]
(12"+=) *(VS 1013-12)* – ('A'original mix).

Nov 87. (7") **MAGIC TOUCH. / THE WIND CHIMES (part 1)** [-] [ ]

Feb 88. (7"/12") *(VS 1047/+12)* **FLYING START. / THE WIND CHIMES (part 2)** [ ] [ ]

Jul 89. (7") *(VS 1189)* **EARTHMOVING. / BRIDGE TO PARADISE** [ ] [ ]
(12"+=/cd-s+=) *(VS T/CD 1189)* – ('A'disco mix).

Jul 89. (cd/c/lp) *(CD/TC+/V 2610)* **EARTHMOVING** [30] [-]
– Holy / Hostage / Far country / Innocent / Runaway son / See the light / Earthmoving / Blue night / Nothing but – Bridge to Paradise. *(re-iss.Apr92 cd/c; OVED CD/C 420) (cd re-iss.Apr97 on 'Virgin-VIP'; CDVIP 169)*

Oct 89. (7") *(VS 1214)* **INNOCENT. / EARTHMOVING (club mix)** [ ] [ ]
(12"+=/cd-s+=) *(VS T/CD 1214)* – ('A'extended).

Jun 90. (cd/c/lp) *(CD/TC+/V 2640)* **AMAROK** [49] [-]
– Amarok (part 1) / Amarok (part 2). *(re-iss.Apr92 cd/c; OVED CD/C 422)*

— with **SIMON PHILLIPS** – drums / **DAVE LEVY** – bass / **MICKEY SIMMONDS** – keyboards / **ANDY LONGHURST** – keyboards / **COURTNEY PINE** – sax

Jan 91. (7"/12"/cd-s; as MICHAEL OLDFIELD) **HEAVEN'S OPEN. / EXCERPT FROM AMAROK** [ ] [-]

Feb 91. (cd/c/lp; as MICHAEL OLDFIELD) *(CD/TC+/V 2653)* **HEAVEN'S OPEN** [ ] [-]
– Make make / No dream / Mr. Shame / Gimme back / Heaven's open / Music from the balcony. *(re-iss.Apr92 cd/c; OVED CD/C 419)*

— solo playing most instruments, except some guests & a bagpipe band.

W.E.A. Reprise

Sep 92. (cd)(lp/c) *(4509 90618-2)(WX 2002/+C)* **TUBULAR BELLS II** [1] [ ]
– Sentinel / Dark star / Clear light / Blue saloon / Sunjammer / Red dawn / The bell / Weightless / The great pain / Sunset door / Tattoo / Altered state / Maya gold / Moonshine.

Sep 92. (7"/c-s/cd-s) *(YZ 698/+C/CD)* **SENTINEL (SINGLE RESTRUCTION). / EARLY STAGES** [10] [ ]

Dec 92. (7"/c-s) *(YZ 708/+C)* **TATTOO. / SILENT NIGHT / SENTINEL (live)** [33] [ ]
(cd-ep+=) *(YZ 708CD)* – Live At Edinburgh Castle:- Moonshine / Reprise / Maya gold.

Apr 93. (7"/c-s) *(YZ 737/+C)* **THE BELL. / SENTINEL** [50] [ ]
(cd-s+=) *(YZ 737CD)* – ('A'-3 mixes).
(cd-s) *(YZ 737??)* – (5-'A'mixes).

Nov 94. (cd/c) *(4509 98581-2/-4)* **THE SONGS OF DISTANT EARTH** [24] [ ]
– In the beginning / Let there be light / Supernova / Magellan / First landing / Oceania / Only time will tell / Prayer for the Earth / Lament for Atlantis / The chamber / Hibernaculum / Tubular world / The shining ones / Crystal clear / The sunken forest / Ascension / A new beginning. *(re-iss.Oct95; same)*

Dec 94. (c-s) *(YZ 871C)* **HIBERNACULUM / MOONSHINE** [47] [ ]
(cd-s+=) *(YZ 871CDX)* – Solution hoedown / Jungle.
(cd-s) *(YZ 871CD)* – ('A'side) / The spectral army / The song of the boat men.

Aug 95. (c-s) *(YZ 880C)* **LET THERE BE LIGHT (Indian Lake mix) / LET THERE BE LIGHT (BT's entropic dub)** [51] [ ]
(12") *(YZ 880T)* – ('A'-BT's pure luminescence remix) / ('A'-Hardfloor mix) / ('A'club mix).
(cd-s) *(YZ 880CD)* – (above club mix) repl.by – ('A'-Ultraviolet mix).

Sep 96. (cd/c) *(0630 15896-2/-4)* **VOYAGER** [12] [ ]
– The song of the sun / Celtic rain / The hero / Women of Ireland / The voyager / She moves through the fair / Dark island / Wild goose flaps its wings / Flowers of the forest / Mont St Michel.

Mar 97. (c-s) *(WEA 093C)* **WOMEN OF IRELAND / ('A'mix)** [ ] [ ]
(12"+=/cd-s+=) *(WEA 093 T/CD)* –

- compilations, etc. -

— on 'Virgin' unless otherwise mentioned

Nov 76. (4xlp-box) *(VBOX 1)* **BOXED** [22] [-]
– (TUBULAR BELLS / HERGEST RIDGE / OMMADAWN / + COLLABORATIONS (singles, etc.) *(re-iss.1985 4xlp/4xc; VBOX/TCVX 1) (4xcd-box Jul87; CDBOX 1)*

Dec 78. (7"ep/12"ep) *(VS/+T 238)* **TAKE 4** [72] [-]
– Portsmouth / In dulce jubilo / Wrekorder wrondo / Sailor's hornpipe.

Oct 85. (cd/c/d-lp) *(CD/C+/MOC 1)* **THE COMPLETE MIKE OLDFIELD** [36] [-]
– Arrival / In dulce jubilo / Portsmouth / Jungle gardenia / Guilty / Blue Peter / Waldberg (the peak) / Etude / Wonderful land / Moonlight shadow / Family man / Mistake / Five miles out / Crime of passion / To France / Shadow on the wall / Excerpt from Tubular Bells / Sheba / Mirage / Platinum / Mount Tiede / Excerpt from Ommadawn / Excerpt from Hergest Ridge / Excerpt from Incantations / Excerpt from Killing Fields.

Jun 88. (3"cd-ep) *(CDT 7)* **MOONLIGHT SHADOW (extended) / RITE OF MAN / TO FRANCE / JUNGLE GARDENIA** [ ] [-]

Jun 88. (cd-video) *(080446-1)* **THE WIND CHIMES (Soundtrack 1986)** [ ] [-]

Nov 90. (3xcd-box) *(TPAK 15)* **COLLECTORS' EDITION** [ ] [-]
– (THE ORCHESTRAL TUBULAR BELLS / OMMADAWN / HERGEST RIDGE)

Nov 90. (3xcd-box) *(TPAK 16)* **COLLECTORS' EDITION** [ ] [-]
– (QE2 / PLATINUM / FIVE MILES OUT)

Dec 90. (7"/c-s) **ETUDE. / GAKKAEN** [ ] [-]
(12"+=/cd-s+=) – ('A'extended) (with "ONO GAGUKU KAI").

— (The above 'A'side was now used on TV ad for 'Nurofen'.)

Sep 93. (cd/c/d-lp) *(VT CD/MC/LP 18)* **ELEMENTS: THE BEST OF MIKE OLDFIELD** [5] [ ]
– Tubular bells – opening theme / Family man / Moonlight shadow / Heaven's open / Five miles out / To France / Foreign affair / In dulce jubilo / Shadow on the wall / Islands / Etude / Sentinel / Ommadawn – excerpt / Incantations part four – excerpt / Amarok – excerpt / Portsmouth.

Sep 93. (4xcd-box) *(CDBOX 2)* **ELEMENTS – MIKE OLDFIELD 1973-1991** [ ] [ ]
– (all TUBULAR BELLS & other album excerpts, plus singles to 1991)

Oct 93. (c-s) *(VSC 1477)* **MOONLIGHT SHADOW / MOONLIGHT SHADOW (extended version)** [52] [ ]
(cd-s+=) *(VSCDT 1477)* – In The Pool (Instrumental) / Bones (Instrumental).

Nov 93. (c-ep/cd-ep) **THE MIKE OLDFIELD CHRISTMAS EP** [ ] [-]
– In dulci jubilo / Portsmouth / etc.

OLIVER

Born: OLIVER CHAPLIN, Wales, UK. In 1973, OLIVER went into the studio with his brother CHRIS CHAPLIN, who had worked as a surface sound engineer for the BBC (JIMI HENDRIX, etc). His only album to surface was the self-financed, 'STANDING STONE' (1974), a quality piece that mixed progressive blues, psychedelia and folk; the experimental side of PINK FLOYD was how it was described. OLIVER passed up a chance to sign for 'Virgin', reluctant to be part of rat race record industry. Although the album has since been re-released, it is still worth over £200 (£300 if it comes in a blue sleeve).

Recommended: STANDING STONE (*8)

OLIVER CHAPLIN – vocals, instruments

Olive not issued

1974. (lp) *(OL 1)* **STANDING STONE** [ ] [-]
– Freezing cold like an iceburg / Flowers on a hill / Primrose / Orbit your factory / In vain / Cat and the rat. *(re-iss.1992 on 'Tenth Planet'; TP 001) (cd-iss.1995 on 'Wooden Hill'+=; WHCD 001)–* (6 extra).

Yoko ONO

Born: 18 Feb'33, Japan. She moved to New York City at the end of the 40's and was soon writing poems, joining the bohemian set. In the 60's, she branched into art/film making, meeting Beatle JOHN LENNON at one of her exhibitions. After/during his separation from wife Cynthia in 1968, LENNON invited YOKO to spend some time with him, subsequently recording an album together, 'TWO VIRGINS'. Deemed unlistenable by critics, the album's sound was compared to an experimental track on The BEATLES' "White Album", 'REVOLUTION #9'. The record was sold in a brown paper bag, due to the cover shot which showed JOHN and YOKO naked.
in the 60's and met JOHN LENNON in 1968. An UNFINISHED MUSIC NO.2

set, 'LIFE WITH THE LIONS', was issued in 1969. She also married JOHN in Gibraltar on the 20th of March '69, subsequently forming The PLASTIC ONO BAND with her new husband and releasing a number of hit singles (e.g. 'GIVE PEACE A CHANCE', 'COLD TURKEY' and 'INSTANT KARMA!'). During this period, The BEATLES had another massive hit with the LENNON-penned, 'THE BALLAD OF JOHN AND YOKO', detailing their constant harassment by the press. In a short space of time, the pair had become one of music's most high profile couples attracting the attention of the world's media (another dual lp, 'THE WEDDING ALBUM' was released late '69). Early in 1971, she debuted with her first solo album, 'YOKO ONO: PLASTIC ONO BAND', which was soon followed by the extremely weird, 'FLY' album. The latter contained the ode to her son, 'DONT WORRY KYOKO', together with the poignant 'MRS. LENNON'. She combined solo activities with her PLASTIC ONO BAND work and an album, 'SOMETIME IN NEW YORK CITY', was trailed by her part in the success of the festive classic, 'HAPPY XMAS (WAR IS OVER)'. Early in 1973, she released what has come to be regarded as her finest hour, 'APPROXIMATELY INFINITE UNIVERSE' (backed by the band, ELEPHANT'S MEMORY), an uncompromising but starkly beautiful piece of proto-feminist rock. With her previous solo albums only managing to scrape a US Top 200 placing, she delivered her fourth set, 'FEELING THE SPACE', a record that fared even worse. Her domestic life was equally rocky as this point, having split with JOHN early in 1974. They reconciled at the end of the year after she watched one of JOHN's famous last performances. She fell pregnant soon after, giving birth to their son, SEAN, on JOHN's 35th birthday on the 9th of October. After a 5-year hiatus from the music business, both were back with the collaborative single, '(JUST LIKE) STARTING OVER'. A JOHN & YOKO album, 'DOUBLE FANTASY', was issued soon after, featuring a welcome return to form on such tracks as LENNON's 'WOMAN', 'BEAUTIFUL BOY' and her own 'KISS KISS KISS'. Tragically, their comeback was short-lived following LENNON's death at the hands of crazed gunman, Mark Chapman on the 8th of December, 1980. Ironically enough, she had her first taste of success soon after, when she hit the singles chart with 'WALKING ON THIN ICE', a prelude to her cross-Atlantic Top 50 album, 'SEASON OF GLASS'. YOKO released two further albums in the 80's, signing to 'Capitol' in 1995 for her comeback, 'RISING', (O No!).

Recommended: WALKING ON THIN ICE (*6)

YOKO ONO – vocals / **JOHN LENNON** – guitar / **KLAUS VOORMAN** – bass / **RINGO STARR** – drums

Apple Apple

Jan 71. (lp) *(SAPCOR 17) <3373>* **YOKO ONO & THE PLASTIC ONO BAND**
– Why / Why not / Greenfield morning I pushed on empty baby carriage all over the city / Aos / Touch me / Paper shoes. *(cd-iss.Jun97 on 'Rykodisc'; RCD 10414)*

— added DEREK & THE DOMINOES musicians featuring ERIC CLAPTON

Oct 71. (7") *(APPLE 38) <1839>* **MRS. LENNON. / MIDSUMMER NEW YORK**

Nov 71. (d-lp) *(SAPTU 101/2) <3380>* **FLY**
– Midsummer New York / Mindtrain / Mind holes / Don't worry Kyoko / Mrs. Lennon / Hirake / Toilet piece – Unknown / O'wind (body is the scar of your mind) / Air male (tone deaf jam) / Don't count the waves / You / Fly / Telephone piece.

Jan 72. (7") *(APPLE 41) <1846>* **MIND TRAIN. / LISTEN THE SNOW IS FALLING**

— now backed by group ELEPHANT'S MEMORY

Nov 72. (7") *<1853>* **NOW OR NEVER. / MOVE ON FAST** -

Feb 73. (d-lp) *(SAPD 01001) <3399>* **APPROXIMATELY INFINITE UNIVERSE**
– Yang Yang / Death of Samantha / I want my love to rest tonight / What did I do! / Have you seen a horizon lately / Approximately infinite universe / Peter the dealer / Song for John / Cat man / What a bastard the world is / Waiting for the sunrise / I felt like smashing my face in a clear glass window / Winter song / Is winter here to stay? / Kite song / What a mess / Shiranakatta (I didn't know) / Air talk / I have a woman inside my soul / Move on fast / Now or never / Looking over from my hotel window.

Apr 73. (7") *(APPLE 47) <1859>* **DEATH OF SAMANTHA. / YANG YANG** Feb73

— now with numerous session people

Nov 73. (7") *(APPLE 48)* **RUN RUN RUN. / MEN MEN MEN** -

Nov 73. (lp) *(SAPCOR 26) <3412>* **FEELING THE SPACE**
– Growing pain / Yellow girl / Coffin car / Woman of Salem / Run run run / If only / A thousand times yes / Straight talk / Angry young woman / She hits back / Woman power / Men men men.

Dec 73. (7") *<1867>* **WOMAN POWER. / MEN MEN MEN** -

— She reunited in 1980 with JOHN LENNON on the album, 'DOUBLE FANTASY'. Sadly this was their last recording together (see above).

Geffen Geffen

Feb 81. (7") *(K 79202) <49638>* **WALKING ON THIN ICE. / IT HAPPENED** 35 58
(c-s+=) *(K 79202T)* – Hard times are over.

Jun 81. (lp/c) *(K/K4 99164) <2004>* **SEASON OF GLASS** 47 49
– Goodbye sadness / Mindweaver / Even when you're far away / Nobody sees me like you do / Turn of the wheel / Dogtown / Silver horse / I don't know why / Extension 33 / No, no, no / Will you touch me? / She gets down on her knees / Toyboat / Mother of the universe.

Aug 81. (7") *<2224>* **NO, NO, NO. / WILL YOU TOUCH ME?** -

Polydor Polydor

Feb 82. (7"/12") **NEVER SAY GOODBYE. / LONELINESS** -

Dec 82. (7") *(POSP 541)* **MY MAN. / LET THE TEARS DRY** Nov82

Dec 82. (lp/c) *(POLD/+C 5073) <6364>* **IT'S ALRIGHT (I SEE RAINBOWS)** 98
– My man / Never say goodbye / Spec of dust / Loneliness / Tomorrow may never come / It's alright / Wake up / Let the tears dry / Dream love / I see rainbows.

— Early in 1984, another JOHN & YOKO posthumous album, 'MILK AND HONEY', was released, hitting UK No.3 + US No.11.

Nov 85. (7") **HELL IN PARADISE. / ('A'instrumental)**

Nov 85. (lp/c/cd) *(827 530-1/-4/-2)* **STAR PEACE**
– Hell in Paradise / I love all of me / Children power / Rainbow revolution / King of the zoo / Remember raven / Cape Clear / Sky people / You and I / It's gonna rain (living on tiptoe) / Star peace / I love you, Earth.

Capitol Capitol

Jan 96. (cd) *(CDEST 2276)* **RISING**
– Warzone / Wouldnit / Ask the dragon / New York woman / Talking to the universe / Turned the corner / I'm dying / Where do we go from here / Kurushi / Will I / Rising / Goodbye, my love / Revelations.

– compilations, etc. –

on 'Rykodisc' unless mentioned otherwise

Mar 92. (6xcd-box) *<(RCD 102 24/29)>* **ONOBOX**

May 92. (cd/c) *<(RCD/RAC 20230)>* **WALKING ON THIN ICE** (best of above boxed set)
– Walking on thin ice / Even when you're far away / Kiss kiss kiss / Nobody sees me like you do / Yang yang / No no no / Death of Samantha / Mind weaver / You're the one / Spec of dust / Midsummer New York / Don't be scared / Sleepless nights / Kite song / She gets down on her knees / Give me something / Hell in Paradise / Woman power / O'oh. *(cd re-iss.Mar97; same)*

ONYX

Formed: Wadebridge, Cornwall, England . . . late '66 originally as The RICK AND THE HAYSEEDS. A popular live attraction, they were snapped up by 'Pye' records, who released their debut 45, 'YOU'VE GOTTA BE WITH ME'. It was played on Radio One but found no glory, like the rest of their output, which was mainly sugar-coated psychedelia. After a brief change of their moniker to SALAMANDER in 1970, the group returned with two more progressive efforts.

Recommended: the third single, which is quite rare (£40)

TONY PRIEST – vocals / **ALAN HODGE** – guitar / **STEVE COTTON** – organ / **DICK BLAND** – bass / **ROGER DELL** – drums

Pye not issued

Mar 68. (7") *(7N 17477)* **YOU'VE GOTTA BE WITH ME. / IT'S ALL PUT ON** -

Nov 68. (7") *(7N 17622)* **MY SON JOHN. / STEP BY STEP** -

Jun 69. (7") *(7N 17668)* **TAMARIS KHAN. / SO SAD INSIDE** -

C.B.S. not issued

Nov 69. (7") *(4635)* **TIME OFF. / MOVIN' IN** -

Jul 70. (7"; as SALAMANDER) *(5102)* **CRYSTAL BALL. / BILLY** -

Parlophone not issued

Feb 71. (7") *(R 5888)* **OUR HOUSE. / AIR** -

May 71. (7") *(R 5906)* **THE NEXT STOP IS MINE. / WHAT'S THAT YOU SAY** -

— split after above

OPAL BUTTERFLY

Formed: London, England ... 1968 by RICHARD BARDEY, TOM DOHERTY and SIMON KING. They released two 45's for 'CBS' (now quite collectable), the second being a WHO cover, 'MARY ANNE WITH THE SHAKEY HAND', before employing the services of LEMMY and RAY MAJOR. A third single, 'YOU'RE A GROUPIE GIRL', was also featured in the late 1969 film, 'Groupie Girl'. The group were basically another psychedelic stepping stone for HAWKWIND bound LEMMY.

Recommended: no albums, but singles are okay.

ALAN LOVE + ROBBIE MILNE – vocals + guitar / **TOM DOHERTY** – guitar, bass / **RICHARD BARDLEY** – bass / **SIMON KING** – drums

C.B.S. not issued

Jan 69. (7") *(3576)* **BEAUTIFUL BIEGE. / SPEAK UP** -

Dec 69. (7") *(3921)* **MARY ANNE WITH THE SHAKEY HAND. / MY GYRATION OR?** -

— **LEMMY** (b. IAN KILMINSTER) – guitar, vocals, repl. LOVE

— **RAY MAJOR** – guitar, vocals, repl. MILNE

Polydor not issued

Aug 70. (2058 041) **YOU'RE A GROUPIE GIRL. / GIGGING SONG** -

— RAY MAJOR joined HACKENSACK, and later joined MOTT THE HOOPLE

— split when LEMMY joined HAWKWIND

OPEN MIND

Formed: London, England ... 1968 by TERRY MARTIN and MIKE BRANCACCIO. Signing to 'Philips' in 1969, they released two singles (the excellent 'MAGIC POTION'; now worth over £100), marking them out as one of the great lost guitar-picking psychedelic bands of that era. Maybe it was a couple of years too late, or even two years ahead, to gain any respect from the buying public. Expect to pay over £300 for this superb piece, although to listen to it, just buy its much cheaper re-issue.

Recommended: THE OPEN MIND (*9)

MIKE BRANCACCIO – vocals, guitar / **TERRY MARTIN** – guitar, vocals / **TIMOTHY DU FEU** – bass / **PHIL FOX** – drums

Philips not issued

May 69. (7") *(BF 1790)* **HORSES AND CHARIOTS. / BEFORE MY TIME**

Jul 69. (lp) *(SBL 7893)* **THE OPEN MIND**
– Dear Louise / Try another day / I feel the same way too / My mind cries / Can't you see / Thor the thunder god / Horses and chariots / Before my time / Free as the breeze / Girl I'm so alone / Soul and my will / Falling again. *(re-iss.Apr86 on 'Antar'+=; ANTAR 2)*– Magic potion / Cast a spell.

Aug 69. (7") *(BF 1805)* **MAGIC POTION. / CAST A SPELL**

— disappeared from sight after above

ORANGE PEEL

Formed: Germany ... 1969 by 17-year old CURT CRESS, plus PETER BISCHOF, LESLIE LINK, HEINI MONN and RALPH WILTHEISS. Unusually for a German progressive band of their ilk, they released a one-off single in 1969, 'I GOT NO TIME'. The self-titled album was delivered the following year and contained four tracks of heavy, rough'n'ready prog-rock which were almost wholly instrumental. Most of the members went on to further projects as detailed below.

Recommended: ORANGE PEEL (*7)

PETER BISCHOF – vocals, percussion / **CURT CRESS** – drums, percussion / **LESLIE LINK** – guitar / **HEINI MOHN** – bass / **RALPH WILTHEISS** – organ

Admiral not issued

1969. (7") *(AD 1136)* **I GOT NO TIME. / SEARCHING FOR A PLACE TO HIDE** German

Bellaphon not issued

1970. (lp) *(BLPS 19036)* **ORANGE PEEL** German
– You can't change them all / Faces that I used to know / Tobacco road / We still try to change.

— peeled off after above. MOHN joined EPSILON, while CRESS then BISCHOF joined jazz/funk rock outfit EMERGENCY. CRESS went onto PASSPORT, ATLANTIS and a few others.

ORGANISATION (see under ⇒ KRAFTWERK)

ORIGINAL DOWNTOWN SYNCOPATORS (see under ⇒ GEESIN, Ron)

OTHER HALF

Formed: Los Angeles, California, USA ... 1967 by RANDY HOLDEN (formerly of The SONS OF ADAM), alongside CRAIG TARWATER and MIKE PORT. Three 45's and an album appeared on the low-key 'Acta' label, leading to a deal with 'GNP Crescendo'. The resulting 45, 'MR. PHARMICIST' was an excellent psyche/garage song, later covered by UK indie act The FALL. However, after it undeservedly flopped, they bowed out. Note: There was another OTHER HALF from New Haven, Connecticut, who released an eponymous privately pressed lp.

Recommended: THE OTHER HALF (*6) / MR. PHARMICIST (*7)

RANDY HOLDEN – guitar (ex-SONS OF ADAM) / **CRAIG TARWATER** – guitar (ex-SONS OF ADAM) / **MIKE PORT** – bass (ex-SONS OF ADAM) / **JEFF NOWLEN** – drums

not issued Acta

1967. (7") *<801>* **WONDERFUL DAY. / FLIGHT OF THE DRAGON LADY**

1967. (7") *<806>* **NO DOUBT ABOUT IT. / I NEED YOU**

— new members **J. WESTEN, BLOWN & WOODY** repl. CRAIG + MIKE

1968. (7") *<825>* **OZ LEE EAVES DROPS. / MORNING FIRE**

1968. (lp) *<38004>* **THE OTHER HALF**
(re-iss.1982 on 'Line' Germany; LMS 3024)

not issued GNP Crescendo

1968. (7") *<378>* **MR. PHARMACIST. / I'VE COME SO FAR**

— when RANDY joined BLUE CHEER, the other half of four-fifths! fell apart

– compilations, etc. –

1980's. Eva; (lp) *(12003)* **MR. PHARMACIST & THE LOST SINGLES** French
– (intro) / Feathered fish / Flight of the dragon lady / Wonderful day / I need you / Oz Lee eaves drops / I've come so far / Mr. Pharmacist / Bad day / Morning fire / What can I do for you, first half / What can I do for you, the other half / No doubt about it / It's too hard (without you) / I know. *(cd-iss.May94; 842093)*

OUTCASTS

Formed: San Antonio, Texas ... 1965 by JIM CARSTEN, DENNY TURNER, EUGENE CARLSON, RICKY WRIGHT and JIM RYAN. Their debut was best forgotten, especially when their second, 'I'M IN PITTSBURGH (AND IT'S RAINING)' became one of the best garage/psych songs of its time. More nuggets were to follow as well as some inspired covers (i.e. 'ROUTE 66' and 'SMOKESTACK LIGHTNIN'). • **Trivia:** There were also a handful of other US bands of the same name, who released singles during this period.

Recommended: the 'Askel' singles.

JIM CARSTEN / DENNY TURNER / EUGENE CARLSON / RICKY WRIGHT / JIM RYAN

not issued Outcast

1965. (7") *<6865>* **NOTHING EVER COMES EASY. / ORIENTAL EXPRESS**

— also joined at times by **LINDA PIERRE KING** – vocals

not issued Askel

1966. (7") *<102>* **I'M IN PITTSBURGH (AND IT'S RAINING). / PRICE OF VICTORY**

1966. (7") *<104>* **I'LL SET YOU FREE. / EVERYDAY**

1966. (7") *<107>* **ROUTE 66. / EVERYDAY**

not issued Gallant

1967. (7") *<101>* **1523 BLAIR. / SMOKESTACK LIGHTNING**

— split after above, although they did re-surface a decade later when they backed The KICKS on their version of 'I'M IN PITTSBURGH'.

OUT OF FOCUS

Formed: Munich, Germany . . .1969 and comprising musicians as detailed below. Signed to the 'Kuckuck' label, the band emerged in 1970 with their debut album, 'WAKE UP'. Generally held to be a classic of the German progressive genre, it was notable for its innovative use of rhythm and the breathtaking dexterity of the musicians. The German sense of humour was also lurking in the lyrics, NEUMULLER'S distinctive vocal giving the whole thing a surreal feel. The self-titled follow-up album was released in 1972 and was more experimental, many songs featuring hypnotic, drawn out instrumental passages. Even more far reaching in its vision was 1972's double album, 'FOUR LETTER MONDAY AFTERNOON', which added such instrumental exotica as bassoon and trumpet. The band split after this mammoth opus with DRECHSLER going off to join EMBRYO, later releasing an album with the group KONTRAST.

Recommended: WAKE UP (*8) / OUT OF FOCUS (*6) / FOUR LETTER MONDAY AFTERNOON (*7)

MORAN NEUMULLER – vocals, sax, flute / **REMIGIUS DRECHSLER** – guitar / **HENNES HERING** – organ, piano / **STEPHAN WISHEU** – bass / **KLAUS SPORI** – drums

Kuckuck not issued

1971. (lp) *(2375 006)* **WAKE UP** German
– See how a white negro flies / God save the queen, cried Jesus / Hey John / No name / World's end / Dark, darker. *(re-iss.1990; 11006-1) (cd-iss.1992 on 'Ohrwashl')*

1971. (lp) *(2375 010)* **OUT OF FOCUS** German
– What can a poor boy do (but to be a streetfighting man) / It's your life / Whispering / Blue Sunday morning / Fly bird fly / Television programm. *(cd-iss.1992 on 'Ohrwashl')*

— added **PETER DECHANT** – acoustic guitar / **INGO SCHMIDT NEUHAUS** – saxophones / **MICHAEL THATCHER** – organ / **JIMMY POTIVKA** – trumpet / **HERMANN BREUER** – bassoon / **ROMAN LANGHANS** – organ

1972. (d-lp) *(2640 101)* **FOUR LETTER MONDAY AFTERNOON** German
– L.S.B. / Tsajama / Black card / Where have you been / Huchen 55, A-55, D. *(cd-iss.1992 on 'Ohrwashl')*

— split in 1973. REMIGIUS was a short-time member of EMBRYO, and later released an album with KONTRAST.

OXFORD CIRCLE

Formed: Sacramento, California, USA . . . 1966 by DEHNER PATTEN, JIM KEYLOR and PAUL WHALEY, who were managed by GARY YODER. They signed a one-off deal to 'World United' records (run by The NEW BREED), securing at least two and a half minutes worth of greatness with the issue of the marvellous psyche/garage 45, 'FOOLISH WOMAN'. It led to a series of gigs supporting the likes of GRATEFUL DEAD, although the band had a limited shelf-life, YODER and PATTEN stepping on to KAK (oops!). With another two talented musicians; JOSEPH DAMRELL and CHRISTOPHER LOCKHEAD, they signed to 'Epic', releasing a flop 45, 'EVERYTHING'S CHANGING'. This single subsequently featured on their promising, eponymous psychedelic album. It has since become very rare, due to some great tracks, 'I'VE GOT TIME', 'DISBELIEVIN' and the hippy/space-rock of 'ELECTRIC SAILOR'.

Recommended: the single / KAK (*6)

DEHNER PATTEN – guitar / **JIM KEYLOR** – bass / **PAUL WHALEY** – drums

not issued World United

Oct 66. (7") *<1002>* **FOOLISH WOMAN. / MIND DESTRUCTION**

— split when KEYLOR joined The FAMILY TREE and ROXY, WHALEY joined ROXY.

KAK

GARY YODER – vocals, guitars / **DEHNER PATTEN** – lead guitar, vocals / **JOSEPH DAMRELL** – bass, sitar, vocals / **CHRISTOPHER LOCKHEAD** – drums, tabla, mouth organ, percussion

not issued Epic

Jan 69. (7") *<10383>* **EVERYTHING'S CHANGING. / (part 2)**

May 69. (7") *<10446>* **I'VE GOT TIME. / DISBELIEVIN'**

Jun 69. (lp) *<BN 26429>* **KAK**
– HCO 97658 / Everything's changing / Electric sailor / Disbelievin' / I've got time / Flowing by / Bryte 'n clear day / Trieulogy: Golgotha – Mirage – Rain / Lemonaide kid.

— split when YODER moved on to BLUE CHEER

PACIFIC DRIFT

Formed: London, England . . . 1969, as jazzy, progressive outfit, SPONGE, by BARRY REYNOLDS, LAWRENCE ARENDES, GRAHAM HARROP and BRIAN SHAPMAN. They had previously backed up pop singer, DAVE BERRY, on his single, 'Huma Luma'. PACIFIC DRIFT's debut 45, 'WATER WOMAN', a cover of a SPIRIT / JAY FERGUSON song, was a nice piece of psychedelia, although they took a more bluesy, progressive pop-trip with their album, 'FEELIN' FREE'. It used a few WILLIAM BLAKE poems, 'GARDEN OF LOVE' and 'GRAINS OF SAND', side by side with other creative melodies.

Recommended: FEELIN' FREE (*6)

BRIAN SHAPMAN – keyboards, vocals / **BARRY REYNOLDS** – guitar, vocals / **GRAHAM HARROP** – guitar, bass / **LAWRENCE ARDENES** – drums, percussion, vocals (ex-WIMPLE WINCH, ex-JUST FOUR MEN)

Deram Nova | not issued

Jan 70. (lp) *(SND 13)* **FEELIN' FREE** ☐ -
– Plaster caster's U.S.A. / Tomorrow morning brings / Feelin' free / Just another girl / Garden of love / Norman / Grain of sand / Greta the legend / Going slow / God has given me / Happy days.

Deram | Deram

Jun 70. (7") *(DM 304)* <85063> **WATER WOMAN. / YES YOU DO** ☐ ☐

— disappeared from sight after above

PAINTED FACES

Formed: Fort Myers, Florida, USA . . . 1966, by New Orleans born BRUCE MORFORD and JERRY TURANO. They were a mysterious act, combining frat-rock garage with hints of British beat, although their first 45, the classic 'ANXIOUS COLOR', was full of LSD connotations, much loved by a small cult following. Two further singles in 1968 were also flops; they subsequently retired at a young age. • **Trivia:** The BIRDMEN OF ALKATRAZ did a cover of 'ANXIOUS COLOR'.

Recommended: the debut single

BRUCE MORFORD – bass / **JERRY TURANO** – guitar / + 2

not issued | Manhatten

Jul 67. (7") <803> **ANXIOUS COLOR. / THINGS WE SEE** - ☐
Jan 68. (7") <811> **I THINK I'M GOING MAD. / I LOST YOU IN MY MIND** - ☐
May 68. (7") <818> **DON'T SAY SHE'S GONE. / IN THE HEAT OF THE NIGHT** - ☐

— split and disappeared from sight

PANAMA LTD JUG BAND

Formed: England. Their eponymous debut album was produced by none other than a pre-punk JOHN PEEL. A quirky hybrid of folk/jug band stylings and progressive rock, the album had a unique sound. By the release of 1970's 'INDIAN SUMMER', the group had shortened their name to PANAMA LTD., dropping the jug influence and adopting a sound more akin to the avante-rock of CAPTAIN BEEFHEART. The album sold poorly, however, and the band split soon after.

Recommended: INDIAN SUMMER (*6)

LIZ HANNS – vocals / **GARY COMPTON, RON NEEDS, BRIAN STRACHAN + DENNIS PARKER** – instruments

Harvest | not issued

Sep 69. (lp) *(SHVL 753)* **PANAMA LTD JUG BAND** ☐ -
– 38 plug / Going to Germany / Canned heat / Viola Lee / Alabamy bound / Overseas stomp / Round and round / Cocaine habit / Wilcat squall / Don't you ease me in / Rich girl / Sundown / Jailhouse / Guitar king / Railroad.

Nov 69. (7") *(HAR 5010)* **LADY OF SHALLOTT. / FUTURE BLUES** ☐ -

— **ANNE MATTHEWS** – vocals, repl. HANN

Jul 70. (7"; as PANAMA LTD.) *(HAR 5022)* **ROUND AND ROUND. / ROTTING WOODEN IN A WHITE COLLARS GRAVE** ☐ -
Sep 70. (lp; as PANAMA LTD.) *(SHVL 779)* **INDIAN SUMMER** ☐ -
– Moonshine / Set me free / Citadel chapters / The woman I love / Dangle wind / Eastern man / Indian summer / Future / Darkness brings / Laughing.

— Split after above all retired except HOZZELL who formed SCREW

PANCAKE

Formed: Germany ... 1974 as the brainchild of WALTER NEGELE. Recruiting HAMPY NERLICH, TOMMY METZGER, WERNER BAUER and GUNTHER KONOPIK (replaced RAINER ROHM), the band recorded their debut album, 'ROXY ELEPHANT' (1976). The record showcased the band's commercially orientated progressive guitar sound which drew comparisons with similar 70's acts of the same ilk, both German and English. PANCAKE were subsequently off the menu for a short while until NEGELE created a new recipe with different ingredients, courtesy of a returning RAINER ROHM, HEINZ BERTSCH, PETER INDRAK and HANS DERER. 'OUT OF THE ASHES' (1977) introduced a more poppy, synth-driven sound while 1979's third and final helping of PANCAKE was the similarly synth-orientated 'NO ILLUSIONS' and was recorded using yet another line-up, NEGELE and DERER recruiting BIGGY ZMIERCZAK, RALF SCHIEBE and ULI FRANK.

Recommended: ROXY ELEPHANT (*8) / OUT OF THE ASHES (*6) / NO ILLUSIONS (*6)

WALTER NEGELE – guitar / **TOMMY METZGER** – guitar, vocals / **HAMPY NERLICH** – vocals / **WERNER BAUER** – bass / **GUNTHER KONOPIK** – drums; repl. RAINER ROHM

Private Press | not issued

Feb 76. (lp) *(Z 33000)* **ROXY ELEPHANT** - - German
– Heartfire / Roltreppe / Aeroplane / End of the day / Remember / Long life / Harmony / Roxy elephant. *(re-press.1976 on 'Pancake'; PCR 1001RE) (re-iss.1976 on 'Offers'; OMP 7602) (re-iss.1978 on 'Blubber Lips'; BL 804)*

— split for a while until **NEGELE** re-formed with returning **RAINER ROHM** – vocals, percussion / + new **HEINZ BERTSCH** – keyboards, synthesizer / **PETER INDRAK** – bass, violin / **HANS DERER** – drums, percussion

Blubber Lips | not issued

1978. (lp) *(BL 801)* **OUT OF THE ASHES** - - German
– Painted rush-hour / Arctic Ocean: Fool's nightmare – Back in the reality / Cakey funk / Rainbow suite: Introduction – Colours in the rain – Winds of Thor – The new day – Gone with the wind / Out of the ashes.

— **NEGELE + DERER** assembled a new line-up (yet again!); **BIGGY ZMIERCZAK** (b. Poland) – vocals / **RALF SCHEIBE** – bass, vocals / **ULI FRANK** – keyboards, vocals

1979. (lp) *(BL 809)* **NO ILLUSIONS** - - German
– Just miss your smile / Fire and rain song / Dream-Delta-Land (part 1 &2) / No touch of illusions / Autumn leaves / I try.

— disappeared after above

PARAMOUNTS (see under ⇒ PROCOL HARUM)

PARLIAMENT (see under ⇒ CLINTON, George)

PARZIVAL

Formed: Bremen, Germany ... 1971 by LOTHAR SIEMS, THOMAS OLIVER and WALTER QUINTUS. The former two had played together in mid-60's outfit, The CHAMBERLAINS, before joining Walter's QUINTUS QUARTET. Adopting the PARZIVAL moniker in 1971, they released their debut album, 'LEGEND', the same year. An enduring folk-rock record that included English folk revival bands among its references, the album was embellished by a wistful string section. A one-off single followed in 1972, 'ONE DAY', while their second and final album, the neo-classical/folk 'BA-ROCK' (ouch!) hit the shelves in 1973. Although a second cellist augmented the line-up for this record, the overall sound was more rock than folk.

Recommended: LEGEND (*7) / BA-ROCK (*7)

LOTHAR SIEMS – guitar, vocals / **WALTER QUINTUS** – violin, bass, organ, piano / **THOMAS OLIVER** – drums, vocals, percussion / guests **MATTHIAS MULLER-MENCHENS** – flute, piano / **JOACHIM REICHHOLD** – cello / **HANS JASPERS** – viola

Telefunken | not issued

1971. (lp) *(SLE 14635)* **LEGEND** - - German
– Marshy legend / Resignation / 8 years later / Senseless No.6 / Wall bungalow / Empty land / Groovy inside.

— added **WALTER V. SEYDLITZ** – cello / plus guests **MATTHIAS** (as MAT ME MILLER) + **HARALD KONIETKO** – bass, vocals

1972. (7") **ONE DAY. / SOULS MARRIED TO THE WIND** - - German
1972. (lp) *(SLE 14685)* **BA-ROCK** - - German
– Stories / Black train / Mrs. Virgin / Frank supper / Scarlet horses / It's a pity / Thought / Paradise.

— split after above

- compilations, etc. -

1975. (d-lp) *Nova; (6.28337)* **A GERMAN ROCK LEGEND** (both albums) [-] [-] German
1981. (lp) *Telefunken; (6.24610AG)* **ROCK IN DEUTSCHLAND VOL.9** [-] [-] German

Mike PATTO

Born: MICHAEL PATRICK McGRATH, 22 Sep'42, Glasgow, Scotland. In 1966, he joined London outfit The BO STREET RUNNERS, debuting as MIKE 'Too Much' PATTO on their (Beatles-penned) fourth single, 'DRIVE MY CAR' (Columbia; DB 7901). He subsequently went on to a short-lived stint with CHICAGO LINE, before forming the Southport-based, psychedelic outfit, TIMEBOX. The band released a series of singles on 'Deram' (one of them, 'BEGGIN'', was a FOUR SEASONS cover), before evolving into the more musically serious PATTO. Their self-titled debut was an accomplished set of jazz-rock experimentation, which failed to achieve any commercial success. After a further two albums, PATTO joined SPOOKY TOOTH for their 'MIRROR' (1974) album before forming BOXER. In 1977, he joined HINKLEY'S HEROES, although he subsequently died from throat cancer a couple of years later. • **Songwriters:** DON'T MAKE PROMISES (Tim Hardin) / A WOMAN THAT'S WAITING (Ivan Zagni / Tim Hinkley) / etc. • **Trivia:** Debut single worth over £45. All PATTO lp's are worth over £25; the highest being 'HOLD YOUR FIRE' at £100.

Recommended: HOLD YOUR FIRE (*6)

CHICAGO LINE

MIKE PATTO – vocals (ex-BREAKAWAYS) / **TIM HINKLEY** – organ (ex-BO STREET RUNNERS) / **LOUIS CENNAMO** – bass / **MIKE FALLANA** – sax (ex-GEORGIE FAME & THE BLUE FLAMES) / **VIV PRINCE** – drums (ex-PRETTY THINGS)

Philips | not issued

1966. (7") *(BF 1488)* **JUMP BACK. / SHIMMY SHIMMY KO KO BOP** [ ] [-]

MIKE PATTO

Columbia | not issued

Dec 66. (7") *(DB 8091)* **CAN'T STOP TALKING 'BOUT MY BABY. / LOVE** [ ] [-]

TIMEBOX

— not with PATTO at this stage / line-up; **OLLIE HALSALL** – guitar, vibes / **CHRIS HOLMES** – keyboards / **CLIVE GRIFFITHS** – bass / **JOHN HALSEY** – drums (ex-FENDER'S ORIOLES)

Piccadilly | not issued

Feb 67. (7") *(7N 35369)* **I'LL ALWAYS LOVE YOU. / SAVE YOUR LOVE** [ ] [-]
Apr 67. (7") *(7N 35379)* **SOUL SAUCE. / I WISH I COULD JERK LIKE MY UNCLE CYRIL** [ ] [-]

— added **MIKE PATTO** – vocals

Deram | Deram

Oct 67. (7") *(DM 153)* **DON'T MAKE PROMISES. / WALKING THROUGH THE STREETS OF MY MIND** [ ] [ ]
Jun 68. (7") *(DM 194)* **BEGGIN'. / A WOMAN THAT'S WAITING** [38] [ ]
Nov 68. (7") *(DM 219)* **GIRL DON'T MAKE ME WAIT. / GONE IS THE SAD MAN** [ ] [ ]
Mar 69. (7") *(DM 246)* **BAKED JAM ROLL IN YOUR EYE. / POOR LITTLE HEARTBREAKER** [ ] [ ]
Oct 69. (7") *(DM 271)* **YELLOW VAN. / YOU'VE GOT THE CHANCE** [ ] [ ]

PATTO

PATTO, HALSALL, GRIFFITHS + HALSEY

Vertigo | not issued

Dec 70. (lp) *(6360 016)* **PATTO** [ ] [ ]
– The man / Hold me back / Time to die / Red glow / San Antone / Government man / Money bag / Sittin' back easy. *(cd-iss.1990's on 'Repertoire'; REP 4446)*

— added briefly **BERNIE HOLLAND** – guitar (he left to join JODY GRIND)

Dec 71. (lp) *(6360 032)* **HOLD YOUR FIRE** [ ] [ ]
– Hold your fire / You, you point your finger / How's your father / See you at the dance tonight / Give it all away / Air raid shelter / Tell me where you've been / Magic door. *(cd-iss.1990's on 'Repertoire'; REP 4360)*

Island | Island

Oct 72. (lp) *(ILPS 9210)* **ROLL 'EM SMOKE 'EM PUT ANOTHER LINE OUT** [ ] [ ]
– Flat footed woman / Singing the blues on reds / Mummy / Loud green song / Turn turtle / I got rhythm / Peter Abraham / Cap'n P and the Atto's (sea biscuits part 1 & 2).
Dec 72. (7") *<1208>* **SINGING THE BLUES ON REDS. / MUMMY** [-] [ ]

— Disbanded and HALSALL joined TEMPEST. PATTO joined SPOOKY TOOTH for one album 'THE MIRROR' (1974).

Good Ear | not issued

Aug 74. (7"; MIKE PATTO) *(EAR 106)* **SITTING IN THE PARK. / GET UP & DIG IT** [ ] [-]

BOXER

MIKE PATTO – vocals, keyboards / **OLLIE HALSALL** – guitar, keyboards / **KEITH ELLIS** – bass (ex-KOOBAS, ex-VAN DER GRAAF GENERATOR) / **TONY NEWMAN** – drums (ex-JEFF BECK, ex-MAY BLITZ)

Virgin | Virgin

Jan 76. (7") *(VS 135)* **ALL THE TIME IN THE WORLD. / DON'T WAIT** [ ] [-]
Feb 76. (lp) *(V 2049)* **BELOW THE BELT** [ ] [ ]
– Shooting star / All the time in the world / California calling / Hip kiss / More than meets the eye / Waiting for a miracle / Loony Ali / Save me / Gonna work out fine / Town drunk.
Apr 76. (7") *<9506>* **ALL THE TIME IN THE WORLD. / SAVE ME** [-] [ ]

— added guest (at first) **CHRIS STAINTON** – keyboards (ex-GREASE BAND)

Oct 76. (lp; w-drawn) *(V 2073)* **BLOODLETTING** [-] [-]
– Hey bulldog / The blizzard / Rich man's daughter / Big city fever / The loner / Why pick on me / Love has got me / Dinah-Low / Teachers.
Dec 76. (7") *<9509>* **HEY BULLDOG. / LOONY ALI** [-] [ ]

— **PATTO + STAINTON** recruited **ADRIAN FISHER** – guitar (ex-SPARKS) / **TIM BOGART** – bass, vocals (ex-VANILLA FUDGE) / **EDDIE TUDURI** – drums (they repl. HALSALL; who joined KEVIN AYERS / ELLIS + NEWMAN)

Epic

Jul 77. (lp) *(EPC 82151)* **ABSOLUTELY** [ ] [ ]
– Fool in love / Red light flyer / Big Lucy / No reply / Can't stand what you do / As God's my judge / Rich man's daughter / Everybody's a star / Hand on your heart. *(free 7") (SHOTS 1)* – NO REPLY
Aug 77. (7") *(EPC 5540)* **EVERYBODY'S STAR. / CAN'T STAND WHAT YOU DO** [ ] [ ]

— PATTO split band and joined HINKLEY'S HEROES, but sadly he was diagnosed with terminal throat cancer and died 4 March 1979.

- compilations, etc. -

Oct 95. (cd) *Mercury; (58 696-2)* **SENSE OF THE ABSURD** [ ] [-]

PEANUT BUTTER CONSPIRACY

Formed: California, USA . . . . 1966 out of the group, The ASHES, by the group's songwriters, AL BRACKETT and JOHN MERRILL. The aforementioned outfit, released two singles and an eponymous album, before changing their group name and relocating to San Francisco. They then found vocalist, SANDI ROBINSON, releasing their debut album, 'THE PEANUT BUTTER CONSPIRACY IS SPREADING' in 1967. Boasting a slick production (courtesy of GARY USHER), with some fine orchestration, it was warmly received by the critics, although it only managed to scrape into the US Top 200. ROBINSON's dreamy vocal chords were highlighted on the trippy, flower-power tune, 'WHY DID I GET SO HIGH?'. A disappointing second set, 'THE GREAT CONSPIRACY', was followed in 1969 by 'FOR CHILDREN OF ALL AGES', although they disbanded soon after.

Recommended: THE PEANUT BUTTER CONSPIRACY IS SPREADING (*7)

ASHES

PAT TAYLOR – vocals / **JOHN MERRILL** – guitar / **AL BRACKETT** – bass / **JIM VOIGHT** – drums; who repl. SPENCER DRYDEN, who joined JEFFERSON AIRPLANE

not issued | Vault

1966. (7") *<924>* **IS THERE ANYTHING I CAN DO? / EVERY LITTLE PRAYER** [-] [ ]
Oct 66. (lp) *<125>* **THE ASHES** [-] [ ]
Dec 66. (7") *<936>* **DARK ON YOU NOW. / ROSES GONE** [-] [ ]

PEANUT BUTTER CONSPIRACY

— **BARBARA ROBINSON** – vocals + **LANCE FENT** – harmonica, guitar; repl. TAYLOR

not issued | Vault

Nov 66. (7") *<933>* **TIME IS AFTER YOU. / FLOATING DREAM** [-] [ ]

C.B.S. | Columbia

May 67. (lp) *<9454>* **THE PEANUT BUTTER CONSPIRACY IS SPREADING** [-] [ ]
– It's a happening thing / Then came love / You can't be found / Twice is life / Second hand man / Why did I get so high / Dark on you now / Market place / You should know / Most up till now / You took too much.
Jul 67. (7") *(CBS 2981) <43985>* **IT'S A HAPPENING THING. / TWICE IS LIFE** [ ] [93] Feb67
Jul 67. (7") *<44063>* **DARK ON YOU KNOW. / THEN CAME LOVE** [-] [ ]

— **BILL WOLF** – guitar, harmonica, repl. FENT

Jun 68. (7") *(CBS 3543) <44356>* **TURN ON A FRIEND. / CAPTAIN SANDWICH** [ ] [ ] Jan68
Jun 68. (lp) *(63277) <9590>* **THE GREAT CONSPIRACY** [ ] [ ] Feb68
– Turn on a friend / Lonely leaf / Pleasure / Too many do / Living, loving life / Invasion of the poppy people / Captain living dream / Ecstasy / Time is after you / Wonderment.
Aug 68. (7") *<44667>* **I'M A FOOL. / IT'S SO HARD** [-] [ ]

— **RALPH SCHUCKETT** – keyboards / **PETE McQUEEN + MICHAEL STEVENS** – drums, repl. WOLF + VOIGHT

London | Challenge

Feb 69. (lp) *<2000>* **FOR CHILDREN ALL AGES** [-] [ ]
– Now / The loudness of your silence / It's alright / What did I do wrong / Out in the cold again / Back in L.A. / Gonna get you home / Have a little faith / Try again / Think.
Oct 69. (7") *(HLH 10290) <500>* **BACK IN L.A. / HAVE A LITTLE FAITH** [ ] [ ]

— Split the scene after above.

- others, etc. -

1971. (7"; as ASHES) *Vault; <973>* **HOMEWARD BOUND. / SLEEPING SERENADE** [-] [ ]

PEARLS BEFORE SWINE

Formed: New York City, New York, USA . . . mid 60's, by TOM RAPP and a bunch of unknown surf/pop musicians. RAPP's only claim to fame was finishing above BOB DYLAN in a local talent contest. Signed to the avant-garde 'ESP' label (home to FUGS), they cut two albums of folky-pop psychedelia, 'ONE NATION UNDERGROUND' (1967) and 'BALAKLAVA' (1968), the former featuring a cover of SAXIE DOWELL's 'PLAYMATE', the latter a version of LEONARD COHEN's 'SUZANNE'. The records were characterised by flowing arrangements, influenced in their own by JACQUES BREL. Switching to 'Reprise' the following year, they hit the high spot of No.200 with their third album, 'THESE THINGS TOO'. They subsequently recorded a few dismal albums in Nashville with session men from AREA CODE 615, although it was clear RAPP wasn't making the grade and he "dropped out". • **Songwriters:** Most by RAPP, some with other members.

Recommended: ONE NATION UNDERGROUND (*7)

TOM RAPP – vocals, guitars / **WAYNE HARLEY** – autoharp, banjo, mandolin, vibraphone, harmony / **LANE LEDERER** – bass, guitar, English horn, percussion / **ROGER CRISSINGER** – organ

Fontana E.S.P.

1967. (7") <4554> **DROP OUT! / MORNING SUN**

1967. (lp) <*ESPS 1054*> **ONE NATION UNDERGROUND**
– Another time / Playmate / Ballad of an amber lady / (Oh dear) Miss Morse / Drop out! / Morning song / Regions of May / Uncle John / I shall not care / The surrealist waltz. *(UK-iss.1968; STL 5505) (re-iss.Apr97 on 'Get Back'; GET 1008)*

—— **JIM BOHANNON** – organ, piano repl. CRISSINGER.

Jul 69. (lp) *(STL 5503)* <*ESPS 1075*> **BALAKLAVA** Dec68
– Trumpeter Landfrey / Translucent carriages / Images of April / There was a man / I saw the world / Guardian angels / Suzanne / Lepers and roses / Florence Nightingale / Ring thing. *(re-iss.Apr97 on 'Get Back'; GET 1010)*

—— **RAPP + HARLEY** added **ELIZABETH NOYES** – vocals / **JIM FAIRS** – guitars / **GRADY TATE** – drums / **BILL SALTER** – bass / **RICHARD GREENE** – violin / **ERIC GALE** – guitar / plus members of AREA CODE 615

Reprise Reprise

Aug 69. (7") <*0873*> **THESE THINGS TOO. / IF YOU DON'T WANT TO**

Sep 69. (lp) <*(RSLP 6364)*> **THESE THINGS TOO**
– Footnote / Sail away / Look into her eyes / I shall be released / Frog in the window / I'm going to city / Man in the tree / If you don't want to (I don't mind) / Green and blue / Mon amour / Wizard of Is / Frog in the window / When I was a child / These things too.

—— now without HARLEY

Oct 70. (7") <*0949*> **THE JEWELLER. / ROCKET MAN**

Dec 70. (lp) <*(RSLP 6405)*> **THE USE OF ASHES**
– The jeweler / From the movie / Rocket man / God save the child / Song about a rose / Tell me why / Margery / The old man / Riegel / When the war began.

—— now trio of **TOM + ELIZABETH** plus **DAVID NOYES** – vocals

1971. (lp) <*(RSLP 6442)*> **CITY OF GOLD**
– Sonnet 65 / Once upon a time / Rain drops / City of gold / Nancy / Seasons in the sun / My father / The man / Casablanca / Wedding / Did you dream of.

—— DAVID repl. by many session men

1971. (lp) <*(RSLP 6467)*> **BEAUTIFUL LIES YOU COULD LIVE IN**
– Snow queen / A life / Butterflies / Simple things / Everybody's got pain / Bird on a wire / Island lady / Come to me / Freedom / She's gone / Epitaph.

TOM RAPP

with many session people

not issued Reprise

1972. (lp) <*MS 2069*> **TOM RAPP (FAMILIAR SONGS)**
– Grace Street / The jeweler / Rocket man / Snow queen / If you don't want to (I don't mind) / Charley and the lady / Margery / Full phantom five – I shall not care / These things too / Sail away.

not issued Blue Thumb

1973. (lp) <*BTS 44*> **STARDANCER**
– Fourth day of July / For the dead in space / The baptist / Summer of '55 / Tiny song / Stardancer / Marshall / Why should I care / Touch tripping / Les ans.

1974. (lp) <*BTS 56*> **SUNFOREST**

—— RAPP moved to Scandinavia or The Netherlands.

– compilations, etc. –

May 81. (d-lp) *Adelphi; (AD 4111)* **BEST OF PEARLS BEFORE SWINE**

PEDAL POINT (see under ⇒ FOCUS)

David PEEL & THE LOWER EAST SIDE

Formed: New York, USA . . .1968 by namesake DAVID PEEL, a political satirist who enlisted some local hippies to play on his 1969 drug-endorsing debut for 'Elektra', 'HAVE A MARIJUANA'. They recorded the album live on the streets of N.Y., although the results were of poor quality. Two others surfacd over the course of the next few years, the final one being produced by JOHN LENNON and YOKO ONO. PEEL went on to release several solo albums, dealing with such pertinent issues as Santa Claus, John Lennon & The Beatles and his hate of Disco music.

Recommended: HAVE A MARIJUANA (*4)

DAVID PEEL – vocals, harmonica, guitar / **BILLY JOE WHITE + LARRY ADAM** – guitar / **GEORGE CORI** – bass / **HAROLD C. BLACK** – tambourine

Elektra Elektra

Jun 69. (lp) *(EKS <74032>)* **HAVE A MARIJUANA** May69
– Mother where is my father? / I like marijuana / Here comes a cop / I've got some grass / Happy mother's day / Up against the wall / I do my bawling in the bathroom / The alphabet song / Show me the way to get stoned / We love you.

—— **HERB BUSHLER** – bass; repl. CORI

—— **DAVID HOROWITZ** – organ + **TOM BARTOLI** – drums; repl. ADAM

Mar 70. (lp) *(2410 001)* <*EKS 74069*> **THE AMERICAN REVOLUTION**
– The Lower East Side / The pledge of allegience / Legalize marijuana / Oink, oink / I want to get high / I want to kill you / Girls, girls, girls / Hey, Mr. Draft Board / God.

not issued Apple

May 72. (lp) <*SW 3391*> **THE POPE SMOKES DOPE**
– I'm a runaway / Everybody's smokin' marijuana / "F" is not a dirty word / The hippie from New York City / McDonald's farm / The ballad of New York City – John Lennon – Yoko Ono / The ballad of Bob Dylan / The Chicago conspiracy / The hip generation / I'm gonna start another riot / The birth control blues / The Pope smokes dope.

DAVID PEEL

with various session people

not issued Orange

1974. (lp) <*ORA 711*> **SANTA CLAUS ROOFTOP JUNKIE**
– Cockroach / Smack freak blues / Rock'n'roll rip-off / The narco is a pusher / The schools of corruption / Santa Claus – Rooftop junkie / Who stole John F. Kennedy's brain / I'm going insane / The ballad of A.J. Weberman / Benedict McCartney – Judas Ringo – B.S. Harrison / Watergate (I didn't do it) / Jingle bells war.

1975. (lp) <*ORA 713*> **AN EVENING WITH DAVID PEEL (live)**
– Hippie from New York City / Have a marijuana / Santa Claus – Rooftop junkie / Bring back The Beatles / The Pope smokes dope / Song on the spot / (Who stole J.F. Kennedy's brain) / I do my bawling in the bathroom / Up against the wall / Coconut grove / Rock and roll rip-off / Auld Lang Syne.

1977. (lp) <*NR 6*> **BRING BACK THE BEATLES**
– The Beatles pledge of allegience / Bring back The Beatles / Coconut grove / Imagine / Turn me on / Lollipop fish / The wonderful worlf of Abbey Road / The ballad of James Paul McCartney / With a little help from my friends / My fat budgie / Keep John Lennon in America (the John Lennon interview) / B-E-A-T-L-E-S.

1978. (lp) <*NR 7*> **KING OF PUNK**
– The Devil's prayer / King of punk / Uptight Manhattan / Marijuana / Murder burgers / Punk rock / In the beginning / The master race / Who killed Brian Jones / He's called a cop / A mother mother F.

1980. (lp) <*NR 8*> **JOHN LENNON FOR PRESIDENT**
– The John Lennon for President speech / The John Lennon for President speech 1 / The Yoko Ono interview / Ameika / The rock'n'roll preamble – John Lennon for President speech / The John Lennon for President speech 2 / Imagine / The John & Yoko interview / The John Lennon for President speech (acoustic) / Imagine (whispered by TINY TIM).

1981. (lp) <*666*> **DEATH TO DISCO**
– I hate disco / Junk rock / I hate you / Disco sucks / Up against the wall – D.F. / Rock'n'roll forever / Death to disco / Baby, I can't take it / Blood murder / Disco taps.

—— Must have given us all a rest.

PELL MELL

Formed: Marsburg, Germany . . . 1971 by THOMAS SCHMITT, OTTO PUSCH, RUDOLF SCHON, JORG GOTZFRIED and MITCH KNIESMEIJER. Peddling English-influenced art-rock with distinct classical pretensions, the band's PETER HAWKE-produced debut album (named after their home city), 'MARBURG' (1972) was released on the 'Bacillus' label. The record's five tracks were almost wholly instrumental, dominated by PUSCH's churning hammond work. For 1973's follow-up, 'FROM THE NEW WORLD', PUSCH was replaced with DIETRICH T. NOLL, although PUSCH's contributions to the record remained intact and the album mined a roughly similar seam to the debut. With RALPH LIPPMANN replacing NOLL on keys and another keyboard player, CHERRY HOCHDORFER, recruited along with bassist JORG GOTZFRIED, the band eventually recorded their third album in 1975. Released the following year on the 'Venus' label, 'RHAPSODY' was a typically self-indulgent 70's record dominated by pretentious classical adaptations. 'ONLY A STAR' was a more spontaneous affair and a career best for PELL MELL although they split the same year. THOMAS SCHMITT released a further self-titled lp in 1980 under the name SKYRIDER, later resurrecting the PELL MELL moniker for the 'MOLDAU' album the following year.

Recommended: MARBURG (*6) / ONLY A STAR (*6)

THOMAS SCHMITT – vocals, violin, guitar, mellotron / **OTTO PUSCH** – organ, piano / **RUDOLF SCHON** – vocals, recorder, guitar / **JORG GOTZFRIED** – bass / **MITCH KNIESMEIJER** – drums

Bacillus not issued

1972. (lp) *(BLPS 19090)* **MARBURG** Germany
– The clown and the queen / The Moldau / Friend / City monster / Alone.

—— **DIETRICH T. NOLL** – keyboards; repl. PUSCH (was still on half of album) / GOETZFRIED also departed

Philips not issued

1973. (lp) *(6305 193)* **FROM THE NEW WORLD** German
– From the new world / Toccata / Suite (parts 1 & 2).

—— **RALPH LIPPMANN** – vocals, guitars, keyboards; repl. NOLL

—— added **CHERRY HOCHDORFER** – keyboards (ex-FRAME) / **GOTZ DRAEGER** – bass

Venus not issued

1976. (lp) *(VB 76-1PM)* **RHAPSODY** - - German
– Rhapsody: Frost of an alien darkness – Wanderer – Can Can / Prelude / Desert in your mind / The riot / Paris the past.

— **WOLFGANG CLAUS** – drums; repl. MITCH

1978. (lp) *(1003)* **ONLY A STAR** - - German
– Count down / Daydreamer / Only a star / Across the universe / Disillusion / Trailers in movie halls / Phoebus is dead.

— split and SCHMITT formed below act

SKYRIDER

THOMAS SCHMITT – guitar, bass, keyboards, violin, vocals / **MICHAEL GREBE** – vocals / **RALPH FRICKE** – guitar / **OTTO PUSCH** – keyboards / **STEPHAN REHLICH** – bass / **WERNER ETTLING** – drums

P.M. not issued

1980. (lp) *(not known)* **SKYRIDER** - - German
– On my line (part 1) / Skyrider / Great beautiful crime / Time of the season / Written on a granite hill / I don't want to leave you know / On my line (part 2) / Up to sky / Love's in my eyes / Save two birds / Fighter of the sun.

PELL MELL

SCHMITT / FRICKE / + KLAUS NASS – drums

Cain not issued

1981. (lp) *(CL 5821)* **MOLDAU** - - German
– Moldau: Moldau part 1 – The farmer's wedding – The nymph dance Moldau part two / Gliding / Dark valley parts 1-4.

— retired after above. There was another PELL MELL, who were an instrumental group from Portland, USA. They released a 12-year in the making 'THE BUMPER CROP' for 'SST' early in '88.

P.F.M.

Formed: Milan, Italy . . .1971 out of pop group QUELLI, by FLAVIO PREMOLI, FRANCO MUSSIDA, FRANZ DI CICCIO and MAURO PAGANI. Having thought of the name PREMIATA FORNERIA MARCONI (thankfully shortened to P.F.M.), they released two worthy, British-influenced "flash-rock" albums, bringing them massive sales in Italy. Having commissioned former KING CRIMSON lyricist, PETE SINFIELD to write for them in English, they signed a healthy deal with ELP's new 'Manticore' label. Later in '73, the first result, 'PHOTOS OF GHOSTS' (with SINFIELD also on production), hit the US Top 200. They continued in the same prog-rock vein, bringing in new bassist DIVAS for the 1974 follow-up, 'THE WORLD BECAME THE WORLD'. Their third UK/US album, 'P.F.M. COOK', was recorded live on their first major North American tour, and this too made the Top 200. They returned to Milan, enlisting new vocalist BERNARDO LANZETTI to aid with the group's first attempts in writing in English. The album, 'CHOCOLATE KINGS', was a large disappointment which led to PAGANI departing. One more album, 'JET LAG', surfaced in 1977 before the group went into session work. • **Trivia:** CLAUDIO FABI co-produced their first two Italian lp's.

Recommended: PHOTOS OF GHOSTS (*7) / THE WORLD BECAME THE WORLD (*6) / CHOCOLATE KINGS (*5)

FLAVIO PREMOLI – keyboards, synthesizers, vocals / **FRANCO MUSSIDA** – guitar, mandolin, vocals / **MAURO PAGANI** – flute, violin, vocals / **GIORGIO PIAZZA** – bass, vocals / **FRANZ DI CIOCCIO** – drums, vocals

Numero Uno not issued

Feb 72. (lp) *(ZSLN 55055)* **STORIA DI UN MINUTO** - - Italy
– Introduzione / Impressioni di Settembre / E festa / Dove . . . quando . . .(part I & II) / La carrozza di Hans / Grazie davvero. *(UK-iss.Nov90 on 'Great Expectations' cd/c/lp; PIP CD/MC/LP 011)*

Nov 72. (lp) *(ZSLN 55155)* **PER UN AMICO** - - Italy
– Appena un poco / Generale! / Per un amico / Il banchetto / Geranio. *(UK-iss.Nov90 on 'Great Expectations' cd/c/lp; PIP CD/MC/LP 012)*

Manticore Manticore

Sep 73. (lp) *(K 43502)* <66668> **PHOTOS OF GHOSTS**
– River of life / Celebration / Photos of ghosts / Old rain / Il banchetto / Mr. 9 till 5 / Promenade the puzzle. *(re-iss.Aug87; same) (re-iss.Nov90 on 'Great Expectations' cd/c/lp; PIP CD/MC/LP 010)*

Nov 73. (7") *(K 13501)* **CELEBRATION. / OLD RAIN**

— **PATRIC DJIVAS** – bass, vocals repl. PIAZZA

Mar 74. (lp) *(K 53502)* *<66673>* **THE WORLD BECAME THE WORLD**
– The mountain / Just look away / The world became the world / Four holes in the ground / Is my face on straight / Have your cake and beat it.

Apr 74. (7") *(K 13505)* **THE WORLD BECAME THE WORLD. / LA CAROZZA DI HANS**

Nov 74. (7") *(K 13506)* **FOUR HOLES IN THE GROUND./ THE WORLD BECAME THE WORLD** -

Jan 75. (lp) *(K 53506)* <502> **COOK (live in Toronto & New York)**
– Four holes in the ground / Dove . . . Quando / Just look away / Celebration / Mr. 9 till 5 / Alta Loma 9 till 5.

— added **BERNARDO LANZETTI** – vocals, guitar

Manticore Asylum

Mar 76. (lp) *(K 53508)* *<7E 1071>* **CHOCOLATE KINGS**
– From under / Harlequin / Chocolate kings / Out of the roundabout / Paper charms. *(re-iss.Sep90 on 'Great Expectations' cd/c/lp; PIP CD/MC/LP 009)*

Jun 76. (7") *(K 13514)* **CHOCOLATE KINGS. / HARLEQUIN**

Jul 77. (lp) *(K 53511)* *<7E 1101>* **JET LAG**
– Peninsula / Jet lag / Storia in 'la' breakin' in / Cerco la lingua / Meridiani / Left-handed theory / Traveller.

— Disbanded after PAGANI departed. The rest all returned to stay permanently in Italy. They recorded 2 more albums in the late 70's for local 'Zoo' records; 'PASSPARTU' *(34032)* & 'SUONARESUONARE' *(34092)*. In 1979, MUSSIDA + DJIVAS sessioned for PABLO CONTE. The latter was heard on JOHNNY TAME's album 'Indistinct Horizon' in 1980. In the same year, DI CIOCCIO, MUSSIDA + DJIVAS augmented FABRIZIO DE ANDRE in 1979 lp 'In Concerto'. PAGANI was to co-produce & session for the same solo artist on his 1984 lp 'Creuza De Ma', which also featured MUSSIDA.

Anthony PHILLIPS

Born: c.1950, London, England. A founder member of GENESIS from its embryonic inception in 1965, The ANON. Guitarist PHILLIPS, departed prior to the release of their late 1970 album, 'TRESPASS', having contributed some of its material. Nicknamed ANT, he studied music and graduated with a teaching degree in the mid-70's. He was, at times, still working with GENESIS bassman, MIKE RUTHERFORD, these recordings finally surfacing early in 1977 as the heavily orchestrated 'THE GEESE & THE GHOST' album. It featured a guest vocal spot for PHIL COLLINS, which also surfaced on his debut single B-side, 'GOD IF I SAW HER NOW'. He signed to 'Arista' records in 1978, completing the follow-up, 'WISE AFTER THE EVENT', which was also issued in the States on a limited picture disc. PHILLIPS continued to work on several further solo albums, none of which won any commercial favour. In the early 90's, he signed a long-term deal with 'Virgin' records, who decided to re-issue his complete back catalogue. A new album, 'SLOW DANCE', failed to impress anyone, including his record company who abruptly dropped him.

Recommended: HARVEST OF THE HEART (*6)

ANTHONY PHILLIPS – guitar, bass, keyboards, percussion, vocals, etc. with **MIKE RUTHERFORD** – guitar, bass, etc / **PHIL COLLINS** – vocals / + wind musicians

Hit & Run Passport

Mar 77. (lp) *(HIT 001)* *<PP 98020>* **THE GEESE & THE GHOST**
– Wind-tales / Which way the wind blows / Henry, portrait from Tudor times: Fanfare – Lutes chorus misty battlements – Henry goes to war – Death of a knight – Triumphant return (Henry; portraits from Tudor times) / God if I saw her now / Chinese mushroom cloud / The geese & the ghost (part 1 & 2) / Collections / Sleepfall: The geese fly west. *<US re-iss.1977 on 'P.V.C.'; PVC 8905> (pic-cd-iss.1985; PVCD 8905) (cd-iss.Dec90 on 'Virgin'+=; CDOVD 315)*– Master of time (demo).

Vertigo not issued

1977. (7") *(6837 406)* **COLLECTIONS. / GOD IF I SAW HER NOW** -

— now with **THE VICAR** – vocals / **MIKE GILES** – drums / **JOHN G. PERRY** – bass / **MEL COLLINS** – sax / **VIC STENCH** – cello, bass / **HUMBERT RUSE** – percussion / etc.

Arista Passport

May 78. (lp,US-pic-lp> *(SPART 1063)* *<PB 9829>* **WISE AFTER THE EVENT**
– We're all as we lie / Birdsong / Moonshooter / Wise after the event / Pulling faces / Regrets / Greenhouse / Paper chase / Now what (are they doing to my little friends?). *(cd-iss.Mar91 on 'Virgin'+=; CDOVD 322)*– Squirrel.

Jun 78. (7"m) *(ARIST 192)* *<79114>* **WE'RE ALL AS WE LIE. / SQUIRREL / SITARS AND NEBULOUS**

Feb 79. (lp) *(SPART 1085)* *<PB 9834>* **SIDES**
– Um & aargh / I want your love / Lucy will / Side door / Holy deadlock / Sisters of Remindum / Bleak house / Magdalen / Nightmare. *(cd-iss.Apr96 on 'Blueprint'+=; BP 213CD)*– Magdalen (instrumental).

Mar 79. (lp) *(ARIST 252)* **UM & AARGH. / SOUVENIR** -

R.C.A. P.V.C.

1979. (lp-ltd.) *(AFLP 1)* **PRIVATE PARTS AND PIECES** (rec.1972-76)
– Beauty and the beast / Field of eternity / Tibetan Yak-music / Lullaby – Old Father Time / Harmonium in the dust / Treganna afternoons / Reaper / Autumnal / Flamingo / Seven long years. *(cd-iss.Jan96 on 'Blueprint'+=; BP 202CD)*– Silver song (demo).

Oct 80. (lp) *<PVC 7913>* **PRIVATE PARTS & PIECES II: BACK TO THE PAVILION** (rare material) -
– Salmon leap – Parting thistle – Electric reaper – Amorphous, cadaverous and nebulous – Salmon's last sleepwalk (Scottish suite) / Lindsay / K2 / End of the season (postitude) / Heavens / Spring meeting / Romany's aria / China man / Nocturne / Magic garden / Von Runkel's Yorker music / Will o' the wisp / Tremulous / I saw you today / Back to the pavillion / An illusion. *(UK cd-iss.Jan96 on 'Blueprint'; BP 203CD)*

— now with **RICHARD SCOTT** – percussion, effects, vocals / **MORRIS PERT** – percussion

Jun 81. (lp/c) *(RCA LP/K 5036)* **1984** -
– Prelude '84 / 1984 (parts 1 & 2) / Anthem 1984. *(cd-iss.Mar91 on 'Virgin'; CDOVD 321)*

Jul 81. (7") *(RCA 102)* **PRELUDE '84. / ANTHEM 1984** -

— next with **ENRIQUE BERRO GARCIA** – guitar

Oct 82. (lp/c) *(INT S/K 5228)* *<PVC 8908>* **PRIVATE PARTS & PIECES III: ANTIQUES**
– Hurlingham suite: Ivied castles – Frosted windows – Bandido – Church bells at sunset / Suite in D-minor: Whirlpool, Cobblestones, Catacombs / Danse nude / Esperansa / Elegy / Otto's face / Sand dunes / Old wives tales / Motherforest. *(cd-iss.Mar96 on 'Blueprint'; BP 204CD)*

Street Tunes Passport

Feb 84. (12"m) *(JJ 102-12)* **SALLY. / EXOCET / THE WOMEN WERE WATCHING** -

Mar 84. (lp) *(STLP 013)* *<PB 6023>* **INVISIBLE MEN** Dec83
– Sally / Golden bodies / Going for broke / It's not easy / Traces / Guru / My time has come / Love in a hot air ballooon / I want your heart / Falling for love / The women were watching. *(cd-iss.Mar96 on 'Blueprint'+=; BP 211CD)*– Exocet / Trail of tears / Alex / The ballad of Penlee.

Cherry Red P.V.C.

1984. (lp) *<PVC 8919>* **PRIVATE PARTS & PIECES IV: A CATCH AT THE TABLES** -

– Arboretum suite: Set piece / Over the gate / Flapjack / Lights over the wall / Earth man / Dawn over the lake / Bouncer / Eduardo / Heart of darkness / The sea and the armadillo / Sistine / Erotic strings / A catch at the tables. *(UK cd-iss.Apr96 on 'Blueprint'; BP 205CD)*

1984. (lp) *<PVC 8926>* **PRIVATE PARTS & PIECES V: TWELVE** [-] [ ]
– January / February / March / April / May / June / July / August / September / October / November / December. *(UK cd-iss.Apr96 on 'Blueprint'; BP 206CD)*

Sep 85. (lp) *(BRED 66)* **HARVEST OF THE HEART** (compilation) [ ] [-]
– Trail of tears / Esperansa / Salmon leap / Flap Jack / Bouncer / Beaty and the beast / Amorphous, cadaverous and Nebulous / Salmon's last sleepwalk / Exotic strings / Bandido / Sistine / Lindsay / Over the gate / The Sean and the armadillo / Lights on the hill.

1986. (lp) *<PVC 8946>* **PRIVATE PARTS & PIECES VI: IVORY MOON** [-] [ ]
– Sea-dogs motoring suite: Sunrise over Sienna – Basking shark – Sea dogs air – Safe havens / Tata's theme (from Masquerade) / Winter's thaw / The old house / Moonfall (from Masquerade) / Rapids / Let us now make love. *(UK cd-iss.Apr96 on 'Blueprint'; BP 207CD)*

not issued Audion

1987. (lp/cd) *<SYN/+CD 308>* **PRIVATE PARTS & PIECES VII: SLOW WAVES, SOFT STARS** [-] [ ]
– Flight of the snow petrel (glacier bay) – Flight of the white birds (blizzard mountain) – Flight of the albatross (ice island) – White Heaven – Cathedral of ice (ice flight) / Beachrunner / End of the affair / The golden pathway / Behind the waterfall (from 'Return to the heart') / Carnival / Through the black hole / Pluto garden / Sospirando / Elevenses / Goodbye serenade / Bubble squeak / Vanishing streets / Slow waves, soft stars. *(UK cd-iss.May96 on 'Blueprint'; BP 208CD)*

P.R.T. not issued

Nov 88. (7"pic) *(PYS 18)* **THE ANTHEM FROM TARKA. / THE RISING SPRING** [ ] [-]
(cd-s+=) *(PYD 18)* – Excerpt from Tarka (movement 1 & 3) / ('A'extended).

— (above credited with HARRY WILLIAMSON and from album 'TARKA' lp/c/cd; *PYL/PYC/PYD 18)*

Virgin Virgin

Sep 90. (cd) *(CDV 2638)* **SLOW DANCE** [ ] [ ]
(re-iss.Mar96 on 'Blueprint'; BP 213CD)

Progressive not issued

Mar 92. (cd) *(PRO 012)* **FINGER PAINTING** [ ] [-]
– God's chosen park suite: Processional – Meditation – Cave painting / Tropical moon over Dorking suite: Estrangement – Myra's dream – Reconciliation / Three piece suite: To the shine – Through the forest – Towards the light / Land of dragons (part 1) – Kiles – Harbour at sunset – ance of the crabs – Sand octopus and the king crabs / Do the shrimps know they're Chinese / Land of dragons (part 2) / Force majeure / Mountain voices / Lord of the smoking mirror / Sea horses / Dungeons / Between the rings / Evening ascent / Streamer / After the rain / Rottweiler / Sad fish / A song / Fountain pool / C.Q. / Boulevard of fallen leaves / And a prayer / Tierra del fuego / aradise found.

Resource not issued

Jun 94. (cd) *(RES 102CD)* **SAIL THE WORLD (MUSIC FROM THE WHITBREAD RACE 1993-94)** [ ] [-]
– Opening theme / Fat work / Dark seas / Cool sailing / Wildlife choir / I wish this would never end / Salsa / Opening theme (demo mix) / Roaring forties / Lonely whales / Icebergs / Majestic whaes / In the southern ocean / The Freemantle doctor / Long way from home / Wildlife flotilla / Big combers / Col sailing II / Cape Horn / Amongst mythical birds / Salsa II / Into the tropics / In the doldrums / Heading for home and victory. *(re-iss.Apr97; same)*

Brainworks not issued

Jun 94. (cd) *(BWKD 212)* **MISING LINKS VOL.2 (THE SKY ROAD)** [ ] [-]
– Exile / Lifeboat suite / The bitter suite / Across the River Styx / A flock of souls / Along the towpath / The sky road / Tears on a rainy day / Tiwai: Island of the apes / Wild voices, quiet water / Suite / Serenita / Time piece / Field of eternity / The beggar and the thief.

Voiceprint not issued

Feb 95. (cd; ANTHONY PHILLIPS & HARRY WILLIAMSON) *(VP 189CD)* **GYPSY SUITE** [ ] [-]
– Gypsy suite: First light – Siesta – Evening circle – The crystal ball / The early years – Streams river & salmon hunting – Dunes & estuary – Moonfield – ostscript (Tarka). *(re-iss.Mar97; same)*

– compilations, etc

Oct 95. (cd) *Blueprint; (BP 201CD)* **ANTHOLOGY** [ ] [-]
May 96. (cd) *Blueprint; (BP 218CD)* **LIVING ROOM CONCERT** [ ] [-]

PHLUPH

Formed: Boston, Massachusetts, USA ... 1967 by BENSON BLAKE IV, JOHN PELL, JOEL MASIANO and LEE DUDLEY. They were responsible for only one 45 and what is now regarded as an excellent self-titled album. It was full of trippy psychedelia, at times verging on pop. Sadly, it was their only long-playing vinyl offering.

Recommended: PHLUPH (*7)

BENSON BLAKE IV / JOHN PELL / JOEL MAISANO / LEE DUDLEY

not issued Verve

1967. (7") *<10564>* **ANOTHER DAY. / DOCTOR MIND** [-] [ ]
1968. (lp) *<V6-5054>* **PHLUPH** [-] [ ]
– Doctor Mind / It takes a lot to laugh, it takes a train to cry / In her way / Another day / Girl in tears / Ellyptical machine / Lovely lady / Death of a nation / Love eyes / Patterns.

— split after above

PINK FAIRIES

Formed: London, England ... 1966 as The SOCIAL DEVIANTS, by RUSSELL HUNTER, MICK FARREN – vocals, SID BISHOP – guitar, CORD REES – bass and two others. In 1967, they shortened to their name to The DEVIANTS, luckily finding a millionaire who put up the cash for an album, 'PTOOF', which sold reasonably well on mail order. With DUNCAN SANDERSON replacing CORD, and the recruitment of a new manager (Canadian Jamie Mandelkau), they issued a second lp, 'DISPOSABLE', another effort showcasing their heavily percussive prog-rock set. Early in '69, PAUL RUDOLPH replaced BISHOP, their third lp, 'DEVIANTS', being issued by 'Transatlantic'. When FARREN left to go solo in October '69, the new line-up (HUNTER, SANDERSON & RUDOLPH) augmented SHAGRAT member TWINK on his debut 'Polydor' album, 'THINK PINK'. The latter had already initiated the idea of The PINK FAIRIES in Colchester, subsequently teaming up with the aforesaid trio under that name. TWINK had also drummed at various stages with The IN-CROWD (who evolved into TOMORROW), and The PRETTY THINGS. Early in 1971, The PINK FAIRIES unleashed their first official 'Polydor' single, 'THE SNAKE', preceding the hippie celebration of the 'NEVER NEVER LAND' album. Their 1972 follow-up, 'WHAT A BUNCH OF SWEETIES', (recorded without TWINK, who had briefly formed The STARS together with another acid casualty, SYD BARRETT) scraped into the UK Top 50. With numerous personnel changes, they decided to disband in March '74, although many re-incarnations lay ahead (for touring purposes only, mainly with friends HAWKWIND).

Recommended: FLASHBACK: PINK FAIRIES (*7)

DEVIANTS

DUNCAN SANDERSON – bass / **SID BISHOP** – guitar, sitar / **MICK FARREN** – vocals, piano / **CORD REES** – bass, guitar / **RUSS HUNTER** – drums

Underground not issued

1967. (lp) *(IMP 1)* **PTOOFF!** [ ] [-]
– Opening / I'm coming home / Child of the sky / Charlie / Nothing man / Garbage / Bun / Deviation street. *(re-iss.May69 on 'Decca' mono/stereo; LK-R/SKL-R 4993) (re-iss.Dec83 on 'Psycho'; PSYCHO 16) (cd-iss.Nov92 on 'Drop Out'; DOCD 1988) (cd re-iss.Sep95 on 'Alive';)*

— **PAUL RUDOLPH** – guitar repl. CORD

Stable not issued

Oct 68. (lp) *(SLE 7001)* **DISPOSABLE** [ ] [-]
– Somewhere to go / Sparrows and wires / Jamie's song / You've got to hold on / Fire in the city / Let's loot the supermarket / Papa-oo-Mao-Mao / Slum lord / Blind Joe McTurk's last session / Normality jam / Guaranteed too dead / Sidney B. Goode / Last man.

Nov 68. 7") *(STA 5601)* **YOU'VE GOT TO HOLD ON. / LET'S LOOT THE SUPERMARKET** [ ] [-]

— now a trio of SANDERSON, RUDOLPH + HUNTER when BISHOP left, FARREN went solo and released lp in 1970 'MONA (THE CARNIVEROUS CIRCUS).'

Transatlantic not issued

Jan 70. (lp) *(TRA 204)* **THE DEVIANTS** [ ] [-]
– Billy the monster / Broken biscuits / First line / The people suite / Rambling 'B'ask transit blues / Death of dream machine / Play time / Black George does it weith his mouth / Junior narco raiders / People of the city / Metamorphosis exploration. *(re-iss.1978 on 'Logo'; MOGO 4001) (re-iss.Oct88 on 'Demon'; DEMON 8)*

TWINK

TWINK (b. JOHN ADLER) – drums, vocals (ex-SHAGRAT) (solo, with DEVIANTS)

Polydor not issued

Jan 71. (lp) *(2343 032)* **THINK PINK** [ ] [-]
– Coming of the other side / Ten thousand words in a cardboard box / Dawn of magic / Tiptoe on the highest hill / Fluid / Mexican grass war / Rock an' roll the joint / Suicide / Three little piggies / Sparrow is a sign. *(re-prom.Apr71; same)*

PINK FAIRIES

PAUL RUDOLPH – guitar, vocals / **DUNCAN SANDERSON** – bass, vocals / **RUSSELL HUNTER** – drums now with **TWINK**

Polydor Polydor

Jan 71. (7") *(2058 059)* **THE SNAKE. / DO IT** [ ] [-]
May 71. (lp,pink-lp) *(2383 045)* **THE NEVER NEVER LAND** [ ] [ ]
– Do it / Heavenly man / Say you love me / War girl / Never never land / Track one side two / Thor / Teenage rebel / Uncle Harry's last freak-out / The dream is just beginning.

— Trimmed to a trio when TWINK joined STARS, before flitting to Morocco. His spot filled by guest **TREVOR BURTON** – guitar (ex-MOVE)

Jul 72. (lp) *(2383 132)* **WHAT A BUNCH OF SWEETIES** [48] [ ]
– Right on, fight on / Portobello shuffle / Marilyn / The pigs of Uranus / Walk, don't run / Middle run / I went up, I went down / X-ray / I saw her standing there.

— **MICK WAYNE** – guitar, vox (ex-JUNIOR'S EYES) repl. RUDOLPH (to UNCLE DOG)

Nov 72. (7") *(2059 302)* **WELL WELL WELL. / HOLD ON** [ ] [-]

— **LARRY WALLIS** – guitar, vocals (ex-UFO, ex-SHAGRAT, ex-BLODWYN PIG) repl. MICK. (trio now consisted of LARRY, DUNCAN + RUSSELL)

Jun 73. (lp) *(2383 212) <5537>* **KINGS OF OBLIVION** [ ] [ ]
– City kids / I wish I was a girl / When's the fun begin / Chromium plating / Raceway / Chambermaid / Street urchin.

— broke-up Mar74, although **DUNCAN, RUSSELL, PAUL, TWINK & LARRY** re-formed for one-off reunion gig at The Roundhouse 13th Jul'75. Autumn 1975, they officially re-united w / **DUNCAN, RUSSELL & LARRY.** When they added (mid'76) **MARTIN STONE** – guitar (ex-CHILI WILLI, ex-MIGHTY BABY, ex-ACTION, etc.) they returned to studio.

Stiff not issued

Sep 76. (7") *(BUY 2)* **BETWEEN THE LINES. / SPOILING FOR A FIGHT** [ ] [-]

— Break-up again, and LARRY went solo in 1977.

TWINK & THE FAIRIES

— solo with ex-PINK FAIRIES (**PAUL RUDOLPH**; who had been recently seen in HAWKWIND, etc. / **DUNCAN + RUSSELL**)

Chiswick not issued

Feb 78. (12"ep) *(SWT 26)* **DO IT '77. / PSYCHEDELIC PUNKAROO / ENTER THE DIAMONDS** ☐ [-]

— Disbanded once again when TWINK moved to Belguim. DUNCAN joined The LIGHTNING RAIDERS.

MICK FARREN

with **TWINK** – drums, percussion, vocals / **SHAGRAT THE VAGRANT** – vocals, percussion / **STEVE HAMMOND** – guitar / **JOHNNY GUSTAFSON** – bass / **PETE ROBINSON** – keyboards

Transatlantic not issued

Apr 70. (lp) *(TRA 212)* **MONA (THE CARNIVEROUS CIRCUS)** ☐ [-]
– Mona (a fragrant) / Carniverous circus part 1: The whole thing starts – But Charlie it's still moving – Observe the ravens – Society 4 the horsemen – Summertime blues / Carniverous circus part 2: Don't talk to Mary – You can't move me – In my window box – An epitaph can point the way – Mona (the whole trip). *(re-iss.Mar84 on 'Psycho'; PSYCHO 20)*

Stiff not issued

Nov 77. (7"ep; MICK FARREN & DEVIANTS) *(LAST 4)* **SCREWED UP** ☐ [-]
– Outragious contagious / Let's loot the supermarket / Screwed up / Shock horror

— now with **WILKO JOHNSON** – guitar / **ALAN POWER** – drums / **ANDY COLQUHOUN** – bass / **WILL STALL** – brass / **CHRISSIE JANE + SONJA KRISTINA** – backing vox.

Logo not issued

1978. (lp) *(LOGO 2010)* **VAMPIRES STOLE MY LUNCH MONEY** ☐ [-]
– Trouble coming every day / Half price drinks / I don't want to go this way / I want a drink / Son of a millionaire / Zombie (live) / Bela Lugosi / People call you crazy / Fast Eddie / Let me in damn you / Self destruction / Drunk in the morning.

1978. (7") *(GO 321)* **HALF PRICE DRINKS. / I DON'T WANT TO GO THIS WAY** ☐ [-]

May 79. (7") *(GO 345)* **BROKEN STATUE. / IT'S ALL IN THE PICTURE** ☐ [-]

DEVIANTS

— re-formed with **MICK FARREN** – vocals / **LARRY WALLIS + WAYNE KRAMER** – guitar / **DUNCAN SANDERSON** – bass / **GEORGE BUTLER** – drums

Psycho not issued

May 84. (lp) *(PSYCHO 25)* **HUMAN GARBAGE** (live at Dingwalls '84) ☐ [-]
– Outragious contagious / Broken statue / Ramblin' Rose / Hey thanks / Screwed up / I wanna drink / Takin' LSD / Police car / Trouble coming every day.

– compilations, etc. –

Sep 92. (cd) *Drop Out; (DOCD 1989)* **PARTIAL RECALL** ☐ [-]
– (from DEVIANTS 3 / VAMPIRES / all 'MONA; THE CARNIVOROUS CIRCUS')

Jun 97. (cd; MICK FARREN & THE DEVIANTS) *Captain Trip; (CTCD 046)* **FRAGMENTS OF BROKEN DREAMS** ☐ [-]

MICK FARREN'S TIJUANA BIBLE

Big Beat not issued

Feb 93. (cd) *(CDWIK 117)* **GRINGO MADNESS** ☐ [-]
– Leader hotel / Mark of Zorro / Lone sungularity / Solitaire devil / Spider kissed / Jezebel / Long walk with the devil / Jumping Jack Flash / Movement of the whores on Revolution Plaza / Hippie death cult / Last night the Alhambra burned down / Eternity is a very long time / Memphis psychosis / Riot in Cell Block #9.

PINK FAIRIES

— re-formed 1987 with **TWINK, LARRY, RUSSELL, ANDY + SANDY** (aka DUNCAN)

Demon not issued

Oct 87. (lp/cd) *(FIEND/+CD 105)* **KILL 'EM AND EAT 'EM** ☐ [-]
– Broken statue / Fear of love / Undercover of confusion / Waiting for the ice-cream to melt / Taking LSD / White girls on amphetamine / Seeing double / Fool about you / Bad attitude / I might be lying. *(cd re-iss.May97; VEXCD 16)*

— Once again, bit the dust, and TWINK joined MAGIC MUSCLE who made live lp in 1989 'ONE HUNDRED MILES BELOW'. TWINK released another solo lp 'MR.RAINBOW', and then 'MAGIC EYE' both in 1990 for 'Woronzow' label.

– compilations, others, etc. –

Jul 75. (lp) *Flashback-Polydor; (2384 071)* **PINK FAIRIES** ☐ [-]
– The snake / City kids / Wargirl / Portobello shuffle / Heavenly man / Do it / pigs of Uranus / Well well well / Chromium plating / I went up, I went down / Say you love me / Street urchin.

Jun 82. (m-lp) *Big Beat; (WIK 14)* **AT THE ROUNDHOUSE (live July '75)** ☐ [-]
– City kids / Waiting for the man / Lucille / Uncle Harry's last freakout / Going down.

Oct 84. (m-lp) *Big Beat; (NED 9)* **PREVIOUSLY UNRELEASED** ☐ [-]
– As long as the price is right / Waiting for the lightning to strike / Can't find a lady / No second chance / Talk of the Devil / I think it's coming back again.

Oct 90. (cd/c) *Polydor; (843894-2/-4)* **THE BEST OF THE PINK FAIRIES** ☐ [-]

Jul 91. (cd) *Big Beat; (CDWIK 965)* **LIVE AT THE ROUNDHOUSE / PREVIOUSLY UNRELEASED / TWINK & THE FAIRIES (ep)** ☐ [-]

Jan 96. (cd) *H.T.D.; (HTDCD 46)* **OUT OF THE BLUE AND INTO THE PINK** ☐ [-]

TWINK

Twink not issued

Mar 86. (7") *(TWK 1)* **APOCALIPSTIC. / HE'S CRYING** ☐ [-]

Jul 86. (12"ep) *(TWK 2)* **SPACE LOVER (Rock'n'roll mix 1 & 2). / ('A'-percussion mix) / ('A'-psychedelic mix) / ('A'instrumental)** ☐ [-]

Jun 87. (7") *(TWK 3)* **DRIVING MY CAR. / WAR GIRL** ☐ [-]

Mar 90. (lp/cd) *(TWK LP/CD 1)* **MR. RAINBOW** ☐ [-]
– Psychedelic punkaroo / Baron Saturday / Teenage rebel / Mr. Rainbow / Seize the time / The snake / Three jolly little dwarfs / Waygirl / Balloon burning / Do it.

Jun 90. (7") *(7TWK 5)* **PSYCHEDELIC PUNKAROO. /** ☐ [-]
(12"+=) *(12TWK 5)* –

PINK FLOYD

Formed: London, England . . . 1965 initially as The ABDABS by ROGER WATERS, RICHARD WRIGHT and NICK MASON, (with others; CLIVE METCALFE – bass, KEITH NOBLE and JULIETTE GALE on vocals). The latter three were dismissed, when the band enlisted SYD BARRETT and adopted the moniker PINK FLOYD (the name taken from bluesmen PINK ANDERSON and FLOYD COUNCIL). In March '66, they secured a residency at the Marquee Club, where their Sunday afternoon gigs were described as "spontaneous underground". Having played the UFO club late in 1966, they were subsequently signed to EMI's 'Columbia' records by their new management team of Peter Jenner and Andrew King. PINK FLOYD's March '67 debut outing, 'ARNOLD LAYNE' (about a transvestite washing-line thief), surprisingly escaped a BBC ban. One of the first missives from the psychedelic underground to reach the Top 20, it was characterised by SYD's whimisically affected vocals. On the 29th of April, they were top of the bill at Alexandria Palace's 14-hour Technicolour Dream, one of the psychedelic era's most infamous events. Their follow-up, 'SEE EMILY PLAY' (originally titled 'GAMES FOR MAY'), hit the Top 10, preceding their classic debut album, 'THE PIPER AT THE GATES OF DAWN' (a pioneering work in the sense that it contained no singles). The collection dominated by BARRETT's eccentric songwriting, it featured the cosmic 'ASTRONOMY DOMINE' alongside the acid-fuelled space-rock of 'INTERSTELLAR OVERDRIVE'. These were contrasted with idiosyncratic ramblings like 'BIKE', 'MATILDA MOTHER' and 'SCARECROW'. Their third 45, 'APPLES AND ORANGES', suprisingly flopped late in 1967, BARRETT's mental condition deteriorating rapidly due to his excessive use of LSD. He increasingly missed shows and studio sessions, PINK FLOYD bringing in DAVE GILMOUR (an old school-friend of SYD's) to compensate. In the April '68, BARRETT was asked to leave the group, retreating to a life of reclusiveness in his mother's Cambridge home. It was widely speculated that PINK FLOYD would be creatively bankrupt without SYD, especially after a further single, 'IT WOULD BE SO NICE', flopped. However, WATERS and WRIGHT took up the reins on the bulk of the songwriting duties, the band soon unleashing their second, more percussive effort, 'A SAUCERFUL OF SECRETS'. Released to ecstatic reviews, the album repeated the debut's success. The tracks, 'SET THE CONTROLS FOR THE HEART OF THE SUN', 'LET THERE BE MORE LIGHT' and SYD's harrowing farewell, 'JUGBAND BLUES' being the undisputed highlights. On the 29th of June, they played their first free concert at London's Hyde Park, alongside JETHRO TULL and ROY HARPER. They finished the year with another flop single, 'POINT ME AT THE SKY', their last in the UK for 11 years. They now concentrated on albums, releasing the under par soundtrack to the Barbet Schroeder- directed 'MORE'. It was basically an instrumental set, 'CIRRUS MINOR' being the standout track of the Top 10 album. Later in '69, they moved to EMI's new 'Harvest' label, issuing the part live, part solo, double album, 'UMMA GUMMA'. Each member contributed a piece of individually credited material, the best being WATERS' bizarre creation, 'SEVERAL SPECIES OF SMALL FURRY ANIMALS GATHERED TOGETHER IN A CAVE AND GROOVING WITH A PICT'. The live disc combined the cream of their sprawling stage improvisations, 'CAREFUL WITH THAT AXE, EUGENE' making its first album appearance. In the autumn of 1970, they released their fifth album, 'ATOM HEART MOTHER' (their first No.1), a record consisting of one patchy, experimental, side of more conventionally structured songs, while the other was a side-long collage with RON GEESIN playing on the title track. The trumpeter was to collaborate with ROGER WATERS the same year, on a soundtrack for the Roy Battersby documentary film, 'THE BODY'. On the 15th of May '71, PINK FLOYD played at the Crystal Palace Garden Party, introducing a new piece of music, 'RETURN TO THE SUN OF NOTHING', which, in six months time, became 'ECHOES'. This composition subsequently took up a whole side of their Top 3 album, 'MEDDLE', which also featured 'ONE OF THESE DAYS', 'A PILLOW OF WINDS' and 'FEARLESS' (the latter notable for its sample of the Anfield Kop). The following year, their most recent recordings were used on another Schroeder film, 'La Vallee', the album being released as 'OBSCURED BY CLOUDS', and although disappointing many die hard FLOYD fans, it cracked the Top 50 in the States. The same year, the group premiered their own music film, 'LIVE AT POMPEII', in Edinburgh. In March 1973, after its spectacular January showing at the Planetarium, the masterpiece, 'DARK SIDE OF THE MOON', was unveiled. A meticulous concept set which the band had worked on for over a year, it dealt with such taboo themes as lunacy, depression and death. These subjects were dealt with on such compelling tracks as 'US AND THEM', 'BREATHE', 'TIME' and the Top 20 US hit 'MONEY'. Scaling both the UK and US charts, the album went on to amass sales of over 10 million, incredibly residing in the chart for nearly 300 consecutive weeks. It has subsequently become regarded by many as the greatest album of all time, breathing new life into stereo headphones. They returned to London's Earl's Court for a spectacular laser show, featuring the albums' all-girl backing singers, The BLACKBERRIES. In 1974, they did a benefit gig, raising £10,000 for their recently disabled friend, ROBERT WYATT (NICK MASON also producing his 'Rock Bottom' album). In the summer of '75, their majestic Knebworth Festival performance previewed another best selling album and subsequent chart-topper, 'WISH YOU WERE HERE'. The record featured some of PINK FLOYD's most enduring songs including the space-jazz ode to SYD BARRETT, 'SHINE ON YOU CRAZY DIAMOND', the oppressive futurism of 'WELCOME TO THE MACHINE', the ROY HARPER-sung 'HAVE A CIGAR' and the wistful melancholy of the title track. It was rounded off by a reprised version of 'SHINE ON', the recording sessions blessed with a rare visit by the song's subject, SYD. Late in 1976, they let loose their 40-foot inflatable pig after a promotional session for their forthcoming 'ANIMALS' album sleeve shot. The Civil Aviation Authority was alerted to warn pilots of the danger, but it was never found. However, the Top 3 album was sighted in shops early the following year. While MASON had produced albums for The DAMNED ('Music For Pleasure') and STEVE HILLAGE ('Green'), GILMOUR and WRIGHT released their own solo albums in 1978, 'DAVID GILMOUR' and 'WET DREAM' respectively. FLOYD returned in late 1979 with a new ROGER WATERS-penned concept double, 'THE WALL', which spawned a decidly unfestive Christmas chart topper in the lugubrious 'ANOTHER BRICK IN THE WALL (PART II)'. This was another unrelentingly cynical concept piece, centering on the life of PINK, a disillusioned pop star. The next few years were spent making it into a film, directed by Alan Parker and issued in 1982 (BOB GELDOF played the main character). By the time of its release, WRIGHT had already left the band after quarrelling with WATERS. In Spring 1983, they/WATERS issued a comeback album of sorts, 'THE FINAL CUT', which again hit UK No.1. However, it was found overbearingly depressing, derided by critics as a poor "son of The Wall". The year ended with WATERS recording a solo album, 'THE PROS AND CONS OF HITCH HIKING', subsequently fighting GILMOUR and MASON in court for the use of the PINK FLOYD name. In 1984, GILMOUR released his second solo album, 'ABOUT FACE', followed a year later by a NICK MASON / RICK FENN set, 'PROFILES'. With WATERS finally leaving in 1986, WRIGHT returned a year later to boost their ever-impressive live shows (which helped them win the court battle with WATERS). PINK FLOYD returned with an extended GILMOUR-led line-up in 1987 on the Top 3 album, 'A MOMENTARY LAPSE OF REASON', which produced a couple of minor hit singles, 'ON THE TURNING AWAY' and 'ONE SLIP'. A live double album, 'THE DELICATE SOUND OF THUNDER' (which, ironically enough, sounded more PINK FLOYD than ever before). A seven year studio hiatus was broken in 1994 with the release of chart-topper 'THE DIVISION BELL', regarded by long-time fans as a return to form. • **Trivia:** MASON also made a 30-minute autobiographical film, 'Life Could Be A Dream' with his other outlet, racing driving, the main feature. In 1995, GILMOUR featured on JOHN 'RABBIT' BUNDRICK's ambient album, 'Dream Jungle'.

Recommended: THE DARK SIDE OF THE MOON (*10) / MEDDLE (*9) / THE PIPER AT THE GATES OF DAWN (*9) / WISH YOU WERE HERE (*10) / THE WALL (*8) / ATOM HEART MOTHER (*8) / ANIMALS (*8) / A SAUCERFUL OF SECRETS (*8) / UMMA GUMMA (*8) / THE DELICATE SOUND OF THUNDER (*7) / THE DIVISION BELL (*7)

SYD BARRETT (b. ROGER KEITH BARRETT, 6 Jan'46) – vocals, guitar / **RICHARD WRIGHT** (b.28 Jul'45, London) – keyboards / **ROGER WATERS** (b. GEORGE WATERS, 9 Sep'44, Surrey, England) – bass, vocals, percussion / **NICK MASON** (b.27 Jan'45, Birmingham, England) – drums, percussion

Columbia Tower

Mar 67. (7") *(DB 8156)* <333> **ARNOLD LAYNE. / CANDY AND THE CURRANT BUN** [20] [ ]

Jun 67. (7") *(DB 8214)* <356> **SEE EMILY PLAY. / SCARECROW** [6] [ ]

Aug 67. (lp; mono/stereo) *(SX/SCX 6157)* **THE PIPER AT THE GATES OF DAWN** [6] [-]
– Astronomy domine / Lucifer Sam / Matilda mother / Flaming / Pow R. Toc H. / Take up thy stethoscope and walk / Interstellar overdrive / The gnome / Chapter 24 / Scarecrow / Bike. *(re-iss.May83 on 'Fame' lp/c; FA/TCFA 3065) (cd-iss.Feb87; CDP 746384-2) (re-iss.Oct94 on 'E.M.I.' cd/c; CD/TC EMD 1073)*

Nov 67. (lp) <5093> **PINK FLOYD** (nearly as above) [-] [ ]

Nov 67. (7") *(DB 8310)* **APPLES AND ORANGES. / PAINTBOX** [ ] [-]

Jan 68. (7") <378> **FLAMING. / THE GNOME** [-] [ ]

— added **DAVID GILMOUR** (b. 6 Mar'44, Cambridge, England) – guitar who soon repl. BARRETT who later went solo.

Apr 68. (7") *(DB 8401)* <426> **IT WOULD BE SO NICE. / JULIA DREAM** [ ] [ ]

Jun 68. (lp; mono/stereo) *(SX/SCX 6258)* **A SAUCERFUL OF SECRETS** [9] [ ]
– Let there be more light / Remember a day / Set the controls for the heart of the sun / Corporal Clegg / A saucerful of secrets / See saw / Jugband blues. *(re-iss.Aug86 on 'Fame' lp/c; FA/TCFA 3163) (cd-iss.Feb87; CDP 746383-2) (re-iss.Jul94 on 'E.M.I.' cd/c; CD/TC EMD 1063)*

Jul 68. (7") <440> **LET THERE BE MORE LIGHT. / REMEMBER A DAY** [-] [ ]

Dec 68. (7") *(DB 8511)* **POINT ME AT THE SKY. / CAREFUL WITH THAT AXE, EUGENE** [ ] [-]

Jul 69. (lp/c) *(SCX/TCSCX 6346)* **MORE (soundtrack)** [9] [ ]
– Cirrus minor / The Nile song / Crying song / Up the Khyber / Green is the colour / Cymbaline / Party sequence / Main theme / Ibiza bar / More blues / Quicksilver / A Spanish piece / Dramatic theme. *(cd-iss.Apr87; CDP 746386-2) (re-iss.Sep95 on 'E.M.I.' cd/c; CD/TC EMD 1084)*

Harvest Harvest

Nov 69. (d-lp)(d-c) *(SHDW 1-2)(TC2SHWD 4501)* <388> **UMMA GUMMA** (live */ others solo) [5] [74]
– Astronomy domine * / Careful with that axe, Eugene * / Set the control for the heart of the sun * / A saucerful of secrets * / RICHARD WRIGHT:- Sysyphus (parts 1-4) / ROGER WATERS:- Grantchester Meadows / Several species of small furry animals gathered together in a cave and grooving with a pict / DAVID GILMOUR: – The narrow way (parts 1-3) / NICK MASON:- The Grand Vizier's garden party – part 1; Entrance – part 2; Entertainment / part 3; Exit. *(d-cd-iss.Mar87; CDS 746404-2) (re-iss.Oct94 on 'E.M.I.' d-cd/d-c; CD/TC EMD 1074)*

Oct 70. (lp/c) *(SHVL/TCSHVL 781)* <382> **ATOM HEART MOTHER** [1] [55]
– Atom heart mother; (a) Father's shout – (b) Breast milky – (c) Mother fore – (d) Funky dung – (e) Mind your throats please – (f) Remergence / If / Summer '68 / Fat old Sun / Alan's psychedlic breakfast / Rise and shine / Sunny side up / Morning glory. *(cd-iss.Mar87; CDP 746381-2) (re-iss.Oct94 on 'E.M.I.' cd/c; CD/TC EMD 1072)*

— (above featured **RON GEESIN** – horns, co-writer)

Nov 71. (lp/c) *(SHVL/TCSHVL 795)* <832> **MEDDLE** [3] [70]
– One of these days / A pillow of winds / Fearless (interpolating 'You'll never walk alone') / San Tropez / Seamus / Echoes. *(re-iss.Nov83 on 'Fame' lp/c; ATAK/TCATAK 35) (cd-iss.Aug84; CDP 746034-2) (re-iss.cd Apr89 on 'Mobile Fidelity'; UDCD 518) (re-iss.Aug94 on 'E.M.I.' cd/c; CD/TC EMD 1061)*

Dec 71. (7") <3240> **ONE OF THESE DAYS. / FEARLESS** [-] [ ]

Jun 72. (lp/c) *(SHVL/TCSHVL 4020)* <11078> **OBSCURED BY CLOUDS** [6] [46]
– Obscured by clouds / When you're in / Burning bridges / The gold it's in the . . . / Wots . . . uh the deal / Mudmen / Childhood's end / Free four / Stay / Absolute curtains. *(cd-iss.Apr87; CDP 746385-2) (re-iss.Sep95 on 'E.M.I.' cd/c; CD/TC EMD 1083)*

Jul 72. (7") <3391> **FREE FOUR. / STAY** [-] [ ]

Mar 73. (lp/c) *(SHVL/TCSHVL 804)* <11163> **THE DARK SIDE OF THE MOON** [2] [1]
– Speak to me / Breathe / On the run / Time / The great gig in the sky / Money / Us and them / Any colour you like / Brain damage / Eclipse. *(cd-iss.Aug84; CDP 746001-2) (re-iss.cd.Mar93; same); hit UK No.4) (re-iss.Jul94 on 'E.M.I.' cd/c; CD/TC EMD 1064) (re-iss.Feb97 on 'E.M.I.'; LPCENT 11)*

May 73. (7") <3609> **MONEY. / ANY COLOUR YOU LIKE** [-] [13]

Oct 73. (7") <3832> **US AND THEM. / TIME** [-] [ ]

Harvest Columbia

Sep 75. (lp/c) *(SHVL/TCSHVL 814)* <33453> **WISH YOU WERE HERE** [1] [1]
– Shine on you crazy diamond (parts 1-5) / Welcome to the machine / Have a cigar / Wish you were here / Shine on you crazy diamond (parts 6-9). *(cd-iss.Aug84; CDP 746035-2) (re-iss.Jul94 on 'E.M.I.' cd/c; CD/TC EMD 1062)*

Oct 75. (7") <10248> **HAVE A CIGAR. / SHINE ON YOU CRAZY DIAMOND (excerpt)** [-] [ ]

Jan 77. (lp/quad-lp/c) *(SHVL/Q4SHVL/TCSHVL 815)* <34474> **ANIMALS** [2] [3] Feb77
– Pigs on the wing (part 1) / Dogs / Pigs (three different ones) / Sheep / Pigs on the wing (part 2). *(cd-iss.Jul86; CDP 746128-2) (re-iss.Jul94 on 'E.M.I.' cd/c; CD/TC EMD 1060)*

Nov 79. (7") *(HAR 5194)* <11187> **ANOTHER BRICK IN THE WALL (PART 2). / ONE OF MY TURNS** [1] [1] Jan80

Dec 79. (d-lp/d-c) *(SHWD/TC2SHWD 411)* <36183> **THE WALL** [3] [1]
– In the flesh / The thin ice / The happiest days of our lives / Another brick in the wall (part 2) / Mother / Goodbye blue sky / Empty spaces / Young lust / One of my turns / Don't leave me now / Another brick in the wall (part 3) / Goodbye cruel world / Hey you / Is there anybody out there? / Nobody home / Vera / Comfortably numb / The show must go on / Run like hell / Waiting for the worms / Stop / The trial / Outside the wall. *(d-cd-iss.Sep84; CDS 746036-2) (re-iss.UK & US Jul90;) (re-iss.Oct94 on 'E.M.I.' cd/c; CD/TC EMD 1071)*

Apr 80. (7") <11265> **RUN LIKE HELL. / DON'T LEAVE ME NOW** [-] [53]

Jun 80. (7") <11311> **COMFORTABLY NUMB. / HEY YOU** [-] [ ]

Jun 82. (7") <03118> **ONE OF MY TURNS. / ANOTHER BRICK IN THE WALL (part 2)** [-] [ ]

Jul 82. (d-lp) **SOUNDTRACK FROM THE FILM 'THE WALL'** [ ] [ ]
– (tracks from above + new singles)

Aug 82. (7") *(HAR 5222)* <01342> **WHEN THE TIGERS BROKE FREE. / BRING THE BOYS BACK HOME** [39] [ ]

— Now just main trio **WATERS, GILMOUR, MASON.**(WRIGHT left to form ZEE) guests on lp were **ANDY BROWN** – organ, **RAY COOPER** – perc., **MICHAEL KAMEN** – piano, **RALPH RAVENSCROFT** – saxophone.

Mar 83. (lp/c) *(SHPF/TCSHPF 1983)* <38243> **THE FINAL CUT** [1] [6]
– The post war dream / Your possible pasts / One of the few / The hero's return / The gunners dream / Paranoid eyes / Get your filthy hands off my desert / The Fletcher memorial home / Southampton dock / The final cut / Not now John / Two suns in the sunset. *(cd-iss.Jul86; CDP 746129-2) (re-iss.Oct94 on 'E.M.I.' cd/c; CD/TC EMD 1070)*

May 83. (7") *(HAR 5224)* <03905> **NOT NOW JOHN. / THE HERO'S RETURN (pts.1 & 2)** [30] [ ]
(12"+=) *(12HAR 5224)* – ('A'version).

— **MASON** and **GILMOUR** recruited new members below to replace WATERS who went solo. **TIM RENWICK** – guitar (ex-SUTHERLAND BROTHERS & QUIVER, ex-TV SMITH) / **GUY PRATT** – bass (ex-KILLING JOKE, ex-ICEHOUSE) / **SCOTT PAGE** – saxophone / **RICK WRIGHT** – keyboards also returned p/t.

E.M.I. Columbia

Sep 87. (lp/c/cd) *(EMD/TCEMD/CDEMD 1003)* <40599> **A MOMENTARY LAPSE OF REASON** [3] [3]
– Signs of life / Learning to fly / The dogs of war / One slip / On the turning away / Yet another movie / Round and around / A new machine (part 1) / Terminal frost / A new machine (part 2) / Sorrow.

Sep 87. (12"pink-ep) *(EMP 26)* <07363> **LEARNING TO FLY (edit) / ONE SLIP (edit). / TERMINAL FROST (lp version)** [ ] [70]
(cd-ep+=) *(CDEM 26)* – Terminal frost (DYOL version).

Dec 87. (7"/7"pink) *(EM/+P 34)* <07660> **ON THE TURNING AWAY. / RUN LIKE HELL (live)** [55] [ ]
(12"+=/cd-s+=) *(12/CD EM 34)* – ('A'live).

Jun 88. (7"/7"pink) *(EM/+G 52)* **ONE SLIP. / TERMINAL FROST** [50] [ ]
(12"+=/12"w-poster+=)(cd-s+=) *(12EM/+P 52)(CDEM 52)* – Dogs of war (live).

Nov 88. (d-lp/d-c/d-cd) *(EQ/TCEQ/CDEQ 5009)* <44484> **THE DELICATE SOUND OF THUNDER (live)** [11] [11]
– Shine on you crazy diamond / Learning to fly / Yet another movie / Round and

around / Sorrow / The dogs of war / On the turning away / One of these days / Time / Wish you were here / Us and them * / Money / Another brick in the wall (part 2) / Comfortably numb / Run like hell. *(d-cd+= *)*

— with **GILMOUR, MASON + WRIGHT** plus **GUY PRATT / TIM RENWICK / BOB EZRIN** – keyboards, percussion / **DICK PARRY** – tenor sax / **GARY WALLIS** – percussion / **JON CARIN** – programming + add.keyboards / + backing vocalists

Apr 94. (cd/c/lp) *(CD/TC+/EMD 1055)* **THE DIVISION BELL** 1 1
– Cluster one / What do you want from me / Poles apart / Marooned / A great day for freedom / Wearing the inside out / Take it back / Coming back to life / Keep talking / Lost for words / High hopes.

May 94. (c-s/7"colrd) *(TC+/EMS 309)* **TAKE IT BACK. / ('A'mix)** 23 73
(cd-s+=) *(CDEMS 309)* – Astronomy Domine (live).

Oct 94. (c-s/7") *(TC+/EMS 342)* **HIGH HOPES. / KEEP TALKING** 26
(12"+=/cd-s+=) *(12/CD EMS 342)* – One of these days.

Jun 95. (d-cd/d-c/q-lp)(video) *(CD/TC+EMD 1078)(MVD 4914363)* **PULSE (live)** 1 1
– Shine on you crazy diamond / Astronomy domine / What do you want from me / Learning to fly / Keep talking / Coming back to life / Hey you / A great day for freedom / Sorrow / High hopes / Another brick in the wall (part 2) / One of these days *[not on cd]* / Speak to me / Breathe / On the run / Time / The great gig in the sky / Money / Us and them / Any colour you like / Brain damage / Eclipse / Wish you were here / Comfortably numb / Run like hell.

– compilations, etc. –

May 71. (lp) *Starline; (SRS 5071) / Harvest; <759>* **RELICS** 32
– Arnold Layne / Interstellar overdrive / See Emily play / Remember a day / Paintbox / Julia dream / Careful with that axe, Eugene / Cirrus minor / The Nile song / Biding my time / Bike. *(re-iss.Oct78 on 'Music For Pleasure' lp/c; MFP/TCMFP 50397)*

Jan 74. (d-lp)(d-c) *Harvest; (SHDW 403)(TC2EXE 1013) <11257>* **A NICE PAIR** 21 36 Dec73
– (THE PIPER AT THE GATES OF DAWN / A SAUCERFUL OF SECRETS)

Dec 79. (11xlp-box) *Harvest; (PF 11)* **THE FIRST XI (67-77)**

Nov 81. (lp/c) *Harvest; (SHVL/TCSHVL 822) <37680>* **A COLLECTION OF GREAT DANCE SONGS** (remixes) 37 31
– One of these days / Money / Another brick in the wall (part 2) / Wish you were here / Shine on you crazy diamond / Sheep. *(re-iss.1985 on 'Fame' lp/c; ATAK/TCATAK 31) (cd-iss.Nov88; CDP 790732-2)*

Nov 81. (7"w-drawn) *Harvest; (HAR 5217)* **MONEY. / LET THERE BE MORE LIGHT** - -

Jun 83. (lp) *Capitol; <12276>* **WORKS (68-73)** - 68

Nov 91. (12"/cd-s) *See For Miles; (SEA/+CD 4)* **TONITE LET'S ALL MAKE LOVE IN LONDON** -

Nov 92. (9xcd-box) *E.M.I.; (PFBOX 1)* **SHINE ON**
– (A SAUCERFUL OF SECRETS – MOMENTARY LAPSE . . . + rare singles)

Nov 93. (cd) *See For Miles; (SFM 2)* **TONITE LET'S ALL MAKE LOVE IN LONDON . . . PLUS** -
– Interstellar overdrive / Nick's boogie / (interviews with David Hockney & Lee Marvin).

Nov 95. (cd) *See For Miles; (SFMCD 3)* **LONDON '66-'67** -
– Interstellar overdrive / Nick's boogie.

DAVID GILMOUR

solo with **MICK WEAVER** – keyboards / **RICK WILLIS** – bass / **JOHN WILLIE WILSON** – drums

Harvest Columbia

Jun 78. (lp/c) *(SHVL/TCSHVL 817) <35388>* **DAVID GILMOUR** 17 29
– Mihalis / There's no way out of it / Cry from the street / So far away / Short and sweet / Raise my rent / No way / Deafinitely / I can't breathe anymore. *(re-iss.1983 on 'Fame' lp/c; FA/TCFA 4130791)*

Jun 78. (7") *(HAR 5167) <10803>* **THERE'S NO WAY OUT OF IT. / DEAFINATELY**

— Now with various sessioners incl.STEVE WINWOOD, JEFF PORCARO & JON LORD

Feb 84. (7"/ext.12") *(HAR/12HAR 5226)* **BLUE LIGHT. / CRUISE** 62

Mar 84. (lp/c)(cd) *(SHSP 24-0079-1/-4)(CDP 746031-2) <39296>* **ABOUT FACE** 21 32
– Until we sleep / Murder / Love on the air / Blue light / Out of the blue / All lovers are deranged / You know I'm right / Cruise / Let's get metaphysical / Near the end. *(re-iss.Mar87 on 'Fame' lp/c; FA/TCFA 3171)*

May 84. (7"/7"pic-d) *(HAR/+P 5229)* **LOVE ON THE AIR. / LET'S GET METAPHYSICAL**

RICHARD WRIGHT

solo with **SNOWY WHITE** – guitar / **MEL COLLINS** – saxophone / **LARRY STEELE** – bass / **REG ISADORE** – drums

Harvest Columbia

Sep 78. (lp/c) *(SHVL/TCSHVL 818)* **WET DREAM**
– Medterranean c / Against the odds / Cat cruise / Summer elegy / Waves / Holiday / Mad Yannis dance / Drop in from the top / Pink's song / Funky deux.

— In 1984, he formed ZEE duo, and returned to FLOYD later in the 80's.

— with **DAVE HARRIS** – guitar, vocals, keyboards, synth (ex-FASHION)

Apr 84. (7"/ext.12"; by ZEE) *(HAR/12HAR 5227)* **CONFUSION. / EYES OF A GYPSY**

Apr 84. (lp/c; by ZEE) *(SHSP 240101/-1/-4)* **IDENTITY**
– Confusion / Voices / Private person / Strange rhythm / Cuts like a diamond / By touching / How do you do it / Seems we are dreaming.

E.M.I. Columbia

Oct 96. (cd/c) *(CD/TC+/EMD 1098)* **BROKEN CHINA** 61
– Breaking water / Night of a thousand furry toys / Hidden fear / Runaway / Underground / Satellite / Woman of custom / Interlude / Black cloud / Far from the harbour wall / Drowning / Reaching for the rail / Blue room in Venice / Sweet July / Along the shoreline / Breakthrough.

NICK MASON

solo with **CARLA BLEY** and **ROBERT WYATT**

Harvest Columbia

May 81. (lp/c) *(SHSP/TCSHSP 4116) <37307>* **FICTITIOUS SPORTS**
– Can't get my motor to start / I was wrong / Siam / Hot river / Boo to you too / Do ya / Wervin' / I'm a mineralist.

Aug 85. (lp; by NICK MASON & RICK FENN) *(MAF 1) <40142>* **PROFILES**
– Malta / Lie for a lie / Rhoda / Profiles (part 1 & 2) / Israel / And the address / Mumbo jumbo / Zip code / Black ice / At the end of the day / Profiles (part 3).

Sep 85. (7"; by NICK MASON & RICK FENN) *(HAR 5238)* **LIE FOR A LIE. / AND THE ADDRESS**
(12"+=) *(12HAR 5238)* – Mumbo jumbo.

PLASTIC ONO BAND (see under ⇒ LENNON, John)

PLASTIC PENNY

Formed: London, England . . . 1967 from The UNIVERSALS, by MICK GRABHAM and NIGEL OLSSON (were not part of CHRIS LAMB & THE UNIVERSALS). They had backed Scottish singer, GIDIAN (r.n. JAMES POLLACK), on a 1966 single, 'FEELING', releasing two singles for Larry Page's 'Page One' label the following year before teaming up with ex-CIRCLES men, PAUL RAYMOND and BRIAN KEITH. Their debut 45, 'EVERYTHING I AM' (originally recorded by The BOX TOPS), hit the UK Top 10 early in 1968, although this was to give them the dreaded one hit wonder tag. After the failure of the BILL MARTIN / PHIL COULTER-penned follow-up, BRIAN KEITH quit to go solo, while the band took on a more psychedelic pop approach. The debut album saw a risky break away from conventional styles with superb guitar interplay from GRAHAM RAYMOND (although their cover of The BEATLES' 'STRAWBERRY FIELDS FOREVER' was better left unheard). Other fruitless stabs at the singles market, together with the music press tagging them as "a sub-standard MOVE", led the band to call it a day. The last two patchy albums contained insipid covers of 'HOUND DOG' and 'McARTHUR PARK', doing the band no favours. Nevertheless, each individual went on to greater "rock" things in the 70's (see below).

Recommended: TWO SIDES OF . . . (*6)

BRIAN KEITH – vocals (ex-CIRCLES) / **MICK GRABHAM** – guitar (ex-UNIVERSALS) / **PAUL RAYMOND** – organ, vocals (ex-CIRCLES) / **TONY MURRAY** – bass / **NIGEL OLSSON** – drums, vocals (ex-UNIVERSALS)

Page One Page One

Nov 67. (7") *(POF 051)* **EVERYTHING I AM. / NO PLEASURE WITHOUT PAIN MY LOVE** 6 -
(re-iss.Feb75 on 'D.J.M.'; DJS 10353)

Mar 68. (7") *(POF 062)* **NOBODY KNOWS IT. / JUST HAPPY TO BE WITH YOU** -

— now without BRIAN KEITH, who went solo, releasing 3 singles for the same label

Apr 68. (lp) *(POLS 005)* **TWO SIDES OF A PENNY** -
– Everything I am / Wake me up / Never my love / Genevieve / No pleasure without pain my love / So much older now / Mrs. Grundy / Take me back / I want you / It's a good thing / Strawberry fields forever. *(cd-iss.1993 on 'Repertoire'; REP 4368-WP)*

Jul 68. (7") *(POF 079) <21005>* **YOUR WAY TO TELL ME TO GO. / BABY YOU'RE NOT TO BLAME**

Jan 69. (7") *(POF 107)* **HOUND DOG. / CURRENCY** -

Feb 69. (lp) *(POLS 014)* **CURRENCY** -
– *(cd-iss.1993 on 'Repertoire'; REP 4369-WP)*

— **CHRIS LAIN** – bass repl. TONY MURRAY who joined The TROGGS

Jul 69. (7") *(POF 146)* **SHE DOES. / GENEVIEVE** -

Apr 70. (lp) *(POS 611)* **HEADS YOU WIN, TAILS I LOSE** -

— split after above out-takes album. GRABHAM formed COCHISE and then joined PROCOL HARUM. RAYMOND joined CHICKEN SHACK then SAVOY BROWN. OLSSON joined SPENCER DAVIS GROUP and then ELTON JOHN.

PLUTO

Formed: London, England . . . early 70's, by PAUL GARDNER, ALLAN WARNER, MICHAEL WORTH and DEREK JARVIS. They jumped on the progressive rock bandwagon, soon jumping back off following the release of a couple of singles and a patchy eponymous album. Their best track, 'I REALLY WANT IT', was issued as a single and featured JOHN GILBERT on vocals, although this boogie-type rock didn't win any new fans. • **Trivia:** Watch out for others groups/artists of the same name.

Recommended: PLUTO (*5)

PAUL GARDNER – vocals, guitar / **ALLAN WARNER** – guitar, vocals / **MICHAEL WORTH** – bass / **DEREK JARVIS** – drums

Dawn not issued

Oct 71. (7") *(DNS 1017)* **RAG A BONE JOE. / STEALING MY THUNDER** -

Dec 71. (lp) *(DNLS 3030)* **PLUTO** -
– Crossfire / And my old rocking horse / Down and out / She's innocent / Road to glory / Stealing my thunder / Beauty queen / Mister Westwood / Rag a bone Joe / Bare lady. *(re-iss.Sep89 on 'See For Miles' lp/cd+=; SEE/+CD 265)*– I really want it / Something that you loved.

Jun 72. (7") *(DNS 1026)* **I REALLY WANT IT. / SOMETHING THAT YOU LOVED** -

Warners / not issued

1973. (7") *(K 16311)* **MOCKINGBIRD HILL. / PLUTO'S THEME** [ ] [-]

— split after above

POETS

Formed: Glasgow, Scotland . . .1961 by GEORGE GALLAGHER, JOHN DAWSON, TONY MYLES, HUME PATON and ALAN WEIR. They became residents at the Flamingo Ballroom prior to being discovered by ROLLING STONES' manager ANDREW LOOG OLDHAM, who subsequently signed them in 1964 to his management and production company. Resplendent in their velvet suits and frilly shirts, their debut, 'NOW WE'RE THRU', just missed out on a Top 30 placing. Their blend of R&B songs (self-penned and covers), went some way towards breaking them outside of Scotland. They never had another hit, even when OLDHAM transferred them to his 'Immediate' label. Their ever-changing line-ups didn't help matters, and by 1967 none of the originals remained, even FRASER WATSON (a member from a year ago) bailing out. OLDHAM too lost interest, and without him, they signed a one-off deal with 'Decca', releasing 'WOODEN SPOON'. This was flipped over for the excellent Eastern psychedelic gem of a B-side, 'IN YOUR TOWER'. The A-side was written by their manager ERIC WOOLFSON and UNIT 4+2's TOMMY MOELLER. Their last two singles in 1971 were set up by DJ, TONY MEEHAN for a Strike Cola plug. • **Trivia:** All 45's except their hit debut, are now worth over £25; the highest being 'WOODEN SPOON' at £80.

Recommended: IN YOUR TOWER (*7)

GEORGE GALLAGHER – vocals / **HUME PATON** – lead guitar, vocals / **TONY MYLES** – guitar / **JOHN DAWSON** – bass / **ALAN WEIR** – drums

Decca / Dyno-vox

Oct 64. (7") *(F 11995) <201>* **NOW WE'RE THRU. / THERE ARE SOME** [31] [ ]

Feb 65. (7") *(F 12074)* **THAT'S THE WAY IT'S GOT TO BE. / I'LL CRY WITH THE MOON** [ ] [-]

Jul 65. (7") *(F 12195)* **I AM SO BLUE. / I LOVE HER STILL** [ ] [-]

— **FRASER WATSON** – guitar (ex-ARROWS), repl. MYLES

Immediate / not issued

Oct 65. (7") *(IM 006)* **CALL AGAIN. / SOME THINGS I CAN'T FORGET** [ ] [ ]

Jun 66. (7") *(IM 024)* **BABY DON'T YOU DO IT. / I'LL COME HOME** [ ] [ ]

— (late '66) no originals remaining just **FRASER** who recruited **ANDI MULVEY** – vocals / **IAN McMILLAN** – guitar / **NORRIE McLEAN** – bass / **RAYMOND DUFFY** – drums

Decca / not issued

Feb 67. (7") *(F 12569)* **WOODEN SPOON. / IN YOUR TOWER** [ ] [ ]

— **DOUGIE HENDERSON** – drums, repl. JIM BREAKEY who repl. DUFFY

— **HUGHIE NICHOLSON** – guitar, repl. WATSON who joined PATHFINDERS

— **JOHNNY MARTIN** – organ, repl. MULVEY

Pye / not issued

Dec 68. (7") *(7N 17668)* **LOCKED IN A ROOM. / ALONE AM I** [ ] [-]

Strike Cola / not issued

1971. (7") *(SC 1)* **HEYLA HOLA. / FUN BUGGY** [ ] [-]

1971. (7") *(SC 2)* **SHEW BLEW A GOOD THING. / OUT TO LUNCH** [ ] [-]
(re-iss.Nov71 on 'United Artists'; UP 35308)

— Finally disbanded disjointed group. HUGHIE joined MARMALADE replacing JUNIOR CAMPBELL. He with McMILLAN later formed BLUE, after former had been a part of CODY.

– compilations, etc. –

Jun 97. (cd) *Strike; (STRIKE 901)* **IN YOUR TOWER** [ ] [-]

Iggy POP

Born: JAMES JEWEL OSTERBERG, 21 Apr'47, Ypsilanti, Michigan, USA. The son of an English father and American mother, he joined The IGUANAS as a drummer in 1964. They issued a cover of Bo Diddley's 'MONA', which was limited to 1,000 copies sold at gigs. The following year, he became IGGY POP and joined The PRIME MOVERS with bassist RON ASHETON, although they folded, IGGY subsequently moving to Chicago. In 1967, he returned to Michigan and formed The (PSYCHEDELIC) STOOGES with RON and his drummer brother SCOTT. They were soon joined by DAVE ALEXANDER, IGGY making his celluloid debut in the avant-garde film, 'Francois De Moniere' with girlfriend NICO. In 1968, the band gigged constantly, on one occasion IGGY being charged with indecent exposure. The following year, A&R man Danny Fields, while looking to sign MC5, instead signed The STOOGES to 'Elektra', furnishing them with a $25,000 advance. Their eponymous debut (produced by JOHN CALE – another VELVET UNDERGROUND connection), later proved to be way ahead of its time. Tracks such as; 'NO FUN', '1969' and 'I WANNA BE YOUR DOG', were howling proto-punk, garage classics, later covered by The SEX PISTOLS, SISTERS OF MERCY and SID VICIOUS! respectively. The album just failed to secure a Top 100 placing, the second album faring even worse commercially, although it was hailed by the more diserning critics of the day as a seminal work. From the primal nihilism of 'DIRT', to the psychedelic kiss-off, 'I FEEL ALRIGHT (1970)', it seemed, to the The STOOGES at least, that flower-power had never happened. They were subsequently dropped by their label, following drug-related problems and dissension in the ranks. IGGY moved to Florida, becoming a greenkeeper while taking up golf more seriously, a healthier pastime than his penchant for self-mutilation. In 1972, he had a chance meeting with DAVID BOWIE and manager TONY DeFRIES, who persuaded IGGY to reform his STOOGES and sign a MainMan management deal, this in turn leading to a 'C.B.S.' contract. After his/their flawed classic, 'RAW POWER' (not one of BOWIE's best productions), they folded again, citing drugs as the cause. It was, however, even more of an embryonic punk record, the amphetamine rush of 'SEARCH AND DESTROY' highly influential on the "blank generation" that would trade-in their STEELY DAN albums for anything with two chords and a sneering vocal. In 1975, IGGY checked in to a psychiatric institute, weaning himself off heroin. His only true friend, BOWIE, who regularly visited him in hospital, invited him to appear on his 'LOW' album. He signed to 'R.C.A.' (home of BOWIE) in 1977, issuing the BOWIE-produced debut solo album, 'THE IDIOT', which, due to the recent "new wave" explosion, broke him into the UK Top 30 and US Top 75. It contained the first BOWIE/POP collaboration, 'CHINA GIRL', later a smash hit for BOWIE. His second solo release, 'LUST FOR LIFE' (also produced by BOWIE in '77), was another gem, again deservedly reaching the UK Top 30 (the title track was later resurrected in 1996 after appearing on the soundtrack to the cult Scottish movie, 'Trainspotting'). In 1979, IGGY moved to 'Arista' records, shifting through various infamous personnel, although his commercial appeal was on the wane (this period will be featured in greater detail in the GREAT ALTERNATIVE & INDIE ROCK DISCOGRAHY). In 1987, his revival of a 1957 Johnny O'Keefe hit, 'REAL WILD CHILD', gave him his first UK Top 10 hit. The proclaimed "Godfather Of Punk" was at last gaining some belated recognition for his pioneering style. • **IGGY covered;** SOMETHING WILD (John Hiatt) / LIVIN' ON THE EDGE OF THE NIGHT (Rifkin / Rackin) / LOUIE LOUIE (Kingsmen) / SEX MACHINE (James Brown). • **Trivia:** In 1987, IGGY made a cameo appearance in the film, 'The Color Of Money'. In 1990, his film & TV work included, 'Cry Baby', 'Shannon's Deal', Tales From The Crypt' & 'Miami Vice'. In 1991, he starred in the opera! 'The Manson Family'.

Recommended: THE STOOGES (*8) / FUN HOUSE (*10) / RAW POWER (*7) / solo:- THE IDIOT (*9) / LUST FOR LIFE (*9) / BLAH-BLAH-BLAH (*7) / INSTINCT (*8) / BRICK BY BRICK (*7) / AMERICAN CAESAR (*6)

STOOGES

IGGY POP – vocals / **RON ASHETON** (b. RONALD RANKLIN ASHETON JR., 17 Jul'48, Washington, D.C.) – guitar / **DAVE ALEXANDER** (b. DAVID MICHAEL ALEXANDER, 3 Jun'47, Ann Arbor) – bass / **SCOTT ASHETON** (b. SCOTT RANDOLPH ASHETON, 16 Aug'49, Washington) – drums

Elektra / Elektra

Sep 69. (lp) *<EKS 74051>* **THE STOOGES** [ ] [ ] Aug69
– 1969 / I wanna be your dog / We will fall / No fun / Real cool time / Ann / Not right / Little doll. *(re-iss.Mar77; K 42032) <US cd-iss.1988; 74051-2> (cd-iss.Nov93; 7559 60667-2)*

Oct 69. (7") *<EK 45664>* **I WANNA BE YOUR DOG. / 1969** [-] [ ]

— added guests **STEVE MACKAY** – saxophone / **BILL CHEATHAM** – 2nd guitar

Dec 70. (lp) *<EKS 74071>* **FUN HOUSE** [ ] [ ]
– Down on the street / Loose / T.V. eye / Dirt / I feel alright (1970) / Fun house / L.A. blues. *(re-iss.Mar77; K 42051) <US cd-iss.1988; 74071-2> (cd-iss.Nov93; 7559 60669-2)*

Dec 70. (7") *<EKM 45695>* **I FEEL ALRIGHT (1970). / DOWN ON THE STREET** [-] [ ]

— Break-up in 1972. Soon **IGGY** re-formed with **SCOTT** and **RON** (now bass)

IGGY AND THE STOOGES

JAMES WILLIAMSON – guitar repl. DAVE (died 10 Feb'75)

C.B.S. / Columbia

Jun 73. (lp) *(CBS 65586) <KC 32111>* **RAW POWER** [ ] [ ] May73
– Search and destroy / Gimme danger / Hard to beat * / Penetration / Raw power / I need somebody / Shake appeal / Death trip. *(re-iss.May77 on 'CBS-Embassy'; 31464)*, hit UK No.44, *track repl. by – Your pretty face is going to Hell. *(re-iss.Nov81; CBS 32081) <US cd-iss.1988 on 'Columbia'; > (UK re-iss.May89 on 'Essential' cd/c/lp; ESS CD/MC/LP 005) (cd-iss.all tracks) (re-iss.May94 on 'Columbia' cd/c; 485176-2/-4)*

Jun 73. (7") *<45877>* **SEARCH AND DESTROY. / PENETRATION** [-] [ ]

— added **SCOTT THURSTON** – keyboards (on last 1974 tour, before disbanding) The ASHETONS formed The NEW ORDER (US version), with RON moving on to DESTROY ALL MONSTERS who had three 45's for UK label 'Cherry Red' in the late 70's.

– compilations, others, etc. –

1977. (white-d-lp) *Visa; <IMP 1015>* **METALLIC K.O.** [-] [ ]
– Raw power / Head on / Gimme danger / Rich bitch / Cock in my pocket / Louie Louie. *(originally issued 1976 on French 'Skydog'; SGIS 008) (re-iss.May88 as 'METALLIC KO x 2' on 'Skydog' lp/cd; 62232-1/2) (cd-iss.Sep94; same) (re-iss.Sep96 on 'Dressed To Kill'; DTKLP 001)*

1977. (7"ep) *Bomp; <EP 113>* **I'M SICK OF YOU** [-] [ ]
– I'm sick of you / Tight pants / Scene of the crime.

1977. (7"ep; by IGGY POP & JAMES WILLIAMSON) *Bomp; <EP 114>* **JESUS LOVES THE STOOGES** [-] [ ]
– Jesus loves the Stooges / Consolation prizes / Johanna. *(re-iss. 10"ep.Nov94;)*

1977. (7") *Siamese; <PM 001>* **I GOT A RIGHT. / GIMME SOME SKIN** [-] [ ]
(UK-iss.Dec95 on 'Bomp';)

Feb 78. (lp,green-lp; as IGGY POP with JAMES WILLIAMSON) *Radar; (RAD 2) / Bomp; <BLP 4001>* **KILL CITY** [ ] [ ] Nov77

– Sell your love / Kill city / I got nothin' / Beyond the law / Johanna / Night theme / Night theme reprise / Master charge / No sense of crime / Lucky monkeys / Consolation prizes. *(re-iss.! on 'Elektra';) (cd-iss.Feb89 on 'Line'; LICD 9.00131) (cd-iss.Jan93;) (re-iss.10"lp Feb95 on 'Bomp';)*

Apr 78. (7") *Radar; (ADA 4)* **KILL CITY. / I GOT NOTHIN'** [ ] [-]
1978. (7"ep) *Skydog; (SGIS 12)* **(I GOT) NOTHING** [-] [-] France
– I got nothing / Gimme danger / Heavy liquid.
Aug 80. (lp/c) *Elektra; (K/K4 52234) <EF 7095>* **NO FUN** (1969-70 best of THE STOOGES) [ ] [ ]
1983. (lp) *Invasion; <E 1019>* **I GOT A RIGHT** [-] [ ]
1987. (lp) *Revenge; (MIG 2)* **I GOT A RIGHT** [-] [-] France
1987. (7") *Revenge; (SS 1)* **I GOT A RIGHT. / NO SENSE OF CRIME** [-] [-] France
1987. (7") *Revenge; (BF 50) KILL CITY. / I'M SICK OF YOU* [-] [-] France
Dec 87. (lp) *Fan Club; (FC 037)* **RUBBER LEGS** [-] [-] France
– Rubber legs / Open up and bleed / Johanna / Cock in my pocket / Head on the curb / Cry for me. *(free 7")–* GIMME DANGER (live). / I NEED SOMEBODY (live) *(cd-iss.Apr97 on 'Last Call'; 422248)*
1988. (cd-ep) *Revenge; (CAX 1)* **PURE LUST** [-] [-] France
– I got a right / Johanna / Gimme some skin / I got nothing.
1988. (cd-ep) *Revenge; (CAX 2)* **RAW POWER** [-] [-] France
– Raw power / Head on the curb / Purple haze / Waiting for the man.
1988. (12"pink-ep,cd-ep) *Revenge; (CAX 3)* **GIMME DANGER** [-] [-] France
– Gimme danger / Open up and bleed / Heavy liquid / I got nothing / Dynamite boogie.
1988. (7") *Revenge; (SS 6)* **JOHANNA. / PURPLE HAZE** [-] [-] France
Sep 88. (pic-lp; as IGGY & THE STOOGES) *Revenge; (LPMIG 6)* **DEATH TRIP** [-] [-] France
May 88. (cd; as IGGY & THE STOOGES) *Revenge; (HTM 16)* **OPEN UP AND BLEED** [-] [-] France
(re-iss.Feb96 on 'Bomp' cd/lp; BCD/BLP 4051) (cd re-iss.Jul96; 890016)
Dec 88. (lp; as IGGY & THE STOOGES) *Revenge; (MIG 7)* **LIVE AT THE WHISKEY A GO-GO** [ ] [-]
(cd-iss.Nov94 & Feb97; 895104F)
Dec 88. (lp; as IGGY & THE STOOGES) *Electric; (190069)* **RAW STOOGES VOL.1** [-] [-] German
Dec 88. (lp; as IGGY & THE STOOGES) *Electric; (190070)* **RAW STOOGES VOL.2** [-] [-] German
May 92. (cd) *Line; (LICD 921175)* **I'M SICK OF YOU / KILL CITY** [ ] [-]
Jun 94. (cd; IGGY & THE STOOGES) *New Rose; (890028)* **MY GIRL HATES MY HEROIN** [ ] [-]
(re-iss.Feb97 on 'Wrote Music'; 7890028)
Jul 94. (cd; IGGY & THE STOOGES) *New Rose; (642100)* **NIGHT OF DESTRUCTION** [ ] [-]
Jul 94. (cd; IGGY & THE STOOGES) *New Rose; (642042)* **TILL THE END OF THE NIGHT** [ ] [-]
(re-iss.Apr97; same)
Sep 94. (cd; IGGY & THE STOOGES) *New Rose; (642011)* **LIVE 1971 & EARLY LIVE RARITIES (live)** [ ] [-]
(re-iss.Apr97; same)
Sep 94. (cd; IGGY & THE STOOGES) *New Rose; (895002)* **RAW MIXES VOL.1** [ ] [-]
Sep 94. (cd; IGGY & THE STOOGES) *New Rose; (895003)* **RAW MIXES VOL.2** [ ] [-]
Sep 94. (cd; IGGY & THE STOOGES) *New Rose; (895004)* **RAW MIXES VOL.3** [ ] [-]
Feb 95. (10"lp/cd) *Bomp; (BLP/BCD 4049)* **ROUGH POWER** [ ] [-]
— Also in France; **THE STOOGES**(12"ep) / **SHE CREATURES OF HOLLYWOOD HILLS**
Jul 96. (cd) *Revenge; (642050)* **WILD ANIMAL (live 1977)** [ ] [-]
Jul 96. (cd) *Revenge; (893334)* **PARIS HIPPODROME 1977 (live)** [ ] [-]
Jul 96. (cd; as IGGY & THE STOOGES) *Trident; (PILOT 008)* **YOUR PRETTY FACE IS GOING TO HELL** [ ] [-]
Mar 97. (cd; IGGY & THE STOOGES) *Bomp; (BCD 4063)* **YEAR OF THE IGUANA** [ ] [-]
Apr 97. (cd; STOOGES) *Arcade; (301563-2)* **THE COMPLETE RAW MIXES** [ ] [-]

— IGGY POP solo releases were of the punk/hard rock variety and can be found in The GREAT ROCK DISCOGRAPHY or forthcoming GREAT INDIE / ALTERNATIVE ROCK DISCOGRAPHY. Couldn't put IGGY's STOOGES under S due to typesetting problems that would arise in the future.

POPOL VUH

Formed: Munich, Germany . . .1969 by FLORIAN FRICKE, who had just acquired a Moog synthesizer after completing a classical piano course at the Freiburg Music School and travelling around the equator. FRICKE was born in 1944 at Lake Constanz on the Swiss/German border. He found the name POPOL VUH (meaning God, The Universe and Everything; from the holy book of the Quechua Incas or the Mayan Book Of The Dead) and recruited HOLGER TRULZSCH – percussion (from AMON DUUL II) and FRANK FIEDLER – synthesizers, to record the early 70's debut lp, 'AFFENSTUNDE' (meaning 'the time of the man, the ape'). Another album of trance meditation, 'IN PHARAOH'S GARDEN', was followed by a guest appearance for FRICKE on TANGERINE DREAM's 'Zeit' double set. In 1973, his director/friend, WERNER HERZOG, premiered his 'AGUIRRE, WRATH OF GOD' feature film, containing a POPOL VUH soundtrack which surfaced on vinyl three years later. Early in '73, on 'HOSIANNA MANTRA', FRICKE discarded electronics for more sedate mantra vocals and conventional instruments (played by himself and two new members, DJONG YUN and CONNY VEIT). Half a year later, with FRICKE handling most of the vocals, they were joined by another former AMON DUUL II member, DANNY FICHELSCHER, who replaced YUN on the album, 'SELIGPREISUNG' ('Beatitudes'). Their style around this era, drew from PINK FLOYD and TANGERINE DREAM, while also creating their own blend of ritualistic and Eastern (Tibetan) experimentation. A year later, YUN re-joined, replacing VEIT for the yet another release, 'EINSJAGER & SIEBENJAGER' ('One Soldier & Seven Soldiers'). In 1975, the trio unleashed their best work so far and their first for 'United Artists' (not outside Germany); 'DAS HOHELIED SALOMOS' ('The Holy Song Of Solomon'). The following two years were spent on WERNER HERZOG projects. The first, in 1977, was 'SIGNET, DENN DER GESANG VERTREIBT DIE WOLFE' ('Sing, Then The Song Which Dispels The Wolf'), which was also given the title 'HERZ AUS GLAZ', so called due to the name of the UK version, translated as 'Heart Of Glass'. The second project, 'NOSFERATU' (a re-make of the 1922 horror classic, but now starring Klaus Kinski) was issued in 1978, but in two versions; 'NOSFERATU – ON THE WAY TO A LITTLE WAY' and 'BRUDER DES SCHATTENS – SONNES DES LICHTS'. Another classic work, 'DIE NACHT DER SEELE: TANTRIC SONGS', saw him expand his personnel to a sextet. In 1979, yet another AMON DUUL II former member, RENATE KNAUP replaced YUN for 'LETZTE TAGE, LETZTE NACHTE' ('Last Days, Last Nights'). After work in 1982 on another awe-inspiring HERZOG film project, 'FITZCARRALDO', in which tragedy upon tragedy struck the crew and cast, POPOL VUH faded into near obscurity during the remainder of the decade. • **Songwriters:** FRICKE. • **Trivia:** FRICKE cameo'd in WERNER HERZOG's 1975 film, 'The Enigma Of Kaspar Hauser'.

Recommended: AGUIRRE (*7) / EINJAGER UND SIEBENJAGER (*8) / AGAPE AGAPE (*8)

FLORIAN FRICKE – moog synthesizer / **HOLGER TRULZSCH** – percussion (ex-EMBRYO) / **FRANK FIEDLER** – synthesizers

Liberty — not issued
Jan 71. (lp) *(83460)* **AFFENSTUNDE** [-] [-] German
– Ich mache einen Spiegel: 1- Dream (part 4) / 2- Dream (part 5) / 3- Dream (part 49) / Affenstunde. *(cd-iss.1991 on German 'Bell'; BLR 84706)*

Pilz — not issued
Apr 72. (lp) *(20-21276-9)* **IN DEN GARTEN PHARAOS** [-] [-] German
– In den Garten Pharaos / Vuh. *(re-iss.1974 on 'PDU Pid'; SQ 6009) (UK-iss.Apr97 on 'Think Progressive'; EFA 03534-1)*

— **FRICKE** recruited new members **CONNY VEIT** – guitar / **DJONG YUN** – vocals / plus guests **KLAUS WIESE** – tamboura / **FRITZ SONNLEITER** – violin / **ROBERT ELISCU** – oboe

Jan 73. (lp) *(20-29143-1)* **HOSIANNA MANTRA** [-] [-] German
– Ah / Kyrie / Hosianna mantra / Das 5. buch mose / Abschied / Segnung / Andacht / Nicht hoch im Himmel. *(re-iss.1974 on 'Kosmische Musik'; 840.061) (re-iss.1981 on 'Celestial Harmonies'; CEL 004)*

— **DANIEL FICHELSCHER** – guitar, drums, congas (ex-AMON DUUL II), repl. YUN

Kosmischen Musik — not issued
Sep 73. (lp) *(KM 58.009)* **SELIGPREISUNG** [-] [-] German
– Selig sind, die da hungern, selig sind, die da duersten nach gerechtigkeit, ja, sie sollen satt werden / Tanz der Chassidm / Selig sind, die da hier weinen, ja, sie sollen spaeter lachen / Selig sind, die da willig arm sind, ja, ihrer ist das Himmelreich / Selig sind, die da leid klagen, ja, sie sollen getroestet werden / Selig sind, die Sanftmuetigen, ja, sie werden einst sie Erde erben / Selig sind, die da reinen Herzens sind, ja, sie sollen Gottes kinder heissen, Agnus Dei, Agnus Dei. *(re-iss.1975 on 'Kosmischen Musik'; 840.102)*

— **FRICKE + FICHELSCHER** + returning **YUN**

Jun 74. (lp) *(58017)* **EINSJAGER & SIEBENJAGER** [-] [-] German
– Kleiner kriege / King Minos / Morgengruss / Wuerfelspiel / Gutes land / Einsjager & Siebenjager. *(UK-iss.Jun97 on 'Bernhard'; KM 58017)*

U.A. — not issued
May 75. (lp) *(UAS 29781)* **DAS HOHELIED SALOMOS** [-] [-] German
– Steh auf, zieh mich dir nach / Du schonste der weiber / In den nachten auf den gassen 1 / Du sohn Davids 1 / In den nachten auf den gassen 2 / Der winter ist vorbei / Deine liebe ist susser als wein / Du sohn Davids 2 / Du tranke mich mit deinen kussen. *(re-iss.1982 on 'WEA'; K 58423)*

— added **AL GROMER** – sitar / **TED DE JONG** – tamboura

1976. (lp) *(UAS 29916)* **LETZTE TAGE – LETZTE NAECHTE** [-] [-] German
– Der grosse kriege / Oh, wie nah ist der weg hibab / Oh, wie weit ist der weg hinauf / In deine hande / Kyrie / Haram dei haram dei haram dei ra / Dort ist der Weg / Letzte tage letzte nachte.

Kosmische — not issued
1976. (lp) *(940.119/120)* **YOGA** [-] [-] German
– Discover cosmic – Popol Vuh.

— **MATTHIAS VON TIPPEELSKIRCH** – flute, repl. YUN + JONG

Brain — not issued
1977. (lp) *(0060.079)* **SINGET, DENN DER GESANG VERTREIBT DIE WOLFE** [-] [-] German
– Engel der gegenwart / Blatter aus dem buch der kuehnheit / Das lied von den hohen bergen / Huter der schwelle / Der ruf / Singet, denn der gesang vertreibt die Woelfe / Gemeinschaft.

— In 1978, the soundtrack to 'NOSFERATU: ON THE WAY TO A LITTLE WAY' was issued; German imp. 'P.D.U.'; *Pld.A 7028).*

Nov 78. (lp) *(0060.167)* **BRUDER DES SCHATTENS – SONNE DES LICHTS** [-] [-] German
– Bruder des schattens – Sonne des lichts / Hore, der du wagst / Das schloss des irrtums / Die umkehr.

— Expanded line-up; **FRICKE, FISCHELSCHER, GROMER, RENATE KNAUP / + DJONG YUN** – vocals / **SUSAN GOETTING** – oboe

1979. (lp) *(0060.242)* **DIE NACHT DER SEELE: TANTRIC SONGS** [-] [-] German
– Mantram der erdberuhrung / Engel der luft / Mit handen, mit fussen / Wo bist du, der du uberwunden hast? / Gesegnet du, bei deiner ankunft? / Mantram der erdberuhrung II / Im reich der schatten / Wanderer durch die nacht / Mantram der herzberuhrung / Auf dem weg / Mantram der herzberuhung II / In der halle des lernens.

Innovative — not issued
Jan 81. (lp) *(KS-80.007)* **SEI STILL, WISSE ICH BIN** [-] [-] German

– Wehe khorazin / Und als er sah es geht dem ende zu / Garten der Gemeinschaft / Gemeinsam assen sie das Brot / Lass los / Gemeinsam tranken sie den wein / . . .Als lebten die Engel auf Erden. *(re-iss.1985 on 'Racket'; RRK 15029)*

Z.Y.X. — not issued

1982. (lp) *(20.021)* **FITZCARRALDO (Soundtrack)** [-] [-] German
– (excerpts from above 2 albums)

— **FRICKE, KNAUP, FICHELSCHER + CONNY VEIT** + guest **BERND WIPPICH** – guitar

Uniton — not issued

1983. (lp) *(U 015)* **AGAPE-AGAPE, LOVE-LOVE** [-] [-] Norway
– Hand in hand / They danced, they laughed, as of old / Love life death / The Christ is near / Love-love / Behold, the drover summonds / Agape-agape / Why do I still sleep.

Cicado — not issued

1985. (lp) *(C 001)* **SPIRIT OF PEACE** [-] [-] Norway
1987. (lp) *Milan; (881309)* **COBRA VERDE (Soundtrack)** [-] [-] German
1988. (lp) *(C 011)* **DER GASANG DER ENGEL** [-] [-] German

— FRICKE and group seem to have dissolved from new record releases.

- compilations, others, etc. -

Jan 76. (lp) *Kosmische; (840.103)* **(Music From The Film) AGUIRRE** [-] [-] German
– Aguirre 1 / Morgengruss 2 / Aguirre 2 / Agnus Dei / Vergegenwaertigung. *(UK cd-iss.Jan97 on 'Spalax'; SPALAX 14974)*
1981. (lp) *Celestial Harmonies; (CEL 006)* **TANTRIC SONGS** [-] [-] German
– edited; 'DIE NACHT DER SEELE: TANTRIC SONGS' & edited 'BRUDER DES SCHATTENS'.
1982. (lp) *PDU; (Pld.A 7028)* **POPOL VUH – SOUNDTRACKS** [-] [-] German
1984. (lp) *Celestial Harmonies; (CEL 008/9)* **IN THE GARDENS OF PHARAOHS/ AGUIRRE** [-] [-] German
1985. (lp) *Nexus; (K22P 471) BNOSFERATU – MUSIC FROM THE WERNER HERZOG FILM* [-] [-] German
1988. (cd) *Cicado; (CACD 01)* **GESANG DER GESANGE (71-74)** [-] [-] Norway
Feb 90. (cd) *Silva Screen; (CDCH 042)* **THE BEST OF POPOL VUH** [-]
1991. (cd) *Celestial Harmonies; (13006-2)* **TANTRIC SONGS (compilation) / HOSIANNA MANTRA** [-] [-] German
1991. (cd) *Bell; (BLR 84710)* **THE BEST OF WERNER HERZOG FILMS** [-] [-] German

— In 1992, mostly all were issued on cd in France for 'Spalax' catalogue numbers between *(14205 – 14219)*

others, etc

1994. (cd) *Spalax; (14875)* **IN DEN GARTEN PHARAOS** [-] [-] France
1994. (cd) *Spalax; (14876)* **FITZCARRALDO** [-] [-] France

PRETTY THINGS

Formed: Dartford, Kent, England . . . 1963 by DICK TAYLOR and PHIL MAY. The former had once been a member of LITTLE BOY BLUE & THE BLUE BOYS, an embryonic version of The ROLLING STONES. The pair added BRIAN PENDLETON, JOHN STAX and PETE KITLEY, the latter being replaced by drummer VIV PRINCE. Taking their name from a BO DIDDLEY song, they soon signed to 'Fontana', employing the management team of Bryan Morrison and James Duncan, the latter of whom wrote their summer '64 debut Top 50 hit, 'ROSALYN'. Their pure roots/R&B follow-up, 'DON'T BRING ME DOWN' (which drew inspiration from black American blues artists of the 50's) dented the UK Top 10, preceding their eponymous Top 10 album in early '65. Unlike the STONES (of whom they were dubbed by the press as uglier cousins), their hits had dried up by 1967, due to a misguided foray into psychedelia. Later that year, they moved to 'Columbia' records, releasing two flop 45's, before they embarked on their most ambitious project so far, 'S.F. SORROW'. It was the first ever "rock opera", inspiring PETE TOWNSHEND (The Who) to write his legendary 'Tommy'. The album was a commercial flop and critically lambasted by the press, although it has since become regarded as an innovative piece of work that was essential to the development of "rock" music. During its recording, TAYLOR left to become a producer, the band folding but regrouping for a heavier 'Harvest' set, 'PARACHUTE' (1970). They struggled on regardless, subsequently signing for LED ZEPPELIN's heavyweight 'Swan Song' label in '74. Two mediocre albums followed before they the band split in '76 after their remaining founder member, MAY, departed. They reformed many times and still tread the boards on the blues circuit alongside members of The YARDBIRDS. • **Songwriters:** Most by PHIL MAY, except covers; PRETTY THING + ROADRUNNER + MONA (Bo Diddley) / CRY TO ME (Bert Berns) / A HOUSE IN THE COUNTRY (Ray Davies; Kinks) / REELIN' AND ROCKIN' (Chuck Berry) / I'M A KING BEE (Muddy Waters) / SHAKIN' ALL OVER (Johnny Kidd & The Pirates) / etc. • **Trivia:** The group made cameo appearances in the films, 'What's Good For The Goose' (1969 w /Norman Wisdom) and 'The Monster Squad' (1980 w /Vincent Price). They were given a tribute by BOWIE in 1973, when he covered their first two hits on his 'PIN-UPS' album.

Recommended: THE PRETTY THINGS (*7) / S.F. SORROW (*7) / PARACHUTE (*6) / THE THINGS (*7)

PHIL MAY (b. 9 Nov'44, Kent, England) – vocals / **DICK TAYLOR** (28 Jan'43) – lead guitar / **BRIAN PENDLETON** (b.13 Apr'44, Wolverhampton, England) – rhythm guitar / **JOHN STAX** (b.JOHN FULLEGAR, 6 Apr'44) – bass / **VIV PRINCE** (b. 9 Aug'44, Loughborough, Leicestershire, England) – drums (PETE KITLEY, then VIV ANDREWS sessioned on 1st-two 45's)

Fontana — Fontana

Jun 64. (7") *(TF 469) <1916>* **ROSALYN. / BIG BOSS MAN** [41] Oct64
Oct 64. (7") *(TF 503) <1941>* **DON'T BRING ME DOWN. / WE'LL BE TOGETHER** [10] Jan65
Feb 65. (7") *(TF 537) <1508>* **HONEY I NEED. / I CAN NEVER SAY** [13]
Mar 65. (lp) *(TL 5239) <67544>* **THE PRETTY THINGS** [6]
– Roadrunner / Judgement day / 13 Chester street / Honey I need / Big city / Unkown blues / Mama, keep your big mouth shut / Oh baby doll / She's fine she's mine / Don't you lie to me / The Moon is rising / Pretty thing. *(re-iss.Jul90 lp/c/cd; 646054-1/-4/-2)*
Jul 65. (7") *(TF 585) <1518>* **CRY TO ME. / JUDGEMENT DAY** [28]
Dec 65. (7") *(TF 647) <1540>* **MIDNIGHT TO SIX MAN. / CAN'T STAND THE PAIN** [46]
Dec 65. (lp) *(TL 5280)* **GET THE PICTURE**
– Get the picture / You don't believe me / We'll play house / Can't stand the pain / Rainin' in my heart / Buzz the jerk / London town / You'll never do it to me baby / Cry to me / I had a dream / Gonna find me a substitute / I want your love. *(re-iss.Mar84; 6438 214) (cd-iss.Jul90; 846459-2)*

— **SKIP ALAN** (b. ALAN ERNEST SKIPPER, 11 Jun'44) – drums repl. PRINCE on some

Fontana — Blue Thumb

Apr 66. (7") *(TF 688)* **COME SEE ME. / £.s.d.** [43]
Jul 66. (7") *(TF 722)* **A HOUSE IN THE COUNTRY. / ME NEEDING YOU** [50]
Dec 66. (7") *(TF 773)* **PROGRESS. / BUZZ IN THE JERK**
Apr 67. (7") *(TF 829)* **CHILDREN. / MY TIME**
May 67. (lp; stereo/mono) *(S+/TL 5425)* **EMOTIONS** [-]
– Death of a socialite / Children / The sun / There will never be another day / House of ten / Out in the night / One long glance / Growing in my mind / Photographer / Bright lights of the city / Tripping / My time / A house in the country / Me needing you / Progress. *(re-iss.Apr91;)*

— **PHIL + DICK** were left to recruit new members **JOHN POVEY** (b.20 Aug'44) – keyboards, vocals (ex-FENMEN) repl. PENDLETON / **WALLY ALLEN** – bass, vocals (ex-FENMEN) repl. SKIP / **MITCH MITCHELL** – (session) drums repl. SKIP

Columbia — Rare Earth

Nov 67. (7") *(DB 8300)* **DEFLECTING GREY. / MR. EVASION** [-]

— **BOBBIE GRAHAM** – drums (also on session) repl. MITCHELL

Feb 68. (7") *(DB 8353)* **TALKIN' ABOUT THE GOOD TIMES. / WALKING THROUGH MY DREAMS** [-]

— **JOHN 'TWINK' ADLER** – percussion, vocals (ex-TOMORROW, etc) repl. GRAHAM

Nov 68. (7") *(DB 8494) <5005>* **PRIVATE SORROW. / BALLROOM BURNING**
Dec 68. (lp; mono/stereo) *(SX/SCX 6306) <506>* **S.F. SORROW** Feb70
– S.F. sorrow / Bracelets of fingers / She says good morning / Private sorrow / Balloon burning / Death / Baron Saturday / I see you / The journey / Well of destiny / Trust / Old man going / Lonliest person. *(re-press.1970; same) (re-iss.Oct87 on 'Edsel'; XED 236) (cd-iss.Oct90; EDCD 236)*

— **SKIP ALAN** – drums, vocals (returned from SUNSHINE) repl. TWINK who joined PINK FAIRIES (new one joining MAY, POVEY and ALLEN plus below) **VICTOR UNITT** – guitar, vocals (ex-EDGAR BROUGHTON) repl. TAYLOR (⇒ producer)

Harvest — Rare Earth

Apr 70. (7") *(HAR 5016)* **THE GOOD MR. SQUARE. / BLUE SERGE BLUES**
Jun 70. (lp) *(SHVL 774) <515>* **PARACHUTE** [43]
– Parachute / Scene 1: The good Mr. Square, she was tall, she was high / Rare Earth / In the square, the letter, rain / Miss Fay regrets / Cries from the midnight circus / Grass / Sickle clowns / She's a lover / What's the use. *(re-iss.Sep88 on 'Edsel' lp/cd; ED/+CD 289)*

— **PETER TOLSON** (b.10 Sep'51, Bishops Stortford, England) – guitar, vocals (ex-EIRE APPARANT) repl. UNITT (who returned to EDGAR BROUGHTON BAND)

Oct 70. (7") *(HAR 5031)* **OCTOBER 26. / COLD STONE**
May 71. (7"m) *(HAR 5037)* **STONE-HEARTED MAMA. / SUMMERTIME / CIRCUS MIND**

— **STUART BROOKS** – bass, vocals repl. WALLY who went into producing

Warners — Warners

Dec 72. (lp) *(K 46190) <2680>* **FREEWAY MADNESS**
– Love is good / Havana bound / Peter / Rip off train / Over the Moon / Religion's dead / Country road / All night sailor / Onion soup / Another bowl?
Jan 73. (7") **OVER THE MOON. / HAVANA BOUND** [-]

— added **GORDON EDWARDS** (b.26 Dec'46, Southport, England) – keyboards (to **MAY, ALAN, POVEY, TOLSON and BROOKS)**

Swan Song — Swan Song

Oct 74. (lp) *(SSK 59400) <8411>* **SILK TORPEDO**
– Dream / Joey / Maybe you tried / Atlanta / L.A.N.T.A. / Is it only love / Come home / Bridge of God / Singapore silk torpedo / Belfast cowboy / Bruise in the sky.
Dec 74. (7") *(K 19401)* **JOEY. / IS IT ONLY LOVE**
Jun 75. (7") *(K 19403)* **I'M KEEPING. / ATLANTA**

— **JACK GREEN** (b.12 Mar'51, Glasgow, Scotland) – bass, vocals (also as EDWARDS, ex-SUNSHINE) repl. BROOKS

Aug 75. (7") *(K 19404) <70107>* **JOEY. / COME HOME MOMMA**
Feb 76. (7") *(K 19405)* **SAD EYE. / REMEMBER THAT BOY** [-]
Apr 76. (7") **REMEMBER THAT BOY. / IT ISN'T ROCK'N'ROLL** [-]
May 76. (lp) *(SSL 59401) <8414>* **SAVAGE EYE** Feb 76
– Under the volcano / My song / Sad eye / Remember that boy / It isn't rock'n'roll / I'm keeping / It's been so long / Drowned man / Theme for Michelle.
May 76. (7") *(K 19406)* **TONIGHT. / IT ISN'T ROCK'N'ROLL** [-]

— Last original PHIL MAY went solo augmented by the FALLEN ANGELS (see below). POVEY also departed leaving only 4 (SKIP, PETER, JACK and GORDON) calling themselves METROPOLIS between mid '76-late'77. JACK also joined T.REX and GORDON went to The KINKS.

PHIL MAY & THE FALLEN ANGELS

with **MICKEY FINN** – guitar (ex-T.REX) / **BILL LOVELADY** – guitar / **BRIAN JOHNSTON** – keyboards (ex-STREETWALKERS) / **WALL ALLEN** – bass / **CHICO GREENWOOD** – drums / etc.

Philips — not issued

1978. (lp) *(6410 969)* **PHIL MAY & THE FALLEN ANGELS** [-] [-] Dutch
– Fallen angels / California / 13 floor suicide / Dance again / Shine on baby / My

good friend / Cold wind / I keep on / Dogs of war / Girl like you. *(UK-iss.1982;) (re-iss.Feb85;)*

PRETTY THINGS

re-formed ex-members in 1980. (**PHIL MAY, DICK TAYLOR, JOHN POVEY, PETER TOLSON, WALLY ALLEN** and **SKIP ALAN**)

Warners Warners

Aug 80. (lp) *(K 56842) <3466>* **CROSS TALK**
– I'm calling / Edge of the night / Sea of blue / Office love / Lost that girl / Bitter end / Falling again / It's so hard / She don't / No future.

Aug 80. (7") *(K 17670)* **I'M CALLING. / SEA OF BLUE**

— Disbanded 1981, but re-formed briefly as . . .

ZAC ZOLAR AND ELECTRIC BANANA

Butt not issued

1984. (7") **TAKE ME HOME. / JAMES MARSHALL**

— (above appeared on 'Minder' TV series) *(re-iss.Aug86 on 'Shanghai'; MGLS 2)*

PRETTY THINGS

re-formed by **MAY + TAYLOR** in 1984. Now with **JOE SHAW** – guitar / **DAVE WINTOUR** – bass / **KEVIN FLANAGAN** – saxophone / **JOHN CLARKE** – drums

Big Beat not issued

Aug 84. (lp) *(WIK 24)* **LIVE AT THE HEARTBREAK HOTEL (live)**
– Big boss man / Midnight to six man / I'm a king bee / Honey I need / Shakin' all over / Rosalyn / Roadrunner / Mama keep your big mouth shut / Raining in my heart / Reelin' and rockin' / Don't bring me down / Mona.

— **ROLF TER VELD** – bass + **BERTRAM ENGEL** – drums (ex-UDO LINDENBERG, ex-PANIKORCHESTER) repl.WINTOUR, FLANAGAN + CLARKE

In-Akustik not issued

Jun 88. (cd) *(INAK 8708)* **OUT OF THE ISLAND**
– Cry to me / Baby doll / She's fine, she's mine / Get the picture / Havana bound / Can't stop / Loneliest person / £.s.d. / Private sorrow / The moon is rising / Big city / Cause and effect / Well known blues / You don't believe me / Judement day. *(re-iss.May95; same)*

— **MAY + TAYLOR** again re-formed them again in 1989, with new **GLEN MATLOCK** – bass, vocals (ex-SEX PISTOLS, ex-RICH KIDS) / **FRANK HOLLAND** – guitar, keyboards / **BOBBY WEBB** – keyboards, vocals / **MARK ST. JOHN** – drums, bass, vocals

Trax not issued

Sep 89. (7") *(7TX 12)* **EVE OF DESTRUCTION. / GOIN' DOWNHILL**
(12"+=) *(12TX 12)* – Can't stop.

— (on tour) **STEVE BROWNING** – bass repl. MATLOCK

— Re-formed again in 1991, with **PHIL MAY / DICK TAYLOR** (ex-MEKONS) / **JIMMY McCARTY** (ex-YARDBIRDS) / **RICHARD HITE** (ex-CANNED HEAT)

PRETTY THINGS & THE YARDBIRD BLUES BAND

Super-blues-group / collab with ex-YARDBIRDS and plenty covers

Demon not issued

Oct 91. (cd) *(FIENDCD 708)* **CHICAGO BLUES JAM 1991**
– Can't judge the book / Down in the bottom / Hush hush / Can't hold out / Spoonful / She fooled me / Time is on my side / Scratch my back / Long tall Shorty / Diddley daddy / Ain't got you / Caress my baby / Here's my picture / Chain of fools / Don't start crying now.

Feb 94. (cd) *(FIENDCD 748)* **WINE, WOMEN & WHISKEY**
– Wine, women and whiskey / Sure look good to me / No questions / The amble / It's all over now / Bad boy / Spoonful (bare bones remix) / French champagne / My back scratcher / Can't hold out (big city remix) / Diddley daddy (street corner remix) / I'm cryin' / Gettin' all wet.

PRETTY THINGS 'N MATES (WITH MATTHEW FISHER)

featuring a plethora of famous cover versions

Kingdom not issued

May 94. (cd) *(CDKVL 9031)* **A WHITER SHADE OF DIRTY WATER**
– He's waitin' / Strychnine / Pushing too hard / Kicks / Candy / Louie, Louie / 96 tears / Let's talk about girls / Sometimes good guys don't wear black / I'm a man / Red river rock / Midnight to 6 man '93.

PRETTY THINGS

not issued Medicine

1994. (7") **HAVANA BOUND. / RELIGION'S DEAD**

— re-formed again 1995, **MAY, TAYLOR, POVEY, ALEN, ALAN + HOLLAND**

Fragile not issued

Oct 95. (d-cd) *(FRA 005D)* **UNREPENTANT – BLOODY BUT UNBOWED**

Jun 96. (7"pic-d) *(FRPS 006)* **EVE OF DESTRUCTION. / ROSALYN / PASSION OF LOVE**

– compilations, others, etc. –

Dec 64. (7"ep) *Fontana; (TE 17434)* **PRETTY THINGS**

Aug 65. (7"ep) *Fontana; (TE 17442)* **RAINING IN MY HEART**

Jan 66. (7"ep) *Fontana; (TE 17472)* **ON FILM**

1967. (lp) *Wing; (WL 1167)* **BEST OF THE PRETTY THINGS**

1968. (lp) *Phonogram;* **GREATEST HITS**
(cd-iss.1991 on 'Carnaby';)

Jun 69. (7") *Fontana; (TF 1024)* **ROSALYN. / DON'T BRING ME DOWN**

Jun 75. (d-lp) *Harvest; (SHDW 406) / Rare Earth; <R7 549>* **REAL PRETTY:- S.F. SORROW / PARACHUTE** 1976

Jul 77. (lp) *Harvest; (SHSM 2022)* **SINGLES A's & B's**

1976. (d-lp) *Sire; <SASH 37132>* **THE VINTAGE YEARS**

1979. (lp; as ELECTRIC BANANA) *Butt; (NOTT 001)* **THE SEVENTIES** (with various artists)

1980. (lp; as ELECTRIC BANANA) *Butt; (NOTT 003)* **THE SIXTIES** (with various artists)

— Film music lp's as ELECTRIC BANANA on 'De Wolfe':- 1967; ELECTRIC BANANA *(DWSLP 3280)* / 1968; MORE ELECTRIC BANANA *(DWSLP 3281)* / 1969; EVEN MORE ELECTRIC BANANA *(DWSLP 3282)* / 1973; THE RETURN OF THE ELECTRIC BANANA (DWSLP 3283) / 1973; HOT LICKS *(DWSLP 3284)*

Mar 82. (lp/c) *See For Miles; (CM/+K 103)* **THE PRETTY THINGS 1967-1971**
(cd-iss.Oct89; SEECD 103)

Jul 82. (7") *Old Gold; (OG 9237)* **DON'T BRING ME DOWN. / HONEY I NEED**

Jun 84. (lp) *Edsel; (ED 139)* **LET ME HEAR THE CHOIR SING**

Feb 86. (lp) *Bam Caruso; (KIRI 032)* **CLOSED RESTAURANT BLUES**

May 86. (lp/c) *Harvest; (EMS/TCEMS 1119)* **CRIES FROM THE MIDNIGHT CIRCUS** (1968-1971)

Nov 88. (cd) *Radioactive; (HORN 004)* **THE PRETTY THINGS**

Aug 91. (cd) *Repertoire; (REP 4089WZ)* **MORE ELECTRIC BANANA**

Apr 92. (cd) *Band Of Joy; (BOJCD 3)* **ON AIR**

Mar 94. (cd/c) *Spectrum; (550 186-2/-4)* **MIDNIGHT TO 6**

Jun 97. (cd) *See For Miles; (SEECD 476)* **THE EP COLLECTION**

PRINCIPAL EDWARDS MAGIC THEATRE

Formed: at Exeter University, England . . . 1969 by hippie students BINDY BOURQUIN, DAVID JONES, MARTIN STELLMAN, ROOT CARTWRIGHT (all co-composers), plus JEREMY ENSOR. They took the group name from the head honcho at their Uni, setting sail on a multi-media trip with costumes, dancers and lightshows. Signing to JOHN PEEL's 'Dandelion' label, they released their original 'SOUNDTRACK', which highlighted the beautiful crystal clear vox of VIVIENNE McAULIFFE. Space-folk for the Glastonbury set, it was followed in 1971 by 'THE ASMOTO RUNNING BAND', a concept piece which didn't live up to their last effort. Only two original members remained (JONES and BOURQUIN) by the time they signed to 'Deram' in 1973. After two singles that year, they isued their last album, 'ROUND ONE', produced by PINK FLOYD's NICK MASON.

Recommended: SOUNDTRACK (*7) / THE ASMOTO RUNNING BAND (*5)

VIVIENNE McAULIFFE – vocals / **MARTIN STELLMAN** – vocals / **DAVID JONES** – vocals, percussion / **ROOT CARTWRIGHT** – guitar / **BINDY BOURQUIN** – violin, keyboards, recorder / **JEREMY ENSOR** – bass / with other dancers, choreographed by GILLIAN HADLEY

Dandelion Columbia

Jul 69. (7") *(S 4405)* **BALLAD OF THE BIG COW GIRL AND A MERE BOY. / LAMENT FOR THE EARTH**

Aug 69. (lp) *(S 63752) <D 9103>* **SOUNDTRACK**
– Enigmatic insomniac machine / Sacrifice / The death of Don Quixote / Third sonnet to sundry notes of music / To a broken guitar / Pinky: A mystery-cycle.

— added **ROGER SWALLOW** – drums

Jan 71. (lp) *(DAN 8002)* **THE ASMOTO RUNNING BAND**
– McAlpine's dream / McAlpine verses the Asmoto / The Asmoto Running Band / Asmoto celebration / Further Asmoto celebration / Total glycerol Esther / Freef (R') all / The Kettering song / Weirdsong of breaking through at last.

— **JONES + BOURQUIN** recruited new members; **NICK PALLETT** – guitar, vocals / **RICHARD JONES** – vocals, bass / **GEOFF NICHOLS** – drums

Deram not issued

Jun 73. (7") *(DM 391)* **CAPTAIN LIFEBOY. / NOTHING**

Sep 73. (7") *(DM 398)* **WEEKDAZE. / WHIZZMORE KID**

1974. (lp; as PRINCIPAL EDWARDS) *(SML 1108)* **ROUND ONE**
– Average chap / Halibut rock / Milk and honeyland / The whizzmore kid / Juggernaut / Dear Mrs. O'Reilly / Triplets / The rise of the glass-white gangster: Moody as a shark on heat – Lady of danger – Glass-white gangster – Sirens – Mechanical madness.

— split after poor showing of above

– compilations, etc. –

Jan 95. See For Miles; (cd) *(SEECD 412)* **SOUNDTRACK / THE ASMOTO RUNNING BAND**

PROCOL HARUM

Formed: Southend, Essex, England . . . 1959 as The PARAMOUNTS, by five schoolboys; BOB SCOTT, GARY BROOKER, ROBIN TROWER, CHRIS COPPING and MICK BROWNLEE. They played a number of local gigs, BROOKER soon taking over vocal chores when SCOTT failed to show. In 1962, they left school and acquired manager Peter Martin. The following year, with a few personnel changes, the band signed to EMI's 'Parlophone' label, soon hitting the UK Top 40 with an R&B cover of The COASTERS' 'POISON IVY'. Their follow-up, a re-working of THURSTON HARRIS's 'LITTLE BITTY PRETTY ONE', failed to emulate their minor earlier success, and, after a few more covers, they folded in late summer '66. • **Note other covers:** I FEEL GOOD ALL OVER (Drifters) / I'M THE ONE WHO LOVES

YOU (Major Lance) / BAD BLOOD (Coasters) / BLUE RIBBONS (Jackie DeShannon) / CUTTIN' IN (Johnny Guitar Watson) / YOU'VE NEVER HAD IT SO GOOD (P.F.Sloan). In 1967, BROOKER and lyricist KEITH REID advertised in the Melody Maker for musicians, soon settling with MATTHEW FISHER, RAY ROYER, DAVE KNIGHTS and BOBBY HARRISON. They became PROCOL HARUM (taking the name from the Latin "procul", meaning "far from these things"), and with help from producer Denny Cordell, they unleashed their mesmeric debut 45, 'A WHITER SHADE OF PALE', for 'Deram'. Adapted from a classical suite by BACH (No.3 in d major; 'Air On A G String'), its neo-gothic/baroque organ refrain combined with REID's extremely surreal lyrics to create a quasi-psychedelic million seller (stayed at No.1 for 6 weeks in the UK charts). With record company pressures to tour, ROYER and HARRISON departed from the group, replaced by former PARAMOUNTS; TROWER and WILSON. Later that year, they moved with producer CORDELL to 'Regal Zonophone', having another major stab at the Top 10 with 'HOMBURG'. The increasingly enjoyed greater success Stateside and by 1970, the band's line-up was identical to the earlier PARAMOUNTS of '63 (see above). In 1972, with their live album riding high in the charts, they resurrected their old 1967 number, 'CONQUISTADOR', subsequently a major hit on both sides of the Atlantic. PROCOL HARUM continued to gain respect from US and Canadian audiences, although the single, 'PANDORA'S BOX', in 1975, gave them a renewed UK chart thrust. Its parent album, 'PROCOL'S NINTH', also returned them to The Top 50, including a cover of The BEATLES' 'EIGHT DAYS A WEEK'. After another patchy album, BROOKER split the band, joining the ERIC CLAPTON BAND before going solo. Like many other rock dinosaurs, the band reformed for a one-off album in the early 90's, surprising many with its inclusion of ROBIN TROWER (he had already established himself as a guitar hero in the 70's & 80's).

Recommended: THE COLLECTION (*8) / BROKEN BARRICADES (*7).

PARAMOUNTS

GARY BROOKER (b.29 May'45) – vocals, keyboards / **ROBIN TROWER** (b. 9 Mar'45) – guitar / **DIZ DERRICK** – bass repl. CHRIS COPPING who went to Leicester University (Sep63) / **B.J. WILSON** (b.18 Mar'47) – drums repl. MICK BROWNLEE (Jan63).

Parlophone / not issued

Dec 63. (7") *(R 5093)* **POISON IVY. / I FEEL GOOD ALL OVER** [35] [-]
Feb 64. (7") *(R 5107)* **LITTLE BIT PRETTY ONE. / A CERTAIN GIRL** [ ] [-]
Jun 64. (7") *(R 5155)* **I'M THE ONE WHO LOVES YOU. / IT WON'T BE LONG** [ ] [-]
Nov 64. (7") *(R 5187)* **BAD BLOOD. / DO I** [ ] [-]
Mar 65. (7") *(R 5272)* **BLUE RIBBONS. / CUTTIN' IN** [ ] [-]
Oct 65. (7") *(R 5351)* **YOU'VE NEVER HAD IT SO GOOD. / DON'T YA LIKE MA LOVE** [ ] [-]

PROCOL HARUM

BROOKER with also **MATTHEW FISHER** (b. 7 Mar'46) – organ (ex-SCREAMING LORD SUTCH) / **RAY ROYER** (b. 8 Oct'45) – guitar / **DAVE KNIGHTS** (b.28 Jun'45) – bass / **BOBBY HARRISON** (b.28 Jun'43) – drums / **KEITH REID** (b.10 Oct'46) – lyrics

Deram / Deram

May 67. (7") *(DM 126)* <7507> **A WHITER SHADE OF PALE. / LIME STREET BLUES** [1] [5]
<US re-iss.Jan73 on 'A&M'; 1389>

— **ROBIN TROWER** – guitar (ex-PARAMOUNTS) repl. ROYER who formed FREEDOM / **B.J. WILSON** – drums (ex-PARAMOUNTS) repl. HARRISON who also formed FREEDOM

Regal Zonophone / A&M

Sep 67. (7") *(RZ 3002)* <885> **HOMBURG. / GOOD CAPTAIN CLACK** [6] [34]
(re-iss.Oct75 on 'Fly'; BUG 2)
Dec 67. (lp) *(LRZ 1001)* <18008> **PROCOL HARUM** [ ] [47] Sep67
– A whiter shade of pale / Conquistador / She wandered through the garden fence / Something following me / Mabel / Cerdes (outside the gate of) / Homburg / Christmas camel / Kaleidoscope / Salad days / Good Captain Clack / Repent Walpurgis. *(re-iss.May85 as 'A WHITER SHADE OF PALE' on 'Sierra' lp/c; FEDB/CFEDB 5008) (cd-iss.Jun97 as 'A WHITER SHADE OF PALE' on 'Repertoire'; RR 4666)*
Apr 68. (7") *(RZ 3007)* <927> **QUITE RIGHTLY SO. / IN THE WEE SMALL HOURS OF SIXPENCE** [50] [ ]
Dec 68. (lp; stereo/mono) *(S+/LRZ 1004)* <SP 4151> **SHINE ON BRIGHTLY** [ ] [24] Oct68
– Quite rightly so / Shine on brightly / Skip softly (my moonbeams) / Wish me well / Rambling on / Magdalene (my regal zonophone) / In held twas I:- a) Glimpses of Nirvana – (b) Twas tea-time at the circus – (c) In the Autumn of my madness – (d) Look to your soul – (e) Grand finale. *(re-iss.Sep85 on 'Sierra' lp/c; FEDB/CFEDB 5026) (cd-iss.Nov92 on 'Castle'; CLACD 321) (cd re-iss.Jun97 on 'Repertoire'; RR 4667)*
May 69. (lp) *(SLRZ 1009)* <SP 4179> **A SALTY DOG** [27] [32]
– A salty dog / The milk of human kindness / Too much between us / The Devil came from Arkansas / Boredom / Juicy John Pink / Wreck of the Hesperus / All this and more / Crucifiction Lane / Pilgrim's progress. *(re-iss.1971 on 'Music For Pleasure'; MFP 5275) (re-iss.May85 on 'Sierra' lp/c; FEDB/CFEDB 5012) (cd-iss.1986 on 'Mobile Fidelity'; MFCD 823) (cd re-iss.Jul92 on 'Castle'; CLACD 289)*
Jun 69. (7") *(RZ 3019)* **A SALTY DOG. / LONG GONE CREEK** [44] [-]
Jul 69. (7") <1111> **THE DEVIL CAME FROM KANSAS. / BOREDOM** [-] [ ]

— **CHRIS COPPING** – organ, bass (ex-PARAMOUNTS) repl. FISHER + KNIGHTS

Jun 70. (7") <1218> **WHISKEY TRAIN. / ABOUT TO DIE** [-] [ ]
Jun 70. (lp) *(SLRZ 1014)* <SP 4261> **HOME** [49] [34]
– Whiskey train / Dead man's dream / Still there'll be more / Nothing that I didn't know / About to die / Barnyard story / Piggy pig pig / Whaling stories / Your own choice. *(re-iss.Apr89 on 'Castle' lp/c/cd; CLA LP/MC/CD 142)*

Chrysalis / A&M

Jun 71. (lp) *(ILPS 9158)* <SP 4294> **BROKEN BARRICADES** [42] [32] May71
– Simple sister / Broken barricades / Memorial drive / Luskus Delph / Power failure / Song for a dreamer / Playmate of the mouth / Poor Mohammed. *(re-iss.1974 lp/c; CHS/ZCHS 1057)*
Jun 71. (7") <1264> **BROKEN BARRICADES. / POWER FAILURE** [-] [ ]
Oct 71. (7") <1287> **SIMPLE SISTER. / SONG FOR A DREAMER** [-] [ ]

— **DAVE BALL** (b.30 Mar'50) – guitar repl. ROBIN TROWER (later solo) / added **ALAN CARTWRIGHT** (b.10 Oct'45) – bass (to **BROOKER, COPPING, WILSON, REID + BALL)**

Apr 72. (lp) *(CHR 1004)* <SP 4335> **PROCOL HARUM IN CONCERT WITH THE EDMUNTON SYMPHONY ORCHESTRA (live)** [48] [5]
– Conquistador / Whaling stories / A salty dog / All this and more / In held 'twas I; a) Glimpses of Nirvana – (b) 'Twas teatime at the circus – (c) In the Autumn of my madness – (d) I know if I'd been wiser – (e) Grand finales.
May 72. (7") <1347> **CONQUISTADOR (live). / A SALTY DOG (live)** [-] [16]
Jul 72. (7") *(CHR 2003)* **CONQUISTADOR (live). / LUSKUS DELPH** [22] [-]

Chrysalis / Chrysalis

Mar 73. (lp/c) *(<CHR/ZCHR 1037>)* **GRAND HOTEL** [ ] [21]
– Grand hotel / Toujours l'amour / A rum tale / T.V. Ceaser / A souvenir of London / Bringing home the bacon / Robert's box / For licorice John / Fires (which burnt brightly) / Robert's box. *(cd-iss.Oct95 on 'Essential'; ESMCD 290)*
Apr 73. (7") *(CHS 2010)* **ROBERT'S BOX. / A RUM TALE** [ ] [-]
Apr 73. (7") <2011> **BRINGING HOME THE BACON. / TOUJOURS L'AMOUR** [-] [ ]
Aug 73. (7") <2013> **GRAND HOTEL. / FIRE'S (WHICH BURNT BRIGHTLY)** [-] [ ]
Aug 73. (7") *(CHS 2015)* **A SOUVENIR OF LONDON. / TOUJOURS L'AMOUR** [ ] [-]

— **MICK GRABHAM** – guitar (ex-PLASTIC PENNY, ex-COCHISE) repl. BALL to BEDLAM

Apr 74. (lp/c) *(<CHR/ZCHR 1058>)* **EXOTIC BIRDS AND FRUIT** [ ] [86]
– Nothing but the truth / Beyond the pale / As strong as Samson / The idol / The thin edge of the wedge / Monsieur R. Monde / Fresh fruit / Butterfly boys / New lamps for old. *(cd-iss.Oct95 on 'Essential'; ESMCD 291)*
Apr 74. (7") *(CHS <2032>)* **NOTHING BUT THE TRUTH. / DRUNK AGAIN** [ ] [ ]
Jul 75. (7") *(CHS <2073>)* **PANDORA'S BOX. / THE PIPER'S TUNE** [16] [ ]
Aug 75. (lp/c) *(<CHR/ZCHR 1080>)* **PROCOL'S NINTH** [41] [52]
– Pandora's box / Fools gold / Taking the time / The unquiet zone / The final thrust / I keep forgetting / Without a doubt / The piper's tune / Typewriter torment / Eight days a week. *(cd-iss.Oct95 on 'Essential'; ESMCD 292)*
Oct 75. (7") *(CHS 2079)* **THE FINAL THRUST. / TAKING THE TIME** [ ] [-]
Jan 76. (7") *(CHS 2084)* **AS STRONG AS SAMSON. / THE UNQUIET ZONE** [ ] [-]

— **PETE SOLLEY** – keyboards (ex-ARTHUR BROWN, ex-SNAFU, ex-CHRIS FARLOWE) repl. CARTWRIGHT (COPPING now bass only)

Jan 77. (7") <2115> **WIZARD MAN. / SOMETHING MAGIC** [-] [ ]
Feb 77. (7") *(CHS 2138)* **WIZARD MAN. / BACKGAMMON** [ ] [-]
Mar 77. (lp/c) *(<CHR/ZCHR 1130>)* **SOMETHING MAGIC** [ ] [ ]
– Something magic / Skating on thin ice / Wizard man / The mark of the claw / Strangers in space / The worm and the tree. *(cd-iss.Oct95 on 'Essential'; ESMCD 293)*

— Disbanded mid-77. WILSON joined JOE COCKER. GRABHAM to MICKEY JUPP. GARY BROOKER joined ERIC CLAPTON band and went solo. PROCOL HARUM re-formed Oct'91, TIM RENWICK instead of TROWER.

PUPILS (see under ⇒ EYES)

PURE FOOD & DRUGS ACT (see under ⇒ MANDEL, Harvey)

PURPLE GANG

Formed: Manchester, England . . . 1967 by PETER WALKER, DEE JAY ROBINSON, ANK LANGLEY, GEOFF BOURJER/BOWYER and JAMES JOE BEARD, all students from the nearby Stockport College Of Art. Their debut jugband 45, 'GRANNY TAKES A TRIP', was taken on board by the English "underground" scene due to its unintentional LSD connotation. This drug reference resulted in a ban from the BBC. Although not a psychedelic band, they took a heavier approach on their one and only album, 'THE PURPLE GANG STRIKES' in 1968.

Recommended: THE PURPLE GANG STRIKES (*6)

LUCIFER (b. PETER WALKER) – vocals, kazoo / **DEE JAY ROBINSON** (b.GERRY) – mandolin, harmonica / **ANK LANGLEY** – jug / **GEOFF BOURJER** – piano, washboard / **JAMES JOE BEARD** – guitar / **TONY MOSS** – bass

Big T / not issued

Jan 68. (7") *(BIG 101)* **GRANNY TAKES A TRIP. / BOOTLEG WHISKY** [ ] [-]
Jun 68. (7") *(BIG 111)* **KISS ME GOODNIGHT SALLY GREEN. / AUNTIE MONICA** [ ] [-]

— now without LANGLEY + MOSS

Trans-atlantic / not issued

1968. (lp) *(97006)* **THE PURPLE GANG STRIKES** [ ] [-]
(re-iss.Nov86 as 'GRANNY TAKES A TRIP' on 'Razor'; RAZ 22)

— **IRISH ALEX** – washboards, drums repl. LUCIFER

— they split soon after above

? & THE MYSTERIANS

Formed: Saginaw, Michigan, USA . . . 1964, after abandoning the name XYZ and their Texan homeland. Early in 1966, their manager, LILY GONZALES, dispatched 750 copies of their first single, '96 TEARS'. This organ-dominated, garage classic sparked off interest from major US record company, 'Cameo', who re-issued it later in the year and it subsequently topped the US charts. They had their last chart appearance with 'I NEED SOMEBODY', before a string of flops over the course of the next few years. • **Songwriters:** RUDY MARTINEZ penned except; SHOUT (Isley Brothers) / etc. • **Trivia:** In 1967, The SEMI-COLONS featured The MYSTERIANS' on two of their instrumental tracks. ALICE COOPER later covered 'I NEED SOMEBODY', while STRANGLERS were one of several major artists to resurrect '96 TEARS'.

Recommended: 96 TEARS (*6)

? (aka RUDY MARTINEZ, 1945, Mexico) – vocals / **FRANK RODRIGUEZ JNR.** (b. 9 Mar'51, Crystal City, Texas) – Farfisa organ / **FRANK LUGO** (b. FRANCISCO HERNANDEZ LUGO, 15 Mar'47, Weslaco, Texas) – bass / **LARRY BORJAS** – guitar / **ROBERT MARTINEZ** – drums

not issued / Pa-Go-Go

Jan66. (7"; as The MYSTERIANS) <*102*> **96 TEARS. / MIDNIGHT HOUR** [-] [ ]

Cameo Parkway / Cameo

Sep 66. (7") <*(C 428)*> **96 TEARS. / MIDNIGHT HOUR** [37] [1] Jan66

— **BOBBY BALDERRAMA** (b.27 Feb'50, O'Donnell, Texas) – guitar repl. ROBERT / **EDDIE SERRATO** (b. 5 Dec'45, Encial, Texas) – drums repl. LARRY

— Both of the outgoing members were drafted into the army.

Nov 66. (lp) <*C 2004*> **96 TEARS** [-] [66]
– I need somebody / Stormy Monday / You're telling me lies / Ten o'clock / Set aside / Upside / Don't tease me / Don't break this heart of mine / Why me / Midnight hour / 96 tears. *(UK-iss.Jun97 on 'Anthology'; ANT 3021)*

Dec 66. (7") <*(C 441)*> **I NEED SOMEBODY. / '8' TEEN** [ ] [22]

Feb 67. (7") <*(C 467)*> **CAN'T GET ENOUGH OF YOU, BABY. / SMOKES** [ ] [ ]

Apr 67. (7") <*(C 479)*> **GIRL (YOU CAPTIVATE ME). / GOT TO** [ ] [ ]

Jun 67. (lp) <*2006*> **ACTION** [-] [ ]
– Girl (you captivate me) / Can't get enough of you baby / Got to / I'll be back / Shout / Hangin' on a string / Smokes / It's not easy / Don't hold it against me / Just like a rose / Do you feel it. *(UK cd-iss.Jun97 on 'Move'; MOVE 3001)*

Jul 67. (7") <*(C 496)*> **DO SOMETHING TO ME. / LOVE ME BABY** [ ] [ ]

— label 'Cameo Parkway' folded early in '68.

not issued / Capitol

May 68. (7") <*2162*> **MAKE YOU MINE. / I LOVE YOU BABY** [-] [ ]

not issued / Tangerine

Dec 68. (7") <*989X*> **AIN'T IT NO SHAME. / TURN AROUND, BABY** [-] [ ]

not issued / Super K

Jan 69. (7") <*SK 102*> **SHA LA LA. / HANG IN** [-] [ ]

— Disbanded in 1969, although they re-united in 1975.

not issued / Chicory

1972. (7") <*410*> **TALK IS CHEAP. / SHE GOES TO CHURCH ON SUNDAY** [-] [ ]

not issued / Luv

1973. (7"ltd.) <*159*> **FUNKY LADY. / HOT'N'GROOVIN'** [-] [ ]

— Disbanded once again, although they did do concerts early 1980.

– compilations, etc. –

Jul 76. (7") *London; (HLU 10534)* **96 TEARS. / '8' TEEN** [ ] [-]

1983. (7") *Abkco; <4020>* **96 TEARS. / CAN'T GET ENOUGH OF YOU, BABY** [-] [ ]

1983. (7") *Abkco; <4033>* **I NEED SOMEBODY. / GIRL (YOU CAPTIVATE ME)** [-] [ ]

1985. (c) *R.O.I.R.; <A-137>* **THE DALLAS REUNION TAPES – 96 TEARS FOREVER** [-] [ ]
(cd-iss.Feb90 on 'Danceteria'; DANCD 032) (lp-iss.Sep90; DAN 032)

QUICKSILVER MESSENGER SERVICE

Formed: San Francisco, California, USA . . . late 1964 by JIM MURRAY, JOHN CIPOLLINA, DAVID FREIBERG and CASEY SONOBAN. Also present at their early rehearsals were SKIP SPENCE and DINO VALENTI, who was later jailed for possession of drugs. In June '65, CIPOLLINA, MURRAY and FREIBERG were joined by GREG ELMORE and GARY DUNCAN (both from The BROGUES, who released a few US 45's in 1965). Two years later, they received a great reception at The Monterey International Pop Festival, although MURRAY left when the group signed to 'Capitol'. They had previously recorded two tracks, 'CODINE' and 'BABE, I'M GONNA LEAVE YOU', for the (late '67) Various Artists soundtrack album, 'REVOLUTION' on 'United Artists'. In the summer of '68, they finally released their eponymous debut, which, amid much anticipation, reached the US Top 75. Their 1969 follow-up, 'HAPPY TRAILS', featuring a 25-minute improvised version of BO DIDDLEY's 'WHO DO YOU LOVE', crashed into the US Top 30. Apparently as close an appropriation of what it was actually like to have your ears massaged/assaulted in the San Francisco ballrooms as you're likely to hear, the part-live album nevertheless sounds dated. Although NICKY HOPKINS impressed with THE ROLLING STONES, his addition to the QUICKSILVER line-up for 1969's 'SHADY GROVE' didn't create the musical spark the band needed and with VALENTE back in the fold after his stint in prison, things went downhill. He came to dominate the band's output over the remainder of their career, his average material dulling the spontaneity that had characterised QUICKSILVER's earlier work and effecting a transformation in their sound from psychedelic rock to workmanlike rock'n'roll. While the band had their sole top 50 hit with 'FRESH AIR' in 1970, the album it was taken from and the rest of their 70's output was bog standard stuff which suffered from the aforementioned lack of honed songwriting and a constantly changing line-up. THE QUICKSILVER MESSENGER SERVICE finally delivered its last lacklustre communication in 1975 after a 3-year hiatus, CIPOLLINA going off to join MAN, FREIBERG joining STARSHIP. • **Songwriters:** CIPOLLINA + FREIBERG, until VALENTI's virtual take-over in 1970 as alter-ego JESSE ORIS FARROW (although others still individually contributed). • **Trivia:** Debut album was produced by NICK GRAVENITES and HARVEY BROOKS of ELECTRIC FLAG.

Recommended: HAPPY TRAILS (*7) / WHAT ABOUT ME (*6) / THE ULTIMATE JOURNEY (*7)

JOHN CIPOLLINA (b.24 Aug'43, Berkeley, Calif.) – guitar, vocals (ex-DEACONS) / **GARY DUNCAN** (b. GARY GRUBB, 4 Sep'46) – guitar, vocals repl. SKIP SPENCE / **DAVID FREIBERG** (b.24 Aug'38, Boston, Mass.) – bass, vocals / **GREG ELMORE** (b. 4 Sep'46, San Diego, Calif.) – drums repl. CASEY SONOBAN

Capitol / Capitol

May 68. (lp) <*(ST 2904)*> **QUICKSILVER MESSENGER SERVICE** [ ] [63]
– Pride of man / Light your windows / Dino's song / Gold and silver / It's been too long / The fool. *(re-iss.Jul86 on 'Edsel'; ED 200) (cd-iss.Mar89; CDP 791146-2) (cd-iss.Jul92 on 'Edsel'; EDCD 200)*

Jun 68. (7") <*2194*> **PRIDE OF MAN. / DINO'S SONG** [-] [ ]

Nov 68. (7") <*2320*> **BEARS. / STAND BY ME** [-] [ ]

Mar 69. (lp) <*(EST 120)*> **HAPPY TRAILS** [ ] [27]
– Who do you love suite:- Who do you love (pt.1) – Who do you love – Where do you love – How do you love – Which do you love – Who do you love (pt.2) / Mona / Maiden of the Cancer Moon / Calvary / Happy trails. *(re-iss.Jun81 on 'Greenlight' lp/c; GO/TC-GO 2012) (cd-iss.Mar89; CDP 791215-2) (cd re-iss.Dec92 on 'Beat Goes On'; BGOCD 151)*

Jul 69. (7") <*2557*> **WHO DO YOU LOVE (edit). / WHICH DO YOU LOVE** [-] [91]

— **NICKY HOPKINS** (b.24 Feb'44, London, England) – keyboards (ex-STEVE MILLER BAND) repl. DUNCAN

Nov 69. (7") <*2670*> **HOLY MOLY. / WORDS CAN'T SAY** [-] [ ]

Dec 69. (lp) <*(EST 391)*> **SHADY GROVE** [ ] [25]
– Shady Grove / Flute song / Three or feet from home / Too far / Holy Moly / Joseph's coat / Flashing lonesome / Words can't say / Edward, the mad shirt grinder. *(re-iss.Feb87 on 'Edsel'; XED 208) (cd-iss.Sep90; EDCD 208)*

Feb 70. (7") <*2800*> **SHADY GROVE. / THREE OR FOUR FEET FROM HOME** [-] [ ]

— added now officially ex-part time member **DINO VALENTI** (b. CHESTER POWERS, 7 Nov'43, Danbury, Connecticut) – guitar, vocals / **GARY DUNCAN** – guitar, vocals returned to 6-piece w / **JOHN, NICKY, DAVID + GREG**

Aug 70. (lp) <*(EA-ST 498)*> **JUST FOR LOVE** [ ] [27]
– Wolf run (part 1) / Just for love (part 1) / Cobra / The hat / Freeway flyer / Gone again / Fresh air / Just for love (part 2) / Wolf run (part 2). *(cd-iss.Dec92 on 'Beat Goes On'; BGOCD 141)*

Sep 70. (7") <*2920*> **FRESH AIR. / FREEWAY FLYER** [-] [49]

— **MARK NATALFIN** – keyboards (ex-PAUL BUTTERFIELD) repl. (on 3 tracks) HOPKINS. Also on below lp: **JOSE RICO REYES** – percussion / **MARTINE FIERRO** – wind / **RON TAORMINA** – saxes / **FRANK MORIN** – sax / **PAT O'HARA** – trombone / **KEN BALZELL** – trumpet

Feb 71. (lp) <*(EA-ST 630)*> **WHAT ABOUT ME** [ ] [26] Jan71
– What about me / Local color / Baby baby / Won't kill me / Long haired lady / Subway / Spindrifter / Good old rock and roll / All in my mind / Call on me. *(re-iss.Jul89 on 'Beat Goes On'; BGOLP 58) (cd-iss.Oct90; BGOCD 58)*

Mar 71. (7") <*3046*> **WHAT ABOUT ME. / GOOD OLD ROCK AND ROLL** [-] [100]

— Now a quintet when CIPOLLINA left to form COPPERHEAD / **MARK RYAN** – bass (ex-COUNTRY JOE & THE FISH) repl. DAVID to JEFFERSON STARSHIP

Nov 71. (lp) <*(SW 819)*> **QUICKSILVER** [ ] [ ]
– Hope / I found love / Song for Frisco / Play my guitar / Rebel / Fire Brothers /

Out of my mind / Don't cry my lady love / The truth. *(cd-iss.Jan94 on 'Beat Goes On'; BGOCD 217)*

Nov 71. (7") *<3233>* **HOPE. / I FOUND LOVE** -

— **CHUCK STEAKS** – organ repl. NATAFLIN

May 72. (lp) *<(ST 11002)>* **COMIN' THRU**
– Doin' time in the U.S.A. / Chicken / Changes / California state correctional facility blues / Forty days / Mojo / Don't lose it. *(cd-iss.Jul91 on 'Beat Goes On' lp/cd; BGO/+CD 88)*

May 72. (7") *<3349>* **DOIN' TIME IN THE U.S.A. / CHANGES** -

— Mid'72, contributed 2 tracks for live lp 'The Last Days Of Fillmore'.

— (May73) **JOHN NICHOLAS** – bass (ex-IT'S A BEAUTIFUL DAY) repl. RYAN / added **HAROLD ACEVES** – 2nd drummer (6-piece DINO, GARY, GREG + CHUCKS)

— (Feb74) **BOB HOGAN** – keyboards (ex-MILES DAVIS) repl. STEAKS / **SKIP OLSEN** – bass repl. BOB FLURIE who had repl. JOHN NICHOLAS

— (Mar75) **DINO, GARY, GREG, SKIP** plus the returning **JOHN CIP . . . + DAVID** on tour / added **MICHAEL LEWIS** – piano

Oct 75. (lp) *<(ST 11462)>* **SOLID SILVER** 89
– Gypsy lights / Heebie jeebies / Cowboy on the run / I heard you singing / Worryin' shoes / The letter / They don't know / Flames / Witches' moon / Bittersweet Moon. *(cd-iss.Sep93 on 'Edsel'; EDCD 376)*

Nov 75. (7") *(CL 15859) <4206>* **GYPSY LIGHTS. / WITCHES MOON**

— Had already broke-up, after brief re-union. CIPOLLINA joined MAN. He was to die 30 May'89 of emphysema lung disease. FREIBERG returned to STARSHIP. In 1987, GARY DUNCAN resurrected QUICKSILVER MESSENGER SERVICE for an album 'PEACE BY PIECE'. Unfortunately on the 29th May 1989, CIPOLLINA died from emphysema. All group members, included others from The GRATEFUL DEAD, JEFFERSON AIRPLANE and (HUEY LEWIS &) THE NEWS, played benefit in San Francisco.

– compilations, others, etc. –

Oct 73. (lp) *Capitol; (STSP 13) <ST 11165>* **ANTHOLOGY** May73
– Pride of man / Dino's song / Fool / Bears / Mona / Edward, the mad shirt grinder / Three or four feet from home / Fresh air / Just for love / Spindrifter / Local color / What about me / Don't cry my lady love / Hope / Fire brothers / I found love. *(cd-iss.Jun95 on 'Beat Goes On'; BGOCD 270)*

Sep 83. (d-lp) *Psycho; (PSYCHO 10)* **MAIDEN OF THE CANCER MOON** (live Fillmore, Jun'68) -

Apr 86. (lp) *See For Miles; (SEE 61)* **THE ULTIMATE JOURNEY** -
– Who do you love / Pride of man / Codine / Dino's song / Gold and silver / Joseph's coat / Shady grove / Fresh air / Too far / Stand by me / What about me / Mona. *(cd-iss.Aug93; SEECD 61)*

Aug 91. (d-cd) *Rhino;* **SONS OF MERCURY (THE BEST OF QUICKSILVER MESSENGER SERVICE 1968-1975)** -

QUIET SUN (see under ⇒ ROXY MUSIC)

QUINTESSENCE

Formed: Notting Hill, London, England . . .1968 by SHAMBU BABAJI and RAJA RAM, plus others who were auditioned through an ad in Melody Maker. They first came to light in 1969 with their debut album, 'IN BLISSFUL COMPANY'. A fusion of Eastern religious chanting and improvised jazz-rock, the record prepared fans for the spiritual union of their gigs. Their eponymous second album took them from the underground to the mainstream, mantras such as 'SHIVA'S CHANT' and 'HIGH ON MT. KOILASH' imprinting the group in the psychedelic consciousness of the pseudo-hippie set. Two more UK Top 50 albums followed in the early 70's, although none were as groundbreaking as the second set. • **Songwriters:** BABAJI + RAM.

Recommended: IN BLISSFUL COMPANY (*6) / QUINTESSENCE (*6) / DIVE DEEP (*5)

RAJA RAM (b. RON ROTHFIELD, Melbourne, Australia) – vocals, flute, percussion / **SHIVA SHANKAR** (b. PHIL JONES) – vocals, keyboards / **ALAN MOSTERT** – lead guitar / **MAHA DEV** (b. DAVE CODLING) – rhythm guitar / **SHAMBU BABAJI** – bass / **JAKE MILTON** – drums

Island / Cotilion

1969. (lp) *(ILPS 9110)* **IN BLISSFUL COMPANY** -
– Giants / Manco capac / Body / Ganga mai / Chant / Pearl and bird / Notting Hill Gate / Midnight mode. *(re-iss.1974; same)*

Jan 70. (7") *(WIP 6075)* **NOTTING HILL GATE. / MOVE INTO THE LIGHT** -

Jun 70. (lp) *(ILPS 9128)* **QUINTESSENCE – OPEN UP TO YOU** 22
– Jai jai jai jai rama hi jai / Rama bhagata hanuman ji jai / Jai Shiva Shankar Kailash Pati / Jai jai Gauri ma parvati / Raghu Pati Raghaw Raja jam / Patita pa wan Sita Ram / Sri Krishna Godvinde Hare Murare / He nath Narian Vasudeva / Om Buddha om mane ne padme hum / Om Brahma Vishnu Sadasiva / Sarada Devi Ki Jai Ho om namo / Bhagvate Ramakrishnaya. *(re-iss.1974 as 'JESUS BUDDHA MOSES'; same)*

Mar 71. (lp) *(ILPS 9143)* **DIVE DEEP** 43
– Dive deep / Dance for the one / Brahman / The seer / Epitaph for tomorrow / Sri ram chant. *(re-iss.1974; same)*

Neon / not issued

Nov 71. (7") *(NE 1003)* **SWEET JESUS. / YOU NEVER STAY THE SAME** -

RCA Victor / not issued

May 72. (lp) *(SF 8273)* **SELF** 50
– (Olympic Studios 1972):- Cosmic surfer / Wonders of the universe / Vishnu-narain / Hallelujad / Celestial procession / Self / (Live at Exeter University 11 December 1971):- Freedom / Water goddess.

— now a quartet when DEV + SHIVA vacated. The latter formed KALA, who made one eponymous lp in 1973 for 'Bradley's'; *(BRADL 1002)*. Around the same time, they released a single; 'TRAVELLING HOME'./ 'STILL GOT TIME'; *(BRAD 302)*

Dec 72. (lp) *(SF 8317)* **INDWELLER**
– Jesus my life / Butterfly music / It's all the same / Indweller / Holy roller / Portable realm / Sai Baba / On the other side of the wall / Dedication / Bliss trip / Mother of the universe.

— Disbanded in 1973. SHIVA went on to form their kindred spirit, KALA. JAKE MILTON later joined BLURT?

– compilations, etc. –

Apr 93. (cd) *Drop Out; (DOCD 1986)* **EPITAPH FOR TOMORROW** -
– Giants / Body / Ganga mai / Chant / Notting Hill Gate / Midnight mode / Jesus, Buddha, Moses, Guaranga / Only love / St. Pancras / Infinitum / Dive deep / Tai ram / Epitah for tomorrow / Sri ram chant.

May 95. (cd) *Drop Out; (DOCD 1982)* **SELF / INDWELLER** -

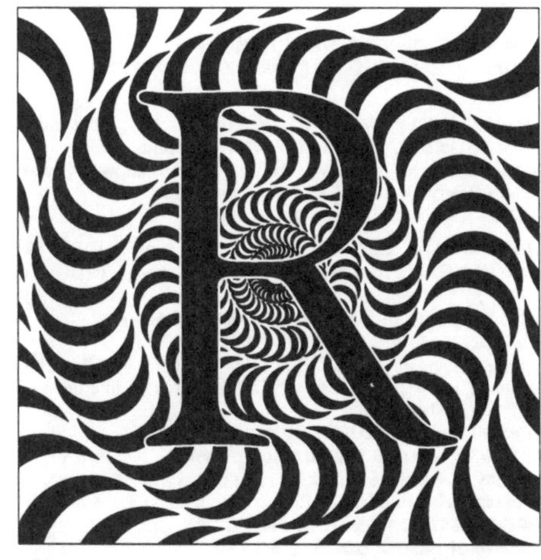

RAINBOW FFOLLY

Formed: London, England ... 1967 by brother JOHN and RICHARD DUNSTERVILLE. Signed to 'Parlophone', they took the same psychedelic path as their more famous labelmates, The BEATLES. The band combined sophisticated melodies, intertwined with experimental sound-effects on their one and only album, 'SALLIES FFORTH'. It has subsequently become quite a collector's piece changing hands for over £100. They also issued one single, the song 'DRIVE MY CAR' on the B-side was not the LENNON / McCARTNEY original.

Recommended: SALLIES FFORTH (*6)

RICHARD DUNSTERVILLE – vocals, guitar / **JOHN DUNSTERVILLE** – guitar, vocals / **ROGER NEWELL** – bass, vocals / **STEWART OSBORN** – drums, vocals

Parlophone | not issued

May 68. (7") *(R 5701)* **GO GIRL. / DRIVE MY CAR** | | -

May 68. (lp; mono/stereo) *(PMC/PCS 7050)* **SALLIES FFORTH** | | -
– She's alright / I'm so hapy / Montgolfier '67 / Drive my car / Goodbye / Hey you / Sun sing / Sun and sand / Labour exchange / They'm / No / Sighing game / Come on go.

— split sometime 1968, JOHN and ROGER later surfacing as session men for RICK WAKEMAN (Journey To The Centre Of The Earth, etc.)

RAMASES

Born: MICHAEL RAPHAEL, Sheffield, England. The former central-heating salesman signed as RAMASES to 'CBS' in 1968, and issued two singles (the first worth £75) before releasing a third in 1969 for 'Major Minor'. In 1971, he was signed to 'Vertigo' and, with the help of 10CC, he completed his debut, the instrumental Eastern album, 'SPACE HYMNS'. This also featured a sleeve design by ROGER DEAN, famous for his YES artwork.

Recommended: SPACE HYMNS (*6)

RAMASES (MICHAEL RAPHAEL) – sitar; with various personnel

C.B.S. | not issued

Sep 68. (7"; as RAMASES & SELKET) *(3717)* **CRAZY ONE. / MIND'S EYE** | | -

Major Minor | not issued

Apr 70. (7"; as RAMASES & SELEKA) *(MM 704)* **LOVE YOU. / GOLD IS THE RING** | | -

— w/ 10CC members; **GRAHAM GOULDMAN, KEVIN GODLEY, LOL CREME + ERIC STEWART** on their usual instruments

Vertigo | not issued

Aug 71. (lp) *(6360 046)* **SPACE HYMNS** | | -
– Life child / Hello mister / And the whole world / Quasar one / You're the only one Joe / Earth people / Molecular delusion / Balloon / Dying swan year 2000 / Jesus come back / Journey to the inside. *(re-iss.1974; same)*

Philips | not issued

Dec 71. (7") *(6113 003)* **JESUS COME BACK. / HELLO MISTER** | | -

— now w/ **SELKET** – vocals, guitar / **JO ROMERO** – guitar, tabla / **BON BERTLES** – sax / **PETE KINGSMAN + COLIN THURSTON** – bass / **BARRY KIRSCH** – piano, synthesizers / **ROGER HARRISON** – drums, percussion / **KAY GARNER + SUE GLOVER + SUNNY LESLIE** – vocals

1975. (lp) *(6360 115)* **GLASS TOP COFFIN** | | -
– Golden landing / Long long time / Now Mona Lisa / God voice / Mind island / Only the loneliest feeling / Sweet reason / Stepping stones / Salesman / Children of the green earth / Glass top coffin / Golden landing (part 2).

— unheard of since his last album.

RAMSES

Formed: Germany . . . late 1972 by HERBERT NATHO and HANS-DIETER KLINKHAMMER. By 1974, they'd enlisted WINIFRIED and NORBERT LANGHORST, plus REINHARD SCHROTER, the completed line-up which played on the 1976 debut, 'LA LEYLA'. The album was similar in style to English symphonic rock groups like ELP, although their sound was less intense and more accessible. The follow-up, 'ETERNITY RISE' (1978), carried on where the debut left off although by 1979, founder members NATHO and KLINKHAMMER had departed. The LANGHORST brothers duly recruited HERBERT WOLFLAST and MATTHIAS MOLLER for 1981's 'LIGHT FANTASTIC', but the album was poorly received and the band split soon after its release.

Recommended: LA LEYLA (*7)

HERBERT NATHO – vocals / **HANS DIETER KLINKHAMMER** – bass / **WINFRIED LANGHORST** – keyboards, vocals / **NORBERT LANGHORST** – guitars / **REINHARD SCHROTER** – drums, percussion

Sky | not issued

Jan 76. (lp) *(002)* **LA LEYLA** | - | - German
– Devil inside / La Leyla / Garden / War / Someone like you / American dream.

1978. (lp) *(020)* **ETERNITY RISE** | - | - German
– City life / Only yesterday / Time / Windy / Agitationplay / Eternity rise.

— **HERBERT WOLFLAST** – bass, guitar, vocals; repl. KLINKHAMMER

— **MATTHIAS MOLLER** – keyboards; repl. NATHO

1981. (lp) *(060)* **LIGHT FANTASTIC** | - | - German
– Sorry ma / Transport of joy / Force of habit / The light fantastic / Earth in the dark / Carry on / Across the Everglades.

— folded soon after

Tom RAPP (see under ⇒ PEARLS BEFORE SWINE)

RARE BIRD

Formed: England . . .1969 by STEVE GOULD and DAVE KAFFINETTE. Late in 1969, they issued their eponymous debut, which included 'SYMPATHY', a surprise UK and Euro hit early the following year. They were subsequently managed by TONY STRATTON-SMITH, releasing a follow-up album, 'AS YOUR MIND FLIES BY' (1970). More ambitious in its reach, the album saw the band stray into self-indulgence with the side-long 'FLIGHT'. After a change of line-up and record label (they moved to 'Polydor') the band released a clutch of albums throughout the first half of the 70's, eventually splitting in 1976.

Recommended: SYMPATHY (*6)

STEVE GOULD – vocals, saxophone, bass / **DAVE KAFFINETTI** – piano / **GRAHAM FIELD** – organ / **MARK ASHTON** – drums, vocals

Charisma | Probe

Nov 69. (lp) *(CAS 1005)* <4514> **RARE BIRD** | | Feb70
– Iceberg / Times / You went away / Melanie / Beautiful Scarlet / Sympathy / Natures fruit / Bird on a wing / God of war.

Jan 70. (7") *(CB 120)* **SYMPATHY. / DEVIL'S HIGH CONCERN** | 27 | -

Apr 70. (7") <477> **SYMPATHY. / BEAUTIFUL SCARLET** | - |

Charisma | A.B.C.

Nov 70. (lp) *(CAS 1011)* <716> **AS YOUR MIND FLIES BY** | |
– What you want to know / Down on the floor / Hammerhead / I'm thinking / As your mind flies by / Vacuum / New Yorker / Central Park.

Jan 71. (7") *(CB 138)* <11284> **WHAT YOU WANT TO KNOW. / HAMMERHEAD** | |

— **FRED KELLY** – drums, repl. ASHTON

— **SETH CURTIS** – guitar + **NICK POTTER** – bass, repl. FIELD who formed FIELDS. In 1971, they made an eponymous album for 'C.B.S.'; *(69009)*, and also a single; 'FRIENDS OF MINE'./ 'THREE MINSTRELS'; *(7555)*.

Polydor | Polydor

1972. (lp) *(2442 101)* <5530> **EPIC FOREST** | | Jul73
– Title No.1 again (birdman) / You went away / Fears of the night / Her darkest hour / Baby listen / Epic forest / Hey man / Turn it all around / Turning the lights out / House in the city. *(w-free 7"ep) (2814 011)* **ROADSIDE WELCOME. / FOUR GREY WALLS / YOU'RE LOST**

1972. (7") <15079> **BIRDMAN. / (part 2)** | - |

— **KEVIN LAMB** – vocals / **AL MATTHEWS + SAMMY ABU + PAUL HOLLAND** – congas, percussion, repl. CURTIS + POTTER

Sep 73. (7") *(2058 402)* **VIRGINIA. / LONELY STREET** | |

Sep 73. (lp) *(2383 211)* <6502> **SOMEBODY'S WATCHING** | |
– Somebody's watching / Third time around / Turn your head / More and more / Hard time / Who is the hero / High in the morning / Dollars.

Nov 73. (7") <15087> **SOMEBODY'S WATCHING. / (part 2)** | - |

— **ANDY RAE** – bass, repl. MATTHEWS, ABU + HOLLAND

Jun 74. (7") *(2058 471)* **BODY AND SOUL. / REDMAN** | |

Jun 74. (lp) *(2383 274)* <6506> **BORN AGAIN** | |
– Body and soul / Live for each other / Diamonds / Reaching you / All that I need / Redman / Peace of mind / Harlem / Lonely street / Last tango in Beulah.

May 75. (7") *(2058 591)* **DON'T BE AFRAID. / PASSIN' THROUGH** | |

— Disbanded in 1975 and GOULD joined RUNNER

– compilations, others, etc. –

Apr 72. (7"ep) *Charisma; (CB 179)* **SYMPATHY / DEVIL'S HIGH CONCERN. / WHAT DO YOU WANT TO KNOW / HAMMERHEAD** | | -

Jun 75. (lp) *Polygram; (9299 008)* <4514> **SYMPATHY & OTHERS** | | -

1975. (7") *Charisma; (CB 262)* **SYMPATHY. / BEAUTIFUL SCARLET** | | -
(re-iss.Sep79 + Jul82 on 'Old Gold'; OG 9040)

Aug 76. (lp) *Charisma; (CS 4)* **SYMPATHY** | | -

– Sympathy / You went away / Nature's fruit / Bird on a wing / What you want to know / Beautiful Scarlet / Hammerhead / I'm thinking / As your mind flies by. *(re-iss.Sep83 lp/c; CHC/+MC 6) (cd-iss.Apr90; CDOVD 280)*

1977. (lp) *Polydor Special; (2384 078)* **RARE BIRD** [ ] [-]

RASCALS

Formed: New York City, New York, USA ... 1964 by ex-JOEY DEE & THE STARLIGHTERS members FELIX CAVALIERE, EDDIE BRIGATI and GENE CORNISH. They recruited past friend of FELIX's and jazz sessioner, DINO DANELLI. After meeting promoter/manager Sid Bernstein, they secured a contract with 'Atlantic' records and, as a reference to their youthful years, they adopted the name, The YOUNG RASCALS. On the 15th of August, 1965, they supported The BEATLES at their final live concert at The Shea Stadium. To end the year, they issued a near US Top 50 entry, 'I AIN'T GONNA EAT MY HEART OUT ANYMORE'. Their follow-up in 1966, 'GOOD LOVIN', smashed into the No.1 spot, the first of a string of hits during the 60's. In 1968, they moved from a white soul/R&B sound to a hip flower-power style, renaming themselves as The RASCALS in acknowledgement of their new-found maturity. They went on to score with a series of pop-orientated bubblegum psychedelia, the biggest being 'PEOPLE GOT TO BE FREE" (1968). • **Songwriters:** CAVALIERE-BRIGATI penned except; I AIN'T GONNA EAT MY HEART OUT ANYMORE (Pam Sawyer & Lori Burton) / GOOD LOVIN' (Rudy Clark & Artie Resnick) / etc. • **Trivia:** Early in 1968, while on tour in Florida, their trailer broke down and they were the subject of an anti-rock music backlash from local rednecks. After their escape, they always toured with at least one black supporting act in way of protest.

Recommended: IN RETROSPECTIVE (*5)

YOUNG RASCALS

FELIX CAVALIERE (b.29 Nov'44, Pelham, N.Y.) – vocals, keyboards / **EDDIE BRIGATI** (b.22 Oct'46, Garfield, New Jersey) – vocals, percussion / **GENE CORNISH** (b.14 May'45, Ottowa, Canada) – guitar / **DINO DANELLI** (b.23 Jul'45, New York City) – drums

Atlantic Atlantic

Dec 65. (7") *(AT 4059) <2312>* **I AIN'T GONNA EAT OUT MY HEART ANYMORE. / SLOW DOWN** [ ] [52]

Mar 66. (7") *(AT 4082) <2321>* **GOOD LOVIN'. / MUSTANG SALLY** [ ] [1]

Jun 66. (7") *(584 024) <2338>* **YOU BETTER RUN. / LOVE IS A BEAUTIFUL THING** [ ] [20]

Jun 66. (lp; mono/stereo) *(587/588 012) <SD 8123>* **THE YOUNG RASCALS** [ ] [15] May66

– Slow down / Baby let's wait / Just a little / I believe / Do you feel it / Good lovin' / Like a rolling stone / Mustang Sally / I ain't gonna eat out my heart anymore / In the midnight hour.

Sep 66. (7") *(584 050) <2353>* **COME ON UP. / WHAT IS THE REASON** [ ] [43]

Dec 66. (7") *(584 067)* **TOO MANY FISH IN THE SEA. / NO LOVE TO GIVE** [ ] [-]

Feb 67. (7") *(584 081) <2377>* **I'VE BEEN LONELY TOO LONG. / IF YOU KNEW** [ ] [16] Jan67

Feb 67. (lp; mono/stereo) *(587/588 060) <SD 8134>* **COLLECTIONS** [ ] [14] Jan67

– What is the reason / Since I fell for you / Lonely too long / No love to give / Mickey's monkey – Love lights / Come on up / Too many fish in the sea / More / 1956 / Love is a beautiful thing / Land of 1000 dances.

Apr 67. (7") *(584 111) <2401>* **GROOVIN'. / SUENO** [8] [1]

Jul 67. (7") *(584 128) <2424>* **A GIRL LIKE YOU. / IT'S LOVE** [37] [10]

Aug 67. (lp; mono/stereo) *(587/588 074) <SD 8148>* **GROOVIN'** [ ] [4]

– A girl like you / Find somebody / I'm so happy now / Sueno / How can I be sure / Groovin' / If you knew / I don't love you anymore / You better run / A place in the sun / It's love.

Sep 67. (7") *<2438>* **HOW CAN I BE SURE. / I'M SO HAPPY NOW** [-] [4]

Sep 67. (7") *(584 138)* **HOW CAN I BE SURE. / I DON'T LOVE YOU ANYMORE** [ ] [-]

Dec 67. (7") *(584 161) <2463>* **IT'S WONDERFUL. / OF COURSE** [ ] [20]

RASCALS

Apr 68. (7") *(584 182) <2493>* **A BEAUTIFUL MORNING. / RAINY DAY** [ ] [3]

Apr 68. (lp; mono/stereo) *(587/588 098) <SD 8169>* **ONCE UPON A DREAM** [ ] [9] Mar68

– Intro / Easy rollin' / Rainy day / Please love me / It's wonderful / I'm gonna love you / My Hawaii / My world / Silly girl / Singin' the blues too long / Sattva / Finale: Once upon a dream.

Jul 68. (7") *(584 210) <2537>* **PEOPLE GOT TO BE FREE. / MY WORLD** [ ] [1]

Aug 68. (lp; mono/stereo) *(587/588 120) <SD 8190>* **TIME PEACE – THE RASCALS' GREATEST HITS** (compilation) [ ] [1] Jul68

– How can I be sure / Groovin' / I've been lonely too long / In the midnight hour / I ain't gonna eat my heart out anymore / Good lovin' / You better run / Come on up / Mustang Sally / Love is a beautiful thing / A girl like you / It's wonderful / Easy rollin' / Beautiful morning. *(cd-iss.May95 on 'Rhino'; 7567 81441-2)*

Nov 68. (7") *<2584>* **A RAY OF HOPE. / ANY DANCE'LL DO** [-] [24]

Feb 69. (7") *(584 255) <2599>* **HEAVEN. / BABY I'M BLUE** [ ] [39]

Apr 69. (d-lp) *(588 183) <SD 8201>* **FREEDOM SUITE** [ ] [17] Mar69

– America the beautiful / Me and my friends / Any dance'll do / Look around / A ray of hope / Island of love / Of course / Love was so easy to give / People got to be free / Baby I'm blue / Heaven / Adrian's birthday / Boom / Cute.

May 69. (7") *(584 274) <2634>* **SEE. / AWAY AWAY** [ ] [27]

Sep 69. (7") *(584 292) <2664>* **CARRY ME BACK. / REAL THING** [ ] [26]

Dec 69. (lp) *(588 210) <SD 8246>* **SEE** [ ] [45]

– See / I'd like to you home / Remember me / I'm blue / Stop and think / Temptations 'bout to get me / Nubia / Carry me back / Away away / Real thing / Death's reply / Hold on.

Jan 70. (7") *(584 307) <2695>* **HOLD ON. / I BELIEVE** [ ] [51]

Aug 70. (7") *(2091 029) <2743>* **GLORY, GLORY. / YOU DON'T KNOW** [ ] [58] Jul70

— (above featured backing by SWEET INSPIRATIONS gospel choir)

Jan 71. (lp) *(2400 113) <SD 8276>* **SEARCH AND NEARNESS** [ ] [ ]

– Right on / I believe / Thank you baby / You don't know / Mama / Almost home / The letter / Ready for love / Fortunes / Glory, glory.

Jan 71. (7") *<2773>* **RIGHT ON. / ALMOST HOME** [-] [ ]

— **ROBERT POPWELL** (b. Daytona, Florida) – bass repl. EDDIE / **BUZZY FEITEN** – guitar repl. GENE / added **ANN SUTTON** (b. Pittsburgh, Pennsylvania) – vocals

C.B.S. Columbia

Jun 71. (7") *(CBS 7363) <45400>* **LOVE ME. / HAPPY SONG** [ ] [95]

Jun 71. (lp) *(CBS 66292) <30462>* **PEACEFUL WORLD** [ ] [ ]

– Sky trane / In and out of love / Bit of Heaven / Love me / Peaceful world / Mother Nature land / Icy water / Happy song / Love letter / Little dove / Visit to Mother Nature land / Getting nearer.

Dec 71. (7") *(CBS 7672) <45491>* **LUCKY DAY. / LOVE LETTER** [ ] [ ]

Apr 72. (lp) *(CBS 64756) <31103>* **THE ISLAND OF REAL** [ ] [ ]

– Lucky day / Saga of New York / Be on the real side / Jungle walk / Brother Tree / Island of real / Hummin' song / Echoes / Buttercup / Time will tell / Lament.

Apr 72. (7") **BROTHER TREE. / SAGA OF NEW YORK** [-] [ ]

Jun 72. (7") *<45600>* **HUMMIN' SONG. / ECHOES** [-] [ ]

Aug 72. (7") **JUNGLE WALK. / SAGA OF NEW YORK** [-] [ ]

— Disbanded May'72. DANELLI re-united with CORNISH to form BULLDOG. In 1978, also as a 5-piece they became FOTOMAKER. When they split DANELLI joined LITTLE STEVEN & THE DISCIPLES OF SOUL. POPWELL joined The CRUSADERS in 1976.

– compilations, others, etc. –

Mar 67. (7") *Atlantic; (584 085)* **I AIN'T GONNA EAT OUT MY HEART. / GOOD LOVIN'** [ ] [-]

Jul 71. (7") *Atlantic; (2091 103)* **GROOVIN'. / YOU BETTER RUN** [ ] [-]

1973. (lp) *Midi; (30049)* **STAR COLLECTION** [ ] [-]

Jul 92. (cd) *Raven-Topic; (RV 1015)* **IN RETROSPECTIVE** [ ] [-]

– I ain't gonna eat out my heart anymore / Slow down / Good lovin' / Mustang Sally / You better run / Come on up / Love is a beautiful thing / What is the reason? / I've been lonely too long / Baby let's wait / Groovin' / A girl like you / How can I be sure? / It's wonderful / Beautiful morning / It's love / Easy rollin' / Rainy day / Silly girl / People got to be free / A ray of hope / Heaven / See / Carry me back / Glory glory.

Aug 93. (d-cd) *Rhino; (8122 71077-2)* **ANTHOLOGY** [ ] [ ]

— for CAVALIERE solo releases, see GREAT ROCK DISCOGRAPHY

RAW MATERIAL

Formed: London, England ... late 60's by MIKE FLETCHER, COLIN CATT, DAVE GREEN, PAUL YOUNG and PHIL GUNN. Their debut album, released in 1969, was basically a prog-rock affair, which featured their best know track, 'TIME AND ILLUSION'. Following on a change of label, they emerged with a much more sophisticated approach, 1971's 'TIME IS RARE', brought back memories of early PINK FLOYD.

Recommended: RAW MATERIAL ALBUM (*5) / TIME IS RARE (*6)

COLIN CATT – vocals, keyboards / **DAVE GREEN** – guitar / **MICK FLETCHER** – saxophone, flute, vocals (ex-STEAM) / **PHIL GUNN** – bass, guitar / **PAUL YOUNG** – percussion

Evolution not issued

Sep 69. (7") *(E 2441)* **TIME AND ILLUSION. / BOBO'S PARTY** [ ] [-]

Dec 69. (7") *(E 2445)* **HI THERE HALLELUJAH. / DAYS OF THE FIGHTING COCK** [ ] [-]

1970. (7") *(E 2449)* **TRAVELLER MAN. / (part 2)** [ ] [-]

1970. (lp) *(Z 1006)* **RAW MATERIAL ALBUM** [ ] [-]

– Time and illusion / I'd be delighted / Fighting cock / Pear on an apple tree / Future recollections / Traveller man / Destruction of America.

— added **CLIFF HAREWOOD** – lead guitar

RCA Neon not issued

Nov 71. (lp) *(NE 8)* **TIME IS RARE** [ ] [-]

– Ice queen / Empty house / Insolent lady: By the way – Small thief – Insolent lady / Miracle worker / Religion / Sun god: Awakening – Realisation – Worship.

Dec 71. (7") *(NE 1002)* **RIDE ON PONY. / RELIGION** [ ] [-]

— split after when GREEN joined DEEP FEELING, then SHOOT

RED CRAYOLA

Formed: Houston, Texas, USA ...1966 by MAYO THOMPSON with STEVE CUNNINGHAM and RICK BARTHELME. Signed to local label 'International Artists', they made two classy albums, 'PARABLE OF ARABLE LAND' and 'GOD BLESS THE RED CRAYOLA AND ALL WHO SAIL WITH IT' before disbanding. These consisted of textured, avant-garde psychedelia, a precursor to the likes of PERE UBU and TORTOISE. In 1972, MAYO released a solo album before moving to England five years later to resurrect the band. They signed to JAKE RIVIERA's 'Radar' label, debuting once again with a single, 'WIVES IN ORBIT'. The band also released a comeback album, 'SOLDIER TALK'. In the 80's, MAYO merged his ART & LANGUAGE outfit with RED CRAYOLA to release two albums for 'Rough Trade'; 'KANGAROO' & 'BLACK SNAKES'. MAYO then worked with The RAINCOATS and EPIC SOUNDTRACKS (ex-SWELL MAPS), before embarking on production work for The CHILLS. He relocated to Dusseldorf,

Germany, where he completed the 1989 album, 'MALEFACTOR ADE'. This was augmented by RUDIGER CARL, for whom MAYO returned the compliment on his COWWS Quintet project. In 1994, THE RED KRAYOLA released yet another (eponymous) comeback album. • **Songwriters:** MAYO THOMPSON except a few covers. • **rivia:** ROKY ERICKSON (13th Floor Elevators) guested on debut album.

Recommended: PARABLE OF ARABLE LAND (*7) / GOD BLESS THE RED CRAYOLA AND ALL WHO SAIL WITH IT (*7) / THE RED KRAYOLA (*6)

MAYO THOMPSON – vocals, guitar / **STEVE CUNNINGHAM** – bass / **RICK BARTHELME** – drums

not issued Int.Artists

1967. (lp) *<IA-LP 2>* **PARABLE OF ARABLE LAND (WITH THE FAMILIAR UGLY)** [-] [ ]
– Free form freakout; (a) Hurricane fighter pilot – (b) Transparent radiation – (c) War sucks – (d) Pink stainless tail – (e) Parable of arable land / Former reflections enduring doubt. *(UK-iss.1978 on 'Radar'; RAD 12) (re-iss.Jan88 on 'Decal'; LIK 20)*

— **TOMMY SMITH** – drums, repl. RICK (also added guest HOLLY PRITCHETT – vox)

1968. (lp) *<ALP 7>* **GOD BLESS THE RED CRAYOLA AND ALL WHO SAIL WITH HER** [-] [ ]
– Say hello to Jamie Jones / Music / The shirt / Listen to this / Save the house / Victory garden / Coconut hotel / Sheriff Jack / Free piece / Ravi Shankar: Parachutist / Dairy maid's lament / Big / Leejol / Sherlock Holmes / Dirth of tilth / Tina's gone to have a baby / The jewels of the Madonna / Green of my pants / Night song. *(UK-iss.Jun79 on 'Radar'; RAD 16)*

— Split in 1970. MAYO THOMPSON went solo in '72 but his 'CORKY'S DEBT' remained unreleased.

ART & LANGUAGE / RED CRAYOLA

MAYO + JESS CHAMBERLAIN

not issued Music Language

1976. (lp) *<1848>* **CORRECTED SLOGANS** [-] [ ]
– Maharashta / Keep all your friends / Imagination 1 & 2 / Coleridge vs. Martineau / An exemplification / Postscript to SDS infiltration / War dance 1 & 2 / An harangue / Ergastulum / The mistakes of Trotsky / The smophoriazusae / Louis Napoleon / Seven compartments / Petrichenko / Don't talk to sociologists / What are the inexpensive things the panel most enjoys an international / History / Organisation / It's an illusion / Penny capitalists / Plekhanov / Natura facit saltus.

RED CRAYOLA

In 1977, they re-formed with **MAYO + CHAMBERLAIN / + CHRISSIE THOMPSON** (Mayo's wife) – vox / **PERE UBU: DAVID THOMAS** – vocals, **TONY MAIMONE** – bass, **ALLEN RAVENSTINE** – sax, **SCOTT KRAUSE** – drums, **TOM HERMAN** – guitar / **LORA LOGIC** – sax (of ESSENTIAL LOGIC) / **DICK CUTHELL** – trumpet

Radar not issued

Oct 78. (7"red) *(ADA 22)* **WIVES IN ORBIT. / YIK YAK** [ ] [-]

Mar 79. (lp) *(RAD 18)* **SOLDIER TALK** [ ] [-]
– March No.12 / On the brink / Letter bomb / Conspirator's oath / March No.14 / Soldier talk / Discipline / X / An opposition spokesman / Uh, knowledge dance / Wonderland.

— **MAYO, ALLEN + LORA** with **EPIC SOUNDTRACKS** – drums (ex-SWELL MAPS) / **GINA BIRCH** (of RAINCOATS) + **BEN ANNESLEY** – bass

Rough Trade not issued

Aug 79. (12") *(RT 026)* **MICRO CHIPS & FISH. / THE STORY SO FAR** [ ] [-]

ART & LANGUAGE / RED CRAYOLA

Oct 80. (7") *(RT 054)* **BORN IN FLAMES. / SWORD OF GOD** [ ] [-]

May 81. (lp)(c) *(ROUGH 19)(COPY 005)* **KANGAROO** [ ] [-]
– Kangaroo / Portrait of V.L. Lenin in the style of Jackson Pollock (parts 1 & 2) / Marches nos.23, 24 & 25 / Born to win (transactional analysis with Gestalt experiments) / Keep all your friends / The milkmaid / The principles of party organisation / Prisoner's model / The mistakes of Trotsky / 1917 / The tractor driver / Plekhanov. *(c+=)–* An old man's dream / If she loves you.

Jul 81. (7") *(RT 073)* **AN OLD MAN'S DREAM. / THE MILKMAID** [ ] [-]

RED CRAYOLA – ART & LANGUAGE

CHRIS TAYLOR – drums, repl. EPIC, GINA + LORA

Recommended Ralph

Sep 83. (lp) *(ALRC 1949)* <002> **BLACK SNAKES** [ ] [ ]
– Black snakes / Ratman, the weight watcher / The sloths / The jam / Hedges / A portrait of V.L. Lenin in the style of Jackson Pollock (part 1) / Future pilots / A portrait of you / Words of love / Cafe twenty-one / Gynaecology in ancient Greece.

RED CRAYOLA

JESSE CHAMBERLAIN – drums, returned to repl. TAYLOR + ANNESLEY

Pure Freude not issued

1984. (lp) *(PF36 CK18)* **THREE SONGS ON A TRIP TO THE UNITED STATES (live)** [-] [-] German
– Monster one / California girl / Caribbean postcard / Discipline / X / Wives in orbit / Ergastulum / A portrait of you.

Glass not issued

Mar 89. (lp/cd) *(GLA LP/CD 035)* **MALEFACTOR ADE** [ ] [-]

RED KRAYOLA

— **THOMPSON** with **JIM O'ROURKE** – guitar (b. Chicago) / **JOHN McENTIRE** – Moog synthesizer (of TORTOISE) / plus + or '96 **MICHAEL BALDWIN / WERNER BUTTNER / DAVID GRUBBS / GEORGE HURLEY / LYNN JOHNSTON / HEI HAN KHIANG / ALBERT OEHLEN / JIM O'ROURKE / STEPHEN PRINA / ELISA RANDAZZO / MARY LASS STEWART / TOM WATSON / CHRISTOPHER WILLIAMS**

Drag City Drag City

1994. (cd) <> **THE RED KRAYOLA** [ ] [ ]

1996. (cd) *<(DC 98CD)>* **HAZEL** [ ] [ ]
– I'm so blase / Duck & cover / Duke of Newcastle / Decaf the planet / GAO / Larking / Jimmy too bad / Falls / We feel fine / 5123881 / Hollywood / Another song, another Satan / Boogie / Dad / Father Abraham / Serenade.

– compilations, etc. –

Apr 90. (cd) *Decal; (CDLIK 65)* **THE PARABLE OF ARABLE LAND / GOD BLESS THE RED CRAYOLA AND ALL WHO SAIL WITH IT** [ ] [-]

RED NOISE (see under ⇒ NELSON, Bill)

Lou REED

Born: LOUIS FIRBANK, 2 Mar'42, Freeport, Long Island, New York, USA. In 1958, he formed The JADES, who released two REED-penned singles, 'LEAVE HER FOR ME' / 'SO BLUE' and 'LEAVE HER FOR ME' / 'BELINDA' for 'Time' and 'Dot' respectively. Late in '64, he joined the 'Pickwick' stable of writers, achieving a local minor hit when The PRIMITIVES issued his 'The Ostrich' / 'Sneaky Pete' 45. Later in the year, he helped for the seminal VELVET UNDERGROUND. An integral part of the group's songwriting prowess, he departed in September 1970, going solo and signing to 'R.C.A.'. His eponymous 1972 debut (with Richard Robinson on production), scraped into the US Top 200, gaining nothing in renewed respect. Later that year, helped by stablemates DAVID BOWIE and MICK RONSON, he unleashed 'TRANSFORMER', gaving him his first major triumph when it reached the Top 30 on both sides of the Atlantic. It was boosted by 'WALK ON THE WILD SIDE' (a superb Top 20 single), the piano-led melancholy of 'PERFECT DAY', the raw glam of 'VICIOUS' and one-that-got-away 'SATELLITE OF LOVE'. His next album, 'BERLIN' (1973), although unfairly panned by US critics, still managed a Top 10 placing in Britain. On reflection, its subject matter of suicide and child neglect ('THE BED' and 'THE KIDS') didn't help win any new friends and it still stands as one of the most unrelentingly bleak listens in the history of rock. After the claustrophobic confessions of BERLIN, the live 'ROCK 'N' ROLL ANIMAL' (1974) album must have come as something of a relief to R.C.A. A technically faultless back-up band roared through a selection of old VELVETS numbers with REED hollering over the top, and while the set represented something of a concession to commercial credibility (by REED's standards anyway) it captured little of the VELVET UNDERGROUND's subtlety. It also saw REED sinking further into self-parody, hamming up his studied image of sleazy decadence to the max. 'SALLY CAN'T DANCE', released later the same year, was REED in full emotionless flight, an icy collection of biting cynicism that included the infamous 'ANIMAL LANGUAGE' track. But laughing LOU hadn't played his ace card yet, that musical two fingered salute fell to 1975's 'METAL MACHINE MUSIC', the one everyone talks about but have never had the will or mental endurance to listen to the whole way through. A double album of impenetrable feedback noise interspersed with inhuman screams, hums etc., the record successfully alienated most of REED's long suffering fans amid critical meltdown. In true contrary style, he sashayed sweetly back with the mellow 'CONEY ISLAND BABY' (1976), although the lyrics remained as brutally frank as ever. His first record for 'Arista', 'ROCK 'N' ROLL HEART' (1976) was indeed as vacantly awful as the title suggests, though the punk-inspired 'STREET HASSLE' (1978) showcased a re-energised REED, most impressively on the malicious guitar workout of 'DIRT' and the swaggering title track. After a tedious live album, REED started to show uncharacteristic signs of maturity in both his music and lyrics with 'THE BELLS' (1979) and 'GROWING UP IN PUBLIC' (1980). At the turn of the 80's, he hooked up with former Void-Oid, ROBERT QUINE, a partnership that resulted in one of the most consistent and accomplished sets in REED's solo career, 'THE BLUE MASK'. Newly married and back at his original stable, 'R.C.A.', REED proffered more domestic lyrical fare alongside darker musings. QUINE remained for one more studio album, the similarly focused 'LEGENDARY HEARTS', before breaking ranks. 1984's 'NEW SENSATIONS' was fairly low-key while 'MISTRIAL' (1986) saw REED introduce a few drum machine tracks in typical 80's style. These were competent albums but hardly essential and only the most devout REED believer could've predicted the creative, commercial and critical renaissance that would ensue with 1989's 'NEW YORK' album. A skeletal strum-athon, this was LOU REED in the raw with the sparsest of musical accompaniment. Back on familiar territory, his sardonic tales of the Big Apple's seedier side made for compelling listening. 'SONGS FOR DRELLA' (1990), a collaboration with JOHN CALE, was a heartfelt tribute to ANDY WARHOL, while 'MAGIC AND LOSS' (1992) was a sincere series of stark meditations on life and death. Despite an ill-advised VELVET UNDERGROUND reunion, REED retained critical favour, going on to release another well-received album in 1996, 'SET THE TWILIGHT REELING'. • **Songwriters:** REED compositions except, SEPTEMBER SONG (Kurt Weill) / SOUL MAN (Sam & Dave). In 1979 and 1980, he co-wrote with MICHAEL FORFARA plus other group members. The single, 'CITY LIGHTS', was co-written with NILS LOFGREN.

• **Trivia:** Surprisingly in 1973, WALK ON THE WILD SIDE was not banned from airplay. It contained lyrics "giving head", which had been overlooked by unstreet-wise cred. radio producers. LOU has been married twice, first to cocktail waitress, Betty on the 9th of January '73, then to Sylvia Morales on the 14th of February '80. He played guitar and composed four tracks on NICO'S 'Chelsea Girl' lp in 1967. Nine years later he produced NELSON SLATER'S 'Wild Angel' album, also contributing guitar, piano and vocals. In 1979 and 1981 he co-composed with NILS LOFGREN and KISS on their 'NILS' and 'THE ELDER' albums respectively. In the late 80's, he guested for RUBEN BLADES and his old friend MAUREEEN TUCKER. He was also backing vocalist on SIMPLE MINDS' 'This is Your Land' / DION'S 'King of The New York Streets' and TOM TOM CLUB'S version of 'Femme Fatale'.

Recommended: TRANSFORMER (*9) / BERLIN (*7) / RETRO (*8) / THE BLUE MASK (*7) / NEW YORK (*9) / MAGIC AND LOSS (*8) / SONGS FOR DRELLA (*7) / SET THE TWILIGHT REELING (*8)

LOU REED – vocals, guitar (ex-VELVET UNDERGROUND) / with **STEVE HOWE** – guitar / **RICK WAKEMAN** – keyboards (both of YES) / **CLEM CATTINI** – drums (ex-TORNADOES)

R.C.A. R.C.A.

Jun 72. (7") *<0727>* **GOING DOWN. / I CAN'T STAND IT** [-] [ ]
Jul 72. (lp) *(SF 8281) <4701>* **LOU REED** [ ] [ ] Jun72
– I can't stand it / Going down / Walk and talk it / Lisa says / Berlin / I love you / Wild child / Love makes you feel / Ride into the Sun / Ocean.
Aug 72. (7") *(RCA 2240) <0784>* **WALK AND TALK IT. / WILD CHILD** [ ] [ ]

— now with **MICK RONSON** – guitar / **HERBIE FLOWERS + KLAUS VOORMANN** – bass / **JOHN HALSEY + RITCHIE DHARMA + BARRY DE SOUZA** – drums / **RONNIE ROSS** – saxophone / **DAVID BOWIE** – backing vocals, producer

Nov 72. (lp) *(LSP 4807) <4807>* **TRANSFORMER** [13] [29]
– Vicious / Andy's chest / Perfect day / Hangin' round / Walk on the wild side / Make up / Satellite of love / Wagon wheel / New York telephone conversation / I'm so free / Goodnight ladies. *(re-iss.Feb81 lp/c; INT S/K 5061); hit UK No.91) (re-iss.1984 lp/c; NL/NK 83806) (cd-iss.1985 + Oct87; PD 83806)*
Nov 72. (7") *(RCA 2303) <0887>* **WALK ON THE WILD SIDE. / PERFECT DAY** [10] [16]
(re-iss.May79 on 'RCA Gold'; GOLD 5)
Feb 73. (7") *<0964>* **SATELLITE OF LOVE. / WALK AND TALK IT** [-] [ ]
Mar 73. (7") *(RCA 2318)* **SATELLITE OF LOVE. / VICIOUS** [ ] [-]
Apr 73. (7") *<0054>* **VICIOUS. / GOODNIGHT LADIES** [-] [ ]

— all new band **DICK WAGNER + STEVE HUNTER** – guitar (both ex-ALICE COOPER) / **STEVE WINWOOD** – keyboards / **JACK BRUCE** – bass / **AYNSLEY DUNBAR** – drums / etc.

Oct 73. (7") *<0172>* **HOW DO YOU THINK IT FEELS. / LADY DAY** [-] [ ]
Oct 73. (lp) *(RS 1002) <0207>* **BERLIN** [7] [98]
– Berlin / Lady day / Men of good fortune / Caroline says I / How do think it feels / Oh Jim / Caroline says II / The kids / The bed / Sad song. *(re-iss.Oct81 lp/c; INT S/K 5150) (re-iss.1984 lp/c; NL/NK 84388) (cd-iss.Jun86; PD 84388)*
Feb 74. (7") *(APBO 0221)* **CAROLINE SAYS I. / CAROLINE SAYS II** [ ] [-]

— **PRAKASH JOHN** – bass (ex-ALICE COOPER) repl. TONY LEVIN / **JOSEF CHIROWSKY** – keyboards / **WHITNEY GLEN** – drums (ex-ALICE COOPER)

Feb 74. (lp/c) *(APL 1/4 0472) <0472>* **ROCK'N'ROLL ANIMAL (live)** [26] [45]
– (intro) – Sweet Jane / Heroin / White light – white heat / Lady day / Rock and roll. *(re-iss.May81 lp/c; INT S/K 5086) (re-iss.1984 lp/c; NL/NK 83664) (cd-iss.Jun86; PD 83664)*
Apr 74. (7") *<(APBO 0238)>* **SWEET JANE (live). / LADY DAY (live)** [ ] [ ]

— **MICHAEL FORFARA** – keyboards repl. JOSEF

Aug 74. (7") *<10053>* **SALLY CAN'T DANCE. / VICIOUS** [-] [ ]
Sep 74. (lp/c) *(APL 1/4 <0611>)* **SALLY CAN'T DANCE** [ ] [10]
– Ride Sally ride / Animal language / Baby face / N.Y. stars / Kill your sons / Billy / Sally can't dance / Ennui. *(cd-iss.Mar87; PD 80611) (re-iss.cd Feb89; ND 90308)*
Oct 74. (7") *(RCA 2467) <10081>* **SALLY CAN'T DANCE. / ENNUI** [ ] [ ]
Mar 75. (lp) *(RS 1007) <0959>* **LOU REED LIVE (live)** [ ] [62]
– Walk on the wild side / I'm waiting for the man / Vicious / Oh Jim / Satellite of love / Sad song. *(re-iss.Feb81 lp/c; INT S/K 5071) (cd-iss.Mar87 + Feb90; ND 83752)*

— LOU now used synthesizer only.

Jul 75. (d-lp) *<(CPL2 1101)>* **METAL MACHINE MUSIC – (THE AMINE B RING)** [ ] [ ]
– Metal machine music A1 / A2 / A3 / A4. *(re-iss.Mar91 on 'Great Expectations' cd/d-c/d-lp; PIPD C/M/L 023)*

— Band now featured **MICHAEL SUCHORSKY** – percussion / **BOB KULICK** – guitar / **BRUCE YAW** – bass

Jan 76. (lp/c) *(RS/ 1035) <0915>* **CONEY ISLAND BABY** [52] [41]
– Crazy feeling / Charley's girl / She's my best friend / Kicks / A gift / Oooh baby / Nobody's business / Coney Island baby. *(re-iss.Mar81 lp/c; INT S/K 5082) (re-iss.1984 lp/c; NL/NK 83807) (cd-iss.Dec86 & Sep89; PD 83807)*
Mar 76. (7") *(RCA 2666) <10573>* **CHARLEY'S GIRL. / NOWHERE AT ALL** [ ] [ ]
May 76. (7") *<10648>* **CRAZY FEELING. / NOWHERE AT ALL** [-] [ ]

Arista Arista

Nov 76. (lp/c) *(ARTY/TC-ARTY 142) <4100>* **ROCK AND ROLL HEART** [ ] [64]
– I believe in love / Banging on my drum / Follow the leader / You wear it so well / Ladies pay / Rock and roll heart / Temporary thing.
Nov 76. (7") *<0215>* **I BELIEVE IN LOVE. / SENSELESSLY CRUEL** [-] [ ]
Apr 77. (7") *(105)* **ROCK AND ROLL HEART. / SENSELESSLY CRUEL** [ ] [-]

— **STUART HEINRICH** – guitar, vocals repl. KULICK / **MARTY FOGEL** – saxophone repl. YAW

Apr 78. (lp/c) *(SPART/TC-SPART 1045) <4169>* **STREET HASSLE** [ ] [89]
– Gimme some good times / Dirt / Street hassle / I wanna be black / Real good time together / Shooting star / Leave me alone / Wait.
Apr 78. (12") **STREET HASSLE. / (same track)** [-] [ ]
Jul 78. (12"ep) *(ARIST12 198)* **STREET HASSLE. / Waiting For The Man + Venus In Furs (by "The VELVET UNDERGROUND")** [ ] [-]

— **ELLARD BOLES** – bass, guitar repl. HEINRICH. (Below released 'RCA' UK)

Mar 79. (d-lp)<red,blue-lp> *(XL 03066) <8502>* **LIVE – TAKE NO PRISONERS (live)** [ ] [ ] Nov78
– Sweet Jane / I wanna be black / Satellite of love / Pale blue eyes / Berlin / I'm waiting for the man / Coney Island baby / Street hassle / Walk on the wild side / Leave me alone.

— **REED** now with **FORFARA, BOLES, SUCHORSKY, FOGEL** and **DON CHERRY** – trumpet

Oct 79. (lp/c) *(SPART/TC-SPART 1093) <4229>* **THE BELLS** [ ] [ ] May 79
– Stupid man / Disco mystic / I want to boogie with you / With you / Looking for love / City lights / All through the night / Families / The bells. *(cd-iss.Aug92; 262 918)*
Jun 79. (7") *<0431>* **CITY LIGHTS. / I WANT TO BOOGIE WITH YOU** [-] [ ]
Oct 79. (7") *(ARIST 308)* **CITY LIGHTS. / SENSELESSLY CRUEL** [ ] [-]

— **CHUCK HAMMER** – synthesizer, guitar repl. FOGEL & CHERRY

May 80. (lp/c) *(SPART/TC-SPART 1131) <9522>* **GROWING UP IN PUBLIC** [ ] [ ]
– How do you speak to an angel / My old man / Keep away / Growing up in public / Standing on ceremony / So alone / Love is here to stay / The power of positive drinking / Smiles / Think it over / Teach the gifted children. *(cd-iss.Aug92; 262 917)*
Jun 80. (7") *<0535>* **THE POWER OF POSITIVE DRINKING. / GROWING UP IN PUBLIC** [-] [ ]

— **ROBERT QUINE** – guitar repl. HAMMER

R.C.A. R.C.A.

Mar 82. (lp/c) *(RCA LP/K 6028) <4221>* **THE BLUE MASK** [ ] [ ] Feb82
– My house / Women / Underneath the bottle / The gun / The blue mask / The gun / The heroine / Waves of fear / The day John Kennedy died / Heavenly arms.
Mar 83. (lp/c) *(RCA LP/K 6071) <4568>* **LEGENDARY HEARTS** [ ] [ ]
– Legendary hearts / Don't talk to me about work / Make up mind / Martial law / The last shot / Turn out the light / ow wow / Betrayed / Bottoming out / Home of the brave / Rooftop garden. *(re-iss.Oct86 lp/c; NL/NK 89843) (re-iss.Apr91 cd/c; ND/NK 89843)*
Apr 83. (7") *<13558>* **MARTIAL LAW. / DON'T TALK TO ME ABOUT WORK** [-] [ ]
Jan 84. (d-lp/c) *(PL/PK 89156)* **LIVE IN ITALY (live)** [ ] [-]
– Sweet Jane / I'm waiting for the man / Martial law / Satellite of love / Kill your sons / Betrayed / Sally can't dance / Waves of fear / Average guy / White light – white heat / Some kinda love / Sister Ray / Walk on the wild side / Heroin / Rock and roll.

— Line-up now **FERNANDO SAUNDERS** – bass, rhythm guitar / **FRED MAHER** – drums / **PETER WOOD** – piano, synthesizer, accordion / **L. SHANKER** – electric violin

Mar 84. (7") *<13841>* **I LOVE YOU SUZANNE. / MY FRIEND GEORGE** [-] [ ]
May 84. (12") *<13849>* **MY RED JOY STICK. / ('A' remix)** [-] [ ]
May 84. (lp/c) *(PL/PK 84998) <4998>* **NEW SENSATIONS** [92] [56]
– I love you, Suzanne / Endlessly jealous / My red joystick / Turn to me / New sensations / Doin' the things that we want to / What becomes a legend most / Fly into the Sun / High in the city / My friend George / Down at the arcade. *(cd-iss.Jul86; PD 84998)*
May 84. (7") *(RCA 417)* **I LOVE YOU, SUZANNE. / VICIOUS** [ ] [-]
(12"+=) *(RCAT 417)* – Walk on the wild side.
Apr 86. (12") *<14427>* **THE ORIGINAL WRAPPER. / (2 'A' versions)** [-] [ ]
Apr 86. (lp/c/cd) *(PL/PK/PD 87190) <7190>* **MISTRIAL** [69] [47]
– Mistrial / No money down / Outside / Don't hurt a woman / Video violence / Spit it out / The original wrapper / Mama's got a lover / I remember you / Tell it to your heart. *(re-iss.Oct88 lp/c/cd; NL/NK/ND 90253)*
Jun 86. (7") *(RCA 501) <14368>* **NO MONEY DOWN. / DON'T HURT A WOMAN** [ ] [ ]
(12"+=) *(RCAT 501) <14388>* – ('A'dub version).

— Next from the film 'Soul Man'.

A&M A&M

Jan 87. (7"; LOU REED & SAM MOORE) *(AM 364)* **SOUL MAN. / Sweet Sarah (by 'Tom Scott')** [30] [ ]
<US-12"+=> – My love is chemical.

— new band **MIKE RATHKE** – guitar / **ROB WASSERMAN** – bass / **FRED MAHER** – drums / **MAUREEN TUCKER** – drums on 2 (ex-VELVET UNDERGROUND)

Sire Sire

Jan 89. (lp/c)(cd) *(WX 246/+C)(925 829-2) <25829>* **NEW YORK** [14] [40]
– Romeo had Juliette / Halloween parade / Dirty Blvd. / Endless cycle / There is no time / The last great American whale / Beginning of a great adventure / Busload of faith / Sick of you / Hold on / Good evening Mr. Waldheim / Xmas in February / Strawman / Dime store mystery. *(re-iss.Feb95 cd/c;)*
Feb 89. (7") **ROMEO HAD JULIETTE. / BUSLOAD OF FAITH (live)** [-] [ ]
Feb 89. (7") *(W 7547)* **DIRTY BLVD. / THE LAST GREAT AMERICAN WHALE** [ ] [-]
(12"+=) *(W 7547T)* – The room.
Apr 90. (cd)(lp/c; by LOU REED / JOHN CALE) *(7599 <26140-2>)(WX 345/+C)* **SONGS FOR DRELLA** [22] [ ]
– Smalltown / Open house / Style it takes / Work / Trouble with classicists / Starlight / Faces and names / Images / Slip away (a warning) / It wasn't me / I believe / Nobody but you / A dream / Forever changed / Hello it's me. *(re-iss.Feb91 & Jan97; same)*

— (above re-united the two VELVET UNDERGROUND members, tributing the recently deceased ANDY WARHOL)

— **MICHAEL BLAIR** – percussion, drums, vocas repl. MAHER

Jan 92. (cd/lp/c) *(7599 <26662-2>)(WX 435/+C)* **MAGIC AND LOSS** [6] [80]
– Dorita – the spirit / What's good – the thesis / Power and glory – the situation / Magician – internally / Sword of Damocles – eternally / Goodby mass – in a chapel bodily termination / Cremation – ashes to ashes / Dreamin' – escape / No chance – regret / Warrior king – revenge / Harry's circumcision – reverie gone astray / Gassed and stoked – loss / Power and glory part II – magic transformation / Magic and loss – the summation. *(cd re-iss.Jan97; same)*
Mar 92. (7"/c-s) **WHAT'S GOOD. / THE ROOM** [ ] [ ]
(12"+=/cd-s+=) – Mary's circumcision / A dream.

— now with just **FERNANDO SAUNDERS** – basses / **TONY 'Thunder' SMITH** – drums / + guest **LAURIE ANDERSON** – backing vocals

WEA / Reprise

Feb 96. (cd/c) *(9362 46159-2/-4)* **SET THE TWILIGHT REELING** [26] [ ]
– Egg cream / NYC man / Finish line / Trade in / Hang on to your emotions / Sex with your parents (motherfucker) part II (live) / Hooky wooky / The proposition / Adventurer / Riptide / Set the twilight reeling.

May 96. (c-s) *(W 0351C)* **HOOKY WOOKY / ON THE RUN** [ ] [ ]
(cd-s) *(W 0351CD)* – ('A'side) / This magic moment / You'll never know you loved.

– compilations, others, etc. –

— Below releases issued on 'RCA' unless mentioned otherwise

Apr 77. (lp/c) *(PL/PK 12001)* *<2001>* **WALK ON THE WILD SIDE – THE BEST OF LOU REED** [ ] [ ]
(cd-iss.Mar87; PD 83753)

Jan 79. (lp/c) *(NL/NK 42731)* **VICIOUS** [ ] [ ]

Dec 80. (d-lp) *Arista; (DARTY 8)* **ROCK AND ROLL DIARY 1967-1980** [ ] [ ]
– (above featured 8 tracks by Velvet Underground)

Aug 81. (7") *RCA Gold; (GOLD 523)* **WALK ON THE WILD SIDE. / VICIOUS** [ ] [-]
(re-iss.Oct86 & Mar89 on 'Old Gold'; OG 9635)

Sep 82. (lp) *(SF 8281)* **I CAN'T STAND IT** [ ] [ ]

Oct 85. (7") *A&M; (AM 283)* **SEPTEMBER SONG. / Oh Heavenly Action (by 'Mark Bingham with Johnny Adams & Aaron Neville')** [ ] [ ]

May 86. (c) *(NK 89895)* **MAGIC MOMENTS** [ ] [-]

Sep 86. (lp/c) *Fame; (FA/TC-FA 3164)* **NEW YORK SUPERSTAR** [ ] [-]

Feb 89. (3"cd-ep) *(PD 49453)* **WALK ON THE WILD SIDE / PERFECT DAY / SATELLITE OF LOVE / VICIOUS** [ ] [ ]

Sep 89. (lp/c/cd) *(PL/PK/PD 90389)* **RETRO** [29] [ ]
– Walk on the wild side / Satellite of love / I love you Suzanne / Wild child / How do you think it feels / Lady day / Coney Island baby / Sweet Jane (live) / Vicious / Sally can't dance / Berlin / Caroline says II / Kill your sons / White light – white heat (live). *(cd+=)*– I'm waiting for the man (VELVET UNDERGROUND) / Heroin (VELVET UNDERGROUND).

Mar 92. (3xcd/3xc) *(PD/PK 90621)* **BETWEEN THOUGHT AND EXPRESSION** [ ] [ ]

REFUGEE (see under ⇒ JACKSON HEIGHTS)

RELEASE MUSIC ORCHESTRA (see under ⇒ TOMORROW'S GIFT)

REMAINS

Formed: Boston, Massachusetts, USA . . . 1964 by BARRY TASHIAN, BILL BRIGGS, VERN MILLER and CHIP DAMIANI. After spending some time in London, they signed to 'Epic', subsequently releasing a few garage/R&B rock/pop singles and an album. They split soon after, although they did guest on the last Beatles tour. • **Songwriters:** TASHIAN except TALKIN' 'BOUT YOU (Chuck Berry) / LUXURY LINER (Gram Parsons) / etc.

Recommended: THE REMAINS (*7)

BARRY TASHIAN – vocals, guitar / **BILL BRIGGS** – keyboards / **VERN MILLER** – bass, brass / **CHIP DAMIANI** – drums

not issued / Epic

1965. (7") *<5-9777>* **I'M TALKING ABOUT YOU. / YOU SAY YOU'RE SORRY** [-] [ ]

1965. (7") *<5-9783>* **WHY DO I CRY. / MY BABE** [-] [ ]

1965. (7") *<5-9842>* **I CAN'T GET AWAY FROM YOU. / BUT I AIN'T GOT YOU** [-] [ ]

1966. (7") *<45-10001>* **DIDDY WAH DIDDY. / ONCE BEFORE** [-] [ ]

1966. (7") *<45-10060>* **DON'T LOOK BACK. / ME RIGHT NOW** [-] [ ]

1966. (lp; mono/stereo) *<LN/BN 26214>* **THE REMAINS** [-] [ ]
– Heart / Lonely weekend / Don't look back / Why do I cry / Diddy wah diddy / You got a hard time coming / Once before / Thank you / Time of day / Say you're wrong. *<US re-iss.1978 on 'Spoonfed'; 3305>*

— disbanded soon after above, although they did re-unite for 1976 single 'LUXURY LINER'. In 1967, BARRY worked with GRAM PARSONS in an embryonic FLYING BURRITO BROTHERS and later became his session man for 'GP' album. In 1970, BARRY started dating singer HOLLY, whom he married two years later. They became a folk/country duo, making several recordings during the next few decades.

– compilations, others, etc. –

1982. (lp) *Eva; (12007)* **DIDDY WAH DIDDY** [-] [-] France

1983. (lp) *Eva; (12024)* **LIVE IN BOSTON** [-] [-] France

1985. (d-lp) *Fan Club; (FC 012)* **THE REMAINS** [-] [-]

1991. (cd) *Epic;* **THE REMAINS** [-] [ ]

RENAISSANCE

Formed: Surrey, England . . . 1969 by KEITH RELF and JIM McCARTY (both ex-YARDBIRDS). They enlisted the beautiful JANE RELF, JOHN HAWKEN, and LOUIS CENNAMO. Signing to 'Island', they released their eponymous debut album, a misguided attempt to combine folk, classical, jazz, blues and rock. The record was met with dismal reviews and a second set due for release, was subsequently shelved when they virtually disbanded. By 1972, the group had evolved with NO original members remaining, ANNIE HASLAM assuming vocal duties. She was backed by JOHN TOUT, ROB HENDRY, JON CAMP and TERRENCE SULLIVAN. After a warmer press reception of their comeback album, 'PROLOGUE', especially in the States where they subsequently relocated, signing to 'Capitol'. Opting for a more quasi-classical sound, ANNIE's vocals (with BETTY THATCHER's lyrics/poems) were a perfect vehicle for their newfound style. They worked hard throughout the mid-70's, 'SCHEHERAZADE & OTHER STORIES' and 'NOVELLA' being their most successful albums to date (both US Top 50). In 1978, they regained their British audience when they had a surprise Top 10 hit with the more folk-orientated 'NORTHERN LIGHTS'. They carried on in this vein, releasing several more albums (including a HASLAM solo effort) and are still going strong today, releasing 'OCEAN GYPSY' in 1997. • **Songwriters:** Originally RELF – McCARTY, until break-up early 70's. By 1973, DUNFORD wrote the music. • **Trivia:** not to be confused with US outfit of same name who released a single in 1969, 'MARY JANE'.

Recommended: DA CAPO – THE STORY OF RENAISSANCE (*8)

KEITH RELF (b.22 Mar'43, London, England) – vocals, mouth harp (ex-YARDBIRDS, ex-Solo, ex-TOGETHER, ex-REIGN) / **JANE RELF** – vocals / **JOHN HAWKEN** – keyboards (ex-NASHVILLE TEENS) / **LOUIS CENNAMO** – bass (ex-CHIGAGO BLUES) / **JIM McCARTY** – drums (ex-YARDBIRDS, ex-TOGETHER)

Island / Elektra

Dec 69. (lp) *(ILPS 9114)* *<74068>* **RENAISSANCE** [60] [ ]
– Kings and queens / Innocence / Islands / Wanderer / Bullet. *(cd-iss.Jan91 on 'Line'; LICD 9004210) (cd re-iss.Jan95 on 'Repertoire'; REP 4512-WY)*

Jan 70. (7") *(WIP 6079)* **THE SEA. / ISLANDS** [ ] [-]

1971. (lp; export) *(HELP 27)* **ILLUSION** [-] [-]
– Love goes on / Golden thread / Love is all / Mr. Pine / Face of yesterday / Past orbits of dust. *(cd-iss.Nov89 on 'Line'; LICD 900425) (cd-iss.Jan95 on 'Repertoire'; REP 4513-WY)*

— They split many times, with McCARTHY joining SHOOT and KEITH RELF becoming producer and joining MEDICINE HEAD. They also changed name to ILLUSION, after above was shelved. Finally evolved again with no!!! originals remaining. RENAISSANCE were now in 1972; **ANNIE HASLAM** – vocals / **JOHN TOUT** – keyboards / **ROB HENDRY** – guitar / **JON CAMP** – bass, vocals / **TERRENCE SULLIVAN** – percussion

Sovereign / Capitol

Oct 72. (lp) *(SVNA 7253)* *<11116>* **PROLOGUE** [ ] [ ]
– Prologue / Kiev / Sounds of the sea / Spare some love / Bound for infinity / Rajah Khan. *(cd-iss.Jun95 on 'Repertoire';)*

Nov 72. (7") *<3487>* **PROLOGUE. / SPARE SOME LOVE** [-] [ ]

— **MICHAEL DUNFORD** – acoustic guitar, vocals (ex-NASHVILLE TEENS), repl. HENDRY

Oct 73. (7") *<3715>* **CARPET OF THE SUN. / BOUND FOR INFINITY** [-] [ ]

Oct 73. (lp) *(SVNA 7261)* *<11216>* **ASHES ARE BURNING** [ ] [ ]
– Can you understand / Let it grow / On the frontier / Carpet of the sun / At the harbour / Ashes are burning. *(cd-iss.Jun95 on 'Repertoire'; REP)*

B.T.M. / Sire

Nov 74. (7") *<714>* **I THINK OF YOU. / MOTHER RUSSIA** [-] [ ]

Mar 75. (lp) *(BTM 1000)* *<6015>* **TURN OF THE CARDS** [ ] [94] Jul74
– Running hard / I think of you / Things I don't understand / Black flame / Cold is being / Mother Russia. *(cd-iss.Sep94 on 'Repertoire'; REP 4491) (cd re-iss.Jan96 on 'H.T.D.'; HTDCD 51)*

Sep 75. (lp) *(BTM 1006)* *<6017>* **SCHEHERAZADE & OTHER STORIES** [ ] [48] Aug75
– Trip to the fair / The vultures fly high / Ocean gypsy / Song of Scheherazade: – Fanfare – The betrayal – The sultan – Love theme – The young prince and princess – Festival preparations – Fugue for the sultans – The festival – Finale. *(cd-iss.Sep94 on 'Repertoire'; REP 4490) (cd re-iss.May96 on 'H.T.D.'; HTDCD 59)*

Sep 76. (d-lp) *(BTM 2001)* *<6029>* **LIVE AT THE CARNEGIE HALL (live)** [ ] [55] Jun76
– Prologue / Ocean gypsy / Can you understand / Carpet of the Sun / Running hard / Mother Russia / Song of Scheherazade: Fanfare – The betrayal – The sultan – Love theme – The young prince and princess – Festival preparations – Fugue for the sultan – The festival – Finale / Ashes are burning. *(d-cd-iss.Sep94 on 'Repertoire'; REP 4506) (re-iss.cd Sep95 on 'H.T.D.'; HTDCD 40) (re-iss.d-lp.Jan96; HTDLP 40)*

Oct 76. (7") *<728>* **CARPET OF THE SUN. / (part 2)** [-] [ ]

Warners / Sire

Aug 77. (lp) *(K 56422)* *<6034>* **NOVELLA** [ ] [46] Feb 77
– Can you hear me / The sisters / Midas man / The captive heart / Touching once (is so hard to keep). *(cd-iss.Jan96; 7599 26516-2)*

Aug 77. (7") *<740>* **THE CAPTIVE HEART. / MIDAS MAN** [-] [ ]

Sep 77. (7") *(K 17012)* **THE CAPTIVE HEART. / BACK HOME ONCE AGAIN** [ ] [-]

Mar 78. (lp) *(K 56460)* *<6049>* **A SONG FOR ALL SEASONS** (Aug78:-) [35] [58]
– Opening out / Day of the dreamer / Closer than yesterday / Kindness (at the end) / Back home once again / She is love / Northern lights / A song for all seasons. *(cd-iss.Jan96; 7599 25959-2)*

May 78. (7") *(K 17177)* *<1022>* **NORTHERN LIGHTS. / OPENING OUT** [10] [ ]

Apr 79. (7") *(K 17353)* **WINTER TREE. / ISLAND OF AVALON** [ ] [-]

May 79. (lp) *(K 56633)* *<6068>* **AZURE D'OR** [73] [ ]
– Jekyll and Hyde / The winter tree / Only angels have wings / Golden key / Forever changing / Secret mission / Kalynda / The discovery / Friends / The flood at Lyons. *(re-iss.Jan88 on 'Thunderbolt' lp/c/cd; THBL/THBC/CDTB 045) (cd re-iss.Jan96; 7599 26517-2)*

Jun 79. (7") *<49041>* **JEKYLL AND HYDE. / FOREVER CHANGING** [-] [ ]

— **PETER GOSLING** – keyboards repl. TOUT

— **PETER BARRON** – percussion repl. SULLIVAN

Illegal / I.R.S.

Sep 81. (7") *(ILS 25)* **FAERIES (LIVING AT THE BOTTOM OF MY GARDEN). / REMEMBER** [ ] [-]

Sep 81. (lp) *(ILP 008)* *<70019>* **CAMERA CAMERA** [ ] [ ]
– Camera camera / Faeries (living at the bottom of my garden) / Remember / Tyrant-Tula / Okichi-San / Jigsaw / Running away from you / Ukraine ways. *(cd-iss.Nov95 on 'H.T.D.'; HTDCD 43)*

Jan 82. (7") *(ILS 27)* **BONJOUR SWANSONG. / UKRAINE WAYS** [ ] [-]

Jan 82. (7") *<9904>* **BONJOUR SWANSONG. / REMEMBER** [-] [ ]

Apr 83. (lp) *(<SP 70033>)* **TIME LINE**
– Flight / Missing persons / Chagrin boulevard / Richard IX / The entertainer / Electric avenue / Majik / Distant horizons / Orient express / Auto-tech. *(cd-iss.Nov95 on 'H.T.D.'; HTDCD 42) (cd re-iss.Jun97 on 'Repertoire'; REP 4655WY)*

Apr 83. (7") *<9914>* **RICHARD IX. / (part 2)**

— Disbanded in 1983.

ANNIE HASLAM

with **ROY WOOD** – instruments, vocals (ex-MOVE, ex-WIZZARD) / **JON CAMP** – bass / **DAVE DONOVAN** – drums / **LOUIS CLARK** – synthesizers.

Warners Sire

Oct 77. (7"; ANNIE HASLAM & ROY WOOD) *(K 17028) <1016>* **I NEVER BELIEVED IN LOVE. / INSIDE MY LIFE**

Jan 78. (7") *(K 17563)* **GOING HOME. / INSIDE MY LIFE**

Apr 78. (lp) **ANNIE IN WONDERLAND**
– Introlise / If I were made of music / I never believed in love / If I loved you / Humicoco / Rockalise / Nature boy / Inside my life / Going home.

— In Aug95, ANNIE HASLAM RENAISSANCE released cd 'BLESSING IN DISGUISE' for 'Thunderbolt'; *CDTB 151)*

RENAISSANCE

MICHAEL DUNFORD re-formed with new female lead singer **STEPHANIE ADLINGTON** – vocals / + **STUART BRADBURY** – guitars / **ANDY SPILLAR** – keyboards, programming / **PHIL MALFORD** – bass / **DAVE DOWLY** – drums

H.T.D. not issued

Jan 95. (cd) *(HTDCD 27)* **THE OTHER WOMAN**
– Deja vu / Love lies, love dies / Don't talk / The other woman / Lock in on love / Northern lights / So blase / Quicksilver / May you be blessed / Somewhere west of here.

— (below could be live or new recordings of old material)

Jun 97. (cd) *(HTDCD 71)* **OCEAN GYPSY**
– Ocean gypsy / Things I don't understand / Young prince and princess / Carpet of the sun / At the harbour / I think of you / Star of the show / Trip to the fair / Great highway.

– compilations, etc –

Jun 95. (d-cd) *Repertoire;* **DA CAPO – THE STORY OF RENAISSANCE**
– Kings and queens / Island / Love goes on / Love is all / Prologue / Bound for infinity / Carpet of the sun / Ashes are burning / Black flame / Running hard / Mother Russia / Africa / Trip to the fair / Ocean gypsy / The young prince and the princess / Midas man / Captive heart / Northern lights / Song for all seasons / Forever changing / Flood at Lyons / Bonjour swansong / Ukraine ways / The entertainer / Writers wronged.

Apr 97. (cd; by ANNIE HASLAM & MIKE DUNFORD) *H.T.D.; (HTDCD 73)* **SONGS FROM RENAISSANCE DAYS**

RESIDENTS

Formed: Shrieveport, Louisiana, USA . . .1966 by mysterious line-up. Soon relocating to San Mateo, California in the early 70's, they made a few untitled homemade recordings. They subsequently sent these to Hal Haverstadt of 'Warners' who promptly returned them, the address marked; 'for the attention of the residents'. Adopting the latter as their moniker, they later issued the two newly named tapes in the early 70's, 'RUSTY COAT HANGER FOR THE DOCTOR' and 'THE BALLAD OF STUFFED TRIGGER' respectively. In 1972, they shifted base to San Francisco, founding the independently distributed 'Ralph' records. Their "real" debut lp, 'MEET THE RESIDENTS' was issued in 1974, its title and cover art a tongue-in cheek take-off of The BEATLES. They then released a series of very limited edition lp's, 'THIRD REICH AND ROLL' in 1976, a collection of mangled 50's and 60's covers, carrying on where FRANK ZAPPA left off (albeit in a much weirder fashion). Later in the year, The RESIDENTS and DEVO competed for the best re-constructed version of The STONES' 'SATISFACTION', however, the latter won out in the end. After more comical parodying of The BEATLES and others, they unleashed the 'ESKIMO' set in 1979. This seminal meisterwork was recorded over a lengthy period of time, weird in the extreme, it featured tribal rhythms behind sub-lingual voices (VIC REEVES in "club style" must have taken inspiration). In 1980, the 'COMMERCIAL ALBUM' was released, containing forty tracks of exactly one minute in length, it was another to explore the barren frontiers of possibilities in music. They continued throughout the 80's with even more obscurity than their earlier 70's work. They were infamous for their hilarious head disguises, which included giant eyeballs, etc. • **Songwriters:** Group penned, except tribute/covers lp's of ELVIS PRESLEY, HANK WILLIAMS, GEORGE GERSHWIN and JAMES BROWN material.

Recommended: THE COMMERCIAL ALBUM (*7) / ESKIMO (*8)

The RESIDENTS (4) – instruments, vocals, noises / assisted by **SNAKEFINGER** (b. PHILIP LITHMAN) (ex-CHILLI WILLI & THE RED HOT PEPPERS)

not issued Ralph

Dec 72. (d-7"ltd) *<RR 1272>* **SANTA DOG**
– Aircraft damage (credited to ARR + OMEGA) / The COLLEGE WALKERS – Lightning /

Feb 74. (lp-ltd) *<RR 0274>* **MEET THE RESIDENTS**
– Boots . . . Numb erone . . . Guylum Bardot . . . Breath and length . . . Consuelo's departure . . . Smelly tongues . . . Rest aria . . . Skratz . . . Spotted pinto bean . . . Infant tango . . . Seasoned greetings . . . N-er-gee (crisis blues). *(re-iss.re-mixed Aug77; RR 0677)*– (lost 7 minutes). *(re-iss.Dec88 on 'Torso' cd/lp; CD/40 416)*

— In Oct'75, they issued 500 copies US of lp 'BLORP ESETTE' for 'LAFMS'; *005>*

Feb 76. (lp-ltd) *<RR 1075>* **THE THIRD REICH AND ROLL**
– Hitler was a vegetarian / Hey Jude / Swastikas on parade / The twist / Land of 1000 dances / Hanky panky. *<re-iss.1978; same>*

Sep 76. (7"ltd) *<RR 0776>* **SATISFACTION. / LOSER = WEED**
<re-iss.Aug78 as 7"yellow; RR 7803>

Jan 77. (7"ep-ltd) *<RR 0377>* **BABYFINGERS**
<re-iss.1979 on 'W.E.I.R.D.' 7"pink; 1>

Feb 77. (lp-ltd) *<RR 1276>* **FINGERPRINCE**
– You yesyesyes / Home age conversation / Godsong / March de la winni / Bos sy / Boo who / Tourniquet of roses / You yesyesyes again / Six things to a cycle. *(re-iss.twice 1978; same) (cd-iss.Dec87 on 'Torso'; TORSOCD 047)*

Aug 77. (7") *<RR 0577>* **(THE BEATLES PLAY THE RESIDENTS AND THE RESIDENTS PLAY THE BEATLES)**
– Beyond the valley of a day in the life /

Feb 78. (7"ep) *<RR 1177>* **DUCK STAB EP**

Oct 78. (lp) *<RR 1174>* **NOT AVAILABLE**
– Edweena / The making of a soul / Ships a going down / Never known questions epilogue. *(UK-iss.cd Sep94 on 'Indigo'; 7539-2)*

Nov 78. (lp) *<RR 0278>* **DUCK STAB / BUSTER AND GLEN**
– Constantinople / Sinister exaggerator / The Booker tease / Blue rosebuds / Laughing song / Bach is dead / Elvis and his boss / Lizard lady / Semolina / Birthday boy / Weight-lifting Lulu / Krafty cheese / Hello skinny / The electrocutioner. *(cd-iss.Jul87 on 'Torso'; TORSOCD 406>*

Dec 78. (7") *<RR 7812>* **SANTA DOG 78. / SANTA DOG**

Aug 79. (lp) *<SM 7908>* **SUBTERRANEAN MODERN**

— more guests **CHRIS CUTLER** – percussion / **DON PRESTON** – synth

Sep 79. (lp,white-lp) *<ESK 7906>* **ESKIMO**
– The walrus hunt / Birth / Arctic hysteria / The angry Angakok / A spirit steals a child / The festival of death. *(cd-iss.Jul87 on 'Torso'; TORSOCD 404) (cd re-iss.1996 on 'Ralph Euro'; CD 016)*

Virgin Ralph

Sep 79. (lp; with SNAKEFINGER) *(VR 3) <DJ 7901>* **NIBBLES** <US title 'PLEASE DO NOT STEAL IT' – DJ compilation> Mar79
– Yesyesyesyes / Santa dog '78 / Gloria / Rest aria / Semolina / The spot / Never known questions / Constantinople / Laughing song / The mocking of a soul / Skratz / Good lovin' / Blue rosebuds / Six things to a cycle / The electrocutioner.

Pre Ralph

Oct 80. (lp) *(PREX 2) <6559>* **THE COMMERCIAL ALBUM**
– Easter woman / Perfect love / Picnic boy / End of home / Amber / Japanes watercolour / Red rider / My second wife / Suburban bathers / Floyd / Dimples and toes / The nameless souls / Die in terror / Love leaks out / Act of being polite / Medicine man / Tragic bells / Loss of innocence / The simple song / Ups and downs / Possessions / Give it someone else / Phantom / Less not more / My work is so behind / Birds in the trees / Handful of desire / Moisture / Love is . . . / Troubled man / La la loneliness / Nice old man / The talk of creatures / Fingertips / In between dreams / Margaret Freeman / The coming of the crow / When we were young.

Oct 80. (7"ep) *(PRE 009)* **THE COMMERCIAL SINGLE**
– Amber / Red rider / Picnic boy / When we were young / Phantom / Moisture.

1980. (12"ep) *<RZ 8006-D>* **DISKOMO**
– Diskomo / Goosebump: Disasterplants – Farmers – Twinkle.

1981. (lp) *<8152>* **MARK OF THE MOLE**
– Hole-worker at the mercies of nature / Voices of the air / The ultimate disaster / Won't you keep us working / First warning / Back to normality / The sky falls / Why are we crying / The tunnels are filling / It never stops / Migration / March to the sea / The observer / Hole-worker's new hymn / Hole-worker's vs Man and machine / Another land / Rumors / Arrival / Deployment / Saturation / The new machine / Idea / Construction / Failure / Reconstruction / Success / Final confrontation / Success / Final confrontation / Driving the moles away / Don't tread on me / The short war / Resolution. *(UK cd-iss.Sep94 on 'Indigo'; 7540-2)*

Ralph Recommended

May 82. (lp) *(RZ 8202)* **THE TUNES OF TWO CITIES** Mar82
– Serenade for Missy / Mousetrap / Smack your lips clap your teeth / A maze of jigsaws / God of darkness / Smokebams / Mourning the undead / Song of the wild / Happy home / The secret seed / The evil disposer.

Jul 83. (12"ep) *(RALPH 1) <RZ 8252>* **INTERMISSION**
– Lights out / Shorty's lament / Moles are coming / Would we be alive / New hymn. *(lp-iss.1989 on 'Torso'; TORSO 33-055)*

1983. (lp) *<RZ 8302>* **RESIDUE OF THE RESIDENTS**
– The sleeper / Whoopy snorp / Kamakazi lady / Boy in love / Shut up! shut up! / Anvil forest / Diskomo / Jailhouse rock / Up & down / Walter Westinghouse / Saint Nix / Open up.

New Ralph New Ralph

Jan 84. (lp; with RENALDO & THE LOAF) *(RR 8351)* **TIME IN LIMBO**

Korova Recommended

Jul 84. (7") *(KOW 36)* **IT'S A MAN'S MAN'S MAN'S WORLD. / I'LL GO CRAZY**

Aug 84. (lp/c) *(KODE/CODE 9) <RZ 8402>* **GEORGE & JAMES** (some live)
– Rhapsody in blue / I got rhythm / Summertime / Live at the Apollo: I'll go crazy / Try me / Think / I don't mind / Lost someone / Please please please / Night train. *(c+=)*– (extra track). *(cd-iss.Sep94 on 'Indigo'; 2122-2)*

DoubleVision Ralph

Dec 84. (lp) *(DV 9) <RZ 8452>* **WHATEVER HAPPENED TO VILENESS FATS**
– Whatever happened to Vileness Fats / Atomic shopping carts / Adventures of a troubled heart / Search for the short man / The importance of evergreen / Broccoli and saxophone / Disguised as meat / Thoughts busily betraying / Lord, it's lonely / The knife fight. *(UK cd-iss.Sep94 on 'Indigo'; 7537-2)*

1985. (lp) *<RZ 8552>* **THE BIG BUBBLE – PART 4 OF THE MOLE TRILOGY**
– Sorry / Hop a little / Go where ya wanna go / Gotta gotta get / Cry for the fire / Die stay-go / Vinegar / Fire fly / The big bubble / Fear for the future / Kula bocca says so. *(cd-iss.Sep94 on 'Indigo'; 7541-2)*

Sep 85. (red-lp) *(DVR 17)* **THE PAL TV LP**
–

not issued Rykodisc

Jan 86. (cd) *<RCD 20012>* **HEAVEN?**
– The importance of evergreen / It's a man's man's man's world / H.E.L.L. no! / Japenese watercolours / I got rhythm / Ups and downs / Serenade for Missy / Eastern woman / Amber / The census taker / Happy home / Crashing / Redrider / Floyd /

The moles are coming / Resolution / Mahogany wood / Simple song / Kula bocca says no / Love leaks out / New hymn / Whater happened to Vileness Fats / Twinkle / Festival of death (excerpt).

Jan 86. (cd) *<RCD 20013>* **HELL!** [-] [ ]
– The ultimate disaster (excerpt) / Lights out / Where is she? / The coming of the crow / Lizard lady / Die interior / Shut up! shut up! / Shorty's lament / Hello skinny / Kamikaze lady / Secret seed / Sonny / Smelly tongues / Monkey and Bunny / Farmers / Satisfaction / Sinister exaggerator / Loss of innocence / The sleeper / Final confrontation (excerpt).

Torso Torso

Oct 86. (d-lp) *(TORSO 33-018) <2614220>* **13TH ANNIVERSARY SHOW (live in Japan & Holland)** [ ] [ ]
– Jailhouse rock / Where is she? / Picnic in the jungle / I got rhythm / Passing in the bottle / Monkey and Bunny / This is a man's man's man's world / Walter Westinghouse / Easter woman guitar solo / Diskomo / Hello skinny / Constantinople / Hop a little / Cry for the fire / Kamikaze. *(cd-iss.Sep94 on 'Indigo'; 7534-2)*

Nov 86. (lp) *<2614202>* **STARS AND HANK FOREVER – THE AMERICAN COMPOSERS SERIES VOL.2** [-] [ ]
– Hey good lookin' / Six more miles / Kaw-liga / Ramblin' man / Jambalaya / John Philip Sousa: Souaside: Nobles of the mystic shrine – The stars and stripes forever – El capitan – The liberty bell – Semper fidelis – Washington post. *(UK-iss.Sep94 on 'Indigo'; 7530-1)*

Dec 86. (7"/12") *(TORSO 7/12 022)* **KAW-LIGA. / ?** [ ] [ ]
(re-iss.Mar89; cd-s; TORSOCD 322)

Jun 87. (7"/12") *(TORSO 7/12 032)* **HIT THE ROAD. / ?** [ ] [ ]

Aug 88. (d-lp/cd/dat) *(TORSO 33/CD/DAT 055) <2614226>* **GOD IN THREE PERSONS** [ ] [ ]
– Hard and tenderly / Devotion / The thing about them / Their early yearsx / Loss of a loved one / The touch / The service / Confused / Fine fat flies / Time / Silver sharp / Kiss of flesh / Pain and pleasure. *(re-iss.lp Sep94 on 'Indigo'; 7531-1)*

1989. (lp/cd) *<2614262>* **THE MOLE SHOW LIVE (live)** [-] [ ]
– Voices of the air / The secret seed / Narration / The ultimate disaster / God of darkness / Migration / Smack your lips clap your feet / Another land / The new machine / Call of the wild / Final confrontation / Satisfaction / Happy home. *(UK cd-iss.Sep94 on 'Indigo'; 7542-2)*

1989. (3"pic-cd-ep) *(TORSOCD 355)* **DOUBLE SHOT / LOSS OF LOVED ONE (extended) / KISS OF FLESH (instrumental)** [ ] [-]

1989. (lp/cd) *<14263-26>* **THE KING AND EYE** [-] [ ]
– Blue suede shoes / Don't be cruel / Heartbreak hotel / All shook up / Return to sender / Teddy bear / Devil in disguise / Stuck on you / Big hunk o' love / A fool such as I / Little sister / His latest flame / Burning love / Viva Las Vegas / Love me tender / Hound dog. *(UK cd-iss.Sep94 on 'Indigo'; 7535-2)*

1989. (cd-ep) *(TORSOCD 421)* **DISKOMO / WHOOPY SNORP / SAINT NIX / DISKOMO LIVE** [ ] [-]

May 90. (7"ep)(12"ep)(cd-ep) **DON'T BE CRUEL. / DISKOMO / DISCO WILL NEVER DIE** [ ] [ ]

1991. (cd)(lp) **FREAKSHOW** [ ] [ ]
– Everyone comes to the freak show / Harry the head / Herman the human mole / Wanda the worm woman / Jack the boneless boy / Benny the bouncing bum / Mickey the mumbling midget / Lillie / Nobody laughs when they leave. *(re-iss.Sep94 on 'Indigo' cd/lp; 2125-2)(7532-1)*

Euro Ralph Ralph

Nov 92. (cd)(c)(lp) **PRESENT OUR FINEST FLOWERS** [ ] [ ]
(re-iss.cd Sep94 on 'Indigo'; 2121-2)

– others, etc. –

Sep 94. (lp)(cd) *Torso; (TORSO 33-199)(7536-2)* **CUBE E** [ ] [ ]
Sep 94. (cd) *Indigo; (2124-2)* **POOR KAW LIGA'S PAIN** [ ] [ ]
Sep 94. (cd/lp) *Indigo; (7543-2/-6)* **POOR KAW LIGA (housey mix)** [ ] [ ]
Oct 94. (cd) *Cargo; (2129-2)* **THE RESIDENTS** [ ] [-]

– compilations, etc.

Oct 84. (lp/c) *Korova; (KODE/CODE 10)* **RALPH BEFORE '84 – VOLUME 1** [ ] [-]
– It's a man's man's man's world / Diskomo / Hello skinny / (I left my heart in) San Francisco / Happy home / Smack your lips / Yesyesyesyes / Jailhouse rock / Monkey and Bunny / Festival of death.

Jan 85. (lp) *Korova; (KODE 12)* **BEFORE RALPH VOLUME 2** [ ] [-]
– Eva's warning / Halloween / Evolution / What use / Mahogany wood / Same ole me / Tritone / Melvyn's repose / Yeti: what are you / Nelda danced at day break / Norrgarden nyvia.

May 97. (4xcd-box) *Cargo; (RESBOX 1)* **25th ANNIVERSARY BOX SET** [ ] [-]

RHYTHM DEVILS (see under ⇒ GRATEFUL DEAD)

Terry RILEY

Born: 24 Jun'35, Colfax, California, USA. Graduating from Berkeley Music College, he played ragtime piano in a San Francisco saloon. In the late 50's, he stayed for a time in Europe while touring Scandivania with various theater projects. He worked with early minimalist, LA MONTE YOUNG, before he set out on his own, recording the 'IN C' album in 1964 (released 1968). This used many musicians and vocalists who performed tunes in staggered sequence over a repetitive array of chords, definitely a precursor to artists such as MIKE OLDFIELD, LAURIE ANDERSON, etc. In 1966, 'REED STREAMS' came out on a small label, leading him to sign for 'Columbia'. Early in the 70's, his work, 'A RAINBOW IN CURVED AIR' and 'CHURCH OF ANTHRAX' (with JOHN CALE) highlighted his style of hypnotic electronics, although he branched out in the 80's, working with Indian vocalist, PANDIT PRANATH. Later in the deaced, his pieces, 'CADENZA ON THE NIGHT PLAIN' and 'SALOME DANCES FOR PEACE', were actually outings by The KRONOS QUARTET, under his name as arranger and composer. An avant-garde pioneer of minimalist muzak, over the years he has inspired a generation of figureheads such as JOHN CALE, LOU REED, DAVID BOWIE, BRIAN ENO, PHILIP GLASS, as well as being a catalyst for "New Age" music.

Recommended: IN 'C' (*7) / A RAINBOW IN CURVED AIR (*7) / PERSIAN SURGERY DERVISHES (*6)

TERRY RILEY – synthesizers, keyboards

not issued Mass Art Inc.

1967. (lp) *<M 131>* **REED STREAMS** [-] [ ]

C.B.S. Columbia

— Early 1971, RILEY was credited on lp 'CHURCH OF ANTHRAX' with JOHN CALE.

Sep 71. (lp) *(CBS 64564) <7315>* **A RAINBOW IN CURVED AIR** [ ] [ ]
– A rainbow in curved air / Poppy Nogood and the phantom band. *(re-iss.Mar82 lp/c; CBS/40 32099) (cd-iss.Oct94 on 'Rewind-Columbia'; 477849-2)*

Sep 71. (lp) *(CBS 64565) <7178>* **IN "C"** (rec.1964) [ ] [ ] 1970
– In "C". *(re-iss.Feb81; CBS 61237) (re-iss.Ma89 on 'Edsel'; ED 314) (re-iss.Nov89 on 'Celestial Harmonies' lp/c/cd; CEL 13026-1/-4/-2)*

Shandar not issued

1972. (d-lp) *(CBS 83501-2)* **PERSIAN SURGERY DERVISHES** [ ] [-]
– *(re-iss.Mar78; same) (cd-iss.Jan94 on 'Tone'; NT 6715)*

Warners not issued

1972. (lp) *(K 46125)* **HAPPY ENDING (Soundtrack)** [-] [-] France
– Happy ending / Journey from a death of a friend.

Stip not issued

1975. (lp) **LIFESPAN (Soundtrack)** [-] [-] Euro
– G. song / Mice / Slow melody in Bhairavi / In the summer / The oldtimer / Delay.

— In 1975, he contributed to Soundtrack 'LE SECRET DE LA VIE' for 'Philips'; *(9120 037).*

C.B.S. Columbia

Aug 80. (lp) *(CBS 73929) <35164>* **SHRI CAMEL** [ ] [ ]
– Anthem of the trinity / Celestial valley / Across the lake of the ancient world / Desert of ice.

Kuckuck not issued

1982. (lp) *(LPKUCK 047)* **DESCENDING MOONSHINE DERVISHES (live 1975)** [-] [-] German
– Descending moonshine dervishes (part 1) / (part 2).

May 84. (lp) *(LPKUCK 067)* **SONGS FOR THE TEN VOICES OF THE TWO PROPHETS** [-] [-] German
– Embroidery / Eastern man / Chorale of the blessed day.

— next featured The KRONOS QUARTET; **DAVID HARRINGTON + JOHN SHERBA** – violin / **HANK DUTT** – viola / **JOAN JEANRENAUD** – cello

Gramavision Nonesuch

Jan 86. (cd; TERRY RILEY & THE KRONOS QUARTET) *(GRCD 7014)* **CADENZA ON THE NIGHT PLAIN** [ ] [ ] 1984
(re-iss.May89 lp/c/cd; 187014-1/-4/-2)

1989. (cd) *<979217-2>* **KRONOS QUARTET PLAYS SALOME DANCES FOR PEACE** [-] [ ]
– Anthem of the great spirit: The summons – Peace dance – Fanfare in the minimal kingdom – Ceremonial night race – At the ancient Aztec corn races – Salome meets wild talker – More ceremonial races – Oldtimers at the races – Half wolf dances mad in moonlight / Conquest of the war demons: Way of the warrior – Salome and the half wolf descend through the gates to the underworld – Breakthrough to the realm of the war demons – Combat dance / Victory: Salome re-enacts for half wolf her deeds of valor – Discovery of peace – The underworld arising / The gift: Echoes of Primondid time – Mongolian winds / The ecstasy: Processional – Seduction of the bear father – The gathering at the summit – Recessional / Good medicine: Good medicine dance.

not issued Celestial Harmonies

May 87. (d-lp/d-c/d-cd) *<LP/MC/CD CEL 018-019>* **THE HARP OF NEW ALBION** [-] [ ]

Pierrot Lun not issued

Jun 97. (cd; as TERRY RILEY & STEFANO SCODANIBBIO) *(AI 008)* **LAZY AFTERNOON AMONG THE CROCODILES** [ ] [-]

– others, etc. –

Oct 95. (cd) *Materiali Sonori; (MASOCD 90070)* **C & EDDY DE FANTI / DJEMBE** [-] [-] Italy

Andy ROBERTS (see under ⇒ LIVERPOOL SCENE)

ROCKIN' HORSE (see under ⇒ 23rd TURNOFF)

Hans-Joachim ROEDELIUS (see under ⇒ CLUSTER)

ROLLING STONES

Formed: London, England ... mid-1962 by JONES, JAGGER and RICHARDS. After a residence at Richmond blues club, 'The Crawdaddy', the band were signed by A&R man DICK ROWE to 'Decca', who had just rejected The BEATLES. Their debut single, a cover of CHUCK BERRY's 'COME ON ', almost hit top 20, and the band were well on the way to crystallising their image as the original bad boys of rock. Hairier, uglier and more rebellious (publicly anyway) than The BEATLES, manager/hustler extrordinaire, ANDREW LOOG OLDHAM, wasted no time in playing the outlaw card for all it was worth. Working the press like a true pro, he elicited a string of publicity grabbing headlines, culminating with the infamous "Would you let your daughter marry a ROLLING STONE?"' Which, of course, made

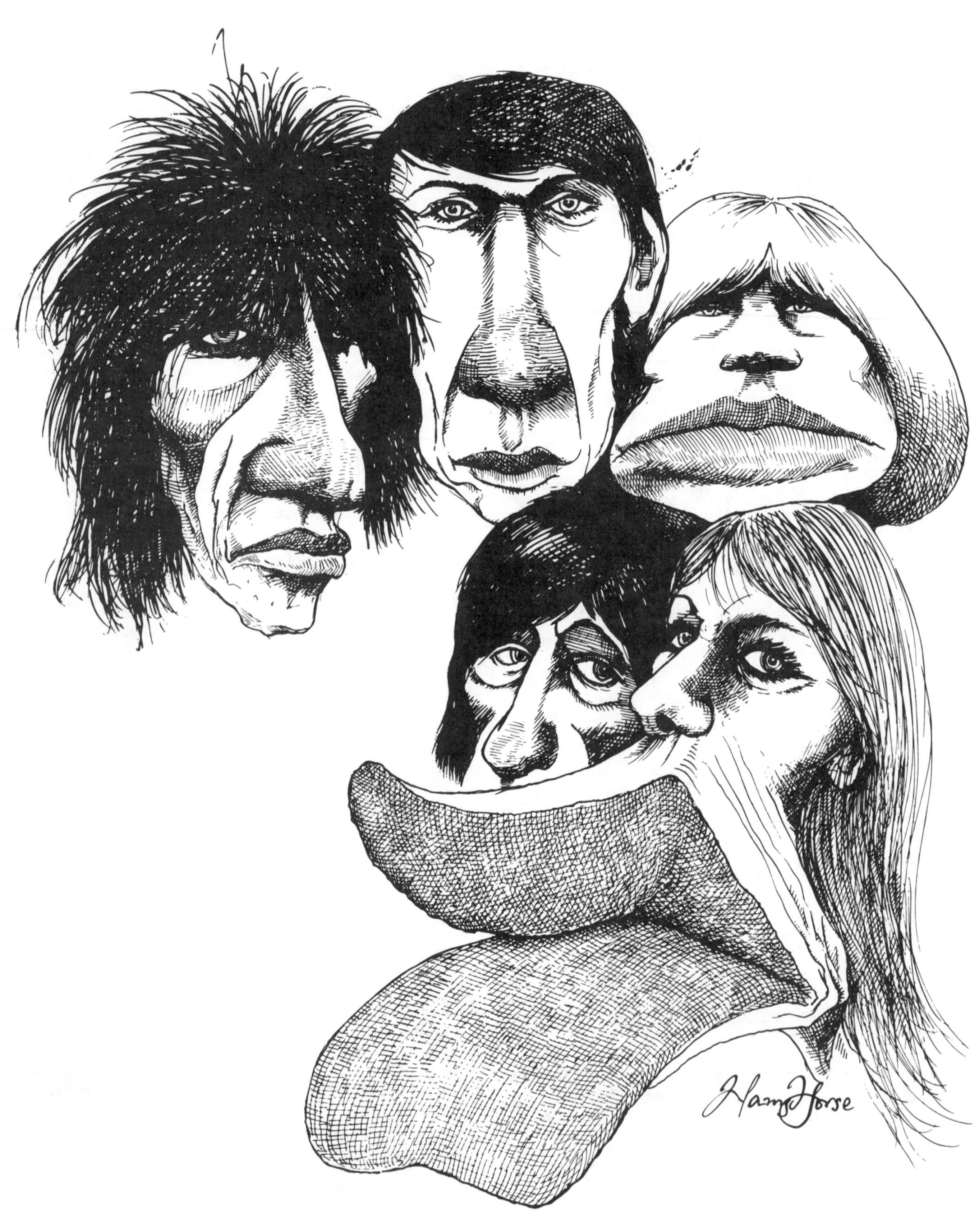

the band even more desirable in the eyes of those self same teenage daughters and as The 'STONES snaked their way across the country the following year on a joint headlining tour with The RONETTES, what had begun as hysteria and isolated fisticuffs had escalated into full – on rioting with promoters quaking in their boots. That summer, they scored their first No.1 single with a cover of BUDDY HOLLY's 'NOT FADE AWAY', now beginning to usurp The BEATLES as the UK's premier knicker-wetting phenomenon. As for the music, the early 'STONES' sound was a fairly derivative take on black America yet it possessed a primal, sexual intensity that made their Merseyside rivals sound like choirboys. Rhythm was everything and in full flight WATT'S fluid, unswerving backbeat locked in perfect unholy union with WYMAN'S bass and RICHARDS' demonic guitar grooves. JONES, meanwhile, casually lashed out searing slide guitar and JAGGER, the blueprint for decades of wannabe's to come, pouted, preened and snarled in equal measure. The first three albums, 'THE ROLLING STONES' (1964), '12 x 5' (1964) and 'THE ROLLING STONES NOW' (1965) were made up largely of R&B and blues covers, the latter marginally topping the other two with the most focused number JAGGERS/RICHARDS had come up with by that point, 'HEART OF STONE' and an electrifying reading of WILLIE DIXON's 'LITTLE RED ROOSTER'. Apparently revealed to KEITH RICHARDS in a dream, one of the most recognisable and famous riffs in rock history formed the core of The 'STONES' breakthrough hit, '(I CAN'T GET NO) SATISFACTION'. Despite the controversial lyrics which earned a boycott from US radio and further enhanced their reputation as leering malcontents, the record hit the top of the charts on both sides of the Atlantic during the summer of '65. This opened the floodgates for a wave of No.1 singles: 'GET OFF MY CLOUD' (1965), '19TH NERVOUS BREAKDOWN' (1966) and 'PAINT IT BLACK' (1966), the latter a brooding psychedelic-tinged stampede that featured some nifty sitar playing by a cross-legged BRIAN JONES. 'AFTERMATH' (1966) was a huge step forward with JONES adding exotic touches in line with his growing admiration for the JouJouka musicians of Morocco. Meanwhile, the JAGGER/RICHARDS songwriting partnership was blossoming, tackling social issues with trenchant ease; 'MOTHER'S LITTLE HELPER' as well as the usual sexual politics; 'UNDER MY THUMB'. It was around this time that JAGGER began assuming the multitude of different masks he would use onstage and off, as one journalist aptly pointed out; "MICK JAGGER was an interesting bunch of guys". His cocky, chameleon-like affectations stood in stark contrast to KEITH RICHARDS' sullen, slightly aloof distance but it was exactly this homo-erotic chemistry that fuelled The STONES and fashioned the decadent legend of 'The Glimmer Twins' as they'd come to be known in the 70's. 'BETWEEN THE BUTTONS' (1967) contained another salacious rebel anthem in 'LET'S SPEND THE NIGHT TOGETHER' alongside the ebb and flow wistfulness of 'RUBY TUESDAY'. By this time, though, the powers that be had had just about enough of these unkempt subversives and their dubious morals. The infamous Redlands drug bust in February '67 was probably the most famous of all The 'STONES' run-in's with the law, although by no means the most serious and in the end, RICHARDS' conviction was quashed on appeal while JAGGER was given a year's probation. Yet only a few days later, MICK talked defiantly to the press about revolution and The 'STONES recorded their acerbic reply to The BEATLES' 'ALL YOU NEED IS LOVE'. With LENNON and McCARTNEY collaborating, the band cut 'WE LOVE YOU'. Allegedly written by JAGGER in jail as a tribute to the fans who had stood by him, it came out sounding like a deliciously snide riposte to the authorities, complete with the sounds of heavy footsteps and a cell door clanging shut. While they were successful with occasional ventures into warped psychedelia, The 'STONES remained first and foremost a rock'n'roll band and their attempt at a psychedelic concept album, 'THEIR SATANIC MAJESTIES REQUEST' (1967) was always destined to sound half-baked at best. The stellar '2000 LIGHT YEARS FROM HOME' and 'SHE'S A RAINBOW' saved the album from being a complete failure although it didn't even come close to rivalling 'SGT. PEPPERS'. A more honest response to The BEATLES' magnum opus, 'BEGGARS BANQUET' (1968) was the first album in a staggering burst of creativity that would see The ROLLING STONES release four of the best albums in the history of rock over a five year period. Preceded by the much needed No.1 hit, 'JUMPIN' JACK FLASH', (which marked the beginning of a fruitful partnership with JIMMY MILLER), the album saw the band realign themselves with roots music to startling effect. At this point The 'STONES' were not simply imitating their heroes of the American South, they had made the music truly their own. Inspired by Mikhail Bulgakov's novel, 'The Master And Margarita', 'SYMPATHY FOR THE DEVIL' was pure malevolent genius, MICK casting himself gleefully in the role of Beelzebub over an irresistable voodoo funk. Similarly controversial were the topical 'STREET FIGHTIN' MAN' and the leering 'STRAY CAT BLUES' which centred on a rock star and an obliging 15 year old groupie, the grinding rhythm oozing illicit sex. These subversive broadsides were alternated with threadbare country blues numbers that, save for JAGGER's barrow boy via Louisiana vocals, sounded so authentic you could almost smell the corn bread. During sessions for the follow-up, 'LET IT BLEED' (1969), BRIAN JONES had left the band and was found dead in controversial circumstances a month later on the 3rd of July, 1969, at his Pooh Corner home. He had never really recovered from having control of the band wrestled from him and his unstable personality buckled under a frightening drug intake. Preceded by The 'STONES' last No.1 single, 'HONKY TONK WOMAN', 'LET IT BLEED' was eventually released the same fateful month as the Altamont disaster and possessed a vivid essence of brooding portent, most obvious on the opening track 'GIMME SHELTER', with its thundering rhythm and near-hysterical urging. 'MIDNIGHT RAMBLER' was equally chilling while RICHARDS made his vocal debut on 'YOU GOT THE SILVER', his voice a ragged sliver of emotive simplicity that stood in direct contrast to MICK's affectations. Closing with the aching desolation of 'YOU CAN'T ALWAYS GET WHAT YOU WANT', the album was another example, if one was needed at all, that The 'STONES' preferred harsh realism to dopey idealism and had never really embraced the hippy philosophy. Perhaps it was fitting then, that The 'STONES' were, quite literally, centre stage when that hopeful euphoria of the 60's finally came to an end during the last bitterly cold days of 1969. As the band played a free gig at a barren speedway track in Altamont, Northern California, poor organisation and delays contributed to bad vibes which were exacerbated by brutal, acid-crazed Hells Angels. Supposedly acting in a security capacity, one of their number ended up stabbing an innocent fan to death while many others were beaten up, The 'STONES' ferried out by helicopter in fear of their lives. By the release of 'STICKY FINGERS' (1971), the dark potency of the previous albums had gone, save for a few tracks, notably MARIANNE FAITHFUL's bleakly beautiful 'SISTER MORPHINE'. The band had pushed things to the limit and from here on in they retreated. Nevertheless, the best was yet to come, and 'STICKY FINGERS' kept 'up the momentum. 'DEAD FLOWERS' was a rollicking country hoedown shot through with typically twisted humour while JAGGER assumed his inimitable Delta Bluesman mantle for the inspired cover of MISSISSIPPI FRED McDOWELL's 'YOU GOT TO MOVE'. Elsewhere, tracks like 'BROWN SUGAR' and 'BITCH' were quintessential 'STONES, revelling in their own mythology. This was also the first stuio material to feature ex-BLUESBREAKER, MICK TAYLOR, who'd joined in '69 as a replacement for BRIAN JONES. Athough his distinctive style was an integral part of the band's early 70's sound, he'd later leave amid growing disatisfaction with the JAGGER/RICHARDS domination of the band. 'EXILE ON MAIN STREET' (1972) remains one of the best double album ever released and quite possibly staking a claim for the best album, bar none, ever released. Big claims, yet this was the pure, unadulterated essence of that cliched thing called rock'n'roll, no cobwebbed history lecture, but a living, breathing, sweating justification for white boys playing the blues. Recorded in a dank, humid basement in RICHARDS' villa in the South of France, the production is so murky that JAGGER's vocals verge on the indecipherable at points and the whole thing seems continually on the brink of collapse. Yet this only serves to enhance the unerringly strong material and elegantly wasted mood of the record. From the aural massage of 'TUMBLING DICE' to the raggedy-assed beauty of 'LOVING CUP', the down home gospel of 'SHINE A LIGHT' to KEITH RICHARDS' off-the-cuff anthem 'HAPPY', The 'STONES, or rock music, for that matter, would never sound so spiritually debauched again. In comparison, 'GOAT'S HEAD SOUP' (1973) was inevitably a let down, the band sounding tired and listless, although JAGGER at least sounded half-convincing on his tender ballad, 'ANGIE'. MICK TAYLOR's last album, 'IT'S ONLY ROCK'N'ROLL' (1974) was 'STONES by numbers and didn't bode well for the coming decade. 'BLACK AND BLUE' (1976) saw ex-FACE, RON WOOD brought into the fold and a half hearted attempt at reggae stylings. By this point, the band were a massive live draw but often sloppy on stage due in no small part to the band's collosal drug intake. It came as little surprise to even the most casual 'STONES observer when, in February 1977, RICHARDS was busted in Toronto holding serious amounts of Class A. Amid alleged rumours of a huge pay-off, KEITH was eventually let off fairly leniently and yet again, the 'STONES lived to fight another day, another 20 years in fact, and counting. Too long some might say, as 'SOME GIRLS' (1978) was the last 'STONES album that actually sounded like they meant it. Although the disco experimentalism of 'MISS YOU' was rather lukewarm, the album contained the last great JAGGER/RICHARDS song, 'BEAST OF BURDEN'. 'EMOTIONAL RESCUE' (1980) was dull and formulaic while 1981's 'TATTOO YOU' redeemed itself slightly with a rawer sound and the sprightly, if cliched hit 'START ME UP'. THE ROLLING STONES were, by now, one of the biggest acts on the stadium rock circuit, particularly in the U.S.A. and although their studio output was stagnating, the band's live show was still worth the admission price, especially now that KEITH had cleaned up his act and could get through a whole set without falling asleep on stage. 'UNDERCOVER' (1984) was a typically ill-advised 80's attempt at experimentation and as such, an unmitigated disaster, while 'DIRTY WORK' (1986) was only marginally less tedious. After a brief lull, the band returned with 1989's 'STEEL WHEELS' and while the single 'MIXED EMOTIONS' was their best in a decade, the album favoured glossy production and slick professionalism over content. With a move to 'Virgin' amid million pound deals, 'VOODOO LOUNGE' was touted as a dangerous return to form. In the event, it was as flaccid and cliched as anything the band had done. The pared down, semi-acoustic 'STRIPPED' (1995) was listenable although as the prospect of a creative rebirth grows ever more remote, maybe one more album would suffice (at the time of writing I'm reviewing a new 'STONES' album).

• **Trivia:** JAGGER's relationship with singer MARIANNE FAITHFULL ended in 1970, when he met Nicaraguan model, Bianca Rosa Perez-Mora and later married her on the 12th of May '71. They split in 1978, probably over Marsha Hunt's allegations that MICK was the father of her child. After a long relationship with Jerry Hall (formerly Bryan Ferry's girlfriend), he later married her on the 21st November '90. JAGGER's film work included:- NED KELLY (1969) / PERFORMANCE (1970) / FITZCARALDO (1981). WYMAN's marriage (since 1959) ended abruptly in the mid-80's, after his 2-year relationship with 16 year-old, Mandy Smith, was revealed in The News

Of The World. They married relatively quietly on the 2nd of June '89, but controversially divorced in 1992, with the now famous Mandy allegedly sueing half a million. • **Songwriters:** JAGGER-RICHARDS mostly except covers; NOT FADE AWAY (Buddy Holly) / ROUTE 66 (Nelson Riddle Orchestra) / I JUST WANT TO MAKE LOVE TO YOU (Willie Dixon) / HONEST I DO (Jimmy Reed) / I NEED YOU BABY (Bo Diddley) / POISON IVY (Coasters) / NOW I'VE GOT A WITNESS ... (Gene Pitney) / LITTLE BY LITTLE (Pitney / Spector) / COME ON + CAROL + YOU CAN'T CATCH ME + TALKIN' 'BOUT YOU + LITTLE QUEENIE + AROUND AND AROUND + BYE BYE JOHNNY (Chuck Berry) / CAN I GET A WITNESS (Holland-Dozier-Holland) / MONEY (Barrett Strong) / I WANNA BE YOUR MAN (Beatles) / LITTLE BY LITTLE (w/Spector) / YOU CAN MAKE IT IF YOU TRY (Gene Allison; hit) / WALKING THE DOG (Rufus Thomas) / SUSIE Q (Dale Hawkins) / UNDER THE BOARDWALK (Drifters) / I CAN'T BE SATISFIED + MANNISH BOY (Muddy Waters) / DOWN HOME GIRL (Jerry Butler) / IT'S ALL OVER NOW (Valentinos) / LITTLE RED ROOSTER (Willie Dixon) / PAIN IN MY HEART + MY GIRL (Otis Redding) / EVERYBODY NEEDS SOMEBODY TO LOVE (Solomon Burke) / DOWN THE ROAD APIECE (?. Raye) / TIME IS ON MY SIDE (Irma Thomas) / SHE SAID YEAH (Jackson/Christy) / I DON'T KNOW WHY (Stevie Wonder) / MERCY, MERCY (Don Covay) / GOOD TIMES (Sam Cooke) / CRY TO ME (Betty Harris; hit) / HITCH HIKE (Marvin Gaye) / THAT'S HOW STRONG MY LOVE IS (?. Jamison) / OH BABY ... (?. Ozen) / PRODIGAL SON (Robert Wilkins) / YOU BETTER MOVE ON (Arthur Alexander) / LOVE IN VAIN (Robert Johnson; trad.) / AIN'T TOO PROUD TO BEG + JUST MY IMAGINATION (Temptations) / I'M A KING BEE + SHAKE YOUR HIPS (Slim Harpo) / CHERRY OH BABY (? reggae) / GOING TO A GO-GO (Smokey Robinson / Miracles) / HARLEM SHUFFLE (Bob & Earl) / TWENTY FLIGHT ROCK (Eddie Cochran) / etc. KEITH RICHARDS solo wrote with JORDAN. RONNIE WOOD covered TESTIFY (Parliaments) / AM I GROOVIN' YOU (Bert Berns) / SEVEN DAYS (Bob Dylan) / SHOW ME (J. Williams).

Recommended: THE ROLLING STONES (*6) / THE ROLLING STONES NO.2 (*7) / OUT OF OUR HEADS (*6) / AFTERMATH (*7) / BETWEEN THE BUTTONS (*6) / THEIR SATANIC MAJESTIES REQUEST (*5) / BEGGARS BANQUET (*9) / LET IT BLEED (*9) / STICKY FINGERS (*8) / EXILE ON MAIN ST. (*10) / ROLLED GOLD (*10) / MADE IN THE SHADE (*6) / GOAT'S HEAD SOUP (*6) / SOME GIRLS (*6) / STEEL WHEELS (*6) / VOODOO LOUNGE (*7)

MICK JAGGER (b.26 Jul'43, Dartford, Kent, England) – vocals, harmonica / **KEITH RICHARDS** (b.18 Dec'43, Dartford) – rhythm guitar / **BRIAN JONES** (b.28 Feb'43, Cheltenham, England) – lead guitar / **CHARLIE WATTS** (b. 2 Jun'41, Islington, London) – drums (ex-BLUES INC.) / **BILL WYMAN** (b.WILLIAM PERKS, 24 Oct'36, Lewisham, London) – bass repl. DICK TAYLOR who later joined PRETTY THINGS / **IAN STEWART** – piano (was 6th member, pushed to the background by manager)

Decca London

Jun 63. (7") *(F 11675)* **COME ON. / I WANT TO BE LOVED** [21] [-]

Nov 63. (7") *(F 11764)* <9641> **I WANNA BE YOUR MAN. / STONED** [12] [ ] Jan64

Feb 64. (7") *(F 11845)* **NOT FADE AWAY. / LITTLE BY LITTLE** [3] [-]

Mar 64. (7") <9657> **NOT FADE AWAY. / I WANNA BE YOUR MAN** [-] [48]

Apr 64. (lp) *(LK 4605)* <375> **THE ROLLING STONES** (US-title 'ENGLAND'S NEWEST HITMAKERS – THE ROLLING STONES) [1] [11] Jun64
– (Get your kicks on) Route 66 / I just want to make love to you / Honest I do / I need you baby (Mona) / Now I've got a witness (like uncle Phil and uncle Gene) / Little by little / I'm a king bee / Carol / Tell me (you're coming back) / Can I get a witness / You can make it if you try / Walking the dog. *(US)*– Not fade away. / – Mona *(re-iss.Jul84 lp/c; LKD/KSDC 4605) (cd-iss.1985 on 'London'; 820 047-2) (re-iss.Jun95 on 'London' cd/c/lp; 844460-2/-4/-1)*

Jun 64. (7") *(F 11934)* <9687> **IT'S ALL OVER NOW. / GOOD TIMES, BAD TIMES** [1] [26] Aug64

Jul 64. (7") <9682> **TELL ME (YOU'RE COMING BACK). / I JUST WANT TO MAKE LOVE TO YOU** [-] [24]

Oct 64. (7") <9708> **TIME IS ON MY SIDE. / CONGRATULATIONS** [-] [6]

Nov 64. (7") *(F 12014)* **LITTLE RED ROOSTER. / OFF THE HOOK** [1] [-]

Nov 64. (lp) <402> **12 x 5** [-] [3]
– Around and around / Confessin' the blues / Empty heart / Time is on my side / Good times bad times / It's all over now / 2120 South Michigan Avenue / Under the boardwalk / Congratulations / Grown up wrong / If you need me / Susie Q. *(UK-iss.Aug84 lp/c; LKD/KDKHAC 5335) (cd-iss.Nov84 on 'London'; 820 048-2) (re-iss.Jun95; 844461-2/-4/-1)*

Jan 65. (lp) *(LK 4661)* **THE ROLLING STONES No.2** [1] [-]
– Everybody needs somebody to love / Down home girl / You can't catch me / Time is on my side / What a shame / Grown up wrong / Down the road apiece / Under the boardwalk / I can't be satisfied / Pain in my heart / Off the hook / Susie Q. *(re-iss.1986;)*

Jan 65. (7") <9725> **HEART OF STONE. / WHAT A SHAME** [-] [19]

Feb 65. (7") *(F 12104)* <9741> **THE LAST TIME. / PLAY WITH FIRE** [1] [9] [96] Mar65

Mar 65. (lp) <420> **THE ROLLING STONES NOW!** [-] [5]
– Everybody needs somebody to love / Down home girl / You can't catch me / Heart of stone / I need you baby (Mona) / Down the road apiece / Off the hook / Pain in my heart / Oh baby (we got a good thing goin') / Little red rooster / Surprise surprise. *(UK-iss.Aug88 cd; 820133-2) (re-iss.Jun95 on 'London' cd/c/lp; 844462-2/-4/-1)*

May 65. (7") *(F 12220)* **(I CAN'T GET NO) SATISFACTION. / THE SPIDER AND THE FLY** [1] [-]

Jun 65. (7") <9766> **(I CAN'T GET NO) SATISFACTION. / THE UNDER ASSISTANT WEST COAST MAN** [-] [1]

Sep 65. (lp; mono/stereo) *(LK/SKL 473)* <429> **OUT OF OUR HEADS** [2] [1] Aug 65
– She said yeah * / Mercy, mercy / Hitch hike / That's how strong my love is / Good times / Gotta get away * / Talkin' 'bout you * / Cry to me / Oh baby (we got a good thing going) * / Heart of stone / The under assistant west coast man / I'm free. *<UK tracks above * were repl. by in US>*– I'm alright (live) / (I can't get no) Satisfaction / Play with fire / The spider and the fly / One more try. *(re-iss.Jul84 lp/c)(cd; LKD/LSLSC 5336)(820 049-2) (re-iss.Jun95 on 'London' cd/c/lp; 844463-2/-4/-1)*

Sep 65. (7") <9792> **GET OFF OF MY CLOUD. / I'M FREE** [-] [1]

Oct 65. (7") *(F 12263)* **GET OFF OF MY CLOUD. / THE SINGER NOT THE SONG** [1] [-]

Nov 65. (lp) <451> **DECEMBER'S CHILDREN (AND EVERYBODY'S)** [-] [4]
– She said yeah / Talkin' 'bout you / You better move on / Look what you've done / The singer not the song / Route 66 (live) / Get off of my cloud / I'm free / As tears go by / Gotta get away / Blue turns to grey / I'm movin' on (live). *(UK-iss.Aug88 cd; 820 135-2) (re-iss.Jun95 on 'London' cd/c/lp; 844464-2/-4/-1)*

Dec 65. (7") <9808> **AS TEARS GO BY. / GOTTA GET AWAY** [-] [6]

Feb 66. (7") *(F 12331)* **19th NERVOUS BREAKDOWN. / AS TEARS GO BY** [1] [-]

Feb 66. (7") <9823> **19th NERVOUS BREAKDOWN. / SAD DAY** [-] [2]

Apr 66. (lp; mono/stereo)(c) *(LK/SKL 4786)(KSKC 4786)* <451> **AFTERMATH** [1] [2] Jul66
– Mother's little helper / Stupid girl / Lady Jane / Under my thumb / Doncha bother me / Goin' home / Flight 505 / High and dry / Out of time / It's not easy / I am waiting / Take it or leave it / Think / What to do. *(US version+=)*– Paint it black. *(re-iss.May85 lp/c)(cd; SKLD/ 4786)(820 050-2) (re-iss.Jun95 on 'London' cd/c/lp; 844466-2/-4/-1)*

May 66. (7") <901> **PAINT IT BLACK. / STUPID GIRL** [-] [1]

May 66. (7") *(F 12395)* **PAINT IT BLACK. / LONG LONG WHILE** [1] [-]

Jul 66. (7") <902> **MOTHER'S LITTLE HELPER. / LADY JANE** [-] [8] [24]

Sep 66. (7") *(F 12497)* <903> **HAVE YOU SEEN YOUR MOTHER BABY, STANDING IN THE SHADOW?. / WHO'S DRIVING YOUR PLANE?** [5] [9]

Nov 66. (lp; mono/stereo)(c) *(TXL/TXS 101)(KSKC 101)* <1> **BIG HITS (HIGH TIDE AND GREEN GRASS)** (compilation) [4] [3] Apr 66
– Have you seen your mother baby, standing in the shadows? / Paint it black / It's all over now / The last time / Heart of stone / Not fade away / Come on / (I can't get no) Satisfaction / Get off my cloud / As tears go by / 19th nervous breakdown / Lady Jane / Time is on my side / Little red rooster. *(re-iss.Jun95 on 'London' cd/c/lp; 844465-2/-4/-1)*

Dec 66. (lp) <493> **GOT LIVE IF YOU WANT IT (live, Royal Albert Hall)** [-] [6]
– Under my thumb / Get off of my cloud / Lady Jane / Not fade away / I've been loving you too long (to stop now) (studio) / Fortune teller (studio) / The last time / 19th nervous breakdown / Time is on my side / I'm alright / Have you seen your mother baby, standing in the shadow? / (I can't get no) Satisfaction. *(UK-iss.Aug88 cd; 820 137-2) (re-iss.Jun95 on 'London' cd/c/lp; 844467-2/-4/-1)*

Jan 67. (7") *(F 12546)* <904> **LET'S SPEND THE NIGHT TOGETHER. / RUBY TUESDAY** [3] [55] [1]

Jan 67. (lp; mono/stereo)(c) *(LK/SKL 4852)(KSKC 4852)* <499> **BETWEEN THE BUTTONS** [3] [2] Feb67
– Yesterday's papers / My obsession / Back street girl* / Connection / She smiled sweetly / Cool, calm and collected / All sold out / Please go home* / Who's been sleeping here? / Complicated / Miss Amanda Jones / Something happened to me yesterday. *(US version*; = tracks repl. by)*
– Let's spend the night together / Ruby Tuesday. *(cd-iss.Jul85; 820 138-2) (re-iss.lp/cd. Dec91 on 'UFO' with free booklet) (re-iss.Jun95 on 'London' cd/c/lp; 844468-2/-4/-1)*

Jul 67. (lp) <509> **FLOWERS** (compilation) [-] [3]
(UK cd-iss.Aug88; 820 139-2) (re-iss.cd Jun95 on 'London')

Aug 67. (7") *(F 12654)* <905> **WE LOVE YOU. / DANDELION** [8] [50] [14]

Nov 67. (7") <906> **SHE'S A RAINBOW. / 2,000 LIGHT YEARS FROM HOME** [-] [25]

Dec 67. (lp; mono/stereo)(c) *(TXL/TXS 103)(KTXC 103)* <2> **THEIR SATANIC MAJESTIES REQUEST** [3] [2]
– Sing this all together / Citadel / In another land / 2,000 man / Sing this all together (see what happens) / She's a rainbow / The lantern / Gomper / 2,000 light years from home / On with the show. *(re-iss.Feb86 lp/c/cd; 820 129-1/-4/-2) (re-iss.Jun95 on 'London' cd/c/lp; 844469-2/-4/-1)*

Dec 67. (7"; by BILL WYMAN) <907> **IN ANOTHER LAND. / THE LANTERN** [-] [87]

May 68. (7") *(F 12782)* <908> **JUMPIN' JACK FLASH. / CHILD OF THE MOON** [1] [3]

Aug 68. (7") <909> **STREET FIGHTING MAN. / NO EXPECTATIONS** [-] [48]

Dec 68. (lp; mono/stereo)(c) *(LK/SKL 4955)(KSKC 4955)* <539> **BEGGARS BANQUET** [3] [5]
– Sympathy for the Devil / No expectations / Dear doctor / Parachute woman / Jigsaw puzzle / Street fighting man / Prodigal son / Stray cat blues / Factory girl / Salt of the Earth. *(cd-iss.Jan83; 800 084-2) (re-iss.Jul84 lp/c; SKDL/KSKC 4955) (re-iss.Jun95 on 'London' cd/c/lp; 844471-2/-4/-1)*

— (Jun69) **MICK TAYLOR** (b.17 Jan'48, Hertfordshire, England) – lead guitar (ex-JOHN MAYALL's BLUESBREAKERS) repl. BRIAN JONES who was found dead by his girlfriend on 3 Jul'69, after a heavy drink/drugs binge.

Jul 69. (7") *(F 12952)* <910> **HONKY TONK WOMEN. / YOU CAN'T ALWAYS GET WHAT YOU WANT** [1] [1]

Sep 69. (lp; mono/stereo)(c) *(LK/SKL 5019)(KSKC 5019)* <3> **THROUGH THE PAST DARKLY (BIG HITS VOL.2)** (compilation) [2] [2]
– Look what you've done / It's all over now / Confessin' the blues / One more try / As tears go by / The spider and the fly / My girl / Paint it black / If you need me / The last time / Blue turns to grey / Around and around. *(re-iss.Jun95 on 'London' cd/c/lp; 844472-2/-4/-1)*

— (all UK singles so far were re-iss.Mar82)

Dec 69. (lp/c) *(SLK/KSKC 5025)* <4> **LET IT BLEED** [1] [3]
– Gimme shelter / Love in vain / Country honk / Live with me / Let it bleed / Midnight rambler / You got the silver / Monkey man / You can't always get what you want. *(cd-iss.Feb86; 820 052-2) (re-iss.Jun95 UK+US on 'London' cd/c/lp; 844473-2/-4/-1)*

— Mid'70, MICK JAGGER finally took the starring role in the film 'Ned Kelly'.

Sep 70. (lp/c) *(SKL/KSKC 5065)* <5> **GET YER YA YA'S OUT** (live, New York, Nov'69) [1] [6] Oct69

– Jumpin' Jack Flash / Carol / Stray cat blues / Love in vain / Midnight rambler / Sympathy for the Devil / Live with me / Little Queenie / Honky tonk women. *(cd-iss.Aug88; 820 131-2) (re-iss.Jun95 on 'London' cd/c/lp; 844474-2/-4/-1)*

— In 1970, MICK JAGGER starred in his second feature film 'Performance'. Below single was his first solo 45 from the film.

Nov 70. (7"; by MICK JAGGER) *(F 13067)* **MEMO FROM TURNER. / ('B'side by 'Jack Nitzsche')** [32] [ ]

Apr 71. (lp/c) *(SKL/KSKC 5084)* **STONE AGE** (compilation) [4] [-]
– Look what you've done / It's all over now / Confessin' the blues / One more try / As tears go by / The spider and the fly / My girl / Paint it black / If you need me / The last time / Blue turns to grey / Around and around.

Rolling Stones | Rolling Stones

Apr 71. (7"m) *(RS 19100)* **BROWN SUGAR. / BITCH / LET IT ROCK** [2] [-]

Apr 71. (lp/c) *(COC/ <59100>)* **STICKY FINGERS** [1] [1]
– Brown sugar / Sway / Wild horses / Can't you hear me knocking? / You gotta move / Bitch / I got the blues / Sister Morphine / Dead flowers / Moonlight mile. *(re-iss.Nov79 on 'E.M.I.'; CUN 59100) <US re-iss.1980; MFSL 1-060> (cd-iss.Nov86 on 'C.B.S.; CK 40488) (re-iss.Nov89 on 'CBS' UK/US lp/c/cd; 450 195-1/-4/-2) (re-iss.cd Jun94 on 'Virgin' UK+US; 7243-8-39504-2-3) (re-iss.Aug94 on 'Virgin' cd/c; CDV/TCV 2730)*

Apr 71. (7") *<19100>* **BROWN SUGAR. / BITCH** [-] [ ]

Jun 71. (7") *<RS 19101>* **WILD HORSES. / SWAY** [-] [28]

Apr 72. (7") *(RS <19103>)* **TUMBLING DICE. / SWEET BLACK ANGEL** [5] [7]

Jun 72. (d-lp/c) *(COC/ 69100) <2900>* **EXILE ON MAIN ST.** [1] [1]
– Rocks off / Rip this joint / Shake your hips / Casino boogie / Tumbling dice / Sweet Virginia / Torn and frayed / Sweet black angel / Loving cup / Happy / Turd on the run / Ventilator blues / I just want to see his face / Let it loose / All down the line / Stop breaking down / Shine a light / Soul survivor. *(re-iss.Nov79 on 'E.M.I.'; CUNSP 69100) (re-iss.Nov89 on 'CBS' lp/c/cd UK/US; 450 196-1/-4/-2) (re-iss.Aug94 on 'Virgin' cd/c; CDV/TCV 2731)*

Jun 72. (7") *<19104>* **HAPPY. / ALL DOWN THE LINE** [-] [22]

Aug 73. (7") *(RS <19105>)* **ANGIE. / SILVER TRAIN** [5] [1]

Sep 73. (lp/c) *(COC/ <59101>)* **GOAT'S HEAD SOUP** [1] [1]
– Dancing with Mr.D / 100 years ago / Coming down again / Doo doo doo doo doo (heartbreaker) / Angie / Silver train / Hide your love / Winter / Can you hear the music / Star star *(re-iss.Nov79 on 'E.M.I.'; CUN 59101) (re-iss.Nov89 on 'CBS' UK/US; 450 207-1/-4/-2) (re-iss.Aug94 on 'Virgin' cd/c; CDV/TCV 2735)*

Jan 74. (7") *<19109>* **DOO DOO DOO DOO DOO (HEARTBREAKER). / DANCING WITH MR.D** [-] [15]

Jul 74. (7") *(RS 19114) <19304>* **IT'S ONLY ROCK'N'ROLL. / THROUGH THE LONELY NIGHTS** [10] [16]

Oct 74. (lp/c) *(COC/ 59103) <79101>* **IT'S ONLY ROCK'N'ROLL** [2] [1]
– If you can't rock me / Ain't too proud to beg / It's only rock'n'roll / Till the next goodbye / Time waits for no one / Luxury / Dance little sister / If you really want to be my friend / Short and curlies / Fingerprint file. *(re-iss.Nov79 on 'E.M.I.'; CUN 59103) (re-iss.Nov89 on 'CBS' UK/US lp/c/cd; 450 202-1/-4/-2) (re-iss.Aug94 on 'Virgin' cd/c; CDV/TCV 2733)*

Oct 74. (7") *(19302>* **AIN'T TOO PROUD TO BEG. / DANCE LITTLE SISTER** [-] [17]

Jun 75. (lp/c) *(COC/ 59104) <79102>* **MADE IN THE SHADE** (compilation) [14] [6]
– Brown sugar / Tumbling dice / Happy / Dance little sister / Wild horses / Angie / Bitch / It's only rock'n'roll (but I like it) / Doo doo doo doo doo (heartbreaker) / Rip this joint. *(re-iss.Nov89 on 'CBS' UK/US lp/c/cd; 450 201-1/-4/-2)*

— (Apr-Dec75) **RON WOOD** – lead guitar (ex-FACES, ex-CREATION, etc) repl. MICK TAYLOR who left Dec74 and later joined JACK BRUCE BAND

Apr 76. (7") *(RS 19121)* **FOOL TO CRY. / CRAZY MAMA** [6] [-]

Apr 76. (7") *<19304>* **FOOL TO CRY. / HOT STUFF** [-] [10] [49]

May 76. (lp/c) *(COC/ 59106) <79104>* **BLACK AND BLUE** [2] [1]
– Hot stuff / The hand of fate / Cherry oh baby / Memory motel / Hey Negrita / Melody / Fool to cry / Crazy mama. *(re-iss.Nov79 on 'E.M.I.; CUN 59106) (re-iss.Nov89 on 'C.B.S.' UK/US; 450 203-1/-4/-2) (re-iss.Aug94 on 'Virgin' cd/c; CDV/TCV 2736)*

Sep 77. (d-lp/d-c) *(COC/ 89101) <9001>* **LOVE YOU LIVE (live)** [3] [5]
– Fanfare for the common man / Honky tonk woman / If you can't rock me / Get off of my cloud / Happy / Hot stuff / Star star / Tumbling dice / Fingerprint file / You gotta me / You can't always get what you want / Mannish boy / Crackin' up / Little red rooster / Around and around / It's only rock'n'roll / Brown sugar / Jumpin' Jack Flash / Sympathy for the Devil. *(re-iss.Nov79 on 'E.M.I.'; CUNSP 69101) (re-iss.Nov89 on 'C.B.S.' UK/US d-lp/c/cd; 450 208-1/-4/-2)*

May 78. (7"/ext.12"pink) *(EMI/12EMI 2802) <19307>* **MISS YOU. / FARAWAY EYES** [3] [1]

Jun 78. (lp/c) *(CUN/ <39108>)* **SOME GIRLS** [2] [1]
– Miss you / When the whip comes down / Just my imagination / Some girls / Lies / Far away eyes / Respectable / Before they make me run / Beast of burden / Shattered. *(re-iss.Nov89 on 'C.B.S' UK/US lp/c/cd; 450 197-1/-4/-2) (re-iss.Aug94 on 'Virgin' cd/c;)*

Sep 78. (7") *<19309>* **BEAST OF BURDEN. / WHEN THE WHIP COMES DOWN** [-] [8]

Sep 78. (7") *(EMI 2861)* **RESPECTABLE. / WHEN THE WHIP COMES DOWN** [23] [-]

Dec 78. (7") *<19310>* **SHATTERED. / EVERYTHING IS TURNING TO GOLD** [-] [31]

Jun 80. (7") *(RSR 105) <20001>* **EMOTIONAL RESCUE. / DOWN IN THE HOLE** [9] [3]

Jul 80. (lp/c) *(CUN/ 39111) <16015>* **EMOTIONAL RESCUE** [1] [1]
– Dance (pt.1) / Summer romance / Send it to me / Let me go / Indian girl / Where the boys go / Down in the hole / Emotional rescue / She's so cold / All about you. *(re-iss.Nov89 on 'C.B.S.' UK/US; 450 206-1/-4/-2) (re-iss.Aug94 on 'Virgin' cd/c; CDV/TCV 2737)*

Sep 80. (7") *(RSR 106) <21001>* **SHE'S SO COLD. / SEND IT TO ME** [33] [26]

Mar 81. (lp/c) *(CUN/ 39112) <16028>* **SUCKING IN THE 70'S** (compilation + new) [ ] [15]
– Shattered / Everything is turning to gold / Hot stuff / Time waits for no one / Fool to cry / Mannish boy / When the whip comes down (live) / I was a dancer (part 2) / Crazy mama / Beast of burden. *(re-iss.Nov89 on 'C.B.S.' UK/US; 450 205-1/-4/-2)*

Aug 81. (7") *(RSR 108) <21003>* **START ME UP. / NO USE IN CRYING** [7] [2]

Sep 81. (lp/c) *(CUN/ 39114) <16052>* **TATTOO YOU** [2] [1]
– Start me up / Hang fire / Slave / Little T & A / Black limousine / Neighbours / Worried about you / Tops / Heaven / No use in crying / Waiting on a friend. *(re-iss.Nov89 on 'C.B.S.' UK/US; 450 198-1/-4/-2) (re-iss.Aug94 on 'Virgin' cd/c; CDV/TCV 2732)*

Nov 81. (7") *(RSR 109) <21004>* **WAITING ON A FRIEND. / LITTLE T & A** [50] [13]

Mar 82. (7") *<21300>* **HANG FIRE. / NEIGHBORS** [-] [20]

Jun 82. (7") *(RSR 110) <21301>* **GOING TO A GO-GO (live). / BEAST OF BURDEN (live)** [26] [25]

Jun 82. (lp/pic-lp/c) *(CUN/+P 39115) <39113>* **STILL LIFE (AMERICAN CONCERTS 1981)** [4] [5]
– Under my thumb / Let's spend the night together / Shattered / Twenty flight rock / Going to a go-go / Let me go / Time is on my side / Just my imagination / Start me up / (I can't get no) Satisfaction / Take the A train / Star-spangled banner. *(re-iss.Nov89 on 'C.B.S.' UK/US; 450 204-1/-4/-2)*

Sep 82. (7") *(RSR 111) <99978>* **TIME IS ON MY SIDE (live). / TWENTY FLIGHT ROCK (live)** [62] [ ]
(12"+=) *(12RSR 111)* – Under my thumb (live).

Nov 83. (7") *(RSR 113) <99813>* **UNDERCOVER OF THE NIGHT. / ALL THE WAY DOWN** [11] [9]
(ext.12"+=) *(12RSR 113)* – Feel on baby (instrumental dub).

Nov 83. (lp/c/cd) *(CUN 165436-1/-4/-2) <90120>* **UNDERCOVER** [3] [4]
– Undercover of the night / She was hot / Tie you up / Wanna hold you / Feel on baby / Too much blood / Pretty beat up / Too tough / All the way down / It must be hell. *(re-iss.Nov89 on 'C.B.S.' UK/US; 450 200-1/-4/-2) (re-iss.Aug94 on 'Virgin' cd/c; CDV/TCV 2741)*

Jan 84. (7"/12"sha-pic-d) *(RSR/+P 114) <99788>* **SHE WAS HOT. / I THINK I'M GOING MAD** [42] [44]

Apr 84. (7") *<99724>* **TOO TOUGH. / MISS YOU** [-] [ ]

Jul 84. (lp/c/cd) *(CUN 1) <90176>* **REWIND 1971-1984 (THE BEST OF THE ROLLING STONES)** (compilation) [23] [86]
– Brown sugar / Undercover of the night / Start me up / Tumbling dice / It's only rock'n'roll (but I like it) / She's so cold / Hang fire / Miss you / Beast of burden / Fool to cry / Waiting on a friend / Angie / Emotional rescue. *(cd+= 2 extra) (re-iss.Nov89 on 'C.B.S.' UK/US; 450 199-1/-4/-2)*

— In 1984, JAGGER guested dual vocals w / MICHAEL JACKSON on The JACKSONS' 'State Of Shock'. He also recorded debut solo album 'She's The Boss', which was released 1985. Later mid'85, he appeared at LIVE AID with DAVID BOWIE duetting on (Martha & The Vandellas) song 'DANCING IN THE STREET'. When issued as a charity single, it made UK No.1 / US No.7 (see BOWIE ⇒).

— 12th Dec'85, IAN STEWART their long-serving 6th member died of a heart attack.

C.B.S. | Rolling Stones

Mar 86. (7"/7"w-poster) *(A/QA 6864) <05802>* **HARLEM SHUFFLE. / HAD IT WITH YOU** [13] [5]
('A'-New York mix; 12"+=/12"w-poster+=) *(TA/QTA 6864)* – ('A'-London mix).

Mar 86. (lp/c/cd) *(CUN/40/CD 86321) <40250>* **DIRTY WORK** [4] [4]
– One hit (to the body) / Fight / Harlem shuffle / Hold back / Too rude / Winning ugly / Back to zero / Dirty work / Had it with you / Sleep tonight. *(re-iss.Nov89 on 'C.B.S.' UK/US; 465 953-1/-4/-2) (re-iss.Aug94 on 'Virgin' cd/c; CDV/TCV 2743)*

May 86. (7"/'A'-London mix-12") *(A/TA 7160) <05906>* **ONE HIT (TO THE BODY). / FIGHT** [ ] [28]

— During this lull in group activity, JAGGER and RICHARDS ventured solo amidst rumours of disbandment. In 1989, they re-surfaced.

Aug 89. (7"/c-s) *(655 193-7/-4) <69008>* **MIXED EMOTIONS. / FANCYMAN BLUES** [36] [5]
(cd-s+=) *(655 193-2)* – Tumbling dice / Miss you.
(cd-s+=) *(655 214-2)* – Shattered / Waiting on a friend.
(12"+=) *(655 193-8)* – ('A'-Chris Kimsey's mix).

Sep 89. (lp/c/cd) *(465 752-1/-4/-2) <45333>* **STEEL WHEELS** [2] [3]
– Sad sad sad / Mixed emotions / Terrifying / Hold on to your hat / Hearts for sale / Blinded by love / Rock and a hard place / Can't be seen / Almost hear you sigh / Continental drift / Break the spell / Slipping away. *(cd re-iss.Dec92;) (re-iss.Aug94 on 'Virgin' cd/c; CDV/TCV 2742)*

Nov 89. (7"/c-s) *(655 422-7/-4) <73057>* **ROCK AND A HARD PLACE. / COOK COOK BLUES** [63] [23]
('A'dance-12"+=) *(655 422-8)* – ('A'-Oh-oh hard dub mix).
(cd-s+=) *(655 448-2)* – It's only rock'n'roll / Rocks off.
(cd-s+=) *(655 448-5)* – Emotional rescue / Some girls.
(12") *(655 422-5)* – ('A'-Michael Brauer mix) / ('A'side) / ('A'-bonus beats mix).

Jun 90. (7") *<73093>* **ALMOST HEAR YOU SIGH. / BREAK THE SPELL** [-] [50]

Jun 90. (7"/c-s) *(656 065-7/-4)* **ALMOST HEAR YOU SIGH. / WISH I'D NEVER MET YOU** [31] [-]
(c-s+=) *(656 065-2)* – Mixed emotions.
(cd-s+=) *(656 065-5)* – Miss you / Waiting on a friend.
(12")(cd-s) – ('A'side) / Beast of burden / Angie / Fool to cry.

Aug 90. (7"/c-s) *(656 122-7/-4)* **TERRIFYING (remix). / ROCK AND A HARD PLACE (remix)** [ ] [ ]
('A'-dance-12"+=) *(656 122-6)* – Harlem shuffle (London mix).
(cd-s) *(655 122-5)* – ('A'side) / Start me up / Shattered / If you can't rock me.

Sony | Sony

Mar 91. (7"/c-s) *(656 756-7/-4) <73742>* **HIGHWIRE. / 2000 LIGHT YEARS FROM HOME (live)** [29] [57]
(12"+=/cd-s+=) *(656 756-6/-2)* – Sympathy for the Devil (live) / I just want to make love to you (live).
(cd-s+=) *(656 756-5)* – Play with fire (live) / Factory girl (live).

Apr 91. (d-cd/cd/c/lp) *(468 135-9/-2/-4/-1)* **FLASHPOINT (live)** [6] [16]
– Start me up / Sad sad girl / Miss you / Ruby Tuesday / Tou can't always get what you want / Factory girl / Little red rooster / Paint it black / Sympathy for the Devil / Brown sugar / Jumpin' Jack Flash / (I can't get no) Satisfaction / Sexdrive (studio) / High wire (studio). *(cd+=)*– Rock and a hard place / Can't be seen.

May 91. (7"/c-s) *(656 892-7/-4)* **RUBY TUESDAY (live). / PLAY WITH FIRE (live)** [59] [ ]
(12"+=) *(656 892-6)* – You can't always get what you want (live) / Rock and a hard place (live).
(3"cd-s+=) *(656 892-1)* – You can't always get what you want (live) / Undercover of the night (live).

(cd-s) *(656 892-5)* – ('A'side) / Harlem shuffle / Winning ugly London mix).

—— In Nov'91, The STONES signed to 'Virgin', and BILL WYMAN soon quit.

Virgin Virgin

Nov 93. (d-lp/c/cd) *(V/TCV/CDV 2726)* **JUMP BACK: THE BEST OF THE ROLLING STONES 1971-1993** (compilation) [16] [ ]
– Start me up / Brown sugar / Harlem shuffle / It's only rock'n'roll (but I like it) / Mixed emotions / Angie / Tumbling dice / Fool to cry / Rock and a hard place / Miss you / Hot stuff / Emotional rescue / Respectable / Beast of burden / Waiting on a friend / Wild horses / Bitch / Undercover of the night. *(re-iss.Oct94 & Jun95;)*

—— WYMAN replaced by sessioners **DARRYL JONES** – bass / **CHUCK LEAVELL** – piano

Jul 94. (7"/c-s) *(VS/+C 1503)* **LOVE IS STRONG. / THE STORM** [14] [93]
(cd-s+=) *(VSCDT 1503)* – So young / ('A'-Bob Clearmountain mix).
(cd-s) *(VSCDX 1503)* – ('A'-Teddy Riley mixes; 5 mixes + other).

Jul 94. (cd/c/d-lp) *(8397821-2/-4/1)* **VOODOO LOUNGE** [1] [2]
– Love is strong / You got me rocking / Sparks will fly / The worst / New faces / Moon is up / Out of tears / I go wild / Brand new car / Sweethearts together / Suck on the jugular / Blinded by rainbows / Baby break it down / Thru and thru. *(cd-rom-iss.Jun95; VMED 2)*

Oct 94. (7"/c-s) *(VS/+C 1518)* **YOU GOT ME ROCKING. / JUMP ON TOP OF ME** [23] [ ]
(cd-s+=) *(VSCDG 1518)* – ('A'-Perfecto mix) / ('A'-sexy dub mix).
(12") *(VST 1518)* – ('A'-Perfecto mix) / ('A'-sexy dub) / ('A'-trance).

Dec 94. (7"/c-s) *(VS/+C 1524)* **OUT OF TEARS. / I'M GONNA DRIVE** [38] [60] Oct94
(cd-s+=/s-cd-s+=) *(VSCD T/X 1524)* – Sparks will fly / ('A'-Bob Clearmountain remix).

Jul 95. (7"/c-s) *(VSP/VSC 1539)* **I GO WILD. / ('A'-Scott Litt remix)** [29] [ ]
(cd-s+=) *(VSCDX 1539)* – ('A'version) / ('A'-Luis Resto straight vocal mix).

Nov 95. (c-s) *(VSC 1562)* **LIKE A ROLLING STONE / BLACK LIMOUSINE / ALL DOWN THE LINE** [12] [ ]
(cd-s+=) *(VSCDT 1562)* – ('A'edit).

Nov 95. (cd/c/d-lp) *(CD/TC+/V 2801)* **STRIPPED (live)** [9] [9]
– Street fighting man / Like a rolling stone / Not fade away / Shine a light / The spider and the fly / I'm free / Wild horses / Let it bleed / Dead flowers / Slipping away / Angie / Love in vain / Sweet Virginia / Little baby.

- compilations, etc. -

—— Below releases issued on 'Decca' UK/ 'Abkco' US unless mentioned

Jan 64. (7"ep) *(DFE 8560)* **THE ROLLING STONES** [ ] [-]
– Bye bye Johnny / Money / You better move on / Poison Ivy. *(re-iss.Mar82) (12"ep-iss.Dec83)*

Aug 64. (7"ep) *(DFE 8590)* **5 X 5** [ ] [-]
– If you need me / Empty heart / 2120 South Michegan Avenue / Confessin' the blues / Around and around. *(re-iss.Mar82) (12"ep-iss.Dec83)*

Jun 65. (7"ep) *(DFE 8620)* **GOT LIVE IF YOU WANT IT! (live)** [ ] [-]
– We want the Stones / Everybody needs somebody to love / Pain in my heart / Route 66 / I'm moving on / I'm alright. *(re-iss.Mar82) (12"ep-iss.Dec83)*

Jul 71. (7"m) *(F 13195)* **STREET FIGHTING MAN. / SURPRISE SURPRISE / EVERYBODY NEEDS SOMEBODY TO LOVE** [21] [-]

Aug 71. (lp/c) *(SLK/KSKC 5101)* **GIMME SHELTER** [19] [-]

Jan 72. (d-lp/c) *<606-7>* **HOT ROCKS 1964-1971** [-] [4]
(UK cd-iss.1983 on 'Decca'; 800 083-2) (re-iss.Jul90 cd/c/lp; 820 140-2/-4/-1) <US cd-iss.1989 on 'Abko'> (re-iss.Jun95 on 'London' cd/c/d-lp; 844475-2/-4/-1)

Feb 72. (lp/c) *(SKL/KSKC 5098)* **MILESTONES** [14] [-]

Jun 72. (7") *(export)* **EVERYBODY NEEDS SOMEBODY TO LOVE. / SURPRISE SURPRISE** [ ] [-]

Nov 72. (lp/c) *(SKL/KSKC 5149)* **ROCK'N'ROLLING STONES** [41] [-]

Dec 72. (lp/c) *<626-7>* **MORE HOT ROCKS (BIG HITS & FAZED COOKIES)** [-] [9]
(UK cd-iss.Aug88; 820 515-2) (re-iss.cd Nov90;) (re-iss.Jun95 on 'London' cd/c; 844478-2/-4)

Apr 73. (7") *(F 13404)* **YOU CAN'T ALWAYS GET WHAT YOU WANT. / SAD DAY** [ ] [42]

Oct 73. (lp/c) *(SKL/KSKC 5173)* **NO STONE UNTURNED** [ ] [-]

May 75. (7") *(F 13584)* **I DON'T KNOW WHY. / TRY A LITTLE HARDER** [ ] [42]

Jun 75. (lp/c) *(SKL/KSKC 5212)* **METAMORPHISIS** (early demos) [45] [8]

Sep 75. (7") *(F 13597)* **OUT OF TIME. / JIVING SISTER FANNY** [45] [81]

Nov 75. (d-lp)(d-c) *(ROST 1-2)(K2R 26)* **ROLLED GOLD – (THE VERY BEST OF THE ROLLING STONES)** [7] [-]
– Come on / I wanna be your man / Not fade away / Carol / It's all over now / Little red rooster / Time is on my side / The last time / (I can't get no) Satisfaction / Get off my cloud / 19th nervous breakdown / As tears go by / Under my thumb / Lady Jane / Out of time / Paint it black / Have you seen your mother baby, standing in the shadows? / Let's spend the night together / Ruby Tuesday / Yesterday's papers / We love you / She's a rainbow / Jumpin' Jack Flash / Honky tonk women / Sympathy for the Devil / Street fighting man / Midnight rambler / Gimme shelter.

Apr 76. (7") *(F 13635)* **HONKY TONK WOMEN. / SYMPATHY FOR THE DEVIL** [ ] [-]
(re-iss.Mar82)

Oct 77. (lp/c) *Arcade; (ADE P/C 32)* **GET STONED** [13] [-]

May 79. (lp) *Rolling Stones; (COC 59107)* **TIME WAITS FOR NO ONE** [ ] [ ]

Aug 80. (12x7"box) *(STONE 1-12)* **BOXED SET SINGLES 1963-1969** [ ] [ ]
– COME ON. / I WANNA BE YOUR MAN // **IT'S ALL OVER NOW. / I WANT TO BE LOVED // (I CAN'T GET NO) SATISFACTION. / LITTLE BY LITTLE // NOT FADE AWAY. / LITTLE RED ROOSTER // THE LAST TIME. / PAINT IT BLACK // GET OFF OF MY CLOUD. / PLAY WITH FIRE // JUMPIN' JACK FLASH. / AS TEARS GO BY // 19th NERVOUS BREAKDOWN. / HAVE YOU SEEN YOUR MOTHER BABY, STANDING IN THE SHADOWS? // LET'S SPEND THE NIGHT TOGETHER. / YOU CAN'T ALWAYS GET WHAT YOU WANT // HONKY TONK WOMAN. / RUBY TUESDAY STREET FIGHTING MAN. / OUT OF TIME // SYMPATHY FOR THE DEVIL. / GIMME SHELTER**

Oct 80. (lp/c) *(TAB/KTBC 1)* **SOLID ROCK** [ ] [-]

Nov 81. (lp/c) *(TAB/KTBC 30)* **SLOW ROLLERS** [ ] [-]

Oct 82. (d-lp/d-c) *K-Tel; (NE2/CE2 201)* **THE STORY OF THE STONES** [24] [-]

Jun 84. (7"/7"sha-pic-d) *Rolling Stones; (SUGAR/+P 1)* **BROWN SUGAR. / BITCH** [ ] [-]

Jan 86. (cd) *(820 141-2)* **HOT ROCKS 1** [ ] [ ] 1985

Jan 86. (cd) *(820 142-2)* **HOT ROCKS 2** [ ] [ ] 1985

Sep 89. (d-lp/d-c/d-cd) *(820 900-1/-4/-2) / Abkco; <1218>* **SINGLES COLLECTION: THE LONDON YEARS** [ ] [91]
(re-iss.Jun95)

Jun 90. (7") *(LON/+CS 264)* **PAINT IT BLACK. / HONKY TONK WOMAN** [61] [-]
(12"+=/remix-12"+=) *(LONX/+R 264)* – Sympathy for the Devil.

Jul 90. (3xcd-box) *Columbia; (466918-2)* **COLLECTOR'S EDITION** [ ] [ ]

Mar 92. (cd/c/lp/video) *Circus;* **LIVE AT THE HOLLYWOOD PALLADIUM DECEMBER 15, 1988 (live)** [ ] [ ]

-solo releases-

—— see book GREAT ROCK DISCOGRAPHY

Mick RONSON

Born: 1946, Hull, England. In 1964, he formed his first band, The RATS, although after a couple of singles over the next few years, they laid low. RONSON re-surfaced the band for a one-off psychedelic track, 'THE RISE AND FALL OF BERNIE GRIPPLESTONE', which, recorded in late '67, only made it to the demo stage. Guitarist RONSON subsequently went into session work, notably for MICHAEL CHAPMAN on his 'Fully Qualified Survivor' album, before his initial association with BOWIE under the group name, HYPE. Around the same time (1971), RONNO made a pro-rock attempt, although the single '4TH HOUR OF MY SLEEP', failed miserably. Alongside drummer WOODY WOODMANSEY on BOWIE's 'Man Who Sold The World', they soon became known as The SPIDERS FROM MARS, named after BOWIE's 1972 album, 'Ziggy Stardust & The Spiders From Mars'. RONSON left for a solo career in 1974 after featuring on late 1973 album, 'Bowie Pin-Ups'. Retained by MainMan productions & 'RCA' records, he issued a solo debut, 'SLAUGHTER ON 10th AVENUE', which featured a version of ELVIS' 'LOVE ME TENDER' and RONSON's most famous track, 'ONLY AFTER DARK'. In between this and his 1975 follow-up, 'PLAY DON'T WORRY', he had a short spell with MOTT THE HOOPLE, who were shortly to disband soon after. Their frontman, IAN HUNTER, who MICK had also toured alongside, formed a partnership with him as The HUNTER-RONSON BAND. For the next decade and a half, RONSON was his guitarist, a dual album, 'YUI ORTA', finally being issued in 1990. MICK's work during this period had included stints with BOB DYLAN on his ROLLING THUNDER REVUE of '75-'76, where he met ROGER McGUINN of The BYRDS. MICK subsequently produced his 'Cardiff Rose' album. He also went on to work in the late 70's for JOHN COUGAR (Chestnut Street Incident), RICH KIDS (Ghosts Of Princes In Towers) and DAVID JOHANSEN (In Style). After a lean spell in the 80's, RONSON returned in 1992, producing MORRISSEY's 'Your Arsenal', and guesting alongside old mates BOWIE and HUNTER at FREDDIE MERCURY's Wembley Tribute, that April. It was rumoured at the time, that MICK was suffering from cancer and he was to die on the 30th of April, 1993, prior to completing most of his long-awaited third album, 'FROM HEAVEN TO HULL', released in 1994. • **Songwriters:** Self-penned except; THE GIRL CAN'T HELP IT (Little Richard) / WHITE LIGHT WHITE HEAT (Velvet Underground) / GROWING UP AND I'M FINE + MOONAGE DAYDREAM (live encore) (Bowie). The RATS covered; PARCHMAN FARM (Mose Allison) / EVERY DAY I HAVE THE BLUES (Arthur Alexander) / SPOONFUL (Willie Dixon) / I'VE GOTTA SEE MY BABY EVERYDAY (Chris Andrews). • **Trivia:** His sister, MARGARET RONSON, provided backing vocals for his debut album. MICK's 80's production work was for the obscure outfits, The PAYOLAS and LOS ILLEGALS.

Recommended: SLAUGHTER ON 10th AVENUE (*6) / PLAY DON'T WORRY (*5)

RATS

MICK RONSON – guitar / + unknown

Oriole not issued

Nov 64. (7") *(CB 1967)* **PARCHMAN FARM. / EVERY DAY I HAVE THE BLUES** [ ] [-]

—— **WOODY WOODMANSEY** – drums repl. ? / (entire new members with RONSON) / included JOHN CAMBRIDGE

Columbia not issued

Mar 65. (7") *(DB 7483)* **SPOONFUL. / I'VE GOT MY EYES ON YOU BABY** [ ] [-]

Jun 65. (7") *(DB 7607)* **I GOTTA SEE MY BABY EVERYDAY. / HEADIN' BACK (TO NEW ORLEANS)** [ ] [-]

—— Disbanded. (see biography for BOWIE details, etc.)

RONNO

MICK RONSON – guitar / **BENNY MARSHALL** / etc.

Vertigo Vertigo

Jul 71. (7") *(6059 029) <100>* **4th HOUR OF MY SLEEP. / POWERS OF DARKNESS** [ ] [ ]

—— He then played on BOWIE albums 'ZIGGY STARDUST', 'ALADDIN SANE' & 'PIN-UPS'.

MICK RONSON

solo with **AYNSLEY DUNBAR** – drums / **TREVOR BOLDER** – bass / **MIKE GARSON** – piano

R.C.A. R.C.A.

Jan 74. (7") *(APBO 212) <0212>* **LOVE ME TENDER. / ONLY AFTER DARK** [ ] [ ]

Mar 74. (lp/c) *(APL/APK 1-0353)* **SLAUGHTER ON 10th AVENUE** 9
– Love me tender / Growing up and I'm fine / Only after dark / Music is lethal / I'm the one / Medley: Pleasure man – Hey ma get papa / Slaughter on 10th Avenue.

Apr 74. (7") *(APBO 5022) <0291>* **SLAUGHTER ON 10th AVENUE. / LEAVE MY HEART ALONE**

— From Sep-Dec'74, RONSON joined MOTT THE HOOPLE, and featured on only one single 'SATURDAY GIGS'. He continued on already recorded 2nd solo album.

Feb 75. (7") *(RCA 2482) <10237>* **BILLY PORTER. / HAZY DAYS**

Feb 75. (lp/c) *(APL/APK 1-0681)* **PLAY DON'T WORRY** 29
– Billy Porter / Angel No.9 / This is for you / White light – white heat / Play don't worry / Hazy days / The girl can't help it / Empty bed (lo me ne andrail) / Woman.

— MICK lost contract, and went off to play for BOB DYLAN, IAN HUNTER, and produce many (see biography). In 1990 he was on record again with IAN HUNTER on album 'YUI ORTA'. (see under ⇒)

Epic Epic

Apr 94. (c-s) *(660358-4)* **DON'T LOOK DOWN. / SLAUGHTER ON 10th AVENUE** 55
(12"+=/cd-s+=) *(660358-6/-2)* – Billy Porter / Love me tender.

— (above with JOE ELLIOTT of DEF LEPPARD on vocals).

May 94. (cd/c/lp) *(474742-2/-4/-1)* **FROM HEAVEN TO HULL**
– Don't look down / Like a rolling stone / When the world falls down / Trouble with me / Life's a river / You and me / Colour me / Takes a long line / Midnight love / All the young dudes.

– compilations, etc. –

May 82. (7") *RCA Gold; (GOLD 546)* **BILLY PORTER. / SLAUGHTER ON 10th AVENUE** -

Sep 94. (d-cd) *Trident; (GY 003)* **ONLY AFTER DARK** -

ROTARY CONNECTION

Formed: Chicago, Illinois, USA . . . 1967 by MARSHALL CHESS, the son of 'Chess' records founder LEONARD CHESS. He assembled a racially mixed, hip bunch of singers and musicians, including MINNIE RIPERTON, BOBBY SIMMS, MITCH ALIOTTA and KENNY VENEGAS. These were complimented by pianist CHARLES STEPNEY, who arranged mainly art-rock & soul versions of rock songs (see below). Their eponymous debut album, released early in 1968, soon climbed the US chart, hitting Top 40. It was a pick'n'mix assortment of progressive psychedelia in the SLY & THE FAMILY STONE mould. Their further releases, 'ALADDIN', etc, had a more basic R&B/soul sound, although they were always rock-based. When the band split in 1971, MINNIE RIPERTON (who had a solo career as ANDREA DAVIS in 1966) backed STEVIE WONDER, then ventured solo again, hitting No.1 (UK 2) with the 1975 beauty, 'LOVING YOU'. However, she was to die of cancer on the 12th of July '79. • **Covers:** LIKE A ROLLIN' STONE (Bob Dylan) / SOUL MAN (Sam & Dave) / RUBY TUESDAY + LADY JANE (Rolling Stones) / RESPECT (Aretha Franklin) / THE WEIGHT (Band) / SUNSHINE OF YOUR LOVE + TALES OF BRAVE ULYSSES + WE'RE GOING WRONG (Cream) / I'VE GOT MY MOJO WORKING (Muddy Waters) / BURNING OF THE MIDNIGHT LAMP (Jimi Hendrix) / etc.

Recommended: ROTARY CONNECTION (*6)

MINNIE RIPERTON (b. 8 Nov'47) – vocals / **SID BARNES** – vocals / **JUDY HAUFF** – vocals / **BOBBY SIMMS** – guitar, vocals / **MITCH ALIOTTA** – bass, vocals / **KENNY VENEGAS** – drums, vocals / **CHARLES STEPNEY** – producer, keyboards, arranger / **MARSHALL CHESS** – producer / **BILL BRADLEY** – electronics

Chess Cadet Concept

Nov 67. (7") *<7000>* **LIKE A ROLLIN' STONE. / TURN ME ON** -

May 68. (7") *(CRS 8072) <7002>* **SOUL MAN. / RUBY TUESDAY** Feb68

Jun 68. (lp) *(CRL 4538) <LPS 312>* **ROTARY CONNECTION** 37 Mar68
– Amen / Rapid transit / Turn me on / Pink noise / Lady Jane / Like a rollin' stone / Soul man / Sursum mentes / Didn't want to have to do it / Black noise / Memory band / Ruby Tuesday / Rotary connection.

— **TOMMY VINCENT** – vocals repl. VENEGAS + BRADLEY

Sep 68. (7") *<7007>* **PAPER CASTLE. / TEACH ME HOW TO FLY** -

Dec 68. (lp) *(CRLS 4547) <LPS 317>* **ALADDIN** Oct68
– Life could / Teach me how to fly / V.I.P. / Let them talk / I took a ride (caravan) / Aladdin / Magical world / I feel sorry / I must be there / Paper castle.

Dec 68. (7") *<7008>* **ALADDIN. / MAGICAL WORLD** -

— **TOM DONLINGER** – vocals / **JIM DONLINGER** – vocals / **JIM NYEHOLT** – vocals; repl. HAUFF, VINCENT + BARNES

Dec 68. (7") *<7009>* **PEACE AT LAST. / SILENT NIGHT CHANT** -

Dec 68. (lp) *<LPS 318>* **PEACE AT LAST** (festive songs) -
(UK-iss.1989 on 'Chess'; GCH 8102)

— **VENEGAS** returned with new vocalists **JOHN STOCKLIN** + **JEREMIAH** to repl. NYEHOLT + DONLINGER's who formed AORTA

Aug 69. (lp) *(CRLS 4551)* **SINGS** Jun69
– Respect / The weight / Sunshine of your love / I've got my mojo working / Burning of the midnight lamp / Tales of brave Ulysses / This town / We're going wrong / The salt of the earth. *(cd-iss.Mar95 on 'Charly'; CDARC 520)*

Oct 69. (7") *(CRS 8103) <7014>* **THE WEIGHT. / RESPECT** Sep69

— now just basically **STEPNEY** + **RIPERTON**

Nov 69. (lp) *<LPS 328>* **DINNER MUSIC** -
– Pointillism / We will be free / Living alone / Lektricks #1 / Country things / Quartet / May our amens be true / Stormy Monday blues / Love me now / Lonely summer / Amuse / Lektricks #2 / Merry prankster / Pump effect / Want you to know.

Jan 70. (7") *(CRS 8106) <7018>* **WANT YOU TO KNOW. / MEMORY BAND** 96 Dec69

Mar 70. (7") *<7021>* **LOVE ME NOW. / MAY OUR AMENS BE TRUE** -

Jun 70. (7") *<7027>* **TEACH ME HOW TO FLY. / STORMY MONDAY BLUES** -

— added **KITTY HAYWOOD, SHIRLEY WAHLS** + **DAVE SCOTT** – vocals / **PHIL UPCHURCH** + **PAT FERRARI** – guitars / **SYDNEY SIMMS** – bass / **DONNY SIMMONS** – drums / **HENRY GIBSON** – congas

Aug 71. (7"; as NEW ROTARY CONNECTION) *<7028>* **HEY LOVE. / IF I SING MY SONG** -

Oct 71. (lp; as NEW ROTARY CONNECTION) *(6310 105) <50006>* **HEY LOVE** Sep71
– If I sing my song / The sea & she / I am the black gold of the sun / Hanging round the bee tree / Hey love / Love has fallen on me / Song for everyman / Love is / Vine of happiness.

— split after above when MINNIE RIPERTON went solo

Michael ROTHER (see under ⇒ NEU!)

ROXY MUSIC

Formed: Newcastle, England . . . 1970 by art school graduate and teacher, BRYAN FERRY alongside GRAHAM SIMPSON. Early in 1971, they invited ANDY MACKAY and electronic wizard BRIAN ENO to join, finally settling with the debut album line-up a year later, when they added PHIL MANZANERA and PAUL THOMPSON. The concept of ROXY MUSIC was the brainchild of FERRY, who attempted to realise his vision of a musical equivalent to the pop art he'd become fascinated with at college. Fashioning the band in an outlandish hybrid of decadent glamour and future shock experimentalism, FERRY made sure ROXY MUSIC would be hot property after only a handful of gigs. At this point, the other prime mover behind ROXY MUSIC was BRIAN ENO, who shaped the band's pioneering sound by wrenching all manner of bizarre electronic noises from his mini-moog, feeding the rest of the instruments through an EMS modular synth and masterminding pre-recorded special effects. Signed to 'Island', the band released their self-titled debut in the summer of 1972. Produced by PETE SINFIELD (the KING CRIMSON lyricist), the album effortlessly fused FERRY's suave crooning, a pulsing rhythm section and ENO's inspired electronic experimentation, garnering rave reviews and defying any attempts to pigeonhole the band's sound. But it was the follow-up single, 'VIRGINIA PLAIN' (1972), which launched the band into pop stardom. A careering blast of avant-pop that managed to incorporate a lyric focussing on one of FERRY's surrealist paintings, the single breached the upper echelons of the charts. By this juncture, SIMPSON had been given his marching orders and the band went through a bewildering succession of personnel changes, FERRY retaining strict control throughout. After another top ten hit with 'PYJAMARAMA' in 1973, ROXY MUSIC released their second album, 'FOR YOUR PLEASURE' later the same year. Juxtaposing the ironic wig-out of tracks like 'DO THE STRAND' and 'BEAUTY QUEEN' with the vivid desolation of 'IN EVERY DREAM HOME A HEARTACHE', the album distilled the essence of FERRY's original vision. ENO left soon after, his more extreme experimental leanings at odds with the direction in which FERRY wanted to take the band. FERRY also began a solo career around this time which he ran in tandem with the band, releasing an album of covers, 'THESE FOOLISH THINGS', in 1973. ROXY MUSIC, meanwhile, released their third masterpiece, 'STRANDED', a month later. The first album to feature new recruit EDDIE JOBSON (ex-CURVED AIR), the record was less confrontational but more assured in terms of songwriting, FERRY excelling himself with the haunted romanticism of 'MOTHER OF PEARL' and the sweeping grandeur of 'A SONG FOR EUROPE'. A typically ROXY slice of ambiguous, discordant pop, the single, 'STREET LIFE', gave the band yet another Top 10 hit. By the following summer, FERRY had another solo album on the shelves; 'ANOTHER TIME, ANOTHER PLACE' saw him revelling in the role of slicked-back sophisticate, while ROXY's 'COUNTRY LIFE' saw the band in rock-out mode on tracks like 'THE THRILL OF IT ALL', while still buffing the sound with an ironic sheen. Despite a promising single, 'LOVE IS THE DRUG', 'SIREN' (1975) found FERRY's studied musings sounding jaded. Less then a year later, the band split, with McKAY and MANZANERA off to work on solo projects while JOBSON joined FRANK ZAPPPA. FERRY, meanwhile, concentrated on his burgeoning solo career, hitting Top 5 with the funky 'LET'S STICK TOGETHER', following it up with the good-time album of the same name, for once going a bit easier on the irony. 'IN YOUR MIND' (1977) kept up the momentum, spawning the hit, 'TOKYO JOE', and seeing FERRY branch out into original material. Recorded in L.A. with aging session musicians, the sober tones of 'THE BRIDE STRIPPED BARE' (1978) was never going to gain much headway during the height of the punk explosion, yet it remains one the more accessible of FERRY's solo albums. The same year, he cannily reformed ROXY MUSIC, 'MANIFESTO' (1979) heralding a smoother, cleaner sound with the emphasis on FERRY's wistful crooning. The singles 'ANGEL EYES' and 'DANCE AWAY' were the first in a string of tortured pop nuggets that breached the upper reaches of the charts at the turn of the decade, the band finally reaching No.1 with their sublime cover of JOHN LENNON's 'JEALOUS GUY' in 1981. 'FLESH AND BLOOD' (1980) and 'AVALON' (1982) were commercial but finely honed and exquisitely melodic, the latter a quintessentially 80's piece of synthesizer sophistication which inspired many 'New wave-futurist' bands of the 80's. On this high note, FERRY disbanded ROXY MUSIC finally in 1982 and resumed his solo career, carving out a niche as a purveyor of refined, complex adult orientated pop on albums 'BOYS AND GIRLS' (1985) and 'BETE NOIR' (1987). TAXI (1993) saw him return to covers material while 'MAMOUNA' (1994) was an accomplished, mature set of original material. • **Songwriters:** FERRY / MANZANERA with contributions from MACKAY and ENO, until the latter bailed out. They covered; IN THE MIDNIGHT HOUR (Wilson Pickett) / EIGHT MILES HIGH (Byrds) / JEALOUS GUY (John Lennon) / LIKE A HURRICANE (Neil Young). • **Trivia:** FERRY married model, Lucy Helmore, on the 26th of June '82 after a 70's relationship with Jerry Hall had finished. He was said to have turned down the Keith Forsey-penned song, 'DON'T YOU FORGET ABOUT ME', a No.1 for SIMPLE MINDS.

Recommended: ROXY MUSIC (*9) / FOR YOUR PLEASURE (*9) / STRANDED (*7) / COUNTRY LIFE (*6) / STREETLIFE compilation (*8)

BRYAN FERRY (b.26 Sep'45, Washington, Durham, England) – vocals, piano / **ANDY MACKAY** (b.23 Jul'46, London, England) – saxophone, oboe, wind inst. / (BRIAN) **ENO** (b.15 May'48, Woodbridge, Suffolk, England) – synthesizers-keyboards / **GRAHAM SIMPSON** – bass, vocals / **PHIL MANZANERA** (b. PHILIP TARGETT-ADAMS, 31 Jan'51, London) – guitar (ex-QUIET SUN) repl. DAVID O'LIST (ex-NICE) who had repl. original ROGER BUNN (Jul'71). / **PAUL THOMPSON** (b.13 May'51, Jarrow, Northumberland, England) – drums repl. original DEXTER LLOYD (Jul71).

Island / Reprise

Jun 72. (lp/c) *(ILPS/ICT 9200) <RS 2114>* **ROXY MUSIC** [10] [ ]
– Bitters end / The bob / Chance meeting / If there is something / Ladytron / Re-make/re-model / 2HB / Would you believe? / Sea breezes. *(re-iss.Feb77 on 'Polydor' lp)(c; 2302 048)(3100 348) (re-iss.Jan87 on 'E.G.' lp/c/cd+=; EG LP/MC/CD 6)*– Virginia Plain. *(re-iss.Sep91 on 'EG';)*

— (May72) **RIK KENTON** (b.31 Oct'45) – bass repl. SIMPSON

Aug 72. (7") *(WIP 6144) <1124>* **VIRGINIA PLAIN. / THE NUMBERER** [4] [ ]

— (Jan73) **JOHN PORTER** – bass repl. KENTON who went solo

Island / Warners

Mar 73. (7") *(WIP 6159)* **PJAMARAMA. / THE PRIDE AND THE PAIN** [10] [ ]
Mar 73. (lp/c) *(ILPS/ICT 9232) <2696>* **FOR YOUR PLEASURE** [4] [ ]
– Do the strand / Beauty queen / Strictly confidential / Editions of you / In every dream home a heartache / The bogus man / Grey lagoons / For your pleasure. *(re-iss.Feb77 on 'Polydor' lp)(c; 2302 049)(3100 349) (re-iss.Jan87 on 'E.G.' lp/c/cd; EG LP/MC/CD 8) (cd+c.Sep91 on 'EG') (re-iss.Feb97 on 'E.M.I.'; LPCENT 19)*
Jul 73. (7") *<7719>* **DO THE STRAND. / EDITIONS OF YOU** [-] [ ]

— (Jul73) **EDDIE JOBSON** (b.28 Apr'55, Billingham, Teeside, England) – keyboards, violin (ex-CURVED AIR) repl. ENO who went solo. session bassmen **JOHN GUSTAFSON** (studio) / **SAL MAIDA** (tour)repl. PORTER (other 5= **FERRY, MANZANERA, MACKAY, JOBSON & THOMPSON)**

Island / Atco

Nov 73. (7") *(WIP 6173)* **STREET LIFE. / HULA KULA** [9] [-]
Nov 73. (lp/c) *(ILPS/ICT 9252) <7045>* **STRANDED** [1] [ ]
– Street life / Just like you / Amazona / Psalm / Serenade / A song for Europe / Mother of pearl / Sunset. *(re-iss.Feb77 on 'Polydor' lp)(c; 2302 050)(3100 350) (re-iss.Jan87 on 'E.G.' lp/c/cd; EG LP/MC/CD 10) (cd+c. Sep91 on 'EG')*

— brought in **JOHN WETTON** (b.1949, Derby, England) – tour bass (ex-FAMILY, ex-KING CRIMSON, etc.) repl. MAIDA

Oct 74. (7") *(WIP 6208)* **ALL I WANT IS YOU. / YOUR APPLICATIONS FAILED** [12] [-]
Nov 74. (lp/c) *(ILPS/ICT 9303) <106>* **COUNTRY LIFE** [3] [37] Jan75
– The thrill of it all / Three and nine / All I want is you / Out of the blue / If it takes all night / Bitter-sweet / Triptych / Casanova / A really good time / Prairie rose. *(re-iss.Feb77 on 'Polydor' lp)(c; 2302 051)(3100 351) (re-iss.Jan87 on 'E.G.' lp/c/cd; EG LP/MC/CD 16) (cd+c.Sep91 on 'EG')*
Nov 74. (7") *<7018>* **THE THRILL OF IT ALL. / YOUR APPLICATIONS FAILED** [-] [ ]
Sep 75. (7") *(WIP 6248)* **LOVE IS THE DRUG. / SULTANESQUE** [2] [-]
Oct 75. (lp/c) *(ILPS/ICT 9344) <127>* **SIREN** [4] [50]
– Love is the drug / End of the line / Sentimental fool / Whirlwind / She sells / Could it hapen to me / Both ends burning / Nightingale / Just another high. *(re-iss.Feb77 on 'Polydor' lp)(c; 2302 052)(3100 352) (re-iss.Jan87 on 'E.G.' lp/c/cd; EG LP/MC/CD 20) (cd+c.Sep91 on 'EG')*
Dec 75. (7") *(WIP 6262)* **BOTH ENDS BURNING. / FOR YOUR PLEASURE** [25] [ ]
Dec 75. (7") *<7042>* **LOVE IS THE DRUG. / BOTH ENDS BURNING** [-] [30]

— **RICK WILLS** – tour bass repl. WETTON who stayed on with FERRY

— Disbanded officially mid'76, leaving behind one more album

Jul 76. (lp/c) *(ILPS/ICT 9400) <139>* **VIVA! ROXY MUSIC (live 1973-1975)** [6] [81]
– Out of the blue / Pjamarama / The bogus man / Chance meeting / Both ends burning / If there is something / In every dream home a heartache / Do the strand. *(re-iss.Feb77 on 'Polydor' lp)(c; 2302 053)(3100 353) (re-iss.Jan87 on 'E.G.' lp/c/cd; EG LP/MC/CD 25) (cd+c.Sep91 on 'EG')*

— After split ANDY MACKAY continued solo work, as did PHIL MANZANERA. EDDIE JOBSON joined FRANK ZAPPA.

— For Bryan FERRY solo, see GREAT ROCK DISCOGRAPHY.

ROXY MUSIC

re-formed with **FERRY, MANZANERA, MACKAY, THOMPSON,** plus **PAUL CARRACK** – studio keyboards (ex-ACE) / **DAVID SKINNER** – tour keyboards / **GARY TIBBS** – bass (ex-VIBRATORS)

Polydor-EG / Atco

Feb 79. (7") *(POSP 32)* **TRASH. / TRASH 2** [40] [-]
Mar 79. (lp/c)(pic-lp) *(POLH/+C 001)(EGPD 001) <114>* **MANIFESTO** [7] [23]
– Manifesto / Trash / Angel eyes / Still falls the rain / Stronger through the years / Ain't that so / My little girl / ance away / Cry cry cry / Spin me round. *(re-iss.Jan87 on 'E.G.' lp/c/cd+=; EG LP/MC/CD 38)*– Angel eyes (12"disco version).
Apr 79. (7") *(POSP 44)* **DANCE AWAY. / CRY CRY CRY** [2] [-]
Apr 79. (7") *<7100>* **DANCE AWAY. / TRASH 2** [-] [44]
Aug 79. (7"/ext.12") *(POSP/+X 67)* **ANGEL EYES. / MY LITTLE GIRL** [4] [-]
May 80. (7") *(POSP 93)* **OVER YOU. / MANIFESTO** [5] [-]
May 80. (lp/c) *(POLH/+C 002) <102>* **FLESH + BLOOD** [1] [35]
– In the midnight hour / Oh yeah (on the radio) / Same old scene / Flesh and blood / My only love / Over you / Eight miles high / Rain rain rain / No strange delight / Running wild. *(re-iss.Jan87 on 'E.G.' lp/c/cd; EG LP/MC/CD 46)*
May 80. (7") *<7301>* **OVER YOU. / MY ONLY LOVE** [-] [80]
Jul 80. (7") *(2001 972)* **OH YEAH (ON THE RADIO). / SOUTH DOWNS** [5] [ ]
Nov 80. (7") *(ROXY 1)* **SAME OLD SCENE. / LOVER** [12] [-]
Dec 80. (7") **IN THE MIDNIGHT HOUR. /** [-] [ ]

— Earlier 1980, CARRACK joined SQUEEZE, and TIBBS joined ADAM & THE ANTS. Session men used at the time **NEIL HUBBARD** – guitar / **ALAN SPENNER** – bass / **ANDY NEWMARK** – drums repl. THOMPSON

E.G. / Warners

Feb 81. (7") *(ROXY 2) <7329>* **JEALOUS GUY. / TO TURN YOU ON** [1] [ ]
Apr 82. (7"/12") *(ROXY/+X 3)* **MORE THAN THIS. / INDIA** [6] [-]
May 82. (lp/c) *(EGHP/+C 50) <23686>* **AVALON** [1] [53]
– More than this / The space between / India / While my heart is still beating / Main thing / Take a chance with me / Avalon / To turn you on / True to life / Tara. *(re-iss.Jan87 on 'E.G.' lp/c/cd; EG LP/MC/CD 50) (re-iss.Apr92 on 'Virgin' lp/c; OVED/+C 397)*
Jun 82. (7") *(ROXY 4)* **AVALON. / ALWAYS UNKNOWING** [13] [ ]
Sep 82. (7"/12") *(ROXY/+X 5)* **TAKE A CHANCE WITH ME. / THE MAIN THING** [26] [-]
Sep 82. (7") *<29978>* **TAKE A CHANCE ON ME. / INDIA** [-] [ ]
Nov 82. (7") *<29912>* **MORE THAN THIS. / ALWAYS UNKNOWING** [-] [ ]

— added **GUY FLETCHER + JIMMY MAELEN** – keyboards / **MICHELLE COBBS + TAWATHA AGEE**

Mar 83. (m-lp/c) *(EGM LP/MC 1) <23808>* **THE HIGH ROAD (live)** [26] [67]
– Can't let go / My only love / Like a hurricane / Jealous guy.

— Had already disbanded again late 1982. MANZANERA and MACKAY became The EXPLORERS, and FERRY went solo again.

– (ROXY MUSIC) compilations, etc. –

— on 'E.G.' unless mentioned otherwise

Oct 77. (7") *Polydor; (2001 739)* **VIRGINIA PLAIN. / PJAMARAMA** [11] [ ]
Nov 77. (lp)(c) *Polydor; (2303 073)(3100 407)* **GREATEST HITS** [20] [ ]
– Virginia Plain / Do the strand / All I want is you / Out of the blue / Pjamarama / Editions of you / Love is the drug / Mother of pearl / Song for Europe / Thrill of it all / Street life. *(re-iss.Jan87 on 'E.G.' lp/cd; EG LP/CD 31)*
Jan 78. (7") *Polydor; (2001 756)* **DO THE STRAND. / EDITIONS OF YOU** [ ] [-]
Dec 81. (7xlp-box/7xc-box) *(EG BS/BC 1)* **THE FIRST SEVEN ALBUMS** [ ] [-]
– (ROXY MUSIC / FOR YOUR PLEASURE / STRANDED / COUNTRY LIFE / SIREN / MANIFESTO / FLESH AND BLOOD).
Nov 83. (lp/c)(cd) *(EG LP/MC 54)(815 849-2) / Atco; <90122>* **THE ATLANTIC YEARS 1973-1980** [23] [ ]
Apr 86. (d-lp/c)(cd) (BRYAN FERRY & ROXY MUSIC) *(EGTV/EGMTV/EGCTV 1) <25857>* **STREETLIFE** [1] [100] Aug89
– Virginia plain / A hard rain's a-gonna fall (BRYAN FERRY) / Pjamarama / Do the strand / These foolish things (BRYAN FERRY) / Street life / Let's stick together (BRYAN FERRY) / Smoke gets in your eyes (BRYAN FERRY) / Love is the drug / Sign of the times (BRYAN FERRY) / Dance away / Angel eyes / Oh yeah / Over you / Same old scene / The midnight hour / More than this / Avalon / Slave to love (BRYAN FERRY) / Jealous guy.
Jun 88. (3"cd-ep) *(CDT 8)* **JEALOUS GUY / LOVER / SOUTHDOWN** [ ] [ ]
Dec 89. (3xc-box/3xcd-box) *(EGBM/EGBC 3)* **ROXY MUSIC – THE EARLY YEARS** [ ] [ ]
– (ROXY MUSIC / FOR YOUR PLEASURE / STRANDED)
Dec 89. (3xc-box/3xcd-box) *(EGBM/EGBC 4)* **ROXY MUSIC – THE LATER YEARS** [ ] [ ]
– (MANIFESTO / FLESH AND BLOOD / AVALON)
Oct 90. (cd/c/d-lp) *(EG CD/MC/LP 77)* **HEART STILL BEATIN' (live in France '82)** [ ] [ ]
Oct 90. (7") **LOVE IS THE DRUG (live). / EDITIONS OF YOU (live)** [ ] [-]
(12"+=/cd-s+=) – Do the strand (live).
Oct 94. (3xcd-box) **THE COMPACT COLLECTION** [ ] [ ]
Nov 95. (4xcd-box) *Virgin; (CDBOX 5)* **THE THRILL OF IT ALL – ROXY MUSIC 1972-1982** [ ] [ ]
Apr 96. (c-ep/12"ep/cd-ep) *Virgin; (VS C/T/CDT 1580)* **LOVE IS THE DRUG (Rollo & Sister Bliss Monster mixes; 3) / ('A'-original version)** [33] [ ]

ANDY MACKAY

Island / not issued

Jun 74. (7") *(WIP 6197)* **RIDE OF THE VALKYRIES. / TIME REGAINED** [ ] [-]
Jun 74. (lp) *(ILPS 9278)* **IN SEARCH OF EDDIE RIFF** [ ] [-]
– The end of the world / Walking the whippet / What becomes of the broken-hearted / An die musik / The hour before dawn / Past, present and future * / Ride of the Valkyries / Summer Sun * / A four-legged friend *. *(re-iss.Feb77 on 'Polydor'; 2302 064)(tracks* repl. by)*– Wild weekend / Pyramid of night / Time regained / The long and winding road.
Aug 75. (7") *(WIP 6243)* **WILD WEEKEND. / WALKING THE WHIPPET** [ ] [-]

— In 1976-77, MACKAY wrote music for hit UK No.1 TV series 'ROCK FOLLIES'.

Bronze / not issued

Oct 78. (lp) *(BRON 510)* **RESOLVING CONTRADICTIONS** [ ] [-]
– Iron blossom / Trumpets on the mountains / Off to work / Unreal city / The Loyang tractor factory / Rivers / Battersea Rise / Skill and sweat / The Ortolan bunting (a sparrow's fall) / The inexorable sequence / A song of friendship (the Renmin hotel) / Medley: Alloy blossom – Trumpets in the Sabu – Green and gold. *(re-iss.Nov90 on 'Expression'; EXPALCD 5)*
Oct 78. (7") *(BRO 64)* **A SONG OF FRIENDSHIP. / SKILL AND SWEAT** [ ] [-]

PHIL MANZANERA

Island Atco

May 75. (lp) *(ILPS 9315) <36113>* **DIAMOND HEAD** 40
– Frontera / Diamond head / Big day / The flex / Same time next week / Miss Shapiro / East of echo / Lagrima / Alma. *(re-iss.Mar77 on 'Polydor'; 2302 062) (re-iss.Jan87 on 'E.G.' lp/cd; EG LP/CD 19)*

— QUIET SUN were formed earlier by **MANZANERA, DAVE JARRETT** – keyboards / **BILL McCORMICK** – bass / **CHARLES HAYWARD** – drums

Help-Island Antilees

Aug 75. (lp; as QUIET SUN) *(HELP 19) <7008>* **MAINSTREAM**
– Sol Caliente / Trumpets with motherhood / Trot / Rongwrong / Bargain classics / R.F.D. / Mummy was an asteroid, daddy was a small non-stick kitchen utensil. *(re-iss.Oct77 on 'Polydor'; 2343 093) (re-iss.Jan87 on 'EG': EGED 4) (cd-iss.Mar97 on 'Blueprint'; BP 246CD)*

— 801 featured **MANZANERA, McCORMICK, ENO** plus **LLOYD WATSON** – guitar / **FRANCIS MONKMAN** – piano, clarinet (ex-CURVED AIR) / **SIMON PHILLIPS** – drums

Island Polydor

Oct 76. (lp; as 801 LIVE) *(ILPS 9444)* **801 LIVE (live)**
– Lagima / T.N.K. (Tomorrow Never Knows) / East of asteroid / Rongwrong / Sombre reptiles / Baby's on fire / Diamond head / Miss Shapiro / You really got me / Third uncle. *(re-iss.Feb77 on 'Polydor'; 2302 044) (re-iss.Jan87 & Mar91 on 'E.G.' lp/c/cd; EG LP/MC/CD 26)*

— retained **McCORMICK**, and brought in **PAUL THOMPSON** – drums (ROXY MUSIC) **SIMON AINLEY** – guitar, vocals / **DAVID SKINNER** – keyboards, vocals / etc.

Polydor Polydor

Sep 77. (7") *(2001 733)* **FLIGHT 19. / CAR RHUMBA** -
Oct 77. (lp) *(2302 074)* **LISTEN NOW!**
– Listen now / Flight 19 / Island / Law and order / ? Que ? / City of light / Initial speed / Postcard love / That falling feeling. *(re-iss.+cd.Jan87 on 'EG')*
Nov 77. (7") **FLIGHT 19. / INITIAL SPEED** -
Feb 78. (7") *(2001 800)* **ISLAND. / DIAMOND HEAD** -

— went solo again, using past QUIET SUN + 801 members.

Nov 78. (lp) *(2302 083) <6147>* **K-SCOPE**
– K-scope / Remote control / Cuban crisis / Hot spot / Numbers / Slow motion T.V. / Gone flying / N-shift / Walking through Heaven's door / You are here.
Nov 78. (7") *(2001 835)* **REMOTE CONTROL. / K-SCOPE** -

EG-Editions not issued

Mar 82. (lp) *(EGED 14)* **PRIMITIVE GUITARS** -
– Criollo / Caracas / La nueva ola / Bogota / Ritmo de Los Angeles / Europe 70-1 / Impossible guitars / Europe 70-1. *(re-iss.Jan87; same)*
Apr 87. (lp/c/cd) *(EG LP/MC/CD 69)* **GUITARISSIMO** (compilation) -
(cd+=/c+=)– (3 extra tracks). *(cd re-iss.Mar91; same)*

Expression not issued

May 90. (7") *(EXPR7 1)* **A MILLION REASONS WHY. / SOUTHERN CROSS** -
(12"+=) *(EXPR12 1)* – Blood brother.
Jun 90. (cd/c/lp) *(EXPAL CD/MC/LP 1)* **SOUTHERN CROSS** -
– A million reasons why / Tambor / The great leveller / Astrud / Southern cross / Guantanemera / Rich and poor / Verde / Dr. Fidel / Venceremos. *(cd re-iss.May97 as 'A MILLION REASONS WHY'; EXVP 1CD)*

The EXPLORERS

PHIL MANZANERA / ANDY MACKAY plus **JAMES WRAITH** – vocals (ex-FLYING TIGERS)

Virgin Virgin

Jun 84. (7"/12") *(VS 687/+12)* **LORELEI. / YOU GO UP IN SMOKE**
Oct 84. (7"/12") *(VS 715/+12)* **FALLING THE NIGHTLIFE. / CRACK THE WHIP**
Apr 85. (7") *(VS 757)* **TWO WORLDS APART. / IT ALWAYS RAINS IN PARADISE**
(12"+=) *(VS 757-12)* – Voodoo isle.
May 85. (cd/c/lp) *(CD/TC+/V 2341)* **THE EXPLORERS**
– Ship of fools / Lorelei / Breath of life / Venus de Milo / Soul fantasy / Prussian blue / Two worlds apart / Robert Louis Stevenson / You go up in smoke. *(re-iss.Jun88 lp/c; OVED/+C 185)*
Jun 85. (7"/12") *(VS 779/+12)* **VENUS DE MILO. / ANOTHER LOST SOUL ON THE RUN**

PHIL MANZANERA & ANDY MACKAY

retained **WRAITH**

Expression Relativity

1988. (cd) **CRACK THE WHIP** -
1989. (cd) **UP IN SMOKE** -
Nov 90. (cd/c/lp) *(EXPAL CD/MC/LP 4)* **MANZANERA / MACKAY** -
– Black gang Chine / Free yourself / Built for speed / Many are the ways / I can be tender / Dreams of the East / Sacrosanct / Every kind of stone / Man with extraordinary ways / Safe in the arms of love / Forgotten man. *(cd-iss.Feb97; same)*
Mar 97. (cd; PHIL MANZANERA & MONCADA) *(EXVP 4CD)* **LIVE AT THE KARL MARX THEATRE (live)** -
– Yo te queria Maria / Mama Hue / Yolanda – Pablo Milanes / Caiman no come caiman / Mi canto sube / Cantar el son de Cuba / Southern cross / Astrud / Musica / Corazon corazon.

Blueprint not issued

Mar 97. (cd; PHIL MANZANERA & JOHN WETTON) *(BP 241CD)* **ONE WORLD** -
– It's just love / Kee on loving yourself / You don't have to leave my life / Suzanne / Round in circles / Do it again / Every trick in the book / One world / Can't let you go / Have you seen her tonight / Talk to me.

– (MANZANERA) compilation –

May 95. (d-cd) *Virgin; (CDVDM 9033)* **THE MANZANERA COLLECTION** -
– Tomorrow never knows (801 LIVE) / Over you (ROXY MUSIC) / Out of the blue (ROXY MUSIC) / Fat lady of Limbourg (801 LIVE) / Impossible guitars (ROXY MUSIC) / Charlie (TIM FINN) / Take a chance with me (ROXY MUSIC) / Frontera (with ROBERT WYATT) / Diamond head (801 LIVE) / Needle in a camel's eye (ENO) / Miss Shapiro (801 LIVE) / The end (NICO) / Gun (JOHN CALE) / Europe 70-1 (PHIL MANZANERA) / / Leyenda / Frontera 91 / Southern cross / Sphinx – :(GUITAR LEGENDS '91) / Amazona (ROXY MUSIC) / A million reasons why (PHIL MANZANERA) / Fifth wheel (TIM FINN) / It's just love / Talk to me / Suzanne – :(WETTON – MANZANERA) / Black gang Chine (MACKAY – MANZANERA) / Lorelei (EXPLORERS) / Criollo (PHIL MANZANERA) / Mama Hue / Corazon corazon – :(MONCADO – MANZANERA) / Flor de Azalea (TANIA LIBERTAD) / Espiritu (SERGIO DIAS – MANZANERA).

RUFUS ZUPHALL

Formed: Aachen, Germany . . . 1971. Their five track debut, 'WEISS DER TEUFEL' (1971), is widely regarded as an early classic of German prog-rock and its extensive use of flute drew comparisons with JETHRO TULL. Like most progressive rock of the time, the album was mostly instrumental in content and possessed of a raw spontaneity. As was the way with these bands, a modified line-up recorded the follow-up, 'PHALLOBST', in 1972. The record was more intricate than the debut, embellished with clavinet and mellotron. Although the band completed demos for a third album, it was never released and RUFUS ZUPHALL split in 1972.

Recommended: WEISS DER TEUFEL (*8) / PHALLOBST (*8)

GUNTER KRAUSE – guitar, vocals / **KLAUS GULDEN** – flute, percussion / **HELMUT LIEBLANG** – bass / **UDO DAHMEN** – drums, tablas

Good Will not issued

1971. (lp) *(10001)* **WEISS DER TEUFEL** - - German
– Weiss der Teufel (inc. 'Summertime') / Knight of the third degree / Freitag / etc. *(re-iss.1989 on 'Little Wing'; LW 1003) (cd-iss.1990's)*

— **THOMAS KITTEL** – guitars, clavinet + **MANFRED SPANGENBERG** – bass; repl. LIEBLANG

Pilz not issued

Dec 71. (lp) *(20.21099-5)* **PHALLOBST** - - German
– Closing time / Wenn schon, denn schon / Schnupfer / Waste land / Makrojel / Prickel prit / Portland town / I'm on my way. *(re-iss.1981; same)*

— bailed out of scene after a concert in June 1972

– compilations, etc. –

1994. (4xlp-box/7") *Little Wing; (LW 1037-1038-1039-1040/1041)* **AVALON AND ON** - - German
– (PHALLOBST / unreleased / demos of 3rd lp / early rare / single)

Todd RUNDGREN

Born: 22 Jun'48, Upper Darby, Pennsylvania, USA. In 1967, he and another ex-WOODY'S TRUCK STOP member, CARSTEN VAN OSTEN, formed The NAZZ (taking the name from a YARDBIRDS b-side). In 1968, after supporting The DOORS a year previously, they signed to 'Screen Gems/Columbia'. An eponymous debut album sold moderately, RUNDGREN leaving the band in the middle of '69, after the completion of two further albums of psychedelic metal. In 1970, he became an in-house producer for Albert Grossman's 'Bearsville', his first job being for The AMERICAN DREAM. Later in the year, he formed his own band, RUNT (his nickname), releasing an album of the same name which spawned his first Top 20 hit, 'WE GOTTA GET YOU A WOMAN'. Following a further RUNT album, he decided to use his own name for future releases. In 1972, after taking over the production duties from GEORGE HARRISON on BADFINGER's 'Straight Up' set, he unleashed a truly wonderful solo debut, 'SOMETHING / ANYTHING'. The double album reached the Top 30, a cut from it, 'I SAW THE LIGHT', making the US Top 20 (a year later Top 40 in the UK). Playing every instrument himself, it encompassed almost every style in the pop/rock pantheon. Among the many highlights were; the aforementioned single, 'HELLO IT'S ME', 'MARLENE', COULDN'T I JUST TELL YOU' and 'COLD MORNING LIGHT'. His next effort, 'A WIZARD, A TRUE STAR' was a wildly ambitious concept piece that attempted to reconstruct psychedelia. Although the record overreached itself, failing commercially as a result, it nevertheless contained a smattering of RUNDGREN gems including 'JUST ONE VICTORY'. Prolific in his songwriting, he returned after only nine months with yet another double set, 'TODD', an unrelentingly snooze-worthy affair. To compliment his wide ranging solo work under many styles, TODD formed a band, UTOPIA, who were a much more free flowing, progressive rock/jazz outfit. Their first self-titled outing was released at the end of '74, while RUNDGREN himself worked on his monumental 'INITITION'. Released in '75, it was largely lambasted by the press, although inside the hour-long lp was the minor classic hit, 'REAL MAN' and the 30-odd minute 'A TREATISE ON COSMIC FIRE' (which was split into three parts). RUNDGREN increasingly seemed to lose his penchant for experimentalism, although UTOPIA's 'RA' album was the exception. The album, 'OOPS! WRONG PLANET' (also 1977), took a more commercial direction, while at the same time, TODD was painstakingly producing MEAT LOAF's grandiose 'Bat Out Of Hell'. For the remainder of the 70's and throughout the first half of the 80's, TODD combined his solo output with UTOPIA releases. Most of these were well-received commercially, although critically, he was often unfairly savaged by the music press. • **Songwriters:** Phenomenal pensmith, although he did fit in a number of near perfect covers; DO YA (Move) / GOOD VIBRATIONS (Beach Boys) / LOVE OF THE COMMON MAN (from West Side Story?) / MOST LIKELY TO GO YOUR WAY (Bob Dylan) / TIN SOLDIER (Small Faces) / STRAWBERRY FIELDS FOREVER + RAIN (Beatles) / IF SIX WAS NINE (Jimi Hendrix) / HAPPENINGS TEN YEARS TIME AGO (Yardbirds) / etc? • **Trivia:** In 1983, TODD co-wrote the Top 20 hit 'KISSING WITH CONFIDENCE' for WILL POWERS (see under Carly SIMON). TODD's others major productions have included GRAND FUNK (1973) / HALL & OATES (1974) / TOM ROBINSON (1978) / TUBES (1979) / PSYCHEDELIC FURS (1982) / etc. Note:- TODD has just released in 1992 a compilation album of his production work.

Recommended: SOMETHING – ANYTHING (*9) / INITIATION (*8) / THE COLLECTION (UTOPIA; *7) / THE EVER POPULAR TORTURED ARTIST (*7) / ANTHOLOGY (*8) / RA (*7)

NAZZ

TODD RUNDGREN – lead guitar, vocals, composer / **ROBERT 'Stewkey' ANTONI** (b.17 Nov'47, Rhode Island, N.Y.) – vocals, piano / **CARSTEN VAN OSTEN** (b.24 Sep'46, New Jersey) – bass, vocals / **THOM MOONEY** (b. 5 Jan'48, Pennsylvania) – drums

Screen Gems | Screen Gems

Sep 68. (7") *(SGC 219 001)* <001> **HELLO IT'S ME. / OPEN MY EYES** [ ] [66]

Apr 69. (lp) *(SGC 221 001)* <SD 5001> **NAZZ** [ ] [ ] Oct68
– Open my eyes / See what you can be / Back of your mind / Hello it's me / Wildwood blues / If that's the way you feel / When I get my plane / The lemming song / Crowded / She's goin' down. *<US re-iss.Oct83 on 'Rhino'; >*

Apr 69. (7") *(SGC 219 002)* <002> **HELLO IT'S ME. / CROWDED** [-] [-]

May 69. (lp,red-lp) *<SD 5002>* **NAZZ NAZZ** [-] [80]
– Forget all about it / Not wrong long / Rain rider / Gonna cry today / Meridian Leeward / Under the ice / Hang on Paul / Kiddie boy / Featherbedding lover / Letters don't count / A beautiful song. *<US re-iss.Oct83 on 'Rhino'; RNLP 109>*

May 69. (7") *(SGC 219 003)* <006> **NOT WRONG LONG. / UNDER THE ICE** [ ] [ ]

Nov 70. (7") *<009>* **SOME PEOPLE. / MAGIC ME** [-] [ ]

Dec 70. (lp,green-lp) *<SD 5003>* **NAZZ III** [-] [ ]
– Some people / Only one winner / Kicks / It's not that easy / Old time lovemaking / Magic me / Loosen up / Take the hand / How can you call that beautiful / Plenty of lovin' / Christopher Colombus / You are my window. *<US re-iss.Nov83 on 'Rhino'; RNLP 111>*

— Had already disbanded early 1970, after completion of III'rd album.

RUNT

was formed by **RUNDGREN** now on – lead vocals, guitar / **TONY SALES** – bass / **HUNT SALES** – drums

not issued | Ampex

Nov 70. (7") *<31001>* **WE GOTTA GET YOU A WOMAN. / BABY LET'S SWING** [-] [20]

Dec 70. (lp) *<10105>* **RUNT** [-] [ ]
– Broke down and busted / Believe in me / We gotta get you a woman / Who's that man / Once burned / Devil's bite / I'm in the cliche / There are no words / Baby let's swing / The last thing you said / Don't tie my hands / Birthday carol. *(UK-iss.Apr72 on 'Bearsville'; K 44505) <US re-iss.Oct87 on 'Rhino'; > (cd-iss.May93 on 'Rhino-Bearsville'; 812270686-2)*

— **N.D.SMART** – drums repl. HUNT who later joined IGGY POP then TIN MACHINE

May 71. (7") *<31002>* **BE NICE TO ME. / BROKE DOWN AND BUSTED** [-] [71]

May 71. (lp) *<10116>* **THE BALLAD OF TODD RUNDGREN** [-] [ ]
– Long flowing robe / The ballad / Bleeding / Wailing wall / The range war / Chain letter / A long time, a long way to go / Boat on the Charles / Be nice to me / Hope I'm around / Parole / Remember me. *(UK-iss.Apr72 on 'Bearsville'; K 45506) <US re-iss.Oct87 on 'Rhino'; > (cd-iss.May93 on 'Rhino-Bearsville'; 812271109-2)*

Aug 71. (7") *<31004>* **A LONG TIME, A LONG WAY TO GO. / PAROLE** [-] [92]

TODD RUNDGREN

now completely solo except for one side of the d-lp which was frequented by session people.

Bearsville | Bearsville

Mar 72. (d-lp) *(K 65501)* <2066> **SOMETHING / ANYTHING** [ ] [29]
– I saw the light / It wouldn't have made any difference / Wolfman Jack / Cold morning light / It takes two to tango (this is for the girls) / Sweeter memories / (intro) Breathless / The night the carousel burned down / Saving grace / Marlene / Song of the Viking / I went to the mirror / Black Maria / One more day (one word) / Couldn't I just tell you / Torch song / Little red lights / Dust in the wind / Piss Aaron / Hello it's me / Some folks is even whiter than me / You left me sore / Slut. *<US re-iss.Nov87 on 'Rhino'; > (re-iss.Jul89 on 'Essential' d-lp/c/cd; ESD LP/MC/CD 007) (re-iss.Jun93 on 'Rhino-Bearsville'; 812271107-2)*

Mar 72. (7") *<0003>* **I SAW THE LIGHT. / BLACK MARIA** [-] [16]

Mar 72. (7") *(K 15502)* **I SAW THE LIGHT. / MARLENE** [ ] [-]

Jul 72. (7") *<0007>* **COULDN'T I JUST TELL YOU. / WOLFMAN JACK** [-] [93]

May 73. (7"m) *(K 15506)* **I SAW THE LIGHT. / BLACK MARIA / LONG FLOWING ROBE** [36] [-]
(re-iss.Nov76)

Jun 73. (lp) *(K 45513)* <213> **A WIZARD, A TRUE STAR** [ ] [86]
– International feel / Never never land / Tic tic tic it wear off / You need your head / Rock and roll pussy / Dogfight giggle / You don't have to camp around / Flamingo / Zen archer / Just another onionhead – Da da Dali / When the shit hits the fan – Sunset Blvd. / Le feel internacionale / Sometimes I don't know what to feel / Does anybody love you? / I'm so proud – Ooh ooh baby – La la means I love you – Cool jerk / Is it my name? / Just one victory. *(re-iss.Nov80 on 'Island'; IRSP 10) (re-iss.Apr89 on 'Castle' lp/c/cd; CLA LP/MC/CD 134) (re-iss.May93 on 'Rhino-Bearsville' cd; 812270864-2)*

Oct 73. (7") *(K 15509)* **WE GOTTA GET YOU A WOMAN. / COULDN'T I JUST TELL YOU** [ ] [-]

Dec 73. (7") *(K 15513)* <0009> **HELLO IT'S ME. / COLD MORNING LIGHT** [ ] [5] Sep73

Dec 73. (7") *<0015>* **SOMETIMES I DON'T KNOW WHAT TO FEEL. / DOES ANYONE LOVE YOU?** [-] [ ]

— He now used many musicians that were to appear as first UTOPIA incarnation

Mar 74. (d-lp) *(K 85501)* <6952> **TODD** [ ] [54]
– How about a little fanfare? / I think you know / The spark of life / An elpee's worth of toons / A dream goes on forever / Lord Chancelor's nightmare song / Drunken blue rooster / The last ride / Everybody's going to Heaven / King Kong reggae / Number one lowest common denominator / Useless begging / Sidewalk cafe / Izzat love / Heavy metal kids / In and out of Chakras we go / Don't you ever learn / Sons of 1984. *(re-iss.Dec89 on 'Castle' d-lp/c/cd; CLD LP/MC/CD 177) (re-iss.May93 on 'Rhino-Bearsville' cd; 812271108-2)*

May 74. (7") *(K 15515)* <0020> **A DREAM GOES ON FOREVER. / HEAVY METAL KIDS** [ ] [69]

— **TODD** formed UTOPIA with **MOODY KLINGMAN** – keyboards / **RALPH SHUCKETT** – bass / **JOHN SIEGLER** – bass, cello / **M.FROG LABAT** – synthesizers (TODD also released solo material)

Nov 74. (lp; by TODD RUNDGREN'S UTOPIA) *(K 55501)* <6954> **TODD RUNDGREN'S UTOPIA** [ ] [34]
– Utopia (theme) / Freak parade / Freedom fighter / The ikon. *(re-iss.cd May93 on 'Rhino-Bearsville'; 812270865-2)*

Feb 75. (7"; by TODD RUNDGREN) *(K 15519)* <0301> **WOLFMAN JACK. / BREATHLESS** [ ] [ ] 1974

Jun 75. (lp; by TODD RUNDGREN) *(K 55504)* <6981> **INITIATION** [ ] [86]
– Real man / Born to synthesize / The death of rock and roll / Eastern intrigue / Initiation / Fair warning / A treatise on cosmic fire (intro- Prana): (a) The fire of mind or solar fire – (b) The fire of spirit or electric fire – (c) The internal fire or fire by friction / (outro- Prana). *(cd-iss.May93 on 'Rhino-Bearsville'; 812270866-2)*

Sep 75. (7"; by TODD RUNDGREN) *(K 15521)* <0304> **REAL MAN. / PRANA** [ ] [83]

— trimmed slightly when LABAT departed.

Oct 75. (lp; as TODD RUNDGREN'S UTOPIA) *(K 55508)* <6961> **ANOTHER LIVE (live)** [ ] [66]
– Another life / The wheel / The seven rays / (intro) – Mister Triscuts / West Side Story theme / Something's coming / Just one victory / Heavy metal kids / Do ya / Just one victory. *(cd-iss.Aug93 on 'Rhino-Bearsville'; 812270867-2)*

TODD RUNDGREN

Apr 76. (lp) *(K 55510)* <6963> **FAITHFUL** [ ] [54]
– Happenings ten years time ago / Good vibrations / Rain / Most likely you go your way and I'll go mine / If six was nine / Strawberry fields forever / Black and white / Love of the common man / When I pray / Cliche / The verb "to love" / Boogies (hamburger hell). *(cd-iss.Jun93 on 'Rhino-Bearsville'; 812270868-2)*

Jun 76. (7") *<0309>* **GOOD VIBRATIONS. / WHEN I PRAY** [-] [34]

Jun 76. (7") *(K 15524)* **LOVE OF THE COMMON MAN. / GOOD VIBRATIONS** [ ] [-]

Nov 76. (7") *<0310>* **LOVE OF THE COMMON MAN. / BLACK AND WHITE** [-] [ ]

UTOPIA

with **TODD** now completely changed line-up into **ROGER POWELL** – keyboards (from late '75) / **JOHN 'Willie' WILCOX** – drums / **KASIM SULTON** – bass

Jan 77. (lp) *(K 55514)* <6965> **RA** [27] [79]
– (overture) / Communion with the sun / Magic dragon theatre / Jealousy / Eternal love / Sunburst finish / Hiroshima / Singing and the glass guitar. *(cd-iss.May93 on 'Rhino-Bearsville'; 812270869-2)*

Feb 77. (7") *(K 15531)* <0317> **COMMUNION WITH THE SUN. / SUNBURST FINISH** [ ] [ ]

— TODD played/produced 'BAT OUT OF HELL' album for MEAT LOAF, which included some UTOPIANS and was massive seller from 1978 onwards.

Sep 77. (lp) *(K 55517)* <6970> **OOPS! WRONG PLANET** [59] [73]
– Trapped / Windows / Love in action / Crazy lady blue / Back on the street / Marriage of Heaven and Hell / The martyr / Abandon city / Gangrene / My angel / Rape of the young / Love is the answer. *(cd-iss.Jun93 on 'Rhino-Bearsville'; 812270870-2)*

Oct 77. (7") *(K 15536)* <0321> **LOVE IS THE ANSWER. / THE MARRIAGE OF HEAVEN AND HELL** [ ] [ ]

TODD RUNDGREN

Apr 78. (lp) *(K 55521)* <6981> **HERMIT OF MINK HOLLOW** [42] [36]
– All the children sing / Can we still be friends / Hurting for you / Too far gone / Onomatopoeia / Determination / Bread / Bag lady / You cried wolf / Lucky guy / Out of control / Fade away. *(cd-iss.May93 on 'Rhino-Bearsville'; 812270784-2)*

May 78. (7") *(K 15539)* <0324> **CAN WE STILL BE FRIENDS. / DETERMINATION** [ ] [29]
<some US copies had 'OUT OF CONTROL' on B-side>

Jul 78. (7") *<0330>* **YOU CRIED WOLF. / ONOMATOPOEIA** [-] [ ]

Nov 78. (7") *(K 15543)* **ALL THE CHILDREN SING. / BAG LADY** [ ] [-]

Dec 78. (d-lp) *(K 65511)* <6986> **BACK TO THE BARS (live)** [ ] [75]
– Real man / Love of the common man / The verb "to love" / Love in action / A dream goes on forever / Sometimes I just don't know what to think / The range war / Black and white / The last ride / Cliche / Don't you ever learn / Never never land / Black Maria / Zen archer / Medley: I'm so proud – Ooh ooh baby – La la means I love you / I saw the light / It wouldn't have made any difference / Eastern intrigue / Initiation / Couldn't I just tell you / Hello it's me. *(cd-iss.Jun93 on 'Rhino-Bearsville'; 812271109-2)*

Feb 79. (7") *<0335>* **IT WOULDN'T HAVE MADE ANY DIFFERENCE. / DON'T YOU EVER LEARN** [-] [ ]

UTOPIA

Island Bearsville

Jan 80. (lp/c) *(ILPS/ZCI 9602) <6991>* **ADVENTURES IN UTOPIA** [57] [32]
– The road to Utopia / You make me crazy / Second nature / Set me free / Caravan / Last of the new wave riders / Shot in the dark / The very last time / Love alone / Rock love. *(cd-iss.May93 on 'Rhino-Bearsville'; 812270872-2)*

Mar 80. (7") *(WIP 6581) <49180>* **SET ME FREE. / UMBRELLA MAN** [ ] [27]

May 80. (7") *<49247>* **THE VERY LAST TIME. / LOVE ALONE** [-] [76]

Oct 80. (lp) *(ILPS 9642) <3487>* **DEFACE THE MUSIC** [ ] [65]
– I just want to touch you / Crystal ball / Where does the world go to hide / Silly boy / Alone / That's not right / Take it home / Hoi poloi / Life goes on / Feel too good / Always late / All smiles / Everybody else is wrong. *(cd-iss.May93 on 'Rhino-Bearsville'; 812270873-2)*

Oct 80. (7") *<49545>* **SECOND NATURE. / YOU MAKE ME CRAZY** [-] [ ]

Nov 80. (7"ep) *(IEP 12)* **I JUST WANT TO TOUCH YOU EP** [ ] [-]
– I just want to touch you / Silly boy / Life goes on / All smiles.

Dec 80. (7") *<49579>* **I JUST WANT TO TOUCH YOU. / ALWAYS LATE** [-] [ ]

TODD RUNDGREN

Feb 81. (7") *<49696>* **TIME HEALS. / TINY DEMONS** [-] [ ]

Feb 81. (lp) *(ILPS 9567) <3522>* **HEALING** [ ] [48]
– Healer / Pulse / Flesh / Golden goose / Compassion / Shine / Healing (part 1, 2 & 3). *(free-7"ltd.w.a.)–* TIME HEALS. / TINY DEMONS *(re-iss.Dec81 on 'Avatar' lp/c; AALP/BHS 3522) (cd-iss.May93 on 'Rhino-Bearsville'; 812270874-2)*

Jan 82. (7") *<49771>* **COMPASSION. / HEALING** [-] [ ]

UTOPIA

Avatar Bearsville

Mar 82. (lp) *(BRK <3666>)* **SWING TO THE RIGHT** [ ] [ ]
– Swing to the right / Lysistrata / The up / Junk rock (million monkeys) / Shinola / For the love of money / Last dollar on Earth / Fahrenheit 451 / Only human / One world. *(cd-iss.Mar93 on 'Rhino-Bearsville'; 812270785-2)*

Apr 82. (7") *<50062>* **ONE WORLD. / SPECIAL INTEREST** [-] [ ]

May 82. (7") *(AAA 126)* **ONE WORLD. / JUNK ROCK (MILLION MONKEYS)** [ ] [-]

Jun 82. (7") *<29947>* **LYSISTRATA / JUNK ROCK (MILLION MONKEYS)** [-] [ ]

Nov 82. (7"ep) *(AVAB 1)* **TIME HEALS / TINY DEMONS / I SAW THE LIGHT / CAN WE STILL BE FRIENDS** [ ] [-]

Epic Network

Nov 82. (7") *(EPCA 2972) <69859>* **FEET DON'T FAIL ME NOW. / FORGOTTEN BUT NOT GONE** [ ] [82]

Nov 82. (lp/c) *(EPC/40 25207) <60183>* **UTOPIA** [ ] [84]
– Libertine / Bad little actress / Feet don't fail me now / Neck on up / Say yeah / Call it what you will / I'm looking at you but I'm talking to myself / Hammer in the heart / Burn three times / There goes my inspiration. *(w/ free UK+US m-lp)–* Princess of the universe / Infrared and ultraviolet / Forgotten but not gone / Private Heaven / Chapter and verse. *(cd-iss.Aug93 on 'Rhino-Bearsville'; 812270713-2)*

Jan 83. (7") *<69859>* **HAMMER IN MY HEART. / I'M LOOKING AT YOU BUT I'M TALKING TO MYSELF** [-] [ ]

TODD RUNDGREN

Lamborghini Bearsville

Mar 83. (7") *<29686>* **BANG THE DRUM ALL DAY. / CHANT** [-] [63]

Aug 83. (lp/c) *(LMGLP/ZCLMG 2000) <23732>* **THE EVER POPULAR TORTURED ARTIST EFFECT** [ ] [66] Feb83
– Hideaway / Influenza / Don't hurt yourself / There goes my baybay / Tin soldier / Emperor of the highway / Bang the drum all day / Drive / Chant. *(cd-iss.Jun93 on 'Rhino-Bearsville'; 812270876-2)*

Aug 83. (7") *(LMG 1)* **BANG THE DRUM ALL DAY. / DRIVE** [ ] [-]

Sep 83. (7") *<29759>* **HIDEAWAY. / EMPEROR OF THE HIGHWAY** [-] [ ]

UTOPIA

W.E.A. Passport

Apr 84. (lp/c) *(WX 4/+C) <6029>* **OBLIVION** [ ] [74]
– Itch in my brain / Love with a thinker / Bring me my longbow / If I didn't try / Too much water / Maybe I could change / Crybaby / Welcome to my revolution / Winston Smith takes it on the jaw / I will wait.

May 84. (7") *(YZ 5) <7923>* **CRYBABY. / WINSTON SMITH TAKES IT ON THE JAW** [ ] [ ]

Jul 84. (7") *(YZ 11)* **LOVE WITH A THINKER. / WELCOME TO MY REVOLUTION** [ ] [-]

Food For Thought Passport

Jun 85. (lp/c) *(GRUB 5) <6044>* **POV** [ ] [ ] May 85
– Play this game / Style / Stand for something / Secret society / Zen machine / Mated / Wildlife / Mimi gets mad / Mystified / More light.

Jun 85. (7") *(YUM 107)* **MATED. / MAN OF ACTION** [ ] [-]

Jun 85. (7") *<7927>* **MATED. / STAND FOR SOMETHING** [-] [ ]

— (Oct85) TODD is credited on duet with BONNIE TYLER on single 'LOVING YOU IS A DIRTY JOB'.

TODD RUNDGREN

Warners Warners

Oct 85. (7") *(W 8852) <28821>* **SOMETHING TO FALL BACK ON. / LOCKJAW** [ ] [ ]
(12"+=) *(WT 8862)* – ('A'dance mix).

Nov 85. (lp/c) *(925128-1/-4) <25128>* **A CAPPELLA** [ ] [ ]
– Blue Orpheus / Johnee Jingo / Pretending to care / Hodja / Lost horizon / Something to fall back on / Miracle in the bazaar / Lockjaw / Honest work / Mighty love.

— Early in 1986, UTOPIA split and ROGER POWELL went solo. TODD returned to solo work in 1988 augmented by **ROSS VALORY** – bass (ex-JOURNEY) / **PRAIRIE PRINCE** – drums (ex-TUBES) (same label)

May 89. (lp/c/cd) *(K 92588-1/-4/-2) <25881>* **NEARLY HUMAN** [ ] [ ]
– The want of a nail / The waiting game / Parallel lines / Can't stop running / Unloved children / Fidelity / Feel it / Hawking / I love my life. *(cd+=)–* Two little Hitlers.

May 89. (7") *<22868>* **PARALLEL LINES. / I LOVE MY LIFE** [-] [ ]

Feb 91. (cd/c/lp) *(7599-26478-2/-4/-1) <26478>* **SECOND WIND** [ ] [ ]
– Change myself / Love science / Who's sorry now / The smell of money / If I have to be alone / Love in disguise / Kindness / Public servant / Goya's eyes / Second wind.

Jun 93. (cd/c) *<(8122-71185-2/-4)>* **REDUX '92: LIVE IN JAPAN (Utopia live)** [ ] [ ]
– Fix your gaze / Zen machine / Trapped / Princess of the universe / Abandon city / Hammer in my heart / Swing to the right / Ikon / Hiroshima / Back on the street / Only human / Love in action / Caravan / Last of the new wave riders / One world / Love is the answer.

Food For Thought Warners

Sep 94. (d-cd/d-c) *(CD/C+/GRUB 30)* **NEW WORLD ORDER / LITE** [ ] [ ]
– Worldwide epiphany / New world order / Worldwide epiphany / Day job / Property / Fascist Christ / Love thing / Time stood still / Proactivity / No world order / World epiphany / Time stood still / Love thing / Time stood still / World made flesh / Fever broke. *(d-cd+=)–* (10 different versions of above).

– compilations, etc. –

1984. (lp; by NAZZ) *Rhino; <RNLP 116>* **THE BEST OF NAZZ** [-] [ ]

Nov 87. (lp/c/cd; UTOPIA) *Passport; <PB/+C/CD 6053>* **TRIVIA** [-] [ ]

Feb 88. (d-lp/c/cd; by TODD RUNDGREN) *Raw Power; (RAW LP/TC/CD 035)* **ANTHOLOGY** [ ] [ ] 1989
– Can we still be friends / All the children sing / Too far gone / Sweet memories / It wouldn't have made any difference / Hello it's me / I saw the light / Just one victory / Love of the common man / The verb 'to love' / Sometimes I don't know what to feel / Couldn't I just tell you / Tiny demons / Initiation / Real man / A long time a long way to go / Long flowing robe / Compassion / We gotta get you a woman / A dream goes on forever / The last ride / Don't you ever learn / Bang the drum all day / Zen archer.

Mar 88. (d-lp/d-c/d-cd; by RUNT /+/ TODD RUNDGREN) *That's Original; (TFO LP/MC/CD 3)* **RUNT / HERMIT OF MINK HOLLOW** [ ] [-]

Mar 88. (d-lp/d-c/d-cd; by UTOPIA) *That's Original; (TFO LP/MC/CD 9)* **OOPS! SORRY WRONG PLANET / ADVENTURES IN UTOPIA** [ ] [-]

Jun 88. (d-lp/d-c/d-cd; by UTOPIA) *Castle; (CCS LP/MC/CD 181)* **THE UTOPIA COLLECTION** [ ] [-]
– Where does the world go to hide / Freedom fighters / All smiles / Lysistrata / Always late / Love in action / Rock love / Set me free / The seven rays / Traped / Swing to the right / One world / Heavy metal kids / The very last time / Crazy lady blue / Feel too good / Love alone / Love is the answer.

Sep 88. (cd-ep) *Special Edition; (CD 3-6)* **BANG THE DRUM ALL DAY / I SAW THE LIGHT / CAN WE STILL BE FRIENDS / ALL THE CHILDREN SING** [ ] [-]

Oct 88. (7") *Old Gold; (OG)* **I SAW THE LIGHT. / (other artist)** [ ] [-]

1989. (d-lp; by TODD RUNDGREN) *Rhino; <R1 71491>* **ANTHOLOGY (1968-1985)** [-] [ ]
(UK-iss.d-cd Aug93 on 'Rhino-Bearsville';)

Apr 92. (cd) *Rhino; <R2>* **AN ELPEE'S WORTH OF PRODUCTIONS** (various) [ ] [-]

May 95. (cd; by UTOPIA) *Rhino;* **ANTHOLOGY** [ ] [-]

RUPERT'S PEOPLE

Formed: London, England . . . Spring 1967 by producer/manager FRANK FENTER, who wanted a sideline to his FLEUR DE LYS group. With guitarist/friend ROD LYNTON, he wrote 'HOLD ON', which was intended for FENTER's South African protege, SHARON TANDY. LYNTON wrote its eventual PROCOL HARUM-inspired psychedelic A-side, 'REFLECTIONS OF CHARLES BROWN', which became a hit all over Europe but not in Britain. The line-up at this time was; vocalist CHRIS ANDREWS, ADRIAN CURTIS, TONY DANGERFIELD, JOHN BANKS and session man PETE SOLLEY, although they all departed when the singer said he disliked the song (now a collector's piece). LYNTON then formed a new RUPERT'S PEOPLE with an entirely different personnel that consisted of DAI JENKINS, RAY BEVERLEY, STEVE BRINDELL, JOHN TOUT and ROD LYNTON. Two 45's followed, although they were of the bubblegum psychedelic variety, the second of which leant on The BEATLES too much.

Recommended: the debut single.

CHRIS ANDREWS – vocals / **ADRIAN CURTIS** – guitar / **TONY DANGERFIELD** – bass / **JOHN BANKS** – drums / guest **PETE SOLLEY** – organ

Columbia not issued

Jul 67. (7") *(DB 8226)* **REFLECTIONS OF CHARLES BROWN. / HOLD ON** [ ] [-]

— the quartet returned to various session work, ADRIAN joined GUN

— new line-up; **ROD LYNTON** – lead guitar, vocals / **DAI JENKINS** – guitar, vocals / **RAY BEVERLEY** – bass, vocals / **JOHN TOUT** – keyboards / **STEVE BRENDELL** – drums

Oct 67. (7") *(DB 8278)* **A PROLOGUE TO A MAGIC WORLD. / DREAM IN MY MIND** [ ] [-]

Mar 68. (7") *(DB 8362)* **I CAN SHOW YOU. / I'VE GOT THE LOVE** [ ] [-]

— split soon after above. TOUT was later to resurface in RENAISSANCE

Mike RUTHERFORD (see under ⇒ GENESIS)

Mitch RYDER

Born: WILLIAM LEVISE JR., 26 Feb'45, Hamtramck, Michigan, USA. In 1963, after leaving local group The PEPS, he formed BILLY LEE & THE RIVIERAS who recorded two singles for local labels, becoming MITCH RYDER & THE DETROIT WHEELS in 1965. On the recommendation of DJ, Dave Prince, they were signed by producer Bob Crewe to his 'New Voice' label. Their second 45, 'JENNY TAKES A RIDE!' (a medley of oldies 'C. C. Rider' & 'Jenny Jenny'), scraped into the US Top 10, and was the first of a string of hits up to 1968. His old blue-eyed soul/R&B style (modelled on JAMES BROWN) was subsequently replaced after he formed DETROIT, a metal-heavy/blues act who produced one eponymous album in 1971. He left the outfit after alleged in-fights, re-emerging some time later with the album, HOW I SPENT MY VACATION' (1978). Early in 1984, he returned to the singles chart with, 'WHEN YOU WERE MINE', SPRINGSTEEN now using some of his repertoire on his stage shows. RYDER is still going strong in the 90's, his most recent work being, 'RITE OF PASSAGE' (1994). • **Songwriters:** Mainly revivals of 50's rock'n'roll medleys; LITTLE LATIN LUPE LU (Righteous Brothers) / JENNY JENNY (Little Richard) / DEVIL WITH THE BLUE DRESS ON (Shorty Long) / C. C. RIDER (Chuck Willis) / THREE LITTLE FISHES (hit; Kay Lyser) / WHAT NOW MY LOVE (Gilbert Becaud) / YOU ARE MY SUNSHINE (Jimmie Davis) / WHEN YOU WERE MINE (Prince) / etc, etc. • **Trivia:** Took the name MITCH RYDER, from a phone directory. His 1983 album for 'Riva' was produced by JOHN COUGAR MELLENCAMP.

Recommended: REV UP – THE BEST OF MITCH RYDER (*6) / NEVER KICK A SLEEPING DOG (*6)

BILLY LEE & THE RIVIERAS

MITCH RYDER – vocals / with **JIM McCARTY** (b.1947) – guitar / **JOE KUBERT** – guitar / **EARL ELLIOTT** (b.1947) – bass / **JOHN "BEE" BADANJEK** (b.1948) – drums

not issued | Carrie

1962. (7") **FOOL FOR YOU. / THAT'S THE WAY IT'S GONNA BE** [–] [ ]

not issued | Hyland

1964. (7") **WON'T YOU DANCE WITH ME. / YOU KNOW** [–] [ ]

MITCH RYDER & THE DETROIT WHEELS

Stateside | New Voice

Jun 65. (7") <801> **I NEED YOU. / I HOPE** [–] [ ]

Jan 66. (7") (SS 481) <806> **JENNY TAKES A RIDE! / BABY JANE** [33] [10] Nov65

Apr 66. (7") (SS 498) <808> **LITTLE LATIN LUPE LU. / I HOPE** [48] [17] Feb66

May 66. (lp; stereo/mono) *(SSL/SL 10178)* <2000> **TAKE A RIDE** [ ] [78] Feb66
– Jenny take a ride! / Come see about me / I'll go crazy / Please, please, please / Shake a tail feather / Let your lovelight shine / I hope / Just a little bit / Sticks and stones / Bring it on home to me / Baby Jane (Mo-Mo Jane) / I got you. *(cd-iss.Jan94 on 'Sundazed'; CDSC 6007)*

Jun 66. (7") (SS 521) <811> **BREAKOUT. / I NEED HELP** [ ] [62] May66

Jul 66. (7") <814> **TAKIN' ALL I CAN GET. / YOU GET YOUR KICKS** [–] [100]

Oct 66. (7") (SS 549) <817> **DEVIL WITH A BLUE DRESS ON – GOOD GOLLY MISS MOLLY (medley). / I HAD IT MADE** [ ] [4]

Dec 66. (lp; stereo/mono) *(SSL/SL 10189)* <2002> **BREAKOUT . . . !!!** [ ] [23] Aug66
– Little Latin Lupe Lu / Breakout / In the midnight hour / Walking the dog / I had it made / So papa do / I like it like that / You got your kicks / Shakin' with Linda / Stubborn kind of fellow / Any day now / I need help. *(cd-iss.Jan94 on 'Sundazed'; CDSC 6008)*

— **JIM McCALLISTER** – bass repl. ELLIOTT who was drafted

Feb 67. (7") (SS 596) <820> **SOCK IT TO ME – BABY!. / I NEVER HAD IT BETTER** [ ] [6]

Apr 67. (7") (SS 2023) <822> **TOO MANY FISH IN THE SEA – THREE LITTLE FISHES (medley). / ONE GRAIN OF SAND** [ ] [24]

Apr 67. (lp; stereo/mono) *(SSL/SL 10204)* <2003> **SOCK IT TO ME!** [ ] [34]
– Sock it to me baby! / I can't hide it / Takin' all I can get / Slow fizz / Walk on by / Devil with the blue dress on / Good golly Miss Molly / I never had it better / Shakedown / A face in the crowd / I'd rather go to jail / Wild child. *(US cd-iss.Jan94 on 'Sundazed'; CDSC 6009)*– (with extra 3 tracks).

MITCH RYDER

solo, groomed for the Las Vegas cabaret circuit.

Jun 67. (7") (SS 2037) <824> **JOY. / I'D RATHER GO TO JAIL** [ ] [41]

Stateside | Dyno Voice

Sep 67. (7") (SS 2063) <901> **WHAT NOW MY LOVE. / BLESSING IN DISGUISE** [ ] [30]

Nov 67. (lp; stereo/mono) *(SSL/SL 10229)* <31901> **WHAT NOW MY LOVE** [ ] [ ]
– Let it be me / I make a fool of myself / Born to lose / If you go away / What now my love / Whole lotta shakin' goin' on / Sally go round the roses / Brown-eyed handsome man / I need lovin' you / That's it . . . I quit..

Jan 68. (7") (SS 2096) <905> **(YOU'VE GOT) PERSONALITY – CHANTILLY LACE (medley). / I MAKE A FOOL OF MYSELF** [ ] [87]

1968. (7") <916> **I NEED YOUR LOVIN'. / THE LIGHTS OF NIGHT** [–] [ ]

1968. (7") <934> **RING YOUR BELL. / BABY I NEED YOUR LOVIN' – THEME FOR MITCH** [–] [ ]

— now backed by BOOKER T & THE MG'S

not issued | Dot

1969. (lp) <25963> **THE DETROIT – MEMPHIS EXPERIMENT** [–] [ ]
– Liberty / Eenie meenie minie moe / Boredom / Push aroun' / Sugar bee / I get hot / I believe / Direct me / Long, long time / Raise your hand / Wear and tear on my heart / Meat. *(cd-iss.Aug91 on 'Repertoire'; REP 4117WZ)*

1969. (7") <17290> **SUGAR BEE. / I BELIEVE (THERE MUST BE SOMEONE) (WE THREE)** [–] [ ]

1969. (7") <17325> **DIRECT ME. / LONG, LONG TIME** [–] [ ]

DETROIT

RYDER with **JOHN BADANJEK** – drums / **BRETT TUGGLE** – guitar / **JIM McCARTY + STEVE HUNTER** – guitar / **HARRY PHILIPS** – keyboards / **W.R. COOKE** – bass / **DIRTY ED** – percussion

Paramount | Paramount

Nov 71. (7") <0051> **I CAN'T SEE NOBODY. / ?** [–] [ ]

Dec 71. (lp) *(SPFL 277)* <6010> **DETROIT** [ ] [ ]
– Long neck goose / Is it you (or is it me) / It ain't easy / Rock'n'roll / Let it rock / Drink / Box of old roses / I found a love. *(cd-iss.1988 +=;)*– Gimme shelter.

1972. (7") *(PARA 3022)* <0094> **IT AIN'T EASY. / LONG NECK GOOSE** [ ] [ ]

1972. (7") <0133> **ROCK 'N' ROLL. / BOX OF OLD ROSES** [ ] [ ]

1972. (7") <0158> **GIMME SHELTER. / OO LA LA LA DEE DA DOO** [–] [ ]

— In 1972, he retired from music business due to throat infection. BADANJEK + McCARTY later formed the ROCKETS.

MITCH RYDER

returned w/new backing band **RICHARD SCHEIN & WAYNE GABRIEL** – guitars / **BILLY CSERNITS** – keyboards / **MARK GOUGEON** – bass / **WILSON OWENS** – drums

Line | Seeds & Stems

1978. (lp) *(5002)* <7801> **HOW I SPENT MY VACATION** [–] [ ] German
– Tough kid / Dance ourselves to death / Passions wheel / Cherry poppin' / Freezin' in Hell / Nice'n'easy / The Jon / Falling forming / Poster.

— **JOE GUTC** – guitar repl. WAYNE

1979. (12"ep) *(3004)* **ROCK'N'ROLL LIVE (live)** [–] [–]
– Rock & roll / Soul kitchen.

1980. (lp) *(5046)* <7804> **NAKED BUT NOT DEAD** [–] [ ] German
– Ain't nobody white / Corporate song / War / Future looks brite / I got mine / Spitting lizard / True love / I don't wanna hear it / Hometown. *(cd-iss. 1992 w/1979 lp)*

1980. (7"ep) *(3013)* **WE'RE GONNA WIN** [–] [ ]

1981. (lp) *(5100)* **GOT CHANGE FOR A MILLION** [–] [–] German
– My heart belongs to me / Back at work / That's charm / Red scar eyes / Bang bang / Betty's too tight / Ich bin aus America / Bare your soul / We're gonna win.

1982. (d-lp) *(8001)* **LIVE TALKIES (live)** [–] [–] German
– It's all over now / Corporate song (it's not for me) / Bang bang / Subterranean homesick blues / Er ist nicht mein praesi dent / Take me to the river / Tough kid / Red scar eyes / Liberty / Ain't nobody white / Nice and easy / Long tall Sally / I'm gonna be a wheel someday. *(free 7"m)*– Wicked messenger / True love. *(cd-iss.1989; LICD 900413)*

— **AL WOTTON** – drums repl. OWENS.

Safari | not issued

Sep 82. (lp) **SMART ASS** [ ] [–]
– Hot house / You better stop / Try and must / Code dancing / Tape's rolling / One room world / Hands high / It keeps you alive / Berlin.

— now w/**LARRY CRANE + MIKE WANCHIC** – guitars / **KENNY ARONOFF** – drums / **MARK GOUGEON** – bass / **HARRY PHILLIPS** – organ

Towerbell | Riva

Oct 83. (lp/c) *(TOWLP/ZCTOW 5)* <7503> **NEVER KICK A SLEEPING DOG** [ ] [ ] Jul83
– B.I.G.T.I.M.E / When you were mine / A thrill is a thrill (w/ MARIANNE FAITHFULL) / Come again / Cry to me / The thrill of it all / Stand / Rue de Thahir / Code dancing. *(cd-iss. 1987 on 'Line')*

Nov 83. (7") *(TOW 44)* <213> **WHEN YOU WERE MINE. / COME AGAIN** [ ] [87] Jul83

1984. (7") **THE THRILL OF IT ALL. / ?** [–] [ ]

— **OWENS** returned to replace WOTTON

— **ROBERT GILLESPIE** – guitar repl. SCHEIN

Line | not issued

1986. (cd) *(LICD 900181)* **IN THE CHINA SHOP** [–] [–] German
– Where is the next one coming from? / Like a worm / Rock 'n' roll skin / All the way / Looks are deceiving / I'm not sad tonite / End of the line / Uncle Sam & the Russian bear / Young blood.

— **JOHN BADANJEK** – drums repl. OWENS

1988. (cd) *(LICD 900538)* **RED BLOOD & WHITE MINK (live)** [–] [–] German
– Little Latin Lupe Lu / Rock & roll / Heart of stone / Gimme shelter / War / Freezin' in hell / Bang bang / Red scar eyes / Where's the next one coming from? / I feel good / Bridge of sympathy / Big time / Ain't nobody white / Berlin.

— with **JOE GUTC + RAY GOODMAN** – guitar / **DENNIS "MOON" WEZALIS** – keyboards / **BARRY GEORGE** – bass / **DANNY McALEER** – drums

Apr 92. (cd) *(LICD 901180)* **LA GASH** [ ] [ ]
– It must be in her genes / Argyle / Do you feel alright? / Child of rage / Bye-bye love / Dr. Margaret Smith / It's your birthday / Arms without love / Correct me if I'm wrong / One thing / Almost bigamy / The terrorist. *(some w/ extra tracks)*; – Long neck goose / Devil with the blue dress on – Good golly Miss Molly.

Sep 94. (cd) *(901285)* **RITE OF PASSAGE** [ ] [ ]
– See her again / Sex you up / Actually 101 / It wasn't me / We are helpless / Into the blue / Mercy / Too sentimental / Let it shine / Hermasn's garden / I'm starting all over again / By the feel.

– compilations, others, etc. –

— below released on 'New Voice' unless stated otherwise

Oct 67. (7") <826> **YOU ARE MY SUNSHINE. / WILD CHILD** [–] [88]

Nov 67. (lp) <2004> **ALL MITCH RYDER HITS!** (solo + band) [–] [37]
– Devil with the blue dress on & Good golly Miss Molly / Jenny take a ride / Joy / Breakout / In the midnight hour / Sock it to me – baby! / Little Latin Lupe Lu / Takin' all I can get / Too many fish in the sea & Three little fishes / I'd rather go to jail / Shake a tail feather.

1967. (lp) *Bell; (1335)* **ALL TIME HEAVY HITS** [ ] [–]

1968. (7") <828> **COME SEE ABOUT ME. / A FACE IN THE CROWD** [–] [ ]

1968.	(7") *<830>* **RUBY BABY & PEACHES ON A CHERRY TREE. / YOU GET YOUR KICKS**	-	
1968.	(lp) *Crewe; <1335>* **SINGS THE HITS**	-	
1971.	(7") *Avco; (4550)* **JENNY TAKES A RIDE!. / I NEVER HAD IT BETTER**		
1972.	(lp) *Virgo; (15163)* **GREATEST HITS**	-	
Mar 75.	(7") *Disco D;* **YOU GET YOUR KICKS. / BREAKOUT**		-
Oct 80.	(7") *Classic Cuts;* **JENNY TAKE A RIDE. / (other artist?)**		-
Apr 83.	(10"lp/c) *P.R.T.; (DOW/ZCDOW 5)* **WHEELS OF STEEL**		-
Jan 90.	(cd/c/lp) *Roulette; (CD/TC+/ROU 5003)* **REV UP – THE BEST OF MITCH RYDER & THE DETROIT WHEELS**		-
	– Jenny take a ride / Little Latin lupe lu / Shakin' with Linda / I like it like that / I had it made / Breakout / Shake a tail feather / Devil with a blue dress on / Good golly Miss Molly / Sock it to me baby / Too many fish in the sea / Three little fishes / I'd rather go to jail / Ooh papa doo / I hope / I never had it better. (cd+=) – Takin' all I can get / You get your kicks / Sticks and stones / Baby Jane (Mo-Mo Jane) / Joy / Just a little bit.		
1990.	(cd) *Line;* **THE BEAUTIFUL TOULANG SUNSET**	-	
Mar 92.	(d-cd) *Line; (LICD 921192)* **HOW I SPENT MY VACATION / NAKED BUT NOT DEAD**		-
Nov 92.	(cd/c) *Connoisseur; (CSAP CD/MC 111)* **DOCUMENT SERIES PRESENTS MITCH RYDER & THE DETROIT WHEELS**		-
Mar 95.	(cd) *Rhino; <R2 71872>* **DEVIL WITH A BLUE DRESS ON**	-	
May 97.	(cd/lp; DETROIT & MYTCH RYDER) *Total Energy; (NER 3010 CD/LP)* **GET OUT THE VOTE**		-

SALVATION

Formed: San Francisco, USA . . . 1967 by AL LINDE and JOE TATE, former garbageman and cesspool worker respectively. They were joined by TEDDY STEWART and later ARTIE McLEAN and ATHUR RESNICK. With their psychedelic, live-in tour bus in tow and after completing a few concerts at the Golden Gate Park, they were offered a deal with 'ABC'. Their eponymous debut showed them in fine form, highlighting good-time songs 'WHAT DOES AN INDIAN LOOK LIKE?' and 'THE VILLAGE SHUCK' alongside the more breezily psychedelic, 'THINK TWICE', which should have been a hit. Another album appeared the following year (1969), featuring the more experimental 'SALVATION JAM', with brilliant keyboard-wizardry from RESNICK.

Recommended: SALVATION (*6) / GYPSY CARNIVAL CARAVAN (*7)

AL LINDE – vocals / **JOE TATE** – guitar / **ARTHUR RESNICK** – organ (ex-THIRD RAIL) / **ARTIE McLEAN** – bass / **TEDDY STEWART** – drums

U.A. / A.B.C.

1968. (7") *<11025>* **THINK TWICE. / LOVE COMES IN FUNNY PACKAGES** [-] [ ]

1969. (lp) *(UAS 29062) <S 623>* **SALVATION** [ ] [ ] 1968
– Think twice / The village shuck / Cinderella / She said yeah / What does an Indian look like? / etc.

Oct 69. (7") *(UP 35048)* **CINDERELLA. / THE VILLAGE SHUCK** [ ] [-]

— **RICK LEVIN** – drums; repl. STEWART

1969. (lp) *<S 653>* **GYPSY CARNIVAL CARAVAN** [-] [ ]
– Hollywood 1923 / Handles of care / Yuk yuk / In the evening / Salvation jam / Come on over here / What'll I do 42.

— disbanded after above

Ed SANDERS (see under ⇒ FUGS)

SANTANA

Formed: San Francisco, California, USA . . . October '66 as The SANTANA BLUES BAND, by Mexican-born CARLOS SANTANA. The guitarist's distinctly pure, fluid sound was backed by a constantly changing personnel over the years, though the best work was driven by the powerhouse rhythm section of drummer, MICHAEL SHRIEVE, and percussionist JOSE 'CHEPITO' AREAS. A compelling fusion of Latin stylings and psychedelic-tinged blues jamming, the band's early work has often been copied but rarely equalled. In 1968, the BLUES BAND part of the name was jettisoned and under the more effective moniker of SANTANA they played San Francisco's Fillmore West. Later the same year, CARLOS guested on the album, 'THE LIVE ADVENTURES OF AL KOOPER AND MIKE BLOOMFIELD' which brought him to the attention of 'Columbia' records. Following a show-stopping performance at The Woodstock Festival, their long-awaited eponymous debut album cracked the US Top 5 in late '69. The record, together with their next two follow-up albums, 'ABRAXAS' (1970) and 'SANTANA III' (1971), secured SANTANA's position as one of US rock's leading lights, the latter two sets hitting No.1 in America as well as spawning the hits 'BLACK MAGIC WOMAN', 'EVERYBODY'S EVERYTHING' and a dazzling, frenetic cover of TITO PUENTE's 'OYE COMO VA'. Following an indulgent live set featuring BUDDY MILES, SANTANA released 'CARAVANSERAI' in 1972, a transitional piece that signalled a tentative move away from blues towards the jazz-fusion that would come to characterise most of the band's later 70's output. Around this time CARLOS became a devotee of Indian guru, SRI CHIMNOY, recording the 'LOVE DEVOTION SURRENDER' (1973) album with the similarly converted JOHN McLAUGHLIN. A contemplative piece of ethereal jazz, it had a spiritual partner in the following year's 'ILLUMINATIONS', recorded with fellow CHIMNOY disciple and jazz composer ALICE COLTRANE. Meanwhile, the SANTANA band released 'WELCOME' (1973) and 'BORBOLETTA' (1974), which further explored complex jazz textures, although 1976's 'AMIGOS' returned to a more grounded Latin-rock sound. It was short-lived though, and late 70's albums such as 'MOONFLOWER' (1977) and 'INNER SECRETS' (1978) bordered on the snooze-worthy with their directionless experimentation. 'ZEBOP' (1981) began the new decade on a high note, a masterful set that spawned the US hit single, 'WINNING'. The 80's also saw a solo effort, 'HAVANNA MOON' (1983) and the grammy-award winning 'BLUES FOR SALVADOR' (1987) as well as a film score for 'La Bamba'. Following a deal with 'Polydor', SANTANA has continued his prolific output, releasing the 'BROTHERS' album in 1994, a collaboration with sibling JORGE. • **Songwriters:** CARLOS penned with group, except covers:- JIN-GO-LA-BA (Michael Babatunde Olatunji) / BLACK MAGIC WOMAN (Fleetwood Mac) / GYPSY WOMAN (Curtis Mayfield) / PEACE ON EARTH (Alice Coltrane) / STORMY (Classics IV) / SHE'S NOT THERE (Zombies) / WELL ALL RIGHT (Buddy Holly) / ONE CHAIN (Four Tops) / WINNING (Russ Ballard) / THIRD STONE FROM THE SUN (Jimi Hendrix) / WHO'S THAT LADY (Isley Brothers) / FULL MOON (Paola Rustichelli) / RIGHT ON (Marvin Gaye) / I'VE BEEN TO THE MOUNTAIN TOP (. . . King) / etc. • **Trivia:** In 1973, CARLOS married Urmila, a Sri Chimnoy devotee. He also became highly religious, changing his name to DEVADIP, which means 'The Light Of The Lamp Supreme'. In the mid-70's, Bill Graham took over the management of SANTANA. For lovers of anything SANTANA, his brother JORGE (in Latin-rock band MALO) had success in April '72 with an eponymous album, which hit US No.14. A single lifted from it, 'SALI VECITO', made No.18. MALO went on to release three more 'Warner Bros.' albums; DOS (1972) / EVOLUTION (1973) + ASCENSION (1974).

Recommended: SANTANA (*7) / ABRAXAS (*8) / SANTANA III (*6) / CARAVANSERAI (*8) / VIVA! SANTANA (*8)

CARLOS SANTANA (b.20 Jul'47, Autlan de Navarro, Mexico. Raised in Tijuana then San Francisco, USA) – lead guitar / **GREGG ROLIE** (b.17 Jun'47, Seattle, Washington) – keyboards, vocals / **DAVID BROWN** (b.15 Feb'47, New York) – bass repl. GUS RODRIGUES (in 1967) / **MIKE SHRIEVE** (b. 6 Jul'49, San Francisco) – drums repl. BOB LIVINGSTONE (in '67). He had repl. ROD HARPER / **JOSE CHEPITO AREAS** (b.25 Jul'46, Leon, Nicaragua) – percussion / **MIKE CARABELLO** (b.18 Nov'47, San Francisco) – congas repl. TOM FRAZER – guitar

C.B.S. / Columbia

Oct 69. (7") *(CBS 4593)* **PERSUASION. / SAVOR** [ ] [-]

Oct 69. (7") *<45010>* **JIN-GO-LA-BA. / PERSUASION** [-] [56]

Nov 69. (lp) *(CBS 63015) <9781>* **SANTANA** [26] [4] Sep69
– Waiting / Evil ways / Shades of time / Savor / Jin-go-la-ba / Persuasion / Treat / You just don't care / Soul sacrifice. *(re-iss.Mar70; CBS 63815)r (re-iss.Mar81 lp/c; CBS/40 32003) (cd-iss.May87; CD 63815) (re-iss.cd May92)*

Jan 70. (7") *<45069>* **EVIL WAYS. / WAITING** [-] [9]

Apr 70. (7") *(CBS 4940)* **EVIL WAYS. / JIN-GO-LA-BA** [ ] [-]

Nov 70. (lp) *(CBS 64087) <30130>* **ABRAXAS** [7] [1] Sep 70
– Singing winds, crying beasts / Black magic woman – Gypsy queen / Oyo como va / Incident at Neshabur / Se a cabo / Mother's daughter / Samba pa ti / Hope you're feeling better / El Nicoya. *(re-iss.Mar81 lp/c; CBS/40 32032) (cd-iss.Mar86; CD 64087) (re-iss.cd Mar91; CD 32032)*

Dec 70. (7") *(CBS 5325) <45270>* **BLACK MAGIC WOMAN. / HOPE YOU'RE FEELING BETTER** [ ] [4] Nov70

Mar 71. (7") *(CBS 7046) <45330>* **OYE COMO VA. / SAMBA PA TI** [ ] [13] Feb71

— added **NEAL SCHON** (b.27 Feb'54) – guitar / **COKE ESCOVEDO** (b. THOMAS ESCOVEDO, 30 Apr'41, Calif.) – percussion

Oct 71. (lp) *(CBS 69015) <30595>* **SANTANA III** [6] [1]
– Batuka / No one to depend on / Taboo / Toussaint l'overture / Everybody's everything / Guajira / Everything's coming our way / Jungle strut / Para los rumberos. *(re-iss.Mar82 lp/c; CBS/40 32058) (cd-iss.Mar87; CD 69015) (re-iss.Jun94 on 'Columbia' cd/c; 476830-2)*

Nov 71. (7") *(CBS 7546) <45472>* **EVERYBODY'S EVERYTHING. / GUAJIRA** [ ] [12] Oct71

Mar 72. (7") *(CBS 7842) <45552>* **NO ONE TO DEPEND ON. / TABOO** [ ] [36] Feb72

Jul 72. (lp; by CARLOS SANTANA & BUDDY MILES) *(CBS 65142) <31308>* **CARLOS SANTANA & BUDDY MILES! LIVE! (live)** [29] [8]
– Marbles / Lava / Evil ways / Faith interlude / Them changes / Free form funkafide filth. *(re-iss.Sep84 lp/c; CBS/40 32271)*

Oct 72. (7"; by CARLOS SANTANA & BUDDY MILES) *(CBS 8338) <45666>* **EVIL WAYS (live). / THEM CHANGES (live)** [ ] [84] Aug72

— **ARMANDO PERAZA** – percussion repl. CARABELLO and ESCOVEDO (latter died 30 Apr'85) / **TOM RUTLEY** – bass repl. BROWN

Nov 72. (lp) *(CBS 65299) <31610>* **CARAVANSERAI** [6] [8]
– Eternal caravan of reincarnation / Waves within / Look up (to see what's coming down) / Just in time to see the sun / Song of the wind / All the love of the universe / Future primitive / Stone flower / La fuente del ritmo / Every step of the way. *(re-iss.Nov81 lp/c; CBS/40 32060) (cd-iss.1988; CD 65299)*

Jan 73. (7") *<45753>* **LOOK UP (TO SEE WHAT'S COMING DOWN). / ALL THE LOVE OF THE UNIVERSE** [-] [ ]

Jul 73. (lp; by CARLOS DEVADIP SANTANA AND MAHAVISHNU JOHN McLAUGHLIN) *(CBS 69073) <32034>* **LOVE DEVOTION SURRENDER** [7] [14]
– A love supreme / Naima / The lie divine / Let us go into the house of the Lord / Meditation. *(re-iss.Oct92 & Jun94 on 'Columbia' cd/c; 982830-2/-4)*

— (above album featured below newcomers (**RAUCH + LEWIS**) + **PERAZA, JAN HAMMER** – keyboards / **BILLY COBHAM** – drums / **LARRY YOUNG** – keyboards)

— **CARLOS** retained **AREAS, PERAZA + SHRIEVE** and brought in newcomers **TOM COSTER** – keyboards, vocals repl. ROLIE who also formed JOURNEY / **RICHARD KERMODE** – keyboards repl. SCHON who also formed JOURNEY / **DOUG RAUCH** – bass repl. RUTLEY / added **LEON THOMAS** – vocals / **JAMES MINGO LEWIS** – congas

Nov 73. (lp) *(CBS 69040) <32445>* **WELCOME** [8] [25]
– Going home / Love, devotion and surrender / Samba de sausalito / When I look into your eyes / Yours is the light / Mother Africa / Light of life / Flame-sky / Welcome.

(re-iss.1984 lp/c; CBS/40 32194)

Nov 73. (7") *(CBS 1925) <45999>* **WHEN I LOOK INTO YOUR EYES. / SAMBA DE SAUSALITO** [ ] [ ]

Sep 74. (lp; by TURIYA ALICE COLTRANE & DEVADIP CARLOS SANTANA) *(CBS 69063) <32900>* **ILLUMINATIONS** [40] [79]
– Guru Sri Chimnoy aphorism / Angel of air – Angel of water / Bliss: The eternal now / Angel of sunlight / Illuminations. *(cd-iss.Mar96 on 'Columbia'; 483810-2)*

— above w/ **ALICE** – keyboards, etc.

— **GREG WALKER** – vocals + sessioners repl. KERMODE, LEWIS and THOMAS

Nov 74. (lp/c) *(CBS/40 69084) <33135>* **BORBOLETTA** [18] [20] Oct74
– Spring manifestations / Canto de los flores / Life is anew / Give and take / One with the Sun / Aspirations / Practice what you preach / Mirage / Here and now / Flor de canela / Promise of a fisherman / Borboletta. *(re-iss.Nov83 lp/c; CBS/40 32157) (re-iss.cd Nov93 on 'Sony Collectors';)*

Nov 74. (7") *(CBS 2829)* **PRACTICE WHAT YOU PREACH. / CANTO DE LOS FLORES** [ ] [-]

Jan 75. (7") *(CBS 3005) <10073>* **MIRAGE. / FLOR DE CANELA** [ ] [ ]

Mar 75. (7") *<10088>* **GIVE AND TAKE. / LIFE IS ANEW** [-] [ ]

— (Below triple album was issued initially in Japan 1973)

Dec 75. (t-lp) *(CBS 66325)* **LOTUS (live)** [ ] [ ]
– Meditation / Going home / A-1 funk / Every step of the way / Black magic woman – Gypsy queen / Oye como va / Yours is the light / Batuka / Xibaba (she-ba-ba) / Savor / Stone flower / (introduction) / Castillos de arena (pt.1) / Waiting / Se a cabo / Samba pa ti / Toussaint l'overture / Incident at Neshabur. *(re-iss.Dec90 d-cd/d-c; 467943-2/-4)*

— **LEON NDUGU CHANCLER** – drums repl. SHRIEVE and AREAS / **IVORY STONE** – bass repl. RAUCH

Mar 76. (7") *(CBS 4143) <10421>* **EUROPA. / TAKE ME WITH YOU** [ ] [ ] Nov76

Apr 76. (lp/c) *(CBS/40 86005) <33576>* **AMIGOS** [21] [10]
– Dance sister dance (baila mi Hermana) / Take me with you / Let me / Gitano / Tell me are you tired / Europa (Earth's cry, Heaven's smile) / Let it shine. *(re-iss.Jun84 lp/c; CBS/40 32476) (cd-iss.Mar87; CD 86005) (re-iss.cd Jun92)*

May 76. (7") *(CBS 4335) <10336>* **LET IT SHINE. / TELL ME ARE YOU TIRED** [ ] [77]

Aug 76. (7") *(CBS 4512) <10353>* **DANCE SISTER DANCE (BAILA MI HERMANA). / LET ME** [ ] [ ]

— **JOSE AREAS** returned to repl. PERAZA / **PABLO TELEZ** – bass repl. STONE

Dec 76. (lp/c) *(CBS/40 86020) <34423>* **FESTIVAL** [27] [27]
– Carnaval / Let the children play / Jugando / Carnival / Give me love / Verao Vermelho / Let the music set you free / Revelations / Reach up / The river / Try a little harder / Maria Caracoles.

Jan 77. (7") *(CBS 4927)* **REVELATIONS. / REACH UP** [ ] [-]

Jan 77. (7") *<10524>* **REVELATIONS. / GIVE ME LOVE** [-] [ ]

Mar 77. (7") *(CBS 5102) <10481>* **LET THE CHILDREN PLAY. / CARNAVAL** [ ] [ ]

— Trimmed slightly when CHANCLER vacated

Sep 77. (7") *(CBS 5671) <10616>* **SHE'S NOT THERE. / ZULU** [11] [27]

Oct 77. (d-lp/c) *(CBS/40 88272) <34914>* **MOONFLOWER (live + studio)** [7] [10]
– Dawn – Go within / Carnaval / Let the children play / Jugando / I'll be waiting / Zulu / Bahia / Black magic woman – Gypsy queen / Dance sister dance (baila mi Hermana) / Europa (Earth's cry, Heaven's smile) / She's not there / Flor de Luna (Moonflower) / Soul sacrifice / Heads, hands & feet / El Morocco / Transcendance / Savor / Toussaint l'overture. *(re-iss.Apr85 d-lp/c; CBS/40 86098) (cd-iss.Apr89; CD 33280) (re-iss.cd Jun96; 463370-2)*

Jan 78. (7") *(CBS 6055)* **BLACK MAGIC WOMAN (live). / TRANSCENDANCE** [ ] [-]

Jan 78. (7") *<10677>* **BLACK MAGIC WOMAN (live). / I'LL BE WAITING (live)** [-] [ ]

Aug 78. (7"; by CARLOS SANTANA) *(CBS 6520)* **I'LL BE WAITING. / FLOR DE LUNA (MOONFLOWER)** [ ] [-]

— **CARLOS** retained only **WALKER + COSTER** and introduced **ARMANDO PERAZA** returned to repl. AREAS / **DAVID MARGEN** – bass repl. TELLEZ / added **GRAHAM LEER** – drums / **CHRIS RHYME** – keyboards / **RAUL REKOW** – percussion / **CHRIS SOLBERG** – guitar, keyboards, vocals

Oct 78. (7") *<10839>* **WELL ALL RIGHT. / JERICHO** [-] [69]

Oct 78. (7") *(CBS 6755)* **WELL ALL RIGHT. / WHAM!** [53] [-]
(12"+=) *(CBS12-6755)* – Life is a lady – Holiday.

Nov 78. (lp/c) *(CBS/40 86075) <35600>* **INNER SECRETS** [17] [27]
– Dealer / Spanish rose / Well all right / One chain (don't make no prison) / Stormy / Open invitation / Wham! / The facts of love / Life is a lady – Holiday / Move on. *(cd-iss.1986 & Jun92; CD 86075)*

Jan 79. (7") *(CBS 6998)* **ONE CHAIN (DON'T MAKE NO PRISON). / MOVE ON** [ ] [-]

Jan 79. (7") *<10873>* **STORMY. / MOVE ON** [-] [32]

Mar 79. (lp/c; by CARLOS SANTANA) *(CBS/40 86037) <35686>* **ONENESS: SILVER DREAMS, GOLDEN REALITY** [55] [87]
– The chosen hour / Arise awake / Light versus darkness / Jim Jeannie / Transformation day / Victory / Silver dreams golden smiles / Cry of the wilderness / Guru's song / Oneness / Life is just a passing parade / Golden dawn / Free as the morning sun / Song for Devadip. *(cd-iss.Mar97 on 'Columbia'; 487238-2)*

Apr 79. (7") *<10938>* **ONE CHAIN (DON'T MAKE NO PRISON). / LIFE IS A HOLIDAY** [-] [59]

— **ALEX LIGERTWOOD** – vocals (ex-BRIAN AUGER) repl. WALKER / **ALAN PASQUE** – keyboards, vocals repl. COSTER + RHYME

Oct 79. (7") *(CBS 7971) <11144>* **YOU KNOW THAT I LOVE YOU. / AQUA MARINE** [ ] [35]

Oct 79. (lp/c) *(CBS/40 86098) <36154>* **MARATHON** [28] [25]
– Marathon / Lightning in the sky / Aqua marine / You know that I love you / All I ever wanted / Stand up – Runnin' / Summer lady / Love / Stay / Hard times. *(cd-iss.May87; CD 86098)*

Feb 80. (7") *(CBS 8160)* **ALL I EVER WANTED. / LOVE** [57] [-]

Feb 80. (7") *<11218>* **ALL I EVER WANTED. / LIGHTNING IN THE SKY** [-] [ ]

Jun 80. (7") *(CBS 8649)* **AQUA MARINE. / STAND UP – RUNNIN'** [ ] [-]

Sep 80. (d-lp/d-c; by CARLOS SANTANA) *(CBS/40 84514) <36590>* **THE SWING OF DELIGHT** [65] [65]
– Swapan tari / Love theme from 'Sparticus' / Phuler Matan / Song for my brother / Jharna kala / Gardenia / La Llave / Golden hours / Shere Khan, the tiger.

— (above featured The MILES DAVIS QUINTET of the 60's)

— added **ORESTES VILATO** – percussion / **RICHARD BAKER** – keyboards

Apr 81. (7") *(A-1139) <01050>* **WINNING. / BRIGHTEST STAR** [ ] [17]

Apr 81. (lp/c) *(CBS/40 84946) <37158>* **ZEBOP!** [33] [9]
– Changes / E papa re / Primera invasion / Searchin' / Over and over / Winning / Tales of Kilimanjaro / The sensitive kind / American gypsy / I love you much too much / Brightest star / Hannibal. *(cd-iss.Dec85; CD 84946)*

Jun 81. (7") *(A-1388)* **CHANGES. / AMERICAN GYPSY** [ ] [-]

Sep 81. (7") *(A-1556) <02178>* **THE SENSITIVE KIND. / AMERICAN GYPSY** [ ] [56] Jul81

Jan 82. (7") *<02519>* **SEARCHIN'. / TALES OF KILIMANJARO** [-] [ ]

— **CARLOS** retained only **LEAR, MARGEN, BAKER + VILATO**

Aug 82. (lp/c) *(CBS/40 85915) <38122>* **SHANGO** [35] [22]
– The Nile / Hold on / Night hunting time / Nowhere to run / Nueva York / Oxun / Body surfing / What does it take / Let me inside / Warrior / Shango. *(cd-iss.1983; CD 85914)*

Aug 82. (7") *<03160>* **HOLD ON. / OXUN** [-] [15]

Nov 82. (7") *<03376>* **NOWHERE TO RUN. / NUEVA YORK** [-] [66]

CARLOS SANTANA

solo, featuring **WILLIE NELSON, BOOKER T.JONES & The FABULOUS THUNDERBIRDS**

Apr 83. (7") *<03925>* **WATCH YOUR STEP. / TALES OF KILIMANJARO** [-] [ ]

Apr 83. (7") *(A-3330)* **WATCH YOUR STEP. / LIGHTNIN'** [ ] [-]

Apr 83. (lp/c) *(CBS/40 25350) <38642>* **HAVANA MOON** [84] [31]
– Watch your step / Lightnin' / Who do you love / Mudbone / One with you / Ecuador / Tales of Kilimanjaro / Havana Moon / Daughter of the night / They all went to Mexico / Vereda tropical. *(cd-iss.May87' CD 25350)*

May 83. (7") *(A-3359)* **THEY ALL WENT TO MEXICO. / MUDBONE** [ ] [-]

Jun 83. (7") *<04034>* **HAVANA MOON. / LIGHTNIN'** [-] [ ]

SANTANA

CARLOS only retained **VILATO** plus sessioners

Mar 85. (7") *(A-4514) <04758>* **SAY IT AGAIN. / TOUCHDOWN RAIDERS** [ ] [46] Feb85
(12"+=) *(TA-4514)* – She's not there / ('A'instrumental).

Mar 85. (lp/c) *(CBS/40 86307) <39527>* **BEYOND APPEARANCES** [58] [50]
– Breaking out / Written in sand / How long / Brotherhood / Spirit / Say it again / Who loves you / I'm the one who loves you / Touchdown raiders / Right now. *(cd-iss.Mar86; CD 86307)*

May 85. (7") *(A-6284)* **HOW LONG. / RIGHT NOW** [ ] [-]
(12"+=) *(TA-6284)* – She's not there.

May 85. (7") *<04912>* **I'M THE ONE WHO LOVES YOU. / RIGHT NOW** [-] [ ]

— **CARLOS** re-united **GREGG ROLIE, MIKE SHRIEVE, JOSE AREAS** +sessioners

Feb 87. (lp/c/cd) *(450 500-1/-4/-2) <40272>* **FREEDOM** [ ] [95]
– Vera Cruz / She can't let go / Once it's gotcha / Love is you / Songs of freedom / Deeper, dig deeper / Praise / Mandela / Before we go / Victim of circumstance.

May 87. (7"/12") *(650417-7/-6) <06654>* **VERA CRUZ. / MANDELA** [ ] [ ] Mar87

May 87. (7") *<07038>* **VERA CRUZ (remix). / MANDELA** [-] [ ]

Jul 87. (7") *<07140>* **PRAISE. / LOVE IS YOU** [-] [ ]

— SANTANA touring band **ROLIE, CHESTER THOMPSON** – keyboards / **TOM COSTER** – synthesizers / **ALFONSO JOHNSON** – bass / **GRAHAM LEER** – drums / **BUDDY MILES** – vocals / **ARMANDO PERAZA, PAUL REKOW + ORESTES VILATO** – percussion

Nov 87. (lp/c/cd; by CARLOS SANTANA) *(460 258-1/-4/-2) <40875>* **BLUES FOR SALVADOR** [ ] [ ]
– Bailando / Aquatic park / Bella / I'm gone / 'Trane / Deeper, dig deeper / Mingus / Now that you know / Hannibal / Blues for Salvador.

— (above featured mainly session people)

— **CARLOS** retained **THOMPSON + PERAZA,** plus recruited **BENNY RIETVELD** – bass / **ALEX LIGERTWOOD** – vocals, guitar / **WALFREDO REYES** – drums, timbales, perc with host of guests (over 15).

Jun 90. (cd/c/lp) *(466913-2/-4/-1) <46065>* **SPIRITS DANCING IN THE FLESH** [68] [85]
– Let there be light – Spirits dancing in the flesh / Gypsy woman / It's a jungle out there / Soweto (African libre) / Choose / Peace on Earth . . . Mother Earth . . . Third stone from the Sun / Full Moon / Who's that lady / Jin-go-la-ba / Goodness and mercy.

Jun 90. (7") *(656027-7)* **GYPSY WOMAN. / GOODNESS AND MERCY** [ ] [ ]
(12"+=/cd-s+=) *(656027-6/-2)* – Black magic woman (live) / Oye como va (live) / She's not there (live).

— Next with samples from MILES DAVIS and JOHN COLTRANE.

Polydor Polydor

Apr 92. (cd/c/d-lp) *(513197-2/-4/-1) <513197>* **MILAGRO** [ ] [ ]
– Medley:- Introduction by BILL GRAHAM – Milagro / Medley:- I've been to the mountain top – Somewhere in Heaven / Medley:- Saja – Right on / Your touch / Life is for living / Red prophet / Aqua que va ceer / Make somebody happy / Free all the people (South Africa) / Medley:- Gypsy – Grajoonca / We don't have to wait / Adios.

Nov 93. (cd/c) *(521 082-2/-4)* **SACRED FIRE** (live in S. America) [ ] [ ]
– Angels all around us / Vive le Vada (life is for living) / Esperando / No one to depend on / Black magic woman – Gypsy queen / Oye como va / Samba pa ti / Guajira / Make somebody happy / Toussaint l'overture / Soul sacrifice / Don't try this at home / Europa / Jingo-la-ba.

— now with brother **JORGE** – guitar (ex-MALO)

Island Island

Sep 94. (cd/c; by SANTANA BROTHERS) *(CID/ICT 8034)* **BROTHERS** [ ] [ ]
– Transmutation industrial / Thoughts / Luz amor y vida / En aranjouz con tu amour / Contigo / Blues Latino / La olaza / Brujo / The trip / Reflections / Morning in Marin.

– (SANTANA) compilations, others, etc. –

on 'CBS/ Columbia' until mentioned otherwise.

Mar 73. (7") *(CBS 1155)* **OYE COMO VA. / BLACK MAGIC WOMAN** [ ] [-]
(re-iss.Feb76; CBS 3950)

Aug 74. (lp/c) *(CBS/40 69081) <3050>* **SANTANA'S GREATEST HITS** [14] [17] Jul74
– Evil ways / Jin-go-la-ba / Hope you're feeling better / Samba pa ti / Persuasion / Black magic woman / Oye como va / Everything's coming up roses / Se a cabo / Everybody's everything. *(cd-iss.Jun87; CD 69081) (re-iss.Feb88 lp/c; CBS/40 32386)*

Sep 74. (7") *(CBS 2561) <46067>* **SAMBA PA TI. / INCIDENT AT NESHABUR** [27] [ ]
(re-iss.Feb79; CBS 7063)

Oct 80. (t-lp) *(CBS 66354)* **BOX SET** (first 3 albums) [ ] [ ]

Jul 84. (7") *(A-4587)* **SHE'S NOT THERE. / SAMBA PA TI** [ ] [-]

Feb 86. (12"ep) *Old Gold; (OG 4005)* **SAMBA PA TI / JIN-GO-LA-BA. / SHE'S NOT THERE / EVIL WAYS** [ ] [-]

Oct 86. (lp/c/cd) *K-Tel; (NE1/CE2/NCD3 338)* **VIVA! SANTANA – THE VERY BEST OF SANTANA** [50] [-]

Jan 88. (7") *Old Gold; (OG 9753)* **SAMBA PA TI. / SHE'S NOT THERE** [ ] [-]

May 88. (cd) *Arcade; (ADEHCD 828-0)* **THE VERY BEST OF SANTANA – VOLUME ONE** [ ] [-]

May 88. (cd) *Arcade; (ADEHCD 828-1)* **THE VERY BEST OF SANTANA – VOLUME TWO** [ ] [-]

Jun 88. (d-lp/c/d-cd) *That's Original; (TFO LP/MC/CD 14)* **WELCOME / CARLOS SANTANA & BUDDY MILES LIVE** [ ] [-]

Oct 88. (t-lp/d-c/d-cd) *(462500-1/-4/-2) <44344>* **VIVA! SANTANA** (best + live) [ ] [ ]
– Everybody's everything / Black magic woman – Gypsy queen / Guajira / Jungle strut / Jingo / Ballin' / Bambara / Angel Negro / Incident at Neshabur / Just let the music speak / Super boogie – Hong Kong blues / Song of the wind / Abi cama / Vitalo / Paris finale / Brotherhood / Open invitation / Aqua marine / Dance, sisters, dance / Europa / Peraza 1 / She's not there / Bambele / Evil ways / Daughter of the night / Peraza II / Black magic woman – Gypsy woman (live) / Oyo como va / Persuasion / Soul sacrifice. *(d-cd re-iss.Jun97; same)*

May 89. (3"cd-ep) **BLACK MAGIC WOMAN / SAMBA PA TI / OYE COMO VA / JIN-GO-LA-BA** [ ] [-]

Jun 89. (lp/cd) *Thunderbolt; (THBVL/CDTB 071)* **PERSUASION** [ ] [-]

Jan 90. (lp/cd) *Thunderbolt; (THBVL/CDTB 079)* **LATIN TROPICAL** [ ] [-]

Oct 90. (cd) *Thunderbolt; (CDTB 087)* **ACAPULCO SUNRISE** [ ] [-]

May 92. (cd) *Traditional Line; (TL 1315)* **LIVE IN MONTREUX 1971 (live)** [ ] [-]

Jun 92. (cd/c) *(468267-2/-4)* **THE BEST OF SANTANA** [ ] [ ]
(re-iss.Oct94; same)

Mar 93. (d-cd) *(465221-2)* **SANTANA / ABRAXAS** [ ] [ ]

May 93. (cd) *F.N.A.C.;* **NINETEEN SIXTY EIGHT** [ ] [-]

Sep 93. (cd/c) *Sony Collectors; (983259-2/-4)* **SALSA, SAMBA & SANTANA** [ ] [-]

Nov 93. (d-cd) *Sound Wings; (ACD 23057-2)* **SAMBA PA TI** [ ] [-]

Feb 94. (cd) *Thunderbolt; (CDTB 502)* **EVOLUTION** [ ] [-]

Mar 94. (cd) *Charly; (CDCD 1168)* **SOUL SACRIFICE** [ ] [-]

Apr 94. (3xcd) *Pulsar;* **THE SUPER COLLECTION** [ ] [-]

Jul 94. (cd/c) *Success;* **AS YEARS GO BY** [ ] [-]

Jul 94. (cd/c) *Success;* **SANTANA JAM** [ ] [-]

Jul 94. (cd/c) *Success;* **EVERY DAY I HAVE THE BLUES** [ ] [-]

Jul 94. (cd/c) *Success;* **WITH A LITTLE HELP FROM MY FRIENDS** [ ] [-]

Oct 94. (cd) *Charly; (CDCD 1187)* **LATIN ROCK FUSIONS** [ ] [-]

Feb 95. (cd/c) *B.A.M.;* **PEARLS OF THE PAST** [ ] [-]

Apr 95. (cd/c) *Muskateer; (MU 5/4 025)* **THE EARLY YEARS** [ ] [-]

Sep 95. (3xcd-box) *Legacy-Columbia; (C3K 64605)* **DANCE OF THE RAINBOW SERPENT** [ ] [-]

Oct 95. (cd/c) *Collectors Choice; (462563-2/-4)* **SAMBA PA TI** [ ] [-]

Nov 95. (3xcd-box) *The Collection; (KBOX 346)* **THE COLLECTION** [ ] [-]

Mar 97. (d-cd) *Legacy; (485106-2)* **LIVE ROCK . . . AT FILLMORE (live)** [ ] [-]

Apr 97. (cd) *(CDX 32386)* **THE VERY BEST** [ ] [-]

May 97. (cd) *C.M.C.; (100182)* **ACAPULCO SUNRISE** [ ] [-]

May 97. (cd) *C.M.C.; (101182)* **LIVE** [ ] [-]

May 97. (d-cd) *Laserlight; (24359)* **SANTANA** [ ] [-]

May 97. (cd) *Experience; (EXP 027)* **SANTANA VOL.1** [ ] [-]

May 97. (cd) *Experience; (EXP 028)* **SANTANA VOL.2** [ ] [-]

— Note: Most albums up to 1974, were also issued on quad-lp. SUCH IS LIFE album late '93, must have been by other band of same name.

Julian Jay SAVARIN
(see under ⇒ JULIAN'S TREATMENT)

Sky SAXON (see under ⇒ SEEDS)

SCHICKE, FURS & FROHLING

Formed: Germany . . . 1975. Their debut album, 'SYMPHONIC PICTURES' (1976), introduced the band as one of the most accomplished purveyors of late 70's symphonic rock and the record was dominated by mellotron and neo-classical string stylings. The follow-up albums, 'SUNBURST' (1977) and 'TICKET TO EVERYWHERE' (1979) contained material of a similar, if not quite so inspired nature, and by the release of the latter lp, SCHICKE had already departed to join HOLDERLIN. FURS and FROHLING continued as a duo, releasing three albums before splitting in the early 80's.

Recommended: SYMPHONIC PICTURES (*8) / SUNBURST (*6) / TICKET TO EVERYWHERE (*6)

EDUARD SCHICKE – drums, percussion, xylophone / **GERHARD FURS** – keyboards / **HEINZ FROHLING** – bass, guitar, mellotron

Brain not issued

1976. (lp) *(60.010)* **SYMPHONIC PICTURES** [-] [-] German
– Tao / Solution / Dialog / Sundrops / Pictures.

1977. (lp) *(60.068)* **SUNBURST** [-] [-] German
– Wizard / Autumn sun in cold water / Artificial energy / Driftin' / Troja / 1580 / Explorer.

1979. (lp) *(60.173)* **TICKET TO EVERYWHERE** [-] [-] German
– Open doors / Songs from India / Ticket to everywhere / Spain Spain Spanish / Here and now / Slow motion / Folk'n'roll.

— SCHICKE had already took off for HOLDERLIN

FURS & FROHLING

1978. (lp) *(60.105)* **AMMERLAND** [-] [-] German
– Ammerland / Gentle breeze / Dance of the leaves / Street dance / Sarabande / Circles of live / Every land tells a story.

— added guests **JAN GROENINK** – drums / **DETLEF WIEDEKE** – bass-drums, percussion, vocals

1980. (lp) *(60.223)* **STRINGS** [-] [-] German
– Roundabout / Morning bird / Dancing colours / Artificial force / Strings / Happiness / Open valley / Sassa.

— still with guest **DETLEF**

1981. (lp) *(60.333)* **DIARY** [-] [-] German
– Late in the evening / All Hallow's eve dream / On my pillow / Prelude / Back and again / Argo / China puppet / Green island / Mind games.

— split after above. Sadly, FURS died in November '92.

– compilations, etc. –

1993. (d-cd) *Laser's Edge;* **COLLECTED WORKS** (first 3 lp's) [-] [-] German

Irmin SCHMIDT (see under ⇒ CAN)

Conrad SCHNITZLER

Born: 1937, Dusseldorf, Germany. After studying under KARL-HEINZ STOCKHAUSEN and performing with electronic pioneers TANGERINE DREAM and CLUSTER, SCHNITZLER released his solo debut, 'SCHWARZ' in 1971. The follow-up, 'ROT' (1972), was groundbreaking in its electronic experimentation but in common with his other two earliest releases, was issued in a strictly limited quantity (all three were included in a further limited edition boxed set in 1974). 'CON' (1978), was SCHITZLER's other significant release of the 70's, a cleaner version of his earlier avant-garde knob twiddling. He changed tack completely on 1981's 'CON 3', a proto-new beat outing in collaboration with ex-TON STEINE SCHERBEN member, WOLFGANG SEQUENZA. Throughout the 80's, SCHNITZLER continued to release a bewildering array of obscure albums and cassettes, mostly covering his familiar territory of abstract, avant-garde electronica.

Recommended: ROT (*6) / CON (*6) / CONSTELLATIONS (*5)

CONRAD SCHNITZLER – electronics; with on first MOEBIUS & ROEDELIUS

Block not issued

1971. (ltd-lp; as ERUPTION) *(KS 1001)* **SCHWARZ** [-] [-] German

1972. (ltd-lp; as MEDITATION) *(KS 1002)* **ROT** [-] [-] German
– Meditation / Kraut rock.

1973. (ltd-lp) *(KS 1003)* **BLAU** [-] [-] German
– Die rebellen haben sich in der Bergen Versteckt / Jupiter.

1974. (3xlp-box+cass) **WORK IN PROGRESS** [-] [-] German
– (first 3 albums + a live cassette)

Barclay not issued

1978. (ltd-lp) *(90184)* **CON** [-] [-] France
– Electric garden / Ballet statique / Zug / Metail I / Black nails. *(re-iss.1978 on German & dist.US 'Egg'; 660052)*

R.C.A. not issued

1980. (m-lp) *(5908)* **AUF DEM SCHWARZEN KANAL** [-] [-] German

— next with **WOLF SEQUENZA** – drums (ex-TON STEINE SCHERBEN) / guest vocals by **GILLI SCHNITZLER** – wife or daughter ?

Sky not issued

1981. (lp) *(061)* **CON 3** [-] [-] German
– Komm mit nach Berlin / Kohlen / Nachte in Kreuzberg / Hong Kong / Wer sind wir denn / Coca / Seemannslied / Das tier / Tanze im Regen.

Block not issued

1981. (ltd-lp) *(KS 1004)* **CONSEQUENZ** [-] [-] German
– Fata Morgana / Weiter / Tape 5 / Bilgenratte / Afghanistan / Lugen haben kurze Beine / Nachte in Kreuzberg / Humpf / M5 – 477 / Pendel / Wer geht da / Copacabana.

Uniton not issued

1981. (lp) *(U 002)* **CONAL** [-] [-] Norway
– N1 (21.45) / N2 (21.50).

C.T. not issued

1981. (ltd-lp) *(CT 1001)* **CONTEMPORA** [-] [-] German

not issued D.Y.S.

1981. (ltd-lp) *(DYS 04)* **CONTROL** (rec.1978-81) [-] [ ]
– Control A / Control B.

Private Press not issued

1981. (lp) *(GS 1001)* **CONRAD & SOHN** [-] [-] German

— above with his son **GREGOR SCHNITZLER** – vocals

1982. (lp) *(GS 1002)* **CONVEX** [-] [-] German
– Convex 1 / Convex 2.

not issued C.B.S.

1982. (m-lp) *(3218)* **BERLIN EXPRESS** [-] [ ]

Block not issued

1983. (lp) *(EB 110)* **GELB** (rec.1974) [-] [-] German
– (12 pieces of untitled music).

1983. (lp) *(EB 111)* **GRUN** (rec.1976 & 1980) [-] [-] German
– Der Riesen und seine Frau / Bis die blaue Blume blut.

Private not issued

Jul 84. (lp) *(none)* **1.7.84** [-] [-] German

1986. (lp) *(1-86.103)* **CONCERT (live)** [-] [-] German

— next with **WOLF SEQUENZA** again

Esplendor Geometrico not issued

1987. (lp) *(EG 006)* **CON & SEQUENZA** [-] [-] Spain

1987. (lp) *(EG 009)* **CONGRATULACION** [-] [-] Spain

Badlands not issued

1988. (cd) *(BAD 005)* **CONSTELLATIONS** [-] [-] France

— next was a collaboration with **GEN KEN MONTGOMERY**

Conrad Schnitzler not issued

1989. (lp) **NEW DRAMATIC ELECTRONIC MUSIC** [-] [-] German

— seems to have disappeared from scene, making only the odd home-made recording

Eberhard SCHOENER

Born: 13 May'38, Stuttgart, Germany. After a distinguished career conducting classical music, SCHOENER was allegedly the first person to introduce the Moog synthesizer to Germany and subsequently promote its use. His debut album, 'DIE SCHACHTEL' (1971), featured electronic adaptations as did 1973's charmingly titled 'DESTRUCTION OF HARMONY'. 'A DAY'S LULLABY' (1972) meanwhile, was comprised of similarly adapted American folk and country material! 'MEDITATION' (1974) was his first original piece and he worked with JON LORD on a rock/classical fusion album, 'WINDOWS', the same year. Also working on this project were such esteemed rock luminaries as DAVID COVERDALE and GLENN HUGHES. 'BALI-AGUNG' (1976) was an attempt to mix Balinese folk music and rock, featuring PETE YORK and SIEGFRIED SCHWAB whom he'd maintained from the 'WINDOWS' sessions while his later attempts at classical/rock concept albums featured various members of The POLICE. This dynamic and highly influential artist continued to produce challenging albums right up until the end of the 80's.

Recommended: MEDITATION (*6)

EBERHARD SCHOENER – keyboards, Moog synthesizer

Reprise not issued

1971. (lp) **DIE SCHACHTEL** [-] [-] German

1972. (lp) *(REP 44143)* **A DAY'S LULLABY** [-] [-] German
– A day's lullaby – Dawn city / Some day soon / A day's lullaby – Morning / You ain't going nowhere / A day's lullaby – Children's hour / Candy man / A day's lullaby – Reading children / Kite song / A day's lullaby – Day fall / Good goodbye / A day's lullaby (part A, B, C, D, E) / Storm / Pancake – Brazierre – Burger / Abilene auction / The lady and the loom / From a hill / Night's lullaby / Friend and me.

Ariola not issued

1973. (lp) *(80847)* **DESTRUCTION OF HARMONY** [-] [-] German
– Bach: H-Moll suite / Ouveture; 1. Teil – 2. Teil – Electronic kontrapunkt – 3. Teil – 4. Teil – Electronickontrapunkt / Rondeau – Einleitung / Ron Deau – Sarabande / Bouree / Bouree nachspiel / Polonaise / Polonaise – Electronic kontrapunkt / Double Polonaise / Menuet – Einleitung / Menuet.

1974. (lp) *(87131)* **MEDITATION** [-] [-] German
– Music for meditation 1 / Music for meditation 2.

— also in '74, he collaborated with JON LORD on album 'Windows'. From these sessions he retained **PETE YORK** – percussion, drums + other **SIEGRIED SCHWAB** – guitar

Harvest not issued

1976. (lp) *(062-29647)* **BALI-AGUNG** [-] [-] German
– Tjandra / Rawana / Nadi / Surija / Ramayana / Ketjak-rock / Agung raka-dalang / Gong-gede.

— SCHOENER was a conductor for The MUNICH KAMMEROPER, who made 2 German-only albums in 1977 'BASTIEN UND BASTIENNE' & 'DER SCHAUSPIELDIREKTOR' for 'E.M.I.' *(065-30231) & (065-30232)*

— now with **ANDY SUMMERS** – guitar (of The POLICE) / **HANSI STROER** – bass, guitar, piano / **NIPPI NOYA** – percussion / **RAIMUND ELLEDER** – keyboards

Harvest not issued

1977. (lp) *(064-32526)* **TRANCE-FORMATION** [-] [-] German
– Falling in trance / Shape of things to come / Frame of mind / Signs of emotion / Trance-formation.

Ariola not ussued

1978. (lp) *(28706)* **THE BOOK** [-] [-] German
– Creation / Paradise / The flood / Genesis / Exodus / Old pictures / To Anthony B, a feeling of passion / Bruckner's seventh – The adagio.

— now with **OLAF KUBLER** – sax / + also POLICE members **STING** – bass / **STEWART COPELAND** – drums

E.M.I. not issued

1978. (lp) *(066-32839)* **FLASHBACK** [-] [-] German
– Trans-Am / Why don't you answer / Only the wind / Powerslide / Flashback / Epilogue / Rhine-Bow / Lorelei / Magma.

Harvest Harvest

1979. (lp) *(064-45234)* *<12171>* **VIDEO MAGIC** [-] [ ]
– Octogon / Speech behind speech / Natural high / Code word Elvis / Video magic / Night bound city / San Francisco city / San Francisco waitress / Koan.

Oct 79. (lp/c) *(SHSM/TC-SHSM 2030)* **VIDEO FLASHBACK** [ ] [-]
(compilation of last 2)
– Trans-Am / Only the wind / Speech behind speech / Koan / Octogon / Frame of mind / Signs of emotions / Code word Elvis / Video magic.

Jan 80. (7") *(HAR 5196)* **VIDEO MAGIC. / CODE WORD ELVIS** [ ] [-]

— with **OLAF** plus **CLARE TORY** – vocals / **IAN BAIRNSON** – guitar / **PETE YORK** – drums / **MORRIS PERT** – percussion / etc

1980. (lp) *(064-45879)* **EVENTS** [-] [-] German
– Fairlight 80 / Margret / A l'ombre de jeunes filles en fleurs / When coburs die / Gam-bang / Events – A la recherche du temps perdu / Inversion / Magical echoes le temps retrouve.

1981. (lp) *(064-46049)* **TIME SQUARE** [-] [-] German
– Radiant women / The nine lives of a cat / Gramercy park hotel / Da da / Voyage / Take the zoom / Time Square / Ich schau'ins licht.

— above featured former hit singer **ESTHER OFARIM** who collaborated with EBERHARD SCHOENER

— added **JOHN GIBLIN** – bass / **MICHAEL GOLTZ** – guitar / etc

Phonogram not issued

1982. (lp; by EBERHARD SCHOENER & ESTHER OFARIM)
(6435 173) **COMPLICATED LADIES** [-] [-] German
– Call the circus / Du / Complicated ladies / Kannst du mir erklaren / Radio on / Ballerina / Einmal nur / Love was a run / Vergessenes lachen.

— added on session HAZEL O'CONNOR – vocals / MEL COLLINS – sax

Mercury not issued

1983. (lp/c) *(814 167-1/-4)* **SPURENSICHERUNG** [-] [-] German
– Spuren / Sunday morning in Manhattan / Systeme / Twilight in Venice / Hotel Reforma / Realzeit / Ein markt in Mexiko / Butterflies / Tao / Wege zum machhapocharp.

— EBERHARD formed his SYSTEM with **JENS FISCHER** – guitar / **GEORGE KOCHBECK** – keyboards, synth / **DARIO DOMINGUES** – flute

1985. (lp/c/cd) *(826 147-1/-4/-2)* **EBERHARD SCHOENER SYSTEM** [-] [-] German
– Morning has broken / Canon / Nights in white satin / Vario del plazas / Magic mountains / Adagio G-moll / Angie / Michelle / Die zwei gesichter des Januar.

— added **UDO DAHMEN** – percussion, drums / **KLAUS KREUZEDER** – sax / **SUNNYI MELLES** – vocals

1986. (cd) *(830 376-2)* **BON VOYAGE** [-] [-] German
– Bon voyage / Rondo Bavarese / Duo in D / I'll wait for you / Trio in D / Poem / Pavane.

1987. (cd) *(830-824-2)* **SCHOENER, STING & SUMMERS** [-] [-] German

— as mentioned, another credited collaboration with the POLICEmen

C.B.S. not issued

1989. (d-cd) *(465544-2)* **DAS ERBE DER GULDENBURGS** [-] [-] German
– Guldenburg – serenade / Nane's concerto / Russian melody / Fruhling in Petersburg / Fantasia cantabile / Intermezzo in E / Andante cantabile / Schleswig Holsten – suite / Macho / Martin's song / Twilight on the beach / Russian melody II / Adel verpflichtet – Musik auf Achloss Guldenburg / Kindheit in Moskau / Nocturno / Agressione / Andante cantabile II / Time of love / Journey of memory / Der clan / Tears in the rain / Russian melody III / Epilog der Guldenburgs.

— nothing to speak of in the 90's

Klaus SCHULZE

Born: Aug'47, Germany. At the age of twenty, having become a proficient drummer, he formed his first musical project, PSY FREE, which included guitarist ALEX CONTI and CURLY CURVE. In the summer of '69, he joined TANGERINE DREAM, releasing only one album, 'ELECTRONIC MEDITATION', before his abrupt departure. Creating a new outfit, ASH RA TEMPEL, he completed only one classic, eponymous space-rock album, leaving to pursue a solo career soon after. Come the Spring of '72, he had recorded his debut album, 'IRRLICHT'. Released soon after, this organ-dominated record drew comparisons to minimalists, JOHN CAGE, KARL-HEINZ STOCKHAUSEN and TERRY RILEY. After participating in an ensemble of Germany musicians, The COSMIC JOKERS, he was back with a second set, the double 'CYBORG'. This was the first in a series of electronic avant-classics, the best of these being the 1975 set, 'PICTURE MUSIC', although 1976's lengthy 'TIMEWIND' has stood the test of time. His later albums developed similar neo-classical themes, "new-age" music inspiring him to further push his own musical boundaries. KLAUS has also worked with a plethora of other artists of the same ilk, including KITARO (with whom he recorded 'Nipponjin' in '75), ARTHUR BROWN (his experimental period!) and RAINER BLOSS.

Recommended: CYBORG (*7) / PICTURE MUSIC (*7) / BLACKDANCE (*7) / TIMEWIND (*6) / MOONDAWN (*6) / MIRAGE (*5) / X (*5) / AUDENTITY (*5) / BABEL (*5) / MIDITERRANEAN PADS (*5)

KLAUS SCHULZE – keyboards, synthesizers, guitar, percussion

Ohr not issued

1972. (lp) *(556022)* **IRRLICHT** [-] [-] German
– Satz Ebene / Satz gewitter / Satz exil sils Maria.

1973. (d-lp) *(KM 2-58005)* **CYBORG** [-] [-] German
– Synphaera / Conphaera / Chromengel / Neu ronengesang.

Brain not issued

1973. (lp) *(40146)* **PICTURE MUSIC** [-] [-] German
– Totem / Mental door. *(UK cd-iss.May87 on 'The CD Label'; CDTL 002) (cd re-iss.Jun91 on 'Thunderbolt'; CDTB 098)*

Caroline not issued

1975. (lp) *(CA 2003)* **BLACK DANCE** [ ] [-]
– Ways of changes / Some velvet phasing / Voices of syn. *(iss. on 'Brain' Germany; 60406) (UK re-iss.Mar84 on 'Virgin'; OVED 23) (cd-iss.Jun88 on 'Virgin'; CDCA 2003)*

1975. (lp) *(1075)* **TIMEWIND** [-] [-] German
– Bayreuth return / Wahnfried. *(UK-iss.Mar84 on 'Virgin'; OVED 24) (cd-iss.Jun88 on 'Virgin'; CDCA 2006)*

— added **HARALD GROSSKOPF** – drums

1976. (lp) *(0001 088)* **MOONDAWN** [-] [-] German
– Floating / Mindphaser. *(re-iss.1979; same) (cd-iss.Feb91 on 'Thunderbolt'; CDTB 093)*

Jan 77. (lp) *(60040)* **MIRAGE** [-] [-] German
– Velvet voyage: 1984 – Aeronef – Eclipse – Exvasion – Lucidinterspace – Destinationvoid / Crystal lake: Xylophones – Cromwaves – Willowdreams – Liquidmirrors – Spring dance. *(cd-iss.Nov86 on 'Thunderbolt' lp/c/cd; THBL/THBC/CDTB 033)*

Island | not issued

1977. (lp) *(ILPS 9510)* **BODY LOVE (Soundtrack)** [ ] [-]
– Stardancer / Blanche / P.T.O. *(iss.'Brain' Germany; 60047) (cd-iss.May86; 811 385-2) (cd re-iss.Jan92 on 'Thunderbolt'; CDTB 123)*

1977. (lp) *(60097)* **BODY LOVE – VOL.2** [-] [-] German
– Nowhere – Nowhere / Stardancer II / Moogetique.

1978. (d-lp) *(80023)* **"X"** [-] [-] German
– Friedrich Nietzsche / Georg Traki / Frank Herbert / Friedemann Bach / Ludwig II Von Bayem / Heinrich Von Kleist. *(d-cd Apr96 on 'Thunderbolt'; CDTB 501)*

— now w/ **ARTHUR BROWN** – vocals (ex-CRAZY WORLD OF . . .) / **WOLFGANG TIEPOLD** – cello

May 80. (lp) *(0060 225)* **DUNE** [-] [-] German
– Dune / Shadows of ignorance. *(cd-iss.May86; 811 842-2)*

— now with **GROSSKOPF + BROWN**

1980. (d-lp) *(80048)* **LIVE (live)** [-] [-] German
– Bellistique / Sense / Heart / Dymagic.

completely solo.

Dec 80. (lp) *(0060 353)* **DIG IT** [-] [-] German
– Death of an analogue / Weird caravan / The looper isn't a hooker / Synthasy. *(cd-iss.1988 on 'Metrognome'; 811 658-2) (cd re-iss.Mar94 on 'Thunderbolt'; CDTB 144)*

— now with **MICHAEL SHRIEVE** – percussion (ex-SANTANA) / **WOLFGANG TIEPOLD** – cello

D.J.M. | not issued

Oct 82. (lp/c) *(DJF20/DJH40 579)* **TRANCEFER** [ ] [-]
– A few minutes after Trancefer / Silent running. *(iss.'I.C.' Germany; KS 80014) (cd-iss.1988 on 'Brain'; 823 605-2) (cd re-iss.Jun94 on 'Thunderbolt'; CDTB 146)*

— added **RAINER BLOSS** – glockenspiel (ex-TANGERINE DREAM)

I.C. | not issued

1983. (d-lp) *(KS 80025/26)* **AUDENTITY** [-] [-] German
– Cellistica / Tango-Saty / Amourage / Ophey Lissem / Spielglocken / Sebastian im Traum. *(cd-iss.1986 on 'Innovative'; IC 349 923)* (cd re-iss.1988 on 'Roadrunner'; *RR 349923) (d-cd Feb95 on 'Thunderbolt'; CDTB 505)*

— now without SHRIEVE + TIEPOLD

1983. (d-lp; by KLAUS SCHULZE & RAINER BLOSS) *(KS 80040-41)* **DZIEKUJE POLAND (live)** [-] [-] German
– Katowice / Warsaw / Lodz / Gdansk / Dziekuje. *(d-cd-iss.Sep94 on 'Thunderbolt'; CDTB 504)*

— added **ERNST FUCHS** – vocals, lyrics

Inteam | not issued

Apr 84. (lp) *(INT 200001)* **APHRICA** [ ] [-]
– Aphrodite / Brothers and sisters / Africa.

— **MICHAEL GARVENS** – vocals, repl. FUCHS

Apr 84. (lp; KLAUS SCHULZE & RAINER BLOSS) *(INT 200002)* **DRIVE INN** [-] [-] German
– Drive Inn / Sightseeing / Truckin' / Highway / Racing / Road clear / Drive out. *(re-iss.Sep85 on 'Thunderbolt'; THBL 2028) (cd-iss.May86; CDTB 2028)*

— now all solo

1984. (lp) *(ID 200003)* **ANGST (Soundtrack)** [-] [-] German
– Pain / Memory / Surrender / Beyond / Freeze. *(UK-iss.Feb86 lp/cd on 'Thunderbolt'; THBL/CDTB 2027)*

— added **ULLI SCHOBER** – percussion

Brain | not issued

1985. (lp/cd) *(827673-1/-2)* **INTERFACE** [-] [-] German
– On the edge / Colours in the darkness / The beat planante / Interface.

— added **ANDREAS GROSSER** – keyboards

Venture | not issued

Oct 87. (cd/c/lp) *(CD/TC+/VE 5)* **BABEL** [ ] [-]
– Nebuchadnezzar's dream / Foundation / The tower raises / First clouds / Communication problems / The gap of alienation / Immuring insanity / Heaven under feet / Deserted stones / Facing abandoned tools / Vanishing memories / Sinking into oblivion / Far from Earth.

Thunderbolt | not issued

Apr 87. (lp/cd) *(THBL/CDTB 039)* **DREAMS** [ ] [-]
– A classical move / Five to four / Dreams / Flexible / Klaustrophony. *(iss.'Brain' Germany lp/cd; 831206-1/-2)*

Aug 88. (lp/cd) *(THBL/CDTB 2061)* **EN=TRANCE** [ ] [-]
– FM delight / Velvet system / En=trance / A-numerique. *(iss.'Brain' Germany; 835159-2)*

Jan 90. (cd/lp) *(CDTB/THBL 081)* **MIDITERRANEAN PADS** [ ] [-]
– Decent changes / Miditerranean pads / Percussion planante. *(iss.'Brain' Germany; 841864-2)*

Venture | not issued

Nov 90. (d-cd) *(CDVED 903)* **DRESDEN PERFORMANCE / THE DRESDEN IMAGINARY SCENES** [ ] [-]
– Dresden I (live) / Dresden III / Dresden V / Dresden II (live) / Dresden IV.

Jun 91. (cd) *(CDVE 906)* **BEYOND RECALL** [ ] [-]
– Grongo Nero / Trancess / Brave old sequence / The big fall / Airlight.

Nov 92. (cd/c) *(CD/TC VE 917)* **ROYAL FESTIVAL HALL VOL.2 (live)** [ ] [-]
– Ancient ambience / Gothic ground / In days of yore / Pavane and Galliard / Dusty spiderwebs and a shorn monk / Basse danse join medieval maracas / Primeval murmur / Pedal away (castle rock) / Anchorage / Variation on B.F.

Apr 93. (cd) *(CDVE 918)* **THE DOME EVENT** [ ] [-]
– The dome event / After eleven.

Fax | not issued

Feb 96. (cd; KLAUS SCHULZE / BILL LASWELL / PETE NAMLOOK) *PK 08108)* **DARK SIDE OF THE MOOG 4** [ ] [-]

– compilations, etc. –

Oct 94. (cd) *Thunderbolt; (CDTB 504)* **POLAND LIVE '83 (live)** [ ] [-]

SEASTONES (see under ⇒ GRATEFUL DEAD)

SECONDHAND (see under ⇒ SEVENTH WAVE)

SEEDS

Formed: Los Angeles, California, USA . . . 1965 by obscure solo artist, SKY SAXON, who had released a number of low-key singles. The SEEDS signed to 'GNP Crescendo' in 1965, cracking the charts early in 1967, when a re-issue of their second 45, '(YOU'RE) PUSHIN' TOO HARD', hit the US Top 40. A wired, deceptively simple slice of garage-psych, the single remains the definitive SEEDS track and a blueprint for the punk movement of the following decade. Their next 45, 'CAN'T SEEM TO MAKE YOU MINE' (their original debut), also gave them a Top 50 hit, although they found it hard to maintain this short run of success. Previously, they had released two seminal albums (both in '66), 'THE SEEDS' and 'A WEB OF SOUND', full of weird, psychotic blues highlighting SKY's dememted vocal sermonising on such reliable topics as sex, drugs and of course, rock'n'roll. Their third album, 'FUTURE', was a more exotic trip into flower-power, two tracks, 'MARCH OF THE FLOWER CHILDREN' and 'A THOUSAND SHADOWS' (their last hit) glaringly over-blown on the production front. SKY subsequently sacked the rest of the band, his new formation, SKY SAXON BLUES BAND, making another album, 'A FULL SPOON OF SEEDY BLUES' in 1967. A revamped SEEDS with SKY at the helm once again, subsequently fell back into the underground scene, only managing to release a handful of 45's and a live album. In the 80's, SKY issued a number of solo albums under many guises, i.e. SKY SUNLIGHT SAXON & THE STARRY SEEDS BAND.

Recommended: EVIL HOODOO (*7)

LITTLE RICHIE MARSH

(aka SKY SAXON)

not issued | Ava

1961. (7") **GOODBYE. / CRYING INSIDE MY HEART** [-] [ ]

not issued | Shepherd

1962. (7") **THEY SAY. / DARLING I SWEAR IT'S TRUE** [-] [ ]

SKY SAXON

not issued | Conquest

1962. (7") **THEY SAY. / GO AHEAD AND CRY** [-] [ ]

— For the rest of 1962, SKY SAXON formed his ELECTRA FIRES. The following 2 years he founded SKY SAXON & The SOUL ROCKERS.

The SEEDS

were formed at the beginning of '65 by **SKY SAXON** – vocals, bass, saxophone / plus **JAN SAVAGE** – guitar / **DARYL HOOPER** – keyboards / **RICK ANDRIDGE** – drums

Vocalion | GNP Crescendo

Jun 65. (7") <354> **CAN'T SEEM TO MAKE YOU MINE. / I'LL TELL MYSELF (or) DAISY MAE** [-] [ ]
(re-iss.Apr67; same); hit No.41>

Nov 65. (7") <364> **(YOU'RE) PUSHIN' TOO HARD. / OUT OF THE QUESTION** [-] [ ]

Apr 66. (lp) *<GNP 2023>* **THE SEEDS** [-] [ ]
– Can't seem to make you mine / No escape / Lose your mind / Evil hoodoo / Girl I want you / Pushin' too hard / Try to understand / Nobody spoil my fun / It''s a hard life / You can't be trusted / Excuse excuse / Fallin' in love. *<US re-iss.1988 lp/cd; GNP S/D 2023> (UK-iss.Feb84 on 'Line'; LLP 5021) (cd-iss.Sep89 on 'Line'; IMCD 900167)*

Aug 66. (7") <370> **TRY TO UNDERSTAND. / THE OTHER PLACE** [-] [ ]

Oct 66. (7") *(VN 9277)* <372> **PUSHIN' TOO HARD. / TRY TO UNDERSTAND** [ ] [36]

— added **HARVEY SHARPE** – bass

Oct 66. (lp) *(VAN 8062)* *<GNP 2033>* **A WEB OF SOUND** [ ] [ ]
– Mr. Farmer / Pictures and designs / Tripmaker / I tell myself / A faded picture / Rollin' machine / Just let go / Up in her room. *<US re-iss.Oct75; same> (re-iss.Feb84 on 'Line'; OLLP 5024) <US re-iss.1988 lp/cd; GNP S/D 2033>*

Feb 67. (7") <383> **MR. FARMER. / UP IN HER ROOM (or) NO ESCAPE** [-] [86]

May 67. (7") *(VN 9287)* **CAN'T SEEM TO MAKE YOU MINE. / DAISY MAE** [ ] [-]

Jun 67. (7") <394> **A THOUSAND SHADOWS. / MARCH OF THE FLOWER CHILDREN** [-] [72]

Aug 67. (lp; mono/stereo) *(VAN/SAVN 8070)* *<GNP 2038>* **FUTURE** [ ] [87]
– Introduction / March of the flower children / Travel with your mind / Out of the question / Painted doll / Flower lady & her assistant / Now a man / A thousand shadows / Two fingers pointing at you / Where is the entrance way to play / Six dreams / Fallin'. *<US re-iss.1988 lp/cd; GNP S/D 2038> (cd re-iss.Sep91 on 'Line'; IMCD 900173)*

Nov 67. (7") <398> **THE WIND BLOWS YOUR HAIR. / SIX DREAMS** [-] [ ]

— now without departing HARVEY

1967. (lp; as SKY SAXON BLUES BAND) *<GNP 2040>* **A FULL SPOON OF SEEDY BLUES** [-] [ ]
– Pretty girl / Moth and the flame / I'll help you / Cry wolf / Plain spoken / The gardener / One more time blues / Creepin' about / Buzzin' around. *<re-iss.Sep76;*

same> <US re-iss.1988 lp/cd; GNP S/D 2040>

—— basically **SKY SAXON** + session people

1968. (lp) *<GNP 2043>* **RAW AND ALIVE (MERLIN'S MUSIC BOX) (live)** [-] [ ]
– Introduction by Humble Harv / Mr. Farmer / No escape / Satisfy you / Night time girl / Up in her room / Gypsy plays his drums / Can't seem to make you mine / Mumble and bumble / Forest outside your door / 900 million people daily all making love / Pushin' too hard. *<US re-iss. 1988 lp/cd; GNP S/D 2043>*

1968. (7") *<408>* **SATISFY YOU (live). / 900 MILLION PEOPLE DAILY MAKING LOVE (live)** [-] [ ]

1969. (7") *<422>* **FALLIN' OFF THE EDGE OF THE WORLD. / WILD BLOOD** [-] [ ]

not issued — M.G.M.

1971. (7") *<14163>* **BAD PART OF TOWN. / WISH ME UP** [-] [ ]

1971. (7") *<14190>* **LOVE IN A SUMMER BASKET. / DID HE DIE** [-] [ ]

not issued — Productions Unlimited

1972. (7") *<22>* **SHUCKIN' AND JIVIN'. / YOU TOOK ME BY SURPRISE** [-] [ ]

—— SKY SAXON folded SEEDS and formed various bands SKY SUNLIGHT / SUNLIGHT / SKY SUNLIGHT SAXON.

SKY SAXON

New Rose — not issued

Nov 84. (lp) *(ROSE 36)* **MASTERS OF PSYCHEDELIA** [ ] [-]

Aug 86. (lp) **A GROOVY THING** [ ] [-]

Dec 88. (lp/cd; as SKY SUNLIGHT SAXON & FIRE WALL) *(ROSE 155/+CD)* **IN SEARCH OF BRIGHTER COLOURS** [ ] [-]
– I hear the mountains crash / Lightning lightning / Put something sweet between your lips / Barbie doll look / The big screen / Baby baby / Come on pretty girl / Kick kick / Paisley rocker / Come a here right now.

SKY SUNLIGHT SAXON

& THE STARRY SEEDS BAND:- ELLIOTT INGBAR / MARS BONFIRE / RON BUSHY / RAINBOW STARDUST

Psycho — not issued

Feb 85. (m-lp) *(PSYCHO 29)* **STARRY RIDE** (various aggregations) [ ] [-]
– Starry ride / I'm in love with life / Drums, stars & guitars / 24 hour rocker.

Fierce — not issued

1987. (7") *(FRIGHT 009)* **DOG = GOD** [ ] [-]

Line — not issued

Jun 87. (lp; as SKYLIGHT SKY SAXON) *(40029-1)* **TAKES ON GLORY** [ ] [-]
– As much as I love you / Born to be wild / In Paradise / Swim / Aphrodite / Sodom & Gomorrah / 30 seconds over Hollywood / Love dog / Wish me up / Statue of stone / Picnic in the grass / Pushin' too far too hard / Skid row children.

—— **SKY + MARS** now with **TOM AZEVEDO** – guitar / **GARY STERN** – bass, guitar / **PAUL SCHOFIELD** – drums

not issued — Pinpoint

1989. (lp) **JUST IMAGINE** [-] [ ]
– Black & red / Focus point / Wild roses / Just imagine / Black beans / Some people / Million miles / World tribute / Thriller riff / Mr.Farmer.

– (SEEDS) compilations, etc. –

Sep 76. (lp) *GNP Crescendo; (lp)* **THE SEEDS IN CONCERT (live)** [-] [ ]

1977. (lp) *GNP Crescendo; (GNP S/S 2107)* **FALLIN' OFF THE EDGE** [-] [ ]

Aug 78. (lp) *Sonet; (SNTF 746)* **LEGENDARY MASTER RECORDINGS** [ ] [-]

Apr 88. (lp/cd) *Bam Caruso; (KIRI 082/+CD)* **EVIL HOODOO** [ ] [-]
– March of the flower children / The wind blows your hair / Tripmaker / Try to understand / Evil hoodoo / Chocolate river / Pushing too hard / Falling off the edge / Mr. Farmer / Up in her room / Can't seem to make you mine / Pictures and designs / Flower lady and her assistant / Rollin' machine / Out of the question / Satisfy you. *(pic-lp Jan89 on 'Strange Things'; STRANGEP 1) (cd re-iss.Jul91 on 'Drop Out'; DOCD 1998)*

Apr 88. (7") *Bam Caruso; (OPRA 091)* **PUSHIN' TOO HARD. / GREENER DAY** [ ] [-]

Nov 91. (cd) *Drop Out; (DOCD 1992)* **A FADED PICTURE** [ ] [-]
– (FIRE ESCAPE – Psychotic Reaction / SEEDS – RAW AND ALIVE – LIVE AT MERLIN'S MUSIC BOX)

Mar 94. (cd) *Drop Out; (DOCD 1984)* **TRAVEL WITH YOUR MIND** [ ] [ ]
(re-iss.Jul95 on 'GNP Crescendo'; GNPD 2218)

May 94. (cd; SEEDS / SKY SAXON) *Eva; (84210)* **BAD PART OF TOWN / LIVE ALBUM BEDTIME** [ ] [-]

SEVENTH WAVE

Formed: London, England . . . 1967 as SECONDHAND, by KEN ELLIOT and KIERAN O'CONNOR. They released two albums in the space of three years; full of prog-rock leanings, they also showed a poetic side, obviously influenced by JIMI HENDRIX or even ARTHUR BROWN. A third album came out as CHILLUM, both members moving on to form an even more confusing act; FUNGUS, who after one privately pressed 45 in 1973, became SEVENTH WAVE. The single, 'PREMONITIONS', surfaced on the first of their two albums, the 'Metropolis'-inspired 'THINGS TO COME'. • **Trivia:** The SECONDHAND albums are nearly worth £100.

Recommended: REALITY (Secondhand; *5) / DEATH MAY BE YOUR SANTA CLAUS (Secondhand; *5) / THINGS TO COME (*4)

SECONDHAND

KEN ELLIOT – vocals, keyboards / **BOB GIBBONS** – lead guitar / **NICK SOUTH** – bass / **KIERAN O'CONNOR** – drums

Buddah — not issued

1968. (lp) *(583 045)* **REALITY** [ ] [-]
– Fairy tale / Rhubarb! / Denis James the clown / Steam tugs / Good old '59 (we are slowly gettin' older) / The world will end yesterday / Denis James (ode to D.J.) / Mainliner / Reality / Bath song. *(cd-iss.1994 on 'Essex'; ESSEX 1006CD)*

—— (early copies of above were credited to MOVING FINGER on the sleeve)

1969. (7") *(56306)* **A FAIRY TALE. /** [ ] [-]

—— **ROB ELLIOT** – vocals + **MOGGY MEAD** – guitar + **GEORGE HART** – bass, violin, vocals; repl. GIBBONS + SOUTH

—— In the early 70's, the band played on two albums by ANDREAS THOMOPOULOS; 'SONGS OF THE STREET' (MR 1) / 'BORN OUT OF THE TEARS OF THE SUN' (MR 4).

Mushroom — not issued

1971. (lp) *(MR 6)* **DEATH MAY BE YOUR SANTA CLAUS** [ ] [-]
– Funeral / Hangin' on an eyelid / Lucifer and the egg / Somethin' you got / Cyclops / Sic transit Gloria Mundi / Revelations ch.16 vs, 9-21 / Take to the skies / Death may be your Santa Claus / Baby you are another monster. *(cd-iss.1991 on 'UFO'; BFTP 004CD) (cd re-iss.Jun97 on 'See For Miles'; SEECD 479)*

1971. (lp; as CHILLUM) *(MR 11)* **CHILLUM** [ ] [-]

SEVENTH WAVE

KEN ELLIOT – synthesizers, piano, clavinet, vocals / **KEIRAN O'CONNOR** – drums, percussion, xylophone, vibes, mellotron

Gull — Janus

Oct 74. (lp) *(GULP 1001) <7009>* **THINGS TO COME** [ ] [ ]
– Sky scraper / Metropolis / Intercity water rat / Escalator / Old dog song / Smog, fog and sunset / Fail to see / Premonition / Festival / Eversolightly / Communication Skyways / Things to come / 199 / Dance of the Eloi. *(re-iss.Sep77;)*

Nov 74. (7") *(GULS 10)* **FAIL TO SEE. / THINGS TO COME** [ ] [-]

—— added **PETER LEMER + BRIAN GOULD + HUGH BANTON** – keyboards / **PEPI LEMER** – vocals / **STEVE COOK** – bass / **CHRIS ANSON** – synthesizers / **TONY UTER + TONY ELLIOT** – percussion

Sep 75. (lp) *(GULP 1010) <7021>* **PSI-FI** [ ] [ ]
– Return to Foreverland / Roads to Rome / Manifestations / Loved by you / Only the beginning / Aether anthem / Astral animal / El Tuto / Camera obscura / Star palace of the sombre warrior. *(re-iss.Sep77)*

Sep 75. (7") *(GULS 17)* **MANIFESTATIONS. / ONLY THE BEGINNING (part 1)** [ ] [-]

—— When they split, PETER LEMER joined The BAKER GURVITZ ARMY.

– compilations, etc. –

Apr 97. (lp) *Corduroy; (CORD 016)* **ALWAYS OFFSHORE** [ ] [-]

SHADOWS OF KNIGHT

Formed: Chicago, Illinois, USA . . . 1965 by JIM SOHNS, WARREN ROGERS, JERRY McGEORGE, NORM GOTSCH and TOM SCHIFFOUR. That year, they signed to Bill Traut & George Badowski's 'Dunwich' label. Their debut single, the Van Morrison-penned 'GLORIA', gave them a US Top 10 triumph, although after one more hit, 'OH YEAH', success eluded them. Pioneers of garage punk, these two singles were inspired by BO DIDDLEY-like R&B rhythms, although by 1968, the band's sound had been tempered by a pop industry sound (copyright of The KASENETZ-KATZ production). • **Songwriters:** Group compositions except; GLORIA (Them) / OH YEAH + GOT MY MOJO WORKING (Muddy Waters) / HOOCHIE COOCHIE MAN + I JUST WANNA MAKE LOVE TO YOU + SPOONFUL (Willie Dixon) / BOOM BOOM (John Lee Hooker) / I'M NOT TALKIN' (Yardbirds) / BAD LITTLE WOMEN (Wheels) / TOMORROW'S GONNA BE ANOTHER DAY (Boyce-Hart) / • **Trivia:** Their final sessions were at Paragon studios in May 1970, although they did re-form for live gigs in the 70's.

Recommended: GEE-EL-O-ARE-I-AY (*8)

JIM SOHNS – vocals / **WARREN ROGERS** – lead guitar / **JERRY McGEORGE** – rhythm guitar / **NORM GOTSCH** – bass / **TOM SCHIFFOUR** – drums

Atlantic — Dunwich

Jan 66. (7") *<45-116>* **GLORIA. / SPANIARD AT THE DOOR** [-] [10]

Mar 66. (7") *(AT 4085)* **GLORIA. / DARK SIDE** [ ] [-]
<US-iss.1971 on 'Atlantic'; 13138>

—— **JOE KELLEY** – lead guitar repl. GOTSCH (WARREN now bass)

May 66. (lp) *<SD 666>* **GLORIA** [-] [46]
– Gloria / Light bulb blues / I got my mojo working / Dark side / Let it rock / Oh yeah / It always happens that way / You can't judge a book (by looking at the cover) / I just want to make love to you / Bad little woman / Gospel zone / Hey Joe / I'll make you sorry / Peepin' and hidin' / Tomorrow's going to be another day / Spoonful. *(UK-iss.Mar79 on 'Radar'; ADA 11)*

Jul 66. (7") *(584 021) <45-122>* **OH YEAH. / LIGHT BULB BLUES** [ ] [39] May66

Sep 66. (7") *(584 045) <45-128>* **BAD LITTLE WOMAN. / GOSPEL ZONE** [ ] [91] Aug66

Dec 66. (7") *<45-141>* **I'M GONNA MAKE YOU MINE. / I'LL MAKE YOU SORRY** [-] [90]

Jan 67. (lp) *<SD 667>* **BACK DOOR MEN** [-] [ ]
– Bad little women / Gospel zone / The behemoth / Three for love / Hey Joe / I'll make you sorry / Peepin' and hidin' / Tomorrow's going to be another day / New York bullseye / High blood pressure / Spoonful.

Mar 67. (7") *<45-151>* **THE BEHEMOTH. / WILLIE JEAN** [-] [ ]

—— **DAVE 'The Hawk' WOLINSKI** – keyboards repl. ROGERS (drafted)

—— (Jul67) **JIM SOHNS** now sole survivor, with hired session musicians. (McGEORGE joined H.P. LOVECRAFT)

Sep 67. (7") *(584 136) <45-167>* **SOMEONE LIKE ME. / THREE FOR LOVE** [ ] [ ] Aug67

— (1968) **SOHNS** brought in **JOHN FISHER / DAN BAUGHMAN / WOODY WOODRUFF / KENNY TURKIN**

Buddah | Team

Dec 68. (7") *(201 024)* <*520*> **SHAKE. / FROM WAY OUT TO WAY UNDER** [ ] [46] Oct68

not issued | Super K

1969. (7") <*8*> **TAURUS. / MY FIRE DEPARTMENT NEEDS A FIREMAN** [-] [ ]

1969. (7") <*10*> **RUN RUN BILLY PORTER. / MY FIRE DEPARTMENT NEEDS A FIREMAN** [-] [ ]

1969. (lp) <*SKS 6002*> **THE SHADOWS OF KNIGHT** [-] [ ]
– Follow / Alone / Times & places / I am what I am / Uncle Wiggley's airship / I wanna make you all mine / Shake revisited '69 / I'll set you free / Under acoustic control / Bluebird / Back door man.

not issued | Atco

1969. (7") <*6634*> **GLORIA '69. / SPANIARD AT MY DOOR** [-] [ ]

Jun 70. (7") <*6676*> **I AM THE HUNTER. / WARWICK COURT AFFAIR** [-] [ ]

— Disbanded 1970, although SOHNS re-united them for one-off tour in 1974.

– compilations, others, etc. –

Apr 85. (lp) *Edsel; (ED 157)* **GEE-EL-O-ARE-I-AY** [ ] [-]
– Gloria / Light bulb blues / I got my mojo working / Dark side / Let it rock / Oh yeah / It always happens that way / You can't judge a book by the cover / I just wanna make love to you / Bad little woman / Gospel zone / Hey Joe / I'll make you sorry / Peepin' and hidin' / Tomorrow's gonna be another day / Spoonful.

Nov 92. (cd) *Sundazed;* **RAW 'N ALIVE AT THE CELLAR, CHICAGO 1966 (live)** [ ] [-]

SHIVA'S HEADBAND

Formed: Austin, Texas, USA ... mid-'67 by SPENCER PERSKIN, a classically-trained violinist who had spent the last year in San Francisco. While there, he turned down the chance of joining MOTHER EARTH, having guested on their first album, 'Living With The Animals'. SHIVA'S HEADBAND's debut, 'KALEIDOSCOPTIC', sold moderately well, leading to them relocating to San Francisco after they were signed to the major 'Capitol' label. They stayed there long enough to record an album, 'TAKE ME TO THE MOUNTAINS' (1970), a surprising set highlighting SPENCER's excellent violin playing. They then returned to Texas and pressed up limited copies of their next album, 'COMIN' TO A HEAD', and although sporadic recordings continued well into the 80's, they couldn't recapture the promise of the first album.

Recommended: TAKE ME TO THE MOUNTAINS (*6)

SPENCER PERSKIN – violin, vocals / **SUSAN PERSKIN** – vocals / **SHAWN SIEGEL** – keyboards / **KENNY PARKER** – bass / **JERRY BARNETT** – drums / **BOB TONREID** – guitar

not issued | Ignite

1968. (7") <*681*> **KALEIDOSCOPTIC. / SONG FOR PEACE** [-] [ ]

— **ROBERT GLADWIN** – guitar, bass; repl. TONREID

— **RICHARD FINNEL** – drums; repl. BARNETT

not issued | Capitol

1970. (lp) <*ST 538*> **TAKE ME TO THE MOUNTAINS** [-] [ ]
– My baby / Take me to the mountains / Homesick armadillo blues / Ripple / Song for peace / Ebeneezer / North Austin strut / Come with me / Good time / Kaleidoscoptic.

not issued | Armadillo

1970. (7") <*811*> **TAKE ME TO THE MOUNTAINS. / LOSE THE BLUES** [-] [ ]

— **JERRY BARNETT** – drums (returned) to repl. FINNEL

— **ISIAH TITTER** – pedal steel, guitar; repl. GLADWIN

— **MIKE COOPER** – bass + **ED VIZARD** – sax; repl. PARKER

1972. (7") **SUCH A JOY. / COUNTRY BOY** [-] [ ]

1972. (lp) <*ASLP 001*> **COMIN' TO A HEAD** [-] [ ]
– Such a joy / Hungry ghost / My girlish days / Anyone / Denton / California mountain klopper / Country boy / A rockslide / Baby what you didn't / Someone / Tennessee waltz.

— **SPENCER, SUSAN + SHAWN** recruited new line-up; **JERRY BAZIL** – drums / **ROBERT FLYNN Jr.** – guitar / **BRIAN MOORE** – bass

not issued | Ape

1976. (7") <*6*> **DON'T BLAME ME. / EXTENSION** [-] [ ]

1977. (lp) <*1001*> **PSYCHEDELIC YESTERDAY** [-] [ ]

— **HANK MILLER** – guitar; repl. FLYNN

— **STEVE NAVARRO** – bass; repl. MOORE

— added **MAUREEN SIEGEL** – vocals

not issued | Moontower

1985. (lp) **IN THE PRIMO OF LIFE** [-] [ ]

— finished recording after above

SILOAH

Formed: Munich, Germany ... 1970, the brainchild of THOM ARGAUER. The band released two obscure albums, 'SAUREADLER' in 1970 and 'SUKRAMGURK PLAYIN' in 1972. The former was an acoustic based psychedelic exploration while the latter was a driving, 60's style psych-garage classic, dominated by frantic organ sounds. Needless to say, the second album featured a different line-up from the first while both albums are highly sought after by collectors.

Recommended: SAUREADLER (*5) / SUKRAMGURK PLAYIN' (*8)

THOM ARGAUER – guitars, vocals / **TINY** – vocals, shinai / **WOLFGANG** – bass / **MANUELA** – percussion, tambourine / guests incl. members of AMON DUUL II

Car | not issued

1970. (lp) *(1558 015)* **SAUREADLER** [-] [-] German
– Aluminium wind / etc. *(cd-iss.1993 on 'Lost Pipe Dreams')*

— **ARGAUER** (keyboards, vocals) brought in **FLORIAN LABER** – bass, vocals / **MARKUS KRUG** – drums / **BLACKY ZUMSTEIN** – percussion

Blues & Underground | not issued

1972. (lp) *(1558 025)* **SUKRAMGURK PLAYIN'** [-] [-] German
– Milk blue mind / Magic carpet ride to the Alps / Feast of the pickpockets / Stony / A landlady's dessert. *(cd-iss.1993 on 'Lost Pipe Dreams')*

— lost themselves again after above

SILVER APPLES

Formed: New York, USA ... 1967 by DAN TAYLOR and SIMEON. A strange couple, who combined vocals with electronics and drums. They signed to US 'Kapp' records for a mildly successful eponymous debut which made US the Top 200 lists. 'CONTACT', in 1969, was their final fling, although this is now regarded as a near-forgotten classic. The record experimented with sci-fi synths and mystical hippydom, although not sacrificing melody. • **Songwriters:** The duo. • **Trivia:** Some 80's/90's outfits unearthed their dog-eared SILVER APPLES records, unleashing their own versions of; A POX ON YOU (Scientists), etc, taken from a tribute mini-lp in late '95, 'ELECTRONIC EVOCATIONS'.

Recommended: SILVER APPLES (*7) / CONTACT (*8)

DAN TAYLOR – vocals, percussion, drums / **SIMEON** – vocals, electronics / with poetry by **STANLEY WARREN**

not issued | Kapp

Jul 68. (lp) <*KS 3562*> **SILVER APPLES** [-] [ ]
– Oscillations / Dancing gods / Dust / Program / Velvet cave / Whirly-bird / Misty mountain / Lovefingers / Seagreen serenades. *(UK-iss.Jun97; same)*

1969. (lp) <*KS 3584*> **CONTACT** [-] [ ]
– You and I / Water / Ruby / Gypsy love / You're not foolin' me / I have known love / A pox on you / Confusion / Fantasies. *(the 2 on cd-iss.1994 on 'T.R.C.';)*

— split and virtually disappeared from scene for over 20 years

not issued | Enraptured

1996. (7) **FRACTAL FLOW. / LOVEFINGERS** [-] [ ]

Richard SINCLAIR'S CARAVAN OF DREAMS (see under ⇒ CARAVAN)

SIREN (see under ⇒ COYNE, Kevin)

SKIP BIFFERTY

Formed: Newcastle, England ... Spring 1966, out of beat combo, The CHOSEN FEW, by MICKEY GALLAGHER, TOMMY JACKMAN, JOHN TURNBULL and COLIN GIBSON. From 1962 to 1965, without the latter two but boasting ALAN HULL (later of LINDISFARNE) at the helm, they played residencies at The Manhole and The Key. Two 45's were released, the latter without HULL, who had left to pursue a solo career. A new vocalist, GRAHAM BELL, took over as the group evolved into the pop-psychedelic, SKIP BIFFERTY, releasing an energetic debut, 'ON LOVE', in the summer of '67. They played many Marquee dates, moving to nearby Putney where they built up an underground following. Their melodic overtones were loved by The SMALL FACES (STEVE MARRIOTT & RONNIE LANE), who produced their 1968 effort, 'MAN IN BLACK'. An eponymous album followed, although a conflict with manager DON ARDEN resulted in the band changing their moniker to HEAVY JELLY. However, another group of that name brought litigation and they folded in early '69. Songwriters TURNBULL and GALLAGHER joined the Robbins Music Company and from this outlet, their new group, ARC, released one album early in 1971. Soon after this, they were re-united with GRAHAM BELL for one album as BELL & ARC, the record featuring their version of LEONARD COHEN's 'SO LONG, MARIANNE'. BELL became a solo artist, while the other two later joined IAN DURY & THE BLOCKHEADS. • **Covers:** SO LONG, MARIANNE (Leonard Cohen).

Recommended: SKIP BIFFERTY (*6) / BELL & ARC (*5)

CHOSEN FEW

ROD HOOD – vocals / **ALAN HULL** – guitar, vocals / **MICKEY GALLAGHER** – keyboards / **BUMPER BROWN** – bass / **TOMMY JACKMAN** – drums

Pye | not issued

1965. (7") *(7N 15905)* **IT WON'T BE AROUND YOU ANYMORE. / BIG CITY** [ ] [-]

ERNIE BELL – vocals repl. HOOD

JOHN TURNBULL – guitar, vocals repl. HULL who went solo

COLIN GIBSON – bass / **MICKIE THE VEG** – sax repl. BROWN

1965. (7") *(7N 15942)* **SO MUCH TO LOOK FORWARD TO. / TODAY, TONIGHT & TOMORROW** [ ] [-]

SKIP BIFFERTY

— **GRAHAM BELL** – vocals repl. ERNIE + MICKIE

RCA Vic. not issued

Aug 67. (7") *(RCA 1621)* **ON LOVE. / COVER GIRL**
Nov 67. (7") *(RCA 1648)* **HAPPY LAND. / REASON TO LIVE**
Jul 68. (7") *(RCA 1720)* **MAN IN BLACK. / MR. MONEY MAN**
Sep 68. (lp; mono/stereo) *(RD/SF 7941)* **SKIP BIFFERTY**
– Mr. Money man / Jeremy Carabine / When she comes to stay / Guru / Come around / Time track / Gas board under dog / Inside the secret / Orange lave / Planting bad seeds / Yours for at least 24 / Follow the path of the stars / Prince Germany the first / Clearway 52. *(re-iss.Jun97 on 'Essex'; ESSEX 1016LP)*

Island not issued

1968. (7"; as HEAVY JELLY) *(WIP 6049)* **I KEEP SINGING THAT SAME OLD SONG. / BLUE**

— got into litigation over the use of the HEAVY JELLY name. They lost! GRAHAM BELL joined EVERY WHICH WAY.

ARC

TURNBULL + GALLAGHER with **TOM DUFFY** – bass, vocals / **DAVE MONTGOMERY** – drums, percussion

Decca not issued

Jan 71. (lp) *(SKL-R 5077)* **ARC AT LAST**
– Let your love run through / It's gonna rain / Four times eight / An ear ago / Great lager street / Hello, hello, Monday / Perfectly happy man / Sophie's cat / You're in the garden.

— **ROB TAIT** – drums repl. MONTGOMERY

BELL & ARC

— re-united with **GRAHAM BELL** – vocals (now a quintet, although many session men were included including two later members below)

Charisma Columbia

Jun 71. (7") *(CB 170)* **SHE BELONGS TO ME. / DAWN**
Jul 71. (lp) *(CAS 1053)* **BELL & ARC**
– High priest of Memphis / Let your love run free / Keep a wise mind / So long, Marianne / She belongs to me / Yat rock / Dawn / Children of the north prison / Everyday.
Sep 71. (7") <45541> **SHE BELONGS TO ME. / EVERYDAY**
Nov 71. (7") <45587> **HIGH PRIEST OF MEMPHIS. / SO LONG, MARIANNE**

— split late 1971, after **ALAN WHITE** (later YES) had repl. JOHN WOODS, who had repl. TAIT (to South Africa). TURNBULL later joined GLENCOE, while GALLAGHER joined PARRISH & GURVITZ then FRAMPTON'S CAMEL.

LOVING AWARENESS

TURNBULL + GALLAGHER plus **NORMAN WATT-ROY** – bass, vocals (ex-GLENCOE, ex-GREATEST SHOW ON EARTH) / **CHARLEY CHARLES** – drums

More Love not issued

Sep 76. (lp) *(ML 001)* **LOVING AWARENESS**

— this was the embryonic BLOCKHEADS, soon to backing band of IAN DURY

SKYRIDER (see under ⇒ PELL MELL)

SLAPP HAPPY

Formed: based Germany . . .late 1971 by English-born film score composer, ANTHONY MOORE, New Yorker PETER BLEGVAD and German chanteuse, DAGMAR KRAUSE. They assembled at UWE NETTELBECK's "Wumme" studio and with augmentation from some members of FAUST (who he also managed and produced), recorded a debut album, 'SORT OF'. The record was a near unclassifiable, quirky creation of avant-garde material. In 1974, they surfaced on Richard Branson's 'Virgin' records (home of FAUST, HENRY COW, TANGERINE DREAM, MIKE OLDFIELD, etc.) with the release of their eponymous follow-up. The next project, 'DESPERATE STRAIGHTS', in 1975, was credited alongside HENRY COW, who augmented their follow-up, 'IN PRAISE OF LEARNING'. Following its release, DAGMAR remained with HENRY COW after BLEGVAD and MOORE took the SLAPP HAPPY name for themselves. However, no further recordings were forthcoming until an isolated one-off single, 'EVERYBODY'S SLIMMIN', appeared in 1983.

Recommended: SORT OF (*6) / SLAPP HAPPY (*6) / DESPERATE STRAIGHTS (*6)

ANTHONY MOORE – piano, vocals, guitar / **PETER BLEGVAD** – guitar, vocals, saxophone, clarinet / **DAGMAR KRAUSE** – vocals, piano; with guests **GUNTHER WUSTHOFF** – sax / **HEAN HERVE PERON** – bass / **WERNER DIERMAIER** – drums

Polydor not issued

1972. (lp) *(2310 204)* **SORT OF**
– Just a conversation / Paradise express / I got evil / Little girl's world / Tutankhamun / Mono plane / Blue flower / I'm all alone / Who's gonna help me now / Small hands of store / Sort of / Heading for Kyoto. *(re-iss.Sep86 on 'Recommended'; RRS 5)*

— In 1973, BLEGVAD moonlighted with his friends FAUST.

Virgin not issued

1974. (lp) *(V 2014)* **SLAPP HAPPY**
– Casablanca Moon / Me and Parvati / Mr. Rainbow / Michelangelo / The drum / A little something / The secret / Dawn / Half-way there / Charlie 'n' Charlie / Slow Moon's rose. *(re-iss.1983 as 'CASABLANCA MOON' on 'Recommended'; RR 5)*
1974. (7") *(VS 105)* **CASABLANCA MOON. / SLOW MOON'S ROSE**

— with HENRY COW; **FRED FRITH** – guitar, violin / **TIM HODGKINSON** – clarinet, piano / **JOHN GREAVES** – bass, piano / **CHRIS CUTLER** – drums; plus others **GEOFF LEIGH** – flute / **LINDSAY COOPER** – wind (old & new HENRY COW members respectively) / **PIERRE MOERLEN** – percussion (of GONG) / **MONGEZI FEA** – trumpet / **NICK EVANS** – trombone

Feb 75. (lp; SLAPP HAPPY & HENRY COW) *(V 2024)* **DESPERATE STRAIGHTS**
– The owl / A worm is at work / Bad alchemy / Europa / Desperate straights / Riding tigers / Apes in capes / Strayed / Giants / Excerpt from 'The Messiah' / In the sickbay / Caucasian lullaby / Some questions about hats.
Jul 75. (7") *(VS 124)* **JOHNNY'S DEAD. / MR. RAINBOW**

— sadly folded after above. Lost DAGMAR KRAUSE to HENRY COW. She later teamed up with KEVIN COYNE on album 'BABBLE' *(Virgin; V 2128)*

— trio re-formed in 1983.

Half Cut not issued

Jun 83. (7") *(HC 001)* **EVERYBODY'S SLIMMIN' (EVEN MEN AND WOMEN). / BLUE-EYED VILLAIN**

– compilations, etc. –

Sep 93. (cd) *Virgin; (CDOVD 441)* **CASABLANCA MOON / DESPERATE STRAIGHTS**

ANTHONY MOORE

Polydor not issued

1971. (lp) *(2310 062)* **PIECES FROM THE CLOUDLAND BALLROOM**
1972. (lp) *(2310 079)* **SECRETS OF THE BLUE BAG**

Virgin not issued

1976. (lp) *(V 2057)* **OUT**
– Stitch in time / Thousand ships / The river / Please go / You tickle / Lover of mine / Johnny's dead / Dreams of his laughter / Catch a falling star / Wrong again / Driving blind / The pilgrim. *(cd-iss.Jun97 on 'Voiceprint'; VP 165CD)*
Apr 76. (7") *(VS 144)* **CATCH A FALLING STAR. / BACK TO THE TOP**

Quango not issued

1979. (lp; as A.MORE) *(HMG 98)* **FLYING DOESN'T HELP**
– Judy / Get down / Ready ready / Useless moments / Lucia / Caught being in love / Time less strange / Girl it's your time / War / Just us / Twilight.
1980. (7"; as A.MORE) *(HMGS 10)* **JUDY. / LUCIA**

— with **ORB** – drums, percussion, sax, piano / **LE CRETIN BLEU** – organ, guitar, synthesizers, percussion / **LU** – sax / **MATT** – bass / **KATH** – vocals

Do It not issued

Aug 81. (7") *(DUN 16)* **WORLD SERVICE. / DIVING GIRLS**
1981. (lp) *(RIDE 7)* **WORLD SERVICE**
– Run right back / Pieces of the puzzle / World service / Fat fly / Broke'n idle / Outta angels / The argument / Nowhere to go.
May 82. (7") *(DUN 22)* **WORLD SERVICE. / RUN RIGHT BACK**

Parlophone not issued

Jun 84. (7") *(R 6072)* **INDUSTRIAL DRUMS. / THE CONFERENCE**
(12"+=) *(12R 6072)* – Elephants & castles.
1984. (7") *(R 6081)* **THE ONLY CHOICE. / O FOR THE OCEAN**
(12"+=) *(12R 6081)* – Judy Judy.

PETER BLEGVAD

Virgin not issued

1977. (lp; by JOHN GREAVES & PETER BLEGVAD) **KEW, RHONE**

Recommended not issued

1980. (1-sided etched-7") *(RRA 5.75)* **ALCOHOL**

— with **JOHN GREAVES** – piano, synth / **DAVID LORD** – synthesizers / **JAKKO M. JAKSZYK** – guitar / **DAVE STEWART** – synthesizers, co-producer / **ANDY PARTRIDGE** – synthesizers, co-producer / **ANTON FIER** – drums / **COLIN MOULDING** – bass / **GEORGIE BORN** – cello / etc

Virgin not issued

Sep 83. (7") *(VS 630)* **KAREN. / LONELY TOO**
Dec 83. (lp) *(V 2284)* **THE NAKED SHAKESPEARE**
– How beautiful you are / Karen / Lonely too / First blow struck / Weird monkeys / The naked Shakespeare / Irma / Like a baby / Powers in the air / You can't miss it / Vermont / Blue-eyed William. *(re-iss.1988; OVED 174) (cd-iss.Apr91 & Mar94; CDV 2284)*
Jan 84. (7") *(VS 655)* **HOW BEAUTIFUL YOU ARE. / VERMONT**

— **KRISTOFFER BLEGVAD** – vocals, guitar, repl. DAVE STEWART

— guests **MANNY ELIAS / GARY BARNACLE / GUY EVANS / GLENN TILBROOK**

Apr 85. (7") *(VS 753)* **PRETTY U AND UGLY I. / MAJOR MINOR**
(12"+=) *(VS 753-12)* – How Beautiful you are.
Jul 85. (7") *(VS 798)* **SPECIAL DELIVERY. / MEET THE RAIN**
(12"+=) *(VS 798-12)* – Karen.

— now with brother + **CHRIS STAMEY** (ex-dB's) / **ANTON FIER**

Aug 85. (lp/c) *(V/TCV 2352)* **KNIGHTS LIKE THIS**
– Special delivery / Face off / Let him go / Incinerator / Pretty U and ugly I / Always be new to me / Last man / Meet the rain / The wooden pyjamas / Marlene. *(re-iss.1988; OVED 168)*
Apr 86. (lp; PETER BLEGVAD & JOHN GREAVES) *(OVED 171)* **KEW RHONE**
– Good evening / Twenty two proverbs / Exhuming the first American (seven scenes from the above painting) / Kew Rhone / Pipeline / Catalogue of fifteen objects and their titles / One footnote (to Kew Rhone) / Three tenses onanism / Nine mineral emblems / Apricot / Gegenstand.

— joined The GOLDEN PALOMINOS for the album 'BLAST OF SILENCE'.

Recommended not issued

Jul 88. (lp) *(RER 34)* **DOWNTIME**

(cd-iss.Feb93 on 'R.E.R.'; PBCD 1)

Silvertone not issued

Sep 90. (lp/c/cd) *(ORE/+C/CD 511)* **KING STRUT & OTHER STORIES** [ ] [-]
– King Strut / Gold / Meantime / On obsession / Not weak enough / Swim / Northern lights / Chicken / Real slap in the face / Shirt and comb / Stranger to myself / King Strut (reprise).

Sub Rosa not issued

Jan 95. (cd; PETER BLEGVAD & JOHN GREAVES) *(SR 75CD)* **UNEARTHED** [ ] [-]

Recommended not issued

Jun 96. (cd) *(RERPB 2CD)* **JUST WOKE UP** [ ] [-]

— He also made 'LOCUS SOLUS' with JOHN ZORN on 'Rfit', and joined The LODGE for album 'SMELL OF A FRIEND'.

DAGMAR KRAUSE

Spoken word; the first Brecht songs with music by Kurt Weill and Hanns Eisler.

Hannibal not issued

Jan 86. (lp/c) *(HN BL/BC 1317)* **SUPPLY AND DEMAND** [ ] [-]
– Supply and demand (the trader's song) / Epitaph 1919 / German miserere / O falladah die du hangest! / Alabama song / Hollywood elegies / Surabaya Johnny / Moritat / Matrosen tango / Lily of Hell / Song of the Moldau / Pavel's prison song / Easter Sunday, 1935 / At Potsdam 'Unter den eichen' / Der song von Mandalay / Benares song. *(cd-iss.May89; HNCD 1317) (German version – iss.Jan87 as 'ANGEBOT & NACHFRAGE' lp/c; HN BL/BC 1317D)*

Antilles not issued

Sep 88. (lp/c/cd) *(AN/+C/CD 8739)* **TANK BATTLES: THE SONGS OF HANNS EISLER** [ ] [-]
– Song of the whitewash / You have to pay / Ballad of the sack slingers / The perhaps song / Mankind / Song of a German mother / Bankenlied / Und endlich stirbt / Mother's hands / Genevieve: Ostern ist ball sur Seine / The trenches / (I read about) Tank battles / Chanson Alemande / Mother Beimlein / Rat men – The nightmare / Bettelied / Change the world – It needs it / Failure in loving / Ballad of (bourgeois) welfare / Berlin 1919 / Homecoming / To a little radio. *(cd re-iss.May97 on 'Blueprint'; BP 138CD)*

SLY & THE FAMILY STONE

Formed: San Francisco, California, USA . . . 1966, initially as The STONERS by former DJ/Producer, SLY STONE (born SYLVESTER STEWART) with brother FREDDIE, sister ROSEMARY and cousin LARRY GRAHAM. They adopted the name SLY & THE FAMILY STONE after gigging around local bars/clubs in Oakland and in 1967 they signed to 'Epic', releasing their debut album, 'A WHOLE NEW THING'. The record introduced the superfly new sound created by one of the first inter-racial, inter-gender and inta-drugs outfits to emerge between the rock/soul divide. With SLY casting himself HENDRIX-like in the role of Afro-American uber-hippie, he and his family were pioneers of the "Psychedelic Soul" movement, re-influencing old hands like The TEMPTATIONS and The ISLEY BROTHERS. Their breakthrough came with the 1968 single, 'DANCE TO THE MUSIC', a skilfully honed melange of doo-wop, soul and acid-funk that shook even the most stoned of hippy asses. The album of the same name followed later that year, crystallising the bands distinctive cross-over sound. Possibly their finest moment, the irresistable swing of 'EVERYDAY PEOPLE' was almost gospel-like in its passionate intensity. The single's B-side, 'SING A SIMPLE SONG', was similarly evangelical and illustrated that musically, at least, in The FAMILY STONE all the soul brothers and sisters were born equal. Each family member was given a fair deal in the mix, both instrumentally and vocally, and along with the band's unique hyrid of styles, this musical equanimity defined their sound. The classic 'STAND' (1969) album fully captured this collective, celebratory fanfare, including the aforementioned tracks as well as the 15-minute bass-heavy pulse of 'SEX MACHINE'. It also introduced SLY's penchant for mordant humour with 'DON'T CALL ME NIGGER, WHITEY'. As the 60's dream turned sour, this penchant would become ever more pronounced, 'HOT FUN IN THE SUMMERTIME' (1969) a wry observation on America's summer of discontent. Come 1970, SLY had moved to L.A. where he immersed himself in cocaine and the vacuum of the back-slapping Hollywood elite. 'THANK YOU (FALLETTINME BE MICE ELF AGIN)' (1970) was an edgy piece of taut funk that inicated the way SLY was headed. Partly composed in SLY's infamous drug den of a motorhome, where he lived gypsy-style around L.A., 'THERE'S A RIOT GOIN' ON' finally appeared in 1971. Reflecting the drug-induced paranoia and detachment of the recording sessions, most of the tracks were blurred snatches of dirty, slow burning funk, topped off by SLY's ravaged vocal chords. The deceptively laid-back groove of 'FAMILY AFFAIR' belied a grim lyrical content which extended to the whole album. From his embalming cocoon of Grade-A narcotics, SLY gave a hazily cynical commentary on the decline of American civilisation and the album remains a darkly brooding classic. With drug busts, financial pressures and hassles from militant black nationalists who didn't care for SLY's racially mixed philosophy, it was two years before 'FRESH' (1973) was released. While the sound recalled the band's effervescent charisma of old, a distinct edginess remained in the watertight grooves. The cool pop-funk of 'IF YOU WANT ME TO STAY' (1973) was the 'FAMILY STONE's last top 20 single. 'SMALL TALK' (1974) was almost overwhelmingly bland save for the title track and from there on in, SLY lost it big time. A drug casualty of the saddest order, SLY's latter 70's output was unremarkable at best. • **Songwriters:** All by SLY and group except; I CAN'T TURN YOU LOOSE (Otis Redding) / YOU REALLY GOT ME (Kinks). • **Trivia:** On the 5th of June '74, SLY married Kathy Silva on stage at Madison Square Garden. Two months earlier, she had borne him his first child, Bubb Ali (all three pictured on the album cover of 'SMALL TALK'). She divorced SLY in '75, and he filed for bankruptcy early '76.

Recommended: STAND (*9) / THERE'S A RIOT GOIN' ON (*9) / TAKIN' YOU HIGHER – THE BEST OF (*8)

SLY STONE (b. SYLVESTER STEWART, 15 Mar'44, Dallas, Texas) – vox, guitar, keyboards (ex-SLY & THE MOJO MEN) / **FREDDIE STONE** (b. FRED STEWART, 5 Jun'46, Dallas) – guitar / **CYNTHIA ROBINSON** (b.12 Jan'46, Sacramento, Calif.) – trumpet / **ROSEMARY STONE** (b. ROSEMARY STEWART, 21 Mar'45, Vallejo, Calif.) – vocals, piano / **LARRY GRAHAM** (b.14 Aug'46, Beaumont, Texas) – bass / **JERRY MARTINI** (b. 1 Oct'43, Colorado) – saxophone / **GREG ERRICO** (b. 1 Sep'46) – drums

not issued Loadstone

1966. (7") *<3951>* **I AIN'T GOT NOBODY. / I CAN'T TURN YOU LOOSE** [-] [ ]

Columbia Epic

1967. (lp) *<30333>* **A WHOLE NEW THING** [-] [ ]
– Underdog / If this room could talk / Run run run / Turn me loose / Let me hear it from you / Advice / I cannot make it / Trip to your heart / I hate to love her / Bad risk / That kind of person / Day. *(cd-iss.Jul95 on 'Epic'; EK 66424)*

1967. (7") *<10229>* **(I WANT TO TAKE YOU) HIGHER. / UNDERDOG** [-] [ ]

Mar 68. (7") *(DB 8369) <10256>* **DANCE TO THE MUSIC. / LET ME HEAR IT FROM YOU** [ ] [8] Jan68

Direction Epic

Jun 68. (7") *(58-3568)* **DANCE TO THE MUSIC. / LET ME HEAR IT FROM YOU** [7] [-]

Sep 68. (lp) *(8-63412) <26371>* **DANCE TO THE MUSIC** [ ] [ ] Apr68
– Dance to the music / (I want to take you) Higher / I ain't got nobody (for real) / Dance to the medley: Music is alive – Dance in – Music lover / Ride the rhythm / Color me true / Are you ready / Don't burn baby / I'll never fall in love again. *(re-iss.Oct73 on 'Embassy'; EMB 31030) (cd-iss.Jul94 on 'Epic'; 480906-2)*

Sep 68. (7") *(58-3707) <10353>* **M'LADY. / LIFE** [32] [93]
[93] Jun68

Jan 69. (lp) *(8-63461) <26397>* **M'LADY** (US-title 'LIFE') [ ] [ ] Nov68
– Dynamite! / Chicken / Plastic Jim / Fun / Into my own thing / Harmony / Life / Love city / I'm an animal / M'lady / Jane is a groupie.

Mar 69. (7") *(58-3938) <10407>* **EVERYDAY PEOPLE. / SING A SIMPLE SONG** [36] [1]
[89] Nov68

May 69. (7") *(58-4279) <10450>* **STAND!. / I WANT TO TAKE YOU HIGHER** [ ] [22]
[60] Apr69
<re-prom.May70 but flipped over, hit US No.38>

Jul 69. (lp) *(8-63655) <26456>* **STAND!** [ ] [13] Apr69
– Stand! / Don't call me nigger, Whitey / I want to take you higher / Somebody's watching you / Sing a simple song / Everyday people / Sex machine / You can make it if you try. *(cd-iss.Feb95 on 'Epic'; EK 64422)*

Aug 69. (7") *(58-4471) <10497>* **HOT FUN IN THE SUMMERTIME. / FUN** [ ] [2]

Feb 70. (7") *(58-4782) <10555>* **THANK YOU (FALLETTINME BE MICE ELF AGIN). / EVERYBODY IS A STAR** [ ] [1] Dec69

C.B.S. Epic

May 70. (7") *(5054)* **I WANT TO TAKE YOU HIGHER. / YOU CAN MAKE IT IF YOU TRY** [ ] [-]

Jan 71. (lp) *(EPC 69002) <30325>* **GREATEST HITS** (compilation) [ ] [2] Oct70
– I want to take you higher / Everybody is a star / Stand / Life / Fun / You can make it if you try / Dance to the music / Everyday people / Hot fun in the summertime / M'lady / Sing a simple song / Thank you (falletinme be mice elf agin). *(<quad-lp 1975; EQ 30325>) (re-iss.Mar81 on 'Epic'; EPC 32029) (re-iss.Jun90 on 'Epic' cd/c/lp; EPC 462524-2/-4/-1)*

Epic Epic

Nov 71. (7") *(EPC 7632) <10805>* **FAMILY AFFAIR. / LUV 'N' HAIGHT** [15] [1] Oct71

Jan 72. (lp/c) *(EPC/40 64613) <30986>* **THERE'S A RIOT GOIN' ON** [31] [1] Nov71
– Luv 'n' haight / Just like a baby / Poet / Family affair / Africa talks to you 'The Asphalt Jungle' / Brave & strong / Smilin' / Time / Spaced cowboy / Runnin' away / Thank you for talkin' to me Africa. *(UK-iss.w/free ltd.7"ep & newspaper) (re-iss.Feb86 on 'Edsel' lp/c; XED/CED 165) (cd-iss.Jan91; EDCD 165) (re-iss.May94 cd/c; 467063-2/-4)*

Mar 72. (7") *(EPC 7810) <10829>* **RUNNIN' AWAY. / BRAVE & STRONG** [17] [23] Jan72

Apr 72. (7") *<10850>* **SMILIN'. / LUV 'N' HAIGHT** [-] [42]

— (Jan73) **RUSTEE ALLEN** – bass repl. LARRY (formed GRAHAM CENTRAL STATION) **ANDY NEWMARK** – drums repl. ERRICO. / added **PAT RICCO** – saxophone

Jun 73. (lp/c) *(EPC/40 69039) <32134>* **FRESH** [ ] [7]
– In time / If you want me to stay / Let me have it all / Frisky / Thankful 'n' thoughtful / The skin I'm in / I don't know (satisfaction) / Keep on dancin' / Que sera sera / If it were left up to me / Babies makin' babies. *(re-iss.May87 on 'Edsel' lp/c/cd; XED/CED/EDCD 232) (cd re-iss.Sep96 on 'Columbia'; 485170-2)*

Aug 73. (7") *(EPC 1655) <11017>* **IF YOU WANT ME TO STAY. / THANKFUL 'N' THOUGHTFUL** [ ] [12] Jun73

Oct 73. (7") *<11060>* **FRISKY. / IF IT WERE LEFT UP TO ME** [-] [79]

Jan 74. (7") *(EPC 1981)* **QUE SERA SERA. / IF IT WERE LEFT UP TO ME** [ ] [-]

— **BILL LORDAN** – drums repl. NEWMARK who became session man

Jul 74. (lp/c) *(EPC/40 69070) <32930>* **SMALL TALK** [ ] [15]
– Small talk / Say you will / Mother beautiful / Time for livin' / Can't strain my brain / Loose booty / Holdin' on / Wishful thinking / Better thee than me / Livin' while I'm livin' / This is love.

Jul 74. (7") *(EPC 2530) <11140>* **TIME FOR LIVIN'. / SMALL TALK** [ ] [32]

Jan 75. (7") *(EPC 1882) <50033>* **LOOSE BOOTY. / CAN'T STRAIN MY BRAIN** [ ] [84] Oct84

SLY STONE

Oct 75. (lp/c) *<EPC/40 69165> <33835>* **HIGH ON YOU** [ ] [45]
– I get high on you / Crossword puzzle / That's lovin' you / Who do you love /

Green-eyed monster girl / Organize / Le lo li / My world / So good to me / Greed.

Oct 75. (7") *(EPC 3596)* <*50135*> **I GET HIGH ON YOU. / THAT'S LOVIN' YOU** [ ] [52] Sep75

Dec 75. (7") <*50175*> **LE LO LI. / WHO DO YOU LOVE** [-] [ ]

Mar 76. (7") <*50201*> **CROSSWORD PUZZLE. / GREED** [-] [ ]

SLY & THE FAMILY STONE

— reformed with last line-up

Dec 76. (lp/c) *(EPC/40 81641)* <*33698*> **HEARD YA MISSED ME, WELL I'M BACK** [ ] [ ]
– Heard ya missed me, well I'm back / What was I thinkin' / In my head / Sexy situation / Blessing in disguise / Everything in you / Mother is a hippie / Let's be together / The thing / Family again.

Feb 77. (7") <*50331*> **FAMILY AGAIN. / NOTHING LESS THAN HAPPINESS** [-] [ ]

Warners Warners

Sep 79. (7") *(K 17474)* <*49062*> **REMEMBER WHO YOU ARE. / SHEER ENERGY** [ ] [ ]

Oct 79. (lp/c) *(K/K4 56640)* <*3303*> **BACK ON THE RIGHT TRACK** [ ] [ ]
– Remember who you are / Back on the right track / If it's not addin' up . . . / The same thing (makes you laugh, makes you cry) / Shine it on / It takes all kinds / Who's to say / Sheer energy. *(cd-iss.Jan96; 7599 26858-2)*

Dec 79. (7") <*49132*> **THE SAME THING (MAKES YOU LAUGH, MAKES YOU CRY). / WHO'S TO SAY** [-] [ ]

— In 1981, SLY guested on album 'THE ELECTRIC SPANKING OF WAR BABIES' by George Clinton's FUNKADELIC.

– compilations, etc. –

— on 'Epic' unless stated otherwise

1972. (lp; by SLY STONE) *Sculpture;* <*SCP 2001*> **RECORDED IN SAN FRANCISCO: 1964-67** [-] [ ]

Mar 73. (7") *(EPC 1148)* **FAMILY AFFAIR. / DANCE TO THE MUSIC** [ ] [-]

Feb 75. (7"ep) *(EPC 3048)* **DANCE TO THE MUSIC / COLOUR ME TRUE. / STAND! / RIDE THE RHYTHM** [ ] [-]

May 75. (d-lp) *(EPC 22004)* <*33462*> **HIGH ENERGY** [ ] [ ]
– (A WHOLE NEW THING / LIFE)

1975. (7") <*50119*> **HOT FUN IN THE SUMMERTIME. / FUN** [-] [ ]

1975. (7") *(152282)* **DANCE TO THE MUSIC. / LIFE** [ ] [-]

1975. (7") *(152302)* **HOT FUN IN THE SUMMERTIME. / M'LADY** [ ] [-]

1975. (7") *(152317)* **FAMILY AFFAIR. / RUNNIN' AWAY** [ ] [-]

1975. (7") *(152331)* **IF YOU WANT ME TO STAY. / FRISKY** [ ] [-]

Jan 77. (7") *(EPC 4879)* **DANCE TO THE MUSIC. / I WANT TO TAKE YOU HIGHER** [ ] [-]

Mar 79. (7") *(EPC 7070)* **DANCE TO THE MUSIC. / STAND!** [ ] [-]

Nov 79. (7") *(EPC 8017)* <*50795*> **DANCE TO THE MUSIC. / SING A SIMPLE SONG** [ ] [ ]

Jan 80. (lp) *(EPC 83640)* <*35974*> **TEN YEARS TOO SOON** (disco remixes) [ ] [ ]

Aug 80. (7") *(EPC 8853)* **DANCE TO THE MUSIC. / EVERYDAY PEOPLE** [ ] [-]
(re-iss.Jul82 on 'Old Gold'; OG 9188)

May 82. (d-lp) *(EPC 22119)* <*37071*> **ANTHOLOGY** [ ] [ ] Dec81
(re-iss.Sep87 lp/c; 460175-1/-4)

Sep 87. (7") *Portrait; (SLY 1)* **DANCE TO THE MUSIC. / FAMILY AFFAIR** [ ] [ ]
(12"+=) *(SLYT 1)* – Everyday people / Runnin' away.

Apr 91. (cd/c) *Thunderbolt; (CDTB/THBC 119)* **FAMILY AFFAIR** [ ] [-]

Nov 91. (cd/c) *Castle; (CCS CD/MC 307)* **THE COLLECTION** [ ] [-]

Dec 91. (cd) *Thunderbolt; (CDTB 129)* **IN THE STILL OF THE NIGHT** [ ] [-]

Jul 92. (cd/c) *Sony; (471758-2/-4)* **TAKIN' YOU HIGHER – THE BEST OF SLY & THE FAMILY STONE** [ ] [ ]
– Dance to the music / I want to take you higher / Family affair / Thank you (falletinme be mice elf agin) / I get high on you / Stand / M'lady / Skin I'm in / Everyday people / Sing a simple song / Hot fun in the summertime / Don't call me nigger, Whitey / Brave & strong / Life / Everybody is a star / If you want me to stay / (You caught me) Smilin' / Que sera sera / Running away / Family affair (remix). *(cd re-iss.Oct94 on 'Epic'; 477506-2)*

Feb 94. (cd/c) *Javelin; (HAD CD/MC 119)* **SPOTLIGHT ON SLY & THE FAMILY STONE** [ ] [-]

Mar 94. (cd) *Charly;* **REMEMBER WHO YOU ARE** [ ] [-]

Sep 94. (cd) *Ace; (CDCHD 539)* **PRECIOUS STONE: IN THE STUDIO WITH SLY STONE** (rec.1963-65) [ ] [-]

Dec 94. (cd/c) *Prestige; (CD/CAS SGP 0125)* **EVERY DOG HAS IT'S DAY** [ ] [-]

Feb 95. (cd; by SLY STONE & THE MOJO MEN) *(KLMCD 005)* **PEARLS FROM THE PAST** [ ] [-]

— Thunderbolt records issued 2 albums of SLY STONE productions in Apr87 + Oct87 respectively, named 'DANCE TO THE MUSIC' & 'FAMILY AFFAIR'.

SLY STONE

Warners Warners

Mar 83. (lp) *(923700-1)* <*23700-1*> **AIN'T BUT THE ONE WAY** [ ] [ ]
– L.O.V.I.N.U. / One way / Ha ha, hee hee / Hobo Ken / Who in the funk do you think we are / You really got me / Sylvester / We can do it / High, y'all. *(cd-iss.Jan96; 7599 23700-2)*

— In 1984, SLY joined BOBBY WOMACK on tour. He later guested on JESSE JOHNSON's 'A&M' US No.53 hit single 'Crazay' (Oct86) *AM 360* /<*2878*>.

not issued A&M

Oct 86. (7") <*2890*> **EEK-A-BO-STATIK. / BLACK GIRLS (RAE DAWN CHONG)** [-] [ ]

Dec 86. (7"w/ MARTHA DAVIS) **STONE LOVE AND AFFECTION. / BLACK GIRLS (RAE DAWN CHONG)** [-] [ ]

SMALL FACES

Formed: East London, England . . . mid '65 by RONNIE LANE, KENNY JONES and JIMMY WINSTON, who subsequently found lead singer and ex-child actor, STEVE MARRIOTT. After a successful residency at Leicester Square's Cavern Club, the band were snapped up by 'Decca' records as potential usurpers to The WHO's mod crown. Their debut single, 'WHATCHA GONNA DO ABOUT IT' (1965) graced the Top 20 with its roughshod R&B and amid the ensuing attention the band received, WINSTON was kicked out after shamelessly trying to promote himself as the lynchpin of the group. With IAN McLAGAN drafted in as a replacement, the band hit Top 3 with the 'SHA LA LA LA LEE' (1966) single. Despite the cliched boy-meets-girl lyric, the record was a wildly exhilirating rush of amphetamine pop and suddenly The SMALL FACES were big news. After another Top 10 single and a critically acclaimed eponymous debut album, the band were being mentioned in the same breath as The BEATLES and The ROLLING STONES. Indeed, in August '66 they deposed The Fab Four's 'ELEANOR RIGBY' at the top of the charts with 'ALL OR NOTHING'. Come 1967, the band had left 'Decca' and signed with ANDREW LOOG-OLDHAM's 'Immediate' label, releasing 'HERE COMES THE NICE'. The single marked a change in direction and in keeping with the times, was vaguely psychedelic. After a similarly adventurous second album that bore a decidedly unadventurous title ('SMALL FACES' yet again), the band released their most well-known track, the slightly twee, deeply dippy 'ITCHYCOO PARK' (later reduced to dross by M-PEOPLE). Next came the abrasive 'TIN SOLDIER' (1967) single after which the band began working on their psychedelic masterpiece, 'OGDEN'S NUT GONE FLAKE' (1968). An engaging blend of trippy R&B and cockney charm, the album's influence was far reaching and it gets re-issued with the same tireless regularity as 'OCEAN WELLER SCENE' namedrop the band. Timeless as it was, the record proved to be the group's swansong and after a few singles, including the gorgeous 'AFTERGLOW (OF YOUR LOVE)' (1969), the band split with MARRIOTT flouncing off to form HUMBLE PIE. Meanwhile JONES, LANE and McLAGAN ditched the psychedelic overtones, recruited RON WOOD and ROD STEWART, renaming the band The FACES; lad-rock was born! The FACES peddled a distinctive strain of ramshackle, boozy, bluesy rock that was apparently best heard in a live setting surrounded by sweaty males. Their debut, 'FIRST STEP' (1970), was a boisterous statement of intent which included the ragged charm of 'THREE BUTTON HAND ME DOWN' and a raw cover of DYLAN's 'WICKED MESSENGER'. 'LONG PLAYER' (1971) was equally ballsy, while 'A NOD IS AS GOOD AS A WINK . . .TO A BLIND HORSE' (1971) saw the band in full flight, WOOD going hell for leather on 'MISS JUDY'S FARM' and the gloriously un-PC raunch of 'STAY WITH ME'. The McLAGAN/LANE penned 'YOU'RE SO RUDE' was a leering gem and LANE excelled himself with the lovely 'DEBRIS'. As STEWART's solo career skyrocketed, the band began to splinter, unbalanced by ROD's high profile. After the slightly disappointing 'OOH LA LA' (1973) album, LANE left to go solo, The FACES basically becoming STEWART's backing band and after a final below par live album, RON WOOD left for The ROLLING STONES. There was a brief SMALL FACES reunion (minus LANE) in the late 70's and although the band had a deal with 'Atlantic', no commercial success was forthcoming. JONES went on to join The WHO, while MARRIOTT re-formed HUMBLE PIE but any chances of a further reunion were dealt a fatal blow in 1991 when MARRIOTT tragically died in a fire at his Essex home. After a respectable, if hardly commercial solo career, RONNIE LANE finally succumbed to Multiple Sclerosis earlier this year (1997). A sad end for two pioneering musicians who, through both The FACES and The SMALL FACES, heavily influenced the course of popular music; stand up BLUR, PULP, OASIS, PRIMAL SCREAM, The BLACK CROWES etc. • **Songwriters:** MARRIOTT and LANE except; WHATCHA GONNA DO ABOUT IT (Ian Samwell-Smith; their early producer) / SHA-LA-LA-LA-LEE (c.Kenny Lynch & Mort Schuman) / EVERY LITTLE BIT HURTS (Brenda Holloway) / TAKE THIS HURT OFF ME (Don Covay) / YOU'VE REALLY GOT A HOLD ON ME (Miracles) / etc. The FACES covered MAYBE I'M AMAZED (Paul McCartney) / I WISH IT WOULD RAIN (Temptations) / etc. • **Trivia:** The FACES had come together initially as the supergroup, QUIET MELON, which included ART WOOD, LONG JOHN BALDRY and JIMMY HOROWITZ.

Recommended: THERE ARE BUT FOUR SMALL FACES (*7) / OGDENS' NUT GONE FLAKE (*8) / THE ULTIMATE COLLECTION (*7)

STEVE MARRIOTT (b.30 Jan'47, Bow, London) – vocals, guitar (ex-solo artist) / **JIMMY WINSTON** (b. JAMES LANGWITH, 20 Apr'45, Stratford, London) – organ / **RONNIE LANE** (b. 1 Apr'45, Plaistow, London) – bass, vocals / **KENNEY JONES** (b.16 Sep'48, Stepney, London) – drums

Decca Press

Aug 65. (7") *(F 12208)* <*45-9794*> **WHATCHA GONNA DO ABOUT IT?. / WHAT'S A MATTER, BABY** [14] [ ] Jan66

— **IAN McLAGAN** (b.12 May'45, Hounslow, England) – keyboards repl. WINSTON who went solo

Nov 65. (7") *(F 12276)* **I'VE GOT MINE. / IT'S TOO LATE** [ ] [-]

Jan 66. (7") *(F 12317)* <*45-9826*> **SHA-LA-LA-LA-LEE. / GROW YOUR OWN** [3] [ ] Apr66

May 66. (7") *(F 12393)* <*45-5007*> **HEY GIRL. / ALMOST GROWN** [10] [ ] Jul66

May 66. (lp) *(LK 4790)* **SMALL FACES** [3] [-]
– Shake / Come on children / You better believe it / It's too late / One night stand / Whatcha gonna do about it? / Sorry she's mine / E to D / You need loving / Don't stop what you're doing / Own up / Sha-la-la-la-lee. *(cd-iss.Jul88 on 'London' 820*

572-2)(+=)
– What's a matter baby / I've got mine / Grow your own / Almost grown.

Decca RCA Vic.

Aug 66. (7") *(F 12470) <47-8949>* **ALL OR NOTHING. / UNDERSTANDING** [1] [ ] Sep66
Nov 66. (7") *(F 12500) <47-9055>* **MY MIND'S EYE. / I CAN'T DANCE WITH YOU** [4] [ ] Dec66
Feb 67. (7") *(F 12565)* **I CAN'T MAKE IT. / JUST PASSING** [26] [-]
Apr 67. (7") *(F 12619)* **PATTERNS. / E TO D** [ ] [-]
May 67. (lp) *(LK 4879)* **FROM THE BEGINNING** (out-takes, demos, etc) [17] [-]
– Runaway / My mind's eye / Yesterday, today and tomorrow / That man / My way of giving / Hey girl / Tell me have you ever seen me? / Come back and take this hurt off me / All or nothing / Baby don't do it / Plum Nellie / Sha-la-la-la-lee / You really got a hold on me / Whatcha gonna do about it?. *(re-iss.Aug84; DOA 2) (cd-iss.Jan89 on 'London' w/ extra tracks; 820 766-2)*

Immediate Immediate

Jun 67. (7") *(IM 050) <1902>* **HERE COMES THE NICE. / TALK TO YOU** [12] [ ]
Jun 67. (lp; mono/stereo) *(IMLP/IMSP 008)* **SMALL FACES** [12] [-]
– Green circles / Become like you / Get yourself together / All our yesterdays / Talk to you / Show me the way / Up the wooden hills to Bedfordshire / Eddie's dreaming / (Tell me) Have you ever seen me / Something I want to tell you / Feeling lonely / Happy boys happy / Things are going to get better / My way of giving. *(cd-iss.May91 as 'GREEN CIRCLES (FIRST IMMEDIATE ALBUM)' on 'Sequel'; NEXCD 163) (+=)–* Green circles (take 2) / Donkey rides, a penny, a glass / Have you ever seen me (take 2). *(cd re-iss.Apr97 on 'Essential'; ESMCD 476)*
Aug 67. (7") *(IM 052) <501>* **ITCHYCOO PARK. / I'M ONLY DREAMING** [3] [16] Nov67
Nov 67. (7") *(IM 062) <5003>* **TIN SOLDIER. / I FEEL MUCH BETTER** [9] [73] Mar68
(re-iss.May75; IMS 100)
Feb 68. (lp) *<Z12-52-002>* **THERE ARE BUT FOUR SMALL FACES** [-] [ ]
– Here comes the nice / All or nothing / Lazy Sunday / Sha-la-la-la-lee / Collibosher / The Autumn stone / Whatcha gonna do about it? / My mind's eye / Itchyco Park / Hey girl / The universal / Runaway / Call it something nice / I can't make it / Afterglow (of your love) / Tin soldier.
Apr 68. (7") *(IM 064) <5007>* **LAZY SUNDAY. / ROLLIN' OVER** [2] [ ]
(re-iss.Oct82; same)
Jun 68. (lp; mono/stereo) *(IMLP/IMSP 012) <Z12-52-008>* **OGDENS' NUT GONE FLAKE** [1] [ ]
– Ogden's nut gone flake / Afterglow (of your love) / Long agos and worlds apart / Rene / Son of a baker / Lazy Sunday / Happiness Stan / Rollin' over / The hungry intruder / The journey / Mad John / Happy days / Toy town. *<US re-iss.Mar73 on 'Abkco'; 4225> (re-iss.Dec75; IML 1001) (re-iss.Jun77; IML 2001) (re-iss.export Aug78 on 'Charly'; CR 300015) (re-iss.Mar80 on 'Virgin'; V 2159) (re-iss.Oct86 on 'Castle' lp/cd+=; CLA LP/CD 116)–* Tin soldier (live). *(re-cd-iss.in box Feb91 on 'Castle'; CLACT 016) (cd re-iss.Feb97 on 'Original Recordings'; ORRLP 001) (cd re-iss.Apr97 on 'Essential'; ESMCD 477)*
Jul 68. (7") *(IM 069) <5009>* **THE UNIVERSAL. / DONKEY RIDES, A PENNY, A GLASS** [16] [ ]
Nov 68. (7") *<5012>* **THE JOURNEY. / MAD JOHN** [-] [ ]
Mar 69. (7") *(IM 077) <5014>* **AFTERGLOW (OF YOUR LOVE). / WHAM BAM, THANK YOU MAM** [36] [ ]
Mar 69. (d-lp) *(IMAL 01/02)* **THE AUTUMN STONE** (rarities, live, etc) [ ] [ ]
– Here comes the nice / The Autumn stone / Collibosher / All or nothing / Red balloon / Lazy Sunday / Rollin' over / If I were a carpenter / Every little bit hurts / My mind's eye / Tin soldier / Just asking / Call it something nice / I can't make it / Afterglow (of your love) / Sha-la-la-la-lee / The universal / Itchycoo Park / Hey girl / Wide eyed girl / On the wall / Whatcha gonna do about it / Wham bam thank you mam. *(re-iss.Jul84; IMLD 1) (re-iss.May86 on 'Castle' lp/c/cd; CLA LP/MC/CD 114) (re-iss.1991) (cd re-iss.Apr97 on 'Essential'; ESMCD 478)*

— Disbanded Mar'69. STEVE MARRIOTT formed HUMBLE PIE. The remaining members became The FACES.

— SMALL FACES re-formed by **JONES, McLAGAN** + re-instated **MARRIOTT** incomer **RICKY WILLS** – bass (ex-Peter FRAMPTON'S CAMEL, ex-ROXY MUSIC, etc)

Atlantic Atlantic

Jul 77. (7") *(K 10983)* **LOOKIN' FOR A LOVE. / KO'D (BY LUV)** [ ] [ ]
Aug 77. (lp/c) *(K/K4 50375) <SD 19113>* **PLAYMATES** [ ] [ ]
– High and happy / Never too late / Tonight / Say larvee / Find it / Lookin' for a love / Playmates / Drive in romance / This song's just for you / Smilin' in tune. *(cd-iss.Jun92 on 'Repertoire';)*
Nov 77. (7") *(K 11043)* **STAND BY ME (STAND BY YOU). / HUNGRY AND LOOKING** [ ] [ ]

— added on tour **JIMMY McCULLOCH** (b.1953, Glasgow, Scotland) – guitar (of WINGS)

Jun 78. (7") *(K 11173)* **FILTHY RICH. / OVER TOO SOON** [ ] [ ]
Sep 78. (lp/c) *(K/K4 50468) <SD 19171>* **78 IN THE SHADE** [ ] [ ]
– Over too soon / Too many crossroads / Let me down gently / Thinkin' about love / Stand by me (stand by you) / Brown man do / Soldier / Reel sour / You ain''t seen nothin' yet / Filthy rich. *(cd-iss.Nov93 on 'Repertoire';)*

— Disbanded again mid'78. KENNY JONES joined The WHO. McCULLOCH died 27th Sep'79. MARRIOTT re-formed HUMBLE PIE. He was to tragically die in his Essex home after it went on fire 20 Apr'91. More recently, in fact just as this books deadline approached, founder member RONNIE LANE finally died in June '97, after 18 years suffering from multiple sclerosis.

– compilations, others, etc. –

Jun 72. (7") *Pride; <1006>* **RUNAWAY./ SHAKE** [-] [ ]
Jul 72. (lp) *Pride; <PRD 0001>* **EARLY YEARS** [-] [ ]
Dec 72. (lp) *Pride; <PRD 0014>* **THE HISTORY OF THE SMALL FACES** [-] [ ]
1974. (lp) *M.G.M.; <M3P 4955>* **ARCHETYPES** [-] [ ]
Jun 77. (lp) *Decca; (ROOTS 5)* **ROCK ROOTS: THE SMALL FACES** ('A'&'B'sides) [ ] [-]
Sep 77. (7"m) *Decca; (F 13727)* **SHA-LA-LA-LA-LEE. / WHAT'CHA GONNA DO ABOUT IT / ALL OR NOTHING** [ ] [-]
(re-iss.Mar82)
Sep 79. (7"ep) *Decca; (FR 13864)* **THE LONDON BOYS EP** [ ] [-]
– (shared EP w/ DAVID BOWIE, DOBIE GRAY, BIRDS)
Mar 81. (lp) *Decca; (TAB 16)* **SHA-LA-LA-LA-LEE** [ ] [-]
Nov 75. (7") *Immediate; (IMS 102)* **ITCHYCOO PARK. / MY MIND'S EYE** [9] [-]
Dec 75. (7") *Immediate; (IMS 701)* **LAZY SUNDAY. / THE AUTUMN STONE** [ ] [-]
(re-iss.Sep81; same)
Mar 76. (7") *Immediate; (IMS 106)* **LAZY SUNDAY. / (TELL ME) HAVE YOU EVER SEEN ME** [36] [-]
Jul 76. (lp) *Immediate; (IML 1008)* **MAGIC MOMENTS** [ ] [-]
Jan 78. (lp/c) *Immediate; (IML/IMC 2008)* **GREATEST HITS** [ ] [-]
May 75. (d-lp) *Sire; (3709/2)* **VINTAGE YEARS – THE IMMEDIATE STORY VOL.2** [-] [ ]
Aug 78. (lp) *Charly; (CR 300025)* **LIVE UK 1969 (live)** [ ] [-]
May 80. (lp) *New World; (NW 6001)* **THE SMALL FACES** (shared w / AMEN CORNER) [ ] [-]
Jul 80. (lp/c) *Virgin; (V/TCV 2166)* **BIG HITS** [ ] [-]
Jul 80. (7"m) *Virgin; (VS 367)* **TIN SOLDIER. / TIN SOLDIER (live) / RENE (live)** [ ] [-]
Oct 80. (lp) *Virgin; (T/TCV 2178)* **FOR YOUR DELIGHT THE DARLINGS OF WAPPING WHARF LAUNDERETTE** [ ] [-]
1982. (lp) *Accord; (SN 7157)* **BY APPOINTMENT** [ ] [-]
Oct 83. (7") *Old Gold; (OG 9343)* **ALL OR NOTHING. / MY MIND'S EYE** [ ] [-]
Oct 83. (7") *Old Gold; (OG 9344)* **SHA-LA-LA-LA-LEE. / WHAT'CHA GONNA DO ABOUT IT** [ ] [-]
1984. (d-lp) *Compleat; <672 004-1>* **BIG MUSIC – A COMPLEAT COLLECTION** [-] [ ]
Nov 84. (lp) *Astan; (20049)* **GOLDEN HITS** [ ] [-]
Jan 85. (7") *Old Gold; (OG 9465)* **LAZY SUNDAY. / TIN SOLDIER** [ ] [-]
Jan 85. (7") *Old Gold; (OG 9466)* **ITCHYCOO PARK. / HERE COMES THE NICE** [ ] [-]
Oct 85. (lp) *Platinum; (PLP 29/LP 24045)* **SORRY SHE'S MINE** [ ] [-]
Nov 85. (d-lp/c/cd) *Castle; (CCS LP/MC/CD 108)* **SMALL FACES COLLECTION** [ ] [-]
(re-iss.cd Oct91; same)
Jun 86. (12"ep) *Archive 4; (TOF 103)* **CLASSIC CUTS** [ ] [-]
– Itchycoo park / Lazy Sunday / Here comes the nice / Sha-la-la-la-lee.
Sep 86. (lp/c) *Showcase; (SHLP 145)* **QUITE NATURALLY** [ ] [-]
(cd-iss.Dec87; SHCD 145)
Jan 88. (lp/cd) *Big Time; (261 552-1/-2)* **20 GREATEST HITS** [ ] [-]
May 88. (3"cd-ep) *Castle Special Edition; (CD 3-9)* **ITCHYCOO PARK / LAZY SUNDAY / ALL OR NOTHING (live) / AUTUMN STONE** [ ] [-]
Jul 88. (lp/c) *Knight; (KN LP/C 10007)* **NIGHTRIDING** [ ] [-]
Feb 89. (cd-ep) *Old Gold; (OG 6119)* **ITCHYCOO PARK / LAZY SUNDAY / TIN SOLDIER** [ ] [-]
Apr 89. (lp/c/cd) *Castle; (CLA LP/MC/CD 146)* **GREATEST HITS** [ ] [-]
Jan 90. (cd) *O.N.N. Range; (ONN 65)* **GREATEST HITS** [ ] [-]
May 90. (cd/c/d-lp) *Castle TV; (CTV CD/MC/LP 004)* **THE ULTIMATE COLLECTION** [ ] [-]
(cd re-iss.Dec91 as 'THE COMPLETE COLLECTION'; CCSCD 302)
Jun 90. (cd/c/lp) *See For Miles; (SEE 293/+C/CD)* **THE SINGLES A's & B's** [ ] [-]
(cd+= extra tracks)
Sep 90. (cd) *Success; (SUC 2198)* **LAZY SUNDAY** [ ] [-]
(re-iss.Sep92 on 'Pickwick';)
1990. (cd) *Ariola Express; (ARICD 973)* **LAZY SUNDAY** [ ] [-]
Aug 91. (cd) *Dojo; (DOJOCD 60)* **QUITE NATAURALLY RARE** [ ] [-]
1992. (cd) *Sony; <52427>* **ALL OR NOTHING** [-] [ ]
May 93. (cd/c) *Spectrum; (550 047-2/-4)* **IT'S ALL OR NOTHING** [ ] [-]
Sep 93. (cd/c) *Laserlight; (CD/MC 12208)* **ITCHYCOO PARK** [ ] [-]
Mar 94. (cd/c) *Laserlight; (CD/MC 12221)* **HERE COMES THE NICE** [ ] [-]
Apr 94. (cd-ep) *Disky; (DISK 4504)* **HIT SINGLE COLLECTABLES** [ ] [-]
– Itchycoo Park / Tin soldier / Lazy Sunday.
May 94. (cd) *Arc; (TOP 940500)* **GREATEST HITS** [ ] [-]
Mar 95. (cd) *Mastertone; (10065)* **ITCHYCOO PARK** [ ] [-]
Jul 95. (cd) *Summit; (SUMCD 4001)* **THE BEST OF THE SMALL FACES** [ ] [-]
Aug 95. (cd) *It's Music; (22579)* **THE SMALL FACES** [ ] [-]
Jul 95. (cd) *Repertoire; (REP 4429-WO)* **BOXED** [ ] [-]
Oct 95. (cd) *Abracadabra; (AB 3034)* **ITCHYCOO PARK** [ ] [-]
Nov 95. (4xcd-box) *Charly; (IMMBOX 1)* **THE IMMEDIATE YEARS** [ ] [-]
May 96. (d-cd/d-c/d-lp) *Deram; (844583-2/-4/-1)* **THE DECCA ANTHOLOGY 1965-1967** [66] [-]
Jan 97. (d-cd) *Charly; (CPCD 82602)* **THE VERY BEST OF THE SMALL FACES** [ ] [-]

SMOKE

Formed: Yorkshire, England . . . 1965 out of one-off outfit, The SHOTS, by MICK ROWLEY, MAL LUKER, PHIL PEACOCK, JOHN 'ZEKE' LUND and GEOFF GILL. They came under the wing of self-made millionaire ALAN BRUSH, who fancied himself as a manager but was shocked when debut, 'KEEP A HOLD OF WHAT YOU'VE GOT', failed to sell. Early in 1967, with new producer MONTY BABSON and new name SMOKE, they had their first and only excursion into UK Top 50 with the flower-power flavoured 'MY FRIEND JACK'. It might have gained a higher placing but for it being banned from airplay due to the lyrics " . . . eats sugar lumps" (drug connotations). It became a massive hit on the continent, gaining support from pirate radio stations and leading to a German-only album release, 'IT'S SMOKE TIME'. The follow-up, 'IF THE WEATHER'S SUNNY', failed to break through and a series of quirky flops superseded another 1967-68 combo; CHORDS FIVE, a BABSON MORGAN studio outfit which didn't include ROWLEY. The early 70's saw a single from each year, none of which were of any note. • **Trivia:**

Not to be confused with the US group of same name, who were on 'Universal' & 'Sidewalk' in '68.

Recommended: IT'S SMOKE TIME (*5)

MICK ROWLEY – vocals / **MAL LUKER** – lead guitar / **PHIL PEACOCK** – rhythm guitar / **JOHN 'ZEKE' LUND** – bass / **GEOFF GILL** – drums

Columbia / not issued

Oct 65. (7"; as SHOTS) *(DB 7713)* **KEEP A HOLD OF WHAT YOU'VE GOT. / SHE'S A LIAR** [ ] [-]

— now without PEACOCK

Feb 67. (7") *(DB 8115)* **MY FRIEND JACK. / WE CAN TAKE IT** [45] [-]

Aug 67. (7") *(DB 8252)* **IF THE WEATHER'S SUNNY. / I WOULD IF I COULD, BUT I CAN'T** [ ] [-]

Gull / not issued

1967. (lp) *(INT 128301)* **MY FRIEND JACK** [-] [-] German
– My friend Jack / Waterfall / You can't catch me / High in a room / Wake up Cherylina / Don't lead me on / We can't take it / If the weather's sunny / I wanna make it with you / It's getting closer / It's just your way of loving / I would if I could but I can't. *(UK-iss.May88 on 'Morgan Blue Town'; MBT 5001) (cd-iss.1987 as '. . .IT'S SMOKE TIME' on 'Avenue'; 826524)*

Island / not issued

May 67. (7"; as CHORDS FIVE) *(WI 3044)* **I'M ONLY DREAMING. / UNIVERSAL VAGRANT** [ ] [-]

Nov 67. (7") *(WIP 6023)* **IT COULD BE WONDERFUL. / HAVE SOME MORE TEA** [ ] [-]

Mar 68. (7"w-drawn) *(WIP 6031)* **UTTERLY SIMPLE. / SYDNEY GILL** [-] [-]

Polydor / not issued

May 68. (7"; as CHORDS FIVE) *(56261)* **SAME OLD FAT MAN. / HOLD ON TO EVERYTHIN' YOU'VE GOT** [ ] [-]

Revolution Pop / not issued

1970. (7") *(REVP 1002)* **DREAMS OF DREAMS. / MY BIRTH** [ ] [-]

Pageant / not issued

1971. (7") *(SAM 101)* **RIDE RIDE RIDE. / GUY FAWKES** [ ] [-]

Regal Zonophone / not issued

1972. (7") *(RZ 3071)* **SUGAR MAN. / THAT'S WHAT I WANT** [ ] [-]

Decca / not issued

Jan 74. (7") *(FR 13484)* **SHAGALAGALU. / GIMME GOOD LOVING** [ ] [-]

Jun 74. (7") *(FR 13514)* **MY LULLABY. / LOOKING HIGH** [ ] [-]

— split after above single again failed to sell

SOFT MACHINE

Formed: Canterbury, England . . . 1966 by ex-WILDE FLOWERS members ROBERT WYATT and KEVIN AYERS, who met up with Australian beatnik, DAEVID ALLEN and former Oxford University student MIKE RATLEDGE. The others members of The WILDE FLOWERS (PYE HASTINGS & RICHARD COUGHLAN) went on to form CARAVAN. A trip to Majorca in 1966 by ALLEN and AYERS led to a chance meeting with a monied, freak-friendly American by the name of Wes Brunson, who agreed to finance the first incarnation of SOFT MACHINE, the fondly named MR. HEAD. Moving to London, the band regrouped and after phoning WILLIAM BURROUGHS to ask his permission, adopted the SOFT MACHINE moniker. Together with PINK FLOYD, the band formed the vanguard of the psychedelic revolution, playing such legendary London gigs as the International Times launch at the Roundhouse. Early in 1967, they were signed to 'Polydor' by CHAS CHANDLER, who employed the services of SOFTS fan JIMI HENDRIX on the B-side of their debut single, 'LOVE MAKES SWEET MUSIC' (1967). The single was basically a pop song and not entirely representative of the band's live free-form improvisation that took its cue from the avant-jazz of artists like ORNETTE COLEMAN and JOHN COLTRANE. After a gig in St. Tropez (where they played an hour long version of AYERS' 'WE DID IT AGAIN' to the assembled Parisian elite), ALLEN was refused re-entry to the UK due to an expired visa, remaining in France and subsequently forming uber-hippies, GONG. Pared down to a trio, SOFT MACHINE underwent a gruelling tour of America supporting JIMI HENDRIX. During a short break in the middle of the tour, the band recorded their eponymous debut for 'PROBE' records, a US-only affair which incredibly, still hasn't had a full UK release almost 30 years on. A pioneering hybrid of psychedelic jazz improvisation, the album was the first and last to feature KEVIN AYERS, who took off for IBIZA at the end of the US tour. Recruiting HENDRIX roadie HUGH HOPPER, the band recorded another album for 'Probe' to fulfill contractual obligations. 'SOFT MACHINE VOL.2' (1969) was another idiosyncratic classic, containing a backwards rendition of the alphabet and a multitude of highbrow cultural references. Employing such live instrumentation as saxophone, trombone and cornet, the band increasingly moved towards jazz fusion and 'THIRD' (1970) was largely instrumental, save for WYATT's sublime meditation, 'MOON IN JUNE'. The other band members refused to have any serious involvement with the song, a crucial factor in WYATT's eventual split from the group. As SOFT MACHINE moved further into tepid jazz-rock territory, WYATT became increasingly frustrated and was eventually pushed out after 'FOURTH' (1971). While WYATT went on to form MATCHING MOLE before going solo, SOFT MACHINE released a further clutch of noodling albums before splitting in 1981. • **Songwriters:** Either AYERS (on debut lp only), WYATT (on first four albums only), or RATLEDGE and group. • **Trivia:** A John Peel session was recorded on the 21st of June '69 with their seminal 7-piece line-up. They were the first "rock" act to play the normally orchestrated 'Proms' at London's Albert Hall (1970). Non-originals, RATLEDGE and JENKINS became ADIEMUS, who had a UK Top 50 hit with their self-titled single (the theme from the TV ad for Delta Airlines), which featured vocalist MIRIAM STOCKLEY.

Recommended: THE SOFT MACHINE (*6) / VOLUME 2 (*6) / THIRD (*7) / FOURTH (*6) / SIX (*5) / SEVEN (*4) / THE PEEL SESSIONS (*6)

MIKE RATLEDGE – keyboards / **DAEVID ALLEN** (b. Australia) – guitar / **KEVIN AYERS** (b.16 Aug'45, Herne Bay, England) – bass, vocals (ex-WILDE FLOWERS) / **ROBERT WYATT** (b. ROBERT ELLIDGE, Bristol, England) – drums, vocals (ex-WILDE FLOWERS) / Note:- Other original American-born guitarist LARRY NOLAN left before debut 45.

Polydor / not issued

Feb 67. (7") *(56151)* **LOVE MAKES SWEET MUSIC. / FEELIN' REELIN' SQUEELIN'** [ ] [-]

— trimmed to a trio, when DAEVID ALLEN went to France to form GONG. He was deputised on tour only by ANDY SUMMERS. First 2 albums guest **BRIAN HOPPER** – saxophone (ex-WILDE FLOWERS)

Probe / Probe

Nov 68. (7") <452> **JOY OF A TOY. / WHY ARE WE SLEEPING** [-] [ ]

Dec 68. (lp) <PLP 4500> **THE SOFT MACHINE** [-] [ ]
– Hope for happiness / Joy of a toy / Hope for happiness (reprise) / Why am I so short? / So boot if at all / A certain kind / Save yourself / Priscilla / Lullabye letter / We did it again / Plus belle qu'une poubelle / Why are we sleeping / Box 25-4 LID. *(UK-iss.Mar87 on 'Big Beat' lp/c; WIK A/C 57)*

— **HUGH HOPPER** – bass (ex-WILDE FLOWERS) repl. AYERS who'd went solo

Apr 69. (lp) *(SPB 1002)* <PLP 4505> **SOFT MACHINE VOL.2** [ ] [ ]
– Pataphysical introduction (part I) / A concise British alphabet (part I) / Hibou, Anemone and bear / A concise British alphabet (part II) / Hulloder / Dada was here / Thank you Pierrot Lunaire / Have you ever been green? / Pataphysical introduction (part II) / Out of tunes / As long as he lies perfectly still / Dedicated to you but you weren't listening / Fire engine passing with bells clanging / Pig / Orange skin food / A door opens and closes / 10.30 returns to the bedroom. *(re-iss.1974 on 'ABC'; ABCL 5004) (re-iss.May87 on 'Big Beat' lp/c; WIK A/C 58)*

— added **ELTON DEAN** – saxophone (ex-BLUESOLOGY) / **LYN DOBSON** – flute, sax / **NICK EVANS** – trombone + **MARK CHARIG** – cornet (ex-BLUESOLOGY) both left before 3rd album. Added guests **JIMMY HASTINGS** – wind / **A.B. SPALL** – violin

C.B.S. / Columbia

Jun 70. (d-lp) *(66246)* <30339> **THIRD** [18] [ ]
– Facelift / Slightly all the time / Moon in June / Out-Bloody-Rageous. *(re-iss.Jun88 on 'Decal' lp/c; LIKD/TCLIKD 35) (cd-iss.Mar93 on 'Beat Goes On'; BGOCD 180) (cd re-iss.Jul96 on 'Columbia'; 471407-2)*

— Now quartet, when LYN departed. Guests **HASTINGS + ALAN SKIDMORE** – sax

Feb 71. (lp) *(64280)* <30754> **FOURTH** [32] [ ]
– Teeth / Kings and queens / Fletcher's blemish / Virtually (parts 1-4). *(cd-iss.Apr93 on 'Sony Europe') (re-iss.cd Oct95 on 'One Way')*

— **JOHN MARSHALL + PHIL HOWARD** – drums (shared) repl. WYATT who went solo. **ELTON DEAN** added electric piano + **ROY BABBINGTON** – double bass (guested 3)

Jun 72. (lp) *(64806)* <31604> **FIFTH** [ ] [ ]
– All white / Drop / Mc / As if / LBO / Pigling bland / Bone. *(re-iss.1979 on 'CBS-Embassy'; 31748) (cd-iss.Apr93 on 'Sony Europe') (re-iss.Sep95 on 'One Way')*

— **KARL JENKINS** – piano, saxophone repl. DEAN who stayed with JUST US (above newcomer alongside **RATLEDGE, HOPPER + MARSHALL)**

Feb 73. (d-lp) *(68214)* <32260> **SIX** (half live) [ ] [ ]
– Fanfare / All white / Between / Riff / 37 and a half / Geseolveut / E.P.V. / Lefty / Stumble / 5 from 13 (for Phil Seaman with love and thanks) / Riff II / The soft weed factor / Stanley stamps gibbon album (for B.O.) / Chloe and the pirates / 1983. *(cd-iss.Apr93 on 'Sony Europe')*

— **ROY BABBINGTON** – bass (guest) repl. HUGH HOPPER who went solo

Oct 73. (lp) *(65799)* <32716> **SEVEN** [ ] [ ]
– Nettle bed / Carolyn / Day's eye / Bone fire / Tarabos / D.I.S. / Snodland / Penny hitch / Block / Down the road / The German lesson / The French lesson. *(cd-iss.Apr93 on 'Sony Europe')*

— added **ALAN HOLDSWORTH** – guitar

Harvest / not issued

Apr 75. (lp) *(SHSP 4044)* **BUNDLES** [ ] [-]
– Hazard profile (parts 1-5) / Gone sailing / Bundles / Land of the bag snake / The man who waved at trains / Peff / Four gongs two drums / The floating world. *(re-iss.1989 on 'See For Miles' lp/cd; SEE/+CD 283)*

— With last original RATLEDGE going solo and HOLDWORTH joining GONG, the remainder **(BABBINGTON, JENKINS + MARSHALL)** were joined by **ALAN WAKEMAN** – saxophone + **JOHN ETHERIDGE** – guitar

Jun 76. (lp) *(SHSP 4056)* **SOFTS** [ ] [-]
– Aubade / The tale of Taliesyn / Bab ban Caliban / Song of Aeolus / Out of season / Second bundle / Kayoo / The Camden tandem / Nexus / One over the eight / Etika. *(reiss.Jan90 on 'See For Miles' lp/cd; SEE/+CD 285)*

— **RIC SAUNDERS** – violin + **STEVE COOKE** – bass repl. WAKEMAN + BABBINGTON

Mar 78. (lp) *(SHSP 4083)* **ALIVE AND WELL – RECORDED IN PARIS** [ ] [-]
– White kite / Eos / Odds, bullets and blades (part 1 & 2) / Song of the sunbird / Puffin, huffin' / Number three / The nodder / Surrounder silence / Soft space. *(cd-iss.Mar90 on 'See For Miles'; SEECD 290) (cd re-iss.Nov95 on 'One Way';)*

Apr 78. (7") *(HAR 5155)* **SOFT SPACE. / (part 2)** [ ] [-]

— Folded 1979, but re-formed for one-off studio outing below. Musicians:- **ETHRIDGE, MARSHALL, HOLDSWORTH** plus sessioners **DICK MORRISSEY** – saxophone / **ALAN PARKER** – guitar / **JOHN TAYLOR** – keyboards / **RAY WARLEIGH** – flute / **JACK BRUCE** – bass

E.M.I. / not issued

Mar 81. (lp) *(EMC 3348)* **THE LAND OF COCKAYNE** [ ] [-]
– Over 'n' above / Lotus groves / Isle of the blessed / Panoramania / Behind the crystal curtain / Palace of glass / Hot biscuit slim / (Black) Velvet mountain / Sly monkey / A lot of what you fancy.

— finally disbanded after above.

– compilations, others, etc. –

Oct 74. (d-lp) *A.B.C.; (ABC 602)* **THE SOFT MACHINE COLLECTION**
– (1st 2 albums) *(cd-iss.1990's on 'Big Beat'; CDWIKD 920)*

1976. (lp) *De Wolfe; (3331)* **RUBBER RIFF**
(cd-iss.Nov94 on 'Voiceprint'; VP 190CD)

Jan 77. (lp) *Charly; (CR 30014)* **AT THE BEGINNING**
– That's how much I need you now / Save yourself / I should've / Jet propelled photographs / When I don't want you / Memories / You don't remember / She's gone / I'd rather be with you. *(re-iss.Mar83; CR 30196) (re-iss.Sep87 as 'JET PROPELLED PHOTOGRAPH' on 'Decal'; LIK 35) (cd-iss.Sep89 as 'JET PROPELLED PHOTOGRAPH' on 'Decal'; LIKCD 197) (re-iss.cd Sep95 on 'Spalax';)*

Mar 77. (t-lp) *Harvest; (SHTW 800)* **TRIPLE ECHO**

Aug 88. (cd/lp) *Reckless; (CD+/RECK 5)* **LIVE AT THE PROMS (live)**

Sep 90. (cd/c/d-lp) *Strange Fruit; (SFR CD/MC/LP 201)* **THE COMPLETE PEEL SESSIONS**

Dec 90. (cd/c/d-lp) *Castle; (CCS CD/MC/LP 281)* **THE UNTOUCHABLE COLLECTION (75-78)**

May 91. (cd/c) *Elite; (ELITE 006 CD/MC)* **AS IF**
– Facelift / Slightly all the time / Kings and queens / Drop / Chloe and the pirates / As if. *(cd-iss.Sep93; same)*

Aug 92. (3xcd-box) *Magpie; (MAGPIE 2)* **SOFTS / ALIVE & WELL / BUNDLES**

Apr 93. (m-cd) *Windsong; (WINCD 031)* **BBC RADIO 1 LIVE IN CONCERT (live)**

Jun 94. (cd) *Windsong; (WINCD 056)* **BBC RADIO 1 LIVE IN CONCERT (live)**

Jan 95. (cd) *Movieplay Gold; (MPG 74033)* **LIVE AT THE PARADISO**

Jun 95. (cd) *C5; (C5MCD 623)* **THE BEST OF SOFT MACHINE: THE HARVEST YEARS**
(re-iss.May97; same)

Jun 97. (cd) *Spalax; (14557)* **LONDON 1967**

SONICS

Formed: Tacoma, Washington, USA . . . 1964 by brothers LARRY and ANDY PARYPA, ROB LIND, GERRY ROSLIE and BOB BENNETT. Signing to the local 'Etiquette' label, they released their debut single, 'KEEP A KNOCKIN'. The record's B-side, 'THE WITCH', was a pioneering garage-punk classic which gained the band some degree of noteriety and a cult following in the Pacific Northwest. A further string of 45's, mostly covers, failed to break the band nationally, only 'PSYCHO' achieving a modicum of success locally. Their third album, 'INTRODUCING THE SONICS' (1967) was their first release for a major label, although the band subsequently split, only to reform a few times in the 70's. At the turn of the decade, with new wave still very much in vogue, The SONICS re-formed for a one-off album, 'SINDERELLA'.

Recommended: PSYCHO-SONIC (*6)

ROB LIND – vocals, sax, harmonica / **LARRY PARYPA** – lead guitar, vocals / **GERRY ROSLIE** – organ, piano, vocals / **ANDY PARYPA** – bass, vocals / **BOB BENNETT** – drums

not issued / Etiquette

1964. (7") *<11>* **KEEP A KNOCKIN'. / THE WITCH**
1965. (7") *<16>* **BOSS HOSS. / THE HUSTLER**
1965. (7") *<18>* **SHOT DOWN. / DON'T BE AFRAID OF THE DARK**
1965. (7") *<22>* **DON'T BELIEVE IN CHRISTMAS. / (b-side by The WAILERS)**
1966. (7") *<23>* **LOUIE LOUIE. / CINDERELLA**
1966. (lp) *<024>* **HERE ARE THE SONICS**
(UK-iss.Aug86 on 'Fan Club'; FC 017) (cd-iss.with below tracks Feb88; FC 017CD)
1966. (lp) *<027>* **SONICS BOOM**
(UK-iss.Jan87 on 'Fan Club'; FC 020)

not issued / Jerden

1966. (7") *<809>* **LOVE LIGHTS. / YOU GOT YOUR HEAD ON BACKWARDS**
1966. (7") *<810>* **THE WITCH. / LIKE NO OTHER MAN**
1966. (7") *<811>* **PSYCHO. / MAINTAINING MY COOL**
1967. (lp) *<7007>* **INTRODUCING THE SONICS**

— **JIM BRADY** – vocals, repl. LIND

not issued / Piccadilly

1967. (7") *<244>* **LOST LOVE. / ANY WAY THE WIND BLOWS**

not issued / Uni

1967. (7") *<55039>* **ANY WAY THE WIND BLOWS. / LOST LOVE**

not issued / Buckshot

1973. (lp) *<001>* **EXPLOSIVES**

not issued / Burdette

1975. (7") *<106>* **DIRTY OLD MAN. / BAMA LAMA BAMA LOO**

— disbanded after above. Re-formed in the 80's with **GARY ROSLIE + GEORGE WALLACE** – guitar, vocals / **GEORGE CROWE** – bass / **MICHAEL GONE** – guitar / **BILL SHAW** or **JAMES N. BUTSCH** – drums / **LES KINGBEARD** – sax

not issued / Bomp

1980. (lp) *<4011>* **SINDERELLA**
(UK cd-iss.Jan97; BCD 4011)

– compilations, etc. –

1977. (lp) *S.R.T.; <77079>* **SONICS**
1979. (7") *Great Northwest; <702>* **THE WITCH. / BAMA LAMA BAMA LOO**
1979. (lp) *First; <7715>* **ORIGINAL NORTHWEST PUNK**
1980. (lp) *First; <7719>* **UNRELEASED**

Nov 87. (lp) *Fan Club; (FC 033)* **LIVE FANZ ONLY**

Mar 88. (lp) *Line; (LILP 400387)* **FULL FORCE (THE BEST OF THE SONICS)**

Jun 88. (lp) *Bam Caruso; (KIRI 104)* **PSYCHO**

Mar 93. (cd) *Big Beat; (CDWIKD 115)* **PSYCHO-SONIC**
– The witch / Do you love me / Roll over Beethoven / Boss Hoss / Dirty robber / Have love will travel / Psycho / Money (that's what I want) / Walking the dog / Night time is the right time / Strychnine / Good golly Milly Molly / The hustler / Psycho (live) / Sinderella / Don't be afraid of the dark / Skinny Minnie / Let the good times roll / Don't you just know it / Jenny Jenny / He's waitin' / Louie Louie / Since I fell for you / Hitch hike / It's all right / Shot down / Keep a knockin' / The witch (live) / The witch (version 2).

SONS OF ADAM

Formed: Los Angeles, California, USA . . . mid-60's by RANDY HOLDEN, MICHAEL STUART, CRAIG TARWATER and MIKE PORT. They were regarded as one of the best garage outfits around L.A., their first 45 being their version of ARTHUR LEE's 'FEATHERED FISH' (1966). They signed to 'Decca' in 1967 but after two more flops, they evolved into NEW WING, who were similarly unsuccessful. In 1968, HOLDEN, TARWATER and PORT became The OTHER HALF, who finally got around to releasing an album before HOLDEN careered off to join BLUE CHEER.

Recommended: SONS OF ADAM EP (*6)

RANDY HOLDEN – guitar / **CRAIG TARWATER** – guitar / **MIKE PORT** – bass, vocals / **MICHAEL STUART** – drums

not issued / Alamo

1966. (7") *<5473>* **FEATHERED FISH. / BABY SHOW THE WORLD**

not issued / Decca

1967. (7") *<31887>* **TAKE MY HAND. / TOMORROW'S GONNA BE ANOTHER DAY**
1967. (7") *<31995>* **YOU'RE A BETTER MAN THAN I. / SATURDAY'S SON**

— **DAVY PETERS** – vocals; repl. STUART who joined LOVE

not issued / Pentacle

1967. (7"; as The NEW WING) *<101>* **THE THINKING ANIMAL. / MY PETITE**
1968. (7"; as The NEW WING) *<104>* **BROWN EYED WOMAN. / I NEED LOVE**

— HOLDEN, TARWATER and PORT joined The OTHER HALF, the former moving onto BLUE CHEER.

– compilations, etc. –

1980. (12"ep) *Moxie; <1032>* **SONS OF ADAM**

SOPWITH CAMEL

Formed: San Francisco, California, USA . . .mid 60's by PETER KRAEMER and TERRY MacNEIL. They first came to light early in '67 at the height of the West Coast flower-power boom. Their debut 45, 'HELLO HELLO', stormed the charts, finally climbing into the Top 30, although their follow-up, 'POSTCARD FROM JAMAICA', only scraped into the 100. Eccentric, in fact neo-vaudeville, they exhibited traces of light psychedelia alongside sheer self-indulgence on their poorly received eponymous debut album. This only managed to dent the Top 200 and not surprisingly, they disbanded the following year, later returning with another effort in 1973. Most people would have settled for one hump rather than two. • **Songwriters:** MacNEIL-KRAEMER and a few by SIEVERS.

Recommended: SOPWITH CAMEL (*5)

PETER KRAEMER – vocals, flute, keyboards / **TERRY MacNEIL** – keyboards, guitar / **WILLIAM SIEVERS** – guitar / **MARTIN BEARD** – bass / **NORMAN MAYELL** – drums, sitar

Kama Sutra / Kama Sutra

Feb 67. (7"; as The SOPWITH "CAMEL") *(KAS 205) <KA-217>* **HELLO HELLO. / TREADIN'** 26 Dec66

Mar 67. (7"; as The SOPWITH "CAMEL") *<KA-224>* **POSTCARD FROM JAMAICA. / LITTLE ORPHAN ANNIE** 88

Jun 67. (7") *<KA-236>* **SAGA OF THE LOW DOWN LET DOWN. / THE GREAT MORPHEUM**

Oct 67. (lp) *<KLPS 8060>* **SOPWITH CAMEL**
– Hello hello / Frantic desolation / Saga of the low down let down / Little orphan Annie / You always tell me baby / Maybe in a dream / Cellophane woman / Things that I could do with you / Walk in the park / The Great Morpheum / Postcard from Jamaica. *<US re-iss.1973 as 'HELLO HELLO'; KSBS 2063> (UK-iss.May86 as 'FRANTIC DESOLATION' on 'Edsel'+=; ED 185)*– Treadin'. *(UK cd-iss.Apr90 as 'HELLO HELLO AGAIN' on 'Sequel'; NEMCD 601)*

— split after above. MAYELL joined BLUE CHEER and sessioned for NORMAN GREENBAUM. Re-formed in 1973 without SIEVERS.

Reprise / Reprise

1973. (lp) *(K 44251) <MS 2108>* **THE MIRACULOUS HUMP RETURNS FROM THE MOON**
– Fazon / Coke, suede and waterbeds / Dancin' wizard / Sleazy Street / Orange peel / Oriental fantasy / Sneaky Smith / Monkeys on the Moon / Astronaut food / Brief symponia. *(re-iss.1988 on 'Edsel'; XED 205)*
1973. (7") *<1179>* **FAZON. / SLEAZY STREET**

— deserted the music scene once again. NORMAN sessioned for WILLIAM TRUCKAWAY on his 1976 lp 'Breakaway'.

SORROWS

Formed: Coventry, England . . . 1963 by DON MAUGHN, BRUCE FINLEY, PHILIP PACKHAM, WEZ PRICE and PHILIP WITCHER. Early in 1965, they debuted with their R&B/mod-pop 45, 'I DON'T WANNA BE FREE'. This, and their follow-up, 'BABY', failed to spark any interest, although the primal raunch of 'TAKE A HEART' propelled the band to the outer regions of the Top 20. However, subsequent releases, including an album, failed to cut any commercial ice. Their final 45 in the summer of '67, 'PINK, PURPLE, YELLOW AND RED' was a storming piece of freakbeat that served as a fitting epitaph for this influential band. DON left to pursue a solo career, leaving the rest to relocate to Italy temporarily, where the UK hit had become an Italian one. DON, who had now changed his second name to FARDON, had a major US Top 20 hit with 'INDIAN RESERVATION' (1967). It took some time for the single to gain recognition in Britain, eventually hitting Top 3 in 1970. The song was subsequently covered by The RAIDERS, who topped the US charts with it in 1971. • **Trivia:** The SORROWS' only lp is now worth around £100 mint, while the non-charting 45's fetch over £20.

Recommended: PINK, PURPLE, YELLOW & RED (*6)

DON MAUGHAN – vocals / **PIP WHITCHER** – lead guitar / **WEZ PRICE** – rhythm guitar / **PHIL PACKMAN** – bass / **BRUCE FINLEY** – drums

Piccadilly | not issued

Jan 65. (7") *(7N 35219)* **I DON'T WANNA BE FREE. / COME WITH ME** [ ] [-]
Apr 65. (7") *(7N 35230)* **BABY. / TEENAGE LETTER** [ ] [-]
Aug 65. (7") *(7N 35260)* **TAKE A HEART. / WE SHOULD GET ALONG FINE** [21] [-]
Oct 65. (7") *(7N 35277)* **YOU'VE GOT WHAT I WANT. / NO, NO, NO, NO** [ ] [-]
Nov 65. (lp) *(NPL 38023)* **TAKE A HEART** [ ] [-]
– Baby / No, no, no, no / Take a heart / She's got the action / How love used to be / Teenage letter / I don't wanna be free / Don't sing no sad songs for me / Cara-Lin / We should get along fine / Come with me / Let me in. *(cd-iss.1990's on 'Repertoire'+=; REP 4093)*– You've got what I want / Let the love live / Pink, purple, yellow and red / My gal / Nimm mein herz / Sei mein girl / Mi si spezza il cuore / Vivi.
Apr 66. (7") *(7N 35309)* **LET THE LOVE LIVE. / DON'T SING NO SAD SONGS FOR ME** [ ] [-]
Aug 66. (7") *(7N 35336)* **LET ME IN. / HOW LOVE USED TO BE** [ ] [-]
Jun 67. (7") *(7N 35385)* **PINK, PURPLE, YELLOW AND RED. / MY GAL** [ ] [-]

—— Split in 1967. DON as DON FARDON went solo.

– compilations, etc. –

Nov 87. (lp) *Bam Caruso; (KIRI 089)* **PINK, PURPLE, YELLOW & RED** [ ] [-]
– Take a heart / Pink, purple, yellow and red / I don't wanna be free / Don't sing no sad songs for me / My gal / Baby / No no no no / Cara-Lin / You've got what I want / Let the love live / Let me in / Come with me / How love used to be / Teenage letter / We should get along fine / She's got the action. *(cd-iss.Jul91 on 'Drop Out'+=; DOCD 1994)*
Apr 91. (cd) *Sequel; (NEXCD 165)* **THE SORROWS** [ ] [-]

DON FARDON

Pye Int. | GNP Crescendo

Oct 67. (7") *(7N 25437)* <405> **(THE LAMENT OF THE CHEROKEE) INDIAN RESERVATION. / DREAMIN' ROOM** [ ] [20] Aug68
(re-iss.Oct68; 7N 25475) (re-iss.1979 & 1982 on 'Old Gold'; OG 9034)
1968. (7") <418> **HOW DO YOU BREAK A BROKEN HEART. / TAKE A HEART** [-] [ ]
1968. (lp) <2044> **THE LAMENT OF THE CHEROKEE** [-] [ ]
1968. (7") <421> **SALLY GOES ROUND THE MOON. / HOW DO YOU BREAK A BROKEN HEART** [-] [ ]
1968. (7") <424> **RUNNING BEAR. / RUBY'S PICTURE** [-] [ ]
Jan 69. (7") *(7N 25483)* **WE CAN MAKE IT TOGETHER. / COMING ON STRONG** [ ] [-]
Mar 69. (7") *(7N 25486)* **GOOD LOVIN'. / RUBY'S PICTURE ON THE WALL** [ ] [ ]

Youngblood | Decca

Jul 69. (7") *(YB 1003)* **I'M ALIVE. / KEEP ON LOVING ME** [ ] [-]
Oct 69. (7") *(YB 1007)* **IT'S BEEN NICE LOVING YOU. / LET THE LOVE LIVE** [ ] [-]
Apr 70. (7") *(YB 1010)* **BELFAST BOY. / ECHOES OF THE CHEERS** [32] [ ]
Jul 70. (lp) *(YB 4)* <75225> **I'VE PAID MY DUES** [ ] [ ]
– Belfast boy / Hudson Bay / (The lament of the Cherokee) Indian reservation / New York City / I'm alive / Take a heart / I need somebody / 6:10 Phoenix / Keep on loving me / Sally goes round the Moon.

Youngblood | Chelsea

Jul 70. (7") *(YB 1013)* <0115> **DELTA QUEEN. / HOMETOWN BABY** [ ] [86] Mar73
Sep 70. (7") *(YB 1015)* **INDIAN RESERVATION. / HUDSON BAY** [3] [ ]
Dec 70. (lp) *(SSYB 13)* **RELEASED** [ ] [ ]
– (The lament of the Cherokee) Indian reservation / Riverboat / California maiden / Hudson Bay / Mississippi woman / New York City / Miami sunset / 6:10 Phoenix gone / Cheyene / San Diego.
Feb 71. (7") *(YB 1021)* **GIRL. / SANDIAGO** [ ] [-]
1973. (7") *(YB 1027)* **FOLLOW YOUR DRUM. / GET AWAY JOHN** [ ] [-]
Sep 73. (7") *(YB 1055)* **LADY ZELDA. / LOUISIANA** [ ] [ ]
Apr 74. (7") *(YB 1071)* **RUNNING BEAR. / ST.MATTHEW, ST.MARK, ST.LUKE, ST.JOHN** [ ] [ ]

M.C.A. | M.C.A.

Mar 76. (7") *(MCA 233)* **JUDY MAE. / DADDY'S SONG** [ ] [ ]

—— must have retired from music.

– other (DON FARDON) releases, etc. –

Aug 84. (7") *Youngblood; (YB 0087)* **INDIAN RESERVATION. / DON'T DO THAT** [ ] [-]
Feb 90. (lp/cd) *C5; (C5/+CD 540) / GNP Crescendo; <GNPS 2044>* **THE BEST OF DON FARDON** [ ] [ ]
– Indian reservation / Gimme gimme good lovin' / The letter / Treat her right / I'm alive / Follow your drum / Delta queen / Running bear / Belfast boy / Take a heart / Lola / It's been nice loving you / Hudson Bay / On the beach / Tobacco road / California maiden / Coming on strong / Mr. Station master / Miami sunset / Riverboat.
May 97. (cd/c) *Prestige; (CDS/CASS GP 0353)* **THE NEXT CHAPTER** [ ] [-]

SPARROW (see under ⇒ STEPPENWOLF)

Alexander SPENCE (see under ⇒ MOBY GRAPE)

SPIRIT

Formed: Los Angeles, California, USA . . . 1964 as The RED ROOSTERS, by RANDY CALIFORNIA and his middle-aged, shaven-headed stepfather, ED CASSIDY. The band split in late '65 and later reformed as SPIRITS REBELLIOUS in the Spring of '67, CALIFORNIA returning from New York where he'd traded axe licks with, and been heavily influenced by, a young JIMI HENDRIX. Along with ex-ROOSTERS, MARK ANDES, JOHN LOCKE and JAY FERGUSON, the band became SPIRIT and signed to LOU ADLER's 'Ode' records. Their eponymous debut was released soon after, a mellow melange of jazz and trippy, bluesy rock that marked the band out from the bulk of the folk-rock pack in the L.A. of 1968. SPIRIT also looked different, CASSIDY resembling some ageing hippy Kojak. With the exuberant 'I GOT A LINE ON YOU' single from the follow-up album, 'THE FAMILY THAT PLAYS TOGETHER' (1969), the band scored an unexpected Top 30 hit, although the bulk of the record explored the grey area where jazz, rock and psychedelia met. 'CLEAR SPIRIT' (1969) displayed a harder-edged sound but the band didn't really come into their own until they were paired with NEIL YOUNG producer DAVID BRIGGS and recorded the psychedelic masterwork, 'TWELVE DREAMS OF DR. SARDONICUS' (1971). From the pastoral psychedelia of 'NATURE'S WAY' to the more direct approach of 'MORNING WILL COME' and 'MR. SKIN', this was CALIFORNIA at his most creative in terms of both songwriting and guitar playing. Although it was critically acclaimed upon release, it failed to sell in any great quantity and FERGUSON left shortly after to form JO JO GUNNE. With CALIFORNIA laid up after a road accident and ED CASSIDY the only original remaining member involved in the 'FEEDBACK' (1972) album, it came as no surprise when the record was a resounding failure, creatively, critically and commercially. This was, in effect, the end of the line for the band although a bogus SPIRIT sprang up to haunt them, fronted by the STAEHELY brothers who'd played on 'FEEDBACK'. Meanwhile, CALIFORNIA recorded a minor classic of a solo album, 'KAPT. KOPTER AND THE (FABULOUS) TWIRLYBIRDS'. A rough-hewn set of psychedelic garage-rock, the record featured some inspired covers including The BEATLES' 'RAIN ' and 'DAY TRIPPER'. The original SPIRIT line-up reformed in the mid-70's and recorded a series of albums for 'Mercury', which tried and failed to capture the original vibe. After yet another split and reformation, the band resurrected Kapt. Kopter and recorded a cod-concept album, 'JOURNEY TO POTATOLAND', in 1981 before breaking up again. In the way of these things, the band reformed with differing line-ups throughout the 80's, CALIFORNIA also recording two solo albums. The long 'SPIRIT'-ual journey finally came to an end when CALIFORNIA was tragically drowned off the coast of the Hawaiian island of Molokai, on the 1st January of 1997. • **Songwriters:** CALIFORNIA and group, except YESTERDAY (Beatles) / HEY JOE (hit; Jimi Hendrix; c.William Roberts). CALIFORNIA covered solo:- MOTHER AND CHILD REUNION (Paul Simon) / ALL ALONG THE WATCHTOWER (Bob Dylan) / WILD THING (Troggs). • **Trivia:** MARK ANDES played on BORIS PICKETT & THE CRYPT KICKER 5's hit single, 'Monster Mash'. LED ZEPPELIN (Jimmy Page), must have listened to 1968 track, 'TAURUS', before writing 'Stairway To Heaven' (listen?).

Recommended: TWELVE DREAMS OF DOCTOR SARDONICUS (*8) / THE BEST OF SPIRIT (*8) / POTATOLAND (*9)

RANDY CALIFORNIA (b. RANDALL CRAIG WOLFE, 20 Feb'51) – guitar, vox / **JAY FERGUSON** (b. JOHN ARDEN FERGUSON, 10 May'47, Burbank, Calif.) – vocals / **MARK ANDES** (b.19 Feb'48, Philadelphia) – bass (ex-YELLOW BALLOON, w /JAY) / **ED CASSIDY** (b. 4 May'22, Chicago, Illinois) – drums (ex-NEW JAZZ TRIO) / **JOHN LOCKE** (b.25 Sep'43) – keyboards (ex-NEW WORLD JAZZ CO.)

C.B.S. | Ode

Jun 68. (lp) *(63278)* <44004> **SPIRIT** [ ] [31] Jan68
– Fresh garbage / Uncle Jack / Mechanical world / Taurus / Straight arrow / Topango windows / Gramophone man / Water woman / Great canyon fire in general / Elijah / Girl in your eyes. *(re-iss.Apr79 as 'THE FIRST OF SPIRIT' on 'CBS-Embassy'; 31693) (re-iss.Apr89 on 'Edsel' lp/c/cd; ED/+MC/CD 311) (re-iss.cd Aug95; 480965-2)*
Jun 68. (7") *(3523)* <257-108> **UNCLE JACK. / MECHANICAL WORLD** [ ] [ ]
Feb 69. (7") *(3880)* <257-115> **I GOT A LINE ON YOU. / SHE SMILED** [ ] [25] Dec68
Apr 69. (lp) *(63523)* <44014> **THE FAMILY THAT PLAYS TOGETHER** [ ] [22] Jan69
– I got a line on you / Poor Richard / Aren't you glad / It shall be / The drunkard / It's all the same / Dream within a dream / Jewish / So little to say / Silky Sam.

<US re-iss.Jul72; > (re-iss.Mar86 on 'Edsel' lp/c/cd+=; XED/CED/EDCD 162)– She smiles / Darlin'. *(cd re-iss.Sep94 on 'Rewind';)*

Aug 69. (7") *(4511)* **DARK EYED WOMAN. / ICE** -

Sep 69. (7") *(4565) <257-122>* **DARK EYED WOMAN. / NEW DOPE AT TOWN**

Oct 69. (lp) *(63729) <44016>* **CLEAR SPIRIT** 55 Jul69

– Dark eyed woman / Apple orchard / So little time to fly / Groundhog / Cold wind / Policeman's ball / Ice / Give a life, take a life / I'm truckin' / Clear / Caught / New dope in town. *(re-iss.Mar88 on 'Edsel' lp/cd; ED/+CD 268)*

Jan 70. (7") *(4773) <257-128>* **1984. / SWEET STELLA BABY** 69 Dec69

C.B.S. Epic

Sep 70. (7") *(5149) <10648>* **ANIMAL ZOO. / RED LIGHT, ROLL ON** 97 Aug70

Oct 70. (7") *<10685>* **MR. SKIN. / SOLDIER** -

Epic Epic

Feb 71. (lp) *(EPC 64191) <30267>* **TWELVE DREAMS OF DR. SARDONICUS** 63 Dec70

– Nothing to hide / Nature's way / Animal zoo / Love has found a way / Why can't I be free / Mr. Skin / Space child / When I touch you / Sweet worm / Life has just begun / Morning will come / Soldier. *(re-iss.Mar81 lp/c; EPC/40 32006) (re-iss.Apr89 on 'Edsel' lp/c/cd; ED/+MC/CD 313) (re-iss.cd Aug93; 468030-2) (re-iss.cd Apr94; 476603-2)*

— (Dec70) **JOHN ARLISS** – bass repl. FERGUSON and ANDES who formed JO JO GUNNE (May71) **CASSIDY + LOCKE** recruited new men **AL STAEHELY** – bass (ex-PUMPKIN) / **J.CHRISTIAN** (b.CHRIS STAEHELY) – guitar repl. ARLISS + RANDY who went solo

May 72. (7") *(EPC 8083)* **CADILLAC COWBOYS. / DARKNESS** -

Jun 72. (lp) *(EPC 64507) <31175>* **FEEDBACK** 63 Mar72

– Chelsea girl / Cadillac / Cowboys / Puesta del scam / Ripe and ready / Darkness / Earth shaker / Mellow morning / Trancas fog-out / The witch.

— (Aug72) Now a totally 'bogus' SPIRIT, fronted by The STAEHELY brothers. **STU PERRY** – drums repl. CASSIDY (see further below), and LOCKE who went solo. An album 'STA-HAY-LEE', included CASSIDY and LOCKE surfaced in US later? CHRIS was another to join JO JO GUNNE. Regarded as the 'real SPIRIT'

RANDY CALIFORNIA

(solo!) with **TIM McGOVERN** – drums, vocals / **CHARLIE BUNDY** – bass, b.vox / **HENRY MANCHOVITZ** (aka MITCH MITCHELL) – drums / **CLIT McTORIUS** (aka NOEL REDDING) – bass / guests **CASS STRANGE** (aka ED CASSIDY) – bass / **FUZZY KNIGHT** (aka ARRY WEISBER) – keyboards

Sep 72. (7") *<10927>* **WALKIN' THE DOG. / LIVE FOR THE DAY** -

Sep 72. (lp) *(EPC 65381) <31755>* **KAPTAIN KOPTER AND THE (FABULOUS) TWIRLY BIRDS**

– Downer / Devil / I don't want nobody / Day tripper / Mother and child reunion / Things yet to come / Rain / Rainbow. *(re-iss.Jun80 on 'C.B.S.' lp/c; CBS/40 31829) (re-iss.Nov85 on 'Edsel'+=; ED 164)–* Walkin' the dog / Live for the day. *(cd-iss.Aug93 & May97 on 'Edsel'; EDCD 164)*

— In 1973, CALIFORNIA attempted suicide by jumping off Chelsea Bridge.

SPIRIT

— after a few other line-up's in 1974, settled with **CASSIDY, CALIFORNIA + MARK ANDES** who repl. FUZZY KNIGHT. **JOHN LOCKE** re-joined for short spell, until he went into sessions. Also ANDES (who joined FIREFALL) were repl. by **BARRY KEANE** – bass

Mercury Mercury

Jun 75. (d-lp) *(6672 012) <804>* **SPIRIT OF '76**

– America the beautiful / The times they are a-changin' / Victim of society / Lady of the lakes / Tampa man / Mounalo / What do I have / Sunrise / Walking the dog / Joker on the run / When? / Like a rolling stone / Once again / Feeling in time / Happy / Jack Bond (part 1) / Mr. Road / Thank you Lord / Urantia / Guide me / Veruska / Hey Joe / Jack Bond (part 2) / The star spangled banner. *(re-iss.May88 on 'Edsel'; DED 251) (cd-iss.Mar93;)*

Aug 75. (7") *<73697>* **AMERICA THE BEAUTIFUL. / THE TIMES THEY ARE A-CHANGIN' / LADY OF THE LAKES** -

— added **MATT ANDES** – guitar (ex-JO JO GUNNE)

Oct 75. (lp) *<SRM1 1053>* **SON OF SPIRIT** -

– Holy man / Looking into darkness / Maybe you'll find / Don't go away / Family / Magic fairy princess / Circle / The other song / Yesterday / It's time now. *(UK-iss.May89 on 'Great Expectations' lp/cd; PIP LP/CD 2)*

Oct 75. (7") *<73722>* **HOLY MAN. / LOOKING INTO DARKNESS** -

Jul 76. (lp) *<(SRM1 1094)>* **FURTHER ALONG**

– Further along / Atomic boogie / World eat world dog / Stoney night / Pineapple / Colossus / Mega star / Phoebe / Don't look up your door / Once with you / Diamond spirit / Nature's way.

Sep 76. (7") *<73837>* **FURTHER ALONG. / ATOMIC BOOGIE** -

— Now just a trio, when MARK re-joined FIREFALL and MATT & JOHN also left.

Apr 77. (lp) *(9100 036) <SRM1 1133>* **FUTURE GAMES (A MAGICAL KAHVANA DREAM)**

– CB talk / Stars are love / Kahouna dream / Brued my brain / Bionic unit / So happy now / All along the watchtower / Would you believe / Jack Bond speaks / Star Trek dreaming / Interlude XM / China doll / Hawaiian times / Gorn attack / Interlude 2001 / Detroit City / Freak out frog / The Romulan experiences / Monkey see, monkey do / Mt. Olympus / The journey of Nomad / Ending. *(re-iss.May89 on 'Great Expectations' lp/c/cd; PIP LP/MC/CD 3)*

May 77. (7") *(6167 519)* **ALL ALONG THE WATCHTOWER. / FURTHER ALONG** -

— **LARRY KNIGHT** – bass returned to repl. KEENE

Illegal Potato

Dec 78. (7") *(IL 007)* **NATURE'S WAY (live). / STONE FREE (live)** -

Jan 79. (lp) *(ILP 001) <PR 2001>* **SPIRIT LIVE** (live 11th Mar'78, Rainbow, London)

– Rock and roll planet / Nature's way / Animal zoo / 1984 / Looking down / It's all the same / I got a line on you / These are words / Hollywood dream.

— Disbanded yet again late 1978, RANDY formed own band with **STEVE LAURA** – bass / **JACK WILLOUGHBY** – drums.

— they re-formed to re-record old unissued lost album below. **CALIFORNIA & CASSIDY** (alias KAPTAIN KOPTER & COMMANDER CASSIDY) enlisted **GEORGE VALUCK, JOHN LOCKE, MIKE BUNNELL + KARI NILE** – keys / **JEFF JARVIS, MIKE THORNBURGH + CHUCK SNYDER** – horns / **JOE GREEN** – strings

Beggars Banquet Rhino

Apr 81. (lp) *(BEGA 23)* **JOURNEY TO POTATOLAND** 40

– We've got a lot to learn / Potatolandland theme / Open up your heart / Morning light / Potatoland prelude / Potatoland intro / Turn to the right / Donut house / Fish fry road / Information / My friend. *(re-iss.1988 += on 'Chord' lp/c/cd; CHORD/+TC/CD 010) (re-iss.cd Jan91 on 'Line'; LICD 90009-2)*

Apr 81. (7") *(BEGA 45)* **WE'VE GOT A LOT TO LEARN. / FISH FRY ROAD** -

Jun 81. (7") *(BEGA 56)* **TURN TO THE RIGHT. / POTATOLAND THEME** -

— Band toured 1981:- **CALIFORNIA, CASSIDY, VALUCK + STEVE LAURA** (aka LIBERTY)

RANDY CALIFORNIA

— solo including all present SPIRIT members and some past.

Apr 82. (lp) *(BEGA 36)* **EURO-AMERICAN**

– Easy love / Fearless leader / Five in the morning / Skull and crossbones / Breakout / Hand gun (toy guns) / This is the end / Mon ami / Rude reaction / Calling you / Wild thing. *(free w/7") (RAN 1)* – SHATTERED DREAMS. / MAGIC WAND

Apr 82. (7") *(BEG 76)* **HAND GUNS (TOY GUNS). / THIS IS THE END**

Aug 82. (7") *(BEG 82)* **ALL ALONG THE WATCHTOWER. / RADIO MAN**

(12"+=) *(BEG 82T)* – Breakout / Killer weed.

SPIRIT

— originals re-formed re-recording material from that era.

Mercury Mercury

Jan 84. (7") *(MER 151)* **1984. / ELIJAH**

(12"+=) *(MERX 151)* – I got a line on you.

Mar 84. (lp) *(MERL 35)* **THE THIRTEENTH DREAM** (remixes)

– Black satin nights / Mr. Skin / Mechanical world / Pick it up / All over the world / 1984 / Uncle Jack / Natures way / Fresh garbage / I got a line on you. *(c+=)–* Elijah. *(cd-iss.Jul84; 818 514-2)*

Apr 84. (7"/6") *(MER 162/+6)* **FRESH GARBAGE. / MR. SKIN**

RANDY CALIFORNIA

— solo with live + studio **MIKE SHEPHERD** – bass / **NEIL MURRAY + ADRIAN LEE + NEAL DOUGHTY** – keyboards / **CURLY SMITH** – drums live: **SCOTT MONAHAN** – keys / **LES WARNER** – drums

Vertigo Mercury

May 85. (7") *(VER 16)* **RUN TO YOUR LOVER. / SECOND CHILD**

(12"+=) *(VERX 16)* – Shane.

Jun 85. (lp/c) *(VERL 19)* **RESTLESS**

– Run to your lover / Restless nights / Second child / Jack Rabbit / Shane / One man's Heaven / Murphy's law / Camelot / Battle march of the overlords / Childhood's end.

Jun 85. (7") *(VER 21)* **JACK RABBIT. / SUPER CHILD**

Line not issued

1986. (lp) **SHATTERED DREAMS** - - German

– Hey Joe (live) / Shattered dreams / All along the watchtower / Don't bother me / Downer / Second child / Man at war / Killer weed / Hand guns (toy guns) / Radio man / Run to your lover.

— In Apr'89, RANDY appeared on Various Artists live d-lp,c,cd,video 'NIGHT OF THE GUITAR', which was on next label.

RANDY CALIFORNIA'S SPIRIT

— gigged with various line-ups, until in 1989 settled with **RANDY, ED + SCOTT** plus **MIKE BUNNELL** – bass

I.R.S. I.R.S.

Jun 89. (7") *(EIRS 117)* **HARD LOVE. / THE PRISONER**

(12"+=) *(EIRST 117)* – Hey Joe.

Aug 89. (lp/c/cd) *(EIRS A/ICD 1014)* **RAPTURE IN THE CHAMBERS**

– Hard love / Love tonight / Thinking of / Rapture in the chambers / Mojo man / Contact / The prisoner / One track mind / Enchanted forest / Human sexuality / Shera, princess of power / End suite.

— now without BUNNELL

not issued W.E.R.C. C.R.E.W.

1995. (cd) *<22003>* **SPIRIT LIVE AT LA PALOMA** -

– Life has just begun / Sadana / Mr. Skin / Hey Joe / I got a line on you / Prelude – Nothin' to hide / Like a rolling stone / Going back to Jones / Living in this world / Magic wand / Give a life take a life / La Paloma jam / 1984 / Jamaica jam / Super la Paloma jam / Nature's way.

— SCOTT repl. by **MATT ANDES** – slide guitar / **STEVE LORIA** – bass / **RACHEL ANDES** (daughter of MATT) – vocals

1996. (cd) **CALIFORNIA BLUES** -

– California blues / Look over yonder / The river / Call on me / Crossroads / Song for Clyde / Pawn shop blues / Sigar mama / Red house / Gimme some lovin' / We believe / One world / Like a dog / oem for John Lennon / Shoes back on (live '67) / Tell everyone (live '67) / Soundtrack for a moth (live '67).

— On 1st Jan'97, RANDY was drowned after surfing with his teenage sons.

– compilations, others, etc. –

— on 'Epic' unless mentioned otherwise

Aug 73. (d-lp) *<31457>* **SPIRIT. / CLEAR SPIRIT** -

Oct 73. (7") *(EPC 7082) <10701>* **MR. SKIN. / NATURE'S WAY** 92

Oct 73. (lp) *(EPC 65585) <32271>* **THE BEST OF SPIRIT** Jul73 *(re-iss.Sep84; EPC 32516)* <US re-iss.May89; >

Dec 91. (d-cd/d-c) *Columbia; (471268-2/-4)* **TIME CIRCLE (1968-72)** – (first 4 albums)

Jan 92. (cd/c) *Castle; (CCS CD/MC 319)* **THE COLLECTION** | - | -

Feb 92. (cd) *Outline; (OLCD 991133)* **CHRONICLES 1967-1982** | - | -

Mar 94. (cd) *Line; (LICD 9000920)* **ADVENTURES OF KAPTAIN KOPTER & COMMANDER CASSIDY IN POTATOLAND** | | -

SPONTANEOUS COMBUSTION

Formed: London, England . . .1971 by brothers TRISTIAN and GARY MARGETTS, plus TONY BROCK. Plucked from obscurity by GREG LAKE, he subsequently produced their eponymous debut, which unsurprisingly, sounded not dissimilar to the progressive rock of EMERSON, LAKE & PALMER. A year later, their second album, 'TRIAD' covered the same territory, although it did contain a version of 'SABRE DANCE'. • **Trivia:** The second lp is now worth £30 mint, and rising.

Recommended: SPONTANEOUS COMBUSTION (*6) / TRIAD (*5)

TRISTIAN MARGETTS – vocals, bass / **GARY MARGETTS** – guitar, vocals / **TONY BROCK** – drums

Harvest | Capitol

Nov 71. (7") *(HAR 5046)* **LONELY SINGER. / 200 LIVES / LEAVING** | - | -

Jan 72. (lp) *(SHVL 801)* <11021> **SPONTANEOUS COMBUSTION**
– Speed of light / Listen to the wind / Leaving / 200 lives / Down with the Moon / Reminder. *(cd-iss.Feb97 & Jun97 on 'See For Miles'+=; SEECD 472)*– TRIAD

Oct 72. (7") *(HAR 5060)* **GAY TIME NIGHT. / SPACESHIP** | - | -

Oct 72. (lp) *(SHVL 805)* <11095> **TRIAD**
– Spaceship / Brainstorm / Child life / Love and laughter / Pan / Rainy day / Monolith (parts 1-3).

Jan 73. (7") *(HAR 5066)* **SABRE DANCE. / (part 2)** | - | -

1973. (7") <3558> **RAINY DAY. / CHESSBOARD** | - |

— split in 1973. BROCK later joined STRIPER, The BABYS, before being part of the ROD STEWART backing band in the 80's.

TIME

TRISS + GARY / + ALEC JOHNSON – guitar, vocals / **JODE LEIGH** – drums, percussion

Buk | not issued

1975. (lp) *(BULP 2005)* **TIME** | | -
– Shady lady / Turn around / Violence / Yesterday, today, tomorrow / Dragonfly / Liar / Hideout / Steal away.

— TRIS joined The GREG LAKE BAND.

SPOOKY TOOTH

Formed: based London, England . . . out of LUTHER GROSVENOR's 1964 outfit The V.I.P.'s, soon adding MIKE HARRISON and GREG RIDLEY. In 1967, they evolved into ART and were joined by MIKE KELLIE. After one flop album, 'SUPERNATURAL FAIRY TALES' and the addition of American GARY WRIGHT, they became SPOOKY TOOTH. Staying with 'Island' records, they released their debut in '68, 'IT'S ALL ABOUT A ROUNDABOUT'. In common with labelmates, TRAFFIC, the band were produced by the legendary JIMMY MILLER, subsequently drawing unfair comparisons with the STEVE WINWOOD outfit. A second set, 'SPOOKY TWO', followed the same pattern, although it fared better commercially in the States where it hit the Top 50. The stand-out tracks were 'EVIL WOMAN' and 'BETTER BY YOU, BETTER THAN ME'. Their hard-rock sound was bent a little to incorporate electronics wizard, PIERRE HENRY, on the 1970 album, 'CEREMONY', which also hit US Top 100. Following the departure of GARY WRIGHT (who formed his WONDERWHEEL), the band split, the remnants of the band recording another 1970 set, 'THE LAST PUFF'. Late in 1972, after WRIGHT and HARRISON had abandoned their own solo projects, SPOOKY TOOTH delivering a new album the following year, 'YOU BROKE MY HEART SO I BUSTED YOUR JAW' (obviously the band had never heard of the "Zero Tolerance" campaign). Further albums failed to re-kindle the spark of old, even when they recruited veteran, MIKE PATTO. After their swansong, 'THE MIRROR' (1974), GARY WRIGHT went on to a very successful FM-orientated solo career, 'THE DREAM WEAVER' nearly topping the charts in America. • **Songwriters:** WRIGHT wrote most of material, except a soliary cover; I AM THE WALRUS (Beatles), taken from 'Island's 1970 compilation, 'Bumpers'.

Recommended: THE BEST OF SPOOKY TOOTH (*7)

The V.I.P.'s

LUTHER GROSVENOR (b.23 Dec'49) – guitar, vocals (ex-HELLIONS) / **FRANK KENYON** – rhythm guitar / **JIMMY HENSHAW** – guitar / **WALTER JOHNSTONE** – drums

R.C.A. | not issued

Nov 64. (7") *(RCA 1427)* **DON'T KEEP SHOUTING AT ME. / SHE'S NO GOOD** | | -

— **MIKE HARRISON** (b. 3 Sep'45, Carlisle, England) – vocals, piano (ex-RAMRODS) / **GREG RIDLEY** (b.23 Oct'41, Cumberland, England) – bass (ex-RAMRODS) both repl. JIMMY

C.B.S. | not issued

Jan 66. (7"; miscredited to VIPPS) *(202031)* **WINTERTIME. / ANYONE** | | -

Island | not issued

Oct 66. (7") *(WI 3003)* **I WANNA BE FREE. / DON'T LET IT GO** | | -

Feb 67. (7") *(WIP 6005)* **STRAIGHT DOWN TO THE BOTTOM. / IN A DREAM** | | -

ART

(same label) **MIKE KELLIE** (b.24 Mar'47, Birmingham, England) – drums repl. WALTER

Aug 67. (7") *(WIP 6019)* **WHAT'S THAT SOUND (FOR WHAT IT'S WORTH). / ROME TAKE AWAY THREE** | | -

Dec 67. (lp) *(ILP 967)* **SUPERNATURAL FAIRY TALES** | | -
– I think I'm going weird / What's that sound (for what it's worth) / African thing / Room with a view / Flying anchors / Supernatural fairy tale / Love is real / Come on up / Brothers, dads & mothers / Talkin' to myself / Alive not dead / Rome take away three. *(re-iss.1975; ILPS 967) (cd-iss.Nov92 on Drop Out)*

— That year, the group also appeared on album 'Featuring The Human Host And The Heavy Metal Kids' by 'HAPSHASH & THE COLOURED COAT'. They recorded 5 or 6 French-only 45's between 1966-68.

SPOOKY TOOTH

HARRISON now on keyboards / added **GARY WRIGHT** (b.26 Apr'45, Englewood, New Jersey) – vocals, organ

Island | Mala

Jan 68. (7") *(WIP 6022)* <587> **SUNSHINE HELP ME. / WEIRD**

Jun 68. (lp; mono/stereo) *(ILP/+S 9080)* **IT'S ALL ABOUT A ROUNDABOUT**
– Society's child / Love really changed me / Here I lived so well / Too much of nothing / Sunshine help me / It's all about a roundabout / Tobacco road / It hurts so much / Forget it, I got it / Bubbles. *<US-iss.Jun 71 as 'TOBACCO ROAD' for 'A&M'; > (cd-iss.Jan96 on 'Edsel'; EDCD 467)*

Jun 68. (7") *(WIP 6037)* <12013> **LOVE REALLY CHANGED ME. / LUGER'S GROVE**

Sep 68. (7") *(WIP 6046)* <1202> **THE WEIGHT. / DO RIGHT PEOPLE**

Island | A&M

Mar 69. (lp) *(ILPS 9098)* <4194> **SPOOKY TWO** | | 44 Jul 69
– Waitin' for the wind / Feelin' bad / I've got enough heartaches / Evil woman / Lost in my dream / Better by you, better than me / Hangman hang my shell on a tree.

Jun 69. (7") *(WIP 6060)* **SON OF YOUR FATHER. / I'VE GOT ENOUGH HEARTACHES** | | -

Jul 69. (7") <1110> **I'VE GOT ENOUGH HEARTACHES. / FEELIN' BAD** | - |

Nov 69. (7") <1144> **WAITIN' FOR THE WIND. / THAT WAS ONLY YESTERDAY** | - |

— trimmed to quartet (**GROSVENOR, WRIGHT, HARRISON & KELLIE**), after RIDLEY joined HUMBLE PIE. Below **PIERRE HENRY** was avant-garde electronic wizard.

Jan 70. (lp; as SPOOKY TOOTH with PIERRE HENRY) *(ILPS 9107)* <4225> **CEREMONY** | | 92 Mar70
– Have mercy / Jubilation / Confession / Prayer / Offering / Hosana.

— GARY vacated to form WONDERWHEEL who made 2 albums on 'A&M';- EXTRACTION (1971) and FOOTPRINT (1972). He was replaced by **HENRY McCULLOCH** – guitar + **ALAN SPENNER** – bass, vocals (both ex-JOE COCKER's GREASE BAND)

Jul 70. (lp) *(ILPS 9117)* <4266> **THE LAST PUFF** | | 84 Aug70
– I am the walrus / The wrong time / Something to say / Nobody there at all / Down river / Son of your father / The last puff. *(cd-iss.Feb96 on 'Edsel'; EDCD 468)*

— **JOHN HAWKEN** – keyboards + **STEVE THOMPSON** – bass repl. last newboys to J.COCKER

— Disbanded Autumn 1970. KELLIE joined (PETER) FRAMPTON'S CAMEL. THOMPSON joined STONE THE CROWS and HAWKEN went to ILLUSION. GROSVENOR released solo lp 'UNDER OPEN SKIES' in Oct71, before joining STEALER'S WHEEL. In mid'73, he became ARIEL BENDER and joined MOTT THE HOOPLE. MIKE HARRISON went solo forming own band JUNKYARD ANGEL. They issued 2 albums for 'Island'; MIKE HARRISON (1971) and SMOKESTACK LIGHTNIN' (1972).

— In 1973, **HARRISON + WRIGHT** re-formed SPOOKY TOOTH with **MICK JONES** (b.27 Dec'44) – guitar / **BRYSON GRAHAM** – drums (both ex-WONDERWHEEL) / **IAN HERBERT** – bass (ex-JUNKYARD ANGELS).

Island | A&M

May 73. (lp) *(ILPS 9227)* <4385> **YOU BROKE MY HEART SO I BUSTED YOUR JAW** | | 84
– Cotton growing man / Old as I was born / This time around / Holy water / Wildfire / Self seeking man / Times have changed / Moriah.

Aug 73. (7") <1466> **COTTON GROWING MAN. / TIMES HAVE CHANGED** | - |

— **MIKE KELLIE** returned to repl. BRYSON / **CHRIS STEWART** – bass repl. IAN

Island | Island

Oct 73. (7") *(WIP 6168)* **ALL SEWN UP. / AS LONG AS THE WORLD KEEPS ON TURNING** | | -

Nov 73. (lp) *(ILPS 9255)* <9337> **WITNESS** | | 99
– Ocean of power / Wings on my heart / Things change / As long as the world keeps on turning / Don't ever stray away / All sewn up / Dream me a mountain / Sunlight of my mind / Pyramids.

Dec 73. (7") <1219> **ALL SEWN UP. / THINGS CHANGE** | - |

— **MIKE PATTO** (b.22 Sep'42) – vocals (ex-TIMEBOX) / **KEITH ELLIS** – bass (ex-VAN DER GRAAF GENERATOR) repl. HARRISON (who went solo) **+ STEWART.** (May74) **WRIGHT, PATTO + JONES** enlisted **BRYSON GRAHAM** – drums returned to repl. KELLIE who joined ONLY ONES. **VAL MOORE** – bass repl. ELLIS to sessions.

Good Earth | Island

Aug 74. (7") <004> **THE MIRROR. / HELL OR HIGH WATER** | - |

Aug 74. (7") *(EAR 109)* **TWO TIME LOVE. / THE HOOFER** | | -

Sep 74. (lp) *(EARL 2001)* <ILPS 9292> **THE MIRROR**
– Hell or high water / I'm alive / The mirror / The hoofer / Fantasy satisfier / Two time love / Kyle / Woman and gold / Higher circles. *(re-iss.May79 on 'Charly'; CD 1032) (cd-iss.Feb93; CDCD 1032) (cd-iss.Jan91 on 'Line'; LICD 9000900)*

Feb 75. (7") *(EAR 607)* **FANTASY SATISFIER. / THE HOOFER** [ ] [-]

—— Inevitably bit the dust for final time in 1975. JONES joined The LESLIE WEST BAND and later FOREIGNER. PATTO formed BOXER, BRYSON joining ALVIN LEE BAND. PATTO died of throat cancer on the 4th of March '79.

- compilations, others, etc. -

Feb 75. (7"; as ART) *Island; (WIP 6224)* **WHAT'S THAT SOUND (FOR WHAT IT'S WORTH). / FLYING ANCHORS** [ ] [-]

Mar 76. (lp) *Island; (ILPS 9368)* **THE BEST OF SPOOKY TOOTH** [ ] [-]
– Tobacco Road / Better by you, better than me / It's all about a roundabout / Waitin' for the wind / The last puff / Evil woman / That was only yesterday / I am the walrus / Self seeking man / All sewn up / Times have changed / As long as the world keeps turning / The weight. *(cd-iss.Nov89; IMCD 74) (cd re-iss.May94; 842688-2)*

—— WRIGHT went solo and had huge success in America

Chris SQUIRE (see under ⇒ YES)

SRC

Formed: Detroit, Michigan, USA . . . 1967 by brothers GLENN and GARY QUACKENBUSH, plus STEVE LYMAN and SCOTT RICHARDSON. In fact, they were actually a sextet, an archetype psychedelic rock band whose eponymous debut album broke into the US Top 200. Guitarist GARY QUACKENBUSH was excellent throughout a now long-lost 45, 'BLACK SHEEP', which inspired groups like FEVER TREE to branch out. The second album, 'MILESTONES', fared even better commercially, combining two classical pieces 'IN THE HALL OF THE MOUNTAIN GRILL' – 'BOLERO', a short trip into neo-classical. However album number three was critically lambasted and they were soon dropped by 'Capitol'.

Recommended: REVENGE OF THE QUACKENBUSH BROTHERS (*6)

SCOTT RICHARDSON – vocals / **GLENN QUACKENBUSH** – keyboards / **GARY QUACKENBUSH** – guitar / **STEVE LYMAN** – guitar, vocals / **ROBIN DALE** – bass, vocals / **E.G. CLAWSON** – drums, percussion

not issued — A-2

1967. (7") <301> **I'M SO GLAD. / WHO IS THAT GIRL** [-] [ ]

1967. (7"; as SCOTT CASE) <402> **GET THE PICTURE. / I NEED YOU** [-] [ ]

Capitol — Capitol

Jan . (lp; stereo/mono) <(S+/T 2991)> **SRC** [ ] [ ] Sep68
– Black sheep / Daystar / Exile / Maionette / Onesimpletask / Paragon council / Refugeve / Interval.

Jan 69. (7") *(CL 15576)* <2327> **BLACK SHEEP. / MORNING MOOD** [ ] [ ] Sep68

—— **AL WILMOT** – bass, vocals, repl. DALE

Feb 69. (7") <2457> **TURN INTO LOVE. / UP ALL NIGHT** [-] [ ]

Aug 69. (lp; mono/stereo) <*(ET/E-ST 134)*> **MILESTONES** [ ] [ ] Jun69
– No secret destination / Show me / Eye of the storm / I remember your face / In the hall of the mountain king – Bolero / Checkmate / Our little secret / Turn into love / Up all night / The angel song.

—— **RAY GOODMAN** – guitar, repl. GARY + STEVE

1970. (7") <2726> **MY FORTUNE'S COMING TRUE. / NEVER BEFORE NOW** [-] [ ]

1970. (lp; mono/stereo) *(ET/E-ST <273>)* **TRAVELLER'S TALE** [-] [ ]
– A new crusader / Street without a name / Midnight fever / Never before now / By way of you / Diana / Across the land of light / The offering.

not issued — Big Casino

1971. (7") <1001> **BORN TO LOVE. / BADAZZ SHUFFLE** [-] [ ]

not issued — Rare Earth

1972. (7"; as BLUE SCEPTER) <5040> **OUT IN THE NIGHT. / GYPSY EYES** [-] [ ]

- compilations, etc. -

Mar 87. (lp) *Bam Caruso; (KIRI 054)* **REVENGE OF THE QUACKENBUSH BROTHERS** [ ] [-]
– Daystar / Midnight fever / Across the land of light / I remember your face / Marionette / By way of you / Exile / A new crusader / Black sheep / Never before now.

1988. (7") *Bam Caruso; (OPRA 063)* **BLACK SHEEP. / Brain:- Nightmares In Red** [ ] [-]

STAMPFEL & WEBER (see under ⇒ HOLY MODAL ROUNDERS)

STANDELLS

Formed: Los Angeles, California, USA . . . 1962 by LARRY TAMBLYN (brother of actor RUSS), TONY VALENTINE, GARY LANE and GARY LEEDS. After the introduction of singer DICK DODD, they signed to 'Liberty', where they released a clutch of forgettable singles starting with novelty type 'PEPPERMINT BEATLES' (1964). An album, released the following year, 'IN PERSON AT P.J.'s', was littered with throwaway college-rock cover versions. Early in 1966, after teaming up with writer/producer ED COBB, they hovered outside the US Top 10 hit with the COBB-penned classic, 'DIRTY WATER'. This took garage-punk to the masses, who were still waiting for another 'Louie Louie' to emerge. An album of the same name nearly hit the Top 50, COBB's songs interspersed with covers of 'PAINT IT BLACK' (Rolling Stones), 'WILD THING' (Troggs) and a re-working of the classic blues number, 'ST. JAMES INFIRMARY'. Two further slices of high-octane R&B/garage followed, both only managing minor chart placings. In 1967, the band appeared in the exploitation film, 'Riot On Sunset Strip', although this was a backdrop to the flower-power of the era. Personnel changes dogged their final outings; one interesting member, LOWELL GEORGE, joined them on the cabaret circuit before he went to other more fruitful pastures (i.e. The MOTHERS OF INVENTION and LITTLE FEAT). • **Covers:** LOUIE LOUIE (Kingsmen) / SO FINE (Johnny Otis) / I'LL GO CRAZY (James Brown) / MONEY (Barrett Strong) / BIG BOSS MAN (Willie Dixon) / BONY MORONIE (Larry Williams) / HEY JOE (hit; Jimi Hendrix) / MY LITTLE RED BOOK (Bacharach-David) / 19th NERVOUS BREAKDOWN + PAINT IT BLACK (Rolling Stones) / LAST TRAIN TO CLARKSVILLE (hit; Monkees) / WILD THING (Troggs) / SUNSHINE SUPERMAN (Donovan) / SUNNY AFTERNOON (Kinks) / ELEANOR RIGBY (Beatles) / BLACK IS BLACK (Los Bravos) / SUMMER IN THE CITY (Lovin' Spoonful) / WHEN I WAS A COWBOY (Leadbelly) / 99 AND A HALF WON'T DO (Wilson Pickett) / etc. • **Trivia:** CHER supplied backing vox on their SONNY BONO-produced 45, 'THE BOY NEXT DOOR'. Late in 1965, DEWEY MARTIN was a brief member, before joining BUFFALO SPRINGFIELD.

Recommended: THE BEST OF THE STANDELLS (*6)

LARRY TAMBLYN – vocals, organ (ex-Solo artist) / **TONY VALENTINE** (b. Italy) – guitar / **GARY LANE** – bass / **GARY LEEDS** (b. New York) – drums

Linda — not issued

1963. (7"; as LARRY TAMBLYN & THE STANDELLS) <112> **YOU'LL BE MINE SOMEDAY. / THE GIRL IN MY HEART** [-] [ ]

—— **DICK DODD** – vox, drums repl. LEEDS (to JOHNNY RIVERS then WALKERS BROTHERS)

Liberty — Liberty

Jul 64. (7") <55680> **PEPPERMINT BEATLES. / THE SHAKE** [-] [ ]

Sep 64. (7") *(LIB <55722>)* **HELP YOURSELF. / I'LL GO CRAZY** [ ] [ ]

Nov 64. (7") <55743> **LINDA LOU. / SO FINE** [-] [ ]

1965. (lp; mono/stereo) *(LBY 1243)* <LRP3/LST7 384> **THE STANDELLS IN PERSON AT P.J.'S (live)** [ ] [ ] Nov64
– Help yourself / So fine / You can't do that / What have I got of my own / Money (that's what I want) / I'll go crazy / Bony Moronie / Ooh poo pah doo / Linda Lou / Louie Louie. <*US re-iss.1966 as 'LIVE AND OUT OF SIGHT' on 'Sunset' mono/stereo; SUM1/SUS5 186*>- (3rd & 4th tracks repl. by)- Peppermint Beatles / The Shake.

not issued — Vee Jay

1965. (7") <643> **THE BOY NEXT DOOR. / B.J. QUETZAL** [-] [ ]

1965. (7") <679> **DON'T SAY GOODBYE. / BIG BOSS MAN** [-] [ ]

not issued — M.G.M.

1966. (7") <13350> **SOMEDAY YOU'LL CRY. / ZEBRA IN THE KITCHEN** [-] [ ]

Capitol — Tower

Apr 66. (7") *(CL 15446)* <185> **DIRTY WATER. / RARI** [ ] [11]

Jun 66. (lp; mono/stereo) <*T/ST 5027*> **DIRTY WATER** [-] [52]
– Dirty water / Little Sally tease / Black is black / Barracuda / Animal girl / St. James infirmary / Try it / Summer in the city / Why did you hurt me / Rari / Paint it black / Medication / Why pick on me / Sunny afternoon / Mr. Nobody / Wild thing. *(cd-iss.Apr94 on 'Sundazed'+=; CDSC 6019)*– My little red book / Mainline / Have you ever spent the night in jail.

Aug 66. (7") <257> **SOMETIMES GOOD GUYS DON'T WEAR WHITE. / WHY DID YOU HURT ME?** [-] [43]

Oct 66. (7") <282> **WHY PICK ON ME?. / MR. NOBODY** [-] [54]

1966. (lp; mono/stereo) <*T/ST 5044*> **WHY PICK ON ME / SOMETIMES GOOD GUYS DON'T WEAR WHITE** [-] [ ]
– Why pick on me / Paint it black / Mi hai fatto innamorate / I hate to leave / Black hearted woman / Sometimes good guys don't wear white / Girl and the moon / Looking at tomorrow / Mr. Nobody / My little red book / Mainline / Have you ever spent the night in jail. *(UK cd-iss.Apr94 on 'Sundazed'+=; CDSC 6020)*– Our candidate / Don't say nothing at all / Boy who is lost.

—— **DAVE BURKE** – bass repl. LANE

Nov 66. (lp; mono/stereo) <*T/ST 5049*> **HOT ONES** [-] [ ]
– Last train to Clarksville / Wild thing / Sunshine Superman / Sunny afternoon / Lil' Red Riding Hood / Eleanor Rigby / Black is black / Summer in the city / 19th nervous breakdown / Dirty water. *(UK cd-iss.Apr94 on 'Sundazed'+=; (CDSC 6021)*– .

Nov 66. (7") <310> **TRY IT. / POOR SHELL OF A MAN** [-] [ ]

—— **JOHN FLECK** – bass repl. BURKE

Jan 67. (7"; as SLLEDNATS) <312> **DON'T TELL ME WHAT TO DO. / WHEN I WAS A COWBOY** [-] [ ]

Mar 67. (7") <314> **RIOT ON SUNSET STRIP. / BLACK HEARTED WOMAN** [-] [ ]

Nov 67. (7") <348> **CAN'T HELP BUT LOVE YOU. / 99 AND A HALF WON'T DO** [-] [78]

Jan 68. (lp; mono/stereo) <*T/ST 5098*> **TRY IT** [-] [ ]
– Can't help but love you / 99 and a half won't do / Trip to Paradise / St. James Infirmary / Try it / Barracuda / Did you ever have that feeling / All fall down / Poor shell of a man / Riot on Sunset Strip. *(UK cd-iss.Apr94 on 'Sundazed'+=; CDSC 6022)*– Get away from here / Animal girl / Soul drippin' / Can you dig it.

1968. (7") <398> **ANIMAL GIRL. / SOUL DRIPPIN'** [-] [ ]

—— Disbanded early '68, although in the early 70's VALENTINO and TAMBLYN re-formed. In the 80's, DODD was again added to 3 originals.

- compilations, etc. -

1966. (7") *Sunset;* <61000> **OOH POO PAH DOO. / HELP YOURSELF** [-] [ ]

1982. (lp) *Rhino;* <RNLP 107> **THE BEST OF THE STANDELLS** [-] [ ]
<*re-iss.1986; RNLP 70176*>

1984. (lp) *Rhino;* <RNLP 115> **RARITIES** [-] [ ]

Oct 92. (cd) *Big Beat; (CDWIKD 110)* **DIRTY WATER** [ ] [-]

Mar 93. (cd) *Big Beat; (CDWIKD 112)* **HOT ONES / TRY IT** [ ] [-]

Jun 93. (cd) *Big Beat; (CDWIKD 113)* **RARITIES / RIOT ON SUNSET STRIP** [ ] [-]

Jun 93. (cd) *Big Beat; (CDWIKD 114)* **IS THIS THE WAY YOU GET YOUR HIGH** [ ] [-]
Nov 94. (cd) *Eva; (EVA 842121B5)* **DIRTY WATER / THE HOT ONES** [ ] [-]
Sep 95. (7") *Sundazed;* **SITTING THERE STANDING. /** [ ] [-]

DICK DODD

went solo augmented by ED COBB

not issued | Attarack

1967. (7") *<102>* **GUILTY. / REQUIEM: 820 LATHAM** [-] [ ]

not issued | Tower

Dec 67. (7") *<447>* **LITTLE SISTER. / LONELY WEEKENDS** [-] [ ]
Feb 68. (7") *<490>* **FANNY. / DON'T BE ASHAMED TO CALL MY NAME** [-] [ ]
Feb 68. (lp) *<ST 5142>* **THE FIRST EVOLUTION OF DICK DODD** [-] [ ]

STATUS QUO

Formed: London, England ... 1962 as The SPECTRES, by schoolboys ALAN LANCASTER, ALAN KEY, MIKE ROSSI (aka FRANCIS) and JESS JAWORSKI. They subsequently added JOHN COUGHLAN to replace BARRY SMITH, and, by the mid-60's were playing a residency at Butlin's holiday camp, where ROY LYNES took over from JESS. In July '66, they signed to 'Piccadilly' records but failed with a debut 45, a Leiber & Stoller cover, 'I (WHO HAVE NOTHING)'. They released two more flops, before they changed name in March '67 to The TRAFFIC JAM. After one 45, they chose an alternative moniker, The STATUS QUO, due to the more high profile TRAFFIC making the charts. In October '67, MIKE ROSSI reverted back to his real Christian name, FRANCIS, the band adding a second guitarist, RICK PARFITT. Now re-signed to 'Pye' records, they unleashed their first single, 'PICTURES OF MATCHSTICK MEN', giving them a breakthrough into the UK Top 10 (it also hit No.12 in the States – their only Top 50 hit). This was an attempt to cash-in on the hugely popular psychedelic scene, an enjoyable pastiche nevertheless, which remains of their most enduring, timeless songs. The following year, they were again in the Top 10 with 'ICE IN THE SUN', another taken from the same blueprint. Soon after, the band shed their psychedelic trappings, opting instead for a blues/boogie hard rock sound a la CANNED HEAT. After two more Top 30 hits in the early 70's, their biggest and best being, 'DOWN THE DUSTPIPE', they jumped ship in 1972, signing to 'Vertigo' records. With their trademark blue jeans and (sometimes) white T-shirts, they became one of the top selling bands of the 70's, continuing their success into the 80's. Their 3-chord-wonder barrage of rock'n'roll had few variations throughout their career, although their constant critical onslaught was not really deserved until the 90's. The 'ANNIVERSARY WALTZ' pop medleys making them sound more like CHAS & DAVE. • **Songwriters:** LANCASTER or ROSSI or PARFITT. In the early 70's, ROSSI and tour manager BOB YOUNG took over duties. Covered; SPICKS AND SPECKS (Bee Gees) / GREEN TAMBOURINE (Lemon Pipers) / SHEILA (Tommy Roe) / ICE IN THE SUN + ELIZABETH DREAMS + PARADISE FLAT + others (Marty Wilde – Ronnie Scott) / JUNIOR'S WAILING (Steamhammer) / DOWN THE DUSTPIPE (Carl Grossman) / THE PRICE OF LOVE (Everly Brothers) / ROADHOUSE BLUES (Doors) / WILD SIDE OF LIFE (Tommy Quickly) / ROCKIN' ALL OVER THE WORLD (John Fogerty) / THE WANDERER (Dion) / IN THE ARMY NOW (Bolland-Bolland) / RESTLESS (Jennifer Warnes) / WHEN YOU WALK IN THE ROOM (Jackie DeShannon) / FUN, FUN, FUN (Beach Boys) / I CAN HEAR THE GRASS GROW (Move) / YOU NEVER CAN TELL (Chuck Berry) / GET BACK (Beatles) / SAFETY DANCE (Men Without Hats) / RAINING IN MY HEART (Buddy Holly) / DON'T STOP (Fleetwood Mac) PROUD MARY (Creedence Clearwater Revival) / LUCILLE (Little Richard) / JOHNNY AND MARY (Robert Palmer) / GET OUT OF DENVER (Bob Seger) / THE FUTURE'S SO BRIGHT (Timbuk 3) / ALL AROUND MY HAT (Steeleye Span) / etc. • **Trivia:** In 1985, the group with LANCASTER still in tow, played The LIVE AID Wembley concert.

Recommended: QUOTATIONS VOL.1 (THE EARLY YEARS) (*6) / 12 GOLD BARS (*7)

MIKE ROSSI (b. FRANCIS, 29 Apr'49, Forest Hill, London) – vocals, guitar / **ROY LYNES** (b.25 Oct'43, Surrey, Kent) – organ, vocals repl. JESS JAWORSKI / **ALAN LANCASTER** (b. 7 Feb'49, Peckham, London) – bass, vocals / **JOHN COGHLAN** (b.19 Sep'46, Dulwich, London) – drums repl. BARRY SMITH

Piccadilly | not issued

Sep 66. (7"; as The SPECTRES) *(7N 35339)* **I (WHO HAVE NOTHING). / NEIGHBOUR, NEIGHBOUR** [ ] [-]
Nov 66. (7"; as The SPECTRES) *(7N 35352)* **HURDY GURDY MAN. / LATICA** [ ] [-]
— (above was not the DONOVAN song)
Feb 67. (7"; as The SPECTRES) *(7N 35368)* **(WE AIN'T GOT) NOTHIN' YET. / I WANT IT** [ ] [-]
Jun 67. (7"; as TRAFFIC JAM) *(7N 35386)* **ALMOST THERE BUT NOT QUITE. / WAIT JUST A MINUTE** [ ] [-]

The STATUS QUO

— added **RICK PARFITT** (b. RICHARD HARRISON, 12 Oct'48, Woking, Surrey) – guitar, vocals / MIKE now **FRANCIS ROSSI**

Pye | Cadet Concept

Nov 67. (7") *(7N 17449) <7001>* **PICTURES OF MATCHSTICK MEN. / GENTLEMAN JOE'S SIDEWALK CAFE** [7] [12] May68
Apr 68. (7") *(7N 17497) <7015>* **BLACK VEILS OF MELONCHOLY. / TO BE FREE** [ ] [ ] Jul69
Aug 68. (lp) *(NSPL 18220)* **PICTURESQUE MATCHSTICKABLE MESSAGES FROM THE STATUS QUO** (US-title 'MESSAGES FROM THE STATUS QUO') [ ] [ ]
– Black veils of melончoly / When my mind is not live / Ice in the Sun / Elizabeth dreams / Gentleman Joe's sidewalk cafe / Paradise flat / Technicolour dreams / Spicks and specks / Sheila / Sunny cellophane skies / Green tambourine / Pictures of matchstick men. *(re-iss.Oct87 on 'P.R.T.' lp/c/cd; PYL/PYM/PYC 6020) (cd re-iss.Dec89 on 'Castle'; CLACD 168)*
Aug 68. (7") *(7N 17581) <7006>* **ICE IN THE SUN. / WHEN MY MIND IS NOT ALIVE** [8] [70]
Jan 69. (7"w-drawn) *(7N 17650)* **TECHNICOLOR DREAMS. / PARADISE FLAT** [-] [-]
Feb 69. (7") *(7N 17665)* **MAKE ME STAY A BIT LONGER. / AUNTIE NELLIE** [ ] [-]
Mar 69. (7") *<7010>* **TECHNICOLOR DREAMS. / SPICKS AND SPECKS** [-] [ ]
May 69. (7") *(7N 17728)* **ARE YOU GROWING TIRED OF MY LOVE. / SO ENDS ANOTHER LIFE** [46] [-]
Sep 69. (lp) *(NSPL 18301)* **SPARE PARTS** [ ] [-]
– Face without a soul / You're just what I'm looking for / Mr.Mind detector / Antique Angelique / So ends another life / Are you growing tired of my love / Little Miss Nothing / Poor old man / The clown / Velvet curtains / When I awake / Nothing at all. *(re-iss.Oct87 on 'P.R.T.' lp/c/cd; PYL/PYM/PYC 6021) (re-iss.Aug90 on 'Castle' cd/c/lp; CLA CD/MC/LP 205)*
Oct 69. (7") *(7N 17825) <7017>* **THE PRICE OF LOVE. / LITTLE MISS NOTHING** [ ] [ ]

Pye | Janus

Mar 70. (7") *(7N 17907)* **DOWN THE DUSTPIPE. / FACE WITHOUT A SOUL** [12] [ ]
Sep 70. (lp) *(NSPL 18344) <3018>* **MA KELLY'S GREASY SPOON** [ ] [ ]
– Spinning wheel blues / Daughter / Everything / Shy fly / (April) Spring, Summer and Wednesdays / Junior's wailing / Lakky lady / Need your love / Lazy poker blues / Is it really me? – Gotta go home. *(re-iss.Oct87 on 'P.R.T.'; PYL/PYM/PYC 6022) (cd re-iss.Dec89 on 'Castle'; CLACD 169)*

— For further STATUS QUO releases; see GREAT ROCK DISCOGRAPHY

Endle ST. CLOUD

Formed: Austin, Texas, USA ... 1968 as the group ENDLE ST. CLOUD IN THE RAIN. ENDLE recruited some musicians from other local bands, including PETE BLACK (from LOST & FOUND), who had also recorded for 'International Artists'. They debuted with the very rare 45, 'TELL ME ONE MORE TIME', which didn't sell in any great quantity. An album, 'THANK YOU ALL VERY MUCH', surfaced in 1970 and contained some fine acid-country tracks, including two borrowed from LOST & FOUND; 'PROFESSOR BLACK' & 'COME THROUGH'. ENDLE's avant-garde work surfaced again on a project, POTTER ST. CLOUD, which re-united him with EAST SIDE KIDS guitarist, DAVE POTTER.

Recommended: THANK YOU ALL VERY MUCH (*5)

ENDLE ST. CLOUD – vocals / **PETE BLACK** – guitar (ex-LOST & FOUND) / **D.F. POTTER** – bass (ex-EAST SIDE KIDS) / **A. MELLINGER** – drums (ex-IGUANAS; not same as IGGY POP's first band)

not issued | Int.Artists

1968. (7") *<129>* **TELL ME ONE MORE TIME. / QUEST FOR BEAUTY** [-] [ ]
1970. (lp) *<IA-LP 12>* **THAN YOU ALL VERY MUCH** [-] [ ]
– Street corner preacher / Who should you like to be today / This is love / Professor Black / Laughter / Jessica / Come through / She wears it like a badge.
1970. (7") *<139>* **SHE WEARS IT LIKE A BADGE. / LAUGHTER** [-] [ ]

— ENDLE formed new outfit with POTTER, plus **JAMES HARRELL** – vocals, bass, guitar / **DANNY BAKER** – vocals, piano, organ / **GENE TREEK** – vocals, guitar

not issued | Mediarts

1971. (lp; as POTTER ST. CLOUD) *<41-7>* **POTTER ST. CLOUD** [-] [ ]
– Sunshine on a rainy day / It's time to climb / Pretty flowers / Open letter / Peace and war / He's gonna clobber you / Mean man / Jessie John / Gentle wind / Sam.

— disappeared from sight once again

STEPPENWOLF

Formed: Toronto, Canada ... 1966 as blues band SPARROW, by JOHN KAY, plus MICHAEL MONARCH, GOLDY McJOHN, RUSHTON MOREVE and JERRY EDMONTON. After one-off 45 for 'Columbia', they soon relocated to Los Angeles following a brief stay in New York. There, they met producer Gabriel Mekler, who gave them the STEPPENWOLF name (after a Herman Hesse novel). They quickly signed to 'Dunhill' and recorded their eponymous 1968 debut, which included that summer's No.2 classic biker's anthem, 'BORN TO BE WILD'. This success resurrected the albums' appeal, which finally climbed to the higher echelons of the charts. The track was subsequently used on the 1969 film, 'Easy Rider', alongside another from the debut; 'THE PUSHER'. While both songs were enjoyable, hot-wired romps through dusty blues-rock terrain, the pseudo-intellectual musings and less than inspired songwriting of JOHN KAY made the multitude of subsequent STEPPENWOLF releases hard going. Nevertheless, the band hit US Top 3 with the colourful psychedelia of the 'MAGIC CARPET RIDE' (1968) single, its parent album, 'STEPPENWOLF THE SECOND' (1969) notching up a similar placing in the album charts. By the early 70's, the band were experiencing diminishing chart returns and split after the 1972 concept album, 'FOR LADIES ONLY'. KAY recorded a couple of solo albums before reforming STEPPENWOLF in 1974. Signed to 'C.B.S.' then 'Epic', the band failed to resurrect their early momentum, although they continued to inflict their tired biker-rock on an oblivious music world right up until the 90's. • **Songwriters:** KAY written, except; THE PUSHER + SNOW BLIND FRIEND (Hoyt Axton) / SOOKIE SOOKIE (Don Covay) / BORN TO BE WILD (Dennis Edmonton; Jerry's brother) / I'M MOVIN' ON (Hank Snow) / HOOCHIE COOCHIE MAN (Muddy Waters). • **Trivia:** BORN TO BE WILD coined a new rock term in the their lyrics "heavy metal thunder". Early in 1969, they contributed some songs to another cult-ish film, 'Candy'.

Recommended: BORN TO BE WILD: A RETROSPECTIVE (*8)

JOHN KAY (b. JOACHIM F. KRAULEDAT, 12 Apr'44, Tilsit, Germany) – vox, guitar / **MICHAEL MONARCH** (b. 5 Jul'50, Los Angeles, California, USA) – guitar / **GOLDY McJOHN** (b. JOHN GOADSBY, 2 May'45) – organ / **RUSHTON MOREVE** (b.1948, Los Angeles) – bass / **JERRY EDMONTON** (b. JERRY McCROHAN, 24 Oct'46, Canada) – drums, vocals

C.B.S. | Columbia

1966. (7"; as The SPARROW) *(202342) <43755>* **TOMORROW'S SHIP. / ISN'T IT STRANGE** [ ] [ ]

1967. (7"; as The SPARROW) *<43960>* **GREEN BOTTLE LOVER. / DOWN GOES YOUR LOVE LIFE** [-] [ ]

1967. (7"; as JOHN KAY) *<44769>* **TWISTED. / SQUAREHEAD PEOPLE** [-] [ ]

— **JOHN RUSSELL MORGAN** – bass repl. MOREVE. He was killed in car crash on 1st Jul'81.

R.C.A. | Dunhill

Nov 67. (7") *<4109>* **A GIRL I KNOW. / THE OSTRICH** [-] [ ]

Apr 68. (7") *(RCA 1679) <4123>* **SOOKIE SOOKIE. / TAKE WHAT YOU NEED** [ ] [ ] Jan68

May 68. (lp; mono/stereo) *(RD/SF 7974) <50029>* **STEPPENWOLF** [ ] [6] Jan68
– Sookie Sookie / Everybody's next one / Berry rides again / Hoochie coochie man / Born to be wild / Your wall's too high / Desperation / The pusher / A girl I knew / Take what you need / The ostrich. *(re-iss.Apr70 on 'Stateside'; SSL 5020); hit No.59 (re-iss.Jun87 on 'M.C.A.' lp/c; MCL/+C 1857) (cd-iss.Jul87; CMCAD 31020) (re-iss.Apr92 cd/c; MCL D/C 19019)*

Aug 68. (7") *(RCA 1735) <4138>* **BORN TO BE WILD. / EVERYBODY'S NEXT ONE** [ ] [2] Jun68
(re-iss.May69 on 'Stateside'; SS 8017); hit No.30

Stateside | Dunhill

Oct 68. (7") *(SS 8003) <4160>* **MAGIC CARPET RIDE. / SOOKIE SOOKIE** [ ] [3] Sep68
(re-iss.Sep69; SS 8027)

Jan 69. (lp; stereo/mono) *(S+/SL 5003) <50053>* **STEPPENWOLF THE SECOND** [ ] [3] Nov68
– Faster than the speed of life / Tighten up your wig / None of your doing / Spiritual fantasy / Don't step on the grass, Sam / 28 / Magic carpet ride / Disappointment / Number (unknown) / Lost and found by trial and error / Hodge, Podge strained through a Leslie / Resurrection / Reflections. *(cd-iss.Jun87 on 'M.C.A.'; CMCAD 31021)*

— **LARRY BYROM** (b.27 Dec'48, USA) – guitar repl. MONARCH / **NICK ST.NICHOLAS** (b. KLAUS KARL KASSBAUM, 28 Sep'43, Pion, Germany) – bass repl. RUSSELL

Mar 69. (7") *(SS 8013) <4182>* **ROCK ME. / JUPITER CHILD** [ ] [10] Feb69

Jun 69. (lp; stereo/mono) *(S+/SL 5011) <50060>* **AT YOUR BIRTHDAY PARTY** [ ] [7] Mar69
– Don't cry / Chicken wolf / Lovely meter / Round and down / It's never too late / Sleeping dreaming / Jupiter child / She'll be better / Cat killer / Rock me / God fearing man / Mango juice / Happy birthday.

May 69. (7") *<4192>* **IT'S NEVER TOO LATE. / HAPPY BIRTHDAY** [-] [51]

Aug 69. (7") *<4205>* **MOVE OVER. / POWER PLAY** [-] [31]

Dec 69. (7") *<4221>* **MONSTER. / BERRY RIDES AGAIN** [-] [39]

Jan 70. (7") *(SS 8035)* **MONSTER. / MOVE OVER** [ ] [-]

Jan 70. (lp) *(SSL 5021) <50066>* **MONSTER** [43] [17] Nov69
– Monster / Suicide / America / Draft resister / Power play / Move over / Fag / What would you do (if I did that to you) / From here to there eventually. *(cd-iss.Sep91 on 'Beat Goes On'; BGOCD 126)*

Mar 70. (7") *(SS 8038)* **THE PUSHER. / YOUR WALL'S TOO HIGH** [ ] [-]

Jun 70. (7") *(SS 8049) <4234>* **HEY LAWDY MAMA. / TWISTED** [ ] [35] Apr70

Jun 70. (d-lp) *(SSL 5029) <50075>* **STEPPENWOLF 'LIVE' (live)** [16] [7] Apr70
– Sookie Sookie / Don't step on the grass, Sam / Tighten up your wig / Hey lawdy mama / Magic carpet ride / The pusher / Born to be wild / Monster / Draft resister / Power play / Corrina, Corrina / Twisted / From here to there eventually. *(re-iss.Oct74 on 'A.B.C.'; ABCL 5007)*

Sep 70. (7") *(SS 8056) <4248>* **SCREAMING NIGHT HOG. / SPIRITUAL FANTASY** [ ] [62] Aug70

Probe | Dunhill

Nov 70. (7") *(PRO 510) <4261>* **WHO NEEDS YA. / EARSCHPLITTENLOUDENBOOMER** [ ] [54]

Nov 70. (lp) *(SPBA 6254) <50090>* **STEPPENWOLF 7** [ ] [19]
– Ball crusher / Forty days and forty nights / Fat Jack / Renegade / Foggy mental breakdown / Snow blind friend / Who needs ya / Earschplittenloudenboomer / Hippo stomp.

Mar 71. (7") *(PRO 525) <4269>* **SNOW BLIND FRIEND. / HIPPO STOMP** [ ] [60] Feb71

— **KENT HENRY** – guitar repl. BYROM

— **GEORGE BIONDO** (b. 3 Sep'45, Brooklyn, N.Y.) – bass repl. NICK

Jul 71. (7") *(PRO 534) <4283>* **RIDE WITH ME. / FOR MADMEN ONLY** [ ] [52]

Oct 71. (7") *(PRO 544) <4292>* **FOR LADIES ONLY. / SPARKLE EYES** [ ] [64]

Oct 71. (lp) *(SPBA 6260) <50110>* **FOR LADIES ONLY** [ ] [54]
– For ladies only / I'm asking / Snakes and chains / Tenderness / The night time's for you / Jadet strumpet / Sparkle eyes / Black pit / Ride with me / In hopes of a garden.

— Disbanded Feb'72, EDMUNTON and McJOHN formed MANBEAST.

JOHN KAY

went solo, augmented by **KENT HENRY + GEORGE BIONDO** plus **HUGH SULLIVAN** – keyboards / **PENTII WHITNEY GLEN** – drums / etc. (same label)

Apr 72. (lp) *(1054) <50120>* **FORGOTTEN SONGS AND UNSUNG HEROES** [ ] [ ]
– Many a mile / Walk beside me / You win again / To be alive / Bold marauder / Two of a kind / Walking blues / Somebody / I'm moving on.

Apr 72. (7") *<4309>* **I'M MOVIN' ON. / WALK BESIDE ME** [-] [52]

Jul 72. (7") *<4319>* **YOU WIN AGAIN. / SOMEBODY** [-] [ ]

Jul 73. (7") *<4351>* **MOONSHINE. / NOBODY LIVES HERE ANYMORE** [-] [ ]

Jul 73. (lp) *(6274) <50147>* **MY SPORTIN' LIFE** [ ] [ ]
– Moonshine / Nobody lives here anymore / Drift away / Heroes and devils / My sportin' life / Easy evil / Giles of the river / Dance to my song / Sing with the children.

Sep 73. (7") *(PRO 601) <4360>* **EASY EVIL. / DANCE TO MY SONG** [ ] [ ]

STEPPENWOLF

re-formed (**KAY, McJOHN, EDMUNTON, BIONDO**) plus **BOBBY COCHRAN** – guitar repl. KENT (first and last with horn section)

C.B.S. | Mums

Oct 74. (lp) *(80358) <33093>* **SLOW FLUX** [ ] [47] Sep74
– Gang war blues / Children of the night / Justice don't be slow / Get into the wind / Jeraboah / Straight shootin' woman / Smokey factory blues / Morning blue / A fool's factory / Fishin' in the dark.

Oct 74. (7") *(MUM 2679) <6031>* **STRAIGHT SHOOTIN' WOMAN. / JUSTICE DON'T BE SLOW** [ ] [29] Sep74

Jan 75. (7") *<6034>* **GET INTO THE WIND. / MORNING BLUE** [-] [ ]

Apr 75. (7") *(MUM 3147) <6036>* **SMOKEY FACTORY BLUES. / A FOOL'S FANTASY** [ ] [ ]

— **ANDY CHAPIN** – keyboards repl. McJOHN who went solo

Aug 75. (7") *(MUM 3470) <6040>* **CAROLINE (ARE YOU READY). / ANGEL DRAWERS** [ ] [ ]

Sep 75. (lp) *(69151) <34120>* **HOUR OF THE WOLF** [ ] [ ]
– Caroline (are you ready for the outlaw world) / Annie, Annie over / Two for the love of one / Just for tonight / Hard rock road / Someone told a lie / Another's lifetime / Mr. Penny pincher.

— **WAYNE COOK** – keyboards repl. ANDY

Epic | Epic

May 77. (lp) *(81328) <34120>* **SKULLDUGGERY** [ ] [ ]
– Skullduggery / Roadrunner / Rock and roll song / Train of thought / Life is a gamble / Pass it on / Sleep / Lip service.

Dec 77. (lp) *<34382>* **REBORN TO BE WILD** (remixes) [-] [ ]
– Straight shootin' woman / Hard rock road / Another's lifetime / Mr. Penny pincher / Smokey factory blues / Caroline / Get into the wind / Gang war blues / Children of night / Skullduggery.

— Disbanded yet again.

JOHN KAY

with **LARRY BYROM** – slide guitar / **MAC McANALLY** – guitar / **CLAYTON IVEY** – keyboards / **BOB WRAY** – bass / **ROGER CLARK** – drums

Mercury | Mercury

Jun 78. (lp) *(9110 054) <1-3715>* **ALL IN GOOD TIME** [ ] [ ]
– Give me some news I can use / The best is barely good enough / That's when I think of you / Ain't nobody home / Ain't nothin' like it used to be / Business is business / Show me how you'd like it done / Down in New Orleans / Say you will / Hey, I'm alright.

Jun 78. (7") *<74004>* **GIVE ME SOME NEWS I COULD USE. / SAY YOU WILL** [-] [ ]

Jun 78. (7") *(6167 683)* **GIVE ME SOME NEWS I CAN USE. / BUSINESS IS BUSINESS** [ ] [-]

— In the early 80's, KAY and group toured as

JOHN KAY & STEPPENWOLF

with **MICHAEL PALMER** – guitar / **BRETT TUGGLE** – keyboards / **CHAD PERRY** – bass / **STEVEN PALMER** – drums

not issued | Allegiance

Dec 81. (lp) **LIVE IN LONDON (live)** [-] [ ]
– Sookie Sookie / Give me news I can use / You / Hot night in a cold town / Ain't nothin' like it used to be / Magic carpet ride / Five finger discount / Hey lawdy mama / Business is business / Born to be wild / The pusher.

Dec 81. (7") *<3909>* **HOT TOME IN A COLD TOWN. /** [-] [ ]

— **WELTON GITE** – bass repl. CHAD / added **MICHAEL WILK** – keyboards

not issued | CBS-Sony

1983. (lp) *<DIDZ 10010>* **WOLFTRACKS** [-] [ ]
– All I want is all you got / None of the above / You / Every man for himself / Five finger discount / Hold your head up / Hot night in a cold town / Down to earth / For rock'n'roll / The balance. *(UK-iss.May97 as 'FIVE FINGER DISCOUNT' on 'C.M.C.'; 10045-2)*

— now with **ROCKET RITCHOTTE** – guitar, vocals + **MICHAEL WILK** – keyboards, bass / **RON HURST** – drums, vocals. Finally issued new material 1988.

Disky | Qwil

May 88. (lp/c/cd) *(979209-1/-4/-2) <1560>* **ROCK & ROLL REBELS** [ ] [ ] Sep87
– Give me life / Rock'n'roll rebels / Hold on / On a mission / Everybody knows you / Rock steady / Replace the face / Turn out the lights / Give me news I can use / Rage.

I.R.S. | I.R.S.

Aug 90. <(cd/c/lp)> *(241066-2/-4/-1)* **RISE & SHINE** [ ] [ ]
– Let's do it all / Time out / Do or die / Rise & shine / The wall / The daily blues / Keep rockin' / Rock'n'roll war / Sign on the line / We like it, we love it (we want more of it).

– compilations, others, etc. –

— on 'Probe' UK / 'Dunhill' US unless mentioned otherwise

Jul 69. (lp) *Stateside; (5015) / Dunhill; <50060>* **EARLY STEPPENWOLF** 29
(live from 1967 as The SPARROW)
– Power play / Howlin' for my baby / Goin' upstairs / Corina Corina / Tighten up your wig / The pusher.

Mar 71. (lp) *(SPB 1033) <50099>* **STEPPENWOLF GOLD** 24
– Born to be wild / It's never too late / Rock me / Hey lawdy mama / Move over / Who needs ya / Magic carpet ride / The pusher / Sookie Sookie / Jupiter's child / Screaming night hog. *(re-iss.Oct74 on 'A.B.C.'; ABCL 8613) (re-iss.Aug80 on 'M.C.A.'; 1502) (re-iss.Aug81 lp/c; MCM/+C 1619) (re-iss.Jan83 on 'Fame' lp/c; FA/TCFA 3052)*

Jul 72. (lp) *(SPB 1059) <50124>* **REST IN PEACE** 62 Jun72

Mar 73. (lp) *(SPB 1071) <50135>* **16 GREATEST HITS** Feb73
(re-iss.Oct74 on 'A.B.C.'; ABCL 5028) (cd-iss.Feb91 on 'M.C.A.'; MCAD 37049)

Jun 80. (7") *M.C.A.; (MCA 614)* **BORN TO BE WILD. / THE PUSHER**
(re-iss.Apr83 on 'Old Gold'; OG 9323)

Jul 85. (lp/c) *M.C.A.; (MCM/+C 5002)* **GOLDEN GREATS**
– Born to be wild / Magic carpet ride / Rock me / Move over / Hey lawdy mama / It's never too late / Who needs you? / Monster / Snow blind friend / The pusher / Sookie sookie / Jupiter's child / Screaming dog night / Ride with me / For ladies only / Tenderness.

1991. (cd) *M.C.A.;* **BORN TO BE WILD: A RETROSPECTIVE** -

Aug 91. (cd/c) *Knight; (KN CD/MC 10022)* **NIGHTRIDING** -

Apr 93. (cd) *Movieplay Gold; (MPG 74016)* **BORN TO BE WILD** -

Jan 94. (cd) *Legacy;* **TIGHTEN UP YOUR WIG – THE BEST OF JOHN KAY & SPARROW**

May 97. (cd) *Experience; (EXP 029)* **STEPPENWOLF** -

Stephen STILLS / MANASSAS (see under ⇒ CROSBY, STILLS, NASH)

Sly STONE (see under ⇒ SLY & THE FAMILY STONE)

STOOGES (see under ⇒ POP, Iggy)

STRAWBERRY ALARM CLOCK

Formed: Santa Barbara, California, USA . . . 1966 originally known as The IRRIDESCENTS, a surf-pop outfit who released one rare single before leader MARK WEITZ changed their name to THEE SIXPENCE. Three singles were issued in 1966, after which they changed name again, this time to the more flowery STRAWBERRY ALARM CLOCK. By the end of 1967, they were top of the US charts with their breezy, quasi-psychedelic anthem, 'INCENSE & PEPPERMINTS' (16 year-old GREG MUNFORD (of The SHAPES) provided the vox). After a hit album of the same title and another Top 30 single, 'TOMORROW', they faded into obscurity, only maintaining a slight foothold in the charts with 'HAIR' (the musical) song, 'GOOD MORNING STARSHINE'. • **Trivia:** In 1968, they contributed three tracks to the 'Psych-Out' film soundtrack on 'Sidewalk' records. The band also appeared in Russ Meyer's skin-flick, 'Beyond The Valley Of The Dolls' in 1970.

Recommended: STRAWBERRIES MEAN LOVE (*7)

LEE FREEMAN – vocals, rhythm guitar, harmonica / **MARK WEITZ** – organ, piano, vocals / **ED KING** – lead guitar, vocals / **GARY LOVETRO** – bass, vocals / **GEORGE BUNNELL** – bass, vocals, effects / **RANDY SEOL** – drums, percussion, vocals

not issued / All American

1966. (7"; as THEE SIXPENCE) *<313>* **MY FLASH ON YOU. / FORTUNE TELLER** -

1966. (7"; as THEE SIXPENCE) *<333>* **IN THE BUILDING. / HEY JOE** -

1967. (7"; as THEE SIXPENCE) *<353>* **HEART FULL OF RAIN. / NEXT PLANE HOME** -

Aug 67. (7") *<333>* **INCENSE & PEPPERMINTS. / THE BIRDMAN OF ALCATRASH** -

Pye Int. / Uni

Oct 67. (7") *(7N 25436) <55018>* **INCENSE & PEPPERMINTS. / THE BIRDMAN OF ALKATRASH** 1 Sep67

Nov 67. (lp) *(NSPL 28106) <73014>* **INCENSE & PEPPERMINTS** 11 Oct67
– The world's on fire / Birds in my tree / Lose to live / Strawberries mean love / Rainy day mushroom pillow / Paxton's back street carnival / Hummin' happy / Pass time with Sac / Incense & peppermints / Unwind with the clock.

—— now without LOVETRO

Jan 68. (7") *(7N 25446) <55046>* **TOMORROW. / BIRDS IN THE TREES** 23 Dec67

Mar 68. (lp) *<73025>* **WAKE UP, IT'S TOMORROW** -
– Nightmare of percussion / Soft skies, no lies / Tomorrow / They saw the fat one coming / Curse of the witches / Sit with the guru / Go back (you're going the wrong way) / The pretty song from Psych-Out / Sitting on a star / Black butter – past / Black butter – present / Black butter – future.

Apr 68. (7") *(7N 25456) <55055>* **SIT WITH THE GURU. / THE PRETTY SONG FROM PSYCH-OUT** 65 Mar68

Aug 68. (7") *<55076>* **BAREFOOT IN BALTIMORE. / ANGRY YOUNG MAN** - 67

Nov 68. (lp) *<73035>* **WORLD IN A SEA SHELL** -
– Sea shell / Blues for a young girl gone / An angry young man / A million miles away / Home sweet home / Lady of the lake / Barefoot in Baltimore / Wooden woman / Heated love / Love me again / Eulogy / Shallow impressions.

Nov 68. (7") *<55093>* **SEA SHELL. / PAXTON'S BACKSTREET CARNIVAL** -

—— **JIMMY PITMAN** – guitar, vocals + **GENE GUNNELS** – drums repl. BUNNELL + SEOL

Mar 69. (7") *<55113>* **MISS ATTRACTION. / STAND BY** -

M.C.A. / Uni

Nov 69. (7") *(MU 1080) <55125>* **GOOD MORNING STARSHINE. / ME AND THE TOWNSHIP** 87 May69

Jan 70. (lp) *<73054>* **GOOD MORNING STARSHINE** -
– Me and the township / Off ramp road ramp / Small package / Hog child / Miss Attraction – Good morning Starshine – Miss Atrraction / Write your name in gold / (You put me on) Standby / Dear Joy / Changes.

Jan 70. (7") *<55158>* **CHANGES. / DESIREE** -

Apr 70. (7") *<55185>* **SMALL PACKAGE. / STARTING OUT THE DAY** -

Jun 70. (7") *<55190>* **I CLIMBED THE MOUNTAIN. / THREE** -

Sep 70. (7") *<55218>* **CALIFORNIA DAY. / THREE** -

Dec 70. (7") *<55241>* **GIRL FROM THE CITY. / THREE** -

Mar 71. (lp) *<73074>* **THE BEST OF STRAWBERRY ALARM CLOCK** (compilation) -

—— **PAUL MARSHALL** – guitar, vocals repl. PITMAN + WEITZ

not issued / Vocalion

1971. (lp) *<73915>* **CHANGES** -

—— Disbanded 1971 and ED KING later joined LYNYRD SKYNYRD. All the rest seemed to disappear from music scene.

– compilations, etc. –

Mar 87. (m-lp/c) *Big Beat; (WIK/+C 56)* **STRAWBERRIES MEAN LOVE** -
– Incense & peppermints / Rainy day mushroom pillow / Sit with the guru / Tomorrow / Black butter – present / Love me again / The pretty song (from 'Psych-Out'). *(cd iss.Jan92; WIKCD 56)*

STREETMARK

Formed: Germany ... 1975 by DOROTHEA RAUKES, THOMAS SCHREIBER, GEORG BUSCHMANN, WOLFGANG WESTPHAL and HANS SCHWEISS. This line-up recorded the debut 1976 album, 'NORDLAND', a neo-classical, progressive outing which featured a distinctly Germanic cover version of The BEATLES' 'ELEANOR RIGBY'! MANFRED KNAUF and WOLFGANG REICHMANN then replaced WESTPHAL and BUSCHMANN respectively, the latter going off to form the pomp-pop act, STRAIGHT SHOOTER. 'EILEEN' (1977) is widely held to be the highlight of STREETMARK's career and it stands up well alongside similar symphonic rock releases of the period. The disillusioned REICHMANN left soon after and by the time of 1979's 'DRY', the line-up was considerably altered. This led to a more commercial sound, also evident on the 80's albums, 'SKY RACER' (1981) and 'DREAMS' (1986), recorded after a further line-up change.

Recommended: NORDLAND (*6) / EILEEN (*8) / DRY (*5)

GEORG BUSCHMANN – vocals / **DOROTHEA RAUKES** – keyboards / **THOMAS SCHREIBER** – guitars / **WOLFGANG WESTPHAL** – bass / **HANS SCHWEISS** – drums, percussion

Sky / not issued

1976. (lp) *(003)* **NORDLAND** - - German
– House of three windows: House for hire – Green velvet curtains – Eleanor Rigby / Amleth saga / Italian concert in rock / Nordland: Waves & visions – Lyster fjord – Ladoga reality airport.

—— **WOLFGANG RIECHMANN** – vocals, synthesizers, guitar; repl. BUSCHMANN who formed heavy-pop outfit STRAIGHT SHOOTER

—— **MANFRED KNAUF** – bass; repl. WESTPHAL

1977. (lp) *(011)* **EILEEN** - - German
– Crazy notion: Crazy notion – I like you – All day long / Passage / Sea of melted lead / Tomorrow / Eileen / Dreams / Choral.

—— **WINFRIED KOWALLIK** – guitar; repl. REICHMANN who completed a solo album 'WUNDERBAR', before he was brutally murdered on 21st August 1978.

—— **BOGDAN SKOWRONEK** – drums, percussion; repl. SCHWEISS

—— now without KOWALLIK + KNAUF (guest on album JURGEN PLUTA)

1979. (lp) *(023)* **DRY** - - German
– Intro / Welcome / Sunny queen / Lovers / Drifting / Disco dry / Watch out.

—— **RAUKES + SKOWRONEK** recruited **DICKIE HANK** – guitar / **STEPHAN JEHRING** – bass, vocals

1981. (lp) *(050)* **SKY RACER** - - German
– We have won / I will follow you / Lullaby / When you got that feeling / Stick to reggae / Sky racer / Settlers to the west / You want it / Streaming.

Jan 86. (lp) *(101)* **DREAMS** - - German

—— split after above

STRING DRIVEN THING

Formed: Glasgow, Scotland . . .mid-'68 by husband and wife team, CHRIS and PAULINE ADAMS. With percussionist JOHN MANNION in tow, they released a very limited eponymous album, followed by the 1970 single, 'AN-OTHER NIGHT'. Moving away from their earlier harmony-driven sound, the ADAMS' enlisted the help of violinist GRAHAM SMITH and all-rounder COLIN WILSON, delivering another eponymous album in 1972. Now signed to 'Charisma' records, they issued an even better follow-up, 'THE MACHINE THAT CRIED' and lent a hit, 'IT'S A GAME', to tartan popstars The BAY CITY ROLLERS. Astonishingly, The ADAMS' subsequently left the band they had formed, GRAHAM SMITH now taking up the reins, complemented by a host of musicians with who he released a further couple of albums.

Recommended: STRING DRIVEN THING (1972) (*6) / THE MACHINE THAT

CRIED (*7)

CHRIS ADAMS – guitar, vocals / **PAULINE ADAMS** – vocals / **JOHN MANNION** – percussion

Concord not issued

1970. (ltd-lp) *(CON 1001)* **STRING DRIVEN THING**
– July morning / Say what you like / Magic garden / Wonderful places / I don't wanna make up / City man / Another night in this old city / That's me lady / Catch as catch can / No more you and I / Lie back and let it happen / One of the lonely people.

May 70. (7") *(CON 7)* **ANOTHER NIGHT. / SAY WHAT YOU LIKE**

—— Split but the ADAMS' re-formed 1972.

—— added **GRAHAM SMITH** – violin / **COLIN WILSON** – bass, guitar, banjo

Charisma Charisma

Sep 72. (lp) *(CAS 1062)* **STRING DRIVEN THING**
– Circus / Fairground / Hooked on the road / Easy to be free / Jack Diamond / Let me down / Very last blue yodell / My real hero / Regent St incident / Where are you. *(re-iss.Aug76; same)*

Jan 73. (7") *(CB 203)* **CIRCUS. / MY REAL HERO**

—— added **BILLY FAIRLEY** – drums, percussion

Sep 73. (7") *(CB 215)* **IT'S A GAME. / ARE YOU A ROCK'N'ROLLER**

1973. (lp) *(CAS 1070)* <6063> **THE MACHINE THAT CRIED**
– Heartfeeder / To see you / Night club / Sold down the river / Two timin' Rama / Travelling / People on the street / The house / The machine that cried / Going down. *(cd-iss.1990's on 'Repertoire'; REP 4207) (cd re-iss.Jun97 on 'Ozit' official version; OZCD 00021)*

Mar 74. (7") *(CB 223)* **I'LL SING ONE FOR YOU. / TO SEE YOU**

—— Amazingly the ADAMS' departed from their own group, alongside COLIN and BILLY. This left behind **GRAHAM SMITH** who recruited **ALUN ROBERTS** – guitar, vocals / **KIMBERLEY BEACON** – vocals / **JAMES EXELL** – bass, vocals / **COLIN FAIRLEY** – drums, vocals / **ALAN SKIDMORE** – saxophone / **KENNY ROWE + GRAHAM WHITE** – vocals

Charisma 20th Cent

Nov 74. (7") *(CB 239)* **KEEP ON MOVIN'. / MRS. O'REILLY**

Nov 74. (lp) *(CAS 1097)* <470> **PLEASE MIND YOUR HEAD**
– Overdrive / Without you / Josephine / Mrs. O'Reilly / Man of means / Black eyed queen / Keep on movin' / Timpani for the Devil / To know you is to love you.

Feb 75. (7") *(CB 247)* <2202> **OVERDRIVE. / TIMPANI FOR THE DEVIL**

—— session man **COLIN WOOD** – piano, repl.SKIDMORE, ROWE + WHITE

Jan 76. (lp) *(CAS 1112)* <503> **KEEP YER 'AND ON IT**
– Starving in the tropics / Call out for mercy / Chains / Things we said today / But I do / Old friends / Ways of a woman / Part of it / Stand back in amazement.

Feb 76. (7") *(CB 276)* **BUT I DO. / STAND BACK IN AMAZEMENT**

Sep 76. (7") *(CB 286)* **CRUEL TO FOOL. / JOSEPHINE**

Oct 76. (7") <2300> **CRUEL TO FOOL. / SAIL AWAY**

—— Split after SMITH joined VAN DER GRAAF GENERATOR + PETER HAMMILL. He later emigrated to Iceland.

– compilations, etc. –

Jul 95. (cd) *Terrapin Truckin'; (TRUCKCD 023)* **SUICIDE LIVE BERLIN '94 (live)**
(cd-iss.Jun97 on 'Ozit'; OZCD 00018)

SUN RA

Born: HERMAN BLOUT, 22 May 1914, Birmingham, Alabama, USA. A child prodigy, he was bought a piano for his 10th birthday by his parents, which he immediately learned to play, while composing some early songs. Majoring at Alabama A&M University, he later went under the name SONNY LEE, playing with a swing band led by FLETCHER HENDERSON. In 1948, he changed his name by deedpoll to LE SONNY'RA, soon shortened to SUN RA. Around this time, he claimed to have been born on Saturn and despatched to Earth as the "creator of the omniverse". By the mid-50's, he had assembled his "ARKESTRA", which included a nucleus of talented musicians; JOHN GILMORE, MARSHALL ALLEN and PAT PATRICK, fusing together be-bop jazz (influenced by THELONIUS MONK or DUKE ELLINGTON), with exotic worldly avant-garde. His/their first recordings were rare, free-form jazz affairs, the band's sound evolving following his move to New York in the early 60's. SUN RA's cult appeal grew, especially after introducing the Moog synthesizer when recording for underground 'E.S.P.' label (home of FUGS). His concerts were of the cosmic funk variety, subsequently developed by the great FUNKADELIC via GEORGE CLINTON. In 1974, the death of his idol DUKE ELLINGTON, seemed to inspire a onslaught of shows, reviving the great man's work (albeit faster and more furiously uptempo). In the late 80's, after releasing many albums over the previous two decades, he signed to UK indie, 'Blast First' (at the time, home to such indie noise merchants as SONIC YOUTH, DINOSAUR JR and The BUTTHOLE SURFERS!), which issued his 1989 and retrospective and a new live album, 'OUT THERE A MINUTE' and 'LIVE IN LONDON 1990' respectively. This led to a contract with his first major, 'A&M', although it was clear his health was fading after suffering a few strokes. On the 4th of July '92, he opened for SONIC YOUTH at New York's Central Park, entering the stage on a wheelchair. He returned to his birthplace late in '92 after he suffered a third stroke, and on the 30th of May that year, he died. However, his band, under GILMORE's leadership, continued to play SUN RA's music.

Recommended: THE HELIOCENTRIC WORLDS OF SUN RA, I (*9) / THE HELIOCENTRIC WORLDS OF SUN RA II (*8) / SUNRISE IN DIFFERENT DIMENSIONS (*7) / COSMIC TONES FOR MENTAL THERAPY (*7) / BLUE DELIGHT (*8)

SUN RA – piano (with session people)

not issued Saturn

1955. (7"; by The COSMIC RAYS) *<SR 401/402>* **DREAMING. / DADDY'S GONNA TELL YOU NO LIE**

1956. (7"; by The COSMIC RAYS with LE SUN RA and his ARKESTRA) *<B 222/223?* **BYE BYE. / SOMEBODY'S IN LOVE**

1956. (7"; as LE SUN-RA and his ARKISTRA) *<Z 222>* **MEDICINE FOR A NIGHTMARE. / URNACK**

1956. (7") **A CALL FOR ALL DEMONS. / EMON'S LULLABY**

1956. (7") **SATURN. / SUPERSONIC JAZZ**

1956. (7") *<Z 1111>* **SUPER BLONDE. / SOFT TALK**

1957. (lp) *<H70 P0216>* **SUPER-SONIC JAZZ**
– India / Sunology / Advice to medics / Sunology part II / Kingdom of Not / Portrait of the living sky / Blues at midnight / El is a sound of joy. *<cd-iss.May92 on 'Evidence'; ECD 22015>*

1959. (7") **SATURN. / VELVET**

1959. (7") *'ROUND MIDNIGHT. / BACK IN YOUR OWN BACKYARD*

1959. (lp) *<K 70 P 359 0-1>* **JAZZ IN SILHOUETTE**
– Hours after / Horoscope / Images / Blues at midnight / Enlightenment / Saturn / Velvet / Ancient Aiethopia.
(cd-iss.May92 on 'Evidence'; 22012-2>

—— note:- SUN RA & HIS ARKESTRA also backed YOCHANAN on a few singles

1960. (7") *<874>* **OCTOBER. / ADVENTUR IN SPACE**

1960. (7") *<SA-1001>* **THE BLUE SET. / BIG CITY BLUES**

1961. (7") *<L08W-0114-5>* **SPACE LKONELINESS. / STATE STREET**

1961. (lp) *<HK 5445>* **SUN RA AND HIS SOLAR ARKESTRA VISIT PLANET EARTH; WE TRAVEL THE SPACEWAYS**
– Eve / Interplanetary music / Tapestry from an asteroid / Velvet / We travel the spaceways / Space loneliness.

1964. (lp) *<408>* **COSMIC TONES FOR MENTAL THERAPY**
– And otherness / Thither and yon / Adventure – Equation / Moon dance / Voice of space.

1964. (lp) *<KH 9876>* **OTHER PLANES OF THERE**
– Other planes of there / Sound spectra / Sketch / Pleasure / Spiral galaxy. *<cd-iss.Nov92 on 'Evidence'; ECD 22037-2>*

1960's. (lp) *<9954>* **SECRETS OF THE SUN**
– Friendly galaxy / Solar differentials / Space aura / Love in outer space / Reflects motion / Solar symbols.

1960's. (lp) *<9956>* **ART FORMS OF DIMENSION TOMORROW**
– Cluster of galaxies / Ankh / Solar drums / The outer heavens / Infinity of the universe / Lights on a satellite / Kosmos in blue.

not issued E.S.P.

1965. (lp) *(ESP 1014)* **THE HELIOCENTRIC WORLDS OF SUN RA, VOLUME I**
– Heliocentric / Outer nothingness / Other worlds / The cosmos / Of heavenly things / Nebulae / Dancing in the sun. *(UK-iss.Apr81; same) (cd-iss.Dec94; ESP 1014-2) (re-iss.Apr97 on 'Get Back'; GET 1004)*

1966. (lp) *(ESP 1017)* **THE HELIOCENTRIC WORLDS OF SUN RA, VOLUME II**
– The sun myth / A house of beauty / Cosmic chaos. *(UK-iss.Apr81; same) (cd-iss.Dec94; ESP 1017-2) (re-iss.Apr97 on 'Get Back'; GET 1005)*

1968. (lp) *(ESP 1045)* **NOTHING IS** (rec.May '66)
– Dancing shadows / Imagination / Exotic forest / Sun Ra and his band from outer space / Shadow world / Theme of the stargazers / Outer spaceways incorporated / Next stop Mars. *(UK-iss.Sep84 as 'DANCING SHADOWS' on 'Happy Bird'; B 90130) (cd-iss.Sep92 on 'Giants Of Jazz And Blues'; 30013) (original:- re-iss.Apr97 on 'Get Back'; GET 1007)*

not issued Saturn

1968. (7") *<3066>* **THE BRIDGE. / ROCKET NUMBER NINE**

1968. (7") *<911-AR>* **BLUES ON PLANET MARS. / SATURN MOON**

1969. (lp) *<ESR 507>* **ATLANTIS** (rec.1967)
– Atlantis / Mu / Lemuria / Yucatan / Bimini. *(UK cd-iss.Nov93 on 'Evidence'+=; ECD 22067-2)– Yucatan (Impulse version).*

1969. (lp) *<ESR 508>* **HOLIDAY FOR SOUL DANCE**
– Early Autumn / But not for me / Day by day / Holiday for strings / Dorothy's dance / I loves you orgy / Body and soul / Keep your sunny side up. *(UK cd-iss.May92 on 'Evidence'; ECD 22011-2)*

1969. (lp) *<SR 509>* **MONORAILS AND SATELLITES** (rec.1966)
– Spacetowers / Cognition / Skylight / The alter destiny / Easy street / Blue differentials / Monorails and satellites / The galaxy way. *(UK cd-iss.May92 on 'Evidence'; ECD 22013-2)*

1970's. (lp) *<SR 512>* **SOUND SUN PLEASURE!!** (rec.1959)
– 'Round midnight / You never told me that you care / Hour of parting / Back in your own backyard / I could have danced all night. *(UK cd-iss.May92 on 'Evidence'; ECD 22014-2)*

1970's. (lp) *<SR 519>* **MONORAILS AND SATELLITES VOL.II** (rec.1966)
– Astro vision / The ninth eye / Solar boats / Perspective prisms of Is / Calundronius.

1970's. (lp) *<ESR 520>* **CONTINUATION** (rec.1968-69)
– Continuation to / Jupiter festival / Biosphere blues / Intergalaxtic research / Earth primitive Earth / New planet.

1970's. (lp) *<ESR 521>* **MY BROTHER THE WIND**
– My brother the wind / Intergalactic II / To nature's god / The code of independence.

1970's. (lp) *<ESR 523>* **MY BROTHER THE WIND, VOLUME II**
– Somewhere else / Contrast / The wind speaks / Sun thoughts / Journey to the stars / World of the myth "I" / The design cosmos II / Otherness blue / Somebody else's world / Pleasant twilight / Walking on the Moon. *(UK cd-iss.Nov92 on 'Evidence'; ECD 22040-2)*

1970's. (lp) *<ESR 532>* **BAD AND BEAUTIFUL** (rec.late '61)
– The bad and the beautiful / Ankh / Search light blues / Exotic two / On the blue side / And this is my beloved.

Byg Actuel not issued

1972. (lp; as SUN RA & HIS SOLAR-MYTH ARKESTRA) *(529.340)* **THE SOLAR MYTH APPROACH VOL.1** (rec.1968-1970) France
– Spectrum / Realm of lightning / The satellites are spinning / Legend / Seen III, took 4 / They'll come back / The adventures of Bugs Hunter. *(UK-iss.Feb78 on 'Infinity'; AFF 10)*

1971. (lp; as SUN RA & HIS SOLAR-MYTH ARKESTRA) *(529.341)* **THE SOLAR MYTH APPROACH VOL.2** (rec.1968-70) [-] [-] France
– Scene 1, take 1 / Outer spaceways incorporated / The utter nots / Interpretation / Ancient Ethiopia / Strange worlds / Pyramids. *(UK-iss.1983 on 'Affinity'; AFF 76)*

Delmark Delmark

1974. (lp; as SUN RA ARKESTRA) *(DL 411)* **SUN SONG** [ ] [ ]
– Brainville / Call for all emons / Transition / Possession / Street named Hell / Lullaby for Brainville / Future / Swing a little taste / New horizons / Fall off the log / Sun song. *<US-iss.Dec94; DDCD 411>*

1974. (lp; as SUN RA ARKESTRA) *(DL 414)* **SOUND OF JOY** [ ] [ ]
<US-iss.Dec94; DDCD 414>

Improvising Artists not issued

1978. (lp) *(37.38-50)* **SOLO PIANO, VOLUME 1** [ ] [-]
– Sometimes I feel like a motherless child / Cosmo rhythmatic / Yesterdays / Romance of two planets / Irregular galaxy / To a friend. *(cd-iss.Nov92; 123850-2)*

1978. (lp) *(37.38-58)* **ST. LOUIS BLUES: SOLO PIANO (VOLUME 2)** [ ] [-]
– Ohosnisixaeht / St. Louis blues / Three little words / Sky and sun / I am we are I / Thoughts on thoth. *(cd-iss.Nov93; 123858-2)*

Cobra not issued

1979. (lp; as SUN RA ARKESTRA) *(COB 37001)* **COSMOS EQUATION** (rec.August '76) [ ] [-]
– The mystery of two / Interstellar low ways / Neo project No.2 / Cosmos / Moonship journey / Journey among the stars / Jazz from an unknown planet. *(cd-iss.Sep92 on 'Giants Of Jazz And Blues'; 30011)*

Inner City not issued

Apr 79. (lp) *(IC 1039)* **SUN RA** [ ] [-]
– For the sunrise / Of the other tomorrow / From out where others dwell / On sound infinity spheres / The house of eternal being / Gos of the thunder rain / Lights on a satellite / Take the 'A' train / Prelude / El is the sound of joy / Encore 1 / Encore 2 / We travel the spaceways.

not issued Hat Hut

1980. (lp; as SUN RA ARKESTRA) *<2R 17>* **SUNRISE IN DIFFERENT DIMENSIONS** [-] [ ]
– Lights from a hidden sun / Pin-points of spiral prisms / Silhouettes of the shadow world / Cocktails for two / 'Round midnight / Lady bird – Half Nelson / Big John's special / Yeah man! / Love in outer space * / Provocative celestials / Disguised gods in skullduggery rendezvous / Queer notions / Limehouse blues / King Porter stomp / Take the A train / Lightnin' / On Jupiter * / A helio-hello and goodbye too!. *(cd-iss.Dec91 – =*; ARTCD 6099)*

Y not issued

Sep 82. (lp) *(Y 19LP)* **STRANGE CELESTIAL ROAD** (rec.July '79) [ ] [-]
– Celestial road / Say / I'll wait for you. *<US-iss.1988 on 'Rounder' lp/c; ROUNDER 3035/+C> (cd-iss.1990's cd/c; ROU CD/C 3035)*

Nov 83. (12"; as SUN RA ARKESTRA) *(RA 1)* **NUCLEAR WAR. / SOMETIMES I'M HAPPY** [ ] [-]

Affinity not issued

1983. (lp) *(AFF 76)* **SOLAR-MYTH APPROACH VOL.2** [ ] [-]
– The utter nots / Outer spaceways (inc. Scene 1, take 1) / Pyramids / Interpretation / Ancient Ethiopia / Strange worlds. *(cd-iss.both VOLS Jan90; CDAFF 76)*

Praxis not issued

May 84. (lp) *(CM 106)* **SUN RA ARKESTRA MEETS SALAM RAGAB IN EGYPT** [-] [-] Greece
– Egypt strut / Dawn / (three others by SALAH RAGAB and The CAIRO JAZZ BAND)

Happy Bird not issued

Sep 84. (lp) *(B 90131)* **OTHER WORLDS** [ ] [-]
– Heliocentric / Other nothingness / Other worlds / The cosmos / Of heavenly things / Nebulae dancing in the sun.

Sep 84. (lp) *(B 90132)* **THE SUN MYTH** [ ] [ ]
– The sun myth / House of beauty / Cosmic chaos. *(cd-iss.Sep92 on 'Giants Of Jazz And Blues'; 30012)*

Saturn – Recommended not issued

Feb 86. (lp) *(SRRRD 1)* **COSMOS SUN CONNECTION** (live 1984) [ ] [-]
– Fate in a pleasant mood / Cosmo journey blues / Cosmo sun connection / Cosmonaut astronaut rendezvous / As space ships aproach / Pharoah's den.

not issued Meltdown

1987. (lp) *<MPA-1>* **JOHN CAGE MEETS SUN RA** [-] [ ]
– John Cage meets Sun Ra. *<cd-iss.Jan97; MPA-1CD>*

Sep 87. (lp; as SUN RA & HIS COSMO DISCIPLINE ARKESTRA) *Leo; (LR 149)* **NIGHT IN EAST BERLIN (live June '86)** [ ] [-]
– Mystic prophecy / Beyond the wilderness of shadows / Prelude to a kiss / Interstellar low ways / Space is the place – We travel the spaceways / The shadow world / Rocket number nine – Second stop is Jupiter. *(cd-iss.1987 on 'Leo'; LR 149)*

Black Saint not issued

1987. (cd) *(120 101-2)* **REFLECTIONS IN BLUE** [-] [-] Italy
– State street Chicago / Nothin' from nothin' / Yesterdays / Say it isn't so / I dream too much / Reflection in blue.

1987. (cd) *(120 111-2)* **HOURS AFTER** [-] [-] Italy
– But not for me / Hours after / Beautiful love / Dance of the extra terrestrians / Love on a faraway planet.

A&M A&M

Feb 89. (lp/c/cd) *(AMA/AMC/CDA 5260)* **BLUE DELIGHT** [ ] [ ]
– Blue delight / Out of nowhere / Sunrise / They dwell on other planes / Gone with the wind / Your guest is as good as mine / Nashira / Days of wine and roses.

Jul 90. (cd) *(75021 5324)* **PURPLE NIGHT** [ ] [ ]
– Journey towards stars / Friendly galaxy / Love in outer space / Stars fell on Alabama / Of invisible them / Neverness / Purple night blues.

not issued Leo

1991. (cd) *<LR 188>* **FRIENDLY GALAXY** [-] [ ]
– Intro percussion / Prelude to a kiss / Blue Lou / Lights on a satellite / Alabama / Fate in a pleasant mood / We travel the spaceways / Space is the place / Saturn rings / Friendly galaxy / They'll come back.

1991. (d-cd) *<LR 210/211>* **PLEIADES** [-] [ ]
– Pleiades / Mythic 1 / Sun procession / Lights on a satellite / Love in outer space / Planet Earth day / Mythic 2 / Blue Lou / Prelude #7 in A major.

1991. (d-cd) *<LR 214/215>* **LIVE AT THE HACKNEY EMPIRE (live)** [-] [ ]
– Astro black / Other voices / Planet Earth day / Prelude to a kiss / Hocus pocus / Love in outer space / Blue Lou / Face the music / String singhs / Discipline 27-II / I'll wait for you / East of the sun / Somewhere over the rainbow / Frisco fog / Sunset on the Nile / Skimming and loping / Yeah man! / We travel the spaceways / They'll come back.

1992. (cd) *<LR 230>* **SECOND STAR TO THE RIGHT (SALUTE TO WALT DISNEY)** (rec.April '89) [-] [ ]
– The forest of no return / Someday my prince will come / Frisco fog / Wishing well / Zip-adee-doo-dah / Second star to the right / Heigh ho! heigh ho! / Whistle while you work.

Black Saint not issued

Jan 92. (cd) *(12012-2)* **MAYAN TEMPLES** (rec.1990) [-] [-] Italy
– Dance of the language barrier / Bygone / Discipline No.1 / Alone together / Prelude to stargazers / Mayan temples / I'll never be the same / Stardust from tomorrow / El is a sound of joy / Time after time / Opus in springtime / Theme of the stargazers / Sunset on the Nile.

Blast First not issued

Jan 92. (cd-s; w/2 videos) *(BFFPCD 101)* **COSMIC VISIONS** [ ] [-]
– I am the instrument.

not issued Enja

Jul 92. (cd) *<7071>* **DESTINATION UNKNOWN** (rec. Switzerland) [-] [ ]
– Carefree / Echoes of the future / Prelude to a kiss / Hocus pocus / Theme of the stargazers / Interstellar low ways / Destination unknown / The satellites are spinning / S'wonderful / Space is the place – We travel the spaceways.

—— SUN RA died on the 30th of May 1993.

not issued Rounder

Jan 94. (cd) *<ROU 3124>* **AT THE VILLAGE VANGUARD (live)** [-] [ ]
– 'Round midnight / Sun Ra blues / Autumn in New York / S'wonderful / Theme of the stargazers.

– others, etc –

—— In Sep'79, he and WALT DICKERSON released 'VISIONS' rec.11 Jul'78 on Steeplechase'; *SCS 1126)*

Jan 85. (lp; as SUN RA & HIS ARKESTRA) *Black Lion; (BLP 30103)* **PICTURES OF INFINITY – IN CONCERT (live 1968)** [ ] [-]
– Somewhere there / Outer spaceways incorporated / Saturn / Song of the sparer / Spontaneous simplicity. *(cd-iss.Feb94+=; BLCD 760191)*– Intergalactic motion (aka-Ankhnaton).

Mar 88. (lp; as SUN RA & HIS ARKESTRA) *Leo; (LR 154)* **LOVE IN OUTER SPACE (live in Utrecht December '83)** [ ] [-]
– Along came Ra / Discipline 27 / Blues Ra / Big John's special / Fate in a pleasant mood / 'Round midnight / Love in outer space – Space is the place. *(cd-iss.Sep88; CDLR 154)*

Mar 89. (lp/c/cd) *Blast First; (BFFP 42/+C/CD)* **OUT THERE A MINUTE** (rec.in New York 1965-) [ ] [ ]
– Love in Outer Space / Somewhere in Space / Dark clouds with silver linings / Jazz and romantic sounds / When angels speak of love / Cosmo enticement / Song of tree and forest / Other worlds / Journey outward / Lights on a satellite / Starships and solar boats / Out there a minute.

May 92. (cd) *Jazz View; (COD 007)* **FOUNDATION NIGHTS VOL.2** [-] [-] German

Nov 92. (cd) *Evidence; <ECD 22036-2>* **COSMIC TONES FOR MENTAL THERAPY / ART FORMS OF DIMENSIONS TOMORROW** [-] [ ]

Nov 92. (cd) *Evidence; <ECD 22038-2>* **WE TRAVEL THE SPACEWAYS / BAD AND BEAUTIFUL** [-] [ ]

Nov 92. (cd) *Evidence; <ECD 22039-2>* **SUN RA VISITS PLANET EARTH / INTERSTELLAR LOW WAYS** (rec.1956-58) [-] [ ]
– Two tones / Saturn / Reflections in blue / El Viktor / Planet Earth / Eve / Overtones of China.

May 93. (cd) *Savoy Jazz; (SV 0213)* **THE FUTURISTIC SOUNDS OF SUN RA** (rec.Oct'61) [ ] [ ]
– Bassism / Of sounds and something else / What's that? / Where is tomorrow? / The beginning / China gate / New day / Tapestry from an asteroid / Jet flight / Looking outward / Space jazz reverie.

1993. (cd/c) *Rounder; (ROU CD/C 3036)* **SOMEWHERE ELSE** [ ] [ ]
– Priest / Discipline – Tall trees in the sun / S'wonderful / Hole in the sky / Somewhere else (part 1 & 2) / Stardust for tomorrow / Love in outer space / Everything is space / Tristar.

Nov 93. (cd) *Evidence; <ECD 22066-2>* **ANGELS AND DEMONS AT PLAY / THE NUBIANS OF PLUTONIA** (rec.1956-60) [-] [ ]

Nov 93. (cd) *Evidence; <ECD 22068-2>* **FATE IN A PLEASANT MOOD / WHEN SUN COMES OUT** (1960-63) [-] [ ]

Nov 93. (cd) *Evidence; <ECD 22069-2>* **THE MAGIC CITY** (rec.1965) [-] [ ]
– The magic city / The shadow world / Abstract "I" / Abstract eye.

Nov 93. (cd) *Evidence; <ECD 22070-2>* **SPACE IS THE PLACE (original soundtrack)** (rec.1972) [-] [ ]
– It's after the end of the world / Under diferent stars / Discipline 33 / Watusi / Calling planet Earth / I am the alter-destiny / The satellites are spinning (take 1) / Cosmic forces / Outer spaceways incorporated (take 3) / We travel the spaceways / The overseer / Blackman – Love in outer space / Mysterious crystal / I am the brother of the wind / We'll wait for you / Space is the place.

Feb 94. (d-cd; as SUN RA ARKESTRA) *D.I.W.; (DIW 388-2)* **LIVE FROM SOUNDSCAPE (live November 1979)** [-] [-] Japan
– The possibility of altered destiny / Astro black / Pleiades / We're living in the space age / Keep your sunny side up / Discipline #27 / Untitled improvisation / Watusi / Space is the place / We travel the spaceways / Angel race / Destination unknown / On Jupiter.

1994. (7"; 33rpm) *<DEP 1-1>* **QUEER NOTIONS. / PRELUDE No.7** [-] [-] Japan

1994. (7"; 33rpm) *<DEP 1-2>* **EAST OF THE SUN. / FRISCO FOG** [-] [-] Japan

1994. (7"; 33rpm) *<DEP 1-3>* **OPUS SPRINGTIME. / COSMOS SWING BLUES** [-] [-] Japan

Mar 94. (cd) *D.I.W.; (DIW 824)* **COSMO OMNIBUS IMAGIABLE ILLUSION: LIVE AT PIT-INN, TOKYO (live 8 August, 1988)** [-] [-] Japan
– Introduction – Cosmo approach prelude / Angel race – I'll wait for you / Can you take it? / If you came from nowhere here / Astro black / Prelude to a kiss / Interstellar low ways.

Jun 96. (cd) *Blast First; (BFFP 60CD)* **LIVE IN LONDON 1990 (live at The Mean Fiddler, 11 June 1990)** [ ] [-]
– Frisco / Shadow world / For the blue people / Prelude to a kiss / Down here on the ground / Blue delight / Cosmo song / Space chants.

May 97. (d-cd; SUN RA & HIS INTERGALAXTIC ARKESTRA) *Leo; (CDLR 235-236)* **STARDUST FROM TOMORROW** [ ] [-]

SVENSK

Formed: Bournemouth, England . . . 1967 by the duo of JASON PAUL and ROGER HOPKINS. They hired the local church organ to aid with the recording of their classic debut single, 'DREAM MAGAZINE', which became an underground favourite due to its psychedelic hybrid of WHO ('Pictures Of Lily') and PROCOL HARUM ('A Whiter Shade Of Pale'). Their follow-up bombed miserably and HOPKINS bailed out of the music business, PAUL, meanwhile, attempted a very brief solo career.

Recommended: the debut single, which might be worth something now!

JASON PAUL – vocals, guitar / **ROGER HOPKINS** – organ

		Page One	Fontana
Aug 67.	(7") *(POF 036) <1615>* **DREAM MAGAZINE. / GETTING OLD**		
Dec 67.	(7") *(POF 050)* **YOU. / ALL I HAVE TO DO IS DREAM**		-

— HOPKINS quit, leaving PAUL to go solo

		Pye	not issued
Mar 69.	(7"; by JASON PAUL) *(7N 17710)* **SHINE A LITTLE LIGHT INTO MY ROOM. / PARADISE PUDDING**		-

Steve SWINDELLS (see under ⇒ HAWKWIND)

SYN

Formed: London, England . . . early '67 by former public school choirboy CHRIS SQUIRE and PETE BANKS alongside three others, STEVE NARDELLI, ANDREW JACKMAN and CHRIS ALLEN. They subsequently left their Tamla/mod/R&B background behind, opting instead for a new flower-power sound. Beginning a Marquee residency, they eventually secured a contract with 'Deram'. Two singles, 'CREATED BY CLIVE' and '14-HOUR TECHNICOLOUR DREAM', surfaced that year, although an eponymous album was shelved after their demise some months later. The singles soon became very rare (now worth over £60), due to two of the group mentioned already forming YES.

STEVE NARDELLI – vocals / **PETE BANKS** – guitar / **CHRIS SQUIRE** – bass / **ANDREW JACKMAN** – organ / **CHRIS ALLEN** – drums

		Deram	Deram
Jun 67.	(7") *(DM 130) <7510>* **CREATED BY CLIVE. / GROUNDED**		
Sep 67.	(7") *(DM 145)* **14-HOUR TECHNICOLOUR DREAM. / FLOWERMAN**		-

— (Jan'68) BANKS and SQUIRE teamed up with JON ANDERSON to form MABEL GREER'S TOY SHOP, which virtually evolved into YES

SYNDICATE OF SOUND

Formed: San Jose, California, USA . . . 1964 by DON BASKIN, JOHN SHARKEY, JIM SAWYERS, BOB GONZALES and JOHN DUCKWORTH. They made an obscure 45 for the 'Scarlet' label in 1965, before unleashing the excellent suburban, garage-punk classic, 'LITTLE GIRL', which, when picked up by the 'Bell' label, hit Top 10 in the summer of '66. It obviously borrowed a riff or two from The LEAVES' 'Hey Joe', typical of the sound of '66 that was also encompassed by COUNT FIVE, STANDELLS and CHOCOLATE WATCH BAND. An album of the same name was a disappointment, both critically and commercially, only hitting the US Top 200 for two weeks after their follow-up 45, 'RUMOURS', made the Top 100. It contained a version of CHUCK BERRY's 'ALMOST GROWN', alongside BEATLES or even HOLLIES-type numbers. More chart attempts were made but they faded away, until that is, 'BROWN PAPER BAG' gave them their final hit in the Spring of 1970. A disastrous signing to 'Capitol' soon led to the band's rapid demise, although they did release one single, 'YOU'RE LOOKIN FINE'. They were revived late in 1977, when "new wave" outfit, The BANNED, made the UK Top 40 with their version of 'LITTLE GIRL' (which they had heard on a DEAD BOYS album).

Recommended: LITTLE GIRL (*6)

DON BASKIN (b. 9 Oct'46, Honolulu, Hawaii) – vocals / **JIM SAWYERS** – lead guitar / **JOHN SHARKEY** (b. 8 Jun'46, Los Angeles, California) – rhythm guitar / **BOB GONZALES** – bass / **JOHN DUCKWORTH** (b.18 Nov'46, Springfield, Missouri) – drums

		not issued	Scarlet
Nov 65.	(7") *<503>* **PREPARE FOR LOVE. / TELL THE WORLD** *<re-is.Dec65 on 'Del-Fi'; 4304>*	-	

		Stateside	Bell
Jun 66.	(7") *(SS 523) <640>* **LITTLE GIRL. / YOU** *<above was originally issued for local 'Hush 'label'; 228>*		8 May66
Sep 66.	(7") *(SS 538) <646>* **RUMOURS. / THE UPPER HAND**		55 Aug66
Sep 66.	(lp) *(SSL 10185) <6001>* **LITTLE GIRL** – Little girl / Rumours / Almost grown / Dream baby / Big boss man / I'm alive / Is you is or is you ain't my baby / So alone / Witch / You / That kind of man / Lookin' for the good times (the robot). *(UK cd-iss.Jun97 on 'Sundazed'; SC 6120)*		Aug66
Jan 67.	(7") *<655>* **GOOD TIME MUSIC. / KEEP IT UP**	-	
May 67.	(7") *<666>* **MARY. / THAT KIND OF MAN**	-	

— officially disbanded in 1967, although they re-formed in 1969

		not issued	Buddah
Mar 70.	(7") *<156>* **BROWN PAPER BAG. / REVERB BEAT**	-	73
Jul 70.	(7") *<183>* **MEXICO. / FIRST TO LOVE YOU**	-	

		not issued	Capitol
1970.	(7") *<2426>* **YOU'RE LOOKING FINE. / CHANGE THE WORLD**	-	

— they finally split in 1970

– compilations, etc. –

1988.	(lp) *Performance; <PERF 388>* **SYNDICATE OF SOUND**	-	

TANGERINE DREAM

Formed: Berlin, Germany . . . Autumn 1967 by art student EDGAR FROESE, who took the name, TANGERINE DREAM, from lyrics used in The BEATLES' classic, 'Lucy In The Sky With Diamonds'. He was invited to play some classical improvisations by surrealist painter SALVADOR DALI in his Spanish villa, EDGAR subsequently going through many egotistical rock musicians before he finally met KLAUS SCHULZE in '69. Together, they soon found KONRAD SCHNITZLER and JOSEPH BEUYS, who, with other guests, worked on the sessions for the 1970 debut, 'ELECTRONIC MEDITATION'. With others going solo, EDGAR then found CHRIS FRANKE and another album, 'ALPHA CENTAURI' surfaced for UK 'Polydor'. In 1972, PETER BAUMANN joined for their third album, 'ATEM', the record heavily playlisted on John Peel's night-time Radio One show and leading to new entrepeneur, Richard Branson, signing them to his 'Virgin' label. Surprisingly, the following year, 'PHAEDRA' made it into the UK Top 40 lists, much aided by the fact 'Virgin' was now an influential part of the British/continental scene. With this album, TANGERINE DREAM made a departure from their PINK FLOYD-like experimentalism, discovering picturesque, electronic waves of sound, rhythmically haunting and repetitive. 'RUBYCON' (1975) was similarly influential, although from there on in the band started to gravitate towards soundtrack work, their atmospheric mood pieces fitting the genre with ease. Over the course of the following decade, they recorded music for such diverse screen projects as 'SORCERER' (1977), 'THIEF' (1981), 'RISKY BUSINESS' (1983) and 'FIRESTARTER' (1984), although their music increasingly verged upon "New Age" sterility.

Recommended: PHAEDRA (*9) / RUBYCON (*9) / RICOCHET (*8) / STRATOSFEAR (*7) / SORCEROR (*7)

EDGAR FROESE (b. 6 Jun'44, Tilsit, Germany) – guitar, piano, organ (ex-The ONES) / **VOLKER HOMBACH** – flute, violin / **KIRT HERKENBERG** – bass / (Mar69) / **SVEN JOHANNSON** – drums repl. LANSE HAPRHASH

— In 1970, after HOMBACH became film cameraman for W.R.FASSBINDER, and brief wind instrumentalist STEVE JOLIFFE departed to join STEAMHAMMER. Group reformed **EDGAR FROESE** brought in newcomers **KLAUS SCHULTZE** (b. 4 Aug'47) – drums, percussion / **CONRAD SCHNITZLER** – cello, flute, violin. with guests **JIMMY JACKSON** – organ / **THOMAS VON KEYSERLING** – flute

Ohr / not issued

Jun 70. (lp) *(OMM 556 004)* **ELECTRONIC MEDITATION** [-] [-] German
– Geburt (Genesis) / Reise durch ein brennendes gehirn (Journey through a burning brain) / Kalter rauch (Cold smoke) / Asche zu asche (Ashes to ashes) / Auferstehung (Resurrection). *(UK cd-iss.Jan87 on 'Jive'; CTANG 4) (cd re-iss.Feb96 on 'Essential'; ESMCD 345)*

— **FROESE** added bass to repertoire, and again supplanted new members **CHRISTOPHER FRANKE** (b. 6 Apr'53) – drums, percussion, synthesizer repl. CONRAD / **STEVE SCHROEDER** – organs repl. KLAUS SCHULTZE who went solo / added new guests **UDO DENNEBORG** – flute, words / **ROLAND PAULICK** – synthesizer

Apr 71. (lp) *(OMM 556 012)* **ALPHA CENTAURI** [-] [-] German
– Sunrise in the third system / Fly and collision of Comas Sola / Alpha Centauri. *(UK-iss.Nov73 on 'Polydor Super'; 2383 314) (cd-iss.Jan87 on 'Jive'; CTANG 5) (re-iss.cd Feb96 on 'Essential'; ESMCD 346)*

— **PETER BAUMANN** – synthesizer, organ repl. SCHROYDER (guested on below)

Feb 72. (7") *(OSS 7006)* **ULTIMA THULE (teil 1). / ULTIMA THULE (teil 2)** [-] [-] German

— More guests were added on next; **FLORIAN FRICKE** – synthesizers / cellists / **CHRISTIAN VALBRACHT / JOCKEN VON GRUMBCOW / HANS JOACHIM BRUNE / JOHANNES LUCKE**

Feb 72. (d-lp) *(OMM 2-556 021)* **ZEIT** [-] [-] German
– 1st movement: Birth of liquid plejades / 2nd movement: Nebulous dawn / 3rd movement: Origins of supernatural probabilities / 4th movement: Zeit. *(UK-iss.Jun76 on 'Virgin'; VD 2503) (cd-iss.Jan87 on 'Jive'; CTANG 3) (cd re-iss.Feb96 on 'Essential'; ESMCD 347)*

Mar 73. (lp) *(OMM 556 031)* **ATEM** [-] [-] German
– Atem / Fauni-Gena / Wahn / Circulation of events. *(UK-iss.Nov73 on 'Polydor Super'; 2383 297) (cd-iss.Jan87 on 'Jive'; CTANG 2) (re-iss.cd Feb96 on 'Essential'; ESMCD 348)*

— In Aug'73, they recorded 'GREEN DESERT' album, unreleased until 1986.

Virgin / Virgin

Mar 74. (lp/c) *(V/TCV 2010) <13108>* **PHAEDRA** [15] [ ]
– Phaedra / Mysterious semblance at the strand of nightmares / Movements of a visionary / Sequent C. *(re-iss.Mar84 lp/c; OVED/+C 25) (cd-iss.Jul87; CDV 2010) (cd re-iss.Feb95; TAND 5)*

— **MICHAEL HOENIG** – synthesizer repl. BAUMANN (on tours only 1974-75)

Mar 75. (lp/c) *(V/TCV 2025) <13166>* **RUBYCON** [12] [ ]
– Rubycon (part 1) / Rubycon (part 2). *(re-iss.Mar84 lp/c; OVED/+C 27) (cd-iss.Jul87; CDV 2025) (cd re-iss.Feb95; TAND 6)*

Dec 75. (lp/c) *(V/TCV 2044)* **RICOCHET (live at Liverpool, Coventry & Yorkminster Cathedrals)** [40] [ ]
– Ricochet (part 1) / Ricochet (part 2). *(re-iss.Mar84 lp/c; OVED/+C 26) (cd-iss.Jul87; CDV 204) (cd re-iss.Feb95; TAND 7)*

— **BAUMANN** re-united with outfit, to depose HOENIG

Nov 76. (lp/c) *(V/TCV 2068) <34427>* **STRATOSFEAR** [39] [ ]
– Stratosfear / The big sleep in search of Hades / 3 a.m. at the border of the marsh from Okefnokee / Invisible limits. *(cd-iss.Jul87; CDV 2068) (re-iss.Aug88 lp/c; OVED/+C 70) (cd re-iss.Feb95; TAND 8)*

Jul 77. (lp/c) *(MCF/+C 2806) <2277>* **SORCERER (Soundtrack)** [25] [ ]
– Main title / Search / The call / Creation / Vengeance / The journey / Grind / Rain forest / Abyss / The mountain road / Impressions of Sorcerer / Betrayal (Sorcerer's theme). *(re-iss.Feb82 lp/c; MCL/+C 1646) (cd-iss.Aug92; MCLD 19159)*

— (above lp & below 45, were from the MCA film 'Wages Of Fear')

Aug 77. (7") *<40740>* **BETRAYAL. / GRIND** [-] [ ]

Nov 77. (d-lp/d-c) *(VD/TCVD 2506) <35014>* **ENCORE (live)** [55] [ ]
– Cherokee lane / Moonlight / Coldwater canyon / Desert dream. *(cd-iss.Jul87; CDV 2506) (cd re-iss.Apr95; TAND 1)*

Jan 78. (7") *(VS 199)* **ENCORE. / HOBO MARCH** [ ] [-]

Mar 78. (7") *<9516>* **MOONLIGHT. / COLDWATER CANYON** [-] [ ]

— **STEVE JOLIFFE** – vocals, keyboards, wind returned after several years to repl. BAUMANN who went solo. Added **KLAUS KRIEGER** – drums

Mar 78. (lp/c) *(V/TCV 2097)* **CYCLONE** [37] [ ]
– Bent cold sidewalk / Rising runner missed by endless sender / Madrigal meridian. *(cd-iss.Jul87; CDV 2097) (re-iss.Aug88 lp/c; OVED/+C 71) (cd re-iss.Apr95)*

Feb 79. (lp,clear-lp/c) *(V/TCV 2111)* **FORCE MAJEURE** [26] [ ]
– Force majeure / Cloudburst flight / Thru metamorphic rocks. *(cd-iss.Jul87; CDV 2111) (re-iss.Aug88 lp/c; OVED/+C 111) cd re-iss.Apr95; TAND 10)*

— (now trio) **FROESE + FRANKE** recruited **JOHANNES SCHMOELLING** – keyboards

May 80. (lp/c) *(V/TCV 2147)* **TANGRAM** [36] [ ]
– Tangram set 1 / Tangram set 2. *(cd-iss.Oct85; CDV 2147) (re-iss.Aug88 lp/c; OVED/+C 112) (cd-iss.Apr95; TAND 11)*

Virgin / Elektra

Apr 81. (lp/c) *(V/TCV 2198) <521>* **THIEF (Soundtrack)** [43] [ ]
– Beach theme / Dr. Destructo / Diamond diary / Burning bar / Scrap yard / Trap feeling / Igneous / Confrontation. *(re-iss.Aug88 lp/c; OVED/+C 72) (cd-iss.Jun88; CDV 2198) (cd re-iss.Aug95; TAND 12)*

Sep 81. (lp/c) *(V/TCV 2212) <557>* **EXIT** [43] [ ]
– Kiev mission / Pilots of purple twilight / Chronozon / Exit / Network 23 / Remote viewing. *(re-iss.Aug88 lp/c; OVED/+C 166) (cd-iss.Aug88; CDV 2212) (re-iss.cd Aug95; TAND 13)*

Sep 81. (7") *(VS 444)* **CHRONOZON. / NETWORK 23** [ ] [-]

Apr 82. (lp/c) *(V/TCV 2226)* **WHITE EAGLE** [57] [ ]
– Midnight in Tulo / Convention of the 24 / White eagle / Mojave plan. *(re-iss.Aug88 lp/c; OVED/+C 150) (cd-iss.Aug88; CDV 2226) (cd re-iss.Aug95; TAND 2)*

Dec 82. (lp/c) *(V/TCV 2257)* **LOGOS – LIVE (At The Dominion)** [ ] [ ]
– Logos part 1 / Logos part 2 / Dominion. *(re-iss.Apr86 lp/c; OVED 167) (cd-iss.Jun88; CDV 2257) (re-iss.cd Aug95; TAND 3)*

1983. (lp/c) *<STV/CTV 81207>* **WAVELENGTH (Soundtrack)** [-] [ ]
– Alien voices / Wavelength (main title) / Desert drive / Mojave (end title) / Healing / Breakout / Alien goodbyes / Spaceship / Church theme / Sunset drive / Airshaft / lley walk / Cyro lab / Running through the hills / Campfire theme / Mojave (end title reprise). *(UK cd-iss.Oct90 also on 'Varese Sarabande'; VCD 47223)*

Oct 83. (lp/c/cd) *(V/TCV/CDV 2292)* **HYPERBOREA** [45] [ ]
– No man's land / Hyperborea / Cinnamon road / Sphinx lightning. *(re-iss.Jun88 lp/c; OVED/+C 175) (re-iss.cd Aug95; TAND 4)*

Dec 83. (lp/c) *(V/TCV 2302)* **RISKY BUSINESS (Soundtrack)** [ ] [ ]
– The dream is always the same / No future / Love on a real train / Guido the killer pimp / Lana / (tracks by other artists; PHIL COLLINS / JOURNEY / MUDDY WATERS / JEFF BECK / BOB SEGER). *(cd-iss.May87; CDV 2302) (re-iss.Apr90 lp/c; OVED/+C 2302)*

M.C.A. / M.C.A.

Jul 84. (lp/c) *(MCF/+C 3233)* **FIRESTARTER (Soundtrack)** [ ] [ ]
– Crystal voice / The run / Test lab / Charley the kid / Escaping point / Rainbirds move / Burning force / Between realities / Shop territory / Flash final / Out of the heat. *(re-iss.Jan89; MCA/+C 6163) (cd-iss.Apr90; DMCL 1899)*

Jive Electro / Relativity

Sep 84. (7"/7"sha-pic-d) *(JIVE/+P 74)* **WARSAW IN THE SUN. / POLISH DANCE** [ ] [ ]
(12"+=) *(JIVET 74)* – ('A'-part 2) / Rare bird.

Oct 84. (d-lp/d-pic-lp/c) *(HIP/+X/C 22)* **POLAND – THE WARSAW CONCERT (live)** [90] [ ]
– Poland / Tangent / Barbakane / Horizon. *(cd-iss.1988; CHIP 22) (re-iss.cd May96 on 'Essential'; ESMCD 365)*

— (below album released on 'Heavy Metal' UK / 'EMI America' US)

Feb 85. (lp/pic-lp/c) *(HMI HP/PD/MC 29) <ST 17141>* **FLASHPOINT (Soundtrack)** [ ] [ ] Dec84
– Going west / Afternoon in the desert / Plane ride / Mystery tracks / Lost in the dunes / Highway patrol / Love phantasy / Madcap story / Dirty cross-roads / Flashpoint. *(cd-iss.Apr87; HMI XD 29) (re-iss.cd Sep95 on 'One Way';)*

Aug 85. (lp/c) *(HIP/+C 26)* **LE PARC** [ ] [ ]
– Bois de Boulogne (Paris) / Central Park (New York) / Gaudi Park (Guell Garden, Barcelona) / Tiergarten (Berlin) / Zen Garden (Myoonj, Temple Kyoto) / Le Parc (L.A. Streethawk) / Hyde Park (London) / The Cliffs of Sydney (Sydney) / Yellowstone Park (Rocky Mountains). *(cd-iss.Mar88; CHIP 26) (re-iss.cd May96 on 'Essential'; ESMCD 364)*

— guest on above album **CLARE TORY** – vocals

Aug 85. (7") *(JIVE 101)* **STREETHAWK. / TIERGARTEN** [ ] [ ]

(12"+=) *(JIVET 101)* – Gaudi Park / Warsaw in the sun (part 1 & 2).

1985. Virgin; (lp) *(207 212-620)* **HEARTBREAKERS (soundtrack)** - - German
– Heartbreakers / Footbridge to Heaven / Twilight painter / Gemeni / Rain in N.Y. city / Pastime / The loser / Breathing the night away / Desire / Thorny affair / Daybreak. *(UK cd-iss.Jun95 on 'Silva Screen'; FILMCD 163)*

—— **PAUL HASLINGER** – multi-instrumentalist repl. SCHMOELLING who went solo

Jul 86. (lp/c)(cd) *(HIP/+C 40)(CHIP 40)* **UNDERWATER SUNLIGHT** 97
– Song of the whale / From dawn . . . to dusk / Ride on the ray / Dolphin dance / Underwater sunlight / Scuba scuba. *(cd re-iss.May96 on 'Essential'; ESMCD 366)*

Aug 86. (12"ep) *<88561-8120-1>* **DOLPHIN DANCE. / DOLPHIN SMILE / SONG OF THE WHALE** -

Jun 87. (lp/c)(cd) *(HIP/+C 47)(CHIP 47)* **TYGER** 88
– Tyger / London / Alchemy of the heart / Smile. *(cd+=)*– 21st century common man I & II. *(cd re-iss.May96 on 'Essential'; ESMCD 367)*

—— guest vox – BERNADETTE SMITH

Jun 87. (7") *(JIVE 143)* **TYGER. / 21st CENTURY COMMON MAN II**
(12"+=) *(JIVET 143)* – ('A'extended).

1987. (lp) *<47357>* **THREE O'CLOCK HIGH (Soundtrack shared with SYLVESTER LEVAY)** -
– It's Jerry's day today / 46-32-15 / No detention / Any school bully will do / Go to the head of the class / Sit / The fight / Jerry's decisions / The fight is on / Paper / Big bright brass knuckles / Buying paper like it's going out of style / Dangerous trend / Who's chasing who? / Bonding by candlelight / You'll never believe it / Starting the day off right / Weak at the knees / Kill him (the football dummy) / Not so quiet in the library – Get lost in a crowd / Something to remember me by / Arrival. *(UK cd-iss.Oct90 also on 'Varese Sarabande'; VCD 47307)*

Apr 88. (lp/c)(cd) *(HIP/+C 62)(CHIP 62)* **LIVE MILES (live)**
– Live miles: (part 1) – The Albuquerque concert / Live miles: (part 2) – The West Berlin concert. *(re-iss.cd May96 on 'Essential'; ESMCD 368)*

Silva Screen / Silva Screen

Feb 88. (lp/c/cd) *(<FILM/+C/CD 026>)* **NEAR DARK (Soundtrack)** Nov87
– Cabeb's blues / Pick up at high noon / Rain in the third house / Bus station / Good times / She's my sister / Father and son / Severin dies / Flight at dawn / Mae's transformation / Mae comes back. *(re-iss.Jun90; same)*

Jul 88. (lp/c/cd) *(<FILM/+C/CD 027>)* **SHY PEOPLE (Soundtrack)** Nov87
– Shy people / Joe's place / The harbor / Nightfal / Dancing on a white moon / Civilized illusion's / Swamp voices / Transparent days / Shy people (reprise).

—— now a duo of **FROESE + HASLINGER**

Arista / Private Music

Feb 89. (lp/c/cd) *(209/409/259 557) <2042-1/-4/-2 P>* **OPTICAL RACE** Aug88
– Marakesh / Atlas eyes / Mothers of rain / Twin soul tribe / Optical race / Cat scan / Sun gate / Turning of the wheel / The midnight trail / Ghtrezi (long song).

Jul 89. (lp/c/cd) *<209/409/259 887>* **MIRACLE MILE** -
– Teetering scales / One for the book / After the call / On the spur of the moment / All of a dither / Final statement. *(re-iss.cd Feb96; 260.016)*

Dec 89. (lp/c/cd) *<210/410/260 103>* **LILY ON THE BEACH** -
– Too hot for my chinchilla / Lily on the beach / Alaskan summer / Desert drive / Mount Shasta / Crystal curfew / Paradise cove / Twenty nine palms / Valley of the kings / Radio city / Blue mango cafe / Gecko / Long island sunset.

Nov 90. (cd/lp) *(261/211 105)* **MELROSE**
– Melrose / Three bikes in the sky / Dolls in the shadow / Yucatan / Electric lion / Rolling down Cahenga / Art of vision / Desert train / Cool at heart.

Silva Screen / Silva Screen

Mar 91. (cd) *(FILMCD 079)* **DEAD SOLID PERFECT (Soundtrack)**
– Theme from Dead Solid Perfect / In the pond / Beverly leaves / Of cads and caddies / (Tournament montage) / A whore in one / Sand trap / In the rough / Nine iron / US Open / My name is bad hair / In the hospital room / Welcome to Bushwood / Deja vu / Birdie / Divot / Kenny and Donny montage / Phone to Beverly / Nice shots / Sinking putts / Kenny's winning shot.

Oct 91. (cd) *(FILMCD 080)* **THE PARK IS MINE**

—— Now a duo of **FROESE + JEROME FROESE** his son and **LINDA SPA** – sax / **ZLASLO PERICA** – synth.

Feb 92. Essential; (cd/c/lp) *(ESM CD/MC/LP 403)* **ROCKOON**
– Big city dwarves / Red roadster / Touchwood / Graffiti sreeet / Funky Atlanta / Spanish love / Lifted veil / Penguin reference / Body corporate / Rockoon / Girls on Broadway. *(re-iss.cd Feb96; same)*

Dec 92. (cd) *(FILMCD 121)* **DEADLY CARE (Soundtrack)**
– Main theme / Paddles – Stolen pills / A strong drink – A bad morning / Wasted and sick / Hope for future / The hospital in bed / Annie and father / More pills / In the Head nurse's – At the father's grave / Clean and sober.

Miramar / Miramar

Jul 93. (cd) **CANYON DREAMS**
– Shadow flyer / Canyon carver / Water's gift / Canyon voices / Sudden revelation / A matter of time / Purple nightfall / Colorado dawn.

Oct 93. (cd)(c) **220 VOLT LIVE (live)**
– Oriental haze / Two bunch palms / 220 volt / Homeless / Treasure of innocence / Sundance kid / Backstreet hero / The blue bridge / Hamlet / Dreamtime / Purple haze.

CoastCoast / Miramar

Nov 94. (cd) *(CTCZ 108)* **TURN OF THE TIDES**
– Pictures at an exhibition / Firetongues / Galley slave's horizon / Death of a nightingale / Twilight brigade / Jungle journey / Midwinter night / Turn of the tides. *(re-iss.Nov96; same)*

Amp / Miramar

Sep 95. (cd) **TYRANNY OF BEAUTY**
–
(re-iss.Oct96 on 'Tangerine Dream Int.'; TDI 002CD)

When!

Sep 96. (cd) *(WENCD 011)* **GOBLINS CLUB**
– Towards the evening star / At Darwin's motel / On Crane's passage / Rising haul in silence / United goblin's parade / Lamb with radar eyes / Elf June and the midnight patrol / Sad Merlin's Sunday.

Mar 97. (c-s) *(WENM 1022)* **TOWARDS THE EVENING STAR / ('A'mix)** -
(12"+=/cd-s+=) *(WEN T/X 1022)* – ('A'remixes).

Tadream / not issued

Jun 97. (cd) *(TDI 007CD)* **OASIS** -
– Flashblood / Zion / Reflections / Cliff dwellers / Waterborne / Cedar breaks / Summer storm / Hopi mesa heart.

– compilations, others, etc. –

—— on 'Virgin' unless mentioned otherwise

Jul 76. (d-lp) *(VD 2504)* **ATEM / ALPHA CENTAURI** -

Dec 80. (4xlp-box) *(VBOX 2)* **TANGERINE DREAM '70-80** -

Nov 85. (t-lp/d-c/d-cd) *(TDLP/TDC/CDTD 1)* **DREAM SEQUENCE** -
(re-iss.d-cd Apr92; same)

Mar 86. (6xlp-box) *Jive Electro; (TANG 1)* **IN THE BEGINNING** -
– (ELECTRONIC MEDITATION / ALPHA CENTAURI / ZEIT (d-lp) / ATEM / GREEN DESERT)

May 86. (lp) *M.C.A.; <6165>* **LEGEND (Soundtrack with other artists)** - 96
– Unicorn theme / Blue room / Darkness / The dance / Goblins / Fairies / The kitchen (medley).

1986. (lp) *(207684620)* **PERGAMON – LIVE AT THE PALAST DER REPUBLIK** *(live & originally issued in East Germany 1980 as 'QUICHOTTE'; Amiga 855891)* - - German
(UK cd-iss.May96 as 'PERGAMON' on 'Essential'; ESMCD 413)

Dec 86. (cd) *Zomba; (CTANG 1)* **GREEN DESERT** (rec.1973) -
(re-iss.May89 on 'Jive' lp/c; HOP/+C 226) (re-iss.Feb96 on 'Essential'; ESMCD 349)

Mar 87. (d-lp/c/cd) *(CCS LP/MC/CD 161)* **THE TANGERINE DREAM COLLECTION** -

Nov 89. (lp/c)(cd) *Jive; (HIP/+C 75)(CHIP 75)* **THE BEST OF TANGERINE DREAM**

Nov 90. (3xcd-box) *(TPAK 11)* **COLLECTORS' EDITION** -
– (CYCLONE / FORCE MAJEURE / ENCORE)

Oct 91. (cd/c) *Music Club; (MC CD/TC 034)* **FROM DAWN . . . TILL DUSK 1973-88** -

Feb 93. (cd) *Private Music; (01005 82105-2)* **THE PRIVATE MUSIC OF TANGERINE DREAM** -

Mar 93. (cd) *Silva Screen; (FILMCD 125)* **DREAM MUSIC**
– from films; THE PARK IS MINE / DEADLY CARE / DEAD SOLID PERFECT.

Oct 94. (5xcd-box) *(CDBOX 4)* **TANGENTS** -

Mar 95. (cd) *Emporio; (EMPRCD 564)* **ATMOSPHERICS** -

Nov 95. (cd) *Silva Screen; (FILMCD 166)* **DREAM MUSIC 2** -

Dec 95. (d-cd) *Essential; (EDFCD 353)* **BOOK OF DREAMS** -
– (THE PINK YEARS: 1970-1973) // THE BLUE YEARS: 1983-1987)

Jul 96. (cd) *Tangerine Dream Int.; (TDI 001CD)* **THE DREAM MIXES** -

Nov 96. (5xcd-box) *Essential; (ESFCD 420)* **THE DREAM ROOTS COLLECTION** -

EDGAR FROESE

—— solo (all music by himself)

Virgin / Virgin

Jun 74. (lp) *(V 2016) <13111>* **AQUA**
– NGC 891 / Upland / Aqua / Panorphelia. *(re-iss.Mar84; OVED 20) (cd-iss.Jun87; CDV 2016)*

Sep 75. (lp) *(V 2040)* **EPSILON IN MALAYSIAN PALE** -
– Epsilon in Malaysian pale / Maroubra Bay. *(re-iss.Mar84; OVED 22) (cd-iss.Jun87; CDV 2040)*

1976. Brain; (lp) *(60.008)* **MACULA TRANSFER** - - German
– Os / Af / Pa / Quantas / If. *(re-iss.Mar82; 0060.008)*

Jan 78. (d-lp) *(VD 2507)* **AGES** -
– Metropolis / Era of the slaves / Tropic of Capricorn / Nights of automatic women / Icarus / Childrens deeper study / Ode to Granny "A" / Pizarro and Atahwallpa / Golgatha and the circle closes. *(cd-iss.Jun97; CDOVD 480)*

Sep 79. (lp) *(V 2139)* **STUNTMAN** -
– Stuntman / It would be like Samoa / Detroit snackbar dreamer / Drunken Mozart in the desert / A Dali-esque sleep fuse / Scarlet score for Mescalero. *(re-iss.Mar84; OVED 21) (cd-iss.Jun87 & Mar94; CDV 2139)*

Oct 82. (lp) *(V 2255)* **KAMIKAZE 1989 (Soundtrack)** -
– Videophonic / Vitamen 'C' / Krismopompas / Polizei disco / Intuition / Polizei therapie center / Blauer panther / Schlangenbad / Underwarter tod / Flying kamikaze / Der konzern / Der 31. stock. *(re-iss.Aug88; OVED 125) (cd-iss.Aug88; CDV 2255)*

Aug 83. (lp) *(V 2277)* **PINNACLES** -
– Specific gravity of smile / The light cone / Walkabout / Pinnacles. *(re-iss.Aug88; OVED 144) (cd-iss.May88; CDV 2277)*

– FROESE compilations, others –

Aug 82. (lp) *Virgin; (V 2197)* **SOLO 1974-1979** -
(re-iss.Mar84; OVED 21) (cd-iss.Aug88; CDV 2197)

Jun 95. (d-cd) *Ambient; (AMBT 5)* **BEYOND THE STORM** -

TEA AND SYMPHONY

Formed: Birmingham, England . . . late 60's by JAMES LANGSTON, JEFF DAW and NIGEL PHILLIPS. They were part of the 'Big Bear' management team, augmented at times by musicians BOB LAMB and MICK HINCKS (from LOCOMOTIVE). Their 1969 debut, 'AN ASYLUM FOR THE MUSICALLY INSANE', was an exotic, self-indulgent offering, sadly ignored by the buying public, as was their more basic second album, 'JO SAGO'. Most of the band went on to greater things.

Recommended: AN ASYLUM FOR THE MUSICALLY INSANE (*7) / JO SAGO (*6)

JAMES LANGSTON – vocals, guitar, wind / **JEFF DAW** – guitar, flute, vocals / **NIGEL PHILLIPS** – drums, percussion, keyboards, vocals / augmented by **BOB LAMB** – drums / **MICK HINKS + RON CHESTERMAN** – bass / **GUS DUDGEON** – percussion

Harvest / not issued

Jul 69. (7") *(HAR 5005)* **BOREDOM. / ARMCHAIR THEATRE** -

Nov 69. (7") *(SHVL 761)* **AN ASYLUM FOR THE MUSICALLY INSANE** -
– Armchair theatre / Feel now so cool / The wind / Sometime / Maybe my mind

with egg / The come on / Tenor in my soul / Travellin' shoes / Winter / Nothing will come of nothing.

— added **BOB WILSON + DAVE CARROLL** – guitars; repl. the guests

Nov 70. (lp) *(SHVL 785)* **JO SAGO** [ ] [-]
– Miniature / Myada / Journey / Brother / African paprika / Fairground suite / Desperate oil / Umbilical Bill / Goodnight / Try your luck / Yourself / Green fingered – Redhanded / Seasons turn to one / View to the sky / Nortihorticulturalist / Dangling.

— broke-up in 1971, when WILSON, CARROLL + LAMB joined IDLE RACE, who became The STEVE GIBBONS BAND. LANGSTON later formed MEAN STREET DEALER and joined ROY HARPER.

TEMPEST (see under ⇒ COLOSSEUM)

TEMPTATIONS

Formed: Birmingham, Alabama, USA ... 1960, initially as The ELGINS, by EDDIE KENDRICKS and PAUL WILLIAMS (from The PRIMES), plus MELVIN FRANKLIN and OTIS WILLIAMS (from The DISTANTS). They moved to Detroit in 1961 after two flop 45's for 'Miracle'. Securing a deal with the Berry 'Gordy' label (aka Tamla Motown), they finally scored their first US hit in 1964 with 'THE WAY YOU DO THE THINGS YOU DO'. By early 1965, 'MY GIRL' had given them their first chart topper. Penned by SMOKEY ROBINSON (who dominated most of the band's songwriting during this period), the song was the first in an incredible run of chart hits that included 'IT'S GROWING', 'SINCE I LOST MY BABY' and 'MY BABY', all released in 1965. Though the act were 'manufactured' to a certain degree by 'Motown', they posessed an impressive three-pronged vocal attack in DAVID RUFFIN's gravel-flecked rasp, EDDIE KENDRICKS' high tenor and PAUL WILLIAMS' heavy baritone. But it was RUFFIN's vocals which were pushed to the fore as producer NORMAN WHITFIELD began to lead the group's sound in a rougher direction, 'AIN'T TOO PROUD TO BEG' (1966), an early example of what was to come. As the band enjoyed a further string of hits including '(I KNOW) I'M LOSING YOU)' (1966), 'YOU'RE MY EVERYTHING' (1967) and 'I WISH IT WOULD RAIN' (1968), RUFFIN became increasingly jealous of the way DIANA ROSS was being nurtured for solo stardom by 'Motown', things coming to a head when RUFFIN failed to show for a gig. The group duly sent him packing, recruiting DENNIS EDWARDS and with the 'CLOUD NINE' (1969) single, hitched a ride on the magic roundabout of "psychedelic soul" pioneered by SLY STONE's thrilling honky hybrids. With WHITFIELD and his partner BARRETT STRONG penning most of the material, the band released a clutch of hard-hitting, socially aware classics like 'PSYCHEDELIC SHACK' (1970), 'BALL OF CONFUSION (THAT'S WHAT THE WORLD IS TODAY)' (1970), the funk getting dirtier and nastier with the hard-bitten tale of a broken home, 'PAPA WAS A ROLLING STONE' (1972). KENDRICKS departed in 1971 after his swansong for the band, 'JUST MY IMAGINATION (RUNNING AWAY WITH ME)' and PAUL WILLIAMS left later the same year, the band drafting in replacements DAMON HARRIS and RICHARD STREET. While the singles dried up, in the pop charts at least, the band still shifted albums up until the late 70's. As their creative muse began to falter, the band extricated itself from 'Motown' and despite a well-received self-produced album, 'THE TEMPTATIONS DO THE TEMPTATIONS' (1976), their two albums for 'Atlantic', 'HEAR TO TEMPT YOU' (1978) and 'BARE BACK' (1978) were marred by insipid disco stylings. EDWARDS had been absent for these albums (replaced by LOUIS PRICE), although he returned towards the end of the decade and the band hooked up with 'Motown' again for a comeback single, 'POWER' (1980) which scraped into the charts. RUFFIN and KENDRICKS returned to the fold for a short-lived reunion in 1982 and following their departure, OTIS WILLIAMS and MELVIN FRANKLIN carried the TEMPTATIONS flame through the 80's and beyond, completing studio and live work with a changing cast of musicians. Although they were inducted into the Rock'n'Roll Hall Of Fame in 1989, the band were merely retreading their 60's heyday, cabaret style. With KENDRICKS dying of cancer in 1992 and MELVIN FRANKLIN dying three years later, WILLIAMS is the sole remaining member from the original line-up. • **Covered:** THE WEIGHT (Band) / I'LL TRY SOMETHING NEW (Miracles) / I'M GONNA MAKE YOU LOVE ME (Madeleine Bell) / etc. • **Trivia:** In 1987, actor and fan, BRUCE WILLIS, invited The TEMPTATIONS to sing back-up on his hit version of The DRIFTERS' 'Under The Boardwalk'.

Recommended: PSYCHEDELIC SHACK (*8) / CLOUD NINE (*8)

MELVIN FRANKLIN (b. DAVID ENGLISH, 12 Oct'42, Montgomery, Alabama) – vocals / **OTIS WILLIAMS** (b. OTIS MILES, 30 Oct'49, Texarkana, Texas) – vocals / **ELDRIDGE BRYANT** – vocals

— From 1960 to late 60's had a string of 45's, many of them soul hits for 'Tamla'.

— line-up update:- **MELVIN FRANKLIN, OTIS WILLIAMS, EDDIE KENDRICKS, PAUL WILLIAMS + DENNIS EDWARDS**

Aug 69. (7") *(TMG 707)* <7081> **CLOUD NINE. / WHY DID SHE HAVE TO LEAVE ME (WHY DID SHE HAVE TO GO)** [15] [6] Oct68

Sep 69. (lp; stereo/mono) *(S+/TML 11109)* <939> **CLOUD NINE** [32] [4] Mar69
– Cloud nine / I heard it through it the grapevine / Why did she have to leave me (why did she have to go) / Runaway child, running wild / Love is a hurtin' thing / Hey girl / I need your lovin' / Don't let him take your love from me / Gonna keep on tryin' till I win your love / I gotta find away (to get you back). *(re-iss.Oct81 lp/c; STML/CSTML 5020) (cd-iss.Aug93; 530153-2)*

Nov 69. (7") *(TMG 716)* <7084> **RUNAWAY CHILD, RUNNING WILD. / I NEED YOUR LOVIN'** [ ] [6] Feb69

Jan 70. (7") *(TMG 722)* <7093> **I CAN'T GET NEXT TO YOU. / RUNNING AWAY (AIN'T GONNA HELP ME)** [13] [1] Aug69

Feb 70. (lp; stereo/mono) *(S+/TML 11133)* <949> **PUZZLE PEOPLE** [20] [5] Oct69
– I can't get next to you / Hey Jude / Don't let the Joneses get you down / Message from a black man / It's your thing / Little green apples / You don't love me no more / Running away (ain't gonna help you) / Since I've lost my baby / Slave / That's the way love is. *(re-iss.Mar82 lp/c; STML/CSTMS 5050)*

Apr 70. (lp; stereo/mono) *(S+/TML 11141)* <953> **LIVE AT THE (LONDON'S) TALK OF THE TOWN (live)** [ ] [21] Aug70
– I'm gonna make you love me / The impossible dream / Run away child running wild / Don't let the Joneses get you down / Love theme from Romeo & Juliet / I can't get next to you / This guy's in love with you / I've got to be me / I'm losing you / Cloud nine / Everything is going to be alright. *(re-iss.Jan79 on 'Music For Pleasure' lp/c; MFP/TCMFP 50419)*

Jun 70. (7") *(TMG 741)* <7096> **PSYCHEDELIC SHACK. / THAT'S THE WAY LOVE IS** [33] [7] Jan70

Jun 70. (lp) *(STML 11147)* <947> **PSYCHEDELIC SHACK** [56] [9] Mar70
– Psychedelic shack / Hum along and dance / War / It's summer / You make your own Heaven and Hell right here on Earth / You need love like I do (don't you) / Take a stroll thru your mind / Friendship train. *(re-iss.Mar82 lp/c; STMS/CSTMS 5051)*

Sep 70. (7") *(TMG 7049)* <7099> **BALL OF CONFUSION (THAT'S WHAT THE WORLD IS TODAY). / IT'S SUMMER** [7] [3] May70

— The TEMPTATIONS continued to have more hits during the 70's and 80's, but they reverted increasingly back to soul/pop. (see GREAT ROCK DISCOGRAPHY for details)

THEM

Formed: Belfast, N.Ireland ... 1963 by VAN MORRISON, BILLY HARRISON, ALAN HENDERSON, ERIC WRIXEN and RONNIE MELLINGS. After their debut single flopped, producers TOMMY SCOTT and BERT BERNS, recruited session men JIMMY PAGE (future LED ZEPPELIN) and PETER BARDENS (future CAMEL) to feature on their hot-wired cover of BIG JOE WILLIAMS' 'BABY PLEASE DON'T GO', the single rocketing into the Top 10 in early '65. The B-side, 'GLORIA' was even more primal, a riotous piece of garage that inspired generations of spotty youths to pick up guitars and has subsequently been covered by everyone from The SHADOWS OF KNIGHT to The DOORS and PATTI SMITH. Although the band found it difficult to equal this incredible double shot, their next single, 'HERE COMES THE NIGHT' climbed to No.2 in the UK charts. The eponymous debut album followed later that summer and although it failed to chart, it was a precocious collection of early VAN-penned originals and incendiary covers. Their fame was short-lived though, as successive singles failed to chart and the second album, 'THEM AGAIN' (1966) lacked the consistency of its predecessor. There were occasional flashes of VAN's maverick genius and it was clear he was the lynchpin holding the thing together. When he left to go solo in 1966, the band inevitably split, only to reform a number of times (minus VAN) around differing line-ups, trading on past glories but predictably producing no new material of any great note. • **Songwriters:** MORRISON penned (until his departure), except HERE COMES THE NIGHT + (IT WON'T HURT) HALF AS MUCH + few early songs (Bert Berns). DON'T START CRYING NOW (Slim Harpo) / BABY PLEASE DON'T GO (Big Joe Williams) / DON'T LOOK BACK (John Lee Hooker) / I PUT A SPELL ON YOU (Screaming Jay Hawkins) / IT'S ALL OVER NOW, BABY BLUE (Bob Dylan), etc.

Recommended: THE COLLECTION (*8)

VAN MORRISON (b.GEORGE IVAN, 31 Aug'45) – vocals, harmonica / **BILLY HARRISON** – guitar / **ERIC WRIXEN** – piano, keyboards / **RONNIE MELLINGS** – drums / **ALAN HENDERSON** (b.26 Nov'44) – bass

Decca Parrot

Aug 64. (7") *(F 11973)* <9702> **DON'T START CRYING NOW. / ONE TWO BROWN EYES** [ ] [ ]

— **JACKIE McAULEY** – organ + **PATRICK McAULEY** – organ repl. ERIC and RONNIE WRIXEN who joined The WHEELS, while MELLINGS became a milkman.

Dec 64. (7") *(F 12018)* <9727> **BABY PLEASE DON'T GO. / GLORIA** [10] [93] Mar65
<US re-dist.Apr66, flipped over; hit 71> (re-iss.Jul73 on 'Deram'; DM 394) (re-iss.May82; F 13923) (re-iss.Oct83 on 'Old Gold'; OG 9341)

Mar 65. (7") *(F 12094)* <9747> **HERE COMES THE NIGHT. / ALL FOR MYSELF** [2] [24] May65
(re-iss.Sep73 on 'Deram'; DM 400)

Jun 65. (lp; mono/stereo) *(LK 4700)* <PS/PAS 6/7 1005> **THEM** [ ] [54] Jul65
– Here comes the night *[US-only]* / Mystic eyes / If you and I could be as two / Little girl / Just a little bit / I gave my love a diamond (UK-only) / Go on home baby / Gloria / You just can't win / Don't look back / I like it like that / Bright lights big city / My little baby *[UK-only]* / Route 66. *(cd-iss.Feb89 on 'London'; 820 563-2)*

— above lp featured sessioners **PETER BARDENS** – keyboards + **JIMMY PAGE** – guitar

— **PETER BARDENS** – keyboards + **JOHN WILSON** (b. 6 Nov'47) – drums now repl. The McAULEY's who formed The BELFAST GYPSIES

Jun 65. (7") *(F 12175)* **ONE MORE TIME. / HOW LONG BABY?** [ ] [-]

Aug 65. (7") *(F 12215)* <9784> **(IT WON'T HURT) HALF AS MUCH. / I'M GONNA DRESS IN BLACK** [ ] [ ]

Nov 65. (7") *(F 12281)* <9796> **MYSTIC EYES. / IF YOU AND I COULD BE AS TWO** [ ] [33] Oct65

— **MORRISON, HENDERSON + WILSON** were joined by **RAY ELLIOTT** (b.13 Sep'43) – piano, sax repl. BARDENS to solo & later CAMEL / **JIM ARMSTRONG** (b.24 Jun'44) – guitar repl. HARRISON

Jan 66. (lp; mono/stereo) *(LK 4751)* <PS/PAS 6/7 1008> **THEM AGAIN** [ ] [ ]
– Could you would you / Something you got / Call my name / Turn on your love light / I put a spell on you / I can only give you everything / My lonely sad eyes / I

got a woman / Out of sight / It's all over now, baby blue / Bad or good / How long baby / Hello Josephine / Don't you know / Hey girl / Bring 'em on in. *(cd-iss.Feb89 on 'London'; 820 564-2)*

Mar 66. (7") *(F 12355)* *<9819>* **CALL MY NAME. / BRING 'EM ON IN**

— (Jan 66) **TERRY NOONE** – drums repl. WILSON later to TASTE (RORY GALLAGHER) Apr 66, **DAVE HARVEY** – drums repl. NOONE.

May 66. (7") *(F 12403)* *<3003>* **RICHARD CORY. / DON'T YOU KNOW**

— Disbanded mid 1966 when VAN MORRISON went solo. In 1967, they re-formed. **KEN McDOWELL** – vocals repl. him

Major Minor / not issued

1967. (7") *(MM 509)* **GLORIA. / FRIDAY'S CHILD**

1967. (7") *(MM 513)* **THE STORY OF THEM. / (part 2)**

not issued / Tower-Capitol

Jan 68. (lp) *<ST 5104>* **NOW AND THEM**
– I'm your witch doctor / What's the matter baby / Truth machine / Square room / You're just what I was looking for today / Dirty old man / At the age of sixteen / Nobody loves you when you're down and out / Walking the Queen's garden / I happen to love you / Come to me. *(UK-iss.Dec88 on 'Zap!'; ZAP 6)*

Feb 68. (7") *<384>* **WALKING IN THE QUEEN'S GARDEN. / HAPPEN TO LOVE YOU**

Apr 68. (7") *<407>* **SQUARE ROOM. / BUT IT'S ALRIGHT**

— trimmed to a quartet when ELLIOTT departed

Nov 68. (lp) *<ST 5116>* **TIME OUT! TIME IN FOR THEM**
– Time out for time in / She put a hex on you / Bent over you / Waltz of the flees / Black widow spider / We've all agreed to help / Market place / Just one conception / Young woman / The moth. *(UK-iss.Dec88 on 'Zap!'; ZAP 7)*

Nov 68. (7") *<461>* **WALTZ OF THE FLIES. / WE ALL AGREED TO HELP**

Mar 69. (7") *<493>* **DARK ARE THE SHADOWS. / CORINA**

— added on session **JERRY COLE** – guitar, vocals / **JOHN STARK** – drums (tour) In 1969, ARMSTRONG, ELLIOT, McDOWELL went off to Chicago to form The TRUTH alongside bassman CURTIS BACHMAN and rummer RENO SMITH. An album 'TRUTH OF TRUTHS' surfaced in 1971 for US 'Oak'. In March '95, an exploitation cd 'OF THEM AND OTHER TALES' was released for 'Epilogue' *(EPI 003)*

not issued / HappyTiger

1970. (lp) *<HT 1004>* **THEM**
– I keep singing / Lonely weekends / Take a little time / You got me good / Jo Ann / Memphis lady / In the midnight hour / Nobody cares / I am waiting / Just a little.

1970. (7") *<525>* **I AM WAITING. / LONELY WEEKENDS**

1970. (7") *<534>* **MEMPHIS LADY. / NOBODY CARES**

1971. (lp; as THEM featuring ALAN HENDERSON) *<HT 1012>* **THEM IN REALITY**
– Gloria / Baby please don't go / Laugh / Let my song through / California man / Lessons of the sea / Rayn / Back to the country / Can you believe.

— **THEM** re-formed originals **HENDERSON, HARRISON & WRIXEN + MEL AUSTIN** – vocals / **BILLY BELL** – drums

Decca / not issued

1979. (lp) **SHUT YOUR MOUTH**
– Hamburg connection / I'm a lover not a worker / Shut your mouth / Needed on the farm / Streetwalking lady / Firewater / Child of the sixties / Slowdown / Losing you / Weekend entertainer / Holy roller / Cincinnati diceman.

— Split 1979 after **JIM ARMSTRONG** – guitar + **BRIAN SCOTT** – keyboards, flute repl. WRIXEN + HARRISON. The latter became BILLY WHO

– compilations, others, etc. –

on 'Decca' UK / 'Parrot' US, unless otherwise mentioned

Feb 65. (7"ep) *(DFE 8612)* **THEM**
– Don't start crying now / Philosophy / One two brown eyes / Baby please don't go.

Jan 69. (7") *(F 12875)* **GLORIA. / HERE COMES THE NIGHT**
<US re-iss.1977 on 'London'; 59028>

Feb 70. (lp; stereo/mono) *(S+/PA 86)* **THE WORLD OF THEM**

Aug 72. (7"; as VAN MORRISON & THEM) *<365>* **GLORIA. / IF YOU AND I COULD BE AS TWO**

Oct 73. (d-lp; as THEM FEATURING VAN MORRISON) *(DPA 3001-2)* *<BP 71053-4>* **THEM FEATURING VAN MORRISON** Jul72
– Don't start crying now / Baby please don't go / Here comes the night / One more time / It won't hurt half as much / Mystic eyes / Call my name / Richard Cory / One two brown eyes / All for myself / If you and I could be as two / Don't you know / Friday's child / The story of Them (part 1) / Philosophy / How long baby / I'm gonna dress in black / Bring 'em on in / Little girl / I gave my love a diamond / Gloria / You just can't win / Go on home baby / Don't look back / I like it like that / Bright lights big city / My little baby / Route 66.*(re-iss.Jul82; lp/c TAB/KTBC 45) (cd-iss.1987 on 'London'; 810 165-2)*

1974. (lp) *London; <APS 639>* **BACKTRACKIN'**

May 76. (lp/c) *(ROOTS/KRTC 3)* **ROCK ROOTS**

1977. (lp) *London; <LC 50001>* **THE STORY OF THEM FEATURING VAN MORRISON**

Oct 83. (7") *Old Gold; (OG 9342)* **HERE COMES THE NIGHT. / (B-side by Ten Years After)**

Aug 86. (d-lp/d-c; as THEM featuring VAN MORRISON) *Castle; (CCS LP/MC 131)* **THE COLLECTION**
(cd-iss.Aug92;)

Sep 87. (lp/c) *See For Miles; (SEE/+K 31)* **THE SINGLES**

Jan 91. (7"/c-s) *London; (LON/+C 292)* **BABY PLEASE DON'T GO. / GLORIA** 65
(12"+=/cd-s+=) *(LON X/CD 292)* – Mystic eyes.

Apr 97. (cd) *Spalax; (14967)* **REUNION CONCERT (live)**

THIRD BARDO

Formed: New York, USA . . . early 1967 by JEFFREY MOON, who named the band from a line in 'The Tibetan Book Of The Dead'. They only released one 45, although it has since become a much-sought-after classic and is worth mentioning here. 'I'M FIVE YEARS AHEAD OF MY TIME' was written by RUSTY EVANS (of The DEEP / FREAK SCENE) and VICTORIA PIKE, who was married to THIRD BARDO's producer Teddy Randazzo. Released on his 'Roulette' label, it was a haunting, fuzztone psyche-garage song, that The CRAMPS might later have been proud of. In fact, it was covered in the 80's by The NOMADS.

Recommended: the single (both sides)

JEFFREY MOON (b. NEUFELD) – vocals, guitar / **RICKY GOLDCLANG** – lead guitar / **RICHY SESLOWE** – rhythm guitar / **DAMIAN KELLY** – bass / **BRUCE GINSBERG** – drums

not issued / Roulette

Jul 67. (7") *<4742>* **I'M FIVE YEARS AHEAD OF MY TIME. / MY RAINBOW LIFE**

— after their split, JEFFREY released an album under the pseudonym CHRIS MOON

– compilations, etc. –

1994. (7"ep) *Here 'Tis;* **THE THIRD BARDO**
– I'm five years ahead of my time / Lose your mind / Dawn of tomorrow / I can understand your problem.

THIRD EAR BAND

Formed: Canterbury, England . . . 1968 originally as GIANT SUN TROLLEY and HYDROGEN JUKEBOX. They went through several personnel changes, before settling with GLENN SWEENEY, RICHARD COFF, PAUL MINNS and MEL DAVIS. Signing to 'Harvest', they kicked off in 1969 with the wholly instrumental, acoustic set, 'ALCHEMY'. Their next self-titled album fared better, even reaching the lower rungs of the Top 50. They split a few years later, after completing the soundtrack to Roman Polanski's 'MACBETH' film. Returning to the fold late in the 80's, they went on to complete two albums for the Italian market. • **Songwriters:** Group. • **Trivia:** Disc jockey, JOHN PEEL, played jews harp on their debut album.

Recommended: ALCHEMY (*6)

GLENN SWEENEY – tabla, percussion / **RICHARD COFF** – violin, viola / **PAUL MINNS** – oboe, recorder / **MEL DAVIS** – cello

Harvest / not issued

Jul 69. (lp) *(SHVL 756)* **ALCHEMY**
– Mosaic / Ghetto raga / Druid one / Stone circle / Egyptian book of the dead / Area three / Dragon lines / Lark rise. *(re-iss.Sep88 on 'Drop Out'; DO 1999) (cd-iss.1990's; DOCD 1999)*

— **URSULA SMITH** – cello, repl. DAVIS

Jun 70. (lp) *(SHVL 773)* **THIRD EAR BAND** 49
– Air / Earth / Fire / Water. *(cd-iss.Jan91 on 'Beat Goes On'; BGOCD 89) (re-iss.Apr97; BGOLP 89)*

— **DENIM BRIDGES** – guitar / **PAUL BUCKMASTER** – cello, bass, guitar / **SIMON HOUSE** – violin, synthesizer (ex-HIGH TIDE); repl. COFF + SMITH who formed COSMIC OVERDOSE

Mar 72. (lp) *(SHSP 4019)* **MUSIC FROM MACBETH (soundtrack)**
– Overture / The beach / Lady Macbeth / Inverness: Macbeth's return – The preparation – Fanfare – Duncan's arrival / The banquet / Dagger & death / At the well – The prince's escape – Coronation – Come sealing tonight / Court dance / Fleance / Grooms' dance / Bear baiting / Ambush – Banquo's ghost / Going to bed – Blind man's bluff – Requiescant / Sere and yellow leaf / The cauldron / Prophesies / Wicca way. *(re-iss.Jan89 & Apr97 on 'Beat Goes On'; BGOLP 61) (cd-iss.Jul90; BGOCD 61)*

— changed their name to The ELECTRIC EAR BAND in 1973, but never released 'NEW WORLDS' album. SIMON HOUSE joined DAVID BOWIE's band. **GLEN SWEENEY** re-formed THIRD EAR BAND, and brought in **MICK CARTER** – guitar / **NEIL BLACK** – violin / **LYN DOBSON** – vocals, flute, wind synthesizer

Materiali Sonori / not issued

Jul 89. (lp) *(MASO 33047)* **LIVE GHOSTS** Italy
– Hope mosaic / Druid three / Ghetto raga / Live ghosts.

Jun 95. (cd) *(MASO 90045)* **BRAIN WAVES**
– Sirocco song / Midnight drums / Spell of the voodoo / Dances with dolphins / Water into wine / Alchemical raga / Psychedelic trance dance.

Blueprint / not issued

Apr 97. (cd) *(BP 257CD)* **NEW AGE MAGICAL MUSICAL**
– Gog and Magog / Flight of the coven / Dance of the elves / Atlantis rising / Midnight on Mars.

– compilations, etc. –

Mar 76. (lp) *Harvest; (SHSM 2007)* **EXPERIENCE**
– Ghetto raga / Stone circle / Area 111 / Earth / Overture – The beach / Groom's dance / The cauldron.

13th FLOOR ELEVATORS

Formed: Austin, Texas, USA . . . 1965 by ROCKY ERICKSON and TOMMY HALL, together with STACY SUTHERLAND, BENNY THURMAN and JOHN IKE WALTON. ERICKSON had originally written and recorded 'YOU'RE GONNA MISS ME' with his first band, The SPADES, the single being released on the small 'Zero' label. A local hit, the record gained national notoriety in early '66 after being picked up by the 'International Artists' label. Around this time, self-styled psychedelic explorer, TOMMY HALL, had introduced ERICKSON to the aforementioned musicians (all three were ex-LINGSMEN) and The 13th FLOOR ELEVATORS were launched into orbit. The frenzied garage thrash of 'YOU'RE GONNA MISS ME' stood out from the pack by dint of ERICKSON's apocalyptic vocal threats and HALL's bizarre amplified jug playing. In addition to his idiosyncratic musical accompaniment, HALL penned most of the lyrics, setting out his agenda according to the chemically-enhanced evolution-of-man ethos espoused by the likes of acid guru, TIM LEARY. Debuting with 'THE PSYCHEDELIC SOUNDS OF THE 13TH FLOOR ELEVATORS' in 1966, the band had unleashed nothing less than a musical manifesto for mind expansion. But if the idea was to promote the use of halucinogenics, then the sirens on the DMT-tribute, 'FIRE ENGINE', surely encouraged any sane person never to go near the stuff, sounding more like the tortured wailing of lost, limbo-locked souls. Likewise 'MONKEY ISLAND', with ERICKSON howling like a man possessed. Elsewhere on the album, tracks like 'ROLLERCOASTER' and 'REVERBATION (DOUBT)' made for thrilling, if uneasy listening, and it was obvious that a trip to the 13th floor with ROCKY and Co. was somewhat different from the rosy hue that the psychedelic experience had taken on in popular mythology. The follow-up, 'EASTER EVERYWHERE' (1967), was a slightly more contemplative affair, opening with the hypnotic brilliance of 'SLIP INSIDE THIS HOUSE' (the subject of an equally essential 90's interpretation by PRIMAL SCREAM) through the trippy 'SHE LIVES (IN A TIME OF HER OWN)' and on to the frantic 'LEVITATION'. Inevitably, the Texan police were none too amused with the band's flagrant advocacy of drugs and after escalating harassment, ERICKSON found himself in court shortly after the album's release. Charged with possession of a small amount of hashish, he was faced with a choice of jail or mental hospital and rather unadvisedly chose the latter. This effectively signalled the end for the band, although a disappointing live album was released the following year and a final studio album appeared in 1969. ' BULL OF THE WOODS' was made up largely of SUTHERLAND-penned tunes although it contained the sublime 'MAY THE CIRCLE REMAIN UNBROKEN', ERICKSON's vocal all the more haunting in light of his tragic incarceration. Subjected to years of mind-numbing drugs and electro shock therapy, ROCKY was finally released in 1972 after a judge declared him sane. Ironically no doubt somewhat less sane after this experience, ERICKSON started making music again, forming a band, BLEIB ALIEN, and immersing himself in B-movie horror nonsense. After a stint in the studio with fellow Texan, DOUG SAHM, of SIR DOUGLAS QUINTET fame, ERICKSON released the inspired psychosis of the 'RED TEMPLE PRAYER (TWO HEADED DOG)' single in 1975. An album, 'ROCKY ERICKSON AND THE ALIENS' surfaced in 1980 and included such wholesome fare as 'DON'T SHAKE ME LUCIFER', 'CREATURE WITH THE ATOM BRAIN' and 'STAND FOR THE FIRE DEMON'. Yet this was no po-faced heavy-metal posturing, ERICKSON actually believed what he was singing about, lending the record a certain level of intensity, despite the cliched hard rock backing. A series of singles and compilations appeared sporadically throughout the 80's, and after ERICKSON was hospitalised again for a short period, 'Warner Bros.' executive and longtime ELEVATORS fan, BILL BENTLEY, masterminded a tribute album, 'Where The Pyramid Meets The Eye', featuring the likes of The JESUS AND MARY CHAIN and JULIAN COPE. Although a collection of early material, 'ALL THAT MAY DO MY RHYME', appeared in 1975 on The BUTTHOLE SURFERS' 'Trance Syndicate' label, ERICKSON appears to have no interest in writing new material. Music biz legend paints the man as an acid casualty, and while he definately appears to live in a world of his own making, his wayward genius continues to win the respect and admiration of fans the world over. • **Songwriters:** ERICKSON penned except; I'M GONNA LOVE YOU TOO (Buddy Holly) / etc.

Recommended: THE PSYCHEDELIC SOUNDS OF (*8) / EASTER EVERYWHERE (*7) / BULL OF THE WOODS (*6) / THE BEST OF . . . (*8)

The SPADES

—— (had already recorded a single 'I NEED A GIRL', before 17 year-old ROKY joined) **ROKY ERICKSON** (b. ROGER KYNARD ERICKSON, 15 Jul'47, Dallas, Texas) – vocals, harmonica / **JOHN KERNEY** – guitar, vocals

not issued | Zero

1965. (7") *<10002>* **YOU'RE GONNA MISS ME. / WE SELL SOUL** [-] [ ]

13th FLOOR ELEVATORS

—— were formed by **ROKY** and **STACEY SUTHERLAND** – lead guitar (ex-LINGSMEN) / **BENNY THURMAN** – bass, electric violin (ex-LINGSMEN) / **JOHN IKE WALTON** – drums (ex-LINGMEN) / **TOMMY HALL** – blow jug, lyrics

not issued | Contact

Jan 66. (7") *<5269>* **YOU'RE GONNA MISS ME. / TRIED TO HIDE** [-] [ ]
<re-iss.Apr66 on 'Hanna Barbara'; HBR 492> <re-iss.Jun66 on 'International Artists'; 107>; hit No.55> (UK-iss.Nov78 on 'Radar' 7"green; ADA 13)

—— **RONNIE LEATHERMAN** – bass repl. BENNY who formed PLUM NELLY

not issued | Int.Artists

Aug 66. (lp) *<IALP 1>* **THE PSYCHEDELIC SOUNDS OF** [-] [ ]
– You're gonna miss me / Roller coaster / Splash 1 / Don't fall down / Reverberation (doubt) / Fire engine / Thru the rhythm / You don't know / Kingdom of Heaven / Monkey island / Tried to hide. *<re-iss.1977; same> (UK-iss.Nov78 on 'Radar'; RAD 13) (re-iss.Feb88 on 'Decal'; LIK 19)*

Oct 66. (7") *<111>* **REVERBERATION (DOUBT). / FIRE ENGINE** [-] [ ]

—— **DAN GALINDO** – bass + **DANNY THOMAS** – drums repl. RONNIE + JOHN IKE

Feb 67. (7") *<113>* **I'VE GOT LEVITATION. / BEFORE YOU ACCUSE ME** [-] [ ]

Apr 67. (lp) *<IALP 5>* **EASTER EVERYWHERE** [-] [ ]
– Slip inside the house / Slide machine / She lives in a time of her own / Nobody to love / It's all over now, baby blue / Earthquake / Dust / I've got levitation / I had to tell you / Postures (leave your body behind). *<re-iss.1977; same> (UK-iss.May79 on 'Radar'; RAD 15) (re-iss.Apr88 on 'Decal'; LIK 28)*

Oct 67. (7") *<121>* **SHE LIVES (IN A TIME OF HER OWN). / BABY BLUE** [-] [ ]

Dec 67. (7") *<122>* **SLIP INSIDE THIS HOUSE. / SPLASH 1** [-] [ ]

—— Disbanded early '68, due to ROKY being imprisoned for possession of a miniscule of hash. He once escaped but was then kept there for another 3 years, and suffered thorazine plus electric shock treatment. **DUKE DAVIS** – bass had briefly repl. GALINDO. DANNY THOMAS and DUKE were to become The GOLDEN DAWN. The original 13th FLOOR ELEVATORS reformed in 1972. In 1984, they gigged again with line-up (ERICKSON, WALTON, LEATHERMAN and GREG 'Catfish' FORREST-guitar). In Autumn 1978, STACEY was shot dead by his wife.

– others, compilations, etc. –

on 'International Artists' unless otherwise mentioned

1968. (lp) *<IALP 8>* **LIVE** (studio out-takes, b-sides, demos; with false applause) [-] [ ]
– Before you accuse me / She lives in a time of her own / Tried to hide / You gotta take that girl / I'm gonna love you too / Everybody needs somebody to love / I've got levitation / You can't hurt me anymore / Roller coaster / You're gonna miss me. *(UK-iss.May88 on 'Decal'; LIK 30)*

1968. (7") *<126>* **MAY THE CIRCLE BE UNBROKEN. / I'M GONNA LOVE YOU TOO** [-] [ ]

1969. (lp) *<IALP 9>* **BULL OF THE WOODS** (rec.early'68) [-] [ ]
– Livin' on / Barnyard blues / Till then / Never another / Rose and the thorn / Down by the river / Scarlet and gold / Street song / Doctor Boom / With you / May the circle remain unbroken. *(UK-iss.Jul88 on 'Decal'; LIK 40)*

1969. (7") *<130>* **LIVIN' ON. / SCARLET AND GOLD** [-] [ ]

Oct 78. (7"ep) *Austin; <RE 1>* **YOU REALLY GOT ME. / WORD / ROLL OVER BEETHOVEN** [-] [ ]

1985. (lp) *Texas Archives; <TAR LP-4>* **FIRE IN MY BONES** [-] [ ]

1987. (lp) *Texas Archives; <TAR LP-7>* **ELEVATOR TRACKS (some live 1966)** [-] [ ]

1988. (lp) *Big Beat; (WIK 82)* **I'VE SEEN YOUR FACE BEFORE** (live bootleg '66) [ ] [-]
(cd-iss.Jun89; CDWIK 82)

1988. (lp) *13th Hour; <(13-LP-1)>* **DEMOS EVERYWHERE** (US-title 'THE ORIGINAL SOUND OF . . .') [ ] [ ]

Nov 88. (cd) *Charly; (CDCHARLY 150)* **EASTER EVERYWHERE / BULL OF THE WOODS** [ ] [-]

Jun 89. (cd) *Charly; (CDCHARLY 159)* **THE PSYCHEDELIC SOUNDS OF / LIVE** [ ] [-]

Aug 91. (4xcd-box) *Decal; (LIKBOX 2)* **THE COLLECTION** [ ] [-]
– (all 1960's albums)
<In 1979, these appeared on a 12-lp box of 'International Artists'>

Jul 93. (cd) *Thunderbolt; (CDTB 124)* **OUT OF ORDER (LIVE AT THE AVALON BALLROOM)** [ ] [-]

Jun 94. (cd) *Thunderbolt; (CDTB 147)* **LEVITATION – IN CONCERT (live)** [ ] [-]

Apr 95. (cd) *Thunderbolt; (CDTB 153)* **THE REUNION CONCERT** [ ] [-]

Jan 96. (cd) *Nectar; (NTMCD 516)* **THE BEST OF THE 13th FLOOR ELEVATORS** [ ] [-]

ROKY ERICKSON

not issued | Mars

1975. (7"; with BLIEB ALIEN) *<1000>* **RED TEMPLE PRAYER (TWO HEADED DOG). / STARRY EYES** [-] [ ]

Virgin | Rhino

Sep 77. (7") *(VS 180) <003>* **BERMUDA. / INTERPRETER** [ ] [ ]

Sponge | not issued

Dec 77. (7"ep) *(101)* **TWO HEADED DOG / I HAVE ALWAYS BEEN HERE BEFORE. / MINE, MINE, MIND / CLICK YOUR FINGERS APPLAUDING THE PLAY** [-] [-] France

ROKY ERICKSON AND THE ALIENS

—— with **DUANE ASLAKSEN** – guitar / **STEVE BURGESS** – bass / **ANDRE LEWIS** – keyboards / **FUZZY FURIOSO** – drums / **BILL MILLER** – autoharp

C.B.S. | Columbia

Aug 80. (7") *(CBS 8888)* **CREATURE WITH THE ATOM BRAIN. / THE WIND AND MORE** [ ] [-]

Aug 80. (lp) *(CBS 84463)* **ROKY ERICKSON & THE ALIENS** [ ] [-]
– Two headed dog / I think of demons / Don't shake me Lucifer / I walked with a zombie / Night of the vampire / Cold night for alligators / White faces / Creatures with the atom brain / Mine, mine, mind / Stand for the fire demon. *(re-iss.Jan87 as 'I THINK OF DEMONS' on 'Edsel'; ED 222) (. . . cd-iss.Jun97; EDCD 528)*

Oct 80. (7") *(CBS 9055)* **MINE MINE MIND. / BLOODY HAMMER (long version)** [ ] [-]

ROKY ERICKSON

not issued | 415 Records

1981. (lp) *<0005>* **THE EVIL ONE** [-] [ ]
<cd-iss.1987 was a compilation on 'Enigma-Pink Dust'; 72212-2>

not issued | Dynamite

1984. (7") *<DY 002>* **DON'T SLANDER ME. / STARRY EYES** [-] [ ]

New Rose | not issued

1985. (m-lp) *(ROSE 69)* **CLEAR NIGHT FOR LOVE** [-] [-] France
– You don't love me yet / Clear night for love / The haunt / Starry eyes / Don't slander me.

One Big Guitar | Live Wire

Apr 86. (12") *(OBG 004T) <LW 5>* **THE BEAST. / HEROIN (live)** [ ] [ ] Nov85

Demon | Enigma

Jan 87. (lp) *(FIEND 66) <72109-1>* **GREMLINS HAVE PICTURES (live 1975-1982 with his bands)** [ ] [ ] Nov86

(cd-iss.Oct90 with extra tracks; FIENDCD 66)

Jun 87. (lp) *(FIEND 86)* **DON'T SLANDER ME** [ ] [-]
– (contains some of 'THE EVIL ONE' lp)

Fan Club / not issued

Sep 87. (lp) *(FC 030)* **THE HOLIDAY INN TAPES** [ ] [-]

— next with **WILL SEXTON + CHRIS HOLYHAUS** – guitar / **FREDDIE KRC** – drums

1988. (lp) *(FC 046)* **LIVE AT THE RITZ (live Feb'87)** [ ] [-]
– You're gonna miss me / Don't slander me / Don't shake me Lucifer / Night of the vampire / Two headed dog / Splash 1 / Take a good look at yourself / Clear night for love / Bloody hammer.

— next with **ET** (aka EVILHOOK WILDLIFE) **BRIAN S.CURLEY / KERRY GRAFTON / TIM GAGAN + DAVE CAMERON**

Fundamental / not issued

Feb 88. (12") *(PRAY 007)* **CLEAR NIGHT FOR LOVE. / YOU DON'T LOVE ME YET** [ ] [-]

not issued / Rok

Dec 88. (7"ep) <88> **ACOUSTIC EP** [-] [ ]

Sympathy.. / Sympathy..

1992. (7") **HASN'T ANYONE TOLD YOU. / THE INTERPRETER** [ ] [ ]

Trance / Trance

Nov 94. (7"ltd.) *(TR 28)* **WE ARE NEVER TALKING. / PLEASE JUDGE (acoustic version)** [ ] [ ]

Jan 95. (lp/cd) *(TR 33/+CD)* **ALL THAT MAY DO MY RHYME** [ ] [ ]

– compilations, others, etc. –

Aug 87. (lp/pic-lp) *5 Hours Back; (TOCK 007/+P)* **CASTING THE RUNES** [ ] [-]

— (above live Nov79 with The EXPLOSIVES; aka **CAM KING** – lead guitar / **WILLIE COLLIE** – bass / **FREDDIE KRC** – drums)

Mar 88. (lp) *5 Hours Back; (TOCK 010)* **OPENERS** [ ] [-]

Jun 88. (red-lp) *5 Hours Back; (TICK 001)* **TWO TWISTED TALES** (interview) [ ] [-]

1988. (cd) *Fan Club; (ROKY 1)* **CLICK YOUR FINGERS APPLAUDING THE PLAY** [ ] [-]

May 92. (cd/c) *Swordfish; (SFMD CD/LP 001)* **MAD DOG** (1976-83) [ ] [-]

Oct 92. (cd/lp) *New Rose; (422404)* **LIVE DALLAS 1979 (live with The NERVEBREAKERS)** [ ] [-]

Feb 93. (cd) *Swordfish; (SFMCD 2)* **LOVE TO SEE YOU BLEED** [ ] [ ]
– Bloody hammer / Every time I look at you / Miss Elude / Haunt / Laughing things / You don't love me yet / Creature with the atom brain / I think of demons / Two headed dog / Red temple prayer / Bumblebee zombie / Click your fingers applauding / The play / Mine mine mind / Things that go bump in the night / Here today . . . gone tomorrow / Realise your my sweet brown angel eyes / I love to see you bleed / Please don't kill my baby.

THUNDERCLAP NEWMAN

Formed: London, England . . . 1969, devised by PETE TOWNSHEND (of The WHO), who brought in the trio of ANDY NEWMAN, JOHN 'SPEEDY' KEEN and JIMMY McCULLOCH. Their debut single, the pop psychedelia of 'SOMETHING IN THE AIR', soon topped the charts, and when it was used on the movie, 'The Magic Christian', it shot into US Top 40. It took a whole year for their next release, 'ACCIDENTS', which only managed to scrape into the UK Top 50. Their 1970 album flopped, as did their next two singles. • **Songwriters:** ANDY NEWMAN, except ROCK AROUND THE CLOCK (Bill Haley).

Recommended: HOLLYWOOD DREAM (*5)

ANDY 'THUNDERCLAP' NEWMAN – vocals, piano / **SPEEDY KEEN** (b. JOHN) – drums, vocals, guitar / **JIMMY McCULLOCH** (b.13 Aug'53, Glasgow, Scotland) – guitar

Track / Track

May 69. (7") *(604 031)* <2656> **SOMETHING IN THE AIR. / WILHELMINA** [1] [37] Aug69
<US re-iss.Oct70; 2769>

Jun 70. (7") *(2094 001)* **ACCIDENTS. / I SEE IT ALL** [46] [ ]

Sep 70. (lp) *(2406 003)* <8264> **HOLLYWOOD DREAM** [ ] [ ]
– Hollywood 1 / The reasons / Open the door, Homer / Look around / Accidents / Wild country / When I think / The old cornmill / I don't know / Hollywood dream / Hollywood 2 / Something in the air.

Nov 70. (7") *(2094 002)* **WILD COUNTRY. / HOLLYWOOD** [ ] [ ]
(re-iss.1979; 2095 002)

Jan 71. (7") *(2094 003)* **THE REASON. / STORMY PETREL** [ ] [ ]

— split in 1971 when SPEEDY KEEN went solo. He was soon to release album 'PREVIOUS CONVICTIONS'. JIMMY McCULLOCH went onto have stints with STONE THE CROWS, PAUL McCARTNEY & WINGS, etc. He overdosed in London on 27th Sep'79.

ANDY NEWMAN

1971. (lp) *(2406 103)* **RAINBOW** [ ] [ ]
– That's what I like about you / Rock around the clock / After tonight / Water music / Arctic sunset / Apalachian champagne / Collage / Red skies / Oh baby take it away / Suzy Wong.

– compilations, etc. –

Oct 71. (7"ep) *Track; (2094 011)* **SOMETHING IN THE AIR. / (other 3 tracks by John's Children / Arthur Brown / Jimi Hendrix)** [ ] [-]

Sep 75. (7") *Track; (2094 017)* **SOMETHING IN THE AIR. / ('Fire' by Crazy World Of Arthur Brown)** [ ] [-]

May 84. (7") *Old Gold; (OG 9435)* **SOMETHING IN THE AIR. / ACCIDENTS** [ ] [-]

TIME (see under ⇒ SPONTANEOUS COMBUSTION)

TIMEBOX (see under ⇒ PATTO, Mike)

TIN MACHINE (see under ⇒ BOWIE, David)

TINTERN ABBEY

Formed: London, England . . . 1967 by DAN SMITH, DAVID MacTAVISH, STUART MacKAY and JOHN DALTON. They named themselves after an Arthurian legend and although the quartet only left a solitary single behind, both the A and B side left the listener awe-struck. The A-side, cheekily called 'BEESIDE', was a great example of UK psychedelia, while the B-side, 'VACUUM CLEANER', showed off some fine fuzztone guitar, backed by crashing cymbals and writer MacTAVISH's effective vox.

Recommended: the single (now worth over £100), which has also appeared on several artists' collections, notably 'The British Psychedelic Trip, Vol.1' and 'The Perfumed Garden' cd's.

DAVID MacTAVISH – vocals / **DAN SMITH** – lead guitar / **STUART MacKAY** – bass / **JOHN DALTON** – drums

Deram / not issued

Dec 67. (7") *(DM 164)* **BEESIDE. / VACUUM CLEANER** [ ] [-]

— (Jan'68) **PAUL BRETT** – lead guitar (ex-ARTHUR BROWN) repl. DAN

— split later in the year, with the new member joining VELVET OPERA before going solo. MacTAVISH later repl. PETE FRENCH in BIG BERTHA.

TITUS GROAN

Formed: London, England . . . 1969 by STUART COWELL, JOHN LEE, TONY PRIESTLAND and JIM TOOMEY. They named themselves after the main character in a Mervyn Peake gothic fantasy novel, from which they also lifted a song title, 'HALL OF BRIGHT CARVINGS'. The track was included on their eponymous debut album in 1970. Progressive rock they certainly were, with lengthy uncomplicated pieces falling short of real excitement and passion. A single, 'OPEN THE DOOR HOMER' (a precursor to The Simpsons perhaps?), also failed to hit the mark, although their album has since become quite collectable.

Recommended: TITUS GROAN (*5)

STUART COWELL – vocals, keyboards, guitar / **JOHN LEE** – bass / **TONY PRIESTLAND** – sax, flute, oboe / **JIM TOOMEY** – drums

Dawn / not issued

Nov 70. (7"m) **(DNX 2503) OPEN THE DOOR HOMER. / WOMAN OF THE WORLD / LIVERPOOL** [ ] [-]

Nov 70. (lp) *(DNLS 3012)* **TITUS GROAN** [ ] [-]
– It wasn't for you / Hall of bright carvings: i) Theme, ii) In the dusty high – Vaulted hall, iii) The burning, iv) The theme / Liverpool / I can't change / It's all up with us / Fuschia. *(re-iss.Sep89 on 'See For Miles' lp/cd+=; SEE/+CD 260)*– Open the door Homer / Woman of the world.

— split early in 1971. TOOMEY later re-surfaced in The TOURISTS, which included ANNIE LENNOX and DAVE STEWART.

TOMITA

Born: ISAO TOMITA, 1932, Tokyo, Japan. He graduated in art from Tokyo University, although music was his main interest, especially of the electronic variety. Having already completed some choral suites, he was commissioned to write the theme music for the 1964 Tokyo Olympic Games, and was soon invited to compose for his country's Philharmonic Orchestra. By the early 70's, he had established his synthesized Plasma Music, the label 'R.C.A.' impressed with the results. They issued his first work, 'SNOWFLAKES ARE DANCING' in the US, an interpretation of music by the classical composer, DEBUSSY. Its sales rapidly rose, resulting in the UK distributing it under the R.C.A. subsidiary, 'Red Seal'. Having already made the Top 60 lists in America, its simplistic childlike approach on excerpts, 'ARABESQUE NO.1', 'CLAIR DE LUNE' and 'GOLLIWOG'S CAKEWALK', breathed new life into DEBUSSY's work. In fact, TOMITA's further mid-70's albums did the same for MUSSOURGSKY, STRAVINSKY and GUSTAV HOLST. TOMITA's interpretation of the latter's 'PLANET SUITE', angered the composer's daughter, Imogen, leading to her serving an injunction and halting its release in Britain for a few months in early '77. It was his last major seller, although he completed more work in the same vein during the following decade.

Recommended: SNOWFLAKES ARE DANCING (*7)

TOMITA – synthesizers, electronics

Red Seal / R.C.A.

May 74. (lp/c) *(ARL-1 <0488>)* **SNOWFLAKES ARE DANCING** [17] [57] Aug74
– Snowflakes are dancing (children's corner, No.4) / Reverie / Gardens in the rain (Estampes, No.3) / Clair de Lune (suite Bergamasque, No.3) / Arabesque No.1 / The engulfed cathedral (preludes, book 1, No.10) / Golliwog's cakewalk (children's corner, No.6) / Footprints in the snow (preludes, book 1, No.6). *(re-iss.Sep81 on 'R.C.A.'; lp/c; PL/PK 84587) (cd-iss.1984; RD 84587) (cd re-iss.Oct91 on 'RCA*

Victor'; GD 60579)

Apr 75. (7") *(RCA 2547) <0308>* **CLAIR DE LUNE. / ARABESQUE No.1** [ ] [ ]

Jun 75. (7") *<10083>* **SNOWFLAKES ARE DANCING. / ARABESQUE NO>1** [-] [ ]

Aug 75. (lp/c) *(ARL-1 <0838>)* **PICTURES AT AN EXHIBITION** [42] [49] May75
– Promenade: The gnome – The old castle – Tuileries / Bydlo / Ballet of the chicks in their shells / The two Jews / Limogues / Catacombs / Cum mortius in Ligua Mortua / The hut of Baba Yaga / The great gate of Kiev. *(re-iss.Sep81 on 'R.C.A.; lp/c; RCA LP/K 3010) (re-iss.1985 lp/c/cd; PL/PK/RD 80838) (cd re-iss.Oct91 on 'RCA Victor'; GD 60576)*

Sep 75. (7") *<10240>* **THE HUT OF BABA YAGA. / PROMENADE: THE GNOME** [-] [ ]

Dec 75. (7") *<10296>* **GREAT GATES OF KIEV. / THE HUT OF BABA YAGA** [-] [ ]

Feb 76. (lp/c) *(ARL-1 <1312>)* **FIREBIRD** [ ] [71]
– Firebird suite: Introduction & Dance of the Firebird – Round of the princesses – Infernal dance of King Kastchei – Berceuse and finale / Prelude a l'apres midi d'un faune / Night on the bare mountain. *(re-iss.May82 on 'R.C.A.' lp/c; RL/RK 11718) (cd-iss.Oct91 on 'RCA Victor'; GD 60578)*

Apr 76. (7") *<10683>* **FIREBIRD SUITE: INFERNAL DANCE OF KING KASTCHEI. / FIREBIRD SUITE: FINALE** [-] [ ]

Apr 77. (lp/c) *(RL/RK 11919) <1919>* **HOLST: THE PLANETS** [41] [67] Jan77
– Mars: The bringer of war / Venus: The bringer of peace / Mercury: The winged messenger / Jupiter: The bringer of jollity / Saturn: The bringer of old age / Uranus: The magician / Neptune: The mystic. *(re-iss.Aug85 on 'R.C.A.' lp/c; RL/RK 81919) (cd-iss.Oct91 on 'RCA Victor'; GD 60518)*

May 77. (7") *<10819>* **THE PLANETS: MARS. / THE LANETS: VENUS** [-] [ ]

Feb 78. (7") *(PB 9207)* **STAR WARS. / GIRL WITH FLAXEN HAIR** [ ] [-]

Feb 78. (lp/c) *(RL/RK 42652) <2616>* **KOSMOS** [ ] [ ]
– Star Wars – main title / Space fantasy: Also Sprach Zarathustra – Ride of the Valkyries – Tannhaeser overture – Also Sprach Zarathustra / The unanswered question / Solvejg's song / Hora staccato / The sea named "Solaris". *(re-iss.May82 on 'R.C.A.' lp/c; RL/RK 42652) (cd-iss.Oct91 on 'RCA Victor'; GD 82616)*

Feb 79. (lp/c) *(RL/RK 12885) <2885>* **THE BERMUDA TRIANGLE** [ ] [ ]
– A space ship lands emitting silvery light / Electromagnetic waves descend / A world of different dimensions / The giant pyramid and its ancient people / Venus in a space uniform shining in fluorescent light / Space children in the underground kingdom called Agharta / The Earth – A hollow vessel / The song of Venus / Dawn over the triangle and mysterious electric waves / The dazzling cylinder that crashed in Tunguska, Siberia / The harp of the ancient people with songs of Venus & Space children / The visionary flight to the 1448 nebular group of the Bootes. *(re-iss.1984 on 'R.C.A.' lp/c; PL/PK 82885)*

Jan 80. (7") *(PB 9498)* **RAVEL: BOLERO. / ('A'version)** [ ] [-]
(12"+=) *(PT 9498)* – Space children in the underground kingdom called Agharta.

Jan 80. (7") *<11901>* **BOLERO (LOVE MUSIC). / PAVAN FOR A DEAD PRINCESS** [-] [ ]

Feb 80. (lp/c) *(RL/RK 13412) <3412>* **RAVEL: BOLERO** [ ] [ ]
– Ravel / Daphnis and Chloe: Suite No.2 / Pavan for a dead princess / Bolero / Mother Goose suite. *(cd-iss.Dec84 on 'R.C.A.'; RD 83412)*

Jul 82. (lp/c) *(RS/+K 9005)* **GROFE / GRAND CANYON** [ ] [ ]
– Sunrise / Painted desert / On the trail / Sunset / Cloudburst. *(re-iss.Jul84 on 'R.C.A.'; PL 84317)*

R.C.A. R.C.A.

Aug 84. (lp/c) *(PL/PK 85037)* **SPACE WALK . . . IMPRESSIONS OF AN ASTRONAUT** [ ] [ ]
– Opening the hatch / Leaving the ship / Floating free / Somersaults in Space / The orb of beauty / Get to work / No sound in space / The orderly beauty of Space / Co-ordinated activity / Fantasies of science friction / Thoughts of home / Survival through technology / Unsettling peace / The unanswered question.

Nov 84. (lp/c/cd) *(PL/PK/PD 85184)* **DAWN CHORUS** [ ] [ ]
– Adagio of the sky / Cosmic chorale / Vocalise / Canon of three stars / Dawn chorus / Whistle train / Pegasus / Velax pulsar.

Dec 85. (cd) *(RD 85461)* **THE MIND OF THE UNIVERSE (live at Linz)** [ ] [ ]
– Auszuge aus Werken von Strauss, Holst, Ravel, Beethoven, Stravinsky, Wagner, Prokofiev.

1988. (cd) *(RD 87717)* **BACK TO THE EARTH (live)** [ ] [ ]
– Werke von Bach, Dukas, Mahler, Strauss, Holst, Debussy, Gershwin.

– compilations, etc. –

May 79. (lp) *R.V.C.; (7564-5)* **SOUND CREATURE** [-] [-] Japan

Feb 80. (lp/c) *Red Seal-RCA; (RL/RK 43076)* **TOMITA'S GREATEST HITS** [66] [ ]
(re-iss.Sep81 on 'R.C.A.'; RCA LP/K 3037)

1988. (cd) *R.C.A.; (PD 89381)* **BEST OF TOMITA** [ ] [ ]

TOMORROW

Formed: London, England . . . 1964 as FOUR + ONE, by JOHN 'JUNIOR' WOOD and SIMON 'BOOTS' ALCOT, who soon recruited Dagenham born singer KEITH WEST and drummer KEN LAWRENCE. After covering a ROLLING STONES song for 'Parlophone', they were advised to change their name to the more fashionable, The IN-CROWD (after a Dobie Gray soul number). Their first soul/mod 45 (a Marvin Gaye cover), 'THAT'S HOW STRONG MY LOVE IS', breached the Top 50, although it was pursued by two flops later in 1965 (both included new guitarist, STEVE HOWE). A quiet year followed, until they returned in 1967 complete with new image, new direction, new drummer (TWINK) and new name; TOMORROW. Their first psychedelic single, 'MY WHITE BICYCLE', was surely in the one-that-got-away category, although it did surface six years later as a Top 10 smash for NAZARETH. Another flop 45 surfaced later in the year and was tailed early the next by an eponymous album, although by this time they had missed the psychedelic love boat and the record sunk without trace. The reasons were simple for the public reaction, as KEITH WEST had also released his solo single in the summer of '67. 'EXCERPT FROM A TEENAGE OPERA' (aka 'Grocer Jack') had made him a star overnight when it peaked at No.2. Suddenly requests for KEITH WEST and TOMORROW to tour were so demanding, that they even wanted this 4-piece to play the hit, although it was originally recorded in the studio with a full orchestra! It was inevitable that they would disband after the albums' release. KEITH WEST continued for a short spell as a solo artist, while TWINK joined The PRETTY THINGS and HOWE formed BODAST before joining YES. • **Songwriters:** Group penned except; STRAWBERRY FIELDS FOREVER (Beatles). • **Trivia:** All produced by MARK WRITZ even WEST's poppy solo stuff.

Recommended: TOMORROW (*7)

FOUR + ONE

KEITH WEST – vocals / **JOHN 'JUNIOR' WOOD** – rhythm guitar, vocals / **SIMON ALCOT** – bass / **KEN LAWRENCE** – drums

Parlophone not issued

Jan 65. (7") *(R 5221)* **TIME IS ON MY SIDE. / DON'T LIE TO ME** [ ] [-]

The IN-CROWD

(same line-up & label)

Apr 65. (7") *(R 5276)* **THAT'S HOW STRONG MY LOVE IS. / THINGS SHE SAYS** [48] [-]

— added **STEVE HOWE** – guitar (ex-SYNDICATS), who soon repl. ALCOT

Sep 65. (7") *(R 5328)* **STOP! WAIT A MINUTE. / YOU'RE ON YOUR OWN** [ ] [-]

Nov 65. (7") *(R 5364)* **WHY MUST THEY CRITICIZE? / I DON'T MIND** [ ] [-]

TOMORROW

'TWINK' JOHN ADLER – drums (ex-FAIRIES) repl. LAWRENCE

Parlophone Capitol

May 67. (7") *(R 5597)* **MY WHITE BICYCLE. / CLAREMONT LAKE** [ ] [ ]
(re-iss.Oct69; R 5813)

Sep 67. (7") *(R 5627)* **REVOLUTION. / THREE JOLLY LITTLE DWARFS** [ ] [-]

Feb 68. (lp; mono/stereo) *(PMC/PCS 7042)* **TOMORROW** [ ] [-]
– My white bicycle / Colonel Brown / Real life permanent dream / Shy boy / Claremont Lake / Revolution / The incredible journey of Timothy Chase / Aunty Mary's dress shop / Strawberry fields forever / Three jolly little dwarfs / Now your time has come / Hallucinations. *(re-iss.Jun76 on 'Harvest'; SHSP 2010) (re-iss.Dec86 on 'Decal'; LIK 2) (cd-iss.Sep90 & Feb97 on 'See For Miles'; SEECD 314)*

— Disbanded soon after above. (note: MY WHITE BICYCLE was re-issued in Oct83 by 'Old Gold' label with track by LOVE SCULPTURE on the flip). BODAST were formed by STEVE HOWE who recorded an lp, although this stayed unreleased until 'Cherry Red' records 'THE BODAST TAPES' in 1982; *(BRED 12)*. It is now on cd (May90) with 2 extra tracks as 'THE EARLY YEARS – STEVE HOWE WITH BODAST' on 'C5' lp/cd; *C5/+CD 528)*

AQUARIAN AGE

TWINK + WOOD (same label and arrangement)

May 68. (7") *(R 5700)* **10,000 WORDS IN A CARDBOARD BOX. / GOOD WIZARD MEETS NAUGHTY WIZARD** [ ] [-]

KEITH WEST

Parlophone Capitol

Jul 67. (7") *(R 5623)* **EXCERPT FROM "A TEENAGE OPERA". / Mark Writz Orchestra: THEME FROM "A TEENAGE OPERA"** [2] [ ]

Nov 67. (7") *(R 5651)* **SAM (FROM "A TEENAGE OPERA"). / Mark Writz's Mood Mosaic: THIMBLE FULL OF PUZZLES** [38] [ ]

Jul 68. (7") *(R R 5713)* **ON A SATURDAY. / THE KID WAS A KILLER** [ ] [-]

Deram not issued

Oct 73. (7") *(DM 402)* **RIDING FOR A FALL. / DAYS ABOUT TO RAIN** [ ] [-]

Feb 74. (7") *(DM 410)* **HAVIN' SOMEONE. / KNOW THERE'S NO LIVIN' WITHOUT YOU** [ ] [-]

Kuckuck not issued

Sep 74. (lp) *(2375 023)* **WHEREVER MY LOVE GOES** [-] [-] German

Pink Elephant not issued

Sep 74. (7") *(PE 22868)* **THE POWER AND THE GLORY. / LIET MOTIF** [-] [-] Dutch

– compilations, etc. –

Jun 72. (7") *Parlophone; (R 5957)* **EXCERPT FROM " A TEENAGE OPERA". / SAM** [ ] [-]

Jul 81. (7") *Video; (VID 02)* **EXCERPT FROM "A TEENAGE OPERA". / COUNT ON ME** [ ] [-]

TOMORROW'S GIFT

Formed: Germany . . . ? This female fronted band released their self-titled debut album in 1972, a long-winded double set with typically progressive instrumental solos. The original band split in 1972, although RURUP and KIEFER recruited new members for another album, 'GOODBYE FUTURE' (1973). The KONRAD PLANK-produced album was markedly different in style, incorporating experimental jazz-rock and fusion. After further line-up changes, the band became RELEASE MUSIC ORCHESTRA, cutting a handful of albums for 'Brain' records.

Recommended: TOMORROW'S GIFT (*7)

ELLEN MEYER – vocals / **CARLO KARGES** – guitar, percussion / **MANFRED 'MANNE' RURUP** – keyboards / **WOLFGANG TRESCHER** – flute / **BERND KIEFER** – bass / **GERD PAETZKE** – drums; repl. OLAF CASALICH

Plus / not issued

1972. (d-lp) *(1-2)* **TOMORROW'S GIFT** [-] [-] German
– Riddle in a swamy / Prayin' to Satan / One of the narrow minded thoughts / Tenakel gang / The first seasons after the destruction / How you want to live / Grey aurora / Ants / Breeds there a man / King in a nook / Sandy concert / Enough to write a song about or two / Second song. *(cd-iss.Jun97 on 'Second Battle'; SB 017)*

— **WOLFGANG 'ZABBA' LINDNER** – drums (ex-SPHINX TUSH) repl. GERD, MEYER, TRESCHER + (KARGES; he joined NOVALIS, EXTRABREIT, then NENA)

Aamok-Spiegelei / not issued

1973. (lp) *(28515-5U)* **GOODBYE FUTURE** [-] [-] German
– Jazzi jazzi / Der geiger fliegt vorbei / Allerheilligen / Wienersatz / Naturgemaess / Didden fur dunden.

— above recorded late 1972. Early in '73, they added **ULI TREPTE** – guitar (ex-GURU GURU), but they soon changed their name to . . .

RELEASE MUSIC ORCHESTRA

— **RURUP, KIEFER + LINDNER** brought in **NORBERT JACOBSON** – sax, clarinet; repl. TREPTE

Brain / not issued

1974. (lp) *(1056)* **LIFE** [-] [-] German
– Eroeffnung / Tibba Tibana / Revue in blau / Damaskus / Rot wild / Der traum des Herrn P. / Zemas Rut / Morgengabe.

— **HOLGER DUNKEL** – bass, acoustic guitar; repl. KIEFER

— added **MARGIT MAYA HABERLAND** – percussion, vocals, acoustic guitar / also guest saxophonists **JOHANNES PAPPERT** (of KRAAN) + **JOCHEN PETERSEN** (of IKARUS, of RANDY PIE)

1975. (lp) *(1072)* **GARUDA** [-] [-] German
– Slapstick / Zwischenspiel – Holger / Torso im Sommerwind / Zwischenspiel – Norbert / Rallye Dallye / Zwischenspiel – Manne / Garuda / Zwischenspiel – Margit / Mama Kubu.

— **FRANK FISCHER** – bass; repl. JACOBSEN + DUNKEL

— guests; **MIKE GONG + CARLO KARGES** – guitar

1976. (lp) *(1083)* **GET THE BALL** [-] [-] German
– Mestaloggo / Sundance / Get the ball / Blackbird / Atlantis / Chambre separee.

— **WOLFGANG THIERFELDT** – drums; repl. LINDNER

— **GUNTHER REGER** – sax, clarinet; repl. MARGIT

— added **TOMMY GOLDSCHMIDT** – percussion (ex-KARTHAGO, ex-GURU GURU) + guest **HANS BEHRENDT** – percussion

1978. (lp) *(60.115)* **BEYOND THE LIMIT** [-] [-] German
– Up by the riverside / Madow / Gettin' together / Jungle nights / New morning / Mainstreet joker / Beyond the limit.

1979. (lp) *(60.194)* **NEWS** [-] [-] German
– Catch up / Pat smile / Don / Tai Ming / Sombras / Kymerian ship / Rubber stamp.

— became anonymous once more when they disbanded

TON STEINE SCHERBEN

Formed: Berlin, Germany . . . 1967 as performance group, HOFFMAN'S COMIC THEATER, by RALPH MOEBIUS and RALPH STEITZ. After a one-off single in 1970, the group adopted the TON STEINE SCHERBEN moniker and along with LOKOMOTIVE KREUZBERG, were one of Germany's foremost political rock bands. Courting controversy and gaining a reputation for concerted political agitation, the band's debut lp, 'WARUM GEHT ES MIR SO DRECKIG' (1971), was released amid much anticipation. Hard hitting both lyrically and musically, it established TON STEINE SCHERBEN as one of Germany's first proto-punk bands. They also pre-empted the SEX PISTOLS infamous T.V. appearance by a number of years, when a member of the band's commune wielded an axe in a live studio discussion! After much name changing and line-up altering, the band released the 1972 follow-up, 'KEINE MACHT FUR NIEMAND'. A double set, it was more progressive, featuring instrumental embellishments like flute and bassoon. After yet more line-up changes, the band cut 'WENN DIE NACHT AM TIEFSTEN' (1975), another double which was less politically aggressive. Although they continued to release material throughout the 80's, the early spark wasn't rekindled.

Recommended: WARUM GEHT ES MIR SO DRECKIG? (*6) / KEINE MACHT FUR NIEMAND (*7) / WENN DIE NACHT AM TIEFSTEN (*8)

RALPH MOEBIUS – vocals, guitar, keyboards / **RALPH STEITZ** – guitar / **KAI SICHTERMANN** – bass / **WOLFGANG SEIDEL** – drums

unknown / not issued

1970. (7"; as HOFFMANN'S COMIC THEATER) *(none)* **MACHT KAPUTT WAS EUCH KAPUTT MACHT. / WIR STREIKEN** [-] [-] German

David Volksmund / not issued

Sep 71. (lp) *(008)* **WARUM GEHT ES MIR SO DRECKIG?** [-] [-] German
– Ich will nicht werden was mein alter ist / Warum geht es mir so dreckig / Der kampf geht weiter / Macht kaputt was euch kaputt macht / Sklaven handler / Alles verandertsich / Solidaritaet / Mein name ist Mensch.

— WOLFGANG (aka WOLF SEQUENZA) left at end of 1971, joined CON SCHNITZLER. Others changed names (bar KAI); MOEBIUS to **RIO REISER** and STEITZ to **R.P.S. LANRUE**. They collected a new line-up; **JORG SCHLOTTERER** – flute, bassoon, percussion / **OLAF LITZAU** – drums / **NIKEL PALLAT** – vocals / **JOCHEN PETERSON** – sax

1972. (d-lp) *(TSS 17-L1)* **KEINE MACHT FUR NIEMAND** [-] [-] German
– Wir mussen hier raus / Feierabend / Die letzte schlacht gewinnen wir / Paul Panzers blues / Menschenjaeger / Allein machen sie dich ein / Schritt fur Schritt ins Paradies / Keine macht fur niemand / Der traum ist aus / Mensch Meier / Komm schlaf bei mir / Rauch-Haus song. *(cd-iss.1989 on 'EFA'; EFA 2007)*

— as HOFFMANN's COMIC THEATER & DIE BREMER STADTMUSIKANTEN, they issued 1973 album 'HR FRESSACK' on 'Rothkehlchen' label.

— **KLAUS 'FUNKY' GOTZNER** – drums; repl. LITZAU

— **WERNER GOTZ** – bass, sax; repl. SICHTERMANN

— **VEGAS VON TRANTOR** – percussion; repl. PETERSON

1975. (d-lp) *(L 49)* **WENN DIE NACHT AM TIEFSTEN** [-] [-] German
– Heut' nacht / Samstag nachmittag / Guten morgen / Durch die wuste / Nimm' den hammer / Ich geh' weg / Halt dich an deiner liebe fest / Wir sind im licht / Wenn die nacht am tiefsten / Land in sicht / Komm an Bord / Steig ein.

— In 1976, HOFFMANN'S COMIC THEATER came out with 2 other albums 'TEUFFEL, HAST DU WIND' & 'PARANOIA'.

— next with BRUHWARM; aka DANNY, CORNY & KLAUS

April / not issued

1977. (lp; as BRUHWARM & TON STEINE SCHERBEN) *(0006)* **MANNSTOLL** [-] [-] German
– Mannercharme / Immer wieder ficken / Ich freu' mich schon auf Dienstag / Mittendrin im jugendrausch / Fummelrock / I stand on you / Kommen sie schnell (hallo hallo) / Geistersongs / Boogie anal / Zimt und Schweiss / Wir mussen ja nicht / Ach muder mann / Tango.

Schneeball / not issued

1980. (lp; as BRUHWARM & TON STEINE SCHERBEN) *(0016)* **ENTARTET** [-] [-] German
– Sie ham mir ein gefuhl geklaut / Komm zu mir / Raus / Grete Heiser und zara frustra: Madel, was bist du progressiv / Wann wann wann / Heute blasen wir den marsch / Bisex-boogie / Heterrorist / Shit-hit.

— **REISER, LANRUE, GOTZNER, SICHTERMANN, SCHLOTTERER, SEQUENZA** added **KLAUS VAN VELZEN** – sax (ex-BRUHWARM)

David Volksmund / not issued

1981. (d-lp) *(DVP 001)* **TON STEINE SCHERBEN IV** [-] [-] German
– Morgenlicht / Happy – End / Gold / Ich hab nix / S.N.A.F.T. / Alles ist richtig / Niemand liebt mich / Kribbel krabbel / Da / S' is eben so / Der turm sturzt ein / Bleib wo du bist / Wie in den tagen midians / Sumpf schlock / Jenseits von Eden / Heimweh / Filmkuss / Der fremde aus Indien / Ebbe & Flut / Kleine freuden.

— **MARTIN PAUL** – keyboards; repl. VELZEN, SEQUENZA + SCHLOTTERER

1983. (lp) *(DVP 009)* **SCHERBEN** [-] [-] German
– Wo sind wir jetzt / Verboten / Sternschnuppen / Regentag / Lass uns ein wunder sein / Mama war so / Tanz / Traum ohne stern / La response / Mole hill rockers / Hauab / Fieber / Ardistan / Bist du's.

— added **DIRK SCHLOMER** – guitar + **RICHARD HERTEN** – percussion

1985. (lp) *(DVP 013)* **IN BERLIN '84 (live)** [-] [-] German
– Ich will nicht werden was mein alter ist / Verboten / Feierabend / Heut' nacht / Raus (aus dem ghetto) / Ich will ich sein / Shit-hit / Jenseits von Eden / La response / Keine macht fur niemand.

— above was their last outing on record

– compilations, etc. –

1981. (lp) *Teldec; (6.24606)* **AUSWAHL 1970-1981** [-] [-] German

TONTO'S EXPANDING HEAD BAND

Formed: USA . . .early 70's by ROBERT MARGOULEFF and MALCOLM CECIL. The former had worked on/produced the late 60's debut of LOTHAR & THE HAND PEOPLE. They signed to 'Embryo' (licenced to Atlantic) and squeezed out the cult-to-be 'ZERO TIME'. This impressed STEVIE WONDER, who invited them to play synthesizers on his classic 'Innervisions' album in 1973. This resulted in masses of session work, notably for LITTLE FEAT's equally prestigious 'Dixie Chicken' and ERIC KAZ's 'Cul De Sac'. A second album finally appeared in 1974, but TONTO took off to produce CHRIS RAINBOW's 'Home Of The Brave', BILLY PRESTON's 'It's My Pleasure' and more by STEVE HILLAGE and JOAN BAEZ. Pioneers of melancholy space-rock, their Eastern-influenced ambient music was just the job for astronauts and Indian takeaway delis. • **Songwriters:** MARGOULEFF – CECIL. • **Trivia:** TONTO stands for:- The Original New Tibrel Orchestra.

Recommended: ZERO TIME (*7)

ROBERT MARGOULEFF – Moog synthesizer, voicebox / **MALCOLM CECIL** – Moog synthesizer, voicebox

Atlantic / Embryo

1971. (lp) *(2400 150)* *<SD 732>* **ZERO TIME** [ ] [ ]
– OUTSIDE:- Cybernaut / Jetsex / Timewhys / INSIDE:- Aurora / Riversong / Tama. *(re-iss.1974; K 40251) <US re-iss.1975 on as 'ROBERT MARGOULEFF AND MALCOLM CECIL – TONTO'S EXPANDING HEAD BAND on 'Atlantic'; SD 18123>*

— expanded with **MICHAEL CEMBALO + MARLO HENDERSON** – guitar / **REGGIE McBRIDE** – bass / **STEVE GADD** – drums / **ARMAND HABDURIAN** – percussion

Polydor / not issued

1974. (lp; as TONTO) *(2383 308)* **IT'S ABOUT TIME** [ ] [-]

— split after above.

Viceroy Viceroy

Jan 97. (cd) *(VIN 60362)* **TONTO RIDES AGAIN**

TOUCH

Formed: Portland, Oregon, USA . . . 1968 by former members of DON & THE GOODTIMES; DON GALLUCI, JEFF HAWKS and JOEY NEWMAN. The aforementioned outfit was formed by GALLUCI and as their moniker suggested they were a good-time band, that is, until 1967, when they branched out into more pop psychedelia. The singles of this era, 'I COULD BE SO GOOD TO YOU' and 'HAPPY AND ME' both hit the US Hot 100, with the parent album reaching No.109. TOUCH followed on with a more exploratory psychedelia which fused together avant-garde jazz and progressive-rock. This was much in evidence on the 'DOWN AT CIRCES PLACE' track, which you could find on the 1969'20/20 SOUND' album. HAWKS voice was very strong, reminiscent of TIM BUCKLEY. • **Note:** Not to be confused with another US band from St. Louis, who released very rare material, including an album and a version of The DOORS' 'Light My Fire'.

Recommended: THIS IS TOUCH (*6)

DON AND THE GOODTIMES

DON GALLUCI – keyboards (ex-KINGSMEN) / **BOB HOLDEN** – drums / **DON McKINNEY** – sax, vocals / **PETE OULETTE** – guitar / **DAVE CHILDS** – bass

not issued Wand

1964. (7") *<165>* **TURN ON SONG. / MAKE IT** -

— **JIM VALLEY** – guitar; repl. OULETTE + McKINNEY

1965. (7") *<184>* **STRAIGHT SCEPTRE. / THERE'S SOMETHING ON YOUR MIND** -

not issued Jerden

1965. (7") *<762>* **LITTLE SALLY TEASE. / YOU'LL NEVER WALK ALONE** -

not issued Dunhill

1965. (7") *<4008>* **LITTLE SALLY TEASE. / LITTLE GREEN THING** -

1965. (7") *<4015>* **I'LL BE DOWN FOREVER. / BIG BIG KNIGHT** -

1966. (7") *<4022>* **HEY THERE, MARY MAE. / SWEETS FOR MY SWEET** -

— **CHARLIE COE** – guitar; repl. VALLEY (swopped over from PAUL REVERE & THE RAIDERS)

not issued Jerden

1966. (7") *<805>* **BLUE TURNS TO GREY. / I'M REAL** -

1966. (7") *<808>* **YOU WERE A CHILD. / I HATE TO HATE YOU** -
<re-iss.1966 on 'Piccadilly'; 223>

not issued Wand

1966. (lp) *<WDS 679>* **WHERE THE ACTION IS** -

— **RON OVERMAN** – bass; repl. CHILDS

— **JOEY NEWMAN** – guitar; repl. COE

— added **JEFF HAWKS** – vocals, guitar

Columbia Epic

Jun 67. (7") *(DB 8199) <10145>* **I COULD BE SO NICE TO YOU. / AND IT'S SO GOOD** 56 Apr67

Jul 67. (lp) *<BN 26311>* **SO GOOD** -
– I could be so good to you / The music box / I could never be / Gimme some lovin' / If you lover her, cherish her and such / With a girl like you / My color song / And it's so good / Sweet, sweet, mama / Good day sunshine.

Sep 67. (7") *(DB 8266) <10199>* **HAPPY AND ME. / IF YOU LOVE HER, CHERISH HER AND SUCH** 98 Jul67

Nov 67. (7") *<10241>* **SALLY! (STUDIO A AT 6 O'CLOCK IN THE MORNING). / BAMBII** -

Feb 68. (7") *<10280>* **MAY MY HEART BE CAST INTO STONE. / BALL OF FIRE** -

not issued Burdette

1968. (7") *<3>* **COLORS OF LIFE. / YOU DID IT BEFORE** -

— they virtually into . . .

TOUCH

GALLUCI, HAWKS + NEWMAN enlisted **BRUCE HAUSER** – bass, vocals / **JOHN BORDONARO** – drums, vocals

Deram Coliseum

Mar 69. (7") *(DM 243) <2712>* **MISS TEACH. / WE FEEL FREE**

Mar 69. (lp; mono/stereo) *(DML/SML 1033)* **THIS IS TOUCH** <US-title'20/20 SOUND'>
– We feel fine / Friendly birds / Miis Teach / Spiritual death of Howard Greer / Down at Circes places / Alesha and others / Seventy-five.

— when they split GALLUCI became house producer for 'Elektra' and was last seen in the real estate business. HAWKS and HAUSER formed STEPSON and later in 1974 teamed back up with NEWMAN in BLUE MOUNTAIN EAGLE.

– compilations, etc. –

1968. (lp; by DON AND THE GOODTIMES) *Burdette; <300>* **GREATEST HITS** -

1982. (lp; by DON AND THE GOODTIMES) *Piccadilly; <3394>* **GOODTIME MUSIC** -

TRACTOR

Formed: England . . . early 70's as The WAY WE LIVE by JIM MILNE and STEVE CLAYTON. Another to gain a deal with Radio One DJ, John Peel, on his newly founded label, 'Dandelion'. In 1971, they released 'A CANDLE FOR JUDITH', which later became a rare collector's piece, as did their similarly PINK FLOYD-inspired follow-up. This came out under the new heavy name of TRACTOR, when they signed to 'Polydor' in 1972 (listeners were surprised when they discovered TRACTOR were not a larger band). However, with loads of other progressive outfits around at the time, they were overlooked. • **Songwriters:** MILNE – CLAYTON.

Recommended: A CANDLE FOR JUDITH (*7) / TRACTOR (*7)

JIM MILNE – vocals, guitar, multi / **STEVE CLAYTON** – percussion, drums / with **DAVE ADDISON** – bass

Dandelion Warners

Jan 71. (lp; as THE WAY WE LIVE) *(DAN 8004) <49004>* **A CANDLE FOR JUDITH**
– King Dick II / Squares / Seiderial / Angle / Storm / Willow / Madrigal / The way ahead.

— later in 1971, The WAY WE LIVE backed Leeds folk artist BEAU on his 'CREATION' lp, also on 'Dandelion'; *DAN 8006)*

Polydor not issued

Mar 72. (7") *(2001 282)* **STONE GLORY. / MARIE / AS YOU SAY** -

1972. (lp) *(2310 217)* **TRACTOR** -
– All ends up / Little girl in yellow / The watcher / Ravencroft's 13 bar boogie:- Shubunkin – Hope in favour – Everytime it happens / Make the journey. *(re-iss.Jul83 on 'Thunderbolt'; THBL 002)*

— split in 1972, although JIM MILNE later retained group name

UK not issued

Mar 75. (7") *(UK 93)* **ROLL THE DICE. / VICIOUS CIRCLE** -

Polydor not issued

Nov 77. (7"; as JIM MILNE & TRACTOR) *(2058 942)* **NO MORE ROCK & ROLL. / NORTHERN CITY** -
(re-iss.1981 as TRACTOR on 'Cargo'; CRS 002)

Birds Nest not issued

Aug 79. (7"; by JIM MILNE) *(BN 122)* **WHO AM I. / TRICK OF THE LIGHT** -

Roach not issued

Oct 81. (7") *(RR 2)* **AVERAGE MAN'S HERO. / BIG BIG BOY** -

– compilations, etc. –

Nov 94. (cd) *See For Miles; (SEECD 409)* **A CANDLE FOR JUDITH / TRACTOR** -

Jul 95. (cd) *Ozit; (OZITCD 00019)* **WORST ENEMIES** -
– Lost on the ocean / Average man's hero / Suicidal / Argument for one / Word games / Trick of the light / Scotch boulevard / No more rock'n'roll / Peterloo. *(re-iss.Jun97; same)*

TRAFFIC

Formed: based Midlands, England . . . April '67, by STEVE WINWOOD, DAVE MASON, JIM CAPALDI and CHRIS WOOD. Initially, TRAFFIC purveyed musically accomplished, thinking man's psychedelia, debuting with the yearning 'PAPER SUN' (1967) single after signing to 'Island'. Utilising MASON's lilting, sitar-like guitar playing, the record perfectly anticipated the mood of the times and duly hit the Top 5. Dippy but delightful, the follow-up, 'HOLE IN MY SHOE' (1967) (later covered with great affection by NIGEL PLANER aka 'NEIL' of 'Young Ones' comedy fame) hit No.2 and after their third Top 10 hit in a row, 'HERE WE GO ROUND THE MULBERRY BUSH' (from the film of the same name), the band released their debut album, 'MR FANTASY' (1967). The record was a well crafted melting pot of ideas and genres put through the psychedelic blender and given a soulful reading by WINWOOD's wholesome vocal chords. The conspicuous absence of any of the previous hit singles, however, signalled that, as was the wont of group in those serious muso days, TRAFFIC wished to be considered an 'Albums' band. Around this time, MASON split, only to return another six months later whence the band fashioned their second album, 'TRAFFIC' (1968), a marked progression that highlighted the band's instrumental dexterity and flowering songwriting talent. Once again, MASON came up with one of the record's most memorable tunes, 'FEELIN' ALRIGHT', later covered by JOE COCKER amongst others. The ever dependable MASON upped sticks and left once more during the recording of TRAFFIC's third album, 'LAST EXIT' (1969). Aptly titled, this careless rag-bag of below par live and studio tracks did indeed mark the end of MASON's time with the band (save for a brief spell of live work in the early 70's), in fact the end of the band itself, for the time being at least. After a spell in short-lived 'supergroup', BLIND FAITH, WINWOOD went in to the studio to commence the recording of a mooted solo album with a working title of 'MAD SHADOWS'. When WOOD and CAPALDI were drafted in for work on the sessions, the project became a fully fledged TRAFFIC concern. The resulting album, re-titled 'JOHN BARLEYCORN MUST DIE' (1970) was a triumphant return to form, mixing up folk, R&B and jazz into a prog-rock classic. In the year or so before their next album, the band recruited bassist RICK GRECH (ex-FAMILY/BLIND FAITH), African percussionist REEBOP KWAKU-BAAH, drummer JIM GORDON (ex-DEREK AND THE DOMINOES) and their old mucker DAVE MASON. 'WELCOME TO THE CANTEEN' (1971) was fairly heavy going but no less self-indulgent than your average early 70's live effort, while the next studio outing, 'THE LOW SPARK OF HIGH HEELED BOYS' (1971) saw the band add to their not inconsiderable studio accomplishments despite the cringe-inducing title. DAVID HOOD and ROGER HAWKINS (both of whom had played on CAPALDI's solo project, 'OH HOW WE DANCED') replaced GRECH and GORDON for 1973's 'SHOOT OUT AT THE FANTASY FACTORY'. The 'Muscle

Shoals' veterans had tightened up the rhythm section considerably, cutting it on stage and in the studio, as evidenced by the best live album of TRAFFIC's career, 'ON THE ROAD' (1973). By 1974's 'WHEN THE EAGLE FLIES', TRAFFIC were beginning to sound congested, finally stalling the following year. CAPALDI and WINWOOD both went on to successful solo careers, resurrecting TRAFFIC briefly in 1994. WINWOOD's output, in particular was undeniable coffee table rock at its shiniest, though surprisingly, he was given top billing at the 1997 Glastonbury festival. In the event he didn't show, apparently due to illness, his place taken by KULA SHAKER. • **Songwriters:** Individually or group compositions, except GIMME SOME LOVIN' (Spencer Davis Group). CAPALDI covered LOVE HURTS (Everly Brothers).

Recommended: MR FANTASY (*6) / TRAFFIC (*7) / LAST EXIT (*5) / JOHN BARLEYCORN MUST DIE (*7) / WELCOME TO THE CANTEEN (*5) / THE LOW SPARK OF THE HIGH HELED BOYS (*6) / SHOOT OUT AT THE FANTASY FACTORY (*6) / ON THE ROAD (*6) / SMILING PHASES (*8)

STEVE WINWOOD (b.12 May'48, Birmingham, England) – vocals, keyboards (ex-SPENCER DAVIS GROUP) / **DAVE MASON** (b.10 May'47, Worcester, England) – guitar, vocals (ex-HELLIONS) / **JIM CAPALDI** (b.24 Aug'44, Evesham, England) – drums, vocals (ex-HELLIONS) / **CHRIS WOOD** (b.24 Jun'44, Birmingham) – flute, sax (ex-SOUNDS OF BLUE)

Island / U.A.

May 67. (7") *(WIP 6002)* <50195> **PAPER SUN. / GIVING TO YOU** [5] [94] Aug67

Aug 67. (7") *(WIP 6017)* <50218> **HOLE IN MY SHOE. / SMILING PHASES** [2] [ ]

Nov 67. (7") *(WIP 6025)* <50232> **HERE WE GO ROUND THE MULBERRY BUSH. / COLOURED RAIN** [8] [ ]

Dec 67. (lp; mono/stereo) *(ILP/+S 9061)* <6651> **MR. FANTASY** [8] [88] Apr68
– Heaven is in your mind / Berkshire poppies / House for everyone / No name, no face, no number / Dear Mr. Fantasy / Dealer / Utterly simple / Coloured rain / Hope I never find me there / Giving to you. <*US version* +=)– Paper sun / Hole in my shoe. *(re-iss.1970; same) (re-iss.Feb87 lp/c; ILPM/ICM 9061) (cd-iss.Nov87; CID 9061) (cd re-iss.Sep89; IMCD 43) (US version-iss.Aug92; 3DCID 1003)*

Feb 68. (7") *(WIP 6030)* **NO NAME, NO FACE, NO NUMBER. / ROAMIN' IN THE GLOAMIN' WITH 40,000 HEADMEN** [40] [-]

Feb 68. (7") <50261> **NO NAME, NO FACE, NO NUMBER. / HEAVEN IS IN YOUR MIND** [-] [ ]

Sep 68. (7") *(WIP 6041)* <50460> **FEELIN' ALRIGHT. / WITHERING TREE** [ ] [ ]

Oct 68. (lp; mono/stereo) *(ILPS 9081/+T)* <6676> **TRAFFIC** [9] [17]
– You can all join in / Pearly queen / Don't be sad / Who knows what tomorrow may bring / Feelin' alright / Vagabond virgin / Forty thousand headmen / Cryin' to be heard / No time to live / Means to an end. *(re-iss.Feb87 lp/c; ILPM/ICM 9081) (cd-iss.Nov87; CID 9081) (cd re-iss.Sep89; IMCD 45)*

Dec 68. (7") *(WIP 6050)* **MEDICATED GOO. / SHANGHAI NOODLE FACTORY** [ ] [-]

Jan 69. (7") <50500> **MEDICATED GOO. / PEARLY QUEEN** [-] [ ]

— Below album was recorded before their split late 1968.

May 69. (lp; mono/stereo) *(ILP/+S 9097)* <6702> **LAST EXIT (some live)** [ ] [19]
– Just for you / Shanghai noodle factory / Something's got a hold of my toe / Withering tree / Medicated goo / Feelin' good / Blind man. *(cd-iss.May88; CID 9097) (cd re-iss.Sep89; IMCD 41)*

Oct 69. (lp; mono/stereo) *(ILP/+S 9112)* <5500> **THE BEST OF TRAFFIC** (compilation) [ ] [48]
– Paper Sun / Heaven is in your mind / No face, no name, no number / Coloured rain / Smiling phases / Hole in my shoe / Medicated goo / Forty thousand headmen / Feelin' alright / Shanghai noodle factory / Dear Mr. Fantasy. *(cd-iss.Mar93; IMCD 169)*

— In 1969, WINWOOD formed BLIND FAITH with ERIC CLAPTON and GINGER BAKER. WOOD also joined the latter's group AIRFORCE. WOOD, MASON and CAPALDI then formed WOODEN FROG. DAVE MASON went solo as TRAFFIC re-formed as a trio.

Jul 70. (lp) *(ILPS 9116)* <5504> **JOHN BARLEYCORN MUST DIE** [5] [11]
– Glad / Freedom rider / Empty pages / Stranger to himself / John Barleycorn / Every mother's son. *(re-iss.Sep86 lp/c/cd; ILPM/ICM/CID 9116) (cd-iss.Sep89; IMCD 40)*

Aug 70. (7") <50692> **EMPTY PAGES. / STRANGER TO HIMSELF** [-] [74]

— added **RIC GRECH** (b. 1 Nov'46) – bass (ex-FAMILY, ex-BLIND FAITH, ex-GINGER BAKER'S AIRFORCE) / **REEBOP KWAKU-BAAH** (b. Konongo, Ghana) – percussion (ex-GINGER BAKER'S AIRFORCE) / **JIM GORDON** – drums (ex-DEREK & THE DOMINOES) / **DAVE MASON** guested on some live.

Sep 71. (lp) *(ILPS 9166)* <5550> **WELCOME TO THE CANTEEN (live)** [ ] [26]
– Medicated goo / Sad and deep as you / Forty thousand headmen / Shouldn't have took more than you gave / Dear Mr. Fantasy / Gimme some lovin'. *(cd-iss.May88; CID 9166) (cd re-iss.Sep89; IMCD 39)*

Oct 71. (7") <50841> **GIMME SOME LOVIN'. / (part 2)** [-] [68]

Island / Island

Dec 71. (lp/c) *(ILPS.ZCI 9180)* <9306> **THE LOW SPARK OF THE HIGH HEELED BOYS** [ ] [7]
– Hidden treasure / The low spark of the high heeled boys / Rock & roll stew / Many a mile to freedom / Light up or leave me alone / Rainmaker. *(re-iss.Sep86 lp/c; ILPM/ICM 9180) (cd-iss.Nov87; CID 9180) (cd re-iss.Sep89; IMCD 42)*

Jan 72. (7") <1201> **ROCK & ROLL STEW. / (part 2)** [-] [93]

— **DAVID HOOD** – bass + ROGER HAWKINS – drums (both of JIM CAPALDI band) repl. JIM GORDON and GRECH. (The latter formed KGB)

Feb 73. (lp/c) *(ILPS/ZCI 9224)* <9323> **SHOOT OUT AT THE FANTASY FACTORY** [ ] [6]
– Shoot out at the fantasy factory / Roll right stone / Evening blue / ragic magic / Uninspired (sometimes I feel so). *(cd-iss.May88; CID 9224) (cd re-iss.Sep89; IMCD 44)*

— added **BARRY BECKETT** – keyboards

Oct 73. (d-lp)(d-c) *(ILSD 2)(ZCID 102)* <9336> **ON THE ROAD (live)** [40] [29]
– Glad / Freedom rider / Tragic magic / (Sometimes I feel so) Uninspired / Shoot out at the fantasy factory / Light up or leave me alone / The low spark of the high heeled boys. *(cd-iss.Jun88; CIDD 2) (cd re-iss.Aug91 & Apr94; IMCD 183)*

Dec 73. (7") <50883> **GLAD. / (part 2)** [-] [ ]

— **WINWOOD, CAPALDI & WOOD** enlisted **ROSKO GEE** – bass (ex-GONZALES)

Island / Asylum

Sep 74. (lp/c) *(ILPS/ZCI 9273)* <7E 1020> **WHEN THE EAGLE FLIES** [31] [9]
– Walking in the wind / Something new / Dream Gerrard / Memories of a rock'n'roller / When the eagle flies / Graveyard people / Love. *(cd-iss.Jun88; CID 9273) (re-iss.Aug91 cd)(c; IMCD 142)(ICM 9273)*

Oct 74. (7") *(WIP 6207)* **WALKING IN THE WIND. / WALKING IN THE WIND (instrumental)** [ ] [ ]

— Disbanded early 1975. STEVE WINWOOD went solo, also collaborating with STOMU YAMASHTA. WOOD and GEE took up session work. On 12 Jul'83, CHRIS WOOD died of liver failure. JIM CAPALDI continued his solo career

— (see GREAT ROCK DISCOGRAPHY)

– compilations, etc. –

— on 'Island' unless stated otherwise

May 74. (7") **HOLE IN MY SHOE. / HERE WE GO ROUND THE MULBERRY BUSH** [-] [ ]

May 75. (lp) *United Artists;* <4211> **HEAVY TRAFFIC** [-] [ ]

Sep 75. (lp) *United Artists;* <LA 526> **MORE HEAVY TRAFFIC** [-] [ ]

Mar 78. (7"ep,7"pic-d-ep) *(IEP 7)* **EXTENDED PLAY** [ ] [-]
– I'm a man / Hole in my shoe / Gimme some lovin' / No name, no face, no number.

Jun 92. (d-cd) *(IMCD 158)* **SMILING PHASES** [ ] [-]
– Paper sun / Hole in my shoe / Smiling phases / Heaven is in your mind / Coloured rain / No face, no name, no number / Here we go round the mulbury bush / Dear Mr. Fantasy / You can all join in / Feelin' alright / Pearly queen / Forty thousand headmen / Vagabond virgin / Shanghai noodle factory / Withering tree / Medicated goo / Glad / Freedom rider / Empty pages / John Barleycorn / The low spark of the high heeled boys / Light up or leave me alone / Rock & roll stew / Shoot out at the fantasy factory / Walking in the wind / When the eagle flies.

TRAFFIC

— **WINWOOD + CAPALDI** re-formed for studio.

Virgin / Virgin

May 94. (cd/c) *(CD/TC V 2727)* **FAR FROM HOME** [29] [ ]
– Riding high / Here comes a man / Far from home / Nowhere is their freedom / Holy ground / Some kinda woman / Every night, every day / This train won't stop / State of grace / Mosambique.

May 94. (7"/c-s) *(VS/+C 1494)* **HERE COMES A MAN. / GLAD (live)** [ ] [ ]
(cd-s+=) *(VSCDG 1494)* – ('A'mix).

Sep 94. (c-s) *(VSC 1506)* **SOME KINDA WOMAN. / FORTY THOUSAND HEADMEN (live)** [ ] [ ]
(cd-s+=) *(VSCDX 1506)* – Low spark of high heeled boys (live)/ ('A'mix).

TRASHMEN

Formed: Minneapolis / St.Paul , Minnesota, USA . . . 1962 by quartet; DAL WINSLOW, TONY ANDREASON, BOB REED and STEVE WAHRER. They quickly grew into an in-demand live act on the local circuit and soon signed to the 'Garrett' label in 1963. At the end of the year, they set free 'SURFIN' BIRD', probably the first ever garage-rock track, which, with its growling vox and driving surf-beat, hit the US Top 5. It borrowed very heavily from soul/doo-wop outfit The RIVINGTONS 'PAPA-OOM-MOW-MOW' and 'THE BIRD'S THE WORD', becoming a novelty hit after its successor 'BIRD DANCE BEAT', also hit the Top 30. However, the formula became too derivative for many and a lost legal battle over the song rights with The RIVINGTONS, led to a quick demise. Their top song has been rehashed (or re-trashed some might say) by many, the best being The CRAMPS' version under the title, 'SURFIN' BIRD (THE BIRD'S THE WORD)'.

Recommended: SURFIN' BIRD (*5)

DAL WINSLOW (b. 1942) – vocals, guitar / **TONY ANDREASON** (b. 1943) – guitar / **BOB REED** (b. 1942) – bass / **STEVE WAHRER** (b. 1942) – drums

Stateside / Garrett

Jan 64. (7") *(SS 255)* <4002> **SURFIN' BIRD. / KING OF THE SURF** [ ] [4] Nov63

Feb 64. (lp) <*LP-GAS 200*> **SURFIN' BIRD** [-] [48]
– Surfin' bird / Misirlou / Money / Tube city / Kuk / It's so easy / King of the surf / Henrietta / Malaguena / My Woodie / Bird bath / The sleeper. *(UK-iss.Nov87 on 'Soma'; same)*

Mar 64. (7") *(SS 276)* <4003> **BIRD DANCE BEAT. / BONE** [ ] [30] Jan64

1964. (7") <4005> **BAD NEWS. / ON THE MOVE** [-] [ ]

1964. (7") <4010> **PEPPERMINT MAN. / NEW GENERATION** [-] [ ]

1964. (7") <4012> **WHOA DAD. / WALKIN' MY BABY** [-] [ ]

not issued / Argo

1965. (7") <5516> **BIRD '65. / UBANGI STOMP** [-] [ ]

— recorded a single in 1965 for 'Tribe' US (unknown)

not issued / Bear

1966. (7") <1966> **KEEP YOUR HANDS OFF MY BABY. / LOST ANGEL** [-] [ ]

— split in 1967. WAHRER died of throat cancer on 21st Jan'89.

– compilations, etc. –

Jul 88. (lp) *Garrett;* <300> **20 BIGGEST HITS** [-] [ ]

Jan 94. (cd) *Sundazed; (CDSC 11006)* **LIVE BIRD 1965-1967 (live)** [ ] [-]

T.REX (see under ⇒ BOLAN, Marc)

TRITONUS

Formed: Germany . . . 1974 by PETER K. SEILER together with RONALD BRAND and CHARLIE JOST. Coming from a classical background, SEILER attempted to create symphonic rock in the mould of such English exponents as ELP. The 1975 self-titled debut album was competent although the follow-up, 'BETWEEN THE UNIVERSE' (1976) was generally more accomplished with sharper songwriting and arrangements. TRITONUS split in 1978 as SEILER began to devote most of his time to collaborations with other musicians.

Recommended: TRITONUS (*5) / BETWEEN THE UNIVERSE (*7)

PETER K. SEILER – organ, piano, synthesizer / **RONALD BRAND** – bass, vocals, guitar / **CHARLIE JOST** – drums, percussion

BASF | not issued

1975. (lp) *(17.22384-1)* **TRITONUS** [-] [-] German
– Escape and no way out / Sunday waltz / Lady Madonna / Far in the sky / Gliding / Lady Turk.

—— **BERNHARD SCHUH** – drums, percussion; repl. JOST

—— added guest **GEFF HARRISON** – vocals (ex-TWENTY SIXTY SIX AND THEN, ex-KING PING MEH)

1976. (lp) *(CC 229467)* **BETWEEN THE UNIVERSE** [-] [-] German
– Between the universe / Mars detection / The day awakes / The day works / The day rests.

—— they split in 1978, when SEILER was working with MICHAEL BUNDT (ex-NINE DAYS' WONDER). He re-surfaced as a new-age synthesist in the 80's

TRIUMVIRAT

Formed: Germany . . . early 70's by JURGEN FRITZ, together with DICK FRANGENBERG and HANS BATHELT. HANS PAPE joined the following year and played on the debut album, 'MEDITERRANEAN TALES' (1972). The album was dominated by symphonic keys and although the arrangements were somewhat elaborate, the sound was fairly accessible. So accessible, in fact, that the band's follow-up, the appallingly titled 'ILLUSIONS ON A DOUBLE DIMPLE' (1974) entered the American charts. 'SPARTACUS' (1975) was similarly successful in the States, breaching the Top 30 and marking a creative peak for the band. Subsequent albums such as 'OLD LOVES DIE HARD' (1976) and 'POMPEII' (1977) became increasingly easy listening in style amid constantly changing line-ups. Falling out of favour with their original fan base, the band split soon after 1980's 'RUSSIAN ROULETTE'.

Recommended: SPARTACUS (*6)

JURGEN FRITZ – keyboards, synthesizers, percussion, vocals / **HANS PAPE** – bass, vocals / **HELMET KOLLEN** – guitar, vocals / **HANS BATHELT** – drums, percussion

Harvest | Capitol

Nov 72. (lp) *(062-29441)* **MEDITERRANEAN TALES** [-] [-] German
– Across the waters / Overture / Taxident / Mind tripper / 5 o'clock tea / Satan's breakfast / Underture / Eleven kids / E minor 5-9 minor 5 / Broken mirror.

—— although HANS PAPE featured on below, he had actually departed. Below featured choir; ULLA WIESNER, BRIGETTE THOMAS + HANNA DOLITZSCH

Oct 74. (lp) *(SHSP 4030)* *<11311>* **ILLUSIONS ON A DOUBLE DIMPLE** [ ] [55] Jul74
– Illusions on a double dimple: Flashback – Schooldays – Triangle – Illusions – Dimplicity – Last dance / Mister ten per cent: Maze – Dawning – Bad deal – Roundabout – Lucky girl – Million dollars.

Jul 75. (lp) *(SHSP 4048)* *<11392>* **SPARTACUS** [ ] [27] May75
– The capitol of power / The school of instant pain: Proclamation – The gladiator's song – Roman entertainment – The battle / The walls of doom / The deadly dream of freedom / The hazy shades of dawn / The burning sword of Capua / The sweetest sound of liberty / The march to the eternal city: Dusty road – Italian improvisation – First success – The superior force of Rome – A broken dream – Finale.

Jul 75. (7") *<3947>* **DIMPLICITY. / MILLION DOLLARS** [-] [ ]

—— **BARRY PALMER** – vocals + **DICK FRANGENBERG** – bass, repl. KOLLEN

Aug 76. (lp) *<11551>* **OLD LOVES DIE HARD** [-] [85]
– I believe / A day in the life / The history of mystery (part 1 & 2) / A cold worried old lady / Panic on 5th Avenue / Old lovers die hard.

—— **DIETER PETEREIT** – bass, repl. FRANGENBERG

—— **CURT CRESS** – drums, percussion, repl. BATHELT

Nov 77. (lp) *<11697>* **POMPEII** [-] [ ]
– The earthquake / Journey of a fallen angel / Viva Pompeii / The time of your life / The rich man & the carpenter / Dance on the volcano / Vesuvius / The hymn.

—— **FRITZ** added **DAVID HANSELMAN** – vocals / **WOLFGANG MAUS** + **ED CARTER** – vocals / **JURGEN FRITZ** – keyboards / **WERNER KOPAL** – bass / **MATTHIAS HOLTMANN** – drums / **MALANDO GASSAMA** – percussion

Nov 78. (lp) *<11862>* **A LA CARTE** [-] [ ]
– Waterfall / Late again / Jo Ann Walker / For you / I don't even know your name / A Bavarian in New York / Original soundtrack / Darlin' / Good-bye.

Jan 79. (7") *<4700>* **WATERFALL. / JO ANN WALKER** [-] [ ]

—— **FRITZ** again with new line-up; **ARNO STEFFEN** – vocals / **TIM MAY** – guitar / **STEVE LUKATHER** – bass, guitar (of TOTO) / **JEFF PORCARO** – drums (of TOTO) / **NEAL STUBENHAUS** – bass / **ALAN ESTES** – percussion / **MIKE GONG** – guitar / **DAVID HUNGATE** – bass / **PETE CHRISTLIEB** – sax / **ROBERT GREENIDGE** – steel drums

Jan 80. (lp) *(064-45834)* **RUSSIAN ROULETTE** [-] [-] German
– Party life / You can't catch me / Games / Cooler / The ballad of Rudy Torner / We're rich on what we've got / Twice / Rien ne vas plus / Roxy / Russian roulette.

—— split soon after above

TROGGS

Formed: Andover, Hampshire, England . . . 1964 briefly as The TROGLODYTES, by REG BALL (PRESLEY), CHRIS BRITTON, PETE STAPLES and RONNIE BOND. In 1965, they were signed by KINKS manager, Larry Page, who leased them to 'C.B.S.' in early '66 for the debut single, 'LOST GIRL'. Their second 45, 'WILD THING', with TV exposure on 'Thank Your Lucky Stars', gave them a No.2 hit, which also went on to become a US No.1. This primal three-chord assault carried on where 'LOUIE LOUIE' left off, the band taking on American garage-rock in a bizarre inversion of the British invasion. It has since become one of the most covered songs ever, a blueprint for almost any band with a guitar and an amp that went up to 11. They then went No.1 with the harmony-laden, 'WITH A GIRL LIKE YOU', which again featured PRESLEY's grizzled drawl of a vocal. Their next single, 'I CAN'T CONTROL MYSELF', gave them their third consecutive Top 3 hit, closely followed by another CHIP TAYLOR-penned song (like 'WILD THING'), 'ANY WAY THAT YOU WANT ME'. They continued in their bid for chart domination with a further string of Top 50 hits, the band's sound rapidly evolving with the onset of psychedelia. One of the aforementioned 45's, 'LOVE IS ALL AROUND', became an even bigger smash in 1994, when Scots popsters WET WET WET took it to the top for several weeks. This subsequently furnished PRESLEY with enough money to indulge his crop circle obsession. Previously in 1990, The TROGGS' profile was raised somewhat, through a collaboration with R.E.M. on an album, 'AU' (this also featured 'LOVE IS ALL AROUND'). • **Songwriters:** PRESLEY was the main writer, except HI HI HAZEL (Geno Washington) / GOOD VIBRATIONS (Beach Boys) / I CAN'T GET NO SATISFACTION (Rolling Stones) / THE KITTY CAT SONG (Hal Roach-Allen Toussaint) / RIDE YOUR PONY (Aaron Neville) / EVIL (. . . Singleton) / LOUIE LOUIE (Richard Berry) / JAGUAR AND THUNDERBIRD + MEMPHIS + NO PARTICULAR PLACE TO GO (Chuck Berry) / GOT LOVE IF YOU WANT IT (Slim Harpo) / WALKING THE DOG (Rufus Thomas) / etc. • **Trivia:** Their 1990's reformation included collaborations with R.E.M. on single 'Nowhere Road'.

Recommended: BEST OF THE TROGGS (*7)

REG BALL (b.12 Jun'43; became REG PRESLEY after hit) – vocals, ocamna / **CHRIS BRITTON** (b.21 Jun'45, Watford, England) – guitar repl. TONY MANSFIELD / **PETE STAPLES** (b. 3 May'44) – bass (ex-TEN FOOT FIVE) repl. DAVID WRIGHT / **RONNIE BOND** (b. 4 May'43) – drums

C.B.S. | not issued

Feb 66. (7") *(202038)* **LOST GIRL. / THE YELLA IN ME** [ ] [-]

Fontana | Fontana

Apr 66. (7") *(TF 689)* *<1548>* **WILD THING. / FROM HOME** [2] [1] Jun66
<above & below 'A' was also double 'A'side on 'Atco'; 6415>

Jul 66. (7") *(TF 717)* *<1552>* **WITH A GIRL LIKE YOU. / I WANT YOU** [1] [29]

Jul 66. (lp; stereo/mono) *(S+/TL 5355)* **FROM NOWHERE . . . THE TROGGS** [6] [-]
– Wild thing / The kitty cat song / Ride your pony / Hi hi Hazel / I just sing / Evil / The yella in me / With a girl like you / Our love will still be there / Louie Louie / Jingle jangle / When I'm with you / From home / Jaguar and Thunderbird / I can't control myself / Night of the long grass. *(cd-iss.1989; 832957-2)*

Aug 66. (lp) *<67556><Atco; SD 33193>* **WILD THING** [-] [52]
– Wild thing / From home / Just sing / Hi hi Hazel / Lost girl / Evil / With a girl like you / I want you / Your love / Our love will be there.

Page One | Atco

Sep 66. (7") *(POF 001)* *<6444>* **I CAN'T CONTROL MYSELF. / GONNA MAKE YOU MINE** [2] [43]
<also on US 'Fontana'; 1557>

Page One | Fontana

Dec 66. (7") *(POF 010)* *<1585>* **ANY WAY THAT YOU WANT ME. / 6-5-4-3-2-1** [8] [ ] Apr67

Feb 67. (7") *(POF 015)* *<1576>* **GIVE IT TO ME. / YOU'RE LYIN'** [12] [ ]

Feb 67. (lp) *(POL 001)* **TROGGLODYNAMITE** [10] [-]
– I can only give you everything / Last summer / Meet Jacqueline / Oh no / It's too late / No.10 Downing Street / Mona / I want you to come into my life / Let me tell you babe / Little Queenie / Cousin Jane / You can't beat it / Baby come closer / It's over.

May 67. (7") *(POF 022)* *<1593>* **NIGHT OF THE LONG GRASS. / GIRL IN BLACK** [17] [ ] Jun67

Jul 67. (lp) *(FOR 001)* **BEST OF THE TROGGS** (compilation) [24] [-]
– Night of the long grass / Gonna make you / Anyway that you want me / 6-5-4-3-2-1 / I want you / With a girl like you / I can't control myself / Girl in black / Give it to me / You're lying / From home / Wild thing. *(re-iss. Feb85 on 'Rhino'+ 1988 on 'Bigtime')*

Jul 67. (7") *(POF 030)* **HI HI HAZEL. / AS I RIDE BY** [42] [-]

Oct 67. (7") *(POF 040)* *<1607>* **LOVE IS ALL AROUND. / WHEN WILL THE RAIN COME** [5] [7] Feb68

Dec 67. (lp; mono/stereo) *(POL/S 003)* **CELLOPHANE** [ ] [-]
– Little red donkey / Too much of a good thing / Butterflies and bees / All of my time / Seventeen / Somewhere my girl is waiting / It's showing / Her emotion / When will the rain come / My lady / Come the day / Love is all around.

Feb 68. (7") *(POF 056)* **LITTLE GIRL. / MAYBE THE MADMEN** [37] [-]

May 68. (7") *(POF 064)* **SURPRISE SURPRISE. / MARBLES AND SOME GUM?** [ ] [-]

May 68. (lp) *<67576>* **LOVE IS ALL AROUND** [-] [ ]
– Love is all around / Night of the long grass / Gonna make you / Anyway that you want me / 6-5-4-3-2-1 / When will the rain come / Little girl / I can't control myself / Girl in black / Give it to me / Cousin Jane.

Aug 68. (7") *(POF 082)* *<1622>* **YOU CAN CRY IF YOU WANT TO. / THERE'S SOMETHING ABOUT YOU** [ ] [ ]

Sep 68. (7") *<1630>* **SURPRISE SURPRISE. / COUSIN JANE** [-] [ ]

Oct 68. (7") *(POF 092)* *<1634>* **HIP HIP HOORAY. / SAY DARLIN'!** [ ] [ ]

Dec 68. (lp) *(POLS 012)* **MIXED BAG** [ ] [-]

Page One | Page One

Jan 69. (7") *(POF 114)* **EVIL WOMAN. / SWEET MADELAINE** [ ] [-]

Jan 69. (lp) *(FOR 007)* **BEST OF THE TROGGS VOL.II** (compilation) [ ] [-]
– I can only give you everything / Meet Jacqueline / Jingle jangle / I want you to come into my life / Cousin Jane / Louie Louie / Love is all around / From home / Jaguar and the thunderbird / Hi hi Hazel / Mona.

Feb 69. (7") *<21026>* **EVIL WOMAN. / HEADS OR TAILS** -

— Split Mar'69.

Mar 69. (7"; by RONNIE BOND) *(POF 123)* **ANYTHING FOR YOU. / CAROLYN** -

Apr 69. (7"; by REG PRESLEY) *(POF 131)* **LUCINDA LEE. / WICHITA LINEMAN** -

— CHRIS BRITTON also issued solo album 'AS I AM' in 1969.

— The TROGGS re-formed. **TONY MURRAY** – bass (ex-PLASTIC PENNY) repl. PETE

Feb 70. (7") *(POF 164) <21030>* **EASY LOVIN'. / GIVE ME SOMETHING**

1970. (lp) *(POS 602)* **TROGGLOMANIA (live)**
– Give it to me / Jingle jangle / No.10 Downing Street / Wild thing / Oh no / Last Summer / Anyway that you want me / Hi hi Hazel / With a girl like you / Mona / Baby come closer / Cousin Jane / I can't control myself / I want you to come into my life / I just sing.

May 70. (7") *(POF 171) <21032>* **LOVER. / COME NOW**

Jul 70. (7") *(POF 182) <21035>* **THE RAVER. / YOU**

— **RICHARD MOORE** – guitar repl. BRITTON

D.J.M. Silverline

1970. (lp) *(DJML 009)* **CONTRASTS** (1966-70)
– I can't control myself / The raver / Surprise, surprise (I need you) / Evil woman / Lover / Wild thing / Love is all around / Little girl / You can cry if you want to / I've waited for someone / Easy loving / Any way that you want me *(re-iss.Nov76; same)*

Jun 71. (7") *(DJS 248)* **LAZY WEEKEND. / LET'S PULL TOGETHER**

Jam not issued

Nov 72. (7"m) *(JAM 25)* **WILD THING (new version). / WITH A GIRL LIKE YOU / LOVE IS ALL AROUND** -

Pye Pye

1972. (7") *(7N 45147)* **EVERYTHING'S FUNNY. / FEELS LIKE A WOMAN** -

Pye Bell

1973. (7") *(7N 45244) <45405>* **LISTEN TO THE MAN. / QUEEN OF SORROW**

Oct 73. (7") *(7N 45295) <45426>* **STRANGE MOVIES. / I'M ON FIRE**

Penny Farthing Pye

Dec 74. (7") *(PEN 861)* **GOOD VIBRATIONS. / PUSH IT UP TO ME**

May 75. (7") *(PEN 884)* **WILD THING (reggae version). / JENNY COME DOWN** -

Jul 75. (7") *(PEN 889)* **SUMMERTIME. / JENNY COME DOWN** -

1975. (lp) *(PEN 543)* **TROGGS**
– I got lovin' if you want it / Good vibrations / No particular place to go / Summertime / Satisfaction / Full blooded band / Memphis Tennessee / Peggy Sue / Jenny come down / Wild thing.

Nov 75. (7") *(PEN 901)* **(I CAN'T GET NO) SATISFACTION. / MEMPHIS, TENNESSEE** -

Jun 76. (lp) *(PELS 551)* **THE TROGGS TAPES** -
– Get you tonight / We rode through the night / A different me / Downsouth to Georgia / Gonna make you / Supergirl / I'll buy you an island / Rolling stone / After the rain / Rock and roll lady / Walkin' the dog.

Jun 76. (7") *(PEN 919)* **I'LL BUY YOU AN ISLAND. / SUPERGIRL** -

1977. (7") *(PEN 929)* **FEELING FOR LOVE. / SUMMERTIME** -

Raw not issued

1978. (7") *(RAW 25)* **JUST A LITTLE TOO MUCH. / THE TRUE TROGG TAPES** -

— added **COLIN 'Dill' FLETCHER** – rhythm guitar

Max's Kansas City Basement

Mar 81. (lp) *(MKC 100)* **LIVE AT MAX'S KANSAS CITY (live)** 1980
– Got love if you want it / Satisfaction / Love is all around / Feels like a woman / Strange movies / Summertime / Walking the dog / Memphis / No particular place to go / Wild thing / Gonna make you. *(cd-iss.Oct94 on 'President'+=; MKCD 1001)–* I do I do / Call me.

New Rose not issued

Mar 82. (lp) *(ROSE 4)* **BLACK BOTTOM** -
(cd-iss.Mar85; ROSE 4CD)

Mar 82. (7") *(NEW 6)* **I LOVE YOU BABY. /** -

Stage Coach not issued

May 82. (7") *(MAIL 38)* **BLACK BOTTOM. / WITH YOU** -

10-Virgin not issued

1984. (7") *(TEN 21)* **EVERY LITTLE THING. / BLACKJACK AND POKER** -
(7"pic-d+=/12"+=) *(TEN T/Y 21)* – With a girl like you.

— In 1986, REG featured on SUZI QUATRO's version of 'WILD THING'.

— **PRESLEY + BOND** recruited **PETER LUCAS** – bass / **DAVE MAGGS** – drums

Big Wave not issued

Nov 89. (7"/12") *(BWR/+T 27)* **WILD THING '89. / FROM HOME** -

New Rose not issued

May 90. (lp/cd) *(ROSE/+CD 186)* **AU** -
– Always something there to remind me / Walking the dog / Wild thing / Love is all around / With a girl like you / I can't control myself / Strange movies / Maximum overdrive / The Disco Kid versus Sid Chicane / What you doing here. *(re-iss.cd Dec95 on 'Javelin'; HADCD 195)*

— now without BOND

Essential Rhino

Feb 92. (7"/c-s/12"/cd-s) **DON'T YOU KNOW. / NOWHERE ROAD**

Mar 92. (cd/c/lp) *(ESS CD/MC/LP 180)* **ANTHENS ANDOVER**
– Crazy Annie / Together / Tuned into love / Deja vu / Nowhere road / Dust bowl / I'm in control / Don't you know / What's your game / Suspicious / Hot stuff. *(cd re-iss.Aug96; same)*

Lifetime not issued

Nov 92. (7"/c-s; by TROGS featuring OLIVER REED & HURRICANE HIGGINS) *(LIF/+C 37)* **WILD THING. / ('A'mix)** -
(12"+=/cd-s+=) *(LIF T/CD 37)* – ('A'original). *(re-is.Oct94; same)*

Weekend not issued

Oct 93. (7"/c-s/cd-s; TROGGS featuring WOLF) **WILD THING. / (other by EDWIN STARR & SHADOW)** 69 -

– compilations, etc. –

1966. (7"ep) *Page One; (POE 001)* **TROGGS TOPS** -

1967. (7"ep) *Page One; (POE 002)* **TROGGS TOPS VOLUME 2** -

1969. (7") *Page One; (POF 23126)* **WILD THING. / I CAN'T CONTROL MYSELF** -

Nov 75. (lp) *D.J.M.; (DJML 26047)* **WITH A GIRL LIKE YOU** -

1976. (d-lp) *Sire; <SASH 3714-2>* **VINTAGE YEARS** -

Jul 76. (lp) *D.J.M.; (44314)* **THE (ORIGINAL) TROGGS TAPES** -

Nov 81. (c) *D.J.M.; (TWO 410)* **VOLUME 1 / VOLUME 2** -

Jul 82. (7") *Old Gold; (OG 9001)* **WILD THING. / WITH A GIRL LIKE YOU** -
(re-iss.Nov85 & Jun88; same)

Jul 82. (7") *Old Gold; (OG 9024)* **I CAN'T CONTROL MYSELF. / GIVE IT TO ME** -

Jul 82. (7") *Old Gold; (OG 9038)* **LOVE IS ALL AROUND. / ANY WAY THAT YOU WANT ME** -

Jan 84. (7"/12") *D.J.M.; (DJS/DJR 6)* **WILD THING. / I CAN'T CONTROL MYSELF / LOVE IS ALL AROUND** -

Aug 84. (lp) *Action Replay; (ARLP 103)* **ROCK IT BABY** -

Nov 84. (lp/c) *Astan; (2/4 0046)* **GOLDEN HITS . . . TROGGS** -

Feb 85. (lp/c) *Rhino; <RN LP/C 118>* **THE BEST OF THE TROGGS** -
(UK-iss.1988 on 'Big Time' lp/c/cd; 221/211/261 526)

Apr 85. (c) *Autograph; (ASK 779)* **HOT DAYS** -

Aug 87. (lp) *Konnexion; (KOMA 788021)* **WILD THINGS** -
(re-iss.Jul89 on 'See For Miles' lp/cd; SEE/+CD 256)

Aug 87. (lp/c) *Masters; (MA/+MC 928487)* **GREATEST HITS** -

Oct 88. (lp/c) *BR Music; (BR LP/MC 28)* **GREATEST HITS** -

Dec 88. (cd) *Spectrum; (SPEC 85031)* **14 GREATEST HITS** -

Oct 89. (lp/c/cd; shared with DAVE DEE, DOZY, BEAKY, MICK & TICH) *Platinum; (PLA T/C/CD 3908)* **DOUBLE HITS COLLECTION** -

Oct 90. (cd) *O.B.J.; (OR 0112)* **WILD THING** -
(re-iss.Jun96 on 'Music De Luxe'; MSCD 030)

May 91. (cd/c) *Fontana; (848 164-2/-4)* **HIT SINGLE ANTHOLOGY** -

— In 1991, WILD THING was re-issued on 'Fontana'.

May 92. (cd-ep) *Old Gold; (OG 6164)* **WILD THING / WITH A GIRL LIKE YOU / I CAN'T CONTROL MYSELF** -

Feb 93. (3xcd-box) *Fontana; (514 423-2)* **ARCHAEOLOGY** -

Nov 93. (cd) *Fat Boy;* **THE VERY BEST OF THE TROGGS** -

Mar 94. (cd) *Charly; (CDCD 1147)* **WILD THING** -

Jul 94. (cd/c) *Polygram TV; (522 739-2/-4)* **GREATEST HITS** 27 -

Aug 94. (cd) *Wisepack; (LECD 074)* **LEGENDS IN MUSIC** -

Feb 95. (cd) *B.A.M.; (KLMCD 030)* **PEARLS OF THE PAST** -

Apr 95. (cd/c) *Muskateer; (MU 5/4 022)* **GREATEST HITS – WILD THING** -

Jul 95. (cd) *Summit;* **THE BEST OF THE TROGGS** -

Aug 95. (cd/c) *Spectrum; (551045-2/-4)* **LOVE IS ALL AROUND** -
(cd re-iss.Apr97 on 'Music'; CD 6065)

Sep 95. (cd/c) *Hallmark;* **THEIR GREATEST HITS** -

Jun 96. (cd/c) *Music Club; (MC CD/TC 242)* **ATHENS GEORGIA AND BEYOND** -

Nov 96. (cd) *See For Miles; (SEECD 453)* **THE E.P. COLLECTION** -

Feb 97. (cd) *Beat Goes On; (BGOCD 340)* **FROM NOWHERE / TROGGLODYNAMITE** -

Apr 97. (cd/c) *Prism; (PLA TCD/C 203)* **WILD THING** -

Apr 97. (cd) *Beat Goes On; (BGOCD 343)* **CELLOPHANE / MIXED BAG** -

Apr 97. (cd) *Prestige; (CDSGP 0337)* **ALL THE HITS PLUS MORE** -

TUCKY BUZZARD (see under ⇒ END)

Nik TURNER (see under ⇒ HAWKWIND)

TURTLES

Formed: Westchester, Los Angeles, California, USA . . . 1961, as The NIGHTRIDERS, by HOWARD KAYLAN and MARK VOLMAN. Two years later, with additional members, AL NICHOL, CHUCK PORTZ and DON MURRAY, they became The CROSSFIRES and released two singles. In 1965, Ted Feigen, co-owner of the 'White Whale' label, signed them, manager Reb Foster re-christening the band The TYRTLES, in line with local folk-rock big cheeses, The BYRDS. Although this was speedily altered to The TURTLES, it was obvious the band were infatuated with their L.A. rivals on the evidence of their debut single, an inspired cover of DYLAN's 'IT AIN'T ME BABE' (1965). Despite two more hits penned by "protest" writer P.F. Sloan, 'LET ME BE' and 'YOU BABY' in 1966, the band's albums stiffed. They also apparently turned down Sloan's 'EVE OF DESTRUCTION', later covered to great success by ex-CHRISTY MINSTREL, BARRY McGUIRE. The TURTLES soon decided that earnest folk-protest wasn't their bag anyway, and they found their true calling with the arrival of flower power in 1967, taking the classic hippy-pop of 'HAPPY TOGETHER' to No.1 in America. They followed-up with the equally effervescent 'SHE'D RATHER BE WITH ME', later that summer. Branching out from the patented TURTLES sound, the band released an eccentric concept album, 'THE TURTLES PRESENT THE BATTLE OF THE BANDS' (1969). An entertaining collection of easy going parody, it spawned the single 'ELENORE' (1968). With the band line-up in continual flux, The TURTLES recorded one more album, the RAY DAVIES-produced 'TURTLE SOUP' (1969), before finally bowing out with a belated cover of 'EVE OF DESTRUCTION' in 1970. KAYLAN and VOLMAN metamorphasised into FLO & EDDIE, lending their satirical expertise to FRANK ZAPPA before venturing out on their own. • **Songwriters:** Some by group members, except covers; LET ME BE + YOU BABY (P.F.Sloan) / HAPPY TOGETHER + SHE'D RATHER BE WITH ME (Gary Bonner-Alan Gordon) / THE STORY OF ROCK AND ROLL (Nilsson) / LADY-O (Judee Sill) / etc. • **Trivia:** In 1976, KAYLAN & VOLMAN wrote the score and dialogue for the adult animated film, 'Cheap'. In 1989, the pair sued DE LA SOUL for sampling a piece of 'YOU SHOWED ME' on their 'Transmitting Live From Mars'.

Recommended: HAPPY TOGETHER (THE VERY BEST OF) (*6)

HOWARD KAYLAN (b. HOWARD KAPLAN, 22 Jun'47, New York City) – saxophone / **MARK VOLMAN** (b.19 Apr'47, Los Angeles) – saxophone / **AL NICHOL** (b.31 Mar'46, Winston-Salem, New Connecticut) – guitar, piano / **JIM TUCKER** (b.17 Oct'46, Los Angeles) – guitar / **CHUCK PORTZ** (b.28 Mar'48, Santa Monica, Calif.) – bass / **DON MURRAY** (b. 8 Nov'45) – drums

not issued | Capco

1963. (7"; as CROSSFIRES) <104> **FIBERGLASS JUNGLE. / DR. JEKYLL & MR. HYDE** [-] [ ]

not issued | Lucky Token

1964. (7"; as CROSSFIRES) <112> **THAT'LL BE THE DAY. / ONE POTATO TWO POTATO** [-] [ ]

KAYLAN + VOLMAN now on dual vox

Pye Int. | White Whale

Sep 65. (7") *(7N 25320)* <222> **IT AIN'T ME BABE. / ALMOST THERE** [ ] [8] Jul65

Oct 65. (lp) *<WWS 7111>* **IT AIN'T ME BABE** [-] [98]

– Wanderin' kind / It was a very good year / Your maw said you cried / Eve of destruction / Glitter and gold / Let me be / Let the cold winds blow / It ain't me babe / A walk in the sun / Last laugh / Love minus zero / Like a rolling stone. *(UK cd-iss.Nov93 on 'Repertoire';)*

Jan 66. (7") *(7N 25341)* <224> **LET ME BE. / YOUR MA SAID YOU CRIED (IN YOUR SLEEP LAST NIGHT)** [ ] [29] Oct65

Immediate | White Whale

Apr 66. (7") *(IM 031)* <227> **YOU BABY. / WANDERIN' KIND** [ ] [20] Jan66

Jun 66. (lp) *<WWS 7112>* **YOU BABY LET ME BE** [-] [ ]

– Flyin' high / I know that you'll be there / House of pain / Just a room / I need someone / Let me be / Down in suburbia / Give love a trial / You baby / Pall bearing, ball bearing world / All my problems / Almost there. *(cd-iss.Jan94 on 'Repertoire';)*

Jun 66. (7") <231> **GRIM REAPER OF LOVE. / COME BACK** [-] [81]

—— **JOHN BARBATA** (b. 1 Apr'46, New Jersey) – drums (ex-SENTINELS) repl. DON MURRAY / **CHIP DOUGLAS** – bass had replaced PORTZ before he too was deposed by recent writer **JIM PONS** – bass (ex-LEAVES)

London | White Whale

Jul 66. (7") <234> **WE'LL MEET AGAIN. / OUTSIDE CHANCE** [-] [ ]

Sep 66. (7") <237> **MAKIN' MY MIND UP. / OUTSIDE CHANCE** [-] [ ]

Nov 66. (7") *(HLU 10095)* <238> **CAN I GET TO KNOW YOU BETTER? / LIKE THE SEASONS** [ ] [89] Oct66

Feb 67. (7") <244> **HAPPY TOGETHER. / LIKE THE SEASONS** [-] [1]

Mar 67. (7") *(HLU 10115)* **HAPPY TOGETHER. / WE'LL MEET AGAIN** [12] [-]

May 67. (lp) *(HA-U 8330)* *<WWS 7114>* **HAPPY TOGETHER** [ ] [25] Apr67

– Makin' my mind up / Guide for the married man / Think I'll run away / The walking song / Me about you / Happy together / She'd rather be with me / Too young to be the one / Person without a care / Like the seasons / Rugs of woods and flowers. *(cd-iss.Jun93 on 'Repertoire';)*

Jun 67. (7") *(HLU 10135)* <249> **SHE'D RATHER BE WITH ME. / THE WALKING SONG** [4] [3] May67

Jun 67. (7") <251> **GUIDE FOR THE MARRIED MAN. / THINK I'LL RUN AWAY** [-] [ ]

—— Now a quintet (**KAYLAN, VOLMAN, NICHOL, PONS + BARBATA**), when TUCKER left

Sep 67. (7") *(HLU 10153)* <254> **YOU KNOW WHAT I MEAN. / RUGS OF WOODS AND FLOWERS** [ ] [12] Jul67

Nov 67. (7") *(HLU 10168)* <260> **SHE'S MY GIRL. / CHICKEN LITTLE WAS RIGHT** [ ] [14]

Dec 67. (lp) *<WWS 7115>* **THE TURTLES! GOLDEN HITS (compilation)** [-] [7]

– It ain't me babe / Let me be / You baby / Outside chance / Grim reaper of love / Can I get to know you better / Happy together / She'd rather be with me / You know what I mean / Is it any wonder / So goes love.

Mar 68. (7") *(HLU 10184)* <264> **SOUND ASLEEP. / UMBASSA AND THE DRAGON** [ ] [57] Feb68

Jun 68. (7") *(HLU 10207)* **THE STORY OF ROCK AND ROLL. / CAN'T YOU HEAR THE COWS** [ ] [48]

Sep 68. (7") *(HLU 10223)* <276> **ELENORE. / SURFER DAN** [7] [6]

Dec 68. (7"; as CHRISTMAS SPIRIT) <290> **CHRISTMAS IS MY TIME OF YEAR. / WILL YOU STILL BELIEVE IN ME** [-] [ ]

—— (above with LINDA RONSTADT)

Jan 69. (lp; mono/stereo) *(HA-U/SH-U 8376)* *<WWA 7118>* **THE TURTLES PRESENT THE BATTLE OF THE BANDS** [ ] [ ] Oct68

– The opening: The battle of the bands / The last thing I remember / Elenore / Too much heartsick feeling / Oh daddy / Buzzsaw / Surfer Dan / I'm chief Kamanawanalea (we're the royal Macadamia nuts) / You showed me / Food / Chicken Little was right / The closing: Earth anthem (all). *<US re-iss.May86 on 'Rhino'; >*

Jan 69. (7") *(HLU 10251)* <292> **YOU SHOWED ME. / BUZZ-SAW** [ ] [6] Dec68

—— **JOHN SEITER** – bass (ex-SPANKY & OUR GANG) repl. BARBATA who later joined JEFFERSON STARSHIP

May 69. (7") <306> **HOUSE ON THE HILL. / COME OVER** [-] [ ]

Jun 69. (7") *(HLU 10279)* <308> **YOU DON'T HAVE TO WALK IN THE RAIN. / COME OVER** [ ] [51] May69

Oct 69. (7") *(HLU 10291)* <326> **LOVE IN THE CITY. / BACHELOR MOTHER** [-] [91]

Oct 69. (lp) *<WWS 7124>* **TURTLE SOUP** [-] [ ]

– Come over / House on the hill / She always leaves me laughing / How you love me / Torn between temptations / Love in the city / Bachelor mother / John and Julie / Hot little hands / Somewhere Friday nite / Dance this dance with me / You don't have to walk in the rain *<re-iss.May86 on 'Rhino'; RNLP 70157> (UK cd-iss.Oct93 on 'Repertoire';) (cd re-iss.Jan97 on 'Sundazed'; SC 6086)*

Dec 69. (7") <334> **LADY-O. / SOMEWHERE FRIDAY NIGHT** [-] [78]

Feb 70. (7") <341> **WE AIN'T GONNA PARTY NO MORE. / WHO WOULD EVER THINK THAT I WOULD MARRY MARGARET** [-] [ ]

Apr 70. (lp) *<WWS 7127>* **THE TURTLES! MORE GOLDEN HITS (compilation)** [-] [ ]

– We ain't gonna party no more / The story of rock and roll / You showed me / Sound asleep / You don't have to walk in the rain / Who would ever think that I would marry Margaret / She's my girl / Elenore / Lady-O / Hot little hands / Love in the city / Cat in the window.

Apr 70. (7") <350> **IS IT ANY WONDER? / WANDERIN' KIND** [-] [ ]

Jun 70. (7") <355> **EVE OF DESTRUCTION. / WANDERIN' KIND** [-] [100]

Aug 70. (7") <364> **ME ABOUT YOU. / THINK I'LL RUN AWAY** [-] [ ]

1970. (lp) *<WWS 7133>* **WOODEN HEAD** [-] [ ]

– I can't stop / She'll come back / Get away / Wrong from the start / I get out of breath / We'll meet again / On a summer's day / Come back / Say girl / Tie me down. *<re-iss.Jul84 on 'Rhino'; RNLP 154> (cd-iss.Jan94 on 'Repertoire';) (cd re-iss.Jan97 on 'Sundazed'; SC 6087)*

—— When their Spring album 'SHELLSHOCK' was not completed due to displeasure with 'White Whale', they split. It was later issued in 1987 on 'Rhino'. Their last single above was actually first heard on debut 1965 lp. KAYLAN & VOLMAN (and later PONS) joined FRANK ZAPPA's MOTHERS OF INVENTION and appeared on 3 albums; 'Chunga's Revenge', 'Fillmore East, June 1971' & 'Just Another Band From L.A.'. Due to legalities, the two were now billed as The PHLORESCENT LEECH & EDDIE. In 1971, they provided guest backing on tracks by T.REX, noteably the hits 'Hot Love' & 'Get It On'. They formed duo in 1972.

MARK VOLMAN & HOWARD KAYLAN

with band **JIM PONS** – bass / **DON PRESTON** – keys / **AYNSLEY DUNBAR** – drums (all ex-FRANK ZAPPA) / **GARY ROWLES** – guitar (ex-LOVE)

Reprise | Reprise

1972. (lp) *(K 44201)* <2097> **THE PHLORESCENT LEECH & EDDIE** [ ] [ ]

– Flo and Eddie's theme / Thoughts have turned / It never happened / Burn the house / Lady blue / Strange girl / Who but I / Been born again / Goodbye surprise / Nikki hoi / Really love / Feel older now / There you sit lonely.

1972. (7") <1113> **GOODBYE SURPRISE. / NIKKI HOI** [-] [ ]

FLO & EDDIE

VOLMAN & KAYLAN

Reprise | Reprise

May 73. (lp) *(K 44234)* <2141> **FLO & EDDIE** [ ] [ ]

– Days / You're the lady / Soundtrack from Carlos the bull / Afterglow / Best part of breaking up / The Sanzini brothers / Another pop stars life / Just another town / Marmendy Hill.

May 73. (7") *(K 14261)* <1142> **AFTERGLOW. / SOUNDTRACK FROM CARLOS AND DE BULL**

Aug 73. (7") <1160> **YOU'RE A LADY. / IF WE ONLY HAD THE TIME** [-] [ ]

C.B.S. | Columbia

Oct 75. (7") *(2753)* <10204> **LET ME MAKE LOVE TO YOU. / COME TO MY RESCUE – WEBELOS**

Dec 75. (lp) <33554> **ILLEGAL, IMMORAL AND FATTENING** [-] [ ]

– Illegal, immoral and fattening / Rebecca / Kama Sutra time / The Sanzini brothers return / Livin' in the jungle / Cheap / The Kung Fu killer / Eddie are you kidding / The pop star massage unit / Let me make love to you / There's no business like show business.

Feb 76. (7") *(3972)* <10264> **REBECCA. / ILLEGAL, IMMORAL & FATTENING** [ ] [ ]

Nov 76. (lp) *(81509)* <33262> **MOVING TARGETS** [ ] [ ]

– Elenore / Moving targets / Mama, open up / Love you gave away / Hot / Best friends / Best possible me / Keep it warm / Guns / Sway when you walk.

Nov 76. (7") <10425> **ELENORE. / THE LOVE YOU GAVE AWAY** [-] [ ]

Feb 77. (7") <10458> **HOT. / KEEP IT WARM** [-] [ ]

—— The pair became guest vocalists for BLONDIE, ALICE COOPER, etc, before returning in 1981, with reggae back-up **UZZIAH STICKY THOMPSON** – percussion / **ALSTON BARRETT** – bass / **AUGUSTUS PABLO** – keyboards / **CARLTON SANTA DAVIS** – drums / etc.

not issued | Epiphany

1981. (lp) <ELP 4010> **ROCK STEADY WITH FLO & EDDIE** [-] [ ]

—— In 1982, the pair re-formed as The TURTLES, but only for tours.

– (TURTLES) compilations, others, etc. –

May 67. (7") *Pye International; (7N 25421)* **LET ME BE. / ALMOST THERE** [ ] [-]

Mar 75. (d-lp) *Philips; (9299 425) / Sire; <SASN 3703-2>* **HAPPY TOGETHER AGAIN:- THE TURTLES' GREATEST HITS** [ ] [ ] Dec74

Apr 75. (7") *Philips; (6078 426)* **SHE'D RATHER BE WITH ME. / THERE YOU SIT LONELY** [ ] [ ]

Jul 82. (7") *Old Gold; (OG 9155)* **ELENORE. / SHE'D RATHER BE WITH ME** [ ] [-]

Jul 82. (7") *Old Gold; (OG 9157)* **HAPPY TOGETHER. / YOU BABY** [ ] [-]

1982. (7",7"clear-box) *Rhino;* **TURTLES** [-] [ ]

1982. (7"sha-pic-d-ep) *Rhino; <RNPD 901>* **TURTLES 1968** [-] [ ]

1982. (7"sha-pic-d-ep) *Rhino;* **TURTLESIZED** [-] [ ]

1986. (cd) *Rhino; <RNCD 5160>* **20 GREATEST HITS** [-] [ ]

1987. (lp) *Rhino; <RNLP 70155>* **CHALON ROAD** [-] [ ]

– She's my girl / You know what I mean / Sound asleep / Can't you hear the cows / The last thing I remember (the first thing I knew) / Umbassa and the dragon / The story of rock and roll / Outside chance / Chicken little was right / The owl / To see the sun.

1987. (lp) *Rhino; <RNLP 70158>* **SHELLSHOCK** [-] [ ]

– Goodbye surprise / Like it or not / There you sit lonely / We ain't gonna party no more / Cat in the window / Lady-o / Can I go on / Dance this dance / You want to be a woman / If we only had the time / Gas money / Teardrops / Who would you ever think that I would marry Margaret.

Dec 88. (cd) *Spectrum; (SPEC 85024)* **20 GOLDEN HITS** ☐ -

Jan 90. (d-cd/d-c) *Mainline; (260 421-2/-4)* **20 GOLDEN CLASSICS** ☐ -

Sep 91. (cd/c) *Music Club; (MC CD/TC 046)* **HAPPY TOGETHER (THE VERY BEST OF THE TURTLES)** ☐ -

– Happy together / She'd rather be with me / Too young to be one / Me about you / Think I'll run away / Can I get to know you better / Guide for the married man / Elenore / It ain't me babe / You baby / Let me be / She's my gal / You don't have to walk in rain / You know what I mean / Lady O / You showed me / There you sit lonely / Outside chance / Buzz saw / Sound asleep.

Feb 93. (cd) *Repertoire; (REP)* **CLASSIC HITS** ☐ -

Sep 93. (cd) *Repertoire; <REP>* **ELENORE** ☐ -

Oct 94. (cd/c) *Laserlight; (12/72 380)* **CALIFORNIA GOLD (HAPPY TOGETHER AGAIN LIVE)** ☐ -

Mar 95. (cd) *Rhino; <R2 71873>* **LOVE SONGS** - ☐

TWENTY SIXTY SIX AND THEN

Formed: Germany . . . early 70's by English-born GEFF HARRISON, GAGEY MROZECK, STEVE ROBINSON, VEIT MARVOS, DIETER BAUER and KONSTANTIN BOMMARIUS. This short-lived band released only one album, 1972's 'REFLECTIONS ON THE FUTURE'. A German rock classic, the album was dominated by psychedelic effects, spiralling organ riffs and opressive guitar workouts. The record was a commercial failure however, although many of the band members went on to more fruitful projects.

Recommended: REFLECTIONS OF THE FUTURE (*9)

GEFF HARRISON (b. England) – vocals / **GAGEY MROZECK** – guitars / **STEVE ROBINSON** (b. RAINER GEYER) – synthesizer, keyboards / **VEIT MARVOS** – keyboards, vocals / **DIETER BAUER** – bass / **KONSTATIN BOMMARIUS** – drums

U.A. / not issued

1972. (lp) *(UAS 29314)* **REFLECTIONS ON THE FUTURE** ☐ -

– At my home / Autumn / Butterking / Reflections of the future / How do you feel. *(re-iss.1989 on 'Second Battle'; SB 001) (re-iss.1991 as 1 + half lp+=; SBT 001)–* The way I feel today (original long version) / At my home (alternate version) / Spring. *(cd-iss.1994; SBT 001CD) (cd re-iss.Jun97; SB 025)*

—— split a few months after above. STEVE joined NINE DAYS' WONDER, then AREA. GEFF and GAGEY joined KIN PING MEH. VEIT recorded with EMERGENCY, MIDNIGHT CIRCUS and TIGER B. SMITH. KONSTATIN went on to ABACUS, then KARTHAGO.

23rd TURNOFF

Formed: Liverpool, England . . . 1966 by JIMMY CAMPBELL and some former members of The KIRKBYS; JOHN LLOYD, ALBY POWER and KENNY GOODLASS, who had released a debut 45, 'IT'S A CRIME' (which has since become quite collectable). They named the new outfit after a turnoff on the M6 just outside their hometown. Signing to the up and coming 'Deram', they created their melancholic psychedelic masterpiece, 'MICHAEL ANGELO', in 1967. However, the record was their only outing under this banner as CAMPBELL took off on a folk-rock venture, making three albums in the process, while also joining duo ROCKIN' HORSE alongside other Scouser, BILLY KINSEY. This band (who were neigh good) made one album, 'YES IT IS', in 1970, which has since become, like the others, quite pricey to buy.

Recommended: their single / Jimmy Campbell: SON OF ANASTASIA (*5)

JOE MOROUTH – vocals repl. GERRY SAVAGE / **JIMMY CAMPBELL** – guitar / **JOHN LLOYD** – guitar / **ALBY POWER** – bass / **KENNY GOODLASS** – drums

R.C.A. / not issued

1967. (7"; as KIRKBYS) *(RCA 1542)* **IT'S A CRIME. / I'VE NEVER BEEN SO MUCH IN LOVE** ☐ -

Deram / not issued

Sep 67. (7") *(DM 150)* **MICHAEL ANGELO. / LEAVE ME HERE** ☐ -

JIMMY CAMPBELL

—— went solo on vocals & guitar

Fontana / not issued

Mar 69. (7") *(TF 1009)* **ON A MONDAY. / DEAR MARGE** ☐ -

Apr 69. (lp) *(STL 5508)* **SON OF ANASTASIA** ☐ -

– When I sit down to reason / Mother's boy / Another Vincent Van Gogh / Penny in my pocket / Bright side of the hill / Dear Margie / Lyanna / They all came marching home / On a Monday / Lovely Elisa Cope is dead / You'll break my heart in two / Tremendous commercial potential / Adrian Henri's party night / Another springtime's passed me by / Michaelangelo / Painting a sign.

Feb 70. (7") *(TF 1076)* **LYANNA. / FRANKIE JOE** ☐ -

Jul 70. (7") *(6007 025)* **DON'T LEAVE ME NOW. / SO LONELY WITHOUT YOU** ☐ -

Vertigo / not issued

Sep 70. (lp) *(6360 010)* **HALF BAKED** ☐ -

– Green eyed American actress / Loving you is all I do / So lonely without you / In my room / That's right that's me / I will not mind / Dulcie / Forever grateful / Half baked / Closing down the shop / Don't leave me now.

May 72. (lp) *(6308 100)* **JIMMY CAMPBELL'S ALBUM** ☐ -

– By the light of the lamp / Salvation Army citadel / Snow covered street / Paris, you're in Paris / Darling sweetheart / April morning / Something in the wind / Maudie / Baby, walk out with your darling man / It's just like a girl / It never rains but it pours / When you're coming home.

ROCKIN' HORSE

JIMMY CAMPBELL – vocals, guitar / **BILLY KINSEY** – bass, vocals (ex-MERSEYS)

Philips / not issued

Sep 71. (7") *(6006 156)* **BIGGEST GOSSIP IN TOWN. / YOU SAY** ☐ -

Nov 71. (lp) *(6308 075)* **YES IT IS** ☐ -

– Yes it is / You're spending all my Monday / You say / Baby walk out with your darlin' man / Oh Carol / I'm so sad / Don't you ever think I cry / Stayed out late last night / Delicate situation / Son, son / I'm trying to forget you / Golden opportunity / Julian the hooligan.

Mar 72. (7") *(6006 200)* **JULIAN THE HOOLIGAN. / STAYED OUT LATE LAST NIGHT** ☐ -

Randy's / not issued

1973. (7") *(RAN 535)* **I'M SO FED UP. / (part 2)** ☐ -

—— CAMPBELL ceased to do any more recording after third solo album

TWINK (see under ⇒ PINK FAIRIES)

T.2. (see under ⇒ BULLDOG BREED)

ULTIMATE SPINACH

Formed: Boston, Massachusetts, USA ... 1967 originally out of UNDERGROUND CINEMA by mainman IAN BRUCE-DOUGLAS, with vocalist BARBARA HUDSON, plus GEOFFREY WINTHROP, KEITH LAHTEINEN and RICHARD NESS. Changing their name on the advice of producer ALAN LORBER, they signed to 'M.G.M.' and released their debut album, 'ULTIMATE SPINACH 1' (1968). A densely psychedelic affair, maybe ULTIMATE MUSHROOM would've been a more appropriate name for this lot. Described as being part of the 'Bosstown sound', the band competed with the likes of San Franciscan outfits ORPHEUS and BEACON STREET UNION. Their follow-up album, 'BEHOLD AND SEE' (1968), continued in a similar fashion, the beautiful BARBARA HUDSON giving flight to her soaring vocals on 'MIND FLOWERS' and 'VISIONS OF YOUR REALITY'. BRUCE-DOUGLAS left soon after and the final album, the self-titled 'ULTIMATE SPINACH' (1969) was extremely lacklustre. • **Songwriters:** BRUCE-DOUGLAS, until his departure in 1969 when BARBARA was left with group name on third lp.

Recommended: ULTIMATE SPINACH (*7)

IAN BRUCE-DOUGLAS – vocals, keyboards, guitar, sitar, harmonica, flute, etc / **BARBARA HUDSON** – vocals, guitar, kazoo / **GEOFFREY WINTHROP** – lead vocals, guitar, sitar / **KEITH LAHTEINEN** – vocals, drums, tabla / **RICHARD NESS** – bass

M.G.M. M.G.M.

Jun 68. (lp; mono/stereo) *(MGM-C/+S 8071) <SE 4518>* **ULTIMATE SPINACH** [ ] [34] Feb68
– Ego trip / Sacrifice of the Moon (in four parts) / Plastic raincoats – Hung up minds / (Ballad of the) Hip death goddess / Your head is reeling / Dove in hawk's clothing / Baroque £1 / Funny freak parade / Pamela. *(cd-iss.May95 on 'Big Beat'; CDWIKD 142)*

Dec 68. (lp; mono/stereo) *(MGM-C/+S 8094) <SE 4570>* **BEHOLD & SEE** [ ] [ ] Nov68
– Behold and see (Gilded lamp of the cosmos) / Visions of your reality / Mind flowers / Where you're at / What you're thinking of (Jazz thing) / Fragmentary march of green / Suite: Genesis of beauty (in four parts) / Fifth horseman of the apocalyse. *(cd-iss.Nov95 on 'Big Beat'; CDWIKD 148)*

— **BARBARA** with newcomers **JEFF 'Skunk' BAXTER** – guitar, steel guitar, vibes, vocals / **TED MYERS** – vocals, guitar (ex-CHAMAELEON CHURCH) / **TONY SCHEUREN** – keyboards, guitar (ex-CHAMAELEON CHURCH) / **MIKE LEVINE** – bass / **RUSS LEVINE** – drums

Nov 69. (lp) *<SE 4600>* **ULTIMATE SPINACH** [-] [ ]
– (Just like) Romeo & Juliet / Some days you just can't win / Daisy / Sincere / Eddie's rush / Strangle life tragicomedy / Reasons / Happiness child / Back door blues / The world has just begun.

Nov 69. (7") *<14023>* **(JUST LIKE) ROMEO & JULIET. / SOME DAYS YOU JUST CAN'T WIN** [-] [ ]

— Disbanded when little interest was shown for 3rd lp. BAXTER later joined STEELY DAN and The DOOBIE BROTHERS.

- compilations, etc. -

Jun 96. (cd) *Big Beat; (CDWIKD 165)* **IN SEARCH OF ULTIMATE SPINACH / SPINACH UNDONE** [ ] [-]

UNITED STATES OF AMERICA

Formed: New York, USA ... 1968, by Californians JOSEPH BYRD and DOROTHY MOSKOWITZ, who enlisted GORDON MARRON, RAND FORBES and CRAIG WOODSON. Main songwriter BYRD, who had worked under critic/composer, VIRGIL THOMPSON while studying composition in the Big Apple. This experience led him to explore more adventurous sounds, MOSKOWITZ providing a more balanced approach with her sculpted vocals. Their one and only eponymous album proved to be one of the era's more fruitful attempts to merge avant-garde electronics with idiosyncratic, psychedelic rock and featured the quirky track, 'I WON'T LEAVE MY WOODEN WIFE FOR YOU, SUGAR'. Sadly, this was to be their only album, although BYRD re-appeared the following year with his bunch of FIELD HIPPIES.

Recommended: THE UNITED STATES OF AMERICA (*7)

DOROTHY MOSKOWITZ – vocals / **JOSEPH BYRD** – keyboards, electronics / **GORDON MARRON** – electric violin, synrhesizer / **RAND FORBES** – bass / **CRAIG WOODSON** – drums, percussion / with guest **ED BOGAS** – keyboards

C.B.S. Columbia

1968. (lp) *(CBS 63340) <9614>* **THE UNITED STATES OF AMERICA** [ ] [ ]
– The American metaphysical circus / Hard coming love / Cloud song / The garden of earthly delights / I won't leave my wooden wife for you, sugar / Where is yesterday / Coming down / Love song for the dead Che / Stranded in time / The American way of love. *(re-iss.May87 on 'Edsel'; ED 233) (cd-iss.Feb90; EDCD 233)*

Oct 68. (7") *(CBS 3745)* **THE GARDEN OF EARTHLY DELIGHTS. / LOVE SONG FOR THE DEAD CHE** [ ] [-]

— split and BYRD formed The FIELD HIPPIES in 1969, releasing one album for 'Columbia'; 'THE AMERICAN METAPHYSICAL CIRCUS' *<CBS 7317>*

UPP (see under ⇒ CLARK - HUTCHINSON)

UTOPIA (see under ⇒ AMON DUUL II)

UTOPIA (see under ⇒ RUNDGREN, Todd)

VAMP (see under ⇒ CLARK-HUTCHINSON)

VAN DER GRAAF GENERATOR

Formed: Manchester, England . . . 1967 by PETER HAMMILL, CHRIS 'JUDGE' SMITH and NICK PEAME, who met at Manchester University. A one-off 45, 'THE PEOPLE YOU WERE GOING TO', surfaced in 1968, before they disbanded. Re-grouping soon after with a slightly modified line-up, HAMMILL and SMITH enlisted the more experienced KEITH ELLIS, GUY EVANS and NICK BANTON. However, it wasn't long before SMITH left HAMMILL as the focal point and sole remaining founder member. This line-up recorded what was initially intended to be a HAMMILL solo album, 'AEROSOL GREY MACHINE', which surprisingly only saw a full release in the States. It was a remarkable debut, showcasing cuts such as 'NECROMANCER', 'RUNNING BACK' and 'AFTERWARDS', in which HAMMILL exercised his wide-ranging vocal talent to startling effect. A change of line-up ensued, with NIC POTTER (like EVANS, he had played in The MISUNDERSTOOD) replacing the JUICY LUCY bound ELLIS. Signing to 'Charisma', they released their conceptual follow-up, 'THE LEAST WE CAN DO IS WAVE TO EACH OTHER', which dented the UK Top 50 in early 1970. The album saw the band developing a hybrid of pseudo-gothic lyrics and progressive rock styles, the stand-out tracks being 'REFUGEEES' and 'AFTER THE FLOOD'. POTTER departed during their next project, 'H TO HE', a record which featured the services of the (then) in-demand guitarist ROBERT FRIPP (KING CRIMSON). He also contributed session work to their subsequent effort, 'PAWN HEARTS' (1971), which included the 20-minute piece, 'A PLAGUE OF LIGHTHOUSE KEEPERS'. The composition traversed a varying degree of moods and tempos, hitting a breathtaking finale. After a GEORGE MARTIN (yes, that one!) penned 45, 'THEME ONE', failed to sell, they disbanded for the second time in the summer of '72. With the help of some VAN DER GRAAF members, HAMMILL had previously recorded a solo album, 'FOOL'S MATE', returning to the studio once again for a follow-up, 'CHAMELEON IN THE SHADOW OF THE NIGHT', released in 1972. For a few years, HAMMILL continued in an increasingly experimental and inventive vein, much in evidence on his 1975 album, 'NADIR'S BIG CHANCE'. VAN DER GRAAF reformed around this time, releasing three albums during the next two years, one of which was the highly regarded 'WORLD RECORD' (1976). After the plug was finally pulled on the 'GENERATOR, HAMMILL went to work on a series of solo albums, bringing in his group K. His work was quite prolific in the 80's and was virtually VAN DER GRAAF in all but name. He has been an inspiration to many alternative acts, JOHN LYDON citing HAMMILL's vocal technique as a guiding influence. • **Trivia:** Named after a generator built by Dr. Robert Jemison Van Der Graaf.

Recommended: AEROSOL GREY MACHINE (*8) / VITAL (*7) / WORLD RECORD (*8) / PETER HAMMILL – NADIR'S BIG CHANCE (*7).

PETER HAMMILL (b. 5 Nov'48, London, England) – vocals, guitar, piano /**NICK PEAME** – organ / **CHRIS JUDGE SMITH** – drums, vocals, oricanos

Polydor / Mercury

Jan 69. (7") *(56758)* **PEOPLE YOU WERE GOING TO. / FIREBRAND** [ ] [-]

— **HUGH BANTON** – keyboards, repl. PEAME

— added **KEITH ELLIS** – bass (ex-KOOBAS) / **GUY EVANS** – drums (ex-MISUNDERSTOOD)

— Now a quartet when CHRIS formed HEEBALOB. He later wrote for HAMMILL

not issued / Mercury

Jan 69. (lp) *<SR 61238>* **AEROSOL GREY MACHINE** [-] [ ]
– Afterwards / Orthenthian St. (part 1 & 2) / Running back / Into a game / Aerosol grey machine / Black smoke yen / Aguarian / Necromancer / Octopus. *(UK-iss.Feb75 on 'Fontana'; 6430 083) (cd-iss.Mar97 on 'Repertoire'+=; RR 4647)*– People you were going to / Firebrand. *(cd re-iss.May97 on 'Fie!'+=; FIE 9116)*– Ferret / Featherbird / Giant squid.

Apr 69. (7") *<72979>* **AFTERWARDS. / NECROMANCER** [-] [ ]

— **NIC POTTER** – bass (ex-MISUNDERSTOOD) repl. ELLIS who joined JUICY LUCY / added **DAVE JACKSON** – saxophone (ex-HEEBALOB)

Charisma / Dunhill

Feb 70. (lp) *(CAS 1007)* **THE LEAST WE CAN DO IS WAVE TO EACH OTHER** [47] [ ]
– Darkness / Refugees / White hammer / Whatever would Robert have said / Out of my book / After the flood. *(re-iss.Aug82 lp/c; CHC/+MC 5) (cd-iss.Apr87; CASCD 1007)*

Apr 70. (7") *(CB 122)* **REFUGEES. / THE BOAT OF MILLIONS OF YEARS** [ ] [ ]

— A quartet again, when POTTER left only completing half of next album. Guest on next 2 albums **ROBERT FRIPP** – guitar (of KING CRIMSON)

Dec 70. (lp) *(CAS 1027) <50097>* **H TO HE, WHO AM THE ONLY ONE** [ ] [ ]
– Killer / House with no door / The emperor in his war-room: The emperor – The room / Lost: Dance in sand and sea – Dance in frost / The pioneers over C. *(re-iss.Jun81 & Sep83 on 'Polydor'; 6321 126) (cd-iss.Nov88; CASCD 1027)*

Charisma / Mercury

Oct 71. (lp) *(CAS 1051)* **PAWN HEARTS** [ ] [-]
– Lemmings / Man-erg / A plague of lighthouse keepers: 1) Eyewitness – 2) Pictures – Lighthouse – 3) Eyewitness – 4) S.H.M. – 5) Presence of the night – 6) Kosmos tours – 7) (Custards) Last stand – 8) The clot chickens – 9) Lands End – 10) We go now. *(re-iss.Oct86; CHC 54) (cd-iss.Apr88; CASCD 1051)*

Feb 72. (7") *(CB 175)* **THEME ONE. / W** [ ] [ ]

PETER HAMMILL

had by this went solo when VAN DER GRAAF split. He continued to use VDGG members.

Charisma / Charisma

Jul 71. (lp) *(<CAS 1037>)* **FOOL'S MATE** [ ] [ ]
– Imperial zeppelin / Candle / Happy / Solitude / Vision / Re-awakening / Sunshine / Child / Summer song (in the autumn) / Viking / The birds / I once wrote some poems. *(re-iss.Sep83 lp/c; CHC/+MC 2) (cd-iss.Oct88; CASCD 1037)*

May 73. (lp) *(<CAS 1067>)* **CHAMELEON IN THE SHADOW OF THE NIGHT** [ ] [ ]
– German overalls / Slender threads / Rock and role / In the end / What's it worth / Easy to slip away / Dropping the torch / In the black room / The tower. *(cd-iss.Apr89; CASCD 1067)*

Feb 74. (lp) *(<CAS 1083>)* **THE SILENT CORNER AND THE EMPTY STAGE** [ ] [ ]
– Modern / Wilhemina / The lie (Bernini's Saint Teresa) / Forsaken gardens / Red shift / Rubicon / A louse is not a home. *(re-iss.Oct86; CHC 61) (cd-iss.Nov88; CASCD 1083)*

Sep 74. (lp) *(<CAS 1089>)* **IN CAMERA** [ ] [ ]
– Ferret and featherbed / (No more) The sub-mariner / Tapeworm / Again / Faintheart and the sermon / The comet, the course. the tail / Gog Magog (in bromine chambers). *(re-iss.Nov80 on 'Polydor'; 9198 770) (re-iss.Aug88 lp/c; CHC/+MC 33) (cd-iss.Nov88; CASCD 1089)*

Feb 75. (lp) *(<CAS 1099>)* **NADIR'S BIG CHANCE** [ ] [ ]
– Nadir's big chance / The institute of mental health's burning / Open your eyes / Nobody's business / Been alone so long / Pompeii / Shingle song / Airport / People you were going to / Birthday special / Two or three spectres. *(re-iss.Mar83 lp/c; CHC/+MC 19) (cd-iss.Nov88; CASCD 1099)*

Apr 75. (7") *(CB 245)* **BIRTHDAY SPECIAL. / SHINGLE SONG** [ ] [ ]

— **HAMMILL, BANTON, JACKSON + EVANS** reformed

VAN DER GRAAF GENERATOR

Charisma / Mercury

Oct 75. (lp) *(CAS 1109) <1069>* **GODBLUFF** [ ] [ ]
– The undercover man / Scorched Earth / Arrow / The sleepwalkers. *(re-iss.Mar83 lp/c; CHC/+MC 13) (cd-iss.Apr88; CASCD 1109)*

Apr 76. (lp)(c) *(CAS 1116)(7208 605) <1096>* **STILL LIFE** [ ] [ ]
– Pilgrims / Still life / La rossa / My room (waiting for Wonderland) / Childlike faith in childhood's end. *(re-iss.Oct86; CHC 55) (cd-iss.Apr87; CASCD 1116)*

Oct 76. (lp)(c) *(CAS 1120)(7208 610) <1116>* **WORLD RECORD** [ ] [ ]
– When she comes / A place to survive / Masks / Meurglys III (the songwriters guild) / Wondering. *(re-iss.Aug88; CHC 62) (cd-iss.1988; CASCD 1120)*

Oct 76. (7") *(CB 297)* **WONDERING. / MEURGLYS III** [ ] [ ]

VAN DER GRAAF

GRAHAM SMITH – violin (ex-STRING DRIVEN THING) repl. JACKSON / **NIC POTTER** – bass returned after US session work to repl. BANTON

Sep 77. (lp) *(CAS 1131)* **THE QUIET ZONE – THE PLEASURE DOME** [ ] [ ]
– Lizard play / The habit of the broken heart / The siren song / Last frame / The wave / Yellow fever (running) / The sphinx in the face / Chemical world / The sphinx returns. *(re-iss.1987 lp/c; CHC/+MC 32) (cd-iss.1987; CASCD 1131)*

— added **DAVE JACKSON** who returned w / **CHARLES DICKIE** – cello, piano

Charisma / P.V.C.

Jul 78. (d-lp) *(CVLD 101)* **VITAL (live)** [ ] [ ]
– Ship of fools / Still life / Mirror images / Medley: Parts of A plague of lighthouse keepers and Sleepwalkers / Pioneers over C / Door / Urban / Nadir's big chance. *(cd-iss.Apr89; CVCLD 101) (re-iss.cd Mar94 on 'Virgin';)*

– compilations, etc. –

Aug 72. (lp) *Charisma; (CS 2)* **68-71** [ ] [-]
Aug 80. (lp/c) *Charisma; (BG/+C 3)* **REPEAT PERFORMANCE** [ ] [-]
– Afterwards / Refugees / The boat of millions of years / W / White hammer / Necromancer / The Emperor in his war room / The empereor / The room / Manerg. *(c+=)*– The clot thickens (extended).
Mar 83. (d-c) *Charisma; (CASMC 106)* **PAWN HEARTS / STILL LIFE** [ ] [-]
May 85. (lp) *Demi-Monde; (DM 003)* **TIME VAULTS** (rare) [ ] [-]
(cd-iss.Apr97 on 'Spalax'; 14847)
Feb 87. (cd) *Virgin; (COMCD 2)* **FIRST GENERATION** [ ] [-]
Feb 87. (cd) *Virgin; (COMCD 3)* **SECOND GENERATION** [ ] [-]
May 88. (lp/cd) Thunderbolt; (THBL/CDTB 042) **NOW AND THEN** [ ] [-]
Sep 93. (cd) *Virgin; (CDVM 9026)* **I PROPHESY DISASTER** [ ] [-]
Jun 94. (cd) *Band Of Joy; (BOJCD 008)* **MAIDA VALE** [ ] [-]

PETER HAMMILL

went solo after split.

Charisma Charisma

Sep 76. (lp) *(<CAS 1125>)* **OVER**
– Crying wolf / Autumn / Time heals / Alice (letting go) / This side of the looking-glass / Betrayed (on Tuesdays she used to) / Yoga / Lost and found. *(cd-iss.Feb91; CASCD 1125)*

Charisma P.V.C.

Sep 78. (lp) *(CAS 1137) <2202>* **THE FUTURE NOW**
– The future now / Still in the dark / Mediaevil / A motor-bike in Africa / The cut / Palinurus / Pushing thirty / The second hand / Trappings / The mousetrap (caught in) / Energy vampires / If I could. *(re-iss.Oct86; CHC 59) (cd-iss.Nov88; CASCD 1137)*

Nov 79. (lp) *(CAS 1146) <2205>* **pH7**
– My favourite / Careering / Porton Down / Mirror images / Handicap and equality / Not for Keith / The old school tie / Time for a change / Imperial walls / Mr. X gets tense / Faculty X. *(cd-iss.Apr89; CASCD 1146)*

Nov 79. (7"; as RICKY NADIR) *(CB 339)* **THE POLAROID. / THE OLD SCHOOL TIE** -

Mercury not issued

1980. (lp) *(6302 067)* **A BLACK BOX** - - Europe
– Golden promise / Losing faith in words / The Jargon king / Fog walking / The spirit / In slow time / The wipe / Flight: Flying blind – White cave fandango – Control – Cockpit – Silk worm wings / Nothing is nothing – A black box. *(UK-iss.Jun83; same) (re-iss.Aug88 on 'Virgin' lp/cd; OVED/CDOVD 140)*

Virgin not issued

May 81. (7") *(VS 424)* **MY EXPERIENCE. / GLUE** -
Jun 81. (lp) *(V 2205)* **SITTING TARGETS** -
– Breakthrough / My experience / Ophelia / Empress's clothes / Glue / Hesitation / Sitting targets / Stranger still / Sign / What I did for love / Central hotel. *(re-iss.Aug88; OVED 139) (cd-iss.Oct88; CDV 2205) (re-iss.cd Mar94;)*

— **HAMMILL** with **GUY EVANS / NIC POTTER** plus **JOHN ELLIS** – guitar (ex-VIBRATORS), formed **K**

Naive not issued

Sep 82. (7") *(NAV 3)* **PARADOX DRIVE. / NOW MORE THAN EVER** -
Oct 82. (lp/c) *(NAV L/C 1)* **ENTER K** -
– Paradox Drive / The unconscious life / Accidents / The great experiments / Don't tell me / She wraps it up / Happy hour / Seven wonders. *(cd-iss.May92 on 'Fie!'; FIE 9101)*

Sep 83. (lp) *(NAVL 3)* **PATIENCE** -
– Labour of love / Film noir / Just good friends / Jeunesse D'Oree / Traintime / Now more than ever / Comfortable / Patient. *(cd-iss.May92 on 'Fie!'; FIE 9102) (above 2 re-iss.Jan86 on 'Spartan' d-lp/d-c; SPD P/C 1)*

Sep 83. (7") *(NAV 8)* **FILM NOIR. / SEVEN WONDERS** -

Foundry not issued

Feb 85. (d-lp) *(FONDL 1)* **THE MARGIN (live)** -
– Future now / Porton Down / Stranger still / Sign / The Jargon king / The second hand / Empress's clothes / The sphinx in the face / Labour of love / Sitting targets / Patience / Flight. *(cd-iss.Feb91 on 'Virgin'; CDOVD 345)*

Mar 86. (lp/c) *(FOND L/C 3)* **SKIN** -
– Skin / After the show / Painting by numbers / Shell / All sais and done / A perfect date / Four pails / New lover. *(cd-iss.Nov87 on 'Line'; DACD 900145) (cd re-iss.Feb91 on 'Virgin'; CDOVD 344)*

Mar 86. (7") *(FOUND 3)* **PAINTING BY NUMBERS. / YOU HIT ME WHERE I LIVE** -
(ext.12"+=) *(FOUND 3-12)* – Shell.

Virgin not issued

Nov 86. (lp/c) *(V/TCV 2409)* **AND CLOSE AS THIS** -
– Too many of my yesterdays / Faith / Empire of delight / Silver / Beside the one you love / Other old cliches / Confident / Sleep now. *(cd-iss.Nov88; CDV 2409) (cd re-iss.1989 on 'Line'; DACD 900254)*

Red Hot not issued

Jun 88. (c/cd; PETE HAMMILL & GUY EVANS) *(ZCRH/CDR 102)* **SPUR OF THE MOMENT** -
– Sweating it out / Little did he know / Without a glitch / Anatol's proposal / You think not? / Multiman / Deprogramming Archie / Always so polite / An imagined brother / Bounced / Roger and out. *(re-iss.May93;)*

Enigma Enigma

Nov 88. (lp/c/cd) *(ENVLP/TCENV/CDENV 512)* **IN A FOREIGN TOWN**
– Hemlock / Invisible ink / Sci-finance (re-visited) / This book / Time to burn / Auto / Vote brand X / Sun City night life / The play's the thing / Under cover names. *(c+=/cd+=)*– Smile / Time to burn (instrumental). *(re-iss.cd Jun95 on 'Fie!';)*

Feb 90. (cd/c/lp) *(CDENV/TVENVENVLP 1003)* **OUT OF WATER**
– Evidently goldfish / Not the man / No Moon in the water / Our oyster / Something about Ysabel's dance / Green fingers / On the surface / A way out. *(re-iss.cd Jun95 on 'Fie!';)*

Some Bizzare not issued

Nov 91. (cd/c/lp) *(SBZ CD/MC/LP 007)* **THE FALL OF THE HOUSE OF USHER** -
– An unenviable role / That must be the house / Architecture / The sleeper / One thing at a time / I shun the light / Leave this house / Dreaming / A chronic catalepsy / The herbalist / The evil that is done / Five years ago / It's over now / An influence / no rot / She is dead / Beating of the heart / The haunted palace / I dared not speak / She comes towards the door / The fall.

Fie! not issued

Mar 92. (cd/c) *(FIE/+C 9103)* **FIRESHIPS** -
– I will find you / Curtains / His best girl / Oasis / Incomplete surrender / Fireship / Given time / Reprise / Gaia.

Mar 93. (cd/c) *(FIE/+C 9104)* **THE NOISE** -
– Kick to kill the kiss / Like a shot / The entertainer / Noise / Celebrity kissing / Where the mouth is / Great European department store / Planet Coventry / Primo on the carpet.

Nov 93. (cd; as PETER HAMMILL & THE NOISE) *(FIE 9106)* **THERE GOES THE DAYLIGHT** -
– Sci-finance (revisited) / The habit of a broken heart / Sign / I will find you / Lost and found / Planet Coventry / Empress's clothes / Cat's eye – Yellow fever / Primo on the parapet / Central hotel.

Sep 94. (cd) *FIE 9107)* **ROARING FORTIES** -
– Sharply unclear / The gift of fire / You can't want what you always get / A headlong stretch / Your tall ship.

Jun 95. (d-cd) *(FIE 9110)* **ROOM TEMPERATURE LIVE (live)** -
– Wave / Just good friends / Vision / Time to burn / Four pails / The comet, the course, the tail / Ophelia / Happy hour / If I could / Something about Ysabel's dance / Patient / Cat's eye, yellow fever (running) / Running / Skin / Hemlock / Our oyster / Unconscious life / After the snow / Way out / Future now / Traintime / Modern.

Mar 96. (cd) *(FIE 9111)* **X MY HEART** -
– Better time / Amnesiac / Ram origami / Forest of pronouns / Earthbound / Narcissus (bar & grill) / Material possession / Come clean.

Sine not issued

Sep 96. (cd) *(SINE 006)* **TIDES** -

– (PETER HAMMILL) compilations, etc. –

1978. (lp) *G.I.R.; <9211 1016>* **VISION** -
1983. (c) *Sofa;* **LOOPS AND REELS** -
(cd-iss.Nov93 on 'Fie!'; FIE 9105)

Aug 84. (lp) *Charisma; (CAS 1166)* **THE LOVE SONGS** (remixes) -
– Just good friends / My favourite / Been alone so long / Ophelia / Again / If I could / Vision / Don't tell me / The birds / (THis side of) The looking glass. *(re-iss.Jun88 lp/c; CHC/+MC 69) (cd-iss.Nov88; CASCD 1166)*

May 85. (7") *Charisma; (CB 414)* **JUST GOOD FRIENDS. / ('A'instrumental)** -
Jul 93. (cd) *Virgin; (CDVM 9017)* **THE CALM (AFTER THE STORM)** -
Jul 93. (cd) *Virgin; (CDVM 9018)* **THE STORM (BEFORE THE CALM)** -
Jan 95. (cd) *Golden Hind; (GH 70112)* **OFFENSICHTLLICH GOLDFISCH** -
– Offensichtilich goldfisch / Dich zu finden / Die kalte killt den kub / Favorit / Kaufhaus Europa / Der larm / Oase / Die prominenz kubt sich / Die tunte verlischt / Auto (wieder im wagen) / Gaia / Schlaft nun.

Nov 95. (cd) *Strange Fruit; (SFRCD 136)* **THE PEEL SESSIONS** -
Jan 96. (cd) *Virgin; (CDOVD 460)* **AFTER THE SHOW** -

VANGELIS

Born: EVANGELOS PAPATHANASSIOU, 29 Mar'43, Volos, Greece. A child prodigy, the young VANGELIS was performing his own compositions in front of a large audience from the age of six. Groomed by his artistic parents, he subsequently studied classical music alongside other areas of the Arts at The Academy Of Fine Arts in Athens. Having already cultivated a love of jazz, like many other budding musicians of the day, he was inspired by the revoltionary pop takeover of The BEATLES. In 1963, he duly instigated a 6-piece beat combo, The FORMINX, who scored a major hit in Greece with the single, 'YENKA BEAT'. They continued for four years, becoming one of their country's leading popular music acts and initiated a dance craze with their biggest hit, 'JERONIMO YANKA' in 1965. Following the band's demise, VANGELIS PAPATHANASSIOU took on board a more keyboard-orientated style, the result being a solo single, 'THE CLOCK', in 1968. Working with him at this time were drummer LUCAS SIDERAS and vocalist/bassist DEMIS ROUSSOS, this trio soon evolving into APHRODITE'S CHILD. A classical adaptation of PACHELBEL's 'Canon' (similar in style to PROCOL HARUM's 'A Whiter Shade Of Pale'), 'RAIN AND TEARS' was released by 'Mercury' in 1968, the single denting the UK Top 30 after being a Europe-wide hit. An album soon followed, 'END OF THE WORLD', being an unlikely hybrid of progressive rock and Latin-styled folk. Further singles appeared, although VANGELIS was eager to branch into more complex solo work. He scored the soundtrack for a soft-porn movie, 'Sex Power', released under the name, 'L'APOCALYPSE DES ANIMAUX' (1971). The following year, APHRODITE'S CHILD surfaced from their Paris studio, delivering the double set, '666', which explored the Bible's Book Of Revelations against a prog-rock backdrop. It was a critical success, although DEMIS ROUSSOS took off for a fruitful solo career (e.g. the chart-topper, 'Forever And Ever'). VANGELIS signed to 'R.C.A.' in 1974, enjoying a revived chart success with his UK debut for the label, 'HEAVEN AND HELL' (1975), which featured vocals by JON ANDERSON (of YES fame) on the track 'SO LONG AGO, SO CLEAR'. 'ALBEDO 0.39' (1976) was an overly ambitious, jazzy concept album while 'BEAUBOURG' (1978) saw VANGELIS in similarly abstruse territory, the album featuring only one track, divided into two parts. In 1979, he again hooked up with JON ANDERSON to form the duo JON AND VANGELIS, recording three successful albums, 'SHORT STORIES' (1980), 'SEE YOU LATER' (1980) and 'THE FRIENDS OF MR. CAIRO' (1981), before splitting in 1983. Meanwhile, VANGELIS recorded his masterstroke with the 1981 soundtrack, 'CHARIOTS OF FIRE'. The regal, whooshing electronica of the title track was an international smash, leading to more soundtrack work for a host of movies throughout the 80's and 90's, including 'MASK' (1985), 'ANTARTICA' (1988) and '1492: THE CONQUEST OF PARADISE' (1992). He also recorded a further one-off album with JON ANDERSON in 1991, 'PAGE OF LIFE'. • **Trivia:** In 1975, he was asked but refused to take the place of RICK WAKEMAN in YES, instead of PATRICK MORAZ. In 1985, he also wrote the ballet score for new version of 'Frankenstein'.

Recommended: HEAVEN & HELL (*8) / CHARIOTS OF FIRE (*7)

FORMINX

VANGELIS – keyboards / **TASSOS PAPASTHAMATIS** – vocals / **VASILLIS BAKOPOULOS** – rhythm guitar / **SOTORIS ARNIS** – bass / **KOSTAS SKODOS** – drums / **NIKOS MASTORASKIS** – co-songs

Vocalion not issued

Apr 65. (7") *(V 9235)* **JENKA BEAT. / GERONIMO JENKA** -

— also released a number of Greek 45's, an album finally surfacing in 1975.

APHRODITE'S CHILD

VANGELIS PAPATHANASSIOU (b. EVANGELOS, 15 Jun'47, Velos) – keyboards, wind, percussion / **DEMIS ROUSSOS** (b.15 Jun'47, Alexandria, Egypt) – vocals, bass / **LUCAS SIDERAS** (b. 5 Dec'44, Athens) – drums, vocals

Mercury Mercury

Oct 68. (7") *(MF 1039)* **RAIN AND TEARS. / DON'T TRY TO CATCH A RIVER** [30] [ ]

Feb 69. (7") *(MF 1075)* **END OF THE WORLD. / YOU ALWAYS STAND IN THE WAY** [ ] [ ]

Feb 69. (lp) *(SMCL 20140)* **END OF THE WORLD / RAIN AND TEARS** [ ] [ ]
– End of the world / Don't try to catch a river / Mister Thomas / Rain and tears / The grass is not green / Valley of sadness / You always stand in my way / The shepherd and the Moon / Day of the fool.

Polydor Polydor

Jun 69. (7") *(BM 56769) <15005>* **I WANT TO LIVE. / MAGIC MIRROR** [ ] [ ]

Nov 69. (7") *(BM 56785)* **LET ME LOVE, LET ME LIVE. / MARIE JOLIE** [ ] [-]

Mar 70. (7") *(BM 56791)* **IT'S FIVE O'CLOCK. / FUNKY MARY** [ ] [-]

Jan 70. (lp) *(238 4005)* **IT'S FIVE O'CLOCK** [ ] [-]
– It's five o'clock / Wake up / Take your time / Annabella / Let me love, let me live / Funky Mary / Good time so fine / Marie Jolie / Such a funny night. *(re-iss.Jul78 on 'Impact'; 6886 650)*

1970. (7") *(6033 003)* **SPRING, SUMMER, WINTER AND FALL. / AIR** [-] [-] France

— Disbanded for a time, until reappeared adding **SILVER KOULOURIS** – guitar, percussion. Guests **HARRIS HALKITIS** – bass, saxophone, percussion, vocals / **MICHEL RIPOCHE** – trombone, saxophone/ **JOHN FORST** – narration / **YANNIS TSAROUCHIS** – Greek text / **IRENE PAPAS** – vox on (1).

Vertigo Vertigo

Jun 72. (d-lp) *(6673 001) <500>* **666** [ ] [ ]
– The system / Babylon / Loud, loud, loud / The four horsemen / The lamb / The seventh seal / Aegian Sea / Seven bowls / The wakening beast / Lament / The marching beast / The battle of the locusts / Do it / Tribulation / The beasts / Ofis / / Seven trumpets / Altamont / The wedding of the lamb / The capture of the beast / oo / Hic and nunc / All the seats were occupied / Break. *(re-iss.Feb77; 6641 581)* (re-iss.May83 on 'Impact' d-lp/c; *6673/7528 001)*

Aug 72. (7") *<107>* **BREAK. / BABYLON** [-] [ ]
(UK-iss.Jun75; 6032 900)

— Disbanded again in 72/73. VANGELIS went solo, as did DEMIS ROUSSOS.

– compilations, others –

Jun 75. (lp) *Vertigo; (6333 002)* **THE BEST OF APHRODITE'S CHILD FEATURING DEMIS ROUSSOS** [ ] [-]

Jun 75. (lp) *Philips; (6483 025)* **RAIN AND TEARS** [ ] [-]
(re-iss.Aug81 as 'GREATEST HITS 1968-1970' on 'Fontana' lp/c; 6420 006)(7240 955)

VANGELIS

VANGELIS – keyboards, synthesizers (ex-APHRODITE'S CHILD, ex-FORMYNX)

Charly not issued

1971. (lp) *(CRL 5013)* **THE DRAGON** [ ] [-]
– The dragon / Stuffed aubergine / Stuffed tomato. *(re-iss.1980)*

Polydor not issued

1973. (lp) *(2489 113)* **L'APOCALYPSE DES ANIMAUX (Soundtrack)** [ ] [-]
– L'apocalypse des animaux / Generique / La petite fille / De la mer / Le singe blue / L'ours musicien / La mort / Du loop / Creation du monde / La mer recommences. *(re-iss.Oct76 + Apr84 lp/c; SPE LP/MC 72)((cd-iss.1988; 831 503-2)*

— He now moved to London and signed to . . .

Vertigo Vertigo

1974. (lp) *(6499 693) <1019>* **EARTH**
– Come on / We were all uprooted / Sunny Earth / He-o / Ritual / Let it happen / The city / My face in the rain / Watch out / A song.

R.C.A. R.C.A.

Nov 75. (lp/c) *(RS 1025) <5110>* **HEAVEN & HELL** [31] [ ]
– Heaven and Hell pt.1 – Bacchanale symphony to the powers of B – 2nd movement – 3rd movement – So long ago so clear * / Heaven and Hell pt.2 – Intestinal heart – Needles and bones – 12 o'clock – Aries – Away. *(re-iss.Sep81; 3012) (re-iss.1984 lp/c; PL/PK 70009) (re-iss.Oct86 lp/c; NL/NK 71148) (cd-iss.Sep89; ND 71148)*

— above featured The ENGLISH CHAMBER CHOIR and VANA VEROUTIS – lead vocals (track* was first to use vocals of **JON ANDERSON** (of YES)

Aug 76. (7") *<10733>* **SO LONG AGO, SO CLEAR. / HEAVEN AND HELL THEME** [-] [ ]

Sep 76. (lp/c) *(RS/RC 1080) <5136>* **ALBEDO 0.39** [18] [ ]
– Pulstar / Freefall / More tranquilillitatis / Main sequence / Sword of Orion / Alpha / Nucleogenesis (pt.1 & 2) / Albedo 0• 39. *(re-iss.Sep81 lp/c; RCA LP/K 3017) (re-iss.Sep89 lp/c/cd; NL/NK/ND 74208)*

Oct 76. (7") *(RCA 2762) <10882>* **PULSTAR. / ALPHA** [ ] [ ]

Dec 77. (lp/c) *(PL2 5116) <2627>* **SPIRAL** [ ] [ ]
– Spiral / Ballad / Dervish D / To the unknown man / 3 plus 3. *(re-iss.Sep81 + Nov84 lp/c; NL/NK 70568) (cd-iss.Oct89; ND 70568)*

Jan 78. (7") *(PB 5064)* **TO THE UNKNOWN MAN. / (part 2)** [ ] [-]

Jul 78. (lp/c) *(PL2/PK2 5155) <3020>* **BEAUBOURG** [ ] [ ]
– Beaubourg (part 1) / Beaubourg (part 2). *(re-iss.Sep86 on 'Fame' lp/c; FA/TC-FA 3168) (re-iss.Feb90 cd/c; ND/NK 74516)*

Polydor Polydor

Apr 79. (lp/c) *(POLD/+C 5018) <6199>* **CHINA** [ ] [ ]
– Chung Kuo / The long march / The dragon / The plum blossom / The Tao of love / The little fete / Yin and Yang / Himalaya / Summit. *(re-iss.Aug83 lp/c)(cd; SPE LP/MC 19)(813653-2)*

May 79. (7") *(POSP 57)* **THE LONG MARCH. / (part 2)** [ ] [-]

JON & VANGELIS

JON = **JON ANDERSON** – vocals (also of YES)

Polydor Polydor

Dec 79. (7") *(POSP 96) <2098>* **I HEAR YOU NOW. / THUNDER** [8] [58] Aug80

Jan 80. (lp/c) *(POLD/+C 5030) <PD1 6272>* **SHORT STORIES** [4] [ ]
– Curious electic / Each and everyday / Bird song / I hear you now / The road / Far away in Bagdhad / Love is / One more time / Thunder / A play within a play. *(cd-iss.1983; 800027-2) (re-iss.Jun87 lp/c; SPE LP/MC 105)*

Feb 80. (7") *<2130>* **ONE MORE TIME. / THE ROAD** [-] [ ]

VANGELIS

solo (same label until stated)

Jun 80. (7") *(2001 973)* **MY LOVE. / DOMESTIC LOGIC 1** [ ] [-]

Nov 80. (lp)(c) *(2302 101)(3100 567)* **SEE YOU LATER** [ ] [ ]
– I can't take it anymore / Multitrack suggestion / Memories of green / Not a bit – all of it / Suffocation / See you later.

Mar 81. (lp/c) *(POLS/+C 1026) <PD1 6335>* **CHARIOTS OF FIRE (Original Motion Picture Soundtrack)** [5] [1] Oct81
– Titles / Five circles / Abraham's theme / Eric's theme / 100 metres / Jerusalem / Chariots of fire. *(re-iss.Apr84; POLD 5160); hit UK No.39) (cd-iss.1983; 8000202-2)*

Apr 81. (7") *(POSP 246) <2189>* **CHARIOTS OF FIRE – TITLES. / ERIC'S THEME** [12] [1] Dec81
(re-prom.UK Feb82 hit UK No.41 & re-iss.Aug84; same)

JON & VANGELIS

May 81. (7") *(POSP 258) <2181>* **THE FRIENDS OF MR. CAIRO. / BESIDE** [ ] [ ]

Jul 81. (lp/c) *(POLD/+C 5039) <PD1 6326>* **THE FRIENDS OF MR. CAIRO** [6] [64]
– The friends of Mr. Cairo / Back to school boogie / Outside of this (inside of that) / State of independence / Beside / The Mayflower. *(cd-iss.May83; 800021-2) (re-iss.Oct89 lp/c; POLD/+C 5053)*

Jul 81. (7") *(POSP 323)* **STATE OF INDEPENDENCE. / BESIDE** [ ] [ ]

Nov 81. (7") *(JV 1)* **I'LL FIND MY WAY HOME. / BACK TO SCHOOL BOOGIE** [6] [-]

Apr 82. (7") *<2205>* **I'LL FIND MY WAY HOME. / I HEAR YOU NOW** [-] [51]

— In 1982, he wrote unissued vinyl score for film 'Blade Runner'.

May 83. (7") *(JV 3)* **AND WHEN THE NIGHT COMES. / SONG IS** [ ] [-]

May 83. (lp/c)(cd) *(POLH/+C 4)(813174-2) <813174>* **PRIVATE COLLECTION** [22] [ ]
– He is sailing / And when the night comes / Deborah / The king is coming / Horizon.

Jul 83. (7") *(JV 4)* **HE IS SAILING. / POLANAISE** [61] [ ]
(12"+=) *(JVX 4)* – Song is.

— Above was last collaboration between the duo, until 1991.

Aug 84. (7"/12") *(JV/+X 5)* **STATE OF INDEPENDENCE. / THE FRIENDS OF MR. CAIRO** [67] [ ]

Aug 84. (lp/c/cd) *(POLH/+C 6)(821929-2)* **THE BEST OF JON & VANGELIS** (compilation) [42] [ ]
– Italian song / I'll find my way home / State of independence / One more time / Play within a play / The friends of Mr. Cairo / Outside of this (inside of that) / He is sailing / I hear you now.

VANGELIS

continued solo. BOUNTY Soundtrack was also unissued. He continued to write unissued soundtracks throughout the 80's as well as below.

Oct 84. (lp/c)(cd) *(POLH/+C 11)(823396-2)* **SOIL FESTIVITIES** [55] [ ]
– Movements 1-5. *(re-iss.Jun87 lp/c; SPE LP/MC 106)*

Mar 85. (lp/c)(cd) *(POLH/+C 19)(825245-2)* **MASK (Soundtrack)** [69] [ ]
– Movements 1-6.

Deutsche not issued

Mar 85. (lp/c/cd) *(415196-1/-4/-2)* **INVISIBLE CONNECTIONS** [-] [-]
– Invisible connections / Atom blaster / Thermo vision.

1986. (lp/c/cd) **RHAPSODIES** [ ] [ ]
– Ti ipermacho stratigo / O! gliki mou ear / Ton nimfona sou vlepo / Rapsodia / Tin oreotita tis partenias sou / Christos anesti / Asma asmaton.

Arista Arista

Sep 88. (lp/c/cd) *(209/409/259 149)* **DIRECT** [ ] [ ]
– The motion of stars / The will of the wind / Metallic rain / Elsewhere / Glorianna (hymn a la femme) / Rotations logic / The oracle of Apollo / Ave / First approach / Dial out / Intergallactic radio station / Message.

Sep 88. (c-s) *(111 767)* **WILL OF THE WIND / INTERGALACTIC RADIO STATION** [ ] [-]
(12"+=/cd-s+=) *(611/661 767)* – Metallic rain.

East West Atlantic

Nov 90. (cd)(lp/c) *(903173026-2)(WX 398/+C)* **THE CITY** [ ] [ ]
– Dawn / Morning papers / Nerve centre / Side streets / Good to see you / Twilight / Red lights / Procession. *(re-iss.cd Nov93 & Feb95; same)*

Oct 92. (cd)(c) *(4509 91014-2)(WX 497C)* **1492: THE CONQUEST OF PARADISE (Soundtrack)** [33] [ ]
– Opening theme / 1492: The conquest of Paradise / Monastery of la Rabida / City of Isabel / Light and shadow / Deliverance / West across the ocean sea / Eternity / Hispanola / Moxica and the horse / 28th parallel / Pinta, Nina, Santa Maria (into eternity) *(re-iss.cd Jun94)*.

Oct 92. (7"/c-s) *(YZ 704C)* **CONQUEST OF PARADISE. / MOXICA AND THE HORSE** [60] [ ]
(cd-s+=) *(YZ 704CD)* – Line open / Landscape. *(re-iss.May95; same)*

Mar 93. (c-s/cd-s) *(YZ 736 C/CD)* **28th PARALLEL / WEST ACROSS THE OCEAN SEA** [ ] [ ]

Oct 95. (c-s) *(EW 007C)* **VOICES / VOICES II (ECHOES)** [ ] [ ]
(cd-s+=) *(EW 007CD)* – Voices III.

Feb 96. (cd/c) *(0630 12786-2/-4)* **VOICES** [58] [ ]

— above featured PAUL YOUNG on vocals

Mar 96. (c-s; as VANGELIS & STINA NORDENSTAM) *(EW 031C)* **ASK THE MOUNTAINS / SLOW PIECE** [ ] [ ]
(cd-s+=) *(EW 031CD)* – ('A'-Album version).

Apr 96. (cd/c) *(531154-2/-4)* **PORTRAIT (SO LONG AGO, SO CLEAR)** (compilation) [14] [ ]
– To the unknown man / Italian song / Pulstar / La petite fille de la mer / Alpha / I hear you now / I'll find my way home / State of indepenence / Himalaya / Conquest of Paradise / Hymn / Antartica / Sauvage et beau / Chariots of fire / So long ago, so clear.

JON & VANGELIS

re-united in '91.

Arista Arista

Aug 91. (7") **WISDOM CHAIN. / PAGE OF LIFE** [ ] [ ]
(cd-s+=) – ('A'full version) / Sing with your eyes.

Sep 91. (cd/c/lp) *(261/411/211 373)* **PAGE OF LIFE** [ ] [ ]
– Wisdom chain / Page of life / Money / Garden of senses / Is it love / Anyone can light a candle / Journey to Ixtlan / Shine for me / Genevieve.

– compilations, others, etc. –

— on 'R.C.A.' unless mentioned otherwise

1978. (lp/c) *(PL2 5174)* **THE BEST OF VANGELIS** [ ] [ ]
(re-iss.Sep81 lp/c; RCA LP/K 3028) (cd-iss.May93; 74321 13885-2)

May 78. (cd) *Affinity; (AFF 11)* **HYPOTHESIS** (rec.1971) [ ] [-]

Jul 81. (7") *B.B.C.; (BBC 1)* **HEAVEN AND HELL, THIRD MOVEMENT (THEME FROM THE BBC-TV SERIES – THE COSMOS). / ALPHA** [48] [-]

Aug 81. (lp) *Polydor; (AFL1 4003)* **OPERA SAUVAGE – COSMOS** [-]
(re-iss.Nov84 lp/c; SPE LP/MC 81) (cd-iss.1987; 829663-2) <US-iss.Dec86; 829663> hit No.42>

Aug 82. (d-c; JON & VANGELIS) *Polydor; (3574 139)* **SHORT STORIES / THE FRIENDS OF MR. CAIRO** [ ] [-]

Nov 82. (d-lp/d-c) *(RCA LP/K 1002-3) <4397>* **TO THE UNKNOWN MAN VOLS.1 & 2** [ ] [-]

1982. (7") *<13402>* **TO THE UNKNOWN MAN. / (part 2)** [-] [ ]

Nov 82. (t-lp) *Polydor; (BOX 1)* **CHARIOTS OF FIRE / CHINA / OPERA SAUVAGE** [ ] [-]

1983. (lp) *(PL 30036)* **THE SAVAGE BEAST** [ ] [-]

Jun 84. (c) *(NK 70345)* **MAGIC MOMENTS** [ ] [-]

Jul 84. (lp) *(NL 70078)* **GREATEST HITS** [ ] [-]

1984. (7") *B.B.C.; (RESL 144)* **FRAME OF THE DAY: BBC SNOOKER THEMES (TO THE UNKNOWN MAN) (part 1). / (part 2)** [ ] [-]

Jun 88. (7"; JON & VANGELIS) *Old Gold; (OG 9785)* **I HEAR YOU NOW. / I'LL FIND MY WAY HOME** [ ] [-]

Nov 88. (lp/c/cd) *Polydor; (815 732-1/-4/-2)* **ANTARTICA (Original Soundtrack)** [ ] [-]

Jul 89. (lp/c)(cd) *Polydor; (LP/MC VGTV 1)(839518-2)* **THEMES** [ ] [ ]
– (excerpts from films, including some from previously unissued)

Oct 89. (cd-box/c-box) *(VGPK 1)* **SPIRAL / ALBEDO 0• 39 / HEAVEN AND HELL** [ ] [-]

Apr 93. (cd) *C.A.M.;* **ENTENDS-TU LES CHEINS** [ ] [-]

Jun 94. (cd/c) *East West; (4509 96574-2/-4)* **BLADE RUNNER (Soundtrack)** [20] [ ]

Aug 94. (cd/c) *(74321 22415-2/-4)* **THE COLLECTION** [ ] [-]

Sep 94. (cd/c; JON & VANGELIS) *Spectrum; (550196-2/-4)* **CHRONICLES** [ ] [-]

Apr 95. (cd) *(74321 25954-2)* **ALBEDO 0.39 / HEAVEN AND HELL** [ ] [-]

Jun 96. (cd) *Camden; (74321 39337-2)* **GIFT . . . THE BEST OF VANGELIS** [ ] [-]

Aug 96. (cd/c) *Autograph; (MAC CD/MC 246)* **CHARIOTS OF FIRE (THE MUSIC OF VANGELIS)** [ ] [-]

VANILLA FUDGE

Formed: New York City, New York, USA . . . 1965 as The PIGEONS. They became VANILLA FUDGE in late '66, and after their debut at The Village Theater (Fillmore East), they were signed up by 'Atlantic'. Their po-faced, psychedelic-symphonic rock often degenerated into dirty, leaden dirges and VANILLA SLUDGE would've been a more accurate name for this proto-metal band. Nevertheless, in 1967 they were unique, if nothing else than for their unqualified heaviness and they enjoyed chart success with their first release, a characteristically over the top and drawn out rendition of The SUPREMES' 'YOU KEEP ME HANGIN' ON'. The self-titled debut album followed later that summer and contained similarly overblown and amusing covers, The BEATLES' 'ELEANOR RIGBY' and 'TICKET TO RIDE' among them. Follow-up albums were inconsistent, the band's original material falling woefully short of matching the strength of the covers they'd made their name with and, after the band split in mid '69 , TIM BOGERT and CARMINE APPICE formed the short lived CACTUS with RUSTY DAY and JIM McCARTY. Purveying straight-down-the-line hard rock, the band cut three albums, 'CACTUS' (1970), 'ONE WAY . . .OR ANOTHER' (1971) and 'RESTRICTIONS' (1972) before BOGERT and APPICE joined JEFF BECK in the supergroup BECK, BOGERT & APPICE. • **Songwriters:** STEIN or group compositions, with mainly other covers :- BANG BANG (Cher) / SEASON OF THE WITCH (Donovan) / I CAN'T MAKE IT ALONE (Goffin-King) / THE WINDMILLS OF YOUR MIND (Legrand-Bergyan). CACTUS also covered several standards. • **Trivia:** In the summer of '69, they played the Seattle Pop Festival at Woodenville, Washington.

Recommended: THE BEST OF (PSYCHEDELIC SUNDAE) (*8)

MARK STEIN (b.11 Mar'47, Bayonne, New Jersey) – vocals, organ / **VINCE MARTELL** (b.11 Nov'45, Bronx, N.Y.) – guitar, vocals / **TIM BOGERT** (b.27 Aug'44) – bass, vocals / **CARMINE APPICE** (b.15 Dec'46, Staten Island, N.Y.) – drums, vocals

Atlantic Atco

Jun 67. (7") *<6590>* **YOU KEEP ME HANGIN' ON. / COME BY DAY, COME BY NIGHT** [-] [67]
<US re-prom.Jul68, hit No.6>

Jul 67. (7") *(584 123) <6590>* **YOU KEEP ME HANGIN' ON. / TAKE ME FOR A LITTLE WHILE** [18] [-]

Sep 67. (lp; mono/stereo) *(587/588 086) <33224>* **VANILLA FUDGE** [31] [6]
– Ticket to ride / People get ready / She's not there / Bang bang / Illusions of my childhood (parts 1-3) / You keep me hangin' on / Take me for a little while / Eleanor Rigby. *(cd-iss.May93; 7567 90390-2)*

Oct 67. (7") *(584 139)* **ILLUSIONS OF MY CHILDHOOD. / ELEANOR RIGBY** [ ] [-]

Feb 68. (lp; mono/stereo) *(587/588 100) <33237>* **THE BEAT GOES ON** [ ] [17]
– Sketch / Variation on a theme from Mozart's Divertimento No.13 in F / Old black Joe / Don't fence me in / 12th Street rag / In the mood / Hound dog / I want to hold your hand – I feel fine – Day tripper – She loves you / The beat goes on / Beethoven's fur Elise and theme from Moonlight Sonata / The beat goes on / Voices in time: – Neville Chamberlain – Winston Churchill – F.D. Roosevelt – Harry S. Truman – John F.Kennedy / Merchant / The game is over / The beat goes on. *(cd-iss.Jun92 & Jul93 on 'Repertoire'+=;)–*

Apr 68. (7") *(584 179) <6554>* **WHERE IS MY MIND?. / THE LOOK OF LOVE** [ ] [73] Jan68

Jun 68. (lp; mono/stereo) *(587/588 110) <33244>* **RENAISSANCE** [ ] [20]
– The sky cried – When I was a boy / Thoughts / Paradise / That's what makes a man / The spell that comes after / Faceless people / Season of the witch. *(cd-iss.Jul93 on 'Repertoire'+=; REP 4126)–* You keep me hangin' on (7" version) / Come by day, come by night / People.

Sep 68. (7") *<6616>* **TAKE ME FOR A LITTLE WHILE. / THOUGHTS** [-] [38]

Nov 68. (7") *<6632>* **SEASON OF THE WITCH. / (part 2)** [-] [65]

Atco Atco

Feb 69. (lp) *(228 020) <33278>* **NEAR THE BEGINNING** (half studio / half live) [ ] [16]
– Shotgun / Some velvet morning / Where is happiness / Break song. *(cd-iss.Jul93 on 'Repertoire' +=)–* Look of love.

Mar 69. (7") *(584 257) <6655>* **SHOTGUN. / GOOD GOOD LOVIN'** [ ] [68]

Jun 69. (7") *<6679>* **SOME VELVET MORNING. / PEOPLE** [-] [ ]

Jul 69. (7") *(584 276)* **SOME VELVET MORNING. / THOUGHTS** [ ] [-]

Oct 69. (lp) *(228 029) <33303>* **ROCK & ROLL** [ ] [34]
– Need love / Lord in the country / I can't make it alone / Street walking woman / Church bells of St. Martin's / The windmills of your mind / If you gotta make a fool of somebody. *(cd-iss.Jul93 on 'Repertoire'+=; REP 4168)–* Good good lovin' / Shotgun / Where is my mind / Need love (7" version).

Nov 69. (7") *<6703>* **I CAN'T MAKE IT ALONE. / NEED LOVE** [-] [ ]

Jan 70. (7") *<6728>* **LORD IN THE COUNTRY. / THE WINDMILLS OF YOUR MIND** [-] [ ]

— Had already folded mid '69. STEIN formed BOOMERANG and MARTELL retired.

CACTUS

were formed Feb'70 by **BOGERT & APPICE** with **RUSTY DAY** – vocals, mouth harp (ex-AMBOY DUKES / TED NUGENT) / **JIM McCARTY** – guitar (not of YARDBIRDS)

Atlantic Atco

Jul 70. (lp) *(2400 020) <SD 33340>* **CACTUS** [ ] [54]
– Parchman farm / My lady from south of Detroit / Bro. Bill / You can't judge a book by the cover / Let me swim / No need to worry / Oleo / Feel so good. *(cd-iss.Jan96; 7567 80290-2)*

Oct 70. (7") *<6792>* **YOU CAN'T JUDGE A BOOK BY THE COVER. / BRO BILL** [-] [ ]

Mar 71. (7") *<6811>* **LONG TALL SALLY. / ROCK'N'ROLL CHILDREN** [-] [ ]

Jul 71. (lp) *(2400 114) <SD 33356>* **ONE WAY . . . OR ANOTHER** [ ] [88] Mar71
– Long tall Sally / Rock out whatever you feel like / Rock'n'roll children / Big mam boogie / Feel so bad / Hometown bust / One way . . .or another.

Sep 71. (7") *<6842>* **TOKEN CHOKIN'. / ALASKA** [-] [ ]

— (May71) added **DUANE HITCHINGS** – piano

Jan 72. (7") *<6872>* **EVIL. / SWEET SIXTEEN** [-] [ ]

Apr 72. (lp) *(K 40307) <SD 33377>* **RESTRICTIONS** [ ] [ ] Nov71
– Restrictions / Token chokin' / Guiltness glider / Evil / Alaska / Sweet sixteen / Bag drag / Mean night in Cleveland. *(cd-iss.Jul93 on 'Repertoire')*

— **PETE FRENCH** – vocals (ex-ATOMIC ROOSTER) McCARTY and DAY

Oct 72. (lp) *(K 50013) <SD 7011>* **'OT & SWEATY** (live/studio) [ ] [ ]
– Swim / Bad mother boogie / Our lil' rock and roll thing / Bad stuff / Bring me down / Bedroom Mazurka / Telling you / Underneath / The arches.

Oct 72. (7") *<6901>* **BAD MOTHER BOOGIE. / BRINGING ME DOWN** [-] [ ]

— Disbanded and DUANE retained some of name NEW CACTUS BAND issuing an album, 'SON OF CACTUS' and single 'BILLIE GYPSY WOMAN' in 1973. TIM and CARMINE teamed up with JEFF BECK ⇒ in supergroup BECK, BOGERT & APPICE. CARMINE joined MIKE BLOOMFIELD's band KGB in the mid-70's. He later joined ROD STEWART and in the 80's with RICK DERRINGER formed DNA.

VANILLA FUDGE

re-formed originals 1982 and again in 1984.

Atco Atco

Jul 84. (lp/c) *(90149-1/-4)* **MYSTERY** [ ] [ ]
– Golden age dreams / Jealousy / Mystery / Under suspicion / It gets stronger / Walk on by / My world is empty / Don't stop now / Hot blood / The stranger.

Jul 84. (7") *<99729>* **MYSTERY. / THE STRANGER** [-] [ ]

— Folded again, although they briefly got together for Atlantic 40 year bash mid-'88.

– compilations, others, etc. –

1970. (lp; as PIGEONS) *Wand; <687>* **WHILE THE WORLD WAS EATING** [-] [ ]

1974. (lp) *Midi; (MID 0033)* **STAR COLLECTION** [ ] [-]

1982. (lp/c) *Atco;* **GREATEST HITS** [-] [ ]

1991. (cd) *Rhino;* **VANILLA FUDGE LIVE (live)** [-] [ ]

Mar 93. (cd) *Atlantic; (8122 71154-2)* **THE BEST OF VANILLA FUDGE (PSYCHEDELIC SUNDAE)** [ ] [ ]

– You keep me hangin' on / Where is my mind? / The look of love / Ticket to ride / Come by day, come by night / Take me for a little while / That's what makes a man / Season of the witch / Shotgun / Thoughts / Faceless people / Good good lovin' / Some velvet morning / I can't make it alone / Lord in the country / Need love / Street walking woman / All in your mind.

Aug 95. (cd) *Atlantic; (7567 90006-2)* **THE BEST OF VANILLA FUDGE** ☐ [-]
Jul 94. (cd/c) *Success;* **YOU KEEP ME HANGIN' ON** ☐ [-]
Jul 96. (cd; CACTUS) *Atlantic; (8122 72411-2)* **CACTOLOGY** ☐ ☐

Thijs VAN LEER (see under ⇒ FOCUS)

VEJTABLES

Formed: San Francisco, California, USA . . . as a 5-piece, by BOB BAILEY, NED HOLLIS and female drummer JAN ERRICO (ASHTON), a novelty for the time although the UK had an equivalent in The HONEYCOMBS. They secured a residency at the Morocco Room in San Mateo, leading to a deal with 'Autumn' records (home of The BEAU BRUMMELS). Becoming quite a live attraction, they soon released their debut 45, 'I STILL LOVE YOU', which bubbled under the Hot 100 for a number of weeks. Like many others around at the time, it fused the styles of The BEATLES and The BYRDS and was showcased on the Lloyd Thaxton Show. Their follow-up, 'THE LAST THING ON MY MIND', was from the pen of TOM PAXTON and to promote it, they supported the likes of The BEACH BOYS and The YARDBIRDS. In April 1966, they played at The Battle Of The Bands contest in L.A., the winners being The DOORS. When their label got into financial problems, JAN ASHTON took off for a brief solo outing, leaving BOB and FRANK to record what was to become their best song yet. 'FEEL THE MUSIC' was a raga-punk style song, simulating heavy sitar-like guitars rounded off with a crashing cymbal.

Recommended: their final single

BOB BAILEY – vocals, tambourine / **REESE SHEETS** – lead guitar; repl. BOB COLE / **NED HOLLIS** – guitar, organ / **FRANK SMITH** – bass; repl. RON who had repl. RICK DEY (to WILDE KNIGHTS) / **JAN ERRICO** – drums (soon became JAN ASHTON)

Pye Int. Autumn

Nov 65. (7") *(7N 25339) <15>* **I STILL LOVE YOU. / ANYTHING** ☐ ☐ Oct65
Jan 66. (7") *<23>* **THE LAST THING ON MY MIND. / MANSIONS OF TEARS** [-] ☐

— **JIM SAWYERS**– lead guitar (ex-OTHER SIDE; from San Jose) repl. SHEETS

— JAN departed after above and released a single 'COLD DREARY MORNING', before joining The MOJO MEN. SAWYERS joined The SYNDICATE OF SOUND, while BAILEY and SMITH were now a duo.

not issued Uptown

1966. (7") *<741>* **FEEL THE MUSIC. / SHADOWS** [-] ☐

VELVET OPERA

Formed: London, England . . . 1966, out of JAYMES FENDA & THE VULCANS by JOHN FORD, COLIN FORSTER and RICHARD HUDSON. They had previously won a TV contest 'Ready Steady Win', before choosing the name, ELMER GANTRY'S VELVET OPERA. A psychedelic/soul-styled single, 'FLAMES', was boosted by appearances on BBC Radio 1's Top Gear in 1967, although it failed to chart. The following year, an excellent album surfaced, although GANTRY left to pursue a solo career while the rest cut the name down to The VELVET OPERA. A prog-rock album, 'RIDE THE HUSTLER'S DREAM', made it to the shops in '69, although they folded when HUDSON and FORD joined The STRAWBS. While HUDSON-FORD were enjoying chart success, GANTRY was scoring a one-hit wonder in 1976 with 'WHY DID YOU DO IT' while in the outfit, STRETCH.

Recommended: ELMER GANTRY'S VELVET OPERA (*7) / RIDE THE HUSTLER'S DREAM (*5)

ELMER GANTRY'S VELVET OPERA

ELMER GANTRY – vocals, guitar / **COLIN FORSTER** – guitar / **JOHN FORD** – bass / **RICHARD HUDSON** – drums

Direction Epic

Nov 67. (7") *(58-3083)* **FLAMES. / SALISBURY PLAIN** ☐ ☐
May 68. (7") *(58-3481)* **MARY JANE. / DREAMY** ☐ ☐
Jul 68. (lp) *(8-63300) <26415>* **ELMER GANTRY'S VELVET OPERA** ☐ ☐
– Intro – Mother writes / Mary Jane / But I was cool / Walter Sly meets Bill Bailey / Air / Lookin' for a happy life / Flames / What's the point of leaving / Long nights of summer / Dream starts / Reaction of a young man / Now she's gone.

— **PAUL BRETT** – guitar, repl. FORSTER (later that year BRETT joined FIRE, before forming PAUL BRETT'S SAGE)

Jan 68. (7") *(58-3924)* **VOLCANO. / A QUICK 'B'** ☐ ☐

VELVET OPERA

HUDSON / FORD / FORSTER / + JOHN JOYCE – vocals, guitar, repl. GANTRY

C.B.S. Columbia

May 69. (7") *(CBS 4189)* **ANNA DANCE SQUARE. / DON'T YOU REALIZE** ☐ ☐
Dec 69. (lp) *(CBS 63692)* **RIDE A HUSTLER'S DREAM** ☐ [-]
– Ride a hustler's dream / Statesboro' blues / Money by / Black Jack Davy / Raise the light / Raga / Anna dance square / Depression / Don't you realize / Warm day in July / Eleanor Rigby.

Feb 70. (7") *(CBS 4802)* **BLACK JACK DAVY. / STATESBORO' BLUES** ☐ [-]

Spark not issued

Nov 70. (7") *(SRL 1045)* **SHE KEEPS GIVING ME THESE FEELINGS. / THERE'S A HOLE IN MY POCKET** ☐ [-]

— After a time in STRAWBS, HUDSON-FORD formed their own hit duo.

– compilations, etc. –

Feb 96. (cd) *See For Miles; (SEECD 437)* **THE VERY BEST OF ELMER GANTRY & VELVET OPERA** ☐ [-]
– (virtually every track and 4 unreleased)

VELVETT FOGG

Formed: London, England . . . 1968 by PAUL EASTMONT, FRANK WILSON, KEITH LAW and MULLETT POLLARD. In 1969, they released an album of organ-based progressive-rock, with sleevenotes by fan/DJ, JOHN PEEL. It contained two covers, 'NEW YORK MINING DISASTER 1941' (Bee Gees) and 'COME AWAY MELINDA' (Tim Rose), alongside the classier 'YELLOW CAVE WOMAN' and 'WIZARD OF GOBSOLOD'. Their up-to-date '69 version of The TORNADOS' 'TELSTAR' was issued together with another instrumental cut, 'OWED TO THE DIP', from their only album. • **Trivia:** The cover of the album featured a face-painted band alongside two face/body-painted females.

Recommended: VELVETT FOGG (*6)

PAUL EASTMONT – vocals / **FRANK WILSON** – organ / **KEITH LAW** – drums / **MULLETT POLLARD** – guitar ?

Pye not issued

Jan 69. (7") *(7N 17673)* **TELSTAR '69. / OWED TO THE DIP** ☐ [-]
Jan 69. (lp) *(NSPL 18272)* **VELVETT FOGG** ☐ [-]
– Yellow cave woman / New York mining disaster 1941 / Wizard of Gobsolod / Once among the trees / Lady Caroline / Come away Melinda / Owed to the dip / Within the night / Plastic man. *(re-iss.Sep89 on 'See For Miles' lp/cd+=; SEE/+CD 259)*– Telstar '69.

— split in 1969, when EASTMONT joined The GHOST. WILSON was to surface in heavy outfit WARHORSE.

VELVET UNDERGROUND

Formed: New York City, New York, USA . . . early 1965, by LOU REED and JOHN CALE, who nearly hit as The PRIMITIVES with the single, 'The Ostrich'. They met modern pop artist, ANDY WARHOL, who invited German chanteuse NICO to join the set-up alongside STERLING MORRISON and MO TUCKER. Early in 1966, they signed to 'MGM-Verve', and soon began work on what was to be their debut album, 'THE VELVET UNDERGROUND AND NICO'. The album was a revelation, strikingly different from the love and peace psychedelia of the day, The VELVETS vision was decidedly darker and more disturbing. Combining sublime melodies and nihilistic noise, it featured eleven superb ahead-of-their-time classics, notably the brutally frank and frenetic 'HEROIN', the S&M 'VENUS IN FURS' and the garage raunch of 'WAITING FOR THE MAN'. It also contained three NICO sung beauties, 'FEMME FATALE', 'ALL TOMORROW'S PARTIES' and 'I'LL BE YOUR MIRROR'. The record only managed a brief stay in the US Top 200, as did the 1967 follow-up, 'WHITE LIGHT, WHITE HEAT', which included the 17-minute white noise freak-out of 'SISTER RAY'. With CALE now out of the picture, the focus fell on REED's songwriting for the self-titled third album. An altogether mellower set of more traditionally structured songs, the highlight was undoubtedly REED's beautiful lullaby, 'PALE BLUE EYES'. The band's last studio album, 'LOADED', was the closest The VELVET UNDERGROUND ever came to mainstream rock and an indicator of the direction REED would take in his solo career. 'SWEET JANE' and 'ROCK 'N' ROLL' marked his creative peak, a final glorious burst of guitar noise before the group disbanded and the myth started to crystallise. And that was that. Except it wasn't, not come 1992 anyway, when many a precious, pasty faced obsessive went even whiter with horror as The VELVET UNDERGROUND reformed. Many more fans, however, eagerly shelled out their hard earned cash for a reunion tour and album as CALE and REED became buddies once more. The live shows were apparently rather joyous and the accompanying vinyl document, 'LIVE MCMXCII' (1993), was an enjoyable romp through all the favourites. After the death of STERLING MORRISON in 1995, however, the prospect of further VELVETS activity looks doubtful. Yet despite the reunion, despite LOU REED's dodgy hairdo, despite everything, The VELVET UNDERGROUND of the 60's remain perenially cool and insidiously influential. Basically, alternative music begins and ends with VU and they have been cited as the inspiration for punk rock. A decade after that, a generation of indie groups (i.e. JESUS & MARY CHAIN, early PRIMAL SCREAM, MY BLOODY VALENTINE, etc.) paid barely disguise homage to their heroes. • **Songwriters:** REED compositions, except some by group. Many rock acts have covered their material, but so far not surprisingly, none have managed to score a major chart hit yet. • **Miscellaneous:** In 1990, REED and CALE re-united on a tribute album to the deceased ANDY WARHOL. NICO had earlier died on the 18th of July '88 after suffering a brain haemorrhage due to a fall from her bike while on holiday in Ibiza. • **Trivia:** The debut lp sleeve,

featured a gimmick peeling banana skin sticker. They reformed for a gig in Paris, 15 June 1990. UK's Channel 4, featured a night-long session of all their previous work.

Recommended: THE VELVET UNDERGROUND AND NICO (*10) / WHITE LIGHT – WHITE HEAT (*9) / V.U. (*7) / THE VELVET UNDERGROUND (*7).

LOU REED (b. LOUIS FIRBANK, 2 Mar'44, Long Island, N.Y.) – vocals, guitar (ex-JADES, ex-PRIMITIVES) / **JOHN CALE** (b. 9 Dec'42, Garnant, Wales) – bass, viola, vocals, etc. / **STERLING MORRISON** – guitar / **MAUREEN TUCKER** – drums / plus **NICO** (b. CHRISTA PAFFGEN, 16 Oct'38, Cologne, Germany) – vocals (also – Solo artist)

Verve Verve

Oct 66. (7") *<10427>* **ALL TOMORROW'S PARTIES. / I'LL BE YOUR MIRROR** -

Dec 66. (7") *<10466>* **SUNDAY MORNING / FEMME FATALE** -

Oct 67. (lp; stereo/mono) *(S+/VLP 9184) <5008>* **THE VELVET UNDERGROUND AND NICO** Dec66
– Sunday morning / I'm waiting for the man / Femme fatale / Venus in furs / Run run run / All tomorrow's parties / Heroin / There she goes again / I'll be your mirror / Black angel's death song / European son to Delmore Schwartz. *(re-iss.Oct71 on 'M.G.M.; 2315 056) (re-iss.Aug83 on 'Polydor' lp/c; SPE LP/MC 20) (cd-iss.1986 on 'Polydor'; 823 290-2) (cd re-iss.May96 on 'Polydor'; 531 250-2)*

— Trimmed to a quartet when NICO preferred the solo life

Jan 68. (7") *<10543>* **WHITE LIGHT – WHITE HEAT. / HERE SHE COMES NOW** -

Mar 68. (7") *<10560>* **I HEARD HER CALL MY NAME. / HERE SHE COMES NOW** -

Jun 68. (lp; stereo/mono) *(S+/VLP 9201) <5046>* **WHITE LIGHT / WHITE HEAT** Dec67
– White light – white heat / The gift / Lady Godiva's operation / Here she comes now / I heard her call my name / Sister Ray. *(re-iss.Oct71 on 'MGM Select'; 2353 024) (re-iss.Apr84 on 'Polydor' lp/c; SPE LP/MC 73) (cd-iss.1986 on 'Polydor'; 825 119-2) (cd re-iss.May96 on 'Polydor'; 531 251-2)*

— **DOUG YULE** – bass, vocals, keyboards, guitar repl. CALE who went solo

M.G.M. M.G.M.

Apr 69. (lp) *(CS 8108) <4617>* **THE VELVET UNDERGROUND** Mar 69
– Candy says . . . / What goes on / Some kinda love / Pale blue eyes / Jesus / Beginning to see the light / I'm set free / That's the story of my life / The murder mystery / Afterhours. *(re-iss.Nov71 on 'MGM Select'; 2353 022) (re-iss.Mar76;) (re-iss.Sep83 on 'Polydor'; SPE LP/MC 39) <US re-iss.Apr85; 815454> (cd-iss.May96 on 'Polydor'; 531 252-2)*

May 69. (7") *<14057>* **JESUS. / WHAT GOES ON** -

— **BILLY YULE** – drums repl. TUCKER who had a baby. **MO TUCKER** returned in 1970 and BILLY only appeared on MAX's live album (see compilations)

Atlantic Cotillion

Jan 71. (7") *<44107>* **WHO LOVES THE SUN? / OH! SWEET NUTHIN'** -

Apr 71. (lp) *(2400 111) <9034>* **LOADED** Aug70
– Who loves the sun? / Sweet Jane / Rock and roll / Cool it down / New age / Head held high / Lonesome cowboy Bill / I found a reason / Train around the bend / Oh! sweet nuthin'. *(re-iss.1972 lp/c; K/K4 40113) (cd-iss.Jun88 on 'Warners') (cd-iss.Feb93 on 'Warners') (d-cd-iss.May97 as 'LOADED (THE FULLY LOADED EDITION)' on 'Rhino'+=; 812272563-2)*– (diff.mixes & demos, etc.)

Apr 71. (7") *(2091 008)* **WHO LOVES THE SUN. / SWEET JANE** -

— (Aug70) now with no originals The **YULE's** brought in newcomers **WALTER POWERS** – bass repl. LOU REED who went solo in 1971. (1971) **WILLIE ALEXANDER** – guitar repl. MORRISON who took a doctorate in English. MO TUCKER finally departed to raise her new family and eventually had five children in total, before going solo in 1980.

Polydor not issued

Feb 73. (lp) *(2383 180)* **SQUEEZE** -
– Little Jack / Mean old man / She'll make you cry / Wordless / Dopey Joe / Crash / Friends / Jack and Jane / Send no letter / Louise.

— Folded soon after above, DOUG sessioned for ELLIOTT MURPHY and later joined AMERICAN FLYER.

— VELVET UNDERGROUND re-formed in 1993; **REED, CALE, MORRISON & TUCKER**

Sire Sire

Oct 93. (d-cd/d-c) *(9362 45464-2/-4)* **LIVE MCMXCII (live)** 70
– We're gonna have a good time together / Venus in furs / Guess I'm falling in love / After hours / All tomorrow's parties / Some kinda love / I'll be your mirror / Beginning to see the light / The gift / I heard her call my name / Femme fatale / Hey Mr. Rain / Sweet Jane / Velvet nursery rhyme / White light – white heat / I'm sticking with you / Black angel's death song / Rock'n'roll / I can't stand it / I'm waiting for the man / Heroin / Pale blue eyes / Coyote.

Feb 94. (7"/c-s) *(W 0224/+C)* **VENUS IN FURS (live). / I'M WAITING FOR THE MAN (live)** 71
(cd-s+=) *(W 0224CD)* – Heroin (live) / Sweet Jane (live).

— On the 30th August 1995, STERLING MORRISON died of lymponia.

— Group inducted into the Rock'n'roll Hall Of Fame, and performed 'LAST NIGHT I SAID GOODBYE TO A FRIEND', REED's tribute to recently deceased STERLING.

– compilations, others, etc. –

Dec 71. (d-lp) *M.G.M.; (2683 006)* **ANDY WARHOL'S VELVET UNDERGROUND FEATURING NICO** -
– I'm waiting for the man / Candy says / Run, run, run / White light – white heat / All tomorrow's parties / Sunday morning / I heard her call my name / Femme fatale / Heroin / Here she comes now / There she goes again / Sister Ray / Venus in furs / European son / Pale blue eyes / Black angel's death song / Beginning to see the light.

Aug 72. (lp) *Atlantic; (K 30022) / Cotillion; <9500>* **LIVE AT MAX'S KANSAS CITY (live 22 Aug'70)** May72
– I'm waiting for the man / Sweet Jane / Lonesome Cowboy Bill / Beginning to see the light / I'll be your mirror / Pale blue eyes / Sunday morning / New age / Femme fatale / After hours. *(cd-iss.Jun93 on 'Warners'; 7567 90370-2)*

Jun 73. (7"m; as LOU REED & VELVET UNDERGROUND)
M.G.M.; (2006 283) **CANDY SAYS. / I'M WAITING FOR THE MAN / RUN RUN RUN** -

Aug 73. (7") *Atlantic; (K 10339)* **SWEET JANE (live). / ROCK AND ROLL** (live) -

Oct 73. (lp) *Verve; (2315 258) / Pride; <0022>* **THE VELVET UNDERGROUND AND LOU REED** -

1974. (lp) *M.G.M.; <4950>* **ARCHETYPES** -

1976. (ltd-7"m) *A.E.B.;* **FOGGY NOTION – INSIDE YOUR HEART. / I'M STICKING WITH YOU / FERRYBOAT BILL** -

Feb 79. (d-lp) *Mercury; (6643 900) <SRM2 7504>* **1969 – THE VELVET UNDERGROUND LIVE (live)** Apr74
– I'm waiting for the man / Lisa says / What goes on / Sweet Jane / We're gonna have a real good time together / Femme fatale / New age / Rock and roll / Beginning to see the light / Ocean / Pale blue eyes / Heroin / Some kinda love / Over you / Sweet Bonnie Brown – It's just too much / I'll be your mirror / White light – white heat. *(re-iss.Nov84; PRID 7) (re-iss.1987; 834 823-1) (re-iss.1988 as 'VOL.1' & 'VOL.2' cd/c; 834823-2/-4 & 834824-2/-4)*

Nov 80. (d-lp)(d-c) *Polydor; (2664 438)(3578 485)* **GREATEST HITS** -

Oct 82. (12"ep) *Polydor; (POSPX 603)* **HEROIN / VENUS IN FURS. / I'M WAITING FOR THE MAN / RUN RUN RUN** -

Feb 85. (lp/c) *Polydor; (POLD/+C 5167) <823721>* **V.U.** (rare rec.68-69) 47 85
– I can't stand it / Stephanie says / She's my best friend / Lisa says / Ocean / Foggy notion / Temptation inside your heart / One of these days / Andy's chest / I'm sticking with you. *(cd-iss.Jun87; 825 092-2)*

May 86. (5xlp-box)(5xcd-box) *Polydor; (VUBOX 1)(815 454-2)* **BOXED SET**
– (first 3 albums, plus V.U. & ANOTHER VIEW)

Aug 86. (lp/c/cd) *Polydor; (829 405-1/-4/-2)* **ANOTHER VIEW**
– We're gonna have a good time together / I'm gonna move right in / Hey Mr. Rain (version 1) / Ride into the Sun / Coney Island steeplechase / Guess I'm falling in love / Hey Mr. Rain (version 2) / Ferryboat Bill / Rock and roll (original).

Feb 88. (12") *Old Gold; (OG 4049)* **I'M WAITING FOR THE MAN. / HEROIN** -

Mar 88. (12") *Old Gold; (OG 4051)* **VENUS IN FURS. / ALL TOMORROW'S PARTIES** -

Sep 88. (lp) *Plastic Inevitable; <FIRST 1>* **THE VELVET UNDERGROUND ETC.** -
– The ostrich / Cycle Annie / Sneaky Pete / Noise.

Sep 88. (lp) *Plastic Inevitable; <SECOND 1>* **THE VELVET UNDERGROUND AND SO ON** -
– It's alright (the way you live) / I'm not too sorry / Stephanie says.

Oct 89. (lp/c/cd) *Verve; <(841 164-1/-4/-2)>* **THE BEST OF THE VELVET UNDERGROUND (THE WORDS AND MUSIC OF LOU REED)**
– I'm waiting for the man / Femme fatale / Run run run / Heroin / All tomorrow's parties / I'll be your mirror / White light – white heat / Stephanie says / What goes on / Beginning to see the light / Pale blue eyes / I can't stand it / Lisa says / Sweet Jane / Rock and roll.

Oct 95. (cd/c) *Global; (RAD CD/MC 21)* **THE BEST OF LOU REED & VELVET UNDERGROUND** 56 -

Oct 95. (4xcd-box) *Polydor; (527887-2)* **PEEL SLOWLY AND SEE** -

— (see also LOU REED discography for other tracks on comps & B's)

— Also tribute albums 'HEAVEN AND HELL' 1, 2 & 3 were isued Oct'90-Feb'92, all on 'Imaginary' records, as was another '15 MINUTES'.

VIRGINIA TREE (see under ⇒ GHOST)

VIRUS

Formed: Germany . . . 1970, by BERNE HOHMANN, WERNER MONKA, JORG-DIETER KRAHE, REINHOLD SPIEGEFELD and WOLFGANG RIEFE. The first of this brief band's two albums stands as one of the best early psychedelic/progressive recordings. Aptly titled 'REVELATION', it emerged in 1970 to general acclaim and its reputation has matured with age. Taking its cue from the pioneering late 60's/early 70's work of many British bands, the album even included a neo-classical adaptation of The ROLLING STONES' 'PAINT IT BLACK'. By the release of 'FOR THOUGHTS', the following year, the band personnel had changed and the style of the album was more straight-ahead hard rock. The record failed to match the intensity or inventiveness of the debut and VIRUS faded into obscurity.

Recommended: REVELATION (*9) / THOUGHTS (*6)

BERND 'MOLLE' HOHMANN – vocals, flute / **WERNER MONKA** – guitar / **JORG-DIETER KRAHE** – organ / **REINHOLD SPIEGELFELD** – bass / **WOLFGANG RIEKE** – drums

BASF not issued

1970. (lp) *(ORC 15)* **REVELATION** - - German
– Revelation / Burning candle / Nur noch zwei lichtjahre. *(cd-iss.1991 on 'Second Battle'; SB 015)*

— **KRAHE + RIEKE** recruited **BERND ROSNER** – guitar / **WERNER VOGT** – bass, guitar, vocals / **JURGEN SCHAFER** – bass, vocals / **AXEL NIELING** – drums (HOHMANN joined WEED)

Pilz not issued

1971. (lp) *(20.21102-9)* **THOUGHTS** - - German
– King Heroin / Mankind, where do you go to / Theme / Old time movie / Butterflies / Take your thoughts / Sittin' & smokin' / Going on / Deeds of the past / My strand-eyed girl. *(cd-iss.1991 on 'Ohrwashl';)*

— disappeared from the scene

Mark VOLMAN & Howard KAYLAN (see under ⇒ TURTLES)

Rick WAKEMAN

Born: 18 May'49, Perivale, Middlesex, England. Aged 16, he attended The Royal College of Music, although interest in playing live and doing sessions led to him dropping out. His in-demand pop session work (i.e. WHITE PLAINS, EDISON LIGHTHOUSE, etc.), saw him working on albums by CAT STEVENS, DAVID BOWIE, T.REX, etc. In 1970, he joined The STRAWBS, but the following year he couldn't turn down YES, as they matched his classical ambitions. He was an on-off YES member during the 70's, subsequently starting his own solo career on 'A&M' records. Prior to this, he had augmented The JOHN SCHROEDER ORCHESTRA on the 1971 'Polydor lp, 'PIANO VIBRATIONS'; (2460 135). Taking themes of history, fiction and legend, he released three well-received (at the time) Top 10 albums between 1973-1975. His second album, 'JOURNEY TO THE CENTRE OF THE EARTH' (an adaptation of the Jules Verne classic), was premiered live at The Royal Festival Hall in January '74, topping the UK charts upon its release that year. With orchestra and choir in tow, he performed it at an open-air Crystal Palace Garden Party, subsequently touring the show around major US venues. His virtuoso, exhibitionist keyboard-playing and flash-rock image (long blonde hair and ankle-length silver capes) was perfectly suited to the live arena, a comparison that could be made with the other famous keys-basher of the era, KEITH EMERSON. Nevertheless, this gruelling tour took its toll, when RICK suffered a minor heart attack nearing the end of the pocket-draining extravaganza. On his recovery, he released the third of these epics, 'KING ARTHUR' in 1975, regarded by many as overblown pomp-rock, although it did have its redeeming moments (i.e. 'MERLIN THE MAGICIAN' and 'SIR LANCELOT & THE BLACK KNIGHT'). Following a move into soundtrack work, notably on Ken Russell's 'LISZTOMANIA' (starring ROGER DALTREY) and 'WHITE ROCK' (a docu-film focussing on the 1976 Winter Olympics), he found time to squeeze in his fourth studio set, 'NO EARTHLY CONNECTION', a record that still managed a Top 10 placing. WAKEMAN returned in 1977 with his ' . . . CRIMINAL RECORD', which was a failure both critically and commercially, leading to public attention drifting somewhat, thus his steady decline. He continued to release a plethora of albums, most taking a neo-classical rock/pop or new-age stance. He will probably be remembered in the next century, not for his theatrical rock indulgence, but for the romantic classical style he helped revive. • **Songwriters:** All his own work, interspersed with little snatches of past classical works. • **Trivia:** Most distinguished session work included; LIFE ON MARS (David Bowie) / CHANGES (Black Sabbath) / MORNING HAS BROKEN (Cat Stevens) / LOU REED's debut album. WAKEMAN was married in the 70's to Ros and settled down in a Buckingham mansion alongside his collection of Rolls Royce's. The couple had three children before their divorce. In the 80's, RICK married ex-model, NINA CARTER, (also of twin-sister outfit, BLONDE ON BLONDE). He fathered another two kids (so far), later finding Christianity. BILL ODDIE (of the GOODIES TV programme) contributed vocals on WAKEMAN's 'JOURNEY' and 'CRIMINAL RECORD'.

Recommended: THE SIX WIVES OF HENRY VIII (*8) / JOURNEY TO THE CENTRE OF THE EARTH (*6) / THE MYTHS & LEGENDS OF KING ARTHUR . . . (*6)

RICK WAKEMAN – keyboards (a member of YES; Aug71-Jun74, Nov76-Mar80, 1990+)

— now used various YES people on sessions plus numerous choirs & ensembles.

A&M A&M

Feb 73. (lp/c) *(AMLH/ 64361)* **THE SIX WIVES OF HENRY VIII** 7 30
– Catherine of Aragon / Anne of Cleves / Catherine Howard / Jane Seymour / Anne Boleyn / Catherine Parr. *(quad-lp; QU-84361) (cd-iss.1988; CDA 3229) (re-iss.cd Aug89; 393 229-2) (re-iss.cd Jan92; CDMID 136)*

Mar 73. (7") *(AMS 7061)* **CATHERINE. / ANNE** -

— (below A-side was an excerpt of 'CATHERINE PARR')

— Introduced **ASHLEY HOLT** – vocals / **ROGER NEWELL** – bass / **BARNEY JAMES** – drums / plus The ENGLISH ROCK ENSEMBLE with The LONDON SYMPHONY ORCHESTRA. Narration by actor DAVID HEMMINGS.

May 74. (lp/c) *(AMLH/ 63621)* **JOURNEY TO THE CENTRE OF THE EARTH** 1 3
– The journey / Recollections / The battle / The forest. *<US quad-lp 1974; SPQU 3621> (re-iss.Feb85 on 'Hallmark' lp/c; SHM/HSC 3164) (cd-iss.Jan88; CDA 3156) <US cd-iss.1988 on 'Mobile Fidelity'; MFCD 848> (re-iss.cd Jan92; CDMID 161) (re-iss.May93 on 'Spectrum' cd/c; 550 061-2/-4)*

Oct 74. (7") **THE JOURNEY. / THE RETURN** -

Dec 74. (7") **THE BATTLE. / AND NOW A WORD FROM OUR SPONSOR** -

Apr 75. (lp/c) *(AMLH/ 64515)* **THE MYTHS AND LEGENDS OF KING ARTHUR AND THE KNIGHTS OF THE ROUND TABLE** 2 21
– Arthur / Lady of the lake / Guinevere / Sir Lancelot & the Black Knight / Merlin the magician / Sir Galahad / The last battle. *<US quad-lp 1975; SPQU 54515> (cd-iss.1988; CDA 3230) (re-iss.cd; CDMID 135)*

Jun 75. (7") **MERLIN THE MAGICIAN. / SIR GALAHAD** -

— (below 1975 releases with ROGER DALTREY on vocals)

Nov 75. (lp) *(AMLH 64546)* **LISZTOMANIA (Soundtrack)**
– Rienzi / Chopsticks fantasia / Love's dream / Dante period / Orpheus song / Hell / Hibernation / Excelsior song / Master race / Rape, pillage and clap funerailles / Free song / Peace at last.

Nov 75. (7") *(AMS 7206)* **ORPHEUS SONG. / LOVE'S DREAM**

— For North & South American tour he trimmed his ENGLISH ROCK ENSEMBLE down to **ASHLEY HOLT** – vocals / **JOHN DUNSTERVILE** – guitar / **ROGER NEWELL** – bass / **TONY FERNANDEZ** – drums / **REG BROOKS + MARTYN SHIELDS** – brass section

Apr 76. (lp/c) *(AMLK/ 64583)* **NO EARTHLY CONNECTION** 9 67
– Music reincarnate: (part 1) The warning – (part 2) The maker – (part 3) The spaceman – (part 4) The realization – (part 5) The reaper / The prisoner / The lost cycle.

Jan 77. (lp/c) *(AMLH/ 64614)* **WHITE ROCK (Film Soundtrack)** 14
– White rock / Searching for gold / The loser / The shoot / Lax'x / After the ball / Montezuma's revenge / Ice run. *(cd-iss.1988; CDA 4614)*

— (above from 1976 Winter Olympics docu-film, narrated by James Coburn)

Jun 77. (7") *<1937>* **AFTER THE BALL. / WHITE ROCK** -

Nov 77. (lp/c) *(AMLH/ 64660)* **RICK WAKEMAN'S CRIMINAL RECORD** 25
– Statute of justice / Crime of passion / Chamber of horrors / Birdman of Alcatraz / The breathalizer / Judas Iscariot. *(re-iss.Mar82 lp/c; AMID/CMID 125)*

Apr 79. (7") *(AMS 7435)* **BIRDMAN OF ALCATRAZ (theme from My Son My Son). / FALCONS DE NEIGE** -

Apr 79. (7") *<2010>* **BIRDMAN OF ALCATRAZ. / AND NOW A WORD FROM OUR SPONSOR** -

May 79. (d-lp/c) *(AMLX/CXM 68508)* **RHAPSODIES** 25
– Pedra da Gavea / Front line / Bombay duck / Animal showdown / Big Ben / Rhapsody in blue / Wooly Willy tango / The pulse / Swan lager / March of the gladiators / Flacons de Neige / The flasher / The palais / Stand by / Sea horses / Half holiday / Summertime.

May 79. (7"/7"pic-d) *(AMS/+P 7436)* **ANIMAL SHOWDOWN. / SEA HORSES** -

Nov 79. (7") *(AMS 7497)* **SWAN LAGER. / WOOLLY WILLY TANGO** -

Feb 80. (7") *(AMS 7510)* **I'M SO STRAIGHT I'M A WEIRDO. / DO YOU BELIEVE IN FAIRIES?** -

WEA not issued

Oct 80. (7") *(K 18354)* **THE SPIDER. / DANIELLE** -

featured **FERNANDEZ / STEVE BARNACLE** – bass / **GARY BARNACLE** – sax / **TIM STONE** – guitar / etc.

Charisma Charisma?

Jun 81. (lp)(c) *(CDS 4022)(7144 136)* **1984** 24
– 1984 overture – part 1 & 2 / War games / Julia / The hymn / The room – part 1 & 2 / Robot man / Sorry / No name / 1984 / Forgotten memories / The proles / 1984. *(re-iss.Jun88; CHC 41)*

— (below vocals by; CORI JOSIAS)

Jul 81. (7"; by The RICK WAKEMAN BAND) *(CB 384)* **JULIA. / SORRY** -

Nov 81. (7"; by The RICK WAKEMAN BAND) *(CB 392)* **ROBOT MAN. / 1984 OVERTURE (part 1)** -

Jan 82. (lp) *(CLASS 12)* **THE BURNING (soundtrack)** -
– Themes from 'The Burning' / The chase continues / Variations on the fire / Sheer terror and more / The burning (end title theme) / Campfire story / The fire / Doin' it / Devil's creek breakdown / The chase / Sheer terror.

Moon not issued

Nov 82. (7") *(LUNA 6)* **I'M SO STRAIGHT I'M A WEIRDO. / MAYBE '80 (edit)** -

Dec 82. (lp/c) *(LUNLP/ZCLUN 1)* **ROCK'N'ROLL PROPHET** (rec.1979) -
– I'm so straight I'm a weirdo / The dragon / Dark / Maybe '80 / Early warning / Spy of '55 / Do you believe in fairies? / Rock'n'roll prophet. *(cd-iss.Apr93 on 'President'; RWCD 12)(+=)–* Return of the prophet / Alpha sleep / March of the child soldiers / Stalemate.

— solo with music from 1982 football World Cup in Spain

Charisma not issued

Apr 83. (7") *(CB 411)* **LATIN REEL (theme from G'OLE). / NO POSSIBLA** -

Apr 83. (lp/c) *(CAS/+MC 1162)* **G'OLE (film soundtrack)** -
– International flag / The dove / Wayward spirit / Red island / Latin reel (theme from G'ole) / Spanish holiday / No possibla / Shadows / Black pearls / Frustration / Spanish montage / G'ole.

Jun 83. (lp) *(CAS 1163)* **THE COST OF LIVING**
– Twij / Pandomonia / Gone but not forgotten / One for the road / Bedtime stories / Happening man / Shakespeare's run / Monkey nuts / Elegy (written in a country church yard). *(re-iss.Aug88; CHC 63) (cd-iss.Jun97 on 'Griffin'; GCDWR 1892)*

— Oct '84, WAKEMAN collaborated on album BEYOND THE PLANETS by KEVIN PEEK (Sky); hit UK No.64

— His Spring 1985 tour band: **TONY FERNANDEZ** – drums / **CHAS CRONK** – bass / **RICK FENN** – lead guitar / **GORDON NEVILLE** – vocals / **LYNN SHEPHERD** – b.vocals

President not issued

Dec 84. (7") *(WAKE 1)* **GLORY BOYS. / GHOST OF A ROCK AND ROLL STAR** -
(12"+=) *(12WAKE 1)* – Elgin mansions.

Mar 85. (lp/c) *(RW/+K 1)* **SILENT NIGHTS** [ ] [-]
– Tell 'em all you know / The opening line / The opera / Man's best friend / Glory boys / Silent nights / Ghost of a rock and roll star / The dancer / That's who I am. *(cd-iss.Jan87; RWCD 1)*– Elgin mansions.

Jun 85. (7"/12") *(WAKE/12WAKE 2)* **THE THEME FROM 'LYTTON'S DIARY'. / DATABASE** [ ] [-]

Dec 85. (lp) *(RW 2)* **LIVE AT HAMMERSMITH (live)** [ ] [-]
– Arthur / Three wives of Henry VIII / The journey / Merlin the magician. *(cd-iss.Jun87; RWCD 2) (re-iss.Nov93)*

Coda | not issued

Apr 86. (lp/c)(cd) *(NAGE/+C 10)(NAGE 10CD)* **COUNTRY AIRS** [ ] [-]
– Dandelion dreams / Stepping stones / Ducks and drakes / Morning haze / Waterfalls / Quite valleys / Nature trail / Heather carpets / Wild moors / Lakeland walks. *(re-iss.Oct92 on 'Art Of Language' cd/c; NAGE 102CD) (re-iss.re-recorded cd Dec92 on 'President'; RWCD 10)* – The spring / Green to gold / Harvest festival / The glade.

Apr 86. (7") *(CODS 19)* **WATERFALLS. / HEATHER CARPETS** [ ] [-]

Stylus | not issued

Nov 86. (d-lp/d-c/d-cd) *(SMR/SMC/SMD 729)* **THE GOSPELS** [94] [-]
– The baptism / The welcoming / The sermon on the mount / The Lord's Prayer / The way / The road to Jerusalem / Trial and error / Galilee / The gift / The magnificat / Welcome a star / Power (the acts of the apostles) / The word / The hour / The children of mine / The last verse. *(re-iss.d-cd Mar94 on 'Fragile'; BM 2-3)*

President | not issued

Mar 87. (lp/c/cd) *(RW/+K/CD 3)* **CRIMES OF PASSION (Soundtrack)** [ ] [-]
– It's a lovely life (featuring MAGGIE BELL) / Eastern shadows / Joanna / The stretch / Policeman's ball / Stax / Taken in hand / Paradise lost / The box / Web of love. *(cd+=)*– Dangerous woman (featuring MAGGIE BELL). *(re-iss.cd Feb93)*

Aug 87. (lp/c/cd) *(RW/+K/CD 4)* **THE FAMILY ALBUM** [ ] [-]
– Adam (Rick's second son) / Black Beauty (black rabbit) / Jemma (Rick and Nina's daughter) / Benjamin (Rick's third son) / Oscar (Rick & Nina's son) / Oliver (Rick's eldest son) / Nina (Rick's wife) / Chloe (German shepherd) / Rookie (cat) / Tilly (Golden Retriever) / Mum / Dad. *(c+=)*– Wiggles (black & white rabbit). *(cd++=)*– The day after the fair / Mackintosh.

Feb 88. (lp/c/cd; RICK WAKEMAN & RAMON REMEDIOS) *(RW/+K/CD 5)* **A SUITE OF GODS** [ ] [-]
– Dawn of time / The oracle / Pandora's box / Chariot of the sun / The flood / The voyage of Ulysses / Hercules.

Apr 88. (lp/c/cd; RICK WAKEMAN & TONY FERNANDEZ) *(RW/+K/CD 6)* **ZODIAQUE** [ ] [-]
– Sagittarius / Capricorn / Gemini / Cancer / Pisces / Aquarius / Aries / Libra / Leo / Virgo / Taurus / Scorpio.

— retained **FERNANDEZ** + recruited **DAVEY PATON** – bass / **JOHN KNIGHTSBRIDGE** – guitar (2) / guest vocals **TRACEY ACKERMAN + ASHLEY HOLT. below vocals by ROY WOOD (A-side) / JOHN PARR (B-side)**

Jul 88. (7") *(WAKE 3)* **CUSTER'S LAST STAND. / OCEAN CITY** [ ] [-]

Jul 88. (lp/c/cd) *(RW/+K/CD 7)* **TIME MACHINE** [ ] [-]
– Custer's last stand / Ocean city / Angel of time * / Slaveman * / Ice / Open up your eyes * / Elizabethan rock / Make me a woman * / Rock age *. *(cd has extended versions of *)*

Nov 89. (lp/c/cd) *(RW/+K/CD 8)* **SEA AIRS** [ ] [-]
– Harbour lights / The pirate / Storm clouds / Last at sea / The mermaid / Waves / The fisherman / Flying fish / The Marie Celeste / Time and tide / The lone sailor / The sailor's lament.

Nov 90. (lp/c/cd) *(RW/+K/CD 9)* **NIGHT AIRS** [ ] [-]
– The sad dream / Twilight / The sleeping child / Mr. Badger / Jack Frost / The lone star / Rain shadows / Fox by night / Night owls / An evening romance.

— (in the US; he released cd 'IN THE BEGINNING' for 'Asaph'; *<AR-1049>*, which received a UK date Dec91). In 1991, the 'Badger' label issued cassette 'THE SUN TRILOGY'; *AMB 4MC)*

Ambient | not issued

Nov 90. (cd) *(AMB1-MCD)* **ASPIRANT SUNSET** [ ] [-]
– Floating clouds / Still waters / The dream / The sleeping village / Sea of tranquility / Peace / Sunset / Dying embers / Dusk / Evening moods. *(re-iss.1992 on 'Rio Digital'; RIOCD 1008) (re-iss.Jun93 on 'President'; RWCD 18)*

Nov 90. (cd) *(AMB2-MCD)* **ASPIRANT SUNRISE** [ ] [-]
– Thoughts of love / Gentle breezes / Whispering cornfields / Peaceful beginnings / Dewy morn / Musical dreams / Distant thoughts / The dove / When time stood still / Secret moments / Peaceful. *(re-iss.1992 on 'Rio Digital'; RIOCD 1009) (re-iss.Jun93 on 'President'; RWCD 17)*

Jan 91. (lp/cd; by RICK WAKEMAN & MARIO FASCIANO) *(A-IOM-2/+CD)* **BLACK KNIGHTS IN THE COURT OF FERNINAND IV** [ ] [-]
(re-iss.cd Nov92 on 'Rio Digital'; RIOCD 1002) (re-iss.cd Jun94 on 'West Coast'; WCPCD 1009)

Feb 91. (lp/cd) *(A-IOM-2/+CD)* **PHANTOM POWER** [ ] [-]
– The visit / Heaven / The rat / The stiff / Evil love / The voice of love / Heat of the moment / Fear of love / The love trilogy:- One night – The dream sequence – One night of love / The hangman / The sand-dance / You can't buy my love / Phantom power / The chase. *(re-iss.cd Nov92 on 'Rio Digital'; RIOCD 1003)*

May 91. (lp/cd) *(A-IOM-3/+CD)* **SOFTSWORD: KING JOHN AND THE MAGNA CHARTER** [ ] [-]
– Magna charter / After prayers / Battle sonata / The siege / Rochester college / The story of love (King John) / March of time / Don't fly away / Isabella / Softsword / Hymn of hope. *(re-iss.cd Nov92 on 'Rio Digital'; RIOCD 1001) (re-iss.cd Feb94 on 'President'; RWCD 24)*

Sep 91. (lp/cd) *(A-IOM-5/+CD)* **A WORLD OF WISDOM** [ ] [-]
(re-iss.cd Feb94 on 'D-Sharp'; DSHCD 7013)

— (above credited to veteran English comedian/singer NORMAN WISDOM)

Oct 91. (7"; by RICK WAKEMAN featuring CHRISSIE HAMMOND) *(A-IOMS 1)* **DON'T FLY AWAY. / AFTER PRAYERS** [ ] [-]

Nov 91. (cd) **2000 A.D. INTO THE FUTURE** [ ] [-]
– Into the future / Toward peace / 2000 A.D. / A.D rock / The time tunnel / Robot dance / A new beginning / Forward past / The seventh dimension. *(re-iss.Dec92 on 'Rio Digital'; RIOCD 1007) (re-iss.Sep93 on 'President'; RWCD 21)*

Rio Digital | not issued

1992. (cd) *(RIOCD 1010)* **AMBIENT SUNSHADOWS** [ ] [-]
– The nightwind / Churchyard / Tall shadows / Shadowlove / Melancholy mood / Mount Fuji by night / Hidden reflections / The evening harp / The moonraker pond / The last lamplight / Japanese sunshadows. *(re-iss.Jul93 as 'ASPIRANT SUNSHADOWS' on 'President'; RWCD 19)*

Nov 92. (cd; RICK WAKEMAN & ADAM WAKEMAN) *(RIOCD 1011)* **WAKEMAN WITH WAKEMAN** [ ] [-]
– Lure of the wild / The beach comber / Meglomania / Raga and rhyme / Sync or swim / Jigajig / Caesarea / After the atom / The suicide shuiffle / Past and present / Paint it black. *(re-iss.Feb93 on 'President'; RWCD 11)*

— (above was with son ADAM)

Myrrh | not issued

May 93. (cd) *(MYRCD 1296)* **PRAYERS** [ ] [-]
–

President | not issued

May 93. (cd) *(RWCD 16)* **HERITAGE SUITE** [ ] [-]
– The chasms / Thorwald's cross / St.Michael's isle / Spanish head / The Ayres / Mona's isle / The Dhoon / The bee orchid / Chapel Hill / The Curraghs / The painted lady / The Peregrine falcon.

Aug 93. (cd) *(RWCD 17)* **AFRICAN BACH** (rec.& rel.South Africa 1991) [ ] [-]
– African Bach / Message of mine / My homeland / Liberty / Anthem / Brainstorm / Face in the crowd / Just a game / Africa east / Don't touch the merchandise.

Nov 93. (cd; by WAKEMAN WITH WAKEMAN) *(RWCD 22)* **NO EXPENSE SPARED** [ ] [-]

May 94. (cd-ep; by RICK WAKEMAN & HIS BAND) *(WAKEY 4)* **LIGHT UP THE SKY / SIMPLY FREE / STARFLIGHT / THE BEAR** [ ] [ ]

Nov 94. (cd; by WAKEMAN WITH WAKEMAN) *(RWCD 25)* **ROMANCE OF THE VICTORIAN AGE** [ ] [-]
– Burlington arcade / If only / The last teardrop / Still dreaming / Memories of the Victorian age / Lost in words / A tale of love / Mysteries unfold / Forever in my heart / Days of wonder / The swans / Another mellow day / Dance of the elves.

Jun 95. (cd) *(RWCD 27)* **THE SEVEN WONDERS OF THE WORLD** (with narration) [ ] [-]
– The Pharoahs Of Alexandria / The Colossus Of Rhodes / The Pyramids Of Egypt / The Gardens Of Babylon / The Temples Of Artemis / The Statue Of Zeus / The Mausoleum At Halicarnassus.

Jul 95. (cd) *(DSHLCD 7018)* **CIRQUE SURREAL – STATE CIRCUS OF IMAGINATION** [ ] [-]

— (above released on 'D-Sharp' label)

Oct 95. (cd) *(RWCD 28)* **VISIONS** [ ] [-]

Nov 96. (cd; by RICK & ADAM WAKEMAN) *(RWCD 30)* **VIGNETTES** [ ] [-]
– Waiting alone / Wish I was you / Sun comes crying / A breath of Heaven / Moment in time / Artist's dream / Change of face / Madman blues / A painting of our love / Riverside / Need you / Simply acoustic / Just another tear.

Hope | not issued

Mar 97. (cd) *(HRHCD 004)* **LIGHT AT THE END OF THE TUNNEL** [ ] [-]

Mar 97. (cd) *(HRHCD 005)* **CAN YOU HEAR ME?** [ ] [-]

– compilations, others, etc. –

1978. (lp) *A&M; (AMLX 68447)* **THE ROYAL PHILHARMONIC ORCHESTRA PERFORMING BEST KNOWN WORKS OF RICK WAKEMAN** [ ] [-]

May 81. (d-c) *A&M; (CAMCR 8)* **THE SIX WIVES OF HENRY VIII / THE MYTHS AND LEGENDS OF KING ARTHUR . . .** [ ] [-]

Feb 89. (4xcd-box) *A&M; (RWCD 20)* **20th ANNIVERSARY** [ ] [-]
– (THE SIX WIVES OF HENRY VIII / JOURNEY TO THE CENTRE OF THE EARTH / THE MYTHS AND LEGENDS OF KING ARTHUR AND THE KNIGHTS OF THE ROUND TABLE / WHITE ROCK)

Mar 83. (d-c) *Charisma; (CASMC 111)* **1984 / THE BURNING** [ ] [-]

May 91. (cd) *Ambient; (A-IOM-4CD)* **THE PRIVATE COLLECTION** [ ] [-]
(re-iss.Nov92 on 'Rio Digital'; RIOCD 1004) (re-iss.Feb94 on 'President'; RWCD 23)

Oct 91. (d-cd) *Ambient; (AMB5-MCD)* **THE CLASSICAL CONNECTION** [ ] [-]
(re-iss.Dec92 on 'Rio Digital'; RIOCD 1005) (re-iss.1-cd May93 on 'President'; RWCD 13)

Oct 91. (cd) *Ambient; (A-IOM-6MCD)* **THE CLASSICAL CONNECTION II** [ ] [-]
(re-iss.Dec92 on 'Rio Digital'; RIOCD 1006) (re-iss.May93 on 'President'; RWCD 14)

Sep 93. (cd) *Icon; (ICONCD 005)* **THE VERY BEST OF RICK WAKEMAN – CHRONICLES** [ ] [-]
– (see below cd for tracks, although not YES songs)

Dec 93. (d-cd) *Fragile; (CDFRL 001)* **RICK WAKEMAN'S GREATEST HITS** (some with YES) [ ] [-]
– Roundabout / Wondrous stories / Don't kill the whale / Going for the one / Siberian khatru / Madrigal / Starship trooper/ / Overture / The journey / The Hansbach / Lost in time / The recollection / Stream of voices / The battle / Liddenbrook / The forest / Mount Etna / Journey's end / Sea horses / Catherine of Aragon / Gone but not forgotten / Merlin the magician.

Apr 94. (cd/c) *Prestige; (CDSGP 115)* **THE CLASSIC TRACKS** [ ] [-]

Jun 94. (d-cd; WAKEMAN WITH WAKEMAN) *Cyclops; (CYCLD 006)* **THE OFFICIAL LIVE BOOTLEG** [ ] [-]
(re-iss.Mar95 on 'Griffin'; GCDRW 156)

Dec 94. (cd; as RICK WAKEMAN & THE ENGLISH ROCK ENSEMBLE) *Windsong; (WHISCD 007)* **LIVE ON THE TEST (live)** [ ] [-]

Jun 95. (cd) *Disky; (RPCD 13)* **ROCK AND POP LEGENDS** [ ] [-]

Sep 95. (cd) *Hope; (HR 001)* **THE NEW GOSPELS** [ ] [-]

Oct 95. (cd) *Essential; (ESSCD 322)* **THE PIANO ALBUM – LIVE (live)** [ ] [-]

May 97. (cd) *RP Media; (CDRPM 0018)* **TRIBUTE** [ ] [-]

WALLENSTEIN

Formed: Germany . . . 1971 initially as BLITZKRIEG, by classically-trained songwriter, JURGEN DOLLASE, who brought in American BILL BARONE, Dutchman JERRY BERKERS and German HARALD GROSSKOPF. Due to another UK group of the same name, they had to change moniker to WALLENSTEIN which delayed the release of their self-titled debut. Mostly instrumental, it was from the PINK FLOYD mould, symphonic and part of the "space rock" scene. The follow-up, 'MOTHER UNIVERSE' (complete with a picture of DOLLASE's grandmother on the cover), was another electric gem, although it did have its quieter folky moments (BERKERS eventually taking off into the singer/songwriter world). DOLLASE and GROSSKOPF went into sideline projects, notably The COSMIC JOKERS alongside WALTER WEGMULLER and SERGIUS GOLOWIN. However, this period brought forth another fine work in the shape of 'COSMIC CENTURY', sadly their last interstellar journey into symphonic rock. In 1975, they became a little more conventional, borrowing an easier-on-the-ear fusion of jazz and rock for the album, 'STORIES, SONGS & SYMPHONIES'. DOLLASE's failure to recapture the excellence of their first three efforts, led to him abandoning studio work, only re-appearing for live appearances. Things improved slightly in 1977 when 'R.C.A.' took them on, only to deliver some disappointing soft-rock albums, starting with 'NO MORE LOVE' (featuring on the cover a man with no genitalia). He sacked all the group in 1978, recruiting a more lightweight line-up, highlighted on some pop-rock/disco albums!

Recommended: BLITZKRIEG (*8) / MOTHER UNIVERSE (*8) / COSMIC CENTURY (*7)

JURGEN DOLLASE – keyboards, mellotron, vocals / **BILL BARONE** – guitars, vocals / **JERRY BERKERS** – bass, vocals / **HARALD GROSSKOPF** – drums, percussion

Pilz / not issued

Nov 71. (lp) *(20.29064-6)* **BLITZKRIEG** [-] [-] German
– Lunetic / The theme / Manhattan project / Audiences. *(cd-iss.1990's;)*

1972. (lp) *(20.29113-8)* **MOTHER UNIVERSE** [-] [-] German
– Mother Universe / Braintrain / Shakespearesque / Dedicated to mystery land / Relics of the past / Golden antenna. *(cd-iss.1990's;)*

— **DIETER MEIER** – bass + **JOACHIM REISER** – violin, percussion; repl. BERKERS who went solo (album 'UNTERWEGS')

Kosmische Musik / not issued

Dec 73. (lp) *(KM 58.006)* **COSMIC CENTURY** [-] [-] German
(cd-iss.1990's;)

— **JURGEN PLUTA** – bass, percussion; repl. MEIER

1975. (lp) *(KM 58.014)* **STORIES, SONGS & SYMPHONIES** [-] [-] German
– The priestess / Stories, songs and symphonies / The banner / Your lunar friends / Sympathy for Bela Bartok. *(cd-iss.1990's;)*

— split for a few years until **DOLLASE + PLUTA** re-grouped with **GERD KLOCKER** – guitar, vocals / **NICKY GEBHARD** – drums, percussion, vocals (BARONE returned to the U.S., GROSSKOPF joined KLAUS SCHULZE and ASH RA)

R.C.A. / not issued

Jan 78. (lp) *(PL 30010)* **NO MORE LOVE** [-] [-] German
– Seventy-seven / Backstreet dreamer / I can't loose / No more love / Jo Jo / On an eagle's wing.

— **DOLLASE** completely changed line-up, bringing in **KIM MERZ** – vocals / **PETE BROUGH** – guitar, vocals / **MICHAEL DOMMERS** – guitar, vocals / **TERRY PARK** – bass / **CHARLY TERSTAPPEN** – drums, percussion

1978. (lp) *(PL 30045)* **CHARLINE** [-] [-] German
– Charline / Fire in the rain / Life is true in London town / Red wine for the judge / All good children (part 1) / Midnight blue / Sally don't mind / All good children (part 2) / Strong and steady / Oldtime cafe.

1979. (7") *(Gem-RCA; GEMS 8)* **CHARLINE. / ALL GOOD CHILDREN** [ ] [-]

1979. (lp) *(PL 30061)* **BLUE EYED BOYS** [-] [-] German
– I wanna live / When the night grows / Votre for the blue eyed boys / If / Rock and roll is all I love / Come back / 1917 / Don't let it be / Little boy / Will you.

Harvest / not issued

1980. (lp) *(064-45932)* **FRAULEINS** [-] [-] German
– Woman in love / Rock high / Father and son / Born in the city / Lay down / Stay on your own / We need your love / I'll be around / Welcome tonight / Downtown.

— now without BROUGH

1981. (lp) *(064-46307)* **SSSSS . . .TOP** [-] [-] German
– You need a friend / Questions / Turn around / The girl from San Yanaro / Who needs you / Pork music / Yesterday's pictures / The bastard / Rod, the mod and his banana cans / Change / Stop and say.

— split after above

WALRUS

Formed: London, England . . . 1970 by main songwriter STEVE HAWTHORN and NOEL GREENAWAY. A progressive-rock act, they added brass for a more jazzy feel, although it was JOHN SCATES guitar work that was the highlight on their eponymous album. It featured the choice single, 'WHO CAN I TRUST?' and a cover version of TRAFFIC's 'COLOURED RAIN'.

Recommended: WALRUS (*6)

NOEL GREENAWAY – vocals / **STEVE HAWTHORN** – bass / **JOHN SCATES** – guitars / **BARRY PARFITT** – keyboards / **NICK GABB** – drums / **DON RICHARDS** – trumpet / **BIL HOAD** – woodwind, saxophones / **ROY VOCE** – tenor sax

Deram / Deram

Aug 70. (7") *(DM 308)* <85065> **WHO CAN I TRUST? / TOMORROW NEVER COMES** [ ] [ ]

Jan 71. (7") *(DM 323)* <85071> **NEVER LET MY BODY TOUCH THE GROUND. / WHY?** [ ] [-]

Jan 71. (lp) *(SML 1072)* **WALRUS** [-] [-]
– Who can I trust? / Rags and old iron / Blind man / Roadside / Why? / Turning monologue – Woman – Turning / Sunshine needs me / Coloured rain – Mother's dead face in memoriam – Coloured rain / Tomorrow never comes.

— soon disbanded after above

Bob WEIR (see under ⇒ GRATEFUL DEAD)

WEST COAST POP ART EXPERIMENTAL BAND

Formed: Los Angeles, California, USA . . . 1964 as The SNOWMAN, by BOB MARKLEY, with brothers DAN and SHAUN HARRIS. They soon adopted the name, WEST COAST POP ART EXPERIMENTAL BAND and issued a privately pressed lp in 1966. Subsequently signing to 'Reprise', they were allowed considerable freedom to express their blend of what their name suggested. A "real" debut, 'PART ONE', featured some real gems, such as 'TRANSPARENT DAY', 'HELP I'M A ROCK' and 'SHIFTING SANDS'. The second and third volumes were a little less ambitious, although the second did contain what should have been a single, 'TRACY HAD A HARD DAY SUNDAY'. One 45 that did surface, 'SMELL OF INCENSE', was later recorded by The ABSTACTS and later SOUTHWEST FOB. A fourth and final album, 'WHERE'S MY DADDY', sold very poorly and it was clear the experiment had failed.

Recommended: TRANSPARENT DAY (*6)

MICHAEL LLOYD – keyboards, guitar, vocals / **DANNY HARRIS** – guitar, vocals / **BOB MARKLEY** – drums, producer / **SHAUN HARRIS** – guitar, bass, vocals / **DENNIS** – bass

not issued / Fifo

1966. (lp-ltd) <*M 101*> **WEST COAST POP ART EXPERIMENTAL BAND** [-] [ ]
– Somethin' you got / Work song / Louie Louie / You really got me / If you want this love / Baby blue / She belongs to me / Insanity / Don't break my balloon / I won't hurt you / Don't let anything!!! stand in your way. <*re-press.1994 lp/cd+=*>– (extra B-sides). *(re-iss.Jun97 on 'Sundazed' cd/d-lp; SC/SLP 11047)*

— now without MICHAEL + DENNIS

Reprise / Reprise

1967. (7") <*0552*> **1906. / SHIFTING SANDS** [-] [ ]

1967. (lp) <*RS 6247*> **PART ONE** [-] [ ]
– Shifting sands / I won't hurt you / Help I'm a rock / Will you walk with me / Transparent day / Leiyla / Here's where you belong / If you want this love / 'Scuse me Miss Rose / High coin / 1906.

1967. (7") <*0776*> **SMELL OF INCENSE. / UNFREE CHILD** [-] [ ]

1967. (lp) <*RS 6270*> **VOL.2 - SECOND** [-] [ ]
– In the arena / Suppose they gave a war and no one comes / Buddha / Smell of incense / Overture – WCAPAEB part II / Queen nymphet / Unfree child / Carte blanche / Delicate fawn / Tracy had a hard day Sunday.

1968. (lp) <*(RS 6298)*> **VOL.3 - A CHILD'S GUIDE TO GOOD & EVIL** [ ] [ ]
– Eighteen is over the hill / In the country / Ritual No.1 / Our drummer always plays in the nude / As the world rises and falls / Until the poorest people have no money to spend / Watch yourself / A child's guide to good and & evil / Ritual No.2 / Child of a few hours is burning to death / As kind as summer / Anniversary of World War III.

not issued / Amos

1969. (lp) <*AAS 7004*> **WHERE'S MY DADDY** [-] [ ]
– Where's my daddy / Where money rules everything / Hup two hup two / My dog back home / Give me your lovething / Outside – Inside / Everyone's innocent daughter / Free as a bird / Not one bummer / Have you met my pet pig / Coming of age in L.A. / Two people.

— split after above. MARKLEY released a solo album before going into production. In 1973, SHAUN HARRIS released an eponymous country-rock lp.

- compilations, etc. -

1982. (lp) *Sawfly;* <*SAW 8001*> **WEST COAST POP EXPERIMENTAL BAND** [-] [ ]

May 86. (lp/c) *Edsel; (ED/CED 180)* **WEST COAST POP EXPERIMENTAL BAND** [ ] [-]
– Shifting sands / I won't hurt you / 1906 / Will you walk with me / Transparent day / Leiyla / Here's where you belong / High coin / Suppose they give me a war and no-one comes / Buddha / Smell of incense / Overture – WCAPAEB part II / Carte blanche / If you want this love / Help I'm a rock.

Jun 97. (cd) *Head; (3096)* **VOL.2 & VOL.3** [ ] [-]

Alan WHITE (see under ⇒ YES)

WHITE NOISE

Formed: England . . . 1969 by DAVID VORHAUS; an electronic synth man who employed the services of likeminded musicians to complete his 'Island' debut, 'AN ELECTRIC STORM'. Lambasted at the time for its basic experimentation and lush exotica, it soon became acknowledged in the 70's for its pioneering "new age" approach, probably half a decade ahead of its time. In fact, that was the time he set about recording and releasing his long-awaited but disappointing follow-up, 'WHITE NOISE II'. In 1980, he started the decade with the 'III' set, much of the material treading familiar territory. He has since gone back underground. • **Songwriters:** VORHAUS collaborates with either DERBYSHIRE, McDONALD or DUNCAN.

Recommended: AN ELECTRIC STORM (*7)

DAVID VORHAUS – effects, synthesizers / with **DELIA DERBYSHIRE + BRIAN HODGSON** – electronics / **PAUL LYTTON** – percussion / **ANNIE BIRD + VAL SHAW + JOHN**

WHITMAN – vocals

Island / Antilles

1969. (lp) *(ILPS 9099) <7011>* **AN ELECTRIC STORM** [ ] [ ] 1976
– Love without sound / My game of loving / Here come the fleas / Firebird / Your hidden dreams / The visitation / Black mass electric storm in Hell.

— now just VORHAUS

Virgin / not issued

1975. (lp) *(V 2032)* **WHITE NOISE 2** [ ] [-]
– Concerto for synthesizer: Movements 1-3. *(cd iss.Jun97; CDV 2032)*

— added guests vocalist **LINDA HAYES + PETE BROWN**

Pulse / not issued

1980. (lp) *(002)* **WHITE NOISE III** [-] [-] German
– Countdown / Lift off / Afterburn / Burn 2 / Orbit / Leaving song / Deep space drift / Meteor storm / Disorientation / Time traveller / Space warp / Voices / Heavy breathing / Black hole blues / Nine dimensions / Nebulous meets Nebula / The Cygnus constellation.

— now again out of sight, man!

WHO

Formed: Chiswick & Hammersmith, London, England ... 1964 as The HIGH NUMBERS, by ROGER DALTREY, PETE TOWNSHEND, JOHN ENTWISTLE and DOUG SANDERS. After making his impromptu mid-set debut at an early gig, manic sticksman, KEITH MOON, was immediately recruited in favour of the struggling SANDERS. At his first show proper, MOON reportedly mystified colleagues by roping his drums to some pillars before the show. All became clear when the drummer proceeded to knock seven shades of proverbial shit out of them during a solo, the kit actually bouncing off the floor! And thus was completed the line-up that would make their mark as one of the most pivotal, not to mention aggressive bands in rock history. Manager PETE MEADON introduced the band to the burgeoning "Mod" scene and shaped their image accordingly as a musical voice for the sharply dressed, scooter-riding young rebels, a movement that TOWNSHEND in particular felt a strong affinity with, and whose frustrations he'd document in his early, indignant blasts of raw rock'n'roll. A strutting, gloriously arrogant piece of R&B, the band's debut one-off 45 for 'Fontana', 'I'M THE FACE', was released the same month as the experienced managerial team of KIT LAMBERT and CHRIS STAMP took the reins from MEADON and began a concerted campaign for chart domination. Later that year, the band were re-christened The WHO and by this time had begun to perfect their powerful stageshow, TOWNSHEND developing his ferocious "windmilling" power-chord guitar style while the band courted controversy and delighted crowds by smashing their instruments in a cathartic rage. Rejected by major labels, they eventually secured a deal with 'Decca' US, through producer SHEL TALMY. Released in Britain via 'Decca's' UK subsidiary, 'Brunswick', 'I CAN'T EXPLAIN' (1965) introduced a more melodic sound and gave the band their first chart hit. The single climbed into the top 10 after TV appearances on 'Ready Steady Go' (which later adopted the track as its theme tune) and Top Of The Pops, 'ANYWAY, ANYHOW, ANYWHERE' following it later that summer. For most people however, The WHO really arrived with the seminal rebel anthem, 'MY GENERATION'. A stuttering, incredibly focused piece of amphetamine aggression, it galvanised legions of disaffected youths and only The SEX PISTOLS ever equalled it for sheer snide factor. It reached No.2 and was closely followed by the similarly titled debut album which included 'THE KIDS ARE ALRIGHT', probably TOWNSHEND's most explicit alignment with his "Mod" following. But if the kids were alright, The WHO's deal with SHEL TALMY certainly wasn't, or at least that's what the band thought, and after releasing their next single, 'SUBSTITUTE' (1966), on a new label, they became embroiled in a court battle over TALMY's right to produce the group. Despite TALMY winning a royalty on all the band's recordings for another five years, The WHO came out fighting, releasing a string of hits including 'I'M A BOY' (1966), 'HAPPY JACK' (1966) and the wistful ode to masturbation, 'PICTURES OF LILY' (1967). The title track from 'A QUICK ONE' (1966) was a patchy, prototype of the rock opera concept TOWNSHEND would later refine towards the end of the decade. Elsewhere on the album, tracks like ENTWISTLE's 'BORIS THE SPIDER' and TOWNSHEND's 'HAPPY JACK' possessed the same quirky Englishness that was the essence of The KINKS, and The WHO only really began to make some headway in America after their incendiary performance at The Monterey Pop Festival in the summer of '67. 'THE WHO SELL OUT' (1967), a mock concept album, contained the sublime 'I CAN SEE FOR MILES', a spiralling piece of neo-psychedelia that had a spiritual partner in the equally trippy 'ARMENIA CITY IN THE SKY'. With 'TOMMY' (1969), TOWNSHEND ushered in the dreaded concept of the 'Rock Opera'. Yet with his compelling story of a "deaf, dumb and blind kid" who finds release through pinball, he managed to carry the whole thing off. 'PINBALL WIZARD' and 'SEE ME, FEEL ME' were classic TOWNSHEND. The album was even made into a film by maverick director Ken Russell and later into a successful West End show. After this artful tour de force, the band released the legendary 'LIVE AT LEEDS' (1970) album while they worked on TOWNSHEND's latest idea, the 'LIFEHOUSE' project. An ambitious attempt at following up 'TOMMY', the venture was later aborted, although some of the material was used as the basis for the landmark 'WHO'S NEXT' album. Released in 1971, the record heralded a harder rocking sound with the anthemic 'WON'T GET FOOLED AGAIN' and 'BABA O'REILLY'. Immaculately produced, it still stands as The WHO's most confident and cohesive work and only No.1 album. TOWNSHEND finally created a follow-up to TOMMY with 'QUADROPHENIA' in 1973. A complex, lavishly embellished piece that saw him retrospectively examining the Mod sub-culture he'd so closely identified with. The project was later made into a film, inspiring a whole new wave of neo-Mod bands at the turn of the decade. 'THE WHO BY NUMBERS' (1975) was exactly that, a confused set that found the band treading water while trying to find direction in a music scene that was to become increasingly dominated by punk rock. While 'WHO ARE YOU' (1978) sounded more assured, the album's release was marred by the death of KEITH MOON, whose hard drinking and drugging ways finally proved his undoing. Speculation of a split was rife but ex-FACE, KENNY JONES, was drafted in and the band eventually came up with 'FACE DANCES' in 1981. Neither this album, nor 1982's 'IT'S HARD' were successful in rekindling The WHO spark of old and, already demoralised after a number of fans were crushed at a gig in Cincinatti, the band finally called it a day in 1983. The WHO have since occasionally reformed for one-off live appearances including 'Live Aid' and as DALTREY has mainly concentrated on his acting career, TOWNSHEND is the only ex-WHO member who's maintained a serious solo career. His most recent release was the critically acclaimed 'PSYCHODERELICT' (1993) album which was a rock opera of sorts updated for the 90's and included material from the shelved 'LIFEHOUSE' project. **DALTREY's filmography:** LISZTOMANIA (1975) / THE LEGACY (1979) / McVICAR (1980) / BUDDY (1991 TV serial + 1992 film). • **Songwriters:** TOWNSHEND wrote most of material except, I'M THE FACE (Slim Harpo's 'Got Live If You Want It') / I'M A MAN (Bo Diddley) / IN THE CITY (Speedy Keen; aka of Thunderclap Newman) / BARBARA ANN (Beach Boys) / BABY DON'T YOU DO IT (Marvin Gaye) / THE LAST TIME + UNDER MY THUMB (Rolling Stones) / SUMMERTIME BLUES (Eddie Cochran). KEITH MOON's only album was comprised wholly of cover versions. DALTREY's solo career started with songs written for him by LEO SAYER and DAVE COURTNEY. • **Trivia:** DALTREY continues to run a trout farm in Dorset. The WHO were inducted into the Guinness Book Of Records after performing the loudest concert (120 decibels) at Charlton Athletic's Football Club.

Recommended: MY GENERATION (*7) / A QUICK ONE (*6) / THE WHO SELL OUT (*7) / TOMMY (*8) / THE WHO LIVE AT LEEDS (*8) / WHO'S NEXT (*10) / QUADROPHENIA (*9) / THE WHO BY NUMBERS (*5) / WHO'S BETTER WHO'S BEST (*8) / Pete Townshend:- EMPTY GLASS (*7)

ROGER DALTREY (b. 1 Mar'45) – vocals / **PETE TOWNSHEND** (b.19 May'45) – guitar, vocals / **JOHN ENTWISTLE** (b. 9 Oct'44) – bass, vocals / **KEITH MOON** (b.23 Aug'47) – drums, vocals repl. DOUGIE SANDON

Fontana / not issued

Jul 64. (7"; as The HIGH NUMBERS) *(TF 480)* **I'M THE FACE. / ZOOT SUIT** [ ] [-]
(re-iss.Feb65) (re-iss.Mar80 on 'Back Door', hit UK No.49) (US re-iss.Mar80 as The WHO on 'Mercury')

Brunswick / Decca

Jan 65. (7") *(05926) <31725>* **I CAN'T EXPLAIN. / BALD HEADED WOMAN** [8] [93] Feb65
(US re-iss.1973 on 'MCA')

May 65. (7") *(05935)* **ANYWAY ANYHOW ANYWHERE. / DADDY ROLLING STONE** [10] [-]

Jun 65. (7") *<31801>* **ANYWAY ANYHOW ANYWHERE. / ANYTIME YOU WANT ME** [-] [ ]

Oct 65. (7") *(05944)* **MY GENERATION. / SHOUT & SHIMMY** [2] [-]

Nov 65. (7") *<31877>* **MY GENERATION. / OUT IN THE STREET** [-] [74]

Dec 65. (lp) *(LAT 8616) <74664>* **MY GENERATION** [5] [ ]
– Out in the street / I don't mind / The good's gone / La-la-la-lies / Much too much / My generation / The kid's are alright / Please please please / It's not true / I'm a man / A legal matter / The ox. *(US title 'THE WHO SING MY GENERATION') (UK re-iss.Oct80 on 'Virgin' lp/c; V/TCV 2179)*– (hit UK No.20) *(cd-iss.1990;)*

Reaction / Decca

Mar 66. (7") *(591 001) <6409>* **SUBSTITUTE. / WALTZ FOR A PIG ("The WHO ORCHESTRA")** [5] [ ]

— (some copies 'INSTANT PARTY' or 'CIRCLES' on b-side)

<above on US 'Atco'; re-iss.Aug67; 6509>

Aug 66. (7") *(591 004) <32058>* **I'M A BOY. / IN THE CITY** [2] [ ] Dec66

Dec 66. (7") *(591 010)* **HAPPY JACK. / I'VE BEEN AWAY** [3] [-]

Dec 66. (lp) *(593 002) <74892>* **A QUICK ONE** <US-title 'HAPPY JACK'> [4] [67] May67
– Run run run / Boris the spider / Whiskey man / I need you / Heatwave / Cobwebs and strange / Don't look away / See my way / So sad about us / A quick one, while he's away. *(re-iss.Aug88 on 'Polydor' lp/c)(cd); (SPE LP/MC 114)(835 782-2) (cd re-iss.Jun95 & Apr97; 527758-2)*

Mar 67. (7") *<32114>* **HAPPY JACK. / WHISKEY MAN** [-] [24]

Track / Decca

Apr 67. (7") *(604 002) <32156>* **PICTURES OF LILY. / DOCTOR DOCTOR** [4] [51] Jun67

Jul 67. (7") *(604 006)* **THE LAST TIME. / UNDER MY THUMB** [44] [-]

Oct 67. (7") *(604 011)* **I CAN SEE FOR MILES. / SOMEONE'S COMING** [10] [-]

Oct 67. (7") *<32206>* **I CAN SEE FOR MILES. / MARY ANN WITH THE SHAKY HANDS** [-] [9]

Jan 68. (lp; mono/stereo) *(612/613 002) <74950>* **THE WHO SELL OUT** [13] [48]
– Armenian city in the sky / Heinz baked beans / Mary-Anne with the shaky hands / Odorono / Tattoo / Our love was, is / I can see for miles / I can't reach you / Medac / Silas Stingy / Sunrise / Tattoo / Rael. *(re-iss.Aug88 on 'Polydor' lp/c)(cd; (SPE LP/MC 115) (cd re-iss.Jun95 & Apr97 on 'Polydor'; 527 759-2)*

Mar 68. (7") *<32288>* **CALL ME LIGHTNING. / DR. JEKYLL & MR. HIDE** [-] [40]

Jun 68. (7") *(604 023)* **DOGS. / CALL ME LIGHTNING** [25] [-]

Jul 68. (7") *<32362>* **MAGIC BUS. / SOMEONE'S COMING** [-] [25]

Oct 68. (7") *(604 024)* **MAGIC BUS. / DR. JEKYLL & MR. HIDE** [26] [-]

Oct 68. (lp) *<75064>* **MAGIC BUS – (THE WHO ON TOUR) (live)** [-] [39]

– Disguises / Run run run / Dr. Jekyll & Mr. Hyde / I can't reach you / Our love was, is / Call me Lightning / Magic bus / Someone's coming / Doctor doctor / Bucket T. / Pictures of ily.

Nov 68. (lp; mono/stereo) *(612/613 006)* **DIRECT HITS** (compilation) □ -

– Bucket T. / I'm a boy / Pictures of Lily / Doctor doctor / I can see for miles / Substitute / Happy Jack / The last time / In the city / Call me Lightning / Mary-Anne with the shaky hand / Dogs.

Mar 69. (7") *(604 027) <32465>* **PINBALL WIZARD. / DOGS (part 2)** 4 19

<US re-iss.1973 on 'MCA'>

May 69. (d-lp) *(613 013-014) <7205>* **TOMMY** 2 4

– Overture / It's a boy / 1921 / Amazing journey / Sparks / Eyesight for the blind / Miracle cure / Sally Simpson / I'm free / Welcome / Tommy's holiday camp / We're not gonna take it / Christmas / Cousin Kevin / The acid queen / Underture / Do you think it's alright / Fiddle about / Pinball wizard / There's a doctor / Go to the mirror / Tommy can you hear me / Smash the mirror / Sensation. *(re-iss.Jul84 on 'Polydor'; 2486 161/2) (d-cd-iss.Apr89; 800 077-2)*

Jul 69. (7") *<32519>* **I'M FREE. / WE'RE NOT GONNA TAKE IT** - 37

Mar 70. (7") *(604 036) <32670>* **THE SEEKER. / HERE FOR MORE** 19 44

May 70. (lp) *(2406 001) <79175>* **LIVE AT LEEDS (live)** 3 4

– Magic bus / My generation / Shakin' all over / Substitute / Summertime blues / Young man blues. *(re-iss.Nov83 on 'Polydor' lp/c; SPE LP/MC 50) (cd-iss.May88 on 'Polydor'; 825 339-2) (cd re-iss.Feb95 on 'Polydor', hit No.59 & Apr97; 527 169-2)*

Jul 70. (7") *(2094 002)* **SUMMERTIME BLUES (live). / HEAVEN AND HELL** 38 -

Jul 70. (7") *<32708>* **SUMMERTIME BLUES (live). / HERE FOR MORE** - 27

Sep 70. (7") *<32729>* **SEE ME, FEEL ME. / WE'RE NOT GONNA TAKE IT / OVERTURE FROM TOMMY** - 12

<US re-iss.1973 on 'MCA'>

Sep 70. (7"w-drawn) *(2094 004)* **SEE ME, FEEL ME. / OVERTURE FROM TOMMY** - -

Jul 71. (7") *(2094 009) <32846>* **WON'T GET FOOLED AGAIN. / I DON'T EVEN KNOW MYSELF** 9 15

Sep 71. (lp) *(2408 102) <79182>* **WHO'S NEXT** 1 4 Aug71

– Baba O'Riley / Getting in tune / Love ain't for keeping / My wife / The song is over / Bargain / Going mobile / Behind blue eyes / Won't get fooled again. *(re-iss.Nov83 on 'Polydor' lp/c)(cd; SPE LP/MC 49)(813 651-2) (cd re-iss.Aug96; 527760-2)*

Oct 71. (7") *(2094 012)* **LET'S SEE ACTION. / WHEN I WAS A BOY** 16 -

Nov 71. (7") *<32888>* **BEHIND BLUE EYES. / MY WIFE** - 34

Dec 71. (lp/c) *(2406/3191 006) <79184>* **MEATY, BEATY, BIG AND BOUNCY** (compilation) 9 11 Nov71

– I can't explain / The kids are alright / Happy Jack / I can see for miles / Pictures of Lily / My generation / The seeker / Anyway, anyhow, anywhere / Pinball wizard / A legal matter / Boris the spider / Magic bus / Substitute / I'm a boy. *(re-iss.1974)*

Jun 72. (7") *(2094 102) <32983>* **JOIN TOGETHER. / BABY DON'T YOU DO IT** 9 17

— In Oct72, PETE TOWNSHEND was another like ENTWISTLE to issue debut solo album 'WHO CAME FIRST'. It scraped into UK Top30. He issued more throughout 70's-80's (see . . .) In Apr'73, ROGER DALTREY hit the singles chart with GIVING IT ALL AWAY. It was a cut from debut album DALTREY.

Jan 73. (7") *(2094 106) <33041>* **RELAY. / WASPMAN** 21 39 Dec72

Track M.C.A.

Oct 73. (7") *(2094 115)* **5:15. / WATER** 20 -

Oct 73. (7") *<40152>* **5:15. / LOVE REIGN O'ER ME** - □

Nov 73. (d-lp) *(2657 002) <10004>* **QUADROPHENIA** 2 2

– I am the sea / The real me / Quadrophenia / Cut my hair / The punk and the godfather / I'm one / Dirty jobs / Helpless dancer / Is it in my head? / I've had enough / 5:15 / Sea and sand / Drowned / Bell boy / Doctor Jimmy / The rock / Love, reign o'er me. *(re-iss.Sep79 on 'Polydor' d-lp)(d-c; 2657013)(3526001) (d-cd-iss.Jan87 on 'Polydor'; 831074-2)*

Nov 73. (7") *<40152>* **LOVE, REIGN O'ER ME. / WATER** - 76

Jan 74. (7") *<40182>* **THE REAL ME. / I'M ONE** - 92

— In Apr75, KEITH MOON was the last WHO member to release solo vinyl. The dismal 'TWO SIDES OF THE MOON' sold poorly.

Polydor M.C.A.

Oct 75. (lp/c) *(2490/3194 129) <2161>* **THE WHO BY NUMBERS** 7 8

– Slip kid / However much I booze / Squeeze box / Dreaming from the waist / Imagine a man / Success story / They are all in love / Blue, red and grey / How many friends / In a hand or a face. *(re-iss.Mar84 lp/c; SPE LP/MC 68) (cd-iss.Jul89; 831552-2)*

Jan 76. (7") *(2121 275) <40475>* **SQUEEZE BOX. / SUCCESS STORY** 10 16 Nov75

Aug 76. (7") *<40603>* **SLIP KID. / DREAMING FROM THE WAIST** - □

Sep 76. (d-lp)(d-c) *(2683 069)(3519 020)* **THE STORY OF THE WHO** (compilation) 2 -

– Magic bus / Substitute / Boris the spider / Run run run / I'm a boy / Heatwave / My generation / Pictures of Lily / Happy Jack / The seeker / I can see for miles / Bargain / Squeeze box / Amazing journey / The acid queen / Do you think it's alright / Fiddle about / Pinball wizard / I'm free / Tommy's holiday camp / We're not gonna take it / See me, feel me / Summertime blues / Baba O'Riley / Behind blue eyes / Slip kid / Won't get fooled again.

Jul 78. (7") *(WHO 1) <40948>* **WHO ARE YOU?. / HAD ENOUGH** 18 14

— On 5th Aug'78, manager PETE MEADON committed suicide.

Sep 78. (lp/c)<US-red/pic-lp> *(WHOD/+C 5004) <3050>* **WHO ARE YOU** 6 2

– New song / Had enough / 905 / Sister disco / Music must change / Trick of the light / Guitar and pen / Love is coming down / Who are you. *(re-iss.Aug84 lp/c; SPE LP/MC 77) (cd-iss.Jul89; 831557-2)*

— After a party on 7th Sep'78, KEITH MOON died on an overdose of heminevrin.

Dec 78. (7") *<40978>* **TRICK OF THE LIGHT. / 905** - □

— Early'79, **KENNY JONES** (b.16 Sep'48) – drums (ex-SMALL FACES, ex-FACES) took place of KEITH. Added 5th tour member **JOHN 'Rabbit' BUNDRICK** – keyboards

Polydor Warners

Feb 81. (7") *(WHO 4) <49698>* **YOU BETTER YOU BET. / THE QUIET ONE** 9 18

Mar 81. (lp/c) *(WHOD/+C 5037) <3516>* **FACE DANCES** 2 4

– You better you bet / Don't let go the coat / Cache cache / The quiet one / Did you steal my money / How can you do it alone / Daily records / You / Another tricky day. *(re-iss.May88 lp/c; SPE LP/MC 112) (re-iss.cd Jun93;) (cd re-iss.May97; 537695-2)*

May 81. (7") *(WHO 5) <49743>* **DON'T LET GO THE COAT. / YOU** 47 84

Sep 82. (lp/c) *(WHOD/+C 5066) <23731>* **IT'S HARD** 11 8

– Athena / It's your turn / Cooks county / It's hard / Dangerous / Eminence front / I've known no war / One life's enough / One at a time / Why did I fall for that / A man is a man / Cry if you want. *(cd-iss.1983 & Jun93; 800 106-2) (cd re-iss.May97; 537696-2)*

Sep 82. (7"/7"pic-d) *(WHO/+P 6)* **ATHENA. / A MAN IS A MAN** 40 -

(12"+=/12"pic-d+=) *(WHO X/PX 6)* – Won't get fooled again.

Sep 82. (7") *<29905>* **ATHENA. / IT'S YOUR TURN** - 28

Dec 82. (7") *<29814>* **EMINENCE FRONT. / ONE AT A TIME** - 68

Feb 83. (7") *<29731>* **IT'S HARD. / DANGEROUS** - □

— They officially split late 1983 from studio work. They occasionally returned for one-off live work.

– other compilations, etc. –

below 4 on 'Brunswick' label.

Mar 66. (7") *(05956)* **A LEGAL MATTER. / INSTANT PARTY** 32 -

Aug 66. (7") *(05965)* **THE KIDS ARE ALRIGHT. / THE OX** 41 -

Aug 66. (7") *<31988>* **THE KIDS ARE ALRIGHT. / A LEGAL MATTER** - □

Nov 66. (7") *(05968)* **LA LA LA LIES. / THE GOOD'S GONE** □ -

Nov 66. (7"ep) *Reaction; (592 001)* **READY STEADY WHO** □ -

– Circles / Disguises / Batman / Bucket 'T' / Barbara Ann. *(re-iss.Nov83 on 'Reaction-Polydor'; WHO 7); hit 58*

Nov 70. (7"ep) *Track; (2252 001)* **EXCERPTS FROM "TOMMY"** □ -

– See me, feel me / I'm free / Christmas / Overture from Tommy.

Oct 74. (lp/c) *Track; (2406/3191 116) <2126>* **ODDS AND SODS** (rarities) 10 15

– Postcard / Now I'm a farmer / Put the money down / Little Billy / Too much of anything / Glow girl / Pure and easy / Faith in something bigger / I'm the face / Naked eye / Long live rock. *(re-iss.cd Jun93;)*

Nov 74. (7") *Track; <40330>* **POSTCARD. / PUT THE MONEY DOWN** - □

Dec 74. (d-lp)(d-c) *Track; (2683 038)(3533 022) <4067>* **A QUICK ONE / THE WHO SELL OUT** □ □

— below with guest singers ELTON JOHN, TINA TURNER, OLIVER REED, ANN-MARGRET, etc

Aug 75. (d-lp)(d-c) *Polydor; (2657 007) <9502>* **TOMMY (Film Soundtrack)** 30 2 Mar75

– Prologue / Captain Walker – It's a boy / Bernie's holiday camp / 1951 – What about the boy? / Amazing journey / Christmas / Eyesight to the blind / Acid queen / Do you think it's alright / Cousin Kevin / Do you think it's alright / Fiddle about / Do you think it's alright / Sparks / Extra, extra, extra / Pinball wizard / Champagne / There's a doctor / Go to the mirror / Tommy can you hear me / Smash the mirror / I'm free / Mother and son / Sensation / Miracle cure / Sally Simpson / Welcome / T.V. studio / Tommy's holiday camp / We're not gonna take it / Listening to you – See me, feel me.

— Note; below on 'Polydor' UK/ 'MCA' US, unless mentioned otherwise

Oct 76. (7"m) *(2058 803)* **SUBSTITUTE. / I'M A BOY / PICTURES OF LILY** 7 -

Apr 79. (7"m) *(WHO 2) <41053>* **LONG LIVE ROCK. / I'M THE FACE / MY WIFE** 48 54

Jun 79. (d-lp)(d-c)<US-pic-d-lp> *(2675 179)(3577 343) <11005>* **THE KIDS ARE ALRIGHT** 26 8

– (some live tracks with interviews) *(re-iss.cd Jun93)*

Sep 79. (7") *<2022>* **I'M ONE. / 5:15** □ 45 b-side

Sep 79. (d-lp)(d-c) *(2625 037)(3577 352) <6235>* **QUADROPHENIA (Film Soundtrack)** 23 46

– (includes tracks by other artists)

Feb 81. (lp)(c) *(2486 140)(3195 235)* **MY GENERATION (compilation)** □ -

Oct 81. (lp) *<12001>* **HOOLIGANS** - 52

(UK-iss.Dec88;)

Feb 83. (d-c) *(3577 378)* **WHO'S NEXT / THE WHO BY NUMBERS** □ -

Feb 83. (d-c) **WHO ARE YOU / LIVE AT LEEDS** □ -

May 83. (lp) *<5408>* **WHO'S GREATEST HITS** - 94

Aug 83. (lp)/(c) *(SPE LP/MC 9) <2311 132><3100 630>* **RARITIES VOL.1 (1966-68)** □ □ Oct82

Aug 83. (lp/c) *(SPE LP/MC 10)* **RARITIES VOL.2 (1970-73)** □ □ Oct82

(re-iss.cd+c.VOL.1 & 2 Jan91)

Nov 84. (d-lp/d-c) *(WHO/+C 1) <8018>* **WHO'S LAST** 48 81

(cd-iss.Dec88; DWHO 1)

Nov 84. (7") *(MCA 927)* **TWIST AND SHOUT. / I CAN'T EXPLAIN** □ -

Nov 84. (lp/c)(cd) *(WHOH/+C 17)(815 965-2)* **THE SINGLES** □ -

Oct 85. (d-lp/d-c) *Impression; (IMDP/IMDK 1)* **THE WHO COLLECTION** 44 -

(d-cd-iss.Oct88; IMCD 41)

Aug 85. (lp/c) *Karusel Gold; (825 746-1/-4)* **THE BEST OF THE SIXTIES** □ -

Apr 86. (lp/c) *Arcade; (ADAH/+C 427)* **GREATEST HITS** □ -

Feb 88. (7") *(POSP 907)* **MY GENERATION. / SUBSTITUTE** 68 □

(12"+=/c-s+=/cd-s+=) *(POSPX/POSPC/POCD 907)* – Baba O'Riley / Behind blue eyes.

Mar 88. (lp/c)(cd) *(WTV/+C 1)(835 389-2)* **WHO'S BETTER WHO'S BEST** 10 □

– My generation / Anyway, anyhow, anywhere / The kids are alright / Substitute / I'm a boy / Happy Jack / Pictures of Lily / I can see for miles / Who are you / Won't get fooled again / Magic bus / Pinball wizard / I'm free / I can't explain / See me feel me / Squeeze box / Join together / You better you bet. *(cd+=)*– Baba O'Riley.

Jun 88. (7") *(POSP 917)* **WON'T GET FOOLED AGAIN. / BONEY MORONIE (live)** □ □

(ext-12"+=/cd-s+=) *(POSPX/POCD 917)* – Dancing in the street (live) / Mary Ann with the shaky hand.

Oct 88. (lp/c/cd) *(SPE LP/MC/CD 116) <5641>* **WHO'S MISSING** □ □ Dec85

Mar 90. (7") *Virgin; (VS 1259)* **JOIN TOGETHER. / I CAN SEE FOR MILES** □ □

(12"+=) *(VST 1259)* – Behind blue eyes.

(cd-s++=) *(VSCD 1259)* – Christmas.

Mar 90. (cd/d-c/d-lp) *Virgin; (CD/TC+/VDT 102) / M.C.A.; <19501>* **JOIN TOGETHER** 59 □

– (contains some solo material)

Jul 94. (4xcd-box) *(521751-2)* **30 YEARS OF MAXIMUM R&B** 48

Jul 96. (7"/c-s) *(863918-7/-4)* **MY GENERATION. / PINBALL WIZARD (live)** 31 -

(cd-s+=) *(854637-2)* – Boris the spider.

Aug 96. (cd/c) *(533150-2/-4)* **MY GENERATION – THE VERY BEST OF THE WHO** 11

– I can't explain / Anyway, anyhow, anywhere / My generation / Substitute / I'm a boy / Boris the spider / Hapy Jack / Pictures of Lily / I can see for miles / Magic bus / Pinball wizard / The seeker / Baba O'Riley / Won't get fooled again / Let's see action / 5.15 / Join together / Squeeze box / Who are you / You better you bet.

— for WHO solo material (see GREAT ROCK DISCOGRAPHY)

WILD TURKEY

Formed: based ... London, England ... early 70's by former JETHRO TULL guitarist GLENN CORNICK and GARY PICKFORD-HOPKINS. A mainstream progressive-rock outfit, they released two albums in their brief career span. They were lambasted at the time for sounding too run-of-the-mill, although 'A UNIVERSAL MAN' from their second set was a stand-out track.

Recommended: BATTLE HYMN (*6) / TURKEY (*5)

GARY PICKFORD-HOPKINS – vocals, guitar (ex-EYES OF BLUE, ex-ANCIENT GREASE, ex-BIG SLEEP) / **TWEKE LEWIS** – guitar / **JON BLACKMORE** – guitar / **GLENN CORNICK** – bass, keyboards, guitar (ex-JETHRO TULL) / **JEFF JONES** – drums, percussion

Chrysalis Reprise

Oct 71. (lp) *(CHR 1002)* <2070> **BATTLE HYMN**

– Butterfly / Twelve streets of cobbled black / Dulwich fox / Easter psalm / To the stars / Sanctuary / One sole survivor / Battle hymn / Gentle rain / Sentinel. *(cd-iss.Sep91 on 'Edsel'; EDCD 337)*

— **MICK DYCHE** – guitar, vocals + **STEVE GURL** – piano (ex-BABE RUTH) repl. BLACKMORE

1972. (7") *(CHS 2004)* **GOOD OLD DAYS. / LIFE IS A SYMPHONY**

Sep 72. (lp) *(CHR 1010)* **TURKEY** -

– Good old days / Tomorrow's friend / A universal man / Eternal mother / The return / Chuck stallion and the mustangs / The street / See you next Tuesday / Telephone. *(cd-iss.May95 on 'Edsel'; EDCD 424)*

— split when TWEKE joined MAN. CORNICK formed German outfit KATHARGO, before joining PARIS. He re-formed WILD TURKEY in the mid-90's.

H.T.D. not issued

Apr 96. (cd) *(HTDCD 58)* **STEALER OF YEARS** -

Brian WILSON (see under ⇒ BEACH BOYS)

WIMPLE WINCH

Formed: Liverpool, England ... 1961 as DEE FENTON & THE SILHOUETTES (actually their Greek-born frontman's DEMETRIUS CHRISTOPHOLUS' stage name). The line-up was completed by PETE TURNER, HARRY BEAR, LAWRENCE ARDENES and JOHN KELMAN. Two years later, they became The FOUR JUST MEN, although on the verge of releasing their debut beat 45, 'THAT'S MY BABY' for 'Parlophone', they were served with an injunction by another group of the same name. After being left in the stalls for a few months, the group returned under the slightly changed moniker, The JUST FOUR MEN. Another single in 1965, 'THERE'S NOT ONE THING', also flopped and it was thought another name change to WIMPLE WINCH would improve matters. Forsaking beat/R&B for freakbeat psychedelia, they released a few (now much sought after) 45's for 'Fontana', the best being their third of 1966, 'RUMBLE ON MERSEY SQUARE SOUTH'. They split in 1967, having just survived a fire at 'The Sinking Ship' club in Stockport (a long-time residency), which saw them losing their equipment. CHRISTOPHOLUS went onto appear in a number of stage shows in London's West End, including 'Hair', 'Jesus Christ Superstar', and 'Joseph & His Amazing Technicolour Dream Coat'.

Recommended: THE WIMPLE WINCH STORY (*6)

JUST FOUR MEN

DEMETRIUS CHRISTOPHOLUS – vocals, guitar / **PETER TURNER** – guitar / **LALLY SCOTT** – guitar; repl. JOHN KELMAN, who joined FREDDIE STARR & THE MIDNIGHTERS / **HARRY BEAR** – bass / **LAWRENCE ARDENES** – drums

Parlophone not issued

1964. (7"w-drawn; as FOUR JUST MEN) *(R 5186)* **THAT'S MY BABY. / THINGS WILL NEVER BE THE SAME** - -

1964. (7") *(R 5208)* **THAT'S MY BABY. / THINGS WILL NEVER BE THE SAME** -

1965. (7") *(R 5241)* **THERE'S NOT ONE THING. / DON'T COME ANY CLOSER** -

— **BARRY ASHALL** – bass, repl. KEITH SHEPPARD, who repl. BEAR

WIMPLE WINCH

— **KELMAN** re-joined to repl. LALLY

Fontana not issued

Apr 66. (7") *(TF 686)* **WHAT'S BEEN DONE. / I REALLY LOVE YOU** -

Jun 66. (7") *(TF 718)* **SAVE MY SOUL. / EVERYBODY'S WORRIED 'BOUT TOMORROW** -

Jan 67. (7") *(TF 781)* **RUMBLE ON MERSEY SQUARE SOUTH. / TYPICAL BRITISH WORKMANSHIP** -

above mispressed with diff. B-side, & worth over £200

— soon split ... LAWRENCE became LAWRENCE KING and joined PACIFIC DRIFT

– compilations, etc. –

Apr 92. (lp) *Bam Caruso; (KIRI 104)* **THE WIMPLE WINCH STORY VOLUME TWO '66-'68 – THE PSYCHEDELIC YEARS** -

Aug 94. (cd) *Bam Caruso; (KIRI 107CD)* **THE WIMPLE WINCH STORY 1963-1968** -

WIND

Formed: Germany ... as the stupidly named CORPORAL GANDER'S FIRE DOG BRIGADE. They were strictly a hard-rock covers act, completing versions of Black Sabbath's 'PARANOID', Smiley Lewis' 'I HEAR YOU KNOCKIN' alongside their own compositions on a poor album, 'ON THE ROCKS'. Changing their name to WIND, they released the 'SEASONS' album the same year, a somewhat more accomplished work which focussed on a distinctive style of heavy progressive rock with folk leanings, often juxtaposing the contrasting sounds within the same song. The follow-up, 'MORNING' (1972), was a considerably more mellow affair, maintaining the folky lilt but dropping the heavy guitar in favour of gentle mellotron stylings. The band split soon after as their contract with 'C.B.S.' came to an end.

Recommended: SEASONS (*9) / MORNING (*7)

THOMAS LEIDENBERGER – guitar, vocals / **ANDREAS BUELER** – bass, vocals / **LUCIAN BUELER** – keyboards, vocals / **LUCKY SCHMIDT** – drums, percussion, mellotron

Europa not issued

Jan 71. (lp; as CORPORAL GANDER'S FIRE DOG BRIGADE) *(E 460)* **ON THE ROCKS** - - German

– Paranoid / I hear you knockin' / Come back here / On the rocks / Hey you / Stealer / Run for life / Do you think it's right / Love song / Don't tell me.

— added **STEVE LEISTNER** – vocals

Plus not issued

1971. (lp) *(3)* **SEASONS** - - German

– What do we do now / Now it's over / Romance / Springwind / Dear little friend / Red morningbird. *(cd-iss.1991 on 'Second Battle'; SB 016)*

C.B.S. not issued

1972. (lp) *(65007)* **MORNING** - - German

– Morning song / The princess and the minstrel / Dragon's maid / Carnival / Schlittenfahrt / Puppet master / Tommy's song.

— split after above.

WINTERGARDEN (see under ⇒ NINE DAYS' WONDER)

WISHBONE ASH

Formed: Torquay, Devon, England ... summer 1969 out of the EMPTY VESSELS, by MARTIN TURNER and STEVE UPTON. They quickly moved to London with two new members; ANDY POWELL and TED TURNER (no relation). In 1970, they signed to 'M.C.A.' and delivered their eponymous debut into the UK Top 40. They were described at the time as Britain's answer to The ALLMAN BROTHERS, albeit with a mystical lyrical element. Fusing heavy-rock with fine harmonies and self-indulgent solos, the second album, the Top 20 'PILGRIMAGE' was more of the same. Their third album, 'ARGUS' (1972) broke them through big time, a compelling hybrid of arcane medieval themes and water-tight prog-rock. This classic Top 3 album featured, 'WARRIOR', 'THE KING WILL COME' and 'THROW DOWN THE SWORD' alongside the more freely flowing, 'BLOWIN' FREE' (a record that should have given them a hit). 'WISHBONE FOUR' was completed the following year, a mellower set with a rootsier country-rock feel, especially on the track, 'BALLAD OF THE BEACON'. After a double live set in '73, they took an even more down-home approach on 'THERE'S THE RUB', although it did contain one highlight, 'F*U*B*B*' (Fucked Up Beyond Belief). Although they managed to retain some (very!) loyal fans, by the end of the decade they had lost all their credibility when most of the original members left. In 1981, they even drafted in folky/new-age vocalist, CLAIRE HAMILL, in an attempt to develop other areas of their sound. They are still treading the boards, churning out new versions of their once classic songs, two live albums of recent material being recorded in Chicago and Geneva respectively. • **Songwriters:** Group compositions / TURNER's.

Recommended: CLASSIC ASH (*8) / ARGUS (*9) / LIVE DATES (*8) / PILGRIMAGE (*6)

MARTIN TURNER (b. 1 Oct'47) – vocals, bass / **ANDY POWELL** (b. 8 Feb'50) – guitar, vocals repl. GLEN TURNER (no relation) / **TED TURNER** (b.DAVID, 2 Aug'50) – guitar, vocals (ex-KING BISCUIT) / **STEVE UPTON** (b.24 May'46, Wrexham, Wales) – drums

M.C.A. Decca

Dec 70. (lp) *(MKPS 2014)* <75249> **WISHBONE ASH** 34

– Blind eye / Lady Whiskey / Error of my ways / Queen of torture / Handy / Phoenix. *(re-iss.Feb74 lp/c; MCG/TCMCG 3507) (re-iss.1980; MCA 2343) (cd-iss.Jul91) (cd-iss.Dec94 on 'Beat Goes On';)*

Jan 71. (7") *(MK 5061)* <32826> **BLIND EYE. / QUEEN OF TORTURE**

Sep 71. (lp) *(MDKS 8004)* <75295> **PILGRIMAGE** 14

– Vas dis / The pilgrim / Jail bait / Alone / Lullaby / Valediction / Where were you tomorrow. *(re-iss.Feb74 lp/c; MCG/TCMCG 3504) (re-iss.Dec83 lp/c; MCL/+C 1762) (cd-iss.Jul91; DMCL 1762) (cd re-iss.1990's; MCLD 19084) (+=)–* Baby what you want me to do / Jail bait (live).

Oct 71. (7") *<32902>* **JAIL BAIT. / VAS DIS** [-] [ ]

May 72. (lp) *(MDKS 8006) <75437>* **ARGUS** [3] [ ]
– Time was / Sometime world / Blowin' free / The king will come / Leaf and stream / Warrior / Throw down the sword. *(re-iss.Feb74 lp/c; MCG/TCMCG 3510) (re-iss.Feb84 lp/c; MCL/+C 1787) (re-iss.1987 on 'Castle' lp/c; CLA LP/MC 140) (cd-iss.1991; DMCL 1787) (cd re-iss.1990's; MCLD 19085)*

Jun 72. (7") *(MKS 5097) <33004>* **BLOWIN' FREE. / NO EASY ROAD** [ ] [ ]

M.C.A. M.C.A.

May 73. (lp) *(MDKS 8011) <327>* **WISHBONE FOUR** [12] [44]
– So many things to say / Ballad of the beacon / No easy road / Everybody needs a friend / Doctor / Sorrel / Sing out the song / Rock'n'roll widow. *(re-iss.Feb74 lp/c; MCG/TCMCG 3505)*

Jul 73. (7") *<40041>* **ROCK'N'ROLL WIDOW. / NO EASY ROAD** [-] [ ]

Jul 73. (7") *(MUS 1210)* **SO MANY THINGS TO SAY. / ROCK'N'ROLL WIDOW** [ ] [-]

Dec 73. (d-lp) *(ULD 1-2) <2-8006>* **LIVE DATES (live)** [ ] [82] Nov73
– The king will come / Warrior / Throw down the sword / Rock'n'roll widow / Ballad of the beacon / Baby what you want me to do / The pilgrim / Blowin' free / Jail bait / Lady Whiskey / Phoenix. *(re-iss.Jun74 d-lp/c; MCSP/+C 254)*

— (Jun74) **LAURIE WISEFIELD** – guitar (ex-HOME) repl. TED who found religion

Nov 74. (7") *(MCA 165)* **HOMETOWN. / PERSEPHONE** [ ] [-]

Nov 74. (lp/c) *(MCF/TCMCF 2585) <464>* **THERE'S THE RUB** [16] [88]
– Silver shoes / Don't come back / Persephone / Hometown / Lady Jay / F*U*B*B.

Feb 75. (7") *(MCA 176) <40362>* **SILVER SHOES. / PERSEPHONE** [ ] [ ]

— added on session **PETER WOODS** – keyboards

M.C.A. Atlantic

Mar 76. (lp/c) *(MCF/TCMCF 2750)* **LOCKED IN** [36] [ ]
– Rest in peace / No water in the well / Moonshine / She was my best friend / It started in Heaven / Half past lovin' / Trust in you / Say goodbye.

Nov 76. (lp/c) *(MCG/TCMCG 3523) <18200>* **NEW ENGLAND** [22] [ ]
– Mother of pearl / (In all of my dreams) You rescue me / Runaway / Lorelei / Outward bound / Prelude / When you know love / Lonely island / Candle-light. *(re-iss.Jul82 lp/c; MCL/+C 1699)*

Nov 76. (7") *(MCA 261)* **OUTWARD BOUND. / LORELEI** [ ] [-]

M.C.A. M.C.A.

Sep 77. (7") *(MCA 326)* **FRONT PAGE NEWS. / DIAMOND JACK** [ ] [-]

Oct 77. (lp/c) *(MCG/+C 3524) <2311>* **FRONT PAGE NEWS** [31] [ ]
– Front page news / Midnight dancer / Goodbye baby, hello friend / Surface to air / 714 / Come in from the rain / Right or wrong / Heart beat / The day I found your love / Diamond Jack. *(re-iss.Feb82 lp/c; MCL/+C 1655)*

Oct 77. (7") *<40829>* **FRONT PAGE NEWS. / GOODBYE BABY, HELLO FRIEND** [-] [ ]

Nov 77. (7") *(MCA 327)* **GOODBYE BABY, HELLO FRIEND. / COME IN FROM THE RAIN** [ ] [-]

Sep 78. (7"/12") *(MCA/12MCA 392)* **YOU SEE RED. / BAD WEATHER BLUES (live)** [ ] [-]

Oct 78. (lp/c) *(MCG/+C 3528) <3060>* **NO SMOKE WITHOUT FIRE** [43] [ ]
– You see red / Baby, the angels are here / Ships in the sky / Stand and deliver / Anger in harmony / Like a child / The way of the world / A stormy weather. *(w/free live 7")–* COME IN FROM THE RAIN. / LORELEI

Aug 79. (7") *(MCA 518)* **COME ON. / FAST JOHNNY** [ ] [ ]

Jan 80. (7") *<41214>* **HELPLESS. / INSOMNIA** [-] [ ]

Jan 80. (7") *(MCA 549)* **LIVING PROOF. / JAIL BAIT (live)** [ ] [-]

Jan 80. (lp/c) *(MCF/TCMCF 3052)* **JUST TESTING** [41] [ ]
– Living proof / Haunting me / Insomnia / Helpless / Pay the price / New rising star / Masters of disguise / Lifeline.

Apr 80. (7"/12") *(MCA/+T 577)* **HELPLESS (live). / BLOWIN' FREE (live)** [ ] [-]

Oct 80. (lp/c) *(MCG/+C 4012)* **LIVE DATES II (live)** [40] [ ]
– Doctor / Living proof / Runaway / Helpless / F*U*B*B / The way of the world. *(ltd. w/free live lp) (re-iss.Jun84; MCL 1799)*

— **JOHN WETTON** – bass, vocals (ex-URIAH HEEP, ex-FAMILY, ex-KING CRIMSON) repl. MARTIN TURNER to production. / added **CLAIRE HAMILL** – vocals (solo artist)

Mar 81. (7") *(MCA 695)* **UNDERGROUND. / MY MIND IS MADE UP** [ ] [-]

Apr 81. (lp/c) *(MCF/+C 3103)* **NUMBER THE BRAVE** [61] [ ]
– Loaded / Where is the love / Underground / Kicks on the street / Open road / Get ready / Rainstorm / That's that / Rollercoaster / Number the brave.

May 81. (7") *(MCA 726/+/MCL 14)* **GET READY. / KICKS ON THE STREET** [ ] [-]

May 81. (7") *<51149>* **GET READY. / LOADED** [-] [ ]

— **UPTON, POWELL + WISEFIELD** recruited new member **TREVOR BOLDER** – bass (ex-SPIDERS FROM MARS / Bowie, ex-URIAH HEEP, etc. repl. WETTON to ASIA, etc.

A.V.M. Fantasy

Oct 82. (7") *(WISH 1)* **ENGINE OVERHEAT. / GENEVIEVE** [ ] [-]

Nov 82. (lp/c) *(ASH/+C 1) <F 9629>* **TWIN BARRELS BURNING** [22] [ ] 1983
– Engine overheat / Can't fight love / Genevieve / Me and my guitar / Hold on / Streets of shame / No more lonely nights / Angels have mercy / Wind up. *(cd-iss.Aug93 on 'Castle'; CLACD 389)*

Dec 82. (7") *(1002)* **NO MORE LONELY NIGHTS. / STREETS OF SHAME** [ ] [-]

— **MERVYN 'Spam' SPENCER** – bass (ex-TRAPEZE) repl. BOLDER to URIAH HEEP

Neat not issued

Jan 85. (lp/pic-lp/c) *(NEAT/+P/C 1027)* **RAW TO THE BONE** [ ] [-]
– Cell of fame / People in motion / Don't cry / Love is blue / Long live the night / Rocket in my pocket / It's only love / Don't you mess / Dreams (searching for an answer) / Perfect timing. *(re-iss.Aug93 on 'Castle'; CLACD 390)*

— **ANDY PYLE** – bass (ex-SAVOY BROWN, ex-BLODWYN PIG) repl. SPENCE

— Originals (**ANDREW, STEVE, MARTIN & TED**) reformed WISHBONE ASH.

I.R.S.-MCA I.R.S.-MCA

Feb 88. (lp/c/cd) *(MIRF/CMIRF/DMIRF 1028)* **NOUVEAU CALLS** (instrumental) [ ] [ ]
– Tangible evidence / Closseau / Flags of convenience / From Soho to Sunset / Arabesque / In the skin / Something's happening in Room 602 / Johnny left home without it / The spirit flies free / A rose is a rose / Real guitars have wings. *(re-iss.1990 lp/c/cd; ILP/+MC/CD 39)*

May 88. (7") *(IRM 164)* **IN THE SKIN. / TANGIBLE EVIDENCE** [ ] [ ]

— In Apr89, TED & ANDY guested on their labels' Various Artists live cd,c,d-lp, video 'NIGHT OF THE GUITAR'.

I.R.S. I.R.S.

Jun 89. (7") *(EIRS 104)* **COSMIC JAZZ. / T-BONE SHUFFLE** [ ] [ ]
(12"+=) *(EIRST 104)* – Bolan's monument.

Aug 89. (lp/c/cd) *(EIRSA/+C/CD 1006) <82006>* **HERE TO HEAR** [ ] [ ]
– Cosmic jazz / Keeper of the light / Mental radio / Walk on water / Witness on wonder / Lost cause in Paradise / Why don't we / In the case / Hole in my heart (part 1 & 2).

— **RAY WESTON** – drums repl. MARTIN

May 91. (lp/c/cd) *(EIRSA/+C/CD 1045)* **STRANGE AFFAIR** [ ] [ ]
– Strange affair / Wings of desire / Dream train / You / Hard times / Standing in the rain / Renegade / Say you will / Rollin' / Some conversion.

— **POWELL + TED TURNER + RAY** bring in **ANDY PYLE** – bass / **DAN C.GILLOGLY** – keyboards

Permanent Griffin

Mar 92. (cd/c/lp) *(PERM CD/MC/LP 6)* **THE ASH LIVE IN CHICAGO (live)** [ ] [ ] 1994

Hengest not issued

Mar 96. (cd) *(HNRCD 03)* **LIVE IN GENEVA (live)** [ ] [-]

– compilations, others, etc. –

— on 'M.C.A.' unless stated otherwise

Apr 77. (7"ep) *(MCA 291)* **PHOENIX. / BLOWIN' FREE / JAIL BAIT** [ ] [-]

May 77. (lp/c) *(MCF/TCMCF 2795)* **CLASSIC ASH** [ ] [ ]
– Blind eye / Phoenix / The pilgrim / Blowin' free / The king will come / Rock'n'roll widow / Persephone / Outward bound / Throw down the sword (live). *(re-iss.Aug81 lp/c; MCL/+C 1621) (re-iss.Jan83 on 'Fame' lp/c; FA/TCFA 3053)*

Jan 82. (lp) *(5283-27126)* **HOT ASH** [-] [ ]

Apr 82. (d-c) *(MCA 2103)* **PILGRIMAGE / ARGUS** [ ] [-]

May 82. (lp) *(MCF 3134)* **THE BEST OF WISHBONE ASH** [ ] [-]

Oct 91. (cd) *Windsong; (WINCD 004)* **LIVE IN CONCERT (live)** [ ] [-]

1993. (d-cd) *<MCAD2 10765>* **TIME WAS** (w/ remixed 'ARGUS') [ ] [-]

Mar 94. (cd/c) *Nectar; (NTR CD/MC 014)* **BLOWIN' FREE – THE VERY BEST OF WISHBONE ASH** [ ] [-]

Sep 94. (cd/c) *(MCLD/MCLC 19249)* **THERE'S THE RUB / LOCKED IN** [ ] [-]

Nov 94. (cd) *Start; (HP 93452)* **IN CONCERT** [ ] [-]

Jan 97. (cd) *Receiver; (RRCD 216)* **LIVE – TIMELINE (live)** [ ] [-]

WITTHUSER & WESTRUPP

Formed: Essen, Germany ... 1970 after WALTER WESTRUPP provided backing on BERND WITTHUSER's solo album, 'LIEDER VON VAMPIREN, NONNEN UND TOTEN' (they had busked together in the mid-60's). WESTRUPP had also been leader of The NIGHT REVELLER SKIFFLE GROUP in the second half of the 60's, while WITTHUSER had been manager of the 'Podium' folk club. The album was nothing startling, full of short, sharp, acoustic folk songs that were quickly forgotten, although the album is now a collector's item, especially if you held on to the free gimmick balloon on its sleeve. In 1971, they were jointly credited on the "follow-up"; 'TRIPS UND TRAUME', an exceptional piece of baroque psychedelia, cosmically in-tune to British folk-rock counterparts, The INCREDIBLE STRING BAND, offering such gems as 'ORIENTA' and the celebrated drug-anthem, 'NIMM EINEN JOINT, MEIN FREUND'. Two albums in quick succession followed, providing more cosmic progressive-rock, but their "trip" was all over in 1973, when sessions/jams with SERGIUS GOLOWIN and WALTER WEGMULLER split them apart.

Recommended: TRIP UND TRAUME (*9) / DER JESUSPILZ (*7) / BAUER PLATH (*7)

BERND WITTHUSER – vocals, guitar, harmonica / **WALTER WESTRUPP** – trombone, bassoon, xylophone, trumpet, percussion, ukelele

Ohr not issued

1970. (lp; by BERND WITTHUSER) *(OMM 56 002)* **LIEDER VON VAMPIREN, NONNEN UND TOTEN** [-] [-] German
– Dracula / Das stille grab / Wir moechten dieses lied noch singen / Kann die klage deuten wer? / Ich bin dahn / Welcher wechsel doch im leben / Leis ertoent die abendglocke / Hinueber wall ich / Wenn ich ein froehlicher waer / Die beschwoerung / Liebeslied / Die lille vom see / Wer schwimmt dort?

— next with guests BERND ROLAND & RENEE ZUCKER

1971. (lp) *(OMM 56 016)* **TRIPS UND TRAUME** [-] [-] German
– Lasst uns auf die reise gehen / Trip po nova / Orienta / Illusion / Karlchen / Englischer walzer / Nimm einen joint, mein freund.

— added guests DIETER DIERKS – mellotron / GILLE LETTMANN – windspiel

Pilz not issued

1972. (lp) *(20.21098-7)* **DER JESUSPILZ – MUSIK VOM EVANGELIUM** [-] [-] German
– Liturgie / Schoepfung / Erleunchtung und berufung: Versammlung – Bekenntnis – Die Aussendung / Nehmet hin esset / Besuch aus dem kosmos.

— added guests GILLE & DIETER plus JULIAN DOLLASE – keyboards, synthesizer / JERRY BERKERS – bass / HARALD GROSSKOPF – percussion (all from WALLENSTEIN)

1972. (lp) *(20.29115-4)* **BAUER PLATH** [-] [-] German

– Zu den jahreszeiten / Vision 1 / Der rat der motten / Bauer plath / Die schluesselblume / Das maerchen vom koenigssohn.

Kosmische Musik — not issued

1974. (d-lp) *(KM 58.004)* **LIVE '68-'73 (live)** — German
– Die jahreszeiten / Lasst uns auf die reise gehen / Karlchen / Die schlusselblume / Der Franziskanermunch / Helena / Der rat der motten / Wenn ich ein wenig frohlicher war / Wenn hoch die Sonne / Erfindung des Dieterichs / Leise ertont die Abendglocke / Liebeslied / Wer das Schneiden hat Erfunden / Karakulschaf / Nimm einen joint, mein freund / Ich mochte dieses lied noch singen.

— split just prior to above release. WESTRUPP teamed up with former folk outfit (KATTONG) member FRANK BAIER. As DIE WALTER HC MEIER PUMPE, they released two albums in the mid 70's, 'UNTERWEGS' *(Der Andere Song 25795)* & 'PUMPT DEN SKIFFLE AUS DEM BODEN' *Songbird 1C062-31140)*. Another 'DAT MUSS DOCH AUCH WAT SPACKEN BRINGEN' as BAIER-WESTRUPP was issued in 1976 on 'Plane'; *S 66601)*. FRANK BAIER went solo in 1981.

BERND WITTHUSER

Zyx — not issued

1985. (lp) *(20045)* **ALTE REZEPTE** — German
– Parade / Schwankende gestalten / Eidechsen – Galopp / Ich sag dir sowas wie goodbye / Alte rezepte (tiel 1 & 2) / Schiffbruch / Ich kuss dich hier / Abmarsch.

WORLD OF OZ

Formed: Birmingham, England . . . 1967 by CHRISTOPHER ROBIN (real name?!), GEOFF NICHOLLS, TONY CLARKSON and ROB MOORE. They found themselves under the wing of manager BARRY CLASS, releasing their 'Deram' debut, 'THE MUFFIN MAN' (based on the children's nursery rhyme). Although full of sugary pop psychedelia, the B-side provided a more lyrical waxing for the discerning ear. A few more nauseating pop singles turned up in 1968/69, which also appeared on their only eponymous album. The line-up had changed by then, although the record did contain one gem; the Indian-flavoured 'LIKE A TEAR'.

Recommended: THE WORLD OF OZ (*5)

CHRISTOPHER ROBIN – vocals, guitar, piano / **GEOFF NICHOLLS** – guitar, organ / **TONY CLARKSON** – bass (ex-NICKY JAMES MOVEMENT, ex-ZEUS) / **ROB MOORE** – drums

Deram — Deram

May 68. (7") *(DM 187) <85029>* **THE MUFFIN MAN. / PETER'S BIRTHDAY**
Aug 68. (7") *(DM 205) <85034>* **KING CROESUS. / JACK**
Feb 69. (7") *(DM 233)* **WILLOW'S HARP. / LIKE A TEAR**

— **DAVID KUBINEC** – guitar, tabla organ (ex-PIECES OF MIND) repl. NICHOLLS

— **DAVID REA** – drums repl. MOORE

1969. (lp; mono/stereo) *(DML/SML 1034)* **THE WORLD OF OZ**
– The muffin man / Bring the ring / Jackie / Beside the fire / The hum-gum tree / With a little help / We've all seen the Queen / King Croesus / Mandy-Ann / Jack / Like a tear / Willow's harp.

1969. (7") *<85043>* **MANDY-ANN. / BESIDE THE FIRE**

— split after above. KUBINEC went into sessions for JOHN CALE and RAINBOW, and released solo material for 'A&M' in the late 70's.

Richard WRIGHT (see under ⇒ PINK FLOYD)

WRITING ON THE WALL

Formed: Edinburgh, Scotland . . . 1966 as The JURY, by JAKE SCOTT, BILL SCOTT, JIMMY HUSH and WILLY FINLAYSON. They found vocalist LINNIE PATTERSON, formerly part of mod/soul outfit The EMBERS (who released one single in 1963). LINNIE then joined THREE'S A CROWD, who issued the 45, 'LOOK AROUND THE CORNER', in '66. The JURY were initially managed by TAM PATON (later boss of The BAY CITY ROLLERS, until London-born BRIAN WALDMAN took over). The name change came about in late '67 to match their influence of West Coast psychedelia. WALDMAN then opened a club in London, calling it MIDDLE EARTH. Using the same name, he also set up a label and issued a debut 45, 'CHILD ON A CROSSING', in late '69. An album, 'THE POWER OF THE PICTS', soon followed, but an offer from an American promotor was refused unwisely by WALDMAN, who wanted his complete roster taken on. The record was a heavy doom-laden, progressive rock effort, fusing CREAM / YARDBIRDS, ARTHUR BROWN, IRON BUTTERFLY and BLACK SABBATH. Late in 1970, they entered the studio with BOWIE, although the only fruits of these sessions were some rough demos. Early the following year, after a John Peel session, LINNIE and SMIGGY left, although they did persuade FINLAYSON to return. In the summer of '72, they played in front of over 60,000 people at Brazil's Rio Song Festival, which was also televised for South American TV. Although the Brazilians hailed them as heroes, the band returned to London and obscurity. They released one more single, containing the excellent B-side, 'BUFFALO', but the "writing was on the wall" as they say, after their equipment and transport was stolen. • **Songwriters:** Group with DONALD CAMERON (my former music teacher at Woodlands High, who died in the early 80's).

Recommended: THE POWER OF THE PICTS (*7)

ROBERT 'Smiggy' SMITH – guitar (ex-EMBERS) repl. WILLY FINLAYSON (mid-69) / **BILL SCOTT** – keyboards / **JAKE SCOTT** – bass, vocals / **JIMMY HUSH** – drums / **LINNIE PATTERSON** – vocals

Middle Earth — not issued

Oct 69. (7") *(MDS 101)* **CHILD ON A CROSSING. / LUCIFER'S CORPUS**
Nov 69. (lp) *(MDLS 303)* **THE POWER OF THE PICTS**
– It came on a Sunday / Mrs. Coopers pie / Ladybird / Aries / Bogeyman / Shadow of man / Taskers successor / Hill of dreams / Virginia Water. *(cd-iss.1991 on 'Repertoire'; REP 8002SP) (German cd on 'Green Tree'; GTR 001)(+=)*– Child on a crossing / Lucifer's corpus.

— now without SMIGGY and LINNIE. They both teamed up with JIMMY BAIN to form STREETNOISE. LINNIE joined BEGGAR'S OPERA, while SMIGGY joined BLUE. They were both replaced by returning **WILLIE FINLAYSON**. In the mid-90's, LINNIE died of asbestosis.

Pye — not issued

Jun 73. (7") *(7N 45251)* **MAN OF RENOWN. / BUFFALO**

— split when only JAKE SCOTT and JIMMY HUSH remained. FINLAYSON joined BEES MAKE HONEY, taking his song 'BURGHLEY ROAD'. He went on to form MEAL TICKET.

– compilations, etc. –

Jun 97. (lp) *Pie & Mash; (PAM 003)* **RARITIES FROM THE MIDDLE EARTH**
Oct 95. (lp) *Tenth Planet; (TP 017)* **CRACKS IN THE ILLUSION OF LIFE: A HISTORY OF WRITING ON THE WALL**
Jul 96. (lp) *Tenth Planet; (TP 018)* **BURGHLEY ROAD: THE BASEMENT SESSIONS**

Robert WYATT

Born: ROBERT ELLIDGE, 28 Jan'45, Bristol, England. While at school he formed The WILDE FLOWERS with the HOPPER brothers, which soon spliced into two groups, CARAVAN and SOFT MACHINE. The latter was the band WYATT joined in 1966, but after four albums ('THE SOFT MACHINE', 'VOLUME 2', 'THIRD' & 'FOURTH'), he estranged himself from the group in '71, forming his own MATCHING MOLE. The previous year, his record label 'C.B.S.', had issued his first solo album, 'THE END OF THE EAR', which was assisted by fellow SOFT MACHINE members supplying the jazz-rock feel. In the summer of '73, WYATT was paralysed from the waist down after falling from a window, convalescing for several months at Stoke Mandeville hospital. He returned the following year (now confined to a wheel-chair), his single, a version of The MONKEES' 'I'M A BELIEVER' hitting the Top 30. Richard Branson had given him a break on 'Virgin' records earlier in the year, WYATT subsequently critically heralded for his NICK MASON-produced album, 'ROCK BOTTOM' (1974). The set featured such gems as 'SEA SONG' and 'LITTLE RED RIDING HOOD HITS THE ROAD (in two parts). His second for the label, 'RUTH IS STRANGER THAN RICHARD' (1975), showed an even deeper side, WYATT covering CHARLIE HAYDEN's jazz track, 'SONG FOR CHE'. In 1977, he had another stab at the pop charts, a dire cover version of CHRIS ANDREWS' 'YESTERDAY MAN' being his final recording for some time. He signed to indie, 'Rough Trade' in 1980, releasing a number of singles prior to his comeback album, 'NOTHING CAN STOP US NOW' (1982). This featured his classy re-working of ELVIS COSTELLO and CLIVE LANGER's 'SHIPBUILDING'. In 1983, through constant airplay by Radio 1 DJ John Peel, the anti-Falklands war song gained a Top 40 placing. He continued to spread his political messages through his music, although he has never been one to preach, his songs retaining an intensely personal quality. • **Songwriters:** WYATT penned except: GRASS (Ivor Cutler) / STRANGE FRUIT (Billie Holliday) / AT LAST I AM FREE (Chic) / STALIN WASN'T STALLIN' (Golden Gate Quartet) / BIKO (Peter Gabriel). • **Trivia:** WYATT also provided session drums for SYD BARRETT (1969) / KEVIN AYERS (early 70's) / HENRY COW (1975) / NICK MASON (1981) / RAINCOATS (1981 and '83).

Recommended: NOTHING CAN STOP US (*8) / ROCK BOTTOM (*7) / GOING BACK A BIT: A LITTLE HISTORY OF ROBERT WYATT (*8)

ROBERT WYATT (solo) – vocals, drums (ex-SOFT MACHINE) w / **DAVID SINCLAIR** – oboe (of CARAVAN) / **MARK CHARIG** – cornet (of SOFT MACHINE) / **ELTON DEAN** – sax / plus **NEVILLE WHITEHEAD** – bass / **CYRIL AYERS** – percussion

C.B.S. — Columbia

Oct 70. (lp) *(64189) <31846>* **THE END OF AN EAR**
– Las Vegas tango (part 1) / To Mark everywhere / To saintly Bridget / To Oz alien Daevyd and Gilly / To Nick everyone / To caravan and Brother Jim / To the old world (thank you for the use of your body) / To Carla, Marsha and Caroline (for making everything beautifuller) / Las Vegas tango (part 2). *(re-iss.Aug80 on 'Embassy' lp/c; CBS/40 31846) (cd-iss.Apr93 on 'Sony Europe')*

MATCHING MOLE

WYATT with retained guest **D.SINCLAIR** and band **DAVE McRAE** – keyboards / **BILL McCORMICK** – bass (ex-QUIET SUN) / **PHIL MILLER** – guitar (ex-DYBLE, COXHILL & THE MB's) (same label)

Apr 72. (lp) *(64850) <32148>* **MATCHING MOLE**
– O Caroline / Instant pussy / Signed curtain / Part of the dance / Instant kitten / Dedicated to Hugh, but you weren't listening / Beer as in braindeer / Immediate curtain. *(re-iss.Mar82; CBS 32105) (cd-iss.Mar93 on 'Beat Goes On'; BGOCD 175)*
Apr 72. (7") *(8101)* **O CAROLINE. / SIGNED CURTAIN**
Oct 72. (lp) *(65260)* **MATCHING MOLE'S LITTLE RED RECORD**
– Gloria gloom / God song / Flora fidgit / Smoke signal / Starting in the middle of the day we can drink all our politics away / Marchides / Nan's true hole / Righteous

rumba / Brandy as in Benji. *(cd-iss.Jul93 on 'Beat Goes On'; BGOCD 174) (cd re-iss.Mar97 on 'Columbia Rewind'; 471488-2)*

— In the summer of '73, WYATT was paralysed from the waist down after falling from a window. After a year convalescing, but still in a wheelchair;

ROBERT WYATT

returned as solo vocalist. He was augmented by guests/friends **FRED FRITH** – percussion / **HUGH HOPPER** – bass / **GARY WINDO** – wind / **LAURIE ALLEN** – drums / **MIKE OLDFIELD** – guitar / **RICHARD SINCLAIR** – bass / **IVOR CUTLER** – vox, keyboards / **ALFREDA BENGE** – vocals

Virgin Virgin

Jul 74. (lp/c) *(V/TCV 2017) <13112>* **ROCK BOTTOM** ☐ ☐
– Sea song / A last straw / Little Red Riding Hood hit the road (part 1) / Alifib / Alife / Little Red Riding Hood hit the road (part 2). *(cd-iss.Feb89; CDV 2017)*

Sep 74. (7") *(VS 114)* **I'M A BELIEVER. / MEMORIES** 29 ☐

— **WYATT** retained **FRITH, ALLEN & WINDO** and contributions from **PHIL MANZANERA** – guitar / **BILL McCORMICK** – bass / **BRIAN ENO** – synthesizers / **JOHN GREAVES** – bass / **MONEZI FEZI** – trumpet / **GEORGE KHAN** – saxophone

May 75. (lp/c) *(V/TCV 2034)* **RUTH IS STRANGER THAN RICHARD** ☐ ☐
– Muddy house: (a) Solar flames – (b) Five black notes and one white tone – (c) Muddy mouth / Soup song / Sonia / Team spirit 1 & 2 / Soup for Che. *(cd-iss.Feb89; CDV 2034)*

Apr 77. (7") *(VS 115)* **YESTERDAY MAN. / SONJA** ☐ -

— accompanied only by **McCORMICK** – bass / **HARRY BECKETT** – flugelhorn (B-side)

Rough Trade not issued

Mar 80. (7") *(RT 037)* **ARAUCO. / CAIMENERA** ☐ -

— now used only **MOGOTSI MOTHLE** – double bass / **FRANK ROBERTS** – keyboards

Nov 80. (7") *(RT 052)* **AT LAST I AM FREE. / STRANGE FRUIT** ☐ -

Feb 81. (7") *(RT 046)* **STALIN WASN'T STALLIN'. / STALINGRAD (P. Blackman)** ☐ -

— now with **ESMAIL SHEK** – tabla / **KADIR DURUESH** – shenzi

Aug 81. (7") *(RT 81)* **GRASS. / TRADE UNION (Dishari featuring Abdus Salique)** ☐ -

Apr 82. (lp) *(ROUGH 35)* **NOTHING CAN STOP US** ☐ -
– Born again cretin / At last I am free / Quantanera / Grass / Stalin wasn't stalling / The red flag / Strange fruit / Arauco / Strange fruit / Trade union / Stalingrad. *(re-iss.Apr83 lp+=/c+=; ROUGH/+C 35)*– Shipbuilding. *(cd-iss.May87; ROUGHCD 35)*

— Above album featured musicians as 1980-82.

— In Apr'82, WYATT was credited on BEN WATT ep 'SUMMER INTO WINTER'.

— guests **STEVE NIEVE** – piano / **MARK BEDDERS** – double bass / **MARTIN HUGHES** – drums / **CLIVE LANGER** – organ / **ELVIS COSTELLO** – b.vox

Aug 82. (7") *(RT 115)* **SHIPBUILDING. / MEMORIES OF YOU** ☐ -
(12"-iss.Nov82+=; RTT 115)– Round midnight. *(re-iss.Apr83; same); hit No.35)*

— now with ? plus **HUGH HOPPER,** etc.

May 84. (m-lp) *(ROUGH 40)* **THE ANIMAL FILM (Soundtrack)** ☐ -
– (no tracks listed) *(cd-iss.Jul94)*

Aug 84. (12"ep) *(RTT 149)* **WORK IN PROGRESS** ☐ -
– Biko / Amber and the amberines / Yolanda / Te rescuerdo Amanda.

Oct 85. (7"/12"; ROBERT WYATT with The SWAPO SINGERS) *(RT/+T 168)* **THE WIND OF CHANGE. / NAMIBIA** ☐ -

Rough Trade Gramavision

Dec 85. (lp/c) *(ROUGH/+C 69)* **OLD ROTTENHAT** ☐ ☐
– Alliance / The United States of amnesia / East Timor / Speechless / The age of self / Vandalusia / The British road / Mass medium / Gharbzadegi / P.I.A. *(cd-iss.Nov86; ROUGHCD 69)*

Sep 91. (cd/c/lp; one-side with BENGE) *(R 274-2/-4/-1* **DONDESTAN** ☐ ☐
– Costa / The sight of the wind / Worship / Catholic architecture / Shrink rap / Left on man / Lisp service / CP jeebies / Dondestan.

Blueprint not issued

Nov 92. (cd+book) *(BP 108CD)* **A SHORT BREAK** ☐ -
– A short break / Tubab / Kutcha / Ventilatir / Unmasked. *(re-iss.Apr96; same)*

Rough Trade not issued

Aug 94. (cd) *(R 3112)* **FLOTSAM AND JETSAM** ☐ -

– compilations, others, etc. –

Mar 81. (d-lp) *Virgin; (VGD 3505)* **ROCK BOTTOM / RUTH IS STRANGER THAN RICHARD** ☐ -

Apr 82. (7"ep; ROBERT WYATT & MEMBERS OF CAST) *Virgin; (VS 499)* **FROM MAN TO WOMAN** ☐ -

Dec 84. (lp) *Rough Trade; (RTSP 25)* **1982-1984** - ☐

Feb 85. (12") *Recommended; (RE 1984)* **THE LAST NIGHTINGALE. / ON THE BEACH AT CAMBRIDGE** ☐ -

— next 'B'side by "The GRIMETHORPE COLLIERY BAND".

Sep 85. (7") *T.U.C.;* **THE AGE OF SELF. / RAISE YOUR BANNERS HIGH** ☐ -

Sep 87. (12"ep) *Strange Fruit; (SFPS 037)* **THE PEEL SESSIONS** (10.9.74) ☐ -
– Soup song / Sea sing / Alife / I'm a believer.

Jan 93. (cd) *Rough Trade; (R 2952)* **MID EIGHTIES** ☐ ☐

Jul 94. (cd; MATCHING MOLE) *Windsong; (WINCD 063)* **BBC RADIO 1 LIVE IN CONCERT (live)** ☐ -

Jul 94. (d-cd) *Virgin; (CDVM 9031)* **GOING BACK A BIT: A LITTLE HISTORY OF . . .** ☐ -

XHOL

Formed: Germany . . . 1967 as SOUL CARAVAN. Under this name, the band cut an early soul influenced album in 1967, 'GET IN HIGH', on 'C.B.S.'. After modifying their name to XHOL CARAVAN, they produced one of the first German progressive albums in 1969's 'ELECTRIP'. As the name might suggest, it was fairly psychedelic in nature, adding multi-coloured brush strokes to the inspired jazz fusion contained within its grooves. 'HAU-RUK' (1970) was an instrumental-led piece of live improvisation, the band splitting soon after its release. A posthumous album was released in 1972, the quaintly titled 'MOTHERFUCKERS GMBH & CO KG'.

Recommended: ELECTRIP (*7)

TIM BELBE – tenor sax / **HANSI FISCHER** – flutes, saxophones / **OCKI BREUERN** – organ, electric piano, tuba / **KLAUS BRIEST** – bass / **SKIP ROGERS** – drums / + **PETER MEISEL** – keyboards

C.B.S. / not issued

1967. (lp; as SOUL CARAVAN) *(63268)* **GET IN HIGH** - / - German

Hansa / not issued

1969. (lp; as XHOL CARAVAN) *(80099)* **ELECTRIP** - / - German
– Electric fun fair / Pop games / All green / Raise up high / Walla mashalla.

— MEISEL left / FISCHER departed for EMBRYO

Ohr / not issued

Sep 70. (lp) *(OMM 56.014)* **HAU-RUK** - / - German
– Breit / Schaukel.

— disbanded after above, leaving behind next album inked on cover "2 YEARS OLD"

1972. (lp) *(OMM 556 024)* **MOTHERFUCKERS GMBH & CO KG** - / - German
– Radio / Leistungsprinzip / Orgelsold / First day / Grille / Love potion 25.

— all disappeared from the scene

XIT

Formed: Albuquerque, New Mexico . . . 1966 as LINCOLN ST. EXIT, by Sioux indians MICHAEL MARTIN, R.C. GARISS, JOMAC SUAZO and LEEJA HERRERA. They were basically garage rockers inspired by their native American roots, explored in greater depth when they became XIT in 1971. 'PLIGHT OF THE RED MAN', in 1972, was their first release under this moniker, although it was their third effort, 'ENTRANCE', that made its mark. It was not a new album, the material comprised from the mid to late 60's. This was probably their finest example of psychedelia, the best track being 'SUNDAY DREAM'.

Recommended: PLIGHT OF THE RED MAN (*5) / ENTRANCE (*7)

LINCOLN ST. EXIT

MICHAEL MARTIN – vocals, lead guitar / **R.C. GARISS** – lead guitar / **JOMAC SUAZO** (b. JOMAC) – bass / **LEEJA HERRERA** – drums, percussion

not issued / Lance

1966. (7") *<109-100>* **WHO'S BEEN DRIVING MY LITTLE YELLOW TAXI CAB. / PAPER LACE** - /

not issued / Ecco

1967. (7") *<ER 1001>* **THE BUMMER. / SUNNY SUNDAY DREAM** - /

not issued / unknown

1968. (7") **WHATEVER HAPPENED . . . / (part 2)** - /

not issued / Souled Out

1968. (7") *<104>* **MISSISSIPPI RIVERBOAT GAMBLIN' MAN. / ST. LOUIS MAMA** - /

not issued / Mainstream

1969. (7") *<722>* **SOULFUL DRIFTER. / TIME HAS COME, GONNA DIE** - /

1970. (lp) *<S-6126>* **DRIVE IT** - /
– Man machine / Dirty mother blues / Got you babe / Teacher teacher / Soulful drifter / Time has come gonna die / Going back home / Straight shootin' man / Phantom child.

XIT

same line-up

Rare Earth / Rare Earth

1972. (lp) *(SREA 4002)* *<R 536>* **PLIGHT OF THE RED MAN**
– Beginning / At peace / I was raised / Nikaa shil hozho (I'm happy about you) / The coming of the white man / War cry / Someday / End.

1972. (7") *<5044>* **NIHAA SHIL HOZHO (I'M HAPPY ABOUT YOU). / END** - /

— **TOM BEE** – vocals, percussion; repl. MARTIN

1973. (lp) *<R 545>* **SILENT WARRIOR** - /
– We live / Awakening / Birth / Reservation of education / Color nature gone / Cement prairie / Young warrior / Anthem of the American Indian.

1974. (7") *<5058>* **RESERVATION OF EDUCATION. / COLOR NATURE GONE** - /

— now just trio of **BEE, SUAZO + WILLIAM JOHNSON** – lead guitar

not issued / Canyon

1978. (lp) *<C 721>* **RELOCATION** - /
– Dark-skin woman / Nothing could be a finer than a 49'er / Riding song / Sweethearted love song / Rainbow rider / Let my people dance / Christopher Colombus / Relocation / Sunrise vision.

— disappeared after above and haven't been spotted since (sorry!?!)

– compilations, etc. –

1974. (lp) *Canyon; <714>* **ENTRANCE (THE SOUND OF EARLY XIT)** - /

1983. (7"m; by LINCOLN ST. EXIT) *Psych-Out; <101>* **HALF A DREAM. / SUNNY SUNDAY / WHATEVER HAPPENED TO BABY JESUS** - /

Stomu YAMASH'TA

Born: TSUTOMU YAMASHITA, 15 Mar'47, Kyoto, Japan. His father was the leader of the Kyoto Philharmonic Orchestra, leading to him studying percussion in his early teens at the Kyoto Academy of Music. In the mid-60's, he arrived in the States, having already performed his first concert as a soloist. Around this time, he also wrote two scores, 'YOJIMBO' & 'SANJURO', for the great film director, KUROSAWA. Having adapted his more westernised classical/jazz style, he worked with composers PETER MAXWELL DAVIES and HANS WERNE HENZE, who created the 'CONTEMPORARY' piece for him under the 'L'OISEAU-LIVRE' banner/label in 1972. YAMASH'TA's "floating music" concept was a hybrid of Eastern rock and neo-classical Western styles which led to a contract with 'Island'. In 1973, they issued 'MAN FROM THE EAST', a record well-received by the British press. In 1975, his music was used on the film, 'The Man Who Fell To Earth', which starred DAVID BOWIE. It led to collaborations with the likes of STEVE WINWOOD, MIKE SHRIEVE, KLAUS SCHULZE, GARY BOYLE (ex-Isotope) and MURRAY HEAD. He returned to more classical themes in the 80's, having set up his own "new age" company, CELESTIAL HARMONIES.

Recommended: FLOATING MUSIC (*6) / EAST WIND (*6)

STOMU YAMASH'TA – percussion, instruments

Decca-L'Oiseau-Livre — not issued

1972. (lp) *(DSLO 01)* **CONTEMPORARY** [ ] [-]
– Hans-Werner Henze: Prison song / Toru Takemitsu: Seasons / Peter Maxwell Davies: Turris campanarum sonatium.

Barclay — Vanguard

1972. (lp) *(16063) <VSD 79343>* **RED BUDDHA** [-] [ ] France
– Red buddha / As expanding as.

— now augmented by various musicians, including **MORRIS PERT** – percussion / **GARY BOYLE** – guitar / **ROBIN THOMPSON** – sax / **PETER ROBINSON** – piano / **HISAKO YAMASH'TA** – violin / etc

Island — Island

1973. (lp) *(ILPS 9228)* **THE MAN FROM THE EAST (soundtrack)** [ ] [-]
– Scoop / Ana Orori / What a way to live in modern times / My little partner / Mandala / Memory of Hiroshima / Mountain pass.

1973. (lp) *(86455)* **FLOATING MUSIC** [-] [-] German
– Poker dice / Keep in lane / Xingu / One way.

Dec 73. (lp) *(ILPS 9242)* **EAST WIND** [ ] [-]
– Freedom is frightening / Rolling nuns / Pine on the horizon / Wind words.

Jun 74. (lp) *(ILPS 9269)* **ONE BY ONE** [ ] [-]
– One by one / Hey man / One by one (reprise) / Black flame / Rain race / Tangerine beach / Superstar / Loxy cycle / Nuremberb ring / Seasons / Accident / At Tangerine Beach.

Mar 75. (lp) *(ILPS 9319)* **RAINDOG** [ ] [-]
– Dunes / 33 & 1/3 / Rainsong / The monk's song / Shadows / Ishi.

— **STEVE WINWOOD** – vocals, keyboards / **MICHAEL SHRIEVE** – drums / with also **KLAUS SCHULZE** – keyboards / **PAT THRALL + AL DiMEOLA + PHIL MANZANERA** – guitar / **ROSCO GEE** – bass

Jun 76. (lp/c; STOMU YAMASH'TA / STEVE WINWOOD / MICHAEL SHRIEVE) *(ILPS/ZCI <9387>)* **GO** [ ] [60]
– Solitude / Nature / Air over / Crossing the line / Stellar / Man of Leo / Space theme / Sace requiem / Space song / Carnival / Ghost machine / Surfspin / Time is here / Winnerloser.

— **JESS RODEN** – vocals / **DONI HARVEY** – guitar, vocals / **PAUL JACKSON** – bass / **PETER ROBINSON** – keyboards, vocals; repl. WINWOOD (now solo) / no MANZANERA, GEE, THRALL

Arista — Arista

Jul 77. (lp) *(SPARTY 1011) <4138>* **GO TOO** [ ] [ ]
– Prelude / See you before / Madness / Mysteries of love / Wheels of fortune / Beauty / You and me / Ecliptic.

— below recorded 1976; **JEROME RIMSON** – bass, repl. GEE + MANZANERA

Island — Island

Apr 78. (d-lp) *(ISLD 10)* **GO LIVE (FROM PARIS) (live 1976)** [ ] -
– Space song / Carnival / Wind spin / Ghost machine / Surfspin / Time is here / Winnerloser / Solitude / Nature / Air voice / Crossing the line / Man of Leo / Stellar / Space requiem.

May 78. (12") *(IPR 2014)* **CROSSING THE LINE (live). / WINNERLOSER (live)** [ ] [-]

— returned to Japan for several years

— with **TAKASHI KOKUBO + SEN IZUMI** – synths / **PAUL BUCKMASTER** & orchestra

Kuckuck — not issued

Aug 85. (lp) *(626154)* **SEA AND SKY** [-] [-] German
– A photon / Appeared / And / Touched / Ah . . . / Time / To see / To know. *(UK cd-iss.Jun87; CDKUCK 072) (UK lp/c 1988; LP/MC KUCK 072)*

– compilations, etc. –

1973. (lp) *Help-Island; (HELP 12)* **COME TO THE EDGE** [ ] [-]

YARDBIRDS

Formed: Richmond, Surrey, England ... 1963, by KEITH RELF and PAUL SAMWELL-SMITH (both ex-METROPOLITAN BLUES QUARTET) together with JIM McCARTY, CHRIS DREJA and ANTHONY TOPHAM. The latter was soon replaced by ERIC CLAPTON and after a residency at Richmond's 'Crawdaddy' club backing bluesman, SONNY BOY WILLIAMSON, the YARDBIRDS were signed up by EMI's 'COLUMBIA' label in early '64. After two well received singles that year, 'I WISH YOU WOULD' and 'GOOD MORNING LITTLE SCHOOLGIRL', the band released the acclaimed 'FIVE LIVE YARDBIRDS' the following year. Recorded at London's Marquee club, the album was a thrilling snapshot of the group's pioneering, souped-up blues and R&B sound. Although it contained no original material, the band marked interpretations of standards like 'SMOKESTACK LIGHTNING' and 'RESPECTABLE' with an indelible stamp. But this line-up promptly came to an end upon the release of the classic 'FOR YOUR LOVE' (1965) single. Considering the record a betrayal of the band's blues roots, CLAPTON upped sticks and left for JOHN MAYALL'S BLUESBREAKERS. Enter JEFF BECK, another supremely gifted guitarist, and the band embarked upon the most successful period of their career, notching up hits with the likes of 'HEART FULL OF SOUL', 'EVIL HEARTED YOU', 'STILL I'M SAD' and 'SHAPES OF THINGS'. BECK had brought a new spirit of experimentation to the band and employed such psychedelic tactics as Eastern-style guitar mantras, distortion and Gregorian Chant. With 'THE YARDBIRDS' (1966), the band further embraced psychedelia and the album stands as a career pinnacle, innovative while maintaining the essence of their R&B heritage. This was especially evident on the single, 'OVER UNDER SIDEWAYS DOWN' (1966), which was backed by another of the album's best tracks, the self explanatory 'JEFF'S BOOGIE'. SAMWELL-SMITH, who'd produced the album, departed soon after and was replaced by yet another future guitar God, JIMMY PAGE. Soon shifting from bass to co-lead alongside BECK, the new line-up cut the electrifying psychedelia of 'HAPPENINGS TEN YEARS AGO' (1966). This honeymoon period was short-lived however, as BECK parted ways with the band during a particularly laborious US tour. 'LITTLE GAMES' (1967) was an ill-advised attempt at commerciality while covers of MANFRED MANN's 'HA! HA! SAID THE CLOWN' and NILSSON's 'TEN LITTLE INDIANS' were equally puzzling. Though these releases achieved a modicum of success in America, the band split in mid '68, PAGE and DREJA going on to form The NEW YARDBIRDS which in turn evolved into LED ZEPPELIN. The inevitable reunion took place in the mid-80's and under the BOX OF FROGS moniker, a line-up of BECK, McCARTY, DREJA, SAMWELL-SMITH, RORY GALLAGHER and MAX MIDDLETON cut a self-titled album in 1984 and the 'STRANGE LAND' lp in 1986. • **Songwriters:** RELF wrote some, except covers, I WISH YOU WOULD (Billy Boy Arnold) / SMOKESTACK LIGHTNING (Howlin' Wolf) / A CERTAIN GIRL (Ernie K-Doe) / GOOD MORNING LITTLE SCHOOLGIRL (Don & Bob) / TRAIN (Johnny Burnette) / FOR YOUR LOVE + HEART FULL OF SOUL (c. Graham Gouldman, ⇒ 10cc) / I'M A MAN (Bo Diddley) / THE SUN IS SHINING (Elmore James) / plus loads of other blues greats. • **Trivia:** Made two group appearances in the 66/67 films 'SWINGING LONDON' & 'BLOW-UP'. Early in 1966, manager GIORGIO GOMELSKY was replaced by SIMON NAPIER-BELL.

Recommended: THE VERY BEST OF THE YARDBIRDS (*9)

KEITH RELF (b.22 Mar'43, Richmond) – vocals, harmonica / **ERIC CLAPTON** (b.30 Mar'45, Ripley, England) – lead guitar, vocals repl. ANTHONY TOPHAM / **CHRIS DREJA** (b.11 Nov'45, Surbiton, Surrey) – rhythm guitar / **PAUL SAMWELL-SMITH** (b. 8 May'43, Richmond) – bass / **JIM McCARTY** (b.25 Jul'43, Liverpool) – drums

Columbia — Epic

Jun 64. (7") *(DB 7283) <9709>* **I WISH YOU WOULD. / A CERTAIN GIRL** [ ] [ ] Oct64

Oct 64. (7") *(DB 7391)* **GOOD MORNING LITTLE SCHOOLGIRL. / I AIN'T GOT YOU** [44] [-]

Feb 65. (lp) *(33SX 1677)* **FIVE LIVE YARDBIRDS (live)** [ ] [-]
– Too much monkey business / I got love if you want it / Smokestack lightning / Good morning little schoolgirl / Respectable / Five long years / Pretty girl / Louise / I'm a man / Here 'tis. *(re-iss.Aug79 on 'Charly' lp)(c; CR 30173)(CFK 1017) (re-iss.Aug89; LIK 55) (cd-iss. on 'Charly'; CDCHARLY 182)*

Mar 65. (7") *(DB 7499) <9790>* **FOR YOUR LOVE. / GOT TO HURRY** [3] [6] May65
(re-iss.Aug76 on 'Charly'; CYS 1012)

Jul 65. (lp; mono/stereo) *<LN24/BN26 167>* **FOR YOUR LOVE** [-] [96]
– For your love / I'm not talking / Putty (in your hands) / I ain't got you / Got to hurry / I ain't done wrong / I wish you would / A certain girl / Sweet music / Good morning little schoolgirl / My girl Sloopy.

— (Mar65) **JEFF BECK** (b.24 Jun'44, Surrey) – lead guitar repl. CLAPTON who joined

JOHN MAYALL's BLUESBREAKERS. He later formed CREAM and went solo

Jul 65. (7") *(DB 7594)* *<9823>* **HEART FULL OF SOUL. / STEELED BLUES** 2 9

Oct 65. (7") *(DB 7706)* **EVIL HEARTED YOU. / STILL I'M SAD** 3 -
(re-iss.Jul82 on 'Old Gold'; OG 9111)

Nov 65. (7") *<9857>* **I'M A MAN. / STILL I'M SAD** - 17

Jan 66. (lp; mono/stereo) *(export; SCXC 28) <LN24/BN26 177>* **HAVING A RAVE UP WITH THE YARDBIRDS (live)** - 53 Dec65
– You're a better man than I / Evil hearted you / I'm a man / Still I'm sad / Heart full of soul / The train kept a-rollin' / Smokestack lightning / Respectable / I'm a man / Here 'tis. *(last 4 tracks from 'FIVE LIVE YARDBIRDS')*

Feb 66. (7") *(DB 7848)* **SHAPES OF THINGS. / YOU'RE A BETTER MAN THAN I** 3 -

Mar 66. (7") *<10006>* **SHAPES OF THINGS. / NEW YORK CITY BLUES** - 11

— (Feb66) **JIMMY PAGE** (b. 9 Jan'44, Middlesex, England) – guitar (ex-session man, solo artist) repl. SAMWELL-SMITH who became producer. (DREJA moved to bass) KEITH issued solo 45 in May.

May 66. (7") *(DB 7928) <10035>* **OVER, UNDER, SIDEWAYS, DOWN. / JEFF'S BOOGIE** 10 13 Jun66

Jul 66. (lp; mono/stereo) *(SX/SCX 6063) <LN24/BN26 210>* **THE YARDBIRDS** (US title 'OVER UNDER SIDEWAYS DOWN') 20 52
– Lost women / Over, under, sideways, down / The Nazz are blue / I can't make your way / Rack my mind / Farewell / Hot house of Omagarashid / Jeff's boogie / He's always there / Turn into earth / What do you want / Ever since the world began. *(re-iss.Feb83 as 'ROGER THE ENGINEER' on 'Edsel' lp; mono/stereo)(c; ED 116 M/S)(CED 116) (cd-iss.1986+=; EDCD 116)*– Happenings ten years time ago / Psycho daisies. *(cd-iss.Feb92 on 'Raven-Topic' US version;)*

Oct 66. (7") *(DB 8024)* **HAPPENINGS TEN YEARS TIME AGO. / PSYCHO DAISIES** 43 -

Nov 66. (7") *<10094>* **HAPPENINGS TEN YEARS TIME AGO. / THE NAZZ ARE BLUE** - 30

— (Oct66) Trimmed to a quartet when JEFF BECK left to go solo.

Apr 67. (7") *(DB 8165) <10156>* **LITTLE GAMES. / PUZZLES** 51

Apr 67. (lp; mono/stereo) *<LN24/BN26 246>* **GREATEST HITS** (compilation) - 28
– Shapes of things / Still I'm sad / New York City blues / For your love / Over, under, sideways, down / I'm a man / Happenings ten years time ago / Heart full of soul / Smokestack lightning / I'm not talking.

Jun 67. (7") *<10204>* **HA HA SAID THE CLOWN. / TINKER, TAILOR, SOLDIER, SAILOR** - 45

Aug 67. (lp; mono/stereo) *<LN24/BN26 313>* **LITTLE GAMES** - 80
– Little games / Smile on me / White summer / Tinker, tailor, soldier, sailor / Glimpses / Drinking muddy water / No excess baggage / Stealing, stealing / Only the black rose / Little soldier boy. *(UK-iss.May85 on 'Fame' lp/c; FA 41 3124-1/-4) (re-iss.Apr91 on 'E.M.I.'; CDEMS 1389) (cd re-iss.Oct96 on 'Gold'; CDGOLD 1068)*

Oct 67. (7") *<10248>* **TEN LITTLE INDIANS. / DRINKIN' MUDDY WATER** - 96

Mar 68. (7"w-drawn) *(DB 8368) <10303>* **GOODNIGHT SWEET JOSEPHINE. / THINK ABOUT IT** -

— Disbanded mid'68. PAGE and DREJA formed NEW YARDBIRDS, but when DREJA departed, PAGE formed LED ZEPPELIN. RELF and McCARTY formed the original RENAISSANCE. On 14 May'76, RELF was electrocuted when touching a faulty amp. In the early 90s, McCARTY was also part of PRETTY THINGS / YARDBIRD BLUES BAND collaboration.

– other compilations, etc. –

— on 'Columbia' unless stated otherwise

Oct 65. (7"ep) *(SEG 8421)* **FIVE YARDBIRDS** -
– My girl Sloopy / I'm not talking / I ain't done wrong / (1).

Jan 67. (7"ep) *(SEG 8521)* **OVER UNDER SIDEWAYS DOWN** -

Jan 66. (lp; mono/stereo) *Fontana; (TL 5277) / Mercury; <MG2/SR6 1071>* **SONNY BOY WILLIAMSON AND THE YARDBIRDS (live)** Feb66
– Bye bye bird / Mr. Downchild / The river Rhine / 23 hours too long / Out on the water coast / Baby don't worry / Pontiac blues / Take it easy baby / I don't care no more / Do the Weston. *(re-iss.1968; SFJL 960) (re-iss.Jun75 on 'Philips'; 6435 011)*

Jun 71. (lp) *Regal Starline; (SRS 5069)* **REMEMBER ... THE YARDBIRDS** -

1971. (lp) *<KE 30615>* **LIVE YARDBIRDS FEATURING JIMMY PAGE** -

1972. (lp) *Epic;* **YARDBIRDS' FAVORITES** -

Dec 76. (7"ep) *Charly; (CEP 110)* **THE YARDBIRDS** -

Aug 77. (lp) *Charly; (CR 30012)* **THE YARDBIRDS FEATURING ERIC CLAPTON** -
(re-iss.Mar83; CR 30194) (re-iss.Mar94 on 'Laserlight' cd/c;) (re-iss.cd Apr95 as 'ERIC CLAPTON & THE YARDBIRDS' on 'Top Masters';)

Aug 77. (lp) *Charly; (CR 30013)* **THE YARDBIRDS FEATURING JEFF BECK** -
(re-iss.Mar83; CR 30195) (re-iss.Feb85 on 'Cambra'; CR 107)

Dec 77. (d-lp) *Charly; (CDX 1)* **SHAPES OF THINGS** -

Feb 82. (10"lp) *Charly; (CFM 102)* **THE SINGLE HITS** -

Jul 82. (7") *Old Gold; (OG 9109)* **FOR YOUR LOVE. / HEARTFUL OF SOUL** -

Feb 83. (7"mono) *Edsel; (E 5005)* **OVER, UNDER, SIDEWAYS, DOWN. / PSYCHO DAISIES** -

Jun 83. (lp) *Charly; (CFF 7001)* **OUR OWN SOUND** -

Mar 84. (7"ep/c-ep) *Scoop; (7RS/7SC 5036)* **6 TRACK HITS** -
– Evil hearted you / Smokestack lightning / A certain girl / For your love / Shapes of things / Louise.

May 84. (7"mono) *Edsel; (E 5007)* **RACK MY MIND. / JEFF'S BOOGIE** -

Nov 84. (lp-box) *Charly; (BOX 104)* **SHAPES OF THINGS – COLLECTION OF CLASSIC RECORDINGS 1964-66** -
– (lp's) THE FIRST RECORDINGS / SONNY BOY WILLIAMSON & . . . / FIVE LIVE YARDBIRDS / FOR YOUR LOVE / HAVING A RAVE . . . / SHAPES OF THINGS / ODDS AND SODS *(4xcd-box Jun91 on 'Decal'; CDLIKBOX 1)*

Nov 84. (lp/c) *Topline; (TOP/KTOP 103)* **FOR YOUR LOVE** (not US version) -

1986. (cd) *Charly; (CDCHARLY 8)* **GREATEST HITS** (not US version) -

1986. (d-lp/d-c) *Castle; (CCS LP/MC 141)* **THE YARDBIRDS COLLECTION** -
(cd-iss.1988; CCSCD 141)

1986. (lp) *Showcase; (SHLP 108)* **GOT LIVE IF YOU WANT IT (credited ERIC CLAPTON)** -

Apr 87. (cd) *Topline; (TOPCD 501)* **CLASSIC CUTS** -

1989. (7"ep) *Old Gold; (OG 6118)* **FOR YOUR LOVE** -

Sep 89. (d-lp/c) *Decal; (LIKD/TCLIK 56)* **THE STUDIO SESSIONS 1964-1967** -
(cd-iss. on 'Charly'; CDCHARLY 187)

Sep 89. (lp/c) *Decal; (LIK/TCLIK 58)* **THE FIRST RECORDINGS – LONDON 1963** -
(cd-iss. on 'Charly'; CDCHARLY 186)

Oct 89. (lp/c/cd) *Instant; (INS/TCINS/CDINS 5012)* **HITS AND MORE** -

Jun 91. (cd) *Music Club; (MCCD 023)* **THE VERY BEST OF THE YARDBIRDS** -
– For your love / Heart full of soul / Good morning little schoolgirl / Still I'm sad / Evil hearted you / A certain girl / Jeff's blues / I wish you would / New York City / I'm not talking / You're a better man than I / Shapes of things / I'm a man / Boom boom / Smokestack lightning (live) / Let it rock (live) / You can't judge a book by it's cover (live) / Who do you love (live) / Too much monkey business (live) / Respectable (live) / Pretty girl (live) / Stroll on.

Apr 91. (cd/c/lp) *Band Of Joy; (BOJ CD/MC/LP 20)* **ON AIR** (65-67) -

Jul 92. (cd) *Repertoire;* **25 GREATEST HITS** -

Sep 92. (cd; by JIM McCARTY & CHRIS DREJA) *Promised Land; (PL 202020)* **YARDBIRDS' REUNION CONCERT (live)** -

Oct 92. (cd) *E.M.I.;* **LITTLE GAMES, SESSIONS & MORE** -

Apr 93. (cd) *Pulsar;* **GREATEST HITS** (not US version) -

Apr 93. (4xcd-box) *Decal; (CDLIKBOX 3)* **THE BLUES WAILING YARDBIRDS – THE COMPLETE GIORGIO GOMELSKY SESSIONS** -

Sep 93. (cd/c) *Laserlight; (12/72 206)* **HEART FULL OF SOUL** -

Nov 93. (cd) *Charly; (CDCD 1145)* **FOR YOUR LOVE (Featuring ERIC CLATON)** -

Apr 94. (cd) *Charly; (CDRB 4)* **HONEY IN YOUR HIPS** -

Aug 95. (cd/c) *Pickwick; (PWK S/MC 4273)* **GOOD MORNING LITTLE SCHOOLGIRL** -
(re-iss.Feb97 on 'Carlton' cd/c; 303600090-2/-4)

Aug 96. (cd/c) *Hallmark; (30522-2/-4)* **THE YARDBIRDS WITH ERIC CLAPTON (14 BLUES BOOM STANDARDS)** -

Nov 96. (cd) *Experience; (EXP 048)* **THE YARDBIRDS** -

Jan 97. (cd) *Charly; (CPCD 82452)* **THE BEST OF THE YARDBIRDS** -

Mar 97. (cd) *Nectar; (NTMCD 527)* **THE BEST OF THE LEGENDARY YARDBIRDS** -

Jun 97. (cd) *Summit; (SUMCD 4115)* **THE VERY BEST OF . . .** -

KEITH RELF

— solo, when a YARDBIRD.

Columbia Epic

May 66. (7") *(DB 7920) <10044>* **MR.ZERO. / KNOWING** 50

Jan 67. (7") *(DB 8084) <10110>* **SHAPES IN MY MIND. / BLUE SANDS**

REIGN

— were formed by **RELF + McCARTY** plus **ROBIN LEMESWRIER**

Regal Zonophone not issued

Nov 68. (7") *(RZ 3028)* **LINE OF LEAST RESISTANCE. / NATURAL LOVING WOMAN** -

TOGETHER

— (McCARTY & RELF) with sessioners.

Columbia not issued

1968. (7") *(DB 8491)* **HENRY'S COMING HOME. / LOVE MUM AND DAD** -

— They evolved into RENAISSANCE the following year. McCARTY joined SHOOT in 1972 and made 1 album 'ON THE FRONTIER' for 'Capitol'. In 1976 he formed ILLUSION with JOHN KNIGHTSBRIDGE, HAWKEN and CENNAMO. The latter had previously been in ARMAGEDDON with KEITH RELF. On 22 Jul'83, The YARDBIRDS re-formed with **McCARTY, DREJA, SAMWELL-SMITH, KNIGHTSBRIDGE** plus 2 vocalists **JOHN FIDDLER** (ex-MEDICINE HEAD) + **MARK FELTON** (ex-NINE BELOW ZERO). Evolved into

BOX OF FROGS

— KNIGHTSBRIDGE and FELTON having been replaced by guests **JEFF BECK** – guitar / **RORY GALLAGHER** – guitar / **MAX MIDDLETON** – keyboards

Epic Epic

Jun 84. (7") *(A 4562)* **BACK WHERE I STARTED. / THE EDGE**
(12"+=) *(TA 4562)* – Nine lives.

Jul 84. (lp/c) *(EPC/40 25996)* **BOX OF FROGS** 45
– Back where I stand / Harder / Another wasted day / Love inside you / The edge / Two steps ahead / Into the dark / Just a boy again / Poor boy. *(cd-iss.Oct93 on 'Sony Europe')*

Aug 84. (7") *(A 4678)* **INTO THE DARK. / X TRACKS**
(12"+=) *(TA 4678)* – X tracks (Medley of tracks).

— Trimmed to quartet of **FIDDLER, McCARTY, DREJA + SAMWELL-SMITH**

Jun 86. (7") *(A 7248)* **AVERAGE. / STRANGE LAND**
(12"+=) *(TA 7248)* – Keep calling.

Jun 86. (lp/c) *(EPC/40 26375)* **STRANGE LAND**

– Strange land / Get it while you can / You mix me up / House on fire / Average / Hanging from the wreckage / Heart full of soul / Asylum. *(cd-iss.Jul94 on 'Sony Europe';)*

YELLOW PAYGES

Formed: Fort Worth, Texas, USA . . . late 1966 by BILL HAM and BOB BARNES. The former had played in the wild garage outfit, The NOMADS, who released a few singles in the mid-60's; 'I SAW YOU GO' and 'BE NICE'. After a few singles on 'Showplace', they signed to 'Uni', releasing a string of singles, none of which breached the Hot 100. They were a mixture of hard rock and slow, ballady psychedelia, much in evidence on their only album in 1969, 'VOLUME ONE'.

Recommended: VOLUME ONE (*6)

DAN HORTTER – vocals, harmonica / **BILL HAM** – guitar, vocals (ex-NOMADS, ex-ROCKS) / **DONNIE DACUS** – lead guitar / **BOB BARNES** – bass (ex-THOSE GUYS) / **DAN GORMAN** – drums

not issued Showplace

1967. (7") *<WS 216>* **NEVER SEE THE GOOD IN ME. / SLEEPING MINDS** [-] [ ]
1967. (7") *<WS 217>* **JEZEBEL. / WE GOT A LOVE IN THE MAKIN'** [-] [ ]

Uni Uni

1967. (7") *<55043>* **OUR TIME IS RUNNING OUT. / SWEET SUNRISE** [-] [ ]
1968. (7") *<55072>* **CHILDHOOD FRIENDS. / JUDGE CARTER** [-] [ ]

—— now without DACUS who joined The STEPHEN STILLS BAND, before later replacing the deceased TERRY KATH in the top group CHICAGO

1968. (7") *<55089>* **CROWD PLEASER. / YOU'RE JUST WHAT I WAS LOOKING FOR TODAY** [-] [ ]
1969. (7") *<55107)* **NEVER PUT AWAY MY LOVE FOR YOU. / THE TWO OF US** [-] [ ]
1969. (7") *<55153>* **VANILLA ON MY MIND. / WOULD YOU MIND IF I LOVED YOU?** [-] [ ]
1969. (lp) *<73045>* **VOLUME ONE** [-] [ ]
– The two of us / Little woman / Friends / Boogie woogie baby / Crowd pleaser / Crowd pleaser / Moon fire / Devil woman / Never put away my love for you / I'm a man / Here 'tis.
1969. (7") *<55176>* **SLOW DOWN. / FRISCO ANNIE** [-] [ ]
Jan 70. (7") *(UN 516) <55192>* **FOLLOW THE BOUNCING BALL. / LITTLE WOMAN** [ ] [ ]
1970. (7") *<55225>* **I'M A MAN. / HOME AGAIN** [-] [ ]

—— when they split, HAM became a producer, notably for ZZ TOP. GORMAN played with heavy act BANDIT.

YES

Formed: London, England . . . mid '68 by veterans of the 60's beat era; JON ANDERSON and CHRIS SQUIRE. They added BILL BRUFORD, PETE BANKS and TONY KAYE, soon signing to 'Atlantic' after opening for CREAM at their farewell concert at London's Royal Albert Hall. In the summer of 1969, their self-titled debut album was released, a set of original material such as 'SURVIVAL', interspersed with two covers ('I SEE YOU' – Byrds & 'EVERY LITTLE THING' – Beatles). In 1970, the follow-up, 'TIME AND A WORD', also included a version of Stephen Stills' 'NO OPPORTUNITY NECESSARY', alongside the more accomplished title track and the single, 'SWEET DREAMS'. A UK Top 50 hit, it was surpassed early the next year by 'THE YES ALBUM', their first release to feature the innovative guitar-work of STEVE HOWE; BANKS having moved on to the group FLASH. The record featured four meticulously-crafted tracks, 'YOURS IS NO DISGRACE', 'STARSHIP TROOPER', 'PERPETUAL CHANGE' and 'I'VE SEEN ALL GOOD PEOPLE', which went some way to crystallising the typical YES sound, ANDERSON's high-pitched choirboy vocals providing the focal point. The more stylish and flamboyant keyboard-wizard, RICK WAKEMAN was then drafted in to replace KAYE on their 4th album, 'FRAGILE'. A little self-indulgent, it nonetheless garnered widespread critic acclaim and was the first to feature ROGER DEAN's fantasy sleeve artwork. The record's sales were boosted by the Top 20 smash, 'ROUNDABOUT', a US-only single in 1972. Later in the year, they unleashed their progressive tour de force, 'CLOSE TO THE EDGE', an exuberant, atmospheric set which utilised a high-tech multi-layered sound. A triple live set, 'YESSONGS', peaked at No.1 in the UK, also hitting Top 20 in America. During this period, they returned with a double studio concept piece, 'TALES FROM TOPOGRAPHIC OCEANS' which was subsequently lambasted by certain sections of the music press for its overly long tracks. This, and other minor details (such as WAKEMAN not toeing the vegetarian line and being partial to a few beers), led to his departure (he had already released a solo album 'THE SIX WIVES OF HENRY VIII'). His replacement was PATRICK MORAZ (ex-REFUGEE) who took over in time for the 1974 album, 'RELAYER'. Each of the individual group members then took the opportunity to have their own solo outing (see below for details). In 1977, when punk rock was king, YES re-grouped once more with RICK WAKEMAN back in the fold for comeback album, 'GOING FOR THE ONE'. By this stage, the pomp-rock excesses had been slimmed down somewhat to accommodate a more commercial sound, much in evidence on the hit single (first in the UK), 'WONDROUS STORIES'. They failed to emulate this success, critically at least, on their follow-up, 'TORMATO', although it did provide a minor hit, 'SAVE THE WHALE'. In the early 80's, two of their most fundamental creative forces, WAKEMAN and ANDERSON, split ranks, leaving YES to pick up the pieces. However, fans were aghast at the pieces they picked up, i.e. The BUGGLES (TREVOR HORN and GEOFFREY DOWNES), who had previously topped the pop charts with the novelty hit, 'Video Killed The Radio Star'. Despite the initial shock, fans still parted with their hard-earned cash for the resultant 'DRAMA' album. YES split again in 1982, when HOWE and DOWNES joined the soon-to-be successful British supergroup ASIA. ANDERSON returned from a solo career (including a lucrative collaboration with VANGELIS on the hit 45 'I Hear You Now') to a newly reformed YES the following year. The new line-up also included old hands TONY KAYE, CHRIS SQUIRE, ALAN WHITE and a new guitarist, the South African born TREVOR RABIN. Retaining TREVOR HORN on production duties only, they recorded the '90125' album, which spawned the US No.1, 'OWNER OF A LONELY HEART. After RABIN dominated the songwriting on their 1987 set, 'THE BIG GENERATOR', ANDERSON departed yet again. Over the next two years, a bitter dispute was fought over the rights to the YES name. SQUIRE and the last remaining members in 1987 won, while ANDERSON, BRUFORD, WAKEMAN & HOWE were forced to record a surprisingly successful album under their own surnames. Come 1991, the two opposing camps had reconciled their differences, recording the appropriately-titled 'UNION' together. The '90125' line-up was then resurrected for the 1994 'TALK' album, a more lightweight affair which was yet another pointless exercise in dinosaur rock. • **Other covers:** I'M DOWN (Beatles) / SOMETHING'S COMING (Sondheim-Bernstein) / AMERICA (Simon & Garfunkel) / AMAZING GRACE (trad).

Recommended: CLOSE TO THE EDGE (*10) / THE YES ALBUM (*10) / YESSONGS (*9) / GOING FOR THE ONE (*8) / TALES FROM TOPOGRAPHIC OCEANS (*8) / RELAYER (*8) / FRAGILE (*7) / CLASSIC YES (*9)

JON ANDERSON (b.25 Oct'44, Accrington, England) – vocals (ex-WARRIORS, ex-MABEL GREER'S TOY SHOP) / **TONY KAYE** (b.11 Jan'46, Leicester, England) – keyboards (ex-FEDERALS, ex-BITTER SWEET) / **PETER BANKS** (b. 7 Jul'47, Barnet, England) – guitar (ex-SYN, ex-MABEL GREER'S TOYSHOP) / **CHRIS SQUIRE** (b. 4 Mar'48, Nth. London) – bass, vocals (ex-SYN, ex-MABEL GREER'S TOYSHOP) / **BILL BRUFORD** (b.17 May'48, Seven Oaks, London, England) – drums, percussion (ex-SAVOY BROWN BLUES BAND)

Atlantic Atlantic

Jun 69. (7") *(584 280)* **SWEETNESS. / SOMETHING'S COMING** [ ] [-]
Jul 69. (lp) *(588 190) <8243>* **YES** [ ] [ ] Oct69
– Beyond and before / I see you / Yesterday and today / Looking around / Harold land / Every little thing / Sweetness / Survival. *(re-iss.Dec71 lp/c; K/K4 40034) (cd-iss.Oct94 on 'East West'; 7567 82680-2)*
Oct 69. (7"w-drawn) *(584 298)* **LOOKING AROUND. / EVERYDAYS** [-] [-]
Jan 70. (7") *<2709>* **SWEETNESS / EVERY LITTLE THING** [-] [ ]
Mar 70. (7") *(584 323)* **TIME AND A WORD. / THE PROPHET** [ ] [-]
Jun 70. (lp) *(2400 006) <8273>* **TIME AND A WORD** [45] [ ] Nov70
– No opportunity neccessary, no experience needed / Then / Everydays / Sweet dreams / The prophet / Clear days / Astral traveller / Time and a word. *(re-iss.Dec71 lp/c; K/K4 40085) (cd-iss.Oct94 on 'East West'; 7567 82681-2)*
Jun 70. (7") *(2091 004)* **SWEET DREAMS. / DEAR FATHER** [ ] [-]

—— **STEVE HOWE** (b. 8 Apr'47) – guitar (ex-TOMORROW, ex-IN CROWD, ex-SYNDICATS, ex-BODAST) repl. BANKS who joined BLODWYN PIG and later FLASH

Mar 71. (lp) *(2400 101) <8283>* **THE YES ALBUM** [7] [40] May71
– Yours is no disgrace / The clap / Starship trooper; (a) Life seeker – (b) Disiilusion – (c) Wurm / I've seen good people (a) Your move – (b) All good people / A venture / Perpetual change. *(re-iss.Dec71 lp/c; K/K4 40106) (cd-iss.Jul87; SD 19131-2) (cd re-iss.Aug94 on 'East West'; 7567 82665-2)*
Aug 71. (7") *<2819>* **YOUR MOVE. / THE CLAP** [-] [40]
<re-iss.1974; 3141>

—— **RICK WAKEMAN** (b.18 May'49) – keyboards (ex-STRAWBS) repl. KAYE who formed BADGER

Nov 71. (lp) *(2401 019) <7211>* **FRAGILE** [7] [4] Jan72
– Roundabout / Cans and Brahms / We have Heaven / South side of the sky / Five per cent of nothing / Long distance runaround / The fish (Shindleria Praematurus) / Mood for a day / Heart of the sunrise. *(re-iss.Dec71 lp/c; K/K4 50009) (cd-iss.Dec86; K2 50009) (cd re-iss.Aug94 on 'East West'; 7567 82667-2)*
Jan 72. (7") *<2854>* **ROUNDABOUT. / LONG DISTANCE RUNAROUND** [-] [13]
Jul 72. (7") *<2899>* **AMERICA. / TOTAL MASS RETAIN** [-] [46]
Sep 72. (lp/c) *(K/K4 50012) <7244>* **CLOSE TO THE EDGE** [4] [3]
– Close to the edge; (a) The solid time of change – (b) Total mass retain – (c) I get up I get down – (d) Seasons of man / And you and I; (a) Cord of life – (b) Eclipse – (c) The preacher the teacher – (d) The apocalypse / Siberian Khatru. *(cd-iss.Dec86; K2 50012) (cd re-iss.Aug94 on 'East West'; 7567 82666-2)*
Oct 72. (7") *<2920>* **AND YOU AND I (part II). / (part I)** [-] [42]

—— (Aug72) **ANDERSON, HOWE, WAKEMAN + SQUIRE** brought in **ALAN WHITE** (b.14 Jun'44, Pelton, Durham, England) – drums (ex-John Lennon's PLASTIC ONO BAND, ex-HAPPY MAGAZINE) repl. BRUFORD who joined KING CRIMSON, etc. (both appeared on live album below)

May 73. (t-lp/d-c) *(K/K4 60045) <100>* **YESSONGS (live)** [1] [12]
– (opening excerpt from 'Firebird Suite') / Siberian Khatru / Heart of the sunrise / Perpetual change / And you and I; (a) Cord of life – (b) Eclipse – (c) The preacher the teacher – (d) The apocalypse / Mood for a day / (excerpts from 'The Six Wives Of Henry VIII') / Roundabout / I've seen all good people; Your move – All good people / Long distance runaround / The fish (Shindleria Praematurus) / Close to the edge (a) The solid time of change – (b) Total mass retain – (c) I get up I get down – (d) Seasons of man / Yours is no disgrace / Starship trooper (a) Life seeker – (b) Disillusion – (c) Wurm. *(d-cd-iss.Feb87; K2 60045) (re-iss.d-cd Oct94 on 'East West'; 7567 82682-2)*
Dec 73. (d-lp/c) *(K/K4 80001) <2908>* **TALES FROM TOPOGRAPHIC OCEANS** [1] [6]
– The revealing science of God / The remembering / The ancient / Ritual. *(cd-*

iss.Sep89; K 781325) (re-iss.d-cd Oct94 on 'East West'; 7567 82683-2)

Jan 74. (7") *(K 10407)* **ROUNDABOUT (live). / AND YOU AND I (live)** □ -

— **PATRICK MORAZ** (b.24 Jun'48, Morges, Switzerland) – keyboards (ex-REFUGEE) repl. WAKEMAN who continued solo

Nov 74. (lp/c) *(K/K4 50096) <18122>* **RELAYER** 4 5 Dec74
– The gates of delirium / Sound chaser / To be over. *(cd-iss.Jul88; K2 50096) (re-iss.cd Oct94 on 'East West'; 7567 82664-2)*

Dec 74. (7") *<3222>* **SOON (from 'Gates of Delirium'). / SOUND CHASER** - □

— Temporarily disbanded to release solo albums.

STEVE HOWE

augmented by **WHITE, BRUFORD, MORAZ** + many including **GRAEME TAYLOR** – guitar / **MALCOLM BENNETT + COLIN GIBSON** – bass / **DAVID OBERLE** – drums

Atlantic Atlantic

Nov 75. (lp/c) *(K/K4 50151) <SD 18154>* **BEGINNINGS** 22 63
– Doors of sleep / Australia / The nature of the sea / The lost symphony / Beginnings / Will o' the wisp / Ram / Pleasure stole the night / Break away from it all. *(cd-iss.Oct94 on 'East West'; 7567 80319-2)*

CHRIS SQUIRE

augmented by **BILL BRUFORD** – drums / **ANDREW BRYCE JACKMAN + BARRY ROSE** – keyboards / **MEL COLLINS** – sax / **PATRICK MORAZ** – keyboards, synthesizers / **JIMMY HASTINGS** – flute

Atlantic Atlantic

Nov 75. (lp/c) *(K/K4 50203) <SD 18159>* **FISH OUT OF WATER** 25 69
– Hold out your hand / You by my side / Silently falling / Lucky seven / Safe (canon song). *(cd-iss.Feb96 on 'WEA'; 7567 81500-2)*

ALAN WHITE

augmented by **PETER KIRTLEY** – guitar, vocals / **COLIN GIBSON** – bass / **KENNY CRADDOCK** – keyboards, vocals / **ANDY PHILIPS** – steel drums / **ALAN MARSHALL** vocals / **HENRY LOWTHER** – trumpet / **STEVE GREGORY + BUD BEADLE** – wind

Atlantic Atlantic

Mar 76. (lp/c) *(K/K4 50217) <SD 18167>* **RAMSHACKLED** 41 □
– Oooh! baby (going to pieces) / One way rag / Avakak / Spring – Song of innocence / Giddy / Silly woman / Marching into a bottle / Everybody / Darkness (parts 1, 2 & 3). *(cd-iss.Jan96 on 'WEA'; 7567 80396-2)*

Apr 76. (7") *(K 10747)* **OOOH! BABY (GOING TO PIECES). / ONE WAY RAG** □ -

JON ANDERSON

augmented **BRIAN GAYLOR** – synths / **KEN FREEMAN** – strings

Atlantic Atlantic

Jun 76. (lp/c) *(K/K4 50261) SD 18180>* **OLIAS OF SUNHILLOW** 8 47
– Ocean song / Meeting (Garden of Geda) – Sound of the galleon / Dance of Ranyart – Olias (to build the Moorglade) / Qoquag en transic – Naon – Transic to / Flight of the Moorglade / Solid space / Moon Ra – Chords – Song of search / To the runner. *(cd-iss.Feb96 on 'WEA'; 7567 80273-2)*

Oct 76. (7") *(K 10840>* **FLIGHT OF THE MOORGLADE. / TO THE RUNNER** □ -

— PATRICK MORAZ also hit UK Top 30 with his 'I, PATRICK MORAZ' album for 'Charisma'. He had now departed YES to continue solo work & join MOODY BLUES.

YES

re-formed the 1973 line-up w / **RICK WAKEMAN** returning, to repl. MORAZ

Jul 77. (lp/c/3x12") *(K/K4/DSK 50379) <19106>* **GOING FOR THE ONE** 1 8
– Going for the one / Turn of the century / Parallels / Wondrous stories / Awaken. *(cd-iss.Jul88; K2 50379) (cd re-iss.Aug94 on 'East West'; 7567 82670-2)*

Sep 77. (12"blue) *(K 10999)* **WONDROUS STORIES. / PARALLELS** 7 -

Sep 77. (7") *<3416>* **WONDEROUS STORIES. / AWAKEN** - □

Nov 77. (12") *(K 11047)* **GOING FOR THE ONE. / AWAKEN (part 1)** 24 -

Sep 78. (7") *(K 11184)* **DON'T KILL THE WHALE. / ABILENE** 36 -

Sep 78. (lp/c) *(K/K4 50518) <19202>* **TORMATO** 8 10
– Future times / Rejoice / Don't kill the whale / Madrigal / Release, release / Arriving UFO / Circus of Heaven / Onward / On the silent wings of freedom. *(cd-iss.Aug94 on 'East West'; 7567 82671-2)*

Nov 78. (7") *<3534>* **RELEASE, RELEASE. / DON'T KILL THE WHALE** - □

— They shocked their fans, when they replaced (solo seeking once more) WAKEMAN and ANDERSON with (ex-BUGGLES duo) :-**TREVOR HORN** (b.15 Jul'49, Hertfordshire, England) – vocals, bass / + **GEOFF DOWNES** – keyboards

Aug 80. (lp/c) *(K/K4 50736) <16019>* **DRAMA** 2 18
– Machine messiah / White car / Does it really happen? / Into the lens / Run through the light / Tempus fugit. *(cd-iss.Oct94 on 'East West'; 7567 82685-2)*

Oct 80. (7") *(K 11622) <3767>* **INTO THE LENS. / DOES IT REALLY HAPPEN?** □ □

Jan 81. (7") *<3801>* **RUN THROUGH THE LIGHT. / WHITE CAR** - □

— YES split again.

Nov 81. (7"; CHRIS SQUIRE & ALAN WHITE / or / CAMERA) *(K 11695)* **RUN WITH THE FOX. / RETURN OF THE FOX** □ -

— above partnership brought back **ANDERSON + KAYE,** plus newcomer **TREVOR RABIN** (b.13 Jan'54, Johannesburg, South Africa) – guitar, vocals. They repl. DOWNES + HOWE (to ASIA) / and HORN who was retained as producer.

Atco Atco

Nov 83. (7"/7"colrd-sha-pic-d/c-s) *(B9817/+P/C) <99817>* **OWNER OF A LONELY HEART. / OUR SONG** 28 1

Nov 83. (lp/c/cd) *(790 125-1/-4/-2) <90125>* **90125** 16 5
– Owner of a lonely heart / Hold on / It can happen / Changes / Cinema / Leave it / Our song / City of love / Hearts.

Mar 84. (7") *(B 9787) <99787>* **LEAVE IT. / LEAVE IT (acappella)** 56 24
(12"+=) *(B 9787T)* – ('A'version).
(c-s+=)<US cd-s+=> *<B 9789C>* – ('A'-hello goodbye mix) / Owner of a lonely heart.

Jun 84. (7") *(B 9745) <99745>* **IT CAN HAPPEN. / IT CAN HAPPEN (live)** □ 51

Mar 86. (m-lp/c) *(790 474-1/-4) <90474>* **9012LIVE – THE SOLOS (live)** 44 81 Dec85
– Hold on / Si / Solly's beard / Soon / Changes / Amazing Grace / Whitefish.

Sep 87. (7") *(A 9449) <99449>* **LOVE WILL FIND A WAY. / HOLY LAMB** 73 30
(ext.12"+=) *(A 9449T)* – ('A'-Rise & fall mix).

Sep 87. (lp/c)(cd) *(WX 70/+C)(790 522-2) <90522>* **BIG GENERATOR** 17 15
– Rhythm of love / Big generator / Shoot high aim low / Almost like love / Love will find a way / Final eyes / I'm running / Holy love.

Dec 87. (12"ep) *<99419>* **RHYTHM OF LOVE (dance mix) – ('A'move mix) / ('A'dub) / CITY OF LOVE** (live) - 40

— In-house squabbles led to splinter of YES . . .

ANDERSON BRUFORD WAKEMAN HOWE

Arista Arista

Jun 89. (lp/c/cd) *(209/409/259 970) <90126>* **ANDERSON BRUFORD WAKEMAN HOWE** 14 30
– Themes: Sound – Second attention – Soul warrior / Fist of fire / Brother of mine: The big dream – Nothing can come between us – Long lost brother of mine / Quartet: I wanna learn – She gives me love – Who was the first – I'm alive / Birthright / The meeting / Teakbois / Order of the universe: Order theme – Rock gives courage – It's so hard to grow – The universe / Let's pretend. *(lp tracks edited) (re-iss.Dec91 cd/c; 262/412 155)*

Jun 89. (7") *(112444)* **BROTHER OF MINE. / THEMES: SOUND** 63 -
(12"+=) *(612379)* – Themes: Second attention – Soul warrior.
(3"cd-s+=/5"cd-s+=)(10"+=)(c-s+=) *(1/6 62379)(260018)(410017)* – Vultures (in the city).

Jun 89. (cd-s) *<9852>* **BROTHER OF MINE: THE BIG DREAM – NOTHING CAN COME BETWEEN US – LONG LOST BROTHER OF MINE / VULTURES** - □

Aug 89. (7") *<9898>* **LET'S PRETEND. / QUARTET: I'M ALIVE** - □

Nov 89. (7"/c-s) *(112618)* **ORDER OF THE UNIVERSE. / FIST OF FIRE** □ -
(12"+=)(cd-s+=) *(612618)(662693)* – ('A'extended).

YES

now settled dispute by combining last line-up of **ANDERSON, BRUFORD, HOWE, WAKEMAN** with present YES men **SQUIRE, WHITE, RABIN + KAYE**

Arista Arista

May 91. (cd/c/lp) *(261/411/211 558) <8643>* **UNION** 7 15
– I would have waited forever / Shock to the system / Masquerade / Lift me up / Without hope you cannot start the day / Saving my heart / Miracle of life / Silent talking / The more we live-let go / Dangerous / Holding on / Evensong. *(c+=/cd+=)*– Angkor wat / Take the water to the mountain / Give and take.

Jun 91. (7") **SAVING MY HEART. / LIFT ME UP (edit)** □ -
(12"+=/cd-s+=) – America.

Aug 91. (7") *<2218>* **LIFT ME UP. / GIVE AND TAKE** - 86

Nov 91. (c-s) **SAVING MY HEART. / THE MORE WE LIVE – LET GO** - □

Victory London

Mar 94. (cd/c) *(828 489-2/-4)* **TALK** 20 33
– Calling / I am waiting / Real love / State of play / Walls / Where will you be / Endless dream (Silent spring – Talk – Endless dream).

Essential Rykodisc

Oct 96. (cd/c) *(EDF CD/MC 417)* **KEYS TO ASCENSION (live)** 48 99
– Siberia / Revealing science / America / Onward / Awaken / Roundabout / Starship trooper / Be the one / That, that is.

– compilations, others, etc. –

Note; on 'Atlantic' unless otherwise stated.

Feb 75. (lp/c) *(K/K4 50048) <18103>* **YESTERDAYS** (early rare) 27 17
– America / Looking around / Time and a word / Sweet dreams / Then / Survival / Astral traveller / Dear father. *(re-iss.cd Oct94)*

Dec 81. (lp/c) *(K/K4 50842) <19320>* **CLASSIC YES** □ □
– Heart of the sunrise / Wondrous stories / Yours is no disgrace / Roundabout / Starship trooper (a) Life seeker (b) Disillusion (c) Wurm / Long distance runaround / The fish (schindleria praematurus) / And you and I; (a) Cord of life (b) Eclipse (c) The preacher the teacher (d) The apocalypse / I've seen all good people; (a) Your move (b) All good people. *(w/free 7")* ROUNDABOUT (live). / I'VE SEEN ALL GOOD PEOPLE (live) *(cd-iss.Dec86; 250842-2) (re-iss.cd Oct94 on 'East West'; 7567 82687-2)*

Dec 80. (d-lp/c) *Atco; (K 60142) <510>* **YESSHOWS (live 1976-1978)** 22 43
(cd-iss.Oct94; 7567 91747-2)

Oct 82. (d-c) *(K4 60166)* **FRAGILE / CLOSE TO THE EDGE** □ -

Aug 91. (4xcd-box) *Atco; (<7567 91644-2>)* **YESYEARS** □ □

Oct 91. (d-cd/d-c/t-lp) *East West; (<7567 91747-2/-4/-1>)* **THE YES STORY** □ □

Nov 91. (7"/c-s) *East West; (B 8713/+C)* **OWNER OF A LONELY HEART. / ('A'-wonderous mix)** □ □
(12"/cd-s) *(B 8713 T/CD)* – ('A'side) / ('A'-Not Fragile mix) / ('A'-Move Yourself mix) / ('A'-Close To The Edge mix).

Sep 93. (cd) *Connoiseur; (VSOPCD 190)* **FAMILY ALBUM AFFIRMATIVE** (YES family tree) □ -
– Small beginnings (FLASH) / Feels good to me (BRUFORD) / Catherine Howard / Merlin the magician (RICK WAKEMAN) / Ocean song / All in a matter of time (JON ANDERSON) / I HEAR YOU NOW (JON & VANGELIS) / SPRING SONG OF INNOCENCE (ALAN WHITE) / Nature of the sea / Ram (STEVE HOWE) / Cahcaca (PATRICK MORAZ) / Hold out your hand (CHRIS SQUIRE) / Wind of change (BADGER) / Etoile noir (TREVOR RABIN).

Sep 93. (cd/c) *(7567 82517-2/-4)* **HIGHLIGHTS – THE VERY BEST OF YES** □ □

Dec 93. (d-cd/video) *Fragile;* **AN EVENING OF YES MUSIC . . . PLUS** □ □

— for other solo releases; see GREAT ROCK DISCOGRAPHY

Neil YOUNG

Born: 12 Nov'45, Toronto, Canada. He was raised in Winnipeg until 1966, when he drove to America in his Pontiac hearse. NEIL had cut his teeth in local instrumental outfit, The SQUIRES, who released one '45 'THE SULTAN'. / 'AURORA' for 'V' records in September '63. The following year, NEIL formed The MYNHA BIRDS and joined forces with RICKY JAMES MATTHEWS (later to become RICK JAMES). Although many songs were recorded, only one saw light of day; 'MYNHA BIRD HOP' for 'Columbia' Canada. They signed to 'Motown' (first white people to do so) but were soon dropped when they found out that RICKY had dodged the draft. He subsequently met up with past acquaintance, STEPHEN STILLS, and formed BUFFALO SPRINGFIELD. Constant rivalry led to YOUNG departing for a solo venture after signing for new label, 'Reprise', in Spring '68. His eponymous debut with arranger/producer JACK NITSCHE, then DAVID BRIGGS, was finally issued in early 1969. A fragile, acoustic affair, the album was a tentative start to YOUNG's mercurial solo career, songs like 'THE OLD LAUGHING LADY' and 'THE LONER' hinting at the genius to come. The album was also a guinea pig for 'Warners' (then) new 'CSG' recording process, YOUNG later complaining bitterly about the resulting sound quality. 'EVERYBODY KNOWS THIS IS NOWHERE' (1969), however, was the sound of YOUNG in full control. Hooking up with a bunch of hard-bitten rockers going by the name of CRAZY HORSE, the record marked the beginning of a long and fruitful partnership that's still going strong almost thirty years on. With 'CINNAMON GIRL', DOWN BY THE RIVER' and 'COWGIRL IN THE SAND', this bruising musical synergy saw YOUNG scaling cathartic new heights and the guitar interplay would become a template for the primal improvisation of YOUNG's live work. Although 'AFTER THE GOLDRUSH' (1970) was partly recorded with CRAZY HORSE and featured the blistering 'SOUTHERN MAN', most of the album was by turns melancholy, bittersweet and charming in the style of the gorgeous ballad, 'HELPLESS', he'd contributed some months earlier to the CSN&Y album, 'DEJA VU'. 'BIRDS' and 'I BELIEVE IN YOU' stand as two of the most poignant love songs of YOUNG's career while the title track was a compelling lament of surreal poetry, based on a script written by actor DEAN STOCKWELL. The album gave YOUNG his breakthrough, going Top 10 in Britain and America but it was the 1972 single, 'HEART OF GOLD' and subsequent album, 'HARVEST', which made YOUNG a household name. Most of the tracks were recorded in Nashville with a band called The STRAY GATORS, piano and production duties falling to JACK NITZSCHE. His biggest selling album to date, the finely crafted country crooning of 'OUT ON THE WEEKEND' and 'HEART OF GOLD' was the closest YOUNG ever came to MOR and true to contrary style, the next few years saw him trawling the depths of his psyche for some of the most uncompromising and uncommercial material of his career. After the fierce sonic assault of the live 'TIME FADES AWAY' (1973) album, YOUNG went back into the studio with CRAZY HORSE to record a tribute to DANNY WHITTEN, their sad-voiced singer who'd overdosed on heroin the previous year. Just as YOUNG was due to begin recording, another of his friends, BRUCE BERRY (STEPHEN STILLS' GUITAR ROADIE), succumbed to smack and the morose, drunken confessionals that resulted from those sessions eventually appeared a couple of years later as the 'TONIGHT'S THE NIGHT' (1975) album. Arguably YOUNG's most essential release, this darkly personal chronicle of drug oblivion veered from the resigned melancholy of 'ALBUQUERQUE' to the detached, twisted country of 'TIRED EYES', while the visceral catharsis of 'COME ON, BABY, LET'S GO DOWNTOWN' (an earlier live recording with a WHITTEN vocal) cranked up the guitars to match the unrelenting intensity level. Following 'Warners' reluctance to release the album, YOUNG set about writing yet another batch of hazy confessionals upon his return from touring the 'TONIGHT'S THE NIGHT' material. Deeply troubled by his increasing estrangement from actress CARRIE SNODGRASS (with whom he'd had a son, ZEKE), he shacked himself up in his new Malibu pad and penned 'ON THE BEACH' (1974). When every other rock star in L.A. was desperately trying to forget they'd ever hung out with CHARLES MANSON, YOUNG wrote 'REVOLUTION BLUES' in response to the Manson Family killings. 'AMBULANCE BLUES' was just as darkly compelling and the album remains an obscure classic. After a brief, ill-starred reunion with CROSBY, STILLS & NASH, YOUNG came up with a set entitled 'HOMEGROWN', which 'Warners' deemed too downbeat to release. Instead, they relented to the belated issue of 'TONIGHT'S THE NIGHT'. Come 1975, YOUNG was back in the studio with CRAZY HORSE, who'd recently recruited FRANK 'PANCHO' SAMPEDRO on guitar as a permanent replacement for WHITTEN. The resulting album, 'ZUMA' (1975), bore the first raw fruits of this new guitar partnership, the lucid imagery and meditative ruminations of 'CORTEZ THE KILLER' bringing the album to a darkly resonant climax while 'DON'T CRY NO TEARS' and 'BARSTOOL BLUES' found YOUNG more animated then he'd sounded for years. Following a disappointing album, 'LONG MAY YOU RUN' (1976), and aborted tour with STEPHEN STILLS, YOUNG cut the 'AMERICAN STARS 'N' BARS' (1977) album. A competent set of country rock, the record featured one of his best loved songs, an aching, soaring testament to the power of romantic obsession entitled 'LIKE A HURRICANE'. With 'COMES A TIME' (1978), he reverted to 'HARVEST'-style mellow country, duetting with then girlfriend, NICOLETTE LARSON. But YOUNG's more abrasive side couldn't be suppresed for long and, rejuvenated by the energy of the punk explosion, YOUNG reunited with CRAZY HORSE once more for the 'RUST NEVER SLEEPS' (1979) album. An electrifying set of passionate rockers and lean acoustic songs, it included such enduring live favourites as 'MY MY, HEY HEY (OUT OF THE BLUE)/(INTO THE BLACK)' (written about SEX PISTOL, JOHNNY ROTTEN) and the wounded 'POWDERFINGER'. The former was YOUNG's own comment on the "live fast, die young" rock'n'roll school of thought (it came back to haunt him when KURT COBAIN quoted the song in his suicide note). 'LIVE RUST' (1979) was the corrosive companion album capturing NEIL YOUNG & CRAZY HORSE live in all their frayed magnificence. Towards the end of 1978, YOUNG's new love, PEGI MORTON, had borne him a second child, BEN. While YOUNG's first son, ZEKE, had been born with cerebral palsy, BEN was a spastic. A stunned YOUNG began to clam up emotionally, with the result that much of his 80's work sounded confused and directionless. After 'REACTOR' (1981) stiffed, YOUNG moved to 'Geffen' where he recorded 'TRANS' (1983), an album that attempted to reflect his son's communication problems. Using a vocoder, YOUNG succeeded in rendering the lyrics almost unintelligible and while the album was alnmost universally panned, tracks like 'TRANSFORMER MAN' remain oddly affecting. The remainder of his time at 'Geffen' marked an all-time low in his career, both commercially and creatively, during which time he made ill-advised forays into rockabilly and stagnant, MOR country as well as making embaressing pro-Reagan statments in interviews. Testing his fans to the limit, he was eventually sued by 'Geffen' for making records that didn't sound like NEIL YOUNG! He didn't really get back on track until 1989's 'FREEDOM' album, 'ROCKIN' IN THE FREE WORLD' and 'CRIME IN THE CITY' marking YOUNG's return to searing rock'n'roll. With CRAZY HORSE, he cut 'RAGGED GLORY' (1990) the following year, a frenetic guitar mash-up that was staggering in its intensity for such an elder statesman of rock. 'WELD' (1991), a live document of the subsequent tour, saw YOUNG championed by the new "grunge" vanguard and revered once more by the indie/rock press as the epitome of guitar cool. Influenced by SONIC YOUTH (who supported him for part of the tour), he even recorded a CD collage of feedback, 'ARC', available in a limited quantity as a bonus disc with the 'WELD' double set. His critical rebirth now complete, 'HARVEST MOON' (1992) gave him his biggest commercial success since the 70's. A lilting, careworn set of country-folk, it was billed as a belated follow-up to 1972's 'HARVEST'. Of course, the MTV 'UNPLUGGED' (1993) set was now obligatory, but rather than give the audience a predictable run through of acoustic numbers, he presented radically altered versions of old numbers like 'TRANSFORMER MAN' and 'LIKE A HURRICANE'. 'SLEEPS WITH ANGELS' (1994) was a downbeat elegy for KURT COBAIN while 'MIRRORBALL' (1995) was a misguided collaboration with grunge band, PEARL JAM. The 'DEAD MAN' soundtrack was interesting although 'BROKEN ARROW' (1996) and the live 'YEAR OF THE HORSE' (1997) were given short shrift by the press. In truth, the records were far too inconsistent to warrant parting with hard earned cash. New fans could do worse than starting with the 'DECADE' (1977) compilation, a stunning triple set (double CD) gathering the best of YOUNG's earlier work and including such obscure gems as the beautiful 'WINTERLONG'. There are also rumours of a comprehensive boxed set in the offing although there were 'rumours' about a CD reissue of 'ON THE BEACH', and that was four years ago! (take note Warner~s!). While YOUNG seems to be in a bit of a rut at present, and detractors peddle their predictable NEIL 'OLD' jokes, few would doubt the possibility of a blinding return to form or dispute that it's just a matter of when, rather than if. • **Songwriters:** As said, 99% of material is his own with contributions from CRAZY HORSE members, except; FARMER JOHN (Harris-Terry). The album 'EVERYBODY'S ROCKIN'' was full of covers.

Recommended: HARVEST (*10) / AFTER THE GOLDRUSH (*10) / RUST NEVER SLEEPS (*9) / ZUMA (*9) / HARVEST MOON (*9) / RAGGED GLORY (*8) / WELD (*9) / SLEEPS WITH ANGELS (*9) / MIRRORBALL (*8) / EVERYBODY KNOWS THIS IS NOWHERE (*8) / TONIGHT'S THE NIGHT (*9) / DECADE (*8) / ON THE BEACH (*8) / LIVE RUST (*7) /

NEIL YOUNG – vocals, guitar (ex-BUFFALO SPRINGFIELD) with **JIM MESSINA** – bass / session men, etc.

Reprise Reprise

Jan 69. (lp) <*(RSLP 6317)*> **NEIL YOUNG** ☐ ☐
– The Emperor of Wyoming / The loner / If I could have her tonight / I've been waiting for you / The old laughing lady / String quartet from Whiskey Boot Hill / Here we are in the years / What did I do to my life / I've loved her so long / The last trip to Tulsa. *(re-iss.1971 lp/c; K/K4 44059) (cd-iss.1987; K2 44059)*

Mar 69. (7") <*0785*> **THE LONER. / SUGAR MOUNTAIN** [-] ☐

Sep 69. (7") *(RS 23405)* **THE LONER. / EVERYBODY KNOWS THIS IS NOWHERE** ☐ [-]

NEIL YOUNG with CRAZY HORSE

— with **DANNY WHITTEN** – guitar / **BILLY TALBOT** – bass / **RALPH MOLINA** – drums / **BOBBY NOTKOFF** – violin

Jul 69. (lp) <*(RSLP 6349)*> **EVERYBODY KNOWS THIS IS NOWHERE** ☐ [24] May69
– Cinnamon girl / Everybody knows this is nowhere / Round and round (it won't be long) / Down by the river / The losing end (when you're on) / Running dry (requiem for the rockets) / Cowgirl in the sand. *(re-iss.1971 lp/c; K/K4 44073) (cd-iss.1988; K2 44059)*

Jul 69. (7") <*0836*> **DOWN BY THE RIVER (edit). / THE LOSING END (WHEN YOU'RE ON)** [-] ☐

— Late 1969, NEIL YOUNG was also added to CROSBY, STILLS, NASH (& YOUNG).

Aug 70. (7") *(RS 23462)* **DOWN BY THE RIVER (edit). / CINNAMON GIRL (alt.take)** ☐ [-]

Crazy Horse
LOUD

NEIL YOUNG

— with **NILS LOFGREN** – guitar (of GRIN) repl. NOTKOFF

Aug 70. (7") *<0898>* **OH LONESOME ME (extended). / I'VE BEEN WAITING FOR YOU (alt.mix)** [-] [ ]

Sep 70. (lp) *<(RSLP 6383)>* **AFTER THE GOLD RUSH** [7] [8]
– Tell me why / After the gold rush / Only love can break your heart / Southern man / Till the morning comes / Oh lonesome me / Don't let it bring you down / Birds / When you dance I can really love / I believe in you / After the goldrush / Cripple Creek ferry. *(re-iss.1971 lp/c; K/K4 44088) (cd-iss.Jul87; K2 44088)*

Sep 70. (7") *(RS 20861)* **OH LONESOME ME (extended). / SUGAR MOUNTAIN** [ ] [-]

Jun 70. (7") *<0911>* **CINNAMON GIRL (alt.mix). / SUGAR MOUNTAIN** [-] [55]

Oct 70. (7") *(RS 20958) <0958>* **ONLY LOVE CAN BREAK YOUR HEART. / BIRDS** [ ] [33]

Jan 71. (7") *<0992>* **WHEN YOU DANCE I CAN REALLY LOVE. / SUGAR MOUNTAIN** [-] [93]

Feb 71. (7") *(RS 23488)* **WHEN YOU DANCE I CAN REALLY LOVE. / AFTER THE GOLDRUSH** [ ] [-]

— solo with The STRAY GATORS. (CRAZY HORSE now recorded on their own). NEIL's musicians: **JACK NITZSCHE** – piano / **BEN KEITH** – steel guitar / **TIM DRUMMOND** – bass / **KENNY BUTTREY** – drums. guests included **CROSBY, STILLS & NASH, LINDA RONSTADT, JAMES TAYLOR** plus The LONDON SYMPHONY ORCHESTRA

Feb 72. (7") *(K 14140) <1065>* **HEART OF GOLD. / SUGAR MOUNTAIN** [10] [1]

Mar 72. (lp/c) *(K/K4 54005) <MS 2032>* **HARVEST** [1] [1]
– Out on the weekend / Harvest / A man needs a maid / Heart of gold / Are you ready for the country? / Old man / There's a world / Alabama / The needle and the damage done / Words (between the lines of age). *(cd-iss.May83; K 244131)*

Apr 72. (7") *(K 14167) <1084>* **OLD MAN. / THE NEEDLE AND THE DAMAGE DONE** [ ] [31]

Jun 72. (7"; by NEIL YOUNG & GRAHAM NASH) *<1099>* **WAR SONG. / THE NEEDLE AND THE DAMAGE DONE** [-] [61]

— **JOHNNY BARBATA** – drums (ex-CROSBY, STILLS & NASH) repl. BUTTREY

Sep 73. (lp/c) *(K/K4 54010) <MS 2151>* **TIME FADES AWAY (live)** [20] [22]
– Time fades away / Journey through the past / Yonder stands the sinner / L.A. / Love in mind / Don't be denied / The bridge / Last dance.

Oct 73. (7") *<1184>* **TIME FADES AWAY (live). / LAST TRIP TO TULSA (live)** [-] [ ]

— now used session people including **CRAZY HORSE** members **BEN KEITH** – steel guitar had now repl. WHITTEN who o.d.'d August 1972.

Jul 74. (7") *(K/K4 54014) <R 2180>* **ON THE BEACH** [42] [16]
– Walk on / See the sky about to rain / Revolution blues / For the turnstiles / Vampire blues / On the beach / Motion pictures / Ambulance blues.

Jul 74. (7") *(K 14360) <1209>* **WALK ON. / FOR THE TURNSTILES** [ ] [69]

— Had just earlier in 1974, re-united with CROSBY, STILLS & NASH

— recorded solo lp in '73. Musicians: **NILS LOFGREN / BEN KEITH / BILLY TALBOT / RALPH MOLINA**

Jun 75. (lp/c) *(K/K4 54040) <MS 2221>* **TONIGHT'S THE NIGHT** [48] [25]
– Tonight's the night (part I) / Speakin' out / World on a string / Borrowed tune / Come on baby let's go downtown / Mellow my mind / Roll another number (for the road) / Albuquerque / New mama / Lookout Joe / Tired eyes / Tonight's the night (part II). *(cd-iss.Jul93; 7599 27221-2)*

NEIL YOUNG with CRAZY HORSE

— (Mar75) **FRANK 'Poncho' SAMPEDRO** – guitar, vocals repl. KEITH + LOFGREN The latter earlier went solo, and later joined BRUCE SPRINGSTEEN band.

Nov 75. (lp/c) *(K/K4 54057) <MS 2242>* **ZUMA** [44] [25]
– Don't cry no tears / Danger bird / Pardon my heart / Lookin' for a love / Barstool blues / Stupid girl / Drive back / Cortez the killer / Through my sails. *(cd-iss.Jul93; 7599 27222-2)*

Mar 76. (7") *<K 14416> <1344>* **LOOKIN' FOR A LOVE. / SUGAR MOUNTAIN** [ ] [ ] Dec75

Mar 76. (7") *<1350>* **DRIVE BACK. / STUPID GIRL** [-] [ ]

May 76. (7") *(K 14431)* **DON'T CRY NO TEARS. / STUPID GIRL** [ ] [-]

— Mid 1976, he teamed up as STILLS-YOUNG BAND with STEPHEN STILLS on album 'LONG MAY YOU RUN'; *K/K4 54081 <MS 2253>*. (see under ⇒ CROSBY, STILLS, NASH & YOUNG).

Jun 77. (lp/c) *(K/K4 54088) <MSK 2261>* **AMERICAN STARS 'N BARS** [17] [21]
– The old country waltz / Saddle up the Palomino / Hey babe / Hold back the tears / Bite the bullet / Star of Bethlehem / Will to love / Like a hurricane / Homegrown. *(cd-iss.Dec96; 7599 27234-2)*

Jul 77. (7") *<1390>* **HEY BABE. / HOMEGROWN** [-] [ ]

Sep 77. (7") *(K 14482) <1391>* **LIKE A HURRICANE (edit). / HOLD BACK THE TEARS** [ ] [ ]

NEIL YOUNG

— solo with loads on session incl.**NICOLETTE LARSON** – vox

Oct 78. (7") *<1395>* **COMES A TIME. / MOTORCYCLE MAMA** [-] [ ]

Oct 78. (lp/c) *(K/K4 54099) <2266>* **COMES A TIME** [42] [7]
– Goin' back / Comes a time / Look out for my love / Lotta love / Peace of mind / Human highway / Already one / Field of opportunity / Motorcycle mama / Four strong winds. *(cd-iss.Jul93; 7599 27235-2)*

Nov 78. (7") *(K 14493)* **FOUR STRONG WINDS. / MOTORCYCLE MAMA** [57] [-]

Dec 78. (7") *<1396>* **FOUR STRONG WINDS. / HUMAN HIGHWAY** [-] [61]

NEIL YOUNG with CRAZY HORSE

— (YOUNG w / **SAMPEDRO, TALBOT & MOLINA**)

Jun 79. (lp/c) *(K/K4 54105) <2295>* **RUST NEVER SLEEPS** [13] [8]
– My my, hey hey (out of the blue) / Thrasher / Ride my llama / Pocahontas / Sail away / Powderfinger / Welfare mothers / Sedan delivery / Hey hey, my my (into the black). *(cd-iss.Jul93; 7599 27249-2)*

Aug 79. (7") *(K 14498) <49031>* **HEY HEY, MY MY (INTO THE BLACK). / MY MY, HEY HEY (OUT OF THE BLUE)** [ ] [79]

Nov 79. (d-lp/d-c) *(K/K4 64041) <2296>* **LIVE RUST (live)** [55] [15]
– Sugar mountain / I am a child / Comes a time / After the gold rush / My my, hey hey (out of the blue) / When you dance I can really love / The loner / The needle and the damage done / Lotta love / Sedan delivery / Powderfinger / Cortez the killer / Cinnamon girl / Like a hurricane / Hey hey, my my (into the black) / Tonight's the night. *(re-iss.cd Jul93; 7599 27250-2)*

Dec 79. (7") *<49189>* **CINNAMON GIRL (live). / THE LONER (live)** [-] [ ]

NEIL YOUNG

— solo with **TIM DRUMMOND + DENNIS BELFIELD** – bass / **LEVON HELM + GREG THOMAS** – drums / **BEN KEITH** – steel, dobro / **RUFUS THIBODEAUX** – fiddle

Oct 80. (lp/c) *(K/K4 54109) <2297>* **HAWKS & DOVES** [34] [30]
– Little wing / The old homestead / Lost in space / Captain Kennedy / Stayin' power / Coastline / Union power / Comin' apart at every nail / Hawks & doves.

Nov 80. (7") *(K 14508) <49555>* **HAWKS & DOVES. / UNION MAN** [ ] [ ]

Feb 81. (7") *<49641>* **STAYIN' POWER. / CAPTAIN KENNEDY** [-] [ ]

NEIL YOUNG with CRAZY HORSE

— (see last CRAZY HORSE line-up)

Oct 81. (lp/c) *(K/K4 54116) <2304>* **RE• AC• TOR** [69] [27]
– Opera star / Surfer Joe and Moe the sleaze / T-bone / Get back on it / Southern Pacific / Motor city / Rapid transit / Shots.

Nov 81. (7"/10"shaped-red) *<498 70/95>* **SOUTHERN PACIFIC. / MOTOR CITY** [-] [70]

Jan 82. (7") *<50014>* **OPERA STAR. / SURFER JOE AND MOE THE SLEAZE** [-] [ ]

NEIL YOUNG

— solo adding synthesizers, drum machine (sessioners) **BRUCE PALMER** – bass (ex-BUFFALO SPRINGFIELD)

Geffen Geffen

Jan 83. (7") *(GEF 2781) <29887>* **LITTLE THING CALLED LOVE. / WE R IN CONTROL** [ ] [71] Dec82

Jan 83. (lp/c) *(GEF/+C 25019) <2018>* **TRANS** [29] [19]
– Little thing called love / Computer age / We r in control / Transformer man / Computer cowboy (aka Syscrusher) / Hold on to your love / Sample and hold / Mr. Soul / Like an Inca. *(re-iss.Sep86 lp/c; 902018-1/-4) (cd-iss.Apr97; GFLD 19357)*

Jan 83. (12") *<20105>* **SAMPLE AND HOLD (extended). / MR SOUL (extended) / SAMPLE AND HOLD** [-] [ ]

Feb 83. (7") *<29707>* **MR. SOUL. / MR. SOUL (part 2)** [-] [ ]

— w / **BEN KEITH** – guitar / **TIM DRUMMOND** – bass / **KARL HIMMEL** – drums / **LARRY BYROM** – piano, vocals / **RICK PALOMBI + ANTHONY CRAWFORD** – b.vocals

Sep 83. (lp/c; as NEIL & THE SHOCKING PINKS) *(GEF/+C 25590) <4013>* **EVERYBODY'S ROCKIN'** [50] [46] Aug83
– Betty Lou's got a new pair of shoes / Rainin' in my heart / Payola blues / Wonderin' / Kinda fonda Wanda / Jellyroll man / Bright lights, big city / Cry, cry, cry / Mystery train / Everybody's rockin'. *(re-iss.Sep86 lp/c/cd; 904013-1/-4/-2)*

Sep 83. (7") *(GEF 3581) <29574>* **WONDERIN'. / PAYOLA BLUES** [ ] [ ]

Oct 83. (7") *<29433>* **CRY, CRY, CRY. / PAYOLA BLUES** [-] [ ]

— Jul85, with country singer WILLIE NELSON he duets on his ARE THERE ANY MORE REAL COWBOYS single issued on 'Columbia'.

— solo again with loads of session people.

Aug 85. (lp/c) *(GEF/40 26377) <24068>* **OLD WAYS** [39] [75]
– The wayward wind / Get back to the country / Are there any more real cowboys? / Once an angel / Misfits / California sunset / Old ways / My boy / Bound for glory / Where is the highway tonight? *(cd-iss.Apr97; GFLD 19356)*

Sep 85. (7") *<28883>* **BACK TO THE COUNTRY. / MISFITS** [-] [ ]

Nov 85. (7") *<28753>* **OLD WAYS. / ONCE AN ANGEL** [-] [ ]

— w / **STEVE JORDAN** – drums, synths, vox / **DANNY KORTCHMAR** – guitar, synth

Aug 86. (lp/c/cd) *(924109-1/-4/-2) <24109>* **LANDING ON WATER** [52] [46]
– Weight of the world / Violent side / Hippie dream / Bad news beat / Touch the night / People on the street / Hard luck stories / I got a problem / Pressure / Drifter. *(re-iss.Apr91;) (cd-iss.Nov96; GED 24109)*

Sep 86. (7"/12") *(GEF/+T 7) <28623>* **WEIGHT OF THE WORLD. / PRESSURE** [ ] [ ] Jul86

NEIL YOUNG & CRAZY HORSE

— (see last **CRAZY HORSE, + BRYAN BELL** – synth)

May 87. (lp/c)(cd) *(WX 108/+C)(924154-2) <24154>* **LIFE** [71] [75]
– Mideast vacation / Long walk home / Around the world / Inca queen / Too lonely / Prisoners of rock'n'roll / Cryin' eyes / When your lonely heart breaks / We never danced.

Jun 87. (7") *<28196>* **MIDEAST VACATION. / LONG WALK HOME** [-] [ ]

Jun 87. (7") *(GEF 25)* **LONG WALK HOME. / CRYIN' EYES** [ ] [-]

NEIL YOUNG & THE BLUENOTES

— with **SAMPEDRO** – keyboards plus others **CHAD CROMWELL** – drums / **RICK ROSAS** – bass / **STEVE LAWRENCE** – tenor sax / **BEN KEITH** – alto sax / **LARRY CRAIG** – baritone sax / **CLAUDE CAILLIET** – trombone / **JOHN FUMO** – trumpet / **TOM BRAY** – trumpet

Reprise Reprise

Apr 88. (7") *<27908>* **TEN MEN WORKIN'. / I'M GOIN'** [-] [ ]

May 88. (lp/c/cd) *(WX 168/+C)(925719-2) <25719>* **THIS NOTE'S FOR YOU** [56] [61]

– Ten men workin' / This note's for you / Coupe de ville / Life in the city / Twilight / Married man / Sunny inside / Can't believe you're lyin' / Hey hey / One thing. *(re-iss.cd Feb95)*

May 88. (7") *<27848>* **THIS NOTE'S FOR YOU (live). / THIS NOTE'S FOR YOU** [-] [ ]

—— Nov88, NEIL re-joined CROSBY, STILLS, NASH & YOUNG for 'AMERICAN DREAM' lp.

NEIL YOUNG

—— solo again with **SAMPEDRO, ROSAS, CROMWELL,** etc.

Oct 89. (lp/c/cd) *(WX 257/+C)(K 925899-2) <25899>* **FREEDOM** [17] [35]
– Rockin' in the free world / Crime in the city (sixty to zero part 1) / Don't cry / Hangin' on a limb / Eldorado / The ways of love / Someday / On Broadway / Wreckin' ball / No more / Too far gone / Rockin' in the free world (live). *(re-iss.cd/c Feb95)*

Apr 90. (7") *(W 2776) <22776>* **ROCKIN' IN THE FREE WORLD. / ('A'live)** [ ] [ ] Aug89
(12"+=/cd-s+=) *(W 2776 T/CD)* – Cocaine eyes.

NEIL YOUNG & CRAZY HORSE

—— with **SAMPEDRO, TALBOT + MOLINA**

Sep 90. (cd)(lp/c) *(7599-26315-2)(WX 374/+C) <26315>* **RAGGED GLORY** [15] [31]
– Country home / White line / Fuckin' up / Over and over / Love to burn / Farmer John / Mansion on the hill / Days that used to be / Love and only love / Mother Earth (natural anthem). *(re-iss.cd/c Feb95)*

Sep 90. (cd-s) *<7599-21759-2>* **MANSION ON THE HILL (edit) / MANSION ON THE HILL / DON'T SPOOK THE HORSE** [-] [ ]

Oct 91. (d-cd/d-c/d-lp) *<(7599 26671-2/-4/-1)>* **WELD (live)** [20] [ ]
– Hey hey, my my (into the black) / Crime in the city / Blowin' in the wind / Live to burn / Welfare mothers / Cinnamon girl / Mansion on the hill / F+!£in' up / Farmer John / Cortez the killer / Powderfinger / Love and only love / Roll another number / Rockin' in the free world / Like a hurricane / Tonight's the night. *(free-cd-ep w.a.+=)*– ARC EP – (feedback).

NEIL YOUNG

solo, with The STRAY GATORS (**KENNY BUTTREY, TIM DRUMMOND, BEN KEITH & SPOONER OLDHAM**) plus **JAMES TAYLOR, LINDA RONSTADT, NICOLETTE LARSON, ASTRID YOUNG & LARRY CRAGG** – backing vocals

Oct 92. (cd/c/lp) *(9362 45057-2/-4/-1)* **HARVEST MOON** [9] [16]
– Unknown legend / From Hank to Hendrix / You and me / Harvest moon / War of man / One of these days / Such a woman / Old king / Dreamin' man / Natural beauty.

Feb 93. (7"/c-s) *(W 0139/+C)* **HARVEST MOON. / WINTERLONG** [36] [ ]
(cd-s+=) *(W 0139CD)* – Deep forbidden lake / Campaigner.
(cd-s) *(W 0139CDX)* – ('A'side) / Old king / The needle and the damage done / Goin' back.

Jun 93. (cd/c/lp) *<(9362 45310-2/-4/-1)>* **UNPLUGGED** [4] [23]
– The old laughing lady / Mr. Soul / World on a string / Pocahontas / Strongman / Like a hurricane / The needle and the damage done / Helpless / Harvest Moon / Transformer man / Unknown legend / Look out for my love / Long may you run / From Hank to Hendrix.

Jul 93. (7"/c-s) *(W 0191/+C)* **THE NEEDLE AND THE DAMAGE DONE (live). / YOU AND ME** [75] [ ]
(cd-s+=) *(W 0191CD)* – From Hank to Hendrix.

Oct 93. (7"/c-s) *(W 207/+C)* **LONG MAY YOU RUN (live). / SUGAR MOUNTAIN (live)** [71] [ ]
(cd-s+=) *(W 0207CD)* – Cortez the killer (live) / Cinnamon girl (live).

Feb 94. (7"/c-s) *(W 0231/+C)* **ROCKIN' IN THE FREE WORLD. / ('A'mixes)** [ ] [ ]
(cd-s+=) *(W 0231CD)* – Weld.

Apr 94. (7"/c-s) *(W 0242/+C)* **PHILADELPHIA. / SUCH A WOMAN** [62] [ ]
(12"+=/cd-s+=) *(W 0242 T/CD)* – Stringman (unplugged).

—— Above 'A'side was another to be taken from the film 'Philadelphia'.

NEIL YOUNG & CRAZY HORSE

Aug 94. (cd/c/d-lp) *<(9362 45749-2/-4/-1)>* **SLEEPS WITH ANGELS** [2] [9]
– My heart / Prime of life / Drive by / Sleeps with angels / Western hero / Change your mind / Blue Eden / Safeway cart / Train of love / Trans Am / Piece of crap / A dream that can last. *(re-iss.Jan97; same)*

Aug 94. (c-s/cd-s) *(W 0261 C/CD)* **PIECE OF CRAP / TONIGHT'S THE NIGHT** [ ] [ ]

Oct 94. (c-s) *(W 0266C)* **MY HEART / ROLL ANOTHER NUMBER (FOR THE ROAD)** [ ] [ ]
(cd-s+=) *(W 0266CD)* – Tired eyes.

Nov 94. (c-s) **CHANGE YOUR MIND / SPEAKIN' OUT** [ ] [ ]
(cd-s+=) – ('A'full version).

Neil YOUNG

—— with backing from all of PEARL JAM; 8th track written w/ EDDIE VEDDER

Jun 95. (cd/c/lp) *<(9362 45934-2/-4/-1)>* **MIRRORBALL** [4] [5]
– Song X / Act of love / I'm the ocean / Big green country / Truth be known / Downtown / What happened yesterday / Peace and love / Throw your hatred down / Scenery / Fallen angel.

Sep 95. (c-s) *(W 0314C)* **DOWNTOWN / BIG GREEN COUNTRY** [ ] [ ]
(cd-s+=) *(W 0314CD)* – ('A'-lp version).

Feb 96. (cd) *<(9362 46171-2)>* **Music From And Inspired By The Motion Picture DEAD MAN** [ ] [ ]

—— above was instrumental YOUNG, and based on Jim Jarmusch's film starring Johnny Depp.

NEIL YOUNG WITH CRAZY HORSE

Jun 96. (cd/c) *<(9362 46291-2/-4)>* **BROKEN ARROW** [17] [31]
– Big time / Loose change / Slip away / Changing highways / Scattered (let's think about livin') / This town / Music arcade / Baby what you want me to do.

Jun 97. (cd/c) *<(9362 46652-2/-4)>* **YEAR OF THE HORSE (live)** [36] [57]
– When you dance / Barstool blues / When your lonely heart breaks / Mr. Soul / Big time / Pocahontas / Human highway / Slip away / Scattered / Danger bird / Prisoners / Sedan delivery.

– compilations, others, etc. –

Note; on 'Reprise' until otherwise stated.

1971. (7") *<0746>* **CINNAMON GIRL (alt.mix). / ONLY LOVE CAN BREAK YOUR HEART** [-] [ ]

Nov 72. (d-lp) *(K 64015) <2XS 6480>* **JOURNEY THROUGH THE PAST (Soundtrack featuring live & rare material with past bands)** [ ] [45]
– For what it's worth – Mr. Soul / Rock & roll woman / Find the cost of freedom / Ohio / Southern man / Are you ready for the country / Let me call you sweetheart / Alabama / Words / Relativity invitation / Handel's Messiah / King of kings / Soldier / Let's go away for a while.

Jan 73. (7") *<1152>* **HEART OF GOLD. / OLD MAN** [-] [ ]

Mar 74. (7") *(K 14319)* **ONLY LOVE CAN BREAK YOUR HEART. / AFTER THE GOLDRUSH** [ ] [-]

May 74. (7"ep) *(K 14350)* **SOUTHERN MAN / TILL MORNING COMES. / AFTER THE GOLDRUSH / HEART OF GOLD** [ ] [-]

Nov 77. (t-lp) *(K 54088) <3RS 2257>* **DECADE** [46] [43]
– Down to the wire + Burned + Mr.Soul + Broken arrow + Expecting to fly (BUFFALO SPRINGFIELD) / Sugar mountain / I am a child / The loner / The old laughing lady / Cinnamon girl / Down by the river / Cowgirl in the sand / I believe in you / After the goldrush / Southern man / Helpless + Ohio (CROSBY, STILLS, NASH & YOUNG) / A man needs a maid / Harvest / Heart of gold / Star of Bethlehem / The needle and the damage done / Tonight's the night (part 1) / Turnstiles / Winterlong / Deep forbidden lake / Like a hurricane / Love is a rose / Cortez the killer / Campaigner / Long may you run (w / STEPHEN STILLS). *(re-iss.d-cd Jul93)*

Jan 78. (7") *<1393>* **SUGAR MOUNTAIN. / THE NEEDLE AND THE DAMAGE DONE** [-] [ ]

Oct 82. (d-c) *(K4 64043)* **NEIL YOUNG / EVERYBODY KNOWS THIS IS NOWHERE** [ ] [-]

Oct 82. (d-c) *(K4 64044)* **AFTER THE GOLDRUSH / HARVEST** [ ] [-]

Feb 87. (cd) *(925271-2)* **THE BEST OF NEIL YOUNG** [ ] [ ]

Jan 93. (cd) *Movieplay Gold; (MPG 74011)* **THE LOST TAPES** [ ] [-]

Jan 93. (cd/c) *Geffen; (GED/GEC 24452)* **LUCKY THIRTEEN** (80's material) [69] [ ]
– Sample and hold / Transformer man / Depression blues / Get gone / Don't take your love away from me / Once an angel / Where is the highway tonight / Hippie dream / Pressure / Around the world / East vacation / Ain't it the truth / This note's for you. *(cd re-iss.Sep96; GFLD 19328)*

—— Note that 1980's 'Where The Buffalo Roam' film contained several YOUNG songs

YOUNGBLOODS

Formed: New York City, New York, USA . . . 1965 by solo artist JESSE COLIN YOUNG, who had just released two albums, 'THE SOUL OF A CITY BOY' and 'YOUNGBLOOD', the second featuring LOVIN' SPOONFUL's JOHN SEBASTIAN on dobro. The following year, The YOUNGBLOODS, with JERRY CORBITT, JOE BAUER and BANANA, issued their first single, 'GRIZZLY BEAR', which bubbled under the US Top 50. An eponymous debut was quickly followed by a second set, 'EARTH MUSIC', and was again produced by FELIX PAPPALARDI (of The RASCALS). YOUNG moved to the West Coast, where the band recorded their finest hour, the hippie-inspired 'ELEPHANT MOUNTAIN' album, containing a later hit, 'DARKNESS, DARKNESS'. Another re-issue of their old 1967 single, 'GET TOGETHER' crashed the charts, subsequently hitting the Top 5 in the summer of '69 (KURT COBAIN later subverting the lyrics for the track 'Territorial Pissings'). The YOUNGBLOODS carried on for a few more years, JESSE COLIN YOUNG taking off for a lucrative country/folk solo career. He hit the US Top 50 with many albums during the 70's.

Recommended: FROM THE GASLIGHT TO THE AVALON compilation (*6)

JESSE COLIN YOUNG

(b. PERRY MILLER, 11 Nov'44, New York City, USA)

not issued Capitol

1964. (lp) *<2070>* **THE SOUL OF A CITY BOY** [-] [ ]
– Four in the morning / You gotta fix it / Rye whiskey / Who a baby / Susanne / Black eyed Susan / Same old man / Drifter's patrol / Stranger love / I think I'll take to whiskey. *<US re-iss.Feb74; 11267>*

—— augmented by **JOHN SEBASTIAN** – harmonica / **PETE CHILDS** – guitar / **GEORGE DUVIVER** – bass / **OSIE JOHNSON** – drums

not issued Mercury

1965. (lp) *<SR 61005>* **YOUNGBLOOD** [-] [ ]
– Rider / Doc Geiger / Lullabye / Brother can you spare a dime / Trouble in mind / Little Suzie / Nobody's dirty business / Green hill mountain home / Summer rain / Walking off the blues / Cotton eyed Joe.

YOUNGBLOODS

JESSE COLIN YOUNG – vocals, guitar, bass / **JERRY CORBITT** (b. Tipton, Georgia) – guitar, bass / **JOE BAUER** (b.26 Sep'41, Memphis, Tenn.) – drums / **BANANA** (b. LOWELL LEVINGER, 1946, Cambridge, Mass.)

R.C.A. R.C.A.

Nov 66. (7") *<9015>* **GRIZZLY BEAR. / THE TEARS ARE FALLING** - 52

Feb 67. (7") *<9142>* **MERRY-GO-ROUND. / FOOLIN' AROUND** -

Mar 67. (lp) *<LSP 3724>* **THE YOUNGBLOODS** -
– Grizzly bear / All over the world (la-la) / Statesboro blues / Get together / One note man / Other side of this life / Tears are falling / Four in the morning / Foolin' around (the waltz) / Ain't that lovin' you, baby / C.C. rider. *(UK-iss.Apr88 on 'Edsel'; ED 271) (cd-iss.Apr91; EDCD 271)*

May 67. (7") *<9222>* **EUPHORIA. / THE WINE SONG** -

Aug 67. (7") *<9264>* **GET TOGETHER. / ALL MY DREAMS BLUE** - 62

Jan 68. (7") *<9360>* **I CAN TELL. / FOOL ME** -

Jan 68. (lp) *<LSP 3865>* **EARTH MUSIC** -
– Euphoria / All my dreams blue / Too much monkey business / Dreamer's dream / Sugar babe / Long and tall / I can tell / Don't play games / The wine song / Fool me / Reason to believe. *(UK-iss.Apr88 on 'Edsel'; ED 274) (cd-iss.Apr91;* EDCD 274)

May 68. (7") *<9422>* **DREAMER'S DREAM. / QUICKSAND** -

— now without CORBITT who later went solo

Apr 69. (7") *(1821) <0129>* **DARKNESS, DARNESS. / ON SIR FRANCIS DRAKE**
(re-iss.Apr70; 1955) <0342>– <hit No.86>

1969. (lp) *(SF 8026) <LSP 4150>* **ELEPHANT MOUNTAIN** Apr69
– Darkness, darkness / Smug / On Sir Francis Drake / Sunlight / Double sunlight / Beautiful / Turn it over / Rain song / Trillium / Quicksand black / Mountain breakdown / Sham / Ride the wind. *(re-is.May88 on 'Edsel'; ED 276) (cd-iss.Apr91; EDCD 276)*

Sep 69. (7") *(1877) <9752>* **GET TOGETHER. / BEAUTIFUL** 5 Jun69

Sep 69. (7") *<0270>* **SUNLIGHT. / TRILLIUM** -

Dec 69. (7") *<0465>* **SUNLIGHT. / REASONS TO BELIEVE** -

1970. (lp) *(LSA 3012) <SP 4399>* **THE BEST OF THE YOUNGBLOODS** (compilation) Aug70
– Get together / Darkness, darkness / Sunlight / Grizzly bear / Euphoria / Wine song / C.C. rider / Sugar babe / Sham / Quicksand.

— added **MICHAEL KANE** – bass

Warners Warners

Dec 70. (lp) *<(WS 1878)>* **ROCK FESTIVAL** 50 Oct70
– It's a lovely day / Faster all the time / Prelude / On beautiful Lake Spenard / Josiane / Sea cow boogie / Fiddler a dram / Misty roses / Interludes / Peepin' 'n' hidin' (baby, what you want me to do) / Ice bag.

1970. (7") *<7404>* **PEACE SONG. / FREE IN THE AIR** -

May 71. (7") *<(WB 7445)>* **HIPPIE FROM OLEMA. / MISTY ROSES**

Sep 71. (7") *(K 16098) <7499>* **IT'S A LOVELY DAY. / ICE BAG**

Dec 71. (lp) *(K 46100) <RBS 2563>* **RIDE THE WIND (live)** Jul71
– Ride the wind / Sugar babe / Sunlight / The dolphin / Get together / Beautiful. *(cd-iss.Oct94 on 'Line'; LECD 901021)*

1972. (lp) *<(RBS 2566)>* **GOOD AND DUSTY** Nov71
– Stagger Lee / That's how strong my love is / Willie and the hand jive / Circus face / Hippie from Olema / Good and Dusty / Let the good times roll / Drifting & drifting / Pontiac blues / The moonshine is the sunshine / Will the circle be unbroken / I'm a hog for you baby / Light shine.

1972. (7") *<7563>* **LIGHT SHINE. / WILL THE CIRCLE BE UNBROKEN** -

1972. (7") *<7660>* **KIND HEARTED WOMAN. / RUNNING BEAR** -

1972. (lp) *<(RBS 2653)>* **HIGH ON A RIDGE TOP** Dec72
– Speedo / She caught the Katy & left a mule to ride / Going by the river / Running bear / I shall be released / Dreamboat / She came in through the bathroom window / Donna / La bamba / Kind hearted woman.

— BAUER went solo, while other original formed BANANA & THE BUNCH

— JESSE COLIN YOUNG continued to release many albums, although most of them were in the folk/country mould.

– (YOUNGBLOODS) compilations, etc. –

Jan 72. (lp) *RCA Victor; (SF 8218) <4561>* **SUNLIGHT** Aug71
– Sunlight / Reason to believe / Foolin' around (the waltz) / Statesboro blues / On Sir Francis Drake / One note man / Dreamer's dream / Ain't that lovin' you, baby / I can tell / Long and tall.

1972. (lp) *R.C.A.; <6051>* **THIS IS . . .** -

Oct 87. (lp) *Edsel; (ED 244)* **POINT REYES STATION** -
– It's a lovely day / She caught the Katy & left me a mule to ride / Dreamboat / Running bear / Light shine / That's how strong my love is / Will the circle be unbroken / La bamba / Circus face / Fiddler a dram / Faster all the time / Get together / Sugar babe.

Jul 88. (lp/c) *Decal; (LIK/TCLIK 38)* **FROM THE GASLIGHT TO THE AVALON** -
– Grizzly bear / All over the world / Get together / The other side of life / Merry go round / Euphoria / I can tell / Sugar babe / Wine song / Darkness, darkness / Sunlight / Double sunlight / Sham / Ride the wind.

YOUNG RASCALS (see under ⇒ RASCALS)

Frank ZAPPA

Born: FRANK VINCENT ZAPPA, 21 Dec'40, Baltimore, Maryland, USA, from Sicilian and Greek parents, who moved to California in 1950. In 1956, he formed The BLACKOUTS with school chum DON VAN VLIET (aka CAPTAIN BEEFHEART). After marrying in the late 50's, he wrote a soundtrack for B-movie, 'The World's Greatest Sinner'. In 1963, after writing another B-movie soundtrack, 'Run Home Slow', he set up his own Studio Z. He also initiated local groups, The MASTERS and The SOUL GIANTS, who recorded some extremely rare 45's. In 1964, he was arrested and sentenced to 10 days in prison and put on probation for 3 years, having made a pornographic tape. He moved to Los Angeles and reformed The SOUL GIANTS, who soon evolved into The MOTHERS OF INVENTION. Early in 1966, after a residency at The Whiskey A-Go-Go, they were signed to 'M.G.M.' by producer Tom Wilson. Their debut album (a double!), 'FREAK OUT!', peaked at No.130 in the States, an avant-garde, satirical piece, that combined psych-pop/rock of songs such as, 'WHO ARE THE BRAIN POLICE' and 'HELP, I'M A ROCK'. The following year (1967), FRANK and his MOTHERS, unleashed another set of weird but wonderful songs on the 'ABSOLUTELY FREE' album. This contained seminal work with equally bizarre titles, 'CALL ANY VEGETABLE', 'SON OF SUZY CREAMCHEESE' and 'BROWN SHOES DON'T MAKE IT', the album nearly scratching the surface of the Top 40. On the 23rd of September '67, The MOTHERS played London's Albert Hall with a 15-piece orchestra, an arrangement he would take further on future albums. His third album, 'WE'RE ONLY IN IT FOR THE MONEY' was an obvious swipe at The BEATLES and their sleeve design for 'Sgt. Pepper's'. This was certainly FRANK and the band's most inventive work to date, the album taking a uniquely anti-drug/hippie stance. The tracks 'LET'S MAKE THE WATER TURN BLACK', 'MOM AND DAD' and 'FLOWER PUNK' being his swipe at America and the 60's counter-cultural establishment. His work continued apace, 'LUMPY GRAVY', 'CRUISING WITH RUBEN AND THE JETS' and 'UNCLE MEAT' all hitting the shelves in the space of a year. Late in 1969, FRANK released his first solo album, 'HOT RATS', which gave him deserved widespread critical acclaim, hitting Top 10 in Britain! The album forsook doo-wop and sardonic pastiche, for a more rock-based guitar extravaganza, the tracks 'PEACHES EN REGALIA' and the BEEFHEART-led 'WILLIE THE WIMP', becoming future ZAPPA jewels. For a few years to come, he combined MOTHERS albums with solo releases (normally with his entourage anyway), the best of these came in the form of live sets, including the double, 'FILLMORE EAST – JUNE 1971'. His commercial fortunes declined however, until The MOTHERS (who had just re-united) came back with the almost pornographic, 'OVERNITE SENSATION', which included the squealing, 'DINAH MOE HUMM'. A year later in 1974, he attacked the US charts once more with the Top 10 return to form, 'APOSTROPHE (')', which featured the cautionary, 'DON'T EAT THE YELLOW SNOW'. His work was now gaining more attention and a live album with his old buddy CAPTAIN BEEFHEART, reconciled their egotistical differences. In 1976, after securing a new deal with 'Warners', he unleashed another fine effort, 'ZOOT ALLURES', which contained some more risque ditties in the shape of the rocking, 'DISCO BOY' and 'FRIENDLY LITTLE FINGER'. After releasing a few instrumental albums, he was back again in 1979 with the 'SHEIK YERBOUTI' set, which included another dig at dance music, 'DANCIN' FOOL' and the cheeky 'BOBBY BROWN GOES DOWN'. The album 'JOE GARAGE' (ACTS 1, II & III) was split over two albums and a lot more was to come in the 80's. Although his work was still quite excellent during this period (i.e. 'SHIP ARRIVING TOO LATE TO SAVE A DROWNING WITCH' and 'THE MAN FROM UTOPIA' being his best), he returned to his favourite pastime of jazz and classical. In the early 90's, he was diagnosed with prostate cancer, and sadly he was to die on the 4th of December '93. • **Songwriters:** ZAPPA compositions, augmented by MOTHERS. Covered WHIPPING POST (Allman Brothers Band) / STAIRWAY TO HEAVEN (Led Zeppelin) / etc. • **Trivia:** In 1969, he married for a second time and was soon the father of sons, DWEEZIL (who became a guitarist in the 80's), AHMET RODAN, and daughters MOON UNIT and DIVA. In 1976, ZAPPA produced GRAND FUNK on their lp, 'Good Singin', Good Playin'.

Recommended: FREAK OUT (*9) / ABSOLUTELY FREE (*8) / WE'RE ONLY IN IT FOR THE MONEY (*8) / HOT RATS (*9) / ZOOT ALLURES (*8) / TINSEL TOWN REBELLION (*8) / THEM OR US (*9) / THING FISH (*6) / STRICTLY COMMERCIAL – THE BEST OF FRANK ZAPPA (*9)

The MOTHERS OF INVENTION

FRANK ZAPPA – guitar, vocals / with **RAY COLLINS** – vocals (had been temp.repl. by JIM GUERCIO; later a producer) / **ELLIOTT INGBER** – guitar repl. JIM FIELDER + STEVE MANN who had repl. HENRY VESTINE. Before he moved onto CANNED HEAT he had repl. MOTHERS original ALICE STUART. / **ROY ESTRADA** – bass / **JIM BLACK** – drums

Verve | Verve-MGM

1966. (7") *<10418>* **HELP, I'M A ROCK. / HOW COULD I BE SUCH A FOOL?** [-] [ ]

Nov 66. (7") *(VS 545)* **IT CAN'T HAPPEN HERE. / HOW COULD I BE SUCH A FOOL?** [ ] [-]

1966. (7") *<10458>* **TROUBLE EVERY DAY. / WHO ARE THE BRAIN POLICE?** [-] [ ]

Mar 67. (lp; stereo/mono) <US; d-lp+=*> *(S+/VLP 9154) <5005>* **FREAK OUT!** [ ] [ ] Aug66

– Hungry freaks, daddy / I ain't got no heart / Who are the brain police? / Go cry on somebody else's shoulder * / Motherly love / How could I be such a fool * / Wowie Zowie / You didn't try to call me / Any way the wind blows * / I'm not satisfied / You're probably wondering why I'm here / Trouble comin' every day / Help, I'm a rock / The return of the son of monster magnet. *(UK re-iss.Dec71 on 'Verve-Polydor' d-lp; 2683 004) (cd-iss.Oct87 on 'Zappa'; CDZAP 1) <Rykodisc'US> (cd re-iss.May95 on 'Rykodisc'; RCD 10501)*

— **JIM 'MOTORHEAD' SHERWOOD** – sax repl. INGBER who joined FRATERNITY OF MAN. He later changed his name and joined CAPTAIN BEEFHEART / added **BILLY MUNDI** – drums / **DON PRESTON** – keyboards / **BUNK GARDNER** – horns

Apr 67. (7") *(VS 557)* **BIG LEG EMMA. / WHY DON'T YOU DO ME RIGHT?** [ ] [-]

Oct 67. (lp; stereo/mono) *(S+/VLP 9174) <5013>* **ABSOLUTELY FREE** [ ] [41] May67

– Plastic people / The duke of prunes / Amnesia vivace / The Duke regains his chops / Call any vegetable / Invocation and ritual dance of the young pumpkin / Soft-cell conclusion and ending of side 1 / America drinks / Status back baby / Uncle Bernie's farm / Son of Suzy Creamcheese / Brown shoes don't make it / America drinks and goes home. *(re-iss.Jun72 on 'Verve-Polydor'; 2317 035) (cd-iss.Jan89 on 'Zappa'; CDZAP 12) ('Rykodisc' US version +=) (cd re-iss.May95 on 'Rykodisc'+=; RCD 10502)* – Big leg Emma / Why don'tcha do me right?.

— **ZAPPA, ESTRADA, MUNDI, PRESTON, GARDNER & JIMMY CARL BLACK** plus **IAN UNDERWOOD** – piano, wind repl. COLLINS

Dec 67. (7") *<10570>* **MOTHER PEOPLE. / LONELY LITTLE GIRL (version)** [-] [ ]

Jun 68. (lp; stereo/mono) *(S+/VLP 9199) <5045>* **WE'RE ONLY IN IT FOR THE MONEY** [32] [30] Jan68

– Are you hung up? / Who needs the peace corps? / Concentration Moon / Mom and dad / Telephone conversation / Bow tie daddy / Harry, you're a beast / What's the ugliest part of your body? / Absolutely free / Flower punk / Hot poop / Nasal retentive calliope music / Let's make the water turn black / The idiot bastard son / Lonely little girl / Take your clothes off when you dance / What's the ugliest part of your body (reprise) / Mother people / The chrome plated megaphone of destiny. *(re-iss.Jun72 on 'Verve-Polydor'; 2317 034) (re-iss.cd/c/lp Apr95 on 'Rykodisc'; RCD/RAC/RALP 10503)*

— (now with The ABNUCEALS EMUUKHA ELECTRIC SYMPHONY

ORCHESTRA & CHORUS; a 50+ piece orchestra incl. GARDNER + GUERIN + some other MOTHERS in choir)

Oct 68. (lp; stereo/mono; by FRANK ZAPPA) *(S+/VLP 9223)* *<8741>* **LUMPY GRAVY** [ ] [ ] May68
– Lumpy gravy (part one): The way I see it, Barry – Duodenum – Oh no – Bit of nostalgia – It's from Kansas – Bored out 90 over – Almost Chinese – Switching girls – Oh no again – At the gas station – Another pickup – I don't know if I can go through this again / Lumpy gravy (part two): Very distrautening – White ugliness – Amen – Just one more time – A vicious circle – King Kong – Drums are too noisy – Kangaroos – Envelopes the bath tub – Take your clothes off. *(re-iss.Jun72 on 'Verve-Polydor'; 2317 046) (cd-iss.Apr95 on 'Rykodisc'; RCD 10504)*

— **ARTHUR TRIPP III** – drums repl. MUNDI who formed RHINOCEROS / added again **RAY COLLINS** – vocals

Dec 68. (7") **DESERI. / JELLY ROLL GUM DROP** [-] [ ]

Feb 69. (lp; stereo/mono) *(S+/VLP 9237) <5055>* **CRUISING WITH RUBEN & THE JETS** [ ] [ ] Nov68
– Cheap thrills / Love of my life / How could I be such a fool / Deseri / I'm not satisfied / Jelly roll gum drop / Anything / Later that night / You didn't try to call me / Fountain of love / No no no / Anyway the wind blows * / Stuff up the cracks. *(re-iss.Jun73 on 'Verve-Polydor'; 2317 069) (cd-iss.Oct87 on 'Zappa'; CDZAP 4) ('Rykodisc'US) (re-iss.cd May95 on 'Rykodisc'; RCD 10505)*

Apr 69. (lp; stereo/mono) *(S+/VLP 9239) <5068>* **MOTHERMANIA: THE BEST OF THE MOTHERS** (compilation) [ ] [ ] Mar68
– Brown shoes don't make it / Mother people / Duke of prunes / Call any vegetable / The idiot bastard son / It can't happen here / You're probably wondering why I'm here / Who are the brain police? / Plastic people / Hungry freaks, daddy / America drinks and goes home. *(re-iss.Feb72 on 'Verve-Polydor'; 2317 047) (re-iss.Jul73 on 'Verve-Polydor'; 2352 017)*

— added **RUTH KOMANOFF** (UNDERWOOD) – marimba, vibes / **NELCY WALKER** – soprano vocals (on 2)

Transatlantic Bizarre

Sep 69. (d-lp) *(TRA 197) <2024>* **UNCLE MEAT** [ ] [43] Apr69
– Uncle Meat (main title theme) / The voice of cheese / Nine types of industrial pollution / Zolar Czakl / Dog breath in the year of the plague / The legend of the golden arches / Louie Louie (at the Royal Albert Hall in London) / The dog breath variations / Sleeping in a jar / Our bizarre relationship / The Uncle Meat variations / Electric Aunt Jemima // Prelude to King Kong / God bless America (live at the Whisky A Go Go) / A pound for a brown on the bus / Ian Underwood whips it out (live on stage in Copenhagen) / Mr. Green genes / We can shoot you / If we'd all been living in California / The air / Project X / Cruising for burgers / Uncle Meat film excerpt part I * / Tengo na minchia tanta * / Uncle Meat film excerpt part II * / King Kong itself (as played by The Mothers in a studio) / King Kong II (it's magnificence as interpreted by Dom Dewild) / King Kong III (as Motorhead explains it) / King Kong IV (the Gardner varieties) / King Kong V (as played by 3 deranged good humor trucks) / King Kong VI (live on a flat bed diesel in the middle of a race track at a Miami pop festival . . . the Underwood ramifications). *(d-cd-iss.Oct87 on 'Zappa' +=; CDZAP 3) (cd-iss.May95 on 'Rykodisc'; RCD 10506-7)*

Sep 69. (7") *<0840>* **MY GUITAR. / DOG BREATH** [-] [ ]

FRANK ZAPPA

— solo guitar w/ **UNDERWOOD** plus **CAPTAIN BEEFHEART** – vocals / **JEAN-LUC PONTY + SUGAR-CANE HARRIS** – violin / **MAX BENNETT + SHUGGY OTIS** – bass / **PAUL HUMPHREY + RON SELICO + JOHN GUERIN** – drums

Reprise Reprise

Jan 70. (7") *<0889>* **PEACHES EN REGALIA. / LITTLE UMBRELLAS** [-] [ ]

Feb 70. (lp) *(RSLP <6356>)* **HOT RATS** [9] [ ] Oct69
– Peaches en regalia / Willie the pimp / Son of Mr. Green genes / Little umbrellas / The Gumbo variations / It must be a camel. *(re-iss.Jul71; K 44078) (remixed cd-iss.Oct87 on 'Zappa'; CDZAP 2) (cd-iss.May95 on 'Rykodisc'; RCD 10508)*

The MOTHERS OF INVENTION

— (see last MOTHERS line-up) + add **BUZZ GARDNER** – horns / **SUGAR-CANE HARRIS** – violin (now without KOMANOFF)

Mar 70. (lp) *(RSLP <6370>)* **BURNT WEENY SANDWICH** [17] [94] Feb70
– WPLJ / Igor's boogie – phase 1 / Overture to a holiday in Berlin / Theme from Burnt Weenie Sandwich / Igor's boogie – phase 2 / Holiday in Berlin, full blown / Aybe sea / The little house I used to live in / Valarie. *(re-iss.Jul71; K 44083) (cd-iss.Nov91 on 'Zappa'; CDZAP 35) (re-iss.cd May95 on 'Rykodisc'; RCD 10509)*

Mar 70. (7") *<0892>* **WPLJ. / MY GUITAR** [-] [ ]

— (below album used rare material from 1967-69, as The MOTHERS OF INVENTION officially disbanded Oct69) guest LOWELL GEORGE – guitar

Sep 70. (lp) *(RSLP <2028>)* **WEASELS RIPPED MY FLESH** [28] [ ]
– Didja get any onya? / Directly from my heart to you / Prelude to the afternoon of a sexually aroused gas mask / Toads of the short forest / Get a little / Eric Dolphy memorial barbecue / Dwarf Nebula processional march and dwarf Nebula / My guitar wants to kill your mama / oh no / The Orange County lumber truck / Weasels ripped my flesh. *(re-iss.Jul71; K 44019) (cd-iss.May95 on 'Rykodisc'; RCD 10510)*

— LOWELL and ROY formed LITTLE FEAT. ART TRIPP became ED MARIMBA and joined CAPTAIN BEEFHEART & HIS MAGIC BAND. BUNK GARDNER and JIMMY CARL BLACK formed GERONIMO BLACK.

FRANK ZAPPA

— formed solo band with **IAN UNDERWOOD, SUGAR-CANE HARRIS & MAX BENNETT.** He introduced **JEFF SIMMONS** – bass / **JOHN GUERIN** – drums / **AYNSLEY DUNBAR** – drums / **GEORGE DUKE** – keyboards, trombone / **MARK VOLMAN + HOWARD KAYLAN** (aka The PHLORESCENT LEECH AND EDDIE) – vocals (ex-TURTLES)

Nov 70. (lp) *(RSLP <2030>)* **CHUNGA'S REVENGE** [43] [ ]
– Transylvania boogie / Road ladies / Twenty small cigars / The Nancy and Mary music (part 1, 2 & 3) / Tell me you love me / Would you go all the way? / Chunga's revenge / The clap / Rudy wants to buy yez a drink / Sharleena. *(re-iss.Jul71; K 44020) (cd-iss.Jun90 on 'Zappa'; CDZAP 23) (cd-iss.May95 on 'Rykodisc'; RCD 10511)*

Nov 70. (7") *<0967>* **TELL ME YOU LOVE ME. / WOULD YOU GO ALL THE WAY?** [-] [ ]

The MOTHERS

— re-formed early 1971 and retained **DON PRESTON** – mini moog / **DUNBAR / VOLMAN & KAYLAN** — and recruited **JIM PONS** – bass (ex-TURTLES) / **BOB HARRIS** – keyboards

Aug 71. (lp) *(K 44150) <2042>* **FILLMORE EAST - JUNE 1971 (live)** [ ] [38]
– Little house I used to live in / The mud shark / What kind of girl do you think we are? / Bwana Dik / Latex solar beef / Willie the pimp (part 1) / Do you like my new car? / Happy together / Lonesome electric turkey / Peaches en regalia / Tears began to fall. *(cd-iss.Jun90 on 'Zappa'; CDZAP 29) (cd re-iss.May95 on 'Rykodisc'; RCD 10512)*

Aug 71. (7") *(K 14100) <1052>* **TEARS BEGAN TO FALL. / JUNIER MINTZ BOOGIE** [ ] [ ]

FRANK ZAPPA

— solo, with MOTHERS:- **IAN + RUTH UNDERWOOD / GEORGE DUKE / AYNSLEY DUNBAR / VOLMAN + KAYLAN / MARTIN LICKERT** – bass / guests were **JIM PONS + JIMMY CARL BLACK / THEODORE BIKEL** – narrator + ROYAL PHILHARMONIC ORCHESTRA

U.A. U.A.

Oct 71. (d-lp) *(UDF 50003) <9956>* **200 MOTELS (live studio soundtrack)** [ ] [59]
– Semi-fraudulent – Direct-from-Hollywood overture / Mystery roach / Dance of the rock & roll interviewers / This town is a sealed tuna sandwich (prologue) / Tuna fish promenade / Dance of the just plain folks / This town is a sealed tuna fish sandwich (reprise) / The sealed tuna bolero / Lonesome cowboy Burt / Touring can make you crazy / Would you like a snack? / Redneck eats / Centerville / She painted up her face / Janet's big dance number / Half a dozen provocative squats / Mysterioso / Shove it right in / Lucy's seduction of a bored violinist & postlude / I'm stealing the towels / Dental hygeine dilemma / Does this kind of life look interesting to you? / Daddy, daddy, daddy / Penis dimension / What will this evening bring me this morning / A nun suit painted on some old boxes / Magic fingers / Motorhead's midnight ranch / Dew on the newts we got / The lad searches the night for his newts / The girl wants to fix him some broth / The girl's dream / Little green scratchy sweaters & corduroy ponce / Strictly genteel (the finale). *(re-iss.Jan89 on 'M.C.A.' d-lp/c; MCA/+C 24183)*

Oct 71. (7") *<50857>* **MAGIC FINGERS. / DADDY, DADDY, DADDY** [-] [ ]

Nov 71. (7") *(UP 35319)* **WHAT WILL THIS EVENING BRING ME THIS MORNING?. / DADDY, DADDY, DADDY** [ ] [-]

— now with a plethera of musicians (see next solo also), including some MOTHERS

Reprise Reprise

Aug 72. (lp) *(K 44203) <2094>* **WAKA/JAWAKA: HOT RATS** [ ] [ ]
– Big Swifty / Your mouth / It just might be a one-shot deal / Waka-Jawaka. *(cd-iss.Jan89 on 'Zappa'; CDZAP 10) (re-iss.cd May95 on 'Rykodisc'; RCD 10516)*

— (above featured **PRESTON, DUNBAR, DUKE, SIMMONS** & others also on next).

The MOTHERS

— recorded live 7th August'71. (see last ZAPPA line-up) Re-formed earlier that year minus BOB HARRIS

Reprise Bizarre

Jun 72. (lp) *(K 44179) <2075>* **JUST ANOTHER BAND FROM L.A.** [ ] [85]
– Billy the mountain / Call any vegetable / Eddie, are you kidding? / Magdalena / Dog breath. *(cd-iss.Jun90 on 'Zappa'; CDZAP 10515) (cd re-iss.May95 on 'Rykodisc'; RCD 10515)*

— The MOTHERS added **TONY DURAN** – slide guitar / **ERRONEOUS** – bass repl. SIMMONS / **KEN SHROYER** – trombone / **JOEL PESKIN** – tenor saxophone / **SAL MARQUEZ** – timpani / **BILL BYERS** – trombone / **MIKE ALTSCHUL** – wind / **JANET NEVILLE-FERGUSON** – vocals / **CHUNKY** – vocals / **EARL DUMLER, FRED JACKSON + TONY ORTEGA** – wind / **ERNIE WATTS** – sax / **ERNIE TACK + MALCOLM McNABB** – horns / **JOHNNY ROTELLA, BOB ZIMMITTI + LEE CLEMENT** – percussion / **JOANNE CALDWELL McNABB** – violin

Dec 72. (lp) *(K 44209)* **THE GRAND WAZOO** [ ] [-]
– The grand Wazoo / For Calvin (and his next two hitch-hikers) / Cletus-awreetus-awrightus / Eat that question / Blessed relief. *(cd-iss.Sep90 on 'Zappa'; CDZAP 31) (cd re-iss.May95 on 'Rykodisc'; RCD 10517)*

Dec 72. (7") *<1127>* **CLETUS-AWREETUS-AWRIGHTUS. / EAT THAT QUESTION** [-] [ ]

— **ZAPPA** brought back **IAN + RUTH UNDERWOOD** (They were on '72 tour) / **GEORGE DUKE / JEAN-LUC PONTY / SAL MARQUEZ.** He introduced **TOM FOWLER** – bass / **BRUCE FOWLER** – trombone / **RALPH HUMPHREY** – drums

DiscReet DiscReet

Jan 73. (lp) *(K 41000) <2149>* **OVERNITE SENSATION** [ ] [32]
– Camarillo brillo / I'm the slime / Dirty love / Fifty-fifty / Zomby woof / Dinah-Moe humm / Montana. *<cd-iss.Oct87 w / 'APOSTROPHE' tracks on 'Rykodisc'> (cd-iss.Jul90 on 'Zappa'; CDZAP 36) (re-iss.cd/c Apr95 on 'Rykodisc'; RCD/RAC 10518)*

Feb 73. (7") *<1180>* **I'M THE SLIME. / MONTANA** [-] [ ]

FRANK ZAPPA

— solo retaining current MOTHERS. He also brought back past MOTHERS: **AYNSLEY DUNBAR / RAY COLLINS / ERRONEOUS / JOHN GUERIN / SUGAR CANE HARRIS / RUBEN GUEVARA + ROBERT CAMARENA** – b.vocals (of RUBEN &..JETS) **NAPOLEON BROCK** – saxophone / guest **JACK BRUCE** – bass (ex-CREAM)

May 74. (lp/c) *(K/K4 59201) <2175>* **APOSTROPHE'** [ ] [10] Apr74
– Don't eat the yellow snow / Nanook rubs it / St. Alphonzo's pancake breakfast / Father O'Blivion / Cosmik debris / Excentrifugal forz / Apostrophe / Uncle Remus / Stink-foot. *(re-iss.cd/c Apr95 on 'Rykodisc'; RCD/RAC 10519) (cd-version-iss.Jun96; RCD 80519)*

Aug 74. (7") *<1312>* **DON'T EAT THE YELLOW SNOW. / COSMIK DEBRIS** [-] [86]

Aug 74. (7") *(K 19201)* **COSMIK DEBRIS. / UNCLE REMUS** [ ] [-]

Sep 74. (7") *(K 19202)* **DON'T EAT THE YELLOW SNOW. / CAMARILLO BRILLO** [ ] [-]

— were now basically **GEORGE DUKE / TOM FOWLER / NAPOLEON / RUTH UNDERWOOD** and new drummer **CHESTER THOMPSON**. Temp. old members were also used **DON PRESTON / BRUCE + WALT FOWLER / JEFF SIMMONS + RALPH HUMPHREY**

Oct 74. (d-lp/c; ZAPPA / MOTHERS) *(K/K4 69201) <2202>* **ROXY & ELSEWHERE (live + unreleased)** ☐ 27 Sep74
– Preamble / Penguin in bondage / Pygmy twylyte / Dummy up / Preamble / Village of the sun / Echidna's arf (of you) / Don't you ever wash that thing? / Preamble / Cheepnis / Son of Orange County / More trouble every day / Be-bop tango (of old Jazzmen's church). *(cd-iss.Feb92 on 'Zappa'; CDZAP 39) (re-iss.cd/c May95 on 'Rykodisc'; RCD/RAC 10520)*

— temp.members above repl. by **JOHNNY GUITAR WATSON** – vocals / **JAMES YOUMAN** – bass / **BLOODSHOT ROLLIN RED** (DON WATSON) – harmonica

Aug 75. (lp; by FRANK ZAPPA & THE MOTHERS OF INVENTION) *(K 59207) <2216>* **ONE SIZE FITS ALL** ☐ 26
– Inca roads / Can't afford no shoes / Sofa No.1 / Po-jama people / Florentine pogen / Evelyn, a modified dog / San Ber'dino / Andy / Sofa No.2. *(cd-iss.Jan89 on 'Zappa'; CDZAP 11) (re-iss.cd May95 on 'Rykodisc'; RCD 10521)*

Sep 75. (7"; by FRANK ZAPPA & THE MOTHERS OF INVENTION) *(K 19205)* **STINK-FOOT. / DU BIST MEIN SOFA** ☐ -

— next a collaboration with **CAPTAIN BEEFHEART** with also **DUKE / FOWLER's / BROCK / THOMPSON** plus **TERRY BOZZIO** – drums / **DENNY WALLEY**– slide guitar

Nov 75. (lp; by FRANK ZAPPA, CAPTAIN BEEFHEART & THE MOTHERS) *(K 59209; w-drawn) <2234>* **BONGO FURY (live + 2 studio)** - 66
– Debra Kadabra / Caroline hard-core ecstasy / Sam with the showing scalp flat top / Poofter's froth Wyoming plans ahead / 200 years old / Cucamonga / Advance romance / Man with the woman head / Muffin man. *(cd-iss.Jan89 on 'Zappa'; CDZAP 15) <US 'Rykodisc'; RY 10097> (re-iss.cd May95 on 'Rykodisc'; RCD 10522)*

FRANK ZAPPA

— finally disbanded The MOTHERS and went solo. Augmented by **TERRY BOZZIO** – drums / **ROY ESTRADA, DAVE PARLATO + RUTH UNDERWOOD** – marimba, synth / **DAVEY MOIRE** – b.vocals / **LU ANN NEIL** – harp / **ANDRE LEWIS** – backing vocals

Warners Warners

Oct 76. (7") *<8296>* **FIND HER FINER. / ZOOT ALLURES** - ☐
Nov 76. (lp/c) *(K/K4 56298) <2970>* **ZOOT ALLURES** ☐ 61
– Wind up workin' in a gas station / Black napkins / The torture never stops / Ms. Pinky / Find her finer / Friendly little finger / Wonderful wino / Zoot allures / Disco boy. *(cd-iss.Jun90 on 'Zappa'; CDZAP 22) (re-iss.cd May95 on 'Rykodisc'; RCD 10523)*
Dec 76. (7") *<8342>* **DISCO BOY. / MS. PINKY** - ☐

— His basic band were **EDDIE JOBSON** – keyboards, violin (ex-ROXY MUSIC) / **RAY WHITE** – guitar, vocals / **PAT O'HEARN** – bass / **RUTH UNDERWOOD** – / **TERRY BOZZIO** – drums. Plus brass section – **RANDY + MICHAEL BRECKER / LOU MARINI / RONNIE CUBER / TOM MALONE / DAVID SAMUELS** – percussion

DiscReet DiscReet

Jun 78. (d-lp) *(K 69204) <2290>* **ZAPPA IN NEW YORK (live 1976)** 55 57
– Titties & beer / Cruisin' for burgers * / I promise not to come in your mouth / Punky's whips *[not on some]* / Honey, don't you want a man like me? / The Illinois enema bandit // I'm the slime * / Pound for a brown * / Manx needs women / The black page drum solo – Black page £1 / Big leg Emma / Sofa / Black page £2 / The torture never stops * / The purple lagoon – approximate. *(cd-iss.Sep91 on 'Zappa'; CDDZAP 37) (cd re-iss.May95 on 'Rykodisc'+= *; RCD 10524-5)*
Nov 78. (lp/c) *(K/K4 59210) <2291>* **STUDIO TAN** (2 instrumental 74-76) ☐ ☐
– The adventures of Greggery Peccary / Revised music for guitar and low budget orchestra / Lemme take you to the beach / RDNZL. *(cd-iss.May95 on 'Rykodisc'; RCD 10526)*
Feb 79. (lp/c) *(K/K4 59211) <2292>* **SLEEP DIRT** (mostly instrumental 74-76) ☐ ☐
– Filthy habits / Flambay / Spider of destiny / Regyptian strut / Time is money / Sleep dirt / The ocean is the ultimate solution. *(cd-iss.Oct91 on 'Zappa'; CDZAP 43) (cd re-iss.May95 on 'Rykodisc'; RCD 10527)*

— He retained only **BOZZIO + O'HEARN,** bringing back **NAPOLEON, ANDRE LEWIS + MOIRE.** New musicians:- **ADRIAN BELEW** – rhythm guitar, some lead vox / **TOMMY MARS** – keyboards, vocals / **PETER WOLF** – keyboards / **ED MANN** – percussion, vocals / **RANDY THORNTON** – b.vocals / **DAVID OCKER** – clarinet (1)

Zappa-CBS Zappa

Mar 79. (d-lp/d-c) *(CBS/40 88339) <1501>* **SHEIK YERBOUTI** 32 21
– I have been in you / Flakes / Broken hearts are for assholes / I'm so cute / Jones crusher / What ever happened to all the fun in the world / Rat tomago / Wait a ninute / Bobby Brown goes down / Rubber shirt / The Sheik Yerbouti tango / Baby snakes / Tryin' to grow a chin / City of tiny lites / Dancin' fool / Jewish princess / Wild love / Yo' mama. *(re-iss.Feb86 on 'E.M.I.' d-lp/d-c; EN/TCEN 5001) (cd-iss.Apr88; CDEN 5001) (cd re-iss.Jun91 on 'Zappa'; CDZAP 28) (re-iss.cd/c May95 on 'Rykodisc'; RCD/RAC 10528)*
Apr 79. (7") *(SCBS 7261) <10>* **DANCIN' FOOL. / BABY SNAKES** ☐ 45

— **WARREN CUCURULLO** – rhythm guitar repl. BELEW (later to BOWIE + TALKING HEADS) **/IKE WILLIS** – lead vocals / **ARTHUR BARROW** – bass repl. O'HEARN / **VINNIE COLAIUTA** – drums repl. TERRY BOZZIO. Others in line-up **DALE BOZZIO** – vocals / **DENNIS WALLEY** – slide guitar / **MARGINAL CHAGRIN** – sax / **WOLF + MANN.**

Sep 79. (lp/c) *(CBS/40 86101) <1603>* **JOE'S GARAGE ACT I** 62 27
– Central scrutinizer / Joe's garage / Catholic girls / Crew slut / Fembot in a wet T-shirt / On the bus / Why does it hurt when I pee? / Lucille has messed my mind up / Scrutinizer postlude. *<d-cd-iss.Oct87 on 'Rykodisc'; RCD 10060> (UK d-cd-iss.Sep90 on 'Zappa'; CDZAP 20) (d-cd re-iss.May95; RCD 10530-31)*
Jan 80. (7") **JOE'S GARAGE. / CENTRAL SCRUTINIZER** - ☐
Jan 80. (7") *(SCBS 7950)* **JOE'S GARAGE. / CATHOLIC GIRLS** ☐ -

— now without DALE, MARS + CHAGRIN

Jan 80. (d-lp/d-c) *(CBS/40 88475) <1502>* **JOE'S GARAGE ACT II & III** 75 53
– ACT II:- A token of my extreme / Stick it out / Sy Borg / Dong work for Yuda / Keep it greasey / Outside now / ACT III:- He used to cut the grass / Packard goose / Watermelon in Easter hay / A little green Rosetta. *<US d-cd-iss.Oct87 on 'Rykodisc'; RCD 10061>*
Jun 80. (7") *(SCBS 8652) <ZR 1001>* **I DON'T WANT TO GET DRAFTED. / ANCIENT ARMAMENTS** ☐ ☐

— now with **STEVE VAI + RAY WHITE + IKE WILLIS** – rhythm guitar, vocals / **TOMMY MARS** – keyboards / **BOB HARRIS** – keyboards, trumpet, high vox / **ED MANN / BARROW** – bass / **COLAIUTA / WOLF**

Barking Pumpkin-CBS Barking Pumpkin-CBS

May 81. (d-lp/d-c) *(CBS/40 88516) <37336>* **TINSELTOWN REBELLION (live)** 55 66
– Fine girl / Easy meat / For the young sophisticate / Love of my life / I ain't got no heart / Panty rap / Tell me you love me / Now you see it – now you don't / Dance contest / The blue light / Tinseltown rebellion / Pick me, I'm clean / Bamboozled by love / Brown shoes don't make it / Peaches III. *(re-iss.Feb86 on 'E.M.I.' d-lp/d-c; EN/TCEN 5002) (d-cd-iss.Apr88; CDEN 5002) (cd-iss.Jun90 on 'Zappa'; CDZAP 26) (re-iss.cd May95 on 'Rykodisc'; RCD 10532)*

— **JIMMY CARL BLACK** – guest vocals returned (+ daughter MOON, son AHMET) to repl. CUCURULLO / WOLF / COLAIUTA and O'HEARN. new members:- **DAVID OCKER** – – clarinet / **PAT O'HEARN** – bass / **SHERWOOD** – sax (returned) / **DAVID LOGEMAN** – drums

Oct 81. (d-lp/d-c) *(CBS/40 88560) <37537>* **YOU ARE WHAT YOU IS** 51 93
– Teenage wind / Harder than your husband / Doreen / Goblin girl / Theme from the 3rd movement of sinister footwear / Society pages / I'm a beautiful guy / Beauty knows no pain / Charlie's enormous mouth / Any downers? / Conehead / You are what you is / Mudd club / The meek shall inherit nothing / Dumb all over / Heavenly bank account / Suicide chump / Jumbo go away / If only she woulda / Drafted again. *(re-iss.Feb86 on 'E.M.I.' d-lp/d-c; EN/TCEN 5000) (d-cd-iss.Apr88; CDEN 5000) (cd-iss.Jun90 on 'Zappa'; CDZAP 27) (re-iss.cd May95 on 'Rykodisc'; RCD 10536)*
Nov 81. (12"pic-d) *<BPRP 114>* **GOBLIN GIRL. / PINK NAPKINS** - ☐
Feb 82. (7") *(A 1622)* **YOU ARE WHAT YOU IS. / HARDER THAN YOUR HUSBAND** ☐ ☐
(12"pic-d+=) *(A12 1622)* – Pink napkins / Soup'n'old clothes.

— added **SCOTT THUNES** – bass / **CHAD WACKERMAN** – drums / **BOBBY MARTIN** – keyboards, sax / vocalists ROY ESTRADA, LISA POPIEL / MOON, who replaced WALLEY, LOGEMAN, SHERWOOD, OCKER, STEWART, BLACK + AHMET

Jun 82. (lp/c) *(CBS/40 85804) <38066>* **SHIP ARRIVING TOO LATE TO SAVE A DROWNING WITCH** 61 23
– No not now / Valley girl / I come from nowhere / Drowning witch / Envelopes / Teen-age prostitute. *(free 7"w.a.) (XPS 147)* – SHUT UP 'N' PLAY YER GUITAR. / VARIATION ON THE C. SANTANA SECRET *(re-iss.Feb86 on 'E.M.I.' lp/c; EMC/TCEMC 3501) (re-iss.Jun87 on 'Fame' lp/c; FA/TCFA 3180) (cd-iss.Aug91 on 'Zappa'; CDZAP 42) (re-iss.cd May95 on 'Rykodisc'; RCD 10537)*
Jul 82. (7")(12") *<02972><03069>* **VALLEY GIRL. / YOU ARE WHAT YOU IS** - 32
Aug 82. (7"; by FRANK & MOON ZAPPA) *(A 2412) <02972>* **VALLEY GIRL. / TEENAGE PROSTITUTE** ☐ -

— **MYRTY KRYSTALL** – sax repl.MOON + POPIEL / **DICK FEGY** – mandolin / also added **CRAIG STEWARD** – harmonica

Jun 83. (lp/c) *(CBS/40 25251) <38403>* **THE MAN FROM UTOPIA** 87 ☐
– Cocaine decisions / Sex / Tink walks amok / The radio is broken / We are not alone / The dangerous kitchen / The man from Utopia meets Mary Lou / Stick together / The jazz discharge party hats / Luigi & the wise guys * / Moggio. *(re-iss.Feb86 on 'E.M.I.' lp/c; EMC/TCEMC 3500) (re-iss.Apr88 on 'Fame' lp/c)(cd; FA/TCFA 3203)(CDP 790074-2) (cd-iss.Feb93 on 'Zappa'+= *; CDZAP 53) (re-iss.cd May95 on 'Rykodisc'; RCD 10538)*

— **JOHNNY GUITAR WATSON + NAPOLEON MURPHY BROCK** – vocals repl. STEWARD, FEGY, KRISTALL (+ COLAIUTA) other guest his son DWEEZIL ZAPPA – guitar solos (2)

E.M.I. Rykodisc

Sep 84. (7") *(EMI 5499)* **BABY TAKE YOUR TEETH OUT. / STEVIE'S SPANKING** ☐ ☐
Oct 84. (d-lp/d-c) *(FZD/+TC 1) <R 40027>* **THEM OR US** 53 ☐
– The closer you are / In France / Ya hozna / Sharleena / Sinister footwear II / Truck driver divorce / Stevie's spanking / Baby take your teeth out / Marqueson's chicken / Planet of my dreams / Be in my video / Them or us / Frogs with dirty, little lips / Whippin' post. *(cd-iss.Apr88; CDEN 24) (cd re-iss.Apr91 on 'Zappa'; CDZAP 30) (re-iss.cd May95 on 'Rykodisc'; RCD 10543)*
1984. (lp) **FRANCESCO ZAPPA** - ☐
(UK cd-iss.May92 on 'Zappa'; CDZAP 48) (cd re-iss.May95 on 'Rykodisc'; RCD 10546)

— (above was conducted by FRANK, and taken from pieces of music from an Italian musician circa 1973-1988)

— **ZAPPA** with band: **VAI, MARS, WHITE, MANN, WACKERMAN, BARROW, THUNES** plus **STEVE DE FURIA & DAVID OCKER** – synclavier programmer. Characters: **IKE WILLIS** (Thing Fish) / **TERRY BOZZIO** (Harry) / His wife **DALE BOZZIO** (Rhonda) / **NAPOLEON MURPHY BROCK** (Evil Prince) / **BOB HARRIS** (Harry as a boy) / **JOHNNY GUITAR WATSON** (Brown Moses) / **RAY WHITE** (Owl Gonkwin Jane Cowhoon)

E.M.I. Capitol

Mar 85. (t-lp/d-c) *(EX240294-1/-4) <R 10020>* **THING FISH** ☐ ☐
– Prologue / The mammy nuns / Harry & Rhonda / Galoot up-date / The 'torchum' never stops / That evil prince / You are what you is / Mudd club / The meek shall inherit nothing / Clowns on velvet / Harry-as-a-boy / He's so gay / The massive improve'lence / Artificial Rhonda / The crab-grass baby / The white boy troubles / No not now / Briefcase boogie / Brown Moses / Wistful wit a fist-full / Drop dead / Won ton on. *(d-cd-iss.Apr88; CDFZ 3) (d-cd-iss.Feb90 on 'Zappa'; CDDZAP 21) (re-iss.d-cd May95 on 'Rykodisc'; RCD 10544-45)*

— In Jun'85, PIERRE BOULEZ released his versions of ZAPPA, under the title 'THE PERFECT STRANGER – BOULEZ CONDUCTS ZAPPA'. Later issued in the UK on cd on 'Rykodisc'; *RCD 10542)*

— musicians; as last but without BOZZIO's, BARROW, BROCK, HARRIS **BOBBY MARTIN** – vocals, keyboards repl. DE FURIA + OCKER

Mar 86. (lp/c) *(EMC/TCEMC 3507) <ST 74203>* **FRANK ZAPPA MEETS THE MOTHERS OF PREVENTION** ☐ ☐

– Porn wars / We're turning again / Alien orifice / Aerobics in bondage / I don't even care * / Little beige sambo / What's new in Baltimore / One man, one vote * / H.R. 2911 *. *(cd-iss.Sep90 on 'Zappa'; CDZAP 33)*– repl. Porn wars; w/ *) *(cd-iss.May95 on 'Rykodisc' all tracks; RCD 10547)*

— now ZAPPA on synclavier only + one live from '82. others:- **VAI, WHITE, MARS, MARTIN, MANN, THUNES, WACKERMAN**

Dec 86. (lp/c) *(EMC/TCEMC 3521)* **JAZZ FROM HELL** ☐ ☐
– Night school / The Beltway bandits / While you were art II / Jazz from Hell / G-spot tornado / Damp ankles / St.Etienne / Massaggio galore. *(cd-iss.Sep90 on 'Zappa'; CDZAP 32) (cd-iss.May95 on 'Rykodisc'; RCD 10549)*

— **FRANK** still with **WILLIS, WACKERMAN, THUNES, MANN, MARTIN,** plus new **MIKE KENEALLY** – guitar, synth., vocals repl. VAI who went solo, etc. / **WALT FOWLER** – trumpet / **BRUCE FOWLER** – trombone / **PAUL CARMAN** – alto sax / **ALBERT WING** – tenor sax / **KURT McGETTRICK** – baritone sax / guest vox – **ERIC BUXTON**

Zappa Zappa

Dec 88. (lp/c/cd) *(ZAPPA/TZAPPA/CDDZAP 14)* **BROADWAY THE HARD WAY (live)** ☐ ☐
– Elvis has just left the building / Planet of the baritone women / Any kind of pain / Dickie's such an asshole / When the lie's so big / Rhymin' man / Promiscuous / The untouchables / Why don't you like me? * / Bacon fat * / Stolen moments * / Murder by numbers * / Jezebel boy * / Outside now * / Hot plate heaven at the green hotel * / What kind of a girl? * / Jesus thinks you're a jerk. *(cd+= *) (re-iss.cd May95 on 'Rykodisc'; RCD 10552)*

— Late '91, it was announced FRANK had been diagnosed with prostrate cancer. He was to die of this on 4th Dec'93.

Feb 93. (12"/cd-s) *(12/CD FRANK 101)* **STAIRWAY TO HEAVEN. / BOLERO** ☐ ☐

— next with the ENSEMBLE MODERN, conducted by himself & PETER RUNDEL

Oct 93. (cd/c) *(CDZAP/TZAPPA 57)* **YELLOW SHARK (live)** ☐ ☐
– Intro / Dog breath variations / Uncle Meat / Outrage at Valdez / Times beach II / III revised / The girl in the magnesium dress / Be bop tango / Ruth is sleeping / None of the above / Pentagon afternoon / Questi cazzi di piccione / Times beach III / Food gathering in post industrial America 1992 / Welcome to the united States / Pound for a brown / Exercise 4 / Get Whitey / G-spot tornado. *(re-iss.cd/c May95 on 'Rykodisc'; RCD/RAC 40560)*

— an opera-pantomime with pre-recorded voices and music supplied by THE PIANO PEOPLE: **F.Z. / SPIDER / JOHN / MOTORHEAD / LARRY / ROY / LOUIS / MONICA / GILLY / GIRL 1 / GIRL 2 / MOON / MIKE / ALI / TODD / DARYL / JESUS**

Feb 95. (d-cd/d-c) *(CDDZAP/TZAPPA 56)* **CIVILIZATION PHAZE III** ☐ ☐
– ACT ONE; This is phaze III / Put a motor in yourself / Oh-umm / They made me eat it / Reagan at Bitburg / A very nice body / Navanax / How the pigs' music works / Xmas values / Dark water / Amnerika / Have you ever heard their band / Religious superstition / Saliva can only take so much / Buffalo voice / Someplace else right now / Get a life / A kayak (on snow) / N-lite (I) Negative light (II) Venice submerged (III) The new world order (IV) The lifestyle you deserve (V) Creationism (VI) He is risen / / ACT TWO; I wish Motorhead would come back / Secular humanism / Attack! attack! attack! / I was in a drum / A different octave / This ain't CNN / The pigs' music / A pig with wings / This is all wrong / Hot & putrid / Flowing inside-out / I had a dream about that / Gross man / A tunnel into muck / Why not? / Put a little motor in 'em / You're just insultin' me, aren't you! / Cold light generation / Dio fa / That would be the end of that / Beat the reaper / Waffenspiel.

– compilations, others, etc. –

1975. (lp; by ZAPPA & THE MOTHERS) *Verve-Polydor; (2352 057)* **ROCK FLASHBACKS** ☐ [-]

Jun 79. (lp/c) *DiscReet; (K/K4 59212) <2294>* **ORCHESTRAL FAVORITES (live 1975)** ☐ ☐
– Strictly genteel / Pedro's dowry / Naval aviation in art? / Duke of prunes / Bogus pomp. *(cd-iss.May95 on 'Rykodisc')*

— Next vocal-less **ZAPPA** – lead guitar plus usual ensemble.

Aug 82. (t-lp) *Barking Pumpkin-CBS; (66368)* **SHUT UP 'N PLAY YER GUITAR** (rec.1977-80 live) ☐ ☐
– Five, five, five / Hog heaven / Pink napkins / Stucco homes / Variations on the C. Santana secret chord progression / Gee I like your pants / Soup 'n old clothes / The deathless horsie / Shut up 'n play yer guitar (x2) / Heavy duty Judy / The return of shut up 'n play yer guitar / Canard du joir / While you were out / Pinocchio's furniture / Beat it with your fist / Why Johnny can't read / Canarsie / Treacherous cretins. *(re-iss.Apr88 on 'E.M.I.' t-lp/d-cd; FZAP/CDFZ 2) (d-cd-re-iss.Jan90 on 'Zappa'; CDDZAP 19) (re-iss.t-cd May95 on 'Rykodisc'; RCD 10533-34-35)*

Feb 86. (cd) *E.M.I.; (CDP 746188-2)* **DOES HUMOR BELONG IN MUSIC** ☐ ☐
(re-iss.Apr95 on 'Rykodisc' cd/c; RCD/RAC 10548)

Jul 87. (lp-box) *Barking Pumpkin; (BPR 7777)* **OLD MASTERS – BOX ONE** ☐ ☐
– FREAK OUT / ABSOLUTELY FREE / WE'RE ONLY IN IT FOR THE MONEY / LUMPY GRAVY / CRUISIN' WITH RUBEN & THE JETS / (Mystery Disc – rare).

Jul 87. (lp-box) *Barking Pumpkin; (BPR 8888)* **OLD MASTERS – BOX TWO** ☐ ☐
– UNCLE MEAT / HOT RATS / BURNT WEENIE SANDWICH / WEASELS RIPPED MY FLESH / CHUNGA'S REVENGE / LIVE AT THE FILLMORE EAST / JUST ANOTHER BAND FROM L.A. / (Mystery Disc – live in London 1968).

Oct 87. (cd) *Rykodisc; <RCD 40025>* **APOSTROPHE / OVERNIGHT SENSATION** [-] ☐

Oct 87. (3"cd-ep) *Rykodisc;* **PEACHES EN REGALIA / I'M NOT SATISFIED / LUCILLE HAS MESSED UP MY MIND** [-] ☐

Nov 87. (lp-box) *Barking Pumpkin; (BPR 9999)* **OLD MASTERS – BOX THREE** ☐ ☐
– OVERNITE SENSATION / ONE SIZE FITS ALL / WAKA JAWAKA / THE GRAND WAZOO / APOSTROPHE / BONGO FURY / ZOOT ALLURES / ROXY AND ELSEWHERE.

Jan 88. (lp/c/cd) *Zappa; (ZAPPA/TZAPPA/CDDZAP 5)* **THE LONDON SYMPHONY ORCHESTRA VOL.II** (out-takes from'200 MOTELS') ☐ ☐
– Bob in Dacron / Strictly genteel / Bogus bomp. *(cd+=)*– (2 extra tracks).

Apr 88. (d-lp/c/cd) *Zappa/ US= Barking Pumpkin; (ZAPPA/TZAPPA/CDDZAP 6)* **GUITAR** (rec.live 1979-84) [82] ☐
– Sexual harassment in the workplace / Which one is it? * / Republicans / Do not pass go / Chalk pie * / In-a-gadda-Stravinsky * / That's not really reggae / When no one was no one / Once again, without the net / Outside now (original solo) / Jim and Tammy's upper room / Were we ever really safe in San Antonio? / That ol' G minor thing again / Hotel Atlanta incidentals * / That's not really a shuffle * / Move it or park it / Sunrise redeemer // Variations on sinister £3 * / Orrin Hatch on skis * / But who was Fulcanelli? / For Duane / Goa / Winos do not march / Swans? what swans? * / Too ugly for show business * / Systems of edges / Do not try this at home * / Things that look like meat / Watermelon in Easter hay / Canadian customs * / Is that all there is? * / It ain't necessarily the St. James Infirmary *. *(cd+= *) (re-iss.cd May95 on 'Rykodisc'; RCD 10550-51)*

Apr 88. (cd) *EMI/ US= Capitol;* **THE MAN FROM UTOPIA / SHIP ARRIVING TOO LATE TO SAVE THE DROWNING WITCH** ☐ [-]

Apr 88. (2xt-lp-box) *E.M.I.; (FZAP 1)* **JOE'S GARAGE ACTS I / II / III / SHUT UP AND PLAY YER GUITAR** ☐ ☐

Apr 88. (d-lp) *Zappa; (ZAPPA 7)* **YOU CAN'T DO THAT ON STAGE ANYMORE SAMPLER** ☐ ☐
(d-cd-iss.Jan90; CDZAP 7)

Apr 88. (3"cd-s) *Rykodisc;* **SEXUAL HARASSMENT IN THE WORKPLACE / WATERMELON IN EASTER HAY** [-] ☐

May 88. (3"cd-s) *Rykodisc;* **ZOMBY WOOF / YOU DIDN'T TRY TO CALL ME** [-] ☐

May 88. (3"cd-s) *Rykodisc;* **MONTANA (WHIPPING FLOSS) / CHEEPNIS** [-] ☐

May 88. (d-cd) *Zappa; (CDZAP 8)* **YOU CAN'T DO THAT ON STAGE ANYMORE VOL.2** ☐ ☐
(re-iss.Jul95 on 'Rykodisc'; RCD 10561-62)

May 88. (cd) *E.M.I.; (CDP 790078-2)* **ZAPPA MEETS THE MOTHERS OF PREVENTION / JAZZ FROM HELL** ☐ [-]

Oct 88. (d-cd) *Zappa; (CDDZAP 9)* **YOU CAN'T DO THAT ON STAGE ANYMORE VOL.2** ☐ ☐
(re-iss.May95 on 'Rykodisc'; RCD 10563-64)

Dec 88. (d-cd) *Zappa; (CDZAP 13) / Rykodisc; <RCD 40024>* **WE'RE ONLY IN IT FOR THE MONEY / LUMPY GRAVY** ☐ ☐

Jan 89. (cd) *Zappa; (CDZAP 16)* **BABY SNAKES** (live 1977) ☐ ☐
(re-iss.May95 on 'Rykodisc'; RCD 10539)

Jan 90. (t-cd) *Zappa; (CDDZAP 20)* **JOE'S GARAGE ACT I / II / III** ☐ [-]

— FRANK decided to bootleg the bootleggers by releasing 10 best sellers that had fleeced him in the past. They were limited on 'Rhino'.

Apr 91. (d-cd/d-c) *Zappa; (CDDZAP/TZAPPA 38)* **THE BEST BAND YOU NEVER HEARD IN YOUR LIFE** (live 1988) ☐ ☐
(re-iss.May95 on 'Rykodisc'; RCD 10653-54)

Jun 91. (d-cd/d-c) *Zappa; (CDDZAP/TZAPA 41)* **MAKE A JAZZ NOISE HERE** (live 1988) ☐ ☐
(re-iss.d-cd May95 on 'Rykodisc'; RCD 10555-56)

Jun 91. (d-cd) *Zappa; (CDDZAP 17)* **YOU CAN'T DO THAT ON STAGE ANYMORE VOL.3** ☐ ☐
(re-iss.d-cd May95 on 'Rykodisc'; RCD 10565-66)

Jun 91. (d-cd/d-c) *Zappa; (CDDZAP/TZAPPA 40)* **YOU CAN'T DO THAT ON STAGE ANYMORE VOL.4** ☐ ☐
(re-iss.May95 on 'Rykodisc'; RCD 10567-68)

Note; below former bootleg releases on 'Essential-Zappa' UK/ 'Rykodisc' US. Released Aug91 as 'BEAT THE BOOTS' 10-lp box; *70907*

Sep 91. (cd) *(ESMCD 956) <70537>* **AS AN AM (live 1981)** ☐ ☐
Sep 91. (cd) *(ESMCD 957) <70538>* **THE ARK (live Boston 1968)** ☐ ☐
Sep 91. (cd) *(ESMCD 958) <70539>* **FREAKS & MOTHERFU*£'%!** ☐ ☐
Sep 91. (cd) *(ESMCD 959) <70540>* **UNMITAGATED AUDACITY** ☐ ☐
Sep 91. (d-cd) *(ESMCD 960) <70541>* **ANYWAY THE WIND BLOWS** ☐ ☐
Sep 91. (cd) *(ESMCD 961) <70542>* **'TIS THE SEASON TO BE JELLY** ☐ ☐
Sep 91. (cd) *(ESMCD 962) <70543>* **SAARBRUCKEN 1978** ☐ ☐
Sep 91. (cd) *(ESMCD 963) <70544>* **PIQUANTIQUE** ☐ ☐
(above 'Essential' releases of 1991 were re-iss.May97; same)

May 92. (cd) *Zappa; (CDZAP 49)* **BOULEZ CONDUCTS ZAPPA: THE PERFECT STRANGER** (Various Artists) ☐ ☐
(re-iss.May95 on 'Rykodisc'; RCD 10542)

Jul 92. (8xcd-box/7xc-box/11xlp-box) *Rykodisc; <R2/R4/R1 70372>* **BEAT THE BOOTS II** [-] ☐
– (DISCONNECTED SYNAPSES / TENGO NA MINCHIA TANTA / ELECTRIC AUNT JEMIMA / AT THE CIRCUS / SWISS CHEESE (double) / FIRE (double) / OUR MAN IN NIRVANA / CONCEPTUAL CONTINUITY)

Nov 92. (d-cd) *Zappa; (CDDZAP 55)* **PLAYGROUND PSYCHOTICS** (live 1971) ☐ ☐
(re-iss.May95 on 'Rykodisc'; RCD 10557-58)

Nov 92. (d-cd) *Zappa; (CDDZAP 46)* **YOU CAN'T DO THAT ON STAGE ANYMORE VOL.5** ☐ ☐
(re-iss.May95 on 'Rykodisc'; RCD 10569-70)

Nov 92. (d-cd) *Zappa; (CDDZAP* **YOU CAN'T DO THAT ON STAGE ANYMORE VOL.6** ☐ ☐
(re-iss.May95 on 'Rykodisc'; RCD 10571-72)

Mar 93. (cd) *Zappa; (CDZAP 51)* **AHEAD OF THEIR TIME** (live 1968) ☐ ☐
(re-iss.May95 on 'Rykodisc'; RCD 10559)

Jul 93. (12"/cd-s) *Zappa; (12/CD FRANK 102)* **VALLEY GIRLS. / YOU ARE WHAT YOU IS** ☐ ☐

Apr 95. (d-cd) *Rykodisc; (RCD 10540-41)* **LONDON SYMPHONY ORCHESTRA VOLUMES 1 & 2** ☐ ☐

May 95. (cd; w/mag) *Sonora;* **MAGAZINE & CD** ☐ ☐

Aug 95. (cd/c/d-lp) *Rykodisc; (RCD/RAC/RALP 40600)* **STRICTLY COMMERCIAL (THE BEST OF FRANK ZAPPA)** [45] ☐
– Peaches en regalia / Don't eat the yellow snow / Dancin' fool / San Ber'dino / Dirty love / My guitar wants to kill your mama / Cosmik debris / Trouble every day / Disco boy / Fine girl / Sexual harassment in the workplace / Let's make the water turn black / I'm the slime / Joe's garage / Bobby Brown goes down / Montana / Valley girl / Be in my video / Muffin man.

Feb 96. (cd/c) *Rykodisc; (RCD/RAC 40573)* **THE LOST EPISODES** ☐ ☐
Sep 96. (t-cd) *Rykodisc; (RCD 10574-75)* **LATHER** ☐ ☐
Apr 97. (cd) *Rykodisc; (RCD 10577)* **HAVE I OFFENDED SOMEONE?** ☐ [-]

ZOMBIES

Formed: St. Albans, England ... 1963 by ROD ARGENT, COLIN BLUNSTONE, HUGH GRUNDY and PAUL ATKINSON. In early 1964, after winning a local band competition, they signed to 'Decca' and soon had a massive worldwide hit with the classic 'SHE'S NOT THERE'. With its distinctive churning organ and portentous overtones, the single instantly marked the band out from the rest of the Brit-Beat pack, especially in America where the song climbed to No.2. The equally classy 'TELL HER NO', again reaped success across the Atlantic but strangely stiffed in the UK. Despite a fine debut album, 'BEGIN HERE' (1965) and a string of well-crafted singles, the band met with zero success in the UK and even their early success in America wasn't repeated. 'Decca' duly declined to renew their contract and they signed to 'C.B.S.' in 1967. Although The ZOMBIES split in frustration before its release, 'ODESSEY AND ORACLE' (deliberate spelling mistake!) was their masterstroke. A concept album of sorts, the record boasted an exquisitely arranged combination of sublime harmonies and jazz-inflected instrumentation, BLUNSTONE's unmistakable high vocals floating overhead. Though the album barely scraped into the top 100, it was an ironic twist of fate when the compelling 'TIME OF THE SEASON' single became an American million seller. The band reformed briefly (minus BLUNSTONE and WHITE) and released a couple of singles without success, ARGENT going on to form, funnily enough, ARGENT, while BLUNSTONE carved out a fairly successful solo career. • **Songwriters:** ARGENT-WHITE penned, except for the ubiquitous covers; GOT MY MOJO WORKING (Muddy Waters) / YOU'VE REALLY GOT A HOLD ON ME (Smokey Robinson) / ROADRUNNER (Bo Diddley) / SUMMERTIME (Gershwin) / GOIN' OUT OF MY HEAD (Little Anthony & The Imperials) / etc. • **Trivia:** Early in 1966, they made a cameo appearance in the film, 'Bunny Lake Is Missing'. They were known as the most intelligent pop group of the mid-60's, after leaving school with over fifty 'O' and 'A' levels between them.

Recommended: ODESSEY & ORACLE (*8) / COLLECTION (*7)

COLIN BLUNSTONE (b.24 Jun'45, Hatfield, England) – vocals / **ROD ARGENT** (b.14 Jun'45, St.Albans) – piano, keyboards, vocals / **PAUL ATKINSON** (b.19 Mar'46, Cuffley, England) – guitar / **CHRIS WHITE** (b. 7 Mar'43, Barnet, England) – bass repl. PAUL ARNOLD / **HUGH GRUNDY** (b. 6 Mar'45, Winchester, England) – drums

Decca / Parrot

Jul 64. (7") *(F 11940)* <9695> **SHE'S NOT THERE. / YOU MAKE ME FEEL GOOD** [12] [2] Oct64

Oct 64. (7") *(F 12004)* **LEAVE ME BE. / WOMAN** [ ] [-]

Jan 65. (7") *(F 12072)* <9723> **TELL HER NO. / WHAT MORE CAN I DO** [42] [6]

Mar 65. (7") *(F 12125)* <9747> **SHE'S COMING HOME. / I MUST MOVE** [ ] [58]

Apr 65. (lp) *(LK 4679)* <7001> **BEGIN HERE** <US-title 'THE ZOMBIES'> [ ] [39] Feb65
– Roadrunner / Summertime / I can't make up my mind / The way I feel inside / Work 'n' play / You've really got a hold on me / She's not there / Sticks and stones / Can't nobody love you / Woman / I don't want to know / I remember when I loved her / What more can I do / I got my mojo working. *(re-iss.Nov84; DOA 4) (re-iss.Jul86 on 'See For Miles' US version) (cd-iss.Aug92 on 'Repertoire'+=;)–* You make me feel good / Leave me be / Tell her no / She's coming home / I must move / Kind of girl / It's alright with me / Sometimes / Whenever you're ready / I love you / Is this the dream / Don't go away / Remember you / Just out of reach / Indication / How we were before / I'm going home.

Jun 65. (7") <9769> **I WANT YOU BACK AGAIN. / ONCE UPON A TIME** [-] [95]

Sep 65. (7") *(F 12225)* <9786> **WHENEVER YOU'RE READY. / I LOVE HER** [ ] [ ]

Nov 65. (7") *(F 12296)* <9821> **IS THIS A DREAM. / DON'T GO AWAY** [ ] [ ] Apr66

Jan 66. (7") *(F 12322)* <9797> **REMEMBER YOU. / JUST OUT OF REACH** [ ] [ ]

Jun 66. (7") *(F 12426)* <3004> **INDICATION. / HOW WE WERE BEFORE** [ ] [ ]

Nov 66. (7") *(F 12495)* **GOTTA GET A HOLD OF MYSELF. / THE WAY I FEEL INSIDE** [ ] [-]

Mar 67. (7") *(F 12584)* **GOIN' OUT OF MY HEAD. / SHE DOES EVERYTHING FOR ME** [ ] [-]

May 67. (7") *(F 12798)* **I LOVE YOU. / THE WAY I FEEL INSIDE** [ ] [-]

C.B.S. / Columbia

Sep 67. (7") *(2960)* **FRIENDS OF MINE. / BEECHWOOD PARK** [ ] [-]

Nov 67. (7") *(3087)* <44363> **CARE OF CELL 44. / MAYBE AFTER HE'S GONE** [ ] [ ]
(re-iss.Mar74 on 'Epic';)

—— Disbanded late 1967, although postumous release below resurrected group in 1969.

C.B.S. / Date

Apr 68. (lp; stereo/mono) *(S+/BPG 63280)* <4013> **ODYSSEY AND ORACLE** [ ] [95] Mar69
– Care of Cell 44 / A rose for Emily / Maybe after he's gone / Beechwood park / Brief candles / Hung up on a dream / Changes / I want her she wants me / This will be our year / Butcher's tale (Western Front 1914) / Friends of mine / Time of the season. *(re-iss.Dec86 on 'Razor';) (cd-iss.Aug92 on 'Repertoire'+=)–* I call you mine / She loves the way they love her / Imagine the swan / Smokey day / If it don't work out / I know she will / Don't cry for me / Walking in the sun / Conversation off Floral Street / I want you back again / Gotta get hold of myself / Goin' out of my head / She does everything for me / Nothing's changed / I could spend the day / Girl help me.

Apr 68. (7") *(3380)* <1604> **TIME OF THE SEASON. / I'LL CALL YOU MINE** [ ] [ ]

Jul 68. (7") <1612> **THIS WILL BE OUR YEAR. / BUTCHERS TALE (WESTERN FRONT 1914)** [-] [ ]

Feb 69. (7") <1628> **TIME OF THE SEASON. / FRIENDS OF MINE** [-] [3]

—— (Mar69) With them riding high in US Top 3, they decided to re-form but without BLUNSTONE (who went solo) / WHITE (who went into producing) + ATKINSON. ARGENT + GRUNDY recruited **RICK BIRKETT** – guitar / **JIM RODFORD** – bass

May 69. (7") <1644> **IMAGINE THE SWAN. / CONVERSATIONS OF FLORAL STREET** [-] [ ]

Jul 69. (7") <1648> **IF IT DON'T WORK OUT. / DON'T CRY FOR ME** [-] [ ]

—— Didn't last long, when ROD and JIM decided to form ARGENT. The ZOMBIES reformed for one-off in the early 90's

Essential / Rykodisc

Apr 91. (cd/c/lp) *(ESS CD/MC/LP 131)* **NEW WORLD** [ ] [-]
– New world (my America) / Love breaks down / I can't be wrong / Lula Lula / Heaven's gate / Time of the season / Moonday morning dance / Blue / Losing you / Alone in Paradise / Knowing you / Love conquers all / Nights on fire. *(cd re-iss.Jun94 on 'Castle'; CLACD 348)*

– compilations, others, etc. –

1965. (7"ep) *Decca; (DFE 8598)* **THE ZOMBIES** [ ] [-]
– Kinda girl / Sometimes / It's alright / Summertime.

Sep 70. (lp) *Decca; (SPA 85)* **THE WORLD OF THE ZOMBIES** [ ] [-]

Jan 74. (d-lp) *Epic; (EPC 65728)* **TIME OF THE ZOMBIES** [ ] [-]

Sep 75. (7") *Epic;* <11145> **TIME OF THE SEASON. / IMAGINE THE SWAN** [ ] [ ]

May 76. (lp) *Decca; (ROOTS 2)* **ROCK ROOTS – THE ZOMBIES** [ ] [-]

Feb 82. (lp/c) *Decca; (TAB/KTBC 34)* **SHE'S NOT THERE** [ ] [-]
(cd-iss.1988 as 'MEET THE ZOMBIES' on 'Razor'; RAZCD 34)

Oct 83. (7") *Old Gold; (OG 9346)* **SHE'S NOT THERE. / TIME OF THE SEASON** [ ] [-]

Feb 86. (lp) *Rhino; (RNLP 120)* **LIVE ON THE BBC 1965-67 (live)** [ ] [-]

Sep 87. (lp/c) *See For Miles; (SEE/K 30)* **THE SINGLES A's & B's** [ ] [-]
(cd-iss.Sep88 & May97; SEECD 30)

1988. (3"cd-ep) *Special Edition; (CD3-12)* **THE ZOMBIES EP** [ ] [-]
– She's not there / Time of the season / Tell her no / I got my mojo working.

Aug 88. (d-lp/c/cd) *Castle; (CCS LP/MC/CD 196)* **THE COLLECTION** [ ] [-]
– Goin' out of my head / Leave me be / Gotta get a hold on myself / I can't make up my mind / Kind of girl / Sticks and stones / Summertime / Woman / I got my mojo working / Roadrunner / You really got a hold on me / Nothing's changed / You make me feel good / She's not there / Don't go away / How we were before / Tell her no / Whenever you're ready / Just out of reach / Remember you / Indication / She does everything for me / Time of the season / I love you.

Mar 89. (cd-ep) *Old Gold; (OG 6123)* **SHE'S NOT THERE. / (2 other tracks by Moody Blues + Easybeats)** [ ] [-]

Apr 89. (cd) *Impact; (IMCD 9.00691)* **THE ZOMBIES COLLECTION VOL.1** [ ] [-]

Apr 89. (cd) *Impact; (IMCD 9.00692)* **THE ZOMBIES COLLECTION VOL.2** [ ] [-]
(re-iss.together for 'Line'; LICD 90061/2)

May 89. (m-lp/cd) *Razor; (RAZ M/CD 41)* **FIVE LIVE ZOMBIES (live)** [ ] [-]

Jun 90. (cd/c) *Knight; (KN CD/MC 10015)* **GOLDEN DECADE OF THE ZOMBIES** [ ] [-]

Feb 91. (cd/c) *Music Club; (MC CD/TC 002)* **BEST OF THE ZOMBIES** [ ] [-]

Jul 91. (3xcd-box) *Razor; (RAZCDBOX 1)* **THE ZOMBIES** [ ] [-]

Jun 92. (cd/c) *op Almanac; (PA CD/MC 7003)* **ZOMBIES FEATURING COLIN BLUNSTONE & ROD ARGENT** [ ] [-]

Nov 92. (cd) *See For Miles; (SEECD 358)* **THE EP COLLECTION** [ ] [-]

Feb 95. (cd/c) *More Music; (MO CD/MC 3009)* **THE ZOMBIES 1964-67** [ ] [-]

Aug 95. (cd-s) *Old Gold; (OG 6305-2)* **SHE'S NOT THERE / LEAVE ME BE** [ ] [-]

Sep 95. (cd-s) *Old Gold; (OG 6326-2)* **TIME OF THE SEASON / TELL HER NO** [ ] [-]

SECTION II

RETRO-PSYCHEDELIA

The 100 or so entries in this section have been selected because of their role in the development of post-punk psychedelia. They were separated from the main body of the book to distinguish two markedly different eras. The groups/artists were chosen on the basis of their ability to incorporate and develop their own blend of psychedelia, drawing on the fundamental experimentation of their 60's counterparts. While the first part of the book focused on psychedelia's early stages and its subsequent evolution into other styles of music (i.e. garage, progressive, experimental, ambient and new-age), the second illustrates how the essence of psychedelia has been translated by modern artists over the last two decades. After punk-rock had run its course, many types of retro styles began to emerge. Mod, ska and new romantic aside, psychedelia was alive and kicking in the early 80's, when bands like The TEARDROP EXPLODES (featuring of course the loopy JULIAN COPE), the equally manic ROBYN HITCHCOCK (from 70's punksters The SOFT BOYS) and The COCTEAU TWINS became indie faves. Over in the States, bands like HUSKER DU, DINOSAUR JR and SONIC YOUTH began fusing hardcore punk with traces of psychedelia, while acts like The RAIN PARADE, The DREAM SYNDICATE and The LONG RYDERS created a more faithful reproduction of classic 60's rock/pop, drawing on the more mellow aspects of The VELVET UNDERGROUND and experimenting with country-rock. While the British indie scene continued to flirt with 60's sounds, the most interesting nouveau psychedelia was created by bands like The JESUS & MARY CHAIN, MY BLOODY VALENTINE (hopefully their 7-year itch will produce an album next year!) and PRIMAL SCREAM. The latter group rapidly developed their sound and were soon at the forefront of the UK indie/dance crossover as the 80's turned into the 90's, The STONE ROSES also emerging as a trippy blueprint for the majority of today's guitar bands. While indie music evolved into the much maligned 'shoegazing' scene (bands like RIDE, SLOWDIVE and SWERVEDRIVER), the most obvious parallel to the chemically imbalanced 60's scene was the burgeoning dance culture. Given that the drug of choice was ecstasy rather than LSD, 'acid-house' employed hypnotic, repetitive rhythms in an attempt to recreate and heighten the mind state of the 'E' user in the same way that 60's musicians strived to express the consciousness-altering effects of an acid trip. After a marathon dancing session, ravers needed a soundtrack to 'chill-out' to, a whole new scene springing up as a result. The most visible act to emerge was undoubtably The ORB, who concocted a soothing balm of ambient, cosmic beats and PINK FLOYD-style weirdness. Other outfits to incorporate intelligent psychedelia into a dance structure (something that TANGERINE DREAM had pioneered in the 70's) included the likes of ORBITAL, UNDERWORLD and former indie psych-pop stars The SHAMEN. Across the water, the dance scene didn't quite have the same impact, although acts like DE LA SOUL and The BEASTIE BOYS emerged with their own particular takes on psychedelic hip-hop. Black urban American music was the basis of the British trip-hop phenomena of the mid 90's, artists like MASSIVE ATTACK, TRICKY and PORTISHEAD (all putting Bristol on the musical map) combining hip-hop, soul and jazz with heavy psychedelic overtones. With trippy music continuing to make its presence felt, the past two years (1996/97) have seen a proverbial smorgasbord of talented acts all interpreting psychedelia in their own particular spaced-out way – stand up THE VERVE, SPIRITUALIZED, STEREOLAB, BECK and not forgetting the Welsh wizardry of GORKY'S ZYGOTIC MYNCI.

Obviously any history of psychedelic music is subjective, and the author makes no apologies for any omissions, as these were a personal choice. At the same time, any suggestions as to how it could be improved are welcome. C'mon though, it's only £14.99, what do you want, blood?

BRENDON GRIFFIN and the rebel M.C.

Ed ALLEYNE-JOHNSON

Born: Oxford, England. Modern composer and virtuoso of a (guitar-sounding) 5-string electric violin, he cut his teeth by guesting on NEW MODEL ARMY's 1989 album, 'Thunder & Consolation'. ED then formed his own Oxford-based label, 'Equation', debuting in 1993 with 'PURPLE ELECTRIC VIOLIN CONCERTO'. Following-up with the sublime, 'ULTRAVIOLET' album, he had his first taste of success, scraping into the Top 75. With each track taking a colour of the spectrum, the record conveyed an atmospheric beauty and melancholic grace. His next release, 'FLY BEFORE DAWN' (1995), was a collaboration with his wife DENYZE. • **Songwriters:** Self-composed except SOMEBODY TO LOVE (Grace Slick). • **Trivia:** His grandfather PA ALLEYNE also played violin.

Recommended: ULTRAVIOLET (*8)

ED ALLEYNE-JOHNSON – electric violin, digital voice

Equation-China | not issued

Feb 93. (cd/c) *(EQ CD/TC 001)* **PURPLE ELECTRIC VIOLIN CONCERTO** □ -
– Oxford suite / Inner city music / Improvisation / Concrete Eden.

Mar 93. (cd-ep) *(EQCD 1)* **OXFORD SUITE** □ -

Jun 94. (cd/c) *(EQ CD/TC 002)* **ULTRAVIOLET (live)** 68 -
– White (intro) / Red / Orange / Yellow / Green / Blue / Indigo / Violet / Ultraviolet.

Jul 94. (cd-ep) *(EQCD 2)* **RED** □ -
– Red / Orange / Yellow / Violet.

Wingspan | not issued

Aug 95. (cd/c; ED ALLEYNE-JOHNSON & DENYZE) *(WING CD/MC 001)* **FLY BEFORE DAWN** □ -
– 3rd eye / Fly before dawn / All a dream / Winter sun / Men-an-tol / God's viewpoint / Summerland / Forest Hill / Wheel of fortune / Lion mountain / UFO / Somebody to love.

ALONE AGAIN OR (see under ⇒ SHAMEN)

ALTAMONT (see under ⇒ PORCUPINE TREE)

APHEX TWIN

Born: RICHARD D. JAMES, 1971, Cornwall, England. Isolated in the wilds of the South West, James began his precocious electronic tinkering at an early age. In true bedroom boffin style, he made his first recordings using customised analog synths at a cherubic 14 years old. Credited to AFX, his first release was 'ANALOGUE BUBBLEBATH VOL.1' (1991), released on the small dance indie label, 'Rabbit City'. The record created something of a buzz but it was 'DIDGERIDOO', included on 'ANALOGUE BUBBLEBATH VOL.2' (1991) which had legendary dance label 'R&S' chasing JAMES' signature. A sinister, didgeridoo-driven bpm marathon, it still sounds unique today. 'XYLEM TUBE' (1992) wasn't quite so scary while 'SELECTED AMBIENT WORKS '85-'92' (1992) was a largely beatless compilation containing some of his earliest creations. Signing to 'Warp', he recorded 'SURFING ON SINE WAVES' (1992) under the pseudonym POLYGON WINDOW. The album spawned the punishing rhythmical workout of the 'QUOTH' (1993) single, its dark intensity recalling 'DIGERIDOO'. By this point, APHEX TWIN was something of a cause celebre among the press, the indie papers surpisingly vocal in their support. With previous single releases, JAMES had missed the top 40 by a small margin but 'ON' (1993) gave him his first chart hit, reaching No.32. The second volume of 'SELECTED AMBIENT WORKS' was released the following year, the record concentrating on darker, more avant-garde material. This went down none too well with the critics and a backlash started to form. Silencing at least some of his detractors with 1995's 'I CARE BECAUSE YOU DO', the record featured equally dark but more consumer friendly fare reflecting the (then) current penchant for trip hop. With 1996's 'RICHARD D. JAMES' album, the boy wonder explored drum 'n' bass textures replete with lush strings and the requisite exotic electronica. He remains one of electronic music's most enduring enigmas and anyone who drives a tank around their back garden sporting a 3-week old chin growth should definately get our vote. • **Songwriters:** Ideas JAMES; sampled various and covered; FILM ME (Luxuria) / ONE DAY (Bjork). • **Trivia:** Was credited on SEEFEEL's 12" 'Time To Find Me (remixes)'.

Recommended: SELECTED AMBIENT WORKS '85-'92 (*7)

RICHARD D. JAMES (aka The APHEX TWIN) – keyboards, synthesizer

Rabbit City | not issued

Dec 91. (12"ep; as AFX) *(CUT 001)* **ANALOGUE BUBBLEBATH VOL.1** □ -

Dec 91. (12"promo) *(009)* **ANALOGUE BUBBLEBATH VOL.2 (DIDGERIDOO 'Aboriginal' mix)** - -
(re-iss.1993 as 12"ep; CUT 002)

Outer Rhythm – R&S | not issued

Apr 92. (12"ep) *(RSUK 12)* **ANALOGUE BUBBLEBATH VOL.2** 55 -
– Didgeridoo / Flaphead / Isoproplex.
(cd-ep+=) *(RSUK 12CD)* – Analogue bubblebath 1.

Jul 92. (12"ep/cd-ep) **XYLEM TUBE EP** □ -

Nov 92. (cd/c/d-lp) *(AMB 3922 CD/MC/LP)* **SELECTED AMBIENT WORKS '85-'92** □ -
– Xtal / Tha / Pulsewidth / Ageispolis / I won't let the Sun go down on me / Greencalx / Heliosphan / We are the music makers / Schotkey / Hedphelym / Delphium / Actium / Ptolemy.

Warp | Wax Trax!

Dec 92. (cd/c/clear-lp; as POLYGON WINDOW) *(WARP CD/MC/LP 7)* **SURFING ON SINE WAVES** □ -
– Polygon window / Audax powder / Quoth / If it really is me / Supremacy II / UT 1 – Dot / (0.07) / Quixote / Quino – Phec. *(cd re-iss.Apr96; same)*

Mar 93. (12"ep/cd-ep; as POLYGON WINDOW) *(WAP 33/+CD)* **QUOTH / IKEATA. / QUOTH (wooden thump mix) / QUOTH (bike pump meets bucket)** 49 -

— In Jul'93, he teamed up with SEEFEEL on 'PURE / IMPURE' EP for 'Too Pure' 12"/cd-s; *PURE/+CD 025)*

Dec 93. (12"ep/cd-ep) *(WAP 39/+CD)* **ON. / 73 YIPS. / D-SCAPE / XEPHA** 32 □
(12"ep/cd-ep) *(WAP 39 R/CDR)* – ('A'-D-Scape mix) / ('A'-Reload mix) / ('A'-M-21Q) / ('A'-28 mix).

Mar 94. (d-cd/d-c/2xd-lp) *(WARP CD/MC/LP 21)* **SELECTED AMBIENT WORKS VOLUME II** 11 □
– (12 + 13 of mostly untitled tracks; 1 of them 'Blue Calx')

Mar 95. (12"ep/cd-ep) *(WAP 60/+CD)* **VENTOLIN / ('A'-Salbutanol mix) / ('A'-Marazanovose mix) / ('A'-Plain-an-guarry mix) / ('A'-The Coppice mix) / ('A'-Crowsnegods mix)** 49 □
(12"ep/cd-ep; remixes) *(WAP 60 R/CDR)* – ('A'-Wheeze mix) / ('A'-Carnarack mix) / ('A'-Cyclob mix) / ('A'-Deep gong mix) / ('A'-Asthma beats mix).

Apr 95. (cd/c/d-lp) *(WARP CD/MC/LP 30)* **. . .I CARE BECAUSE YOU DO** 24 □
– Acrid avid Jan Shred / The waxen path / Wax the nip / Icct Hedral / Ventolin / Come on you slags / Start as you mean to go one / Wet tip hen ax / Mookid / Alberto Balsan / Cow cud is a twin / Next heap with.

Aug 95. (12"ep/cd-ep) *(WAP 63/+CD)* **DONKEY RHUBARB EP** □ □
– Icct Hedral (credited with PHILIP GLASS) / Pancake lizard / Mass observation (the crackdown) / Film me and finish off / One day (Sabres of Paradise mix) / Vaz deferenz.

Oct 96. (12"/cd-s) *(WAP 78/+CD)* **GIRL/BOY EP** 64 □
– Girl/boy (NLS mix) / Milk man / Inkey $ / Girl/boy (#18 snare rush mix) / Beatles under my carpet / Girl/boy (redruth mix).

Nov 96. (cd/c/lp) *(WARP CD/MC/LP 43)* **RICHARD D. JAMES ALBUM** 62 □
– 4 / Cornish acid / Peek 824545201 / Fingerbob / Corn mouth / To cure a weakling child / Goon gumpos / Yellow calx – Girl/boy song / Local fock witch.

– compilations, others, etc. –

(all on 'Rephlex' unless mentioned otherwise)

1992. (d-12"ep; as Q-CHASTIC) *(002EP)* **Q-CHASTIC EP** □ -

1994. (12"; as KOSMIC KOMMANDO) *(CAT 007)* **THE KOSMIC KOMMANDO** □ -
(also issued 1994 same label; MC 202)

1994. (12"ep/cd-ep) *(CAT 008/+CD)* **ANALOGUE BUBBLEBATH VOL.3** □ -
– (track numbers)

1994. (12"; as CAUSTIC WINDOW) *(CAT 009)* **JOYREX 1. / JOYREX 2** □ -

Aug 94. (12"ep/cd-ep; as AFX) *(CAT 019/+CD)* **ANALOGUE BUBBLEBATH VOL.4** □ -
– I / II / III / IV.

Jan 95. (blue-d-lp/c/cd) *R&S; (RS 95035/+MC/CD)* **CLASSICS** 24 □
– Digeridoo / Flaphead / Phloam / Isoproplex / Polynomial-C / Tamphex / Phlange phace / Dodeccaheedron / Analogue bubblebath / En trance to exit / AFX 2 / Metapharstic / Digeridoo (live).

APOLLO XI (see under ⇒ ORB)

A PRIMARY INDUSTRY (see under ⇒ ULTRAMARINE)

A.R. KANE

Formed: East London, England . . . 1986 by ALEX AYULI and RUDI TAMBALA. They signed a one-off deal with 'One Little Indian', debuting in the indie charts with the 'WHEN YOU'RE SAD' EP in 1987. Described in the press as a unique fusion of COCTEAU TWINS meeting MILES DAVIS and ROBERT WYATT, their ROBIN GUTHRIE (Cocteau Twins)-produced follow-up, 'LOLITA', came out on '4 a.d.'. This led to a one-off collaboration with the label's COLOUR BOX; M/A/R/R/S. This project soon rose to No.1 simultaneously in the UK pop, dance and indie charts with the techno/dub classic 'PUMP UP THE VOLUME' (by the end of the year, it also hit No.13 in the States). During this fruitful period, they moved to 'Rough Trade', who issued their first long player '69'. This, together with their late 1989 follow-up, 'i', again topped the indie chart, although little was heard of them until they returned in 1994 with the album, 'NEW CLEAR CHILD'.

Recommended: 69 (*8) / i (*8) / NEW CLEAR CHILD (*6)

ALEX AYULI – guitars, etc / **RUDI TAMBALA** – guitars, etc

O. L. Indian | not issued

Feb 87. (12"ep) *(12TP 2)* **WHEN YOU'RE SAD. / WHEN YOU'RE SAD / THE HAUNTING** □ -
(re-iss.Aug87; same)

4 a.d. | not issued

Jul 87. (12"ep) *(BAD 704)* **LOLITA. / SADO-MASOCHISM IS A MUST / BUTTERFLY COLLECTOR** □ -

— (above was to have been issued May87; *12TP 8)*

Rough Trade | Rough Trade

Apr 88. (12"ep) *(RTT 201)* **UP HOME. / BABY MILK SNATCHER / W.O.G.S.** — -

Jun 88. (lp/c/cd) *(ROUGH/+C/CD 119)* **69** — -
– Crazy blue / Suicide kiss / Baby milk snatcher / Scab / Sulliday / Dizzy / Spermwhale trip over / The sun falls into the sea / The Madonna is with child / Spanish quay (3).

Nov 88. (7") *(RT 231)* **GREEN HAZED DAZE. / IS THIS IT?** — -
(12"ep+=) *(RTT 231)* **LOVESICK EP** – Sperm travels like a juggernaut / Is this dub?.

Jul 89. (7"/12"plays-@48rpm) *(RT/+T 239)* **POP. / WHAT'S ALL THIS THEN?** — -
(cd-s+=) *(RT 239CD)* – Snow joke.

Oct 89. (d-lp/c/cd) *(ROUGH/+C/CD 139)* **i** — -
– Snow joke / Off into space / Hello / Crack up / Yeti / What's all this then? / Honeysuckleswallow / In a circle / Insect love / Miles apart / Sugar wings / Down / And I say / Catch my drift / A love from outer space / Timewind / Conundrum / Long body / Fast kg / Pop / Mars / Spook/ Back home / Super vixens / Sorry / Challenge.

May 90. (m-cd/m-lp) *(RT CD/CMC/D 171)* **REM'I'XES** (6 remixes) — -
– Miles apart / Crack up / Crack up (space mix) / Sugarwings / Love from Outer Space / Catch my drift.

not issued | Luaka Bop

1992. (cd) **AMERICANA** (compilation of first 2 albums) - —

3rd Stone | 3rd Stone

Oct 94. (cd) *(STONE 11CD)* **NEW CLEAR CHILD**
– Deep blue breath / Grace / Tiny little drop of perfumed time / Surf motel / Gather / Honey be (for Stella) / Cool as moons / Snow White's world / Pearl / Sea like a child.

B

BANCO DE GAIA

Formed: Leamington Spa, London, England . . . late 80's, as nom de plume for metal guitarist TOBY MARKS, resident dub DJ at 'Club Dog' dance evenings. This genre hopping gypsy was known to scour the globe for obscure ethnic music and exotic samples, first surfacing in the early 90's on three various artists compilations, one of which was Planet Dog's (their new label) 'FEED YOUR HEAD'. He also issued a few cassette-only long-players, 'MEDIUM' & 'FREEFORM FLUTES AND FADING TIBETANS', before finally making his official debut in 1993 with the 'DESERT WIND' EP. His first "proper" album, 'MAYA', followed in 1994, an ethnic-ambient sample fest which topped the indie charts, even nudging into the mainstream charts. 95's 'LAST TRAIN TO LHASA' consolidated his respected position in the nouveau-hippy dance scene and MARKS toured his live show around the festival circuit. A Glastonbury set was released in the summer of '96, while the fest took a year off. • **Trivia:** Group name means "World Bank". MARKS has mixed SENSER ('Stacked up') / LEVELLERS ('This Garden').

Recommended: MAYA (*6) / LAST TRAIN TO LHASA (*6)

TOBY MARKS – keyboards, synthesizers, guitars

Planet Dog | not issued

Nov 93. (12"/cd-s) *(BARK 001 T/CDS)* **DESERT WIND (sunset mix). / GAMELAH / SHANTI (Soup Dragons mix)** — —

Feb 94. (cd/c/d-lp) *(BARK CD/MC/LP 003)* **MAYA** 34 —
– Heliopolis / Mafich Arabi / Sunspot / Gamelah (dub 3) / Qurna (Mister Christian on the decks) / Sheesha / Lai lah (V1.oo) / Shanti (red with white spots edit) / Maya. *(lp-iss.Jun94 w/free lp+=)*– Gamelah / Shanti / Darkside / Data inadequate.

Oct 94. (12"ep/cd-ep) *(BARK 004 T/CDS)* **HELIOPOLIS (Michael Dog mix) / ('A'-Liquid light mix) / ('A'-Redwood mix) / ('A'original mix)** — —

Apr 95. (cd-s) *(BARK 010CDS)* **LAST TRAIN TO LHASA (original mix) / ('A'-extended ambient mix)** — -
(12"+=) *(BARK 010T)* – ('A'-radio edit).

May 95. (d-cd/d-c/t-lp) *(BARK CD/MC/LP 011)* **LAST TRAIN TO LHASA** 31 -
– Last train to Lhasa / Kuos / China (clouds not mountains) / Amber / Kincajou (small and cuddly mix) / White paint / 887 (structure) / Kuos (gnomes mix) / Kincajou (duck! asteroid) / Eagle (small steppa mix). *(cd/lp w/free cd/lp) (BARK CD/LP 011S)*– China (follow the red brick road mix) / Amber (insect intelligence) / 887 (darkside return).

Jul 95. (12"ep) *(BARK 017T)* **KINCAJOU (Oliver Lieb mix). / KINCAJOU (Here Comes The Norse Gods mix) / KINCAJOU (Speed J mix)** — —
(cd-ep+=) *(BARK 017CD)* – ('A'lp version).

Jul 96. (cd) *(BARKCD 021)* **LIVE AT GLASTONBURY (live)** — -
– Last train to Lhasa / Mafich Arabi / Amber / White paint / Kincajou / Buos / 887 / Heliopolis / Data inadequate.

— about to release album 'BIG MEN CRY' in July '97

BEASTIE BOYS

Formed: Greenwich Village, New York, USA . . . 1981 by ADAM YAUCH and MIKE DIAMOND. They recruited ADAM HOROWITZ to replace 2 others (see below), and after two US indie releases they signed to 'Def Jam', the label run by The BEASTIE's friend and sometime DJ, RICK RUBIN. RUBIN paired with the BEASTIE BOYS was a match made in Heaven (or Hell, if you were unfortunate enough to own a Volkswagon) and the debut album 'LICENSED TO ILL' (1986) was the first real attempt to create a white, rock-centric take on of Afro-American Hip Hop. At turns hilarious and exhilirating, RUBIN and the BEASTIE's shared taste in classic rock was evident with samples from the likes of AC/DC and LED ZEPPELIN along with the theme tune from American TV show 'Mr. Ed'. With snotty rapping and riff-heavy rhymes, tracks like 'FIGHT FOR YOUR RIGHT (TO PARTY) and 'NO SLEEP TILL BROOKLYN' stormed the charts on both sides of the Atlantic, 'LICENSED TO ILL' becoming the fastest selling debut in 'Columbia's history. The record turned the band into a phenomenon and in 1987 they undertook a riotous headlining tour. Courting controversy wherever they played, the band were savaged by the press, a dispute with 'Def Jam' not helping matters any. Despite all the upheaval, by the release of 'PAUL'S BOUTIQUE' in 1989, the group's profile was negligible and the album was more or less passed over. A tragedy, as it remains one of Hip Hops lost gems, a widescreen sampladelic collage produced by the ultra-hip DUST BROTHERS (U.S.). Bypassing the obvious guitar riffs for samples of The BEATLES, CURTIS MAYFIELD and PINK FLOYD along with a kaleidoscopic array of cultural debris and hip references, the album was a funky tour de force. After another extended sabbatical during which the group relocated to California, the BEASTIE BOYS returned in 1992 with 'CHECK YOUR HEAD'. Hipness and attitude were still there in abundance but by now, the group were using live instrumentation. Despite veering from all out thrash to supple funk, the record was a success and only the BEASTIE BOYS could get away with a TED NUGENT collaboration ('THE BIZ VS THE NUGE'). ILL COMMUNICATION (1994) developed this strategy to stunning effect. From the irresistable funk of 'SURE SHOT' and 'ROOT DOWN' to the laid back swing of 'GET IT TOGETHER' and 'FLUTE LOOP', this was the group's most mature and accomplished work to date. The hardcore was still there, 'TOUGH GUY' and 'HEART ATTACK MAN' but it was offset by the sombre strings of 'EUGENE'S LAMENT' and the mellow 'RICKY'S THEME'. A double A-side 'GET IT TOGETHER' and the screachingly brilliant 'SABOTAGE' (complete with entertaining cop-pastiche video) returned them quite rightly back into the UK Top 20. From the artwork to the meditative feel of the music (well O.K., maybe not the punk numbers) it was no surprise that YAUCH had become a buddhist and the band subsequently played a high profile benefit for the oppressed nation of Tibet. Ever industrious, the group also started their own label and fanzine 'Grand Royal', signing the likes of LUSCIOUS JACKSON and the now tedious BIS. • **Songwriters:** Although they released little cover versions, they sampled many LED ZEPPELIN songs. In 1992, they covered JIMMY JAMES (Jimi Hendrix) + TIME FOR LIVIN' (Stewart Frontline), and collaborated with NISHITA. • **Trivia:** ADAM HOROWITZ is the son of playwrite ISRAEL. Volkswagen car owners were up in arms when fans of the group tore by the thousands, the "VW" metal emblems which they wore round their necks. HOROWITZ played a cameo role in TV serial 'The Equalizer' (circa '88).

Recommended: LICENSED TO 'ILL (*8) / PAUL'S BOUTIQUE (*7) / CHECK YOUR HEAD (*7) / ILL: COMMUNICATION (*9)

'MCA' ADAM YAUCH (b. 5 Aug'65, Brooklyn, New York) – vocals / **'MIKE D' MIKE DIAMOND** (b.20 Nov'66, New York) – vocals / **KATE SCHELLENBACH** (b. 5 Jan'66, New York City) – drums / **JOHN BERRY** – guitar

Rat Cage | Rat Cage

Nov 82. (12"ep) *<MOTR 21>* **POLLY WOG STEW** — —
– Riot fight / Transit cop / Holy snappers / Egg raid on mojo / Beastie Boys / Jimi / Ode to . . . / Michelle's farm.
(UK-iss.Apr88 +c-s)(re-iss.12"ep/c-ep/cd-ep Feb93)

— **KIND AD-ROCK – ADAM HOROWITZ** (b.31 Oct'67, New York City) – vocals, guitar (ex-The YOUNG & THE USELESS) repl.BERRY + SCHELLENBACH (she later joined LUSCIOUS JACKSON)

Aug 83. (7") *<MOTR 26>* **COOKIE PUSS. / BEASTIE REVOLUTION** - —
(UK-iss.Jan85 + Jul87; MOTR 26 C/CD) (cd-ep-iss.Dec87;) (re-issues +=)– Bonus bater / Cookie dub / Censored. *(re-iss.12"ep/c-ep/cd-ep Feb93; same)*

added guest **RICK RUBIN** – scratcher DJ

Def Jam | Def Jam

Oct 85. (7") **ROCK HARD. / ?** - —

Jan 86. (7"/12") *(A/TA 6686)* **SHE'S ON IT. / SLOW AND LOW** — —

May 86. (7") *(A 7055)* **HOLD IT, NOW HIT IT. / ('A'-acappella)** — —
(12"+=) *(TA 7055)* – ('A'instrumental).

Sep 86. (7") *(650114-7)* **SHE'S ON IT. / SLOW AND LOW** — —
(12"+=) *(650114-6)* – Hold it, now hit it.

Nov 86. (7") *(650169-7) <06341>* **IT'S THE NEW STYLE. / PAUL REVERE** — —
(12"+=) *(650169-6)* – ('A'&'B'instrumentals).
(d12"++=) *(650169-?)* – Hold it, now hit it / Hold it, now hit it (Acapulco version) / Hold it, now hit it (instrumental).

Nov 86. (lp/c/cd) *(450 062-1/-4/-2) <40238>* **LICENSED TO 'ILL** 7 1
– Rhymin and stealin' / The new style / She's crafty / Posse in effect / Slow ride / Girls / (You gotta) Fight for your right (to party) / No sleep till Brooklyn / Paul Revere / Hold it now, hit it / Brass monkey / Slow and low / Time to get ill. *(re-iss.Nov89 on 'Capitol'; 460949-1) (re-iss.Jun94 cd/c; 460949-2/-4) (cd-iss.Jul95; 527 351-2)*

Dec 86. (7") *<06595>* **(YOU GOTTA) FIGHT FOR YOUR RIGHT (TO PARTY). / PAUL REVERE** - 7

Feb 87. (7") *(650418-7)* **(YOU GOTTA) FIGHT FOR YOUR RIGHT (TO PARTY). / TIME TO GET ILL** 11 -
(12"+=) *(650418-6)* – No sleep till Brooklyn.

Apr 87. (7") *<06675>* **NO SLEEP TILL BROOKLYN. / SHE'S CRAFTY** - —

May 87. (7"/7"sha-pic-d/12") *(BEAST/+P/T 1)* **NO SLEEP TILL BROOKLYN. / POSSE IN EFFECT** 14 -

Jul 87. (7"/12") *(BEAST/+T 2)* **SHE'S ON IT. / SLOW AND LOW** 10 —

Sep 87. (7"/7"sha-pic-d) *(BEAST/+P 3)* **GIRLS. / SHE'S CRAFTY** 34 —
(12"+=) *(BEASTQ 3)* – Rock hard.

Mar 88. (7") *<07020>* **BRASS MONKEY. / POSSE IN EFFECT** [-] [48]

— no more RICK RUBIN as DJ

Capitol Capitol

Jul 89. (7") *(CL 540) <44454>* **HEY LADIES. / SHAKE YOUR RUMP** [36]
(12"ep+=/cd-ep+=) *(12/CD CL 540)* **LOVE AMERICAN STYLE** – 33% God / Die yourself in '89 (just do it).

Jul 89. (cd/c/lp) *(DE/TC+/EST 2102) <91743>* **PAUL'S BOUTIQUE** [44] [14]
– To all the girls / Shake your rump / Johnny Ryall / Egg man / High plains drifter / The sound of science / 3-minute rule / Hey ladies / 5-piece chicken dinner / Looking down the barrel of a gun / Car thief / What comes around / Shadrach / Ask for Janice / B-boy bouillabaisse:- (a) 59 Chrystie Street, (b) Get on the mic, (c) Stop that train, (d) A year and a day, (e) Hello Brooklyn, (f) Dropping names, (g) Lay it on me, (h) Mike on the mic, (i) A.W.O.L.

Aug 89. (7") *<44472>* **SHADRACH. /** [-]

— Trio now also on instruments; MCA – bass / **AD ROCK** – keyboards / **MIKE D** – drums

Apr 92. (12"ep/c-ep) *(12/TC CL 653)* **PASS THE MIC** [47]
– Pass the mic / Time for living / Drunken praying mantis style / Professor Booty.
(cd-ep+=) *(CDCL 653)* – Nethy's girl.

May 92. (cd/c/d-lp) *(CD/TC+/EST 2171) <98938>* **CHECK YOUR HEAD** [10]
– Jimmy James / Funky boss / Pass the mic / Gratitude / Lighten up / Finger lickin' good / So what'cha want / The biz vs. the Nuge (with TED NUGENT) / Time for livin' / Something's got to give / Blue nun / Stand together / Pow / The maestro / Groove Holmes / Live at PJ's / Mark on the bus / Professor Booty / In 3's / Mamaste. *(re-iss.Sep94)*

Jun 92. (12"white-ep) *(12CL 665)* **FROZEN METAL HEAD EP** [55] [-]
– Jimmy James / The blue nun / Drinkin' wine.
(cd-ep+=) *(CDCL 665)* – Jimmy James (original).

Jun 92. (c-ep) *<15847>* **SO WHAT'CHA WANT / ?** [-] [93]

Grand Royale Capitol

May 94. (cd/c/d-lp) *(CD/TC+/EST 2229)* **ILL: COMMUNICATION** [10] [1]
– Sure shot / Tough guy / Freak freak / Bobo on the corner / Root down / Sabotage / Get it together / Sabrosa / The update / Futterman's rule / Alright hear this / Eugene's lament / Flute loop / Do it / Rick's theme / Heart attack man / The scoop / Shambala / Bodhisattva vow / Transitions. *(lp re-iss.Apr97 on 'Grand Royale'; GR 006LP)*

Jul 94. (c-s/7"green) *(TC+/CL 716)* **GET IT TOGETHER. / SABOTAGE / DOPE LITTLE SONG** [19]
(10") *(10CL 716)* – (1st 2 tracks) / ('A'buck wild remix) / ('A'instrumental).
(cd-s) *(CDCL 716)* – (1st 2 tracks) / ('A'remix) / Resolution time.

Nov 94. (7"maroon) *(CL 726)* **SURE SHOT. / MULLET HEAD** [27]
(10"+=) *(10CL 726)* – ('A'mix) / The vibes.
(cd-s+=) *(CDCL 726)* – Son of neck bone / (2-'A'remixes).

Jun 95. (m-cd/m-c/m-lp) *(CD/TC+/EST 2262) <>* **ROOT DOWN EP** (some live) [23] [50]
– Root down (free zone mix) / Root down / Root down (PP balloon mix) / Time to get ill / Heart attack man / The maestro / Sabrosa / Flute loop / Time for livin' / Something's got to give / So what'cha want. *(m-lp-iss.Apr97 on 'Grand Royale'; GR 018)*

Mar 96. (cd/c) *(CD/TC EST 2281) <>* **THE IN SOUND FROM WAY OUT!** (instrumental) [45] [45]
– Groove Holmes / Sabrosa / Namaste / Pow / Son of neckbone / In 3's / Eugene's lament / Bobo on the corner / Shambala / Lighten up / Ricky's theme / Transitions / Drinkin' wine.

– compilations, etc. –

Feb 94. (cd/c) *Honey World; (CD/TC EST 2225) / Capitol;* **SOME OLD BULLSHIT** [46]
– (compilation of 1st 2 EP's)

BECK

Born: BECK HANSEN, 8 Jul'70, Los Angeles, California, USA. After absorbing the strains of primitive country blues artists like LEADBELLY and MISSISSIPPI JOHN HURT, along with the aural terrorism of hardcore noise, the 17-year old BECK relocated to New York in 1989 to try his hand on the post-punk East Village folk scene. Broke, he retired to L.A., setting himself up in the (now) trendy Silverlake district, playing low key gigs in local coffeehouses. Spotted by 'Bongload' owner TOM ROTHROCK, he was offered some studio time and the resulting sessions produced the 'LOSER' (1993) single. Caned by L.A.'s alternative radio stations, its popularity led to BECK signing with 'Geffen'. 'LOSER' (1994) in its re-issued, major label form went top 20 in both Britain and America, its slow burning hip hop blues turning the rosy cheeked BECK into an overnight slacker anti-hero. The 'MELLOW GOLD' (1994) album went some way towards crystallising BECK's skewed vision of a modern folk music that encapsulated roots blues, hip hop, country, noise-core and psychedelia. While the record went on to sell half a million copies, BECK's unique contract allowed him the option of recording for other labels. 'STEREOPATHIC SOUL MANURE' (1994) was a U.S. only release of rough early material on the small 'Flipside' label, while 'ONE FOOT IN THE GRAVE' (1995) was a mainly acoustic set released on CALVIN JOHNSON's 'K' records, its stark harmonica-driven title track remaining a highlight of the BECK live experience. Any dubious whispers of one-hit wonder were cast aside with the release of 1996's 'ODELAY', a record that topped many end of year polls and turned BECK into the music world's coolest hep cat. Garnering gushing praise from the dance, rock and hip hop communities alike, the album's effortless fusion of disparate styles was breathtaking. The cut'n'paste surrealism of the lyrics flourished imagery of a lucidness to match BOB DYLAN's 60's work and indeed, the gorgeously bittersweet 'JACKASS' used DYLAN's 'IT'S ALL OVER NOW BABY BLUE' as a shimmering harmonic backdrop. The album segued smoothly from distortion and dissonance into downhome steel guitar hoedown, all the while retaining an irresistably funky backbeat. For now, this pop auteur/wunderkid can do no wrong, his live experience is a dayglo potted history of American music and any readers who were lucky enough to catch his glorious set at the Chelmsford V97 festival, will know that BECK doesn't take too kindly to bottle throwing eunuchs! • **Songwriters:** BECK writes most of his material, some with KARL STEPHENSON. 'LOSER' used a sample of DR.JOHN's 'I Walk On Guilded Splinters'. • **Trivia:** The 'Geffen Rarities Vol.1' album of various artists, featured the BECK track, 'Bogusflow'.

Recommended: MELLOW GOLD (*7) / ODELAY (*9)

BECK – vocals, acoustic guitar with guests **RACHEL HADEN** – drums, vocals / **ANNA WARONKER** – bass, vocals / **PETRA HADEN** – violin, vocals / **MIKE BOITO** – organ / **DAVID HARTE** – drums / **ROB ZABRECKY** – bass

not issued Bongload

1993. (12") *<BL 5>* **LOSER. /** [-]

1993. (7") *<BL 11>* **STEVE THREW UP. /** [-]
(both above UK-iss.Jan95; same)

not issued Sonic Enemy

1993. (cd) **GOLDEN FEELINGS** [-]

not issued Fingerpaint

1993. (cd) **A WESTERN HARVEST FIELD BY MOONLIGHT** [-]

Geffen Geffen

Feb 94. (7"/c-s) *(GFS/+C 67)* **LOSER. / ALCOHOL / FUME** [15] [10]
(cd-s) *(GFSTD 67)* – ('A'side) / Totally confused / Corvette bumper / MTV makes me want to smoke crack.

Mar 94. (cd/c/lp) *(GED/GEC/GEF 24634) <BL 012 CD/C>* **MELLOW GOLD** [41] [13]
– Loser / Pay no mind (snoozer) / Fuckin with my head (mountain dew rock) / Whiskeyclone, Hotel City 1997 / Soul suckin jerk / Truckdrivin neighbors downstairs (yellow sweat) / Sweet sunshine / Beercan / Steal my body home / Nitemare hippy girl / Motherfuker / Blackhole. *(hidden track cd+=)*– Analog odyssey. *(lp re-iss.Apr97 on 'Bongload'; BL 012LP)*

May 94. (c-s/cd-s) **BEERCAN /** [-]

May 94. (7"/c-s) *(GFS/+C 73)* **PAY NO MIND (SNOOZER). / SPECIAL PEOPLE** [-]
(12"+=/cd-s+=) *(GFST/+D 73)* – Trouble all my days / Supergold (sunchild).

not issued Flipside

1994. (cd) *<FLIP 60>* **STEREOPATHETIC SOUL MANURE** [-]
–
(UK-iss.Dec95; same)

K K

Nov 95. (cd) *(KLP 28CD)* **ONE FOOT IN THE GRAVE**
(lp-iss.Jun97; KLP 28)

D.G.C. D.G.C.

Jun 96. (c-s) *(GFSC 22156)* **WHERE IT'S AT / ('A'mix)** [35] [75]
(12"+=/cd-s+=) *(GFST/+D 22156)* – ('A'mixes).

Jun 96. (cd/c; as BECK!) *(GED/GEC 24908) <BL 030 CD/C>* **ODELAY** [18] [16]
– Devils haircut / Hotwax / Lord only knows / The new pollution / Derelict / Novacane / Jack-ass / Where it's at / Minus / Sissyneck / Readymade / High 5 (rock the catskills) / Ramshackle / Diskobox. *(lp-iss.Apr97 on 'Bongload'; BL 030LP)*

Nov 96. (c-s) *(GFSC 22183)* **DEVILS HAIRCUT / ('A'mix)** [22]
(cd-s) *(GFSTD 22183)* – ('A'mixes).
(cd-s) *(GFSXD 22183)* –

Mar 97. (7"/c-s) *(GFS/+C 22205)* **THE NEW POLLUTION / RICHARD'S HAIRPIECE (remix)** [14] [78]
(12"+=/cd-s+=) *(GFST/+D 22205)* – Lemonade. *(rel.Europe 12" May97 on 'Play It Again Sam'; 22300)*

May 97. (7"/c-s) *(GFS/+C 22253)* **SISSYNECK. / THE NEW POLLUTION (remix)** [30]
(cd-s+=) *(GFSTD 22253)* – Feather in your cap.

BEDHEAD

Formed: Texas, USA ... 1991 by BUBBA KADANE and brother MATT. In 1994, they finally released their debut, 'WHAT FUN LIFE WAS', for The BUTTHOLE SURFERS' label, 'Trance Syndicate'. Two years went by before their follow-up, 'BEHEADED', gained some belated press recognition. • **Style:** Slo-core, melancholy psychedelia-influenced rock, similar to LOW and even sleepier than The RED HOUSE PAINTERS. • **Songwriters:** BUBBA and MATT.

Recommended: WHAT FUN LIFE WAS (*6) / BEHEADED (*7)

BUBBA KADANE – vocals / **MATT KADANE** – guitar / **TENCH COXE** – guitar / **KRIS WHEAT** – bass / **TRINI MARTINEZ** – drums

Trance Syndicate Trance Syndicate

Apr 94. (lp/cd) *(TRANCE 21/+CD)* **WHAT FUN LIFE WAS**

Nov 94. (cd-ep) *(TR 28CD)* **4 SONG CD E.P.**

Mar 96. (10"/cd-s) *(TR 42/+CD)* **THE DARK AGES**

Rough Trade Mayking

Sep 96. (cd/lp) *(R 405-2/-1)* **BEHEADED**
– Beheaded / The rest of the day / Left behind / What's missing / Smoke / Burned out / Roman candle / Withdrew / Felo de sen / Lares and Penatia / Lost me works.

BEL CANTO (see under ⇒ BIOSPHERE)

BEVIS FROND

Formed: Walthamstow, London, England ... 1987 by NICK SALOMAN, who had been part of the duo NICK & DICK, who became ODDSOCKS in 1975. They made one album, 'MEN OF THE MOMENT', for the 'Sweet Folk'

label. In 1980, NICK formed the 5-piece, VON TRAPP FAMILY, which made an EP, 'BRAND NEW THRILL'. Two years later, the band became ROOM 13, releasing another single, 'MURDER MYSTERY'. Unfortunately, NICK was seriously injured in a motorcycle accident, using the compensation money to finance his next project, the solo BEVIS FROND. Early in 1987, he was back on vinyl with the 'MIASMA' album, released on his own 'Woronzow' label and loved by music critics. Another two albums, 'INNER MARSHLAND', and 'BEVIS THROUGH THE LOOKING GLASS', were issued during that year and several others followed, although he kept a low profile. In the late 80's, he also set up his own underground magazine 'Ptolemaic Terrascope'. In 1990, he recorded a collaboration album, 'MAGIC EYE', with the legendary PINK FAIRIES drummer TWINK. • **Style:** Psychedelic guitar-rock act, led by the quintessential English eccentric SALOMAN, whose influences ranged from JIMI HENDRIX and CREAM to folky-punk! • **Songwriters:** SALOMAN except; XPRESS MAN (Groundhogs) / POSSESSION (Iron Butterfly) / SUMMER HOLIDAY EP (Cliff & The Shadows) / etc.

Recommended: MIASMA (*8) / A GATHERING OF FRONDS (*7) / NEW RIVER HEAD (*8)

NICK SALOMAN – vocals, guitar / + 4 others

Woronzow | not issued

1980. (7"ep; as VON TRAPP FAMILY) *(W 001)* **BRAND NEW THRILL. / DREAMING / NO REFLEXES** ☐ -

SALOMAN + 2 others

1982. (12"; as ROOM 13) *(W 002)* **MURDER MYSTERY. / NEED SOME DUB** ☐ -

NICK SALOMAN – vocals, instruments

Mar 87. (lp) *(W 003)* **MIASMA** ☐ -
– Garden gate / She's in love with time / Wild mind / Wild afterthought / Splendid isolation / The Earl of Walthamstow / The Newgate wind / Release yourself / Maybe / Ride the train of thought / Confusion days. *(re-iss.Jul89 on 'Reckless'; RECK 13) (cd-iss.Mar89+=; CDRECK 13)*– Rat in a waistcoat / In another year / Mudman / Now you know / 1970 home improvements.

Aug 87. (lp) *(W 004)* **INNER MARSHLAND** ☐ -
– Cries from the inner marshland / Termination station grey / Window eye / Once more / Defoliation part one / Reflections in a tall mirror / Hey Mr. Undecided / I've got eyes in the back of my head / Minsmere sphagnum Sienese acid blues / Defoliation part two / I can't get into your scene / Song for the sky / The shrine. *(re-iss.Jul89 on 'Reckless'; RECK 14) (cd-iss.Mar89; CDRECK 14)*

Dec 87. (d-lp) *(W 005)* **BEVIS THROUGH THE LOOKING GLASS – THE GREAT MAGNET DISASTER** ☐ -
– 1970 home improvements / Now you know / The shrine / Rat in a waistcoat / In another year / Express man / Mudman / Song for the sky / Purtle sline / I can't get into your scene / Soot / Die is cast / Alistair Jones.
(re-iss.Dec88 on 'Reckless'; RECKD 9)

Jun 88. (lp) *(W 006)* **ACID JAM** ☐ -

— BEVIS featured on OUTSKIRTS OF INFINITY lp 'Lord Of The Dark Skies' *W 007)*

Aug 88. (lp) *(W 008)* **TRIPTYCH** ☐ -
– Into the cryptic mist / Debbie's new song for drums / Lights are changing / Gemini machine / Phil exorcises the Daemons / Old man blank / The daily round / Hurt goes on / Corinthian / Nowhere fast / Tangerine infringement beak / Hey Joe / Purtle sline / Soot / Long journey into light. *(re-iss.Mar89 on 'Reckless' cd/lp; CD+/RECK 15)*

— used occasional musician; **MARTIN CROWLEY** – drums / **SHAW + GOODWAY**

Reckless | Reckless

Jul 89. (cd/lp) *(CD+/RECK 17)* **THE AUNTIE WINNIE ALBUM** ☐ ☐
– Malvolios dream – Journey to Pikes / Foreign laugh / Down again / Will to lose / Repressor / Winters blues / The mizmaze / Close / Without mind / City of the sun / Die is cast / The miskatonic variations.

Feb 90. (cd/lp) *(CD+/RECK 18)* **ANY GAS FASTER** ☐ ☐
– Lord Plentiful reflects / Rejection day (a.m.) / Ear song / This corner of England / Legendary / When you wanted me / Lost rivers / Somewhere else / These dark days / Head on a pole / Your mind's gone grey / Old sea dog / Rejection day (p.m.) / Olde world.

Oct 90. (12"ep) *(12RECK 20)* **EAR SONG / OLDE WORLDE. / I'VE GOT EYES IN THE BACK OF MY HEAD (live) / MEDIAEVAL SIENESE ACID BLUES (live) / OLDE WORLDE (live) / RADIO BLOODBEAST (live)** ☐ -

Woronzow | not issued

Feb 91. (lp/cd; by BEVIS & TWINK) **MAGIC EYE** ☐ ☐
– Sorrow remembered / Flying igloos / The fairy / She darks the sun / Eclipse / Fractured sky / Black queen / Gryke / Bag drip.

Sep 91. (d-lp/cd) *(W 016/+CD)* **NEW RIVER HEAD** ☐ ☐
– White sun / Drowned / She's entitled to / Waving / New river head / Wild jack hammer / He'd be a diamond / Undertaker / Stain on the sun / Thankless task / Mistatonic variations II / It won't come again / Chinese burn / God speed you to earth.

Nov 92. (lp/cd) *(W 018/+CD)* **LONDON STONE** ☐ -

Jul 93. (7"ep) *(W 020)* **SUMMER HOLIDAY EP** ☐ -
– Summer holiday / Big news / Dancing shoes / Round and round.

Oct 93. (d-lp/cd) *(W 021/+CD)* **IT JUST IS** ☐ ☐
– Can't stop lying / Time-share heart / Idiot dance / Desperate / What's it all about / Day one / Let me live / Terrible day / Dreamboat sinking / A sorry tale / Human overload / I can't catch up with you / Hit the lights / Everyday sunshine / Not for now / All gone / Time piece / And then?

Oct 94. (lp/cd) *(W 022/+CD)* **SPRAWL** ☐ -
– I know we're going / Awake! / Love you more / The puller / Oh Gideon / Right on (hippie dream) / I bought my love a lapdog / New Alexandria / Anodyne – See you.

— live band included; **ANDY WARD** – drums (ex-CAMEL) / **ADRIAN SHAW** – bass / **RIC GUNTHER + MARTIN CROWLEY** occasional drums

Oct 95. (d-lp/cd) *(W 026/+CD)* **SUPERSEEDER** ☐ -
– Superseded / Dolly bug / Stoned train driver / Animal tracks / Jaye / I can't cry / Could be / Flashy / Golden walks of London / House of mountains / The queen of May / Sue me / Loveland / Could you fly higher?

Oct 96. (lp/cd) *(W 028/+CD)* **SON OF WALTER** ☐ -
–

Spare Me | not issued

Apr 97. (7") *(SPAREME 004)* **LITTLE TOWN PIER. /** ☐ -

– compilations, etc –

May 92. (cd) *Reckless; (CDRECK 25)* **A GATHERING OF FRONDS** ☐ -
– Down in the well / Mother dust / Cuvie / Blurred vision / Solar marmalade / Son of many mothers / Hillview (PARTHENOGENTICK BROTHERHOOD) / Bad time / High in a flat / Snow / Express man / African violet / Possession / Visions (through dilated eyes) (VACANT PLOT) / Somewhere else / Alistair Jones.

1990's. (7") *(HELPF 101)* **AFRICAN VIOLET. / The Steppes: History Hates No Man** ☐ -

BIOSPHERE

Formed: Tromso, Norway . . . early 90's by GEIR JENSSEN, whose previous work was in the late 80's with group BEL CANTO and his own BLEEP. BEL CANTO released a few albums, before BLEEP came out with three singles and a Norwegian-only album, 'THE NORTH POLE BY SUBMARINE' in 1990. Its inspiration came from him taking part in an Arctic archaelogical expedition during which he was exposed to the elements, thus his subsequent interest in short-wave radio listening. BIOSPHERE's debut album, 'MICROGRAVITY', saw light a few years later. His/their UK debut, 'PATASHNIK', gave him a brief Top 50 entry early in '94, later used on a Levi's jeans TV ad. He collaborated with PETE NAMLOOK on the 'FIRE OF ORK' album, scoring a soundtrack for the Norwegian film, 'Evige Stjerner', and producing work for an exhibition at the Norwegian Ministry Of Arts. After a busy year, JENSSEN then took off to scale mountains in Nepal, and upon his return he re-formed BEL CANTO, having just signed to 'Warners'. • **Style:** Time-transported ambient/techno-punk, whose stage appearance consisted of him sitting "lotus-position" wearing an EXPLOITED T-shirt and smoking a spliff. Two-note ostinatos were soon bolstered by the proverbial bass-drum explosion. • **Songwriters:** JENSSEN or with DRECKER and JOHANSON in BEL CANTO. • **Trivia:** JENSSEN also guested on a release by The HIGHER INTELLIGENCE AGENCY.

Recommended: PATASHNIK (*7)

BEL CANTO

GEIR JENSSEN – synthesizer / **ANNELI DRECKER** – vocals, synthesizer / **NILS JOHANSEN** – mellotron, bass, flute, synthesizer

Crammed Discs | not issued

Mar 88. (lp/cd) *(CRAM/+CD 057)* **WHITE OUT CONDITION** ☐ -
– Blank sheets / Dreaming girl / Without you / Capio / Agassiz / Klooberdanz / White out condition / Baltic icebreaker / Upland.

1988. (7") *(CRAM 15-457)* **WHITE OUT CONDITION. / DREAMING GIRL** ☐ -

Dec 88. (lp/cd) *(CRAM/+CD 065)* **BIRDS OF PASSAGE** ☐ -
– Look 3 / Dewy fields / Continuum / The suffering / The glassmaker / Piemie on the moon / Intravenous / Oyster / Birds of passage / A shoulder to the wheel / Time without end.

Apr 92. (cd) *(CRACD 077)* **SHIMMERING, WARM AND BRIGHT** (compilation) ☐ -

BLEEP

GEIR JENSSEN – synthesizer

Sampler Et Sans Reproches | not issued

Feb 89. (12") *(12SSR 91)* **SURE BE GLAD WHEN YOU'RE DEAD. / I SAIS BLEEP** ☐ -

1989. (12") **IN YOUR SYSTEM. /** - - Norway

1990. (12") **A BITE OF AMC. /** - - Norway

1990. (lp/cd) **THE NORTH POLE BY SUBMARINE** - - Norway

1990. (12") **THE LAUNCHPAD. /** - - Norway

BIOSPHERE

Apollo | not issued

May 93. (12") *(APOLLO 007)* **BABY INTERPHASE. /** ☐ -

Jun 93. (lp/cd) *(AMB/+CD 3921)* **MICROGRAVITY** ☐ -
– Microgravity / Baby satelite / Tranquilizer / The fairytale / Cloudwalker II / Cygnus – A / Baby interphase / Biosphere.

Feb 94. (cd/cd/c/d-blue-lp) *(AMB 3927 CD/CDX/MC/X)* **PATASHNIK** 50 -
– Phantasm / Startoucher / Decryption / Novelty waves / Patashnite / Mir / The shield / Seti project / Mastigoth / Botancal dimensions / Caboose / Entrance.

Feb 94. (12"/cd-s) *(APOLLO 012/+CD)* **SETI PROJECT / THE FAIRY TALE (remix). / ('A'remix) / CLOUD X-3** ☐ -

Apr 95. (12"/c-s/cd-s) *(APOLLO 020/+MC/CD)* **NOVELTY WAVES / ('A'-Arctic mix) / ('A'-Darkroom mix) / ('A'-Mark Bell mix) / ('A'-Higher Intelligence Agency mix).**
(cd-s) *(APOLLO 020CDX)* – ('A'side) / Baby satellite (live) / Patashnik / Baby interphase.

BEL CANTO

— re-formed same line-up

Atlantic | Atlantic

Feb 96. (c-s) *(A 8128C)* **RUMOUR. / ('A'version)** ☐ ☐
(12"+=/cd-s+=) *(A 8128 T/CD)* – (2 other mixes).

May 96. (cd/c) *(7567 92617-2/-4)* **MAGIC BOX** ☐ ☐
– Kiss of Spring / Bombay / Rumour / Magic box / Free lunch in the jungle / Sleepwalker / Big belly butterfly / Magic box II.

BIOSPHERE

All Saints / not issued

Jun 97. (cd) *(ASCD 033)* **SUBSTRATA** [ ] [-]
– As the sun kissed the horizon / Poa alpina / Chukhung / Things I tell you / Times when I know you'll be sad / Hyperborea / Kobresia / Antennaria / Uva-ursi / Sphere of no-form / Silene.

BIRDSONGS OF THE MESOZOIC (see under ⇒ MISSION OF BURMA)

BLACK DOG

Formed: London, England . . .1989 by ED HANDLEY, KEN DOWNIE and ANDY TURNER. Taking the term "faceless techno" to new and obscure heights, BLACK DOG remain something of an enigma. Rarely giving personal interviews, the group prefer to remain anonymous and let their subtle blend of cerebral, jazzy techno do the talking instead. BLACK DOG released their debut lp on 'Warp' in 1993, 'TEMPLE OF TRANSPARENT BALLS', having already appeared on the label's 1991 sampler 'ARTIFICIAL INTELLIGENCE' alongside such knob-twiddling luminaries as RICHIE HAWTIN, SPEEDY J and APHEX TWIN. The collective released another couple of albums for 'Warp', the most recent, 'SPANNERS' (1995) taking pride of place in 'MUZIK' magazine's top 20 albums of 1995. Simultaneously, they've released a string of well-recieved EP's under aliases on labels such as 'Rising High' and CARL CRAIG's 'Planet E'. They have also mixed for the likes of BJORK and many others.

Recommended: SPANNERS (*8)

Warp / not issued

Feb 93. (cd/c/d-lp; as BLACK DOG PRODUCTIONS) *(WARP CD/MC/LP 8)* **BYTES** [ ] [ ]
– Object Orient / Caz / Cercenes ex novum / Phil; (1) Focus Mel (2) Olivine (3) Clan Mongol nordes (4) Yamenn (5) Fight the hits (6) Merck (7) Jauqq 3 4 heart. *(re-iss.Apr96; same)*

Oct 93. (cd/c/lp) *(GPR CD/MC/LP 1)* **TEMPLE OF TRANSPARENT BALLS** [ ] [-]

— (above on 'G.P.R.)

1994. (cd/c/d-lp) **PARALLEL** [ ] [-]
(re-iss.Nov95)

Feb 95. (cd/c/d-lp) *(PUP CD/MC/LP 1)* **SPANNERS** [31] [ ]

Jul 96. (cd/c/d-lp) *(PUP CD/MC/LP 2)* **MUSIC FOR ADVERTS (AND SHORT FILMS(** [ ] [-]

G.P.R. / not issued

Dec 96. (12"ep) *(GENPX 017)* **COST II** [ ] [-]
– The actor and audience / On the dance scene at all times.

BLEEP (see under ⇒ BIOSPHERE)

BLUR

Formed: Colchester, Essex, England . . . 1989 by DAMON ALBARN, GRAHAM COXON, ALEX JAMES and DAVE ROWNTREE. Initially they went under the moniker of SEYMOUR before opting for The GREAT WHITE HOPES. Finally settling with BLUR, they soon were on the books of David Balfe's 'Food' label, a subsidiary of Parlophone. There, they secured their first UK Top 50 entry with 'SHE'S SO HIGH', an early PINK FLOYD-influenced tune, that rode the coat-tails of the baggy brigade. With the ghost of SYD BARRETT even more pronounced, they created one of the more psychedelic singles of the era in 'THERE'S NO OTHER WAY', the record hitting Top 10 in '91. Another single, 'BANG', preceded their debut album, 'LEISURE', a record that received mixed reviews at the time. Still mainly a singles orientated outfit, they progressed dramatically with the much-improved, 'MODERN LIFE IS RUBBISH' (1993) album, which featured some classy tracks including the hits, 'FOR TOMORROW', 'CHEMICAL WORLD' and 'SUNDAY SUNDAY'. Although they had come on leaps and bounds creatively, this wasn't translated into sales. With the release of 'GIRLS AND BOYS', however, they embarked upon a commercial renaissance that saw the record become their biggest hit to date. It was the opening track on the critically approved 'PARKLIFE' album, which also spawned further hits, 'TO THE END' and the title track (co-sung with actor PHIL DANIELS). By this point they had evolved into a mod-ish indie-pop combo, ALBARN supplying the cockney barra-boy delivery over a musical backdrop that drew from the rich English pop heritage, once the domain of such luminaries as The SMALL FACES and The KINKS. The following year, 1995, saw them win the battle to the coveted No.1 spot with 'COUNTRY HOUSE', beating rivals OASIS who were sharpening their tongues for an onslaught of media slagging. However, BLUR lost ground in the credibility stakes, when their 'GREAT ESCAPE' album failed to impress the critics. OASIS, on the other hand, were scaling new heights with their 2nd album. 1997 marked a slight return to favour, both the single, 'BEETLEBUM', and their eponymous 5th album hitting pole position. • **Songwriters:** Group songs, ALBARN lyrics. Covered MAGGIE MAY (Rod Stewart) / LAZY SUNDAY (Small Faces). • **Trivia:** DAMON's father KEITH ALBARN used to be the manager of 60's rock outfit The SOFT MACHINE.

Recommended: LEISURE (*6) / MODERN LIFE IS RUBBISH (*8) / PARKLIFE (*10) / THE GREAT ESCAPE (*7) / BLUR (*8)

DAMON ALBARN (b.23 Mar'68, Whitechapel, London) – vocals / **GRAHAM COXON** (b.12 Mar'69, Germany) – guitars / **ALEX JAMES** (b.21 Nov'68, Dorset, England) – bass, vocals / **DAVE ROWNTREE** (b. 8 Apr'63) – drums

Food-EMI / S.B.K.

Oct 90. (c-s/7") *(TC+/FOOD 26)* **SHE'S SO HIGH. / I KNOW** [48] [-]
(12") *(12FOOD 26)* – ('A'-Definitive) / Sing / I know (extended).
(cd-s) *(CDFOOD 26)* – ('A'side) / I know (extended) / Down.

Apr 91. (c-s/7") *(TC+/FOOD 29)* <07374> **THERE'S NO OTHER WAY. / INERTIA** [8] [82] Dec91
(ext.12"+=/cd-s+=) *(12/CD FOOD 29)* – Mr.Briggs / I'm all over.
(12") *(12FOODX 20)* – ('A'remix). / Won't do it / Day upon day (live).

Jul 91. (c-s/7") *(TC+/FOOD 31)* **BANG. / LUMINOUS** [24] [ ]
(ext.12"+=) *(12FOOD 31)* – Explain / Uncle Love.
(cd-s+=) *(CDFOOD 31)* – Explain / Beserk.

Aug 91. (cd/c/lp) *(FOOD CD/TC/LP 6)* **LEISURE** [7] [ ]
– She's so high / Bang / Slow down / Repetition / Bad day / Sing / There's no other way / Fool / Come together / High cool / Birthday / Wear me down.

Mar 92. (c-s/7") *(TC+/FOOD 37)* **POPSCENE. / MACE** [32] [ ]
(12"+=) *(12FOOD 37)* – I'm fine / Garden central.
(cd-s+=) *(CDFOOD 37)* – Badgeman Brown.

Apr 93. (c-s) *(TCFOOD 40)* **FOR TOMORROW. / INTO ANOTHER / HANGING OVER** [28] [ ]
(12"+=) *(12FOOD 40)* – Peach.
(cd-s) *(CDFOOD 40)* – ('A'extended) / Peach / Bone bag.
(cd-s) *(CDSFOOD 40)* – ('A'side) / When the cows come home / Beachcoma / For tomorrow (acoustic).

May 93. (cd/c/lp) *(FOOD CD/TC/LP 9)* **MODERN LIFE IS RUBBISH** [15] [ ]
– For tomorrow / Advert / Colin Zeal / Pressure on Julian / Star shaped / Blue jeans / Chemical world / Sunday Sunday / Oily water / Miss America / Villa Rosie / Coping / Turn it up / Resigned.

Jun 93. (7"red) *(FOODS 45)* **CHEMICAL WORLD. / MAGGIE MAY** [28] [ ]
(12"/cd-s) *(12/CD FOOD 45)* – ('A'side) / Es Schmecht / Young and lovely / My ark.
(cd-s) *(CDFOODS 45)* – ('A'side) / Never clever (live) / Pressure on Julian (live) / Come together (live).

Oct 93. (7"yellow) *(FOODS 46)* **SUNDAY SUNDAY. / TELL ME, TELL ME** [26] [ ]
(12") *(12FOODS 46)* – ('A'side) / Long legged / Mixed up.
(cd-s) *(CDFOODS 46)* – ('A'side) / Dizzy / Fried / Shimmer.
(cd-s) *(CDFOODX 46)* – ('A'side) / Daisy bell / Let's all go The Strand.

Mar 94. (7"/c-s) *(FOODS/TCFOOD 47)* **GIRLS AND BOYS. / MAGPIE / PEOPLE IN EUROPE** [5] [59] Jun94
(cd-s) *(CDFOOD 47)* – ('A'side) / People in Europe / Peter Panic.
(cd-s) *(CDFOODS 47)* – ('A'side) / Magpie / Anniversary waltz.

Apr 94. (cd/c/lp) *(FOOD CD/TC/LP 10)* **PARKLIFE** [1] [ ] Jun94
– Girls and boys / Tracy Jacks / End of a century / Park life / Bank holiday / Bad head / The debt collector / Far out / To the end / London loves / Trouble in the message centre / Clover over Dover / Magic America / Jubilee / This is a low / Lot 105.

May 94. (c-s) *(TCFOOD 50)* **TO THE END / GIRLS AND BOYS (Pet Shop Boys remix) / THREADNEEDLE STREET** [16] [ ]
(12"/cd-s) *(12/CD FOOD 50)* – (1st 2 tracks; 2 versions of 2nd).
(cd-s) *(CDFOODS 50)* – ('A'side) / Threadneedle Street / Got yer.

— (above featured LETITIA of STEREOLAB. Next with actor PHIL DANIELS.

Aug 94. (c-s/cd-s) *(TC/CDS FOOD 53)* **PARKLIFE. / SUPA SHOPPA / THEME FROM AN IMAGINARY FILM** [10] [ ]
(12") *(12FOOD 53)* – (1st 2 tracks) / To the end (French version).
(cd-s) *(CDFOOD 53)* – (1st track) / Beard / To the end (French version).

Nov 94. (c-s/7") *(TCFOOD/FOODS 56)* **END OF A CENTURY. / RED NECKS** [19] [ ]
(cd-s+=) *(CDFOOD 56)* – Alex's song.

Aug 95. (c-s/7") *(TC+/FOOD 63)* **COUNTRY HOUSE. / ONE BORN EVERY MINUTE** [1] [ ]
(cd-s+=) *(CDFOOD 63)* – To the end (with FRANCOISE HARDY).
(cd-ep) *(CDFOODS 63)* ('A'live) / Girls and boys (live) / Parklife (live) / For tomorrow (live).

Sep 95. (cd/c/lp) *(FOOD CD/MC/LP 14)* **THE GREAT ESCAPE** [1] [ ]
– Stereotypes / Country house / Best days / Charmless man / Fade away / Top man / The universal / Mr. Robinson's quango / He thought of cars / It could be you / Ernold Same / Globe alone / Dan Abnormal / Entertain me / Yuko and Hiro.

Nov 95. (c-s) *(TCFOOD 69)* **THE UNIVERSAL / ENTERTAIN ME (the live it! remix)** [5] [ ]
(cd-s+=) *(CDFOODS 69)* – Ultranol / No monsters in me.
(cd-ep) *(CDFOOD 69)* – ('A'live) / Mr. Robinson's quango (live) / It could be you (live) / Stereotypes (live).

Feb 96. (c-s/7") *(TC+/FOOD 73)* **STEREOTYPES. / THE MAN WHO LEFT HIMSELF / TAME** [7] [ ]
(cd-s+=) *(CDFOOD 73)* – Ludwig.

Apr 96. (c-s/7") *(TC+/FOOD 77)* **CHARMLESS MAN. / THE HORRORS** [5] [ ]
(cd-s+=) *(CDFOOD 77)* – A song / St. Louis.

— BLUR were joint winners (with rivals OASIS; NOEL) of the Ivor Novello Award for songwriter of the year.

May 96. (d-cd; ltd on 'EMI Japan') *(TOCP 8400)* **LIVE AT THE BUDOKAN (live)** [-] [-]

— ALEX JAMES helped to form one-off indie supergroup ME ME ME alongside JUSTIN WELCH (Elastica –), STEPHEN DUFFY and CHARLIE BLOOR. Had a UK Top 20 hit in Aug'96 with 'HANGING AROUND'.

Jan 97. (c-s/cd-s/7") *(TC/CD+/FOOD 89)* **BEETLEBUM. / ALL YOUR LIFE / A SPELL FOR MONEY** [1] [ ]
(cd-s) *(CDFOODS 89)* – ('A'side) / Woodpigeon song / ('A'-Mario Caldato Jr mix) / ('A'-dancehall mix).

Feb 97. (cd/c/lp) *(FOOD CD/TC/LP 19)* **BLUR** [1] [61]
– Beetlebum / Song 2 / Country sad ballad man / M.O.R. / On your own / Theme from retro / You're so great / Death of a party / Chinese bombs / I'm just a killer for your love / Look inside America / Strange news from another star / Movin' on / Essex dogs.

Apr 97. (c-s) *(TCFOOD 93)* **SONG 2 / GET OUT OF CITIES** [2] [ ]
(cd-s+=) *(CDFOODS 93)* – Polished stone.
(cd-s) *(CDFOOD 93)* – ('A'side) / Bustin' & dronin' / Country sad ballad man (live acoustic).

Jun 97. (7") *(FOOD 98)* **ON YOUR OWN. / POP SCENE (live) / SONG 2 (live)** 5
(cd-s+=) *(CDFOOD 98)* – On your own (live).
(cd-s) *(CDFOODS 98)* – ('A'side) / Chinese bombs (live) / Moving on (live) / MOR (live).

BONGWATER

Formed: New York, USA . . . 1987 by MARK KRAMER and actress ANN MAGNUSON, who he had met while working in the latter's PULSALLAMA band. KRAMER founded his new indie label, 'Shimmy Disc', releasing the mini-lp, 'BREAKING NO NEW GROUND'. This featured a cover of The MONKEES' 'PORPOISE SONG' and avant-garde guitarist FRED FRITH. The 1988 follow-up, 'DOUBLE BUMMER' featured more inspired covers including GARY GLITTER's 'ROCK & ROLL PART 2', JOHNNY CASH's 'THERE YOU GO' and an outrageous version of LED ZEPPELIN's 'DAZED AND CONFUSED' (re-born/aborted as DAZED AND CHINESE). They satirized many styles and cultures, nobody (even DAVID BOWIE) being safe from their merciless humour. KRAMER moonlighted with other projects, producing just about anyone who was anyone (i.e. GALAXIE 500, URGE OVERKILL and DOGBOWL) from the US indie world, while also finding time to play with B.A.L.L. The albums, 'THE POWER OF PUSSY' (1991) and 'THE BIG SELL-OUT' (1992), showed KRAMER and MAGNUSON at their most wilfully perverse/diverse. The neo-narrative, seductive/soft-core vox of ANN lent a shimmering, psychedelic beauty to proceedings, even on their version of FRED NEIL's 'EVERYBODY'S TALKIN'. Sadly, their partnership came to an abrupt halt, both taking off on solo flights. • **Songwriters:** KRAMER – music / MAGNUSON – lyrics (later a few with HUDSON), except RIDE MY SEE-SAW (Moody Blues) / WE DID IT AGAIN (Soft Machine) / JUST MAY BE THE ONE (Monkees) / SPLASH 1 (13th Floor Elevators) / THE DRUM (Slapp Happy) / KISSES SWEETER THAN WIRE (Newman – Campbell) / BEDAZZLED (from the film) / ONE SO BLACK (Dogbowl) / LOVE YOU TOO + RAIN (Beatles) / REAGANATION (Fugs). • **Trivia:** ANN's acting C.V. included a TV sitcom, 'Anything But Love', and a film, 'Making Mr Right'.

Recommended: THE POWER OF PUSSY (*7) / THE BIG SELL-OUT (*8)

KRAMER – guitar, other instruments, vocals (of-B.A.L.L., ex-SHOCKABILLY, ex-BUTTHOLE SURFERS) / **ANN MAGNUSON** – vocals / guest **FRED FRITH** – guitar (ex-HENRY COW)

Shimmy Disc / Shimmy Disc

Feb 88. (m-lp) *(SHIMMY 002)* **BREAKING NO NEW GROUND** Nov87
–

— the duo added **DAVE RICK** – guitar (was part-time) / **DAVID LICHT** – drums, percussion

Feb 89. (lp) *(SDE 8801) (SHIMMY 011)* **DOUBLE BUMMER**
– Lesbians of Russia / Frank / We did it again / Homer / Joy ride / Decadent Iranian country club / David Bowie wants ideas / Rock & roll (part 2) / Just may be the one / There you go / Shark / Jimmy / Crime / Pornography / Dazed and Chinese / Bullaby / So help me God / His old look / Stone / Number / Love you too / Reaganation / Double birth / Bruce / Pool / Rain.

— In 1989, he and JAD FAIR (of HALF JAPANESE) released album 'ROLL OUT THE BARREL' *(SDE 8802)*

Apr 90. (cd/lp) *(SDE 9017/+CD)* **TOO MUCH SLEEP**
– The living end / The drum / Mr & Mrs Hell / Too much sleep / Talent is a vampire / Psychedelic sewing room / Slash one / He loved the weather / Teena stays the same / One hand on the road / Khomeini died tonight / One so black / No trespassing.

— Late in 1990, KRAMER collaborated with CARNEY & HILD on 'cd 'HAPPINESS FINALLY CAME TO THEM'. Just earlier, he and REBBY SHARP issued 'IN ONE MOUTH AND OUT THE OTHER' *(SHIMMY 033)*

Feb 91. (lp/cd) *(SHIMMY 040/+CD)* **THE POWER OF PUSSY**
– The power of pussy / Great radio / What if? / Kisses sweeter than wine / Chicken pussy / White rental car blues / Nick Cave dolls / Bedazzled / Obscene and pornographic art / Connie / What kind of man reads Playboy / I need a new tape / Women tied up in knots / Junior / Mystery hole / Time is coming / Polar song.

— **RANDOLPH A. HUDSON III** – guitars, devices, repl. DAVE RICK

— **DOGBOWL** also provided live guitar

Mar 92. (lp/cd) *(SDE 9239/+CD)* **THE BIG SELL-OUT**
– Ye olde backlash / The real thing / Free love messes up my life / You're like me now / I wanna talk about it now / What's big in England now? / Schmoozedance / Celebrity compass / When Johnnie dies / The big sell-out / Over the credit line / Flop sweats / Holding hands / Flute of shame / On the cusp of 1970 / Her litigious nature / Love song / Everybody's talking.

— dropped out of scene man. ANN signed a solo contract with 'Geffen'. This led to a bitter lawsuit, between her and the now solo KRAMER, which led to his label folding.

KRAMER

1992. (cd; as KRAMER & DAEVID ALLEN) **WHO'S AFRAID**
Jun 93. (d-cd/d-c/d-lp) *(SHIMMY 055 CD/MC/LP)* **THE GUILT TRIP**
1995. (lp/cd) *(SHIMMY 075/+CD)* **SECRET OF COMEDY**
Mar 97. (cd; KRAMER & DAVID HILD) *(SHIMMY 087CD)* **RUBBER HAIR**

BOO RADLEYS

Formed: Liverpool, England . . . 1988, by schoolmates SICE and MARTIN CARR. Another friend, TIM BROWN, was invited to join after teaching MARTIN how to play guitar. They took the group name from a weird character in the film, 'To Kill A Mockingbird'. The quartet was complete when they found drummer STEVE HEWITT. They worked hard on the Mersey gig circuit but no major deal was forthcoming. Come 1990, they finally found a home with small indie label, 'Action', who released their debut lp 'ICHABOD AND I'. On its merit, they were invited by the illustrious DJ John Peel to session for Radio 1. This led to a signing for 'Rough Trade', who issued 3 popular EP's between late 1990 & 91. They then moved to 'Creation', their psychedelic, BYRDS-influenced jangle-pop soon making them favourites of the music press (Singles Of The Week, etc). The release of 1992's 'EVERYTHING'S ALRIGHT FOREVER' and the following years' masterful 'GIANT STEPS' album infused their sugary pop with screeching guitars and jagged brass accompaniment. The latter secured them their first Top 20 placing, the tracks 'I HANG SUSPENDED', 'BARNEY (. . . AND ME)' and 'LAZARUS' being effervescent highlights. Early to rise in '95, they scored their first Top 10 hit with 'WAKE UP BOO!', taken from their similarly titled No.1 album. The single was subsequently spoiled after it was played to death as the theme tune for ITV's Breakfast TV. In 1996, SICE (aka EGGMAN) released a patchy solo album, while The BOOS returned with another slice of nostalgic pop, 'C'MON KIDS'. • **Songwriters:** CARR lyrics / group music, except TRUE FAITH (New Order) / ALONE AGAIN OR (Love) / ONE OF US MUST KNOW (Bob Dylan) / THE QUEEN IS DEAD (Smiths). • **Trivia:** MERIEL BARHAM of The PALE SAINTS provided vocals on 2 tracks for GIANT STEPS album. ED BALL (ex-TV PERSONALITIES) often made guest appearances.

Recommended: EVERYTHING'S ALRIGHT FOREVER (*7) / GIANT STEPS (*9) / WAKE UP! (*8) / C'MON KIDS (*6) / FIRST FRUITS (EGGMAN; *5)

SICE (b. SIMON ROWBOTTOM, 18 Jun'69, Wallasey, England) – vocals, guitar / **MARTIN CARR** (b.29 Nov'68, Thurso, Scotland) – guitar / **TIM BROWN** (b.26 Feb'69, Wallasey) – bass / **STEVE DREWITT** (b. Northwich, England) – drums

Action / not issued

Jul 90. (lp) *(TAKE 4)* **ICHABOD AND I** -
– Eleanor everything / Bodenheim Jr. / Catweazle / Sweet salad birth / Hip clown rag / Walking 5th carnival / Kaleidoscope / Happens to us all.

— **ROB CIEKA** (b. 4 Aug'68, Birmingham, England) – drums repl. DREWITT to BREED

Rough Trade / not issued

Oct 90. (12"ep/cd-ep) *(RTT 241/+CD)* **KALEIDOSCOPE EP** -
– Kaleidoscope / How I feel / Aldous / Swansong.
Apr 91. (12"ep/cd-ep) *(R 201127-10/-13)* **EVERY HEAVEN EP** -
– The finest kiss / Tortoiseshell / Bluebird / Naomi.
Sep 91. (12"ep/cd-ep) *(R 275-0/-3)* **BOO UP! EP (Peel sessions)** -
– Everybird / Sometime soon she said / Foster's van / Song for up!.

Creation / Columbia

Feb 92. (12"ep)(cd-ep) *(CRE 128T)CRESCD 124)***ADRENALIN EP** -
– Lazy day / Vegas / Feels like tomorrow / Whiplashed.
Mar 92. (cd/c/lp) *(CRE CD/MC/LP 120)* **EVERYTHING'S ALRIGHT FOREVER** 55
– Spaniard / Towards the light / Losing it (song for Abigail) / Memory babe / Skyscraper / I feel nothing / Room at the top / Does this hurt / Sparrow / Smile fades fast / Firesky / Song for the morning to sing / Lazy day / Paradise.
Jun 92. (7") *(CRE 128)* **BOO! FOREVER. / DOES THIS HURT** 67 -
(12"+=)(cd-s+=) *(CRE 128T)(CRESCD 128)* – Buffalo Bill / Sunfly II: Walking with the kings.
Nov 92. (7") *(CRE 137)* **LAZARUS. / LET ME BE YOUR FAITH** 76 -
(12"+=)(cd-s+=) *(CRE 137T)(CRESCD 137)* – At the sound of speed / Petroleum.

— added **STEVE KITCHEN** – trumpet, flugel horn / **JACKIE ROY** – clarinet / **LINDSAY JOHNSTON** – cello

Jul 93. (7") *(CRE 147)* **I HANG SUSPENDED. / RODNEY KING (St. Etienne mix)** 77 -
(12"+=)(cd-s+=) *(CRE 147T)(CRESCD 147)* – As bound a stomorrow / I will always ask where you have been though I know the answer.
Jul 93. (cd/c/d-lp) *(CRE CD/MC/LP 149)* **GIANT STEPS** 17
– I hang suspended / Upon 9th and Fairchild / Wish I was skinny / Leaves and sand / Butterfly McQueen / Rodney King (song for Lenny Bruce) / Thinking of ways / Barney (. . . and me) / Spun around / If you want it, take it / Best lose the fear / Take the time around / Lazarus / One is for / Run my way runway / I've lost the reason / The white noise revisited.
Oct 93. (7"/c-s) *(CRE/+CD 169)* **WISH I WAS SKINNY. / PEACHY KEEN** 75 -
(12"+=)(cd-s+=) *(CRE 169T)(CRESCD 169)* – Furthur / Crow eye.
Feb 94. (7"/c-s) *(CRE/+CS 178)* **BARNEY (. . .AND ME). / ZOOM** 48 -
(12"+=)(cd-s+=) *(CRE 178T)(CRESCD 178)* – Tortoiseshell / Cracked lips, homesick.
May 94. (7") *(CRE 187)* **LAZARUS. / (I WANNA BE) TOUCHDOWN JESUS** 50 -
(12"+=) *(CRE 187T)* – ('A'-Secret Knowledge mix) / ('A'-Ultramarine radio mix).
(cd-s+=) *(CRESCD 187)* – ('A'acoustic) / ('A'-St. Etienne mix).
(cd-s) *(CRESCD 187X)* – ('A'-Secret Knowledge mix) / ('A'-Ultramarine mix) / ('A'-Augustus Pablo mix) / ('A'-12"mix).
Feb 95. (c-s) *(CRECS 191)* **WAKE UP BOO! / JANUS** 9
(cd-s+=) *(CRESCD 191)* – Blues for George Michael / Friendship song.
(12") *(CRE 191T)* – Wake up Boo!: Music for astronauts / Janus / Blues for George Michael.
(cd-s) *(CRESCD 191X)* – Wake up Boo!: Music for astronauts / . . .And tomorrow the world / The history of Creation parts 17 & 36.
Mar 95. (cd/c/lp) *(CRE CD/MC/LP 179)* **WAKE UP!** 1
– Wake up Boo! / Fairfax scene / It's Lulu / Joel / Find the answer within / Reaching out from here / Martin, Doom! it's 7 o'clock / Stuck on amber / Charles Bukowski is dead / 4am conversation / Twinside / Wilder.
May 95. (c-s) *(CRECS 202)* **FIND THE ANSWER WITHIN / DON'T TAKE YOUR GUN TO TOWN** 37 -
(cd-s+=) *(CRESCD 202)* – Wallpaper.
(12"++=) *(CRE 202T)* – The only word I can find / Very together.
(cd-s) *(CRESCD 202X)* – ('A'-High Llamas mix) / The only word I can find / Very together.

Jul 95. (c-s) *(RECS 211)* **IT'S LULU / THIS IS NOT ABOUT ME** [25] [ ]
(cd-s+=) *(CRESCD 211)* – Reaching out from here (the High Llamas mix / Martin, doom! it's seven o'clock (Stereolab mix).
(cd-s) *(CRESCD 211X)* – ('A'side) / Joel (Justin Warfield mix) / Tambo / Donkey.
Sep 95. (c-s/7") *(C+/CRE 214)* **FROM THE BENCH AT BELVIDERE. / HI FALUTIN'** [24] [ ]
(cd-s+=) *(CRESCD 214)* – Crushed / Nearly almost time.
Aug 96. (7") *(CRE 220)* **WHAT'S IN THE BOX? (SEE WHATCHA GOT). / BLOKE IN A DRESS** [25] [ ]
(cd-s+=) *(CRESCD CRESCD 220)* – Flakes / ('A'-Kris Needs mix).
(cd-s) *(CRESCD 220X)* – ('A'side) / Atlantic / The absent boy / Annie and Marnie.
Sep 96. (cd/c)(d-lp) *(CRECD/CCRE 194)(CRELP 194L)* **C'MON KIDS** [20] [ ]
– C'mon kids / Meltin's worm / Melodies for the deaf / Get on the bus / Everything is sorrow / Bullfrog green / What's in the box? (see whatcha got) / Four saints / New Brighton promenade / Fortunate sons / Shelter / Ride the tiger / One last hurrah. *(lp w/free 7")* SKYWALKER. / FRENCH CANADIAN BEAN SOUP
Oct 96. (7") *(CRE 236)* **C'MON KIDS. / SPION COP** [18] [ ]
(cd-s+=) *(CRESCD 236)* – Too beautiful / Bullfrog green (ultra living mix).
• (cd-s) *(CRESCD 236X)* – ('A'side) / Nothing to do but scare myself / From the bench at Belvidere (Ultramarine mix) / Fortunate sons (Greg Hunter remix).
Jan 97. (7") *(CRE 248)* **RIDE THE TIGER. / VOTE YOU** [38] [ ]
(cd-s) *(CRESCD 248)* –
(cd-s) *(CRESCD 248X)* –

EGGMAN

— i.e. SICE with **ROB LIEKA** – drums / **ED BALL** – bass / **SEAN JACKSON** – lead guitar / **TIM BROWN** – piano, etc / others

Creation Rykodisc

May 96. (7"/c-s) *(CRE/+CS 225)* **NOT BAD ENOUGH. / IDENTIKIT** [ ] [-]
(cd-s+=) *(CRESCD 225)* – We won the war.
May 96. (cd/lp)(c) *(CRE CD/LP 201)(CCRE 201)* **FIRST FRUITS** [ ] [ ]
– Purple patches / Tomas / That's that then (for now) / Not bad enough / The funeral song / Replace all your lies with truth / Out of my window / Look up / I'll watch your back / First fruits fall.

BOY HAIRDRESSERS

(see under ⇒ TEENAGE FANCLUB)

BUTTHOLE SURFERS

Formed: San Antonio, Texas, USA . . . 1980 originally as The ASHTRAY BABY HEELS by ex-accountant GIBBY (son of US children's TV presenter "Mr. Peppermint") and PAUL LEARY, who met at Trinity College, San Antonio. By 1983, they had signed to JELLO BIAFRA's (Dead Kennedys) label, 'Alternative Tentacles'. Around the mid-80's, they gigged heavily in Britain due to lack of Stateside interest, and this, together with radio play from John Peel, helped them make it into the UK indie charts. In 1987, they unleashed the brilliantly crazed 'LOCUST ABORTION TECHNICIAN', complete with a parody of BLACK SABBATH's 'SWEET LEAF', the humourously titled 'SWEAT LOAF'. Also deep inside its nightmarish musical grooves was their gem, 'TWENTY TWO GOING ON TWENTY THREE', a track that made John Peel's Festive 50. A longer sojourn in Britain culminated in some riotous, oversubscribed London gigs. The follow-up, 'HAIRWAY TO STEVEN' (another piss-take; this time of LED ZEPPELIN – Stairway To Heaven), deliberately left the tracks nameless (instead using obscene looking symbols) as a twisted tribute to ZEPPELIN's "untitled" symbols album. 1990 saw them shift to a more commercial sound with 'PIOUGHD' (which means "pissed-off" in Red Indian), which featured a re-working of DONOVAN's 'HURDY GURDY MAN'. Having signed to 'Capitol' in 1992, they were back to their abrasive sound of old with the JOHN PAUL JONES-produced album, 'INDEPENDENT WORM SALOON'. This, together with their previous effort, had given them their first taste of chart success in Britain, this being well surpassed in 1996 when 'ELECTRICLARRYLAND' hit the US Top 30. It was due, no doubt, to a surprise domestic hit with 'PEPPER'. • **Style:** Heavy psychedelia that mixed noise, confusion and futuristic art-punk. The manic GIBBY, (complete with loudspeaker, etc), was always offensive and disturbing, while their weird stage act included the nude dancer, KATHLEEN. She covered herself in green jello while GIBBY simulated sex with her! GIBBY was well-known for other stage antics; pissing in plastic baseball bats ('piss wands') and annointing the audience at the front. There have been other obscenities, too rude to print here (no need to mention President Carter's creamy briefcase). • **Songwriters:** GIBBY and co., except AMERICAN WOMAN (Guess Who). P covered DANCING QUEEN (Abba).

Recommended: BROWN REASONS TO LIVE (*5) / REMBRANDT PUSSYHORSE (*6) / LOCUST ABORTION TECHNICIAN (*8) / HAIRWAY TO STEVEN (*7) / PHIOGHD (*6) / INDEPENDENT WORM SALOON (*7) / ELECTRICLARRYLAND (*7)

GIBBY HAYNES (b. GIBSON JEROME HAYNES, 1957) – vocals / **PAUL LEARY** (b.1958) – guitar / **KING COFFEY** – drums repl. ? / **ALAN ?** – bass

Alt.Tent. Alt.Tent.

Apr 84. (m-lp) *(VIRUS 32)* **BUTTHOLE SURFERS** <'BROWN REASONS TO LIVE; US-title> [ ] [ ] 1983
– The Shah sleeps in Lee Harvey's grave / Hey / Something / Bar-b-que / Pope / Wichita cathedral / Suicide / The legend of Anus Presley. *(re-iss.Sep93 as 'BROWN REASONS TO LIVE' brown-lp; same)*
Jan 85. (12"ep) *(VIRUS 39)* **LIVE PCPPEP (live)** [ ] [ ]
– (contains most of last m-lp).

— **TERENCE** – bass repl. ALAN (?)

Fundamental Touch & Go

Apr 85. (7") **LADY SNIFF. / ?** [-] [ ]
Jul 85. (lp) *(SAVE 5)* **PSYCHIC . . . POWERLESS . . . ANOTHER MAN'S SAC** [ ] [ ] 1984
– Concubine / Eye of the chicken / Dum dum / Woly boly / Negro observer / Butthole surfer / Lady sniff / Cherub / Mexican caravan / Cowboy Bob / Gary Floyd. *(cd-iss.Jan88+=)*– CREAM CORN FROM THE SOCKET OF DAVIS

— **MARK KRAMER** – bass (of SHOCKABILLY) repl. TREVOR who had repl. TERENCE

Oct 85. (12"ep) *(PRAY 69)* **CREAM CORN FROM THE SOCKET OF DAVIS** [ ] [ ]
– Moving to Florida / Comb – Lou Reed (two parter) / Tornados.

R.R.E. Touch & Go

Apr 86. (lp) *(RRELP 2)* <*TGLP 8*> **REMBRANDT PUSSYHORSE** [ ] [ ]
– Creep in the cellar / Sea ferring / American woman / Waiting for Jimmy to kick / Strangers die / Perry / Whirling hall of knives / Mark says alright / In the cellar. *(cd-iss.May88; RRECD 2)*

— **JEFF 'TOOTER' PINKUS** – bass repl. KRAMER who formed BONGWATER

Blast First Blast First

Mar 87. (lp/c/cd) *(BFFP 15/+C/CD)* **LOCUST ABORTION TECHNICIAN** [ ] [ ]
– Sweat loaf / Graveyard 1 / Pittsburgh to Lebanon / Weber / Hay / Human cannonball / U.S.S.A. / Theoman / Kintz / Graveyard 2 / 22 going on 23 / The G-men.

— added **THERESA NERVOSA (NAYLOR)** – 2nd drummer / **KATHLEEN** – naked dancer (above with GIBBY, PAUL, COFFEY and PINKUS)

Apr 88. (lp/cd) *(BFFP 29/+CD)* **HAIRWAY TO STEVEN** [ ] [ ]
– Hairway part 1 / Hairway part 2 / Hairway part 3 / Hairway part 4 / Hairway part 5 / Hairway part 6 / Hairway part 7 / Hairway part 8 / Hairway part 9. *(9 tracks marked rude symbols as titles)*
Aug 89. (12"ep/10"ep/cd-ep) *(BFFP 41/+T/CD)* **WIDOWERMAKER** [ ] [ ]
– Bong song / 1401 / Booze tobacco / Helicopter.

— now without THERESA

Rough Trade Rough Trade

Nov 90. (7") *(RT 240)* **THE HURDY GURDY MAN. / BARKING DOGS** [ ] [ ]
(12"+=/cd-s+=) *(RTT 240/+CD)* – ('A'-Paul Leary remix).
Feb 91. (cd/c/lp) *(R 2081260-2/-4/-1)* <*RTE R2601*> **PIOUGHD** [68] [ ]
– Revolution pt.1 & 2 / Lonesome bulldog pt.1 & 2 / The hurdy gurdy man / Golden showers / Lonesome bulldog pt.3 / Blindman / No, I'm iron man / Something / P.S.Y. / Lonesome bulldog pt.IV. *(cd+=)*– Barking dogs. *(cd-iss.Dec 94 on 'Danceteria';)*

— In Apr'92, GIBBY guested for MINISTRY on single 'Jesus Built My Hotrod'.

Capitol Capitol

Mar 93. (cd/c/lp) *(CD/TC+/EST 2192)* <*98798*> **INDEPENDENT WORM SALOON** [73] [ ]
– Who was in my room last night / The wooden song / Tongue / Chewin' George Lucas' chocolate / Goofy's concern / Alcohol / Dog inside your body / Strawberry / Some dispute over T-shirt sales / Dancing fool / You don't know me / The annoying song / Dust devil / Leave me alone / Edgar / The ballad of a naked man / Clean it up.
May 96. (cd/c/d-lp) *(CD/TC+/EST 2285)* <*29842*> **ELECTRICLARRYLAND** [ ] [31]
– Birds / Cough syrup / Pepper / Thermador / Ulcer breakout / Jingle of a dog's collar / TV star / My brother's wife / Ah ha / The Lord is a monkey / Let's talk about cars / L.A. / Space.
Sep 96. (7") *(CL 778)* **PEPPER. / HYBRID** [59] [ ]
(cd-s+=) *(CDCL 778)* – Pepper (Butcha' Bros remix) / The Lord is a monkey.

– compilations, others, etc. –

Jun 89. (d-lp/cd) *Latino Bugger; (LBV ?)* **DOUBLE LIVE (live)** [ ] [-]
Nov 94. (7"/7"pic-d) *Trance Syndicate; (TR 30/+PD)* **GOOD KING WENCENSLAUS. / THE LORD IS A MONKEY** [ ] [-]
Apr 95. (cd) *Trance Syndicate; (TR 35CD)* **THE HOLE TRUTH & NOTHING BUTT!** (early demos) [ ] [-]

JACK OFFICERS

off-shoot with **GIBBY, JEFF & KATHLEEN**

Naked Brain Shimmy Disc

Dec 90. (lp/c/cd) *(NBX 003/+C/CD)* **DIGITAL DUMP** [ ] [ ]
– Love-o-maniac / Time machine pt.1 & 2 / L.A.name peanut butter / Do it / Swingers club / Ventricular retribution / 6 / Don't touch that / An Hawaiian Christmas song / Flush.

PAUL LEARY

Rough Trade Capitol

Apr 91. (cd/c/lp) *(R 2081263-2/-4/-1)* **THE HISTORY OF DOGS** [ ] [ ]
– The birds are dying / Apollo one / Dalhart down the road / How much longer / He's working overtime / Indians storm the government / Is it milky / Too many people / The city / Fine home.

DRAIN

aka **KING COFFEY + DAVID McCREETH** (ex-SQUID)

Trance Syndicate Trance Syndicate

Apr 91. (12")(cd-s) **A BLACK FIST** [ ] [ ]
Mar 92. (lp/cd) *(TR 11/+CD)* **PICK UP HEAVEN** [ ] [ ]
– National anthem / Crawfish / Martyr's road / Non compis mentis / Funeral pyre / Ozark monkey chant / Instant hippie / Flower mound / Every secret thing / The ballad of Miss Toni Fisher.
Apr 96. (cd) *(TR 49CD)* **OFFSPEED & IN THERE** [ ] [ ]

P

— formed 1993 by **GIBBY + JOHNNY DEPP** – bass, guitar (yes! the actor & beau of supermodel Kate Moss) / **BILL CARTER** – bass / **SAL JENCO** – drums

Capitol Capitol

Feb 96. (cd/c/lp) *(CD/TC PCS 7379) <7243 8 32942-2/-4/-1>* **P** [ ] [ ]
– I save cigarette butts / Zing Splash / Michael Stipe / Oklahoma / Dancing queen / Jon Glenn (megamix) / Mr Officer / White man sings the blues / Die Anne / Scrapings from ring / The deal.

C

CARDINAL

Formed: Boston, Massachusetts, USA . . . mid 90's by San Franciscan music student ERIC MATTHEWS and Australian RICHARD DAVIS. They got together after listening to each other's recent demo tapes. DAVIS, in his early 30's, had previously worked with garage retro band The MOLES. Early in 1995, The CARDINAL released their own eponymous album which featured the single, 'DREAM FIGURE'. The future of CARDINAL seems uncertain, MATTHEWS subsequently going on to release an acclaimed solo debut, 'IT'S HEAVY IN HERE', for cult label 'Sub Pop'. • **Style:** Psychedelic duo using diversive instrumentation alongside an orchestra. MATTHEWS was described as the new NICK DRAKE or even The BLUE NILE, with his melancholy vox. • **Songwriters:** Most by DAVIS, some with MATTHEWS. Covered SINGING TO THE SUNSHINE (US-band; Mortimer). ERIC MATTHEWS:- A CERTAIN KIND (Soft Machine).

Recommended: CARDINAL (*7) / IT'S HEAVY IN HERE (ERIC MATTHEWS *8)

MOLES

RICHARD DAVIS – vocals, electronics, instruments

not issued Seaside

1992. (lp) **UNTUNE THE SKY** [-] [ ]

Fire

Oct 94. (cd) *(FIRECD 42)* **INSTINCT** [ ] [ ]
– Minor royal march / Eros lunch (1963) / Already in black / Instinct / Cars for Kings Cross / Cassic pesk / Raymond, did you see the red queen? / Treble metal / The crasher.

— split when DAVIS formed The CARDINAL with ERIC

CARDINAL

ERIC MATTHEWS (b. Portland, Oregon) – vocals, trumpet / **RICHARD DAVIS** – instruments

Dedicated Flydaddy

1995. (cd-s) **DREAM FIGURE. /** [ ] [ ]
Feb 95. (cd) *(DED CD/LP 018)* **CARDINAL** [ ] [ ]
– If you believe in Christmas trees / Last poems / Bog mine / You've lost me there / Public melody #1 / Dream figure / Tough guy tactics / Angel darling / Singing to the sunshine / Silver machines.

ERIC MATTHEWS

Sub Pop Sub Pop

Feb 96. (7") *(SP 319)* **FANFARE. / LIDS, NAILS, SCREWS** [ ] [ ]
(cd-s+=) *(SPCD 319)* – A certain kind / Distant mother reality (S H mix).
Nov 95. (lp/c/cd) *(SP/+MC/CD 312)* **IT'S HEAVY IN HERE** [ ] [ ]
– Fanfare / Forging plastic rain / Soul nation select them / aith to day / Angels for crime / Fried out broken girl / Lust takes time / Hop and tickle / Three-cornered moon / Distant mother reality / Flight and lion / Poison will pas me / Sincere sensation / Fanfare (reprise).

RICHARD DAVIS

Flydaddy Flydaddy

1996. (cd-ep) *(BRRC 1004-2)* **CHIPS RAFFERTY / 6/4 ON / IN BETWEEN MOODS / CARS FOR KINGS CROSS / ALREADY IN BLACK** [ ] [ ]
1996. (cd/lp) *(FLY 016-2/-1)* **THERE'S NEVER BEEN A CROWD LIKE THIS** [ ] [ ]
– Transcontinental / Sign up maybe for being / 6/4 on / Chips Rafferty / Why not bomb the movies / Jubilee / In between moods / Hard river / Topple into my fantasy / Showtime.

CHAPTERHOUSE

Formed: Reading, England . . . late '87 by ANDREW SHERRIFF, STEPHEN PATMAN, SIMON ROWE, JON CURTIS and ASHLEY BATES. After thoroughly polishing their sound in the studio, they went on tour supporting SPACEMEN 3. Moving to London in 1990, they signed to the newly formed 'Dedicated' label. After a series of EP's, they cracked the UK charts with the album, 'WHIRLPOOL'. Courted by the music press initially, they released a further album, 'BLOOD MUSIC', before suffering a critical backlash as the shoegazing scene fell out of favour. • **Style:** Drew similarities to SLOWDIVE, MY BLOODY VALENTINE and RIDE, but with a psychedelic/noise lo-fi veneer. • **Songwriters:** All SHERRIFF or PATMAN or combined. Covered; RAIN (Beatles) / LADY GODIVA'S OPERATION (Velvet Underground).

Recommended: WHIRLPOOL (*6)

STEPHEN PATMAN (b. 8 Nov'68, Windsor, England) – vocals, guitar / **ANDREW SHERRIFF** (b. 5 May'69, Wokingham, England) – vocals, guitar / **SIMON ROWE** (b.23 Jun'69) – guitar / **ASHLEY BATES** (b. 2 Nov'71) – drums / **RUSSELL BARRETT** (b. 7 Nov'68, Vermont, USA) – bass (ex-BIKINIS) repl. JON CURTIS

Dedicated not issued

Aug 90. (12"ep/cd-ep) *(STONE 001 T/CD)* **FREE FALL** [ ] [-]
– Falling down / Need (somebody) / Inside of me / Sixteen years.
Nov 90. (7") *(STONE 002)* **SOMETHING MORE. / RAIN** [ ] [-]
(12"ep+=/cd-ep+=) **SUNBURST EP** (STONE 002 T/CD) – Satin safe / Feel the same.
Mar 91. (7") *(STONE 003)* **PEARL. / COME HEAVEN** [67] [-]
(12"+=) *(STONE 003T)* – In my arms.
(cd-s++=) *(STONE 003CD)* – Pearl (edit).
Apr 91. (cd/c/lp) *(DED CD/MC/LP 001)* **WHIRLPOOL** [23] [-]
– Brother / Pearl / Autosleeper / Treasure / Falling down / April / Guilt / If you want me / Something more. *(free-ltd.one-sided-12"w-lp)*– DIE DIE DIE
Oct 91. (12"ep/cd-ep) *(HOUSE 001/+CD)* **MESMERISE. / PRECIOUS ONE / SUMMER CHILL / THEN WE'LL RISE** [60] [-]
Jul 93. (7"purple) *(HOUSE 003)* **SHE'S A VISION. / DON'T LOOK NOW** [ ] [-]
(12"+=) *(HOUSE 003T)* – ('B'-sitar trance mix) / For what it's worth (demo).
(cd-s+=) *(HOUSE 003CD)* – ('B'-sitar trance mix) / Deli (dark jester mix).
Aug 93. (7") *(HOUSE 004)* **WE ARE THE BEAUTIFUL. / AGE** [ ] [ ]
(12"colrd+=/cd-s+=) *(HOUSE 004 T/CD)* – Frost.
Sep 93. (cd/c/lp) *(DED CD/MC/LP 11)* **BLOOD MUSIC** [ ] [-]
– Don't look now / There's still life / We are the beautiful / Summer's gone / Everytime / Deli / On the way to fly / She's a vision / Greater power / Confusion trip / Love forever.

— Sank without trace after lukewarm reviews of above album.

Nov 96. (d-cd) *(DEDCD 025)* **ROWNDERBOWT** (compilation) [ ] [-]

CHARLATANS

Formed: Northwich, Cheshire, England . . . late 1989 by MARTIN BLUNT, ROB COLLINS, JON BROOKES and JON BAKER. They soon found a frontman in singer TIM BURGESS and after a few attempts at getting a record deal, they set up their own 'Dead Dead Good' label. Early in 1990, they scored a massive indie hit with the 'INDIAN ROPE' single. Following the explosion of the "Madchester" scene, the label was taken over by the Beggars Banquet subsidiary, 'Situation 2', for whom they recorded their first Top 10 hit, 'THE ONLY ONE I KNOW'. Another hammond-driven classic, 'THEN', preceded a late summer chart topping debut album, 'SOME FRIENDLY'. A relatively quiet year followed, during which MARTIN BLUNT nearly retired due to severe depression. However, it was actually BAKER who departed after playing at London's Royal Albert Hall. Come 1992, MARK COLLINS was drafted in and things look brighter when the single, 'WEIRDO', gave them another Top 20 hit. Their second album, however, ('BETWEEN 10TH AND 11TH'), was given the thumbs down by the music press, hence its failure to secure a respectable chart placing. This was not the only setback that year, as ROB COLLINS was charged with aiding and abetting an armed robbery. A year later, although maintaining his innocence, he was sentenced to several months in jail, later being released in early 1994 on good behavior. 'CAN'T GET OUT OF BED', saw them return in fine style, and was lifted from the Top 10 album 'UP TO OUR HIPS'. TIM then moonlighted on singles by SAINT ETIENNE and The CHEMICAL BROTHERS, before the group were back to their best on the eponymous 1995 album. From its retro cover art, to the 'Sympathy For The Devil'-style single, 'JUST WHEN YOU'RE THINKIN' THINGS OVER', the album was an obvious homage to The ROLLING STONES. Tragically, on 23rd of July '96, ROB COLLINS was killed when his car spun off a road in Wales. The coroners report concluded that he was the driver and also that he had twice the legal amount of alcohol in his blood. They had just recorded their fifth album, 'TELLIN' STORIES', preceded by their biggest hit singles to date, 'ONE TO ANOTHER' and 'NORTH COUNTRY BOY'. • **Songwriters:** Group compositions except; I FEEL MUCH BETTER ROLLING OVER (Small Faces). On their eponnymous 1995 album, the track 'HERE COMES A SOUL SAVER' featured a guitar riff remarkably similar to that of PINK FLOYD's 'Fearless' (from 'Meddle' 1971).

Recommended: SOME FRIENDLY (*8) / BETWEEN 10th & 11th (*5) / UP TO OUR HIPS (*7) / THE CHARLATANS (*8) / TELLIN' STORIES (*8)

TIM BURGESS (b.30 May'68) – vocals (ex-ELECTRIC CRAYONS) repl. BAZ KETTLEY / **ROB COLLINS** (b.23 Feb'63) – organ / **JON BAKER** (b.1969) – guitar / **JON BROOKS** (b.1969) – drums / **MARTIN BLUNT** (b.1965) – bass (ex-MAKIN' TIME, ex-TOO MUCH TEXAS w / TIM)

Dead Dead Good not issued

Feb 90. (7") *(GOOD ONE SEVEN)* **INDIAN ROPE. / WHO WANTS TO KNOW** [89] [-]
(12"+=) *(GOOD ONE TWELVE)* – You can talk to me. *(re-iss.Jul91 12"/cd-s; GOOD 1 T/CD,* hit No.57) *(re-iss.cd-s Oct96)*

Situation 2 Beggars Banquet

May 90. (7") *(SIT 70)* **THE ONLY ONE I KNOW. / EVERYTHING CHANGED** [9] [ ]

(12"+=) *(SIT 70T)* – Imperial 109.
(cd-s++=) *(SIT 70CD)* – You can talk to me.

Sep 90. (7"/c-s) *(SIT 74/+C)* **THEN. / TAURUS MOANER** [12] [ ]
(12"+=/cd-s+=) *(SIT 74 T/CD)* – ('A'-alternate take) / ('B'instrumental).

Oct 90. (lp/c/cd/s-lp) *(SITU 30/+MC/CD/R)* <2411> **SOME FRIENDLY** [1] [73]
– You're not very well / White shirt / Opportunity / Then / 109 pt.2 / Polar bear / Believe you me / Flower / Sonic / Sproston Green. *(cd+=)*– The only one I know. *(cd re-iss.Sep95 on 'Beggars Banquet'; BBL 30CD)*

Feb 91. (7"/c-s) *(SIT 76/+CS)* **OVER RISING. / WAY UP THERE** [15] [ ]
(12"/c-s+=/cd-s+=) *(SIT 76 T/TC/CD)* – Happen to die / Opportunity Three (re-work).

— **MARK COLLINS** – guitar (ex-CANDLESTICK PARK) repl. BAKER

Oct 91. (7"/c-s) *(SIT 84/+C)* **ME IN TIME. / OCCUPATION H. MONSTER** [28] [ ]
(12"+=/cd-s+=) *(SIT 84 T/CD)* – Subtitle.

Feb 92. (7"/c-s) *(SIT 88/+C)* **WEIRDO. / THEME FROM 'THE WISH'** [19] [ ]
(12"+=/cd-s+=) *(SIT 88 T/CD)* – Sproston Green (U.S. remix) / ('A'-alternate take).

Mar 92. (lp/c/cd) *(SITU 37/+MC/CD)* <61108> **BETWEEN 10th AND 11th** [21] [ ]
– I don't want to see the lights / Ignition / Page one / Tremelo song / The end of everything etc / Subtitle / Can't even be bothered / Weirdo / Chewing gum weekend / (No one) Not even the rain. *(re-iss.cd Sep95 on 'Beggars Banquet'; BBL 37CD)*

Jun 92. (c-s) *(SIT 97C)* **TREMELO SONG (alternate take) / THEN (live) / CHEWING GUM WEEKEND (live) / TREMELO SONG** [44] [ ]
(12") *(SIT 97T)* – Happen to die (unedited) repl. last version.
(cd-s) *(SIT 97CD1)* – ('A'side) / Happen to die (unedited) / Normality swing (demo).
(cd-s) *(SIT 97CD2)* – ('A'live April '92) / Then (live) / Chewing gum weekend (live).

— ROB COLLINS was imprisoned in Sep'93 for taking part in a robbery. (see above) He had already recorded below while awaiting trial, and was free just in time to feature on Top Of The Pops.

Beggars Banquet | Beggars Banquet

Jan 94. (7"/c-s) *(BBQ 27/+C)* **CAN'T GET OUT OF BED. / WITHDRAWN** [24] [ ]
(12"+=/cd-s+=) *(BBQ 27 T/CD)* – Out.

Mar 94. (cd-ep) *(BBQ 31CD)* **I NEVER WANT AN EASY LIFE IF ME AND HE WERE EVER TO GET THERE / ONLY A BOHO / SUBTERRAINEAN / CAN'T GET OUT OF BED (demo)** [38] [-]

Mar 94. (cd/c/lp) *(BBQ CD/MC/LP 147)* **UP TO OUR HIPS** [8] [ ]
– Come in number 21 / I never want an easy life / If me and he were ever to get there / Can't get out of bed / Feel flows / Autograph / Jesus hairdo / Up to our hips / Patrol / Another rider up in flames / Inside – looking out. *(re-iss.cd Sep95; BBL 147CD)*

Jun 94. (c-s) *(BBQ 32C)* **JESUS HAIRDO / PATROL (Dust Brothers mix)** [48] [ ]
(12"+=) *(BBQ 32T)* – Feel flows (the carpet kiss mix).
(cd-s+=) *(BBQ 32CD1)* – Stir it up / Feel flows (Van Basten mix).
(cd-s) *(BBQ 32CD2)* – ('A'side) / I never want an easy life / Another rider up in flames / Up to our hips (BBC Radio 1 live sessions).

Dec 94. (7"/c-s) *(BBQ 44/+C)* **CRASHIN' IN. / BACK ROOM WINDOW** [31] [ ]
(12"+=/cd-s+=) *(BBQ 44 T/CD)* – Green flashing eyes.

May 95. (7"/c-s) *(BBQ 55/+C)* **JUST LOOKIN'. / BULLET COMES** [32] [ ]
(cd-s+=) *(BBQ 55CD)* – Floor nine.

Aug 95. (c-s) *(BBQ 60C)* **JUST WHEN YOU'RE THINKIN' THINGS OVER / FRINCK / YOUR SKIES ARE MINE** [12] [ ]
(cd-s+=) *(BBQ 60CD)* – Chemical risk (toothache remix).
(12") *(BBQ 60T)* – (first 2 tracks) / Chemical risk dub (toothache remix) / Nine acre dust (Dust Brothers mix).

Aug 95. (cd/c/d-lp) *(BBQ CD/MC/LP 174)* **THE CHARLATANS** [1] [ ]
– Nine acre court / Feeling holy / Just lookin' / Crashin' in / Bullet comes / Here comes a soul saver / Just when you're thinkin' things over / Tell everyone / Toothache / No fiction / See it through / Thank you. *(d-lp+=)*– Chemical risk (toothache remix).

— On 23rd July '96, ROB COLLINS was killed in a car crash (see above).

Aug 96. (7"/c-s/cd-s) *(BBQ 301/+C/CD)* **ONE TO ANOTHER. / TWO OF US / REPUTATION** [3] [ ]

— **MARTIN DUFFY** – keyboards (of PRIMAL SCREAM) augmented

Mar 97. (7"/c-s/cd-s) *(BBQ 309/+C/CD)* **NORTH COUNTRY BOY. / AREA 51 / DON'T NEED A GUN** [4] [ ]

Apr 97. (cd/c/lp) *(BBQ CD/MC/LP 190)* **TELLIN' STORIES** [1] [ ]
– With no shoes / North country boy / Tellin' stories / One to another / You're a big girl now / How can you leave us / Area 51 / How high / Only teethin' / Get on it / Rob's theme / Two of us / Reputation.

Jun 97. (7"/c-s) *(BBQ 312/+C)* **HOW HIGH. / DOWN WITH THE MOOK** [6] [ ]
(cd-s+=) *(BBQ 312CD)* – Title fight.

CHEMICAL BROTHERS

Formed: North London, England . . .1992 by DJ's ED SIMONS and TOM ROWLANDS. The pair had met at Manchester University, and, discovering a shared love of techno and classic hip hop, they set about creating their own club night, 'NAKED UNDER LEATHER'. The logical next step was to cut their own record and with 'SONG TO THE SIREN', they successfully blended their myriad inluences into an abrasive chunk of freak-beat techno. Wildly impressed, 'Junior Boys Own' maestro ANDY WEATHERALL released the single in early 1993, the more discerning underground D.J.'s of the time caning the track at club nights across the country. The record was credited to The DUST BROTHERS, the name SIMONS and ROWLANDS assumed for their DJ work. Later the same year, they released the '14th Century Sky' EP which included the definitive 'CHEMICAL BEATS'. 'MY MERCURY MOUTH' from the 1994 EP of the same name was equally impressive and by this point the DUST BROTHERS had become one of the hippest name-drops among the dance cognoscenti. Their seminal reworking of SAINT ETIENNE's 'Like a motorway', together with a DJ spot on PRIMAL SCREAM's 1994 tour further increased their profile and it wasn't long before the major record labels came sniffing round. Signing to 'Virgin', they released 'LEAVE HOME' in 1995, following it up with the top ten debut album, 'EXIT PLANET DUST'. The duo were now trading under the moniker of The CHEMICAL BROTHERS following objections from The DUST BROTHERS (U.S), a highly rated hip hop production team (Responsible for the BEASTIE BOYS' classic, 'Paul's Boutique'). For the most part, the debut was an unrelenting, exhilirating, rollercoater ride of breakbeat techno, only letting up on 'ALIVE: ALONE' (featuring a BETH ORTON vocal) and the TIM BURGESS (of CHARLATANS fame) collaboration, 'LIFE IS SWEET'. The 'LOOPS OF FURY EP' was as uncompromising as the title suggests while the 'SETTING SUN' (featuring NOEL GALLAGHER on vocals) single gave the CHEMICALS' their first No.1 later that year. The track featured a 'TOMMORROW NEVER KNOWS'-style rhythm pattern, the folow-up album, 'DIG YOUR OWN HOLE' (1997), similarly psychedelic in its reach. Using samples from 60's theramin pioneers LOTHAR AND THE HAND PEOPLE, and featuring a guest spot from MERCURY REV's JONATHAN DONOHUE, the album was more thrillingly diverse than the debut. With a mind bending live show, universal critical acclaim and even a burgeoning Stateside career, for the moment, The CHEMICAL BROTHERS can do no wrong. • **Songwriters:** ROWLANDS-SIMONS except samples of Blake Baxters 'Brothers Gonna Work It Out' on 'LEAVE HOME'/ Borrowed SWALLOW's; 'Peekaboo' & 'Follow Me Down'.

Recommended: EXIT PLANET DUST (*9) / DIG YOUR OWN HOLE (*9)

DUST BROTHERS

TOM ROWLANDS + ED SIMONS – synthesizers, etc

Junior Boys Own | not issued

1993. (12") *(JBO 10)* **SONG TO THE SIREN. / SONG TO THE SIREN (Sabres Of Paradise mixes)** [ ] [-]

1993. (12"ep) *(COLLECT 004)* **14th CENTURY SKY EP** [ ] [-]
– Chemical beats / One too many mornings / Dope coil / Ref jazz.

— (above issued on 'Boys Own')

May 94. (12"ep) *(JBO 20)* **MY MERCURY MOUTH EP** [ ] [-]
– My mercury mouth / If you kling to me I'll kling to you / Dust up beats.

CHEMICAL BROTHERS

TOM ROWLANDS + ED SIMONS with voices by **TIM BURGESS** (CHARLATANS) + **BETH ORTON** (solo artist)

Virgin | Virgin

Jun 95. (12"/cd-s) *(CHEMS T/D 1)* **LEAVE HOME (Sabres Of Paradise mix). / LEAVE HOME (Underworld mix) / LET ME IN MATE** [17] [ ]
(12") *(CHEMSTX 1)* –

Jun 95. (cd/c/d-lp) *(XDUST CD/MC/LP 1)* **EXIT PLANET DUST** [9] [ ]
– Leave home / In dust we trust / Song to he siren / Three little birdies down beats / Fuck up beats / Chemical beats / Chico's groove / One too many mornings / Life is sweet / Playground for a wedgeless firm / Alive alone.

Aug 95. (12") *(CHEMSD 2)* **LIFE IS SWEET. / ('A'-Daft Punk remix) / ('A'-remix 1) / ('A'-remix 2)** [25] [ ]
(cd-s) *(CHEMSD 2)* – ('A'-remix 1, repl.by) Leave home (terror drums).
(cd-s) *(CHEMSDX 2)* – ('A'remix 1) / If you kling to me I'll klong to you / Chico's groove (mix 2).

Jan 96. (12"ep/cd-ep) *(CHEMS T/D 3)* **LOOPS OF FURY EP** [13] [ ]
– Chemical beats (Dave Clarke remix) / Loops of fury / (The best part of) Breaking up / Get up on it like this.

Oct 96. (c-s/12"/cd-s) *(CHEMS C/T/D 4)* **SETTING SUN. / ('A'extended & instrumental mixes) / BUZZ TRACKS** [1] [ ]

— above featured NOEL GALLAGHER (Oasis) on vocals/ co-writer

Mar 97. (12"/cd-s) *(CHEMS T/D 5)* **BLOCK ROCKIN' BEATS. / PRESCRIPTION BEATS / MORNING LEMON** [1] [ ]
(cd-s) *(CHEMSDX 5)* – ('A'mixes).

Apr 97. (cd/c/d-lp) *(XDUST CD/MC/LP 2)* **DIG YOUR OWN HOLE** [1] [14]
– Block rockin' beats / Dig your own hole / Elektrobank / Piku / Setting sun / It doesn't matter / Don't stop the rock / Get up on it like this / Lost in the k-hole / Where do I begin / The private psychedelic reel.

CHILLS

Formed: Dunedin, Christ Church, New Zealand . . .1980 by MARTIN PHILLIPS together with ex-SAME members RACHEL PHILLIPS and JANE DODD. After signing to local label 'Flying Nun', they created a stir with their debut 45, 'ROLLING MOON', subsequently winning many fans in the UK with their follow-up, 'PINK FROST'. However tragedy struck in July 1983, when drummer MARTYN BULL died of cancer. This triggered a series of line-up changes, numerous and complex enough to give Pete Frame (writer of Rock Family Trees) nightmares! In 1987, they moved (as did part of Flying Nun) to London, releasing their first "proper" album, 'BRAVE WORDS'. Although very dissappointing, it did result in a contract with 'Slash' records and a remarkable comeback album, 'SUBMARINE BELLS', early in 1990. Throughout the 90's, they've only surfaced with one album, 'SOFT BOMB', and by'95, MARTIN PHILLIPS was thinking about a solo career. • **Style:** Pounding organ sound, influenced by garage/psychedelia and 'Pebbles/Nuggets' groups of the US mid-60's. Imagine SYD BARRETT being backed by BYRDS or The VELVET UNDERGROUND. • **Songwriters:** PHILLIPS penned. • **Trivia:** MARTIN played keyboards on The CLEAN's debut Flying Nun 45 'Tally Ho'.

Recommended: KALEIDOSCOPE WORLD (*8) / SUBMARINE BELLS (*7)

MARTIN PHILLIPS – vocals, guitar / **PETER GUTTERIDGE** – guitar (ex-CLEAN) / **ALAN HAIG** – drums (ex-RED TAPE) / **FRASER BATTS** – keyboards, guitar (ex-BORED GAMES), repl. RACHEL / **TERRY MOORE** – bass (ex-BORED GAMES), repl. PETER + JANE

Flying Nun not issued

Jan 82. (d12"ep) **DUNEDIN EP** [-] [-] New Z.
– Satin doll / Kaleidoscope world / (+ 6 other tracks by New Zealand groups The VERLAINES, STONES + The SNEAKY FEELINGS).

— **RACHEL PHILLIPS** – keyboards, returned to replace FRASER

— **MARTYN BULL** – drums, repl. HAIG

May 82. (7"m) **ROLLING MOON. / BITE / FLAME THROWER** [-] [-] New Z.

— **PETER ALLISON** – keyboards, repl. RACHEL

Jul 82. (7") **PINK FROST. / PURPLE GIRL** [-] [-] New Z.

— **ALAN HAIG** – drums, returned to repl. deceased MARTYN BULL

— **MARTIN KEAN** – bass, repl. TERRY

Jan 84. (7") **DOLEDRUMS. / HIDDEN BAY** [-] [-] New Z.

— **MARTIN PHILLIPS, PETER ALLISON + ALAN HAIG** brought back **TERRY MOORE** – bass, to repl. KEAN

Dec 84. (12"ep) *(COLD 004)* **THE LOST EP** [-] [-] New Z.
– This is the way / Never never go / Dream by dream. *(UK-iss.Mar86; same)*

Creation not issued

Feb 86. (m-lp) *(CRELP 008)* **KALEIDOSCOPE WORLD** (compilation) [ ] [-]
– Kaleidoscope world / Satin doll / Frantic drift / Rolling moon / Bite / Flame thrower / Pink frost / Purple girl. *(re-iss.Dec87 on 'Flying Nun'; FNE 13) (w/free 7"ep)* **THE LOST EP** *(cd-iss.Nov92 +=; FNE 13CD)*– This is the way / Never never go / Don't even know her name / Bee bah bee bah bee boe / Whole weird world / Dream by dream / Doledrums / Hidden bay / I love my leather jacket / The great escape.

— **CAROLINE EASTER** – drums (ex-VERLAINES), repl. ALAN HAIG

Flying Nun Rough Trade

Mar 87. (12") *(FNUK 7)* **I LOVE MY LEATHER JACKET. / THE GREAT ESCAPE** [ ] [-]

Aug 87. (12") *(FNUK 11T)* **THE HOUSE WITH A HUNDRED ROOMS. / LIVING IN A JUNGLE** [ ] [-]

Sep 87. (lp) *(FNE 12)* **BRAVE WORDS** [ ] [-]
– Push / Rain / Speak for yourself / Look for the good in others . . . / Wet blanket / Ghosts / Party in my heart / Dan Destiny & the silver dawn / Night of the chill blue / 16 heart throbs / Brave words / Dark carnival / Creep. *(cd-iss.Sep89 & Nov92 +=; FNE 12CD)*– House with a hundred rooms / Living in a jungle.

— (Sep'88 line-up) **MARTIN PHILLIPS** – vocals, guitar / **ANDREW TODD** – keyboards, vocals / **JUSTIN HARWOOD** – bass, vocals / **JAMES STEVENSON** – drums

Slash Slash

Mar 90. (7") *(LASH 22)* **THE HEAVENLY POP HIT. / WHOLE LOT OF NONE** [ ] [ ]
(12"+=/cd-s+=) *(LAS HX/CD 22)* – Ways watching / Water wolves.

Mar 90. (cd/c/lp) *(828 191-2/-4/-1) <26130-1>* **SUBMARINE BELLS** [ ] [ ]
– The Heavenly pop hit / Tied up in chain / The oncoming day / Part past part fiction / Singing in my sleep / I soar / Dead web / Familiarity breeds contempt / Don't be a memory / Efforence and deliquence / Sweet times / Submarine bells.

Aug 92. (cd/c/lp) *(828 322-2/-4/-1)* **SOFT BOMB** [ ] [ ]
– The male monster from the Id / Background affair / Ocean ocean / Soft bomb / There is no harm in trying / Strange case / Soft bomb II / So long / Song for Randy Newman etc / Sleeping giants / Double summer / Sanctuary / Halo fading / There is no point in trying / Entertainer / Water wolves / Soft bomb III.

— JUSTIN joined LUNA 2 with former GALAXIE 500 member DEAN WAREHAM.

– compilations, etc –

Feb 95. (lp/cd) *Flying Nun; (FN/+CD 306)* **HEAVENLY POP HITS** [ ] [-]

Sep 96. (cd) *Flying Nun; (FNCD 303)* **SUNBURNT** [ ] [-]

CHOO CHOO TRAIN (see under ⇒ VELVET CRUSH)

CINDYTALK

Formed: London, England . . . 1984 as studio outfit by GORDON SHARPE and DAVID CLANCY, both ex-members of young Edinburgh punk outfit The FREEZE. After only a few 45's, the broke up and SHARPE was called up to aid THIS MORTAL COIL. In 1984, SHARPE surfaced again with his new venture CINDYTALK. The album 'CAMOUFLAGE HEART' was poorly received, so SHARPE returned to the studio for three years, to complete the follow-up; a double-album 'IN THIS WORLD'. An album in the early 90's was another progression, but this was surpassed with the 1995 effort 'WAPPINSCHAW'. This was a return to his Scottish roots and featured readings by long-time SNP affiliated novelist ALISDAIR GRAY. References were made to outside heroes like SITTING BULL and WOLFE TONE, among others. • **Style:** Ambient atmospherics using powerful chants. • **Songwriters:** SHARPE except trad; HUSH.

Recommended: IN THIS WORLD (*6) / WAPPINSCHAW (*6)

FREEZE

GORDON SHARPE – vocals / **DAVID CLANCY** – guitar, vocals / **KEITH GRANT** – bass, vocals / **GRAEME RADIN** – drums

A1 not issued

Aug 79. (7") *(A 11)* **IN COLOUR** [ ] [-]
– Paranoia / For J.P.'s / Psychodalek nightmares.

Apr 80. (7") *(A 11 S1)* **CELEBRATION. / CROSS-OVER** [ ] [-]

— split in 1981. A few years later, SHARPE guested for 4ad conglomerate THIS MORTAL COIL. He provided vox for the track 'KANGAROO' (a cover taken from BIG STAR) on album 'It'll End In Tears'.

CINDYTALK

GORDON SHARPE – vocals, piano / **DAVID CLANCY** – guitar / **JOHN BYRNE** – bass / **KINNISON** – drums

Midnight Music not issued

Sep 84. (lp) *(CHIME 00.065)* **CAMOUFLAGE HEART** [ ] [-]
– It's luxury / etc. *(cd-iss.1988; CHIME 006CD) (cd re-iss.Oct96 on 'Touch'; TOUCH 3CD)*

— **SHARPE** with **BYRNE** – instruments / **ALIK WRIGHT** – instruments / **DEBBIE WRIGHT** – vocals, instruments

Mar 88. (d-lp/cd) *(CHIME 027/028CD)* **IN THIS WORLD** [ ] [-]
– In this world / Janey's love / Gift of a knife / Playtime / The room of delight / Touched / Circle of shit / My sun / The beginning of wisdom / No serenade / Sight after sight / Angels of ghosts / Through water / Cherish / Homeless / Still whisper / In this world. *(cd re-iss.Oct96 on 'Touch'; TOUCH 2CD)*

Jan 91. (lp/c/cd) *(CHIME 103/+CC/CD)* **THE WIND IS STRONG** [ ] [-]
– Landing / First sight / To the room / Waiting / Through flowers / Second sight / Through the forest / Arrival / Is there a room for hire / Choked I / Choked II / Dream ritual / Fuck you Mrs. Grimace / On snow moor / Angel wings.

Jan 94. (12"/cd-s) *(DONG 76/+CD)* **SECRETS & FALLING** [ ] [-]

Touch not issued

Oct 96. (7") *(FEEL 001)* **PRINCE OF LIES. / MUSTER** [ ] [-]
(cd-s) *(TOUCHED 1)* –

Oct 96. (lp/cd) *(TOUCH/+CD 1)* **WAPPINSCHAW** [ ] [ ]
– A song of changes / Empty hand / Return to pain / Wheesht / Snow kisses / Secrets and falling / Disappear / Traum lose nacht / And now in sunshine / Prince of lies / Hush.

COCTEAU TWINS

Formed: Grangemouth, Scotland . . . late 1981 when the (then) trio (ELIZABETH FRASER, ROBIN GUTHRIE and WILL HEGGIE) visited London to hand DJ John Peel a demo tape. He booked them for sessions on his Radio 1 night time show and they subsequently signed to IVO WATT-RUSSELL's indie label, '4 a.d.'. Their debut offering, 'GARLANDS', was quickly recorded, hitting the shops 10 days later. Resisting many offers from the majors, they were back in the studio again for 1983's 'LULLABIES' EP and 'HEAD OVER HEELS' album. After a support slot to OMD, WILL HEGGIE left, making the long trip back north to set up his own outfit, LOWLIFE. Around the same time ROBIN and LIZ hit No.1 in the indie charts when guesting for 'IVO/4 a.d.' ensemble THIS MORTAL COIL on 'SONG TO THE SIREN'. It was mistakenly thought by many that this was a COCTEAU TWINS offshoot, rather than IVO's project. This idea was laid to rest after the album, 'IT'LL END IN TEARS', was issued in '84. Meanwhile, The COCTEAU TWINS, were back with another gem, 'TREASURE', which saw newcomer SIMON RAYMONDE on bass. It was their first taste of Top 30 success, but they easily surpassed this with the 1986 Top 10 effort 'VICTORIALAND'. An abortive film project collaboration with HAROLD BUDD was issued at the end of the year as they headed towards an increasingly "New Age"-style sound. Two more classics, 'BLUE BELL KNOLL' and 'HEAVEN OR LAS VEGAS' were released over the next half decade, both finding a home in the US charts for 'Capitol' records. In 1992, they finally succumbed to signing for 'Fontana' in the UK, leading to a comeback album, 'FOUR CALENDAR CAFE' in '93. The following year saw LIZ guest on FUTURE SOUND OF LONDON's ambient venture, 'Lifeforms'. After another 3-year hiatus, The COCTEAUS were once again up there challenging the alternative music scene with 'MILK AND KISSES'. • **Style:** Pastel and picturesque beauty, fused with LIZ's intentionally incoherent but heart-felt vox. • **Songwriters:** All by COCTEAU TWINS • **Trivia:** ROBIN has produced many '4.a.d.' outfits, and also The GUN CLUB in 1987. An item for some time, LIZ and ROBIN became parents in 1989. Early in 1991, LIZ was surprisingly, but not undeservedly nominated for Best Female Vocalist at the 'Brit' awards.

Recommended: TREASURE (*9) / VICTORIALAND (*8) / GARLANDS (*7) / HEAD OVER HEELS (*8) / BLUE BELL KNOLL (*7) / HEAVEN OR LAS VEGAS (*7) / THE PINK OPAQUE (*8) / MILK AND KISSES (*7)

ELIZABETH FRASER (b.29 Aug'63) – vocals / **ROBIN GUTHRIE** (b. 4 Jan'62) – guitar, drum programming, keyboards / **WILL HEGGIE** – bass

4 a.d. Relativity

Jul 82. (lp) *(CAD 211)* **GARLANDS** [ ] [-]
– Blood bitch / Wax and wane / But I'm not / Blind dumb deaf / Grail overfloweth / Shallow than halo / The hollow men / Garlands. *(c-iss.Apr84 +=; CADC 211)*– Dear heart / Blind dumb deaf / Hearsay please / Hazel. *(cd-iss.1986 ++=; CAD 211CD)*– Speak no evil / Perhaps some other acorn.

Sep 82. (12"ep) *(BAD 213)* **LULLABIES** [ ] [-]
– It's all but an ark lark / Alas dies laughing / Feathers-Oar-Blades.

Mar 83. (7") *(AD 303)* **PEPPERMINT PIG. / LAUGH LINES** [ ] [-]
(12"+=) *(BAD 303)* – Hazel.

— Trimmed to a duo, when HEGGIE left to form LOWLIFE

Oct 83. (lp) *(CAD 313)* **HEAD OVER HEELS** [51] [-]
– When mama was moth / Sugar hiccup / In our anglehood / Glass candle grenades / Multifoiled / In the gold dust rush / The tinderbox (of a heart) / My love paramour / Musette and drums / Five ten fiftyfold. *(c-iss.Apr84 +=; CADC 313) (cd-iss.1986 +=; CAD 313CD)*– SUNBURST AND SNOWBLIND EP

Oct 83. (12"ep) *(BAD 314)* **SUNBURST AND SNOWBLIND** [ ] [-]

– Sugar hiccup / From the flagstones / Because of whirl-Jack / Hitherto.

— added **SIMON RAYMONDE** (b. 3 Apr'62, London, England) – bass, keyboards, guitar (ex-DROWNING CRAZE)

Apr 84. (7") *(AD 405)* **PEARLY DEWDROPS DROP. / PEPPER-TREE** [29] [-]
(12"+=) *(BAD 405)* – The spangle maker.

Nov 84. (lp/c) *(CAD/+C 412)* **TREASURE** [29] [-]
– Ivo / Lorelei / Beatrix / Persephone / Pandora – for Cindy / Amelia / Aloysius / Cicely / Otterley / Donimo. *(cd-iss.1986; CAD 412CD)*

Mar 85. (7") *(AD 501)* **AIKEA-GUINEA. / KOOKABURRA** [41] [-]
(12"+=) *(BAD 501)* – Rococo / Quiquose.

Nov 85. (12"ep) *(BAD 510)* **TINY DYNAMITE** [52] [-]
– Pink orange red / Ribbed and veined / Sultitan Itan / Plain tiger.

Nov 85. (12"ep) *(BAD 511)* **ECHOES IN A SHALLOW BAY** [65] [-]
– Great spangled fritillary / Melonella / Pale clouded white / Eggs and their shells *(cd-iss.Oct86 +=; BAD 510/511)*– TINY DYNAMITE

— **RICHARD THOMAS** – saxophone, bass (of DIF JUZ) repl. SIMON who fell ill.

Apr 86. (lp/c)(cd) *(CAD/+C 602)(CAD 602CD)* **VICTORIALAND** [10] [ ]
– Lazy calm / Fluffy tufts / Throughout the dark months of April and May / Whales tales / Oomingmak / Little Spacey / Feet-like fins / How to bring a blush to the snow / The thinner the air.

— **SIMON RAYMONDE** returned repl.temp. RICHARD (back to DIF JUZ)

Oct 86. (7") *(AD 610)* **LOVE'S EASY TEARS. / THOSE EYES, THAT MOUTH** [53] [-]
(12"+=) *(BAD 610)* – Sigh's smell of farewell.

— next was a one-off collaboration with label new signing **HAROLD BUDD** – piano

Nov 86. (lp/c)(cd; by HAROLD BUDD, ELIZABETH FRASER, ROBIN GUTHRIE, SIMON RAYMONDE) *(CAD/+C 611)(CAD 611CD)* **THE MOON AND THE MELODIES** [46] [-]
– Sea, swallow me / Memory gongs / Why do you love me? / Eyes are mosaics / She will destroy you / The ghost has no home / Bloody and blunt / Ooze out and away, one how.

4 a.d. Capitol

Sep 88. (lp/c/dat)(cd) *(CAD/+C/T 807)(CAD 807CD)* <C1/C4/C?/C2 90892> **BLUE BELL KNOLL** [15] [ ]
– Blue bell knoll / Athol-brose / Carolyn's fingers / For Phoebe still a baby / The itchy glowbo blow / Cico buff / Suckling the mender / Spooning good singing gum / A kissed out red floatboat / Ella megablast burls forever.

Oct 88. (7") **CAROLYN'S FINGERS. / BLUE BELL KNOLL** [-] [ ]

— In Apr'90, LIZ was heard on Ian McCulloch's (ex-ECHO & THE BUNNYMEN) 'Candleland' single.

Aug 90. (7"/c-s) *(AD 0011/+C)* **ICEBLINK LUCK. / MIZAKE THE MIZAN** [38] [ ]
(12"+=/cd-s+=) *(AD 0011 T/CD)* – Watchiar.

Sep 90. (cd)(lp/c) *(CAD 0012CD)(CAD/+C 0012)* <C2/C1/C4 93669> **HEAVEN OR LAS VEGAS** [7] [99]
– Cherry coloured funk / Pitch the baby / Iceblink luck / Fifty-fifty clown / Heaven or Las Vegas / I wear your ring / Fotzepolitic / Wolf in the breast / Road, river and rail / Frou-frou foxes in midsummer fires.

— on U.S. tour, augmented by **MITSUO TATE + BEN BLAKEMAN** – guitars

Fontana Capitol

Sep 93. (7"/c-s) *(CT/+C 1)* **EVANGELINE. / MUD AND LARK** [34] [ ]
(12"pic-d+=/cd-s+=) *(CT X/CD 1)* – Summer-blink.

Oct 93. (cd/c/lp) *(518259-2/-4/-1)* <C2/C4/C1 99375> **FOUR CALENDAR CAFE** [13] [78]
– Know who you are ate every age / Evangeline / Blue beard / Theft and wandering around lost / Oil of angels / Squeeze-wax / My truth / Essence / Summerhead / Pur.

Dec 93. (cd-s) *(COCCD 1)* **WINTER WONDERLAND. / FROSTY THE SNOWMAN** [58] [ ]

— (above festive tracks, deleted after a week in UK Top 60)

Feb 94. (7"/c-s) *(CT/+C 2)* **BLUEBEARD. / THREE SWEPT** [33] [ ]
(12"+=) *(CTX 2)* – Ice-pulse.
(cd-s++=) *(CTCD 2)* – ('A'acoustic).

Sep 95. (7"//7"/cd-ep) *(CCT//CTT/CTCD 3)* **TWINLIGHTS** [59] [ ]
– Rilkean heart / Golden-vein // Pink orange red / Half-gifts.

Oct 95. (12"ep/cd-ep) *(CT X/CD 4)* **OTHERNESS** (An Ambient EP) [59] [ ]
– Feet like fins / Seekers who are lovers / Violaine / Cherry coloured funk.

Mar 96. (cd-ep) *(CTCD 5)* **TISHBITE / PRIMITIVE HEART / FLOCK OF SOUL** [34] [ ]
(12"ep/cd-ep) *(CT X/DDD 5)* – (title track) / Round / An Elan.

Apr 96. (cd/c/lp) *(514 501-2/4/-1)* <37049-2/-4/-1> **MILK & KISSES** [17] [99]
– Violaine / Serpent skirt / Tishbite / Half-gifts / Calfskin smack / Rilkean heart / Ups / Eperdu / Treasure hiding / Seekers who are lovers. *(also ltd.cd; 532 363-2)*

Jul 96. (12") *(CTX 6)* **VIOLAINE. / ALICE** [56] [ ]
(cd-s+=) *(CTDD 6)* – Circling girl.
(cd-s) *(CTCD 6)* – ('A'side) / Tranquil eye / Smile.

– compilations, others, etc. –

Dec 85. (cd) *4 a.d.; (CAD 513CD) / Relativity;* <ENC 8040> **THE PINK OPAQUE** [ ] [ ] Sep85
– The spangle maker / Millimillenary / Wax and wane / Hitherto / Pearly-dewdrops' drops (12" Version) / From the flagstones / Aikea-Guinea / Lorelei / Pepper-tree / Musette and drums.

Nov 91. (10xcd-ep-box) *Capitol; (CTBOX 1)* **THE SINGLES COLLECTION** [ ] [-]
– (above featured previous 9 singles + new 1) (sold separately Mar92)

COIL

Formed: London, England . . .1983 by JOHN BALANCE and PETER 'SLEAZY' CHRISTOPHERSON. The latter had been a graphic designer for Hypgnosis (album sleeves for PINK FLOYD and LED ZEPPELIN) in the 70's, before becoming part of THROBBING GRISTLE, and later co-founder of PSYCHIC TV (with TG mainman GENESIS P. ORRIDGE). PETER had just departed from the latter to become a pop video maker, but chose to return to the studio in 1984 to record with BALANCE, the 17-minute single 'HOW TO DESTROY ANGELS'. Soon after its release, they found CLINT RUIN (aka JIM 'FOETUS' THIRLWELL), who produced their debut album 'SCATOLOGY', aided by expanding line-up of STEPHEN E. THROWER, GAVIN FRIDAY (Virgin Prunes) and ALEX FERGUSSON. Next up, was the single 'PANIC', which was backed by a cover of GLORIA JONES 'TAINTED LOVE' (more recently covered by SOFT CELL). In fact, they used MARC ALMOND on an accompanying video, which was widely banned. During this time, they had worked with gay film-maker DEREK JARMAN on soundtrack 'The Angel Conversation'. In 1986, they shared billing with BOYD RICE (NON) on album 'NIGHTMARE CULTURE. STEPHEN was now a full-time member and two more releases appeared in '86; ep 'THE ANAL STAIRCASE' and lp 'HORSE ROTORVATOR'. In 1987, they worked on the Clive Barker soundtrack for the horror movie 'HELLRAISER', and released the out-takes as an 10"ep. That year, they incorporated OTTO AVERY into the line-up for 'GOLD IS THE METAL' album, but little was heard from them until a compilation was released in 1990. In 1994, they were snapped up by TRENT REZNOR, who signed to his new 'Eksaton' label. • **Style:** In the 90's, they moved away from industrial ritual experimentation, incorporating sexual arcane ambience, to a more dark techno/rave-ish sound. • **Songwriters:** BALANCE – CHRISTOPHERSON except WHO BY FIRE (Leonard Cohen). • **Note:** Not to be confused with late 70's COIL, who released 'MOTOR INDUSTRY' single.

Recommended: HORSE ROTORVATOR (*6) / THE CONSEQUENCES OF RAISING HELL (*9) / UNNATURAL HISTORY (*6) / LOVE'S SECRET DOMAIN (*7)

JOHN BALANCE – guitar, bass, vocals, piano (also of CURRENT 93) / **PETER 'SLEAZY' CHRISTOPHERSON** – drum programming (ex-PSYCHIC TV, ex-THROBBING GRISTLE)

Himalaya not issued

Jun 84. (12"one-sided) *(LAY 005)* **HOW TO DESTROY ANGELS** [ ] [-]
(cd-iss.1988+=; LAY 005CD)– Absolute elsewhere. *(cd re-iss.Oct96 on 'Threshold'=; LOCICD 5)*– The sleeper / Remotely / The sleeper II / Tectonic plates / Dismal orb.

— added guests **STEPHEN E. THROWER** – clarinet, percussion (of POSSESSION) / **ALEX FERGUSSON** – guitar (of PSYCHIC TV) / **GAVIN FRIDAY** – vocals (of VIRGIN PRUNES) / **CLINT RUIN** – synthesizers

Force & Form/K422 not issued

Feb 85. (lp) *(FKK 1)* **SCATOLOGY** [ ] [-]
– Ubu noir / Panic / At the heart of it all / Tenderness of wolves / The spoiler / Clap / Aqua regis / Restless day / Solar lodge / The S.W.B.P. / Godhead = deadhead / Cathedral in flames. *(cd-iss.Dec88; FKK 001CD)(+=)*– Tainted love.

May 85. (12",12"red) *(FFK 512)* **PANIC. / TAINTED LOVE / AQUA REGIS** [ ] [-]

— In 1986, shared billing with BOYD RICE on album 'NIGHTMARE CULTURE'.

— added **STEPHEN E. THROWER** – wind, percussion

Dec 86. (12"ep,12"clear-ep) *(ROTA 121)* **THE ANAL STAIRCASE. / BLOOD FROM THE AIR / RAVENOUS** [ ] [-]

Jan 87. (lp) *(ROTA 1)* **HORSE ROTORVATOR** [ ] [-]
– The anal staircase / Slur / Babylero / Ostia / Herald / Penetralia / Circles of mania / Blood from the air / Who by fire / The golden section / The first five minutes after death. *(cd-iss.Jan88; ROTA 1CD)(+=)*– Ravenous.

Solar Lodge Torso

Jan 88. (lp) *(SL 1)* **MUSIC FOR COMMERCIALS** [ ] [-]

Jun 88. (10"m-lp; some colrd) *(COIL 001)* **THE CONSEQUENCES OF RAISING HELL** [ ] [-]
– Hellraiser theme / The hellbound heart / Box theme / No new world / Attack of the Sennapods / Main title. *(re-iss.as 'HELLRAISER' Feb89 c/cd; COIL C/CD 001)(+=)*– MUSIC FOR COMMERCIALS

— added **OTTO AVERY**

Threshold House Torso

Sep 88. (lp,red-lp,clear-lp/cd) *(LOCI/+CD 1)* **GOLD IS THE METAL** [ ] [-]
– The last rites of spring / Paradisiac / Thump / For us they will / The broken wheel / Boy in a suitcase / Golden hole / Cardinal points / Red slur / . . .Of free enterprise / Aqua regalia / Metal in the head / Either his, or yours / Chickenskin / Soundtrap / The first five minutes after violent death. *(cd+=)*– The wheal / Hellraiser. *(lp's w/ free 7")*– THE WHEEL. / THE WHEAL *(re-iss.1990 on 'Normal' lp/cd; NORMAL/+CD 77) (lp w/ free 7")*– THE WHEEL. / KEEL HAULER *(re-iss.cd May94 on 'Normal'; same) (cd re-iss.Oct96; same)*

1990. (7") *(SX 002)* **WRONG EYE. / SCOPE** [ ] [-]

— (above issued on 'Shock')

Dec 90. (12") *(LOCI 3)* **WINDOWPANE. / WINDOWPANE** [ ] [-]

Torso Wax Trax!

May 91. (lp/cd) *(TORSO/+CD 181)* <WAXCD 7143> **LOVE'S SECRET DOMAIN** [ ] [ ] 1989
– Disco hospital / Teenage lightning / Things happen / The snow / Dark river / Where even the darkness / Something to see / Windowpane / Further back and faster / Lorca not Orca / Love's secret domain.

Aug 91. (12"ep/cd-ep) *(TORSO/+CD 180)* **THE SNOW REMIXES** [ ] [-]
– (6 remixes from last album by JACK DANGERS + DREW McDOWELL)

1992. (7") **AIRBORNE BELLS. / IS SUICIDE A SOLUTION** [ ] [-]

— above issued on 'Clawfist'

Nov 92. (cd) *(LOCICD 4)* **STOLEN AND CONTAMINATED KISSES** [ ] [-]
(cont. 'HOW TO DESTROY ANGELS') (cd re-iss.Oct96; same)

1994. (12"blue) *(LOCIS 1)* **THEMES FROM BLUE 1. / THEMES FROM BLUE 2** [ ] [-]

Eskaton Eskaton

1994. (12") *(ESKATON 001)* **NASA ARAB. / FIRST DARK RIDE** [ ] [-]

1994. (12") *(ESKATON 002)* **BEAUTIFUL CATASTROPHE** [ ] [-]

– Protection / Glimpse / Crawling sirit / PHILM #1.
1995. (10"ep,10"clear-ep; by COIL & ELPH) *(ESKATON 003)* **PHILM. / STATIC ELECTRICIAN / RED SCRATCH** [ ] [-]
1995. (cd/lp) *(ESKATON 006/007)* **WORSHIP THE GLITCH** [ ] [-]

– compilations, etc. –

Dec 89. (cd) *Threshold House; (LOCICD 2)* **UNNATURAL HISTORY** [ ] [-]
1995. (cd) *Threshold House; (LOCICD)* **UNNATURAL HISTORY VOL.2** [ ] [-]
1995. (d-cd) *Threshold House;* **THE SOUND OF MUSIC** (film music) [ ] [-]
Apr 97. (cd) *Threshold House; (LOCICD 12)* **UNNATURAL HISTORY VOL.3 (JOYFUL PARTICIPATION IN THE SORROWS OF THE WORLD)** [ ] [-]

Julian COPE

Born: 21 Oct'57, Bargeld, Wales although he was raised in Liverpool, England. His first foray into the music business was with CRUCIAL THREE, alongside IAN McCULLOCH and PETE WYLIE. In the Autumn of '78 he formed The TEARDROP EXPLODES, originally named A SHALLOW MADNESS with MICK FINKLER and PAUL SIMPSON. In late '78 a deal was inked with local UK indie label, 'Zoo', and after three critically acclaimed singles, they transferred to the major label, 'Mercury,' in July 1980. They scored their first hit with 'WHEN I DREAM', from the classic album, Top 30 'KILIMANJARO'. Early in 1981, they cashed-in when 'REWARD' delivered them a Top tenner. 'TREASON', the next 45, didn't emulate this feat, although it still managed a Top 20 placing. Their second album, 'WILDER' was another commercial success, although it lacked the bite of its predecessor. A few minor hits followed over the next year and a bit, but it was clear JULIAN was gearing up for a solo career. Remaining with 'Mercury' records, he released two albums in 1984, 'WORLD SHUT YOUR MOUTH' and 'FRIED', both receiving a lukewarm response from the music press. He then signed for 'Island' in 1985, leaving behind the unissued (until 1990) 'SKELLINGTON' lp. Around the same time he suffered a marriage break-up and drug problems, although he re-married in 1986. Re-emerging triumphantly in 1986, he scored with the Top 20 hit 45, 'WORLD SHUT YOUR MOUTH' (curiously enough, the song wasn't included on the 1984 album of the same name). The single was a taster for the following year's comeback album 'SAINT JULIAN', a record which almost gave him his first solo top ten hit. A disappointing pop album, 'MY NATION UNDERGROUND', lent his street cred a bitter blow and he retreated somewhat with two (meant for mail-order) 1990 albums 'SKELLINGTON' & 'DROOLIAN'. He returned in fine fashion a year later with the splendid double, 'PEGGY SUICIDE', a record that targeted pollution and even the dreadful Tory poll tax (something he protested against vehemently). In 1992, he brought back his old influences (CAN, FAUST, "Kraut-rock") with 'JEHOVAKILL'. Creatively, the album was an admirable effort although it bombed both commercially and critically. This was his last for Island, who dropped him unceremoniously after he recorded the 'RITE' cd-album for German release. In 1994, he signed with 'Echo' and returned with two mediocre and great albums respectively; 'AUTOGEDDON' &'20 MOTHERS' (1995). • **Style:** Keyboard-biased (TEARDROP EXPLODES) were mostly influenced by 60's pop psychedelia, sounding like a modern, post-new wave SCOTT WALKER. On-stage like antics cutting his stomach (IGGY POP-like) in, and singing perched on a high pole in, saw him develop a weird new character. Often he perfomed through his alter-ego (SQWUBBSY a seven foot giant) at work. • **Songwriters:** COPE penned except; READ IT IN BOOKS (co-with; Ian McCulloch). He wrote all material, except NON-ALIGNMENT PACT (Pere Ubu) / BOOKS (Teardrop Explodes). • **Trivia:** The album DROOLIAN, was released as part of a campaign to free from jail ROKY ERICKSON (ex-13th FLOOR ELEVATORS). In '90, COPE took part in the Anti-Poll tax march from Brixton to Trafalgar Square.

Recommended: PEGGY SUICIDE (*8) / SAINT JULIAN (*7) / FLOORED GENIUS (*9) / WORLD SHUT YOUR MOUTH (*8) / FRIED (*7) / MY NATION UNDERGROUND (*6) / JEHOVAHKILL (*7) / 20 MOTHERS (*8) / TEARDROP EXPLODES:- KILIMANJARO (*9) / WILDER (*7)

TEARDROP EXPLODES

JULIAN COPE (b.21 Oct'57, Bargoed, Wales) – vocals, bass / **PAUL SIMPSON** – keyboards / **MICK FINKLER** – guitar / **GARY DWYER** – drums

Zoo | not issued

Feb 79. (7"m) *(CAGE 003)* **SLEEPING GAS. / CAMERA CAMERA / KIRBY WORKERS' DREAM FADES** [ ] [-]

— **GERARD QUINN** – keyboards repl. SIMPSON who formed The WILD SWANS

May 79. (7") *(CAGE 005)* **BOUNCING BABIES. / ALL I AM IS LOVING YOU** [ ] [-]

— **DAVID BALFE** – keyboards (ex-LORI & THE CHAMELEONS, ex-BIG IN JAPAN, ex-THOSE NAUGHTY LUMPS) repl. QUINN who joined The WILD SWANS

Mar 80. (7") *(CAGE 008)* **TREASON (IT'S JUST A STORY). / READ IT IN BOOKS** [ ] [-]

— **ALAN GILL** – guitar (ex-DALEK I) repl. FINKLER now (COPE, DWYER, BALFE + GILL)

Mercury | Mercury

Sep 80. (7") *(TEAR 1)* **WHEN I DREAM. / KILIMANJARO** [47] [ ]
Oct 80. (lp) *(6359 035) <4016>* **KILIMANJARO** [24] [ ]
– Ha, ha, I'm drowning / Sleeping gas / Treason (it's just a story) / Second head / Poppies in the field / Went crazy / Brave boys keep their promises / Bouncing babies / Books / Thief of Baghdad / When I dream. *(re-iss.Mar81 lp/c +=; 6359/7150 035)*– Reward. *(re-iss.Jul84 lp/c; PRICE/PRIMC 59) (re-iss.May89 lp/c/cd; 836 897-1/-4/-2)*

— (below trumpet by RAY MARTINEZ)

Jan 81. (7") *(TEAR 2)* **REWARD. / STRANGE HOUSE IN THE SNOW** [6] [ ]
Apr 81. (7") *(TEAR 3)* **TREASON (IT'S JUST A STORY). / USE ME** [18] [ ]
(12"+=) *(TEAR 3-12)* – Traison (c'est juste une histoire).
Jun 81. (7") *(TEAR 4)* **POPPIES IN THE FIELD. / HA HA I'M DROWNING** [ ] [ ]
(d7"+=) *(TEAR 44)* – Bouncing babies / Read it in books.

— **TROY TATE** – guitar, vocals (ex-INDEX, ex-SHAKE) repl. GILL

Sep 81. (7") *(TEAR 5)* **PASSIONATE FRIEND. / CHRIST VS. WARHOL** [25] [ ]

— on session/gigs **ALFIE ALGIUS** (b.Malta) – bass / **JEFF HAMMER** – keyboards

Nov 81. (lp/c) *(6359/7150 056) <4035>* **WILDER** [29] [ ]
– Bent out of shape / Tiny children / The culture bunker / Falling down around me / Passionate friend / Colours fly away / Pure joy / Seven views of Jerusalem / The great dominions / Like Leila Khaled said / . . .And the fighting takes over. *(re-iss.Jun87 lp/c; PRICE/PRIMC 112) (re-iss.May89 lp/c/cd; 836 896-1/-4/-2)*
Nov 81. (7") *(TEAR 6)* **COLOURS FLY AWAY. / WINDOW SHOPPING FOR A NEW CROWN OF THORNS** [54] [ ]
(12"+=) *(TEAR 6-12)* – East of the equator.

— **DAVID BALFE** returned

— **RON FRANCOIS** – bass (ex-SINCEROS) repl. guests

Jun 82. (7"/7"g-f) *(TEAR 7/+G)* **TINY CHILDREN. / RACHEL BUILT A STEAMBOAT** [44] [ ]
(12"+=) *(TEAR 7-12)* – Sleeping gas (live).

— now trio of **COPE, DWYER + BALFE** plus session man **FRANCOIS** — TROY TATE went solo and joined FASHION

Mar 83. (7") *(TEAR 8)* **YOU DISAPPEAR FROM VIEW. / SUFFOCATE** [41] [ ]
(d7"+=/12"+=) *(TEAR 88/8-12)* – Soft enough for you / Ouch monkey's / The in-psychlopedia.

— Disbanded early '83. BALFE went into producing films and music. JULIAN COPE went solo augmented by DWYER.

– compilations, others, etc. –

Jun 85. (7") *Mercury; (TEAR 9)* **REWARD (remix). / TREASON (IT'S JUST A STORY)** [ ] [-]
(12"+=) *(TEAR 9-12)* – Strange house in the snow / Use me.
Jan 90. (7") *Fontana; (DROP 1)* **SERIOUS DANGER. / SLEEPING GAS** [ ] [-]
(12"+=)(c-s+=/cd-s+=) *(DROP 1-12)(DRO MC/CD 1)* – Seven views of Jerusalem.
Mar 90. (cd/c/lp) *Fontana; (842 439-2/-4/-1)* **EVERYBODY WANTS TO SHAG THE TEARDROP EXPLODES** (long lost 3rd album) [72] [-]
– Ouch monkey's / Serious danger / Metranil Vavin / Count to ten and run forever / In-psychlopaedia / Soft enough for you / You disappear from view / The challenger / Not only my friend / Sex / Terrorist / Strange house in the snow.
Apr 90. (7") *Fontana; (DROP 2)* **COUNT TO TEN AND RUN FOR COVER. / REWARD** [ ] [-]
(12"+=)(cd-s+=) *(DROP 2-12)(DROCD 2)* – Poppies / Khaled said.
Jan 91. (cd/c/lp) *Document; (DCD/DMC/DLP 004)* **PIANO** [ ] [-]
– (early 'Zoo' material)

JULIAN COPE

with **GARY DWYER / STEVE CREASE + ANDREW EDGE** – drums / **STEPHEN LOWELL** – lead guitar / **RON FRANCOIS** – bass / **KATE ST. JOHN** – oboe

Mercury | Mercury

Nov 83. (7") *(COPE 1)* **SUNSHINE PLAYROOM. / HEY HIGH CLASS BUTCHER** [64] [ ]
(12"+=) *(COPE 1-12)* – Wreck my car / Eat the poor.
Feb 84. (lp/c) *(MERL/+C 37)* **WORLD SHUT YOUR MOUTH** [40] [ ]
– Bandy's first jump / Metranil Vavin / Strasbourg / An elegant chaos / Quizmaster / Kolly Kibber's birthday / Sunshine playroom / Head hang low / Pussy face / The greatness and perfection of love / Lunatic and fire pistol. *(cd-iss.1986; 818 365-2)*
Mar 84. (7") *(MER 155)* **THE GREATNESS AND PERFECTION OF LOVE. / 24a VELOCITY CRESCENT** [52] [ ]
(12"+=) *(MERX 155)* – Pussyface.
Nov 84. (lp/c) *(MERL/+C 48)* **FRIED** [87] [ ]
– Reynard the fox / Bill Drummond said / Laughing boy / Me singing / Sunspots / Me singing / Bloody Assizes / Search party / O king of chaos / Holy love / Torpedo. *(cd-iss.1986; 822 832-2)*
Feb 85. (7") *(MER 182)* **SUNSPOTS. / I WENT ON A CHOURNEY** [ ] [ ]
(d7"+=) *(MER 182-2)* – Mik mak mok / Land of fear.

— **COPE** recruited Americans **DONALD ROSS SKINNER** – guitar / **JAMES ELLER** – bass / **DOUBLE DE HARRISON** – keyboards / **CHRIS WHITTEN** – drums

Island | Island

Sep 86. (7") *(IS 290) <99479>* **WORLD SHUT YOUR MOUTH. / UMPTEENTH UNNATURAL BLUES** [19] [84] Feb87
(d7"+=) *(ISB 290)* – ('A'-Trouble Funk remix) / Transportation.
(c-s+=) *(CIS 290)* – I've got levitation / Non-alignment pact.
(12"++=) *(12IS 290)* – (all extra above).
Jan 87. (7") *(IS 305)* **TRAMPOLENE. / DISASTER** [ ] [ ]
(7"ep+=/12"ep+=) *(ISW/12IS 305)* – Mock Turtle / Warwick the kingmaker.
Feb 87. (m-lp) *<90560>* **JULIAN COPE** [-] [ ]
– World shut your mouth / Transportation / Umpteenth unnatural blues / Non-alignment pact / I've got levitation.
Mar 87. (lp/c/cd) *(ILPS/ICT/CID 9861) <90571>* **SAINT JULIAN** [11] [ ]
– Trampolene / Shot down / Eve's volcano (covered in sin) / Spacehopper / Planet ride / Trampolene / World shut your mouth / Saint Julian / Pulsar NX / Space hopper / Screaming secrets / A crack in the clouds. *(re-iss.Aug91 cd)(c; IMCD 137)(ICM 2023)*
Apr 87. (7") *(IS 318)* **EVE'S VOLCANO (COVERED IN SIN). / ALMOST BEAUTIFUL CHILD** [ ] [ ]
(12"+=) *(12IS 318)* – Pulsar NX (live) / Shot down (live).
(12"+=) *(12ISX 318)* – Spacehopper – Annexe / ('B'side; pt.II).
(cd-s++=) *(CID 318)* – (all 3 extra above).

— **DAVE PALMER** – drums (studio) / **MIKE JOYCE** – drums (tour) repl. WHITTEN / added **RON FAIR** – keyboards / **ROOSTER COSBY** – percussion, some drums

Sep 88. (7") *(IS 380)* **CHARLOTTE ANNE. / CHRISTMAS MOURNING** [35] [ ]
(12"+=/12"pic-d+=/pic-cd-s+=) *(12IS/12ISP/CIDP 380)* – Books / A question of temptation.

Oct 88. (lp/c/cd) *(ILPS/ICT/CID 9918)* <91025> **MY NATION UNDERGROUND** [42] [ ]
– 5 o'clock world / Vegetation / Charlotte Anne / My nation underground / China doll / Someone like me / Easter everywhere / I'm not losing sleep / The great white hoax. *(re-iss.Aug91 cd/c;)*

Nov 88. (7") *(IS 399)* **5 O'CLOCK WORLD. / S.P.Q.R.** [42] [ ]
(10"+=/12"+=/pic-cd-s+=) *(10IS/12IS/CIDP 399)* – Reynard in Tokyo (extended live).

Jun 89. (7") *(IS 406)* **CHINA DOLL. / CRAZY FARM ANIMAL** [53] [ ]
(10"+=/10"pic-d+=/12"+=) *(10IS/10ISP/12IS 406)* – Desi.
(cd-s++=) *(CID 406)* – Rail on.

— **COPE** retained **SKINNER & COSBY** plus **J.D.HASSINGER** – drums / **TIM** – keyboards / **BRAN** – bass (both of Guernsey)

Jan 91. (7"/c-s) *(IS/CIS 483)* **BEAUTIFUL LOVE. / PORT OF SAINTS** [32] [ ]
(12"+=/cd-s+=) *(12IS/CID 483)* – Love L.U.V. / Unisex cathedral.
(12"pink+=) *(12ISX 483)* – Love L.U.V. / Dragonfly.

Mar 91. (cd/c/d-lp) *(CID/ICT/ILPSD 9977)* **PEGGY SUICIDE** [23] [ ]
– Pristeen / Double vegetation / East easy rider / Promised land / Hanging out & hung up on the line / Safesurfer / If you loved me at all / Drive, she said / Soldier blue / You . . . / Not raving but drowning / Head / Leperskin / Beautiful love / Uptight / Western Front 1992 CE / Hung up & hanging out to dry / The American Lite / Las Vegas basement. *(cd re-iss.Aug94; IMCD 188)*

Apr 91. (7"/c-s) *(IS/CIS 492)* **EAST EASY RIDER. / BUTTERFLY E** [51] [ ]
(12"+=/cd-s+=) *(12IS/CID 492)* – Almost live / Little donkey.
(12"pic-d+=) *(12ISX 492)* – Easty Risin' / Ravebury stones.

Jul 91. (7"/c-s) *(IS/CIS 497)* **HEAD. / BAGGED – OUT KEN** [57] [ ]
(12"+=/cd-s+=) *(12IS/CID 497)* – Straw dogs / Animals at all.

Oct 92. (7"/c-s) *(IS/CIS 545)* **FEAR LOVES THE SPACE. / SIZEWELL B.** [42] [ ]
(12"pic-d+=) *(12ISX 545)* – I have always been here before / Gogmagog.

Oct 92. (cd/c/d-lp) *(514052-2/-4/-1)* **JEHOVAHKILL** [20] [ ]
– Soul desert / No harder shoulder to cry on / Akhenaten / The mystery trend / Upwards at 45<< >> / Cut my friends down / Necropolis / Slow rider / Gimme back my flag / Poet is priest / Julian H Cope / The subtle energies commission / Fa-fa-fa-fine / Fear loves this place / Peggy Suicide is missing. *(cd re-iss.Aug94; IMCD 189)*

— Next was last in the 90's album trilogy about pollution. Its theme this time was the car, (coincidentally he had just passed his driving test). It featured usual musicians.

Echo / Def American

Jul 94. (cd/c/lp) *(ECH CD/MC/LP 001)* **AUTOGEDDON** [16] [ ]
– Autogeddon blues / Don't call me Mark Chapman / Madmax / I gotta walk / Ain't no gettin' round gettin' round / Paranormal in the West Country / Paranormal / Archdrude's roadtrip / Kar-ma-kanik / Ain't but the one way / Starcar.

Aug 95. (7"/c-s) *(ECS/+MC 11)* **TRY TRY TRY / WESSEXY** [24] [ ]
(cd-s+=) *(ECSCD 11)* – Baby, let's play vet / Don't jump me, mother.

Aug 95. (cd/c/d-lp) *(ECH CD/MC/LP 005)* **20 MOTHERS** [20] [ ]
– Wheelbarrow man / I wandered lonely as a child / Try try try / Stone circles 'n' you / Queen – Mother / I'm your daddy / Highway to the sun / 1995 / By the light of the Silbury moon / Adam and Eve hit the road / Just like Pooh Bear / Girl-call / Greedhead detector / Don't take roots / Senile get / The lonely guy / Cryingbabiessleeplessnights / Leli B. / Road of dreams / When I walk through the land of fear.

Jul 96. (7"ep/cd-ep) *(ECS/+CDX 022)* **I COME FROM ANOTHER PLANET, BABY. / HOW DO I UNDERSTAND MY MOTORMAN? / IF I COULD DO IT ALL OVER AGAIN, I'D DO IT OVER YOU** [34] [ ]
(cd-s) *(ECSCD 022)* – Ambulance: Weesex post-ambient therapy.

Sep 96. (c-s/cd-s) *(ECS/+CD 025)* **PLANETARY SIT-IN. / TORCH** [34] [ ]
(cd-s+=) *(ECSCX 025)* – Cummer in summertime / Radio sit-in.

Oct 96. (cd/c/lp) *(ECH CD/MC/LP 12)* **INTERPRETER** [39] [ ]
– I come from another planet, baby / I've got my TV and my pills / Planetary sit-in / Since I lost my head, it's awl-right / Cheap new age fix / Battle for the trees / Arthur / Spacerock with me / Re-directed male / Maid of constant sorrow / Loveboat / Dust.

– compilations, others, etc. –

Feb 85. (7"; as RABBI JOSEPH GORDON) *Bam Caruso; (NRICO 30)* **COMPETITION. / BELIEF IN HIM** [ ] [-]

May 90. (cd/lp) *Copeco-Zippo; (JUCD/JULP 89)* **SKELLINGTON** (1985 lost lp) [ ] [-]
– Doomed / Beaver / Me & Jimmy Jones / Robert Mitchum / Out of my mind on dope and speed / Don't crash here / Everything playing at once / Little donkey / Great white wonder / Incredibly ugly girl / No how, no why, no way, no where, no when / Comin' soon.

Jul 90. (cd/lp) *Mofo-Zippo; (MOFOCO CD/LP 90)* **DROOLIAN** [ ] [-]

Jul 92. (c-s/7") *Island; (C+/IS 534)* **WORLD SHUT YOUR MOUTH (remix). / DOOMED** [44] [ ]
(12"+=/cd-s+=) *(12/CD IS 534)* – Reynard the fox / The elevators / Levitation.

Aug 92. (cd/c/d-lp) *Island; (CID/ICT/ILPSD 8000)* **FLOORED GENIUS – THE BEST OF JULIAN COPE AND THE TEARDROP EXPLODES 1981-1991** [22] [ ]
– Reward / Treason / Sleeping gas / Bouncing babies / Passionate friend / The great dominions (; all TEARDROP EXPLODES) / The greatness & perfection of love / An elegant chaos / Sunspots / Reynard the fox / World shut your mouth / Trampolene / Spacehopper / Charlotte Anne / China doll / Out of my mind on dope & speed / Jellypop perky Jean / Beautiful love / East easy rider / Safesurfer.

Nov 92. (d-cd) *Island; (ITSCD 11)* **SAINT JULIAN / MY NATION UNDERGROUND** [ ] [-]

Nov 93. (cd/lp) *Night Tracks; (CD/LP NT 003)* **BEST OF THE BBC SESSIONS 1983-91 (FLOORED GENIUS VOL.2)** [ ] [-]

Jun 97. (cd) *Island; (IMCD 251)* **THE FOLLOWERS OF SAINT JULIAN** [ ] [-]

CRASH (see under ⇒ ULTRA VIVID SCENE)

CYPRESS HILL

Formed: Los Angeles, California, USA . . . 1988 by MUGGS, B.REAL and SEN DOG. In the early 90's, after signing to US 'Columbia' label through their own 'Ruffhouse' label, the hard-core rappers cracked the Top 40 with their eponymous debut. The album contained the single, 'I COULD JUST KILL A MAN', alongside the dirty, trippy narcotica of tracks like 'ULTRAVIOLET DREAMS' and 'SOMETHING FOR THE BLUNTED'. With B-REAL's sneering intonation and the bass-heavy production, CYPRESS HILL were instantly recognisable. Tireless advocators of marijuana use (and legalisation), most of the band's music was so cluastrophobically heavy it sounded like they'd been stoned since birth. Influenced by the infamous 'Rodney King' incident in L.A., the follow-up album, 'BLACK SUNDAY' (1993) took a decidedly darker turn, gangsta-like bravado ('LICK A SHOT', 'COCK THE HAMMER', 'A TO THE K') interspersing the trademark homages to hash. 'INSANE IN THE BRAIN' (1993) was the first in a string of U.K. hit singles and the band consolidated their success in Britain by playing at a number of predominantly white rock festivals, proving their crossover appeal. 'CYPRESS HILL III (TEMPLES OF BOOM)' (1996) upped the gangsta ante with such subtle fare as 'KILLAFORNIA' and 'KILLA HILL NIGGAS' although the hopelessly stoned vibe was still sufficiently alive and kicking (or head bowed and nodding) to satisfy fans. • **Songwriters:** Group penned. I AIN'T GOIN' OUT LIKE THAT sampled; THE WIZARD (Black Sabbath) / WHEN THE SH-- GOES DOWN sampled; DEEP GULLY (Outlaw Blues Band) / LIL' PUTOS sampled; ODE TO BILLY JOE (Bobbie Gentry) / etc. • **Trivia:** MUGGS also produced HOUSE OF PAIN, BEASTIE BOYS and ICE CUBE.

Recommended: BLACK SUNDAY (*8) / CYPRESS HILL (*7) / III – TEMPLES OF BOOM (*6)

B-REAL (b. LOUIS FREESE, 2 Jun'70) – vocals / **SEN DOG** (b. SENEN REYES, 20 Nov'65, Cuba) – vocals / **DJ MUGGS** (b. LARRY MUGGERUD, 28 Jan'68, Queens, N.Y.) – DJ, producer

Ruffhouse Columbia / Ruffhouse Columbia

Dec 91. (c-s) **HAND ON THE PUMP. / REAL ESTATE** [-] [ ]
(12"+=) – ('A'instrumental).

Jan 92. (cd/c/lp) *(468893-2/-4/-1)* <47889> **CYPRESS HILL** [ ] [31] Nov91
– Pigs / How I could just kill a man / Hand on the pump / Hole in the head / Ultraviolet dreams / Light another / The phuncky feel one / Break it up / Real estate / Stoned is the way of the walk / Psycobetabuckdown / Something for the blunted / Latin lingo / The funky Cypress Hill shit / Tres equis / Born to get busy. *(cd re-iss.May94 & Feb97; same)*

Feb 92. (7") <73930> **HOW I COULD JUST KILL A MAN. / THE PHUNKY FEEL ONE** [-] [77] [94]

1992. (12"ep/cd-ep) **HAND ON THE PUMP (Mugg's extended mix) / ('A'-instrumental) / HAND ON THE GLOCK** [-] [ ]

1992. (12"ep/cd-ep) **LATIN LINGO (Prince Paul mix) / STONED IS THE WAY OF THE WALK (reprise) / HAND ON THE GLOCK** [-] [ ]

Jul 93. (c-s) *(659533-4)* <77135> **INSANE IN THE BRAIN (radio version). / WHEN THE SH-- GOES DOWN (radio version)** [32] [19]
(12"+=/cd-s+=) *(659533-6/-2)* – ('A'instrumental).

Jul 93. (cd/c/lp) *(474075-2/-4/-1)* **BLACK SUNDAY** [13] [1]
– I wanna get high / I ain't goin' out like that / Insane in the brain / When the sh--goes down / Lick a shot / Cock the hammer / Interlude / Lil' putos / Legalize it / Hits from the bong / What go around come around, kid / A to the K / Hand on the glock / Break 'em off some.

Sep 93. (c-s) *(659670-8)* **WHEN THE SH-- GOES DOWN (extended). / LATIN LINGO / HOW COULD I JUST KILL A MAN (the Killer mix)** [19] [ ]
(12"+=/cd-s+=) *(659670-6/-2)* – ('A'instrumental) / The phunky feel one (extended).

Dec 93. (c-s) *(659690-4)* **I AIN'T GOIN' OUT LIKE THAT. / HITS FROM THE BONG** [15] [65]
(12"+=/cd-s+=) *(659690-6/-2)* – When the sh-- goes down (Diamond D mix).

Feb 94. (c-s) *(660176-4)* **INSANE IN THE BRAIN. / STONED IS THE WAY OF THE WALK** [21] [ ]
(12"+=) *(660176-6)* – Latin lingo (Prince Paul mix).
(cd-s) *(660176-2)* – ('A'side) / Something for the blunted.

Apr 94. (c-s) *(660319-4)* **LICK A SHOT (Baka Boys remix). / I WANNA GET HIGH** [20] [ ]
(12"+=/cd-s+=) *(660319-6/-2)* – Scooby Doo.

Sep 95. (c-s) *(662354-4)* **THROW YOUR SET IN THE AIR / KILLA HILL NIGGAS** [15] [45]
(12"+=/cd-s+=) *(662354-6/-2)* – ('A'-Slow roll remix) / ('B'instrumental).

Oct 95. (cd/c/d-lp) *(478127-2/-4/-1)* **CYPRESS HILL III / TEMPLES OF BOOM** [11] [3]
– Spark another owl / Throw your set in the air / Stoned raiders / Illusions / Killa hill niggas / Boom biddy bye bye / No rest for the wicked / Make a move / Killafornia / Funk freakers / Locotes / Red light visions / Strictly hip hop / Let it rain / Everybody must get stoned. *(d-cd+=/t-lp+=; 478127-9/-0)–* DJ MUGGS BUDDHA MIX:- Hole in the head – How could I just kill a man – Insane in the brain – Stoned is the way of the walk – Hits from the bong – Hand on the pump – Real estate – I wanna get high.

Feb 96. (12"ep) *(662905-6)* **ILLUSIONS / THROW YOUR SET IN THE AIR (radio version). / ILLUSIONS (harpsicord mix) / ILLUSIONS (harpsicord instrumental)** [23] [ ]
(cd-ep) *(662905-2)* –

— SEN DOG went solo (DOGWOOD) and was repl. by DJ SCANDALOUS

Jun 96. (cd-ep) **BOOM BIDDY BYE BYE** [-] [87]

Aug 96. (m-cd/m-c/m-lp) *(485230-2/-4/-1)* **UNRELEASED & REVAMPED EP** [29] [21]
–

D

DAMON & NAOMI (see under ⇒ GALAXIE 500)

DARKSIDE

Formed: Rugby, England . . . late '89 by ex-SPACEMEN 3 members PETE BASSMAN BAINES and STEWART ROSCO ROSSWELL. Signing to 'Situation 2', they debuted the following Spring with an EP, 'HIGH RISE LOVE'. Later that year, an album 'ALL THAT NOISE' hit the indie charts. However, the dream was over by '92. • **Style:** Doors-influenced ambience, cloaked with a soundtrack feel. • **Songwriters:** Group except covers; BRIGHT LIGHTS BIG CITY (Jimmy Reed).

Recommended: ALL THAT NOISE (*6)

PETE (BASSMAN) BAINES – vocals, bass (ex-SPACEMEN 3) / **STEWART (ROSCO) ROSSWELL** – keyboards (ex-SPACEMEN 3) / KEVIN COWAN – guitar / **CRAIG WAGSTAFF** – drums (joined 1991)

Situation 2 not issued

Apr 90. (12"ep) *(SIT 068T)* **HIGH RISE LOVE. / THE KILLING TIME / CAN'T THINK STRAIGHT** ☐ -

Aug 90. (12"/cd-s) *(SIT 72 T/CD)* **WAITING FOR THE ANGELS. / SWEET VIBRATIONS** ☐ -

Nov 90. (lp/c)(cd/pic-lp) *(SIT U/C 29)(SITU 29 CD/P)* **ALL THAT NOISE** ☐ -
– Guitar voodoo / Found love / She don't come / Good for me / Love in a burning universe / All that noise / Spend some time / Don't stop the rain / Soul deep / Waiting for the angels.

1991. (lp; mail-order) *(DARK 2)* **PSYCHEDELIZE SUBURBIA** - -

—— (above and below on 'Acid Ray' records)

Nov 91. (12"ep/cd-ep) *(DARK 3)* **ALWAYS PLEASURE** ☐ -

Jan 92. (lp/c)(cd/pic-lp) *(SIT U/C 34)(SITU 34 CD/P)* **MELOMANIA** ☐ -
– Always pleasure / Feeling flow / Tornado / This mystic morning / Someday / Are you for real / 24 hours / Cry for me / Rise.

Jun 92. (12"ep/cd-ep) *(SIT 95 T/CD)* **MAYHEM TO MEDIATE** ☐ -
– Straightest shot / This time is mine / Heart of the sun / This mystic morning (remix) / This mystic morning (instrumental dub) / Cry for me (remix).

Bomp Bomp

Jul 93. (7") *(BMP 141)* **LUNAR SURFING EXPERIMENT** ☐ ☐

—— split after above.

DAS DAMEN

Formed: Arizona, USA . . . mid 80's by JIM WALTERS, ALEX TOTINO, PHIL LEOPOLD VON TRAPP and LYLE HYSEN. After an initial eponymous release on 'Ecstatic Peace', they signed to 'SST', former home of HUSKER DU, MEAT PUPPETS and fIREHOSE. In 1987, they unleashed the sublime 'JUPITER EYE' album, a record of quasi-hardcore, that touched on garage psychedelia. This sound was even more pronounced on the follow-up album, 'TRISKAIDEKAPHOBE' and the EP 'MARSHMALLOW CONSPIRACY'. On the latter, the band ploughed through a manic re-working of The BEATLES' 'MAGICAL MYSTERY TOUR. However, this was their last decent effort before signing to 'What Goes On', then 'City Slang', in the early 90's.

Recommended: JUPITER EYE (*6) / TRISKAIDEKAPHOBE (*6)

JIM WALTERS – vocals, guitar / **ALEX TOTINO** – guitar, vocals / **PHIL LEOPOLD VON TRAPP** – bass, vocals / **LYLE HYSEN** – drums, electronics

not issued Ecstatic Peace

1986. (lp) *<004>* **DAS DAMEN** - ☐
– Tsava / Trick question / Slave bird / House of mirrors / How do you measure / Behind my eyes. *<US re-iss.1988 on 'SST' lp/c; SST 040/+C)*

S.S.T. S.S.T.

1987. (lp/c) *(SST 095/+C)* **JUPITER EYE** ☐ ☐
– Gray isn't black / Quarter after eight / Trap door / Where they all went / Name your poison / Impasse / Raindance / Do / Girl with the hair.

Aug 88. (lp) *(SST 190)* **TRISKAIDEKAPHOBE** ☐ ☐
– Spiderbirds / Reverse into tomorrow / Pendant / Seven / Five five five / Firejoke / Bug / Siren plugs / Up for the ride / Ruby Woodpecker / Candy korn.

Dec 88. (m-lp/c/cd) *(SST/+C/CD 218)* **MARSHMALLOW CONSPIRACY EP** ☐ ☐

1989. (cd) **MOUSETRAP** ☐ ☐
– Noon daylight / Mirror leaks / Twenty four to zero / Somewhere, sometime / Demagnetized / Hey angel / Sad mile / Please please me / Click.

What Goes On What Goes On

1989. (7") *(GOES ON 16)* **NEON DAYLIGHT. / GIVE ME EVERYTHING** ☐ ☐

City Slang City Slang

1991. (cd) *(SLANG 10)* **HIGH ANXIETY** ☐ ☐
– The promise / Chaindrive (a slight return) / The outsider / Thrilled to the marrow / Silence.

—— disbanded after above

Richard DAVIS (see under ⇒ CARDINAL)

DEAD CAN DANCE

Formed: Melbourne, Australia . . .1982 by Anglo-Irish decendents BRENDAN PERRY and LISA GERRARD. After one homeland recording (very limited for 'Fast Forward' cassette mag), they came to London where they were signed to up and coming indie '4 a.d.', by owner IVO WATTS-RUSSELL. Their eponymous 1984 debut was critically acclaimed and soon soared to the higher regions of the indie charts. With a 15-piece ensemble, they selected a few venues for concerts, but never toured consistantly. After several albums, they secured a Top 50 spot in 1993 with 'INTO THE LABYRINTH'. LISA then released a few solo outings, one under the pseudonym of ELIJAH'S MANTLE. • **Style:** Deeply gothic with ambient overtones. Wailing Eastern diva-type vocals (OFRA HAZA) and COCTEAU TWINS / JOY DIVISION like backing. • **Songwriters:** GERRARD / PERRY (some w/ others & some trad samples). • **Trivia:** Engineered by JOHN A. RIVERS. They also can be heard on '4 a.d.' amalgam THIS MORTAL COIL and also featured 2 tracks on various lp 'LONELY AS AN EYESORE'.

Recommended: DEAD CAN DANCE (*8) / SPLEEN AND IDEAL (*7) / WITHIN THE REALM OF A DYING SUN (*8) / THE SERPENT'S EGG (*8) / AION (*7) / A PASSAGE IN TIME (compilation *8) / INTO THE LABYRINTH (*8) / TOWARD THE WITHIN (*7) / SPIRITCHASER (*8)

BRENDAN PERRY – multi-instrumentalist, vocals / **LISA GERRARD** – vocals, percussion / **PETER ULRICH** – percussion, drums, tapes with **JAMES PINKER** – timpani, mixer / **SIMON RODGER** – trombone; plus **MARTIN McCARRICK + GUY FERGUSON** – cello / **CAROLYN LOSTIN** – violin / **RICHARD AVISON** – trombone / **TONY AYERS** – timpani / **ANDREW NUTTER** – soprano vox

4 a.d. Rough Trade

Feb 84. (lp) *(CAD 404)* **DEAD CAN DANCE** ☐ -
– A passage in time / Threshold / The trial / Frontier / Ocean / Fortune / East of Eden / The fatal impact / Wild in the woods / Musical eternal. *(cd-iss.Feb87; CAD 404CD)*– (includes below EP).

Sep 84. (12"ep) *(BAD 408)* **THE GARDEN OF ARCANE DELIGHTS** ☐ -
– Carnival of light / The arcane / Flowers of the sea / In power we entrust the love advocated.

Nov 85. (lp/c)(cd) *(CAD/+C 512)(CAD 512CD)* **SPLEEN AND IDEAL** ☐ -
– De profounds (out of the depths of sorrow) / Ascension / Circumradiant dawn / The cardinal sin / Mesmerism / Enigma of the absolute / Advent / Avatar / Indoctrination. *(cd+=)*– This tide / A design for living.

—— now a basic duo of **BRENDAN + LISA** when ULRICH departed (SIMON + JAMES formed HEAVENLY BODIES). Retained **FERGUSON + AVISON** and recruited **ALISON HARLING + EMLYN SINGLETON** – violin / **PIERO GASPARINI** – viola / **TONY GAMMAGE + MARK GERRARD** (bother) – trumpet / **RUTH WATSON** – oboe, bass trombone / **JOHN + PETER SINGLETON** – trombone / **ANDREW CAXTON** – tuba, bass trombone

Jul 87. (lp/c)(cd) *(CAD/+C 705)(CAD 705CD)* **WITHIN THE REALM OF A DYING SUN** ☐ ☐
– Dawn of the Iconoclast / In the wake of adversity / New age / Summoning of the muse / Anywhere out of the world / Cantara / Windfall / Xavier / Persephone (the gathering of flowers).

—— **LISA + BRENDAN** brought in **DAVID NAVARRO SUST** (retained **ALISON + TONY**), new **REBECCA JACKSON** – violin / **SARAH BUCKLEY + ANDREW BEESLEY** – violas

Oct 88. (lp/c)(cd) *(CAD/+C 808)(CAD 808CD)* **THE SERPENT'S EGG** ☐ ☐
– The host of Seraphim / Orbis de Ignis / Severance / Chant of the Paladin / The writing on my father's hand / Echolalia / In the kingdom of the blind, the one-eyed are kings / Song of Sophia / Mother tongue / Ullysses.

Jul 90. (cd)(lp/c) *(CAD 0007CD)(CAD/+C 0007)* **AION** ☐ ☐
– The arrival and the reunion / Saltarello / Mephisto / The song of the Sibyl / Fortune presents gifts not according to the book / As the bell rings the maypole spins / The end of the words / Black Sun / Wilderness / The promised womb / The garden of Zephirus / Radharc.

Oct 91. (cd)(c) *(CAD 1010CD)(CADC 1010)* **A PASSAGE IN TIME** (part compilation) ☐ ☐
– Salterello / Song of Sophia / Ullyses / Cantara / The garden of Zephirus / Enigma of the absolute / Wilderness / The host of Seraphim / Anywhere out of the world / The writing on my father's hand / Severance / The song of the Sibyl (traditional version; Catalan 16th Century) / Fortune presents gifts not according to the book / In the kingdom of the blind the one-eyed are kings / Bird / Spirit.

Sep 93. (cd)(c)(d-lp) *(CAD 3013CD)(CADC 3013)(DAD 3013) <45384>* **INTO THE LABYRINTH** 47 ☐
– Yulunga (spirit dance) / The ubiquitous Mr. Lovegrove / The wind that shakes the barley / The carnival is over / Ariadne / Saldek / Towards the within / Tell me about the forest (you once called home) / The spider's Stratagem / Emmeleia / How fortunate the man with none. *(d-lp+=)*– Bird / Spirit.

Oct 94. (cd)(d-lp/c) *(DAD 4015CD)(DAD/+C 4015) <45769>* **TOWARD THE WITHIN** ☐ ☐
– Rakim / Persian love song / Desert song / Yulunga (spirit dance) / Piece for solo flute / The wind that shakes the barley / I am stretched on your grave / I can see now / American dreaming / Cantara / Oman / Song of the Sibyl / Tristan / Sanveen / Don't fade away.

Jun 96. (c/cd)(d-lp) *(CAD 6008/+CD)(DAD 6008) <46230>* **SPIRITCHASER** 43 75
– Nierika / Song of the stars / Indus / Song of the dispossessed / Dedicaci outr / The snake and the Moon / Song of the Nile / Devorzhum.

– compilations, etc. –

1991. (cd) *Emperion;* **THE HIDDEN TREASURES** (out-takes, live, rare) ☐ -

LISA GERRARD

— with The VICTORIAN PHILHARMONIC ORCHESTRA. She had worked on the scores for 'Oedipus Rex' and 'Baraku', while sidelining with ELIJAH'S MANTLE.

Aug 95. (cd)(c) *(CAD 5009CD)(CADC 5009)* **THE MIRROR POOL**
– Violina: The last embrace / La Bas: Song of the drowned / Persian love song: The silver gun / Sanvean: I am your shadow / The rite / Ajhon / Glorafin / Majhnavea's music box / Largo / Werd / Laurelei / Celon / Ventelas / Swans / Nilleshna / Gloradin.

DE LA SOUL

Formed: Amityville, Long Island, New York, USA . . . 1987 by DAVID JOLICOEUR (TRUGOY THE DOVE), KELVIN MERCER (POSDNOUS) & VINCENT MASON (PACEMASTER MASE). They quickly set about writing their soon-to-be critically acclaimed cross-Atlantic debut album, '3 FEET HIGH AND RISING', which made the Top 30 in the Spring of '89. Produced by STETSASONIC's PRINCE PAUL, it featured cameos from A TRIBE CALLED QUEST, JUNGLE BROTHERS (their inspiration) and QUEEN LATIFAH. Their much-anticipated but disappointing 1991 follow-up, 'DE LA SOUL IS DEAD,' accurately predicted their fate. Nevertheless, the album sold respectively and on reflection, many critics acknowledged that it contained some disturbing but poignant messages. On '93's 'BUHLOONE MINDSTATE', DE LA SOUL were back on top form once again, firing subtly subversive broadsides at the white middle class ruling system. • **Style:** Psychedelic hip-hop rappers, influenced a little by the mid 80's urban scene. Dressed mostly in baggy sportswear, they infused their lyrics with a pseudo flower-power, visionary attitude, termed as 'daisy-age'. These hip hop gypsies sampled everything from JAMES BROWN (again!) to STEELY DAN, the latter on debut hit 'ME MYSELF AND I'.

Recommended: 3 FEET HIGH AND RISING (*9) / DE LA SOUL IS DEAD (*6) / BUHLOONE MINDSTATE (*6) / STAKES IS HIGH (*7)

TRUGOY THE DOVE (b. DAVID JOLICOEUR, 21 Sep'68, Brooklyn) – vocals / **POSDNOUS** (b. KELVIN MERCER, 17 Aug'69, Bronx) – vocals / **PACEMASTER MASE** (b. VINCENT MASON, 24 Mar'70, Brooklyn) – DJ

Tommy Boy | Tommy Boy

Jul 88. (7") **PLUG TUNIN'. / FREEDOM OF SPEAK** [-]

Oct 88. (7") <(TB 917)> **JENIFA (TAUGHT ME). /**

Big Life | Tommy Boy

Mar 89. (lp/c/cd) *(DLS LP/MC/CD 1) <TB/+C/CD 1019>* **3 FEET HIGH AND RISING** [13] [24]
– Intro / The magic number / Change in speak / Cool breeze on the rocks / Can you kep a secret / Jenifa (taught me) / Ghetto thang / Transmitting live from Mars / Eye know / Take it off / A little bit of soap / Tread water / Say no go / Do as De La does / Plug tunin' / De La orgee / Buddy / Description / Me myself and I / This is a recording for living in a fulltime era I can do anything / D.A.I.S.Y. age / Potholes in my lawn. *(cd re-iss.Jan96; DLSCD 1) (cd re-iss.Jun97 +=; TBCD 1019)*– Plug tunin' (12"mix).

Mar 89. (7") *(BLR 7) <7926>* **ME MYSELF AND I. / BRAIN WASHED FOLLOWER** [22] [34] Feb89
(12"+=) *(BLR 7T)* – Ain't hip to be labelled a hippie / What's more.
(cd-s+=) *(BLR 7CD)* – Ain't hip to be labelled a hippie / ('A'version).
(12"+=) *(BLR 7R)* – ('A'remixes).

Jun 89. (7"/7"pic-d) *(BLR 10/+P)* **SAY NO GO. / THEY DON'T KNOW THAT THE SOUL DON'T GO FOR THAT** [18]
(12"+=/cd-s+=) *(BLR 10 T/CD)* – ('A'versions).
(12"+=) *(BLR 10R)* – ('A'remixes).

Sep 89. (7"/7"pic-d/c-s) *(BLR 13/+P/C)* **EYE KNOW. / THE MACK DADDY ON THE LEFT** [14]
(12"+=/cd-s+=) *(BLR 13 T/CD)* – ('A'versions).

Dec 89. (7"/c-s) *(BLR 14/+MC)* **THE MAGIC NUMBER. / BUDDY** [7]
(12"+=/cd-s+=) *(BLR 14 T/CD)* – Ghetto thang.
(12"+=) *(BLR 14R)* – ('A'remixes).

— In Mar'90, DE LA SOUL were credited on QUEEN LATIFAH's UK Top 20 single 'MAMA GAVE BIRTH TO THE SOUL CHILDREN' *(Gee Street; GEE 26)*

Apr 91. (7"/c-s) *(BLR 42/+MC)* **RING RING RING (HA HEY HEY). / PILES AND PILES OF DEMO TAPES BI DA MILES** [10]
(12") *(BLR 42T)* – ('A'extended) / Afro connection of a mis / ('A'-sax version).
(cd-s+=) *(BLR 42CD)* – ('A'-party mix).

May 91. (cd/c/d-lp) *(BLR CD/MC/LP 8) <TB/+C/CD 1029>* **DE LA SOUL IS DEAD** [7] [26]
– Intro / Oodles of O's / Talkin' bout hey love / Pease porridge / (skit 1) / Johnny's dead aka Vincent Mason (live from the BK lounge) / A roller skating jam named 'Saturdays' (disco fever edit) / WRMS' dedication to the bitty / Bitties in the BK lounge / (skit 2) / Let, let me in / Rap de rap show / Millie pulled a pistol on Santa / (skit 3) / Pass the plugs / Ring ring ring (ha ha hey) / WRMS: Cat's in control / (skit 4) / Shwingalokate / Fanatic of the B word / Keepin' the faith / (skit 5). *(cd re-iss.Jan96; DLSCD 8)*

Jul 91. (7"/c-s) *(BLR 55/+MC)* **A ROLLER SKATING JAM CALLED 'SATURDAYS'. / WHAT YOUR LIFE CAN TRULY BE** [22]
(12"+=/cd-s+=) *(BLR 55 T/CD)* – ('A'-disco mix) / Who's skatin'.

Nov 91. (7"/c-s) *(BLR 64/+MC)* **KEEPIN' THE FAITH (remix). / ('A'instrumental)** [50]
(12"+=) *(BLR 64T)* – Roller skating jam called 'Saturdays' / Ring ring ring (ha ha hey).
(cd-s) *(BLR 64CD)* – (2 'A'versions) / ('A'instrumental) / ('A' funky mix).

Sep 93. (7"/c-s) *(BLR/+C 103) <7586>* **BREAKADAWN. / EN FOCUS (vocal version)** [39] [76]
(12"+=/cd-s+=) *(BLR T/CD 103)* – ('A'mixes).

Oct 93. (cd/c/lp) *(BLR CD/MC/LP 25)* **BUHLOONE MIND STATE** [37] [40] Sep93
– Intro / Eye patch / En focus / Patti Dooke / I be blowin' / Long Island wildin' / Ego trippin' / Paul Revere / Three days later / Area / I am I be / In the woods / Breakadawn / Dave has a problem . . . seriously / Stone age / Lonely days.

— In Mar'94. they teamed up with TEENAGE FANCLUB on the single 'FALLIN' *(Epic 660262-4/-2)*. From the rap-rock film 'Judgement Night'.

Nov 95. (12"/cd-s) *(BLR T/D 132)* **ME MYSELF & I. /**

Tommy Boy | Tommy Boy

Jun 96. (c-s) *(TBC 7730)* **STAKES IS HIGH / ('A'-UK clean version)** [55]
(cd-s) *(TBCD 7730)* – ('A'side) / ('A'extended) / ('A'-DJ original) / The bizness.
(12") *(TBV 7730)* – ('A'extended) / ('A'-DJ original) / ('A'-album version) / ('A'-acapella).

Jul 96. (cd/c/d-lp) *(TB CD/C/V 1149)* **STAKES IS HIGH** [42] [13]
– Intro / Supa emcees / The bizness (featuring COMMON SENSE) / Wonce again Long Island / Dinninit / Brakes / Dog eat dog / Baby baby baby ooh baby / Long Island degrees / Betta listen / Itsoweezee (HOT) / 4 more (featuring ZHANE) / Big brother beat (featuring MOS DEF) / Down syndrome / Pony ride (featuring TRUTH ENOLA) / Stakes is high / Sunshine. *(cd re-iss.Feb97; same)*

Mar 97. (c-ep/12"ep/cd-ep) *(TB C/V/CD 7779)* **4 MORE / BABY BABY BABY OOH BABY. / ITZSOWEEZEE / SWEET DREAMS** [52]

DINOSAUR JR.

Formed: Amherst, Massachusetts, USA . . . 1983 by J.MASCIS. Initially recording hardcore punk under the DEEP WOUND moniker, the band recruited PATRICK MURPHY and metamorphosised into DINOSAUR. Their self-titled debut album appeared in 1985, a raw blueprint for their distinctive candy-coated noise rock that was good enough to secure an American tour support slot with SONIC YOUTH. After protestations from aging West Coast rockers DINOSAUR, J.MASCIS' crew added the JR. part of their name. Subsequently recording one album for 'SST', 'YOU'RE LIVING ALL OVER ME' (1987), the band further developed their melodic distortion although it was the 'FREAK SCENE' (1988) single, their debut for 'Blast First', which saw DINOSAUR JR. pressed to the cardigan-clad bosoms of the nations pre-baggy indie kids.. A wildly exhilirating piece of pristine pop replete with copious amounts of intoxicating noise pollution, MASCIS' go-on-impress-me vocals epitomised the word slacker when that dubious cliche was still gestating in some hack's subconscious. The follow-up album, 'BUG' (1988) was arguably the band's finest moment, perfectly crafted pop spiked with scathing slivers of guitar squall. BARLOW departed soon after the album's release, going off to form SEBADOH while MASCIS' mob came up with a wonderfully skewed cover of The CURE's 'JUST LIKE HEAVEN'. DON FLEMING (of GUMBALL fame) and JAY SPIEGEL featured on DINOSAUR JR.'s major label debut for 'WEA' subsidiary 'Blanco Y Negro', 'THE WAGON' (1991). Another slice of cascading noise-pop, the single raised expectations for the follow-up album 'GREEN MIND' (1991). More or less a MASCIS solo album, it failed to live up to its promise although by the release of 1993's 'WHERE YOU BEEN', MASCIS had found a permanent bassist in MIKE JOHNSON. Their most successful album to date, DINOSAUR JR. at last reaped some rewards from the grunge scene they'd played a major role in creating. With both JOHNSON and MASCIS releasing solo albums in 1996, DINOSAUR JR. have been conspicuous by their absence of late. • **Songwriters:** MASCIS wrote all, except JUST LIKE HEAVEN (Cure) / LOTTA LOVE (Neil Young) / QUICKSAND (David Bowie) / I FEEL A WHOLE LOT BETTER (Byrds) / GOIN' BLIND (Kiss) / HOT BURRITO 2 (Gram Parsons). J. MASCIS solo:- EVERY MOTHER'S SON (Lynyrd Skynyrd) / ANTICIPATION (Carly Simon). • **Trivia:** In Jun'91, MASCIS moonlighted as a drummer with Boston satanic hard-core group UPSIDE DOWN CROSS, who made one self-titled album Autumn '91 on 'Taang!'. He also wrote songs and made a cameo appearance in the 1992 film 'Gas, Food, Lodging'.

Recommended: BUG (*8) / YOU'RE LIVING ALL OVER ME (*6) / GREEN MIND (*6) / WHERE YOU BEEN? (*7)

LOU BARLOW (b.17 Jul'66, Northampton, Mass.) – guitar / **J. MASCIS** (b. JOSEPH, 10 Dec'65) – drums / **CHARLIE NAKAJIMA** – vox / **SCOTT HELLAND** – bass

not issued | Radiobeat

Dec 83. (7"ep; as DEEP WOUND) *<RB 002>* **I SAW IT** [-]
– I saw it / Sisters / In my room / Don't need / Lou's anxiety song / Video prick / Sick of fun / Deep wound / Dead babies.

— **J.MASCIS** – vocals, guitar, percussion / **LOU BARLOW** – bass, ukelele, vocals / added **MURPH** (b. EMMETT "PATRICK" MURPHY, 21 Dec'64) – drums (ex-ALL WHITE JURY)

not issued | Homestead

Jun 85. (lp; as DINOSAUR) *<HMS 015>* **DINOSAUR** [-]
– Forget the swan / Cats in a bowl / The leper / Does it float / Pointless / Repulsion / Gargoyle / Several lips / Mountain man / Quest / Bulbs of passion.

Mar 86. (7"; as DINOSAUR) *<HMS 032>* **REPULSION. / BULBS OF PASSION** [-]

S.S.T. | S.S.T.

Mar 87. (12"ep) *<SST 152>* **DINOSAUR JR.** [-]
– Little fury things / In a jar / Show me the way. *(cd-ep iss.Dec88; SSTCD 152)*

Jul 87. (m-lp/c) *(SST/+C 130)* **YOU'RE LIVING ALL OVER ME**
– Little fury things / Kracked / Sludgefeast / The lung / Raisans / Tarpit / In a jar / Lose / Poledo / Show me the way. *(cd-iss.Oct95;)*

BlastFirst | S.S.T.

Sep 88. (7") *(BFFP 30)* **FREAK SCENE. / KEEP THE GLOVE**
(US-iss.7",7"green; SST 220)

Oct 88. (lp/c/cd) *(BFFP 31/+C/CD)* **BUG**
– Freak scene / No bones / They always come / Yeah we know / Let it ride / Pond song / Budge / The post / Don't.

— **DONNA BIDDELL** – bass (ex-SCREAMING TREES) repl. BARLOW who formed SEBADOH

Apr 89. (7"/etched-12"/cd-s) *(BFFP 47 S/T/CD) <SST 244>* **JUST LIKE HEAVEN. / THROW DOWN / CHUNKS (A Last Rights Tune)** [78] Feb 90

(US version 12"ep+=/c-ep+=/cd-ep+=) (SST/+C/CD 244)– Freak scene / Keep the glove.

— DONNA left and was repl. by **DON FLEMING** – guitar + **JAY SPIEGEL** – drums (both B.A.L.L.)

Glitterhouse Sub Pop

Jun 90. (7"/7"white) (GR 0097) <SP 68> **THE WAGON. / BETTER THAN GONE** [-] [ ]

— In Oct 90, J.MASCIS and other ex-DINOSAUR JR member FLEMING + SPIEGEL, made an album 'RAKE' as VELVET MONKEYS (aka B.A.L.L. + friends).

Blanco Y Negro Sire

Jan 91. (7"/c-s) (NEG 48/+C) **THE WAGON. / THE LITTLE BABY** [49] [ ]
(12"+=/cd-s+=) (NEG 48 T/CD) – Pebbles + weeds / Quicksand.

Feb 91. (lp/c/cd) (BYN 24/+C/CD) **GREEN MIND** [36] [ ]
– The wagon / Puke + cry / Blowing it / I live for that look / Flying cloud / How'd you pin that one on me / Water / Muck / Thumb / Green mind.

Aug 91. (7"/c-s) (NEG 52/+C) **WHATEVER'S COOL WITH ME. / SIDEWAYS** [ ] [ ]
(12"+=/cd-s+=) (NEG 52 T/CD) – Thumb (live) / Keep the glove (live).

— **MASCIS + MURPH** introduced new member **MIKE JOHNSON** (b.27 Aug'65) – bass

Nov 92. (7") (NEG 60) **GET ME. / HOT BURRITO #2** [44] [ ]
(c-s+=/12"+=/cd-s+=) (NEG 60 C/T/CD) – Qwest (live).

Jan 93. (7") (NEG 61) **START CHOPPIN'. / TURNIP FARM** [20] [ ]
(10"+=/12"+=/cd-s+=) (NEG 61 TEP/T/CD) – Forget it.

Feb 93. (lp/c/cd) (BYN 28/+C/CD) **WHERE YOU BEEN?** [10] [50]
– Out there / Start choppin' / What else is new? / On the way / Not the same / Get me / Drawerings / Hide / Goin' home / I ain't sayin'.

Jun 93. (7"/c-s/12") (NEG 63/+C/T) **OUT THERE. / KEEBLIN' (live) / KRACKED (live)** [44] [ ]
(10"+=) (NEG 63TE) – Post.
(cd-s++=) (NEG 63CD) – Quest (live).
(cd-s) (NEG 63CDX) – ('A'side) / Get me / Severed lips / Thumb (radio sessions).

— now without MURPH

Aug 94. (7"/c-s) (NEG 74/+C) **FEEL THE PAIN. / GET OUT OF THIS** [25] [ ]
(10"etched+=/cd-s+=) (NEG 74 TE/CD) – Repulsion (acoustic).

Sep 94. (cd/c/lp) (4509 96933-2/-4/-1) **WITHOUT A SOUND** [24] [44]
– Feel the pain / I don't think so / Yeah right / Outta hand / Grab it / Even you / Mind glow / Get out of this / On the brink / Seemed like the thing to do / Over your shoulder.

Feb 95. (7"green/c-s) (NEG 77 X/C) **I DON'T THINK SO. / GET ME (live)** [67] [ ]
(cd-s+=) (NEG 77CD) – What else is new? / Sludge.

Mar 97. (c-s/12"/cd-s) (NEG 103 C/T/CD) **TAKE A RUN AT THE SUN. / DON'T YOU THINK IT'S TIME** [53] [ ]

Mar 97. (cd/c/lp) (0630 18312-2/-4/-1) **HAND IT OVER** [ ] [ ]
– Take a run at the sun / Never bought it / Nothin's goin' on / I'm insane / Can't we move this alone / Sure not over you / Loaded / Mick / I know yer insane / Gettin' rough / Gotta know.

MIKE JOHNSON

Atlantic Atlantic

Apr 96. (cd/c) <(7567 92669-2/-4)> **YEAR OF MONDAYS** [ ] [ ]

J. MASCIS

WEA WEA

May 96. (cd/c) **J. MASCIS** [ ] [ ]

DOME (see under ⇒ WIRE)

DRAIN (see under ⇒ BUTTHOLE SURFERS)

DREAM SYNDICATE

Formed: Los Angeles, California, USA . . . 1981 by STEVE WYNN and KENDRA SMITH. The former had previously cut his teeth with SID GRIFFIN in an embryonic LONG RYDERS. They soon completed the line-up with KARL PRECODA and DENNIS DUCK. After an untitled mini-lp back home, they caught the interest of UK indie, 'Rough Trade', in 1983, who released their debut full-length album 'THE DAYS OF WINE AND ROSES'. Cut from a distinctly rougher-hewn cloth than most of the band's 'Paisley Underground' contemporaries, the album's dark intensity caused enough of a stir to eventually get them snapped up by 'A&M'. By the release of their major label debut, 'MEDICINE SHOW' (1984), KENDRA SMITH had been replaced by DAVE PROVOST. Although more mainstream than its predecessor, the album still showed the ragged influence of NEIL YOUNG and THE VELVET UNDERGROUND and while it didn't accrue the success it was probably due, its critical acclaim paved the way for other majors to give them a shot at the big league. After a final album for 'A&M', the compilation of early live material, 'IT'S NOT THE NEW DREAM SYNDICATE ALBUM' (1985), the band released their next studio offering on 'Chrysalis', 1986's 'OUT OF THE GREY'. Despite the more commercial, straight ahead rock sound of the record, success continued to elude the band and they split in early 1989 after releasing a final well-recieved album for 'Enigma', 'GHOST STORIES'. • **Songwriters:** Most written by WYNN, except covers CINNAMON GIRL (Neil Young) / MR. SOUL (Buffalo Springfield). GUTTERBALL mainly WYNN with HARVEY or McCARTHY. • **Trivia:** Early '85, STEVE WYNN was also in DANNY & DUSTY duo alongside old cohort DAN STUART (of GREEN ON RED).

Recommended: THE DAYS OF WINE AND ROSES (*7) / THE MEDICINE SHOW (*7) / OUT OF THE GREY (*6)

STEVE 'DUSTY' WYNN (b.21 Feb'60, Santa Monica, Calif.) – vocals / **KARL PRECODA** (b.1961) – guitar / **DENNIS DUCK** (b.25 Mar'53) – drums / **KENDRA SMITH** (b.14 Mar'60, San Diego, Calif.) – bass / guest on below; **TOM ZVONCHECK** – keyboards

not issued Down There

Dec 82. (m-lp) <VEX 10> **THE DREAM SYNDICATE** [-] [ ]
– Sure thing / Some kinda itch / That's what you always say / When you smile. (UK-iss.Jun85 on 'Zippo'; ZANE 001) (cd-iss.Aug92; VEXCD 10)

Rough Trade Ruby

Nov 83. (lp) (ROUGH 53) **THE DAYS OF WINE AND ROSES** [ ] [ ]
– Tell me when it's over / Definitely clean / That's what you always say / Then she remembers / Halloween / When you smile / Until lately / Too little, too late / The days of wine and roses. (re-iss.Jan87 on 'Slash'; 23844-1) (cd-iss.Jan95 on 'Normal'; NORMAL 176CD)

Dec 83. (12"ep) (RTT 121) **TELL ME WHEN IT'S OVER. / SOME KINDA ITCH (live) / MR. SOUL (live) / SURE THING (live)** [ ] [ ]

— **DAVE PROVOST** – bass repl. KENDRA (she joined RAINY DAY then OPAL) (appeared on live album early '84) and later went solo

A&M A&M

Jun 84. (lp/c) (AMLX/CXM 64990) **MEDICINE SHOW** [ ] [ ]
– Still holding on to you / Daddy's girl / Burn / Armed with an empty gun / Bullet with my name on it / The medicine show / John Coltrane stereo blues / Merrittville.

Feb 85. (lp) (AMLH 12511) **IT'S NOT THE NEW DREAM SYNDICATE ALBUM (live)** [ ] [ ]
– Tell me when it's over / Bullet with my name on it / Armed with an empty gun / The medicine show / John Coltrane stereo blues.

— added **PAUL B. CUTLER** (b. 5 Aug'54, Phoenix, Arizona) – lead guitar + **MARK WALTON** (b. 9 Aug'59, Fairfield, Calif.) – bass, repl. PRECODA + PROVOST

Chrysalis Chrysalis

Jun 86. (lp/c) (CHR/ZCHR 1539) **OUT OF THE GREY** [ ] [ ]
– Out of the grey / Forest for the trees / 50 in a 25 zone / Boston / Slide away / Dying embers / Now I ride alone / Dancing blind / You can't forget. (cd-iss.1987; CCD 1539) (re-iss.Oct87 on 'Big Time' lp/c; ZL/ZK 71457X)

Big Time Big Time

Sep 87. (12"ep) (ZT 41420) **50 IN A 25 ZONE. / DRINKING PROBLEM / BLOOD MONEY / THE LONELY BULL** [ ] [ ]

— now quartet (**WYNN, CUTLER, PROVOST + DUCK**) when PREGODA departed

Enigma-Virgin Enigma

Sep 88. (lp/c/cd) (ENVLP/TCENV/CDENV 506) <73341-1/-4/-2> **GHOST STORIES** [ ] [ ]
– The side I'll never show / My old haunts / Loving the sinner, hating the sin / Whatever you please / Weathered and torn / See that my grave is kept clean / I have faith / Some place better than this / Black / When the curtain calls. (cd re-iss.Sep95 on 'Restless'; 72758-2)

Nov 88. (7") (ENV 6) **I HAVE FAITH. / NOW I RIDE ALONE** [ ] [ ]
(12"+=) (ENVT 6) – I ain't living long like this.

— split early 1989, when WYNN decided to venture solo.

He released a number of albums, the first two being 'KERSOSENE MAN' and 'DAZZLING DISPLAY'. He also formed GUTTERBALL with Long Ryder; STEPHEN McCARTHY.

– compilations etc. –

Jun 89. (lp/cd) Enigma-Virgin; (ENVLP/CDENV 531) / Restless; <72293-2> **LIVE AT RAJI'S (live at Hollywood Jan'85)** [ ] [ ]
– Still holding on to you / Forest for the trees / Until lately / That's what you always say / Burn / Merritville / The days of wine and roses / The medicine show / Halloween / Boston / John Coltrane stereo blues. (re-iss.Jun90 on 'Demon' lp/cd; DFIEND/FIENDCD 176)

Sep 89. (lp) Another Cowboy; (ANOTHER 1) **IT'S TOO LATE TO STOP NOW** [ ] [-]

Apr 90. (d-lp/cd) Demon; (FIEND/+CD 170) **LIVE AT RAJI'S / GHOST STORIES** [ ] [ ]

Nov 93. (cd) Normal; (NORMAL 156CD) **THE LOST TAPES 1985-1988** [ ] [-]

DUET EMMO (see under ⇒ WIRE)

DUKES OF STRATOSPHEAR (see under ⇒ XTC)

DURUTTI COLUMN

Formed: Manchester, England . . . early 1978 by VINI REILLY, CHRIS JOYCE and DAVE ROWBOTHAM. That year they signed to Tony Wilson's indie label 'Factory', but split in mid-79 leaving VINI REILLY to pick up the pieces. They took their name from the 1930's art-terrorists, Situationiste Internationale and after free time given by label boss TONY WILSON under the wing of producer MARTIN HANNETT, VINI finally came up with DURUTTI's debut 'THE RETURN OF . . .'. This was a brilliant introduction to his minimalist yet effective guitar improvisations, but its gimmick sandpaper sleeve was not the toast of the record retailers, who had to protect their stock from its glassy debris. He soon supported on tour fellow Mancunian JOHN COOPER CLARKE, PAULINE MURRAY and even JOHN MARTYN, while recording the follow-up, 'L.C.'. However, ill-health was to dog him yet again, and it took a few years to record 'ANOTHER SETTING'. The above recordings featured eccentric percussionist BRUCE MITCHELL of former parody-rock outfit, ALBERTOS. He has since become a stalwart on all VINI's/DURUTTI's work. In 1986, VINI took a trip to California, where he invited punkess DEBI DIAMOND to sing on a version of JEFFERSON AIRPLANE's 'White Rabbit'. After the release of a further album, 'GUITAR AND OTHER MACHINES' REILLY was invited by old NOSEBLEEDS chum MORRISSEY, to play guitar pieces on his 1988 solo debut, 'VIVA HATE'. In 1990, DURUTTI COLUMN returned in fine style with 'OBEY THE TIME', but it was the last for Factory, as the label went bankrupt in '92. Under the control of 'Polygram', the imprint was once again under way in 1994 as 'Factory Too', and a happier VINI unleashed another textured beauty, 'SEX AND DEATH'. • **Style:** Picturesque and dreamy, jazzy, guitar-based outfit. • **Songwriters:** All composed by REILLY, except cover; I GET ALONG WITHOUT YOU VERY WELL (Hoagy Carmichael). • **Miscellaneous:** On 8 Nov'91, original member DAVE ROWBOTHAM was axed to death by an as yet undiscovered murderer.

Recommended: THE RETURN OF (*9) / VALUABLE PASSAGES (*8) / L.C. (*7) / DOMO ARIGATO (*7) / SEX AND DEATH (*7) / VINI REILLY (*7)

VINI REILLY (b. Aug'53) – guitar (ex-NOSEBLEEDS, ex-V2) / **DAVE ROWBOTHAM** – guitar / **CHRIS JOYCE** – drums / **BRUCE MITCHELL** – percussion / also **TONY BOWERS** – bass / **PHIL RAINFORD** – vocals (left Jul78)

— recorded for Various Artists EP – A FACTORY SAMPLER. Split mid'79, DAVE, CHRIS and TONY joined The MOTHMEN. **VINI REILLY** now brought in **MARTIN HANNETT** – switches, producer (ex-INVISIBLE GIRLS (JOHN COOPER CLARKE) with **PETER CROOKS** – bass / **TOBY** (b.PHILIP TOMANOV) – drums / **GAMMER** – melody

Factory | not issued

Feb 80. (lp) *(FACT 14)* **THE RETURN OF THE DURUTTI COLUMN** □ –
– Sketch for Summer / Requiem for a father / Katherine / Conduct / Beginning / Jazz / Sketch for winter / Collette / In "D". *(w/ free testcard flexi by MARTIN HANNETT)* **FIRST ASPECT OF THE SAME THING. / SECOND ASPECT OF THE SAME THING** *(re-iss.Jul80 lp/c; FACT 14/+C)*

— **VINI** on his own, featured **PHIL RAYNHAM** – vocals

Nov 80. Factory Benelux; (12") *(FACBN 2)* **LIPS THAT WOULD KISS (FORM PRAYERS TO BROKEN STONE). / MADELEINE** – – Belguim
(re-iss.Mar81; FACBN 2-005) (re-iss.cd-ep Mar91; FBN 2CD)

Mar 81. Sordide Sentimentale; (7"ltd) *(SS 45-005)* **ENIGMA. / DANNY** – – Italy

— now just a duo when **VINI** – guitars, now on extra vocals & keyboards / added **BRUCE MITCHELL** – percussion (ex-ALBERTOS Y LOST TRIOS PARANOIAS)

Sep 81. (lp/c) *(FACT 44/+C)* **LC** □ –
– Sketch for dawn 1 / ~Portrait for Frazier / Jacqueline / Messidor / Sketch for dawn 2 / Never known / The act committed / Detail for Paul / The missing boy / The sweet cheat gone.

— VINI completely solo.

1982. Factory Benelux; (7"ltd) *(FBN 100)* **FOR PATTI. / WEARINESS AND FEVER** – – Belguim

Mar 82. Factory Benelux; (12"ep) *(FBN 10)* **DEUX TRIANGLES** – – Belguim
– Favourite painting / Zinni / Piece for out of tune grand piano.

— added guests **LINDSAY WILSON** – vocals / **MAUNAGH FLEMING** – cor anglais

Aug 82. (7") *(FAC 64)* **I GET ALONG WITHOUT YOU VERY WELL. / PRAYER** □ –

— **VINI** now augmented by **MERVYN FLETCHER** – saxophone / **TONY BOWERS** – bass / **CHRIS JOYCE** – drums / **TIM KELLETT** – trumpet (all ex-MOTHMEN)

Aug 83. (lp/c) *(FACT 74/+C)* **ANOTHER SETTING** □ –
– Prayer / Bordeaux / The beggar / The response / For a western / Francesca / Smile in the crowd / Dream of a child / Spent time / You've heard it before / Second family.

— **VINI** retained **MERVYN** and **TIM.** (TONY & CHRIS later joined SIMPLY RED with TIM). **BRUCE MITCHELL** rejoined (he had always been part of live set-up) / **MAUNAGH FLEMING** rejoined with new guests **CAROLINE LAVELLE** – cello / **RICHARD HENRY** – trombone / **BLAINE REININGER** – viola/violin (of TUXEDO MOON)

Dec 84. (lp/c) *(FACT 84/+C)* **WITHOUT MERCY** □ –
– Face 1 / Face 2.

— Now just basically **VINI** with **BRUCE** with old friends augmenting

Mar 85. (12"ep) *(FAC 114)* **SAY WHAT YOU MEAN, MEAN WHAT YOU SAY** □ –
– Goodbye / The room / E.E. / A little mercy / Silence / Hello.

Aug 85. (video-cd) *(FACD 144)* **DOMO ARIGATO (live Japan)** □ –
– Sketch for Summer / Mercy theme / Sketch for dawn / E.E. / Little mercy / Jacqueline / Dream of a child / Mercy dance / The room / Blind elevator girl / Tomorrow / Belgian friends / Missing boy / Self-portrait / (audience noise).

Mar 86. Factory Benelux; (7") *(FBN 51)* **TOMORROW. / TOMORROW (live)** – – Belguim
(12"+=) *(FBN 51)* – All that love and maths can do.

Mar 86. (lp)(cd) *(FBN 36)(FACD 154)* **CIRCUSES AND BREAD** □ –
– Pauline / Tomorrow / Dance 2 / For Hilary / Street fight / Royal infirmary / Black horses / Dance 1 / Blind elevator girl – Osaka. *(cd+=)*– (last 45). *(cd-iss.Nov93 on 'Crepescule';)*

— **VINI** with **MITCHELL, KELLETT, JOHN METCALFE**

Oct 86. Materiali Sonori; (12") *(MASO 70003)* **GREETINGS THREE** – – Italy
– Florence sunset / All that love and maths can do / San Giovanni dawn / For friends in Italy.

Aug 87. (12"ep; w/ DEBI DIAMOND) *(FAC 184)* **THE CITY OF OUR LADY** □ –
– Our lady of the angels / White rabbit* / Catos con guantes.

Dec 87. (cd-ep) *(FACD 194)* **OUR LADY OF THE ANGELS / CATOS CON GUANTAS / WHEN THE WORLD (Newson mix)** □ –

— **VINI + BRUCE** were joined by guests **TIM KELLETT** (of SIMPLY RED) (1 track.) / **STANTON MIRANDA** – vocals (solo artist – 2 tracks.) **POL** – vocals (3 tracks.) / **STEPHEN STREET** – bass (1 track.) **JOHN METCALFE** – viola (1 track.) / **ROB GREY** – mouth organ

Nov 87. (lp/cd)(c/dat) *(FAC T/D 204)(FACT 204 C/D)* **THE GUITAR AND OTHER MACHINES** □ –
– When the world / Arpeggiator / What is it to me (woman) / U.S.P. / Red shoes / Jongleur grey / Bordeaux sequence / Miss Haynes / Don't think you're funny / English tradition landscape / Pol in 'B'. *(cd+=)*– Dream topping / You won't feel out of place / 28 Oldham Street.

Dec 87. (7"flexi) *(FAC 214)* **THE GUITAR AND OTHER MARKETING DEVICES** □ –
– Jongleur grey / Bordeaux sequence / English landscape tradition / U.S.P.

— added **ROBERT NEWTON** plus **DV8 PHYSICAL THEATRE**

Apr 88. (cd-s-video) *(FACDV 194)* **WHEN THE WORLD (soundtrack) / WHEN THE WORLD (lp) / FINAL CUT / WHEN THE WORLD (video)** □ –

Dec 88. (3"cd-ep) *(FACD 234)* **WOMAD LIVE (live)** □ –
– Otis / English landscape tradition / Finding the sea / Bordeaux.

Mar 89. (lp/cd)(dat) *(FAC T/CD 244)(FACT 244D)* **VINI REILLY** □ □
– Homage to Catalonea / Opera II / People's pleasure park / Pol in G / Love no more / Opera I / Finding the sea / Otis / They work every day / Requiem again / My country. *(lp w/ free 7" with MORRISSEY) (FAC 244+)* – I KNOW VERY WELL HOW I GOT MY NOTE WRONG *(cd w/ free 3"cd-ep) (FAC 244+)* – (above) / Red square / William B.

— Included sampled voices of OTIS REDDING, ANNIE LENNOX and TRACY CHAPMAN. **VINI** added **PAUL MILLER**

Dec 90. (cd/lp)(c/dat) *(FAC D/T 274)(FACT 274 C/D)* **OBEY THE TIME** □ □
– Vino della easa Bianco / Fridays / Home / Art and freight / Spanish reggae / Neon / The warmest rain / Contra-indications / Vino della casa rosso.

Feb 91. (12"ep/cd-ep) *(FAC/+D 284)* **THE TOGETHER MIX. / CONTRA INDICATIONS (version) / FRIDAYS (up-person mix)** □ –

Jun 91. Materiali Sonori; (cd)(lp) *(CDMASO 90024)(33-065)* **DRY** – – Italy
(cd+=)– WOMAD LIVE (tracks).

— **VINI, BRUCE** w / guests **PETER HOOK** – bass (of NEW ORDER) + **MARTIN JACKSON** – keyboards (ex/of-SWING OUT SISTER)

Factory Too | not issued

Nov 94. (cd) *(FACD 201)* **SEX AND DEATH** □ –
– Anthony / The rest of my life / For Colette / The next time / Beautiful lies / My irasable friend / Believe in me / Fermina / Where I should be / Fado / Madre mio / Blue period.

Les Disques Du Crepescule | not issued

May 96. (cd) *(TWI 9762)* **FIDELITY** □ –

– compilations, etc. –

Jun 83. V.U.; (lp) *(VINI 1)* **LIVE AT THE VENUE (live VINI & BRUCE)** □ □
– Sketch for summer / Conduct / Never known / Jacqueline / Party / etc.

Dec 85. Fundacao Atlantica; (lp) *(1652071)* **AMIGOS EM PORTUGAL / DEDICATIONS FOR JACQUELINE** – – Port.
– Friends in Portugal / Small girl by a pool / Crumpled dress / Sara and Tristana / Nighttime Estoril / Lisbon / To end with / Wheels turning / Favourite descending intervals / Saudade / Games of rhythm / Lies of mercy.

Dec 86. Factory; (lp/cd)(d-c) *(FAC T/D 164)(FACT 164C)* **VALUABLE PASSAGES** □ –
– Sketch for summer / Conduct / Sketch for winter / Lips that would kiss / Belgian friends / Danny / Piece for out-of-tune piano / Never know / Jacqueline / Missing boy / Prayer / Spent time / Without mercy stanzas 2-8 & 12-15 / Room / Blind elevator girl / Tomorrow / LFO MOD.

Nov 87. R.O.I.R.; (c) *(A-152)* **THE DURUTTI COLUMN LIVE AT THE BOTTOM LINE, NEW YORK (live)** □ –
(re-iss.May93 & Feb95 cd/c; A-152 CD/C)

Mar 88. Factory; (4xcd-box) *(FACD 224)* **THE DURUTTI COLUMN – THE FIRST FOUR ALBUMS** □ –

Dec 89. Spore; (ltd-cd) *(CD 1)* **THE SPORADIC RECORDINGS** □ –

Sep 94. Materiali Sonori; (cd) *(90037)* **RED SHOES** □ –

DUST BROTHERS
(see under ⇒ CHEMICAL BROTHERS)

E

EAT STATIC **(see under ⇒ OZRIC TENTACLES)**

Damon EDGE **(see under ⇒ CHROME)**

EGGMAN **(see under ⇒ BOO RADLEYS)**

F

Th' FAITH HEALERS

Formed: Camden, London, England . . .late 80's by ROXANNE STEPHEN and TOM CULLINAN. They were one of the first bands on the roster of the (then) new indie label,'Too Pure' (run by RICHARD ROBERTS and PAUL COX), for whom they released their debut EP, 'POP SONG'. A few more EP's under their belt, they finally released a debut album proper in 1992,

'LIDO'. Well-received by the music press, it fashioned its own unique hybrid of post-modern nostalgic rock. By 1994, however, they had called in the doctor. • **Style:** Repetitive arty experimental rock'n'roll, that drifted between STEREOLAB and HAWKWIND. • **Songwriters:** TOM penned most, except cover MOTHER SKY (Can) / etc. • **Trivia:** ROXANNE guested on MOOSE's 'XYZ' album from 1992.

Recommended: LIDO (*7) / IMAGINARY FRIEND (*5)

ROXANNE STEPHEN – vocals / **TOM CULLINAN** – guitar / **BEN HOPKIN** – bass / **JOE DILWORTH** – drums (also of STEREOLAB)

Too Pure / not issued

Jul 90. (12"ep) *(PURE 2)* **POP SONG. / DELORES / SLAG** [ ] [-]
Feb 91. (12"ep) *(PURE 3)* **PICTURE OF HEALTH** [ ] [-]
– Gorgeous blue flower in my garden / Not a God / God.
Jan 92. (12"ep) *(PURE 6)* **IN LOVE** [ ] [-]
– Reptile smile / Super / Lovely.
Apr 92. (cd) *(31023)* **L'** (singles compilation) [ ] [-]
Jun 92. (lp/cd) *(PURE/+CD 12)* **LIDO** [ ] [-]
– This time / Word of advice / Hippy hole / Don't Jones me / Love song / Mother sky / It's easy being you / Spin half.
Oct 92. (12"ep/cd-ep) *(PURE/+CD 15)* **MR. LITANSKI** [ ] [-]
– Oh baby / Moona-Inna-Joona / My loser / Reptile smile.
Feb 93. (cd-ep) *(PURECD 18)* **DON'T JONES ME / GORGEOUS BLUE FLOWER / OH BABY / MY LOSER** [ ] [-]
Oct 93. (lp/cd) *(PURE/+CD 27)* **IMAGINARY FRIEND** [ ] [ ]
– Sparkingly chime / Heart fog / See-saw / Kevin / The people / Curly lips / Everything, all at once forever / Run out groove.

Clawfist / not issued

Mar 94. (7") *(XPIG 23)* **S.O.S. / ('B'side by Mambo Taxi)** [ ] [-]
— split soon after above

FEELIES

Formed: Hoboken, New Jersey, USA ...1978 by GLENN MERCER and BILL MILLION. They emerged from the garage and played the CBGB's in the late 70's, which led to a one-off single ('RAISED EYEBROWS') with the UK label, 'Rough Trade'. Early the next decade, they unleashed their debut album for UK 'Stiff'; 'CRAZY RHYTHMS', although this failed to sell due to non-interest in publicity and no support tour. This in turn, led to their 5-album contract being torn up. They then went off into various side projects, only surfacing occasionally to play on holiday weekends. This hiatus resulted in them joining old high school mates The TRYPES, who released the 1984 EP, 'THE EXPLORERS HOLD' on the FEELIES' label, 'Coyote'. In 1983, they found fellow songwriter DAVID WECKERMAN (of YUNG WU), who helped them write the score for the film 'Smithereens'. The following year, they featured as The WILLIES in Jonathan Demme's film 'Something Wild'. In the film they covered 'I'M A BELIEVER', 'FAME' & 'BEFORE THE NEXT TEARDROP FALLS'. In 1986, PETER BUCK (R.E.M.) heard they were back together, and asked to produce their return album 'THE GOOD EARTH'. It was worth the six year wait, and it even re-vitalised them into a tour of Europe early the next year. In 1988, they signed to a major (A&M) and hit the lower regions of the US chart with third album 'ONLY LIFE'. They recorded one more, before MERCER and WECKERMAN took off; later to surface as WAKE OOLOO. • **Style:** Described as the new VELVET UNDERGROUND, due to their sparse two-chord harmonies and jerky pop rhythms. • **Songwriters:** MERCER, except several covers including; EVERYBODY'S GOT SOMETHING TO HIDE + SHE SAID SHE SAID (Beatles) / SEDAN DELIVERY (Neil Young).

Recommended: CRAZY RHYTHMS (*7) / THE GOOD EARTH (*8)

GLEN MERCER – vocals, guitar, drums / **BILL MILLION** – percussion, guitar, vocals / **KEITH CLAYTON** – bass, drums, vocals / **VINNIE DeNUNZIO** – drums

Rough Trade / not issued

Sep 79. (7") *(RT 24)* **RAISED EYEBROWS. / FA CE-LA** [ ] [-]
— **ANTON FIER** – drums, repl. VINNIE who later formed CERTAIN GENERALS / added guests **ARTHUR ADAMS + ROLAND BAUTISTA** – guitars

Stiff / not issued

Jan 80. (7";w-drawn) *(BUY 65)* **EVERYBODY'S GOT SOMETHING TO HIDE. / ORIGINAL LOVE** [-] [-]
Jan 80. (lp/c) *(SEEZ/ZSEEZ 20)* **CRAZY RHYTHMS** [ ] [-]
– The boy with the perpetual nervousness / Fa ce-la / Loveless love / Forces at work / Original love / Everybody's got something to hide / Moscow nights / Raised eyebrows / Crazy rhythms. *(re-iss.Nov87 on 'Line' lp/cd; XILP4/LICD9 00168)* *<US-iss.1991 on 'A&M'>*
— rested/split for a time, when ANTON joined PERE UBU
— **GLENN, BILL, KEITH / + STANLEY DEMESKI** – drums / **DAVE WECKERMAN** – percussion

Rough Trade / Coyote-Twin/Tone

Sep 86. (lp) *(ROUGH 104)* **THE GOOD EARTH** [ ] [ ]
– On the roof / The high road / The last round up / Slipping (into something) / When company comes / She said, she said / Let's go / Two rooms / The good earth / Tomorrow today / Slow down / Sedan delivery. *(cd-iss.Nov87 on 'Line'; LICD 900428)*
Nov 86. (12"ep) *(RTT 180)* **NO ONE KNOWS EP** [ ] [-]
– The high road / She said she said / Slipping (into something) / Sedan delivery.
— In 1987, (WECKERMAN's) YUNG WU released US lp 'SHORE LEAVE' for 'Coyote-Twin/Tone'.
— **BRENDA SAUTER** – bass, vocals, repl. CLAYTON

A&M / Coyote-A&M

Apr 89. (lp/c/cd) *<(AMA/AMC/CDA 5214)>* **ONLY LIFE** [ ] [ ] Nov88
– It's only life / Too much / Deep fascination / Higher ground / The undertow / For a while / The final word / Too far gone / Away / What goes on.
Feb 91. (cd/lp) *(<7502 15344-2/-1)>* **TIME FOR A WITNESS** [ ] [ ]
— disbanded in 1991. STANLEY joined LUNA 2 with former GALAXIE 500 member DEAN WAREHAM. SAUTER joined SPEED THE PLOUGH and later WILD CARNATION.

WAKE OOLOO

MERCER + WECKERMAN / +

Pravada / Pravada

Dec 94. (cd) *<(EFA 26207-2)>* **HEAR NO EVIL** [-] [ ]

House In Motion / Pravada

Jul 95. (cd) *<EFA 06197-2>* **WHAT ABOUT IT** [ ] [ ]

Konkurrent / Pravada

Sep 96. (cd) *(K 171CD)* **STOP THE RIDE** [ ] [ ]

FFWD (see under ⇒ ORB)

FLAMING LIPS

Formed: Oklahoma City, Oklahoma, USA . . . early 80's by COYNE brothers WAYNE and MARK, who reputedly stole instruments from a church hall. After a rare and weird EP in 1985, MARK left brother WAYNE to recruit new members for the 'Enigma' album, 'HEAT IT IS'. Their next 'OH MY GAWD!!!' in '87, saw them strike with many poetic assaults, including the near 10-minute track 'ONE MILLION BILLIONTH OF A MILLISECOND ON A SUNDAY MORNING'. Their reputation grew, with wild, climactic live appearances, highlighting albums 'TELEPATHIC SURGERY' and 'IN A PRIEST-DRIVEN AMBULANCE (WITH SILVER SUNSHINE STARES)'. Phew!!!. Signed to 'Warners' in 1992, and between appearing at the Reading Festival, they released 'HIT TO DEATH IN THE FUTURE HEAD' and the US No.108 (!) album 'TRANSMISSIONS FROM THE SATELLITE HEART'. By the mid-90's, they had secured weirdo posterity, after giving birth to the drug-orientated narrative track, 'WATERBUG'. • **Style:** Avant-garde psychedelic BARRETT /FLOYD inspired, whose barrage of sound was described as JESUS & MARY CHAIN meeting BLACK FLAG or DEAD KENNEDYS. • **Songwriters:** Coyne-English-Ivins except; SUMMERTIME BLUES (Eddie Cochran) / WHAT'S SO FUNNY 'BOUT PEACE, LOVE & UNDERSTANDING (Brinsley Schwarz) / STRYCHNINE (Sonics) / AFTER THE GOLD RUSH (Neil Young).

Recommended: OH MY GAWD!!! (*7) / TELEPATHIC SURGERY (*6) / IN A PRIEST-DRIVEN AMBULANCE (*7) / HIT TO DEATH IN THE FUTURE HEAD (*7)

MARK COYNE – vocals / **WAYNE COYNE** – guitar / **MICHAEL IVINS** – bass / **RICHARD ENGLISH** – drums

not issued / Lovely Sorts Of Death

1985. (7"green-ep) *<L-19679>* **THE FLAMING LIPS E.P.** [ ] [ ]
– Bag full of thoughts / Out for a walk / Garden of eyes – Forever is a long time / Scratching the door / My own planet. *(re-iss.1986 red-ep; same) (re-iss.1987 on 'Pink Dust' 7"ep/c-ep; 731881-1/-4)*
— **WAYNE** now on vox, when MARK departed

Enigma / Restless

Nov 86. (white-lp,lp/c/cd) *(72173-1/-4/-2)* **HEAR IT IS** [ ] [ ]
– With you / Unplugged / Trains, brains and rain / Jesus shootin' heroin / Just like before / She is death / Charles Manson blues / Man from Pakistan / Godzilla flick / Staring at sound – With you.
(cd+=)– Bag full of thoughts / Out for a walk / Garden of eyes – Forever is a long time / Scratching the door / My own planet / Summertime blues.
Nov 87. (clear-lp,lp/c/cd) *<72207-1/-4/-2>* **OH MY GAWD!!!** [-] [ ]
– Can't exist / Can't stop the spring / Ceiling is bending / Everything's explodin' / Love yer brain / Maximum dream for Evil Knievel / Ode to CC / One million billionth / Prescription: Overkill / Thank.
Feb 89. (lp/c/cd) *(ENVLP/TCENV/CDENV 523) <72350-1/-4/-2>* **TELEPATHIC SURGERY** [ ] [ ]
– Drug machine / Michael time to wake up / Miracle on 42nd Street / UFO story / Shaved gorilla / Begs and achin' / Right now / Hare Krishna stomp wagon / Chrome plated suicide / Redneck school of technology / Spontaneous combustion of John / The last drop of morning dew.
— **JONATHAN PONEMANN** – guitar + **JOHN DONAHUE** – guitar

City Slang / Sub Pop

Jun 89. (7"m) *(EFA 40153) <SP-28>* **DRUG MACHINE / STRYCHNINE. / (WHAT'S SO FUNNY ABOUT) PEACE, LOVE AND UNDERSTANDING** [ ] [ ] Jan89
— **NATHAN ROBERTS** – drums repl. ENGLISH
Jan 91. (12"ep) *(EFA 04063-05)* **UNCONSCIOUSLY SCREAMIN' EP** [ ] [ ]
Feb 91. (pink-lp,lp/c/cd) *(SLANG 005/+C/CD)* **IN A PRIEST-DRIVEN AMBULANCE (WITH SILVER SUNSHINE STARES)** [ ] [ ]
– Shine on sweet Jesus – Jesus song No.5 / Unconsciously screamin' / Rainin' babies / Take Meta Mars / Five stop Mother Superior rain / Stand in line / God walks among us now / Jesus song No.6 / There you are / Jesus song No.7 / Mountain song / Wonderful world. *(cd re-iss.Sep96 on 'Restless'; 72359-2)*

Warners / Warners

Aug 92. (cd/c/lp) *(CD/MC/LP 5628)* **HIT TO DEATH IN THE MAJOR HEAD** [ ] [ ]
– Talkin' about the deathporn immorality (everyone wants to live forever) / Hit me

like you did the first time / The Sun / Felt good to burn / Gingerale afternoon (the astrology of a Saturday) / Halloween on the Barbary Coast / The magician vs. the headache / You have to be joking (autopsy of the Devil's brain) / Frogs / Hold your head. *(re-iss.Apr95)*

— **RONALD JONES** – guitar repl. JOHN who joined MERCURY REV

— **STEVEN DROZD** – drums repl. NATHAN

Jun 93. (cd/c/lp) *(9362 45334-2/-4/-1)* **TRANSMISSIONS FROM THE SATELLITE HEART** [ ] [ ]
– Turn it on / Pilot can at the queer of God / Oh my pregnant head (labia in the sunlight) / She don't use jelly / Chewin' the apple of your eye / Superhumans / Be my head / Moth in the incubator / Plastic Jesus / When yer twenty-two / Slow nerve action.

Aug 94. (7"/c-s) *(WO 246/+C)* **SHE DON'T USE JELLY. / TURN IT ON (bluegrass version)** [ ] [55]
(cd-s+=) *(WO 246CD)* – Translucent egg.
(cd-s) *(WO 246CDX)* – ('A'side) / The process / Moth in the incubator.

Sep 95. (cd/c) *(9362 45911-2/-4)* **CLOUDS TASTE METALLIC** [ ] [ ]
– The abandoned hospital ship / Psychiatric explorations of the fetus with needles / Placebo headwood / This here giraffe / Brainville / Guy who lost a headache and accidentally saves the world / When you smile / Kim's watermelon gun / They punctured my yolk / Lightning strikes the postman / Christmas at the zoo / Evil will prevail / Bad days (aurally excited version).

Dec 95. (c-s) *(W 0322C)* **BAD DAYS / GIRL WITH HAIR LIKE AN EXPLOSION** [ ] [ ]
(cd-s+=) *(W 0322CD)* – She don't use jelly / Giraffe (demo).
(cd-s) *(W 0322CDX)* – ('A'side) / Ice drummer / When you smiled I lost my only idea / Put the water bug in the policeman's ear.

Mar 96. (cd-s) *(W 0335CD)* **THIS HERE GIRAFFE / JETS pt.2 (MY TWO DAYS AS AN AMBULANCE DRIVER) / LIFE ON MARS** [72] [ ]
(c-s/cd-s) *(W 0335 C/CDX)* – ('A'side) / The sun / Hit me like you did the first time.

— above was the first ever shaped cd single.

Aug 96. (3D-cd-s) *(W 0370CD)* **BRAINVILLE / EVIL WILL PREVAIL (live) / WATERBUG (live)** [ ] [ ]
(c-s/cd-s) *(W 0370 C/CDX)* – ('A'side) / Brainville (live) / Raindrops keep falling on my head.

FLUKE

Formed: Beaconsfield, Buckinghamshire, England . . .mid 1989 by the trio of MIKE BRYANT, MICHAEL TOURNIER and JONATHAN FUGLER. They emerged with the white label 12", 'THUMPER!', before creating a stir via club favourite, 'JONI', which sampled JONI MITCHELL's 'Big yellow taxi' single. In 1990, after a debut gig at a 'Boy's Own' label rave, they signed to 'Creation'. Early the following year saw the release of their first album, 'THE TECHNO ROSE OF BLIGHTY', paving the way for a major signing to Virgin subsidiary, 'Circa'. 1993's 'SIX WHEELS ON MY WAGON' cemented the band's reputation as critical darlings of intelligent electronica, spawning dancefloor hits 'GROOVY FEELING' and 'ELECTRIC GUITAR'. Crossover success finally came with the 'BULLET' EP, reaching No.23 in the summer of '95. This was later consolidated by their first top 20 hit, the throbbing 'ATOM BOMB', at the tail end of last year. With the success of acts like UNDERWORLD and LEFTFIELD, it remains to be seen whether FLUKE (often courted by the same indie press that fawned over the aforementioned bands) can break out of the dance margins. • **Style:** Electronic dance pop/rock similar to the CABS or YELLO. • **Songwriters:** Group – sampled many including TALK TALK's 'Life's What You Make It'/ STEVE HILLAGE's 'Hello Dawn'/ BILL NELSON's 'When Your Dream Of Perfect Beauty Comes True'/ etc. • **Trivia:** Have been house remixers for TEARS FOR FEARS, TALK TALK, WORLD OF TWIST, etc.

Recommended: SIX WHEELS ON MY WAGON (*7) / OTO (*6)

MIKE BRYANT (b. 1 May'60, High Wycombe) – synthesizer/ **MICHAEL TOURNIER** (b.24 May'63, High Wycombe) – synthesizer/ **JONATHAN FUGLER** (b.13 Oct'2, St.Austell, Cornwall, England) – synthesizer

Fluke / not issued

Sep 89. (12") *(FLUKE 001T)* **THUMPER!. / COOL HAND FLUTE** [ ] [-]

Taxi / not issued

May 90. (12") **JONI (mixes)** [ ] [-]

Creation / not issued

Oct 90. (7") *(CRE 090)* **PHILLY. / TAXI** [ ] [-]
(12")(cd-s) *(CRE 090T)(CRESCD 090)* – ('A'side) / ('A'-amorphous mix) / ('A'-Jamoeba mix) / ('A'-Jameteur mix).

Feb 91. (cd/lp)(c) *(CRE CD/LP 072)(C-CRE 072)* **THE TECHNO ROSE OF BLIGHTY** [ ] [-]
– Philly / Glorious / Cool hand Fluke / Joni / Easy peasy / Phin / Jig / Taxi / Coolest.

Virgin / not issued

Nov 91. (12"ep/cd-ep) **THE BELLS. / (other mixes)** [ ] [-]

Nov 91. (cd/lp) *(FLUKD/FLUKE 1)* **OUT (IN ESSENCE)** [ ] [-]
– Pan Am into Philly / Pearls of wisdom / The bells:- Heresy – Garden of Blighty.

— added **JULIAN NUGENT** – synthesizer

Circa / Virgin

Mar 93. (12"ep/cd-ep) *(YR T/CD 103)* **SLID (glid) / (4 other mixes; No guitars / Glidub / PDFMIX / Scat and sax frenzy mix)** [59] [ ]

Jun 93. (12"ep/c-ep) *(YR T/C 104)* **ELECTRIC GUITAR (vibrochamp). / ('A'-superhound mix) / ('A'-headstock mix)** [58] [ ]
(cd-ep+=) *(YRCD 104)* – ('A'-sunburst mix) / ('A'-hot tube mix).
(12"ep) *(YRTX 104)* – ('A'side) / (above 2 mixes).

Sep 93. (7"ep/c-ep) *(YR/+C 106)* **GROOVY FEELING (Toni Bell's single scoop) / ('A'-Make mine a 99 mix) / ('A'-Nutty chip cornet mix)** [45] [ ]
(12"ep+=/cd-ep+=) *(YR T/CD 106)* – ('A'-Lolly gobble choc bomb) / ('A'-screwball mix).

Oct 93. (cd/c/d-lp) *(CIR CDX/C/CA 27)* **SIX WHEELS ON MY WAGON** [41] [ ]
– Groovy feeling – Make mine a 99 / Letters / Glidub / Electric guitar – Humbucker / Top of the world / Slid – PDFMONE / Slow motion / Spacey (Catch 22 dub) / Astrosapiens / Oh yeah / Eko / Life support. (cd/d-lp w/free cd/lp) – THE TECHNO ROSE OF BLIGHTY

Apr 94. (c-ep/cd-ep) *(YR C/CD 110)* **BUBBLE (speakbubble). / ('A'-stuntbubble mix) / ('A'-burstbubble mix)** [37] [ ]
(12"+=) *(YRT 110)* – ('A'-Braillbubble mix).

Jul 95. (12"ep/cd-ep) *(YR T/CD 121)* **BULLET / ('A'-Dust Brothers (US) mix) / ('A-Empirion mix) / ('A'-Atlas space odyssey mix)** [23] [ ]
(cd-ep+=) *(YRCDX 121)* – ('A'-Bullion mix) / ('A'-percussion cap mix) / ('A'-cannonball mix) / ('A'-bitter mix).

Aug 95. (cd/c/lp) *(CIR CD/C/CA 31)* **OTO** [44] [ ]
– Bullet / Tosh / Cut / Freak / Wobbler / Squirt / O.K. / Setback.

Nov 95. (12"ep) *(YRT 122)* **TOSH / (mixes; gosh / mosh / cosh / posh)** [32] [ ]
(cd-ep) *(YRCD 122)* – ('A'mixes; Nosh / Dosh / Josh / Shriekbackwash).
(cd-ep) *(YRCDX 122)* – ('A'mixes; Mosh / Gosh / Nosh / Dosh).

Nov 96. (12"ep/cd-ep) *(YR T/CD 125)* **ATOM BOMB /** [20] [ ]
(cd-ep) *(YRCDX 125)* –

May 97. (12"/cd-s) *(YR T/CD 126)* **ABSURD. /** [25] [ ]
(cd-s) *(YRCDX 126)* – ('A'mixes; Reeferendrum / Whitewash / Mighty Dub Katz dub / Headrillaz vox).

– compilations, etc. –

Dec 94. Strange Fruit; (cd/lp) *(SFMCD/SFPMA 215)* **THE PEEL SESSIONS** [ ] [-]
– Thumper / Taxi / Jig / Our definition of jazz / The bells / The allotment of Blighty / Time keeper.

FLYING SAUCER ATTACK

Formed: Bristol, England ... 1992 by DAVE PEARCE and RACHEL BROOK, who had just dropped out of LYNDA'S STRANGE VACATION. Their first releases were limited singles for 'Heartbeat-F.S.A.', beginning with the debut, 'SOARING HIGH'. In 1994, they signed to 'Domino', where they debuted with the single 'LAND BEYOND THE SUN'. This year also marked their first live gigs, which they were augmented by ex-LYNDA'S STRANGE VACATION members MATT ELLIOT and KATE WRIGHT. The former worked under the THIRD EYE FOUNDATION banner releasing 'SEMTEX' in '96, while he, RACHEL and KATE had surfaced as MOVIETONE. • **Style:** Influenced by arty lo-fi psychedelia; SYD BARRETT, WIRE and Kraut-rock (especially CAN and POPOL VUH), although a hint of JOHN COLTRANE-style experimental jazz was in evidence. • **Songwriters:** PEARCE or duo, except OUTDOOR MINER (Wire) / THE DROWNERS (Suede).

Recommended: DISTANCE (*8) / FURTHER (*7) / CHORUS (*7)

DAVE PEARCE – slide guitar, etc / **RACHEL BROOK** – vocals, etc.

Heartbeat / not issued

Mar 93. (ltd-7") *(FSA 6)* **SOARING HIGH. / STANDING STONE** [ ] [-]

Jun 93. (ltd-7") *(FSA 61)* **WISH. / OCEANS** [ ] [-]

Nov 93. (lp) *(FSA 62)* **FLYING SAUCER ATTACK** [ ] [-]
– My dreaming hill / A silent tide / Moonset / Make my dream / Wish / Popol Vuh 2 / The drowners / Popol Vuh 1 / Still / The season is ours. *(cd-iss.Aug94 & Dec96 on 'V.H.F.'; VHF 11CD)*

Domino / Drag City

Oct 94. (ltd-7"/7") *(RUG 23/+X)* **LAND BEYOND THE SUN. / EVERYWHERE WAS EVERYTHING** [ ] [-]

Oct 94. (cd/lp) *(WIG CD/LP 12)* **DISTANCE** (compilation) [ ] [-]
– Oceans / Standing stone / Crystal shade / Instrumental wish / Distance / November mist / Soaring high / Oceans 2.

Apr 95. (ltd-7") *(PUNK 008)* **BEACH RED LULLABY. / SECOND HOUR** [ ] [-]

— (above single issued for 'Planet')

Apr 95. (cd/lp) *(WIG CD/LP 20)* **FURTHER** [ ] [-]
– Rainstorm blues / In the light of time / Come and close my eyes / For silence / Still point / Here I am / To the shore / She is the daylight.

Sep 95. (7") *(RUG 41)* **OUTDOOR MINER. / PSYCHIC DRIVING** [ ] [-]
(cd-s+=) *(RUG 41CD)* – Land beyond the sun / Everywhere was everything.

Nov 95. (cd/lp) *(WIG CD/LP 22)* <DC 87CD> **CHORUS** (compilation of singles & sessions) [ ] [-]
– Feedback song / Light in the evening / Popol Vuh III / Always / Feedback song (demo) / Second hour / Beach red lullaby / There but not there / February 8th / There dub.

Nov 96. (cd-s)<12"> *(RUG 48CD)* <DC 109> **SALLY FREE AND EASY / THREE SEAS** [ ] [ ]

VHF / VHF

Jan 97. (12"ep/cd-ep) *(VHF 26/+CD)* **GOODBYE EP** [ ] [-]

1997. (7") **AT NIGHT. / FROM HERE TO NOW OTHERWISE** [-] [ ]

— (above issued on 'Enraptured')

John FRANKOVIC (see under ⇒ PLASTICLAND)

FREEZE (see under ⇒ CINDYTALK)

FREUR (see under ⇒ UNDERWORLD)

FUTURE SOUND OF LONDON

Formed: London, England ... 1991 as HUMANOID by Manchester dance duo of GARY COCKBAIN & BRIAN DOUGANS. They created one of the all-time great acid-house records with the 1988 UK Top 20 hit, 'STAKKER HUMANOID'. This outfit spawned other projects; SEMI REAL, YAGE, METROPOLIS + ART SCIENCE TECHNOLOGY before 'Virgin' signed the duo as FUTURE SOUND OF LONDON in 1991. Early the following year, their fourth effort, the seminal 'PAPUA NEW GUINEA', was very reminiscent of ENO & DAVID BYRNE's proto-ambient work, although it possessed an overtly commercial appeal. 'LIFEFORMS', in 1994, was a 90 minute atmospheric chill-out epic which careered into the Top 10 and featured a guest vocal spot from LIZ FRASER (Cocteau Twins). To complete the year, they conducted a pioneering experiment by playing gigs down a ISDN line, issuing the results as a cd-album. In 1996, prior to the 'DEAD CITIES' double-album, they returned to the singles charts with the moody classic, 'MY KINGDOM'. • **Style:** Modern ambient conceptual soundscapes of gothic beauty, reminiscent of early TANGERINE DREAM. • **Songwriters:** DOUGANS / COCKBAIN except FLAK; co-written w / ROBERT FRIPP plus WILLIAMS / GROSSART / THOMPSON / NIGHTINGALE. OMNIPRESENCE co-wriiten with KLAUS SCHULZE. MY KINGDOM sampled VANGELIS & ENNIO MORRICONE. • **Trivia:** Augmented on NOMAD's single 'Your Love Has Lifted Me', SYLVIAN-FRIPP's album 'Darshan' and APOLLO 440's 'Liquid Cool'.

Recommended: ACCELERATOR (*7) / LIFEFORMS (*8)

HUMANOID

GARRY COCKBAIN (b. Bedford, England) – keyboards / **BRIAN DOUGANS** (b.Scotland) – keyboards

Westside | not issued

Oct 88. (7") *(WSR 12)* **STAKKER HUMANOID. / (part 2)** [6] [-]
(12"+=/3"cd-s+=) *(WSR T/CD 12)* – ('A'-open mix).
(re-iss.8 mixes Jul92 on 'Jumpin' & Pumpin' 12"ep/cd-ep; 12/CD TOT 27); hit No.40 (note 7"+c-s+cd-s; original part 2 was repl. by 'A'-Smart Systems remix)

Apr 89. (7") *(WSR 14)* **SLAM. / BASS INVADERS** [54] [-]
(12"+=/cd-s+=) *(WSR T/CD 14)* – ('A'dub mix) / ('A'-hip house).

Humanoid | not issued

Aug 89. (7") *(HUM 1)* **TONIGHT. /** [ ] [-]
(12"+=/cd-s+=) *(HUM 1/+12/CD)* –

Oct 89. (lp/c/cd) *(HUMAN/ZCHUM/CDHUM 1989)* **GLOBAL** [ ] [-]
–

Apr 90. (12"ep) *(HUMT 2)* **THE DEEP (3 mixes). / CRY BABY** [ ] [-]

Debut | not issued

1990. (12"; as ART SCIENCE TECHNOLOGY) *(DEBTX 3100)*
A.S.T. / ESUS FLOW [ ] [-]

FUTURE SOUND OF LONDON

same line-up as above.

Jumpin' & Pumpin' | not issued

1991. (12"ep) *(12TOT 11)* **PULSE EP** [ ] [-]
1991. (12"ep) *(12TOT 15)* **PRINCIPLES OF MOTION EP** [ ] [-]
1991. (12"ep) *(12TOT 16)* **PULSE 3** [ ] [-]
Feb 92. (12"ep) *(TOT 17)* **PAPUA NEW GUINEA (Dali mix) / ('A'dumb child of a Q mix) / ('A'-Qube mix)** [22] [ ]
(12"ep/c-ep/cd-ep) *(12/TC/CD TOT 17)* – (the remixes by Andy Weatherall & Graham Massey). *(re-iss.May95 12"cd-s; 12TOT/CDSTOT 17) (12" re-issjun97; 12TOT 17R)*
1992. (12"ep) *(12TOT 18)* **SMART SYSTEMS EP** [ ] [-]
1992. (12") *(12TOT 25)* **PULSE 4** [ ] [-]
Jun 92. (cd/c/lp) *(CD/MC/LP TOT 2)* **ACCELERATOR** [75] [ ]
– Expander / Stolen documents / While others cry / Calcium / It's not my problem / Papau New Guinea / Moscow / 1 in 8 / Pulse state / Central industrial. *(cd re-iss.Aug94 +=; CDTOT 2R)*– Expander (remix) / Moscow (remix).

— above featured **BASIL CLARKE** – vocals (ex-YARGO)

1992. (12"ep) **EXPANDER (remix). / MOSCOW (remix) / CENTRAL INDUSTRIAL (remix)** [ ] [ ]
(cd-ep+=) – *('A'radio remix). (re-iss.Jul94 12"/cd-s; 12/CDS TOT 37); hit UK 72)*

Quigly | not issued

Jun 93. (lp/c; as AMORPHOUS ANDROGYNOUS) *(LP/TC EBV 1)* **TALES OF EPHIDRINA** [ ] [ ]
– Swab / Mountain goat / In mind / Ephidrina / Auto pimp / Pod room / Fat cat.
Aug 93. (12"ep/cd-ep; as AMORPHOUS ANDRONGYNOUS) **ENVIRONMENTS** [ ] [-]

Virgin | Virgin

Oct 93. (12"/c-s) *(VS T/C 1478)***CASCADE. / ('A'-parts 2-5)** [27] [ ]
(cd-s+=) *(VSCDT 1478)* – ('A'-short form mix).
May 94. (d-cd/c/d-lp) *(CD/TC+/V 2722)* **LIFEFORMS** [6] [ ]
– Cascade / Ill flower / Flak / Bird wings / Dead skin cells / Lifeforms / Eggshell / Among myselves / / Domain / Spineless jelly / Interstat / Vertical pig / Cerebral / Life form ends / Vit / Omnipresence / Room 208 / Elaborate burn / Little brother.
Aug 94. (7"/c-s) *(VS P/C 1484)* **LIFEFORMS. / ('A'alternative mix)** [14] [ ]
(12"+=/cd-s+=) *(VS/+T/CDT 1484)* – ('A'-paths 1-7).

— (above featured LIZ FRASER (of COCTEAU TWINS) on vocals)

Dec 94. (cd/c/d-lp) *(CD/TC+/VX 2755)* **I.S.D.N.** [62] [ ]
– Just a f***in' idiot / Far out son of lung and the ramblings of a madman / Appendage / Slider / Smokin' Japanese babe / You're creeping me out / Eyes-pop-skin-explodes-everybody's dead / It's my mind that works / Dirty shadows / Tired of bugs / Egypt / Are they fighting us? / Hot knives. *(re-iss.Jun95 with 3 new remixed tracks, hit No.44)*

— (In 1994, they were also at times, abbreviated to F.S.O.L.)

May 95. (12"ep/c-ep/cd-ep) *(VS T/C/CDT 1540)* **FAR OUT SON OF LUNG AND THE RAMBLINGS OF A MADMAN. / SNAKE HIPS / SMOKIN' JAPANESE BABE / AMOEBA** [22] [ ]
Oct 96. (12") *(VST 1605)* **MY KINGDOM (parts 1-4)** [13] [ ]
(c-s+=/cd-s+=) *(VS C/CDT 1605)* – (part 5).
Oct 96. (cd/c) *(CD/TC+/V 2814)* **DEAD CITIES** [26] [ ]
– Herd killing / Dead cities / Her face forms in summertime / We have explosive / Everyone in the world is doing something without me / My kingdom / Max / Antique toy / Quagmire / In a state of permanent abyss / Glass / Yage / Vit drowning / Through your gills I breathe / First death in the family. *(d-cd-iss.; CDVX 2814)*
Apr 97. (12"/cd-s) *(VST/VSCDT 1616)* **WE HAVE EXPLOSIVE. /** [12] [ ]
(cd-s) *(VSCDX 1616)* –

G

GALAXIE 500

Formed: Boston, Massachusetts, USA ... mid-80's by ex-Harvard College student DEAN WAREHAM, plus NAOMI YANG and DAMON KRUKOWSKI. They soon moved to New York where they met KRAMER (ex-BUTTHOLE SURFER and Shimmy Disc label boss), who produced their 1987 album 'TODAY'. In 1989 they signed to 'Rough Trade' and with KRAMER at the controls yet again, they unleashed their flawed epic, 'ON FIRE'. They subsequently gained a lot of fans in the UK, although their homebase critics found a way to lambast WAREHAM's limited vocals at every opportunity. He and the other two (DAMON & NAOMI) went their separate ways early in 1991, after their 3rd album, 'THIS IS OUR MUSIC, failed to register any apraisal. WAREHAM produced his mates, MERCURY REV ('Car Wash Hair' EP), and was soon to be part of indie supergroup LUNA, who signed to 'Elektra'. After a patchy, unsettling debut, they reached higher standards with the 1994 follow-up, 'BEWITCHED', a record which saw veteran VELVET UNDERGROUND guitarist STERLING MORRISON come out of retirement. Meanwhile, DAMON & NAOMI (also as PIERRE ETOILE) stayed with KRAMER who produced their 1992 album 'MORE SAD HITS'. • **Style:** Lo-Fi anti-rock psychedelia, which was reminiscent of JONATHAN RICHMAN being backed by The VELVET UNDERGROUND. LUNA were somewhat similar although a little lighter and jazzier, lying somewhere between heroes LOU REED and TOM VERLAINE (who guested in 1994). • **Songwriters:** Group, except a RUTLES cover!, plus LISTEN THE SNOW IS FALLING (Yoko Ono) / DON'T LET OUR YOUTH GO TO WASTE (Jonathan Richman) / HERE SHE COMES NOW (Velvet Underground) / CEREMONY (New Order) / ISN'T IT A PITY (George Harrison). LUNA group covered INDIAN SUMMER (Beat Happening) / RIDE INTO THE SUN (Velvet Underground) / SEASON OF THE WITCH (Donovan) / IN THE FLESH (Blondie). MAGIC HOUR covered AMERICA (Traffic Sound).

Recommended: ON FIRE (*8) / Luna; BEWITCHED (*7)

(MICHAEL) DEAN WAREHAM (b. 1 Aug'63, Wellington, New Zealand) – vox, guitar / **NAOMI YANG** (b.15 Sep'64) – bass, vocals / **DAMON KRUKOWSKI** (b. 6 Sep'63) – drums, percussion

Shimmy Disc | Aurora

Apr 89. (lp)(cd) *(SCHEMER 8905)(SDE 8908)* <AU 002> **TODAY** [ ] [ ] Oct87
– Flowers / Pictures / Parking lot / Don't let our youth go to waste / Temperature's rising / Oblivious / It's getting late / Instrumental / Tugboat. *(cd+=)*– King of Spain / Crazy. *(cd re-iss.Apr97 on 'Rykodisc'; RCD 10356)*

Rough Trade | Rykodisc

Oct 89. (lp/c/cd) *(ROUGH/+C/CD 146)* **ON FIRE** [ ] [ ]
– Blue thunder / Tell me / Snowstorm / Strange / When will you come home / Decomposing trees / Another day / Leave the planet / Plastic bird / Isn't it a pity. *(cd re-iss.Apr97 on 'Rykodisc'; RCD 10357)*
Feb 90. (7") *(RT 246)* **CEREMONY. / BLUE THUNDER** [ ] [ ]
(12"+=/cd-s+=) *(RTT 246/+CD)* – Cold night / Victory garden.
mid 90. (7"ltd) *(CAFF 8)* **RAIN. / DON'T LET OUR YOUTH GO TO WASTE** [ ] [-]

— (above 45 on 'Caff' records)

Sep 90. (12"/cd-s) *(RTT 249/+CD)* **FOURTH OF JULY. / HERE SHE COMES NOW** [ ] [ ]
Oct 90. (cd/c/lp) *(CDR/RC/R 156)* **THIS IS OUR MUSIC** [ ] [ ]
– Fourth of July / Hearing voices / Spook / Summertime / Way up high / Listen, the snow is falling / Sorry / Melt away / King of Spain, part two. *(other cd-iss.; CDR 156L) (cd re-iss.Apr97 on 'Rykodisc'; RCD 10358)*

— In Spring '91, DEAN WAREHAM departed to work on solo project and guest for MERCURY REV. Nearly a year later, he issued single 'ANAESTHESIA' / 'I CAN'T WAIT' / 'TOMATO PEOPLE' for 'Mint Tea'; . This was augmented by JUSTIN HARWOOD (Chills), JIMMY CHAMBERS (Mercury Rev) and BYRON GUTHRIE (Ultra Vivid Scene). DAMON & NAOMI became PIERRE ETOILE and went in studio with Boston musicians.

– compilations, others –

Sep 96. Rykodisc; (4xcd-box) *(RCD 10355)* **4CD BOX SET** [ ] [ ]
– (TODAY / ON FIRE / THIS IS OUR MUSIC / UNCOLLECTED).
Apr 97. Rykodisc; (cd) *(RCD 10363)* **COPENHAGEN** [ ] [ ]
– Decomposing trees / Fourth of July / Summertime / Sorry / When will you come home / Spook / Listen, the snow is falling / Here she comes now / Don't let our youth go to waste.

LUNA

DEAN WAREHAM – vocals, guitar / **JUSTIN HARWOOD** – bass (ex-CHILLS) / **STANLEY DEMESKI** – drums (ex-FEELIES)

Rough Trade Rough Trade

Jan 92. (12"ep/cd-ep; as LUNA 2) *(R 2973/+CD)* **INDIAN SUMMER / EGG NOG. / RIDE INTO THE SUN / THAT'S WHAT YOU ALWAYS SAY**

Elektra Elektra

Aug 92. (12"ep/cd-ep; as LUNA 2) *(EKR 169 T/CD)* **SMILE / SLASH YOUR TIRES. / HEY SISTER (demo) / ROLLERCOASTER** [ ] [-]

Aug 92. (cd/c; as LUNA 2) *(7559 61360-2/-4)* **LUNAPARK**
– Slide / Anaesthesia / Slash your tires / Crazy people / Time / Smile / I can't wait / Hey sister / I want everything / Time to quit / Goodbye / We're both confused.

Mar 94. (cd/c; as LUNA 2) *(7559 61617-2/-4)* **BEWITCHED**
– California (all the way) / Tiger Lily / Friendly advice / Bewitched / This time around / Great Jones Street / Going home / Into the fold / I know you tried / Sleeping pill.

— added **SEAN EDEN** – guitar

Beggars Banquet Beggars Banquet

Apr 95. (12"ep/cd-ep) *(BBQ 56 T/CD)* **BONNIE AND CLYDE EP**
– Bonnie and Clyde / Chinatown / Thank you for sending me an angel.

— above w/ guest LAETITIA SADLER – vocals (of STEREOLAB)

Aug 95. (cd/c/lp) *(BBQ CD/MC/LP 178)* **PENTHOUSE**
– Chinatown / Sideshow by the seashore / Moon palace / Double feature / 23 minutes in Brussels / Lost in space / Rhythm king / Kalanazoo / Hedgehog / Freakin' and peakin' / Bonnie and Clyde (The Clyde Barrow version).

Nov 95. (7") *(BBQ 59)* **HEDGEHOG. / 23 MINUTES IN BRUSSELS**
(cd-s+=) *(BBQ 59CD)* – No regrets / Happy New Year.

Sep 96. (10"/cd-s) *(BBQ 302 TT/CD)* **SEASON OF THE WITCH / INDIAN SUMMER. / LOST IN SPACE / 23 MINUTES IN BRUSSELS**

Apr 97. (7") *(TRDSC 005)* **IN THE FLESH. / EARLY MORNING** [ ] [-]

— (above issued on 'Trade 2')

Jun 97. (7") *(BBQ 313)* **IHOP. /**
(cd-s+=) *(BBQ 313CD)* –

Jun 97. (cd-ep) *(KAR 036)* **LUNA EP** [ ] [-]

— (above on 'No.6' label)

DAMON & NAOMI

Rough Trade Rough Trade

Jul 91. (12"ep/cd-ep; as PIERRE ETOILE) *(R 272-0/-3)* **IN THE SUN. / 1969 / THIS CAR CLIMBED MT. WASHINGTON**

Shimmy Disc Shimmy Disc

Nov 92. (lp/c/cd) *(SHIMMY 058/+MC/CD)* **MORE SAD HITS**
– E.T.A. / Little red record co. / Information age / Laika / This car climbed Mt.Washington / Astrafiammante / Boston's daily temperature / (Scene change) / Sir Thomas and Sir Robert / Once more / This changing world / Memories.

Sub Pop Sub Pop

Nov 95. (lp/cd) *(SP 322/+b)* **THE WONDROUS WORLD OF DAMON & NAOMI**

MAGIC HOUR

WAYNE ROGERS – vocals (from TWISTED VILLAGE & CRYSTALIZED MOVEMENTS stable) / **KATE BIGGAR / DAMON KRUKOWSKI / NAOMI YANG**

Che Twisted Village

Oct 94. (cd/lp) *(che 20 cd/lp)* **NO EXCESS IS ABSURD**
– Isn't a way / Always leaving never / Sally free and easy / After tomorrow / Lower / World of one / The last mistake / Heads down #2.

Nov 94. (10") *(che 18)* **AFTER TOMORROW. /**

May 95. (7") *(che 29)* **I HAD A THOUGHT. / AMERICA**

Jun 95. (cd/lp) *(che 30 cd/lp)* **WILL THEY TURN YOU ON OR WILL THEY TURN YOU OFF**
–

1997. (cd) **MAGIC HOUR** [-] [ ]

— DAMON & NAOMI have now become a duo again.

DAMON & NAOMI

Earworm Earworm

Apr 97. (7") *(WORM 3)* **NAVIGATOR. /**

Elefant Elefant

Jun 97. (12") *(ER 306)* **PIERRE ETOILE**

GAME THEORY

Formed: Sacramento, California, USA . . . early 80's by SCOTT MILLER, NANCY BECKER, FRED JUHOS and MICHAEL IRWIN. MILLER had previously been part of ALTERNATIVE LEARNING, which numbered NANCY's brother JOZEF BECKER (later of TRUE WEST and THIN WHITE ROPE). Their 1982 debut album, 'BLAZE OF GLORY', led MICHAEL QUERCIO (of THREE O'CLOCK) to produce their 1983 EP, 'DISTORTION'. This job was taken over by MITCH EASTER (button pusher for R.E.M. and dB's) onwards from the 1985 work, 'REAL NIGHT TIME'. Their next album, 'THE BIG SHOT CHRONICLES', was unfairly dismissed by the buying public, and throughout the remainder of the 80's the band were sadly content to tread water. In the early 90's, MILLER was back again with his new outfit, The LOUD FAMILY, who had completed four albums by 1996. • **Style:** Psychedelic Paisley power-pop. • **Songwriters:** MILLER, some with JUHOS, until his departure. Covered YOU CAN'T HAVE ME (Big Star) / I WANT TO HOLD YOUR HAND (Beatles) / COULDN'T I JUST TELL YOU (Todd Rundgren).

Recommended: THE BIG SHOT CHRONICLES (*7)

SCOTT MILLER – vocals, guitar, synthesizers / **NANCY BECKER** – keyboards / **FRED JUHOS** – bass, vocals / **MICHAEL IRWIN** – drums

not issued Rational

1982. (lp) **BLAZE OF GLORY** [-] [ ]

1983. (7"ep) **POINTED ACCOUNTS OF PEOPLE YOU KNOW** [-] [ ]

1983. (7"ep) **DISTORTION** [-] [ ]
(cd-iss.as 'DISTORTION OF GLORY' Feb94 on 'Alias'; A 048D) contained all below tracks)
– Something to show / Tin scarecrow / White blues / Date with an angel / Mary Magdalene / The young drug / Bad year at the U.C.L.A. / All I want is everything / Stupid heart / Sleeping through Heaven / It gives me chills / T.G.A.R.T.G. / Dead center / Penny, things won't / Metal and glass exact / Selfish again / Life in July / Shark pretty / Nine lives to Rigel 5 / The Red Baron / Kid Convenience / Too late for tears.

1984. (lp) **DEAD CENTER** [-] [ ]
– (compilation of 2 ep's above; issued on 'Lolita').

1985. (lp) <72002-1> **REAL NIGHTTIME** [-] [ ]
– Here comes everybody / 24 / Waltz the halls always / I mean it this time / Friend of the family / If and when it all falls apart / Curse of the frontierland / Rayon Drive / She'll be a verb / Real nighttime / You can't have me / I turned her away / Any other hand / I want to hold your hand / Couldn't I just tell you. *(UK cd-iss.Feb94 on 'Alias'; A 047D)*

— **DONNETTE THAYER** – guitar, vocals, piano (ex-VEIL) + **GIL RAY** – drums, repl. JUHOS

Enigma Enigma

Nov 86. (lp) <(3210-1)> **THE BIG SHOT CHRONICLES**
– Here it is tomorrow / Where you going Northern / I've tried subtlety / rica's word / Make any vows / Regenisraen / Crash into June / Book of millionaires / The only lesson learned / Too closely / Never mind / Like a girl Jesus / Girl W / A guitar / Come home with me / Seattle / Linus and Lucy / Faithless. *(cd-iss.Feb94 on 'Alias'; A 046D)*

Dec 87. (lp) <(3280-1/-2)> **LOLITA NATION**
– What's the frequency / Not because you can / Shard / Go ahead, you're dying to / Dripping with looks / Exactly what we don't want to hear / We love you Carol and Alison / The waist and the knees / Nothing new / The world's easiest job / Look away / Slip / The real Sheila.

— **SHELLEY LA FRENIERE** – vocals, keyboards, repl. NANCY

— **GILLAUME GASSAUN** – bass, repl. IRWIN

Oct 88. (cd/c/lp) *(CD/TC+/ENV 507)* <73350-1> **TWO STEPS FROM THE MIDDLE AGES**
– Room for one more, honey / What the whole world wants / Picture of agreeability / Amelia have you lost / Rolling with the moody girls / Wyoming / In a Delorean / You drive / Leilan / Wish I could stand or have / Don't entertain me twice / Throwing the election / Initations week.

— **MILLER + RAY** (now guitar, keyboards) were joined by **QUERCIO + BECKER** (of THIN WHITE ROPE). THAYER went onto HEX with CHURCH singer STEVE KILBEY.

— This line-up only lasted until the early 90's, when even MILLER left to form own outfit The LOUD FAMILY.

– compilations, etc. –

1990. (cd) *Enigma; <D21S-75351-2>* **TINKER TO EVERS TO CHANCE**
– Beach state rocking / Band year at UCLA / Sleeping through Heaven / Something to show / Penny, things won't / Metal and glass exact / Shark pretty / Nine lives to Rigel 5 / The Red Baron / Curse of the frontier land / I turned her away / Regenisraen / Erica's word / Crash into June / Like a girl Jesus / We love you, Carol and Alison / The real Sheila / Together now, very minor / Room for one more, honey / Leilani / Throwing the election.

LOUD FAMILY

SCOTT MILLER – vocals, guitar, etc

Alias Alias

Feb 93. (lp/cd) *(A 033/+D)* **PLANTS AND BIRDS AND THINGS**
– He do the police in different voices / Sword swallower / Aerodeleria / Self righteous boy reduced to tears / Jimmy still comes around / Take me down (too halloo) / Don't thank me all at once / Idiot son / Some grand vision of motives and irony / Spot the set-up / Inverness / Rosy overdrive / Slit my wrists / Isaac's law / The second grade applauds / Last honest face / Even you / Ballad of how you can all shut up / Give in world.

Sep 93. (7") *(A 043S)* **TAKE ME DOWN. / THE COME ON**

Dec 93. (m-lp/m-cd) *(A 055/+D)* **SLOUCHING TOWARDS LIVERPOOL**
– Take me down / The come on / Back of a car / Slit my wrists (live) / Aerodeliri (live) / Erica's word (live in studio).

Jan 95. (lp/cd) *(A 060/+D)* **THE TAPE OF ONLY LINDA**
– Soul drain / My superior / Marcia and Etrusca / Hyde Street virgins / Baby hard-to-be-around / It just wouldn't be Christmas / Better nature / Still its own reward / For beginners only / Ballet hetero.

Aug 96. (cd) *(A 098D)* **INTERBABE CONCERN**
– Sodium laureth sulfate / North San Bruno dishonor trip / Don't respond, she can tell / I'm not really a spring / Rise of the chokehold princess / Such little non-believers / Softest hip of her baby tongue / Screwed over by stylist introverts / Top dollar survivalist hardware / Not expecting both contempo and classique / I no longer fear the headlines / Hot roux avec lying sweet talk / Uncle Lucky / Just gone / Asleep and awake on the man's freeway / Where they go back to school but get depressed / Where they sell antique food / Where the flood waters soak their belongings / Where they walk over Saint Therese.

Lisa GERRARD (see under ⇒ DEAD CAN DANCE)

GORKY'S ZYGOTIC MYNCI

Formed: Camarthen, South Wales ... early 90's by EUROS CHILD, RICHARD JAMES and JOHN LAWRENCE. Naming themselves after the Russian writer MAXIM GORKY, they were signed to the Bangor-based 'Ankst' label by owner ALUN LLWYD and issued their 1992 debut 45, 'PATIO'. Two years later, their first album 'TATAY', found favour in the indie circuit, while they toured supporting The FALL. They were banned in some Welsh clubs for combining the Welsh and English language. Two brilliant singles were released in 1995; 'MISS TRUDY' (from 'LLANFROG' EP) and the classic 'IF FINGERS WERE XYLOPHONES', while they progressed with their second album proper, 'BWYD TIME', in 1995 (another in 1994; 'PATIO' was demos, etc from '91-93). Early in '96, they inked a deal with the major 'Fontana' label, through A&R man Steve Greenberg. Their first single for the label, 'PATIO SONG', was their initial breakthrough into the UK Top 50. In April '97, it featured with 15 others, on their best offering to date; 'BARAFUNDLE'. • **Style:** Youthful Welsh-language psychedelic/folk/pop-rock outfit, influenced by INCREDIBLE STRING BAND, early SOFT MACHINE, or the medieval GRYPHON. • **Songwriters:** Mostly EUROS CHILDS, some by or with JOHN LAWRENCE and RICHARD JAMES, and a few by MEGAN. Covered; WHY ARE WE SLEEPING? (Soft Machine) / O CAROLINE (Matching Mole).

Recommended: TATAY (*6) / PATIO (*5) / BWYD TIME (*6) / INTRODUCING (*6) / BARAFUNDLE (*9)

EUROS CHILDS – vocals, keyboards, synthesizer / **RICHARD JAMES** – guitars, bass / **JOHN LAWRENCE** – bass, guitars, keyboards/ **MEGAN CHILDS** – violin / **OSIAN EVANS** – drums

Ankst / not issued

1993. (10"lp) *(ANKST 40)* **PATIO** [ ] [-]
– Peanut dispenser / Lladd eich gwraig / Dafad yn sirad / Mr Groovy / Ti! Moses / Barbed wire / Miriam o Farbel / Oren, mefus a chadno / Gwallt rhegi Pegi / Sally Webster / Diamonds o Monte Carlo / Siwt nofio. *(re-iss.Jan95 & Apr97 cd+=/c+=; ANKST 055 cd/c)*– Blessed are the meek / Reverend Oscar Marzaroli / Oren, mefus a chadno / Dean ser / Siwmper heb grys / Llenni ar gloi / Anna apera / Siwf nofio / Hi ar gan.

Mar 94. (cd/c) *(ANKST 047 cd/c)* **TATAY** [ ] [-]
– Thema o cartref (Theme from home) / Beth sy'n digwydd i'r fuwch (What happens to the cow?) / Tatay / Y ffordd oren (Orange way) / Gwres prynhawn (Afternoon heat) / Amsermaemaiyndod (When May comes) – Cinema / O, Caroline / Naw.e.pimp (Nine for a pimp) / Kevin Ayers / When you hear the captain sing / O, Caroline II / Tatay (moog mix) / Anna apera:- a. Anna apera – b. Gegin nos (Night kitchen) – c. Silff ffenest (Window sill) – d. Backward dog. *(re-iss.Apr97; same)*

Jun 94. (7") *(ANKST 048)* **MERCHED YN GWALLT EI GILYDD. / BOCS ANGELICA / WHEN YOU LAUGH AT YOUR OWN GARDEN IN A BLAZER** [ ] [-]
(cd-s+=) *(ANKST 048cd)* – *(re-iss.Apr97; same)*

Nov 94. (7") *(ANKST 053)* **THE GAME OF EYES. / PENTREF WRTH Y MOR** [ ] [-]
(cd-s+=) *(ANKST 053cd)* – Cwpwrdd soldwrn. *(re-iss.Apr97; same)*

— **EUROS ROWLANDS** – percussion, drums, repl. EVANS

Mar 95. (10"ep/cd-ep) *(ANKST 056/+cd)* **LLANFWROG EP** [ ] [-]
– Miss Trudy / Eira / Mthu aros tan haf / Why are we sleeping? *(re-iss.Apr97; same)*

Jun 95. (7") *(ANKST 058)* **GEWN NI GORFFEN. / 12 IMPRESSIONISTIC SOUNDSCAPES** [ ] [-]

Jul 95. (lp/c/cd) *(ANKST 059/+c/cd)* **BWYD TIME** [ ] [-]
– Bwyd time / Miss Trudy / Paid cheto ar Pam (Don't cheat on Pam) / Oraphis yndelphie / Eating salt is easy / Gewn ni gorffen (Let's finish) / Iechyd da (Good health) / Ymwelwyr a gwrachod (Visitors and witches) / The telescope and the bonfire / The man with salt hair / The game of eyes / Blood chant / Ffarm-wr. *(re-iss.Apr97; same)*

Nov 95. (7") *(ANKST 064)* **IF FINGERS WERE XYLOPHONES. / MOON BEATS YELLOW** [ ] [-]
(cd-s+=) *(ANKST 064cd)* – Pethau. *(re-iss.Apr97; same)*

Jul 96. (10"ep/cd-ep) *(ANKST 068/+cd)* **AMBLER GAMBLER EP** [ ] [-]
– Lucy's hamper / Heart of Kentucky / Sdim yr adar yn canu / 20. *(re-iss.Apr97; same)*

Fontana / Mercury

Sep 96. (cd) *(532 818-2)* **INTRODUCING** (compilation) [ ] [-]

Oct 96. (7") *(GZMX 1)* **PATIO SONG. / NO ONE LOOKED AROUND** [41] [ ]
(cd-s+=) *(GZMCD 1)* – Morwyr o hyd yn lad eu hun y tir.

Mar 97. (7"/c-s/cd-s) *(GZM/+MC/CD 2)* **DIAMOND DEW. / QUEEN OF GEORGIA / TEARS IN DISGUISE** [42] [-]

Apr 97. (cd/c) *(534 769-2/-4)* **BARAFUNDLE** [46] [ ]
– Diamond dew / The barafundle bumbler / Starmoonsun / Patio song / Better rooms . . . / Heywood lane / Pen gwag glas / Bola bola / Cursed, coined and crucified / Sometimes the father is the son / Meirion Wylit / The wizard and the lizard / Miniature kingdoms / Dark night / Hwyl fawr i pawb / Wordless song.

Jun 97. (7"/c-s) *(GZM/+MC 3)* **YOUNG GIRLS & HAPPY ENDINGS. / DARK NIGHT** [49] [ ]
(cd-s) *(GZMCD 3)* –

GREEN ON RED

Formed: Tucson, Arizona, USA ... 1979 by DAN STUART, CHRIS CACAVAS, JACK WATERSON and VAN CRISTIAN. The latter was replaced by ALEX MacNICOL prior to the release of their eponymous mini-lp for STEVE WYNN's 'Down There' label. Their debut album, 'GRAVITY TALKS' (1984), drew comparisons with NEIL YOUNG's more rockyoutings, moving away from the ramshackle garage of their earlier releases. This influence was even more evident on their 1985 offering 'GAS FOOD LODGING', which featured the distinctive guitar style of the newly recruited CHUCK PROPHET. Signing to 'Mercury' the same year, they released the disappointing 'NO FREE LUNCH', an album that saw the band attempting a BYRDS-like country sound, and even included a WILLIE NELSON cover 'AIN'T IT FUNNY NOW'. After the similarly poor 'THE KILLER INSIDE ME' in 1987, the group disbanded although DAN and CHUCK re-formed, using session players to flesh out the sound. Always on the verge of a commercial breakthrough, they were dogged by label failures and by the time of 1989's 'HERE COME THE SNAKES', the band had signed to 'China' in the UK although the record, which showcased a bolshier, heavy guitar sound, was previously to have been issued in August '88 by the soon-to-be bust 'Red Rhino' records. Undaunted, the band played a blinding live set in London, documented on 'LIVE AT THE TOWN AND COUNTRY' (1989). The band issued another three albums (including AL KOOPER-produced 'SCAPEGOATS') to no commercial success and after the ironically titled 'TOO MUCH FUN' (1992), PROPHET and STUART went on to releaseswell-received solo albums. • **More covers:** KNOCKIN' ON HEAVEN'S DOOR (Bob Dylan) / SMOKESTACK LIGHTNIN' (Howlin' Wolf) / RAINY DAYS AND MONDAYS (Carpenters).

Recommended: GAS FOOD LODGING (*8) / GRAVITY TALKS (*7) / GREEN ON RED (*6) / ROCK'N"ROLL DISEASE – THE BEST OF GREEN ON RED (*7)

DAN STUART – vocals, guitar / **CHRIS CACAVAS** – keyboards / **JACK WATERSON** – bass / **ALEX MacNICOL** – drums, repl. VAN CRISTIAN

not issued / Private

1981. (12"ep) *<none>* **TWO BIBLES** [-] [ ]

not issued / Down There

1982. (m-lp) **GREEN ON RED (UNTITLED)** [-] [ ]
– Death and angels / Hair and skin / Black night / Illustrated crawling / Aspirin / Lost world / Apartment 6. *(UK-iss.Jun85 on 'Zippo'; ZANE 002)*

Slash / Slash

Aug 84. (lp) *(SR 207) <23964-1>* **GRAVITY TALKS** [ ] [ ] 1983
– Gravity talks / Old chief / 5 easy pieces / Deliverance / Over my head / Snake bite / Blue parade / That's what you're here for / Brave generation / Abigail's ghost / Cheap wine / Narcolepsy. *(re-iss.Jan87 lp/c; SLM P/C 16)*

— added **CHUCK W. PROPHET** – steel guitar, vocals

Zippo / Enigma

May 85. (lp/c) *(ZONG/+CASS 005) <ST 74249>* **GAS FOOD LODGING** [ ] [ ] 1986
– That's what dreams / Black river / Hair of the dog / This I know / Fading away / Easy way out / Sixteen ways / The drifter / Sea of Cortez / We shall overcome. *(cd-iss.1990 on 'Enigma';)*

— **KEITH MITCHELL** – percussion repl. ALEX

Mercury / Mercury

Oct 85. (m-lp/c) *(MERM/+C 78) <82646-1>* **NO FREE LUNCH** [99] [ ]
– Time ain't nothing / Honest man / Ballad of Guy Fawkes / No free lunch / Funny how time slips away / Jimmy boy / Keep on moving. *(c+=)*– Smokestack lightning.

Nov 85. (7") *(MER 202)* **TIME AIN'T NOTHING. / NO FREE LUNCH** [ ] [ ]

Feb 87. (7") *(GOR 1)* **CLARKSVILLE. / NO DRINKIN'** [ ] [ ]
(12"+=) *(GOR 1-12)* – Broken.

Mar 87. (lp/c)(cd) *(GOR LP/MC 1)(839122-2) <830912-2>* **THE KILLER INSIDE ME** [ ] [ ]
– Clarksville / Mighty gun / Jamie / Whispering wind / Ghost hand / Sorry Naomi / No man's land / Track you down (his master's voice) / Born to fight / We ain't feee / The killer inside me. *(cd+=)*– NO FREE LUNCH (m-lp)

Jun 87. (7") *(GOR 2)* **BORN TO FIGHT. / DON'T SHINE YOUR LIGHT ON ME** [ ] [ ]
(ext.12"+=) *(GOR 2-12)* – While the widow weeps.

— Disbanded late 1987, DAN and CHUCK reformed and brought in new sessioners. WATERSON released an album 'WHOSE DOG' in 1988, while CHRIS CACAVAS & THE JUNKYARD LOVE released self-titled one in 1989.

China / Restless

Apr 89. (7") *(CHINA 16)* **KEITH CAN'T READ. / THAT'S THE WAY THE WORLD GOES ROUND / VAYA CON DIOS** [ ] [ ]
(12") *(CHINX 16)* – (1st & 3rd tracks) / Tenderloin.

Apr 89. (lp/c/cd) *(839294-1/-4/-2) <72351-1>* **HERE COME THE SNAKES** [ ] [ ]
– Keith can't read / Rock and roll disease / Morning blue / Zombie for love / Broken radio / Change / Tenderloin / Way back home / We had it all / D.T. blues.

Aug 89. (ltd; 10"lp/c) *(841013-0/-4)* **LIVE AT THE TOWN & COUNTRY CLUB (live)** [ ] [-]
– 16 ways / Change / DT blues / Fading away / Morning blue / Are you sure Hank done it this way / Zombie for love / Hair of the dog. *(c+=)*– Rock and roll disease / We had it all.

— duo now with **RENE COMAN** – upright bass, bass / **MIKE FINNEGAN** – keyboards / **DAVID KEMPER** – drums, percussion / plus **BERNIE LEADON** – mandolin, acoustic guitar (4) / **PAT DONALDSON** – bass (4) / **SPOONER OLDHAM** – piano (3)

China / Catalina

Oct 89. (7") *(CHINA 21)* **THIS TIME AROUND. / FADING AWAY (live)** [ ] [ ]
(12"+=/cd-s+=) *(CHINX/CHICD 21)* – 16 ways (live).

Nov 89. (lp/c/cd) *(841720-1/-4/-2) <841519-2>* **THIS TIME AROUND** [ ] [ ]
– This time around / Cool million / Rev. Luther / Good patient woman / You couldn't get arrested / The quarter / Foot / Hold the line / Pills and booze / We're all waiting. *(free-7"w.a.)*– MORNING BLUE / ROCK AND ROLL DISEASE. / (interview) *(re-iss.Jul91 cd/c; WOL CD/MC 1019)*

Dec 89. (7") *(CHINA 22)* **YOU COULDN'T GET ARRESTED. / BROKEN RADIO** [ ] [ ]
(ext.12"/ext.cd-s) *(CHINX/CHICD 22)* – Hair of the dog.

— DAN and CHUCK recruit **MICHAEL RHODES** – bass / **DAREN HESS** – drums

Mar 91. (7") **LITTLE THINGS. / CHERRY KIND** [ ] [ ]
(12"+=/cd-s+=) – Sun goes down / Waiting for love.

Mar 91. (cd/c/lp) *(WOL CD/MC/LP 1001)* **SCAPEGOATS** [ ] [-]
– A guy like me / Little things in life / Two lovers (waitin' to die) / Gold in the

graveyard / Hector's out / Shed a tear (for the lonesome) / Blowfly / Sun goes down / Where the rooster crows / Baby loves her gun.

Jun 91. (7") **TWO LOVERS (WAITIN' TO DIE). / KEITH CAN'T READ**

Sep 91. (cd/c/lp) *(WOL/+MC/CD 1021)* **THE BEST OF GREEN ON RED** (compilation)
– Time ain't nothing / Born to fight / Hair of the dog / Keith can't read / Morning blue / This time around / Little things in life / You couldn't get arrested / That's what dreams / Zombie for love / Baby loves her gun.

— added **J.D. FOSTER**

Oct 92. (lp/c/cd) *(WOL/+MC/CD 1029)* **TOO MUCH FUN**
– She's all mine / Frozen in my headlights / Love is insane / Too much fun / The getaway / I owe you one / Man needs woman / Sweetest thing / Thing or two / Hands and knees / Wait and see / Rainy days and Mondays.

– compilations, others, etc. –

Sep 91. (cd/c) *Music Club; (MC CD/TC 037) / Rhino;* **THE LITTLE THINGS IN LIFE**

May 92. (cd) *Mau Mau; (MAUCD 612)* **GAS FOOD LODGING / GREEN ON RED** | – |

Jun 94. (cd) *China; (WOLCD 1047)* **ROCK'N'ROLL DISEASE – THE BEST OF . . .**

— DAN STUART also had appeared on album below.

DANNY & DUSTY

DUSTY being STEVE WYNN of DREAM SYNDICATE. Augmented by LONG RYDERS:- SYD GRIFFIN, TOM STEVENS + STEVE McCARTHY, plus DENNIS DUCK of DREAM SYNDICATE + CHRIS CACAVAS of GREEN ON RED

Nov 85. (lp) *Zippo; (ZONG 007)* **THE LOST WEEKEND**
– Down to the bone / The word is out / Song for the dreamers / Miracle mile / Baby, we all gotta go down / The king of the losers / Send me a postcard / Knockin' on Heaven's door.

— DAN was also guest on two of NAKED PREY albums. CHRIS guested on the GIANT SAND album 'VALLEY OF RAIN' in Mar'86. In Sep'90, CHUCK PROPHET issued solo album 'BROTHER ALDO' for 'Fire'. In 1993 for 'China', he issued 'BALINESE DANCER' foolowed by in '95; 'FEAST OF HEARTS'. Meanwhile CACAVAS on 'Normal' released 'PALE BLONDE HELL' (1994) & 'NEW IMPROVED PAIN' (1995).

DAN STUART

Normal

Jul 94. (cd; by AL PERRY & DAN STUART) *(NORMAL 169CD)* **RETRONEUVO**
– Daddy's girl / Hermit of Jerome / I could run / Little slant 6 / Sick and tired / Better than I did / Mamcita / Eyes of a fool / Empty chair / Lone wolf.

Jul 95. (cd) *(NORMAL 189CD)* **CANO'WORMS**
– Panhandler / Home after dark / La pasionara / Who needs more / What a day / Expat blues / Waterfall / In Madrid / Filipina stripped / Can't get through / The greatest.

GRID

Formed: based London, England . . . Spring 1990, by DAVE BALL (ex-SOFT CELL), and former music journalist RICHARD NORRIS after meeting in Ibiza about nine months earlier. Both having had already signed to 'WEA' in 1988, writing ads for Wow-Ball, TSB and Shell, they released their debut single on 'East West'. Top 60 breakthrough 'FLOATATION' showcased their innovative strand of electronic head music and the album 'ELECTRIC HEAD' (1990) further crystallized their sound. The title said it all, really, CAN-like electronica imbued with a narcotic, narcoleptic ambience. A couple of months later, they let their freak flag fly by working with infamous (now sadly deceased) psychedelic zealot TIMOTHY LEARY on the 'ORIGINS OF DANCE' 12" (Evolution; EVO 1). The follow-up album 'FOUR FIVE SIX' (1992) saw the band move to 'Virgin' and enlist an array of guest musicians including ROBERT FRIPP and the inimatable ZODIAC MINDWARP. This gave their trippy techno a more structured, focused sound and while artistically it was definitely a leap forward, the album failed to cut it commercially. After moving to 'RCA's 'DeConstruction' the band emerged with a radical new sound via 1993's 'TEXAS COWBOYS' single. A tongue-in-cheek high energy stormer, the track was a massive dancefloor smash, especially in the gay clubs and its hock-laden pop appeal was enough to see it climb to No.21 in the charts. An innovative novelty, their next single, 'SWAMP THING' (1994), blended the seemingly unblendable, bluegrass techno had arrived! A simple down home banjo riff over a funky, pumping beat powered the song into the Top 5, maybe CATTLE GRID would've been a more appropriate moniker for the group at this juncture. The album 'EVOLVER' arrived in September of the same year, reaching Top 20 in the charts but receiving a bit of a lukewarm critical reception, a bit miffed at their musical u-turn. After the twisting acidic throb of their next single 'ROLLERCOASTER', they immersed themselves in live work and remixes, already having done jobs for ART OF NOISE, SOFT CELL (remixes obviously), ERASURE, HAPPY MONDAYS, JESUS LOVES YOU, WORLD OF TWIST and The BHUNDU BOYS.

Recommended: ELECTRIC HEAD (*6) / FOUR FIVE SIX (*6) / EVOLVER (*7)

DAVE BALL – keyboards, synthesizers (ex-SOFT CELL) / **RICHARD NORRIS** – DJ, vocals, keyboards, synthesizers, guitar (ex-PSYCHIC TV) with **SACHA REBECCA SOUTER** – vocals / **COBALT STARGAZER** (of ZODIAC MINDWARP) / **JULIAN STRINGLE** – clarinet / **ANDY MURRAY** – slide guitar / **GUY BARKER** – trumpet / etc

East West East West

Jun 90. (7"/c-s) *(YZ 475/+C)* **FLOATATION (Andrew Weatherall remix). / ('A'-Richard Norris mix)** | 60 |
(12"+=/cd-s+=) *(YZ 475 T/CD)* – ('A'mixes).

Sep 90. (7"/c-s) *(YZ 498/+C)* **A BEAT CALLED LOVE. / ('A'original studio)** | 64 |
(12"+=) *(YZ 498T)* – Floatation (Olimax and DJ Shapps remix).
(cd-s) *(YZ 498CD)* – ('A'side) / ('A'club mix) / ('A'dub mix).

Oct 90. (cd/c/lp) *(9031 71457-2/-4/-1)* **ELECTRIC HEAD**
– One giant step / Interference / Are you receiving / Islamatron / The traffic / Driving instructor / A beat called love / The first stroke / Central locking / Intergalactica / Beautiful & profound / This must be Heaven / Machine delay / Doctor Celine / Typical Waterloo sunset / Strange electric Sun / Floatation. *(cd+=/c+=)*– Virtual.

— In Nov 90, they remixed STEX (a soul trio, which featured JOHNNY MARR), on their single 'Still Feel The Rain'.

Virgin Virgin

Sep 91. (12"/cd-s) **BOOM! (freestyle mix). / ('A'-707 mix) / Bonus BOOM! beats**

Jul 92. (c-s/12"/cd-s) *(VS C/T/CD 1421)* **FIGURE OF 8. / ('A'mixes)** | 50 |
(12") *(VSTG 1421)* – ('A'remixes by Todd Terry).

Sep 92. (12"/cd-s) *(VS T/CD 1427)* **HEARTBEAT. / BOOM! (space cadet mix)** | 72 |

— next feat. guests **ROBERT FRIPP** – guitar / **COBALT STARGAZER + ZOD** (of ZODIAC MINDWARP) / **RUN RA / DIETER MEIER** – keyboards (of YELLO) / **P.P. ARNOLD** – vocals

Oct 92. (cd/c/lp) *(CD/TC+/V 2696)* **FOUR FIVE SIX**
– Face the Sun / Ice machine / Crystal clear / Aquarium / Instrument / Heartbeat / Oh six one / Figure of eight / Boom! / Leave your body / Fire engine red.

Mar 93. (12") *(VST 1442)* **CRYSTAL CLEAR. / ('A'mix)** | 27 |
(c-s+=/12"+=/cd-s+=) *(VS C/TX/CD 1442)* – (4 more 'A'mixes).

deConstruction-RCA R.C.A.

Oct 93. (7"/c-s) *(74321 16776-7/-4)* **TEXAS COWBOYS. / RISE** | 21 |
(12"+=) *(74321 16776-1)* – ('A'mix).
(cd-s++=) *(74321 16776-2)* – Cheerleader song.

May 94. (c-s) *(74321 20584-4)* **SWAMP THING. / ('A'mix)** | 3 |
(12"+=) *(74321 20584-1)* – ('A'mix).
(cd-s++=) *(74321 20584-2)* – ('A'other mix).

Sep 94. (c-s) *(74321 23077-4)* **ROLLERCOASTER. / ('A'-Justin Robertson mix)** | 19 |
(12"+=) *(74321 23077-1)* – ('A'-Global Communication mix).
(cd-s) *(74321 23077-2)* – ('A'side) / ('A'-Nemesis mix) / ('A'-Lionrock house of sound of Didsbury mix) / ('A'-Lionrock toolbag mix) / ('A'-The Global Communication yellow submarine re-take).

Sep 94. (cd/c/lp) *(74321 22718-2/-4/-1)* **EVOLVER** | 14 |
– Wake up / Rollercoaster / Swamp thing / Throb / Rise / Shades of sleep / Higher peaks / Texas cowboys / Spin cycle / Golden dawn.

Nov 94. (c-s) *(74321 24403-4)* **TEXAS COWBOYS. / ('A'mix)** | 17 |
(12"+=) *(74321 24403-1)* – (2 more 'A'mixes).
(cd-s++=) *(74321 24403-2)* – (2 more 'A'mixes; now 6 in total).

Sep 95. (c-s) *(74321-4)* **DIABLO / ('A'-Acapulco mix)** | 32 |
(12") *(74321-1)* – ('A'side) / ('A'-Atomic bidet mix) / ('A'-Devil rides out mix) / ('A'-Devil dubs out mix).
(cd-s) *(74321-2)* – (all 5 mixes).

Sep 95. (cd/c/d-lp) *(74321 27670-2/-4/-1)* **MUSIC FOR DANCING** (remixes) | 67 |
– Floatation (the subsonic Grid mix) / Crystal clear (456 mix) / Boom! (freestyle mix) / Figure of 8 (tribal trance mix) / Rollercoaster (nemesis mix) / Texas cowboys (ricochet mix) / Swamp thing (southern comfort mix) / Crystal clear (prankster prophet mix) / Figure of 8 (Todd's master dub) / Diablo (the Devil rides out mix) / Rollercoaster (the yellow submarine re-take).

H

Grant HART (see under ⇒ HUSKER DU)

HE SAID (see under ⇒ WIRE)

HIS NAME IS ALIVE

Formed: Livonia, Michigan, USA . . . 1987 by WARREN DEFERER with schoolfriends ANGELA CAROZZO and KARIN OLIVER. Over the course of the next few years, they issued much homegrown material, the last being 'EUTECTIC', commissioned for the Harbinger Dance Company. In 1990, they re-appeared on the UK label '4 a.d.' for their British debut, 'LIVONIA'. • **Style:** English sounding minimal rock outfit playing ethnic folk through echo chambers, something like COCTEAU TWINS fused with ENO. • **Songwriters:** DEFERER wiyh in '96; SMITH & MASTERS, except MAN ON A SILVER MOUNTAIN (Rainbow).

Recommended: LIVONIA (*8) / STARS ON ESP (*7)

WARREN DEFERER (b.1969) – guitar, bass, vocals, samples / **KARIN OLIVER** – vocals, guitar / **ANGELA CAROZZO** – vocals

not issued own label

1987. (c-ep) **RIOTOUSNESS AND POSTROPHE** | – |
1987. (lp) **HIS NAME IS ALIVE** | – |
1988. (c) **I HAD SEX WITH GOD** | – |
1988. (lp) **EUTECTIC** | – |

4 a.d. 4 a.d.

Jun 90. (lp/cd)(c) *(CAD 0008/+CD)(CADC 0008)* **LIVONIA**
– As we could ever / E-Nicolle / If July / Some and I / E-Nicolle / Caroline's

supposed demon / Fossil / Reincarnation / You and I have seizures / How ghosts affect seizures / How ghosts affect relationships / Darkest dreams.

— CAROZZO departed and was repl. by **DENISE JAMES** – vocals / **MELISSA ELLIOTT** – guitar / **JYMN AUGE** – guitar / **DAMIAN LANG** – drums

Sep 91. (lp/cd)(c) *(CAD 1013/+CD)(CADC 1013)* **HOME IS IN YOUR HEAD**
– This week / Eyes were / Charmer / Hope (song of schizophrenia) / Feathers (song of schizophrenia) / Well (song of schizophrenia) / Something / Ice / Married / Finger / Home / People / Eyes are / Birds / Chances / Mescalina / Sitting / Very bad / Beautiful / Tempe / Spirit / Fish eye / Dreams.

Apr 92. (12"ep/cd-ep) *(BAD 2005/+CD)* **THE DIRT EATERS EP**
– Man on a silver mountain / Are we still married / Is this the way the tigers? / We hold the land in great esteem.

Apr 93. (lp/cd)(c) *(CAD 3006/+CD)(CADC 3006)* **MOUTH BY MOUTH**
– Baby fish mouth / Lip / Cornfield / In every Ford / Lord, make me a channel of your peace / Drink, dress and ink / Where knock is open wide / Can't go wrong without you / Jack rabbits / Sort of / Sick / Blue moon / Ear / Lemon ocean / The torso / The dirt eaters.

— **DEFERER with SMITH + MASTERS**

Jun 96. (lp/cd) *(CAD 6010/+CD)* **STARS ON ESP**
– Dub love letter / This world is not my home / Bad luck girl / What are you wearing tomorrow / The bees / What else is new list / Wall of speed / Universal frequencies / The sand that holds the lakes in place / I can't live in this world anymore / Answer to rainbow at midnight / Famous goodbye king / Across the street / Movie / Last one.

Jun 96. (7") *(AD 6007)* **UNIVERSAL FREQUENCIES. / SUMMER OF ESP** -
(cd-s+=) *(BAD 6007CD)* –

Motorway / not issued

Apr 97. (7"ep; with LITTLE PRINCESS) *(MOTOR 016)* **PET FARM EP** -

Robyn HITCHCOCK

Born: 3 Mar'53, East Grinstead, London, England. Aged 21, he went to find the home of his idol SYD BARRETT in Cambridge, but ended up busking. He then formed a number of bands in 1976, including The WORST FEARS, The BEETLES, MAUREEN & THE MEATPACKERS and finally by the end of the year; DENNIS AND THE EXPERTS, who were the embryonic SOFT BOYS. Alongside ROBYN were ALAN DAVIES, ANDY METCALFE and MORRIS WINDSOR. In March '77 they were offered a deal with indie label 'Raw', who soon issued their debut release, 'GIVE IT TO THE SOFT BOYS EP'. The record included three trash-punk songs, one of which was 'WADING THROUGH A VENTILATOR'. KIMBERLEY REW replaced DAVIES, before they embarked on a UK tour supporting ELVIS COSTELLO and The DAMNED. This led to a contract with 'Radar', although after one 45 and many disagreements, they left. In 1979, they issued a debut album, 'A CAN OF BEES', on their own 'Two Crabs'. The record was a resounding failure although it has since been the subject of many re-issues in different versions. In 1980, they established themselves, critically at least, with the follow-up, 'UNDERWATER MOONLIGHT'. However, by the following year, they had split-up, even though they were well-received on a US tour. HITCHCOCK then completed a solo album, 'BLACK SNAKE DIAMOND ROLE', containing the cult classics, 'BRENDA'S IRON SLEDGE' and the single, 'THE MAN WHO INVENTED HIMSELF'. After the disastrous STEVE HILLAGE-produced 'GROOVY DECAY' in 1982, ROBYN decided enough was enough. That was until 1984, when he returned with the acoustic gem, 'I OFTEN DREAM OF TRAINS'. This saw him bring back The SOFT BOYS, but under the guise of ROBYN HITCHCOCK & THE EGYPTIANS. In 1985, their first product, 'FEGMANIA!', hit the shops, and songs like 'THE MAN WITH THE LIGHTBULB HEAD' & 'EGYPTIAN CREAM', ressurected public favour. After a few more albums in the mid-80's, he and his band were signed to 'A&M', the resulting album, 'GLOBE OF FROGS', worthy of anything he'd previously recorded. It brought recomendations from R.E.M., who were longtime fans of HITCHCOCK. His band became firm faves on the US college circuit, especially when indie idols MICHAEL STIPE and PETER BUCK guested on the two mediocre either-side-of-the-decade albums 'QUEEN ELVIS' & 'PERSPEX ISLAND'. In 1993, he returned to his manic style of old with the highly regarded 'RESPECT', subsequently undergoing a creative renaissance of sorts. He even re-united The SOFT BOYS early in 1994 for some Bosnia benefits concerts. • **Style:** Initially "New Wave" rock, influenced by West Coast psychedelia. Lyrically as daft as SYD BARRETT, with tongue-in-cheek humour that could even outstrip CAPTAIN BEEFHEART. • **Songwriters:** HITCHCOCK, some with KIMBERLEY REW (in SOFT BOYS).

Recommended: UNDERWATER MOONLIGHT (*8) / THE SOFT BOYS 1976-81 (*8) / I OFTEN DREAM OF TRAINS (*7) / FEGMANIA! (*8) / GLOBE OF FROGS (*7) / RESPECT (*8)

SOFT BOYS

ROBYN HITCHCOCK – vocals, guitar, bass / **ALAN DAVIS** – guitar / **ANDY METCALFE** – bass / **MORRIS WINDSOR** (aka OTIS FAGG) – drums

Raw / not issued

Jul 77. (7"ep) *(RAW 5)* **GIVE IT TO THE SOFT BOYS** -
– Wading through a ventilator / The face of death / Hear my brane. *(re-iss.Oct79; RAW 37)*

— **KIMBERLEY REW** – guitar, harmonica, vocals repl. DAVIS

Radar / not issued

May 78. (7") *(ADA 8)* **(I WANT TO BE AN) ANGELPOISE LAMP. / FAT MAN'S SON** -

Two Crabs / not issued

Feb 79. (lp) *(AUL 709)* **A CAN OF BEES** -
– Give it to the soft boys / The pigworker / Human music / Leppo and the jooves / The rat's prayer / Do the chisel / Sandra's having her brain out / The return of the sacred crab / Cold turkey / Skool dinner blues / Wading through a ventilator. *(re-iss.Feb80 on 'Aura'; AUL 709) (re-iss.Jun84 on 'Two Crabs'; same) (cd-iss.Feb95 on 'Rhino'+=;)–* Leppo and the jooves / Sandra's having her brain out / Skool dinner blues / Fatman's son / (I want to be an) Angelpoise lamp / Ugly Nora. *(cd re-iss.May96 on 'Rykodisc'; RCD 20231)*

— In Oct'79, 'Raw' quickly withdrew release of 45 'WHERE ARE THE PRAWNS'; *RAW 41)*

— **MATTHEW SELIGMAN** – bass, keyboards (ex-SW9) repl. ANDY to FISH TURNED HUMAN

Armageddon / Armageddon

Jun 80. (7"ep) *(AEP 002)* **NEAR THE SOFT BOYS** -
– Kingdom of love / Vegetable man / Strange.

Jul 80. (lp) *(ARM 1)* **UNDERWATER MOONLIGHT** -
– I wanna destroy you / Kingdom of love / Positive vibrations / I got the job / Insanely jealous / Tonight / You'll have to go sideways / Old pervert / The queen of eyes / Underwater moonlight. *(cd-iss.Feb95 on 'Rhino'+=;)–* Vegetable man / Strange / Only the stones remain / Where are the prawns / Dreams / Black snake diamond role / There's nobody like you / Song No.4. *(cd re-iss.May96 on 'Rykodisc'; RCD 20232)*

Aug 80. (7") *(AS 005)* **I WANNA DESTROY YOU. / (I'M AN) OLD PERVERT (DISCO)** -

Oct 81. (7") *(AS 029)* **ONLY THE STONES REMAIN. / THE ASKING TREE**

Mar 82. (lp) *(BYE 1)* **TWO HALVES FOR THE PRICE OF ONE** (half live) Oct81
– Only the stones remain / Where are the prawns / The bells of Rhymney / There's nobody like you / Innocent box / Black snake diamond role / Underwater moonlight / Astronomy domine / Outlaw blues / Mystery train. *<US-title; ONLY THE STONES REMAIN>*

— Disbanded in 1982, SELIGMAN who joined The THOMPSON TWINS

– compilations, others, etc –

1982. (7"w/mag) *Bucketful Of Brains; (BOB 1)* **LOVE POISONING. / WHEN I WAS A KID** - -

Nov 83. (7") *Midnight Music; (DING 4)* **HE'S A REPTILE. / SONG NO.4** -

Nov 83. (7") *Midnight Music; (CHIME 0002)* **INVISIBLE HITS** -
– Wey-wey-hep-uh-hole * / Have a heart Betty (I'm not fireproof) * / The asking tree / Muriel's hoof / The rout of the clones / Let me put it next to you / When I was a kid * / Rock & roll toilet * / Love poisoning * / Empty girl / Blues in the dark / He's a reptile. *(cd-iss.Feb95 on 'Rhino" +=;)–* (alt.takes of *). *(cd re-iss.May96 on 'Rykodisc'; RCD 20233)*

Aug 85. (lp/pic-lp) *De Laurean; (SOFT 1/+P)* **WADING THROUGH A VENTILATOR** -

1987. (7"flexi; w-mag) *Bucketful Of Brains; (BOB 17)* **DECK OF CARDS. / Robyn Hitchcock & Peter Buck: FLESH NO.1** - -

Dec 87. (lp) *Midnight Music; (MOIST 4)* **LIVE AT THE PORTLAND ARMS (live)** -

1989. (7"yellow,7"white; ltd) *Overground; (OVER 4)* **THE FACE OF DEATH. / THE YODELLING HOOVER** -

Sep 93. (d-cd) *Rykodisc; (RCD 10234-35)* **1976-81** -
– (mostly all of their material).

ROBYN HITCHCOCK

was already solo, using session people, including most ex-SOFT BOYS

Armageddon / not issued

Apr 81. (7") *(AS 008)* **THE MAN WHO INVENTED HIMSELF. / DANCING ON GOD'S THUMB** -
(free 7"flexi w-above) (4SPURT 1) IT'S A MYSTIC TRIP. / GROOVING ON AN INNER PLANE

May 81. (lp) *(ARM 4)* **BLACK SNAKE DIAMOND ROLE** -
– The man who invented himself / Brenda's iron sledge / Do policemen sing? / The lizard / Meat / Acid bird / I watch the cars / Out of the picture / City of shame / Love. *(re-iss.May86 on 'Aftermath'; AFT 1) (cd-iss.1988; AFTCD 1) (cd re-iss.Feb95 on 'Rhino-Sequel'+=; RSACD 819)–* Dancing on God's thumb / Happy the golden prince / I watch the cars / It was the night / Grooving on an inner plane.

— now w / **SARA LEE** – bass / **ANTHONY THISTLETWAITE** – sax / **ROD JOHNSON** – drums repl. SELIGMAN to THOMAS DOLBY (and REW who re-joined The WAVES, who added Czech KATRINA; now KATRINA & THE WAVES)

Albion / not issued

Mar 82. (7") *(ION 103)* **AMERICA. / IT WAS THE NIGHT / HOW DO YOU WORK THIS THING** -

Mar 82. (lp) *(ALB 110)* **GROOVY DECAY** -
– Night ride to Trinidad / Fifty-two stations / Young people scream / The rain / America / The cars she used to drive / Grooving on an inner plane / St. Petersburg / When I was a kid / Midnight fish. *(some with free various 'Albion' artists; RH track '52 STATIONS') (re-iss.Dec85 on 'Midnight Music'; CHIME 00.15) (cd-iss.Nov89 & Oct94 on 'Line'; ALCD 9.000008) (cd-iss.Feb95 as 'GRAVY DECO (THE COMPLETE GROOVY DECAY / DECOY SESSIONS)' on 'Rhino-Sequel'+=; RSACD 820)–* (extra mixes)

Midnight Music / Slash

Nov 82. (7"m) *(DING 2)* **EATEN BY HER OWN DINNER. / LISTENING TO THE HIGSONS / DR. STICKY** -
(12"ep; Oct86) *(DONG 2)* – ('A'side) / Grooving on an inner plane / Messages of the dark / The abandoned brain / Happy the golden prince.

— now w / **WINDSOR + METCALFE / + ROGER JACKSON** – keyboards

Aug 84. (lp) *(CHIME 00.05S)* **I OFTEN DREAM OF TRAINS** -
– Nocturne / Uncorrected personality traits / Sounds great when you're dead / Flavour of night / This could be the day / Trams of old London / Furry green atom bowl / Heart full of leaves / Autumn is your last chance / I often dream of trains. *(cd-iss.Oct86; CHIME 00.05CD) (cd re-iss.Feb95 on 'Rhino-Sequel'+=; RSACD 821)–* Ye sleeping knights of Jesus / Sometimes I wish I was a pretty girl / Cathedral / Mellow together / Winter love / The bones in the ground / My favourite buildings / I used to say I love you.

Nov 84. (12"m) *(DONG 8)* **THE BELLS OF RHYMNEY / FALLING LEAVES. / WINTER LOVE / THE BONES IN THE GROUND**

ROBIN HITCHCOCK & THE EGYPTIANS

— same as solo line-up

Mar 85. (lp) *(CHIME 00.08)* **FEGMANIA!**
– Egyptian cream / Another bubble / I'm only you / My wife and my dead wife / Goodnight I say / The man with the lightbulb head / Insect mother / Strawberry mind / Glass / The fly / Heaven. *(cd-iss.1986 +=; CHIME 00.08CD)* – The bells of rhymney / Dwarfbeat / Some body. *(re-iss.Mar95 on 'Rhino-Sequel'+=; RSACD 822)*– Egyptian cream (demo) / Heaven (live) / Insect mother (demo) / Egyptian cream (live) / The pit of souls: I) The plateau – II) The descent – III) The spinal dance – IV) Flight of the iron lung.

May 85. (12"m) *(DONG 12)* **HEAVEN. / DWARFBEAT / SOME BODY**

Midnight Relativity

Oct 85. (lp/c) *(CHIME 00.15 S/C)* **GOTTA LET THIS HEN OUT (live)**
– Sometimes I wish I was a pretty girl / Kingdom of love / Acid bird / The cars she used to drive / My wife and my dead wife / Brenda's iron sledge / The fly * / Only the stones remain * / Egyptian cream * / Leppo & the Jooves / America / Heaven / Listening to The Higsons / Face of death. *(cd-iss.Oct86 += *; CHIME 00.15CD) (re-iss.cd Mar95 on 'Rhino-Sequel'; RSACD 823)*

Feb 86. (12"ep) *(DONG 17)* **BRENDA'S IRON SLEDGE (live). / ONLY THE STONES REMAIN (live) / THE PIT OF SOULS (part I-IV)**

Mar 86. (pic-lp)(c) *(BM 80)(BMC 80-4) <EMC 8074>* **EXPLODING IN SILENCE**

Glass Fish Relativity

Jun 86. (lp) *(MOIST 2)* **INVISIBLE HITCHCOCK** (compilation)
– All I wanna do is fall in love / Give me a spanner, Ralph / A skull, a suitcase, and a long red bottle of wine / It's a mystic trip / My favourite buildings / Falling leaves / Eaten by her own dinner / Pits of souls / Trash / Mr. Deadly / Star of hairs / Messages of dark / Vegetable friend / I got a message for you / Abandoned brain / Point it at gran / Let there be more darkness / Blues in A. *(re-iss.cd Mar95 on 'Rhino-Sequel'+=; RSACD 825)*– Listening to the higsons / Dr. Sticky.

Sep 86. (lp/cd) *(MOIST 3/+CD)* **ELEMENT OF LIGHT**
– If you were a priest / Winchester / Somewhere apart / Ted, Woody and Junior / The president / Raymond Chandler evening / Bass / Airscape / Never stop bleeding / Lady Waters & the hooded one / The black crow knows / The crawling / The leopard / Tell me about your drugs. *(re-iss.cd Mar95 on 'Rhino-Sequel'+=; RSACD 824)* – The can opener / Raymond Chandler evening (demo) / President (demo) / If you were a priest (demo) / Airscape (live) / The leopard (demo).

Jan 87. (7") *(OOZE 1)* **IF YOU WERE A PRIEST. / THE CRAWLING**
(12"+=) *(OOZE 1T)* – Tell me about your drugs / The can opener.

A&M A&M

Feb 88. (lp/c/cd) *<(AMA/AMC/CDA 5182)>* **GLOBE OF FROGS**
– Trapped flesh Mandela / Vibrating / Balloon man / Luminous rose / Sleeping with your devil mask on / Unsettled / Flesh number one / Chinese bones / A globe of frogs / Beatle Dennis / The shapes between us / Turn to animals.

Apr 88. (7") **GLOBE OF FROGS. / BALLOON MAN**

— still with **METCALFE + WINDSOR** + guest **PETER BUCK** – guitar (of R.E.M.)

Jul 89. (7") **MADONNA OF THE WASPS. / RULING CLASS**
(12"+=/cd-s+=) – Veins of the queen (royal mix) / Freeze (shatter mix).

Dec 89. (lp/c/cd) *<395241-1/-4/-2>* **QUEEN ELVIS**
– Madonna of the wasps / The Devils coachman / Wax doll / Knife / Swirling / One long pair of eyes / Veins of the Queen / Freeze / Autumn sea / Superman. *(cd+=)*– Veins of the Queen (royal mix) / Freeze (shatter mix).

ROBIN HITCHCOCK

Glass Fish Twin/Tone

Nov 90. (lp/cd) *(MOIST 8/CD)* **EYE**
– Cynthia mask / Certainly clickot / Queen Elvis / Flesh cartoons / Chinese water python / Executioner / Linctus House / Sweet ghosts of light / College of ice / Transparent lover / Beautiful girl / Raining twilight coast / Clean Steve / Agony of pleasure / Glass hotel / Satellite / Aquarium / Queen Elvis II. *(UK cd-iss.Mar95 on 'Rhino-Sequel'+=; RSACD 826)*– Raining twilight coast (demo) / Agony of pleasure (demo) / Queen Elvis III (demo).

Go! Discs Twin/Tone

Oct 91. (cd/c) *(828 292-2/-4)* **PERSPEX ISLAND**
– Oceanside / So you think you're in love / Birds in perspex / Ultra unbelievable love / Vegetations and dines / Lysander / Child of the universe / She doesn't exist / Ride / If you go away / Earthly Paradise.

Jan 92. (7") *(GOD 65)* **SO YOU THINK YOU'RE IN LOVE. / WATCH YOUR INTELLIGENCE**
(12"+=/cd-s+=) *(GOD X/CD 65)* – Dark green energy.

— (above featured STIPE + BUCK of R.E.M.)

1993. (cd/c; with ARCHIE ROACH) *(RHE CD/MC 1)* **RESPECT**
– The yip song / The arms of love / The moon inside / Railway shoes / When I was dead / The wreck of Arthur Lee / Driving aloud (radio storm) / erpnt at the gates of wisdom / Then you're dust / Wafflehead.

Rhino-Sequel Rykodisc

Mar 95. (cd) *(RSACD 827)* **YOU & OBLIVION** 1994
– You've got / Don't you / Birdshead / She reached for a light / Victorian squid / Captain Dry / Mr. Rock I / August hair / Take your knife out of my back / Surgery / The dust / Polly on the shore / Aether / Fiend before the shrine / Nothing / Into it / Stranded in the future / Keeping still / September clones / Ghost ship / You & me / If I could look.

Feb 95. (cd-ep) *(CDSEQ 2)* **MY WIFE AND MY DEAD WIFE / I SOMETHING YOU / ZIPPER IN MY SPINE / MAN WITH A WOMAN'S SHADOW**

W.E.A. Warners

Aug 96. (cd/c) *(9362 46302-2/-4)* **MOSS ELIXIR**
– Sinister but she was happy / The Devil's radio / Heliotrope / Alright, yeah / Filthy bird / The speed of things / Beautiful queen / Man with a woman's shadow / I am not me / De Chirico Street / You and oblivion / This is how it feels.

– his compilations, etc. –

May 83. (12"ep) *Albion; (12ION 1036)* **NIGHT RIDE TO TRINIDAD (long version). / KINGDOM OF LOVE / MIDNIGHT FISH**

1984. (7"flexi; w-mag) *Bucketful Of Brains; (BOB 8)* **HAPPY THE GOLDEN PRINCE**

Jun 94. (cd) *Strange Roots; (ROOTCD 001)* **KERSHAW SESSIONS**

Mar 95. (cd) *Rhino-Sequel;* **RARE & UNRELEASED**

HUMANOID
(see under ⇒ FUTURE SOUND OF LONDON)

HUSKER DU

Formed: St. Paul, Minnesota, USA ... 1978 by MOULD, HART and NORTON. In 1980-82, they issued a few 45's and a live lp 'LAND SPEED RECORD', on their own label, 'New Alliance'. The record typified the band's early uncompromising hardcore which was often tediously workmanlike in its adherence to the steadfast confines of the genre. 'EVERYTHING FALLS APART' (1983) was also unflinching in its intensity and it was all the more surprising when the band showed glimmers of noise-pop greatness on their 1983 debut for 'SST', 'METAL CIRCUS'. They consolidated this by cross fertilising the previously polarised worlds of psychedelia and hardcore punk on an electrifying cover of The BYRDS' 'EIGHT MILES HIGH' (1984). The follow-up double set, 'ZEN ARCADE' (1984) was a further giant step for hardcore kind. A concept album no less, the twin songwriting attack of MOULD and HART was becoming sharper and even the sprawling, unfocused feel of the whole affair wasn't enough to blunt the edges of songs like 'WHATEVER' and 'TURN ON THE NEWS'. The songwriting on 'NEW DAY RISING' (1985) was even more trenchant, the band's adrenaline fuelled pop-core hybrid developing at breakneck speed. 'FLIP YOUR WIG' (1985), the band's last indie release, marked a stepping stone to their major label debut for 'Warners', 'CANDY APPLE GREY' (1986). While HART perfected HUSKER DU's melodic dischord on tracks like 'DEAD SET ON DESTRUCTION', MOULD showcased darkly introspective, acoustic elegies 'TOO FAR DOWN' and 'HARDLY GETTING OVER IT'. The more musically-challenged among HUSKER DU's following were none too taken with this new fangled unplugged business although the album was released to unanimous critical acclaim. The band's swansong, 'WAREHOUSE: SONGS AND STORIES' (1987) was the culmination of a decade's experimentation and possessed an unprecedented depth, clarity and consistence. By the time of its release, though, tension in the band was reaching breaking point and HUSKER DU was disbanded in 1987. While GRANT HART and BOB MOULD went on to solo careers, as well as respectively forming NOVA MOB and SUGAR, they were always better together and the magic of HUSKER DU is inestimable in its influence on a generation of alternative guitar bands. • **Songwriters:** MOULD-HART compositions except; SUNSHINE SUPERMAN (Donovan) / TICKET TO RIDE + SHE'S A WOMAN + HELTER SKELTER (Beatles) / EIGHT MILES HIGH (Byrds). NOVA MOB covered I JUST WANT TO MAKE LOVE TO YOU (Willie Dixon) / SHEENA IS A PUNK ROCKER (Ramones). Solo GRANT HART covered SIGNED D.C. (Love). • **Trivia:** HUSKER DU means; DO YOU REMEMBER in Swedish.

Recommended: NEW DAY RISING (*7) / FLIP YOUR WIG (*7) / ZEN ARCADE (*8) / CANDY APPLE GREY (*8) / WAREHOUSE (*9)

BOB MOULD (b.12 Oct'60, Malone, N.Y.) – vocals, guitar, keyboards, percussion / **GRANT HART** (b. GRANTZBERG VERNON HART, 18 Mar'61) – drums, keyboards, percussion, vocals / **GREG NORTON** (b.13 Mar'59, Rock Island, Illinois) – bass

not issued Reflex

1980. (7") *<38285>* **STATUES. / AMUSEMENT (live)**

Alt.Tent. New Alliance

1982. (lp) *(VIRUS 25) <NAR 007>* **LAND SPEED RECORD (live)**
– All tensed up / Don't try to call / I'm not interested / Big sky / Guns at my school / Push the button / Gilligan's Island / MTC / Don't have a life / Bricklayer / Tired of doing things / You're naive / Strange week / Do the bee / Ultracore / Let's go die / Data control. *(re-iss.Nov88 on 'S.S.T.'; SST 195) (re-iss.cd/c/lp Oct95)*

1982. (7"m) *<NAR 010>* **IN A FREE LAND. / WHAT DO I WANT? / M.I.C.**

not issued Reflex

Jul 83. (lp) *<D>* **EVERYTHING FALLS APART**
– From the gut / Blah, blah, blah / Punch drunk / Bricklayer / Afraid of being wrong / Sunshine Superman / Signals from above / Everything falls apart / Wheels / Obnoxious / Gravity. *(cd-iss.May93 on 'WEA'+=; 8122 71163-2)* – In a free land / What do I want / M.I.C. / Statues / Let's go die / Amusement (live) / Do you remember?

S.S.T. S.S.T.

Dec 83. (m-lp) *<(SST 020)>* **METAL CIRCUS**
– Real world / Deadly skies / It's not funny anymore / Diane / First of the last calls / Lifeline / Out on a limb.

Apr 84. (7"colrd) *(SST 025)* **EIGHT MILES HIGH. / MASOCHISM WORLD**
(cd-s iss.Dec88; SST 025CD)

Sep 84. (d-lp) *<(SST 027)>* **ZEN ARCADE**
– Something I learned today / Broken home, broken heart / Never talking to you again / Chartered trips / Dreams reoccurring / Indecision time / Hare Krishna / Beyond the threshold / Pride / I'll never forget you / The biggest lie / What's going on / Masochism world / Standing by the sea / Somewhere / One step at a time / Pink turns to blue / Newest industry / Monday will never be the same / Whatever / The tooth fairy and the princess / Turn on the news / Reoccurring dreams. *(cd-iss.Oct87; SST 027CD) (re-iss.cd/c/d-lp Oct95 & Jun97; same)*

Feb 85. (lp) <(SST 031)> **NEW DAY RISING**
– New day rising / Girl who lives on Heaven Hill / I apologize / Folklore / If I told you / Celebrated summer / Perfect example / Terms of psychic warfare / 59 times the pain / Powerline / Books about UFO's / I don't know what you're talking about / How to skin a cat / Watcha drinkin' / Plans I make. *(cd-iss.Oct87; SST 031CD) (re-iss.cd/c/lp Oct95; same)*

Aug 85. (7") <(SST 051)> **MAKE NO SENSE AT ALL. / LOVE IS ALL AROUND (MARY'S THEME)**

Oct 85. (lp) <(SST 055)> **FLIP YOUR WIG**
– Flip your wig / Every everything / Makes no sense at all / Hate paper doll / Green eyes / Divide and conquer / Games / Find me / The baby song / Flexible flyer / Private plane / Keep hanging on / The wit and the wisdom / Don't know yet. *(cd-iss.Oct87; SST 055CD) (re-iss.cd/c/lp Oct95; same)*

Warners Warners

Feb 86. (7") *(W 8746)* **DON'T WANT TO KNOW IF YOU ARE LONELY. / ALL WORK NO PLAY**
(12"+=) *(W 8746T)* – Helter skelter (live).

Mar 86. (lp/c) *(WX 40/+C)* <25385> **CANDY APPLE GREY**
– Crystal / Don't want to know if you are lonely / I don't know for sure / Sorry somehow / Too far down / Hardly getting over it / Dead set on destruction / Eiffel Tower high / No promises have I made / All this I've done for you. *(cd-iss.Nov92; 7599 25385-2)*

Sep 86. (7") *(W 8612)* **SORRY SOMEHOW. / ALL THIS I'VE DONE FOR YOU**
(d7+=/12"+=) *(W 8612 F/T)* – Flexible flyer / Celebrated summer.

Jan 87. (7") *(W 8456)* **COULD YOU BE THE ONE. / EVERYTIME**
(12"+=) *(W 8456T)* – Charity, chastity, prudence, hope.

Jan 87. (d-lp/d-c) *(925544-1/-4)* <25544> **WAREHOUSE: SONGS & STORIES** 72
– These important years / Charity, chastity, prudence and hope / Standing in the rain / Back from somewhere / Ice cold ice / You're a soldier / Could you be the one? / Too much spice / Friend, you've got to fall / Visionary / She floated away / Bed of nails / Tell you why tomorrow / It's not peculiar / Actual condition / No reservations / Turn it around / She's a woman (and now he is a man) / Up in the air / You can live at home. *(cd-iss.Oct92; 7599 25544-2)*

Jun 87. (7") *(W 8276)* **ICE COLD ICE. / GOTTA LETTA**
(12"+=) *(W 8276T)* – Medley.

– compilations, etc. –

May 94. Warners; (cd/c) <(9362 45582-2/-4)> **THE LIVING END (live)**
– New day rising / Heaven Hill / Standing in the rain / Back from somewhere / Ice cold ice / Everytime / Friend you're gonna fall / She floated away / From the gut / Target / It's not funny anymore / Hardly getting over it / Terms of psychic warfare / Powertime / Books about UFO's / Divide and conquer / Keep hangin' on / Celebrated summer / Now that you know me / Ain't no water in the well / What's goin' on / Data control / In a free land / Sheena is a punk rocker.

— Disbanded in 1987 after manager DAVID SAVOY Jr. committed suicide. GRANT HART went solo in '89, as did BOB MOULD. In 1992 he formed SUGAR.

GRANT HART

S.S.T. S.S.T.

Oct 89. (7"ep/cd-ep) *(SST 219/+CD)* **2541. / COME HOME / LET'S GO** -

Nov 89. (lp/cd) <(SST 215/+CD)> **INTOLERANCE**
– All of my senses / Now that you know me / The main / Roller risk / Fanfare in D major (come, come) / You're the victim / 2541 / Anything / She can see the angels coming / Reprise.

May 90. (12"ep/cd-ep) *(SST 262/+CD)* **ALL OF MY SENSES. / THE MAIN (edit) / SIGNED D.C.**

NOVA MOB

(GRANT HART) & his group:- **TOM MERKL** – bass / **MICHAEL CRECO** – drums

RoughTrade RoughTrade

Feb 91. (cd/c/lp) *(R 2081261-2/-4/-1)* **THE LAST DAYS OF POMPEII**
– Introduction / Woton / Getaway (gateway) in time / Admiral of the sea (79 a.d. version) / Wernher Von Braun / Space jazz / Where you grave land (next time you fall off of yo) / Over my head / Admiral of the sea / Persuaded / Lavender and grey / Medley:- The last days of Pompeii / Benediction.

Feb 91. (12"ep/cd-ep) **ADMIRAL OF THE SEA (first avenue mix) / ('A' milk off mix) / THE LAST DAYS OF POMPEII (mix) / GETAWAY IN TIME (instrumental) / I JUST WANT TO MAKE LOVE TO YOU (live)**

— **MARK RELISH** – drums repl. CRECO

Southern Big Store

Jul 92. (cd-ep) <EFA 04669CD> **SHOOT YOUR WAY TO FREEDOM / BALLAD NO.19 / OH! TO BEHOLD / CHILDREN IN THE STREET**

— **HART** with **CHRIS HENSLER** – guitar / **TOM MERKL** – bass / **STEVE SUTHERLAND** – drums

World Service Restless

May 94. (cd/lp) *(1571744-2/-1)* **NOVA MOB**
– Shoot your way to freedom / Puzzles / Buddy / See and feel and know / Little Miss Information / I won't be there anymore / Please don't ask / The sins of their sons / Beyond a reasonable doubt / I was afraid – Coda.

Sep 94. (cd-ep) **OLD EMPIRE / PLEASE DON'T ASK / LITTLE MISS INFORMATION / BEYOND A REASONABLE DOUBT**

Dec 95. (cd; GRANT HART) <(RTD 1573096-2)> **ECCE HOMO** (live)
– Ballad No.19 / 2541 / Evergreen / Memorial drive / Come come / Pink turns to blue / She floated away / The girl who lives on Heaven hill / Admiral of the sea / Back somewhere / Last days of Pompeii / Old Empire / Never talking to you again / Please don't ask / The main.

I

INSPIRAL CARPETS

Formed: Manchester, England . . . 1980 initially as The FURS, by schoolboy GRAHAM LAMBERT. He was joined in the mid-80's by STEPHEN HOLT, TONY WELSH and CHRIS GOODWIN. In 1986, as The INSPIRAL CARPETS, they replaced GOODWIN and WELSH, with CRAIG GILL, DAVE SWIFT and CLINT BOON. Early in '87, they recorded a version of 'GARAGE' for a 7" flexi-disc given free with 'Debris' magazine. After gigs supporting the WEDDING PRESENT, JAMES, STONES ROSES and The SHAMEN, they issued their official debut, the 'PLANE CRASH EP' in mid-'88 for indie, 'Playtime' records. Early in 1989, they set up their own 'Cow' label, after their distributers 'Red Rhino' went bust. At the same time, HOLT and SWIFT left to form The RAINKINGS, and were replaced by HINGLEY and WALSH. After a late 1988 recording, 'TRAIN SURFING EP' was issued, they recorded the 808 STATE-produced 'JOE' single/EP. In late 1989, they had their first UK Top 50 entry with 'MOVE', which led to Daniel Miller of 'Mute' records giving them & 'Cow' a record deal. In April 1990, they broke into UK Top 20 with the poignant single, 'THIS IS HOW IT FEELS', pushing their debut album, 'LIFE', to No. 3. They continued with a run of hit singles that included, 'SHE COMES IN THE FALL', 'CARAVAN' and 'DRAGGING ME DOWN', the latter two featured on the Top 5 album, 'THE BEAST INSIDE' (1991). The following year, with a further clutch of hit singles under their belt, they scraped into the Top 20 with 'REVENGE OF THE GOLDFISH', a weaker effort. A year of reflection in 1993 preceded a return to form with a MARK E. SMITH (The Fall) collaboration 45, 'I WANT YOU' (now featured on a certain TV ad). This helped the album, 'DEVIL HOPPING', reach the Top 10 but when their next single, 'UNIFORM', failed to even dent the Top 50, they were unceremoniously dropped by their label, 'Mute'. The band split soon after, leaving behind the customary cash-in compilation. • **Style:** Heavy, organ-orientated psychedelic-pop group, who lay somewhere between The DOORS and The FALL. • **Songwriters:** Group penned except; 96 TEARS (? & The Mysterians) / GIMME SHELTER (Rolling Stones) / TAINTED LOVE (Soft Cell) / PARANOID (Black Sabbath). • **Trivia:** To promote debut album, they employed the services of the Milk Marketing Board who ran a TV ad on their bottles. Early 1990, they penned 'THE 8.15 FROM MANCHESTER' (theme) from children's Saturday morning TV show.

Recommended: LIFE (*8) / THE BEAST INSIDE (*7) / REVENGE OF THE GOLDFISH (*6) / DEVIL HOPPING (*5)

GRAHAM LAMBERT (b.10 Jul'64, Oldham, England) – guitar / **STEPHEN HOLT** – vocals / **DAVE SWIFT** – bass repl. TONY WELSH / **CRAIG GILL** (b. 5 Dec'71) – drums repl. CHRIS GOODWIN who joined ASIA FIELDS (later BUZZCOCKS F.O.C. and The HIGH) / added **CLINT BOON** (b.28 Jun'59, Oldham) – organ, vocals

Playtime not issued

Jul 88. (7"ltd.) *(AMUSE 2)* **KEEP THE CIRCLE AROUND. / THEME FROM COW** -
(12"ep+=) **PLANE CRASH EP** (AMUSE 2T) – Seeds of doubt / Garage full of flowers / 96 tears.

Cow not issued

Mar 89. (12"ep) *(MOO 2)* **TRAIN SURFING** -
– Butterfly / Causeway / You can't take the truth / Greek wedding song.

— **TOM HINGLEY** (b. 9 Jul'65, Oxford, England) – vocals (ex-TOO MUCH TEXAS) repl. HOLT who formed RAINKINGS **MARTIN WALSH** (b. 3 Jul'68) – bass (ex-NEXT STEP) repl. SWIFT who formed RAINKINGS

May 89. (12"ep) *(MOO 3)* **JOE. / COMMERCIAL MIX / DIRECTING TRAFFIK / COMMERCIAL RAIN** -

May 89. (c;ltd) *(DUNG 4)* **DEMO CASSETTE** (rec.Dec'87) -
– Keep the circle around / Seeds of doubt / Joe / Causeway / 26 / Inside my head / Sun don't shine / Theme from Cow / 96 tears / Butterfly / Garage full of flowers.

Aug 89. (7") *(DUNG 5)* **FIND OUT WHY. / SO FAR** -
(12"+=/cd-s+=) *(DUNG 5 T/CD)* – Plane crash (live).

Oct 89. (7"/s7") *(DUNG 6/+X)* **MOVE. / OUT OF TIME** 49 -
(12"+=/cd-s+=) *(DUNG 6 T/CD)* – Move in.

Cow-Mute Sire

Mar 90. (7") *(DUNG 7)* **THIS IS HOW IT FEELS. / TUNE FOR A FAMILY** 14
(12"+=/cd-s+=) *(DUNG 7 T/CD)* – ('A'extended) / Seeds of doubt.
(c-s+=) *(DUNG 7MC)* – ('A'extended) / Whiskey.
(12") *(DUNG 7R)* – ('A'-Robbery mix) / ('B'drum mix).

Apr 90. (lp/c/cd) *(DUNG 8/+C/CD)* **LIFE** 2
– Real thing / Song for a family / This is how it feels / Directing traffik / Besides me / Many happy returns / Memories of you / She comes in the fall / Monkey on my back / Sun don't shine / Inside my head / Move * / Sackville. *(cd+= *)* <US++=>– Commercial rain / Weakness / Biggest mountain / I'll keep it in mind.

Jun 90. (7") *(DUNG 10)* **SHE COMES IN THE FALL. / SACKVILLE** 27
(12"+=/cd-s+=) *(DUNG 10 T/CD)* – Continental reign (version).
(12"+=) *(DUNG 10R)* – ('A'acappella version).

Nov 90. (7"ep/12"ep) *(DUNG 11/+T)* **ISLAND HEAD** 21
– Biggest mountain / I'll keep it in mind / Weakness / Gold to . . .
(cd-ep+=) *(DUNG 11CD)* – Mountain sequence.

Mar 91. (7") *(DUNG 13)* **CARAVAN. / SKIDOO** 30
(7"/12") *(DUNG 13 R/T)* – ('A'side) / ('B'-Possession mix).
(cd-s) *(DUNG 13CD)* – ('A'-What noise rethink mix) / ('B'side).

Apr 91. (lp/c/cd) *(DUNG 14/+C/CD)* **THE BEAST INSIDE** 5
– Caravan / Please be cruel / Born yesterday / Sleep well tonight / Grip / Beast inside /

Niagara / Mermaid / Further away / Dreams are all we have.
Jun 91. (7"/c-s) *(DUNG/ 15)* **PLEASE BE CRUEL. / THE WIND IS CALLING YOUR NAME** 50
(12"+=/cd-s+=) *(DUNG 15 T/CD)* – St.Kilda (version).
Feb 92. (7") *(DUNG 16)* **DRAGGING ME DOWN. / I KNOW I'M LOSING YOU** 12
(12"+=/cd-s+=) *(DUNG 16 T/CD)* – (2 other 'A'mixes).
May 92. (7") *(DUNG 17)* **TWO WORLDS COLLIDE. / BOOMERANG** 32
(12"+=/cd-s+=) *(DUNG 17 T/CD)* – ('A'-Mike Pickering remix).
Sep 92. (7") *(DUNG 18)* **GENERATIONS. / ('A'remix)** 28
(c-s) *(DUNG 18C)* – Lost in space again.
(12"/cd-s) *(DUNG 18 T/CD)* – ('A'side) / She comes in the fall (live) / Move (live) / Directing traffik (live).
(cd-s) *(DUNG 18CDR)* – ('A'side) / Joe (live) / Commercial rain (live) / Butterfly (live).
Oct 92. (lp/c/cd) *(DUNG 19/+C/CD)* **REVENGE OF THE GOLDFISH** 17
– Generations / Saviour / Bitches brew / Smoking her clothes / Fire / Here comes the flood / Dragging me down / A little disappeared / Two worlds collide / Mystery / Rain song / Irresistable force.
Nov 92. (c-ep/12"ep) *(DUNG 20 C/T)* **BITCHES BREW / TAINTED LOVE. / BITCHES BREW (Fortran 5 remix) / IRRESISTABLE FORCE (Fortran 5 mix)** 36
(cd-ep+=) *(DUNG 20CD)* – Mermaid (live) / Born yesterday (live) / Sleep well tonight (live).
(cd-ep+=) *(DUNG 20CDR)* – Dragging me down (live) / Smoking her clothes (live) / Fire (live).

— parted company with 'Cow' co-founder/manager Anthony Boggiano.

May 93. (7"/c-s) *(DUNG 22/+C)* **HOW IT SHOULD BE. / IT'S ONLY A PAPER MOON** 49
(12"+=/cd-s+=) *(DUNG 22 T/CD)* – I'm alive.
Jan 94. (7"/c-s) *(DUNG 23/+C)* **SATURN 5. / PARTY IN THE SKY** 20
(cd-s+=/12"+=) *(DUNG 23 T/CD)* – ('A'mixes).
(cd-s) *(DUNG 23CDR)* – ('A'side) / Well of seven heads / Two cows / Going down.
Feb 94. (7"/c-s; by INSPIRAL CARPETS featuring MARK E. SMITH) *(DUNG 24/+C)* **I WANT YOU. / I WANT YOU (version)** 18
(cd-s+=) *(DUNG 24CD)* – We can do everything / Inside of you.
(cd-s) *(DUNG 24CDR)* – ('A'side) / Dragging me down / Party in the sky / Plutoman.
Mar 94. (lp/c/cd) *(DUNG 25/+C/CD)* **DEVIL HOPPING** 10
– I want you / Party in the sky / Plutoman / Uniform / Lovegrove / Just Wednesday / Saturn 5 / All of this and more / The way the light falls / Half way there / Cobra / I don't want to go blind. *(w / free ltd-cd of 'BBC SESSIONS' or free ltd.red-10"lp)*
Apr 94. (7"/c-s/cd-s) *(DUNG 26/+C/CD)* **UNIFORM. / PARANOID** 51
(cd-s) *(DUNG 26 CDR)* – ('A'side) / Paranoid (Collapsed Lung mix).
Aug 95. (7"m) *(DUNG 27L)* **JOE (acoustic). / SEEDS OF DOUBT / WHISKEY** 37
(7"m) *(DUNG 27R)* – Joe (live) / Sackville (live) / Saviour (live).
(cd-s) *(DUNG 25CD)* – ('A'side) / I want you / I'll keep it in mind / Tainted love.
Sep 95. (cd/c/d-lp) *(CD/C+/MOOTEL 3)* **THE SINGLES** (compilation) 17
– Joe / Find out why / Move / This is how it feels / (extended) / She comes in the fall / Commercial reign / Sackville / Biggest mountain / Weakness / Caravan / Please be cruel / Dragging me down / Two worlds collide / Generations / Bitches brew / How it should be / Saturn 5 / I want you / Uniform.

— Had already been dropped from the 'Mute' roster late in 1994.

– compilations, etc. –

Jul 89. (12"ep/cd-ep) *Strange Fruit; (SFPS/+CD 072)* **THE PEEL SESSIONS** -
– Out of time / Directing traffic / Keep the circle around / Gimme shelter.
Aug 92. (cd/10"lp) *Strange Fruit;* **PEEL SESSIONS** -

— also released import 7"colrd/12"colrd/pic-cd-s 'GIMME SHELTER'.

IRRESISTIBLE FORCE

Formed: based; London, England . . . late 80's by one-man unit MIXMASTER MORRIS. He had worked as a DJ in the early 80's, before experimenting with samples. He's said to have been influenced by the ambient/psyche world after taking LSD at a concert by veteran minimalist STEVE REICH. He struck up a relationship with PSYCHIC TV leader GENESIS P. ORRIDGE, which led him to work with The SHAMEN (most noteably the now deceased WILL SINOTT). A few 45's came out in 1988/89 under the banner of The IRRESISTIBLE FORCE. In 1991, he scored a minor dance hit with the SUN RA-inspired 'SPACE IS THE PLACE', while a year later, his debut long-play venture 'FLYING HIGH' graced both rave-floor and chill-out bedsitters alike. He then worked with DR. ALEX PATERSON and fellow ambient acolyte PETE NAMLOOK on two separate projects, before he followed-up in 1994 with his 2nd album 'GLOBAL CHILLAGE'. • **Style:** He phrased the term 'I Think Therefore I Ambient', which says a lot for his post-KRAFTWERK / SHAMEN / SUN RA influences. • **Songwriters:** Himself and samples. • **Trivia:** Worked on COLD CUT (Autumn Leaves), LLOYD COLE (My Bag) & BANG BANG MACHINE.

MIXMASTER MORRIS – electronics, samples, keyboards, etc.

Red Mega-phone / not issued
May 88. (12") *(DMT 001)* **I WANT YOU. /** -
Freestyle / not issued
Jul 89. (12") *(12BBBK 7)* **FREESTYLE. /** -
Rising High
1991. (12") *(RSN 5)* **SPACE IS THE PLACE. / ('A'-ambient)** -
Nov 92. (cd/c/d-lp) *(RSN CD/MC/LP 5)* **FLYING HIGH** -
– Spiritual high / Sky high / Flying high / High frequency / Symphony in E / Mountain high (live).
1993. (12") *(RSN 11)* **UNDERGROUND. / ('A'mix)** -

— In 1993, with PETER NAMLOOK, MIXMASTER MORRIS released 'DREAM FISH' on 'Rising High'; *RSN CD/LP 9)*. NAMLOOK's label 'Ambient World' re-issued it Oct96; *AW 012CD)*

— Later, with DR. ALEX PATERSON (of The ORB), MIXMASTER MORRIS released cd 'MIGMAG LIVE! VOL.9' *(MMLCD 019)*

Nov 94. (cd/d-lp) *(RSN CD/LP 24)* **GLOBAL CHILLAGE**
-

— FRASER CLARK v THE IRRESISTIBLE FORCE issued 12"; WAR AND PEACE for 'Evolution' *(EVO 2)*

J

JACK OFFICERS (see under ⇒ BUTTHOLE SURFERS)

JESUS & MARY CHAIN

Formed: East Kilbride, Scotland . . . 1983, by brothers WILLIAM and JIM REID, who took their name from a line in a Bing Crosby film. After local Glasgow gigs, they moved to Fulham in London, having signed for Alan McGhee's independent 'Creation' label in May'84. Their debut SLAUGHTER JOE-produced 45, 'UPSIDE DOWN', soon topped the indie charts, leading to WEA subsidiary label, 'Blanco Y Negro', snapping them up in early 1985. They hit the UK Top 50 with their next single, 'NEVER UNDERSTAND', and they were soon antagonising new audiences, crashing gear after 20 minutes on set. Riots ensued at nearly every major gig, and more controversy arrived when the next 45's B-side 'JESUS SUCKS', was boycotted by the pressing plant. With a new B-side, the single 'YOU TRIP ME UP', hit only No.55, but was soon followed by another Top 50 hit in October, 'JUST LIKE HONEY'. A month later they unleashed their debut album, 'PSYCHOCANDY', and although this just failed to breach the UK Top 30, it was regarded by many (NME critics especially) as the album of the year. Early in '86, BOBBY GILLESPIE left to concentrate on his PRIMAL SCREAM project and soon after, JAMC hit the Top 20 with the softer single, 'SOME CANDY TALKING'. In 1987 with new drummer JOHN MOORE, the single 'APRIL SKIES' and album 'DARKLANDS' both went Top 10. Later that year, they remixed The SUGARCUBES' classic 'Birthday' single.'BARBED WIRE KISSES' (1988) was a hotch-potch of B-sides and unreleased material, essential if only for the anarchic trashing of The Beach Boys' 'SURFIN' U.S.A.'. By the release of the 'AUTOMATIC' album in 1989, the Reid brothers had become the core of the band, enlisting additional musicians as needed. The record sounded strangely muted and uninspired although the 'ROLLERCOASTER' EP and subsequent tour (alongside MY BLOODY VALENTINE and a pre-'PARKLIFE' BLUR) were an improvement. True to controversial style, the band returned to the singles chart in 1992 with the radio un-friendly, post-industrial mantra, 'REVERENCE'. Perhaps the last great piece of venom-spewing noise the 'MARY CHAIN produced, the follow-up album, 'HONEY'S DEAD', was tame in comparison. No surprise then, that it recieved mixed reviews although there were a few low key highlights, notably the melodic bubblegum grunge of 'FAR GONE AND OUT'. After 1993's 'SOUND OF SPEED' EP, the band hooked up with MAZZY STAR'S Hope Sandoval for 'STONED AND DETHRONED', a mellow set of feedback free strumming. While still echoing the brooding portent of the THE VELVETS, the style of the record was more 'PALE BLUE EYES' than 'SISTER RAY'. Predictably, the band were seen as having 'sold out' by Indie-Rock dullards and a 1995 single 'I HATE ROCK 'N' ROLL' didn't even scrape the top 50. • **Style:** Initially a noisy post-punk outfit who screeched with feedback. Described as VELVET UNDERGROUND meeting The SEX PISTOLS, they soon mellowed at times into romantic garage type rock. • **Songwriters:** All written by JIM and WILLIAM except; VEGETABLE MAN (Syd Barrett) / SURFIN' USA (Beach Boys) / WHO DO YOU LOVE (Bo Diddley) / MY GIRL (Temptations) / MUSHROOM (Can) / GUITAR MAN (Jerry Lee Hubbard) / TOWER OF SONG (Leonard Cohen) / LITTLE RED ROOSTER (Willie Dixon) / (I CAN'T GET NO) SATISFACTION (Rolling Stones) / REVERBERATION (13th Floor Elevators) / GHOST OF A SMILE (Pogues) / ALPHABET CITY (Prince) / NEW KIND OF KICK (Cramps). • **Trivia:** Their 1986 single 'SOME CANDY TALKING' was banned by Radio 1 DJ Mike Smith, due to its drug references. The following year in the States, they were banned from a chart show due to their blasphemous name. Although yet not overwhelming, their success in the US, have made albums reach between 100 & 200. On 1994's 'STONED AND DETHRONED', they were joined by William's girlfriend HOPE SANDOVAL (of MAZZY STAR).

Recommended: PSYCHOCANDY (*10) / DARKLANDS (*8) / AUTOMATIC (*7) / HONEY'S DEAD (*8) / BARBED WIRE KISSES (*7)

JIM REID (b.29 Dec'61) – vox, guitar / **WILLIAM REID** (b.28 Oct'58) – guitar, vox / **MURRAY DALGLISH** – drums (bass tom & snare) / **DOUGLAS HART** – bass

Creation / not issued
Nov 84. (7") *(CRE 012)* **UPSIDE DOWN. / VEGETABLE MAN** -
(12"+=) *(CRE 012T)* – ('A' demo).

— **BOBBY GILLESPIE** – drums (ex-WAKE, of PRIMAL SCREAM) repl. DALGLISH who formed BABY'S GOT A GUN

Blanco Y Negro / Reprise

Feb 85. (7") *(NEG 8)* **NEVER UNDERSTAND. / SUCK** 47 –
(12"+=) *(NEGT 8)* – Ambition.

Jun 85. (7") *(NEG 13)* **YOU TRIP ME UP. / JUST OUT OF REACH** 55 –
(12"+=) *(NEGT 13)* – Boyfriend's dead.

Oct 85. (7") *(NEG 017)* **JUST LIKE HONEY. / HEAD** 45 –
(12"+=) *(NEGT 17)* – Just like honey (demo) / Cracked.
(d7"+=) *(NEGF 17)* – ('A'demo) / Inside me.

Nov 85. (lp/c) *(BYN/+C 11) <25383>* **PSYCHOCANDY** 31 –
– Just like honey / The living end / Taste the floor / Hardest walk / Cut dead / In a hole / Taste of Cindy / Never understand / It's so hard / Inside me / Sowing seeds / My little underground / You trip me up / Something's wrong. *(cd-iss.Aug86 & Jan97 +=; K 242 000-2)*– Some candy talking.

— **JOHN LODER** – drums (on stage when BOBBY was unavailable)

Jul 86. (7") *(NEG 19)* **SOME CANDY TALKING. / PSYCHO CANDY / HIT** 13 –
(12"+=) *(NEGT 19)* – Taste of Cindy.
(d7"+=) *(NEGF 19)(SAM 291)* – Cut dead (acoustic) / You trip me up (acoustic) / Some candy talking (acoustic) / Psycho candy (acoustic).

— now basic trio of **JIM**, **WILLIAM** and **DOUGLAS** brought in **JOHN MOORE** (b.23 Dec'64, England) – drums repl. GILLESPIE (who was busy with PRIMAL SCREAM) / **JAMES PINKER** – drums (ex-DEAD CAN DANCE) repl. MOORE now on guitar

Apr 87. (7") *(NEG 24)* **APRIL SKIES. / KILL SURF CITY** 8 –
(12"+=) *(NEGT 24)* – Who do you love.
(d7"+=) *(NEGF 24)* – Mushroom / Bo Diddley is Jesus.

Aug 87. (7") *(NEG 25)* **HAPPY WHEN IT RAINS. / EVERYTHING IS ALRIGHT WHEN YOU'RE DOWN** 25 –
(ext.12"+=) *(NEGT 25)* – Happy place / F-Hole.
(ext.10"+=) *(NEGTE 25)* – ('A'demo) / Shake.

— trimmed to basic duo of REID brothers.

Sep 87. (lp/c)(cd) *(BYN/+C 25)(K 242 180-2) <25656>* **DARKLANDS** 5 –
– Darklands / Deep one perfect morning / Happy when it rains / Down on me / Nine million rainy days / April skies / Fall / Cherry came too / On the wall / About you. *(cd re-iss.Nov94; K 242 180-2)*

Oct 87. (7"/7"g-f) *(NEG/+F 29)* **DARKLANDS. / RIDER / ON THE WALL (demo)** 33 –
(12"+=/12"g-f+=) *(NEGTF 29)* – Surfin' U.S.A.
(10"+=/cd-s+=) *(NEG TE/CD 29)* – Here it comes again.

— **DAVE EVANS** – rhythm guitar repl. MOORE who formed EXPRESSWAY

Mar 88. (7") *(NEG 32)* **SIDEWALKING. / TASTE OF CINDY (live)** 30 –
(12"+=) *(NEGT 32)* – ('A'extended) / April skies (live).
(cd-s++=) *(NEGCD 32)* – Chilled to the bone.

Apr 88. (lp/c)(cd) *(BYN/+C 29)(K 242 331-2) <25729>* **BARBED WIRE KISSES** (part compilation) 9 –
– Kill Surf City / Head / Rider / Hit / Don't ever change / Just out of reach / Happy place / Psychocandy / Sidewalking / Who do you love / Surfin' USA / Everything's alright when you're down / Upside down / Taste of Cindy / Swing / On the wall. *(c+=/cd+=)*– Cracked / Here it comes again / Mushroom / Bo Diddley is Jesus. *(cd re-iss.Jan97; same)*

— In Nov'88, DOUGLAS HART moonlighted in The ACID ANGELS, who released 7"promo 'SPEED SPEED ECSTASY' on 'Product Inc.'; *FUEL 1)*

Nov 88. (7") **KILL SURF CITY. / SURFIN' USA (summer mix)** - –

— Basically REID brothers, HART and EVANS. (added **RICHARD THOMAS** – drums) / **BEN LURIE** – rhythm guitar repl. EVANS

Sep 89. (7") *(NEG 41)* **BLUES FROM A GUN. / SHIMMER** 32 -
(10"+=) *(NEG 41TE)* – Break me down / Penetration.
(12"+=/c-s+=) *(NEG 41 T/C)* – Penetration / Subway.
(3"cd-s+=) *(NEG 41CD)* – Penetration / My girl.

Oct 89. (lp/c)(cd) *(BYN/+C 20)(K 246 221-2) <26015>* **AUTOMATIC** 11 –
– Here comes Alice / Coast to coast / Blues from a gun / Between planets / UV ray / Her way of praying / Head on / Take it / Halfway to crazy / Gimme hell. *(cd re-iss.Jan97; same)*

Nov 89. (7") *(NEG 42)* **HEAD ON. / IN THE BLACK** 57 -
(12"+=) *(NEG 42T)* – Terminal beach.
(3"cd-s++=) *(NEG 42CD)* – Drop (acoustic re-mix).
(7") *(NEG 42XB)* – ('A'side). / DEVIANT SLICE
(7") *(NEG 42Y)* – ('A'side). / I'M GLAD I NEVER
(7") *(NEG 42Z)* – ('A'side). / TERMINAL BEACH

Mar 90. (7") **HEAD ON. / PENETRATION** - –

Aug 90. (7") *(NEG 45)* **ROLLERCOASTER. / SILVER BLADE** 46 –
(12"+=) *(NEG 45T)* – Tower of song.
(7"ep++=/cd-ep++=) *(NEG 45 D/CD)* – Low-life.

— Trimmed again, when THOMAS joined RENEGADE SOUNDWAVE on U.S.tour. HART became video director. The **REID** brothers and **BEN** recruited **MATTHEW PARKIN** – bass + **BARRY BLACKER** – drums (ex-STARLINGS)

Blanco Y Negro / Def American

Feb 92. (7") *(NEG 55)* **REVERENCE. / HEAT** 10 –
(12"+=/cd-s+=) *(NEG 55 T/CD)* – ('A'radio remix) / Guitar man.

Mar 92. (cd/c/lp) *(9031 76554-2/-4/-1) <26830>* **HONEY'S DEAD** 14 –
– Reverence / Teenage lust / Far gone and out / Almost gold / Sugar Ray / Tumbledown / Catchfire / Good for my soul / Rollercoaster / I can't get enough / Sundown / Frequency. *(cd re-iss.Jan97; same)*

Apr 92. (7") *(NEG 56)* **FAR GONE AND OUT. / WHY'D DO YOU WANT ME** 23 –
(12"+=/cd-s+=) *(NEG 56 T/CD)* – Sometimes you just can't get enough.

Jun 92. (7") *(NEG 57)* **ALMOST GOLD. / TEENAGE LUST (acoustic)** 41 –
(12"+=) *(NEG 57T)* – Honey's dead.
(gold-cd-s+=) *(NEG 57CD)* – Reverberation (doubt) / Don't come down.

Jun 93. (7"ep/c-ep/10"ep/cd-ep) *(NEG 66/+C/TE/CD)* **SOUND OF SPEED EP** 30 –
– Snakedriver / Something I can't have / White record release blues / Little red rooster.

Jul 93. (cd/c/lp) *(4509 93105-2/-4/-1)* **THE SOUND OF SPEED** (part comp '88-'93) 15 –
– Snakedriver / Reverence (radio mix) / Heat / Teenage lust (acoustic version) / Why'd you want me / Don't come down / Guitar man / Something I can't have / Sometimes / White record release blues / Shimmer / Penetration / My girl / Tower of song / Little red rooster / Break me down / Lowlife / Deviant slice / Reverberation / Sidewalking (extended version). *(cd re-iss.Jan97; same)*

— next album feat. guest vox HOPE SANDOVAL (Mazzy Star) + SHANE McGOWAN. **STEVE MONTI** – drums repl. BLACKER

Jul 94. (7"/c-s) *(NEG 70/+C)* **SOMETIMES ALWAYS. / PERFECT CRIME** 22 96
(10"+=/cd-s+=) *(NEG 70 TE/CD)* – Little stars / Drop.

Aug 94. (cd/c/lp) *(4509 93104-2/-4/-1) <45573>* **STONED AND DETRONED** 13 98
– Dirty water / Bullet lovers / Sometimes always / Come on / Between us / Hole / Never saw it coming / She / Wish I could / Save me / Till it shines / God help me / Girlfriend / Everybody I know / You've been a friend / These days / Feeling lucky. *(cd re-iss.Jan97; same)*

Oct 94. (7"/c-s) *(NEG 73/+C)* **COME ON. / I'M IN WITH THE OUT-CROWD** 52 –
(cd-s+=) *(NEG 73CD)* – New York City / Taking it away.
(cd-s) *(NEG 73CD)* – ('A'side) / Ghost of a smile / Alphabet city / New kind of kick.

Jun 95. (c-ep/12"ep/cd-ep) *(NEG 81 C/TEX/CD)* **I HATE ROCK'N'ROLL / BLEED ME. / 33 1-3 / LOST STAR** 61 –

– compilations etc. –

Sep 91. (m-lp/m-c/m-cd) *Strange Fruit; (SFP MA/MC/CD 210)* **THE PEEL SESSIONS (1985-86)** – -
– Inside me / The living end / Just like honey / all / Hapy place / In the rain.

Jun 94. (cd+book) *Audioglobe;* **LIVE (live)** – -

Mike JOHNSON (see under ⇒ DINOSAUR JR)

K

Edward KA-SPEL (see under ⇒ LEGENDARY PINK DOTS)

KRAMER (see under ⇒ BONGWATER)

KULA : SHAKER

Formed: Highgate, London, England . . .mid 90's out of mods The KAYS by CRISPIAN MILLS. They played down the fact his mother was the famous English actress HAYLEY MILLS (daughter of SIR JOHN MILLS). In the late 80's, CRISPIAN and ALONZA BEVIN set up a school group, The LOVELY LADS, later becoming The OBJECTS. In 1995, after jointly winning the 'In The City' new band competition and a Glastonbury appearance, KULA SHAKER signed to 'Columbia', through A&R man Ronnie Gurr. They debuted that Xmas with the limited edition single, 'TATTVA'. Their first single proper, 'GRATEFUL WHEN YOU'RE DEAD', was a tribute of sorts to the late, great JERRY GARCIA and earned them their first Top 40 hit. Their follow-up, a re-vamped version 'TATTVA', fared even better, making the Top 5. 'HEY DUDE', the next single, kept up the momentum, reaching No.2 following a blinding 'T In The Park' appearance in Scotland (they returned there in 1997 as headliners). CRISPIAN MILLS' songwriting was heavily influenced by a combination of classic 60's psychedelia and grandoise 70's rock, much in evidence on their debut album 'K' (1996). Relying on similar Eastern influences as 'TATTVA', 'GOVINDA' was another slice of elaborate, but cliched psychedelia, while 'HUSH' (1997) was workman-like in its similarity to the DEEP PURPLE version of the JOE SOUTH original.

Recommended: K (*7)

CRISPIAN MILLS – vocals, guitars / **ALONZA BEVIN** – bass, piano, tabla, vocals / **JAY DARLINGTON** – keyboards / **PAUL WINTERHART** – drums

Columbia / Columbia

Dec 95. (ltd;7"/cd-s) *(KULA 71/CD1)* **TATTVA (Lucky 13 mix)/ HOLLOW MAN (part II)** – -

Apr 96. (c-s) *(KULAMC 2)* **GRATEFUL WHEN YOU'RE DEAD – JERRY WAS THERE. / ANOTHER LIFE** 35 –
(cd-s+=) *(KULACD 2)* – Under the hammer.

Jun 96. (7") *(KULA 3)* **TATTVA. / TATTVA ON ST. GEORGE'S DAY / DANCE IN YOUR SHADOW** 4 –
(cd-s) *(KULACD 3)* – (first & third tracks) / Moonshine / Tattva (lucky 13).
(cd-s) *(KULACD 3K)* – (second & third tracks) / Red balloon (Vishnu's eyes).

Aug 96. (7"/c-s) *(KULA/+MC 4)* **HEY DUDE. / TROUBLED MIND** 2 –
(cd-s+=) *(KULACD 4)* – Grateful when you're dead (Mark Radcliffe session) / Into the deep (Mark Radcliffe session).
(cd-s) *(KULACD 4K)* – ('A'side) / Tattva / Drop in the sea / Crispian reading from the Mahabharata.

Sep 96. (cd/c/lp) *(SHAKER CD/MC/LP 1)* **K** 1 –
– Hey dude / Knight on the town / Temple of the everlasting light / Govinda / Smart dogs / Magic theatre / Into the deep / Sleeping jiva / Tattva / Grateful when you're dead – Jerry was there / 303 / Start all over / Hollow man (parts 1 & 2). *(also ltd-cd; SHAKER CD1K)*

Nov 96. (c-s) *(KULAMC 5)* **GOVINDA / GOKULA** 7 –
(cd-s+=) *(KULACD 5)* – Hey dude (live) / Alonza Bevan's The Leek.

('A'-Hari & St.George mix-cd-s+=) *(KULACD 5K)* – ('A'-Monkey Mafia Pigsy's vision) / ('A'-Monkey Mafia Ten to ten version).
(7"mail-order+=) *(KULA 75)* – Temple of everlasting light.

Feb 97. (c-s) *(KULAMC 6)* **HUSH / RAAGY ONE (WAITING FOR TOMORROW)** [2] [ ]
(cd-s+=) *(KULACD 6)* – Knight on the town (live) / Smart dogs (live).
(cd-s+=) *(KULACD 6K)* – Under the hammer (hold on to the magical key) / Govinda (live).

L

LABRADFORD

Formed: Richmond, Virginia, USA . . . 1991, by MARK NELSON and CARTER BROWN. They set-up CARTER's Moog Synthesizer in MARK's house and eventually acquired gigs supporting low-grade Virginia punk bands. In 1992, Chicago-based label 'Kranky' took up an option to sign them, soon releasing 'PRAZISION'. After its cult success, they retreated back home, but were lured to sign for New Zealand-based label 'Flying Nun' in the UK. The label subsequently released a follow-up album, 'A STABLE REFERENCE', in 1995. Another two-year hiatus was again worth the wait, when, in November '97, 'Blast First' issued their eponymous third effort. • **Style:** Drummerless Krautrock, likened to CLUSTER, SPACEMEN 3 and MAIN. Space-rock dreamscapes of ambient drones of uneasy-listening, resurrecting the nearly forgotten Moog synthesizer. • **Songwriters:** MARK lyrics / CARTER + MARK tunes.

Recommended: PRAZISION (*7) / A STABLE REFERENCE (*8) / LABRADFORD (*8)

CARTER BROWN – synthesizers / **MARK NELSON** – vocals, guitars, tapes / (ROBERT DONNE was only part-time until later)

Flying Nun / Kranky

1992. (cd-s) **EVERLAST /** [ ] [ ]
1993. (cd/lp) **PRAZISION** [-] [ ]
– Listening in depth / Accelerating in depth / Splash down / Disremembering / Experience the gated oscillator / Soft return / Sliding grass / C of people / New listening / Gratitude / Skyward with motion / Everlast. *(UK-iss.Feb96 lp/cd; FN/+CD 342)*

— added **ROBERT DONNE** – bass (ex-BREADWINNER)

Jun 95. (lp/cd) *(FN/+CD 329)* **A STABLE REFERENCE** [ ] [ ]
– Mas / El Lago / Streamlining / Banco / Eero / Balanced on its own flame / Star City, Russia / Comfort / SEDR 77.

Duophonic / not issued

Feb 96. (10") *(DS 4512)* **SCENIC RECOVERY. / UNDERWOOD 5IVE** [ ] [-]

Blast First / Kranky

Nov 96. (lp/cd) *(BFFP 136/+CD)* **LABRADFORD** [ ] [ ]
–

Trance Syndicate / Trance Syndicate

Jun 97. (12"; as LABRADFORD & STARS OF THE LID) *(TR 60)* **KAHANEK INCIDENT VOL.3** [ ] [ ]

Paul LEARY (see under ⇒ BUTTHOLE SURFERS)

LEFTFIELD

Formed: London, England . . . 1990 by ex-teacher of English NEIL BARNES and PAUL DALEY, formerly of Balearic housers A MAN CALLED ADAM. Barnes had previously released the 'Mississippi Burning'-sampling 'NOT FORGOTTEN' on dance indie Outer Rhythm and when the single became an underground club hit, contractual problems ensued. Undeterred, the duo kept a high profile with remix work (including David Bowie and Inner City) before setting up the Hard Hands label and cutting two singles in 1992, 'RELEASE THE PRESSURE' and 'SONG OF LIFE', the latter a slow building progressive house epic which further enhanced their dancefloor reputation and nudged into the lower regions of the pop charts. But the song that really branded LEFTFIELD into the musical consciousness of the nation was the pounding crossover hit, 'OPEN UP'. A collaboration with P.I.L.'s JOHN LYDON, his blood curdling wail of 'BURN HOLLYWOOD BURN' was scarier than Michael Bolton's mullet cut and was enough to have the video banned from ITV's Chart Show. Spookily enough, the song was released at the same time as a spate of Californian fires . . . The single was a corking tune into the bargain and climbed to No.13 in the charts. The debut album, 'LEFTISM' was greeted with critical plaudits galore upon its release in 1995, reaching No.3 in the U.K. and even being nominated for The Mercury Music Prize . An exhilirating cross-fertilisation of musical stylings, the album took pumping techno trance as its base ingredient, interspersing this with everything from cerebral sonic tapestries ('MELT') to dark, foreboding drum 'n' bass ('STORM 3000'). It contained all the aforementioned singles (save the earlier 'NOT FORGOTTEN') as well as a vocal-led collaboration with goth goddess Toni Halliday. LEFTFIELD enjoyed further chart success with tracks and remixes from the album and contributed material to both the 'Shallow Grave' and 'Trainspotting' film soundtracks. A nationwide tour and a series of legendary festival appearances in 1996 cemented their position as one of the key players in the new techno vanguard alongside Underworld, Prodigy et al. • **Songwriters:** BARNES / DALEY / guests and some samples. • **Trivia:** Their label 'Hard Hands' run by manager LISA HORRAN, also included acts VINYL BLAIR, DELTA LADY, DEE PATTEN and SCOTT HARRIS.

Recommended: LEFTISM (*9)

NEIL BARNES – DJ, percussion, synthesizers / **PAUL DALEY** – samples (ex-A MAN CALLED ADAM)

Outer Rhythm / not issued

Mar 90. (12") *(FOOT 3)* **NOT FORGOTTEN. / PATELL'S ON THE CASE / ('A'version)** [ ] [-]
Feb 91. (12") *(FOOT 9)* **NOT FORGOTTEN (Hard Hands mix). / MORE THAN I KNOW** [ ] [-]
(12") *(FOOT 9R)* – ('A'&'B'remixes).

Hard Hands / not issued

Aug 92. (12"ltd.; featuring EARL SIXTEEN) *(HAND 001T)* **RELEASE THE PRESSURE (3 track vocal)** [ ] [-]
(12"ltd.) *(HAND 001R)* – Release the dubs (instrumental mixes).
Nov 92. (12"ltd.) *(HAND 002T)* **SONG OF LIFE. / FANFARE OF LIFE / DUB OF LIFE** [59] [-]
(12") *(HAND 002R)* – ('A'-3 Underworld mixes).
(cd-s) *(HAND 002CD)* – ('A'side) / Fanfare of life / Release the dub.
Dec 92. (cd) *(OUTERCD 1)* **BACKLOG** (compilation of above material on 'Outer Rhythm') [ ] [-]

— Below single with JOHN LYDON (of PUBLIC IMAGE LTD) on vocals

Nov 93. (7"/c-s; as LEFTFIELD / LYDON) *(HAND 9/+MC)* **OPEN UP (radio edit). / ('A'instrumental)** [13] [ ]
(12"+=)(cd-s+=) *(HAND 9 T/CD)* – ('A'vocal 12"mix) / ('A'-Dervish overdrive mix) / ('A'-Andrew Weatherall mix) / ('A'-Dust Brothers mix).
(12") *(HAND 9R)* – ('A'remixes).
Jan 95. (cd/c/d-lp) *(HAND CD/MC/LP 2/+D)* **LEFTISM** [3] [ ]
– Release the pressure / Afro-left / Melt / Song of life / Original / Black flute / Space shanty / Inspection (check one) / Storm 3000 / Open up / 21st century poem. *(iss.Apr95, 3x12"+=) (HANDLP 2T)*– Half past dub. *(cd w/ bonus disc)* – Afro-left (Afro-ride) / Release the pressure (release one) / Original (live dub) / Filter fish / Afro-left (Afro-Central) / Release the pressure (release four).

— Below single as featured TONI HALLIDAY (ex-CURVE) on vocals

Mar 95. (c-ep/cd-ep; as LEFTFIELD & HALLIDAY) *(HAND 18 MC/CD)* **ORIGINAL / ('A'-live mix) / ('A'jam mix) / FILTER FISH** [18] [-]
(12"ep) *(HAND 18T)* – ('A'-Drift version) – repl. ('A'live)
Jul 95. (12"ep/c-ep/cd-ep; LEFTFIELD featuring DJUM DJUM) *(HAND 23 T/MC/CD)* **AFRO-LEFT EP** [22] [ ]
– Afro left / Afro ride / Afro sol / Afro central.
Jan 96. (c-s) *(HAND 29MC)* **RELEASE THE PRESSURE (remix 96 vocal): RELEASE ONE / RELEASE TWO** [13] [ ]
(12"+=) *(HAND 29T)* – Release four.
(cd-s++=) *(HAND 29CD)* – Release three.

LEGENDARY PINK DOTS

Formed: London, England . . . late 1980 by EDWARD KA-SPEL and PHILIP KNIGHT (aka THE SILVERMAN). They released their debut album, 'BRIGHTER NOW', for the Birmingham-based indie label, 'Phaze', but moved to The Netherlands in 1985, after 'THE TOWER' album was neglected. Signing to Belgium's 'Play It Again Sam' the same year, they issued the first of several albums, 'FACES IN THE FIRE'. Around the same time, KA-SPEL moonlighted as a solo artist, releasing the first of many albums, 'LAUGH CHINA DOLL'. He also collaborated with SKINNY PUPPY on their TEARGARDEN project. Various personnel came and went, and in the 90's they came up with their best efforts to date, 'THE MARIA DIMENSION' and 'THE SHADOW WEAVER'. The latter was promoted by a US tour, after having previously been prevented due to the "lack of artistic merit" rule! • **Style:** Experimental exploratory electro-psychedelic outfit, influenced by FAUST or CAN backed by HILLAGE or BARRETT-inspired KA-SPEL. • **Songwriters:** Group.

Recommended: THE TOWER (*7) / STONE CIRCLES (*7) / THE MARIA DIMENSION (*8) / THE SHADOW WEAVER (*7) / 9 LIVES TO WONDER (*7)

EDWARD KA-SPEL (as D'ARCHANGEL) – vocals, instruments / **PHILIP KNIGHT** (as THE SILVERMAN) – keyboards, tapes, samples

Phaze / not issued

Jan 82. (lp) *(IPNER 1)* **BRIGHTER NOW** [ ] [-]
– Red castles / Louder after six / The wedding / Apocalypse then / Legacy / City ghosts / Hanging gardens / Soma bath / Premonition four. *(re-iss.Jun86 on 'Terminal Kaleidoscope'; TK 001)*

— added **ROLAND CALLOWAY** (as PRUUMPTJE JUSTE) – bass / **STRET MAJEST** – guitars / **APRIL ILIFFE** – vocals, keyboards

Aug 83. (lp) *(PHA 2)* **CURSE** [ ] [-]
– Love puppets / Wallpurges night / Lisa's party / Arzhklahh Olgevezh / Pruumptje kurss / Waving at the aeroplanes / Hiding / Doll's house / The palace of love / Stoned obituary. *(re-iss.Dec86 on 'Terminal Kaleidoscope'; TK 002) (cd-iss.Aug88; TK 002CD)*

— added **PAT PAGANINI** (aka WRIGHT) – violin, keyboards, vocals

May 84. (lp) *(PHA 3)* **THE TOWER** [ ] [-]
– Black zone / Break day / Tower one / Vigil-anti / A lust for powder / Poppy day / Tower two / Astrid / Rope and glory / Tower three / Tower four / Tower five. *(cd-iss.Aug88 with 'BRIGHTER NOW' on 'Terminal Kaleidoscope'; TK 003CD)*

Ding Dong / not issued

Jan 85. (lp) *(DDD 3333)* **THE LOVERS** [-] [-] Dutch
– MMMmmmmmmmmmm / Geisha mermaid / The heretic / Jungle / The lovers (part 1) / Silverture / Flowers for the silverman / The lovers (part 2). *(cd-iss.1990 on 'Play It Again Sam'+=; CDBIAS 156)*– Curious guy / Premonition 16.

Play It Again Sam / S.P.V.

Jun 84. (lp) *(BIAS 01)* **FACES IN THE FIRE** [ ] [-]
– Blasto / Love in a plain brown envelope / Sleeso / Neon gladiators / Kitto / Eight minutes to live. *(cd-iss.Aug88; CDBIAS 001)*

— added **GRAHAM WHITEHEAD** –

Sep 85. (d-lp) *(BIAS 12)* **ASYLUM** [ ] [-]
– Echo police / Gorgon Zola's baby / Fifteen flies in the marmalade / Femme mirage / The hill / Demonism / Prisoner / So gallantly screaming / I am the way, the truth, the light / Agape / Golden dawn / The last straw / A message from our sponsor / Go ask Alice / This could be the end. *(cd-iss.Mar88; CDBIAS 012)*

— added **HANS MEYER** – saxophone, flute, electronics / **BOB PISTOOR** – guitar, bass (to KA-SPEL, THE SILVERMAN)

Aug 86. (12") *(BIAS 030)* **CURIOUS GUY. / PREMONITION 16** [ ] [-]

Nov 86. (lp) *(BIAS 041)* **ISLAND OF JEWELS** [ ] [-]
– Tower six / The red and the black / The dairy / Emblem parade / Jewel on an island / Rattlesnake arena / The shock of contact / Jewel in the crown / Our lady in chambers / Our lady in Kharki / Our lady in darkness / The guardians of Eden. *(cd-iss.1988; CDBIAS 041)*

Oct 87. (12"ep) *(BIAS 074)* **UNDER GLASS. / THE LIGHT IN MY LITTLE GIRL'S EYES / THE PLASMA TWINS** [ ] [-]

Nov 87. (cd/lp) *(CD+/BIAS 080)* **ANY DAY NOW** [ ] [ ]
– Casting the runes / A strychnine kiss / Laguna beach / The gallery / Neon mariners / True love / The peculiar funfair / Waiting for the cloud / Cloud zero / Under glass / The light in my little girl's eyes / The plasma twins.

Nov 88. (lp) *(BIAS 101)* **STONE CIRCLES** (compilation) [ ] [-]
– Love puppets / Black zone / Golden dawn / Curious day / The hanging gardens / Fifteen flies / Our lady in darkness / Apocalypse / Gladiators (version). *(cd-iss.Apr89; CDBIAS 101)*

Jul 89. (cd/c/lp) *(CD/C+/BIAS 103)* **THE GOLDEN AGE** [ ] [-]

Oct 89. (12"ep/cd-ep) *(BIAS 109/+CD)* **BLACK-LIST. / METHODS / OUR LADY OF CERVETORI** [ ] [-]

1989. (cd/lp) **GREETINGS 9** [ ] [-]

— (above issued for 'Soleilmoon')

Feb 90. (12"ep/cd-ep) *(BIAS)* **PRINCESS COLDHEART / THE PLEASURE PALACE. / THE COLLECTOR / C.V.A.** [ ] [-]

Mar 90. (cd/c/lp) *(CD/C+/BIAS 149)* **THE CRUSHED VELVET APOCALYPSE** [ ] [ ]
– I love you in your tragic beauty / Green gang / Hellsville / Hellowe'en / The safe way / Just a lifetime / he death of Jack The Ripper / New tomorrow. *(cd+=)*– Princess Coldheart / The pleasure palace / The collector / C.V.A.

— **KA-SPEL, KNIGHT + PISTOOR** added **NIELS VAN HOORNBLOWER** – wind, bass

Mar 91. (cd/lp) *(CD+/BIAS 184)* **THE MARIA DIMENSION** [ ] [ ]
– Disturbance / Pennies for Heaven / The third secret / The grain kings / The ocean cried "blue murder" / Belladonna / A space between / Evolution. *(cd w/free cd-ep+=)*– I DREAM OF GEANNIE / LITTLE OYSTER / SHE GAVE ME AN APPLE / STIRRED BUT NOT SHAKEN / WHERE NO MAN *(cd+=)*– Cheraderama / Lilith / Fourth secret / Expresso noir / Home / Crushed velvet.

Sep 92. (cd) *(BIAS 225CD)* **SHADOW WEAVER** [ ] [ ]
– Zero zero / Guilty man / Ghosts of unborn children / City of needles / Stitching time / Twilight hour / Key to heaven / Laughing guest / Prague Spring / Leper colony.

— **RYAN MOORE** – bass (of TEARGARDEN) repl. PISTOOR

— added **MARTYN DE KLEER** – guitar

Mar 93. (cd) *(BIAS 236CD)* **MALACHAI** (Shadow Weaver pt.2) [ ] [ ]
– Joey the canary / Kingdom of the flies / Encore une fois / Wildlife estate / Pavane / Window of the world / On the boards / We bring the day / Paris 4 a.m.

— with drummer **CEVIN KEY** (of SKINNY PUPPY)

Mar 94. (cd) *(BIAS 280CD)* **NINE LIVES TO WONDER** [ ] [ ]
– Madame Guillotine / On another shore / Softly softly / Crumbs on the carpet / Hotel Z / Oasis Malade / A crack in melancholy time / Siren / The angel trail / Nine shades to a circle / A terra firma welcome.

Terminal Kaleidoscope / not issued

1994. (ltd-cd) **FOUR DAYS** [ ] [-]

1995. (d-cd) **CHEMICAL PLAYSCHOOL VOLS 8/9** [ ] [-]
– A triple moon salute / etc

Staalplaat / not issued

Sep 95. (cd) *(STCD 099)* **FROM HERE YOU'LL WATCH THE WORLD GO BY** [ ] [-]
– A velvet resurrection / Friend / etc

Soleilmoon / not issued

1995. (cd) **REMEMBER ME THIS WAY** [ ] [-]

– compilations, etc –

on 'Play It Again Sam' unless mentioned otherwise

Jul 83. (cd) *Third Man Tapes; (TMT 08)* **BASILISK** [ ] [-]

Nov 88. (lp) *Materiali Sonori; (MASO 70009)* **LEGENDARY PINK DOTS** [-] [-] Italy

1989. (3xlp-box/d-cd) *(BIAS 834/+CD)* **THE LEGENDARY PINK BOX** [ ] [-]

1996. (cd) *Terminal Kaleidoscope;* **PRAYER FOR ARCADIA** [ ] [-]

Aug 96. (cd) *(BIAS 325CD)* **CANTA MIENTRAS PUEDAS** ('90–'95) [ ] [-]
– Belladonna / I love you in your tragic beauty / Green gang / Princess coldheart / Disturbance / The grain kings / Prague spring / A triple moon salute / Joey the canary / Siren / The angel trail / A velvet resurrection (version) / Friend (version).

May 97. (cd) *R.O.I.R.; (RUSCD 8231)* **UNDER TRIPLE MOONS** (very early material) [ ] [-]

EDWARD KA-SPEL

with **PATRICK Q. WRIGHT** – violin, keyboards, vocals / **PATRICK WRIGHT** – guitars, keyboards

In-Phaze / not issued

Jun 84. (12") *(HAZ 6)* **DANCE, CHINA DOLL. /** [ ] [-]

Sep 84. (lp) *(PHA 6)* **LAUGH CHINA DOLL – NOTHING ELSE** [ ] [-]
– Lilith's daughter / Eye contact / Lady sunshine / Find the lady / Requiem / Suicide pact / Paradise then / Irrational anthem / Lisa's funeral / The glass moved by itself / Atomic roses. *(cd-iss.Jan90 on 'Licensed'; LD 894) (cd re-iss.Sep95 on 'Staalplaat'; STCD 090)*

— now with **LADY SUNSHINE** (EDWARD's wife ELKE KA-SPEL) – vocals / **HERO WOUTERS** – keyboards / **NEEL HOLST** – saxophone / **MATTHIEU KEIZER** – percussion

Scarface / not issued

Aug 85. (lp) *(FACE 13)* **EYES! CHINA DOLL** [ ] [-]
– Mirror soul / Avengelist / God in a cupboard / Blowing bubbles (part 2) / Six cats on a dead man's chest / "Joey" – the video / The char char / Intermezzo / Hotel Blanc.

— with **STAPLETON + SUNSHINE + WRIGHT**(latter as PAGANINI)

Torso / not issued

Mar 86. (lp) *(TORSO 33-013)* **CHYCKK CHINA DOLL** [-] [-] Dutch
– Lines / The infinity waltz / Prelude for a splash / The price of salvation / Chyekk 1 / Lisa's christening / Chyekk 2 / Beautiful naked / Klazh, Tristurr / Lisa's resurrection / The power, the power / The glory, the glory. *(cd-iss.Nov88; TORSO CD013)*

Play It Again Sam / not issued

1989. (lp) **PERHAPS WE'LL ONLY SEE A THIN BLUE LINE** [ ] [-]

SPV / not issued

Oct 91. (cd) *(TM 92671)* **TANITH & THE LION TREE** [ ] [-]

Staalplaat / not issued

1994. (cd) **LYVV CHINA DOLL** [ ] [-]

1995. (d-cd) **AAZHYDD / CHYCKK CHINA DOLL** [ ] [-]

Soleilmoon / not issued

Feb 96. (cd) *(SOL 29CD)* **DOWN IN THE CITY OF HEARTBREAK & NEEDLES** [ ] [-]

Staalplaat / not issued

Feb 96. (cd) *(1009)* **KHATACLIMICI CHINA DOLL** [ ] [-]

Terminal Kaleidoscope / not issued

1996. (cd) **THE SCRIPTURES OF ILLUMINA** [ ] [-]

SILVERMAN

Terminal Kaleidoscope / not issued

1996. (cd) **DREAM CELL** [ ] [-]

— Also, RYAN MOORE as TWILIGHT CIRCUS released 2 cd's 'IN DUB' (1995) & 'OTHER WORLDS OF DUB' both for 'M Records – Terminal Kaleidoscope'. Other members of LPD collaborated with CHRISTOPH & ANDREAS HEEMANN became MIMIR. Issued 'MIMIR' (1991) & 'MIMYRIAD' (1993) on 'Streamline' See SKINNY PUPPY for TEARGARDEN releases.

LEMON INTERRUPT (see under ⇒ UNDERWORLD)

LFO

Formed: Sheffield, England . . .1990 by MARK BELL and JEZ VARLEY. After two hit singles, 'LFO' and 'WE ARE BACK', they received critical plaudits for the excellent 'FREQUENCIES' album. Early in 1992, they played a rave gig at 'La Grande Arche de la Defence' in Paris. Going to Germany soon after, they recorded with KRAFTWERK and remixed YELLOW MAGIC ORCHESTRA. The group started recording a follow-up album, 'ADVANCE', in 1993, but its release was delayed many times. A single, 'TIED UP', did reach the shops in late 1994, but its length disqualified it from the charts. The album finally made an appearance in early '96, three years late, but worthy of another near Top 40 position. • **Style:** Described as The STONE ROSES of techno, although influences lay in KRAFTWERK or YMO. • **Songwriters:** Duo; except on debut with WILLIAMS. • **Trivia:** Also had solo outings; JEZ as G-MAN and MARK as FAWN, COUNTERPOINT or CLARK. Remixed many others including SABRES OF PARADISE (Tow Truck) / RADIOHEAD (Planet Telex) / BIOSPHERE, ART OF NOISE and AFRIKA BAMBAATAA's re-working of classic 'Planet Rock'.

Recommended: FREQUENCIES (*8) / ADVANCE (*7)

MARK BELL (b. 1972) – electronics / **JEZ VARLEY** (b. 1972) – electronics / augmented live by WILD PLANET: **SIMON HARTLEY + RITCHIE BROOK**

Warp / Tommy Boy

Jul 90. (12") *(WAP 5)* **L.F.O. / TRACK 4** [12] [-]
(12"+=) *(WAP 5R)* – Probe (the Cuba edit).
(cd-s++=) *(WAP 5CD)* – Mentok 1.

Jun 91. (12") *(WAP 14)* **WE ARE BACK. / NURTURE** [47] [-]
(cd-s+=) *(WAP 14CD)* – We are back (remix) / Push.
(12") *(WAP 14R)* – ('A'remixes).

Jul 91. (cd/c/d-lp) *(WARP CD/MC/LP 3)* **FREQUENCIES** [42] [-]
– Intro / L.F.O. / Simon from Sydney / Nurture / Freeze / We are back / Tan ta ra / You have to understand / El ef oh! / Love is the message / Mentok 1 / Think a moment. *(cd+=/c+=)*– Groovy distortion / Track 14. *(cd re-iss.Apr96; same)*

Jan 92. (12"ep/cd-ep) *(WAP 17/+CD)* **WHAT IS HOUSE E.P.** [62] [-]
– Tan ta ra / Mashed potato / What is house / Syndrome.

— MARK BELL joined FEEDBACK (aka WILD PLANET) for a single 'I'm for Real'.

Nov 94. (12"/cd-s) *(WAP 56/+CD)* **TIED UP (Spiritualized Electric Mainline remix). / NURTURE** [ ] [-]
(12") *(WAP 56R)* – ('A'remixes).

Jan 96. (cd/c/d-lp) *(WARP CD/MC/LP 29)* **ADVANCE** [44] [ ]
– Advance / Shut down / Loch Ness / Goodnight Vienna / Tied up / Them / Ultra

schall / Shove piggy shove / Psychodelik / Jason Vorhees / Forever / Kombat drinking.

Richard LLOYD (see under ⇒ TELEVISION)

LONG RYDERS

Formed: Paisley, Los Angeles, California, USA ... Mar'82 out of The UNCLAIMED by SID GRIFFIN, BARRY SKANK, MATT ROBERTS and STEVE WYNN. The latter soon formed his own band, DREAM SYNDICATE, and was superseded by STEPHEN McCARTHY. This aggregation made an ep for 'Moxie', which included the tracks 'Time to Time' and 'Deposition Central'. As The LONG RYDERS (named after Walter Hill film 'The Long Riders), they issued a debut, '10-5-60', on their own 'Jem' label, a distinctive hybrid of jagged garage rock, psychedelia and country. While the band were lumped in with their mates under the catch-all term, 'Paisley Underground', The LONG RYDERS always wore their country influences more proudly. 'NATIVE SONS' (1984), their debut for 'ZIPPO', marked the fruition of that experimentation, a finely hewn tapestry of alternative country which featured GENE CLARK on the keening 'IVORY TOWER'. Heralded by the critics, the band signed to 'Island' in 1985 and recorded a further two albums, 'STATE OF OUR UNION' (1985) and 'TWO FISTED TALES' (1987). More overtly country and lyrically politically pointed than their previous efforts, the latter proved to be the band's swansong and they split the following year. SID GRIFFIN subsequently relocated to London where he concentrated on his band The COAL PORTERS. The man has also helped to keep the 'Cosmic American Music' flame burning by penning a GRAM PARSONS biog and he continues to write for various music mags. • **Style:** Psychedelic turned countryfied rock outfit, similar to The BYRDS or FLYING BURRITO BROTHERS & idol GRAM PARSONS. • **Songwriters:** GRIFFIN-McCARTHY compositions, except YOU'RE GONNA MISS ME (13th Floor Elevators) / I SHALL BE RELEASED + MASTERS OF WAR (Bob Dylan) / DIRTY OLD TOWN (Ewan MacColl) / PRISONERS OF ROCK'N'ROLL (Neil Young) / ANARCHY IN THE UK (Sex Pistols) / PUBLIC IMAGE (P.I.L. w/ STEVE MACK of THAT PETROL EMOTION on vox). • **Trivia:** Will Birch produced them in 1985. SID, STEPHEN + TOM featured on 'Zippo' lp THE LOST WEEKEND by DANNY & DUSTY. They also guested on DREAM SYNDICATE album 'Medicine Show'.

Recommended: 10-5-60 (*6) / NATIVE SONS (*8) / STATE OF OUR UNION (*6)

SID GRIFFIN (b.18 Sep'55, Louisville, Kentucky) – vocals, guitar / **STEPHEN McCARTHY** (b.12 Feb'58, Richmond, Virginia) – steel guitar, vocals, repl. STEVE WYNN (to DREAM SYNDICATE) / **DES BREWER** – bass repl. BARRY SKANK / **MATT ROBERTS** – drums

not issued — P.V.C.

1983. (m-lp) <PVC 5906> **10-5-60** [-] [ ]
– Join my gang / I don't care what's right, I don't care what's wrong / 105-60 / And she rides / Born to believe in you. *(UK-iss.1985 on 'P.V.C.'; PVC 50) (re-iss.Nov85 on 'Zippo'+=; ZANE 004)*– The trip. *(cd-iss.Aug87 on 'Zippo'; CMCAD 31038)*

— **TOM STEVENS** (b.17 Sep'56, Elkhart, Indiana) – drums repl. DON McCALL who had repl. DES BREWER

— **GREG SOWDERS** (b.17 Mar'60, La Jolla, Calif.) – drums, repl. ROBERTS

Zippo — Frontier

Nov 84. (lp) *(ZONG 004) <4606-1>* **NATIVE SONS** [ ] [ ] 1983
– Final wild sun / Still by / Ivory tower / Run Dusty run / (Sweet) Metal revenge / Fair game / Tell it to the judge on Sunday / Too close to the light / Wreck of the 809 / Never get to meet the man / I had a dream. *(cd-iss.Jan88; ZONGCD 003)*– (w/ last m-lp tracks). *(cd re-iss.Jun96 on 'Diablo'; DIAB 821)*

Apr 85. (7") *(ZIPPO 45-2)* **I HAD A DREAM. / TOO CLOSE TO THE LIGHT (Buckskin mix)** [ ] [ ]

Island — Island

Sep 85. (7") *(IS 237)* **LOOKING FOR LEWIS & CLARK. / CHILD BRIDE** [59] [ ]
(d7"+=/10"+=) *(ISD/10IS 237)* – Southside of the story / If I were a bramble and you were a rose.

Oct 85. (lp/c) *(ILPS/ICT 9802) <422842863-1>* **STATE OF OUR UNION** [66] [ ]
– Looking for Lewis & Clark / Lights of downtown / WDIA / Mason-Dixon line / Here comes that train again / Years long ago / Good times tomorrow, hard times today / Two kinds of love / You just can't ride the boxcars anymore / Capturing the flag / State of my union. *(cd-iss.Mar95 on 'Prima'+=; SID 003)*– If I were a bramble and you were a rose / Southside of the story / Child bride / Christmas in New Zealand.

Jun 87. (lp/c/cd) *(ILPS/ICT/CID 9869) <422842864-1>* **TWO FISTED TALES** [ ] [ ]
– Gunslinger man / I want you bad / A stitch in time / The light gets in the way / Prairie fire / Baby's in toyland / Long short story / Man of misery / Harriet Tubman's gonna carry me home / For the rest of my life / Spectacular fall. *(cd re-iss.cd Mar96 on 'Prima'+=; SID 005)*– Ring bells / Time keeps travelling / State of our union (live) / Baby we've all got to go down (live).

Jun 87. (7") *(IS 330)* **I WANT YOU BAD. / RING BELLS** [ ] [ ]
(12"+=) *(12IS 330)* – State of our union.

— The split New Year '88. In Spring '90, GRIFFIN formed country-rock band The COAL PORTERS, who released first album 'REBELS WITHOUT APPLAUSE' in 1992. McCARTHY later appeared in GUTTERBALL with STEVE WYNN. GRIFFIN released a solo album in 1997.

– compilations, others, etc. –

Jan 91. (cd) *Overground; (OVER 16CD)* **METALLIC B.O.** (covers) [ ] [-]
– You're gonna miss me / Route 66 / Brand new headache / Prisoners of rock'n'roll / Dirty old town / Billy Jean / Circle round the sun / Six days on the road / Anarchy in the U.K. / Masters of war / Sandwich man / Blues theme / P.I.L. theme / I shall be released. *(re-iss.Dec94; same)*

May 94. (cd) *Windsong; (WINCD 058)* **BBC RADIO 1 LIVE IN CONCERT (live)** [ ] [-]

LOOP

Formed: Croydon, London, England ... 1986 by ROBRT HAMPSON, who replaced the old rhythm section for JOHN WILLS and NEIL MacKAY. They issued their own releases on 'Head' records, their debut album seeing the light of day in November 1987. A remshackle affair, it nevertheless sowed the seeds for 1989's 'FADE OUT'. Released on the small indie label, 'Cheree', the album showcased the band's queasily churning, endlessly repetitive riffs enveloping HAMPSON's broooding vocals. The sound and atmosphere conjured up nothing less than a hallcinogenic fever and indeed, the band's alleged stated intention was to sonically reproduce an acid trip gone wrong. While their indie compadres were getting 'sorted' during the supposed second summer of love, Loop concerned themselves with darkness and despair and it was obvious they never really fitted with the mood of the times. Their swansong, 'A GILDED ETERNITY', was a distillation of their sound, a hypnotic trip to the scarier side of the human psyche. In early 1991 they finally split with McKAY and WILLS going off to form the rockier HAIR AND SKIN TRADING COMPANY. HAMPSON and newcomer SCOTT DAWSON formed the tripped-out MAIN, releasing 'HYDRA' in November, the first of a series of long E.P.'s and mini-albums that were more sculptured trance-ambient than the SPACEMEN 3/MC5 hybrid of LOOP. Throughout the last half of 1995, their unique 'HERTZ' series demonstrated their continuing break from the rock world. • **Songwriters:** All penned by HAMPSON and group, except MOTHER SKY (Can) / CINNAMON GIRL (Neil Young).

Recommended: ETERNAL – THE SINGLES (*7) / A GILDED ETERNITY (*7) / Main:- FIRMAMENT (*6) / MOTION POOL (*7) / LIGATURE (*6) / FIRMAMENT II (*7)

ROB 'Josh' HAMPSON – vocals, guitar / **JAMES** – guitar / **GLEN** – bass repl. PHILIP KING (ex-SERVANTS) / **JOHN WILLS** – drums (ex-SERVANTS)

Head — not issued

Jan 87. (12"m) *(HEAD 5)* **16 DREAMS. / HEAD ON / BURNING WORLD** [ ] [-]

Jun 87. (7"pic-d) *(HEAD 7L)* **SPINNING. / SPINNING (part 2)** [ ] [-]
(12") *(HEAD 7)* – ('A'side) / Deep hit / I'll take you there.

Nov 87. (lp) *(HEADLP 1)* **HEAVEN'S END** [ ] [-]
– Soundhead / Straight to your heart / Forever / Heaven's end / Too real to feel / Fix to fall / Head on / Carry me / Rocket U.S.A. / Spinning / Brittle head girl. *(cd-iss.Mar88; HEADCD 1) (re-iss.Jul91 & Mar94 on 'Reactor' cd/c/lp ; REACTOR CD/C/LP 001)*

— **NEIL MacKAY** – bass repl. GLEN / **SCOTT DOWSON** – guitar repl. JAMES

Chapter 22 — not issued

Apr 88. (7") *(LCHAP 27)* **COLLISION. / CRAWLING HEART** [ ] [-]
(12"+=) *(12CHAP 27)* – Thief of fire / Thief.

Cheree — not issued

1988. (7"flexi) *(CHEREE 1)* **SOUNDHEAD (live). / (other by The TELESCOPES)** [ ] [-]

— Trimmed to trio, when NEIL departed

Dec 88. (12"m) *(12CHAP 32)* **BLACK SUN. / CIRCLE GRAVE / MOTHER SKY** [ ] [-]

Jan 89. (2x12"lp/lp/c/cd) *(CHAP LLP/LP/C/CD 34)* **FADE OUT** [51] [-]
– Black sun / This is where you end / Fever knife / Torched / Fade out / Pulse / Vision strain / Got to get it over / Collision / Crawling heart / Thief of fire / Thief (motherfucker) / Mother sky. *(cd re-iss.Nov92 on 'Reactor'+=; REACTORCD 004)*– Where you end.

Situation 2 — not isssued

Nov 89. (7") *(SIT 64)* **ARC-LITE (SONAR). / ARC-LITE (RADIATED)** [ ] [-]
(12"+=/cd-s+=) *(SIT 64 T/CD)* – Sunburst.

Jan 90. (cd)(c/2x12"m-lp) *(SITU 27CD)(SIT C/U 27)* **A GILDED ETERNITY** [39] [ ]
– Vapour / Afterglow / The nail will burn / Blood / Breathe into me / From centre to wave / Be here now. *(free-7"w/above)*– SHOT WITH A DIAMOND. / THE NAIL WILL BURN (BURN OUT) *(cd++=)*– Arc-lite (sonar). *(cd re-iss.Sep95 on 'Beggars Banquet'; BBL 27CD)*

— Disbanded early in 1991; WILLS founded HAIR & SKIN TRADING CO (with McKAY)

– compilations, others, etc. –

Aug 88. (lp) *Head; (HEADLP 2)* **THE WORLD IN YOUR EYES** [ ] [-]
– 16 dreams / Head on / Burning world / Rocket U.S.A. / Spinning / Deep hit / I'll take you there / Brittle head girl / Burning prisma / Spinning (spun out). *(re-iss.Jul91 & Mar94 on 'Reactor' cd/c/lp; REACTOR CD/C/LP 002)*

Nov 89. (lp) *Chapter 22; (CHAPLP 44)* **ETERNAL – THE SINGLES 1988** (all Chapter 22 singles) [ ] [-]

May 91. (cd/c/2x12"m-lp) *Reactor; (REACTOR CD/C/LP 003)* **WOLF FLOW** (The John Peel sessions 1987-91) [ ] [-]
– Soundhead / Straight to your heart / Rocket U.S.A. / Pulse / This is where you end / Collision / From centre to wave / Afterglow / Sunburst. *(re-iss.Mar94 on 'Reactor'; same)*

Mar 94. (cd/lp) *Reactor; (REACTOR CD/LP 5)* **DUAL** [ ] [-]

MAIN

were founded by **HAMPSON + DOWSON**

Situation 2 — not issued

Nov 91. (12"ep) *(SIT 83T)* **HYDRA** [ ] [-]
– Flametracer / Time over (dub) / Suspension.

May 92. (12"ep) *(SIT 89T)* **CALM** [ ] [-]

– There is only light / Remain / Feed the collapse / Sever.
(cd-ep+=) *(SITL 89CD)* – Thirst.

—— HAMPSON joined GODFLESH, when MAIN split temporarily.

Beggars Banquet | Beggars Banquet

Jul 93. (12"ep/cd-ep) *(BBQM 18 T/CD)* **DRY STONE FEED** [ ] [-]
– Cypher / Above axis / Blown / Pulled from the water / Dry stone feed.

Aug 93. (cd-ep) *(BBQ 19CD)* **FIRMANENT (cloudscape). / CYPHER (pentode) / HEAT REALM (shortwave) / SUSPENSION (hyaline) / CODE RAYS** [ ] [ ]
(re-iss.Oct94; 12"ep/cd-ep as 'LIGATURE'; BBQM 43 T/CD)

Apr 94. (cd/3x12"m-lp) *(BBQ CD/LP 148)* **MOTION POOL** [ ] [ ]
– VII / Rail / Crater star / Core / Spectra decay / Rotary eclipse / Reformation / Heat realm / VIII / Liquid reflection.

Nov 94. (cd) *(BBQCD 168)* **FIRMAMENT II** – (part IX, X) [ ] [ ]
Jun 95. (cd-ep) *(HERTZ 1)* **CORONA** – (part I & II) [ ] [-]
Aug 95. (cd-ep) *(HERTZ 2)* **TERMINUS** – (part I, II & III) [ ] [-]
Sep 95. (cd-ep) *(HERTZ 3)* **MASER** – (part I, II, III & IV) [ ] [-]
Oct 95. (cd-ep) *(HERTZ 4)* **HALOFORM** – (part I, II, III) [ ] [-]
Nov 95. (cd-ep) *(HERTZ 5)* **KAON** – (part I, II, III, IV & V) [ ] [-]
Dec 95. (cd-ep) *(HERTZ 6)* **NEPER** – (part I, II & III) [ ] [-]
Jan 96. (cd/d-lp) *(HERTZ 16 CD/LP)* **HERTZ** [ ] [-]
– (the 'HERTZ' singles)
Nov 96. (cd) *(BBQCD 179)* **FIRMAMENT 3** [ ] [-]

LOUD FAMILY (see under ⇒ GAME THEORY)

LOW

Formed: Minnesota, USA . . . 1993 by Mormons ALAN SPARHAWK, his wife MIMI PARKER, and ZAK SALLY. Their early efforts, 'I COULD LIVE IN HOPE' and 'LONG DIVISION', were almost ignored, although people pricked up their ears for the low-key classic album, 'THE CURTAIN HITS THE CAST' (1996). They subsequently completed a few UK gigs to promote it later that summer, later cutting a 'Sub Pop' 45, 'VENUS'. • **Style:** Melancholy ambient lo-fi rock. • **Songwriters:** Group except SUNSHINE (Mitchell – Davis) / JACK SMITH (Supreme Dicks) / Transmission (Joy Division).

Recommended: I COULD LIVE IN HOPE (*7) / LONG DIVISION (*6) / THE CURTAIN HITS THE CAST (*7)

ALAN SPARHAWK – vocals, guitar / **ZAK SALLY** (r.n. NICHOLS) – bass / **MIMI PARKER** – drums

Quigley | Quigley

Aug 94. (cd) <*(QUIGD 5)*> **I COULD LIVE IN HOPE** [ ] [ ]
– Words / Fear / Cut / Slide / Lazy / Lullaby / Sea / Down / Drag / Rope / Sunshine.

Vernon Yard | Vernon Yard

1995. (cd) <*YARDCD 014*> **LONG DIVISION** [-] [ ]
– Violence / Below and above / Shame / Throw out the line / Swingin' / See-through / Turn / Caroline / Alone / Streetlight / Stay / Take. *(UK-iss.Feb97; same)*

Hi-Rise | not issued

Feb 96. (cd-ep) *(FLATSCD 24)* **TRANSMISSION EP** [ ] [-]
– Transmission / Bright / Cardine / Hands / Jack Smith / Untitled.

—— NICHOLS repl. by **MICHELETI**

May 96. (cd-ep) *(YARD 022CD)* **FINALLY** [ ] [ ]
– Anon / Tomorrow one / Prisoner / Turning over.

Aug 96. (d-lp/cd) *(YARD/+CD 018)* **THE CURTAIN HITS THE CAST** [ ] [ ]
– Anon / The plan / Over the ocean / Mom says / Coat tails / Standby / Laugh / Lust / Stars gone out / Same / Do you know how to waltz / Dark. *(d-lp+=)*– Prisoner / Tomorrow one.

Nov 96. (7"/cd-s) *(YARD 024/+CD)* **OVER THE OCEAN. / CIOLENCE / BE THERE** [ ] [ ]

Sub Pop | Sub Pop

Jun 97. (7") *(SP 392)* **VENUS. / BOYFRIEND** [ ] [ ]

LUNA (see under ⇒ GALAXIE 500)

M

MAGIC HOUR (see under ⇒ GALAXIE 500)

MAIN (see under ⇒ LOOP)

J. MASCIS (see under ⇒ DINOSAUR JR)

MASSIVE ATTACK

Formed: Bristol, England . . . 1988 by 3-D, MUSHROOM and DADDY G. They had founded their own label, 'Wild Bunch' (named after the loose Bristol collective of DJ's, producers and musicians of which MASSIVE ATTACK were an integral part) five years earlier, later snapped up by Virgin subsidiary 'Circa' in 1990. Their second single, 'UNFINISHED SYMPATHY', although suffering an undignified name change (to MASSIVE) due to the Gulf War, crashed into the top 20. Featuring the velvet tones of Shara Nelson and some luxuriant string arrangements, the song remains timeless and is oft cited as one of the best singles ever made. This was quickly followed up by the classic debut, 'BLUE LINES', which made the UK Top 20 lists in Spring '91. Alongside the aforementioned NELSON, the record featured guests vocalists TRICKY and dub reggae veteran HORACE ANDY. NELSON and TRICKY subsequently departed for solo careers, and all was quiet from the MASSIVE' camp until the Autumn of '94, when they re-surfaced with the NELLEE HOOPER (Soul II Soul)-produced album, 'PROTECTION'. It featured the hits; 'SLY', 'PROTECTION' (with TRACY THORN on vox) and the spooky bass-psyche of 'KARMACOMA' as well as the aching 'BETTER THINGS' (also featuring TRACY THORN). The album was later remixed by London dub producer The MAD PROFESSOR, who gave it a bowel quaking reworking early in '95 as 'NO PROTECTION'. • **Style:** Soulful, Hip hop & urban dub-jungle dance trio, revered by music press and public alike. • **Songwriters:** Group except; BE THANKFUL FOR WHAT YOU'VE GOT (William DeVaughn) / LIGHT MY FIRE (Doors). Sampled JAMES BROWN, PIECES OF A DREAM, YOUNG HOLT TRIO. • **Trivia:** Remixed PETER GABRIEL, LES NEGRESSES VERTES.

Recommended: BLUE LINES (*10) / PROTECTION (*9) / NO PROTECTION (*8; MASSIVE ATTACK V MAD PROFESSOR)

3-D (b. DEL NAJA) – vocals / **MUSHROOM** (b. A.VOWLES) – keyboards / **DADDY-G** (b. MARSHALL) – keyboards

Warners | Warners

Jul 88. (12") *(MASS 001)* **ANY LOVE. / ('A'mix)** [ ] [ ]

—— w / **SHARA NELSON** – vocals / **NELLEE HOOPER** – programmer / arranger

Wild Bunch-Circa | Virgin

Nov 90. (7"/c-s) *(WBR S/C 1)* **DAYDREAMING. / ('A'instrumental)** [ ] [ ]
(12"+=/cd-s+=) *(WBR T/X 1)* – Any love (2).
(12") *(WBR TX 1)* – ('A'-luv it mix) / ('A'-Brixton bass mix) / ('A'-luv it dub).

Feb 91. (7"/c-s; as MASSIVE) *(WBR S/C 2)* **UNFINISHED SYMPATHY. / ('A'-Nellee Hooper mix)** [13] [ ]
(12"/cd-s) *(WBR T/X 2)* – ('A'side) / ('A'-Paul Oakenfold mix) / ('A'-P.O. instrumental) / ('A'instrumental).

—— Below also featured **HORACE ANDY** – vox

Apr 91. (cd/c/2x12"lp) *(WBR CD/MC/LP 1)* **BLUE LINES** [13] [ ]
– Safe from harm / One love / Blue lines / Be thankful for what you've got / Five man army / Unfinished sympathy / Daydreaming / Lately / Hymn of the big wheel. *(re-iss.Sep96; same); hit UK 21)*

May 91. (7"/c-s) *(WBR S/C 3)* **SAFE FROM HARM. / ('A'version)** [25] [ ]
(cd-s+=) *(WBRX 3)* – ('A'-Perfecto mix).
(12") *(WBRT 3)* – ('A'-Perfecto mix) / ('A'dub mix) / ('A'instrumental).

Feb 92. (7"ep/c-ep/12"ep/cd-ep) *(WBR S/C/T/X 4)* **MASSIVE ATTACK** [27] [ ]
– Hymn of the big wheel / Home of the whale / Be thankful / Any love.

—— now w / **TRACY THORN** (Everything But The Girl) **/ NICOLETTE / TRICKY + HORACE ANDY** – vocals. **CRAIG ARMSTRONG** – piano / **CHESTER KAMEN** – guitar / **ROB MERRIL** – drums

Sep 94. (cd/c/lp) *(WBR CD/MC/LP 2)* **PROTECTION** [4] [ ]
– Protection / Karmacoma / Three / Weather storm / Spying glass / Better things / Eurochild / Sly / Heat miser / Light my fire (live).

Oct 94. (c-s/cd-s) *(WBR C/X 5)* **SLY / ('A'mix by UNDERDOG) / ('A'-Mad Professor mix) / ('A'-Tim Simenon mix)** [24] [ ]
(12"s+=/cd-s+=) *(WBR T/DX 5)* – (extra-'A'mix).

Jan 95. (cd-s; by MASSIVE ATTACK with TRACY THORN) *(WBRDX 6)* **PROTECTION / ('A'-J.Swift mix) / THREE (Don T's house mix)** [14] [ ]
(c-s/cd-s) *(WBR C/X 6)* – (1st 2 tracks) / ('A'-Radiation for the nation mix) / ('A'-Eno mix).
(12"+=) *(WBRT 6)* – ('A'-Mad Professor mix).

Feb 95. (cd/c/lp; as MASSIVE ATTACK VS MAD PROFESSOR) *(WBR CD/MC/LP 3)* **NO PROTECTION** [10] [ ]
– Radiation ruling the nation (Protection) / Bumper ball dub (Karmacoma) / Trinity dub (Three) / Cool monsoon (Weather storm) / Eternal feedback (Sly) / Moving dub (Better things) / I spy (Spying glass) / Backward sucking (Heat miser).

Mar 95. (12"ep) *(WBRT 7)* **KARMACOMA. / ('A'-Napoli trip mix) / ('A'-Unkle mix) / BLACKSMITH – DAYDREAMING** [28] [ ]
(cd-ep+=) *(WBRX 7)* – ('A'-Portishead experience mix) / ('A'-Bumper ball mix).
(c-ep++=/cd-ep++=) *(WBR C/DX 7)* – ('A'-Portishead mix).

—— Stop press:- July '97. Returned with a near Top 10 hit single 'RISINGSON', from their forthcoming album.

Eric MATTHEWS (see under ⇒ CARDINAL)

MAZZY STAR

Formed: Santa Monica, Los Angeles, California, USA . . . by veteran of the Paisley circuit, DAVID ROBACK and the young HOPE SANDOVAL. She had met him around six years before, after friend KENDRA SMITH (in RAINY DAY with ROBACK), had introduced them. She joined ROBACK's outfit OPAL, but after a tour, they split in 1987, only to re-form as MAZZY STAR at the beginning of '89. The results came out in 1990 as 'SHE HANGS BRIGHTLY', and surprised many who thought anything new in dark psychedelia could not be surpassed. In 1993, their second album 'SO TONIGHT THAT I MIGHT SEE' cracked the US Top 50, and paved the way for a gorgeously languid hit single, 'FADE INTO YOU'. • **Style:** Part acoustic psychedelic / part melancholy folk rock outfit, with dreamy haunting soft-VELVETS side. • **Songwriters:** SANDOVAL / ROBACK except covers; BLUE FLOWER (Slapp Happy) / I'M GONNA BAKE MY BISCUIT (McCoy) / I'M SAILIN' (Lawler) / FIVE STRING SERENADE (. . . Lee) / GIVE YOU MY LOVIN' (. . . Gomez). RAINY DAY covered I'LL KEEP IT WITH MINE (Nico) / SLOOP JOHN B. (Beach Boys) / I'LL BE YOUR MIRROR (Velvet Underground). • **Trivia:** HOPE SANDOVAL guested on The JESUS & MARY CHAIN's 1994 single 'SOMETIMES ALWAYS'.

Recommended: SO TONIGHT THAT I MIGHT SEE (*8) / SHE HANGS BRIGHTLY (*8)

RAINY DAY

DAVID ROBACK – guitar, vocals, piano, bass (ex-RAIN PARADE) / **WILL GLENN** – violin, cello (of RAIN PARADE) / **MICHAEL QUERICO** – vocals, bass, guitar (of THREE O'CLOCK) / **MATT PIUCCI** – guitar (of RAIN PARADE) / **KENDRA SMITH** – bass, vocals + **KARL PRECODA** – guitar + **DENNIS DUCK** – drums (3 of DREAM SYNDICATE) / **ETHAN JAMES** – keyboards / + **SUSANNA HOFFS** + **VICKI PETERSON** – backing vocals (of BANGLES)

Rough Trade / Llama

Apr 84. (lp) *(ROUGH 70) <E-1024>* **RAINY DAY** [ ] [ ]
– I'll keep it with mine / John Riley / Flying on the ground is wrong / Sloop John B. / Holocaust / On the way home / I'll be your mirror / Rainy day, dream away.

Jun 84. (7") *(RT 140)* **I'LL KEEP IT WITH MINE. / HOLOCAUST** [ ] [ ]

OPAL

DAVID ROBACK / + KENDRA SMITH – bass

One Big Guitar

1986. (12"ep) *(OBG 002T)* **NORTHERN LINE. / EMPTY BOTTLES / SOUL GIVER** [ ] [ ]

— split but left compilation below . . .

— when KENDRA left ROBACK, he introduced friend **HOPE SANDOVAL** – vocals, guitar (ex-GOING HOME)

Rough Trade / not issued

Sep 87. (lp; w-drawn) **HAPPY NIGHTMARE BABY** [-] [-]

Nov 89. (cd/c/lp) *(CD/C+/ROUGH 128)* **EARLY RECORDINGS** [ ] [-]
– Empty box blues / She's a diamond / My only friend / Empty bottles / Grains of sand / Brigit on Sunday / Northern line / Strange delight / Fell from the sun / Harriet Brown / Lullabye / All souls. *(cd+=)–* Hear the wind blow.

MAZZY STAR

— **ROBACK + SANDOVAL** added guest drummer **CLAY ALLISON**

Rough Trade / Rough Trade

Apr 90. (cd/c/lp) *(CD/TC+/R 158)* **SHE HANGS BRIGHTLY** [ ] [ ]
– Halah / Blue flower / Ride it on / She hangs brightly / I'm sailin' / Give you my lovin' / Be my angel / Taste of blood / Ghost highway / Free / Before I sleep. *(re-iss.May93 + Sep94 on 'Capitol' cd/c; CD/TC EST 2196)*

Capitol / Capitol

Oct 93. (cd/c/lp) *(CD/TC+/EST 2206) <98253>* **SO TONIGHT THAT I MIGHT SEE** [68] [36]
– Fade into you / Bells ring / Mary of silence / Five string serenade / Blue light / She's my baby / Unreflected / Wasted / Into dust / So tonight that I might see. *(re-iss.Jun94; same)*

Aug 94. (cd-s) *(CDCL 720)* **FADE INTO YOU / BLUE FLOWER / I'M GONNA BAKE MY BISCUIT** [48] [44]
(10") *(10CL 720)* – ('A'side) / Five string serenade / Under my car / Bells ring (acoustic).

— The track 'TELL ME NOW' featured in the film 'Batman Forever' and the was on B-side of U2's 'Hold Me, Kiss Me, Kill Me!'.

Oct 96. (7"/cd-s) *(CL/CDCLS 781)* **FLOWERS IN DECEMBER. / TELL YOUR HONEY / HAIR AND SKIN** [40] [ ]
(cd-s) *(CDCL 781)* – ('A'side) / Ride it on (live) / Had a thought.

Nov 96. (cd/c) *(CD/TC+/EST 2288)* **AMONG MY SWAN** [57] [68]
– Disappear / Flowers in December / Rhymes of an hour / Cry cry / Take everything / Still cold / All your sisters / I've been let down / Roseblood / Happy / Umbilical / Look on down from the bridge.

MEAT PUPPETS

Formed: Tempe, Phoenix, Arizona, USA . . . 1980 by brothers CURT and CRIS KIRKWOOD. They were soon snapped up by rising US indie label 'SST' in 1981, after a debut on their own label. Their first recording for the company, 'MEAT PUPPETS 1' (1982), was a demanding blast of howling noise and twisted country that barely hinted at the compelling sound they'd invent with the follow-up 'MEAT PUPPETS II' (1983). A hybrid of mystical GRATEFUL DEAD-like psychedelia that short-fused hardcore punk rock and the country-boy slur of CRIS, the record was the blueprint for most of their subsequent output. 'UP ON THE SUN' (1985) was slightly more polished and saw the band garner snowballing critical acclaim. By the release of 'MIRAGE' (1987), the band had fully realised their desert-rock vision with a collection of weather beaten, psychedelic country classics; tracks like 'BEAUTY' and 'CONFUSION FOG' rank among the MEAT PUPPET's best. Yet the record failed to sell and the band returned to a rawer, ZZ TOP-influenced sound on 'HUEVOS'. This album, together with the more mainstream 'MONSTERS' (1989) and continuing critical praise led to a deal with 'London'. Their major label debut, 'FORBIDDEN PLACES' (1991) was accomplished but lacked the high-noon intensity of their earlier work. After a step-up from KURT COBAIN (see below), the raw 'NO JOKE' (1995) album at last saw The MEAT PUPPETS reaping some financial rewards, sales of the album going on to break the half million mark. • **Songwriters:** Most by CURT, some with CRIS or DERRICK. Covered TUMBLIN' TUMBLEWEEDS (Bob Nolan). • **Trivia:** On 18 Nov'93, CURT & CRIS guested with NIRVANA's on an unplugged MTV spot. The tracks they performed were 'PLATEAU', 'OH ME' & 'LAKE OF FIRE'.

Recommended: UP ON THE SUN (*8) / MONSTERS (*8) / TOO HIGH TO DIE (*7) / FORBIDDEN PLACES (*6) / MIRAGE (*9)

CURT KIRKWOOD (b.10 Jan'59, Amarillo, Texas) – guitar, vocals / **CRIS KIRKWOOD** (b.22 Oct'60, Amarillo) – vocals, bass, rhythm guitar / **DERRICK BOSTROM** (b.23 Jun'60, Phoenix) – drums

not issued / World Inv.

Sep 81. (7"ep) **IN A CAR / BIG HOUSE. / DOLFIN FIELD / OUT IN THE GARDINER / FOREIGN LAWNS** [-] [ ]
(cd-ep iss.Nov88 on 'S.S.T.'; SST 044CD)

S.S.T. / S.S.T.

Jan 82. (m-lp) *<SST 009>* **MEAT PUPPETS I** [-] [ ]
– Reward / Love offering / Blue green god / Walking boss / Melons rising / Saturday morning / Our friends / Tumblin' tumbleweeds / Milo, Sorghum and maize / Meat puppets / Playing dead / Litterbox / Electromud / The goldmine. *(re-iss.May93 lp/c/cd; SST 009/+C/CD)*

Apr 84. (lp) *<(SST 019)>* **MEAT PUPPETS II** [ ] [ ] 1983
– Split myself in two / Magic toy missing / Lost plateau / Aurora Borealis / We are here / Climbing / New gods / Oh, me / Lake on fire / I'm a mindless idiot / The whistling song. *(re-iss.May93 lp/c/cd; SST 019/+C/CD)*

Apr 85. (lp) *<(SST 039)>* **UP ON THE SUN** [ ] [ ]
– Up on the Sun / Maiden's milk / Away / Animal kingdom / Hot pink / Swimming ground / Bucket head / Too real / Enchanted pork fist / Seal whales / Two rivers / Creator. *(cd-iss.Sep87; SST 039CD) (re-iss.May93 cd/c; SST 039 CD/C)*

Aug 86. (m-lp) *<(SST 049)>* **OUT MY WAY** [ ] [ ]
– She's hot / Out my way / Other kinds of love / Not swimming ground / Mountain line / Good golly Miss Molly. *(cd-iss.Sep87; SST 049CD) (re-iss.May93 cd/c; SST 049 CD/C)*

Apr 87. (lp/cd) *<(SST 100/+CD)>* **MIRAGE** [ ] [ ]
– Get on down / Love your children forever / Liquery / Confusion fog / Look at the rain / I am a machine / Quit it / Beauty / etc.**** *(re-iss.May93 cd/c; SST 100 CD/C)*

Oct 87. (lp/cd) *<(SST 150/+CD)>* **HEUVOS** [ ] [ ]
– Paradise / Look at the rain / Bad love / Sexy music / Crazy / Fruit / Automatic mojo / Dry rain / I can't be counted on at all. *(re-iss.May93 cd/c; SST 150 CD/C)*

Oct 87. (12") *<(PSST 150)>* **I CAN'T BE COUNTED ON AT ALL. / PARADISE** [ ] [ ]

Oct 89. (lp/cd) *<(SST 253/+CD)>* **MONSTERS** [ ] [ ]
– Attacked by monsters / Light / Meltdown / In love / The void / Touchdown king / Party till the world obeys / Flight of the fire weasel / Strings on your heart / Like being alive.

Nov 90. (d-lp/cd) *<(SST 265/+CD)>* **NO STRINGS ATTACHED** (compilation) [ ] [ ]
– Big house / In a car / Tumblin' tumbleweeds / Reward / The whistling song / New gods / Lost / Lake of fire / Split myself in two / Up on the Sun / Swimming ground / Maiden's milk / Bucket head / Out my way / Confusion fog / I am a machine / Quit it / Beauty / Look at the rain / I can't be counted on at all / Automatic mojo / Meltdown / Like being alive / Attacked by monsters.

London / London

Nov 91. (cd/c/lp) **FORBIDDEN PLACES** [ ] [ ]
– Sam / Nail it down / This day / Open wide / Another Moon / That's how it goes / Whirlpool / Popskull / No longer gone / Forbidden places / Six gallon pie.

Mar 94. (cd/c/lp) *(828484-2/-4/-1)* **TOO HIGH TO DIE** [ ] [62]
– Violet eyes / Never to be found / We don't exist / Severed goddess head / Flaming heart / Shine / Backwater / Roof with a hole / Station / Things / Why / Evil love / Comin' down / Lake of fire.

Jul 94. (c-s/cd-s) **BACKWATER. / ?** [ ] [47]

Oct 95. (cd/c) *(828665-2/-4)* **NO JOKE!** [ ] [ ]
– Scum / Nothing / Head / Taste of the sun / Vampires / Predator / Poison arrow / Eyeball / For free / Cobbler / Inflamable / Sweet ammonia / Chemical garden.

MERCURY REV

Formed: Buffalo, New York, USA . . . 1988 by JONATHAN DONAHUE, DAVID BAKER, SEAN MACKIOWIAK, DAVE FRIDMANN, JIMMY CHAMBERS and SUZANNE THORPE, who claimed they had all met while attending a psychiatric hospital. Admittedly, their sound was certainly deliciously deranged enough for this explanation of their secret history. Just over two years of rehearsals passed, before they finally surfaced with the mini-lp 'YERSELF IS STEAM'. Perhaps the most immaculate marriage of searing noise and crystalline pop ever commited to vinyl, it was given a resounding thumbs-up by the British press and record buying public alike. After a hypnotic appearance at the Reading Festival in August 1991, the record was re-issued. Later that year, an EP, 'CAR WASH HAIR' was recorded with DEAN WAREHAM (of GALAXIE 500), although their volatile infighting led to break-up rumours. These were soon silenced when they were snapped up by 'Beggars Banquet' and in mid- '93, they unleashed a follow-up album, 'BOCES', its self-indulgent beauty nudging the record into the UK Top 50 lists. The following year, a single, 'EVERLASTING ARM', appeared, but the band were constantly at each others throats and it was clear their days were numbered. In 1995, their last great, although more accessible album, 'SEE YOU ON THE OTHER SIDE', drew the curtains on another wasted band. • **Style:** Freaky guitar-angst rock outfit, mixing psychedelia, noise, film dialogue and exhilirating experimentation, only previously matched by The FLAMING LIPS. Other indie influences were apparent (i.e. BIRTHDAY PARTY, STUMP, VERY THINGS & MY BLOODY VALENTINE). • **Songwriters:** Group penned, except IF YOU WANT ME TO STAY (Sly Stone) / SHHH – PEACEFUL (Miles Davis). • **Trivia:** ALAN VEGA (ex-Suicide) appeared on their 1994 single 'EVERLASTING ARM'.

Recommended: YERSELF IS STEAM (*9) / BOCES (*7) / SEE YOU ON THE OTHER SIDE (*8)

DAVID BAKER – vocals / **JONATHAN DONAHUE** – vocals, guitar / **SEAN 'Grasshopper' MACKIOWIAK** – guitar / **DAVID FRIDMANN** – bass / **JIMMY CHAMBERS** – drums / **SUZANNE THORPE** – woodwind

Mint Films Mint Films

Feb 91. (m-cd/m-c/m-lp) *(MINT CD/C/LP 4)* **YERSELF IS STEAM**
– Space patrol / Uh . . . . . . it's out there / I better (let my pants back on / My mom is coming over. *(re-iss.Sep91)*

Nov 91. (12"ep/cd-ep) *(MINT 5 T/CD)* **CAR WASH HAIR (the bee's chasing me) Full pull / CHASING A BEE (demo) / CONEY ISLAND CYCLONE (demo)**

Rough Trade not issued

Apr 92. (7") *(45REV 6)* **IF YOU WANT ME TO STAY. / THE LEFT-HANDED RAYGUN OF PAUL SHARITS (RETIREMENT JUST LIKE THAT)** -

Beggars Banquet Columbia

Nov 92. (12"/cd-s) *(BBQ 1/+CD)* **CHASING A BEE. / CONEY ISLAND CYCLONE**

Nov 92. (cd/c/lp) *(BBQ CD/MC/LP 125)* **MERCURY REV** (compilation)
– If you want me to stay / Shhh – Peaceful – Very sleepy rivers / Frittering / Coney Island cyclone / Car was hair / Syringe mouth / Blood on the moon / Chasing a girl (inside a car). *(w/free cd+=)* **LEGO MY EGO** – Chasing a bee / Syringe mouth / Coney Island cyclone / Blue and black / Sweet oddysee of a commercial t' th' center of yer heart / Frittering / Continuous trucks and thunder under a mother's smile / Very sleepy rivers.

Mar 93. (10"/cd-s) *(BBQ 5 T/CD)* **THE HUM IS COMING FROM HER. / SO THERE (with ROBERT CREELY)**

May 93. (7") *(BBQ 14)* **SOMETHING FOR JOEY. / THREE SPIDER'S EGGS (Live)**
(12"+=) *(BBQ 14/+T)* – Suzanne peels out.
(cd-s++=) *(BBQ 14CD)* – Noise. *(re-iss.Jul93)*

Jun 93. (cd/c/lp) *(BBQ CD/MC/LP 140)* **BOCES** 43
– Meth of a rockette's kick / Trickle down / Bronx cheer / Boys peel out / Downs are feminine balloons / Something for Joey / Snorry mouth / Hi-speed boats / Continuous drunks and blunders / Girlfren.

— now without BAKER, who became SHADY and released solo album 'WORLD', which included members of SWERVEDRIVER and The BOO RADLEYS

Jun 94. (12"white/cd-s) *(BBQ 37 T/CD)* **EVERLASTING ARM. / DEAD MAN**

May 95. (cd/c/lp)(pic-lp) *(BBQ CD/MC/LP 176)(BBQ 176P)* **SEE YOU ON THE OTHER SIDE**
– Empire state (Sun house in excelsis) / Young man's stride / Sudden ray of hope / Everlasting arm / Racing the tide / Close encounters of the third grade / A kiss from an old flame (a trip to the Moon) / Peaceful night.

— already split late '94. Some were already splintered as HARMONY ROCKETS, who released 1993 single 'SKELETON MAN' and went onto release 1995 album 'PARALYZED MIND OF THE ARCHANGEL VOID' for 'Big Cat'. However, MERCURY REV were to re-surface as a duo (DONAHUE & GRASSHOPPER) in summer of '97. They had signed to RICHARD BRANSON's new 'V2' label and were contacting veterans LEVON HELMS & GARTH HUDSON (The Band), plus ZOOT ROLLO HORN (ex-Captain Beefheart). DONAHUE and MERCURY REV collaborated on CHEMICAL BROTHERS 'Dig Your Own Hole' track 'Private Psychedelic Reel'.

Roger MILLER (see under ⇒ MISSION OF BURMA)

MISSION OF BURMA

Formed: Boston, Massachusetts, USA . . . 1979, from the ashes of The MOVING PARTS by the classically trained ROGER MILLER and CLINT CONLEY. They soon found a further two members, MARTIN SWOPE and PETE PRESCOTT, who supplied the rhythm behind their classic debut 45, 'ACADEMY FLIGHT SONG' in 1980. A mini-lp, 'SIGNALS' was issued in '81, blessing the music world with the seminal 'THAT'S WHEN I REACH FOR MY REVOLVER'. Unfortunately, after an astounding debut album, 'VS.', in 1982, they had to retire, due to MILLER's tinnitus (a hearing disorder). • **Style:** Noisy wall-of-sound breakneck guitar punk-pop, likened to WIRE, HUSKER DU or MC5. MARTIN SWOPE provided loud tapings. • **Songwriters:** CONLEY or MILLER. • **Trivia:** R.E.M. covered 'ACADEMY FLIGHT SONG' for a b-side in 1989, while more recently MOBY charted with 'THAT'S WHEN I REACH FOR MY REVOLVER'.

Recommended: MISSION OF BURMA (*9; 1988 cd)

ROGER MILLER (b.24 Feb'52, Ann Arbor, Michigan) – guitar, vox / **CLINT CONLEY** (b.16 May,55, Indianapolis, Indiana) – bass, vox / **PETE PRESCOTT** (b.26 Oct'57, Nantucket Island, Mass.) – drums (ex-MOLLS) / **MARTIN SWOPE** (b. 1 Jun'55, Ann Arbor) – tapes

not issued Ace Of Hearts

Jun 80. (7") *<AHS 104>* **ACADEMY FLIGHT SONG. / MAX ERNST** -

1981. (m-lp) *<AHS 10006>* **SIGNALS, CALLS, AND MARCHES** -
– That's when I reach for my revolver / Outlaw / Fame and fortune / This is not a photograph / Red / All world cowboy romance.

1982. (lp) **VS.** -
– Forget / Laugh the world away / OK – No way / Secrets / Train / Trem two / New nails / Dead pool / Learn how / Mica / Weatherbox / The ballad of Johnny Burma / Einstein's day / Fun world / That's how I escaped my certain fate / Go fun burn man / 1970.

— split to MILLER's tinnitus, although he did release quieter solo stuff and form BIRDSONGS OF THE MESOZOIC, with SWOPE. PRESCOTT had formed and continued to tour with VOLCANO SUNS (an SST label band who in 1989 released d-lp,cd 'THING OF BEAUTY'; *SST 257)*. CONLEY later produced for YO LA TENGO.

– compilations, etc. –

Nov 85. (lp) *New Rose; (ROSE 76)* **THE HORRIBLE TRUTH ABOUT BURMA**

1987. (m-lp) *Taang!; (TAANG 20)* **MISSION OF BURMA EP** -
(UK cd-iss.Jun92; TAANG 20CD)

1988. (cd) *Rykodisc; <RCD 40072>* **MISSION OF BURMA** -
– Academy fight song / That's when I reach for my revolver / Outlaw / Fame and fortune / This is not a photograph / Red / All world cowboy romance / Forget / Laugh the world away / Ok no way / Secrets / Train / Trem two / New nails / Dead pool / Learn how / Mica / Weatherbox / The ballad of Johnny Burma / Einstein's day / Fun world / That's how I escaped my certain fate / Go fun burn man / 1970. *(re-iss.Jun92 & Mar94 cd/c; RCD4/RACS 0072)*

Mar 89. (lp) *Taang!; (TAANG 24)* **FORGET**
(re-iss.Jan93 lp/cd; TAANG 024/+CD)

Sep 90. (cd) *Emergo; (EM 94081) / Relix; <983608>* **LET THERE BE BURMA**
– Execution / Progress / Playland / House flaming / Eyes of men / Manic incarnation / Anti-aircraft warning / Active in the yard / Hunt again / Smoldering fuselage / Head over head / Forget / This is not a photograph / Peking spring / Dumbells / Dirt / Sing-a-long / He is – she is / Black board / Go fun burn man / Nu disco / Foreign country / Einstein's day.

BIRDSONGS OF THE MESOZOIC

ROGER MILLER – keyboards, percussion, vocals / **MARTIN SWOPE** – tapes, guitar, cymbals / **RICK SCOTT** – organ / **ERIK LINDGREN** – synthesizers (of SPACE NEGROS, ex-FAMILY FUN) / guest **PETE PRESCOTT** – percussion

not issued Ace Of Hearts

1983. (m-lp) *<AHS 1008>* **BIRDSONGS OF THE MESOZOIC EP** -
– Sound valentine / Transformation of Oz / Drift / The orange ocean / Triassic Jurassic, Cretaceous.

not issued Rykodisc

1986. (cd) *<RCD 20073>* **SONIC GEOLOGY** -
– Shiny golden snakes / Ptoccata / Waterwheel / Pulse piece / The rite of spring / The orange ocean / The tyger / Scenes from a . . . / The beat of the Mesozoic (part 1) / International tours / Drift / Final motif / Theme from Rocky and Bullwinkle / The fundamental / Sound valentine / The common sparrow / Lost in the B-zone / Triassic, Jurassic, Cretaceous. *(UK-iss.Apr92; same)*

not issued C.U.N.

1989. (cd) *<RUNE 19>* **FAULTLINE** -
– The true wheelbase / They walk among us / Coco Boudakian / I don't need no crystal ball / Chariots of fire / Magic fingers / Faultline / On the street where you live / Maybe I will / There is no one / Slo-boy / Pterobold / Just say yes.

ROGER MILLER

Fundamental Fundamental

1988. (lp) *(SAVE 054)* **THE BIG INDUSTRY**
– Portrait of a mechanical dog / Boil away / Hammers / Upon this boat in the sea / The age of reason / Groping hands / Manic depression / The big industry / We don't know why.

NO MAN IS ROGER MILLER

S.S.T. S.S.T.

Jul 89. (lp/c/cd) *(SST/+C/CD 243)* **WIN! INSTANTLY!**
– Run water, run water / No man's landing / Calling the animals / Scratch / This is not a photograph / The promised land / The quarry / Renegades / Volumptuous airplane.

1990. (7") *(SST 912)* **DIAMOND BACK. /** -

Sep 90. (lp/c/cd) *(SST/+C/CD 267)* **WHAMON EXPRESS**

1991. (lp/c/cd) *(SST/+C/CD 281)* **HOW THE WEST WAS WON**

— An entirely different NO MAN; the UK one featuring STEVEN WILSON of PORCUPINE TREE released stuff from 1989 onwards (mostly for 'One Little Indian' label).

ROGER MILLER

New Alliance New Alliance

Apr 91. (lp/c/cd) *(NAR/+C/CD 051)* **XYLYL & A WOMAN IN HALF**

Apr 94. (cd) *(NAR 097CD)* **OH, GUITARS ETC**
– We grind open (in) / Meltdown man / Chinatown samba / Firetruck / Cosmic battle / You son of a bitch / War bolts / Fun world reductions / Space is the place / Forest / Kalgastak.

S.S.T. S.S.T.

Oct 94. (cd/c; as ROGER MILLER'S EXQUISITE COMPANY) *(SST 307 CD/C)* **UNFOLD**

Sep 95. (cd/c) *(SST 318 CD/CA)* **ELEMENTAL GUITAR**

MOBY

Born: RICHARD MELVILLE HALL, 11 Sep'65, Darien, Connecticut, USA. After being raised by his middle-class mother, he joined hardcore outfit The VATICAN COMMANDOES, which led to him having a brief stint in the similar FLIPPER. He didn't record anything with the band and moved back to New York to become a DJ, making hardcore techno/dance records under the guise of BRAINSTORM and UHF3, etc. He subsequently became a mixer for The PET SHOP BOYS, ERASURE and MICHAEL JACKSON, before and during his return into solo work in the early 90's. His UK debut, 'GO', hit the Top 10 in October '91, having just breached the charts 3 months earlier. Sampling the 'Twin Peaks' theme, the song was a compelling piece of techno-pop that remains a dancefloor favourite. Little was subsequently heard of him barring a few US imports, although this led to UK semi-indie, 'Mute', taking him on board in mid'93. First up was his near Top 20 single, 'I FEEL IT', beginning a series of hits, albeit sporadic. Early in 1995, his album 'EVERYTHING IS WRONG' had critics lavishing praise on the man for his combination of acid-dance and ambience. In 1996, his 'ANIMAL RIGHTS' follow-up added a new dimension; heavy industrial punk-metal which gave him a new found 'Kerrang' audience. • **Style:** From dance to ambient/techno hardcore and grunge punk. • **Songwriters:** Himself and a few with singer MIMI GOESE 'Into The Blue' + 'When It's Cold I'd Like To Die'. Other singers on 1995 album; ROZZ MOREHEAD / MYIM ROSE / NICOLE ZARAY / KOOKIE BANTON / SAUNDRA WILLIAMS. Samples BADALAMENTI's 'Twin Peaks' on 'GO'. Covered NEW DAWN FADES (Joy Division) / THAT'S WHEN I REACH FOR MY REVOLVER (Mission Of Burma). • **Trivia:** RICHARD is a Christian vegan. In 1992 he remixed JAM & SPOON's club smash 'STELLA', which had sampled his 'GO'. He also provided vox for RECOIL's 1992 album 'Bloodline'. MOBY also remixed B-52's, ESKIMOS AND EGYPT, LFO, FORTRAN 5, ORBITAL, ENO, PET SHOP BOYS + The OTHER TWO.

Recommended: THE STORY SO FAR (*6) / EVERYTHING IS WRONG (*9) / ANIMAL RIGHTS (*8)

MOBY – vocals, keyboards, etc.

Outer Rhythm / Instinct

Jul 91. (12") *(FOOT 15)* **GO (analog mix). / ('A'-Night time mix)/ ('A'-Soundtrack mix)** [46] [ ]
(12") *(FOOT 15R)* – ('A'side) / ('A'-video aux w/ LYNCH & BADALAMENTI) / ('A'-Rain forest mix).
(cd-s) *(FOOT 15CD)* – ('A'side) / ('A'-Low spirit mix) / ('A'-Woodtick mix). *(re-iss.Oct91, hit No.10; same)*

1992. (cd) **MOBY** [-] [ ]

1992. (cd) **AMBIENT** [-] [ ]
– My beautiful blue sky / Heaven / Tongues / J Breas / Myopia / House of blue leaves / Bad days / Piano & string / Sound / Dog / 80 / Lean on me. *(UK-iss.Oct93 on 'Equator Arctic' cd/c/lp; ATLAS CD/MC/LP 002)*

Equator Arctic / Instinct

Jun 93. (c-s) *(AXISMC 001)* **I FEEL IT. / THOUSAND** [38] [ ]
(12"/cd-s) *(AXIS T/CD 001)* – (3-'A'mixes).
(12") *(AXISM 001)* – ('A'remixes).

Aug 93. (cd/c/lp) *(ATLAS CD/MC/LP 001)* **THE STORY SO FAR** [ ] [ ]
– Ah ah / I feel it / Everything / Help me to believe / Go (woodtick mix) / Yeah / Drop a beat (the new version) / Thousand / Slight return / Go (sublimal mix unedited version) / Stream. *(cd+=)*– Mercy.

Mute / Elektra

Sep 93. (c-s) *(CMUTE 158)* **MOVE (YOU MAKE ME FEEL SO GOOD). / ('A'-disco threat mix)** [21] [ ]
(12"/cd-s) *(12/CD MUTE 158)* – ('A'side) / ('A'-Subversion) / ('A'-xtra mix) / ('A'-MK-Blades mix).
(cd-s) *(LCDMUTE 158)* – ('A'side) / All that I need is to be loved / Unloved symphony / Rainfalls and the sky shudders.
(12") *(L12MUTE 158)* – (last track repl. by)- Morning dove.

May 94. (c-s) *(CMUTE 161)* **HYMN – THIS IS MY DREAM (extended) / ALL THAT I NEED IS TO BELOVED (H.O.S. mix)** [31] [ ]
(cd-s+=) *(CDMUTE 161)* – ('A'-European edit) / ('A'-Laurent Garnier mix).
(12") *(12MUTE 161)* – ('A'extended) / ('A'-Laurent Garnier mix) / ('A'-Upriver mix)/ ('A'-Dirty hypo mix).
(cd-s) *(LCDMUTE 161)* – Hymn (alternate quiet version 33 mins).

Oct 94. (c-s) *(CMUTE 173)* **FEELING SO REAL. / NEW DAWN FADES** [30] [ ]
(cd-s+=) *(CDMUTE 173)* – ('A'-Unashamed ecstatic piano mix) / ('A'-Old skool mix).
(cd-s) *(LCDMUTE 173)* – ('A'-Westbam remix) / ('A'-Ray Keith remix) / ('A'dub mix) / Everytime you touch me (remix parts).
(12") *(12MUTE 173)* – ('A'side) / (4-versions from cd's above).

Feb 95. (c-s/7"dinked) *(C+/MUTE 176/+D)* **EVERYTIME YOU TOUCH ME / THE BLUE LIGHT OF THE UNDERWATER SUN** [28] [ ]
(cd-s+=) *(CDMUTE 176)* – ('A'-Beatmasters mix) / ('A'-competition winner; Jude Sebastian mix) / ('A'Freestyle mix).
(cd-s++=) *(LCDMUTE 176)* – ('A'-Uplifting mix).
(12") *(12MUTE 176)* – ('A'-Sound Factory mix) / ('A'-SF dub) / ('A'-Follow me mix) / ('A'-Tribal mix).

Mar 95. (cd/c/d-lp) *(CD/C+/Stumm 130)* **EVERYTHING IS WRONG** [21] [ ]
– Hymn / Feeling so real / All that I need is to be loved / Let's go free / Everytime you touch me / Bring back my happiness / What love? / First cool hive / Into the blue / Anthem / Everything is wrong / God moving over the face of the waters / When it's cold I'd like to die. *(cd/c w/free cd/c) (XLCD/XLC+/Stumm 130)*– Underwater (parts 1-5).

Jun 95. (c-s) *(CMUTE 179)* **INTO THE BLUE / ('A'-Shining mix)** [34] [ ]
(cd-s+=) *(LCDMUTE 179)* – ('A'-Summer night mix) / ('A'-Beatmasters mix).
(12"/cd-s) *(12/CD MUTE 179)* – ('A'-Beastmasters mix) / ('A'-Jnr Vasquez mix) / ('A'-Phil Kelsey mix) / ('A'-Jon Spencer Blues mix).

Jan 96. (cd/c) *(XLStumm 130)* **EVERYTHING IS WRONG – MIXED AND REMIXED** [25] [ ]

— The track 'GOD MOVING OVER THE FACE OF THE WATERS' was used for the Rover 400 TV commercial. Toyota had earlier sampled his 'GO'.

Aug 96. (12") *(12MUTE 184)* **THAT'S WHEN I REACH FOR MY REVOLVER. / ('A'-Rollo & Si Star Bliss mix)** [50] [ ]
(cd-s) *(CDMUTE 184)* – ('A'side) / Lovesick / Displaced / Sway.
(cd-s) *(LCDMUTE 184)* – ('A'side) / Every one of my problems / God moving over the face of the waters (dark mix).

Oct 96. (cd/c/d-lp) *(CD/C+/Stumm 150)* **ANIMAL RIGHTS** [38] [ ]
– Now I let it go / Come on baby / Someone to love / Heavy flow / You / My love will never die / Soft / Say it's all mine / That's when I reach for my revolver / Face it / Living / Love song for my mom. *(cd w/free cd)* **LITTLE IDIOT** (LCDStumm 150) – Degenerate / Dead city / Walnut / Old / A season in Hell / Love song for my mom / The blue terror of lawns / Dead sun / Reject.

Nov 96. (12"ep) *(12MUTE 200)* **COME ON BABY / LOVE HOLE / WHIP IT / GO / ALL THAT I NEED TO BE IS LOVED / HYMN** [ ] [ ]
(cd-ep) *(CDMUTE 200)* – ('A'-Eskimos And Egypt mix) / ('A'-Crystal method mix) / ('A'-Eskimos And Egypt extended).

– compilations, specials, etc

Nov 93. (12") *Mute; (12NEMY 2)* **ALL THAT I NEED IS TO BE LOVED. / (3 other 'A'mixes)** [ ] [-]

Sep 94. (c-s) *Mute; (CNOCAR 1)* **GO (woodtick mix). / ('A'-Low spirit mix)** [ ] [-]
(12"+=) *(12NOCAR 1)* – ('A'-Voodoo chile mix).
(12"+=) *(12LNOCAR 1)* – ('A'-Appathoski mix) / ('A'-Amphemetix mix).
(cd-s+=) *(CDNOCAR 1)* – ('A'-Delirium mix).

Mar 95. (10"ltd.) *Soapbar; (SBR 15)* **FEELING SO REAL (mixes)** [ ] [-]

MOISTBOYZ (see under ⇒ WEEN)

MOJAVE 3 (see under ⇒ SLOWDIVE)

MOLES (see under ⇒ CARDINAL)

Thurston MOORE (see under ⇒ SONIC YOUTH)

MOOSE

Formed: London, England . . . Spring 1990 by KEVIN 'Moose' (his nickname). KEVIN completed the line-up with DAMIEN WARBUTTON and RUSSELL YATES. They quickly signed to 'Hut' (home of SMASHING PUMPKINS) and unleashed their well-received debut EP, 'JACK', early in 1991, before supporting CHAPTERHOUSE. The following year, their series of EP's were broken by a debut album, 'XYZ', its sales unfortunately not enough to prevent the Virgin subsidiary dropping them. However, they charted new territory with 'Play It Again Sam', who issued what would have been their final outing, 'HONEY BEE', but for 1996's return, 'LIVE A LITTLE, LOVE A LOT'. • **Style:** Pioneers of the shoe-gazing fraternity, they were also characterised by their fusing of HUSKER DU and TIM BUCKLEY, also GRAM PARSONS and LED ZEPPELIN! In 1993, they moved away from indie-rock ground to more C&W-tinged folk and heavy soul. • **Songwriters:** McKILLOP on own or with YATES, group music except covers; EVERYBODY'S TALKIN' (Fred Neil). • **Trivia:** The PIXIES' KIM DEAL produced their debut. RUSSELL was also part of STEREOLAB live act in Spring 1991. TIM GANE of said outfit, augmented on stage with bassist MICK (ex-MODERN ENGLISH). McKILLOP also moonlights with SEE SEE RIDER. DOLORES from The CRANBERRIES and ROXANNE from Th' FAITH HEALERS guested on their 1992 MITCH EASTER produced album 'XYZ'.

Recommended: XYZ (*8) / HONEY BEE (*6)

RUSSELL YATES – vocals, guitar / **KEVIN McKILLOP** – guitar / **DAMIEN WARBURTON** – drums

Hut / Caroline

Mar 91. (12"ep/cd-ep) *(HUT T/CD 3)* **THE JACK E.P.** [ ] [ ]
– Jack / Ballad of Adam and Eve / Boy / I'll take tomorrow.

Jun 91. (7") *(HUT 5)* **SUZANNE. / BUTTERFLY COLLECTOR** [ ] [ ]
(12"ep+=/cd-ep+=) **COOL BREEZE** (HUT T/CD 5) – Untitled love song / Speak to me.

— **LINCOLN FONG** – bass repl. MICK CONROY who joined STEREOLAB then formed TREETOP

Nov 91. (7"ep/12"ep/cd-ep) *(HUT/+T/CD 8)* **REPRISE EP** [ ] [ ]
– Last night I fell again / This river will never run dry / Do you remember? / Reprise.

Jan 92. (m-cd) *(HUTCD 11)* **SONNY AND SAM** (1991 ep's) [ ] [ ]

— **RICHARD THOMAS** – drums (ex-JESUS & MARY CHAIN, ex-DIF JUZ) repl. DAMIEN

Aug 92. (7") *(HUT 020)* **LITTLE BIRD (ARE YOU HAPPY IN YOUR CAGE?). / WHERE DO I GO?** [ ] [ ]
(12"+=) *(HUT 020T)* – Theme from Ace Conroy.
(cd-s++=) *(HUT 020CD)* – ZYX.

Sep 92. (cd/c/lp) *(HUT CD/MC/LP 55)* **XYZ** [ ] [ ]
– Soon is never soon enough / I'll see you in my dreams / High flying bird / Screaming / Friends / XYZ / Slip & slide / Little bird / Don't bring me down / Polly / The whistling song / Everybody's talking / Sometimes loving is the hardest thing. (cd+=/c+=/free-7"w-lp)– This river is nearly dry (live).

Cool Badge / not issued

Feb 93. (12"ep/cd-ep) **LIQUID MAKE-UP EP** [ ] [ ]
– I wanted to see you to see if I wanted you / There's a place / Ramon.

— added **ROXANNE STEPHEN, JOE DILWORTH, RUSSELL FONG + STEVEN YOUNG**

Play It Again Sam / not issued

Sep 93. (12"ep/cd-ep) *(BIAS/+CD 254)* **UPTOWN INVISIBLE / CALL IT WHAT YOU WANT, ANYTHING. / NEVERGREEN / TOWER OF CRUMBS** [ ] [ ]

Oct 93. (cd/lp) *(BIAS 260 CD/LP)* **HONEY BEE** [ ] [ ]
– Uptown invisible / Meringue / Mondo cane / You don't listen / Joe Courtesy / Asleep at the wheel / I wanted to see you to see if I wanted you / Around the warm bed / Stop laughing / Dress you the same / Hold on. (lp w /free lp)

Mar 94. (12"ep/cd-ep) *(BIAS 264/+CD)* **BANG BANG EP** [ ] [ ]

– I wanted to see you to see if I wanted you / Welcome to the mind of Mr. Breeders / Following in my own footsteps / Sexy M.O.R. (take your clothes off).

Feb 96. (cd) *(BIAS 320CD)* **LIVE A LITTLE, LOVE A LOT** [ ] [-]
– Play God / The man who hanged himself / First balloon to Nice / Rubdown / Poor man / Eve in a dream / Old man Time / Love on the dole / So much love so little time / Last of the good old days / Regulo 7.

MY BLOODY VALENTINE

Formed: Dublin, Ireland ... 1984 by KEVIN SHIELDS and COLM CUSACK. Late that year, they went to Germany and recorded a mini-lp 'THIS IS YOUR BLOODY VALENTINE', for the small 'Tycoon' records. It was issued the next year, but only 50 copies seemed to emerge (now very rare). They moved to London and soon issued the 'GEEK!' EP for 'Fever'. After more 45's for 'Kaleidoscope' then 'Lazy' (home of The PRIMITIVES), they were transferred to 'Creation' in 1988 by SLAUGHTER JOE FOSTER (ex-TV PERSONALITIES). They finally made the breakthrough in 1990, when the 'GLIDER' EP nearly went Top 40in the UK. The following year, they released their most challenging and inventive track to date in 'TO HERE KNOWS WHEN' from the 'TREMOLO' EP. The song either enveloped you in its blissful noise or you thought it was just out of bloody tune, there was no middle ground. 'Loveless', the lp follow-up, was a revelation. Its undulating noisescapes sounded not-of-this-earth and 'Creation' were saddled with an astronomical studio bill to match, almost going bankrupt as a result. They subsequently signed to 'Island' records, and five years on, fans are still awaiting some product. Their reclusive silence makes The STONE ROSES look prolific, although few doubt their potential to return with a masterpiece. • **Style:** Twangly fuzzy IGGY POP-like beginnings, they progressed into dreamy psychedelia and uncompromising non-rock, with a new concept and language of sound. • **Songwriters:** SHIELDS writes most of material, with words after 1987 by BILINDA. Covered MAP REF 41 (Wire). • **Trivia:** A track 'SUGAR' was given away free with 'The Catalogue' magazine of Feb '89.

Recommended: LOVELESS (*9) / ISN'T ANYTHING (*8) / ECSTASY AND WINE (*7)

KEVIN SHIELDS (b.21 May'63, Queens, New York) – guitar, vocals, occasional bass / **DAVE CONWAY** – vocals / **COLM CUSACK** (b. COLM MICHAEL O'CIOSOIG, 31 Oct'64) – drums / **TINA** – keyboards

Tycoon | not issued

1985. (m-lp) *(ST 7501)* **THIS IS YOUR BLOODY VALENTINE** [-] [-] German
– Forever and again / Homelovin' guy / Don't cramp my style / Tiger in my tank / The love gang / Inferno / The last supper.

— **DEBBIE GOOGE** (b.24 Oct'62, Somerset, England) – bass repl. TINA

Fever | not issued

Apr 86. (12"ep) *(FEV 5)* **GEEK!** [ ] [-]
– No place to go / Moonlight / Love machine / The sandman never sleeps.

Jun 86. (7") *(FEV 5X)* **NO PLACE TO GO. / MOONLIGHT** [ ] [-]

Kaleidoscope Sound | not issued

Oct 86. (12"ep) *(KS 101)* **THE NEW RECORD BY MY BLOODY VALENTINE** [ ] [-]
– Lovelee sweet darlene / By the danger in your eyes / On another rainy Sunday / We're so beautiful.

Lazy | not issued

Feb 87. (7") *(LAZY 04)* **SUNNY SUNDAE SMILE. / PAINT A RAINBOW** [ ] [-]
(12"+=) *(LAZY 04T)* – Kiss the eclipse / Sylvie's head.

— **BILINDA BUTCHER** (b.16 Sep'61, London, England) – vocals, guitar repl. CONWAY

Nov 87. (m-lp) *(LAZY 08)* **ECSTASY** [ ] [-]
– (Please) Lose yourself in me / The things I miss / I don't need you / Clair / (You're) Safe in your sleep / She loves you no less / Strawberry wine / Lovelee sweet darlene.

Nov 87. (12"m) *(LAZY 07)* **STRAWBERRY WINE. / NEVER SAY GOODBYE / CAN I TOUCH YOU** [ ] [-]

Creation | Relativity

Jul 88. (7") *(CRE 055)* **YOU MADE ME REALISE. / SLOW** [ ] [-]
(12"+=) *(CRE 055T)* – Thorn / Cigarette in your bed / Drive it all over me. *(re-iss.Mar90 as cd-ep; CRECD 55)*

Oct 88. (7") *(CRE 061)* **FEED ME WITH YOUR KISSES. / EMPTINESS INSIDE** [ ] [-]
(12"+=) *(CRE 061T)* – I believe / I need no trust. *(re-iss.Mar90 as cd-ep; CRECD 61)*

Nov 88. (lp/cd)(c) *(CRELP 040/+CD)(C-CRELP 040)* **ISN'T ANYTHING** [ ] [ ]
– Soft as snow (but warm inside) / Lose my breath / Cupid come / (When you wake) You're still in a dream / No more sorry / All I need / Feed me with your kiss / Sue is fine / Several girls galore / You never should / Nothing much to lose / I can see it (but I can't feel it). *(free 7"w/ lp)*– INSTRUMENTAL. / INSTRUMENTAL

Creation | Sire

Apr 90. (7"ep/12"ep)(cd-ep) *(CRE 73/+T)(CRESCD 73)* **GLIDER** [41] [ ]
– Soon / Glider / Don't ask why / Off your face.

Feb 91. (7"ep/12"ep)(cd-ep) *(CRE 085/+T)(CRESCD 085)* **TREMOLO** [29] [ ]
– To here knows when / Swallow / Honey power / Moon song.

Nov 91. (cd/lp)(c) *(CRE CD/LP 060)(C-CRELP 060)* **LOVELESS** [24] [ ]
– Only shallow / Loomer / Touched / To here knows when / When you sleep / I only said / Come in alone / Sometimes / Blown a wish / What you want / Soon.

— During there long hiatus, KEVIN SHIELDS contributed (1996) to an album 'Beyond The Pale' by EXPERIMENTAL AUDIO RESEARCH. It also featured SONIC BOOM (ex-SPACEMEN 3), KEVIN MARTIN (of GOD) & EDDIE PREVOST (of AMM).

– compilations, others, etc. –

Feb 89. (lp/cd) *Lazy; (LAZY 12/+CD)* **ECSTASY AND WINE** [ ] [-]
– Strawberry wine / Never say goodbye / Can I touch you / She loves you no less / The things I miss / I don't need you / Safe in your sleep / Clair / You've got nothing / Lose yourself in me.

N

NEARLY GOD (see under ⇒ TRICKY)

NO MAN (see under ⇒ PORCUPINE TREE)

NO MAN IS ROGER MILLER (see under ⇒ MISSION OF BURMA)

NOTHING BUT HAPPINESS (see under ⇒ ULTRA VIVID SCENE)

NOVA MOB (see under ⇒ HUSKER DU)

OPAL (see under ⇒ MAZZY STAR)

ORB

Formed: South London, England ... 1989 by remix supremo and ex-KILLING JOKE roadie Dr. ALEX PATERSON. Working as an A&R bod for ambient label EG (home to he likes of BRIAN ENO), PATTERSON began recording similar ambient sounds in his spare time. He hooked up with the KLF's JIMMY CAUTY in 1988 and recorded an EP, 'KISS', using samples from NEW YORK's Kiss FM. The duo traded under the ORB moniker (which PATTERSON had taken from the WOODY ALLEN sci-fi film 'Sleepers') and released the record the following year on the 'WAU!Mr Modo' label, a joint venture between PATTERSON and ex-KILLING JOKE bassist YOUTH. Around this time the multi-talented PATTERSON was doing a spot of DJ'ing in the chill-out room of PAUL OAKENFOLD's Land of Oz club, where, in a well documented incident, he met STEVE HILLAGE (ex-GONG). The two struck up an immediate friendship (HILLAGE no doubt impressed by the fact that PATTERSON had been spinning one of his old tracks at the time) and a series of mutual collaborations ensued. Meanwhile, the ORB carved out a place in the cobwebbed corners of music history by making what was arguably the first ever ambient dance track, entitled, pause for breath, 'A HUGE EVER GROWING PULSATING BRAIN THAT RULES FROM THE CENTRE OF THE ULTRAWORLD'. The psychedelic/progressive rock influence was glaringly obvious, not only in the overblown title but in the slowly shifting rhythms and tripped-out dub effects. The ORB's heavy use of samples continued, this time running into trouble with MINNIE RIPPERTON's 'LOVING YOU'. Come 1990, the band found themselves in the enviable position of being in-demand remixers and amid their growing reputation released another single, the celestial 'LITTLE FLUFFY CLOUDS'. This time penned by PATTERSON/YOUTH, the single saw the ORB run into sample trauma again, with RICKIE LEE JONES reportedly none too happy that her, frankly, out-of-it sounding tones were used on the single. During the sessions for the single, PATTERSON met a young engineer, THRASH, who would go on to become a fully fledged ORB member in late '91 as a replacement for the recently departed CAUTY. The much anticipated debut album, 'ADVENTURES BEYOND THE ULTRAWORLD', released in April '91 on Big Life, was a sprawling double set of blissed-out almost-beats and shimmering ambience. It was also a catalyst for the burgeoning ambient scene that would spawn the likes of MIXMASTER MORRIS and the APHEX TWIN, the music spilling out of chill-out rooms across the country into fully paid-up ambient club nights. In June '92, the ORB stormed into the top 10 with the 'BLUE ROOM' single. At a record breaking 39 minutes long, it wasn't exactly radio-friendly although the band 'performed' it on Top Of The Pops, sitting nonchalantly playing chess and the act's cult popularity saw the subsequent album, 'UFORB', go straight in at No.1. Following a dispute with YOUTH, PATTERSON signed with Island, fighting a protracted battle for the ORB name which he eventually won. His first release for the label was a live album, imaginatively titled 'LIVE '93', and culled from the legendary ORB stage show at various locations around the globe. A collaboration with German techno exponent THOMAS FEHLMAN resulted in the harder sounding 'POMMEFRITZ' album which included such wonderfully titled tracks as 'MORE GILLS, LESS FISHCAKES'. Another two albums, 'ORBUS TERRARUM' (1995) and 'ORBLIVION' (1997) ploughed similarly obscure furrows and divided critical opinion, although both hit top 20. Along with the likes of PRIMAL SCREAM, the ORB helped define an era, bringing overt pychedelia back into the pop charts and updating the genre for the 90's. • **Songwriters:** Most by WESTON and PATERSON. • **Trivia:** The ORB have remixed many including 'Mute' label stars; DEPECHE MODE / ERASURE & WIRE. In 1992, they caused upset in the Asian community by using their religious chants.

Recommended: UF ORB (*9) / ADVENTURES BEYOND THE ULTRAWORLD (*9) / POMME FRITZ (*6) / ORBLIVION (*7)

ALEX PATERSON – synth, keyboards / with **JIM CAUTY**

Wau! Mr Modo | not issued

May 89. (ltd.12"ep; as ROCKMAN ROCK & LX DEE) *(MWS 010T)* **KISS EP** [ ] [-]
– Kiss your love / Suck my kiss mix / The roof is on fire / Ambiorix mix.

Oct 89. (12"ep) *(MWS 017T)* **A HUGE EVER GROWING PULSATING BRAIN THAT RULES FROM THE CENTRE OF THE ULTRAWORLD: LOVIN' YOU (Orbital mix). / ('A'bucket and spade mix) / WHY IS 6 SCARED OF 7?** [ ] [-]

Big Life | Mercury

Jun 90. (12"ep) *(BLR 270T)* **(above with new vocals)** [ ] [-]
(cd-ep) *(BLR 270CD)* – (above) / Loving you (ambient house).

Jul 90. (12"ep/cd-ep) *(BLR 27 T/CD)* **(above remixed) / ('A'-9 a.m. radio mix) / ('A'-Aubrey mix I)** [ ] [-]

Nov 90. (7") *(BLR 33)* **LITTLE FLUFFY CLOUDS. / ('A'-Ambient mix Mk.1)** [ ] [ ]
(dance mix-12"ep+=/cd-ep+=) *(BLR 33 T/CD)* – Into the fourth dimension (Essenes beyond control).
(12"ep) *(BLR 33R)* – ('A'side) / ('A'-drum & vox version) / Into the fourth dimension.

— In Nov90, they collaborated on STEVE HILLAGE's SYSTEM 7 release 'Sunburst'.

— CAUTY was replaced by **STEVE HILLAGE** – guitar (ex-Solo artist, ex-GONG) / **MIQUETTE GIRAUDY** (ex-GONG) / **ANDY FALCONER**

Apr 91. (d-cd/d-c/d-lp) *(BLR CD/MC/LP 5)* **ADVENTURES BEYOND THE ULTRAWORLD** [29] [ ] Nov 91
– Little fluffy clouds / Earth (Gaia) / Supernova at the end of the universe / Back side of the Moon / Spanish castles in space / Perpetual dawn / Into the fourth dimension / Outlands / Star 6 & 7 8 9 / A huge ever growing pulsating brain that rules from the centre of the Ultraworld.

Jun 91. (7"/c-s) *(BLR 46/+C)* **PERPETUAL DAWN (SOLAR YOUTH). / STAR 6&789 (phase II)** [61] [ ]
(cd-ep+=) *(BLR 46CD)* – Perpetual dawn: Solar flare.
(12"ep+=) *(BLRT 46)* – (above version) / ('B'side) / ('A'-Ultrabass 1 mix).
(12"ep) *(BLR 46R)* – ORB IN DUB: Towers of dub (ambient mix) / Perpetual dawn (ultrabass II). *(re-iss.Jan94; same)*– (hit No.18)

— In Nov91, SYSTEM 7 issued another release on '10-Virgin'; 'Miracle'.

Dec 91 (cd/c/lp) *(BLR CD/MC/LP 14)* **THE AUBREY MIXES: THE ULTRAWORLD EXCURSIONS** (deleted after 1 day) [44] [ ]
– Little fluffy clouds / (Pal Joey mix) / Black side of the moon (Steve Hillage remix) / Spanish castles in Spain (Youth remix) / Outlands (Ready made remix) / A huge ever growing pulsating brain (Jim Caldy & Dr. Alex Patterson remix).

— **PATERSON** now with **THRASH (KRISTIAN WESTON)** – guitars, synthesizers, samplers, percussion, plus guests **YOUTH, STUART McMILLAN, GUY PRATT, JAH WOBBLE, STEVE HILLAGE, MIQUETTE GIRAUDY, THOMAS FEHLMANN, GREG HUNTER, ORDE MEIKLE, TOM GREEN, MARNEY PAX.**

Jun 92. (12"ep) *(BLRT 75)* **THE BLUE ROOM (part 1). / (part 2)** [8] [ ]
(cd-ep) *(BLRDA 75)* – The blue room (40 minute version).
(cd-ep) *(BLRDB 75)* – The blue room (radio 7) / The blue room (excerpt 605) / Towers of dub (Mad Professor mix).

Jul 92. (d-cd/d-c/t-lp) *(BLR CD/MC/LP 18)* **UF ORB** [1] [ ]
– O.O.B.E. / U.F. Orb / Blue room / Towers of dub / Close encounters / Majestic / Sticky end. *(free live lp at some shops 'Soundtrack To The Film: ADVENTURES BEYOND THE ULTRAWORLD: PATTERNS & TEXTURES') (re-iss.Apr96 on 'Island; (cd)(c) IMCD 219)(ICM 8033)*

Oct 92. (c-s) **ASSASSIN (the oasis of rhythm mix)** [12] [ ]
(12"ep+=/cd-ep+=) *(BLR T/DA 81)* – U.F. ORB (Bandulu remix).
(cd-ep) *(BLRDB 81)* – ('A'-radio 7 mix) / ('A'-another live version) / ('A'-Chocolate hills of Bohol mix).

Nov 93. (c-ep/12"ep/cd-ep) *(BLR C/T/D 98)* **LITTLE FLUFFY CLOUDS. / ('A'mixes)** [10] [ ]

Island | Island

Nov 93. (d-cd/d-c/q-lp) *(CIDD/ICTT/ILPSQ 8022)* **LIVE 93 (live)** [23] [ ]
– Plateau / The valley / Oobe / Little fluffy clouds / Star 6, 7, 8 & 9 / Towers of dub / Spanish castles in space / The blue room / Perpetual dawn / Assassin / Outlands / A huge ever pulsating brain that rules from the centre of the ultraworld. *(d-cd-iss.Mar97; IMCD 245)*

Jun 94. (cd/c/lp) *(ORB CD/MC/LP 1)* **POMMEFRITZ** [6] [ ]
– Pommefritz / More gills less fishcakes / We're paste to be grill you / Banger'n'chips / Allers ist schoen / His immortal logness.

— now w /out KRIS WESTON, who was repl. (after 1995 recording by) **ANDY HUGHES**

Mar 95. (cd/cd/c/d-lp) *(CID/CIDX/ICT/ILPSD 8037)* **ORBUS TERRARUM** [20] [ ]
– Valley / Plateau / Oxbow lakes / Montagne d'or (der gute berg) / White river junction / Occidental / Slug dub.

May 95. (c-s) *(CIS 609)* **OXBOW LAKES / ('A'-Everglades mix)** [38] [ ]
(12"+=) *(12IS/CID 609)* – ('A'-Sabres No.1 mix).
(12") *(12ISX 609)* – ('A'-Carl Craig psychic pals family wealth plan mix) / ('A'-Evensong string arrangement mix).
(cd-s) *(CIDX 609)* – (all 5 mixes above).

— In Jul'96, the label 'Deviant' released various artists compilation of their mixes 'AUNTIE AUBREY'S EXCURSIONS BEYOND THE CALL OF DUTY'.

— line-up **LX PATERSON / ANDY HUGHES / THOMAS FEHLMANN**

Jan 97. (12"/cd-s) *(12IS/CID 652)* **TOXYGENE. / DELTA Mk.II** [4] [ ]
(cd-s) *(CIDX 652)* – ('A'side) / Rose tinted.

Feb 97. (cd/c/d-lp) *(CID/ICT/ILPSD 8055)* **ORBLIVION** [19] [ ]
– Delta mk II / Ubiquity / Asylum / Bedouin / Molten love / Pi / S.A.L.T. / Toxygene / Log of deadwood / Secrets / Passing of time / 72.

May 97. (12"/cd-s) *(12IS/CID 657)* **ASYLUM. / ('A'-Blood Sugar's mix 1) / ('A'-Andrea Parker's Bezirkskrankenhams mix)** [20] [ ]
(cd-s) *(CIDX 657)* –

– compilations, others, etc. –

Nov 91. (cd/c/lp) *Strange Fruit; (SFR CD/MC/LP 118)* **THE PEEL SESSIONS** [ ] [-]
– A huge ever growing brain that rules from the centre of the ultraworld. *(re-iss.Apr96; same)*

APOLLO XI

DR. ALEX PATERSON + guest **BEN WATKINS** (of SUNSONIC)

Wau! Mr Modo | not issued

Feb 91. (12"/cd-s) *(APOLLO 11/+CD)* **PEACE (IN THE MIDDLE EAST) / ('A'-Sea Of Tranquility mix). / ('A'radio) / ('A'-Is This Really The Orb mix?)** [ ] [-]

F.F.W.D.

aka **ROBERT FRIPP / THOMAS FEHLMANN / KRIS WESTON / DR.ALEX PATERSON**

Intermodo | Intermodo

Aug 94. (cd/c/d-lp) *(INTA 001 CD/TC/LP)* **F.F.W.D.** [48] [ ]
– Hidden / Lucky saddle / Drone / Hempire / Collosus / What time is clock / Can of bliss / Elauses / Meteor storm / Buckwheat and grits / Klangtest / Suess wie eine nuss.

ORBITAL

Formed: Seven Oaks, London, England . . . late 80's by brothers PHIL and PAUL HARTNOLL. United by a shared love of electro and punk, they were inspired by the outdoor party scene of '89 and named themselves after the infamous circular motorway which ravers used in delirious pursuit of their next E'd-up shindig. A home produced 4-track demo, 'CHIME', brought the band almost instant fame and remains one of their best loved songs. Originally released on the small 'Oh-Zone' label, the track was given a full release in March 1990 on 'London' offshoot 'Ffrr', it's subtly euphoric charms elevating 'CHIME' into the top 20 and the brothers onto a memorable 'Top Of The Pops' appearance where they sported defiant 'No Poll Tax' t-shirts. Although dance culture has since become increasingly politiscized as a result of heavy handed legislation, it was unusual at the time for a techno act to be so passionately anti-establishment, an ethos the HARTNOLL brothers had carried over from their punk days and which would become a recurring theme throughout their career. Meanwhile, ORBITAL followed their debut with a trio of largely instrumental, synth-driven singles, the highlight being the pounding white noise of the BUTTHOLE SURFERS-sampling 'SATAN'. The track reached No.31 upon its release in August '91 although a subsequent live version stormed into the top 5 earlier this year. Their untitled debut album, released in September of the same year, showcased cerebral electronic soundscapes which nevertheless retained a melancholy, organic warmth while their live shows moved feet and minds en masse. Alongside events like the Shamen's Synergy, which attempted to mix the spectacle of rock 'n' roll with the communal energy of house, ORBITAL were pivotal in pioneering dance music in the live evironment. Rather than reproducing the songs live on stage, they improvised, restructuring tracks which had been pre-set into sequencers. This spontaneity was enhanced by an innovative light show utilising state of the art technology, a heady combination that saw ORBITAL headline the Glastonbury festival two years running during the mid-90's. They were no less effective in the studio and their second untitled album was a finely tuned extension of the debut, encompassing such exotica as a sample from an Australian pedestrian crossing (!) With their third long player, 1994's cynically titled 'SNIVILISATION', the music took on an uneasy paranoia, seething with a bitter undercurrent that railed against the state of humanity in general, as well as issues closer to home such as the much hated Criminal Justice Bill. The record also introuced elements of drum 'n' bass, a dalliance that continued with their 'IN SIDES' album. Preceded by the near-half hour strangeness of 'THE BOX' single, the record marked the pinnacle of ORBITAL's sonic explorations, a luminous trip to the final frontiers of electronica. In spite of their experimentalism, a loyal following ensures that the duo are never short of chart success, the 'IN SIDES' album reaching No.5, while this year alone has seen ORBITAL go top 3 in the singles chart twice. First with the aforementioned live version of 'SATAN' and then with their celebrated remake of 'THE SAINT'. • **Songwriters:** The duo, except cover of THE SAINT (E. Astley) and noted samples; O EUCHARI (performed by Emily Van Evera). • **Trivia:** Vox on tracks 'SAD BUT TRUE' & 'ARE WE HERE?' by ALISON GOLDFRAPP.

Recommended: UNTITLED (ORBITAL 1) (*7) / UNTITLED (ORBITAL II) (*7) / SNIVILIZATION (*8) / IN SIDES (*9)

PHIL HARTNOLL – keyboards / **PAUL HARTNOLL** – keyboards

Oh-Zone | not issued

Jan 90. (12"ep) *(ZONE 001)* **CHIME. / DEEPER (full version)** [ ] [-]

Ffrr-London | London

Mar 90. (7"/c-s) *(F/FCS 135)* **CHIME. / DEEPER** [ ] [-]
(cd-ep+=) *(FCD 135)* – ('A'version).
(12"ep) *(FX 135)* – ('A'-JZM remix) / ('A'-Bacardi mix).

Jul 90. (7"ep) *(F 145)* **OMEN. / 2 DEEP / OPEN MIND** [ ] [-]
(cd-ep) *(FCD 145)* – (1st & 3rd track) / ('A'edit)
(12"ep) *(FX 145)* – Omen: The chariot / The tower / Wheel of fortune / The fool.
(12"ep) *(FXR 145)* – ('A'remixes).

Jan 91. (7") *(F 149)* **SATAN. / BELFAST** [31] [-]
(12"ep+=/cd-ep+=) *(FX/FCD 149)* – L.C.1. *(cd-ep re-iss.Aug95 on 'Internal'; LIECD 25)*
(12"ep) *(FXR 149)* – ('A'-rhyme & reason mix) / L.C.2 (outer limits mix) / Chime.

Aug 91. (12") *(FX)* **MIDNIGHT. / CHOICE** [ ] [-]
(12"ep) *(FX)* – Midnight (Sasha mix) / Choice (Orbital & Eye & I mix).
(cd-ep+=) *(FCD)* – Analogue test Feb'90. *(re-iss.Aug95 on 'Internal'; LIECD 26)*

Sep 91. (cd/c/lp) *(828 248-2/-4/-1)* **UNTITLED (ORBITAL 1)** [71] [ ]
– The moebius / Speed freak / Oolaa / Desert storm / Fahrenheit 303 / Steel cube idolatry / High rise / Chime (live) / Midnight (live) / Belfast / Macrohead. *(cd w-out last track, repl. by)*– I think it's disgusting. *(c+=)*– Untitled. *(re-iss.Apr96 & Apr97 on 'Internal' cd/c; TRU CD/MC 9)*

Feb 92. (12"ep) *(FX 181)* **MUTATIONS (I): OOLAA (Joey Beltram remix) / OOLAA (Meat Beat Manifesto mix) / CHIME (Joey Beltram). / SPEED FREAK (Moby mix)** [24] [-]
(12"ep) *(FX 181)* – MUTATIONS (II): Chime (Ray Keith mix) / Chime (Crime remix) / Steel cube idolatory / Farenheit 303.
(cd-ep) *(FCD 181)* – Oolaa (Joey Beltram mix) / Chime (Ray Keith mix) / Speed freak / Fahrenheit 303.

Internal | Ffrr-London

Sep 92. (12"ep/cd-ep) *(LIARX/LIECD 1)* **RADICCIO EP** [37] [ ]
– Halycon / The naked and the dead / Halycon. *(cd-ep re-is.Aug95; LIECD 27)*

Apr 93. (12"ep/c-ep) *(LIARX/LIEMC 7)* **LUSH 3-1. / LUSH 3-2 / LUSH 3-3 (Underworld mix)** [ ] [-]
(12"ep) *(LIAXR 7)* – LUSH 3-4 (Psychick Warriors Ov Gaia) / LUSH 3-5 (CJ Bollard).
(cd-ep) *(LIECD 7)* – (all 5 tracks).

Jun 93. (cd/c/lp) *(TRU CD/MC/LP 2)* **UNTITLED (ORBITAL II)** [28] [-]
– Time becomes / Planet of the shapes / Lush 3-1 / Lush 3-2 / Impact (the Earth is burning) / Remind / Walk now . . . / Monday / Halycon + on + on / Input out. *(re-iss.Aug95; same)*

Mar 94. (cd-ep/12"ep) *(LIECD/LIARX 12)* **THE JOHN PEEL SESSIONS EP** [ ] [-]
– Lush (Euro-tunnel disaster '94) / Walk about / Semi detached / Attached.
(cd-ep) **DIVERSIONS EP** (LIEDC 12) – Impact USA / Lush 3 (Euro-Tunnel disaster '94) / Walkabout / Lush 3-5 (CJ Bolland) / Lush 3-4 (Warrior drift) / Lush 3-4 (Underworld).

Aug 94. (cd/c/d-lp) *(TRU CD/MC/LP 5)* **SNIVILIZATION** [4] [ ]
– Forever / I wish I had duck feet / Sad but true / Crash and carry / Science friction / Philosophy by numbers / Kein trink wasser / Quality seconds / Are we here? / Attached. *(re-iss.Aug95 & Apr97; same)*

Sep 94. (12"ep/c-ep) *(LIARX/LIEMC 15)* **ARE WE HERE? EP** [33] [ ]
– Are we here?: Who are they? – Do they here? – They did it (mix).
(cd-ep+=/s-cd-ep+=) *(LIE CD/DC 15)* – Are we here?: What was that? – Criminal Justice bill? – Industry standard?.

— In May'95, they covered THERAPY?'s 'Belfast' on special cd-s which hit UK No.53. THERAPY? gave us interpretation of 'INNOCENT X'.

Aug 95. (d7"ep/12"ep/cd-ep/s-cd-ep) *(LIE/LIARX/LIECD/LIEDP 23)* **UNTITLED EP** [ ] [-]
– Times fly (slow) / Sad but new / Times fly (fast) / The tranquilizer.

— (above was not eligible for UK chart position due to it's length)

Apr 96. (12"/cd-s) *(LIARX/LIECD 30)* **THE BOX. / THE BOX** [11] [ ]
(cd-s+=) *(LICDP 30)* – (2 extra mixes).

Apr 96. (cd/cd/c/3x12"lp) *(TRU DC/CD/MC/LP 10)* **IN SIDES** [5] [ ]
– The girl with the sun in her head / P.E.T.R.O.L. / The box / Dwr budr / Adnan's / Out there somewhere? *(cd re-iss.Apr97 on 'Dutch East India'; 124129CD)*

Jan 97. (cd-s) *(LIECD 37)* **SATAN (live at New York) / OUT THERE SOMEWHERE (live at New York)** [3] [ ]
(cd-s) *(LICDP 37)* – ('A'-live at Chelmsford) / Lush 3 (live at Boston) / The girl with the sun in her head (live at Boston).
(cd-s) *(LICDD 37)* – ('A'-Industry standard edit) / Chime (live at Chelmsford) / Impact (live at Chelmsford).

— (due to length above actually also hit No.48 in the UK album charts)

FFRR | London

Apr 97. (c-s/12"/cd-s) *(FCS/FX/FCD 296)* **THE SAINT / THE SINNER** [3] [ ]
(cd-s+=) *(FCDP 296)* – Belfast (live) / Petrol (live).

OZRIC TENTACLES

Formed: London, England . . . after meeting at Stonehenge in 1982. Brothers ED and ROLY WYNNE, together with the others, decamped to Trowbridge, Somerset, in the early 90's, having issued their second album proper (a double), 'ERPLAND', on manager JOHN BENNETT's own 'Dovetail' label. Their unashamedly retro style was developed over six low key cassette-only releases throughout the 80's and countless festival appearances. The afore-mentioned double album, 'ERPLAND', released in 1990, distilled the essence of their sprawling open-ended jams into an epic of ethnic-inflected trip-rock. Coming on like a younger, hipper Hawkwind, the band fitted neatly into the crusty/rave crossover scene, galvanising space cadets the length and breadth of the country. Taking the OZRIC's occasional ambient techno dabbling to its ultimate conclusion, PEPLAR and HINTON formed EAT STATIC along with new recruit STEVE EVERITT. They peddled beat-friendly trance-athons that eschewed high minded techno purism for lyrics that centred on aliens, UFO's etc. After the success of the 'ABDUCTION' (1993) and 'IMPLANT' (1994) albums, PEPLAR and HINTON left OZRIC TENTACLES to make their new act a full time concern, releasing a string of well-recieved EP's. Meanwhile, the OZRIC's brushed aside a sneering music press and stormed into the top 20 with the 'JURASSIC SHIFT' album in 1993. Their grassroots following of crusties and students accounting largely for this sudden leap into the spotlight, the follow-up album, 'ABORESCENCE' (1994) also gained a respectable chart placing. After riding out a near fatal bankruptcy following a copyright run-in with Kellog's (the band had designed the 6-CD retrospective of their earlier work in the guise of a cereal packet) and a financially draining American tour, the band bounced back with the psychotropic explorations of the 'BECOME THE OTHER' (1995) album. • **Songwriters:** Group / or ED and JOIE. • **Trivia:** JOIE bet their record company that aliens!!! would land on Earth by the year 2000.

Recommended: STRANGEITUDE (*7) / JURASSIC SHIFT (*7) / ARBORESCENCE (*7)

ED WYNNE – guitar, synthesizers / **ROLY WYNNE** – bass / **JOIE 'OZROONICULATOR' HINTON** – synthesizers / **NICK 'TIG' VAN GELDER** – drums / **GAVIN GRIFFITHS** – guitar / added in 1983; **TOM BROOKES** – synthesizers / **PAUL HANKIN** – percussion

— In 1984, GRIFFITHS left to form ULLINATORS, and a year later BROOKES also left. HINTON sidelined with group ULLINATORS and OROONIES. Released cassette-only albums which I think were untitled.

— **MERV PEPLER** – drums, percussion repl. VAN GELDER

Demi-Monde | not issued

Feb 89. (lp) *(DMLP 1017)* **PUNGENT EFFULGENT** [ ] [-]
– Dissolution (the clouds disperse) / 0-1 / Phalam dawn / The domes of G'bal / Shaping the pelm / Ayurvedic / Kick muck / Agog in the ether / Wreltch. *(re-iss.Mar91 on 'Dovetail' cd/c/lp; DOVE CD/MC/LP 2)*

Dovetail | not issued

Nov 90. (cd)(d-lp) *(DOVE CD/MC/LP 1)* **ERPLAND** [ ] [-]
– Eternal wheel / Toltec spring / Tidal convergence / Sunscape / Mysticum Arabicola / Crackerblocks / The throbbe / Erpland / Valley of a thousand thoughts / Snakepit / Iscence / A gift of wings.

Jul 91. (12"/cd-s) *(DOVE EST/CD 3)* **SPLOOSH!. / LIVE THROBBE** [ ] [-]

Aug 91. (cd/c/lp) *(DOVE CD/MC/LP 3)* **STRANGEITUDE** [70] [-]
– White rhino tea / Sploosh / Saucers / Strangeitude / Bizzare bazaar / Space between your ears. (cd+=) – Live Throbbe.

— **STEVE EVERETT** – synthesizers repl. BROOKES

— added **MARCUS CARCUS** – percussion / **JOHN EGAN** – flute

Jan 92. (d-cd) *(DOVECD 4)* **AFTERWISH** (compilation 1984-1991) [ ] [ ]
– Guzzard / Chinatype / The sacred turf / Og-ha-be / Thyroid / Omnidibectional Bhadba / Afterwish / Velmwend / Travelling the great circle / Secret names / Soda water / Fetch me the pongmaster / Zall! / Abul Hagag / It's a hup ho world / The dusty pouch / Thrashing breath texture / Floating seeds / Invisible carpet / The code for Chickendon / Kola b'pep / Mae Hong song / Symetricum / Jabular / Sliding and gliding.

Apr 92. (cd/c/d-lp) *(DOVE CD/MC/LP 5)* **LIVE UNDERSLUNKY (live)** [ ] [-]
– Dot thots / Og-ha-be / Erpland / White rhino tea / Bizzare bazaar / Sunscrape / Erpsongs / Snake pit / Kick muck / 0-1 / Ayurvedic.

— **ZIA** – bass repl. ROLY (late'92)

— (5-piece **ED, JOIE, JON, MERV + ZIA**)

Apr 93. (cd/c/lp) *(DOVE CD/MC/LP 6)* **JURASSIC SHIFT** [11] [-]
– Sun hair / Stretchy / Feng Shui / Jurassic shift / Pteranodon / Train oasis / Vita voom.

Jul 94. (cd/c/lp) *(DOVE CD/MC/LP 7)* **ARBORESCENCE** [18] [ ]
– Astro Cortez / Yog-bar-og / Arborescence / Al-salooq / Dance of the Loomi / Myriapod / There's a planet here / Shima Koto.

— JOIE + MERV were now EAT STATIC full-time. They had splintered as said outfit since summer '92.

Oct 95. (cd/c) *(DOVE CD/MC 8)* **BECOME THE OTHER** [ ] [-]
– Og-ha-be / Shards of ice / Sniffing dog / Music to gargle at / Ethereal cereal / Atmosphear / Ulluvar gate / Tentacles of Erpmiad / Trees of eternity / Mescalito / Odhanshan / Become the other / Gnuthlia / Sorry style / The Aun shuffle.

– compilations, etc. –

on 'Dovetail' unless mentioned otherwise

Nov 93. (6xcd-box) *(DOVEBOX 1)* **VITAMIN ENHANCED** [ ] [-]
– (the 6 cd's below)

Feb 94. (cd) *(OTCD 1)* **ERPSONGS** [ ] [-]

Feb 94. (cd) *(OTCD 2)* **TANTRIC OBSTACLES** [ ] [-]

Feb 94. (cd) *(OTCD 3)* **LIVE ETHEREAL CEREAL** [ ] [-]

Feb 94. (cd) *(OTCD 4)* **THERE IS NOTHING** [ ] [-]

Feb 94. (cd) *(OTCD 5)* **SLIDING GLIDING WORDS** [ ] [-]

Feb 94. (cd) *(OTCD 6)* **THE BITS BETWEEN THE BITS** [ ] [-]

EAT STATIC

JOIE + MERV + STEVE

CJP | not issued

1991. (12"; as COSMIC JOURNEY PROJECT) *(CJP 1)* **BASS PROBE** [ ] [-]

Static Music | not issued

1992. (12") *(AR 1)* **INANNA. /** [ ] [-]

H.A.B. | not issued

1992. (12") *(HAB 1)* **MONKEY MAN. /** [ ] [-]

Alien | not issued

1992. (c) *(ARO 1C)* **PREPARE YOUR SPIRIT** [ ] [-]
– Hallucinate / Fudge / Wormlips / Instinct / Eat-Static / Destroy / Raga / Almost human / Om machine / Cyper-funk / The watcher / Higher-state / Woman is life / Medicine wheel / Fourt dimension.

Nov 92. (12"ep/cd-ep) *(ARO/+CD 2)* **ALMOST HUMAN / FOURTH DIMENSION. / PUPAE (THE LOCUST SONG) / MOTHER PLANET** [ ] [-]

Ultimate-Planet Dog | not issued

Apr 93. (12") *(BARK 001V)* **INTRUSION (mixes)** [ ] [-]

May 93. (cd/c/lp) *(BARK CD/MC/LP 1)* **ABDUCTION** [62] [-]
– Prana / Gulf breeze / Kalika / Splitting world / Kinetic flow / Forgotten rites / Abduction / Intruder / Xenomorph / Inner peace.

Nov 93. (12"ep/cd-ep) *(BARK 2 T/CDS)* **LOST IN TIME. / GULF BREEZE / THE BRAIN** [ ] [-]

Mar 94. (12"ep/cd-ep) *(BARK 002/+CD)* **GULF BREEZE (remix). / ('A'-Ashoshashoz mix) / ('A'-Cat mix)** | | -
Jun 94. (cd)(c)(lp) **IMPLANT** | 13 |
– Implant.
Jul 94. (12"/cd-s) *(BARK 003 T/CD)* **SURVIVORS** | | -
Mar 95. (c-ep/12"ep/d12"ep/cd-ep) *(BARK 009 MCS/T/TS/CDS)* **EPSYLON EP** | | -
– Epsylon / Dionsyiac / Peeou / Undulattice.
Feb 96. (cd-ep) *(BARK 016CDS)* **BONY INCUS EP** | | -
–
Feb 97. (12"ep/cd-ep) *(BARK 024 T/CD)* **HYBRID** | 41 |
(cd-ep) *(BARK 024CDX)* –
(12"ep) *(BARK 024TX)* –

P

P (see under ⇒ BUTTHOLE SURFERS)

Andy PARTRIDGE (see under ⇒ XTC)

PERE UBU

Formed: Cleveland, Ohio, USA ... Sep'75 out of ROCKET FROM THE TOMBS, by DAVID THOMAS (aka CROCUS BEHEMOTH; his alter-ego) and PETER LAUGHNER. They recruited other musicians; TIM WRIGHT, ALLEN RAVENSTINE, TOM HERMAN plus SCOTT KRAUSS, and took their name from a play by French writer Alfred Jarry. THOMAS formed his own 'Hearthan' label, and issued a classic debut, '30 SECONDS OVER TOKYO', leading to gigs at Max's Kansas City in New York in early '76. Another gem, 'FINAL SOLUTION', was unleashed soon after, although LAUGHNER departed for the 3rd & 4th rare 45's 'STREET WAVES' & 'THE MODERN DANCE'. The latter was the name of their debut album released early in '78. It was clearly a break from the "New Wave", echoeing as it did a revival of the avant-garde (CAPTAIN BEEFHEART and early ROXY MUSIC). On the strength of this masterwork, they signed to the major 'Chrysalis' label, and six months later, wowed the music world with another abstract beauty, 'DUB HOUSING'. After the dissappointing 'NEW PICNIC TIME', however, they were unceremoniously dropped by their label. They subsequently found a home with UK indie, 'Rough Trade', but two poorly-received albums later they split. For the next five years, THOMAS embarked on an equally weird and anti-commercial solo venture, taking some of UBU with him. In 1987, they recorded a comeback album, 'THE TENEMENT YEARS', which was released the following year. This treaded the same path, the band releasing sub-standard albums (bar 'CLOUDLAND'), until their final blast, 'RAYGUN SUITCASE', in 1995. • **Style:** Surrealistic, avant-garde, anti-rock'n'roll collective, capturing an array of influences, (see above). The large-framed eccentric, DAVID THOMAS, never quite appealed commercially, although the music press and night time Radio 1 DJ John Peel gave them acolade and deserved airplay. • **Songwriters:** All group compositions, except MIRROR MAN (Captain Beefheart) / DOWN BY THE RIVER (Neil Young). THOMAS collaborated with others on solo work and covered SLOOP JOHN B. (Beach Boys).

Recommended: TERMINAL TOWER: AN ARCHIVAL COLLECTION (*9) / THE MODERN DANCE (*9) / DUB HOUSING (*7) / NEW PICNIC TIME (*7) / CLOUDLAND (*6) / RAYGUN SUITCASE (*7). DAVID THOMAS & THE PEDESTRIANS:- THE SOUND OF THE SAND (*6) / VARIATIONS ON A THEME (*6).

DAVID THOMAS (b.14 Jun'53) – vocals / **PETER LAUGHNER** (b.1953) – guitar / **TIM WRIGHT** – bass, guitar / **TOM HERMAN** (b.19 Apr'49) – guitar, bass / **SCOTT KRAUSE** (b.19 Nov'50) – drums / **ALLEN RAVENSTINE** (b. 9 May'50) – synthesizer

not issued | Hearthan

Dec 75. (7"ltd) *<HR 101>* **30 SECONDS OVER TOKYO. / HEART OF DARKNESS** | - |

— **DAVE TAYLOR** – synthesizer repl. RAVENSTINE

Mar 76. (7"ltd) *<HR 102>* **FINAL SOLUTION. / CLOUD 149** | - |

— **ALLEN RAVENSTINE** – synthesizer returned to repl. TAYLOR / **ALAN GREENBLATT** – guitar repl. LAUGHNER who formed FRICTION (he died of drug & alcohol abuse 22nd June '77)

— **TONY MAIMONE** (b.27 Sep'52) – bass, piano repl. WRIGHT who joined DNA. (GREENBLATT left also) (were now a quintet with **THOMAS, HERMAN, KRAUSE, MAIMONE** and **RAVENSTINE**)

Nov 76. (7"ltd) *<HR 103>* **STREET WAVES. / MY DARK AGES** | - |
Aug 77. (7"ltd) *<HR 104>* **THE MODERN DANCE. / HEAVEN** | - |

Mercury | Blank

Apr 78. (lp) *(9100 052) <001>* **THE MODERN DANCE** | | Jan78
– Non-alignment pact / The modern dance / Laughing / Street waves / Chinese radiation / Life stinks / Real world / Over my head / Sentimental journey / Humor me. *(re-iss.Jan81 on 'Rough Trade'; ROUGH 22) (re-iss.Feb88 on 'Fontana' lp/cd; SF LP/CD 3)*

Radar | not issued

Apr 78. (12"ep) *(RDAR 1)* **DATAPANIK IN THE YEAR ZERO (remixes compilation)** | | -

– Heart of darkness / 30 seconds over Tokyo / Cloud 149 / Untitled / Heaven.

Chrysalis | Chrysalis

Nov 78. (lp) *(CHR 1207)* **DUB HOUSING**
– Navy / On the surface / Dub housing / Cagliari's mirror / Thriller / I will wait / Drinking wine Spodyody / Ubu dance party / Blow daddy-o / Codex. *(cd-iss.Mar89 on 'Rough Trade'; ROUGHCD 6002)*
Sep 79. (lp) *(CHR 1248)* **NEW PICNIC TIME**
– One less worry / Make hay / Goodbye / The voice of the sand / Jehovah's kingdom comes / Have shoes will walk / 49 guitars and 1 girl / A small dark cloud / Small was fast / All the dogs are barking. *(cd-iss.Mar89 on 'Rough Trade'; ROUGHCD 6003)*
Oct 79. (7"m) *(CHS 2372)* **THE FABULOUS SEQUEL (HAVE SHOES WILL WALK). / HUMOR ME (live). / THE BOOK IS ON THE TABLE**

— **MAYO THOMPSON** (b.26 Feb'44) – guitar, vocals (ex-RED CRAYOLA) repl. HERMAN who went solo

Rough Trade | not issued

Jun 80. (7") *(RT 049)* **FINAL SOLUTION. / MY DARK AGES** | | -
Sep 80. (lp) *(ROUGH 14)* **THE ART OF WALKING** | | -
– Go / Rhapsody in pink / Arabia * / Miles * / Misery goats / Loop / Rounder / Birdies / Lost in art / Horses / Crush this horn. *(re-iss.1981; same)*– Arabian nights / Tribute to Miles; repl. *) *(cd-iss.Apr89 tracks as re-issue; ROUGHCD 14)*
Feb 81. (7") *(RT 066)* **NOT HAPPY. / LONESOME COWBOY DAVE** | | -
May 81. (lp) *(ROUGH 23)* **390<< >> OF SIMULATED STEREO – UBU LIVE: VOLUME 1 (live 76-79)** | | -
– Can't believe it / Over my head / Sentimental journey / 30 seconds over Tokyo / Humor me / Real world / My dark ages / Street waves / Laughing / Non-alignment pact / Heart of darkness / The modern dance. *(cd-iss.Apr89; ROUGHCD 23)*

— added **ANTON FIER** (b.20 Jun'56) – drums, percussion (ex-FEELIES) / guest **EDDIE THORNTON** – trumpet

Jun 82. (lp) *(ROUGH 33)* **SONG OF THE BAILING MAN** | | -
– The long walk home / Use of a dog / Petrified / Stormy weather / West Side story / Thoughts that go by steam / Big Ed's used farms / A day such as this / The vulgar boatman bird / My hat / Horns are a dilemma. *(cd-iss.Apr89; ROUGHCD 33)*

— Split mid'82. MAYO returned to RED CRAYOLA (which also incl. most UBU's) **KRAUSE** and **MAIMONE** formed HOME AND GARDEN, (see below for more).

DAVID THOMAS & THE PEDESTRIANS

Rough Trade | Recommended

Dec 81. (12"ep; by DAVID THOMAS) *(TRADE 5-12)* **VOCAL PERFORMANCES** | | -

— included **THOMPSON, KRAUSE, FIER & RAVENSTINE** plus **CHRIS CUTLER** (b. 4 Jan'47) – drums / **JOHN GREAVES** – bass (both ex-HENRY COW) / **PHILIP MOXHAM** – multi (ex-YOUNG MARBLE GIANTS) / **RICHARD THOMPSON** – guitar

Jan 82. (lp) *(ROUGH 30)* **THE SOUND OF THE SAND AND OTHER SONGS OF THE PEDESTRIANS**
– The birds are good ideas / Yiki Tiki / The crickets in the flats / Sound of the sand / The new atom mine / Big dreams / Happy to see you / Crush this horn – part 2 / Confuse did / Sloop John B. / Man's best friend.
Oct 82. (7") **PETRIFIED. / ?** | - |

— w/ **CHRIS CUTLER & LINDSAY COOPER** – bassoon (ex-MIKE OLDFIELD)

Feb 83. (lp; DAVID THOMAS & HIS LEGS) *(DTLP)* **WINTER COMES HOME (live Munich, 1982)** | | -
– A day such as this / Winter comes home / West side story / Sunset / Stormy weather / Poetic license / Rhapsody in pink / Dinosaurs like me / Petrified / Bones in action / Contrasted views of the archaeopterix.

— added **RICHARD THOMPSON** etc. (CUTLER, COOPER)

Dec 83. (lp) *(ROUGH 60)* **VARIATIONS ON A THEME** | | -
– A day at the Botanical Gardens / Pedestrians walk / Bird town / The egg and I / Who is it / Song of hoe / Hurry back / The ram / Semaphore.

— **TONY MAIMONE** – bass repl. GREAVES who joined The FLYING LIZARDS

Rough Trade | Rough Trade

May 85. (lp) *(ROUGH 80)* **MORE PLACES FOREVER** | | -
– Through the magnifying glass / Enthusiastic / Big breezy day / About true friends / Whale head king / Song of the bailing man / The farmer's wife / New broom.

DAVID THOMAS & THE WOODEN BIRDS

(**DAVID** retained **MAIMONE** and **CUTLER**) brought in **RAVENSTINE** again. (**DAVID HILD** – accordion of LOS LOBOS guested)

Apr 86. (lp) *(ROUGH 90)* **MONSTER WALKS THE WINTER LAKE**
– My theory of similtanious similtude – Red tin bus / What happened to me / Monster walks the winter lake / Bicycle / Coffee train / My town / Monster Magge king of the seas / Monster thinks about the good days / What happened to us.

— **JIM JONES** (b.12 Mar'50) – guitar was added

Mar 87. (lp) *(ROUGH 120)* **BLAME THE MESSENGER**
– The long rain / My town / King Knut / A fact about trains / When love is uneven / Storm breaks / Having time / Velikovsky / The two-step.

PERE UBU

(**THOMAS, RAVENSTINE, MAIMONE, CUTLER, JONES** and **KRAUSE**)

Fontana | Enigma

Mar 88. (lp/c)(cd) *(SF LP/MC 5)(834 537-2)* **THE TENEMENT YEAR**
– Something's gotta give / George had a hat / Talk to me / Busman's honeymoon / Say goodbye / Universal vibration / Miss you / Dream the Moon / Rhythm kind / The hollow Earth / We have the technology.
Jul 88. (7") *(UBU 1)* **WE HAVE THE TECHNOLOGY. / THE B-SIDE**
(12"+=/cd-s+=) *(UBU 1-12/CD1)* – The postman drove a caddy / ('A'-different mix).

— **ERIC DREW FELDMAN** (b.16 Apr'55) – drums (ex-CAPTAIN BEEFHEART) repl. RAVENSTINE + CUTLER

Fontana | Mercury

Mar 89. (7") *(UBU 2)* **WAITING FOR MARY (WHAT ARE WE DOING HERE?). / WINE DARK SPARKS**
(12"+=/cd-s+=) *(UBU 2-12/CD2)* – Flat.

May 89. (lp/c/cd) *(838 237-1/-4/-2)* **CLOUDLAND**
– Breath / Bus called happiness / Race the sun / Waiting for Mary / Cry / Flat * / Ice cream truck / Lost nation road / Monday night / Pushin' / The wire * / The waltz. *(cd+= *)*

Jun 89. (7") *(UBU 3)* **LOVE LOVE LOVE. / FEDORA SATELLITE**
(cd-s+=) *(UBUCD 3)* – Say goodbye.
(12") *(UBU 3-12)* – ('A'-cajun house mix) / ('A'132 bpm mix) / ('A'side).

Oct 89. (7") *(UBU 4)* **BREATH. / BANG THE DRUM**
(12"+=) *(UBU 4-12)* – Over my head (live) / Universal initiation (live).
(cd-s+=) *(UBUCD 4)* – Humor me (live).

Mar 91. (7") *(UBU 5)* **I HEAR THEY SMOKE THE BARBEQUE. / INVISIBLE MAN**
(12"+=/cd-s+=) *(UBU 5-12/CD5)* – Around the fire.

May 91. (cd/c/lp) *(848 564-2/-4/-1)* **WORLDS IN COLLISION**
– Oh Catherine / I hear they smoke the barbeque / Turpentine / Goodnight Irene / Mirror man / Cry cry / World's in collision / Life of Riley / Over the Moon / Don't look back / Playback / Nobody knows / Winter in the Netherlands.

May 91. (7") *(UBU 6)* **OH CATHERINE. / LIKE A ROLLING STONE**
(12"+=/cd-s+=) *(UBU 6-12/CD6)* – Down by the river.

Fontana Imago

Jan 93. (cd/c) *(514159-2/-4)* **THE STORY OF MY LIFE**
– Wasted / Come home / Louisiana train wreck / Fedora satellite II / Heartbreak garage / Postcard / Kathleen / Honey Moon / Sleep walk / The story of my life / Last will and testament.

—— **THOMAS / KRAUSS / JONES / TEMPLE / YELLIN**

Cooking V.

Aug 95. (cd) *(COOKCD 089)* **RAY GUN SUITCASE**
– Folly of youth / Electricity / Beach Boys / Turquoise fins / Vacuum in my head / Memphis / Three things / Horse / Don't worry / Ray gun suitcase / Surfer girl / Red sky / Montana / My friend is a stooge for the media priests / Down by the river II.

Oct 95. (cd-ep) *(FRYCD 043)* **FOLLY OF YOUTH / BALL 'N' CHAIN (jam) / DOWN BY THE RIVER II (demo) / MEMPHIS (demo)**

– compilations, others, etc. –

Nov 85. (lp) *Rough Trade; (ROUGH 83)* **TERMINAL TOWER: AN ARCHIVAL COLLECTION** -
– (early 'Hearthan' sides + rare)

Mar 89. (cd) *Rough Trade; (ROUGHCD 93)* **ONE MAN DRIVES WHILE THE OTHER MAN SCREAMS – LIVE VOL.2: PERE UBU ON TOUR** -

Nov 95. (4x7"box) *Cooking Vinyl; (FRY 045)* **THE HEARTHAN SINGLES** -

Nov 95. (d-cd) *Movieplay Gold; (MPG 74178)* **MODERN DANCE / TERMINAL TOWER** -

Sep 96. (5xcd-box) *Cooking Vinyl;* **DATAPANIK IN THE YEAR ZERO** -
– (first 5 albums + 1 free rarities album)

DAVID THOMAS

Cooking V.

Sep 96. (cd; DAVID THOMAS & TWO PALE BOYS) *(COOKCD 105)* **EREWHON**
– Obsession / Planet of fols / Nowheresville / Fire / Lantern / Morbid sky / Weird cornfields / Kathlen / Highway 61 revisited.

Jun 97. (5xcd-box) *(HR 110)* **MONSTER** (compilation of all work) -

PLASTICLAND

Formed: Milwaukee, Wisconsin, USA . . . 1980 by GLENN REHSE and JOHN FRANKOVIC, who had actually played together in a mid-60's garage band. They played some live psychedelic (PINK FLOYD / CREATION-like) shows, but by the early 70's they had "progressed" into rock outfit, WILLIE THE CONQUEROR. Influenced by Britain's new-found love of "Krautrock", they became AROUSING POLARIS, although it wasn't long before another quarrel split them apart. With PLASTICLAND, they were once again reunited, taking their first fruitful sojourn into the studio with the single, 'MINK DRESS'. With punk-rock out of the way, they fashioned themselves in 60's Carnaby Street wares although this image didn't go down too well back home in Milwaukee. In 1982 they made an appearance on "Battle Of The Garages", which led to a self-issued EP, 'POP! OP DROPS'. A debut album, 'COLOR APPRECIATION', was released for the French 'Lolita' label, and its flowing dramas and sense of the absurd led to a deal with 'Enigma' in 1985. Their first outing for the label, 'WONDER WONDERFUL WONDERLAND', was lush Lewis Carroll-style fantasy, although ignored producer PAUL CUTLER (of DREAM SYNDICATE) might disagree. Their next groovy offering, 'SALON', in 1987, showed a shift to more "Psychedelic Shack"-style R&B/soul although they refused to do a promotional tour, giving their label the "old age" excuse (they were now over 40!). Despite developing musically with some awe-inspiring, occasional gigs (complete with go-go dancers), they were dropped. This led to semi-retirement, the band only surfacing to play reunion gigs although they backed veteran TWINK on his live album. In 1994, their 1991 recorded comeback album, 'DAPPER SNAPPINGS', was finally released by the German 'Repulsion' label. More releases are in the pipeline, although FRANKOVIC is now part-time solo, while other offshoots The GOTHICS and FABULON TRIPTOMETER are also underway. • **Songwriters:** REHSE-FRANKOVIC except covers ALEXANDER (Pretty Things) / etc.

Recommended: PLASTICLAND (*6) / WONDER WONDERFUL WONDERLAND (*7) / SALON (*6) / DAPPER SNAPPINGS (*6) / John Frankovic:- UNDER THE WATER LILY (*6)

GLENN REHSE – vocals, guitar, keyboards / **JOHN FRANKOVIC** – bass, vocals, percussion, bouzouki / **DAN MULLEN** – guitar, vocals / **BRIAN RITCHIE** – drums

Scadillac Scadillac

Jan 81. (7") *<SC-1001>* **MINK DRESS. / OFFICE SKILLS** -

—— **ROB McCUEN** – drums, repl. RITCHIE who joined VIOLENT FEMMES

May 81. (12"ep) *<SC-1002>* **VIBRASONGS FROM . . . POP! OP DROPS** -
– Too many fingers / Standing in a room / The prince's playground / Pushy.

Mar 84. (7") *<(SC 05)>* **EUPHORIC TRAPDOOR SHOES. / RAT TAIL COMB**

Lolita not issued

1984. (lp) **COLOR APPRECIATION** - - France
– Alexander / The garden in pain / Rat tail comb / etc. *<US-iss.1985 as 'PLASTICLAND'; > (UK-iss.Feb87 on 'Bam Caruso'; KIRI 034)*

Pink Dust-Enigma Pink Dust-Enigma

1985. (lp) *(70063-1)* **WONDER WONDERFUL WONDERLAND** -
– No shine for the shoes / Gloria Knight / Transparencies, friends / Fairytale hysteria / Don't let it all pass by / The gingerbread house / Flower scene / Processes of the silverness / Non-stop kitchen / Grassland of reeds and things / Gloria Knight (reprise) / Wonder wonderful wonderland.

—— **VICTOR DEMICHI** – drums, repl. McCUEN

Jun 87. (lp) *(ENIG 2179-1) <72179-1>* **SALON**
–

Repulsion not issued

1991. (12"ep) *(EFA 15651)* **LET'S PLAY POLLYANNA / RADIANT FUZZBOX WIG. / KALEIDOSCOPIC GLANCE / ENCHANTED FORESTRY** -

Feb 95. (cd) *(EFA 15660-2)* **DAPPER SNAPPINGS**

– compilations, etc. –

1995. (cd) ; **MINK DRESS AND OTHER CATS**

JOHN FRANKOVIC

Midnight Midnight

1994. (cd) **UNDER THE WATER LILY**

PLASTIKMAN

Born: RICHIE HAWTIN, c.1971, Canada. Frequenting the techno clubs of DETROIT as a teenager, HAWTIN eventually hooked up with fellow DJ, JOHN AQUAVIVA, and cut the track, 'ELEMENTS OF MIND', under the STATES OF MIND moniker. It was the first release on the fledgling 'PLUS 8' label, a joint project run by HAWTIN and AQUAVIVA to showcase likeminded talent. The PLASTIKMAN alter ego was duly adopted by HAWTIN to showcase his own particular mind scrambling take on acid techno, debuting with the infamous 'SHEET ONE' album. A blistering assault of bowel-quaking 303 mayhem, the record courted controversy as a fan was arrested when police mistook the LSD blotter-sheet style of the cover artwork for the real thing. Undaunted, HAWTIN continued apace with remix work and music of a more cerebral nature under the FUSE moniker. 'MUSIK', 'SHEET ONE's follow-up, mined a slightly more musical seam than its predecessor, although tracks like 'PLASTIK', with its subliminal spookiness, still made for decidedly uneasy listening.

Recommended: SHEET ONE (*7) / MUSIK (*7)

RICHIE HAWTIN – electronics, keyboards

Nova Mute Plus 8

Oct 93. (cd/lp) *(NOMU 22 CD/LP)* **SHEET ONE** -
–

Oct 93. (12") *(12NOMU 28)* **SPASTIK. / HELIKOPTER** -

Nov 93. (12") *(12NOMU 25)* **KRAKPOT. / ELEKTROSTATIK** -

Apr 94. (cd-s) *(CDNOMU 30)* **RECYCLED PLASTIK EP** -

Oct 94. (12"/cd-s) *(12/CD NOMU 34)* **PLASTIQUE. / FREEK / ETHNIK** -

Nov 94. (lp/c/cd) *(NOMU 37/+C/CD)* **MUSIK** -

May 97. (12"/cd-s) *(12/CD NOMU 36)* **SICKNESS. / PANIKATTACK / SLAK/KRIKET – LIVE a SPASTIK**

PORCUPINE TREE

Formed: 1989 by STEVEN WILSON, a self-taught guitarist and keysman. He had originally surfaced in the duo ALTAMONT (in 1983 aged 15), issuing the cassette, 'PRAYER FOR THE SOUL' (half solo, half with SI VOCKINGS on keyboards). Released on 'Acid Tapes', it featured lyrics by the label's owner, ALAN DUFFY (later 'Imaginary' records). Concurrent with this duo was the heavier KARMA, who also released a few private tapes; 'THE JOKE'S ON YOU' (1983) & 'THE LAST MAN TO LAUGH' (1985), before splitting in 1986. Several tracks from these were to take on a new lease of life with PORCUPINE TREE. STEVEN then compiled a progressive rock compilation, 'EXPOSURE', which featured several new bands, plus his new concept NO MAN IS AN ISLAND EXCEPT THE ISLE OF MAN on the track, 'From A Toyshop Window'. He shortened the name slightly for another compilation, 'DOUBLE EXPOSURE', and added ex-PLENTY frontman TIM BOWNESS on the song 'Faith's Last Doubt'. They continued for two years and issued a few items for 'Plastic Head', including two tracks for the label's 'EXPOSE IT' various album. His next venture, PORCUPINE TREE (also with ALAN DUFFY) continued in the same vein, releasing the cassette-only 'TARQUIN'S SEA-

WEED FARM', featuring a PRINCE cover, 'The Cross'. Two more cassettes surfaced in the early 90's; 'LOVE, DEATH AND MUSSOLINI' and 'THE NOSTALGIA FACTORY', whose tracks appeared on the excellent 1992 debut album, 'ON THE SUNDAY OF LIFE'. A single, 'VOYAGE 34' (a 30 minute track), was issued soon after and STEVEN continued with NO MAN, who had also expanded into a band featuring members of JAPAN (STEVE JANSEN, RICHARD BARBIERI & MICK KARN). STEVEN returned the favour in 1994 when he featured on two of their albums, 'Seed' & 'Stone To Flesh' (the latter without KARN). In 1996, PORCUPINE TREE were back on form with 'SIGNIFY', while his NO MAN had signed to '3rd Stone', releasing the more commercial 'WILD OPERA'. • **Style:** Ambient retro-progressive/psychedelic outfit, akin to PINK FLOYD fused with HAWKWIND and rave! • **Songwriters:** WILSON; except NO MAN covers COLOURS (Donovan). NO MAN was a group thing. • **Trivia:** PORCUPINE TREE are also alter-ego The INCREDIBLE EXPANDING MINDFUCK.

Recommended: ON THE SUNDAY OF LIFE (*9) / SIGNIFY (*7)

ALTAMONT

STEVEN WILSON + ALAN DUFFY

Acid Tapes not issued

1983. (c) *(TAB 004)* **PRAYER FOR THE SOUL** ☐ -
1985. (c) *(TAB 010)* **EVERYDAY HEROES** (compilation) ☐ -

— also with KARMA who also released private cassettes (see above).

NO MAN

STEVEN WILSON – guitar, keyboards / **TIM BOWNESS** – vocals / **BEN COLEMAN** – violin

Plastic Head not issued

Jun 89. (12"ep; as NO MAN IS AN ISLAND) *(PLASS 012)* **THE GIRL FROM MISSOURI / FOREST ALMOST BURNING. / NIGHT SKY SWEET EARTH / THE BALLET BEAST** ☐ -

Hidden Art not issued

Jul 90. (7") *(HA 4)* **COLOURS. / COLOURS (remodelled)** ☐ -

Probe Plus not issued

Nov 90. (12"ep) *(PP 27T)* **COLOURS. / DRINK JUDAS / COLOURS (remodelled)** ☐ -

O. L. Indian not issued

Jul 91. (12"ep/cd-ep) *(57TP 12/7CD)* **DAYS IN THE TREES EP** ☐ -
– Days in the trees (Mahler / Ives / Bartok / Reich versions).

Apr 92. (m-lp/m-cd) *(TPLP 47 M/CD)* **LOVESIGHS – AN ENTERTAINMENT** ☐ -
– Heartcheat pop / Days in the trees (Mahler) / rink Judas / Heartcheat motel / Kiss me stupid / Colours / Iris Murdoch cut me up / Days in the trees (Reich).

— added JAPAN (RAIN TREE CROW) members **STEVE JANSEN** – drums / **RICHARD BARBIERI** – keyboards / **MICK KARN** – bass

Sep 92. (12"ep/cd-ep) *(63TP 12/7CD)* **OCEAN SONG. / BACK TO THE BURNING SHED / SWIRL** ☐ -

Jan 93. (cd-ep mail-order) *(73TP 7CD)* **SWEETHEART RAW / BLEED / SAY BABY SAY GOODBYE** - -

Mar 93. (12"ep/cd-ep) *(83TP 12/7CD)* **ONLY BABY (Move For Me) / ONLY BABY (Breathe For Me) / ONLY BABY (Be For Me) / LONG DAY FALL** ☐ -

May 93. (d-lp/c/cd) *(TPLP 57/+C/CD)* **LOVEBLOWS AND LOVECRIES – A CONFESSION** ☐ -
– Loveblow / Only baby / Housekeeping / Sweetheart raw / Lovecry / Tulip / Break Heaven / Beautiful and cruel / Painting Paradise / Heaven's break. *(ltd.cd w/ free cd) (TPLP 57CDL)*- **LOVESIGHS**

Jun 93. (12"/cd-s) *(93TP 12/7CD)* **PAINTING PARADISE. / HEAVEN TASTE** ☐ -

— JAPAN members dislodged by ROBERT FRIPP (King Crimson) – guitar

Jun 94. (d-lp/c/cd) *(TPLP 67/+C/CD)* **FLOWERMOUTH** ☐ -
– Angel gets caught in the beauty trap / You grow more beautiful / Animal ghost / Soft shoulders / Shell of a fighter / Teardrop falls / Watching over me / Simple / Things change.

— now without COLEMAN

Hidden Art not issued

Oct 95. (cd) *(HI-ART 1)* **HEAVEN TASTE** ☐ -
(re-iss.Oct96; same)

Oct 95. (cd) *(HI-ART 2)* **FLOWERMIX** ☐ -
(re-iss.Oct96; same)

3rd Stone not issued

May 96. (cd-ep) *(STONE 026CD)* **HOUSEWIVES HOOKED ON HEROIN / HIT THE CEILING / HOUSEWIVES HOOKED ON METHADONE (Scanner mix) / URBAN DISCO / WHERE I'M CALLING FROM** ☐ -

Aug 96. (cd) *(STONE 027CD)* **WILD OPERA** ☐ -
– Radiant city / Pretty genius / Infant phenomenon / Sinister jazz / Housewives hooked on heroin / Libertino libretto / Taste my dream / Dry cleaning Ray / Sheep loop / My rival Trevor / Time travel in Texas / My revenge on Seattle / Wild opera.

May 97. (7"ltd) *(STONE 034S)* **DRY CLEANING RAY. / TIME TRAVEL IN TEXAS / WATCHING OVER ME** ☐ -

Jun 97. (cd) *(STONE 035CD)* **DRY CLEANING RAY** ☐ -
– Dry cleaning Ray / Sweetside silver night / Jack the sax / Diet mothers / Urban disco / Punished for being born / Knightlinger / Evelyn (the song of slurs) / Sicknote.

PORCUPINE TREE

STEVEN WILSON – guitar, keyboards, vocals

Delerium C&S

1991. (ltd.c) *(DELC 0002)* **TARQUIN'S SEAWEED FARM** (originally very ltd.50 in 1989) - -

— LOVE, DEATH AND MUSSOLINI cassette released 1990 but only 10 copies.

1991. (ltd.c) *(DELC 0003)* **THE NOSTALGIA FACTORY** (originally very ltd.50 in 1990) - -

May 92. (cd/d-lp) *(DELEC CD/LP 008D)* **ON THE SUNDAY SIDE OF LIFE** ☐ -
– Music for the head / Jupiter island / Third eye surfer / On the Sunday side of life . . . / The nostalgia factory / Space transmission / Message from a self-destructing turnip / Radioactive toy / Nine cats / Hymn / Footprints / Linton Samuel Dawson / And the swallows dance above the sun / Queen quotes Crowley / No luck with rabbits / Begonia seduction scene / This long silence / It will rain for a million years.

Nov 92. (12"ep/cd-ep) *(DELEC EP/CDEP 010)* **VOYAGE 34 PHASE 1. / PHASE 2** ☐ -

— added **COLIN EDWIN** – bass / **CHRIS MAITLAND** – drums / **RICHARD BARBIERI** – keyboards

Jun 93. (cd/lp) *(DELEC CD/LP 020)* **UP THE DOWNSTAIR** ☐ -
– What are you listening to / Synesthesia / Monuments burn into moments / Always never / Up the downstair / Not beautiful anymore / Siren / Small fish / Burning sky / Fadeaway.

Nov 93. (12"ep) *(DELEC EP 007)* **VOYAGE 34 REMIX: PHASE 3 (Astralasia Dreamstate). / PHASE 4 (A New Civilisation)** ☐ -

Oct 94. (12"ep/cd-ep) *(DELEC EP/CDEP 032)* **STARS DIE. / MOONLOOP** ☐ -

Oct 94. (cd-ep) <*CS 2024-2*> **STARS DIE / MOONLOOP / ALWAYS NEVER** - ☐

Jan 95. (cd,pic-cd/lp/blue-lp) *(DELEC CD/LP 028/+L)* **THE SKY MOVES SIDEWAYS** ☐ -
– The sky moves sideways (part one) / Dislocated day / Moon touches your shoulder / Prepare yourself / The sky moves sideways (part two). *(cd+=)*– Moonloop.

Apr 96. (12"ep) *(DELEC EP 049)* **WAITING PHASE 1 / WAITING PHASE 2. / COLOURFLOW IN MIND / FUSE THE SUN** ☐ -
(cd-ep) *(DELEC CDEP 049)* – (Phase 1 & 2) / The sound of no-one listening.

Sep 96. (cd/d-lp) *(DELEC CD/LP 045)* **SIGNIFY** ☐ -
(d-lp+=)– The sound of no-one listening.

– compilations, others, etc –

Aug 94. (cd) *Magic Gnome; (MG 4299325)* **YELLOW HEDGEROW DREAMSCAPE** ☐ -
– Mute / Landscape / Prayer / Daughters in excess / Delightful suicide / Split image / No reason to live, no reason to die / Wastecoat / Towel / Execution of the will of the Marquis De Sade / Track eleven / Radioactive toy / An empty box / The cross / Yellow hedgerow dreamscape / Music for the head.

Oct 94. (10"m-lp) *Lazy; (LE 3094)* **STAIRCASE INFINITIES** ☐ -
(cd-iss.Oct95 on 'Blueprint'; BP 217CD)

PORTISHEAD

Formed: Bristol, England . . . 1993 by duo GEOFF BARROWS and BETH GIBBONS. After working as MASSIVE ATTACK's studio runner and writing one of the better songs on NENEH CHERRY's 'HOMEBREW' album, BARROWS recruited covers band stalwart GIBBONS and the band signed to 'Go! Discs' off-shoot 'Go! Beat'. Named after BARROW's faded seaside resort hometown of Portishead near Bristol, the group debuted with a short film, 'TO KILL A DEAD MAN'. A retro spy movie pastiche, the film (which starred Portishead in an acting capacity) and its accompanying soundtrack were indicative of the cinematic melodrama which would chracterise the band's groundbreaking debut. Released in August '94 amid much anticiption, and preceeded by the singles 'NUMB' and 'SOUR TIMES', 'DUMMY' was a wracked, claustrophobic melange of painfully slow hip hop rhythms, droning hammond, knife-edge guitar and rumbling bass. Spiced with a sprinkling of obscure samples and topped off by the sublime lament of GIBBONS' vocals, the sound PORTISHEAD had created was one of the most striking definitions of the phenomena that would come to be known as 'Trip Hop'. Along with MASSIVE ATTACK, TRICKY et al., the band insisted the label was a lazy attempt at pigeonholing but what really set PORTISHEAD apart was simply the otherness of their sound, a strange grace that made the unrelenting lyrical bleakness and despair bearable. Who knows, winning the Mercury Music Prize in 1995 may have cheered them up a bit, although a cover of 'SHINY HAPPY PEOPLE' looks unlikely. • **Songwriters:** BARLOW-GIBBONS, but most with UTLEY. Sample; MORE MISSION IMPOSSIBLE (Lalo Schifrin) / SPIN IT JIG (Smokey Brooks) / ELEGANT PEOPLE (Weather Report) / MAGIC MOUNTAIN (War) / I'LL NEVER FALL IN LOVE AGAIN (Johnnie Ray; at slow speed!) / ISAAC MOODS (Isaac Hayes). • **Trivia:** Have remixed for the likes of DEPECHE MODE (In Your Room) / RIDE (I Don't Know Where It Comes From) / GRAVEDIGGAZ (Nowhere To Run).

Recommended: DUMMY (*10)

BETH GIBBONS – vocals / **GEOFF BARLOW** (b.1971) – programming, synthesizer with **ADRIAN UTLEY** – guitar, bass / **CLIVE DEAMER** – drums / **DAVE McDONALD** – nose flute / **RICHARD NEWELL** – drum programme / **NEIL SOLMAN** – synthesizers, organ / **ANDY HAGUE** – trumpet

Go Beat Go! Discs

Jun 94. (c-s) *(GODMC 114)* **NUMB / NUMBED IN MOSCOW** ☐ ☐
(12"+=/cd-s+=) *(GOD X/CD 114)* – Revenge of the numbed / Numb: Earth under / Extra numb.
(cd-s++=) *(GOLCD 114)* – A tribute to Monk and Cantella.

Aug 94. (c-s) *(GODMC 116)* **SOUR TIMES / SOUR SOUR TIMES** 57 ☐
(12"+=) *(GODX 116)* – Lot more / Sheared times.
(cd-s++=) *(GODCD 116)* – Airbus reconstruction.
(cd-s) *(GOLCD 116)* – ('A'side) / It's a fire / Pedestal / Theme from 'To Kill A Dead Man'.
(re-iss.Apr95, hit UK No.13/ issued US hit 53)

Aug 94. (cd/c/lp) *(<828552-2/-4/-1>)* **DUMMY** 2 79 Jan95
– Mysterons / Sour times / Strangers / It could be sweet / Wandering star / Numb / Roads / Pedestal / Biscuit / Glory box.

Oct 94. (c-s) *(GODMC 120)* **GLORY BOX / ('A'version)** 13
(12"+=/cd-s+=) *(GOD X/CD 120)* – ('A'versions).

—— BARROW guested on EARTHLING's 1996 minor hit album 'Radar'.

Jun 97. (12"ltd) *(571277-1)* **COWBOYS** -

—— above will be included on their forthcoming album.

PRIMAL SCREAM

Formed: Glasgow, Scotland . . . mid'84 by JESUS & MARY CHAIN drummer BOBBY GILLESPIE. Signing to JAMC's label, 'Creation', in 1985, they cut two singles, GILLESPIE leaving The 'MARY CHAIN after the debut, 'ALL FALL DOWN' (1985). The first album, 'SONIC FLOWER GROOVE' (1987), was recorded by the current band line-up core of ANDREW INNES, ROBERT 'THROB' YOUNG and MARTIN DUFFY (save MANI, ex-STONE ROSES, who joined up in 1996) along with an ever-changing array of additional musicians. Released on 'Creation' boss ALAN McGEE's 'WEA' subsidiary label, 'Elevation', the album saw the band pretty much live up to their name, a primitive take on raw ROLLING STONES, STOOGES etc. with a bit of BYRDS jingle jangle thrown in. This sound served the band well through their second album, PRIMAL SCREAM (1989) until the release of 'LOADED' in early 1990. Back at 'CREATION' and enamoured with the Acid House explosion, the band had enlisted the esteemed ANDREW WEATHERALL to remix 'I'M LOSING MORE THAN I'LL EVER HAVE' from the second lp. More a revolution than a remix, WEATHERALL created the stoned funk shuffle of 'LOADED', in the process bringing indie and rave kids together on the same dancefloor for the first time. PRIMAL SCREAM were now set on pushing the parameters of rock, releasing a trio of singles that defined an era, 'COME TOGETHER' (1990) was 90's style hedonist gospel that converted even the most cynical of rock bores while 'HIGHER THAN THE SUN' (1991) was perhaps the 'SCREAM's stellar moment, a narcotic lullaby beamed from another galaxy. Combining all the aforementioned tracks with a trippy 13TH FLOOR ELEVATORS cover, a heavyweight dub workout and a clutch of STONES-like beauties, 'SCREAMADELICA' (1991) was flawless. Opening with the euphoric 'MOVIN' ON UP' (the best song the 'STONES never wrote), the album effortlessly proved that dance and rock were essentially carved out of the same soulful root source, a seam that's been mined by any artist that's ever mattered. A landmark album, 'SCREAMADELICA' was awarded the Mercury Music prize in 1992 and for sheer breadth of vision the record has yet to meet its match in the 90's. Inevitably, then, the GEORGE DRAKOULIAS-produced follow-up, 'GIVE OUT BUT DON'T GIVE UP' (1994) was a disappointment in comparison. Recorded in MEMPHIS, the record saw PRIMAL SCREAM trying far too hard to achieve a roughshod R&B grit. Where before they had made The STONES' sound their own, now they came across as mere plagiarists, and over-produced plagiarists at that. Granted, the likes of 'JAILBIRD' and 'ROCKS' were funkier than any of the insipid indie competition around at the time and GILLESPIE's epileptic handclap routine was always more endearing than the run-of-the-mill rock posturing. Rumours of severe drug abuse abounded at this point and few were shocked when, in January 1994, it emerged that DUFFY had survived a near fatal stabbing in America. For the next couple of years, the band kept a fairly low profile, only a contribution to the 'Trainspotting' soundtrack and an unofficial Scottish 'Euro '96' single confirmed the 'SREAM were still in existence. But while Scotland stumbled to defeat (again!!), PRIMAL SREAM cleaned up their act and recorded the wonderful 'VANISHING POINT' (1997). Apparently cut as an alternative soundtrack to cult 70's road movie 'Kowalski', this album was the true follow-up/comedown to the psychedelic high of 'SCREAMADELICA'. 'OUT OF THE VOID' was the band's darkest moment to date while the title track and 'STUKA' were fractured, paranoid psych-outs. Only the vintage screenshow of 'GET DUFFY' and the mellow 'STAR' offered any respite. Big on dub and low on derivation, the album was a spirited return to form for one of Scotland's most enduring and groundbreaking bands. • **Songwriters:** GILLESPIE, YOUNG and BEATTIE, until the latter's replacement by INNES. Covered CARRY ME HOME (Dennis Wilson) / UNDERSTANDING (Small Faces) / 96 TEARS (? & The Mysterians) / KNOW YOUR RIGHTS (Clash).

Recommended: SCREAMADELICA (*10) / PRIMAL SCREAM (*8) / GIVE OUT BUT DON'T GIVE UP (*7).

BOBBY GILLESPIE (b.22 Jun'64) – vocals (ex-WAKE) (also drummer of JESUS & MARY CHAIN) / **JIM BEATTIE** – guitar / **ROBERT YOUNG** – bass / **TOM McGURK** – drums / **MARTIN ST.JOHN** – tambourine

Creation / not issued

May 85. (7") *(CRE 017)* **ALL FALL DOWN. / IT HAPPENS** -

—— added **PAUL HARTE** – rhythm guitar (GILLESPIE left JESUS & MARY)

Apr 86. (7") *(CRE 026)* **CRYSTAL CRESCENT. / VELOCITY GIRL** -
(12"+=) *(CRE 026T)* – Spirea X.

—— **STUART MAY** – rhythm guitar (ex-SUBMARINES) repl. HARTE (Dec86) / **ANDREW INNES** – rhythm guitar (of REVOLVING PAINT DREAM) repl. MAY / Guest drummers **PHIL KING** (studio) + **DAVE MORGAN** (tour) repl. McGURK

Elevation / not issued

Jun 87. (7") *(ACID 5)* **GENTLE TUESDAY. / BLACK STAR CARNIVAL** -
(12"+=) *(ACID 5T)* – I'm gonna make you mine.

Sep 87. (7") *(ACID 5)* **IMPERIAL. / STAR FRUIT SURF RIDER** -
(12"+=/s12"+=) *(ACID 5T/+W)* – So sad about us / Imperial (demo).

Oct 87. (lp/c)(cd) *(ELV 2/+C)(242-182-2)* **SONIC FLOWER GROOVE** 62
– Gentle Tuesday / Treasure trip / May the sun shine bright for you / Sonic sister love / Silent spring / Imperial / Love you / Leaves / Aftermath / We go down slowly. *(re-iss.Jul91)*

—— (Jun87) **GAVIN SKINNER** – drums repl. ST.JOHN

—— (Feb88) Now a trio **GILLESPIE, YOUNG + INNES** augmented by **JIM NAVAJO** – guitar. (BEATTIE formed SPIREA X, and SKINNER also left)

—— (Feb89) added **HENRY OLSEN** – bass (ex-NICO) / **PHILIP 'TOBY' TOMANOV** – drums (ex-NICO, ex-DURUTTI COLUMN, ex-BLUE ORCHIDS)

Creation / Sire

Jul 89. (7") *(CRE 067)* **IVY IVY IVY. / YOU'RE JUST TOO DARK TO CARE**
(12"+=)(cd-s+=) *(CRE 067T)(CRESCD 067)* – I got you split wide open over me.

Sep 89. (lp/c/cd) *(CRE LP/C/CD 054)* **PRIMAL SCREAM**
– Ivy Ivy Ivy / You're just dead skin to me / She power / You're just too dark to care / I'm losing more than I'll ever have / Gimme gimme teenage head / Lone star girl / Kill the king / Sweet pretty thing / Jesus can't save me. *(free 7"ltd.)*– SPLIT WIDE OPEN (demo). / LONE STAR GIRL (demo)

—— trimmed to a trio again (**GILLESPIE, YOUNG + INNES**)

Feb 90. (7") *(CRE 070)* **LOADED. / I'M LOSING MORE THAN I'LL EVER HAVE** 16
(ext.12"+=/'A'Terry Farley remix-12"+=)(ext.cd-s+=) *(CRE 070 T/X)(CRESCD 070)* – Ramblin' Rose (live).

Jul 90. (7"/c-s)(ext.12")(ext.cd-s) *(CRE/+CS 078)(CRE 078T(CRESCD 078)* **COME TOGETHER (Terry Farley mix). / COME TOGETHER (Andrew Weatherall mix)** 26
(12") *(CRE 078X)* – ('A'-HypnotoneBrainMachine mix) / ('A'-BBG mix).

Jun 91. (7"/ext.12") *(CRE 096/+T)* **HIGHER THAN THE SUN. / ('A' American Spring mix)** 40
(cd-s+=) *(CRESCD 096)* – Higher than the Orb.

—— guest spot on above from **JAH WOBBLE** – bass

Aug 91. (7"/ext.12")(c-s) *(CRE 110/+T)(CRECS 110)* **DON'T FIGHT IT, FEEL IT. / ('A'scat mix featuring Denise Johnson)** 41
(cd-s+=) *(CRESCD 110)* – ('A'extended version).

Sep 91. (cd/c/d-lp) *(CRE CD/C/LP 076)* **SCREAMADELICA** 8
– Movin' on up / Slip inside this house / Don't fight it, feel it / Higher than the Sun / Inner flight / Come together / Loaded / Damaged / I'm comin' down / Higher than the Sun (a dub symphony in two parts) / Shine like stars.

Jan 92. (7"ep/c-ep) *(CRE/+CS 117)* **DIXIE-NARCO EP** 11
– Movin' on up / Carry me home / Screamadelica.
(12"ep+=)(cd-ep+=) *(CRE 117T)(CRESCD 117)* – Stone my soul.

—— In Jan'94, MARTIN DUFFY was stabbed in Memphis, although he recovered soon after.

—— Line-up:- **GILLESPIE, YOUNG, INNES, DUFFY + DAVID HOOD + DENISE JOHNSON** + guest **GEORGE CLINTON** – vocals

Mar 94. (7"/c-s) *(CRE/+CS 129)* **ROCKS. / FUNKY JAM** 7
(12")(cd-s) *(CRE 129T)(CRESCD 129)* – ('A'side) / Funky jam (hot ass mix) / Funky jam (club mix).

Apr 94. (cd/c/lp) *(CRE CD/C/LP 146)* **GIVE OUT, BUT DON'T GIVE UP** 2
– Jailbird / Rocks / (I'm gonna) Cry myself blind / Funky jam / Big jet plane / Free / Call on me / Struttin' / Sad and blue / Give out but don't give up / I'll be there for you.

Jun 94. (7"/c-s) *(CRE/+CS 145)* **JAILBIRD. / ('A'-Dust Brothers mix)** 29
(12"+=) *(CRE 145T)* – ('A'-Toxic Trio stay free mix) / ('A'-Weatherall dub chapter 3 mix).
(cd-s++=) *(CRESCD 145)* – ('A'-Sweeney 2 mix).

Nov 94. (7"/c-s) *(CRE/+CS 183)* **(I'M GONNA) CRY MYSELF BLIND (George Drakoulias mix). / ROCKS (live)** 51
(cd-s+=) *(CRESCD 183)* – I'm losing more than I'll ever have (live) / Struttin' (back in our minds) (Brendan Lynch remix).
(10") *(CRE 183X)* – ('A'side) / Struttin' (back in our minds) (Brendan Lynch remix) / Give out, but don't give up (Portishead remix) / Rockers dub (Kris Needs mix).

Jun 96. (c-s/cd-s; PRIMAL SCREAM, IRVINE WELSH AND ON-U SOUND PRESENT . . .) *(CRECS-CRESCD 194)* **THE BIG MAN AND THE SCREAM TEAM MEET THE BARMY ARMY UPTOWN (mixes:- full strength fortified dub / electric soup dub / a jake supreme)** 17 -

—— In Oct'96, GILLESPIE, INNES, YOUNG & DUFFY were joined by **MANI MOUNFIELD** – bass (ex-STONE ROSES)

May 97. (c-s) *(CRECS 245)* **KOWALSKI / 96 TEARS** 8
(cd-s+=) *(CRESCD 245)* – Know your rights / ('A'-Automator mix).

Jun 97. (c-s) CRECS 263) **STAR / JESUS** 16
(cd-s+=) *(CRESCD 263)* – Rebel dub / How does it feel to belong.
(12"+=) *(CRE 263T)* – ('A'mixes).

—— (above 2 singles from the forthcoming album 'VANISHING POINT' Jul97)

R

RAIN PARADE

Formed: Los Angeles, California, USA . . . 1981 as The SIDEWALKS by Minneapolis college mates DAVID ROBACK and MATT PIUCCI. They also numbered DAVID's younger brother STEVEN and WILL GLENN, before they opted for a name change. Their vinyl debut came with the BYRDS-like 'WHAT'S SHE DONE TO YOUR MIND' in 1982 while they found a permanent drummer in EDDIE KALWA. DAVID moonlighted with another project, RAINY DAY, but a disappointing covers album was soon forgotten when 'EMERGENCY THIRD RAIL POWER TRIP' hit the shops. The record gained a UK release on Demon's off-shoot 'Zippo' label, as did their 1984 mini-lp 'EXPLOSIONS IN THE GLASS PALACE'.This was recorded without co-leader DAVID, however, who had left earlier in the year. 'Island' records gave them their break in '85 but surely damaged their growing reputation when they rush-released a live-set recorded in Japan, 'BEYOND THE SUNSET'. With MATT and STEVEN the sole remaining members, they recruited JOHN THOMAN and MARK MARCUM although the 1986 album, 'CRASHING DREAM', was appropriately titled, Island soon ditching them. They took a two-year hiatus before going back into the studio to finish off a double album. It never found its way to the shops, as PIUCCI joined a re-formed CRAZY HORSE, while the rest became VIVA SATURN. • **Style:** "Paisley Underground" psychedelia with tints of early PINK FLOYD or TELEVISION. • **Songwriters:** All written by the ROBACKS and group, except AIN'T THAT NOTHIN' (Television).

Recommended: EMERGENCY THIRD RAIL POWER TRIP (*8) / EXPLOSIONS IN THE GLASS PALACE (*7) / CRASHING DREAM (*7)

DAVID ROBACK – vocals, guitar, percussion / **MATT PIUCCI** – guitar, vocals, sitar / **WILL GLENN** – keyboards / **STEVEN ROBACK** – bass, vocals / **EDDIE KALWA** – drums

not issued Llama

1982. (7") **WHAT'S SHE DONE TO YOUR MIND?. / ?** [-]

Zippo Enigma

Aug 84. (lp) *(ZING 001) <ENIGMA 19>* **EMERGENCY THIRD RAIL POWER TRIP** 1983
– Talking in my sleep / This can't be today / I look around / 1 hr. half ago / Carolyn's song / What she's done to your mind / Look at Merri / Saturday's asylum / Kaleidoscope / Look both ways.

— trimmed to a quartet when DAVE left to form RAINY DAY (later OPAL). He is now part of duo MAZZY STAR

1984. (m-lp) *(ZANE 003)* **EXPLOSIONS IN THE GLASS PALACE**
– You are my friend / Prisoners / Blue / Broken horse / No easy way down.

Feb 85. (7") *(ZIPPO 45-1)* **YOU ARE MY FRIEND. / THIS CAN'T BE TODAY** 1984

— **MARK MARCUM** – drums repl. KALWA

— added **JOHN THOMAN** – guitar, vocals

Island Island

Jun 85. (lp/c) *(IMA/IMC 17)* **BEYOND THE SUNSET** (live in Tokyo 1984) 78
– Night shade / Prisoners / This can't be today / Blue / Eyes closed / Ain't that nothin' / Don't feel bad / 1 hr. 1/2 ago / Blue / No easy way down / Cheap wine.

Oct 85. (lp/c) *(ILPS/ICT 9805)* **CRASHING DREAM**
– Depending on you / My secret country / Don't feel bad / Mystic green / Sad eyes kill / Shoot down the railroad man / Fertile crescent / Invisible people / Gone west / Only business.

— Disbanded when PIUCCI formed GONE FISHIN', then joined CRAZY HORSE

- compilations, others, etc. -

Feb 92. (cd) *Mau Mau; (MAUCD 610)* **EMERGENCY THIRD RAIL POWER TRIP / EXPLOSIONS IN THE GLASS PALACE** [-]

VIVA SATURN

STEVEN ROBACK / JOHN THOMAN / MARK MARCUM

World Service World Service

Jun 89. (lp) *(SERVS 003)* **VIVA SATURN**
– So glad / Brought it on yourself / Remember I'm dead / Old world / Wild town.

Normal

May 94. (m-cd) *(NORMAL 139CD)* **SOUNDMIND**

Restless Restless

Jul 95. (cd) *(72909-2)* **BRIGHTSIDE**
– Send a message / Black cloud / Brightside / Here comes April / Abondoned car string me out a line / Mourn the light / Distracted / Nothing helps / Heart of you / One for my baby.

RAINY DAY (see under ⇒ MAZZY STAR)

Lee RANALDO (see under ⇒ SONIC YOUTH)

RED HOUSE PAINTERS

Formed: San Francisco, California, USA . . . 1989 by MARK KOZELEK, who had earlier sang in GOD FORBID. After moving from Ohio to Atlanta he met ANTHONY KOUTSOS who helped him form RED HOUSE PAINTERS. They relocated again, this time to San Francisco, where they met GORDON MACK and JERRY VESSEL. Their demos found their way to the doors of UK's '4 a.d.' via the ears of MARK EITZEL (American Music Club). The early 1990 demos soon became their well-recieved debut album, 'DOWN COLORFUL HILL'. In 1993, they released two self-titled albums, the first of which made the UK Top 75 lists. They then took a 2-year hiatus away from the music business, returning with 'OCEAN HOUSE'. On the strength of this release they secured a deal with 'Island' records and 'SONGS FOR A BLUE GUITAR' was again well-received by critics although it failed commercially. • **Style:** Moody alternative pastel-rock outfit, fronted by the drug & drink-free KOZELEK. • **Songwriters:** All by KOZELEK, except 'Dragonflies' by ROBYN RIEL-NAIL. Covers; I AM A ROCK (Paul Simon) / STAR SPANGLED BANNER (US National Anthem) / SHOCK ME (Kiss) / LONG DISTANCE RUNAROUND (Yes). • **Trivia:** Their UK first gig (very rare) was at The Borderline in London in the Autumn of '92.

Recommended: RED HOUSE PAINTERS (*9; Jun93 double album) / DOWN COLORFUL HILL (*8) / OCEAN BEACH (*7) / SONGS FOR A BLUE GUITAR (*8)

MARK KOZELEK – vocals / **GORDON MACK** – guitar / **JERRY VESSEL** – bass / **ANTHONY KOUTSOS** – drums

4 a.d. 4 a.d.

Sep 92. (cd)(lp/c) *(CAD 2014CD)(CAD/+C 2014)* **DOWN COLORFUL HILL**
– 24 / Medicine bottle / Down colourful hill / Japanese to English / Lord kill the pain / Michael.

Jun 93. (cd)(d-lp/c) *(DAD 3008CD)(DAD/+C 3008)* **RED HOUSE PAINTERS** 63
– Grace cathedral park / Down through / Katy song / Mistress / Things mean a lot / Funhouse / Take me out / Rollercoaster / New Jersey / Dragonflies / Mistress (piano version) / Mother / Strawberry hill / Brown eyes.

Oct 93. (cd)(m-lp/c) *(CAD 3016CD)(CAD/+C 3016)* **RED HOUSE PAINTERS** 68
– Evil / Bubble / I am a rock / Helicopter / New Jersey / Uncle Joe / Blindfold / Star spangled banner.

Feb 94. (12"ep/cd-ep) *(BAD 4004/+CD)* **SHOCK ME / SHOCK ME (mix). / SUNDAYS AND HOLIDAYS / THREE-LEGGED CAT**

Mar 95. (cd)(c)(2x10"lp) *(CAD 5005CD)(CADC 5005)(DAD 5005)* **OCEAN BEACH**
– Cabezon / Summer dress / San Geronimo / Shadows / Over my head / Red carpet / Brockwell Park / Moments / Drop. *(lp+=)*– Long distance runaround.

Island Island

Jul 96. (cd/c) *(CID/ICT 8050)* **SONGS FOR A BLUE GUITAR**
– Have you forgotten / Song for a blue guitar / Make like paper / Priest alley song / Trailways / Feel the rain fall / Long distance runaround / All mixed up / Revelation Big Sur / Silly love songs / Another song for a blue guitar.

RED RED MEAT

Formed: Chicago, Illinois, USA . . . 1992 by TIM, GLEN, TIM and BRIAN, singer TIM also being a pop video maker for the likes of VERUCA SALT. Their eponymous 1993 debut didn't quite set the world alight, although a deal with 'Sub Pop' won the band a new audience. They played at the opening party of controversial Spanish director PEDRO ALMODOVAR's film, 'Kika', in New York, although their rock set wasn't quite appreciated by the arty dance crowd. A 1994 album, 'JIMMYWINE MAJESTIC', was highly regarded by many critics, although they topped this a year later with the semi-classic 'BUNNY GETS PAID'. • **Style:** Lo-fi psychedelic grunge-blues, brooding, laid-back and eerily melancholic. • **Songwriters:** RUTILLI + some with rest of band. Covered CARPET OF HORSES (Polara).

Recommended: JIMMYWINE MAJESTIC (*6) / BUNNY GETS PAID (*7)

TIM – vocals / **GLEN** – guitar / **TIM** – bass / **BRIAN** – drums (RUTILLI, JOHNSON, GIRARD + HURLEY

not issued Red Red Meat

1993. (cd) *<RRM 001>* **RED RED MEAT** [-]
– Robo sleep / Snowball / Molly's on the rag / Flossy / Idaho durt / Cellophane / Grief giver / Rabbit eyed / Hot nickety monkey / Nice round numbers / X-diamond cutter blues / Stare box. *(UK-iss.Feb95 on 'Sub Pop';)*

Sub Pop Sub Pop

Sep 93. (7") *(SP 232S)* **FLANK. /**

Mar 94. (lp/cd)(c) *(SP/+CD 119300)(SP 243A)* **JIMMYWINE MAJESTIC**
– Flank / Stained and lit / Braindead / Smokey Mtn. cool dip / Moon calf tripe / Cillamange / Ball / Lather / Rusted water / Gorshin / Dowser / Comes / Roses.

— **DECK** repl. JOHNSON

Oct 94. (7"/10") *(SP 272)* **IDIOT SON. / GAUZE**
(10"+=) *(SP 139/343)* – Mouse-ish.

Oct 95. (lp/cd) **(SP 318/+b) BUNNY GETS PAID**
– Carpet of horses / Chain chain chain / Rosewood, Wax, Voltz + Glitter / Buttered / Gauze / Idiot son / Variations on Nadia's theme / Oxtail / Sad cadillac / Taxidermy blues in reverse / There's always tomorrow.

Nov 96. (7") *(SP 376)* **THERE'S A STAR ABOUT THE MANGER TONIGHT. /**

Feb 97. (cd-s) *(SPCD 387)* **THERE'S A STAR ABOUT THE MANGER TONIGHT /**

- others, etc

1997. (7") *Generator;* **LISTENING NOW. / Polara: Carpet Of Horses** [-]

RIDE

Formed: Oxford, England . . . 1988 by local art college students MARK GARDENER, ANDY BELL and LAURENCE COLBERT. They drafted in STEVE QUERALT and journalist/manager Dave Newton who subsequently secured them some London gigs. These led to a deal with 'Creation' records and they released their eponymous debut EP early in 1990, the record quickly selling out of its limited number and squeezing into the UK Top 75. The disc showcased the band's spiralling guitar-scapes and contained an early classic in the cathartic 'DRIVE BLIND'. It was hotly pursued by two further Top 40 EP's, 'PLAY' & 'FALL', the latter containing their best track to date (at that point) in 'TASTE'. Come October, they nearly secured a Top 10 place with their stunning debut album, 'NOWHERE'. 1991 was spent in the studio (excluding Reading Festival), and the fruits were heard early in '92 on their superb 8-minute single 'LEAVE THEM ALL BEHIND'. This slow burning psychedelic epic gave them their first Top 10 entry and was a prelude to their second album, 'GOING BLANK AGAIN'. The record went Top 5, despite being derided by certain music critics. Frictions began to appear and it was thought a two-year sabbatical would solve the problem. BELL took time off to help out his Swedish wife and stablemate IDHA (OVELIUS) on her debut album. In 1994, RIDE were back with 'CARNIVAL OF LIGHT', but again they received lukewarm reviews. Early the next year, GARDENER took off to the States, leaving them all behind (ouch!). Their swansong, 'TARANTULA' was annoyingly deleted after one week, as BELL and GARDENER considered separate solo ventures. • **Style:** Solemn and dreamy ("shoegazing") psychedelic rock band, taking influences from The BYRDS, STOOGES and The JESUS & MARY CHAIN. • **Songwriters:** Lyrics MARK or ANDY / group compositions except covers EIGHT MILES HIGH (Byrds) / THE MODEL (Kraftwerk) / HOW DOES IT FEEL TO FEEL (Creation) / THAT MAN (Small Faces) / UNION CITY BLUE + ATOMIC (Blondie). • **Trivia:** In 1991, they headlined the Slough Music Festival in front of over 8,000 fans.

Recommended: NOWHERE (*8) / GOING BLANK AGAIN (*7) / TARANTULA (*6)

MARK GARDENER – vocals, guitar / **ANDY BELL** – guitar, vocals / **STEPHAN QUERALT** – bass / **LAURENCE COLBERT** – drums

Creation | Creation

Jan 90. (12"ep)(cd-ep) *(CRE 072T)(CRESCD 072)* **RIDE** [71] [-]
– Chelsea girl / Drive blind / Close my eyes / All I can see. *(re-iss.Oct90; same)*

Apr 90. (12"ep)(cd-ep) *(CRE 075T)(CRESCD 075)* **PLAY** [32] [ ]
– Like a daydream / Silver / Furthest sense / Perfect time.

Oct 90. (12"ep)(cd-ep) *(CRE 087T)(CRESCD 087)* **FALL** [34] [ ]
– Dreams burn down / Taste / Here and now / Nowhere.

Oct 90. (cd/lp)(c) *(CRE CD/LP 74)(CREC 74)* **NOWHERE** [11] [ ]
– Seagull / Kaleidoscope / Polar bear / Dreams burn down / In a different place / Decay / Paralysed / Vapour trail. *(cd+=)*– Taste / Here and now / Nowhere.

Mar 91. (c-ep)(12"ep)(cd-ep) *(CRECS 100)(CRE 100T)(CRESCD 100)* **TODAY FOREVER** [14] [ ]
– Unfamiliar / Sennen / Beneath / Today.

Feb 92. (c-ep)(12"ep)(cd-ep) *(CRECS 123)(CRE 123T)(CRESCD 123)* **LEAVE THEM ALL BEHIND. / CHROME WAVES / GRASSHOPPER** [9] [ ]

Mar 92. (cd/2x12"lp)(c) (CRE CD/LP 124)(CCRE 124) **GOING BLANK AGAIN** [5] [ ]
– Leave them all behind / Twisterella / Not fazed / Chrome waves / Mouse trap / Time of her life / Cool your boots / Making Jusy smile / Time machine / OX4.

Apr 92. (c-ep)(12"ep)(cd-ep) *(CRECS 150)(CRE 150T)(CRESCD 150)* **TWISTERELLA / GOING BLANK AGAIN. / HOWARD HUGHES / STAMPEDE** [36] [ ]

— In Oct'93, 'Fright' records issued 'UNION CITY BLUE' *(FRIGHT 060)*

Nov 92. (cd) *<CRECD 126>* **SMILE** (first 2 EP's) [-] [ ]

Apr 94. (12"ep/12"clear-ep)(cd-ep) *(CRE 155T/+C)(CRESCD 155)* **BIRDMAN / ROLLING THUNDER 2. / LET'S GET LOST / DON'T LET IT DIE** [38] [ ]

Jun 94. (7"/c-s) *(CRE/+MC 184)* **HOW DOES IT FEEL TO FEEL? / CHELSEA GIRL** [58] [ ]
(12")(cd-s) *(CRES 184T)(CRESCD 184)* – ('A'side) / Walkabout / At the end of the universe.

Jun 94. (pic-cd/d-lp)(c) *(CRE CD/LP 147)(C-CRE 147)* **CARNIVAL OF LIGHT** [5] [ ]
– Moonlight medicine / 1000 miles / From time to time / Natural grace / Only now / Birdman / Crown of creation / How does it feel to feel? / Endless road / Magical spring / Rolling thunder / I don't know where it comes from.

Sep 94. (c-s) *(CRECS 189)* **I DON'T KNOW WHERE IT COMES FROM. / TWISTERELLA** [46] [ ]
(12")(cd-s) *(CRE 189T)(CRESCD 189)* – ('A'side) / Drive blind / From time to time / How does it feel to feel (live w / The CREATION).
(cd-s) *(CRESCD 189R)* – ('A'-Apollo 11 mix) / Moonlight medicine (ride on the wire mix by Portishead) / A journey to the end of the universe (version).

— split officially early '96. MARK citing ANDY's near takeover of vocal duties.

Feb 96. (12"ep/cd-ep) *(CRE 199T)(CRESCD 199)* **BLACK NITE CRASH** [67] [ ]

Mar 96. (cd/lp)(c) *(CRE CD/LP 180)(CCRE 180)* **TARANTULA** [21] [-]
– Black nite crash / Sunshine – Nowhere to run / Dead man / Walk on water / Deep inside my pocket / Mary Anne / Castle on the hill / Gonna be alright / Dawn patrol / Ride the wind / Burnin' / Starlight motel.

— above was only available for 1 week only

— On the 30th June (last day of book deadline folks!) MARK GARDENER released his limited solo cd-single 'MAGDALEN SKY / CAN'T LET IT DIE' for Oxford-based 'Shifty Disco' *(DISCO 9706)*.

Fierce | not issued

Apr 97. (7"ltd) *(FRIGHT 060)* **UNION CITY BLUE. / ATOMIC** [ ] [-]

S

SABRES OF PARADISE

Formed: Hounslow, London, England . . . early 90's by mixer to the masses, ANDY WEATHERALL. He had previously completed remix work for SECRET KNOWLEDGE, WAXWORTH INDUSTRIES, CORRIDOR, etc, before he met NINA WALSH at his "Shoom" evenings. She had worked with the 'Boys Own' stable and YOUTH, before setting up the 'Sabrettes' label with ANDY. This operation also included GARY BURNS, JAGZ KOONER and DJ ALEX KNIGHT. In 1993 they completed their debut album, 'SABRESONIC', which broke the Top 30 aided by the excellent top techno track of that year; 'SMOKEBELCH II'. This was followed by the churning techno hip-hop of 'THE THEME' in 1994 although the 'HAUNTED DANCEHALL' album, released later that year, failed to break into the Top 50. The SABRETTES (WEATHERALL & WALSH)'s label released several techno opuses by INKY BLACKNUSS, VOODOO PEOPLE, and a collective various artists album, 'PINK ME UP', in 1994. • **Style:** Ambient-techno mixer of atmospheric grandeur. • **Songwriters:** WEATHERALL with samples, except UNITED (Throbbing Gristle). • **Trivia:** WEATHERALL's numerous later remixes have included ONE DOVE / BJORK / LEFTFIELD-LYDON / JAMES / ESPIRITU / THERAPY? / BOMB THE BASS & K-CLASS.

Recommended: SABRESONIC (*8) / HAUNTED DANCEHALL (*7)

ANDY WEATHERALL – keyboards, synthesizers / **NINA WALSH** – vocals / **JAGZ KOONER** – keyboards, synthesizers / **GARY BURNS** – keyboards, synthesizers

Sabres Of Paradise | not issued

Feb 93. (12") *(PT 001)* **UNITED (Andrew Weatherall mix)** [ ] [-]

Sep 93. (12") *(PT 009)* **SMOKEBELCH II (entry). / SMOKEBELCH II (exit)** [55] [ ]
(cd-s+=) *(PT 009CD)* – ('A'mix).
(12") *(PT 009R)* – ('A'-David Holmes mix) / ('A'-flute mix).

Oct 93. (cd/c/lp) *(WARP CD/MC/LP 16)* **SABRESONIC** [29] [ ]
– Still fighting / Smokebelch I / Clock factory / Ano electric endante / R.S.D. / Inter-Lergen-Tan-Ko / Ano electro allegro.

Mar 94. (12"ep/cd-ep) *(PTO 14/+CD)* **THE THEME. / RETURN OF CARTER & EDGE 6 (original mix)** [56] [ ]
(10") *(PT 014R)* – ('A'-Underdog Vs Sabres) / ('A'version).

Warp | Warp

Sep 94. (10"ep/12"ep) *(10+/WAP 50)* **WILMOT. / WILMOT MEETS LORD SCRUFFAGE / SIEGE REFRAIN** [36] [ ]
(c-ep+=/cd-ep+=) *(WAP 50 MC/CD)* – ('A'edit).

Nov 94. (cd/c/d-lp) *(WARP CD/MC/LP 26)* **HAUNTED DANCEHALL** [58] [ ]
– Bubble and slide / Bubble and slide II / Duke of Earlsfield / Flight path estate / Planet D / Wilmot / Tow truck / Theme / Theme 4 / Return to Planet D / Ballad of Nicky McGuire / Jacob Street 7 a.m. / Chapel Street Market 9 a.m. / Haunted dancehall.

May 95. (12"ltd.) *(WAP 62)* **TOW TRUCK (Depth Charge remix). / TOW TRUCK (Chemical Brothers remix)** [ ] [-]

May 95. (10"ltd.) *(10WAP 62)* **DUKE OF EARLSFIELD (LFO remix). / BUBBLE & SLIDE (Nightmares On Wax remix)** [ ] [-]

May 95. (7"ltd.) *(7WAP 62)* **HAUNTED DANCEHALL (In The Nursery mix)** [ ] [-]

May 95. (m-cd) *(WARPCD 31)* **VERSUS** [ ] [-]
– (all 3 similtaneous releases + extra Depth Charge mix).

Jul 95. (cd/c/d-lp) *(WARP CD/MC/LP 34)* **SABRESONIC II** [ ] [ ]
– Smokebelch II / Inter Lergen ten k.o. II / Return of Carter / Still fighting / Smokebelch II / Edge 6 / Clock factory / R.S.D. / Smokebelch II (David Holmes mix).

Special Emissions | not issued

Sep 96. (7"etched) *(SE 011)* **YSAEBUD** [ ] [-]

Waxworth | not issued

Oct 96. (12"ep) *(WB 001)* **ROY REVISITED EP** [ ] [-]

SEEFEEL

Formed: London, England . . . 1992 by JUSTIN FLETCHER and MARK CLIFFORD. The college students soon found DARREN 'Delores Throb' SEYMOUR, but were still in need of a singer. Another to answer a wanted ad was SARAH PEACOCK who soon assumed vocal duties for the 1993 debut, 'MORE LIKE SPACE EP'. Radio One DJ JOHN PEEL subsequently found it hard to distinguish what speed to play it at! (33 or 45rpm). Signed to the same label ('Too Pure') as PJ HARVEY, STEREOLAB, TH' FAITH HEALERS, they tried to break away from the inevitable pigeonholing on a collaboration with APHEX TWIN, the 'PURE, IMPURE EP'. His Sheffield based label, 'Warp', took them on in 1994, releasing their second, more sculpted album, 'SUCCOUR'. • **Style:** Textured pop-rock, moving away from JESUS & MARY CHAIN / MY BLOODY VALENTINE influences to more COCTEAU TWINS and chill-out droning dance. • **Songwriters:** CLIFFORD.

Recommended: QUIQUE (*8) / SUCCOUR (*7)

SARAH PEACOCK – vocals, guitars / **MARK CLIFFORD** – guitars / **DARREN SEYMOUR** – bass / **JUSTIN FLETCHER** – drums

Too Pure | not issued

Mar 93. (12"ep/cd-ep) *(PURE/+CD 20)* **MORE LIKE SPACE E.P.** [ ] [-]
– More like sace / Time to find me (come inside) / Come alive / Blue easy sleep.

Jun 93. (12"ep) *(PURE 23)* **PLAINSONG E.P.** [ ] [-]
– Plainsong / Moodwing / Minky starshine.

Jul 93. (12"ep; with APHEX TWIN) *(PURE 25)* **REMIXES E.P.** [ ] [-]
– Time to find me (AFX fast mix) / Time to find me (AFX slow mix) / Plainsong (sinebubble embossed dub).
(m-cd) **PURE, IMPURE** (PURE/+CD 25) – (the two 12"ep's above).

Oct 93. (cd/c/lp) *(PURE CD/MC/LP 28)* **QUIQUE** [ ] [-]
– Climatic phase 3 / Polyfusion / Industrious / Imperial / Plainsong / Charlotte's mouth / Through you / Filter dub / Signals.

Warp | not issued

May 94. (12"ep/cd-ep) *(WAP 45/+CD)* **STARETHROUGH / ACR EYES. / SPANGLE / LUX 1** [ ] [-]

Sep 94. (10"/cd-s) *(10+/WAP 53/+CD)* **FRACTURE. / TIED** [ ] [-]

Mar 95. (cd/c/d-lp) *(WARP CD/MC/LP 28)* **SUCCOUR** [ ] [-]

– Meal / Extract / When face was pace / Fracture / Gatha / Ruby-ha / Rupt / Vex / Cut / Utreat / (Tempean).

— Taking time off for CLIFFORD to release solo album 'DISJEKTA', while the three others are moonlighting as SIREN.

Rephlex not issued

Nov 96. (cd/lp) *(CAT 038 CD/LP)* **CH-VOX** [ ] [-]

SHAMEN

Formed: Aberdeen, Scotland ... 1984 as ALONE AGAIN OR (named after a LOVE track from '67) by COLIN ANGUS and McKENZIE brothers DEREK and KEITH. After two singles (one for 'Polydor'; DREAM COME TRUE), they became The SHAMEN, releasing the singles 'YOUNG TILL YESTERDAY' (1986) and 'SOMETHING ABOUT YOU' (1987) on their own 'Moksha' label. The debut album, 'DROP' (1987), followed soon after and at this point the band were touting a fairly derivative indie take on classic West coast psychedelia combined with overtly political/drug orientated lyrics. As Angus became increasingly preoccupied with the nascent dance scene, however, DEREK McKENZIE split ranks and was replaced by WILL SINOTT. After the controversial single, 'JESUS LOVES AMERIKA' (1988), ANGUS and SINOTT relocated to LONDON, immersing themselves in the burgeoning acid house scene. The 'SHAMEN VS BAM BAM' (1988) moved the duo ever further into electronic territory and though the 'IN GORBACHEV WE TRUST' (1989) album fitted with the indie/dance crossover zeitgeist, The SHAMEN were one of the only acts to take the phenomenon to its ultimate conclusion. After a last outing for 'Moksha', the band signed to the 'One Little Indian' label in 1989. Their second single for the label, 'PROGEN' (1990), finally saw The SHAMEN make their mark on the dance scene. Although it barely scraped into the charts, the track was huge on the club scene and climbed to No.4 upon its re-release (in remixed form) the following year. In addition to this pivotal track, the album 'EN-TACT' (1990), contained the liquid psychedelia of 'HYPERREAL' (featuring the velvet tones of Polish singer PLAVKA) and the dancefloor manifesto of 'MAKE IT MINE', both minor hit singles. Having initially had DJ EDDIE RICHARDS play acid house ar their gigs, The SHAMEN had now developed the 'Synergy' live experience, a pioneering integration of live electronica and top flight DJ's (including the likes of MIXMASTER MORRIS and PAUL OKENFOLD) that attmepted to create a cultural fusion between the excitement of live performance and the communal vibe of the party scene. Just as the band were beginning to realise their dreams, WILL SINOTT drowned while swimming off the coast of The Canary Islands in May '91. ANGUS eventually decided to carry on and recruited RICHARD WEST aka Mr C, a veteran of the house scene, having DJ'd at the seminal RIP club. He was a natural choice, having rapped on the revamped 'PROGEN' single and collaborated on the 'Synergy' gigs, his inimitable cockney patois possessing a ragamuffin charm. He was also visually striking and along with SOUL FAMILY SENSATION singer JHELISSA ANDERSON, would become the public face of the The SHAMEN, ANGUS cannily content to communicate with the media via E-mail. The 'L.S.I. (LOVE, SEX, INTELLIGENCE)' (1992) single introduced a more commercial sound to the new look SHAMEN, as did the unashamed pop/dance of controversial hit, 'EBENEEZER GOODE' (1992) (the question of whether Mr C did actually sing 'E's are good' was endlessly debated by those tireless moral guardians of the nation's wellbeing). Many longtime fans couldn't stomach the new sound although the band gained a whole new following of pop kids enamoured with cheeky chappy Mr C. The million selling 'BOSS DRUM' (1992) album combined the aforementioned chart fodder with typically SHAMEN-esque communiques on ~'Archaic Revivals' and the like (i.e.'RE-EVOLUTION', the title track etc.). 1995 saw ex-SOUL II SOUL chanteuse VICTORIA WILSON JAMES replace ANDERSON and a new album in the shops, 'AXIS MUTATIS'. Although the record included the celebratory dance pop of single 'DESTINATION ESCHATON', overall it was more cerebral with a companion ambient album, 'ARBOR BONA/ARBOR MALA', released at the same time. 'HEMPTON MANOR' (1996) carried on The SHAMEN's overriding theme of transformation through mind altering substances and although the media profile of the band has shrunk considerably over the last couple of years, The SHAMEN have kept fans abreast of their activities with a rather fabby self-produced internet web-site, 'Nemeton'. • **Songwriters:** All written by COLIN and DEREK, until latter's departure and replacement by the late WILL SINNOTT. ANGUS & WEST took over in '91. Covered; GRIM REAPER OF LOVE (Turtles) / FIRE ENGINE + SLIP INSIDE THIS HOUSE (13th Floor Elevators) / LONG GONE (Syd Barrett) / SWEET YOUNG THING (Monkees) / PURPLE HAZE (Jimi Hendrix). • **Trivia:** In Apr'88, they were dropped from a McEwans lager TV ad, because of their then anti-commercial approach.

Recommended: IN GORBACHEV WE TRUST (*7) / BOSS DRUM (*8) / EN-TACT (*9) / AXIS MUTATIS (*7) / ARBOR BONA/ARBOR MALA (*7)

ALONE AGAIN OR

COLIN ANGUS (b.24 Aug'61) – keyboards / **DEREK McKENZIE** (b.27 Feb'64) – vocals, guitar / **KEITH McKENZIE** (b.30 Aug'61) – drums

All One not issued

Dec 84. (7") *(ALG 1)* **DRUM THE BEAT (IN MY SOUL). / SMARTIE EDIT** [ ] [-]

All One – Polydor not issued

Mar 85. (7") *(ALG 2)* **DREAM COME TRUE. / SMARTER THAN THE AVERAGE BEAR** [ ] [-]
(12") *(ALGX 2)* – ('A'-Splintered version) / ('B'-Ursa Major) / Drum the beat (shall we dance?).

SHAMEN

— added **ALISON MORRISON** – bass, keyboards

One Big Guitar not issued

Apr 86. (12"ep) *(OBG 003T)* **THEY MAY BE RIGHT ... BUT THEY'RE CERTAINLY WRONG** [ ] [-]
– Happy days / Velvet box / I don't like the way the world is turning.

— **PETER STEPHENSON** (b. 1 Mar,62, Ayrshire) – keyboards repl. ALISON

Moksha not issued

Nov 86. (7"m) *(SOMA 1)* **YOUNG TILL YESTERDAY. / WORLD THEATRE / GOLDEN HAIR** [ ] [-]
(12"m) *(SOMA 1T)* – (first 2 tracks) / It's all around / Strange days dream.

May 87. (7") *(SOMA 2)* **SOMETHING ABOUT YOU. / DO WHAT YOU WILL** [ ] [-]
(12"+=) *(SOMA 2T)* – Grim reaper of love.

Jun 87. (lp/c) *(SOMA LP/C 1)* **DROP** [ ] [-]
– Through with you / Something about you / Four letter girl / The other side / Passing away / Young till yesterday / Happy days / Where do you go / Through my window / I don't like the way the world is turning / World theatre / Velvet box. *(c+=)*– Do what you will. *(cd-iss.Nov88 ++=; SOMACD 1)*– Strange days dream. *(re-iss.Jan92 on 'Mau Mau' lp/c/cd; MAU/+MC/CD 613)*

Sep 87. (7") *(SOMA 3)* **CHRISTOPHER MAYHEW SAYS. / SHITTING ON BRITAIN** [ ] [-]
(12"+=) *(SOMA 3T)* – Fire engine / Christopher Mayhew says a lot.

— **WILL SINNOTT** (b.23 Dec'60, Glasgow, Scotland) – bass repl. DEREK (COLIN now vocals, guitar)

Feb 88. (7") *(SOMA 4)* **KNATURE OF A GIRL. / HAPPY DAYS** [ ] [-]
(12"+=) *(SOMA 4T)* – What's going down / Sub knature of a girl.

Ediesta not issued

Jun 88. (7") *(CALC 069)* **JESUS LOVES AMERIKA. / DARKNESS IN ZION** [ ] [-]
(12"+=) *(CALCT 069)* – Do what you will.
(cd-s++=) *(CALCCD 069)* – Sub knatural dub.

— now a duo of **COLIN + WILL**

Desire not issued

Nov 88. (12"; as SHAMEN VS BAM BAM) *(WANTX 10)* **TRANSCENDENTAL. / ('A'-housee mix)** [ ] [-]

Demon not issued

Jan 89. (lp/c/cd) *(FIEND/+C/CD 666)* **IN GORBACHEV WE TRUST** [ ] [-]
– Synergy / Sweet young thing / Raspberry infundibulum / War prayer / Adam Strange / Jesus loves Amerika / Transcendental / Misinformation / Raptyouare / In Gorbachev we trust / (Fundamental). *(c+=)*– Resistance (once again). *(cd+=)*– Yellow cellaphane day / Mayhew speaks out.

— added **SANDRA** – percussion

Moksha not issued

Apr 89. (7") *(SOMA 6)* **YOU, ME & EVERYTHING. / RERAPTYOUARE** [ ] [-]
('A'-Evil edits; 12"+=/cd-s+=) *(SOMA 6 T/CD)* – Ed's bonus beats.

May 89. (10"m-lp/c/cd) *(SOMA LP/C/CD 3)* **PHORWARD** [ ] [-]
– You, me & everything (else) / Splash 2 / Negation state / Reraptyouare / SDD 89 / Phorward. *(free 7")*– (The S&N Sessions) *(c+=/cd+=)*– Happy days / Knature of a girl.

— **JOHN DELAFONS** – percussion repl. SANDRA

O. L. Indian Epic

Nov 89. (12"ep/cd-ep) *(30TP 12/7CD)* **OMEGA AMIGO / OMEGA A. / OMEGA PRE-MIX / PH 1** [ ] [-]

Mar 90. (7") *(36 TP7)* **PRO>GEN (Beatmasters mix). / ('A'dub version)** [55] [-]
(12") *(36 TP12L)* – ('A'-C-mix F+) / ('B'side) / Lightspan (Ben Chapman mix).
(c-s++=) *(36 TP7C)* – ('A'-Paul Oakenfold 'Land Of Oz' mix).
(12") *(36 TP12)* – (above mix) / Lightspan (Ben Chapman mix).
(cd-s) *(36 TP7CD)* – (above 2 mixes) / ('A'-Steve Osborne mix).

Sep 90. (7"/c-s) *(46 TP7/+C)* **MAKE IT MINE (Lenny D vox). / ('A'-Evil Ed mix)** [42] [ ] Feb92
(12"/cd-s) *(46TP 12/7CD) <742 36/41>* – ('A'-Lenny D mix) / ('A'-Progress mix) / ('A'-Lenny D vox) / Something wonderful.
(12") *(46 TP12L)* – ('A'-Evil Ed mix) / ('A'-Outer Limits mix) / Pro>gen (Land of Oz mix) / ('A'-Micro minimal mix).

Oct 90. (cd)(c)(2x12"lp) *(TPLP 22 CD/MC/SP)* **EN-TACT** [31] [ ]
– Human N.R.G. / Pro>gen (land of Oz) / Possible worlds / Omega amigo / Evil is even / Hypereal / Lightspan / Make it mine V 2.5 / Oxygen restriction / Here are my people (orbital delays expected). *(cd+=)*– (Oxygen reprise (V 2.0 mix) / Human NRG (Massey mix) / Make it mine (pirate radio mix) / (etc.) *(re-iss.Nov90 lp; TPLP 22)*

Mar 91. (7"/c-s) *(48 TP7/+C)* **HYPERREAL (William Orbit mix). / ('A'-lp version)** [29] [ ]
(12") *(48 TP12)* – ('A'versions incl. Maguire + dub) / In the bag.
(cd-s) *(48 TP7CD)* – ('A'versions incl. Meatbeat Manifesto mix) / In the bag.
(12") *(48 TP12L)* – ('A'-Meatbeat Manifesto mixes) / ('A'-Maguire + Dirty dubbing mixes).

— (above featured **PLAVKA** (b. Poland) – vocals)

— On the 23 May'91, WILL drowned while on holiday in Ibiza.

Jul 91. (7"/c-s) *(52 TP7/+C)* **MOVE ANY MOUNTAIN – PROGEN '91 (Beatmasters edit). / ('A'-The Goat From The Well Hung Parliament mix)** [4] [38] Nov91
(12") *(52 TP12) <74043>* – ('A'-mixes; Landslide / Devil / Rude / R.I.P. in the Land Of Oz).
(cd-s) *(52 TP7CD) <74044>* – ('A'mixes; Beatmasters / Landslide / F2 Mello / Mountains in the sky).

Sep 91. (3xlp/c/cd) *(TPLP 32/+MC/CD)* **PROGENCY** [23] [ ]

– Progency (8 versions).

— New line-up **COLIN** plus **MR.C** – vocals, rhythm / **+ JHELSA ANDERSON** – backing vox (ex-SOUL FAMILY SENSATION) / **BOB BREEKS** – live keyboards / **GAVIN KNIGHT** – live drums / **RICHARD SHARPE** – occasional analogue

Jun 92. (7"/12") *(68 TP 7/12) <74437>* **L.S.I. (LOVE SEX INTELLIGENCE). / POSSIBLE WORLDS** [6] [ ]
(c-s+=/cd-s+=) *(68 TP 7 C/CD)* – Make it mine (Moby mix).

Aug 92. (7"/c-s) *(78 TP7/+C)* **EBENEEZER GOODE. / ('A'dub)** [1] [ ]
(12"+=/cd-s+=) *(78 TP 12/7CD)* – ('A'mix) / L.S.I. (mix).

Oct 92. (lp/c/cd) *(TPLP 42/+C/CD)* **BOSS DRUM** [3] [ ]
– Boss drum / L.S.I.: Love Sex Intelligence / Space time / Librae solidi denari / Ebeneezer Goode (Beatmasters mix) / Comin' on / Phorever people / Fatman / Scientas / Re: evolution.

Oct 92. (7"/c-s) *(88 TP 7/+C)* **BOSS DRUM. / OMEGA AMIGO** [4] [ ]
(cd-s+=) *(88 TP7CD)* – (3 'A'mixes).
(12"-2 diff.) *(88 TP12)* – (5 'A'mixes either J.Robertson or Beatmasters).
(cd-s++=) *(88 TP7CDL)* – ('A'-Steve Osbourne mixes & Youth).

Dec 92. (7"ep/c-ep/12"ep/cd-ep) *(98 TP 7/7C/12/CD)* **PHOREVER PEOPLE. / ('A'dub + 'A'-Hyperreal orbit mix)** [5] [ ]
(cd-s++=) *(98 TP7CDL)* – ('A'mixes).

Feb 93. (c-s; as SHAMEN with TERENCE McKENNA) *(118 TP7C)* **RE:EVOLUTION / ('A'mix)** [18] [ ]
(12"+=/cd-s+=) *(118 TP 12/7CD)* – ('A'mixes).

Oct 93. (c-ep/12"ep/cd-ep) *(108 TP 7C/12/7CD)* **THE S.O.S. EP** [14] [ ]
– Comin' on / Make it mine / Possible worlds.
(cd-ep) *(108 TP7CDL)* – ('A'mixes).

— now with vocalist **VICTORIA WILSON-JAMES**

Aug 95. (c-s) *(128 TP7C)* **DESTINATION ESCHATON (Beatmasters mix) / ('A'-Deep melodic mix)** [15] [ ]
(cd-s) *(128 TP7CD)* – ('A'-Shamen acid: Escacid) / (2 'A'-Hardfloor mixes).
(cd-s) *(128 TP7CDL)* – (2 'A'-Basement Boys mixes) / (3 'A'-Beatmasters mixes).

Oct 95. (c-s) *(138 TP7C)* **TRANSAMAZONIA (Beatmasters mix) / ('A'-Visnadi mix) / ('A'-Watershed instrumental) / ('A'-LTJ Bukin mix)** [28] [ ]
(12"+=) *(138 TP12)* – ('A'-Deep dish mix).
(cd-s) *(138 TP7CD)* – (6 'A'mixes including; Alex Party Aguirre / Zion Train).
(cd-s+=) *(138 TP7CDL)* – ('A'-Nuv Idol mix).

Oct 95. (d-lp/c/cd) *(TPLP 52/+C/CD)* **AXIS MUTATIS** [27] [ ]
– Destination Eschaton / Transamazonia / Conquistador / Mauna Kea to Andromeda / Neptune / Prince of Popacatapertl / Heal the separation / Persephone's quest / Moment / Axis mundi / Eschaton omega (deep melodic techno). *(cd/c/d-lp with other cd/c/d-lp) (TPLP 52 CDL/CL/L)* **ARBOR BONA / ARBOR MALA** – Asynptotic Escaton / Sefirotic axis (a)(b)(c) Formation (d) Action / Extraterrestrial / Deneter / Beneath the underworld / Xochipilis return / Rio Negro / Above the underworld / A moment in dub / Pizarro in Paradiso / West of the underworld / Anticipation Escaton (be ready for the storm) / Out in the styx.

Feb 96. (c-s) *(158 TP7C)* **HEAL (THE SEPARATION) / ('A'mix)** [31] [ ]
(cd-s+=) *(158 TP7CD)* – ('A'mixes).
(cd-s) *(158 TP7CDL)* – ('A'mix).

Oct 96. (3x12"lp/c/cd) *(TPLP 62/+C/CD)* **HEMPTON MANOR** [ ] [ ]
– Freya / Urpflanze / Cannabeo / Khat / Bememe / Indica / Rausch / Kava / El-fin / Monoriff.

Dec 96. (c-s) *(169 TP7C)* **MOVE ANY MOUNTAIN '96 / ('A'mix)** [35] [ ]
(12"/cd-s) *(169 TP 12P/7CD)* –
(cd-s) *(169 TP7CDL)* –

– compilations, others, etc. –

Aug 88. (lp/c)(cd) *Materiali Sonori; (MASO 33041/+C)(MASOCD 9008)* **STRANGE DAY DREAMS** [-] [-] Italy
(re-iss.cd Oct91 imported) (re-iss.Jan93; same)

Dec 89. (m-lp/cd) *Communion; (COMM 4 LP/CD)* **WHAT'S GOING DOWN** [-] [ ]

Nov 93. (cd/c/lp) *Band Of Joy; (BOJ CD/MC/LP 006)* **ON AIR (live session)** [61] [-]

Jan 97. (cd/c) *One Little Indian; (TPLP 72 CD/C)* **THE COLLECTION** [ ] [ ]

Jan 97. (cd/c) *One Little Indian; (TPLP 72 CDR/CR)* **THE SHAMEN REMIX COLLECTION – STARS ON 45** [ ] [ ]

SILVERMAN (see under ⇒ LEGENDARY PINK DOTS)

SLIPSTREAM

Formed: Rugby, England . . . 1993 by MARK REFOY of SPIRITUALIZED. Early in 1994, they signed to the indie label, 'Che', releasing 3 singles over the course of the following year, the last of which was a version of KRAFTWERK's 'COMPUTER LOVE'. Their eponymous ZION TRAIN!-produced album came out soon after, in March '95, featuring some fine acoustic PINK FLOYD / CAN-ish styled songs. Later that year, two more singles preceded a compilation, although all has been quiet on the SLIPSTREAM front of late.

Recommended: SLIPSTREAM (*6)

MARK REFOY – vocals, guitar / **IAN ANDERSON** – guitar / **GARY LENNON** – bass / **STEVE BESWICK** – drums

Kinglake / not issued

1993?. (7") *(KLR 006)* **YOUR STAR IS FALLING** [ ] [-]

Che / not issued

Jul 94. (7") *(che 14)* **SUNDOWN. / SWEET MERCY / IT'S TRUE SHE SAID** [ ] [-]

Oct 94. (7") *(che 19)* **YOUR PRESENCE. / GIVE IT SOME TIME** [ ] [-]
(cd-s+=) *(che 19cd)* – Kornbus / I saw your face.

Feb 95. (7") *(che 21)* **COMPUTER LOVE. /** [ ] [-]

Mar 95. (cd/c/lp) *(che 22 cd/mc/lp)* **SLIPSTREAM** [ ] [-]
– Harmony / Riverside / Pulsebeat / One step ahead / Sensurround / Computer love / Sweet mercy / Feel good again / Sundown / She passes by.

Sep 95. (7") *(che 35)* **UP IN HEAVEN. / HEARING VOICES** [ ] [-]

Sep 95. (7") *(che 36)* **COME BACK. / LATE TOO LATE** [ ] [-]

Dec 95. (cd) *(che 37cd)* **SIDE EFFECTS** (singles compilation) [ ] [-]

SLOWDIVE

Formed: Thames Valley, Reading, England . . . 1990 by schoolfriends RACHEL GOSWELL and NEIL HALSTEAD. They duly recruited NICK CHAPLIN and belatedly accepted a final member, CHRISTIAN SAVILLE, who had been desperate to join them. After only a handful of gigs, they signed to Alan McGee's 'Creation' label, where they debuted with a self-titled EP. Early the next year, they scored another massive alternative chart hit with 'MORNINGRISE'. Their third EP, 'HOLDING OUR BREATH', nearly cracked the UK Top 50 with the debut album 'JUST FOR A DAY', accomplishing this feat later that year. However, emerging grunge acts like NIRVANA, were to aid SLOWDIVE's downfall, well at least in the music press stakes where 'shoegazing' bands were now looked down upon. After an 18-month hiatus, they returned with the follow-up, 'SOUVLAKI', but it was clear from their poor sales, they had left it too long. An EP (their 5th) entitled '5EP', showed greater promise, using techno acts RELOAD and BANDULU to boost their now ambient direction. After their third and probably their best work, 'PYGMALION', in 1995, they were dropped by their burgeoning record label. NEIL and RACHEL were soon back with MOJAVE 3, which was actually a 5-piece. • **Style:** Shimmering, distortion-happy, guitar-based outfit, complete with splendid atmospheric harmonies. Their sound lay somewhere between MY BLOODY VALENTINE, The JESUS & MARY CHAIN and other "shoegazers" (RIDE and MOOSE) of that early 90's era. • **Songwriters:** HALSTEAD – GOSWELL mostly penned, except GOLDEN HAIR (Syd Barrett).

Recommended: JUST FOR A DAY (*6) / SOUVLAKI (*5) / PYGMALION (*7) / Mojave 3:- ASK ME TOMORROW (*6)

RACHEL GOSWELL (b.16 May'71, Hampshire, England) – vocals, guitar / **NEIL HALSTEAD** (b. 7 Oct'70, Luton, England) – vocals, guitar / **CHRISTIAN SAVILLE** (b. 6 Dec'70, Bury, England) – guitar / **NICK CHAPLIN** (b.23 Dec'70, Slough, England) – bass / **NEIL CARTER** (ex-COLOUR MARY), who had repl. original ADRIAN SELL

Creation / Creation

Nov 90. (12"ep)(cd-ep) *(CRE 093T)(CRESCD 093)* **SLOWDIVE:- AVALYN I. / SLOWDIVE:- AVALYN II** [ ] [-]

— **SIMON SCOTT** (b. 3 Mar'71, Cambridge, England) – drums (ex-CHARLOTTES), repl. NEIL CARTER

Feb 91. (12"ep)(cd-ep) *(CRE 098T)(CRESCD 098)* **MORNINGRISE. / SHE CALLS / LOSING TODAY** [ ] [-]

Jun 91. (7") *(CRE 112)* **CATCH THE BREEZE. / SHINE** [52] [ ]
(12"ep+=)(cd-ep+=) **HOLDING OUR BREATH** (CRE 112T)(CRESCD 112) – Albatross / Golden hair.

Aug 91. (cd/lp)(c) *(CRE CD/LP 094)(CCRE 094)* **JUST FOR A DAY** [32] [ ]
– Spanish air / Cedlia's dream / Catch the breeze / Ballad of Sister Sue / Erik's song / Waves / Brighter / The sadman / Primal.

1992. (cd/lp) **BLUE DAY** [-] [ ]
– Slowdive:- Avalyn I / Morningrise / She calls / Losing today / Shine / Albatross.

— now without CHAPLIN

May 93. (12"ep)(cd-ep) *(CRE 119T)(CRESCD 119)* **OUTSIDE YOUR ROOM** [69] [ ]
– Alison / So tired / Souvlaki space station / Moussaka chaos.

Jun 93. (cd/lp)(c) *(CRE CD/LP 139)(CCRE 139)* **SOUVLAKI** [51] [ ]
– Alison / Machine gun / 40 days / Sing / Here she comes / Souvlaki space station / When the Sun hits / Altogether / Melon yellow / Dagger.

Nov 93. (12"ep)(cd-ep) *(CRE 157T)(CRESCD 157)* **5 EP** [ ] [ ]
– Bandulu (in mind mix) / (open mind mix) / (in mind mix) / Reload (remix – the 147 take).
(12"ep)(cd-ep) *(CRE 157TR)(CRESCD 157R)* – ('A'-other mixes).

Feb 95. (cd/lp)(c) *(CRE CD/LP 168)(CCRE 168)* **PYGMALION** [ ] [ ]
– Rutty / Crazy for you / Miranda / Trellisaze / Cello / Jay's heaven / Visions of L.A. / Blue skied and clear / All of us.

MOJAVE 3

— **RACHEL + NEIL** plus **IAN McCUTCHEON** – drums, percussion / **CHRISTOPHER ANDREWS** – piano / + **SIMON ROWE** – guitar / **AUDREY RILEY** – cello

4 a.d. / 4 a.d.

Oct 95. (lp/cd) *(CAD 5013/+CD)* **ASK ME TOMORROW** [ ] [ ]
– Love songs on the radio / Sarah / Tomorrow's taken / Candle song 3 / You're beautiful / Where is the love / After all / Pictures / Mercy.

SOFT BOYS (see under ⇒ HITCHCOCK, Robyn)

SONIC BOOM (see under ⇒ SPACEMEN 3)

SONIC YOUTH

Formed: New York City, New York, USA . . . early 1981 by THURSTON MOORE and KIM GORDON. They replaced an early embryonic rhythm section with LEE RANALDO and RICHARD EDSON. After numerous releases on various US indie labels (notably Glenn Branca's 'Neutral' records), they signed to 'Blast First'in the U.K. First up for the label was 'BAD MOON RISING' in 1985, showing them at their most menacing and disturbing, especially on the glorious 'DEATH VALLEY 69' (a macabre reference to killer Charles Manson) with LYDIA LUNCH providing dual vox. They subsequently secured a US deal with 'S.S.T.', heralding yet another socially passionate thrash effort with 'EVOL'. A sideline project, CICCONE YOUTH, saw KIM and the lads plus MIKE WATT (of fIREHOSE), take off MADONNA's 'INTO THE GROOVE(Y)', which became a surprise dancefloor fave. Two more classic pieces, 'SISTER' (1987) & 'DAYDREAM NATION' (1988), finally secured them a major deal with 'D.G.C.' (David Geffen Company). In the early 90's, they smashed into the UK Top 40 with the album 'GOO', featuring a cameo by CHUCK D (of PUBLIC ENEMY) on the track/single 'KOOL THING'. The album, which sweetened their garage-punk/art-noise collages with melodic hooks, also included their deeply haunting tribute to KAREN CARPENTER, 'TUNIC (SONG FOR KAREN)'. They supported PUBLIC ENEMY that year, also stepping out with NEIL YOUNG on his 'Ragged Glory' tour in '91 (much to the distaste of YOUNG's more conservative fans!). In 1992, many thought 'DIRTY' to be a disappointment, the record being overproduced and overtaken by their new rivals and labelmates NIRVANA. By the mid-90's, they had returned to ground roots with acoustic psychedelia and the albums, 'EXPERIMENTAL JET SET' and 'WASHING MACHINE' were again lauded by the alternative music press. All members had also taken on side solo projects, KIM featuring in all-star punk-grunge affair, FREE KITTEN. • **Songwriters:** MOORE / RANALDO / GORDON compositions, except I WANNA BE YOUR DOG (Stooges) / TICKET TO RIDE + WITHIN YOU WITHOUT YOU (Beatles) / BEAT ON THE BRAT (Ramones) / TOUCH ME, I'M SICK (Mudhoney) / ELECTRICITY (Captain Beefheart) / COMPUTER AGE (Neil Young). Their off-shoot CICCONE YOUTH covered INTO THE GROOVE (Madonna) / ADDICTED TO LOVE (Robert Palmer) / IS IT MY BODY (Alice Cooper) / PERSONALITY CRISIS (New York Dolls) / CA PLANE POUR MOI (Plastic Bertrand). • **Trivia:** Early in 1989, they were featured on hour-long special TV documentary for Melvyn Bragg's 'The South Bank Show'.

Recommended: BAD MOON RISING (*8) / EVOL (*8) / SISTER (*9) / DAYDREAM NATION (*9) / GOO (*9) / DIRTY (*7) / WASHING MACHINE (*8)

THURSTON MOORE (b.25 Jul'58, Coral Gables, Florida) – vocals, guitar / **KIM GORDON** (b.28 Apr'53, Rochester, N.Y.) – vocals, bass / **LEE RANALDO** (b. 3 Feb'56, Glen Cove, N.Y.) – vocals, guitar repl. ANN DEMARIS / **RICHARD EDSON** – drums repl. DAVE KEAY

Neutral / not issued

Feb 84. (m-lp) *(ND 01)* **SONIC YOUTH (live)** [-] [-] German
– The burning spear / I dreamt I dreamed / She's not alone / I don't want to push it / The good and the bad. *(re-iss.cd Oct87 on 'S.S.T.'; SSTCD 097)*

— **JIM SCLAVUNOS** – drums repl. EDSON

Feb 84. (lp) *(ND 02)* **CONFUSION IS SEX** [-] [-] German
– Inhuman / The world looks red / Confusion is next / Making the nature scene / Lee is free / (She's in a) Bad mood / Protect me you / Freezer burn / I wanna be your dog / Shaking Hell. *(re-iss.cd Oct87 on 'S.S.T.'; SSTCD 096)*

— **BOB BERT** – drums repl. SCLAVUNOS (still featured on 2 tracks)

Zensor / not issued

Oct 83. (m-lp) *(ZENSOR 10)* **KILL YR. IDOLS** [-] [-] German
– Protect me you / Shaking Hell / Kill yr. idols / Brother James / Early American.

not issued / Ecstatic Peace

1984. (c) *<none>* **SONIC DEATH (SONIC YOUTH LIVE)** [-] [ ]
– Sonic Death (side 1) / Sonic Death (side 2). *(UK cd-iss.Jul88 on 'Blast First'; BFFP 32CD>*

not issued / Iridescence

Dec 84. (12"; by SONIC YOUTH & LYDIA LUNCH) *<I-12>*
DEATH VALLEY '69. / BRAVE MEN (RUN IN MY FAMILY) [-] [ ]

Blast First / Homestead

Mar 85. (lp) *(BFFP 1)* **BAD MOON RISING** [ ] [ ]
– Intro / Brave men rule / Society is a hole / I love her all the time / Ghost bitch / I'm insane / Justice is might / Death valley '69. *(cd-iss.Nov86+=; BFFP 1CD)*– Satan is boring / Flower / Halloween.

Jun 85. (12"ep; by SONIC YOUTH & LYDIA LUNCH) *(BFFP 2) <I-12>* **DEATH VALLEY '69. / I DREAMT I DREAMED / INHUMAN / BROTHER JAMES / SATAN IS BORING** [ ] [-]

Jan 86. (12",12"yellow) *(BFFP 3)* **HALLOWEEN. / FLOWER** [-] [ ]

Jan 86. (7") *(BFFP 3)* **FLOWER. / REWOLF (censored)** [ ] [-]
(12") – ('A'side) / Satan is boring (live).

Mar 86. (etched-12") *(BFFP 3-B)* **HALLOWEEN II** [ ] [-]

— **STEVE SHELLEY** (b.23 Jun'62, Midland, Michigan) – drums repl. BOB BERT who joined PUSSY GALORE

Blast First / S.S.T.

May 86. (lp)(c) *(BFFP 4/+C)* **EVOL** [ ] [ ]
– Green light / Star power / Secret girl / Tom Violence / Death to our friends / Shadow of a doubt / Marilyn Moore / In the kingdom / Madonna, Sean and me. *(cd-iss.Nov86+=; BFFP 4CD)*– Bubblegum.

Jul 86. (7") *(BFFP 7)* **STAR POWER. / BUBBLEGUM** [ ] [ ]
(12"+=) *(BFFP 7T)* – Expressway.

— added guest **MIKE WATT** – bass (of fIREHOSE)

Nov 86. (12"; as CICCONE YOUTH) *(BFFP 8)* **INTO THE GROOVE(Y). / TUFF TITTY RAP / BURNIN' UP** [ ] [ ]

Jun 87. (lp/c/cd) *(BFFP 20/+C/CD)* **SISTER** [ ] [ ]
– White cross / (I got a) Catholic block / Hot wire my heart / Tuff gnarl / Kotton crown / Schizophrenia / Beauty lies in the eye / Stereo sanctity / Pipeline – killtime / PCH. *(cd+=)*– Master-Dik (original).

Jan 88. (12") *(BFFP 26T)* **MASTER-DIK. / BEAT ON THE BRAT / Under the influence of The Jesus And Mary Chain: Ticket to ride** [ ] [ ]

Jan 88. (lp/c/cd; as CICCONE YOUTH) *(BFFP 28/+C/CD)* **THE WHITEY ALBUM** [63] [ ]
– Needle-gun (silence) / G-force / Platoon II / Macbeth / Me & Jill / Hendrix Cosby / Burnin' up / Hi! everybody / Children of Satan / Third fig / Two cool rock chicks / Listening to Neu! / Addicted to love / Moby-Dik / March of the Ciccone robots / Making the nature scene / Tuff titty rap / Into the groovey.

Feb 88. (d-one-sided-7"on 'Fierce') *(FRIGHT 015-016)* **STICK ME DONNA MAGICK MOMMA / MAKING THE NATURE SCENE (live)** [ ] [-]
(also soon issued as normal-7")

Blast First / Torso

Oct 88. (d-lp/c/cd) *(BFFP 34/+C/CD) <2602339>* **DAYDREAM NATION** [99] [ ]
– Teenage riot / Silver rocket / The sprawl / 'Cross the breeze / Eric's trip / Total trash / Hey Joni / Providence / Candle? / Rain king / Kissability / Trilogy: The wonder – Hyperstation – Eliminator Jr.

— Late in '88, KIM teamed up with LYDIA LUNCH and SADIE MAE to form one-off project HARRY CREWS. Their live appearences were issued in Apr 90 as 'NAKED IN GARDEN HILLS' for 'Big Cat' UK + 'Widowspeak' US.

Feb 89. (12") *(BFFP 46)* **TOUCH ME, I'M SICK. / (Halloween; by MUDHONEY)** [ ] [ ]

W.E.A. / D.G.C.

Jun 90. (cd/c/lp) *(7599 24297-2/-4/-1) <24297>* **GOO** [32] [96]
– Dirty boots / Tunic (song for Karen) / Mary-Christ / Kool thing / Mote / My friend Goo / Disappearer / Mildred Pierce / Cinderella's big score / Scooter + Jinx / Titanium expose. *(re-iss.cd Oct95 on 'Geffen'; GFLD 19297)*

Sep 90. (7")(c-s) **KOOL THING. / THAT'S ALL I KNOW (RIGHT NOW)** [ ] [ ]
(12"+=) – ('A'demo version).
(cd-s++=) – Dirty boots (rock & roll Heaven version).

— In Autumn '90, THURSTON was part of 'Rough Trade' supergroup VELVET MONKEYS.

D.G.C. / D.G.C.

Apr 91. (m-lp/m-c/m-cd) *(DGC/+C/D 21634)* **DIRTY BOOTS** (all live, except the title track) [69] [ ]
– Dirty boots / The bedroom / Cinderella's big scene / Eric's trip / White kross. *(re-iss.cd Apr92; DGLD 19060)*

— Early in '92, THURSTON and STEVE also teamed up with RICHARD HELL's off-shoot group The DIM STARS.

Jun 92. (7") *(DGCS 11)* **100%. / CREME BRULEE** [28] [ ]
(10"orange+=/12"+=) *(DGC V/T 11)* – Hendrix necro.
(cd-s++=) *(DGCTD 11)* – Genetic.

Jul 92. (d-lp/c/cd) *(DGC/+C/D <24485>)* **DIRTY** [6] [83]
– 100% / Swimsuit issue / Theresa's sound-world / Drunken butterfly / Shoot / Wish fulfillment / Sugar Kane / Orange rolls, angel's spit / Youth against fascism / Nic fit / On the strip / Chapel Hill / JC / Purr / Creme brulee. *(d-lp+=)* – Stalker. *(re-iss.cd Oct95; GFLD 19296)*

Geffen / D.G.C.

Oct 92. (7") *(GFS 26)* **YOUTH AGAINST FASCISM. / PURR** [52] [ ]
(10"colrd+=) *(GFSV 26)* – ('A'version).
(12"++=/cd-s++=) *(GFST/+D 26)* – The destroyed room (radio version)

Apr 93. (7"/c-s) *(GFS/+C 37)* **SUGAR KANE. / THE END OF THE END OF THE UGLY** [26] [ ]
(10"blue+=/cd-s+=) *(GFS V/TD 37)* – Is it my body / Personality crisis.

Apr 94. (10"silver/c-s/cd-s) *(GFS V/C/TD 72)* **BULL IN THE HEATHER. / RAZORBLADE** [24] [ ]

May 94. (cd/c/blue-lp) *(GED/GEC/GEF 24632) <24632>* **EXPERIMENTAL JET SET, TRASH AND NO STAR** [10] [34]
– Winner's blues / Bull in the heather / Starfield road / Skink / Self-obsessed and sexxee / Bone / Androgynous mind / Quest for the cup / Waist / Doctor's orders / Tokyo eye / In the mind of the bourgeois reader / Sweet shine.

— In Sep 94; 'A&M' released CARPENTERS tribute album, which contained their single 'SUPERSTAR'. It was combined with also another cover from REDD KROSS, and reached UK No.45.

— early '95, FREE KITTEN (aka KIM, JULIE CAFRITZ, MARK IBOLD + YOSHIMI) released album 'NICE ASS'. An EP 'PUNKS SUING PUNKS' was released on 'Wiiija' Feb'96.

Oct 95. (cd/c/d-lp) *(GED/GEC/GEF 24925) <24825>* **WASHING MACHINE** [39] [58]
– Becuz / Junkie's promise / Saucer-like / Washing machine / Unwind / Little trouble girl / No queen blues / Panty lines / Becuz coda / Skip tracer / The diamond sea.

Apr 96. (12"/cd-s) *(GRS T/D 22132)* **LITTLE TROUBLE GIRL. / MY ARENA / THE DIAMOND SEA (edit)** [ ] [ ]

Sonic Youth / Sonic Youth

Jun 97. (12"ep/cd-ep) *(SYR 1/+CD)* **SYR VOL.1** [ ] [ ]
– Anagrama / Improvisation ajout'e / Tremens / Mieux: de corrosion.

– compilations, others, etc. –

Feb 92. (cd) *Sonic Death;* **GOO DEMOS LIVE AT THE CONTINENTAL CLUB (live)** [ ] [ ]

Mar 95. (cd/c) *Blast First; (BFFP 113 CD/C)* **CONFUSION IS SEX / KILL YR IDOLS** [ ] [-]

Mar 95. (cd) *Warners-Rhino; (8122 71591-2)* **MADE IN THE U.S.A.** (1986 soundtrack) [ ] [ ]

Apr 95. (cd) *Blast First; (BFFP 119CD)* **SCREAMING FIELDS OF SONIC LOVE** [ ] [-]

May 97. (pic-lp) *Sonic Death; (SYLB 1)* **LIVE IN BREMEN (live)** [ ] [-]

LEE RANALDO

Blast First / S.S.T.

Jul 87. (m-lp/c) *(BFFP 9/+C)* **FROM HERE ⇒ ETERNITY** [ ] [ ]
– Time stands still / Destruction site / Ouroboron / Slodrown / New groove loop / Florida flower / Hard left / Fuzz-locusts / To Mary / Lathe speaks / The resolution / King's egg. *(re-iss.May93 on 'S.S.T.' lp/c/cd; SST 113/+C/CD)*

not issued

1995. (cd) **EAST JESUS** [-] [ ]

THURSTON MOORE

Geffen D.G.C.

May 95. (cd/c/d-lp;colrd 3-sides) *(GEF/GEC/GED 24810)* **PSYCHIC HEARTS**
– Queen bee and her pals / Ono soul / Psychic hearts / Pretty bad / Patti Smith math scratch / Blues from beyond the grave / See-through play-mate / Hang out / Feathers / Tranquilizor / Staring statues / Cindy (rotten tanx) / Cherry's blues / Female cop / Elergy for all dead rock stars.

Victo Victo

Mar 97. (cd) *(VICTOCD 045)* **PIECE FOR JETSUN DOLMA**

Corpus Hermeticum Corpus Herme

Apr 97. (cd) *(HERMES 011)* **KLANGFARBENMELODIE**

Father Yod Father Yod

May 97. (cd; THURSTON MOORE & PHIL MILSTEIN) *(HOTYOD 1)* **SONGS WE TAUGHT THE LORD VOL.2** [-]

SPACEMEN 3

Formed: Rugby, Warwickshire, England . . . 1983 by SONIC BOOM (PETE KEMBER) and JASON PIERCE. They enlisted PETE BAINES and ROSCO as a rhythm section and through their manager, Gerald Palmer, they signed to indie label, 'Glass'. In 1986, they debuted with 'SOUND OF CONFUSION', a primal embryo for "shoegazers" to come. Their follow-up, 'THE PERFECT PRESCRIPTION', set the world alight (well! the indie world anyway), with some clever retro, 'WALKIN WITH JESUS' (again!), 'TRANSPARENT RADIATION' and 'TAKE ME TO THE OTHER SIDE'. In 1989, they were back again with a third set, 'PLAYING WITH FIRE', featuring the 10-minute squall of 'SUICIDE', and 'REVOLUTION', later covered by MUDHONEY. SONIC BOOM's heroin addiction was taking its toll during the early 90's, and with JASON having found SPIRTITUALIZED, the group were heading for their own proverbial rocket ship once more. Their final outing in 1991, 'RECURRING' was a slight disappointment. By this point, SONIC had gone solo, soon going under the guise of SPECTRUM. His debut was followed by two albums of patchy, yet somewhat appealing albums, 'SOUL KISS (GLIDE DIVINE)' & 'HIGH LOWS AND HEAVENLY BLOWS' between '92 & '94. • **Style:** Psychedelic pulsating garage-noise outfit, intertwined with melancholy bursts of beauty and experimentation. • **Songwriters:** KEMBER or PIERCE material until the 90's when KEMBER penned all. Covered; IT'S ALRIGHT (Bo Diddley) / CHE + ROCK'N'ROLL IS KILLING MY LIFE (Suicide) / WHEN TOMORROW HITS (Mudhoney) / COME TOGETHER + STARSHIP (MC5) / MARY-ANNE (. . .Campbell) / ROLLER COASTER (13th Floor Elevators).

Recommended: SOUND OF CONFUSION (*7) / THE PERFECT PRESCRIPTION (*8) / PLAYING WITH FIRE (*8) / SPECTRUM (SONIC BOOM; *5) / SOUL KISS (GLIDE DIVINE) (SPECTRUM; *6) / HIGH LOWS AND HEAVENLY BLOWS (SPECTRUM; *6)

SONIC BOOM (b. PETE KEMBER, 19 Nov'65) – vocals / **JASON PIERCE** (b.19 Nov'65) – guitar / **STEWART (ROSCO) ROSSWELL** – keyboards / **PETE (BASSMAN) BAINES** – bass

Glass not issued

Jun 86. (lp) *(GLA 018)* **SOUND OF CONFUSION** [-]
– Losing touch with my mind / Hey man / Roller coaster / Mary Anne / Little doll / 2:35 / O.D. catastrophe. *(re-iss.Sep89 on 'Fire' lp/c/cd; REFIRE CD/MC/LP 5)*

Dec 86. (12"m) *(GLAEP 105)* **WALKIN' WITH JESUS (SOUND OF CONFUSION). / ROLLERCOASTER / FEEL SO GOOD** [-]

Jul 87. (12"m) *(GLAEP 108)* **TRANSPARENT RADIATION / ECSTASY SYMPHONY / TRANSPARENT RADIATION (FLASHBACK). / THINGS'LL NEVER BE THE SAME / STARSHIP** [-]

Aug 87. (lp/c) *(GLA LP/MC 026)* **THE PERFECT PRESCRIPTION** [-]
– Take me to the other side / Walkin' with Jesus / Ode to street hassle / Ecstasy – Symphony / Feel so good / Things'll never be the same / Come down easy / Call the doctor / Soul 1 / That's just fine. *(re-iss.Dec89 on 'Fire' lp/c/cd; REFIRE LP/MC/CD 6)*

Mar 88. (12") *(GLASS 12-054)* **TAKE ME TO THE OTHER SIDE. / SOUL 1 / THAT'S JUST FINE** [-]

Jul 88. (lp/cd) *(GLA LP/CD 030)* **PERFORMANCE** (live 1988 Holland) [-]
– Mary-Anne / Come together / Things'll never be the same / Take me to the other side / Roller coaster / Starship / Walkin' with Jesus. *(re-iss.May91 on 'Fire' cd/c/lp; REFIRE CD/MC/LP 11)*

— **WILLIE B. CARRUTHERS** – bass / **JON MATLOCK** – drums repl. ROSCO + BAINES who formed The DARKSIDE

Fire not issued

Nov 88. (7") *(BLAZE 29S)* **REVOLUTION. / CHE** [-]
(12"+=/cd-s+=) *(BLAZE 29 T/CD)* – May the circle be unbroken.

Feb 89. (lp/c/cd) *(FIRE LP/MC/CD 16)* **PLAYING WITH FIRE** [-]
– Honey / Come down softly to my soul / How does it feel? / I believe it / Revolution / Let me down gently / So hot (wash away all my tears) / Suicide / Lord can you hear me. *(free-12"ep/cd-ep+=)*– Starship / Revolution / Suicide (live) / Repeater / Live intro theme (xtacy).

Jul 89. (7") *(BLAZE 36S)* **HYPNOTIZED. / JUST TO SEE YOU SMILE HONEY (part 2)** [-]
(12"+=/3"cd-s+=) *(BLAZE 36 T/CD)* – The world is dying.
(free 7"flexi w.a) *(CHEREE 5)* – EXTRACTS FROM A CONTEMPORARY SITAR EVENING (with other artists).

Jan 91. (7") *(BLAZE 41)* **BIG CITY. / DRIVE** [-]
(12"+=/cd-s+=) *(BLAZE 41 T/CD)* – Big City (everybody I know can be found here).
(12"w-drawn) *(BLAZE 41TR)* – ('A'remix) / I love you (remix).

Feb 91. (cd/lp)(s-lp) *(FIRE CD/LP 23)(FIRELP 23S)* **RECURRING** [46] [-]
– Big city (everybody I know can be found here) / Just to see you smile (orchestral) / I love you / Set me free – I've got the key / Set me free (reprise) / Feel so bad (reprise) / Hypnotized / Sometimes / Feelin' just fine (head full of shit) / Billy Whizz – blue 1. *(cd+=)*– When tomorrow hits / Why couldn't I see / Just to see you smile (instrumental) / Feel so sad (demo) / Drive.

— Had already folded June '90.

– compilations, etc. –

Dec 90. (cd/d-lp) *Fierce; (FRIGHT 042/+CD)* **DREAM WEAPON / ECSTASY IN SLOW MOTION** [-]
(re-iss.Nov95 on 'Space Age' cd/d-lp; ORBIT 001 CD/LP)

Nov 94. (cd) *Bomp; (BCD 4047)* **TAKING DRUGS TO MAKE MUSIC TO TAKE DRUGS TO** [-]

May 95. (cd/lp) *Sympathy For The Record Industry; (SFTRI 1368 CD/LP)* **FOR ALL FUCKED UP CHILDREN OF THE WORLD**

May 95. (cd) *Bomp; (BCD 4044)* **SPACEMEN ARE GO!**

Jun 95. (cd/d-lp) *Fire; (FLIP CD/DLP 003)* **TRANSLUCENT FLASHBACKS** [-]

Oct 95. (cd) *Fierce; (FRIGHT 063)* **THE CHOICE IS REVOLUTIONORHERION** [-]

Nov 95. (cd/d-lp) *Space Age; (ORBIT 002 CD/LP)* **LIVE IN EUROPE 1989 (live)** [-]

Mar 97. (d-cd) *Nectar; (NTMCDD 534)* **1 + 1 = 3** [-]

SONIC BOOM

(PETE KEMBER solo with **WILLIE B. CARRUTHERS** and also **PHIL PARFITT + JO WIGGS** of PERFECT DISASTER)

Silvertone not issued

Oct 89. (12"ep/cd-ep) *(ORE/+CD 11)* **ANGEL. / ANGEL (version) / HELP ME PLEASE** [-]

Feb 90. (cd/c/lp) *(ORE CD/MC/LP 506)* **SPECTRUM** [65] [-]
– Pretty baby / If I should die / Lonely avenue / Help me please / Angel / Rock'n'roll is killing my life / You're the one. *(free 10" w-lp) (SONIC 1)*– DRONE DREAM EP: OCTAVES. / TREMELOS

Apr 91. (7"; gig freebie) *(SONIC 2)* **(I LOVE YOU) TO THE MOON AND BACK. / CAPO WALTZ (live)** [-] [-]

— SONIC BOOM has now featured in E.A.R. (EXPERIMENTAL AUDIO RESEARCH), who after first low-key album 'MESMERISED' in 1994 on 'Sympathy For The Record Industry), released for 'Big Cat' the 1996 lp/cd 'BEYOND THE PALE' *(ABB 96/+CD)*. It featured KEVIN SHIELDS (of; we still think; MY BLOODY VALENTINE),KEVIN MARTIN (of GOD) and EDDIE PREVOST.

— In Mar 92, HONEY TONGUE (aka MATTOCK + WIGGS) released lp 'NUDE NUDES' on 'Playtime'; *AMUSE 012CD)*

SPECTRUM

KEMBER, CARRUTHERS, etc

Silvertone Silvertone

Jun 92. (7") *(ORE 41)* **HOW YOU SATISFY ME. / DON'T GO (instrumental 2)** [-]
(12"clear+=/cd-s+=) *(ORE 41 T/CD)* – My life spins around your every smile / Don't go (instrumental 1).

Jun 92. (cd/c/lp) *(ORE CD/C/LP 518)* **SOUL KISS (GLIDE DIVINE)** [-]
– How you satisfy me / Lord I don't even know my name / The drunk suite (overture) / Neon sigh / Waves wash over me / (I love you) To the Moon and back / My love for you never died away but my soul gave out and wit / Sweet running water / Touch the stars / Quicksilver glide divine / The drunk suite / Phase me out (gently). *(re-iss.Apr95; same)*

Sep 92. (7") *(ORE 44)* **TRUE LOVE WILL FIND YOU IN THE END. / MY LIFE SPINS AROUND YOUR EVERY SMILE** [70] [-]
(12"/cd-s) *(ORE T/CD 44)* – ('A'side) / To the moon and back / Waves wash over me.

Aug 93. (7") *(ORE 56)* **INDIAN SUMMER. / BABY DON'T YOU WORRY (California lullabye)**
(12"+=/cd-s+=) *(ORE T/CD 56)* – It's alright / True love will find you in the end.

Oct 94. (12"ep/cd-ep) *(ORE T/CD 65)* **UNDO THE TABOO / IN THE FULLNESS OF TIME. / TURN THE TIDE (SUB AQUA) / GO TO SLEEP** [-]

Nov 94. (cd/lp) *(ORE CD/LP 532)* **HIGHS LOWS AND HEAVENLY BLOWS**
– Undo the taboo / Feedback / Then I just drifted away / Take your time / Soothe me / All night long / Don't pass me by / I know they say / Take me away.

— Note; Not to be confused with dance outfit, who released 'SKY ABOVE' & 'BRAZIL'.

SPACE TIME CONTINUUM

Formed: San Francisco, California, USA . . . 1993 by former jazz session drummer JONAH SHARP, who collaborated with TERENCE McKENNA (an ethnobotanist, described as the TIMOTHY LEARY of the 90's). His books about propsychedelia and its culture; 'True Hallucinations', 'The Archaic Revival' & 'The Food Of The Gods', were to Americans, what IRVINE WELSH's 'Trainspotting' was to Scotland or the UK. SHARP was the main part of this outfit, and he finally gained a UK release for his third effort, 'emiT ecapS'. • **Style:** Techno-trip, with psychedelic variations. • **Songwriters:** SHARP.

Recommended: SEA BISCUIT (*6) / ALIEN DREAMTIME (*6) / REMIT RECAPS (*7)

JONAH SHARP – synthesizers, DJ, keyboards, drums

Source Caroline

1994. (cd) **SEA BISCUIT** [-]

Sep 94. (12"ep; by JONAH SHARP) *(EFA 00637-6)* **FLURESCENCE E.P.**

1994. (cd) **ALIEN DREAMTIME** [-] [ ]
–

— Late in '95, he collaborated with PETE NAMLOOK on album ''WECHSELSPANNUNG' for 'Fax'; *PW 023CD)*

Reflective Caroline

Oct 95. (12"ep) *(REF 013)* **KAIRO EP** [ ] [-]
Jan 96. (cd/s-cd/d-lp) *(REF CD/SCD/LP 7)* **emiT ecapS** [ ] [ ]
–
Oct 96. (12") *(REF 015)* **emiT ecapS Vol.1** [ ] [-]
Oct 96. (12") *(REF 016)* **emiT ecapS Vol.2** [ ] [-]

SPECTRUM (see under ⇒ SPACEMEN 3)

SPEED THE PLOUGH

Formed: Haledon, New Jersey, USA ... 1982 as The TRYPES, by BAUMGARTNER who had been school friends of new wave/psychedelic outfit The FEELIES. When The FEELIES, (BILL MILLION & GLEN MERCER) decided to take a hiatus in 1983/84, they guested on the EP, 'THE EXPLORER'S HOLD. They also played together on Sunday nights at the local Peanut Gallery bar, a series dubbed, "Music For Neighbors". In 1986 when The FEELIES sorted out their problems, the TRYPES became SPEED THE PLOUGH. Many gigs later, their first album was issued in 1989, a set of avant-garde psychedelia, drawing inspiration from RAVI SHANKAR, BRIAN ENO and PHILIP GLASS. Three more apeared in the first half of the 90's, the best of which was 1995's 'MARINA'. • **Songwriters:** BAUMGARTNER and a few with BARNES.

Recommended: SPEED THE PLOUGH (*6) / MARINA (*7)

BAUMGARTNER with GLEN MERCER + BILL MILLION (of The FEELIES)

not issued Coyote

1984. (12"ep; as TRYPES) **THE EXPLORER'S HOLD** [-] [ ]

— now without part-time FEELIES, who re-joined said outfit

East Side Digital East Side Digital

1991. (cd) <> **SPEED THE PLOUGH** [ ] [ ] 1989
–

— now with **BRENDA SAUTER** – bass (ex-FEELIES)

1991. (cd) **WONDER WHEEL** [-] [ ]
–
1993. (cd) **MASON'S BOX** [-] [ ]
–
Jul 96. (cd) *<(ESD 81102)>* **MARINA** [ ] [ ] 1995
– ust a little / Written each day / Said and done / Once in a while / Late birds / A saint restored / High wine / Love song / Bayswater lane / A hard friend to keep / Hourglass / In the atmosphere / Marina.

— SAUTER was also part of WILD CARNATION, who issued one US album 'TRICYCLE' for 'Delmore' in 1995.

SPIRITUALIZED

Formed: Rugby, England ... 1990, initially as a side project for JASON 'SPACEMAN' PIERCE, who was soon to split from SONIC BOOM and SPACEMEN 3. He retained JON MATTOCK and WILLIE B. CARRUTHERS from the latter outfit and set about getting to grips with a new 90's psychedelia. Their first release was a version of The TROGGS' 'ANYWAY THAT YOU WANT ME', which squeezed into the UK Top 75. The dedut album, 'LAZER GUIDED MELODIES', was awash with VELVET-tones, recycled, and heavily distorted. A three year hiatus did not deter the British buying public, who also assured the follow-up, 'PURE PHASE', of a Top 30 placing in 1995. It was blessed with a more soulful vibe, while the majestic, lo-fi rhythm lifted it from an ambient crypt. In June '97, they returned to the fold (albeit a month after schedule) with their third album, 'LADIES AND GENTLEMEN WE ARE FLOATING IN SPACE B P'. The delay was due to ELVIS PRESLEY's team of whatnots objecting to the sample of 'Can't Help Falling In Love'. Nevertheless, the album, complete with bizarre prescription pill cd packaging, duly floated into the UK Top 5. Described by one reviewer as 'album of the decade', the record met with almost universal praise while its blissful melange of retro-psych, ambient noise and gospel was a heady tonic for the Dad-rock by numbers peddled by most 'indie' bands. • **Songwriters:** PIERCE, except more covers; BORN NEVER ASKED (Laurie Anderson). • **Trivia:** In the early 90's, they headlined at the ICA Rock Week sponsored by 'Irn Bru'.

Recommended: LAZER GUIDED MELODIES (*8) / PURE PHASE (*8) / LADIES AND GENTLEMEN WE ARE FLOATING IN SPACE B P (*10)

JASON PIERCE – guitar / **WILLIE B. CARRUTHERS** – bass / **JON MATTOCK** – drums plus girlfriend **KATE RADLEY** – organ, keyboards, vocals / **MARK REFOY** – guitar, dulcimer

Dedicated not issued

Jun 90. (7") *(ZB 43783)* **ANYWAY THAT YOU WANT ME. / STEP INTO THE BREEZE** [75] [-]
(12"+=/cd-s+=) *(ZT/ZD 43784)* – ('B'-part 2).
(12") *(ZT 43780)* – ('A'remix) / ('B'-parts 2-3) / ('A'demo).
Jun 91. (7") *(FRIGHT 053)* **FEEL SO SAD. / I WANT YOU** [ ] [-]
(above is a gig freebie given away by 'Fierce' re-iss.Apr97)
Aug 91. (7") *(SPIRIT 002)* **RUN. / I WANT YOU** [59] [-]
(12"+=/cd-s+=) *(SPIRIT 002 T/CD)* – Luminescent (stay with me) / Effervescent.
Nov 91. (7") *(SPIRIT 003)* **WHY DON'T YOU SMILE NOW. / SWAY** [ ] [-]
(12"+=/cd-s+=) *(SPIRIT 003 T/CD)* – ('A'extended).
Apr 92. (cd/c/2x12"lp) *(DED CD/MC/LP 004)* **LAZER GUIDED MELODIES** [27] [ ]
– You know it's true / If I were with her now / I want you / Run / Smiles / Step into the breeze / Symphony space / Take your time / Shine a light / Angel sigh / Sway / 200 bars. *(free-7" at 'Chain With No Name' shops)*– ANY WAY THAT YOU WANT ME / WHY DON'T YOU SMILE NOW
Jul 92. (7"red) *(SPIRIT 005)* **MEDICATION. / SMILES (Peel session)** [55] [-]
(12"+=) *(SPIRIT 005T)* – Feel so sad (Peel session) / Angel sigh.
(cd-s++=) *(SPIRIT 005CD)* – Space (instrumental).
Jun 93. (mail-order cd) *(SPIRIT 006CD)* **F***ED UP INSIDE** [-] [-]
Oct 93. (7") *(SPIRIT 007)* **GOOD TIMES / LAY BACK IN THE SUN** [49] [ ]
(12"ep+=/cd-ep+=) *(SPIRIT 008 T/CD)* – Electric Mainline 1 + 2.

— now without REFOY, who formed SLIPSTREAM. They issued two albums for 'Che' in 1995; 'SLIPSTREAM' & 'SIDE EFFECTS'.

SPIRITUALIZED ELECTRIC MAINLINE

— **SPACEMAN (JASON) + KATE RADLEY** – keyboards, vox / **SEAN COOK** – bass, harmonica / plus **MARK REFOY** – guitar (guest only) / **JON MATTOCK** – percussion / **LEON HUNT** – banjo / **STEWART GORDON** – violin / **THE BALANESCU QUARTET** – strings / + others on wind instruments

Jan 95. (cd-ep) *(SPIRIT 009CD)* **LET IT FLOW / DON'T GO / STAY WITH ME / DON'T GO / STAY WITH ME (THE INDIVIDUAL)** [30] [ ]
(cd-ep) *(SPIRIT 009CD2)* – ('A'side) / Take good care of it / Things will never be the same / Clear rush.
(cd-ep) *(SPIRIT 009CD3)* – ('A'side) / Medication / Take your time / Smile.
(3xbox-cd-ep/10"ep) *(SPIRIT 009BOX/T)* – (all above).
Feb 95. (cd/c/d-lp) *(DED CD/MC/LP 017)* **PURE PHASE** [20] [ ]
– Medication / The slide song / Electric phase / All of my tears / These blues / Let it flow / Take good care of it / Born never asked / Electric mainline / Lay back in the sun / Good times / Pure phase / Spread your wings / Feel like goin' home.
Nov 95. (cd-ep) *(74321 31178-2)* **LAY BACK IN THE SUN / THE SLIDE SONG / SPREAD YOUR WINGS / LAY BACK IN THE SUN** [ ] [ ]

SPIRITUALIZED

— **DAMON REECE** – percussion + guests, repl. MATTOCK, HUNT + GORDON

Dedicated R.C.A.

Jun 97. (cd/c/lp) *(DED CD/MC/LP 034)* **LADIES AND GENTLEMEN WE ARE FLOATING IN SPACE B P** [4] [ ]
– Ladies and gentlemen we are floating in space / Come together / I think I'm in love / All of my thoughts / Stay with me / Electricity / Home of the brave / The individual / Broken heart / No god only religion / Cool waves / Cop shoot cop . . .

STEREOLAB

Formed: South London, England ... late 1990, by ex-indie stalwart TIM GANE (mainman for McCARTHY), who invited girlfriend LAETITIA SADIER to join. They soon completed the initial line-up with MARTIN KEAN and JOE DILWORTH (other past indie veterans), subsequently forming their own label, 'Duophonic Super 45s'. The group released three 45's ('SUPER 45', 'SUPER ELECTRIC' & 'STUNNING DEBUT ALBUM') in 1991, the second of which was for the 'Too Pure' label (these have re-instated vinyl as worthy product, whether for limited edition collectors or just vinyl junkies who hate cd's). The following year, they topped the indie charts with their actual "stunning debut album", 'PENG!'. During this period, the couple introduced four new members; MARY HANSEN, SEAN O'HAGAN, DUNCAN BROWN and ANDY RAMSAY, who helped them with a busy touring schedule. In 1993, they signed to 'Elektra' in the States for a 6 figure-sum, while in the UK, they released several more 45's! and an album, 'TRANSIENT RANDOM NOISE BURSTS WITH ANNOUNCEMENTS', which, like the classy single, 'JENNY ONDIOLINE', scraped into the UK charts (the track was premiered on Channel 4's "The Word" programme). 1994 saw them unsurprisingly hit the UK Top 20 with another double album, 'MARS AUDIAC QUINTET'. Two years later, with their best offering to date, 'EMPEROR TOMATO KETCHUP', they had established themselves as leaders of the "Metronomic Underground" scene, as the opening track suggested. • **Style:** Eclectic ambient-boogie outfit, influenced by minimalists VELVET UNDERGROUND, JOHN CAGE, NEU!, SPACEMEN 3 and mid-60's BEACH BOYS!. Lushly fronted by SAINT ETIENNE-like (at times) French vox of LAETITIA (pronounced Le-ti-seaya). • **Songwriters:** GANE songs / SADIER lyrics.

Recommended: PENG! (*7) / TRANSIENT RANDOM ... (*8) / MUSIC FOR THE AMORPHOUS BODY STUDY CENTER (*8) / MARS AUDIO QUINTET (*8) / EMPEROR TOMATO KETCHUP (*9)

TIM GANE (b. 1966) – guitar, vox organ, guitar (ex-McCARTHY) / **LAETITIA SADIER** (b. 1968, Paris, France) – vocals, vox organ, guitar, tambourine, moog / **REBECCA MORRIS** – vocals / **JOE DILWORTH** – drums (of TH' FAITH HEALERS)

Duophonic not issued

May 91. (10"ep-mail order) *(DS45-01)* **SUPER 45** [ ] [-]
– The light (that will cease to fail) / Au grand jour / Brittle / Au grand jour!.

— added **MARTIN KEAN** (b.New Zealand) – guitar (ex-CHILLS) / **RUSSELL YATES** – live guitar (of MOOSE). **MICK CONROY** (ex-MOOSE) was also a live member early '92.

Nov 91. (7"clear,7"colrd) *(DS45-02)* **STUNNING DEBUT ALBUM: Doubt / Changer** [ ] [-]

Too Pure Slumberland

Sep 91. (10"ep) *(PURE 4)* **SUPER ELECTRIC / HIGH EXPECTATION. / THE WAY WILL BE OPENING / CONTACT** [ ] [-]

Apr 92. (cd-ltd.) <*Slumberland 22*> **SWITCHED ON** (compilation) [-] [ ]
– Super electric / Doubt / Au grand jour / The way will be opening / Brittle / Contract / Au grand jour / High expectation / The light that will cease to fail / Changer. *(UK-iss.Mar97 on 'Dupophonic' cd/lp; TBC 25/24)*

— GINA departed after above. (when did she join?)

May 92. (cd,c,lp) *(PURE 11)* **PENG!** [ ] [-]
– Super falling star / Orgiastic / Peng! 33 / K-stars / Perversion / You little shits / The seeming and the meaning / Mellotron / Envivez-vous / Stomach worm / Surrealchemist.

— added **MARY HANSEN** – vocals, tambourine, guitar / **ANDY RAMSAY** – percussion, vox organ, bazouki repl. DILWORTH

Sep 92. (10"ep,10"clear-ep,cd-ep) *(PURE 14)* **LOW FI / (VAROOM!). / LAISSER-FAIRE / ELEKTRO (HE HELD THE WORLD IN HIS IRON GRIP)** [ ] [-]

— added **SEAN O'HAGAN** – vox organ, guitar (ex-MICRODISNEY, ex-HIGH LLAMAS)

Feb 93. (7",7"pink) <*Slumberland 24*> **JOHN CAGE BUBBLEGUM. / ELOGE D'EROS** [-] [ ]

— added **DUNCAN BROWN** – bass, guitar, vocals

Mar 93. (cd,c,m-lp) *(PURE 19)* **THE GROOP PLAYED SPACE AGE BACHELOR PAD MUSIC** [ ] [-]
– Avant-garde M.O.R. / Space age bachelor pad music (mellow) / The groop play chord X / Space age bachelor pad music / Ronco symphony / We're not adult orientated / UHF-MFP / We're not adult orientated (new wave).

Duophonic Elektra

Aug 93. (10"ep/cd-ep) *(DUHF D/CD 01)* **JENNY ONDIOLINE / FRUCTION / GOLDEN BALL / FRENCH DISCO** [75] [ ]

Sep 93. (cd/c/2xlp) *(DUHF CD/DMC/D 02)* **TRANSIENT RANDOM-NOISE BURSTS WITH ANNOUNCEMENTS** [62] [ ]
– Tone burst / Our trinitone blast / Pack yr romantic mind / I'm going out of my way / Golden ball / Pause / Jenny Ondioline / Analogue rock / Crest / Lock-groove lullaby.

Nov 93. (7") *(DUHF D01P)* **FRENCH DISKO (new version). / JENNY ONDIOLINE** [ ] [-]

— added **KATHERINE GIFFORD** – synthesizers, keyboards

Jul 94. (7"ltd) *(DUHFD 04S)* **PING PONG. / MOOGIE WONDERLAND** [45] [ ]
(10"+=/cd-s+=) *(DUHF D/CD 04)* – Pain et spectacles / Transcoma (live).

Aug 94. (cd/c/d-lp) *(DUHF CD/MC/D 05)* **MARS AUDIAC QUINTET** [16] [ ]
– Three-dee melodie / Wow and flutter / Transona five / Des etoiles electroniques / Ping pong / Anamorphose / Three longers later / Nihilist assault group / International colouring contest / The stars of our destination / Transporte sans bouger / L'enfer des formes / Outer accelerator / New orthophony / Fiery yellow. *(free clear-7" w/d-lp + cd-s on cd) (DUHF D/CD 05X)*– Klang-tang / Ulaan batter.

Oct 94. (7"ltd) *(DUHFD 07S)* **WOW AND FLUTTER. / HEAVY DENIM** [70] [ ]
(10"+=/cd-s+=) *(DUHF D/CD 07)* – Nihilist assault group / Narco Martenot.

Apr 95. (10"ep/cd-ep) *(DUHF D/CD 08)* **AMORPHOUS BODY STUDY CENTRE** [59] [-]
– Pop quiz / The extension trip / How to explain your internal organs overnight / The brush descends the length / Melochord seventy five / Space moment.

Sep 95. (cd/c/colrd-d-lp) *(DUHF CD/MC/D 09)* **REFRIED ECTOPLASM (SWITCHED ON – VOLUME II)** (compilation) [30] [-]
– Harmonium / Lo boob oscillator / Mountain / Revox / French disko / Exploding head movie / Eloge d'eros / Tone burst (country) / Animal or vegetable (a wonderful wooden reason) / John Cage bubblegum / Sadistic / Farfisa / Tempter.

— **GANE / SADIER / HANSEN / RAMSAY + BROWN** added **MORGANE LHOTE** (guests; SEAN O'HAGAN / JOHN McINTYRE (of TORTOISE) + RAY DICKARTY)

Feb 96. (7") *(DUHFD 10S)* **CYBELE'S REVERIE. / BRIGITTE** [62] [ ]
(10"+=/cd-s+=) *(DUHF D/CD 10)* – Les yper yper sound / Young lungs.

Mar 96. (d-lp/c/cd) *(DUHF D/MC/CD 11)* **EMPEROR TOMATO KETCHUP** [27] [ ]
– Metronomic underground / Cybele's reverie / Percolator / Les ypersound / Spark plug / Olv 26 / The noise of carpet / Tomorrow is already here / Emperor tomato ketchup / Monstre sacre / Motoroller scalatron / Slow fast Hazel / Anonymous collective.

Apr 96. (12"ltd.) *(DS 3311)* **SIMPLE HEADPHONE MIND. / (other track by NURSE WITH WOUND)** [ ] [-]
(re-iss.Jun97; same)

— now without BROWN, who was repl. by **RICHARD HARRISON**

Sep 96. (7";on 'Lissys') *(LISS 15)* **SHE USED TO CALL ME SADNESS. /** [ ] [-]

Nov 96. (7"ep)(12"ep/cd-ep) *(DUHFD 14S)(DUHF D/CD 14)* **FLUORESCENCES EP** [ ] [-]
– Fluorescences / Pinball / You used to call me sadness / Soop groove *2.

Dec 96. (12"; STEREOLAB & WAGON CHRIST) *(DUHFD 15)* **METROGNOMIC UNDERGROUND. /** [ ] [-]

– more very limited singles, etc. –

Jun 92. (7"pink) *B.M.I.; (BMI 025)* **THE LIGHT (THAT WILL CEASE TO FAIL). / AU GRAND JOUR** [ ] [-]

Jul 92. (7"colrd) *Duophonic; (DS45-04)* **HARMONIUM. / FARFISA** [ ] [-]

Oct 93. (10"ep) *Clawfist; (Clawfist 20)* **CRUMB DUCK (with NURSE WITH WOUND)** [ ] [-]
– Animal or vegetable / Exploding head movie.

Oct 93. (7"clear) *Sub Pop; (<SP 107/283>)* **LE BOOB OSCILLATOR. / TEMPTER** [ ] [ ]

Nov 93. (7") *Teenbeat; <Teenbeat 121>* **MOUNTAIN. / ('B'by Unrest)** [-] [ ]

STONE ROSES

Formed: Sale & Chorley, Gtr.Manchester, England ... 1984 by IAN BROWN, JOHN SQUIRE, RENI, ANDY COUZENS and PETER GARNER who took their name from a group called ENGLISH ROSE and The ROLLING STONES. After a MARTIN HANNETT produced 45, they signed a one-off deal with 'Black' records and in 1988, were snapped up by ANDREW LAUDER's 'Jive' subsidiary, 'Silvertone'. They soon became darlings of the music press after the indie success of the single, 'ELEPHANT STONE' (1988), a gloriously uplifting piece of pristine pop. Propelled by RENI's consummate drumming and featuring SQUIRE's dizzy, spiralling guitar, the track was a blueprint for the group's eponymous debut album, released the following year. Surely a contender for album of the decade, the record was flawless, from the ominous opening bass rumble of 'I WANNA BE ADORED' to the orgasmic finale of 'I AM THE RESURRECTION'. This life-affirming hybrid of BYRDS-style psychedelia and shuffling rhythmic flurries remains the definitive indie album, its all-pervading influence more pronounced with each successive crop of guitar bands. Incredibly, the band topped the magic of their debut with the 'FOOL'S GOLD' single, which exploded into the Top 10 later that year. A seminal guitar-funk workout, it was the crowning glory of the 'Baggy' movement with which The STONE ROSES had become so closely affiliated, and marked a creative highpoint in their career. After a few one-off shows (that have since achieved almost mythical status) and a solitary single, 'ONE LOVE', the following year, the band went to ground. In the five years that followed, the band fought a protracted court battle with 'Silvertone', eventually signing with 'Geffen' for a reported record sum of $4,000,000. After much speculation and intrigue into when or if a follow-up would finally appear, the appropriately title 'SECOND COMING' was eventually released in 1994. A month previously, they had enjoyed a return to the singles chart with the ZEPPELIN-esque 'LOVE SPREADS'. On the album, the effervescent pop of old took second place to riff-heavy guitar workouts, alienating many of their original fans. Nevertheless, the blistering funk-rock of 'BEGGING YOU' partly made up for any excess noodling by SQUIRE. As the STONES ROSES faithful dusted down their flares and beany hats in readiness for the band's headlining spot at the 1995 Glastonbury festival, they were again bitterly disappointed. At the last minute the band pulled out, apparently due to SQUIRE breaking his collarbone, young pretenders OASIS stealing the show in their absence. They had failed to seize the moment and from here on in, it was all downhill. Despite an ecstatically received Winter tour, SQUIRE shocked the music world by departing the following Spring (RENI had already quit a year earlier). BROWN and MANI bravely soldiered on for a headlining appearance at the 1996 Reading Festival but were given a critical mauling (particularly by the NME), finally splitting later that year. It was a sorry, messy end for a band that had seemed, at one point, to be on the brink of world domination and it remains a bitter irony that their duller Manchester progeny, OASIS, seem to have inherited the success that tragically eluded the 'ROSES. While SQUIRE has gone on to relative success with The SEAHORSES, their sound pales next to the magic of The STONE ROSES, a band that remain as fondly remembered as any in the history of rock. • **Songwriters:** Mainly SQUIRE but with other members also collaborating. The SEAHORSES was mainly SQUIRE, except a few by HELME. one with FLETCHER. NOEL GALLAGHER (Oasis) co-wrote 'LOVE ME AND LEAVE ME'. • **Trivia:** Their debut album artwork was a pastiche of a Jackson Pollock splatter job painted by the multi-talented SQUIRE.

Recommended: THE STONE ROSES (*10) / SECOND COMING (*8) / SEAHORSES: DO IT YOURSELF (*8)

IAN BROWN (b.20 Feb'63, Ancoats, Manchester) – vocals / **JOHN SQUIRE** (b.24 Nov'62, Broadheath, Manchester) – guitar, vocals / **PETER GARNER** – rhythm guitar / **ANDY COUZENS** – bass / **RENI** (b. ALAN WREN, 10 Apr'64) – drums

Thin Line not issued

Sep 85. (12") *(THIN 001)* **SO YOUNG. / TELL ME** [ ] [-]

— now a quartet, when PETER departed.

Revolver not issued

May 87. (12"m) *(12REV 36)* **SALLY CINNAMON. / HERE IT COMES / ALL ACROSS THE SAND** [ ] [-]
(re-iss.Feb89; same) (re-iss.Dec89 cd-ep+=; CDREV 36); hit No.46)– ('A'demo).

— (1987) **GARY 'Mani' MOUNFIELD** (b.16 Nov'62, Crumpsall, Manchester) – bass, vocals repl. COUZENS who later joined The HIGH.

Silvertone Silvertone

Oct 88. (7") *(ORE 1)* **ELEPHANT STONE. / THE HARDEST THING IN THE WORLD** [ ] [-]
(12"+=) *(ORE 1T)* – Full fathoms five. *(re-iss.Feb90 c-s/cd-s; ORE 1 C/CD); hit No.8.*

Mar 89. (7") *(ORE 2)* **MADE OF STONE. / GOING DOWN** [ ] [-]
(12"+=) *(ORE 2T)* – Guernica. *(re-iss.Mar90 c-s/cd-s; ORE 2 C/CD); hit No.20.*

Apr 89. (lp/c/cd) *(ORE LP/MC/CD 502)* <*1184*> **THE STONE ROSES** [19] [86]
– I wanna be adored / She bangs the drum / Waterfall / Don't stop / Bye bye badman / Elizabeth my dear / (Song for my) Sugar spun sister / Made of stone / Shoot you down / This is the one / I am the resurrection. *(re-iss.Aug91 as 2x12"+=;)*– Elephant stone / Fool's gold. *(cd re-iss.Mar97; same)*

Jul 89. (7"/7"s) *(ORE/+X 6)* **SHE BANGS THE DRUM. / STANDING HERE** [36] [-]
(12"+=/12"s+=) *(ORE T/Z 6)* – Mersey Paradise.
(c-s++=/cd-s++=) *(ORE C/CD 6)* – Simone. *(re-entered chart Mar90; hit No.34)*

Silvertone Jive

Nov 89. (7"/ext.12") *(ORE/+T 13)* **FOOL'S GOLD. / WHAT THE WORLD IS WAITING FOR** [8] [ ]
(c-s+=/cd-s+=) *(ORE C/CD 13)* <*1315*> – ('A'extended). *(flipped over re-entered chart Sep90; hit No.22) (re-iss.remix May92, hit No.73)*
(12") *(ORET 13)* – ('A'-The Top Won mix) / ('A'-The Bottom Won mix).

Jul 90. (7"/c-s/12"/cd-s) *(ORE/+C/T/CD 17)* <*1399*> **ONE LOVE. / SOMETHING'S BURNING** [4] [ ]

Sep 91. (7"/c-s) *(ORE/+C 31)* **I WANNA BE ADORED. / WHERE ANGELS PLAY** [20] [-]
(12"+=/cd-s+=) *(ORE T/CD 31)* – Sally Cinnamon (live).

1991. (c-ep) <*1301*> **I WANNA BE ADORED / (long version) / GOING DOWN SIMONE** [-] [ ]

Jan 92. (7"/c-s) *(ORE/+C 35)* **WATERFALL (remix). / ONE LOVE (remix)** [27] [ ]
(12"+=/cd-s+=) *(ORE T/CD 35)* – ('A'&'B'extended versions).

Apr 92. (7"/c-s) *(ORE/+C 40)* **I AM THE RESURRECTION. / ('A'-Pan & scan radio version)** [33] [ ]
(12"+=) *(ORET 40)* – Fool's gold (The Bottom Won mix).
(cd-s++=) *(ORECD 40)* – ('A'-5:3 Stoned Out club mix).

Jul 92. (cd/c/lp) *(ORE CD/C/LP 521)* **TURNS INTO STONE** (demos & rare) [32] [ ]
– Elephant stone / The hardest thing in the world / Going down / Mersey Paradise / Standing here Where angels play / Simone / Fools gold / What the world is waiting for / One love / Something's burning. *(cd re-iss.Mar97; same)*

Geffen Geffen

Nov 94. (7"/c-s) *(GFS/+C 84)* **LOVE SPREADS. / YOUR STAR WILL SHINE** [2] [ ]
(cd-s+=) *(GFST 84)* – Breakout.
(12"++=) *(GFSTD 84)* – Groove harder.

Dec 94. (cd/c/lp) *(GED/GEC/GEF 24503)* **SECOND COMING** [4] [47] Jan95
– Breaking into Heaven / Driving south / Ten storey love song / Daybreak / Your star will shine / Straight to the man / Begging you / Tightrope / Good times / Tears / How do you sleep? / Love spreads. *(cd+=)* – (untitled hidden track No.90).

Feb 95. (7"/c-s) *(GFS/+C 87)* **TEN STOREY LOVE SONG. / RIDE ON** [11] [ ]
(12"+=/cd-s+=) *(GFST/+D 87)* – Moses.

— In Apr'95, RENI quit and was replaced by **ROBERT MADDIX** (ex-GINA GINA).

Oct 95. (c-s) *(GFSC 22060)* **BEGGING YOU / ('A'-Chic mix)** [15] [ ]
(cd-s+=) *(GFSTD 22060)* – ('A'-Stone Corporation mix) / ('A'-Lakota mix) / ('A'-Young American primitive remix).
(12") *(GFST 22060)* – ('A'-Carl Cox mix) / ('A'-Development Corporation mix).

— Late in March '96, SQUIRE left to pursue new venture SEAHORSES. The STONE ROSES continued on and in Aug'96, they recruited **AZIZ IBRAHIM** (ex-SIMPLY RED) / **NIGEL IPPINSON** – keyboards

— They officially split in Nov'96, after MANI joined PRIMAL SCREAM.

– compilations, etc. –

on 'Silvertone' unless mentioned; who else?

Jan 92. (8xcd-s-box-set) *(SRBX 1)* **SINGLES BOX** [ ] [-]

Nov 92. (10x12"box-set) *(SRBX 2)* **SINGLES BOX** [ ] [-]

Apr 95. (c-s) *(OREC 71)* **FOOL'S GOLD '95 / ('A'extended mix)** [23] [ ]
(12"+=/cd-s+=) *(ORE T/CD 71)* – ('A'-Tall Paul remix) / (A'-Cricklewood Ballroom mix).

May 95. (cd/c/lp) *(ORE CD/C/ZLP)* **THE COMPLETE STONE ROSES** [4] [ ]

Dan STUART (see under ⇒ GREEN ON RED)

SUN DIAL

Formed: South London, England . . .1985 out of MODERN ART by GARY RAMON. They/he had issued a few limited edition releases on 'Color Disc'; 1986 7" 'DREAMS TO LIVE'. / 'BEAUTIFUL TRUTH' / 1987 lp 'STEREOLAND' / 1989 one-sided-7"clear-flexi freebie 'PENNY VALENTINE'. / 'ONE-WAY TICKET' / 1989 German-lp 'ALL ABOARD THE MIND TRAIN', re-iss.cd/lp Sep94 on 'Acme' (8007 CD/LP). These recordings featured drummers DAVE MORGAN (Weather Prophets) and ED KENT plus GERALD on guitar and occasional saxophone. GARY and SUN DIAL came onto the scene in the early 90's, when they unleashed the 12", 'EXPLODING IN YOUR MIND'. This appeared on 'Tangerine'; a label formed by record dealer HUGO CHAVEZ-SMITH. Its very limited release was rectified when MARK HEYWARD of Vinyl Experience record store, set up 'UFO' records to create an outlet for SUN DIAL recordings. The group subsequently expanded into a quartet (briefly a 5-piece) after their debut album, 'OTHER WAY OUT' was re-issued in 1991. In 1993, they signed to semi-major, 'Beggars Banquet', releasing the album, 'LIBERTINE'. • **Style:** Guitar-noise experimentalists like 60's STOOGES fusing JESUS & MARY CHAIN with SPACEMEN 3 or LOOP. • **Songwriters:** RAMON except covers; CIRCLE SKY (Monkees) / MAGIC POTION (Open Mind) / ONLY A NORTHERN SONG (Beatles) / etc? • **Trivia:** OTHER WAY OUT was voted best album in Italian magazine, 'Rockerilla'. OVERSPILL was produced by VIC KEARY, boss of Mushroom records, the first person to record MARC BOLAN solo.

Recommended: OTHER WAY OUT (*8)

GARY RAMON – guitar with **DAVE MORGAN** – drums / **TONY CLOUGH** – keyboards, flute

UFO not issued

Jan 91. (12"ep/cd-ep) *(45002 T/CD)* **EXPLODING IN YOUR MIND (edit). / OTHER SIDE / PLAINS OF NAZCA (edit)** [ ] [-]

— Note: the unreleased test pressing of above was on 'Tangerine' *(TAN111)*

— Below album was also released on 'Tangerine' in 1990.

Apr 91. (pic-cd/c) *(UFO 1 CD/MC)* **OTHER WAY OUT** [ ] [-]
– Plains of Nazca / Exploding in your mind / Magic flight / She's looking all around / World without time / Lorne blues. *(cd+=)*– Visitation / Other side. *(re-iss.cd 1994 on 'Acme'++=; AC8003CD)*
– Slow motion / Fountain.

— **JOHN PELLECH** – drums repl. MORGAN

— **CHRIS DALLEY** – bass + **NIGEL CARPENTER** – guitar (both ex-BIKINIS) repl.CLOUGH
, who joined SPIRAL SKY

Sep 91. (12"ep,12"orange-ep/cd-ep) *(45002 T/CD)* **OVERSPILL** [ ] [-]
– Fireball/ Only a northern song / Never fade / Overspill.

Mar 92. (clear-lp/cd) *(UFO 8/+CD)* **REFLECTER** [ ] [-]
– Reflecter / Easy for you / I don't mind / Slow motion / Tremelo / Never fade / Sunstroke / Mind train. *(ltd-cd+=) (UFO 8XCD)*– Reflecter 2.

Jul 92. (12"green-ep/cd-ep) *(45008 T/CD)* **FAZER** [ ] [-]
– I don't mind / Let it go / Out of place / Easy fazer.

— above featured **MICKY MANN** (of The SHAMEN)

— **CRAIG ADRIENNE** – drums repl. PELLECH

Beggars Banquet Beggars Banquet

Jun 93. (lp/c/cd) *(BBQ/+C/CD 138)* **LIBERTINE** [ ] [ ]
– Send / Going down / Watch you smile / Deep inside / Everything you see / Dual / Hold on / Around and around / Star baby / Believer.

Oct 93. (7"ep/cd-ep) *(BBQ 51/+CD)* **GOING DOWN / WATCH YOU SMILE. / JEWEL / STARBABY (live)** [ ] [-]

— now w/out DALLEY + CARPENTER, they had become a trio.

Jun 95. (cd) *(BBQCD 173)* **ACID YANTRA** [ ] [ ]
– Red sky / Apollo / 3000 miles / Are you supernatural? / Bad drug / Fly into the sun / Rollercoaster / Nova / Yantra jam.

Jun 95. (12"/cd-s) *(BBQ 54/+CD)* **BAD DRUG. / FAIRGROUND** [ ] [-]

– compilations, etc. –

1994. Acme; (bootleg-cd,lp) *(AC 8001)* **RETURN JOURNEY** (rec.1991 lost 2nd lp) [ ] [-]

SWERVEDRIVER

Formed: Oxford to Camden, London, England . . . late 1989 initially as SHAKE APPEAL, by ADAM FRANKLIN, JIMMY HARTRIDGE, GRAHAM BONNAR and spokesman ADRIAN VINES. This outfit issued one 7" in 1988, 'GIMME FEVER' for 'No Town'; (NO 002). SWERVEDRIVER signed to 'Creation' in the early 90's and broke with 'SON OF MUSTANG FORD' & 'RAVE DOWN'. In 1991, they scored a minor UK hit with their third EP 'SANDBLASTED', which preceded their Top 50 debut album, 'RAISE'. Although they supported the likes of The WONDER STUFF, they were lawded as the new UK "great white hopes" of the metal world! They toured the States in 1992 with SOUNDGARDEN, but this took its toll, causing BONNER to quit. They subsequently returned home and were soon another member down, when VINES couldn't cope. Their next set, 'MEZCAL HEAD', in 1993 was produced by ALAN MOULDER, who had worked with the top-rated SMASHING PUMPKINS. It didn't set the industry alight, and by the release the more solid follow-up, 'EJECTOR SEAT RESERVATION', in 1995, they were dropped by their label. However, they are working out a new deal with 'Geffen', who might release something by late '97. • **Style:** "Shoegazing" grunge-rock inspired by JESUS & MARY CHAIN, although tighter and heavier in melody. • **Songwriters:** HARTLIDGE / FRANKLIN penned except; JESUS (Velvet Underground).

Recommended: RAISE (*8) / EJECTOR SEAT RESERVATION (*7)

ADAM FRANKLIN (b.19 Jul'68, Essex, England) – vocals, guitar / **JIMMY HARTRIDGE** (b.27 Nov'67, Oxfordshire, England) – guitar / **ADRIAN 'ADI' VINES** (b.25 Jan'68, Yorkshire, England) – bass / **GRAHAM BONNAR** (b.28 Apr'67, Glasgow, Scotland) – drums, vocals (ex-UT)

Creation A&M

Jul 90. (7"ep/12"ep)(cd-ep) *(CRE 079/+T)(CRESCD 079)* **SON OF MUSTANG FORD / VOLCANO TRASH. / KILL THE SUPERHEROES / JUGGERNAUT RIDE** [ ] [-]

Nov 90. (7"ep/12"ep)(cd-ep) *(CRE 088/+T)(CRESCD 088)* **RAVE DOWN / SHE'S BESIDE HERSELF. / AFTERGLOW / ZED HEAD** [ ] [-]

Jul 91. (7"ep/12"ep)(cd-ep) *(CRE 102/+T)(CRESCD 102)* **SANDBLASTED / OUT. / FLAWED / LAZE IT UP** [67] [ ]

Sep 91. (cd/lp)(c) *(CRE CD/LP 093)(C-CRE 093)* **RAISE** [44] [ ]
– Sci-flyer / Pole-up / Son of Mustang Ford / Deep seat / Rave down / Sunset / Feel so reel / Sandblasted / Lead me where you dare. *(free-12"w.a.)*– SURF TWANG. / DEEP TWANG

May 92. (7") *(CRE 120)* **NEVER LOSE THAT FEELING. / SCRAWL AND SCREAM** [62] [ ]
(12"+=)(cd-s+=) *(CRE 120T)(CRESCD 120)* – The watchman's hands / Never learn.

— ADI left in Sep'92. He was soon replaced by **JEZ** – drums

Aug 93. (7") *(CRE 136)* **DUEL. / PLANES OVER THE SKYLINE** [60] [ ]
(12"+=)(cd-s+=) *(CRE 136T)(CRESCD 136)* – Year of the girl.

Sep 93. (cd/lp)(c) *(CRE CD/LP 143)(C-CRE 143)* **MEZCAL HEAD** [55] [ ]
– For seeking heat / Duel / Blowin' cool / MM abduction / Last train to Satansville / Mary and Maggie / A change is gonna come / Girl on a motorbike / Duress / You find it everywhere.

Feb 94. (12"ep)(cd-ep) *(CRE 174T)(CRESCD 174)* **LAST TRAIN TO SATANSVILLE / JESUS. / SATANSVILLE REVISITED / LAND OF THE LOST** [ ] [ ]

Jul 94. (7") *(FLOWER 004)* **MY ZEPHYR (SEQUEL). / MARS** [ ] [-]

— (above 45 was a one-off for 'Flower Shop' records)

Jun 95. (12"white-ep)(c-ep/cd-ep) *(CRE 179T)(CRE CS/SCD 179)* **LAST DAY ON EARTH / MAELSTROM / I AM SUPERMAN / THE DIRECTORS CUT OF YOUR LIFE** [ ] [-]

Aug 95. (cd/lp)(c) *(CRE CD/LP 157)(C-CRE 157)* **EJECTOR SEAT RESERVATION** [ ] [-]
– Single factor salute / Bring me the head of the fortune teller / The other Jesus / Song of Jaguar E / I am Superman / Bubbling up / Ejector seat reservation / How does it feel to like Candy? / Last day on Earth / The birds. *(c+=/cd+=)*– Untitled / So downhearted. *(w/free-7")*– FLAMING HEART / PLAN 7 SATELLITE 10.

Echostatic not issued

Jan 97. (d7") *(ECHO 09-10)* **SPLIT SINGLE (with SOPHIA)** [ ] [-]

A&M A&M

Feb 97. (7"/c-s) *(582130-7/-4)* **MAGIC BUS. /** ☐ ☐
(cd-s+=) *(582131-2)* –

Sessions not issued

Jun 97. (7") *(7SMS 07)* **93 MILLION MILES FROM THE SUN (AND COUNTING). /** ☐ -

SYSTEM 7 (see ⇒ HILLAGE, Steve)

— (actually in first part of book)

T

TEARDROP EXPLODES (see under ⇒ COPE, Julian)

TEENAGE FANCLUB

Formed: Glasgow, Scotland ... 1989 although earlier they had posed as The BOY HAIRDRESSERS. After a one-off single, 'GOLDEN SHOWERS' (1988), bassist GERRY LOVE was recruited and BRENDAN O'HARE replaced FRANCIS McDONALD (who went off to join that other Glasgow institution, The PASTELS) on the drums. As TEENAGE FANCLUB, they cut the inspired chaos of the 'EVERYTHING FLOWS' (1990) single and followed it up with the debut album, 'A CATHOLIC EDUCATION' later the same year. The term slacker rock was surely coined with this bunch of cheeky Glaswegian wide boys in mind and if it was lazy to compare their honey-in-the-dirt melodic dischord with Dinosaur Jr., that was nothing compared to the laid back, laissez faire philosophy that fuelled (if that's not too strong a word) TEENAGE FANCLUB'S ramshackle racket, both on stage and in the studio. By the release of the DON FLEMING-produced 'BANDWAGONESQUE' (1991), ('THE KING' was a sub-standard effort released to fulfill contractual obligations), the band were sounding more professional, crafting an album of langourous harmonies and chiming guitar that was a thinly veiled homage to BIG STAR as well as taking in such obvious reference points as The BYRDS, The BEACH BOYS, BUFFALO SPRINGFIELD etc. Ironically, rather than propelling TEENAGE FANCLUB into the big league, the album seemed instead to merely rekindle interest in BIG STAR's back catalogue and after a honeymoon period of being indie press darlings, the backlash was sharp and swift. The fact that the self-produced 'THIRTEEN' (1993) lacked their trademark inspired sloppiness didn't help matters any. Not that the band were overly concerned, they crafted modern retro more lovingly than most and had a loyal following to lap it up. The FANNIE's further developed their niche with 'GRAND PRIX' (1995) and if it was that reliably trad, West Coast via Glasgow roots sound you were after then TEENAGE FANCLUB were your band. While they wear their influences more proudly than any other group, (O.K., so I forgot about OASIS ...) they do it with such verve and style that it'd be churlish to write them off as mere plagiarists and they remain one of Scotland's best loved exports. Their latest effort, 'SONGS FROM NORTHERN BRITAIN' (1997) was their most considered release to date, sharpening up their sound and arrangements to an unprecedented degree. But if that's what it takes to come up with something as engagingly swoonsome as 'I DON'T CARE' or 'IS THAT ENOUGH', no one's going to make much of a fuss. • **Songwriters:** BLAKE or BLAKE-McGINLEY or group compositions except; DON'T CRY NO TEARS (Neil Young) / THE BALLAD OF JOHN AND YOKO (Beatles) / LIKE A VIRGIN (Madonna) / LIFE'S A GAS (T.Rex) / FREE AGAIN + JESUS CHRIST (Alex Chilton) / CHORDS OF FAME (Phil Ochs) / BAD SEEDS (Beat Happening) / HAVE YOU EVER SEEN THE RAIN? (Creedence Clearwater Revival) / BETWEEN US (Neil Innes) / FEMME FATALE (Velvet Underground). • **Trivia:** ALEX CHILTON (ex-BOX TOPS) guested on 1992 sessions and contributed some songs.

Recommended: BANDWAGONESQUE (*8) / THIRTEEN (*7) / GRAND PRIX (*9)

NORMAN BLAKE (b.20 Oct'65, Bellshill, Scotland) – vocals, guitar (ex-BMX BANDITS) / **RAYMOND McGINLEY** (b. 3 Jan'64, Glasgow) – bass, vocals / **FRANCIS McDONALD** (b.21 Nov'70, Bellshill, Scotland) – drums / **JOE McALINDEN** – violin / **JIM LAMBIE** – vibraphone

53rd & 3rd not issued

Jan 88. (12"; as BOY HAIRDRESSERS) *(AGARR 12T)* **GOLDEN SHOWERS. / TIDAL WAVE / THE ASSUMPTION AS AN ELEVATOR** ☐ -

— **NORMAN + RAYMOND** – guitars, vocals plus **GERARD LOVE** (b.31 Aug'67, Motherwell, Scotland) – bass, vocals / **BRENDAN O'HARE** (b.16 Jan'70, Bellshill, Scotland) – bass repl. McDONALD who joined The PASTELS

Paperhouse Matador

Jun 90. (7"m) *(PAPER 003)* **EVERYTHING FLOWS. / PRIMARY EDUCATION / SPEEEDER** ☐ ☐
(cd-ep+=) *(PAPER 003CD)* – Don't Cry No Tears. *(rel.Feb91)*

Jul 90. (cd/c/lp) *(PAP CD/MC/LP 004)* **A CATHOLIC EDUCATION** ☐ -
– Heavy metal / Everything flows / Catholic education / Too involved / Don't need a drum / Critical mass / Heavy metal II / Catholic education 2 / Eternal light / Every picture I paint / Everybody's fun. *(re-iss.cd Mar95)*

Oct 90. (one-sided-7") *(PAPER 005)* **THE BALLAD OF JOHN AND YOKO** ☐ -

Nov 90. (7") *(PAPER 007)* **GOD KNOWS IT'S TRUE. / SO FAR GONE** ☐ ☐
(12"+=/cd-s+=) *(PAPER 007 T/CD)* – Weedbreak / Ghetto blaster.

Creation Geffen

Aug 91. (cd/lp) *(CRE CD/LP 096)* **THE KING (instrumental)** 53 ☐
– Heavy metal 6 / Mudhoney / Interstellar overdrive / Robot love / Like a virgin / The king / Opal inquest / The ballad of Bow Evil (slow and fast) / Heavy metal 9.

— (above originally only meant for US ears, deleted after 24 hours)

Aug 91. (7") *(CRE 105)* **STAR SIGN. / HEAVY METAL 6** 44 -
(12"+=)(cd-s+=) *(CRE 105T)(CRESCD 105)* – Like a virgin / ('A'demo version).
(7"ltd) *(CRE 105L)* – ('A'side) / Like a virgin.

Oct 91. (7"/c-s) *(CRE/+CS 111)* **THE CONCEPT. / LONG HAIR** 51 -
(12"+=)(cd-s+=) *(CRE 111T)(CRESCD 111)* – What you do to me (demo) / Robot love.

Nov 91. (cd)(c/lp) *(CRECD 106)(C+/CRE 106)* **BANDWAGONESQUE** 22 ☐
– The concept / Satan / December / What you do to me / I don't know / Star sign / Metal baby / Pet rock / Sidewinder / Alcoholiday / Guiding star / Is this music?.

Jan 92. (7"/c-s) *(CRE/+CS 115)* **WHAT YOU DO TO ME. / B-SIDE** 31 ☐
(12"+=)(cd-s+=) *(CRE 115T)(CRESCD 115)*– Life's a gas / Filler.

Jun 93. (7"/c-s) *(CRE/+CS 130)* **RADIO. / DON'S GONE COLUMBIA** 31 ☐
(12"+=)(cd-s+=) *(CRE 130T)(CRESCD 130)* – Weird horses / Chords of fame.

Sep 93. (7"/c-s) *(CRE/+CS 142)* **NORMAN 3. / OLDER GUYS** 50 ☐
(12"+=)(cd-s+=) *(CRE 142T)(CRESCD 142)* – Golden glades / Genius envy.

Oct 93. (cd)(c/lp) *(CRECD 144)(C+/CRE 144)* **THIRTEEN** 14 ☐
– Hang on / The cabbage / Radio / Norman 3 / Song to the cynic / 120 minutes / Escher / Commercial alternative / Fear of flying / Tears are cool / Ret live dead / Get funky / Gene Clark.

— In Mar'94, they teamed up with DE LA SOUL on single 'FALLIN''. This was from the rock-rap album 'Judgement Day' on 'Epic' records (hit UK 59).

— **PAUL QUINN** – drums (ex-SOUP DRAGONS) repl. O'HARE

Mar 95. (7"/c-s) *(CRE/+CS 175)* **MELLOW DOUBT. / SOME PEOPLE TRY TO FUCK WITH YOU** 34 ☐
(cd-s+=) *(CRESCD 175)* – Getting real / About you.
(cd-s) *(CRESCD 175X)* – ('A'side) / Have you ever seen the rain? / Between us / You're my kind.

May 95. (7"/c-s) *(CRE/+CS 201)* **SPARKY'S DREAM. / BURNED** 40 ☐
(cd-s+=) *(CRESCD 201)* – For you / Headstand.
(cd-s) *(CRESCD 201X)* – ('A'-alternative version) / Try and stop me / That's all I need to know / Who loves the sun.

May 95. (cd)(c/lp) *(CRECD 173)(C+/CRE 173)* **GRAND PRIX** 7 ☐
– About you / Sparky's dream / Mellow doubt / Don't look back / Verisinilitude / Neil Jung / Tears / Discolite / Say no / Going places / I'll make it clear / I gotta know / Hardcore – ballad. *(lp w/free 7")* – DISCOLITE (demo). / I GOTTA KNOW (demo)

Aug 95. (7"/c-s) *(CRE/+CS 210)* **NEIL JUNG. / THE SHADOWS** 62 ☐
(cd-s+=) *(CRESCD 210)* – My life / Every step is a way through love.
(cd-s) *(CRESCD 210X)* – ('A'side) / Traffic jam / Hi-fi / I heard you looking.

Dec 95. (7"ep/c-ep/cd-ep) *(CRE/+CS/SCD 216)* **TEENAGE FANCLUB HAVE LOST IT EP (acoustic)** 53 -
– Don't look back / Everything flows / Starsign / 120 mins.

Jun 97. (cd-s) *(CRESCD 228)* **AIN'T THAT ENOUGH /** 17 ☐
(cd-s) *(CRESCD 228X)* – ('A'side) / Femme fatale / Jesus Christ.

– compilations, others, etc. –

May 92. (7") *K; <IPU 26>* **FREE AGAIN. / BAD SEEDS** - ☐

Nov 92. (12"ep/cd-ep) *Strange Fruit; (SFPS/+CD 081)* **THE JOHN PEEL SESSION** ☐ -
– God knows it's true / Alcoholiday / So far gone / Long hair.
(re-iss.Dec93 & Jul95; same)

Mar 95. (cd/c) *Fire; (FLIPCD 002)* **DEEP FRIED FANCLUB** ☐ -
– Everything flows / Primary education / Speeeder / Critical mass (orig.) / The ballad of John and Yoko / God knows it's true / Weedbreak / So far gone / Ghetto blaster / Don't cry no tears / Free again / Bad seed.

Apr 97. (cd0 *Nectar; (NTMCD 543)* **FANDEMONIUM** ☐ -

TELEVISION PERSONALITIES

Formed: Chelsea, London, England . . . 1976 by schoolmates DAN TREACY and EDWARD BALL. They soon found JOE FOSTER, plus the brothers JOHN and GERARD BENNETT. After originally going under the moniker TEEN 78, they came up with the name TV PERSONALITIES, parading themselves as HUGHIE GREEN, BRUCE FORSYTHE, BOB MONKHOUSE, RUSSELL HARTY and NICHOLAS PARSONS. Their first 45, '14th FLOOR', was released in the early summer of 1978, and with help from John Peel who playlisted it, sold all its 867 copies. They soon formed their own 'King's Road' label, (distributed initially by 'Rough Trade') and released an EP, 'WHERE'S BILL GRUNDY NOW?', which included the superb title track, alongside another gem, 'PART-TIME PUNKS'. Around this time ED and GERARD were also part of The O-LEVEL, who, after one 45, became The TEENAGE FILMSTARS (with DAN & JOE). In 1980, after a short retirement, they gigged for the first time and issued the 'SMASHING TIME' single. A year later, DAN and ED set up their own label, 'Whaam!', but were forced to fold it after a few releases due to pressure from pop duo, WHAM. In 1985, they chose another name, 'Dreamworld', but this too became defunct, even after signing The MIGHTY LEMON DROPS. They broke their long silence in early 1990, when 'Fire' records finally issued the remarkable 'PRIVILEGE'. By 1992's 'CLOSER TO GOD', they had lost their initial impact and TREACY became more heavily into drugs, leading to bouts of depression and little creative output. In the Autumn of '95, he was back to his near best with the sarcastic 'I WAS A MOD BEFORE YOU WERE A MOD'. • **Style:** D-I-Y punk outfit influenced initially by The SEX PISTOLS and, by the late 70's, SYD BARRETT. However, they never gained more than cult attraction. • **Songwriters:** DAN and ED penned most, until latters' departure. Covered BIKE (Pink Floyd) / NO ONE'S LITTLE GIRL (Raincoats) / SEASONS IN

THE SUN (Jacques Brel). • **Trivia:** DAN once tried to decapitate MARK SHEPPARD while in the studio, but producer DALE GRIFFIN locked him in the cupboard!

Recommended: AND DON'T THE KIDS JUST LOVE IT (*8) / PRIVILEGE (*8) / YES DARLING, BUT IS IT ART? (*7)

DAN TREACY – vocals / **EDWARD BALL** – organ, vocals / **JOE FOSTER** – guitar / **JOHN BENNETT** – bass / **GERARD BENNETT** – drums

W1 Teen not issued

May 78. (7"; as TV PERSONALITIES) *(SRTS-CUS 77089)* **14th FLOOR. / OXFORD STREET** [ ] [-]
(re-iss.Aug89 on 'Overground', 7" + yellow or white; OVER 03)

— now as trio (ED, DAN & JOE)

Kings Road not issued

Nov 78. (7"ep) *(LYN 5976-7)* **WHERE'S BILL GRUNDY NOW?** [ ] [-]
– Part-time punks / Where's Bill Grundy now? / Happy families / Posing at the Roundhouse. *(re-iss.Nov79 on 'Rough Trade'; RT 033)*

— disbanded for a year. **MARK 'EMPIRE' SHEPPARD** – drums (of SWELL MAPS)

Rough Trade not issued

Jul 80. (7") *(RT 051)* **SMASHING TIME. / KING AND COUNTRY** [ ] [-]

— JOE FOSTER left and soon became The MISSING SCIENTISTS who released a 45 in Sep80 'BIG CITY BRIGHT LIGHTS'. / 'DISCOTEQUE X', which featured DAN TREACY and DANIEL MILLER of Mute label.

Jan 81. (lp; as TV PERSONALITIES) *(ROUGH 24)* **AND DON'T THE KIDS JUST LOVE IT** [ ] [-]
– I know where Syd Barrett lives / This angry silence / The glittering prizes / Silly girl / Jackanory stories / Geoffrey Ingram / La grande illusion / Look back in anger. *(re-iss.Jan84; same) (cd-iss.Aug91 on 'Fire'; REFIRECD 7)*

Feb 81. (7") *(RT 063)* **I KNOW WHERE SYD BARRETT LIVES. / ARTHUR THE GARDENER** [ ] [-]

— were now just **DAN + EMPIRE** + new bassman BERNARD COOPER (ED BALL had formed The TIMES.)

Whaam! not issued

May 81. (7"; as GIFTED CHILDREN) *(WHAAM 001)* **PAINTING BY NUMBERS. / LICHTENSTEIN GIRL** [ ] [-]

— **ED** returned on guitar & bass. SLAUGHTER JOE FOSTER also returned.

Jan 82. (lp) *(WHAAM 3)* **MUMMY YOU'RE NOT WATCHING ME** [ ] [-]
– Adventure playground / A day in heaven / Scream quietly / Mummy you're not watching me / Brians magic ear / Where the rainbow ends / David Hockney's diaries / Painting by numbers / Lichtenstein painting / Magnificent dreams If I could write poetry. *(re-iss.Jun86 on 'Dreamworld'; BIG DREAM 4) (re-iss.Sep91 on 'Fire' cd/lp; REFIRE CD/LP 8)*

Aug 82. (lp) *(BIG 5)* **THEY COULD HAVE BEEN BIGGER THAN THE BEATLES** [ ] [-]
– Three wishes / David Hockney's diary / In a perfumed garden / Flowers for Abigail / King and country / The boy in the Paisley shirt / Games for boys / Painter man / Psychedelic holiday / 14th floor / Sooty's disco party / Makin time / When Emily cries / The glittering prizes / Anxiety block / Mysterious ways.. *(re-iss.Jun86 on 'Dreamworld'; BIG DREAM 2) (re-iss.Sep91 on 'Fire' cd/lp; REFIRE CD/LP 9)*

Sep 82. (7"m) *(WHAAM 4)* **THREE WISHES. / GEOFFREY INGRAM / AND DON'T THE KIDS JUST LOVE IT** [ ] [-]

— **DAN + ED** added **DAVE MUSKER** – organ / **JOE FOSTER** – guitar / **MARK FLUNDER** – bass / (JOWE HEAD repl. MARK who joined ROBYN HITCHCOCK)

Rough Trade not issued

Dec 83. (7") *(RT 109)* **A SENSE OF BELONGING. / PARADISE ESTATE** [ ] [-]

— (below lp should have been issued by 'Whaam!' in Nov83)

Illuminated not issued

Jan 85. (lp) *(JAMS 37)* **THE PAINTED WORD** [ ] [-]
– Stop and smell the roses / The painted word / A life of her own / Bright sunny smiles / Mentioned in dispatches / A sense of belonging / Say you won't cry / Someone to share my life with / You'll have to scream louder / Happy all the time / The girl who had everything / Paradise estates / Back to Vietnam. *(re-iss.Sep91 on 'Fire' cd/lp; REFIRE CD/LP 10)*

— now with **JOWE HEAD** – bass / **JEFF BLOOM** – drums (FOSTER became SLAUGHTER JOE and MUSKER formed JASMINE MINKS. ED continued with The TIMES and later went solo

Dreamworld not issued

Feb 86. (12"m) *(DREAM 4)* **HOW I LEARNED TO LOVE THE . . .BOMB! / THEN GOD SNAPS HIS FINGERS. / NO YOU'RE JUST BEING RIDICULOUS** [ ] [-]

Nov 86. (7"m) *(DREAM 10)* **HOW I LEARNED TO LOVE THE BOMB. / GROCER'S DAUGHTER / GIRL CALLED CHARITY** [ ] [-]

— (next album was to have been issued a year earlier on 'Dreamworld')

— **JOWE HEAD** – bass (ex-SWELL MAPS) repl. BALL.

Fire not issued

Oct 89. (7") *(BLAZE 37S)* **SALVADOR DALI'S GARDEN PARTY. / ROOM AT THE TOP OF THE STAIRS** [ ] [-]
(12"+=) *(BLAZE 37T)* – This time there is no happy ending / Part one: Fulfilling the contractual obligations.

Dec 89. (ltd.7") *(CAFF 5)* **I STILL BELIEVE IN MAGIC. / RESPECTABLE** [ ] [-]

— (above single on 'Caff' label)

Feb 90. (cd/c/lp) *(FIRE CD/MC/LP 21)* **PRIVILEGE** [ ] [-]
– Paradise is for the blessed / Conscience tells me no / All my dreams are dead / The man who paints the rainbows / Sad Mona Lisa / Sometimes I think you know me / Privilege / Good and faithful servant / My hedonistic tendencies / Salvador Dali's garden party / What if it's raining? / The engine driver song / Better than I know myself. *(c+=/cd+=)*– (3 tracks).

Sep 91. (12"ep/cd-ep) *(BLAZE 48 T/CD)* **STRANGELY BEAUTIFUL / REACHING FOR THE STARS. / NOT EVEN A MAYBE / ('A'-Chill out mix)** [ ] [-]

Feb 92. (7") **SHE NEVER READ MY POEMS. / ?** [ ] [-]
(12"+=/cd-s+=) – ?

Seminal Twang not issued

Sep 92. (7"/cd-s) **WE WILL BE OUR GURUS. / AN EXHIBITION BY JOAN MIRO / LOVE IS BETTER THAN WAR** [ ] [-]

Oct 92 (cd/c/d-lp) *(FIRE CD/MC/LP 032)* **CLOSER TO GOD** [ ] [-]
– You don't know how lucky you are / Hard luck story No. 30 / Little works of art / Razorblades and lemonade / Coming home soon / Me and big ideas / Honey for the bears / I see myself in you / Goodnight Mr. Spaceman / My very nervous breakdown / We will be your gurus / You are special and you always will be / Not for the likes of us / You're younger than you know / Very dark today / I hope you have a nice day / Baby you're only as good as you should be / Closer to God.

May 93. (7"/cd-s) *(BLAZE 65)* **GOODNIGHT MR. SPACEMAN. / IF I WAS YOUR GIRLDRIEND** [ ] [-]
(cd-s+=) *(BLAZE 65CD)* – She loves it when he sings like Elvis / ('A'-Lost in space mix).

Vinyl Japan not issued

May 94. (12"ep/cd-ep) **FAR AWAY AND LOST IN JOY / I DON'T WANT TO LIVE THIS LIFE. / DO YOU KNOW WHAT THEY'RE SAYING ABOUT ME NOW? / I GET FRIGHTENED** [ ] [-]

Oct 95. (12"ep/cd-ep) *(TASK/+CD 048)* **DO YOU THINK IF YOU WERE BEAUTIFUL YOU'D BE HAPPY / HE USED TO PAINT IN COLOURS / WHO WILL BE YOUR PRINCE / I SUPPOSE YOU THINK IT'S FUNNY** [ ] [-]

Overground not issued

Sep 95. (lp/cd; as TV PERSONALITIES) *(OVER 41/+CD)* **I WAS A MOD BEFORE YOU WAS A MOD** [ ] [-]
– As John Belushi said / I was a mod before you were a mod / A stranger to myself / Little Woody Allen / A long time gone / Evan doesn't ring me anymore / Things have changed since I was girl / Haunted / I can see my whole world crashing down / Something flew over my head / Everything she touches turns to gold. *(re-iss.Jun97; same)*

Twist not issued

Jan 96. (7"m) *(TWIST 20)* **SEASONS IN THE SUN. / BIKE / NO ONE'S LITTLE GIRL** [ ] [-]

– compilations, etc. –

1985. (lp) *Pastell; (POW 2)* **CHOCOLAT-ART (A TRIBUTE TO JAMES LAST) (live Germany 1984)** [-] [-] German
(re-iss.Jul93 cd/lp; POW 2)

Aug 91. (lp/cd; as TV PERSONALITIES) *Overground; (OVER 21/+CD)* **CAMPING IN FRANCE (live '85)** [ ] [-]

1994. (lp/cd; as TV PERSONALITIES) *Overground; (OVER 30/+CD)* **HOW I LEARNED TO LOVE THE BOMB** [ ] [-]
(re-iss.Jun97; same)

Feb 95. (cd) *Fire; (FLIPCD 001)* **YES DARLING BUT IS IT ART?** [ ] [-]

Mar 96. (cd; as TV PERSONALITIES) *Overground; (OVER 48CD)* **TOP GEAR** [ ] [-]

Jun 97. (cd; as TV PERSONALITIES) *Overground; (OVER 52/+CD)* **PAISLEY SHIRTS & MINI SKIRTS** [ ] [-]

THIN WHITE ROPE

Formed: Davis, Sacramento, California, USA . . . 1984 by mainman GUY KYSER. Their debut album, 'EXPLORING THE AXIS', found its way into the hands of Demon off-shoot label, 'Zippo', who issued it in '85. However, it took until 1987's MOONHEAD', for them to gain recognition. 'IN THE SPANISH CAVE' followed a year later as their European popularity soared (at least critically). They subsequently signed to 'RCA' in 1989, but mediocre albums resulted in their demise by '92. KYSER went back to university to gain a degree, while maintaining his songwriting skills, augmented by his girlfriend. • **Style:** Retro psyche/country act that drew from the new guitar movement pioneered by RAIN PARADE and LONG RYDERS, for which they suffered an initial press backlash. • **Songwriters:** KYSER penned except; ROAD-RUNNER (Bo Diddley) / AIN'T THAT LOVIN' YOU BABY (Jimmy Reed) / TOWN WITHOUT PITY (hit; Gene Pitney) / SOME VELVET MORNING (Lee Hazlewood) / YOO DOO RIGHT (Can) / THE MAN WITH THE GOLDEN GUN (John Barry) / BORN TO FLAMES (13th Floor Elevators) / OUTLAW BLUES (Bob Dylan) / EYE (Foster Children) / THEY'RE HANGING ME TONIGHT (Love – Wolpert) / HERE SHE COMES NOW (Velvet Underground) / etc. • **Trivia:** Took their name from William Burroughs' description of ejaculation.

Recommended: MOONHEAD (*8) / IN THE SPANISH CAVE (*7)

GUY KYSER – vocals, guitar / **ROGER KUNKEL** – guitar / **STEPHEN TESLUK** – bass, who repl. KEVIN STAYHODOR / **JOZEF BECKER** – drums, repl. FRANK FRENCH (ex-TRUE WEST)

Zippo Frontier

Sep 85. (lp/c) *(ZONG/+CASS 006)* <FRO 1015> **EXPLORING THE AXIS** [ ] [ ]
– Down in the desert / Disney girl / Soundtrack / Lithium / Dead grammas on a train / The three song / Eleven / Roger's tongue / The real west / Exploring the axis. *(cd-iss.Jul90; ZONGCD 006) (cd re-iss.Apr97 on 'Diablo'+=; DIAB 824)*– BOTTOM FEEDERS

Jan 87. (lp) *(ZONG 017)* <FRO 1020> **MOONHEAD** [ ] [ ]
– Not your fault / Wire animals / Take it home / Thing / Moonhead / Wet heart / Mother / Come around / If those tears / Crawl piss freeze. *(w/free-flexi-7")*
– WIRE ANIMALS. / WET HEART *(cd-iss.Jul90 +=; ZONGCD 017)*– Waking up / Valley of the bones / Atomic imagery / Ain't that lovin' you baby. *(cd re-iss.Apr97 on 'Diablo'+=; DIAB 825)*

Sep 87. (m-lp) *(ZANE 005)* **BOTTOM FEEDERS** (rare, etc.) [ ] [ ]
– Ain't that loving you baby / Macy's window / Waking up / Valley of the bones / Atomic imagery / Rocket U.S.A. (live).

— now without JOZEF who joined GAME THEORY (now full-time)

Demon Frontier

Mar 88. (lp/cd) *(FIEND/+CD 114)* **IN THE SPANISH CAVE** [ ] [ ]

– Mr. Limpet / Ring / It's o.k. / Ahr-Skidar / Red sun / Elsie crashed the party / Timing / Astronomy / Wand / July. *(cd+=)*– BOTTOM FEEDERS (m-lp) *<US-c++=>*– Munich Eunich.

Oct 88. (m-lp) *(VEX 8)* **RED SUN** [-]
– Red sun / Town without pity / The man with the golden gun / They're hanging me tonight / Some velvet morning / Red sun (original). *(cd-iss.May92;)*

R.C.A. R.C.A.

May 90. (cd/c/lp) *(PD/PK/PL 90469) <9994-2/-4/-1>* **SACK FULL OF SILVER** Feb90
– Hidden lands / Sack full of silver / You do right (can) / The napkin song / Americana – The ghost / Whirling Dervish / The tiggle song / Diesel man / On the floe. *(re-iss.Jul92 on 'Frontier' clear-lp; 34638-1)*

Sub Pop Sub Pop

Apr 91. (7") **ANTS ARE CAVEMEN. / LITTLE DOLL (live)**

Frontier Frontier

May 91. (m-cd/m-lp) *(FCD/FLP 1035)* **SQUATTERS RIGHTS**
– Caravan / Roadrunner / Film theme / May this be love / Everybody's been burned / I knew I'd want you.

Aug 91. (cd/c/lp) *(34632-2/-4/-1)* **THE RUBY SEA**
– The ruby sea / Tina and Glen / Puppet dog / Bartender's rag / Midwest flower / Dinosaur / The lady vanishes / Up to midnight / Hunter's moon / Christmas skies / The fish song / The clown song.

—— Disbanded on 28th June 1992, after their last concert below.

Mar 93. (d-cd/d-c/d-lp) *(34642-2/-4/-1)* **THE ONE THAT GOT AWAY (live)**
– Down in the desert / Disney girl / Eleven / Not your fault / Wire animals / Take it home / Mr. Limpet / Elsie crashed the party / Red sun / Some velvet morning / Triangle song / Yoo doo right / Tina & Glen / Napkin song / Ants are cavemen / Fish song / Bartender's rag / Hunter's moon / Astronomy / Outlaw blues / It's o.k. / Wreck of the ol' 97 / Roadrunner / Munich Eunich / Silver machine / The clown song.

Dec 93. (7"ltd.) **MOONHEAD. / ?** [-]

Munster Munster

May 94. (cd/lp) *(MR 047 CD/LP)* **WHEN WORLDS COLLIDE**

– compilations, etc

Feb 95. (cd/lp) *Frontier-RCA; (31064-2/-1)* **SPOOR**
– Radio afternoon / Town without pity / Red sun / The man with the golden gun / They're hanging me tonight / Some velvet morning / Ants are caveman / Little doll / Outlaw blues / Born to flames / Eye / Skinhead / Tina and Glen / Munich Eunich / God rest ye merry gentlemen / Here she comes now.

THIS MORTAL COIL

Formed: London, England . . . 1983 by IVO WATTS-RUSSELL, aided by producer JOHN FRYER. IVO employed many singers and musicians from their '4 a.d.' stable, including ELIZABETH FRAZER and ROBIN GUTHRIE (of COCTEAU TWINS) on their debut 45, 'SONG TO THE SIREN'. A year later, a larger ensemble was represented on the hit debut album, 'IT'LL END IN TEARS'. Sporadic recordings followed, as IVO continued to expand his record company with new US acts; The PIXIES, THROWING MUSES, etc. The 1986 follow-up, 'FILIGREE & SHADOW', with new singer DOMINIC APPLETON, also made the charts, but it was five years before their third set, 'BLOOD'. • **Style:** Atmospheric and inspiring gothic-rock, that at times delved into the past for mystical but effective covers. • **Songwriters:** IVO and some 4 a.d. musicians, except; SONG TO THE SIREN + MORNING GLORY (Tim Buckley) / GATHERING DUST + 16 DAYS (Modern English) / ANOTHER DAY (Roy Harper) / COME HERE MY LOVE (Van Morrison) / DRUGS (Talking Heads) / HELP ME LIFT YOU UP (Mary Margaret O'Hara) / LATE NIGHT (Syd Barrett) / YOU AND YOUR SISTER (Chris Bell) / I AM THE COSMOS (Big Star) / NATURE'S WAY (Spirit) / others by GENE CLARK, etc. • **Trivia:** One of their singers from 1991; HEIDI BERRY had releases on 'Creation'.

Recommended: IT'LL END IN TEARS (*8) / FILIGREE & SHADOW (*7) / BLOOD (*7)

IVO WATTS-RUSSELL (b.1955) – tapes, loops, etc. / **JOHN FRYER** – instruments, producer with **COCTEAU TWINS:- ELIZABETH FRAZER** – vox / **ROBIN GUTHRIE** – guitar

4 a.d. Relativity

Sep 83. (7") *(AD 310)* **SONG TO THE SIREN. / 16 DAYS (reprise)** [66]
(12"+=) *(BAD 310)* – Gathering dust.

—— (above 'B'sides featured **ROBBIE GREY** – vocals (of MODERN ENGLISH) (below 'A'side featured **MARTIN McCARRICK** – cello, strings (of WILLING SINNERS; MARC ALMOND) / **GORDON SHARPE** – vocals (of CINDY TALK) / **SIMON RAYMONDE** – guitar, tapes (of COCTEAU TWINS)

Aug 84. (7") *(AD 410)* **KANGAROO. / IT'LL END IN TEARS** [-]

Below album feat. said musicians, plus **GINI BALL** – violin (of WILLING SINNERS) / DEAD CAN DANCE: **LIZA GERRARD** – accordion, vocals / **BRENDAN PERRY** – bass drone, drum / **PETER ULRICH** – percussion / COLOUR BOX: **STEVEN YOUNG** – piano / **MARTYN YOUNG** – sitar, guitar, bass / X-MAL DEUTSCHLAND: **MANUELA RICKERS** – guitar / WOLFGANG PRESS: **MARK COX** – organ / **HOWARD DEVOTO** – vocals (ex-MAGAZINE)

Oct 84. (lp/c) *(CAD/+C 411)* **IT'LL END IN TEARS** [38]
– Kangaroo / Song to the siren / Holocaust / FYT / Fond affections / The last ray / Waves become wings / Another day / Barramundi / Dreams made flesh / Not me / A single wish. *(cd-iss.1986; CAD 411CD)*

—— Retained guests **SIMON RAYMONDE / PETER ULRICH / MARK COX / STEVEN YOUNG** plus new BREATHLESS: **DOMINIC APPLETON** – vocals / **RICHENEL** – vocals / DIF JUZ: **DAVID CURTIS** – guitar / **ALAN CURTIS** – guitar / **RICHARD THOMAS** – saxophone / **MODERN ENGLISH: ANDREW GRAY** – guitar / / **JEAN** – vocals / **ALISON LIMERICK** – vocals / **CAROLINE SEAMAN** – vocals / **KEITH MITCHELL** – guitar / **DIERDRE RUTOWSKI** – backing vocals / **LOUISE RUTOWSKI** – backing vocals / **KEITH MITCHELL** – guitar / **NIGEL K.HINE** – guitar / **CHRIS PYE** – guitar / **JOHN TURNER** – organ, keyboards / **TONY WAEREA** – didgeridoo / **ANNE TURNER + LES McKUEN** – choir

Sep 86. (d-lp/c)(cd) *(DAD/+C 609)(DAD 609CD)* **FILIGREE & SHADOW** [53]
– Velvet belly / The jeweller / Ivy and neet / Meniscus / Tears / Tarantula / My father / Come here my love / At first, and then / Strength of strings / Morning glory / Inch-blue / I want to live / Mama K I / Filigree & shadow / Firebrothers / Thais I / I must have been blind / A heart of glass / Alone / Mama K II / The horizon bleeds and sucks its thumb / Drugs / Red rain / Thais II.

Sep 86. (ltd-10") *(BAD 608)* **COME HERE MY LOVE. / DRUGS** [-]

—— They used past musicians, plus **CAROLINE CRAWLEY, KIM DEAL + TANYA DONELLY, DOMINIC APPLETON, HEIDI BERRY + The RUTOWSKI's,** etc.

Apr 91. (d-lp/c/cd) *(DAD/+C/CD 609)* **BLOOD** [28]
– The lacemaker / Mr. Somewhere / Ardialu / With tomorrow / Loose joints / You and your sister / Nature's way / I come and steal at every door / Bitter / Baby Ray baby / Several times / The lacemaker II / Late night / Ruddy and wretched / Help me lift you up / Carolyn's song / DD and E / Til I gain control again / Dreams are like water / I am the cosmos / (Nothing but) Blood.

—— above could be their last release

David THOMAS (see under ⇒ PERE UBU)

TORTOISE

Formed: Chicago, Illinois, USA . . . 1990 by DOUG McCOMBS and JOHN HERNDON, who started jamming together with JOHN McENTIRE, BUNDY K. BROWN and DAN BITNEY. They released a number of EP's, before finally unleashing their eponymous debut in '94. This was remixed by STEVE ALBINI on the following years' blistering EP, 'RHYTHMS, RESOLUTIONS & CLUSTERS'. In 1996, their second album, 'MILLIONS NOW LIVING WILL NEVER DIE', showed them at their best again, especially on the ever-lasting track 'DJED'. This track was given different treatment, when it was radically remixed for the 'Mo Wax' label. • **Style:** Experimental arcane post-rock in the mould of MAIN, THIS HEAT or prog-rock YES, with added cut'n'mix trip-hop. A jazz-rock frenzy of NEU! and avant-garde post-Krautrock. • **Songwriters:** McINTYRE and group. • **Trivia:** McENTIRE was also part-time member of The RED CRAYOLA and The SEA AND CAKE.

Recommended: TORTOISE (*5) / MILLIONS NOW LIVING WILL NEVER DIE (*8)

JOHN McENTIRE – synthesizers, drums, vibraphone (ex-ELEVENTH DREAM DAY, ex-BASTRO) / **BUNDY K. BROWN** – guitar, bass / **DOUG McCOMBS** – bass / **JOHN HERNDON** – drums, synthesizers, vibraphone / **DAN BITNEY** – synthesizers, percussion / 6th member **CASEY** – soundman

not issued Soul Static

1994. (7") *<SOUL 7>* **WHY WE FIGHT. / WHITEWATER** [-]
(UK-iss.Jan95; same)

City Slang Thrill Jockey

Jan 95. (cd/lp) *(EFA 04950-2/-1) <THRILL 013>* **TORTOISE**
– Magnet pulls through / Night air / Ry Cooder / Onions wrapped in rubber / Tin cans and twine / Spiderwebbed / His second story island / On noble / Flyrod / Cornpole brunch. *(cd-iss.remixed May97; TKCB 71016) (lp re-iss.Jun97 on 'Thrill Jockey'; THRILL 013)*

Apr 95. (12") *(Dodgey Beast; DS 3309)* **GAMARA. / CLIFF DWELLER SOCIETY**
(12") *(DS 3309S)* –

Jun 95. (cd/lp) *(EFA 04957-2/-1)* **RHYTHMS, RESOLUTIONS & CLUSTERS EP** (remixes)

—— **DAVE PAJO** – guitar (ex-SLINT) repl. BROWN

Jan 96. (cd/lp) *(EFA 04972-2/-1)* **MILLIONS NOW LIVING WILL NEVER DIE**
– Djed / Glass museum / A survey / The taut and the tame / Dear grandma and grandpa / Along the banks of rivers. *(cd-iss.Japanese version May97; TKCB 70931)*

Apr 96. (12"ep) *(SHELL 001)* **DJED (remix). /**

Jul 96. (12"ep; by TORTOISE VS OVAL) *(SHELL 002)* **MUSIC FOR WORK GROUPS EP**
– Bubble economy (mix by Marcus Popp) / Learning curve (mix by Marcus Popp).

Sep 96. (12"ep; by TORTOISE VS SPRING HEEL JACK) *(SHELL 003) <TJ 124>* **GALAPAGOS (Spring Heel Jack remix). / REFERENCE RESISTANCE GATE (Jim O'Rourke remix)**
(re-iss.Jun97 on 'Thrill Jockey'; TJ 124)

Nov 96. (12"ep; by TORTOISE VS LUKE VIBERT) *(SHELL 004) <TJ 125>* **THE TAUT AND THE TAME**

May 97. (cd) *(TKCB 70932)* **DIGEST COMPENDIUM OF . . .**

TRICKY

Born: 1969, Knowle West, Bristol, England. After a troubled youth growing up on one of BRISTOL's poorer housing estates, ADRIAN THAWES began spending less time lawbreaking and more time busying himself with the city's club culture, helping run sound systems and hanging out with The WILD BUNCH, a loose collective of musicians and DJ's that icluded MASSIVE ATTACK and famed producer NELLEE HOOPER. In between trips to court in OXFORD, where he was defending an assault charge, TRICKY KID (as he was nicknamed by his Bristolian cohorts) occasionally collaborated with MASSIVE ATTACK on their seminal 'BLUE LINES' album, contributing stoned raps on several tracks. He also contributed to MASSIVE's follow-up, 'PROTECTION', although his first solo effort was a 'Betty Blue'-sampling track entitled 'LOYALTY IS VALUABLE', engineered by future PORTISHEAD mainman GEOFF BARROWS and featured on the 1991 Sickle Cell charity album, 'HARD SELL', alongside the likes of MASSIVE ATTACK, SMITH & MIGHTY etc. Yet the track that brought him to the attention of a discerning public was the sublime claustrophobia of 'AFTERMATH'. Eventually released in early '94, the track had previously been recorded a couple of years earlier with TRICKY's musical partner, MARTINA, predating the trip-hop scene that TRICKY would later be lumped in with. Next came the jarring loops and nervous paranoia of 'PONDEROSA', another taster for the pioneering debut album, 'MAXINQUAYE' (1994), released later that summmer. A dense, brooding collection of slow motion beat-poetry from the darkside, the record was immediately hailed as a classic. Taking bastardised hip-hop beats as his raw material then suffocating them with layers of samples, disjointed rhythms, freak instrumental lines and obscure noises, TRICKY created music that was wired yet lethargic, with lyrics equally contradictory and ambiguous to match. Collaborating with TERRY HALL, NENEH CHERRY and ALISON MOYET amongst others, TRICKY released his 'NEARLY GOD' project in 1996. The album revisited the dark intensity of 'MAXINQUAYE' without quite the same effect, possibly a case of too many cooks (or too many spliffs) spoiling the broth. 'PRE-MILLENNIUM TENSION', released later the same year, was on a par with 'MAXINQUAYE' and if it didn't exactly break new ground, the album illustrated that TRICKY's wellspring of paranoid psychosis is far from running dry. Tracks like 'BAD THINGS', 'MAKES ME WANNA DIE' and 'MY EVIL IS STRONG' speak for themselves, and though it's a well worn cliche, it would appear that this man really does suffer for his art. Then again, maybe he shouldn't smoke so much. • **Songwriters:** Self-penned & samples except; BLACK STEEL (Public Enemy) / PONDEROSA (co-with HOWIE B) / HELL IS ROUND THE CORNER (same source that PORTISHEAD found 'Glory Box'?)

Recommended: MAXINQUAYE (*9) / NEARLY GOD (*8)

TRICKY – vocals / with **MARTINE** – vocals

4th & Bro. | 4th & Bro.

Jan 94. (7") *(BRW 288)* **AFTERMATH. / ('A'-I could be looking for people mix)** [69] [ ]
(12"+=) *(12BRW 288)* – ('A'mix).
(cd-s++=) *(BRCD 288)* – ('A'mix).

Apr 94. (7") *(BRW 299)* **PONDEROSA. / ('A'-Dobie's roll pt.1 mix)** [ ] [ ]
(12"+=/cd-s+=) *(12BRW/BRCD 299)* – (3 'A'mixes; Ultragelic / Original / Dobie's roll pt.2).

Jan 95. (7"/c-s) *(BR W/CA 304)* **OVERCOME. / ABBA ON FAT TRACKS** [34] [ ]
(12"+=/cd-s+=) *(12BRW/BRCD 304)* – ('A'-Zippy & Bungle mix).

— guests on below ALISON GOLDFRAPP + RAGGA – vocals / PETE BRIQUETTE – bass / MARK SAUNDERS – keyboards / FTV – guitar, drums / TONY WRAFTER – flute / JAMES STEVENSON – guitar

Feb 95. (cd/c/lp) *(BR CD/CA/LP 610)* **MAXINQUAYE** [3] [ ]
– Overcome / Ponderosa / Black steel / Hell is round the corner / Pumpkin / Aftermath / Abbaon fat tracks / Brand new you're retro / Suffocated love / You don't / Strugglin' / Feed me.

Mar 95. (c-s) *(BRCA 320)* **BLACK STEEL. / ('A'-Been caught stealing mix)** [28] [ ]
(12"+=/cd-s+=) *(12BRW/BRCD 320)* – ('A'live) / ('A'-In the draw mix).
(cd-s++=) *(BRCDX 320)* – ('A'edit).

Jul 95. (7"pic-d-ep/12"red-ep/cd-ep; as TRICKY VS. THE GRAVEDIGGAZ) *(BRW/12BRW/BRCD 326)* **THE HELL E.P.** [12] [ ]
– Hell is round the corner (original) / ('A'-Hell and water mix) / Psychosis / Tonite is a special nite (chaos mass confusion mix).

Nov 95. (c-s) *(BRCA 330)* **PUMPKIN / MOODY BROODY BUDHIST CAMP / NEW KINGDOM** [26] [ ]
(cd-s+=) *(BRCD 330)* – Brand new you're retro (Alex Reece mix).
(12"colrd) *(12BRW 330)* – ('A'side) / (above track) / Slick 66.

NEARLY GOD

TRICKY with **TERRY HALL / MARTINA / BJORK / NENEH CHERRY / ALISON MOYET + CATH COFFEY**

Durban Poison

Apr 96. (7") *(DP 003)* **POEMS / CHILDREN'S STORY** [28] [ ]
(12"+=/cd-s+=) *(DP X/CD 003)* – ('A'extended).

Apr 96. (cd/c/lp) *(DP CD/MC/LP 1001)* **NEARLY GOD** [11] [ ]
– Tattoo / Poems / Together now / Keep your mouth shut / I be the prophet / Make a chane / Black cofee / Bubbles / I sing for you / Yoga.

— above was to have been under his DURBAN POISON project.

— Aug 96, TRICKY PRESENTS GRASS ROOTS 12"ep for 'Ultra'.

TRICKY

4th & Bro. | 4th & Bro.

Oct 96. (7"pic-d) *(BRW 340)* **CHRISTIANSANDS. / FLYNN** [36] [ ]
(12"+=/cd-s+=) *(12BRW/BRCD 340)* – Ghetto youth.

Nov 96. (cd/c/lp) *(BR CD/CA/LP 623)* **PRE-MILLENNIUM TENSION** [30] [ ]
– Vent / Christiansands / Tricky kid / Bad dreams / Makes me wanna die / Ghetto youth / Sex drive / Bad things / Lyrics of fury / My evil is strong / Piano. *(d-cd-iss.; BRCDX 623)*

— late '96, featured on the hit single by GARBAGE; 'Milk'.

Jan 97. (cd-ep) *(BRCDX 341)* **TRICKY KID. / MAKES ME WANNA DIE (Tricky's extremix) / GRASS ROOTS** [28] [ ]
(12"ep+=) *(12BRW 341)* – Smoking Beagles (Sub Sub vs Tricky).
(cd-ep) *(BRCD 341)* – ('A'side) / Devils helper / Smoking Beagles (Sub Sub vs Tricky) / Suffocated love (live on 'Later with Jools').

Apr 97. (cd-s) *(BRCDX 348)* **MAKES ME WANNA DIE / MAKES ME WANNA DIE (The Weekend mix – remixed by The Stereo MC's) / PIANO (the Green sticky mix remixed by A Guy Called Gerald)** [29] [ ]
(12"clear+=) *(BRX 348)* – Here comes the aliens (AFRIKA IZLAM & TRICKY).
(cd-s) *(BRCD 348)* – ('A'side) / ('A'acoustic) / Here come the aliens (AFRIKA IZLAM & TRICKY).

U

ULTRAMARINE

Formed: Chelmsford, Essex, England . . . 1984 as A PRIMARY INDUSTRY by IAN COOPER and PAUL HAMMOND, with JEMMA, GUY and SIMON. In the early 90's, IAN and PAUL became ULTRAMARINE after basing themselves in Leamington Spa. They were showered with praise during 1992, after the release of their album, 'EVERY MAN AND WOMAN IS A STAR'. Just prior to this, they had taken a canoe trip with the band, AMERICA's organist DEWEY BUNNELL. In the Autumn of '93, they managed to scrape into the UK Top 50 with the SOFT MACHINE-influenced, 'UNITED KINGDOMS' album, which featured veteran Canterbury legend ROBERT WYATT. They took another about turn in 1995, with the release of the uninspiring US West Coast type album, 'BEL AIR'. • **Style:** Electronic/dance, left-field of Balearic, with distinctive fairground organ, samples and the influence of KEVIN AYERS, who provided them with some of his old lyrics in 1991. A PRIMARY INDUSTRY were of the avant-garde, noise merchant variety. • **Songwriters:** COOPER-HAMMOND, except HEART OF GLASS (Blondie) / HYMN (Kevin Ayers). ULTRAMARINE of '93, included co-writing and singing contributions from wheel-chair bound veteran ROBERT WYATT. • **Trivia:** Another group (foreign?) named ULTRAMARINE issued 2 albums 'DE' & 'E SI MALA' 1990-1993.

Recommended: EVERY MAN AND WOMAN IS A STAR (*8) / UNITED KINGDOMS (*8)

A PRIMARY INDUSTRY

IAN COOPER – acoustic guitar, keyboards, prog. / **PAUL HAMMOND** – bass, keyboards, programming / **JEMMA** – vocals / **GUY** – keyboards / **SIMON** – drums

Les Tempes Modernes | not issued

Nov 84. (7") *(CSBTV:V)* **AT GUNPOINT. / PERVERSION** [ ] [-]
(re-iss.Feb86 on 'N.I.S.S.' 12"; C88TV)

Sweatbox | not issued

Nov 85. (12"ep) *(SOX 007)* **7 HERTZ** [ ] [-]
– Cicatrice / Obeah / Biting back / Bled dry.

Oct 86. (lp) *(SAX 015)* **ULTRAMARINE** [ ] [-]
– Body blow / Beacon Hill / Shear / Sans orange / Cicatrice / Watchword weal / Gush / Raw umber / Silesia / Rose madder.

Jul 87. (7") *(OX 22)* **HEART OF GLASS. / WHERE IS YOUR VORTEX** [ ] [-]
(12") *(BOX 25)* – ('A'extended) / ('A'extended).

Mar 88. (m-lp) *(BOX 26)* **WYNDHAM LEWIS** [ ] [-]
– The liquid brown detestable Earth Fokker Bomb shit / The song of the militant romance / If so the man you are / End of enemy interlude / Merde alors!

— Disbanded after above, IAN and PAUL became . . .

ULTRAMARINE

COOPER + HAMMOND

Sweatbox | not issued

Jun 89. (m-lp) *(BOX 28)* **WYNDHAM LEWIS** [ ] [-]
– (the re-issue of A PRIMARY INDUSTRY m-lp)

Crepuscule | not issued

Mar 90. (lp/cd) *(TWI 894/+CD)* **FOLK** [ ] [-]
– Lobster / Antiseptic / Bronze eye / Bastard folk / Bullprong / Softspot / Vulfar streak / The golden target. *(re-iss.cd Nov94 on 'Offshore'+=; OSHCD 1)*– Stella / Interstellar.

Dancydopedia | not issued

Sep 90. (12"ep) *(DAN 002)* **STELLA. / INTERSTELLAR / ULTRABASS (Eddy De Cierca mix)** [ ] [-]

Brainiak | not issued

May 91. (12") *(BAUBJ 11)* **STELLA CONNECTS. / STELLA BREATHS** [ ] [-]

Oct 91. (12"ep) *(BRAINK 019)* **WEIRD GEAR. / WEIRD GEAR (version) / BRITISH SUMMERTIME** [ ] [-]

Dec 91. (cd/m-lp) *(BRAIN KCD/MKLP 21)* **EVERY MAN AND WOMAN IS A STAR** [ ] [-]
– Discovery / Weird gear / Pansy / Money / Stella / Geezer / Panther / British summertime / Lights in my brain / Canoe trip / Skyclad / Gravity. *(re-iss.& re-mixed Jul92 on 'Rough Trade' cd)(lp+=; R 292)(RT 896)*– Nova Scotia / Saratoga.

Rough Trade | Dali

May 92. (7"ltd.) *(45REV 7)* **SARATOGA. / NOVA SCOTIA** [ ] [-]

Nov 92. (12"ep/cd-ep) *(R 294-0/-3)* **NIGHTFALL IN SWEETLEAF** [ ] [-]
– Panther (Coco Steel remix) / Lights in my brain (Spooky mix) / Geezer (Sweet Exorcist mix).

Mar 93. (12"ep)(cd-ep) *(066324)(PRCD 8737)* **WEIRD GEAR (remix) / LIGHTS IN MY BRAIN (Spooky mix) / GEEZER (Sweet Exorcist mix) / PANTHER (Coco Steel & Lovebomb mix) / OUTRO** [-] [ ]

— now with **ROBERT WYATT** – vocals ('A'above) / **SIMON KAY** – Hammond organ / **JIMMY HASTINGS** – clarinet, flute, piccolo, sax / **JIM RATTIGAN** – accordion / **ROBERT ATCHISON** – violin / **PHIL JAMES** – trumpet, harmonica / **PAUL**

JOHNSON – percussion

Blanco Y Negro / Warners

Jul 93. (7"/c-s) *(NEG 65/+C)* **KINGDOM. / GOLDCREST** [46]
(12"/cd-s) *(NEG 65 T/CD)* – ('A'side) / ('B'extended) / ('A'extended mix).

Aug 93. (cd/c/lp) *(4509 93425-2/-4/-1)* **UNITED KINGDOMS** [49]
– Source / Kingdom / Queen of the Moon / Prince Rock / Happy land / Urf / English heritage / Instant kitten / The badger / Hooter / Dizzy fox / No time. *(cd re-iss.Jan97; same)*

Jan 94. (c-ep/12"ep/cd-ep) *(NEG 67 CD/T/CD)* **THE BAREFOOT EP** [61]
– Happy land / Hooter / The badger.

Jan 95. (c-s) *(NEG 76C)* **HYMN (David McAlmont mix) / HYMN (Kevin Ayers mix) / BASE ELEMENT** [ ] [-]
(cd-s+=) *(NEG 76CD1)* – (first & last track) / Our love / Love life.
(12") *(NEG 76T)* – Hymn (U-ziq mix) / Hymn (Luke Slater mix) / Our love / Love life.
(cd-s) *(NEG 76CD2)* – Hymn (U-ziq mix) / Hymn (Luke Slater mix) / Hymn (Paul Sampson's lullabye mix) / Hymn (Sugar J mix) / Hymn (Mouse On Mars: a sleep mix) / Hymn (Ultramarine & Kevin Ayers version).

Aug 95. (cd/c/clear-d-lp) *(0603 11206-2/-4/-1)* **BEL AIR**
– Welcome / Buena vista / Maxine / Pioneer spirit / Mutant / Fantasy filter / 78 / I got sane / Schnaltz / Citizen / Alter ego / Free radical / Harmony Street / K-V / Escape velocity / Rainbow brew / Everyone in Brazil. *(cd re-iss.Jan97; same)*

— next featuring DAVID McALMONT

Dec 95. (12"ep/c-ep) *(NEG T/C)* **HYMN / STRONGER TO WACK / GATED LATIN / WINDING RHODES**
(cd-ep) *(NEGCD)* – ('A'mixes).

ULTRA VIVID SCENE

Formed: New York, USA . . .1988 by KURT RALSKE, who flitted between the local jazz and hardcore scenes. He then moved to London, England in '86, forming the bands, NOTHING BUT HAPPINESS and CRASH. Having gained a contract with the UK label, '4 a.d.', he returned to New York, where he formed UVS and it wasn't long before his eponymous HUGH JONES-produced debut scaled the UK indie charts. Immediately previous to this, he released the 'SHE SCREAMED' EP, which included his tribute to HANK WILLIAMS and The MARQUIS DE SADE; 'NOT IN LOVE (HIT BY A TRUCK)'. The follow-up album in 1990, fared even better, and was given recognition by the US college circuit. He finally gave up solo/group work, moving into production work for singer LIDA HUSIK after 1992's disappointing 'REV' album. • **Style:** Bubblegum ambient sound influenced by JESUS & MARY CHAIN / MY BLOODY VALENTINE, but tackling issues such as sex, schizophrenia and suicide. • **Songwriters:** RALSKE. • **Trivia:** 1990 album produced by HUGH JONES.

Recommended: ULTRA VIVID SCENE (*8) / JOY 1967-1990 (*7)

NOTHING BUT HAPPINESS

KURT RALSKE (b. 1967) – guitar / **DAVID MAREADY BOWAN / BILL GERSTALL / LYNN CUTHBERTSON**

Remorse / Justine

Jun 86. (7") *(LOST 1)* <JUS 002> **COULDN'T MAKE YOU MINE. / NARCOTICS DAY** Feb89

Mar 87. (lp) *(REMLP 1)* **DETOUR**
– For waitress friends / Striped songs / Battle hymn / Buried in the flowers / Facsimile / Don't laugh / Couldn't make you mine / My summer dress / Blue kiss / Narcotics day.

CRASH

had already been formed by **KURT** plus **MARK DUMAIS** – vocals, guitar, main songwriter / **BILL CAREY** – guitar (ex-EXCENTRICKS) / **ADAM WRIGHT** – bass / **BYRON GUTHRIE** – drums

Remorse / Justine

Nov 86. (12"ep) *(LOST 2)* <JUS 001> **DON'T LOOK NOW (NOW!). / INTERNATIONAL VELVET / DON'T LOOK NOW (acoustic)** Jun88

Nov 86. (12"ep) *(LOST 4)* **ALMOST. / MY MACHINE / ON AND ON (version)** [ ] [-]

Feb 87. (lp) *(REMLP 2)* **I FEEL FINE** [ ] [-]
– Almost / Craig egg / International velvet / I go round / Superfly / Everything under the sun / I feel fine / My machine / On and on / Rings, chains and groups / Get set / John stood by / What I found.

Aug 87. (7") *(LOSS 6)* **BRIGHT COLOURED LIGHTS. / IN MY HEAD** [ ] [-]

— Disbanded soon after above. BYRON joined JOHN MOORE'S EXPRESSWAY and CAREY joined SOMETHING PRETTY BEAUTIFUL. It was an entirely different CRASH that issued for 'Creation', a single 'SUNBURST' early '89.

ULTRA VIVID SCENE

KURT RALSKE – vocals, everything (solo)

4 a.d. / Columbia

Aug 88. (12"ep/cd-ep) *(BAD 806/+CD)* **SHE SCREAMED / WALKIN' AFTER MIDNIGHT / NOT IN LOVE (HIT BY A TRUCK)** [ ] [-]

Oct 88. (lp/c)(cd) *(CAD/+C 809)(CAD 809CD)* **ULTRA VIVID SCENE** [ ] [-]
– She screamed / Crash / You didn't say please / Lynne-Marie 2 / Nausea / Mercy seat / Dream of love / Lynne-Marie / This isn't real / The whore of God / Bloodline / How did it feel / Hail Mary. *(cd+=)*– (1 track).

1989. (7") <JUS 003> **SLOW YOU DOWN. / TOTALLY FREE** [-] [ ]

— added **KRISTAN KRAMER** – bass / **MAZORA CREAGER** – cello, vocals / + there turning **BYRON GUTHRIE** – drums

Mar 89. (7") *(AD 906)* **MERCY SEAT. / CODINE** [ ] [-]
(12"+=/cd-s+=) – H like in Heaven / ('A'-lp version).

Jul 89. (7"ltd.shop-freebie) *(AD 908)* **SOMETHING TO EAT. / H LIKE IN HEAVEN** [-] [-]

— **KURT** retained **BYRON** + recruited **COLLIN RAE** – rhythm guitar / **ANN HOLLIS** – bass

Apr 90. (7"ep/c-ep/12"ep/cd-ep) *(BAD/+C/T/CD 0004)* <73371> **STARING AT THE SUN / THREE STARS (*** version). / CRASH / SOMETHING BETTER**

Apr 90. (cd)(lp/c) *(CAD 0005CD)(CAD/+C 0005)* **JOY 1967-1990** [ ] [-]
– It happens every time / Staring at the sun / Three stars / Special one / Grey turns white / Poison / Guilty pleasure / Extra ordinary / Beauty No.2 / The kindest cut / Praise the law / Lightning.

Nov 90. (7")<cd-ep> *(AD 0016)* <73534> **SPECIAL ONE. / KIND OF A DRAG** [ ] [-]

— **RALSKE** recruited entire new line-up; **JACK DALEY** – bass / **JULIAN KLEPACZ** – drums

Oct 92. (cd)(lp/c) *(CAD 2017CD)(CAD/+C 2017)* **REV** [ ] [-]
– Candida / Cut-throat / Mirror to mirror / The portion of delight / Thief's love song / How sweet / Medicating angels / Blood and thunder / This is the way.

Feb 93. (12"ep/cd-ep) **BLOOD AND THUNDER (remix) / DON'T LOOK NOW (NOW!). / CANDIDA (theme from 'Red Pressure Mounting') / WINTER SONG** [ ] [-]

— As said, KURT concentrated on production demands.

UNDERWORLD

Formed: Romford, London, England . . . 1987 by RICK SMITH, KARL HYDE, ALFIE THOMAS and BRYN BURROWS, who had all been in Cardiff outfit FREUR (which was actually a symbol translated into a word!; no, PRINCE wasn't the first!). Even before this, RICK and KARL had played in synth-pop band, The SCREEN GEMS. In 1987, they took on the more conventional moniker, UNDERWORLD and hit America in the late 80's after signing for Seymour Stein's 'Sire' records. After a No.1 smash, 'RADAR', in Australia, they toured the States supporting EURYTHMICS, but it was clear this was not the direction for them. After recruiting DJ DARREN EMERSON, the band signed with the 'Boys Own' label, releasing the seminal techno crescendo of 'REZ' in February '93. They followed this up with the critically acclaimed, early '94 album, 'DUBNOBASSWITHMYHEADMAN', a nouveau-psychedelic classic climaxing with the delirious trance-athon of 'COWGIRL'. However, their big break came with the track 'BORN SLIPPY', a song featured on the 'Trainspotting' soundtrack. When re-released as a single in 1996, the track stormed to No.2, boosting sales of their recently released follow-up album, 'SECOND TOUGHEST IN THE INFANTS'. The band remain one of Britain's best loved techno acts, and with the Stateside success of The PRODIGY, there's still a chance that the band might break in America. • **Songwriters:** SMITH / HYDE / THOMAS then SMITH / HYDE / EMERSON. • **Trivia:** Produced by RUPERT HINES in 1988. HYDE worked on a 1991 'Paisley P.' album with TERRI NUNN (ex-Berlin). GEOFF DUGMORE (ex-ART OF NOISE) was a guest on 1989 album. Also appeared on WILLIAM ORBIT's 'Watch From A Vine Leaf' & ORBITAL's 'Lush 3' and remixed BJORK's 'Human Behaviour'.

Recommended: DUBNOBASSWITHMYHEADMAN (*8) / SECOND TOUGHEST IN THE INFANTS (*8)

FREUR

RICK SMITH – keyboards, vocals / **KARL HYDE** – vocals, guitar / **ALFIE THOMAS** – guitar, vocals / **JOHN WARWICKER LE BRETON** – synthesizers / **BRYN B. BURROWS** – drums

C.B.S. / Epic

Mar 83. (7"pic-d/ext.12") *(WA/A13 3141)* **DOOT DOOT. / HOLD ME MOTHER** [59]

Jun 83. (7"/7"pic-d) *(A/WA 3456)* **MATTERS OF THE HEART. / YOU'RE A HOOVER**
(12"+=) *(TA 3456)* – ('A'extended).

Sep 83. (7")(12") **RUNAWAY. / YOU'RE A HOOVER**

Nov 83. (lp/c) *(CBS/40 25522)* **DOOT DOOT**
– Doot doot / Runaway / Riders in the night / Theme from the film of the same name / Tender surrender / Matters of the heart / My room / Steam machine / Whispering / All too much.

Jan 84. (7"/ext.12") *(A/TA 4073)* **DOOT DOOT. / HOLD ME MOTHER**

Apr 84. (7") *(A 4333)* **RIDERS IN THE NIGHT. / INNOCENCE**
(12"+=) *(TA 4333)* – This is the way I like to live my life.

— added **JAKE BOWIE** – bass

Oct 84. (7") *(A 4726)* **DEVIL AND DARKNESS. / JAZZ 'N' KING**
(12"+=) *(TX 4726)* – ('A'extended).

Feb 85. (7") *(A 4983)* **LOOK IN THE BACK FOR ANSWERS. / HEY HO AWAY WE GO**
(12"+=) *(TX 4983)* – Uncle Jeff.

Feb 85. (lp/c/cd) **GET US OUT OF HERE**
– Look in the back for answers / Emeralds and pearls / Kiss me / A.O.K.O. / The Devil and darkness / The piano song / Happiness / Endless groove / This is the way I'd like to live my life / Bella Donna.

UNDERWORLD

BAZ ALLEN – bass repl. JOHN

Sire / Sire

Mar 88. (lp/c/cd) *(925627-1/-4/-2)* **UNDERNEATH THE RADAR**
– Glory! glory! / Call me No.1 / Rubber ball (space kitchen) / Show some emotion / Underneath the radar / Miracle party / I need a doctor / Bright white flame / Pray / The God song.

Jul 88. (7") *(W 7968)* **UNDERNEATH THE RADAR. / BIG RED X** [ ] [74] Apr88

(12"+=) *(W 7968T)* – ('A'dub version).
Aug 88. (7") **SHOW SOME EMOTION. / SHOCK THE DOCTOR** [-] [ ]

— **PASCAL CONSOLI** – percussion, drums repl. BURROWS who joined WORLDWIDE ELECTRIC

Aug 89. (7"/c-s) *(W 2854/+C)* **STAND UP. / OUTSKIRTS** [ ] [67]
(12") *(W 2854T)* – Stand up (and dance) / Stand up (ya house) / Outskirts.
(cd-s) *(W 2854CD)* – (all mixes & B-side)
Sep 89. (lp/c)(cd) *(WX 289/+C)(K 925945-2)* **CHANGE THE WEATHER** [ ] [ ]
– Change the weather / Stand up / Fever / Original song / Mercy / Mr. Universe / Texas / Thrash / Sole survivor / Beach.
Nov 89. (7") **CHANGE THE WEATHER. / TEXAS** [-] [ ]

— ALLEN + CONSOLI became D-INFLUENCE

UNDERWORLD

— **SMITH + HYDE** brought in **DARREN EMERSON** (b.1970, Essex) – keyboards

Boys Own | Sire

Dec 92. (12"ep/cd-ep) **DIRTY. / DIRTY GUITAR** [ ] [-]
Feb 93. (12"ep/cd-ep) **REZ. / WHY WHY WHY** [ ] [-]
Jul 93. (12"ep/cd-ep) *(BOIX 13/+CD)* **MMM . . . SKYSCRAPER I LOVE YOU. / ('A'-Telegraph mix 6.11.92) / ('A'-Jamscraper mix)** [ ] [ ]
Sep 93. (12"/12"pink)(cd-s) *(Collect 002/+P)* **REZ. / COWGIRL** [ ] [ ]
(re-iss.Aug95 on 'Junior Boys Own'; JBO 1001)

Junior Boys Own | not issued

1993. (12"; as LEMON INTERRUPT) *(JBO 12-002)* **ECLIPSE. / BIGMOUTH** [ ] [-]
1993. (12"; as LEMON INTERRUPT) *(JBO 7-12)* **DIRTY / MINNEAPOLIS. / MINNEAPOLIS (AIRWAVES)** [ ] [-]
Dec 93. (12"/cd-s) *(JBO 17/+CD)* **SPIKEE. / DOGMAN GO WOOF** [60] [ ]
Feb 94. (cd/c/d-lp) *(JBO CD/CS/LP 1)* **DUBNOBASSWITHMYHEADMAN** [12] [ ]
– Dark and long / Mmm . . . skyscraper I love you / Surfboy / Spoonman / Tongue / Dirty epic / Cowgirl / River of bass / ME. *(cd re-iss.May97; same)*
Jun 94. (cd-ep) *(JBO 19CDS)* **DARK & LONG (mixes)** [57] [ ]
– Hall's mix / Dark train / Most 'ospitable / 215 miles.
(12") *(JB 019)* – ('A'-spoon deep mix) / ('A'-thing in a back mix).
(12") *(JB 019X)* – ('A'-dark train mix) / ('A'-Burt's mix).
May 95. (12") *(JBO 29)* **BORN SLIPPY (telenatic). / COWGIRL (Vinjer mix)** [52] [ ]
(12") *(JBO 29R)* – ('A'side) / ('A'-Nuxx mix).
(cd-s) *(JBO 29CDS)* – (above 2) / ('A'side again).
Mar 96. (cd/c/d-lp) *(JBO CD/MC/LP 4)* **SECOND TOUGHEST IN THE INFANTS** [9] [ ]
– Juanita / Kiteless / To dream of love / Banstyle – Sappys curry / Confusion the waitress / Rowla / Pearl's girl / Air towel / Blueski / Stagger. *(cd re-iss.May97; same)*
May 96. (12"ep) *(JBO 38)* **PEARL'S GIRL. / MOSAIC / DEEP ARCH** [24] [ ]
(cd-ep) *(JBO 38CDS1)* – ('A'-Carp Dreams . . . Koi) / Oich oich / Cherry pie.
(cd-ep) *(JBO 38CDS2)* –

— next used in the film 'Trainspotting' (cult book by Scotsman Irvine Welsh).

Jul 96. (12"/cd-s) *(JBO 44/+CDS1)* **BORN SLIPPY. / ('A'mixes)** [2] [ ]
(cd-s) *(JBO 38CDS2)* – ('A'side) / ('A'-Deep pan mix) / ('A'-Darren Price mix) / ('A'-Darren Price remix).
Oct 96. (12"/cd-s) *(JBO 45/+CDS1)* **PEARL'S GIRL. / ('A'mixes)** [22] [ ]
(cd-s) *(JBO 45CDS2)* – ('A'mixes).

V

Sven VATH

Born: Frankfurt, Germany. Starting out as a conventional DJ in his father's pub, he later joined The OFF, who had one major Euro hit with 'ELECTRIC SALSA'. This set-up also included MICHAEL MUNZING and LUCA ANZILOTTI, who were responsible for dance/rave outfit SNAP! He subsequently initiated his own labels, 'Harthouse', 'Recycle Or Die' and, for his own releases; 'Eye Q', which was subsequently licensed to 'WEA' in 1993. That year, after hitting the dancefloors with 'BARBARELLA' (including a sample of JANE FONDA's dialogue from the 1969 film), he unleashed his Indian/Eastern-inspired debut album, 'ACCIDENT IN PARADISE'. The album showcased VATH's compellingly eclectic style which drew from such esoteric sources as TANGERINE DREAM, YELLOW MAGIC ORCHESTRA, JEAN MICHEL JARRE, THE ORB and of course, house music. Lifted from it, the singles 'L'ESPERANZA' and the title track, both hit the Top 75. He followed this up a year later with 'THE ROBOT, THE HARLEQUIN AND THE BALLET DANCER', an album which inspired a set of remixes in 1995.
• **Songwriters:** VATH – HILDENBEUTEL. • **Trivia:** Recycle Or Die label introduced two other artists RALF HILDENBEUTEL and OLIVER LIEB.

Recommended: ACCIDENT IN PARADISE (*7)

SVEN VATH – keyboards, synthesizers, tapes

Eye-Q WEA | Warners

May 93. (cd/c/lp) *(4509 93989-2/-4/-1)* **ACCIDENT IN PARADISE** [ ] [ ]
– Ritual of life / Caravan of emotions / L'Esperanza / Sleeping invention / Mellow illusion / Merry-go-round somewhere / An accident id Paradise / Drifting like whales in the darkness / Coda. *(cd+=/c+=)*– L'esperanza (single edit) / Tribal of life (Tribal acid mix).
Jul 93. (7"/c-s) *(YZ 757/+C)* **L'ESPERANZA. / ('A'mix)** [63] [ ]
(12"/cd-s) *(YZ 757 T/CD)* – ('A'mixes).
Oct 93. (12"ep) *(YZ 778T)* **AN ACCIDENT IN PARADISE (4 mixes)** [57] [ ]
(cd-s+=) *(YZ 778CD)* – ('A'mix).
Sep 94. (cd/c/lp) *(4509 97534-2/-4/-1)* **THE ROBOT, THE HARLEQUIN & THE BALLET DANCER** [ ] [ ]
– Intro / Harlequin plays bells / Harlequin – The beauty and the beast / Harlequin's meditation / The birth of Robby / Robot / Ballet romance / Ballet fusion / Ballet dancer.
Oct 94. (7"/c-s) *(YZ 857/+C)* **HARLEQUIN – THE BEAUTY AND THE BEAST** [72] [ ]
(12"+=/cd-s+=) *(YZ 857 T/CD)* – ('A'mixes).
Feb 95. (12"/c-s) *(YZ 897 T/C)* **BALLET IN FUSION. / ('A'mix)** [ ] [ ]
(cd-s+=) *(YZ 897CD)* – ('A'mix).
Apr 95. (cd) *(4509 99702-2)* **TOUCH THEMES OF HARLEQUIN** (remixes) [ ] [-]
(d-lp-iss.Mar96 on 'Eye Q'; EYEUKLP 001)

VELVET CRUSH

Formed: Providence, New York, then settling in Boston, USA . . . 1988 as CHOO CHOO TRAIN by PAUL CHASTAIN, JEFFREY BORCHARDT and RIC MENCK. They made 2 singles, 'THE BRIAR ROSE' & 'HIGH' for the UK indie label, 'Subway', before they changed the group name to the slightly less childish HONEYBUNCH. In the early 90's, they were back as VELVET CRUSH, a beat/psychedelic fusion of FLAMIN' GROOVIES, BIG STAR and The REPLACEMENTS. First up was a TENNAGE FANCLUB number 'EVERYTHING FLOWS', a track that led them to sign for Alan McGee's 'Creation' label. In 1991, they unleashed their debut album 'IN THE PRESENCE OF GREATNESS'. • **Songwriters:** Group except ONE HUNDRED YEAR (Gram Parsons) / EVERYTHING FLOWS (Teenage Fanclub) / WHY NOT YOUR BABY (Gene Clark).

Recommended: IN THE PRESENCE OF GREATNESS (*7) / TEENAGE SYMPHONIES TO GOD (*6)

CHOO CHOO TRAIN

PAUL CHASTAIN – vocals, bass / **JEFFREY BORCHARDT** – guitar, vocals / **RIC MENCK** – drums

Subway | not issued

Jul 88. (12"ep) *(SUBWAY 20T)* **THE BRIAR ROSE** [ ] [-]
– Briar rose / Big blue buzz / Nothing else! / Flower field / Every little knight / Catch another breath.
Nov 88. (7") *(SUBWAY 23)* **HIGH. / WISHING ON A STAR** [ ] [-]
(12"+=) *(SUBWAY 23T)* – My best friend / When Sunday comes / Parasol!

— took new name HONEYBUNCH, before going into a little hibernation

VELVET CRUSH

Seminal Twang | not issued

Jun 91. (7") **EVERYTHING FLOWS. /** [ ] [-]

Creation | not issued

Oct 91. (cd/c) *(CRECD/C-CRE 109)* **IN THE PRESENCE OF GREATNESS** [ ] [-]
– Window to the world / Drive me down / Ash and earth / White soul / Superstar / Blind faith / Speedway baby / Stop / Asshole / Die a little every day.
Apr 92. (7") *(CRE 122)* **WINDOW TO THE WORLD. / ATMOSPHERE** [ ] [-]
(12"ep)(cd-ep) **THE POST GREATNESS E.P.** (CRE 122T)(CRESCD 122) – The gentle breeze / Butterfly position.

— added guest **DAVE GIBBS** – guitar (of GIGOLO AUNTS)

Oct 92. (12"ep)(cd-ep) *(CRE 139T)(CRESCD 139)* **DRIVE ME DOWN (SOFTLY). / ATMOSPHERE / SLIP AWAY** [ ] [-]
Jun 94. (7") *(CRE 146)* **HOLD ME UP. / DON'T YOU SLIP AWAY FROM ME** [ ] [-]
(12"+=)(cd-s+=) *(CRE 146T)(CRESCD 146)* – One hundred year from now.
Jul 94. (cd/lp)(c) *(CRECD/CRELP/C-CRE 130)* **TEENAGE SYMPHONIES TO GOD** [ ] [ ]
– Hold me up / My blank pages / Why not your baby / Time wraps around you / Atmosphere / #10 / Faster days / Somethings goota give / This life is killing me / Weird summer / Star trip / Keep on lingerin'.

– compilations, etc. –

Mar 92. (lp/cd; by CHOO CHOO TRAIN) *Suborg; (SUBORG 015/+CD)* **BRIAR HIGH** (THE 1988 SINGLES) [ ] [-]

VERVE

Formed: Wigan, England . . . 1990 by local college lads RICHARD ASHCROFT, NICK McCABE, SIMON JONES and PETER SALISBURY. They were soon supporting the likes of RIDE and SPIRITUALIZED, signing to 'Hut' in 1991. The following year, they released three singles, the spiralling psychedelia of 'ALL IN THE MIND', 'SHE'S A SUPERSTAR' & 'GRAVITY GRAVE'. In early summer of '93, they had a minor hit with 'BLUE', a taster for the debut album, 'A STORM IN HEAVEN', which made the UK Top 30. The album delivered on the promise of the early singles; an amorphous melange of trippy rock and liquid space-jazz ambience. Ambitious and cocksure, they toured the States, subsequently coming unstuck with US label VERVE, who forced them to slightly change their name to THE VERVE. In

1995, they unleashed a second album, 'A NORTHERN SOUL', a much darker, more intense affair featuring more conventional song structures. Although the album went top 20, they announced they were splitting several months later, the 'HISTORY' single apparently their swan song. Just when the band were poised to enter the big league, it looked as if they'd missed the boat, McCABE and ASHCROFT's quarreling, together with well documented drug problems, seemingly to blame for the band's demise. By February '97, however, they got it together sufficiently to reform and their first single of the year was to many, their best song yet, the grandiose, string-laden 'BITTER SWEET SYMPHONY'. The song crashed into the UK chart at No.2 thanks to a glorious video featuring an angry jaywalking ASHCROFT barging into everyone in sight! • **Songwriters:** Group. • **Trivia:** RICHARD believes in astral travel. His nickname is MAD RICHARD, enough said!

Recommended: A STORM IN HEAVEN (*7) / A NORTHERN SOUL (*8)

RICHARD ASHCROFT (b. 1971) – vocals / **NICK McCABE** – guitar / **SIMON JONES** – bass / **PETER SALISBURY** – drums

Hut | Vernon Yard

Mar 92. (12"ep/cd-ep) *(HUT T/CD)* **ALL IN THE MIND. / ONE WAY TO GO / A MAN CALLED SUN** [ ] [-]

Jun 92. (12"/cd-s) *(HUT T/CD 16)* **SHE'S A SUPERSTAR. (8+mins) / FEEL (10+mins)** [66] [-]

Oct 92. (10"ep/12"ep/cd-ep) *(HUT)* **GRAVITY GRAVE / ENDLESS LIFE / A MAN CALLED SUN (live) / SHE'S A SUPERSTAR (live)** [ ] [-]

Nov 92. (m-cd) *(<HUTUS 1>)* **THE VERVE E.P.** (compilation) [ ] [ ]
– Gravity grave / A man called Sun / She's a suprstar / Endless life / Feel.

Hut | Caroline

May 93. (12"ep) *(HUT 29)* **BLUE. / TWILIGHT / WHERE THE GEESE GO** [69] [ ]
(10"ep+=/cd-ep+=) *(HUT T/CD 29)* – No come down.

Jun 93. (cd)(c/lp) *(CDHUT 10)(HUT MC/LP 10)* **A STORM IN HEAVEN** [27] [ ]
– Star sail / Slide away / Already there / Beautiful mind / The Sun, the sea / Virtual world / Make it 'til Monday / Blue / Butterfly / See you in the next one (have a good time).

Sep 93. (7"ep/12"ep/cd-ep) *(HUT/+T/CD)* **SLIDE AWAY. / MAKE IT 'TIL MONDAY (acoustic) / VIRTUAL WORLD (acoustic)** [ ] [ ]

May 94. (cd) *(CDHUT 18)* **NO COMEDOWN** (rare / b-sides) [ ] [-]

THE VERVE

Apr 95. (7") *(HUT 54)* **THIS IS MUSIC. / LET THE DAMAGE BEGIN** [35] [ ]
(12"+=/cd-s+=) *(HUT T/CD 54)* – You and me.

Jun 95. (7"green/c-s) *(HUT/+C 55)* **ON YOUR OWN. / I SEE THE DOOR** [28] [ ]
(cd-s+=) *(HUTCD 55)* – Little gun / Dance on your bones.

Jul 95. (cd)(c/d-lp) *(CDHUT 27)(HUT MC/LP 27)* **A NORTHERN SOUL** [13] [ ]
– A new decade / This is music / On your own / So it goes / A northern soul / Brainstorm interlude / Drive you home / History / No knock on my door / Life's an ocean / Stormy clouds / Stormy clouds (reprise).

Sep 95. (c-s) *(HUTC 59)* **HISTORY / BACK ON MY FEET AGAIN** [24] [ ]
(cd-s+=) *(HUTCD 59)*
– On your own (acoustic) / Monkey magic (Brainstorm mix).
(cd-s) *(HUTDX 59)* – ('A'extended) / Grey skies / Life's not a rehearsal.

— originals re-formed adding **SIMON TONG**

Jun 97. (7") *(HUTLH 82)* **BITTER SWEET SYMPHONY / SO SISTER** [2] [ ]
('A'extended; cd-s+=) *(HUTDX 82)* – Echo bass.
(c-s/cd-s) *(HUT C/DG 82)* – ('A'side / Lord I guess I'll never know / Country song / ('A'radio version).

VIVA SATURN (see under ⇒ RAIN PARADE)

WAKE OOLOO (see under ⇒ FEELIES)

WEEN

Formed: New Jersey, USA ... early 1985 by 14-year-old MICKEY MELCHIONDO and AARON FREEMAN (alias DEAN and GENE WEEN). They worked together in a farm commune on a 4-track cassette machine for the last half of the 80's. The first fruits of this were released as a double album in 1990; 'GOD WEEN SATAN – THE ONENESS'. Its underground cult success led KRAMER of BONGWATER to put out 'THE POD', named after the home they had just been evicted from. After a brief stint on 'Sub Pop', they were signed to 'Elektra' in 1993, Creation off-shoot 'August' subsequently taking up an option on their album, 'PURE GUEVA'. They were later dropped by the label although 'Flying Nun' UK division released their next effort, 'CHOCOLATE AND CHEESE'. The duo recruited a full band after a hip-hop attempt as The MOIST BOYS for The BEASTIE BOYS' 'Grand Royale' label. 1996's '12 COUNTRY GREATS' was psychedelic country of the weirdo variety, shot through with WEEN's inimitable warped humour. • **Songwriters:** The duo except SHOCKADELICA (Prince).

Recommended: GOD WEEN SATAN – THE ONENESS (*8) / THE POD (*7) / PURE GUAVA (*6) / CHOCOLATE AND CHEESE (*6)

DEAN WEEN (b. MICHAEL MELCHIONDO) – vocals, guitar, etc / **GENE WEEN** (b. AARON FREEMAN) – vocals, guitar, etc

Twin/Tone | Twin/Tone

1990. (cd/d-lp) *(TTR 89186-2/-1)* **GOD WEEN SATAN – THE ONENESS** [ ] [ ]
– Birthday boy / Blackjack / Quelch the weazel / Marble tulip juicy tree / Puffy cloud / Nan / Lick the palm for Guava / Mushroom festival in Hell / L.M.L.Y.P. / Papa zit / Old man thunder / Up on the hill / Wayne's pet youngin' / Nicole / Common bitch / El camino / Old Queen Cole / You fucked up / Tick / I got a weazel / I'm in the mood / Fat Lenny / Cold + wet / Bumble bee / Don't laugh (I love you) / Never squeal on the pusher. *(re-iss.cd Jul95; same)*

Shimmy Disc | Shimmy Disc

1991. (cd/d-lp) *(SDE 9238 DD/DLP)* **THE POD** [ ] [ ]
– Strap on the jammy pack / Dr. Rock / Frank / Sorry Charlie / Pollo Asado / Right to the ways and the rules of the world / Captain Fantasy / emon sweat / Molly / Can u taste the waste / Don't sweat it / Laura / Boing / Oh my dear / Sketches of winkle / Alone / Moving away / She fucks me / Pork roll egg and cheese / The stallion (part 2). *(re-iss.Apr95 on 'Flying Nun' d-lp/cd; FN/+CD 322)*

— 1992, 'SKYCRUISER' released on 'Sub Pop'

Creation – August | Elektra

Jan 93. (cd/lp) *(RUST 002 CD/LP)* **PURE GUAVA** [ ] [ ]
– Little Birdy / Tender situation / The stallion (part 3) / Big Jim / Push th' little daisies / The going gets tough from the getgo / Reggaejunkiejew / I play it off legit / Pumpin' 4 the man / Sarah / Springtime / Flies on my dick / I saw Gene cryin' in his sleep / Touch my tooter / Mourning glory / Loving u thru it all / Hey fat boy (asshole) / Don't get 2 close (2 my fantasy) / Poop ship destroyer.

Aug 93. (12"/cd-s) *(CAUG 004 T/CD)* **PUSH TH' LITTLE DAISIES / MANGO WOMAN. / PUERTO RICAN POWER (parts 1 & 2) / ODE TO RON** [ ] [ ]

1994. (7"white) **I'M FAT. /** [ ] [ ]

— above featured **CALVIN CELSIUS** – vocals

Flying Nun | Flying Nun

Jan 95. (7") *(FN 321)* **VOODOO LADY. / BUENAS TARDES, AMIGO** [ ] [ ]
(cd-s+=) *(FNCD 321)* – There's a pig / Valleso.
(7") *(FNSP 321)* – ('A'side) / Cover it with gas and set it on fire.

Jan 95. (d-lp/cd) *(FN/+CD 314)* **CHOCOLATE AND CHEESE** [ ] [ ]
– Take me away / Spinal menegitis / Freedom of '76 / I can't put my finger on it / A tear for eddie / Roses are free / Baby back / Mister, would you please help my pony? / Drifter in the dark / Voodoo lady / Joppa road / Candi / Buenas tardes, amigo / The HIV song / What Deaner was talkin' about / Don't spit when you eat.

Apr 95. (7") *(FN 327)* **FREEDOM OF '76. / POLLO ASADO** [ ] [ ]
(cd-s+=) *(FNCD 327)* – ('A'-Shaved dog mix) / Now I'm freaking own.
(7") *(FNSP 327)* – ('A'-Shaved dog mix) / Bakersfield.

Jul 96. (7") *(FN 387)* **YOU WERE THE FOOL. /** [ ] [ ]
(cd-s+=) *(FNCD 387)* –
(7") *(FNS 387)* –

Aug 96. (lp/s-lp/c/cd) *(FN/+SP/MC/CD 386)* **12 COUNTRY GREATS** [ ] [ ]
– I'm holding you / Japanese cowboy / Piss up a rope / I don't want to leave you on the farm / Pretty girl / Powder blue / Mister Richard smoker / Help me scrape the mucus of my brain / You were the fool / Fluffy.

MOISTBOYZ

DEAN & GENE WEEN splinter group remixed by The BEASTIE BOYS on their label.

Grand Royale | Grand Royale

Apr 97. (lp/cd) *(GR 004/+CD)* **MOISTBOYZ** [ ] [ ] 1996

WIRE

Formed: London, England ... October '76, by GRAHAM LEWIS, COLIN NEWMAN, BRUCE GILBERT and ROBERT GOTOBED. They made their vinyl debut in April '77, when ears were subjected to their punk anthems, '12XU' and 'LOWDOWN' on the seminal Various Artists lp, 'LIVE AT THE ROXY'. The EMI backed label 'Harvest', desperate for some hip punk credibility, decided to give WIRE a contract. Unsuccessful with their first single attempt ('MANNEQUIN'), they unleashed the Mike Thorne-produced 'PINK FLAG' at the end of '77. It contained 21 short, sharp shocks of minimalist punk rock/new wave, possessed of a musical intelligence that dwarfed their more retro-fixated contemporaries. Early in 1978, they followed this with the classic 'I AM THE FLY', lyrically a simple piece of what can only be described as progressive punk. After another unsuccessful stab at the charts with 'DOT DASH', they returned with an even better second set', the oblique, atmospheric 'CHAIRS MISSING', which deserved better than its Top 50 placing. It featured the classic avant-punk tunes, 'PRACTICE MAKES PERFECT', 'I FEEL MYSTERIOUS TODAY' and the hit 45, 'OUTDOOR MINER'. In the Autumn of '79, their third set, '154' hit the Top 40, showing in great style, an even more experimental side to the one-time three-chord wonders. Sadly, however, it was their final outing for 'Harvest', the group moving on to the more appropriate indie label 'Rough Trade', who released the 1981 single, 'OUR SWIMMER'. An anti-commercial, unproduced live set appeared around the same, the band members having already taken off for solo projects. One of these, DOME (aka GILBERT & LEWIS), had been in the pipeline for some time, while NEWMAN went onto indie success with several albums. In 1986, the much-in-demand WIRE returned, completing a few EP's for top indie, 'Mute' before the following year's 'THE IDEAL COPY' album. They continued to gain cult success, which even spread across the Atlantic to the

States, the band signing to 'Enigma'. In 1991, GOTOBED departed, thus they became WIR, their last album that year being, 'THE FIRST LETTER', which dissappointed many of their most ardent fans. For the remainder of the 90's, all took on individual projects, all of course, fairly obscure. • **Songwriters:** Group compositions. • **Trivia:** COLIN NEWMAN produced The VIRGIN PRUNES in 1982 and FAD GADGET in 1984. He moved to India at this time, returning after a few years to live in Belguim, where he founded 'Crammed Discs' records.

Recommended: PINK FLAG (*8) / CHAIRS MISSING (*10) / 154 (*7) / ON RETURNING (*8) / THE IDEAL COPY (*8). Best solo:- COLIN NEWMAN – NOT TO (*6)

COLIN NEWMAN (b.16 Sep'54, Salisbury, England) – vox, guitar, keyboards / **BRUCE GILBERT** (b.18 May'46, Watford, England) – guitar, vocals, synths. / **GRAHAM LEWIS** (b.22 Feb'53, Grantham, England) – bass, vocals, synthesizers / **ROBERT GOTOBED** (b. MARK FIELD, 1951, Leicester, England) – drums, percussion (ex-SNAKES, ex-ART ATTACKS) / **GEORGE GILL** – guitar (left before debut)

Harvest Harvest

Nov 77. (7"m) *(HAR 5144)* **MANNEQUIN. / 12XU / FEELING CALLED LOVE** –

Nov 77. (lp/c) *(SHSP/TC-SHSP 4076)* **PINK FLAG**
– Reuters / Field day for the Sundays / Three girl rhumba / Ex-lion tamer / Lowdown / Start to move / Brazil / It's so obvious / Surgeon's girl / Pink flag / The commercial / Straight line / 106 beats that / Mr. Suit / Strange / Fragile / Mannequin / Different to me / Champs / Feeling called love / 12XU. *(cd-iss.1990+=;)*– Options R. *(re-iss.cd Aug94 on 'E.M.I.'; CDGO 2063)*

Feb 78. (7") *(HAR 5151)* **I AM THE FLY. / EX-LION TAMER** –

Jun 78. (7") *(HAR 5161)* **DOT DASH. / OPTIONS R** –

Sep 78. (lp/c) *(SHSP/TC-SHSP 4093)* **CHAIRS MISSING** 48
– Practice makes perfect / French film blurred / Another the letter / Men 2nd / Marooned / Sand in my joints / Being sucked in again / Heartbeat / Mercy / Outdoor miner / I am the fly / I feel mysterious today / From the nursery / Used to / Too late. *(cd-iss.1990 +=;)*– Go ahead / A question of degree / Former airline. *(re-iss.cd Aug94 on 'E.M.I.'; CDGO 2065)*

Jan 79. (7",7"white) *(HAR 5172)* **OUTDOOR MINER. / PRACTICE MAKES PERFECT** 51

Harvest Warners

Jun 79. (7") *(HAR 5187)* **A QUESTION OF DEGREE. / FORMER AIRLINE** –

Sep 79. (lp/c) *(SHSP/TC-SHSP 4105)* **154** 39
– I should have known better / Two people in a room / The 15th / The other window / Single k.o. / A touching display / On returning / A mutual friend / Blessed state / Once is enough / Map reference 41<< >>N, 93<< >>W / Indirect enquiries / 40 versions. *(free-7"ep w.a) (Dome; PSR 444)*– Song 2 / Get down (parts 1 & 2) / Let's panic / Later / Small electric piece. *(cd-iss.1990 += 7"ep above;) (re-iss.cd Aug94 on 'E.M.I.'; CDGO 2064)*

Oct 79. (7") *(HAR 5192)* **MAP REFERENCE 41<< >>N 93<< >>W. / GO AHEAD** –

— In 1980, WIRE also diversed into own activities; GILBERT & LEWIS became CUPOL and DOME, etc. The pair also joined THE THE. COLIN NEWMAN went solo taking ROBERT GOTOBED with him. The latter also became member of FAD GADGET. (see further on for these activities)

Rough Trade not issued

May 81. (7") *(RT 079)* **OUR SWIMMER. / MIDNIGHT BAHNHOF CAFE** –

Jul 81. (lp) *(ROUGH 29)* **DOCUMENT AND EYEWITNESS: ELECTRIC BALLROOM (live)** –
– 5 10 / 12XU (fragment) / Underwater experiences / Zegk hoqp / Everything's going to be nice / Instrumental (thrown bottle) / Piano tuner (keep strumming those guitars) / And then . . . / We meet under tables / Revealing trade secrets / Eels sang lino / Eastern standard / Coda. *(free 12"m-lp)* **DOCUMENT AND EYEWITNESS: NOTRE DAME HALL (live)** – Underwater experiences / Go ahead / Ally in exile / Relationship / Our swimmer / Witness to the fact / 2 people in a room / Heartbeat. *(re-iss.1984 lp/c; same/ COPY 004) (cd-iss.Apr91 on 'Grey Area-Mute'; WIRE 80CD)*

Mar 83. (12"m) *(RTT 123)* **CRAZY ABOUT LOVE. / SECOND LENGTH (OUR SWIMMER) / CATAPULT 30** –

— WIRE were now back to full-time membership.

Mute Enigma

Nov 86. (12"ep) *(12MUTE 53)* **SNAKEDRILL** –
– A serious of snakes / Advantage in height / Up to the Sun / Drill.

Mar 87. (7") *(MUTE 57)* **AHEAD. / FEED ME (live)** –
(12"+=) *(12MUTE 57)* – Ambulance chasers (live) / Vivid riot of red (live).

Apr 87. (cd/c/lp) *(CD/C+/STUMM 42)* <273270> **THE IDEAL COPY** 87
– Points of collapse / Ahead / Madman's honey / Feed me / Ambitious / Cheeking tongues / Still shows / Over theirs. *(cd+=)*– Ahead II / SNAKEDRILL EP tracks.

Mar 88. (7") *(MUTE 67)* **KIDNEY BONGOS. / PIETA**
(3"cd-s+=) *(CDMUTE 67)* – Drill (live).
(12"++=) *(12MUTE 67)* – Over theirs (live).

May 88. (cd/c/lp) *(CD/C+/STUMM 54)* <73314-1> **A BELL IS A CUP . . . UNTIL IT IS STRUCK**
– Silk skin paws / The finest drops / The queen of Ur and the king of Um / Free falling divisions / It's a boy / Boiling boy / Kidney bongos / Come back in two halves / Follow the locust / A public place. *(cd+=)*– The queen of Ur and the king of Um (alternate take) / Pieta / Over theirs (live) / Drill (live).

Jun 88. (7") *(MUTE 84)* **SILK SKIN PAWS. / GERMAN SHEPHERDS**
(12"+=) *(12MUTE 84)* – Ambitious (remix).
(3"cd-s+=) *(CDMUTE 84)* – Come back in two halves.

Apr 89. (7"clear; withdrawn) *(MUTE 87)* **EARDRUM BUZZ. / THE OFFER** 68
(12"+=) *(12MUTE 87)* – It's a boy (instrumental).
(cd-s) *(CDMUTE 87)* – ('A'side) / Silk skin paws / A serious of snakes / Ahead (extended).
(live-12") *(LMUTE 87)* – BUZZ BUZZ BUZZ – Eardrum buzz / Ahead / Kidney bongos.

Mute Mute

May 89. (cd/c/lp) *(CD/C+/STUMM 66)* <73516-2> **IT'S BEGINNING TO AND BACK AGAIN (live)**
– Finest drops / Eardrum buzz / German shepherds / Public place / It's a boy / Illuminated / Boiling boy / Over theirs / Eardrum buzz (12"version) / The offer / In vivo.

Jul 89. (7") *(MUTE 98)* **IN VIVO. / ILLUMINATED**
(12"+=/cd-s+=) *(12/CD MUTE 98)* – Finest drops (live).

May 90. (7"; w-drawn) *(MUTE 107)* **LIFE IN THE MANSCAPE. / GRAVITY WORSHIP** –
(12"+=/cd-s+=) *(12/CD MUTE 107)* – Who has wine.

May 90. (cd/c/lp) *(CD/C+/STUMM 80)* <73559-2> **MANSCAPE**
– Patterns of behaviour / Goodbye ploy / Morning bell / Small black reptile / Torch it / Other moments / Sixth sense / What do you see? / Where's the deputation? / You hung your lights in the trees – A craftman's touch. *<US cd+=>*– Life in the manscape / Stampede / Children of groceries.

Apr 91. (cd/c/lp) *(CD/C+/STUMM 74)* **DRILL**
– (7 versions of out-takes from last album)

WIR

Slightly different name when GOTOBED left.

Sep 91. (7") **SO AND SLOW IT GOES. / NICE FROM HERE**
(12") – ('A'side) / ('A'-Orb mix) / Take it (for greedy)
(cd-s+=) – (all 4 tracks).

Oct 91. (cd/c/lp) *(CD/C+/STUMM 87)* **THE FIRST LETTER**
– Take it (for greedy) / So and slow it goes (extended) / A bargain at 3 and 20 yeah! / Rootsi-rootsy / Ticking mouth / It continues / Looking at me (stop!) / Naked, whooping and such-like / Tailor made / No cows on the ice / A big glue canal.

– compilations, others, etc. –

Mar 86. (m-lp) *Pink; (PINKY 7)* **PLAY POP** –

Aug 86. (lp) *Dojo; (DOJOLP 36)* **IN THE PINK (live)** –

Nov 87. (12"ep) *Strange Fruit; (SFPS 041)* **THE PEEL SESSIONS** (18.1.78) –
– I am the fly / Culture vultures / Practice makes perfect / 106 beats that.

Jul 89. (cd)(c/lp) *Harvest; (CDP 792 535-2)(TC+/SHSP 4127) / Restless; <72358-1>* **ON RETURNING (1977-1979)**
– 12XU / It's so obvious / Mr. Suit / Three girl rhumba / Ex lion tamer / Lowdown / Strange / Reuters / Feeling called love / I am the fly / Practise makes perfect / French film blurred / I feel mysterious today / Marooned / Sand in my joints / Outdoor miner / A question of degree / I should have known better / The other window / 40 versions / A touching display / On returning. *(cd+=)*– Straight line / 106 beats that / Field day for the Sundays / Champs / Dot dash / Another the letter / Men 2nd / Two people in a room / Blessed state.

Feb 90. (cd/c/lp) *Strange Fruit; (SFR CD/MC/LP 108)* **DOUBLE PEEL SESSIONS** –
(cd re-iss.May96; same)

May 93. (cd/c/d-lp) *Mute; (CD/C+/STUMM 116)* **1985-1990 THE A LIST** –

Sep 94. (cd; w/book) *Audioglobe; (SCONC 25)* **EXPLODING VIEWS** –

May 95. (cd) *E.M.I.; (CDGO 2066)* **BEHIND THE CURTAIN** –

Dec 95. (12"; WIR30 with HAFLER TRIO) *Touch; (TONE 5)* **THE FIRST LAST NUMBER / LAST LAST NUMBER** –

May 96. (cd) *W.M.O.; (WMO 004CD)* **TURNS AND STROKES** –
(d-lp-iss.Apr97; same)

COLIN NEWMAN

(solo playing most instruments) **with ROBERT GOTOBED** – drums / **DESMOND SIMMONDS** – bass, guitar / **BRUCE GILBERT** – guitar / **MIKE THORNE** – keyboards

Beggars Banquet not issued

Oct 80. (lp) *(BEGA 20)* **A-Z** –
– I waited for ages / And jury / Alone / Order for order / Image / Life on deck / Troisieme / S-S-S-Star eyes / Seconds to last / Inventory / But no / B. *(re-iss.Sep88 on 'Beggars Banquet-Lowdown' lp/c/cd; (BBL/+C 20/+CD)*

Nov 80. (7"m) *()* **B. / CLASSIC REMAINS / ALONE ON PIANO** –

Mar 81. (7") *(BEG 52)* **INVENTORY. / THIS PICTURE** –

— **COLIN** played everything.

4.a.d. not issued

Aug 81. (lp) *(CAD 108)* **PROVISIONALLY TITLED THE SINGING FISH** –
– Fish 1 / Fish 2 / Fish 3 / Fish 4 / Fish 5 / Fish 6 / Fish 7 / Fish 8 / Fish 9 / Fish 10. *(d-cd-iss.Jan88 +=; CAD 108)*– NOT TO (lp tracks) / Not to (remix) / You and your dog / The grace you know / H.C.T.F.R. / No doubt.

— added **DES SIMMONDS + SIMON GILHAM** – bass, vocals

Jan 82. (lp) *(CAD 201)* **NOT TO** –
– Lorries / Don't bring reminders / You me and happy / We meet under tables / Safe / Truculent yet / 5'10 / 1, 2, 3, beep beep / Not to / Indians / Remove for improvement / Blue Jay way.

May 82. (7") *(AD 209)* **WE MEANS WE STARTS. / NOT TO (remix)** –

Crammed Discs not issued

Sep 86. (lp) *(CRAM 045)* **COMMERCIAL SUICIDE** –
– Their terrain / 2-sixes / Metakest / But I . . . / Commercial suicide / I'm still here / Feigned hearing / Can I explain the delay / I can hear you . . .

Oct 86. (7") *(CRAM 1345-7)* **FEIGNED HEARING. / I CAN'T HEAR YOU . . .** –

Aug 87. (12") *(CRAM 051)* **INTERVIEW. / INTERVIEW** –

May 88. (7") *(CRAM 1745-7)* **BETTER LATE THAN NEVER. / AT LAST** –

May 88. (lp/c/cd) *(CRAM 058/+C/CD)* **IT SEEMS** –
– Quite unrehearsed / Can't help being / The rite of life / An impressive beginning / It seems / Better late than never / Not being in Warsaw / At rest / Convolutions / Round and round. *(w/ free label 'Various Artists' lp)*

Swim not issued

May 95. (12") **VOICE. /** –

CUPOL

GILBERT & LEWIS under many guises (not initially chronological)

4.a.d. not issued

Jul 80. (12"ep) *(BAD 9)* **LIKE THIS FOR AGES. / KLUBA CUPOL** (20min@'33rpm) –

GILBERT & LEWIS

		4 a.d.	not issued
Nov 80.	(m-lp) *(CAD 16)* **3R4** – Barge calm / 3,4 / Barge calm / R.		-
Aug 81.	(7") *(AD 106)* **ENDS WITH THE SEA. / HUNG UP TO DRY WHILE BUILDING AN ARCH**		-

— In May88, a cd-compilation '8 TIME' was issued by duo on '4 a.d.'; *CAD 16CD)*

DOME

		Dome	not issued
Aug 80.	(lp) *(DOME 1)* **DOME 1** – Cancel your order / Cruel when complete / And then . . . / Here we go / Rolling upon my day / Say again / Lina sixup / Airmail / Ampnoise / Madmen. *(free-7")*– SO. / DROP		-
Feb 81.	(lp) *(DOME 2)* **DOME 2** – The red tent 1 + 2 / Long lost life / Breathless / Reading Prof. B / Ritual view / Twist up / Keep it.		-
Oct 81.	(lp) *(DOME 3)* **DOME 3** – Jasz / Ar-gu / An-an-an-d-d-d / Ba-dr / D-o-bo / Na-drm / Dasz / Ur-ur / Danse / Roor-an.		-

(above with also **RUSSELL MILLS** – percussion / **DANIEL MILLER** – saxophone / **E.C.RADCLIFFE** – guitar / **PETER PRINCE** – drums)

— (1 & 2 and 3 & 4 were re-issued on 2 cd's for 'Grey Area-Mute' Aug92; *DOME 12CD & DOME 34CD)*

Apr 83.	(lp; by BRUCE GILBERT) **TO SPEAK** – To speak / To walk, to run / To duck, to dive / This / Seven year / Atlas. *(iss.Sep84 as 'WILL YOU SPEAK THIS WORD?' on 'Uniton'; U 011)*		-

GILBERT, LEWIS & MILLS

		Cherry Red	not issued
May 82.	(lp) *(BRED 27)* **MZUI (WATERLOO GALLERY)** – Mzui (part 1) / Mzui (part 2).		-
		W.M.O.	not issued
Dec 95.	(cd) **PACIFIC / SPECIFIC**		-

P'O

		Court	not issued
Jan 83.	(lp) *(COURT 1)* **WHILST CLIMBING THIEVES VIE FOR ATTENTION**		-

DUET EMMO

— **GILBERT & LEWIS** augmented by **DANIEL MILLER** (label boss)

		Mute	not issued
Aug 83.	(7") *(MUTE 25)* **OR SO IT SEEMS. / HEART OF HEARTS (OR SO IT SEEMS)**		-
Aug 83.	(lp) *(STUMM 11)* **OR SO IT SEEMS** – Hill of men / Or so it seems / Friano / The first person / A.N.C. / Long sledge / Gatemmo / Last's card / Heart of hearts. *(cd-iss.Aug92 on 'Grey Area-Mute'; CDSTUMM 11)*		-

BRUCE GILBERT

		Mute	not issued
Sep 84.	(lp) *(STUMM 18)* **THIS WAY** – Work for do you me / I did / Here visit. *(cd-iss.with next; CDSTUMM 18)*		-
Mar 87.	(lp) *(STUMM 39)* **THE SHIVERING MAN** – Angel food / The shivering man / Not in the feather / There are / Hommage / Eline Court li / Epitaph for Henran Brenlar.		-
Jan 91.	(cd/lp) *(CD+/STUMM 71)* **INSIDING (excerpts from 'SAVAGE WATER')** – Side 1 / Side 2 / Bloodlines (ballet).		-
Aug 91.	(cd/lp) *(CD+/STUMM 91)* **MUSIC FOR FRUIT** – Music for fruit / Push / You might be called.		-
Oct 95.	(7") **BI YO YO. /**		-

— (above single on 'Sub Pop')

Mar 96.	(cd) *(CDSTUMM 117)* **AB OVO**		

HE SAID

(aka **GRAHAM LEWIS** solo) augmented by **JOHN FRYER** – drum prog.

		Mute	not issued
Oct 85.	(7"/12") *(7/12 MUTE 41)* **ONLY ONE I. / ONLY ONE I**		-
Apr 86.	(7") *(7MUTE 43)* **PUMP. / PUMP (instrumental)** (12"+=) *(12MUTE 43)* – To and fro.		-
Aug 86.	(7") *(7MUTE 48)* **PULLING 3 G's. / PALE FEET** (12"+=) *(12MUTE 48)* – ('A'&'B'extended versions).		-

— added **BRUCE GILBERT** – guitar / **NIGEL H. KIND** – guitar / **E.C. RADCLIFFE** – prog. / **ANGELA CONWAY** – backing vocals / **ENO** (guested on 1)

Oct 86.	(cd/c/lp) *(CD/C+/STUMM 29)* **HAIL** – Kidnap yourself / Only one I / Pump / I fall in your arms / Do you mean that? / Flagwearing / Shades to escape / Pale feet.		-
Nov 88.	(7"/12") *(MUTE/12MUTE 73)* **COULD YOU?. / HE SAID . . . SHE SAID**		-
Feb 89.	(cd/c/lp) *(CD/C+/STUMM 57)* **TAKE CARE** – Could you? / ABC Dicks love / Watch-take-care / Tongue ties / Not a soul / Halfway house / Get out of that rain / Hole in the sky.		-

X

XTC

Formed: Swindon, Wiltshire, England . . . 1976 after 3 years of calling themselves The HELIUM KIDZ. Not an early version of acid house as the name might suggest, XTC traded in a quirky blend of pop that owed more to quintessential English psychedelia than the nihilistic three chord assault of their punk peers. Nevertheless, they were picked up by 'Virgin' in the signing scramble that followed The SEX PISTOLS early success in 1977. The debut album, 'WHITE MUSIC' (1978), introduced their tentative art-pop sound, PARTRIDGE's songwriting talent much in evidence even at this early stage. The JOHN LECKIE (STONE ROSES, RADIOHEAD,etc.) produced 'GO 2' (1978) was a more sonically adventurous follow-up, heavily influenced by BRIAN ENO and moulding their pop with quirky electronica. Soon after the record's release, ANDREWS left to join ROBERT FRIPP's 'LEAGUE OF GENTLEMEN' and was replaced by DAVE GREGORY. The new improved unit cut the successful 'DRUMS AND WIRES' (1979) album which spawned a top 20 hit single, the hypnotic, MOULDING-penned 'MAKING PLANS FOR NIGEL'. The rest of the tracks were just as catchy in their distinctive, left-of-centre way. This signalled the onset of a punishing touring/recording schedule during which time the band released a succession of impressive singles, some of which went top 20 and an album, 'BLACK SEA' (1980), that hinted at the psychedelic nostalgia which would characterise their later output. 'ENGLISH SETTLEMENT' (1982) is generally held to be band's finest hour. A double set, the record artfully blended rustic folk, ethnic rhythms and synthesizer pop, all shot through with the spectral hue of psychedelia. Although the stellar single, 'SENSES WORKING OVERTIME' was one of the band's biggest hits and XTC looked to be headed for the big time, PARTRIDGE, never comfortable with live performance, was dreading the inevitable round of touring. In the event, after a few disastrous shows he decided he could suffer it no longer and shortly after, announced that the band would never tour again. CHAMBERS promptly left, unhappy with such a prospect and although PARTRIDGE was now suffering from Agoraphobia, the band struggled on. With no full-time drummer and a string of producers, 'MUMMER' (1983) and 'THE BIG EXPRESS' (1983) were inconsistent and lacking in direction although 'EVERYDAY STORY OF SMALLTOWN' from the latter set was a charming piece of nostalgia-pop. It was clear the band needed some fresh inspiration and with the help of JOHN LECKIE they cut the '25 O'CLOCK' mini-album in 1985 under the pseudonym DUKES OF STRATOSPHERE. More overtly psychedelic than any previous XTC material, PARTRIDGE was given free range to indulge his obvious passions. Re-energised, the band were paired with TODD RUNDGREN for 'SKYLARKING' (1986) and although there were some well documented clashes between PARTRIDGE and the maverick American, the resultant album was a triumphant return to form. Embellishing the gentle hybrid of 'ENGLISH SETTLEMENT' with a 'PET SOUNDS'-like sonic richness, the album spawned the sultry single 'GRASS'. Its B-side, the semi-acoustic sweep of 'DEAR GOD' was picked up by American radio, with the end result that 'SKYLARKING' was a considerable stateside success. After a final DUKES OF STRATOSPHERE album, 'PSONIC PSUNSPOT', XTC began work on the 'ORANGES AND LEMONS' set. Released in 1989, the album was another resounding success, creatively at least, and spawned the charming 'MAYOR OF SIMPLETON' single. While the album was a relative success in America, it failed to make any lasting impact in the U.K. and after 'NONESUCH' (1992) stiffed completely, XTC faded into obscrity. Although sightings are rare, PARTRIDGE has surfaced occasionally, notably on the HAROLD BUDD collaboration, 'THROUGH THE HILL', in 1994. • **Songwriters:** Either penned by PARTRIDGE or MOULDING or both. Covered ALL ALONG THE WATCHTOWER (Bob Dylan) / ELLA GURU (Captain Beefheart).

Recommended: ENGLISH SETTLEMENT (*8) / WHITE MUSIC (*8) / THE COMPACT XTC – THE SINGLES 1978-1985 (*9) / DRUMS AND WIRES (*8) / SKYLARKING (*7) / ORANGES AND LEMONS (*7)

ANDY PARTRIDGE (b.11 Dec'53) – vocals, guitar / **COLIN MOULDING** (b.17 Aug'55) – bass, vocals / **BARRY ANDREWS** (b.12 Sep'56, London) – keyboards repl. JONATHAN PERKINS / **TERRY CHAMBERS** (b.18 Jul'55) – drums

		Virgin	Virgin-Epic
Oct 77.	(7") *(VS 188)* **SCIENCE FRICTION. / SHE'S SO SQUARE** (12"ep+=) *(VS 188-12)* **3-D** – Dance band.		-
Jan 78.	(7") *(VS 201)* **STATUE OF LIBERTY. / HANG ON TO THE NIGHT**		-
Feb 78.	(lp/c) *(V/TCV 2095)* **WHITE MUSIC** – Radios in motion / Cross wires / This is pop? / Do what you do / Statue of liberty / All along the watchtower / Into the atom age / I'll set myself on fire / I'm bugged / New town animal in a furnished cage / Neon shuffle. *(re-iss.Mar84 lp/c; OVED/+C 60) (cd-iss.Mar87 +=; CDV 2095)*– Science friction / She's so square / Dance band / Hang on to the night / Heatwave / Traffic light rock / Instant tunes.	38	
Apr 78.	(7") *(VS 209)* **THIS IS POP?. / HEATWAVE**		-
Oct 78.	(7") *(VS 231)* **ARE YOU RECEIVING ME. / INSTANT TUNES**		-
Oct 78.	(lp/c) *(V/TCV 2108)* **GO 2** – Mekanic dancing (oh we go!) / Battery brides / Buzzcity talking / Crowded room / The rhythm / Beatown / My weapon / Life is good in the greenhouse / Jumping in Gomorrah / My weapon / Super-tuff. *(free-12"ep w/ lp)* **GO +** – Dance with me	21	

Germany / Beat the bible / A dictionary of modern marriage / Clap, clap, clap / We kill the beast. *(re-iss.Mar84 lp/c; OVED/+C 61) (cd-iss.Jul87 +=; CDV 2108)*– Are you receiving me.

— **DAVE GREGORY** – synthesizers, guitar repl. ANDREWS who joined LEAGUE OF GENTLEMEN (w/ ROBERT FRIPP). He later went solo and formed SHRIEKBACK

May 79. (7",7"clear) *(VS 259)* **LIFE BEGINS AT THE HOP. / HOMO SAFARI** [54] [-]

Virgin / Virgin Atlantic

Aug 79. (lp/c) *(V/TCV 2129)* *<VA 13134>* **DRUMS AND WIRES** [34] [ ]
– Making plans for Nigel / Helicopter / Life begins at the hop / When you're near me I have difficulty / Ten feet tall / Roads girdle the globe / Reel by reel / Millions / That is the way / Outside world / Scissor man / Complicated game. *(free-7"w/ lp)*– LIMELIGHT. / CHAIN OF COMMAND *(re-iss.1986 lp/c; OVED/+C 113) (cd-iss.Jun88 +=; CDV 2129)*– Limelight / Chain of command.

Sep 79. (7"m) *(VS 282)* **MAKING PLANS FOR NIGEL. / BUSHMAN PRESIDENT (HSS 2) / PULSING, PULSING** [17] [-]

Nov 79. (7") **TEN FEET TALL. / HELICOPTER / THE SOMNAMBULIST** [-] [ ]

Feb 80. (7"m) *<VA 67009>* **MAKING PLANS FOR NIGEL. / THIS IS POP? / MEKANIC DANCING (OH WE GO!)** [-] [ ]

Mar 80. (7") *(VS 322)* **WAIT TILL YOUR BOAT GOES DOWN. / TEN FEET TALL (U.S. version)** [ ] [ ]

Aug 80. (7") *(VS 365)* **GENERALS AND MAJORS. / DON'T LOSE YOUR TEMPER** [32] [ ]
(d7"+=) *(VS 365)* – Smokeless zone. / The somnambulist.

Sep 80. (lp/c) *(V/TCV 2173)* *<VA 13147>* **BLACK SEA** [16] [41]
– Respectable Street / General and majors / Living through another Cuba / Love at first sight / Rocket from a bottle / No language in our lungs / Towers of London / Paper and iron (notes and coins) / Burning with optimism's flames / Sgt. Rock (is going to help me) / Travels in Nihilon. *(re-iss.1986 lp/c; OVED/+C 83) (cd-iss.Mar87 +=; CDV 2172)*– Smokeless zone / Don't lose your temper / The somnambulist.

Oct 80. (7") *(VS 372)* **TOWERS OF LONDON. / SET MYSELF ON FIRE (live)** [31] [ ]
(d7"+=) *(VS 372)* – Battery brides (live) / Scissor man.

Oct 80. (7"; as The COLONEL) *(VS 380)* **TOO MANY COOKS IN THE KITCHEN. / I NEED PROTECTION** [ ] [-]

— (above by The COLONEL; aka MOULDING + CHAMBERS)

Nov 80. (7") *(RSO 71)* **TAKE THIS TOWN. / (b-side by The Ruts)** [ ] [ ]

— (above single was from 'Times Square' film soundtrack on 'R.S.O.')

Dec 80. (7") **LOVE AT FIRST SIGHT. / ROCKET FROM A BOTTLE** [-] [ ]

Jan 81. (7"m) *(VS 384)* **SGT. ROCK (IS GOING TO HELP ME). / LIVING THROUGH ANOTHER CUBA (live) / GENERALS AND MAJORS (live)** [16] [ ]

Mar 81. (7"m) *(VS 407)* **RESPECTABLE STREET. / STRANGE TALES, STRANGE TAILS / OFFICER BLUE** [ ] [ ]

Virgin / Epic

Jan 82. (7"m) *(VS 462)* **SENSES WORKING OVERTIME. / BLAME THE WEATHER / TISSUE TIGERS** [10] [-]
(12"+=) *(VS 462-12)* – Egyptian solution (HSS 3).

Feb 82. (d-lp/c)<US-lp> *(V/TCV 2223)* *<37943>* **ENGLISH SETTLEMENT** [5] [48] Mar82
– Runaways / Ball and chain / Senses working overtime / Jason and the Argonauts / No thugs in our house / Yacht dance / All of a sudden (it's too late) / Melt the guns / ** Leisure * / It's nearly Africa * / Knuckle down * / Fly on the wall * / ** Down in the cockpit * / English roundabout / Snowman. *<US single-lp version omits *>* *(cd-iss.Jun88; CDV 2223)*; omits tracks **)

Mar 82. (7"m) *(VS 482)* **BALL AND CHAIN. / PUNCH AND JUDY / HEAVEN IS PAVED WITH BROKEN GLASS** [58] [ ]
(12"+=) *(VS 482-12)* – Cockpit dance mixture.

May 82. (7"ep,9"ep) *(VS 490)* **NO THUGS IN OUR HOUSE / CHAIN OF COMMAND. / LIMELIGHT / OVER RUSTY WALLS** [ ] [-]

May 82. (7") **SENSES WORKING OVERTIME. / ENGLISH ROUNDABOUT** [-] [ ]

Nov 82. (lp/c) *(V/TCV 2251)* **WAXWORKS** (A-sides compilation) [54] [-]
(free lp w/ above) **BEESWAX** (B-sides) (re-iss.Dec82 lp/c; *OVED/+C 9)*

— Trimmed to basic trio of **PARTRIDGE, MOULDING + GREGORY** plus on session **PETER PHIPPES** – drums (ex-GLITTER BAND) (CHAMBERS emigrated to Australia)

Virgin / Geffen

Apr 83. (7") *(VS 553)* **GREAT FIRE. / GOLD** [ ] [-]
(12"+=) *(VS 553-12)* – Frost circus (HSS 5) / Procession towards learning land (HSS 6).

Jul 83. (7"/7"pic-d) *(VS/+Y 606)* **WONDERLAND. / JUMP** [ ] [ ]

Aug 83. (lp/c) *(V/TCV 2264)* *<4027>* **MUMMER** [51] [ ]
– Beating of hearts / Wonderland / Love on a farmboy's wages / Great fire / Deliver us from the elements / Human alchemy / Ladybird / In loving memory of a name / Me and the wind / Funk pop a roll. *(re-iss.1986 lp/c; OVED/+C 142) (cd-iss.Mar87 +=; CDV 2264)*– Frost circus (HSS 5) / Jump / Toys / Gold / Procession towards learning land (HSS 6) / Desert island.

Sep 83. (7") *(VS 613)* **LOVE ON A FARMBOY'S WAGES. / IN LOVING MEMORY OF A NAME** [50] [ ]
(d7"+=) *(VS 613)* – Desert island / Toys.
(12") *(VS 613-12)* – ('A'side) / Burning with optimism's flames (live / English roundabout (live) / Cut it out (live).

Nov 83. (7"; as THREE WISE MEN) *(VS 642)* **THANKS FOR CHRISTMAS. / COUNTDOWN TO CHRISTMAS PARTYTIME** [ ] [-]

Sep 84. (7") *(VS 709)* **ALL YOU PRETTY GIRLS. / WASHAWAY** [55] [ ]
(12"+=) *(VS 709-12)* – Red brick dream.

Oct 84. (lp/c) *(V/TCV 2325)* *<24054>* **THE BIG EXPRESS** [38] [ ]
– Wake up / All you pretty girls / Shake you donkey up / Seagulls screaming kiss her, kiss her / This world over / The everyday story of Smalltown / I bought myself a liarbird / Reign of blows / You're the wish you are I had / I remember the sun / Train running low on soul coal. *(cd-iss.1987 +=; CDV 2325)*– Red brick dreams / Washaway / Blue overall. *(re-iss.1988 lp/c; OVED/+C 182)*

Oct 84. (7"/12") *(VS 721/+12)* **THIS WORLD OVER. / BLUE OVERALL** [ ] [ ]

Jan 85. (7"m) *(VS 746)* **WAKE UP. / TAKE THIS TOWN / MANTIS ON PAROLE (HSS 4)** [ ] [ ]
(12"+=) *(VS 746-12)* – Making plans for Nigel / Sgt. Rock (is going to help me) / Senses working overtime.

— **IAN GREGORY** (DAVE's brother) – drums repl. PHIPPES

DUKES OF STRATOSPHEAR

Apr 85. (7") *(VS 763)* **THE MOLE FROM THE MINISTRY. / MY LOVE EXPLODES** [ ] [-]

Apr 85. (m-lp/c) *(WOW/+C 1)* **25 O'CLOCK** [ ] [ ]
– 25 o'clock / Bike ride to the Moon / My love explodes / What in the world . . . / Your gold dress / The mole from the ministry.

XTC

Aug 86. (7") *(VS 882)* **GRASS. / DEAR GOD** [ ] [ ]
(12"+=) *(VS 882-12)* – Extrovert.

Oct 86. (lp/c/cd) *(V/TCV/CDV 2399)* *<24117>* **SKYLARKING** [90] [70]
– Summer's cauldron / Grass / The meeting place / That's really super, Supergirl / Ballet for a rainy day / 1000 umbrellas / Season cycle / Earn enough for us / Big day / Another satellite / Mermaid smiled * / The man who sailed around his soul / Dying / Sacrificial bonfire. *<re-iss.1987; 'Dear God' repl. *>*

Jan 87. (7"/7"clear) *(VS/+Y 912)* **THE MEETING PLACE. / THE MAN WHO SAILED AROUND HIS SOUL** [ ] [ ]
(12"+=) *(VS 912-12)* – Terrorism.

Jun 87. (7") *(VS 960)* **DEAR GOD. / BIG DAY** [ ] [ ]
(12"+=) *(VS 960-12)* – Another satellite (live).
(cd-s) *(CDEP 3)* – ('A'side) / Homo safari series (HSS 1-6):- Homo safari / Bushman president / Egyptian solution / Mantis on parole / Frost circus / Procession towards learning land.

Jul 87. (7") **DEAR GOD. / MERMAID SMILED** [-] [ ]

DUKES OF STRATOSPHEAR

Jul 87. (7"/7"colrd) *(VS/+Y 982)* **YOU'RE A GOOD MAN ALBERT BROWN (CURSE YOU RED BARREL). / VANISHING GIRL** [ ] [-]
(12"+=) *(VS 982-12)* – The mole from the ministry / My love explodes.

Aug 87. (lp/colrd-lp/c) *(V/VP/TCV 2440)* **PSONIC PSUNSPOT** [ ] [ ]
– Vanishing girl / Have you seen Jackie? / Little lighthouse / You're a good man Albert Brown (curse you red barrel) / Collideascope / You're my drug / Shiny cage / Brainiac's daughter / The affiliated / Pale and precious.

1989. (cd) *(COMCD 11)* **CHIPS FROM THE CHOCOLATE FIREBALL** [ ] [ ]
– (25 O'CLOCK / PSONIC PSUNSPOT)

XTC

— **PAT MASTELOTTO** – drums (of MR. MISTER) repl. IAN

Jan 89. (7") *(VS 1158)* **THE MAYOR OF SIMPLETON. / ONE OF THE MILLIONS** [46] [72]
(12"+=) *(VST 1158)* – Ella guru.
(3"cd-s) *(VSCD 1158)* – ('A'side) / Ella guru / Living in a haunted heart / The good thing.
(12") *(VSR 1158)* – ('A'side) / Dear God / Senses working overtime / Making plans for Nigel.

Feb 89. (d-lp/c/cd) *(V/TCV/CDV 2581)* *<24218>* **ORANGES AND LEMONS** [28] [44]
– Garden of earthly delights / The Mayor of Simpleton / King for a day / Here comes President Kill again / The loving / Poor skeleton steps out / One of the millions / Scarecrow people / Merely a man / Cynical days / Across this antheap / Hold me my daddy / Pink thing / Miniature sun / Chalkhills and children. *(re-iss.Oct89, 3xcd-ep-box; CDVT 2581)*

Apr 89. (7") *(VS 1177)* **KING FOR A DAY. / HAPPY FAMILIES** [ ] [-]
(12"+=) *(VST 1177)* – ('A'extended).
(c-s+=) *(VSC 1177)* – Generals and majors / Towers of London.
(3"cd-s) *(VSCD 1177)* – ('A'extended) / ('A'side) / My paint heroes (home demo) / Skeletons (home demo).

Aug 89. (7") *(VS 1201)* **THE LOVING. / CYNICAL DAYS** [ ] [ ]
(c-s) *(VSC 1201)* – ('A'side) / The world is full of angry young men.
(12"/cd-s) *(VS T/CD 1201)* – (all 3 tracks).

Sep 89. (cd-ep) *<9-21236-2>* **KING FOR A DAY (Czar mix) / ('A' Versailles mix) / TOYS / DESERT ISLAND** [-] [ ]

Mar 92. (7"/c-s) *(VS/+C 1404)* **THE DISAPPOINTED. / THE SMARTEST MONKEYS** [33] [ ]
(10"+=) *(VST 1404)* – Humble Daisy.
(cd-s++=) *(VSCD 1404)* ('B'demo).

May 92 (cd/c/d-lp) *(CD/TC+/V 2699)* *<24474>* **NONESUCH** [28] [97]
– The ballad of Peter Pumpkinhead / My bird performs / Dear Madam Barnum / Humble Daisy / The smartest monkeys / The dismal / Holly up on poppy / Crocodile / Rook / Omnibus / That wave / Then she appeared / War dance / Wrapped in grey / The ugly underneath / Bungalow / Books are burning.

Jun 92. (7"/c-s) *(VS/+C 1415)* **THE BALLAD OF PETER PUMPKINHEAD. / WAR DANCE** [71] [ ]
(cd-s+=) *(VSCD1 1415)* – Down a peg (demo) / ('A'demo).
(cd-s+=) *(VSCD2 1415)* – My bird performs (demo) / Always winter never Christmas (demo).

– compilations, others, etc. –

— on 'Virgin' unless otherwise mentioned

Jan 87. (cd) *(CDV 2251)* **THE COMPACT XTC – THE SINGLES 1978-1985** [ ] [-]
– Science friction / Statue of liberty / This is pop? / Are you receiving me / Life begins at the hop / Making plans for Nigel / Wait till your boat goes down / Generals and majors / Towers of London / Sgt. Rock (is going to help me) / Senses working overtime / Ball and chain / Great fire / Wonderland / Love on a farmboy's wages / All you pretty girls / This world over / Wake up.

Jul 88. (3"cd-ep) *(VSCDT 9)* **SENSES WORKING OVERTIME / BLAME THE WEATHER / TISSUE TIGERS** [ ] [-]

Nov 88. (7") *Old Gold; (OG 9819)* **MAKING PLANS FOR NIGEL. / SENSES WORKING OVERTIME** [ ] [-]

Aug 90. (cd) *(CDOVD 308)* **EXPLODE TOGETHER (THE DUB EXPERIMENTS 78-80)** [ ] [-]

– (included the ANDY PARTRIDGE album below)

Aug 90. (cd) *(CDOVD 311)* **RAG & BONE BUFFET** (rare) [ ] [-]
(c-iss.Mar91)

Nov 94. (cd) *Night Tracks; (CDNT 008)* **DRUMS AND WIRELESS: BBC RADIO SESSIONS 77-89** [ ] [-]

Sep 96. (cd/c) *(CD/TC VD 2811)* **FOSSIL FUEL: THE XTC SINGLES 1977-92** [33] [ ]
– (nearly same tracks as 1987 collection + add more recent) *(d-cd; CDVDX 2811)*

MR. PARTRIDGE

Feb 80. (lp/c) *(V/TCV 2145)* **TAKE AWAY (THE LURE OF SALVAGE)** [ ] [-]
– Commerciality / The day the pulled the North Pole down / Cairo / Madhattan / The forgotten language of light / Steam fist futurist / The rotary / Shore leave ornithology (another 1950) / I sit in the snow / Work away Tokyo day / New broom. *(re-iss.Aug88; OVED 130)*

— In Jun'94, ANDY PARTRIDGE co-released with HAROLD BUDD the cd 'THROUGH THE HILL' for 'All Saints' label.

— Also in '94, PARTRIDGE with MARTIN NEWELL, issued album 'THE GREATEST LIVING ENGLISHMAN' for 'Pipeline'.

Y

YO LA TENGO

Formed: Hoboken, New Jersey, USA ... 1984 by IRA KAPLAN and GEORGIA HUBLEY, who advertised for musicians. Finally, through much time and varied personnel, they stabilised their line-up with DAVE SCHRAMM and MIKE LEWIS. This configuration recorded the 1986 debut album, 'RIDE THE TIGER', introducing the band's countrified acouistic-rock which drew on the likes of VELVET UNDERGROUND, LOVE and RAIN PARADE. Following the departure of SCHRAMM and LEWIS, KAPLAN assumed writing duties for 'NEW WAVE HOT DOGS', providing the band with their first of many credible and critically acclaimed albums. 1989's 'PRESIDENT YO LA TENGO' was more experimental while 'FAKEBOOK' (1990) was a beguiling album of rootsy covers (see below). Throughout the 90's, the band have released a string of albums for 'City Slang', taking an increasingly left-field direction. • **Songwriters:** SCHRAMM on debut / taken over by KAPLAN. Covered; KICK ME HARD (NBRQ) / YELLOW SARONG (Scene Is Now) / THE ONE TO CRY (Escorts) / HERE COMES MY BABY (Cat Stevens) / EMULSIFIED (Rex Garvin & The Mighty Carvers) / GRISELDA (Peter Stampfel) / SPEEDING MOTORCYCLE (Daniel Johnston) / ANDALUCIA (John Cale) / OKLAHOMA, U.S.A. (Kinks) / TRIED SO HARD (Flying Burrito Brothers) / YOU TORE ME DOWN (Flamin' Groovies) / A HOUSE IS NOT A MOTEL (Love) / I THREW IT ALL AWAY (Bob Dylan) / IT'S ALRIGHT (Velvet Underground) / THE WHOLE OF THE LAW (Only Ones) / DREAMING (Blondie) / etc. • **Trivia:** Duetted with TARA KEY for the film 'I Shot Andy Warhol'. Hip film director Hal Hartley is a big fan, often using the band's music in his movies.

Recommended: NEW WAVE HOT DOGS (*6) / FAKEBOOK (*7) / PRESIDENT YO LA TENGO (*6) / THAT IS YO LA TENGO (*7) / PAINFUL (*7) / ELECTR-O-PURA (*6)

IRA KAPLAN – guitar, vocals / **GEORGIA HUBLEY** – drums, vocals / +2 (guitarist + bassist)

Shigaku Shigaku

Nov 85. (7") **THE RIVER OF WATER. / A HOUSE IS NOT A MOTEL** [-] [ ]

— **DAVE SHRAMM** – vocals, guitar repl.

— **MIKE LEWIS** – bass repl.

Feb 87. (lp) *(SHIGLP 2)* **RIDE THE TIGER** [ ] [ ] 1986
– The cone of silence / The evil that men do / The fcrest green / The pain of pain / The way some people die / The empty pool / Alrok's bells / Five years / Screaming dead balloons / Living in the country. *(cd-iss.1990's; EFA 0491827)*

— **STEPHEN WICHNEWSKI** – bass repl. LEWIS + SCHRAMM

What Goes On Restless

Nov 87. (lp) *(GOESON 13)* **NEW WAVE HOT DOGS** [ ] [ ]
– Clunk / Did I tell you / House fall down / Lewis / Lost in Bessemer / It's alright / The way that you live / 3 blocks from Groove Street / Let's compromise / Serpentine / A shy dog / No water / The story of jazz.

May 89. (lp) *(GOESON 28)* **PRESIDENT YO LA TENGO** [ ] [ ]
– Barnaby, hardly working / Drug test / The evil that men do / Orange song / Alyda / The evil that men do / I threw it all away. *(cd-iss.Aug94 on 'City Slang'+=; EFA 049252-2)*– NEW WAVE NEW DOGS

— **AL GRELLER** – double bass, repl. WICHNEWSKI

City Slang Bar/None

1990. (lp/cd) *<SLANG 003/+CD>* **FAKEBOOK** [-] [ ]
– Can't forget / Griselda / Here comes my baby / Barnaby, hardly working / Yellow sarong / You tore me down / Emulsified / Speeding motorcycle / Tried so hard / The summer / Oklahoma, U.S.A. / What comes next / The one to cry / Andalucia / Did I tell you / What can I say. *(UK-iss.1990's; EFA 04062-26)*

— **GENE HOLDER** – producer (also last one), bass repl. STEPHEN

City Slang City Slang

Jul 91. (lp/cd) *(EFA 04068/+CD) <SLANG 009>* **WHAT IS YO LA TENGO** [ ] [ ]
– Detouring America with horns / Upside down / Mushroom cloud of hiss / Swing for life / Five cornered drone (crispy duck) / Some kinda fatigue / Always something / 86 second blowout / Out the window / Sleeping pill / Satellite.

— added **JAMES McNEW** – bass

Alias City Slang

May 92. (cd-ep) *(A 026CD) <SLANG 021>* **UPSIDE DOWN / (THE) FARMER'S DAUGHTER / OUT OF CONTROL / UPSIDE DOWN (ONE MORE TIME) / SUNSQUASHED** [ ] [ ]

Jun 92. (lp/cd) *(A 021/+CD) <SLANG 26>* **MAY I SING WITH YOU** [ ] [ ]
– Out the window / Swing for life / Walking away from you / Five cornered drone (crispy duck) / Fog over Frisco.

City Slang City Slang

Sep 93. (cd/c/lp) *(EFA 04927-2/-4/-1)* **PAINFUL** [ ] [ ]
– Big day coming / From a motel 6 / Double dare / Superstar – Watcher / Nowhere near / Sudden organ / A worrying thing / I was the fool beside you far too long / The whole of the law / Big day coming / I heard you looking.

Matador Matador

Nov 93. (7") *(OLE 060-7)* **SHAKER. / FOR SHAME OF DOING WRONG (demo)** [ ] [ ]
(cd-s+=) *(OLE 060-2)* – What she wants.

Apr 94. (cd-s) *(OLE 080-2)* **FROM A MOTEL 6 / ASHES ON THE GROUND / NUTRICIA** [ ] [ ]

City Slang Matador

Apr 95. (7") *(EFA 04954-7)* **TOM COURTNEY. / THE BIOSEXUAL BOOGIE** [ ] [ ]
(cd-s+=) *(EFA 04954-2)* – Treading water / Bad politics / My hearts reflection.

Apr 95. (cd/lp) *(04955-2/-1)* **ELECTR-O-PURA** [ ] [ ]
– Pablo and Andrea / etc

Matador Matador

Dec 96. (d-cd) *(OLE 194-2)* **GENIUS + LOVE = YO LA TENGO** (compilation) [ ] [ ]
– Evanescent psychic pez drop / emons / Fog over Frisco / Too late / Hanky panky nohow / Something to do / Ultra-powerful short wave radio picks up music from Venus / Up to you / Somebody's baby / Walking away from you / Artificial heart / Cast a shadow / I'm set free / Barnaby, hardly working / Some kinda fatigue / Speding motorcycle / Her grandmother's gift / From a motel 6 / Gooseneck problem / Surfin' with the Shah / Ecstacy blues / Too much (part 1) / Blitzkreig bop / One self: Fish girl / Enough / Drum solo / From a motel 6 / Too much (part 2) / Sunsquashed.

Feb 97. (7") *(WORM 4)* **BLUE-GREEN ARROW. /** [ ] [ ]

— (above on 'Earworm' / below 45 on 'Planet')

Mar 97. (7"ltd) *(PUNK 016)* **ROCKET NO.9. / ('A'mix)** [ ] [-]

Apr 97. (12") *(OLE 2501)* **AUTUMN SWEATER (remixes)** [ ] [ ]

Apr 97. (cd/lp) *(222 2/1)* **I CAN HEAR THE HEAR BEATING AS ONE** [ ] [ ]
– Return to hot chicken / Moby octopad / Sugarcube / Damage / Deeper into movies / Shadows / Stockholm syndrome / Autumn sweater / Little Honda / Green arrow / One PM again / Lie and how we told it / Center of gravity / Spec bebop / We're an American band / My little corner of the world.

YOUR DESERT ISLAND DISC(S)

– tracks you would take on a trip –

If you could make an imaginary various-artists CD that typified PSYCHEDELIC music of the 60's, what would you pick? (personal choices of course). Do the same for PROGRESSIVE & EXPERIMENTAL music of the 60's/70's, then RETRO-PSYCHEDELIC music (late 70's/80's/90's). You can also give the 3 discs a title. You're allowed 70 minutes total running time maximum, and select in order of preference (i.e. track 1 being your favourite). If you can't be bothered finding out the time of the song, just write down around 20 (10 for Progressive & Experimental). Below is an example, picking only one song per artist/group and making sure the running time is in brackets (approximate if you want; but mark *). When you've finished all or any of the 3 lists, send them c/o Martin Strong's Desert Island Discs, CANONGATE BOOKS, 14 HIGH STREET, EDINBURGH, EH1 1TE. The best – or most interesting – from each section will receive a copy of THE GREAT ROCK DISCOGRAPHY (edition 4), which will hit the shops in the Autumn of 1998.

CLASSIC PSYCHEDELIA OF THE 60's

1:- PINK FLOYD – Astronomy Domine <4.30*> / 2:- The JIMI HENDRIX EXPERIENCE – Purple Haze <3.00*> / 3:- CAPTAIN BEEFHEART & HIS MAGIC BAND – Electricity <3.05> / 4:- The VELVET UNDERGROUND – Venus In Furs <5.09> / 5:- LOVE – 7 And 7 Is <2.30*> / 6:- The BYRDS – Eight Miles High <3.37> / 7:- The INCREDIBLE STRING BAND – A Very Cellular Song <10.00*> / 8:- IRON BUTTERFLY – In-A-Gadda-Da-Vida <single edit; 2.53> / 9:- The FEVER TREE – San Francisco Girls (Return Of The Native) <3.00*> / 10:- The DOORS – The End <11.50> / 11:- The SMALL FACES – Lazy Sunday <3.00*> / 12:- TYRANNOSAURUS REX – Debora <2.30*> / 13:- FRANK ZAPPA – Peaches En Regalia <4.00*> / 14:- The BEATLES – Helter Skelter <3.30*> / 15:- The ROLLING STONES – Paint It Black <3.30*> / 16:- The ELECTRIC PRUNES – I Had Too Much to Dream (Last Night) <2.54> / 17:- JEFFERSON AIRPLANE – White Rabbit <2.32> / 18:- DONOVAN – Hurdy Gurdy Man <3.00*> / 19:- The MISUNDERSTOOD – Children Of The Sun <3.00*> / 20:- The SYNDICATE OF SOUND – Little Girl <2.30*>.

CLASSIC PROGRESSIVE ROCK OF THE 70's

1:- PINK FLOYD – Echoes < > / 2:- YES – And You And I < > / 3:- GENESIS – The Battle Of Epping Forest < > / 4:- WISHBONE ASH – Throw Down The Sword < > / 5:- EMERSON, LAKE & PALMER – Abaddon's Bolero < > / 6:- ENO – In Dark Skies < > / 7:- TANGERINE DREAM – Mysterious Semblance At The Strand Of Nightmares < > / 8:- DAVID BOWIE – Sense Of Doubt < > / 9:- KRAFTWERK – The Hall Of Mirrors < > / 10:- ROXY MUSIC – The Bogus Man < >.

CLASSIC (retro) PSYCHEDELIA (post-punk)

1:- The ORB – Little Fluffy Clouds < > / 2:- MY BLOODY VALENTINE – To Here Knows When < > / 3:- SONIC YOUTH – Death Valley '69 < > / 4:- MERCURY REV – Very Sleepy Rivers < > / 5:- WIRE – I Am The Fly < > / 6:- GORKY'S ZYGOTIC MYNCI – Diamond Dew < > / 7:- TELEVISION PERSONALITIES – I Know Where Syd Barrett Lives < > / 8:- TORTOISE – Djed < > / 9:- BUTTHOLE SURFERS – 22 Going On 23 < > / 10:- ROBYN HITCHCOCK – Brenda's Iron Sledge < > / 11:- The GRID – Rollercoaster < > / 12:- HUSKER DU – Find Me < > / 13:- STONE ROSES – Fool's Gold < > / 14:- ORBITAL – Are We Here? / 15:- JULIAN COPE – Greatness And Perfection Of Love < > / 16:- BLUR – There's No Other Way < > / 17:- MASSIVE ATTACK – Karmacoma < > / 18:- STEREOLAB – Metrognome Underground < > / 19:- RIDE – Leave Them All Behind < > / 20:- FLAMING LIPS – Waterbug < >.

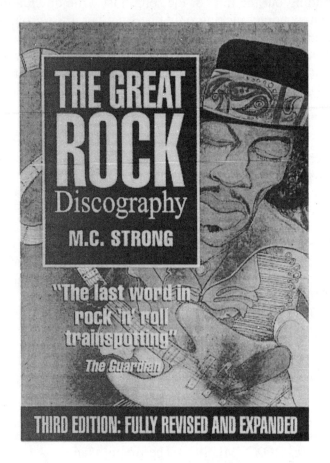